THE
ALL ENGLAND
LAW REPORTS
1982

Volume 3

Editor
PETER HUTCHESSON LL M
Barrister, New Zealand

Assistant Editor
BROOK WATSON
of Lincoln's Inn, Barrister
and of the New South Wales Bar

Consulting Editor
WENDY SHOCKETT
of Gray's Inn, Barrister

London
BUTTERWORTHS

ENGLAND: Butterworth & Co (Publishers) Ltd
                88 Kingsway, London WC2B 6AB

AUSTRALIA: Butterworths Pty Ltd
                271–273 Lane Cove Road, North Ryde, NSW 2113
                Also at Melbourne, Brisbane, Adelaide and Perth

CANADA: Butterworth & Co (Canada) Ltd
                2265 Midland Avenue, Scarborough, Ont M1P 4S1

                Butterworth & Co (Western Canada) Ltd
                409 Granville Street, Ste 856, Vancouver, BC V6C 1T2

NEW ZEALAND: Butterworths of New Zealand Ltd
                33–35 Cumberland Place, Wellington

SINGAPORE: Butterworth & Co (Asia) Pte Ltd
                Crawford Post Office Box 770, Singapore 9119

SOUTH AFRICA: Butterworth & Co (South Africa) (Pty) Ltd
                Box 792, Durban

USA: Mason Publishing Co
                Finch Bldg, 366 Wacouta Street, St Paul, Minn 55101

                Butterworth (Legal Publishers) Inc
                15014 NE 40th, Suite 205, Redmond, Wash 98052

                Butterworth (Legal Publishers) Inc
                381 Elliot Street, Newton, Upper Falls, Mass 02164

©

Butterworth & Co (Publishers) Ltd

1982

ISBN 0 406 85145 X

Typeset by CCC, printed and bound in Great Britain by William Clowes (Beccles) Limited, Beccles and London

REPORTERS
House of Lords

Mary Rose Plummer Barrister

Privy Council

Mary Rose Plummer Barrister

Court of Appeal, Civil Division

Mary Rose Plummer Barrister
Frances Rustin Barrister
Diana Procter Barrister

Henrietta Steinberg Barrister
Diana Brahams Barrister
Patricia Hargrove Barrister

Sophie Craven Barrister

Court of Appeal, Criminal Division

N P Metcalfe Esq Barrister
Sepala Munasinghe Esq Barrister
Dilys Tausz Barrister

Jacqueline Charles Barrister
April Weiss Barrister
Raina Levy Barrister

Chancery Division

Jacqueline Metcalfe Barrister
Evelyn M C Budd Barrister
Hazel Hartman Barrister
Azza M Abdallah Barrister

Queen's Bench Division

David Bartlett Esq Barrister
M Denise Chorlton Barrister

J M Collins Esq Barrister
K Mydeen Esq Barrister

Family Division

Bebe Chua Barrister

Admiralty

N P Metcalfe Esq Barrister

Revenue Cases

Rengan Krishnan Esq Barrister
Edwina Epstein Barrister

Courts-Martial Appeals

N P Metcalfe Esq Barrister

European Cases

Andrew Durand Esq Barrister

MANAGER

John W Wilkes Esq

House of Lords

The Lord High Chancellor: Lord Hailsham of St Marylebone

Lords of Appeal in Ordinary

Lord Diplock
Lord Fraser of Tullybelton
Lord Keith of Kinkel
Lord Scarman
Lord Roskill

Lord Bridge of Harwich
Lord Brandon of Oakbrook
Lord Brightman
Lord Templeman
(appointed 30 September 1982)

Court of Appeal

The Lord High Chancellor

The Lord Chief Justice of England: Lord Lane
(President of the Criminal Division)

The Master of the Rolls

Lord Denning (retired 29 September 1982)
Sir John Francis Donaldson (appointed 30 September 1982)
(President of the Civil Division)

The President of the Family Division: Sir John Lewis Arnold

The Vice-Chancellor: Sir Robert Edgar Megarry

Lords Justices of Appeal

Sir John Frederick Eustace Stephenson
Sir Frederick Horace Lawton
Sir Roger Fray Greenwood Ormrod
  (retired 29 September 1982)
Sir George Stanley Waller
Sir James Roualeyn Hovell-Thurlow-
  Cumming-Bruce
Sir Edward Walter Eveleigh
Sir Sydney William Templeman
  (appointed Lord of Appeal in Ordinary,
  30 September 1982)
Sir John Francis Donaldson
  (appointed Master of the Rolls,
  30 September 1982)
Sir Desmond James Conrad Ackner

Sir Robin Horace Walford Dunn
Sir Peter Raymond Oliver
Sir Tasker Watkins VC
Sir Patrick McCarthy O'Connor
Sir William Hugh Griffiths
Sir Michael John Fox
Sir Michael Robert Emanuel Kerr
Sir John Douglas May
Sir Christopher John Slade
Sir Francis Brooks Purchas
  (appointed 30 September 1982)
Sir Robert Lionel Archibald Goff
  (appointed 30 September 1982)
Sir George Brian Hugh Dillon
  (appointed 30 September 1982)

Chancery Division

The Lord High Chancellor

The Vice-Chancellor

Sir Peter Harry Batson Woodroffe Foster
Sir John Norman Keates Whitford
Sir Ernest Irvine Goulding
Sir Raymond Henry Walton
Sir Nicolas Christopher Henry Browne-
Wilkinson
Sir John Evelyn Vinelott
Sir George Brian Hugh Dillon
(appointed Lord Justice of Appeal,
30 September 1982)

Sir Martin Charles Nourse
Sir Douglas William Falconer
Sir Jean-Pierre Frank Eugene Warner
Sir Peter Leslie Gibson
Sir David Herbert Mervyn Davies
Sir Jeremiah LeRoy Harman
(appointed 15 November 1982)

Queen's Bench Division

The Lord Chief Justice of England

Sir John Thompson
Sir Helenus Patrick Joseph Milmo
(retired 29 September 1982)
Sir Joseph Donaldson Cantley
Sir Hugh Eames Park
Sir Bernard Caulfield
Sir Hilary Gwynne Talbot
Sir William Lloyd Mars-Jones
Sir Ralph Kilner Brown
Sir Peter Henry Rowley Bristow
Sir Hugh Harry Valentine Forbes
Sir Neil Lawson
Sir David Powell Croom-Johnson
Sir Leslie Kenneth Edward Boreham
Sir Alfred William Michael Davies
Sir John Dexter Stocker
Sir Kenneth George Illtyd Jones
Sir Haydn Tudor Evans
Sir Peter Richard Pain
Sir Kenneth Graham Jupp
Sir Robert Lionel Archibald Goff
(appointed Lord Justice of Appeal,
30 September 1982)
Sir Stephen Brown
Sir Roger Jocelyn Parker
Sir Ralph Brian Gibson
Sir Walter Derek Thornley Hodgson
Sir James Peter Comyn
Sir Anthony John Leslie Lloyd

Sir Frederick Maurice Drake
Sir Brian Thomas Neill
Sir Michael John Mustill
Sir Barry Cross Sheen
Sir David Bruce McNeill
Sir Harry Kenneth Woolf
Sir Christopher James Saunders French
Sir Thomas Patrick Russell
Sir Peter Edlin Webster
Sir Thomas Henry Bingham
Sir Iain Derek Laing Glidewell
Sir Henry Albert Skinner
Sir Peter Murray Taylor
Sir Murray Stuart-Smith
Sir Christopher Stephen Thomas Jonathan
Thayer Staughton
Sir Donald Henry Farquharson
Sir Anthony James Denys McCowan
Sir Iain Charles Robert McCullough
Sir Hamilton John Leonard
Sir Alexander Roy Asplan Beldam
Sir David Cozens-Hardy Hirst
Sir John Stewart Hobhouse
Sir Michael Mann
(appointed 30 September 1982)
Sir Andrew Peter Leggatt
(appointed 30 September 1982)
Sir Michael Patrick Nolan
(appointed 8 November 1982)

Family Division

The President of the Family Division

Sir John Brinsmead Latey
Sir Alfred Kenneth Hollings
Sir Charles Trevor Reeve
Sir Francis Brooks Purchas
(appointed Lord Justice of Appeal,
30 September 1982)
Dame Rose Heilbron
Sir Brian Drex Bush
Sir Alfred John Balcombe
Sir John Kember Wood

Sir Ronald Gough Waterhouse
Sir John Gervase Kensington Sheldon
Sir Thomas Michael Eastham
Dame Margaret Myfanwy Wood Booth
Sir Anthony Leslie Julian Lincoln
Dame Ann Elizabeth Oldfield Butler-Sloss
Sir Anthony Bruce Ewbank
Sir John Douglas Waite
Sir Anthony Barnard Hollis
(appointed 30 September 1982)

CITATION

These reports are cited thus:

[1982] 3 All ER

REFERENCES

These reports contain references to the following major works of legal reference described in the manner indicated below.

Halsbury's Laws of England

The reference 35 Halsbury's Laws (3rd edn) 366, para 524, refers to paragraph 524 on page 366 of volume 35 of the third edition, and the reference 26 Halsbury's Laws (4th edn) para 577 refers to paragraph 577 on page 296 of volume 26 of the fourth edition of Halsbury's Laws of England.

Halsbury's Statutes of England

The reference 5 Halsbury's Statutes (3rd edn) 302 refers to page 302 of volume 5 of the third edition of Halsbury's Statutes of England.

The Digest

References are to the blue band replacement volumes and the green band reissue volumes of The Digest (formerly the English and Empire Digest), and to the continuation volumes.

The reference 48 Digest (Repl) 645, 6207 refers to case number 6207 on page 645 of Digest Blue Band Replacement Volume 48.

The reference 36(2) Digest (Reissue) 764, 1398 refers to case number 1398 on page 764 of Digest Green Band Reissue Volume 36(2).

The reference Digest (Cont Vol E) 640, 2392a refers to case number 2392a on page 640 of Digest Continuation Volume E.

Halsbury's Statutory Instruments

The reference 20 Halsbury's Statutory Instruments (4th reissue) 302 refers to page 302 of the fourth reissue of volume 20 of Halsbury's Statutory Instruments; references to subsequent reissues are similar.

Cases reported in volume 3

Digest of cases reported in volume 2

CORRIGENDA

[1982] 1 All ER
p 807. **R v Beck.** Line *h* 4: for 'what the accused had said' read 'what the accomplice had said'.

[1982] 3 All ER
p 389. **Tommey v Tommey.** Line *j* 2: for 'not' read 'now'.
p 730. **R v Waveney District Council, ex p Bowers.** Lines *a* 2 and *a* 3 should read: '. . . in the context of this legislation vulnerable means less able to fend for oneself . . .'

Sudbrook Trading Estate Ltd v Eggleton and others

HOUSE OF LORDS
LORD DIPLOCK, LORD FRASER OF TULLYBELTON, LORD RUSSELL OF KILLOWEN, LORD SCARMAN AND
LORD BRIDGE OF HARWICH
23, 24, 25, 29 MARCH, 8 JULY 1982

*Option – Option to purchase – Tenant's option conferred by lease – Uncertainty of option –
Option to purchase at price to be fixed by valuers nominated by parties – Tenant seeking to
exercise option – Landlord refusing to appoint valuer – Tenant asking court to order specific
performance or to appoint valuer – Whether option uncertain – Whether court should order
specific performance – Whether court having power to appoint valuer.*

By a lease dated 23 March 1949 the predecessors in title of the lessors granted the lessees'
predecessors in title a lease of property to expire on 24 December 1997. A clause in the
lease gave the lessees an option to purchase the reversion in fee simple at a price to be
agreed by two valuers, one to be nominated by the lessors and the other by the lessees
and, in default of agreement, by an umpire to be appointed by the valuers, a minimum
purchase price being specified in the clause. By three other leases in 1956, 1966 and 1968,
adjoining properties were demised by the lessors' predecessors in title to the lessees'
predecessors in title for varying terms ending on 24 December 1997. Each lease contained
an option to purchase the reversion on almost identical terms, save for differences in the
minimum purchase price. When the lessees sought to exercise the options in December
1979 the lessors claimed that the option clauses were void for uncertainty and refused to
appoint a valuer. On the lessees' application, the judge declared that the options to
purchase were valid and had been effectively exercised. On the lessors' appeal, the lessees
contended that the court should direct the lessors to appoint a valuer, or should itself
appoint one if they refused, or should remedy the machinery provided in the leases and
determine a fair purchase price. The lessors contended that the options were unenforceable
as there was no contract of sale since the purchase price had not been fixed. The lessors
further contended that the court had no power to grant a mandatory order and could not
itself appoint a valuer or determine a fair price. The Court of Appeal allowed the lessors'
appeal, holding that where the agreement was on the face of it incomplete until
something else had been done, whether by further agreement between the parties or by
the decision of an arbitrator or valuer, there was no complete agreement which the court
could enforce. The lessees appealed.

Held (Lord Russell dissenting) – The appeal would be allowed and the options would
be ordered to be specifically performed for the following reasons—
(1) Where the machinery by which the value of a property was to be ascertained was
subsidiary and non-essential to the main part of an agreement for the sale and purchase
of the property at a fair and reasonable price, the court could, if the machinery for
ascertaining the value broke down, substitute other machinery to ascertain the price in
order to ensure that the agreement was carried out. Since the contract between the parties
provided that the price was to be determined by valuers, it necessarily followed that the
contract was a contract for sale at a fair and reasonable price assessed by applying objective
standards, and on the exercise of the option clauses a complete contract for the sale and
purchase of the freehold reversion was constituted; it was unrealistic to treat the

machinery provided by the option clauses for ascertaining the price as an essential term
of the contract when it merely consisted of provision for the appointment of valuers and *a*
an umpire, none of whom was named or identified. The only reason the machinery had
not been implemented was the lessors' own breach of contract in refusing to appoint
their valuer. It followed that, since such machinery was not essential, there was no reason
why the court should not substitute its own machinery (see p 4 *e f*, p 5 *e f*, p 6 *j* to p 7 *f*, p
9 *b c*, p 10 *d* to *j*, p 12 *b c e f*, p 13 *d* to *g* and p 14 *a* to *c*, post); *Agar v Macklew* (1825) 2 Sim
& St 418 and *Vickers v Vickers* (1867) LR 4 Eq 529 overruled.   *b*

(2) Where an agreement which would otherwise be unenforceable for want of
certainty or finality in an essential stipulation had been partly performed so that the
intervention of the court was necessary in aid of a grant that had already taken effect, the
court would strain to supply the want of certainty even to the extent of providing a
substitute machinery. It followed that, since the option was one term of the lease which
had been in force for several years when the option under the contract was exercised, the *c*
resulting agreement was not entirely separate from the partly performed contract of lease
(see p 4 *e f*, p 7 *e f*, p 11 *a* to *d*, p 12 *e f*, p 13 *d* to *h* and p 14 *b c*, post); *Gregory v Mighell*
(1811) 18 Ves 328, *Dinham v Bradford* (1869) LR 5 Ch App 519 and *Beer v Bowden* (1976)
[1981] 1 All ER 1070 followed.

(3) Where the valuation provisions related to a subsidiary part of a wider contract
which was itself valid and enforceable, the court would take steps to prevent the wider *d*
contract being rendered unenforceable by a failure of the machinery for the subsidiary
part. Since the mode of valuation provided for was not the very essence and substance of
the contract, the court could accordingly substitute machinery to prevent the contract
being rendered unenforceable, and in the circumstances the appropriate means to enforce
the contract would be to order an inquiry into the fair value of the reversions (see p 4 *e f*,
p 7 *c e f*, p 10 *a* to *d*, p 11 *e* and *j*, p 12 *a* to *f*, p 13 *d e* and p 14 *b c*, post); *Dinham v Bradford* *e*
(1869) LR 5 Ch App 519, *Richardson v Smith* (1870) LR 5 Ch App 648, *Smith v Peters* (1875)
LR 20 Eq 511 and *Talbot v Talbot* [1967] 2 All ER 920 followed.

Decision of the Court of Appeal [1981] 3 All ER 105 reversed.

Notes

For the need for certainty in the terms of a contract, see 9 Halsbury's Laws (4th edn) para *f*
266, and for cases on the subject, see 12 Digest (Reissue) 24–26, *13–21*.

Cases referred to in opinions

Agar v Macklew (1825) 2 Sim & St 418, 57 ER 405, 44 Digest (Repl) 9, *25*.
Beer v Bowden (1976) [1981] 1 All ER 1070, [1981] 1 WLR 522, CA.
Dinham v Bradford (1869) LR 5 Ch App 519, LC, 36(2) Digest (Reissue) 727, *1091*.   *g*
Foley v Classique Coaches Ltd (1929) [1934] 2 KB 17, HL.
Gregory v Mighell (1811) 18 Ves 328, 34 ER 341, 31(1) Digest (Reissue) 67, *500*.
Hall v Warren (1804) 9 Ves 605, [1803–13] All ER Rep 57, 32 ER 738, 44 Digest (Repl)
    39, *274*.
Milnes v Gery (1807) 14 Ves 400, [1803–13] All ER Rep 369, 33 ER 574, 40 Digest (Repl)
    16, *46*.   *h*
Richardson v Smith (1870) LR 5 Ch App 648, LC and LJJ, 40 Digest (Repl) 79, *604*.
Selkirk (Earl) v Nasmith (1778) Mor 627.
Smith v Peters (1875) LR 20 Eq 511, 40 Digest (Repl) 80, *605*.
Talbot v Talbot [1967] 2 All ER 920, [1968] Ch 1, [1967] 3 WLR 438, CA, Digest (Cont
    Vol C) 1060, *427a*.
Vickers v Vickers (1867) LR 4 Eq 529, 40 Digest (Repl) 17, *55*.   *j*

Appeal

Sudbrook Trading Estate Ltd (the lessees) appealed with leave of the House of Lords
granted on 11 June 1981 against the order of the Court of Appeal (Cumming-Bruce,
Templeman and Oliver LJJ) ([1981] 3 All ER 105, [1981] 3 WLR 361) dated 17 March

a 1981 allowing the appeal of William Vernon Eggleton, Thomas Harraden Drew Keck and Alan Gibson Keddie (the lessors) and quashing the declarations granted by Lawson J sitting as an additional judge of the Chancery Division at Bristol on 17 November 1980 that the option clauses in four leases dated 23 March 1949, 18 November 1955, 30 August 1966 and 26 July 1968 and made between the respective predecessors in title of the lessors and of the lessees conferred on the lessees valid options to purchase the reversions in fee simple of properties in High Orchard Street, Gloucester and (ii) that the options in

b the 1955, 1966 and 1968 leases had been validly and effectively exercised. The facts are set out in the opinion of Lord Diplock.

Peter Millett QC and *Martin Roth* for the lessees.
Edward Nugee QC and *Roger Kaye* for the lessors.

c Their Lordships took time for consideration.

8 July. The following opinions were delivered.

d **LORD DIPLOCK.** My Lords, the appellants (the lessees) are lessees of four adjacent industrial premises in Gloucester under four separate leases entered into in 1949, 1955, 1966 and 1968 respectively for various terms of years all of which expire on the same date, viz 24 December 1997. Each lease contained a clause in identical terms, save as to the minimum purchase price, which purported to confer on the lessees an option to purchase the freehold reversion to the premises from the lessors of whom the respondents, who are trustees, are the successors in title. These option clauses were in the following

e terms, which are taken from the 1955 lease, and the words on which the instant appeal will turn are italicised:

'AND IT IS HEREBY AGREED AND DECLARED . . .
    9. *That if the Lessees shall desire to purchase the reversion in fee simple in the premises hereby demised* and having paid all rent then due and duly performed and observed the convenants and conditions on their part herein contained *shall* at any time not

f later than six months before the expiration of the said term but after the expiration of the first twenty one years thereof and during the life of the survivor of the Lessors children Susan Margaret Keck Valerie Josephine Keck Rosemary Veronica Keck and Jeremy Hamilton Halls Keck *give to the Lessor notice in writing to that effect the Lessees shall be the purchasers of such reversion as from the date of such notice at such price not being less than twelve thousand pounds as may be agreed upon by two Valuers one to be nominated*

g *by the Lessor and the other by the Lessees or in default of such agreement by an Umpire appointed by the said Valuers* subject to the conditions following namely:—(a) The purchase money shall be paid and the purchase completed on such one of the quarterly days appointed for payment of rent as shall happen next after the expiration of six calendar months from the date of such notice (b) The Lessees shall pay all rent up to the day appointed for completion of the purchase including the

h rent due on that day (c) The title shall commence with a Trust Deed made the Ninth day of August One thousand eight hundred and ninety eight between Matthews and Company Limited of one part and Albert Estcourt William Henry Isaac Pryer and John Albert Matthews of the other part (d) The sale shall in other respects be subject to the Law Society's Conditions of Sale (according to the edition current at the date of such notice) so far as the same are applicable to a private sale.'

j What, one may ask, could be clearer, fairer or more sensible than that?
    After expiry of the first 21 years of the term the lessees gave to the lessors notice in writing of their desire to purchase the reversion in fee simple to the 1955, 1966 and 1967 leases and nominated their own valuer. They requested the lessors to nominate their valuer; but this the lessors refused to do. Hence these proceedings.

By their statement of claim, dated 29 February 1980, the lessees claimed against the lessors the following relief:

a

'1. Declarations that upon the true construction of:—(i) the 1949 Lease (ii) the 1955 Lease (iii) the 1966 Lease (iv) the 1968 Lease the said clauses therein respectively contained confer on the Plaintiff valid options to purchase the reversions in fee simple in the premises thereby respectively demised

2. Declarations that upon such construction as aforesaid and in the events which have happened the options contained in:—(i) the 1955 Lease (ii) the 1966 Lease (iii) the 1968 Lease have been validly and effectually exercised

b

3. Declarations that the contracts constituted by the exercise of the options contained in:—(i) the 1955 Lease (ii) the 1966 Lease (iii) the 1968 Lease ought to be specifically performed and carried into execution in accordance with the conditions contained in the respective clauses of such Leases

4. That directions may be given as to the nomination of a Valuer or Valuers by or on behalf of the Defendants

c

5. All such further directions and inquiries as may be requisite

6. Damages in addition to specific performance

7. Further or other relief

8. Costs.'

d

Lawson J, before whom the action was heard in Bristol in November 1980, where he sat as an additional judge of the Chancery Division, made the first two declarations sought but declined at that stage to grant any of the other relief claimed. His attitude may be summarised as being 'wait and see', and he gave liberty to apply.

What did happen, though not without some waiting, was that the lessors sought and obtained leave to appeal out of time to the Court of Appeal against this judgment. The Court of Appeal in a unanimous judgment delivered by Templeman LJ allowed the appeal, holding, with expressed regret, that they were bound by an unbroken series of authorities, starting as long ago as *Milnes v Gery* (1807) 14 Ves 400, [1803–13] All ER Rep 369, to allow the appeal. For my part, I think they were so bound. Templeman LJ's judgment refers to and incorporates an adequate and lucid statement of the facts and rationes decidendi of all the relevant authorities. My noble and learned friend Lord Fraser in his speech, with which I would express my entire agreement, also cites the most important of them. I do not propose to refer to them individually myself since I accept that the principles that they establish are accurately summarised by Templeman LJ in the following passage of his judgment (the 'essential term' referred to being, in the instant case, the purchase price of the reversion in fee simple to the lease) [1981] 3 All ER 105 at 114–115, [1981] 3 WLR 361 at 373):

e

f

g

'First, in ascertaining the essential terms of a contract, the court will not substitute machinery of its own for machinery provided by the parties, however defective that machinery may prove to be. Second, where machinery is agreed for the ascertainment of an essential term, then until the agreed machinery has operated successfully, the court will not decree specific performance, since there is not yet any contract to perform. Third, where the operation of the machinery is stultified by the refusal of one of the parties to appoint a valuer or an arbitrator, the court will not, by way of partial specific performance, compel him to make an appointment. All three of these principles stem from one central proposition, that where the agreement on the face of it is incomplete until something else has been done, whether by further agreement between the parties or by the decision of an arbitrator or valuer, the court is powerless, because there is no complete agreement to enforce . . .'

h

j

The authorities binding on the Court of Appeal in which these principles are established do not include any decisions of this House. Even before the change of practice of this House, announced in 1966 (see *Note* [1966] 3 All ER 77, [1966] 1 WLR 1234), they would not have been binding on your Lordships. It is open to the House to consider whether in

the 1980s it remains consistent with a just and rational system of law to continue to apply
a those principles to an option to purchase land granted in terms similar to those used in
the option clauses that are the subject matter of this appeal, so as to enable the grantor,
by the simple expedient of refusing to appoint a valuer, to deprive the grantee of any
legal right to obtain title to the land. If a majority of your Lordships are convinced, as I
am, that to do so would be to administer not justice but injustice then, despite the
antiquity and consistency of the previous authorities, it will be the duty of this House to
b overrule them.

The option clause in each lease was obviously intended by both parties to the lease to
have legal effect, that is to say to create legally enforceable rights and obligations. What
other reason could there be for going to the trouble of inserting those elaborate and
carefully drafted provisions in the lease?

The option clause cannot be classified as a mere 'agreement to make an agreement'.
c There are not any terms left to be agreed between the parties. In modern terminology, it
is to be classified as a unilateral or 'if' contract. Although it creates from the outset a right
on the part of the lessees, which they will be entitled, but not bound, to exercise against
the lessors at a future date, it does not give rise to any legal obligations on the part of
either party unless and until the lessees give notice in writing to the lessors, within the
stipulated period, of their desire to purchase the freehold reversion to the lease. The
d giving of such notice, however, converts the 'if' contract into a synallagmatic or bilateral
contract, which creates mutual legal rights and obligations on the part of both lessors and
lessees.

The first obligation on each of them, once the contract has become synallagmatic, is to
appoint their respective valuers to fix what is the fair and reasonable price for the
reversion. That this is a primary obligation under the contract follows from the use of
e the words 'to be nominated', but it would, in my view, also be a necessary implication to
give business efficacy to the option clause. The requirement that the price to be so fixed
is one that will be fair and reasonable as between lessors and lessees appears to me to be a
necessary implication from the description 'valuers' applied to the persons by whom the
price is to be fixed by agreement between them, if possible, and from the description
'umpire' applied to the person by whom the price is to be fixed if the valuers cannot
f agree. The term 'valuer' (with a capital 'V' at any rate) is used nowadays to denote a
member of a recognised profession comprised of persons possessed of skill and experience
in assessing the market price of property, particularly real property.

The obligation of both lessors and lessees on appointing their respective valuers is to
instruct them to carry out the functions for which the option clause requires that they
should be appointed, viz to try to reach agreement with one another on a price for the
g reversion that is fair and reasonable as between the lessors and the lessees and, failing
such agreement, to agree on and appoint a suitably qualified impartial person to fix such
price.

The option clause, to which the lessors and lessees alone are parties, cannot of itself
impose on the valuers any legal duty to endeavour to reach agreement with one another
as to a fair and reasonable price for the reversion or, if they fail to do so, to agree on what
h person is to be appointed by them jointly as umpire to fix the price. But that this, which
is stressed in several of the cases cited by Templeman LJ, presents an obstacle to
compelling performance of the contract contained in the option clause is a proposition
that on examination proves, in my opinion, to be illusory. If a valuer appointed by the
lessors or lessees does not carry out the instructions given him by his appointor, but in
default of agreement with his fellow valuer on the price, fails to agree with him on the
j person to be appointed as umpire, the valuer will be in breach of his own contract with
his appointor; his appointment can be revoked and a fresh valuer, who will comply with
his instructions, appointed in his stead. In the (improbable) event contemplated, in my
view it would by necessary implication be a contractual duty owed by the lessors and
lessees to one another under the option clause to adopt this course.

So if both lessors and lessees carry out their primary contractual obligations to one another, under the option clause, the result will be a conveyance by the lessors to the lessees of the reversion in fee simple to the demised premises on the completion date *a* fixed for completion by para (b) of the clause at a price agreed on between valuers appointed by each party or failing such agreement determined by an umpire appointed jointly by the valuers. Until such conveyance and payment the contract remains executory; but so does any other contract for the sale of land. What Templeman LJ refers to in his summary of the effect of the authorities as the one central proposition from which the three principles that he states all stem, viz until the price has been fixed by the *b* method provided for in the contract 'there is no complete agreement to enforce' (see [1981] 3 All ER 105 at 115, [1981] 3 WLR 361 at 373), involves a fundamental fallacy. A contract is complete as a contract as soon as the parties have reached agreement as to what each of its essential terms is or can with certainty be ascertained, for it is an elementary principle of the English law of contract id certum est quod certum reddi potest. True it is that the agreement for the sale of land remains executory until transfer of title to the *c* land and payment of the purchase price; but if this is the sense in which the agreement is said not to be complete it is only executory contracts that do require enforcement by the courts; and such enforcement may either take the form of requiring a party to perform his primary obligation to the other party under it (specific performance) or, if he has failed to perform a primary obligation, of requiring him to perform the secondary obligation, that arises only on such failure, to pay monetary compensation (damages) to *d* the other party for the resulting loss that he has sustained.

My Lords, the real issue in this case is not whether the option clause when brought into operation by written notice given by the lessees to the lessors converted an 'if' contract into a synallagmatic contract for the sale of the reversion in fee simple in the promises that are the subject of the lease, of which the lessors were in breach at the date of the commencement of the proceedings before Lawson J by their refusal to appoint a *e* valuer and are now in further breach by their failure to convey the fee simple to the lessees on the date fixed for completion by that clause. For reasons that I have already given I have no doubt that it did; but the real issue is whether the court has jurisdiction to enforce the lessors' primary obligation under the contract to convey the fee simple by decreeing specific performance of that primary obligation, or whether its jurisdiction is limited to enforcing the secondary obligation arising on failure to fulfil that primary *f* obligation, by awarding the lessees damages to an amount equivalent to the monetary loss they have sustained by their inability to acquire the fee simple at a fair and reasonable price, i e for what the fee simple was worth. Since if they do not acquire the fee simple they will not have to pay that price, the damages for loss of such a bargain would be negligible and, as in most cases of breach of contract for the sale of land at a market price by refusal to convey it, would constitute a wholly inadequate and unjust remedy for the *g* breach. That is why the normal remedy is by a decree for specific performance by the vendor of his primary obligation to convey, on the purchaser's performing or being willing to perform his own primary obligations under the contract.

Why should the presence in the option clause of a convenient and sensible machinery for ascertaining what is a fair and reasonable price, which the lessors, in breach of their contractual duty, prevent from operating, deprive the lessees of the only remedy which *h* would result in justice being done to them? It may be that where on the true construction of the contract the price to be paid is not to be a fair and reasonable one assessed by applying objective standards used by valuers in the exercise of their professional task but a price fixed by a named individual applying such subjective standards as he personally thinks fit, and that individual, without being instigated by either party to the contract of sale, refuses to fix the price or is unable through death or disability to do so, the contract *j* of sale is thereupon determined by frustration. But such is not the present case. In the first place the contract on its true construction is in my view a contract for sale at a fair and reasonable price assessed by applying objective standards. In the second place the only thing that has prevented the machinery provided by the option clause for ascertaining the fair and reasonable price from operating is the lessors' own breach of contract in refusing to appoint their valuer. So if the synallagmatic contract created by a the exercise of the option were allowed to be treated by the lessors as frustrated the frustration would be self-induced, a circumstance which English law does not allow a party to a contract to rely on to his own advantage. So I see no reason why, because they have broken one contractual obligation, the lessors should not be ordered by the court to perform another contractual obligation on their part, namely to convey the fee simple in the premises to the lessees against payment of a fair and reasonable price assessed by applying the objective standards to which I have referred.

b   As regards the assessment of the fair and reasonable price to be paid by the lessees on specific performance of the contract to convey, the lessors have clearly waived their contractual right to have that price assessed by the machinery for which the option clause provides. The lessees in their turn are content also to waive their corresponding right to use that machinery. This will leave it to the court itself to determine on the expert evidence of valuers what is the fair and reasonable price. In these circumstances I do not

c find it necessary to decide whether in the absence of such waiver by the lessees the court would have jurisdiction to compel the lessors to appoint a valuer; but it must not be taken that I am accepting that it would not. I do not accept as fit for survival in a civilised system of law any of the three principles extracted from the authorities that are summarised in the passage that I have quoted from the judgment of Templeman LJ.

My Lords, I would have hesitated long before overruling such a long and consistent

d line of authorities if I thought that people had arranged their affairs and dealt with their property on the basis that those authorities correctly stated what is the existing law; but when honest parties to a contract for the sale of land or an option to enter into such a contract have in the past inserted provisions for the ascertainment of the purchase price similar to the emphasised words included in the option clause in the instant case they must have intended to create legal rights to have those provisions acted on by both parties

e and not flouted by either party at his own sweet will, otherwise there is no point in inserting them at all. So, to overrule the old authorities will be to give effect to the intentions of those who have made use of such provisions in contracts that have been entered into before the decision of this House in the instant appeal.

For these reasons and those given by Lord Fraser I would allow the appeal and make the following order:

f
'DECLARE that on the true construction of each of the four leases in the statement of claim mentioned the clauses therein respectively contained confer on the plaintiff valid options to purchase the reversions in fee simple in the premises thereby respectively demised

AND DECLARE that on the true construction thereof and in the events which have

g happened the options respectively contained in the three of such leases defined in the statement of claim as the 1955 lease, the 1966 lease and the 1968 lease have been validly and effectively exercised

ORDER that the contracts constituted by the exercise of the options respectively contained in the said three leases be specifically performed and carried into execution in accordance with the conditions contained in the respective clauses of such leases

h AND ORDER that the following inquiries shall be made, that is to say: 1. AN INQUIRY what is the fair valuation of each of the reversions in fee simple in the premises respectively demised by the said three leases, the amount of such valuation in each case to be certified; 2. AN INQUIRY whether a good title can be made to each of such reversions

AND IN CASE it shall appear that a good title can be made to each of the said

j reversions ORDER that the plaintiff be at liberty to prepare proper conveyances (to be settled by the court in case the parties differ) to itself of such reversions in consideration of the following sums respectively, that is to say (a) in the case of the 1955 lease the fair valuation of the reversion in the premises thereby demised certified as aforesaid or the sum of £12,000, whichever be the greater (b) in the case of the 1966 lease the fair valuation of the reversion in the premises thereby demised certified as aforesaid, (c) in the case of the 1968 lease the fair valuation of the

reversion in the premises thereby demised certified as aforesaid or the sum of
£21,500, whichever be the greater   *a*

AND ORDER that the first and second defendants do execute the said conveyances
in respect of the reversions in the premises comprised in the 1955 lease and the 1966
lease and that the first and third defendants do execute the said conveyance in
respect of the reversion in the premises comprised in the 1968 lease

AND ORDER that the plaintiffs' costs in the courts below be taxed by the taxing
master and their costs in this House be taxed by the Clerk of the Parliaments and   *b*
that the said costs when taxed be deducted from the amount of the said purchase
moneys when computed as aforesaid provided that such costs to be deducted as
aforesaid shall be limited to the plaintiffs' costs in this House and the Court of
Appeal and one-half of their costs of the action down to and including the judgment
of Lawson J

AND UPON the plaintiff paying to the defendants at a time and place to be fixed by   *c*
the court the balance of the amount of such purchase moneys after such deduction
as aforesaid ORDER that the defendants do deliver to the plaintiff the three said
conveyances together with all deeds and writings in their possession dealing solely
with the said premises and giving an acknowledgment of the right of the plaintiff
to production and delivery of copies of and undertaking for the safe custody of deeds
relating also to other property as provided by s 64 of the Law of Property Act 1925   *d*

AND THE PARTIES are to be at LIBERTY TO APPLY to the High Court.'

LORD FRASER OF TULLYBELTON. My Lords, the appellants (the lessees) are
the tenants in four leases, by each of which they were granted an option to purchase the
freehold reversion of the leased premises at a valuation. The lessees have exercised the
options, but the respondents (the lessors), who are the landlords, contend that the options   *e*
are unenforceable. The questions now to be determined, therefore, are whether the
options are valid and enforceable, and, if so, how they should be enforced.

The leases relate to adjacent industrial premises in Gloucester. They were granted at
different dates, but for terms which all expire on 24 December 1997 at yearly rents
which are subject to periodical review. The leases are all in substantially the same form.
For reasons that are not now material the option contained in the earliest lease, that dated   *f*
23 March 1949, had not been exercised when the writs in these proceedings were issued,
but it has been subsequently exercised and there is now no relevant distinction between
that option and the other three. The clause in the 1949 lease, cl 11, has been taken as
typical of them all. It entitled the lessees to purchase the reversion in fee simple, on
certain conditions which were all satisfied—

> 'at such price not being less than Seventyfive thousand pounds as may be agreed   *g*
> upon by two valuers one to be nominated by the Lessor and the other by the Lessee
> or in default of such agreement by an Umpire appointed by the said Valuers . . .'

The lessors contend that the options are void for uncertainty on the ground that they
contain no formula by which the price can be fixed in the event of no agreement being
reached, and that they are no more than agreements to agree. The lessors have therefore   *h*
declined to appoint their valuer. The machinery provided in the leases has accordingly
become inoperable.

In these proceedings the lessees seek a declaration that the options are valid, that they
have been validly and effectively exercised, and that the contents constituted by the
exercise ought to be specifically performed. As regards the mode of performance, the
main argument for the lessees is that the court should order such inquiries as are   *j*
necessary to ascertain the value of each of the properties. Lawson J decided the question
of principle in favour of the lessees, but his decision was reversed by the Court of Appeal
which held that the options were unenforceable. Templeman LJ, who delivered the
judgment of the Court of Appeal, made a full review of the English authorities and the
conclusion which he drew from them was, in my opinion inevitably, adverse to the

lessees' contentions. The fundamental proposition on which he relied was, in his own
a words—

> 'that where the agreement on the face of it is incomplete until something else has
> been done, whether by further agreement between the parties or by the decision of
> an arbitrator or valuer, the court is powerless, because there is no complete agreement
> to enforce . . .'

b (See [1981] 3 All ER 105 at 115, [1981] 3 WLR 361 at 373.)

I agree that that is the effect of the earlier decisions but, with the greatest respect, I am
of opinion that it is wrong. It appears to me that, on the exercise of the option, the
necessary preconditions having been satisfied, as they were in this case, a complete
contract of sale and purchase of the freehold reversion was constituted. The price, which
was of course an essential term of the contract, was, for reasons which I shall explain,
c capable of being ascertained and was therefore certain. Certum est quod certum reddi
potest: see *Foley v Classique Coaches Ltd* (1929) [1934] 2 KB 17 at 21 per Viscount Dunedin.

The courts have applied clauses such as those in the present case in a strictly literal way
and have treated them as making the completion of a contract of sale conditional on
agreement between the valuers either on the value of the property or, failing that, on the
choice of an umpire. They have further laid down the principle that where parties have
d agreed on a particular method of ascertaining the price, and that method has for any
reason proved ineffective, the court will neither grant an order for specific performance
to compel parties to operate the agreed machinery nor substitute its own machinery to
ascertain the price, because either of these clauses would be to impose on parties an
agreement that they had not made. That was decided by Grant MR in *Milnes v Gery*
(1807) 14 Ves 400, [1803–13] All ER Rep 369, and his decision has been accepted ever
e since. The basis of his decision is sufficiently explained by the following sentences from
his opinion (14 Ves 400 at 406, 409, [1803–13] All ER Rep 369 at 370, 371):

> 'The only agreement, into which the Defendant entered, was to purchase at a
> price, to be ascertained in a specified mode. No price having ever been fixed in that
> mode, the parties have not agreed upon any price. Where then is the complete and
f > concluded contract which this Court is called upon to exercise? . . . In this case the
> Plaintiff seeks to compel the Defendant to take this estate at such price as a Master
> of this Court shall find it to be worth; admitting, that the Defendant never made
> that agreement; and my opinion is that the agreement he has made is not
> substantially, or in any fair sense, the same with that; and it could only be by an
> arbitrary discretion that the Court could substitute the one in the place of the other.'

g
That view had not always been followed in previous cases in England: see *Hall v Warren*
(1804) 9 Ves 605, [1803–13] All ER Rep 57, where the seller had become insane and
could not name his valuer but Grant MR held that a mode of ascertaining the value
'equivalent, and as effectual and fair' as that which had been agreed on might be found.
In Roman law there had been doubt about the position when a sale was made at a price
h to be fixed by a third party, until Justinian laid down that the contract became complete
only when the third party had fixed the price (Just Inst 3.23.1), but that rule was not
followed by the Scottish court in *Earl of Selkirk v Nasmith* (1778) Mor 627.

So far as England is concerned, the decision in *Milnes v Gery* seems to have been treated
as settling the law on this point, and in *Agar v Macklew* (1825) 2 Sim & St 418 at 423, 57
ER 405 at 407 Leach V-C said:

j
> 'I consider it to be quite settled that this Court will not entertain a bill for the
> specific performance of an agreement to refer to arbitration; nor will, in such case,
> substitute the Master for the arbitrators, which would be to bind the parties contrary
> to their agreement.'

Although the Vice-Chancellor referred to 'arbitrators' their function was to act as what

would now be called valuers. The rule being settled, it is unnecessary for me to refer to
later decisions when it has been applied.   *a*

While that is the general principle it is equally well established that, where parties
have agreed to sell 'at a fair valuation' or 'at a reasonable price' or according to some
similar formula, without specifying any machinery for ascertaining the price, the
position is different. As Grant MR said in *Milnes v Gery* 14 Ves 400 at 407, [1803–13] All
ER Rep 369 at 371:

> 'In that case no particular means of ascertaining the value are pointed out: there   *b*
> is nothing therefore precluding the Court from adopting any means adapted to that
> purpose.'

The court will order such inquiries as may be necessary to ascertain the fair price: see
Talbot v Talbot [1967] 2 All ER 920, [1968] Ch 1.

I recognise the logic of the reasoning which has led to the courts refusing to substitute   *c*
their own machinery for the machinery which has been agreed on by the parties. But
the result to which it leads is so remote from that which parties normally intend and
expect, and is so inconvenient in practice, that there must in my opinion be some defect
in the reasoning. I think the defect lies in construing the provisions for the mode of
ascertaining the value as an essential part of the agreement. That may have been perfectly
true early in the nineteenth century, when the valuer's profession and the rules of   *d*
valuation were less well established than they are now. But at the present day these
provisions are only subsidiary to the main purpose of the agreement, which is for sale
and purchase of the property at a fair or reasonable value. In the ordinary case parties do
not make any substantial distinction between an agreement to sell at a fair value, without
specifying the mode of ascertaining the value, and an agreement to sell at a value to be
ascertained by valuers appointed in the way provided in these leases. The true distinction   *e*
is between those cases where the mode of ascertaining the price is an essential term of the
contract and those cases where the mode of ascertainment, though indicated in the
contract, is subsidiary and non-essential: see *Fry on Specific Performance* (6th edn, 1921)
paras 360, 364. The present case falls, in my opinion, into the latter category. Accordingly,
when the option was exercised, there was constituted a complete contract for sale, and
the clause should be construed as meaning that the price was to be a fair price. On the   *f*
other hand, where an agreement is made to sell at a price to be fixed by a valuer who is
named, or who, by reason of holding some office such as auditor of a company whose
shares are to be valued, will have special knowledge relevant to the question of value, the
prescribed mode may well be regarded as essential. Where, as here, the machinery
consists of valuers and an umpire, none of whom is named or identified, it is in my
opinion unrealistic to regard it as an essential term. If it breaks down there is no reason   *g*
why the court should not substitute other machinery to carry out the main purpose of
ascertaining the price in order that the agreement may be carried out.

In the present case the machinery provided for in the clause has broken down because
the lessors have declined to appoint their valuer. In that sense the breakdown has been
caused by their fault, in failing to implement an implied obligation to co-operate in
making the machinery work. The case might be distinguishable in that respect from   *h*
cases where the breakdown has occurred for some cause outside the control of either
party, such as the death of an umpire, or his failure to complete the valuation by a
stipulated date. But I do not rely on any such distinction. I prefer to rest my decision on
the general principle that, where the machinery is not essential, if it breaks down for any
reason the court will substitute its own machinery.

The question has apparently never been considered by your Lordships' House, but it   *j*
has been regarded as settled at least since the case of *Agar* in 1825 in England and also in
other countries whose law is based on English law, including Australia, New Zealand,
Canada and some of the states in the United States of America. In these circumstances I
would not have felt it right to depart from the rule which has been so long and so widely
accepted were it not that, in addition to my clear opinion that the existing rule is not

a appropriate in present day conditions, there are other considerations tending to justify a departure from precedent. These are as follows.

1. The rule established by *Milnes* and *Agar* has not been extended, but has been to some extent whittled away by exceptions. One of these exceptions is where an agreement has been partly performed. It was expressed by Templeman LJ in the Court of Appeal in the following words which I gratefully adopt ([1981] 3 All ER 105 at 115, [1981] 3 WLR 361 at 373):

b
'... where an agreement which would otherwise be unenforceable for want of certainty or finality in an essential stipulation has been partly performed so that the intervention of the court is necessary in aid of a grant that has already taken effect, the court will strain to the utmost to supply the want of certainty even to the extent of providing a substitute machinery.'

c An example was *Gregory v Mighell* (1811) 18 Ves 328, 34 ER 341, where a tenant had been in possession of premises for 11 years under a lease which provided for a fair rent to be fixed by two valuers or their umpire, but no rent had been fixed in that way. The tenant admitted that some rent must be due and the court ordered that it should be fixed by the master. The recent case of *Beer v Bowden* (1976) [1981] 1 All ER 1070, [1981] 1 WLR 522 is another example of the exception. No doubt these were stronger cases than
d the present to justify intervention by the court, but the present case is not entirely outside the exception because the option is one term of the lease which has been in force for some years. When the option is exercised in accordance with cl 11, the resulting agreement is not entirely separate from the partly performed contract of lease.

2. A second exception applies where the valuation provisions relate to a subsidiary part of a wider contract which is itself valid and enforceable. The court will take steps to
e prevent the wider contract being rendered unenforceable by a failure of the machinery for the subsidiary valuation. Thus in *Smith v Peters* (1875) LR 20 Eq 511 there was an agreement for sale of the lease of a public house at a fixed price and of the household furniture, fixtures and other effects at a fair valuation to be made by a named valuer. The seller obstructed the valuer in the performance of his duty. Jessel MR said (at 513) that 'There is no evidence that the value of the fixtures and furniture was so large as to be an
f essential portion of the contract', and he decreed specific performance and made a mandatory order compelling the vendor to permit the valuer to enter the premises for the purpose of valuing the fixtures and furniture. Similarly in *Richardson v Smith* (1870) LR 5 Ch App 648 a contract for the sale of a valuable estate included an agreement that certain furniture and other articles of much less value should be taken by the purchaser at a valuation to be made by valuers mutually agreed on. The vendor refused to appoint
g a valuer and refused to complete any part of the contract. The court made an order for specific performance of the contract except for the part relating to the furniture and other articles which was severed. Lord Hatherley LC said (at 651):

'In this case an attempt is made to push the doctrine of *Milnes* v. *Gery*, which has already been certainly carried quite far enough, to an extent which would be utterly unwarrantable, and which, if it were permitted, would induce vendors who are
h desirous of retaining the power of escaping from their contracts to introduce provisions for the valuation of some minor part of the subject matter of the contract in such a mode that they might at any time escape from the performance of the agreement as to the main subject of the contract simply by setting up an act of their own in wrong of the purchaser, and refusing to appoint a valuer... Then could
j either the purchaser or the seller play fast and loose as long as he pleased with the agreement and get off the bargain by not naming a valuer?'

These observations are applicable in principle to a case where the mode of valuation specified in the contract is not essential to the main purpose of the contract.

Dinham v Bradford (1869) LR 5 Ch App 519 partakes of both the exceptions to which I have referred. In that case a partnership agreement provided that, on dissolution of the partnership, one partner should purchase the interest of the other at a valuation to be made by two valuers, one appointed by each partner, but no provision was made to *a* appoint an umpire. It was held that the court would carry the partnership agreement into effect by ascertaining the value of the share. Lord Hatherley LC said (at 523):

> 'If the valuation cannot be made *modo et forma*, the Court will substitute itself for the arbitrators. It is not the very essence and substance of the contract, so that no contract can be made out except through the medium of the arbitrators. Here the property has been had and enjoyed, and the only question now is, what is right and *b* proper to be done with regard to settling the price?'

Similarly here the mode of valuation provided for is not the very essence and substance of the contract.

3. Departure from precedent on the question raised in this appeal is not likely to create a 'danger of disturbing retrospectively the basis on which contracts, settlements of *c* property and fiscal arrangements have been entered into' (see *Note* [1966] 3 All ER 77, [1946] 1 WLR 1234) to borrow the language of the practice direction explaining the condition on which your Lordships' House would not regard itself as bound by its own previous decisions, I do not believe that honest persons are in the habit of making agreements containing option clauses in terms such as those now under consideration, on the basis and with the intention that the option will be unenforceable. On the *d* contrary. I think they would generally be astonished to be told that the exercise of the option had not brought about a complete contract.

The appropriate means for the court to enforce the present agreements is in my opinion by ordering an inquiry into the fair value of the reversions. That was the method used in *Talbot v Talbot* [1967] 2 All ER 920, [1968] Ch 1. The alternative of ordering the lessors to appoint a valuer would not be suitable because, in the event of the order not *e* being obeyed, the only sanction would be imprisonment for contempt of court, which would clearly be inappropriate.

For these reasons the decisions in *Agar v Macklew* (1825) 2 Sm & St 418, 57 ER 405 and *Vickers v Vickers* (1867) LR 4 Eq 529 should in my opinion be overruled. I agree with the order proposed by my noble and learned friend Lord Diplock allowing this appeal.

f

LORD RUSSELL OF KILLOWEN. My Lords, it appears to be generally accepted that the law as previously understood since at least the early nineteenth century is in favour of the respondents (the lessors) and of the decision of the Court of Appeal. It is proposed by the majority of your Lordships to assert that that previous understanding was erroneous. I cannot agree.

Basically the assumption is made that the parties intended that the exercise of the *g* option should involve payment of a 'fair price' or a 'fair value'. Of course parties to such a contract could in terms so agree, and I am not concerned to deny that in such a case a court could enforce the contract by ascertainment of a fair price or fair value, treating specific provisions in the contract for methods (which proved to be unworkable) of ascertaining that fair price or valuation as being inessential. But that is not this case. Why should it be thought that potential vendor and purchaser intended the price to be 'fair'? *h* The former would intend the price to be high, even though 'unfairly' so. And the latter vice versa. Vendors and purchasers are normally greedy.

If the theory that the contract can be construed as if it were a contract *in terms* for ultimate sale and purchase at a fair price or value is wrong, specific performance cannot be ordered, on well-established principles. Assuming refusal by the vendor to appoint a valuer to be a breach of contract, damages cannot be other than nominal; and I do not *j* understand it to be suggested that the court can nominate a person as 'vendor's valuer', or order nomination of a valuer by the vendors on pain of contempt of court should the order not be obeyed.

In my opinion this case is an example of the long established and quite sound principle that if A agrees to sell Blackacre to B the contract must provide for the price to be paid

either in express terms or by the establishment of agreed machinery *which is bound to work*
a by which the price can be ascertained. If the machinery is not so bound to work the party
taking ultimate advantage of its deficiencies is not to be castigated as having taken some
unfair advantage, as though he had from the outset plotted to do so. If the tackle is not
in order from the start it cannot be assumed that either party then knew it.

I do not propose to examine the relevant authorities stretching through generations of
distinguished judges in this field. They have been fully discussed in the judgment of the
b Court of Appeal which was given by Templeman LJ. It will have been noted that the
strength of the mainstream of authority is accentuated by the exceptions diverted from
it; for example, if there is undoubtedly a tenancy the court *must* fix a proper rent or if a
sale of Blackacre involves chattels or stock at a valuation the court will in one form or
another ensure that the main object (the sale of Blackacre at a stated price) is not stultified
by a sidewind problem of valuation. But the mainstream has flowed on, and I know of
c no adequate reason in 1982 for damming it. Indeed I mistrust profoundly the possible
flooding.

I felt considerable sympathy for counsel for the lessors when he was told that he had
all the law on his side, but was (in effect) facing the prophets. (This is a paraphrase of my
own remark in argument, when he was told that he had all equity behind him and I
intervened to suggest that he had less in front of him.)
d   In the result I would dismiss this appeal. I can only exclaim with Macduff: 'What! all
my pretty chickens and their dam At one fell swoop?' (Macbeth IV.3.218).

LORD SCARMAN. My Lords, I would allow the appeal. I agree with the speeches
delivered by my noble and learned friends Lord Diplock and Lord Fraser, and with the
order proposed by them. I added a few observations only because we are departing from
e a rule which has been accepted as good law for more than 150 years.

The question for decision is as to the true construction to be placed on an option
granted to a lessee to buy the freehold reversion. The terms of the option have been set
out in full by my noble and learned friend Lord Diplock. Were the parties agreeing to a
sale 'at a fair valuation', ie 'at a reasonable price'? Or were they treating their chosen
mode of ascertaining the price as being of the essence of their contract? What was the
f object of their contract? A fair and reasonable price? Or a price reached only by the
means specified?

Unembarrassed by authority, I would unhesitatingly conclude that the parties intended
that the lessee should pay a fair and reasonable price to be determined as at the date when
he exercised the option. The valuation formula was introduced into the contract merely
as a convenient way of ascertaining the price at that future time. Should we be deterred
g from so construing the provision by the existence of a line of authority stretching back
over 150 years in which provisions remitting to a valuer or arbitrator the ascertainment
of a price have been construed as making the machinery of ascertainment an essential
term of the contract?

I think not. Indeed I challenge the relevance of ancient authority when construing the
terms of the formula used in these leases. I agree with the comments of my noble and
h learned friends on the injustice which can arise by applying old cases when what has to
be construed is a modern contract.

In my view, no 'judicial valour' (a quality greatly admired by Sir Frederick Pollock) is
needed to overrule a line of authority which never reached this House and which,
properly considered, is concerned not so much with principle as with construction. We
would be doing a public disservice if, in deference to ancient law, we were to invalidate a
j simple, sensible and practical formula for ascertaining a fair and reasonable price. In
today's conditions a valuation by professional valuers achieves exactly that.

LORD BRIDGE OF HARWICH. My Lords, your Lordships are invited to overrule
a line of authority originating with the decision of Grant MR in *Milnes v Gery* (1807) 14
Ves 400, [1803–13] All ER Rep 369 and continuing unbroken ever since. The principal

decisions and their effect are comprehensively and accurately reviewed in the unanimous judgment of the Court of Appeal, which rightly regarded itself as bound to decide against *a* the appellants (the lessees). Your Lordships are not so bound, and being convinced, in agreement with the majority of your Lordships, that there are compelling reasons why the principles laid down by the line of authority in question should no longer be regarded as good law I had intended to write a speech attempting to express those reasons in my own words.

I have now had the advantage of reading in draft the speeches of my noble and learned *b* friends Lord Diplock, Lord Fraser and Lord Scarman, and finding in them the grounds for allowing this appeal so fully, so clearly and so convincingly expressed I am satisfied that anything I might add would be mere repetition. For the reasons given in those speeches I too would allow the appeal and I concur in the order proposed by Lord Diplock.

c

Appeal allowed.

Solicitors: *Field, Fisher & Martineau*, agents for *Rickerbys*, Cheltenham (for the lessees); *Stevensons*, agents for *Taynton & Son*, Gloucester (for the lessors).

Mary Rose Plummer   Barrister. *d*

Head v Head

e

FAMILY DIVISION
REEVE AND SHELDON JJ
29 MARCH 1982

Injunction – Husband and wife – Domestic violence – Attachment of power of arrest to injunction *f* *– Committal to custody for breach of protection order – Whether 'committal to custody' the same as imprisonment – Whether magistrates having power to order consecutive periods of custody for separate breaches of protection order – Domestic Proceedings and Magistrates' Courts Act 1978, ss 16(6), 18 – Magistrates' Courts Act 1980, ss 63(3), 133(1).*

Sentence – Imprisonment – Magistrates' court – Consecutive terms – Committal to custody for *g* *breach of injunction in domestic proceedings – Whether committal to custody in domestic proceedings the same as imprisonment – Whether magistrates having power to order consecutive periods of custody for separate breaches of injunction – Magistrates' Courts Act 1980, ss 63(3), 133(1).*

The wife obtained an order in a magistrates' court under s 16(6) of the Domestic *h* Proceedings and Magistrates' Courts Act 1978 restraining the husband from using or threatening violence against her. The magistrates attached a power of arrest to the order under s 18 of the 1978 Act. Subsequently the wife made a complaint that the husband had committed breaches of the protection order. On the hearing of that complaint the magistrates found that on two separate occasions the husband had assaulted or molested the wife and threatened her with violence, and on the same day the magistrates made *j* separate orders under s 63(3)ᵃ of the Magistrates' Courts Act 1980 committing the husband to custody for a period of six weeks. The magistrates further ordered that the two periods of six weeks' custody were to run consecutively. The husband appealed to

---

a Section 63(3), so far as material, is set out at p 16 *d e*, post

a
the Divisional Court against the committal orders on the ground, inter alia, that the
magistrates had no power to order the two periods of custody to run consecutively.

Held – The power which magistrates had by virtue of s 133(1)[b] of the 1980 Act to impose
consecutive terms of 'imprisonment' did not apply to an order for committal to custody
made under s 63(3) of that Act because, although prison was the eventual destination of
a person committed to custody under s 63(3), 'committal to custody' within s 63(3) was

b
not the same as 'imprisonment'. Since there was no power to order consecutive committal
orders, every committal order made under s 63(3) had to take effect from the day the
order was made and since the committal orders had been made on the same day the
periods of committal should have been ordered to run concurrently rather than
consecutively. The appeal would therefore be allowed (see p 16 j and p 17 b d f, post).

B (B) v B (M) [1969] 1 All ER 891 applied.

c
Per curiam. Magistrates making orders under the 1978 Act and consequential
committal orders under the 1980 Act should have a note prepared of the evidence given
before them so that if there is an appeal against the period of the committal to custody
the appeal court can properly determine whether that period was just (see p 17 d to f,
post).

d **Notes**
For enforcement by magistrates of orders other than for payment of money by committal
to custody, see 29 Halsbury's Laws (4th edn) para 446.

For the meaning of commit to custody, see ibid para 443.

For the Domestic Proceedings and Magistrates' Courts Act 1978, ss 16, 18, see 48
Halsbury's Statutes (3rd edn) 761, 764.

e
For the Magistrates' Courts Act 1980, ss 63, 133, see 50(2) ibid 1495, 1558.

Case referred to in judgments
B (B) v B (M) [1969] 1 All ER 891, [1969] P 103, [1969] 2 WLR 62, 27(2) Digest (Reissue)
1006, 8076.

f **Originating motion**
By a motion dated 17 March 1982 Leslie John Head (the husband) appealed against orders
of the Grays Magistrates' Court dated 16 February 1982 committing him to custody for
consecutive periods of six weeks for two breaches of a protection order made on 4 January
1982 not to use or threaten violence against Brenda Rose Head, his wife. The facts are set
out in the judgment of Sheldon J.

g
John Bassett for the husband.
The wife did not appear.

SHELDON J delivered the first judgment at the invitation of Reeve J. On 18 December
1981 at Grays Magistrates' Court, on an ex parte application by the wife, the justices, as it

h
appears, found that she had been assaulted and physically injured by her husband, that it
was likely that it would happen again, and that she was in imminent danger of physical
injury. Accordingly, they made an expedited order under s 16(6) of the Domestic
Proceedings and Magistrates' Courts Act 1978 restraining him from using or threatening
to use further violence against her or against any of their four children. They also
attached to that order a power of arrest under s 18 of the Act. As that, however, was an

j
'expedited order' which would cease to have effect at the latest at the end of 28 days from
the date on which it was made, the matter was considered further by the justices, on a
non-expedited basis, on 4 January 1982 when a protection order was made in similar

---

b   Section 133(1), so far as material, is set out at p 16 f, post

terms, although fortified by an order prohibiting the husband from entering the
matrimonial home, but without the addition of a power of arrest under s 18.   *a*

On 20 January, however, on the wife's application under s 18(4) of the 1978 Act for an
order for her husband's arrest for having disobeyed the order of 4 January the justices
made such an order coupled with a direction that he should be released on bail on his
own recognisance in the sum of £100 pending the hearing of the complaint.

At that hearing on 16 February the wife's complaints of breaches by her husband of
the order of 4 January 1982 were three, of which the first and last were that on 15 January   *b*
he had obtained entry to the matrimonial home and had assaulted her and molested her,
and that on 8 February, in the precincts of the magistrates' court, he had threatened to
'get his boys to beat her up'.

The justices found that those first and third complaints had been proved and
accordingly, for each breach of the order, committed the husband to custody for a period
of six weeks, such periods being ordered to run consecutively. The husband has now   *c*
sought the leave of this court to appeal out of time against both those orders, on the
grounds (1) that the justices had no power to order that the periods of custody should be
consecutive and (2) that, in any event, the overall and individual periods of custody were
excessive. That second ground of appeal, however, has not now been pursued.

That this court has jurisdiction in this connection is not disputed; we are satisfied,
moreover, that that is so, from the combined effects of the Administration of Justice Acts   *d*
1960 and 1970 and the Magistrates' Courts Act 1980. Accordingly we granted the
husband leave to appeal out of time, and, having done so, with the consent of both
parties, have treated this hearing as that of the appeal.

Section 63(3) of the Magistrates' Courts Act 1980, so far as it is material to this case, is
in these terms:

> 'Where any person disobeys an order of a magistrates' court made under an Act   *e*
> passed after 31st December 1879 to do anything other than the payment of money
> or to abstain from doing anything the court may ... (b) commit him to custody
> until he has remedied his default or for a period not exceeding 2 months ...'

By s 150(1):

> '... "commit to custody" means commit to prison or, where any enactment   *f*
> authorises or requires committal to some other place of detention instead of
> committal to prison, to that other place ...'

By s 133(1):

> 'A magistrates' court imposing imprisonment on any person may order that the
> term of imprisonment shall commence on the expiration of any other term of   *g*
> imprisonment imposed by that or any other court ...'

By s 150(1):

> '... "impose imprisonment" means pass a sentence of imprisonment or fix a term
> of imprisonment for failure to pay any sum of money, or for want of sufficient
> distress to satisfy any sum of money, or for failure to do or abstain from doing   *h*
> anything required to be done or left undone ...'

But by that same section—

> '"sentence" does not include a committal in default of payment of any sum of
> money, or for want of sufficient distress to satisfy any sum of money, or for failure
> to do or abstain from doing anything required to be done or left undone ...'   *j*

In my opinion, this somewhat convoluted series of provisions leads to the conclusion
that, although prison or any other appropriate place of detention would be the eventual
destination of anyone 'committed to custody' under s 63(3), or who receives 'a sentence
or term of imprisonment' under any other section of the Act, a 'committal to custody' is
not the same as 'imprisonment'.

a It follows in my view that the provisions of s 133(1), which enables a magistrates' court to impose consecutive sentences of imprisonment, have no application to committals to custody under s 63(3), so that every such committal must take effect from the day on which it is ordered.

I am fortified in this conclusion by the decision in *B (B) v B (M)* [1969] 1 All ER 891, [1969] P 103 which reached a similar conclusion in regard to s 54(3) of the Magistrates' Courts Act 1952 and s 39 of the Criminal Justice Act 1967, which dealt with suspended **b** sentences. Those provisions have now been superseded respectively by s 63(3) of the Magistrates' Courts Act 1980, to which I have already referred, and, as regards suspended sentences, by s 22 of Powers of Criminal Courts Act 1973 which enables such sentences to be imposed by a court 'passing a sentence of imprisonment for a term of not more than two years'. Section 57 of the 1973 Act, moreover, also distinguishes a sentence of imprisonment from a committal 'for failure to do or abstain from doing anything **c** required to be done or left undone'.

In the result, in my opinion, the husband's contention is correct, that the two periods of a committal should have been imposed concurrently and not consecutively.

As to the other ground of appeal, I would add only that, in my opinion if it had not been abandoned by the husband, it would have been difficult if not impossible for us to have considered it on its merits having regard to the complete absence before us of any **d** information as to the justices' findings of fact either as to the events that preceded the orders made under the Domestic Proceedings and Magistrates' Courts Act 1978 or as to the subsequent events. For my part I see no reason why in this as in other cases the justices should not produce a note of the evidence that was put before them and on which they decided to commit the husband as they did and of their reasons for so doing.

e **REEVE J.** I agree that the justices had no power to commit this appellant to custody for two consecutive periods and I entirely agree with the reasons given by Sheldon J.

With regard to the practice that appears to obtain before this bench of justices I would only add this, that it seems to me extremely desirable that a note should be given of the evidence because, if an appeal is to be taken against the period of committal to custody it is quite impossible to judge whether that period is just or unjust unless one knows what **f** evidence has been given before the justices so that one can judge in its context the appropriateness of the length of the period of committal to custody. For that reason I would say that it was extremely desirable that the justices should, as a matter of practice, have a note of the evidence prepared in these cases.

The result is that the appeal is allowed, the order of the justices will be varied so that the two periods of committal will be ordered to run concurrently instead of consecutively.

Appeal allowed. Order of justices varied.

Solicitors: *Sanders & Co*, Grays Thurrock (for the husband).

Bebe Chua   Barrister.

Afovos Shipping Co SA v Pagnan and another
The Afovos

COURT OF APPEAL, CIVIL DIVISION

LORD DENNING MR, GRIFFITHS AND KERR LJJ

1, 2 MARCH 1982

Shipping – Time charterparty – Withdrawal of vessel for non-payment of hire – Punctual payment – Anti-technicality clause – Owners to give 48 hours' notice of withdrawal of ship – Payment not made on due date – Owners giving notice of withdrawal of ship if payment not received – Notice of withdrawal given at end of banking hours on due date of payment – Whether default occurring at end of banking hours or at midnight on due date – Whether owners' notice to rectify valid – Whether terms of notice sufficiently clear.

By a time charterparty dated 8 February 1978 in the New York Produce Exchange form, the owners chartered a vessel to the charterers for a period of two years. Under the terms of the charterparty hire was payable semi-monthly in advance at a designated bank in London. In the event of the charterers failing to pay the hire punctually and regularly, the owners were to be at liberty to withdraw the vessel from hire. The charterparty further provided by cl 31, an 'anti-technicality' clause, that if the hire was not received 'When . . . due' the owners were to give the charterers 48 hours' notice to rectify the default before exercising the right of withdrawal. The charterers paid hire punctually until the end of May 1979 but the credit transfer from the charterers' bank of the next instalment, due on 14 June, did not reach the owners' bank on that date because of an error by both banks. At 1640 hrs on 14 June the owners' agents sent a telex to the charterers stating that they had been instructed 'in case we do not receive the hire which is due today' to give notice to the charterers under cl 31 of the charterparty of withdrawal of the vessel. The instalment due was not received by the owners within 48 hours of the telex and the owners accordingly claimed to be entitled to withdraw the vessel. The charterers, relying on the general rule that payment was not due until midnight on the due date for payment, contended that the telex sent by the owners' agents was premature and that, in any event, the telex was insufficiently clear in its terms for it to be an effective notice under cl 31. The owners claimed that, where payment was to be made to a specified bank, the time at which hire became overdue was the time at which normal banking hours closed. The judge held that the hire was due on the last day for payment and that a notice given at any time on that day constituted a proper notice to rectify. The judge accordingly held that the owners were entitled to withdraw the vessel. The charterers appealed.

Held – The appeal would be allowed for the following reasons—

(1) Applying the general rule of law that when payment had to be made on a certain day it could, in the absence of any usage to the contrary, be made at any time up to midnight of that day, the charterers were not in default until midnight on the due date for payment, even though payment was to be made at a London bank whose normal banking hours ended before that time. It followed that notice to rectify could not be given under cl 31 of the charterparty in advance of midnight on 14 June. Accordingly the notice given by the owners' agents was premature and therefore ineffective (see p 21 *f* to p 22 *b* and *h*, p 23 *g* to *j*, p 25 *c f*, p 26 *b* to *j* and p 27 *b*, post); *Startup v Macdonald* (1843) 6 Man & G 593 applied; *Maredelanto Compania Naviera SA v Bergbau-Handel GmbH, The Mihalis Angelos* [1970] 3 All ER 125 considered.

(2) (Per Lord Denning MR and Griffiths LJ) Furthermore, notice to rectify given under an anti-technicality clause had to be clear, definite and absolute and could only be issued

after a breach of the obligation to pay the hire. Since the notice given by the owners'
a agents was a conditional notice intended to operate if payment was not received it was
thus capable of being construed as being merely a warning that notice of withdrawal
would be given if payment of hire was not made in time rather than as an unambiguous
statement of intention to withdraw the vessel. It followed therefore that the notice was
not an effective notice under cl 31, and the owners were accordingly not entitled to
withdraw the vessel from hire (see p 22 *c g h* and p 25 *c* to *f*, post).

b
Notes

For withdrawal of a ship for non-payment of hire, see 35 Halsbury's Laws (3rd edn) 281,
para 423, and for cases on the subject, see 41 Digest (Repl) 229, 532–539.

Cases referred to in judgments

c *Empresa Cubana de Fletes v Lagonisi Shipping Co Ltd* [1971] 1 All ER 193, [1971] 1 QB 488,
[1971] 2 WLR 221, CA, Digest (Cont Vol D) 819, 482a.
Italmare Shipping Co v Ocean Tanker Co Inc, The Rio Sun [1982] 1 All ER 517, [1982] 1 WLR
158, CA.
Mardorf Peach & Co Ltd v Attica Sea Carriers Corp of Liberia, The Laconia [1977] 1 All ER
545, [1977] AC 850, [1977] 2 WLR 286, HL; *rvsg* [1976] 2 All ER 249, [1976] QB 835,
d [1976] 2 WLR 668, CA, Digest (Cont Vol E) 547, 539d.
Maredelanto Compania Naviera SA v Bergbau-Handel GmbH, The Mihalis Angelos [1970] 3 All
ER 125, [1971] 1 QB 164, [1970] 3 WLR 601, CA, 12 Digest (Reissue) 420, 3059.
Startup v Macdonald (1843) 6 Man & G 593, 134 ER 1029, Ex Ch, 12 Digest (Reissue)
396, 2886.

e ### Cases also cited

A/S Tankexpress v Compagnie Financiere Belge des Petroles SA [1948] 2 All ER 939, [1949]
AC 76, HL.
Bremer Handelsgesellschaft mbH v Vanden Avenne-Izegem PVBA [1978] 2 Lloyd's Rep 109,
HL.
Fox v Jolly [1916] 1 AC 1, HL.
f *Momm v Barclays Bank International Ltd* [1976] 3 All ER 588, [1977] QB 790.
Toepfer v Cremer [1975] 2 Lloyd's Rep 118, CA.

Appeal

Romano Pagnan and Pietro Pagnan, trading as R Pagnan & Flli, the charterers, appealed
from the decision of Lloyd J dated 19 June 1980 declaring (i) that Afovos Shipping Co
g SA, the owners of the motor vessel Afovos were entitled under the terms of a charterparty
dated 8 February 1978 to withdraw the vessel from service, (ii) that the owners had given
valid notice of withdrawal under the terms of the charterparty and (iii) that they had
effectively withdrawn the vessel. The facts are set out in the judgment of Lord Denning
MR.

h Kenneth Rokison QC and Richard Wood for the charterers.
Anthony Hallgarten QC and Martin Moore-Bick for the owners.

LORD DENNING MR. In time charterparties there is very often a clause giving the
shipowners the right to withdraw the vessel from service in case the charterer fails to
make regular and punctual payments of hire. This is called a 'withdrawal clause'. When
j market rates are rising shipowners look at the time of payment very keenly. If the
charterer falls behind, even by a second or two by the slightest mischance, the shipowner
will seize the opportunity and issue a notice of withdrawal. As a rule there is no actual
withdrawal because of the difficulties which would arise for the cargo owners, with the
bills of lading, and the like. After the notice of withdrawal is given, in nine cases out of
ten the parties agree to go on just as before. If it turns out that notice of withdrawal was

rightly given, the charterer will pay the increased market rate. If it was wrongly given, then the rate remains the same.   *a*

In order to avoid the strict and literal interpretation which the House of Lords has given to the effect of the withdrawal clause, in many cases an anti-technicality clause has been introduced into charterparties. It is that clause, in the charterparty in this case, which comes for consideration today.

Before I come to deal with the interpretation of this clause, I will set out the facts of the case. The charterparty was dated 8 February 1978. It was between owners in Panama   *b* (Afovos Shipping Co, a Greek group) and charterers in Padua, Italy (the Pagnan brothers, a well-known Italian firm of charterers). The charterparty was for two years, three months more or less in charterers' option. Delivery was made on 14 February 1978. It was on the New York Produce Exchange form. Clauses 5 and 31 are the two clauses in question in this case. Clause 5 says:

> 'Payment of said hire to be made in London to the FIRST NATIONAL BANK OF   *c* CHICAGO, 1, Royal Exchange Building, Cornhill, London EC3P 3DR for the credit of ANGELICOUSSIS SHIPHOLDING GROUP LIMITED, account No. 6060202036 in cash in United States Currency, semi-monthly in advance . . . otherwise failing the punctual and regular payment of the hire . . . the Owners shall be at liberty to withdraw the vessel from the service of the Charterers . . .'
>   *d*

That is the withdrawal clause. Then cl 31, the anti-technicality clause, was added in type:

> 'When hire is due and not received the Owners, before exercising the option of withdrawing the vessel from the Charter-Party, will give Charterers fortyeight hours notice, Saturdays, Sundays and Holidays excluded and will not withdraw the vessel if the hire is paid within these fortyeight hours.'
>   *e*

The semi-monthly payment which gave rise to this case was due on 14 June 1979. The charterers made arrangements in good time with their bank at Padua for the payment to be made. On 11 June 1979 Pagnan sent this message to Credito Italiano in Padua:

> 'Please arrange for the following telex remittance on our instructions and for our account: U.S.$53,308 (fifty three thousand three hundred and eight United States   *f* dollars) in favour of: ANGELICOUSSIS SHIPHOLDING GROUP LIMITED . . .'

I will not read the whole telex: but it was in exact conformity with the clause. Payment was to be made through the First National Bank of Chicago in London 'as payment hire vessel "AFOVOS"'. They enclosed the charterparty which they asked to be returned to them duly validated.
                                                                                        g
Credito Italiano in Padua did everything in order to get the payment through in due time. They sent a telex to the First National Bank of Chicago in London, and a telex to the bank in Chicago itself asking them to credit the London bank with $53,308.

Although everything was done in due time, a misfortune occurred. The owners' bank had three telex numbers in the directory of telexes. Anyone who wanted to telex them in London could operate any of those numbers. Unfortunately the last of the three   *h* numbers had been given up in 1975. But the directory of telexes had not been rectified accordingly. The result was that after Credito Italiano in Padua had dialled the first two numbers and failed to get through, they then tried the third number. That number had been given to a firm of sand suppliers in Reigate in Surrey. So the telex message did not get to the First National Bank of Chicago in London at all. It was an error. The Italian bank did not check to see if the message had got through. So both banks were to blame   *j* for the credit transfer not arriving in London in due time by 14 June. We now know that the mistake was discovered later and the credit transfer was made on 19 June. But that is said to be too late.

I now come to the crucial matters in dispute in this case. The first is the telex which is said to be a good notice of withdrawal. It was sent at 1640 hrs on 14 June:

a 'Owners have instructed us that in case we do not receive the hire which is due today, to give charterers notice as per cl. 31 of the charter party for withdrawal of the vessel from their service.'

That was sent at 1640 hrs on Thursday, 14 June. Friday, 15 June, came and went. The Saturday and Sunday, 16 and 17 June, were excluded. Then on Monday, 18 June, at 1920 hrs this telex was sent by the owners:

b 'Please note that owing to charterers failure to pay hire due on the 14 June 79 punctually as per the above quoted charter party owners having already given charterers forty-eight hours notice under clause of the charter party have now withdrawn vessel from service of charterers as from 1900 hours London time 18th June 79.'

c It was signed by Mr Kohler, a director of the Agelef Shipping Co, by authority of the owners.

That withdrawal was not operated because, by arrangement between the parties, the vessel continued in service. It was left to the decision of the courts whether the withdrawal was effective, in which case a higher market rate would have to be paid. If it was ineffective, the lower rate of hire would be payable. We are told that the difference comes to $2½m.

d The judge held that the withdrawal was effective and good. There was argument before him whether there should be relief from forfeiture. He held that, in the circumstances, there should not be. He held in favour of the owners that the higher market rate should be payable after the date of withdrawal. Now there is an appeal to this court.

e As I have said, the case depends on the construction of cll 5 and 31. It is largely a matter of impression. The judge said in his judgment:

'By cl 31 notice may be given as soon as hire is "due". When is hire "due" under the charterparty? It seems to me that it is due on the last day for payment. It follows that the notice could be given at any time on 14 June. By 15 June the hire was not due but overdue.'

f I am sorry to say that I cannot agree with that interpretation of the anti-technicality clause. Clause 5 of the charterparty states that the owners shall be at liberty to withdraw the vessel 'failing the punctual and regular payment of the hire'. When does the failure occur? It seems to me that, in this case, the failure occurred at midnight on 14–15 June. The general rule of law was well stated by Patteson J in *Startup v Macdonald* (1843) 6 Man & G 593 at 619, 134 ER 1029 at 1040:

g 'I apprehend the general rule of law to be, that where a thing is to be done on a certain day, it may be done at any time before twelve o'clock at night, unless there be any particular usage [to the contrary].'

h So in this case the last moment for payment was at midnight on 14 June unless there was any usage to the contrary. What would be usage to the contrary? It is suggested that in ordinary banking practice in London the telexes would only be received and processed on that day if they had been received by 3 pm within banking hours. The judge said that they might be processed in exceptional circumstances, on a special request, up until 5 pm when the banks close. But they would not be processed except in the most unusual circumstances after 5 pm.

j Although that may be well understood to be normal banking practice, nevertheless it seems to me that the general rule of law applies that a default only occurs at midnight on the due date for payment.

I now turn to cl 31. Reading into it the general rule of law, it seems to me that the clause should be interpreted in this way: when hire is due and is not received by midnight on 14–15 June the owners, before exercising the option of withdrawing the vessel, will give the charterers 48 hours' notice etc. It seems to me that the notice cannot be given in advance of midnight. It may be that the owner can see beforehand that the transfer   *a* cannot be processed on that day. Nevertheless, he must wait. A parallel situation arose-in *Maredelanto Compania Naviera SA v Bergbau-Handel GmbH, The Mihalis Angelos* [1970] 3 All ER 125, [1971] 1 QB 164, where the majority of the court held that there could not be an anticipatory determination of the contract even though it was impossible for the vessel to get there in time. In order to operate the cancelling clause, the owners had to wait until the failure occurred.   *b*

It seems to me that a like principle applies here. The notice could not be given until after the last moment for payment, ie midnight on 14 June.

That is sufficient to decide this case. Suppose that after midnight a good notice was given, the 48 hours would not expire until midnight on Monday, because Saturday and Sunday were excluded. The notice was bad because it was given too soon.

But I think that the charterers' second point was right. This notice was a conditional   *c* notice. It was only to operate 'in case we do not receive payment'. That is not a good notice. A notice must be clear, definite and absolute and given at a time after the default has occurred.

This is almost the first anti-technicality clause we have had to consider. But we did consider it in *Italmare Shipping Co v Ocean Tanker Co Inc, The Rio Sun* [1982] 1 All ER 517 at 522, [1982] 1 WLR 158 at 164, where I agreed with the arbitrator when he said: *d*

'A notice under cl 30 [cl 31 in this case] need not be legally perfect in its draftsmanship, but it must be clear beyond doubt that the owners are putting the charterers on notice that, if the correct hire is not paid within the 48 hours' grace, they will withdraw the vessel.'

That seems to me to be the right approach to these clauses. They are inserted in case   *e* something has gone wrong causing the charterer to fail to make payment on the due date. The notice is to be given to the charterer so that he may have an opportunity of putting things right within 48 hours. The anti-technicality clause comes in to relieve the charterer from forfeiture.

The judge went into the question of relief against forfeiture. But that does not arise in the present case. This question was raised in *Mardorf Peach & Co Ltd v Attica Sea Carriers*   *f* *Corp of Liberia, The Laconia* [1977] 1 All ER 545, [1977] AC 850 by the House of Lords. It was not raised in the Court of Appeal (see [1976 2 All ER 249, [1976] 2 QB 835), but, when I was drafting my judgment, I wrote a passage saying that I was in favour of granting relief from forfeiture. My two colleagues (Lawton and Bridge LJJ), however, told me that I had better not include that passage, because the point had not been argued before us. I gave way to their wishes and excluded it from my judgment. So that trifling   *g* contribution to law reform is lost to the law reports!

To return to the anti-technicality clause, the withdrawal notice cannot be given until after the default has occurred. It cannot be given conditionally. It has to be clear, definite and absolute. The owners in this case did not give a good notice. So they cannot claim to withdraw the vessel.

I would allow the appeal and find in favour of the charterers.   *h*

GRIFFITHS LJ. As appears from the facts stated by Lord Denning MR, the charterers through no fault of their own failed to pay one instalment of hire in time. It should have been paid not later than 14 June 1979 but, due to a chapter of accidents, it was not received by the owners until after the owners had given notice of withdrawal of the vessel as from 1920 hrs on Monday, 18 June. If the owners were entitled to withdraw the   *j* vessel, this mistake in payment will, we are told, cost the charterers some $US2½m, because rates were much higher in June 1979 than at the time the vessel was originally chartered in February 1978. The $2½m represents the additional sum that would have to be paid to charter the ship for the remaining period of the charterparty at the then market rate as opposed to the contract rate.

This is one of those cases where owners seek to withdraw the vessel not because of any
a genuine fear that the charterers will not pay the hire, but because if they can take
advantage of a late payment of hire, however trivial the time, they will be able to
renegotiate the remainder of the hire at the prevailing higher market rate. I do not
suggest in saying that that the owners were guilty of any sharp practice. Indeed the judge
has gone out of his way expressly to exonerate them of any such suggestion; it was just a
matter of business, a matter of very hard business.

b Clause 5 of the charterparty gives the owner the right to withdraw the vessel failing
punctual payment of hire. The courts have construed such a clause as meaning that the
owner can without notice withdraw his vessel if for whatever reason the payment of hire
is late no matter how short the period of delay may be. So, for a trivial delay, resulting
from a genuine mistake, causing no hardship to the owners, the charterer may suffer a
grievous loss. In order to mitigate the obvious hardship to charterers of such a rule, the
c commercial community now incorporates in charterparties a further clause, known as
an anti-technicality clause, which requires the owner to give the charterers notice of late
payment and a further short period to make payment before the vessel can be withdrawn.

This appeal is concerned with the true construction of the anti-technicality clause in
this charterparty. But before turning to that clause it is first necessary to consider cl 5
which imposes the liability to pay hire. It reads:

d
'Payment of said hire to be made in London to the FIRST NATIONAL BANK OF
chicago, 1, Royal Exchange Buildings, Cornhill, London EC3P 3DR for the credit
of ANGELICOUSSIS SHIPHOLDING GROUP LIMITED, account No. 6060202036 in cash in
United States Currency, semi-monthly in advance, and for the last half month part
or same the approximate amount of hire, and should same not cover the actual time,
hire is to be paid for the balance day by day, as it becomes due, if so required by
e Owners, unless bank guarantee or deposit is made by the Charterers, otherwise
failing the punctual and regular payment of the hire, or bank guarantee, or on any
breach of this Charter Party, the Owners shall be at liberty to withdraw the vessel
from the service of the Charterers, without prejudice to any claim they (the Owners)
may otherwise have on the Charterers.'

f Because payment has to be made to a London bank the owners submit that the last
moment for payment of a semi-monthly instalment is at the close of banking hours on
the last date for payment. In this case they say that means either 3.00 pm on 14 June at
which time the bank ceases to take money over the counter or, alternatively, some later
time before 4.40 pm, by which time they say no money could realistically have been
paid by telex to the owner's account.

g The general rule is that when a payment has to be made on a certain day it can be
made at any time up to midnight on that day: see *Startup v Macdonald* (1843) 6 Man & G
593, 134 ER 1029. Provided the charterers have paid before midnight on 14 June then,
applying the general rule, they have paid the instalment semi-monthly in advance as
prescribed by the charterparty; and for myself I can see no reason to cut down that period
because payment has to be made to a named bank. It is of course true that in the ordinary
h course of things payment to be effective will have to be made during banking hours, but
in an emergency it is not difficult to envisage special arrangements being made for the
bank to receive a payment after hours, especially if a sum such as $2½m may depend on
the making of such an arrangement.

Although this point was not argued before them, Donaldson J in *Empresa Cubana de
Fletes v Lagonisi Shipping Co Ltd* [1971] 1 QB 488 at 493 and Lord Russell in *Mardorf Peach
j & Co Ltd v Attica Sea Carriers Corp of Liberia, The Laconia* [1977] 1 All ER 545 at 565,
[1977] AC 850 at 887 both assumed that the charterers had until midnight on the last
day to make payment, and I would so construe the charterers' obligation in this clause. It
seems to me far preferable that so important an obligation, with such momentous
consequences hanging on its discharge, should be fixed at the certain time of midnight
rather than it should depend on the particular hours of business of a particular bank

named in the charterparty which are likely, of course, to vary from country to country
and even from bank to bank and to be a ready source of confusion.   *a*
  I turn now to the anti-technicality clause. It reads:

> 'When hire is due and not received the Owners, before exercising the option of
> withdrawing the vessel from the Charter-Party, will give Charterers fortyeight
> hours notice, Saturdays, Sundays and Holidays excluded and will not withdraw the
> vessel if the hire is paid within these fortyeight hours.'   *'b*

  The owners purported to give notice under cl 31 at 1640 hrs on 14 June. Assuming
for the moment that the form of the notice was good, the charterers say it was premature
because the owners cannot give notice until the charterers are in breach of their obligation
to pay. The purpose of the notice, say the charterers, is firstly to inform the charterer that
he has failed to make a payment by the due date and then to give him a period of 48
hours' grace in which to pay. At first blush it might appear rather naive to say that the   *c*
charterers need to be told that they have not paid the owners. But this is not the case;
payments of this kind are normally made by telex through a number of banks, and it
may well be that through some slip-up the money does not arrive in the owner's account
as quickly as the charterer has the right to expect. Once the charterer has instructed his
bank to pay, he has no further direct control over the payment which is then in the
banking chain. The charterer in this case gave his bank in Italy instructions to pay on 11   *d*
June, which should have been ample time for payment to be made by 14 June, but, as
we know, payment was not made by 18 June. I therefore accept that charterers do require
to be told by the owners that payment has not been received. There is little point in
telling the charterer that payment has not been received until the time for payment has
expired; if the charterer is told that payment has not been received before the time for
payment has expired, he may not realise the urgency of the matter and continue to   *e*
expect that the payment will be credited in time. On the other hand, if he is told after
the time for payment has expired, he will realise he is in breach and has only 48 hours in
which to save himself.
  The owners submit that the object of the clause is not to give the charterers a period of
48 hours' grace after breach of their obligation but to give a warning to the charterers on
the last day that payment is due that if they do not pay in 48 hours the vessel will be   *f*
withdrawn. If this is the right construction, it leaves the charterer in the difficulty of not
knowing whether or not the owners have in fact received payment, and gives a shorter
period than 48 hours to rectify any failure to meet his obligation to make payment.
  In my judgment the opening words of cl 31 show that the charterers' construction is
correct. What is meant by 'When hire is due and not received'? I accept counsel for the
charterers' construction that it means that the hire ought to have been paid and has not   *g*
been paid; or, to put it another way, that the hire has not been paid by the deadline. To
say that the hire is due on 14 June and therefore that a notice can be given at any time on
that day fails to give any proper weight to the words 'and not received'. If at 9.00 am on
14 June the owner were to say to the charterer, 'I have not received the hire,' the charterer,
knowing that he had given his bank instructions some days before, might reply, 'So what
is the fuss? You'll get it in time.' It is only after the time for payment has passed that the   *h*
fact that the money has not been received becomes of contractual significance. I have no
doubt that the words are intended to be of contractual significance and only by adopting
the charterers' construction is this achieved.
  Support for the charterers' construction is also to be derived from the use of the word
'before' in the phrase 'before exercising the option', which presupposes that but for the
need to give 48 hours' notice the owner would have the right to withdraw the vessel.   *j*
And such a right only arises under cl 5 once the time for payment of the instalment of
hire is passed and the charterer is in breach of his obligation.
  Then I ask myself: which result are commercial men likely to have intended? A
construction that results in a simple situation expressed thus: 'You haven't paid up when
you should have done; pay in 48 hours or lose the ship'? Or a construction that gives this
result: 'I warn you that, although the final time for payment has not yet arrived, I have

not yet received payment, and if I do not receive payment when I should, then you will
a lose the ship if you don't pay me what you owe me in the extra time this notice gives you
which is calculated by adding to your deadline for payment so many hours of this 48-
hour notice as have not expired by the final time for payment'? I suppose they would
prefer the first construction.

Finally, if notice can be given before the charterer is in default, it does little more than
add some unspecified period of less than 48 hours to the time for payment. It does not
b give the charterer notice that he is in default, nor does it give him a period of grace.

We were also referred to the decision of the majority of the Court of Appeal in
Maredelanto Compania Naviera SA v Bergbau-Handel GmbH, The Mihalis Angelos [1970] 3 All
ER 125, [1971] 1 QB 164, but I do not myself think that much is to be learned from a
decision on the construction of a different clause in another charterparty. But at least it
can be said that, if anything, it supports rather than detracts from the charterers'
c argument.

I would therefore hold that the notice given at 1640 hrs on 14 June was not a notice
pursuant to cl 31 because such a notice can only be issued after breach of the obligation
to pay the hire. It must therefore follow that the owners were not entitled to withdraw
the vessel on Monday, 18 June.

If necessary I would also hold that the telex sent at 1640 hrs on 14 June was not a
d sufficient notice. It reads:

> 'Owners have instructed us that in case we do not receive the hire which is due
> today, to give charterers notice as per cl. 31 of the charter party for withdrawal of
> the vessel from their service.'   .

This notice does not say that there has been a failure to pay in time; it is capable of
e being construed as a warning that if payment is not made in time a notice of withdrawal
will be given. Withdrawal is so serious a matter for the charterer that it is the duty of the
owner to give a clear and unambiguous notice of his intention to withdraw the ship. It
should state that payment has not been received and give the charterer 48 hours to pay
or lose the ship: see the observations of Lord Denning MR in *Italmare Shipping Co v Ocean
Tanker Co Inc, The Rio Sun* [1982] 1 All ER 517 at 522, [1982] 1 WLR 158 at 164. Of
f course no special wording is required, but it is surely not too much to expect men of
commerce dealing in huge sums to make their meaning clear.

I would allow the appeal.

KERR LJ. I agree that this appeal should be allowed, and only add some remarks of my
g own in deference to Lloyd J since we are differing from him.

The object of cl 31, the so-called anti-technicality clause, is clearly to mitigate the
strictness of the primary clause, cl 5, which entitles the owners to withdraw without
notice 'failing the punctual . . . payment of hire'. It obliges the owners to give to the
charterers a further chance of paying within the time limited by a 48-hour notice, and it
was common ground before us that the 48 hours start to run from the time of the notice
h (whether when sent or received does not arise here) and not from some later time.

The judge focused on the words 'When hire is due' and on the fact, with which I agree,
that in ordinary parlance the hire was 'due' on 14 June. He therefore based his reasoning
on the view that the notice could be given at any time on 14 June. Counsel for the
owners then logically had to submit, as he did, that the notice could have been given as
early as, say, 8.00 am, with the result that the 48-hour notice period would begin to run
j as from then.

However, I cannot agree with this first step of the argument in the light of the
remainder of the clause and of its clear business purpose, and it does not appear to me,
with respect, that any sufficient weight was given to these by the judge. The very next
words, 'and not received', by themselves suggest that at least the business part of the 'due'
day, 14 June, if not the whole day until midnight, must have passed before the notice
can be given. But, if there were any remaining doubt, this is in my view conclusively

resolved by the following words which go still further in indicating the business purpose
of the clause. The words 'before exercising the option of withdrawing the vessel' throw   a
one back to cl 5 and to the question: when would the owners' option of withdrawing the
vessel have first arisen but for cl 31? As Lord Wilberforce said in *Mardorf Peach & Co Ltd
v Attica Sea Carriers Corp of Liberia, The Laconia* [1977] 1 All ER 545 at 550, [1977] AC 850
at 870, an owner has to show that the conditions necessary to entitle him to withdraw
have been strictly complied with. In my view this right did not arise until the charterers
were clearly in breach, and the charterers were not in breach of their obligation to pay   b
the hire until midnight of the final or 'due' day, 14 June. In the absence of a binding
custom to the contrary, the general rule is that, if an act must be done on or before a
certain day, there is no breach until midnight of the last day; albeit that, where
performance requires the co-operation of another party, the obligee cannot complain if
the other party is unavailable at a time of day which is unreasonable in the circumstances:
see *Startup v Macdonald* (1843) 6 Man & G 593, 134 ER 1029. This conclusion accords   c
with what was said both by Donaldson J in *Empresa Cubana de Fletes v Lagonisi Shipping Co
Ltd* [1971] 1 QB 488 at 493, and by Lord Russell in *The Laconia* [1977] 1 All ER 545 at
565, [1977] AC 850 at 887, and also with what one would expect from the wording of
the charter and the policy of the law which generally takes no account of broken days,
viz that the charterers were not in breach until the whole of 14 June had passed.

It follows in my judgment that the owners' option to withdraw under cl 5 did not   d
arise until immediately after midnight on 14–15 June and that the 48 hours' notice
under cl 31 could equally not be given before then.

This construction gives certainty and clarity to the clause. The owners' construction,
on the other hand, creates uncertainty for at least two reasons. First, it leaves it open to
the owners to determine arbitrarily as from any time on 14 June when the 48 hours are
to begin and therefore to end. Second, it enables the owners to give the notice at a time   e
when it may as yet be uncertain whether or not the hire will still be received on 14 June,
whereas the clear object of cl 31 is that the notice is only to be given when the hire is
both due and unreceived. This double condition cannot be satisfied with total certainty
until midnight, and the commercial probabilities would depend on when a particular
bank ceased to process incoming telexes on a particular day. The latter time is flexible
and uncertain and in my view produces an unsatisfactory criterion in any event. But,   f
even if one takes the probable close of all banking business as the criterion, the owners'
primary argument postulates, as already mentioned, that on the true construction of
cl 31 the notice could in fact have been given at any earlier time on that day, when the
hire might well still be received thereafter, and this I cannot accept.

I therefore conclude that on the true construction of cl 31 a notice under this provision
could not be given before midnight on 14 June. But even if I should be wrong about   g
this, I would also reject the owners' alternative argument that the notice given at 1640
hrs was given at a time when the charterers were in breach by reference to the commercial
possibilities. On the findings of Lloyd J as to the practice of this particular bank, a notice
given at 1640 hrs was in my view still premature, because by then it had not yet become
wholly impossible for the hire to be received thereafter. In this connection the close of
all banking business is not to be equated with ordinary banking hours for transactions   h
over the counter, and on the judge's findings the close of all banking business for the
purposes of receiving and processing transfers of money by telex had not yet necessarily
and finally occurred by 1640 hrs. It should also be noted that the wording of the notice
itself does not exclude the possibility of the hire still being received thereafter.

Finally, I do not accept that the earliest permissible time for giving the cl 31 notice can
be advanced by relying on the doctrine of anticipatory breach. This may arise in the   j
context of repudiation. But there was clearly no repudiation by the charterers in this
case.

In these circumstances, I find it unnecessary to deal with counsel for the charterers'
further argument that this was in any event only a provisional or conditional notice,
because in my view this really stands or falls with the view which one takes in the first
place whether the notice could have been given at any time on 14 June, which I have

a rejected. It seems to me that the argument merely serves to demonstrate the difficulties which arise if the notice can be given when it is still uncertain whether the hire will be received or not, since the notice is then likely to be expressed in a conditional sense, as here, so as to lead to uncertainty. Still less do I find it necessary to deal with any issue concerning the possibility of relief against forfeiture in this context, which has not been argued and does not in my view arise.

Accordingly I would allow this appeal.

b
Appeal allowed. Leave to appeal to the House of Lords refused.

6 May. The Appeal Committee of the House of Lords granted the owners leave to appeal.

Solicitors: *Middleton, Potts & Co* (for the charterers); *Constant & Constant* (for the owners).

c
Diana Procter   Barrister.

d
R v Reilly

COURT OF APPEAL, CRIMINAL DIVISION
KERR LJ, PETER PAIN AND BELDAM JJ
16 MARCH 1982

e *Criminal law – Bankruptcy order – Jurisdiction to make order – Conviction of conspiracy to defraud – Acts committed in pursuance of conspiracy resulting in loss – Whether loss suffered 'as a result of the offence' of conspiracy – Powers of Criminal Courts Act 1973, s 39(1)(a).*

Crown Court – Order – Amendment – Jurisdiction – Criminal bankruptcy order – Judge imposing sentence on accused for conspiracy to defraud – Judge making criminal bankruptcy order against accused after pronouncement of sentence – Whether judge having jurisdiction to *f* *'vary' sentence by making criminal bankruptcy order – Courts Act 1971, s 11(2).*

On 25 March 1981 the appellant, a company director, pleaded guilty in the Crown Court to, inter alia, four counts of conspiracy to defraud the Inland Revenue. In the course of the hearing counsel for the Crown indicated that he intended to apply to the court for a criminal bankruptcy order to be made against the appellant. On the following day the *g* judge sentenced the appellant to concurrent terms of three years' imprisonment on each count, disqualified him for five years from participating in the management of any company, and ordered him to contribute to the costs of his legally-aided defence, but stated that he did not intend to make a criminal bankruptcy order. Thereupon counsel for the Crown reminded the judge that there was an application for a criminal bankruptcy order before the court and after some discussion about making such an order the judge *h* adjourned the hearing for a short time to enable counsel to place further material before the court relative to such an order. After the adjournment the judge made a criminal bankruptcy order in the sum of £178,000 against the appellant under s 39ᵃ of the Powers of Criminal Courts Act 1973. The appellant appealed against the order on the ground that the judge had no jurisdiction to make it, submitting (i) that s 39 of the 1973 Act did not give the court power to impose a criminal bankruptcy order in respect of a conviction *j* for an offence of conspiracy to defraud, because loss resulting from acts done in pursuance of a conspiracy was suffered as a result of the acts themselves and not the offence of conspiracy (which was merely an agreement to do those acts) and therefore the loss had not been suffered 'as a result of the offence', that being a precondition set out in s 39(1)(a)

---

a   Section 39, so far as material, is set out at p 30 *b c*, post

to the imposition of a criminal bankruptcy order, and (ii) that the judge had completed sentencing before the adjournment and was not entitled, under the power in s 11(2)[b] of *a* the Courts Act 1971 to 'vary' a sentence within 28 days of it being imposed, fundamentally to change and increase the severity of the sentence already imposed by adding the criminal bankruptcy order.

Held – The appeal would be dismissed for the following reasons—

(1) Where conspirators agreed as part of a conspiracy to commit acts which were liable *b* to cause loss or damage to another and the acts were in fact committed as part of the conspiracy any loss or damage thereby suffered was, on the commonsense meaning of the words, suffered 'as a result of the offence' within s 39(1)(a) of the 1973 Act. Furthermore, the conspiracy continued to exist while the acts were being carried out even though the offence of conspiracy was committed and completed when the conspirators made their agreement, and therefore loss or damage arising out of the actions of the conspirators was suffered 'as a result of' the conspiracy. The judge had *c* therefore had jurisdiction under s 39(1) to impose a criminal bankruptcy order on the accused (see p 34 *j* to p 35 *b* and *f g*, post); DPP v Doot [1973] 1 All ER 940, dictum of Lawton LJ in *R v Thomson Holidays Ltd* [1974] 1 All ER at 829 and *R v Howell* (1978) 66 Cr App R 179 applied; dictum of Lord Diplock in *R v Cuthbertson* [1980] 2 All ER at 405 explained.

(2) Further, applying a wide interpretation of the power to 'vary' a sentence contained *d* in s 11(2) of the 1971 Act, which was not, therefore, limited to the alteration of mere slips of the tongue or memory but which included, as a matter of law, any variation of sentence which might be made in the circumstances of a particular case, the judge had had jurisdiction under s 11(2) to impose a criminal bankruptcy order on the appellant after the completion of sentence on him (see p 31 *h*, p 32 *c* to *f* and p 35 *g*, post); *R v Sodhi* (1978) 66 Cr App R 260 and dicta of Lord Scarman and Lord Edmund-Davies in *R v* *e* *Menocal* [1979] 2 All ER at 516, 520–521 applied; *R v Grice* (1977) 66 Cr App R 167 not followed.

Notes

For criminal bankruptcy orders, see 11 Halsbury's Laws (4th edn) para 803.

For variation of a sentence imposed by the Crown Court, see ibid para 333–350.   *f*

For the Courts Act 1971, s 11, see 41 Halsbury's Statutes (3rd edn) 299.

For the Powers of Criminal Courts Act 1973, s 39, see 43 ibid 334.

As from 1 January 1982 s 11 of the 1971 Act was replaced by s 47 of the Supreme Court Act 1981.

Cases referred to in judgment

DPP v Doot [1973] 1 All ER 940, [1973] AC 807, [1973] 2 WLR 532, HL, 14(1) Digest *g* (Reissue) 120, 801.

R v Cuthbertson [1980] 2 All ER 401, [1981] AC 470, [1980] 3 WLR 89, HL.

R v Gleaves (21 April 1977, unreported), CA.

R v Grice (1977) 66 Cr App R 167, CA.

R v Howell (Anthony) (1978) 66 Cr App R 179, CA.

R v Menocal [1979] 2 All ER 510, sub nom *Customs and Excise Comrs v Menocal* [1980] AC *h* 598, [1979] 2 WLR 876, HL, Digest (Cont Vol E) 154, 9188a.

R v Sodhi (1978) 66 Cr App R 260, CA.

R v Thomson Holidays Ltd [1974] 1 All ER 823, [1974] QB 592, [1974] 2 WLR 371, CA, Digest (Cont Vol D) 985, 1100d.

Case also cited   *j*

R v Newsome, R v Browne [1970] 3 All ER 455, [1970] 2 QB 711, CA.

Appeal

On 25 March 1981 in the Crown Court at Willesden (sitting at Acton) before his Honour Judge Palmer and a jury the appellant, William Joseph Thomas Reilly, pleaded guilty to

b   Section 11(2), so far as material, is set out at p 31 *b c*, post a four counts of conspiracy to defraud the Inland Revenue and three counts of making false statements in his tax returns. On 26 March he was sentenced to concurrent terms of three years' imprisonment on each count and in addition was disqualified for five years from participating in the management of any company and ordered to contribute towards the costs of his legally-aided defence. On the same day, after a short adjournment, the judge, in relation to the counts of conspiracy to defraud, made a criminal bankruptcy order pursuant to s 39 of the Powers of Criminal Courts Acts 1973. The appellant

b appealed against the bankruptcy order on the ground that the judge did not have jurisdiction to make it because (1) having completed the pronouncement of the sentence before the adjournment, thereafter the judge did not have jurisdiction under s 11 of the Courts Act 1971 to alter the sentence pronounced by imposing the criminal bankruptcy order and (2) under s 39 of the 1973 Act there was no power to make a criminal bankruptcy order in relation to conspiracy offences. The facts are set out in the judgment

c of the court.

Brian Leary QC and Robin C Griffiths (assigned by the Registrar of Criminal Appeals) for the appellant.
Alan Hitching for the Crown.

d
KERR LJ delivered the following judgment of the court: On 25 March 1981 the appellant pleaded guilty in the Crown Court at Willesden (sitting at Acton), before his Honour Judge Palmer, to a number of offences in relation to the Inland Revenue. He pleaded guilty to four offences of conspiracy to defraud the Inland Revenue under counts 2, 3, 4 and 5, and to three further offences of making false statements in his tax returns

e under counts 8, 9 and 10. He also asked for two other similar offences to be taken into consideration.

He was sentenced to concurrent terms of three years' imprisonment on each count. In addition he was disqualified from participating in the management of any company for a period of five years. In relation to the counts of conspiracy to defraud, a criminal bankruptcy order was made against him in the total sum of £178,000 in favour of the

f Inland Revenue. He was also ordered to contribute £250 towards his legally aided defence.

It is unnecessary for the purposes of the present appeal, which relates solely to the criminal bankruptcy order, to go into the facts at any length. He appeals to this court in relation to that order by leave of the single judge.

Very briefly the facts are that between May 1975 and April 1980 the appellant carried

g on business ostensibly through the medium of a number of companies as a supplier of labour to the construction industry. The position in relation to that is that following the Finance Act 1971, when sub-contractors such as the appellant were paid, income tax was to be deducted at source. That was the procedure for paying self-employed construction workers on what is usually known as 'the lump'. However, in the case of a corporate supplier of labour, such as the appellant purported to be, gross payments could still be

h made, since it was then the responsibility of the payee to make the appropriate deductions.

Counts 2 and 3 concerned the appellant's operations in the name of two companies (Roseville Contractors Ltd and Lamadale Ltd) during different periods when he was engaged to supply labour to a company called E W Avent Ltd, from whom he received gross payments without any deduction of tax and he then failed to make the necessary deductions, being a director of both those companies.

j Counts 4 and 5 were similar in relation to two other companies (Lurkhurst Builders Ltd and Lobtone Ltd). There, although the appellant was not a director, he was a guarantor of the companies and clearly acted in the everyday management of both of them.

I need not go further into counts 8, 9 and 10, which related to failing to make appropriate tax returns, save to say that they related to another business, that of an insurance broker.

It is also unnecessary in the present context to say anything about the appellant's antecedents, save to say that the nature of the offences certainly would not make a *a* criminal bankruptcy order inappropriate if there was power to make it.

This appeal relates to the submission that for two reasons there is no power to make such an order.

The power to make a criminal bankruptcy order arises under s 39 of the Powers of Criminal Courts Act 1973. I must read parts of that provision. Subsection (1) provides:

> 'Where a person is convicted of an offence before the Crown Court and it appears *b* to the court that (*a*) as a result of the offence, or of that offence taken together with any other relevant offence or offences, loss or damage (not attributable to personal injury) has been suffered by one or more persons whose identity is known to the court; and (*b*) the amount, or aggregate amount, of the loss or damage exceeds £15,000; the court may, in addition to dealing with the offender in any other way (but not if it makes a compensation order against him), make a criminal bankruptcy *c* order against him in respect of the offence or, as the case may be, that offence and the other relevant offence or offences.'

Then I go to sub-s (3), which provides:

> 'A criminal bankruptcy order shall specify—(*a*) the amount of the loss or damage appearing to the court to have resulted from the offence or, if more than one, each *d* of the offences; (*b*) the person or persons appearing to the court to have suffered that loss or damage; (*c*) the amount of that loss or damage which it appears to the court that that person, or each of those persons, has suffered; and (*d*) the date which is to be the relevant date for the purpose of the exercise by the High Court of its powers under paragraph 10 of Schedule 2 to this Act in relation to dispositions made by the offender, being the date which appears to the court to be the earliest date on which *e* the offence or, if more than one, the earliest of the offences, was committed.'

Then it is necessary to read s 40(1), which provides: 'No appeal shall lie against the making of a criminal bankruptcy order.'

Pausing there, what is said in this case is that notwithstanding s 40(1) of the 1973 Act, an appeal (or something in the nature of an appeal) lies in this case because there was no *f* jurisdiction to make this criminal bankruptcy order. It has rightly not been submitted on behalf of the Crown that if there was no jurisdiction then this court could not interfere. Clearly, if there was no jurisdiction the order would be a nullity and would have to be set aside.

Pursuant to s 39(3), the judge made the following criminal bankruptcy order: in relation to Roseville Contractors Ltd, the earliest date of the offence committed was 1 *g* May 1975 and the tax loss was £55,000. In relation to Lamadale Ltd, the date was 30 September 1977, the sum being £8,000. In relation to Lurkhurst Builders Ltd, the date was 1 October 1977 and the sum was £80,000, and in relation to Lobtone Ltd, the date was 1 August 1978 and the sum £35,000. This made a total tax loss of £178,000. The loser (the person injured or damaged in each case) was stated to be the Inland Revenue. Accordingly a criminal bankruptcy order in the total sum of £178,000 was made against *h* the appellant, which is now the subject matter of this appeal.

There are two grounds on which this appeal is put forward. The first arises as follows. Although counsel for the Crown had at an early stage of the hearing, when the appellant pleaded guilty, made it clear that he would invite the court to make a criminal bankruptcy order, this was not in fact done when the judge came to sentence the appellant. He then sentenced him to three years' imprisonment concurrent, as I have *j* already said, as well as to the disqualification under the Companies Act 1948. I need not read what he said on that occasion. But he then also said that he did not propose to make any criminal bankruptcy order and he dealt with the costs, as I have already mentioned. Having said that, and, on the face of it, completed the pronouncement of the sentence, he was reminded by counsel on behalf of the Crown that there was an application for a

criminal bankruptcy order and counsel asked to be heard about that. There was some
a discussion about it and a measure of objection on behalf of the appellant.

Then, after a short adjournment, when certain further material was placed before the
court, the criminal bankruptcy order, in the terms which I have already mentioned, was
made.

The first ground of this appeal is that the judge, having completed the pronouncement
of the sentence, had no jurisdiction to make the criminal bankruptcy order, or, at any
b rate, should not have done so, in the light of certain authorities to which I will refer in a
moment. These turn on s 11(2) of the Courts Act 1971. Section 11(2) provides, so far as
relevant:

'. . . a sentence imposed, or other order made, by the Crown Court when dealing
with an offender may be varied or rescinded by the Crown Court within the period
c   of 28 days beginning with the day on which the sentence or other order was imposed
or made . . .'

In the present case the variation (consisting of the addition of the criminal bankruptcy
order) was made on the same day after only a short adjournment. But what is said is that
the proper interpretation of that provision is that there should be no fundamental change
d of mind, to use the phrase which was used by counsel on behalf of the appellant, by
adding to or varying a sentence, so as to make it more severe, once the sentence has been
pronounced. The case on which counsel for the appellant mainly relied for that
proposition was R v Grice (1977) 66 Cr App R 167. That was a case in which a court,
having imposed no prison sentence on a defendant in relation to a charge of unlawful
sexual intercourse with his adopted daughter, aged 16, then came to hear that, contrary
e to an undertaking which he had given to the court, he had contacted her. The court
called him back and purported then to vary the previous sentence by imposing a sentence
of immediate imprisonment. That was strongly criticised by this court, consisting of
Roskill, Waller LJJ and Ackner J, in relation to the facts of that case. It was said that what
had been done in that case, substantially increasing the sentence (indeed altering it
fundamentally), was not something which should be done under the power to vary
f within that provision. However, not only were the facts of that case wholly different
from those of the present case, since they concerned events which came to light after the
sentence had been pronounced, but the authority of that case has also been very
substantially affected by two subsequent decisions: one of this court and one of the House
of Lords.

The first of these is R v Sodhi (1978) 66 Cr App R 260. In that case the defendant had
g been convicted and sentenced to six months' imprisonment for malicous wounding.
When his medical condition in prison then gave rise to concern, he was brought back
and the court, acting under s 11(2) of the Courts Act 1971, varied the sentence to a
hospital order under s 60 of the Mental Health Act 1959, together with a restriction
order.

In giving the judgment of this court in that case Lawton LJ referred to R v Grice (1977)
h 66 Cr App R 167. Without it being necessary to go through what he said, it is clear that
this court then took a wider view of the meaning of the word 'varied' in s 11(2). In effect
it was held that 'varied' bore its ordinary meaning and that, while caution no doubt has
to be exercised in applying s 11(2), there was no limit as a matter of law on the variation
which might be made in the circumstances of a particular case.

One then comes finally to the decision of the House of Lords in R v Menocal [1979] 2
j All ER 510, [1980] AC 598. That case, apart from the very important feature concerning
the chronology, was somewhat similar to the present case, because a monetary order was
added to the sentence after this had been pronounced. The case arose under the Misuse
of Drugs Act 1971, the defendant having been arrested at an airport when she arrived,
carrying cocaine. She then had a sum of money in excess of £4,000 in her handbag. She
was charged and convicted on an offence under the 1971 Act concerning the importation

of cocaine. Her sentence was pronounced on 31 January 1977, but on 9 May 1977, and therefore nearly 3½ months later, the same judge purported to make an order under s 27   *a* of the 1971 Act, or alternatively under s 43 of the Powers of Criminal Courts Act 1973, for the forfeiture of the money which had been found in the defendant's handbag at the time of her arrest. It can be seen at once that the power in that case purported to be exercised well outside the period of 28 days. While most of the argument concerned the question whether this order of forfeiture was properly describable as a sentence, which is not relevant for present purposes, a number of statements were made concerning s 11(2),   *b* which are of considerable importance for present purposes. I attach great weight to them, seeing that they are statements made in the House of Lords, albeit, as counsel for the appellant reminded us, that they were strictly obiter. The main point of the decision was undoubtedly that there was no jurisdiction because the period of 28 days had expired.

The views concerning s 11(2) which were then expressed cannot be ignored on the ground that they were obiter, particularly in view of what had already been said in *R v*   *c* *Sodhi* (1978) 66 Cr App R 260. Again without reading at length, it is clear from the speeches of Lord Salmon and of Lord Edmund-Davies ([1979] 2 All ER 510 at 516, 520–521, [1980] AC 598 at 607, 611–612) that the narrow interpretation of the powers under s 11(2) which had been adopted in *R v Grice* (1977) 66 Cr App R 167, was not considered to be correct. Once again the word 'varied' was given its ordinary meaning. Both Lord Salmon and Lord Edmund-Davies, with whom both Lord Fraser and Lord Keith agreed,   *d* made it clear that if the order of forfeiture in that case had been made within 28 days, it would have been entirely appropriate. Lord Edmund-Davies expressly said, contrary to what had been said in *R v Grice*, to which he referred, that the power should not be restricted to mere slips of the tongue or slips of memory. He also made it clear that it is proper for the prosecution, albeit of course within the time limit, to go back to the court to ask for a variation after sentence, if in all the circumstances the prosecution takes the   *e* view that it is proper to do so.

Having reviewed those authorities, it appears to us clear almost beyond argument that the judge in this case had jurisdiction to make the order which he made. Seeing that he had jurisdiction (and indeed in our view he was perfectly right on the merits of the case to make the order) it follows from s 40(1) of the 1973 Act that there is no appeal against his order on that ground.   *f*

That disposes of the first point of this appeal.

I then turn to the second (and more substantial) one: more substantial in the sense that it is one of greater general importance. What is said is that this criminal bankruptcy order was made in relation to offences of conspiracy to defraud and that it is in the nature of a conspiracy, and I hope I do justice to the argument, that it consists merely of an agreement to do something, whereas the loss in question, on which the criminal   *g* bankruptcy order was founded, is something which does not result from the agreement which is the conspiracy itself, but from an act or acts done pursuant to that conspiracy, when those acts have not been the subject matter of any charge, let alone conviction. That is the nature of the argument. Ultimately its correctness or otherwise, apart from certain authorities to which I will refer, must turn on the words 'as a result of the offence' in s 39(1)(*a*).   *h*

The issue is therefore whether an offence of conspiracy to defraud, which (and I must not beg the question) is followed by loss or damage to somebody is an offence from which that loss or damage can be said to result so as to found a criminal bankruptcy order.

We have been helpfully referred to a number of cases in this connection. The first one is an unreported decision of this court in *R v Gleaves*, a judgment of Parker J, sitting with   *j* Lord Widgery CJ and Park J, on 21 April 1977. That is an interesting case because it concerned a conviction on a count of conspiracy to commit theft. The issue was whether in relation to that offence, of which the accused was convicted, a compensation order could properly be made under s 35 of the Powers of Criminal Courts Act 1973. That provision for present purposes is relevantly similar to s 39 with which we are here concerned. It provides, so far as material, in sub-s (1):

a
> '. . . a court by or before which a person is convicted of an offence, in addition to dealing with him in any other way, may, on application or otherwise, make an order (in this Act referred to as "a compensation order") requiring him to pay compensation for any . . . loss or damage resulting from that offence . . . '

Substituting the words 'as a result of the offence' for the words 'resulting from that offence', as to which I cannot see any distinction, one has the same issue arising in that case as we have here, albeit there in relation to an order for compensation.

b
The argument there put forward was precisely the same as that put forward today. I must read a few lines from the judgment. It referred to the fact that the defendant had money, that is to say the necessary money on which a compensation order could be founded, and went on:

c
> '. . . that is sufficient to found the order, subject to one point which was somewhat faintly suggested by counsel for the defendant, and it may be that it was one of the matters which troubled this court on the last occasion, that there was some point to be made that where there was a conspiracy only, s 35 of the 1973 Act was not in wide enough terms to allow the order to be made. That appears to us to be splitting hairs and the order can be properly, and was properly, made, under s 35.'

d
The argument there put forward was equally that by its nature a conspiracy is not something from which a loss can result on which to found, in that case, an order for compensation, and was rejected in this summary manner.

A further helpful case is the decision of this court in *R v Howell* (1978) 66 Cr App R 179. That was also concerned with an order for compensation, but not in the context of a charge of conspiracy. It was in the context of a charge of receiving stolen goods. The argument was that it could not be said that the loss to the owner resulted from the

e
offence of receiving, because it did not result from the receipt of the goods, but from their subsequent disposition by the accused. That argument was equally rejected by this court. Peter Pain J, giving the judgment of the court, referred to a judgment of Lawton LJ in *R v Thomson Holidays Ltd* [1974] 1 All ER 823, [1974] QB 592, where he had dealt with a somewhat similar issue in relation to causation in the context of a compensation

f
order. Lawton LJ there said ([1974] 1 All ER 823 at 829, [1974] QB 592 at 599):

> 'Parliament, we are sure, never intended to introduce into the criminal law the concepts of causation which apply to the assessment of damages under the law of contract and tort . . . Whenever the making of an order for compensation is appropriate the court must ask itself whether loss or damage can fairly be said to have resulted to anyone from the offence for which the accused has been convicted or has been taken into consideration.'

g
Peter Pain J then said that, looking at the offence of receiving in a commonsense way and giving an appropriate meaning to the words 'resulting from that offence', it seemed plain that the loss could be said to have resulted from the offence of receiving and that it would be far too narrow a construction to say that it only resulted from the subsequent disposition of the goods.

h
However, what counsel for the appellant submits is that these authorities have been weakened, or perhaps even set aside, by some remarks in the speech of Lord Diplock in the House of Lords in *R v Cuthbertson* [1980] 2 All ER 401, [1981] AC 470. That again concerned the Misuse of Drugs Act 1971. It was the well-known case in which there was a far-reaching conspiracy to contravene that Act by manufacturing drugs, which was successful to the extent that the perpetrators made enormous profits from this

j
manufacture and were able to put aside large sums of money. The question was whether it was proper to order a forfeiture under s 27 of the 1971 Act, in particular of the financial proceeds of the conspiracy. Section 27(1), which fell to be construed in that case, reads as follows:

> '. . . the court by or before which a person is convicted of an offence under this Act may order anything shown to the satisfaction of the court to relate to the offence,

to be forfeited and either destroyed or dealt with in such other manner as the court may order.'   *a*

The primary ground stated by Lord Diplock, with which all their Lordships agreed, as to why an order for forfeiture could not properly be made in that case, the charge having been a charge of conspiracy to manufacture drugs, was that conspiracy was not 'an offence under this Act'. The section only gives power to make an order for forfeiture in respect of offences under the Act. He said that it did not matter whether the conspiracy was a conspiracy at common law or under the Criminal Law Act 1977: it was clearly not an offence under the Misuse of Drugs Act 1971. That was the primary ground, and it is clearly irrelevant for present purposes.   *b*

Secondly, however, Lord Diplock gave a further reason for considering that the order of forfeiture could not properly be made.

This really falls into two parts. I must read a few passages from his speech. He said ([1980] 2 All ER 401 at 405, [1981] AC 470 at 473):   *c*

> 'Its [that is the provisions] evident purpose is to enable things to be forfeited so that they may be destroyed or dealt with in some other manner as the court thinks fit. The words are apt and, as it seems to me, are only apt to deal with things that are tangible, things of which physical possession can be taken by a person authorised to do so by the court and which are capable of being physically destroyed by that   *d*
> person or disposed of by him in some other way.'

Pausing there, that clearly has no bearing on the present issue. He then went on to say:

> 'So one limitation on the subject matter of an order for forfeiture is that it must be something tangible. There is also another: that what is forfeited must be shown "to relate" to an offence under the Act *of which a person has been convicted by or before*   *e*
> *the court making the order.* For the purposes of s 27 one is therefore looking for an offence which is not only an offence under the Act but also an offence which in its legal nature is of a kind to which something tangible and thus susceptible to forfeiture can be said to "relate". This cannot, in my view, be properly said of the offence of conspiracy which in its legal nature does not involve any dealing by the offender with anything tangible at all, but consists entirely of an *unperformed*   *f*
> agreement to do so. Whether he performs the agreement or does not is irrelevant to the commission of that offence. If the offender does perform it he commits a separate and distinct offence for which something tangible may quite properly be said to "relate", for that is a verb which in its ordinary meaning has wide connotations.'

I do not think I need read further, since it will be clear from this passage what the   *g*
foundation for the present argument is, which is based on that speech, though it is right to mention that Lord Scarman expressed certain reservations in regard to this passage.

In my view what Lord Diplock said in that case, albeit that it was a further ground of his decision, cannot govern the present context. He was construing s 27 of the 1971 Act. He was particularly concerned, not with words of causation, as in the present case, but   *h*
with the words 'relating to the offence' (I am slightly paraphrasing) and in the context of the need to find something 'tangible', as he put it, which could be forfeited or destroyed. That was the context.

We have to construe the words of s 39 of the 1973 Act in the light of the important authorities, two of them in this court, to which I have already referred. In our view it is clear that if the acts which conspirators agree to do are acts which are liable to cause loss   *j*
or damage someone, and if these acts are in fact done by the conspirators in pursuance of the conspiracy, then, any loss or damaged suffered as the result of those acts is also loss or damage 'as a result of the conspiracy'. That to my mind is the ordinary commonsense meaning of these wide words 'as a result of the offence'. It would be, to use Parker J's words, 'hairsplitting' to construe these words otherwise. Furthermore, although it is clearly the law that the offence of conspiracy is complete once the relevant agreement has

been made, it does not follow that it terminates with the making of the agreement;
a indeed it does not do so. Where the planned acts are in fact carried out, the conspiracy
remains in being. In this sense also, the loss or damage is clearly a result of the conspiracy,
the conspiracy still then being in existence. If authority is needed for that, it will be
found in the decision of the House of Lords in *DPP v Doot* [1973] 1 All ER 940, [1973]
AC 807. That case was concerned with a conspiracy which had been made abroad, in the
sense that the agreement had been made outside the jurisdiction of this court, but acts
b pursuant to it were then done within the jurisdiction. It is clear from the speeches of
Viscount Dilhorne, Lord Pearson and Lord Salmon (see [1973] 1 All ER 940 at 947, 951,
958, [1973] AC 807 at 822, 827, 835–836) that they did not accede to the argument that
a conspiracy was complete in the sense that it could be limited to the making of the
agreement only. In particular Lord Pearson, in the same sense as their other Lordships,
said ([1973] 1 All ER 940 at 951, [1973] AC 807 at 827):

c   'A conspiracy involves an agreement expressed or implied. A conspiratorial
        agreement is not a contract, not legally binding, because it is unlawful. But as an
        agreement it has its three stages, namely (1) making or formation (2) performance
        or implementation (3) discharge or termination. When the conspiratorial agreement
        has been made, the offence of conspiracy is complete, it has been committed, and
d   the conspirators can be prosecuted even though no performance has taken place . . .
        But the fact that the offence of conspiracy is complete at that stage does not mean
        that the conspiratorial agreement is finished with. It is not dead. If it is being
        performed, it is very much alive. So long as the performance continues, it is
        operating, it is being carried out by the conspirators, and it is governing or at any
        rate influencing their conduct. The conspiratorial agreement continues in operation
e   and therefore in existence until it is discharged (terminated) by completion of its
        performance or by abandonment or frustration or however it may be.'

Clearly Lord Diplock in *R v Cuthbertson* did not intend to say anything different;
indeed he referred twice to *DPP v Doot* in his speech; and equally clearly what I have just
read out from Lord Pearson's speech is settled law.

It therefore appears to me that both by reason of the wide words 'as a result of' in their
f ordinary meaning, and because the conspiracy continues to be in existence when the
planned acts are done in pursuance of it, for both those reasons, any loss which results
from the acts which the conspirators agree to do also results from the conspiracy itself.

It follows in our judgment that the judge had jurisdiction in relation to these offences
to make the criminal bankruptcy order. Accordingly the appeal will be dismissed,
technically on the ground that it is governed by s 40 (1) of the 1973 Act, with the result
g that no appeal lies.

Appeal dismissed.

*The court refused leave to appeal to the House of Lords but certified, under s 33(2) of the Criminal
Appeal Act 1968, that the following a point of law of general public importance was involved in
the decision: whether the Crown Court was empowered by s 39 of the Powers of Criminal Courts
Act 1973 to make a criminal bankruptcy order against an offender following his conviction of an
offence of conspiracy to defraud where loss or damage intended or contemplated by the conspirators
had in fact resulted from acts done in pursuance of the conspiracy.*

*6 May. The Appeal Committee of the House of Lords (Lord Diplock, Lord Scarman and Lord
Brightman) dismissed a petition by the appellant for leave to appeal.*

Solicitors: *Solicitor of Inland Revenue.*

Sepala Munasinghe Esq   Barrister.

Chief Constable of Kent v V and another   *a*

COURT OF APPEAL, CIVIL DIVISION
LORD DENNING MR, DONALDSON AND SLADE LJJ
23 APRIL, 6 MAY 1982

Police – Powers – Power to retain property relevant to criminal proceedings – Injunction to *b*
preserve property in hands of another – Accused obtaining money by deception on forged
instruments – Accused paying that money into his own bank account – Police seeking injunction to
freeze money in bank account – Whether police having sufficient interest to apply for injunction
freezing moneys in bank account obtained from another by criminal means – Supreme Court Act
1981, s 37(1).

Injunction – Interlocutory – Preservation of proceeds of crime – Extent of court's powers to grant *c*
injunction in favour of police – Money in bank account – Accused obtaining money by deception
on forged instruments – Accused paying that money into his own bank account – Police seeking
injunction to freeze money in bank account – Whether court having power to grant injunction
sought – Supreme Court Act 1981, s 37(1).

The defendant was charged with forgery and obtaining money by deception on forged *d*
instruments. It was alleged by the police that the defendant had obtained several cheque
books belonging to R, forged her signature and withdrawn sums totalling some £16,000
from her account which he then paid into two accounts at his own bank where, following
subsequent withdrawals and payments in, the money became intermingled with moneys
belonging to others which had possibly been obtained by deception. In order to prevent
the defendant using the money in his accounts, the police, acting in the name of the *e*
chief constable, issued an originating summons seeking an injunction restraining the
defendant from withdrawing money from his two accounts, and the bank from carrying
out any transactions in respect of the accounts or any other accounts which the defendant
had with it. On the hearing of the summons the judge held that he had no jurisdiction
to grant the injunction sought. The police appealed. The questions arose whether, under
its power under s 37(1)ᵈ of the Supreme Court Act 1981 to grant an injunction where it *f*
was 'just and convenient' to do so, the court could grant an injunction freezing the
defendant's bank account on the application of the police, notwithstanding that neither
R nor her bank had applied for such an injunction, and, if so, what the extent of such
jurisdiction was.

Held (Slade LJ dissenting) – The appeal would be allowed for the following reasons— *g*
    (1) The police were under a duty, when they knew or had reason to believe that goods
had been stolen or unlawfully obtained, to apprehend the thief and to recover the goods,
and had an interest on behalf of the public to seize the stolen goods, detain them pending
trial of the defendant and in due course restore them to the rightful owner. Applying
that principle to cases where money had been fraudulently obtained or stolen and the *h*
money could be traced into the bank account of the defendant, the police had a sufficient
interest on behalf of the public at large to obtain an injunction under s 37(1) of the 1981
Act freezing moneys standing to the credit of defendant in a bank account, if and to the
extent that the money could be shown to have been obtained from another in breach of
the criminal law (see p 39 c g h, p 40 h j, p 41 c to g, p 42 h and p 44 d to g, post); *Chic*
Fashions (West Wales) Ltd v Jones [1968] 1 All ER 229 and *West Mercia Constabulary v* *j*
Wagener [1981] 3 All ER 378 applied.
    (2) The police were therefore entitled to an injunction preventing the defendant from
withdrawing the £16,000 belonging to R traceable into his two bank accounts, but (per
Donaldson LJ) the order should be conditional by being restricted to moneys which were
traceable as coming from R's two accounts and should not extend to all moneys therein

---
a Section 37(1) is set out at p 40 *f*, post

or any other moneys belonging to the defendant, the order should further not apply to
a any amount in excess of £16,000 in the accounts, the defendant should be at liberty to
apply to vary the order in so far as it could be shown that moneys in the accounts did not
originate from R's accounts, and the chief constable should be required to issue a writ
seeking a declaration in order to prove his right to detain the moneys transferred from
R's account by forged cheques, which would give R and her bank the opportunity to
intervene to assert their respective interests in the money (see p 42 *f* to *h* and p 45 *a* to *d*,
b post).

Per Lord Denning MR. An injunction obtained by the police freezing a defendant's
bank account should if necessary extend to freezing the proceeds of stolen goods which
have been paid into the account or any other moneys which the police reasonably suspect
of having been stolen or obtained by deception, regardless of the fact that the stolen
moneys may have become intermingled with the defendant's own money, because only
c by freezing the account can the court prevent the defendant from disposing of the money
and evading a future restitution order (see p 41 *h* to p 42 *g*, post); *Malone v Comr of Police
of the Metropolis* [1979] 1 All ER 256 doubted.

Per Donaldson and Slade LJJ. The police are not entitled to obtain an injunction
freezing intangible assets of a defendant, including money in his bank accounts, solely
with a view to providing a fund to satisfy a future restitution, compensation or forfeiture
d order made against the defendant (see p 44 *j* and p 48 *c d*, post); *Malone v Comr of Police of
the Metropolis* [1979] 1 All ER 256 approved.

Per Slade LJ. A chief constable could only have a locus standi to seek an injunction to
freeze moneys standing to the credit of a bank account if he could show that he had a
claim to a present or contingent legal right to have some or all of those moneys actually
paid over to him (see p 47 *d* to *f* and p 48 *h j*, post).

e
Notes
For the grant of interlocutory injunctions generally, see 24 Halsbury's Laws (4th edn)
para 953, and for cases on the subject, see 28(2) Digest (Reissue) 968–980, 67–161.
For the Supreme Court Act 1981, s 37, see 51 Halsbury's Statutes (3rd edn) 632.

f ### Cases referred to in judgments
Banque Belge pour l'Etranger v Hambrouck [1921] 1 KB 321, CA, 35 Digest (Repl) 183, 9.
Beddow v Beddow (1878) 9 Ch D 89, 28(2) Digest (Reissue) 959, 22.
Chic Fashions (West Wales) Ltd v Jones [1968] 1 All ER 229, [1968] 2 QB 299, [1968] 2
    WLR 201, CA, 14(1) Digest (Reissue) 215, *1573*.
Diplock's Estate, Re, Diplock v Wintle [1948] 2 All ER 318, [1948] Ch 465, CA; *affd* sub
g nom *Ministry of Health v Simpson* [1950] 2 All ER 1137, [1951] AC 251, HL, 47 Digest
    (Repl) 532, 4825.
Ghani v Jones [1969] 3 All ER 1700, [1970] 1 QB 693, [1969] 3 WLR 1158, CA, 11 Digest
    (Reissue) 745, 608.
Gouriet v Union of Post Office Workers [1977] 3 All ER 70, sub nom *Gouriet v A-G* [1978] AC
    435, [1977] 3 WLR 300, HL, 16 Digest (Reissue) 265, 2528.
h *Malone v Comr of Police of the Metropolis* [1979] 1 All ER 256, [1980] QB 49, [1978] 3 WLR
    936, Digest (Cont Vol E) 133, *1573a*.
Mareva Compania Naviera SA v International Bulkcarriers SA, The Mareva (1975) [1980] 1
    All ER 213, CA, Digest (Cont Vol E) 331, *79b*.
North London Rly Co v Great Northern Rly Co (1883) 11 QBD 30, CA, 28(2) Digest (Reissue)
    959, 24.
j *R v Metropolitan Police Comr, ex p Blackburn* [1968] 1 All ER 763, [1968] 2 QB 118, [1968]
    2 WLR 893, CA, 14(2) Digest (Reissue) 761, 6346.
R v Uxbridge Justices, ex p Comr of Police of the Metropolis [1981] 3 All ER 129, [1981] QB
    829, [1981] 3 WLR 410, CA; *affg* [1981] 1 All ER 940, [1981] 1 WLR 112, DC.
Siskina (cargo owners) v Distos Compania Naviera SA, The Siskina [1977] 3 All ER 803, [1979]
    AC 210, [1977] 3 WLR 818, HL, Digest (Cont Vol E) 660, 782a.
West Mercia Constabulary v Wagener [1981] 3 All ER 378, [1982] 1 WLR 127.

Case also cited
Chaplin v Boys [1969] 2 All ER 1085, [1971] AC 356, HL.   *a*

Appeal
The plaintiff, the Chief Constable of Kent, appealed against the decision of Beldam J on
16 February 1982 that the injunction granted by Skinner J on 8 February 1982 ordering,
inter alia, (i) that the first defendant, V, be restrained from making or attempting to
make any withdrawals or transfers or other transactions in respect of two bank accounts   *b*
held by the second defendant, Bank of Credit and Commerce International, and (ii) that
the second defendant be restrained from handling or processing or otherwise dealing
with any withdrawals, transfers, payments or any transactions in respect of the first
defendant's bank accounts be continued only until the hearing of the appeal. The facts
are set out in the judgment of Lord Denning MR.

c

David Pitman for the chief constable.
Simon D Brown as amicus curiae.
The first defendant did not appear and the second defendant was not represented.

Cur adv vult

d

6 May. The following judgments were read.

LORD DENNING MR. There was an old lady living in Tunbridge Wells. She had a
good deal of money to her credit in Grindlays Bank, 13 St James Square, London SW1. A
man, V, is charged with wrongfully extracting money from her account. He has not yet
been tried, so you must not take anything against him yet. I would ask the reporters not   *e*
to give his name if they report this case. This is what is alleged against him. It is said that
in October 1981 this man got hold of two or three of the old lady's cheque books. He
forged her signature on cheque after cheque. From October 1981 to January 1982 he
drew cheques every few days for sums of £800 or £900. He drew 21 cheques amounting
in all to £16,001. He paid them into his own bank accounts with the Bank of Credit and
Commerce International, sometimes at their branch in Leadenhall Street and the others   *f*
at their branch in the Cromwell Road. He also paid in other moneys which he had got
from other people; and he had drawn on them from time to time. So you could not tell
which was which.
    Soon afterwards he was found out. He was arrested in London on 28 January 1982.
He was charged with forgery and obtaining money by deception on forged instruments.
The Chief Constable of Kent thought that he might draw out the moneys in the bank so   *g*
that they would be lost beyond recovery. So on 2 February 1982 he issued an originating
summons and applied ex parte for an injunction to restrain him from withdrawing any
moneys from the bank account. Skinner J granted an injunction. He relied on a decision
of Forbes J in *West Mercia Constabulary v Wagener* [1981] 3 All ER 378, [1982] 1 WLR
127. Later on the summons was heard by Beldam J. He held that the court had no
jurisdiction to grant such an injunction but he continued it temporarily pending the   *h*
appeal. This was because the man was allowed out on bail and the judge did not want
him to be able to draw cheques on the account until after the appeal was heard.
    At the hearing before us he was not represented but, as the point was of much
importance, we asked for the assistance of an amicus curiae. Now we have had the benefit
of counsel and are grateful for it. I would first tell of the *West Mercia* case.
    Wagener put advertisements in local newspapers advertising video cassettes for sale at   *j*
low prices, and asking for cheques to be sent in advance. A lot of customers sent cheques.
Wagener paid them into his bank account. But he never sent any cassettes to the
customers. The whole thing was suspected of being a fraud. But the police did not know
the names of the customers. So the chief constable himself applied for an injunction to
'freeze' the bank account. Forbes J granted an injunction.

THE LAW
a *Seizure of goods*

Our books have much in them about the powers of the police to make an arrest of the person of a suspected wrongdoer. There is something in the books of their power to seize and detain stolen goods. But there is nothing at all of their power to seize or detain money in a bank account.

I need say nothing today of the power of the police to arrest a person. I speak first of
b their power to seize or detain goods. This was considered by this court in *Chic Fashions (West Wales) Ltd v Jones* [1968] 1 All ER 229, [1968] 2 QB 299. That case showed that on entering a house with a search warrant or by the occupier's consent the police have power to seize goods which they reasonably believe to have been stolen or obtained fraudulently by deception. They can thereafter detain the goods for such time as is reasonably necessary to complete their investigations into the theft or fraudulent obtaining. If their
c investigations indicate that the goods have been stolen or fraudulently obtained by deception, the police can detain them further so that they can in due course be restored to their rightful owner and, where necessary, be produced as material evidence at the trial of an accused person. But, once it appears that the goods were not stolen or fraudulently obtained and are not needed as evidence, then the police should restore them to the person from whom they were taken: see *Ghani v Jones* [1969] 3 All ER 1700,
d [1970] 1 QB 693, *Malone v Comr of Police of the Metropolis* [1979] 1 All ER 256, [1980] 1 QB 49 and *R v Uxbridge Justices, ex p Comr of Police of the Metropolis* [1981] 1 All ER 940, [1981] QB 829, unless in special circumstances the court directs them to be held until after the trial.

Money in a bank account
e Apply those principles to currency notes. Forbes J in *West Mercia Constabulary v Wagener* put this case: suppose a bank robber steals a million pounds in easily negotiable notes. He puts them into a suitcase and deposits them in a luggage office or in a bank. If the police reasonably believe that they have been stolen or fraudulently obtained, they could, on getting a search warrant or by consent, seize the suitcase and the notes in it. The police could hold them just as any other goods that are believed to have been stolen
f or fraudulently obtained.

Next, suppose that, instead of the thief putting them into a suitcase, he pays them into his own bank account. His account may already be in credit, so that the stolen notes go to swell his credit balance. It may be in overdraft, so that they serve to pay off the overdraft and put him in credit. In either case, in so far as the notes can be traced into his bank account, and are still available to his credit, I am of opinion that the court, at the
g instance of the police, can and should 'freeze' his bank account. If this be so when currency notes are stolen, so also it is when money is abstracted by forgery from the account of the true owner and put by the forger into his own bank account. This 'freezing' is done so as to ensure that the moneys can in due course be restored to the rightful owner. I cannot believe that a thief can get away with his stolen hoard by the simple device of paying it into his own bank account. So long as it can be traced, it can
h be frozen. It may be that 150 years ago the common law halted outside the banker's door, but for the last 100 years, since the fusion of law and equity, it has had the courage to lift the latch, walk in and examine the books: see *Banque Belge pour l'Etranger v Hambrouck* [1921] 1 KB 321 at 335 per Atkin LJ and *Re Diplock's Estate, Diplock v Wintle* [1948] 2 All ER 318, [1948] Ch 465 per Lord Greene MR.

j *Timorous souls*
Some timorous souls are fearful of this extension. They say that the police have no cause of action known to the law so as to come under RSC Ord 29, r 2, and that that is where Forbes J went wrong in the *West Mercia* case [1981] 3 All ER 378 at 382, [1982] 1 WLR 127 at 131; and that the police have no legal or equitable right such as to warrant an injunction under RSC Ord 29, r 1. They pray in aid the classic case of *North London Rly*

Co v Great Northern Rly Co (1883) 11 QBD 30 applied by the House of Lords in *Gouriet v*
Union of Post Office Workers [1977] 3 All ER 70 at 100, 112–113, [1978] AC 435 at 501,   *a*
516 per Lord Diplock and Lord Edmund-Davies and *Siskina (cargo owners) v Distos*
Compania Naviera SA, The Siskina [1977] 3 All ER 803 at 824, [1979] AC 210 at 256 per
Lord Diplock.

But I am glad to say that the reasoning of those cases has now been circumvented by
statute. They were based on the wording of s 25(8) of the Supreme Court of Judicature
Act 1873, which said that—   *b*

> '... an injunction may be granted ... by an *interlocutory* order of the court in all
> cases in which it shall appear to the court to be just or convenient that such order
> should be made ...'

That was re-enacted in s 45(1) of the Supreme Court of Judicature (Consolidation) Act
1925 in these words: *c*

> 'The High Court may grant a mandamus or an injunction or appoint a receiver
> by an *interlocutory* order in all cases in which it appears to the court to be just or
> convenient so to do.'

I have emphasised the word 'interlocutory' because it was the basis of the decision in
the *North London Rly Co* case and following cases. That was pointed out by Lord Diplock   *d*
in *The Siskina* [1977] 3 All ER 803 at 823, [1979] AC 210 at 254 when he said:

> 'That subsection, speaking as it does of *interlocutory* orders, presupposes the
> existence of an action, actual or potential, claiming substantive relief which the
> High Court has jurisdiction to grant and to which the interlocutory orders referred
> to are but ancillary.' (Emphasis mine.)
>   *e*

Section 37 of the Supreme Court Act 1981

Now that reasoning has been circumvented by s 37(1) of the Supreme Court Act 1981,
which came into force on 1 January 1982. It says that:

> 'The High Court may by order (*whether interlocutory or final*) grant an injunction   *f*
> or appoint a receiver in all cases in which it appears to the court to be just and
> convenient to do so.'

The emphasised words in brackets show that Parliament did not like the limitation to
'interlocutory'. It is no longer necessary that the injunction should be *ancillary* to an
action claiming a legal or equitable right. It can stand on its own. The section as it now
stands plainly confers a new and extensive jurisdiction on the High Court to grant an   *g*
injunction. It is far wider than anything that had been known in our courts before.
There is no reason whatever why the courts should cut down this jurisdiction by
reference to previous technical distinctions. Thus Parliament has restored the law to what
my great predecessor Jessel MR said it was in *Beddow v Beddow* (1878) 9 Ch D 89 at 93
and which I applied in the first Mareva injunction case, *Mareva Compania Naviera SA v*
International Bulkcarriers SA (1975) [1980] 1 All ER 213 at 214: 'I have unlimited power   *h*
to grant an injunction in any case where it would be right or just to do so ...' Subject,
however, to this qualification: I would not say the power was 'unlimited'. I think that
the applicant for an injunction must have a sufficient interest in a matter to warrant his
asking for an injunction. Whereas previously it was said that he had to have a 'legal or
equitable right' in himself, now he has to have a locus standi to apply. He must have a
sufficient interest. This is a good and sensible test. It is the self-same test of locus standi   *j*
as the legislature itself authorised in s 31(3) of the Supreme Court Act 1981. Next, it
must be just and convenient that an injunction should be granted at his instance as, for
example, so as to preserve the assets or property which might otherwise be lost or
dissipated. On this principle I think that *The Siskina* would be decided differently today.
The cargo owners had plainly a sufficient interest: it would have been most just and
convenient to have granted an injunction, as I pointed out in this court ([1977] 3 All ER

803 at 808–809, [1979] AC 210 at 228). It was most unjust for the House of Lords to
a refuse it.

Have the police a sufficient interest?
I turn therefore to the crucial question in this case: has the chief constable a sufficient
interest to apply for an injunction? We considered the position of the police in *R v
Metropolitan Police Comr, ex p Blackburn* [1968] 1 All ER 763 at 769, [1968] 2 QB 118 at
b 136, where I said:

> 'I hold it to be the duty of the Commissioner of Police, as it is of every chief
> constable, to enforce the law of the land. He must take steps so to post his men that
> crimes may be detected; and that honest citizens may go about their affairs in peace.'

To this I would now add that it is his duty, once he knows or has reason to believe that
c goods have been stolen or unlawfully obtained, to do his best to discover and apprehend
the thief and to recover the goods. Corresponding to that duty he has a right, or at any
rate an interest, on behalf of the public to seize the goods and detain them pending the
trial of the offender and to restore them in due course to the true owner. In pursuance of
that duty, and of that right and interest, he can apply to the magistrate for a search
warrant and to a High Court judge for an injunction.
d So I hold that the chief constable here has a sufficient right and interest to warrant his
applying to the court.

Applied to a bank account
Apply this to the circumstances of this case. Go back to the suitcase full of stolen
currency notes, belonging to many person who are not yet ascertained. If the thief
e deposits the suitcase with his bank, he is entitled to demand back his suitcase at any time
and the bankers must deliver it to him at his request, unless there is an order of the court
to prevent them doing so. Surely the police can get an injunction to stop the bank
delivering it to him. Just as they can go to a magistrate and get a search warrant, surely
they can go to a High Court judge and get an injunction. If that be correct for the
currency notes in the suitcase, it must also be correct when they are paid into the thief's
f banking account. On an application by the police setting out their reasonable grounds,
the High Court can grant an injunction to prevent the thief drawing on his bank account
and the bank from honouring his cheques, so that in due course the moneys can be
restored to the true owner. Such an injunction is vital as an ancillary support to an order
for restitution under s 28 of the Theft Act 1968. That section enables the court of trial,
on convicting the man, to order the stolen goods or their proceeds, direct or indirect, to
g be restored to the true owner. It would be a mockery of the law if he could always evade
a restitution order by disposing of the goods or their proceeds pending his trial. The
court must have power to grant an injunction to stop him from doing so.

Following the proceeds
Thus far I have considered only those cases where money itself has been stolen or
h fraudulently obtained, and then paid by the thief into his own bank account. But suppose
the thief did not steal money but goods; then sold the stolen goods for cash; and put the
cash into his own bank account. To such a case I would apply the same principle. If and
in so far as the proceeds of stolen goods can be traced into the bank account, then the
court, at the instance of the police, can grant an injunction to prevent their being disposed
of, so that in due course, after the thief's conviction, the proceeds of the theft can be
j restored to the owner of the goods under s 28 of the Theft Act 1968. I know that this
means making the true owner into a secured creditor, but that is just as it should be. Just
as he could have recovered the stolen goods (if he could have traced them to the buyer)
so he should be able to recover the proceeds from the bank account. Section 28 of the
Theft Act 1968 enables the court of trial, on the thief's conviction, to order the return of
the proceeds. It is only right that the police should be able to get an injunction to prevent
him disposing of them meanwhile.

Mixed moneys

There remains the final question: suppose the bank account contains moneys which   *a*
the thief has come by honestly, so that they are really his own moneys, and are then
mixed with moneys which he has come by dishonestly, by theft or fraudulent obtaining.
At the time of his arrest, the police discover that to be the state of his bank account. It is
quite plain that he paid the stolen money into his own bank account so as to avoid
detection. It follows that under s 43 of the Theft Act 1968 the court of trial, on his
conviction, can make an order depriving him of his rights in the stolen money. He   *b*
cannot avoid such an order by mixing it with his own moneys. In order to make the
power under s 43 effective, it is essential that the court should have power to grant an
injunction meanwhile to stop him disposing of any moneys in his account; because, until
trial, it cannot be known how much of it belongs to him personally and how much was
stolen.

Malone's case   *c*

Malone v Comr of Police of the Metropolis [1979] 1 All ER 256, [1980] QB 49 is
distinguishable because the man's own property was separate and distinct from the stolen
property. But, even so, I venture to doubt whether it would be decided in the same way
today, for we have now available the wide provision of s 37 of the Supreme Court Act
1981. It seems to me undesirable that, if a thief is found to have a large sum of money in   *d*
the bank, he should be able to dispose of it completely, send it to a numbered Swiss bank
account, or give it to his accomplices, so as to avoid giving compensation to the people he
has defrauded. By s 35 of the Powers of Criminal Courts Act 1973, the court is given
ample power to make a compensation order requiring the thief, on his conviction, to pay
compensation for any damage that he has done. In order to make this power effective, I
think that under s 37 the court might well feel justified in many cases to grant an   *e*
injunction preventing him from disposing of the money in his bank account pending
his trial. The court could, of course, release to him whatever is necessary for him to spend
on his defence, and so forth.

Applied to this case

Skinner J made an injunction in a wide form restraining any withdrawals from the   *f*
bank account. I think that was entirely justified as an emergency measure. It was quite
right to do it pending further investigation into the source of the moneys. If the accused
man had any special reason for making payments out of it, he had only to ask and only
proper payments would be permitted. The police have already traced £16,001 into the
account. The injunction should certainly be continued so as to prevent the withdrawal
of that sum. It should also be continued as to any further sum which the police may   *g*
reasonably suspect of having been stolen or obtained by deception. There is no evidence,
so far, to this effect. But, in case it should be forthcoming, I would continue the
injunction in its wide form until the trial. If the man is convicted, the trial judge can
make such orders for restitution or for compensation as he thinks proper.

I would, therefore, allow the appeal and continue the injunction in the form granted
by Skinner J, but reserving leave to the man to apply for the release of such sums as he   *h*
may need for his defence, or otherwise.

DONALDSON LJ. Section 37(1) of the Supreme Court Act 1981, re-enacting and
slightly amending parts of s 45(1) of the Supreme Court of Judicature (Consolidation)
Act 1925, authorises the High Court by interlocutory or final order to grant an injunction
'in all cases in which it appears to the court to be just and convenient so to do'. These are   *j*
wide words, but I am quite unable to see how it can appear to the court to be just and
convenient to make such an order, save in the enforcement or protection of a legal or
equitable right or interest. Were it otherwise, every judge would need to be issued with
a portable palm tree.

The first question for consideration is thus whether the Chief Constable of Kent has
any legal or equitable right or interest the enforcement or protection of which would

require the making of the injunctive order claimed in his originating summons. That
a order would impose a total embargo on all withdrawals, transfers or other transactions in
respect of two specified bank accounts of the first defendant, Mr V, with the second
defendant, Bank of Credit and Commerce International. It would also extend to any
other, unspecified, accounts of Mr V with the second defendant.

The facts sworn to in support of the chief constable's claim are essentially that 21
cheques for amounts totalling £16,001 drawn on the account of a Mrs Raikes with
b Grindlays Bank Ltd have been paid to the credit of the two specified accounts of Mr V
and that it appears to the chief constable that these cheques, purporting to be signed by
Mrs Raikes, are forgeries. If he is right, Mrs Raikes may well have a cause of action
against Grindlays Bank requiring it to recredit her account with these sums, or she may
have a cause of action against Mr V. Again, Grindlays Bank may have a cause of action
against Mr V. However, so far as I know, neither Mrs Raikes nor Grindlays Bank has
c sought to assert such causes of action and the chief constable has no right to do so on their
behalf. Furthermore, none of the parties involved in the alleged crimes, whether as
criminals or victims, owes any duty to the chief constable the alleged breach of which
could afford him any cause of action.

In these circumstances, any cause of action must arise out of the chief constable's rights
or duties as such. His duties, which, so far as material, are no greater and no less than
d those of any other police constable, have never been exhaustively defined. It has always
proved unnecessary, difficult and probably unwise to do so and I would certainly not
essay such a feat in this appeal. However, it is clear that they include a duty to use his
best endeavours to detect crime, to bring criminals to justice, to recover stolen property
and to restore it, or make it available for restoration, to the rightful owner. This being
the case, the common law has invested police constables with powers which include a
e right to seize goods which, on reasonable grounds, they believe to be stolen property (see
Chic Fashions (West Wales) Ltd v Jones [1968] 1 All ER 229, [1968] 2 QB 299).

In this appeal we have to consider whether the common law has invested the police
with a similar right in relation to intangibles. So far as the reported cases go, this is to
some extent a novel proposition raised for the first time in *West Mercia Constabulary v
Wagener* [1981] 3 All ER 379, [1982] 1 WLR 127. There Mr Wagener invited the public
f to send cheques to a company which he owned in payment for electronic equipment
which he was offering to sell at below trade prices. The public, blinded by the prospects
of a bargain, accepted the invitation and a number of cheques were received and credited
to the company's bank account. Unfortunately, there was no electronic equipment, and
in due course Mr Wagener was charged with fraudulently obtaining property contrary
to s 20(2) of the Theft Act 1968. The West Mercia Constabulary issued an originating
g summons in reliance on RSC Ord 29, r 2(1)(a), which authorises the court to make an
order for the detention, custody or preservation of any property which is the subject
matter of a cause or matter, or as to which any question may arise therein, or for the
inspection of any such property in the possession of a party to the cause or matter. By the
summons the West Mercia Constabulary claimed orders 'freezing' the company's bank
account, as has the chief constable in the instant case.

h Forbes J granted the order, making it clear that he intended only to 'freeze' the proceeds
of the improperly obtained cheques and that, if the wording of his order had any wider
effect than this, it could and would be corrected under the liberty to apply. In doing so
he did not specifically advert to the fact that RSC Ord 29, r 2(1)(a) is one of a number of
ancillary powers of the High Court designed to enable it to discharge its primary duty of
determining causes or matters. The rule does not of itself give the High Court jurisdiction
j to determine a cause or matter. Accordingly, the judge did not in terms ask himself the
question, 'What is the cause or matter subsisting between the West Mercia Constabulary,
on the one hand, and Mr Wagener and his company on the other in connection with the
determination of which I need to exercise the ancillary power conferred by Ord 29,
r 2(1)(a)?' Had he done so, I think that he would have been driven to conclude that none
was alleged and would have had to consider how Ord 29, r 2(1)(a) came to be applicable.

However, it does not follow from this that his decision was wrong in the result. He

records that all concerned accepted that, if a bank robber stole a million pounds in notes
and deposited them in suitcases in the strong room of a bank, the police, on learning of   *a*
this fact, could have obtained a search warrant, entered the bank and seized the bank
notes with a view not only to using them as evidence in criminal proceedings but also to
their preservation and ultimate restitution to their rightful owners (see [1981] 3 All ER
378 at 382, [1982] 1 WLR 127 at 131). I agree with this statement of the rights of the
police, subject to the qualification that the search warrant, although no doubt necessary
in practice, is not an essential element in the exercise of the right of seizure so long as the   *b*
bank is prepared to allow the police to enter and search the strong room without a
warrant.

Forbes J then further recorded that all concerned agreed that if, instead of depositing
the notes in the bank's strong room, the bank robber had opened an account and paid the
money into that account, no search warrant could be issued. Again I agree, but would
point out that, if the bank robber had been charged, an order could have been obtained   *c*
under the Bankers' Books Evidence Act 1879, which would have had some of the effects
of a search warrant and would have given the police a sight of the account. But what the
police could not do was themselves to seize or freeze the £1m standing to the credit of
the account.

From this it is argued by counsel who has appeared as amicus curiae and to whom I
am greatly indebted for his assistance that the police have no rights in relation to the   *d*
£1m standing to the credit of the account. This I do not accept. It can equally well be
said of the bank from whom the £1m in notes was stolen that it could not seize or freeze
the £1m if it was discovered in the account of a customer of another bank. But the bank
which was the victim of the robbery would quite clearly have a right, having traced the
money, to obtain an order from the court for its return and an order freezing the account
meanwhile. Accordingly it does not seems to me that the mere absence of a self-help   *e*
remedy is conclusive of the absence of a right.

It is at this point that I return to *Chic Fashions (West Wales) Ltd v Jones* [1968] 1 All ER
229, [1968] 2 QB 299. There the common law came to the support of the common weal
and invested the police with a right to seize goods which the courts would, if necessary,
have enforced by mandatory injunction. In the instant appeal I consider that the common
law can and should similarly invest the police with a right to 'detain' moneys standing to   *f*
the credit of a bank account if and to the extent that they can be shown to have been
obtained from another in breach of the criminal law. Only thus will a criminal be
prevented from making the fruits of his crime immune from seizure by the simple
expedient of banking the money. Whether this right can be extended to a case in which
the criminal takes tangible property, converts it into money by selling it and banks the
money is a different question which should I think await decision when it arises. I would   *g*
only mention the problem that, if the right were so extended, the police might have a
double right, to seize the stolen property itself in the hands of the receiver who had
bought it and to freeze the proceeds. This might be difficult to justify.

During the course of the argument consideration was given to whether the police
might not be entitled to something in the nature of a Mareva injunction freezing all the
alleged criminal's assets with a view to providing a fund to satisfy a future restitution,   *h*
compensation or forfeiture order. In this connection we were referred to the decision of
this court in *Malone v Comr of Police of the Metropolis* [1979] 1 All ER 256, [1980] QB 49.
There the police were seeking to retain possession of money which they had seized. The
defendant police commissioner was unable to advance any criminal charge in respect of
the money and sought to retain it, inter alia, for the purpose of satisfying a possible
restitution order under s 28(1)(c) of the Theft Act 1968, as amended, or a compensation   *j*
or forfeiture order under s 35 or s 43 of the Powers of Criminal Courts Act 1973. This
court held that the police had no such right of detention. Although this was an
interlocutory decision of a court of two and so could be reviewed by this court, I would
not wish to do so because I consider the decision to have been correct. If it was correct,
any claim to the more extended right to freeze intangible property not in the possession
of the police for a similar purpose must fail.

I must now return to the order sought to be continued in the instant appeal. In so far
a as it affects all moneys standing to the specified accounts and any other moneys of Mr V,
I think that it is much too wide. It should be confined to moneys in those accounts which
are traceable as coming from the account of Mrs Raikes. Furthermore, I consider that the
chief constable should assert and, if necessary, eventually prove his right to detain these
moneys as being moneys transferred from Mrs Raikes's account by forged cheques and
for that purpose should issue a writ claiming a declaration to this effect, the application
b for an injunction being ancillary thereto. I would allow the appeal to the extent of
granting an injunction limited to restraining any withdrawals, transfers or other dealings
with the specified accounts in so far as the balance to the credit of those accounts is less
than £16,001 or would thereby be reduced below that sum, but the defendants would
have liberty to apply with a view to varying this order in so far as it can be shown that
moneys standing to the credit of the account do not originate from Mrs Raikes's account.
c As a condition of making this order, I should require the chief constable to issue a writ
claiming the declaration to which I have referred. Either Mrs Raikes or Grindlays Bank
or both would be able to intervene in the proceedings to assert their respective interests
in the money, but no doubt the final determination of the proceedings will be postponed
until after the conclusion of the criminal proceedings.

d **SLADE LJ.** I have the misfortune to differ from the conclusion of Lord Denning MR
and Donaldson LJ that this appeal should be allowed. I do so with great diffidence and
regret. This is the greater because I well see the practical advantages of a temporary
freezing of the two bank accounts by a court order, even though I understand that the
conditions under which the accused man has been granted bail may perhaps secure the
like result.
e   Statute or the common law may confer on certain persons or bodies a special right,
beyond that conferred on ordinary citizens, to seek injunctive relief from the court, even
though they may be able to point to no independent legal or equitable right of their own
which is sought to be protected. The Attorney General, for example, has the right to seek
an injunction to restrain a threatened illegal act in his capacity as guardian of the public
interest. Section 222 of the Local Government Act 1972 has given local authorities
f certain powers to prosecute or defend legal proceedings where they consider it expedient
for the promotion or protection of the inhabitants of their area. No authority, however,
has been cited to this court which suggests that the Chief Constable of Kent has been
invested by statute or by common law with any special rights or locus standi to seek
relief from the court by way of injunction as a protector of the public interest.
      With this introduction, I respectfully agree with the following propositions of law,
g which I think all appear from the judgment of Donaldson LJ:
      (1) The court would have no jurisdiction to grant the chief constable any injunctive
relief save in the enforcement or protection of a legal or equitable right. I would add one
or two observations in this context. This qualification on the power to grant injunctions
conferred on the court by s 45 of the Supreme Court of Judicature (Consolidation) Act
h 1925 was referred to by Lord Denning MR in *Mareva Compania Naviera SA v International
Bulkcarriers SA* (1975) [1980] 1 All ER 213 at 214, where he cited the decision in *North
London Rly Co v Great Northern Rly Co* (1883) 11 QBD 30 as authority for the proposition
that 'The court will not grant an injunction to protect a person who has no legal or
equitable right whatever'. Though the innovation embodied in the *Mareva* decision now
enables the court to give effective relief to a plaintiff in a form wider than had previously
been thought permissible, the decision of the House of Lords in *Siskina (cargo owners) v*
j *Distos Compania Naviera SA, The Siskina* [1977] 3 All ER 803, [1979] AC 210 shows that it
can only do so where he shows an apparent pre-existing legal or equitable right which
requires protection. As Lord Diplock said in that case ([1977] 3 All ER 803 at 824, [1979]
AC 210 at 256):

      'A right to obtain an interlocutory injunction is not a cause of action. It cannot
      stand on its own. It is dependent on there being a pre-existing cause of action against

the defendant arising out of an invasion, actual or threatened, by him of a legal or equitable right of the plaintiff for the enforcement of which the defendant is *a* amenable to the jurisdiction of the court. The right to obtain an interlocutory injunction is merely ancillary and incidental to the pre-existing cause of action.'

The correctness of this statement of the law cannot, I think, have been affected by the addition of a reference to a 'final order' in s 37(1) of the Supreme Court Act 1981. That added reference, as I read it, was simply intended to make it explicitly clear that in an *b* appropriate case the court has the jurisdiction to grant a permanent injunction by a final order no less than it has the power to grant an interlocutory injunction by an interlocutory order. It cannot, I think, properly be construed as removing the qualification which the decision of this court in the *North London Rly Co* case establishes as being attached to the apparently very wide discretionary power to grant injunctions conferred on the court by statute.   *c*

(2) The first question for consideration in the present case is thus whether the chief constable has any legal or equitable right, the enforcement or protection of which would require the grant of the injunction sought by his originating summons.

(3) While Mrs Raikes may have a cause of action against Grindlays Bank and that bank may have a cause of action against the accused man, the chief constable has no right to assert either such cause of action.   *d*

(4) In these circumstances, if the chief constable is to succeed on the present motion, any cause of action must be based on his own rights in this capacity.

(5) The decision in *Chic Fashions (West Wales) Ltd v Jones* [1968] 1 All ER 229, [1968] 2 QB 299 establishes that under common law a police officer may seize and take away goods which he believes on reasonable grounds to be stolen property. The more detailed incidents of this right are described in the judgment of Lord Denning MR.   *e*

(6) Since the bank account which the chief constable is attempting to freeze on the present motion constitutes an intangible interest, the relevant question on this appeal must be whether police officers have common law rights in relation to intangible property analogous to those established by the *Chic Fashions* case in relation to tangible property.

(7) If the answer to the last mentioned question were in the negative, the plaintiff *f* could not establish a claim to a legal or equitable right sufficient to enable him to succeed on the present motion. RSC Ord 29, r 2(1), which was relied on by Forbes J in *West Mercia Constabulary v Wagener* [1981] 3 All ER 378, [1982] 1 WLR 127, cannot in my opinion, with deference to him, operate to create a cause of action where none otherwise appears. It is, I think, a merely procedural rule which defines certain remedies which it is open to the court to make available to a party to a cause or matter in an appropriate *g* case; no more than the principle of the *Mareva* decision can it operate to create a cause of action in a case where none otherwise appears. It does not, I think, remove the necessity for an ordinary litigant who is seeking an interlocutory injunction, such as the plaintiff in the present case, to show a claim to a legal or equitable right in support of which the injunction is sought; a mere interest in the broader sense is not in my view enough to give him a locus standi to seek an injunction.   *h*

In the present case Donaldson LJ has observed in relation to the *Chic Fashions* case that—

'the common law came to the support of the common·weal and invested the police with a right to seize goods which the courts would, if necessary, have enforced by mandatory injunction.'   *j*

He has concluded that in the instant appeal—

'the common law can and should similarly invest the police with a right to "detain" moneys standing to the credit of a bank account if and to the extent that they can be shown to have been obtained from another in breach of the criminal law.'

He has expressed the view that the chief constable should assert, and if necessary
a eventually prove, his right to 'detain' the moneys in the two accounts which are traceable
as being moneys transferred from Mrs Raikes's account by forged cheques and for that
purpose should issue a writ claiming a declaration to this effect, the application for an
injunction being ancillary thereto. He takes the view that, at least if a writ were issued
claiming a declaration of that nature, the chief constable would be asserting a claim to a
legal or equitable right sufficient to ground a claim to protection by way of injunction.

b   It is at this crucially important part of the judgment of Donaldson LJ that I find myself,
with all respect to him, driven to a different conclusion. I shall now attempt to state my
reasons.

If this court were to extend the principle of the *Chic Fashions* case by holding that the
chief constable has the right at common law to 'detain' all or part of the moneys standing
to the credit of Mr V's two bank accounts, it would be necessary to consider what would
c be the precise nature of that right which would form the subject matter of the suggested
declaration by the court. It could not be the mere right to come to the court and seek an
injunction freezing the two accounts. Counsel appearing as amicus curiae in his most
helpful argument reminded the court that the right to seek an injunction cannot by itself
constitute an equitable or legal right sufficient to support an application for an injunction.
For the plaintiff to contend otherwise would involve what Lord Diplock described in *The*
d Siskina [1977] 3 All ER 803 at 825, [1979] AC 210 at 257 as 'an attempt to pull oneself up
by one's own bootstraps'.

If therefore the court is to hold that in the present instance the chief constable has a
cause of action sufficient to support an application for an injunction, it seems to me that
it must go to the lengths of holding that, where a chief constable believes on reasonable
grounds that moneys standing to the credit of a bank account are traceable to property
e which has been obtained from another in breach of the criminal law, he has a present or
contingent legal or equitable right to demand that such moneys be *actually paid over to
him*. If, and only if, such were the law, I would see no difficulty in principle in granting
him an interlocutory injunction to protect such a right, by freezing the accounts.

The difficulty, to my mind insuperable, is in surmounting the first hurdle, by
extending the principle of *Chic Fashions* by holding that a chief constable has any present
f or contingent right of the nature last mentioned. The question before the court in that
case was—

> 'whether the common law allows a policeman to seize goods which he finds in
> the possession or custody of a person if he believes, on reasonable grounds, that that
> person has stolen the goods or received them knowing them to be stolen.'

g (See [1968] 1 All ER 229 at 239, [1968] 2 QB 299 at 318 per Salmon LJ.) As I understand
the decision, the basis of it was that a right of seizure and subsequent detention is
necessary, first, in order to preserve material evidence on the prosecution of a criminal
charge against the person from whom they were seized and, second, to ensure that after
the trial they may be restored to their rightful owner (see, for example, [1968] 1 All ER
229 at 236, 238, [1968] 2 QB 299 at 313, 316 per Lord Denning MR and Diplock LJ).

h   I have referred to 'extending' the principle of the *Chic Fashions* case, because there can
be no doubt that this is what this court would be doing if it were to hold that the chief
constable has any legal or equitable right, present or contingent, to demand that any of
the moneys in the two accounts be actually paid over to him in any circumstances
whatsoever. The present case is distinguishable on its facts from that case in at least three
material respects. (1) It concerns intangible property in the form of choses in action,
j rather than tangible property. Intangible rights, such as rights to moneys in a bank
account, are by their very nature incapable of being enforced by taking physical
possession. Without the consent of the other interested parties, they are only enforceable
by legal proceedings. Correspondingly, in the absence of such consent, 'detention' of
intangible rights can only be made possible by an order of the court. (2) It could not, I
think, be seriously suggested that the moneys standing to the credit of the two accounts
require to be paid over to the chief constable for the purpose of providing material

evidence at the trial; and counsel for the chief constable, as I understood him, did not so argue. (3) Even assuming that the police were somehow or other to gain possession of *a* these moneys and were to 'restore' them to the injured party in the event of a conviction of the accused man, the restoration would be of a very different nature from that envisaged by the *Chic Fashions* case. In that case the restoration envisaged related to the actual goods which were believed to have been stolen. In the present case it could at best relate only to moneys representing a chose in action of which the injured party had been deprived. As I understood counsel's argument, the chief constable's concern has hitherto *b* been to preserve the moneys in the accounts not so much for the purpose of enabling himself or the court to engage in some kind of tracing operation, so as to enable some sort of 'restoration' to be made to the injured party as for the purpose of meeting any order for compensation which might hereafter be made under s 35 of the Powers of Criminal Courts Act 1973 in case the accused man should be convicted. The decision of this court in *Malone v Comr of Police of the Metropolis* [1979] 1 All ER 256, [1980] QB 49 *c* clearly establishes that the police do not have the right to seize and detain even tangible assets which represent neither goods alleged to be stolen nor the fruits of such goods if the sole purpose of the detention is to make them available in the event of a conviction to satisfy an order under s 35 or s 43 of 1973 Act or s 28(1)(c) of the Theft Act 1968.

For my own part, and with all respect to those who hold a contrary view, I am not even convinced that the public interest necessarily and unquestionably makes it desirable *d* that the police should have the right to intervene in cases such as the present, where only intangible rights are involved. The existence of such a right would presumably denote the existence of some parallel duty on their part to attempt to secure the preservation of intangible rights which they believe on reasonable grounds to be traceable to other assets taken in breach of the criminal law. In default of co-operation from the alleged guilty party, any attempts to enforce 'detention' of such rights will necessarily involve legal *e* proceedings. While the tracing process involved may be comparatively simple on the particular facts of the present case, there would be many cases where it would be far less simple. The court has no evidence before it as to the extent of the increased burden which would be likely to fall on the police themselves, their legal departments and the courts, if the duty were held to exist and the police were to attempt to discharge it. The practical consequences are not easy to foresee. Though in the *Chic Fashions* case [1968] 1 *f* All ER 229 at 239–240, [1968] 2 QB 299 at 318, as Salmon LJ pointed out, 'common sense and principle' alike suggested that the police must have the power there in question, in the present case they do not seem to me inevitably to point in one direction only. It must be emphasised that the absence of such a power in the police would in no way preclude the injured party himself from coming to the court to seek an order for the preservation of any choses in action in which he could show a prima facie legal or *g* equitable interest. As it happens in the present case, neither Mrs Raikes nor Grindlays Bank, so it appears, have thus far chosen to pursue any remedies which may be available to them. It should not however be assumed that the absence of a remedy for the police themselves in situations such as the present would necessarily mean that in other cases dishonest men would be left free to enjoy their ill-gotten gains pending their trial.

I have already given reasons for concluding that, if he is to be entitled to interlocutory *h* relief, the chief constable must establish a claim to a relevant legal or equitable right in himself and that he can establish this only by showing that he has a claim to a present or contingent legal right to have some or all of the moneys in the two bank accounts actually paid over to him. No authority has been cited which suggests that he has any such right. At the risk of deserving the description of a timorous soul, I find myself driven to the conclusion that (whether or not it might be desirable) the police themselves have no *j* power under the common law to 'detain' intangible assets, even if they have reasonable grounds for supposing that they are traceable to property which has been obtained from another in breach of the criminal law. If, after full consideration of all the consequences, they think it desirable that they should have this right or that new special powers to seek relief by way of injunction, in cases like the present, should be conferred on them, then they should in my opinion seek such powers from Parliament and not from the court.

a For my own part therefore, with great respect to Lord Denning MR and Donaldson LJ and to the persuasive submissions of counsel for the chief constable, I would uphold the order of Beldam J in refusing to continue the subsisting injunction beyond this present appeal. I would do so on the grounds that the chief constable has established no claim to a legal or equitable right sufficient to give him a locus standi to seek an injunction. I would dismiss the appeal accordingly. Since, however, Lord Denning MR and Donaldson LJ take a different view, the appeal will be allowed, though the precise form of the order *b* will no doubt require some further discussion.

Appeal allowed. Injunction granted.

Solicitors: *Sharpe, Pritchard & Co*, agents for *R A Crabb*, Maidstone (for the chief constable); *Treasury Solicitor.*

c Frances Rustin   Barrister.

Savage v Savage

d FAMILY DIVISION AT SWANSEA
WOOD J
23, 29 APRIL 1982

Divorce – Decree absolute – Application for leave to apply for decree to be made absolute – Application made out of time – Cohabitation after decree nisi – Matters to be considered in
e *exercising discretion to grant or refuse application – Matrimonial Causes Rules 1977, r 65(2)*
proviso.

In April 1977, after nine years of marriage, the wife filed a petition for divorce on the ground that the husband's behaviour was such that she could not reasonably be expected to live with him. The wife's case was not very strong, but her petition was undefended *f* and on 21 May 1977 she was granted a decree nisi under the special procedure. After the decree the husband attempted a reconciliation and in June or July 1977 the wife agreed to his return to the matrimonial home (where she was living with the two young children of the marriage) because she wished to give him an opportunity to change his behaviour as he had promised and because she thought his return would benefit the children. The wife's evidence was that all was well for the first five or six months of the *g* reconciliation but that thereafter the husband's behaviour deteriorated and the reconciliation came to an end. However, the parties continued to cohabit and have sexual relations for some 3½ years until February 1981 when, after a single violent incident, the husband left the matrimonial home saying the marriage was over. In June 1981, more than 12 months after the grant of the decree nisi, the wife made an application for the decree to be made absolute. The hearing of the application was delayed because further *h* affidavits were ordered to be sworn by the wife, and it was not until April 1982, nearly five years after the decree nisi, that the application was heard. The registrar referred the application to a judge. The husband did not oppose the application and consented to a rescission of the decree nisi if the court should refuse to make it absolute. At the hearing of the application the wife submitted that, although more than 12 months had elapsed since the decree nisi, the court should exercise its discretion under the proviso to r 65(2)[a] *j* of the Matrimonial Causes Rules 1977 to make the decree absolute because (i) at the date of the application the marriage had broken down because of the husband's behaviour, (ii) the period of reconciliation after the decree nisi had lasted only five or six months and (iii) in all the circumstances it would be wrong to rescind the decree nisi and require the wife to present a fresh petition.

---

a   Rule 65(2), so far as material, is set out at p 51 a, post

Held – In exercising the discretionary jurisdiction which the court had under the proviso
to r 65(2) of the 1977 rules to make a decree absolute notwithstanding that more than 12   *a*
months had elapsed since the decree nisi, the matters to be considered included (a) the
question whether, in the light of the evidence at the date of the application, the decree
nisi had been pronounced on sound evidence and on sound inferences from that evidence,
(b) the period and not merely the quality of the post-decree nisi cohabitation (so that the
fact that the period of reconciliation during the cohabitation had been shortlived was
irrelevant), and (c) public policy, which required that the decree should not be made   *b*
absolute where there was prolonged cohabitation after a decree, since reconciliation was
to be encouraged and should not be constantly threatened by the fact that the decree
might be made absolute. In the light of the circumstances known at the date of the
application, it was clear that the wrong inference had been drawn that the wife could not
reasonably be expected to live with the husband when the decree nisi was pronounced
under the special procedure. Having regard to that, to the long period of the post-decree   *c*
nisi cohabitation, and to public policy, the proper conclusion was that the application for
the decree to be made absolute should be refused and the decree nisi granted in May
1977 rescinded, despite the fact that the court was satisfied that at the date of the
application the marriage had irretrievably broken down because of the husband's
behaviour. The application would therefore be refused (see p 52 *c* to p 53 *c* and *e*, post).

Per curiam. Delay in applying for a decree to be made absolute after the lapse of 12   *d*
months from the decree nisi should not of itself prejudice the applicant if the court
thinks it right on other grounds to make the decree absolute. Where, however, substantial
doubts exist as to the likely outcome of an application for a decree to be made absolute
after the lapse of 12 months from the decree nisi, consideration should be given to
obtaining leave to file a second petition and to bringing it on for hearing, together with
any issues concerning children and financial matters, at the same time as the application   *e*
for the decree to be made absolute (see p 53 *c* to *e*, post).

Court v Court [1982] 2 All ER 531 considered.

Notes

For the grant of a decree absolute on lodging notice, see 13 Halsbury's Laws (4th edn)
para 977.   *f*

For the Matrimonial Causes Rules 1977, r 65, see 10 Halsbury's Statutory Instruments
(4th reissue) 261.

Case referred to in judgment

Court v Court [1982] 2 All ER 531, [1982] 3 WLR 199.

g

Application

Frances Rosina Savage (the wife) applied for leave to make absolute a decree nisi
pronounced in her favour on 27 May 1977. The registrar referred the application to a
judge of the Family Division. The husband did not oppose the application. The facts are
set out in the judgment.

h

Huw Davies for the wife.
E James Holman for the Queen's Proctor as amicus curiae.
The husband did not appear.

Cur adv vult

j

29 April. **WOOD J** read the following judgment: The applicant petitioner, the wife,
was married to the respondent, the husband, on 2 March 1968. She was then aged 18
and he was 24. There are two children of the family, both girls, born respectively on 18
October 1972 and 13 November 1974. On 27 May 1977 she obtained a decree nisi of
divorce on the grounds set out in s 1(2)(*b*) of the Matrimonial Causes Act 1973 and a
declaration was made under s 41 of the 1973 Act in respect of the children. She now

seeks the leave of this court to make that decree absolute under r 65(2) of the Matrimonial
a Causes Rules 1977, SI 1977/344, the proviso to which reads:

> 'Provided that if the notice [of an application to make absolute a decree nisi] is
> lodged more than 12 months after the decree nisi, the registrar may require the
> applicant to file an affidavit accounting for the delay and may make such order on
> the application as he thinks fit or refer the application to a judge.'

b
The district registrar has quite properly referred this matter to a judge of the Family
Division and the Queen's Proctor attends as amicus curiae under s 8(1)(*a*) of the 1973 Act.
Very nearly five years have elapsed since the decree nisi.

The history may be stated quite shortly. Some two years after the marriage the wife
issued a summons in the Swansea Magistrates' Court alleging desertion, which summons
c was dismissed. The husband was then in the merchant navy and had been away for about
11 months. The parties were reconciled. Unfortunately, shortly after that reconciliation
he infected her with venereal disease. That episode was, however, overcome and the two
girls, as will be seen from the dates of birth, were born thereafter. In her petition, which
is undated, but which must have been filed early in April 1977, the wife alleges that the
husband treated her with indifference and with a lack of attention; that he neglected the
d children; that the sexual side of the marriage was unsatisfactory in that he frequently
refused sexual intercourse, that there were financial problems, that he did not help with
the children despite the wife's ill-health and that on 25 March 1977 he refused to
accompany her to a previously arranged social evening, as a result of which there was a
quarrel and on the following day, 26 March, the wife took the children, left and went to
live with relatives in Swansea. Four weeks later she arranged with the husband that she
should move back into the matrimonial home, which was a council house, and that the
e tenancy should be assigned to her. It was some two weeks later that he started to try to
seek a reconciliation. However, he was unsuccessful but continued in his efforts after
decree nisi and by the end of June or early July 1977 he had returned with the wife's
agreement to the matrimonial home and a reconciliation took place.

The wife says that she felt it right to allow her husband an opportunity to live up to
f his promises to change and she thought it would be for the benefit of the children if a
reconciliation took place. She tells me, and I do not doubt her, that things were better for
some five to six months, then started once more to deteriorate. She had not sought the
advice of her solicitors before resuming cohabitation and she did not know that she could
apply for decree absolute within 12 months of the decree nisi. She told me that if she had
known she would have applied for the decree nisi to be made absolute. However, the
fact is that cohabitation continued until an incident of violence took place on 12 February
g 1981, after which the husband declared the marriage to be over, packed his cases and left.

On 1 April 1981 the wife consulted solicitors and early in June 1981 she initiated the
present application, which was then supported by a wholly inadequate affidavit. Since
that time a number of orders have been made and on 30 October 1981 a fuller affidavit
was filed, giving the history of the wife's relationship with the husband from June 1977
to February 1981. Paragraph 2 of that affidavit reads:
h

> 'After the Respondent returned to live with me in or about June 1977 our
> relationship was not too bad for the first few months but after that his behaviour
> gradually deteriorated until it became impossible to live with him.'

Looking to the remainder of the affidavit it is to be noted that the incidents complained
j of start in June 1980 and subject to the last incident of violence substantially extend up
to the end of 1980, at which time the wife was seeking the advice of her doctor. Counsel
for the Queen's Proctor asked the wife some questions from which it was clear that
although the physical side of her marriage remained unsatisfactory after June 1977, she
had, until near the end, been anxious and willing for normal sexual relationships, but
that it was the husband who had often refused. The only incident of violence was that in
February 1981, save that on one occasion the husband had struck the eldest daughter.

The husband does not oppose this application and he would consent to rescission of the decree if I refuse it. I understand it to be common ground that, if in the exercise of *a* my discretion I refuse to make the decree absolute, the decree nisi should be rescinded so that a further petition could be filed at once on which prima facie the wife will succeed.

Counsel for the wife made helpful submissions and I trust that I will show due deference to his arguments if I set them out somewhat shortly. He submitted that the marriage has now clearly broken down; that looking at the whole history the behaviour of the husband has now been such, as indeed he submits it was originally; that the wife *b* cannot reasonably be expected to live with him. Secondly he argues that the justice of the case requires a decree absolute to be granted, that the reconciliation in fact only existed for some five to six months and that it would be wrong to make parties start the proceedings afresh, although at the suggestion of the Queen's Proctor a second petition was in draft and ready for filing.

Counsel for the Queen's Proctor submitted that public policy must play a large part in *c* the decision which the court is asked to reach. He stressed that reconciliation was to be encouraged and that that was shown by the provisions of s 2 of the Matrimonial Causes Act 1973 and also by the fact that a decree absolute could be sought at any time up to 12 months from decree nisi. He submitted, however, that it was wrong that reconciliation, once achieved, should be continued with the threat of a decree nisi hanging over the head of the respondent to the suit. Encouragement should be given to the parties to *d* agree to rescind the decree under r 64 of the Matrimonial Causes Rules 1977. His second main submission was that a stale decree nisi should not be given new life, especially when a prolonged cohabitation had taken place since it was pronounced. The test he proposed was whether the inference drawn by the court originally from the facts that 'the petitioner cannot reasonably be expected to live with the respondent' was still justified in the light of subsequent events. *e*

The present decree nisi was obtained by the special procedure, which itself is no doubt tending to exacerbate a problem which already existed and apparently there are an increasing number of cases similar to the present one of which the Queen's Proctor has knowledge.

I am quite satisfied that at the present time this marriage has irretrievably broken down and that the husband has behaved in such a way that the wife cannot reasonably *f* be expected to live with him, but one of the main issues in the exercise of this discretionary jurisdiction is whether the original decree nisi was pronounced on sound evidence and on sound inferences to be drawn from such evidence. The final phrase of s 1(2)(b) of the 1973 Act is too often overlooked. It is an essential factor.

In looking to the present case it is clear that a parting took place in 1970, after which there was a reconciliation. The original petition does not present a very strong case if one *g* excludes the allegation of the venereal infection which took place shortly after the reconciliation in 1970. The incident which brought matters to a head in March 1977 was a very minor one, and the wife agreed in evidence that the marriage might possibly have continued even after that incident. The period between the original parting and the reconciliation was only some three months. The reconciliation and cohabitation following thereon extended over a very long period of time, some 3½ years, and it was some 2¼ *h* years before any substantial incidents are complained about. The physical side of the marriage also continued, as it had done before, and it was the wife who was always ready and willing for it to take place.

In looking at the period of cohabitation it was argued that the quality of the cohabitation should be examined in each case to see how long the reconciliation continued. I am not convinced that that is the correct approach in view of the wording *j* of many parts of s 2 of the 1973 Act. It is also extremely difficult to assess such a test, and, although cohabitation will always be with the hope of reconciliation, it is the living together which is the period which must be examined, in my judgment. All the factors which I have mentioned above lead me to the inevitable conclusion that the inference originally drawn under the special procedure, that the wife could not reasonably be a expected to live with the husband, was the wrong inference, looked at in the light of all the circumstances now known.

To approach the problem in this way is not to undermine attempts at reconciliation. There is the period of 12 months referred to in the proviso to r 65(2) of the 1977 rules, to which I have already referred, and the periods of time outlined in s 2 of the 1973 Act are within that span; thereafter the court has a discretion. It is perhaps surprising that the substantive law does not direct that a decree nisi shall lapse after a given period, possibly

b two years. This might help to cement any reconciliation which had taken place within that period and to encourage finality where the condition of the marriage was in reality hopeless.

I do not criticise the wife in any way. She is a hard-working, responsible person who has given considerable thought to her family problems and to the best interests of her children, but in exercising my discretion there is an element here of public policy and I

c am quite clear that the proper conclusion is that I must refuse to make the decree absolute. I have been referred helpfully to *Court v Court* [1982] 2 All ER 531, [1982] 3 WLR 199, a decision of Arnold P, which has been of assistance to me in reaching my conclusions. In that case emphasis was laid on the importance of a prompt application at the end of any period of cohabitation after the lapse of 12 months from decree nisi. In this case there has been some considerable lapse of time, but, as many practitioners may

d not be very familiar with this procedure, I do not think that it should prejudice the wife if I thought it right on other grounds to make the decree absolute. Where substantial doubts occur as to the likely outcome of an application such as the present, advisers will no doubt be wise to consider whether application should not be made for leave to file a second petition and perhaps to bring it on for hearing at the same time, together with all issues concerning the children and the financial issues which may not have been agreed.

e It is of course obvious that in any event, whether the decree is made absolute or not, financial issues will have to be decided and by taking this course it may minimise the overall cost of the proceedings to the parties or to the legal aid fund.

I refuse to make the decree absolute and rescind the decree nisi granted on 27 May 1977.

f *Application refused.*

Solicitors: *Peter Williams & Co*, Swansea (for the wife); *Queen's Proctor.*

Bebe Chua   Barrister.

g # R v Goldstein

COURT OF APPEAL, CRIMINAL DIVISION
LORD LANE CJ, LLOYD AND EASTHAM JJ
29 MARCH, 1, 2 APRIL 1982

h *Criminal law – Trial – Evidence in absence of jury – Question of law – Interpretation of EEC Treaty – Question whether prohibition on importation of radiotelephonic apparatus contrary to terms of treaty – Whether question of law to be determined by judge in absence of jury – European Communities Act 1972, s 3(1) – EEC Treaty, art 36.*

j The appellant was charged with being party to the fraudulent evasion of the prohibition on the importation of citizens' band radios imposed by s 7[a] of the Wireless Telegraphy Act 1967 and reg 3[b] of the Radiotelephonic Transmitters (Control of Manufacture and Importation) Order 1968. He did not dispute the facts but pleaded not guilty on the

---

a   Section 7, so far as material, is set out at p 56 a to c, post
b   Regulation 3 is set out at p 56 c d, post

ground that s 7 and reg 3 were inconsistent with, and superseded by, art 30^c of the EEC
Tresty, which prohibitel the imposition of quantitative restrictions on imports between   *a*
member states of the EEC. The Crown submitted that, by virtue of art 36^d of the treaty,
art 30 did not apply because the prohibition on the importation of citizens' band radios
was 'justified on grounds of . . . public policy or public security [or] the protection of . . .
life'. That issue was considered by the judge in the absence of the jury. The judge heard
evidence from three Crown witnesses to the effect that the ban was justified and on the
strength of that evidence ruled that the case came within art 36 and that the trial should   *b*
proceed. The jury were recalled and, after the appellant had formally intimated that he
did not wish to call any evidence, the judge directed them to return a verdict of guilty,
which they did. The appellant appealed against conviction, contending that the issue
whether the prohibition imposed by s 7 and reg 3 was justified under art 36 was an issue
of mixed law and fact and should therefore have been determined on evidence given in
the course of the trial in the presence of the jury.   *c*

Held – Because s 3(1)^e of the European Communities Act 1972 required that any
question as to the meaning or effect of, inter alia, the EEC Treaty was to be 'treated as a
question of law', the judge had been right to deal with the issue of whether art 36 of the
EEC Treaty applied to the prohibition which the appellant was charged with breaching
as if that issue was a question of law, even though it might not be one. Furthermore, the   *d*
evidence given by the Crown witnesses in the jury's absence was not evidence which
related to the guilt or innocence of the appellant (which was a question to be decided by
the jury) but was evidence of facts which determined the existence or non-existence of
the offence and the very power of the court to hear the case at all, which was a question
to be decided by the judge alone. It was irrelevant that the facts had been admitted, the
jury empanelled and the appellant arraigned before the issue was raised (see p 61 *d* to *g*   *e*
and p 62 *f g*, post).

   R v Maywhort [1955] 2 All ER 752 considered.

   Per curiam. Questions concerning the existence of an offence should be raised on a
motion to quash the indictment before arraignment (see p 62 *f*, post).

Notes   *f*
For prohibitions on imports to the United Kingdom from member states of the European
Community, see 12 Halsbury's Laws (4th edn) paras 1054–1063.

   For evidence in the absence of the jury, see 11 ibid para 302, and for cases on the
subject, see 14(2) Digest (Reissue) 827–828, 7097–7098.

   For motions to quash indictments, see 11 Halsbury's Laws (4th edn) para 236, and for
cases on the subject, see 14(1) Digest (Reissue) 325–328, 2532–2595.   *g*

   For the Wireless Telegraphy Act 1967, s 7, see 35 Halsbury's Statutes (3rd edn) 169.

   For the European Communities Act 1972, ss 2, 3, see 42 ibid 80, 84.

   For the EEC Treaty, arts 30, 36, see 42A ibid 525, 528.

Cases referred to in judgment
de Peijper (Adriaan), Re Case 104/75 [1976] ECR 613, CJEC.   *h*
*Firma Denkavit Futtermittel GmbH v Minister für Ernährung, Landwirtschaft und Forsten des
   Landes Nordrhein-Westfalen* Case 251/78 [1979] ECR 3369, CJEC.
DPP v Stonehouse [1977] 2 All ER 909, [1978] AC 55, [1977] 3 WLR 143, HL, Digest
   (Cont Vol E) 129, 744a.
NV United Foods v Belgian State Case 132/80 [1981] ECR 995, CJEC.
Officier van Justitie v Koninklijke Kaasfabriek Eyssen BV Case 53/80 [1981] ECR 409, CJEC.   *j*

---

c   Article 30 is set out at p 56 *g*, post
d   Article 36 provides: 'The provisions of Articles 30 to 34 shall not preclude prohibitions or
      restrictions on imports . . . justified on grounds of . . . public policy or public security; the
      protection of health and life of humans . . .'
e   Section 3(1) is set out at p 61 *b c*, post

R v Dunne (1929) 21 Cr App R 176, CCA, 22 Digest (Reissue) 421, *4235*.

a *R v Jones* [1974] ICR 310, CA, Digest (Cont Vol D) 964, *1458c*.

R v Maywhort [1955] 2 All ER 752, [1955] 1 WLR 848, 15 Digest (Reissue) 1331, *11495*.

R v Reynolds [1950] 1 All ER 335, [1950] 1 KB 606, CCA, 14(2) Digest (Reissue) 827, *7097*.

R v Tymen [1980] 3 CMLR 101, Crown Court at Cardiff.

b **Cases also cited**

Casati (Guerrino), Re criminal proceedings against Case 203/80 [1981] ECR 2595, CJEC.

Hauer (Liselotte) v Land Rheinland-Pfalz Case 44/79 [1979] ECR 3727, CJEC.

Joshua v R [1955] 1 All ER 22, [1955] AC 121, PC.

Knuller (Publishing, Printing and Promotions) Ltd v DPP [1972] 2 All ER 898, [1973] AC 435, HL.

c *R v Sutton* [1969] 1 All ER 928, [1969] 1 WLR 375, CA.

R v Vickers [1975] 2 All ER 945, [1975] 1 WLR 811, CA.

Appeal

On 2 December 1980 in the Crown Court at Ipswich before his Honour Judge Binns and a jury the appellant, Alexander Joseph Goldstein, was convicted of being concerned in

d the fraudulent evasion of the prohibition on the importation of certain radiotelephonic apparatus imposed under s 7 of the Wireless Telegraphy Act 1967 and reg 3 of the Radiotelephonic Transmitters (Control of Manufacture and Importation) Order 1968, SI 1968/61. He was fined £500 with six months' imprisonment in default of payment and ordered to pay £250 towards the costs of the prosecution. He appealed against conviction and sentence. The facts are set out in the judgment of the court.

e

Louis Blom-Cooper QC and *Gordon Bennett* (neither of whom appeared below) (assigned by the Registrar of Criminal Appeals) for the appellant.

John Lindsay QC (who did not appear below) and *John Devaux* for the Crown.

LORD LANE CJ delivered the following judgment of the court: On 2 December 1980

f in the Crown Court at Ipswich the appellant pleaded not guilty to one count of being concerned in the fraudulent evasion of the prohibition on the importation of certain wireless telegraphic apparatus, known familiarly as 'citizens' band' or 'CB' radios. He was found guilty. He was fined £500, to be paid by certain instalments with a sentence of six months' imprisonment in default, and also to pay a sum towards the prosecution costs. He appeals against both conviction and sentence.

g   The facts of the offence alleged against him were simple enough. He arrived by sea at Felixstowe from Antwerp with a motor car on a date in January 1980. He drove towards and into the green area of the customs shed where he was stopped by a customs officer, and he was asked if he had any dutiable goods in his possession, to which he replied, 'No.' The car was then searched and concealed in the floor at the rear of the car were found 50 of these radio sets. He first of all said that he knew nothing about them, but that the car

h he was driving belonged to a man called Hochauser for whom, as a matter of friendship, he had driven across from Antwerp to Felixstowe. He had simply been doing a favour to Hochauser in this way. Eventually, however, he admitted that he knew of the presence of these radios and indeed had himself assisted in the packing of them in the car in the way I have described.

The facts were not in dispute at the trial. Counsel for the defence intimated that he

j did not intend to address the jury, and indeed all the evidence relating to this aspect of the matter was read to the jury. The plea of not guilty, said defending counsel in plain terms to the judge, was based on what he described as a point of law alone. He recognised that the verdict of the jury would be one of guilty or not guilty on the direction of the judge according to the way in which the judge decided the so-called point of law.

The point at issue was whether s 7 of the Wireless Telegraphy Act 1967 and the Radiotelephonic Transmitters (Control of Manufacture and Importation) Order 1968, SI

1968/61, under which the prosecution was brought, were inconsistent with and
superseded by art 30 of the EEC Treaty of 1957.

Section 7 of the Wireless Telegraphy Act 1967, in so far as it is material, provides:

'(1) Where it appears to the Postmaster General to be expedient that the provisions
of this section should apply to wireless telegraphy apparatus of any class or
description for the purpose of preventing or reducing the risk of interference with
wireless telegraphy, he may by order specify apparatus of that class or description
for the purposes of this section.

'(2) Where apparatus of any class or description is for the time being specified by
an order under subsection (1) of this section—(a) no person shall manufacture,
whether or not for sale, any apparatus of that class or description; and (b) the
importation of apparatus of that class or description is hereby prohibited . . .'

Regulation 3 of the Radiotelephonic Transmitters (Control of Manufacture and
Importation) Order 1968 provides:

'Wireless telegraphy apparatus of the following class or description is hereby
specified for the purposes of section 7 of the Wireless Telegraphy Act 1967 namely,
wireless telegraphy apparatus consisting of radio-telephonic apparatus capable of
transmitting on any of the following frequencies, that is to say, on any frequency
between 26·1 and 29·7 megacycles per second or between 88 and 108 megacycles
per second, and notwithstanding that the said apparatus is also capable of
transmitting on other frequencies outside the limits aforesaid.'

These citizens' band radios transmitted on 27 MHz or were apt to interfere with any
harmonics of that particular frequency.

The next enactment to which reference has to be made is the European Communities
Act 1972. Section 2(1) of that Act provides:

'All such rights, powers, liabilities, obligations and restrictions from time to time
created or arising by or under the Treaties, and all such remedies and procedures
from time to time provided for by or under the Treaties, as in accordance with the
Treaties are without further enactment to be given legal effect or used in the United
Kingdom shall be recognised and available in law, and be enforced, allowed and
followed accordingly; and the expression "enforceable Community right" and
similar expressions shall be read as referring to one to which this subsection applies.'

Article 30 of the EEC Treaty provides:

'Quantitative restrictions on imports and all measures having equivalent effect
shall, without prejudice to the following provisions, be prohibited between Member
States.'

The issue which was, by agreement of both parties, dealt with by the judge alone and
not by the jury was whether the Crown could rely on art 36 of the EEC Treaty as
protecting them from the effect of art 30 which I have just read. It was conceded, and
properly conceded, that art 30 on its own would supersede the 1967 Act and the 1968
order because they amounted to quantitative restrictions on the import of this type of
equipment.

The Crown called three witnesses before the judge on this particular point. The effect
of their evidence, if believed, was to show that the use of the citizens' band radio on the
27 MHz waveband was to adversely affect a whole variety of electronic devices which are
in use up and down the length and breadth of this country. But suffice it to mention but
a few. First of all, aircraft instrument landing systems, which operate either on this
wavelength or a harmonic of it; hospital bleep paging systems, whereby doctors and
officials in hospitals can be summoned by a centrally operated radio signal; fire services
and police wavelengths and communication systems; alarm systems which are available
to some old people living on their own to communicate to a central point if they are in

a   need of assistance and so on. There was one particular witness, a Major A, doing service in Northern Ireland. He gave specific evidence that citizens' band radios are a method popular among terrorists in Northern Ireland, both for detonating by remote control explosive devices and for alerting fellow terrorists to police movements and so on, and are therefore, in that part of the United Kingdom, a valuable adjunct to murder and violence.

b   The judge, on the strength of that evidence, came to the conclusion that the defence submission was not correct, and that art 36 did avoid the embarrassment, so to speak, of art 30. Accordingly the matter was one which his court was entitled to try. Perhaps it is necessary at this stage to see the course he actually took thereafter.

The judge completed his judgment on the submission in these words: 'I suppose, expressing it in legal terms, Mr Maidment [who was counsel for the defence] I find that there is a case to answer.' The following exchange then took place:

c

> 'Mr Maidment. In that case, your Honour, the jury will have to come back and it will be a matter, really, for your Honour to direct the jury that as a matter of law there is only one verdict they can bring in.
>
> Judge Binns. I take it I must formally ask you, are you proposing to call any evidence or address the jury?
>
> Mr Maidment. Your Honour, no.
>
> *d*   Judge Binns. Very well, we will have the jury back.'

In short the judge on that basis, plainly by the consent of counsel, directed the jury that in the circumstances they should return a verdict of guilty.

Now by a last minute amendment to the notice of appeal counsel for the appellant raises a number of interesting points which, he submits, show that the conviction cannot *e*   stand. The fresh notice of appeal, no doubt counsel for the appellant's brain-child, only saw the light of day last Monday morning, and we adjourned the matter until today in order to give counsel for the Crown time to marshal more effectively the arguments which he has propounded to us today in answer to counsel for the appellant's submissions.

The first and most important point which counsel for the appellant raises is this: the question whether the prohibition imposed by the regulations of 1968 was justified under *f*   the terms of art 36 was, he submits, a mixed question of fact and law and was therefore a question to be determined by a properly directed jury and not by the decision of the judge alone. In support of that contention he advances the following argument. All admissible evidence given in the course of a criminal trial must be tendered in the presence of the jury for the simple reason that the jury are the masters of fact.

He cites for our benefit the decision in *R v Reynolds* [1950] 1 All ER 335, [1950] 1 KB *g*   606. In that case the judge in the absence of the jury asked questions of a school attendance officer about the reliability of the child complainant with a view to determining whether the child should be sworn or not before the child gave evidence. In the judgment of the court, given by Lord Goddard CJ, there appears this passage ([1950] 1 All ER 335 at 337, [1950] 1 KB 606 at 610):

h

> 'In *R. v. Dunne* ((1929) 21 Cr App R 176), a child of seven was put into the box to be examined on a charge of incest, and the judge had her taken to his room so that he could talk to her and examine her to see whether she understood the nature of an oath. She afterwards gave evidence, but this court quashed the conviction and LORD HEWART, C.J., said (at 178): "It goes without saying that what the judge did in that matter was suggested purely by feelings of kindness and consideration for the youthful witness. The question for this court is, can a conviction stand after an *j*   incident of that kind has occurred? It is admittedly an incident without parallel. Admittedly, nobody in this court, either from his own experience or from researches into the authorities, can adduce any parallel case. In the result, something was said to or by this witness which was not in the hearing or presence of the jury or of the accused. The court is clearly of opinion that, in these cirumstances, the appeal must be allowed and the conviction quashed." No member of this court has ever known

of a case in which a witness has been called to inform the court whether or not a
child is fit to give evidence. I am not saying that there may not be cases—perhaps *a*
this is one—in which the judge or chairman may want some assistance, especially if
he hears that the child is at a particular sort of school. It is not on that ground that
the court thinks that there has been a fatal mistake here. The reason why the court
decided in *R. v. Dunne* that the evidence of the child must be given in the presence
of the jury was because, although the duty of deciding whether the child may be
sworn or not lies on the judge and is not a matter for the jury, it is most important *b*
that the jury should hear the answers which the child gives and see her demeanour
when she is questioned by the court for that enables them to come to a conclusion
as to what weight they should attach to her evidence.'

We agree that apart from obvious exceptions, such as decisions as to the admissibility
of evidence which for clear reasons have to be made in the absence of the jury, all matters *c*
going to the issues raised by the indictment must be dealt with in the presence of the
jury and by evidence given in the presence of the jury. As these two cases, *R v Dunne* and
R v Reynolds, amply demonstrate, this includes questions as to the credibility of the
evidence called to prove the allegations in the indictment.

Secondly, counsel for the appellant submits that the issue whether the 1968 order was
justified by virtue of the terms of art 36 was a question of mixed law and fact, and *d*
therefore one for the jury. In this respect he cites the decision in *DPP v Stonehouse* [1977]
2 All ER 909, [1978] AC 55. The passage which he cited to us was a passage in the opinion
of Lord Diplock, who in certain respects found himself in the minority of their Lordships,
and which reads ([1977] 2 All ER 909 at 918–919, [1978] AC 55 at 69–70):

'There are some crimes whose definition incorporates as a constituent element a
concept which is imprecise in that it involves some matter of degree on which *e*
opinions of reasonable men may differ and as to which the legal training and
experience of a judge does not make his opinion on the matter more likely to be
right than that of a non-lawyer. Under our system of trial by jury the question
whether the facts proved conform to such a concept is one for the jury despite its
involving interpretation of the definition of a crime; because, it being a matter on
which opinions may reasonably differ, an opinion that is shared by at least ten jurors *f*
is thought to be more reliable than that of a single judge. In the crime of attempt
the concept of proximity between the acts of the accused and the complete offence
that he intended to commit involves this kind of imprecision; but the imprecision
is limited in its range. At one extreme it can be said that the particular acts proved
are so remote from the complete offence that no reasonable person could regard
them as sufficiently proximate to conform to the definition of an attempt; at the *g*
other extreme it can be said that they are so immediately connected with it that no
reasonable person could regard them as not conforming to the definition of an
attempt. In directing the jury that the only acts of the accused of which there is
evidence are outside the range of proximity which any reasonable person could
regard as conforming to that concept as a constituent element in the common law
offence of attempt, the judge is exercising his responsibility as controller of the trial *h*
to prevent its resulting in a perverse verdict which would call for correction by the
Court of Appeal under s 2(1)(a) of the Criminal Appeal Act 1968. If the acts of the
accused lay beyond the other extreme of the range of proximity within which any
reasonable person could doubt that they conformed to that concept as a constituent
element in the offence of attempt, a verdict of acquittal on the ground that the acts
of the accused were not sufficiently proximate would also be perverse.' *j*

Here again no one would of course wish to quarrel with the accuracy and lucidity of
that exposition. But to take it out of its context and try and apply it to the totally different
circumstances of the instant case may perhaps be something less than helpful.

Next it is submitted that once the indictment is before the court, as counsel for the
appellant put it, the defendant must be arraigned and tried thereon unless there is a

successful motion to quash, or a plea in bar or the Attorney General enters a nolle
a prosequi, or the indictment discloses an offence which the court has no power to try.
Accordingly, goes the submission, if art 36 raises a pure matter of law, the way of dealing
with it would be by way of motion to quash the indictment before the jury has been
empanelled or the prisoner arraigned.

This is much more a matter of form than a matter of substance. It was by agreement
of all the parties that the point was dealt with as it was, namely by the judge at the close
b of the prosecution case giving his ruling coupled with the appropriate direction to the
jury as invited to do by counsel for the defence and which resulted in a verdict of guilty,
which of course is one of the ways a jury trial can properly come to an end.

It may be that, if it was a matter for the judge, it would have been better to have dealt
with the matter at the outset of the trial before the defendant was arraigned by a motion
to quash. We were referred in this respect to *R v Tymen* [1980] 3 CMLR 101 at 103, in
c which Watkins J, giving the judgment of the court, said: 'If, as a consequence of the way
I deal with this application, it becomes necessary to listen to a motion to quash this
indictment, that I will do.'

We were also referred to a passage in the judgment of James LJ in *R v Jones* [1974] ICR
310 at 320 (the Shrewsbury picket case), in which he said:

d 'We can deal with the last argument at once and shortly. The validity of a count
in an indictment is a question of law. It is a question for the judge. It can never be a
question for the jury. If the judge rules that the count is valid the trial will proceed
on the count as drawn. If the judge is later shown to have been wrong in that ruling,
a conviction on that count may be challenged successfully on appeal to this court.
But there may be cases in which during the presentation or at the end of the Crown
case the evidence discloses a situation not apparent before arraignment. Upon a
e motion to quash a count made before arraignment the judge gives his ruling on the
form and matter on the face of the indictment. Only in one circumstance can the
judge look beyond the indictment to the depositions or statements. That is when
the motion to quash is on the ground that the offence is not disclosed by the
depositions or statements and that there has been no committal for trial of that
offence [and James LJ then cited two cases. He went on:] But when evidence has
f been called, the decision based upon the face of the indictment may be shown to be
wrong. If it then appears that a count is defective in that it contains allegations of
more than one offence it is the duty of the judge to rule that the indictment should
be amended pursuant to section 5(1) of the Indictments Act 1915 by splitting the
offences into different counts if no injustice would be caused or by directing the
prosecution to elect on which offence the trial should proceed. We emphasise that
g the decision at this stage is again one of law for the judge and not of fact for the
jury.'

In the present case, if there had been a motion to quash based in some way on the facts
of the offence charged or the way in which that offence had been committed for trial,
those observations would be in point. Non constat that they are relevant when the issue
h was whether the offence charged existed as an offence at all.

Next counsel for the appellant argues that, even if he is wrong in the foregoing
submissions, yet nevertheless the judge was wrong in his approach to the test of
justification in art 36. We have listened to submissions on the precise meaning of the
word 'justified' in art 36. We have been referred to a very recent decision, *Officier van
Justitie v Koninklijke Kaasfabriek Eyssen BV* [1981] ECR 409, which indicates that the
j meaning of the word 'justified' in that article is 'necessary'. We assume, for the purpose
of argument, that that is the case. The test of necessity, of justification, in the article, so
goes the argument, is not merely whether the prohibition is necessary or justified, but
also whether the means used were necessary; in other words, was the particular
prohibition necessary, or would something less than that prohibition have been enough
to achieve the ends which the particular enactment sought? It is said that the judge never
directed himself on this point.

We were referred to a number of decisions from which we do not feel it necessary to cite. We give their names: *Re Adriaan de Peijper* [1976] ECR 613, *Firma Denkavit* *a* *Futtermittel GmbH v Minister für Ernährung, Landwirtschaft und Forsten des Landes Nordrhein-Westfalen* [1979] ECR 3369 and *NV United Foods v Belgium State* [1981] ECR 995.

We accept the proposition, which is self-evident from the wording of art 36 itself, that the restriction must be bona fide intended to meet the particular danger envisaged in the article. We accept the further proposition contained in this case, that the restriction should not be wider than is reasonably necessary for that purpose. It may be that the *b* judge did not have that latter consideration in mind. Indeed he can scarcely be blamed if he did not, because nobody mentioned it to him.

It is said that the passages in his judgment show that if he had that consideration in mind his decision would have been different. We were referred to a passage from the evidence of Mr Ricketts, who was one of the witnesses called on this question before the judge: *c*

'Q. And has CB radio featured in the planning? A. Not at all in this country. Not at all in the overall world planning of the bands, which are governed by the international body.

Q. Assignment on the 27 MHz has already been made? A. Yes, and citizens' band on that would interrupt and upset all the services on the band which are harmonically *d* related.'

We were referred to a further passage which reads as follows:

'Q. And do I understand you correctly, that because of this situation in Northern Ireland it is impossible to conduct your duties without using the multiples of 27 MHz? A. It is not impossible, it is extremely difficult. Nothing is impossible, but it makes our job very much harder if we cannot use those frequencies.' *e*

The final passage we were referred to reads:

'. . . Operators of radio-controlled model aircraft may, I believe, shortly be allowed to use another frequency for their operations within 27 MHz which would take them out of the way of illicit citizens' band operation but no attempt to my knowledge has been made to alter the frequencies used by the police, fire brigades, *f* hospital paging systems and other services which could be affected by direct radiation or harmonics from citizens' band. It would be a very complicated and expensive job because all those frequencies would have to be put somewhere else and the frequency spectrum is fairly well crowded at the moment.

Q. Yes, but if, as you suggest, there is a potential risk to life and limb would not such cost be justified, if what you are saying is correct? A. I would suggest the best *g* way of dealing with such a problem would be to prevent the use of this illegal radio equipment in the first place.'

If the judge had been alerted to this subsidiary question, as demonstrated from the Common Market cases, and if he had considered them before reaching a conclusion, we do not see how his conclusion could have been any different from the one which he *h* reached. The suggestion that everybody, from aircraft manufacturers, or manufacturers of aircraft avionics, to fire service and the police and the army should alter their frequencies to cater for this situation is, to our mind, quite extraordinary and untenable. Given that the dangers presented by the presence of these devices as spoken to by witnesses existed, which they plainly did, it seems to us that the judge was absolutely correct in coming to the conclusion that nothing short of a ban on import would have *j* any effect on the use of these articles. It is, as the evidence indicates, a practical impossibility to trace these devices. A ban on their use, which apparently exists at the moment, is almost impossible to carry out effectively, and certainly so far as Northern Ireland is concerned, once these devices are in this country there is nothing to stop them, so far as import controls are concerned, from going direct to Ulster. A total ban on

importation, if any restriction is justified under art 36, was, in our judgment, the only
a feasible method of control. In other words it was justified and also necessary.

We do not feel necessary, and we are sure counsel for the appellant will forgive us, to
deal with the subsidiary point which he raised under art 10 of the European Convention
for the Protection of Human Rights and Fundamental Freedoms (Cmnd 8969) relating
to freedom of expression. We say in passing that freedom of expression does not mean
freedom to express yourself on 27 MHz.

b The point in this case, and we return to it, is the first point made by counsel for the
appellant. One starts by looking at the terms of the European Communities Act 1972
itself, and particularly at s 3(1), which reads as follows:

'For the purposes of all legal proceedings any question as to the meaning or effect
of any of the Treaties, or as to the validity, meaning or effect of any Community
instrument, shall be treated as a question of law (and, if not referred to the European
c Court, be for determination as such in accordance with the principles laid down by
and any relevant decision of the European Court).'

It is to be noted, as has been drawn to our attention, that the footnote to this section in
42 Halsbury's Statutes (3rd edn) 85, dealing with 'Any question . . . shall be treated as a
question of law' says this: 'Apart from this provision questions of Community law might
d have been treated as questions of fact to be resolved by the use of expert witnesses . . .'
That, submits counsel for the appellant, is the only purpose of that particular provision.
But if one looks at the wording closely, these matters with which we are concerned here
were legal proceedings. The question was one as to the meaning and effect of art 36 of
the EEC Treaty. This, according to the terms of s 3(1), is to be treated as a question of
law, which means dealt with as if it were a question of law, even though it may not be
e one. That is precisely what his Honour Judge Binns, with the concurrence of counsel,
did. In our view he was correct.

But we do not base our decision primarily on that point. The answer does not rest
solely on the meaning of the words which we have just read in s 3(1). Any conclusion
other than that which we have indicated would, in our judgment, be contrary to
principle. The facts deposed to by the three witnesses called live before the judge to deal
f with the citizens' band radios, and giving evidence relating to the nature and effect of
those pieces of apparatus, were not facts on which the guilt or innocence of the appellant
depended, which facts are plainly for the jury to determine. They were facts which
determined the existence or non-existence of the very power of the court to hear the case
at all. They went to the existence of the offence.

It seems to us that in those circumstances it was not for the jury to decide whether the
g crime existed or not, but for the court itself. This is so whether the facts are admitted or
not. If they are not admitted, then the evidence, as happened here, must be adduced
before the judge, who will decide what is established and what is not, draw the proper
inferences and will come to his conclusion accordingly.

If the contention of the appellant were correct, it would have been improper to put
him in charge of the jury at all. There was no criminal offence which existed to which
h he could be required to plead guilty or not guilty. Therefore the decision is one which
has to be taken by the court and not by the jury.

We have succeeded in discovering only one case, *R v Maywhort* [1955] 2 All ER 752,
[1955] 1 WLR 848, which seems to bear on the question. We have given counsel for the
appellant an opportunity of looking at that authority this afternoon, and he concedes that
that decision is correct. It is a decision by Sellers J on the Welsh Circuit. A passage at the
j outset of his judgment explains the situation with such clarity as no précis could. It reads
([1955] 2 All ER 752 at 753):

'[The defendant] is indicted on three separate charges of fraudulent conversion,
contrary to s. 21 of the Larceny Act, 1916. The charges allege that he, being a trustee
of certain property, fraudulently converted it to his own use. Section 21 of the

Larcency Act, 1916, is the section dealing with conversion by a trustee. The defence have applied to quash the indictment, relying on s. 43(2) of the same Act, which *a* reads: "No person shall be liable to be convicted of any offence against s. 6, s. 7(1), s. 20, s. 21 and s. 22 of this Act upon any evidence whatever in respect of any act done by him, if at any time previously to his being charged with such offence he has first disclosed such an act on oath, in consequence of any compulsory process of any court of law or equity in any action, suit, or proceeding which has been bona fide instituted by any person aggrieved." The procedure for bringing before the *b* court the reliance on s. 43(2) was discussed by counsel for the prosecution and for the defence, and it seemed to me appropriate, although there is no clear precedent to which I have been referred, that a motion to quash could and should be taken before plea and at the outset of the case, because, if the submission that s. 43(2) applies is correct, the court would have no jurisdiction to try the case. If the case had been tried the trial would be a nullity if the submission later succeeded. In regard *c* to the evidence which is to be adduced and the manner of its presentation on such an application, counsel for the defence was content to rely on the evidence in the depositions taken before the justices and the documents which were exhibited. It may be, however [I interpolate, note this] although it is not necessary to decide this in the present case, that other evidence might be brought before the court on such a motion to quash, because, notwithstanding anything that may have been revealed *d* by the defendant in any proceedings such as those referred to in s. 43(2), the charges in an indictment might well be supported by evidence independent of that, and the sub-section expressly states that a person who comes within the sub-section shall not be liable to be convicted "upon any evidence whatever in respect of any act done by him".'

The present case is in certain ways stronger than that case decided by Sellers J, because *e* there the Act provided that no person shall be liable to be convicted of any offence against a particular section, unlike the present case where we are concerned with whether the section, so to speak, exists at all on which any prosecution can be founded or launched. The fact that the jury had already been empanelled and the defendant arraigned before that seems to us to make no difference. That was a matter of form and a matter of form only and a matter of form moreover agreed by defence counsel. It should not be allowed *f* to affect the substance of the matter. However in future it would, in our judgment, be better if matters of this sort were raised on a motion to quash the indictment before arraignment, and the matter can then be decided in the way we have indicated.

For these reasons in our judgment the submissions of counsel for the appellant fail and this appeal, so far as conviction is concerned, must be dismissed.

g

Appeal dismissed.

2 April. The court granted the appellant leave to appeal to the House of Lords and certified, under s 33(2) of the Criminal Appeal Act 1968, that the following point of law of general public importance was involved in the decision: (1) whether the issue whether the prohibition on importation contained in the Radiotelephonic Transmitters (Control of Manufacture and Importation) Order 1968 was ineffective by virtue of arts 30 and 36 of the EEC Treaty was to be decided by the judge alone, whether or not evidence had to be called; (2) whether the answer to question (1) differed depending on whether such issue was raised before or after arraignment.

Solicitors: *Solicitor for the Customs and Excise.*

N P Metcalfe Esq   Barrister.

R v Pitt

COURT OF APPEAL, CRIMINAL DIVISION
KERR LJ, PETER PAIN AND BELDAM JJ
30 MARCH, 2 APRIL 1982

Criminal evidence – Compellability as witness – Spouse as witness for prosecution – Wife competent but not compellable witness against husband – Wife having right to refuse to give evidence up to time she enters witness box – Wife's right not affected by previous witness statement or evidence given in committal proceedings – Effect of wife waiving right to refuse to give evidence against husband.

By reason of her status of being merely a competent and not a compellable witness for the prosecution in criminal proceedings against her husband, the choice which a wife has of refusing to give evidence for the prosecution or waiving the right of refusal and giving evidence against her husband exists right up to the moment she enters the witness box, and is unaffected by whether she has previously made a witness statement or given evidence at the husband's committal proceedings. However, if the wife chooses to waive her right of refusal and give evidence against her husband she becomes an ordinary witness, and having started her evidence she must complete it in the ordinary way; she cannot in such circumstances use the non-compellability of a wife as a witness as a reason for refusing to answer questions put to her by the prosecution, and is, furthermore, liable to be treated as a hostile witness if the nature of her evidence justifies such a course (see p 65 g h and p 66 a to d, post); *Leach v R* [1912] AC 305 and *Hoskyn v Comr of Police for the Metropolis* [1978] 2 All ER 136 applied.

Since a wife who chooses to give evidence for the prosecution against her husband may be treated as a hostile witness, it is desirable that, before she takes the oath and in the absence of the jury, the judge should explain to her that she has the right to refuse to give evidence against her husband but that if she chooses to give evidence against him she will be treated like any other witness and may be treated as a hostile witness (see p 66 d g to j, post); dictum of Darling J in *R v Acaster* (1912) 7 Cr App R at 189 applied.

If the circumstances justify it, the Court of Appeal may, under s 2(1)[a] of the Criminal Appeal Act 1968, set aside a conviction on the ground that it is unsafe or unsatisfactory if the court considers that injustice may have occurred because a wife gave evidence for the prosecution against her husband without appreciating that she had the right to refuse to give evidence against him (see p 66 j, post).

Notes

For evidence by a defendant's spouse in criminal proceedings, see 11 Halsbury's Laws (4th edn) paras 470–471, and for cases on the subject see 14(2) Digest (Reissue) 646–651, 5216–5277.

For the Criminal Appeal Act 1968, s 2, see 8 Halsbury's Statutes (3rd edn) 690.

Cases referred to in judgment

Hoskyn v Comr of Police for the Metropolis [1978] 2 All ER 136, [1979] AC 474, [1978] 2 WLR 695, HL, Digest (Cont Vol E) 143, 5234a.
Leach v R [1912] AC 305, HL, 14(2) Digest (Reissue) 650, 5267.
R v Acaster (1912) 7 Cr App R 187, CCA, 14(2) Digest (Reissue) 650, 5271.
R v Thompson (1976) 64 Cr App R 96, CA, Digest (Cont Vol E) 136, 2785a.

---

a   Section 2(1), so far as material, provides: 'Except as provided by this Act, the Court of Appeal shall allow an appeal against conviction if they think—(a) that the conviction should be set aside on the ground that under all the circumstances of the case it is unsafe or unsatisfactory . . .'

Cases also cited
R v Lapworth [1931] 1 KB 117, [1930] All ER Rep 340, CCA.   *a*
R v Manning [1968] Crim LR 675, CA.

Appeal
On 21 October 1981 in the Crown Court at Chelmsford before his Honour Judge Taylor
and a jury, the appellant, Ian Barry Pitt, was convicted on one count of assault occasioning
actual bodily harm and for that offence, and for breach of a suspended sentence and of a   *b*
community service order, was sentenced in all to 18 months' imprisonment. He appealed
with leave of the single judge against the conviction on the ground that the trial judge
wrongly allowed the appellant's wife, who gave evidence for the Crown against the
appellant, to be treated as a hostile witness. The facts are set out in the judgment of the
court.

Michael Wood (assigned by the Registrar of Criminal Appeals) for the appellant.   *c*
Dorothy Quick for the Crown.

Cur adv vult

2 April. **PETER PAIN J** read the following judgment of the court: On 21 October   *d*
1981 in the Crown Court at Chelmsford, the appellant was found guilty on one count of
assault occasioning actual bodily harm. He was found not guilty on another similar
count. He was sentenced as follows: for assault occasioning actual bodily harm, 18
months' imprisonment; for breach of a suspended sentence, 12 months' imprisonment
concurrent; for breach of a community service order, 3 months' imprisonment   *e*
concurrent. His total sentence was one of 18 months' imprisonment. He now appeals
with the leave of the single judge.
  This was a baby battering case. The Crown case was that on 22 January 1981 Mrs Pitt,
the appellant's wife, was visiting a next door neighbour and the appellant was at home
with their two children, Ian Andrew aged 2½ years and Louise Maria aged 8 months.
From the next door neighbour's house Mrs Pitt heard Louise crying and hurried home.   *f*
She found the baby's face bruised. On 23 January the baby was examined by a doctor
who found bruises and abrasions on her face, eyelids, nose and bridge of the nose. There
was also a swelling of the nose. When questioned about these injuries the appellant
attributed them to her having been hit in the face with a toy telephone by the little boy
. Ian. He claimed that at the time he was asleep and only woke when his wife came home.
This was the subject of count 1.
  Count 2 related to a later remarkably similar incident. On 1 March 1981 the appellant   *g*
telephoned the social workers to say that the baby had again been injured. When one of
the social workers arrived the appellant pointed out to him that had he, the appellant,
caused the injuries he would not have telephoned them. Again it was the baby's face that
had been injured. The appellant said that the baby had been upstairs in her cot, that she
had cried for an hour and that he then went up to her and found her face injured. He
suggested that the injuries had been caused by Ian hitting her in the face with a toy gun.   *h*
The social worker found Ian fast asleep in bed. Mrs Pitt, who had been out, arrived home
and stated in the presence of the appellant that injuries always occurred when she was
out. The baby was examined by a doctor who found multiple small bruises and abrasions
on her forehead, eyelid, nose, cheek and ears. There were at least 12 separate injuries
which had been caused by a minimum of 12 blows. The appellant told the doctor that
the baby was upstairs in her cot and that he was downstairs. She cried, as she often did,   *j*
and he left her to settle down. She did so, but about an hour later she cried again and he
went up to her. He found her injured and he could only assume that the injuries had
been caused by the little boy with a toy gun. He did not say that the baby had cried
continuously for an hour. The doctor was of the opinion that, although the injuries could
have been caused by a two-year-old child with a toy gun, it stretched her imagination to

believe that they had been so caused. She would not have expected so many blows, even
a from an aggressive child, and it assumed too much forward planning, to get the gun and
to climb into the cot, because she was of opinion that the injuries could not have been
caused by him from outside the cot.

The Crown called Mrs Pitt to give evidence. In the course of her evidence-in-chief, she
gave answers which led the Crown to apply to treat her as a hostile witness. The judge
acceded to this application and Mrs Pitt was then cross-examined on the witness statement
b she had made for the purpose of the proceedings. The appellant did not give evidence
but he called his father as a witness that the little boy was insanely jealous of the little
girl. The nature of the defence on count 2 was that the injuries were caused by the little
boy and not by the appellant, who was asleep when the injuries were caused. A number
of points were raised in the grounds of appeal. The only matter which has troubled us is
whether it was right to treat Mrs Pitt, who was not a compellable witness, as hostile. We
c will first dispose of the other matters.

It is asserted that the judge was wrong to reject an application that the two counts on
the indictment should be severed. The judge clearly had a discretion in the matter and,
in view of the similarity of the facts alleged in the two counts, we cannot say that he
exercised his discretion wrongly. In view of the fact that the jury acquitted on count 1, it
is clear that there was no prejudice to the defence.

d Then it is asserted that the judge was wrong in rejecting the defence's submission that
there was no case to answer on count 1, so that the jury in considering count 2 might still
have in mind the evidence on count 1. Again in view of the similarity of the facts we
think the judge was right not to withdraw count 1 from the jury. There was evidence on
which they might have committed on count 1, but they in fact acquitted.

We will now deal with Mrs Pitt's evidence. Paragraphs 2 and 3 of the grounds of
e appeal read that the judge erred:

'(2) by allowing the prosecution leave to treat the [appellant's] wife as hostile,
when she was merely unfavourable to the prosecution; (3) by allowing her to be
treated as hostile when she was a competent but not compellable witness.'

The single judge, when giving leave, approached the problem from a slightly different
f angle. He said:

'Ground 3 is the one which in my view is arguable; I would rephrase it: "that
since the wife was a competent but not a compellable witness she should have been
informed of this before she took the oath and asked whether she was willing to give
evidence."'

g The question raised is one of general importance and we shall deal with it on a broad
basis. As a result of the decisions in *Leach v R* [1912] AC 305 and *Hoskyn v Comr of Police
for the Metropolis* [1978] 2 All ER 136, [1979] AC 474 it is now clear that a wife is a
competent, but not compellable, witness in proceedings against her husband. The choice,
whether to give evidence or not, is hers. She does not lose that choice because she makes
a witness statement or gives evidence at the committal proceedings. She retains the right
h of refusal up to the point when, with full knowledge of that right, she takes the oath in
the witness box. We refer to the speeches of Lord Wilberforce and Lord Salmon in
Hoskyn. Lord Wilberforce said ([1978] 2 All ER 136 at 138, [1979] AC 474 at 483):

'On the other hand, cases must have occurred where, after a charge has been made
and during the period before trial, a wife, in the interests of her marriage, has second
j thoughts and when it comes to the point does not wish to give evidence against her
husband and will only do so under compulsion.'

Lord Salmon said ([1978] 2 All ER 136 at 149, [1979] AC 474 at 495):

'In many such cases, the wife is not a reluctant or unwilling witness; she may
indeed sometimes be an enthusiastic witness against her husband. On the other
hand, there must also be many cases when a wife who loved her husband completely

forgave him, had no fear of further violence, and wished the marriage to continue
and the pending prosecution to fail. It seems to me altogether inconsistent with the   *a*
common law's attitude towards marriage that it should compel such a wife to give
evidence against her husband and thereby probably destroy the marriage.'

Up to the point where she goes into the witness box, the wife has a choice: she may
refuse to give evidence or waive her right of refusal. The waiver is effective only if made
with full knowledge of her right to refuse. If she waives her right of refusal, she becomes   *b*
an ordinary witness. She is by analogy in the same position as a witness who waives
privilege, which would entitle him to refuse to answer questions on a certain topic.

In our view, in these circumstances, once the wife has started on her evidence, she
must complete it. It is not open to her to retreat behind the barrier of non-compellability
if she is asked questions that she does not wish to answer. Justice should not allow her to
give evidence which might assist, or injure, her husband and then to escape from normal   *c*
investigation.

It follows that if the nature of her evidence justifies it, an application may be made to
treat her as a hostile witness. There is, in our view, no objection in law which will
preclude a judge from giving leave to treat as hostile a wife who chooses to give evidence
for the prosecution of her husband. We have not been able to find any direct authority
on this point. This makes it particularly important that the wife should understand
when she takes the oath that she is waiving her right to refuse to give evidence. It points   *d*
to the wisdom of the words of Darling J in *R v Acaster* (1912) 7 Cr App R 187 at 189
when he said:

> 'The only suggestion made for the appellant is founded on a passage which
> occurred in the argument in *Leach's* case in the House of Lords, where the Solicitor-
> General asked whether it was suggested that the prosecution, when a wife came to   *e*
> give evidence, should raise the question whether she knew she could refuse to give
> evidence, and Lord Atkinson said it was for the witness to take the point and the
> Lord Chancellor added "Or for the judge." Speaking for myself, and I think for the
> other members of the Court, in consequence of these observations I shall, when the
> wife—in any case where she is not a compellable witness—comes to give evidence
> against her husband, ask her: "Do you know you may object to give evidence?" and   *f*
> I shall also do so if she is called on behalf of her husband. That, I imagine, is what
> other judges will do for the present, though there is no decision which binds us to
> do it, and the point is open to argument on an appeal to this Court. So far none of
> us here remember to have ever done it, nor did it occur to us before that it was
> necessary.'

That decision is now 70 years old and we cannot say that Darling J's counsel of   *g*
prudence has become a rule of law. Nor do we seek to lay down any rule of practice for
the future. This is an unusual case and we are reluctant to make it the basis for any
general rule. None the less, this case does illustrate very powerfully why it is necessary
for the trial judge to make certain that the wife understands her position before she takes
the oath. Had that been done here, there would have been no difficulty.

It seems to us to be desirable that, where a wife is called as a witness for the prosecution   *h*
of her husband, the judge should explain to her, in the absence of the jury, that before
she takes the oath she has the right to refuse to give evidence, but that if she chooses to
give evidence she may be treated like any other witness.

It has also to be borne in mind that since the decision in *R v Acaster* there has been an
important change in the law. The Court of Appeal may now upset a verdict on the
ground that it was unsafe or unsatisfactory: see the Criminal Appeal Act 1968, s 2(1).   *j*
Should the circumstances of a case justify it, the Court of Appeal may upset a verdict
where it feels that injustice may have occurred because a wife gave evidence without
appreciating that she had a right to refuse to do so.

Should we come to such a conclusion in this case, in the light of the judge's decision
that the prosecution might treat Mrs Pitt as a hostile witness? We were informed by

counsel that both counsel knew that Mrs Pitt had returned to live with her husband and
a that the Pitts used to arrive at court together in the morning. Counsel for the Crown told
us that she took further instructions at the trial and was told that Mrs Pitt was willing to
give evidence, but she could not tell us that Mrs Pitt had been told of her right to refuse
to do so.

Mrs Pitt was called by the Crown in the usual way. Whilst we do not suggest that
counsel were in any way open to criticism, we feel strongly, with the benefit of hindsight,
b that it would have been much better if counsel had told the judge of the wife's position
in the absence of the jury and before she was sworn. It must have been obvious that, as
Mrs Pitt had been reunited with her husband, it was unlikely that she would be willing
to give evidence which could help to send him to prison. Had the judge had the matter
brought to his attention in this way, it seems certain that he would have taken steps to
satisfy himself that Mrs Pitt was really willing to give evidence before she did so.
c   We do not have a transcript of Mrs Pitt's evidence, and we have to rely on the
recollection of counsel as to the gist of it. She had made a witness statement on 5 March
1981, and this formed part of the evidence on which a committal under s 1 of the
Criminal Justice Act 1967 took place. In the course of her evidence-in-chief, she gave
answers which were inconsistent with her witness statement and said that she could not
remember a number of matters which she might have been expected to remember if she
d were trying to tell the whole truth.

The Crown then applied, in the absence of the jury, for leave to treat her as a hostile
witness for the purpose of cross-examining her on her witness statement. It appears from
the transcript that the judge was at first somewhat doubtful about this, but, after going
carefully through his notes of the evidence she had given, he came to the conclusion that
leave should be given. He said:
e
    'I thought at first that what this witness was saying was in answer to perhaps one
    or two questions: "I do not remember"; but, when she says that on so many occasions
    and there is other direct contradiction, I base myself on what the Lord Chief Justice
    says, as reported in para 521. I think she has shown herself decidedly adverse and I
    shall allow cross-examination.'

f   The judge was there referring to para 521 of *Archbold's Pleading, Evidence and Practice
in Criminal Cases* (40th edn, 1979), which refers to *Stephen, Digest of the Law of Evidence*
(12th edn, 1936) art 147, which reads:

    'If a witness appears to the judge to be hostile to the parties calling him, that is to
    say not desirous of telling the truth to the court at the instance of the party calling
g   him, the judge may in his discretion permit examination by such party to be
    conducted in the manner of cross-examination to the extent which the judge
    considers necessary for the purpose of doing justice.'

The conclusion that Mrs Pitt was a hostile witness cannot, in our view, be criticised,
but we are troubled about the decision to give leave to treat her as a hostile witness. It
was only after the judge had given his ruling that defence counsel raised the question of
h whether it was right to give leave to treat a non-compellable witness as hostile. The
Crown then relied on the decision in *R v Thompson* (1976) 64 Cr App R 96, but that seems
to us to have little bearing as it does not relate to a non-compellable witness. In the upshot
the judge said:

j   'In the absence of authority I am not going to make new law. I take the view that
    the point about compellability does not arise at this stage, she having gone so far,
    and, as I said originally, I shall give leave to cross-examine her.'

When she was cross-examined, Mrs Pitt admitted that she had said what was in her
statement. She was not asked whether it was true. She further said that she had now
changed her mind about the appellant's responsibility for the events of 28 February.

We have reached the conclusion that when she went into the witness box Mrs Pitt did not sufficiently appreciate that it was open to her to refuse to give evidence; accordingly, when she gave her evidence, she was trying to shield her husband as far as possible.

In a direction, of which no criticism can be made, the judge advised the jury wholly to disregard Mrs Pitt's evidence. He said:

> 'Now I want to talk to you for a short time about Mrs Pitt. Mrs Pitt was the mother of the little girl who was injured and is the wife of the accused. We need not speculate as to the distress which one assumes that anybody in such circumstances may be undergoing, but you will remember that she gave evidence yesterday about this time, I should think; no, perhaps rather less than 24 hours ago. Then, after you had been out for a short time and came back, you heard that she had made a statement in March, I think on 5 March, within four or five days of this incident occurring, which was inconsistent with the evidence that she gave yesterday. Those inconsistencies were: first, whether or not she had blamed her husband for the instances; whether or not the social worker wanted her to go to hospital; whether or not the husband was fast asleep when she arrived on the scene after the first incident; and whether the conversation of 3 March in which she had said that her husband had said something to her about the hitting ever took place. There were one or two other matters where she said, perhaps not unnaturally, that she did not remember now matters on which her memory was clear in March. Well, now, I have got to tell you something about that. What I tell you about that is this. When a witness is shown to have made previous statements inconsistent with the evidence given by that witness at the trial, the jury should not merely be directed that the evidence given at the trial should be regarded as unreliable, they should also be directed that the previous statements do not constitute evidence on which you can act. If you think for a moment, it is only common sense. So far as Mrs Pitt was concerned, she was not sworn when she gave the statement to the police on 5 March. It was not subject to cross-examination and you must not rely on what she said in that statement as being true. It is probably right also to say that you ought not to rely on what she said yesterday as being true either because it is entirely inconsistent with what she said six months ago when the facts, you may think, were probably more fresh in her mind. Although it is entirely a matter for you, members of the jury, you are the people who judge fact and not me, the advice I would give you (and I think the advice your common sense would give you) is that in the circumstances it is probably very prudent indeed entirely to disregard what she said.'

The judge repeated this advice, shortly, at the end of his summing up. If the jury followed the judge's advice, no harm would have been done. If the jury ignored Mrs Pitt's evidence completely, the result would have been the same as if she had refused to give evidence.

But we cannot be sure that the jury followed this direction. It must have been apparent to them that Mrs Pitt was going back on a statement she had made only five days after the incident, and that she was now reconciled to the appellant. They may well have concluded that she was telling lies at her husband's instigation.

Counsel for the Crown told us that she put the statement to Mrs Pitt virtually line by line. Counsel for the appellant complained that there were four passages in the statement which were particularly prejudicial to the appellant. These were: (1) 'I accused my husband of doing it.' (2) The passage in which Mrs Pitt explained that she blamed her husband on 28 February because of the incident which formed the basis of count 1. (3) 'My son Ian has never hit Louise in front of me and is not an aggressive boy.' (4) 'On 3 March 1981 my husband hit me, and told me to say that little Ian is violent towards Louise but that is not true. I did not agree at first and that is why he hit me. Then I said: "All right", and he has been all right since.'

However carefully the jury were directed that the statement was not evidence, the fact that Mrs Pitt said these things so soon after the incident, and then resiled from them at the trial, may well have affected their minds. We take the view that there is a possibility,

if not a probability, that the minds of the jury were affected by the contents of Mrs Pitt's
a witness statement, which was not evidence, and that consequently the conviction was
unsafe and unsatisfactory.

Counsel for the Crown has argued that none the less we should apply the proviso. She
asserts that, even without Mrs Pitt's evidence, the prosecution would have succeeded. But
it is apparent that a great deal of attention was paid to Mrs Pitt's evidence at the trial. It is
true that there was other evidence on which the appellant might have been convicted if
b Mrs Pitt had refused to go into the witness box, but it has to be remembered that there
was an acquittal on count 1. Without Mrs Pitt's evidence, the trial would have taken a
very different shape and we are quite unable to say that a reasonable jury, properly
directed, would have convicted the appellant.

Accordingly, the appeal will be allowed and the convictions on count 2 and for breach
of suspended sentence and breach of community service order will be quashed.

c

Appeal allowed. Conviction quashed.

Solicitors: *T Hambrey Jones*, Chelmsford (for the Crown).

Jacqueline Charles   Barrister.

d

Rivers v Cutting

COURT OF APPEAL, CIVIL DIVISION
e FOX LJ AND SIR SEBAG SHAW
5 MARCH, 7 APRIL 1982

*Road traffic – Motor vehicle – Abandoned or broken down vehicle on road – Removal – Police
powers of removal – Police power to arrange for removal – Whether police vicariously liable for
negligence of independent contractor engaged to remove abandoned vehicle – Removal and
f Disposal of Vehicles Regulations 1968, reg 4.*

The plaintiff abandoned his motor car on a motorway verge after it had broken down. A
police officer, acting under the power contained in reg 4[a] of the Removal and Disposal of
Vehicles Regulations 1968 to 'remove or arrange for the removal' of a vehicle which had
broken down or been abandoned on a road, arranged for the plaintiff's car to be towed
g away by a local garage. The car was damaged while being removed and the plaintiff
brought an action in the county court against the chief constable of the police officer's
force alleging that the damage had been caused by negligence on the part of the garage
and that the police were vicariously liable for that negligence since the garage was acting
as the agent of the police when removing the vehicle. At the trial of a preliminary issue
the chief constable contended that the garage was an independent contractor. The judge
h upheld that contention. The plaintiff appealed, contending that the power to remove a
vehicle conferred on the police by reg 4 was a power given to the police alone to be
exercised either by themselves or their agents and which could not be delegated to an
independent contractor.

Held – Under reg 4 of the 1968 regulations the police had two separate and distinct
j powers in relation to broken down or abandoned vehicles on a road, namely to remove
the vehicle or to arrange for its removal. In exercising the power to arrange for its
removal, a police constable was under a duty to use reasonable care in the choice of an
independent contractor to do the work, but, provided he did so, he was not then
vicariously liable for any negligence of the contractor in carrying out the removal, save

---

a   Regulation 4, so far as material, is set out at p 71 *c*, post

in those circumstances where a private person would be liable for the acts of an
independent contractor. The plaintiff's appeal would therefore be dismissed (see p 71 *g*   *a*
to p 72 *h*, post).

Notes
For police powers to remove vehicles, see 33 Halsbury's Laws (3rd edn) 541, para 916.
  For the Removal and Disposal of Vehicles Regulations 1968, reg 4, see 10 Halsbury's
Statutory Instruments (4th reissue) 82.   *b*

Interlocutory appeal
By a writ dated 9 July 1980 the plaintiff, Shane Rivers, brought an action against the
defendant, Frederick C Cutting, the Chief Constable of Northampton, alleging that the
defendant was vicariously liable for damage amounting to £716·50 caused when a police
officer arranged for the plaintiff's car to be towed away from where it had been left on   *c*
the M1 motorway. On 29 January 1981 the action was ordered to be transferred to the
Northampton County Court and on 27 April 1981 the registrar ordered the trial of a
preliminary issue. His Honour Judge Rush decided that issue in favour of the defendant
on 21 July 1981. The plaintiff appealed. The facts are set out in the judgment of Fox LJ.

Nigel Murray for the plaintiff.   *d*
Jeremy Roberts for the defendant.

                                                                        Cur adv vult

7 April. The following judgments were read.

                                                                                        e
FOX LJ. In May 1979 the plaintiff's car broke down on the M1 motorway. The plaintiff
abandoned it on the verge. A police officer in the exercise of his powers under the
Removal and Disposal of Vehicles Regulations 1968, SI 1968/43, arranged for the car to
be removed by a local garage, whose employee towed the car away. In the course of the
towing the car was damaged. The plaintiff says that the damage was caused by negligence
in the process of removal. If there was indeed negligence somebody must be liable to the   *f*
plaintiff for the damage caused. The plaintiff contends that the garage was the agent of
the police and therefore, in the present action in the county court, sues the chief constable
of the relevant police authority for damages. The chief constable contends that the garage
was not the agent of the police but an independent contractor for whose default the
police have no vicarious liability. That, it is said, is no hardship on the plaintiff: if those
engaged in the towing were negligent the plaintiff will have a cause of action against the   *g*
garage.
  In the circumstances the registrar directed the following issue to be tried as a
preliminary issue:

  '... whether, when a Chief Constable in exercise of his powers under Regulations
  4 and 6 of the Removal and Disposal of Vehicles Regulations 1968 ... instructs a
  reputable garage to tow away a motor vehicle, he is vicariously liable for any   *h*
  negligence of such garage in the execution of his instructions.'

That issue was tried by his Honour Judge Rush who, on 21 July 1981, made an order
declaring as follows:

  'When any constable in the exercise of his powers under Regulations 4 and 6 of
  the Removal and Disposal of Vehicles Regulations 1968 ... instructs a reputable
  garage to tow away a motor vehicle he is not vicariously liable for any negligence of   *j*
  such garage in the execution of his instructions.'

  From that order the plaintiff appeals. I am not sure that the direction to determine the
issue was a satisfactory mode of proceeding in this case, since it involves the court having
to make a declaration on hypothetical and rather imprecise facts. However, the matter
has now reached this court and we will give the parties such assistance as we can.

The 1968 regulations were made under the provisions of s 20(1) of the Road Traffic
a Regulation Act 1967, which is in the following terms:

'The appropriate Minister may by regulations make provision for the removal of
vehicles which have been permitted to remain at rest—(*a*) on a road in contravention
of any statutory prohibition or restriction, or (*b*) on a road in such a position or in
such condition or in such circumstances as to cause obstruction to other persons
using the road or as to be likely to cause danger to such other persons, or (*c*) on a
b road or on any land in the open air in such a position . . . as to appear . . . to have
been abandoned . . . or which have broken down on a road.'

Regulation 4 of the 1968 regulations provides:

'Except as provided by Regulation 7 of these Regulations, where a vehicle [is
c within one of the three classes of vehicles described in s 20(1)] then, subject to the
provisions of section 20 of the Road Traffic Regulation Act 1967, a constable may
remove or arrange for the removal of the vehicle and, in the case of a vehicle which
is on a road, he may remove it or arrange for its removal from that road to a place
which is not on that or any other road, or may move it or arrange for its removal to
another position on that or another road.'

d
Regulation 7 deals with the Severn Bridge. Regulation 5 deals with the power of local
authorities to remove vehicles. Regulation 6 provides:

'Any person removing or moving a vehicle under the last two preceding
Regulations may do so by towing or driving the vehicle or in such other manner as
he may think necessary and may take such measures in relation to the vehicle as he
e may think necessary to enable him to remove or move it as aforesaid.'

The plaintiff's case in this court is put broadly as follows. (1) Where a duty is imposed
by statute on a person, that person is bound to perform it without negligence. (2) The
obligation to ensure the performance of a statutory duty without negligence cannot be
discharged by delegation of that duty to an independent contractor. (3) Regulation 4, on
f its true construction, gives two separate discretionary powers to the constable. First, he is
given a power to decide whether to remove the vehicle or not. Second, if he determines
to remove it, he may either remove it himself or cause it to be removed. In substance, it
is said, the power to remove is a single power given to the police alone. They may
exercise the power either by themselves or by their agents, but everything which is done
is the act of the police. (4) On the commencement of the removal the constable's duty of
g care to ensure that the removal is effected without negligence will also commence. (5)
The removal was negligently conducted and consequently the constable is liable.

In my opinion the crucial matter is to ascertain the duty which is cast on the police.
We are concerned with reg 4 under which the police acted. I agree with the plaintiff that
the regulation confers two powers, but I do not agree with his identification of those
powers. It seems to me that, in terms and in substance, the regulation confers on the
h police two quite distinct powers, namely a power for the constable to remove the vehicle
himself and a power to arrange for its removal. He can exercise either power. They are
separate. Neither of them is a mere exercise of some wider general power given to the
police to effect a removal. I quite agree that before the constable exercises either power
he must have made up his mind that the vehicle should be removed. But that is not a
power. It is merely the preliminary to the exercise of a power. It does not mean that the
j regulation is to be read as if it simply conferred a power on the constable to remove the
vehicle either by himself or his agents. The regulation does not say that. It is clearly
couched in the form of two separate powers and I can see no reason to construe it
otherwise. It is perfectly sensible and workable on that basis.

If I am correct thus far, the constable exercised no power until he arranged for the
garage to remove the car. The question then is: what was his duty in relation to the
exercise of that power? I think that the duty was to exercise reasonable care in the choice

of the garage. I think that duty is discharged if the garage is selected with due care having regard to the sort of work which it is instructed to undertake.   *a*

The word 'arrange' is very wide and, it seems to me, authorises the appointment of an independent contractor to do the work. If such an appointment is made I see no reason why the police (assuming that they discharge the duty of care in selection which I have mentioned) should incur any greater liability to third parties than any other person who employs an independent contractor.

It is said that the police cannot delegate a statutory duty to an independent contractor   *b* so as to avoid liability for the performance of that duty. I think that is a misconception of the position in the present case. Regulation 4 imposes no duty on the police to remove vehicles. It merely confers powers in relation to their removal. The only duty which it imposes is the duty to exercise those powers properly and with due care. As to delegation, I do not think that any question of delegation arises. The appointment of a contractor to remove the vehicle is not a delegation of the power: it is an actual exercise of the power   *c* itself.

We were referred to s 20(6) of the Road Traffic Regulation Act 1967, which provides that, while a vehicle is in the custody of an authority under the provisions of the Act or regulations made under the Act, then, in general, it is the duty of the authority to take such steps as are reasonably necessary for the safe custody of the vehicle.

I do not think that that takes the matter any further. Once the constable arranges for   *d* an independent contractor, as opposed to an agent, to remove the vehicle it seems to me that so long as the contractor is performing that duty he, and not the constable, has custody of the vehicle. That is necessary to enable him to effect the removal. Regulation 6 will safeguard him from an action for trespass but he will be subject to a common law duty of care in the conduct of the removal.

The result, in my judgment, is that the chief constable's contention is well founded. I   *e* do not find that an unsatisfactory result. An independent contractor is lawfully employed by the police at the public expense. I see no reason why there should not be available to the police, if the contractor acts negligently and damages a third party, whatever defences would be available to a private person employing an independent contractor to perform that task. I say 'whatever defences would be available': the employment of an independent contractor does not necessarily protect the employer from liability in all circumstances,   *f* for example, if the work is inherently dangerous.

In my view, therefore, if a constable in exercise of the powers conferred by reg 4 of the 1968 regulations arranges for the removal of a vehicle by an independent contractor who is chosen with reasonable care having regard to the nature of the work to be done, the constable is not vicariously liable for damage caused by the default of the contractor in carrying out the removal save to such extent, if any, as liability is imposed by law for the   *g* acts of an independent contractor in the circumstances of the case.

We can consider with counsel the appropriate form of order.

SIR SEBAG SHAW. I agree.

Appeal dismissed ; case remitted to county court to be dealt with in accordance with judgment.   *h*

Solicitors: *Jacobs, Blok & Kane* (for the plaintiff); *R C Beadon*, Northampton (for the defendant).

Diana Brahams   Barrister.

a

R v Viola

COURT OF APPEAL, CRIMINAL DIVISION
LORD LANE CJ, SKINNER AND TAYLOR JJ
10 MAY 1982

b *Criminal evidence – Sexual offence – Cross-examination of complainant about previous sexual experience with other men – Restrictions on evidence – When judge should give leave to cross-examine complainant – Whether Court of Appeal entitled to substitute its own conclusion on evidence of complainant's previous sexual experience with other men – Sexual Offences (Amendment) Act 1976, s 2.*

c The appellant was charged with rape. The alleged rape occurred in the complainant's flat shortly before midnight after the appellant, who was acquainted with the complainant, had sought refuge in her flat because he was having trouble with the police over the driving of a car. The only issue at the trial was whether the complainant had consented to sexual intercourse with the appellant. After the complainant had given evidence-in-chief the appellant applied to the trial judge, under s 2[a] of the Sexual Offences

d (Amendment) Act 1976, for leave to cross-examine her regarding two incidents concerning her sexual relations with other men shortly before and shortly after the alleged rape. The judge refused leave to cross-examine the complainant about those incidents because he was not 'satisfied that it would be unfair to [the] defendant to refuse to allow' the cross-examination, within s 2(2) of the 1976 Act. The appellant was convicted. He appealed against the conviction on the ground that the judge erred in law

e in refusing to allow the cross-examination.

Held – (1) The test whether a trial judge should give a defendant leave under s 2(2) of the 1976 Act to cross-examine a complainant about her sexual experience with other men was whether the proposed cross-examination was relevant to the defendant's case according to the common law rules of evidence, and if so whether the judge was satisfied

f that it was more likely than not that the cross-examination, if allowed, might reasonably lead the jury to take a different view of the complainant's evidence. However, since the purpose of s 2 was to protect a complainant from questions which went merely to her credit, as a general rule a judge ought not to allow cross-examination which merely sought to establish that because the complainant had had sexual experience with other men she ought not to be believed under oath. If, on the other hand, the cross-examination

g was relevant to an issue in the trial such as consent, it ought usually to be allowed (see p 76 a c d and p 77 a to g, post); R v Mills (1978) 68 Cr App R 327 followed; R v Lawrence [1977] Crim LR 492 approved.

   (2) A trial judge's decision to exclude or allow the proposed cross-examination under s 2 was an exercise of his judgment, and not of his discretion, and therefore the Court of Appeal, which was in as good a position as the trial judge to reach a conclusion on the

h matter, could substitute its own conclusion for that of the trial judge if it thought that he had been wrong (see p 77 c d and p 78 a b, post); dictum of Roskill LJ in R v Mills (1978) 68 Cr App R at 330 considered.

   (3) In all the circumstances the incidents regarding the complainant's sexual relations with other men were relevant to the issue of consent and could not be regarded as so trivial or of so little relevance to that issue that the judge was entitled to conclude that no injustice would be done to the appellant if cross-examination about them was excluded.

j It followed that the judge had been wrong to exclude the cross-examination, and the appeal would accordingly be allowed and the conviction quashed (see p 78 j to p 79 c and g, post).

---

a   Section 2, so far as material, is set out at p 75 j, post

Notes

For evidence as to the complainant's character at a trial on a charge of rape, see Supplement   *a*
to 11 Halsbury's Laws (4th edn) para 1230.

For the Sexual Offences (Amendment) Act 1976, s 2, see 46 Halsbury's Statutes (3rd
edn) 323.

Cases referred to in judgment

R v Harris (12 June 1979, unreported), CA.   *b*
R v Lawrence [1977] Crim LR 492.
R v Lester (6 May 1980, unreported), CA.
R v Mills (1978) 68 Cr App R 327, CA.

Cases also cited   *c*

DPP v Ping Lin [1975] 3 All ER 175, [1976] AC 574, HL.
R v Fenlon (1980) 71 Cr App R 307, [1980] Crim LR 573, CA.
R v Hinds and Butler [1979] Crim LR 111.
R v Krausz (1973) 57 Cr App R 466, CA.
R v Lillyman [1896] 2 QB 167, [1895–9] All ER Rep 586, CCR.
R v O'Sullivan (27 February 1981, unreported), CA.
R v Riley (1887) 18 QBD 481, 16 Cox CC 191, CCR.   *d*
Ward v James [1965] 1 All ER 568, [1966] 1 QB 273, CA.

Appeal

On 24 February 1982 in the Crown Court at Warwick before Drake J and a jury the
appellant, Michael Viola, was convicted on a majority verdict of rape and was sentenced   *e*
to four years' imprisonment. He applied for leave to appeal against the conviction on the
ground, inter alia, that the trial judge erred in law in refusing to allow an application on
his behalf, under s 2 of the Sexual Offences (Amendment) Act 1976, to cross-examine the
complainant about incidents relating to her sexual experience with persons other than
the appellant. The court granted leave to appeal and treated the application as the hearing
of the appeal. The facts are set out in the judgment of the court.   *f*

Richard Wakerley QC and *J H B Saunders* for the appellant.
B R Escott Cox QC and *D A F Jones* for the Crown.
Allan Green as amicus curiae.

LORD LANE CJ delivered the following judgment of the court: On 24 February 1982   *g*
in the Crown Court at Warwick the applicant was convicted of rape and sentenced to
four years' imprisonment.

He now applies for leave to appeal against that conviction. We give him leave and,
with counsel's consent on his behalf, we treat this as the hearing of the appeal.

The issue for the jury in this case was one of consent and the facts, in so far as they are   *h*
material, were as follows. The complainant was 22 years of age. She lived in a maisonette
in Coventry with two young children of her own. There was no dispute that about half
an hour before midnight on Tuesday, 8 September 1981 the appellant came to her door.
The reason why he had come there was this. He had, it seems, been in some trouble with
the police over the driving of a motor car, and he had parked the vehicle and then thrown
the keys into a doorway. He knocked on the door of the complainant's maisonette in   *j*
order to try, so he said, to find the keys. She by fetching a piece of lighted paper assisted
him in that search and, according to her, let him inside the maisonette in order that he
could look out of the window to see whether the police were still waiting for him or
looking for him. There was a slight acquaintanceship between the two of them. It seems
that he and she on one occasion had danced together.

The complainant's version of events thereafter is this. Once inside, the appellant told

her that he fancied her, sat next to her on the sofa, whereupon she asked him to go and
a got up. Then, according to her, he seized hold of her, butted her in the face with his
head, he pulled her hair and, when she started to scream, he threatened to knock her out
and to stab her. He, according to her, ripped her knickers and when she was on the sofa
he raped her.

On the other hand the appellant's version of events was that when he knocked on the
door in order to get assistance, the complainant invited him in for a drink. They sat on
b the sofa for a while, kissing and so on, and then intercourse took place between them
with her fully consenting to the act.

The first complaint proper made by the complainant herself seems to have been on
Friday, that is some considerable time after the alleged event. It was after that complaint
and after she had been seen by the police on the Friday that she was examined by the
police doctor and also by her own doctor, and it is plain that at that stage she was found
c to have swelling across the bridge of her nose and bruising round the eye.

The police interviewed the appellant on Friday evening. He first of all said that he
never touched her, that he had not been involved in any trouble with the police and
when the complaint was put to him he said that it was all a lie and referred to the
complainant in highly uncomplimentary terms. Then at the police station he changed
his story, admitted that he had had intercourse with the complainant, but that she
d consented to it and, according to the police, he admitted that he had butted her with the
head, but he said that that took place after the intercourse and not before it. The appellant
in evidence denied having made any admissions to the police with regard to butting the
complainant in the face.

There were three defence witnesses who gave evidence that shortly after the alleged
rape and a matter of 48 hours or so before the complainant was examined by the doctors,
e they had seen her and that she had no injuries on her face. Certainly so far as Mr and Mrs
Burns are concerned, they said that she did not appear to have any injuries. The
complainant's boyfriend or ex-boyfriend (there is some dispute as to the precise state of
affairs between them) said that he saw her shortly afterwards and saw a slight scratch on
her nose but no more.

The jury came to the conclusion by a majority verdict that the offence had been made
f out. The principal ground of appeal is that the trial judge was wrong in preventing the
defendant from cross-examining the complainant about three separate matters. The first
matter was a suggestion that, during the afternoon and evening of the Tuesday (it will be
remembered that the rape was alleged to have taken place at very shortly before midnight
on that day) and immediately prior to the alleged act of rape, this complainant was
making sexual advances to two men who visited her flat; the next matter was that during
g the afternoon of 9 September 1981 the complainant had sexual intercourse with her
boyfriend, or recently discarded boyfriend; and finally, on the morning of 9 September,
that would be about eight or nine hours after the alleged act of rape, there was a man in
the complainant's flat on the sofa wearing nothing except a pair of slippers.

So far as this aspect of the appeal is concerned, it raises once again the problem of the
application of s 2 of the Sexual Offences (Amendment) Act 1976. We have to determine
h whether the judge was right or wrong in refusing to allow the suggested questions to be
put. Section 2 of the Act provides:

'(1) If at a trial any person is for the time being charged with a rape offence to
which he pleads not guilty, then, except with the leave of the judge, no evidence
and no question in cross-examination shall be adduced or asked at the trial, by or on
behalf of any defendant at the trial, about any sexual experience of a complainant
j with a person other than that defendant.
(2) The judge shall not give leave in pursuance of the preceding subsection for
any evidence or question except on an application made to him in the absence of the
jury by or on behalf of a defendant; and on such an application the judge shall give
leave if and only if he is satisfied that it would be unfair to that defendant to refuse
to allow the evidence to be adduced or the question to be asked . . .'

It is, we think, apparent from those words, without more, that the first question which the judge must ask himself is this: are the questions proposed to be put relevant according *a* to the ordinary common law rules of evidence and relevant to the case as it is being put? If they are not so relevant, that is the end of the matter.

We have been referred to two unreported cases which are in point so far as that aspect of the matter is concerned: the first is *R v Harris* (a decision of this court on 12 June 1979) and the second is *R v Lester* (again a decision of this court on 6 May 1980).

The second matter which the judge must consider is this. If the questions are relevant, *b* then whether they should be allowed or not will of course depend on the terms of s 2, which limits the admissibility of relevant evidence. That section has been the subject of judicial consideration first of all by May J in *R v Lawrence* [1977] Crim LR 492. A passage, which is taken verbatim from the transcript of his decision, reads (at 493):

> 'The important part of the statute which I think needs construction are the words *c* "if and only if he [the judge] is satisfied that it would be unfair to that defendant to refuse to allow the evidence to be adduced or the question to be asked". And, in my judgment, before a judge is satisfied or may be said to be satisfied that to refuse to allow a particular question or a series of questions in cross-examination would be unfair to a defendant he must take the view that it is more likely than not that the particular question or line of cross-examination, if allowed, might reasonably lead *d* the jury, properly directed in the summing-up, to take a different view of the complainant's evidence from that which they might take if the question or series of questions was or were not allowed.'

That statement was approved by this court in *R v Mills* (1979) 68 Cr App R 327. Roskill LJ giving the judgment of the court said (at 329–330): *e*

> 'The second ground of appeal is different in character. It was alleged that the complainant had had a good deal of earlier sexual experience. As is well known, in former times cross-examination in rape cases was permitted with a view to attacking the character of the complainant on the ground that she had had such previous sexual experience. That practice was the subject of widespread public condemnation *f* and ultimately the Sexual Offences (Amendment) Act 1976 was passed. [Then Roskill LJ read the contents of s 2 and continued:] Application was made during cross-examination of this complainant by [counsel for the applicant] that he should be allowed to cross-examine her as to her antecedent sexual experience. On the face of it such cross-examination would be contrary to section 2(1). Accordingly the learned judge was only empowered by subsection (2) to give leave "if and only if he *g* is satisfied that it would be unfair to that defendant to refuse to allow the evidence to be adduced or the question to be asked." That was therefore the question to which the learned judge had to direct his attention. This section has not yet, as far as this Court is aware, been considered by this Court. It was however considered by May J. a few months before the present trial, in LAWRENCE AND ANOTHER [1977] Crim. L.R. 492, which that learned judge heard at Nottingham Crown Court. [Then Roskill LJ *h* read out the part of the judgment of May J which we have already read, and continued:] This is, as we pointed out to [counsel for the applicant] in the course of argument, essentially a matter for the exercise of discretion by the trial judge within the framework of the Act, bearing in mind that that statutory provision is designed to secure protection for complainants. The learned judge here exercised his discretion after having had that decision of May J. quoted to him. [Counsel for the *j* applicant] found himself unable to say that this was not a matter for the exercise of the learned judge's discretion, but argued that this Court should substitute its own discretion for that of the learned judge. With respect, it would be entirely wrong for us to do so. [Then Roskill LJ said that the court over which he presided felt that the ruling of May J, which they approved, was entirely right, and said:] It would be impossible, and it would be quite wrong, for this Court in any way to seek to disturb

that exercise of discretion which seems to us to be wholly in accordance with section
a   2(1) and (2) of the statute.'

The application was refused.

That approval by this court of the decision in *R v Lawrence* [1977] Crim LR 492 means
that we are bound by the words of May J to which we have referred. In the end the judge
will have to ask himself the question whether he is satisfied in the terms expounded by
May J. It will be a problem for him to apply that dictum to the particular facts of the
b   case. In those circumstances it seems to us it would be both improper and, perhaps more
important, very unwise for us to try to say in advance what may or may not be unfair in
any particular case.

We would further like to say this about the judgment in *R v Mills* (1978) 68 Cr App R
327 and say it with the greatest possible deference to that court. It has been agreed on all
hands, not only by the appellant and by the Crown but also by counsel who has assisted
c   us as amicus curiae, that it is wrong to speak of a judge's 'discretion' in this context. The
judge has to make a judgment whether he is satisfied or not in the terms of s 2. But once
having reached his judgment on the particular facts, he has no discretion. If he comes to
the conclusion that he is satisfied it would be unfair to exclude the evidence, then the
evidence has to be admitted and the questions have to be allowed.

Having said that, when one considers the purposes which lay behind the passing of the
d   1976 Act, as expounded by Roskill LJ, it is clear that it was aimed primarily at protecting
complainants from cross-examination as to credit, from questions which went merely to
credit and no more. The result is that generally speaking (I use these words advisedly, of
course there will always be exceptions) if the proposed questions merely seek to establish
that the complainant has had sexual experience with other men to whom she was not
married, so as to suggest that for that reason she ought not to be believed under oath, the
e   judge will exclude the evidence. In the present climate of opinion a jury is unlikely to be
influenced by such considerations, nor should it be influenced. In other words questions
of this sort going simply to credit will seldom be allowed. That is borne out by the cases
to which we have been referred, not only those which I have cited, but other unreported
cases which have been before this court, to which perhaps it is not necessary to make
f   reference.

On the other hand, if the questions are relevant to an issue in the trial in the light of
the way the case is being run, for instance relevant to the issue of consent, as opposed
merely to credit, they are likely to be admitted, because to exclude a relevant question on
an issue in the trial as the trial is being run will usually mean that the jury are being
prevented from hearing something which, if they did hear it, might cause them to
change their minds about the evidence given by the complainant. But, I repeat, we are
g   very far from laying down any hard and fast rule.

Inevitably in this situation, as in so many similar situations in the law, there is a grey
area which exists between the two types of relevance, namely relevance to credit and
relevance to an issue in the case. On one hand evidence of sexual promiscuity may be so
strong or so closely contemporaneous in time to the event in issue as to come near to, or
indeed to reach the border between mere credit and an issue in the case. Conversely, the
h   relevance of the evidence to an issue in the case may be so slight as to lead the judge to
the conclusion that he is far from satisfied that the exclusion of the evidence or the
question from the consideration of the jury would be unfair to the defendant.

We have had drawn to our attention some of the difficulties which face a judge. It is
perfectly true to say that normally he has to make this decision at an early stage of the
trial. It will be, generally speaking, when the complainant's evidence-in-chief is concluded
j   that counsel, in the absence of the jury, will make the necessary application under s 2. At
this stage it may not be easy for the judge to reach a conclusion, but this is a problem
which is continually being faced by judges, sometimes in even more trying circumstances,
for example, when he is asked to determine whether a count should be tried separately
or whether defendants should be tried separately and so on, before the trial has got under
way at all. He has to reach the best conclusion that he can.

The second matter is: is this court entitled to differ from the conclusions of the trial judge? As already pointed out, this is the exercise of judgment by the judge, not an *a* exercise of his discretion. This court is in many respects in as good a position as the judge to reach a conclusion. The judge has certainly heard the complainant give evidence, but only in chief. So far as the proposed questions are concerned, the statements on which the questions were to be asked or the way in which the matter was going to be put to the jury are presented in exactly the same way to this court as they were to the judge at first instance. We have been told what it was that counsel sought in the course of his *b* submission to the judge and indeed we have been given the statements which were to be the basis of the questions which he was going to ask. So what we have to decide is whether the judge was right or wrong in the conclusion which he reached, applying the test of May J in R v Lawrence [1977] Crim LR 492 at 493. Like so many decisions in the grey area, it is not an easy decision to make. Let me turn therefore to the precise matters about which it was proposed to ask questions. *c*

First of all, the presence of the two men in her maisonette very shortly before the alleged rape took place. The facts of that were apparently these. The two men, whose names are not material, called at the maisonette occupied by the complainant in the hope of finding the complainant's boyfriend, whose name was Willy, present. They arrived some time during the afternoon. They were equipped with a considerable amount of drink, amongst other things a gallon of wine. They discovered that Willy was not there. *d* Nevertheless they went in at the invitation of the complainant. It was not suggested that she knew them very well. Indeed she probably did not, although she was acquainted with them. According to their evidence not only was a good deal of alcohol consumed by them and the complainant, but during the course of the several hours that they were there with her she made sexual advances to them: she suggested that one or other might like to try out her new bed; she made physical contact with one of them by rubbing his *e* back, and so on; in other words she indicated that she would not be averse to sexual intercourse with them. The precise timing is not available, perhaps not surprisingly, but it seems likely that the length of time which elapsed between the departure of these two men and the advent of the appellant was something like an hour and a half. Consequently it is suggested to us, and was suggested to the judge, that in the context of this case this evidence was very much material to an issue in the case, namely the question of consent, *f* owing, inter alia, to the similarity between the entry of these two men to the maisonette and the entry of the appellant and to the close proximity in time of the two incidents.

The next matter was the fact that she had had sexual intercourse with her boyfriend during the afternoon of 9 September, that was about 14 hours after the alleged act of rape. The relevance, it was suggested, in respect of this question was that it was said in the complainant's statement to the police that after the so-called rape her vagina was sore, *g* the inference being that it was because the sexual intercourse had been without consent that she suffered that pain. We are told, although it is not in evidence, that there was some difficulty about the real cause for the girl's soreness; it was suggested perhaps it was the size of the appellant's male member that had caused the soreness rather than the lack of consent.

The final matter which it was sought to introduce was this, that on the morning of 9 *h* September, a very few hours after the alleged act of rape, a woman friend of the complainant had come to her maisonette to pick up the complainant's little boy to take him to school. There was no reason apparently to doubt the veracity of this lady and what she said was that in the maisonette there was lying on the sofa this man naked apart from a pair of slippers.

All those matters have to be read against the somewhat unusual features of this case, *j* the unusual features being first of all the dispute about the injuries, some people saying that they observed them on the Friday, and others apparently saying that they did not earlier on; and the remarkable feature that no complaint was made to anyone apparently between the time of the event at about midnight on Tuesday night and Friday.

In those circumstances it seems to us that the events of the two men in the maisonette a prior to the incident in question and the presence of the naked man in the maisonette immediately after the event are matters which went to the question of consent and were matters which could not be regarded as so trivial or of so little relevance as for the judge to be able to say that he was satisfied that no injustice would be done to the appellant by their exclusion from the evidence. This case differs from those to which we have been referred, because those to which we have been referred were cases when the questions sought to be put in were questions solely as to credit. These questions were not mere b questions as to credit.

It need hardly be said that one differs from a judge in a point such as this with the greatest possible reluctance, and it is only after very serious consideration that we have come to the conclusion that in this particular case the judge was wrong in the conclusion which he reached: he was wrong in respect of the two men in the flat and wrong in respect of the naked man in the flat. We would not say the same of the second of the c three allegations, about sexual intercourse with the boyfriend. If the appeal had rested on that alone, we would not have interfered. We think he was right in the conclusion he reached in respect of that, but he was wrong in respect of the other two.

There are two other grounds of appeal which we can deal with quite shortly. A question arose about whether the prosecution should have been allowed to cross-examine a defence witness as to what the complainant had said to her after the incident took place. d We propose not to waste time on that. It is a trivial matter. Even if we had come to the conclusion that the judge was wrong in what he did, we should have unhesitatingly applied the proviso to s 2(1) of the Criminal Appeal Act 1968. Such irregularity that there was cannot be possibly be called material.

The other point was that evidence was given by the complainant's boyfriend, Willy Mullen, that the complainant had made an allegation to him that she had been raped. e The judge did not direct the jury that what was said by way of complaint to Willy Mullen was not evidence of its truth, and failed to point out to them, so it was suggested, that it was merely evidence of the consistency of the girl's behaviour and no more.

The judge dealt in detail and accurately and carefully with the question of corroboration. It seems to us, that being the case, and the judge having carefully refrained from making any mention to the jury that a complaint could possibly amount to f corroboration, the effect on the jury of the failure specifically to warn them about the value of the complaint was not a matter which could have affected the appellant adversely. It might perhaps have been better if the judge had given that warning. There again if that matter had stood on its own we would not have interfered, and if it were a material irregularity, then we would have applied the proviso to s 2(1) of the Criminal Appeal Act 1968.

g The fact remains that so far as the first ground of appeal is concerned, that must succeed. Accordingly the appeal must be allowed and the conviction quashed.

Appeal allowed ; conviction quashed.

Solicitors: *Varley, Hibbs & Co*, Coventry (for the appellant); *I S Manson*, Birmingham (for the Crown); *Treasury Solicitor*.

N P Metcalfe Esq   Barrister.

Burridge v Burridge

FAMILY DIVISION
ANTHONY LINCOLN J
24 MARCH 1982

Husband and wife – Summary proceedings – Financial provision – Lump sum order – Wife reasonably incurring liabilities in maintaining herself and children of marriage – Husband unemployed and having no capital resources but likely to obtain employment within six weeks – Magistrates making lump sum order against husband for payment of £500 for wife and £250 for children – Sums made payable by instalments and payment postponed for six weeks to enable husband to find employment – Husband failing to comply with order – Whether lump sum order proper if respondent had no capital resources – Whether order exceeding prescribed limit of £500 for lump sum – Whether magistrates should inquire further into husband's resources before enforcing order – Domestic Proceedings and Magistrates' Courts Act 1978, s 2(2)(3).

Following a separation the wife and two young children of the family lived apart from the husband. When the husband failed to maintain the family the wife reasonably incurred substantial debts in maintaining herself and the children. She applied to a magistrates' court for an order for financial provision, on the ground that the husband had failed to provide reasonable maintenance for herself and the children. The husband was unemployed and had no capital resources. On the hearing of the application the husband told the magistrates that he was confident that he could obtain employment within six weeks. The magistrates made a lump sum order against the husband, pursuant to s 2(2)[a] of the Domestic Proceedings and Magistrates' Courts Act 1978, for the payment of £500 for the wife and £125 for each of the two children, but made the lump sum payable by weekly instalments and postponed payment of the instalments for six weeks to enable the husband to find employment. The husband failed to find employment and failed to comply with the lump sum order. The wife sought enforcement of the order and the husband applied to have the order varied. The magistrates varied the order by reducing the size of the instalments. The husband appealed against both the lump sum order and the variation, contending (i) that, by analogy with the practice in divorce proceedings of not making a lump sum order against a spouse who had insufficient assets, the magistrates ought to have exercised their discretion by not making a lump sum order when the husband had no capital resources, and (ii) alternatively, that the order was in effect a lump sum order for £750 which exceeded the limit of £500 imposed by s 2(3)[b] of the 1978 Act on the making of lump sum orders by magistrates.

Held – (1) Since magistrates were expressly empowered by s 2(2) of the 1978 Act to make a lump sum order against a respondent to enable the applicant to meet any liabilities or expenses reasonably incurred in maintaining the applicant or a child of the family, the exercise of that power was not limited either by implication or public policy to cases where the respondent had capital resources. Accordingly, provided the magistrates had regard to the respondent's capacity to pay a lump sum out of income or potential income, they could make a lump sum order against the respondent despite the respondent's lack of capital resources. Since the husband had a potential income from likely employment the magistrates were entitled to make the lump sum order against him (see p 82 j to p 83 d, post); *Wachtel v Wachtel* [1973] 1 All ER 829 considered.

(2) Furthermore, the magistrates had power to order payment of £250 for the children in addition to £500 for the wife, because the wife had incurred the debts for the upkeep of the family as a whole and thus partly for the benefit of the children who were entitled, as well as the wife, to a lump sum order under s 2(2) (see p 83 f, post).

---

a   Section 2(2) is set out at p 82 j, post
b   Section 2(3) is set out at p 83 d e, post

(3) However, the magistrates had been wrong to postpone payment of the instalments
a for six weeks after which time the instalments automatically became payable, since such
an arbitrary time limit could have caused injustice to the husband if, despite all proper
attempts, he failed to obtain employment by the end of that period. In the circumstances,
the lump sum order ought not to be enforced until there was a further inquiry by the
magistrates into the husband's income resources, and to that extent the appeal would be
allowed and the case remitted to the magistrates for further inquiry (see p 83 f to j and p
b 84 a b, post).

Notes

For matrimonial orders in magistrates' courts where there is wilful neglect to maintain,
see 29 Halsbury's Laws (4th edn) para 175.

For the Domestic Proceedings and Magistrates' Courts Act 1978, s 2, see 48 Halsbury's
c Statutes (3rd edn) 736.

Cases referred to in judgment

Wachtel v Wachtel [1973] 1 All ER 829, [1973] Fam 72, [1973] 2 WLR 366, CA, Digest
(Cont Vol D) 425, 6962Aa.
Williams v Williams [1974] 3 All ER 377, [1974] Fam 55, [1974] 3 WLR 379, DC, Digest
d (Cont Vol D) 437, 7854a.

Appeal

By notice of motion dated 19 February 1982 Terence Burridge (the husband) applied for
an order extending the time for bringing an appeal against orders made on 17 March and
27 October 1981 by the Milton Keynes justices sitting at Newport Pagnell ordering him
e to pay by instalments a lump sum of £500 to Susan Barbara Burridge (the wife) and two
further lump sums, each of £125, to the wife for the benefit of the two children of the
marriage, pursuant to s 2(2) of the Domestic Proceedings and Magistrates' Courts Act
1978, and further applied for the orders be set aside. The facts are set out in the judgment.

John Reddish for the husband.
f *Paul Coleridge* for the wife.

ANTHONY LINCOLN J. This is an application by a husband to appeal out of time
against orders made by the Milton Keynes justices at Newport Pagnell on two different
occasions, the first on 17 March 1981 and the second on 27 October 1981. Those hearings
were concerned with complaints on the part of a wife that she was not being reasonably
g maintained, and it is conceded that that was the position. The notice of appeal is dated
19 February 1982. It can therefore be seen that almost a year has now passed since the
initial order was made by the magistrates, and at first sight it seems difficult to justify so
great a delay.

The husband, who has many criminal convictions, had come out of prison towards the
end of 1980. In January 1981 there was a separation of the parties, who had been married
h in 1977; there were two children of that marriage, Zoe born in 1978 now aged three,
and Suzanne born in 1979 now aged two. After three months the complaint came on for
hearing before the magistrates and they made an order, having heard evidence from
both parties, which it is not easy to construe. The effect of it is that they ordered the
husband to pay a lump sum of £500 to the wife and £125 to each child, making £750
in all. They then proceeded to make those lump sum payments payable by instalments,
j the £500 lump sum being payable at £10 a week, commencing from 28 April 1981. The
reason why they did that was because the husband in his evidence had said that although
he was unemployed he hoped to get work within some six weeks. In their reasons the
magistrates stated that what they were doing was this: they were allowing him the time
to find a job within six weeks; they were then ordering him to pay a lump sum by
weekly instalments. This would enable his wife to pay off some fairly substantial debts
which had been properly incurred by her and expenses reasonably defrayed by her in the

maintenance of the family. It is accepted that those debts were outstanding and that he ought at least to contribute to their payment, if not totally to reimburse her for their payment.	*a*

The husband, who was not unacquainted with the law and with the system by virtue of his criminal record, failed to consult the solicitors acting for him in relation to the criminal matters in which he was involved. He appeared in person at the hearing in March 1981. He failed to pay any arrears. He stated that he believed that the order was a conditional order, that is to say that he did not have to pay any money if he failed to get	*b* work within six weeks but if he did get such work then the order was to come into force. That of course was simply not correct. As a result enforcement notices were issued by the wife's solicitors in due course, and they made an application. At long last in July 1981 he consulted his present solicitors. A few days before the second hearing the solicitors, although they did not have the original order in their possession, realised that there had been the order for a lump sum, and the magistrates on 27 October heard an application	*c* for variation of the lump sum order on the basis that the husband was not employed. They varied the instalments by which the lump sum was to be paid.

Still no appeal had been launched in relation to the earlier order, notwithstanding the fact that the solicitors were now fully conversant with its terms and indeed had been arguing the case on the basis of that earlier order. They knew that a lump sum had been ordered, and they took no point on it. However, in due course counsel was consulted,	*d* applications were made for legal aid and the application was granted, and thus it came about that on 19 February 1982 this appeal was at last initiated.

I was minded to refuse the application for leave to appeal out of time, for it seemed to me that it was wholly the fault of the husband. He ought to have consulted his solicitors shortly after, if not before, the hearing in March 1981. He had ample opportunity of finding out whether the order imposed on him on that occasion was one which ought to	*e* have been made or not, and I do not accept that he misunderstood the nature of the order. However, it seemed to me, that having regard to the submissions which have been made by counsel relating to the orders made and the powers of the magistrates in that regard and having regard to the consequences of this order which might well result, if left undisturbed, in the husband being sent to prison yet again, it was right to grant leave to appeal out of time.	*f*

As to the merits, the main argument which was put on behalf of the husband was to this effect: that the husband has no capital resources and there is no evidence that he had any capital in any form whatsoever. The only evidence before the magistrates was to the effect that he had a capacity for work and therefore a potential income, and the magistrates as I have said believed that that potential would be realised within six weeks of the date of the making of the order. Counsel for the husband submitted that the	*g* power undoubtedly granted to the magistrates by the Domestic Proceedings and Magistrates Courts Act 1978, s 2(1)(b) and (d) ought not to have been exercised in the circumstances of this case. If, he says, there are no capital resources, then, he submits, the principle or dictum contained in *Wachtel v Wachtel* [1973] 1 All ER 829, [1973] Fam 72 that a lump sum should only be ordered where capital exists, should be applied in the magistrates' jurisdiction in the same manner. At first sight there is much to be said for	*h* that argument. However, counsel for the wife has drawn my attention to the additional subsections of s 2, in particular sub-s (2), which reads:

'Without prejudice to the generality of subsection (1)(b) or (d) above [which is concerned with the making of lump sum orders], an order under this section for the payment of a lump sum may be made for the purpose of enabling any liability or expenses reasonably incurred in maintaining the applicant, or any child of the	*j* family to whom the application relates, before the making of the order to be met.'

In this case, the liability or expenses reasonably incurred were the debts to which I have already referred. They were debts incurred before the making of the order, which was made in March 1981. And the question arises in this case whether the powers of the

a magistrates are by implication, or ought to be as a matter of public policy, circumscribed
so as to confine the exercise of the power to order lump sums to cases where there is
capital. Counsel for the wife submits that this is not the case. The powers should be left
untrammelled in the manner in which Parliament has left them expressly in the
subsections of s 2; sub-s (2) directly applies to a case such as the present one. With that
submission I agree. It does lead to a rather curious consequence that the order made is
then converted into what looks on the face of it like a periodical payments order, for the
b order made here was that the lump sum should be paid by periodical payments. That is
a necessary consequence of the husband not having any capital resources, but having a
potential income.

Accordingly, I hold that it would not be right to read into s 2(2) any limitation on the
exercise of the power, provided that the magistrates apply the principles laid down by
statute with regard to quantum, and in particular in the circumstances of this case they
c must have regard to the capacity of the husband to pay. They have done so. They must
have regard to the needs of the wife, and they have done so. These are all stated in the
magistrates' reasons, and the notes of evidence justify these reasons. There is no illogicality
in ordering a husband or a wife to pay a lump sum to meet debts which have accumulated
and remain to be paid as a lump sum by one or other of the parties. There is no illogicality
in breaking the lump sum ordered into weekly instalments, to accord with what the
d magistrates find to be the likely income of the payer.

It was also urged on me by counsel for the husband that the magistrates have in effect
transgressed the limits imposed by s 2(3), which provides:

'The amount of any lump sum required to be paid by an order under this section
shall not exceed £500, or such larger amount as the Secretary of State may from
time to time by order fix for the purposes of this subsection.'
e

He argued that the magistrates had in effect, by ordering a lump sum of £500 in
relation to the wife and £125 each in relation to the two children, gone beyond their
powers because the debts are not debts which could have been incurred by the children.
I do not agree. They were debts which were incurred for the upkeep of the family as a
whole, and in part were beneficial to the children, and to that extent the magistrates were
f fully entitled to fix the amounts which they did, even if these were at the very limit laid
down by sub-s (3).

However, that does not conclude the matter. It is conceded by counsel for the wife
that the magistrates were wrong to impose an arbitrary date of six weeks. The husband
had stated that he was confident of obtaining a job within six weeks. He asserted without
any justification that he made that statement under pressure from the magistrates. I find
g that that was a statement made by him freely and in the ordinary course of his evidence,
and that the magistrates were entitled to rely on it. But that does not mean that they
should have postponed the payment of a lump sum to a fixed date in the manner which
they did. Events might show that he could not with the exercise of all possible diligence
obtain employment within six weeks, and that his prediction was wholly unjustified,
that he was over confident. That means that the parties have to go back again to the
h magistrates in order to resolve yet one more issue. It is quite clear that if the present
order stands undisturbed with the arbitrary date incorporated as it now stands the order
would work an injustice on the husband, if it be found by the magistrates that he has
made attempts to find and has not obtained employment after making proper attempts
to do so.

Accordingly, it becomes necessary to remit that limited issue for further inquiry by
j the magistrates in order to ascertain whether he is earning money. Counsel for the
husband submitted at one point in his argument, on the basis of *Williams v Williams*
[1974] 3 All ER 377, [1974] Fam 55, that where a man or a woman is on supplementary
benefit then it must be assumed that he is not working. That assumption cannot be
made in realistic terms in modern conditions. There are many persons who can be shown
to be working and earning money albeit they are on supplementary benefit, and it is for

the magistrates to make inquiry to see whether that is the case or not. For those reasons, whilst rejecting the main contentions of the husband in relation to the powers of the *a* magistrates, I have come to the conclusion that this appeal should be allowed to this limited extent and the matter remitted to the magistrates for further inquiry in relation to his resources. As was pointed out by counsel for the husband in his argument, it is open to them yet again to vary or reduce to a nominal sum the instalments payable, and if the facts justify such reduction I have no doubt that they will make it. For those reasons this appeal is allowed. *b*

Appeal allowed. Case remitted to magistrates for determination of husband's resources.

Solicitors: *Boxall & Boxall*, agents for *Godfrey Davis & Waitt*, Ramsgate (for the husband); *Osborne, Morris*, Bletchley (for the wife).

c

Bebe Chua   Barrister.

Re H (a minor) (adoption: non-patrial)   *d*

FAMILY DIVISION
HOLLINGS J
15, 16 FEBRUARY, 5 MARCH 1982

Adoption – Order – Discretion – Nationality – Immigration control – Application to adopt child *e* *who has been refused admission for settlement – Matters to be considered – Child's welfare to be balanced against reasons and policy for refusal of admission – Whether court entitled to consider afresh matters decided in immigration proceedings – Children Act 1975, s 3 – Statement of Immigration Rules for Control on Entry: EEC and Other Non-Commonwealth Nationals (HC Paper (1972–73) no 81), para 38.* *f*

On 31 December 1978 H, who was then aged 14 and one of a family of nine children in Pakistan whose parents were divorced, was given leave to enter the United Kingdom as a visitor for one month to visit relatives including the applicants, who were his uncle and aunt. H had been rejected by his family in Pakistan and the leave to enter was probably obtained by deception because in fact the applicants intended to adopt him. From the *g* date of his entry H lived with the applicants as a de facto member of their family. The Secretary of State refused an application by the uncle for an extension of H's leave to enter when the reason given was that H wished to see more of England before returning to Pakistan, because he was not satisfied that H was a genuine visitor. In the mean time the uncle notified the local authority of his intention to adopt H and, when he received notice of the Secretary of State's refusal of an extension of H's leave to enter, the uncle *h* requested the Secretary of State to reconsider and extend H's leave until a decision was reached regarding his adoption. The Secretary of State, treating the uncle's application as an application by H for admission to settle in the United Kingdom by adoption, again refused the application, on the ground that he was not satisfied, for the purposes of para 38[a] of the Statement of Immigration Rules for Control on Entry: EEC and Other Non-

j

---

a   Paragraph 38, so far as material provides:'... children under 18 are to be admitted for settlement: (a) if both parents are settled in the United Kingdom ... In this paragraph "parent" ... includes an adoptive parent, but only where there has been a genuine transfer of parental responsibility on the ground of the original parents' inability to care for the child, and the adoption is not one of convenience arranged to facilitate the child's admission.'

Commonwealth Nationals, that there had been a genuine transfer of parental
a responsibility to the adopting parents or that the proposed adoption was not an adoption
of convenience to facilitate H's admission. H appealed under the Immigration Act 1971
but both the adjudicator and the Immigration Appeal Tribunal dismissed the appeal.
The applicants thereupon initiated adoption proceedings in the High Court. The Official
Solicitor was appointed H's guardian ad litem and prepared a confidential report for the
High Court which favoured the adoption of H by the applicants because of the family
b benefits that H would gain and because his return to Pakistan would jeopardise his future
well-being. The Secretary of State opposed the application on the ground that it was
merely a device to circumvent immigration control and obtain, by means other than the
Secretary of State's permission, the right to acquire British nationality and the right of
abode in the United Kingdom. The Secretary of State submitted that, although s 3[b] of the
Children Act 1975 required that the court's 'first consideration' in adoption proceedings
c must be the 'welfare of the child throughout his childhood', nevertheless where the
adoptive child was subject to immigration control the court should, save in the most
exceptional cases, exercise its discretion in the adoption proceedings in accord with para
38 of the immigration rules and should, furthermore, refuse to rehear and determine
matters which had already been decided in immigration proceedings. The applicants
contended that the immigration proceedings were different proceedings between
d different parties and therefore irrelevant in the adoption proceedings.

Held – (1) Since s 3 of the 1975 Act required the court to have regard to 'all the
circumstances' when considering an application for adoption, where the proceedings
concerned a foreign national the court was required to balance the factors in favour of
adoption against the factors relating to immigration and the refusal of admission. Thus,
e on the one hand, the court could not abdicate its responsibility to have regard to the
welfare of the child, and since that was a factor which the Secretary of State and the
immigration authorities were not required to consider the court was not bound by their
decisions and was entitled to consider afresh matters and evidence already considered in
immigration proceedings. On the other hand, the court had to be on guard against the
abuse of the adoption proceedings as a means of obtaining the right of abode and British
f nationality and therefore the court was required to give due consideration and weight to
any decision by the immigration authorities refusing admission and to the policy
underlying such a decision. Moreover, in balancing the minor's welfare against the policy
considerations the court was required to have regard to the fact that the wider the
implications of the policy considerations the less the weight that could be given to the
minor's welfare. Accordingly, the proper approach of the court was that, if the true
g motive of the adoption application was to obtain British nationality and the right of
abode for the minor rather than to promote his general welfare, an adoption order should
be refused; but if part of the motive was to obtain the emotional, social and legal benefits
of adoption for the minor the court was entitled to make an adoption order even if to do
so would override an immigration decision refusing him admission or an immigration
rule (see p 89 *d* to *f* and p 93 *j* to p 94 *f*, post); Re A (an infant) [1963] 1 All ER 531, Re R
h (adoption) [1966] 3 All ER 613, dictum of Lord Denning MR in Re A (an infant), Hanif v
Secretary of State for Home Affairs [1968] 2 All ER at 151 and Re D (an infant) (parent's
consent) [1977] 1 All ER 145 considered.
    (2) On the facts, H's welfare and the findings by the court that H had been rejected by
his parents, that contrary to the Secretary of State's findings, there had been a genuine
transfer of parental responsibility to the applicants and that the adoption was not one of
j convenience had to be weighed against the policy considerations underlying the decision
to refuse admission to H, including the fact that there had been an attempt to deceive the
immigration authorities. In all the circumstances, the welfare considerations should
prevail and an adoption order would therefore be made (see p 95 *d* to *f* and *h*, post).

---

b   Section 3, so far as material, is set out at p 89 *f g*, post

Notes

For the duty in adoption to promote the child's welfare, see 24 Halsbury's Laws (4th edn)   *a*
para 673.

For the Children Act 1975, s 3, see 45 Halsbury's Statutes (3rd edn) 676.

Cases referred to in judgment

A (an infant), Re [1963] 1 All ER 531, [1963] 1 WLR 231, 28(2) Digest (Reissue) 836,
   1402.   *b*

A (an infant), Re, Hanif v Secretary of State for Home Affairs [1968] 2 All ER 145, sub nom
   Re Mohamed Arif (an infant) [1968] Ch 643, [1968] 2 WLR 1290, Ch D and CA, 2 Digest
   (Reissue) 204, 1165.

D (an infant), Re [1958] 3 All ER 716, [1959] 1 QB 229, [1959] 2 WLR 26, CA, 28(2)
   Digest (Reissue) 836, 1401.

D (an infant) (parent's consent), Re [1977] 1 All ER 145, [1977] AC 602, [1977] 2 WLR 79,   *c*
   HL, Digest (Cont Vol E) 320, 1375c..

Hollington v F Hewthorn & Co Ltd [1943] 2 All ER 35, [1943] KB 587, CA, 22 Digest
   (Reissue) 270, 2470.

Official Solicitor v K [1963] 3 All ER 191, [1965] AC 201, [1963] 3 WLR 408, HL, 28(2)
   Digest (Reissue) 912, 2233.

R v Secretary of State for the Home Department, ex p Zamir [1980] 2 All ER 768, [1980] AC   *d*
   930, [1980] 3 WLR 249, HL.

R (adoption), Re [1966] 3 All ER 613, [1967] 1 WLR 34, 28(2) Digest (Reissue) 824, 1357.

Originating summons

By an originating summons dated 12 August 1980 the applicants applied for an adoption
order to adopt their nephew, H, a minor, who was a national of Pakistan. H had been   *e*
refused admission to the United Kingdom to settle by the Secretary of State for the Home
Office and his decision had been upheld on H's appeal to an adjudicator and to the
Immigration Appeal Tribunal. Pursuant to r 18 of the Adoption (High Court) Rules
1976, SI 1976/1645, the Secretary of State had been notified of the adoption proceedings
and under r 19 of the rules had given notice that the Treasury Solicitor wished to attend
the proceedings to be heard on the question whether an adoption order should be made.   *f*
This application was heard in chambers but judgment was given by Hollings J in open
court. The facts are set out in the judgment.

Nicholas Mostyn for the applicants.
E James Hôlman for the Official Solicitor as guardian ad litem of H.
Simon D Brown and *Peter Goldsmith* for the Secretary of State.   *g*

                                                                      Cur adv vult

5 March. **HOLLINGS J** read the following judgment: I am giving the judgment in this
adoption application, which I heard in chambers on 15 and 16 February 1982, in open
court so that it can be reported; but to avoid identification I have referred to the relevant   *h*
persons by initials and this confidentiality must be preserved.

The application came to be made in the following circumstances. On 31 December
1978 H, the second son of nine children of a family in Pakistan, was given leave to enter
the United Kingdom by Home Office immigration control. He was then aged 14, born
in Lahore on 7 November 1964. He told the immigration officer that he wished to visit
his paternal grandparents and his paternal uncle, Dr N, who is the male applicant in these   *j*
proceedings. He was given leave to enter for one month, subject to a condition
prohibiting employment. His grandparents had entered the United Kingdom in 1977
and were settled here and living in Birmingham. Dr N, the male applicant, entered the
United Kingdom from Pakistan in 1968. He studied successfully at Southampton,
Edinburgh and Birmingham Universities obtaining degrees at each, ending with a PhD
in December 1979 in chemical engineering at the last of these universities. His wife, the

female applicant, was a Ugandan Asian. She entered the United Kingdom in 1971. She
a and her husband met while they were studying and married in May 1974.

Dr N has been employed since 1978, and now holds a responsible and well-paid
position in a well-known company as a chemical engineer. He and his wife have a home
in Harrow and have four children of their own aged from six to 1½ years. It was Dr N
who had arranged for his parents, H's grandparents, to enter and settle in the United
Kingdom.

b On entering the United Kingdom in December 1978, H went to live with his uncle in
Harrow. So far, the facts are undisputed. According to H and Dr N, H had sought his
uncle's help because he had been turned out of his home where he lived with his father
and his siblings and was destitute. He and Dr N say that until he was aged 12 he had
lived in Pakistan in the home of his grandparents who had cared for him until they came
to England in 1977. H's parents had been unhappily married and eventually divorced.
c H's mother left Lahore for Karachi, and the nine children of their marriage were left in
the custody of the father in Lahore. H, however, was treated differently from the others,
his father and the other children seeming to blame H as the cause of his parents'
separation. After he was turned out of the home by his father in about September 1978
H claims that he spent the next few months living rough in the streets until he was taken
in by an aunt, and it was she who put him in touch with Dr N, his paternal uncle. Dr N
d sent him the air fare and so he came to England.

On 28 January 1979 Dr N wrote a letter for H to the Home Office asking for an
extension of H's stay. The Home Office on 6 March 1979 asked for reasons, and Dr N in
H's name replied on 22 March 1979 stating where he was living and requesting an
extension of H's stay 'for six months only' adding 'I am requesting this extension merely
to be able to see the cultural and social aspects of life in Britain. I shall be leaving Britain
e by next September'.

Dr N told me that in the meantime he had been holding discussions with the family
in the United Kingdom, and by telephone with some of the family, including H's father,
in Pakistan, with a view to he and his wife adopting H, and it was decided that they
should seek to do this. On 18 March 1979, Dr N wrote to the London Borough of Harrow
Social Services for advice about adoption, and he received advice a few days later. On 16
f April 1979 he gave the London Borough of Harrow notice of his intention to adopt. On
17 April 1979 Dr N wrote again to the Home Office, which is a letter annexed to the
Home Office statement, which has been put in in these proceedings without objection,
requesting the necessary instructions and relevant papers to adopt H and setting out
briefly the circumstances in which H had been rejected by his family. In that letter he
referred to the fact that H had come to the United Kingdom as a visitor about three
g months before and that his passport was already with the Home Office for an extension
of his stay.

The Secretary of State, however, when he considered the application for an extension
was not aware of the letter of the 17 April. This again appears from the Home Office
statement, and on 27 April 1979 he refused the application on the ground that he could
not be satisfied that H was a genuine visitor who would leave at the end of his permitted
h stay or that he would not become a charge on public funds.

On 28 April 1979 Dr N by letter requested the Home Office to reconsider the decision
and extend the time until a decision about adoption was reached. Dr N's application on
behalf of H was ultimately treated by the Secretary of State as an application for
settlement by means of adoption, but the refusal was confirmed on 6 February 1980. An
appeal was lodged on behalf of H. According to the Home Office statement, the Home
j Office made various inquiries and H and Dr N and Mrs N were interviewed, as a result
of which the appeal was rejected by the Secretary of State. Further appeals under the
immigration rules to an adjudicator and to the Immigration Appeal Tribunal were also
rejected, and the grounds of the rejection as notified to H were as follows:

> 'Dr. N has applied on your behalf for a variation of your leave to enter in order to
> adopt you, but the Secretary of State is not satisfied that there has been a genuine

transfer of parental responsibility nor is he satisfied that the adoption is not one of
convenience arranged to enable you to remain in the country.'   *a*

On 13 May 1980 Dr and Mrs N became naturalised United Kingdom citizens. On 12
August 1980 Dr and Mrs N issued the originating summons for adoption of H. In
accordance with the rules, the Official Solicitor was appointed guardian ad litem of H,
and the Official Solicitor took steps to enable him to prepare his confidential report. On
his advice, notice of the hearing of the application was, pursuant to r 18 of the Adoption
(High Court) Rules 1976, SI 1976/1645, served on the Home Office. The Treasury   *b*
Solicitor thereupon gave notice that he wished, as solicitor for the Home Office, to attend
and be heard on the question whether an adoption order should be made, pursuant to
r 19 of the Adoption (High Court) Rules 1976. Accordingly, at the hearing before me
the Secretary of State, the Official Solicitor as guardian ad litem of H, and the applicants
were each represented by counsel and I have been greatly assisted by the argument and
submissions of each of them.   *c*

In the mean time, the Official Solicitor, carrying out the duties placed on him by the
adoption rules, obtained a report from the London Borough of Harrow Social Services
and kept in touch with the progress of the proceedings and appeals under the Immigration
Act 1971. Two letters from the Home Office are annexed to the Official Solicitor's
confidential report dated 22 April and 29 June 1981. In the latter, the Home Office say,
inter alia: *d*

   'It is noted that in your official capacity you are making extensive inquiries . . .
   which seem to be leading towards a favourable outcome for the adoption of H. Be
   that as it may, we would like to put on record our concern from an immigration
   viewpoint that in this case the appellant and his sponsors would have thereby
   succeeded in a significant circumvention of the immigration control and may be an *e*
   example for others to follow.'

No steps have yet been taken by the Home Office to deport H. I understand that this
is partly out of consideration for these proceedings and partly because in any event if, as
is likely, full use were made of the appeal system, H would still today be in the United
Kingdom. H has, ever since 31 December 1978, lived with the applicants. I am satisfied
that he has been in their 'actual custody' throughout this period within the meaning of *f*
s 3 of the Adoption Act 1958, as amended by the Children Act 1975. This is an essential
prerequisite of an adoption order.

The consent of H's parents has been sought by the Official Solicitor. I am satisfied that
H's father has given his written consent with full knowledge of the implications. Having
considered the steps which have been taken by the Official Solicitor to ascertain whether
H's mother consents, I can say that I am satisfied on the evidence in her case too that her *g*
consent has been properly obtained in accordance with s 6 of the Adoption Act 1958 and,
in particular, r 7(2)(b) of the Adoption (High Court) Rules 1976.

If an adoption order is made, this will have the effect of conferring United Kingdom
citizenship and the right of abode or 'patriality' on H, for s 19 of the Adoption Act 1958
confers United Kingdom citizenship on a foreign minor in respect of whom an adoption
order is made in favour of an adopter who is a United Kingdom citizen, as is the case *h*
here; and by s 2(1)(a) of the Immigration Act 1971 the right of abode in the United
Kingdom under that Act is conferred if the person concerned is a United Kingdom
citizen by adoption.

The Official Solicitor as guardian ad litem has the specific duties laid on him by the
rules. He had carried out those duties which include making relevant inquiries and
obtaining relevant reports. He has filed a confidential report to which I think, however, *j*
it is proper that I should refer in part at this stage. The report is by the assistant Official
Solicitor. He says that having completed his inquiries he has ascertained that the
applicants wish to adopt H because of the rejection that he has suffered by his parents
following their divorce, and because they wish to provide him with parental love and a
home. He is satisfied of the stability of the applicants' marriage and that H wishes to be

adopted by the applicants. He states that the Official Solicitor is thus satisfied that an
a adoption order if made will safeguard and promote the child's welfare throughout his
childhood. (This is a reference to s 3 of the Children Act 1975.) He further says that he
has naturally been concerned to ascertain as far as possible whether the principal purpose
of this application could be regarded as an attempt to secure an 'accommodation order'
designed to circumvent the immigration control procedures of this country, and that
although he must concede that his inquiries do not entirely remove his doubts, the
b Official Solicitor is, on balance, of the view on the evidence available to him, that the
applicants can properly be regarded as standing fully in loco parentis to H, that the
benefit which an adoption order would confer on H would not be confined to the
acquisition of British nationality but would give the child social, legal and psychological
benefits of belonging to a family and that the refusal of an adoption order and H's
subsequent removal to Pakistan would be likely to jeopardise considerably H's future
c well-being.

Annexed to the Official Solicitor's report is an account of an interview of the applicants
and H by a representative of the Official Solicitor, and the report of a social worker on
behalf of the London borough of Harrow on the applicants and H, a letter from the
British Consultate General who has interviewed H's mother and given some indication
of her present circumstances in Karachi, a letter from H's father in Lahore, and a report
d of a representative of the Official Solicitor of an interview of H's grandparents in
Birmingham.

The Official Solicitor's report is not, of course, binding on this court, but supplied as it
is pursuant to the duty to do so imposed by the 1975 Act and rules, this court is not only
entitled to but is bound to have regard to its findings and recommendations. This case
therefore demonstrates in acute form the conflict or even collision which can occur and
e seems bound to occur from time to time between immigration policy and procedures
and adoption law and procedures; for as counsel who appears on behalf of the Secretary
of State properly concedes, this court clearly has jurisdiction to consider the adoption
application and to make an adoption order notwithstanding the adverse decision in the
immigration proceedings under the Immigration Act 1971. In exercise of this
jurisdiction, this court has to have regard to the provisions of s 3 of the Children Act
f 1975, which provides:

> 'In reaching any decision relating to the adoption of a child, a court . . . shall have
> regard to all the circumstances, first consideration being given to the need to
> safeguard and promote the welfare of the child throughout his childhood; and shall
> so far as practicable ascertain the wishes and feelings of the child regarding the
> decision and give due consideration to them, having regard to his age and
g > understanding.'

On the other hand, the Secretary of State for his part is responsible for immigration
control and is answerable to Parliament in that respect. With regard to this responsibility,
counsel for the Secretary of State submits that it has two aspects: (1) the formulation of
policy as to the circumstances in which immigration rights and status can properly be
h conferred by adopters; and (2) the responsibility of determining the facts relevant to the
application of the policy.

Counsel for the Secretary of State has, in support of this, referred me to a number of
authorities and to the provisions of the Immigration Act 1971 and the rules made under
it. Two of the authorities are decisions in adoption proceedings in the Chancery Division:
Re A (an infant) [1963] 1 All ER 531, [1963] 1 WLR 231, in which Cross J was the judge,
j and Re R (adoption) [1966] 3 All ER 613, [1967] 1 WLR 34, in which Buckley J was the
judge. In the former case, Cross J refused to make an adoption order in respect of a
French boy aged 20. He found as a fact that the reason why the applicants in that case
wished to adopt him and why he wished to be adopted by them was not that they should
become his parents in the true sense of the word but that he should acquire British
nationality. Cross J pointed out that the benefit to the boy would flow from the fact that

he was being adopted, not from the fact that he was being adopted by particular adopters, and he found that the adoption would be an 'accommodation adoption' and he said it *a* was not difficult to envisage cases in which such adoption would be open to objection on the ground of public policy. The basic objection that Cross J felt to the application was that the applicants were not really in loco parentis to the boy.

In the latter case, Re R (adoption), the subject of the adoption application was a 20-year-old refugee from a totalitarian country. Buckley J found that the minor's parents in the country in question were indifferent to their son's intention to leave them and the *b* country, and kept up no communication with him, and he further found that the applicant was now fully in loco parentis to the minor and that the benefit which adoption, if permitted, would confer on the minor would not be confined to British nationality. It would give him the social and psychological benefits of truly belonging to a family, as a member of it, with the attendant legal status and rights. Buckley J concluded as follows ([1966] 3 All ER 613 at 617–618, [1967] 1 WLR 34 at 41): *c*

'I have, of course, given very careful consideration to the public policy aspect of the matter mentioned by Cross J in Re A (an infant) ([1963] 1 All ER 531, [1963] 1 WLR 231). This aspect, I think makes it incumbent on the court to be particularly circumspect in exercising the jurisdiction under the Act of 1958 when the infant proposed to be adopted is of foreign nationality and, more particularly, when he or *d* she is no longer a young child but is approaching his or her majority. It does not, in my judgment, have the result that the court cannot, or ought not to, exercise the jurisdiction in such a case on the ground that it may thereby usurp the functions of the Home Secretary in relation to naturalisation. I am told that in the present case R's circumstances have been carefully and fully investigated by the appropriate Government department or departments and that no objection on grounds of security or otherwise have been found to R's acquiring British nationality, but no *e* evidence of this has been filed. In these circumstances, I am prepared to make the order asked for, but subject to a certificate being obtained and signed by an appropriate official of the Home Office, or subject to other satisfactory evidence being produced to the court, to the effect that there are no considerations of security or otherwise which ought, in the view of the Home Secretary or some official in his department authorised to deal with such matters, to be brought to the attention of *f* the court before the order is permitted to become effective. If no such certificate or evidence is forthcoming the case must be mentioned to me again in chambers, and it will be for the applicant or the applicant's advisers to obtain the necessary certificate or evidence. [The order will be conditional upon such evidence being produced.]'

g

Both Re A (an infant) and Re R (adoption) were of course decided before the Immigration Act 1971 and are not therefore directly applicable. Counsel for the Secretary of State then referred me to the relevant provisions of the 1971 Act and the rules made under it. Leave to enter the United Kingdom is for initial decision by the immigration officer. Extension of stay after limited leave to enter is for decision by the Secretary of State. Part II of the Act makes comprehensive provision for appeals, to an adjudicator and then to the *h* Immigration Appeals Tribunal. These are appeals on fact as well as law and enable a review of the Secretary of State's discretion. By r 29 of the Immigration Appeals (Procedure) Rules 1972, SI 1972/1684, the appellate authority is empowered to receive evidence relevant to the appeal notwithstanding that it would be inadmissible in a court of law. In the Statement of Immigration Rules for Control on Entry: EEC and Other Non-Commonwealth Nationals (HC Paper (1972–73) no 81), by para 38, it is provided *j* that children are to be admitted for settlement under certain conditions relating to their parents, and it is provided that in that rule 'parent' includes an adoptive parent but only where there has been a genuine transfer of parental responsibility on the ground of the original parent's inability to care for the child, and the adoption is not one of convenience arranged to facilitate the child's admission. (This is the same as the current rule, para 46, which is in Statement of Changes in Immigration Rules (HC Paper (1979–80) no 394).)

Counsel for the Secretary of State referred me to two other reported cases. In *Re A* (*an*
a   *infant*), *Hanif v Secretary of State for Home Affairs* [1968] 2 All ER 145, [1968] Ch 643 the
issue of an originating summons in wardship proceedings was used in an attempt to
obtain a fresh hearing and decision whether an applicant for admission under the
Commonwealth Immigrants Act 1962 was indeed the son of the plaintiffs in the wardship
proceedings. Lord Denning MR said ([1968] 2 All ER 145 at 151, [1968] Ch 643 at 660–
661):

b   'Meanwhile, it is said, he cannot be removed from the jurisdiction without the
        leave of the court because no ward can be removed from the jurisdiction without
        leave. In answer to this argument, two points are taken. First, it is said that once a
        child has been ordered to be removed, there is no jurisdiction to make him a ward
        of court. I do not think it necessary to determine that point. I can well see that there
        may be exceptional cases where such a jurisdiction may be desirable. Second, it is
c   said that at any rate, even if there is jurisdiction it ought not to be exercised in cases
        like the present one. I think that this second submission is correct. It seems to me
        that in the Commonwealth Immigrants Act, 1962, Parliament laid down a full and
        complete code to govern the entry or removal of immigrants from the
        Commonwealth and has entrusted the administration of it to the immigration
        officers. So much so that the courts ought not to interfere with their decisions save
d   in the most exceptional circumstances.'

He then referred to the case of a Pakistani boy and concluded on this aspect ([1968] 2 All
ER 145 at 152, [1968] Ch 643 at 661):

        'So long as they [ie the immigration officers] exercise it honestly and fairly, the
        courts cannot and should not interfere. They will not issue a writ of habeas corpus
e   or certiorari so as to review the decision of the immigration officers. Nor will they
        allow the wardship jurisdiction to be used for a like purpose.'

But, counsel for the Secretary of State concedes, this decision relating to wardship
proceedings as it does has no direct application because the legislation relevant to the
present case expressly envisages that a United Kingdom adoption order can be made to
f   defeat, as it were, the normal procedure of immigration control.

R v Secretary of State for the Home Department, ex p Zamir [1980] 2 All ER 768, [1980]
AC 930 was a case of illegal entry by deception, where the decision of the immigration
officer and of the Secretary of State was sought to be challenged by an application for an
order of judicial review, involving a different consideration, of course, from the
considerations in this case. It was held, and I read from part of the headnote ([1980] AC
g   930 at 931), that—

        'the decision of the Secretary of State to remove the appellant, and the appellant's
        consequent detention, could only be attacked if it could be shown that there had
        been no grounds on which the Secretary of State, through his officers, could have
        acted, or that no reasonable person could have decided as he had done.'

h   I was referred to this authority by counsel for the Secretary of State for the passage in
Lord Wilberforce's speech where he said ([1980] 2 All ER 768 at 772, [1980] AC 930 at
949):

        'The immigration officer, whether at the stage of entry or that of removal, has to
        consider a complex of statutory rules and non-statutory guidelines. He has to act on
        documentary evidence and such other evidence as inquiries may provide. Often
j   there will be documents whose genuineness is doubtful, statements which cannot
        be verified, misunderstandings as to what was said, practices and attitudes in a
        foreign state which have to be estimated. There is room for appreciation, even for
        discretion.'

But again, this decision is not binding in relation to the issues in this case.
In the light of these statutory provisions and the authorities, counsel for the Secretary

of State submits that, while, under s 3 of the Children Act 1975, welfare is the first
consideration, it is not the first and paramount consideration as it is in wardship and   *a*
guardianship proceedings, and that this distinction is reflected in *Re A (an infant)* [1963]
1 All ER 531, [1963] 1 WLR 231 and *Re R (adoption)* [1966] 3 All ER 613, [1967] 1 WLR
34; and further, that *Re A (an infant)* and *Re R (adoption)* show that general policy
considerations can outweigh benefit to the minor. *Re A (an infant)* and *Re R (adoption)*
were decided before the enactment of s 3 of the Children Act 1975. In their time, welfare
was not given by statute in adoption proceedings the same prominence as is given to it   *b*
by s 3 of the 1975 Act. Section 7 of the Adoption Act 1958 was the then relevant section,
and in that section welfare was placed second of three matters in respect of which the
court had to be satisfied before making an adoption order. The first was that the consents
of those whose consent was necessary had been obtained; the second was that the order,
if made, would be for the welfare of the infant; and the third was that the applicant had
not received or any other person made or given or agreed to make or give the applicant   *c*
any payment or reward in consideration of the adoption; and under sub-s (2) it is
provided that in determining whether an adoption order, if made, will be for the welfare
of the infant, the court shall have regard (amongst other things) to the health of the
applicant.

In his judgment in *Re A (an infant)* [1963] 1 All ER 531 at 533, [1963] 1 WLR 231 at
234, Cross J referred to s 7(1) of the 1958 Act of which he said: *d*

'Section 7(1) prescribes certain matters, (a)–(c), of which the court must be satisfied
before it makes an order. Matter (a) is that the necessary consents have been given . . .
Matter (b) is that the order if made will be for the welfare of the infant. The word
"welfare" might perhaps be thought to point rather to the physical or moral well-
being of the infant than to such a benefit as he will secure here if the order is made,
but in the light of *Re D. (an infant)* ([1958] 3 All ER 716, [1959] 1 QB 229), to which   *e*
I shall be referring in a moment, I think that "welfare" simply means "benefit", and,
as I have said, I am satisfied that it will be for the benefit of this young man that I
should make the order.'

Then he referred to the third requisite.

Paragraph 38 of HC Paper (1972–73) no 81 is relevant, counsel for the Secretary of   *f*
State submits, for it is clearly designed to limit the type of adoption order that will give
the same standing to a child abroad as a natural child, and this rule seems to be reflected
in the Secretary of State's revised decision in this case. This rule, he submits, should or
can be used by the Secretary of State as a guide to the policy desired by Parliament, and
should be applied by analogy a fortiori to a United Kingdom adoption case where an
adoption order has not yet been made. So, counsel for the Secretary of State submits, only   *g*
in the most exceptional cases should this court be prepared to sanction the adoption
process in circumstances which do not accord with the basic requirement of para 38,
which is, he submits, that the natural parents should be unable to care for their child,
and otherwise the policy in relation to conferment of patriality by adoption is a matter
which should be left in the province of the Secretary of State.

The second aspect of the Secretary of State's responsibility, the determination of the   *h*
facts relevant to the application of the policy, involves a submission that this court should
not 'rehear' evidence already considered and pronounced on in the immigration
proceedings, which are proceedings conducted in accordance with a comprehensive code
laid down in the 1971 Act and its rules, and reliance is placed on the passages in the
judgments in *Hanif* and *Zamir* to which I have referred. Counsel for the Secretary of State
does not suggest that there is any form of estoppel, but he does submit and point out that   *j*
it is undesirable that there should be a parallel system of adjudication, and also that it
would in most cases be quite impracticable for the Secretary of State to enter into
adoption proceedings and play a full role in them.

Submitting, therefore, that I should at least take into account the actual decision and
the policy considerations which informed it and the findings of primary fact underlying
the decision, though conceding that they should not be regarded as conclusive, counsel

for the Secretary of State did not call any evidence on behalf of the Home Office, nor did
a he cross-examine the evidence of the applicants, and H, which I allowed to be given (at
least as to part) de bene esse pending my final decision.

Before considering these submissions and their implications, I must here interpose to
refer to and consider a different but related submission which has been made by counsel
on behalf of the applicants. This was that I should take quite the opposite view and pay
no regard at all to the decision of the Secretary of State and the adjudicator on the ground
b that it was a decision in proceedings between different parties, on the principle res inter
alios acta alteri nocere non debet and relies on the well-known decision in *Hollington v F
Hewthorn & Co Ltd* [1943] 2 All ER 35, [1943] KB 587, as developed in *Phipson on Evidence*
(12th edn, 1976) paras 1379–1385.

Adoption proceedings are however sui generis and are in substance if not in form non-
adversarial in conception. The minor is represented by a guardian ad litem who is
c enjoined by the rules to make specific, detailed inquiries and to file a confidential report.
This report is rarely revealed, at least in its totality, to the applicants or others who may
be making representations. The court relies on the report of the guardian ad litem and
on reports obtained by him. I have referred to the reports filed in the present case. Much
of the evidence thereby presented to the court is hearsay. When welfare considerations
apply, where the welfare of the minor is paramount as in guardianship or wardship cases,
d or a first consideration as in adoption proceedings, the very welfare of the minor dictates
that regard must be had to every matter which bears on a possible risk or benefit to the
child: see the decision of the House of Lords in *Official Solicitor v K* [1963] 3 All ER 191,
[1965] AC 201, which concerned wardship proceedings. I can see no reason for making
a distinction between reports supplied pursuant to the adoption order and reports
originating in any other way, and plainly a decision after investigation by the Secretary
e of State carrying out his duties under the Immigration Act 1971 must be able to be
received by this court and given due weight and consideration.

Further, by s 3 of the 1975 Act this court is enjoined to take into account 'all the
circumstances' of the case.

To return to the submissions of counsel for the Secretary of State, he urges therefore
that for this court, save in most exceptional cases, to reopen matters otherwise finally
f decided in the immigration proceedings is plainly contrary to the spirit and policy of the
Immigration Act 1971 as laid down by Parliament. The policy with regard to
immigration, and especially national security, are indeed matters to do with the Secretary
of State and not directly with this court. He has further argued that it is at least established
by, in particular, *Re A (an infant)* [1963] 1 All ER 531, [1963] 1 WLR 231 and *Re R
(adoption)* [1966] 3 All ER 613, [1967] 1 WLR 34 that a minimum requirement for an
g adoption order is that the applicant should stand in loco parentis to the minor. I am not
sure that it is right to infer from the judgments in *Re A (an infant)* and *Re R (adoption)*
that being in loco parentis is a minimum requirement in general for an adoption order,
though it was a statutory prerequisite under the Adoption Act 1958, on which both cases
were decided that the minor must have been in the care and possession (that is the
equivalent of 'actual custody' under the present law) of the applicants for a certain period.
h Cross J in the earlier case made reference to 'in loco parentis' in relation to that
requirement and not in regard to the wider aspect. But if the applicants are indeed in
loco parentis to the minor, that is of course a most material factor to be put in the scales
in favour of adoption.

Plainly, in circumstances such as these, the adoption process is open to abuse, not
merely in the form of 'accommodation adoptions' but also even where there is a genuine
j transfer of parental responsibility where it is effected primarily to obtain the crucial
advantage of nationality or patriality, as counsel for the Secretary of State submitted. This
court must be on its guard particularly where, as here, not only is the minor a foreign
national but he is approaching his majority. These are substantial and cogent
considerations which must be taken into account with due regard however to the
requirements of s 3 of the 1975 Act. The immigration authorities and the Secretary of
State are in no way enjoined to have regard themselves to the welfare as such of the

applicant to enter, although as one knows great regard is paid in practice to considerations of humanity so far as is consistent with policy.   *a*

In *Re D (an infant) (parent's consent)* [1977] 1 All ER 145 at 160, [1977] AC 602 at 638 Lord Simon, referring to s 3 of the 1975 Act, said:

> 'In adoption proceedings, the welfare of the child is not the paramount consideration (ie outweighing all others) as with custody and guardianship; but it is the first consideration (ie outweighing any other).'   *b*

Plainly, this court cannot and must not abdicate the responsibility which has been thus laid on it. Equally, it must pay regard to the decision and reasons of the minister on whom Parliament has laid the responsibility of controlling entry into this country. It must however do so without being restricted as to the evidence it hears or the information it relies on. While it should therefore pay such regard as it thinks proper in the light of these considerations to the decisions and reasons of the Secretary of State and the appellate   *c* authorities in the immigration proceedings, it is nevertheless at the end of the day not bound by those decisions or reasons. I firstly rule therefore that this court may hear and act on evidence given by the applicants and H, including evidence which has already been considered in the immigration proceedings.

What then should the approach of this court be in applications of this nature? Clearly, it must pay great regard to the 'immigration decision' and in particular considerations of   *d* public policy and where relevant national security. It must be on its guard against the possibility of abuse; but the mere fact that nationality or patriality would result is not conclusive. It must treat welfare as the first consideration, outweighing any one other factor but not all factors. If the court considers on the evidence and information before it that the true motive of the application is based on the desire to achieve nationality and the right of abode rather than the general welfare of the minor then an adoption order   *e* should not be made. If on the other hand part of the motive, or it may be at least as much, is to achieve real emotional or psychological, social and legal benefit (s 19 apart) of adoption, then an adoption order may be proper, notwithstanding that this has the effect of overriding an immigration decision or even an immigration rule. In every case it is a matter of balancing welfare against public policy, and the wider the implications of the public policy aspect the less weight may be attached to the aspect of the welfare of the   *f* particular individual.

I seek now to apply these considerations to the circumstances of the present application. Firstly, it is plain that there was deception practised by or on behalf of H at least when the application was made for the extension of his stay. Reasons were given which were false, for at that stage an adoption was being considered. Secondly, having heard Dr N and his wife give evidence, I can say that they have satisfied me that they have a genuine   *g* wish for H's own sake to keep him as a member of their family, and I am sure, supported as this is by the Official Solicitor, that they are now in loco parentis to H. Thirdly, notwithstanding the decision and reasons in particular of the adjudicator in the immigration proceedings, I believe H in his account of what happened to him in Pakistan. That is, that he has indeed been rejected by his family, confirmed as this is by the Official Solicitor's inquiries so far as they have been able to go. I have examined the   *h* reasons, particularly of the adjudicator, for finding this application to be in effect bogus. Broadly, they are that the grandparents' application to enter in 1976 had contained a serious misrepresentation of fact, namely the omission of the names of certain relatives from their family tree; and also the omission of the name of the applicant who had been living with them until they left for England. Dr N told me, as he told the interviewing officer, that he had told his parents that there was no point in mentioning H as there was   *j* no evidence to prove he was a member of their family, and there was in any event no intention then that he should come to England. If anything this may seem to confirm that something happened since the grandparents left to make H wish to come to the United Kingdom. The adjudicator gave as another reason that Dr N himself had given false information to the Secretary of State concerning his wife when he had applied for British nationality. No evidence of this is referred to, nor are there any other details, and

it is the fact that Dr and Mrs N have since then been granted United Kingdom citizenship
a by naturalisation.

For my part, I considered Dr N to be truthful and genuine, although of course he was
not subjected to cross-examination on behalf of the Secretary of State, and such questions
as I asked him would not be as searching no doubt as such questioning would have been.
I have little doubt on the evidence, which is supported by the investigations on behalf of
the Official Solicitor and not contradicted by direct evidence, not only that H is now and
b has been for 3½ years a de facto member of the applicants' family, but also that he has
indeed been rejected by his family in Pakistan. I also believe that if he were returned to
Pakistan he would have no home to go to and no means of earning his living. The other
relations who might have been thought willing to take him in have been considered and
convincing reasons given which satisfy me that they are all for one reason or another
unable to do so. He is of course going to be 18 next November. His welfare needs to be
c safeguarded and promoted in the words of s 3 of the 1975 Act 'throughout his childhood'.
It would however be harsh, if not illogical after this lapse of time to reject the application
on the ground that so little of his childhood remains. In neither *Re A (an infant)* [1963] 1
All ER 531, [1963] 1 WLR 231 nor *Re R (adoption)* [1966] 3 All ER 613, [1967] 1 WLR
34 was this factor treated as decisive.

Immigration policy apart, I am satisfied that having regard to all the other
d circumstances, and having regard to H's welfare, an adoption order should be made. This
means, inter alia, that having heard and seen Dr N and H and considered all the material
before me, I am satisfied that contrary to the findings on behalf of the Secretary of State,
there has been a genuine transfer of parental responsibility and that it is not an adoption
application of convenience. I do however find that there was at least deception in the
application for leave to extend H's stay, and probably too in regard to the initial
e application to enter. The refusal of the Secretary of State was not based only on the fact
that deception as to the purpose of entry was practised, but the fact that deception was
practised is clearly relevant to the policy decision whether or not to admit, even given
that there are otherwise valid grounds for giving leave to enter. Deception ought to be
seen not to be tolerated, and when leave to enter is a matter of discretion, deception of
itself may be a proper ground for refusal to exercise the discretion in favour of granting
f leave or granting an extension. But in an adoption application, it must be put in the
scales and weighed against the welfare considerations which have first consideration. In
the present case, in the particular circumstances, in my judgment welfare considerations
must prevail, and an adoption order made.

In conclusion, I wish to stress that this application illustrates the importance where a
foreign national is concerned of notice being given to the Secretary of State pursuant to
g r 18 of the Adoption (High Court) Rules 1976 or the equivalent rule for the county
courts, r 12 of the Adoption (County Court) Rules 1976, SI 1976/1644, so that in every
such case, as was indeed done in this case, the Secretary of State is given the opportunity
of intervening if he wishes, especially so as to ensure that considerations of national
security are not overlooked. This is what Buckley J made provision for at the conclusion
of his judgment which I have quoted in *Re R (adoption)*. Perhaps consideration should be
h given to making an amendment to the rules to cover this aspect specifically.

For these reasons, I grant the adoption order and I further order that, in accordance
with s 21(1) of the Adoption Act 1958, H's name be entered in the Adopted Children
Register together with his date and country of birth as set out in the Official Solicitor's
report.

j   *Adoption order granted. Leave to appeal.*

Solicitors: *Peter Conway & Co,* Wealdstone (for the applicants); *Official Solicitor ; Treasury
Solicitor.*

Bebe Chua   Barrister.

R v Whitehead and others
R v Nicholl and another

COURT OF APPEAL, CRIMINAL DIVISION
DONALDSON, WATKINS LJJ AND STAUGHTON J
1, 2 MARCH, 2 APRIL 1982

Customs and excise – Importation of prohibited goods – Importation of drugs – Evasion of prohibition – Conspiracy to evade prohibition – Institution of proceedings – Accused charged with conspiracy to evade prohibition imposed by misuse of drugs legislation – Underlying offence arising out of breach of customs and excise legislation – Whether order of Commissioners of Customs and Excise required for institution of proceedings – Customs and Excise Act 1952, ss 281(1)(4), 304 – Misuse of Drugs Act 1971, s 3(1)(a) – Criminal Law Act 1977, s 4(3).

The appellants attempted to import large quantities of prohibited drugs into the United Kingdom. They were detained and subsequently charged with two counts of conspiracy to evade the prohibition imposed by s 3(1)(a)[a] of the Misuse of Drugs Act 1971, contrary to s 1(1)[b] of the Criminal Law Act 1977. The particulars given in the counts were that the appellants conspired with others 'fraudulently to evade the prohibition imposed by virtue of Section 3(1)(a) of the Misuse of Drugs Act 1971, namely the importation of a controlled drug ...' The appellants were convicted. They appealed on the ground that the proceedings were invalid because s 3(1)(a) of the 1971 Act did not itself create an offence but merely imposed a prohibition on the importation of controlled drugs, the fraudulent evasion of which was an offence under s 304[c] of the Customs and Excise Act 1952, and therefore, it was submitted, the underlying offence charged was fraudulent evasion under s 304 of the 1952 Act for which an order of the Commissioners of Customs and Excise was required by s 281(1)[d] of that Act before proceedings could be instituted. No such order had been obtained. The appellants further contended that under s 4(3)[e] of the 1977 Act any statutory restriction on the institution of proceedings for an underlying offence without 'consent' also extended to the institution of proceedings for conspiracy to commit the underlying offence.

Held – The appeals would be dismissed for the following reasons—
(1) Where the offence charged was the fraudulent evasion of the prohibition contained in s 3(1)(a) of the 1971 Act on the importation of a controlled drug, the underlying offence arose from a combination of s 3(1)(a) of the 1971 Act and s 304 of the 1952 Act and therefore, although the offence could be described and charged in the indictment as arising under either or both Acts, the underlying offence could not be said to arise solely under the 1971 Act to the exclusion of the 1952 Act. The underlying offence was thus an offence which arose under s 304 of the 1952 Act for which, under s 281(1) of that Act, an order of the commissioners was required before proceedings were instituted, unless the

---

a   Section 3(1) is set out at p 99 *h*, post
b   Section 1(1) is set out at p 99 *d e*, post
c   Section 304, so far as material, provides 'Without prejudice to any other provision of this Act, if any person—(*a*) knowingly ... acquires possession of ... any goods ... with respect to the importation ... of which any prohibition or restriction is for the time being in force [under or by virtue of any enactment]; or (*b*) is, in relation to any goods, in any way knowingly concerned in any fraudulent evasion or attempt at evasion ... of any such prohibition or restriction as aforesaid or of any provision of this Act applicable to those goods, he may be detained and, save where, in the case of an offence in connection with a prohibition or restriction, a penalty is expressly provided for that offence by the enactment or other instrument imposing the prohibition or restriction, shall be liable to a penalty of three times the value of the goods or one hundred pounds, whichever is the greater, or to imprisonment for a term not exceeding two years, or to both.'
d   Section 281, so far as material, is set out at p 101 *c d*, post
e   Section 4(3) is set out at p 101 *e*, post

accused had been detained for that offence, in which case under s 281(4) of the 1952 Act
a the commissioners' order was not required (see p 102 e to h, post); dicta of Lord Salmon
and of Lord Edmund-Davies in *R v Menocal* [1979] 2 All ER at 515, 518 applied; *R v
Williams* [1971] 2 All ER 444 explained.

(2) Although the restriction contained in s 281(1) of the 1952 Act on the institution
of proceedings for an offence under the Customs and Excise Acts without the
commissioners' order did not in terms extend to proceedings for conspiracy to commit
b such an offence, the restriction nevertheless applied to such conspiracy proceedings by
virtue of s 4(3) of the 1977 Act, since the prerequisite of an 'order' of the commissioners
under s 281(1) for the institution of proceedings was the same as the 'consent' required
by s 4(3). An order of the commissioners was therefore required before proceedings
could be instituted charging conspiracy to commit a customs offence. However, s 4(3)
applied s 281(1) as qualified by s 281(4), so that the commissioners' order was not required
c if the accused had been detained for conspiracy to commit a customs offence, and since
the appellants had been so detained an order by the commissioners under s 281(1) was
not required before proceedings for conspiracy were instituted against them (see p 103 b
to e, post).

Per curiam. (1) Section 4(3) of the 1977 Act confers authority on the commissioners
to make an order to institute proceedings in relation to a statutory conspiracy to commit
d an offence under the Customs and Excise Acts (see p 103 e f, post).

(2) It is desirable but not mandatory that an offence of evading the prohibition on the
importation of a controlled drug should be charged under both the Misuse of Drugs Act
1971 and the Customs and Excise Management Act 1979 (see p 102 f and p 103 f, post).

Notes
e For the institution of proceedings for an offence under the Customs and Excise Acts, see
12 Halsburys Laws (4th edn) para 650.

For fraudulent evasion of any prohibition on the importation of goods, see ibid para
642.

For the Customs and Excise Act 1952, ss 281, 304, see 9 Halsbury's Statutes (3rd edn)
186, 201.

f For the Misuse of Drugs Act 1971, s 3, see 41 ibid 882.

For the Criminal Law Act 1977, ss 1, 4, see 47 ibid 145, 149.

For the Customs and Excise Management Act 1979, see 49 ibid 290.

As from 22 February 1979 ss 281 and 304 of the 1952 Act were replaced by ss 145 and
170 of the 1979 Act.

g **Cases referred to in judgment**
R v Menocal [1979] 2 All ER 510, sub nom *Customs and Excise Comrs v Menocal* [1980] AC
598, [1979] 2 WLR 876, HL; rvsg [1978] 3 All ER 961, [1979] QB 46, [1978] 3 WLR
602, CA, Digest (Cont Vol E) 154, 9188a.
R v Williams [1971] 2 All ER 444, [1971] 1 WLR 1029, CA, Digest (Cont Vol D) 157,
1537a.
h
Cases also cited
R v Hall [1891] 1 QB 747.
R v Lennox-Wright [1973] Crim LR 529.

Appeal and application for leave to appeal
j On 25 July 1980 in the Crown Court at Chelmsford before his Honour Judge Greenwood
and a jury Brian Whitehead, Kenneth Johnson and Lewis Nicholl were convicted of,
inter alia, offences of conspiracy to evade the prohibition against the importation of drugs
imposed by s 3(1)(a) of the Misuse of Drugs Act 1971, contrary to s 1(1) of the Criminal
Law Act 1977, and for those and other offences were sentenced to terms of imprisonment.
On 8 October 1980 in the Crown Court at Chelmsford before his Honour Judge Petre,
Lewis Nicholl and Louis Fletcher-Hall pleaded guilty to conspiracy to evade the

prohibition on the importation of drugs and conspiracy to supply controlled drugs. Whitehead appealed and Nicholl and Fletcher-Hall applied for leave to appeal against the *a* convictions for the offences against s 3(1)(*a*) of the 1971 Act and s 1(1) of the 1977 Act on the ground that an order of the Commissioners of Customs and Excise to institute proceedings for those offences had not been obtained, and that without such an order there could be no prosecution for those offences. The facts are set out in the judgment of the court.

b

Dermot Wright (assigned by the Registrar of Criminal Appeals) for Whitehead.
Peter Jackson (assigned by the Registrar of Criminal Appeals) for Nicholl and Fletcher-Hall.
John W Rogers QC and *Keith Simpson* for the Crown.

Cur adv vult   *c*

2 April. **DONALDSON LJ** read the following judgment of the court: On 25 July 1980 before his Honour Judge Greenwood in the Crown Court at Chelmsford, Brian Whitehead and Lewis Nicholl were convicted of various offences concerning the importation and supply of drugs. Whitehead was sentenced to concurrent terms of three years' imprisonment on all charges and Nicholl to concurrent terms of ten years' imprisonment *d* on all charges.

Whitehead now appeals against his conviction by leave of the single judge, who referred an application to appeal against sentence to the full court.

Nicholl applies for an extension of time and for leave to appeal against conviction and sentence, these applications also having been referred to the full court.

On 8 October 1980 Louis Fletcher-Hall and Lewis Nicholl appeared before his Honour *e* Judge Petre in the Crown Court at Chelmsford, each charged with conspiracies to evade the prohibition on the importation of drugs and to supply controlled drugs. Fletcher-Hall pleaded guilty and was sentenced to six years' imprisonment, concurrent on each charge. Nicholl raised a plea of autrefois convict by reason of the July convictions and, when that was rejected by a jury, pleaded guilty and was sentenced to seven years' imprisonment, concurrent on each charge and concurrent with the July sentences. So far *f* as Nicholl was concerned, the judge's intention was that the sentences should be co-extensive with the ten-year sentences. The three years' difference was accounted for by the fact that time spent in custody awaiting trial would count against the ten-year sentence imposed in July but not against that imposed by the judge.

Fletcher-Hall applies for leave to appeal against sentence, his application having been referred to the full court by the single judge who granted a necessary extension of time. *g*

Nicholl applies for leave to appeal against conviction, his application having been referred to the full court. Although he has not formally applied for leave to appeal against sentence, we have borne in mind that if for any reason the effective length of the July sentence was to be reduced he should be granted leave to appeal against the October sentences in order that these might be fully reviewed.

In order to clear the ground, we will deal first with two grounds of appeal advanced by *h* counsel on behalf of Whitehead, which have no relevance in the case of Nicholl.

[The first ground, which applied to all the counts with which Whitehead was charged, was that the judge left to the jury inadmissible evidence from an accomplice. The court held that there was no substance in that ground. The second ground, which applied only to count 3 of the indictment, charging Whitehead, Nicholl and one Kenneth Johnson with conspiring to evade the prohibition on the importation of amphetamine sulphate, *j* was that the evidence in the depositions and statements tendered in the committal proceedings did not justify the inclusion in the indictment of count 3. The court held that in the light of the evidence in the committal proceedings it was open to the jury to infer the commission of the offence charged in count 3 and that in admitting that count the judge had properly exercised his discretion. His Lordship continued:]

That brings us to the remaining ground of appeal, which raises an issue of considerable

difficulty and no little importance. It affects counts 1 and 3, those alleging a conspiracy
a to import cannabis resin and amphetamine sulphate. If good, it should avail Nicholl as
well as Whitehead. The essence of the complaint is that these counts could not be
prosecuted in the absence of an order of the Commissioners of Customs and Excise,
which was not in fact obtained. Both counts are in the same terms, save that count 1
refers to cannabis resin and count 3 to amphetamine sulphate. Count 1 reads as follows:

b
'STATEMENT OF OFFENCE
CONSPIRACY TO EVADE THE PROHIBITION IMPOSED BY SECTION 3(1)(*a*) OF THE MISUSE OF
DRUGS ACT 1971, contrary to Section 1(1) of the Criminal Law Act, 1977.

PARTICULARS OF OFFENCE
BRIAN WHITEHEAD, KENNETH JOHNSON and LEWIS NICHOLL on divers days between the
1st day of January 1976 and the 7th day of August 1977, in the County of Kent and
elsewhere, conspired together and with Alan Edward Whitehead, John Eric Stone,
c Richard William Reeves and with other persons, fraudulently to evade the
prohibition imposed by virtue of Section 3(1)(*a*) of the Misuse of Drugs Act 1971,
namely the importation of a controlled drug, to wit quantities of cannabis resin, a
controlled drug being specified as a Class B drug in Part II of Schedule 2 of the
Misuse of Drugs Act 1971, in respect of the importation of which the said prohibition
was for the time in force.'
d

The relevant provisions of the Criminal Law Act 1977 are ss 1(1) and 4(3), which are
in the following terms:

'**1.**—(1) Subject to the following provisions of this Part of this Act, if a person
agrees with any other person or persons that a course of conduct shall be pursued
which will necessarily amount to or involve the commission of any offence or
e offences by one or more of the parties to the agreement if the agreement is carried
out in accordance with their intentions, he is guilty of conspiracy to commit the
offence or offences in question . . .
4 . . . (3) Any prohibition by or under any enactment on the institution of
proceedings for any offence which is not a summary offence otherwise than by, or
on behalf or with the consent of, the Director of Public Prosecutions or any other
f person shall apply also in relation to proceedings under section 1 above for conspiracy
to commit that offence . . .'

In essence s 1(1) creates a statutory offence of conspiracy where the course of conduct
agreed on would necessarily amount to or involve the commission of another offence,
the 'underlying offence'. Section 4(3) applies to the institution of proceedings for the
g statutory conspiracy the same restrictions as apply to the institution of proceedings for
the underlying offence.
It is next necessary to consider what is the underlying offence in this case. As charged,
it is the evasion of the prohibition imposed by s 3(1)(*a*) of the Misuse of Drugs Act 1971.
Section 3(1) is in the following terms:

h
'Subject to subsection (2) below—(*a*) the importation of a controlled drug; and (*b*)
the exportation of a controlled drug, are hereby prohibited.'

Subsection (2) enables the Secretary of State to except particular controlled drugs from
the prohibition or to licence the import or export of controlled drugs.
Counsel for Whitehead prays in aid a decision of this court in R v Williams [1971] 2 All
ER 444, [1971] 1 WLR 1029. In that case the defendant was charged on indictment with
j 'being knowingly concerned in a fraudulent evasion of the restriction upon importation
of cannabis resin imposed by the Dangerous Drugs Act 1965, contrary to section 304 of
the Customs & Excise Act 1952'. The prohibition referred to was contained in s 2 of the
1965 Act and was expressed in the following terms: 'It shall not be lawful for a person to
import into the United Kingdom a drug to which this Part of this Act applies except
under a licence granted by a Secretary of State.' It is to be noticed that the 1965 Act does
use the words 'it shall not be lawful' which might perhaps be thought to point more

strongly towards creating an offence than the wording of s 3 of the Misuse of Drugs Act 1971, and, in addition, s 16 of the 1965 Act, which sets the scale of penalties, unlike s 25 *a* of and Sch 4 to the 1971 Act, is completely general in its application to offences under the 1965 Act and could well apply to any offence created by s 2.

The point taken in that case on behalf of the defendant Williams was that the proceedings had not been instituted by or with the consent of the Attorney General or the Director of Public Prosecutions, contrary to s 20(1) of the 1965 Act which, in the absence of such consent, prohibits proceedings on indictment 'for an offence against this *b* Act'. Lord Parker CJ, giving the judgment of the court, which also included Widgery LJ and Cooke J, said ([1971] 2 All ER 444 at 446, [1971] 1 WLR 1029 at 1031):

> 'The offence here is an offence against s 304 of the Customs and Excise Act 1952; that provides, so far as it is material: "Without prejudice to any other provision of this Act, if any person . . . (*b*) is in relation to any goods in any way knowingly *c* concerned in any fraudulent evasion or attempt at evasion of any duty chargeable thereon or of any such prohibition or restriction as aforesaid or of any provision of this Act applicable to those goods, he may be detained and, save where, in the case of an offence in connection with a prohibition or restriction, a penalty is expressly provided for that offence by the enactment or other instrument imposing the prohibition or restriction, shall be liable to a penalty of three times the value of the *d* goods or one hundred pounds, whichever is the greater, or to imprisonment for a term not exceeding two years, or to both." It is quite clear, therefore, that that section is providing an offence and a penalty, and the words "any such prohibition or restriction as aforesaid" carry one back to para (*a*) where the prohibition or restriction is one for the time being in force under or by virtue of any enactment with respect thereto. In other words s 304 of the Customs and Excise Act 1952 *e* creates the offence and the penalty, and one only goes to the Dangerous Drugs Act 1965 in order to see what the prohibition is that is imposed in s 2. Further, on the wording of s 20 of the Dangerous Drugs Act 1965 itself, the consent of the Attorney-General is only needed in the case of proceedings by indictment for an offence against that Act, and s 2 to which I have already referred does not create an offence in itself.' *f*

Counsel for Whitehead accordingly submits that s 3(1) of the Misuse of Drugs Act 1971 of itself creates no offence. Its purpose is to impose a statutory prohibition to which s 304(*a*) of the Customs and Excise Act 1952 will refer and the fraudulent evasion of which will constitute an offence under s 304(*b*). The matter does not even stop there, because s 7 of the Dangerous Drugs Act 1967 provides:

> '*Increase of certain penalties under Customs and Excise Act 1952.*—(1) In relation to *g* offences in connection with a prohibition or restriction imposed by section 2, section 7 or section 10 of the principal Act (importation and exportation of certain drugs and other substances), being offences committed after the commencement of this Act, sections 45(1), 56(2) and 304 of the Customs and Excise Act 1952 shall have effect as if for the words "imprisonment for a term not exceeding two years" there were substituted the words "imprisonment for a term not exceeding ten years" . . .' *h*

The relevant words are not 'In relation to offences *under* or *against* section 2 of the principal Act,' but '*in connection with a prohibition or restriction* under' that section and, furthermore, the penalties referred to are not penalties imposed by the principal Act, but penalties imposed by sections of the Customs and Excise Act 1952. With the repeal of the Dangerous Drugs Act 1965 and the substitution of the 1971 Act, a similar approach *j* was adopted by Parliament. Indeed, if regard is had to the sidenote to s 26(1) of the Misuse of Drugs Act 1971, the matter is perhaps even clearer. Section 26 provides:

> '*Increase of penalties for certain offences under Customs and Excise Act 1952.*—(1) In relation to an offence in connection with a prohibition or restriction on importation or exportation having effect by virtue of section 3 of this Act, the following provisions of the Customs and Excise Act 1952, that is to say section 45(1) (improper

a   importation), section 56(2) (improper exportation) and section 304 (fraudulent evasion of prohibition or restriction affecting goods) shall have effect subject to the modifications specified in whichever of subsections (2) and (3) below is applicable in the case of that offence.'

Subsection (2) then increases the maximum term of imprisonment to 14 years. Counsel for Whitehead therefore submits that, although s 3(1) of the 1971 Act is rightly referred to in the indictment as being the section which creates the prohibition, the underlying offence is created by s 304 of the Customs and Excise Act 1952, and not by that section. He then turns to the need for an order from the Commissioners of Customs and Excise authorising the bringing of this charge. This is said to arise under s 281(1) of the 1952 Act and s 4(3) of the Criminal Law Act 1977. Section 281 of the 1952 Act is in the following terms:

c   'Institution of proceedings.—(1) No proceedings for an offence under the customs or excise Acts or for condemnation under the Seventh Schedule to this Act shall be instituted except by order of the Commissioners . . .
         (3) Nothing in the foregoing provisions of this section shall prevent the institution of proceedings for an offence under the customs or excise Acts by order and in the name of a law officer of the Crown in any case in which he thinks it proper that proceedings should be so instituted.
d   (4) Notwithstanding anything in the foregoing provisions of this section, where any person has been detained for any offence for which he is liable to be detained under the said Acts, any court before which he is brought may proceed to deal with the case although the proceedings have not been instituted by order of the Commissioners or have not been commenced in the name of an officer.'

e   Section 4(3) of the 1977 Act provides:

     'Any prohibition by or under any enactment on the institution of proceedings for any offence which is not a summary offence otherwise than by, or on behalf or with the consent of, the Director of Public Prosecutions or any other person shall apply also in relation to proceedings under section 1 above for conspiracy to commit that f   offence.'

This is an impressive argument, but before considering whether it is right, we should refer to another decision of this court. This is R v Menocal [1978] 3 All ER 961, [1979] QB 46, CA; [1979] 2 All ER 510, [1980] AC 598, HL. The defendant had been charged and convicted of an offence under s 304 of the Customs and Excise Act 1952. More than three months later, application was made for an order forfeiting money found in her g   possession on arrest, which the court inferred had been provided to her to assist in the importation of the controlled drug. The order was expressed to be made under s 27 of the Misuse of Drugs Act 1971, or, alternatively, under s 43 of the Powers of Criminal Courts Act 1973. If it was made under the latter section, it was out of time. If made under the former, it seems to have been accepted in the Court of Appeal that it was good. h   Section 27 of the Misuse of Drugs Act 1971 provides that 'the court by or before which a person is convicted of an offence under this Act may order anything . . . to be forfeited' (our emphasis). The issue was thus whether the defendant had been convicted of an offence under the 1971 Act. The court held that she had. No reference was made to R v Williams [1971] 2 All ER 444, [1971] 1 WLR 1029, either in the judgment or, as reported, in the argument.

j   Orr LJ, giving the judgment of the court consisting of himself, Cumming-Bruce LJ and Wein J, said ([1978] 3 All ER 961 at 965, [1979] QB 46 at 53–54):

     '. . . counsel for [the defendant] pointed out that in the count of the indictment to which [the defendant] pleaded guilty the statement of the offence referred to s 304 of the Customs and Excise Act 1952 as amended (as to punishment) by s 26 of the Misuse of Drugs Act 1971, although the particulars of the offence referred to s 3(1) of the 1971 Act, which provides that the importation of a controlled drug is prohibited. It is also relevant in our judgment that it is by virtue of s 22 of and Sch 2 to the 1971 Act that cocaine is classified as a Class A controlled drug. For these *a* reasons, in our judgment, the offence in question arises from a combination of both Acts and can properly be charged under both or either and can equally be said to be an offence arising under both or either, and we reject counsel's argument that the power of forfeiture conferred by s 27 of the 1971 Act is inapplicable in the present case.'

In the House of Lords *R v Williams* again does not appear to have been cited. The *b* House decided, for reasons which are immaterial for present purposes, that the forfeiture order was made without jurisdiction whichever section was prayed in aid. The House did not therefore have to decide whether s 3 of the Misuse of Drugs Act 1971 created an offence. However, Lord Salmon expressly approved of the passage which we have quoted from the judgment of Orr LJ (see [1979] 2 All ER 510 at 515, [1980] AC 598 at 606). Lord Edmund-Davies also expressed the view that this passage correctly stated the law, *c* but he also recorded that the contrary had not been argued (see [1979] 2 All ER 510 at 518, [1980] AC 598 at 609).

It seems to us that the remarks of Lord Salmon and of Edmund-Davies are technically obiter and that we have to consider whether there is any essential conflict between *R v Williams* and *R v Menocal*. We think that there is no such inconsistency. In *R v Williams* this court decided that the 1965 Act did not 'create an offence *in itself*' (see [1971] 2 All *d* ER 444 at 446, [1971] 1 WLR 1029 at 1031; our emphasis). The same can be said of the 1971 Act. *R v Menocal* decided that the offence arose from the combination of the 1971 Act and the Customs and Excise Act 1952. It also decided that an offence so arising could be charged under either Act and 'can . . . be said to be an offence arising under both or either' (see [1978] 3 All ER 961 at 965, [1979] QB 46 at 54). These decisions are not inconsistent with one another or with the expression of view in the House of Lords, *e* provided that it is borne in mind that the offence in law arises from a combination of the two Acts and not from the 1971 Act alone, but that the offence can be *described* or *charged* as an offence arising under either or both Acts. This is not the same as saying that the 1971 Act *creates* an offence either 'in itself' or without reference to the 1952 Act, both of which propositions would be contrary to *R v Williams*. Nor does it involve any denial that it is better to charge an offence under both Acts. *f*

Ignoring for the moment the fact that we are concerned with a conspiracy charge, the question which we have to consider is whether the underlying offence could have been prosecuted otherwise than by order of the commissioners. Subject to s 281(4) of the 1952 Act, to which we shall have to return, we consider that it could not. Where an offence arises under a combination of the provisions of the two Acts, it may well be said that it arises under both or either. But it cannot be said that it arises under one to the exclusion *g* of the other. Accordingly, the underlying offence was, in our judgment, an offence under the Customs and Excise Acts and the institution of proceedings for the underlying offence would have required an order of the commissioners.

We now turn to s 281(4) of the 1952 Act, which we have already quoted. The section as a whole is at first sight rather curious. Proceedings can only be instituted by order of the commissioners, unless the accused has been detained for a customs offence, when no *h* such order is required. At first glance the exception might seem to be as wide as the prohibition, since no one is likely to be prosecuted for a customs offence, at least on indictment, unless he has been detained for that offence. The explanation, as we see it, is that the section is designed only to ensure that proceedings under the 1952 Act are not brought without the commissioners being aware of them. The commissioners will become aware of such proceedings if the proceedings are brought by their order. They *j* should also become aware of them if the accused is detained for any offence under the Act. We say this because s 274 provides wide powers of detention by customs officers and others, but in the case of those who are not customs officers there is an obligation to inform the nearest convenient office of Customs and Excise (see s 274(4)). On the other hand, they might never hear of proceedings begun by summons.

a If therefore Whitehead had been detained for the underlying offence, i e an offence under s 304 of the Customs and Excise Act 1952, the bar on the institution of proceedings imposed by s 281(1) would have been lifted or avoided by s 281(4).

But neither Whitehead nor Nicholl were so detained. They were detained by police officers for the offence of conspiring to evade the prohibition imposed by s 3(1)(a) of the Misuse of Drugs Act 1971, contrary to s 1(1) of the Criminal Law Act 1977. The prohibition on the institution of proceedings contained in s 281(1) of the 1952 Act does

b not in terms apply to such a conspiracy. The problem is whether it is applied by s 4(3) of the Criminal Law Act 1977, which we have already quoted.

Counsel for the Crown submits that it is not so applied because s 281(1) is not, to quote s 4(3), a 'prohibition . . . on the institution of proceedings for any offence . . . otherwise than by . . . consent'. Section 281(1) requires an 'order', not a 'consent'. We do not accept this submission. In this context, 'order' includes 'consent'. The commissioners cannot

c order the institution of proceedings unless they consent to their institution.

Alternatively, on the assumption that s 4(3) of the 1977 Act does apply s 281 of the 1952 Act, counsel for the Crown submits that what s 4(3) applies is not simply s 281(1), but s 281(1) as qualified by s 281(4). This is right. However, s 281 cannot be applied literally. In ordering that s 281 and other similar prohibitions should apply to conspiracy counts, Parliament must have intended that the words in s 281(4), 'where any person has

d been detained for any offence for which *he is liable* to be detained under the said Acts', should be read as 'where any person has been detained for conspiracy to commit any offence for which *he would be liable* to be detained under the said Acts'. Nicholl and Whitehead were so detained. Had they been detained for the substantive offence, s 281 of the 1952 Act would not have required the consent of the commissioners for the institution of proceedings for that offence. Accordingly, reading s 281 of the 1952 Act

e with s 4(3) of the 1977 Act, no consent is required for the institution of the conspiracy proceedings.

In the light of the fact that the matter was said to have been in doubt, we would add that in our judgment s 4(3) also confers authority on the commissioners to make an order in relation to a statutory conspiracy to commit an offence under the Customs and Excise Acts. Finally, perhaps we should record that counsel for the Crown refused to amend the

f indictment to include an express reference to s 304 of the Customs and Excise Act 1952. In our judgment, such an amendment, although perhaps desirable, was not necessary and the absence of any express reference to that Act does not affect the matter one way or the other.

For these reasons the appeal by Whitehead and the application for leave to appeal by Nicholl are dismissed in so far as they relate to their respective convictions before his

g Honour Judge Greenwood.

[The court then considered Nicholl's appeal against sentence, and Whitehead's application for leave to appeal against sentence, passed at the July 1980 trial and dismissed both the appeal and the application. The court went on to consider Nicholl's application for leave to appeal against his conviction in the October 1980 trial, on the ground of autrefois convict by reason of his conviction in the July 1980 trial, and also his application

h for leave to appeal against the sentence passed on him in the October trial, and dismissed both applications. Finally the court considered Fletcher-Hall's application for leave to appeal against the sentence of six years' imprisonment passed on him in the October trial and, treating his application as the hearing of the appeal, reduced his sentence to four years' imprisonment.]

j *Appeals and applications by Whitehead and by Nicholl dismissed. Application by Fletcher-Hall allowed ; sentence varied.*

Solicitors: *Director of Public Prosecutions.*

Jacqueline Charles   Barrister.

Jennings v United States Government

QUEEN'S BENCH DIVISION
ORMROD LJ AND FORBES J
23, 24 MARCH, 6 APRIL 1982

HOUSE OF LORDS
LORD FRASER OF TULLYBELTON, LORD SCARMAN, LORD ROSKILL, LORD BRIDGE OF HARWICH AND
LORD BRIGHTMAN
12, 13, 14, 15, 29 JULY 1982

Extradition – Committal – Extradition crime – Manslaughter – British citizen charged with manslaughter as a result of causing death by driving in California – Whether charge amounting to manslaughter under English law – Whether facts constituting extraditable offence or extradition crime – Extradition Act 1870, s 26 – United States of America (Extradition) Order 1976, Sch 1, art III(1).

The defendant, a British citizen, was involved in a motor accident in California when the car she was driving collided with a cyclist who subsequently died. She was charged in California with 'felony drunk driving' and, in breach of the terms of her bail, she returned to England. The United States government applied to a stipendiary magistrate for the extradition of the defendant based on a charge of manslaughter, in violation of § 192(3)(a)[a] of the Penal Code of California. The magistrate ordered that the defendant be extradited and that she be detained in custody pending extradition. The defendant applied to the Divisional Court for a writ of habeas corpus, contending that the defendant's conduct relied on by the United States government before the magistrate did not amount to an 'extradition crime' within s 26[b] of the Extradition Act 1870 or an 'extraditable offence' under art III(1)[c] of the extradition treaty made in 1972 between the United Kingdom and the United States of America and set out in Sch 1 to the United States of America (Extradition) Order 1976, because the only extradition crime which the defendant's conduct could possibly give rise to was manslaughter and under English law her conduct could only give rise to the offence of causing death by reckless driving, which, although an offence under s 1[d] of the Road Traffic Act 1972 as substituted by s 50 of the Criminal Law Act 1977, was not manslaughter. The defendant further contended that in any event the relevant common law offence of manslaughter had been repealed by the 1977 Act when the offence of causing death by dangerous driving was abolished and the offence of causing death by reckless driving was substituted, and that under art III(1)(c) of the 1972 treaty the defendant's conduct did not amount to a felony under the law of the United States because under Californian law the jury could, by their verdict, recommend a sentence which would result in the offence being treated as a misdemeanour for all purposes. The Divisional Court granted the defendant an order for habeas corpus on the grounds that conduct giving rise to the offence of causing death by reckless driving did not amount to manslaughter under English law and was therefore not an extraditable offence under the 1972 treaty. The United States government appealed.

Held – (1) The offence of causing death by reckless driving was manslaughter under English law, even though it was also a statutory offence under the 1972 Act, because the relevant part of the common law offence of manslaughter had not been abolished by the

---

a   Section 192(3) is set out at p 112 j to p 113 a, post
b   Section 26, so far as material, provides: '. . . The term "extradition crime" means a crime which, if committed in England or within English jurisdiction, would be one of the crimes described in the first schedule to this Act . . .'
c   Article III(1) is set out at p 110 b, post
d   Section 1 is set out at p 114 g, post

a 1977 Act. Accordingly the offence of causing death by reckless driving was an 'extradition crime' within the 1870 Act and an 'extraditable offence' under the 1972 treaty (see p 111 *e f* and p 116 *j* to p 117 *d* and *h*, post).

(2) Under art III(1)(c) of the 1972 treaty, the character of the offence depended on the category into which it fell by Californian law and not on the question of what lesser offence, if any, the defendant might ultimately be convicted of. It followed that, since the offence with which the defendant was charged was a felony under Californian law, it *b* was a felony for the purposes of art III(1)(c). The defendant was therefore subject to extradition. Accordingly, the appeal would be allowed and the magistrate's order restored (see p 111 *e f* and p 117 *d* to *h*, post).

Notes

For extradition crimes generally, see 18 Halsbury's Laws (4th edn) paras 213–217, and *c* for cases on the subject, see 24 Digest (Reissue) 1125–1126, 11946–11956.

For applications for habeas corpus in extradition proceedings, see 18 Halsbury's Laws (4th edn) paras 233–238, and for cases on the subject, see 24 Digest (Reissue) 12194–12211.

For the Extradition Act 1870, s 26, see 13 Halsbury's Statutes (3rd edn) 265.

For the Road Traffic Act 1972, s 1 (as substituted by the Criminal Law Act 1977, s 50), *d* see 47 ibid 1221.

Cases referred to in judgments and opinions

Andrews v DPP [1937] 2 All ER 552, [1937] AC 576, HL, 45 Digest (Repl) 85, *281*.
DPP v Newbury, DPP v Jones [1976] 2 All ER 365, [1977] AC 500, [1976] 2 WLR 918, HL, 15 Digest (Reissue) 1139, *9643*.
e *Henderson v Sherborne* (1837) 2 M & W 236, 150 ER 743, 44 Digest (Repl) 364, *2014*.
Michell v Brown (1858) 28 LJMC 53.
R v Church [1965] 2 All ER 72, [1966] 1 QB 59, [1965] 2 WLR 1220, CCA, 15 Digest (Reissue) 1140, *9656*.
R v Davis (1783) 1 Leach 271, 168 ER 238, 44 Digest (Repl) 364, *2012*.
R v Governor of Pentonville Prison, ex p Ecke (1973) (1981) 73 Cr App R 223, DC, 24 Digest *f* (Reissue) 1126, *11956*.
R v Larkin [1943] 1 All ER 217, [1943] KB 174, CCA, 14(1) Digest (Reissue) 384, *3244*.
R v Lawrence [1981] 1 All ER 974, [1982] AC 510, [1981] 2 WLR 524, HL.
R v Milburn [1974] RTR 431, CA.

Application for habeas corpus

g The defendant, Gail Anne Jennings, applied on 28 April 1981 for a writ of habeas corpus ad subjiciendum directed to the governor of HM Prison Holloway in respect of her committal by Sir Evelyn Russell, the Chief Metropolitan Stipendiary Magistrate, sitting at Bow Street Magistrates' Court on 23 April 1981 on the application of the United States government under an extradition warrant to await her return to the United States of America under s 10 of the Extradition Act 1870. The facts are set out in the judgment of *h* Ormrod LJ.

Mark Littman QC and *John Nutting* for the defendant.
Colin Nicholls QC for the United States government and the governor of Holloway Prison.

Cur adv vult

j

6 April. The following judgments were read.

ORMROD LJ. This is an application for a writ of habeas corpus directed to the Governor of Her Majesty's Prison at Holloway by the defendant, who was committed to prison on 23 April 1981, on the warrant of the stipendiary magistrate at Bow Street, on an

application for extradition by the Deputy District Attorney, County of Los Angeles, State
of California, USA, to the State of California. She was released on bail on an undertaking *a*
to apply for a writ of habeas corpus to this court.

This is a most unusual, and in one respect unique, case. It is common ground that
researches on both sides of the Atlantic show that it is the first occasion on which an
application for extradition has been made in respect of an offence of causing death by the
driving of a motor vehicle. It is unusual in that the facts on which the application is
based occurred as long ago as August 1978, and the defendant is a young woman, now *b*
aged 21 years, of good character as far as the evidence goes.

The facts out of which the application for extradition arises are shortly as follows. At
about 7.30 pm on 21 August 1978 the defendant was driving a Ford Mustang in an
easterly direction along Grand Avenue in the city of El Segundo in California. At the
intersection with Standard Street she attempted to turn left into Standard Street, and in
doing so collided with the rear of another car and drove on down Standard Street, *c*
followed by the other car. At the next intersection, that of Standard Street and Holly
Street, she braked violently but failed to stop at the stop sign, and continued over the
intersection and collided with a cyclist riding along Holly Street, knocking him to the
ground and severely injuring him, as a result of which he died on 13 September 1978.
She was interviewed by a police officer, whom she told that the heel of her shoe had got
jammed under the pedals, preventing her from stopping. He formed the opinion that *d*
she was under the influence of alcohol and, in due course, a blood sample was taken and
found to contain 170 mg of alcohol to 100 ml of blood. She was charged with 'felony
drunk driving', and bailed.

On 7 September 1978 she and her mother boarded a plane for England, where she has
remained ever since.

On 6 June 1979 a charge of 'MANSLAUGHTER, in violation of Section 192, subdivision 3a, *e*
Penal Code of California', that is 'unlawfully killing a human being without malice but
with gross negligence', was added with a view to extradition proceedings. On 24 July
1979 the deputy district attorney initiated extradition proceedings based on this charge.

The validity of the warrant of committal to Holloway prison depends on the provisions
of the Extradition Act 1870 and the terms of the extradition treaty between the
governments of the United Kingdom and of the United States dated 8 June 1972 (Cmnd *f*
5040).

Under the 1870 Act, it must be shown that the conduct relied on by the requesting
state amounts to an 'extradition crime', as defined by s 26 of and Sch 1 to the Act. Under
the 1972 treaty it must be shown that it amounts to an 'extraditable offence' within the
meaning of art III of the treaty.

Counsel for the defendant contends that the conduct disclosed in the evidence before *g*
the stipendiary magistrate does not amount to an extradition crime under the Act or,
alternatively, does not amount to an extraditable offence under the treaty.

An extradition crime is defined in s 26 to mean a crime which, if committed in
England, would be one of the crimes described in Sch 1. The crime which is relied on in
this case is manslaughter, and the schedule provides that the list of crimes therein is to be
construed 'according to the law existing in England . . . at the date of alleged crime'. *h*

Counsel's first submission is that in August 1978 causing death by the driving of a
vehicle was not manslaughter in English law, although, of course, it could amount to the
offence of causing death by reckless driving, contrary to the Road Traffic Act 1972, s 1, as
amended by the Criminal Law Act 1977, s 50. Alternatively, if it could amount in law
to manslaughter, the evidence in this case would not justify committal for trial on such a
charge because in 1978 no reasonable jury would convict the defendant of manslaughter *j*
on such evidence. Thirdly, the evidence before the stipendiary magistrate did not prove
that the conduct alleged amounted to an extraditable offence within the meaning of the
treaty, because it did not amount to manslaughter within the meaning of art III(1) of and
the schedule to the treaty and/or did not amount to a felony in the law of the United
States of America.

The first point raises a question of general importance. The submission is that, leaving
a aside the effect, if any, of s 1 of the Road Traffic Act 1972, in its original form, the
amendment made by the Criminal Law Act 1977 brings the statutory offence precisely
in line with Lord Atkin's dictum on manslaughter by driving in *Andrews v DPP* [1937] 2
All ER 552 at 556, [1937] AC 576 at 583:

> 'The principle to be observed is that cases of manslaughter in driving motor cars
> are but instances of a general rule applicable to all charges of homicide by negligence.
b > Simple lack of care such as will constitute civil liability is not enough. For purposes
> of the criminal law there are degrees of negligence, and a very high degree of
> negligence is required to be proved before the felony is established. Probably of all
> the epithets that can be applied "reckless" most nearly covers the case. It is difficult
> to visualise a case of death caused by "reckless" driving, in the connotation of that
> term in ordinary speech, which would not justify a conviction for manslaughter,
c > but it is probably not all-embracing, for "reckless" suggests an indifference to risk,
> whereas the accused may have appreciated the risk, and intended to avoid it, and yet
> shown in the means adopted to avoid the risk such a high degree of negligence as
> would justify a conviction.'

Read in conjunction with the speeches in the House of Lords in *R v Lawrence* [1981] 1
d All ER 974, [1982] AC 510 and, in particular, with Lord Diplock's construction of
'reckless', the two offences are indistinguishable except in relation to the maximum
penalty, which is five years' imprisonment for the statutory offence, compared to life
imprisonment for manslaughter. Lord Diplock said ([1981] 1 All ER 974 at 982, [1982]
AC 510 at 526):

> 'In my view, an appropriate instruction to the jury on what is meant by driving
e > recklessly would be that they must be satisfied of two things: first, that the defendant
> was in fact driving the vehicle in such a manner as to create an obvious and serious
> risk of causing physical injury to some other person who might happen to be using
> the road or of doing substantial damage to property; and, second, that in driving in
> that manner the defendant did so without having given any thought to the
f > possibility of there being any such risk or, having recognised that there was some
> risk involved, had none the less gone on to take it.'

So, it is argued, there is no room for the common law offence in relation to deaths
caused by driving vehicles; it has been replaced by the statutory offence, and, therefore,
to this extent, manslaughter is an obsolete offence. Had manslaughter been a statutory
offence prior to 1977 there is no doubt that, by the rules of construction, the 1977
g enactment would be held to have impliedly repealed the earlier statute to the extent of
the overlap: see per Lord Abinger CB in *Henderson v Sherborne* (1837) 2 M & W 236 at
239, 150 ER 743 at 744:

> 'If a crime be created by statute, with a given penalty, and be afterwards repeated
> in another statute, with a lesser penalty attached to it, I cannot say that the party
h > ought to be held liable to both.'

And where the same offence is re-enacted with a different punishment it repeals the
former law: see also *Craies on Statute Law* (7th edn, 1971) pp 370–371.

There is no logical reason why the same principle should not apply to a common law
offence. There are, indeed, good practical reasons why it should be applied.

Counsel for the United States government and the prison governor, however, argues
j that it would have been a simple matter for Parliament to have expressly abolished this
kind of manslaughter. He relies on the view of the editor of *Archbold's Pleading, Evidence
and Practice in Criminal Cases* (40th edn, 1979) para 2817a, which reads:

> 'This offence is not intended to be used as an alternative and second charge to
> manslaughter, but is intended to be used as a substitute for it. Charges of

manslaughter arising from the driving of a motor vehicle should be preferred only
in the most serious cases where the offence approximates to murder, e.g., where a   a
policeman is knocked down by reckless driving of a stolen car or there is a very high
degree of negligence.'

Andrews v DPP is cited in support of this view but, with respect, the present problem
was not, and could not have been, in their Lordships' minds in 1937, some 20 years
before the first version of the statutory offence appeared, and 30 years before the present
problem arose. Accordingly, he submits that the common law offence survives to the   b
extent that the prosecution have an option to charge manslaughter in very serious cases.
He referred to some remarks by Roskill LJ in *R v Milburn* [1974] RTR 431 at 434 where
he said:

> 'On the other hand, as this court put to [counsel for the appellant], it is difficult to
> see how, if the appellant had been charged with manslaughter, he could have   c
> avoided pleading guilty; and, had he pleaded guilty to manslaughter, it would have
> been difficult for him (if one ignores the argument based on disparity) to have
> complained of a three years' sentence.'

But it is clear from the context that the judge was thinking purely in terms of sentence
and not about whether an indictment for manslaughter might, or might not, have been
laid in that case. On its facts, it was as bad a case of reckless driving as could be imagined,   d
yet the defendants were charged with the statutory offence.

Formidable difficulties are inherent in the submission of counsel for the United States
government and the prison governor. It involves the concept of degrees of recklessness.
In its uncomplicated form recklessness has caused sufficient trouble; to add to it by
introducing degrees of recklessness would make the task of a judge who has to direct a
jury how to distinguish between the statutory offence and the common law offence   e
extremely difficult and would require the jury to make a pure value judgment without
any scale of values other than the difference in the maximum penalties. The prosecution
would have to make the same value judgment on the same material, so both prosecution
and jury would, inevitably, be brought into the area of sentence, a complete break with
tradition.

Counsel for the defendant's argument is, therefore, a powerful one. For the purposes   f
of this case, however, it is not necessary to make a final decision on it. It is enough to say
that in respect of deaths caused by driving manslaughter has either been replaced or
reduced to vestigial survival by s 1 of the Road Traffic Act 1972, as amended.

This conclusion has a very important bearing on counsel for the defendant's second
and third points. The second point arises under s 10 of the Extradition Act 1870, which
provides: g

> 'In the case of a fugitive criminal accused of an extradition crime, if the foreign
> warrant authorising the arrest of such criminal is duly authenticated, and such
> evidence is produced as (subject to the provisions of this Act) would, according to
> the law of England, justify the committal for trial of the prisoner if the crime of
> which he is accused had been committed in England, the police magistrate shall   h
> commit him to prison, but otherwise shall order him to be discharged . . .'

In deciding whether or not to commit the defendant to prison pending extradition,
the stipendiary magistrate, therefore, has to be satisfied that he would have been justified
by the evidence before him in committing her for trial on a charge of manslaughter had
her conduct taken place in England. This means that he would have to consider the value
judgment which the jury would have to make, assuming that the submission of counsel   j
for the United States government and the prison governor on the first point is accepted.
Clearly, he would have to ask himself whether a reasonable jury, properly directed on
degrees of recklessness, would convict of the major offence on the material before him.
Paragraph 6(1) of the defendant's affidavit in support of her present application suggests
that he did not consider this important point. Had he done so he would have had to hold
that the evidence disclosed an offence under the statute, but without any significantly

aggravating features which would justify a verdict of manslaughter. In exercising his
a function as a modern grand jury, therefore, he would have been obliged to refuse to
commit her for trial for manslaughter.

That is enough to decide this application in the defendant's favour, but it is necessary
to deal also with the third point which involves construction of the relevant provisions
of the treaty.

It is clearly established that in construing and applying the list of offences set out in
b the schedule to the treaty the court is required to treat the language used as expressing
not the technical meanings which lawyers on either side of the Atlantic would
instinctively adopt, but the meanings which the words convey to an intelligent layman:
see *R v Governor of Pentonville Prison, ex p Ecke* (1973) (1981) 73 Cr App R 223 at 227 per
Lord Widgery CJ.

It is a well-known fact that English juries became more and more unwilling to convict
c drivers of the offence of manslaughter, so much so that Parliament, in 1956, found it
necessary to create the statutory offence of causing death by reckless or dangerous driving
with a lesser maximum penalty: see the Road Traffic Act 1956, s 8. It is reasonable to
infer that the public generally (though not necessarily individually) did not perceive
killing by bad driving as conduct meriting the description of manslaughter, with all its
grave implications.

d The evidence in this case shows that juries in the State of California reacted in the same
way, and that it became necessary to amend the Penal Code in much the same way.
Under § 192 of the Penal Code in its unamended form manslaughter was of two kinds,
'voluntary' and 'involuntary'. Voluntary manslaughter was unlawful killing, as in a fight,
without malice; involuntary manslaughter was defined as killing in the commission of
an unlawful act not amounting to felony. Both forms of manslaughter were punishable
e by imprisonment in the state prison which, by definition, makes them felonies in
Californian law.

To get over the difficulty of juries refusing to convict in these cases, the Penal Code
was amended by making special provision for driving cases. Section 192 of the Code now
reads:

f   '*Manslaughter; voluntary, involuntary, and in driving a vehicle defined; construction of
      section*   Manslaughter is the unlawful killing of a human being, without malice. It
      is of three kinds:
      1. Voluntary—upon a sudden quarrel or heat of passion.
      2. Involuntary—in the commission of an unlawful act, not amounting to felony;
      or in the commission of a lawful act which might produce death, in an unlawful
g   manner, or without due caution and circumspection; provided that this subdivision
      shall not apply to acts committed in the driving of a vehicle.
      3. In the driving of a vehicle—(a) In the commission of an unlawful act, not
      amounting to felony, with gross negligence; or in the commission of a lawful act
      which might produce death, in an unlawful manner, and with gross negligence. (b)
      In the commission of an unlawful act, not amounting to felony, without gross
h   negligence; or in the commission of a lawful act which might produce death, in an
      unlawful manner, but without gross negligence . . .'

Section 193 of the Penal Code deals with punishment for each type of manslaughter.
Voluntary and involuntary manslaughter are punishable with from two to six years'
imprisonment in the state prison. Manslaughter by driving a vehicle is punishable, in
the case of an offence within § 192(3)(a), by either imprisonment in the county jail for
j not more than one year, or in the state prison; the jury can recommend, by their verdict,
imprisonment in the county jail, and in such a case the judge is precluded from passing
a sentence of imprisonment in the state prison.

The importance of this amendment for present purposes is that the definition of
'felony' in the law of California is a crime punishable by death or imprisonment in the
state prison. Every other crime is a misdemeanour (see § 17(a)). Where a crime is
punishable at the discretion of the court by imprisonment in the state prison or by fine

or imprisonment in the county jail it is a misdemeanour 'for all purposes' after the imposition of a punishment other than imprisonment in the state prison.

The question, therefore, arises whether, in these circumstances, the evidence establishes, prima facie, an 'extraditable offence' under the 1972 treaty. Article III(1) reads:

'Extradition shall be granted for an act or omission the facts of which disclose an offence within any of the descriptions listed in the Schedule annexed to this Treaty, which is an integral part of the Treaty, or any other offence, if: (a) the offence is punishable under the laws of both Parties by imprisonment or other form of detention for more than one year or by the death penalty; (b) the offence is extraditable under the relevant law, being the law of the United Kingdom or other territory to which this Treaty applies by virtue of sub-paragraph (1)(a) of Article II; and (c) the offence constitutes a felony under the law of the United States of America.'

The only relevant offence listed in the schedule is 'manslaughter', which is to be understood in general, rather than specific and technical, terms. It must be open to question, in the light of experience in both California and England, whether the conduct alleged against the defendant would be regarded by an intelligent layman or diplomat as properly described by the word 'manslaughter'.

So far as the other provisions of art III(1) are concerned, it is doubtful, for reasons already given, whether para (b) is complied with, that is whether the evidence establishes an extradition crime under the Extradition Act 1870. As to para (c) the question whether the acts or omissions relied on amount to a felony within the meaning of this paragraph is also uncertain. What is certain is that, if the defendant is extradited to the State of California and is convicted of the offence with which she is charged, the strong probability is that the jury will recommend imprisonment in the county jail, thus making the offence a misdemeanour, and not a felony or, more accurately, converting it to a misdemeanour by their recommendation. An intelligent layman might well consider, in these circumstances, that her offence does not fall within the description of a felony for the purposes of the treaty. Consequently, the evidence in this case falls short of proving an extradition offence under the treaty.

Alternatively, if the purpose of the schedule is to provide a descriptive list of offences which both countries regard as of sufficient gravity to justify extradition, all the foregoing considerations indicate that the conduct relied on in this case does not reach such a degree of gravity.

For these reasons it has not been established that the defendant is subject to extradition to the United States of America. Her application for an order for habeas corpus, therefore, succeeds and she must be released.

FORBES J. I agree and would just like to add a word because I believe it may be possible to put this case in an alternative way.

I agree entirely that the statutory definition imported into s 1 of the Road Traffic Act 1972 by the Criminal Law Act 1977 is one which is quite indistinguishable from the proper definition of manslaughter. I prefer to think that Parliament, in not abolishing the crime of manslaughter committed in the driving of a motor vehicle, thought that some purpose would be served by preserving it. It is difficult to imagine what that purpose was or in what circumstances a charge of manslaughter arising out of driving a motor vehicle could properly be laid. It may well be that Parliament intended, as the editors of *Archbold's Pleading, Evidence and Practice in Criminal Cases* (40th edn, 1979) para 2817a aver, that such a charge should only be brought in the most serious cases. I am quite sure, however, that it cannot have been intended that a charge of manslaughter should be brought where nothing more than reckless driving can be proved. Some other ingredient must exist to justify such a charge.

If this is so then one must take a fresh look at s 26 of the Extradition Act 1870 and its definition of an extradition crime as one of the crimes described in Sch 1 to that Act. It would be wholly wrong to describe as manslaughter in England a crime which consisted only of driving a motor vehicle recklessly without the additional ingredients, whatever a they may be, the existence of which Parliament thought was sufficient warrant for not abolishing the crime of manslaughter arising out of the driving of a motor vehicle. I can see no trace here of circumstances which might serve to lift this case into the category of manslaughter in England and hence it cannot be described as an extradition crime.

I agree entirely with Ormrod LJ in accepting counsel for the defendant's second and third points. For the reason I have given I think it may be possible to accept his first point also.

b

Application granted. Leave to appeal refused.

Dilys Tausz   Barrister.

Appeal

c The United States government appealed with leave of the House of Lords granted on 6 May 1982 against the decision of the Divisional Court.

Colin Nicholls QC and *R Alun Jones* for the United States government and the governor of Holloway Prison.
Mark Littman QC and *John Nutting* for the defendant.

d

Their Lordships took time for consideration.

29 July. The following opinions were delivered.

LORD FRASER OF TULLYBELTON. My Lords, I have had the benefit of reading in draft the speech prepared by my noble and learned friend Lord Roskill. I agree with
e it, and for the reasons stated in it I would allow this appeal.

LORD SCARMAN. My Lords, I have had the advantage of reading in draft the speech to be delivered by my noble and learned friend Lord Roskill. For the reasons he gives I would allow the appeal.

f **LORD ROSKILL.** My Lords, this appeal by the government of the United States of America which seeks the extradition of the defendant, a British subject, is, of course, of great importance to her but it also raises questions of general importance in connection with the operation of the extradition treaty concluded between the governments of the United Kingdom and of the United States of America on 8 June 1972 (Cmnd 5040). By Order in Council dated 15 December 1976, which took effect on 21 January 1977,
g entitled the United States of America (Extradition) Order 1976, SI 1976/2144, Her Majesty, pursuant to the powers conferred by the Extradition Acts 1870 to 1935, ordered that those Acts should apply to the United States of America in accordance with the treaty. Since the United Kingdom statutory provisions relevant to this appeal will all be found in the Extradition Act 1870 I need hereafter only refer to that statute.

My Lords, this appeal is brought from a decision of the Divisional Court (Ormrod LJ
h and Forbes J) dated 6 April 1982. The Divisional Court refused leave to appeal against that decision but leave was in due course granted by your Lordships' House. The Divisional Court had ordered that a writ of habeas corpus ad subjiciendum should issue in favour of the defendant and that she should be discharged from the custody in which she was then held. The defendant had on 23 April 1981 been committed to prison by the stipendiary magistrate sitting at Bow Street Magistrates' Court on an application for her
j extradition to the State of California made by the Deputy District Attorney, County of Los Angeles in that state. She was subsequently released on bail on her undertaking to apply for a writ of habeas corpus, as in due course she did.

My Lords, the application for the defendant's extradition arose out of events which took place almost four years ago. The defendant was then only some 17 years of age. These were the main allegations. At about 7.30 pm on 21 August 1978, in light conditions which were described as dusk, the defendant was driving a yellow Ford

Mustang car along Grand Avenue in El Segundo, California. Grand Avenue is a dual
carriageway with a central reservation. The defendant was travelling in the eastbound **a**
carriageway. At the intersection of Standard Street, she turned northward, and in doing
so struck the rear of a car travelling in the westbound carriageway of Grand Avenue. She
did not stop but drove off up Standard Street pursued by the car which she had struck at
a speed estimated by one witness as about 40 mph. That witness said she appeared to be
accelerating. The next east-west street crossing Standard Street was Holly Avenue and
this was protected by a stop sign. On approaching the intersection the defendant braked **b**
violently, failed to stop at the stop sign, skidded over the junction and in so doing struck
a 13-year-old boy named Gary Sheehan who was riding his bicycle along Holly Street.
Sheehan was very seriously injured. A police officer who was called to the scene of the
accident stated that the defendant's breath smelt of alcohol. What is described as a 'field
sobriety test' was given. The respondent was then arrested for 'felony drunk driving' and
was taken to a hospital for a blood test which was carried out. The resulting analysis **c**
revealed 0·17 g (ie 170 mg) of alcohol in 100 ml of blood. Driving in this condition was
an offence against § 23101 of the Vehicle Code of the State of California. The defendant
was charged accordingly. She was released on bail. On 7 September 1978 the defendant,
in breach of the terms of her bail, left California by aeroplane for England, accompanied
by her mother. She has remained in this country ever since.

My Lords, on 13 September 1978 Sheehan died, never having recovered consciousness. **d**
The post mortem report with your Lordships' papers reveals the full extent of his grave
injuries.

My Lords, on 6 June 1979 an amended complaint alleging manslaughter of Sheehan
by the defendant was filed in the Municipal Court of Inglewood in the judicial district of
the County of Los Angeles in California. The charge alleged 'MANSLAUGHTER, in violation
of Section 192, Subdivision 3a, Penal Code of California, a felony' on the ground that the **e**
defendant 'did unlawfully kill a human being to wit Gary Sheehan without malice but
with gross negligence ...' The complainant sought a warrant for the arrest of the
defendant, who of course by then had been in England for nearly nine months. It was
that charge which led in due course to the present application for the extradition of the
defendant. In a statement by the Governor of California, with your Lordships' papers,
made under the Great Seal of that state on 14 August 1979, the governor stated that the **f**
purpose of the application was to require the defendant to stand trial for 'the felony
offences of which she stood charged', namely manslaughter and felony drunk driving.
But, recognising that felony drunk driving was not an extraditable offence, the governor
certified that if the defendant were extradited it would not be sought to prosecute her for
the latter offence.

My Lords, I have mentioned that the charge of manslaughter brought against the **g**
defendant was one of unlawful killing without malice by gross negligence contrary to
§192(3)(a) of the Penal Code of the State of California. It will be convenient to set out the
text of §192 of the Code in full:

> '*Manslaughter; voluntary, involuntary, and in driving a vehicle defined; construction of
> section*   Manslaughter is the unlawful killing of a human being without malice. It **h**
> is of three kinds:
>   1. Voluntary—upon a sudden quarrel or heat of passion.
>   2. Involuntary—in the commission of an unlawful act, not amounting to felony;
> or in the commission of a lawful act which might produce death, in an unlawful
> manner, or without due caution and circumspection; provided that this subdivision
> shall not apply to acts committed in the driving of a vehicle.
>   3. In the driving of a vehicle—(a) In the commission of an unlawful act, not **j**
> amounting to felony, with gross negligence; or in the commission of a lawful act
> which might produce death, in an unlawful manner, and with gross negligence. (b)
> In the commission of an unlawful act, not amounting to felony, without gross
> negligence; or in the commission of a lawful act which might produce death, in an
> unlawful manner, but without gross negligence.

a   This section shall not be construed as making any homicide in the driving of a vehicle punishable which is not a proximate result of the commission of an unlawful act, not amounting to felony, or of the commission of a lawful act which might produce death, in an unlawful manner.'

My Lords, it was common ground that, subject to what I am about to say, by the law of California manslaughter is a felony. Further, the remaining relevant provisions of the law of California were not in dispute. The punishment for manslaughter is prescribed

b   by § 193 of the Penal Code of the State of California which your Lordships were told had been amended in 1977. Your Lordships were further told that the relevant maximum punishment for involuntary manslaughter contrary to §192(3)(a) was three years in the state prison (see the affidavit of Mr Billy Webb, the Deputy District Attorney for the County of Los Angeles) but your Lordships were referred to §17 of the Code which when read with §193(c) had the effect, at the date of the alleged offence, that a jury are entitled

c   by their verdict in the event of conviction of this offence to recommend that the punishment should be by imprisonment in the county jail and not in the state prison, whereupon the judge no longer has power to pass a sentence of imprisonment in the state prison, but not so as to prevent him placing a defendant on probation. In the event of such a recommendation by the jury the conviction would not be one of felony but of misdemeanor: see §17(b)(i). Your Lordships were also told that this provision has since

d   been amended.

My Lords, I turn to the relevant English law. I draw attention to the provision in s 26 of the 1870 Act which defines an extradition crime as 'one of the crimes *described* [my emphasis] in the first schedule'. The second crime named in Sch 1 is manslaughter. It seems therefore clear, both from the Act and from art III(1) of the treaty, that the first prerequisite to a successful application for the extradition of the respondent is that the charge against her is of a crime which in England is properly described as manslaughter.

e   The second prerequisite to such an application is that the offence is punishable under English law and under the relevant law of the United States of America (in this case the law of the State of California) by imprisonment for more than one year: see art III(1)(*a*) of the treaty. The third prerequisite is that the offence is a felony under the relevant law of the United States of America, again Californian law: see art III(1)(*c*) of the treaty. The

f   fourth prerequisite is that the evidence produced in support of the application is found to be sufficient to 'justify' (that word is used both in s 10 of the Act and in art IX(1) of the
·   treaty) the committal of the respondent for trial had the alleged offence of manslaughter been committed in England.

My Lords, I propose to consider these four prerequisites in turn. It is, however, the first which has given rise to the greater part of the argument before your Lordships'

g   House. Counsel advanced a formidable argument before your Lordships on behalf of the defendant that the unlawful killing of another by the reckless driving of a motor vehicle on a road was no longer manslaughter by the law of England and had not been manslaughter in England since 1956 or, if that be wrong, at least since 1977.

My Lords, the significance of those two dates is this. The offence of causing the death of another by the reckless or dangerous driving of a motor vehicle on a road was created

h   for the first time in 1956. In 1977 that statutory offence was amended by eliminating dangerous driving and requiring nothing less than reckless driving as the cause of death. Neither of those offences has ever been an extradition crime under the Act or an extraditable offence within the descriptions listed in the schedule to the treaty, nor has either been an offence other than one so listed which fulfills the three requirements of art III(1) of the treaty. It must therefore follow that if counsel's main submission be

j   correct, the application for extradition must fail. This was the view taken by the Divisional Court.

My Lords, counsel's argument was founded on the well-known decision of your Lordships' House in *Andrews v DPP* [1937] 2 All ER 552, [1937] AC 576. Until that decision there had been some doubt whether the killing of another by the dangerous driving of a motor vehicle on a road, being itself an unlawful act, was, without more,

manslaughter. Your Lordships' House unanimously and emphatically held that it was
not. In the leading speech Lord Atkin related the development of the common law a
relating to manslaughter, and observed ([1937] 2 All ER 552 at 554, [1937] AC 576 at
581) that it afforded 'most difficulties of definition, for it concerns homicide in so many
and so varying conditions.' He said ([1937] 2 All ER 552 at 556–557, [1937] AC 576 at
583–584):

> 'For purposes of the criminal law there are degrees of negligence, and a very high b
> degree of negligence is required to be proved before the felony [ie manslaughter] is
> established. Probably of all the epithets that can be applied "reckless" most nearly
> covers the case. It is difficult to visualise a case of death caused by "reckless" driving,
> in the connotation of that term in ordinary speech, which would not justify a
> conviction for manslaughter ... I entertain no doubt that the statutory offence of
> dangerous driving may be committed, though the negligence is not of such a degree
> as would amount to manslaughter if death ensued.'   c

My Lords, that decision of your Lordships' House left the law as it was at that date in
no doubt. It was decided that conviction for what was then popularly called 'motor
manslaughter' could only be justified if reckless driving were proved against the
defendant; proof of dangerous driving was not enough. Thus a clear distinction came to
be drawn between death caused by the dangerous driving of a motor vehicle on a road d
and death so caused by the reckless driving of a motor vehicle on a road.

My Lords, counsel founded his argument on this decision. He submitted that
thenceforward causing death by the reckless driving of a motor vehicle on a road and
'motor manslaughter' were synonymous. It was well known, he said, as indeed is the
fact, that the new statutory offence first introduced in 1956 was introduced because of
the reluctance of juries to convict of manslaughter in these cases. It was also well known e
that from 1956 onwards many offences which before 1956 would have been charged as
'motor manslaughter' were only charged as offences against the statute. 'Motor
manslaughter' virtually disappeared, save perhaps in the gravest cases.

This submission was reinforced by reference to the change in the law effected by s 50
of the Criminal Law Act 1977. Between 1956 and 1977 the statutory offence created by
s 8 of the Road Traffic Act 1956 had first by virtue of s 1 of the Road Traffic Act 1960 and f
then by virtue of s 1 of the Road Traffic Act 1972 (both those were consolidating statutes)
become an offence against s 1 of the latter statute. But s 50 of the 1977 Act drastically
amended s 1 of that statute by providing:

> 'Amendment of Road Traffic Act 1972.—(1) For sections 1 and 2 of the Road Traffic
> Act 1972 (causing death by reckless or dangerous driving, and reckless, and
> dangerous, driving generally) there shall be substituted—   g
>
> "1. Causing death by reckless driving. A person who causes the death of another
> person by driving a motor vehicle on a road recklessly shall be guilty of an offence.
> 2. Reckless driving. A person who drives a motor vehicle on a road recklessly shall
> be guilty of an offence.". . .'

My Lords, it was by virtue of these successive statutory provisions that counsel for the h
defendant argued first that the relevant part of the common law of manslaughter had
been impliedly repealed in 1956 and second, even if that were wrong, that it had certainly
been repealed in 1977 when the offence of causing death by the dangerous driving of a
motor vehicle on a road had been abolished and the offence of causing death by the
reckless driving of a motor vehicle on a road was substituted. What had formerly been
called 'motor manslaughter' by reckless driving of a motor vehicle on the road and j
causing death by such reckless driving were henceforth the same offence. Parliament
could not have intended those two offences, one a common law offence the other a
statutory offence, to co-exist after 1977, and even if there had been no implied repeal of
the relevant part of the common law of manslaughter in 1956 there had certainly been
such an implied repeal in 1977. He relied strongly on the fact that, whereas the

maximum penalty for manslaughter at common law had been imprisonment for life,
a the maximum penalty for the original statutory offence created in 1956 and for the new statutory offence created in 1977 was five years' imprisonment. This was, counsel submitted, another reason why Parliament could not be taken to have intended the two offences to continue to exist together.

My Lords, the evaluation of this argument requires a review of the relevant legislative history leading up to the alteration of the law which took place in 1977. This legislative *b* history does not appear to have been explained to the Divisional Court. It is necessary to begin this review as far back as the Motor Car Act 1903. Section 1(1) of the 1903 Act enacted:

> 'If any person drives a motor car on a public highway recklessly or negligently, or at a speed or in a manner which is dangerous to the public, having regard to all the
> *c* circumstances of the case, including the nature, condition and use of the highway, and to the amount of traffic which actually is at the time, or which might reasonably be expected to be, on the highway, that person shall be guilty of an offence under this Act.'

My Lords, your Lordships will observe the three states of fact which Parliament then envisaged might arise in connection with the driving of motor vehicles on roads. The *d* first was reckless driving. The second was negligent driving. The third was driving at a speed or in a manner which was dangerous to the public.

My Lords, I can pass from the 1903 Act to the Road Traffic Act 1930. The relevant sections of the Act are ss 11, 12 and 15. Section 11(1) provided as follows:

> 'If any person drives a motor vehicle on a road recklessly, or at a speed or in a
> *e* manner which is dangerous to the public, having regard to all the circumstances of the case, including the nature, condition, and use of the road, and the amount of traffic which is actually at the time, or which might reasonably be expected to be, on the road, he shall be liable [to penalties both on summary conviction and on indictment].'

Section 12(1) provided

> *f* 'If any person drives a motor vehicle on a road without due care and attention or without reasonable consideration for other persons using the road he shall be guilty of an offence.'

The section went on to provide suitable penalties. Careless driving was thus for the first time made the subject matter of a separate legislative provision but the former *g* language of the 1903 Act regarding reckless or dangerous driving was in substance preserved. Section 15 created the separate offence of driving under the influence of drink. The penalties for a conviction for an offence against s 11 were comparatively light judged by modern standards but by s 4 of the Road Traffic Act 1934 those penalties were substantially increased.

My Lords, I have already mentioned the creation of the new statutory offence in 1956 *h* and the reason why it was created. I would only emphasise that s 8, in creating this new offence, dealt not only with the offence of causing death by dangerous driving of a motor vehicle on a road but also with the offence of causing such death by reckless driving on a road, though in practice thereafter such offences were, as is well known, usually charged as causing death by dangerous driving rather than causing death by reckless driving. Thus one finds a statutory reference to reckless driving carried right through this *j* legislation from 1903 to 1956 and indeed beyond that year. Counsel for the defendant relied on this fact as showing that the relevant law must be treated as having been changed in relation to causing death by reckless driving in 1956 as well as by causing death by dangerous driving and that that change did not only take place as late as 1977. The 1956 Act was, of course, passed almost 20 years after the decision of your Lordships' House in *Andrews v DPP* [1937] 2 All ER 552, [1937] AC 576.

But, my Lords, in considering this submission it is important to observe one matter in connection with the 1956 Act. Schedule 4, para 5, which deals with disqualifications and *a* endorsements, deals not only with convictions for the new statutory offence but also with 'manslaughter by the driving of a motor vehicle' as among the offences for which disqualification or endorsement may be ordered. This provision was reproduced in the 1960 Act, a consolidating Act: see ss 104 and 111 and Sch 11, paras 1 and 2. These separate manslaughter from the statutory offence and thus treat manslaughter, or in Scotland culpable homicide, as separate from the statutory offence in this connection.   *b*

Similar provision will be found in paras 1 and 2 of Part I of Sch 1 to the Road Traffic Act 1962 dealing with obligatory disqualification. I turn next to the Criminal Law Act 1967. This Act, by s 6(3), created new provisions regarding alternative verdicts. One finds in para 13(1)(e) of Sch 2 another reference to the earlier provision in s 2(3) of the 1960 Act regarding convictions of reckless or dangerous driving on a charge of manslaughter. Finally, in the 1972 Act in the table of punishments, one finds in Sch 4, *c* Part I, para 1 a reference to causing death by reckless or dangerous driving and in Part II to 'Manslaughter or, in Scotland, culpable homicide by the driver of a motor vehicle'.

My Lords, these successive references to manslaughter and indeed to culpable homicide seem to me to put formidable difficulties into the path of counsel for the defendant's main submission. He contended, however, that they did not affect his main submission since the statutory offence was limited to offences on a road to which the public had *d* access. It was that which hitherto had been manslaughter by reckless driving on a road which had in his submission ceased to be a common law offence. The offence of manslaughter by reckless driving might still be required to meet the case of causing death by reckless driving otherwise than on a road, as, for example, on waste ground or on the forecourt of a public house.

Counsel also submitted that the offence of manslaughter remained in full force and *e* effect where the motor vehicle had been used, whether on a road or not, as a deliberate instrument of attack or of causing fright. He instanced cases such as *DPP v Newbury* [1976] 2 All ER 365, [1977] AC 500, *R v Larkin* [1943] 1 All ER 217, [1943] KB 174 and *R v Church* [1965] 2 All ER 72, [1966] 1 QB 59 as cases which, though not themselves involving the use of a motor vehicle, illustrated the circumstances in which unlawful acts involving the use of a motor vehicle and resulting in death might still require the *f* invocation of the common law offence of manslaughter.

My Lords, counsel for the defendant also referred your Lordships to a number of cases in the last century and indeed before on the subject of the implied repeal of an earlier by a later statute, as, for example, *Henderson v Sherborne* (1837) 2 M & W 236, 150 ER 743 and *Michell v Brown* (1858) 28 LJMC 53. An even more striking example can be found in the earlier case of *R v Davis* (1783) 1 Leach 271, 168 ER 238, where a statute creating a *g* capital offence was, perhaps not surprisingly, held to have been impliedly repealed by a later statute carrying a penalty of only £20. My Lords, I do not doubt that the principles applicable to the implied repeal of an earlier by a later statute are well established. But today those old cases must be approached and applied with caution. Until comparatively late in the last century statutes were not drafted with the same skill as today. In a field so complex as the criminal law as it exists today, frequently changing in an ever changing *h* society, a crucial change of this kind was, if counsel's submission is right, left only to implication. The 1977 Act, on s 50 of which counsel relied so strongly as giving rise to an implied repeal of the relevant part of the common law of manslaughter, itself contains an express repeal of the common law offence of conspiracy in clear and explicit language. I refer to s 5 which provides that 'the offence of conspiracy at common law is hereby abolished'. If Parliament had in the 1977 Act intended to abolish the relevant part of the *j* common law offence of manslaughter I should have expected to find a similar provision somewhere in the legislation between 1956 and 1977. My Lords, there is none. On the contrary there are, as I have shown, plenty of indications of an intention that that common law offence should remain fully intact after 1956 and after 1977 as it had before the successive statutory offences had ever been created. The fact that Parliament made it

possible in those years for prosecuting authorities to choose to prosecute for a lesser
a offence carrying a lesser penalty does not seem to me to militate against the correctness
of the view I have formed. No doubt the prosecuting authorities today would only
prosecute for manslaughter in the case of death caused by the reckless driving of a motor
vehicle on a road in a very grave case.

My Lords, I would only add two further observations on this part of the case. First,
s 18 of the Interpretation Act 1978 contains nothing inconsistent with the view which I
b have formed. The protection in the case of what I will call overlapping offences is not to
hold that the more serious has been repealed but in the provision that there must not be
in such a case the infliction of two penalties, one for each such offence. Second, the wide
spectrum of cases embraced by the offence of manslaughter at common law makes it
desirable that that offence with its infinite flexibility should remain and should not be
fragmented as acceptance of counsel's argument would involve.

c I must therefore reject that argument and hold without doubt that the offence of
causing death by reckless driving of a motor vehicle on a road is still manslaughter by
the law of England even though since 1977 it is also a statutory offence. Indeed, although
it was rarely charged as such, it has been a statutory offence since 1956.

My Lords, I can deal much more briefly with the remaining three prerequisites to a
successful application for extradition. As to the second there is no doubt that the offence
d in question of manslaughter is, both in England and California, punishable by
imprisonment for more than one year.

My Lords, the third question gave rise to some controversy. Counsel for the defendant
argued that this type of manslaughter was not a felony in Californian law because of the
power of a jury by their verdict to prevent imprisonment in a state prison and thus, in
the circumstances which I have described by reference to the relevant statutory provisions,
e reduce the offence to a misdemeanour. My Lords, I regret that I am quite unable to
accept this argument. The character of the offence depends on the category into which it
falls by the Californian law and not on the question of what lesser offence a defendant
may ultimately be convicted, if at all.

My Lords, as to the fourth prerequisite it was properly conceded that the evidence
before the stipendiary magistrate would in England justify committal on a charge of
f causing death by reckless driving of a motor vehicle on a road. Since in my view in
English law the ingredients of the statutory offence are coextensive with the ingredients
of the relevant common law offence of manslaughter, the concession inevitably involves
that the evidence would justify committal for manslaughter. The further submission by
counsel on the absence of any finding by the stipendiary magistrate of what counsel
called 'aggravating circumstances' does not arise.

g My Lords, I have therefore reached the conclusion, with great respect to the Divisional
Court, that that court was wrong in the reasons it gave for discharging the warrant of
committal and that the stipendiary magistrate was right in ordering its issue.

In my view the appeal must be allowed and the magistrate's order restored.

LORD BRIDGE OF HARWICH. My Lords, for the reasons given by my noble and
h learned friend Lord Roskill I too would allow this appeal.

LORD BRIGHTMAN. My Lords, I agree with the speech of my noble and learned
friend Lord Roskill and would allow the appeal.

Appeal allowed.

Solicitors: *Director of Public Prosecutions* (for the United States government and the
governor of Holloway Prison); *Herbert Smith & Co* (for the defendant).

Mary Rose Plummer   Barrister.

Re Dallaway (deceased)

CHANCERY DIVISION
SIR ROBERT MEGARRY V-C
22 JUNE, 12 OCTOBER, 17 DECEMBER 1981

*Executor and administrator – Action against – Costs of litigation – Action by beneficiary under
will claiming entire estate – Executor no longer holding any part of estate if beneficiary's action
successful – Whether executor's costs in defending action ought to be paid out of estate – RSC Ord
62, r 6(2).*

By his will the testator, whose only substantial asset was the farm where he lived, left his
entire estate to his ten brothers and sisters equally, and appointed a bank to be his
executor. The testator lived on the farm with one of his brothers and his wife, and by a
codicil to the will left a legacy of £900 to the wife. The testator died in 1978 and in
March 1979 the bank was granted probate of the will and codicil. In November 1979 the
brother and his wife (the claimants) commenced an action against the bank seeking
specific performance of an alleged oral agreement between the testator and the claimants
whereby the testator had agreed to leave his entire estate to the claimants. The other nine
brothers and sisters wished the bank to resist the claim on their behalf. The bank, in
order to protect its right of indemnity against the testator's estate for the costs of the
litigation, took out an originating summons seeking the court's direction whether it
should continue to defend the claimants' action and should counterclaim for possession
of the farm from the claimants. At the hearing of the summons the claimants agreed to
an order authorising the bank to carry on the litigation with them but submitted that
such an order should be on terms that the bank should obtain an indemnity for its costs
from the nine brothers and sisters and should only be entitled to an indemnity out of the
estate for its costs to the extent that it could not recover the costs from them. The
claimants submitted that if they succeeded in the action the entire estate would belong
to them and it would be unjust for the bank to take costs awarded against it out of the
estate and thereby diminish the estate when it would not hold any part of it. The
question arose whether RSC Ord 62, r 6(2)[a], which provided that a trustee or a personal
representative who litigated in that capacity was entitled to take his costs out of the fund
held by him, applied when, if the claimants were to succeed, the bank would not hold
any part of the fund.

Held – Applying the principle that a trustee or a personal representative should be
accorded full protection for costs properly incurred by him, a personal representative
who was a party to proceedings in that capacity was entitled under RSC Ord 62, r 6(2) to
be reimbursed his costs out of the fund held by him, even though the claimant in the
proceedings was a beneficiary under a will who was claiming the entire estate. In such
circumstances the claimant beneficiary was not entitled to an order for costs preserving
the disputed fund intact for him. Accordingly, the bank would not be required to obtain
an indemnity for costs from the nine brothers and sisters and would be directed to
continue to defend the action and to counterclaim on the basis that, subject to any order

---

a   Rule 6(2) provides: 'Where a person is or has been a party to any proceedings in the capacity of
trustee, personal representative or mortgagee, he shall, unless the Court otherwise orders, be
entitled to the costs of those proceedings, in so far as they are not recovered from or paid by any
other person, out of the fund held by the trustee or personal representative or the mortgaged
property, as the case may be; and the Court may otherwise order only on the ground that the
trustee, personal representative or mortgagee has acted unreasonably or, in the case of a trustee or
personal representative, has in substance acted for his own benefit rather than for the benefit of
the fund.'

that the trial judge might make, the bank should be entitled to be indemnified out of
a the estate for all costs for which it was liable in the action even if its defence and
counterclaim failed (see p 121 *f* to *h*, p 122 *f g* and p 123 *b*, post).
   Merry v Pownall [1898] 1 Ch 306 applied.

Notes
For a personal representative's right of indemnity out of the estate for all costs properly
b incurred, see 17 Halsbury's Laws (4th edn) paras 1190, 1492, and for cases on the subject,
see 23 Digest (Reissue) 565–571, 6301–6368.

Cases referred to in judgment
Beddoe, Re, Downes v Cottam [1893] 1 Ch 547, CA, 40 Digest (Repl) 766, 2510.
Eaton (decd), Re, Shaw v Midland Bank Exor and Trustee Co Ltd [1964] 3 All ER 229, [1964]
c   1 WLR 1269, 18 Digest (Reissue) 85, 608.
Ideal Bedding Co Ltd v Holland [1907] 2 Ch 157, 21 Digest (Reissue) 499, 4052.
Kay's Settlement, Re, Broadbent v Macnab [1939] 1 All ER 245, [1939] Ch 329, 40 Digest
   (Repl) 530, 404.
Merry v Pownall [1898] 1 Ch 306, 25 Digest (Reissue) 291, 2624.
Moritz, Re, Midland Bank Exor and Trustee Co Ltd v Forbes [1959] 3 All ER 767, [1960] Ch
d   251, [1959] 3 WLR 939, 18 Digest (Reissue) 85, 607.
Turner, Re, Wood v Turner [1907] 2 Ch 126, 539, CA, 43 Digest (Repl) 325, 3392.

Cases also cited
Bullock v Lloyds Bank Ltd [1954] 3 All ER 726, [1955] Ch 317.
Coverdale v Eastwood (1872) LR 15 Eq 121.
e Dent (a bankrupt), Re, ex p the trustee [1923] 1 Ch 113.
Foster v Royal Trust Co [1950] OR 673.
Holden, Re, ex p Official Receiver (1887) 20 QBD 43, DC.
Wakeham v Mackenzie [1968] 2 All ER 783, [1968] 1 WLR 1175.

Originating summons
f By an originating summons dated 6 March 1981 the plaintiff, Lloyds Bank Ltd (the
bank), the sole executor under the will of a deceased testator, applied for (1) directions
whether it should continue to defend and to counterclaim in an action brought against it
in the Chancery Division of the High Court by the tenth and eleventh defendants to the
summons, Jack Dallaway and Cynthia Jessie Dallaway (the claimants), who were
beneficiaries under the will, (2) an order that the costs of the application should be paid
g by the claimants or that such other provision for the costs of the application should be
made as the court thought fit, and (3) further and other relief. The first to the ninth
defendants to the summons were also beneficiaries under the will. The summons was
heard in chambers but judgment was delivered by Sir Robert Megarry V-C in open court.
The facts are set out in the judgment.

h Jonathan Simpkiss for the bank.
John H Weeks for the claimants.
Malcolm Waters for the first nine defendants.

                                                          Cur adv vult

j
   17 December. **SIR ROBERT MEGARRY V-C** read the following judgment: This
case raises an unusual point under *Re Beddoe, Downes v Cottam* [1893] 1 Ch 547 in relation
to a testator's estate. The testator died on 29 December 1978, and the effect of his will,
dated 4 March 1975, and a codicil, dated 1 June 1978, was that, apart from a legacy of
£900 given by the codicil to a sister-in-law, he left his entire estate equally between his

ten brothers and sisters, all of whom survived him. The estate was sworn at £31,800 gross and £24,483 net. The only substantial asset is the testator's farm of nearly 30 acres in Worcestershire, which was valued for probate at £28,000. The main liability of the estate is for an overdraft which was £7,000 at the testator's death and is now over £9,000. The will appointed Lloyds Bank Ltd as sole executor; and probate of the will and codicil was granted to the bank on 1 March 1979.

Some two or three years before the testator's death, one of his brothers came with his wife to live with the testator at the farm; and they are living there now. The wife is the sister-in-law to whom the testator gave the legacy of £900. The dispute before me arises out of a claim put forward by this brother and his wife. They are respectively the tenth and eleventh defendants to the originating summons which the bank issued on 6 March 1981. The other nine defendants are the other brothers and sisters of the testator (each being entitled to one-tenth of the residue), save that one of the sisters has died and is represented by her executor.

The bank took out the summons because the tenth and eleventh defendants to these proceedings had made a claim against the estate, and on 6 November 1979 had issued a writ against the bank to enforce that claim. For convenience I shall refer to the tenth and eleventh defendants to the summons as the claimants. Their claim is that in 1975 or 1976 the testator orally agreed with them that he would by his will leave them his entire estate, including the farm. If that claim succeeds, then of course there would be nothing for the other nine brothers and sisters; and not surprisingly they wished the bank to resist the claim.

In those circumstances the bank took out the originating summons. It is a Beddoe summons in which are sought directions whether the bank should continue to defend the action, and to counterclaim in it. The counterclaim, of course, is for possession of the farm. The summons first came before me in chambers on 22 June 1981, when Mr Simpkiss appeared for the bank and Mr Weeks appeared for the claimants, counsel for the bank having no objection to the presence or participation of counsel for the claimants. The nine brothers and sisters were not present, and were not represented. They had, indeed, lodged notices of no intention to defend. Counsel for the claimants did not oppose an order being made on the summons which would authorise the bank to carry on the litigation; and he foresaw no difficulty if the claimants' action for specific performance failed, for then in the normal way they would have to pay the costs. But, he said, if the claimants succeeded in the action for specific performance, and an order for costs was made in their favour against the bank, the effect of the bank being able to indemnify itself out of the testator's estate would be that the whole of the costs would fall on the claimants; and that would be most unjust. The practical result would be that, win or lose, the entire costs would have to be borne by the claimants. Therefore, said counsel for the claimants, if the nine brothers and sisters want the bank to resist the action brought by the claimants, they should make themselves responsible for the costs if the action succeeded; for the bank was only a nominal defendant, and what was in substance involved was hostile litigation between the two claimants and the nine brothers and sisters. Accordingly, counsel for the claimants asked for an order in this Beddoe summons that would produce the result that he desired.

When I inquired on the point, it appeared that nothing had been done to bring it to the attention of the nine brothers and sisters that an order of this kind would be sought; and plainly such an order would adversely affect them in a material way. I therefore directed that a letter, to be agreed by counsel, should be sent to the nine brothers and sisters, setting out the issue that had arisen, and stating that they would be given an opportunity of arguing the point. The summons was accordingly stood over, with liberty to restore, and some four months later the matter came back before me, with counsel representing the nine brothers and sisters.

Before I turn to the contentions put before me, I should say something about the action for specific performance. Nothing I say is intended to prejudice the result in that case; but of course in Beddoe applications the court has to form a view about the prospects

of success or failure. The claimants face some obvious difficulties. An allegation that an
oral agreement was made by a deceased person is one which plainly must be examined
carefully. Here, no claim that there was any such agreement was advanced until nearly
five months after the testator's death. At first, nearly two months after the death, the
claimants, through their solicitors, were seeking to purchase the farm. Two months later
they were contending that they had a tenancy of the farm. It was only three weeks after
that that the claimants' solicitors put forward an allegation that the testator had agreed
that if the claimants would give up their home and the male claimant came to work full-
time on the testator's farm, the testator would leave to the claimants the farm and
farmhouse (and not, it may be observed, the whole of his estate). A claim with such a
history obviously requires to be scrutinised with considerable care.

The form of order sought by counsel for the claimants was an order authorising the
bank to carry on the litigation on terms as to costs. Those terms, he said, should be that
if the bank failed in the proceedings, the bank's costs would not be taken out of the estate.
That would leave the bank to obtain a suitable indemnity from the nine brothers and
sisters. Counsel for the claimants accepted that this would be an unusual direction, but
he said that the circumstances were unusual. After some discussion, counsel for the
claimants put forward a modified form of order, namely that the bank should be entitled
to its costs out of the estate only to the extent that these costs could not be recovered from
the nine brothers and sisters.

There does not appear to be any authority directly in point; and for this reason I am
delivering judgment in open court. There are, however, some authorities which provide
a certain amount of assistance. I take it to be axiomatic that, acting with proper prudence,
executors should take proper steps to protect their testator's estate against adverse claims.
However, when there is an adverse claim not merely to a small part of the estate, but to
the whole of it, the executors are in a difficult position; for if the claim succeeds, the
decision establishes that nothing is theirs, and so they hold nothing out of which they
can indemnify themselves for the costs of defending what they believed to be their estate.
Executors who have an estate which is held to consist of nothing can have nothing out of
which they could take their costs. However, in the parallel case of trustees the courts
have tempered this icy logic. It has been held that where a settlement is set aside and so
there is no property out of which the trustees can take their costs as of right, the court
nevertheless has a discretion to allow the trustees to take their costs out of the fund before
handing it over to the successful litigants. It has also been held that in exercising this
discretion, trustees who have acted properly ought to be allowed their costs: see *Merry v
Pownall* [1898] 1 Ch 306 at 310–311. Furthermore, although the trustees may not be
strictly trustees for the successful litigants (a point on which the views of Kekewich J in
Merry v Pownall [1898] 1 Ch 306 at 312 and in *Ideal Bedding Co Ltd v Holland* [1907] 2 Ch
157 at 174 do not appear to be entirely in accord), they are sufficiently trustees of the
fund for them not to be confined to party and party costs.

I can see no reason to distinguish between trustees and executors in this respect, and
no distinction has been suggested. It might be said that the discretion for this purpose
should be the discretion of the trial judge, after all the facts have been ascertained.
However, the difficulty and inconvenience that would be caused by leaving the matter
until the trial are obvious. The bank, and all the beneficiaries, and not least the claimants,
want to know where they are on the point, and counsel for the nine brothers and sisters
and counsel for the claimants joined in seeking a decision now. I think I can properly do
as they ask.

The court has, of course, a general discretion in relation to costs. However, RSC Ord
62, r 6(2) lays down a special rule for any who litigate as, inter alia, trustee or personal
representative. In so far as such a person does not recover his costs from any other person,
he is entitled to take his costs out of the fund held by him unless the court otherwise
orders; and the court can otherwise order only on the ground that he has acted
unreasonably, or in substance for his own benefit, rather than for the benefit of the fund.
If that rule applied to the present case simpliciter, plainly the bank would be entitled to

take its unpaid costs out of the fund; for there is not, and could not be, any suggestion
that the bank was acting unreasonably or for its own benefit. The only thing which   *a*
prevents this rule from applying directly to the present case is the fact that the adverse
claim is to the entire estate vested in the bank, so that it is in doubt whether there is any
fund held by the bank.

I think that a case of this sort should be approached by considering first the general
rule and then examining whether any difference is made by the particular circumstances
of the case. First, suppose that the claim to the estate is made by someone who is not a   *b*
beneficiary under the will. In such a case, the claimant not only would not be present at
the hearing of the Beddoe summons by the executor, but also would in all probability
not even know anything about any such summons. If the claim were one which the
executor ought to resist, the court would give the executor the requisite authority to
resist it, and would allow the executor to take his costs out of the fund even if the claim
succeeded. No question of requiring the beneficiaries under the will to indemnify the   *c*
executor, or to contest the claim themselves, would arise. The claimant would not be
there to seek such an order; and there is nothing in the authorities, or in any principles
that I know of, which would encourage the court to impose any such terms. In pursuing
his claim, the claimant would know that if he succeeded, the executor would in all
normal circumstances be able to recover the costs out of the fund before handing it over,
and the claimant would have to make his calculations on this footing.   *d*

Second, what difference, if any, is there when the claimants are beneficiaries under the
will, as in the present case? One obvious difference is that they will normally be parties
to the Beddoe application, though they will be subject to the usual limitations on their
right to see the evidence and take part in the hearing: see, eg, *Re Eaton (decd), Shaw
v Midland Bank Exor and Trustee Co Ltd* [1964] 3 All ER 229, [1964] 1 WLR 1269, relaxing
to some extent the views expressed in *Re Moritz, Midland Bank Exor and Trustee Co Ltd v*   *e*
Forbes [1959] 3 All ER 767, [1960] Ch 251. I observe that in *Re Kay's Settlement, Broadbent
v Macnab* [1939] 1 All ER 245 at 247, [1939] Ch 329 at 339 it appears that on a Beddoe
application, counsel for the proposed defendant was heard in argument. As parties to the
Beddoe application, the claimants will know what is proposed, and so will have the
opportunity of seeking the sort of order that counsel for the claimants now seeks. Apart
from that, I find it difficult to see what material difference it makes that the claimants   *f*
are beneficiaries under the will. In particular, I cannot see why that circumstance should
give the claimants any right or claim to the sort of order that counsel for the claimants is
seeking, so as to put them in a position which is materially different from that of all other
claimants. The existence of their beneficial interest seems to me to have no relevant
bearing on their status as litigants in relation to the executor's costs. I can see no rational
basis on which it could be said that litigants who are beneficiaries should be entitled to   *g*
an order which will preserve for them the corpus in dispute, while litigants who are not
beneficiaries should be entitled to no such order. Why should the presence or absence of
a £100 legacy transform the position? What if some of the litigants are beneficiaries and
others are not?

Third, I can see grave difficulties in relation to the indemnities which counsel for the
claimants says should be given to the bank by the nine brothers and sisters. If, contrary   *h*
to my opinion, it would be right to require such indemnities to be given, how far ought
the bank to go in enforcing them before resorting to the fund? Must it sue those who do
not pay? Ought it to require the indemnity to be secured in each case? If some of the
nine can give adequate indemnities, but others cannot, must the more prosperous bear
the shares of the less prosperous, in addition to their own? If they are all unable to offer a
satisfactory indemnity, is the bank to be told to abandon the resistance to the proceedings   *j*
by the claimants which otherwise the bank could, and should, offer? Would it be right
to allow the claimants to triumph over the nine brothers and sisters in this way, despite
the need to test the claimants' assertions? I do not say that these questions are all
unanswerable; but it does seem to me that the problems that they pose emphasise the

unsatisfactory nature of the claim put forward by counsel for the claimants. Throughout
a I bear in mind the importance of affording full and proper protection for the costs and
other expenses incurred by trustees and personal representatives who, as such, act
properly: see, e g, *Re Turner, Wood v Turner* [1907] 2 Ch 126.

In the result, I reject the contentions of counsel for the claimants. Subject to any
submissions that there may be on the wording, I propose to give a suitable direction to
the bank to continue to defend and to counterclaim, as sought in para 1 of the summons.
b In giving that direction, I propose to include a provision that, subject to any order made
by the trial judge, the bank will be entitled to be indemnified out of the estate for all
costs for which it is liable, even if the defence or counterclaim, or both, are unsuccessful.
It seems to me to be necessary to make this provision subject to any order of the trial
judge because although as matters stand the bank, on the material before me, is fully
justified in defending and counterclaiming, it is possible that material may emerge
c subsequently which will make it unreasonable for the bank to continue to defend or
counterclaim; and if, despite that, the bank continued with the litigation, no order that I
make now ought to protect it in relation to subsequent costs. In view of this possibility I
propose that my order should take effect only until further order, giving all parties
liberty to apply, and authorising the master to consider and deal with any such
application.

d
Order accordingly

Solicitors: *Gregory Rowcliffe & Co*, agents for *John Stallard & Co*, Worcester (for the bank);
Needham & James, Stratford-upon-Avon (for the claimants); *Gregory Rowcliffe & Co*, agents
for *Hulme & Co*, Worcester, and for *Gordon Jones & Co*, Droitwich (for the first nine
defendants).

Azza M Abdallah   Barrister.

Practice Direction

CHANCERY DIVISION

Practice – Chancery Division – Administrative arrangements – Chancery Chambers – Court file – Issue of process – Fees – Assignment of masters – Ex parte applications – Appeals – Filing of documents – Orders – Judgments by default – Agreed adjournment of motions – Motions judge – Listing – Receivers' accounts – RSC (Amendment No 2) 1982.

1 RSC (Amendment No 2) 1982, SI 1982/1111, the relevant provisions of which come into force on 1 October 1982, provides for extensive changes in the conduct of Chancery business. This direction gives details of the new administrative arrangements in London and, in addition, designates three new trial centres outside London.

2 *Companies Court and bankruptcy business*
Nothing in this direction affects the conduct of proceedings in the Companies Court or bankruptcy business.

3 *Chancery in the provinces*
As from 1 October 1982 the Rules of the Supreme Court will authorise Chancery business to be conducted in Birmingham, Bristol and Cardiff; and it is hereby directed that trials of Chancery proceedings may be held at these places in addition to those specified in the Practice Direction of 10 December 1971 relating to Chancery proceedings outside London ([1972] 1 All ER 103, [1972] 1 WLR 1).
Local arrangements will be made for the hearing of motions and appeals from the decisions of district registrars. Details may be obtained from the relevant courts after 13 September 1982.

4 *Administrative structure in Chancery Chambers*
Four sections have been established to deal with the transaction of business in Chancery Chambers.
(a) The Chancery Chambers (Registry) deals with court files, masters' summonses and the issue of process.
(b) The Drafting Section deals with court attendance and the drafting of orders. Officers sitting in court will be called associates.
(c) The Listing Section deals with (i) setting down of all cases save motions and (ii) listing of all cases except motions and patent actions.
(d) The Accounts Section deals with the examination of accounts and any certificates arising from accounts and inquiries.
The schedule to this direction sets out a full list of the various types of business and the appropriate room for inquiries or the lodging of papers.

5 *The court file*
The court file will be maintained for each case. The documents relevant to a particular case will be kept on the file, including the originating process, copies of civil aid certificates, acknowledgments of service, notices of change of solicitors, summonses, affidavits, pleadings and orders. The master will make his notes on the file and the associate in court will complete a case note, which will also be filed in respect of each hearing, including motions. The court file will normally be kept in the registry (rooms 156 and 157), but it will be sent to the master when required by him. It will also be available in court on the trial of any action or interlocutory application, and it will be used by the Drafting Section when drawing up any order of a judge or master.

6 *Issue of process*
All originating process, that is writs, originating summonses, originating motions and

a petitions, together with Revenue appeals and appeals from the Comptroller-General of Patents, will be issued in room 157. Notices of motion will continue to be lodged with the clerk to the motions judge. Subpoenas and writs of execution will continue to be issued in the Central Office, Action Department.

7   *Payment of fees*
b Fees payable in Chancery proceedings, except for the issue of a subpoena or writ of execution, must be paid in room 157.

8   *Assignment of masters*
Cases will no longer be assigned by reference to groups. All cases which have already been assigned to a master will continue to be dealt with by that master. Cases which are required to be assigned to a master for the first time from 1 October 1982 will be assigned *c* on an alphabetical basis, two masters sharing each division of A–E, F–M and N–Z. The letter which appears as part of the action number and which is assigned at the time of issue of the originating process will decide the appropriate alphabetical division.

Masters' summonses will be issued in room 156, and evidence in support must be filed there. It will not be necessary for copy writs, acknowledgment of service or certificate of non-acknowledgment of service to be produced at the time of issue of a master's *d* summons. The counter positions in room 156 will be marked with the names of the masters and the alphabetical divisions so that litigants or their advisers can identify the point they should attend to issue their summons and have the name of the master and the date of the appointment indorsed.

It is stressed that a case assigned to a master before 1 October 1982 will be retained by that master even if the case letter indicates that it belongs to a different alphabetical *e* division.

9   *Ex parte applications to masters*
If an ex parte application is to be made to a master notice should be given to the summons clerk in room 156 by noon on the day the application is to be made. This can be done by telephone if that is more convenient (01–405 7641 extn 3148). In the case of *f* genuinely urgent applications, notice may be given at any time.

10   *Appeals from masters*
The right of a party to an adjournment from a master to a judge has been replaced by a right of appeal to a judge in chambers.

Two copies of the notice of appeal against the decision of a master must be lodged in *g* room 157 within five days after the judgment, order or decision appealed against was given or made. Notice of appeal will be in Queen's Bench Masters' Practice Form PF 114, save that in place of a fixed date the words 'on a date to be notified' should be inserted. The names, addresses, references and telephone numbers of all solicitors should be shown. Appeals will be entered in the non-witness list and shown on the warned list as for hearing in chambers.

h

11   *Filing of documents*
Documents in Chancery proceedings will not be accepted for filing in room 81 after 30 September 1982. All affidavits filed in room 81 up to and including 30 September 1982 will be retained there and must be bespoken if they are required after that date. If they are then used in proceedings in Chancery they will be retained on the court file after *j* use. Exhibits to affidavits will be retained if they are required for the purposes of drawing up an order, though they will in due course be returned to the parties.

Any documents not in support of a master's summons (see para 8) which parties wish to file and are not handed in during a hearing, whether before a judge or master, must be lodged in room 157.

Office copy documents can be obtained in room 157 on payment of the proper fee.

Stop notices under RSC Ord 50, r 11 and affidavits relating to funds paid into court under the Trustee Act 1925, the Compulsory Purchase Act 1965 and the Lands Clauses Consolidation Act 1845 must be filed in room 157.

12 *Orders made prior to 1 October 1982*

Under the revised RSC Ord 42 the requirement to bespeak an order is abolished for any order made after 30 September 1982, but it will still be necessary to bespeak orders made in court prior to 1 October 1982. The following documents must be lodged in room 188: (a) a statement showing (i) the names of all parties concerned, and whether they are in receipt of legal aid, and (ii) the names of their solicitors, if any, or a statement that they are acting in person; (b) the pleadings, summons, notice or other document on which the order was made; (c) the original writ or other document originating the proceedings, or a duplicate of the last order made in the proceedings; (d) all acknowledgments of service, unless they have already been lodged; (e) all the evidence before the court when the order was made; and (f) the indorsed brief of counsel acting for the party bespeaking the order.

On lodgment of these documents the order will be drawn up, and unless the draftsman has any questions a sealed copy will be sent to the party bespeaking the order.

13 *Orders by masters made after 30 September 1982*

(a) *Interlocutory orders* In every case where a master makes an interlocutory order he will ask the parties whether or not they want the order to be drawn up. If an order is to be drawn up the master will ask the party seeking the order whether he wishes to draw it. If the order is to be drawn up by the court a sealed copy will be sent to the party having carriage of the order.

If the order is to be drawn up by a solicitor it must be lodged in room 180 within seven days.

(b) *Final orders* Final orders made by masters will be drawn up by the court, and unless the draftsman has any questions a sealed copy will be sent to the party having carriage of the order.

14 *Orders by judges made after 30 September 1982*

(a) *Agreed minutes of order* Where a judge directs that minutes of order be agreed and signed by counsel, the agreed minutes may either be handed to the associate in court or else be lodged in room 180. In each case the action number should be shown. Agreed minutes will normally be adopted as the order of the court.

(b) *Drafting by the court* Unless the court directs minutes of order to be produced or that no order need be drawn up the court will draw up the order and send it out without reference to the parties. If the order is unusually complicated it may be necessary to submit a draft to the parties.

(c) *Orders on motion* Where an order has been made on motion any party wishing to have the order drawn up should ask the judge or associate for this to be done. This arrangement is necessary to ensure that the court does not draw up orders which are not required by the parties. This is the only occasion where the court will not draw up a judge's order unless it is requested.

15 *Forms of order*

The form of each order will be simplified. Recitals will be kept to a minimum, and the body of the order will be confined to setting out the decision of the court and the directions required to give effect to it. If on receipt of an order any party is of the opinion that it is not drawn in such a way as to give effect to the decision of the court, prompt notice must be given to the Drafting Section in room 180 and to all other parties setting out the reasons for dissatisfaction. If the differences cannot be resolved the objecting party may apply by motion or by summons for the order to be amended.

16   *Copies of orders*

a   Copies of orders may be obtained from room 157 on payment of the appropriate fee.

17   *Judgments by default*

An application for judgment by default should be presented to room 157 in the first instance, together with an affidavit of service of the writ. It is not necessary to produce a certificate of non-acknowledgment of service.

b

18   *Agreed adjournment of motions*

Parties who wish to take advantage of the procedure for the agreed adjournment of motions (see the Practice Note of 17 April 1976 ([1976] 2 All ER 198, [1976] 1 WLR 441)) must bespeak the court file from room 157 and make their application in accordance with the direction in room 180 at any time between 10 a m and 4.30 p m.

c

19   *Motions judge*

As announced in previous Term Lists, there is now no stand-by judge for the hearing of motions. Instead the Clerk of the Lists will arrange for any necessary assistance to be given by any judge available. Paragraph 2 of the Practice Direction of 23 June 1980 relating to motions in the Chancery Division ([1980] 2 All ER 750, [1980] 1 WLR 751)

d   is varied accordingly.

20   *Listing*

The listing of Revenue appeals and appeals from the Comptroller-General of Patents will be dealt with by the Listing Section in room 163. No other changes in respect of listing have been made.

e

21   *Receivers' accounts*

RSC Ord 30 has been amended to introduce a new approach to the auditing of receivers' accounts. A receiver must submit accounts to such parties at such intervals or on such dates as the court may direct. A party who is dissatisfied with the accounts may give to the receiver and the court a notice specifying the item or items to which objection

f   is taken and requiring the accounts to be lodged with the court within 14 days. Both the accounts and the copy notice must be lodged at room 165.

Examination of the accounts will be limited to the item or items to which objection is taken. A receiver may apply to the court informally for any directions he may require.

22   The following Practice Directions are revoked:

g   Practice Direction of 17 October 1960 relating to the drawing up of procedural orders made in chambers ([1960] 3 All ER 415, [1960] 1 WLR 1166)

Practice Direction of 17 October 1960 relating to minutes of order drawn by counsel ([1960] 3 All ER 416, [1960] 1 WLR 1168)

Practice Direction of 21 December 1960 relating to orders drawn up by Chancery registrars ([1961] 1 All ER 159, [1961] 1 WLR 47)

h   Practice Direction of 24 September 1965 relating to the adjournment of proceedings in chambers in the Chancery Division to the judge ([1965] 3 All ER 306, [1965] 1 WLR 259)

Practice Direction of 18 December 1974 relating to adjournments from Chancery masters to the judge ([1975] 1 All ER 232, [1975] 1 WLR 82)

j   Practice Direction of 12 June 1980 relating to bespeaking judgments and orders in the Chancery Division ([1980] 2 All ER 400, [1980] 1 WLR 754)

By direction of the Vice-Chancellor and with the concurrence of the Lord Chancellor.

EDMUND HEWARD
Chief Master.

29 July 1982

SCHEDULE

Room 156 (Chancery Chambers (Registry))   *a*
  Issue of masters' summonses
  Inquiries regarding masters' summonses
  Bespeaking files for ex parte applications to masters
  Filing affidavits in proceedings before masters
  Applications to serve out of jurisdiction

        b
Room 157 (Chancery Chambers (Registry))
  Issue of all originating process
  Amendment of process
  Payment of fees
  Filing affidavits (other than for proceedings before a master)
  Filing stop notices (RSC Ord 50, r 11)   *c*
  Filing testamentary documents in contested probate cases
  Filing grants lodged under RSC Ord 99, r 7
  Filing acknowledgments of service
  Certification of documents for use abroad
  Applications for office copy documents, including orders
  Judgments by default   *d*
  Filing affidavits relating to funds paid into court under the Trustee Act 1925, the
    Compulsory Purchase Act 1965 and the Lands Clauses Consolidation Act 1845.
  Notices of appeal from decisions of masters

Room 180 (Drafting Section)
  Masters' orders drawn by solicitors   *e*
  Agreed minutes of order
  Questions arising on orders made after 30 September 1982

Room 188 (Drafting Section)
  Bespeaking orders made prior to 1 October 1982
  Questions arising on orders made prior to 1 October 1982   *f*

Room 165 (Accounts Section)
  Bills of costs for assessment
  Small payments (RSC Ord 92)
  Sales by private treaty or auction
  Settlement of advertisements   *g*
  Settlement of payment and lodgment schedules (otherwise than part of an order)
  Accounts of receivers, judicial trustees, guardians and administrators
  Applications relating to security set by the court
  References to taxing masters
  Matters arising out of accounts and inquiries ordered by the court

        h
Room 163 (Listing Section)
  Setting down
  Listing of motions when the clerk to the motions judge is not available (but not
    otherwise)
  All listing save patents actions
  Inquiries regarding Revenue cases and appeals from the Comptroller-General of   *j*
    Patents

Langdale and another v Danby

HOUSE OF LORDS

LORD DIPLOCK, LORD FRASER OF TULLYBELTON, LORD ROSKILL, LORD BRIDGE OF HARWICH AND LORD BRIGHTMAN

23, 24 JUNE, 29 JULY 1982

Court of Appeal – Evidence – Further evidence – Appeal following summary judgment – Objection to evidence – Objection not taken at first opportunity – Evidence in reply filed – Whether objection to admission of evidence waived.

Practice – Summary judgment – Appeal – Further evidence – Admissibility – Evidence available at time of hearing application for summary judgment – Whether hearing application for summary judgment a hearing 'on the merits' – Whether further evidence admissible only on special grounds – RSC Ord 14, Ord 59, r 10(2), Ord 86.

Admission – Counsel – Summary proceedings – Admission on behalf of defendant – Judgment given on basis of admission – Plaintiff spending time and money on enforcing judgment – Whether defendant entitled to withdraw admission.

In 1964 the first plaintiff, a solicitor, and the second plaintiff, his wife, bought an estate which included a cottage for which they had no immediate use. They foresaw, however, that the cottage might in the future provide a home for one of their three young daughters when they grew up and married. They offered the cottage for sale for £2,650 on terms reserving for themselves the right of pre-emption and an option exercisable within 21 years to repurchase the cottage at the same price. The defendant, who was in urgent need of accommodation for himself and his family and who had no money at all, was introduced to the plaintiffs by his employer, C, a builder who had done some work on the cottage. In the result, the defendant purchased the cottage on the plaintiffs' terms, the purchase being financed by a building society mortgage loan of £2,250 with the balance left outstanding and secured to the plaintiffs on a second mortgage. Since the defendant could not afford to employ a solicitor, the first plaintiff agreed to undertake all the necessary conveyancing work for no fee except disbursements. The conveyance, the two mortgage deeds and the deed granting the right of pre-emption and option were all executed in March 1965. In 1979 the plaintiffs sought to exercise the option because they required the cottage for a daughter who was about to be married. The defendant was unwilling to sell and he consulted a number of solicitors. The plaintiffs offered to repurchase the cottage for £6,150 but the offer was refused. Formal notice to exercise the option was given on 2 July 1979, by which time the defendant had employed a solicitor, B, who continued to act for him throughout the subsequent proceedings. On 4 October the defendant commenced proceedings in the county court challenging the validity of the option on the sole ground that it was a clog on the equity of redemption under the second mortgage. On 23 October the plaintiffs swore affidavits asserting that at the time of the 1964 agreement they had made clear to the defendant and his wife that the offer to sell the cottage for £2,650 was only on terms of the right of pre-emption and option to repurchase within 21 years at the same price, that in any event those were the only terms on which they were prepared to sell to anyone and that it was because the defendant could not afford a solicitor that the first plaintiff undertook to do the conveyancing work for no charge except disbursements. Also on 23 October C swore an affidavit deposing that he had been aware of the plaintiffs' terms, that he had told the defendant of them, that after the defendant had agreed the terms with the plaintiffs the defendant had discussed the bargain with him and that he had told the defendant that in the circumstances it was the best the defendant would get. On 29 October the plaintiffs issued a writ in the Chancery Division seeking specific performance of the option

contract, and on 9 November they issued a summons for summary judgment under RSC
Ord 86ᵃ. On 21 November the defendant issued a cross-summons to transfer the High   a
Court proceedings to the county court. Both summonses were adjourned to the judge,
who heard and determined them on 13 December. On the day of the hearing B swore an
affidavit deposing, inter alia, that he had been informed by the defendant that the first
plaintiff explained to the defendant that the purpose of the option was to protect the
plaintiffs as to who would be their neighbour and that if the defendant wanted to sell the
cottage he had to give the plaintiffs the opportunity to buy it first. There was no affidavit   b
from the defendant. At the hearing before the judge, at which B was present, counsel for
the defendant expressly asserted that there was no suggestion of any misconduct against
the plaintiffs and he conceded that the only question to be decided was whether the
option was a clog on the equity of redemption. The judge found in favour of the plaintiffs
and made an order for specific performance. For two years the plaintiffs sought to enforce
the judgment, but the defendant resorted to every conceivable device to deny the   c
plaintiffs the fruits of their judgment for as long as possible, and during that time the
mortgage loans were repaid. The defendant failed to comply with an order to complete
the transaction and give vacant possession on 30 June 1981. In July the conveyance of the
cottage to the plaintiffs was ordered to be and was executed on the defendant's behalf by
a Chancery master, yet the defendant and his wife failed to move. On 17 September a
writ of possession was issued and executed and the defendant and his family were evicted.   d
A few days after the eviction the defendant sought leave to appeal out of time against the
judge's order. Further evidence, in affidavits sworn by the defendant and B on 28
September, was put before the court on the application. The plaintiffs took no objection
to the evidence at that stage, but filed further affidavits in reply. On 6 October the Court
of Appeal granted leave to appeal out of time. At the hearing of the substantive appeal
the plaintiffs contended (i) that RSC Ord 59, r 10(2)ᵇ rendered the further evidence   e
inadmissible in the absence of special grounds and that there were no such special
grounds, and (ii) that the defendant should not be permitted to withdraw the admissions
made on his behalf before the judge. The Court of Appeal rejected those contentions,
holding (i) that it had full discretionary power as to the admission of further evidence
and that in the circumstances the further evidence should be admitted, and (ii) that (a)
admissions by counsel could be withdrawn unless the circumstances gave rise to an   f
estoppel and that in the circumstances no estoppel arose, or (b) the plaintiffs had not acted
to their detriment on the faith of counsel for the defendant's failure to take before the
judge the points taken in the Court of Appeal, or (c) the matter went only to costs and
not substance and could be dealt with separately. The court went on to hold that,
although the judge had been right on the material before him, the further evidence
before it and new points taken on behalf of the defendant which contradicted the express   g
admission before the judge that no impropriety was alleged against the first plaintiff
were grounds for setting aside the judge's order and giving the defendant unconditional
leave to defend. The plaintiffs appealed to the House of Lords. The defendant submitted
that, because objection to the admission of the further evidence had not been taken at
the first opportunity and because further affidavits in reply had been filed by the
plaintiffs, they has waived the objection.   h

Held – The appeal would be allowed for the following reasons—
  (1) The plaintiffs had not waived their objection to the admission of the further
evidence by failing to object to its admission at the first opportunity or by filing further
evidence in reply since whenever the objection was taken the Court of Appeal would
have considered the further evidence de bene esse before deciding on its admissibility   j
and it was only prudent for the plaintiffs to answer the further evidence in case their
objection to its admissibility should fail (see p 132 d to f, p 135 h j and p 140 f g, post).

a   Order 86, so far as material, is set out at p 136 h to p 137 b, post
b   Rule 10(2) is set out at p 135 f, post

(2) On the true construction of RSC Ord 59, r 10(2) an appeal against a summary
a judgment given under RSC Ord 14 or Ord 86 was an appeal from a judgment after a
hearing 'on the merits' since the judge could only give judgment for the plaintiff if he
was satisfied that there were no merits on the defendant's side as to warrant giving leave
to defend. Accordingly Ord 59, r 10(2), which excluded the admission of further evidence
on appeal to the Court of Appeal except on special grounds, was, in its ordinary meaning,
applicable to appeals against summary judgments given for plaintiffs under Ord 14 or
b Ord 86. Furthermore, such a construction was in accordance with the principle that a
successful litigant was not lightly to be deprived of his judgment, a principle of particular
importance to a plaintiff, frequently pursuing a recalcitrant and obstructive defendant,
who had secured a judgment by showing that the defendant had no defence. Where a
plaintiff applied for summary judgment, there was no injustice in requiring the
defendant to use such diligence as was reasonable in the circumstances to put before the
c judge hearing the application, albeit in summary form, all the evidence he relied on in
defence, whereas it would be a great injustice to the plaintiff to allow the defendant to
introduce for the first time on appeal evidence which had been readily available at the
hearing of the application but was not produced. Since the evidence to support the
assertion that the first plaintiff had failed to explain the effect of the option deed to the
defendant was extremely tenuous, it followed that there were no special grounds for
d admitting it, and without it there was no issue to be tried (see p 132 d e, p 137 c to j,
p 138 d, p 139 b c and p 140 f g, post); dicta of Lord Loreburn LC in Brown v Dean [1908–
10] All ER Rep at 662, of Denning LJ in Ladd v Marshall [1954] 3 All ER at 748 and of
Lord Hodson in Skone v Skone [1971] 2 All ER at 586 applied; Robinson v Bradshaw (1883)
32 WR 95 explained.

(3) Since the direct result of the conduct of the defendant's case before the judge was
e to permit the plaintiffs to obtain summary judgment and since the plaintiff had spent
two years and a great deal of money in costs in the course of enforcing the judgment, it
was beyond argument that the plaintiffs would have acted to their detriment if they were
to be denied the benefit of the judgment by allowing the defendant to set up a case which
conflicted radically with the case presented on his behalf before the judge. It followed
that the defendant was estopped from arguing the case on which he succeeded in the
Court of Appeal (see p 132 d e and p 140 a to g, post); H Clark (Doncaster) Ltd v Wilkinson
[1965] 1 All ER 934 distinguished.

Notes
For the power of the Court of Appeal to receive further evidence on an appeal, see 37
Halsbury's Laws (4th edn), para 693, and for cases on the subject, see 51 Digest (Repl)
f 823, 3789–3793.
For appeals against summary judgments, see 26 Halsbury's Laws (4th edn) para 526,
and for cases on the subject, see 50 Digest (Repl) 415–416, 1231–1240.
For admissions by solicitors and counsel, see 3 Halsbury's Laws (4th edn) para 1184
and 17 ibid para 73, and for cases on the subject, see 3 Digest (Reissue) 773, 4712–4714,
and 22 ibid 99–100, 147–148, 684–696, 1206–1215.

Cases referred to in opinions
Brown v Dean [1910] AC 373, [1908–10] All ER Rep 661, HL, 51 Digest (Repl) 865, 4160.
Clark (H) (Doncaster) Ltd v Wilkinson [1965] 1 All ER 934, [1965] Ch 694, [1965] 2 WLR
    751, CA, 3 Digest (Reissue) 773, 4713.
Din v Wandsworth London Borough Council (No 2) [1982] 1 All ER 1022, [1982] 1 WLR
    418, HL.
Ladd v Marshall [1954] 3 All ER 745, [1954] 1 WLR 1489, CA, 51 Digest (Repl) 827,
    3826.
Robinson v Bradshaw (1883) 32 WR 95, DC, 50 Digest (Repl) 415, 1234.
Skone v Skone [1971] 2 All ER 582, [1971] 1 WLR 812, HL, Digest (Cont Vol D) 1062,
    3828c.

Appeal

The plaintiffs, Horace William Langdale and Audrey Alice Langdale, appealed pursuant *a* to leave granted by the Appeal Committee of the House of Lords on 29 March 1982 against the order of the Court of Appeal (Lord Denning MR, Dunn and Fox LJJ) dated 4 December 1981 whereby pursuant to leave granted by the court on 6 October 1981 to appeal out of time it allowed an appeal by the defendant, Tom Danby, against an order made by Oliver J dated 13 December 1979 and varied by an order made by Goulding J dated 19 May 1980 granting the plaintiffs summary judgment under RSC Ord 86 for *b* specific performance of an option to purchase land. The facts are set out in the opinion of Lord Bridge.

John E A Samuels QC and *R F D Barlow* for Mr and Mrs Langdale.
Gerald Godfrey QC and *David L Porter* for Mr Danby.

c
Their Lordships took time for consideration.

29 July. The following opinions were delivered.

LORD DIPLOCK. My Lords, I have had the advantage of reading in advance the speech about to be delivered by my noble and learned friend Lord Bridge. For the reasons *d* he gives I too would allow this appeal.

LORD FRASER OF TULLYBELTON. My Lords, I have had the privilege of reading in draft the speech prepared by my noble and learned friend Lord Bridge. I agree with it, and for the reasons given by him I would allow this appeal.

e
LORD ROSKILL. My Lords, I have had the advantage of reading in draft the speech prepared by my noble and learned friend Lord Bridge. For the reasons given by him, I too would allow this appeal.

LORD BRIDGE OF HARWICH. My Lords, the appellants are Mr and Mrs Langdale. Mr Langdale is a solicitor. Through most of the period covering the events giving rise to *f* this appeal he was a partner in the firm of Payne & Payne, of Hull. He is now a consultant with that firm.

In July 1964 Mr and Mrs Langdale bought an estate near Hull. The estate included a cottage, 33 Dale Road, Elloughton, for which the Langdales had no immediate use. But they foresaw that the day might come when it would provide a home for one of their three young daughters when they grew up and married. They decided to offer the *g* cottage for sale at a price of £2,650 but on terms that they would reserve for themselves the right of pre-emption and an option exercisable within 21 years to repurchase the cottage at the same price. The cottage was put on the market on these terms through estate agents. A Mr and Mrs Ford offered to purchase. The terms of the contract and the option deed were agreed with the Fords' solicitor but contracts were never exchanged. In the event, the Fords could not find the purchase price and the deal fell through. *h*

The respondent, Mr Danby, was then introduced to the Langdales by his employer, a builder named Cogan, who had done some work to the cottage. Mr Danby was in urgent need of accommodation for himself and his family. The upshot of the negotiations was that the cottage was sold by the Langdales to Mr Danby on exactly the same terms as those which had been agreed, subject to contract, with the Fords. But Mr Danby had no money at all. The purchase was financed by a mortgage loan from the Skipton Building *j* Society of £2,250 with the balance of the purchase price and costs, £412 14s 9d, left outstanding and secured to the Langdales by a second mortgage. Moreover, Mr Danby could not even afford to employ a solicitor. Mr Langdale therefore agreed to undertake all the necessary conveyancing work for no fee except disbursements. In the event all that Mr Danby had to pay was £7 16s 0d. The conveyance, the two mortgage deeds and a the deed granting the rights of pre-emption and option were all executed on 12 March 1965.

In 1979 the Langdales, requiring the cottage for a daughter who was about to be married, wished to exercise the option. Mr Danby was unwilling to sell. He evidently consulted a number of solicitors. The Langdales offered to repurchase for £6,150, £3,500 above the option price. This offer was refused. Formal notice to exercise the option was given on 2 July 1979. By this time the solicitor acting for Mr Danby was a Mr

b Bosomworth, then a partner in the firm of Simpson, Curtis & Co, but subsequently practising on his own account as John Bosomworth & Co. He has acted for Mr Danby in this matter ever since.

On 4 October 1979 Mr Danby commenced proceedings in the Beverley County Court challenging the validity of the option on the sole ground that it was a clog on the equity of redemption under the second mortgage. On 29 October 1979 the Langdales issued

c their writ in the Chancery Division claiming specific performance of the option contract. On 9 November 1979 the Langdales issued a summons for summary judgment under RSC Ord 86. On 21 November 1979 Mr Danby issued a cross-summons for transfer of the High Court proceedings to the Beverley County Court. Both summonses came before Master Dyson on 27 November 1979, when they were adjourned to the judge. They were heard and determined by Oliver J on 13 December 1979. In the light of the

d subsequent course of these proceedings, it is of the first importance to notice both the sequence and the substance of the affidavit evidence put before the court on this occasion. No doubt anticipating the issue of both writ and summons for summary judgment, affidavits were sworn in support of the Langdales' claim on 23 October 1979 by both Mr and Mrs Langdale and by Mr Danby's former employer, Mr Cogan. Mr Langdale's affidavit, confirmed by his wife, asserts categorically that at the time of the 1964

e agreement he and his wife made clear to Mr and Mrs Danby that the offer to sell the cottage for £2,650 was only on terms of the right of pre-emption and option to re-purchase within 21 years at the same price, that in any event these were the only terms on which they were prepared to sell to anyone and that it was because Mr Danby could not afford to go to a solicitor that he undertook to have the conveyancing work done for him without charge except for disbursements. The affidavit of the wholly independent

f Mr Cogan is sufficiently important to be worth quoting verbatim. Mr Cogan deposed:

'I knew that the cottage was up for sale because Mr Langdale had told me. I overheard him discussing the cottage with his wife and I asked him afterwards if he had thought about letting it. Mr Langdale told me that he would not consider letting it. I told him that I wanted a house for the defendant. Mr Langdale said that he would let the defendant have the cottage at a reasonable price but that he wanted

g to be able to have the cottage back at the price the defendant was to pay if the defendant wanted to sell or if Mr Langdale wanted it back. I told the defendant about my conversation with Mr Langdale and told him the terms on which he was prepared to sell the house. I suggested that he should go round to see him. Later after the defendant had visited the plaintiffs and agreed the terms of the sale, he discussed the bargain with me and asked my opinion. I told him that it was the best

h thing he could do in the circumstances because I could not help him financially and could not find him a house to rent.'

Presumably with these affidavits before him, Mr Bosomworth swore an affidavit in support of the cross-summons to transfer the High Court proceedings to the county court on 22 November 1979 in which he deposed:

i '. . . the dispute does not appear to give rise to any difficult questions of law, such as would make a High Court trial desirable. It appears, rather, to require the application of well-established principles to facts which will be agreed, or almost agreed.'

Master Dyson having indicated his view that the Langdales were entitled to specific

performance and adjourned the summons to the judge, it was only on the day of the
hearing before Oliver J, 13 December 1979, that Mr Bosomworth swore a further   *a*
affidavit, which contained the following two paragraphs:

> '3. I am informed by the defendant and verily believe that it was explained to the
> defendant by the first named plaintiff that the deed was to protect the plaintiffs as to
> who was to be their neighbour and that if he the defendant wanted to sell the
> property the subject matter of this action he had to give to the plaintiffs the
> opportunity to buy it first . . . 6. In my respectful submission the defendant should   *b*
> have been separately represented in the transaction and that a reasonable option
> would have been to repurchase at a price to be agreed or at a price fixed by an
> independent valuer.'

There was no affidavit from Mr Danby.

Mr Bosomworth was in court at the hearing before Oliver J. As appears from the   *c*
judgment of Oliver J, counsel then appearing for Mr Danby expressly asserted, as he had
before the master, that there was 'no suggestion of any misconduct or anything of that
sort against the plaintiffs, and he then conceded that the only question to be decided was
clog or no clog'. The judge referred to para 6 of Mr Bosomworth's latest affidavit and
added:

> 'It has not been suggested, at any rate up to this stage, that the transaction was in   *d*
> any way open to attack as being induced by undue influence or anything of that
> sort.'

Oliver J decided the 'clog on the equity' point in favour of the Langdales and against
Mr Danby. His decision on this point is now no longer in issue. He accordingly gave
judgment in favour of the Langdales for specific performance.   *e*

It would be tedious in the extreme to rehearse in detail the long history of the
consequential proceedings to which the Langdales were obliged to resort to secure the
enforcement of the judgment given in their favour on 13 December 1979. I hope it is
not unfair to summarise the history by saying that Mr Danby, presumably with the
advice and co-operation of his solicitor, resorted to every conceivable device to deny the
Langdales the fruits of their judgment for as long as possible. In the course of these   *f*
manoeuvres the mortgage loans were repaid. When eventually ordered to complete the
transaction and give vacant possession on 30 June 1981 Mr Danby failed to do so. In July
the conveyance of the cottage to the Langdales was ordered to be and was executed on
Mr Danby's behalf by a Chancery master. Still the Danbys did not move. Eventually a
writ of possession was issued and executed on 17 September 1981 when the Danby
family were evicted amidst a blaze of publicity which one can only suppose had been   *g*
organised by or on behalf of the Danbys and which was calculated to show Mr Langdale
in the worst possible light.

The balance of the purchase price due on completion (a deposit of £265 having been
paid at some earlier stage) was £2,385. But the Langdales' costs of the action, which had
been ordered to be set off against the purchase price, had been taxed at £2,662·91, leaving
a balance due in their favour of £277·91. A substantial proportion of these costs must   *h*
have been incurred since the order of Oliver J. Further costs were incurred by the
Langdales after taxation and before possession was finally obtained. There seems little
prospect of either the certified balance or the further costs ever being recovered.

Within a few days of the Danby's eviction a notice of motion for leave to appeal out of
time against the order of Oliver J was served. On 6 October 1981 the Court of Appeal
(Lord Denning MR, Eveleigh LJ and Sir Stanley Rees) granted that leave. My Lords, with   *j*
the utmost respect, I regard that as a surprising decision. We do not know what the court
was told by counsel, but the affidavit material put before the court on that occasion seems
to me totally deficient of any such explanation or excuse for the delay as to justify
granting an extension of time of nearly two years for appealing against a summary
judgment. An affidavit sworn by Mr Danby, to which I must refer later, has no relevance
to the delay. The affidavit of Mr Bosomworth, so far as relevant to delay at all, said in

effect: (i) junior counsel before Oliver J failed to take the right points; (ii) leading counsel
a in early 1980 had advised against an appeal, but had advised instead an action for damages
for negligence against Mr Langdale's firm (such an action was in fact instituted on 9
January 1981); (iii) after the Danbys' eviction, Mr Bosomworth had decided to take other
advice and had been advised that there were good grounds for appealing. The grant of an
extension of time for appealing is, of course, an exercise of discretion by the Court of
Appeal, but, if there were not more solid grounds for reversing the Court of Appeal's
b decision on the substantive appeal, I should feel it necessary to consider whether the
grant of an extension in this case was not so plainly wrong an exercise of discretion as to
call for reversal by your Lordships' House.

   The substantive appeal was heard by Lord Denning MR, Dunn and Fox LJJ on 19 and
20 November 1981. They gave judgment on 23 November allowing the appeal, setting
aside the judgment of Oliver J and giving Mr Danby unconditional leave to defend. The
c Langdales appeal against that decision by leave of your Lordships' House. Mr Danby, I
should mention, has been legally aided throughout the appellate proceedings and would
presumably continue to be so if the action now proceeded to trial pursuant to the Court
of Appeal's order.

   The Court of Appeal was unanimous in the view that the decision of Oliver J was right
on the material before him. It based its decision on the new evidence which was before
d it in an affidavit sworn by Mr Danby and on new points taken on his behalf which
contradicted the express admission made before Oliver J that no impropriety was alleged
against Mr Langdale.

   The primary and most important question for decision by your Lordships' House is
whether, on hearing an appeal against a summary judgment given in favour of a plaintiff
under RSC Ord 14 or Ord 86, the Court of Appeal has an unfettered discretion to receive
e further evidence or whether it may only do so on special grounds. The question turns on
the true construction of Ord 59, r 10(2), as applied to proceedings under Ord 14 and Ord
86. Order 59, r 10(2), provides:

   'The Court of Appeal shall have power to receive further evidence on questions of
   fact, either by oral examination in court, by affidavit, or by deposition taken before
f   an examiner, but, in the case of an appeal from a judgment after trial or hearing of
   any cause or matter on the merits, no such further evidence (other than evidence as
   to matters which have occurred after the date of the trial or hearing) shall be
   admitted except on special grounds.'

   The course the proceedings took in the Court of Appeal was that the further evidence,
in affidavits sworn by Mr Bosomworth and Mr Danby on 28 September 1981, was put
g before the court on the application for an extension of time. No objection was taken at
that stage. At the substantive hearing the appeal was opened by counsel for Mr Danby
on the basis of the further evidence. It was only when counsel for the Langdales addressed
the court as respondent that he raised the objection that Ord 59, r 10(2), rendered the
evidence in Mr Danby's affidavit inadmissible in the absence of special grounds and that
there were no such special grounds. The point was then fully argued and is dealt with
h expressly in the judgment of Lord Denning MR and, I think, by implication in the
judgments of Dunn and Fox LJJ.

   It was submitted for Mr Danby in your Lordships' House that, both because objection
to the admission of the further evidence was not taken at the first opportunity and
because further affidavits in reply were filed on behalf of the Langdales, they had waived
the objection and could not argue the point under Ord 59, r 10(2), before your Lordships.
j This submission is wholly devoid of substance or merit. The point was clearly taken in
the Court of Appeal. It was not then suggested by counsel for Mr Danby that it was not
open to be taken. Whenever the point had been taken, the Court of Appeal would clearly
have considered the further evidence de bene esse before deciding on its admissibility. It
was only prudent for the Langdales to answer the further evidence, in case their clearly
voiced objection to its admissibility should fail.

   Before turning to the question of construction, I should mention that your Lordships were told from the bar that in recent years it has been treated as settled practice in the Court of Appeal that there is no fetter on the court's discretion to receive further evidence *a* on appeal against a summary judgment. This is evidently the view of Lord Denning MR, who said of counsel for the Langdales' argument on Ord 59, r 10(2):

> 'But that rule and those cases do not apply to summary judgments under Ord 14 or Ord 86. We constantly allow new facts and new points to be raised in this court on appeal from summary judgments, if it be necessary or desirable in the interests of justice.'   *b*

Dunn LJ said:

> 'There has, however, been much more evidence before us which we admitted according to the normal practice set out in *The Supreme Court Practice 1982*, vol 1, para 14/3–4/28, p 178: "... the Court of Appeal has full discretionary power as to admission of further evidence" in Ord 14 proceedings. That also applies to *c* proceedings under Ord 86.'

The full text of the note to Ord 14, rr 3 and 4 in *The Supreme Court Practice* from which Dunn LJ quotes reads as follows:

> '*Evidence on Appeals.*—Should be the same as below; but new affidavits are frequently admitted on appeal to the Judge, and on further appeal a similar *d* indulgence may be granted as a matter of convenience (*Robinson* v. *Bradshaw* ((1883) 32 WR 95)), whilst the Court of Appeal has full discretionary power as to admission of further evidence (O. 59, r. 10(2)).'

Counsel's researches reveal that this note has appeared unaltered in *The Supreme Court Practice* since 1912. It is unfortunately most misleading. The case cited of *Robinson* v *e Bradshaw* is no authority at all for the proposition in the note. It was decided in 1883, when appeals from chambers went not to the Court of Appeal but to the Divisional Court, which was not subject to the rule then in force corresponding to Ord 59, r 10(2). In any event the very short report, without revealing any of the circumstances, merely shows that it was thought 'a matter of convenience' in that case to read the new affidavit tendered.   *f*

Apart from this misleading note, no authority in support of the practice was cited. It does not appear that, before this case, the application of the rule in question (or any of its predecessors in similar terms) to appeal from summary judgments has ever been considered. If, on its true construction the rule requires that on the hearing of such appeals further evidence may only be admitted on special grounds then the rule must prevail and any practice to the contrary must be discontinued.   *g*

Since we are here concerned with proceedings under Ord 86, it will be convenient to set out the relevant provisions of that order, though corresponding provisions can also be found in Ord 14. Order 86 provides as follows:

> '*Application by plaintiff for summary judgment*
> 1.—(1) In any action in the Chancery Division begun by writ indorsed with a claim—(a) for specific performance of an agreement ... for the sale, purchase or *h* exchange of any property ... the plaintiff may, on the ground that the defendant has no defence to the action, apply to the Court for judgment ...
>
> *Manner in which application under rule 1 must be made*
> 2.—(1) An application under rule 1 shall be made by summons supported by an *j* affidavit verifying the facts on which the cause of action is based and stating that in the deponent's belief there is no defence to the action ...
>
> *Judgment for plaintiff*
> 4. Unless on the hearing of an application under rule 1 either the Court dismisses the application or the defendant satisfies the Court that there is an issue or question

a in dispute which ought to be tried or that there ought for some other reason to be a
trial of the action, the Court may give judgment for the plaintiff in the action.

Leave to defend

5.—(1) A defendant may show cause against an application under rule 1 by
affidavit or otherwise to the satisfaction of the Court.

b (2) The Court may give a defendant against whom such an application is made
leave to defend the action either unconditionally or on such terms as to giving
security or time or mode of trial or otherwise as it thinks fit . . .'

When judgment given for a plaintiff under Ord 86, r 4, is under appeal, is this 'an
appeal from a judgment after trial or hearing of any cause or matter on the merits'?
These are the critical words to be construed. There is plainly 'an appeal from a judgment'.
In the light of the distinction drawn in Ord 86, r 4, between 'the hearing of [the]
c application' and 'a trial of the action', the judgment is not 'after trial'; but I can see no
plausible argument that it is not 'after [the] hearing of any cause'. 'Cause', by definition,
includes an action, and since a summary judgment for the plaintiff under Ord 86, r 4,
disposes of the action it can only result from a hearing of the action. The only point of
construction which, at first blush, might seem debatable is whether the hearing is 'on the
merits'. But, on analysis, it seems to me that these words are as clearly apt to embrace a
d hearing under Ord 86 which results in judgment for the plaintiff as the trial of an action.
What the judge must do before he gives judgment for the plaintiff under r 4 is to be
satisfied that the merits of the plaintiff's claim are duly verified as required by r 2 and,
more importantly, that the defendant has failed to mount a sufficient challenge to those
merits on the law or on the facts to show that there is any issue or question in dispute
which ought to be tried. In other words, the judge can only give judgment for the
e plaintiff if satisfied that there are no such merits on the defendant's side as to warrant
giving leave to defend. In the ordinary use of language, a hearing leading to the
conclusion that there are no merits to be tried is just as much a hearing 'on the merits' as
a full scale trial of disputed issues.

I accordingly reach the conclusion that the language of Ord 59, r 10(2), which excludes
the admission of further evidence on appeal to the Court of Appeal except on special
f grounds is, in its ordinary meaning, applicable to appeals against summary judgments
given for plaintiffs under Ord 14 or Ord 86. But I am powerfully reinforced in this
construction of the rule by the consideration that the principle underlying this restrictive
provision applies with at least equal, if not indeed greater, force to a summary judgment
as to judgment after trial. In *Brown v Dean* [1910] AC 373 at 374, [1908–10] All ER Rep
661 at 662 Lord Loreburn LC said:

g
'My Lords, the chief effect of the argument which your Lordships have heard is
to confirm in my mind the extreme value of the old doctrine "Interest reipublicae
ut sit finis litium", remembering as we should that people who have means at their
command are easily able to exhaust the resources of a poor antagonist . . . When a
litigant has obtained a judgment in a Court of justice . . . he is by law entitled not to
h be deprived of that judgment without very solid grounds . . .'

I would paraphrase the first part of this quotation, to bring it up to date, by saying that
'people who have the legal aid fund at their command are easily able to exhaust the
resources of an antagonist who does not qualify for legal aid'. But, leaving that aside, the
principle that a successful litigant is not lightly to be deprived of his judgment seems to
me of particular importance to a plaintiff, frequently pursuing a recalcitrant and
j obstructive defendant, who has secured a judgment by showing that the defendant has
no defence.

The classic statement of what amounts to 'special grounds' within the meaning of Ord
59, r 10(2), comes from the judgment of Denning LJ in *Ladd v Marshall* [1954] 3 All ER
745 at 748, [1954] 1 WLR 1489 at 1491, and was expressly approved by your Lordships'
House in *Skone v Skone* [1971] 2 All ER 582 at 586, [1971] 1 WLR 812 at 815 in the speech

of Lord Hodson with which all the other members of the Appellate Committee agreed.
The statement reads:

'In order to justify the reception of fresh evidence or a new trial, three conditions
must be fulfilled: first, it must be shown that the evidence could not have been
obtained with reasonable diligence for use at the trial: second, the evidence must be
such that, if given, it would probably have an important influence on the result of
the case, although it need not be decisive: third, the evidence must be such as is
presumably to be believed, or in other words, it must be apparently credible, though
it need not be incontrovertible.'

In the situation arising on an appeal to the Court of Appeal from a summary judgment,
the application of these conditions and perhaps the conditions themselves will require
some modification. It may well be that the standard of diligence required of a defendant
preparing his case in opposition to a summons for summary judgment, especially if
under pressure of time, will not be so high as that required in preparing for trial. The
second and third conditions will no doubt be satisfied if the further evidence tendered is
sufficient, according to the ordinary principles applied on applications for summary
judgment, to raise a triable issue. But I can see no injustice at all in requiring a defendant
to use such diligence as is reasonable in the circumstances to put before the judge on the
hearing of the summons, albeit in summary form, all the evidence he relies on in
defence, whereas it would be a great injustice to the plaintiff to allow the defendant to
introduce for the first time on appeal evidence which was readily available at the hearing
of the summons but was not produced.

It follows from what I have said that the Court of Appeal misdirected itself in holding
that it was open to it to admit Mr Danby's affidavit in evidence without special grounds.
Counsel for Mr Danby nevertheless submits that there are special grounds for admission
of that affidavit, alternatively that even without it the original affidavits of Mr
Bosomworth should entitle Mr Danby to unconditional leave to defend. To understand
these submissions, it is necessary to appreciate that the issue of fact sought to be raised is
whether Mr Langdale in 1964 explained to Mr Danby the effect of the option deed. Such
an issue, says counsel for Mr Danby, is of general public importance as reflecting on the
professional conduct of a solicitor and ought not to be shut out by any procedural
technicality.

The affidavit of Mr Danby, sworn on 28 September 1981, is very remarkable. It merely
exhibits a statement which Mr Danby made to Mr Bosomworth on 7 June 1979 and
asserts that the facts in that statement are true. It says further that the earlier statement
was made 'for the purposes of my defence in these proceedings'. This is clearly inaccurate.
The proceedings were not commenced until 29 October 1979. However, this may be of
little significance. So far as I can see, the only paragraph in Mr Danby's statement of
7 June which is of any relevance reads as follows:

'So far as the deed of the 12th March 1965 is concerned, I think that Mr. Langdale
did tell me about this but the impression that I got (and certainly it is still clear in
my mind) was that he was doing this in order to protect himself as to who was to be
his neighbour. It never for one moment crossed my mind that I would not have
complete freedom with regard to the house when I had bought it. All I understood
that I was doing was that if I wanted to move and sell the property I had to give Mr.
Langdale the chance to buy it first.'

This statement was made before the original affidavits of Mr and Mrs Langdale and
Mr Cogan were sworn. Mr Danby has never made an affidavit denying anything said in
those affidavits. The affidavits of Mr Bosomworth sworn on 22 November and 13
December 1979 cannot possibly be read as putting in issue any of the evidence tendered
in support of the Langdales' claim. Moreover, Mr Bosomworth, in his latest affidavit,
though he waives his client's privilege by disclosing a letter he wrote to junior counsel

two days before the hearing before Oliver J, does not disclose what advice counsel gave
a him and offers no explanation of how counsel came to make the express admission both
before the master and the judge that no impropriety was alleged against Mr Langdale.
Your Lordships, in the absence of clear evidence to the contrary, are entitled to assume
that counsel satisfied himself that the admission was, on his own client's version of the
facts, a proper admission to make.

In the light of all these considerations, the evidence to support the assertion that Mr
b Langdale failed to explain the effect of the option deed to Mr Danby is tenuous in the
extreme. Assuming, without accepting, that the conditions for the admission of evidence
on 'special grounds' as laid down in *Ladd v Marshall* and approved in *Skone v Skone* do not
apply when the evidence relates to the propriety of a solicitor's conduct, because that is a
matter of public concern, this principle certainly could only apply when the evidence
was of a solid and substantial character and there was at least *some* sensible explanation of
c why it had previously been held back. Accordingly there are no 'special grounds' for
admitting Mr Danby's affidavit and without it there is no issue to be tried.

Two further matters need to be mentioned.

An argument advanced by counsel for Mr Danby in the Court of Appeal, which was
not renewed in your Lordships House but is reflected in the judgment of Lord Denning
MR, appears to suggest that even if Mr Danby was fully aware of the terms of the option
d Mr Langdale owed him a duty, as his solicitor, to advise him against entering the
transaction as being against his interest. It must be remembered that, according to Mr
Langdale's uncontradicted account, the whole bargain, sale of the cottage at £2,650
subject to reservation of the rights of pre-emption and option for 21 years at the same
price, was first agreed. Second, the finance was arranged. Then and only then did Mr
Danby reveal that he could not afford to employ a solicitor and Mr Langdale agree to do
e the conveyancing work gratuitously, disbursements excepted. To my mind, the
suggestion that at this final stage Mr Langdale was in breach of duty in not advising Mr
Danby to call the whole thing off is untenable.

Finally, it was argued for the Langdales, independently of any other points, that Mr
Danby should not be permitted to withdraw the admissions made on his behalf before
Oliver J. The Court of Appeal unanimously rejected this submission. Lord Denning MR
f and Dunn LJ relied on *H Clark (Doncaster) Ltd v Wilkinson* [1965] 1 All ER 934, [1965] Ch
694. That was a case where an admission made by counsel, without instructions, on the
hearing of a Chancery summons before a district registrar was allowed to be withdrawn
when the summons was adjourned to the judge, on the ground that the other party had
not acted to his detriment on the faith of the mistaken admission. There are many
reasons why, with respect, I regard that case as so far removed from the circumstances of
g the present case as to have no relevance. But let it be assumed that Mr Danby could only
be held bound by counsel's admission that no impropriety of conduct was to be attributed
to Mr Langdale if the Langdales had acted to their detriment on the faith of it, so as to
create an estoppel. The members of the Court of Appeal dealt with this point differently.
Lord Denning MR cited *Clark's* case, said: 'Even admissions by counsel can be withdrawn
unless the circumstances are such as to give rise to an estoppel.' He implies that no
h estoppel arose in the present case, though without explaining why. Dunn LJ said:

'It does not seem to me that it can be said that the plaintiffs acted to their
detriment on the faith of counsel for the defendant's failure to take before the judge
the points now taken in this court. On the contrary, as a result of that, they obtained
summary judgment and ultimately possession of the property, and the subsequent
j delay was caused by the tactics of the defendant and his advisers and not by the way
the case was presented before the judge. These matters might, it seems to me, have
been relevant to the grant of leave to appeal out of time; but, once leave to appeal
was given, two arguable issues having been raised, in my judgment the defendant
is entitled to a trial of those issues.'

Fox LJ said:

> 'Nevertheless, it does not seem to me that a case of prejudice has been disclosed. *a* It is perfectly true that Mr and Mrs Langdale have spent money on costs in pursuing the order they obtained for specific performance. That is a matter which, it seems to me, goes only to costs and not to substance, and I think the matter can be dealt with by considering the question of costs separately.'

My Lords, with all respect, I cannot agree with any of the reasons suggested for holding *b* that the conduct of Mr Danby's case before Oliver J and in particular the admission that no impropriety was attributed to Mr Langdale did not estop Mr Danby from alleging, nearly two years later, that the judgment of Oliver J could be reversed on grounds which were not taken before Oliver J and which directly accused Mr Langdale of improper conduct as a solicitor. In this context, I confess I simply do not understand the distinctions sought to be drawn by Dunn LJ between the conduct of the case before Oliver J and Mr *c* Danby's subsequent delaying tactics or between the grant of leave to appeal out of time and the decision of the appeal itself, or that drawn by Fox LJ between matter going to costs and matter going to substance.

As I see it the direct result of the conduct of Mr Danby's case before Oliver J was to permit the Langdales to obtain summary judgment. They then spent nearly two years in time and a great deal of money in costs in the course of enforcing that judgment. True *d* it is that part, but part only, of the costs so incurred could be and were set off against the balance of the purchase price of the cottage due to Mr Danby, probably Mr Danby's only significant resource. But now, if the Court of Appeal judgment were to stand, the Langdales would face a full scale trial against a legally-aided defendant in which, though they succeeded, they would have little prospect of recovering any of their costs. Looking at this history in a commonsense way, it seems to me beyond argument that the *e* Langdales will have acted to their detriment, on the faith of the conduct of Mr Danby's case which enabled them to obtain summary judgment, by spending large sums to enforce that judgment, if they are now denied the benefit of it by allowing Mr Danby to set up a case which conflicts radically with the case presented on his behalf before Oliver J. Independently of any other ground I would, therefore, hold Mr Danby estopped from arguing the case on which he succeeded in the Court of Appeal. *f*

My Lords, for all these reasons I would allow the appeal, set aside the order of the Court of Appeal and restore the judgment of Oliver J. Bearing fully in mind the recent observations of your Lordships' House, in *Din v Wandsworth London Borough Council (No 2)* [1982] 1 All ER 1022, [1982] 1 WLR 418, this seems to me, subject to any submissions advanced on behalf of the Law Society for which the usual opportunity should be provided, pre-eminently a case where it would be just and equitable to order the costs of *g* the Langdales in the Court of Appeal and this House to be paid out of the legal aid fund pursuant to s 13 of the Legal Aid Act 1974.

LORD BRIGHTMAN. My Lords, I also agree with the speech of my noble and learned friend Lord Bridge and would allow this appeal.

Appeal allowed.

Solicitors: *Warren, Murton & Co*, agents for *Stamp, Jackson & Procter*, Hull (for Mr and Mrs Langdale); *Lake, Parry & Treadwell*, agents for *John Bosomworth & Co*, Leeds (for Mr Danby).

Mary Rose Plummer   Barrister.

Chief Constable of the North Wales Police v Evans

HOUSE OF LORDS

LORD HAILSHAM OF ST MARYLEBONE LC, LORD FRASER OF TULLYBELTON, LORD ROSKILL, LORD BRIDGE OF HARWICH AND LORD BRIGHTMAN

21, 22 JUNE, 22 JULY 1982

Police – Dismissal – Constable – Probationer constable – Chief constable deciding to dispense with services of constable on basis of certain allegations and rumours – Constable informed that if he did not resign he would be dismissed – Constable not given opportunity to refute allegations and rumours – Whether chief constable having absolute discretion to discharge constable – Whether chief constable required to observe rules of natural justice before exercising discretion – Police Regulations 1971, reg 16(1).

Judicial review – Availability of remedy – Mandamus – Wrongful dismissal of police constable – Rules of natural justice not observed in dismissal procedure – Impractical to order reinstatement – Whether mandamus should be issued requiring constable to be reinstated – Whether constable merely entitled to declaration that he was entitled to rights and remedies not including reinstatement.

The respondent was a probationer constable undergoing training with a police force. He received good reports on his progress from his instructors who stated that there was no reason to doubt his becoming a reliable and competent constable. However, during his probationary period, certain rumours started concerning his private life. Those rumours were largely unfounded but, following inquiries made by the respondent's superiors, the chief constable believed them to be true and decided to dispense with the services of the respondent under reg 16(1)[a] of the Police Regulations 1971, which provided for the discharge of a probationer constable if the chief constable considered 'that he [was] not fitted ... to perform the duties of his office or that he [was] not likely to become an efficient or well conducted constable'. The chief constable did not put to the respondent the allegations and rumours on which he based his decision nor did he offer the respondent an opportunity to offer any explanation, but he informed him that if he did not resign he would be discharged. The respondent resigned and began proceedings against the chief constable seeking (i) an order of certiorari to quash the chief constable's decision that the respondent should resign or be discharged, (ii) an order of mandamus requiring the chief constable to reinstate the respondent to the office of police constable, and (iii) a declaration that the chief constable's decision requiring the respondent to resign or be discharged was illegal, ultra vires and void. In an affidavit sworn in the proceedings, the chief constable asserted that reg 16(1) gave him an absolute discretion to dispense with a probationer constable's services. The judge held that the decision of the chief constable did not accord with the standards of fairness that should have been observed, but that no relief should be granted except in regard to costs. The respondent appealed in order to obtain substantive relief. The chief constable cross-appealed. The Court of Appeal confirmed the conclusion of the judge but added a declaration that the decision of the chief constable requiring the respondent to resign or be dismissed was void. The chief constable appealed.

Held – (1) It was plain from the wording of reg 16(1) of the 1971 regulations that the

---

a   Regulation 16(1), so far as material, provides: '... during his period of probation in the force the services of a constable may be dispensed with at any time if the chief officer of police considers that he is not fitted, physically or mentally, to perform the duties of his office, or that he is not likely to become an efficient or well conducted constable.'

power of a chief constable to dispense with the services of a probationer constable was not an absolute discretion, but was to be exercised only after due consideration and *a* determination of whether the constable was fitted to perform the duties of his office or was likely to become an efficient and well conducted constable. The chief constable's decision to force the resignation of the respondent was vitiated by his erroneous assumption that he had an absolute discretion and by his total failure to observe the rules of natural justice in not giving the respondent the opportunity to refute the allegations on which the chief constable relied (see p 144 *b* to *j*, p 145 *e f*, p 146 *h j*, p 147 *a* to *e* and *b* p 154 *a b* and *g* to p 155 *b*, post); dictum of Lord Reid in *Ridge v Baldwin* [1963] 2 All ER at 72 followed.

(2) On the question of the appropriate remedy, the respondent was entitled at least to a declaration that the chief constable had acted unlawfully and in breach of his duty under reg 16 of the 1971 regulations. However, although an order of mandamus to reinstate the respondent was the only satisfactory remedy in consequence of that breach *c* of duty, to make such an order would be impractical and might border on a usurpation of the powers of the chief constable by the court and therefore the court would restrict itself to issuing a further declaration affirming that, by reason of his unlawfully induced resignation, the respondent thereby became entitled to the same rights and remedies, not including reinstatement, as he would have had if the chief constable had unlawfully dispensed with his services under reg 16 (see p 146 *g h*, p 147 *a b* and *h* to p 148 *d*, p 155 *h* *d* *j* and p 156 *a d e* and *g*, post).

Per curiam. Judicial review is not an appeal from a decision but a review of the manner in which the decision was made, and therefore the court is not entitled on an application for judicial review to consider whether the decision itself was fair and reasonable (see p 143 *h*, p 144 *a*, p 146 *h*, p 147 *a b*, p 154 *c* and p 155 *c d*, post).

Per Lord Hailsham LC and Lord Bridge. A chief officer of police who is contemplating *e* dispensing with the services of a probationer constable under reg 16 may delegate the investigation of a specific complaint to a suitable subordinate but (per Lord Bridge) (i) the delegate should make clear to the constable the precise nature of the complaint and that he, the delegate, is acting on behalf of the chief officer of police to hear whatever the constable wishes to say about it, (ii) the delegate should make a full report of what the constable has said, and (iii) the chief officer himself should show the report to the *f* constable and invite any comment on it before reaching any decision under reg 16 (see p 144 *e* to *g* and p 147 *e f*, post).

Notes
For breach of natural justice, see 1 Halsbury's Laws (4th edn) 64, and for cases on the subject, see 1(1) Digest (Reissue) 200–201, 1772–1176. *g*
For the Police Regulations 1971, reg 16, see 17 Halsbury's Statutory Instruments (3rd reissue) 278.

Cases referred to in opinions
Associated Provincial Picture Houses Ltd v Wednesbury Corp [1947] 2 All ER 680, [1948] 1 KB 223, CA, 45 Digest (Repl) 215, *189*. *h*
Ridge v Baldwin [1963] 2 All ER 66, [1964] AC 40, [1963] 2 WLR 935, HL, 37 Digest (Repl) 195, *32*.

Appeal
Philip Meyers, Chief Constable of the North Wales Police, appealed with leave of the House of Lords granted on 13 January 1982 against the order of the Court of Appeal *j* (Lord Denning, MR, Shaw and Ackner LJJ) dated 21 December 1981 in so far as the Court of Appeal (i) allowed an appeal by the respondent, Michael John Evans, against the decision of Woolf J hearing the Divisional Court list on 23 March 1981 whereby he refused to make an order save as to costs on the respondent's application for judicial review by way of orders for certiorari and mandamus and a declaration in respect of the applicant's decision of 7 November 1978 requiring the respondent to resign or be

dismissed from the North Wales Police Force, (ii) dismissed the appellant's cross-appeal,
a and (iii) declared that the appellant's decision of 7 November 1978 was void. The facts
are set out in the opinion of Lord Brightman.

Martin Thomas QC and *Alexander Carlile* for the chief constable.
Roger Gray QC and *Michael Jefferis* for the respondent.

b Their Lordships took time for consideration.

22 July. The following opinions were delivered.

LORD HAILSHAM OF ST MARYLEBONE LC. My Lords, the analysis of the
facts and argument contained in the speech of my noble and learned friend Lord
c Brightman, which I have read in draft, relieve me of much of the labour in this case, and
enable me to reduce the few observations I wish to make to reasonably concise
proportions. I desire, however, to say at the outset that I agree with every word which is
about to fall from my noble and learned friend as to the treatment to which this young
respondent has been subjected by the chief constable. Like my noble and learned friend,
I do not doubt the chief constable's good faith, but in the result, partly as the result of
d muddle, partly as the result of a false view of the law, and partly as the result of a
disregard of the elementary principles of natural justice, I regard the treatment meted
out to this young man as little short of outrageous.
    Briefly, the proceedings originated in an application by the respondent for judicial
review under RSC Ord 53 of a decision by the appellant (then Chief Constable of the
Police Force of North Wales) whereby in November 1978 he had given the respondent,
e at that time a probationary constable, the option of resignation from office or dismissal
on a month's notice under reg 16 of the relevant regulations. In the event, the respondent
had chosen resignation, but had sought relief under RSC Ord 53 on the basis that he had
been treated unfairly and in a manner contrary to natural justice.
    The first observation I wish to make is by way of criticism of some remarks of Lord
Denning MR which seem to me capable of an erroneous construction of the purpose of
f the remedy by way of judicial review under RSC Ord 53. This remedy, vastly increased
in extent, and rendered, over a long period in recent years, of infinitely more convenient
access than that provided by the old prerogative writs and actions for a declaration, is
intended to protect the individual against the abuse of power by a wide range of
authorities, judicial, quasi-judicial, and, as would originally have been thought when I
first practised at the Bar, administrative. It is not intended to take away from those
g authorities the powers and discretions properly vested in them by law and to substitute
the courts as the bodies making the decisions. It is intended to see that the relevant
authorities use their powers in a proper manner.
    Since the range of authorities, and the circumstances of the use of their power, are
almost infinitely various, it is of course unwise to lay down rules for the application of
the remedy which appear to be of universal validity in every type of case. But it is
h important to remember in every case that the purpose of the remedies is to ensure that
the individual is given fair treatment by the authority to which he has been subjected
and that it is no part of that purpose to substitute the opinion of the judiciary or of
individual judges for that of the authority constituted by law to decide the matters in
question. The function of the court is to see that lawful authority is not abused by unfair
treatment and not to attempt itself the task entrusted to that authority by the law. There
j are passages in the judgment of Lord Denning MR (and perhaps in the other judgments
of the Court of Appeal) in the instant case and quoted by my noble and learned friend
which might be read as giving the courts carte blanche to review the decision of the
authority on the basis of what the courts themselves consider fair and reasonable on the
merits. I am not sure whether Lord Denning MR really intended his remarks to be
construed in such a way as to permit the court to examine, as for instance in the present
case, the reasoning of the subordinate authority with a view to substituting its own

opinion. If so, I do not think this is a correct statement of principle. The purpose of judicial review is to ensure that the individual receives fair treatment, and not to ensure *a* that the authority, after according fair treatment, reaches on a matter which it is authorised or enjoined by law to decide for itself a conclusion which is correct in the eyes of the court.

In the instant case I have no doubt that the respondent was not treated fairly by the chief constable. In the first place by his own affidavit the chief constable establishes that he asked himself the wrong question, and, once this has been established, for the purposes *b* of judicial review, that by itself is surely enough to vitiate an impugned decision which is not otherwise self-evidently justified. The relevant regulation enjoined the chief constable to consider whether the respondent was 'fitted physically or mentally to perform the duties of his office' or was likely to 'become an efficient or well-conducted constable' before dispensing with his services. In his affidavit the chief constable claimed that this regulation 'gives me an absolute discretion to dispense with a probationer's *c* services'. In my opinion the discretion, although wide, is not absolute. The chief constable should have directed his mind to the criteria laid down in the regulation in accordance with the appropriate principles of natural justice. He did not do so, and I think it only too likely that it was precisely the belief that his discretion was absolute which led to the cavalier treatment to which, in the event, the respondent was subjected.

To this treatment I now come. Once it is established as was conceded here, that the *d* office held by the chief constable was of the third class enumerated by Lord Reid in *Ridge v Baldwin* [1963] 2 All ER 66 at 72, [1964] AC 40 at 66, it becomes clear, quoting Lord Reid, that there is 'an unbroken line of authority to the effect that an officer cannot lawfully be dismissed without first telling him what is alleged against him and hearing his defence or explanation'. I regard this rule as fundamental in cases of this kind when deprivation of office is in question. I agree with the chief constable's affidavit that 'a *e* formal hearing' may well be unnecessary if by that is meant an oral hearing in every case held before the chief constable himself. But this does not dispense a chief constable from observing the rule laid down by Lord Reid. It may well be also that part or all of the inquiry on the facts may be delegated to a subordinate official, as was done here by the chief constable to the deputy chief constable, though, where this is done, the ultimate decision must not be delegated, and in my view, common prudence should dictate that *f* the report by the delegated officer, in this case the deputy chief constable, or at least its susbstance, should be shown to the officer the subject of review and an opportunity afforded him to comment on it before the final decision is taken by the chief constable himself. This was not done here. Moreover, where there has been delegation, the delegated inquiry itself must be conducted in accordance with Lord Reid's rule, and, where it is not, the ultimate decision, even if not delegated, will almost certainly be *g* vitiated.

Apart from his self misdirection on the scope of his discretion, in the present case the chief constable clearly admitted in his affidavit that he had taken into account matters concerning the domestic life of the respondent, some of which, if properly put to the respondent, might perhaps, after his explanation had been given and heard, have influenced the decision as to whether the respondent was likely to become an efficient or *h* well-conducted constable. But some of the allegations were plainly erroneous and none, whether erroneous or otherwise, was ever put to the respondent at all in connection with the relevant inquiry, whether at the delegated hearing or otherwise. Moreover, it was conceded by counsel for the chief constable that, at the time of the extremely brief interview at which the decision was made by the chief constable, the chief constable had already made up his mind to dispense with the respondent's services on the basis of the *j* report made to him by the deputy chief constable, and the respondent was given no chance to say anything by way of denial of the facts alleged in the report or in mitigation of them.

As an example of the extreme danger of proceeding in this way, it must be observed, that, as one of the two clinching matters which seem to have influenced him, the chief constable says in his affidavit:

'Further, it became known (sic) to Senior Officers that the Applicant and his wife
a   had lived a "hippy" type lifestyle at Tyddyn Mynyddig Farm, Bangor.'

This had never been put to the respondent at all, and had the chief constable or his deputy
to whom he delegated the inquiry taken the trouble to ask the respondent about it, he
would have discovered at once that this allegedly clinching allegation was palpably
untrue, and simply the result of a mistaken address. It was, in short, an utterly incorrect
b   statement relied on precisely owing to the failure of natural justice of which complaint
is made.

   There is room for greater controversy regarding the other matter supposedly clinching.
There was a finding by the deputy who conducted the inquiry that the respondent had
'deliberately flouted' the conditions of tenancy at his council house by keeping dogs in
excess of the number permitted by the council and that this exhibited an attitude to
c   authority improper in a member of the police force. This matter had indeed been put to
the respondent in some form, but there is a conflict of evidence relating to the interview,
of which only the respondent's version is on oath. Without seeking to resolve this
conflict, I am of the opinion that natural justice required that it should have been put
precisely to the respondent that exact compliance with the conditions of tenancy within
the extended time permitted by the council, which at the time of the interview had not
d   yet expired, would probably be a condition of his continuance in office as a probationary
constable. It is clear that this was not done and it is fair to the respondent to say that he
deposed on oath that, had it been put in this way, 'I would have disposed of the dogs'.
Without going into this conclusively, I must express doubt whether, on a fair view of the
evidence, the chief constable, had he applied his mind at all to the correct criteria, or to
the evidence available to him in his file, or had he given the respondent a chance to speak,
e   could possibly have come to the conclusion that the facts relating to this aspect of the
matter betrayed an attitude to authority inconsistent with the view that he could at the
conclusion of his probationary period become an efficient or well-conducted constable,
or that the respondent was in any sense deliberately flouting authority. However this
may be, the decision of the chief constable was, it seems to me, vitiated beyond repair
partly by the fact that the chief constable does not appear to have directed his mind to
f   the correct criteria laid down in the regulations, and partly by the fact that he certainly
took into account matters which were never put to the respondent in connection with
the relevant inquiry, one of which, and not the least important, had it been put, would
have been immediately exposed as nonsense.

   Like my noble and learned friend, I find much more difficulty in deciding the order
which it is appropriate for the House to make in a case such as the present. In *Ridge v
g   Baldwin* [1963] 2 All ER 66, [1964] AC 40, a majority of the House, in not dissimilar
circumstances, granted a declaration that the decision of the watch committee was 'void'.
This was the language adopted by the Court of Appeal in the instant case. Personally, I
find difficulty in applying the language of 'void' and 'voidable' (appropriate enough in
situations of contract or of alleged nullity of marriage) to administrative decisions which
give rise to practical and legal consequences which cannot be reversed. Under pressure,
h   which I have considered to be inappropriate and unfair, the respondent, nearly four years
ago, was compelled to resign as an alternative to dismissal from office. That was in
November 1978. He was then a probationary constable with ten months of service to
run. I am inclined to think that his decision, though made under duress, to pursue the
option of resignation did put an end to the tenure of his office as a constable. If so, a
declaration simply to declare void the decision of the chief constable to offer the
j   respondent a Hobson's choice between resignation and dismissal is a mere brutum
fulmen without practical consequences. This may be illustrated by asking a number of
quasi rhetorical questions. If the decision was 'void', has the respondent been a constable
in the police force in North Wales in the intervening four years and what has happened
to the ten months of uncompleted probationary service? Since the only decision
removing him from office was the decision now impugned has he now become an
established constable? Has he acquired pension rights? Is he entitled to back pay? The

respondent has moved house. We are told that he has found other, though less rewarding, employment in the Civil Service. Can we simply put the clock back as if nothing has *a* taken place? Presumably the respondent has lost much of his training and experience. If he returned, and if he is still a probationary constable, he would still be subject to reg 16 and the possibility, after a fair inquiry, of dismissal on a month's notice. It might well be thought that after what has happened it might be considered by the new chief constable that the respondent could not become an efficient constable or at least not without further training. His counsel said that, if reinstated, he would apply for a transfer to *b* another force. But what possible guarantee have we that another force would now have him, or that the transfer would be in the public interest if it did? These would be matters for the relevant authority. The respondent has not sought damages, which, in my view, might well have proved substantial, and, though the chief constable stated to us that he would be prepared to pay compensation if the appeal went against him on the merits, even in the face of this, the respondent through his counsel, firmly stated that he was not *c* interested in money and simply wanted 'reinstatement' whatever that might mean. This problem did not arise in *Ridge v Baldwin* where the chief constable did not seek reinstatement, and was content with a declaration and his pension rights.

Are we then to leave the respondent wholly without remedy without spelling out the consequences? In that case, the order of the Court of Appeal stands and the decision of the chief constable is declared 'void' without spelling out what this means. It would be *d* possible, of course, simply to quash the decision of the appellant as in the old writ of certiorari. But this, too, would leave the parties without a clue as to their present position or any direction as to their future conduct. But what the respondent wishes is reinstatement. There is no cross appeal, but it must be within the power of your Lordships' House to vary the order of the Court of Appeal. My own belief is that this would have been pre-eminently a case which would have been dealt with most effectively *e* either by re-engagement perhaps on a fresh term, which the chief constable does not offer, or by substantial monetary compensation for which the respondent does not ask. Your Lordships' House is therefore put in a position in which it is compelled to make an order within the limits of the powers given the court by RSC Ord 53 which must in any circumstances be less than satisfactory. I must confess to surprise, and, even to some degree of indignation, that, despite the offer of compensation should the tide of argument *f* go against him, the chief constable gave no instructions to counsel to tender to the respondent the smallest expression of regret at the really extraordinary treatment meted out to him or even the most qualified offer of re-engagement in the face of the respondent's persistent desire to rejoin the force (described in much greater detail and with great restraint by my noble and learned friend). As it is, the order of the Court of Appeal cannot stand unaltered, and the best that your Lordships' House can properly do *g* for the respondent is the course proposed by my noble and learned friend with which I now concur. Happily, the Appeal Committee, as a condition of giving leave to appeal, directed that the chief constable bear the respondent's costs of the appeal in any event.

LORD FRASER OF TULLYBELTON. My Lords, I have had the advantage of reading in draft the speech of my noble and learned friend Lord Brightman, and I agree *h* with it.

I wish to emphasise that the only matter which I am deciding is that the process by which the chief constable reached his decision in this case was unfair in respect that the respondent was never told the reasons why his dismissal was being considered, and that he was given no opportunity of making an explanation about the matters of complaint against him. I am far from saying that, if the procedure had been fair, the chief constable *j* would not have been entitled to reach the decision that he did. Whether the decision itself was fair and reasonable is not a matter that can be raised in the present proceedings, but, having regard to the criticisms of the chief constable's decision made by the Court of Appeal, I think it is only right to say that if he had decided, after hearing the respondent's explanations, that the respondent's conduct in marrying a woman who had been living in the same house as him on the footing that she was his aunt showed that he

a was not likely to become a well conducted constable, I very much doubt whether the
decision could have been said to be unreasonable.

I agree that the two declarations proposed by Lord Brightman should be made.

LORD ROSKILL. My Lords, I have had the advantage of reading in draft the speech
prepared by my noble and learned friend Lord Brightman, with which I agree and I too
would dismiss the appeal.

b
LORD BRIDGE OF HARWICH. My Lords, the facts of this most unhappy case are
fully set out in the speech of my noble and learned friend Lord Brightman. There are
only certain aspects of the case on which I wish to comment.

The chief constable's decision to force the resignation of the respondent was vitiated
both by his erroneous assumption that he had an absolute discretion and by his total
c failure to observe the rules of natural justice. The matters considered fell into two
categories, first the respondent's private life and domestic circumstances, second his
keeping four dogs in the council house rented for his occupation by the police authority.
In the first category, because the chief constable gave the respondent no opportunity to
refute the allegations against him, he acted on false information. If the truth had been
established, the only matters for consideration under this head would have been that the
d respondent was married to a lady some fourteen years older than himself whom he had
previously treated as an aunt, because she had for some years lived as man and wife,
although not married, with the respondent's uncle by whom she had four children. For
my part, I should regard these matters as irrelevant to the question whether the
respondent was likely to become an efficient or well-conducted constable.

With regard to the dogs, I do not dissent from the view that a chief officer of police
e who is contemplating dispensing with the services of a probationer constable under reg
16 of the Police Regulations 1971, SI 1971/156, may delegate to a suitable subordinate
the investigation of a specific complaint with a view to giving the constable a fair
opportunity to meet the allegations made against him. But in the case of such delegation
certain conditions should be observed. First the delegate should make clear to the
constable the precise nature of the complaint and that he, the delegate, is acting on behalf
f of the chief officer of police to hear whatever the constable wishes to say about it. Second,
the delegate should make a full report to the chief officer of what the constable has said.
Third, the chief officer should himself show the report to the constable and invite any
comment on it before reaching any decision under reg 16.

The evidence as to what happened with regard to the respondent's dogs is the least
satisfactory part of this case. The memorandum of 6 November 1978 of the deputy chief
g constable exhibited to the affidavit of the chief constable contains matter which has never
been verified by an affidavit of the deputy chief constable, although much of it is flatly
contradicted by the affidavit of the respondent. Of the three conditions I have referred to
above as necessary to the investigation of a complaint by a delegate of the chief officer of
police, it is doubtful if the first two were observed. It is certain that the third was not.
On the probabilities, it is hard to believe that the respondent, whose dedicated enthusiasm
h for a police career has never been doubted, if faced with the stark alternatives of removing
three of his dogs from his council house or being dismissed from the force, would have
chosen the latter.

My Lords, I agree with my noble and learned friends, the Lord Chancellor and Lord
Brightman, that the most difficult problem posed by this appeal is to decide what remedy
is appropriate and further that the form of declaration made by the Court of Appeal is
i unsatisfactory in that its practical consequences are uncertain. So far as it lies within our
power, we should, above all, make clear to the parties what their respective rights and
obligations are in consequence of any order to be pronounced. There is no doubt in my
mind that the respondent has suffered a grievous wrong. It should not be beyond the
power of the courts to provide a suitable remedy. The respondent has throughout
disclaimed any interest in monetary compensation. What he seeks is reinstatement. This
could only be secured by an order of mandamus requiring the present Chief Constable

of the North Wales Police to reinstate him as a probationer constable who has already completed fourteen months of his probationer service. I have no doubt your Lordships *a* have power to make such an order and was at one time strongly inclined to think that it should be made. I know now that none of your Lordships favour such an order and it would therefore be an empty gesture for me to express a formal dissent on the point. But, that apart, I appreciate the weight of the objections to it. Great practical problems would arise in relation to his training and perhaps other matters from the fact that his service has been interrupted for nearly four years. Moreover, human nature being what *b* it is, if the North Wales Police Force had the respondent forced on them by order of your Lordships' House as the culmination of this lengthy litigation, there would be an obvious danger that an undercurrent of ill-feeling would affect his future relations with his superiors in the force.

I am reluctantly driven to the conclusion that the best service we can render to the respondent, and indeed this is the least we should do, is to make clear to the North Wales *c* Police Force or indeed to any other police force he may now seek to join that he emerges from this litigation with his reputation wholly untarnished, that nothing has ever been proved against him to show that he is unlikely to become an efficient and well-conducted constable, but that, on the contrary, all the formal reports on his work and training during the period of his service in 1977 and 1978 were highly favourable to him.

As regards the formal disposal of the appeal I concur in the order proposed by my *d* noble and learned friend, Lord Brightman.

LORD BRIGHTMAN. My Lords, the issue in this case is whether the Chief Constable of the North Wales Police acted lawfully when he forced a probationer constable to resign his office; and, if not, what remedies can properly be granted to the aggrieved constable. *e*

The matter first came before a Divisional Court of the Queen's Bench Division. It was heard by Woolf J. He came to the conclusion that the decision reached by the chief constable did not accord with the standards of fairness that should have been observed, but held that no relief should be granted except in regard to costs. The constable appealed in order to obtain substantive relief. The chief constable cross-appealed. The Court of Appeal confirmed the conclusion of the Divisional Court but added a declaration that the *f* chief constable's decision to require the constable to resign or be dismissed was void. The chief constable now appeals to your Lordships' House.

My Lords, I will narrate the story as briefly as I can, but some detail is inevitable. In the summer of 1977 the respondent, Mr Michael John Evans, applied to join the North Wales Police. He had an unfortunate upbringing. His father, who had been in the Royal Navy, died when he was five years old. His mother suffered from ill health and was *g* unable to look after him. In consequence, he was brought up in an orphanage until he was 16. In May 1971, when he was about 19, he had a serious motor cycle accident. He received a considerable sum of money as compensation. He was in hospital for almost a year. While there, he was visited and befriended by Miss Margaret Farey. She was a lady who had been living with his uncle for a number of years. There were four children of the liaison. The respondent believed that his uncle and Miss Farey were married. She *h* called herself Mrs Evans and he referred to her as his aunt. At about this time, Miss Farey and the respondent's uncle parted company. After the respondent left hospital he stayed for a while with his grandmother, and later with Miss Farey. He came to know that she was unmarried but he continued to refer to her as his aunt.

The respondent went out to work. He was first first employed as a chauffeur. He then spent a year as an operating theatre technician in a hospital. This was followed by a spell *j* of unemployment. In the autumn of 1976 he accepted an offer of a place at the University College of North Wales, Bangor, beginning in the autumn of 1976. He first lived in lodgings, but later secured the tenancy of a house on a farm near Bangor, where Miss Farey and her two younger children joined him.

The respondent's first year at the university was not a success. He did not achieve the requisite academic standard and he left. He applied to join the North Wales Police. He was interviewed in July 1977 by Police Sergeant Morris. The police sergeant recorded the

a following in his suitability report:

> 'The address where the applicant resides is a house on Tyddyn Mynyddig Farm some two miles from Bangor, which his aunt rents from the owner of the farm. It is a comfortable home, clean and well cared for . . . For the past twelve months he has resided with his aunt, Mrs Margaret Evans at the farm, and it appears that she has been the one person in his life who has cared for him, and encouraged him in
b his studies.'

A fortnight later he was interviewed by Superintendent Ellis. Finally he had a brief interview with the chief constable, the appellant, and was accepted into the force. He was duly sworn into the office of constable on 31 August and became a probationary member of the police force for a period of two years pursuant to reg 15(2) of the Police
c Regulations 1971. He was then just under 25 years of age.

On 5 September he began his initial course of training at the police training centre at Cwmbran. It lasted for two months. He obtained a good report. The commandant of the centre described him as 'a very good prospect with all the attributes to develop into a reliable and competent police officer'. He then spent a month on the beat at Holyhead attached to a tutor constable. He was given a satisfactory report. During this period he
d gave formal notice to his divisional chief superintendent of his intention to be married to 'Miss Margaret Farey of Tyddyn Mynddig Farm' and requested police accommodation. Within a week the deputy chief constable allocated accommodation to him at Llangefni, and changed his station from Holyhead to Llangefni. The accommodation provided was a house belonging to the local council. On 26 January the respondent gave the divisional chief superintendent formal notification of his marriage. This showed that his wife was
e 14 years older than he.

On 31 January 1978 Police Sergeant Roberts, of the Llangefni Police Station made a report to the divisional chief superintendent. He said that as a result of various observations and various rumours spread about the police station, he had decided to make some discreet inquiries about the respondent and his wife. It is a long report. It is sufficient to pick out these items: (1) A year previously a police officer visiting the Evans'
f household about the absence from school of one of the children, had been introduced to the respondent as the stepson of Mrs Evans. (2) Police Sergeant Morris, who had made the suitability report, had been led to believe that Mrs Evans was the respondent's aunt. (3) The respondent's council house was untidy, poorly carpeted and furnished. (4) Despite the poor state of the house, the respondent had just bought a large car and he also owned an almost new Honda motor cycle; and there were four or five dogs in the
g house. (5) It was also within the police sergeant's knowledge that the respondent's referees (in the plural) described him as plausible and possibly dishonest. Inspector Yates added a footnote to the report: (6) Prior to their marriage, the respondent and Mrs Evans resided at a hippy commune at Tyddyn Mynyddig; it was believed that Mrs Evans was the sister of the respondent's mother (and therefore within the prohibited degree of relationship); and there was no proof that Mrs Evans was divorced from her previous
h husband (thus also indicating bigamy).

On 3 February this report was forwarded by the divisional chief superintendent to the deputy chief constable. On 8 February the divisional chief superintendent added fuel to the fire. Current information, he said, suggested that in the past the respondent had had several (query severe) financial difficulties; he was said to be plausible; and he had a medical history of chronic leg injuries.

j On 9 February the deputy chief constable asked the divisional chief superintendent to interview the respondent with a view to resolving the various issues which had recently come to notice. The respondent was summoned to an interview. Superintendent Ellis attended with the divisional chief superintendent. The divisional chief superintendent gave the respondent to believe that the interview was concerned only with a discrepancy in the number of children in the family, in order to ensure that the family would obtain the full benefit of the pension arrangements.

According to the evidence, none of the various items, I am tempted to call them smears, appeared to have been brought out into the open so as to enable the respondent *a* to put the record straight. The rumour that Mrs Evans was still the wife of the respondent's uncle, and the alternative rumour that Mrs Evans was the sister of the respondent's mother, were ultimately laid to rest by an investigation conducted by New Scotland Yard at the request of the divisional chief superintendent. A report of this investigation was made on 19 July. As to the rest of the items: (1) as regards the untidy and poorly equipped house, the respondent and his wife had only just moved in and *b* there is uncontradicted evidence that they had not had time to get their furniture out of store and carpets fitted; (2) there is uncontradicted evidence that the respondent had suffered from no financial difficulties; (3) it was somewhat misleading to record that the respondent's referees (in the plural) had described him as plausible and possibly dishonest. The truth was that one referee, the Dean of the Faculty of Science at Bangor University had concluded his letter as follows: *c*

> 'I believe Evans to be reasonably intelligent and, on first acquaintance, has an outgoing and fairly attractive personality. However, I should say that I doubt somewhat his plausibility. In some ways it is perhaps a minor matter but he tendered a number of excuses about his academic performance which I saw no reason to disbelieve. Quite by accident, as a result of an enquiry from his Local Education Authority, I came to discover that much of what he had said was in fact *d* untrue. When subsequently tackled about this matter he still wished me to believe most of what he had previously told me. He therefore is either dishonest with himself and/or is willing himself to believe a situation exists when it clearly does not. I am sorry to have to report on Evans in this way because I firmly believe he has had a difficult home environment in his earlier days and I think he is deserving of some help.' *e*

(4) The reference to the hippy commune was a most damaging error. Inspector Yates had confused the farm where the respondent lived with another locality where he had never been; (5) the respondent's leg injury had been fully disclosed in his medical report and he had completely recovered from it.

In the meantime the respondent undertook phase 1 of the headquarters training *f* course, a traffic course, an administration course and a CID course. All reports from those instructing him were good.

To go back in time for a moment: in January 1978 when the respondent's house had been allocated to him, the respondent had called at the council's housing department to discover the council's attitude towards the keeping of domestic pets. He had four dogs. He was told that as a rule pets were not allowed, but that the council took no notice *g* unless there were complaints. At a routine meeting with the divisional chief superintendent a little later, the respondent told him about the dogs. The divisional chief superintendent informed him that there was no problem as long as the dogs were kept under control. In the autumn of 1978, acting on information that the respondent had four dogs, a health inspector called at the house. He said that as a rule only one dog was allowed, but it appeared that no actual complaint had been made by anyone. The health *h* inspector agreed that the dogs were well cared for and said that the health department could have no complaint. However, two days later a council official called and told the respondent that he would have to get rid of the dogs.

On 19 October Superintendent Jones of Caernarvon interviewed the respondent as a result of what he had heard about the dogs. On the next day the respondent made a written report to the divisional chief superintendent explaining his predicament. He *j* referred to the interview with Superintendent Jones and added that at this interview he had indicated that he would try to find alternative accommodation, but the possibility of success seemed remote. The respondent handed his memorandum to Superintendent Jones who forwarded it to the divisional chief superintendent with his own covering letter. In his covering letter Superintendent Jones wrongly informed the divisional chief superintendent that prior to being moved to Llangefni the respondent and his family

were living in a hippy commune at Bangor, and added that his wife continued to dress
a in the hippy fashion; and that all the dogs were strays. The respondent denies that his
wife dressed in hippy clothes, and there is undisputed evidence that none of the dogs was
a stray. Superintendent Jones added that he had told the respondent that he had the
alternative of getting rid of three of the dogs or finding alternative accommodation.

On 20 October a routine assessment report was made on the respondent. This followed
the pattern of earlier reports; his appearance and bearing were of high standard; in the
b performance of his duties he got through a great deal of work; he accepted responsibility;
was considerate and firm in his attitude to the public; showed a great deal of interest;
and was well liked and respected by his colleagues. Sergeant Evans, who signed the
assessment, considered that he would do well in his career. Inspector Yates, who endorsed
the assessment, said the respondent showed a great deal of interest and enthusiasm, and
intended to establish a career for himself within the police force. It was Inspector Yates
c who started the damaging canard about the hippy commune. He did not repeat it. But
unfortunately it had already been repeated by Superintendent Jones.

On 23 October the respondent visited the senior management officer of the local
council to discuss the question of the dogs. In a letter of the same day the senior
management officer wrote to the respondent requesting him to find other accommodation
for the animals within the next four weeks, ie by the third week in November.

d On 25 October the respondent reported to his divisional chief superintendent. He said
that he had been given four weeks to leave the council house. That was not an accurate
account of the council's letter, although it would come to the same thing if he adhered to
his expressed intention of not parting with the dogs. The respondent said that he could
see no prospect of finding suitable alternative accommodation.

On 30 October the divisional chief superintendent forwarded the memoranda of 19,
e 20 and 25 October to the deputy chief constable.

On 6 November the deputy chief constable interviewed the respondent. He was told
that there were only two alternatives, that he 'should comply with the conditions of
tenancy or that we should take other action by, e g, terminating his employment'. The
deputy chief constable added in his memorandum of the interview, which he forwarded
to the chief constable, that 'it was very doubtful in my view whether people who
f deliberately flouted conditions of tenancy were suitable to be in the police service'. Your
Lordships may feel that an accusation of deliberately flouting the terms of the tenancy is
an extravagant description of the respondent's conduct in the light of the clear evidence
that he began with a revocable permission to keep the dogs and, though the permission
was then revoked, he still had another fortnight within which to comply with the
council's requirements.

g On 8 November the respondent was summoned to an interview with the chief
constable. He was told by the chief constable that he 'had made a mistake in accepting
him and gave him the opportunity to resign as an alternative to formally dispensing with
his services'. He was given no indication of the reasons for his enforced resignation. The
respondent in his affidavit says this about the interview, and his account is not disputed:

> **h** 'I asked if I could have a reason for this action but he refused outright. I was not
> informed of what was alleged against me nor afforded any opportunity to be heard
> by way of defence or explanation. I asked for time to consider and he said that I
> must let him know by 10 a.m. the following morning. I was not given any
> document recording this decision.'

As a result of the chief constable's threat, the respondent signed on 9 November a formal
j letter of resignation.

At the time of his enforced resignation it should be observed that the respondent still
had a fortnight within which to comply with the council's requirements: that all the
routine reports on his suitability as a police constable had been highly satisfactory, and
likely, viewed in isolation, to lead to his being confirmed in office; and that he was due
in only three weeks' time to attend a routine interview with his divisional chief
superintendent pursuant to the ordinary probationary procedure.

Within a week of his enforced resignation, the respondent applied to join the
Metropolitan Police. The Metropolitan Police, naturally enough, communicated with a
the North Wales Police. The deputy chief constable replied by letter in fairly innocuous
terms. The Chief Constable of the North Wales Police also spoke personally to an assistant
commissioner of the Metropolitan Police. Not surprisingly his application was rejected.
It has no particular importance except to demonstrate the respondent's dedication to
police work, and the then practical impossibility of his regaining acceptance into a police
force.   b
    My Lords, before I conclude this unhappy story, I must turn to the statutory provision.
Regulation 16 of the Police Regulations 1971, which I need not quote verbatim, provides
that during his period of probation in the force, the services of a constable may be
dispensed with at any time if the chief officer of police considers: (1) that he is not fitted,
physically or mentally, to perform the duties of his office; or (2) that he is not likely to
become an efficient constable; or (3) that he is not likely to become a well conducted c
constable.
    It is plain from the wording of the regulation that the power of a chief officer of police
to dispense with the services of a person accepted as a probationer constable is to be
exercised, and exercised only, after due consideration and determination of the specified
questions. It is not a discretion that may be exercised arbitrally and without accountability.
    A year went by. The respondent tried unsuccessfully to pursue a remedy before an d
industrial tribunal. He consulted solicitors and applied for legal aid which took some
time to arrange. On 23 October 1979 his solicitors wrote to the chief constable. They
indicated that he would be seeking judicial review of the decision to dispense with his
services. They asked the chief constable to reconsider his decision. They also requested
disclosure of various reports about him which the respondent knew, or suspected, were
in existence. This request was peremptorily refused in a letter despatched by the chief e
constable two days later.
    In early January 1980 the respondent filed the requisite statement and swore the
requisite affidavit in support of his application for leave to apply for judicial review. At
this time he was still unaware of the facts or supposed facts which had led the chief
constable to force his resignation. So far as he was aware, there was only one matter over
which any problem arose, namely, his ownership of the dogs, of which the North Wales f
Police were aware shortly after he took up accommodation at Llangefni. Leave was given
by a Divisional Court on 29 January. On the following day the respondent issued a notice
of motion seeking (1) an order of certiorari to quash the chief constable's decision of 8
November 1978, (2) an order of mandamus directed to the chief constable requiring his
reinstatement, and (3) a declaration that the decision of the chief constable was illegal,
ultra vires and void. On 8 May 1980 the respondent obtained a consent order for the g
discovery of the documents which he had requested six months earlier.
    On 12 June 1980 the chief constable swore an affidavit in answer to the respondent's
filed statement and affidavit. There are two important matters revealed in the affidavit.
First, the chief constable asserted that reg 16(1) gave him an absolute discretion to
dispense with a probationer's services. Second, in deciding as he did, the chief constable
was principally concerned with three adverse factors: (1) The respondent had married a h
woman much older than himself; she was the former mistress of his uncle; such a
marriage might give rise to some scandal, which would not be in the interests of the
force. (2) The respondent and his wife were keeping four or five dogs in a police/council
house, when there was a permitted limit of one dog. (3) The respondent and his wife had
lived a 'hippy' life style at the Bangor farm.
    The second of these adverse factors was inaccurate, because the dogs were initially kept j
in the house with the council's permission; and that permission was still extant at the
date of the chief constable's decision. The third adverse factor was the result of a complete
misunderstanding and was devoid of all substance.
    The respondent swore an affidavit in reply on 15 January 1981. He furnished his
answers to all the criticisms of which he had by now become aware and he convincingly

disposed of the damaging statement about the previous life style of himself and his wife.
a   Furthermore, he deposed that if he had realised that he had to choose between keeping
his career and keeping the dogs, the dogs would have gone. It is difficult to suppose
otherwise.

The chief constable has never challenged the truth of the respondent's second affidavit.

The motion came before Woolf J on 23 March 1981. The judge found in favour of the
respondent to the extent that he held that the proper approach to this type of case was
b   that the chief constable was bound to act fairly in the course of exercising his statutory
discretion under reg 16; and that the decision which was reached did not accord with the
standards of fairness because the respondent was not given an opportunity to answer the
accusations which led the chief constable to the conclusion which he reached. However,
the judge declined to grant any relief except in costs. His reasoning was this. The court
could give no remedy now which would enable the respondent to serve the period which
c   would have remained if his engagement had not been terminated, because the two year
probationary period had long since expired. Even if that period had not ended, the court
would not in the normal way make an order of mandamus requiring a chief constable to
re-engage a constable. The only order which could be made would be one which would
have required the chief constable to reconsider his decision of 8 November. There was
no purpose to be served by such an order now that the probationary period had expired.
d   To put the matter shortly, an order of mandamus would be contrary to all precedent and
an order of certiorari would be academic. He could not make a declaratory order that the
respondent was still a probationary constable, nor could he make a declaration that the
chief constable's decision was wrong. All that could be declared would be that the
decision had been reached irregularly, and such a declaration would serve no purpose.

My Lords, I must address myself later to the question of remedy. All that I would say
e   at this moment is that it would, to my mind, be regrettable if a litigant who establishes
that he has been legally wronged and particularly in so important a matter as the pursuit
of his chosen profession, has to be sent away from a court of justice empty handed save
for an order for the recoupment of the expense to which he has been put in establishing
a barren victory.

The respondent appealed. By his notice of appeal, he sought an order of certiorari, an
f   order of mandamus and a declaration in the terms set out in his application for leave to
apply for judicial review. The chief constable cross-appealed. He attacked the findings of
the judge. He claimed not only that the decision was fairly reached, but also that the
respondent's office was held during pleasure so that, on established principles, he had no
right to be heard before dismissal.

Before I turn to the judgments in the Court of Appeal, I would make certain
g   observations on the law as I understand it. I turn first to the decision of this House in
Ridge v Baldwin [1963] 2 All ER 66, [1964] AC 40 where I find useful guidance on the
proper approach to this type of case. As was pointed out by Lord Reid, the application of
principles of natural justice to a variety of different situations is likely to lead to varying
definitions of those principles (see [1963] 2 All ER 66 at 71–72, [1964] AC 40 at 64–66).
For example, 'what a minister ought to do in considering objections to a scheme may be
h   very different from what a watch committee ought to do in considering whether to
dismiss a chief constable'. So cases of dismissal need to be considered on their own. Lord
Reid divided these into three categories. First, dismissal of a servant by his master. Here
no relevant question arises whether the master has heard the servant in his defence
unless, presumably, the principle of audi alteram partem has been made a term of the
contract. The question is whether the facts emerging at the trial prove a breach of
j   contract. If so, damages are payable for the breach. Second, dismissal from an office held
during pleasure

> 'It has always been held, I think rightly, that such an officer has no right to be
> heard before he is dismissed, and the reason is clear. As the person having the power
> of dismissal need not have anything against the officer, he need not give any reason.'

(See [1963] 2 All ER 66 at 71, [1964] AC 40 at 65 per Lord Reid.) Third, dismissal from an office where there must be something against the office holder to warrant his dismissal:

> 'There I find an unbroken line of authority to the effect that an officer cannot lawfully be dismissed without first telling him what is alleged against him and hearing his defence or explanation.'

(See [1963] 2 All ER 66 at 72, [1964] AC 40 at 66 per Lord Reid.)

I turn secondly to the proper purpose of the remedy of judicial review, what it is and what it is not. In my opinion the law was correctly stated in the speech of Lord Evershed ([1963] 2 All ER 66 at 91, [1964] AC 40 at 96). His was a dissenting judgment but the dissent was not concerned with this point. Lord Evershed referred to—

> 'a danger of usurpation of power on the part of the courts . . . under the pretext of having regard to the principles of natural justice . . . I do observe again that it is not the decision as such which is liable to review; it is only the circumstances in which the decision was reached, and particularly in such a case as the present the need for giving to the party dismissed an opportunity for putting his case.'

Judicial review is concerned, not with the decision, but with the decision-making process. Unless that restriction on the power of the court is observed, the court will in my view, under the guise of preventing the abuse of power, be itself guilty of usurping power.

I leave these preliminary observations in order to consider the judgments in the Court of Appeal. It was accepted by each member of the court that the case fell within the third of Lord Reid's categories; that the respondent was entitled to a fair hearing; and that he had not had one. However, Lord Denning MR added this:

> 'I go further. Not only must he be given a fair hearing, but the decision itself must be fair and reasonable. That is the protection afforded to every servant who is employed under a contract of service. He is protected against unfair dismissal. No less protection should be afforded to a probationer constable . . . It is my opinion that the chief constable was not justified in dispensing with the services of Constable Evans or in requiring him to resign.'

Shaw and Ackner LJJ concurred.

In his submissions to this House, counsel for the appellant submitted that the chief constable took into account all the matters which appeared on the respondent's file; that he was entitled to rely on the accuracy of the reports of his officers; and that he was not bound to put every adverse point to the respondent.

My Lords, for my part I emphatically reject the approach of the chief constable to his duties under reg 16. He made the fundamental mistake, as appears from his affidavit, of assuming that he had an absolute discretion to discharge the respondent under reg 16, a right to dismiss him at pleasure. That was not his right. His mistake coloured and indeed tainted the decision-making process. His discretion to discharge was a qualified one, exercisable only if he considered that the respondent was not fitted to perform the duties of the office or was not likely to become an efficient constable or a well conducted constable. It is implicit in reg 16 that there must be a fair consideration of the constable's fitness to perform his duties and a fair consideration of the likelihood of his becoming an efficient and well conducted constable. The legality of the choice given to the respondent to resign or be discharged must be judged by the same criteria as would be applied to the legality of discharge without the alternative of resignation; for clearly the chief constable could not use an invalid threat of discharge to compel resignation, as that would be an abuse of power.

As I have indicated, the chief constable forced the respondent's discharge on account of three adverse factors which he believed to exist: the allegedly undesirable marital circumstances, the alleged hippy life style and the alleged flouting of authority. It was the duty of the chief constable to deal fairly with the respondent in relation to the adverse

factors on which he was proposing to act. The chief constable failed in his performance
a of that duty because these supposedly adverse factors were never put to the respondent.
He was given no opportunity to offer one word of explanation. Your Lordships will not
doubt the honesty of the chief constable and that he reached a decision which he truly
believed was in the interests of the North Wales Police on the information that had been
laid before him. But the inescapable fact is that he misunderstood the extent of his
discretion and the nature of his duty under reg 16. The decision-making process was
b therefore defective.

There is however a wider point than the injustice of the decision-making process of
the chief constable. With profound respect to the Court of Appeal, I dissent from the
view that 'Not only must [the probationer constable] be given a fair hearing, but the
decision itself must be fair and reasonable'. If that statement of the law passed into
authority without comment, it would in my opinion transform, and wrongly transform,
c the remedy of judicial review. Judicial review, as the words imply, is not an appeal from
a decision, but a review of the manner in which the decision was made. The statement
of law which I have quoted implies that the court sits in judgment not only on the
correctness of the decision-making process but also on the correctness of the decision
itself. In his printed case counsel for the appellant made this submission:

d 'Where Parliament has entrusted to an administrative authority the duty of
making a decision which affects the rights of an individual, the court's supervisory
function on a judicial review of that decision is limited. The court cannot be
expected to possess knowledge of the reasons of policy which lie behind the
administrative decision nor is it desirable that evidence should be called before the
court of the implications of such policy. It follows that the court ought not to
attempt to weigh the merits of the particular decision but should confine its function
e to a consideration of the manner in which the decision was reached.'

When the sole issue raised on an application for judicial review is whether the rules of
natural justice have been observed, these propositions are unexceptionable. Other
considerations arise when an administrative decision is attacked on the ground that it is
vitiated by self-misdirection, by taking account of irrelevant factors or neglecting to take
f account of relevant factors, or is so manifestly unreasonable that no reasonable authority,
entrusted with the power in question, could reasonably have made such a decision: see
the well known judgment of Lord Greene MR in *Associated Provincial Picture Houses Ltd v
Wednesbury Corp* [1947] 2 All ER 680, [1948] 1 KB 223.

I agree entirely with the Court of Appeal, and indeed with the Divisional Court, that
the respondent did not have the fair hearing to which he was entitled. I differ only from
g the Court of Appeal on the extent of the court's supervisory jurisdiction.

I turn now to the question of remedies. The Court of Appeal granted the respondent a
declaration that the decision requiring the respondent to resign or be dismissed was void.
I feel some misgivings about a declaration in that form, because it is not clear to me what
consequences flow from it. Whatever remedy may be granted by the court in this case, I
think it is highly desirable that the North Wales Police and the respondent should be in
h no doubt how, under the order, they will stand in relation to each other.

The conclusion reached by the Divisional Court, the Court of Appeal and by this
House, if your Lordships are in agreement with me, is that the chief constable acted
unlawfully and in breach of his duty under reg 16 in threatening to dispense with the
respondent's services unless he resigned from the North Wales Police and in thus causing
him to resign. That having been established, the respondent is, in my view, entitled at
j least to a declaration to that effect. But the matter cannot be satisfactorily left there. One
must know what are the consequences that flow from the breach of duty.

One possibility would be to add to that declaration an order of mandamus. The
respondent has one desire and one desire only, namely, to be reinstated in the police
force. This would be secured if an order of mandamus were to issue, directed to the chief
constable now in office, requiring him, for example, to restore the respondent to the
office of probationer constable as held by him on 8 November 1978.

An alternative to an order of mandamus would be a declaration affirming that, by reason of such unlawfully induced resignation, the respondent thereby became entitled *a* to the same rights and remedies, not including re-instatement, as he would have had if the appellant had unlawfully dispensed with his services under reg 16(1). Such a declaration would clarify the status of the respondent vis-à-vis the North Wales Police, and would leave him free to pursue such remedies, short of re-instatement, as may be open to him. I have in mind that under Ord 53, r 7 an applicant for judicial review may claim damages if they are sought in the filed statement and if damages could have been *b* awarded in an action brought for the purpose. I have not, however, addressed my mind to the question whether it is still open to the respondent to apply to amend his filed statement by adding a claim for damages.

It is possible that the respondent would not wish, nor indeed would have any incentive, to pursue a claim for damages. Counsel for the appellant, acting on instructions, told your Lordships that if the decision of your Lordships' House went in favour of the *c* respondent it would be the intention of the North Wales Police to offer him monetary compensation. I trust that the compensation which the chief constable has in mind to offer would be on a generous scale, and amply reflect the fact that the respondent has been unlawfully deprived of his profession as a consequence of the wrongful procedures of the chief constable's predecessor in office.

I feel that the choice of remedy is a difficult one. It is a matter of discretion. From the *d* point of view of the respondent who has been wronged in a matter so vital to his life, an order of mandamus is the only satisfactory remedy. I have been much tempted to suggest to your Lordships that it would in the circumstances be a remedy proper to be granted. But it is unusual, in a case such as the present, for the court to make an order of mandamus, and I think that in practice it might border on usurpation of the powers of the chief constable, which is to be avoided. With some reluctance and hesitation, I feel *e* that the respondent will have to content himself with the less satisfactory declaration that I have outlined.

So far as I am aware, it would be open to the respondent to apply in the ordinary way to re-join the North Wales Police as a new entrant. If the respondent does make such an application, I for my part express the hope that the North Wales Police will give very serious consideration to it. If an objective assessment of his accomplishments and *f* character were made, the North Wales Police might come to the conclusion that a person so dedicated to the profession is police material which ought not lightly to be discarded. They might feel that his re-acceptance would go some way towards remedying the wrong which he has suffered as well as benefiting the force itself. This would be a happy solution, if it could properly be brought about; it would give the respondent the chance which he merits; and the way that I have expressed myself avoids any usurpation of the *g* power of the chief constable, because a decision to accept or reject must lie with him.

My Lords, I would dismiss the appeal but vary the order of the Court of Appeal by substituting the declarations which I have outlined for that which is contained in the order of the Court of Appeal.

Appeal dismissed.   *h*

Solicitors: *Sharpe, Pritchard & Co*, agents for *M H Phillips*, Mold (for the chief constable); *Peter Badham & Co* (for the respondent).

Mary Rose Plummer   Barrister.

a

Ruffle v Rogers and another

COURT OF APPEAL, CIVIL DIVISION
LORD DENNING MR, EVELEIGH AND WATKINS LJJ
10, 11 FEBRUARY 1982

b *Elections – Local government – Ballot papers – Rejection – Ballot paper marked otherwise than by means of a cross – Clear intention to vote for one or other of candidates – Voter writing candidate's name and party instead of marking paper with a cross – Whether ballot paper void – Local Elections (Principal Areas) Rules 1973, r 43(1)(3).*

c *Elections – Local government – Validity of election – Irregularities affecting result – Ballot papers not bearing official mark – Rejection – Rejection having effect that result not a tie and returning officer not deciding between candidates by lot – Whether rejection of ballot papers an act or omission which affected result of election – Representation of the People Act 1949, s 37(1).*

In a local election the result declared was 1,519 votes for the respondent and 1,517 votes for the petitioner. The respondent was declared to be duly elected. Included in the votes for the petitioner was a ballot paper which the voter had filled in by writing the *d* petitioner's name and party instead of merely marking it with a cross. Four other ballot papers were rejected because an election official had omitted to stamp them with the official mark. Three of the rejected votes had been cast for the petitioner and one for the respondent, so that if they had been included the result would have been a tie. In the event of a tie the returning officer would have been required by r 45*a* of the Local Elections (Principal Areas) Rules 1973 to decide between the candidates by lot. The *e* petitioner sought a declaration that the election was invalid because the returning officer had wrongly rejected the four unstamped ballot papers. At the hearing of the petition the respondent contended that the ballot paper filled in with the petitioner's name and party should not have been accepted as a valid vote because the voter who marked the ballot paper could possibly be identified by his handwriting and therefore the ballot paper was void under r 43(1)(c)*b* of the 1973 rules. The petitioner contended that since *f* the way the paper was marked did not 'of itself identify the voter' and since the paper had been marked 'otherwise than by means of a cross' in such a way as to show clearly 'an intention that the vote [should] be for one or other of the candidates' it had been properly accepted as a valid vote under r 43(3)*c* of the 1973 rules. The Divisional Court held that all five disputed votes were valid and that, since the omission by an official to stamp four of the ballot papers had affected the result, it was necessary, under s 37(1)*d* of the *g* Representation of the People Act 1949, to hold a new election. The respondent appealed.

Held – The appeal would be dismissed for the following reasons—
    (1) The mere fact that a voter wrote the name of his chosen candidate on his ballot paper did not of itself invalidate the paper under r 43(1)(c) of the 1973 rules, since a ballot paper was only invalidated if the voter could be clearly identified from what was written. *h* Since the voter's identity could not be discovered and since he had made his intention clear, the ballot paper filled in with the petitioner's name and party was a valid ballot paper under r 43(3) (see p 160 *b e f*, p 161 *b c e h* and p 162 *b*, post); *Woodward v Sarsons* (1875) LR 10 CP 733 and *Duke v St Maur* (1911) 6 O'M & H 228 not followed.
    (2) The failure to stamp the four ballot papers with the official mark was an omission which affected the result of the election within s 37(1) of the 1949 Act, because it

j

---
a   Rule 45, so far as material, is set out at p 160 *j*, post
b   Rule 43(1) is set out at p 159 *g h*, post
c   Rule 43(3) is set out at p 159 *j* to p 160 *a*, post
d   Section 37(1) is set out at p 160 *h*, post

prevented the result of the count from being a tie and accordingly prevented the successful candidate from being chosen by lot in accordance with r 45 of the 1973 rules. It followed that the election should be declared void and that a new election should be held (see p 161 *b c* and p 162 *a b*, post).

a

Notes

For the rejection of ballot papers because of marks of identification, see 15 Halsbury's Laws (4th edn) para 634, and for cases on the subject, see 20 Digest (Reissue) 52–55, *437–* *471.*

b

For the rejection of ballot papers for want of an official mark, see 15 Halsbury's Laws (4th edn) para 632, and for cases on the subject, see 20 Digest (Reissue) 49, *393–401.*

For the Representation of the People Act 1949, s 37, see 11 Halsbury's Statutes (3rd edn) 582.

For the Local Elections (Principal Areas) Rules 1973, r 43, see 7 Halsbury's Statutory Instruments (4th reissue) 37.

c

Cases referred to in judgments

Birmingham Case, Woodward v Sarsons (1875) LR 10 CP 733, 20 Digest (Reissue) 53, *439.*
Exeter Case, Duke v St Maur (1911) 6 O'M & H 228, 20 Digest (Reissue) 52, *438.*
Wigtown District Burgh Case (1874) 2 O'M & H 215.

d

Cases also cited

Clare, Eastern Division Case (1892) 4 O'M & H 162.
Gloucester (County) Cirencester Division Case, Lawson v Charter-Master (1893) 4 O'M & H 194.
Morgan v Simpson [1974] 3 All ER 722, [1975] QB 151, CA.
South Newington (Kingston-upon-Hull) Municipal Election Petition, Re, Lewis v Shepperdson [1948] 2 All ER 503.
Tower Hamlets, Stepney Division Case, Isaacson v Durant (1886) 54 LT 684.

e

f

Appeal

The first respondent, Dudley James Rogers, appealed with leave of the Divisional Court of the Queen's Bench Division against the decision of that court (Kilner Brown and Mais JJ) on 21 December 1981 allowing the petition of Rodney Gerald Ruffle and declaring that a local government election for the constituency of Alphington and St Thomas in Exeter, in the county of Devon, held on 7 May 1981 was void. Both the petitioner and the first respondent were candidates in the election. The second respondent, Alan Edgar Bennett, was the returning officer. The facts are set out in the judgment of Lord Denning MR.

g

Michael Tugendhat for the first respondent.
Ian Karsten for the petitioner.
Julian Sandys for the second respondent.

h

LORD DENNING MR. On 7 May 1981 there was a local election in Exeter. There were four candidates: (1) Humphries (Ecology Party), (2) Rich (Labour), (3) Rogers (Conservative) and (4) Ruffle (Liberal).

One of the voters filled in the ballot paper as follows. On the right hand side, in the appropriate box, after the name 'Ruffle' he wrote the words 'Ruffle Liberal'. He did not make a cross as he ought to have done. During the counting, an objection was taken to that ballot paper. It was overruled by the deputy returning officer. So this ballot paper was counted as one vote for Mr Ruffle (Liberal).

j

The result of the election as the returning officer recorded it was:

a
'Linda Elizabeth Humphries (Ecology Party)   61
Martin Rich (Labour)   1,066
Dudley James Rogers (Conservative)   1,519
Rodney Gerald Ruffle (Liberal)   1,517.'

So the returning officer declared that the Conservative candidate, Dudley James Rogers,
b was elected.

During the counting, however, several ballot papers had been rejected. Four were
rejected because they had not got the official mark stamped on them. The four voters
had put their cross on the ballot papers in the correct way, but they had been rejected
because an official had omitted to stamp them. That omission by an official can be
corrected later, as I will show. On being corrected, it appears that one of those four ballot
c papers was for Mr Rogers (Conservative). The other three were for Mr Ruffle (Liberal). If
those four ballot papers had been counted, it would have meant that Mr Rogers and Mr
Ruffle got equal numbers in the election: 1,520 each. So if the unstamped ballot forms
are counted (as they can be in case of need) the result is a tie.

In these circumstances, Mr Rogers (Conservative) objects now to the ballot paper
marked 'Ruffle Liberal'. He says that it was invalid. If it is invalid, he wins by one vote.

d   Counsel for Mr Rogers, in a very skilful argument before us, drew our attention to a
number of cases. It is clear that before 1948 a ballot paper, so filled in, would have been
invalid.

The first case was *Birmingham Case, Woodward v Sarsons* (1875) LR 10 CP 733. We were
shown an extract from *Schofield's Local Government Elections* (8th edn, 1979) p 365. It
showed photographs of ballot papers which were held to be bad in that case. In two
e examples the voter had not put a cross beside the name 'Sarsons'. He had written in the
name 'Sarsons'. He had written in the name of the candidate for whom he wished to
vote. The court held in 1875, with some hesitation, that that was a bad ballot paper.

The next case was *Exeter Case, Duke v St Maur* (1911) 6 O'M & H 228. One of the
candidates was Mr Henry Edward Duke KC (afterwards the President of the Probate,
Divorce and Admiralty Division). The opposing candidate was Mr Richard Harold St
f Maur. Mr Duke presented an election petition, which was tried by two judges at the
Guildhall, Exeter in 1911. In that case the voter had not been content merely to put a
cross next to Mr Duke's name. He showed his enthusiasm by writing in 'Up Duke'. That
ballot paper was rejected as invalid.

So the law stood until the Representation of the People Act 1948, which amended the
Ballot Act 1872, and was consolidated in 1949. It is now contained in the Local Elections
g (Principal Areas) Rules 1973, SI 1973/179. The important rule is r 43(1). It goes back to
1948. It provides:

'Any ballot paper—(*a*) which does not bear the official mark; or (*b*) on which
votes are given for more candidates than the voter is entitled to vote for; or (*c*) on
which anything is written or marked by which the voter can be identified except
h the printed number on the back; or (*d*) which is unmarked or void for uncertainty;
shall, *subject to the provisions of this rule,* be void and not counted.'

The question in this case is whether the words 'Ruffle Liberal' written on the ballot
paper were something by which the voter can be identified. Looking at the ballot paper,
the only possible way in which the voter could be identified is by his handwriting. Can a
man be identified by his handwriting? The handwriting of some persons is so special or
j so peculiar that the writer can be identified. But that is not this case. This voter could not
be identified by his handwriting.

I turn to r 43(3):

'A ballot paper on which a vote is marked—(*a*) elsewhere than in the proper
place; or (*b*) otherwise than by means of a cross [that is this case]; or (*c*) by more than

one mark; shall not be reason thereof be deemed to be void (either wholly or as respect that vote), if an intention that the vote shall be for one or other of the candidates clearly appears, and the way the paper is marked does not of itself identify the voter and it is not shown that he can be identified thereby.'

It seems to me as plain as can be that, in our present case, the vote was intended for Mr Ruffle (Liberal). We do not know who the voter was. If we did, that would invalidate the ballot paper because of the words 'the way the paper is marked does not of itself identify the voter'. It is clear that that is not so in this case. The handwriting of a voter on a ballot paper does not of itself identify him. It is certainly not shown 'that he can be identified thereby'.

We know that the Conservative candidate thought the voter could be identified in this case. He said to the returning officer: 'I know the man who wrote that. I have been told his name. You check it.' He was supposed to have been a Mr Richard Red of Exeter. But when Mr Red was approached, he said: 'It was not me at all. I voted quite correctly at another station.'

It is clear to me that the new regulations going back to 1948 altered the pre-existing law. It is interesting to note that in *Schofield's Local Government Elections* (8th edn, 1979) p 365 it is said of *Birmingham Case, Woodward v Sarsons*: 'But there are grave doubts whether this now invalidates the vote.' It is also said (at p 369):

'In all cases which have been before the courts in recent years, the judges have all indicated that the voter's franchise should not lightly be lost by declaring a vote to be bad if there is a clear intention shown as to what the voter intended to do.'

In my opinion, since the new rules came into force, *Birmingham Case* and *Exeter Case* are no longer law. The fact that a voter has written in handwriting the name of his chosen candidate, clearly showing that he intended to vote for that candidate, on the correct ballot paper and in the correct place does not invalidate the ballot paper at all.

The voter in this case did not obey the directions. Many people make a slip of some kind. But when the intention is clear, as it was in this case, it seems to me entirely wrong that his vote should not be counted. The voter intended to vote for Mr Ruffle. He made it all the clearer by writing down the name of the candidate he wanted to vote for. He cannot be identified by his handwriting. The ballot paper should not be rejected simply because somebody says that he might possibly be identified by his handwriting. I think that the returning officer was absolutely right to accept the ballot paper as valid.

I now turn to the next point in the case. Four ballot papers were not stamped with the official mark to show that they were properly issued. That mistake was made at the polling booth. The four voters filled in those ballot papers absolutely correctly. They put crosses next to the names of their chosen candidates. It seems to me that those votes certainly ought to be counted whenever the result is so close that it is necessary. Section 37 of the Representation of the People Act 1949 expressly deals with this sort of situation:

'(1) No local government election shall be declared invalid by reason of any act or omission of the returning officer or any other person in breach of his official duty in connection with the election or otherwise of the local elections rules if it appears to the tribunal having cognizance of the question that the election was so conducted as to be substantially in accordance with the law as to elections [as this certainly was] and that the act or omission did not affect its result . . .'

Counsel for Mr Rogers submits that the omission (to stamp the four ballot papers) did not affect the result, which was that the Conservative candidate was elected. I cannot agree with that argument in the slightest. When the four rejected ballot papers are brought in, as they ought to be, the result is a tie. So the result is affected.

Under r 45 of the Local Elections (Principal Areas) Rules 1973 (repealing the 1949 rules), where there is a tie—

'the returning officer shall forthwith decide between those candidates by lot, and proceed as if the candidate on whom the lot falls had received an additional vote.'

a No lot was held in this case, because it did not appear on the count that there was a tie. Now we know that there was a tie. But we do not know if the Conservative candidate or the Liberal candidate would have won. So the result has been affected by those four votes.

In the circumstances, it is quite plain that the election as declared is now found to be invalid, because the Conservative candidate did not win by two votes as announced. When the unstamped ballot papers are taken into account, the result was a tie. So I am afraid that the election must be declared void; and there must be a new election so as to b clear up the position in this part of Exeter.

I think the judge below was quite right. I would dismiss the appeal.

c **EVELEIGH LJ.** I agree. I approach this case by reading r 43 of the Local Elections (Principal Areas) Rules 1973 first and not by looking at the cases as we have been invited to do. The application of r 43(3) to the facts of this case is, in my opinion, straightforward. Taking the words 'Ruffle Liberal' as a vote, as I think it was and which the officer took it to be, then the ballot paper is one on which a vote is marked, in the words of r 43(3)(b), 'otherwise than by means of a cross', namely by handwriting. Then the rule says that the vote—

d 'shall not by reason thereof [that is, by reason of being in handwriting] be deemed to be void . . . if an intention that the vote shall be for one or other of the candidates appears . . .'

That intention does clearly appear. Then there only remains the question: is this a case where 'it is not shown that [the voter] can be identified thereby'?

e Handwriting may be of assistance in identification, but the experience in these courts has shown that in many cases it may be no help at all. The mere fact that it is in handwriting does not of itself show that the voter can be identified. The cases cited to this court in which handwriting has been held to be fatal were all cases before the introduction of the provisions of r 43(3) which I am now construing. They are, therefore, not authorities for the construction of r 43(3) itself. They were concerned to construe s 2 f of the Ballot Act 1872, when that section stood alone without the qualifications introduced by r 43(3). However, in any case, I doubt the correctness of the statement of principle which is to be found in those cases. The first appears in *Wigtown Case* (1874) 2 O'M & H 215 at 217, where Lord Ormidale said:

'The construction which I am disposed to put on the statute is that this name which has been written on the ballot-paper might lead to the identification of the g voter.'

And he later again uses the expression 'might lead to the identification of the voter'. The rule does not say 'might': it says 'can'. Handwriting, as I have said, may be a pointer, but it may not. These doubts were clearly shared by Ridley J in *Exeter Case* (1911) 6 O'M & H 228 at 230, where he said:

h 'In the circumstances I should have thought that the rule might well be drawn not exactly at the line where it was in *Woodward* v. *Sarsons* ((1875) LR 10 CP 733), but at another one, namely, that there must be something in the writing, in the words upon the paper more than the mere handwriting, to give facility of identification of the voter.'

j Therefore we are concerned to decide whether an election which should otherwise be declared invalid shall be saved by s 37 of the Representation of the People Act 1949. That provides in sub-s (1) that it shall not be invalid—

'if it appears to the tribunal having cognizance of the question that the election was so conducted as to be substantially in accordance with the law as to elections and that the act or omission did not affect its result . . .'

There are two conditions to be fulfilled there. The first, in my view, that the election was conducted substantially in accordance with the law as to elections, is fulfilled, but in *a* my opinion the second one is not. As Lord Denning MR has said, had it not been for the irregularity, there would in this case have been a lot; no one can say who would have been the successful candidate. Therefore we cannot be satisfied that the result has not been affected by the irregularity. It prevented the candidate being chosen by lot, and it dictated the choice of Mr Rogers.

I too agree that this appeal should be dismissed. *b*

WATKINS LJ. I agree and I have nothing to add.

Appeal dismissed.

Solicitors: *Kenwright & Cox*, agents for *Crosse & Crosse*, Exeter (for the petitioner); *c* *Penningtons*, agents for *Ford, Simey & Ford*, Exeter (for the first respondent); *Sharpe, Pritchard & Co*, agents for *W A Burkinshaw*, Exeter (for the second respondent).

Frances Rustin Barrister.

d

Bernard v Josephs

COURT OF APPEAL, CIVIL DIVISION
LORD DENNING MR, GRIFFITHS AND KERR LJJ *e*
4, 5, 30 MARCH 1982

Trust and trustee – Constructive trust – Unmarried couple – House acquired by joint efforts for joint benefit – Principles governing apportionment of beneficial interests – Relevance of principles governing rights of husband and wife in matrimonial home – House acquired by engaged couple in joint names – Both going into occupation and letting rooms to meet mortgage instalments – Couple *f* *separating – Man thereafter occupying house alone – Sale of property – Share of proceeds of sale to which woman entitled – Whether order for sale should be made.*

In 1973 the plaintiff and the defendant became engaged and subsequently purchased a house for their joint occupation. The whole of the purchase price was borrowed on mortgage, for which they assumed joint liability, and the house was transferred into *g* their joint names, without any express declaration of trust. They each made an initial contribution to the expenses of the purchase, and the defendant spent a further sum on improvements to enable part of the premises to be let, the resulting rents being used for the mortgage payments. Both the plaintiff and the defendant went out to work and both contributed towards the joint living expenses. In 1976 they separated and the defendant remained in the house and later married another woman. In February 1978 the plaintiff *h* commenced proceedings in the Chancery Division seeking an order for sale of the house and a declaration that she was entitled to a half share of the proceeds. The judge held that, subject to each party receiving credit for their initial contribution towards the expenses of the purchase and to the defendant receiving credit for the sum spent on improving the property, they had an equal share in the proceeds of the house, and, since the purpose for which the house had been acquired was at an end, the house should be *j* sold with vacant possession. The defendant appealed, contending that he should have the major share in the equity and that no order for sale should be made. Pending the hearing of the appeal, the plaintiff indicated that she would not insist on a sale if the defendant purchased her share.

Held – (1) Where a house had been acquired jointly by an unmarried couple but without

any express declaration of trust and the couple lived in it together as if married, the share
a of the beneficial interest in the property to which each was entitled was normally to be
ascertained according to the same principles applicable to a married couple. However
(per Griffiths and Kerr LJJ), the nature of the relationship was an important factor when
considering the inference to be drawn from the way in which the parties had conducted
their affairs and it was essential for the court to be satisfied that the relationship between
the parties was intended to involve the same degree of commitment as a marriage before
b applying the principles applicable to a married couple (see p 167 e to g, p 169 f to h, p 170
a b and p 173 h j, post); Cooke v Head [1972] 2 All ER 38 applied.
   (2) Accordingly, where there was no express declaration of trust there was no
presumption that the parties would always take equal shares; instead, their respective
shares were to be ascertained according to the circumstances and the parties' respective
contributions to the purchase and the joint finances of the home, either (per Lord
c Denning MR and Kerr LJ) by adding up the contributions in cash, in kind or in services
of each party up to the time of the separation and even, where necessary, having regard
to post-separation events, or (per Griffiths LJ) by determining the intention of the parties
at the time of the purchase regarding their respective beneficial interests as evidenced by
their respective contributions both at the time of the purchase and subsequently (see p
166 d e j, p 169 c d, p 170 e to j, p 171 b c and p 173 e to g, post); dictum of Pearson LJ in
d Hine v Hine [1962] 3 All ER at 350, Pettitt v Pettitt [1969] 2 All ER 385, Gissing v Gissing
[1970] 2 All ER 780, Hazell v Hazell [1972] 1 All ER 923 and dictum of Lord Denning
MR in Cooke v Head [1972] 2 All ER at 41–42 considered.
   (3) Since the house had been purchased in the parties' joint names in order to provide
a house for them, since the mortgage was in joint names and since each had contributed
to the purchase price and they had pooled their incomes, the proper inference to be
e drawn was that the parties intended that they should have equal shares in the house
subject to receiving credit for their initial contributions and sums spent on improvements.
Furthermore, since the purpose for which the house had been bought (and for which
there was a trust for sale) was at an end, the judge had been right to make an order for
sale. However, since the plaintiff had agreed to let the defendant remain in the house
and purchase her share, the order would be postponed pending the purchase (see p 167 j
f to p 168 h, p 171 d to p 172 d, p 174 a to h and p 176 g h, post).
   Per Lord Denning MR. Cases concerning homes of unmarried couples should be
brought in the Family Division and not in the Chancery Division because they are so
similar to those concerning husband and wife (see p 168 j, post).

Notes
g For resulting trusts arising out of joint transactions, see 38 Halsbury's Laws (3rd edn)
868, para 1462, and for cases on the subject, see 47 Digest (Repl) 127, 925–927.
   For the determination of property rights between husband and wife, see 22 Halsbury's
Laws (4th edn) para 1030, and for cases on the subject, see 27(1) Digest (Reissue) 305–
315, 2267–2330.

h **Cases referred to in judgments**
Ball, Re, Jones v Jones (1930) 74 SJ 298, 47 Digest (Repl) 412, 3692.
Bedson v Bedson [1965] 3 All ER 307, [1965] 2 QB 666, [1965] 3 WLR 891, CA, 27(1)
   Digest (Reissue) 313, 2316.
Browne (formerly Pritchard) v Prichard [1975] 3 All ER 721, [1975] 1 WLR 1366, CA,
   Digest (Cont Vol D) 427, 6962Add.
j Cobb v Cobb [1955] 2 All ER 696, [1955] 1 WLR 731, CA, 27(1) Digest (Reissue) 309, 2296.
Cooke v Head [1972] 2 All ER 38, [1972] 1 WLR 518, CA, Digest (Cont Vol D) 1008, 927a.
Cowcher v Cowcher [1972] 1 All ER 943, [1972] 1 WLR 425, Digest (Cont Vol D) 394,
   715a.
Crisp v Mullings (1974) 233 EG 511; rvsd (1975) 239 EG 119, CA.
Dennis v McDonald [1981] 2 All ER 632, [1981] 1 WLR 810; affd [1982] 1 All ER 590,
   [1982] 2 WLR 275, CA.

Evers's Trust, Re, Papps v Evers [1980] 3 All ER 399, [1980] 1 WLR 1327, CA.
Farquharson v Farquharson (1971) 115 SJ 444, CA, 27(1) Digest (Reissue) 312, 2308.   *a*
Gissing v Gissing [1970] 2 All ER 780, [1971] AC 886, [1970] 3 WLR 255, HL, 27(1) Digest
   (Reissue) 311, 2303.
Godwin v Bedwell [1982] CA Bound Transcript 185.
Hall v Hall (1981) Times, 4 April, CA.
Hazell v Hazell [1972] 1 All ER 923, [1972] 1 WLR 301, CA, Digest (Cont Vol D) 398,
   2310a.   *b*
Hine v Hine [1962] 3 All ER 345, [1962] 1 WLR 1124, CA, 27(1) Digest (Reissue) 313,
   2315.
Jones v Challenger [1960] 1 All ER 785, [1961] 1 QB 176, [1960] 2 WLR 695, CA, 47
   Digest (Repl) 400, 3595.
Pettitt v Pettitt [1969] 2 All ER 385, [1970] AC 777, [1969] 2 WLR 966, HL, 27 Digest
   (Reissue) 102, 707.   *c*
Rawlings v Rawlings [1964] 2 All ER 804, [1964] P 398, [1964] 3 WLR 294, CA, 27(1)
   Digest (Reissue) 94, 680.
Richards v Dove [1974] 1 All ER 888, Digest (Cont Vol D) 1009, 927b.
Robinson v Robinson (1977) 241 EG 153.
Turner v Morgan (1803) 8 Ves 143, 32 ER 307.
Williams v Williams [1977] 1 All ER 28, [1976] Ch 278, [1976] 3 WLR 494, CA, Digest   *d*
   (Cont Vol E) 255, 662b.
Wilson v Wilson [1963] 2 All ER 447, [1963] 1 WLR 601, CA, 27(1) Digest (Reissue) 93,
   676.

Cases also cited
Burgess v Rawnsley [1955] 3 All ER 142, [1975] Ch 429, CA.   *e*
Fender v Mildmay [1937] 3 All ER 402, [1938] AC 1, HL.

Appeal
The defendant, Dion Emmanuel Josephs, appealed against the decision of his Honour
Judge Mervyn Davies QC sitting as a judge of the High Court on 17 July 1980, whereby
the judge ordered that the beneficial interest in the property known as 177 Dunstan's   *f*
Road, London SE22 was held on equal shares by the defendant and the plaintiff, Maria
Teresa Bernard, that the property be sold with vacant possession, that the defendant give
vacant possession on or before 1 November 1980 and that the net proceeds of sale after
deducting the amounts owing on mortgage and amounts owing to the parties be divided
equally between the parties. The facts are set out in the judgment of Lord Denning MR.

g

John Speed for the defendant.
William Panton for the plaintiff.

Cur adv vult

30 March. The following judgments were read.   *h*

LORD DENNING MR. This is all about a young lady, Maria Teresa Bernard. In
August 1973 it was her 21st birthday. On that very day she became engaged to be
married. It was to Dion Emmanuel Josephs. He was 30. Unknown to her he was already
a married man, not yet divorced. They arranged to get a house to set up home together.
It was 177 Dunstan's Road, London SE22. It was conveyed to them on 21 October 1974   *j*
in their joint names. It was a simple transfer by the vendor as beneficial owner 'to Dion
Emmanuel Josephs and Maria Teresa Bernard', without more, no declaration of trust, or
anything.
    The purchase price was £11,750. The whole of it was raised on mortgage from the
Southwark London Borough Council. They both signed the legal charge to secure it.

They each paid some of the incidental expenses. She paid £200 of her own money. He
a paid £250 and £400 which he borrowed. They went into occupation and lived there
together as man and wife. The house was quite large. So they let off much of it to tenants.
This helped greatly towards the mortgage instalments. Both went out to work. Their
earnings enabled them to pay the rest of the outgoings and food, and so forth. Then after
a year or two they quarrelled. She says that he was violent to her. So in July 1976 she left.
He stayed on in the house. She applied for the house to be sold and for one-half of the
b proceeds. Meanwhile in June 1975 he had got a divorce from his lawful wife. In April
1978 he married another woman. He took her to live with him in the house. They are
childless.

The law
In our time the concept of marriage, I am sorry to say, is being eroded. Nowadays
c many couples live together as if they were husband and wife, but they are not married.
They hope and expect that their relationship will be permanent. They acquire a house in
their joint names. Most of the purchase price is obtained on mortgage in both their
names. They are both responsible for payment of the instalments. Both go out to work.
They pay the outgoings out of their joint resources. One paying for the food and
housekeeping. The other paying the mortgage instalments. And so forth. Just as husband
d and wife do. But later on, for some reason or other, they fall out. They go their own
separate ways. One or other leaves the house. The other stays behind in it. There is no
need to divorce. They just separate. What is to happen to the house? Is it to be sold? If
so, are the proceeds to be divided? And, if so, in what proportion? Or is one of them to
be allowed to stay in it? If so, on what terms? If they had been husband and wife, our
matrimonial property legislation would give the Family Division a very wide discretion
e to deal with all these problems. It is contained in ss 23 to 25 of the Matrimonial Causes
Act 1973. But there is no such legislation for couples like these.

The legislative provision
The legal position is that they hold the house on trust for sale. Section 36(1) of the Law
of Property Act 1925 says:
f
> 'Where a legal estate . . . is beneficially limited to or held in trust for any persons
> as joint tenants, the same shall be held on trust for sale, in like manner as if the
> persons beneficially entitled were tenants in common, but not so as to sever their
> joint tenancy in equity.'

That is followed by sub-s (2) which says:
g
> '. . . under the trust for sale affecting the land the net proceeds of sale, and the net
> rents and profits until sale, shall be held upon the trusts which would have been
> requisite for giving effect to the beneficial interests if there had been an actual
> severance.'

But that does not tell what those beneficial interests shall be.
h   When there is a dispute as to the shares in the house, the parties can apply to the court
for a declaration. After they separate, the appropriate machinery is for one or other to
apply to the court under s 30 of the Law of Property Act 1925. He or she can apply to the
court 'for an order directing the trustees for sale to give effect thereto, and the court may
make such order as it thinks fit'.

j What are their shares?
When the house is conveyed into *joint names*, the question often arises: what are the
shares of the two parties in the house? And at what date are those shares to be ascertained?
If the conveyance contains an express declaration of the shares, that is decisive, as we held
recently in *Godwin v Bedwell* [1982] CA Bound Transcript 185. But often there is, as here,
no such declaration. In such a case it used to be thought that the shares would always be

equal shares. That was the view of Russell LJ in *Bedson v Bedson* [1965] 3 All ER 307 at 318, [1965] 2 QB 666 at 689, when he said:

> 'If there be two beneficial joint tenants, severance produces a beneficial tenancy in common in two equal shares ... by declaration of the beneficial joint tenancy between A and B, their respective rights and titles are no less clearly laid down and established than if there had been a declaration of a beneficial tenancy in common in equal undivided shares.'

Russell LJ had previously said much the same in *Wilson v Wilson* [1963] 2 All ER 447 at 453, [1963] 1 WLR 601 at 609.

But that view has not prevailed. It is because a conveyance into joint names does not necessarily mean equal shares. It is often required by the local council or by the building society when they grant a mortgage, so that they are both responsible for repayment. It is sometimes done on the suggestion of lawyers, without taking into account all the factors, such as their contributions to the purchase money and so forth.

As between husband and wife, when the house is in joint names and there is no declaration of trust, the shares are usually to be ascertained by reference to their respective contributions, just as when it is in the name of one or other only. The share of each depends on all the circumstances of the case, taking into account their contributions at the time of acquisition of the house, and, in addition, their contributions in cash, or in kind, or in services, up to the time of separation. In most cases the shares should be ascertained as at that time. But there may be some cases where later events can be considered. The departing party may only be entitled to one-half, one-quarter or even one-fifth, depending on the contributions made by each and, I would add, all the circumstances of the case. That was the view of this court in *Hine v Hine* [1962] 3 All ER 345, [1962] 1 WLR 1124. The facts of that case show clearly that justice requires that the courts should have a discretion to apportion the shares, and that there should not be a rigid rule of equal shares. I would adopt, in particular, the words of Pearson LJ ([1962] 3 All ER 345 at 350, [1962] 1 WLR 1124 at 1132):

> 'In my judgment, however, the fact that the husband and wife took the property in joint tenancy does not necessarily mean that the husband should have a half interest in the proceeds of the sale now in contemplation. The parties agreed, expressly or by implication from the creation of the joint tenancy, that the house should be the matrimonial home and should belong to both of them (technically to each of them in its entirety) and that, on the death of one it would belong to the other by right of survivorship. They did not, however, make any agreement, or have any common intention, what should happen in the event of the marriage breaking up and the property then being sold. That event was outside the contemplation of the parties. The proper division of the proceeds of sale in that event is left to be decided by the court in this application under s. 17 [of the Married Women's Property Act 1882]. The court has to do this by attributing artificially to the parties a reasonable intention at the time of the transaction in the year 1950, and for this purpose has to take into account not only the nature and form of the transaction, but also (as stated by ROMER, L.J., in *Cobb* v. *Cobb* ([1955] 2 All ER 696 at 699, [1955] 1 WLR 731 at 735)) "the course of conduct of husband and wife (including their respective contributions towards the purchase price) at the time when the home was purchased *and subsequently.*" In my judgment, the principle, which is shortly stated in the maxim "equality is equity", though it affords a just solution in many cases under s. 17, does not in the present case afford a just solution such as the parties can reasonably be taken to have intended.' (My emphasis.)

In that passage Pearson LJ refers to husband and wife, but his reasoning applies also to persons living together, as if husband and wife. We applied it in such a case. In *Cooke v Head* [1972] 2 All ER 38, [1972] 1 WLR 518 the house was in the man's name only, but the woman made such substantial contributions that she was awarded a one-third share. I said ([1972] 2 All ER 38 at 41–42, [1972] 1 WLR 518 at 520–521):

a

'The legal owner is bound to hold the property on trust for them both. This trust does not need any writing. It can be enforced by an order for sale, but in a proper case the sale can be postponed indefinitely. It applies to husband and wife, to engaged couples, and to man and mistress, and may be to other relationships too . . . In the light of recent developments, I do not think it is right to approach this case by looking at the money contributions of each and dividing up the beneficial interest according to those contributions. The matter should be looked at more broadly, just as we do in husband and wife cases. We look to see what the equity is worth at the time when the parties separate. We assess the shares as at that time. If the property has been sold, we look at the amount which it has realised, and say how it is to be divided between them. Lord Diplock in *Gissing v Gissing* [1970] 2 All ER 780 at 793, [1971] AC 886 at 909 intimated that it is quite legitimate to infer that "the wife should be entitled to a share which was not to be quantified immediately on the acquisition of the home but should be left to be determined when the mortgage was repaid or the property disposed of." Likewise with a mistress.'

b

c

That view was confirmed by this court recently in *Hall v Hall* (1981) Times, 4 April. A man and woman lived together for seven years without being married. The house was in the man's name alone. They separated. The woman left. The court ascertained the shares at the date of separation and held that her share was one-fifth. I notice that in that case we referred to cases between husband and wife, and said that the shares are ascertained at the date of divorce. But I do not think that is correct. Their shares should normally be ascertained at the time of separation; not at the date when they acquired the house, but at the date of separation: see *Hazell v Hazell* [1972] 1 All ER 923, [1972] 1 WLR 301. That is the proper date, for only then can the respective contributions be fairly assessed. But later events can be taken into account. And, of course, under the matrimonial legislation, the Family Division can afterwards vary those shares by appropriate transfers.

d

e

In my opinion in ascertaining the respective shares, the courts should normally apply the same considerations to couples living together (as if married) as they do to couples who are truly married. The shares may be half and half, or any such other proportion as in the circumstances of the case appears to be fair and just.

f

Engaged couples

As it happened Parliament had in 1970 passed an Act which put engaged couples on the same footing as husband and wife: see s 2 of the Law Reform (Miscellaneous Provisions) Act 1970. Our decision in *Cooke v Head* does the same for couples living together as if they were husband and wife, even though they have not made any agreement to marry. This is very desirable. There is no good reason for making any difference between the two kinds of case. Especially when their relationship of 'engaged' or 'not engaged' to be married is so often undetermined and indeterminable.

g

Should there be an order for sale?

When the parties separate, each wants to know what is to be done with the house. One or other then makes an application under s 30 of the Law of Property Act 1925. Under it the court has ample power to postpone a sale. I stated the modern approach in *Williams v Williams* [1977] 1 All ER 28 at 30, [1976] Ch 278 at 285:

h

'When judges are dealing with the matrimonial home, they nowadays have great regard to the fact that the house is bought as a home in which the family is to be brought up. It is not treated as property to be sold, nor as an investment to be realised for cash. That was emphasised by this court in the recent case of *Browne v Pritchard* [1975] 3 All ER 721, [1975] 1 WLR 1366. The court, in executing the trust, should regard the primary object as being to provide a home and not a sale. Steps should be taken to preserve it as a home for the remaining partner and children, but giving the outgoing partner such compensation, by way of a charge or being bought out, as is reasonable in the circumstances.'

j

The same approach should be adopted to cases where a man and woman are living together but not married: see *Re Evers's Trust, Papps v Evers* [1980] 3 All ER 399, [1980] 1 WLR 1327. Also when, as here, there are no children. The court can refuse to order a sale at the instance of the outgoing party, even after they separate, if it would be unduly harsh to require the remaining party to vacate, or it can make an order for sale but suspending it on terms.

Turning into money

After ascertaining the shares, the next problem arises when it is to be turned into money. Usually one of the parties stays in the house, paying the mortgage instalments and the rates and other outgoings. The house also increases in value greatly owing to inflation. None of that alters the shares of the parties in the house itself. But it does mean that when the house is sold, or the one buys the other out, there have to be many adjustments made. The value of the house itself is taken at the value at the time of sale or buying out. There must be deducted from it all the money needed to redeem the mortgage. Then the one in possession must be given credit for paying the other's share of the mortgage instalments and be debited with an occupation rent for using the other's share of the house. Other adjustments may be needed for other outgoings. Then the net amount must be divided according to the shares.

Applied to this case

The judge assessed the shares in the house as half and half. He took it at the date of acquisition. But I think on the facts it would be the same (half and half) at the date of separation. Mr Josephs and his present wife have been in the house for over three years now. Miss Bernard has not been in it for five years. It would be unduly harsh to turn Mr Josephs and his wife out of this house, simply in order to provide funds for Miss Bernard. But, seeing that he has the use of her share, it would only be fair that he should pay an occupation rent in respect of it: see *Dennis v McDonald* [1981] 2 All ER 632, [1981] 1 WLR 810; [1982] 1 All ER 590, [1982] 2 WLR 275. No doubt, however, he has been paying the whole of the mortgage instalments and this should be taken into account as well. It may relieve him of paying any occupation rent for her half share.

The problem is to calculate the sum which Mr Josephs should pay to Miss Bernard to buy her out. This is to be done by taking the price obtainable for the house if it were sold now with vacant possession. Then deduct the sum payable to redeem the mortgage. Then deduct one-half of the amount paid by Mr Josephs since the separation for mortgage instalments (deducting, of course, the amount received from the tenants). He should only get credit for one-half, because he has had the benefit of her half share. Then make any other special adjustments.

It is undesirable to spend money on inquiries. On the information given to us, we calculate that the sum payable by Mr Josephs to Miss Bernard is £6,000. An order for sale should be made, but not to be enforced if Mr Josephs pays £6,000 to Miss Bernard within four months. On his paying her that sum, she should transfer all her share in the house to him.

We are told that both sides are legally aided. It looks as if the Law Society will have a charge on Miss Bernard's £6,000 for their costs on her behalf, and a charge on the house for their costs on Mr Josephs's behalf. The allowance of £2,500 is made only to married persons, not to unmarried ones. Each charge will reduce the amounts considerably. But this case will, we hope, be a precedent for others of like nature, so that they can be settled by agreement without recourse to the courts.

One last word: these cases about the home of couples living together are so similar to those of husband and wife that I think they should be started in the Family Division or transferred to it, rather than the Chancery Division.

GRIFFITHS LJ. This appeal presents a problem with which the courts are becoming very familiar. Today more and more people live together without getting married. They

acquire a house in their joint names, and then, when their relationship breaks down and
a they part, they cannot agree who owns the house so they turn to the courts to solve the
question of ownership. In my view the legal principles by which the court must solve
the problem are now well settled and are to be found in two decisions of the House of
Lords: *Pettitt v Pettitt* [1969] 2 All ER 385, [1970] AC 777 and *Gissing v Gissing* [1970] 2
All ER 780, [1971] AC 886.

Before Parliament enacted the Matrominal Causes Act 1973, which now gives the
b court a wide discretion to adjust rights of property on the breakdown of a marriage, the
question of the ownership of the matrimonial home was generally settled on an
application to the court under s 17 of the Married Women's Property Act 1882. In the
case of an unmarried couple the appropriate machinery is to make an application under
s 30 of the Law of Property Act 1925, as was done in this case. Both sections are essentially
procedural: neither gives the judge a wide discretion to decide the question of ownership
c of the house in accordance with his idea what would be 'fair' in all the circumstances.
The respective interests of the parties must be determined by the application of the law
relating to trusts. This is, of course, far easier to say than to do.

The task of the judge is to look at all the evidence placed before him and decide
whether it indicates an intention by the parties that the beneficial ownership of the house
should be held in other than equal shares. It is only in the somewhat unlikely event that
d nothing in the evidence provides a pointer to the intention of the parties that the judge
should decide the case on the basis that the equitable title follows the legal title or to use
another maxim that equality is equity.

In *Pettitt v Pettitt* [1969] 2 All ER 385 at 406, [1970] AC 777 at 813–814 Lord Upjohn
said:

e
> '. . . in the absence of all other evidence, if the property is conveyed into the name
> of one spouse at law that will operate to convey also the beneficial interest and if
> conveyed to the spouses jointly that operates to convey the beneficial interest to the
> spouses jointly, i.e., with benefit of survivorship, but it is seldom that this will be
> determinative.'

See also *Crisp v Mullings* (1975) EG 119.
f The cases that have been decided in the last 30 years provided valuable pointers to the
matters that the courts should or should not take into consideration when assessing the
proportions in which the beneficial interest in the house should be divided. But here I
would like to sound a note of caution. Most of the decided cases have been dealing with
married people. The legal principles to be applied are the same whether the dispute is
between married or unmarried couples, but the nature of the relationship between the
g parties is a very important factor when considering what inferences should be drawn
from the way they have conducted their affairs. There are many reasons why a man and
a woman may decide to live together without marrying, and one of them is that each
values his independence and does not wish to make the commitment of marriage; in
such a case it will be misleading to make the same assumptions and to draw the same
inferences from their behaviour as in the case of a married couple. The judge must look
h most carefully at the nature of the relationship, and only if satisfied that it was intended
to involve the same degree of commitment as marriage will it be legitimate to regard
them as no different from a married couple. Parliament itself has recognised this and has
made specific provision for it by providing in s 2 of the Law Reform (Miscellaneous
Provision) Act 1970 that in the case of engaged couples where the agreement to marry is
terminated 'any rule of law relating to the rights of husbands and wives in relation to
j property in which either or both has or have a beneficial interest . . . shall apply . . .'

Although Miss Bernard claimed that she was officially engaged to Mr Josephs at the
time they bought the house, she did not rely on this section, and accordingly, although
there was some discussion about the effect of the section, its full scope was not examined
and does not fall to be decided in this case, in particular whether it empowers the court
to use all the powers of the Matrimonial Causes Act 1973 to adjust the rights of property

between engaged couples, which it certainly does not possess in the case of couples living together who have not become engaged to marry. There will of course be many cases of *a* couples living together with every intention that the relationship should be permanent and with the same degree of commitment as marriage; they may be unable to marry because one or other cannot obtain a divorce, and in such cases it may be legitimate to regard them in the same way as a married couple. Each case will depend on its own facts, and I only warn against a blithe assumption that all couples living together are to be regarded as no different from a married couple.   *b*

The starting point of an inquiry into the beneficial ownership of a house in joint names must be the conveyance. If the conveyance deals with the beneficial ownership and defines the shares, it is conclusive: see *Pettitt v Pettitt* [1969] 2 All ER 385 at 405, [1970] AC 777 at 813, where Lord Upjohn said:

> 'If the property in question is land there must be some lease or conveyance which shows how it was acquired. If that document declares not merely in whom the legal *c* title is to vest but in whom the beneficial title is to vest that necessarily concludes the question of title as between the spouses for all time, and in the absence of fraud or mistake at the time of the transaction the parties cannot go behind it at any time thereafter even on death or the break-up of the marriage.'

I wish more heed had been paid to the advice to solicitors given by Bagnall J in *Cowcher* *d* *v Cowcher* [1972] 1 All ER 943, [1972] 1 WLR 425, in which he pointed out the wisdom of making an express declaration of the beneficial interests in the property at the time it is bought. The home is usually the most valuable asset of any couple living together and if, when they separate, a legal battle is waged with the aid of legal aid over the ownership of their shares in the house the result is that both of them see a large part of their share of the equity disappear in costs into the maw of the legal aid fund, as indeed will happen in *e* this case.

In the absence of any express declaration as to the beneficial interest, the judge must look to see the respective contributions made towards the purchase price. In the unlikely event that the house was bought without a mortgage, their respective contributions to the purchase price will determine their share in the equity.

If the house has been bought on a mortgage, the inquiry is more difficult. The fact *f* that one party paid the mortgage may indicate that it was recognised by the couple that that party was solely responsible for providing the purchase price and therefore to be regarded as the sole beneficial owner. But often, where a couple are living together and both are working and pooling their resources, which one of them pays the mortgage may be no more than a matter of internal accounting between them. In such a case the judge must look at the contributions of each to the 'family' finances and determine as *g* best he may what contribution each was making towards the purchase of the house. This is not to be carried out as a strictly mathematical exercise; for instance, if the man was ill for a time and out of work so that the woman temporarily contributed more, that temporary state of affairs should not increase her share, nor should her share be decreased if she was temporarily unable to work whilst having a baby. The contributions must be viewed broadly by the judge to guide him to the parties' unexpressed and probably *h* unconsidered intentions as to the beneficial ownership of the house. There is of course an air of unreality about the whole exercise, but the judge must do his best and only as a last resort abandon the attempt in favour of applying the presumption of equality, which may so often give an unfair result.

It emerges clearly from the speeches in *Pettitt v Pettitt* and *Gissing v Gissing* that it is the intention as to the beneficial ownership at the time the house is bought that is crucial, *j* and the contributions made by the parties to the acquisition are examined to establish that intention: see *Pettitt v Pettitt* [1969] 2 All ER 385 at 394, 400, 408, [1970] AC 777 at 800, 807, 816 per Lord Morris, Lord Hodson and Lord Upjohn; and see also *Gissing v Gissing* [1970] 2 All ER 780 at 783, 786, 787, [1971] AC 886 at 898, 900, 902 per Lord Morris, Viscount Dilhorne and Lord Pearson.

It might in exceptional circumstances be inferred that the parties agreed to alter their
a beneficial interests after the house was bought; an example would be if the man bought
the house in the first place and the woman years later used a legacy to build an extra floor
to make more room for the children. In such circumstances the obvious inference would
be that the parties agreed that the woman should acquire a share in the greatly increased
value of the house produced by her money. But this depends on the court being able to
infer an intention to alter the share in which the beneficial interest was previously held;
b the mere fact that one party has spent time and money on improving the property will
not normally be sufficient to draw such an inference: see *Pettitt v Pettitt*. In the absence of
any special circumstances I agree with the judge in this case that the time at which the
beneficial interest crystallises is the time of the acquisition, but to ascertain this he must
look at all the evidence including all the contributions made by the parties. As a general
rule the only relevant contributions will be those up to the date of the separation, but it
c does not necessarily follow that what happens after the separation will in every case be
irrelevant. In my opinion the judge should examine all the evidence placed before him
and not regard the date of separation as a cut-off point. The task imposed on the judge is
so difficult that every scrap of evidence may be of value, and should be available to him.

On the facts of this case I have no doubt that the judge was right to hold that the
beneficial ownership was held in equal shares. The house was bought to provide a home
d for the couple and they lived in it together; it was bought in joint names, the mortgage
was in joint names; the intention was to pay the mortgage by taking in tenants and using
their rent; they pooled their joint income; the girl worked all the time, but the man was
for a period unemployed. They both contributed small sums to the expenses involved in
the purchase: she provided £200 of her own money; he £650, £400 of which he
borrowed.
e   When they parted she left the house and he continued living there and is still living in
the house. He married another woman in 1978 and the mortgage repayments are up to
date. It appears that the rent of tenants has continued to contribute to the cost of the
mortgage.

The judge concluded that the evidence showed that this couple must be regarded as
providing the purchase money in equal shares and that accordingly the beneficial
f ownership of the house must be declared to be held in equal shares, and I agree with
him.

The fact that Mr Josephs paid the mortgage after Miss Bernard left the house was in
this case clearly done for his own convenience and provides no clue to their intentions at
the time they bought the house. I agree that in this case none of the evidence of the
behaviour of the parties after the separation throws any light on the question of the
g beneficial ownership of the house.

Now comes the problem as to the form of order that a judge has power to make on an
application under s 30 of the Law of Property Act 1925. This was recently considered by
the Court of Appeal in *Re Evers's Trust, Papps v Evers* [1980] 3 All ER 399, [1980] 1 WLR
1327.

The court should look at the purpose for which the house was bought in joint names
h and which resulted in its being held on trust for sale. If the purpose of that trust is
exhausted, then the court should make an order directing the sale of the house. This
house was bought to provide a home in which Miss Bernard and Mr Josephs could live
together. Now that they have separated, the purpose of the trust is exhausted, and if Miss
Bernard insisted on sale I can see no legitimate ground on which the court could refuse
to make an order for sale, although it could of course postpone sale for a few months to
j give Mr Josephs a reasonable chance to make other arrangements for his accommodation.
I can see no ground for criticising the judge's order that Mr Josephs should have four
months to vacate the property and that there should then be a sale with vacant possession.

When the proceeds of sale are realised there will have to be equitable accounting
between the parties before the money is distributed. If the woman has left, she is entitled
to receive an occupation rent, but if the man has kept up all the mortgage repayments,

he is entitled to credit for her share of the payments; if he has spent money on recent redecoration which results in a much better sale price, he should have credit for that, not *a* as an altered share, but by repayment of the whole or a part of the money he has spent. These are but examples of the way in which the balance is to be struck. The judge did it in this case; I see nothing wrong in his approach.

Now, it would be a great hardship on Mr and Mrs Josephs if they were to be forced to leave their home to enable it to be sold with vacant possession. Miss Bernard does not wish this misery to be inflicted on them, but she does want a fair sum of money for her *b* share in the value of the house. There is agreement as to the present market value of the house and this court has all the material available to calculate the sum that would represent the present value of her equity in the house after taking into account the equitable accounting to which I have referred. This being so, and because Miss Bernard through her counsel sensibly and compassionately agrees to this course, I accordingly agree with the orders proposed by Lord Denning MR, which will give Mr Josephs the *c* chance to buy Miss Bernard's share for £6,000; but, if he does not pay the money within four months, the house must then be sold with vacant possession and the proceeds distributed as directed by the judge.

KERR LJ. The facts of this case have already been stated in the judgment of Lord Denning MR, but I think that it is necessary to mention some of them in detail, as well *d* as the way in which these were dealt with in the decision of his Honour Judge Mervyn Davies QC, in order to illustrate the problems raised by this appeal.

As frequently happens, the parties decided to buy a house for their joint occupation with the possibility of ultimate marriage in mind, but with no clear agreement or common fixed intention concerning their future. Accordingly, the machinery of adjustment under s 2 of the Law Reform (Miscellaneous Provisions) Act 1970 is *e* unavailable. The house was conveyed to the parties in 1974 under a council transfer as joint owners without any express declaration of trust, and they assumed joint liability under a council mortgage for 100% of the purchase price of £11,750. The plaintiff, Miss Bernard, then contributed £200, and the defendant, Mr Josephs, £650 to the costs incidental to the purchase, the mortgage and the expenses of moving in. Mr Josephs thereafter spent £2,000 on decorations and repairs to enable part of the premises to be *f* let, and the resulting rents were used for the mortgage payments, which were made by him throughout. These were their respective contributions to the acquisition of the property and to its improvement during their cohabitation. They also both contributed to their living expenses during this period. Miss Bernard paid for their food and household necessities, and Mr Josephs paid the electricity and other bills. I only mention the latter contributions in passing, since the judge rightly took no account of these *g* domestic arrangements, which might apply equally to any people living together in, for instance, rented accommodation, and which throw no light on what should be their shares in the property in which they live. This relationship continued for about 18 months until Miss Bernard left against her will, following a serious disagreement in which Mr Josephs appears to have behaved with violence towards her. She was accordingly in the position of having been ousted from the jointly owned property, *h* similarly to the facts in *Dennis v McDonald* [1981] 2 All ER 632, [1981] 1 WLR 810; [1982] 1 All ER 590, [1982] 2 WLR 275, to which I refer further hereafter. Mr Josephs continued to live in the property and, for some time at any rate, to rent out parts of it. He fell into arrears with the mortgage, but successfully resisted a claim for possession by the council by bringing the mortgage payments up to date, as they evidently now are. I will return to the resulting figures in a moment in the context of the judgment given *j* below.

In February 1978 Miss Bernard then issued proceedings in the Chancery Division by originating summons under ss 30 and 203(5) of the Law of Property Act 1925 and s 57 of the Trustee Act 1925 for an order for sale and a declaration that she was entitled to a half share of the proceeds after deduction of the outstanding mortgage. In this connection

it was common ground before us that the balance of the equity value of the house, in
a view of the rise in property prices since 1974, would now be about £15,000. Shortly
after the proceedings began Mr Josephs remarried, having meanwhile obtained his
divorce from a former marriage, and he and his wife are now still living in the house.
No children are involved as the result of either relationship.

Although the action had been commenced by originating summons followed by
(conflicting) affidavits on both sides, it was ordered (pursuant to RSC Ord 28, r 8) that the
b proceedings be continued as if they had been commenced by writ. Pleadings were served
and there was an oral hearing in which all the circumstances were inquired into.
Accordingly, I turn to the judge's decision from which Mr Josephs now appeals on two
main grounds, viz that (i) he should have been awarded the major share of the equity
and (ii) no order for sale should have been made.

First, in the light of the circumstances concerning the acquisition of the property, the
c judge concluded on the evidence that he would not be justified in imputing to the parties
any common intention as to their then respective ownership rights, but that, having
regard to the facts that the property was conveyed to them jointly and that both assumed
joint liability under the mortgage, the house belonged to the parties in equal shares. He
accordingly made a declaration to this effect.

Pausing at this point, although it was strongly contended on behalf of Mr Josephs that
d this was an inequitable result, I have no doubt, in agreement with the judgments which
have already been delivered, that no other conclusion could possibly have been reached
in the circumstances. But I would add two comments, although for the reasons
mentioned hereafter neither affects the outcome of this appeal.

First, if the parties' contributions towards the acquisition of the house had been
substantially unequal, then this would no doubt have been reflected in their respective
e shares in equity, since the absence of any express declaration of trust as to their respective
shares would permit this result. The judge clearly accepted this in principle, as did the
parties on the appeal to this court.

Second, while I agree that the parties' contributions on acquisition necessarily provide
the starting point for the declaration as to what their respective shares should be, I also
respectfully agree with Lord Denning MR that on the authorities as they now stand the
f court should consider the ultimate position concerning the parties' rights in the property
by reference to the time of separation, when one of the parties moves out and the
common purpose of the implied trust thereby generally, but not always, comes to an
end; and further that, for the purposes of equitable accounting, it is also permissible to
have regard to the events concerning the property which have occurred thereafter. In
my view these principles clearly follow from a number of decisions, most of them in this
g court, in which *Gissing v Gissing* [1970] 2 All ER 780, [1971] AC 886, following on *Pettitt
v Pettitt* [1969] 2 All ER 385, [1970] AC 777, has been considered. In relation to married
couples these are in particular *Farquharson v Farquharson* (1971) 115 SJ 444, *Hazell v Hazell*
[1972] 1 All ER 923, [1972] 1 WLR 301 and *Williams v Williams* [1977] 1 All ER 28,
[1976] Ch 278. In relation to unmarried couples the main decisions are *Cooke v Head*
[1972] 2 All ER 38, [1972] 1 WLR 518, *Richards v Dove* [1974] 1 All ER 888 at 894, *Crisp
h v Mullings* (1974) 233 EG 511, reversed on the facts (1975) 239 EG 119, CA, *Robinson v
Robinson* (1977) 241 EG 153, *Re Evers's Trust* [1980] 3 All ER 399, [1980] 1 WLR 1327
and *Hall v Hall* (1981) Times, 4 April.

It follows, in my view, that in principle there should be no difference, as between
married and unmarried persons, in seeking to ascertain their common intention (if any)
as to their respective rights to the property in which they live, and that in both cases it is
j appropriate for this purpose to have regard to their respective contributions up to the
time of separation, and perhaps thereafter, and not merely as at the time of acquisition.
However, in agreement with Griffiths LJ, I also consider that cohabitation in marriage,
in contrast to a less permanently intended relationship, may of course have an important
bearing on the ascertainment of their common intention and on the determination of an
appropriate apportionment of their respective rights to the property in which they live.

I then return to the judgment given in this case. Although the judge concentrated primarily on the rights of the parties as derived from their position as at the time of *a* acquisition, he did not in fact disregard the subsequent events, and in my view it would have been wrong had he done so. Thus, although the parties clearly started on a fifty-fifty basis in their acqusition of the property, subject to the small disparity in their respective contributions at that time, the judge rightly also took account of their contributions to the property up to the time of their separation. In this regard it was irrelevant that Mr Josephs made the mortgage payments, since these were financed out *b* of the rents received for their joint benefit. However, the judge rightly gave credit to Mr Josephs for the £2,000 which he spent on improvements. In respect of the period of cohabitation up to separation, he accordingly gave credit to Miss Bernard for her initial contribution of £200, and to Mr Josephs for his initial contribution of £650 plus the subsequent expenditure on the property of £2,000. However, notwithstanding this relatively small disparity in their respective contributions, he concluded, in effect, that, *c* subject to giving the appropriate credit to each of the parties, their basic share in the equity remained equal. In my view he was clearly correct in this conclusion, both as at the time of acquisition and as at the time of separation. It follows that Mr Josephs's appeal on the first ground must fail.

Next, it is necessary to mention what the judge decided in relation to the events subsequent to the separation. Again, he rightly did not disregard these. Miss Bernard *d* had been ousted from the house against her will, but Mr Josephs continued to make the mortgage payments for which both of them remained liable. On the other hand, Mr Josephs also continued to receive some rents from letting part of the premises. His mortgage payments between the date of separation and the trial were £4,743 and the amount received by way of rent was £2,080, leaving a balance of £2,663 which Mr Josephs paid out of his own pocket during this period. The judge accordingly gave *e* further credit to Mr Josephs for £1,331·50, one-half of this balance, by way of a further adjustment to the parties' equal shares. In my view this was again clearly correct. By allowing only half of this balance to Mr Josephs, the judge in effect made him pay an 'occupation rent': cf *Dennis v McDonald*. Conversely, and in my view equally correctly, by holding that Miss Bernard must give credit for half, but only half, of this balance, the judge treated her as being still entitled to an equal share in the property, but also liable to *f* contribute equally towards the expenses referable to it.

None of these adjustments as such were challenged on the appeal to this court, but it was faintly argued on behalf of Mr Josephs that his post-separation expenditure could also be taken into account in determining what should be the parties' basic equitable shares in the property. In my judgment this is untenable in the present case; since everything which occurred after the separation took place against Miss Bernard's will, *g* the subsequent events could not possibly have any bearing on their common intention as to what should be their respective rights in the property; in the present case any common intention in this regard clearly came to an end with their separation.

There then remains the important question concerning the order for sale which was made by the judge. This was the second ground of appeal by Mr Josephs and it raises the second issue of principle. Again it is important to note what happened, both below and *h* in this court. The judge said:

> 'The plaintiff asks for an order for sale. The purpose for which the house was
> bought in co-ownership is at an end and I see no special reason why the defendant
> should continue to enjoy the house to the exclusion of the plaintiff. There was no
> offer made of any rent or periodic payment or other compensation for the *j*
> defendant's sole occupation. Accordingly, I will order that the property be sold with
> vacant possession. The defendant is to vacate the property within four months so
> that vacant possession may be given by 1 November next.'

Pausing there, I agree that the purpose for which the house was bought in co-ownership came to an end when Miss Bernard moved out. She could obviously never

have intended that it should continue to provide a home of Mr Josephs with his new
a wife. Nor could it be said ever to have been their common intention that, if their
relationship should break down and one of them should move out, let alone unwillingly,
the house should remain available as a home of the other. Accordingly, decisions such as
Re Evers's Trust have no application, and s 30 of the Law of Property Act 1925 must
inevitably come into operation.

In order to follow what happened on the appeal to this court, it is necessary to see how
b s 30 would have operated under the order made by the judge. The house would have
been sold and, before dividing the net proceeds of sale into equal shares, Miss Bernard
would have had to give credit for £3,781·50 against her share. This sum is arrived at as
already explained. Up to the time of the separation, Mr Josephs was given credit for
£2,450, ie the £650 which he provided at the time of acquisition, plus the £2,000 which
he spent on improvements, less the £200 which Miss Bernard provided at the time of
c acquisition. Then, for the period after Miss Bernard had moved out, Mr Josephs was
given credit for half the mortgage payments made by him less half the rents received, ie
£1,331·50, making a total credit of £3,781·50, or, say, £3,800, in favour of Mr Josephs.

In my view this result would have been wholly correct in applying s 30 and ordering
a sale. However, a sale pursuant to s 30 may well entail consequences which neither party
really wants, if some other solution can be found. A forced sale at short notice may fail
d to realise the best price obtainable for both parties in the long term, and it will inevitably
involve immediate expense. Moreover, and above all, in these times of housing shortage,
a sale has the disadvantage that the property ceases to be available as a home for either of
the parties. This is likely to inflict hardship on the occupant and may also not be desired
by the non-occupant if some other equitable financial adjustment can be made. On the
present appeal, all these undesired consequences of a sale in fact ultimately became
e common ground between the parties. However, before turning to what happened, I
think that it is necessary to consider the position in principle as to the extent to which an
application under s 30 may allow some latitude to the court.

As to this, I think it is clear that the concluding words of s 30, 'and the court may make
such order as it thinks fit', confer no powers on the court unless an order for sale is in fact
made. This was the view expressed by Purchas J in *Dennis v McDonald* [1981] 2 All ER
f 632 at 640, [1981] 1 WLR 810 at 819–820, and nothing to the contrary was said in this
court, when an appeal against his award of an 'occupation rent' was dismissed. He said:

> 'I now turn to consider s 30 of the Law of Property Act 1925. Counsel for the
> plaintiff submitted that I can make appropriate orders by virtue of the provision in
> s 30. After considering the wording of this section I have come to the conclusion
> that it does not confer any power on the court to this effect. As was said in argument,
g > the section was really passed for conveyancing purposes to help deal with the flood
> of equitable tenants in common holding under trusts for sale which resulted from
> the passing into law of the Law of Property Act 1925. I do not think that this section
> enables the court to make orders where an order for sale is not made. Only orders
> ancillary to an order for sale which are necessary to implement the sale are envisaged
h > by the words of the section. The words are "*and* the court may make such order as
> it thinks fit" and not "*or* the court may make such other orders" etc. As is explained
> in Megarry and Wade's *Law of Real Property* (4th edn, 1975, p 427) s 30 of the Law
> of Property Act 1925 is the successor to the old Partition Acts and in particular the
> power of sale granted under the Partition Act 1868. In *Turner v Morgan* (1803) 8
> Ves 143 at 145, 32 ER 307 at 308 Lord Eldon LC held the threat of making a
j > partition order over the parties in order to bring them to terms. Although s 30 does
> not grant a power to the court to order the payment of an occupation rent it certainly
> could be used in a manner similar to that adopted by Lord Eldon LC, by means of
> indicating that unless an undertaking to pay an occupation rent was forthcoming
> from the defendant then the order for sale would be made.'

This passage also demonstrates that the threat of making an order for sale under s 30 can be used against the occupant in order to seek to compel him to make an equitable financial adjustment in favour of the party who is out of occupation if the latter does not *a* insist on a sale. However, could the threat of refusing to make an order for sale, or postponing a sale indefinitely, also be used against the non-occupant, unless he agrees, in effect, to allow his interest in the property to be bought out on reasonable terms? As at present advised, I am driven to the conclusion that this would not be possible. Once the purpose of the trust has come to an end, it seems clear that a sale can be insisted on by any of the beneficiaries unless the court considers that it is inequitable for him to want to *b* realise his investment: see the decisions of the majority of this court in *Jones v Challenger* [1960] 1 All ER 785, [1961] 1 QB 176 and *Rawlings v Rawlings* [1964] 2 All ER 804, [1964] P 398 (albeit under s 17 of the Married Women's Property Act 1882), and *Bedson v Bedson* [1965] 3 All ER 307 at 312, [1965] 2 QB 666 at 678 per Lord Denning MR. The fact that these were cases between married couples does not appear to me to make any difference; on the contrary, when property is bought otherwise than as a matrimonial or *c* family home, it seems to me even more difficult to find grounds for refusing an order for sale. It is also interesting to note that in *Turner v Morgan* 8 Ves 143 at 145, 32 ER 307 at 308, the case cited by Purchas J, Lord Eldon LC ended his judgment by saying:

'Out of mercy to the parties I will let it [an order for sale] stand over: but I have no doubt what is to be done, if they will have a decree.'

d

Finally in this connection the decision of Luxmore J in *Re Ball, Jones v Jones* (1930) 74 SJ 298 must also be borne in mind, that the power to postpone a sale under s 25 of the Law of Property Act 1925 cannot prevail when the right to insist on a sale under s 30 has arisen.

However, ultimately these issues did not arise for decision on the present appeal; we heard no full argument on them; and I only venture into this territory with diffidence. *e* The reason why this issue did not arise was that, with the assistance of the court, the parties effectively came to terms to a large extent, and it is to be hoped that the same result may follow in other cases. Miss Bernard very sensibly decided not to insist on a sale, in consideration of being bought out; but there was some argument about the terms. As already mentioned, the equity value of the house was about £15,000 after allowing for the mortgage. On the basis of the financial adjustment made by the judge, *f* Miss Bernard would accordingly have got about £5,600, taking round figures, viz £15,000 less £3,800 equalling £11,200, of which one-half is £5,600. We were told that Mr Josephs had previously offered £5,000, and before us his counsel raised this offer to £5,500. In effect the parties left it to us to determine what would be a fair sum for Mr Josephs to pay, also having regard to the passage of time since the proceedings began. We indicated that in our view £5,000 would produce an equitable result, and Mr Josephs's *g* counsel did not object to this sum if this would avoid the necessity of an order for the sale of the house in any event. We accordingly arrived at the order mentioned by Lord Denning MR on the basis that both parties should regard this as a reasonably satisfactory outcome in all the circumstances. It is to be hoped that this approach may provide an acceptable basis for the resolution of similar cases in the future.

Accordingly, I would dismiss this appeal subject to the substitution of the order *h* mentioned above, not as a matter of law but in view of the course which was taken by both parties on the appeal to this court.

Appeal dismissed.

Solicitors: *Simpson Millar* (for the plaintiff); *Moss Beachley* (for the defendant).

Diana Procter   Barrister.

Re Orwell's Will Trusts
Dixon and others v Blair

CHANCERY DIVISION

VINELOTT J

18 JANUARY, 1 FEBRUARY 1982

Executor and administrator – Executor – Remuneration – Charging clause – Professional charging clause – Charging clause providing that 'any trustee' entitled to charge for services – Literary executor – Whether literary executor a 'trustee' and entitled to charge remuneration for dealing with literary estate.

The husband of the testatrix was a well-known writer who died in 1950 leaving all his literary estate to her absolutely. In 1979 the testatrix made a will in which she appointed the plaintiffs to be her executors and trustees and appointed X to be her literary executor. X was a director of H & Co Ltd, a private company carrying on business as literary agents. The will directed her trustees to give into X's charge all copyrights and other matters comprising her husband's literary estate and further directed that X was to have full power to exploit the literary estate by the grant of publishing rights and licences. After deducting all expenses properly incurred, X was required to pay all sums arising from the administration of the literary estate to the trustees who were to pay the income from the estate to the defendant for life. By cl 16(a), which was a common form charging clause, the will provided that 'Any trustee hereof being a solicitor or other individual engaged in any profession or business shall be entitled to charge and be paid all usual professional or other reasonable and proper charges for any business transacted or services rendered or time spent by him or his firm in connection with the trust powers or provisions . . .' When the testatrix died in 1980 the question arose whether X and H & Co Ltd were entitled under the will to charge and be paid fees and commission for work done by them in connection with the literary estate. The plaintiffs applied to the court for the determination of the questions (i) whether X, as a 'literary executor', was entitled to charge and be paid remuneration under cl 16(a), (ii) whether H & Co Ltd were a 'firm' within the meaning of cl 16(a) and could also charge and be paid remuneration under cl 16(a), and (iii) if so, whether X was bound to account for directors' fees or remuneration received by him from H & Co Ltd.

Held – (1) On the true construction of the will, X was personally entitled to charge for and be paid remuneration for work done by him in connection with the literary estate because in cl 16(a) the testatrix had shown a clear intention to modify the general rule precluding an executor or trustee from charging for work done for an estate, and to give any person appointed by the will to administer the estate or the trusts created by the will the power to charge for work within the description in cl 16(a) irrespective of whether the work was done as an executor or strictly as a trustee (see p 179 *f* and p 180 *b c*, post).

(2) H & Co Ltd were also entitled to charge and be paid remuneration if they were employed by X in the administration of the literary estate because, even if the general rule precluding an executor or trustee charging for his services applied to a private company, such a company were, for the purpose of that rule, to be regarded as equivalent to a partnership, and therefore the terms of cl 16(a) negatived the application of the general rule (see p 179 *f* and p 180 *e* to *g*, post).

(3) X was not bound to account for any remuneration which he received from H & Co Ltd because the principle that a trustee was required to account for any benefit (such as remuneration received as a director of a company) obtained as a result of his position as a trustee did not apply where the only nexus between the trust estate and the benefit or remuneration received by the trustee from the company was that the income of the company comprised the remuneration and commission which the company were entitled to be paid (see p 179 *f g* and p 180 *g h*, post); *Re Gee, Wood v Staples* [1948] 1 All ER 498 distinguished.

Notes

For the remuneration of a personal representative, see 17 Halsbury's Laws (4th edn) paras   *a*
738–746, and for cases on the subject, see 23 Digest (Reissue) 51–62, 578–762.

Cases referred to in judgment

Chapple, Re, Newton v Chapman (1884) 27 Ch D 584, 23 Digest (Reissue) 60, 737.
Gee, Re, Wood v Staples [1948] 1 All ER 498, [1948] Ch 284, 47 Digest (Repl) 248, 2185.

b

Summons

By a summons dated 20 October 1981 the plaintiffs, Michael Dixon, Miriam Gross and
Benita Krystyna George-Perutz, the executors of the will of Sonia Mary Brownell Orwell,
who died on 11 December 1980, sought, inter alia, the determination of the following
questions on the true construction of the will: (i) whether Mark Hamilton, a director of,
and shareholder in, A M Heath & Co Ltd, was entitled, pursuant to his appointment as   *c*
literary executor of the will, to charge and be paid remuneration in accordance with the
provisions of cl 16(a) of the will for any business transacted or services rendered or time
spent by him in connection with such literary executorship and to retain any customary
commission which might be paid to him; and (ii) whether Mark Hamilton was entitled,
pursuant to his appointment as literary executor of the will, to charge and be paid
remuneration in accordance with the provisions of cl 16(a) for any business transacted or   *d*
services rendered or time spent by A M Heath & Co Ltd in connection with such literary
executorship and to retain any customary commission which might be paid to A M
Heath & Co Ltd. The defendant was Richard Blair, who was entitled under the will to
the income from the testatrix's literary estate. The summons was heard in chambers but
judgment on question (1) was given by Vinelott J in open court. The facts are set out in
the judgment.
                                                                                       e

Paul Baker QC and *Michael Driscoll* for the plaintiffs.
Simon Berry for the defendant.

Cur adv vult

f

1 February.   **VINELOTT J** read the following judgment: The first question on the
originating summons before me relates to the construction of a professional charging
clause contained in the will of the testatrix, Sonia Mary Brownell Orwell, the widow of
Eric Arthur Blair, who wrote under and was commonly known by the name George
Orwell. By his will he appointed separate literary executors of the property, assets and
effects of his profession as writer and journalist (defined as his 'literary estate') and gave   *g*
his residuary estate including his literary estate to his widow absolutely. After his death
on 21 January 1950 his literary executors confided the management of his literary estate
to a company, A M Heath & Co Ltd, which carries on business as literary agents. Since
1956 one Mark Hamilton, a director of and a substantial shareholder in A M Heath & Co
Ltd, has had the charge of the management of George Orwell's literary estate. He is now
the chairman and joint managing director of that company.   *h*
    The testatrix made her will on 8 August 1979. By cl 1 she appointed her brother
Michael Dixon and one Miriam Gross and her solicitor Benita Krystyna George-Perutz to
be her executors and trustees, and declared that 'the expression "my Trustees" used in
this my Will and all Codicils hereto shall mean the trustees or trustee for the time being
of this my Will whether original, additional or substituted'. Clause 2(1) reads as follows:
'I APPOINT MARK HAMILTON of A.M. Heath & Co. Limited of 40 William IV Street London   *j*
WC2 (hereinafter called "my Literary Executor") to be my Literary Executor.' By cl 2(2)
she directed her trustees to give into his charge all copyrights, film and television rights
derived from the estate of George Orwell or which had any connection with his literary
works or career and the benefit of all subsisting contracts and book debts owed to her
relating thereto, all of which premises she defined as her 'Literary Estate'. By cl 2(3) she
directed that her literary executor should have full power to exploit her literary estate by

the grant of publishing licences and rights, and further directed by cl 2(3)(iii) that her

a literary executor should—

> 'after deducting all expenses properly incurred by him when called upon by my Trustees and in any event annually give a full accounting for and pay over all sums in his hands arising from the administration or disposal of my Literary Estate to my Trustees.'

b   Then by cl 5 she gave her shares in George Orwell Productions Ltd and her literary estate to her trustees on trust to pay the income to George Orwell's adopted son, Richard, for life, the remainder on trust to pay the income to his named wife during the remainder of her life with remainder to his children. By a codicil to her will dated 26 June 1980 she gave her trustees power to apply all or any part of the trust fund settled by cl 5 of her will which should not at time of application consist of her literary estate or shares of any

c company holding part of her literary estate to Richard or after his death his named wife during her life. The will contained (in cl 16(a)) a common form charging clause which I should read in full:

> 'Any trustee hereof being a solicitor or other individual engaged in any profession or business shall be entitled to charge and be paid all usual professional or other reasonable and proper charges for any business transacted or services rendered or
> d   time spent by him or his firm in connection with the trust powers or provisions hereof whether or not within the usual scope of his profession or business and including acts which a trustee not being in any profession or business could have done personally and may retain any customary share of brokerage or commission which may be paid to him or his firm.'

e   The testatrix's will was proved by the three named executors on 5 May 1981 with power reserved to Mark Hamilton to prove as literary executor. He has not proved the will pending clarification of his power and of the power of A M Heath & Co Ltd to charge and be paid fees and commission if he does prove the will.

Three questions arise on the construction of cl 16(a). First, under cl 16(a) will Mr Hamilton, who was in terms appointed to be the testatrix's literary executor, be entitled

f to charge remuneration at all? Second, if he is entitled to charge and be paid remuneration for work done by him personally, will the company similarly be entitled to charge? Third, if the company is entitled to charge remuneration and does so, will Mr Hamilton be bound to account for any part of any directors' fees or remuneration that he may receive from the company?

It is trite law that an executor or trustee is in general entitled to no allowance for his

g care and trouble. The rule applies to fees charged by a professional man for work done in his professional capacity. The harshness of the rule is normally if not invariably tempered in any well-drawn will or trust instrument by including an express charging clause. Such clauses are strictly construed. For instance, it has been held that a clause authorising a solicitor trustee to charge for his professional services will not authorise him to charge for matters which a layman is able to do personally (see *Re Chapple, Newton v Chapman*

h (1884) 27 Ch D 584). It has been said that a wider form of charging clause entitling a solicitor trustee to charge for such matters ought not to be included except under express instructions given by the client himself with full knowledge of its effect.

What is said in the present case is that on a strict construction cl 16(a) only authorises a trustee and not an executor to charge for his services. However strictly cl 16(a) may be construed, it cannot I think be read as narrowly as that. On that construction the

j testatrix's solicitor, Benita Krystyna George-Perutz, would be unable to charge for work done by her in her capacity as executor but only for work done after she had completed adminstration and assumed office as trustee. The point at which a person appointed executor and trustee ceases to occupy the former and assumes the latter capacity is not always easy to determine. It is no answer to say that under cl 1 the expression 'my Trustees' is so defined as to include the three persons appointed executors and trustees and so authorises the executrix to charge for work done in her capacity as one of the

executors. The power in cl 16(a) is a power for 'Any trustee hereof' to charge and not for
any of 'my Trustees' to charge. If the persons appointed to be executors and trustees are
entitled to charge for all work done in the administration of the estate and of the trusts
thereby constituted, whether in their capacity as executors or trustees, it must I think
follow that Mr Hamilton must equally be entitled to charge for work done in his capacity
as literary executor. His position is a fortiori. In his capacity as literary executor he will
be concerned with the administration of the property settled by cl 5 after the general
administration of the estate has been completed and after the executors have assumed
their role as trustees.

It seems to me that the testatrix in including cl 16(a) must have intended to modify
the general rule which precludes an executor or trustee from charging for work done for
the estate and must have intended to confer power on any person appointed by the will
or subsequently to administer the estate or the trusts created by the will to charge for
work within the description in cl 16(a), whether such work was done as executor or
strictly as trustee. It is said that as regards the literary executor such an intention is
negatived by cl 2(3)(iii), which I have already read. The argument is that by requiring
the literary executor to account for all sums coming into his hands in the administration
of the literary estate after deducting all expenses properly incurred by him, the testatrix
has shown an intention that he was to be entitled to deduct only out-of-pocket expenses.
That argument I think begs the question. If under cl 16(a) the literary executor is entitled
to charge for business transacted and services rendered by him and to retain any
customary commission the charge and commission are part of the expenses properly
incurred by him within cl 2(3)(iii).

The general rule which precludes a trustee from charging for his services extends to
any firm of which he is a partner. So cl 16(a), as is usual in a well-drawn charging clause,
permits a trustee to charge and be paid reasonable and proper charges for business
transacted by him or his firm. It is said that A M Heath & Co Ltd is not a firm in the
ordinary connotation of that word, and that accordingly if it is employed by the literary
executor in the administration of the literary estate it will not be entitled to charge. It is
to my mind doubtful whether the general rule extends to a company of which a trustee
is a director or member, but I do not need to decide this point. While the word 'firm' in
its narrowest sense is apt to describe an unincorporated partnership it is in ordinary usage
frequently applied as a description of a private company such as A M Heath & Co Ltd. If
the general rule applies to such a private company on the footing that it is for this purpose
to be treated as the equivalent of a partnership, then equally the terms of cl 16(a) must in
my judgment suffice to negative the application of the rule in the administration of the
testatrix's estate.

Lastly it is said that Mr Hamilton is bound to account for any remuneration he may
receive from A M Heath & Co Ltd if he is employed in the administration of the literary
estate under the principle explained in Re Gee, Wood v Staples [1948] 1 All ER 498, [1948]
Ch 284. That principle applies where a trustee receives a benefit from a company the
shares of which are comprised in the trust estate. It rests on and exemplifies the wider
principle that a trustee must account for any benefit, such as remuneration as a director
of a company, which he obtained as a result of his position as trustee. It can have no
application where, as here, the only nexus between the benefit or remuneration received
by a trustee from a company and the trust estate is that the income of the company
comprises remuneration and commission which, if I am right on the first two questions,
the company was entitled to charge and be paid.

The originating summons before me raises other questions of an administrative
nature. I will adjourn into chambers and hear argument on those points and will deal
with the costs of the originating summons as a whole.

Declarations accordingly.

Solicitors: *Herbert Smith & Co* (for all parties).

Jacqueline Metcalfe   Barrister.

a   # Re Abbott (a bankrupt), ex parte the trustee of the property of the bankrupt v Abbott

CHANCERY DIVISION
SIR ROBERT MEGARRY V-C AND PETER GIBSON J
20, 21, 22 OCTOBER, 21 DECEMBER 1981

b
Bankruptcy – Avoidance of settlement – Exception – Purchaser in good faith – Settlement made on purchaser in good faith and for valuable consideration – Purchaser for valuable consideration – Matrimonial home – Husband and wife joint owners of matrimonial home – Claim by wife in divorce proceedings for property adjustment order transferring matrimonial home to her – Compromise of claim – Wife relinquishing right to pursue claim in return for sum of money on
c   sale of matrimonial home – Husband adjudicated bankrupt – Whether wife a 'purchaser...for valuable consideration' – Bankruptcy Act 1914, s 42(1) – Matrimonial Causes Act 1973, ss 24, 39.

A wife included in her petition for divorce a claim for a property adjustment order under s 24(1)[a] of the Matrimonial Causes Act 1973 transferring to her the matrimonial home
d   of which she and her husband were the joint owners. Following negotiations between the parties, a compromise was reached which was embodied in a consent order and under which the matrimonial home was to be sold, the wife was to be paid £18,000 from the net proceeds, and the balance, if any, was to be divided equally between the husband and wife. The house was sold, the proceeds exceeding £18,000. Less than two years after the consent order, the husband, who had in fact been insolvent at the date of the divorce
e   petition, was adjudicated bankrupt. His trustee in bankruptcy applied to the court for a declaration that the consent order and/or the carrying into effect of the order was a 'settlement' by the husband of £9,000 on the wife within the meaning of s 42(1)[b] of the Bankruptcy Act 1914 and as such was void against the trustee. The trustee accepted that the wife had not known of the husband's insolvency when she obtained the consent order and that she had acted in good faith, but contended that she was not 'a
f   purchaser... for valuable consideration' within s 42(1) and thereby exempted from the provisions relating to void settlements. The trustee contended that the effect of s 39[c] of the 1973 Act, which provided that a settlement or transfer of property made pursuant to a property adjustment order was not thereby prevented from being a settlement or transfer to which s 42(1) of the 1914 Act applied, was such that a spouse in whose favour a property adjustment order was made was only a 'purchaser... for valuable consideration'
g   if the court ordered not only that a proprietary interest be transferred from the debtor to the purchaser but also that a proprietary interest of substantially equivalent value be transferred by the purchaser to the debtor.

Held – The compromise of a bona fide claim to a property adjustment order under s 24 of the 1973 Act could, for the purposes of s 42(1) of the 1914 Act, constitute the claimant
h   a 'purchaser... for valuable consideration' of what the claimant received under the compromise even though no interest in property was transferred by the purchaser and the consideration provided by the purchaser was not measurable in monetary terms, because, although there had to be a quid pro quo between the parties, that was not

---

j   *a*   Section 24(1), so far as material, provides: 'On granting a decree of divorce ... or at any time thereafter ... the court may make any one or more of the following orders, that is to say—(a) an order that a party to the marriage shall transfer to the other party ... such property as may be so specified, being property to which the first-mentioned party is entitled, either in possession or reversion; (b) an order that a settlement of such property as may be so specified, being property to which a party to the marriage is so entitled, be made to the satisfaction of the court for the benefit of the other party to the marriage ...'

b   Section 42(1), so far as material, is set out at p 183 c, post

c   Section 39 is set out at p 184 b c, post

confined to the exchange of a material asset in return for the asset received. On the facts, the wife was a 'purchaser . . . for valuable consideration' within s 42(1) of the 1914 Act because she had given up her legal right to pursue her claim under s 24 of the 1973 Act in return for the right to part of her husband's share in the net proceeds of sale of the matrimonial home. Accordingly, although the consent order was a 'settlement' for the purposes of s 42(1), it was exempted from the provisions relating to void settlements. The trustee's application would therefore be dismissed (see p 184 *f* to *j*, p 185 *f g*, p 186 *b* to *e* and *j* and p 187 *c* and *g* to *j*, post).

Re Pope, ex p Dicksee [1908] 2 KB 169 applied.
Re Macdonald, ex p McCullum [1918–19] All ER Rep 392 distinguished.
Hance v Harding (1888) 20 QBD 732 considered.

Notes

For the rights of a trustee in bankruptcy in respect of a matrimonial home, see 3 Halsbury's Laws (4th edn) para 594, and for cases on the subject, see 5 Digest (Reissue) 681, 5964–5965.

For settlements made in favour of a purchaser for valuable consideration which are valid against the trustee in bankruptcy, see 3 Halsbury's Laws (4th edn) paras 895, 900, and for cases on the subject, see 5 Digest (Reissue) 899–903, 7415–7442.

For the Bankruptcy Act 1914, s 42(1), see 3 Halsbury's Statutes (3rd edn) 93.
For the Matrimonial Causes Act 1973, ss 24, 39, see 43 ibid 566, 587.

Cases referred to in judgments

Charters, Re, ex p trustee (1923) 8 B & CR 94, 5 Digest (Reissue) 902, 7434.
Cole, Re, Trustee in bankruptcy v Public Trustee [1931] 2 Ch 174, [1931] All ER Rep 663, 5 Digest (Reissue) 902, 7438.
Debtor, Re a, ex p Official Receiver, Trustee of the property of the debtor v Morrison [1965] 3 All ER 453, [1965] 1 WLR 1498, 5 Digest (Reissue) 903, 7441.
Densham (a bankrupt), Re, ex p trustee of the bankrupt v Densham [1975] 3 All ER 726, [1975] 1 WLR 1519, 5 Digest (Reissue) 898, 7414.
Hance v Harding (1888) 20 QBD 732, CA, 5 Digest (Reissue) 900, 7421.
Macdonald, Re, ex p McCullum [1920] 1 KB 205, [1918–19] All ER Rep 392, 5 Digest (Reissue) 902,7439.
Pope, Re, ex p Dicksee [1908] 2 KB 169, CA, 5 Digest (Reissue) 899, 7418.
Pumfrey, Re, ex p Hillman (1879) 10 Ch D 622, CA, 5 Digest (Reissue) 899, 7415.
Windle (a bankrupt) Re, ex p trustee of the bankrupt v Windle [1975] 3 All ER 987, [1975] 1 WLR 1628, 5 Digest (Reissue) 902, 7435.

Cases also cited

Bailey (a bankrupt), Re, ex p trustee of the bankrupt v Bailey [1977] 2 All ER 26, [1977] 1 WLR 278, DC.
Holliday (a bankrupt), Re, ex p trustee of the bankrupt v The bankrupt [1980] 3 All ER 385, [1981] Ch 405, CA.

Appeal

The trustee of the property of Derek John Abbott, a bankrupt, appealed against an order made by his Honour Judge Peck in Reading County Court on 21 July 1981 dismissing an application by the trustee for a declaration that a property adjustment order made in divorce proceedings between the respondent, Phylis Margaret Abbott, and the bankrupt constituted a voluntary settlement within s 42(1) of the Bankruptcy Act 1914 and as such was void against the trustee. The facts are set out in the judgment of Peter Gibson J.

John Vallat for the trustee in bankruptcy.
Jules Sher QC and Reziya Harrison for Mrs Abbott.

Cur adv vult

21 December. The following judgments were read.

a
PETER GIBSON J (delivering the first judgment at the invitation of Sir Robert
Megarry V-C). This is an appeal by the trustee in bankruptcy of Mr Derek Abbott from
an order made on 21 July 1981 by his Honour Judge Peck in the Reading County Court.
By that order an application by the trustee to have a property adjustment order under
the Matrimonial Causes Act 1973 declared void by virtue of s 42 of the Bankruptcy Act
b 1914 was dismissed. The respondent to this appeal is the bankrupt's former wife, Mrs
Phylis Abbott, in whose favour the property adjustment order was made. The material
provisions of s 42 are as follows:

'(1) Any settlement of property, not being a settlement . . . made in favour of a
purchaser or incumbrancer in good faith and for valuable consideration . . . shall, if
the settlor becomes bankrupt within two years after the date of the settlement, be
c void against the trustee in bankruptcy . . .
(4) "Settlement" shall, for the purposes of this section, include any conveyance or
transfer of property.'

The matter arises in this way. The bankrupt married Mrs Abbott on 8 June 1957.
There were three children of the marriage, the youngest being born on 16 December
d 1974. The matrimonial home was at 24 Sedgwell Road, Sonning, Oxfordshire, and was
held in the joint names of Mr and Mrs Abbott. On 18 January 1977 Mrs Abbott
petitioned for divorce on the ground of the bankrupt's adultery. The ancillary relief
sought by Mrs Abbott in her petition included a maintenance order under s 23 of the
Matrimonial Causes Act 1973 and a property adjustment order under s 24 of that Act.
There were negotiations between the bankrupt and Mrs Abbott which were conducted
e for the most part between their respective solicitors. Mrs Abbott sought, inter alia, a
transfer of 24 Sedgwell Road to herself alone, but a compromise was eventually agreed
and the terms were incorporated in a consent order made on 6 December 1978 in the
Reading County Court. It was thereby ordered (so far as material) that 24 Sedgwell Road
should be sold, that from the net proceeds of sale Mrs Abbott should be paid the sum of
£18,000 and that the balance of the net proceeds of sale should be divided equally
f between the bankrupt and Mrs Abbott. In due course the property was sold and the net
proceeds comfortably exceeded £18,000. If, as their joint ownership of the property
prima facie indicated, they were beneficially entitled before the order of 6 December
1978 to the net proceeds in equal shares, the effect of that order was to transfer the right
to £9,000 from the bankrupt to Mrs Abbott.
The bankrupt has admitted knowledge in January 1977 of his insolvency. But the
g trustee does not suggest that Mrs Abbott, when obtaining the consent order, knew of the
bankrupt's insolvency, and he accepts that she acted in good faith. The bankrupt filed his
own bankruptcy petition, and a receiving order and an adjudication order were made on
19 May 1980. His liabilities exceeded his assets at that date by more than £11,000.
On 15 June 1981 the trustee applied to the county court for a declaration that the
consent order of 6 December 1978 and/or the carrying into effect of that order constituted
h and was a settlement of £9,000 by the bankrupt on Mrs Abbott and was void against the
trustee under the provisions of s 42 of the Bankruptcy Act 1914.
Before Judge Peck two issues were debated. One was whether the relevant part of the
consent order was a settlement for the purposes of s 42. The judge held that it was. That
part of his order is not challenged in this court. The other issue was whether Mrs Abbott
was a purchaser for valuable consideration within the meaning of s 42. The judge held
j that she was and that accordingly the trustee's application fell to be dismissed. It is the
second issue which is the subject of this appeal.
Counsel appearing for the trustee puts his case in this way. He says that the statutory
phrase 'purchaser . . . for valuable consideration' must be construed in the context of
bankruptcy, and in that context the compromise of the right of a spouse to seek a
property adjustment order under s 24 of the Matrimonial Causes Act 1973 does not
constitute that spouse a purchaser for valuable consideration. He points to the fact that

the court under s 24 has a wide discretion and that the claimant spouse has no proprietary right to the property the subject of the order until the order is made. He says that in legislating on matrimonial matters Parliament has recognised the special position of bankruptcy and the need to protect creditors, and in this regard he points to s 2(5) of the Matrimonial Homes Act 1967 (whereby a spouse's rights of occupation of the matrimonial home which are a charge on the estate or interest of the other spouse are void against the trustee in bankruptcy of the latter spouse) and in particular to s 39 of the Matrimonial Causes Act 1973. Section 39 reads:

'The fact that a settlement or transfer of property had to be made in order to comply with a property adjustment order shall not prevent that settlement or transfer from being a settlement of property to which section 42(1) of the Bankruptcy Act 1914 (avoidance of certain settlements) applies.'

I shall start by considering the effect of s 39 in the present case, relating as it does to a property adjustment order made under s 24 of the Matrimonial Causes Act 1973. The wording of the section seems to me designed to put beyond doubt that which otherwise might have been in doubt. In the absence of the section it might have been thought that s 42(1) might not apply to a settlement or transfer made pursuant to an order of the court, particularly when the debtor himself could not impugn the settlement or transfer. Section 39 makes clear that the mere fact that there has been a court order does not prevent any such transfer or settlement from being challenged by the trustee under s 42(1). As counsel for the trustee accepts, s 39 does not say that every property adjustment order will be avoided under s 42(1) if the bankruptcy of the person in whose favour the order is made supervenes. But in his submission the words 'a purchaser . . . for valuable consideration' are only satisfied in the case of orders made under the Matrimonial Causes Act 1973 when the court orders not only that a proprietary interest be transferred by the debtor to the purchaser but also that a proprietary interest be transferred by the purchaser to the debtor. Moreover, he says that these proprietary interests must be substantially of equivalent value.

I turn to consider whether the words in question in s 42(1) have the limitations which counsel for the trustee would put on them. Those words have been considered in a number of reported cases to which we were referred. I must consider in some detail three cases relevant to the specific question whether the compromise of a claim can make the claimant a purchaser for valuable consideration, but I think it sufficient to summarise the effect of the other cases as establishing, so far as material, three propositions. (1) The word 'purchaser' in s 42(1) means a buyer in the ordinary commercial sense, that is to say a person providing a quid pro quo: see *Re Pumfrey, ex p Hillman* (1879) 10 Ch D 622, as explained in *Hance v Harding* (1888) 20 QBD 732. (2) The consideration moving from the purchaser need not replace in the hands of the debtor the consideration moving from the debtor: see *Hance v Harding*. The contrary suggestion in *Re a debtor, ex p Official Receiver, Trustee of the property of the debtor v Morrison* [1965] 3 All ER 453 at 457, [1965] 1 WLR 1498 at 1505 by Stamp J, to whom *Hance v Harding* was not cited, is erroneous: see *Re Windle (a bankrupt), ex p trustee of the bankrupt v Windle* [1975] 3 All ER 987 at 994, [1975] 1 WLR 1628 at 1637. (3) The consideration given by the purchaser need not be equal in value to the consideration given by the debtor, though it must be valuable consideration in the commercial sense: see *Re Densham (a bankrupt), ex p trustee of the bankrupt v Densham* [1975] 3 All ER 726, [1975] 1 WLR 1519; thus, where the debtor conveys property subject to a mortgage but having a valuable equity of redemption, a mere covenant of indemnity given by the transferee in respect of the mortgage will not be such consideration: see *Re Windle*.

Counsel appearing for Mrs Abbott submits that the authorities also establish that the compromise of a bona fide claim can constitute the claimant a purchaser for valuable consideration of what he receives under the compromise, even though no interest in property is transferred by the purchaser and the consideration provided by the purchaser is not measurable in money. In particular he relies on the decision of the Court of Appeal

in *Re Pope, ex p Dicksee* [1908] 2 KB 169. In that case a wife threatened to bring divorce
a proceedings against her husband on the ground of his misconduct and to claim a
permanent allowance in the nature of alimony and maintenance. She offered to refrain
from taking those proceedings if the husband would make adequate provision by means
of a settlement for her and her children. The husband agreed, and a settlement was
executed. Within two years the husband was adjudicated bankrupt. Bigham J found as a
fact that the settlement was executed in pursuance of a bargain, and he rejected the
b trustee's application to set aside the settlement under s 47 of the Bankruptcy Act 1883
(the statutory predecessor of s 42) as it was a settlement in favour of a purchaser in good
faith and for valuable consideration. By a majority, the Court of Appeal upheld that
decision. Buckley LJ, however, in his dissenting judgment, held that the purchaser for
valuable consideration had to be a person who had given such a valuable consideration as
justified him being described as a purchaser or buyer, and that this requirement was
c satisfied only when the valuable consideration was money or property or something
capable of being measured by money, and did not extend to the surrender of such a right
as the right to relief for matrimonial offences. Cozens-Hardy MR (with whom Fletcher
Moulton LJ agreed) took a different view. He said that it was plain that there was valuable
consideration, having regard to the finding of the judge as to the bargain. Further he said
(at 173)

d   'I am unable to adopt the view that there must be either money or physical
        property given by the purchaser in order to bring the case within the exception. In
        my opinion the release of a right on the compromise of a claim, not being a merely
        colourable right or claim, may suffice to constitute a person a "purchaser" within
        the meaning of s. 47.'

e   Counsel for the trustee sought to distinguish *Re Pope* on the ground that in that case
the wife was giving up entirely all her rights to relief from the divorce court, whereas in
the present case Mrs Abbott was not giving up her rights to further relief from the court,
as she could go back to the court for further maintenance in appropriate circumstances.
I accept that there is that factual difference between the two cases; but I cannot see why
as a matter of principle it should make any material distinction for present purposes. In
f each case that which was given up was a right to seek from the court the exercise of a
discretion in the wife's favour. In each case the wife had no prior proprietary interest in
the property the subject matter of the settlement in her favour. In each case there was no
transfer of a proprietary interest in property by the wife to the husband as part of the
bargain. In each case there was a compromise of rights not measurable in money terms.
    Re Cole, Trustee in bankruptcy v Public Trustee [1931] 2 Ch 174, [1931] All ER Rep 663
g provides a further illustration of a bona fide compromise of a claim constituting a person
a purchaser for valuable consideration. In that case forfeiture proceedings brought by the
Attorney General in a relator action against a husband and wife had been compromised
on the terms of a settlement by the wife of property for the benefit of her and her unborn
issue. Within two years of the settlement the husband and wife became bankrupt and
their trustee in bankruptcy sought to set aside the settlement under s 42(1). Farwell J
h held that the settlement was made for valuable consideration, the purchasers being the
unborn issue represented by the Attorney General, and that such issue 'bought' the
settlement by giving up their possible right to exclude the wife from benefit in the
forfeiture proceedings.
    The authority which counsel for the trustee described as his best case was *Re Macdonald,
ex p McCullum* [1920] 1 KB 205, [1918–19] All ER Rep 392. In that case a husband had
j by an ante-nuptial settlement settled property on himself for life. After his marriage he
made informal arrangements for the payment of the income of the settlement to his
wife. He and his wife then agreed to separate. Later, at the wife's request, he executed a
deed whereby the income from the settlement became payable to his wife. He also
conferred on her a power of appointment over the capital of the settled property. That
deed was not expressed to be for valuable consideration. The husband subsequently

became bankrupt and the trustee in bankruptcy applied to have the deed declared void under s 42(1). Horridge J made that declaration. As he said, instead of a voluntary allowance to his wife for maintenance, the husband had given her a voluntary settlement; no consideration whatever had been provided by the wife; she had not even bargained that she would not take court proceedings for maintenance. That case is plainly distinguishable, and I cannot see how it affords any help to counsel for the trustee in any of his contentions.

In my judgment, therefore, counsel for Mrs Abbott has made good his submission that the compromise of a claim can constitute the claimant a purchaser for valuable consideration of what the claimant receives by way of compromise. I can find nothing in the authorities that supports the limitations which counsel for the trustee would apply to the words 'purchaser . . . for valuable consideration'. The ratio of the decision of Judge Peck on this point is contained in this passage from his judgment:

'. . . where there is a genuine bona fide compromise in family matters where the parties are at arm's length, the wife is giving up something which can be described as consideration in a commercial sense, she is giving up her rights to pursue her claim under s 24. It is true that she is not giving up a proprietary right and it is right that she may not be giving up right to maintenance and indeed under s 24 she may be recovering more than she has a proprietary right to recover but she has a legal right to continue her claim under s 24 and under that section the court has wide powers as to what it may award and it seems that looked at commercially (using the words in a fairly wide sense) the husband is giving something and the wife is losing something and it seems to me that that is valuable consideration.'

I respectfully agree.

Two other considerations were urged on us by counsel for the trustee. He said that, if the wife's claim had not been compromised but had been fought in the court and the same order had then been made as the consent order, the wife could not have been described as a purchaser for valuable consideration; accordingly, it would be anomalous if by a compromise she improved her position. It is unnecessary, and perhaps undesirable, to decide what would have been the position if, contrary to the facts, there had been no compromise, and I shall say no more on this than that I am not convinced that counsel's premise is correct. The second matter raised by counsel for the trustee is that, if he were wrong on his construction of s 42, that section would have become a dead letter in respect of settlements or transfers pursuant to property adjustment orders under the Matrimonial Causes Act 1973, as in all cases it could be said that the person in whose favour the order was made was a purchaser for valuable consideration. In this context counsel for the trustee relied on what Stamp J had said in the Morrison case [1965] 3 All ER 453 at 457, [1965] 1 WLR 1498 at 1505 was the clear intention of s 42, that is to say to prevent properties bring put into the hands of relatives to the disadvantage of creditors. Whilst I accept that the construction of s 42 which I favour will make it more difficult for trustees in bankruptcy to upset settlements or tansfers made pursuant to property adjustment orders than if the contentions of counsel for the trustee were to prevail, each case must be looked at in the light of its own particular circumstances. It may well be that in many cases it will be possible to avoid such settlements or transfers because the person in whose favour it was made knew of the settlor's or transferor's insolvency at that time and was not acting in good faith. But in any event Parliament has not chosen to modify s 42 in relation to such settlements or transfers, and I do not think that so general a consideration compels the court to give the exception for a purchaser for valuable consideration in s 42 a narrower construction than on the authorities, and in particular Re Pope [1908] 2 KB 169, that exception would otherwise bear. I would dismiss this appeal.

SIR ROBERT MEGARRY V-C. I agree, and have little to add. I do not think that s 39 of the Matrimonial Causes Act 1973 has altered the meaning of the phrase 'purchaser . . . for valuable consideration' in s 42(1) of the Bankruptcy Act 1914 in any

way. If Parliament had intended to alter that meaning, the enactment of s 39 would have
a provided the spur and the occasion for making a specific amendment; and there has been
none.

The question, then, is what that meaning is. Plainly 'good consideration', in the sense
of the natural love and affection that a man has for his wife and children, is not enough.
Nor is a merely nominal consideration, even though it would suffice to support a simple
contract at common law. In the context of the avoidance of settlements by a trustee in
b bankruptcy, a 'purchaser . . . for valuable consideration' must be someone who can not
only be described as being a 'purchaser' but can also be said to have given a consideration
for his purchase which has a real and substantial value, and not one which is merely
nominal or trivial or colourable.

It is in this sense that I understand the use of the phrase about providing a quid pro
quo that is to be found in the authorities. In that phrase, I do not think that the word
c 'quid' is confined to some material asset which can or will replace in the hands of the
debtor the asset of which he has disposed to the purchaser. The doctrine of replacement
which is suggested in *Re a debtor, ex p Official Receiver, Trustee of the property of the debtor v
Morrison* [1965] 3 All ER 453 at 457, [1965] 1 WLR 1498 at 1505 may indeed be a
doctrine which Parliament might have thought it right to enact; but I cannot see any
ground on which it can be suggested that Parliament has done this. If *Hance v Harding*
d (1888) 20 QBD 732, *Re Pope* [1908] 2 KB 169, *Re Charters, ex p trustee* (1923) 8 B & CR 94
and *Re Cole* [1931] 2 Ch 174, [1931] All ER Rep 663, or any combination of them, had
been cited in *Re a debtor, ex p Official Receiver, Trustee of the property of the debtor v Morrison*
[1965] 3 All ER 453, [1965] 1 WLR 1498, I do not think that any doctrine of replacement
would have been suggested. In the face of *Re Windle* [1975] 3 All ER 987 at 994, [1975]
1 WLR 1628 at 1637, that doctrine must now be regarded as being extinct.

e Counsel for the trustee also contended that even if a compromise could constitute
valuable consideration, a compromise of proceedings under s 24 of the 1973 Act such as
was made in the present case did not. The parties, he said, were merely attempting to
prejudge the order that the court would be likely to make in the exercise of its discretion,
so that payment under the compromise was no more than payment of a pre-estimate of
what would have to be paid in any event. I cannot see any special element in s 24 which
f would put a compromise of proceedings under that section in any position which
materially differs from a compromise of other proceedings. In any case, the essence of
most compromises is that each party does worse than he had hoped, and better than he
had feared. No doubt the compromise is effected against a background of some estimate
of the probable result of the case; but that is far from being the whole story. Thus the
spectre of costs will inevitably play its part. In my judgment, a claimant who relinquishes
g the claim in return for the right to a substantial sum of money, whether £9,000 or any
other sum, is a purchaser of that sum for valuable consideration within the meaning of
s 42(1) of the 1914 Act, whether that sum is an accurate or inaccurate estimate of what
the court would award.

In ordinary parlance, of course, one would not describe an outright payment of £9,000
as a 'settlement', any more than one would describe a person as a 'purchaser . . . for
h valuable consideration' of that sum because that person in return gives up some litigious
claim. But the 1914 Act has understandably cast its net wide. Under s 42(4), the payment
is a 'settlement' because that word includes 'any conveyance or transfer of property'; and
under s 167 'property' includes 'money'. For the reasons given by my brother, with these
few additions, I agree that the appeal must be dismissed.

j *Appeal dismissed.*

Solicitors: *Braby & Waller*, agents for *Ratcliffe, Duce & Gammer*, Reading (for the trustee
in bankruptcy); *Clark & Son*, Reading (for Mrs Abbott).

Azza M Abdallah   Barrister.

Chamberlain v Boodle & King (a firm)

COURT OF APPEAL, CIVIL DIVISION
LORD DENNING MR, DUNN AND O'CONNOR LJJ
30, 31 MARCH 1981

Solicitor – Costs – Contentious business – Alleged agreement – Solicitors stating by letter that charges would be made on basis of hourly rates applicable to partners or associates involved – Client replying by letter enclosing advance payment but not expressly assenting to rates proposed – Whether letters constituting a 'contentious business agreement' – Solicitors Act 1974, s 59.

Costs – Taxation – Solicitor – Bill of costs for contentious business – Four bills delivered in successive months – Later bills including amounts of earlier bills as accounts rendered – Taxation demanded within a month of receipt of fourth and final bill – Whether right to taxation extending to all four bills – Solicitors Act 1974, s 70(1).

In November 1978 the plaintiff retained the defendant firm of solicitors to act for him in a complex piece of litigation. On 4 January 1979 the defendants sent him a letter informing him that they would charge for their services 'on the basis of the standard hourly rates applicable to the particular attorneys or solicitors involved in the litigation', that the rates would 'range from £60 to £80 per hour for lawyers of partner status and from £30 to £45 per hour for associates', and that they would render statements at regular intervals. In the mean time they asked him for an advance payment of £2,000. On 24 January the plaintiff sent them a cheque for £1,000 with a covering letter in which he made no reference to the proposed charges but promised to remit the balance in two weeks' time. The defendants continued to act for him and delivered to him bills of costs dated 19 February, 20 March, 30 April and 11 May 1979. Each of the last three bills referred to the account rendered by the preceding one. The litigation was settled between the delivery of the third and fourth bill. The plaintiff failed to pay the sums demanded and applied, within a month of receiving the fourth bill, for the bills to be taxed pursuant to s 70(1)[a] of the Solicitors Act 1974. The defendants contended (i) that the bills were not subject to taxation because the letters of 4 and 24 January constituted a 'contentious business agreement' within ss 59[b] and 60[c] of the 1974 Act, or (ii) alternatively that the four bills were separate bills for the purposes of s 70 and, accordingly, since the plaintiff had not demanded taxation of each of the first three bills within a month of their receipt, no order could be made for their taxation pursuant to s 70(1). The master found that there was a contentious business agreement and gave the defendants liberty to enforce it. The plaintiff appealed to a judge, who held that there was not a contentious business agreement and made an order for taxation, but, in the exercise of his discretion, directed that each side should bear its own costs of the appeal. The defendants appealed to the Court of Appeal on the substantive issue and, by leave of the judge, the plaintiff cross-appealed against the order as to costs.

Held – (1) The defendants' appeal would be dismissed for the following reasons—
    (a) An agreement by letter could only amount to a contentious business agreement if it was specific in its terms and signed by the client. The defendants' letter to the plaintiff and his reply could not constitute such an agreement because the defendants' letter was imprecise as to the amount for which the plaintiff might expect to be liable and (per

---

a   Section 70(1) provides: 'Where before the expiration of one month from the delivery of a solicitor's bill an application is made by the party chargeable with the bill, the High Court shall, without requiring any sum to be paid into court, order that the bill be taxed and that no action be commenced on the bill until the taxation is completed.'
b   Section 59, so far as material, is set out at p 190 b, post
c   Section 60, so far as material, is set out at p 190 c, post

O'Connor LJ) was silent as to disbursements, and the plaintiff in his reply did not
a expressly assent to the rates of charging which the defendants proposed (see p 191 *c* to *h*
and p 192 *g h*, post).

(b) Whether successive bills of costs were to be regarded as instalments of a single bill
or as separate bills depended on whether there were natural breaks in the work done by
the solicitor so that each portion of the work could and should be treated as distinct from
the rest. Since the defendants were engaged on the litigation for under six months and
b since the bills were expressly delivered as part of a running account, they were to be
regarded as a single bill divided into parts. Accordingly the plaintiff was entitled to have
the whole bill taxed (see p 192 *a* to *c* and p *g h*, post); *Re Romer & Haslam* [1893] 2 QB 286
applied.

(2) The plaintiff's cross-appeal would be dismissed because, in the circumstances, the
judge had exercised his discretion properly by ordering each side to bear its own costs
c (see p 192 *e* to *h*, post).

Notes

For agreements between solicitor and client as to remuneration in contentious business,
see 36 Halsbury's Laws (3rd edn) 125–126, paras 167–169, and for cases on the subject,
see 43 Digest (Repl) 137–139, 1237–1253.
d   For the client's right to taxation within one month from delivery of a bill of costs, see
36 Halsbury's Laws (3rd edn) 145, para 192, and for cases on the subject, see 43 Digest
(Repl) 196, 1908–1910.
    For the Solicitors Act 1974, ss 59, 60, 70, see 44 Halsbury's Statutes (3rd edn) 1528,
1529, 1539.

e ### Cases referred to in judgments

Davidsons v Jones-Fenleigh (1980) Times, 11 March, CA.
Pontifex v Farnham (1892) 62 LJQB 344, 43 Digest (Repl) 138, 1249.
Raven, Re, ex p Pitt (1881) 45 LT 742, 43 Digest (Repl) 138, 1245.
Romer & Haslam, Re [1893] 2 QB 286, CA, 12 Digest (Reissue) 586, 4111.

f ### Appeal and cross-appeal

By an originating summons dated 20 June 1979, the plaintiff, Bartlett Beardslee
Chamberlain III, applied for the taxation, pursuant to s 70(1) of the Solicitors Act 1974,
of bills of fees, charges and disbursements delivered to him by the defendants, Boodle &
King (a firm). On 19 November 1979 Master Elton found that a contentious business
agreement existed between the parties and gave the defendants liberty to enter judgment
g for £30,099·49. The plaintiff appealed against that decision. On 21 February 1980 Smith
J allowed the appeal and made an order for taxation but directed that the plaintiff and
defendants should bear their own costs of the application for taxation. The defendants
appealed against that decision and, by leave of the judge, the plaintiff cross-appealed
against the order as to costs. The facts are set out in the judgment of Lord Denning MR.

h   *Nicholas Strauss* for the defendants.
  Jonathan Hirst for Mr Chamberlain.

LORD DENNING MR. This is an unusual case. It is in regard to a solicitor's bill of
costs. The first question which arises is whether there was a contentious business
agreement between the parties such as to satisfy s 59 of the Solicitors Act 1974. If it was
j a contentious business agreement, the client has no right to have the bill taxed. He can
complain afterwards that it is not fair and reasonable. If it were held not to be fair and
reasonable, then it could be set aside and he could have it taxed. But if it were a
contentious business agreement, the immediate effect is that he has no right to taxation.
    The matter arises in this way. At the end of November 1978 a gentleman living in
New Orleans, who goes by the picturesque name of Bartlett Beardslee Chamberlain III,

was in dispute with a Mr Peter Fitzgerald and other persons. There was litigation in the
United States of America and this country. Mr Chamberlain instructed the firm of Messrs   **a**
Boodle & King in regard to the English proceedings. In particular he instructed Mr
Joseph Jaworski, an employee of Messrs Boodle & King. Their practice is at 22 Grosvenor
Square.

Some work was done in December 1978. Then letters passed between the parties,
which I shall read: because it is on the true effect of them that the whole case depends.
But, before I read them, I will read s 59 of the 1974 Act: **b**

> '. . . a solicitor may make an agreement in writing with his client as to his
> remuneration in respect of any contentious business done, or to be done, by him . . .
> providing that he shall be remunerated by a gross sum, or by a salary, or otherwise,
> and whether at a higher or lower rate than that at which he would otherwise have
> been entitled to be remunerated.'
                                                                                            c
At the same time, I will mention s 60, which says:

> '. . . the costs of a solicitor in any case where a contentious business agreement has
> been made shall not be subject to taxation . . .'

I now come to the two letters which are said by the solicitors to amount to a contentious
business agreement. The first is dated 4 January 1979. It is from Messrs Boodle & King   **d**
to Mr Bart Chamberlain:

> 'Boodle & King will bill you for its services rendered on the basis of the standard
> hourly rates applicable to the particular attorneys or solicitors involved in the
> litigation. These rates range from £60 to £80 per hour for lawyers of partner status
> and from £30 to £45 per hour for associates who may be involved. These standard
> rates are reviewed for adjustment on a regular basis, ordinarily at the conclusion of   **e**
> the firm's fiscal year. Statements will be rendered by the firm to you on a regular
> basis, either monthly or quarterly, depending upon the activity generated during
> the applicable period. At this time we would appreciate your sending to us a check
> [sic] representing a retainer in the amount of £2,000 in accordance with our prior
> telephone conversation. This will be treated as an advance payment; our fees in
> accordance with the foregoing schedule will be applied against this retainer. We   **f**
> would appreciate your always remitting to us in pounds sterling if that is convenient.'

Mr Bart Chamberlain replied on 24 January 1979 from New Orleans:

> 'I enclose a bank check for one thousand pounds sterling; this represents one half
> of the retainer payment you have requested. We will remit the balance within two
> weeks. There are several large drafts in the mails to us, but I decided to forward this **g**
> partial payment now so that you would have cash from us to pay some of the out of
> pocket costs incurred in the Peter Fitzgerald matter.'

That really is the substance of the agreement. To complete the story, which is really a
very short one, I should say that bills were sent to Mr Chamberlain. The first was dated
19 February 1979. It totalled £2,373·36, less paid on account £1,000, which came to   **h**
£1,373·36. The second was dated 20 March 1979, which came to a total of £12,041·58.
That brought in the balance from the account rendered. The third was dated 30 April
1979, which brought the total up to £17,523·68. I should add that, before the final bill
was delivered, all the litigation had been settled, rather to the surprise of the parties.
There was no further litigation. That had finished by 8 May. Then the final bill was sent
on 11 May. 'Received on account' was now £3,427·35. But the total bill came to   **j**
£30,099·49.

It is those bills which Mr Chamberlain claims should be taxed. But the solicitors say
that he has no right to have them taxed, because there had been an agreement in writing.

Before I conclude the story, I may say that Mr Chamberlain was not at all polite to the
solicitors about the matter. He wrote a letter saying: '. . . the various attorneys and their

minions are no doubt wringing their hands in collective disgust now that new fees and
a costs will not be incurred through their arcane efforts.'
   That ends the story. I turn to the question which is at the root of this case: was this a
contentious business agreement in writing?
   Going back to the first Act, the Attorneys' and Solicitors' Act 1870, I should like to say
that, to satisfy its terms, the agreement should be clear and represent an agreement in
writing by both parties to the whole of its terms. In *Re Raven, ex p Pitt* (1881) 45 LT 742
b at 743, Fry J said:

> 'The words of the Act are "an agreement in writing". What is an agreement in
> writing? It must be a document which shall show all the terms of the bargain
> between the parties, and show by writing the accession of both parties to those
> terms.'

c To that I would add the subsequent case of *Pontifex v Farnham* (1892) 62 LJQB 344.
   It seems to me that an agreement in writing can be contained in letters. But the letters
ought at least to be signed by the client if he is to be deprived by the agreement of his
right to tax. Further the agreement must be sufficiently specific, so as to tell the client
what he is letting himself in for by way of costs. It seems to me that the letters in this
case do not give the client the least idea of what he is letting himself in for. As counsel
d for Mr Chamberlain said to us, there is a broad band of many uncertainties. Take, for
instance, the rate. It certainly seems high enough to me. It is £60 to £80 an hour. What
rate is to be charged? And for what partner? Of what standard? Then £30 to £45 an
hour for associates who may be involved. Which legal executives? Of what standard?
Which associates? Does it include the typists? That is one of the broad bands which is
left completely uncertain by this agreement. Then there is the hourly rate. That must
e depend on the skill and expertise of the individual partner or associate. A skilled partner
can do the work in half the time of a slow partner. Is the client to be charged double the
rate because a slow partner has been put on the case? These rates per hour are over a
pound a minute. It would seem that there must be a very good system of timing, almost
by stopwatch, if that is to be the rate of payment.
   I only make those observations because it seems to me that this is not an agreement as
f to remuneration at all. It is simply an indication of the rate of charging on which the
solicitors propose to make up their bill. It is by no means an agreement in writing as to
the remuneration. I would add this: the client, in reply, does not agree in express terms
to those rates of charging. He simply says nothing on it. He encloses his cheque for
£1,000 on account, but that is all. There is no express agreement. There is nothing in
writing saying, 'I agree your terms.' It seems to me, on such grounds as these, it is
g impossible to say that this was a contentious business agreement in writing such as to
deprive the client of his right to have it taxed.
   We discussed in the course of the argument the sort of method of remuneration which
could be covered by a contentious business agreement. Such as whether an hourly rate
would come within it. I need say nothing as to that. Also, whether it should be such as
to say whether it is the higher or lower rate of remuneration. I say nothing as to that
h either. Because, to my mind it is plain that this agreement was not a contentious business
agreement in writing such as to satisfy the statute. For this reason I would agree with the
judge that it is not a case in which the client loses his right to taxation. Nor is it necessary
to go into the question of whether it is fair and reasonable, in which case, of course, it
would be set aside. For the purposes of this case, it is sufficient to say that this is not a
contentious business agreement such as to deprive the client of his right to taxation.
j The next point in the case is whether the bills were four separate bills or whether they
were one. If they were four separate bills, the client would have to demand taxation of
each within a month of receipt. If they were one bill, divided into separate parts, as long
as he demands taxation within a month of the final account, then he has a right to
taxation.
   We were referred to one or two cases on this point: first, *Re Romer & Haslam* [1893] 2

QB 286 and the latest was a case in this court on 6 March 1980, *Davidsons v Jones-Fenleigh*
(1980) Times, 11 March. Putting it quite shortly, as Bowen LJ said in *Re Romer & Haslem* a
it is a question of fact whether there are natural breaks in the work done by a solicitor so
that each portion of it can and should be treated as a separate and distinct part in itself,
capable of and rightly being charged separately and taxed separately. Applying that
simple test, it seems to me that over this short time, the end of November 1978 to the
beginning of May 1979, this was one continuous dealing and work done by a solicitor,
not dividing itself naturally or otherwise into any breaks at all. When the bills were b
delivered, they were delivered each time as part of the running account, 'account
rendered' being carried on in each to the next. I agree with the judge on this point too
that this should be regarded as one bill in respect of one complete piece of work, although
divided into parts. As this is one bill, and the client demanded taxation within the
month, he is entitled to have the whole of it taxed.

The only remaining point is on the question of costs. Mr Chamberlain appeals on this c
because the judge made an order that each side should bear their own costs. The judge
gave him leave to appeal on costs. Counsel for Mr Chamberlain said, 'All the costs in this
case were incurred by the solicitors refusing taxation when they ought to have agreed to
it from the beginning.' On the other hand, counsel on behalf of the defendants referred
us to the well-known principle expressed in *The Supreme Court Practice 1982* vol 1, para
62/2/10, p 979: d

'. . . when the Judge, intending to exercise his discretion, has acted on facts
connected with or leading up to the litigation, the Court of Appeal is prohibited by
statute from entertaining an appeal from his decision . . .'

In this case it seems to me that the judge did exercise his discretion on the facts leading
up to the litigation. Mr Chamberlain did not pay the sums on account for which he was e
asked. Bills were running up. The solicitors had to write to him on 4 April 1979 telling
him of the difficulty, and asking him to deal with the charges for the work to be done
from thenceforward. Not only did he not pay them on account the sums for which they
reasonably asked, but, in addition, he wrote the disagreeable letter afterwards in regard
to solicitors who had undoubtedly done a first-class piece of work on his behalf. As far as
I know, the charges for this excellent work in a most complex litigation may be entirely f
fair and reasonable. I may say that the solicitors reduced the charge from the £39,000
which they calculated on the rates to only £30,000. Their charges may be entirely fair
and reasonable, and, in the circumstances, having regard to the conduct of the client,
Smith J made the order that each side should bear their own costs. It seems to me that
this is a case in which we should not interfere with his discretion in regard to the question
of costs. Therefore I would dismiss the cross-appeal. g

DUNN LJ. I agree and I have nothing to add.

O'CONNOR LJ. I agree. I only wish to add that, in coming to the decision that the
letters of 4 and 24 January 1979 do not constitute a contentious business agreement, they
are entirely silent as to how disbursements are to be dealt with and they do not set out h
any plan by which the client could make any reasoned calculation as to what his monthly
or quarterly liability might be.

I agree that both the appeal and the cross-appeal should be dismissed.

Appeal and cross-appeal dismissed.

Solicitors: *Boodle & King* ; *Middleton, Potts & Co* (for Mr Chamberlain).

Diana Procter   Barrister.

Martin Boston & Co (a firm) v Levy and another

CHANCERY DIVISION

WARNER J

14, 15, 18, 19 JANUARY 1982

Solicitor – Costs – Contentious business – Action to recover costs – Action on cheque – Client giving solicitor cheque in payment of costs – Cheque dishonoured on presentation – Solicitor suing on cheque – Whether action on cheque circumventing statutory requirements relating to solicitors' remuneration and therefore barred – Solicitors Act 1974, ss 59, 69.

In 1980 the plaintiffs, a firm of solicitors, acted for the defendants in respect of certain contentious business. The defendants had difficulty in paying the plaintiffs' legal fees and disbursements incurred on behalf of the defendants by the plaintiffs. Following negotiations between the parties in October and November 1980, the defendants agreed by letter dated 24 November 1980 to give the plaintiffs a number of postdated cheques in payment. One such cheque, dated 31 December 1980, for £32,648 was dishonoured on presentation. The plaintiffs, who had not delivered a bill of costs, decided to bring an action against the defendants on the cheque and on 5 and 9 March 1981 they asked the defendants' new solicitors if they had instructions to accept service of process on behalf of the defendants. They received no reply and on 10 March served the writ at the defendants' registered office. Someone at that office erroneously informed the defendants' solicitors that the writ had been served on 13 March. The solicitors accordingly thought that they had until 27 March to deliver an acknowledgment of service, but on 25 March, without prior warning, the plaintiffs applied for and obtained judgment in default of acknowledgment of service of the writ. On 26 March the defendants' solicitors discovered that judgment in default had been obtained when they sought to deliver an acknowledgment of service. On the following day they applied to have the judgment set aside on the ground that a solicitor was only entitled to recover costs in respect of contentious business if he had made a valid contentious business agreement with the client in accordance with s 59(1)[a] of the Solicitors Act 1974 or had delivered a bill of costs in accordance with s 69(1)[b] of that Act and in the absence of such an agreement or a bill of costs the plaintiffs could not circumvent the requirements of s 59 or s 69 by bringing an action on the cheque. The plaintiffs contended (i) that the judgment should not be set aside, because the defendants had no defence to the action since the cheque constituted a separate contract independent of the relationship of solicitor and client subsisting between the parties or any other contract between them, and (ii) that, if the court were to set the judgment aside, it should set it aside on condition that the £32,648 was paid into court, because the agreement of 24 November 1980 had been negotiated over a substantial period of time and the defendants had derived benefits under it, the defendants

---

a   Section 59(1), so far as material, provides: '... a solicitor may make an agreement in writing with his client as to his remuneration in respect of any contentious business done, or to be done, by him ... providing that he shall be remunerated by a gross sum, or by a salary, or otherwise, and whether at a higher or lower rate than that at which he would otherwise have been entitled to be remunerated.'

b   Section 69(1), so far as material, provides: 'Subject to the provisions of this Act, no action shall be brought to recover any costs due to a solicitor before the expiration of one month from the date on which a bill of those costs is delivered ... but if there is probable cause for believing that the party chargeable with the costs—(a) is about ... to become bankrupt or to compound with his creditors, or (b) is about to do any other act which would tend to prevent or delay the solicitor obtaining payment, the High Court may, notwithstanding that one month has not expired from the delivery of the bill, order that the solicitor be at liberty to commence an action to recover his costs and may order that those costs be taxed.'

had deliberately embarked on a course designed to delay payment to the plaintiffs of that
which was due to them and there was evidence that the defendants were insolvent.   *a*

Held – (1) The judgment would be set aside because the defendants had shown that they
had an arguable defence to the action on the cheque on the basis that a solicitor could not
escape from the provisions of ss 59 and 69 of the 1974 Act simply by taking a cheque
from his client and suing on the cheque. Since the defendants had an arguable defence it
was right, therefore, that the issue should be determined at the trial of the plaintiffs'   *b*
action on the cheque (see p 199 *a b* and p 200 *c* to *f*, post); *Ray v Newton* [1913] 1 KB 249,
Stewart-Moore v Sprague (1917) 34 TLR 113 and *Tiverton Estates Ltd v Wearwell Ltd* [1974]
1 All ER 209 considered.

(2) No condition would be imposed on the setting aside of the judgment because, if
the defendants had a good defence to the action, they were entitled to rely on it without
being subjected to an onerous condition which could not have been imposed on them   *c*
but for the fortuitous fact that, in the particular circumstances of the case, judgment had
been obtained against them in default of delivery of an acknowledgment of service (see
p 200 *g* to *j*, post).

Notes
For actions by solicitors to recover costs, see 36 Halsbury's Laws (4th edn) 170–171,   *d*
paras 230–234, and for cases on the subject, see 43 Digest (Repl) 339–347, 3533–3622.
For the Solicitors Act 1974, ss 59, 69, see 44 Halsbury's Statutes (3rd edn) 1528, 1537.

Cases referred to in judgment
Chamberlain v Boodle & King (a firm) [1982] 3 All ER 188, CA.
Clare v Joseph [1907] 2 KB 369, [1904–7] All ER Rep 508, CA, 43 Digest (Repl) 137, 1242.
Lamont (James) & Co Ltd v Hyland Ltd [1950] 1 All ER 341, [1950] 1 KB 585, CA, 51   *e*
    Digest (Repl) 811, 3678.
Nova (Jersey) Knit Ltd v Kammgarn Spinnerei GmbH [1977] 2 All ER 463, [1977] 1 WLR
    713, HL, 3 Digest (Reissue) 75, 389.
Ray v Newton [1913] 1 KB 249, CA, 43 Digest (Repl) 145, 1308.
Stewart-Moore v Sprague (1917) 34 TLR 113, 43 Digest (Repl) 202, 1985.
Tiverton Estates Ltd v Wearwell Ltd [1974] 1 All ER 209, [1975] Ch 146, [1974] 2 WLR   *f*
    176, CA, Digest (Cont Vol D) 116, 602b.

Procedure summons
By a summons dated 27 March 1981 the defendants, Harry Levy and Jet Records Ltd,
applied for an order that a judgment entered on 25 March 1981 in default of delivery of
an acknowledgment of service of a writ served at the second defendant's registered office   *g*
on 10 March 1981 by the plaintiffs, Martin Boston & Co, a firm of solicitors, be set aside,
that the defendants be allowed to serve a defence and that pending the hearing of the
summons all further proceedings on the judgment be stayed. The facts are set out in the
judgment.

Charles Flint for the defendants.   *h*
Jack Hames QC and *Gordon Nurse* for the plaintiffs.

WARNER J. This is a procedure summons in an action brought by Martin Boston &
Co, who are a firm of solicitors, against two of their former clients, namely Mr Harry
Levy, who is also known as Don Arden, and Jet Records Ltd, which I shall call 'JRL'. JRL
is one of a group of companies known as the Jet Records Group and Mr Levy is the   *j*
principal shareholder and a director of JRL. The summons is for an order setting aside a
judgment obtained by the plaintiffs against JRL in default of an acknowledgment of
service of the writ having been delivered in time on its behalf. The relevant dates are
these. The writ was served at the registered office of JRL, which was the office of its
accountants, on 10 March 1981. The statement of claim was served on the following day.
The judgment was entered on 25 March 1981. The defendants' new solicitors, Messrs

Clintons, discovered that it had been entered when, on 26 March 1981, they sought to
a deliver an acknowledgment of service of the writ. On 27 March 1981 they took out this
summons to set aside that judgment. On 13 May 1981 a defence was served on behalf of
Mr Levy.
  The evidence before me shows how the mishap occurred. For some days before the
service of the writ Messrs Clintons were in correspondence with the plaintiffs. In a letter
dated 5 March 1981 the plaintiffs asked Messrs Clintons whether they had instructions
b to accept service of proceedings on behalf of the defendants. In a further letter dated 9
March 1981 the plaintiffs pressed Messrs Clintons for an answer to that question.
Without, however, waiting for the answer, and without any further warning, the
plaintiffs served the writ on JRL in the way I have described. Owing, it seems, to a
mistake on the part of someone in the office of JRL's accountants, Messrs Clintons were
told that the writ had been served on 13 March 1981. They therefore took it that they
c had until 27 March 1981 to deliver the acknowledgment of service. Nor did the plaintiffs
warn Messrs Clintons in any way that they intended to apply for judgment in default.
  The facts of the case are complex and to some extent in dispute. In substance the
plaintiffs' claim is for fees and charges alleged to be due by the defendants to the plaintiffs
for work carried out by the plaintiffs as solicitors for the defendants and other companies
in the Jet Records Group. The plaintiffs allege (and there is some evidence to support the
d allegation, though it is denied by Mr Levy) that it was a term of the agreement under
which the plaintiffs acted for him and for the Jet Records Group that he would be
personally responsible for the plaintiffs' fees and charges incurred on behalf of any
company in the group. There is, however, no allegation that JRL was to be responsible
for any fees or charges other than those that it incurred on its own behalf.
  The plaintiffs' claim against JRL falls into two parts. There is first a claim against JRL
e as the drawer of a cheque for £32,648 which was dishonoured. That cheque had been
handed to the plaintiffs pursuant to an agreement which was embodied in a letter dated
24 November 1980. Second, there is a claim for a total sum of £10,790·50 in respect of
bills rendered by the plaintiffs to JRL (or in one case to Mr Levy and JRL jointly) since 24
November 1980. The judgment recovered by the plaintiffs is for the aggregate of those
two sums, that is £43,438·50, and for interest to be assessed on that amount.
f As regards the sum of £10,790·50, counsel for the plaintiffs concedes that the
judgment should be set aside. He concedes that JRL is entitled to have the bills in
question taxed. He says that, as to that sum, the only question is whether the judgment
should be set aside unconditionally or not. To that question I shall come later.
  As regards the sum of £32,648, however, counsel submits that the judgment should
not be set aside because, he says, as to that sum JRL has no defence to the action. If the
g plaintiffs had not recovered judgment for it in default they would have been entitled to
judgment for it under RSC Ord 14. Counsel's argument, in a nutshell, is that JRL is sued
in respect of that sum on the cheque, and that the cheque constitutes a separate contract
independent of the relationship of solicitor and client that subsisted between the parties
and of any other contract between them. He relies on familiar principles of the law of
bills of exchange illustrated by such cases as *James Lamont & Co Ltd v Hyland Ltd* [1950] 1
h All ER 341, [1950] 1 KB 585 and *Nova (Jersey) Knit Ltd v Kammgarn Spinnerei GmbH*
[1977] 2 All ER 463, [1977] 1 WLR 713. Counsel for the plaintiffs points out that it is
not alleged on behalf of the defendants that the cheque was tainted with fraud, invalidity
or duress, and it was, he submits, supported by sufficient consideration.
  Counsel for the defendants relies on the provisions of the Solicitors Act 1974 as to the
remuneration of solicitors for contentious business (ss 59 ff) as affording JRL a defence
i or, at all events, an arguable defence to the action on the cheque. It is common ground
that some, if not all, of the fees and disbursements covered by the agreement of 24
November 1980 were in respect of contentious business.
  Before I consider the arguments of counsel for the defendants, I must state some facts
about that agreement. The story, so far as directly relevant, starts with a letter dated 14
October 1980 written by Mr Levy to Mr Martin Boston, the senior partner in the
plaintiffs' firm. That letter is in these terms:

'Dear Martin,

Re: Outstanding Accounts   a
I do apologise for all the difficulties that you have had regarding all payments due
to you and particularly all the cheques that have not been paid, but you are, of
course, fully aware of all my difficulties. I therefore agree as at today's date your fees
and profit charges in respect of my personal and companies' matters at the sum of
£45,000 exclusive of V.A.T., disbursements, (including Counsel's fees, travelling
and general expenses and all other out of pocket expenses). I note that you will let   b
me have full details of all your disbursements etc shortly. I further agree to pay the
sum of £45,000 plus disbursements etc by three monthly instalments, that is to pay
£15,000 plus disbursements immediately and the balance outstanding by two equal
monthly instalments. I further agree to pay interest on the total amount outstanding
as mentioned above as from the 1st June 1980 at the rate of 3% above Barclays Bank
Base Rate and will pay such interest within three months from today's date. I   c
formally confirm that I am personally responsible for all the Legal costs and
disbursements that you are incurring or have incurred in relation to all my
companies and all members of my family. [Then there is a sentence which I do not
think is material, and he signs it:]

Yours sincerely
DON ARDEN.'   d

There is a suggestion (though not, I think, any clear evidence) that that letter was
drafted by Mr Boston. I do not think anything turns on whether it was. At all events,
there were further discussions between the parties, and then on 3 November 1980 Mr
Boston wrote to Mr Levy in these terms:

'Dear Don,   e
Outstanding Accounts
I refer to our discussions last Friday night, the 31st ultimo, and I accordingly
confirm our agreement as follows:—1. You will pay the sum of £20,000 within 14
days from the 31st ultimo, that is by Friday the 14th November and on that basis I
will release to you the deeds of Parkside. [That was property belonging to Mr Levy,
over the documents of title to which the plaintiffs claimed a lien for unpaid charges.]   f
2. You will pay a further £10,000 within 14 days thereafter, that is by the 28th
instant. 3. The balance outstanding, which will amount to approximately £31,000
plus accrued interest and other costs and disbursements incurred since the 14th
ultimo will be paid by the end of the year, namely the 31st December 1980. It has
been agreed between us that these payments will be made on their due dates and
you will hand over a series of post-dated cheques to secure the same and there will   g
be no question of any kind whatsoever that these payments will not be met that the
cheques will be dishonoured for any reason and that this arrangement will effectively
clear up on the payments being made all the past situations regarding costs and
disbursements provided of course we deliver to you VAT accounts for these
payments that you are now making. It is further agreed that you will be delivered,
on a monthly basis, details of the time spent by us on your matters and we will be   h
paid regularly every month on interim accounts delivered, for such work done on
your behalf. I further confirm that you have agreed these terms and you have
authorised Colin Newman to confirm the same to me and hand over the post-dated
cheques and I am seeing him today with a view to getting his confirmation of these
terms.

Yours sincerely,   j
MARTIN R. BOSTON.'

Colin Newman is a chartered accountant and a partner in the firm of accountants
acting for Mr Levy and the Jet Records Group.
On 24 November 1980, after further correspondence between the parties, Mr Boston
addressed to Mr Newman the letter that recorded the final agreement. It was in these
terms:

'Dear Colin,

a   *Don Arden Outstanding Costs*
I refer to our various discussions and our meeting today and I accordingly confirm
the present financial position is as follows in accordance with Don's letter to me of
the 14th October last:—

Profit Charges agreed as at 14th October   £45,000·00.
Counsel's fees and other disbursements outstanding   £ 4,300·00.
b   VAT on these amounts   £ 7,395·00.

                                                            £56,695·00.

There is interest on this outstanding balance as from the
1st June 1980 as agreed   £ 5,953·00.
c
                                                            £62,648·00.

There are, in addition, considerable outstanding costs in regard to the
$1,700,000 loan situation and all the other numerous matters we have been dealing
with since the 14th October, but we will render accounts for these shortly and we
d   note that these accounts will be paid immediately. I am accordingly, as arranged,
handing over to you the deeds of Parkside in exchange for a Bankers Draft for
£20,000 and a post-dated cheque dated the 28th instant for £10,000 which will be
met on presentation without any equivocation, and a further post-dated cheque
dated the 31st December 1980 for £32,648 and you have agreed that in no sense
whatsoever will you, on behalf of Don query the accounts or for any reason will the
e   cheques be dishonoured or orders not to pay given to the Bank. I confirm that I
have received a telex from Don confirming that you are fully authorised to confirm
the terms of my letter to him, of the 3rd November 1980, and that you are fully
authorised in this respect to sign a copy of this letter approving the payment
schedule relating to our fees. I enclose herewith a copy of this letter which please be
good enough to sign fully approving and agreeing all the above-mentioned terms.
f   Yours sincerely,
                                                       MARTIN R. BOSTON.'

A copy of that letter was signed by Mr Newman, who confirmed his agreement to its
terms and his authority so to do on behalf of Mr Levy.
At the meeting between Mr Boston and Mr Newman referred to in the letter, Mr
g   Newman handed to Mr Boston the banker's draft for £20,000 and the postdated cheques
for £10,000 and £32,648, and Mr Boston handed to Mr Newman the documents of title
to the Parkside property. The banker's draft and the cheque for £10,000 were duly
honoured, but the cheque for £32,648 was not. It was returned by JRL's bank marked
'Orders not to pay'.
Counsel for the defendants' arguments rest on the premise that under the provisions
h   of the Solicitors Act 1974 a solicitor may only recover his costs in respect of contentious
business if either he has made with his client a valid contentious business agreement in
accordance with s 59 or he has delivered a bill of costs in accordance with s 69. Here no
bill of costs was delivered, so that the plaintiffs are not entitled to the £32,648 unless the
agreement recorded in the letter of 24 November 1980 was a valid contentious business
agreement; and counsel submits, if it was a valid contentious business agreement, the
j   plaintiffs can only enforce it by the procedure prescribed by s 61 of the 1974 Act.
Counsel for the defendants argues, first, that the agreement was not a valid contentious
business agreement because, assuming it to have been made by the plaintiffs with JRL
and not merely with Mr Levy, it was insufficiently specific. In particular, it did not show
how much of the costs to which it related were chargeable to Mr Levy alone or to other
companies in the Jet Records Group, and how much to JRL itself. Nor did it show in
respect of what cases or for what periods those costs were chargeable. For the proposition

that a contentious business agreement must be specific, counsel relies on *Chamberlain v Boodle & King (a firm)* [1982] 3 All ER 188 though the facts of that case were very different **a** from those of this. Because the agreement was not a valid contentious business agreement, counsel for the defendants' first argument continues, it was ineffective, so that there was no consideration to support the cheque for £32,648 drawn pursuant to it. This being an action between the immediate parties to the cheque, the lack of consideration is fatal. Alternatively, counsel submits that, whether or not the agreement was a valid contentious business agreement, the plaintiffs cannot circumvent the requirements of the 1974 Act **b** by bringing an action on the cheque. In support of that proposition he relies on *Ray v Newton* [1913] 1 KB 249.

Counsel for the plaintiffs meets the first of those arguments by submitting that it is founded on the misapprehension that the provisions of the Solicitors Act 1974 on which counsel for the defendants relies are concerned with the validity of agreements between solicitors and their clients as distinct from the enforceability of such agreements. Counsel **c** for the plaintiffs referred me to a passage in *Cordery on Solicitors* (7th edn, 1981) pp 193–195 and to the judgment of Fletcher Moulton LJ in *Clare v Joseph* [1907] 2 KB 369, [1904–7] All ER Rep 508, which seem to me to make it clear that on that point counsel for the plaintiffs is right. Counsel for the defendants founded an argument to the contrary on s 61 of the 1974 Act, but it left me unconvinced. The provisions of the 1974 Act did not, therefore, in my judgment, invalidate the agreement recorded in the letter **d** of 24 November 1980. If counsel for the defendants is right in saying that the agreement did not comply with the requirements of s 59, those provisions merely rendered it unenforceable by an action until the provisions of s 69 had been complied with. If, on the other hand, counsel for the defendants is wrong, and the agreement was a contentious business agreement within s 59, it could not be enforced by an action at all but only by the procedure prescribed by s 61. There was, therefore, no 'total or quantified partial **e** failure of consideration' for the cheque, to use the words of Lord Russell in *Nova (Jersey) Knit Ltd v Kammgarn Spinnerei GmbH* [1977] 2 All ER 463 at 480, [1977] 1 WLR 713 at 732–733. In saying that, I do not overlook counsel for the defendants' contention that the agreement was made between the plaintiffs and Mr Levy alone and was not binding on JRL. But the facts, and, in particular, the wording of Mr Levy's letter of 14 October 1980, do not seem to me consistent with that contention. **f**

Counsel for the defendants' alternative argument is more formidable. Counsel for the plaintiffs sought to meet it by emphasising that the plaintiffs' action was brought on the cheque and that there was no exception in the Bills of Exchange Act 1882 applicable to cheques drawn in favour of solicitors by their clients. He submitted that there were, in effect, three ways in which a solicitor could recover his costs in respect of contentious business. The first was to enter into a contentious business agreement with his client and **g** then make an application under s 61 of the 1974 Act; the second was to deliver a bill of costs and proceed under s 69; and the third was to obtain a cheque from his client and then sue on the cheque. Counsel for the plaintiffs said that, in the third case, the client remained entitled to call for a bill of costs and to have it taxed, or, if the cheque were given under a contentious business agreement, to make an application under s 61, but that until and unless he did so there was no defence to an action against him on the **h** cheque. Thus, he said, in the present case a refusal on my part to set aside the judgment obtained by the plaintiffs would leave it open to JRL to make an application under s 61 or to require the plaintiffs to deliver a bill of costs, and to require it to be taxed, according to whether or not the agreement of 24 November 1980 was a contentious business agreement within s 59. If on such an application or on such a taxation it was found that the amount of the cheque was excessive, the court would order the excess to be repaid to **j** JRL. Manifestly, however, that would not make JRL's position as satisfactory as if effect had been given to the provisions of the 1974 Act before it was required to pay. I observe in particular that where the amount agreed under a contentious business agreement has actually been paid, s 61(5) of the 1974 Act gives the court only a limited power to order repayment by the solicitor. That point is not academic here because it was also a contention of counsel for the plaintiffs that the agreement of 24 November 1980 was, *a* contrary to the submission of counsel for the defendants, a contentious business agreement within s 59.

Another difficulty in counsel for the plaintiffs' way seems to me to lie in the authority relied on by counsel for the defendants, *Ray v Newton* [1913] 1 KB 249, which is a decision of the Court of Appeal. The basis of that decision, as I understand it, is that a solicitor cannot escape from the provisions of the legislation relating to solicitors' remuneration by taking a cheque from his client and suing on the cheque. Of course the

b legislation there in question was different from the legislation now in force. In *Ray v Newton* the defendant relied on s 4 of the Attorneys' and Solicitors' Act 1870, which applied to remuneration for contentious business, and on s 8 of the Solicitors' Remuneration Act 1881, which applied to remuneration for non-contentious business. Counsel for the plaintiffs pointed out to me that s 4 of the 1870 Act provided that the amount payable under an agreement between an attorney or solicitor and his client

c should not be 'received' by the attorney or solicitor until the agreement had been examined and allowed by a taxing officer of the competent court. But s 8 of the 1881 Act only provided, so far as relevant:

d
> '. . . if, under any order for taxation of costs, such agreement being relied upon by the solicitor shall be objected to by the client as unfair or unreasonable, the taxing Master or officer of the Court may inquire into the facts, and certify the same to the Court; and if, upon such certificate, it shall appear to the Court or judge that just cause has been shown either for cancelling the agreement, or for reducing the amount payable under the same, the Court or judge shall have power to order such cancellation or reduction, and to give all such directions necessary or proper for the purpose of carrying such order into effect, or otherwise consequential thereon, as to the Court or judge may seem fit.'

e The Court of Appeal did not rest its decision on one section rather than on the other. On the contrary, Farwell LJ said (at 256) that 'the order should go under both these statutes'. Counsel for the plaintiffs also relied on the fact that in that case the Court of Appeal did not stay the action on the cheque. As to that, Farwell LJ merely said (at 256): 'There is no reason why the defendant should not plead so that he may be ready to go to

f trial the moment this is over.'

Hamilton LJ gave fuller reasons. They amounted to this: that he knew too little about the action on the cheque to express any opinion about its chances of succeeding or failing, and that there might be defences to it other than that which might emerge when a bill of costs had been seen. The significant passage in his judgment, for present purposes, is this (at 258):

g
> 'It is then, as I understand, also suggested that the fact that a bill of exchange has been given for the amount mentioned in the agreement on which the solicitor relies is an answer to the claim for the delivery of the bill of costs. But from this point of view the bill itself is no more than another agreement to pay 2000*l.*, and therefore is as much the subject of investigation as the agreement of March 22, 1910, itself.'

h Counsel for the plaintiffs relied on the decision of Avory J in *Stewart-Moore v Sprague* (1917) 34 TLR 113. That is at first sight a decision in his favour, but it is to my mind an unsatisfactory authority on the present point. In that case a bill of costs had been delivered by the solicitor and the defendant had not disputed it or asked for taxation. He had merely asked for time to pay, and the solicitor had agreed to accept two promissory notes, one payable in three months and one that had not become due when the action was

j brought. Avory J (at 113) treated the case as one in which—

> 'The only question now before him was whether it was a good answer to a claim on a promissory note to say that if it should turn out that the defendant had a right to have the bill taxed and if on taxation something should be struck off the bill, there would be a part failure of the consideration for the note. If there was such a part failure of consideration the proper judgment would be for the amount of the note less the amount by which the consideration had failed.'

He then pointed out (at 113):

'The defendant was really asking that judgment should be given on the note less *a* some amount which it was quite impossible to arrive at. To arrive at it, he would have to decide whether the defendant was entitled to taxation, and also how much would come off the bill on taxation.'

So the case was one where the only defence put forward was that there was a potential (and unquantified) partial failure of consideration for the note. So far as can be discerned *b* from the report there was no reference to any legislation relating to solicitors' remuneration, much less any submission that the action on the note amounted to a circumvention of that legislation. Probably on the facts of that case no such submission would have been sustainable. *Ray v Newton* was cited, but only by counsel for the plaintiff solicitor in reply. Avory J dismissed it as an authority for saying that, whether the defendant might be found entitled to taxation or not, the plaintiff must now have judgment on the note. Clearly, on no careful analysis of *Ray v Newton* could it be considered authority for that proposition.

In the upshot I would be inclined to hold that JRL had a good defence to the action on the cheque, but I must bear in mind that this is only a summons to set aside the judgment obtained by the plaintiffs.

Counsel for the plaintiffs referred me to what was said by Lord Denning MR in *d* *Tiverton Estates Ltd v Wearwell Ltd* [1974] 1 All ER 209 at 213–214, [1975] Ch 146 at 156, and submitted that what divided the parties in this case was a pure question of law, so that, on the basis of what Lord Denning MR there said, I should decide it rather than merely decide whether it was arguable. It may be that if, having heard the argument on the·question, I had been persuaded that the point taken by counsel for the defendants, whilst arguable, was wrong, it would have been right for me to refuse to set aside the judgment, so as to avoid the same argument having to be heard again by another judge. *e* But my inclination at present is, as I have indicated, to think that counsel for the defendants is right. That being so, the proper course is, I think, for me to say no more about it but to set aside the judgment and leave the decision of the point to the trial judge.

Counsel for the plaintiffs submitted that, if I set aside the judgment, I should do so on *f* the condition that JRL paid the whole amount of it or at least £32,648 into court. He gave three reasons. The first was that the agreement of 24 November 1980 was negotiated over a substantial period of time, and that the terms of it were fully accepted by the defendants who had derived benefits from it; the second was that there was evidence before me from which I should draw the inference that the defendants had deliberately embarked on a course designed to delay payment ·to the plaintiffs of what was due to them; and the third was that there was evidence to the effect that JRL was insolvent. *g* Counsel for the plaintiffs submitted that in those circumstances it would be 'just' within the meaning of that term in RSC Ord 13, r 9 that I should require a payment into court. I do not think it would. I think, on the contrary, that it would be unjust to impose that condition on JRL. If JRL has a good defence to this action, it should in my judgment be entitled to rely on it without being subjected to an onerous condition to which it could *h* not have been subjected but for the fortuitous fact that judgment was obtained against it in default of delivery of an acknowledgment of service in the circumstances that I have described. I need not, I think, discuss the cases to which I was referred on this question. It is essentially a question on which what is the right course in any case depends on the particular circumstances of that case. I will, however, hear counsel on the question whether I should impose on JRL strict time limits for the delivery of an acknowledgment *j* of service and the service of a defence, and also of course on the question of costs.

Judgment of 25 March 1981 set aside. Leave to appeal to the Court of Appeal with 28 days' extension of time.

Solicitors: *Clintons* (for the defendants); *Nicholson, Graham & Jones* (for the plaintiffs).

Azza M Abdallah　Barrister.

Junior Books Ltd v Veitchi Co Ltd

HOUSE OF LORDS
LORD FRASER OF TULLYBELTON, LORD RUSSELL OF KILLOWEN, LORD KEITH OF KINKEL, LORD ROSKILL AND LORD BRANDON OF OAKBROOK
20, 21, 22, 29 APRIL, 15 JULY 1982

Negligence – Duty to take care – Defective work or product – Duty to avoid producing defective work or product – Proximity – Defendants laying defective floor in plaintiffs' factory – Defective floor not causing damage to the person or to plaintiffs' other property – No contractual relationship between plaintiffs and defendants – Whether defendants liable to plaintiffs in negligence for cost of replacing defective floor – Whether parties in sufficient proximity for duty of care to arise.

The respondents (the owners) engaged a building company to build a factory for them. In the course of construction the owners' architects nominated the appellants (the sub-contractors) as specialist sub-contractors to lay a concrete floor with a special surface in the main production area of the factory, and the sub-contractors duly entered into a contract with the main contractors to carry out the flooring work. There was, however, no contractual relationship between the sub-contractors and the owners. Two years after the floor had been laid it developed cracks in the surface and the owners were faced with the prospect of continual maintenance costs to keep the floor usable. The owners brought an action against the sub-contractors alleging that the floor was defective because of the sub-contractors' negligence in laying it, and claiming that the sub-contractors were liable for the cost of replacing the floor and for consequential economic loss arising out of the moving of machinery, the closing·of the factory, the payment of wages and overheads, and the loss of profits during the period of replacement. The owners further alleged that it would be cheaper to lay a new floor than to carry out continuous maintenance on the existing floor. The sub-contractors in reply claimed that, in the absence of any contractual relationship between the parties or a plea by the owners that the defective floor was a danger to the health or safety of any person or constituted a risk of damage to any other property of the owners, the owners' pleading did not disclose a good cause of action. The Lord Ordinary and, on appeal, the Court of Session rejected the sub-contractors' contention and held that the owners were entitled to proceed with their action. The sub-contractors appealed, contending, inter alia, (i) that to impose liability on the sub-contractors in the absence of any danger to the person or loss or damage to other property would in effect require sub-contractors and other manufacturers or suppliers of goods or work to give to an indeterminate class of potential litigants the same warranty regarding the fitness of the goods or work as they would be required to do when in a contractual relationship, and (ii) that a duty not to produce a defective article could not have a universally ascertainable standard of care, since whether an article was to be judged defective depended on whether it measured up to the contract under which it was constructed and the terms of that contract would not necessarily be known to the user of the article.

Held (Lord Brandon dissenting) – The appeal would be dismissed for the following reasons—

(1) (Per Lord Fraser, Lord Russell and Lord Roskill) Where the proximity between a person who produced faulty work or a faulty article and the user was sufficiently close, the duty of care owed by the producer to the user extended beyond a duty merely to prevent harm being done by the faulty work or article and included a duty to avoid faults being present in the work or article itself, so that the producer was liable for the cost of remedying defects in the work or article or for replacing it and for any consequential economic or financial loss, notwithstanding that there was no contractual relationship between the parties. Since (a) the owners or their architects had nominated the sub-

contractors as specialist sub-contractors and the relationship between the parties was so
close as to fall only just short of a contractual relationship, (b) the sub-contractors must   a
have known that the owners relied on the sub-contractors' skill and experience to lay a
proper floor, and (c) the damage caused to the owners was a direct and foreseeable result
of the sub-contractors' negligence in laying a defective floor, it followed that the
proximity between the parties was sufficiently close for the sub-contractors to owe a duty
of care to the owners not to lay a defective floor which would cause the owners financial
loss (see p 203 e, p 204 d to h, p 205 b to d, p 213 f to p 214 f and j to p 215 a, post); dicta   b
of Lord Reid in Home Office v Dorset Yacht Co Ltd [1970] 2 All ER at 297 and of Lord
Wilberforce in Anns v Merton London Borough [1977] 2 All ER at 498 applied; dictum of
Stamp LJ in Dutton v Bognor Regis United Building Co Ltd [1972] 1 All ER at 489–490,
Rivtow Marine Ltd v Washington Iron Works [1974] SCR 1189, Caltex Oil (Australia) Pty Ltd
v Dredge Willemstad (1976) 136 CLR 529 and Bowen v Paramount Builders (Hamilton) Ltd   c
[1977] 1 NZLR 394 considered.
    (2) (Per Lord Keith) The sub-contractors were in breach of a duty owed to the owners
to take reasonable care to avoid acts or omissions, including laying a defective floor,
which they ought to have known would be likely to cause the owners economic loss,
including loss of profits caused by the high cost of maintaining a defective floor, and in
so far as the owners were required to mitigate the loss by replacing the floor itself the
cost of replacement was the appropriate measure of the sub-contractors' liability (see   d
p 206 c to j and p 207 f, post).

Notes
For cases in which duty of care arises and for claims in negligence for economic loss, see
34 Halsbury's Laws (4th edn) paras 5–6 and for cases on the subject, see 36(1) Digest
(Reissue) 17–39, 34–123.   e

Cases referred to in opinions.
Anns v Merton London Borough [1977] 2 All ER 492, [1978] AC 728, [1977] 2 WLR 1024,
    HL, Digest (Cont Vol E) 449, 99b.
Batty v Metropolitan Property Realizations Ltd [1978] 2 All ER 445, [1978] QB 554, [1978]   f
    2 WLR 500, CA, 7 Digest (Reissue) 327, 2219.
Bowen v Paramount Builders (Hamilton) Ltd [1977] 1 NZLR 394, NZ CA.
Caltex Oil (Australia) Pty Ltd v Dredge Willemstad (1976) 136 CLR 529, Aust HC, Digest
    (Cont Vol E) 457, *2517a.
Donoghue (or Mc'Alister) v Stevenson [1932] AC 562, [1932] All ER Rep 1, HL, 36(1) Digest
    (Reissue) 144, 562.
Dutton v Bognor Regis United Building Co Ltd [1972] 1 All ER 462, [1972] 1 QB 373, [1972]   g
    2 WLR 299, CA, 36(1) Digest (Reissue) 30, 98.
Dynamco Ltd v Holland & Hannen & Cubitts (Scotland) Ltd 1971 SC 257, Digest (Cont Vol
    D) 717, *2541a.
Heaven v Pender (1883) 11 QBD 503, [1881–5] All ER Rep 35, CA, 36(1) Digest (Reissue)
    7, 11.
Hedley Byrne & Co Ltd v Heller & Parners Ltd [1963] 2 All ER 575, [1964] AC 465, [1963]   h
    3 WLR 101, HL, 36(1) Digest (Reissue) 24, 84.
Home Office v Dorset Yacht Co Ltd [1970] 2 All ER 294, [1970] AC 1004, [1970] 2 WLR
    1140, HL, 36(1) Digest (Reissue) 27, 93.
Morrison Steamship Co Ltd v Greystoke Castle (cargo owners) [1946] 2 All ER 696, [1947] AC
    265, HL, 41 Digest (Repl) 514, 2887.
Mount Albert Borough Council v Johnson [1979] 2 NZLR 234, NZ CA.   j
Rivtow Marine Ltd v Washington Iron Works [1974] SCR 1189, Can SC, 36(1) Digest
    (Reissue) 337, *2779.
Sparham-Souter v Town and Country Developments (Essex) Ltd [1976] 2 All ER 65, [1976]
    QB 858, [1976] 2 WLR 493, CA, 32 Digest (Reissue) 507, 3865.
Spartan Steel and Alloys Ltd v Martin & Co (Contractors) Ltd [1972] 3 All ER 557, [1973]
    QB 27, [1972] 3 WLR 502, CA, 17 Digest (Reissue) 149, 403.

Ultramares Corp v Touche (1931) 255 NY 170.
a *Voli v Inglewood Shire Council* (1963) 110 CLR 74, 7 Digest (Reissue) 451, *2659.
Wimpey Construction (UK) Ltd v Martin Black & Co 1982 SLT 239.
Young & Marten Ltd v McManus Childs Ltd [1968] 2 All ER 1169, [1969] 1 AC 454, [1968]
    3 WLR 630, HL, 7 Digest (Reissue) 436, 2572.

Appeal
b The defenders, Veitchi Co Ltd, appealed against an interlocutor of the Second Division of
the Court of Session in Scotland (the Lord Justice-Clerk (Lord Wheatley), Lord Kissen and
Lord Robertson) dated 1 September 1980 with leave of that court granted on 31 October
1980 refusing the appellants' reclaiming motion against an interlocutor of the Lord
Ordinary (Grieve) dated 22 November 1979 allowing the pursuers, Junior Books Ltd (the
respondents), a proof before answer of their averments in an action in which the
c respondents claimed damages against the appellants for loss and damage which they
claimed to have sustained as a result of the appellants' negligence in laying a floor at the
respondents' factory. The facts are set out in the opinion of Lord Roskill.

W D Cullen QC and A F Rodger (both of the Scottish Bar) for the appellants.
d J Murray QC and J E Drummond Young (both of the Scottish Bar) for the respondents.

Their Lordships took time for consideration.

15 July. The following opinions were delivered.

e **LORD FRASER OF TULLYBELTON.** My Lords, I have had the advantage of
reading in draft the speech of my noble and learned friend Lord Roskill, and I am in full
agreement with his conclusion and with the reasons on which he bases it. I also gratefully
adopt his summary of the facts. It is enough for me to say that the appellants (defenders)
are specialist sub-contractors who laid composition flooring in a factory that was built for
the respondents (pursuers) at Grangemouth between September 1969 and May 1970.
f The respondents aver that the floor is defective, owing to failure by the appellants to take
reasonable care in laying it, and that it will have to be replaced. There was no contractual
relationship between the appellants and the respondents, and for some reason that has
not been explained the respondents have not taken legal proceedings against the main
contractors with whom they did have a contractual relationship. The respondents have
raised this action against the appellants, claiming damages which consist mainly of the
g direct and indirect cost of replacing the floor, the action being founded on averments
that the appellants were negligent in laying the floor. At the present stage of relevancy
these averments must be taken as true. The appeal raises an important question on the
law of delict or, strictly speaking, quasi delict, which is not precisely covered by authority.
The question is whether the appellants having (as must at this stage be assumed)
negligently laid a floor which is defective, but which has not caused danger to the health
h or safety of any person or risk of damage to any other property belonging to the owner
of the floor, may in the circumstances averred by the respondents be liable for the
economic loss caused to them by having to replace the floor.
    The Lord Ordinary (Grieve) and the Second Division answered that question in the
affirmative, and they have allowed to the respondents a proof before answer. The
appellants maintain that the question should be answered in the negative and that the
i action should be dismissed as irrelevant. As I agree with my noble and learned friend
Lord Roskill that the appeal fails, I only add to his speech in order to deal in my own
words with two important matters that arise.
    The first is the concern, which has been repeatedly expressed by judges in the United
Kingdom and elsewhere, that the effect of relaxing strict limitations on the area of
liability for delict (tort) would be, in the words of Cardozo CJ in *Ultramares Corp v Touche*
(1931) 255 NY 170 at 179, to introduce 'liability in an indeterminate amount for an

indeterminate time to an indeterminate class'. This is the floodgates argument, if I may
use the expression as a convenient description, and not in any dismissive or question- *a*
begging sense. The argument appears to me unattractive, especially if it leads, as I think
it would in this case, to drawing an arbitrary and illogical line just because a line has to
be drawn somewhere. But it has to be considered, because it has had a significant
influence in leading judges to reject claims for economic loss which were not consequent
on physical danger to persons or other property of the pursuer/plaintiff. It was the main
reason for rejecting the claim in the Scottish case of *Dynamco Ltd v Holland & Hannen &* *b*
Cubitts (Scotland) Ltd 1971 SC 257, which has recently been followed with some apparent
reluctance by the Lord Ordinary (Maxwell) in *Wimpey Construction (UK) Ltd v Martin
Black & Co* 1982 SLT 239. The floodgates argument was much discussed by the High
Court of Australia in *Caltex Oil (Australia) Pty Ltd v Dredge Willemstad* (1976) 136 CLR
529, where the majority of the court held that there was sufficient proximity between
the parties to justify a claim for economic loss because the defendant knew (in the words *c*
of the headnote) 'that a particular person, not merely as a member of an unascertained
class, [would] be likely to suffer economic loss as a consequence of his negligence'.
Whether the defender's knowledge of the identity of the person likely to suffer from his
negligence is relevant for the present purpose may with respect be doubted and it seems
to be contrary to the views expressed in *Hedley Byrne & Co Ltd v Heller & Partners Ltd*
[1963] 2 All ER 575 at 580, 588, [1964] AC 465 at 482, 494 by Lord Reid and by Lord *d*
Morris. But it is not necessary to decide the question in this appeal because the appellants
certainly knew, or had the means of knowing, the identity of the respondents for whom
the factory was being built. So, if knowledge of the respondents' identity is a relevant
test, it is one that the appellants can satisfy. They can also satisfy most, if not all, of the
other tests that have been suggested as safeguards against opening the floodgates. The
proximity between the parties is extremely close, falling only just short of a direct *e*
contractual relationship. The injury to the respondents was a direct and foreseeable result
of negligence by the appellants. The respondents, or their architects, nominated the
appellants as specialist sub-contractors and they must therefore have relied on their skill
and knowledge. It would surely be wrong to exclude from probation a claim which is so
strongly based, merely because of anxiety about the possible effect of the decision on
other cases where the proximity may be less strong. If and when such other cases arise *f*
they will have to be decided by applying sound principles to their particular facts. The
present case seems to me to fall well within limits already recognised in principle for this
type of claim, and I would decide this appeal strictly on its own facts. I rely particularly
on the very close proximity between the parties which in my view distinguishes this case
from the case of producers of goods to be offered for sale to the public.
   The second matter which might be thought to justify rejecting the respondents' claim *g*
as irrelevant is the difficulty of ascertaining the standard of duty owed by the appellants
to the respondents. A manufacturer's duty to take care not to make a product that is
dangerous sets a standard which is, in principle, easy to ascertain. The duty is owed to all
who are his 'neighbours'. It is imposed on him by the general law and is in addition to
his contractual duties to other parties to the contract. It cannot be discharged or escaped
by pleading that it conflicts with his contractual duty. But a duty not to produce a *h*
defective article sets a standard which is less easily ascertained, because it has to be judged
largely by reference to the contract. As Windeyer J said in *Voli v Inglewood Shire Council*
(1963) 110 CLR 74 at 85, if an architect undertakes 'to design a stage to bear only some
specified weight, he would not be liable for the consequences of someone thereafter
negligently permitting a greater weight to be put upon it'. Similarly a building
constructed in fulfilment of a contract for a price of £100,000 might justly be regarded *j*
as defective, although the same building constructed in fulfilment of a contract for a
price of £50,000 might not. Where a building is erected under a contract with a
purchaser, then, provided the building, or part of it, is not dangerous to persons or to
other property and subject to the law against misrepresentation, I see no reason why the
builder should not be free to make with the purchaser whatever contractual arrangements

about the quality of the product the purchaser wishes. However jerry-built the product,
a the purchaser would not be entitled to damages from the builder if it came up to the
contractual standard. I do not think a subsequent owner could be in any better position,
but in most cases he would not know the details of the contractual arrangements and,
without such knowledge, he might well be unable to judge whether the product was
defective or not. But in this case the respondents, although not a party to the contract
with the appellants, had full knowledge of the appellants' contractual duties, and this
b difficulty does not arise. What the position might have been if the action had been
brought by a subsequent owner is a matter which does not have to be decided now.

For the reasons given by my noble and learned friend Lord Roskill, and for the
additional reasons which I have stated, I would dismiss this appeal.

LORD RUSSELL OF KILLOWEN. My Lords, I have had the advantage of reading
c in draft the speeches prepared by my noble and learned friends Lord Fraser and Lord
Roskill. I agree with them and with their conclusion that this appeal fails. In my
respectful opinion the view of my noble and learned friend Lord Brandon unnecessarily
confines the relevant principles of delict to exclude cases of such immediate proximity as
the present.

d **LORD KEITH OF KINKEL.** My Lords, the respondents own and occupy a factory
in Grangemouth. This factory was constructed for them over a period in 1969 and 1970
under a contract between them and a company called Ogilvie (Builders) Ltd, which I
shall call 'the main contractors'. The respondents' architects nominated the appellants as
specialist sub-contractors for the purpose of laying a floor in the main production area of
the factory. The appellants entered into a contract with the main contractors for the
e carrying out of this work.

According to the respondents' averments the appellants' workmanship was seriously
defective in a number of respects, with the result that after two years the floor began to
develop cracks over the whole of its surface. They say that it requires replacement in
order to avoid the necessity for continual maintenance, which would be more expensive
in the long run. They claim against the appellants for the cost of such replacement,
f together with certain consequential loss which they say they will suffer while the work
of replacement is being carried out. The claim is founded in delict, the respondents
pleading that they have suffered loss through the appellants' negligence and are entitled
to reparation therefor.

The appellants plead that the respondents' averments are irrelevant. The Lord Ordinary
(Grieve) after debate, refused to sustain this plea and allowed a proof before answer. The
g Second Division (the Lord Justice-Clerk (Lord Wheatley), Lord Kissen and Lord
Robertson) refused a reclaiming motion against the Lord Ordinary's interlocutor. The
appellants now appeal to your Lordships' House.

It is a notable feature of the respondents' pleadings that they contain no averment that
the defective nature of flooring has led or is likely to lead to any danger of physical injury
to work people or of damage to property, movable or immovable, other than the floor
h surface itself, or even of economic loss through interruption of production processes. The
only type of pecuniary consequential loss claimed for is that arising out of the need to
replace the flooring. Had there been an averment of any such apprehended danger, I am
of opinion that the respondents' case would have been clearly relevant. There undoubtedly
existed between the appellants and the respondents such proximity of relationship,
within the well-known principle of *Donoghue v Stevenson* [1932] AC 562, [1932] All ER
j Rep 1, as to give rise to duty of care owed by the former to the latter. As formulated in
Donoghue v Stevenson, the duty extended to the avoidance of acts or omissions which
might reasonably have been anticipated as likely to cause physical injury to persons or
property. The scope of the duty has, however, been developed so as to cover the situation
where pure economic loss is to be foreseen as likely to be suffered by one standing in the
requisite degree of proximity (see *Hedley Byrne & Co Ltd v Heller & Partners Ltd* [1963] 2

All ER 575, [1964] AC 465). That case was concerned with a negligent statement made in response to an inquiry about the financial standing of a particular company, in reliance *a* on the accuracy of which the plaintiffs had acted to their detriment. So the case is not in point here except in so far as it established that reasonable anticipation of physical injury to person or property is not a sine qua non for the existence of a duty of care. It has also been established that where a duty of care exists through the presence of such reasonable anticipation, and it is breached, then, even though no such injury has actually been caused because the person to whom the duty is owed has incurred expenditure in *b* averting the danger, that person is entitled to damages measured by the amount of that expenditure (see *Anns v Merton London Borough* [1977] 2 All ER 492 at 505, [1977] AC 728 at 759 per Lord Wilberforce). That is the principle which in my view underlies *Dutton v Bognor Regis United Building Co Ltd* [1972] 1 All ER 462, [1972] 1 QB 373 and *Batty v Metropolitan Property Realizations Ltd* [1978] 2 All ER 445, [1978] QB 554. So in the present case I am of opinion that the appellants in the laying of the floor owed to the *c* respondents a duty to take reasonable care to avoid acts or omissions which they ought to have known would be likely to cause the respondents not only physical damage to person or property but also pure economic loss. Economic loss would be caused to the respondents if the condition of the floor, in the course of its normal life, came to be such as to prevent the respondents from carrying out ordinary production processes on it, or, short of that, to cause the production process to be more costly than it would otherwise *d* have been. In that situation the respondents would have been entitled to recover from the appellants expenditure incurred in relaying the floor so as to avert or mitigate their loss. The real question in the appeal, as I see it, is whether the respondents' averments reveal such a state of affairs as, under the principles I have outlined, gives them a complete right of action. I am of opinion that they have relevantly averred a duty of care owed to them by the appellants, though I think their averments in this respect might have been *e* more precise and better related to the true legal position. It is the averments of loss which cause me some trouble. On the face of it, their averments might be read as meaning no more than that the respondents have got a bad floor instead of a good one and that their loss is represented by the cost of replacing the floor. But they do also aver that the cost of maintaining the floor which they have got is heavy, and that it would be cheaper to take up the floor surface and lay a new one. If the cost of maintaining the defective floor is *f* substantially greater than it would have been in respect of a sound one, it must necessarily follow that their manufacturing operations are being carried on at a less profitable level than would otherwise have been the case, and that they are therefore suffering economic loss. That is the sort of loss which the appellants, standing in the relationship to the respondents which they did, ought reasonably to have anticipated as likely to occur if their workmanship was faulty. They must have been aware of the nature of the *g* respondents' business, the purpose for which the floor was required and the part it was to play in their operations. The appellants accordingly owed the respondents a duty to take reasonable care to see that their workmanship was not faulty, and are liable for the foreseeable consequences, sounding in economic loss, of their failure to do so. These consequences may properly be held to include less profitable operation due to the heavy cost of maintenance. In so far as the respondents, in order to avert or mitigate such loss, *h* incur expenditure on relaying the floor surface, that expenditure becomes the measure of the appellants' liability. On that analysis of the situation, I am of opinion that the respondents have stated a proper case for inquiry into the facts, and that the Lord Ordinary and the Second Division were therefore right to allow a proof before answer. I would accordingly dismiss the appeal.

Having thus reached a conclusion in favour of the respondents on the somewhat *j* narrow ground which I have indicated, I do not consider this to be an appropriate case for seeking to advance the frontiers of the law of negligence on the lines favoured by certain of your Lordships. There are a number of reasons why such an extension would, in my view, be wrong in principle. In the first place, I am unable to regard the deterioration of the flooring which is alleged in this case as being damage to the

respondents' property such as to give rise to a liability falling directly within the principle
a of *Donoghue v Stevenson*. The flooring had an inherent defect in it from the start. The
appellants did not, in any sense consistent with the ordinary use of language or
contemplated by the majority in *Donoghue v Stevenson*, damage the respondents' property.
They supplied them with a defective floor. Such an act can, in accordance with the views
I have expressed above, give rise to liability in negligence in certain circumstances. But it
does not do so merely because the flooring is defective or valueless or useless and requires
b to be replaced. So to hold would raise very difficult and delicate issues of principle having
a wide potential application. I think it would necessarily follow that any manufacturer
of products would become liable to the ultimate purchaser if the product, owing to
negligence in manufacture, was, without being harmful in any way, useless or worthless
or defective in quality so that the purchaser wasted the money he spent on it. One
instance mentioned in argument and adverted to by Stamp LJ in *Dutton v Bognor Regis*
c *United Building Co Ltd* [1972] 1 All ER 462 at 489, [1972] 1 QB 373 at 414 was a product
purchased as ginger beer which turned out to be only water, and many others may be
figured. To introduce a general liability covering such situations would be disruptive of
commercial practice, under which manufacturers of products commonly provide the
ultimate purchaser with limited guarantees, usually undertaking only to replace parts
exhibiting defective workmanship and excluding any consequential loss. There being no
d contractual relationship between manufacturer and ultimate consumer, no room would
exist, if the suggested principle were accepted, for limiting the manufacturer's liability.
The policy considerations which would be involved in introducing such a state of affairs
appear to me to be such as a court of law cannot properly assess, and the question whether
or not it would be in the interests of commerce and the public generally is, in my view,
much better left for the legislature. The purchaser of a defective product normally can
e proceed for breach of contract against the seller who can bring his own supplier into the
proceedings by third party procedure, so it cannot be said that the present state of the law
is unsatisfactory from the point of view of available remedies. I refer to *Young & Martin*
Ltd v McManus Childs Ltd [1968] 2 All ER 1169, [1969] 1 AC 454. In the second place, I
can foresee that very considerable difficulties might arise in assessing the standards of
quality by which the allegedly defective product is to be judged. This aspect is more fully
developed in the speech to be delivered by my noble and learned friend Lord Brandon,
with whose views on the matter I respectfully agree.

My Lords, for the reasons which I have given I would concur in the dismissal of the
appeal.

LORD ROSKILL. My Lords, this appeal against an interlocutor of the Second Division
f of the Court of Session (the Lord Justice-Clerk (Lord Wheatley), Lord Kissen and Lord
Robertson) dated 1 September 1980 refusing a reclaiming motion against an interlocutor
of the Lord Ordinary (Grieve) dated 22 November 1979 raises a question of fundamental
importance in the law of delict. Since it was accepted in the courts below and in argument
before your Lordships' House that there was no relevant difference between the Scots law
of delict and the English law of negligence, it follows that this appeal equally raises a
g question of fundamental importance in the development of the latter law. The defenders,
the appellants before your Lordships' House, tabled a general plea to the relevance of the
pursuer's averments and it was that plea which was debated in both courts below. The
appellants contended that there was no averment in the pursuers' pleadings relevant to
found an action against the defenders in delict and that therefore the action should be
dismissed as irrelevant. The respondents, on the other hand, contended that proof before
h answer should be allowed. Both courts below allowed proof before answer. The Lord
Ordinary started his opinion by stating that there was no Scottish authority directly in
point and, while in argument before your Lordships' House much Scottish, English and
indeed Commonwealth authority was cited, it remains the fact that no decision in any
court that was cited to your Lordships conclusively shows the correct route to be taken,
though many may be said greatly to illuminate that route.

My Lords, since the appeal comes before your Lordships' House in the manner I have
just stated, it follows that the respondents' averments, alleged not to state a relevant case, *a*
must be assumed for present purposes to be correct. Those averments are fully set out in
the record and in the opinion of the Lord Ordinary and to avoid repetion, I gratefully
borrow his statement of them. I need only summarise the bare essentials. The appellants
are specialist contractors in the laying of flooring. They were nominated sub-contractors
under a main building contract concluded between the respondents and some main
contractors. There was no privity of contract between the appellants and the respondents. *b*
The appellants laid flooring in the production area of a factory which was being built for
the respondents at Grangemouth as long ago as 1969 and 1970. In 1972 it is averred that
that flooring showed defects allegedly due either to bad workmanship or bad materials
or both. At the time the pleadings were prepared no repair work had been carried out
but it was averred that the cost of repairs would be some £50,000 to which were added
certain figures which, as the Lord Ordinary said, might reasonably be described as items *c*
of economic or financial loss. The total sum claimed by the respondents was over
£200,000.

My Lords, your Lordships are thus invited to deal with events which happened long
ago. It is difficult to believe that in the intervening period some work has not been done
to this flooring, but no information was vouchsafed as to the course of subsequent events.
The main building contract was not exhibited in the courts below. Your Lordships were *d*
not told whether that contract included as between the main contractors and the
respondents any relevant exceptions clause, nor whether if there were such an exceptions
clause it might be available for the benefit of the appellants. Nor were your Lordships
told why the respondents had chosen to proceed in delict against the appellants rather
than against the main contractors in contract, nor indeed why the main contractors had
not been joined as parties to these proceedings. This economy of fact is in stark contrast *e*
to the wealth of citation of authority of which your Lordships have had the benefit. Thus
the bare point of law has to be decided on an assumption of the truth of the facts pleaded.
But I cannot but suspect that the truth regarding the supposed deficiencies of this flooring
at Grangemouth has long since been either established or disproved. Of those matters
however your Lordships know and have been told nothing. Half a century ago your
Lordships' House decided *Donoghue v Stevenson* [1932] AC 562, [1932] All ER Rep 1 on a *f*
similar plea of irrelevancy. In that case however some 3¾ years only had elapsed between
the purchase of the allegedly offending bottle of ginger beer and the decision of your
Lordships' House.

My Lords, there was much discussion before your Lordships' House as to the effect of
the pleadings. I see no need to discuss them in detail. They seem to me clearly to contain
no allegation that the flooring was in a dangerous state or that its condition was such as *g*
to cause danger to life or limb or to other property of other persons or that repairs were
urgently or imminently required to avoid any such danger, or that any economic or
financial loss had been, or would be, suffered save as would be consequential on the
ultimate replacement of the flooring, the necessity of which was averred in
condescendence VII. The essential feature of the respondents pleading was that it
advanced a claim for the cost of remedying the alleged defects in the flooring itself by *h*
replacement together with resulting or economic or financial loss consequential on that
replacement.

My Lords, it was because of that scope of the respondents' pleading and because that
pleading was limited in this way that the appellants were able to mount their main attack
on those pleadings and to contend that they were, at least in the absence of amendment,
for which no leave has been sought at any stage, irrelevant since the law neither of *j*
Scotland nor of England made the appellants liable in delict or in negligence for the cost
of replacing this flooring or for the economic or financial loss consequent on that
replacement. It was strenuously argued for the appellants that for your Lordships' House
now to hold that in those circumstances which I have just outlined the appellants were
liable to the respondents would be to extend the duty of care owed by a manufacturer

a and others, to whom the principles first enunciated in *Donoghue v Stevenson* have since been extended during the last half century, far beyond the limits to which the courts have hitherto extended them. The familiar 'floodgates' argument was once again brought fully into play. My Lords, although it cannot be denied that policy considerations have from time to time been allowed to play their part in the last century and the present either in limiting or in extending the scope of the tort of negligence since it first developed as it were in its own right in the course of the last century, yet today I think its

b scope is best determined by considerations of principle rather than of policy. The 'floodgates' argument is very familiar. It still may on occasion have its proper place but, if principle suggests that the law should develop along a particular route and if the adoption of that particular route will accord a remedy where that remedy has hitherto been denied, I see no reason why, if it be just that the law should henceforth accord that remedy, that remedy should be denied simply because it will, in consequence of this

c particular development, become available to many rather than to few.

My Lords, I think there is no doubt that *Donoghue v Stevenson* by its insistence on proximity, in the sense in which Lord Atkin used that word, as the foundation of the duty of care which was there enunciated marked a great development in the law of delict and of negligence alike. In passing it should be noted that Lord Atkin emphasised that the laws of Scotland and of England were in that case, as is agreed in the present, identical

d (see [1932] AC 562 at 579, [1932] All ER Rep 1 at 10). But, that advance having been thus made in 1932, the doctrine then enunciated was at first confined by judicial decision within relatively narrow limits. The gradual development of the law will be found discussed by the editor of *Salmond and Heuston on Torts* (18th edn, 1981) pp 289ff. Though initially there is no doubt that, because of Lord Atkin's phraseology in *Donoghue v Stevenson* [1932] AC 562 at 599, [1932] All ER Rep 1 at 20, 'Injury to the consumer's life

e or property', it was thought that the duty of care did not extend beyond avoiding physical injury or physical damage to the person or the property of the person to whom the duty of care was owed, that limitation has long since ceased as Professor Heuston points out in the passage to which I have just referred.

My Lords, in discussion on the later developments of the law the decision of your Lordships' House (albeit by a majority) in *Morrison Steamship Co v Greystoke Castle (cargo*

f *owners)* [1946] 2 All ER 696, [1947] AC 265 is sometimes overlooked. The facts were essentially simple. Two ships collided. For simplicity I will call them A and B. Both ships were to blame, albeit in unequal proportions. The owners of the cargo on ship A became liable to contribution in general average to the owners of ship A. The cargo owners then sued ship B to recover the relevant proportion of that liability for general average contribution. They succeeded in that claim. My Lords, I shall not quote extensively from

g the speeches of either the majority or the minority. Suffice it to say that here the recovery of economic loss was allowed and I do not think that the decision is to be explained simply on some supposed esoteric mystery appertaining to the law regarding general average contribution. It is true that there seems to be little discussion in the speeches regarding the extent of the duty of care, but the very rejection by the majority of the views expressed by Lord Simonds in his dissenting speech that 'nothing would justify

h me in holding that the cargo owner can recover damages from the wrong-doing ship, not because his cargo has suffered damage, but because he has been placed under an obligation to make a general average contribution' (see [1946] 2 All ER 696 at 716, [1947] AC 265 at 307) shows that Lord Simonds at least was appreciating the consequences of the step forward which the majority were then taking. The decision is indeed far from the previously limited application of the doctrine enunciated in *Donoghue v Stevenson*.

j Fifteen years later, in *Hedley Byrne & Co Ltd v Heller & Partners Ltd* [1963] 2 All ER 575, [1964] AC 465, your Lordships' House made plain that the duty of care was not limited in the manner for which the respondents in that appeal had contended. Your Lordships' House held without doubt that economic loss was recoverable without physical damage having been suffered provided that the relevant duty of care had existed and that that duty existed when the party to whom the allegedly negligent advice was

given relied on the 'judgment' or 'skill' (I take those two words from the speech of Lord
Morris [1963] 2 All ER 575 at 594, [1964] AC 465 at 503) of him who gave the advice. I **a**
draw attention without citation to a passage of Lord Hodson ([1963] 2 All ER 575 at 598,
[1964] AC 465 at 509) where he refers to the *Greystoke Castle* case. Two passages in the
speech of Lord Devlin however demand quotation in full. The noble and learned Lord
said ([1963] 2 All ER 575 at 610–611, [1964] AC 465 at 529):

> 'I have had the advantage of reading all the opinions prepared by your lordships **b**
> and of studying the terms which your lordships have framed by way of definition
> of the sort of relationship which gives rise to a responsibility towards those who act
> on information or advice and so creates a duty of care towards them. I do not
> understand any of your lordships to hold that it is a responsibility imposed by law
> on certain types of persons or in certain sorts of situations. It is a responsibility that
> is voluntarily accepted or undertaken either generally where a general relationship,
> such as that of solicitor and client or banker and customer, is created, or specifically **c**
> in relation to a particular transaction.'

Later Lord Devlin said ([1963] 2 All ER 575 at 611, [1964] AC 465 at 530):

> 'I shall therefore content myself with the proposition that wherever there is a
> relationship equivalent to contract there is a duty of care. Such a relationship may **d**
> be either general or particular . . . I regard this proposition as an application of the
> general conception of proximity. Cases may arise in the future in which a new and
> wider proposition, quite independent of any notion of contract, will be needed.
> There may, for example, be cases in which a statement is not supplied for the use of
> any particular person, any more than in *Donoghue v. Stevenson* the ginger beer was
> supplied for consumption by any particular person; and it will then be necessary to **e**
> return to the general conception of proximity and to see whether there can be
> evolved from it, as was done in *Donoghue v. Stevenson*, a specific proposition to fit the
> case.'

My Lords, it was, I think, this development of the law which led Lord Reid in *Home
Office v Dorset Yacht Co Ltd* [1970] 2 All ER 294 at 297, [1970] AC 1004 at 1026–1027 to
say: **f**

> 'In later years there has been a steady trend towards regarding the law of
> negligence as depending on principle so that, when a new point emerges, one should
> ask not whether it is covered by authority but whether recognised principles apply
> to it. *Donoghue v Stevenson* may be regarded as a milestone, and the well-known
> passage in Lord Atkin's speech ([1932] AC 562 at 580, [1932] All ER Rep 1 at 11)
> should I think be regarded as a statement of principle. It is not to be treated as if it **g**
> were a statutory definition. It will require qualification in new circumstances. But I
> think that the time has come when we can and should say that it ought to apply
> unless there is some justification or vital explanation for its exclusion . . . But where
> negligence is involved the tendency has been to apply principles analogous to those
> stated by Lord Atkin . . .' **h**

Similarly, in *Anns v Merton London Borough* [1977] 2 All ER 492 at 498, [1978] AC 728 at
751–752 Lord Wilberforce, approving the earlier decisions of the Court of Appeal in
Dutton v Bognor Regis United Building Co Ltd [1972] 1 All ER 462, [1972] 1 QB 373 and
Sparham-Souter v Town and Country Developments (Essex) Ltd [1976] 2 All ER 65, [1976]
QB 858, said of the trilogy of cases, *Donoghue v Stevenson, Hedley Byrne* and *Dorset Yacht*:
  j
> '. . . the position has now been reached that in order to establish that a duty of care
> arises in a particular situation, it is not necessary to bring the facts of that situation
> within those of previous situations in which a duty of care has been held to exist.
> Rather the question has to be approached in two stages. First one has to ask whether,
> as between the alleged wrongdoer and the person who has suffered damage there is

a   a sufficient relationship of proximity or neighbourhood such that, in the reasonable contemplation of the former, carelessness on his part may be likely to cause damage to the latter, in which case a prima facie duty of care arises. Secondly, if the first question is answered affirmatively, it is necessary to consider whether there are any considerations which ought to negative, or to reduce or limit the scope of the duty or the class of person to whom it is owed or the damages to which a breach of it may give rise . . .'

b   Applying those statements of general principle as your Lordships have been enjoined to do both by Lord Reid and by Lord Wilberforce rather than to ask whether the particular situation which has arisen does or does not resemble some earlier and different situation where a duty of care has been held or has not been held to exist, I look for the reasons why, it being conceded that the appellants owed a duty of care to others not to
c   construct the flooring so that those others were in peril of suffering loss or damage to their persons or their property, that duty of care should not be equally owed to the respondents, who, though not in direct contractual relationship with the appellants, were as nominated sub-contractors in almost as close a commercial relationship with the appellants as it is possible to envisage short of privity of contract, so as not to expose the respondents to a possible liability to financial loss for repairing the flooring should it
d   prove that the flooring had been negligently constructed. It is conceded that if the flooring had been so badly constructed that to avoid imminent danger the respondents had to expend money on renewing it the respondents could have recoverd the cost of so doing. It seems curious that if the appellants' work had been so bad that to avoid immenent danger expenditure had been incurred the respondents could recover that expenditure but that if the work was less badly done so that remedial work could be
e   postponed they cannot do so. Yet this is seemingly the result of the appellants' contentions.

     My Lords, I have already said that there is no decided case which clearly points the way. But it is, I think, of assistance to see how far the various decisions have gone. I shall restrict my citation to the more important decisions both in this country and overseas. In *Dutton*, which, as already stated, your Lordships' House expressly approved in *Anns*,
f   the Court of Appeal held that the plaintiff, who bought the house in question long after it had been built and its foundations inadequately inspected by the defendants' staff, was entitled to recover from the defendants, inter alia, the estimated cost of repairing the house as well as other items of loss including diminution in value. There was in that case physical damage to the house. It was argued that the defendants were not liable for the cost of repairs or diminution in value. This argument was expressly rejected by Lord Denning MR and by Sachs LJ (see [1972] 1 All ER 462 at 474, 480–481, [1972] 1 QB 373
g   at 396, 403–404). Stamp LJ was however more sympathetic to this argument. He said ([1972] 1 All ER 462 at 489–490, [1972] 1 QB 373 at 414–415):

     'It is pointed out that in the past a distinction has been drawn between constructing a dangerous article and constructing one which is defective or of inferior quality. I may be liable to one who purchases in the market a bottle of ginger beer which I
h   have carelessly manufactured and which is dangerous and causes injury to person or property; but it is not the law that I am liable to him for the loss he suffers because what is found inside the bottle and for which he has paid money is not ginger beer but water. I do not warrant, except to an immediate purchaser and then by contract and not in tort, that the thing I manufacture is reasonably fit for its purpose. The submission is I think a formidable one and in my view raises the most difficult
j   point for decision in this case. Nor can I see any valid distinction between the case of a builder who carelessly builds a house which, although not a source of danger to person or property, nevertheless owing to a concealed defect in its foundations starts to settle and crack and becomes valueless, and the case of a manufacturer who carelessly manufactures an article which, though not a source of danger to a subsequent owner or to his other property, nevertheless owing to a hidden defect

quickly disintegrates. To hold that either the builder or the manufacturer was liable, except in contract, would be to open up a new field of liability, the extent of which could not I think be logically controlled, and since it is not in my judgment necessary to do so for the purposes of this case, I do not, more particularly because of the absence of the builder, express an opinion whether the builder has a higher or lower duty than the manufacturer. But the distinction between the case of a manufacturer of a dangerous thing which causes damage and that of a thing which turns out to be defective and valueless lies I think not in the nature of the injury but in the character of the duty. I have a duty not carelessly to put out a dangerous thing which may cause damage to one who may purchase it, but the duty does not extend to putting out carelessly a defective or useless or valueless thing. So again one goes back to consider what was the character of the duty, if any, owed to the plaintiff, and one finds on authority that the injury which is one of the essential elements of the tort of negligence is not confined to physical damage to personal property but may embrace economic damage which the plaintiff suffers through buying a worthless thing, as is shown by the *Hedley Byrne* case.'

Thus it was on the character of the duty that Stamp LJ founded and was able to agree with the other members of the Court of Appeal in that case.

My Lords, a similar question arose some years later in *Batty v Metropolitan Property Realizations Ltd* [1978] 2 All ER 445, [1978] QB 554. By the date of this decision the Court of Appeal had the benefit of the decision in your Lordships' House in *Anns*. Megaw LJ (see [1978] 2 All ER 445 at 456, [1978] QB 554 at 570) regarded the doubts raised by Stamp LJ as resolved by Lord Wilberforce's speech in *Anns*. Once again the argument based on absence of physical damage was advanced, as it had been in *Dutton*. Once again it was rejected, but on the basis that there was in this case as in *Dutton* the requisite degree of physical damage. Bridge LJ ([1978] 2 All ER 445 at 459, [1978] QB 554 at 573) however seems to me to use somewhat wider language and indeed he refers to two sentences at the end of Lord Wilberforce's speech in *Anns* [1977] 2 All ER 492 at 505, [1978] AC 728 at 759 where Lord Wilberforce said: 'Subject always to adequate proof of causation, these damages may include damages for personal injury and damage to property. In my opinion they may also include damage to the dwelling-house itself . . .'

My Lords, I am inclined to think that that last sentence was directed to the facts in *Anns* where there was, as in the other cases to which I have referred, the element of physical damage present due to trouble with the foundations, rather than directed to the full breadth of the proposition for which the respondents in the present appeal contended. None the less the three decisions, *Dutton*, *Anns* and *Batty*, seem to me to demonstrate how far the law has developed in the relevant respect in recent years.

My Lords, I turn next to the three main Commonwealth decisions. They are *Rivtow Marine Ltd v Washington Iron Works* [1974] SCR 1189, a decision of the Supreme Court of Canada, *Caltex Oil (Australia) Pty Ltd v Dredge Willemstad* (1976) 136 CLR 529, a decision of the High Court of Australia, and *Bowen v Paramount Builders (Hamilton) Ltd* [1977] 1 NZLR 394, a decision of the Court of Appeal of New Zealand. All three of these cases were decided before *Anns* reached your Lordships' House.

My Lords, in the first of this trilogy the Supreme Court by a majority held that the manufacturer of a dangerously defective article is not liable in tort to an ultimate consumer or user of that article for the cost of repairing damage arising in the article itself or for such economic loss as would have been sustained in any event as a result of the need to effect repairs. But there was, if I may respectfully say so, a powerful dissenting judgment by Laskin J with which Hall J concurred. The judge posed as the first question (see [1974] SCR 1189 at 1217) whether the defendants' liability for negligence should embrace economic loss where there has been no physical harm in fact. He gave an affirmative answer. After pointing out (at 1221) that the judicial limitation on liability was founded on what I have called 'the floodgates' argument rather than on principle, he adopted the view that economic loss resulting from threatened physical loss from a

negligently designed or manufactured product was recoverable. It was this judgment
a which Lord Wilberforce described in his speech in *Anns* [1977] 2 All ER 492 at 505,
[1978] AC 728 at 759–760 as of strong persuasive force. In the *Caltex* case the High Court
of Australia elaborately reviewed all the relevant English authorities and indeed others as
well. My Lords, I hope I shall not be thought lacking in respect for those elaborate
judgments or failing to acknowledge the help which I have derived from them if I do
not cite from them, for to some extent certain of the difficulties there discussed have
b been subsequently resolved by the decision of this House in *Anns*. In *Bowen*, to which
Lord Wilberforce also referred in *Anns* as having afforded him much assistance, the Court
of Appeal in New Zealand followed the Court of Appeal decision in *Dutton*. Cooke J took
the view that it was enough for the purpose of the case in question to say that the damage
was basically physical. But, as the report shows, he would have been prepared in
agreement with the judgments of Lord Denning MR and of Sachs LJ in *Dutton* to go
c further (see [1977] 1 NZLR 394 at 423).

My Lords, to my mind in the instant case there is no physical damage to the flooring
in the sense in which that phrase was used in *Dutton, Batty* and *Bowen* and some of the
other cases. As my noble and learned friend Lord Russell said during the argument, the
question which your Lordships' House now has to decide is whether the relevant Scots
and English law today extends the duty of care beyond a duty to prevent harm being
d done by faulty work to a duty to avoid such faults being present in the work itself. It was
powerfully urged on behalf of the appellants that were your Lordships so to extend the
law a pursuer in the position of the pursuer in *Donoghue v Stevenson* could in addition to
recovering for any personal injury suffered have also recovered for the diminished value
of the offending bottle of ginger beer. Any remedy of that kind it was argued must lie in
contract and not in delict or tort. My Lords, I seem to detect in that able argument
e reflections of the previous judicial approach to comparable problems before *Donoghue v
Stevenson* was decided. That approach usually resulted in the conclusion that in principle
the proper remedy lay in contract and not outside it. But that approach and its
concomitant philosophy ended in 1932 and for my part I should be reluctant to
countenance its re-emergence some fifty years later in the instant case. I think today the
proper control lies not in asking whether the proper remedy should lie in contract or
f instead in delict or tort, not in somewhat capricious judicial determination whether a
particular case falls on one side of the line or the other, not in somewhat artificial
distinctions between physical and economic or financial loss when the two sometimes go
together and sometimes do not (it is sometimes overlooked that virtually all damage
including physical damage is in one sense financial or economic for it is compensated by
an award of damages) but in the first instance in establishing the relevant principles and
g then in deciding whether the particular case falls within or without those principles. To
state this is to do no more than to restate what Lord Reid said in the *Dorset Yacht* case and
Lord Wilberforce in *Anns*. Lord Wilberforce in the passage I have already quoted
enunciated the two tests which have to be satisfied. The first is 'sufficient relationship of
proximity', the second any considerations negativing, reducing or limiting the scope of
the duty or the class of person to whom it is owed or the damages to which a breach of
h the duty may give rise. My Lords, it is I think in the application of those two principles
that the ability to control the extent of liability in delict or in negligence lies. The history
of the development of the law in the last fifty years shows that fears aroused by the
'floodgates' argument have been unfounded. Cooke J in *Bowen* [1977] 1 NZLR 394 at
472 described the 'floodgates' argument as specious and the argument against allowing a
cause of action such as was allowed in *Dutton, Anns* and *Bowen* as 'in terrorem or
j doctrinaire'.

Turning back to the present appeal I therefore ask first whether there was the requisite
degree of proximity so as to give rise to the relevant duty of care relied on by the
respondents. I regard the following facts as of crucial importance in requiring an
affirmative answer to that question: (1) the appellants were nominated sub-contractors;

(2) the appellants were specialists in flooring; (3) the appellants knew what products were required by the appellants and their main contractors and specialised in the production of those products; (4) the appellants alone were responsible for the composition and construction of the flooring; (5) the respondents relied on the appellants' skill and experience; (6) the appellants as nominated sub-contractors must have known that the respondents relied on their skill and experience; (7) the relationship between the parties was as close as it could be short of actual privity of contract; (8) the appellants must be taken to have known that if they did the work negligently (as it must be assumed that they did) the resulting defects would at some time require remedying by the respondents expending money on the remedial measures as a consequence of which the respondents would suffer financial or economic loss.

My Lords, reverting to Lord Devlin's speech in *Hedley Byrne*, it seems to me that all the conditions existed which give rise to the relevant duty of care owed by the appellants to the respondents.

I then turn to Lord Wilberforce's second proposition. On the facts I have just stated, I see nothing whatever to restrict the duty of care arising from the proximity of which I have spoken. During the argument it was asked what the position would be in a case where there was a relevant exclusion clause in the main contract. My Lords, that question does not arise for decision in the instant appeal, but in principle I would venture the view that such a clause according to the manner in which it was worded might in some circumstances limit the duty of care just as in the *Hedley Byrne* case the plaintiffs were ultimately defeated by the defendants' disclaimer of responsibility. But in the present case the only suggested reason for limiting the damage (ex hypothesi economic or financial only) recoverable for the breach of the duty of care just enunciated is that hitherto the law has not allowed such recovery and therefore ought not in the future to do so. My Lords, with all respect to those who find this a sufficient answer I do not. I think this is the next logical step forward in the development of this branch of the law. I see no reason why what was called during the argument 'damage to the pocket' simpliciter should be disallowed. when 'damage to the pocket' coupled with physical damage has hitherto always been allowed. I do not think that this development, if development it be, will lead to untoward consequences. The concept of proximity must always involve, at least in most cases, some degree of reliance; I have already mentioned the words 'skill' and 'judgment' in the speech of Lord Morris in *Hedley Byrne*. These words seem to me to be an echo, be it conscious or unconscious, of the language of s 14(1) of the Sale of Goods Act 1893. My Lords, though the analogy is not exact, I do not find it unhelpful for I think the concept of proximity of which I have spoken and the reasoning of Lord Devlin in the *Hedley Byrne* case involve factual considerations not unlike those involved in a claim under s 14(1); and as between an ultimate purchaser and a manufacturer would not easily be found to exist in the ordinary everyday transaction of purchasing chattels when it is obvious that in truth the real reliance was on the immediate vendor and not on the manufacturer.

My Lords, I have not thought it necessary to review all the cases cited in argument. If my conclusion be correct, certain of them can no longer be regarded as good law and others may have to be considered afresh hereafter, for example whether the decision of the majority of the Court of Appeal in *Spartan Steel and Alloys Ltd v Martin & Co (Contractors) Ltd* [1972] 3 All ER 557, [1973] QB 27 is correct or whether the reasoning of Edmund-Davies LJ in his dissenting judgment is to be preferred, and whether the decision of the First Division of the Inner House of the Court of Session in *Dynamco Ltd v Holland & Hannen & Cubitts (Scotland) Ltd* 1971 SC 257, a decision given after the *Dorset Yacht* case but before *Anns*, but seemingly without reference to the *Dorset Yacht* case, is correct.

My Lords, for all these reasons I would dismiss this appeal and allow this action to proceed to proof before answer.

My Lords, I would add two further observations. First, since preparing this speech I

have had the advantage of reading in draft the speech of Lord Fraser, with which I agree.
a Second, my attention has been drawn to the decision of the Court of Appeal in New
Zealand in *Mount Albert Borough Council v Johnson* [1979] 2 NZLR 234. The judgment of
Cooke and Somers JJ in which the decision in *Bowen v Paramount Builders (Hamilton) Ltd*
[1977] 1 NZLR 394 is stated to reflect the present law in New Zealand (see [1979] 2
NZLR 234 at 238–239) is consonant with the views I have expressed in this speech.

b **LORD BRANDON OF OAKBROOK.** My Lords, this appeal arises in an action in
which Junior Books Ltd are the pursuers and Veitchi Co Ltd are the defenders. In that
action, which purports to be founded in delict, the pursuers seek reparation from the
defenders for loss and damage which they claim to have suffered by reason of the want
of care of the defenders in laying flooring at the pursuers' factory in Grangemouth.

The defenders made a general challenge to the relevancy of the averments contained
c in the pursuers' condescendence at procedure roll. The question of law raised by that
challenge came first before the Lord Ordinary (Grieve). He decided the question in
favour of the pursuers, and by an interlocutor of 22 November 1979 allowed them a
proof before answer of all their averments. The defenders reclaimed to the Inner House
and by an interlocutor of 1 September 1980 the Second Division, consisting of the Lord
Justice-Clerk (Lord Wheatley), Lord Kissen and Lord Robertson, refused the reclaiming
d motion and affirmed the interlocutor of the Lord Ordinary. The defenders now appeal
from that decision to your Lordships' House.

Avoiding all matters of detail, the averments contained in the condescendence can be
summarised as follows. (1) In 1969–70 the pursuers had built for them by main
contractors a factory in Grangemouth. (2) Earlier, in July 1968, the pursuers' architects
had nominated the defenders as sub-contractors to lay flooring, consisting of a magnesium
e oxychloride composition, in the production area of the factory. (3) The pursuers'
architects, in so nominating the defenders, had relied on the fact that the defenders were
specialists in the laying of flooring. (4) The defenders had accepted the nomination and,
after entering into a contract with the main contractors, laid flooring of the specified
composition in the specified area. (5) It was the duty of the defenders to mix and lay the
flooring with reasonable care. (6) The defenders were in breach of that duty in that they
f failed, in a number of respects, to mix and lay the flooring with reasonable care. (7) In
consequence of that breach of duty by the defenders the flooring began to develop cracks
in 1972 and had gone on cracking more and more ever since. (8) As a result of the
cracking of the flooring the pursuers suffered the following items of damage or loss:
necessary relaying or replacement of the flooring £50,000; storage of books during the
carrying out of the work £1,000; removal of machinery to enable the work to be done,
g £2,000; loss of profits due to disturbance of business £45,000; wages of employees
thrown away £90,000; overheads thrown away £16,000; investigation of necessary
treatment of flooring £3,000. The total of these items was pleaded as £206,000; it is in
fact, although the point is not material, £207,000.

For the purpose of considering the relevancy of the pursuers' averments of fact, it is
necessary to make the assumption that all such averments are true. On the basis of that
h assumption, the dispute between the parties is not whether the defenders owed a duty of
care to the pursuers in connection with the laying of the flooring; the existence of some
duty arising from the proximity of the parties is, rightly in my view, admitted by the
defenders. The dispute is rather concerned with the scope of that admitted duty of care.

For the defenders, on the one hand, it was contended that the duty was limited to a
duty to exercise reasonable care so to mix and lay the flooring as to ensure that it was not
j a danger to persons or property, excluding for this purpose the property brought into
being by the work and labour done, that is to say the flooring itself. For the pursuers, on
the other hand, it was contended that the duty was a duty to exercise reasonable care so
to mix and lay the flooring as to ensure that it was free of any defects, whether dangerous
to persons or property or not; alternatively, if the duty was in principle that put forward

by the defenders, the relevant property, damage to which the defenders were under a duty to exercise reasonable care to avoid, included the property brought into being by *a* the work and labour done, that is to say the flooring itself.

In relation to that dispute it is common ground that, so far as the present case is concerned, there are no material differences between the Scottish law of delict and the English law of negligence, so that authorities relating to the latter are properly to be taken into account in relation to the former. It is further common ground that authorities in Commonwealth countries, the laws of which, in so far as they are not statutory, are *b* derived from the English common law, may usefully be considered, although their value is necessarily persuasive only.

My Lords, it appears to me clear beyond doubt that, there being no contractual relationship between the pursuers and the defenders in the present case, the foundation, and the only foundation, for the existence of a duty of care owed by the defenders to the pursuers, is the principle laid down in the decision of your Lordships' House in *Donoghue* *c* *v Stevenson* [1932] AC 562, [1932] All ER Rep 1. The actual decision in that case related only to the duty owed by a manufacturer of goods to their ultimate user or consumer, and can be summarised in this way: a person who manufactures goods which he intends to be used or consumed by others is under a duty to exercise such reasonable care in their manufacture as to ensure that they can be used or consumed in the manner intended without causing physical damage to persons or their property. *d*

While that was the actual decision in *Donoghue v Stevenson*, it was based on a much wider principle embodied in passages in the speech of Lord Atkin, which have been quoted so often that I do not find it necessary to quote them again here. Put shortly, that wider principle is that, when a person can or ought to appreciate that a careless act or omission on his part may result in physical injury to other persons or their property, he owes a duty to all such persons to exercise reasonable care to avoid such careless act or *e* omission.

It is, however, of fundamental importance to observe that the duty of care laid down in *Donoghue v Stevenson* was based on the existence of a danger of physical injury to persons or their property. That this is so is clear from the observations made by Lord Atkin ([1932] AC 562 at 581–582, [1932] All ER Rep 1 at 11–12) with regard to the statements of law of Brett MR in *Heaven v Pender* (1883) 11 QBD 503 at 509, [1881–5] *f* All ER Rep 35 at 39. It has further, until the present case, never been doubted, so far as I know, that the relevant property for the purpose of the wider principle on which the decision in *Donoghue v Stevenson* was based was property other than the very property which gave rise to the danger of physical damage concerned.

My Lords, I have already indicated my opinion that the wider principle on which the decision in *Donoghue v Stevenson* was based applies to the present case. The effect of its *g* application is that the defenders owed a duty to the pursuers to exercise reasonable care so to mix and lay the flooring as to ensure that it did not, when completed and put to its contemplated use, constitute a danger of physical damage to persons or their property, other than the flooring itself.

The averments contained in the condescendence in the present case do not include any averment that the defects in the flooring complained of by the pursuers either constitute *h* presently, or might reasonably be expected to constitute in the future, a danger of physical damage to persons or their property, other than the flooring itself. In the absence of any averment of that kind, I am of opinion that the averments contained in the condescendence disclose no cause of action in delict and are accordingly irrelevant.

My Lords, a good deal of the argument presented to your Lordships during the hearing of the appeal was directed to the question whether a person can recover, in an action *j* founded on delict alone, purely pecuniary loss which is independent of any physical damage to persons or their property. If that were the question to be decided in the present case, I should have no hesitation in holding that, in principle and depending on the facts of a particular case, purely pecuniary loss may be recoverable in an action

founded on delict alone. Two examples can be given of such cases. First, there is the type
a of case where a person suffers purely pecuniary loss as a result of relying on another
person's negligent misstatements: see *Hedley Byrne & Co Ltd v Heller & Partners Ltd* [1963]
2 All ER 575, [1964] AC 465. Second, there may be a type of case where a person, who
has a cause of action based on *Donoghue v Stevenson,* reasonably incurs pecuniary loss in
order to prevent or mitigate imminent danger of damage to the persons or property
exposed to that danger: see the dissenting judgment of Laskin J in the Canadian Supreme
b Court case of *Rivtow Marine Ltd v Washington Iron Works* [1974] SCR 1189, referred to
with approval in the speech of Lord Wilberforce in *Anns v Merton London Borough* [1977]
2 All ER 492 at 505, [1978] AC 728 at 760.

I do not, however, consider that the question of law for decision in this case is whether
a person can, in an action founded in delict alone, recover for purely pecuniary loss. On
the contrary, I adhere to the nature of the question of law to be decided which I
c formulated earlier, namely what is the scope of the duty of care owed by the defenders
to the pursuers on the assumed facts of the present case?

My Lords, in support of their contentions the pursuers placed reliance on the broad
statements relating to liability in negligence contained in the speech of Lord Wilberforce
in *Anns v Merton London Borough* [1977] 2 All ER 492 at 498, [1978] AC 728 at 751–752:

d 'Through the trilogy of cases in this House, *Donoghue v Stevenson* [1932] AC 562,
[1932] All ER Rep 1, *Hedley Byrne & Co Ltd v Heller & Partners Ltd* [1963] 2 All ER
575, [1964] AC 465 and *Home Office v Dorset Yacht Co Ltd* [1970] 2 All ER 294, [1970]
AC 1004, the position has now been reached that in order to establish that a duty of
care arises in a particular situation, it is not necessary to bring the facts of that
situation within those of previous situations in which a duty of care has been held
to exist. Rather the question has to be approached in two stages. First one has to ask
e whether, as between the alleged wrongdoer and the person who has suffered damage
there is a sufficient relationship of proximity or neighbourhood such that, in the
reasonable contemplation of the former, carelessness on his part may be likely to
cause damage to the latter, in which case a prima facie duty of care arises. Secondly,
if the first question is answered affirmatively, it is necessary to consider whether
there are any considerations which ought to negative, or to reduce or limit the scope
f of the duty or the class of person to whom it is owed or the damages to which a
breach of it may give rise . . .'

Applying that general statement of principle to the present case, it is, as I indicated
earlier, common ground that the first question which Lord Wilberforce said one should
ask oneself, namely whether there is sufficient proximity between the parties to give rise
g to the existence of a duty of care owed by the one to the other, falls to be answered in the
affirmative. Indeed, it is difficult to imagine a greater degree of proximity, in the absence
of a direct contractual relationship, than that which, under the modern type of building
contract, exists between a building owner and a sub-contractor nominated by him or his
architect.

That first question having been answered in the affirmative, however, it is necessary,
h according to the views expressed by Lord Wilberforce in the passage from his speech in
Anns v Merton London Borough quoted above, to ask oneself a second question, namely
whether there are any considerations which ought, inter alia, to limit the scope of the
duty which exists.

To that second question I would answer that there are two important considerations
which ought to limit the scope of the duty of care which it is common ground was owed
i by the defenders to the pursuers on the assumed facts of the present case.

The first consideration is that, in *Donoghue v Stevenson* itself and in all the numerous
cases in which the principle of that decision has been applied to different but analogous
factual situations, it has always been either stated expressly, or taken for granted, that an
essential ingredient in the cause of action relied on was the existence of danger, or the

threat of danger, of physical damage to persons or their property, excluding for this purpose the very piece of property from the defective condition of which such danger, *a* or threat of danger, arises. To dispense with that essential ingredient in a cause of action of the kind concerned in the present case would, in my view, involve a radical departure from long-established authority.

The second consideration is that there is no sound policy reason for substituting the wider scope of the duty of care put forward for the pursuers for the more restricted scope of such duty put forward by the defenders. The effect of accepting the pursuers' *b* contention with regard to the scope of the duty of care involved would be, in substance, to create, as between two persons who are not in any contractual relationship with each other, obligations of one of those two persons to the other which are only really appropriate as between persons who do have such a relationship between them.

In the case of a manufacturer or distributor of goods, the position would be that he warranted to the ultimate user or consumer of such goods that they were as well designed, *c* as merchantable and as fit for their contemplated purpose as the exercise of reasonable care could make them.

In the case of sub-contractors such as those concerned in the present case, the position would be that they warranted to the building owner that the flooring, when laid, would be as well designed, as free from defects of any kind and as fit for its contemplated purpose as the exercise of reasonable care could make it. *d*

In my view, the imposition of warranties of this kind on one person in favour of another, when there is no contractual relationship between them, is contrary to any sound policy requirement.

It is, I think, just worth while to consider the difficulties which would arise if the wider scope of the duty of care put forward by the pursuers were accepted. In any case where complaint was made by an ultimate consumer that a product made by some *e* persons with whom he himself had no contract was defective, by what standard or standards of quality would the question of defectiveness fall to be decided? In the case of goods bought from a retailer, it could hardly be the standard prescribed by the contract between the retailer and the wholesaler, or between the wholesaler and the distributor, or between the distributor and the manufacturer, for the terms of such contracts would not even be known to the ultimate buyer. In the case of sub-contractors such as the *f* defenders in the present case, it could hardly be the standard prescribed by the contract between the sub-contractors and the main contractors, for, although the building owner would probably be aware of those terms, he could not, since he was not a party to such contract, rely on any standard or standards prescribed in it. It follows that the question by what standard or standards alleged defects in a product complained of by its ultimate user or consumer are to be judged remains entirely at large and cannot be given any just *g* or satisfactory answer.

If, contrary to the views expressed above, the relevant contract or contracts can be regarded in order to establish the standard or standards of quality by which the question of defectiveness falls to be judged, and if such contract or contracts happen to include provisions excluding or limiting liability for defective products or defective work, or for negligence generally, it seems that the party sued in delict should in justice be entitled to *h* rely on such provisions. This illustrates with especial force the inherent difficulty of seeking to impose what are really contractual obligations by unprecedented and, as I think, wholly undesirable extensions of the existing law of delict.

By contrast, if the scope of the duty of care contended for by the defenders is accepted, the standard of defectiveness presents no problem at all. The sole question is whether the product is so defective that, when used or consumed in the way in which it was intended *j* to be, it gives rise to a danger of physical damage to persons or their property, other than the product concerned itself.

My Lords, for the reasons which I have given, I would decide the question of relevancy in favour of the defenders and allow the appeal accordingly.

Appeal dismissed.

a

Solicitors: *Macfarlanes*, agents for *McClure, Naismith, Brodie & Co*, Edinburgh (for the appellants); *Beaumont & Son*, agents for *Russel & Aitken WS*, Edinburgh (for the respondents).

Mary Rose Plummer   Barrister.

b

Wilson & Garden Ltd v Inland Revenue Commissioners

c

HOUSE OF LORDS

LORD FRASER OF TULLYBELTON, LORD RUSSELL OF KILLOWEN, LORD LOWRY, LORD ROSKILL AND LORD BRANDON OF OAKBROOK

d 26, 27 APRIL, 8 JULY 1982

Income tax – Close company – Apportionment of income – Relevant income – Maintenance and development of business – Business – Taxpayer company carrying on business as manufacturers of chalkboards – Decline in demand for chalkboards – Taxpayer company planning to acquire motor dealership to improve its trading position – Acquisition of dealership within taxpayer
e *company's objects – Whether acquisition of dealership a 'development' of taxpayer company's business – Whether planned expenditure on acquisition of dealership a 'requirement' of taxpayer company's business – Finance Act 1972, Sch 16, para 8(2).*

The taxpayer company, which carried on business as a manufacturer of chalkboards, was a close company. In the period from 1 July 1972 to 30 June 1977 there was a steady fall
f in the number of chalkboards sold by the taxpayer company, and in 1976 the directors of the company, seeking to find other means of creating profits to maintain the company's trading position, decided to acquire a major motor dealership at a total cost of not more than £110,000. The acquisition of the dealership was intra vires the company's memorandum of association. The company's only previous connection with the motor trade had been its ownership of a number of vehicles for use in connection with its
g business as a manufacturer of chalkboards. In the accounting period to 30 June 1975, the accounts for which were approved by the taxpayer company on 8 October 1976 (the relevant date), the taxpayer company distributed dividends totalling £6,614 out of a profit of £68,573. The question arose whether, for the purposes apportioning the taxpayer company's relevant income in the accounting period to 30 June 1975 in accordance with the Finance Act 1972, Sch 16, para 1*a*, the planned expenditure in
h relation to the dealership was a 'requirement [which was] necessary or advisable for the maintenance and development of [the taxpayer company's] business' within para 8(2)*b* of that schedule. The Crown contended that the words 'such other requirements as may be necessary or advisable for the maintenance and development of that business' in para 8(2)(*a*) referred only to the maintenance and development of the particular business carried on at the time when the relevant income was calculated, and that accordingly the
j acquisition of the dealership was not a business the requirements of which could be taken

---

a Paragraph 1, so far as material, is set out at p 222 *a* to *c*, post
b Paragraph 8(2) is set out at p 222 *j*, post

into account in determining the relevant income of the period in question. The General
Commissioners upheld the Crown's contention, but on an appeal by the taxpayer *a*
company their decision was reversed by the Court of Session. The Crown appealed to the
House of Lords.

Held – In determining what constituted the 'current requirements of the [taxpayer
company's] business' and 'such other requirements as may be necessary or advisable for
the maintenance and development of that business' within para 8(2)(*a*) of Sch 16 to the *b*
1972 Act regard could be had not only to the business which the taxpayer company was
actually carrying on but also to whatever was genuinely in the contemplation of the
taxpayer company at the relevant date as being then required for the future maintenance
and development of the business in whatever form the taxpayer company might think
was desirable. Furthermore, the phrase 'requirements of the business' within para 8(2)(*a*)
connoted something which was continuous and which would or might require *c*
maintaining or developing from time to time, and there was no reason why 'development'
of a business should not include diversification of that business. In the circumstances the
acquisition of the dealership was within the requirements of the taxpayer company's
business under para 8(2)(*a*). The appeal would therefore be dismissed (see p 220 *j* to p 221
b, p 223 *d* to *j* and p 224 *c e g h*, post).
Per curiam. The 'business' of a company is not necessarily merely the application of *d*
shareholders' funds for the generation of profits in accordance with its memorandum of
association (see p 220 *j* to p 221 *b* and p 224 *d e g h*, post).

Notes
For the apportionment of the income of close companies, see 23 Halsbury's Laws (4th
edn) paras 1211–1224. *e*
For the Finance Act 1972, Sch 16, paras 1, 8, see 42 Halsbury's Statutes (3rd edn) 2039,
2046.

Appeal
The Crown appealed from interlocutors of the First Division of the Court of Session as
the Court of Exchequer in Scotland (the Lord President (Lord Emslie), Lord Cameron *f*
and Lord Avonside) dated 19 February and 5 May 1981 ([1981] STC 301) allowing an
appeal by Wilson & Garden Ltd (the taxpayer company) by way of case stated from a
determination of the General Commissioners for the division of Stirling refusing the
taxpayer company's appeal against a notice served on them by the inspector of taxes
under para 15(1) of Sch 16 to the Finance Act 1972 requiring the taxpayer company to
apportion the sum of £51,066 among the participators of the company for the accounting *g*
period to 30 June 1975. The facts are set out in the opinion of Lord Roskill.

The Lord Advocate (Rt Hon Lord Mackay of Clashfern QC), Robert Carnwath and *A C Hamilton*
(of the Scottish Bar) for the Crown.
G W Penrose QC and *J E Drummond Young* (both of the Scottish Bar) for the taxpayer
company. *h*

Their Lordships took time for consideration.

8 July. The following opinions were delivered.

j
LORD FRASER OF TULLYBELTON. My Lords, I have had the advantage of
reading in draft the speech of my noble and learned friend Lord Roskill. I agree with it,
and for the reasons stated in it I would dismiss this appeal.

LORD RUSSELL OF KILLOWEN. My Lords, I have had the advantage of reading

a in draft the speech prepared by my noble and learned friend Lord Roskill. I agree with it
and for the reasons he gives I also would dismiss this appeal.

LORD LOWRY. My Lords, I have had the advantage of reading in draft the speech
about to be delivered by my noble and learned friend Lord Roskill. I agree with his
conclusions, and, for the reasons which he gives, I would dismiss this appeal.

b **LORD ROSKILL.** My Lords, this is an appeal by the Inland Revenue Commissioners
from interlocutors of the First Division of the Court of Session as the Court of Exchequer
in Scotland (the Lord President (Lord Emslie), Lord Cameron and Lord Avonside) ([1981]
STC 301) dated 19 February and 5 May 1981. By those interlocutors the First Division
allowed an appeal by the taxpayer company by way of case stated by the General
Commissioners for the division of Stirling. The taxpayer company had appealed to the
c General Commissioners against a notice served on them by the inspector of taxes under
para 15(1) of Sch 16 to the Finance Act 1972. The General Commissioners had refused
that appeal. On 25 March 1980, before those two interlocutors presently appealed from,
the First Division had during the hearing of the appeal remitted the case to the General
Commissioners on certain matters and in due course the General Commissioners reported
to the First Division on those matters.

d My Lords, the principal question for determination in this appeal arises in this way.
The taxpayer company were a close company for the purposes of s 282(1) of the Income
and Corporation Taxes Act 1970. The taxpayer company had from the 1930s onwards
carried on a business as manufacturers of chalkboards. They still did so at the material
times giving rise to the present dispute. But in the five years from 1 July 1972 to 30 June
1977 there was a steady fall in the number of chalkboards which they sold though it was
e found that that fall was not necessarily matched by a fall in the value of the taxpayer
company's sales or of their trading profit. None the less early in 1976 the taxpayer
company's board of directors came to the conclusion that it was essential for the taxpayer
company to find other means of creating profits in order to maintain their trading
position. Later that year they made inquiries about the acquisition of a major motor
dealership. This was an entirely new departure for the taxpayer company since hitherto
f their connection with the motor trade had been only the ownership of a number of
vehicles which they used in connection with their business of making and selling
chalkboards.

My Lords, the taxpayer company's accounts for the year ending 30 June 1975 were
approved by their directors on 8 October 1976, which I shall call 'the relevant date'. The
accompanying report recommended that out of a profit of £68,573 for that financial
g year dividends totalling £6,614 should be paid. Those accounts were adopted by the
taxpayer company in general meeting on 17 November 1976. Meanwhile on 12
November 1976 the taxpayer company had decided to acquire a Ford retail dealership at
Glenrothes in Fife. This was later acquired at a cost of £109,000. This acquisition had
been in contemplation on the relevant date and it was common ground that the
transaction was intra vires the taxpayer company.

h My Lords, the notice served by the inspector, to which I have referred, showed that
the sum of £51,066 was to be apportioned among participators in respect of the taxpayer
company's financial year ending 30 June 1975. As already stated it was against that notice
that the taxpayer company appealed to the General Commissioners. Whether the First
Division or the General Commissioners were correct must depend on the application to
the facts, which I have summarised, of the relevant statutory provisions on their proper
j construction. It is therefore to these that I now turn.

Section 94 of the Finance Act 1972 provided that Sch 16 to that Act should have effect
instead of certain statutory provisions relating to the charge to income tax in respect of
shortfall in distributions of close companies and apportionment of income of close
companies among participators. It is therefore to Sch 16 that I next turn. The most
relevant provisions of that schedule are as follows:

'PART I

POWERS OF APPORTIONMENT AND CONSEQUENCES OF APPORTIONMENT

Power to apportion excess of company's relevant income over its distributions

1.—(1) Subject to sub-paragraphs (2) and (3) below, the income of a close company for any accounting period may, for the purposes of this Schedule, be apportioned by the inspector among the participators.

(2) Subject to paragraphs 2 and 3 below—(a) an apportionment shall not be made under this paragraph unless the relevant income of the company for the accounting period exceeds its distributions for that period; and (b) the amount apportioned shall be the amount of that excess, and Part II of this Schedule shall have effect for determining the relevant income and distributions of a company for an accounting period and whether or not there is any such excess . . .

Manner of apportionment

4.—(1) Subject to the provisions of this paragraph, any apportionment under paragraph 1 above, including any sub-apportionment of an amount directly or indirectly apportioned to a company, shall be made according to the respective interests in the company in question of the participators . . .

Consequences of apportionment: income tax

5 . . . (2) Where a sum is so apportioned to an individual—(a) it shall be treated for the purpose of computing his total income as income received by him at the end of the accounting period to which the apportionment relates and, subject to section 529 of the Taxes Act, shall be deemed to be the highest part of his total income . . .

PART II

PROVISIONS FOR DETERMINING RELEVANT INCOME AND DISTRIBUTIONS, ETC.

Determination of "relevant income"

8.—(1) Subject to the provisions of this paragraph and of paragraphs 9 and 13 below, the relevant income of a company for an accounting period is—(a) in the case of a company which is a trading company or a member of a trading group, so much of its distributable income for that period as can be distributed without prejudice to the requirements of the company's business; (b) in the case of a company not within paragraph (a) above whose distributable income for that period consists of or includes estate or trading income—(i) so much of the estate or trading income as can be distributed without prejudice to the requirements of the company's business so far as concerned with the activities or assets giving rise to estate or trading income; and (ii) its distributable income, if any, other than estate or trading income; (c) in the case of any other company, its distributable income for that period.

(2) In arriving at the relevant income for any accounting period—(a) where under sub-paragraph (1) above regard is to be had to the requirements of a company's business, regard shall be had not only to the current requirements of the business but also to such other requirements as may be necessary or advisable for the maintenance and development of that business but, for this purpose, the provisions of paragraph 12 below shall apply; (b) the amount of the estate or trading income shall be taken as the amount included in respect of it in the distributable income . . .

Requirements of the company's business

a

12.—(1) For the purposes of paragraph 8(2) above there shall be regarded as income available for distribution and not as having been applied, or as being applicable, to the current requirements of a company's business, or to such other requirements as may be necessary or advisable for the maintenance and development of that business—(a) any sum expended or applied, or intended to be expended or applied, out of the income of the company, otherwise than in pursuance of an

b

obligation entered into by the company before 4th August 1914 ... (b) any sum expended or applied, or intended to be expended or applied, in pursuance or in consequence of any fictitious or artificial transaction ...'

My Lords, though I have for ease of reference set out the foregoing statutory provisions, the all important words are to be found in para 8(2)(a). What, on the facts already

c

summarised, were 'the current requirements of the business' of the taxpayer company and what in this context is meant by 'such other requirements as may be necessary or advisable for the maintenance and development of that business'? Learned counsel were at least agreed on two matters. First, the phrase 'maintenance and development' must be read disjunctively. Second, the date as at which these matters have to be decided, which I have called 'the relevant date', was 8 October 1976, this being the date at which the

d

taxpayer company's board approved the accounts for the financial year ending 30 June 1975.

My Lords, the crucial question is whether in determining what are 'the current requirements of the business' and 'such other requirements as may be necessary or advisable for the maintenance and development of that business' regard is to be had only to the business which the taxpayer is actually carrying on at the relevant date so that the

e

phrase 'the maintenance and development of that business' must be read as referring to, and only to, that business which the taxpayer is then actually carrying on (for brevity I will call this 'the narrow construction') or whether regard may also be had to whatever is genuinely in the contemplation of the taxpayer at the relevant date as being then required for the future maintenance and development of the business in whatever form the taxpayer may think is desirable (I will call this 'the wide construction'). The General

f

Commissioners preferred the narrow construction. The First Division preferred the wide construction.

My Lords, both learned counsel sought support for their respective contentions by reference to other paragraphs of Sch 16. Of course, the crucial phrases must be construed in the context of the schedule as a whole. But, for my part, I do not derive any assistance from those other paragraphs. I ask first what the purpose is of Sch 16. Clearly, it is to

g

prevent the accumulation by close companies of undistributed profits which are in truth income and thereby the conversion of what is in truth income into tax-free capital. Your Lordships were referred by counsel for the taxpayer company to s 21 of the Finance Act 1922, which was the legislative ancestor of the present legislation and was designed to impose liability for supertax on the undistributed income of certain companies; and the proviso to sub-s (1) of s 21 contains language identical with that which now appears in

h

para 8(2) of Sch 16. The language of s 21 clearly shows the legislative purpose of the section and of its statutory successors. My Lords, acceptance of the wide construction does not of itself seem to me to offend against that legislative purpose, for in the instant case its effect would be to enable the taxpayer company to seek to generate further profits, not to seek to capitalise those profits which they have already earned.

My Lords, once it is accepted that the relevant date is a date substantially later than the end of the financial year in question, it seems to me necessarily to follow that events between the end of that financial year and the taking of the crucial decision on the relevant date must be able to be legitimately taken into account. It is easy to envisage many changes in circumstances during that period, which in some cases might well be substantially longer than it was in the present case and which might make it essential in the taxpayer's interest as a matter of prudent business management to take decisions which could not possibly have been envisaged at the end of that financial year. There might have been a complete change during that period in the demand for the taxpayer's *a* products so that commercial prudence would dictate discontinuance and, unless liquidation were to follow, the development of some new line of business. Is this to be regarded as an irrelevant consideration? Or the normal supply to the taxpayer of raw materials might suddenly cease and the only alternative source of supply might be the acquisition of some trading company whose business was not only producing that particular raw material but perhaps other materials or products as well. It is not easy in *b* these circumstances to see why 'current requirements' should not reflect all these matters or why, if as a matter of ordinary commercial prudence distribution of profits is to be restricted in the interests of the sound financing of future developments, the taxpayer should be in peril of the invocation by the Revenue of the provisions of Sch 16. The phrase 'requirements of the business' seems to me to connote something which is continuous and will or may from time to time require maintaining or developing or *c* both. I do not see why 'development' should not include what today is usually called 'diversification'. As my noble and learned friend Lord Brandon pointed out during the argument, the Crown's narrow construction involves that if on the day before the relevant date the new business had already been acquired the taxpayer company would succeed, but if it is only in contemplation on the relevant date the taxpayer company must fail. Such a result seems to me to be indefensible. The language of the statute does *d* not require it. Nor does the legislative purpose of Sch 16 demand it. My Lords, with profound respect I venture to doubt whether the statement in the judgment of the First Division ([1981] STC 301 at 308) that 'The "business" of any company is the application of shareholders' funds for the generation of profit in accordance with its memorandum of association' is necessarily of universal application. But, whether that be so or not, I respectfully agree with the First Division that it is the wide construction which is correct. *e*

My Lords, on this view it becomes unnecessary to deal with the second question which the learned Lord Advocate argued and which arose from a passage in the last paragraph but two of the judgment of the First Division. As to the third question which he argued and which arose out of the findings in the report of the General Commissioners to the First Division following remission on 25 March 1980, I agree that these findings could have been more happily expressed; indeed they were severely criticised by the First *f* Division. But I am inclined to think that the four paragraphs consecutively numbered (1) to (4) (see [1981] STC 301 at 305) must be read cumulatively and that the General Commissioners intended to convey that if their view on the question of construction were wrong, as in my view it was, then taking all four matters into account the taxpayer company's business, on the basis that the wide construction was correct, would be prejudiced by the distribution. The Lord Advocate made it plain that in any event he did *g* not seek further remission on this issue.

I would dismiss this appeal.

LORD BRANDON OF OAKBROOK. My Lords, I have had the advantage of reading in advance the speech prepared by my noble and learned friend Lord Roskill. I agree with it and would dismiss the appeal accordingly. *h*

Appeal dismissed.

Solicitors: *Solicitor of Inland Revenue,* agent for *Solicitor of Inland Revenue (Scotland); Lee, Bolton & Lee,* agents for *Dundas & Wilson CS,* Edinburgh (for the taxpayer company).

Rengan Krishnan Esq   Barrister.

Re Christonette International Ltd

CHANCERY DIVISION
VINELOTT J
27 NOVEMBER 1981, 7 APRIL 1982

Company – Compulsory winding up – Costs – Power to order costs of winding up to be paid out of assets – Priority – Liquidator's costs of unsuccessful action against receiver to set aside debenture – Receiver under debenture appointed before winding-up order made – Receiver realising company's assets and paying preferential debts, his own and petitioner's costs and sum secured by debenture – Payments exhausting proceeds in receiver's hands – Whether liquidator's costs should be paid in priority to sum secured by debenture – Whether assets subject to a floating charge under a debenture remaining 'assets of the company' when charge crystallises and becomes fixed – Whether company can be 'in the course of being wound up' prior to compulsory winding-up order being made or liquidator being appointed – Companies Act 1948, ss 94(1), 319.

In November 1977 and February 1978 a company issued two debentures giving floating charges over all its assets as security for the sums payable under the debentures. On 30 October 1978 the debenture holder gave the company notice calling for payment within seven days of the principal sums secured by the debentures. On 13 December 1978 a creditor's petition to compulsorily wind up the company was presented. Subsequently, on 19 January 1979 the debenture holder appointed a receiver of the company's assets pursuant to the debentures. On 22 January an order was made on the creditor's petition compulsorily winding up the company, and on 16 March a liquidator was appointed. Meanwhile, shortly after he was appointed, the receiver realised the company's assets and under an agreement made in April 1979 sold substantially all the assets to a purchaser. However £35,000 of the purchase price was paid into a deposit account pending the outcome of proceedings by the receiver against a third party to establish ownership of part of the assets sold. Out of the remaining proceeds of sale in his hands the receiver first discharged the preferential debts as specified in s 319(1)[a] of the Companies Act 1948 which were required by s 94(1)[b] of that Act to be paid out of those assets in priority to the

---

a   Section 319, so far as material, provides:
    '(1) In a winding up there shall be paid in priority to all other debts—(a) the following rates and taxes,—(i) all local rates . . . (ii) all income tax, profits tax, excess profits tax or other assessed taxes . . . (b) all wages or salary . . . of any clerk or servant . . . and all wages . . . of any workman or labourer . . . (d) all accrued holiday remuneration becoming payable to any clerk, servant, workman or labourer . . . (e) . . . all the debts specified in [certain enactments relating to social security] (f) . . . all amounts due in respect of any [workmen's] compensation . . .
    (5) The foregoing debts [ie those given priority in s 319(1)] shall—(a) rank equally among themselves and be paid in full, unless the assets are insufficient to meet them, in which case they shall abate in equal proportions; and (b) . . . so far as the assets of the company available for payment of general creditors are insufficient to meet them, have priority over the claims of holders of debentures under any floating charge created by the company, and be paid accordingly out of any property comprised in or subject to that charge.
    (6) Subject to the retention of such sums as may be necessary for the costs and expenses of the winding up, the foregoing debts shall be discharged forthwith so far as the assets are sufficient to meet them . . .'
b   Section 94(1) provides: 'Where, in the case of a company registered in England, either a receiver is appointed on behalf of the holders of any debentures of the company secured by a floating charge, or possession is taken by or on behalf of those debenture holders of any property comprised in or subject to the charge, then, if the company is not at the time in course of being wound up, the debts which in every winding up are under the provisions of Part V of this Act relating to preferential payments to be paid in priority to all other debts, shall be paid out of any assets coming to the hands of the receiver or other person taking possession as aforesaid in priority to any claim for principal or interest in respect of the debentures.'

sums secured by the debentures, then paid his own expenses and remuneration and the
petitioning creditor's taxed costs of his petition, and finally paid the principal sum
secured by the first debenture. Those payments virtually exhausted the proceeds in the
receiver's hands except for the £35,000 on deposit, entitlement to which was disputed
by the purchaser of the company's assets. Shortly after being appointed and with the
authority of the court subsequently obtained, the liquidator, instructed solicitors to bring
an action against the receiver and debenture holder to set aside the debentures and for an
injunction restraining the receiver from making any payments under the debentures
but in May 1979 that action was dismissed with no order as to costs. In May 1981 the
liquidator applied by summons to recover the taxed costs of that action from the receiver,
submitting that by virtue of s 319(5) and (6) the costs, being an expense of the winding
up, were payable out of the assets in the receiver's hands in priority to any sums secured
by the debentures, because (i) s 319 supplemented s 94 and 'the assets of the company' in
the winding up, within s 319(5) and (6), therefore included the assets of the company
which were subject to a floating charge at the date of presentation of the petition to wind
up the company which led to the subsequent winding-up order, in so far as such assets
had not been used by the receiver to pay the preferential debts, (ii) alternatively, the
winding-up order related back to the date of presentation of the petition (13 December
1978) and therefore at the date when the receiver was appointed (19 January 1979) the
company was 'in the course of being wound up' for the purpose of s 94(1) and thus the
application of its assets was governed by s 319 and not by s 94.

Held – The liquidator's application would be dismissed for the following reasons—
    (1) The purpose of s 94(1) of the 1948 Act was that, where a company was not in the
course of being wound up when a receiver was appointed under a debenture, the receiver
nevertheless had to pay out of the assets in his hands, those debts which would have been
preferential debts in a winding up under s 319(1) of that Act in priority to the sums
secured by the debenture, even though on his appointment the assets subject to the
debenture ceased to be assets of the company capable of being dealt with by it for the
purpose of its business. But, notwithstanding the purpose of s 94(1), where a floating
charge under a debenture had crystallised and become fixed before the date of a winding-
up order, the assets comprised in the charge were no longer 'assets of the company' in the
winding up within s 319. It followed that since the floating charges under the debentures
had crystallised and become fixed charges on the appointment of the receiver on 19
January 1979, and therefore before the date (22 January 1979) of the winding-up order,
the proceeds of sale of the company's assets in the receiver's hands were not 'assets of the
company' in the winding up within s 319(5) and (6) and were not, therefore, available
for payment of the liquidator's costs of his action under s 319(6) (see p 230 b to f and
p 231 g, post); Re Griffin Hotel Co Ltd [1940] 4 All ER 324 applied; Re Barleycorn Enterprises
Ltd [1970] 2 All ER 155 considered.
    (2) Furthermore, a company was 'in the course of being wound up' for the purposes
of s 94(1) only after an order for its compulsory winding up had been made or a resolution
to wind it up and appoint a liquidator had been passed, because only then was the
liquidator responsible for the payment of the preferential creditors, whereas s 94 was
dealing with the situation where a liquidator had not been appointed. It followed that,
since the winding-up order had not been made when the receiver was appointed, the
company was 'not . . . in the course of being wound up', within s 94(1), when the receiver
was appointed and thus s 94(1) governed the application of the assets in the receiver's
hands (see p 231 f g, post).

Notes
For payment of preferential debts where a receiver is appointed under a debenture, see 7
Halsbury's Laws (4th edn) para 892, for priority of payments in a winding up, see ibid
para 1316, for cases on preferential payments by a receiver, see 10 Digest (Reissue) 882–
884, 5107–5115, and for cases on distribution of assets in a winding up, see ibid 1215,
1216, 7628–7634.
    For The Companies Act 1948, ss 94, 319, see 5 Halsbury's Statutes (3rd edn) 187, 345.

Cases referred to in judgment

a *Barleycorn Enterprises Ltd, Re, Mathias and Davies (a firm) v Down (liquidator of Barleycorn Enterprises Ltd)* [1970] 2 All ER 155, [1970] Ch 465, [1970] 2 WLR 898, CA, 10 Digest (Reissue) 1089, 6693.
Griffin Hotel Co Ltd, Re, Joshua Tetley & Son Ltd v Griffin Hotel Co Ltd and John Lupton & Son Ltd [1940] 4 All ER 324, [1941] Ch 129, 10 Digest (Reissue) 884, 5115.
Lewis Merthyr Consolidated Collieries Ltd, Re, Lloyds Bank Ltd v The company [1929] 1 Ch
b 498, CA, 10 Digest (Reissue) 883, 5112.

Cases also cited
Colonial Trusts Corp, Re, ex p Bradshaw (1879) 15 Ch D 465.
Crompton & Co Ltd, Re, Player v Crompton & Co Ltd [1914] 1 Ch 954.
Victoria Steamboats Ltd, Re, Smith v Wilkinson [1897] 1 Ch 158.

c
Summons for payment of liquidator's costs
By a summons dated 12 May 1981 the liquidator of Christonette International Ltd (the company) applied for an order that Jitendra Nath Dutta, the receiver of the company appointed under two debentures issued by the company, should pay to the liquidator within seven days the sum of £1,491·01, being the amount of the liquidator's taxed costs
d incurred in retaining solicitors, under retainers dated 30 April and 15 May 1979, in proceedings by the liquidator to set aside the debentures and for an injunction restraining the receiver from making any payment to the debenture holder, and pursuant to the order of the Companies Court dated 16 April 1980, with interest thereon at the rate and for such period as the court determined. The facts are set out in the judgment.

e *David Oliver* for the liquidator.
Hubert Picarda for the receiver.

Cur adv vult

7 April. **VINELOTT J** read the following judgment: This is a summons by the
f liquidator of a company Christonette International Ltd. It raises a question of some importance concerning the proper application of moneys which came into the hands of a receiver appointed by the holder of a debenture creating a floating charge over the assets of the company and which came into the receiver's hands after a petition for the winding up of the company had been presented but before an order for the compulsory winding up of the company had been made.
g The relevant facts can be briefly stated. On 15 November 1977 the company issued a debenture, which I will call the first debenture, whereby the company undertook to pay to a named debenture holder on a specified date or on such earlier date as the principal moneys thereby secured should become payable in accordance with conditions indorsed thereon, the sum of £20,000 with interest. It charged all its undertaking and assets present and future as security therefor. The first debenture was issued subject to a
h number of indorsed conditions. I need only refer to two of them.
Condition 8 provided that the principal moneys thereby secured should become payable if, amongst other things, the debenture holder should give seven days' notice in writing calling for payment. Condition 9 gave the debenture holder power at any time after the principal moneys should have become payable to appoint a receiver and provided that—
j
'all monies received by any such receiver shall, after providing for the matters specified in the first three paragraphs of section 109(8) of the Law of Property Act 1925 and in sections 94 and 319 of the Companies Act 1948, and for all costs charges and expenses of and incidental to the exercise of the receiver's power and subject to the provisions of the Law of Property Act 1925 as to the application of insurance money, be applied in or towards satisfaction of the principal monies and interest secured by this debenture.'

On 6 February 1978 the company issued a further debenture, the second debenture, to secure the payment of a further advance of £15,000 to the same debenture holder. *a* Save that the charge created by the second debenture ranks after the charge created by the first debenture the terms of the second debenture are identical with the terms of the first debenture. Both debentures were duly registered pursuant to s 95 of the Companies Act 1948.

On 30 October 1978 the debenture holder gave the company notice calling for payment of the principal moneys secured by both debentures within seven days. A *b* creditor's petition for the compulsory winding up of the company was presented on 13 December 1978. On 19 January 1979 the debenture holder appointed a receiver and manager. An order was made on 22 January 1979 for the compulsory winding up of the company. Under that order of course one of the official receivers was appointed provisional liquidator. A liquidator was appointed on 16 March 1979.

Shortly after the liquidator had been appointed he instructed solicitors to institute *c* proceedings to set aside the debenture and to apply for an injunction to restrain the receiver from making any payment to the debenture holder. An action was duly commenced on 26 April 1979. By an order dated 18 May 1979 the action was dismissed with no order as to costs. The liquidator had retained solicitors and had commenced the action without the prior authority of the court, but the retainer and the institution of the action were each respectively sanctioned by an order of the Companies Court made on *d* 16 April 1980. The costs have since been taxed. In this summons the liquidator seeks to recover those costs from the receiver.

Following his appointment, the receiver realised the assets of the company. Substantially the whole of the company's assets were sold under an agreement dated 6 April 1979. At that time there was a dispute between the receiver and a third party as to the ownership of certain chattels comprised in the sale. Proceedings had been commenced by the *e* receiver to establish his title to them. Under the agreement of 6 April 1979 the receiver agreed to prosecute the action in accordance with the directions and at the expense of the purchaser. I understand that the action is still pending. It is provided by the agreement that if at first instance the receiver fails to obtain a declaration of his title to the chattels or if the purchaser is previously advised by leading counsel that the receiver does not have title to them he will refund £35,000 of the purchase price to the purchaser. If the *f* receiver obtains the declaration as to title sought in the action but fails to obtain an order for costs he is to bear the first £5,000 of costs. It was further agreed that of the purchase price payable on completion £35,000 would be paid into a deposit account with a named bank and retained so long as the purchaser should have a contingent right to a refund of that amount. Interest on the sum deposited is to be treated as an accretion to the principal sum and refunded or paid to the receiver, as a case may be, with the principal sum. *g*

The receiver has discharged those liabilities of the company which are given preference by the joint effect of ss 94(1) and 319 of the Companies Act 1948 and which, under s 94(1), are payable out of assets coming into his hands in priority to the principal and interest secured by the debenture. He has also paid or retained his own expenses and remuneration. In addition he has paid the petitioner's taxed costs of the petition. Lastly, *h* he has paid the principal sum secured by the first debenture. Those payments have almost exhausted the moneys which have come into his hands, though of course £35,000 is still held in a deposit account under the terms of the agreement of 6 April 1979. If this sum with its accrued interest, which now amounts to a considerable sum, ultimately falls to be paid to the receiver, he will probably have sufficient moneys to pay the principal sum secured by the second debenture with the interest due under both debentures and be left with a surplus for which he will have to account to the liquidator. That surplus *j* may well suffice to meet the costs incurred by the liquidator in the litigation which I have mentioned as well as his other expenses. If the sum of £35,000 with accrued interest ultimately falls to be repaid to the purchaser, there will be no surplus to be paid to the liquidator. The question is whether in these circumstances the receiver should have paid

the principal sum secured by the first debenture before paying the liquidator his taxed
a costs of the action against the receiver.

The case for the liquidator is founded on the decision of the Court of Appeal in *Re
Barleycorn Enterprises Ltd, Mathias and Davies (a firm) v Down (liquidator of Barleycorn
Enterprises Ltd)* [1970] 2 All ER 155, [1970] Ch 465. In that case an order was made for
the compulsory winding up of a company which had issued a debenture creating a
floating charge which was still a floating charge immediately before the winding-up
b order was made. The priority of preferential debts and of the costs and expenses of the
winding up was accordingly governed by s 319 of the 1948 Act. Section 319(5)(b)
specifically provides that in the case of a company registered in England, if the assets of
the company available for general creditors are insufficient to meet debts of the company
which are given priority by s 319(1), those debts are to have priority over the claims of
the holders of a debenture creating a floating charge. The assets of the company in
c question were insufficient to meet the preferential debts which included part of the sum
secured by the floating charge but advanced by the debenture holder (a bank) for the
payment of wages. The question was whether fees charged by a firm of chartered
accountants in preparing a statement of affairs, the amount of which fees had been
approved by the official receiver and which were clearly expenses of the winding up,
took priority over the claims of the preferential creditors.

d Section 319(5) does not specifically refer to the costs and expenses of a winding up,
though the costs and expenses of a winding up are given priority over preferential debts
to the extent of the assets of the company by s 319(6) which, so far as material, provides:

'Subject to the retention of such sums as may be necessary for the costs and
expenses of the winding up, the foregoing debts [that is the debts given priority by
sub-s (1)] shall be discharged forthwith so far as the assets are sufficient to meet them
e ...'

The order in which the costs and expenses of the winding up by the court are to be
paid out of the assets of a company remaining after payment of the fees and expenses
properly incurred in preserving, realising or getting in the assets is in turn governed by
r 195 of the Companies (Winding-up) Rules 1949, SI 1949/330. There the costs and
f expenses of preparing the statement of affairs are given a high priority.

It had been held in a number of cases before the passing of the Preferential Payments
in Bankruptcy Act 1888 (the precursor of s 319(5)(a) and (6) of the Companies Act 1948),
that assets comprised in a floating charge ceased to be assets of the company as soon as the
floating charge crystallised and became a fixed charge, which of course it necessarily does
on the making of a winding-up order if still floating immediately before the order is
g made. But to construe the words 'the assets' in para (a) of sub-s (5) and in sub-s (6) of s 319
as embracing only free assets which at the date of the winding-up order are not subject
to a floating charge produces an obvious absurdity. On that construction the effect of
sub-s (6) is that the costs and expenses of the winding up are given priority over 'the
foregoing debts', that is debts which are made preferential by s 319(1), to the extent that
the company has free assets. To the extent that the assets available for payment of general
h creditors are insufficient to meet preferential debts, that is to the extent that assets not
comprised in the floating charge or not required to meet the debt thereby secured are
insufficient to meet preferential debts, the preferential debts but not the costs and
expenses of the winding up are given priority over the claims of the debenture holder.
In *Re Barleycorn Enterprises Ltd* the Court of Appeal avoided this absurdity by holding
that in the 1888 Act and in the Preferential Payments in Bankruptcy Amendment Act
j 1897, and in the sections of the Companies Act 1948 which successively re-enacted those
Acts and in r 195, of the 1949 rules the word 'assets' is used in a different sense from that
in which it had been used in the previous legislation and so as to include assets comprised
in the floating charge. In *Re Barleycorn Enterprises Ltd*, of course, the floating charge was
still floating immediately before the winding-up order was made and the order of

application of the company's assets was governed by s 319. In the present case the floating charge was crystallised and became a fixed charge when the receiver was appointed and took possession of the assets of the company with a view to realising them for the benefit of the debenture holder. Under s 94 where a company is not in the course of being wound up, it becomes the duty of the receiver to pay in priority to the principal and interest due to the debenture holder debts which in every winding up are 'under the provisions of Part V of this Act relating to preferential payments to be paid in priority to all other debts . . .' The scheme of s 94 is in broad outline to give preference to debts which would have been preferential under s 319 if an order had been made or a resolution passed for the winding up of the company at the time of the appointment of a receiver or of possession being taken on behalf of the debenture holder. As I have said, in the instant case, the receiver has in fact paid all debts to which preference is given by s 94.

It is said on behalf of the liquidator that s 319 supplements s 94 and applies to any assets of the company which were subject to a floating charge at the date of presentation of the petition on which a winding-up order was made so far as not absorbed in making payments which are given preference over the claims of the debenture holder by s 94. Despite counsel for the liquidator's persuasive advocacy I find this an impossible construction. As I see it the purpose of s 94 is to give priority to debts and other liabilities which would have been preferential in a winding-up by reference to the period ending on the appointment of a receiver, or the taking of possession by the debenture holder, notwithstanding that by the appointment of a receiver or the taking of possession by the debenture holder the assets over which the receiver is appointed or of which possession is taken cease to be assets of the company capable of being dealt with by the company for the purposes of its business. I can see nothing in the decision of the Court of Appeal in *Re Barleycorn Enterprises Ltd* inconsistent with that construction of s 94. To the extent that assets of a company are comprised in a floating charge which has not crystallised at the making of a winding-up order those assets are to be treated as assets for the purposes of, amongst other provisions, para (*a*) of sub-s (5) and of sub-s (6) of s 319, and of r 195; but if the floating charge has been crystallised the proceeds of realisation of the assets of the company comprised in it, to the extent that those proceeds are required to meet preferential debts and the claims of the debenture holder, are no longer assets of the company in a subsequent winding up any more than if they had initially been subject to a fixed charge. That construction of s 94 is supported by the decision of Bennett J in *Re Griffin Hotel Ltd, Joshua Tetley & Son Ltd v Griffin Hotel Ltd and John Lupton & Son Ltd* [1940] 4 All ER 324, [1941] Ch 129, a case which was not cited to the court in *Re Barleycorn Enterprises Ltd* and which, on the view I take of the effect of that decision, was not relevant to it. In *Re Griffin Hotel Co Ltd*, the plaintiffs had a debenture which created a floating charge on all the assets of the company which then included an hotel, the Griffin Hotel, which had also been charged by way of collateral security in favour of the plaintiffs. Subsequently the company acquired the leasehold interest in premises known as Spa Plaza Hotel and Laundry which accordingly became subject to the floating charge though ranking after a mortgage thereon. The plaintiffs commenced a debenture holder's action on 9 December 1938 and on the same day obtained ex parte an interim order for the appointment of a receiver of all the assets of the company except the Spa Plaza Hotel and Laundry. Having regard to the prior mortgage that asset was of no value to the debenture holder. The interim order was superseded on 13 December when the interim receiver was appointed receiver without limit of time. A compulsory winding-up order was made on 15 March 1939. Although it is not apparent from the report reference to the records of the court shows that the petition was presented on 9 December 1938, the day on which an interim receiver was appointed. It was served on the company on 13 December, the day on which the interim receiver was appointed receiver. The question which arose was whether debts and liabilities incurred in connection with the carrying on by the company of the business of the Spa Plaza Hotel and Laundry were payable in priority to the debenture holder out of the proceeds of sale of the assets of which a receiver had been appointed. It was argued by the late Mr J A Wolfe for the defendants (see [1941] Ch 129 a at 134) that in s 264(4)(*b*) of the Companies Act 1929, which corresponds to s 319(5)(*b*) of the 1948 Act: 'The expression "any floating charge" includes all floating charges originally created as such, whether or not they have subsequently crystallized.' That is in substance the argument advanced by counsel for the liquidator in the instant case. It was rejected by Bennett J. He said ([1940] 4 All ER 324 at 329, [1941] Ch 129 at 135–136):

> 'In my judgment sect. 264(4)(*b*) operates only if, at the moment of the winding up, there is still floating a charge created by the company, and it gives the preferential
> b creditors a priority only over the claims of the debentureholders in any property which at that moment of time is comprised in or subject to that charge. In the present case, the debenture held by the plaintiffs contained a floating charge over all the borrowers' property. On Dec. 9, 1938, that charge ceased to float upon the property and assets of which Veale was appointed receiver. The charge crystallised, and became fixed on that property and those assets. It remained a floating charge
> c upon any other assets of the borrowers. At the moment before the winding up order was made, the charge still floated over any other assets of the borrowers, and over those other assets, if any, the preferential creditors as defined by sect. 264(1) have a priority over the claims of the plaintiffs by force of the provisions of sect. 264(4). This seems to be a corollary of the proposition established by *Re Lewis Merthyr Consolidated Collieries, Ltd., Lloyds Bank* v. *Lewis Merthyr Consolidated Collieries, Ltd.*
> d ([1929] 1 Ch 498).'

That principal must I think apply a fortiori to the costs and expenses of a winding up. Counsel for the liquidator's alternative submission was that as the winding-up order relates back to the date of the presentation of the petition, the company was not one which when the receiver was appointed was not in the course of being wound up within
e s 94(1). That submission was not advanced in *Re Griffin Hotel Co Ltd*, and indeed it may not have been open to the creditor seeking payment out of the moneys in the hands of the receiver in as much as the petition was presented and the receiver appointed on the same day.

I think the answer to counsel for the liquidator's submission is that the words 'in the course of being wound up' describe the situation of a company after an order for its
f compulsory winding up has been made or a resolution for the winding up of the company and the appointment of a liquidator has been passed. The liquidator, or the provisional liquidator, is then responsible for the payment of the preferential creditors. Section 94 deals with the situation when at the time of the appointment of a receiver or when a debenture holder takes possession of assets of a company no liquidator has been appointed.

g For these reasons I think this application fails and must be dismissed.

Application dismissed.

Solicitors: *D J Freeman & Co* (for the liquidator); *Sampson & Co* (for the receiver).

Jacqueline Metcalfe   Barrister.

R v Clarke (Linda)

a

COURT OF APPEAL, CRIMINAL DIVISION
LORD LANE CJ, DONALDSON LJ AND SKINNER J
20 MAY 1982

Sentence – Suspended sentence – Partial suspension – Matters to be considered by court before
ordering partial suspension of sentence – Circumstances in which partially suspended sentence *b*
appropriate – Whether court can order partial suspension of sentence for offence committed before
court given power to order partial suspension – Criminal Law Act 1977, s 47(1)(8), Sch 14, para
5.

Since the effect of s 47(1)[a] of the Criminal Law Act 1977 (which gives the court power to
order the partial suspension of a prison sentence) is to mitigate punishment and not to *c*
increase it, and since para 5[b] of Sch 14 to that Act (which provides that, subject to certain
exceptions, a provision in that Act which relates to the punishment by way of fine or
imprisonment for any offence is not to affect the punishment for an offence committed
before that provision came into force) was aimed at those provisions of the 1977 Act
which increased maximum sentences and was designed simply to ensure that no
defendant was given a greater sentence than that which was available in respect of his *d*
offence at the time he committed it, it follows that, on the true construction of the 1977
Act, para 5 of Sch 14 does not have the effect of preventing a court from ordering the
partial suspension of a sentence for an offence committed before the date when s 47 was
brought into force. Such a construction also follows from the provision in s 47(8)[c] that
s 47 is to be construed and have effect as if it were contained in the Powers of Criminal
Courts Act 1973, with the result that for the purposes of para 5 of Sch 14 to the 1977 Act *e*
it is to be understood as being a provision not of the 1977 Act but of the 1973 Act (see
p 234 j to p 235 a and h j, post).

Before exercising its power to order that part of a sentence of imprisonment is to be
held in suspense under s 47 of the 1977 Act, the court should ask itself whether the case
is one where a custodial sentence is necessary. If it is not, it should pass a non-custodial
sentence; but, if it is necessary, the court should then ask whether it can make a *f*
community service order as an equivalent to imprisonment or whether the whole
sentence can be suspended. If it can, it should do so; but, if it cannot, it should consider
what is the shortest sentence it can properly impose. It is only where imprisonment is
necessary, where a very short sentence is not enough and where it is not appropriate to
suspend the whole sentence that the court should consider partial suspension, and in such
cases great care must be taken to ensure that the court's power is not used in such a way *g*
as may serve to increase the length of the sentence (see p 236 a to e, post).

Observations on the circumstances in which a partially suspended sentence may be
appropriate (see p 236 e to j, post).

Notes
For suspended sentences of imprisonment, see 11 Halsbury's Laws (4th edn) para 500. *h*
   For the Powers of Criminal Courts Act 1973, see 43 Halsbury's Statutes (3rd edn) 288.
   For the Criminal Law Act 1977, s 47, Sch 14, para 5, see 47 ibid 165, 211.

Case referred to in judgment
R v Houghton, R v Donachie (7 May 1982, unreported), Crown Court at Leeds.

j

---

a Section 47(1) is set out at p 234 d e, post
b Paragraph 5 is set out at p 234 e f, post
c Section 47(8) is set out at p 235 c, post

Appeal against sentence

a On 2 April 1982 at the Crown Court at St Albans before his Honour Judge Watling QC the appellant, Linda Vera Clarke, pleaded guilty to conspiracy to defraud and asked for 25 other offences to be taken into consideration. She was sentenced to 18 months' imprisonment, of which 6 months were to be served immediately and the remaining 12 months to be held in suspense pursuant to s 47 of the Criminal Law Act 1977. She appealed against sentence with the leave of the single judge. The facts are set out in the

b judgment of the court.

Helena Kennedy (assigned by the Registrar of Criminal Appeals) for the appellant.
A G Moses as amicus curiae.

LORD LANE CJ delivered the following judgment of the court: This appeal arises in

c the following circumstances. On 2 April 1982 in the Crown Court at St Albans the appellant pleaded guilty to conspiracy to defraud and was sentenced to 18 months' imprisonment, of which 6 months were to be served immediately, and the remaining 12 months held in suspense, 35 other offences being taken into consideration. She now appeals against that sentence by leave of the single judge.

The facts of the case were that in June, July and August 1981 this woman used stolen

d cheque books and stolen credit cards to obtain property, the vast bulk of which was video tapes, from various concerns in and around St Albans and district and also in London. She was eventually arrested in Charing Cross Road in London in August 1981 and found to be using a stolen Access card. She was searched, as also was her home, and a number of documents were found, including Access cards in names other than her own. She was released on bail.

e Plainly she had been used by a sophisticated organisation as the front operator in this swindle. Although she handled the large sum of £12,000, she derived very little benefit for herself. As happens so often in this type of fraud, those who derived most benefit escaped the clutches of the law. She committed this fraud because she was going through great suffering and financial hardship in her domestic affairs. Another result of that was that she had also defrauded the Department of Health and Social Security by failing to

f declare her earnings, which would have been deducted from the social security payments made to her. For that she was sentenced to the short term of six weeks' imprisonment after the end of the credit card frauds.

The appellant is not the usual kind of feckless woman who sometimes commits this type of fraud. One passage from her social inquiry report reads:

g '[The appellant] would appear to be a hard worker and apart from the obvious breaks to bear children, she has normally been in full or part time employment. Her main employment has been secretarial, mostly legal, but she has had other employments including 4 months in the army which she didn't like. She joined it to leave home, but didn't like the discipline as it would appear that she has been fairly headstrong.'

h It then sets out the matrimonial and emotional difficulties which this unfortunate lady has suffered, and continues:

'[The appellant's] financial problems appear to be great. Her rent is about £40 per week and she is over £400 in arrears. She owes £800 to the L.E.B £350 to SEGAS and has H.P. commitments of £60 per month for a washing machine and a fridge, £5 a week for a Christmas Club and £10 a week for insurances. She would like to

j take employment as a night telephonist with part time secretarial work but would find it difficult to keep her family and meet her debts. [The appellant] fully admits her last offence. She tells me one of the reasons she became in debt was she claims, paying [a man's] motoring fines and other debts. [The appellant] is I understand pleading guilty to the offences before this Court. It would seem that the offence was

the usual "kiting" offence where the vulnerable woman is used to perpetrate the
crime and is paid for her actions. However it is the woman, and not the unnamed   *a*
person (usually male) who is caught and takes the consequences whilst the other
person decamps with the goods. The Court will appreciate that in similar cases [the
appellant] and women like her are the last operatives in a long line of criminal
activity which starts with the sometimes violent removal of women's handbags.'

This court accepts that as a true picture of the circumstances of this case. But for the
term of six weeks' imprisonment that the appellant has already suffered, a partly   *b*
suspended sentence would have been entirely correct and apt. But the appellant has
already served six weeks' imprisonment, albeit for a different offence, to mark the
disapproval of the public, and accordingly we think that the correct course is to suspend
the sentence in whole and not in part.

Before turning to the formal position of the case it is right that we should say two
things. First of all, a preliminary matter has been raised with which we must deal and in   *c*
respect of which we have had the advantage of the help of counsel as amicus curiae. The
problem has been troubling courts up and down the country (and this case gives this
court the first opportunity to give a ruling on it) whether s 47 of the Criminal Law Act
1977, which came into force on 29 March 1982 by virtue of the Criminal Law Act 1977
(Commencement No 11) Order 1982, SI 1982/243, applies to cases where the criminal
offence was committed on a date before 29 March 1982. Section 47(1), which is the   *d*
material provision, reads:

'Where a court passes on an adult a sentence of imprisonment for a term of not
less than six months and not more than two years, it may order that, after he has
served part of the sentence in prison, the remainder of it shall be held in suspense.'

The answer to the question which is posed depends on the interpretation of the   *e*
transitional provisions which are contained in Sch 14 to the Act, para 5 of which reads:

'Except as provided in paragraph 3 above a provision of this Act (other than
section 29 or any provision mentioned in paragraph 4 above) which relates to the
punishment by way of fine or imprisonment for any offence shall not affect the
punishment for an offence committed before that provision comes into force.'   *f*

It is suggested that those words prevent a court from partly suspending a sentence
imposed for an offence committed before the Act came into force on 29 March 1982.
The argument is that s 47 by its wording relates to 'punishment by way of imprisonment
for any offence', and thus cannot affect the punishment for any offence committed before
29 March 1982, as the appellant's offences plainly were

Section 47, however, as counsel as amicus curiae has helpfully pointed out, is something   *g*
of an oddity in the Act. The 1977 Act contains a number of different subjects. Part I deals
with conspiracy, as the heading states. Part II, which is ss 6 to 13, deals with offences
relating to entering and remaining on property, again as the heading shows. Part III deals
with criminal procedure, penalties etc, again as the heading shows. In Part II there is a
whole group of sections, from s 27 to s 33, which deal specifically with penalties under
that particular heading. Some maximum penalties are increased and some are decreased.   *h*
Section 47 does not appear under the heading of penalties at all, but appears under the
heading 'other provisions'. It does not deal with penalties for specific offences or indeed
with any particular type of offence.

It seems clear to us that para 5 of Sch 14 was aimed at those sections under the heading
of penalties which increase maximum sentences, and that it was designed simply to
ensure that no one was given a greater sentence than that which was available in respect   *j*
of his offence at the time he committed it. It would not, we think, have occurred to the
draftsman that the schedule would affect the coming into operation of s 47. The reason
is this: the court which is taking advantage of the wording of s 47 must first of all ask
itself whether a custodial sentence is necessary, and, if so, whether it can be suspended in

toto. It is only in the event of an immediate custodial sentence being required that s 47
a will come into play. The effect of s 47 is to mitigate punishment, not to increase it.
Consequently s 47 is not a provision of the Act which relates to punishment by way of
imprisonment, but one which relates to the opposite, namely the reduction or mitigation
of punishment, and accordingly is not affected by Sch 14.

That is sufficient to decide this point of the case.

b
But counsel as amicus curiae has drawn our attention to another argument which, if
correct, leads to the same conclusion. This argument appears in a judgment delivered by
Glidewell J in *R v Houghton, R v Donachie* (unreported) in the Crown Court at Leeds on 7
May 1982. The judge reached the same conclusion as this court has reached, but he based
his decision primarily on this different basis, namely the wording of s 47(8) of the
Criminal Law Act 1977:

c
'This section and paragraphs 1 to 6 of Schedule 9 to this Act and the Powers of
Criminal Courts Act 1973 shall be construed *and have effect* as if this section and
those paragraphs of the Schedule were contained in that Act.'

In his judgment Glidewell J said on this matter:

'The general provisions relating to the nature of penalties which may be imposed
d by criminal courts on conviction for criminal offences are contained in the Powers
of Criminal Courts Act 1973, a consolidating Act which contains groups of sections
dealing with probation and discharge, community service orders, imprisonment,
borstal training and detention and then six sections, ss 22 to 27, dealing with
suspended sentences of imprisonment. Section 47 is clearly a section of the same
nature as those various provisions in the 1973 Act and of a different kind from any
e of the other provisions of the 1977 Act . . . Counsel for the prosecution argues that
[s 47(8) of the 1977 Act] provides the clue to the problem and I agree with him . . . As
he points out, s 47(8) not merely says that s 47 is to be construed as if it were
contained in the 1973 Act but it shall be construed and have effect as if it were
contained in the 1973 Act. Therefore, he submits and I agree, that the provisions of
s 47, albeit they formed part of an Act passed by Parliament in 1977, are to be read
f as and are part of the 1973 Act. Section 47(8) of the 1977 Act has in my view the
same effect as if the section had started with the words, "There shall be added to the
Powers of Criminal Courts Act 1973 the following section." When one comes to
look back at the provisions of Sch 14 it does appear that, first, there are certain
specific exceptions made clear in the schedule to which the schedule is not applied.
Second, that on the face of it, before one comes to para 5 of the schedule, the
g provisions to which the schedule does apply are those provisions to which I have
already referred in ss 27 to 33 inclusive which increase or decrease maximum
penalties for particular offences with the specified exceptions, and on the face of it
para 5 of the schedule is apt to have effect in relation to those provisions; that is to
say, for an offence committed, for instance, before s 32, which in certain
circumstances increase maximum fines, came into force but tried after that section
h came into force, para 5 of Sch 14 made it clear that it would not be proper to impose
a fine above the old maximum as opposed to the new maximum. But in my view
para 5 of Sch 14 does not bite on s 47 because s 47 is not to be understood as being a
provision of this Act, ie of the 1977 Act.'

We respectfully agree with the judge's ruling and statement and adopt his reasoning
as a further, concurrent, basis for the conclusion which we have reached.
j
Having said this we turn now to consider the new power which has become available
to the court. Although these are early days in the history of the partly suspended sentence,
it may be helpful if we make one or two tentative observations on the subject, realising
that they may very well have to be modified subsequently in the light of the experience
which courts up and down the country, and this court, may gain in the future.

Before imposing a partly suspended sentence the court should ask itself the following question: first of all, is this a case where a custodial sentence is really necessary? If it is *a* not, it should pass a non-custodial sentence; but if it is necessary then the court should ask itself, second, this: can we make a community service order as an equivalent to imprisonment, or can we suspend the whole sentence? That problem requires very careful consideration. It is easy to slip into a partly suspended sentence because the court does not have the courage of its own convictions. That temptation must be resisted. If it is possible to make a community service order or to suspend the whole of the sentence, *b* then of course that should be done. If not, then the third point arises: what is the shortest sentence the court can properly impose? In many cases, of which an obvious example is the case of the first offender for whom a short term of imprisonment is a sufficient shock, without any suspension, that would be enough. Sometimes 14 or 28 days may suffice, which is shorter than the shortest term which is at present available under s 47, which of course is one quarter of 6 months, that is 1½ months. In that case that should be the order *c* of the court, without any partial suspension at all. The imposition of a very short term will also make possible the ordering of a fine or a compensation order in addition, when such a course is appropriate.

If imprisonment is necessary, and if a very short sentence is not enough, and if it is not appropriate to suspend the sentence altogether, then partial suspension should be considered. Great care must be taken to ensure that the power is not used in a way which *d* may serve to increase the length of sentence. It is not possible satisfactorily to forecast the precise way in which the provisions of s 47 might be used. In general the type of case that we have in mind is where the gravity of the offence is such that at least six months' imprisonment is merited, but when there are mitigating circumstances which point towards a measure of leniency not sufficient to warrant total suspension. Examples are always dangerous, but we venture very tentatively to suggest a few: first of all, some *e* serious 'one-off' acts of violence which are usually met with immediate terms of imprisonment; some cases of burglary which at present warrant 18 months' or 2 years' imprisonment, where the offender is suitably qualified in terms of his record; some cases of fraud on public departments or some credit card frauds, where a short immediate sentence would be insufficient; some cases of handling involving medium-range sums of money; some thefts involving breach of trust; some cases of stealing from employers. *f* All these are examples of cases where it may be possible to suspend part of the sentence without harm to the public and with benefit to the prisoner.

We would like to echo the words of the Home Office Advisory Council on the Penal System in their *Sentences of Imprisonment; a review of maximum penalties* (1978) para 282:

> '... we view the partially suspended sentence as a legitimate means of exploiting one of the few reliable pieces of criminological knowledge that many offenders sent *g* to prison for the first time do not subsequently re-offend. We see it not as a means of administering a "short, sharp shock", nor as a substitute for a wholly suspended sentence, but as especially applicable to serious first offenders or first-time prisoners who are bound to have to serve some time in prison, but who may well be effectively deterred by eventually serving only a small part of even the minimum sentence appropriate to the offence. This, in our view, must be its principal role.' *h*

We would like to add another type of offender: prisoners whose last term of imprisonment was some considerable time ago. We think that the power can be used on occasions where something more than a short sentence of immediate imprisonment is required to mark public disapproval and as a deterrent to others, but where the circumstances of the particular offender are such that some short term of immediate *j* imprisonment, coupled with the threat involved in the suspension of the remainder, is enough to punish him for what he has done and to deter him in the future.

Before finally parting with this case we would like to echo the words of the probation officer in this case, who said in a passage in the social inquiry report immediately after that which we have already read:

a   'It is time in my opinion that the London Clearing Banks attempted to make credit cards less open to abuse with the possible introduction of photographs on the card.'

Every day in this court we are now concerned with credit card frauds, and quite plainly they provide a great temptation to people who are minded to commit fraud. It is a great pity that some more effective method of protection cannot be devised to stop as far as possible their being used as a vehicle for fraud.

b   So far as this appellant is concerned, her appeal is allowed. We quash the partially suspended sentence which was imposed, and we substitute for it a term of 18 months' imprisonment suspended for 2 years.

Appeal allowed. Sentence varied.

c   Solicitors: *Treasury Solicitor.*

N P Metcalfe Esq   Barrister.

d   # CBS United Kingdom Ltd v Lambert and another

COURT OF APPEAL, CIVIL DIVISION
LAWTON, TEMPLEMAN AND FOX LJJ
e   19 MAY, 9 JUNE 1982

Injunction – Interlocutory – Danger that defendant may transfer assets out of jurisdiction – Discovery of assets and delivery up of particular asset in aid of Mareva injunction – Defendant involved in large scale infringement of plaintiffs' copyright – Inference that defendant spent money from his unlawful activities on goods easily disposed of – Motor vehicles – Delivery up of motor
f   *vehicles in defendant's possession pending trial – Guidelines for court to follow in ordering delivery up of chattels pending trial.*

The plaintiffs had for many years been trying to safeguard their copyrights in musical recordings which were constantly being infringed by the production and sale of counterfeit records and cassettes. In 1981, in the course of proceedings which they
g   brought against a large scale distributor, they discovered that the defendant was supplying the distributor and others with counterfeit cassettes. In May 1982 the defendant was arrested for handling stolen goods. When the police searched his premises they found a large quantity of labels for cassettes of a kind affixed to counterfeit cassettes. The defendant admitted to the police that he was a record pirate and gave them particulars of his sources of supply for tapes and labels for cassettes and where the unlawful recordings
h   were made. From information which the plaintiffs obtained from the police and from other sources they inferred that the defendant, helped by his wife, was involved in the large scale production, distribution and sale of counterfeit cassettes the scale of which, if proved at a trial, would entitle the plaintiffs to damages in conversion of about £105,000, that the defendant was pretending to be unemployed when he was not and to be receiving social security payments when he had no right to them, that he was spending
j   money on assets such as expensive motor cars which could easily be hidden from creditors and disposed of for cash if the need arose, and that he intended, if his illegal activities in the production of counterfeit cassettes was discovered, to ensure that the owners of the copyrights would be unable to enforce any judgment against him. The plaintiffs therefore decided to bring proceedings against the defendant and his wife to protect their copyrights but in the meantime they applied ex parte for an order restraining the

defendants from selling or disposing of any illicit sound recordings, labels or equipment
used to make the illicit recordings, from removing their assets from the jurisdiction and
requiring the defendants to disclose the full value of their assets and to deliver up the
motor cars in their possession. In making an order on the application the judge refused
to order discovery of assets or the delivery up of the motor cars, since he was concerned
that the defendant might be obliged on an order for discovery to incriminate himself on
the charge of handling stolen goods. The plaintiffs appealed.

Held – In the circumstances it was a clear case for the court to order discovery of assets
and delivery up pending trial of a particular kind of asset because there was reason to
believe that the defendant had put such profits as he had made from infringing the
plaintiffs' copyrights into easily removable and disposable chattels such as motor vehicles,
and, since he claimed to be unemployed, there was no reason to think that he used the
motor vehicles for the purposes of earning his living or that he or his wife would suffer
hardship if an order for their delivery up were made. Moreover, the possibility of self-
incrimination on the charge of handling stolen property was not in the circumstances a
bar to ordering discovery. It followed therefore that the court would allow the appeal,
grant the order sought and order the defendant and his wife to disclose the value, nature
and whereabouts of their assets, including bank and other accounts, and to deliver up,
pending trial, the motor vehicles in their possession, to be kept in a garage chosen by the
plaintiffs' solicitors (see p 242 *b* to *f* and *j* to p 243 *b*, post); *A J Bekhor & Co Ltd v Bilton*
[1981] 2 All ER 565 applied.

Per curiam. The court should apply the following guidelines when deciding whether
to exercise its jurisdiction to order the delivery up of chattels, bearing in mind that
guidelines are not rules of court and that their spirit and not the letter should be kept in
mind—

(1) There should be clear evidence that the defendant is likely, unless restrained by
order, to dispose of or otherwise deal with his chattels in order to deprive the plaintiff of
the fruits of any judgment he may obtain. Moreover, the court should be slow to order
the delivery up of property belonging to the defendant unless there is some evidence or
inference that the property has been acquired by the defendant as a result of his alleged
wrongdoing (see p 243 *b* to *d*, post).

(2) No order should be made for the delivery up of a defendant's wearing apparel,
bedding, furnishings, tools of his trade, farm implements, livestock or any machines
(including motor vehicles) or other goods such as materials or stock-in-trade which it is
likely he uses for the purpose of a lawful business. If the evidence is clear that furnishings
consisting of objets d'art of great value were bought for the purposes of frustrating
judgment creditors they could be included in an order (see p 243 *d e*, post).

(3) All orders should specify as clearly as possible what chattels or classes of chattels are
to be delivered up. A plaintiff's inability to identify what he wants delivered up and why
is an indication that no order should be made (see p 243 *e*, post).

(4) The order must not authorise the plaintiff to enter on the defendant's premises or
to seize the defendant's property save by permission of the defendant (see p 243 *e f*, post).

(5) No order should be made for delivery up to anyone other than the plaintiff's
solicitor or a receiver appointed by the High Court. The court should appoint a receiver
to take possession of the chattels unless satisfied that the plaintiff's solicitor has, or can
arrange, suitable safe custody for what is delivered to him (see p 243 *g h*, post).

(6) The court should follow the court's guidelines for the granting of Mareva
injunctions in so far as they are applicable to chattels in the possession, custody or control
of third parties (see p 243 *h*, post); *Z Ltd v A* [1982] 1 All ER 556 applied.

(7) Provision should always be made for liberty to apply to stay, vary or discharge the
order (see p 243 *h j*, post).

Notes

For Anton Piller orders, see 37 Halsbury's Laws (4th edn) para 372.

For Mareva injunctions, see ibid paras 362–363, 371.

For injunctions restraining the disposition of chattels, see 24 ibid paras 1018–1019,
a and for cases on the subject, see 28(2) Digest (Reissue) 1091–1094, 918–961.

Cases referred to in judgment
Anton Piller KG v Manufacturing Processes Ltd [1976] 1 All ER 779, [1976] Ch 55, [1976] 2
  WLR 162, CA, Digest (Cont Vol E) 338, *1238b*.
Bekhor (A J) & Co Ltd v Bilton [1981] 2 All ER 565, [1981] QB 923, [1981] 2 WLR 601,
b CA.
EMI Records Ltd v Riley [1981] 2 All ER 838, [1981] 1 WLR 923.
Johnson v L & A Philatelico Ltd [1981] FSR 286.
Lister & Co v Stubbs (1890) 45 Ch D 1, [1886–90] All ER Rep 797, CA, 1(2) Digest (Reissue)
  659, 4513.
Z Ltd v A [1982] 1 All ER 556, [1982] QB 558, [1982] 2 WLR 288, CA.

c
Case also cited
A v C [1980] 2 All ER 347, [1981] QB 956.

Interlocutory appeal
The plaintiffs, CBS United Kingdom Ltd, suing on behalf of themselves and on behalf of
d and as representing all other members of the British Phonographic Industry Ltd (BPI),
applied ex parte in the course of an action which they intended to bring against the
defendants, Steven Raymond Lambert and Hilary Lambert, his wife, to protect the
copyrights of the plaintiffs and all other members of BPI in musical recordings for an
order restraining the defendants from, inter alia, (1) doing or authorising the making,
selling, offering for sale, distributing or otherwise parting with possession, power,
e custody or control of, or destroying or defacing, altering or hiding, or removing from
certain named premises or any other premises owned or occupied or used by the
defendants or either of them for storing cassettes or other sound recordings, any
unlicensed sound recordings, labels etc and equipment used or intended to be used for
making such unlicensed sound recordings, (2) passing off or attempting to pass off such
unlicensed sound recordings by making, selling, offering for sale, advertising, distributing
f or otherwise parting with possession of such sound recordings and (3) warning any
person or firm supplied with the illicit goods of the existence of the plaintiffs' proceedings,
and ordering the defendants to disclose the names and addresses of all persons and firms
responsible for supplying or offering to supply such illicit goods, to make and serve on
the plaintiffs' solicitors an affidavit setting out the information required to be given by
the order and exhibiting thereto all documents in the defendants' possession, power,
g custody or control relating thereto and restraining them from removing from the
jurisdiction or otherwise disposing of or dealing in any manner whatsoever with any of
their assets within the jurisdiction or pledging, charging or parting with possession of
the same. On 12 May 1982 Goulding J sitting in camera made the order sought except
in so far as it related to disclosure of the full value of the defendants' assets or to the
delivery into the custody of the plaintiffs' solicitors the motor vehicles in the defendants'
h possession. The plaintiffs appealed to the Court of Appeal. The appeal was heard in
camera, the writ not having been served, but judgment was delivered in open court, the
writ having by then been served. The facts are set out in the judgment of the court.

Robin Jacob QC and *Alistair J McGregor* for the plaintiffs.
The defendants did not appear.

j
At the conclusion of the argument the court made the order sought stating that it would
give its reasons for so doing later.

9 June. **LAWTON LJ** read the following judgment of the court: On 19 May 1982 we
made, on the application ex parte of the plaintiffs in an action which they proposed to
start for the protection of their copyrights, an order the body of which was in the usual

Anton Piller form but, at the end of which, there were Mareva requirements, first, that the defendant should disclose to the plaintiffs' solicitor serving the order the full value, *a* nature and whereabouts of their assets and, second, that they should deliver up to that solicitor all motor vehicles owned by them. Counsel for the plaintiffs told us that this was the first case in which an order in this form had been considered by this court, although in a case at first instance a similar requirement for delivering up had been put into a Mareva injunction: see *Johnson v L & A Philatelico Ltd* [1981] FSR 286. We had to consider whether there is any jurisdiction in the Supreme Court of Judicature to include *b* these requirements in a Mareva injunction and, if there is, whether this was an appropriate case for doing so. The purpose of this judgment is to set out our reasons for making the order.

The plaintiffs claim to represent the members of the British Phonographic Industry Ltd (BPI), which is a company limited by guarantee. We did not consider whether the plaintiffs were entitled to do so. We were informed by counsel for the plaintiffs that a *c* number of representative actions in this form have been started in the Chancery Division and that Dillon J, in *EMI Records Ltd v Riley* [1981] 2 All ER 838, [1981] 1 WLR 923, had granted an injunction and ordered an inquiry as to damages in such an action. Prima facie on this authority the plaintiffs are entitled to sue in a representative capacity; but we did not consider that this occasion, being an ex parte application, was an appropriate one to consider whether the plaintiffs were rightly entitled to sue in such a capacity. *d* Even if they cannot, any defect in the proceedings can probably be cured by joining all the BPI members as plaintiffs. This would put a very long title on the case and result in much pointless typing and consequential time wasting.

The plaintiffs and those whom they claim to represent have for some years past been trying to safeguard their copyrights in musical recordings, mostly of popular songs, which are constantly being infringed by the production and sale of counterfeit records *e* and cassettes. Many of these counterfeits are sold in street markets in the United Kingdom. In the autumn of 1981 it was discovered that there was a large scale distributor of counterfeit cassettes in Southampton. Proceedings were started against him and on 1 December 1981 Goulding J made an Anton Piller order against him and a helper. As a result of those proceedings it became clear that the defendant Steven Lambert had supplied this distributor with counterfeit cassettes. He and his wife, the defendant Hilary *f* Lambert, were known to BPI. In 1977 a recording company had started proceedings against him, his wife and others for infringing copyright in their recordings. An Anton Piller order was made, and on 17 June 1977 the two defendants, by their counsel, gave undertakings to comply with that order pending trial. Another Anton Piller order was made against them on 16 May 1978. These actions were never brought to trial as inquiries seemed to show that the defendants would be unable to pay any money orders *g* which were made against them. It was thought then that Mrs Lambert's father was mainly responsible for the infringements and he had left the United Kingdom. Further, in 1979 the defendant Steven Lambert offered to turn informer against other infringers and did so, thereby revealing that he had an extensive knowledge of how counterfeit cassettes were distributed and to whom.

In the course of following up information obtained as a result of the Anton Piller order *h* made against the Southampton distributor, one of the BPI's investigators visited the defendant Steven Lambert at his home at 145 Chingford Lane, London E4 on 10 March 1982. He questioned the defendant Steven Lambert and inferred from his answers that he had been supplying the Southampton distributor and others with counterfeit cassettes. He noticed that this defendant's house, which later inquiries revealed to be a council house, had recently been completely redecorated, refurnished and carpeted. Much money *j* had clearly been spent on furnishings and a fitted kitchen. The investigator learned later that this defendant was claiming to be unemployed and was then receiving social security payments. Attempts later to test this defendant's story as to where he obtained the cassettes he handed on to the Southampton distributor were unsuccessful. These cassettes purported to be of foreign origin but BPI's researchers had established that they were not.

On 11 May 1982 the plaintiffs' solicitors learned from the police that the defendant
a Steven Lambert had been arrested for handling stolen goods and was in custody. When
his home at 145 Chingford Lane had been searched by the police a large quantity of
labels, estimated to total about 15,000, had been found. These labels were for cassettes
and were of a kind which had been affixed to the kinds of counterfeit cassettes into the
origins of which BPI had been inquiring for some months past. The solicitors were told
by the police that this defendant had admitted to them that he was a 'record pirate' and
b had given them particulars of his sources of supply for tapes and labels for cassettes and
where the unlawful recordings had been made. They also told the solicitors that this
defendant had recently bought a Lotus Elite motor car, registration number OPW 656W
at a cost of £9,000 and a Jaguar motor car of the XJ-6 type which had a T registration
letter. They also said that they believed him to be the owner of two Jensen Healey motor
cars and a Scimitar car. Further, he had rented accommodation at 44A Chingford Mount
c Lane, London E4 which he had shared with a woman who was thought to be his mistress.
From what the plaintiffs had learned and had been told (and I have summarised the
evidence very briefly) they drew the following inferences: first, that from at least
November 1981 the defendant Steven Lambert, helped by his wife, had been engaged in
a large way with the production, distribution and sale of counterfeit cassettes; second,
that the size of his alleged operation, as assessed from the number of labels found and the
d titles on his order forms, was consistent with the production and sale of about 35,000
counterfeit cassettes which, if proved at a trial, would entitle the plaintiffs to damages in
conversion of about £105,000; third, that this defendant was pretending to be
unemployed when he was not and to be receiving social security payments when he had
no right to them; fourth, that he was spending money on assets such as expensive motor
cars, which could easily be hidden from creditors and disposed of for cash if the need
e arose; and, finally, that he intended to do all he could to ensure that, if his illegal activities
in the production of counterfeit cassettes were discovered, the owners of the copyrights
would be unable to enforce any judgment they obtained against him or his wife. In our
judgment, these inferences were justified. On the facts put before us this was not a case
of a plaintiff seeking to freeze a defendant's assets pending trial in anticipation of getting
judgment. It was one which seemed to us to show that the defendant Steven Lambert
f was conducting his affairs with intent to deprive anyone who got judgment against him
of the fruits of victory.

The Mareva injunction was brought into use to make this kind of behaviour in
commercial cases unprofitable.

The history of the development of the Mareva injunction is so well known that there
is, in our opinion, no need to set it out again in this judgment. The jurisdiction of the
g High Court to grant Mareva injunctions is now statutory: see s 37(1) and (3) of the
Supreme Court Act 1981. Subsection (3) is in these terms:

> 'The power of the High Court under subsection (1) to grant an interlocutory
> injunction restraining a party to any proceedings from removing from the
> jurisdiction of the High Court, or otherwise dealing with, assets located within that
> jurisdiction shall be exercisable in cases where that party is, as well as in cases where
h > he is not, domiciled or resident or present within that jurisdiction.'

Since, under sub-s (1), the High Court may by order (whether interlocutory or final)
grant an injunction 'in all cases in which it appears to the court to be just and convenient
to do so', it follows that a Mareva injunction can be granted for the same purposes.
Subsection (3) in terms envisages the granting of a Mareva injunction against a defendant
j to restrain him from dealing with assets within the jurisdiction of the court. The words
'dealing with' are wide enough to include disposing of, selling, pledging or charging; and
there are no limitations put on the word 'assets', from which it follows that this word
includes chattels such as motor vessels, jewellery, objets d'art and other valuables as well
as choses in action. The only restriction there is on the making of a Mareva injunction is
that it must appear to the court to be just and convenient to do so. Whatever may have

been the source of the court's jurisdiction to grant Mareva injunctions before the Supreme
Court Act 1981 came into operation, it is now statutory. It is for the judges to decide on   *a*
the facts of each case whether to exercise the jurisdiction.

A jurisdiction to grant Mareva injunctions, however, is not likely to be of any use to a
plaintiff who believes that he is suing a defendant who intends to deal with his assets in
such a way as to deprive him of the fruits of any judgment he may obtain unless there is
some means of making the defendant disclose what his assets are and whereabouts they
are to be found. In *A J Bekhor & Co Ltd v Bilton* [1981] 2 All ER 565, [1981] QB 923 this   *b*
court decided that the High Court has jurisdiction to order discovery in aid of a Mareva
injunction if it is necessary for the effective operation of the injunction; but the majority
(Stephenson and Ackner LJJ) judged that, on the facts of that case, such an order was
inappropriate. For the purposes of this judgment, in our opinion, it is unnecessary to
consider whether the power to order discovery is derived from s 37(1) of the Supreme
Court Act 1981 or from the inherent jurisdiction of the court. Although in the *A J Bekhor*   *c*
case there was a difference of opinion as to the source of the power, all the members of
this court agreed that there was such a power. It was on this authority that we ordered
the defendants to disclose the full value and whereabouts of their assets.

We were informed that Goulding J, when he heard this application at first instance,
refused to order either discovery or the delivery up of assets, although he was willing to
make, and did make, an order in the usual Anton Piller form. We have not seen any   *d*
transcript of what he said when refusing, in Stephenson LJ's words in the *A J Bekhor* case
[1981] 2 All ER 565 at 586, [1981] QB 923 at 955, 'to pile Piller on Mareva'. We were
told that he was concerned that the defendant Steven Lambert might be obliged by an
order for discovery to incriminate himself, having regard to the fact that he had been
charged with handling stolen property. The judge's attention was not invited to s 31 of
the Theft Act 1968, which provides that a person shall not be excused from answering   *e*
questions in civil proceedings such as these on the ground that to do so might incriminate
him of an offence under that Act. In our judgment, the judge's concern was misplaced.
The possibility of self-incrimination on the facts of this case is no bar to ordering
discovery.

More difficult is the problem when the jurisdiction to order disclosure of assets and
their delivery up should be exercised. For nearly a hundred years now it has been the   *f*
established practice of the courts to refuse injunctions to freeze the assets of a defendant
in anticipation of the plaintiff obtaining judgment against him: see *Lister & Co v Stubbs*
(1890) 45 Ch D 1, [1886–90] All ER Rep 797. The freezing of a defendant's bank account,
in a case where a Mareva injunction is properly granted, may cause a defendant such
hardship that provision should be made for him to withdraw money for ordinary living
expenses: see *Z Ltd v A* [1982] 1 All ER 556 at 565, [1982] QB 558 at 576 per Lord   *g*
Denning MR. Even more hardship might be caused to a defendant who was deprived by
a Mareva injunction of assets which he used for the purpose of living and earning his
livelihood. Even if a plaintiff has good reason for thinking that a defendant intends to
dispose of assets so as to deprive him of his anticipated judgment, the court must always
remember that rogues have to live and that all orders, particularly interlocutory ones,
should as far as possible do justice to all parties.   *h*

In the *Z Ltd* case this court had to consider how justice should be done when, pursuant
to Mareva injunctions, assets in the hands of innocent third parties were frozen. This case
is concerned with assets in the possession of or under the control of the defendants and
with the delivery up, pending trial, of such motor vehicles as the defendants have in
their possession, custody or control. On the evidence put before us ex parte in this case
there was reason to think that the defendant Steven Lambert had put such profits as he   *j*
had made from infringing the plaintiffs' copyrights into easily removable and disposable
chattels such as motor vehicles. There is no reason at present to think that he uses the
motor vehicles he owns for the purposes of earning his living; indeed, he claims to be
unemployed. Neither he nor his wife will suffer hardship pending trial if his motor
vehicles are kept in a garage chosen by the plaintiffs' experienced solicitors. Further, a
man who can buy expensive motor cars, as the defendant Steven Lambert is alleged to
have done, must have access to money and it is improbable that he has confined his

buying for the purpose of acquiring easily disposable assets exclusively to motor cars. It
a follows, in our judgment, that this is the kind of case in which both defendants should
be ordered to disclose the value, nature and whereabouts of their assets, including bank
or other accounts. This, in our judgment, was a clear case for ordering both discovery of
assets and the delivery up pending trial of a particular kind of asset.

In other cases the evidence may not be so clear. It may be helpful if we indicate
guidelines for the making of orders for the delivery up of chattels.

b First, there should be clear evidence that the defendant is likely, unless restrained by
order, to dispose of or otherwise deal with his chattels in order to deprive the plaintiff of
the fruits of any judgment he may obtain. Moreover, the court should be slow to order
the delivery up of property belonging to the defendant unless there is some evidence or
inference that the property has been acquired by the defendant as a result of his alleged
wrongdoing. In the present case, for example, the inference is that the motor vehicles
c which the defendants own could only have been purchased out of the proceeds of sale by
the defendants of articles which infringe the plaintiffs' copyright. The inference is also
that, if the defendants are forewarned or left in possession of the motor vehicles, those
vehicles will be sold on and the proceeds of sale dissipated or hidden so that the plaintiffs
would be deprived not only of damages but also of the proceeds of sale of infringing
articles which belong to the plaintiffs.

d Second, no order should be made for the delivery up of a defendant's wearing apparel,
bedding, furnishings, tools of his trade, farm implements, livestock or any machines
(including motor vehicles) or other goods such as materials or stock-in-trade which it is
likely he uses for the purposes of a lawful business. Sometimes furnishings may consist
of objets d'art of great value. If the evidence is clear that such objects were bought for the
purposes of frustrating judgment creditors they could be included in an order.

e Third, all orders should specify as clearly as possible what chattels or classes of chattels
are to be delivered up. A plaintiff's inability to identify what he wants delivered up and
why is an indication that no order should be made.

Fourth, the order must not authorise the plaintiff to enter on the defendant's premises
or to seize the defendant's property save by permission of the defendant. In *Anton Piller
KG v Manufacturing Processes Ltd* [1976] 1 All ER 779 at 782–783, [1976] Ch 55 at 60
f Lord Denning MR emphasised that the order in that case—

'. . . does not authorise the plaintiffs' solicitors or anyone else to enter the
defendants' premises against their will . . . It only authorises entry and inspection by
the permission of the defendants. The plaintiffs must get the defendants' permission.
But it does do this: it brings pressure on the defendants to give permission. It does
more. It actually orders them to give permission—with, I suppose, the result that if
g they do not give permission, they are guilty of contempt of court.'

The order in the present case was in the same form.

Fifth, no order should be made for delivery up to anyone other than the plaintiff's
solicitor or a receiver appointed by the High Court. The court should appoint a receiver
to take possession of the chattels unless satisfied that the plaintiff's solicitor has, or can
h arrange, suitable safe custody for what is delivered to him.

Sixth, the court should follow the guidelines set out in the *Z Ltd* case in so far as they
are applicable to chattels in the possession, custody or control of third parties.

Finally, provision should always be made for liberty to apply to stay, vary or discharge
the order.

Guidelines are guidelines; they are not rules of court and the spirit of them and not
j the letter should be kept in mind.

Application granted.

Solicitors: *A E Hamlin & Co* (for the plaintiffs).

                                                    Mary Rose Plummer   Barrister.

Babanaft International Co SA v Avant Petroleum Inc
The Oltenia

COURT OF APPEAL, CIVIL DIVISION
STEPHENSON, DONALDSON LJJ AND SIR DAVID CAIRNS
31 MARCH, 7 APRIL 1982

Arbitration – Preliminary question of law – Appeal from decision of High Court – Circumstances in which leave to appeal should be given – Relevance of agreement of all parties to appeal – Application to Court of Appeal for leave to appeal – Procedure on hearing of application – Arbitration Act 1979, s 2.

Arbitration – Commencement – Extension of time fixed by agreement – Circumstances in which court should extend time – Charterparty – Charterers not liable unless claim and supporting documents presented within 90 days – Whether time-barring of claim a matter which could be referred to arbitration – Whether presentation of claim with supporting documents constituting a 'step to commence arbitration' – Arbitration Act 1950, s 27.

By a charterparty dated 12 November 1980 the owners chartered a vessel to the charterers for one voyage. The charterparty provided for arbitration proceedings to be held in London according to English law and further provided, by cl M2, that the charterers were to be released from all liability in respect of any claims by the owners under the charterparty unless a claim was presented to the charterers within 90 days from completion of discharge of the cargo. The vessel completed discharge on 16 December 1980 and on 30 December the owners claimed damages for detention of the vessel at an intermediate port based on loss of daily profit from the use of the vessel. The 90-day period referred to in cl M2 expired on 16 March 1981. On 17 March the owners issued a writ claiming damages for detention of the vessel based not only on loss of profit but also on an allegation that the detention of the vessel had rendered the owners liable to pay damages to a third party. The charterers issued a summons to stay the proceedings, and the claims were referred to arbitration. The charterers contended that, in respect of the claim for loss of profit, the owners had failed to present supporting documents within the 90-day period, and that, in respect of the owners' alleged liability to pay damages to a third party, the owners had failed to present the claim and supporting documents within that period. The owners applied to the High Court seeking (i) the determination under s 2[a] of the Arbitration Act 1979 of a preliminary question of law arising in the course of the reference to arbitration whether the claim for damages for detention was time-barred as contended by the charterers, and (ii) an order under s 27[b] of the Arbitration Act 1950 extending the time for the presentation of the claims and all supporting documents. The owners secured the consent of the charterers under s 2(1)(b) of the 1979 Act to the application under that section. The judge held that cl M2 was a 'one-off' clause and that its effect was to time-bar the owners' claim for loss of profit because no supporting documents had been presented within 90 days and the claim for alleged liability in damages to a third party because no claim and no supporting documents had been presented within 90 days. In respect of the application under s 2 of the 1979 Act, the judge refused leave to appeal to the Court of Appeal, although he certified under s 2(3)(b) of that Act that the question was one of general public importance and, in respect of the application under s 27 of the 1950 Act, the judge refused to make the order sought and, in the exercise of his discretion, refused leave to appeal. The owners applied to the Court of Appeal for leave to appeal.

---

a   Section 2 is set out at p 248 b to e, post
b   Section 27 is set out at p 254 c d, post

Held – The application would be dismissed for the following reasons—

a (1) In the case of an appeal to the High Court under s 1 of the 1979 Act on a question of law arising out of an arbitration award, s 1(3)(*a*) gave the parties an absolute right of appeal if all the parties agreed, but, by virtue of s 1(7), that right did not extend to a further appeal to the Court of Appeal, where, although the wishes of the parties would be a very powerful factor, strict conditions applied. In the case of an appeal to the High Court under s 2 of that Act on a preliminary question of law arising in the course of a *b* reference to arbitration, the High Court was not bound to entertain the appeal notwithstanding any agreement of the parties to appeal, but the judge should only grant leave in exceptional circumstances, as, for example, where the preliminary point of law, if rightly decided, would determine the whole dispute between the parties. It followed, therefore, in view of the difference in the importance accorded to the agreement of the parties to appeal in cases of appeals to the High Court under ss 1 and 2, that, if there were *c* to be any difference in the attitude of the Court of Appeal towards an application for leave to appeal to it under s 2 as compared with one to appeal under s 1, it was that leave to appeal under s 2 was to be less readily given. Section 2 prescribed what was essentially a speedy procedure designed to interrupt the arbitration to the minimum possible extent and was an exception to the general rule that the court did not intervene in the course of an arbitration. The court should consider the application on its general merits and, if not *d* satisfied that the question of law proposed for determination ought to be determined at that stage, refuse the application. In the circumstances the judge had been right to determine that cl M2 was a 'one-off' clause and accordingly to refuse leave to appeal to the Court of Appeal (see p 252 *g* to p 253 *b* and *f* to *g* and p 256 *c d*, post); dictum of Lord Diplock in *Pioneer Shipping Ltd v BTP Tioxide Ltd, The Nema* [1981] 2 All ER at 1039–1040 applied.

e (2) Section 27 of the 1950 Act gave the court power to extend the time limit fixed in an agreement for giving notice to appoint an arbitrator, appointing an arbitrator or taking some other step to commence arbitration if doing so would prevent a claim becoming time-barred. It did not, however, give the court power to extend any other time limits or to extend a time limit for commencing arbitration if in the absence of such extension the claim would remain alive and could be litigated. On the facts, the *f* charterparty between the owners and the charterers did not contain a time limit for commencing arbitration proceedings, and the effect of cl M2 was not to bar claims under the charterparty within 90 days unless all supporting documents were presented. It was not true that if a claim was barred under the charterparty there would be nothing left to arbitrate since the fact that the claim was barred might itself be in dispute and be an issue which could be referred to arbitration. Nor could the presentation of a claim with all *g* supporting documents be regarded as a 'step to commence arbitration proceedings' within s 27 since the presentation of a claim did not necessarily lead to an arbitration and so was not a step to commence arbitration proceedings; the presentation of a claim with all supporting documents was not even a condition precedent to commencing arbitration proceedings since an arbitration could be begun by referring a claim which was bereft of any supporting documents notwithstanding that many were available. In the *h* circumstances there were no grounds for interfering with the judge's exercise of his discretion to refuse to make an order under s 27 (see p 255 *g* to *j* and p 256 *a* to *d*, post); *Nestlé Co Ltd v E Biggins & Co Ltd* [1958] 1 Lloyd's Rep 398 overruled.

Per curiam. Applications for leave to appeal under either s 1 or s 2 of the 1979 Act in commercial arbitrations should be considered in isolation from the appeal itself in order to enable them to be determined much more quickly. In considering such applications *j* it is wholly inappropriate to allow the type of prolonged adversarial argument which is usually deployed when the application for leave is to be followed immediately by the hearing of the appeal if leave is granted; rather, the court will read the judgment sought to be appealed and ask itself questions similar to those which the High Court judge should himself have asked (see p 252 *c d*, p 253 *h j* and p 256 *c d*, post).

Notes

For the extension of time limits contained in arbitration agreements, see 2 Halsbury's

Laws (4th edn) para 544, and for cases on the subject, see 3 Digest (Reissue) 7–9, 40–43, 7–15, 195–205.

For the determination of preliminary points of law in references to arbitration, see Supplement to 2 Halsbury's Laws (4th edn) paras 599–605.2.

For the Arbitration Act 1950, s 27, see 2 Halsbury's Statutes (3rd edn) 457.

For the Arbitration Act 1979, s 2, see 49 ibid 61.

Cases referred to in judgments

A/S Rendal v Arcos Ltd [1937] 3 All ER 577, HL, 22 Digest (Reissue) 160, *1335*.

British Westinghouse Electric and Manufacturing Co Ltd v Underground Electric Rlys Co of London Ltd [1912] AC 673, HL, 3 Digest (Reissue) 181, *1106*.

Metalimex Foreign Trade Corp v Eugenie Maritime Co Ltd [1962] 1 Lloyd's Rep 378, 3 Digest (Reissue) 52, *278*.

Nestlé Co Ltd v E Biggins & Co Ltd [1958] 1 Lloyd's Rep 398, DC, 3 Digest (Reissue) 7, 9.

Pinnock Bros v Lewis and Peat Ltd [1923] 1 KB 690, 3 Digest (Reissue) 41, *200*.

Pioneer Shipping Ltd v BTP Tioxide Ltd, The Nema [1981] 2 All ER 1030, [1982] AC 724, [1982] AC 724, [1981] 3 WLR 292, HL.

Cases also cited

Aries Tanker Corp v Total Transport Ltd [1977] 1 All ER 398, [1977] 1 WLR 185, HL.

Consolidated Investment and Contracting Co v Saponaria Shipping Co, The Virgo [1978] 3 All ER 988, [1978] 1 WLR 987, CA.

Himmerland, The [1965] 2 Lloyd's Rep 353.

Nea Agrex SA v Baltic Shipping Co Ltd [1976] 2 All ER 842, [1976] QB 933, CA.

Rolimpex (Ch E) Ltd v Avra Shipping Co Ltd, The Angeliki [1973] 2 Lloyd's Rep 226.

Smeaton Hanscomb & Co Ltd v Sassoon I Setty, Son & Co (No 2) [1953] 2 All ER 1588, [1953] 1 WLR 1468.

Application for leave to appeal

By notice of motion the plaintiffs, Babanaft International Co SA, the chartered owners of the motor tanker Oltenia, applied to the Court of Appeal for leave to appeal from the orders of Bingham J made on 20 January 1982 whereby he ordered (i) on an originating motion by the owners for the determination of a preliminary question of law arising in the course of an arbitration between the owners as claimants in the arbitration and the defendants, Avant Petroleum Inc, the charterers of the Oltenia, as respondents that, on the true construction of a charterparty dated 12 November 1980 and the facts set out in the pleading between the parties in the arbitration, the owners' claim for damages for detention of the Oltenia was time-barred, and (ii) on an originating summons issued by the owners under s 27 of the Arbitration Act 1950 seeking an extension of time for the presentation of claims and all supporting documents by the owners in respect of their claim that the application be dismissed. The facts are set out in the judgment of Donaldson LJ.

Richard Yorke QC and Richard Aikens for the owners.
David Johnson QC and Timothy Dutton for the charterers.

Cur adv vult

7 April. The following judgments were read.

DONALDSON LJ (delivering the first judgment at the invitation of Stephenson LJ). The proceedings in this court raise two issues of considerable commercial interest and general importance. They concern (i) the principles on which leave to appeal to the Court of Appeal should be granted from a decision of the High Court determining a preliminary point of law pursuant to s 2 of the Arbitration Act 1979 and (ii) the scope of s 27 of the Arbitration Act 1950.

The background

a On 12 November 1980 Babanaft International Co SA, disponent owners of the mt Oltenia, to whom I shall refer as 'the owners', chartered the vessel to Avant Petroleum Inc, to whom I shall refer as 'the charterers', for a voyage from one safe port Soviet Black Sea to one or two safe ports European Mediterranean Sea including Greece and Turkey. The charterparty was on the Asbatankvoy form (October 1977 edn), published by the Association of Ship Brokers and Agents (USA) Inc. That form, as printed, provides by

b cl K that: 'The place of General Average and arbitration proceedings to be London/New York (strike out one).'

The parties modified this printed clause by striking out 'New York' and adding in typescript, the words 'in accordance with English law'.

The printed form also provides space, under the heading 'M. (Special Provisions)', for the parties to include additional clauses. The parties in the event agreed on eight such

c clauses of which only one, M2, is relevant. This provided:

> 'Charterers shall be discharged and released from all liability in respect of any claims Owners may have under this Charter Party (such as, but not limited to, claims for deadfreight, demurrage, shifting expenses or port expenses) unless a claim has been presented to Charterers in writing with all available supporting documents,
>
> d within 90 (ninety) days from completion of discharge of the cargo concerned under this Charter Party.'

The vessel completed discharge at Algeciras on 16 December 1980, and accordingly the 90-day period mentioned in cl M2 expired on 16 March 1981. On 31 December 1980 the owners presented to the charterers a claim for discharging port demurrage with all

e available supporting documents. The validity of this claim is disputed by the charterers, but we are not concerned with it. However, on the previous day the owners had presented a different claim to the charterers, namely one for damages for the detention of the vessel at Augusta. The sum claimed was $US162,341·05 and, broadly speaking, the claim was based on loss of daily profit from the use of the Oltenia.

For reasons which are not apparent, bearing in mind that the charterparty contained

f an arbitration clause, on 17 March 1981 the owners issued a writ out of the High Court indorsed with points of claim. This advanced the claims already notified to the charterers. However, the damages claimed for detention were based not only on loss of profit but also on an allegation that the detention had rendered the owners liable to pay damages to Petroship International SA in the sum of $US130,046·45, being that company's liability for demurrage on another vessel, the Cys Mariner. For present purposes it is sufficient to

g say that the owners were advancing (a) the discharging port demurrage claim, (b) the original (Oltenia loss of daily profit) detention claim and (c) the new (Cys Mariner) detention claim. The first that the charterers heard of the Cys Mariner detention claim was when they received the writ in New York on 6 May 1981.

Predictably a summons was issued to stay the proceedings and in due course the claims were referred to arbitration on the basis of the existing points of claim. In reply to the

h detention claims, the charterers relied, inter alia, on cl M2 alleging, so far as the Oltenia loss of daily profit claim was concerned, that the owners had failed to present documents relating to alleged port disbursements amounting to $US51,000 within the 90-day period and, so far as the Cys Mariner claim was concerned, had failed both to present the claim and to present supporting documents within that period.

The owners then made two originating applications to the High Court. The first

j invited the court to determine a preliminary point of law arising in the course of the reference pursuant to s 2 of the Arbitration Act 1979. The second invited the court to make an order under s 27 of the Arbitration Act 1950 extending the time for the presentation of the detention claims and all available supporting documents.

The preliminary point of law
The preliminary point of law was expressed in the following terms:

'. . . whether upon the true construction of the said Charterparty and the facts set out at paragraphs 9 to 12 of the Points of Claim and paragraph 14 of the Points of *a* Defence and Counterclaim served by the above parties respectively in the above reference, the Plaintiffs/Claimants' claim for damages for detention of the "OLTENIA" is time-barred as alleged by the Defendant/Respondents or at all.'

Section 2 of the Arbitration Act 1979, as amended by the Supreme Court Act 1981, provides as follows:

b

'(1) Subject to subsection (2) and section 3 below, on an application to the High Court made by any of the parties to a reference—(a) with the consent of an arbitrator who has entered on the reference or, if an umpire has entered on the reference, with his consent, or (b) with the consent of all the other parties, the High Court shall have jurisdiction to determine any question of law arising in the course of the reference.

(2) The High Court shall not entertain an application under subsection (1)(a) *c* above with respect to any question of law unless it is satisfied that—(a) the determination of the application might produce substantial savings in costs to the parties; and (b) the question of law is one in respect of which leave to appeal would be likely to be given under section 1(3)(b) above.

(2A) Unless the High Court gives leave, no appeal shall lie to the Court of Appeal from a decision of the High Court to entertain or not to entertain an application *d* under subsection (1)(a) above.

(3) A decision of the High Court under subsection (1) above shall be deemed to be a judgment of the court within the meaning of section 16 of the Supreme Court Act 1981 (appeals to the Court of Appeal), but no appeal shall lie from such a decision unless—(a) the High Court or the Court of Appeal gives leave; and (b) it is certified by the High Court that the question of law to which its decision relates *e* either is one of general public importance or is one which for some other special reason should be considered by the Court of Appeal.'

Section 3 (to which of course reference is made in s 2) relates to exclusion agreements affecting rights under ss 1 and 2 and is immaterial for present purposes.

In the instant case the owners secured the consent of the charterers to their application *f* and were thus able to proceed under s 2(1)(b). In deciding whether or not to grant the application, the judge's discretion was accordingly unfettered by sub-s (2), no doubt because Parliament considered that prima facie it could be left to the parties to consider whether the determination of the question of law at that stage would be likely to lead to a substantial saving in costs (sub-s (2)(a)) and whether it could substantially affect their rights. Nevertheless, it should be emphasised that the High Court has a discretion whether or not to grant such an application. It is a not uncommon experience to be faced *g* in the Divisional Court of the Queen's Bench Division with a question of law stated by justices which, although important as a question, can on the facts found only be answered by saying, 'Well, it all depends.' If such were the position, it would not be suprising if an application were refused notwithstanding the fact that it was supported by both parties. In the instant case Bingham J acceded to the application and was plainly right to do so.

The judge's judgment on the preliminary question of law is a model of clarity and *h* conciseness and I cannot do better than quote it in full:

'[Counsel] for the owners submitted that the clause was on any showing unhappily drafted, there being an obvious lack of correspondence between "any claim" before the bracket and "a claim" after it. But this was a clause inserted exclusively for the benefit of the charterers and any ambiguity should be resolved against them. The *j* natural meaning, and that consistent with authority, was that the owners should within the period communicate the factual ground of the claim (in this case the detention at Augusta) and supply documents relevant to that (such as the log extract to show the existence and period of the detention). This the owners did. Having done so, they were free to raise other claims arising from the same factual premise (such as the Cys Mariner claim). It was not incumbent on the owners to provide full documentation to support a detailed quantification of any claim. This construction was consistent with cl 24, the arbitration clause, which permitted or required the arbitrators on notice to entertain further disputes and differences not previously referred.

[Counsel] for the charterers submitted that the meaning of the clause, despite its obvious want of professional legal draftsmanship, was plain. Charterers were to be discharged and released from all liability in respect of any claim the owners might have under the charterparty unless such claim had been presented to the charterers in writing with all available supporting documents within 90 days. "All available supporting documents" meant exactly what the words said: they included documents supporting the quantum of the claim as well as liability, and were not apt to describe legal summaries or formulations of the claim. This construction involved no inconsistency with cl 24; it merely meant that the charterers would have a defence to new claims introduced into an arbitration at a late stage if proper and timely presentation of the claim in accordance with cl M2 had not taken place.

The commercial intention underlying this clause seems to me plainly to have been to ensure that claims were made by the owners within a short period of final discharge so that the claims could be investigated and if possible resolved while the facts were still fresh (cf *Metalimex Foreign Trade Corp v Eugenie Maritime Co Ltd* [1962] 1 Lloyd's Rep 378 at 386 per McNair J. This object could only be achieved if the charterers were put in possession of the factual material which they required in order to satisfy themselves whether the claims were well founded or not. I cannot regard the expression "all available supporting documents" as in any way ambiguous: documents supporting the owners' claim on liability would of course be included, but so would a document in relation to quantum only, just as a doctor's bill would be a document supporting a claim for damages for personal injury. The owners would not, as a matter of common sense, be debarred from making factual corrections to claims presented in time (as they have done to the claim in para 12(A), nor from putting a different legal label on a claim previously presented, but the owners are in my view shut out from enforcing a claim the substance of which and the supporting documents of which (subject always to de minimis exceptions) have not been presented in time. It is true that the drafting of the clause would give a legal draftsman little cause for pride, but it was obviously not the work of a legal draftsman and that is a good reason for not embarking on any sophisticated legal exegesis. One possible, though strict, interpretation, that the presentation of any claim has the effect of preserving all claims, was not embraced by [counsel for the owners] with any show of enthusiasm, and indeed it borders on the absurd. Clause 24 is not in my judgment inconsistent with my construction: claims could be introduced into an arbitration even though they had not originally been the subject of the arbitration, but the charterers would have a defence if cl M2 had not been complied with.

The interpretation of any clause must of course be governed very largely by the language of the clause itself, but I find some support for my approach to this clause in the House of Lords decision in *A/S Rendal v Arcos Ltd* [1937] 3 All ER 577. The clause in question (numbered 24) in that case was less rigorous than cl M2, in that it provided for notice of a claim to be given within 12 months, with no requirement that supporting documents be submitted. The question was considered whether there had been compliance with the clause if notice had been given of a claim for delay and consequential expenses caused by lack of ice-breaker assistance but not of damage caused by ice to the ship itself. Lord Wright said (at 580): "It is convenient first to state how I construe cl. 24. That clause requires 'notice of claim'. That, in my opinion, does not mean a precisely formulated claim, with full details, but it must be such a notice as will enable the party to whom it is given to take steps to meet the claim, by preparing and obtaining appropriate evidence for that purpose. Thus, in the present case, there was a general claim for damages for breach of the ice clause, with particulars so far as damages were claimed in respect of delay and consequent *a* expenses. The further claim for damage to the ship herself was a claim in respect of the same cause of action, that is, breach of the ice clause, but it involved different issues of fact, estimates of damage, ship surveys, repair accounts and so forth. I think, therefore, that cl. 24 requires a separate notice in respect of such a claim, if the purpose of cl. 24 is to be fulfilled." Lord Maugham observed (at 589): "My Lords, on the first point the Court of Appeal has held that the letter was not a *b* definite notice of claim. For my part, I am in agreement with this view, if it means that the letter lacks definitiveness. But cl. 24 of the charterparty uses no adjective indicating precision as to details or amounts. It is, I think, a sufficient claim under the clause if the shipowner or the charterer, as the case may be, indicates that there will be a claim in respect of an indicated head of damage arising from a breach of a clause in the charterparty." But the plain effect of the present clause, in particular *c* because of its documentary requirement, is that the claim should be presented with at least reasonable precision as to details and amounts.

I have outlined what I consider to be the correct construction of cl M2. Do the charterers establish that they are discharged and released from all liability in respect of the owners' detention claim because the claim was not presented in time? So far as the Cys Mariner demurrage claim in para 12(B) is concerned there can only be an *d* affirmative answer: no claim was presented and no documents directly bearing on this claim were presented within the 90 days. The telex references did not put the charters on notice of this claim, let alone enable them to investigate it. The claim rested on factual premises going well outside the detention claim which was indicated. I am in no doubt that this part of the claim is time-barred under cl M2.

The loss of profit detention claim in para 12(A) is more difficult. The claim *e* certainly was presented, with much supporting documentation. The only omission to which the charterers can point is the documentation supporting the disbursements of $51,000 in two ports. I do not know, and the owners cannot tell me, whether there was or is any documentation to support these disbursements. If there was not, the owners would not be in default under cl M2 because these supporting documents would not have been available. But what if these documents, having been available, *f* were not presented? Would that omission enable the charterers to rely on the time bar? On the one hand, one bears in mind that these disbursements were only one ingredient in the owners' calculation and the clause should not be operated with pedantic literalness. On the other hand, the sum involved is not trivial, it could have a significant effect on the calculation if understated and it is a deduction which the charterers (perhaps bearing in mind Dr Johnson's observation that "Round numbers *g* are always false") might well wish to probe. On balance I have concluded that there were supporting documents which, if available, should have been produced, with the result that the claim is time-barred if they were not. The expression "all available supporting documents" must cover these documents, if available, and I do not think they can be disregarded as de minimis. But whether there is a good defence to this part of the detention claim must await a finding of fact by the arbitrators whether *h* these documents were available.'

Bingham J was then asked to give a certificate under s 2(3) of the 1979 Act and also to give leave to appeal to this court. He said:

'Although cl M2 is a one-off clause it is a variant of a clause that one sees not all that infrequently and I think that by analogy my decision on cl M2 could be relied *j* on in the context of other clauses. Moreover, it could very well be that my decision on cl M2 would affect the use of such a clause. Those are both, in my judgment, reasons why it would be proper for the matter to be considered by the Court of Appeal, if they wish to do so. I further think that in respect of a large claim such as that in para 12(B), and possibly para 12(A) also, there could be ramifications as

between the owners and their advisers and it would be unsatisfactory if that had to
a   be resolved on the basis of any uncertainty as to what the correct law was. I shall
accordingly certify in respect of the notice of motion under s 2(1)(*b*), according to
s 2(3)(*b*), but I shall not, in respect of either the notice of motion or the summons,
give leave. The effect therefore is that the owners are not shut out from going to the
Court of Appeal but they are obliged to seek the leave of the Court of Appeal. My
reason for refusing leave is that I would not wish it to be thought that there was any
b   doubt in my mind as to the answer either on the motion or the summons. Moreover,
so far as s 27 is concerned, it is involving an exercise of my discretion. I think it
would be inappropriate to give leave.'

The judge's certificate cannot be questioned, and I would not wish to do so. However,
I may perhaps be permitted to express surprise if he meant to hold that the size of this
claim or the possible 'ramifications' (I use his word) between owners and strangers to the
c   arbitration brought the question within the category of being one of general public
importance. In argument it was suggested that in this respect Bingham J probably had
in mind that these were special reasons why the question should be considered by the
Court of Appeal. If this were the case, I can only say that it is not reflected in the formal
certificate, which Bingham J probably never saw. The reality may well be that the
learned judge considered these to be makeweight factors.
d

The application for leave to appeal
The owners then applied for leave to appeal following Bingham J's refusal. This is the
first such application to come before this court where the decision in question has been
given in the exercise of the jurisdiction under s 2 of the Arbitration Act 1979. It may
e   therefore be of assistance if I indicate what, in my judgment, is the scope of the inquiry
which this court should make.
In *Pioneer Shipping Ltd v BTP Tioxide Ltd, The Nema*, [1981] 2 All ER 1030, [1982] AC
724 the House of Lords considered what should be the approach of a judge of the High
Court in deciding whether or not to permit leave to appeal to the High Court under s 1
of the 1979 Act. Lord Diplock explained the traditional conflict in this field between the
f   often wholly inconsistent requirements of speedy finality of decision and legal accuracy
of decision. He concluded that the legislative intention of Parliament was to promote
greater finality in arbitral awards than was being achieved prior to the passing of the Act
(see [1981] 2 All ER 1030 at 1039, [1982] AC 724 at 741). With this in mind, Lord
Diplock said ([1981] 2 All ER 1030 at 1039–1040, [1982] AC 724 at 742–743):

g   'Where, as in the instant case, a question of law involved is the construction of a
one-off clause the application of which to the particular facts of the case is an issue
in the arbitration, leave should not normally be given unless it is apparent to the
judge, on a mere perusal of the reasoned award itself without the benefit of
adversarial argument, that the meaning ascribed to the clause by the arbitrator is
obviously wrong; but if on such perusal it appears to the judge that it is possible that
h   argument might persuade him, despite impression to the contrary, that the
arbitrator might be right, he should not grant leave; the parties should be left to
accept, for better or for worse, the decision of the tribunal that they had chosen to
decide the matter in the first instance.'

He then turned to consider questions involving the construction of contracts in
standard terms and said ([1981] 2 All ER 1030 at 1040, [1982] AC 724 at 743):
j
      'For reasons already sufficiently discussed, rather less strict criteria are in my view
appropriate where questions of construction of contracts in standard terms are
concerned. That there should be as high a degree of legal certainty as it is practicable
to obtain as to how such terms apply on the occurrence of events of a kind that it is
not unlikely may reproduce themselves in similar transactions between other parties

engaged in the same trade is a public interest that is recognised by the 1979 Act, particularly in s 4. So, if the decision of the question of construction in the *a* circumstances of the particular case would add significantly to the clarity and certainty of English commercial law it would be proper to give leave in a case sufficiently substantial to escape the ban imposed by the first part of s 1(4), bearing in mind always that a superabundance of citable judicial decisions arising out of slightly different facts is calculated to hinder rather than to promote clarity in settled principles of commercial law. But leave should not be given, even in such a case, *b* unless the judge considered that a strong prima facie case had been made out that the arbitrator had been wrong in his construction; and when the events to which the standard clause fell to be applied in the particular arbitration were themselves one-off events stricter criteria should be applied on the same lines as those that I have suggested as appropriate to one-off clauses.'

If we are to adopt a similar approach in considering whether to grant leave to appeal *c* from a decision of the High Court, whether given under s 1 or under s 2, it would be wholly inappropriate to allow the type of prolonged adversarial argument which is usually deployed where the application for leave is to be followed immediately by the hearing of the appeal if leave is granted. It would rather be for us to read the judgment sought to be appealed and to ask ourselves similar questions to those which the House of Lords has ruled should be asked by judges of the High Court. I say 'similar questions' *d* rather than 'the same questions' because the cause of uniformity of arbitral decision may already have been sufficiently served by a decision of a High Court judge which will bind all arbitrators. A decision of the Court of Appeal will then only be necessary if there is a divergence of opinion between High Court judges, who are not, of course, bound by each others' decisions however much they may respect them.

But counsel for the owners submits that we should not adopt such an approach, at least *e* in the case of an appeal from a decision under s 2 which had been sought by one party with the consent of all other parties. In such a case, he submits, the parties have expressed their preference for legal accuracy and should be allowed to appeal both to this court and to the House of Lords if there is any possibility of inaccuracy.

I do not accept this argument for as least two reasons. First, agreement to the High *f* Court determining a question of law arising during the course of the reference is one thing. Agreeing to an appeal to the Court of Appeal from that determination is quite another and the charterers have never so agreed. Indeed, they opposed this application. Second, and more generally, I do not accept that leave to appeal should more readily be given in a s 2 case than in a s 1 case.

It is true that in the case of an appeal on a question of law arising out of an award (a s 1 case) Parliament has given an absolute right of appeal to the High Court if all parties so *g* agree. But on the wording of sub-s (7) this does not extend to a further appeal to the Court of Appeal. There strict conditions apply, although the wishes of the parties would no doubt be a very powerful factor. That it is, and should be, more difficult to appeal to the Court of Appeal than to the High Court was confirmed by Lord Diplock in *The Nema* [1981] 2 All ER 1030 at 1038, [1982] AC 724 at 740.

By contrast, in the case of an appeal on a preliminary point of law arising in the course *h* of the reference (s 2) Parliament has indicated that the High Court is not bound by the agreement of the parties. The judge has to consider the application on its inherent merits. If he is not satisfied that the question of law proposed for determination ought to be determined at that stage, he should refuse the application. When it comes to an appeal to this court under s 2, the same conditions apply as in the case of a s 1 appeal (cf ss 1(7) and 2(3)). But, in the light of the difference in the importance accorded to the agreement of *i* the parties at the High Court stage, if there is to be any difference in the attitude of this court towards an application for leave to appeal under s 2 as compared with one to appeal under s 1, it must be that leave to appeal under the former is less readily given.

This must be right in principle. Section 2 is the successor in title to the old consultative case, which more aptly describes its nature. Put colloquially, the arbitrator or the parties

nip down the road to pick the brains of one of Her Majesty's judges and, thus enlightened,
a resume the arbitration. It is essentially a speedy procedure designed to interrupt the
arbitration to the minimum possible extent and it is an exception to the general rule that
the courts do not intervene in the course of an arbitration. If, other than in wholly
exceptional cases, it were used to obtain definitive decisions from this court or even the
House of Lords, it would create unacceptable interruptions in the conduct of arbitrations.
The exceptional case which I have in mind is where the preliminary question of law, if
b rightly decided, determines the whole dispute between the parties. In such a case, the
application for leave to appeal should no doubt be considered as if it were one under s 1
and there may be other exceptional cases.

There was also some discussion on the interrelationship between ss 1 and 2 of the 1979
Act in the context of whether it would be possible to seek leave to appeal to the High
Court under s 1, and from that court to this court, on the basis that the arbitrator had
c erred in law in following a decision of the High Court given in the same arbitration
under s 2. It was certainly possible in effect to do so before the passing of the 1979 Act.
The most extreme example is probably to be found in *British Westinghouse Electric and
Manufacturing Co Ltd v Underground Electric Rlys Co of London Ltd* [1912] AC 673. There
the arbitrator stated an award in the form of a consultative case and the Divisional Court
answered the questions of law. The arbitrator then made a final award incorporating the
d decision of the Divisional Court. Application was made to set this award aside on the
ground that it contained an error of law on its face. All the courts held that this procedure
was available to the applicants and the House of Lords indeed set the award aside.

Counsel for the owners rightly pointed out that in an application for leave to appeal
under s 1 on a question of law which had already been decided by the court in the same
arbitration under s 2, the applicant would undertake a considerable burden. This is
e correct. He would have to satisfy the judge that the question was fit for consideration by
a court having power to declare the s 2 decision to have been wrong and, with this in
mind, the judge would normally want to be satisfied that if he gave leave to appeal to the
High Court he would be likely also to certify the question under s 1(7)(b) with a view to
giving the Court of Appeal jurisdiction to entertain a further appeal. But that said, I do
not consider that the s 2 decision would be res judicata. If this is right, it provides an
f additional reason for refraining from allowing a s 2 determination to be appealed save in
exceptional circumstances.

In the instant case we had read the judgment of Bingham J on the construction of
cl M2 before hearing the application. It was a one-off clause even if there are other clauses
in circulation bearing a family relationship. On a perusal of the clause and the judgment,
it was very far from apparent to me that the judge's decision was obviously wrong. On
g the contrary, it bore every indication of being right. As Stephenson LJ and Sir David
Cairns were of the same opinion, counsel for the owners was not allowed to deploy his
arguments on why the decision was wrong, ie to argue the merits of the appeal on the
hearing of the application, although he was, of course, allowed to seek to persuade us that
the appeal was of such a nature that it should be heard irrespective of whether the judge
was right or wrong.

h   The judgment of Bingham J was given on 20 January 1982, and the possibility of an
appeal has only been eliminated three months later. This is much too long an interruption
of a commercial arbitration. No doubt in part this has been due to a lack of appreciation
of the special nature of an application for leave to appeal a decision given under the 1979
Act, which led to the appeal being listed to follow the application for leave. I would hope
that hereafter such applications, whether under s 1 or under s 2, will be considered in
j isolation from the appeal itself and that this will enable them to be determined much
more quickly.

Section 27 of the Arbitration Act 1950
This is an independent appeal by the owners from the refusal of the judge to grant
their application for an extension of time for the presentation of claims and all available
supporting documents. The judge's refusal had two bases. First, he held that he had no

jurisdiction to make such an order in the circumstances of the instant case; and, second, he held that, if he had such jurisdiction, it was a jurisdiction which, in the exercise of his a discretion, should not be exercised in relation to the Oltenia detention claim. He refused leave to appeal because of the alternative discretionary basis of his decision.

In this case our approach to the grant or refusal of leave to appeal was quite different for at least two reasons. First, neither s 1 nor s 2 of the 1979 Act was involved and accordingly the special restrictions imposed by those sections did not apply. Second, the application was scarcely resisted. Whilst we should have been reluctant to have interfered b with the judge's exercise of discretion, we granted the application because counsel for the owners wished to challenge the decision that s 27 had no application and that is a point of the greatest importance to all concerned with arbitration.

Section 27 of the 1950 Act, re-enacting s 16(6) of the Arbitration Act 1934, is in the following terms:

> 'Where the terms of an agreement to refer future disputes to arbitration provide c
> that any claims to which the agreement applies shall be barred unless notice to
> appoint an arbitrator is given or an arbitrator is appointed or some other step to
> commence arbitration proceedings is taken within a time fixed by the agreement,
> and a dispute arises to which the agreement applies, the High Court, if it is of
> opinion that in the circumstances of the case undue hardship would otherwise be d
> caused, and notwithstanding that the time so fixed has expired, may, on such terms,
> if any, as the justice of the case may require, but without prejudice to the provisions
> of any enactment limiting the time for the commencement of arbitration
> proceedings, extend the time for such period as it thinks proper.'

In order to succeed in establishing the jurisdiction of the court to make an order under this section, the owners had to show that cl M2, or the charterparty as a whole including e that clause, provided that claims to which the arbitration agreement applied would be barred—

> 'unless notice to appoint an arbitrator is given or an arbitrator is appointed or
> some other step to commence arbitration proceedings is taken within a time fixed
> by the agreement.' f

This has only to be stated for the owners' difficulties to become obvious. Clause M2 has no apparent connection with the commencement of arbitration proceedings within 90 days or any other time. It appears to relate solely to making a claim in a particular form within a fixed period.

The judge said:

> g
> 'I have much sympathy with the object which the owners seek in principle to
> achieve. Section 27 is a valuable provision, enabling the court to relieve a party from
> the effect of a consensual time limit to which it applies where the interests of justice
> so require. A similar provision was introduced into a different area of the law by s 1
> of the Limitation Act 1975 (and now by s 33 of the Limitation Act 1980). However
> beneficial a short time limit may be in intention, cases can arise in which it can h
> become a source of injustice or even oppression, and I should be pleased to conclude
> that in a case such as the present the court could, if the circumstances warranted it,
> grant relief from the time bar in cl M2. But I can find no warrant in s 27 for such a
> conclusion. A notice clause such as cl M2 is entirely different from the provisions to
> which s 27 applies. So far as I, and counsel, are aware, s 27 has never been applied to
> such a clause.' j

Counsel for the owners accepts that s 27 must be applied according to its terms, but he submits that by reading the contract as a whole, as one must, it is possible to reach the conclusion that the parties have agreed that the owners' claims should be barred if some step to commence arbitration proceedings is not taken within a fixed period. This

involves linking the cl M2 time limit to the arbitration clause and giving a very wide
a construction to the concept of taking a step to commence arbitration proceedings.

I doubt whether the argument could have been advanced with the faintest air of
plausibility but for the discovery since the hearing below of the decision of the Divisional
Court in *Nestlé Co Ltd v E Biggins & Co Ltd* [1958] 1 Lloyd's Rep 398. There a contract for
the sale of coffee provided that, failing amicable agreement, any dispute should be
referred to arbitration in London according to the rules of the Coffee Trade Federation of
b London. Those rules required all arbitrations to be 'claimed within 14 days following
final day of weighing and/or warehousing of the contract goods at port of final
destination'. The contract then provided that 'any claim on quality or condition of the
goods must be made not later than 14 days from final day of weighing and/or discharge
of goods at port of final destination'. Lord Goddard CJ, sitting with Hilbery and Donovan
JJ, in giving the judgment of the court said (at 400):

c
> 'It seems to me that the Court has clear jurisdiction under [s 27] to extend the
> time in which a claim is to be made because the claim is the first step towards
> arbitration. If the claim is not made within 14 days and if the parties go before the
> arbitrator, the objection will at once be taken that the arbitrator cannot make an
> award in favour of the buyer here in question because the claim was not made
> within 14 days. Therefore, it seems to me that, taking the provision in the contract
d > that the making of any claim on quality must be made not later than 14 days from
> a particular date, the making of such a claim is a step to commence proceedings;
> and, therefore, the Court has got jurisdiction to enlarge the time. In fact, I think it
> is just this sort of provision in a contract with which this section is intended to deal.'

The concept of 'claiming arbitration' is well known in the commodity trades. Telex
e messages fly to and fro and at some stage one party or the other says, 'We claim
arbitration.' The arbitration rules of the trade concerned then provide the steps to be
taken by each party. I would therefore accept that in such cases 'claiming arbitration'
may be regarded as a step to commence arbitration proceedings within the meaning of
s 27. I would also accept that, under that particular contract, the claim for quality or
condition had to precede or accompany the claim for arbitration, since arbitration cannot
f be claimed in vacuo: it has to be linked to a specific dispute. Where I have much more
difficulty is in seeing why the making of a claim for quality or condition is a step to
commence arbitration proceedings. It is a condition precedent to such proceedings, but
it does not of itself commence the proceedings or necessarily lead to their being
commenced. The claim may be conceded or settled amicably. In my judgment, the
decision of the Divisional Court was wrong and should be overruled.

g In essence s 27 empowers the court to extend the time fixed for giving notice to
appoint an arbitrator, appointing an arbitrator or taking some other step to commence
arbitration proceedings if doing so will prevent a claim becoming time-barred. It does
not empower the court to extend any other time limits. In parenthesis I would add that
it does not empower the court to extend a time limit for commencing arbitration if, in
the absence of such an extension, the claim would remain alive and could be litigated, as
h was the case, for example, in *Pinnock Bros v Lewis & Peat Ltd* [1923] 1 KB 690.

In the instant case there is no time limit for commencing arbitration proceedings.
Counsel for the owners seeks to overcome this difficulty by submitting that the effect of
cl M2 is to bar claims after 90 days if its conditions are not fulfilled, that if the claim is
barred there is nothing left to arbitrate and that therefore the time for the commencement
of arbitration proceedings is limited by cl M2. Unfortunately for the owners, it is not
j true that the barring of a claim leaves nothing to be referred to arbitration. The fact that
the claim is barred may well be in dispute and this issue can be referred to arbitration.
Indeed, arbitration proceedings were in fact begun in the present case after the expiration
of the 90-day period, but no one has suggested that the arbitrator is without jurisdiction.

Alternatively, counsel for the owners submitted that presenting a claim with all
available supporting documents can itself be regarded as a step to commence arbitration

proceedings and that accordingly cl M2 can be construed as barring claims unless such a step is taken. The answer to this is that presenting a claim with all available supporting   *a* documents does not necessarily lead to an arbitration and so is not a step to commence such proceedings. It is not even a condition precedent to commencing arbitration proceedings, since an arbitration could be begun by referring a claim which was bereft of any supporting documents, notwithstanding that many were available.

This appeal discloses what many may think is a serious gap in the law. Time bar clauses can, as Bingham J pointed out, become a source of injustice or even oppression.   *b* In such cases the courts should not be impotent to grant relief. However, as the law stands, that will be the position if, in order to avoid a barring provision, the claimant is required to take some action other than taking a step to commence arbitration proceedings.

With very considerable reluctance, but without doubt or hesitation, I would dismiss the appeal.   *c*

SIR DAVID CAIRNS. I am in complete agreement with the judgment which has just been delivered, and I have nothing to add.

STEPHENSON LJ. I also am in complete agreement with the judgment of Donaldson LJ, and have nothing to add.   *d*

Appeal dismissed.

Solicitors: *Thomas Cooper & Stibbard* (for the owners); *Coward Chance* (for the charterers).

Sophie Craven   Barrister.

a   # Le Scroog v General Optical Council

PRIVY COUNCIL

LORD FRASER OF TULLYBELTON, LORD KEITH OF KINKEL AND LORD BRIGHTMAN

14, 15 JUNE, 21 JULY 1982

b   *Ophthalmic optician – Erasure of name from register – Infamous conduct in a professional respect – Profession – Infamous – Canvassing by means of a letter – Letters sent to officials of students' union at two colleges – Letters in breach of a previous undertaking to disciplinary committee not to advertise for clients – Letters criticising other members of profession and making careless statement as to price of contact lenses – Prominent advertisements placed in students' magazine and in professional magazine – Whether advertisements 'dignified and restrained' – Opticians*
c   *Act 1958, s 11(1)(b)(3) – General Optical Council (Rules on Publicity) Order of Council 1981, rr 4, 5.*

The disciplinary committee of the General Optical Council charged the appellant, an ophthalmic optician, with infamous conduct in a professional respect by canvassing students at two colleges by means of a letter sent to an official of the students' union at each of the colleges. The letters, which were in breach of an assurance which the appellant
d had previously given to the committee not to canvass for clients, each bore the address of the appellant's firm and stated that his price for soft contact lenses was 'the lowest price to be found in England' and that information concerning prices 'would obviously be of benefit to the public who are open to exploitation by some of England's most expensive practices simply through ignorance'. The appellant later admitted that he did not know if his prices were the lowest in England. The committee also charged the appellant with
e publishing prominent advertisements in a students' magazine and a professional magazine contrary to the General Optical Council (Rules on Publicity) Order of Council 1981, of which r 4[a] provided that all means of giving publicity to a practice or business should be 'of a dignified and restrained character and free from any reference to the efficiency of, or the facilities given by, other registered practitioners' and r 5[b] that
f publication of advertisements in periodicals was restricted to those circulating wholly or mainly among registered opticians, registered medical practitioners and professions ancillary to medicine. The committee found the appellant guilty of the charges and ordered that his name should be erased from the register of ophthalmic opticians in accordance with s 11(1)(b) and (3)[c] of the Opticians Act 1958. The appellant appealed, contending, inter alia, (1) on the charge of infamous conduct, that if the letters constituted
g canvassing the conduct of the appellant in sending them did not amount to 'infamous conduct in a professional respect', and the advice on the law as to the meaning of infamous conduct by a professional man given by the legal assessor to the committee after they had retired to consider their findings was erroneous or misleading, and (2) on the charge of advertising in breach of the rules, that although the appellant's advertisements were prominent they were perfectly proper because the opticians'

h

---

a   Rule 4, so far as material, is set out at p 261 *c*, post
b   Rule 5, so far as material, is set out at p 262 *b c*, post
c   Section 11, so far as material, provides:
    '(1) If any registered optician . . . (b) is judged by the Disciplinary Committee to have been guilty of infamous conduct in any professional respect, the Committee may, if they think fit, direct that his name shall be erased from the register . . .
j   (3) If it appears to the Disciplinary Committee that a registered optician or an enrolled body corporate has contravened or failed to comply with any rules made under section twenty-five of this Act and that the contravention or failure is such as to render the optician unfit to have his name on the register or the body corporate unfit to have its name on the list, the Disciplinary Committee may, if they think fit, direct that the name of the optician or body corporate shall be erased from the register or list . . .'

profession was to be regarded mainly as a trade or business and not as a profession comparable to the medical profession, and that seen in that light the advertisements were *a* of a dignified and restrained character as required by r 4.

Held – The appeal would be dismissed for the following reasons—

(1) Although there was no specific reference to canvassing in the General Optical Council's Notes of Guidance it was clear from the reference therein to the need to maintain the highest standards and from the restriction on advertising contained in the *b* rules on publicity that canvassing might in certain circumstances amount to infamous conduct. In considering whether it did the committee were entitled to take into account the whole circumstances of the canvassing and the terms of the letters themselves. Since the letters were in breach of the solemn assurance which the appellant had given to the committee not to advertise for clients, the committee were entitled to regard it as specially deserving of reprobation. Moreover, the contents of the letters were open to *c* serious objection having regard to the carelessness of the appellant as to the truth of the statement that his price was the lowest in England and the implied criticism of other members of the profession. The advice given by the legal assessor as to the meaning of infamous conduct was not open to criticism on the ground either of insufficiency or inaccuracy because the word 'infamous' was a word implying strong reprobation and the committee would have been aware of that fact. Accordingly the committee were entitled *d* to find that the appellant's conduct had been infamous in a professional respect (see p 260 *a* to 261 *b* and p 262 *f* to *h*, post).

(2) Since Parliament had, by the 1958 Act, entrusted the committee with the duty of setting standards appropriate to the opticians' profession, the committee were the proper tribunal to decide the status of the profession. The committee were not shown to have fallen into error in applying the standard which they considered appropriate for *e* professional persons, and not a purely commercial standard, in judging whether the advertisements were dignified and restrained. Accordingly they were entitled to find that both advertisements contravened the rules in respect that they were not dignified and restrained. Furthermore, the advertisement in the students' magazine would not have been permitted even if the advertisement itself had been dignified and restrained *f* because the magazine circulated mainly among students and students did not constitute a profession (see p 261 *g h* and p 262 *a* and *c* to *h*, post); dictum of Devlin J in *Hughes v Architects' Registration Council of the United Kingdom* [1957] 2 All ER at 442 approved.

Notes

For erasure of registered opticians from register for infamous conduct, see 30 Halsbury's *g* Laws (4th edn) para 506, and for restrictions on advertising, see ibid para 495.

For the Opticians Act 1958, s 11, see 21 Halsbury's Statutes (3rd edn) 765.

Cases referred to in judgment

Allinson v General Council of Medical Education and Registration [1894] 1 QB 750, [1891–4] All ER Rep 768, CA, 33 Digest (Reissue) 296, *2364.* *h*

Hughes v Architects' Registration Council of the United Kingdom [1957] 2 All ER 436, [1957] 2 QB 550, [1957] 3 WLR 119, DC, 7 Digest (Reissue) 465, *2664.*

R v General Council of Medical Education and Registration of the United Kingdom [1930] 1 KB 562, CA, 33 Digest (Reissue) 289, *2334.*

j

Appeal

Edouard Le Scroog appealed against the determination of the disciplinary committee of the General Optical Council on 8 February 1982 that, by reason of findings on that date and on 25 June 1980 of infamous conduct in a professional respect and of findings on the former date of publishing advertisements contrary to the General Optical Council (Rules

on Publicity) Order of Council 1981, SI 1981/522, the name of the appellant should be
a erased from the register. The facts are set out in the judgment of the Board.

John Platts-Mills QC and *Edward Irving* for the appellant.
Roderick Adams for the respondents.

LORD FRASER OF TULLYBELTON. This appeal is from a direction of the
b disciplinary committee of the General Optical Council made on 8 February 1982 to the
effect that, by reason of findings made on that date and on 25 June 1980 of infamous
conduct in a professional respect and of findings on the former date of publishing
advertisements contrary to the General Optical Council (Rules on Publicity) Order of
Council 1981, SI 1981/522, the name of the appellant should be erased from the register.

Their Lordships will refer later to the findings made on 25 June 1980 (the 1980
c findings). They will consider first the findings made on 8 February 1982. On that date
the disciplinary committee had before them a total of six charges against the appellant.
They found four of these charges proved. Two (charges 1 and 2) were of infamous
conduct, the conduct alleged being that the appellant had canvassed students at
Hammersmith and West London College of Further Education and at King's College,
London respectively. Two were breaches of the council's rules on publicity by advertising
d in the University College Hospital magazine Too Much (charge 4) and in the Nursing
Mirror (charge 5). The committee made no finding on the remaining two charges but
ordered that they remain on the file. The effect of that order is that the charges were
adjourned sine die.

The appellant's written case included a complaint that he had not received proper
notice of the hearing on 8 February 1982, but that complaint was expressly abandoned
e at the hearing before this Board and it need not be further considered.

It will be convenient to consider first the two charges of infamous conduct by
canvassing. The facts on which the committee reached their decision were as follows.
The appellant had sent, or caused to be sent, to an official of the students' union at each
of the colleges already mentioned a letter. The letters were in identical terms. They bore
the address of his firm, 'Softlens Practice', and contained, inter alia, the following
f paragraphs:

'Dear Secretary,
We are currently selling soft contact lenses from £55 a pair. As this is the lowest
price to be found in England, it should be of interest to students (indeed, many of
our clients have been students) . . .
Please feel free to convey this information to your students.'
g
The letter was signed by a person named Paterson who, the appellant said, had been
employed by him at the time the letters were sent in January and February 1981. The
appellant admitted having caused the letters to be sent. He also admitted that if they
were unsolicited they would constitute canvassing. His defence was that they had been
sent in answer to requests from the students' unions concerned for information about his
h business, and particularly his prices for contact lenses. There was thus raised an issue of
pure fact whether or not the letters had been sent in answer to requests. The committee
decided that issue against the appellant after hearing evidence from the persons who had
been in charge of the correspondence at the students' unions concerned at the relevant
time to the effect that, so far as they were aware, no request had been made to the
appellant or his firm for information such as that contained in the letter. The witness
j from King's College, London, who had been the secretary of the students' union at the
relevant time, said that when he received the letter he had posted it on the notice-board.
In addition to that evidence there is the fact that, in the opinion of their Lordships, the
terms of the letters are more consistent with their having been unsolicited than with
their having been sent in answer to requests. The appellant gave evidence and said that
the letters would have been sent in response to requests for information about the prices

and services that he offered, but that he did not remember specifically instructing the letters to be sent, and he had 'no idea' whether the requests had been written or oral. In *a* the opinion of their Lordships the weight of the evidence was in favour of the view that the letters had been unsolicited and that they constituted canvassing.

The next question is whether the appellant's conduct in canvassing by sending these letters can properly be described as 'infamous in a professional respect'. The practice of canvassing had been expressly condemned by the General Optical Council in their Notes for Guidance (1977 edn) para 75. In the 1981 edition of the Notes for Guidance there is *b* no specific reference to canvassing but there is a general reference in para 78 to the need for maintaining the highest standards of behaviour. Having regard to these notes and to the prohibition in the rules on publicity of advertising, except in accordance with the rules (to be referred to below), their Lordships have no doubt that canvassing may in certain circumstances amount to infamous conduct. In considering whether it did so in the present case there are two matters which are of particular importance. The first is *c* that one of the 1980 findings had been on a charge of canvassing, and, before that finding was made, the appellant had written to the General Optical Council a letter, dated 18 October 1979, in which he apologised for canvassing and said:

> 'I am truly sorry for what has happened and I am prepared to give the Council my solemn assurance that the activity will not recur. I am also prepared to give my personal and solemn assurance that I shall not, in the future, canvass for clients or *d* participate in selective discount schemes.'

The canvassing referred to in charges 1 and 2 was therefore in breach of that solemn assurance and the committee were entitled to regard it as specially deserving of reprobation for that reason. Second, the terms of the letter sent to the two students' unions were open to serious objection. When the appellant was asked about the statement *e* quoted above, to the effect that his price was 'the lowest price to be found in England', he replied that he did not know if that was correct. In cross-examination he said: 'It may be true, it may also be close to the truth, but it is not a downright and blatant lie.' Such carelessness as to the truth of the statement might properly have been taken into account by the committee. Later in the letter there is a statement to the effect that information concerning prices 'would obviously be of benefit to the public who are open to *f* exploitation by some of England's more expensive practices simply through their ignorance'. That statement implied, as the appellant admitted in cross-examination, that there were opticians who were exploiting the public by reason of the public's ignorance. Such implied criticism of other members is a further objectionable feature of the letter.

Counsel for the appellant submitted that the disciplinary committee were not entitled to have regard to the contents of the letters because the charge was simply that he had been guilty of infamous conduct 'in that [he] canvassed students . . . by means of a letter' *g* without any indication that the terms of the letter were to be relied on. Their Lordships reject that submission. In their view the whole circumstances of the canvassing have to be taken into account including the terms of the letters themselves. For these reasons their Lordships consider that the committee were well entitled to hold that the appellant's conduct in sending the letters had been infamous in a professional respect.

Finally, on the question of infamous conduct, counsel for the appellant submitted that *h* the advice on the law given by the legal assessor to the committee after they had retired to consider their findings was erroneous or at least misleading. The note made by the legal assessor of the advice which he had given is before their Lordships. The note is brief but it refers to judgments given in the courts, and the reference must have been intended, and understood, to have been to cases from which counsel on both sides had quoted *j* passages in the judgments when addressing the committee. These cases were *R v General Council of Medical Education and Registration of the United Kingdom* [1930] 1 KB 562 and *Allinson v General Council of Medical Education and Registration* [1894] 1 QB 750, [1891–4] All ER Rep 768, in which the judges explained that infamous conduct by a professional man means serious misconduct, or conduct which is disgraceful or dishonourable. Even without such instruction from reported cases, it must be obvious to any educated person

that 'infamous' is a word implying strong reprobation, and their Lordships have no doubt
a that the members of the committee were well aware of that fact. In these circumstances,
the advice given by the legal assessor is, in the opinion of their Lordships, not open to
criticism on the ground either of insufficiency or inaccuracy.

The result is that, in the opinion of their Lordships, the committee's findings on the
charges of infamous conduct are not shown to have been in any respect erroneous.

Turning now to the charges relating to advertising in the magazine Too Much and in
b the Nursing Mirror, these are brought under the General Optical Council's (Rules on
Publicity) Order of Council 1981. The advertisements are alleged to have been in breach
of rr 3 and 4, and not to have been within any of the exceptions provided by later rules.
Rule 3 prohibits any means of giving publicity, whether by advertisements or not, except
in accordance with the rules. Rule 4, so far as applicable here, provides as follows:

c   'All means of giving publicity to a practice or business, used by registered
opticians ... shall be of a dignified and restrained character and free from any
reference to the efficiency of, or the facilities given by, other registered opticians ...'

It was contended on behalf of the appellant that the advertisements were not in breach
of these rules, and in particular of r 4, because they were of a dignified and restrained
character as required by that rule. The contention raised a question of taste in which
d there may be room for differences of opinion, but it is a matter of objective fact that the
advertisements complained of were prominent, in the case of the Nursing Mirror
advertisement, the most prominent on the page, and in large type. But they were not the
most prominent or in the largest type of any advertisements in the respective periodicals.
It appears to their Lordships that the solution of this question depends on the view that
is taken of the opticians' profession. If, as the appellant maintained, it is to be regarded
e mainly as a trade or business of selling spectacles and contact lenses, then an 'eye-catching'
advertisement is perfectly proper in accordance with ordinary commercial practice. If, as
the General Optical Council maintain, it is to be regarded primarily as a profession,
comparable to the medical profession, then advertisements by opticians should be
designed merely to impart information, and not to attract attention. The reason is that,
if prominent advertisements are allowed, then advertisers will tend to compete, as
f commercial advertisers do, to have the most attractive and the most effective
advertisement. Counsel for the appellant submitted that opticians were not solely
concerned with rendering a service, such as testing eyesight, but that they also sell goods,
and in that respect their profession differs from the medical profession and from most
other professions. Consequently, he said, it was in the public interest for the appellant to
increase the turnover of his business thereby reducing his overheads and enabling him
g to reduce his charges to the public. That is a possible view, although their Lordships note
in passing that an increased turnover, if it led to improved profits, would also benefit the
appellant. But the answer to the contention is that Parliament has entrusted the
disciplinary committee of the Optical Council with the duty of setting the standards
appropriate to the profession, and in their Lordships' opinion that committee is the
proper tribunal to decide this issue. The appellant, having joined the profession, is bound
h to observe the rules which apply to its members. Their Lordships cannot improve on the
explanation given in relation to the architects' profession by Devlin J in *Hughes v
Architects' Registration Council of the United Kingdom* [1957] 2 All ER 436 at 442, [1957] 2
QB 550 at 561–562, as follows:

j   'If a man joins a profession in which the use of trade weapons is barred, and then
proceeds to employ them, he is taking an unfair advantage over his fellows. They
restrain themselves, believing rightly or wrongly that such restraint is essential to
the good health of the profession as a whole; he gets the benefit of their restraint
and fills his purse at their expense. He is defaulting on the obligation, by which
explicitly or impliedly he undertook to be bound, when they made him of their
company. Such conduct could be thought disgraceful not merely by those of the
profession but by outsiders who were not themselves bound by the same standards.'

In the opinion of their Lordships the committee are not shown to have fallen into error in applying the standard which they considered appropriate for professional persons, and *a* not a purely commercial standard, in judging whether the advertisements were dignified and restrained, and in finding that the advertisements were in breach of the rules.

It was accepted by the General Optical Council that the Nursing Mirror was a periodical in which publication of advertisements by members of the profession was permitted under r 5 of the rules of publicity. Rule 5 is in the following terms:

> 'A registered optician or an enrolled body corporate may publish advertisements *b* or other matter relating to his or its practice or business in periodicals circulating wholly or mainly among registered opticians, registered medical practitioners, pharmaceutical chemists, members of professions ancillary to medicine, manufac- turers of or dealers in optical appliances, or employees of registered opticians or enrolled bodies corporate . . .'

It was argued on behalf of the appellant that the magazine Too Much was also a *c* periodical falling within that rule. Having regard to the view already expressed that both advertisements contravened the rules, in respect that they were not dignified and restrained, nothing turns on this further point, but, as it was argued, it is right that their Lordships should express an opinion on it. In their opinion Too Much does not fall within the class of periodicals referred to in r 5. There was evidence from the former *d* editor of that periodical that 600 copies of the particular issue published in June 1981 were printed, that the number of (clinical) students at University College Hospital at that time was about 130 and that the policy of the publishers was to sell the periodical also to doctors, nurses and other professional persons in order to increase its income. Counsel for the appellant submitted that it had not been shown that the circulation of the magazine was not mainly among members of professions ancillary to medicine. Their *e* Lordships do not accept that submission. The evidence as to the actual circulation of the particular issue was quite inconclusive, but the former editor said that the periodical was written by students for students, and the most cursory examination of its contents bears that out. Having regard to the evidence of the editor, and to the nature of the contents of the periodical, their Lordships consider that the proper conclusion is that it circulated mainly among students. Students do not in the opinion of their Lordships constitute a *f* profession. The periodical is therefore not within r 5 and publication of an advertisement in it would not have been permitted even if the advertisement itself had been dignified and restrained.

For these reasons their Lordships are of opinion that there is no reason for interfering with the finding of the disciplinary committee on the four charges which they heard on 8 February 1982. They were in addition to the 1980 charges which had already been found proved. In terms of the Opticians Act 1958, s 11(1)(*b*) and (3) the only penalty *g* which the disciplinary committee could impose was to order that the appellant's name be erased from the register. That is the order that they made and in their Lordships' opinion it is not open to criticism. They will humbly advise Her Majesty that the appeal should be dismissed.

The appellant must pay the respondent's costs of the appeal.   *h*

Appeal dismissed.

Solicitors: *Gersten & Co* (for the appellant); *Hempsons* (for the respondents).

Mary Rose Plummer   Barrister.

Felix v Shiva

a

COURT OF APPEAL, CIVIL DIVISION
WALLER, EVELEIGH AND ACKNER LJJ
5, 6 MAY 1982

b County court – Jurisdiction – Interim payment – Jurisdiction to order interim payment – County court rules not providing for interim payments – Whether equivalent practice of the High Court applicable – Whether county court having jurisdiction to order interim payment – County Courts Act 1959, s 103 – Administration of Justice Act 1969, s 20 – RSC Ord 29, r 10.

In an action in a county court for possession of land, the landlord applied for an interim payment on account of rent or mense profits to be made to him. The landlord contended that the county court had jurisdiction to order such an interim payment because,
c although there was no express provision in the County Court Rules with respect to the making of orders for interim payment, s 103ᵃ of the County Courts Act 1959 applied 'the general principles of practice in the High Court' to county court proceedings where there was no express provision relating to county court proceedings, and the High Court was given such power by RSC Ord 29, r 10ᵇ. The county court judge made the order sought.
d The tenant appealed, contending that the provisions set out in RSC Ord 29, r 10 could not be described as 'general principles of practice in the High Court' since they were specific rules made by the Supreme Court Rule Committee under the specific power conferred on it by s 20ᶜ of the Administration of Justice Act 1969 to make rules enabling the court to order an interim payment to be made.

e **Held** – Since s 20 of the 1969 Act specifically empowered the County Court Rule Committee to make rules enabling the court to order a party to make an interim payment, that was the only method by which the county court could be invested with jurisdiction to make such orders and the fact that the rule committee had not made the appropriate rules did not mean that there was a lacuna in the county court's jurisdiction which could be filled by using the power contained in s 103 of the 1959 Act. The county
f court judge had therefore had no jurisdiction to order the tenant to make an interim payment. The tenant's appeal would accordingly be allowed (see p 265 c d, p 266 f to j and p 267 b to f, post).

Notes

g For the county court rules and the application of High Court rules in the county court, see 10 Halsbury's Laws (4th edn) para 2.

For the County Courts Act 1959, s 103, see 7 Halsbury's Statutes (3rd edn) 367.

For the Administration of Justice Act 1969, s 20, see 25 ibid 797.

As from 1 January 1982 s 20 of the 1969 Act was amended by the Supreme Court Act 1981, s 152(4) and Sch 7 so as to repeal references therein to the power to make rules of
h the Supreme Court with respect to the making of orders for interim payment. That power is now conferred on the Supreme Court Rule Committee by s 32 of the 1981 Act.

Case referred to in judgments

Moore v Assignment Courier Ltd [1977] 2 All ER 842, [1977] 1 WLR 638, CA, Digest (Cont Vol E) 372, 7626a.

j ### Cases also cited

McCreagh v Frearson (1921) 91 LJKB 365.

---

a   Section 103 is set out at p 264 f, post
b   Rule 10, so far as material, is set out at p 264 g h, post
c   Section 20, so far as material, is set out at p 265 e, post

R v Bloomsbury and Marylebone County Court, ex p Villerwest Ltd [1976] 1 All ER 897,
[1976] 1 WLR 362, CA.
Williamson v Rider [1962] 2 All ER 268, [1963] 1 QB 89, CA.

Interlocutory appeal

The defendant, Bijan Tadayan Shiva, appealed against the order of his Honour Judge
Honig made on 4 March 1982 in the Bloomsbury and Marylebone County Court
whereby the judge ordered the defendant to pay the sum of £4,000 to the plaintiff,
Charles Felix, by way of an interim award in the plaintiff's action against the defendant
for arrears of rent in respect of a flat at 63 Redington Road, London NW3 owned by the
plaintiff as landlord and occupied by the defendant as tenant. The facts are set out in the
judgment of Eveleigh LJ.

Jonathan Arkush for the tenant.
Frank Hinks for the landlord.

EVELEIGH LJ delivered the first judgment at the invitation of Waller LJ. This is an
appeal from the judgment of his Honour Judge Honig made on 4 March 1982, when he
determined that he had jurisdiction in this particular case to make an order for interim
payment of money. The claim was a claim for possession by a landlord, and coupled with
that claim was a claim for arrears of rent and, although we have not had the actual
pleadings, I assume for mesne profits also.

An application was made in the Bloomsbury and Marylebone County Court by the
landlord for an interim payment on account of the rent, or mesne profits. On 4 March
1982 the judge ordered the defendant to make an interim payment to the plaintiff for
£4,000 within 21 days, and it is against that order that the defendant now appeals.

This court has been concerned with a very short point of law, namely: has the county
court power to make such an order? The judge considered that he had jurisdiction, or
the power so to order, because there was a similar power in the High Court which he
regarded as being available to the county court by virtue of s 103 of the County Courts
Act 1959. That section reads:

> 'In any case not expressly provided for by or in pursuance of this Act, this general
> principles of practice in the High Court may be adopted and applied to proceedings
> in a county court.'

The relevant order in the High Court is RSC Ord 29, where, in Part II of that order,
the question of interim payments is dealt with and a procedure is laid down for claiming
an interim payment.

The particular provision under which this application would be made is Ord 29, rr 10
and 12. Rule 10(1) reads:

> 'The plaintiff may, at any time after the writ has been served on a defendant and
> the time limited for him to acknowledge service has expired, apply to the Court for
> an order requiring that defendant to make an interim payment.'

Rule 12 reads:

> 'If, on the hearing of an application under rule 10, the Court is satisfied . . . (b) that
> the plaintiff's action includes a claim for possession of land and, if the action
> proceeded to trial, the defendant would be held liable to pay to the plaintiff a sum
> of money in respect of the defendant's use and occupation of the land during the
> pendency of the action, even if a final judgment or order were given or made in
> favour of the defendant; or (c) that, if the action proceeded to trial the plaintiff
> would obtain judgment against the defendant for a substantial sum of money apart
> from any damages or costs, the Court may, if it thinks fit, and without prejudice to
> any contentions of the parties as to the nature or character of the sum to be paid by
> the defendant, order the defendant to make an interim payment of such amount as

a
it thinks just, after taking into account any set-off, cross-claim or counterclaim on which the defendant may be entitled to rely.'

Argument was addressed to the judge on behalf of the defendant to the effect that s 103 of the County Courts Act 1959 did not apply because the Ord 29 provision for an interim payment could not be described as the general principles of practice in the High Court. Before the judge, and here, we have heard argument as to what is meant by the expression 'the general principles of practice'. We have been referred to some cases which
b
were quoted to us by counsel as aids to understand the meaning of those words.

The words are ones which have given difficulty but they are not easily capable of further definition by a court, any more than the word 'procedure' is. That too has given difficulty in deciding precisely what it means, though many of us, or many of those who have practised in the courts, perhaps by instinct recognise what is meant by 'practice' as opposed to 'procedure', when we come across it.
c
For my part, I would not approach this case by attempting any general definition of those words.

The power of the court to order interim payments may, to some, be seen as a principle of practice. But to others, they may not; but whatever the words 'principles of practice' mean in s 103 I do not think that they are apt to cover the power of the court to make interim payments.
d
My reason for saying that is the legislation that has resulted in RSC Ord 29 of the High Court, which has, in its turn, given the court the power and set out the procedure for interim payments. That legislation is to be found in s 20 of the Administration of Justice Act 1969, s 20(1) which reads:

e
'The power to make rules of court under section 99 of the Judicature Act 1925, and the power to make county court rules under section 102 of the County Courts Act 1959, shall each include power by any such rules to make provision for enabling the court in which any proceedings are pending, in such circumstances as may be specified in the rules, to make an order requiring a party to the proceedings to make an interim payment of such amount as may be specified in the order, either by payment into court or (if the order so provides) by paying it to another party to the
f
proceedings.'

As I have said, rules were made in the High Court.

When the power of s 20 was first invoked by the Rule Committee, it did so to provide for interim payment of damages in personal injury cases; subsequently the rules were extended to apply to a wider field of claims. But I do not think that without special statutory provision the court did have the power to make an interim payment; at least it
g
did not regard itself as having that power, that is clear.

Moreover, the power to make rules of court given by s 99 of the Supreme Court of Judicature (Consolidation) Act 1925 was not regarded as giving the committee power to provide for the court to make interim payments. That seems to me to be a reasonable conclusion from the very fact that Parliament thought it necessary to enact s 20 of the 1969 Act.
h
A similar approach was adopted in *Moore v Assignment Courier Ltd* [1977] 2 All ER 842, [1977] 1 WLR 638. In that case the landlord had issued a writ in the High Court and he claimed an interim payment of the rent. At that date the only power to entertain interim payments was contained in the rules relating to personal injury actions. Megaw LJ said ([1977] 2 All ER 842 at 848, [1977] 1 WLR 638 at 645):

j
'Section 99 of the Supreme Court of Judicature (Consolidation) Act 1925 is the section which primarily gives the Rule Committee its statutory power to make rules. Section 99(1) provides: "Rules of Court may be made under this Act for the following purposes . . ."; and then a number of purposes are set out thereafter. The first, (*a*), begins with these words "For regulating and prescribing the procedure (including the method of pleading) and the practice to be followed in the Court of

Appeal and the High Court respectively in all causes and matters whatsoever ...", and so on. That section is referred to in s 20 of the Administration of Justice Act 1969 which by sub-s (1) provides: "The power to make rules of court under section 99 of the Judicature Act 1925, and the power to make county court rules under section 102 of the County Courts Act 1959, shall each include power by any such rules to make provision for enabling the court in which any proceedings are pending, in such circumstances as may be specified in the rules, to make an order requiring a party to the proceedings to make an interim payment of such amount as may be specified in the order, either by payment into court or (if the order so provides) by paying it to another party to the proceedings." So it appears to me to be clear that the extension of the provisions of s 99 of the 1925 Act was necessary, because the power given by s 99 of the 1925 Act to the Rule Committee to make rules as to procedure was not regarded by Parliament as applying to or governing, or as giving the right to make rules in respect of, this matter, for which the powers are thus specifically extended by s 20(1) of the 1969 Act. That being so, this is a matter which Parliament itself has treated for this purpose as being outside "procedure". But it goes beyond being a question of mere words, or of the meaning of "procedure"—a word which always has to be treated with great care, because it has substantially different meanings in different contexts, and, indeed, at times, to different people in the same context. What matters here, as I see it, is that, Parliament having given to the Rule Committee the specific power to make rules in relation to interim payments, there would have been power in the Rule Committee to make a rule that would, or might, have governed the matter in respect of which counsel for the plaintiff invites us to assume that we have inherent jurisdiction. The very fact that that power has then been expressly given to the Rule Committee indicates, to my mind, that, without action by the Rule Committee, this court does not have such a power. The only exercise of that power hitherto by the Rule Committee, so far as we have been told, is the provision to which Sir John Pennycuick has referred, the new provisions of RSC Ord 29, r 9, which are confined to cases of personal injury claims and claims in respect of death.'

That case clearly established that the court had no inherent jurisdiction to make this kind of order. It would follow that the county court has no inherent jurisdiction to make this kind of order.

It has been submitted by counsel on behalf of the landlord that none the less the rules of the county court are wide enough for it to assume such power by passing the particular rule. Those rules are no different in any relevant respect (relevant to this argument) from those of the High Court, and for myself I would follow the judgment of Megaw LJ in that regard and consequently come to the conclusion that the county court rules would not be wide enough to enable that court to give itself this power.

From that it follows that the power of the county court would have to be found in some specific legislation. Regarding s 20 of the 1969 Act as an empowering section (as I do), the source of the county court's jurisdiction to make an interim order would rest on that section, as I see it, and could be gleaned from nowhere else.

Section 20 does not specifically state that the High Court or the county court shall have the power referred to in that section, but it must, by implication, not merely be regarded as a section giving power to the Rule Committee to make the rules referred to therein, but by implication empowering the High Court and the county court to make interim payments, subject to there first being brought into force rules of court as provided for.

If a power is given by statute, and the statute lays down the way in which that power is to be brought into existence, it must be brought into existence by that method and none other. That seems to me to be the short answer to this case.

The method of investing the county court with the jurisdiction which the landlord claims he has is laid down in s 20. The procedure for investing the court with the power has not yet been adopted, and consequently the county court judge, in my opinion, does not possess the power to make an interim order.

For those reasons I would allow this appeal.

a I would just add one word: counsel on behalf of the landlord has said that the court ought to allow this power to be extended to the county court without the necessary formalities because it would be just to do so. I do not find that argument very persuasive, and the fact that the power has been adopted in the High Court does not necessarily mean that it would have been wise at this time, or at the time when the High Court was given the power, for the county court to assume it. There may be a number of policy decisions relating to the speed with which cases are currently tried in the county court

b and the availability of judges to try cases which would provide a reason for the County Court Rules not yet having brought this power into force. I know not, but we are concerned here, as I see it, with the strict interpretation of the relevant statutory provisions, and, for the reasons which I have stated, I would allow the appeal.

ACKNER LJ. I agree. The county court judge, in his very careful judgment, has not

c dealt specifically with s 20 of the Administration of Justice Act 1969, which, like Eveleigh LJ, I consider provides the answer to the question raised in this appeal. That section gave specific power to the rule committees of the High Court and the county court to make rules in relation to interim payments. That power was not to be found in s 99 of the Supreme Court of Judicature (Consolidation) Act 1925 or s 102 of the County Courts Act 1959.

d The High Court has exercised, through the Rule Committee, the power and, by RSC Ord 29, Part II, has provided a procedure under which interim payments can be obtained.

The County Court Rule Committee has not made any rules. In my judgment this is not a lacuna to be filled by the use of s 103 of the County Courts Act 1959. Parliament clearly intended that, if and when those powers were to be exercised in relation to the county courts, they should be exercised through the County Court Rule Committee. The

e reasons why this has not yet been done might be various; it could be that the Rule Committee is awaiting the necessary extension of the county court jurisdiction to make this desirable; or it may be that they were anxious to see how the matter worked out in the High Court, where it has proceeded by stages; or it may be, in addition, that there are certain particular problems relating to the county court and the county court procedure for which special provision has to be made.

f I also, therefore, would allow this appeal.

WALLER LJ. I agree that this appeal should be allowed, for the reasons given by both Eveleigh and Ackner LJJ.

Appeal allowed.

Solicitors: *Ewart Price & Primhak*, Hampstead (for the tenant); *Michael Shapiro & Co*, Golders Green (for the landlord).

Diana Brahams   Barrister.

Desmond v Thorne and others   *a*

QUEEN'S BENCH DIVISION
TAYLOR J
29 MARCH, 7 APRIL 1982

Criminal law – Libel – Leave to commence proceedings – Discretion of judge – Material judge   *b*
entitled to consider in determining whether criteria for leave existing – Criteria for granting leave
consisting of prima facie case to answer and public interest in institution of criminal proceedings
– Libel by newspaper – Whether proposed plea of justification to be taken into account and
weighed against applicant's evidence – Law of Libel Amendment Act 1888, s 8.

On an application under s 8[a] of the Law of Libel Amendment Act 1888 to a judge in   *c*
chambers for leave to commence a prosecution for criminal libel against a newspaper,
the judge, in exercising his discretion, is required to consider all the circumstances and is
not confined to consideration only of the evidence adduced by the applicant. Accordingly,
in considering whether necessary criteria for the grant of leave exist, namely whether
there is a clear prima facie case against the newspaper and whether the public interest
requires the institution of criminal proceedings, the judge is entitled to take into account
a proposed plea of justification by the newspaper and to weigh the evidence adduced in   *d*
support of that plea against evidence adduced by the applicant proving that the words
complained of were published and that, if they are untrue, they amount to a serious libel
(see p 271 *g* to *j* and p 272 *d e g h*, post).

     Goldsmith v Pressdram Ltd [1977] 2 All ER 557 applied.
     Gleaves v Deakin [1979] 2 All ER 497 considered.

  e

Notes
For criminal libel, see 28 Halsbury's Laws (4th edn) para 5, for criminal proceedings for
libel against newspapers, see ibid paras 280–284, and for cases on the subject, see 32
Digest (Reissue) 333–344, 2765–2879.
     For the Law of Libel Amendment Act 1888, s 8, see 19 Halsbury's Statutes (3rd edn)   *f*
32.

Cases referred to in judgment
Gleaves v Deakin [1979] 2 All ER 497, [1980] AC 477, [1979] 2 WLR 665, HL.
Goldsmith v Pressdram Ltd [1977] 2 All ER 557, [1977] QB 83, [1976] 3 WLR 191, 32
     Digest (Reissue) 343, 2879.
R v Wicks [1936] 1 All ER 384, CCA, 32 Digest (Reissue) 333, 2765.   *g*

Application for leave to institute criminal proceedings
By an application dated 9 December 1981 Paul Desmond applied to a judge in chambers
under the Law of Libel Amendment Act 1888 for leave to commence a prosecution for
criminal libel, in respect of an alleged libel on him published in the Sunday People
newspaper on 15 November 1981, against the first and second respondents, Frank Thorne   *h*
and Len Adams, as the authors of the libel, against the third respondent, Geoffrey
Pinnington, as the editor of the newspaper, and against the fourth respondent, Odham
Newspapers Ltd, as the publishers of the newspaper. The application was heard in
chambers but judgment was given by Taylor J in open court. The facts are set out in the
judgment.

  j

Mr Michael Mullins, solicitor, for the applicant.
Desmond Browne for the respondents.

                                                    Cur adv vult

a   Section 8 is set out at p 271 *d*, post

7 April. **TAYLOR J** read the following judgment: This is an application by Paul
a   Desmond for leave to bring proceedings for criminal libel against the respondents. The
application was made in chambers, but, at the request of counsel, I agreed to give my
decision and reasons in open court. Of the respondents, Frank Thorne and Len Adams
are reporters, Geoffrey Pinnington is the editor, and Odhams Newspapers Ltd are the
proprietors of the Sunday People. No point of distinction has been raised as between the
two reporters and the other respondents. It seems to be alleged that they were all
b   responsible for the publication in that newspaper on Sunday, 15 November 1981 of the
article complained of, which I shall read in full:

> 'BULLY BOASTS "I BEAT UP TRAGIC DEB"
>
>   Society girl Jessica Kitson was constantly beaten up during a stormy love affair
> shortly before her tragic death. And the bully who gave her a mass of bruises claims
> c   that he was trying to frighten her off drugs. "I hate drugs and addicts and when I
> saw the disgusting state she was in I just lost my temper," said Dublin-born Paul
> Desmond between sinking pints of Guinness at his local in Chelsea. "I couldn't help
> myself. I couldn't keep my hands off her. I would beat her up because it was the
> only way I knew to stop her." Three months after former Deb of the Year Jessica
> fled her tormentor, she was found dead at her home in West London. Less than a
> d   month after her death, Desmond was trying to sell his story to Fleet Street for
> £3,000. The Sunday People has not paid Desmond a penny for what he told us.
> Erin Pizzey who took Jessica into her home for battered wives in Chiswick says:
> "Jessica's face was smashed in. She was a real mess. I've seen bad beatings, but this
> was the worst. Any man who could inflict such damage on another human being is
> in need of medical treatment himself." The beatings began last June two weeks after
> e   42-year-old heavy-drinking Desmond moved into Jessica's back street home in
> Shepherd's Bush. "I regularly blacked her eyes—I was so frustrated with her drug-
> taking and drinking," said Desmond. "Then we'd make love. She had lost her sex
> urge because of her drug addiction. I don't suppose we made love more than half a
> dozen times in the two months. Jessica was like a child, crying out for affection. As
> long as I cuddled her in bed at night, what went before meant nothing. She told
> f   me: 'I would not mind if you blacked my eyes every day, as long as you don't reject
> me physically.'" Desmond said that Jessica did manage to kick the habit—for three
> days. Then she went on an "almighty drinking binge." "I kept telling her that if she
> carried on she would be dead in six months," he went on. "But I don't feel a bit
> guilty. I didn't really love her, you see. I was getting over a heavy love affair with a
> girl in Greece. I was attracted to her, but I can't love two women at once. To me
> g   there's nothing like a bit of violence to turn a woman on." The boastful bully also
> claimed that he beat up a couple of men he suspected of supplying Jessica with hard
> drugs. After that, he said, he was afraid Jessica's drug pedlar friends would come
> after him. "I slept with a knife under the pillow;" he said, "and for a time, even
> carried a gun." After her spell at Mrs. Pizzey's Jessica phoned the police that
> Desmond was still threatening her. The drunken Irishman was arrested and fined
> h   £15 at Marylebone Court. In her final weeks Jessica met and fell in love with South
> African Rex Potter and they planned to marry. It was Mr. Potter who found her
> dead at her home in Oaklands Road last month. She was 34. Her three-year-old son
> Wolfe was asleep on the sofa in the next room. Jessica's Godfather was the late Paul
> Getty, once the world's richest man. Her mother was left £469,000 in oil shares and
> £8,000 a year for life in his will. Two days before Jessica died Desmond married,
> j   for £500, a Polish hotel chambermaid who needed a work permit. He said: "For
> five hundred quid, I'd have married a chimpanzee."'

That is the article. It is flanked in that edition of the newspaper by photographs both of
the applicant and of Jessica Kitson.
    I have read the affidavits sworn by the applicant and two witnesses in support of his
application. I have also read the affidavits of the first three respondents and of a number

of witnesses who support them. The following facts are unchallenged: the applicant is a
poet. Miss Jessica Kitson was a god-daughter of the millionaire Paul Getty. In the summer   *a*
of 1981 the applicant was living with Jessica. She was addicted to drugs. On a day in July
the applicant assaulted her so as to cause two black eyes. As a result Jessica went, with her
young son, to Mrs Erin Pizzey's home for battered wives and stayed there between 10
and 15 July. She then returned to the applicant. But he made further threats on her as a
result of which he was brought before the Marylebone magistrates on 16 July. There he
pleaded guilty to a charge of threatening behaviour and was fined. Jessica left him and   *b*
took up with a South African mentioned in the article. There was talk of marriage. She
died on 19 October, aged 34. On 23 October the Daily Mail published an article which
referred to a beating-up by her boyfriend and the stay with Mrs Pizzey, but the applicant's
name was not mentioned. On Friday, 30 October the applicant telephoned the Sunday
People and offered to sell his story if the paper was prepared to pay. As a result the
respondent Adams was dispatched to interview the applicant. Adams was handed a 20-   *c*
page typescript by the applicant, who, according to him, asked for £3,000. There was
then a brief interview and Adams returned to his office with the typescript. He later
telephoned the applicant, offering him £200 for a news story, but that was rejected. On
3 November at an editorial conference the respondent Pinnington decided to publish an
exposé of the applicant, and, following guidelines laid down by the Press Council,
resolved to pay the applicant nothing for what he had written and said. Adams now   *d*
being on holiday, the respondent Thorne was sent on 5 November to conduct a further
interview with the applicant. The interview began in a studio and ended in a public
house. On the return of Adams from holiday he and Thorne produced, together, the
article complained of. It was held over for a week and published on 15 November. The
applicant himself wrote to the respondents complaining of the article. He engaged a
solicitor, who took up the complaint, and he wrote to the Press Council. The summons   *e*
was issued on 9 December.

On these agreed facts, therefore, the applicant accepted that he did, at any rate on one
occasion, assault Jessica severely enough to blacken both her eyes and send her in search
of succour, that he did on another occasion plead guilty to a criminal charge of
threatening her, that hard on her death he did offer to the press, for money, his account
of their stormy relationship. Moreover, he does not challenge that for £500 he married   *f*
a Polish chambermaid who needed a work permit. What he does challenge in his
affidavit, and this forms the basis of the application, is the accuracy of the article as to
what he said when interviewed by Adams and Thorne. In particular, he denies having
assaulted Jessica more than once, or having said that he did. Various remarks are
attributed to him in the article which he never made; others are taken out of context.
The result, he says, was to portray him as a habitually violent drunken bully, a braggart   *g*
who was mercenary, callous and unfeeling. His two witnesses support to a considerable
extent his account of the interviews by Adams and Thorne.

The affidavits sworn on behalf of the respondents, however, support and stand by the
contents of the article, and I am told by counsel that if this application were to be granted
the respondents' intentions are to plead justification. There is, therefore, a head-on
conflict of evidence, except as to the unchallenged facts I have recited. Those include the   *h*
handing over by the applicant to Adams of this 20-page script now exhibited to Mr
Adams's affidavit. That script, which it is accepted was typed with a view to publication
for reward, has this title: 'My life with Jessica Kitson—the "I don't care" girl. I predicted
she would be dead within six months. She died in half that time. By Paul Desmond.'

Counsel appearing on behalf of the respondents has pointed to a number of passages
in the script which he says are to the very same effect as passages complained of as   *j*
fabrications in the article. There are other parts of the script which counsel for the
respondents says are consistent with the reporters' accounts of what was said to them. For
example, there are passages describing, with apparent relish, how the applicant beat up
various men. At another point the applicant opines that there is nothing like a bit of
violence to turn a woman on. It is not necessary for me to go seriatim through the
passages which were relied on by counsel for the respondents.

The precise nature of criminal libel was considered by Wien J in *Goldsmith v Pressdram*
a *Ltd* [1977] 2 All ER 557, [1977] 1 QB 83 and more recently by the House of Lords in
Gleaves v Deakin [1979] 2 All ER 497, [1980] AC 477. It was long thought that to amount
to a crime the libel must be calculated to provoke a breach of the peace. That view was
rejected in *R v Wicks* [1936] 1 All ER 384. The decision in *Wicks's* case was applied in
Goldsmith's case and was approved by the House of Lords in *Gleaves v Deakin*. It is now
clear that the publication of written words which are seriously defamatory is capable of
b amounting to criminal libel. Although Viscount Dilhorne took a contrary view, some of
their Lordships indicated in *Gleaves v Deakin* that the gravity of the libel must be such as
to require the intervention of the Crown in the public interest. Whether that is generally
so does not affect this case, in view of the principles affecting newspaper cases which
certainly do involve consideration of public interest, as I shall indicate later.

It is not disputed here that the respondents published the article complained of.
c Moreover, I think it clear that, if untrue, the article is capable of constituting a serious
libel. It is now therefore necessary, since this case concerns a newspaper, to consider how
to approach the exercise of judicial discretion to allow or disallow the institution of
criminal proceedings.

Section 8 of the Law of Libel Amendment Act 1888 reads:

d
'No criminal prosecution shall be commenced against any proprietor, publisher,
editor, or any person responsible for the publication of a newspaper for any libel
published therein without the order of a Judge at Chambers being first had and
obtained. Such application shall be made on notice to the person accused, who shall
have an opportunity of being heard against such application.'

The proper approach to an application was considered by Wien J in *Goldsmith v*
e *Pressdram Ltd* [1977] 2 All ER 557 at 562, [1977] 1 QB 83 at 88, where he said:

'All the argument in this case has turned on how my discretion should be
exercised. I have been invited by counsel on both sides to lay down principles for
the guidance of others who may have to decide this somewhat difficult question. I
decline to lay down principles for the guidance of others for that would mean that
by so doing I would curtail the discretion that any judge might have in the future.
f The very essence of a discretion is that it is a discretion to be exercised in all the
circumstances of a particular case. The discretion has to be exercised judicially and
not capriciously, but if one were to lay down principles for the guidance of others it
would have the inevitable effect of diminishing the ambit of the discretion that
must be open to every judge who hears an application of this sort. For the benefit of
the parties in this case, and for my own benefit as well, I think I ought to state that
g there are principles that can be extracted from all the cases that have been cited, that
should influence me one way or the other in this particular case . . . First, before a
discretion can be exercised in favour of an applicant who wishes to institute criminal
proceedings in respect of a libel, which he contends is criminal, there must be a clear
prima facie case. What I mean by that is that there must be a case to go before a
criminal court that is so clear at first sight that it is beyond argument that there is a
h case to answer. Secondly, the libel must be a serious one, so serious that it is proper
for the criminal law to be invoked. It may be a relevant factor that it is unusually
likely for the libel to provoke a breach of the peace, although that is not a necessary
ingredient at all. Thirdly, the question of the public interest must be taken into
account, so that the judge has to ask himself the question: "Does the public interest
require the institution of criminal proceedings?" What is not appropriate, in my
j judgment, is the question whether damages might or might not afford an adequate
remedy to a complainant. I consider that that question is irrelevant. Once one
arrives at the conclusion that the criminal law ought to be invoked, then it is not a
private case between individuals: the state has an interest and the state has a part in
it.'

I would adopt every word of that passage. Apart from the three broad principles laid down by Wien J, I agree that it is undesirable to attempt a more detailed formulation of the criteria to be applied in the exercise of an unfettered discretion.

But a dispute has arisen in the present case as to what material a judge is entitled to consider in applying Wien J's three principles. Mr Mullins, on behalf of the applicant, argues that a clear prima facie case involves a consideration only of the evidence of the applicant. He says that once it is proved that the respondents have published the article, and that the article is capable of amounting, if the words are untrue, to a serious libel, the application should be granted without more. He says that the only purpose of s 8 is to guard against a vexatious or frivolous criminal prosecution. In particular, he argues that evidence on behalf of the respondents in support, for example, of a proposed plea of justification ought not to be weighed in the exercise of discretion. He seeks to support that argument by reference to two statutory provisions. By s 6 of the Libel Act 1843, a defence of justification to a charge of criminal libel can be raised on indictment only, and if there is an express plea that the words are true and their publication was for the public benefit. Section 4 of the Newspaper Libel and Registration Act 1881 allows committing justices, in a case against a newspaper, to receive evidence in support of such a proposed plea of justification. If, having heard that evidence, they think there is a strong or probable presumption the jury would acquit, they may dismiss the case.

From these provisions Mr Mullins argues that the first time justification can be considered is at the trial on indictment in most cases and before the committing justices in a newspaper case. Earlier than that, he says, it cannot come into any reckoning. Therefore, in effect, a judge faced with an application under s 8 should wear blinkers and look only at the case for the applicant. In my view this simplistic approach is wholly misconceived. A judge's function under s 8 is to decide whether or not a prosecution should be instituted. To do that, he is entitled, indeed bound, to look at all the circumstances before coming to a conclusion whether there is a clear prima facie case.

It is significant that, before s 8 of the 1888 Act, the equivalent provision was s 3 of the Newspaper Libel and Registration Act 1881. That required leave to be obtained from the Director of Public Prosecutions before a criminal libel could be charged against a newspaper. Because this restriction proved of little practical value, the task was entrusted to a judge in chambers by the later, 1888 Act, by s 8(1). In *Gleaves v Deakin* [1979] 2 All ER 497 at 502, [1980] AC 477 at 488, however, Viscount Dilhorne expressed disapproval of giving a judge the responsibility for the institution of prosecutions and suggested instead that leave of the Attorney General or the Director of Public Prosecutions should be required in all criminal libel cases, a view echoed by all their Lordships and said to be required, moreover, by art 10(2) of the European Convention for the Protection of Human Rights and Fundamental Freedoms (TS 71 (1953); Cmd 8969).

It would be absurd if the Director of Public Prosecutions, in considering whether to institute criminal proceedings, can, and does, look at all the circumstances and probable outcome of a prosecution, but a judge, performing a similar task, must look only at the evidence on one side. I have no doubt that in considering whether there is a clear prima facie case I must look at all the circumstances. Likewise in considering whether the public interest requires the institution of criminal proceedings. Adopting that approach and applying the principles to the facts of the present case, I am far from satisfied that there is here a case so clear as to be, beyond argument, a case to answer. The admitted facts take much of the sting out of the article. The applicant's own script contains passages which tend to confirm both the tenor and some of the detail of the article. The affidavit evidence, not only of the respondents but of independent witnesses, further tends to undermine the reliability of the evidence for the applicant. Furthermore, I am quite satisfied that this is not a case in which the public interest requires the institution of criminal proceedings.

In *Goldsmith's* case the applicant's position was such as to make his integrity a matter of general public interest. The article complained of alleged a conspiracy to pervert the course of justice. The respondents had admitted the article was untrue but had nevertheless pursued a campaign of vilification against the applicant. None of those

elements is present here. Nor are there, in my judgment, any other features in this case
a to justify the bringing of criminal proceedings, let alone require it.
    This application is therefore refused.

Application refused.

Solicitors: *Michael J Mullins & Co* (for the applicant); *Bindman & Partners* (for the
b respondents).

K Mydeen Esq   Barrister.

c

Italmare Shipping Co v Ocean Tanker Co Inc (No 2)

d # The Rio Sun (No 2)

QUEEN'S BENCH DIVISION (COMMERCIAL COURT)
PARKER J
4, 11 NOVEMBER 1981

e *Shipping – Time charterparty – Withdrawal of vessel for non-payment of hire – Notice of*
withdrawal – Charterparty providing that owners to give 48 hours' notice before withdrawing
vessel for non-payment of hire – Charterers notifying owners of claim to set off certain payments
and disbursements against cost of hire – Owners withdrawing vessel without giving notice –
Whether notification of claim to set off amounting to declaration of intention not to pay hire –
Whether charterers waiving right to notice by refusing to pay hire – Whether notification of claim
f *to set off giving rise to promissory estoppel – Whether implied clear and unequivocal representation*
that owners did not need to give notice.

By a time charterparty dated 26 February 1980 in the standard New York Produce
Exchange form but providing for arbitration in London, the owners chartered a vessel to
the charterers for two transatlantic voyages. Under the terms of the charterparty, hire
was payable semi-monthly in advance and, in the event of the charterers failing to pay
g the hire punctually or regularly, the owners were to be at liberty to withdraw the vessel
from the charterers. The charterparty further provided, however, by an 'anti-technicality
clause', that if the hire was not received when due the owners were to give the charterers
48 hours' notice to rectify the default before exercising the right of withdrawal. The
charterers failed to pay an instalment of hire due, and the owners sent a telex to them
stating that their bankers were unable to confirm the receipt of hire and asking for
h details. The charterers replied by telex that they were entitled to set off against the hire
due certain payments and disbursements which more than covered the hire. The owners
thereupon gave notice withdrawing the vessel immediately from the charterers' service
without giving the 48 hours' notice required by the anti-technicality clause. At the
ensuing arbitration, the arbitrator held that, although the owners' telex was insufficient
j notice under the anti-technicality clause, the owners were entitled to insist on
withdrawing the vessel immediately because the charterers had by their telex waived
any right to notice under the anti-technicality clause, since the owners were reasonably
entitled to take the view that such notice would have served no useful purpose because
of the charterers' declared intention not to make any payment. The charterers obtained
leave to appeal. At the hearing of the appeal the owners contended that the charterers'

telex was a clear statement that the charterers would not pay the hire due and therefore
amounted to an implied clear and unequivocal representation that the owners did not
need to give a notice under the anti-technicality clause before exercising their right of
withdrawal. They further contended that they were also absolved from the need to give
notice under the principle that the law did not compel a person to do that which was
useless and unnecessary.

Held – The appeal would be allowed for the following reasons—

(1) The anti-technicality clause required the owners to give the charterers 48 hours'
notice 'to rectify the cause for such delay' and, although the notice did not need to refer
in terms to the anti-technicality clause, it nevertheless had to make clear that the owners
required the cause of the delay to be rectified within 48 hours, failing which the vessel
might be withdrawn. The owners' telex was no more than an inquiry as to what had
happened to the hire, and to construe such an inquiry as a notice to rectify the cause of
the delay would be to deprive the anti-technicality clause of its clearly intended purpose
of providing protection to the charterers against the vessel being suddenly withdrawn
without any warning (see p 277 *e* to *g* and p 279 *f* to *j*, post).

(2) The charterers' telex was merely an explanation of why the hire had not been paid
and, even if it amounted to a declaration of their intention not to pay, it still did not
amount to a clear and unequivocal representation, either expressed or implied, that the
owners need not give notice under the anti-technicality clause before withdrawing the
vessel. The charterers' telex neither constituted a waiver nor gave rise to a promissory
estoppel. Furthermore the owners could not rely on any so-called 'futility principle' that
the law did not compel a person to do that which was useless or unnecessary, because
even if that were a general all-embracing and unqualified principle it did not apply where
one party was seeking to be absolved from complying with a clause inserted for the
benefit of the other party when the other party had not in fact received any benefit from
the clause (see p 278 *b* to *e* and p 279 *b* to *f* and *h j*, post); *Lickiss v Milestone Motor Policies at
Lloyds* [1966] 2 All ER 972 distinguished.

Notes

For waiver generally, see 9 Halsbury's Laws (4th edn) paras 571–574 and 16 ibid para
1471, and for cases on the subject, see 12 Digest (Reissue) 544–545, 3796–3806 and 20
ibid 901–902, 6707–6712.

Cases referred to in judgment

Braithwaite v Foreign Hardwood Co [1905] 2 KB 543, CA, 12 Digest (Reissue) 545, 3801.
Italmare Shipping Co v Ocean Tanker Co Inc, The Rio Sun [1982] 1 All ER 517, [1982] 1 WLR
158, CA.
Lickiss v Milestone Motor Policies at Lloyds [1966] 2 All ER 972, sub nom *Barrett Bros (Taxis)
Ltd v Davies* [1966] 1 WLR 1334, CA, 29 Digest (Reissue) 613, 5346.
Sinason-Teicher Inter-American Grain Corp v Oilcakes and Oilseeds Trading Co Ltd [1954] 3
All ER 468, [1954] 1 WLR 1394, CA, 39 Digest (Repl) 732, 2118.
Woodhouse AC Israel Cocoa Ltd SA v Nigerian Produce Marketing Co Ltd [1972] 2 All ER 271,
[1972] AC 741, [1972] 2 WLR 1090, HL, 3 Digest (Reissue) 186, 1126.

Appeal award

Italmare Shipping Co, the charterers under a time charterparty made in Oslo between
Ocean Tanker Co Inc of Monrovia as disponent owners of the Greek motorship Rio Sun
on 26 February 1980 in the New York Produce Exchange form amended to provide for
arbitration in London, appealed pursuant to the order of Robert Goff J dated 11 June
1981 and affirmed by the Court of Appeal (Lord Denning MR, Shaw and Griffiths LJJ)
([1982] 1 All ER 517, [1982] 1 WLR 158) on 31 July 1981 granting the charterers leave
to appeal against the award of the arbitrator, Mr Clifford A L Clark, dated 3 March 1981
granting the owners a declaration that they had lawfully and properly withdrawn the

a vessel from the service of the charterers on 29 May 1980. The facts are set out in the judgment.

Stewart Boyd QC and Timothy Young for the charterers.
Johan Steyn QC and David Mildon for the owners.

Cur adv vult

b

11 November. **PARKER J** read the following judgment: This is an appeal under the Arbitration Act 1979 from an interim award of Mr Clifford Clark dated 3 March 1981. The relevant facts are very short.

The appellant charterers, Italmare Shipping Co, by a time charterparty dated 26
c February 1980, chartered the motor ship Rio Sun from the respondent owners, Ocean Tanker Co Inc, who were disponent owners. The charter was, initially, for one transatlantic round voyage, but by an addendum dated 21 March 1980 it was extended, at an increased rate of hire, to cover a second round voyage in direct continuation of the first. Hire was payable semi-monthly in advance to Williams & Glyn's Bank Ltd, 5–10 Great Tower Street, London, for the credit of disponent owners. In the events which
d happened, hire was payable on the 6th and the 22nd of each month.

The first round voyage was duly completed at 1700 hrs on 14 May 1980, and the second round voyage commenced at that time. On 6 May the charterers had duly paid the hire at the rate for the first voyage up to 22 May. As that voyage had terminated and the next, at the higher rate, had begun on 14 May, the owners, on 16 May, requested the charterers to include, in the advance payment of hire due on 22 May, the difference
e between the first and second voyage rate for the period from 14 to 22 May.

On 22 May the next instalment of hire fell due, which, together with the amount requested on 16 May, made a total sum then said to be due of $US218,773·75. No payment of that sum, or any part of it, was made by the charterers on that day or at any material time thereafter.

Clause 5 of the charterparty provided that the owners, failing the punctual and regular
f payment of hire, should be at liberty to withdraw the vessel from the service of the charterers without prejudice to any claim the owners might otherwise have against them.

Such liberty was, however, subject to cl 30 (referred to in earlier proceedings as, and generally known as, an anti-technicality clause), which provided as follows:

g 'If hire not received when due, Owners to give Charterers 48 hours notice in order to rectify that cause for such delay, before exercising their rights under clause 5. Charterers liberty to deduct from final hire payment estimated cost of bunkers remaining on board and estimated amount of disbursements for Owners' account for which Charterers have not yet received vouchers, but full supporting documents to be submitted within reasonable time.'

h As from 23 May, the owners thus had the option, subject to giving the necessary notice under cl 30, to withdraw the vessel from the charterers' service. On 27 May at 1418 hrs the owners' brokers telexed (telex A) the charterers' brokers as follows:

'OWNS BANKERS UNABLE CONFIRM RECEIPT HIRE DUE 22/5 TOGETHER WITH BALANCE
DUE FROM PERIOD 6/5 – 22/5 KINDLY URGE ADV FULL DETAILS.'

j At 1605 hrs on the same day the charterers' brokers replied (telex B):

'THKS URS REF PAYMENT CHRTS ARE PRESENTLY CHECKING WITH THEIR BANKERS AND
WILL REVERT SOONEST WE HEAR WITH REQUESTED INFO.'

At 1745 hrs, also on the same day, the charterers' brokers telexed to the owners (telex C) the following provisional statement:

'VESSEL PAIED [sic] TILL 21-5-80. EXECTED [sic] TO BE REDELIVERED TO OWNERS ON 18TH AT LE HAVRE/ROUEN RANGE.

HIRE FM 21–5 TO 18–6 = 28 DAYS × 13950 = DOLL.	390600·00
DIFFERENCE ON PREVIOUS REMITTANCE	7964·38
BONUS FOR HOLDS CLEANING	5000·00

DOLL. 403564·38

LESS 2,50 PCT ADDRESS COMM = DOLL.	9963·86	
BUNKER ON REDELIVERY		
F.O. 200 × 175	350000·00	
D.O. 150 × 350	52500·00	
OFF HIRE AND		
CONSUMPTION AZORES	20000·00	
PROVISIONAL DISBURSEMENT	10000·00	

	DOLL.	442463·86
BALANCE CHARTERERS FAVOUR		38909·48 [sic]

	DOLL.	442463·86	DOLL. 442463·86

BALANCE WILL BE ADJUSTED ON REDELIVERY WHEN WE HAVE EXACT FIGURES FOR BUNKER AND EXACT TIME DELIVERY.'

At 1741 hrs on 29 May the owners' brokers telexed to the charterers' brokers passing on a telex received by them from the owners as follows:

'REFERENCE CLAUSE 30 AND CLAUSE 5 OF C/P AND NOTICE NON RECEIPT HIRE DATED 27TH, HIRE STILL UNRECEIVED THEREFORE, RELUCTANTLY, WE WITHDRAW VSL FROM THE SERVICE OF THE CHARTERERS AND HOLD CHRS RESPONSIBLE FOR ANY DAMAGES WE MAY INCUR.'

The question for determination by the arbitrator was whether the owners were entitled to withdraw the vessel from the service of the charterers when, by their last-mentioned telex, they purported to do so.

The owners contend that they were so entitled on the grounds (i) that telex A was a valid notice under cl 30, (ii) that by telex B the charterers had waived further compliance with cl 30 or were stopped from asserting that telex A was an insufficient notice, (iii) that by telex C the charterers had waived any right to a notice under cl 30, or the owners had been absolved from giving such a notice.

The arbitrator concluded in a reasoned award that telex A was an insufficient notice under cl 30 'being only an enquiry of the Charterers' for full details of the non-receipt of the hire . . .' As to telex B, he said no more (and that in brackets) than that it 'indicated that they [the charterers] were taking it [telex A] as notice under Clause 30 in that they were seeking to rectify the situation'. He concluded, however, that by telex C the charterers—

'had waived any right to a notice under clause 30, as a reasonable Owner would have been entitled to take the view that such a notice would have served no useful purpose in view of the Charterers declared intention not to make any payment.'

Having further held, it is conceded rightly, that the deductions set out in telex C were not permissible and that the hire claimed was correctly due and had not been punctually and regularly paid, the arbitrator awarded by way of declaration that the owners lawfully and properly withdrew the vessel from the service of the charterers on 29 May.

The charterers sought and obtained leave to appeal from this award from Robert Goff J. On the application for leave, the owners do not appear to have argued that telex B was of any significance although they did contend that even if the arbitrator was wrong

as to the effect of telex C the withdrawal was justified on the ground that telex A was a
a   sufficient notice.

The owners appealed to the Court of Appeal against the grant of leave to appeal (see
[1982] 1 All ER 517, [1982] 1 WLR 158). Again it does not appear to have been argued
that telex B was of any significance but the other two points were again canvassed. The
owners' appeal was dismissed, as was a subsequent petition to the House of Lords after
the Court of Appeal had itself refused leave to appeal to that House.

b   Although the possible significance of telex B was apparently mentioned to the
arbitrator, it appears then to have dropped out of the picture until it was raised again by
way of amendment to the owners' motion at the commencement of the hearing before
me. I shall consider it after I have dealt with the other two matters.

Telex A

This was in terms no more than an inquiry as to what had happened to the hire. In the
c   Court of Appeal, Lord Denning MR said in regard to it ([1982] 1 All ER 517 at 522,
[1982] 1 WLR 158 at 164):

'I agree with the arbitrator, Mr Clifford Clark, when he said in this case: "A notice
under cl 30 need not be legally perfect in its draftsmanship, but it must be clear
beyond doubt that the owners are putting the charterers on notice that, if the correct
d   hire is not paid within the 48 hours' grace, they will withdraw the vessel." Applying
these considerations, the [owners'] telex on 27 May was not a notice sufficient to
satisfy cl 30. I think a notice must be as clear as an ultimatum. It must tell the
charterers: "Unless you pay the hire due within 48 hours, we will withdraw the
vessel." The telex here did not do so.'

Shaw LJ agreed with the judgment of Lord Denning MR. Their views, although not
e   expressed to be provisional, must be taken to be so. Nevertheless they are of great weight.
Respectfully, I fully agree with them. Clause 30 requires the owners to give the charterers
48 hours' notice 'in order to rectify the cause for such delay'. I accept the submission that
a notice need not in terms refer to cl 30, but it must make clear that the owners require
the cause of delay to be rectified within 48 hours, failing which the vessel may be
withdrawn. To construe telex A as a notice would be to rob cl 30 of its clearly intended
f   protection to charterers against the vessel being suddenly withdrawn without warning.
A document which says no more than that the hire has not yet been received and requests
information about the position cannot reasonably be interpreted as a notice, 48 hours' or
otherwise, to rectify the cause of the delay.

Telex C

g   Counsel for the charterers submitted that, whether the matter was treated as waiver or
promissory estoppel, it was necessary for it to be shown, at the least, (i) that the telex on
its true construction constituted a clear and unequivocal representation that the charterers
would not insist on compliance with cl 30 or released the owners from their obligation
to comply with that clause, (ii) that the owners, in giving no notice after receipt of that
telex, relied on the representation, (iii) that such reliance was reasonable.

h   These propositions were derived from *Woodhouse AC Israel Cocoa Ltd SA v Nigerian
Produce Marketing Co Ltd* [1972] 2 All ER 271, [1972] AC 741. I accept them. They were
indeed not seriously disputed.

Counsel further submitted that the telex could not be so construed, that even if it
could be it had not been so construed by the arbitrator and that there were in any event
no findings to support reliance on it reasonable or otherwise.

j   For the owners, counsel submitted that the telex should be, and had been, interpreted
by the arbitrator to whose views great weight should on this matter (albeit not on the
matter of telex A) be given, and that if the award, contrary to his submission, was short
of necessary further findings it should be sent back. He put his argument on the first of
the three requirements in this way. The telex, he said, was a clear statement that the
charterers would not pay the hire due, and the arbitrator had so found. Such a statement
contained a necessarily implied clear and unequivocal representation that the owners

need not give a notice under cl 30 before exercising their right of withdrawal under cl 5, and, even if the court would itself construe the telex differently from the arbitrator, it should not interfere unless it concluded that no reasonable arbitrator could have reached the conclusion reached by him.

It is clear that the arbitrator concluded that the telex constituted a declared intention not to pay, but he went no further than this. All he said was that the telex constituted a waiver because a reasonable owner would have been entitled to take the view that such a notice would have served no useful purpose in view of the charterers' declared intention. He did not say that these owners took such a view or that they refrained from giving a notice because they had taken such a view. This is hardly surprising for the withdrawal telex of 29 May shows clearly that owners were acting on the basis that telex A was a valid notice, not that telex C absolved them from giving notice at all. There are thus insufficient findings to support the waiver argument. But, in my judgment, the strong, albeit provisional, views expressed by the Court of Appeal that the arbitrator was wrong on waiver are reinforced by further argument rather than the reverse. There was admittedly no express representation of the required character, and I find it impossible to imply one. The owners had asked to be advised of the situation regarding hire due. They had been told that the charterers were checking and that they would be given the information as soon as possible. They then received telex C. This appears to me to be no more than an explanation why the hire had not been paid. It is accepted that it was an explanation which did not justify non-payment. It may even be that it was a declaration, as at the time it was sent, of an intention not to pay, but I can see no possible ground on which it could be construed as an implied clear unequivocal representation that the owners need not give a cl 30 notice before withdrawing the vessel.

The arbitrator was, in my judgment, clearly wrong in holding that the telex constituted a waiver. Nor did it give rise to any promissory estoppel.

It was no doubt in the realisation that there were well-nigh insuperable difficulties in supporting the award on the basis of either waiver or promissory estoppel that counsel for the owners put forward as his principle argument the contention that the giving of a cl 30 notice was in the present case excused on the basis of an alleged principle of law which he described as the 'futility principle'.

This alleged principle, which was said to be of general application, is founded on the judgment of Lord Denning MR in *Lickiss v Milestone Motor Policies at Lloyds* [1966] 2 All ER 972, [1966] 1 WLR 1334, with which judgment Danckwerts LJ agreed.

In that case, a motor cyclist who had had a collision with a taxi cab was insured at Lloyds. It was a condition of the policy that he should forward immediately any letter, notice of intended prosecution, writ, summons or process relating thereto. The policy provided that due observance and fulfilment of its conditions was a condition precedent to any liability of the underwriters. The motor cyclist received, but did not pass on to his insurers, both a notice of intended prosecution and a summons which was returnable at the magistrates' court on 2 July. On 18 June the insurers were sent by the police a letter informing them that proceedings were pending against the motor cyclist and would be heard on 2 July. As a result, the insurers wrote to the motor cyclist on 23 June stating that they understood proceedings were being taken against him on 2 July, and continuing: 'It would be appreciated if you would let us know why you have not notified us of these proceedings since we will wish to arrange your defence.' The insurers later repudiated liability for non-compliance with the condition requiring that the documents should be forwarded. Lord Denning MR said ([1966] 2 All ER 972 at 975, [1966] 1 WLR 1334 at 1339):

> 'First, it was unnecessary for the motor cyclist to send the documents to the insurers. They had all the relevant facts, and that absolved the motor cyclist from doing more ... Seeing that they had received the information from the police, it would be a futile thing to require the motor cyclist himself to give them the self-same information. The law never compels a person to do that which is useless and unnecessary.'

It is the last sentence quoted which counsel for the owners contends establishes and

clarifies a general principle which had its birth in *Braithwaite v Foreign Hardwood Co*
a [1905] 2 KB 543 and was applied in *Sinason-Teicher Inter-American Grain Corp v Oilcakes
and Oilseeds Trading Co Ltd* [1954] 3 All ER 468, [1954] 1 WLR 1394. Of the two earlier
cases, I say only that I cannot find in them either the birth or subsequent growth of any
such principle as that which, it is said, was enunciated by Lord Denning MR. As to Lord
Denning MR's sentence, it would be going much further than I am confident he intended
if it were to be taken as establishing some general all-embracing unqualified principle. It
b must be taken in its context and not elevated to the status of a principle which would be
unworkable. Taken in context, it does not avail the owners. The essence of the position
in the *Likiss* case was that the insurers, for whose protection the notice requirement was
inserted, had received notice of all the relevant facts from a third party. In the present
case, the charterers were the persons for whose protection the anti-technicality clause was
inserted. The relevant facts for them to know were whether or not the owners intended
c to exercise their option to withdraw if non-payment was not rectified. Neither the
owners nor anyone else had communicated to them on this matter. Indeed, the present
case is wholly different from the *Lickiss* case. There A was absolved from complying with
a clause inserted for the benefit of B on the ground that B had already got from elsewhere
the very benefit for which the clause provided. Here A (the owners) are seeking to be
absolved from complying with a clause inserted for the benefit of B (the charterers)
d notwithstanding that B had not got the benefit of the clause at all. The *Lickiss* case has,
therefore, in my judgment, no application. Lord Denning MR's statement does not apply
to such a case as the present. He would, I think, be surprised to know that it had been
suggested that it did.
    Furthermore, it is to be noted that Lord Denning MR's statement refers to something
which *is* useless and unnecessary, not to something which the party is seeking to be
absolved thinks *would be* useless and unnecessary, or, as the arbitrator says, 'would serve
e no useful purpose'. Hence, even if the futility principle is wider than I believe it to be, it
would still be of no avail to the owners who can point to nothing more than the finding
that *a* reasonable owner *would have* been entitled to form the view that a notice *would
have* served no useful purpose.

Telex B
f I can deal with this very briefly. The telex was sent in answer to a request for
information. It stated merely that the charterers were checking and would revert as soon
as possible. I can see no basis on which the telex can possibly give rise to any waiver or
estoppel in regard to a cl 30 notice.
    I should, in conclusion, mention that counsel for the owners put forward two
alternative contentions with regard to telexes B and C. They are set out in a written
g summary of his submissions, with which he most helpfully supplied me, and which will
be available for the Court of Appeal should the case proceed there for the second time.
This being so, I do not rehearse them. It is sufficient to say that they assert facts which,
contrary to his submissions, are not, in my judgment, to be found in the award, and
which not only could I not find, even if I wanted to, but which are, in my view,
inconsistent with the documents on which the case proceeded.
h The appeal must be allowed, and the award of the arbitrator varied (a) by the deletion
of para 25 (in which the arbitrator found and held that the owners' claim for a declaration
succeeded), (b) by substituting for the declaration in para 26 (that the owners had lawfully
and properly withdrawn the vessel from the charterers' service on 29 May 1980) the
declaration sought in the charterers' motion that the owners did not validly withdraw
the vessel from the charterers' service, and (c) by substituting for the award of costs in
i para 27 the award that the owners bear and pay their own and the charterers' costs of the
reference to be taxed if not agreed, and also do pay the costs of the interim award taxed
and settled at £625, the proviso in that paragraph standing unaltered.

Appeal allowed ; award of arbitrator varied. Leave to appeal to Court of Appeal refused.

Solicitors: *Richards, Butler & Co* (for the charterers); *Coward Chance* (for the owners).

K Mydeen Esq   Barrister.

Beal and others v Beecham Group Ltd   *a*

COURT OF APPEAL, CIVIL DIVISION
STEPHENSON, O'CONNOR LJJ AND SIR STANLEY REES
3, 4, 5, 8 FEBRUARY, 5 APRIL 1982

Industrial relations – Trade union membership and activities – Rights of worker as against
employer – Right to time off for carrying out trade union duties – Attendance at union meeting –   *b*
Meeting to discuss industrial relations strategy – Discussion not wholly confined to topics for
which union recognised by employer – Whether officials entitled to time off with pay to attend
meeting – Employment Protection (Consolidation) Act 1978, s 27(1)(a).

The employer, a large company, was divided into two sub-groups, each of which was
divided into divisions which operated at various sites in the United Kingdom. An   *c*
independent trade union had members in both sub-groups and had an agreement with
the employer covering various negotiating and representational rights. For the purposes
of industrial relations and collective bargaining the work force was divided into 'common
interest groups' and the union set up a national advisory committee (the NAC) for the
purposes of exchanging information between separate establishments and to determine
national policies, although the NAC had no power to negotiate with the employer. In   *d*
December 1978 seven of the company's employees, all of whom were officials of the
union, sought permission to attend, as accredited representatives of various common
interest groups, a meeting of the NAC 'to discuss matters of an industrial relations nature
and to plan a co-ordinated industrial relations strategy'. The employer granted the seven
employees permission to take time off to attend the meeting but without pay. The
employees attended the meeting and subsequently complained to an industrial tribunal   *e*
for an order that they were entitled under s 27ᵃ of the Employment Protection
(Consolidation) Act 1978 to be paid for the time taken off to attend the meeting. The
industrial tribunal found that the attendance by the employees at the NAC meeting was
not an official duty concerned with industrial relations for which, by virtue of s 27(1)(a),
the employees would have been entitled to time off with pay, but was merely a trade
union activity within s 28 of the 1978 Act in connection with which there was no   *f*
obligation on the employer to pay the employees for time taken off. The employees
appealed to the Employment Appeal Tribunal, which held that attendance at the meeting
could amount to the carrying out of a duty concerned with industrial relations. The
appeal tribunal accordingly remitted the case for the industrial tribunal to determine
whether, under s 27(2), it was reasonable in the circumstances for the employer to have
granted the employees time off with pay. The employer appealed, contending that s   *g*
27(1)(a) was concerned primarily with collective bargaining, i e one party making a claim
against another, and that duties 'concerned with industrial relations' within s 27(1)(a) had
to involve the actual transaction of industrial relations business or to have a sufficiently
close and proximate relationship to actual negotiations for them to be properly considered
part of the collective bargaining process. The employer further contended that the duties
carried out had to be consistent with the recognition afforded to the union under the   *h*
agreement with the employer.

Held – The appeal would be dismissed for the following reasons—
    (1) On the true construction of s 27(1)(a) of the 1978 Act, 'industrial relations' was not
limited to collective bargaining or by the terms of the recognition agreement, but was
capable of covering many matters which arose in connection with the relationship   *j*
between an employer and his employees, including meetings of union representatives
which were not meetings of the negotiating body for collective bargaining but were

---

a   Section 27, so far as material, is set out at p 282 *j* to p 283 *c*, post

nevertheless meetings to determine national policies concerned with industrial relations
a within the company (see p 287 *g*, p 289 *b* to *d* and p 291 *c d*, post); dictum of Slynn J in
Sood v GEC Elliott Process Automation Ltd [1980] ICR at 7–8 followed.

(2) In considering what was reasonable in all the circumstances for allowing time off
with pay, s 27(2) of the 1978 Act required that regard was to be had to the Advisory,
Conciliation and Arbitration Service's code of practice, para 13[b] of which showed that a
union meeting could be concerned with industrial relations. Although the code referred
b to collective bargaining in a restricted sense by separating out matters of grievance and
discipline, it showed that preparatory and explanatory work by union officials could be
in fulfilment of duties concerned with industrial relations. It followed that the
Employment Appeal Tribunal had been correct to remit the complaint to the industrial
tribunal for it to determine whether in the circumstances it was reasonable for the
employees to have been granted time off with pay (see p 289 *h j*, p 290 *a* to *f* and p 291 *c*
c d, post).

Notes

For time off to carry out trade union duties, see 16 Halsbury's Laws (4th edn) paras
786:1–786: 3, and for cases on the subject, see 20 Digest (Reissue) 595–596, 4526–4528.

For the Employment Protection (Consolidation) Act 1978, ss 27, 28, see 48 Halsbury's
d Statutes (3rd edn) 478, 480.

Cases referred to in judgments

Depledge v Pye Telecommunications Ltd [1981] ICR 82, EAT.
Menzies v Smith & McLaurin Ltd [1980] IRLR 180, EAT.
Sood v GEC Elliott Process Automation Ltd [1980] ICR 1, EAT.
e *RHP Bearings Ltd v Brookes* [1979] IRLR 452, EAT.
Young v Carr Fasteners Co Ltd [1979] ICR 844, EAT.

Cases also cited

Heatons Transport (St Helens) Ltd v Transport and General Workers' Union [1972] 3 All ER
101, [1973] AC 15, HL.
f *National Union of Gold, Silver and Allied Trades v Albury Bros Ltd* [1979] ICR 84, CA.

Appeal

Beecham Group Ltd (the employers) appealed against the decision of the Employment
Appeal Tribunal (Waterhouse J, Mr J D Anderson and Mr A C Blyghton) on 23 October
1980 whereby it allowed the appeal of the respondents, Nigel Beal, James Scott, Nicholas
Johnson, John Baker, Kenneth Trail, James Clark and Bruce Esler, against the decision of
g an industrial tribunal (chairman Mr D J Savin) on 11 September 1979 dismissing the
respondents' complaints under s 27(7) of the Employment Protection (Consolidation) Act
1978. The facts are set out in the judgment of O'Connor LJ.

Richard Field for the employers.
h *John Hendy* for the respondents.

Cur adv vult

5 April. The following judgments were read.

j **O'CONNOR LJ** (delivering the first judgment at the invitation of Stephenson LJ). The
seven respondents to this appeal were employees of the appellant company (the
employers) and members of the Association of Scientific, Technical and Managerial Staffs
(the union). In November 1978 Mr Sheppard, a full-time official of the union, decided to
hold a one-day meeting in London on 14 December 1978. On 24 November 1978 he

---

b Paragraph 13 is set out at p 289 *e* to *g*, post

wrote to Mr Monks and Mr Jones, personnel directors of two groups within the
employers' organisation: *a*

'I am writing to inform you that I have made preliminary arrangements for an
ASTMS Beecham National Advisory Committee meeting for Thursday December
14th. The purpose of the meeting is to enable representatives from Beecham Group
to discuss matters of an industrial relations nature and to plan a co-ordinated
industrial relations strategy. A copy of the agenda, when available, will be forwarded   *b*
if requested. In view of the ACAS Code of Practice on "Time Off For Trade Union
Officials" and the practice of other companies, e.g. Glaxo, ICI, we hope that this year
there will be no problems in allowing accredited representatives time off with pay
to attend this meeting. It would also be appreciated if unaccredited representatives
(where appropriate) could be allowed time off without pay to attend the meeting as
per past practice in previous years. It is not our intention in 1978/79 to arrange
separate National Advisory Committee meetings for Beecham Products and   *c*
Pharmaceutical Divisions.'

Mr Monks replied on 29 November 1978:

'Thank you for your letter of 24th November. As you are aware, this subject has
been already fully dealt with in previous discussions and correspondence between
the Company and the Association. It is considered that the meeting of Thursday,   *d*
14th December, does not form part of the duties of accredited representatives as set
down in the ACAS Code of Practice "Time off for trade union duties and activities".
However, accredited representatives will be allowed to take time off without pay or
alternatively, as part of any outstanding holiday entitlement. "Unaccredited
representatives" will be allowed to take time off as part of any outstanding holiday
entitlement only, subject to the normal requirements. Would you please supply a   *e*
list of the accredited representatives as soon as possible, so that the necessary
arrangements can be made.'

Mr Jones replied to the same effect. Mr Sheppard made a final attempt to get time off
with pay for his people; he wrote on 11 December 1978:

'I refer to your letter of 29 November in which you refused to allow accredited   *f*
representatives time off with pay to attend the Beecham NAC meeting due to be
held on Thursday, 14 December. We were of course extremely disappointed by
your initial decision on this matter in the light of the ACAS Code of Practice on
time off for trade union officials. We would hope, however, that the initial refusal
to allow the time off with pay may be due to a misunderstanding of the nature of
the NAC meeting. I am listing below the major items which have been submitted   *g*
by the various groups for discussion at the NAC: (1) 1979 Salary Negotiations –
Overall level, differentials and productivity. (2) Pensions. (3) Sickness Benefit. (4)
Holidays. (5) Reduction in Working Week. (6) Health and Safety. (7) Outer London
Weighting Allowance. The prime purpose of the NAC is quite clearly to allow the
representatives, if they so wish, the opportunity of discussing and co-ordinating the
salary and terms and conditions claim for 1979. I would hope that with the new   *h*
information which I have provided you with in the form of the main items for the
agenda you may be in a position to reconsider your decision.'

The employers were unmoved.

The respondents all went to the meeting on 14 December 1978 and in due course
presented complaints to the industrial tribunal under s 27(7) of the Employment   *j*
Protection (Consolidation) Act 1978 asking for an order that they were entitled to be paid
for the time off for the meeting by reason of the provisions of s 27(1), (2) and (3) of the
Act. Those provisions read:

'*Time off for carrying out trade union duties.*—(1) An employer shall permit an
employee of his who is an official of an independent trade union recognised by him

a to take time off, subject to and in accordance with subsection (2), during the employee's working hours for the purpose of enabling him—(a) to carry out those duties of his as such an official which are concerned with industrial relations between his employer and any associated employer, and their employees; or (b) to undergo training in aspects of industrial relations which is—(i) relevant to the carrying out of those duties; and (ii) approved by the Trade Union Congress or by the independent trade union of which he is an official.

b (2) The amount of time off which an employee is to be permitted to take under this section and the purposes for which, the occasions on which and any conditions subject to which time off may be so taken are those that are reasonable in all the circumstances having regard to any relevant provisions of a Code of Practice issued by the Advisory, Conciliation and Arbitration Service under section 6 of the Employment Protection Act 1975.

c (3) An employer who permits an employee to take time off under this section for any purpose shall, subject to the following provisions of this section, pay him for the time taken off for that purpose in accordance with the permission . . .'

There is no dispute that at all material times the respondents were officials of an independent trade union recognised by the employers. The industrial tribunal held that d in attending the meeting the respondents were not 'carrying out duties which are concerned with industrial relations' within s 27(1)(a) and so did not qualify for time off with pay. Having reached that conclusion the industrial tribunal made no finding under s 27(2).

The respondents appealed to the Employment Appeal Tribunal, who held that the industrial tribunal had construed s 27(1) too narrowly and allowed the appeal. It is e pertinent to state that when the case was before the industrial tribunal there was no reported decision of the appeal tribunal on the true construction of s 27 of the 1978 Act. By the time the appeal tribunal heard this appeal there were four decisions of the appeal tribunal, one of which is very important. The employers appeal against the judgment of the appeal tribunal. We are told that this is the first time that this court has had to consider the section.

f The factual background to this case is complex. I cannot do better than adopt the relevant paragraphs in the industrial tribunal's reasons; I read from para 4 onwards:

'4. Although the dispute which gives rise to these complaints is confined to the question of whether these 7 applicants are entitled to be paid for the day on which they were permitted to take time off to attend the NAC meeting, which at first sight might seem to be a simple question, it is in fact a complicated one. It has involved g the Tribunal in a detailed consideration of the facts, including the constitution, status and role of the NAC, the structure of the respondent company and the grouping of its employees into various Common Interest Groups (CIGs) for the purposes of recognition and bargaining and the terms of the agreements entered into by the respondents' sub-groups with the union for representational and bargaining purposes. It has also involved the Tribunal in a consideration of the h meaning of the words used in section 27 and other sections of the 1978 Act and the Code of Practice (Code No 3) issued by the Advisory, Conciliation and Arbitration Service under section 6 of the Employment Protection Act 1975.

5. The respondent company, Beecham Group Ltd, operates all over the world. In the United Kingdom it has some 16,000 employees. Of these some 900 belong to ASTMS. The company is divided into 2 sub-groups, Beecham Pharmaceuticals j ("Pharmaceuticals") and Beecham Products ("Products"). Although not separate legal entities the 2 sub-groups are to all intents and purposes entirely autonomous. Pharmaceuticals is divided into 6 divisions and Products into 5.

6. The applicants in these cases are all employees of Pharmaceuticals. ASTMS is involved in 2 of its divisions, the research division and the UK division. The research division operates at 4 sites, Harlow, Brookham Park, Great Burgh and Walton with

a small operation at Worthing. The UK division operates at 3 sites, Worthing, Crawley and Irvine in Scotland. The Products sub-group operates at various sites *a* including sites at Brentford and Leatherhead.

7. Each sub-group has its own management with a Chairman and Directors. The Personnel Director of Beecham Group Ltd, the respondent company, is Mr Newman. The Personnel Director of Pharmaceuticals is Mr Monks, and of Products Mr Jones. Mr Monks does not report to Mr Newman but to his own management board. His contacts with Mr Newman are infrequent. There is little or no liasion between Mr *b* Monks and Mr Jones. Mr Monks and Mr Jones conduct entirely separately their relations with the various trade unions to which the employees of their sub-groups belong.

8. The only significant matters touching industrial relations in which Beecham Group Ltd is itself directly involved with the employees of the sub-groups are pensions and holidays. As regards pensions it is obviously more sensible and *c* economical for Beecham Group Ltd to deal with this matter, involving as it does the management and investment of substantial funds and the appointment of trustees.

9. The respondents' employees range from highly qualified scientists to manual labourers. For the purposes of industrial relations they are divided into categories called Common Interest Groups (CIGs). This is for the purpose of present and future collective bargaining. One union will represent the employees in one CIG where *d* that union has reached an agreement including bargaining rights with the company. Collective bargaining is dealt with at CIG level.

10. There are 5 CIGs in Pharmaceuticals as follows: (a) The Scientific Executive and Managerial CIG (SEM). In Pharmaceuticals SEM covers employees in Pharmaceuticals across all the sites. There is one other union involved. Pharmaceuticals has concluded an agreement with ASTMS for the SEM group allowing the *e* union representational rights only. (b) The Technical CIG. This covers technicians in Pharmaceuticals across all sites. Pharmaceuticals has concluded a collective agreement with ASTMS giving the union *negotiating* rights in respect of the employees in that common interest group. The agreement dated February 1975 is Exhibit A3 in the exhibits placed before this Tribunal. Where the company and the union has concluded an agreement giving the union bargaining rights there is only *f* one union involved. (c) The Supervisory CIG. This exists at the Irvine site in Scotland only. Here there is a collective agreement between Pharmaceuticals and ASTMS giving the union *negotiating* rights. (d) The Clerical CIG. This again exists at the Irvine, Scotland site only and there is a collective agreement giving the union representational (not negotiating) rights. (e) The Job Evaluation CIG. This covers manual workers and exists at Harlow only. There is a collective agreement between *g* the union and the company giving the union representational rights.

11. In Products there is one CIG for laboratory employees and scientists and ASTMS have a collective agreement with Products giving the union negotiating rights.

12. ASTMS have a strong foothold in Pharmaceuticals going back some years but its involvement in Products is less and of more recent origin. *h*

13. Of the 7 applicants in these cases, 6 belong to the Technicians' CIG and one ... to the Supervisors' CIG.'

The NAC referred to by the industrial tribunal is the Beecham national advisory committee set up by the union. The NAC was created by the union under r 19 of its rules. That rule, although headed 'Sectional Advisory Councils', empowers the national executive committee of the union to set up three different kinds of bodies: *j*
(a) Sectional advisory councils under r 19(1) to (3), which provide:

'(1) It shall be the aim of the Association to ensure that all sections of its membership, in whatever employment, have appropriate access to its policy-making bodies. For this purpose, there shall be established sectional advisory councils where *a* the Association has substantial membership. Each Council shall have a member of the NEC as Chairman and a full-time official as Secretary.

(2) The members engaged in the particular section shall elect their respective Sectional Advisory Councils and the NEC shall determine the method of carrying out the election.

(3) The NEC shall make regulations suitable to each case for the constitution, representation, conduct, scope and expenses of such Councils.'

b (b) Sections of the union under r 19(4) to (21), each of which begins 'The NEC will establish a   Section'. When read in conjunction with r 4(8) to (25), 'Qualifications for membership', these 18 sections seem to represent a take-over by the union of what can be loosely described as in-house employees' associations. These paragraphs provide for a wide variety of organisation for the sections but tell us nothing about their sectional advisory councils and there is no evidence as to which, if any of them, ever got one,

c although r 19(22) clearly envisages that each would have one. It reads:

'It shall be the duty of these Sectional Advisory Councils to be the primary source of advice to the National Executive Council on: (i) the improvement of the terms and conditions of employment of the members engaged in the section covered by the Sectional Advisory Council concerned; (ii) the development of organisation

d amongst the unorganised within the sphere of the Association; and to ensure that the views of the members in the respective sections are made known to the NEC before any decisions which might affect their terms and conditions of service are taken.'

(c) National advisory committees. Rule 19(23) provides:

e 'The NEC will set up National Advisory Committees to cover members working in separate establishments of large industrial organisations, in order that there may be an adequate interchange of information and that policies affecting such members may be nationally determined.'

This paragraph tells us the purpose of an NAC but leaves its constitution to the

f discretion of the NEC.

The Beecham NAC was set up by the NEC at a meeting on 14 July 1973. The relevant minute reads:

'g) National Advisory Councils
The committee AGREED to set up Advisory Councils covering the following concerns:

g
Fisons	NEC Chairman:	Mr. S. Cerrone
Ciba Geigy	„ „	Mr. A. E. Brown
British Petroleum	„ „	Mr. J. Williams
Burmah Castrol	„ „	Mr. J. Williams
Beechams Group	„ „	Mr. K. McAleer

h Additionally, the committee AGREED that the Academics NAC should be chaired by Dr. Ian Gibson. The following motion was then carried unanimously: "National Advisory Council Meetings should only be called in consultation with the NEC Chairman except in an emergency situation".'

There is no provision in r 19, or anywhere else in the rules, enabling the NEC to set up 'National Advisory Councils'. The minute requires correction and as the presumption is

j that the NEC was acting within its powers I am satisfied that it is the word 'Councils' which must be corrected to 'Committees' and not 'National' to 'Sectional'. I say this because I think it is clear that the establishment of a sectional advisory council requires the prior or at least contemporaneous establishment of a section. Assuming, without deciding, that r 19(1) is wide enough to enable the NEC to establish a new section, the constitution of the section has to be spelt out and it is most unlikely that any two, let alone five, sections would have the same constitution (see r 19(4) to (21)). It is not possible to say that the minute of 14 July 1973 was setting up five new sections and apply to them a model constitution, for no model exists. Secondly, in all subsequent documents the Beecham NAC is described as the 'Beecham National Advisory Committee'.

Unfortunately the case, when it was before the industrial tribunal, was argued and in part at least decided on the basis that the NAC was a sectional advisory council. The error arose from a short passage in the cross-examination of Mr Sheppard:

'Q. Look at the ASTMS rules. Rule 19, p 24. When the NAC met on 14 December was it a sectional advisory council? A. Yes, it was. They have been called sectional advisory councils for the last six years.

Q. Does r 19(1) give an overall statement of the functions of the NAC? A. Yes.

Q. That was a function that went to the internal working and regulation of the union, rather than bilateral industrial relations between the union and employers? A. No. Not necessarily. The NAC is an institution provided under the rules and the rules express its function.

Q. Which section does Beecham come under? A. Some of the sections are to have advisory councils.

Q. The sections expressly included in r 19 were not the only ones to have advisory councils? A. Yes.'

It is trite law that it is not for the witness to construe the rules, but in the light of those answers and as no submissions to the contrary were made it is understandable that the industrial tribunal clothed the NAC with the constitution and purposes of a sectional advisory council.

The error was fundamental to the crucial decision paragraph in their reasons, which reads:

'43. Taking into account, therefore, the constitution of the NAC and the role of the NAC as demonstrated by the minutes of the meetings, the status of the persons invited to attend the meeting, the fact that there is no reference to the NAC in the agreements, the fact (as we find) that the information derived from the meeting was not essential to the applicants in the claims made by the representatives following the meeting, and was information which would have been easily and readily disseminated in other ways, the terms of the agreements in relation to time off, the organisation of the employees into CIGs, the terms of reference of the holders of letters of credentials contained in those agreements and all other relevant factors, this Tribunal have come to the conclusion and find as a fact that the attendance at the NAC meeting of 14 December was not an official duty covered by section 27(1). It was a trade union activity. Thus there was no obligation for the respondents to pay the representatives for the time off they were permitted to take to attend the meeting.'

In the present case there is no dispute that the union had members working in separate establishments of the employers who were a large industrial organisation. It follows that the NAC was a properly constituted body under r 19(23). Its purpose was to provide a forum for an adequate exchange of information between the separate establishments and to determine policies affecting the members nationally, that is in the separate establishments nationwide. I am clear that attendance at a meeting of the NAC called solely for the purpose of exchanging information would not qualify for time off with pay under s 27(1) but would qualify for time off without pay under s 28 of the 1978 Act as a trade union activity. The question is whether attendance at a meeting called to determine policies nationally qualifies under s 27(1).

The agenda for the meeting of 14 December 1978, as set out in Mr Sheppard's letters, together with the minutes of the meeting, shows that it was called for both purposes. Any questions of 'prime purpose' or 'real purpose' or 'predominant purpose' are irrelevant to a decision whether the second purpose qualifies under s 27(1). Those questions may be relevant in deciding what is reasonable under s 27(2).

The respondents were officials of an independent trade union recognised by the
a employers; when they attended the meeting for the second purpose, was their attendance,
in the words of the section, 'for the purpose of enabling them to carry out those duties of
theirs as such officials which are concerned with industrial relations between their
employer and its employees'? Of necessity the section requires that the official has some
duties 'concerned with industrial relations between his employer and any associated
employer, and their employees'. Six of the respondents held office on terms agreed
b between the employers and the union in writing in February 1975, when the union was
given full negotiating rights at all sites for the technicians' CIG. The other respondent, a
supervisor from Irvine, held office on like terms. The employers recognised the union as
'the sole bargaining agent for all employees in the technicians' CIG'. The agreement
provided for the election of representatives at each site and for the issue to them of a joint
letter of credentials. There is express permission for time off 'to carry out their duties and
c deal with questions arising from this agreement as shown in Appendix D' (see para 4.6
of the agreement). The joint letter of credentials records that 'the representative agrees to
accept the duties and responsibilities defined in the agreement'. Paragraph 4.8 of the
agreement provides that 'it is agreed that only accredited Representatives can raise issues
and grievances on behalf of members under the terms of this Agreement'. The agreement
and the appendices make detailed provision for the part representatives are to play in
d grievance matters. The only provision for collective bargaining is found at para C in App
E, which reads:

'C. COMPANY-WIDE NEGOTIATIONS
    1. Company-wide negotiations will take place between National representatives
    of the Association and senior management representatives of the Company on
    general salary levels of members and such other items on the terms and conditions
e   of employment as may be mutually agreed between the Company and the
    Association.'

I can find no provision for 'national representatives' in the agreement, but the evidence
is that the representatives took part in the collective bargaining and it is not disputed that
such participation was part of their duty.
f   It will be seen that it was the CIG that was the negotiating body and it is accepted that
when negotiating the representatives were carrying out a duty 'concerned with industrial
relations'. Further, the employers also accept that a meeting of representatives to prepare
themselves for the negotiations and formulate a claim is part of that duty and they have
allowed time off with pay for such meetings.
        It follows that there can be no doubt that the representatives had duties 'concerned
g with industrial relations', and the only question is whether attendance at the NAC
meeting was 'for the purpose of enabling them to carry out those duties'.
        Counsel for the employers submitted (i) that the duties within s 27(1) of the 1978 Act
must involve the actual transaction of industrial relations business or have a sufficiently
close and proximate relationship to actual negotiations for them to be properly considered
part of the collective bargaining process, (ii) that at the heart of s 27(1)(a) is collective
h bargaining, that is one party making a claim on another; the employer has an interest in
orderly and efficient organisation of collective bargaining, and that is the function for
which the employer must pay. In support of these submissions he invokes s 32 of the
1978 Act, which reads:

        'Provisions supplementary to ss 27 to 31.—(1) For the purposes of sections 27 to 31—
        (a) a trade union shall be treated as recognised not only if it is recognised for the
j   purposes of collective bargaining, but also if the Advisory, Conciliation and
        Arbitration Service has made a recommendation for recognition which is operative
        within the meaning of section 15 of the Employment Protection Act 1975 . . . (2) In
        subsection (1)—"collective bargaining" means negotiations related to or connected
        with one or more of the matters specified in section 29(1) of the Trade Union and
        Labour Relations Act 1974; "recognised" means recognised by an employer, or two
        or more associated employers, to any extent for the purposes of collective bargaining.'

Section 29 of the Trade Union and Labour Relations Act 1974 defines 'trade dispute', and the matters specified are wide ranging: terms and conditions of employment, engagement *a* and dismissal of workers, matters of discipline, trade union membership and machinery for negotiation or consultation.

Counsel for the employers submitted further that the duties carried out must be consistent with the recognition afforded to the union. He recognised that for these submissions to succeed it would involve overruling the decision of the appeal tribunal in *Sood v GEC Elliott Process Automation Ltd* [1980] ICR 1. That was a case which bore some *b* similarity to this case. The same union had members employed in GEC Ltd and its subsidiary companies, of which Automation was one. The union had set up an NAC, but in addition they had set up a products advisory committee, whose function was to enable representatives from various subsidiaries and sites producing similar products to meet, exchange information and experience and supply information to the NAC. The question was whether an official attending a meeting of the products advisory committee came *c* within s 27(1)(*a*). The case was decided under the Employment Protection Act, but the wording of the relevant sections, s 57 in particular, is the same. The industrial tribunal decided by a majority that attendance at the products advisory committee was not within the section. On appeal by the employee, counsel for the employers made the same submissions as counsel for the employers has made to us. The appeal tribunal rejected the submissions. Slynn J, giving the judgment of the tribunal, said (at 7–8): *d*

> 'We share the view of the whole of the industrial tribunal that the provision permitting time off for the purpose of enabling a trade union official to carry out his duties does not of itself mean that he is to be allowed paid time off in order to prepare himself or to make himself a better trade union representative. That in our view is covered by section 57(1)(*b*). We also agree with the industrial tribunal that the phrase "industrial relations" is not to be narrowly construed. It is capable of *e* covering many matters which arise in connection with the relationship of employer and employee. We do not accept [counsel for the employers'] argument that the test of an official's duties is to be limited by the recognition. It seems to us that recognition identifies the trade union whose officials are entitled to claim time off under the section. It does not limit those duties to collective bargaining or to the precise terms of the recognition. We think that it is not the intention of Parliament *f* that a trade union official should only have time off for the purpose of meetings with representatives of management. It seems to us that when questions involving industrial relations arise, a union official may well be entitled, as part of his duties, to take part in the planning of strategy and in discussing with other workers who are at the time negotiating with their employers, so long as the latter employers are associated with a particular trade union official's own employers. Nor do we accept *g* the argument that a trade union official is only entitled to take time off for the purpose of negotiating where the employers have laid down the particular industrial relations structure as [counsel for the employers] suggests. It seems to us that the carrying out of the trade union official's duties for the purpose of the section can go wider than that. We do not accept the view of the second member of the industrial tribunal that the fact that these committees are set up purely by the trade unions, *h* and for trade union functions, necessarily means that the duty of an official in connection with them prevents them from being duties concerned with industrial relations. The intention of section 57 of the Employment Protection Act 1975 is that trade union officials should have time off to enable them to perform certain duties. We do not think that Parliament intended we should approach the section on the basis that the words should be narrowly construed. On the other hand it is *j* clear from the words themselves that the duties must concern industrial relations between the official's employer and its employees, and an associated employer and the associated employer's employees, in a case where both employers and both sets of employees are concerned with the particular industrial relations problem. So, if two associated companies are negotiating with the trade union, or are involved in

a
an industrial relations problem which will or may need to be negotiated, then it seems to us that the official's duties in connection with such negotiations may fall within the section. There must however be some limit to the activities which fall within the section. In our view, the test is whether the time off is required to enable the official to carry out his duties in relation to a matter which arises in relations between employees and management. We do not consider that the mere exchange of information between the trade union officials themselves necessarily qualifies,

b
even if those officials represent workers in a particular group of companies.'

The appeal tribunal held that the purpose of the products advisory committee meeting was to exchange information and experience, and so dismissed the appeal. Like the appeal tribunal I do not think it correct to limit 'industrial relations' in s 27 of the 1978 Act to mean collective bargaining as defined in s 32. If that had been the intention of Parliament, s 27 would have read 'concerned with collective bargaining'. I agree with

c
Slynn J that 'industrial relations' in the section are not limited by the terms of the recognition agreement and I am content to adopt the passages from *Sood v GEC Elliott Process Automation Ltd* which I have quoted as correct. The recognition agreement may well be of very great importance when considering what is reasonable under s 27(2): see *Depledge v Pye Telecommunications Ltd* [1981] ICR 82, to which I shall refer later.

In practice matters arising in relations between employees and management are likely

d
to be within the very wide range of collective bargaining as defined in the 1978 Act. In considering what is reasonable in all the circumstances for allowing time off with pay, s 27(2) requires that regard be had to the ACAS Code of Practice 'Time off for Trade Union duties and activities'. Paragraph 13 of the code, 'Trade union officials' duties concerned with industrial relations', reads:

e
'In addition to his or her work as an employee a trade union official may have important duties concerned with industrial relations. An official's duties are those duties pertaining to his or her role in the jointly agreed procedures or customary arrangements for consultation, collective bargaining and grievance handling where such matters concern the employer and any associated employer and their employees. To perform these duties properly an official should be permitted to take reasonable

f
paid time off during working hours for such purposes as (a) collective bargaining with the appropriate level of management; (b) informing constituents about negotiations or consultations with management; (c) meetings with other lay officials or with full-time union officers on matters which are concerned with industrual relations between his or her employer and any associated employer and their employees; (d) interviews with and on behalf of constituents on grievance and

g
discipline matters concerning them and their employer; (e) appearing on behalf of constituents before an outside official body such as an industrial tribunal which is dealing with an industrial relations matter concerning the employer; and (f) explanations to new employees whom he or she will represent of the role of the union in the workplace industrial relations structure.'

h
These provisions, which expressly are not comprehensive, show that the role envisages that what is a union meeting may well be concerned with industrial relations. The code uses collective bargaining in a restricted sense as it separates matters of grievance and discipline, but it shows that what may be called preparatory work and explanatory work by officials may well be in fulfilment of duties concerned with industrial relations.

Counsel for the employers submitted that as the SEM CIG only had representational recognition, and as there were also invited representatives from Products and a non-

j
accredited representative, the NAC meeting could not be a duty for the technicians' representatives within s 27(1)(a). Like the appeal tribunal, I cannot accept this submission. I am not concerned with the position of the SEM representatives, but only with the respondents and if they were attending to enable them to carry out their duties concerned with industrial relations I do not think it matters who else was there. Such factors may well be relevant under s 27(2).

Finally, counsel for the employers submitted that, as the NAC had no negotiating
function with the employers, indeed no function at all with the employers, attending its   *a*
meeting could not be for the purpose of enabling the official to carry out his duties
concerned with industrial relations. Once it is recognised that preparatory work falls
within the discharge of duties concerned with industrial relations, then one looks to see
if the preparatory work had some direct relevance to an industrial relations matter, and
if so it qualifies under s 27(1)(a). As I have said, attending the NAC to exchange
information would not have that direct relevance but to determine policies nationally   *b*
may well be directly relevant, depending on what the policies are. The agenda and
minutes of the meeting show that at least of the policies were concerned with
industrial relations matters that were to go into the 1979 wage claim.

It follows that in my judgment when the respondents attended the NAC meeting it
was for the purpose of enabling them to carry out their duties concerned with industrial
relations.   *c*

It must be remembered that time off under s 27(1) is subject to, and in accordance
with, sub-s (2). This is the safeguard for employers against any attempt by a union to
dress up what is an activity to make it look like a duty concerned with industrial relations.
So too it is under sub-s (2) that the question has to be decided whether it was reasonable
for the respondents to seek time off with pay for the NAC meeting in addition to their
accepted CIG meeting.   *d*

Having reached the conclusion that I have reached on the true function of the NAC,
there is no difficulty in this case. The appeal tribunal recognised that the constitution of
a sectional advisory council might make it difficult to contend that a meeting was within
s 27(1)(a). They recognised from the agenda and minutes that the NAC was not behaving
like a sectional advisory council and decided that the purpose had changed since it was
set up in 1973. They pointed to the change from having a member of the NEC as   *e*
chairman and the change of date to December 'so that the NAC could co-ordinate claims
to be formulated in the following spring'. This is within the second purpose of the NAC
as I have found it to be. The appeal tribunal thereafter correctly decided to allow the
respondents' appeal and remit the matter to the industrial tribunal for consideration
under s 27(2).

In *RHP Bearings Ltd v Brookes* [1979] IRLR 452 the employee, an official of a recognised   *f*
union, attended a meeting of a shop stewards' joint liasion committee and claimed time
off with pay. The employers having refused the employee, he went to the industrial
tribunal who upheld his claim. The Employment Appeal Tribunal allowed the employers'
appeal and sent the case back for rehearing on the ground that the letter summoning the
meeting and the minutes showed that the meeting had two purposes: exchange of
information and some discussion on topics that might be considered as within s 27. And   *g*
the industrial tribunal had not considered the question of how much time off it was
reasonable to award under s 27(2). Bristow J, giving the judgment of the appeal tribunal,
said at the end of his judgment, after pointing out the laborious nature of investigating
item by item the business of a dual purpose meeting (at 454):

> 'The lesson to be drawn from what happened in this case is that where it is   *h*
> proposed to set up a body which is likely in its work to consider matters some of
> which will be within s. 27 and some of which will not, there ought to be negotiaton
> beforehand with a view to agreeing how much of the cost it is reasonable for the
> employer and how much it is reasonable for the union to bear.'

The same lesson is to be drawn from the present case. It is particularly important
where the officials may have to travel a long way to the meeting, as in the present case,   *j*
and may need a whole day off to be at the meeting at all, regardless of the time spent on
considering any topic. *Sood v GEC Elliott Process Automation Ltd* [1980] ICR 1, *RHP Bearings
Ltd v Brookes* [1979] IRLR 452 and this case show the lengthy, burdensome and expensive
outcome of having to investigate the dispute ex post facto as must be done if the dispute
cannot be prevented by prior agreement.

Three further decisions of the Employment Appeal Tribunal were cited to us. The
a first two were *Young v Carr Fasteners Co Ltd* [1979] ICR 844, decided on the same day as
Sood by the same members of the appeal tribunal, and *Menzies v Smith & McLaurin Ltd*
[1980] IRLR 180, both cases of time off for training under s 27(1)(*b*). I can find nothing
in those cases that conflicts with what was said in *Sood* and I get no help from them. I
would, however, draw attention to *Depledge v Pye Telecommunications Ltd* [1981] ICR 82,
another ASTMS case. There the union had called a one-day conference to discuss job
b security in the group's plants in the Cambridge area. The group agreement with the
union provided procedures for such matters but the meeting had been convened outside
the terms of the agreement. Talbot J, giving the judgment of the Employment Appeal
Tribunal, said that, although the meeting fell within s 27(1)(*a*) of the 1978 Act, the
industrial tribunal had been correct in deciding that the employee was not entitled to
time off with pay under s 27(2). In reaching my conclusion that the true construction of
c s 27 is that given by Slynn J in *Sood*, I am fortified by the fact that the judges in the three
subsequent cases of the appeal tribunal were of the same opinion.
I would dismiss this appeal.

SIR STANLEY REES. For the reasons stated by O'Connor LJ I agree that the appeal
should be dismissed. I do not wish to add anything.
d

STEPHENSON LJ. I also agree.

Appeal dismissed. Leave to appeal to House of Lords.

Solicitors: *I M F Balfour*, Brentford (for the employers); *Robin Thompson & Partners* (for
the respondents).

Sophie Craven   Barrister.

Garden Cottage Foods Ltd v Milk Marketing   *a*
Board

COURT OF APPEAL, CIVIL DIVISION
LORD DENNING MR, MAY LJ AND SIR SEBAG SHAW
17, 18 MAY 1982

b

*European Economic Community – Rules on competition – Abuse of dominant position – Remedy –
Statutory undertaking sole supplier in England and Wales of bulk butter – Undertaking selling
butter to 20 distributors in England and Wales including plaintiff for resale to EEC countries –
Undertaking subsequently deciding to limit sale to only four distributors excluding plaintiff –
Decision taken in good faith to protect undertaking's commercial interests – Whether 'abuse . . . of
a dominant position within . . . a substantial part' of Common Market – Whether remedy of *c*
injunction available to plaintiffs – Whether remedy of damages available – EEC Treaty, art 86.*

The defendants, a statutory undertaking, produced all the bulk butter in England and
Wales, that is the butter surplus to the requirements for packaged butter in those
countries, and sold it to distributors in the United Kingdom for resale by them to
countries in the European Economic Community. Prior to 1982 the defendants regularly *d*
supplied 20 distributors in England and Wales with bulk butter for resale to EEC
countries, among them being the plaintiff who, between August 1980 and August 1981,
purchased considerable quantities of bulk butter from the defendants and resold it, at
prices which compared favourably with the prices asked by the other distributors, to,
inter alios, a Dutch customer; in consequence the plaintiff built up a connection and
goodwill with the Dutch customer. In March 1982 the defendants informed the plaintiff *e*
that following review of their sales and marketing strategy they had decided to limit sale
of the bulk butter to only four in England and Wales distributors among whom the
plaintiff was not included, and that in future the plaintiff would have to purchase bulk
butter from those distributors. That meant that the plaintiff would have to pay more for
the butter than he had done when purchasing it direct from the defendants and that he
would be unable to compete with the four distributors when reselling the butter to *f*
purchasers in the EEC. In April 1982 the plaintiff brought proceedings against the
defendants seeking an injunction to restrain them from withholding supplies of butter
from him or otherwise refusing to maintain normal business relations with him, contrary
to art 86[a] of the EEC Treaty, on the ground that the defendants' conduct amounted to an
'abuse . . . of a dominant position within the common market' of the EEC within art 86.
The judge refused to grant an injunction on the ground that, whilst it was arguable that *g*
there had been a breach of art 86, damages were the appropriate remedy since it would
be difficult to frame an injunction in terms sufficiently precise to give the relief sought.
The plaintiff appealed.

Held – The appeal would be allowed for the following reasons—
    (1) Having regard to the volume of the bulk butter produced and supplied for the *h*
Common Market by the defendants, they had, in regard to bulk butter, a 'dominant
position . . . in a substantial part' of the Common Market, within art 86 of the EEC
Treaty. Furthermore, in deciding to limit the sale of bulk butter to four distributors only
it was arguable that the defendants had been guilty of 'abuse' of that dominant market
position within art 86, because, though their decision had been made in good faith, it
had the effect of eliminating the competition of the other 16 distributors, including the *j*
plaintiff, in the bulk butter market and of thereby strengthening the defendants'
dominant position in the market, and in those circumstances the defendants could not
escape liability under art 86 on the ground that their decision had been made merely to

---
a Article 86, so far as material, is set out at p 296 *e f*, post

protect their own commercial interests (see p 296 *g* to *j*, p 297 *c* and *f*, p 298 *a b* and p 299
a   *a b* and *f*, post); *Coöperatieve vereniging 'Suiker Unie' UA v EC Commission* [1975] ECR 1663
and *United Brands Co v EC Commission* [1978] ECR 207 applied.

(2) The remedy of an injunction was available in the English courts to restrain abuse
of a dominant market position contrary to art 86, and, in all the circumstances, an
injunction was the only remedy which would be effective to protect the plaintiff.
Accordingly, an injunction would be granted to restrain the defendants from confining
b   their sales of bulk butter to any particular distributor or from imposing significantly
different terms in relation to the supply of bulk butter to buyers in that market in regard
to price or quantity otherwise than pursuant to ordinary mercantile and commercial
practice (see p 298 *d* to *j* and p 299 *a b e* to *j*, post)

Quaere. Whether a remedy in damages is available for breach of art 86 of the EEC
Treaty (see p 298 *d* and p 299 *b* to *d* and *f*, post).

c
Notes
For abuse of a dominant market position, see Supplement to 38 Halsbury's Laws (3rd
edn) para 185F, and for cases on the subject, see 21 Digest (Reissue) 279–282, 1792–1804.
For the EEC Treaty, art 86, see 42A Halsbury's Statutes (3rd edn) 1183.

d   **Cases referred to in judgments**
Application des Gaz SA v Falks Veritas Ltd [1974] 3 All ER 51, [1974] Ch 381, [1974] 3
    WLR 235, CA, 21 Digest (Reissue) 225, 1571.
Belgische Radio en Televisie v SV SABAM Case 127/73 [1974] ECR 51, CJEC, 21 Digest
    (Reissue) 233, 1599.
Coöperatieve vereniging 'Suiker Unie' UA v EC Commission Joined Cases 40–48, 50, 54–56,
e   111, 113 and 114/73 [1975] ECR 1663, CJEC, 21 Digest (Reissue) 274, 1770.
Garland v British Rail Engineering Ltd Case 12/81 [1982] 2 All ER 402, [1982] 2 WLR 918,
    CJEC and HL.
Macarthys Ltd v Smith Case 129/79 [1981] 1 All ER 111, [1981] QB 180, [1980] 3 WLR
    929, [1980] ECR 1275, CJEC and CA.
United Brands Co v EC Commission Case 27/76 [1978] ECR 207, CJEC, 21 Digest (Reissue)
f   282, 1801.
Valor International Ltd v Application des Gaz SA [1978] 3 CMLR 87, CA.
Worringham v Lloyds Bank Ltd Case 69/80 [1981] 2 All ER 434, [1981] 1 WLR 950, [1981]
    ECR 767, CJEC.

Cases also cited
g   *Bandengroothandel Frieschebrug BV v Nederlandsche Banden-Industrie Michelin NV* (81/969/
    EEC) [1982] 1 CMLR 643, EC Commission.
Island Records Ltd, Ex p [1978] 3 All ER 824, [1978] Ch 122, CA.
Istituto Chemioterapico Italiano SpA v EC Commission Joined Cases 6 and 7/73 [1974] ECR
    223, CJEC.
Lonrho Ltd v Shell Petroleum Co Ltd [1981] 2 All ER 456, [1982] AC 173, HL.
h   *NV Union de Remorquage et de Sauvetage v NV Schelde Sleepvaartbedrijf* [1965] CMLR 251,
    Commercial Court, Antwerp.

Interlocutory appeal
By writ issued on 14 April 1982 the plaintiffs, Garden Cottage Foods Ltd, sought as
against the defendants, the Milk Marketing Board, an injunction restraining the
j   defendants by themselves, their servants, agents or otherwise, from withholding supplies
of butter from the plaintiffs or otherwise refusing to maintain normal business relations
with the plaintiffs contrary to art 86 of the EEC Treaty. By summons dated 15 April
1982 the plaintiffs sought an interim injunction in the terms claimed by the writ. By a
judgment given on 21 April 1982 Parker J refused to grant an interim injunction on the
ground that it would be wrong at that stage to grant such relief since the plaintiffs' proper

remedy lay in damages at the trial of the action. The plaintiffs appealed on the grounds, inter alia, that the judge was wrong in concluding that damages would be an adequate remedy for the loss they had suffered as a result of the defendants' withdrawal of supplies of bulk butter and wrongly exercised his discretion in refusing to grant an interim injunction. The facts are set out in the judgment of Lord Denning MR.

David Vaughan QC and *Peter Langdon-Davies* for the company
Leonard Hoffmann QC and *Francis Jacobs* for the board.

LORD DENNING MR.

Preliminary

It is some years ago now that we considered in this court arts 85 and 86 of the EEC Treaty. It was in *Application des Gaz S A v Falks Veritas Ltd* [1974] 3 All ER 51 at 58, [1974] Ch 381 at 396. I there said:

> 'Articles 85 and 86 are part of our law. They create new torts or wrongs. Their names are "undue restriction of competition within the common market"; and "abuse of dominant position within the common market". Any infringement of those articles can be dealt with by our English courts. It is for our courts to find the facts, to apply the law, and to use the remedies which we have available.'

Three years later in *Valor International Ltd v Application des Gaz S A* [1978] 3 CMLR 87 at 99 Roskill LJ reserved his opinion on the matter. But I still think that what I said was right. It has been reinforced by later decisions in this court as in the House of Lords that the articles of the treaty are part of our own law. They have supremacy over anything in our own municipal law which is inconsistent with them. They can be and are to be enforced by our courts just as any other provisions of our law: see *Macarthys Ltd v Smith* [1981] 1 All ER 111, [1981] QB 180, *Worringham v Lloyds Bank Ltd* [1981] 2 All ER 434, [1981] 1 WLR 950, *Garland v British Rail Engineering Ltd* [1982] 2 All ER 402, [1982] 2 WLR 918. So far as these two arts 85 and 86 are concerned, there is the direct authority of the European Court itself in *Belgische Radio en Televisie v SV SABAM* [1974] ECR 51 at 62–63 where it was said:

> '16. As the prohibitions of articles 85(1) and 86 tend by their very nature to produce direct effects in relations between individuals, these Articles create direct rights in respect of the individuals concerned which the national courts must safeguard.
> 17. To deny ... the national courts' jurisdiction to afford this safeguard, would mean depriving individuals of rights which they hold under the Treaty itself.'

Facts of this case

In this case an English company, Garden Cottage Foods Ltd, comes to these courts, the national courts. They say that the Milk Marketing Board have a dominant position within the Common Market, or a substantial part of it. They complain that the Milk Marketing Board are abusing their dominant position.

The Milk Marketing Board are an undertaking set up by statute. They collect milk from all the farmers in England and Wales. They sell that milk at the best price they can obtain. They turn the surplus into butter and cheese. They package a great deal of the butter and sell it under their own brand names, 'Country Life' and so forth, in England. But there is a large surplus left which is called 'bulk butter'. The bulk butter is not put into packages. It is sold in bulk largely to countries within the Common Market.

It is sold in this way: a representative of the Milk Marketing Board arranges contracts with customers in England and Wales. Those customers buy the bulk butter from the Milk Marketing Board. They then resell it to 'middlemen' in countries such as Holland. It is a term of the resale that the bulk butter is not to be imported back to this country, because, if it were sent back, it would depress the market here.

For many years there have been a number of buyers in England. One concern was

called Staple Dairy Products. Mr Bunch was previously employed by this company.
a Having gained a great deal of expertise in the bulk butter market, he left Staple Dairy
Products and set up his own company, which he operated under the name of Garden
Cottage Foods Ltd. Mr Bunch and his wife carried on the business on their own. They
bought bulk butter from the Milk Marketing Board and resold it overseas. Their major
customer was a Dutch company called J Wijffels BV. We have before us a summary of
all the sales by the Milk Marketing Board to Garden Cottage Foods Ltd since the
b commencement of business. From August 1980 to November 1980 Mr Bunch bought
over 1,200 tonnes of bulk butter for which he paid £2,170,257. From January 1981 to
August 1981 he bought about 10,000 tonnes for which he paid £20,126,854. He resold
that butter overseas. That was his turnover, but Mr Bunch's profit margin was very
small, something like $\frac{1}{4}$%.

In the middle of 1981 there was an unfortunate happening so far as Mr Bunch was
c concerned. A consignment of butter from the Milk Marketing Board was badly packaged.
It became streaky. Mr Bunch arranged to sell it to the Netherlands. They agreed to take
it in its defective condition. But afterwards they changed their minds. They would not
take it. So Mr Bunch had to sell it on the market in this country.

The Milk Marketing Board were displeased. They told Mr Bunch that he should not
have sold the butter in England. There was an inquiry, but in the end all was settled
d satisfactorily. No blame was put onto Mr Bunch. Indeed the Milk Marketing Board paid
compensation of £1,000 to Mr Bunch's company. On 24 August 1981 the bulk butter
manager of Dairy Crest (that is the name under which the Milk Marketing Board sell
their bulk butter) wrote to Mr Bunch, saying:

'... it has been decided to continue to do business with your company in the
normal way ... I hope that we can do business together in future to the satisfaction
e of both parties.'

That sounded very nice; but no business was forthcoming. Months and months passed.
Mr Bunch said that he telephoned every fortnight. He asked: 'Have you got any butter
for sale?' They always said: 'No; I am afraid we have none available.' The matter came to
a head in March 1982 when the Milk Marketing Board (under the heading of 'Dairy
f Crest') wrote to Mr Bunch. They said:

'Dear Mr Bunch

MMB Bulk Butter for Export

Following a detailed review of our sales and marketing strategy we have decided
to appoint 4 independent distributors to handle the sales of our bulk butter for
g export with effect from 1 April 1982.'

They set out the names and addresses of the four independent distributors, which
included Staple Dairy Products Ltd, who had been Mr Bunch's previous employers. Then
they went on:

'We have valued the business which we have done with you in the past and I wish
h to record our appreciation for your efforts in exporting some of our bulk butter. For
the future, you should contact the above distributors to discuss availability of
supplies if you require MMB bulk butter for export. If you wish to discuss any
points about the new arrangements then please contact Malcolm Matthew or me.'

It is quite clear that if Mr Bunch had to buy bulk butter from the four distributors in
j the future, he would have to pay more for it than he did before. The distributors would
have to allow for their own profit margin. This would mean that Mr Bunch would not
be able to compete in the bulk butter market.

Mr Bunch went to see Mr Matthew, the board's representative. They had a meeting
about a week later. He was told that the Milk Marketing Board had previously supplied
bulk butter to 20 distributors, but they had now changed their policy and were only

going to supply the four named distributors. They were not prepared to reconsider their
decision and supply Mr Bunch or his company with bulk butter in the future.   *a*
    At the end of March 1982 Mr Bunch or his advisers bethought themselves of art 86 of
the EEC Treaty, which deals with the abuse of a dominant position. On 14 April 1982
they issued a writ and applied for an injunction asking that the Milk Marketing Board
should be restrained from withholding supplies of butter from them. The solicitors for
the Milk Marketing Board said that the arrangement which their clients had had with
Mr Bunch had no contractual force, and that the appointment of distributors did not   *b*
infringe the provisions of the EEC Treaty.
    The matter came before Parker J. He gave an interesting judgment on the impact of
the Common Market. He thought there was a good arguable case that there had been a
breach of art 86. He said that it was difficult to know what to do in the circumstances,
but he thought that damages might be an adequate remedy. He felt that it was difficult
to frame an injunction in sufficiently precise terms so as to be a ground for relief. In   *c*
those circumstances, he refused to grant an injunction. Now Mr Bunch has come to this
court.

The treaty provisions
    I first refer to art 3 of the treaty. It says:

    '. . . the activities of the Community shall include . . . (*f*) the institution of a   *d*
    system ensuring that competition in the common market is not distorted . . .'

Article 86 says:

    'Any abuse by one or more undertakings of a dominant position within the
    common market or in a substantial part of it shall be prohibited as incompatible
    with the common market in so far as it may affect trade between Member States.   *e*
    Such abuse may, in particular, consist in: (*a*) directly or indirectly imposing unfair
    purchase or selling prices or other unfair trading conditions; (*b*) limiting production,
    markets or technical development to the prejudice of consumers; (*c*) applying
    dissimilar conditions to equivalent transactions with other trading parties, thereby
    placing them at a competitive disadvantage . . .'
                                                                                                 f
Those are instances of the general provision of abuse of a dominant position.

A substantial part
    The first point we have to consider is whether or not England and Wales is 'a substantial
part' of the Common Market. Beyond all doubt, to my mind, so far as bulk butter is
concerned, the Milk Marketing Board are in a dominant position within England and   *g*
Wales. They are the suppliers of 100% of bulk butter. They sell it for distribution
overseas within the Common Market. Although other countries within the Common
Market supply a large amount of bulk butter, nevertheless it seems to me that, because
of the scale of their operations and the amount of bulk butter being distributed in
Europe, the Milk Marketing Board are in 'a dominant position' within a substantial part
of the Common Market.   *h*
    We were referred to a passage in *Coöperatieve vereniging 'Suiker Unie' UA v EC Commission*
[1975] ECR 1663 at 1977 where the court at Luxembourg said that, for the purpose of
determining whether a specific territory is large enough to amount to a substantial part
of the Common Market within the meaning of art 86 of the Treaty, the pattern and
volume of the production and consumption of the product, as well as the habits and
economic opportunities of the vendors and purchasers, must be considered.   *j*
    Applying that test to the case before us, it seems to me that England and Wales was a
substantial part of the Common Market in which the Milk Marketing Board had a
dominant position.

Was there an abuse?
    The next question is whether the Milk Marketing Board have been guilty of any abuse

of that dominant position. It is important to remember that before 1982 the Milk
a Marketing Board had at least 20 customers to whom they were regularly supplying bulk
butter. They were supplying it at competitive prices by ordinary negotiation in the
market. The prices depended on supply and demand and according to the purchaser's
offer and the board's acceptance. Although Mr Bunch had only been a customer of 20
months' standing, he was an established customer with his own connections and
goodwill, particularly his connection with the Dutch purchaser. Mr Wijffels, the Dutch
b purchaser, had the greatest confidence in him and was taking all his supplies from him.
Quite often he purchased bulk butter at a lower price from Mr Bunch than he would
from the other distributors.

That is the background against which the Milk Marketing Board came down with a
thunderbolt. They decided to limit the sale of bulk butter to four distributors only. They
refused to supply bulk butter to the other 16 distributors. They eliminated competition
c in the market. They drove those 16 out of the bulk butter business. I will read the
statement of Mr Bunch in his affidavit of the effect on his trading. He said:

> 'The effect of the Defendants' decision is that henceforth the Plaintiff Company
> will only be able to purchase supplies of butter produced by the Defendants from
> one or more of the four distributors. These distributors have hitherto competed
> drectly with the Plaintiff Company in both tendering for and re-selling butter
d > manufactured by the Defendants and to my knowledge at least two of them also
> deal directly with the Plaintiff Company's major customer in Holland. I verily
> believe that any supplies of butter which the Plaintiff Company may eventually be
> able to purchase from these distributors will be sold to it at a price above that at
> which the distributors have purchased or could purchase the same from the
> Defendants in order to enable them to make a profit. This will mean that the
e > Plaintiff Company will be unable to compete with the distributors on price when
> re-selling the butter to customers and accordingly it may be forced out of business
> as it cannot purchase equivalent supplies of butter from other sources.'

That seems to me to be an abuse of a dominant position. We were referred to several
decisions of the European Court at Luxembourg, but I will only refer to the leading case
f of *United Brands Co v EC Commission* [1978] ECR 207. It covers 140 pages. United Brands
was a big concern which supplied 35% of the world's exports in bananas. It had a
customer in Denmark who offended it. This customer had taken part in an advertising
campaign for a competing brand of bananas. United Brands refused to supply him with
any more bananas. It was held by the European Court that there had been an abuse of a
dominant position. The court said (at 292):

g
> '182. In view of these conflicting arguments it is advisable to assert positively
> from the outset that an undertaking in a dominant position for the purpose of
> marketing a product which cashes in on the reputation of a brand name known to
> and valued by the consumers—cannot stop supplying a long standing customer
> who abides by regular commercial practice, if the orders placed by that customer
> are in no way out of the ordinary.
h > 183. Such conduct is inconsistent with the objectives laid down in article 3(*f*) of
> the Treaty, which are set out in detail in article 86, especially in paragraphs (*b*) and
> (*c*), since the refusal to sell would limit markets to the prejudice of consumers and
> would amount to discrimination which might in the end eliminate a trading party
> from the relevant market.'

j It was said on behalf of United Brands that it was only protecting its own commercial
interests; but the court disposed of the argument in this way (at 293):

> '189. Although it is true, as the applicant points out, that the fact that an
> undertaking is in a dominant position cannot disentitle it from protecting its own
> commercial interests if they are attacked, and that such an undertaking must be
> conceded the right to take such reasonable steps as it deems appropriate to protect

its said interests, such behaviour cannot be countenanced if its actual purpose is to strengthen this dominant position and abuse it.'

a

Applying those principles, I do not think that the Milk Marketing Board can escape by saying they were only protecting their own commercial interests. Although they were acting in good faith by appointing these four distributors, nevertheless the effect of it was to eliminate the competition of the other 16 distributors, and to strengthen their own dominant position. They deliberately refused to supply butter to Mr Bunch, or any of the other 15, whom they had been supplying for some time in the past. That was *b* arguably at any rate an abuse of their dominant position; and the judge so held.

Remedy

The remaining question is the remedy. The judge thought that there would be a remedy in damages and that in the circumstances that would be an adequate remedy. So *c* he refused an injunction.

Counsel for the plaintiff company had told us that in some of the other Common Market countries there have been cases where damages have been granted. He referred us to a recent case in the Commercial Court at Antwerp where there was an inquiry as to damages. I do not think that this is the occasion to decide that point. I think there is a good deal to be said for there being a remedy in damages. But it is not altogether certain. *d*

I think that the only effective remedy available in such a case as this is an injunction. The Common Market Commission have recently considered their own position about their ability to make interim orders. They said that they had power but they preferred it to be done by the national courts. They made a statement on 20 February 1980 in which they said:

'While not relevant to the present case, in general parties should consider whether *e* a similar remedy may not be available from a national court before applying to the Commission—particularly if the national procedures are cheaper or the order more easily policed.'

(See Kerse *EEC Anti-trust Procedure* (1981) App 1, p 322.)

That especially applies to the present case. Undoubtedly the national procedures here *f* for obtaining an injunction are cheaper. The order is more easily policed here by way of seeing that the injunction is obeyed. In the circumstances, I think that there is a remedy by injunction available in our courts to restrain a breach of art 86 of the Treaty, especially as that article says that it 'shall be prohibited'.

Framing an injunction

g

The judge felt that there was much difficulty in framing an injunction. So difficult that he refused it altogether. But we have some help about it. We ourselves can restrain the Milk Marketing Board from limiting their supplies to those four distributors. Other customers should be able to come in and tender for the butter. We can insist on their being allowed to do so on fair terms. We have guidance on this from the Annual Report of the Director General of Fair Trading. He gives an instance of a case which did not *h* come to court but which was settled on the basis of an undertaking given by a company to supply their appliances on terms 'not significantly less favourable than those normally applied to other dealers carrying on business in similar circumstances'. It seems to me that that would be a good way of making the order. The Milk Marketing Board ought to supply bulk butter to the plaintiffs on terms which are not significantly less favourable than those normally applied to other persons, these four distributors or others, either as *j* to quantity or as to price. If this order is obeyed, as it should be, it means that the plaintiffs will not be shut out of business. They will be able to come in as they have done in the past; and their offers will be considered on a fair basis by the Milk Marketing Board.

Counsel for the board said that the Milk Marketing Board have already committed themselves to the four distributors; and it would be very difficult and embarrassing for them to break those commitments. I am afraid that that is a bed of their own making a and they must deal with it as best they can. It seems to me that this is a case where there is evidence at this stage of an abuse of a dominant position; sufficient evidence to warrant the court granting an interim injunction substantially in the terms which I have mentioned.

I would allow the appeal accordingly.

b **MAY LJ.** I agree. I propose to add very little on my own behalf because in interlocutory proceedings generally, and in interlocutory proceedings of this importance, in my opinion the least said the better so far as this court is concerned.

I would merely add this. I am not so doubtful about the availability of a remedy in damages for a breach of the provisions of art 86 of the EEC Treaty as was Lord Denning MR in the judgment which he has just delivered. If art 86, as part of the law of England, as it is, creates a cause of action permitting the grant of an injunction, I think it difficult c to argue that a possible alternative remedy for that cause of action in appropriate circumstances would not be the grant of damages. It is clear from the Belgian case to which Lord Denning MR has referred and also from a German case of which we were told that this is a remedy upheld by the courts of other members of the European Economic Community.

Be that as it may, the contrary is certainly arguable as the law stands at the moment, d particularly when one reads the passage from the judgment of Roskill LJ in *Valor International Ltd v Application des Gaz SA* [1978] 3 CMLR 87 at 99 to which Lord Denning MR referred. I can also see that in cases such as this it may be difficult, and on occasions perhaps impossible, to assess the proper measure of damage for any breach of art 86.

It must also be remembered in the present case that on the material before us it is clear that we are at or near the beginning of the main butter season for 1982. Consequently, e at this stage of this litigation at this time of the year, and having regard to the present development of this branch of the law, I cannot be satisfied that whatever damages might be recoverable for any breach of the provisions of art 86 would in the circumstances of this case provide an adequate remedy.

In those circumstances, I agree that this appeal should be allowed to the extent that an injunction should be granted in the terms referred to by Lord Denning MR.

f

SIR SEBAG SHAW. I agree also that this appeal should be allowed and that an interim injunction should be granted. I have considerable misgivings whether a remedy in damages lies for a contravention of art 86 of the EEC treaty.

The difficulty has been in determining what the form of the injunction should be. Following the indication given by Lord Denning MR in the course of his judgment, I g have ventured on an effort in draftsmanship which may at least provide a basis for agreement by both sides. I suggest that it should read:

'The defendants be restrained whether by themselves [etc] (1) from confining their sales of bulk butter to any particular person or persons, or bodies of persons, or any particular organisation or corporate body; (2) from imposing significantly h different terms in relation to the supply of bulk butter to buyers in the bulk butter market whether as regards price or quantity, otherwise than pursuant to ordinary mercantile and commercial practice.'

That may, I think, overcome the difficulty which presented itself to the judge below, and in that form it may commend itself to both parties as an interim measure.

j *Appeal allowed. Leave to appeal to the House of Lords refused.*

29 July. The Appeal Committee of the House of Lords allowed a petition by the board for leave to appeal.

Solicitors: *Joynson-Hicks & Co* (for the company); *Ellis & Fairbairn*, Thames Ditton (for the board).

Frances Rustin   Barrister.

Benson v Biggs Wall & Co Ltd

QUEEN'S BENCH DIVISION

PETER PAIN J

18, 19 JUNE 1980

Fatal accident – Damages – Loss of future earnings – Survival of claim for benefit of estate – Measure of damages – Principles of assessment – Deductions to be made from estimated net future earnings in arriving at surplus earnings on which award to be based – Living expenses – Method of calculating – Same method to be used as under Fatal Accidents Act in calculating amount of dependency – Living expenses restricted to deceased's own living expenses and not including expenses of maintaining his family – Effect of intestacy on award – Effect of award on division of damages under Fatal Accidents Act between widow and children – Law Reform (Miscellaneous Provisions) Act 1934, s 1(1) – Fatal Accidents Act 1976, s 3.

Fatal accident – Damages – Apportionment of damages between widow and children – Effect on apportionment of claim under Law Reform (Miscellaneous Provisions) Act 1934 for deceased's loss of future earnings in lost years – Fatal Accidents Act 1976, s 3.

The husband was killed in an accident at work for which his employers, the defendants, accepted liability. He died intestate, his earnings being his only estate. His widow brought an action against the defendants claiming (i) damages for herself and her infant son as dependants under the Fatal Accidents Act 1976 and (ii) damages for the benefit of the husband's estate under s 1 of the Law Reform (Miscellaneous Provisions) Act 1934. At the date of the trial the widow was aged 26 and the son aged 17 months. For the purposes of the claim under the 1976 Act it was agreed between the parties that the family's dependency was to be taken as being 70% of the husband's future loss of earnings and that 30% of those earnings represented the husband's own living expenses which were deductible from his earnings in calculating the dependency. It was further agreed that the claim under the 1976 Act should be compromised at £49,000. The claim under the 1934 Act included damages for the husband's loss of earnings in the 'lost years', ie the period of his pre-accident earning life expectancy. In regard to that claim the defendants submitted that the living expenses which had to be deducted from the earnings in the lost years in assessing the recoverable damages were greater than the living expenses deductible in calculating the family's dependency for the purposes of the 1976 Act and included not only the husband's own living expenses but also a reasonable sum for the cost of maintaining his family and that, accordingly, at least 40% of the earnings in the lost years was deductible from those earnings in assessing the recoverable damages under the 1934 Act. The defendants further submitted that in order to reduce the total amount of the damages recoverable under both Acts by the widow, bearing in mind that damages awarded under the 1934 Act were deductible from damages awarded under the 1976 Act, the proportion of the damages awarded under the 1976 Act to be attributed to the son should reflect his genuine dependency and not be fixed at a small notional sum representing the pocket money he would have received from the husband over and above his upkeep and maintenance and that accordingly the proportion of the damages awarded under the 1976 Act which were attributable to the son should be £7,000, and the widow's proportion of those damages should not include the cost of the son's upkeep.

Held – (1) The proportion of the damages awarded under the 1976 Act which were attributable to the son was to be assessed on the basis of his estimated genuine dependency and not merely on his 'pocket money' dependency. Bearing in mind his extreme youth and that there would be a long dependency, the amount of his dependency and thus his damages under the 1976 Act should be £5,000 and the widow's damages under that Act a should be £42,500 (see p 303 *b* to *f*, post); dictum of Boreham J in *Thompson v Price* [1973] 2 All ER at 850 not followed.

(2) The living expenses which had to be deducted from the husband's lost earnings in the lost years in assessing the recoverable damages under the 1934 Act had to be calculated on the same basis as was used in calculating the family's dependency under the 1976 Act. It followed that only the husband's own living expenses, and not the expenses of maintaining his family, could be deducted from his lost earnings in the lost years in

b assessing the damages under the 1934 Act and that, as his own living expenses had been agreed at 30% of his future earning for the purpose of the claim under the 1976 Act, the same proportion of his earnings was deductible as living expenses for the purpose of the claim under the 1934 Act. It followed that the same figure, £49,000, was recoverable under the 1976 Act as was recoverable under the 1934 Act. The £49,000 recoverable under the 1934 Act therefore comprised the husband's estate (see p 304 *b c* and p 305 *b* to

c *f*, post); *Pickett v British Rail Engineering Ltd* [1979] 1 All ER 774 and dictum of Megaw LJ in *Gammell v Wilson* [1980] 2 All ER at 567 applied.

(3) Since the deceased had died intestate the widow's and the son's damages under the 1934 Act were to be determined according to the division of the estate on the intestacy. Under the intestacy the widow was entitled to the first £25,000 of the husband's estate and to a life interest in half the remainder of the estate, ie in £12,000 (the reversion to

d that half of the remainder going to the son) and the son, in addition to the reversion, was entitled to the other half of the remainder on the statutory trusts. It followed that under the 1934 Act and the effect of the intestacy the widow was entitled to damages of £36,750, namely £25,000 plus £11,750 as representing the value of her life interest less the value of the son's reversion (£250), and the son was entitled to damages of £12,250, namely £250, the value of his reversion on the widow's life interest, and £12,000, being

e the value of his entitlement under the intestacy to the other half of the remainder on the statutory trusts. Deducting the wife's damages under the 1934 Act (£36,750) from her damages under the 1976 Act (£42,500), it followed that she was entitled to £5,750 under the 1976 Act in addition to her damages under the 1934 Act. However, the amount of the son's damages under the 1934 Act extinguished his damages of £5,000 under the 1976 Act. Accordingly, the widow was entitled to judgment for the total sum of £54,750,

f namely (i) her damages of £36,750 under the 1934 Act, (ii) her damages of £5,750 under the 1976 Act and (iii) the son's damages of £12,250 under the 1934 Act (see p 305 *f* to p 306 *a*, post).

Notes

For damages under the Fatal Accidents Act 1976, see 34 Halsbury's Laws (4th edn) paras

g 14–15.

For damages for loss of earnings in the lost years, see 12 ibid para 1154.

For the Law Reform (Miscellaneous Provisions) Act 1934, s 1, see 13 Halsbury's Statutes (3rd edn) 115.

For the Fatal Accidents Act 1976, s 3, see 46 ibid 1119.

h **Cases referred to in judgment**

Benham v Gambling [1941] 1 All ER 7, [1941] AC 157, HL, 36(1) Digest (Reissue) 383, 1544.

Gammell v Wilson [1980] 2 All ER 557, [1982] AC 27, [1980] 3 WLR 591, CA; *affd* [1981] 1 All ER 578, [1982] AC 27, [1981] 2 WLR 248, HL.

Kandalla v British Airways Board (formerly British Airways Corp) [1980] 1 All ER 341,

j [1981] QB 158, [1980] 2 WLR 730.

Oliver v Ashman [1961] 3 All ER 323, [1962] 2 QB 210, [1961] 3 WLR 669, CA, 36(1) Digest (Reissue) 313, 1267.

Pickett v British Rail Engineering Ltd [1979] 1 All ER 774, [1980] AC 136, [1978] 3 WLR 995, HL, Digest (Cont Vol E) 459, 1314b.

Rose v Ford [1937] 3 All ER 359, [1937] AC 826, HL, 36(1) Digest (Reissue) 382, 1530.

Thompson v Price [1973] 2 All ER 846, [1973] QB 838, [1973] 2 WLR 1037, 36(1) Digest (Reissue) 365, 1482.

Action

The plaintiff, Janet Mary Benson, the widow and administratrix of the estate of Paul *a*
Geoffrey Benson, deceased, brought an action against the defendants, Biggs Wall & Co
Ltd, claiming damages under the Fatal Accidents Act 1976 for herself and her infant son
and damages under the Law Reform (Miscellaneous Provisions) Act 1934 for the
deceased's estate. Liability was admitted and the only issue was the quantum of the
damages. The facts are set out in the judgment.

b
W R H Crowther QC and *Stephen Archer* for the plaintiff.
Peter Ripman for the defendants.

Cur adv vult

19 June. **PETER PAIN J** read the following judgment: This is an action by the widow *c*
of a Mr Benson who was employed by the defendants on 10 August 1978, when
unhappily he met with a fatal accident. The matter originally came before the court as a
contested case, but I was informed at the beginning of the hearing that liability was no
longer in issue and that on agreed facts I was to be asked to determine certain points of
law.

The widow in this case is now aged 26. Her husband, being born in 1958, was 21 at *d*
the time he met with his fatal accident. So they were a young couple, and the wife was
pregnant at the time of the accident. Happily she did not lose her child, who is a son
born on 30 January 1979. So he is now a 17-month-old baby.

The facts as to dependency are largely agreed. The problem I really have to contend
with is how the calculations now ought to be made, having regard to the Pandora's box
that has been opened by the decision of the House of Lords in *Pickett v British Rail* *e*
Engineering Ltd [1979] 1 All ER 774, [1980] AC 136. The figures had this been an ordinary
what I may call 'traditional' case (certainly traditional so far as counsel for the defendants
and I are concerned: we used to have many together in the past) are these. It is agreed
that the dependency of the family is to be taken as 70% of the husband's earnings, and
that there is effectively no separate estate. So one is concerned with his earnings as being
the only estate. If one takes 70% of what would have been his earnings from the date of *f*
death to the date of trial, one gets a figure of £4,156. As to his future loss of earnings by
comparison with a man in the same grade, the rate as at today is established as £3,947 a
year, 70% of which is £2,763, and it is agreed that there should be 15 years' purchase at
that rate as from today which gives one a figure of £41,445.

I gather that the deceased had good prospects. It is agreed that he had a good chance of
becoming a foreman and earning more money at somewhere about the 35 to 40 age, and *g*
a further sum of £2,500 is to be allowed for that. There is in addition a sum for loss of
expectation of life, the traditional sum, which is taken at £1,250. There is a claim for
£224 funeral expenses, and it is agreed for simplicity of calculation that I can treat that
as being the equivalent of £250 in the rounded sum which the parties were agreed on as
being the traditional basis of calculation. If one adds the £224 into those figures one gets
£49,575, and it is agreed that this whole claim should be compromised at £49,000. It is *h*
necessary for me to approve that; in so far as it is necessary I do.

The only issue on the Fatal Accidents Act calculation is one in which the defendant is
not usually in the least interested, and that is as to the sum to be attributed to the infant.
In the circumstances of this case, as it will turn out, it is clear the defendants are closely
interested in that. Counsel for the plaintiff contended that the sum of £4,000 would be
appropriate. Counsel for the defendants contended that the more appropriate sum would *j*
be £7,000. Counsel for the plaintiff referred me to *Thompson v Price* [1973] 2 All ER 846,
[1973] QB 838, a decision of Boreham J. At the end of that decision Boreham J said
([1973] 2 All ER 846 at 850, [1973] QB 838 at 843):

'I remind myself that in this case the dependency of £9 per week which is
apportioned to the widow does in fact take into account the fact, or assumes, that

she will have to support her infant son. The dependency of £3 per week apportioned
to the child is intended to represent what he would have received over and above
the cost of his keep. In those circumstances, it seems to me that there is no room for
the argument that the son's proportion of damages is to be assessed on the footing
the court takes no account of the remarriage of his mother . . .'

Of course, Boreham J was dealing with a rather different problem. Counsel for the
defendants has contended that this statement, that the mother's dependency includes the
cost of maintaining the son, is not accurate; it is neither the practice nor is it sound in
principle. On that I think counsel is right. Certainly it is my experience in a large
number of these cases, both at the Bar and on the Bench, that one looked at the child's
genuine dependency and not merely at what I might call a 'pocket money' dependency.
That seems to be right in principle, because the function of the court is to safeguard the
child. Even with a mother who is a model one could not effectively safeguard the child
if one treated the child's dependency as being partly included in her figure. The point
being this, that if one leaves the cost of maintaining the child as being included in the
mother's figure that money become hers; she may well spend it on the child, look after
it beautifully, but decide after a short while that it would be to the child's advantage as
well as to her own if she remarries, then unhappily in a year or two she meets with an
accident or something and dies without having taken the precaution of making a will.
Then so far as the Fatal Accidents Act money is concerned which has gone to her, if that
has been saved it will pass to the stepfather so far as the first £25,000 is concerned plus a
life interest in half the remainder. The stepfather, one would hope, would give effect to
the moral claim of the child, but the law is not content to rely on a moral claim.

I think it right to do the best I can to estimate the child's genuine dependency. I am
not prepared to follow *Thompson v Price*. I think the figure of counsel for the defendants
is a bit on the high side if one looks at the realities of the family, and takes account of the
fact that this is a sum which will be held in hand. I take account of the child's extreme
youth which means there will be a long dependency here. I think the right figure for the
child's dependency is £5,000. This means that taking the agreed £49,000 this would be
broken up as to £42,500 to the widow, £250 to funeral expenses, £5,000 damages for
loss of expectation of life.

That is only the beginning of the matter, because the real issue I have to decide is
whether the effect of the decision in *Pickett v British Rail Engineering Ltd* means that the
damages payable under the Law Reform Act are not limited to £1,250 plus the funeral
expenses. Counsel for the plaintiff contends that damages are recoverable in respect of
the earnings in the lost years, and that while in *Pickett's* case the court was dealing with
someone who had survived for a period before he died of the injuries which the
defendant's negligence had inflicted on him, in principle that makes no difference; one
applies exactly the same principle to the person who is killed immediately.

He further contends that by reason of the decision of the Court of Appeal in *Gammell v
Wilson* [1980] 2 All ER 557, [1982] AC 27 the claim is not barred by the wording of s 1(c)
of the Law Reform (Miscellaneous Provisions) Act 1934. He also referred me to the
decision of Griffiths J in *Kandalla v British Airways Board* [1980] 1 All ER 341, [1981] QB
158, which antedated the decision of the Court of Appeal, but was on the same lines as
the decision of the majority in the Court of Appeal. That decision in the Court of Appeal
is a majority decision, and I understand from the best information one has that the case
is probably going to the House of Lords[1]. Counsel for the defendants concedes that so far
as this court is concerned he cannot distinguish the decision in the Court of Appeal and
that in principle counsel for the plaintiff's contention is right, but he says that when one
comes to apply the principles of those two cases one finds that in effect it will not carry
the damages which are payable above the limit of £49,000, which he agrees is payable
anyhow under the Fatal Accidents Act.

The first point he makes is as to the calculation of the earnings in the 'lost years'. I use

---

1   The case was subsequently affirmed: see [1981] 1 All ER 578, [1982] AC 27.

that phrase throughout since it has been used in a number of authorities now. The House of Lords said in *Pickett's* case that the living expenses should be deducted from the loss of earnings in the lost years in order to arrive at the true figure of damages. The House of Lords itself did not attempt any calculations; it remitted the case for further consideration, and it therefore did not have to define any further what it meant by 'living expenses'. When one examines it one sees there is a problem there. Is one to treat that simply as under the Fatal Accidents Act calculation as being those expenses which are specifically referable to the deceased as distinct from family expenses, or is one to look at it as I suppose an accountant might who would attribute to the deceased's expenses not only the cost of fares to work, clothing and so on, but also a fair share of the cost of maintaining the family home where he lived?

It is agreed between the parties that 30% is to be treated for the purposes of the Fatal Accidents Act as the appropriate figure. Counsel for the defendants has contended that for the purposes of *Pickett's* case it ought to be a considerably larger figure; certainly at least 40%. I do not agree with counsel on this argument. The reason I reject his contention is that it seems to me that one has got to look at the decision in *Pickett* in context, and the whole purpose of the decision in *Pickett* was to redress the injustice which was brought about by the decision in *Oliver v Ashman* [1961] 3 All ER 323, [1962] 2 QB 210. I quote the way in which Lord Wilberforce deals with it, because I think that sets the whole context in which Pickett was decided. He said in reference to *Oliver v Ashman* ([1979] 1 All ER 774 at 777–778, [1980] AC 136 at 146–147):

'In 1974, when his symptoms became acute, the deceased was a man of 51 with an excellent physical record. He was a champion cyclist of Olympic standard, he kept himself very fit and was a non-smoker. He was leading an active life and cycled to work every day. He had a wife and two children. There was medical evidence at the trial as to his condition and prospects, which put his then expectation of life at one year: this the judge accepted. There can be no doubt that but for his exposure to asbestos dust in his employment he could have looked forward to a normal period of continued employment up to retiring age. That exposure, for which the defendant accepts liability, has resulted in this period being shortened to one year. It seems, therefore, strange and unjust that his claim for loss of earnings should be limited to that one year (the survival period) and that he should recover nothing in respect of the years of which he has been deprived (the lost years). But this is the result of authority binding on the judge and the Court of Appeal: *Oliver v Ashman*. The present is, in effect, an appeal against that decision. *Oliver v Ashman* is part of a complex of law which has developed piecemeal and which is neither logical nor consistent. Judges do their best to make do with it but from time to time cases appear, like the present, which do not appeal to a sense of justice. I shall not review in any detail the state of the authorities for this was admirably done by Holroyd Pearce LJ in *Oliver v Ashman*. The main strands in the law as it then stood were: (1) the Law Reform (Miscellaneous Provisions) Act 1934 which abolished the old rule actio personalis moritur cum persona and provided for the survival of causes of action in tort for the benefit of the victim's estate; (2) the decision of this House in *Rose v Ford* [1937] 3 All ER 359, [1937] AC 826 that a claim for loss of expectation of life survived under the 1934 Act, and was not a claim for damages based on the death of a person and so barred at common law . . . (3) the decision of this House in *Benham v Gambling* [1941] 1 All ER 7, [1941] AC 157 that damages for loss of expectation of life could only be given up to a conventional figure, then fixed at £200; (4) the Fatal Accidents Acts under which proceedings may be brought for the benefit of dependants to recover the loss caused to those dependants by the death of the breadwinner; The amount of this loss is related to the probable future earnings which would have been made by the deceased during "lost years". This creates a difficulty. It is assumed in the present case, and the assumption is supported by authority, that if an action for damages is brought by the victim during his lifetime, a and either proceeds to judgment or is settled, further proceedings cannot be brought after his death under the Fatal Accidents Acts. If this assumption is correct, it provides a basis, in logic and justice, for allowing the victim to recover for earnings lost during his lost years. This assumption is based on the wording of s 1 of the 1846 Act (now s 1 of the Fatal Accidents Act 1976) and is not supported by any decision of this House. It cannot however be challenged in this appeal, since there is before us no claim under the Fatal Accidents Acts. I think, therefore, that we must for b present purposes act on the basis that it is well founded, and that if the present claim, in respect of earnings during the lost years fails it will not be possible for a fresh action to be brought by the deceased's dependants in relation to them.'

Now that being the whole purpose of the House of Lords, it seems to me it would have been absurd if they had then imported into the calculations to be made some new method of assessing living expenses. There is certainly nothing in the speeches to suggest c that living expenses should be calculated differently from the way in which it is done under the Fatal Accidents Act, so I am bound to agree that equally there is nothing which says it must be done that way, but it is of some significance that in the subsequent case of *Gammell v Wilson* [1980] 2 All ER 557 at 567, [1982] AC 27 at 40 Megaw LJ said in the course of his dissenting judgment:

d   'If damages for loss of income in the lost years were recoverable by the estate in a Law Reform Act action, presumably the same principle of assessment would apply as applied in an action such as *Pickett*'s case. The judge would have to assess what the earnings of the lost years would have been (presumably net of tax). That will often be an extremely difficult task, involving what is truly no more than guesswork in many aspects in many cases. But it is essentially the same task as is required to be e   carried out in assessing the dependency in a Fatal Accidents Act case.'

Therefore, I hold that from the point of view of calculating living expenses one uses the same yardstick as one does under the Fatal Accidents Act, and it follows from the agreement which has been reached as to Fatal Accidents Act damages that the same method should be applied as to the Law Reform Act damages and one arrives at the same overall figure of £49,000.

f Now the deceased died intestate, and there being no other significant estate I have to see how his estate falls to be divided on an intestacy. It is common ground that the effect will be that the first £25,000 goes to the plaintiff, second that the plaintiff has a life interest in half the remainder with the reversion to the son, and third that the other half of the remainder goes to the son on the statutory trusts.

I have no actuarial evidence before me as to the value of the widow's life interest and g the son's reversion in terms of cash today, but after some discussion and there being no formal evidence it was agreed that as the widow is only 26 the value of the son's reversion is very small indeed and I should take that figure as being worth £250, and that, since the life interest and the reversion together, it would seem logically, must amount to the same amount as the capital sum, I should treat the wife's life interest as being worth £11,750.

h In view of the wide powers of maintenance and advancement which accompany the statutory trusts on which the son's share is held, it was agreed that I should treat his interest as being the equivalent of money in hand, so that will be £12,000. Therefore, under the Law Reform Act and the law as to intestacy, the wife will benefit to the extent of £36,750 and the son as to £12,250. The Law Reform Act damages fall to be deducted from the Fatal Accidents Act damages. The widow is entitled to £42,500 under the Fatal j Accidents Act. One sets against that the £36,750 which she is entitled to under the Law Reform Act, and this reduces her entitlement under the Fatal Accidents Act to £6,000. The son is entitled to £5,000 under the Fatal Accidents Act. That sum is entirely extinguished by his claim under the Law Reform Act. The effect of this is that there will be judgment for the plaintiff for £54,750 made up as follows: damages under the Law

Reform Act £36,750, damages under the Fatal Accidents Act £5,750, and the son's damages £12,250. Of course, there will be the appropriate award by way of interest.

Judgment accordingly.

Solicitors: *L Bingham & Co* (for the plaintiff); *Mackrell & Co* (for the defendants).

K Mydeen Esq　Barrister.

Harris v Empress Motors Ltd

QUEEN'S BENCH DIVISION
MCCOWAN J
18, 19, 20, 21 JANUARY 1982

Fatal accident – Damages – Loss of future earnings – Survival of claim for benefit of estate – Measure of damages – Principles of assessment – Deductions to be made from estimated net future earnings in arriving at surplus earnings on which award to be based – Living expenses – Method of calculating – Same method to be used as under Fatal Accidents Act in calculating amount of dependency – Living expenses restricted to deceased's own living expenses – Award not based on proportion of earnings deceased would have saved after deducting whole of his expenditure on himself and his family – Law Reform (Miscellaneous Provisions) Act 1934, s 1(1).

In assessing the damages recoverable by a deceased's estate under the Law Reform (Miscellaneous Provisions) Act 1934 for the deceased's loss of earnings in the 'lost years', ie the period of the deceased's pre-accident earning life expectancy, the deceased's living expenses in those years, which have to be deducted from his net earnings in those years in assessing the recoverable damages, are to be calculated on the same basis as a deceased's living expenses are calculated under the Fatal Accidents Act 1976 in assessing, on the basis of the deceased's future earnings, the amount of a claimant's dependency under the 1976 Act. The deductible living expenses from the earnings in the lost years for the purpose of the 1934 Act are, therefore, merely the living expenses which the deceased would have spent on himself and are not the whole of his expenditure on himself and his family during the lost years. It follows that the basis for an award of damages for lost earnings in the lost years under the 1934 Act is not confined to that proportion of the deceased's earnings which he would have been likely to save, or put indirectly into building up his wealth, after deducting the whole of his expenditure on himself and his family (see p 311 j, post); *Benson v Biggs Wall & Co Ltd* (1980) [1982] 3 All ER 300 followed; *Pickett v British Rail Engineering Ltd* [1979] 1 All ER 774 and *Gammell v Wilson* [1981] 1 All ER 578 considered.

Faced with the situation that a plaintiff by suing under both the 1976 Act and the 1934 Act may be awarded a total sum larger than that which she could be awarded under either Act, judges should no longer be content when making an apportionment under the 1976 Act to fix a small notional sum for the child or children of the deceased's family but should attempt to estimate the child's genuine dependency (see p 311 j to p 312 b, post); *Benson v Biggs Wall & Co Ltd* (1980) [1982] 3 All ER 300 followed.

Notes

For damages for loss of earnings, see 12 Halsbury's Laws (4th edn) para 1154.

For the Law Reform (Miscellaneous Provisions) Act 1934, s 1, see 13 Halsbury's Statutes (3rd edn) 115.

For the Fatal Accidents Act 1976, see 46 ibid 1115.

Cases referred to in judgment

a *Benham v Gambling* [1941] 1 All ER 7, [1941] AC 157, HL, 36(1) Digest (Reissue) 383, 1544.

Benson v Biggs Wall & Co Ltd (1980) [1982] 3 All ER 300.

Gammell v Wilson [1981] 1 All ER 578, [1982] AC 27, [1981] 2 WLR 248, HL; *affg* [1980] 2 All ER 557, [1982] AC 27, [1980] 3 WLR 591, CA.

Oliver v Ashman [1961] 3 All ER 323, [1962] 2 QB 210, [1961] 3 WLR 669, CA, 36(1)
b Digest (Reissue) 313, 1267.

Pickett v British Rail Engineering Ltd [1979] 1 All ER 774, [1980] AC 136, [1978] 3 WLR 995, HL, Digest (Cont Vol E) 459, 1314b.

Skelton v Collins (1966) 115 CLR 94, [1966] ALR 449, HC of Aust, 30 Digest (Reissue) 267, *380.

Sullivan v West Yorkshire Passenger Transport Executive (17 December 1980, unreported),
c QBD.

Action

By a writ dated 15 November 1979 the plaintiff, Susan Harris, the administratrix of the estate of Peter Henry Harris deceased, claimed against the defendants, Empress Motors Ltd (1) damages under the Fatal Accidents Act 1976 for herself, as the deceased's widow,
d and for the two sons of the deceased, Nicholas Harris, born on 11 August 1974 and Timothy Harris born on 22 April 1978, (2) damages under the Law Reform (Miscellaneous Provisions) Act 1934 for the deceased's estate and (3) interest on the damages under the 1934 Act. The facts are set out in the judgment.

Patrick Bennett QC and *Jonathan Acton-Bond* for the plaintiff.
e *C H Whitby QC* for the defendants.

McCOWAN J. The accident in this case occurred on 3 February 1978 and resulting from it the deceased died on 10 February 1978. He was then aged 29, so was his widow. She is now aged 33. They were married in 1969 and they had two children, Nicholas, born on 11 August 1974, now aged 7½, and Timothy, born on 22 April 1978 and now
f nearly four. He was born very shortly after his father's death. As a husband he was, I am satisfied, an utterly sober and responsible man. His wife told me, and I found her a wholly reliable witness, that he did not smoke or gamble and he only drank socially. He provided the home with a freezer, colour television and stereo. He never spent very much on himself. After very properly probing her evidence about these matters counsel for the defendants, as one would expect of him, conceded that it would be reasonable to accept the proportion of his income for the dependency at 75%.
g Specifically as a father, his widow said that the boy whom he lived to know, Nicholas, was the apple of his eye. His accountant spoke of him being anxious to get home early enough in the evening to be able to see Nicholas before he went to bed. Nicholas's clothing, his widow told me, was not stinted in any way. They were considering moving in time to a better house in an area where the education possibilities would be better. As
h she put it, 'We had thought about private education but not come to any conclusion about it. He was the sort of man who would have made sacrifices for his children.'

It also appeared from the evidence that he was the sort of man who took thought for the future. He had started a self-employed person's pension scheme and paid an annual premium of £94. Counsel for the plaintiff relies on that as showing that he would not have had to retire at 65 onto a state pension alone. He was useful about the house. His
j widow said that he did decorations, knocked down a wall, blocked a door, put in a window and laid the lawn. That is lost to the family, and counsel for the plaintiff rightly points out that this factor must be taken into consideration in arriving at the dependency.

[His Lordship reviewed the evidence relating to the deceased's earnings over the four years from his death to the date of the trial and continued:]

Taking account of all the evidence and the risks involved in any business, his record as a worker and what he did in the home, I think a reasonable estimate of his net earnings

over the relevant four years would be as follows: the first year £4,750, the second year
£5,500, the third year £6,250, and the fourth year £7,000, which I calculate to total   *a*
£23,500. Taking the proportion for dependency, which was agreed between the two
sides at 75%, I arrive at a figure for damages under the Fatal Accidents Act to the date of
judgment of £17,625 plus funeral expenses agreed at £226·50, giving a total of
£17,851·50. It was agreed between the parties that interest on whatever figure I found
should be at the rate of 24·79%. I have attempted this calculation. I shall state the figure
that I have arrived at, and will depend on the parties to check it. The figure I arrive at is   *b*
£4,425·38, giving a total of £22,276·88.

I turn to the question of future dependency. Four years have passed since the death. In
all the circumstances, including the ages of the people concerned, the deceased's
willingness to work, his personal pension scheme, etc, I think I should take a multiplier
of a further 12 years and a multiplicand of £7,000, and that is a somewhat easier sum for
me, and I arrive at a figure of £84,000 for future earnings, and 75% of that equals   *c*
£63,000. And assuming that that sum is correct, the total Fatal Accidents Act claim
amounts in my judgment to £85,276·88.

I turn to the claim under the Law Reform (Miscellaneous Provisions) Act 1934. The
following figures are agreed. For loss of expectation of life £1,250, the general damages
£100, and for wages etc £350, giving a total of £1,700.

Then arises the vexed question of the lost years. I was referred to a judgment of Peter   *d*
Pain J in *Benson v Biggs Wall & Co Ltd* (1980) [1982] 3 All ER 300. In that case the value
of the fatal accidents claim was £49,000. Having quoted from the speech of Lord
Wilberforce in the House of Lords in *Pickett v British Rail Engineering Ltd* [1979] 1 All ER
774, [1980] AC 136, Peter Pain J went on (at [1982] 3 All ER 300 at 305–6):

> 'Now that being the whole purpose of the House of Lords, it seems to me it would
> have been absurd if they had then imported into the calculations to be made some   *e*
> new method of assessing living expenses. There is certainly nothing in the speeches
> to suggest that living expenses should be calculated differently from the way in
> which it is done under the Fatal Accidents Act, so I am bound to agree that equally
> there is nothing which says it must be done that way, but it is of some significance
> that in the subsequent case of *Gammell v Wilson* [1980] 2 All ER 557 at 567, [1982]
> AC 27 at 40 Megaw LJ said in the course of his dissenting judgment: "If damages   *f*
> for loss of income in the lost years were recoverable by the estate in a Law Reform
> Act action, presumably the same principle of assessment would apply as applied in
> an action such as *Pickett's* case. The judge would have to assess what the earnings of
> the lost years would have been (presumably net of tax). That will often be an
> extremely difficult task, involving what is truly no more than guesswork in many
> aspects in many cases. But it is essentially the same task as is required to be carried   *g*
> out in assessing the dependency in a Fatal Acccidents Act case." Therefore, I hold
> that from the point of view of calculating living expenses one uses the same yardstick
> as one does under the Fatal Accidents Act, and it follows from the agreement which
> has been reached as to Fatal Accidents Act damages that the same method should be
> applied as to the Law Reform Act damages and one arrives at the same overall figure
> of £49,000. Now the deceased died intestate, and there being no other significant   *h*
> estate I have to see how his estate falls to be divided on an intestacy. It is common
> ground that the effect will be that the first £25,000 goes to the plaintiff, second that
> the plaintiff has a life interest in half the remainder with the reversion to the son,
> and third that the other half of the remainder goes to the son on the statutory trusts.
> I have no actuarial evidence before me as to the value of the widow's life interest
> and the son's reversion in terms of cash today, but after some discussion and there   *j*
> being no formal evidence it was agreed that as the widow is only 26 the value of the
> son's reversion is very small indeed and I should take that figure as being worth
> £250, and that, since the life interest and the reversion together, it would seem
> logically, must amount to the same amount as the capital sum, I should treat the

wife's life interest as being worth £11,750. In view of the wide powers of
maintenance and advancement which accompany the statutory trusts on which the
son's share is held, it was agreed that I should treat his interest as being the equivalent
of money in hand, so that will be £12,000. Therefore, under the Law Reform Act
and the law as to intestacy, the wife will benefit to the extent of £36,750 and the
son as to £12,250. The Law Reform Act damages fall to be deducted from the Fatal
Accidents Act damages. The widow is entitled to £42,500 under the Fatal Accidents
Act. One sets against that the £36,570 which she is entitled to under the Law
Reform Act, and this reduces her entitlement under the Fatal Accidents Act to
£6,000. The son is entitled to £5,000 under the Fatal Accidents Act. That sum is
entirely extinguished by his claim under the Law Reform Act. The effect of this is
that there will be judgment for the plaintiff for £54,750 made up as follows:
damages under the Law Reform Act £36,750, damages under the Fatal Accidents
Act £5,750, and the son's damages at £12,250. Of course, there will be the
appropriate award by way of interest.'

Accordingly Peter Pain J held that in calculating living expenses one uses the same
yardstick under one Act as under the other, and in consequence he arrived at the same
overall figure under each Act. Yet by the plaintiff suing under both Acts a result was
arrived at where a total sum was awarded larger than that awarded under either Act, in
that case £54,750 instead of £49,000. That offends common sense. It does not seem
right that by this means a sum has to be awarded by the court which is larger than the
proper sum due under either Act. It seems unlikely to me that such a result was ever
envisaged by their Lordships in *Pickett*.

Counsel for the defendants suggests one way of dealing with the problem is to follow
the approach of Mustill J in *Sullivan v West Yorkshire Passenger Transport Executive*, a
judgment given by him on 17 December 1980, a transcript of which was supplied to me.
Mustill J said:

'As previously stated, I assume for the purpose of this judgment that the plaintiff
as administrator can claim in respect of the notional earnings of the deceased during
the "lost years", but that a deduction must be made in respect of her notional living
expenses. There is a wide divergence between the parties as to the way in which this
deduction should be computed. The plaintiff says that there should be only a modest
reduction on account of living expenses; but the defendants maintain that the whole
of the deceased's expenditures on herself and her family should be deleted from the
calculation, leaving only that part of her contribution to the joint income which
represents her share of the notional joint family savings. Since the deceased's share
of the savings amounted to only about 10% of her net annual income, it can readily
be seen that the choice between the two alternatives makes a radical difference to
the amount of the recovery; indeed it affects it by a factor of about six . . .
Accordingly, I consider that of the two rival methods, that proposed by the
defendants should be preferred. I am not, however, persuaded that it can be adopted
without qualification. The defendants' argument involves the proposition that there
are three types of expenditure: (1) money spent solely on the deceased before they
reach the family pool; (2) those which go into, and are disbursed from, the pool; (3)
those which are directed into savings. But this is an over simplification, for some of
the disbursements go to increase the deceased's wealth, even if not directly banked
as savings. Mortgage repayments on a house provide an obvious example, for the
estate of the deceased will share the enhanced value of the equity of the repayment.
In the same category, as it would seem to me, are expenditures on the upkeep and
insurance of a valuable asset which will pass on death to the estate. Other examples
may readily be found. So an apportionment of the expenditures from the pool will
have to be made, necessarily on a rough and ready basis, to add to the figure for
direct savings, before a multiplicand can be arrived at on which to base an award in

respect of the lost years. I now turn in the light of these various conclusions to
consider what awards should be made in respect of the two distinct heads of claim.'   *a*

Mustill J went on to calculate that the total recovery under the Fatal Accidents Act
should be a sum of £39,950, after which he turned to the Law Reform Act, and I take up
his judgment again:

> 'Law Reform Act   Here, it can be seen at a glance that if the view which I have
> expressed as to the method of computation is correct, the recovery will fall well   *b*
> short of that under the Fatal Accidents Act. Detailed calculation is therefore
> unnecessary. It is sufficient to say that on the facts of the present case I would assess
> the proportion of the deceased's earnings which went to build up wealth at a figure
> of 15%. During the period up to trial, the amount would have been £1,650. For
> the post trial period, assuming earnings of £6,500 per annum and with a balance
> remaining for the multiplier of 12½ years, this yields a total recovery of £12,185. To   *c*
> this must be added the commuted pension which, roughly discounted for
> advancement, yields £4,750. In addition there is a conventional figure of £1,250
> representing the loss of expectation of life. In total, these components of the Law
> Reform Act claim amount to £23,500 in round figures. Since this is substantially
> less than the amount awarded under the Fatal Accidents Act, it is irrelevant to the
> ultimate measure of recovery.'   *d*

I must consider whether the approach of Mustill J is justified in the light of the
speeches in *Pickett*. I read first from a passage in the speech of Lord Wilberforce ([1979] 1
All ER 774 at 781–782, [1980] AC 136 at 150–151):

> 'My Lords, in the case of the adult wage earner with or without dependants who
> sues for damages during his lifetime, I am convinced that a rule which enables the   *e*
> "lost years" to be taken account of comes closer to the ordinary man's expectations
> than one which limits his interest to his shortened span of life. The interest which
> such a man has in the earnings he might hope to make over a normal life, if not
> saleable in a market, has a value which can be assessed. A man who receives that
> assessed value would surely consider himself and be considered compensated; a man
> denied it would not. And I do not think that to act in this way creates insoluble   *f*
> problems of assessment in other cases. In that of a young child (cf *Benham v Gambling*
> [1941] 1 All ER 7, [1941] AC 157) neither present nor future earnings could enter
> into the matter; in the more difficult case of adolescents just embarking on the
> process of earning (cf *Skelton v Collins* (1966) 115 CLR 94) the value of "lost" earnings
> might be real but would probably be assessable as small. There will remain some
> difficulties. In cases, probably the normal, where a man's actual dependants coincide   *g*
> with those for whom he provides out of the damages he receives, whatever they
> obtain by inheritance will simply be set off against their own claim. If on the other
> hand this coincidence is lacking, there might be duplication of recovery. To that
> extent injustice may be caused to the wrongdoer. But if there is a choice between
> taking a view of the law which mitigates a clear and recognised injustice in cases of
> normal occurrence, at the cost of the possibility in fewer cases of excess payments   *h*
> being made, or leaving the law as it is, I think that our duty is clear. We should
> carry the judicial process of seeking a just principle as far as we can, confident that a
> wise legislator will correct resultant anomalies. [Lord Wilberforce then referred to
> *Skelton v Collins* decided in the High Court of Australia and the judgments therein,
> and continued:] The judgments, further, bring out an important ingredient, which
> I would accept, namely that the amount to be recovered in respect of earnings in the   *j*
> "lost" years should be after deduction of an estimated sum to represent the victim's
> probable living expenses during those years. I think that this is right because the
> basis, in principle, for recovery lies in the interest which he has in making provision
> for dependants and others, and this he would do out of his surplus. There is the
> additional merit of bringing awards under this head into line with what could be
> recovered under the Fatal Accidents Acts.'

a   It is to be noted there that Lord Wilberforce is anticipating that where a man's actual
dependants coincide with those for whom he provides out of the damages he received,
whatever they obtain by inheritance must simply be set off against their own claim. That
reinforces my provisional view that the present anomaly facing me was not anticipated
by Lord Wilberforce. Again, it is apparent that he did not envisage a different method of
deducting living expenses under the two Acts. A similar approach was shown by Lord
Salmon ([1979] 1 All ER 774 at 784, [1980] AC 136 at 154):

b   'I think that in assessing those damages, there should be deducted the plaintiff's
own living expenses which he would have expended during the "lost years" because
these clearly can never constitute any part of his estate. The assessment of these
living expenses may, no doubt, sometimes present difficulties, but certainly no
difficulties which would be insuperable for the courts to resolve, as they always have
done in assessing dependency under the Fatal Accidents Acts.'

c   Again, a similar approach is shown by Lord Edmund-Davies ([1979] 1 All ER 774 at
792, [1980] AC 136 at 163):

        'This House lacks the material to enable it to estimate what would be proper
compensation for the "lost years", and the task will have to be remitted to the
Queen's Bench Division for determination. It is likely to prove a task of some
d   difficulty, though (contrary to the view expressed by Willmer LJ in Oliver v Ashman
[1961] 3 All ER 323 at 338, [1962] 2 QB 210 at 240) the lost earnings are not "far
too speculative to be capable of assessment by any court of law". The only guidance
I can proffer is that, in reaching their final figure, the court should make what it
regards as a suitable deduction for the total sum which Mr Pickett would have been
likely to expend on himself during the "lost years". This calculation, too, is by no
e   means free from difficulty, but a similar task has to be performed regularly in cases
brought under the Fatal Accidents Act.'

    I turn next to Gammell v Wilson, and note in particular a passage in the speech of Lord
Diplock ([1981] 1 All ER 578 at 583, [1982] AC 27 at 65):

        'Here was an obvious injustice which this House remedied by overruling Oliver v
f   Ashman and holding that a living plaintiff could recover damages for loss of earnings
during the lost years, but that in assessing the measure of such damages there should
be deducted from the total earnings the amount that he would have spent out of
those earnings on his own living expenses and pleasures because these would
represent an expense that would be saved in consequence of his death. In the case of
a married man of middle age and of a settled pattern of life, which was the case of
g   Mr Pickett, the effect of this deduction is to leave a net figure which represents the
amount which he would have spent on providing for his wife and any other
dependants, together with any savings that he might set aside out of his income. If
one ignores the savings element, which in most cases would be likely to be small,
this net figure is substantially the same as the damages that would have been
recoverable by the widow under the Fatal Accidents Acts: it represents the
h   dependency. So, in the particular case of Mr Pickett's widow the result was to do
substantial justice.'

    And again, without reading the passage, suffice it for me to draw attention to the
passage in the speech of Lord Scarman ([1981] 1 All ER 578 at 593, [1982] AC 27 at 78–
79) in which it seems to me, once again, that his approach is the same as that of Lord
j   Diplock in Gammell v Wilson and Lord Wilberforce in Pickett.
    I can see no logical justification for a different approach to the expenses to be deducted
under the two Acts. Moreover, having looked at the speeches in Pickett's case and
Gammell's case, I see no justification for it in authority either. Consequently, with respect
to Mustill J, I do not feel able to follow his lead. I think that the approach of Peter Pain J
was right and that I must go through the exercise that he did and which I read from the
transcript of his judgment. However, I also think, as he did, that faced with this situation

a judge should no longer be content, as judges often have been in the past when making an apportionment under the Fatal Accidents Act, to fix a small notional sum for the child or children. I agree with Peter Pain J that an attempt must be made to estimate the child's genuine dependency. Counsel for the plaintiff submits, and I accept, that it is wrong to arrive at an artificial apportionment in order to remedy the anomaly which faces me, which it will be apparent from the terms of my judgment I do not like. But counsel agrees that it is right to estimate the children's genuine dependency. He submits that for that purpose I should ignore the damages for the four years to date because the widow has kept the children at her own expense during that period. He further submits that for the future I should not take more than six years purchase for the boy who is now aged 7½ and not more than ten years for the boy who is now nearly four. I accept those submissions. As to the multiplicand, on the evidence from the widow of the deceased's attitude to and plans for his existing and expected children I would take this at £1,250 each a year.

In the result I apportion under the Fatal Accidents Act as follows: Nicholas £7,500, Timothy £12,500 and the widow £65,276·88.

[Following discussion between his Lordship and counsel on the consequential calculations necessary to determine the final award to the plaintiff under both the Fatal Accidents Act 1976 and the Law Reform (Miscellaneous Provisions) Act 1934, his Lordship awarded the plaintiff £8,276·88 under the 1976 Act (ie £85,276·88 less the gain to the deceased's estate consequent on his death, viz £7,500 for Nicholas, £12,500 for Timothy and £57,000 for the plaintiff) together with £82,325 assessed under the 1934 Act (ie £80,625 for the lost years, £1,250 for loss of expectation of life, £100 general damages and £350 for wages etc), making a total award of £90,601·88 under both Acts.]

Judgment for the plaintiff accordingly.

Solicitors: *Romain, Coleman & Co*, Walthamstow (for the plaintiff); *Edward Lewis & Co* (for the defendants).

K Mydeen Esq   Barrister.

Erven Warnink BV and others v J Townend & Sons (Hull) Ltd and others (No 2)

COURT OF APPEAL, CIVIL DIVISION
LAWTON, TEMPLEMAN AND FOX LJJ
6, 27 MAY 1982

Costs – Interest on costs – Date from which interest payable – Orders for costs made in plaintiffs' favour in passing-off action – Costs not taxed until after House of Lords hearing – Whether interest payable from date of orders or from date of taxation – Whether court has discretion to award interest on costs from date earlier than date of taxation – Judgments Act 1838, ss 17, 18.

The plaintiffs obtained three orders for costs in their favour in a passing-off action in which they succeeded before the trial judge, lost in the Court of Appeal, but succeeded in the House of Lords. The order of the House of Lords included an order that the defendants should pay the plaintiffs' costs in the courts below and, with certain exceptions, in the House of Lords. After the decision of the House of Lords the plaintiffs proceeded to tax their costs of all three hearings and obtained three certificates accordingly. The plaintiffs applied for an order that the defendants pay to them interest at the statutory rate on the taxed costs from the date of the orders for costs. The judge refused their application on the ground that interest on costs under the Judgments Act 1838 ran from *a* the date of the taxing master's certificate and not from the date of the order for costs. The plaintiffs appealed, seeking interest on the costs of the hearings in the court of first instance and in the Court of Appeal from the date of the respective judgments, but not on the costs of the hearing in the House of Lords. The plaintiffs contended that they were entitled to interest from the dates of the orders for costs under the 1838 Act or, alternatively, on the basis that the court had, in special cases, a discretion as to the date from which interest on costs was to be payable.

b

Held – On the true construction of ss 17 and 18*ᵃ* of the 1838 Act interest on an order for costs ran from the date of taxation, and the court had no discretion to award interest from an earlier date. The appeal would accordingly be dismissed (see p 318 *b* and *h* to p 319 *a*, post).

K v K [1977] 1 All ER 576 applied.

c *Boswell v Coaks* (1887) 57 LJ Ch 101 distinguished.

Per curiam. (1) The expression in s 17 of the 1838 Act that interest is payable from 'the time of entering up the judgment' relates to the date on which judgment is pronounced and not to the time of the formal entry in the judgment roll (see p 319 *f g* and p 320 *b c*, post); *Fisher v Dudding* (1841) 3 Man & G 238 and *Parsons v Mather & Platt Ltd* [1977] 2 All ER 715 approved.

d (2) The law has gone too far for the argument that s 17 of the 1838 Act does not apply to costs at all: the courts have accepted since its enactment that s 17 does apply to costs (see p 320 *g*, post).

Notes
For interest on costs, see 26 Halsbury's Laws (4th edn) paras 546, 553, and for cases on the
e date from which interest runs on judgments and orders, see 30 Digest (Reissue) 248–250, 540–564.

For the Judgments Act 1838, ss 17, 18, see 18 Halsbury's Statutes (3rd edn) 9, 11.

Cases referred to in judgment
Boswell v Coaks (1887) 57 LJ Ch 101, CA, 21 Digest (Reissue) 320, 2058.
f *Borthwick v Elderslie Steamship Co Ltd (No 2)* [1905] 2 KB 516, CA, 30 Digest (Reissue) 253, 596.
Erven Warnink BV v J Townend & Sons (Hull) Ltd [1979] 2 All ER 927, [1979] AC 731, [1979] 3 WLR 68, HL, Digest (Cont Vol E) 630, 1494a.
Fisher v Dudding (1841) 3 Man & G 238, 3 Scott NR 516, 133 ER 1131, 30 Digest (Reissue) 248, 548.
g *K v K (divorce costs: interest)* [1977] 1 All ER 576, [1977] Fam 39, [1977] 2 WLR 55, CA, Digest (Cont Vol E) 276, 7415Aa.
Landowners' West of England and South Wales Land Drainage and Inclosure Co v Ashford (1884) 33 WR 41, 30 Digest (Reissue) 249, 560.
Newton v Grand Junction Rly Co (1846) 16 M & W 139, 153 ER 1133, 30 Digest (Reissue) 248, 549.
h *Parsons v Mather & Platt Ltd* [1977] 2 All ER 715, [1977] 1 WLR 855, Digest (Cont Vol E) 354, 549a.
Peirce v Derry (1843) 4 QB 635, 114 ER 1038.
Pyman & Co v Burt and Boulton [1884] WN 100, 30 Digest (Reissue) 249, 581.
Schroeder v Cleugh (1877) 46 LJ QB 365, 30 Digest (Reissue) 249, 559.
Young v Bristol Aeroplane Co Ltd [1944] 2 All ER 293, [1944] KB 718, CA; *affd* [1946] 1 All
j ER 98, [1946] AC 163, HL, 30 Digest (Reissue) 269, 765.

Case also cited
BP Exploration Co (Libya) Ltd v Hunt (No 2) [1982] 1 All ER 925, [1982] 2 WLR 253, HL.

---

a Sections 17 and 18 are set out at p 315 *e* to *g*, post

Interlocutory appeal

The plaintiffs, Erven Warnink BV (a company incorporated under the laws of Holland)   *a*
and Victoria Wine Co Ltd, appealed against the order of Slade J made on 1 May 1981
dismissing the plaintiffs' motion issued on 18 December 1980 by which they sought
interest on the sums due for costs pursuant to orders made in their favour from the date
of those orders in a passing-off action which they brought against the defendants,
J Townend & Sons (Hull) Ltd and H Keeling & Co (a firm). The plaintiffs succeeded
before Goulding J on 29 July 1977, lost in the Court of Appeal (Buckley, Goff LJJ and Sir   *b*
David Cairns) on 19 April 1978, but succeeded in the House of Lords on 21 June 1979
(see [1979] 2 All ER 927, [1979] AC 731). The order of the House of Lords included an
order that the defendants pay the plaintiffs' costs in the courts below and, with certain
exceptions, in the House of Lords. The facts are set out in the judgment of the court.

Simon Thorley for the plaintiffs.
John Hamilton for the defendants.   *c*

Cur adv vult

27 May. **FOX LJ** read the following judgment of the court: The issue in this appeal is
whether the plaintiffs, who obtained certain orders for costs in their favour, are entitled   *d*
to interest on the taxed costs from the date of the orders. Slade J held that they were not.
He decided that the case was covered by the decision of this court in *K v K (divorce costs:
interest)* [1977] 1 All ER 576, [1977] Fam 39.

The action in which the orders were made was a passing-off action which was tried in
the Chancery Division over some 25 days by Goulding J. The plaintiffs lost in the Court
of Appeal, but succeeded in the House of Lords, where the order of Goulding J was   *e*
restored (see [1979] 2 All ER 927, [1979] AC 731).

The judgment of Goulding J was given on 29 July 1977, when he made an order
granting the plaintiffs an injunction, an inquiry as to damages and their taxed costs of
the action. The order of the House of Lords was made on 21 June 1979 and included an
order that the defendants should pay the plaintiffs' costs in the courts below and (with
certain exceptions) in the House of Lords.   *f*

By an order of 18 July 1979 the order of the House of Lords was made an order of the
High Court.

Because an appeal to the Court of Appeal was pending, the plaintiffs did not proceed
to tax their costs after the judgment of Goulding J. That, according to the uncontradicted
evidence of Mr Thum, the plaintiffs' solicitor, is in accordance with the usual practice.

After the decision of the House of Lords the plaintiffs did proceed to tax their costs of   *g*
all three hearings and obtained three certificates accordingly. Those certificates were as
follows: (i) on 25 February 1980 a certificate in the sum of £53,937·16 was granted
pursuant to the order of Goulding J; (ii) on 25 February 1980 a certificate in the sum of
£25,953·22 was granted pursuant to the order of 18 July 1979 in respect of the costs of
the appeal to the Court of Appeal; (iii) on 25 February 1980 a certificate was granted in
the sum of £15,181·31 in respect of the costs of the appeal to the House of Lords.   *h*

The total of the amounts on the three certificates is £95,071·69. The defendants paid
that on 28 March 1980 together with a sum of £982·26 in respect of interest on the taxed
costs (other than costs in the House of Lords) from the date of the relevant certificates to
payment.

The plaintiffs themselves had made various payments to their solicitors on account of
costs during the course of the proceedings. These were as follows: *j*

15 July 1976	£2,000·00
7 July 1977	£3,000·00
20 September 1977	£70,597·24
27 December 1977	£1,000·00
20 April 1978	£33,574·48

a

19 July 1978	£2,000·00
17 November 1978	£500·00
8 October 1979	£34,138·85
	£146,810·57

By the present motion issued on 18 December 1980 the plaintiffs sought an order (a) pursuant to the Judgments Act 1838 or (b) pursuant to the Law Reform (Miscellaneous

b Provisions) Act 1934 or (c) in the exercise of the court's discretion that the defendants pay to the plaintiffs interest at the statutory rate on the sums due for costs pursuant to (i) the order of Goulding J of 29 July 1977 from the date of the order and (ii) the order of the House of Lords of 21 June 1979 from the date it was made an order of the High Court on 18 July 1979.

The claim pursuant to the Law Reform (Miscellaneous Provisions) Act 1934 was not

c pursued before us. Nor was the claim for interest on the costs of the appeal in the House of Lords, since the present practice of the House of Lords is that interest will not be ordered on the costs of an appeal to the House.

In the event, the plaintiffs in this court sought interest from the date of the respective judgments other than interest on the costs of the hearing in the House of Lords (a) under the Judgments Act 1838 or, alternatively, (b) on the basis that, under the decision in *K v*

d *K*, the court has, in special cases, a discretion as to the date from which interest on costs is to be payable.

The material provisions of the Judgments Act 1838 are ss 17, 18 and 20, which are in the following terms:

> '**17.** Every judgment debt shall carry interest at the rate of four pounds per
>
> e centum per annum from the time of entering up the judgment until the same shall be satisfied, and such interest may be levied under a writ of execution on such judgment. [The statutory rate of interest has been increased from time to time.]
>
> **18.** All decrees and orders of courts of equity, and all rules of courts of common law, whereby any sum of money, or any costs, charges, or expences, shall be payable to any person, shall have the effect of judgments in the superior courts of common law, and the persons to whom any such monies, or costs, charges, or expences, shall
>
> f be payable, shall be deemed judgment creditors within the meaning of this Act; and all powers hereby given to the judges of the superior courts of common law with respect to matters depending in the same courts shall and may be exercised by courts of equity with respect to matters therein depending; and all remedies hereby given to judgment creditors are in like manner given to persons to whom any monies, or costs, charges, or expences, are by such orders or rules respectively directed to be
>
> g paid . . .
>
> **20.** Such new or altered writs shall be sued out of the courts of law, equity, and bankruptcy as may by such courts respectively be deemed necessary or expedient for giving effect to the provisions herein-before contained, and in such forms as the judges of such courts respectively shall from time to time think fit to order . . .'

h Section 20 was repealed by the Civil Procedure Acts Repeal Act 1879, s 2 and Sch, Part I.

Assuming that an order for payment of costs to be taxed is a judgment debt within s 17 (a matter to which we will refer again later) we would have supposed that the only question was what is meant in s 17 of the Judgments Act 1838 by the words 'from the time of entering up the judgment'. Do they mean the date when the judgment is

j pronounced or the date when it is actually passed and entered though the judgment on its face may bear the date of pronouncement, or the date when the amount to be paid has actually been assessed by the court? Prima facie that is simply a matter of construction of the 1838 Act. That is not, however, the way in which the matter has developed.

The Court of Chancery evidently regarded s 20 of the 1838 Act as authorising it to make rules that interest on costs should run from the date of the certificate of taxation (the allocatur) and not from the date of entering up the judgment (the incipitur). In *Boswell v Coaks* (1888) 57 LJ Ch 101 at 105 Lindley LJ said:

a

> 'The right to interest on costs depends on the statutory enactment 1 and 2 Vict.
> c. 110 [ie the Judgments Act 1838], ss. 17 and 18, and by section 20 of that Act the
> court is empowered to make orders framing new rules, and under that section the
> Court of Chancery by consolidated orders issued a form of writ of *fi. fa.* according to
> which interest on costs was to run from the date of the Taxing Master's Certificate.'

b

The Court of Common Pleas, however, awarded interest on costs from the date of the incipitur (see *Fisher v Dudding* (1841) 3 Man & G 238, 133 ER 1131), and so did the Court of Exchequer (see *Newton v Grand Junction Rly Co* (1846) 16 M & W 139, 153 ER 1133). The court in the latter case followed *Fisher v Dudding* and made it clear that it was of opinion that *Fisher v Dudding* was rightly decided.

On the other hand, in *Peirce v Derry* (1843) 4 QB 635, 114 ER 1038 the Court of c
Queen's Bench in effect applied the allocatur principle.

The Judicature Acts produced a change. Section 16 of the Supreme Court of Judicature Act 1875 is in the following terms:

> 'The Rules of Court in the First Schedule to this Act shall come into operation at
> the commencement of this Act, and as to all matters to which they extend shall d
> thenceforth regulate the proceedings in the High Court of Justice and the Court of
> Appeal . . .'

Section 33 of the 1875 Act repeals 'Any other enactment inconsistent with' the Act or the Supreme Court of Judicature Act 1873.

The rules in Sch 1 to the 1875 Act contained in App F forms of writ of fieri facias. e
Form 1 directed the sheriff to levy the taxed costs 'together with interest thereon . . . from the   day of   ,† . . .' The latter mark † refers to a footnote which states: 'The date of the certificate of taxation. The writ *must* be so moulded as to follow the substance of the judgment or order.'

The Common Pleas Division in *Schroeder v Cleugh* (1877) 46 LJQB 365 held that the effect of the 1875 Act was that interest on costs ran from the date of the allocatur. Lord f
Coleridge CJ held that the 1875 Act operated as a partial repeal of the Judgments Act 1838. He took it as undisputed that under the latter statute interest would run from the incipitur. Grove J took the view that there was no conflict between the two statutes at all but, if there was, he would want to give further consideration to the question whether the 1875 Act operated as a repeal of the Judgments Act 1838. Denman J took the view that either there was a conflict between the two statutes or there was not. If there was a g
conflict the Judicature Act must prevail.

Schroeder v Cleugh was decided in January 1877. In 1883 new Rules of the Supreme Court came into operation. Appendix H contained forms of writs of fieri facias including writs on an order for costs where the party wishes to execute under a separate writ. Form 1, which relates both to the judgment debt and costs directs the sheriff to levy the judgment debt and the costs in the same form as in App F to the 1875 rules, but with a h
different footnote. The 1883 footnote reads: 'Day of the judgment or order, or day on which money directed to be paid, or day from which interest is directed by the order to run, as the case may be.' Form 2 (the separate writ for costs only) contained no footnote.

This amendment was interpreted as meaning that the new footnote once more altered the law and, at any rate in a case where the debt and costs were issued by a single writ, as providing that interest on costs should run from the date of the incipitur (see *Pyman &* j
Co v Burt and Boulton [1884] WN 100). This was followed in a number of cases including *Landowners' West of England and South Wales Land Drainage and Inclosure Co v Ashford* (1884) 33 WR 41, a decision of Pearson J. That case was followed by North J in *Boswell v Coaks* (1887) 57 LJ Ch 101. He regarded the matter as depending on the rules and the forms which they prescribed. He said (at 103):

'Down to 1875 the Courts took different views. From 1875 to 1883 the Court took the equitable or equity view, and it was during that time that the case of *Schroeder* v. *Cleugh* was decided, and the Court of law, therefore, departing from its habitual practice, adopted that course. Under the Order of 1883 the practice is changed and the *fi. fa.* is now to be drawn as giving interest from the date of the judgment.'

North J's decision was upheld by the Court of Appeal, which, it seems to us, also regarded the matter as depending on the 1883 rules. Cotton LJ said (at 105):

'The previous order altered the common law rule which gave interest as from the date of the judgment. The case of *Schroeder* v. *Cleugh* shews that that order allowed the time at which the interest is to be calculated to be varied to the prejudice of a successful party by postponing the date from which the interest could be claimed . . . Whether it was right or wrong to vary the old rule I give no opinion, but we have this rule which applies here . . .'

And Lindley LJ said (at 105–106):

'Then came the Rules of 1883; they struck out the old rules and made one code applicable to all divisions of the Court, and then we find the writ of *fi. fa.* varied, and the present form made applicable to all divisions under which interest is made to run from the judgment not the allocatur . . . I think that the Rules of 1883 apply, and that the proper form of the writ of *fi. fa.* is that given in Appendix H., under which interest on costs runs from the date of the judgment, and not from the date of the Taxing Master's Certificate.'

Lopes LJ also regarded the case as turning on the 1883 rules.

By RSC (Revision) 1965, Ord 45, r 12 new writs of execution were introduced (App A). Forms 53 and 54 replaced the old Forms 1 and 2 respectively. The forms in fact are unchanged but the footnote to Form 1 has gone.

In that state of the law *K v K* [1977] 1 All ER 576, [1977] Fam 39 came before this court in 1976 on appeal from Baker P. In that case on 17 May 1974, in matrimonial proceedings ultimately transferred to the High Court as regards ancillary relief, the husband was ordered to pay the wife a lump sum of £50,000 on or before 1 September 1974 and also to pay the wife's costs of the proceedings. The husband paid the lump sum by 1 September. The wife's costs were lodged for taxation on 3 October 1974 and the taxation was completed in August 1975, and on 18 August the registrar ordered the husband to pay the amount taxed within 28 days; the husband did so. The wife claimed interest on the taxed costs from 17 May 1974. The claim was quite without merit because the wife had made no payments in respect of her costs until after August 1975. The court, upholding the decision of Baker P, rejected the wife's claim. Lord Denning MR said ([1977] 1 All ER 576 at 580–581, [1977] Fam 39 at 48) that, having got rid of the 1883 note—

'we are entitled to go back to the time before 1883. We can go back to the note which appeared in the 1875 Act, which says that the date to be inserted is "The date of the certificate of taxation". Alternatively, we are entitled to say that the rule of equity should prevail. In the further alternative, we are entitled to apply a little commonsense. Interest should be payable whenever money is "wrongly withheld" from the one who is entitled to it . . . When the sum is unascertained, the debtor cannot be expected to pay it until it is quantified . . . So in all fairness interest should only run from the date of quantification . . .'

Stephenson LJ said ([1977] 1 All ER 576 at 586, [1977] Fam 39 at 55):

'We cannot, in my opinion, declare the allocatur rule to be again the law because it was law before 1883 and the abolition of the 1883 footnote restores the earlier law; for the 1875 footnote, which was the foundation of the earlier law, has not

been put back. We have got to go back to the pre-existing law before the 1875
footnote and that was, as I have shown, not uniform.'

He concluded that there was a vacuum and the court was free to choose the better rule.
He chose the allocatur.

Orr LJ agreed that the court was free to choose between the incipitur rule and the
allocatur rule and had no hesitation in preferring the latter.

In our opinion, *K v K* decides that interest, under the Judgments Act 1838, on an order
for costs runs from the date of taxation. That is binding on us.

It is submitted by counsel for the plaintiffs that *K v K* is inconsistent with *Boswell v
Coaks* and that, under the rule in *Young v Bristol Aeroplane Co Ltd* [1944] 2 All ER 293,
[1944] KB 718, we are entitled to prefer it to the decision in *K v K* and should do so. In
our opinion, there is no inconsistency between the two cases. The court in *Boswell v Coaks*
plainly regarded itself as giving effect to the 1883 rules. At the time of *K v K* the relevant
provisions of the 1883 rules had gone altogether. The court in *K v K* was not giving effect
to the rules. It was deciding what was the effect of the Judgments Act 1838 in the absence
of any material rules. The two courts, therefore, were dealing with quite different
problems.

Second, counsel for plaintiffs contends that the court in any event has a discretion to
award interest on costs from a date earlier than the allocatur and should do so in the
present case because the plaintiffs had, as I have shown, paid out substantial sums in costs
during the course of the proceedings. Counsel for the plaintiffs refers to two passages in
the judgments in *K v K*. First, the passage in the judgment of Lord Denning MR, where
he says ([1977] 1 All ER 576 at 581–582, [1977] Fam 39 at 50):

'The modern rule should be, and is, that interest on costs runs from the date of
the master's certificate of taxation quantifying the same or such other date as may
be ordered as the date on which payment is to be made.'

Counsel for the plaintiffs places emphasis on the latter words. We entirely agree with the
judge, however, that they give no support to the plaintiffs' case. The basis of Lord
Denning MR's judgment is that interest should not run until the debtor wrongfully
withholds payment which, in the case of costs, would not in his view be until after they
were quantified by taxation. Thus, he says ([1977] 1 All ER 576 at 580–581, [1977] Fam
39 at 49):

'So in all fairness interest should only run from the date of quantification . . . That
is admittedly the case with the lump sum of £50,000 which was payable on 1st
September 1974. It should also be the case with the costs . . .'

That does not involve any discretion. In our view, the words 'such other date as may be
ordered' in the first-mentioned passage merely refer to a case where the specific date for
payment is ordered as with the £50,000 in *K v K*.

Counsel for the plaintiffs also relies on the statement of Stephenson LJ where, after
concluding that the court should reimpose the allocatur rule, he said ([1977] 1 All ER
576 at 587, [1977] Fam 39 at 57): 'I hope that any injustice to the payee will be mitigated
by agreement or acceleration of taxation wherever possible, or in special cases by special
order.' Counsel for the plaintiffs emphasises the words 'in special cases by special order'.
If, however, these words were intended (and we doubt if they were) to indicate a
discretion of the court to order retrospectively the payment of interest on costs in respect
of a period prior to taxation, we do not think that they can stand with the judgments of
Lord Denning MR and of Orr LJ, which seem to us to determine that interest on costs
runs from the date of the master's certificate and which contain no reference to any
discretion. And it seems to us unlikely that, if any member of the court in *K v K* was of
opinion that so important a discretion existed, he would not have said so in terms.
Moreover, we do not see what could be the origin of such a discretion. It is not to be
found in the Judgments Act 1838 or the rules nor do the earlier cases suggest its existence.

a   In the circumstances, we agree with the judge that this case is governed by *K v K* and accordingly we dismiss the appeal.

That disposes of the issue in the present case, but we have heard some argument on wider issues, and, in case the matter goes further, we set out below our views on the basis that we were free to consider the matter generally.

The relevant rules of 1883 having gone, there is no rule of court which has a bearing on the matter, and it seems to us that one comes back to the statute. It is a matter of
b   construction of the 1838 Act. Interest is payable from 'the time of entering up the judgment'. As a matter of language taken by itself, we should have said that meant the date of formal entry, in modern terms the date appearing on the 'Entered' stamp which appears on the formal order issued by the court. In *Fisher v Dudding* (1841) 3 Man & G 238, 133 ER 1131, which was followed in *Newton v Grand Junction Rly Co* (1846) 16 M & W 139, 153 ER 1133, that was rejected. Erskine J in *Fisher v Dudding* 3 Man & G 238 at
c   241, 133 ER 1131 at 1132 said:

'We must refer to the state of the law and the practice of the courts, as known to exist at the time of the passing of the [1838 Act], to ascertain what is meant by "entering up the judgment." Looking at the statute, in connexion with the former law and practice, the time from which the interest is to run, appears to be, the time of signing judgment by entering an incipitur in the master's book, and not the time
d   of the formal entry on the judgment roll.'

Maule J (in the report of the case in 3 Scott NR 516 at 520) is reported as saying:

'The whole judgment of the court is supposed to be entered in the Master's book. No formal record is drawn up until it is wanted for some particular purpose; and the entry in the book affords the materials for that more formal record . . . A formal
e   judgment may at any time be drawn up from the Master's book and the postea. Such being the practice, the legislature could never have meant, when they used the words "entering up judgment", the making of a regular record.'

We think that the approach in *Fisher v Dudding* of considering the practice of the court in 1838 was correct and, having regard to the views of Erskine and Maule JJ given in
f   1841 as to what that practice was, we see no reason to depart from their conclusion. Under the modern practice an order of the court takes effect from the day of its date and it is to be dated on the day on which it is pronounced unless the court orders it to be dated earlier or later (see RSC Ord 42, r 3). In practical terms there is no evident advantage in choosing the date of formal entry which may often be delayed for purely administrative reasons in the courts. We would in the circumstances reject the date of entry as the
g   correct date, as did Ackner J in *Parsons v Mather & Platt Ltd* [1977] 2 All ER 715, [1977] 1 WLR 855.

That leaves the much more difficult question whether interest runs from the date the judgment is pronounced or from the date of quantification. We do not think that either rule is satisfactory as to costs in all circumstances. We can see no sensible reason why the appellant wife in *K v K* should have succeeded (as she would have done if the incipitur
h   rule had been applied) or why the present plaintiffs should wholly fail (as they must if the allocatur rule is applied). Nor does it seem to us that either rule is satisfactory in relation to interest generally. The incipitur rule cannot be satisfactorily applied to a judgment for payment at a future date (such as the order for the payment of the £50,000 in *K v K*). Nor can the 'quantification' rule be satisfactorily applied to a judgment for unliquidated damages. It is not a useful approach in such a case to say that a person
j   cannot be expected to pay until the liability has been quantified. The litigant who obtains a judgment for damages to be assessed has already suffered damage at the date when the judgment is pronounced. That he should have to wait for the damages until after they are quantified is necessary, but there is no reason why he should not have interest when, in the end, they are paid. In *Borthwick v Elderslie Steamship Co Ltd (No 2)* [1905] 2 KB 516, the Court of Appeal held that, in the case of a judgment for damages to be assessed,

interest was payable from the date of the judgment. Romer LJ, after saying that the plaintiff was held entitled to recover damages the amount of which remained to be *a* ascertained, continued (at 522):

'The amount has since been ascertained, and must be treated as if it had been mentioned in the judgment of the Court; and the result is that the plaintiff has a judgment for an ascertained sum, dated on the day on which it is pronounced.'

Whichever rule is adopted, therefore, some violence will have to be done to the general *b* principle in order to secure a just result in certain cases.

Returning to the language of the Judgments Act 1838, it seems to us that, if the approach in *Fisher v Dudding* by reference to the practice as to judgments at the time the statute was enacted in 1838 is correct, it follows that the court was correct in deciding in favour of the date of pronouncement as being 'the time of entering up' the judgment. That, in practice, produces a sensible result except in the cases of (a) a judgment for *c* payment of a specific sum at a future date and (b) an order for payment of costs to be taxed where the litigant is seeking interest in respect of a period before the taxation when he had not paid the costs (ie the *K v K* situation).

The first of those cases does not, we think, give rise to difficulty. The litigant manifestly cannot be entitled to interest in such a case except in respect of a period of default after the specified date, and it must be assumed that the 1838 Act was never intended to *d* provide otherwise. If that involves a departure from what would otherwise be the construction of the Act, we think it can be accepted as a proper construction to avoid absurd results.

As regards costs, the purpose of an order for costs is to give an indemnity, or partial indemnity, to the successful litigant in respect of his expenses of the litigation. If, therefore, he has made payments to his lawyers in respect of costs prior to taxation (and *e* it is likely nowadays that he will) it is difficult to see why he should be denied interest as from the judgment or later payment on the amounts from time to time paid (up to the aggregate ultimately allowed on taxation). On the other hand, interest cannot be allowed in the *K v K* situation. It seems to us that the court is entitled to consider the purpose of the statute and to construe it as not permitting interest in such circumstances. If the date of judgment is accepted as the general principle, such a construction would merely be a *f* limitation on the general principle in order to avoid absurd results, just as in the case of interest on a judgment on a fixed sum to be paid at a future date. On this basis both of the cases to which we have referred at (a) and (b) could be accommodated without abandoning the general rule. The only alternative, we think, is to apply the allocatur rule rigidly in the case of costs.

There are two further matters to which we should refer. Counsel for the defendants *g* suggested that s 17 of the Judgments Act 1838 does not apply to costs at all. We think that the law has gone too far for that argument. The courts appear to have accepted since its enactment that s 17 does apply to costs.

There may be a question how far it would be possible to vary the effect of the Judgments Act 1838 by making rules of court. The matter is not material under the present rules and we express no view on it. *h*

Appeal dismissed. Leave to appeal to House of Lords granted.

Solicitors: *Ashurst, Morris, Crisp & Co* (for the plaintiffs); *Gouldens,* agents for *Iveson, Jarratt & Co,* Hull (for the defendants).

Mary Rose Plummer   Barrister.

Potter v Potter

a

COURT OF APPEAL, CIVIL DIVISION
ORMROD, DUNN LJJ AND SIR SEBAG SHAW
21 JUNE 1982

b Divorce – Financial provision – Lump sum order – Factors to be regarded – Application of one-
third rule – Marriage of short duration with no children – Both parties earning – Husband's
principal asset a one-man business which he did not wish to sell – Wife not seeking order for
periodical payments because parties wanted to make a clean break – Wife applying for lump sum
and transfer of husband's interest in matrimonial home – Judge making lump sum order and
ordering transfer of husband's interest in home to wife – Lump sum order based on valuation of
husband's business on a sale together with parties' other capital assets to which one-third rule
c applied – Whether appropriate case for lump sum order in addition to order for transfer of
matrimonial home to wife – Whether one-third rule appropriate guideline in cases involving
distribution of capital as opposed to distribution of income of the parties – Matrimonial Causes
Act 1973, s 25(1).

The husband and wife were married in 1968 when the husband was aged 26 and the
d wife aged 22. The marriage lasted for only six years and in 1974 the husband left the
matrimonial home. The home was in the parties' joint names and worth £25,000. In
1979 the wife was granted a divorce on the basis of the husband's adultery. Although
each party had formed an association with another person neither intended to remarry.
There were no children of the marriage. The wife wished to remain in the matrimonial
home. At the beginning of the marriage the husband was in business in a small way but
e he subsequently built up the business into a very successful, though small, concern of
which he was the sole owner. During the marriage the wife helped him in the business
at weekends. She also contributed to the home out of the wages she earned elsewhere as
a secretary. She continued to work as a secretary after the divorce. The wife applied for
financial relief following the divorce, seeking orders for a transfer of property and a lump
sum from the husband, but she did not seek periodical payments from him because both
f parties wanted a clean break. On the hearing of the application the judge (i) ordered the
husband to transfer his share in the matrimonial home to the wife and (ii) having heard
conflicting expert evidence as to the value of the husband's business and having valued it
at £88,000, and having made findings as to the parties' respective means and the
additional income the wife needed to maintain the same standard of living she had
enjoyed during the marriage, ordered the husband to pay the wife a lump sum of
g £23,900 including £1,400 to cover loss of pension rights. The judge arrived at that
figure by adding together the parties' capital assets, to which he applied the one-third
rule, made a discount for the short duration of the marriage and took into account the
wife's deficiency of income for the purpose of maintaining the standard of living she
enjoyed during the marriage. The husband appealed against the lump sum order,
submitting either that there should be no lump sum order in all the circumstances or
h that the lump sum should be less than the judge awarded.

Held – (1) Even though the marriage had been short and there were no children and the
parties were capable of earning and maintaining themselves, s 25(1)[a] of the Matrimonial

j   a   Section 25(1), so far as material, provides: 'It shall be the duty of the court in deciding whether to
        exercise its powers under section 23(1)(a), (b) or (c) . . . above in relation to a party to the marriage
        and, if so, in what manner, to have regard to all the circumstances of the case including the
        following matters, that is to say—(a) the income, earning capacity, property and other financial
        resources which each of the parties to the marriage has or is likely to have in the foreseeable future;

(Continued on p 322)

Causes Act 1973 required the husband to do more by way of financial provision than merely transfer his share in the matrimonial home to the wife because, under s 25(1), the court in deciding the appropriate financial provision had to have regard to the wife's standard of living during the marriage and, so far as it was practicable and just, place her in the position she would have been in if the marriage had not broken down and the husband had performed his financial obligations to her. It followed that the husband should transfer his share in the matrimonial home to the wife and also pay her a lump sum, but regard was to be had to what it was practicable for him to pay without crippling the income producing asset represented by his business (see p 325 *f g*, p 326 *a* to *d* and p 327 *a b*, post).

(2) In calculating the amount of the lump sum payment the one-third rule ought not to be applied because, although it was a useful guideline where there was a straightforward application for periodical payments and the parties' incomes were readily ascertainable, it was not an appropriate guideline where the redistribution of capital assets was involved. Where the husband's principal asset was a one-man business which he did not intend to sell, the application of the one-third rule was particularly inappropriate because it would involve valuing the business on the basis that it was going to be sold when that would be a useless hypothetical, speculative and unnecessarily costly exercise. The proper approach of the court in calculating the amount of a lump sum payment in such a case was to take the wife's reasonable requirements and to balance them against the husband's ability to pay. That approach involved a general consideration of the husband's resources of income and capital, the liquidity of his assets and the fixing of a lump sum that would not be so large as to cripple his business or to provide the wife with the benefit of the income without resorting to the capital. The calculation to be made was best done by going through the specific provisions in s 25(1) of the 1973 Act (see p 324 *d* to *j*, p 325 *h j* and p 326 *a* to *d* and *f* to *j*, post).

(3) Having regard to the wife's circumstances and the sum necessary to make good her income deficiency, a lump sum of £10,000 would be appropriate and well within the husband's competence to pay from his cash resources without adversely affecting his business. Accordingly, the appeal would be allowed and an order for a lump sum payment of that amount would be substituted for the judge's lump sum order (see p 325 *j* to p 326 *a c d* and p 327 *b*, post).

Notes
For the matters to which the court must have regard in making an order for financial provision, see 13 Halsbury's Laws (4th edn) paras 1060–1066.

For the Matrimonial Causes Act 1973, s 25, see 43 Halsbury's Statutes (3rd edn) 567.

Cases referred to in judgments
Calderbank v Calderbank [1975] 3 All ER 333, [1976] Fam 93, [1975] 3 WLR 586, CA, Digest (Cont Vol D) 422, 6786*b*.
Slater v Slater (1982) Times, 26 March, [1982] CA Bound Transcript 141.

(Continued from p 321)
(*b*) the financial needs, obligations and responsibilities which each of the parties to the marriage has or is likely to have in the forseeable future; (*c*) the standard of living enjoyed by the family before the breakdown of the marriage; (*d*) the age of each party to the marriage and the duration of the marriage . . . (*f*) the contributions made by each of the parties to the welfare of the family, including any contribution made by looking after the home or caring for the family; (*g*) in the case of proceedings for divorce . . . the value to either of the parties to the marriage of any benefit (for example, a pension) which, by reason of the dissolution . . . of the marriage, that party will lose the chance of acquiring; and so to exercise those powers as to place the parties, so far as it is practicable and, having regard to their conduct, just to do so, in the financial position in which they would have been if the marriage had not broken down and each had properly discharged his or her financial obligations and responsibilities towards the other.'

Interlocutory appeal

a   In ancillary proceedings following the parties' divorce his Honour Judge Ewart James
sitting in the Bournemouth County Court on 7 April 1982 ordered the husband to
transfer to the wife his share in the matrimonial home and to pay the wife a lump sum
of £22,500 and a further sum of £1,400 in respect of loss of pension rights, making a
total sum of £23,900, and further ordered taxation of the wife's costs of the application
and that the husband should pay two-thirds of the taxed costs. The husband appealed
b   against that part of the order relating to payment of the lump sum and sought either an
order that no lump sum was payable or that the lump sum payable was less than that
ordered to be paid by the judge. By a respondent's notice the wife sought variation of the
order for costs. The facts are set out in the judgment of Dunn LJ.

Frank Abbott for the husband.
c   *Steven Whitaker* for the wife.

DUNN LJ delivered the first judgment at the invitation of Ormrod LJ. This is an appeal
from an order of his Honour Judge Ewart James sitting in the Bournemouth County
Court on 7 April 1982 whereby he ordered the husband (I shall call the parties husband
and wife although there has been a decree absolute) to transfer his interest in the former
d   matrimonial home to the wife. He also ordered the husband to pay to the wife a lump
sum of £22,500, together with a sum of £1,400 in respect of loss of pension, making a
total of £23,900. The husband now appeals against that order.

The history of the matter is that the parties were married in 1968 when the husband
was 26 and the wife was 22 years old. According to the judge they began to drift apart
after about four years and in 1974 the husband left and set up home elsewhere. They
e   were divorced in 1979 on the basis of the husband's adultery with a woman with whom
he is still friendly and who spends time at a house which he has bought since the
separation. The wife has also formed an association with another man, though both
husband and wife say that they have no intention of remarrying. There are no children.

They are both plainly very able people. The wife worked throughout the marriage
and still works. She is obviously a very competent secretary; she was employed by a well-
f   known firm of estate agents at the time of the marriage, and she then moved to a local
authority where she is now personal secretary to the chairman and chief executive.

The husband has also done very well in business. He has his own photography business.
He was in quite a small way of business at the time of the marriage but he has now built
up the business. He operates it through two separate business names, although he, in
fact, is the person who is responsible for the success of it.

g   The judge found that during the marriage the wife had contributed to the home from
her wages and also helped at weekends and at other times in the business as and when
she could. One of her complaints about the husband was that he neglected her, because
all his time and energies were devoted to the business, and also that he kept her short of
money because he ploughed back any money that he made into the business.

It was against that background that the judge had to consider the matter.

h   The matrimonial home was in their joint names. It was bought for £4,400 with the
assistance of a loan from the husband's grandfather, on which he paid interest. It is a
three bedroomed house and the wife now lives there. She told the judge that she did not
want to move.

The judge having made certain findings of fact as to the means of the parties,
approached the case on the basis of adding together the capital assets of both parties,
j   dividing those assets by one-third, deducting the wife's assets and, having done that
exercise, he arrived at a figure of some £30,000 as being the appropriate figure for the
order. Since the marriage had only lasted six years, the judge felt that that was too high,
so he said that the wife had to be compensated for the deficiency in income which she
had proved. The wife's evidence was that her outgoings exceeded her income by some
£22 a month, and it was accepted that the husband has been making payments in respect

of rates and gas to a total of some £58 a month. The judge accepted that the wife needed some £80 a month in order to keep up her present standard of living. Accordingly, on the basis of some figures which had been put before him, the judge arrived at the figure of £22,500 which he said was the necessary capital to enable this lady to make good the deficiency in income.

The judge justified his original approach of applying the one-third rule by reference to *Slater v Slater* (1982) Times, 26 March, a case in which Arnold P, sitting in this court, is reported as having said:

'The one-third guideline might not be particularly helpful in cases involving very large or very small sums of money, but in cases in between it was still useful . . .'

May LJ is reported as having said:

'. . . although one could not approach the case in a strictly arithmetical way it would clearly be of assistance to the parties' advisers to have as precise a line of approach as was possible.'

Slater v Slater was concerned with periodical payments, and it was in that context that this court made the observations which it did in relation to the one-third guideline. In straightforward cases of applications for periodical payments where the incomes of the parties are readily ascertainable, the one-third guideline is indeed a useful rule of thumb, and one that has been adopted by the profession for many years as a readily ascertainable approach to the kind of income liability under which a husband might be expected to find himself. But this court has said over and over again that in cases involving the redistribution of capital, the one-third approach is not appropriate.

This case is a good example of the practical disadvantage of this approach, because in order to arrive at a figure of a proportion of one-third, a global figure has to be arrived at and where, as in this case, the husband is engaged in a one-man business, that involves a valuation of the business. This is a necessarily hypothetical exercise because the only way that it can be done is for those valuing it to assume that the business would be sold, and that, of course, is the one thing which in fact is not going to happen, and very rarely does happen. This case is a particularly acute example of the result of approaching these cases in this way. No fewer than four accountants were instructed to value this comparatively small business. Three of them were called to give evidence; none of them agreed as to their conclusions, which were hotly contested; there was disagreement as to the proper way of arriving at a figure of goodwill for a business of this kind; there was disagreement as to the proper figure to be attributed to a notional managerial expense which, on one theory it was necessary to deduct before arriving at the goodwill, and there was disagreement whether or not the incidence of capital gains tax and other taxes was a proper deduction from the valuation of the business. We were told that the total cost of this inquiry amounted to some £12,000, the bulk of which no doubt will be payable to the accountants.

At the end of the day, this exercise, namely the detailed valuation of the business, is an almost wholly irrelevant consideration.

In a case of this kind, the proper approach of the court should be to take the wife's reasonable requirements and balance those against the husband's ability to pay. That involves a general consideration of his sources of income and capital and, in particular, of his liquidity. As this court has said many times, the best way to arrive at that is to rehearse the specific provisions of s 25 of the Matrimonial Causes Act 1973, and this I propose quite shortly to do.

In addition to his half share in the matrimonial home, which was valued at £12,500, the husband is possessed of an equity in his new house of £34,250 and £7,500 invested in building society accounts and national savings certificates. He also has a number of life policies with surrender values of £4,800 and a boat, making a total (which was not in dispute) of just under £60,000. In addition to that, he is the sole owner of the business, the position of which is fully reflected in the accounts which were before the court and

which go back to before the marriage. The accounts show an increased turnover over the
a years and an unusually strong cash position in a business of this kind, with credit bank
balances totalling just under £12,000. For the year ending 5 April 1982 the net profit
increased to £22,750 and the drawings have increased to £14,425. The accounts also
show that, over the years, capital on a modest scale was introduced into the business.

In general terms that represents the husband's position. He has only himself to look
after. His lady friend works and earns her own money. He has a motor car on the
b business and his whole life is really entirely involved with his business.

So far as the wife is concerned, she also is not without assets of her own. She has her
half share in the matrimonial home. She has just under £5,000 worth of investments
and £3,500 which represents a loan which she made to her man friend, and she has a
small amount in a building society, making her total assets about £8,400, excluding her
share in the house. Her present income is just under £6,000 gross a year. The judge
c accepted that she had reached her top salary band with the local authority for whom she
works, and that she would not be entitled to any further increment. She is entitled to a
pension, and also to a lump sum payment on her retirement of something more than her
gross annual salary. After deduction of tax and national insurance she is left with about
£330 a month. She has her car expenses and lunches to enable her to earn her income.
She pays about £60 a month for her electricity, telephone and other incidentals and she
d will have to pay the £58 that her husband now pays for her rates and gas. She will be left
with about £115 a month for her food, clothes and hair. It is on that basis that the judge
came to the conclusion that in effect she had a shortfall to cover her husband's payments
and also her money deficiency.

Those are not the only considerations which the court is required to take into account
under s 25. The judge has found that this lady made a contribution to the welfare of the
e family. There is no doubt, as the judge found and it plainly influenced him, that this was
a comparatively short marriage in which there were no children. Counsel for the
husband suggested to us that this was a case of two independent adults, both capable of
earning and looking after themselves. They both made a mistake, so far as this marriage
was concerned, and, provided that the wife had the matrimonial home, which she has as
a result of a transfer of property order, that was all the provision that it was right for the
f husband to make for her, and in effect she should stand on her own feet which, counsel
submitted, she was well able to do; indeed she might be able to obtain better paid
employment than with her present employers. But the answer to that is that the 1973
Act requires that the court should have regard to the standard of living enjoyed by the
parties during the marriage, and there is the provision at the end of s 25 that the court is
under a duty to place both parties, so far as is practicable and just to do so, in the position
g in which they would have been if the marriage had not broken down and each had
performed their financial obligations.

In arriving at the figure which he did, the judge seems to have ignored the fact that on
his order the wife would be able to make good the income deficiency without having
recourse to the capital sum which he ordered. From one point of view it could be said
that the wife's reasonable requirements could be met by an appropriate order for
h periodical payments, but neither party asks for that. Both parties are anxious that there
should be a clean break and, having regard to the comparatively short marriage, no
children, and to the wife's age and ability to earn her own living, it seems to me that that
is a sensible way of approaching the case. But if the case is approached in that way on the
basis of what is the wife reasonably likely to require to make good her income deficiency,
it seems to me that one must amortise the capital payment so that she does not have the
j benefit both of the capital and of the income. It is said that she needs capital for the
maintenance of the house. One thing that was mentioned in particular was some repairs
to the porch; but one must not lose sight of the fact that this is a lady who has a certain
amount of capital of her own in any event.

Approaching the matter in that way, bearing in mind the wife's age, the various
contingencies with which she is likely to be faced and the uncertainties of the future, in

order to make good her income deficiency a capital figure of £10,000 would be appropriate. This is a sum which would be well within the competence of the husband to pay from his cash resources without adversely affecting the business.

In conclusion, I would once again emphasise that it is important, in a case where the capital sum is to be raised by a man engaged in a one-man business (as this man is) that the sum should not be so large as to cripple the income producing asset represented by the business.

Without going into detail, the effect of applying the one-third rule in this case, or, indeed, even of applying the somewhat reduced order which the judge made after looking at the arithmetic under the one-third rule, would have been to have given the wife a total capital of between £57,000 and £58,000 including the house. The business was valued by the judge at £88,000, no regard having been given to the problem of liquidity which faced the husband.

I would accordingly allow this appeal and replace the order for a lump sum payment with one of £10,000.

SIR SEBAG SHAW. I agree, and I would respectfully adopt the approach of Dunn LJ to the problems which present themselves in this appeal. I agree with that approach and with Dunn LJ's resolution of them. I would allow the appeal accordingly.

ORMROD LJ. I agree. I only add a few words of my own as we are differing from the judge.

The case to which he was referred, *Slater v Slater* (1982) Times, 26 March, is an example of the very understandable desire of judges to provide some kind of certainty in these cases if it is possible, and the reason why Arnold P in that case (which was, as Dunn LJ pointed out, a periodical payments' case) reasserted the advantage of the one-third rule was simply that. As he pointed out, it was helpful to practitioners to have a clear understanding of what principles were likely to apply so that they could feel confident as to how to advise their clients, and he added that the 'issues . . . would not be determined by caprice or judicial idiosyncrasy'.

The problem, when one comes to deal with capital, particularly in a case of this kind, is that one cannot use the one-third rule, as Dunn LJ has made clear, until the value of the assets of the parties have been ascertained. This is a highly speculative exercise in a great many cases, particularly where a small business is concerned. Applying the one-third rule to this case would mean that the amount to be paid by the husband would depend on valuations by accountants and here, in this case, the unfortunate judge had before him no less than four different valuations by four different accountants. The spread of the valuations ranged between £10,000 and £40,000 for the goodwill, so that it is wholly illusory to think that, by using the one-third rule in relation to capital, any certainty is achieved. It simply exchanges one uncertainty for another. And there are no indications as to which accountant is more likely to be right, because the whole thing is an imaginary exercise from beginning to end. When one adds the question of capital gains tax, one simply complicates the matter even further. I think it is very unwise, where capital is concerned, to try to work on a one-third basis. It is inevitable that there will be a high degree of uncertainty. We have said before that, however much that is to be regretted, there is no way of avoiding it of which I am aware, and I have never heard anyone suggest a way in which this uncertainty can be reduced. All one can do is to demonstrate, as far as one can, the ways in which the court should approach the problem and leave it to the parties to make the best assessment that they can. But for the concluding words of s 25(1) of the Matrimonial Causes Act 1973, I would have no doubt that this case was not a case for a lump sum at all. The marriage, which has lasted for only six years and in which neither party has suffered any handicaps so far as career or earnings are concerned, and where there are no children, is not one which in the ordinary way in these days should attract very much in the way of payment as between one spouse and the other after the marriage has broken down. However, that is not the principle we a have to apply under the section and, in applying the concluding words of s 25, it is crucial to remember that the phrase is 'so far as it is practicable', and, in most of the cases with which we have to deal in this court, it is that phrase which, in the end, proves decisive of the appeal. In this case the judge did not consider whether it was 'practicable' for the husband to raise £33,000, or what the consequences on the business would be, so that one does not know, except, from looking at the accounts, that it was obviously going to be extremely difficult. The figure which Dunn LJ has suggested is clearly within his

b capacity because there is cash, or assets which may be rendered liquid and available to the amount suggested, and I agree that the appeal should be allowed and the order varied to £10,000.

[Following discussion on costs, his Lordship continued:] On the question of costs, the situation is a little difficult.

In her affidavit the wife asked for a lot of detail about the husband's business, which

c was quite reasonable, and for an accountant to examine the books and business affairs. So far as that is concerned, it is eminently reasonable in a case of this kind. She may have had suspicions that money was being salted away, as so often happens in these cases.

I will not mention a 'without prejudice' letter which was written by the husband on 21 August 1981, but, on 8 March 1982 a true *Calderbank v Calderbank* ([1975] 3 All ER 333, [1976] Fam 93) offer was made by the husband to transfer his share of the house to

d the wife, plus a lump sum of £12,000. That offer was rejected and, as it turns out in this court, the wife has recovered less than that. I think, therefore, that the proper order should be to follow the rule that the wife should have her costs up to that date (8 March 1982) and, subject to what I am going to say in a moment, the husband should have the costs below thereafter.

The problem in this case is that much of the costs have arisen as a result of the conflict

e over the valuation of the goodwill of the business, and we have already commented in the course of our judgments about the relevance of that factor. The position appears to be that originally there was not a very large gap between the wife's accountants' valuation of goodwill and the husband's accountants' valuation of the goodwill so that a compromise was possible but, unfortunately, the husband called in further accountants whose valuation of the goodwill was markedly different from the wife's, and that has led to a

f bitter dispute between them. In those circumstances it seems unreasonable that the wife should have to bear all the heavy costs of the trial, most of which has been taken up in this futile dispute between accountants.

The order I would propose is that, after 8 March 1982, the husband is to have his costs, but the costs are to be limited to the costs of one accountant only and that these costs should also include the costs of applying to this court for leave to appeal out of time.

g There is no reason why that should not have been agreed between the parties.

Appeal allowed. Order for costs in accordance with judgment of Ormrod LJ.

Solicitors: *Watts, Vallance & Vallance*, agents for *Coles*, Poole (for the husband); *Philip Evans & Co*, Bournemouth (for the wife).

Patricia Hargrove   Barrister.

Reid v Reid

a

PRIVY COUNCIL

LORD DIPLOCK, LORD SIMON OF GLAISDALE, LORD KEITH OF KINKEL, LORD SCARMAN AND LORD
BRANDON OF OAKBROOK

2, 3 FEBRUARY, 20 APRIL 1982

New Zealand – Husband and wife – Division of matrimonial property – Distinction between
matrimonial and separate property – Business started after marriage with property belonging to
husband before marriage – Whether proceeds of sale of business available for division in
matrimonial proceedings – Exercise of discretion of local courts – Whether Privy Council should
interfere – Matrimonial Property Act 1976 (NZ), ss 8(e), 9(2).

The husband and wife were married in 1955. A few years after the marriage the husband
started a business with tools and machinery which he had owned before the marriage
and a gift of $1,000 from his mother. He sold the business for $500,000 shortly before
the parties separated in 1976. Proceedings were commenced under the New Zealand
Matrimonial Property Act 1976 in which the question arose whether the proceeds of the
sale of the business were 'matrimonial property' under that Act and therefore divisible
between the husband and wife. Under the 1976 Act matrimonial property, but not
separate property of either spouse, was subject to division between the parties by the
court. Section 8(e)[a] of the Act provided that matrimonial property included 'all property
acquired by either the husband or the wife after the marriage' but did not include
'separate property', which was defined in s 9(1)[b] as being 'all property of either spouse
which [was] not matrimonial property'. Section 9(2) further provided that, subject to
s 8(e), 'all property acquired out of separate property, and the proceeds of any disposition
of separate property, [was] separate property'. Under s 15[c] each spouse was entitled to
share equally in the division of matrimonial property unless the contribution of one to
the matrimonial partnership was clearly greater than that of the other, in which case the
shares were to be determined in accordance with the contribution of each. The trial
judge held that the proceeds of the sale of the business were separate property under the
1976 Act and therefore not divisible between the parties, and ordered that, on the basis
that the husband's contribution to the marriage partnership had been the greater, the
matrimonial property, other than the matrimonial home and family chattels, should be
divided in the proportion of two-thirds to the husband and one-third to the wife. He
further ordered under s 33(3)[d] of the 1976 Act, which empowered the court to make an
order vesting the matrimonial property or any part of it in the husband or the wife, that
the matrimonial home be vested in the husband and the parties' holiday home be vested
in the wife. On appeal, the New Zealand Court of Appeal held that the proceeds of sale
of the business were property 'acquired by either the husband or the wife after the
marriage' and therefore matrimonial property within s 8(e). The court directed that the
matrimonial property should be divided on the basis of 60% to the husband and 40% to
the wife. The Court of Appeal affirmed the order of the trial judge regarding the holiday
home and ordered that unless the parties otherwise agreed all the matrimonial property
should be valued according to the values current on the date of the hearing of the
application for valuation. The husband appealed to the Privy Council against the orders,
contending that since the business had been built up out of his pre-marital property the
proceeds of the sale of the business were 'the proceeds of any disposition of separate
property' within s 9(2). The wife sought leave to cross-appeal against the apportionment
of the matrimonial property.

---

a   Section 8, so far as material, is set out at p 330 g to j, post
b   Section 9, so far as material, is set out at p 330 j to p 331 b, post
c   Section 15, so far as material, is set out at p 332 h j, post
d   Section 33(3), so far as material, is set out at p 334 a, post

Held – The husband's appeal and the wife's application for leave to cross-appeal would
a be dismissed for the following reasons—

(1) Since the proceeds of the sale of the business were apt to be included as matrimonial
property under s 8(e) as 'property acquired by either the husband or the wife after the
marriage' and at the same time could be described as 'the proceeds of [a] disposition of
separate property' under s 9(2) because the business had been built up out of the husband's
pre-marital property, the question whether the proceeds were matrimonial property or
b separate property was to be decided by determining which of the two sections was
paramount. Applying the primary rule of construction that where the words of a statute
were plain and unambiguous effect should be given to the natural sense of the words
used, s 8(e) was clearly intended to override s 9(2), since s 9(2) was expressed to be subject
to s 8(e) while s 8(e), although expressed to be subject to sub-ss (3) to (6) of s 9, was not
expressed to be subject to sub-s (2) of s 9. It followed that the proceeds of sale of the
c business ranked as matrimonial property (see p 331 *b* to *e*, p 332 *c f g* and p 334 *g*, post).

(2) Since the question of apportionment was a discretionary matter which the local
courts were in a superior position to judge, the Privy Council would not interfere in the
exercise of their discretion. Similarly, because the local courts were better placed to
consider the relevant local considerations determining the date to be fixed for valuation,
the Privy Council would not interfere in the exercise of their discretion to determine the
d date of valuation (see p 333 *d* to *j* and p 334 *c f g*, post).

Notes
For the determination of proprietary rights between husband and wife, see 22 Halsbury's
Laws (4th edn) paras 1027–1030, and for cases on the subject, see 27(1) Digest (Reissue)
305–315, 2267–2330.
e   For interference by the Judicial Committee of the Privy Council with a local court's
findings with respect to local matters, see 10 Halsbury's Laws (4th edn) para 821, and for
cases on the subject, see 16 Digest (Reissue) 208–211, 2064–2097.

Cases referred to in judgment
Comr of Stamp Duties v Atwill [1973] 1 All ER 576, [1973] AC 558, [1973] 2 WLR 327,
f   PC.
Courtauld v Legh (1869) LR 4 Exch 126, 3 Digest (Reissue) 188, 1142.
Haldane v Haldane [1975] 1 NZLR 672; *on appeal* [1977] AC 673, [1976] 3 WLR 760, PC,
27(1) Digest (Reissue) 258, *946.
Thompson v Goold & Co [1910] AC 409, HL, 34 Digest (Repl) 652, 4494.

g **Appeal and application for leave to cross-appeal**
Anthony Fulton Reid (the husband) appealed with leave of the Court of Appeal of New
Zealand against the judgments of the Court of Appeal (Woodhouse, Cooke and
Richardson JJ) on 22 August 1979 and 21 November 1980 allowing the appeal of the
respondent, Susan Rosemary Reid (the wife), against the order of Quilliam J dated 21
November 1977 whereby the judge held that the proceeds of sale of shares in a company
h owned by the husband was matrimonial property under s 8(e) of the Matrimonial
Property Act 1976 (NZ) and ordered (i) that all the matrimonial property other than the
matrimonial home and family chattels be divided in the proportions 60% to the husband
and 40% to the wife, (ii) that the family holiday home be vested in the wife and (iii) that
the values current on the date of the hearing of the application for valuation be fixed for
all the matrimonial property unless the parties otherwise agreed. The wife sought special
j leave to cross-appeal, contending that the balance of the matrimonial property should be
divided equally between the parties. The facts are set out in the judgment.

The husband appeared in person.
George Barton (of the New Zealand Bar) as amicus curiae.
Swinton Thomas QC and *Anthony Temple* for the wife.

At the conclusion of argument their Lordships announced that they were of opinion that the appeal and the application for special leave to appeal should both be dismissed and *a* that they would give their reasons for their decision at a later date.

LORD SIMON OF GLAISDALE. This case concerns the interpretation of the New Zealand Matrimonial Property Act 1976 and various orders made thereunder. The matters originally came before Quilliam J on an application by the husband. The New Zealand Court of Appeal (Woodhouse, Cooke and Richardson JJ) allowed an appeal by *b* the wife and dismissed a cross-appeal by the husband. They made an order that current values should be fixed for all matrimonial property. The husband now appeals to Her Majesty in Council and the wife seeks special leave to cross-appeal.

As is usual in litigation of this sort, a great number of issues have been raised as the case has proceeded, and the status and disposal of a wide variety of assets have been in question. Most of these matters have been disposed of as the action has progressed. The *c* issues which have been canvassed before their Lordships and which remain for decision are as follows: 1. are the proceeds (now nearly $500,000) of the sale of shares in a company (Reid Containers Ltd) built up by the husband 'matrimonial property' or the husband's 'separate property' within the meaning of the statute? 2. in what proportions should the matrimonial property be divided between husband and wife? (with this issue is tied up the wife's application for special leave to cross-appeal) 3. should a vesting order stand in *d* favour of the wife in respect of the family holiday home at Paihia? 4. were the Court of Appeal justified in ordering 'current values' to be fixed for all matrimonial property or should the values have been those at the date of the hearing of the husband's application? Their Lordships will consider each of these issues in turn. First, though, they must give some relevant facts. These were fully set out in the judgments below, and can be summarised for the purpose of the instant appeal. *e*

The husband and the wife were married in 1955. They have four children, born respectively in 1956, 1958, 1961 and 1964. Two or three years after the marriage the husband started a business named Reid Containers Ltd with virtually nothing except some old tools and machinery (his own pre-marital property) and a gift to himself from his mother of $1,000. Such was his mechanical and business ability that years later he sold his shares in the business for over $500,000; it is these proceeds which are the subject *f* matter of the first issue. (Their Lordships are in some position to appreciate the husband's capacity, as he conducted his own appeal before them with truly remarkable skill and judgment.) The parties separated in 1976; and the proceedings instantly under review were then started.

1. Construction of the statute: 'matrimonial' or 'separate' property   *g*
   The following are the provisions on which this part of the appeal turns:

     '**8.** *Matrimonial property defined*—Matrimonial property shall consist of—(a) The matrimonial home whenever acquired; and (b) The family chattels whenever acquired; and (c) All property owned jointly or in common in equal shares by the husband and the wife; and (d) All property owned immediately before the marriage by either the husband or the wife if the property was acquired in contemplation of *h* his or her marriage to the other and was intended for the common use and benefit of both the husband and the wife; and (e) Subject to subsections (3) to (6) of section 9 and to section 10 of this Act, all property acquired by either the husband or the wife after the marriage, including property acquired for the common use and benefit of both the husband and the wife out of property owned by either the husband or the wife or both of them before the marriage or out of the proceeds of *j* any disposition of any property so owned . . .
     9. *Separate property defined*—(1) Separate property means all property of either spouse which is not matrimonial property.
     (2) Subject to subsection (6) of this section and to sections 8(e) and 10 of this Act,

all property acquired out of separate property, and the proceeds of any disposition
of separate property, shall be separate property . . .

(6) Subject to section 10 of this Act, any separate property which is or any proceeds
of any disposition of, or any increase in the value of, or any income or gains derived
from, separate property, which are, with the express or implied consent of the
spouse owning, receiving, or entitled to them, used for the acquisition or
improvement of, or to increase the value of, or the amount of any interest of either
the husband or the wife in, any property referred to in section 8 of this Act shall be
matrimonial property.'

Section 10 deals with property acquired by succession or by survivorship or as a
beneficiary under a trust or by gift.

Sections 8(e) and 9(2) are not easy to construe together; and there has understandably
been some difference of judicial opinion. '. . . all property acquired by either the husband
or the wife after the marriage' in s 8(e) is on the face of it apt to include the proceeds of
the shares, which would thus be matrimonial property and subject to division by the
court. On the other hand, the business of Reid Containers was built up out of the
husband's pre-marital property and a personal money gift to himself, so that the words
'the proceeds of any disposition of separate property' in s 9(2) are apt to include the
proceeds of the shares, which would thus be separate property and not subject to division
by the court. So, at its most elemental, the question of construction turns on which is
paramount: s 8(e) or s 9(2)? Of that there can be no doubt. Section 8(e) is 'Subject to
subsections (3) to (6) of section 9 . . .', significantly not to sub-s (2). And, on the other
hand, s 9(2) is 'subject to . . . sections 8(e) . . .', whereas, were s 9(2) to be paramount, the
words would run 'and notwithstanding section 8(e) . . .', a technique the draftsman has
used elsewhere in the Act (see ss 10(3) and 25(3)). So it is clear that s 9(2) is subordinate to
s 8(e).

But, in deference to the able arguments of the husband and of counsel who appeared
as amicus curiae and to the careful and closely reasoned judgment of Quilliam J, their
Lordships turn to examine the issue more narrowly. Quilliam J recognised that 'all
property acquired by either the husband or the wife after the marriage' in s 8(e) were
plain and unambiguous; and that the primary rule of construction would demand that
effect should be given to them in their natural sense (see *Maxwell on Interpretation of
Statutes* (12th edn 1969) pp 28, 43, and the cases there cited). He felt justified in rejecting
this primary rule of construction by two considerations. In the first place, he held, the
second part of s 8(e) (ie following the word 'including') must enlarge the meaning of the
first part, since it must refer—

'to property already referred to (that is, property acquired after marriage) but
which was acquired out of property acquired before marriage. The fact that the
second part is there at all means that, without it, the first part standing alone would
not have achieved the result of making property acquired from assets owned before
marriage into matrimonial property.'

In order to obviate the described redundancy, Quilliam J therefore construed the first
part to read '. . . acquired by either the husband or the wife after the marriage *for the
common use and benefit of both the husband and the wife*' (thereby adopting one of the
constructions urged by the husband). But their Lordships respectfully agree with the
Court of Appeal (per Woodhouse J) that—

'it is quite a common statutory device to add an inclusive clause of specific
description simply to give precautionary emphasis to something which otherwise
might be left open to doubt or argument.'

(In this respect being somewhat similar to a proviso, as to which see *Comr of Stamp Duties
v Atwill* [1973] 1 All ER 576, [1973] AC 558.)

This very word 'including' is palpably used in the way indicated by Woodhouse J in s 18(1)(h), quoted hereafter. Their Lordships moreover agree that, even with the addition of the words italicised above, there will still be a redundancy in the two parts of s 8(e), *a* and also that s 9(2) itself contains a redundancy. Finally, their Lordships have in mind what was said by Lord Mersey in *Thompson v Goold & Co* [1910] AC 409 at 420:

> 'It is a strong thing to read into an Act of Parliament words which are not there, and in the absence of clear necessity it is a wrong thing to do.'

The second reason that impelled Quilliam J to decline to read s 8(e) according to its *b* plain words was that to do so would leave s 9(2) with a very limited scope. But their Lordships respectfully agree with the Court of Appeal that this is understandable in a statute dealing primarily with matrimonial property and not with separate property (cf New Zealand Married Women's Property Act 1884 and its re-enactments: see *Haldane v Haldane* [1977] AC 673 at 688). In any case their Lordships agree that the consideration that s 9(2) is left with an extremely limited scope is inadequate to displace the primary *c* canon of construction according to plain words, reinforced as it is here by the other considerations to which their Lordships have referred.

The husband put his case on construction in two ways alternative to the foregoing. The first, urged before the courts below and rejected both at first instance and on appeal, was to read 'acquired' in s 8(e) as meaning 'acquired *from assets which are not separate property*'. In view of the fact that this construction was accepted neither by the judge nor *d* by the Court of Appeal it will suffice to say that this construction too involves reading in words which are not in the statute.

The same objection applies to the second alternative construction put forward by the husband, this time in his argument before their Lordships. It was that 'acquired' means 'acquired *by his or her own exertion*'. Furthermore, in statutory interpretation there is a presumption against a change in terminological usage: *e*

> '. . . it is a sound rule of construction to give the same meaning to the same words occurring in different parts of an Act of Parliament . . .'

(See *Courtauld v Legh* [1869] LR 4 Exch 126 at 130 per Cleasby B.)

'Acquired' cannot possibly mean 'acquired by his or her own exertion' in s 10, which deals with 'property acquired by succession' etc. Section 10 is actually referred to in both *f* ss 8(e) and 9(2).

Their Lordships therefore agree with the construction put on s 8(e) by all three members of the Court of Appeal, so that the proceeds of the Reid Container shares were 'matrimonial property'.

g

2. *Apportionment*

Quilliam J ordered the matrimonial home and the family chattels to be equally divided in accordance with s 11 of the Act; and his decision in that regard was accepted by the parties.

The division of the balance of the matrimonial property was governed by ss 15 and 18. These read as follows, omitting ss 15(3) and 18(3) as irrelevant: *h*

> '15. *Division of balance of matrimonial property*—(1) Upon the division of matrimonial property . . . each spouse shall share equally in it unless his or her contribution to the marriage partnership has clearly been greater than that of the other spouse.
>
> (2) Where, pursuant to subsection (1) of this section, the spouses do not share equally in the matrimonial property or any part of the matrimonial property, the *j* share of each in the matrimonial property or in that part of it shall be determined in accordance with the contribution of each to the marriage partnership . . .
>
> 18. *Contribution of spouses*—(1) For the purposes of this Act a contribution to the marriage partnership means all or any of the following—(a) The care of any child of

the marriage or of any aged or infirm relative or dependant of the husband or the wife: (b) The management of the household and the performance of household duties: (c) The provision of money, including the earning of income, for the purposes of the marriage partnership: (d) The acquisition or creation of matrimonial property, including the payment of money for those purposes: (e) The payment of money to maintain or increase the value of—(i) The matrimonial property or any part thereof; or (ii) The separate property of the other spouse or any part thereof: (f) The performance of work or services in respect of—(i) The matrimonial property or any part thereof; or (ii) The separate property of the other spouse or any part thereof: (g) The foregoing of a higher standard of living than would otherwise have been available: (h) The giving of assistance or support to the other spouse (whether or not of a material kind), including the giving of assistance or support which—(i) Enables the other spouse to acquire qualifications; or (ii) Aids the other spouse in the carrying on of his or her occupation or business.

(2) There shall be no presumption that a contribution of a monetary nature (whether under subsection (1)(c) of this section or otherwise) is of greater value than a contribution of a non-monetary nature . . .'

Quilliam J held that the contribution of the husband to the marriage partnership had clearly been greater than that of the wife. The Court of Appeal agreed, particularly in the light of their finding that the proceeds of sale of the shares were matrimonial property (see s 18(1)(d)). This is essentially the sort of issue where the courts of the society to which the spouses belong are in a position far superior to that of their Lordships in forming a judgment. Here there were concurrent findings by the trial judge and a Court of Appeal unanimous on this point. Their Lordships hold clearly that this finding must be respected. That disposes of the petition by the wife for special leave to cross-appeal, since its object was to argue for an equal division. Their Lordships will therefore humbly advise Her Majesty that the wife's petition should be dismissed.

Having found that the husband's contribution to the marriage partnership had clearly been greater than that of the wife, Quilliam J held that the matrimonial property (other than the matrimonial home and the family chattels) should be divided in the proportion of two-thirds to the husband and one-third to the wife.

With their finding that the proceeds of the shares were to be included in the matrimonial property falling for division, the Court of Appeal faced an entirely different picture from that which presented itself to Quilliam J and had perforce to exercise their own discretion in the new situation. Woodhouse and Richardson JJ favoured division of 60% to the husband and 40% to the wife; Cooke J (dissenting on this point alone) would have preferred 75% to the husband and 25% to the wife.

What their Lordships have said about the superior advantage of the local court is equally cogent when it comes to an appointment of this sort.

It was urged on their Lordships that there was a minority judgment. This would perhaps justify a closer scrutiny to ensure that no relevant consideration had been omitted by the majority nor any irrelevant consideration taken into account. Their Lordships find none such. In the end it is a question of how the various factors are held to weigh up. Their Lordships are of opinion that there is no ground for interfering with the assessment of the majority.

It was also argued that the starting point of the Court of Appeal should have been Quilliam J's apportionment; and that the Court of Appeal, having found the proceeds of the shares were matrimonial property, should have increased the husband's share in view of s 18(1)(d). Quilliam J's judgment did not go uncriticised in the Court of Appeal in this regard; but their Lordships do not find it necessary to go into that matter, since in their view it would have been a wrong approach to take the apportionment of the trial judge as a starting point. As their Lordships have pointed out, the Court of Appeal had, in the new situation, no alternative to the exercise of their own discretion, a discretion which it would be wrong to fetter in any way.

3. The holiday home

The relevant part of s 33(3) reads:

> 'The Court may make any one or more of the following orders . . . (c) An order vesting the matrimonial property or any part thereof in the husband or in the wife . . .'

Quilliam J made an order vesting the matrimonial home in the husband, who was residing there. In view of the fact that the husband had the matrimonial home, he made an order vesting the holiday home at Paihia in the wife. His judgment in this respect was unanimously upheld by the Court of Appeal. The husband challenged this before their Lordships.

The use of the word 'may' shows that the jurisdiction is discretionary. Their Lordships are again of opinion that it would be wrong to interfere with a matter of discretion in which the trial judge had been unanimously upheld by the Court of Appeal.

The wife will of course have to give credit for 60% of the value of the holiday home (there is also an advance of $50,000 to be repaid).

4. Valuation date

The relevant part of s 2(2) reads:

> 'For the purposes of this Act the value of any property to which an application under this Act relates shall . . . be its value as at the date of the hearing, unless the Court in its discretion otherwise decides.'

The Court of Appeal ordered that current values should be fixed for all matrimonial property unless the parties could otherwise agree, remitting the case to the Supreme Court for this purpose. The husband has included in his challenge that part of their judgment which ordered current values to be put on the matrimonial property.

It is unnecessary to determine whether the 'hearing' of 'an application under this Act' refers to the hearing of the original application invoking the jurisdiction of the court or the hearing of the application for valuation (though their Lordships incline to the former construction), because the Court of Appeal exercised its discretion under the last limb of this subsection, 'unless the Court in its discretion otherwise decides'.

This once again is a matter of discretion in which the court appealed from is much more favourably placed than their Lordships to consider the relevant local considerations (for example, inflationary pressures or other fluctuations in value). Their Lordships therefore decline to interfere with the exercise of the discretion.

Conclusion

In the result their Lordships will humbly advise Her Majesty that the appeal should be dismissed with costs.

Appeal dismissed. Application for special leave to cross-appeal dismissed.

Solicitors: *Allen & Overy* (for the amicus curiae); *Blyth, Dutton, Holloway* (for the wife).

Diana Procter   Barrister.

a   # Astro Exito Navegacion SA v Southland Enterprise Co Ltd and another (Chase Manhattan Bank NA intervening) The Messiniaki Tolmi

b   COURT OF APPEAL, CIVIL DIVISION

STEPHENSON, ACKNER AND O'CONNOR LJJ

3, 4, 8, 9 MARCH, 5 APRIL 1982

Injunction – Interlocutory – Specific performance – Mandatory injunction compelling execution of contractual obligation – Contract for sale of vessel – Letter of credit in payment of purchase
c   *price – Buyers refusing to complete contract – Sellers commencing proceedings for specific performance – Buyers seeking stay of proceedings pending arbitration – Judge granting stay but ordering buyers to sign notice of readiness by certain date failing which notice to be signed by master and ordering letter of credit held by third party to be released – Jurisdiction of court to make order – Jurisdiction of court to order specific performance at interlocutory stage – Whether order enforceable against third party – Supreme Court of Judicature (Consolidation) Act 1925,*
d   *ss 45(1), 47.*

The sellers, a Panamanian company, agreed to sell a vessel to the buyers, a Taiwanese company, in accordance with a memorandum of agreement dated 2 July 1980. The vessel was intended to be broken up by the buyers and the sellers agreed to deliver the vessel to a specified harbour in Taiwan with a valid gas-free certificate and a notice of readiness which was to be countersigned by the buyers. Under the terms of the contract,
e   it was agreed that arbitration of any dispute arising out of the sale was to be in London in accordance with English law. Pursuant to the contract the buyers opened a letter of credit in payment of the purchase price with a bank in Taiwan, and the letter of credit was confirmed by a London bank. The sellers duly delivered the vessel to the Taiwan harbour with a gas-free certificate and gave notice of readiness. The buyers refused to accept the notice on the ground that the gas-free certificate was not valid. They refused
f   to countersign the notice of readiness and purported to cancel the contract. The sellers commenced proceedings in the Commercial Court for specific performance of the contract. The buyers applied for a stay of proceedings pending the outcome of arbitration. On 24 October 1980 the judge stayed the proceedings but on terms which included by way of interim relief granted to the sellers injunctions directing the buyers (i) to countersign the notice of readiness by 28 October 1980, failing which the notice was to
g   be signed by a master of the Supreme Court for and on behalf of the buyers, and (ii) to instruct the Taiwan bank to authorise the London bank to release the moneys secured by the letter of credit, the moneys so released to be lodged in the joint names of the parties' solicitors until further order. The buyers failed to comply with the order on the due date and the notice of readiness was signed by a Supreme Court master and presented to the
h   London bank with the documents necessary to operate the letter of credit. The London bank refused to release the moneys and the letter of credit expired on 30 October. On 10 November the buyers issued a notice of appeal against the order of 24 October and on 12 November commenced proceedings against the London bank in respect of its refusal to pay on the letter of credit. Subsequently the arbitrators awarded damages to the sellers for the buyers' breach of contract. The sellers and the buyers then applied to the Court of
j   Appeal to withdraw the appeal from the order of 24 October, since it had been overtaken by the arbitrators' award. However, the sellers' claim against the London bank remained alive and the London bank accordingly applied to intervene in the appeal in order to be joined as a defendant so that it could pursue the appeal. In the course of the hearing of the London bank's application the bank was granted leave on 4 March under RSC Ord

15, r 6(2)(b)[a] to intervene as a defendant. The court then went on to consider the merits of the London bank's claim that the judge had no jurisdiction to make the order of 24   *a* October, or if he did he ought to have exercised his discretion by refusing to make the order. On the merits, the London bank contended, inter alia, (i) that the judge had no jurisdiction to make the orders because he had purported to grant partial specific performance by way of an interim order, and (ii) that in respect of the order providing for a master[b] to sign the notice of readiness, although the court had power under s 47[b] of the Supreme Court of Judicature (Consolidation) Act 1925 to order a document to be   *b* executed 'where any person neglects or refuses to comply with a judgment or order directing him to execute [the] document', that did not empower the court to make such an order against a third party, and in any event the order should not have been used to validate a document against a third party; furthermore, the order authorising the notice of readiness to be signed by the master was in anticipation of, and did not follow, a neglect or refusal by the London bank to sign the notice of readiness.   *c*

Held – (1) Under the provisions of s 45(1)[c] of the 1925 Act the court had jurisdiction where it appeared just and convenient to do so to order interim relief by granting an interlocutory mandatory injunction to enforce a contractual obligation (see p 347 *j*, post); *Smith v Peters* (1875) LR 20 Eq 511 followed.

(2) The judge had properly exercised his discretion in granting the injunction since   *d* (a) the sellers had performed their obligations under the memorandum of agreement, (b) prima facie the sellers had a good claim to specific performance, (c) there was a serious risk that if the sellers obtained an order for specific performance after the letter of credit was allowed to expire the order would in practice prove to be valueless, (d) the funds resulting from activating the letter of credit would be adequately secured pending the determination of the arbitration proceedings, (e) the London bank, by confirming the   *e* letter of credit, had assumed liability for payment of the price of the vessel, and (f) having regard to all the facts, the London bank's position was no worse than it would have been if the buyers had performed their obligations (see p 348 *a* to *d*, post).

(3) Although the object of an order under s 47 of the 1925 Act was to ensure that the defendant was no better off as a result of his refusal to execute the document, it was also to ensure that the plaintiff was no worse off as a result of the defendant's non-compliance.   *f* Furthermore, the plaintiff's relationship with a third party might be so critical as to justify the use of the order. Therefore, although the London bank was entitled to apply to the judge for a variation or discharge of the order, on the facts it could not contend that the order would cause it any special prejudice. Moreover, the judge had jurisdiction to make the order on concluding that there had been a neglect or refusal to comply with the order. It followed that, although the order was unusual, it was within the jurisdiction   *g* of the judge to make it (see p 348 *h j* and p 349 *g h*, post).

Notes

For the statutory jurisdiction of the court to grant interlocutory injunctions, see 24 Halsbury's Laws (4th edn) paras 917–918, and for cases on interlocutory mandatory injunctions, see 28(2) Digest (Reissue) 995–996, 254–274.   *h*

For injunctions in aid of specific performance, see 24 Halsbury's Laws (4th edn) para 1008, and for cases on the subject, see 28(2) Digest (Reissue) 1061–1062, 772–783.

For Mareva injunctions, see 24 Halsbury's Laws (4th edn) para 1018 and 37 ibid para 362.

For the Supreme Court of Judicature (Consolidation) Act 1925, ss 45, 47, see 25 Halsbury's Statutes (3rd edn) 717, 719.

As from 1 January 1982, ss 45 and 47 of the 1925 Act were replaced by ss 37 and 39 of   *j* the Supreme Court Act 1981.

---

a Rule 6(2), so far as material, is set out at p 340 *e f* and *j*, post

b Section 47 is set out at p 348 *e f*, post

c Section 45(1) is set out at p 346 *h j*, post

Cases referred to in judgments

a   *Astro Exito Navegacion SA v Southland Enterprise Co Ltd* [1981] 2 Lloyd's Rep 595, CA.
Behnke v Bede Shipping Co Ltd [1927] 1 KB 649, [1927] All ER Rep 689, 42 Digest (Repl) 633, 3867.
Gurtner v Circuit [1968] 1 All ER 328, [1968] 2 QB 587, [1968] 2 WLR 668, CA, Digest (Cont Vol C) 1083, 1570a.
Kynaston v East India Co (1819) 3 Swans 248, 36 ER 850.
b   *Savage v Norton* [1908] 1 Ch 290, 3 Digest (Reissue) 511, 3347.
Smith v Peters (1875) LR 20 Eq 511, 3 Digest (Reissue) 104, 543.
Tetra Molectric Ltd v Japan Imports Ltd [1976] RPC 541, CA, Digest (Cont Vol E) 470, 175a.
Vandervell Trustees Ltd v White [1970] 3 All ER 16, [1971] AC 912, [1970] 3 WLR 452, HL, Digest (Cont Vol C) 1084, 1574a.
c   *Wellesley v Wellesley* (1853) De GM & G 537, 43 ER 617, LJJ, 27(1) Digest (Reissue) 271, 2010.

Cases also cited

American Cyanamid Co v Ethicon Ltd [1975] 1 All ER 504, [1975] AC 396, HL.
Associated Bulk Carriers Ltd v Koch Shipping Inc, The Fuohsan Maru [1978] 2 All ER 254, CA.
d   *Bonner v Great Western Rly Co* (1883) 24 Ch D 1, CA.
Gebr Van Weelde Scheepvaart Kantoor BV v Homeric Marine Services Ltd, The Agrabele [1979] 2 Lloyd's Rep 117.
Harbottle (K D) (Mercantile) Ltd v National Westminster Bank Ltd [1977] 2 All ER 862, [1978] QB 146.
Howe Richardson Scale Co Ltd v Polimex-Cekop [1978] 1 Lloyd's Rep 161, CA.
e   *Mundy v Joliffe* (1839) 5 My & Cr 167, 41 ER 334, LC.
Owen (Edward) Engineering Ltd v Barclays Bank International Ltd [1978] 1 All ER 976, [1978] QB 159, CA.
Rasu Maritima SA v Perusahaan Pertambangan Minyak Dan Gas Bumi Negara (Pertamina) and Government of Indonesia (as interveners) [1977] 3 All ER 324, [1978] QB 644, CA.
Sheperd Homes Ltd v Sandham [1970] 3 All ER 402, [1971] Ch 340.
f   *Woodstock Shipping Co v Kyma Compania Naviera SA, The Wave* [1981] 1 Lloyd's Rep 521.
Z Ltd v A [1982] 1 All ER 556, [1982] QB 558, CA.

Interlocutory appeal

g   The first defendants, Southland Enterprise Co Ltd (the buyers), and the second defendants, Nan Jong Iron and Steel Co Ltd (the buyers' agents), appealed against the order of Parker J made on 24 October 1980 on their application to stay proceedings arising from a contract between the buyers and the plaintiffs, Astro Exito Navegacion SA (the sellers), for the purchase of the motor vessel Messiniaki Tolmi in so far as the judge ordered, inter alia, that the proceedings be stayed on terms that the buyers sign a notice of readiness by 28 October 1980, in default of which the notice was to be signed by a master of the Supreme Court, and further, that the buyers authorise Chase Manhattan Bank NA (Chase)
h   to release moneys held by Chase under a letter of credit pursuant to the contract into an account in the joint names of the parties' solicitors until further order. On 28 October 1980, the buyers having failed to sign the notice of readiness, the order was amended to authorise Master Bickford Smith to sign the notice. On 4 March 1982 the buyers and the buyers' agents were granted leave to withdraw from the appeal and Chase was granted leave to intervene in the action as a defendant under RSC Ord 15, r 6(2)(b). The case is
j   reported only on the issue of whether Parker J had jurisdiction to make the order of 24 October 1980, and if so, whether he had exercised his discretion properly in making the order. The facts are set out in the judgment of Ackner LJ.

Leonard Hoffmann QC and *Nicholas Paines* for Chase.
Nicholas Phillips QC and *Steven Gee* for the sellers.
David Hunt for the buyers and the buyers' agents.

4 March. **ACKNER LJ** delivered the first judgment at the invitation of Stephenson LJ. The plaintiffs in this action are a Panamanian company; I shall refer to them hereafter as *a* 'the sellers'. They agreed to sell a Greek motor vessel, the Messiniaki Tolmi of about 51,000 tons, built in 1965, to the first defendants, Southland Enterprise Co Ltd, a Taiwanese company to whom I shall refer hereafter as 'the buyers', in accordance with a memorandum of agreement dated 2 July 1980 at a price equivalent to $US212·50 per lightweight ton. The second defendants acted as their agents and, although joined as defendants, really play no part of any significance in the action. *b*

The vessel was intended to be broken up by the buyers and the vendors agreed to deliver her to Kaohsiung harbour, Taiwan, with a valid gas-free certificate to be approved by the Taiwan authorities. Pursuant to the contract, the buyers opened a letter of credit in payment of the purchase price, which was in excess of $US4m, with Overseas Chinese Commercial Banking Corporation (OCCBC) and that letter of credit was confirmed by the Chase Manhattan Bank in London, referred to hereafter as 'Chase'. *c*

Problems arose in regard to the letter of credit, for this reason, that in the letter of credit, at the instance of the buyers, there had been inserted an additional obligation, namely, that the notice of readiness should be countersigned by the Kaohsiung harbour-master or Lloyds' agents in Taiwan, Jardine Matheson & Co Ltd, Taipei, confirming safe arrival of the vessel inside Kaohsiung harbour and accepted and signed by the second defendants, Nan Jong Iron & Steel Co Ltd, Tainan, Taiwan, on behalf of the buyers. *d*

What so prophetically the sellers anticipated was that that addition to the letter of credit would give rise to serious problems. This appears from a telex which said:

'We agree proposed wording of item/document 6 of the letter of credit except phrase in the bottom reading "Inside Kaohsiung Harbour and accepted and signed by the purchasers" ... which should be definitely deleted as it opposes provisions of the memorandum of agreement in the following respects: (A) "Inside Kaohsiung *e* Harbour" precludes possibility that sellers may deliver vessel and be entitled to the proceeds of the letter of credit in accordance with clause 3 of the memorandum of agreement; and (B) the phrase "Accepted and signed by the purchasers" may through unreasonable refusal of buyers to accept and sign properly given notice of readiness make it impossible for sellers to deliver the vessel and collect purchase price by letter of credit in accordance with the memorandum of agreement.' *f*

As it turned out, it was not possible for a vessel to proceed inside Kaohsiung Harbour unless there was a berth available, and the buyers had to make that provision themselves. However, after protests, the form of the letter of credit was accepted by the sellers, but such acceptance did not imply any waiver of the terms of the memorandum of agreement as to the notice of readiness. *g*

On 22 September 1980 the vessel arrived in the outer harbour of Kaohsiung, and gave notice of readiness. The buyers, however, refused to accept the notice of readiness on the ground that this was not accompanied by a valid gas-free certificate approved by the Taiwan authorities; they contended that the vessel's gas-free certificate had not been approved by the authorities by 30 September, the cancelling date provided in the contract, and purported to cancel the contract. In actual fact, the Taiwan authorities do *h* not formally approve a gas-free certificate; they allow vessels into the harbour so long as they have a gas-free certificate and are satisfied that there is a berth available to which the vessel can proceed.

On 29 September the sellers purported to extend the cancelling date in the contract, which the buyers contended they were not entitled to do. The contract was expressed to be governed by English law, and contained an arbitration clause. On 9 October 1980 the *j* sellers brought proceedings for specific performance of the contract, asking for judgment under RSC Ord 86. The buyers countered by applying to stay the proceedings pending the arbitration.

On 24 October 1980 Parker J announced his intention of staying the action on terms which included making injunctions directing the buyers to countersign the notice of readiness and to instruct OCCBC to authorise Chase to release the moneys secured by the

letter of credit, the moys so released to be lodged in the joint names of the solicitors
a for the buyers and the sellers within the jurisdiction and after being paid into the joint
account was not to be released without further order. I need make little further reference
to the order, save to say that there was also provision for the addition of the words on the
face of the notice of readiness, 'Vessel arrived in outer harbour Kaohsiung'. It was also
provided that in the event of the document, duly signed, not being returned to the
sellers' solicitors in London by 12 noon on 28 October 1980, then a master of the Supreme
b Court should be appointed to carry out the acts in the place of the second defendants on
the other original notice of readiness and to sign the resulting document for the second
defendants on behalf of the buyers. The resulting document signed by the master of the
Supreme Court as aforesaid was to stand as a good and valid document, duly executed by
the second defendants on behalf of the buyers. I emphasise that the letter of credit was
due to expire on 30 October 1980 and accordingly there was need for considerable
c expedition.

On 28 October 1980 the buyers applied to Parker J for a stay of his order on the basis
that they would seek to obtain an extension of the validity of the letter of credit to 12
November 1980; they also applied for an extension of time for complying with the
order. This application was adjourned to see whether the proposed extension of the
validity of the letter of credit could in fact be obtained; in fact, on 28 October the buyers
d did instruct Chase to extend the letter of credit to 12 November, but countermanded
these instructions on the same or the following day. Understandably the buyers did not
pursue their application for a stay of the order on the basis of an extension of the validity
of the letter of credit.

On the afternoon of Tuesday, 28 October 1980 Parker J, on the application of the
sellers, amended the order, having nominated Master Bickford Smith for the purpose of
e carrying out that part of his order relating to the notice of readiness, which acts the
master subsequently performed. On 29 October the sellers presented to Chase what they
regarded as all the documents, including the notice of readiness altered and signed by
Master Bickford Smith, which were necessary to operate the letter of credit. Chase,
however, objected to the documents on a number of specified grounds and returned
them to the sellers.

f On 30 October 1980 the sellers obtained an ex parte order from the Court of Appeal,
authorising Mr Lowe, who is a partner in the firm of solicitors acting for the sellers, to
delete from the sellers' notice of readiness the words 'Vessel arrived in outer harbour
Kaohsiung' which Master Bickford Smith had added on its face pursuant to the order of
Parker J of 24 October. On the same day the sellers again presented to Chase all the
documents, including the notice of readiness in its reamended form, which they regarded
g as necessary to operate the letter of credit. Chase, however, again objected to the
documents on various grounds and returned them. On 30 October 1980 Chase applied
by telex to OCCBC for authority to pay on the letter of credit, but on 3 November
OCCBC sent a telex to Chase, requesting them not to do so. The material words of that
telex are: 'Documents not acceptable due to discrepancies stated in your telex of October
30. Please do not effect payment.'

h In the result, the validity of the letter of credit expired on 30 October in accordance
with its terms. On 10 November 1980 the buyers issued a notice of appeal against the
order of Parker J.

On 29 November 1980 the vessel left Kaohsiung for Hong Kong. On the same day the
sellers purported to treat the conduct of the buyers as a repudiation of the contract for
sale and accepted such repudiation. On 11 December the vessel was resold by the sellers
j at well below the contract price, the market in scrap metal having fallen dramatically
since the contract was made, that being the motivating factor in the conduct of the
buyers as subsequently found by the arbitrators: a matter to which I shall refer later.

Meanwhile, the sellers had begun the arbitration proceedings against the buyers under
cl 14 of the memorandum of agreement, claiming damages for breach of the contract of
sale.

I now proceed to 1981. On 25 September 1981 the sellers sought to stay the appeal

brought against Parker J's decision, on the ground that the buyers were in contempt of
Parker J's order. I need not go into the basis of the Court of Appeal's judgments ([1981] 2   *a*
Lloyd's Rep 595), but the application failed.

On 30 November 1981, following an oral hearing lasting some seven days, a joint
award was made by the arbitrators in favour of the sellers in relation to the claim for
damages, leaving the damages to be subsequently assessed. The substantial dispute
between the parties at the arbitration concerned the gas-freeing of the vessel and the
various gas-free certificates which had been obtained. The arbitrators were satisfied that   *b*
the buyers' conduct in taking points on the gas-free condition of the vessel did not arise
from any genuine apprehension as to such condition but, as I have already indicated, was
motivated by the fall in the price of scrap steel and they wished either to get out of, or
renegotiate, the contract.

What we are concerned with today is an application by the parties, that is the sellers
and the buyers and the second defendants, that the appeal to this court from the order of   *c*
Parker J, the stay of which was refused, be now withdrawn, the issues raised between the
parties having been overtaken and therefore rendered academic by the arbitration award.

However, Chase now seek to be added as defendants to the action in order to prosecute
the appeal with a view to establishing that Parker J had no jurisdiction to make, or
alternatively ought not to have exercised his discretion in favour of making, his order.
The reason for the interest of Chase in keeping the appeal alive is due to the sellers' claim   *d*
against them to enforce the letter of credit.

As long ago as 12 November 1980 the sellers commenced proceedings against Chase.
There has been a voluminous exchange of pleadings, the last move in which occurred as
recently as last month, when OCCBC were added as defendants and reamended points of
claim were delivered. The rule on which counsel on behalf of Chase relies in support of
his application is, of course, RSC Ord 15, r 6(2)(b). He says that he is entitled to rely on   *e*
para (2)(b)(i), which provides:

'At any stage of the proceedings in any cause or matter the court may on such
terms as it thinks just and either of its own motion or on application . . . (b) order
any of the following persons to be added as a party, namely—(i) any person who
ought to have been joined as a party or whose presence before the Court is necessary
to ensure that all matters in dispute in the cause or matter may be effectually and   *f*
completely determined and adjudicated upon . . .'

He relies, in support of invoking that rule, on *Gurtner v Circuit* [1968] 1 All ER 328
esp at 332, [1968] 2 QB 587 esp at 595, where Lord Denning MR said:

'It seems to me that, when two parties are in dispute in an action at law and the   *g*
determination of that dispute will directly affect a third person in his legal rights or
in his pocket, in that he will be bound to foot the bill, then the court in its discretion
may allow him to be added as a party on such terms as it thinks fit. By so doing, the
court achieves the object of the rule. It enables all matters in dispute to "be effectually
and completely determined and adjudicated upon" between all those directly
concerned in the outcome.'   *h*

Counsel for Chase also relies on the much wider words in RSC Ord 15, r 6(2)(b)(ii),
which refer to (I do not need to quote again the preceding words):

'. . . (ii) any person between whom and any party to the cause or matter there
may exist a question or issue arising out of or relating to or connected with any
relief or remedy claimed in the cause or matter which in the opinion of the Court it   *j*
would be just and convenient to determine as between him and that party as well as
between the parties to the cause or matter . . .'

That rule was added in 1971. The addition was made consequent on the decision of
the House of Lords in *Vandervell Trustees Ltd v White* [1970] 3 All ER 16, [1971] AC 912.

a
In that case it had been held that in a dispute between trustees and beneficiaries under the trust the Inland Revenue was not a necessary party within the terms of what is now sub-para (b)(i). Accordingly, it was decided that an order which had been made adding the Inland Revenue as a party to those proceedings was not authorised by the rule as it then stood. Sub-paragraph (b)(ii) was added to widen the discretion of the court, so that the court may add any person such as is described in that sub-paragraph if the question or issue involved is one in which in the opinion of the court it would be just and

b
convenient to determine as between the applicant and a party to the proceedings as well as between the parties to the proceedings themselves.

Counsel for Chase, as a close illustration of how that rule can be applied, invited our attention to *Tetra Molectric Ltd v Japan Imports Ltd* [1976] RPC 541. In that case, as appears from the headnote, in 1971—

c
'the proprietor of a patent relating to piezo-electric smokers' lighters commenced an action for infringement. The defendant, an English company, did not make the lighters in question, but obtained them from a Japanese corporation and acted as a distributor in this country. The Japanese corporation however, agreed to indemnify the defendant and to pay for and conduct the case on its behalf. At the trial of the action the patent was held to be invalid on the ground of obviousness. The patentee appealed. While the appeal was pending a dispute arose between the Japanese

d
corporation and the owners of the defendant company, the former accusing the latter of having misappropriated its trade mark. In November 1975, about two months before the appeal was to be heard, the defendant company intimated to the Japanese corporation that it was no longer interested in resisting the appeal; at the same time it instructed its solicitors to remove their name from the record. On 31st December the defendant company intimated that it did after all intend to resist the

e
appeal. The Japanese corporation, which had appointed a new distributor for its lighters, feeling that its interests were unlikely to be advanced with vigour by the defendant, applied to the Court of Appeal to be joined as respondent to the appeal. It was the intention of the Japanese corporation to be represented by the same counsel and solicitors as had acted for the defendant at first instance. The patentee resisted the application, contending that there was no power to allow the Japanese

f
corporation to intervene and that, even if there was, it had been so dilatory that the application ought to be refused.'

It was held by the Court of Appeal, again quoting from the headnote—

g
'that there was power under Order 15, rule 6(2)(b)(ii), to add the Japanese corporation as respondent, and that the requirements of justice and of the efficient conduct of the hearing of the apppeal required that this should be done on the Japanese corporation giving security for costs.'

I quote but a small part of the judgment of Buckley LJ (at 544):

h
'It has been argued that upon the construction of that paragraph there must be shown to be a question or issue between the applicant—that is Win [the Japanese corporation] in the present case—and the party to the proceedings between whom and the applicant it is said that a question or issue exists; and, of course, that must be so. It seems to me that in the present case there clearly is a question or issue between Win and the plaintiff company in which both parties have an important interest, namely, the validity of the plaintiff's patent and, if it is valid, the question

j
whether Win's product constitutes an infringement of that patent, or any of Win's products constitute an infringement of that patent. It is perfectly true that at the date of the issue of the writ the plaintiff had no cause of action against Win, as I conceive, because Win had not, it would appear, sold any of their lighters in this country. They had sold them in Japan, or outside this country, to persons who imported them into this country and who then sold them on the market here. But

that does not mean that there was not then or there is not now a question or issue
between Win and the plaintiff company which answers to the description contained   *a*
in the sub-paragraph. As I conceive it, Win could have at any time presented a
petition for the revocation of the plaintiff company's patent, or could have instituted
proceedings for a declaration of non-infringement in relation to Win's cigarette
lighters. The validity of the patent and the question of whether Win's lighters
infringe the patent are matters of very considerable commercial importance to Win,
because there is a large market for their lighters in this country, and that is a market   *b*
which they obviously wish to preserve and do not want to be excluded from. So I
find no difficulty myself in saying that there is here such a question or issue as is
referred to in the paragraph.'

Counsel on behalf of the sellers maintains that the bank are seeking to intervene to
promote an appeal from a first instance decision to which they were not a party; this is of
course right. He says that leave to intervene presupposes that there is a process proceeding.   *c*
The object is to avoid a multiplicity of proceedings, and he contends that for RSC Ord
15, r 6(2)(*b*)(ii) to operate, it is necessary to establish that there is an action, or an appeal,
which is proceeding. In my judgment, the mere fact that the buyers wish to withdraw
from the appeal does not assist the sellers. The application which is made by Chase is to
come into these proceedings. If this court were to allow them to enter these proceedings
as they are now constituted, there would clearly be an intervention in a process which is   *d*
proceeding. The fact that thereafter this court might accede to the buyers' application to
withdraw does not in my view defeat the operation of Ord 15, r 6(2)(*b*)(ii).

Counsel for the sellers' next contention on this procedural aspect was that the proper
course which Chase should have taken was to apply to Parker J to lift the injunctions
which he made, they being parties who had an interest which was affected by his order,
but who were not parties to the proceedings in which the order had been made. I accept   *e*
that that was a course which was clearly open to Chase, but I also accept the answer of
counsel for Chase that matters were proceeding so fast that by the time they had sought
to apply to Parker J, everything had become fait accompli. True, even after Master
Bickford Smith had signed the letter of credit and there had been the subsequent
alteration, with the authority of the judge, by Mr Lowe and there had been the
presentations and the refusals by Chase, Chase could have gone back to Parker J and asked   *f*
him to reconsider the justification for his order. But, as I have indicated, it was all
somewhat late in the day. True it is that Chase could have sought earlier to have been
made parties to the appeal. But, until the arbitration proceedings were over, there was
no reason for them to contemplate that the appeal would not proceed effectively, and in
fact, in the judgment of Templeman LJ, in the application by the sellers for a stay of the
buyers' appeal (see *Astro Exito Navegacion SA v Southland Enterprise Co Ltd* [1981] 2 Lloyd's   *g*
Rep 595 at 604), he said:

'The buyers argue that they are entitled to pursue the appeal because that will
assist the Chase Manhattan Bank to resist proceedings which the sellers have brought
against the bank for payment of the monies secured by the letter of credit, the
release of Chase Manhattan Bank will procure the release of OCCBC and that in turn   *h*
will procure the release of any guarantors or securities furnished by unidentified
third parties of an unspecified nature and existence.'

So that although there has been a failure by Chase to apply to Parker J and a failure to
seek to come in on the appeal at an earlier stage, I do not take the view that that should,
if justice and convenience make it desirable, disentitle then from relying on RSC Ord 15,
r 6.   *j*

I come now to the merits. The right place to protect the interest of Chase, if there is
any interest to protect, is, submits counsel for the sellers, in the letter of credit action;
and he makes the significant point that, despite the extensive pleas made in the defence,
it has not yet been pleaded that Parker J had no jurisdiction to make the order. Of course,
if he had no jurisdiction to make the order, it would follow that what he did was a nullity

and the authority of Master Bickford Smith could not then have produced a conforming
document within the requirements of the letter of credit.

a

But counsel for Chase, while accepting that that could be raised in the action, maintains
that what could not be raised was his second ground of attack, namely that if the judge
had jurisdiction to make the order, then he acted wrongly in making the order; he
should have exercised his discretion by refusing to make such an order. Counsel for
Chase argues that, unless Parker J's order is appealed against and this court finds that the

b order, even though there was jurisdiction, was wrongly made, it remains a valid order.
He cannot in the letter of credit action attack it on the basis that it was the result of a
wrongful exercise by the judge of his jurisdiction.

This is not really contested by counsel for the sellers. Counsel for the sellers' contention
essentially is that, given that there was jurisdiction to make the order, and given that the
only criticism that could be made of it was that the learned judge should not have made

c that order, this would be of no consequence. On that hypothesis, the order, once made,
would have given Master Bickford Smith the authority to sign on behalf of the
defendants; the document would have been a conforming document within the
requirements of the letter of credit, and Chase were obliged to honour their obligations
under the letter of credit. If the Court of Appeal decided that the exercise of the discretion
was wrongful, that would not detract from the fact, so he submitted, that as at the date

d when the notice of readiness was presented, there was a proper authority in Master
Bickford Smith to sign the document; there would be, so to speak, no relation back of
the order made in the Court of Appeal.

We have looked at the relevant orders, which are RSC Ord 59, r 13 and Ord 42, r 3.
While it is usual for the order of the Court of Appeal to take effect on the day on which
it is made and not to relate back, there seems to be power, and there is no need for a final

e decision to be made at this stage, in the court to back date its order so that it takes effect
on the day on which the learned judge purported to make his decision.

Accordingly, counsel for Chase is in a position to submit that if Chase are not allowed
to be added as defendants to the action, and therefore to be added as parties to the appeal,
they can only in relation to Parker J's order raise in the letter of credit action want of
jurisdiction. Even if counsel were to be allowed, and he takes the view that he cannot be

f allowed, to raise the issue that the order, although within the court's jurisdiction, was an
order which should not have been made, there would be no right to seek from the trial
judge any backdating of such a decision; backdating could only be achieved by the Court
of Appeal reversing the order of Parker J on the ground of a wrongful exercise of his
discretion and backdating that order; and he thus submits that there would be an
injustice in depriving him of what may be a valid defence to the claim brought against

g his clients under the letter of credit.

I think there is force in this submission. Further, it seems to me that a contrary
decision produces a very odd situation. The commercial judge who tries the letter of
credit action would have the obligation, for all practical purposes, to sit in the capacity of
an appellate court on the order of Parker J although there is already in existence an
effective notice of appeal relating to that order, and the court which should pronounce

h on the validity of the order should be the Court of Appeal.

In all the circumstances, without of course expressing any view, since this has not been
argued before us, on the merits of the points to be canvassed in the appeal, it seems to me
that it would be just and convenient for Chase to be added as parties to the action heard
by Parker J and to be added as parties to the appeal, thus enabling them to deal in the
Court of Appeal, as fully as they may be entitled to, with the validity of the notice of

j readiness, and in particular the validity of the signature of Master Bickford Smith and/or
Mr Lowe on that document.

Accordingly, I would allow the application.

O'CONNOR LJ. For the reasons given by Ackner LJ, I agree that Chase should be
joined as defendants in these proceedings.

STEPHENSON LJ. I also agree. In *Tetra Molectric Ltd v Japan Imports Ltd* [1976] RPC 541, to which Ackner LJ has referred, this court gave a stranger to an action leave to be added as a co-defendant/respondent to an appeal. It must be unusual to allow a stranger to intervene and be added as a co-defendant/appellant in order to be enabled to be substituted as sole appellant if the existing defendant is given leave to withdraw its appeal. But in my judgment counsel for Chase has brought Chase within RSC Ord 15, r 6(2)(b)(ii) and, for the reasons given by Ackner LJ, I agree that he should be given leave to prosecute this appeal should the defendant be given leave to withdraw, or indeed, even if that leave is not granted.

Application by Chase to be added as defendants/appellants granted. First and second defendants' application for leave to withdraw granted.

Having given judgment allowing the first and second defendants to withdraw from the appeal and allowing Chase to intervene in the proceedings, the court heard argument with respect to the issues whether the judge had jurisdiction to make the order of 24 October 1980 and if so, whether he had correctly exercised his discretion in making the order.

Cur adv vult

5 April. **ACKNER LJ** read the following judgment of the court: On 4 March 1982 the application of Chase to be added as defendants in the action and as appellants to this appeal in the place of the buyers and their agents (the first and second defendants, who sought leave to withdraw from the appeal) was allowed for the reasons set out in our extempore judgments of that date. In my judgment I gave some detail of the background to the action and appeal. I do not propose to repeat those facts, save as a matter of convenience, to recall the following points. (1) The letter of credit opened, pursuant to the memorandum of agreement by the buyers of the vessel, with OCCBC for payment of the purchase price was confirmed by Chase. (2) The buyers had inserted additional obligations in the letter of credit not provided for in the memorandum of agreement, namely that the notice of readiness had to be (a) countersigned by the Kaohsiung harbour master or Lloyds' agents, confirming safe arrival inside Kaohsiung harbour, (b) accepted and signed by the buyers' agents, the second defendants, on their behalf. (3) The buyers had refused to accept and sign the notice of readiness on the grounds that it was not accompanied by an acceptable gas-free certificate. When the sellers' summons before Parker J for an order that the buyers do accept and sign the notice was heard, there were clearly strong reasons for suspecting that the buyers' sole motive for refusing to sign was that, since the date of the memorandum of agreement, the bottom had fallen out of the scrap steel market. However, this could not then be established. The subsequent arbitration so found in clear terms. (4) Parker J, on 24 October 1980, on the application of the buyers, stayed the sellers' claim for specific performance of the memorandum of agreement and ancillary relief so that the dispute could go to arbitration, pursuant to the arbitration provision in the memorandum of agreement. However, by way of interim relief, he ordered, inter alia, (i) the second defendants, for and on behalf of the buyers, to sign the notice of readiness and return the same to the sellers' solicitors by 12 noon on 28 October 1980 (the letter of credit was due to expire on 30 October 1980); (ii) in the event of the document not being duly signed and returned by the time and date specified, then a master of the Supreme Court be appointed to carry out the aforesaid acts in place of the second defendants, the resulting document signed by the master to stand as a good and valid document duly executed by the second defendants on behalf of the buyers, (iii) the second defendants, for and on behalf of the buyers, to instruct OCCBC to instruct Chase to release forthwith to the sellers the full amount of the letter of credit, the amount so received to be paid into the joint names of the parties' solicitors, no sum to be paid out other than by agreement of the parties or pursuant to an order of the court. (5) The buyers' agents having failed to comply with the order, Parker J on 28 October amended

it by nominating Master Bickford Smith to sign the notice of readiness, which he did on
a that day. On subsequent days the sellers presented to Chase with what they considered
were all the documents necessary to operate the letter of credit, including the notice of
readiness signed by Master Bickford Smith, but Chase objected to the documents on a
number of specified grounds and returned them to the sellers. (6) Although as long ago
as 12 November 1980 the sellers commenced proceedings against Chase, Chase now seek
to establish in the appeal, with a view to administering the coup de grâce to the sellers'
b claim, that Parker J had no jurisdiction to make, or alternatively ought not to have
exercised his discretion in favour of making, his orders.

It is convenient at this stage to refer to the judgment of Parker J. After summarising
the relevant facts and issues between the parties, he then expressed his view that the
sellers, although unable to sustain a claim for summary judgment for an order of specific
performance, nevertheless had a good arguable case that the vessel was in the right place,
c the gas-free certificate had been approved by the Taiwan authorities and the notice of
readiness was not required to be signed by the buyers. He was, however, obliged by s 1
of the Arbitration Act 1975 to grant a stay pending the arbitration proceedings. There
remained, however, the question whether there should be some interim relief. I now
quote from his judgment:

d   'Turning now to interim relief, this can be put in a number of ways. It can be put
          under s 12(6) of the Arbitration Act 1950, para (f) (securing the amount in dispute
          in the reference) and para (h) (interim injunctions). One power the judge has is to
          impose conditions on leave to defend. The judge also has power to secure that there
          will be money available to meet the plaintiffs' claim if successful. It may be done in
          any one of a number of ways or by a combination of those ways. Money can be
          ordered into court. There can be an injunction of the Mareva type. It can be done
e   by a combination of a restrictive injunction relating to assets and a mandatory
          injunction requiring disclosure of the whereabouts of assets. The purpose is to see
          that the plaintiffs' position is not worsened between the date of the application and
          the date of judgment. In the present case, the letter of credit expires on 30 October
          1980. The letter of credit is confirmed by Chase Manhattan and therefore represents,
          so far as the plaintiffs are concerned, good and solid assets within the jurisdiction.
f   But it will have disappeared if nothing is done . . . To ensure that the plaintiffs are
          protected otherwise than by sensible agreement between the parties, it is for the
          court to make orders to ensure that the money under the letter of credit is preserved
          so that it may be used to meet any judgment for the plaintiffs if they succeed. The
          only way to do it is for the court to make the necessary directions to ensure that the
          bank pays out the money. It would be wrong to stop there. It would be as unfair to
g   the defendants as it is unfair to the plaintiffs if the credit were allowed to expire,
          hence it is necessary for conditions to be attached to ensure that the money released
          is preserved and not used pending resolution of disputes.'

At an earlier stage in his judgment the judge had considered the submission that it
was impossible, or unlikely, that the arbitrators would grant specific performance and
h accordingly that nothing in the nature of specific performance would be granted by way
of interim relief. He accepted that specific performance at the suit of the sellers, even of
a specific vessel, would not normally be given, but he was satisfied that there was no bar
to granting this relief in appropriate cases and, having considered the facts more fully, he
concluded 'that it is strongly arguable that specific performance should be granted here'.
If judicial precedent is required for specific performance of the sale of a ship, it is to be
j found in Behnke v Bede Shipping Co Ltd [1927] 1 KB 649, [1927] All ER Rep 689, a decision
of Wright J.

Did the judge have jurisdiction to make the orders?

The contention of counsel on behalf of Chase, expressed in general terms, is that the
judge has, by cross-breeding between the Mareva jurisdiction and the specific performance
jurisdiction, produced a hybrid which is beyond the court's generative powers. He

contends that the Mareva type of order is clearly not appropriate because it is a negative order, is designed to prevent the dissipation of assets and is aimed at the assets of the defendant in the action. Here the order is a mandatory order, a positive order, and is aimed at the assets of a bank which was not a party to the action. These propositions are, of course, correct. However, the judge, as the terms of his judgment made clear, was not purporting to make a Mareva or a Mareva-type order. But, submits counsel for Chase, the Mareva jurisdiction is the only jurisdiction that can be invoked against the buyers to require them to provide security against the sellers' claim. What the judge has sought to do, despite staying the proceedings for arbitration to take place, is to grant partial specific performance. This is an encroachment, he submits, on the arbitrators' jurisdiction and pre-empts their decision. This he is not entitled to do.

Counsel on behalf of the sellers takes a much simpler approach to the eugenics of the order. He contends that the judge has simply granted an interim mandatory injunction in the nature of an order for specific performance. It is not an order akin to a Mareva injunction, which merely provides, by way of ancillary relief, security for the claim if successful. Parker J's order related to a substantive legal right claimed in the proceedings. It provides interim relief by enforcing, to a limited extent, and subject to specific safeguards, the buyers' contractual obligation as asserted in the points of claim. Paragraph 3 of the points of claim alleges, in terms, that—

'Within three business days of the Vendors or their Agents in Taiwan giving notice to the Purchasers, by letter or telegram, of the vessel's readiness for delivery in accordance with this Agreement and presenting the Gas Free Certificate as per clause 17, the Negotiating Bank shall be instructed by the Purchasers to release the full Letter of Credit amount to the Vendors forthwith.'

He further contends that the interim order was so understood, as is made clear by ground 2 of the notice of appeal of the buyers, now adopted by Chase, which reads:

'That the Learned Judge erred in law in holding that it was appropriate to enforce the Memorandum of Agreement . . . The enforcement of a contract of sale such as the aforesaid by way of equitable relief is inappropriate and/or contrary to the provisions of section 52 of the Sale of Goods Act 1979.'

Counsel for Chase countered by submitting that there is no precedent for making an interim order that provides for partial specific performance. There is, he contended, no instance of an interlocutory order to compel the execution of a contractual obligation, in particular to pay any sum of money. He thus argued that the orders made were not permissible. While conceding that interim mandatory orders are, of course, not infrequently made, he maintained that these were essentially restorative orders, in that they directed a party to restore the status quo which he had disturbed. Subject to the Mareva-type injunction, an order could not be made for the provision of security for a money judgment which the plaintiff might obtain.

Thus the first issue in this appeal crystallises itself into the following question: is there jurisdiction to make such an order at the interlocutory stage?

Section 45(1) of the Supreme Court of Judicature (Consolidation) Act 1925, which replaced s 25(8) of the Supreme Court of Judicature Act 1873, and which since Parker J's judgment has now been re-enacted in s 37(1) of the Supreme Court Act 1981, provides:

'The High Court may grant a mandamus or an injunction or appoint a receiver, by an interlocutory order in all cases in which it appears to the court to be just or convenient so to do.'

In *Fry on Specific Performance of Contracts* (6th edn, 1921) p 544, commenting on s 25(8) of the 1873 Act, it is stated:

'These provisions give the Court a wide if not an unlimited power of granting an injunction at any stage of any case where it would, according to sufficient legal reasons or on settled legal principles, be right or just to do so.'

The power to grant Mareva relief was indeed founded on this subsection. Why should it
not be wide enough, in appropriate cases, to justify an interlocutory mandatory
injunction to enforce part of a contractual obligation?

The industry of junior counsel for the sellers has unearthed *Smith v Peters* (1875) LR 20
Eq 511. Since this is, in our judgment, a case of considerable importance and which does
not appear to have been cited in the past, we feel that we should quote extensively from
it. The headnote reads as follows:

> 'Where an agreement has been entered into for the sale of a house at a fixed price,
> and of the fixtures and furniture therein at a valuation by a person named by both
> parties, and he undertakes the valuation, but if refused permission by the vendor to
> enter the premises for that purpose, the Court will make a mandatory order to
> compel the vendor to allow the entry to enable the valuation to proceed. The Court
> had jurisdiction to make any interlocutory order which is reasonably asked as
> ancillary to the administration of justice at the hearing.'

It was contended for Chase that it was contrary to the practice of the court to make a
mandatory order of this nature on an interlocutory application before the hearing of the
case. It was argued that there was only an incomplete contract, which the court could not
compel the defendants specifically to perform.

Jessel MR said in his judgment (at 512–513):

> 'The first question that I have to consider is, whether this application is in
> accordance with the practice of the Court. I have no hesitation in saying that there
> is no limit to the practice of the Court with regard to interlocutory applications so
> far as they are necessary and reasonable applications ancillary to the due performance
> of its functions, namely, the administration of justice at the hearing of the cause. I
> know of no other limit. Whether they are, or are not, to be granted must of course
> depend upon the special circumstances of the case. But if authority were wanting
> for my guidance in this matter – and I think the principle is so clear that authority
> is not wanting – I might refer to the case which has been mentioned by the Plaintiff's
> counsel, of *Kynaston* v. *East India Company* (3 Swans 248, 36 ER 850), which was an
> application in a tithe suit to inspect the Defendant's house before the hearing, in
> order to ascertain its value. The object in ascertaining its value would be to make a
> decree against the Defendant at the hearing. Here the object of ascertaining the
> value is also to make a decree against the defendant at the hearing. What does Lord
> *Eldon* say? "I have found no case in point but on principle I think the Court has
> authority." Therefore in deciding the question of practice, he only looked at the
> principle. That is what I am going to do. [Having dealt with the facts, Jessel MR
> continued (at 513–514)]: Can it be tolerated, in a country in which violence is not
> allowed, in which Mr. *Lound* and his clerks would not be permitted to force an
> entry, although in pursuance of an agreement, that a Court of justice shall say no
> provision can be made for such a case, and that it shall be permitted to a Defendant
> to say, "Although I have sold this furniture and fixtures at a valuation to be made by
> Mr. *Lound*, a valuer of my own choice, I will at my will and pleasure obstruct Mr.
> *Lound* in the performance of his duty, and prevent his completing the valuation
> which I have already contracted he shall make"? I do not believe it to be the law of
> this Court, and I do not believe it will ever be so decided.'

This provides the precedent that counsel for Chase says was lacking. Here a positive
order, which was not restorative of something that had been wrongfully undone, was
made. It was an interlocutory mandatory order compelling the execution of a contractual
obligation.

We conclude that s 45(1) of the Supreme Court of Judicature (Consolidation) Act 1925
gave the judge jurisdiction to make the order requiring the second defendants to take
the steps described above. We deal later with the amendment of the order which
substituted Master Bickford Smith for the second defendants. If we are right so far, then
there remain two further questions.

The remedy to grant the injunction being discretionary, was the discretion properly exercised?
We are satisfied that, for the following reasons, the answer to this question is clearly in   *a*
the affirmative. (i) Prima facie the sellers had performed their obligations under the
memorandum of agreement. They had taken the vessel to Singapore and had it made
gas-free. They had then sailed her to Kaohsiung harbour. (ii) Prima facie the sellers had a
good claim to specific performance. (iii) Prima facie there was a serious risk that if the
letter of credit, the very security for which the sellers had contracted, was allowed to
expire, then if the sellers obtained an order for specific performance, the order would in   *b*
practice prove valueless. (iv) The funds resulting from activating the letter of credit
would be adequately secured pending the determination of the arbitration proceedings.
(v) Chase, by confirming the letter of credit, had assumed liability for the payment of the
price of the vessel, subject of course to the terms of the letter of credit. It was not to be
assumed that they had done so without adequate security, nor was such a suggestion
advanced before us. In any event, a confirming bank must be taken fully to appreciate   *c*
the consequences of its actions. (vi) Having regard to the facts now known, Chase's
position was no worse than it would have been if the buyers had performed their
obligations. (vii) While the order was certainly an unusual order, it was an unusual case.
It must indeed be rare that, without there being any express provision in the contract,
the operation of the letter of credit could depend on the will of the buyer.

  d

*Ought the order to have provided for the appointment of Master Bickford Smith to sign etc the
notice of readiness?*
Section 47 of the Supreme Court of Judicature (Consolidation) Act 1925, now s 39 of
the Supreme Court Act 1981, provides:

> 'Where any person neglects or refuses to comply with a judgment or order
> directing him to execute any conveyance, contract or other document, or to indorse   *e*
> any negotiable instrument, the High Court may, on such terms and conditions, if
> any, as may be just, order that the conveyance, contract or other document shall be
> executed or that the negotiable instrument shall be indorsed by such person as the
> court may nominate for that purpose, and a conveyance, contract, document or
> instrument so executed or indorsed shall operate and be for all purposes available as
> if it had been executed or indorsed by the person originally directed to execute or   *f*
> indorse it.'

Counsel for Chase submits firstly that the order does not apply as against third parties.
However, the only authority to which he has invited out attention is *Wellesley v Wellesley*
(1853) 4 De G M & G 537, 43 ER 617. In that case a donee of a power of jointuring under
a settlement was ordered, in a specific performance suit instituted by his wife, to execute   *g*
the power by a deed to be approved by a master. The order was made 'without prejudice
to any question as to the validity against any person or persons other than the Earl of
Mornington . . .' (see 4 De G M & G 537 at 542, 43 ER 617 at 619). This, however, was a
special provision inserted for this particular litigation. The words of the section are very
wide and the effect of the document executed pursuant to the order is provided for in
very clear terms.   *h*
Counsel for Chase further submitted that, as a matter of principle, the order should
not be used to validate a document against a third party. If the submission of counsel for
Chase were right this would render the section almost nugatory. The object of the order,
submits counsel for Chase, is to ensure that the *defendant* is no better off as a result of his
refusal to execute the document. However, we accept the submission of counsel for the
sellers, that the object should also be that the plaintiff is no worse off as a result of the   *j*
defendant's non-compliance. The plaintiff's relationship with a third party, as in this
case, may be so critical as to justify the use of the order. Counsel for Chase argues that it
is wrong to give the plaintiffs, by means of this order, a cause of action against a person
who was not a party to the proceedings. This, however, overlooks the entitlement of
Chase (who were kept informed by the sellers from the outset of the proceedings) to

apply to the judge, if there was material to justify such an application, for the variation
a or discharge of the order. For example, as was suggested at one stage, the order might
have prejudiced Chase's right of recovery against OCCBC, if their relationship was
governed by Taiwan law. However, in third party proceedings brought by Chase in the
letter of credit action against OCCBC, the assistant treasurer of Chase deposed in an
affidavit in support of an application for leave to serve the third party notice on OCCBC
out of the jurisdiction, that Chase made two contracts with OCCBC and a contract (the
b letter of credit) with the sellers, 'all of which were made in England and by implication
governed by English law'. In the third party proceedings Chase were claiming to be
indemnified pursuant to their agreement to confirm the letter of credit. There is thus no
basis for Chase contending that the order will cause them any special prejudice. OCCBC
will not, on the material before us, be able to raise any special defence against Chase in
relation to the order, arising out of Taiwan or some other law.

c   The final point taken by counsel for Chase (and he with characteristic realism accepts
it as a technical point of no great merit) is that the order authorising the notice of
readiness to be signed by Master Bickford Smith was in anticipation of, and not after, a
neglect or refusal. This objection was considered in *Savage v Norton* [1908] 1 Ch 290, and
was left open by the judge who said (at 297):

d   'My own opinion is that, on the true construction of s. 14 [of the Supreme Court
of Judicature Act 1884], the circumstance which gives rise to the jurisdiction is the
neglect or refusal, and that the Court, before making the order, ought to satisfy
itself that there has been a neglect or refusal and also as to the circumstances in
which that neglect or refusal has taken place, because the order is only to be made
"on such terms and conditions (if any) as may be just." Therefore, in making the
order, the Court ought to know the circumstances of the refusal or neglect as well as
e the fact that there has been a refusal or neglect. The refusal may, for instance, have
been due to some unforeseen cause, and the party all along may have been willing,
and may still be willing, to comply, but may have been prevented by some
accident—in which case I doubt whether the Court would, after considering the
circumstances of the case, make any order.'

f   However, because of the extreme urgency of the situation, a time limit had to be
imposed in this case and, when Parker J amended the order on 28 October 1980 to
provide for Master Bickford Smith to sign etc the notice of readiness, it is common
ground that he was justified in concluding that there had been a neglect or refusal to
comply with his order of 24 October 1980. Accordingly, there is no question but that he
had jurisdiction to make the order. Although it did not appear on the face of the order
g that Master Bickford Smith had been directed to sign etc the notice of readiness by reason
of a neglect or refusal of the buyers or their agents, Chase would have had no difficulty
in establishing that this was the basis for the order.

     In the result, while we accept that the order was an unusual one, it was not only within
the jurisdiction of the learned judge, but was fully justified by his percipient assessment
of the merits of an unusual dispute.

h   We would accordingly confirm the order and dismiss this appeal.

Appeal dismissed.

29 July. The Appeal Committee of the House of Lords granted Chase leave to appeal.

Solicitors: *Allen & Overy* (for Chase); *Holman, Fenwick & Willan* (for the sellers); *Cameron
& Markby* (for the buyers and the buyers' agents).

                                                  Sophie Craven   Barrister.

Kodros Shipping Corp v Empresa Cubana de Fletes
The Evia

HOUSE OF LORDS

LORD DIPLOCK, LORD ELWYN-JONES, LORD KEITH OF KINKEL, LORD ROSKILL AND LORD BRANDON OF OAKBROOK

5, 6, 7, 29 JULY 1982

Shipping – Charterparty – Safe port – Obligation of charterer to nominate safe port – Prospective safety – Unexpected and abnormal event – Port becoming unsafe after nomination and after arrival – Whether charterer in breach of obligation to nominate safe port – Whether charterer's obligation to nominate safe port amounting to a warranty.

Shipping – Charterparty – Safe port – Insurance – Owner's right to insure vessel against risks of unsafety arising from breach of charterer's duty with respect to safety of vessel – Whether owner's right to insure freeing charterer from liability for risks of unsafety arising after vessel's arrival at port which was prospectively safe at date of nomination.

Shipping – Charterparty – Safe port – Whether port must be politically safe as well as physically safe.

By a time charterparty dated 12 November 1979 in the Baltime form with a London arbitration clause the owners chartered a vessel to the charterers for a period of 18 months, 2 months more or less in the charterers' option. By cl 2 of the charterparty the vessel was to be employed in lawful trades for the carriage of lawful merchandise only 'between . . . safe ports'. By cl 21(A) the vessel was not, without the owners' consent, to be ordered or to continue to any place within a zone which was dangerous as the result of, inter alia, actual or threatened acts of war, and by cl 21(B) the owners were entitled to insure their interests in the vessel should the vessel approach or be brought or ordered within such a zone and to demand a refund of the premium from the charterers. In March 1980 the charterers ordered the vessel to load a cargo of cement and other building materials for carriage from Cuba to Basrah, on the Shatt al-Arab waterway. The vessel arrived in the Shatt al-Arab waterway on 1 July and had to anchor in the river waiting for a berth, her entry being delayed by congestion. She finally berthed on 20 August and, subject to some interruption, completed discharge at 1000 hrs on 22 September. She was, however, unable to sail to continue her chartered service because large-scale hostilities had broken out between Iran and Iraq, the Shatt al-Arab waterway being in the thick of the hostilities. From 22 September no ship of the many then in that area was able to escape, and gradually their crews in whole or in part left them. On 1 October the majority of the vessel's crew were repatriated, leaving only the master and a skeleton crew of about a dozen. The vessel was still trapped in July 1982. The owners claimed time-charter hire from 5 October 1981 (the previous payment covering the period up to and including 4 October 1981) and reimbursement of war risk premiums allegedly incurred by the owners after 28 June 1980. The charterers disputed the claims, contending that the charterparty had been frustrated on 22 September 1980, and on that basis they counterclaimed for overpaid hire. The charterers made a general denial of any liability for the war risk premiums. The dispute was referred to arbitrators, who, on their disagreement, appointed an umpire. The umpire found that Basrah was a safe port for the vessel both when she was ordered to proceed there and when she got there, and that it did not become unsafe until 22 September, by which time it was impossible for the vessel to leave. The umpire accordingly held that there had been no breach of the charterparty by the charterers, that the charterparty had been frustrated and that the

frustration took place on 4 October 1980. On an appeal by the owners, the judge reversed
a that decision, holding that there had been a breach of charterparty by the charterers,
since under cl 2 any port or place to which the vessel was ordered was to be warranted by
the charterers to be safe throughout the period of the vessel's contractual service there,
and that the charterers were debarred from relying on frustration as a defence to the
claim for hire because the frustration was self-induced. On a further appeal by the
charterers, the Court of Appeal held that there had been no breach of the charterparty by
b the charterers, since Basrah had been a safe port when the vessel was ordered there and
the unsafety that arose on the outbreak of hostilities on 22 September 1980 was an
abnormal and extraneous occurrence, for which provision had been made by cl 21(B) of
the charterparty. Although the Court of Appeal upheld the umpire's choice of date for
the frustration of the charterparty, it expressed the view that in arbitrations arising out
of the same events it was desirable that arbitrators should uniformly ascribe the same
c date of frustration. The owners appealed to the House of Lords, contending, inter alia, (i)
that the charterers had employed the vessel at Basrah after that port had become unsafe,
in breach of cl 2, and (ii) that cl 21 did not exempt the charterers from liability for breach
of contract in employing the vessel at an unsafe port within a war zone.

Held – The appeal would be dismissed for the following reasons—
d   (1) A port was not safe unless, in the relevant period of time, the particular ship could
reach it, use it and return from it, without, in the absence of some abnormal occurrence,
being exposed to damage which could not be avoided by good navigation and seamanship.
In exercising his right to order a ship to go to a particular port or place of loading or
discharge, the charterer's contractual promise regarding the safety of that intended port
or place related to the characteristics of the port or place, and meant that when the order
e was given (which was the moment when the relevant employment of the ship began)
that port or place was prospectively safe for the ship to get to, stay at, so far as necessary,
and, in due course, leave; and, so long as those characteristics were, at the time the order
was given, such as to make that port or place prospectively safe in that way, the sudden
occurrence thereafter in spite of them of some unexpected and abnormal event which
created conditions of unsafety where conditions of safety had previously existed and as a
result of which the ship was delayed, damaged or destroyed would not extend the
f charterer's contractual promise to make him liable for any resulting loss or damage,
physical or financial. Were it otherwise the charterer would be made the insurer of such
unexpected and abnormal risks which should properly fall on the ship's insurers under
the policies of insurance the effecting of which was, in the case of the Baltime charterparty,
the owner's responsibility under cl 3 unless the owner chose to be his own insurer in
g those respects. It followed that, since Basrah was prospectively safe at the time of
nomination, and since the unsafety arose after the vessel's arrival and was due to an
unexpected and abnormal event, there was at the former time no breach of cl 2 of the
charterparty by the charterers (see p 353 f to j, p 354 g h, p 360 b to g, p 362 j to p 633 b, p
364 h j, p 366 d e and p 368 e f, post); dictum of Sellers LJ in *Compania Naviera Maropan
SA v Bowaters Lloyd Pulp and Paper Mills Ltd, The Stork* [1955] 2 All ER at 255 applied;
h *Compania Naviera Maropan SA v Bowaters Lloyd Pulp and Paper Mills Ltd, The Stork* [1955]
2 All ER 241, *Reardon Smith Line Ltd v Australian Wheat Board, The Houston City* [1956] 1
All ER 456, *Leeds Shipping Co Ltd v Société Française Bunge, The Eastern City* [1958] 2 Lloyd's
Rep 127, *Tage Berglund v Montoro Shipping Corp Ltd, The Dagmar* [1968] 2 Lloyd's Rep
563, *Unitramp v Garnac Grain Co Inc, The Hermine* [1979] 1 Lloyd's Rep 212 and *Islander
Shipping Enterprises SA v Empresa Maritima del Estado SA, The Khian Sea* [1979] 1 Lloyd's
j Rep 545 distinguished; *Vardinoyannis v Egyptian General Petroleum Corp, The Evaggelos Th*
[1971] 2 Lloyd's Rep 200 considered; *NV Stoomv Maats 'De Maas' v Nippon Yusen Kaisha,
The Pendrecht* [1980] 2 Lloyd's Rep 56 and *Transoceanic Petroleum Carriers v Cook Industries
Inc, The Mary Lou* [1981] 2 Lloyd's Rep 272 disapproved.
    (2) The effect of cl 21 of the charterparty was to give the owners an absolute veto on
employment which would imperil the vessel in the various circumstances for which

cl 21(A) provided. Clause 21(B) also protected the owners in circumstances in which they
had not been able to impose a veto because the dangers had arisen too late for the consent
to be required and given or refused. Furthermore, cl 2 and any other relevant clause,
including cl 21, were to be construed together, and since cl 21 protected the owners by
entitling them to effect extra insurance, including war risks insurance, at the charterers
expense, the charterers were accordingly freed from liability for any unsafety which
arose after the vessel arrived at Basrah (see p 353 *f*, p 354 *g h*, p 367 *f* to *j* and p 368 *e f*,
post).

(3) There were no grounds for saying that the arbitrator was wrong in his choice of
the date of frustration of the charterparty. It was wrong in principle to consider other
awards arising from different questions of fact, and the court would not review the
arbitrator's choice of date by reference to dates chosen by other arbitrators or umpires in
other cases said to raise the same issues (see p 353 *f*, p 354 *g h* and p 368 *a* to *f*, post).

Per curiam. (1) Unless there is something unusual in the relevant express language in
a particular charterparty, the charterer's obligation with respect to the safety of a port at
its time of nomination applies equally to a voyage charterer as to a time charterer (see p
353 *f*, p 354 *g h*, p 364 *j* to p 365 *a* and p 368 *f*, post).

(2) A port is not a 'safe port' unless it is politically safe as well as physically safe (see p
353 *f*, p 354 *g h*, p 366 *e f* and p 368 *f*, post); *Ogden v Graham* (1861) 1 B & S 773 approved.

(3) The use of the word 'warranty' in the expression 'safe port warranty' or 'warranty
of safety', as in the expression 'warranty of seaworthiness', is convenient but is not an
expression of the legal consequences of the so-called warranty (see p 353 *f*, p 354 *g h*, p
366 *f* to *h* and p 368 *f*, post).

Per Lord Diplock and Lord Keith. It is dangerous to assemble together isolated
statements contained in judgments at first instance, each dealing with the facts of a
particular case, and using such statements to build up some novel principle of law
inconsistent with an existing principle which carries with it the authority and approval
of an appellate court (see p 354 *e* to *h*, post).

Observations on the obligations imposed on a time charterer who has ordered a vessel
to a port which, though prospectively safe at the time the order was given, has
subsequently become unsafe (see p 354 *a b* and p 365 *a* to p 366 *b*, post).

Notes

For a charterer's option to name a port of discharge, see 35 Halsbury's Laws (3rd edn)
273, para 413, for what constitutes a safe port and the consequences of nominating an
unsafe port, see ibid 439–441, paras 627–628, and for cases on the subject, see 41 Digest
(Repl) 420–423, 2048–2071.

Cases referred to in opinions

Compania Naviera Maropan SA v Bowaters Lloyd Pulp and Paper Mills Ltd, The Stork [1955]
    2 All ER 241, [1955] 2 QB 68, [1955] 2 WLR 998, CA; *affg* [1954] 3 All ER 563, [1955]
    2 QB 68, [1954] 3 WLR 894, 41 Digest (Repl) 189, 259.
Duncan v Köster, The Teutonia (1872) LR 4 PC 171, PC, 41 Digest (Repl) 379, 1702.
Grace (G W) & Co Ltd v General Steam Navigation Co Ltd, The Sussex Oak [1950] 1 All ER
    201, [1950] 2 KB 383, 41 Digest (Repl) 421, 2056.
Islander Shipping Enterprises SA v Empresa Maritima del Estado SA, The Khian Sea [1979] 1
    Lloyd's Rep 545, CA, Digest (Cont Vol E) 553, 2069a.
Leeds Shipping Co Ltd v Société Française Bunge, The Eastern City [1958] 2 Lloyd's Rep 127,
    CA; *affg* [1957] 2 Lloyd's Rep 153.
National Carriers Ltd v Panalpina (Northern) Ltd [1981] 1 All ER 161, [1981] AC 675,
    [1981] 2 WLR 45, HL.
NV Stoomv Maats 'De Maas' v Nippon Yusen Kaisha, The Pendrecht [1980] 2 Lloyd's Rep 56.
Ogden v Graham (1861) 1 B & S 773, 121 ER 901, 41 Digest (Repl) 422, 2062.
Pioneer Shipping Ltd v BTP Tioxide Ltd, The Nema [1981] 2 All ER 1030, [1982] AC 724,
    [1981] 3 WLR 292, HL.

Reardon Smith Line Ltd v Australian Wheat Board, The Houston City [1956] 1 All ER 456,
[1956] AC 266, [1956] 2 WLR 403, PC; *affg* [1954] 2 Lloyd's Rep 148, Aust HC, 41
Digest (Repl) 326, 1266.
Tage Berglund v Montoro Shipping Corp Ltd, The Dagmar [1968] 2 Lloyd's Rep 563.
Transoceanic Petroleum Carriers v Cook Industries Inc, The Mary Lou [1981] 2 Lloyd's Rep
272.
Unitramp v Garnac Grain Co Inc, The Hermine [1979] 1 Lloyd's Rep 212, CA; *rvsg* [1978] 2
Lloyd's Rep 37.
Vardinoyannis v Egyptian General Petroleum Corp, The Evaggelos Th [1971] 2 Lloyd's Rep
200, Digest (Cont Vol D) 825, 2068a.

Appeal

Kodros Shipping Corp of Monrovia, the owners of the vessel Evia chartered to Empresa
Cubana de Fletes of Havana, Cuba under a time charterparty in Baltime 1939 form
agreed in Greece on 12 November 1979, appealed with the leave of the Court of Appeal
against the decision of that court (Lord Denning MR and Shaw LJ, Ackner LJ dissenting)
([1982] 1 Lloyd's Rep 334) on 5 February 1982 whereby it allowed an appeal by the
charterers and dismissed a cross-appeal by the owners against the decision of Robert Goff
J ([1981] 2 Lloyd's Rep 613) on 6 August 1981 allowing in part an appeal by the owners
against the interim reasoned award of the umpire, Mr Basil Eckersley, dated 20 March
1981 declaring that the charterparty was frustrated on 4 October 1980 and awarding the
owners $US18,000 in respect of additional war risk premiums together with interest.
The facts are set out in the opinion of Lord Roskill.

Johan Steyn QC and *Nicholas Legh-Jones* for the owners.
Nicholas Phillips QC and *Jonathan Sumption* for the charterers.

Their Lordships took time for consideration.

29 July. The following opinions were delivered.

LORD DIPLOCK. My Lords, I agree with the speech to be delivered by my noble and
learned friend Lord Roskill and with the detailed reasons that he will give for dismissing
this appeal.
    For my part, I would regard the nature of the contractual promise by the charterer
that a chartered vessel shall be employed between safe ports (the safe port clause) as
having been well settled for a quarter of a century at the very least. It was correctly and
concisely stated by Sellers LJ in *Leeds Shipping Co Ltd v Société Française Bunge, The Eastern
City* [1958] 2 Lloyd's Rep 127 at 131 in a classic passage which, in its reference to
'abnormal occurrence', reflects a previous statement in the judgment of Morris LJ in
Compania Naviera Maropan SA v Bowaters Lloyd Pulp and Paper Mills Ltd, The Stork [1955]
2 All ER 241 at 255, [1955] 2 QB 68 at 105. Sellers LJ said:

> '. . . a port will not be safe unless, in the relevant period of time, the particular
> ship can reach it, use it and return from it without, in the absence of some abnormal
> occurrence, being exposed to danger which cannot be avoided by good navigation
> and seamanship . . .'

It is with the prospective safety of the port at the time when the vessel will be there for
the loading or unloading operation that the contractual promise is concerned and the
contractual promise itself is given at the time when the charterer gives the order to the
master or other agent of the shipowner to proceed to the loading or unloading port.
    What are the respective rights and duties of charterer and shipowner under a voyage
charter if the port becomes prospectively unsafe by reason of some abnormal occurrence
actually occurring (whether or not to the knowledge of either of them) during the period

of the loading or unloading voyage is not a matter that arises in the instant appeal and I think it would be unwise for your Lordships to express any view about it. In the case of the time charter, however, under which the charterer has power to substitute for his original order to the master to proceed to a particular port and there undertake the loading or unloading operation a fresh order to proceed elsewhere, so long as such fresh order is given at a time when it is possible for the vessel to comply with it, the contractual promise is a continuing one and if an occurrence which at the time of the original order could properly be regarded as abnormal has actually occurred and has rendered the port prospectively unsafe the charterer could not rely on the exception of 'abnormal occurrence' in Sellers LJ's statement of the effect of the safe port clause.

So great is the variety of ports to which chartered vessels are ordered to go, it is not surprising that disputes should arise whether damage sustained by a particular vessel in a particular port on a particular occasion was caused by an 'abnormal occurrence' rather than resulting from some normal characteristic of the particular port at the particular time of year. In cases of this kind, judges, particularly at first instance with their minds directed solely to the particular facts of the case they are deciding, may, not infrequently, in expressing the reasons for their decision, state a proposition of law on which they rely as relevant to the particular case in general terms which omit qualifications to that proposition that would be relevant to other cases, but are not relevant to the case under decision.

The heresy that, in the last decade or so, has been embraced by judges in the Commercial Court in the course of several judgments at first instance, culminating in that of Mustill J in *Transoceanic Petroleum Carriers v Cook Industries Inc, The Mary Lou* [1981] 2 Lloyd's Rep 272 at 277, would have the effect of eliminating the exception based on abnormal occurrence in Sellers LJ's statement of the effect of the safe port clause. These judgments, which are analysed by Lord Roskill in his speech, afford in my view a classic example of the danger of assembling together isolated statements contained in judgments at first instance, each dealing with the facts of a particular case, and using such statements to build up some novel principle of law, inconsistent with an existing principle which carries with it the authority and approval of an appellate court.

It may be because so high a proportion of those judgments of the Commercial Court which turn on the application of well-known principles of law to particular and peculiar facts are reported in a specialised series of reports that this misuse of judgments given at first instance is particularly rife in commercial cases.

On the other aspects of the case dealt with in the speech of my noble and learned friend, there is nothing that I could wish to add.

LORD ELWYN-JONES. My Lords, I have had the advantage of reading in draft the speech prepared by my noble and learned friend Lord Roskill. I agree with it and for the reasons which he gives I would dismiss the appeal.

LORD KEITH OF KINKEL. My Lords, I have had the benefit of reading in draft the speech of my noble and learned friend Lord Roskill. I agree with it, and for the reasons which he gives I, too, would dismiss the appeal. I agree also with the supplementary observations contained in the speech of my noble and learned friend Lord Diplock.

LORD ROSKILL. My Lords, in preparing this speech I have had the great advantage of the help of my noble and learned friend Lord Brandon, and the speech now represents the opinions both of my noble and learned friend and of myself.

My Lords, as a result of the outbreak of hostilities between Iran and Iraq in September 1980, a large number of ships were trapped in the Shatt al-Arab waterway. The appellants had the misfortune to be the owners of such a ship, the Evia, registered in Liberia. The respondents were the time charterers of the Evia under a time charterparty for a period of 18 months, two months more or less at the charterers' option, concluded in Greece and dated 12 November 1979. This time charterparty was in the Baltime 1939 form as

amended in 1950, that form being as is usual substantially amended and with a large
number of typed clauses attached.

My Lords, disputes between the owners and the charterers thereupon arose as to their
respective rights and obligations, as indeed they have done between many other
shipowners and charterers who have found themselves in a similar predicament. The
time charterparty contained a London arbitration clause (cl 23). Pursuant to that clause
the disputes were in due course referred to two arbitrators who appointed Mr Basil
Eckersley as umpire. On the disagreement of the arbitrators, it fell to Mr Eckersley to
decide the disputes, which he duly did on 20 March 1981, attaching to his formal interim
award some 35 pages containing 65 paragraphs of reasons expressed with admirable
clarity.

My Lords, it will be convenient at this point to mention one curious fact about this
case. The principal and most important question argued before your Lordships' House,
namely the effect of the 'safe port' clause in the charterparty, arose only incidentally
before Mr Eckersley. There were no pleadings. The owners' claim was for two sums of
money only, first, time-charter hire from 5 October 1981 onwards. The previous
payment covered the period up to and including 4 October 1981. And, second,
reimbursement of certain war risk premiums allegedly incurred by the owners after 28
June 1980. The charterers challenged these two claims. In answer to the first, they
contended that the charterparty was frustrated on 22 September 1980, adding a counterclaim on that basis for overpaid hire, and in answer to the second made a general denial
of liability. The second issue revolved mainly round questions of quantum and is in no
way relevant to this appeal. But the owners challenged the defence of frustration. They
contended that if the charterparty had been frustrated at any relevant date, that defence
was not open to the charterers, since the assumed frustrating events had been brought
about by the charterers' own breach of the charterparty by ordering the ship to an unsafe
port, namely Basrah. Thus before the umpire the issue principally argued before your
Lordships' House was only raised in answer to the defence of frustration.

My Lords, while the issue of frustration is of course of great importance to these
parties, and no doubt to others similarly placed, the question whether the charterers were
in breach of the charterparty by ordering the Evia to an unsafe port raises questions of
wide general importance, and it was for that reason that your Lordships' House thought
it right to give leave to appeal so that that question might be fully argued and determined,
especially in the light of a number of recent decisions of judges of first instance sitting in
the Commercial Court on this issue, the correctness of which had been challenged. The
obligation of a charterer whether for time or for voyage in relation to the safety of the
port or place to which the ship may be ordered during her chartered service seems never
before to have been considered by your Lordships' House. The principles governing
frustration of contract, however, have very recently been considered twice in your
Lordships' House: first, in National Carriers Ltd v Panalpina (Northern) Ltd [1981] 1 All ER
161, [1981] AC 675 and, second, in Pioneer Shipping Ltd v BTP Tioxide Ltd, The Nema
[1981] 2 All ER 1030, [1982] AC 724. The latter decision had not been announced at the
time of Mr Eckersley's award. Further, though the argument on the appeal against that
award before Robert Goff J for which that judge had previously given leave, also took
place before the date of that decision, judgment was given subsequent to its date (see
[1981] 2 Lloyd's Rep 613). Those principles at any rate should no longer admit of doubt
and were applied at least by the majority of the Court of Appeal from whom this appeal
is now brought.

With this brief introduction, I turn to consider the facts which give rise to this appeal.
In March 1980 the charterers ordered the Evia to load a cargo of cement and other
building materials for carriage from Cuba to Basrah, which is on the west bank of the
Shatt al-Arab waterway. She left Cuba on 28 May 1980, passed through the Suez Canal
on 19–20 June and arrived in the Shatt al-Arab waterway on 1 July. She there anchored
in the river waiting for a berth her entry to which was delayed by congestion. She finally
berthed on 20 August and, subject to some interruption, completed discharge at 1000

hrs on 22 September. In the ordinary course of events, she would then have sailed to
continue her chartered service. Unhappily, she could not do so. By that date, large-scale   *a*
hostilities had broken out between Iran and Iraq, and the area around the Shatt al-Arab
waterway was in what the umpire called in para 3 of his awards 'the thick of those
hostilities'. From 22 September onwards, no ship of the many then in that area was able
to escape. All were trapped. Gradually their crews in whole or in part left them. Only
the master and a skeleton crew of about a dozen remained on board the Evia after 1
October, when the majority of that crew were repatriated. At the date of Mr Eckersley's   *b*
award the Evia was still trapped. Some 16 months later your Lordships were told that
she and the other ships were still there.

My Lords, in paras 14 to 26 (inclusive) of his reasons, Mr Eckersley set out the history,
first down to and then after 23 September 1980. No repetition is now required of that
history. In para 41(iv), after considering the impact of that history on the issues which
he had to decide, Mr Eckersley concluded: *c*

'Basra was a safe port for the vessel both when she was ordered to proceed there
and when she got there. It did not become unsafe until 22 September, and by then
it was impossible for the vessel to leave.'

My Lords, it is by reason of those findings that the principal issue in this appeal arises.

My Lords, Mr Eckersley held, so far as is presently relevant, first, that there was no   *d*
breach of the charterparty by the charterers, second, that the charterparty was frustrated
and, third, that frustration took place on 4 October 1980. He made a declaration
accordingly. I ignore his conclusions on the question of war risk insurance premiums
only because that issue is no longer relevant.

My Lords, in due course Robert Goff J, who had very properly given leave to appeal in
view of the importance of this case, reversed that decision. He held that there was a   *e*
breach of the charterparty by the charterers, and, whilst agreeing with the umpire that
apart from that breach the charterparty would have been frustrated, he held that the
charterers were debarred from relying on frustration as a defence to the claim for hire
because of that breach since the case, as he said, was one of 'self-induced' frustration. The
charterers appealed to the Court of Appeal (Lord Denning MR, Ackner LJ and Sir Sebag
Shaw), which on 5 February 1982 by a majority, Ackner LJ dissenting, held that there   *f*
was no breach of the charterpary by the charterers (see [1982] 1 Lloyd's Rep 334). Mr
Eckersley's award was accordingly restored in the relevant respect.

My Lords, for ease of reference it will be convenient next to set out the more material
clauses of the charterparty:

'IT IS THIS DAY MUTUALLY AGREED between KODROS SHIPPING CORP, OF MONROVIA
owners of the Vessel called "EVIA" (EX-STRANTHTEVIOT) of 10028 tons gross/5581 tons   *g*
net Register, classed Lloyd's+ 100A1 or equivalent and to remain so classed during
the whole currency of this Charter, indicated horse power, carrying guaranteed
14499 tons deadweight on Board of Trade summer freeboard inclusive of bunkers,
stores, provisions and boiler water, having as per builder's plan 729700/643500
cubic-feet grain/bale guaranteed capacity. See also Cl.51 exclusive of permanent
bunkers, which contain about   tons, and fully loaded will be capable On   *h*
delivery and thereafter of maintaining an average speed of 14·5 knots on a
consumption of about 22 tons oil-fuel, max 1500 scs Redwood scale No. 1 plus 1·5/
2 tons Diesel Oil. and EMPRESA CUBANA DE FLETES "CUFLET" of Havana, Cuba Charterers,
as follows:

1. The Owners let and the Charterers hire the Vessel for a period of 18 months   *j*
T/C with two months more or less Charterer's option. calendar months from the
time the Vessel is delivered and placed at the disposal of the Charterers, on dropping
outward pilot Piraeus or if first loading port is on the continent then delivery to be
in direct continuation after completion of discharge of present voyage in Algeria.
Owners to be allowed to drydock on the continent in this case Charterers to declare

prior to complete discharge in Algeria whether vessel will proceed to continent or
not. Drydock in continent to last approx 5 (five) days she being in every way fitted
for ordinary cargo service with full complement of Officers and crew. The Vessel to
be delivered with clean holds and decks not before 25th November 1979.

2. The Vessel to be employed in lawful trades for the carriage of lawful
merchandise only between good and safe ports or places where she can safely lie
always afloat or safe around where vessels of similar size and draft are accustomed to
lie safely. within the following limits: WORLDWIDE TRADING within Institute
Warranty Limits (but Charterers to have the option of breaking these limits, in
which case any extrainsurance on vessel to be for their account but payable only
against original invoices from the underwriters certifying exact amount of
extrainsurance). Israel, Taiwan, USA ports and ports under their jurisdiction to be
excluded. No injurious, inflammable or dangerous goods (such as acids, explosives,
calcium carbide, ferro silicon, naphtha, motor spirit, tar, or any of their products) to
be shipped. See Cl.47

3. The owners to provide and pay for all provisions and wages, for insurance of
the Vessel, for all deck and engine-room stores and maintain her in a thoroughly
efficient state in hull and machinery during service. The Owners to provide one
winchman per winch. If further winchmen are required, or if the stevedores refuse
or are not permitted to work with the Crew, the Charterers to provide and pay
qualified shore-winchmen ...

Master

9. The Master to prosecute all voyages with the utmost despatch and to render
customary assistance with the Vessel's Crew. See Cl. 49 The Master to be under the
orders of the Charterers as regards employment agency, or other arrangements. The
Charterers to indemnify the Owners against all consequences or liabilities arising
from the Master, Officers or Agents signing Bills of Lading or other documents or
otherwise complying with such orders, as well as from any irregularity in the
Vessel's papers or for overcarrying goods. The Owners not to be responsible for
marks, nor for damage to or claims on cargo caused by bad stowage unless this is
due to Master's or Owner's servants fault. See Cl. 43 and also 39. If the Charterers
have reason to be dissatisfied with the conduct of the Master, Officers, or Engineers,
the Owners, on receiving particulars of the complaint, promptly to investigate the
matter, and, if necessary and practicable, to make a change in the appointments ...

Suspension of Hire etc.

11. (A) In the event of drydocking or other necessary measures to maintain the
efficiency of the Vessel, deficiency and/or default of men or Owners' stores,
breakdown of machinery, damage to hull or other accident, either hindering or
preventing the working of the vessel and continuing for more than twelve
consecutive hours, no hire to be paid in respect of any time lost thereby during the
period in which the Vessel is unable to perform the service immediately required,
and if on voyage speed be reduced by defect or breakdown of any part of her hull,
machinery or equipment the time so lost shall be deducted from hire. Any hire paid
in advance to be adjusted accordingly. and costs or any fuel consumed or any
expenses incurred thereof to be deducted from hire. See Cl. 42

(B) In the event of the Vessel being driven into port or to anchorage through
stress of weather, trading to shallow harbours or to rivers or ports with bars or
suffering an accident to her cargo, any detention of the Vessel and/or expenses
resulting from such detention to be for the Charterers' account even if such
detention and/or expenses, or the cause by reason of which either is incurred, be due
to, or be contributed to by, the negligence of the Owners' servants but any
compensation obtainable from underwriters to be credited to Charterers ...

Excluded Ports

15. The Vessel not to be ordered to nor bound to enter: a) any place where fever
or epidemics are prevalent or to which the Master, Officers and Crew by law are not
bound to follow the Vessel b) any ice-bound place or any place where lights,
lightships, marks and buoys are or are likely to be withdrawn by reason of ice on
the Vessel's arrival or where there is risk that ordinarily the Vessel will not be able
on account of ice to reach the place or to get out after having completed loading or
discharging. The Vessel not to be obliged to force ice. If on account of ice the Master
considers it dangerous to remain at the loading or discharging place for fear of the
Vessel being frozen in and/or damaged, he has liberty to sail to a convenient open
place and await the Charterers' fresh instructions. Unforeseen detention through
any of above causes to be for the Charterer's account . . .

War

21. (A) The Vessel unless the consent of the Owners be first obtained not to be
ordered nor continue to any place or on any voyage nor be used on any service
which will bring her within a zone which is dangerous as the result of any actual or
threatened act of war, war hostilities, warlike operations, acts of piracy or of hostility
or malicious damage against this or any other vessel or its cargo by any person, body
or State whatsoever, revolution, civil war, civil commotion or the operation of
international law, nor be exposed in any way to any risks or penalties whatsoever
consequent upon the imposition of Sanctions, nor carry any goods that may in any
way expose her to any risks of seizure, capture, penalties or any other interference
of any kind whatsoever by the belligerent or fighting powers or parties or by any
Government or Ruler.

(B) Should the Vessel approach or be brought or ordered within such zone or be
exposed in any way to the said risks, (1) the Owners to be entitled from time to time
to insure their interests in the Vessel and/or hire against any of the risks likely to be
involved thereby on such terms as they shall think fit, the Charterers to make a
refund to the Owners of the premium on demand; and (2) notwithstanding the
terms of clause 11 hire to be paid for all time lost including any lost owing to loss of
or injury to the Master, Officers, or Crew or to the action of the Crew in refusing to
proceed to such zone or to be exposed to such risks.

[Section (C) deleted].

(D) The Vessel to have liberty to comply with any orders or directions as to
departure, arrival, routes, ports of call, stoppages, destination, delivery or in any
other wise whatsoever given by the Government of the nation under whose flag the
Vessel sails or any other Government or any person (or body) acting or purporting
to act with the authority of such Government or by any committee or person having
under the terms of the war risks insurance on the Vessel the right to give any such
orders or directions.

(E) In the event of the nation under whose flag the Vessel sails becoming involved
in war, hostilities, warlike operations, revolution, or civil commotion, both the
Owners and the Charterers may cancel the Charter and, unless otherwise agreed, the
Vessel to be redelivered to the Owners at the port of destination or, if prevented
through the provisions of section (A) from reaching or entering it, then at a near
open and safe port at the Owners' option, after discharge of any cargo in board.

(F) If in compliance with the provisions of this clause anything is done or is not
done, such not to be deemed a deviation . . .

Arbitration

23. Any dispute arising under the Charter to be referred to arbitration in London
(or such other place as may be agreed) one Arbitrator to be nominated by the
Owners and the other by the Charterers, and in case the Arbitrators shall not agree
then to the decision of an Umpire to be appointed by them, the award of the
Arbitrators or the Umpire to be final and binding upon both parties . . .'

a My Lords, the question whether the charterers were in breach of their obligations under the charterparty so as to debar them from relying on frustration on 4 October 1980 depends on its true construction. Two principal questions of construction arise. First, independently of the provisions of cl 21 of the charterparty, were the charterers in breach of the charterparty in ordering the Evia to Basrah which, though safe when the order was given, became unsafe on 22 September when the ship was still on her chartered service? It was, as I have already stated, on that date that Basrah and the surrounding area

b became involved in hostilities of which I have spoken so that she was henceforth trapped. Second, if apart from cl 21 of the charterparty the charterers would have been in breach in so ordering the ship to Basrah, is the effect of cl 21 to free the charterers from that liability? A third and subsidiary question, which was briefly argued before your Lordships, was whether cl 21 excludes in any event the application of the doctrine of frustration. As already stated, it is the first of these questions which is of wide general

c importance since most charterparties, into whatever class they fall, impose obligations on charterers regarding the safety of the chartered ship during her service under charter. The second question is, of course, of particular importance under this form of time charterparty.

My Lords, I propose to consider first the question which arises on cl 2. It will be convenient to quote again those few words in that clause which are relevant: 'The Vessel

d to be employed ... between good and safe ports ...' Learned counsel were unable to offer any suggestion what in this context the word 'good' added to the word 'safe'. Your Lordships are, I think, all of the like mind. So I will consider only the eight words 'The vessel to be employed ... between ... safe ports ...' The argument for the owners is simple. The relevant restriction during her employment is to safe ports. Her employment took her to Basrah. Basrah, though safe when nominated, on 22 September 1980 became

e and thereafter remained, unsafe. The Evia was trapped. Those eight words applied. The charterers were therefore in breach.

It was this attractively simple answer which appealed to Robert Goff J. He said ([1981] 2 Lloyd's Rep 613 at 620):

f 'The relevant express term provides that the vessel is to be employed only between good and safe ports or places. I have to give those words their natural and ordinary meaning, unless the context otherwise requires; and I am bound to say that on their natural and ordinary meaning they comprise a warranty that any port or place to which the vessel is ordered shall be safe for the vessel throughout the period of the vessel's contractual service there. Furthermore, in my judgment this meaning of the provision is supported by authority. Here, unlike the umpire, I have the benefit of the analysis of the authorities by Mr. Justice Mustill in *Transoceanic Petroleum*

g *Carriers v Cook Industries Inc. (The Mary Lou)* ([1981] 2 Lloyd's Rep 272). With that analysis, I find myself respectfully in agreement; and I most gratefully adopt it.'

The judge also expressed his agreement with the earlier decisions on the same point which Mustill J had cited in that judgment. Put in other words, the judge accepted the owners' argument that there was an absolute continuing contractual promise that at no

h time during her chartered service would the ship find herself in any port which was or had become unsafe for her. Support for this view was said to be derived from a well-known passage in the judgment of Sellers LJ in *Leeds Shipping Co Ltd v Société Française Bunge, The Eastern City* [1958] 2 Lloyd's Rep 127 at 131; the Lord Justice had there said:

'If it were said that a port will not be safe unless, in the relevant period of time, the particular ship can reach it, use it and return from it without, in the absence of

j some abnormal occurrence, being exposed to danger which cannot be avoided by good navigation and seamanship, it would probably meet all circumstances as a broad statement of the law.'

My Lords, unless it can be said, as both Mustill and Robert Goff JJ thought, that this passage in the judgment of Sellers LJ, properly understood, lends support to the view thus accepted by Robert Goff J in the present case, learned counsel for the owners

expressly accepted that, before the first of those recent first-instance decisions, there was
no authority supporting the existence of this suggested absolute continuing contractual *a*
promise. I shall consider later whether this passage does so support the owners' argument
when I consider it in the context of the earlier relevant authorities. But the first question
is whether, apart from authority, these words are to be construed in the manner
suggested. In order to consider the scope of the contractual promise which these eight
words impose on a charterer, it must be determined how a charterer would exercise his
undoubted right to require the shipowner to perform his contractual obligations to *b*
render services with his ship, his master, officers and crew, the consideration for the
performance of their obligation being the charterer's regular payment of time-charter
hire. The answer must be that a charterer will exercise that undoubted contractual right
by giving the shipowner orders to go to a particular port or place of loading or discharge.
It is clearly at that point of time when that order is given that that contractual promise to
the charterer regarding the safety of that intended port or place must be fulfilled. But *c*
that contractual promise cannot mean that that port or place must be safe when that
order is given, for were that so, a charterer could not legitimately give orders to go to an
ice-bound port which he and the owner both knew in all human probability would be
ice-free by the time that vessel reached it. Nor, were that the nature of the promise, could
a charterer order the ship to a port or place the approaches to which were at the time of
the order blocked as a result of a collision or by some submerged wreck or other obstacles *d*
even though such obstacles would in all human probability be out of the way before the
ship required to enter. The charterer's contractual promise must, I think relate to the
characteristics of the port or place in question, and in my view, means that when the
order is given that port or place is prospectively safe for the ship to get to, stay at, so far as
necessary, and, in due course, leave. But if those characteristics are such as to make that
port or place prospectively safe in this way, I cannot think that if, in spite of them, some *e*
unexpected and abnormal event thereafter suddenly occurs which creates conditions of
unsafety where conditions of safety had previously existed and as a result the ship is
delayed, damaged or destroyed that contractual promise extends to making the charterer
liable for any resulting loss or damage, physical or financial. So to hold would make the
charterer the insurer of such unexpected and abnormal risks which in my view should
properly fall on the ship's insurers under the policies of insurance the effecting of which *f*
is the owner's responsibility under cl 3 unless, of course, the owner chooses to be his own
insurer in these respects.

My Lords, it will be seen that in this analysis I have stressed the point of time at which
the order is given as the moment when the relevant obligation of the charterer arises, for
it is then that the relevant employment of the ship will begin. I venture to think this is
plain as a matter of construction. But when one looks at the authorities one sees that they *g*
strongly support the view which I have just expressed. As long ago as 1861 *Ogden v
Graham* 1 B & S 773, 121 ER 901 was decided. The charterparty there in question was a
voyage charterparty. At that date, when the steamship was only beginning to come into
general use, the time charterparty was still a rarity. Under that voyage charterparty the
ship was chartered to go from England to a safe port in Chile with leave to call at
Valparaiso. When she was there, the charterers by their agent ordered her to Carrisal *h*
Bojo there to discharge her cargo. At the time of that order that port was closed by
government order. The ship could not go there without risk of confiscation. That port
was thus 'politically' unsafe to use the adverb often used to describe that type of unsafety.
The ship was delayed until, ultimately when that port was opened, she went there and
discharged. Her owners claimed damages for delay. The case came before a court
comprising Wightman and Blackburn JJ. In agreeing with Wightman J, Blackburn J said *j*
(1 B & S 773 at 780–782, 121 ER 901 at 903–904):

'By the charter-party it is agreed that the vessel shall sail for a safe port in Chili,
with leave to call at Valparaiso, and although it is not in terms so stated, it follows
by necessary implication that the charterers are to name a safe port to the shipowner,

who will then be able to earn his freight by proceeding thither . . . Now, in the
absence of all authority, I think that, on the construction of this charter-party, the
charterers are bound to name a port which, at the time they name it, is in such a
condition that the master can safely take his ship into it; but, if a certain port be in
such a state that, although the ship can readily enough, so far as natural causes are
concerned, sail into it, yet, by reason of political or other causes, she cannot enter it
without being confiscated by the Government of the place, that is not a safe port
within the meaning of the charter-party . . . They [the charterers] were to name a
port which was to be safe at the time they named. They named a port which had
been a safe port and would probably thereafter become a safe port; but if, at the
time they named it, it was a port into which the ship-owner could not take his ship
and earn his freight, it seems to me that they have not complied with the conditions
in the charter-party that they should name a safe port. That being so, they are liable
for damages for not naming a safe port within a reasonable time, and the measure
of damages will be regulated by the detention of the ship at Valparaiso beyond that
time.'

It will be seen that the judge interpreted the relevant obligation with regard to a safe
port in Chile as one which arose at the moment of nomination.

My Lords, I can move forward for nearly a century to the decision of Devlin J in G W
Grace & Co Ltd v General Steam Navigation Co Ltd, The Sussex Oak [1950] 1 All ER 201,
[1950] 2 KB 383. I should make three observations regarding this case at the outset. First,
I shall have to consider it again in connection with the issue arising on cl 21. Second, I
would observe that it was decided before the relevant law was clarified a few years later
in the cases to which I am about to refer, a state of affairs which obviously put the judge
in some difficulty (see [1950] 1 All ER 201 at 205–206, [1950] 2 KB 383 at 395–396).
Third, the matter came before the judge by way of case stated by an arbitrator with the
consequent restriction on any possible review of the findings of fact. I only mention the
decision at this juncture to draw attention to the fact that Devlin J held that it was the
giving of the order to go to an unsafe port which constituted a breach of contract (see
[1950] 1 All ER 201 at 206–207, [1950] 2 KB 383 at 396–397). On the facts found by the
arbitrator, the charterers had known of the danger from ice which was involved in
ordering the Sussex Oak to Hamburg and had given the order to go there knowing of
that danger.

But, my Lords, the basic law regarding the nature of the contractual promise to which
those eight, or other similar words, gives rise, whether in time or voyage charterparties,
remained in doubt until the further decision of Devlin J, affirmed by the Court of
Appeal, in Compania Naviera Maropan SA v Bowaters Lloyd Pulp and Paper Mills Ltd, The
Stork [1955] 2 All ER 241, [1955] 2 QB 68. On the facts found by the judge in that case,
the nominated loading place, Tommy's Arm in Newfoundland, was always inherently
unsafe both at the time of nomination and, indeed, later, at least for a ship of the size of
the Stork, for its permanent characteristics included insufficient room to manoeuvre her
in bad weather, which was regular hazard in that place, and that place was extremely
exposed. The ship grounded and was seriously damaged, and her owners sued the
charterers for breach of the relevant contractual promise as to safety. The main argument
for the charterers, which failed in both courts, was that, even if the loading place were
unsafe, as the judge ultimately found it to be, they were not laible because an order to go
to an unsafe port or place was only a nullity. It was an order which need not be accepted.
But, once accepted, the shipowner must accept the consequences (see [1954] 3 All ER 563
at 566, [1955] 2 QB 68 at 73). It was this argument which was emphatically rejected both
by Devlin J and by the Court of Appeal, who held that the breach lay in nominating an
unsafe port or place, and that when damage followed the obeying of that order the
ordinary rules of the recovery of damages for breach of contract followed. In so holding
both Devlin J and the Court of Appeal accepted as correct the dissenting judgment of
Dixon CJ in the High Court of Australia in Reardon Smith Line Ltd v Australian Wheat

Board, The Houston City [1954] 2 Lloyd's Rep 148, a judgment later upheld by the Judicial
Committee of the Privy Council (see [1956] 1 All ER 456, [1956] AC 266). I need only *a*
refer to, without quoting, the passages in the judgment of Dixon CJ which made it
absolutely plain that the relevant breach was the giving of the order to go to an unsafe
port or berth (see [1954] 2 Lloyd's Rep 148 at 151–152). This passage culminated in the
statement (at 153):

> 'The point which appears to me to be of capital importance in the decision of the
> present case is whether the giving of an order to proceed to a port that is unsafe *b*
> amounts to a breach of obligation on the part of the charterer, and that point appears
> to me to be definitely covered by what has been determined by the general operation
> ascribed to such a clause.'

That passage summarises the view which was subsequently accepted as correct in the
Judicial Committee. But the berth at Geraldton in Western Australia, to which the *c*
Houston City had been ordered by the charterers was, like the loading place of the Stork
in Tommy's Arm, inherently unsafe. In both cases the breach lay in giving the respective
orders to go there. In neither case were the courts concerned to consider in any way what,
if any, were the obligations of the charterer, whether under a time charterparty or a
voyage charterparty, where at the time of nomination the port or place was prospectively
safe but subsequently became unsafe. Indeed, in delivering the opinion of the Privy *d*
Council in *The Houston City* [1956] 1 All ER 456 at 462, [1956] AC 266 at 284, Lord
Somervell expressly declined to express any view on that question, which did not there
arise.

My Lords, it follows that the passage in the judgment of Morris LJ in *The Stork* [1955]
2 All ER 241 at 255, [1955] 2 QB 68 at 105 and the reference in that passage to 'some
abnormal occurrence', it was this passage which was the foundation of the passage in the *e*
judgment of Sellers LJ in *The Eastern City* to which I have already referred, was directed
to a suggested definition of the safe port in the context of a loading port or place which
was inherently unsafe at the time the order was given. It was not directed to the situation
where a port or place inherently safe when the order was given, subsequently, by reason
of some unexpected and abnormal occurrence, became unsafe.

My Lords, the later decision of Pearson J ([1957] 2 Lloyd's Rep 153) and of the Court *f*
of Appeal ([1958] 2 Lloyd's Rep 127) upholding Pearson J in *The Eastern City* laid down
no new principles of law. Both courts simply applied the law then recently laid down in
The Stork to a similar case of Mogador, a port in north-west Africa. That port was also
inherently unsafe at the time of nomination because it was not a port or place which
fulfilled the stated qualifications, and the damage suffered was not due to any unexpected
or abnormal occurrence in an inherently safe port, nor was it due to any negligence of *g*
those on board the Eastern City.

My Lords, even if I had thought some 25 years and more later that those two passages
in the judgments of Morris LJ in *The Stork* and of Sellers LJ in *The Eastern City* were in
any way open to criticism when properly understood in the context of the issues then
before the Court of Appeal in those two cases, which I emphatically do not, I should not
after so long a time be bold enough to suggest to your Lordships that they should be *h*
overruled. The number of charterparties concluded since those cases were decided with
words of the same or of a similar kind included amongst their provisions must be legion.
Those who have since concluded such charterparties must be taken to have known the
effect of those words as laid down in those cases and to have been content with that
interpretation of them. One can often, without the exercise of undue diligence, detect in
charterparties typed additions to printed forms designed to circumvent particular *j*
decisions on printed clauses the consequence of which the parties to that charterparty
seek to avoid. But that has not been the case with the words of the charterparty presently
in question.

My Lords, it follows that that passage of the judgment of Sellers LJ in *The Eastern City*
is no authority for construing those eight or other similar words as giving rise to an

absolute continuing promise of safety by charterers after the order or nomination in
a question has been given subject only to the qualification of some subsequent unexpected
and abnormal occurrence. It further follows from the concession properly made by
learned counsel for the owners that there was no authority supporting the view accepted
both by Robert Goff J in this case and by Mustill J in *The Mary Lou* [1981] 2 Lloyd's Rep
272, other than those recent first-instance cases which I have previously mentioned.

My Lords, the fact that a proposition is novel does not mean that it is incorrect, but it
b does mean that in your Lordships' House it must be closely examined before it can safely
be accepted as a correct statement of the law. The first of these cases is *Vardinoyannis v
Egyptian Petroleum Corp, The Evaggelos Th* [1971] 2 Lloyd's Rep 200, a decision of
Donaldson J on a special case. My Lords, I propose to deal with this and the later cases as
briefly as possible. This case arose out of alleged unsafety at Suez in June 1969. The judge
distinguished between the express promise of safety and what he called the implied
c promise. I confess I am not certain in the context of that case whether that distinction
was correct. But, be that as it may, after holding that the express promise did not help
the owners in establishing liability since Suez was safe at the time of nomination but had
become unsafe, he said that the implied promise was limited to one that the nominated
place was safe at the time of nomination and might be expected to remain so from the
moment of departure and no breach was committed if the place later became unsafe by
d the time of arrival, though the ship need not then enter that place. My Lords, I do not
propose to discuss this case in detail. I think the decision was right but I would respectfully
question its reasoning. In any case, there is nothing in the judge's judgment to support
the view later propounded by Mustill and Robert Goff JJ.

The next decision is also a decision at first instance by Donaldson J. I refer to *Unitramp
v Garnac Grain Co Inc, The Hermine* [1978] 2 Lloyd's Rep 37. This decision was later
e reversed by the Court of Appeal consisting of Lane LJ, Sir David Cairns and myself (see
[1979] 1 Lloyd's Rep 212). Donaldson J said ([1978] 2 Lloyd's Rep 37 at 47):

'The point of the warranty is that it speaks *from* the date of nomination, but it
speaks *about* the anticipated state of the port when the vessel arrives. The charterer's
sole right under a contract in the terms of this charter-party is to nominate a safe
f port and, in nominating a port under the charter-party, he impliedly warrants that
it *is* a safe port. The charterer undertakes that, in the absence of some abnormal
occurrence, the vessel *will* be able, at the relevant times, to reach, use and leave the
port without being exposed to dangers which cannot be avoided by good navigation
and seamanship. The warranty is absolute, but contains within itself the qualification
in relation to abnormal occurrences.' (Donaldson J's emphasis.)

g Later, in his judgment in *The Mary Lou* [1981] 2 Lloyd's Rep 272 at 277 Mustill J after
quoting that passage continued:

'I read this as a statement that under an express warranty of safety, in a case where
the ship does actually proceed to the port, the question is to be judged as at the time
when the vessel is using the port, and not solely at the time of the order: and indeed
this is the only reading which is consistent with the learned Judge's decision that the
h port in question was unsafe. The judgments in the Court of Appeal contain nothing
to the contrary effect.'

My Lords, I regret that I am unable so to interpret what Donaldson J said. If anything
I said in giving the leading judgment in the Court of Appeal in *The Hermine*, when
Donaldson J's judgment was reversed, led Mustill J to think that the Court of Appeal was
j intending to support his interpretation of that passage, I can only suggest that the fault is
mine in the expression of my view in an extempore judgment. My Lords, Donaldson J
had held that the port in question, Destrahan, 140 miles up the Mississippi, was unsafe
because the ship had been delayed after discharge on her voyage downstream by silting
up which had been found as a fact by the arbitrator not to be an abnormal occurrence.
He held that because the ship had been delayed for 'a commercially unacceptable time'

this was a breach of the charterer's contractual promise, the port having been entirely safe at all times in all other relevant respects. The Court of Appeal held that, since the delay was not of a frustrating character, there was no breach of which the owners were entitled to complain. The Court of Appeal was not in any way concerned with the extent of the contractual promise or whether the promise which arose on nomination was an absolute continuing promise, but whether there was a breach of the promise which had arisen on nomination because much later there was temporary delay of a non-frustrating kind. That was the ground on which Donaldson J's judgment was reversed. On rereading my judgment I agree that the passage ([1979] 1 Lloyd's Rep 212 at 217) 'Is it enough for the delay to be "commercially unacceptable" or has the delay got to be of a frustrating nature before the owner can complain of its as creating a breach of the warranty of safety?' might perhaps, with the wisdom of the hindsight of four years, have been better worded if the sentence had concluded 'as constituting or evidencing a breach of the charterer's promise at the time of nomination regarding the future safety of the ship'. But I think that the general intent of that passage, especially in the light of what Lane LJ subsequently said, is without any amendment reasonably plain and, with respect, nothing in any of the judgments of the Court of Appeal in that case is any support for the view later expressed by Mustill J regarding the supposed absolute continuing promise.

My Lords, the next case in the series is *NV Stoomv Maats 'De Maas' v Nippon Yusen Kaisha, The Pendrecht* [1980] 2 Lloyd's Rep 56, a judgment of Parker J. The determination of this case depended on when the cause of action arose. The judge concluded, after a review of authorities (at 63): 'The result of the cases is in my judgment that a breach of cl. 2 [it was cl 2 which contained the relevant contractual promise as to safety by the charterer] can occur at any time . . . up to the time of damage', ie that there was an absolute continuing obligation. Parker J sought to derive support for his conclusion, not only from the cases I have just discussed and I hope explained, but also from two earlier cases, *Tage Berglund v Montoro Shipping Corp Ltd, The Dagmar* [1968] 2 Lloyd's Rep 563 and *Islander Shipping Enterprises SA v Empresa Maritima del Estado SA, The Khian Sea* [1979] 1 Lloyd's Rep 545. But, my Lords, in the former, a decision of Mocatta J, the learned judge had held Cape Chat to be what I have called an inherently unsafe port, like Tommy's Arm and Mogador, because of the absence of a system to warn vessels of the approach of bad weather. *The Khian Sea* is a similar case where absence of a proper system made the wharf in Valparaiso inherently unsafe. My Lords, with respect, Parker J has misunderstood what Lord Denning MR said ([1979] 1 Lloyd's Rep 545 at 547). In that passage he said in terms that there was not an adequate system of ensuring that there was enough sea room for the vessel in question because of two other vessels which had been anchored far too close to her.

My analysis of the recent cases, and the references which I have already made to the judgment of Mustill J in *The Mary Lou* [1981] 2 Lloyd's Rep 272, absolve me from further detailed consideration of his careful judgment in that case. I can only say, with profound respect, that the conclusion he reached (at 277) as to the present state of the law was, in my view, wrong. It follows that, with equal respect, Robert Goff J was wrong to follow Mustill J in the present case, as indeed was Ackner LJ on this issue in his dissenting judgment in the Court of Appeal.

My Lords, on the view of the law which I take, since Basrah was prospectively safe at the time of nomination, and since the unsafety arose after the Evia's arrival and was due to an unexpected and abnormal event, there was at the former time no breach of cl 2 by the charterers, and that is the first ground on which I would dismiss this appeal.

But, my Lords, since your Lordships' House gave leave to appeal in order that this branch of the law should be fully explored, I think your Lordships may wish further to consider whether, notwithstanding the rejection of the views of Mustill and Robert Goff JJ and of Ackner LJ, there is a residual obligation on a charterer, whether for time or voyage, given that he has fully complied with his obligation at the time of nomination. My Lords, unless there is something unusual in the relevant express language used in a particular charterparty, the charterer's obligation at the time of nomination which I have

been discussing must, I think, apply equally to a voyage charterer as to a time charterer.
a But in considering whether there is any residual or remaining obligation after nomination it is necessary to have in mind one fundamental distinction between a time charterer and a voyage charterer. In the former case, the time charterer is in complete control of the employment of the ship. It is in his power by appropriate orders timeously given to change the ship's employment so as to prevent her proceeding to or remaining at a port initially safe which has since it was nominated become unsafe. But a voyage charterer
b may not have the same power. If there is a single loading or discharging port named in the voyage charterparty then, unless the charterparty specifically otherwise provides, a voyage charterer may not be able to order that ship elsewhere. If there is a range of loading or discharging ports named, once the voyage charterer has selected the contractual port or ports of loading or discharge, the voyage charterparty usually operates as if that port or those ports had originally been written into the charterparty, and the charterer
c then has no further right of nomination or renomination. What, then, is the contractual obligation of such charterers whether for time or voyage if the nominated port becomes unsafe after it was nominated?

My Lords, in the case of a time charterer, I cannot bring myself to think that he has no further obligation to the owner even though for the reasons I have given earlier he is not the insurer of the risks arising from the unsafety of the nominated port. Suppose some
d event has occurred after nomination which has made or will or may make the nominated port unsafe. Is a time charterer obliged to do anything further? What is a voyage charterer to do in similar circumstances? My Lords, this problem seems never to have been judicially considered in any detail; indeed, as I have already stated, in *The Houston City* [1956] 1 All ER 456, [1956] AC 266 the Privy Council expressly declined to consider it.

e In my opinion, while the primary obligation of a time charterer under cl 2 of this charterparty is that which I have already stated, namely to order the ship to go only to a port which, at the time when the order is given, is prospectively safe for her, there may be circumstances in which, by reason of a port, which was prospectively safe when the order to go to it was given, subsequently becoming unsafe, cl 2, on its true construction, imposes a further and secondary obligation on the charterer.

f In this connection two possible situations require to be considered. The first situation is where, after the time charterer has performed his primary obligation by ordering the ship to go to a port which, at the time of such order, was prospectively safe for her, and while she is still proceeding towards such port in compliance with such order, new circumstances arise which render the port unsafe. The second situation is where, after the time charterer has performed his primary obligation by ordering the ship to go to a
g port which was, at the time of such order, prospectively safe for her, and she has proceeded to and entered such port in compliance with such order, new circumstances arise which render the port unsafe.

In the first situation it is my opinion that cl 2, on its true construction, (unless the cause of the new unsafety be purely temporary in character) imposes on the time charterer a further and secondary obligation to cancel his original order and, assuming
h that he wishes to continue to trade the ship, to order her to go to another port which, at the time when such fresh order is given, is prospectively safe for her. This is because cl 2 should be construed as requiring the time charterer to do all that he can effectively do to protect the ship from the new danger in the port which has arisen since his original order for her to go to it was given.

In the second situation the question whether cl 2, on its true construction, imposes a
j further and secondary obligation on the time charterer will depend on whether, having regard to the nature and consequences of the new danger in the port which has arisen, it is possible for the ship to avoid such danger by leaving the port. If, on the one hand, it is not possible for the ship so to leave, then no further and secondary obligation is imposed on the time charterer. This is because cl 2 should not be construed as requiring the time charterer to give orders with which it is not possible for the ship to comply, and which

would for that reason be ineffective. If, on the other hand, it is possible for the ship to
avoid the new danger in the port which has arisen by leaving, then a further and *a*
secondary obligation is imposed on the timer chartered to order the ship to leave the port
forthwith, whether she has completed loading or discharging or not, and, assuming that
he wishes to continue to trade the ship, to order her to go to another port which, at the
time when such fresh order is given, is prospectively safe for her. This is again because
cl 2 should be construed as requiring the time charterer to do all that he can effectively
do to protect the ship from the new danger in the port which has arisen since his original *b*
order for her to go to it was given.

My Lords, what I have said with regard to these further and secondary obligations
under cl 2 of this charterparty will apply to any other similarly worded 'safe port' clauses.

My Lords, for the reasons I have given I find it much more difficult to say what are the
comparable obligations under a voyage charterparty at any rate where there is no express
right to renominate. The well-known decision in *Duncan v Köster, The Teutonia* (1872) LR *c*
4 PC 171, a case decided long before the doctrine of frustration assumed its modern
form, has always presented difficulties, and voyage charterparties today almost invariably
contain war and strike clauses which give the shipowners and their masters the right
sometimes to require another nomination and sometimes an unfettered right in any
event to proceed elsewhere. I think, therefore, in a case where only a time charterparty is
involved, it would be unwise for your Lordships to give further consideration to the *d*
problems which might arise in the case of a voyage charterparty and, for my part, I
would leave those problems for later consideration if and when they arise.

My Lords, on the basis that time charterers were potentially under the further and
secondary obligations which I have held that cl 2 may impose on them, it cannot avail
the owners against the charterers since the events giving rise to the unsafety did not
occur until after the Evia had entered Basrah, and an order to leave the port and proceed *e*
to another port could not have been effective.

My Lords, before leaving this part of the case, I would mentioned three further
matters. First, with all respect to Sir Sebag Shaw, I cannot accept (still ignoring cl 21) that
cl 2 only applies to physical unsafety. I think that both as a matter of construction and on
the authorities, of which *Ogden v Graham* (1861) 1 B & S 773, 121 ER 901 is but an
example, though an impressive one, it covers political unsafety as well. Second, it will *f*
have been observed that throughout this judgment I have eschewed the use of the phrases
'safe port warranty' and 'warranty of safety' though the word 'warranty' is often used in
the cases to which I have referred. As with the so-called warranty of seaworthiness, so
with this so-called warranty, its use is historic but, as well-known recent decisions have
shown, inaccurate. So long as it is realised that it is used as a matter of convenience, and
not an expression of the legal consequences of its breach and is not a definition of the *g*
character of the provision under consideration, that use may be convenient. But since
your Lordships are here concerned with statements of principle, I have ventured, at the
risk of accusations of pedantry, to call the obligation under discussion a contractual
promise, for in truth that is what it is rather than a warranty. Third, if it be said that the
imposition of these further and secondary obligations on a time charterer may put him
in difficulties with any sub-time charterer or voyage charterer from him or under any *h*
bills of lading issued by him or at his behest, my answer is that a time charterer would
be prudent to protect himself against the consequences of such possible inconsistencies
by including suitable wording into whatever further contracts he chooses himself to
make or into which the owners, the master or other agent of the owners wish to enter.

My Lords, I now turn to consider the second main question. Does cl 21 operate as a
complete code so that, even if, apart from cl 21, there would be a breach by the time *j*
charterers of cl 2, cl 21 when read with cl 2 casts on the owners and their insurers all risks
of unsafety which arise from the dangers of the nature referred to in cl 21(A) and thus
frees the time charterers from liability for them? My Lords, four observations may be
made at the outset. First, cl 21(A) gives the owners an unqualified right to refuse to
accept orders for the ship to go to or to continue to any place or on any voyage or to be

used in any service which will subject her to any of the dangers to which cl 21(A) refers.
Second, under cl 21(B) the owners can, in the circumstances there prescribed, insure the
ship and charge the premiums to the time charterers. Third, notwithstanding the off-
hire clause (cl 11(A)) the ship is to stay on-hire in the circumstances predicated in
cl 21(B)(2). Fourth, whereas cl 2 bears the rubric 'Trade', cl 21 bears the rubric 'War', and
it is permissible to consider these rubrics when construing these various clauses.

My Lords, whether cl 21 is a complete code and thus exhaustive of the owners' rights
depends on the construction of the time charterparty as a whole. But if the owners are
right that cl 21 leaves the time charterers' obligations under cl 2 in full force and effect,
one remarkable result follows. The time charterers are to repay to the owners the
premiums for the extra insurance, including extra war risk insurance premiums. But, if
the dangers against the risks on which they have paid those premiums materialise and
cause loss or damage to the ship, then the war risk insurers, on payment of the relevant
claim, become subrogated to the owners' right against the time charterers for the assumed
breach of cl 2. My Lords, this result would no doubt be highly attractive to war risk
insurers, but the less fortunate time charterers would have paid the premiums not only
for no benefit for themselves but without shedding any of the liabilities which cl 2
would, apart from cl 21, impose on them. Of course, duplication of rights of recovery is
not unknown. Indeed, it is because of such duplication that subrogation rights can be
enforced.

My Lords, learned counsel for the owners relied on the ice clause (cl 15) and drew
attention to the fact that in *The Sussex Oak* [1950] 1 All ER 201, [1950] 2 KB 383, in
which case, as in the present, the time charterparty was on the Baltime form and was
substantially identical with the present cl 15, a similar argument in relation to the ice
clause failed for the reasons which appear in the report (see [1950] 1 All ER 201 at 204,
[1950] 2 KB 383 at 392). But Devlin J was in that case concerned with the interaction of
cll 2 and 15. He was not concerned with the interaction between cll 2 and 21. I draw
particular attention to the fact that cl 15 imposes an absolute bar on the ship being sent
to fever-ridden or ice-bound ports or the like. Devlin J said that it could not be construed
as overriding cl 2 to the extent of entitling the time charterers to insist on the ship going
to an ice-bound port to which it was unsafe for her to go, merely because the ice
conditions at and in the approaches to Hamburg were extraordinary. It is not necessary
in this appeal to decide whether in this respect the view expressed by Devlin J was correct.

In the instant case cl 21 gives the owners an absolute veto on employment which will
imperil the ship in the various circumstances for which cl 21(A) provides. They can
impose their own terms. Clause 21(B) also protects the owners in circumstances in which,
like the present case, they have not been able to impose a veto because the dangers have
arisen too late for the consent to be required and given or refused. On this matter I
respectfully and entirely agree with Lord Denning MR and Sir Sebag Shaw, and equally
respectfully disagree with Ackner LJ and Robert Goff J. I should add that I regret that I
am unable to follow the reasoning in the last sentence of s 3 of the judgment of Ackner
LJ, which deals with this issue, where he says that in construing cl 2 the insurance
position must be ignored (see [1982] 1 Lloyd's Rep 334 at 349). This suggests that cl 21 is
to be construed in isolation from cl 2. But cl 2 and any other relevant clause must be
construed together and, with all respect to Ackner LJ, it is not the conditions of any
insurance policy which matter but the fact that cl 21 makes provision for the effecting of
extra insurance, including war risks insurance, at the time charterers' expense which is
the relevant consideration. The second ground on which I reject the owners' submissions
is that, in any event, cl 21 frees the charterers from any liability under which they might
otherwise be.

My Lords, the two remaining submissions can be briefly dealt with. Learned counsel
for the owners argued that the effect of cl 21 was to exclude the applicability of the
doctrine of frustration. This argument found no favour with Robert Goff J nor with any
member of the Court of Appeal. I respectfully agree, and were I to elaborate my reasons
I would only be repeating what has been better said in the courts below.

My Lords, finally the date of frustration adopted by Mr Eckersley, namely 4 October 1980, was attacked. Learned counsel for the owners conceded that he could not suggest that Mr Eckersley had in any way misdirected himself, or that no reasonable arbitrator could have selected that date. One has only to read Mr Eckerlsey's reasons to see that he clearly applied his mind to the right tests and reached his conclusion as stated in para 61 after considering all the relevant facts. I find it quite impossible to say that his choice of date was wrong.

My Lords, attempts were made to review this choice of date by reference to dates chosen by other distinguished arbitrators or umpires in other cases said to raise the same issue. Two other arbitrators, or umpires, were said to have chosen 24 November 1980. This date is some seven weeks later than the date chosen by Mr Eckersley. Your Lordships were invited to study the reasons for those other awards which were included with your Lordships' papers and your Lordships declined to do so. My Lords, I am sure that your Lordships were entirely right to adopt that attitude, for it must be wrong in principle to consider other awards arising from different questions of fact. In preparing this speech I have not referred to either of those two awards. Lord Denning MR said that it was desirable for the same result to be reached in similar cases. No doubt in a perfect world that would be right. But in an imperfect world different opinions can be legitimately formed on matters of this kind. Lord Denning MR in his judgment referred to what I had said in *The Nema* [1981] 2 All ER 1030 at 1047, [1982] AC 724 at 752 with the agreement of all my noble and learned friends then sitting, including Lord Diplock, namely that where questions of degree are involved opinions may, and often do, legitimately differ. I am not in the least surprised at this difference of opinion. The charterparties in question may well have been of differing characteristics and of different lengths. The discharge of cargo may have been completed on a different date. The several masters, officers and crew may have left their ships on different dates. A host of differing factors may have arisen, and in common with all your Lordships I resolutely decline to investigate the facts found in other cases to see which choice of date is to be preferred. The choice of date in this case, as in the others, was for the umpire or arbitrator concerned and is not a matter for your Lordships' House. I would dismiss this appeal.

LORD BRANDON OF OAKBROOK. My Lords, as appears from the opening of the speech of my noble and learned friend Lord Roskill, I have had the privilege of participating to some extent in its preparation. I agree with that speech and, for the reasons set out in it, would dismiss this appeal.

Appeal dismissed.

Solicitors: *Ince & Co* (for the owners); *Coward Chance* (for the charterers).

Mary Rose Plummer   Barrister.

Hussain v Hussain

COURT OF APPEAL, CIVIL DIVISION
ORMROD, GRIFFITHS AND SLADE LJJ
25 MAY, 24 JUNE 1982

Marriage – Polygamous – Potentially polygamous – Right to matrimonial relief – Marriage celebrated abroad under law permitting polygamy – Wife domiciled abroad and husband domiciled in England – Neither party permitted by law of their domiciles to marry second spouse during subsistence of marriage – Whether marriage void – Matrimonial Causes Act 1973, ss 11(b)(d), 47.

Both parties to a marriage which took place in Pakistan in 1979 in accordance with Muslim law were Muslims by religion. The wife's ante-nuptial domicile was Pakistan but the husband was domiciled in England. By Muslim law he was permitted to marry a second wife during the subsistence of the marriage but the wife was not allowed to marry a second husband. In 1982 the wife filed a petition in England for a decree of judicial separation. The husband opposed the petition, contending that, as the marriage had taken place under a law which permitted polygamy, it was a 'polygamous marriage' within s 11(d)[a] of the Matrimonial Causes Act 1973, and as such void, and that therefore the court had no jurisdiction to entertain the wife's petition. By s 11(d) a 'polygamous marriage' entered into outside England and Wales after 31 July 1971 was void if 'either party was at the time of the marriage domiciled in England and Wales' and a marriage might be 'polygamous' for the purposes of para (d) even if 'at its inception neither party [had] any spouse additional to the other'. In fact, neither party had had an additional spouse at the time of the marriage. If either of them had had one, the marriage would, in any event, have been invalid under English law because s 11(b) provided that a marriage celebrated after 31 July 1971 should be void where 'at the time of the marriage either party was already lawfully married'.

Held – (1) The fact that the marrige had taken place under a law which permitted polygamy did not necessarily render it void because s 11 of the 1973 Act had to be read in conjunction with s 47(1)[b] of that Act, which provided that the court was not precluded from granting matrimonial relief by reason only that the marriage had been entered into under a law which permitted polygamy. In consequence, when deciding for jurisdictional purposes whether a marriage was monogamous or polygamous, the court no longer had to consider the nature of the ceremony according to the lex loci celebrationis (as it had had to do in cases prior to the passing of the Matrimonial Proceedings (Polygamous Marriages) Act 1972, on which ss 11(d) and 47 of the 1973 Act were based) but merely the capacity of the parties to marry under the laws of their respective domiciles. If one at least of the parties had the capacity to marry a second spouse during the subsistence of the marriage, the marriage was potentially polygamous (see p 371 g to j and p 372 c to f and h, post).

(2) On the facts the marriage of the parties was not potentially polygamous because under the laws of their respective domiciles at the date it had been entered into neither of them could marry a second spouse during the subsistence of the marriage. It followed that the marriage was not void under s 11(d) and that the court had jurisdiction to entertain the wife's petition (see p 371 b to d and p 372 h j, post).

---

a   Section 11, so far as material, is set out at p 371 a, post

b   Section 47(1) provides: 'A court in England and Wales shall not be precluded from granting matrimonial relief or making a declaration concerning the validity of a marriage by reason only that the marriage in question was entered into under a law which permits polygamy.'

Notes

For the jurisdiction of English courts to grant matrimonial relief in cases of polygamous   *a*
marriages, see 8 Halsbury's Laws (4th edn) para 479.

For the Matrimonial Proceedings (Polygamous Marriages) Act 1972, see 42 Halsbury's
Statutes (3rd edn) 760.

For the Matrimonial Causes Act 1973, ss 11, 47, see 43 ibid 553, 597.

Case referred to in judgment   *b*

Hyde v Hyde and Woodmansee (1866) LR 1 P & D 130, [1861–73] All ER Rep 175, 11
    Digest (Reissue) 502, 967.

Interlocutory appeal

Shahid Hussain (the husband) appealed against the order of his Honour Judge Lord dated
22 September 1981 dismissing an appeal by the husband against an order of Mr Registrar   *c*
Lockett dated 20 May 1981 dismissing an application by the husband for leave to file an
answer to a petition by Aliya Hussain (the wife) for a decree of judicial separation and to
set aside a certificate given by the registrar under r 48(1)(a) of the Matrimonial Causes
Rules 1977. The facts are set out in the judgment of the court.

Joyanne Bracewell QC and *Philip Dykes* for the husband.

Joseph Jackson QC and *Mukhtar Hussain* for the wife.   *d*

Cur adv vult

24 June. **ORMROD LJ** read the following judgment of the court: This is an appeal by
the husband, the respondent in the suit, from an order made by his Honour Judge Lord,   *e*
at Manchester County Court on 22 September 1971. The judge had before him an appeal
by the husband from the refusal of the registrar to set aside his certificate under the
Matrimonial Causes Rules 1977, SI 1977/34, r 48(1)(a), and give leave to file an answer
out of time. The case is unusual because, as appears from his affidavit, the husband
wishes to challenge the validity of the marriage and, therefore, the jurisdiction of the
court to entertain the wife's suit. Although in form this is an interlocutory application   *f*
for leave to file an answer out of time, it has been treated by all concerned as though it
were a preliminary issue as to the validity of the marriage, and we shall deal with it in
the same way.

There is no dispute on the facts. The marriage took place on 4 August 1979 at Chirag
Park Shad Bad in the District of Lahore, Pakistan, in accordance with the Muslim Laws
Family Ordinance 1961. Both parties are Muslim by religion. At all material times the   *g*
husband was and is domiciled in England; the wife's ante-nuptial domicile was Pakistan.

It is common ground that under this form of marriage a husband is permitted to
marry a second wife during the subsistence of the marriage, but a wife is not permitted
to marry a second husband. In other words, the personal law of the wife precludes her
from contracting another marriage so long as her present marriage continues.

No evidence of Pakistan law was adduced and for the purpose of this appeal we assume   *h*
that the parties are correct in their understanding of its provisions.

The husband's contention is that the marriage is polygamous and therefore void under
the provisions of s 11(d) of the Matrimonial Causes Act 1973. The judge, in a very careful
judgment, rejected this contention, and, therefore, refused to set aside the registrar's
certificate and refused leave to file an answer out of time, thereby confirming that the
wife was entitled to a decree of judicial separation. (Three years had not elapsed since the   *j*
date of the marriage.)

The question in this appeal is purely one of construction of para (d) of s 11, and it turns
on the meaning to be given to the phrase 'a polygamous marriage' in the context in
which it appears. Section 11, so far as material, is in the following terms:

'A marriage celebrated after 31st July 1971 shall be void on the following grounds
only, that is to say . . . (b) that at the time of the marriage either party was already
lawfully married . . . (d) in the case of a polygamous marriage entered into outside
England and Wales, that either party was at the time of the marriage domiciled in
England and Wales. For the purposes of paragraph (d) of this subsection a marriage
may be polygamous although at its inception neither party has any spouse additional
to the other.'

Counsel for the husband contends that 'a polygamous marriage' refers to the character
and incidents of marriage under the relevant regime. If the regime permits polygamy in
any form, she submits that such marriage is void if either party to it is domiciled in
England or Wales at the date on which it was entered into. Counsel for the wife contends
that it refers not to marriages which may be categorised as polygamous in general terms
but to the particular marriage which is in question. He submits that a marriage which is
not actually polygamous at its inception, and incapable of becoming actually polygamous,
by reason of the personal laws of the parties at the time it was entered into, is not void
under this paragraph. On the facts of this case the husband, by English law, is incapable
of contracting a valid marriage when he is already lawfully married (para (b)), and the
wife, by Pakistan law, cannot marry another man so long as she is married to the
husband, so this marriage can never become polygamous. Consequently, the marriage
was not polygamous at its inception and cannot become polygamous at any time in the
future. It is, therefore, not avoided by para (d) of s 11.

The submission of counsel for the husband is supported by the proposition which
appears in leading textbooks that 'the nature of the ceremony, according to the *lex loci
celebrationis*, and not the personal law of either party, determines whether a marriage is
monogamous or polygamous' (see Dicey and Morris *The Conflict of Laws* (10th edn, 1980)
pp 309–310; but see Cheshire and North *Private International Law* (10th edn, 1979)
p 349). No authority is cited in support of this proposition, but it is clearly derived from
cases concerned with polygamous marriages which were decided before the passing of
the Matrimonial Proceedings (Polygamous Marriages) Act 1972, which radically altered
the law relating to polygamous marriages. Prior to this Act, the law was governed by the
decision in *Hyde v Hyde and Woodmansee* (1866) LR 1 P & D 130, [1861–73] All ER Rep
175 that a 'marriage' which did not create a monogamous union between a man and a
woman was not a marriage at all. Stated, perhaps more precisely, the word 'marriage',
where it appeared in the matrimonial legislation, did not, as a matter of construction,
include any kind of ceremony which did not create a monogamous relationship of the
kind adopted by Christianity. Consequently, in all the cases before 1972 it was the nature
and incidents of the ceremony which were crucial, and these could only be ascertained
by reference to the lex loci celebrationis.

Since the Matrimonial Proceedings (Polygamous Marriages) Act 1972 was passed, the
position is quite different; s 1 provided that a court in England and Wales shall not be
precluded from granting matrimonial relief by reason only that the marriage in question
was entered into under a law which permits polygamy. It is no longer necessary,
therefore, to characterise the nature and incidents of the status created by the lex loci
celebrationis for jurisdiction purposes. The only question is whether the marriage under
consideration is valid by English law, which is a question of capacity. The proposition in
the textbooks, therefore, does not assist the argument of counsel for the husband.

Paragraph (d) of s 11 is not very happily phrased and does not fit in at all well with the
rest of the section, and in the process of consolidation it has become widely separated
from its proper context. It was originally s 4 of the 1972 Act, and was passed to deal with
the new situation created by s 1 of that Act (now s 47 of the 1973 Act). It must be read,
therefore, with s 47.

When these two provisions are read together a significant difference can be seen
between the language used in s 47 and in para (d) of s 11. Section 47 refers to 'a marriage
. . . entered into under a law which permits polygamy'. This is the exact equivalent in

English of the proposition in the textbooks; it clearly refers to the lex loci celebrationis and not the law of either party's domicile. But s 11(d) refers simply to 'a polygamous marriage' and goes on to provide that a marriage may be polygamous although at its inception neither party has an additional spouse.

The argument of counsel for the husband has to overcome the difficulty that, if her construction of para (d) is right, the draftsman used two very different formulations to express the same idea in a short Act, containing only two relevant sections (ss 1 and 4). Had the intention of Parliament been to prevent persons domiciled in England and Wales from entering into marriages under the Muslim Laws Family Ordinance, or under other similar laws which 'permit polygamy', it would have been easy to say so in so many words. On the other hand, once the position of *Hyde v Hyde* had been abandoned, the question of the capacity of persons domiciled in England and Wales to enter into polygamous or potentially polygamous marriages had to be considered. Actually polygamous marriages were already covered by what is now para (b) of s 11, but potentially polygamous marriages were not completely covered by the existing law. The spouse domiciled in England and Wales is, of course, incapable of marrying a second spouse, but if one of the spouses in the first marriage retains a domicile the law of which permits polygamy a situation could arise in which the spouse domiciled in this country becomes a party to a polygamous union. Counsel for the wife submits that s 4 of the 1972 Act (now s 11(d) of the 1973 Act) was passed to prevent this situation from arising. The effect would be that a marriage between a woman domiciled in England and Wales and a man domiciled in Pakistan would be a polygamous marriage because the husband has the capacity, by his personal law, to take a second wife, but not vice versa.

The language used by the draftsman is, at least, consistent with this construction. The insertion of the qualifying words at the end of the section suggests that without them the phrase 'polygamous marriage' would, or might be, confined to a marriage which was actually polygamous at its inception, ie one in which one of the spouses was already married to another spouse. The use of the word 'may' in the qualifying words suggests that the draftsman had some contingency in mind the happening of which would make a marriage between two unmarried persons polygamous, within the meaning of the provision, that is, as it is called, a potentially polygamous marriage. A marriage can only be potentially polygamous if at least one of the spouses has the capacity to marry a second spouse.

On a broader view, it is difficult to conceive any reason why Parliament, in an increasingly pluralistic society, should have thought it necessary to prohibit persons whose religious or cultural traditions accept polygamy from marrying in their own manner abroad simply because they are domiciled in England and Wales. On the other hand, it is obvious that Parliament, having decided to recognise polygamous marriages as marriages for the purposes of our matrimonial legislation, would think it right to preserve the principle of monogamy for persons domiciled here.

Finally, the consequences of accepting the submission of counsel for the husband in this case would be far reaching and very serious. It would mean that all marriages contracted abroad by people domiciled in this country in accordance with the local law would be void if that law permitted polygamy in any form. The repercussions on the Muslim community alone in this country would be widespread and profound.

For these reasons the narrower construction of s 11(d) is to be preferred. On the facts, the marriage in this case is monogamous and should be held to be a valid marriage. The husband's contention, therefore, fails and his appeal should be dismissed. The petition should be restored to the list as soon as possible for the pronouncement of the decree of judicial separation.

Appeal dismissed. Leave to appeal to the House of Lords refused.

Solicitors: *Glickman & Co*, Manchester (for the husband); *Charnley & Afzal*, Manchester (for the wife).

Bebe Chua   Barrister.

a # Worringham and another v Lloyds Bank Ltd

COURT OF APPEAL, CIVIL DIVISION
LORD DENNING MR, SHAW AND TEMPLEMAN LJJ
26, 27, 30 JULY, 5 OCTOBER 1979, 10 DECEMBER 1981

b *Employment – Equality of treatment of men and women – Equal pay for equal work – Pay –
Termination of employment – Contributions to retirement benefits scheme – Employer paying
contributions of female employees under 25 – Other employees paying contributions out of their
salaries by deductions at source made by employer in employees' names – Employees other than
females under 25 entitled on termination of employment to refund of contributions made in their
names – Whether female employees under 25 entitled on termination of employment to sum equal
to amount of contribution refund they would have received if they were male employees engaged*
c *in like work – Equal Pay Act 1970, ss 1(1), 2(5) – EEC Treaty, art 119.*

A bank operated two occupational pension schemes for its staff, one for men and the
other for women. The schemes were funded by contributions made by the members and
the bank. Each member, other than women under 25, was required to contribute 5% of
d his or her salary to the appropriate fund. The 5% contribution was deducted at source
and paid by the bank, in the employee's name, into the fund. The bank instituted salary
schemes under which its female employees under 25 were paid at nationally agreed rates,
while all other staff were paid at those rates plus 5%. Since redundancy payments and
unemployment benefits were determined by reference to gross pay, female employees
who left before the age of 25 were at a disadvantage when compared with their male
e counterparts. They were similarly disadvantaged in respect of mortgage and credit
facilities made available to the bank's employees. Furthermore, male employees who left
the bank's employment were entitled to the transfer to other schemes, or the return to
them, of part of their contributions, including the 5% contribution paid in their name
by the bank. The applicants, two female employees under 25, complained to an industrial
tribunal that the bank had not paid its female staff under 25 years of age the same gross
f salary as that of the male staff of the same age engaged in the same work, in breach of the
Equal Pay Act 1970. The industrial tribunal dismissed the complaint, but its decision
was reversed by the Employment Appeal Tribunal. On an appeal by the bank, the Court
of Appeal referred certain questions to the Court of Justice of the European Communities,
which ruled, inter alia, that a contribution to a retirement benefits schemes paid by an
employer in the name of an employee by means of an addition to his gross salary and
which helped to determine the amount of that salary was 'pay' within art 119[a] of the EEC
g Treaty. On receipt of that ruling by the Court of Appeal,

Held – Pursuant to the equality clause included in the applicants' contracts of
employment by reason of s 1(1)[b] of the 1970 Act and pursuant to art 119 of the EEC
Treaty, on terminating their employment with the bank the applicants were entitled to
h be paid a sum of money equal in amount to the refund of pension contributions in
respect of the period referred to in s 2(5)[c] of the 1970 Act which they would have received

---

a   Article 119, so far as material, provides: '. . . For the purpose of this Article, "pay" means the
     ordinary basic or minimum wage or salary and any other consideration, whether in cash or in
     kind, which the worker receives, directly or indirectly, in respect of his employment from his
     employer . . .'
j   b   Section 1(1) provides: 'If the terms of a contract under which a woman is employed at an
          establishment in Great Britain do not include (directly or by reference to a collective agreement or
          otherwise) an equality clause they shall be deemed to include one.'
     c   Section 2(5) provides: 'A woman shall not be entitled, in proceedings brought in respect of a failure
          to comply with an equality clause (including proceedings before an industrial tribunal), to be
          awarded any payment by way of arrears of remuneration or damages in respect of a time earlier
          than two years before the date on which the proceedings were instituted.'

if they had been male employees employed on like work in whose names contributions had been paid to a retirement benefits scheme by the bank, subject in each case to *a* statutory and other lawful deductions, and a declaration in those terms would be made (see p 375 *d* to *h*, post).

Notes

For equal treatment of men and women as regards terms and conditions of employment, see 16 Halsbury's Laws (4th edn) para 767, and for cases on the subject, see 20 Digest *b* (Reissue) 579–595, 4466–4523.

For the Equal Pay Act 1970, ss 1, 2 (as amended by the Sex Discrimination Act 1975), see 45 Halsbury's Statutes (3rd edn) 290, 292.

For the EEC Treaty, art 119, see 42A ibid 779.

Case referred to in judgments

c

Macarthys Ltd v Smith Case 129/79 [1981] 1 All ER 111, [1981] QB 180, [1980] 3 WLR 929, [1980] ECR 1275, CJEC and CA, 20 Digest (Reissue) 583, 4476.

Cases also cited

Amies v Inner London Education Authority [1977] 2 All ER 100, CA.
Bulmer (H P) Ltd v J Bollinger SA [1974] 2 All ER 1226, [1974] Ch 401, CA.   *d*
Clay Cross (Quarry Service) Ltd v Fletcher [1979] 1 All ER 474, [1978] 1 WLR 1429, CA.
Defrenne (Gabrielle) v Sabena Case 149/77 [1978] ECR 1365, CJEC.
Early (Charles) & Marriott (Witney) Ltd v Smith [1977] 3 All ER 770, [1978] QB 11, EAT.
Garland v British Rail Engineering Ltd [1979] 2 All ER 1163, [1979] 1 WLR 754, CA.
Halcyon Skies, The [1976] 1 All ER 856, [1977] QB 14.
R v Chief Immigration Officer, Heathrow Airport, ex p Salamat Bibi [1976] 3 All ER 843, *e*
     [1976] 1 WLR 979, CA.
Shields v E Coomes (Holdings) Ltd [1979] 1 All ER 456, [1978] 1 WLR 1408, CA.
Van Duyn v The Home Office Case 41/74 [1975] 3 All ER 190, [1975] Ch 358, CJEC.

Appeal

Lloyds Bank Ltd (the bank) appealed against the decision of the Employment Appeal *f* Tribunal (Kilner Brown J, Mr S C Marley and Mrs M E Sanderland) dated 9 November 1978 allowing an appeal by the applicants, Susan Jane Worringham and Margaret Humphreys, against the decision of an industrial tribunal (chairman Mr G E Heggs) sitting in London on 19 September 1977 dismissing the consolidated complaints of the applicants that the bank was in breach of the clause guaranteeing equal pay for men and women incorporated by virtue of s 1(2)(a) of the Equal Pay Act 1970 in their contracts of *g* employment. On 5 October 1979 the Court of Appeal referred certain questions as to the interpretation of art 119 of the EEC Treaty and EEC Council Directives 75/117 and 76/207 to the Court of Justice of the European Communities for a preliminary ruling under art 177 of the Treaty. On 11 March 1981 the European Court ruled on those questions (see Case 69/80 [1981] 2 All ER 434, [1981] 1 WLR 950). On the receipt of the answers by the Court of Appeal, the parties requested the court to make declaration in terms they *h* had agreed.

David Hunter QC and Charles Bennett for the bank.
Anthony Lester QC and Christopher Carr for the applicants.

LORD DENNING MR. This case was referred by us to the Court of Justice of the *j* European Communities for certain questions to be answered. It was in relation to two occupational pension schemes for the permanent staff of Lloyds Bank. One scheme was for the men, the other for the women. But there was a difference in respect of those under 25 years of age. The men had to contribute 5% of their salary from the commencement of their employment, whereas the women did not contribute until they *a* reached the age of 25. The men were paid 5% more then the women to bring their take-home pay up to that of the women's. Questions were referred to the European Court to see whether there was an infringement of art 119 of the EEC Treaty which provides for equal pay for equal work.

The first question was:

b 'Are (a) contributions paid by an employer to a retirement benefits scheme or (b) rights and benefits of a worker under such a scheme, "pay" within the meaning of art 119 of the EEC Treaty?'

The European Court answered only question 1(a). They said ([1981] 2 All ER 434 at 446, [1981] 1 WLR 950 at 968):

c 'In view of all these facts, it is therefore necessary to reply to question 1(a) that a contribution to a retirement benefits scheme which is paid by the employer in the name of the employees by means of an addition to the gross salary and which helps to determine the amount of that salary is "pay" within the meaning of the second paragraph of art 119 of the EEC Treaty. In view of this reply, there is no need to examine the second part of the first question, question 1(b), which is subsidiary to question 1(a).'

d In view of that answer, the case comes back to us to decide what should be done. The parties have agreed that this declaration should be made:

e 'A declaration that, pursuant to the equality clause included in the applicants' contracts of employment by reason of s 1(1) of the Equal Pay Act 1970, as amended, and pursuant to art 119 of the EEC Treaty, on terminating their employment with the respondents, the applicants were entitled to be paid a sum of money equal in amount to the refund of pension contributions in respect of the period referred to in s 2(5) of the 1970 Act which they would have received if they had been male employees employed on like work in whose name contributions had been paid to a retirement benefits scheme by the respondents (subject in each case to statutory and other lawful deductions).'

f It is only necessary in this case for that declaration to be made by this court. As the women have succeeded, they should have their costs in this court.

The question has been mooted whether the effect of the decision of the European Court is to displace s 6(1A)(b) of the Equal Pay Act 1970 as part of English law, because, as we said in *Macarthys Ltd v Smith* [1981] 1 All ER 111, [1981] QB 180 community law now has priority. It is unnecessary to go further into that question today because the European Court has limited its answer in the way in which I have stated. All we need to *g* today is to make the declaration accordingly.

SHAW LJ. I agree.

TEMPLEMAN LJ. I agree and would only add this, that in fact the European Court *h* also answered another question by saying that art 119 of the treaty may be relied on before the national courts (see [1981] 2 All ER 434 at 447, [1981] 1 WLR 950 at 970).

Declaration accordingly.

Solicitors: *Geoffrey Johnson* (for the bank); *Lawford & Co* (for the applicants).

Frances Rustin   Barrister.

Practice Note   *a*

COURT OF APPEAL, CIVIL DIVISION
DONALDSON MR, O'CONNOR AND DILLON LJJ
4 OCTOBER 1982

Court of Appeal – Practice – Civil Division – New practice and procedure – Registrar –
Functions – Leave to appeal and time limit for notice of appeal – Listing and setting down appeals *b*
– Respondent's notice – Amendment of notices – List of forthcoming appeals – Directions by
registrar – Applications and references to single judge – Constitution of Court of Appeal – RSC
Ord 59.

DONALDSON MR made the following statement at the sitting of the court: Before   *c*
we begin the day's work, for my part I should like to take this opportunity of welcoming
Mr Registrar Adams, who has joined the Civil Division of the Court of Appeal as its first
registrar. I should also like to explain, albeit briefly, how and why that office has been
created.

For a long time the delay in hearing civil appeals has been causing considerable anxiety.
In February 1978, when there were about 650 appeals awaiting hearing, a committee   *d*
was appointed under the chairmanship of Lord Scarman to examine ways and means of
relieving the pressure. After a detailed study of the procedures of the court, it made a
number of recommendations. The two most important were the creation of the office of
registrar and a change in the law to enable a single judge of the Court of Appeal to deal
with procedural matters. Both these recommendations required legislation to implement
them, and until the passing of the Supreme Courts Act 1981 little progress could be   *e*
made. Meanwhile the number of appeals outstanding at the end of last term had risen to
only just short of 1,000.

The essence of the Scarman Committee's recommendations was that better use must
be made of time, the court's time, counsel's and solicitors' time and the parties' time. It
identified four main sources of wasted time. The first stemmed from a failure by the
parties, particularly if they were acting in person, to provide the court with all the   *f*
documentation necessary for the hearing of the appeal or to do so in time and in a logical
and legible form. This failure led to appeals being adjourned when called on for hearing
or to the court taking much longer than should have been necessary in hearing the appeal
itself. The second consisted in the requirement that at least two Lords Justices should
consider and determine procedural applications. The third was the absence of a flexible
and co-ordinated listing system for the whole Civil Division. This resulted in the parties   *g*
and their advisers being kept waiting if the previous appeal took longer than expected
and to judicial time being wasted if the previous appeal was disposed of more quickly
than expected. The fourth, and potentially the most important because of the number of
people involved, was the length of oral hearings.

With the passing of the Supreme Court Act 1981 the making of an order authorising
the constitution of a Court of Appeal consisting of two judges for the hearing of certain   *h*
types of appeal, the making of important changes in RSC Ord 59 and the appointment
of the registrar of the Civil Division, we are now for the first time able to tackle the
problems which the Scarman Committee identified. However, and this is really of
fundamental importance, it must be understood that there is no perfect ready-made
solution. We have to experiment in order to evolve practices and procedures which give
the greatest balance of advantage for the parties to appeals and their legal representatives,   *j*
for those awaiting the hearing of appeals and last, but by no means least, for the orderly
development of the law. In this latter context, it must not be forgotten that in most cases
the Court of Appeal is the ultimate appellate court and it is its decisions which determine
the law to be applied by all other courts.

In all this we shall need, and I know that we shall receive, the fullest co-operation and
a   assistance from the two branches of the legal profession and from all others concerned.
With this in mind I have already met the Chairman of the Bar Council and the President
of the Law Society with a view to arranging regular and frequent consultation and we
shall welcome any and every constructive suggestion from any informed source.

Mr Adams, as the court's first registrar, has a formidable task, but happily he has the
advantage of experience of both sides of the Bench, if I can put it that way. He has
b   practised at the Bar and he has occupied the judicial office of a Special Commissioner of
Income Tax. Under the revised Ord 59 he has certain important judicial functions, but
initially at least much of his time will necessarily be taken up in creating a new
administrative infrastructure for the court. In addition, he will have the task of ensuring
that parties and their advisers have complied with the rules and furnish the court with
all the necessary documents so that there shall be no delay when the case is called on. He
c   will also seek to assist all those, whether professionally qualified or not, who are
unfamiliar with the practice and procedure of the court.

One of his most important and, I think, arduous duties will be to act as the listing
officer of the court. The establishment of a co-ordinated listing system will, without
doubt, improve the service which the court can offer to the public, but there will
inevitably be teething troubles. These will be discussed with both sides of the profession
d   and I am confident that an effective and acceptable system will emerge.

Compared with other legal systems, the Court of Appeal has remarkably few judges
and they must be used to the best advantage. Accordingly, we hope to make the fullest
possible use of the new power to constitute two-judge courts. Nevertheless, there will be
cases in which, although there is jurisdiction for two judges to hear an appeal, it would
be in the public interest that they be heard by a court of three. Only experience will
e   show where the dividing line should be drawn. The new powers of the single judge
should also make a substantial contribution towards making better use of judicial time.
For example, today there are two two-judge courts in session and in addition two Lords
Justices are exercising the powers of a single judge of the Court of Appeal. As the registrar
will also be hearing applications which would previously have required the attention of
at least two Lords Justices, we are now in effect sitting in nine divisions today whereas
f   the maximum number which had ever sat in the past was six.

This brings me to the question of whether it may not be possible to make more
economical use of time spent in court. Such time, it must be remembered, is relatively
very expensive because it involves the attendance not only of the judges but also of
counsel, solicitors and often the parties. The Scarman Committee considered and rejected
a change to the system of written briefs and limitations on the time allowed for argument
g   which is the practice in some other jurisdictions. They did so on the ground that,
although such an approach has advantages, it is alien to the British tradition of oral
presentation and argument and is not necessarily less expensive because of the time
which has to be devoted to preparing highly complex briefs.

However, the Scarman Committee suggested that substantial savings in this expensive
time could be achieved if, before the oral hearing began, the judges were able to inform
h   themselves of the general background to the dispute, the decision of the court below and
the effective grounds of appeal. With this in mind it recommended an adaptation of the
system of perfected grounds of appeal which is in use in the Criminal Division. The
judges would come into court having read the judgment under appeal together with the
perfected grounds of appeal or some analogous guide to the issues in the appeal and
counsel would be able to dispense with any lengthy opening as well as being able to
j   display greater brevity in the argument itself.

We, for our part, fully accept the committee's approach. It is in everyone's interest that
the cost of litigation should be reduced by a better use of time. Under the revised Ord 59
the registrar can give directions as to the documentation to be made available to the court
before the hearing and appeals can be listed in such a way as to give the judges time to

read appropriate parts of that documentation before the oral hearing begins. What can and cannot profitably be preread by the judges will vary from appeal to appeal, as will the best method of informing the judges of the issues in the appeal. In some cases it may well be that the original notice of appeal and the judgment appealed from may suffice. In others it may be desirable to ask for a perfected notice of appeal or even a skeleton of the argument for both parties. This is an area where there is really immense scope for innovation, experiment, trial and, let me stress quite inevitably also, error. But, with the assistance of counsel and solicitors engaged in particular appeals and that of both sides of the profession on a more general basis, there can be no doubt but that very worthwhile improvements can be made.

On the conclusion of the oral argument, there is again scope for some saving in expensive time. Where a court has reserved judgment and put its reasons into writing, both the public interest and the interests of the parties may be better served if the judgments are not read out and that instead the result of the appeal be announced in open court, with or without a brief summary of the reasons, and that copies of the full judgments be handed to counsel, the law reporters and the members of the press present in court as representing the public. Circumstances vary from appeal to appeal and what course should be adopted in any particular appeal must be a matter for decision by the judges who have heard that appeal. For present purposes it is sufficient to say that this method of saving not only time and expense to the parties, but also judicial time which can be better devoted to hearing further appeals, will certainly be borne in mind by all the judges of the court.

In this context may I return to RSC Ord 59? The changes in the rules are, of course, incorporated in a statutory instrument (see RSC (Amendment No 2) 1981, SI 1981/1734), but they require some study (as I know to my cost) before their significance becomes apparent. In the circumstances, it seems to me that it might be helpful if I were to explain their effect, but to do so orally in court would be to commit the very sin which we are all trying to eliminate, the misuse of time. The more detailed explanation of the changes has been put into writing and will be handed to the law and other reporters present in court today. Copies have already been provided to the Bar Council and to the Law Society.

In conclusion may I proclaim my personal belief, shared I know by all members of the Court of Appeal (we discussed the matter at a meeting on Friday), that the members of the legal profession, whether judges, counsel or solicitors, have a common interest in providing and a common determination to provide the best possible service to the public. I do most earnestly ask all concerned to monitor the results of these changes and to let the court know to what extent they are successful and how further improvements can be made. Constructive criticism and suggestions will always be welcome. But, without a two-way exchange of ideas, we shall achieve little; on the other hand, with such an exchange of ideas, I have no doubt that we can achieve improvements in the civil appellate system of which we may all be justly proud.

Diana Procter   Barrister.

THE NEW PRACTICE AND PROCEDURE OF THE COURT OF APPEAL

An informal commentary on the more important changes

References
Unless otherwise stated, references are to the rules of RSC Ord 59, as amended.

Leave to appeal
Applications for leave to appeal to the Court of Appeal will be heard by a single judge of the court sitting in chambers. No appeal will lie from his decision (see the Supreme Court Act 1981, s 54(6)).

Notice of appeal

a   Heretofore the time for serving notice of appeal has varied according to the nature of the appeal. In future there will be a single time limit of four weeks from the date on which the judgment or order of the court below was signed, entered or otherwise perfected, unless this limit is abridged or extended by order of the court below, the registrar, the single judge of the Court of Appeal or the Court of Appeal (see r 4(1)). The only exception will be social security appeals with a six-week limit. Applications for leave

b   to serve notice of appeal out of time will be heard by the registrar. In view of the importance of parties knowing whether a judgment is final or is still subject to possible appeal, it will only be in exceptional cases that such leave will be granted.

  The content of the notice of appeal is much more important than is generally realised. A notice of appeal which complies fully with r 3 will both define and confine the area of controversy on the hearing of the appeal, thus saving both time and expense to the

c   parties. It is intended that wherever possible the members of the court will have read the notice of appeal and any respondent's notice and the reasons for the judgment under appeal before the appeal is called on and a properly drawn notice of appeal will enable counsel to come at once to the central issues without any or any prolonged opening. Failure to give the court this essential assistance by means of a carefully drawn notice of appeal may well lead to special orders being made in relation to time wasted and

d   additional costs incurred.

The list of appeals

  Rule 3(4) requires the notice of appeal to specify the list of appeals in which the appellant proposes that the appeal shall be set down. There are final and interlocutory lists of the following descriptions which are self-explanatory:

e

      Chancery Division
      Chancery Division (in Bankruptcy)
      Revenue Paper
      Family Division
      Queen's Bench Division
      Queen's Bench Division (Admiralty)

f   Queen's Bench Division (Commercial Court)
      Queen's Bench Division (Divisional Court)
      County Courts
      County Courts (Divorce)
      County Courts (Admiralty)
      Appeal Tribunals (Land)

g   Appeal Tribunals (Patent)
      Appeal Tribunals (Employment)
      Appeal Tribunal (Social Security Commission)
      Restrictive Practices Court.

  In the light of experience the number of lists may require alteration from time to

h   time, but full notice will be given of any change. Meanwhile it is only necessary to mention that appeals from the Commercial Court and from the Queen's Bench Divisional Court, both of which were formerly submerged in the general Queen's Bench Division lists, now have their own final and interlocutory lists.

Setting down the appeal

j   Rule 5 requires the appellant to 'set down' the appeal within seven days after the service of the notice of appeal on the parties. The time limit is important and will be strictly enforced. Any application for an extension of time must be made to the registrar. 'Setting down' means filing the notice of appeal with the court, accompanied by the documents specified in r 5(1). The registrar and his staff will have to be satisfied that the required documentation is complete and will not hesitate to reject any notice where this is not the case. When they are so satisfied, the appeal will be given a serial number identifying the list in which it will be included and its position in that list. This list is not to be confused with the 'list of forthcoming appeals' in which appeals are included at a slightly later stage.

Respondent's notice

Rule 6 makes provision for the service of a respondent's notice within 21 days after the service of the notice of appeal. The content of any such notice is as important as that of the notice of appeal and for the same reason, it defines and confines the scope of the argument on the appeal, enables the members of the court to inform themselves in advance of the hearing of what the appeal is about and so saves both time and expense. Again the time limit is important and will be strictly enforced, any application for an extension of time being made to the registrar unless the appeal is before the court itself at the time when the application is made.

Amendment of notice of appeal and respondent's notice

It is most desirable that both notices of appeal and respondent's notices should be full and accurate when first served. This should not be too difficult, since the judgment under appeal and the proceedings which led to it will be fresh in everyone's mind. Nevertheless it can happen that, on reflection, it is thought desirable to amend such notices. Rule 7 allows this to be done without leave at any time before the appeal first appears in the list of forthcoming appeals. Thereafter leave will be required and application should be made to the registrar on notice to all other parties, unless the appeal is already before the court for some other purpose. The registrar will require good reasons to be shown why the amendment was not made before the appeal appeared in the list of forthcoming appeals and to be satisfied that the application has been made at the earliest possible moment.

Appearance of appeal in the list of forthcoming appeals

This is the second of the key stages in an appeal, the first being the service of the notice of appeal and the third the appearance of the appeal in the warned list. Ultimately it will follow as soon after the appeal is set down as is reasonable, bearing in mind the steps which the appellant is then required to take. However, until the backlog of appeals has been reduced, there will be some cases in which there is a rather greater interval. The registrar is considering whether, and how, it will be possible to give solicitors advance notice that an appeal is to appear in the list of forthcoming appeals. However, it is the responsibility of the parties and their advisers to watch the Daily Cause List in which the list of forthcoming appeals will periodically be published.

Once an appeal appears in the list of forthcoming appeals, the appellant has seven days in which to lodge the various documents specified in r 9.

Although the rules do not at present so require, it would greatly assist the efficient running of the court if, at the same time as they are lodging documents pursuant to r 9, appellants would provide an estimate of how much in-court time is likely to be needed for the hearing. In putting forward this estimate they should consult the respondents or their representatives, and all concerned will no doubt wish to seek the views of counsel who will be appearing. It would also assist the court if appellants would indicate which counsel are being instructed by them and, where known, by the respondents. This will make it easier for the registrar when listing to take such accounts as is possible of counsel's other commitments, although it will be appreciated that this is only one factor amongst many which have to be considered if the current delays are to be eliminated and eliminated quickly.

It may be thought that seven days from the date when an appeal appears in the list of forthcoming appeals is rather a short time in which to do a lot of work, since the

documentation required is substantially all that which will be needed for the hearing of
a   the appeal. It is indeed a short time, but it must be remembered that parties and their
advisers are free to file these documents as early as they like and the earlier that they in
fact do so the better. As a matter of good practice they should start assembling the
documents as soon as the appeal has been set down.

In the past much time has been wasted because appellants have failed to file all the
appropriate documents, have filed an inadequate number of copies or have failed to
b   ensure that bundles are properly paginated and are legible throughout. In the light of
the contribution which this has made to the delay in hearing appeals, a serious view will
be taken of any failure by appellants to comply with their obligations in this respect.

Directions by the registrar

Rule 9 has been amended so as to include a new para (3) in the following terms:

c
'After the documents have been lodged the registrar shall give such directions in
relation to the documents to be produced at the appeal, and the manner in which
they are to be presented, and as to other matters incidental to the conduct of the
appeal, as appear best adapted to secure the just, expeditious and economical disposal
of the appeal.'

d   This is perhaps the most important single change in the rules. The conduct of appeals
by way of oral hearing lies at the heart of the English tradition and practice and neither
the Scarman Committee nor anyone else has suggested that it should be abandoned in
favour of a system of written appeals supplemented by oral hearings which are subject to
strict time limits, as is the practice in some other jurisdictions. Nevertheless, an oral
hearing involving the presence of the members of the court, shorthand writers, court
e   staff, counsel, solicitors and, sometimes, the parties is extremely expensive in terms of
time and therefore of money. Furthermore, time, and particularly judicial time, is a
scarce commodity of which the best possible use should be made if the current level of
delay is to be reduced. The problem is how to achieve a proper balance between what
can be done by way of prereading by the members of the court in their rooms, which
involves only judicial time, and what must be left to oral presentation and argument in
f   court which involves the time of many others.

There can never be any single universal answer. Every appeal is different, although
patterns do emerge. Rule 9(3) therefore contemplates that once the documentation is
complete the registrar, either at the request of the parties or of his own motion, shall
consider whether any special directions can be given which will expedite the hearing and
render it less costly. We have as yet little experience of how this will work, although in
g   exceptional cases it has in the past been attempted with some success by the court itself.
The Scarman Committee suggested the use of 'perfected grounds of appeal' on the lines
of those used in the Criminal Division of the Court of Appeal. These grounds of appeal
often refer to the key authorities which will be relied on and to the portions of the
summing up and evidence which are relevant to each ground of appeal. They permit
members of the court to preread the relevant material, much of which is non-
h   controversial, and, thus informed, to consider and adjudicate on the basis of a much
abbreviated oral argument and to do so in a fraction of the time which would be necessary
if they took their places in court knowing nothing of the appeal. In the context of civil
appeals, it may be possible to use 'perfected grounds of appeal', but another possibility,
which may be better, is for the parties to provide the court in advance with a skeleton
outline of their respective arguments annotated by reference to the documents and
j   authorities. The probability is that different approaches will be found appropriate to
different types of appeal, but only time and experience will show which is the best
method or methods.

What needs to be said now, and said with all possible emphasis, is that the better use
of time is in the interests of everyone: the parties to the appeal, their advisers, parties to
other appeals which will be delayed if time is not used to the best advantage and the

public at large which has an interest in the efficient administration of justice. Accordingly, the members of the court look forward with some confidence to all concerned giving serious thought to, and, where appropriate, discussing with the registrar, how each individual appeal can best be presented. The registrar will be ready and willing to assist at any stage, but the appropriate moment will probably be at or about the time when an appeal appears in the list of forthcoming appeals. The Bar Council and the Law Society will not be concerned with individual appeals, but there will be the fullest and most frequent consultation with them as to what experiments are worth trying and as to the success of those experiments. As experience is built up, and in the light of that experience, we have no doubt the rate of disposal of appeals can be increased without detriment to, and even with an improvement in, the quality of the justice which is administered.

The single judge of the Court of Appeal

In the past a court consisting of at least two judges has had to consider incidental applications, such as those for leave to appeal, for the imposition or removal of orders staying execution or for the grant, variation or discharge of injunctions pending appeal. This represented an extravagant use of judicial time and r 10(9) will now enable all these matters to be considered and disposed of by a single judge sitting in chambers. All such applications will be made by motion (see r 14(1)).

Internal appeals and referrals

The amended Ord 59 gives the registrar power to refer matters to a single judge and the single judge power to refer matters to the Court of Appeal (see r 14(9) and (10)). It also gives a right of appeal to the single judge from any determination of the registrar and from any determination of the single judge to the Court of Appeal. However, in respect of a determination by the registrar, there is no right of appeal to the Court of Appeal without the leave of that court if the registrar's determination has been reviewed by the single judge (see r 14(11) and (12)). Nevertheless, the advantages of the new system would be substantially eroded if appeals became a matter of course and parties and their advisers should give serious consideration to where their best interests lie before launching such appeals.

Listing of appeals for hearing, 'the warned list'

The science, or more accurately the art, of a successful listing officer consists of an ability to quantify the unquantifiable and to predict the unpredictable. Factors of which he has to take account are the availability of judges, the availability of counsel, the speed with which the judges concerned will wish the argument to be presented, the inherent complexity of the appeal, the loquacity of counsel and the relative urgency of the appeal both objectively and in the eyes of the parties. If, against this background, a listing officer is instructed to give fixed dates for the hearing of all appeals and to specify far in advance by which court the appeal will be heard, the result is inevitable. Either he will overestimate the hearing time needed for appeals and there will be gaps in the list which are too short to be filled by taking in other appeals or he will underestimate and the fixed dates will not be met. Both have been happening, thereby causing delay and inconvenience to all concerned. Some new approach must be adopted, at least on an experimental basis.

The most obviously necessary change, and one recommended by the Scarman Committee, is to list for the Civil Division of the Court of Appeal as a whole and not for particular courts. This gives greater flexibility and will enable appeals originally destined for court A, whose cases are overrunning, to be switched to court B, where an appeal has been withdrawn or for some other reason judges have become available. This recommendation is being implemented and the registrar will be the listing officer for the whole of the Civil Division.

The next aspect which needs to be looked at is the concept of all or the vast majority of

appeals being given fixed dates and given them far in advance of the hearing of the
a appeal. Clearly parties to appeals, and more particularly those appearing for them, have
to be able to plan their work and need to know with a greater or lesser degree of precision,
according to circumstances, when an appeal will be heard. But giving fixed dates, which
because they are fixed must be very far ahead and well spaced out if they are to be
guaranteed, is no real service to the parties. On the other hand, failing to space the appeals
out and instead giving fixed dates to a consecutive series of appeals will almost inevitably
b lead to a failure to meet some or all of these dates and that is worse than useless.
Nevertheless, despite the difficulties inherent in a fixed date system, where appeals have
already been given fixed dates, this commitment will be honoured if at all possible.

The reality is surely that only the most urgent appeals need to be heard with very short
notice of the time of hearing and only a minority of appeals need to be allotted a fixed
and guaranteed date far in advance. An obvious example of the latter category is the
c exceptionally heavy appeal on which counsel, and to a lesser extent the court, will have
to work for an extended period before the oral hearing begins. Listing is not unlike
weather forecasting. The further away you are from the date for hearing, the more
difficult it is to identify it precisely. But as you approach that day it becomes more and
more possible to do so and, in effect, to give a fixed date. Between the extremes of the
very urgent appeal which must be heard almost at once, thus precluding substantial
d notice, and the exceptionally heavy case which requires long notice of a more or less fixed
date, it may well be possible to meet the legitimate needs of the parties and of their
advisers and also the public interest in reducing the number of appeals awaiting hearing
by a system of long-range forecasting coupled slightly later with a more or less precise
indication of the date for the hearing.

The maximum possible direct and continuing contact will be maintained between the
e court and the parties to appeals which are ready for hearing in order that they shall be
heard as quickly as possible and with the minimum conflict with other commitments.
However, it is only fair to the registrar and his staff to point out that the task of
establishing an entirely new office, creating a new administrative infrastructure for the
court and also a new centralised system of listing will involve great problems for them in
the initial stages and there are bound to be teething troubles. In future communications
f should be easier than heretofore, because telex is being installed in the Royal Courts of
Justice. This will be the subject of a separate announcement.

Notwithstanding such communication, some form of published 'warned list'
containing appeals to be heard in the immediate future will still be needed. The existing
warned list was designed to operate in connection with the unamended rules and is now
inappropriate. Furthermore, cases appeared in it so long before they were likely to be
g heard that parties and their advisers, not unreasonably, did not regard themselves as
being warned of anything. A new warned list will be published containing the appeals
which are both ready for hearing and have already been given fixed dates, together with
some other appeals of an urgent character. Meanwhile, consideration will be given to
what are the appropriate criteria for including appeals in a new-style warned list.

In taking a fresh look at listing in the context of a new centralised system, the registrar
h and the court will be looking to both sides of the profession for constructive suggestions,
advice and assistance, and experience shows that we shall not look in vain. This is
supremely an area where it is necessary to try and to err before an effective system can be
evolved.

Constitution of courts
j   Section 54(4) of the Supreme Court Act 1981 and the Court of Appeal (Civil Division)
Order 1982, SI 1982/543, have authorised the constitution of courts consisting of two
judges instead of three in certain specified circumstances, mainly appeals from
interlocutory decisions, which includes most family and divorce matters, and appeals
from the county courts. If the very serious backlog of appeals is to be reduced, it is

essential that the fullest use be made of this power. The main theoretical objection to an
appellate court of two judges is that they might disagree. Should this be likely to occur, *a*
it would be possible to relist the appeal for argument before a differently constituted
court of three, but experience in the Divisional Court of the Queen's Bench Division
suggests that this is most unlikely to occur in other than an insignificant number of cases.
Nevertheless it will sometimes happen that, whilst an appeal is of such a nature that there
is jurisdiction for a two-judge court to hear it, it is well recognised that, despite the need
to make the best possible use of the available judge power, there are some appeals falling *b*
within the jurisdiction of a two-judge court which raise issues of such complexity or
general importance that a three-judge court is desirable. Should this appear to the
registrar to be the case, he will list the appeal for hearing by a three-judge court. Should
it appear to the parties that this is the case, they will be free to apply to the registrar for a
special listing before a three-judge court, but it is hoped that they will only adopt this
course if there are really good reasons for so doing.   *c*

Oral hearings
    It is hoped and expected that early consideration by the parties of the extent to which
judges can profitably read papers before the hearing and the assistance of the registrar at
the stage at which an appeal appears in the forthcoming list of appeals will enable the
length of the oral hearing to be considerably reduced and that all concerned will know in *d*
advance what is expected of them. However, the way in which the hearing is conducted
will, as always, be a matter to be determined by the members of the court hearing the
appeal, and if it appears to them that the directions which have been given were mistaken
or need to be supplemented the court will take the appropriate action.

Written judgments   *e*
    Where the court has prepared written judgments, consideration will be given by the
judges concerned to the advantage of giving copies to counsel, the law reporters and the
representatives of the press present in court instead of reading the judgments aloud.
However, where this is done, it must be understood that the purpose for which the copies
are handed down is strictly limited, namely to save the parties the expense involved in
prolonging the hearing, to allow the time saved to be devoted to deciding other appeals, *f*
to enable the representatives of the parties to make any necessary application following
the announcement of the decision and to enable the law reporters and press to report the
appeal in the same was as they would have done if the judgments had been read out in
court. Copies so handed down must not be reproduced without the leave of the court
and the only recognised record of the written judgments will be that contained in the
official transcript which will be obtainable from the court shorthand writers and will *g*
record not only the written judgments but also the exchanges between the court and
counsel which follow the judgments being handed down.

Tommey v Tommey

a

FAMILY DIVISION
BALCOMBE J
25 FEBRUARY, 10 MARCH 1982

b

Divorce – Financial provision – Consent order – Setting aside order – Jurisdiction – Consent order incorporating terms agreed between spouses – Spouse subsequently alleging that agreement had been obtained as a result of undue influence by other spouse – Whether undue influence a ground for setting aside the consent order.

Early in 1974 relations between a husband and wife began to deteriorate. The wife committed adultery in March of that year, became pregnant and in June had the
c
pregnancy terminated. In September 1974 the husband and wife agreed that he would present a petition for divorce based on her adultery, that she would not defend the petition and that he would pay her a lump sum of £8,000 in return for her interest in the matrimonial home and 'in full and final satisfaction' of any financial claim by her. The petition subsequently presented by the husband included the terms of the agreement regarding ancillary relief. By the time the petition came on for hearing on 18 February
d
1975 the wife had transferred her interest in the matrimonial home to the husband in return for the payment of the £8,000. The judge granted the decree nisi and by consent made an order that all further financial claims regarding the wife be dismissed. The decree nisi was made absolute on 4 April 1975. Three years later the wife asked the court to set aside the consent order on the ground that it was based on an agreement which the husband had induced her to make at a time when she was in a highly emotional state
e
and unfit to make any major decision, and to consider afresh all ancillary matters arising from the decree nisi. The question arose whether a consent order obtained in matrimonial proceedings could be set aside for undue influence.

Held – Unlike consent orders in other types of litigation which derived their force and effect from the parties' agreement, a consent order embodying financial arrangements
f
between the parties to a divorce derived its legal effect from the order itself and not from the parties' agreement, and could not be impeached, after the pronouncement of a decree absolute, on the ground of undue influence in the way in which consent orders in other types of litigation could. A consent order in divorce proceedings could therefore only be invalidated on the same grounds as non-consensual matrimonial orders. Whether those grounds should be extended to include undue influence depended on balancing the need
g
to provide a remedy for a wrong and protect a weaker spouse from exploitation by a stronger spouse against the need to encourage finality and certainty in matrimonial proceedings. Since it was the policy of the law to encourage a clean break after divorce, the balance was in favour of not extending the grounds for setting aside a non-consensual matrimonial order, and accordingly, even if the wife established undue influence, it would not be a ground for setting aside the consent order (see p 390 *d e*, p 391 *b c* and *j* to
h
p 392 *a* and *d* and p 393 *d* to *j*, post).
   Minton v Minton [1979] 1 All ER 79 applied.
   Thwaite v Thwaite [1981] 2 All ER 789 followed.
   Aspden (Inspector of Taxes) v Hildesley [1982] 2 All ER 53 considered.

Notes
j
For consent orders embodying spouses' agreement on financial provision, see 13 Halsbury's Laws (4th edn) para 1158.

Cases referred to in judgment
Allcard v Skinner (1887) 36 Ch D 145, [1886–90] All ER Rep 90, CA, 12 Digest (Reissue) 126, 689.

Allsopp v Allsopp (1981) 11 Fam Law 18, [1980] CA Transcript 495.

Ampthill Peerage Case [1976] 2 All ER 411, [1977] AC 547, [1976] 2 WLR 777, HL, 32
Digest (Reissue) 22, 156.

Aspden (Inspector of Taxes) v Hildesley [1982] 2 All ER 53, [1982] 1 WLR 264.

Backhouse v Backhouse [1978] 1 All ER 1158, [1978] 1 WLR 243, Digest (Cont Vol E) 273,
6962Adf.

Dean v Dean [1978] 3 All ER 758, [1978] Fam 161, [1978] 3 WLR 288, Digest (Cont Vol
E) 265, 6631a.

de Lasala v de Lasala [1979] 2 All ER 1146, [1980] AC 546, [1979] 3 WLR 390, PC, Digest
(Cont Vol E) 354, 708a.

Edgar v Edgar [1980] 3 All ER 887, [1980] 1 WLR 1410, CA.

Hip Foong Hong v H Neotia & Co [1918] AC 888, PC, 51 Digest (Repl) 741, 3283.

Huddersfield Banking Co Ltd v Henry Lister & Son Ltd [1895] 2 Ch 273, [1895–9] All ER Rep
868, CA, 51 Digest (Repl) 733, 3231.

Jonesco v Beard [1930] AC 298, [1930] All ER Rep 483, HL, 51 Digest (Repl) 741, 3285.

Minton v Minton [1979] 1 All ER 79, [1979] AC 593, [1979] 2 WLR 31, HL, Digest (Cont
Vol E) 268, 6702a.

Shaw, Re, Smith v Shaw [1918] P 47, CA, 28(1) Digest (Reissue) 291, 986.

Thwaite v Thwaite [1981] 2 All ER 789, [1982] Fam 1, [1981] 3 WLR 96, CA.

Preliminary issue

On 23 October 1974 Eric Leslie Tommey (the husband) filed a petition for divorce and
included in it the terms of an agreement he had made with Cynthia Dorothy Joan
Tommey, his wife, on 2 September 1974 regarding ancillary relief. When the petition
came on for hearing in the Luton County Court on 18 February 1975 his Honour Judge
Kingham granted a decree nisi and by consent made an order embodying such terms of
the agreement as had not already been fulfilled and dismissing all further financial claims
by the wife. The decree nisi was made absolute on 4 April 1975. The consent order was
subsequently varied, by consent, on 8 July 1975 and 14 September 1976. On 5 December
1978 the wife applied, under CCR Ord 37, to the Luton County Court for an order (i)
setting aside the orders of 18 February 1975, 8 July 1975 and 14 September 1976 to the
extent that her financial claims had been dismissed and in so far as they related to the
matrimonial home and her rights to ancillary relief and (ii) for a new trial of all matters
relating to her rights to ancillary relief. The grounds for her application were (i) that the
order of 18 February 1975 was based on an agreement obtained as a result of undue
influence by the husband, (ii) that the judge had made the order of 18 February 1975 in
ignorance of the relevant facts and (iii) that the husband had never filed an affidavit of
means. On 1 February 1979 Judge Kingham ordered that there should be a hearing on
the preliminary issue of whether the wife could rely on undue influence. He gave
directions for discovery, ordered inspection and filing of evidence on the preliminary
issue and transferred the case to the High Court under r 81 of the Matrimonial Causes
Rules 1977. On 3 April 1980 the wife issued a summons in the High Court seeking an
order that there should be a trial on the preliminary issue. On 27 June 1980 Sheldon J
ordered that there should be a trial of the following issues: whether the wife was entitled
on any of the grounds set out in her application of 3 April 1980 to have the order of 18
February 1975, in so far as it dismissed all claims by her then outstanding for financial
relief, set aside and to have such claims, or any of them, reopened. The facts are set out in
the judgment.

Christopher Cousins for the wife.
E James Holman as amicus curiae.
The husband did not appear.

Cur adv vult

10 March. **BALCOMBE J** read the following judgment: Mr and Mrs Tommey (whom
a I shall call respectively 'the husband' and 'the wife') were married in 1962. There were
three children of the marriage: two boys, born in 1965 and 1967, and a girl, born in
1973.

In August 1973 the parties moved into a new house which cost £43,000 and was
conveyed to them as beneficial joint tenants. It does not appear that any mortgage was
taken out to assist with the acquisition of this house.

b Early in 1974 relations between the husband and wife started to deteriorate. In March
1974 the wife committed adultery and, as a result, became pregnant. The pregnancy was
terminated in June 1974. It is the wife's case that, as a result of her matrimonial
difficulties, her adulterous affair, her pregnancy and its subsequent termination, she was,
during the summer and autumn of 1974, in a highly emotional state and unfit to make
any major decision. It is also the wife's case that in discussion she had with the husband
c on the subject of divorce he threatened to allege that she was an unfit mother and to
oppose her claim for the custody of the children.

Eventually they agreed terms: the husband would present a petition based on the
wife's adultery; the wife would not defend that petition. The wife should have custody
of the children with reasonable access to the husband. The husband should pay reasonable
maintenance for the children (which was agreed initially at the rate of £5 per week). The
d husband should pay to the wife a lump sum of £8,000 in return for all her interests in
the matrimonial home and 'in full and final satisfaction of any claim for financial benefit
or provision for herself'. The wife accepted these terms against the express advice of her
solicitors, and an agreement was concluded on 2 September 1974. It is now the wife's
case that she was induced to enter into this agreement as a result of undue influence
exercised by the husband. In support of that case, she has filed an affidavit making a
e number of detailed allegations against the husband and his solicitor. The husband has
filed an affidavit denying these allegations.

In October 1974 the wife consulted her then solicitors about financial provision for
herself and the children, but was advised that the agreement of 2 September was binding
on her.

On 23 October 1974 the husband presented his petition based on the wife's adultery
f and the substance of the agreement mentioned above was set out in para 8 of the petition.
On 9 January 1975 the wife's solicitors returned the acknowledgment of service, which
stated that she did not intend to defend the case but wished to make application for
ancillary relief. However, at no time did the wife give notice of her intention to apply
for ancillary relief.

On 18 February 1975 the husband's petition came on for hearing before his Honour
g Judge Kingham at Luton County Court, when both sides were legally represented. The
judge granted the decree nisi, gave a certificate of satisfaction under s 41 of the
Matrimonial Causes Act 1973 and, by consent, gave custody of the three children to the
wife with reasonable access to the husband and, again by consent, ordered that all further
financial claims regarding the wife be dismissed. It appears that the wife's transfer of her
interest in the matrimonial home, and the payment to her of £8,000, had already taken
h place outside court. The judge was not told that the wife's agreement to the financial
arrangements was against the advice of her solicitors. No evidence as to means had been
filed by either party. The decree was made absolute on 4 April 1975.

Subsequently the wife's relationship with the co-respondent broke down and, with the
consent of the husband, she moved back with the children into Amberley Close, the
house which had been the matrimonial home before the move in August 1973, and
j which still belonged to the husband's company. This position was regularised by an order
of the registrar dated 8 July 1975 when the husband undertook to provide Amberley
Close as a home for the wife and the children, he being responsible for the rent and rates,
repairs and external decorations, and there was a consent order that the husband should
pay the sum of £5 per week in respect of each of the three children. That order was
varied by consent on 14 September 1976 when the husband was relieved of his

responsibility to pay the general and water rates on Amberley Close, and the maintenance
for the children was increased to the sum of £766 p a for each child.

By 1977 the wife found herself in financial difficulties and consulted new solicitors.
She was advised that she could not upset the financial agreement made at the time of the
divorce. However, she consulted her present solicitors in June 1978 when she received
different advice and on 5 December 1978 she issued an application in the Luton County
Court to have the orders of 18 February 1975, 8 July 1975 and 14 September 1976 set
aside to the extent that her financial claims had been dismissed and in so far as they
related to Amberley Close and her rights to ancillary relief and asking for a new trial of
all matters relating to her rights to ancillary relief.

The grounds for the application were set out in considerable detail, but may be
summarised as follows: (i) undue influence; (ii) that the judge made the order of 18
February 1975 in ignorance of the relevant facts; (iii) that the husband had never filed an
affidavit of means. Although the notice of application does not say so in terms, I was told
by the wife's counsel, that the application was made under CCR Ord 37, which empowers
the judge to order a new trial.

The application came before his Honour Judge Kingham on 1 February 1979, when
he ordered that there be a hearing on the preliminary issue whether the wife can rely on
undue influence. He gave directions for discovery, ordered inspection and filing of
evidence on the preliminary issue and transferred the action to the High Court under
r 81 of the Matrimonial Causes Rules 1977, SI 1977/344. Further delay occurred while
the wife sought, and eventually obtained, legal aid.

On 3 April 1980 the wife issued a summons in the High Court for an order that there
be a trial on the preliminary issue, the wife's advisers doubting whether an order made
in the county court could effectively direct the trial of a preliminary issue in the High
Court. That summons came before Sheldon J on 27 June 1980, when the judge ordered
that there be a trial of the following issues, namely—

'whether the [wife] is entitled upon the grounds or any of them set out in the
[wife's] application dated 3 April 1980 to have the order herein dated 18 February
1975 insofar as it dismissed all claims by her then outstanding for financial relief,
set aside, and for such claims, or any of them, now to be re-opened.'

The grounds set out in the application of 3 April 1980, apart from one ground which
was based on an error of fact and has since been abandoned, may be summarised in the
same way as those set out in the application of 5 December 1978, namely (i) undue
influence; (ii) unawareness of relevant facts on the part of the judge who made the order;
(iii) failure by the husband to file an affidavit of means. There was still further delay
while evidence was filed in accordance with directions given by Sheldon J, but, eventually,
the preliminary issue came before me for hearing on 20 January 1982.

In the mean time, the husband had failed to give instructions to his solicitors, who had
taken themselves off the record, and he did not appear before me. It soon became
apparent to me that the preliminary issue raised questions of considerable difficulty and
I adjourned the matter for further argument in open court, with the assistance of counsel
as amicus curiae. The matter came back before me on 25 February, when Mr Holman
appeared as amicus, instructed by the Treasury Solicitor. I would like to express the
gratitude of the court for the very considerable assistance afforded by him.

There is a short answer to the question framed by the order of 27 June 1980, namely
that in proceedings as at present constituted the wife is not entitled to have the order of
18 February 1975 set aside: see *de Lasala v de Lasala* [1979] 2 All ER 1146 at 1155, [1980]
AC 546 at 561 where Lord Diplock, in delivering the judgment of the Privy Council,
said:

'Where a party to an action seeks to challenge, on the ground that it was obtained
by fraud or mistake, a judgment or order that finally disposes of the issues raised
between the parties, the only ways of doing it that are open to him are by appeal

from the judgment or order to a higher court, or by bringing a fresh action to set it
aside.'

This is a restatement of a long-settled rule.

In *Jonesco v Beard* [1930] AC 298 at 300, [1930] All ER Rep 483 at 484 Lord Buckmaster,
delivering the leading judgment in the House of Lords, said:

> 'It has long been the settled practice of the court that the proper method of
> impeaching a completed judgment on the ground of fraud is by action in which, as
> in any other action based on fraud, the particulars of the fraud must be exactly given
> and the allegation established by the strict proof such a charge requires.'

Assuming that there is jurisdiction to set aside an order on the ground that it was
obtained by undue influence, the same considerations apply as to an action based on
fraud.

To this general rule there are certain exceptions. (i) If the order is in the substantive,
and not merely the procedural, sense interlocutory. This was accepted by Lord Diplock,
who, in the passage from the judgment in *de Lasala v de Lasala* immediately following
that set out above, said:

> 'The test whether a judgment or order finally disposes of the issues raised between
> the parties is not determined by enquiring whether for the purposes of rules of
> court relating to time or leave to appeal it attracts the label "final" or "interlocutory".
> The test is: has the court that made the order a continuing power to vary its terms,
> as distinct from making orders in aid of enforcing those terms under a liberty to
> apply?'

An example of the application of this exception is afforded by the decision in *Allsop v
Allsop* (1981) 11 Fam Law 18. (ii) Special reasons which permit a departure from the
established practice (see *Hip Foong Hong v Neotia & Co* [1918] AC 888, as explained in
Jonesco v Beard [1930] AC 298 at 301, [1930] All ER Rep 483 at 484). *Allsop v Allsop* is also
an example of the application of this exception since in that case both Ormrod and
Brandon LJJ gave as an alternative ground for their decision, as appears clearly from the
full transcript of the judgments, the fact that the husband in that case had admitted the
facts which gave rise to the charge of fraud (so that there was no issue of fact in dispute)
and had consented to the original order being set aside although he had subsequently
withdrawn that consent. Accordingly, there was no necessity for the procedural
safeguards afforded by an action with pleadings, discovery etc. (iii) Possibly, where the
original order is still executory and the basis on which it was made has altered (see *Thwaite
v Thwaite* [1981] 2 All ER 789, [1982] Fam 1).

None of these exceptions applies in the present case. In regard to the wife's claim for
financial provision the order of 18 February 1975 was final in every sense of the word.
The issues of fact are hotly disputed, as appears from the affidavits already filed.
Accordingly, the procedure adopted in this case, an application for a new trial under CCR
Ord 37 was wrong. I have considered whether it might be possible to let the action go
ahead by giving directions now for pleading and discovery, but I cannot see that any
advantage will be gained, or costs saved, thereby. If there are to be pleadings and
discovery (and possibly interrogatories) it seems to me that it is best that they should take
place in the context of the well-settled procedure of an action commenced by writ and
not in the context of some ad hoc procedure constituted for the purposes of a particular
case.

However, it does not seem to me to be right to answer the question solely on the
procedural point and leave the wider and more important questions as to jurisdiction
unanswered, especially as I have not had the benefit of full argument. Accordingly, I
propose to consider whether there is jurisdiction to set aside the order of 18 February
1975 on any of the grounds set out in the application of 3 April 1980, assuming that the
wife adopts the correct procedure for that purpose.

One of the grounds can be disposed of shortly, namely the husband's failure to file an affidavit of means. Since the wife never served a notice in respect of an application for ancillary relief, the husband never became subject to an obligation to file an affidavit of means (see r 73(2) of the Matrimonial Causes Rules 1977). So his failure to file such an affidavit cannot be the subject of complaint.

Nor is there any substance in another ground, namely ignorance of relevant facts on the part of the judge. A judge who is asked to make a consent order cannot be compelled to do so: he is no mere rubber stamp. If he thinks there are matters about which he needs to be more fully informed before he makes the order, he is entitled to make such inquiries, and require such evidence to be put before him, as he considers necessary. But, per contra, he is under no obligation to make inquiries or require evidence. He is entitled to assume that parties of full age and capacity know what is in their own best interests, more especially when they are represented before him by counsel or solicitors. The fact that he was not told facts which, had he known them, might have affected his decision to make a consent order cannot of itself be a ground for impeaching the order. Accordingly, the wife is not entitled on this ground to have the order of 18 February 1975 set aside.

There remains the ground of undue influence, and this poses a much more difficult question. Until recently it was considered well-settled law that a consent order can be set aside on any ground which would invalidate the agreement embodied in the order (see *Huddersfield Banking Co Ltd v Henry Lister & Son Ltd* [1895] 2 Ch 273, [1895–9] All ER Rep 868). There can be no doubt that undue influence would be such a ground.

However, in *Thwaite v Thwaite* [1981] 2 All ER 789, [1982] Fam 1 the Court of Appeal, in a considered judgment, held that a distinction must be made between consent orders generally and consent orders in the matrimonial jurisdiction. The contractual basis of matrimonial consent orders is to be disregarded and they must be dealt with in the same way as non-consensual orders (see *Thwaite v Thwaite* [1981] 2 All ER 789 at 794, [1982] Fam 1 at 8 per Ormrod LJ who gave the judgment of the court). This is a decision which is binding on me.

Thus far I have been reading from a prepared judgment. When I came into court this morning to deliver this judgment, my attention was drawn to *Aspden (Inspector of Taxes) v Hildesley* [1982] 2 All ER 53, [1982] 1 WLR 264, which has been reported since the argument took place before me in this case. That is a decision of Nourse J in a tax case. He said ([1982] 2 All ER 53 at 56, [1982] 1 WLR 264 at 265):

'The question in this case is whether capital gains tax was payable on a transfer of a joint interest in property pursuant to a consent order made in 1976 on the granting of a decree nisi for the dissolution of the taxpayer's marriage. The General Commissioners for the St Martin-in-the-Fields division held that tax was not payable, and the Crown now appeals to this court. The taxpayer is Major Raymond James Hildesley. He was formerly married to Mrs Eileen Dolores Hildesley. They separated in June 1970, and in 1975 the taxpayer commenced divorce proceedings. Since 1964 the taxpayer and Mrs Hildesley had been the joint legal and beneficial owners of 21 Westmoreland Terrace, Pimlico, but it was not at any material time the only or main residence of either of them. On 12 February 1976 Dunn J, on the making of the decree nisi, ordered that certain terms be filed and made a rule of court. Those terms took the form of cross-undertakings followed by a consent order. The convenient course is to refer first to paras 1, 2 and 3 of the consent order. Paragraph 1 ordered the taxpayer to transfer forthwith to Mrs Hildesley "all his interest both legal and equitable" in 21 Westmoreland Terrace. Paragraph 2 ordered the taxpayer to make periodical payments to Mrs Hildesley at the rate of £2,500 per annum payable monthly, less tax, from decree absolute during a period which I need not specify. Paragraph 3 ordered that the foregoing financial provision was in satisfaction of all Mrs Hildesley's claims for ancillary relief and against the taxpayer's estate.'

The judge then set out the undertakings which were incorporated in the terms, and continued ([1982] 2 All ER 53 at 58, [1982] 1 WLR 264 at 268–269):

a 'Counsel for the Crown accepts that the Crown's success in these proceedings depends on its being able to establish that the disposal took place on 12 February 1976 because otherwise there can have been no disposal during the year of assessment 1975–76. That involves a consideration of the Finance Act 1971, Sch 10, para 10 . . . In the light of the provisions I have read counsel for the Crown has to show, first, that the order of 12 February 1976 was a contract and, second, that it was not conditional within para 10(2). As to the first of these matters counsel for the Crown

b referred me to the recent case in the Court of Appeal of *Thwaite v Thwaite* [1981] 2 All ER 789, [1981] 3 WLR 96, in which it was held that where parties to matrimonial proceedings agreed terms, and by consent those terms were embodied in an order of the court, the legal effect of their agreement derived from the court's order and not from contract. However, it is clear that the consent order there in question had been made after decree absolute, and in the light of ss 23(5) and 24(3) of the

c Matrimonial Causes Act 1973 I do not think that either that case or *de Lasala v de Lasala* [1979] 2 All ER 1146, [1980] AC 546, a decision of the Privy Council on which the court of Appeal based itself, is to be taken as a decision on the effect of a consent order made before decree absolute. In such a case the matter would appear to rest on contract in accordance with the normal rule which was recognised by the Court of Appeal in *Thwaite v Thwaite*. Moreover, in this case the order was not a full

d consent order but an order that the agreed terms "be filed and made a Rule of Court". That is a very familiar formula in the Family Division. It seems clear from the decision of the Court of Appeal in *Re Shaw, Smith v Shaw* [1918] P 47, and in particular from the judgment of Warrington LJ (at 53–54), that the effect of an order in that form is that the obligation remains contractual. In all the circumstances it seems to me to be clear that the consent order of 12 February 1976 was a contract

e within para 10 of Sch 10 to the Finance Act 1971.'

Section 23(5) of the Matrimonial Causes Act 1973 provides:

'Without prejudice to the power to give a direction under section 30 . . . where an order is made under subsection (1)(*a*), (*b*) or (*c*) above on or after granting a decree of divorce or nullity of marriage, neither the order nor any settlement made in
f pursuance of the order shall take effect unless the decree has been made absolute.'

Section 23, of course, deals with powers to make orders for periodical payments and lump sum payments, secured or unsecured; and s 24 deals with property transfer.

In the present case, the order of 18 February 1975 was not a positive order under either s 23 or s 24, but was simply an order that all further financial claims regarding the wife be dismissed. So one way in which this case might be distinguished from *Aspden*
g *(Inspector of Taxes) v Hildesley* is on that ground. Another is on the ground that there the terms were filed and made a rule of court; that was not the case here.

It seems to me to be important that on a question as fundamental as this the law should not be bedevilled by fine distinctions. I have to say that, if Nourse J was going further in *Aspden (Inspector of Taxes) v Hildesley* than was necessary for the case before him, then I
h would, with respect, dissent from his conclusion, because a decision of a judge of co-ordinate jurisdiction, while of the greatest persuasive authority, is not binding on me.

However, it is relevant to note that all that Nourse J was concerned to decide in *Aspden (Inspector of Taxes) v Hildesley* was the effect of the consent order of Dunn J on 12 February 1976 (the date it was made), and before decree absolute was granted. He was concerned with its effect during the financial year of assessment 1975–76, which ended on 5 April.
j If he was intending to say no more than this, that as at that date (12 February 1976) and pending decree absolute the order was contractual in its effect, I would respectfully agree with him. But, if he is intending to say that after the decree has been made absolute the order still remains contractual, then I would, respectfully, disagree, because it seems to me that a decision in those terms would be inconsistent with the decision of the Court of Appeal in *Thwaite v Thwaite* [1981] 2 All ER 789, [1982] Fam 1, which is binding on both of us. Accordingly, having considered *Aspden (Inspector of Taxes) v Hildesley*, it does not

seem to me to alter the basis of the judgment which I have already prepared. I now propose to continue reading from that judgment.

It follows, therefore, that a matrimonial consent order cannot be impeached on grounds sufficient to invalidate the underlying agreement, unless those grounds would also suffice to invalidate a non-consensual order.

I turn, therefore, to consider whether undue influence is a ground on which a non-consensual matrimonial order could be set aside, although I find it difficult to conceive of circumstances where undue influence could affect the making of a non-consensual order. Counsel have not been able to find any authority directly in point. In *de Lasala v de Lasala* [1979] 2 All ER 1146, [1980] AC 546 Lord Diplock referred to two grounds on which an order may be set aside, namely fraud or mistake. But, as was pointed out by the Court of Appeal in *Thwaite v Thwaite* [1981] 2 All ER 789 at 794, [1982] Fam 1 at 8, those grounds are not exclusive. So the question is an open one. Undue influence is closely akin to fraud (see *Allcard v Skinner* (1887) 36 Ch D 145, [1886–90] All ER Rep 90, and, in particular, the judgment of Lindley LJ (36 Ch D 145 at 182–183, [1886–90] All ER Rep 90 at 99–100). Fraud is clearly recognised as a ground on which an order, consensual or non-consensual, can be set aside. So it would involve no great development of the existing law to hold that undue influence is a ground on which a matrimonial order can be set aside.

I accept a submission of counsel acting as amicus curiae that whether that development should take place involves considerations of policy. In my judgment, this involves holding a balance between two important principles which are often expressed by the Latin phrases: ubi jus ibi remedium and interest reipublicae ut sit finis litium.

The first principle, that the law should provide a remedy for wrongs, suggests that in the case of matrimonial orders which are obtained as a result of undue influence the law should intervene to protect the weaker spouse from exploitation by the stronger. In *Edgar v Edgar* [1980] 3 All ER 887 at 894, [1980] 1 WLR 1410 at 1418 Ormrod LJ referred to the 'situation with which all experienced practitioners are familiar, where one spouse takes an unfair advantage of the other in the throes of marital breakdown, a time when emotional pressures are high and judgment apt to be clouded'. I made a similar point in *Backhouse v Backhouse* [1978] 1 All ER 1158 at 1166, [1978] 1 WLR 243 at 251. One suspects that cases where unfair pressure has been brought to bear and which come to the attention of the court are but the tip of the iceberg. Nevertheless, there is a locus poenitentiae in these cases. If a wife, as in the present case, contends that she has been induced to enter into an improvident agreement or transaction by reason of undue influence exercised by her husband, she may still proceed with a claim for financial relief under ss 23 and 24 of the Matrimonial Causes Act 1973 and the existence of the agreement, though relevant, is not decisive (see *Dean v Dean* [1978] 3 All ER 758, [1978] Fam 161; *Edgar v Edgar* [1980] 3 All ER 887, [1980] 1 WLR 1410). It will be a rare case where undue influence can be shown to exist right up to the making of the order. Indeed, the evidence in the present case suggests that, by the time the matter came before the court in February 1975, the wife had ceased to be subject to the alleged influence of the husband and consented to the order because she was advised, mistakenly if her allegations were justified, that she could not resile from her agreement.

The second principle is that to which Lord Simon referred in his speech in *Ampthill Peerage Case* [1976] 2 All ER 411 at 423, [1977] AC 547 at 575:

'There is a fundamental principle of English law (going back to Coke's Commentary on Littleton (1809) p 303) generally expressed by a Latin maxim which can be translated: "It is in the interest of society that there should be some end to litigation." This fundamental principle finds expression in many forms . . . But the fundamental principle that it is in society's interest that there should be some end to litigation is seen most characteristically in the recognition by our law— by every system of law—of the finality of a judgment. If the judgment has been obtained by fraud or collusion it is considered as a nullity and the law provides

machinery whereby its nullity can be so established. If the judgment has been
obtained in consequence of some procedural irregularity, it may sometimes be set
aside. But such exceptional cases apart, the judgment must be allowed to conclude
the matter. That, indeed, is one of society's purposes in substituting the lawsuit for
the vendetta.'

To the like effect is Lord Wilberforce ([1976] 2 All ER 411 at 417–418, [1977] AC 547 at
569):

> 'English law, and it is safe to say, all comparable legal systems, place high in the
> category of essential principles that which requires that limits be placed on the
> rights of citizens to open or to reopen disputes . . . Any determination of disputable
> fact may, the law recognises, be imperfect: the law aims at providing the best and
> safest solution compatible with human fallibility and having reached that solution
> it closes the book . . . For a policy of closure to be compatible with justice, it must
> be attended with safeguards: so the law allows appeals; so the law, exceptionally,
> allows appeals out of time; so the law still more exceptionally allows judgments to
> be attacked on the ground of fraud . . . But these are exceptions to a general rule of
> high public importance, and as all the cases show, they are reserved for rare and
> limited cases, where the facts justifying them can be strictly proved.'

In balancing these two contrasting principles, I have come to the conclusion that the
latter should prevail. I accept that it is highly undesirable that, at a time of matrimonial
breakdown, the stronger party should be able to exploit the weaker, and that the law
should make provision to prevent such exploitation wherever possible. Nevertheless, the
ability of a party to resile from an agreement made as a result of undue influence, and to
seek an independent decision from the court, provides a safety net which should be large
enough to catch most cases of exploitation. To balance the rare case that may slip through
the net, one must weigh the harm which could be caused to many innocent persons if
orders once made and long acted on could be challenged. The fact that the challenge
might ultimately be unsuccessful is no answer. Another fact well known to practitioners
in this field is the emotional strain caused by constant litigation, and the heavy financial
burden of such litigation.

I have also been influenced by the consideration that fraud, in its strict legal sense, is a
well-defined and understood concept. If fraud, as a ground for setting aside a matrimonial
order, were extended to include undue influence, where should one draw the line? What
about other forms of pressure or exploitation? The wife who is in receipt of legal aid and
uses that fact as a bargaining counter with the husband who has to pay his own costs. Or
the husband who accepts a disadvantageous financial settlement rather than risk his
access to the children being disturbed. One can envisage endless possibilities of further
litigation. In my judgment the policy of the law in this field should be to encourage
finality and certainty, the 'clean break' as in *Minton v Minton* [1979] 1 All ER 79, [1979]
AC 593, and to prefer that principle even if it means that the occasional 'hard case' will
be without remedy.

Accordingly I hold that undue influence, even if established, would not be a ground
for setting aside the order of 18 February 1975 and I answer the question posed by para
(1) of the order of 27 June 1980 by declaring that the respondent wife is not entitled, on
any of the grounds set out in her application dated 3 April 1980, to have the order of 18
February 1975 set aside.

Order accordingly.

Solicitors: *Babington-Browne & Co* (for the wife); *Treasury Solicitor*.

Bebe Chua   Barrister.

Paal Wilson & Co A/S v Partenreederei Hannah Blumenthal
The Hannah Blumenthal

COURT OF APPEAL, CIVIL DIVISION

LORD DENNING MR, GRIFFITHS AND KERR LJJ

24, 25, 26 FEBRUARY, 26 MARCH 1982

Arbitration – Practice – Want of prosecution – Inordinate and inexcusable delay – Delay making fair arbitration impossible – Repudiation – Frustration – Parties under mutual duty to co-operate in keeping arbitration moving – Delay occurring before mutual obligation arising – Delay entirely caused by one party – Whether delay amounting to repudiation of arbitration agreement – Whether agreement to arbitrate frustrated.

In 1969 the sellers agreed to sell a vessel to the buyers under a contract which provided that any dispute arising out of the sale was to be settled by arbitration in London by a single arbitrator or, if the parties could not agree on a single arbitrator, by three arbitrators, one appointed by each party and one appointed by an outside body. Over two years after the sale the buyers informed the sellers that they had a 'number of complaints' about the vessel and some months later commenced arbitration proceedings by appointing an arbitrator. The sellers also appointed an arbitrator but a third arbitrator was never appointed. In 1974 the buyers delivered their points of claim alleging that the sellers had made a false representation or warranty prior to the execution of the contract regarding the vessel's speed and engine performance. Four months later the sellers delivered their defence in which they denied the claim. Nothing further happened in the arbitration for two years and nine months and thereafter further substantial periods of delay caused by the buyers occurred in the course of the preliminary steps before trial. As a result, by July 1980, some 11 years after the sale, there had occurred periods of delay in the arbitration amounting to seven years and nine months. In July 1980 the buyers proposed that a date of hearing be fixed for the arbitration. The sellers thereupon issued a writ seeking (i) a declaration that the arbitration agreement had been discharged by, inter alia, the buyers' repudiation or by frustration and (ii) an injunction restraining the buyers from taking any further steps in the arbitration. The judge held, inter alia, that he was bound by House of Lords authority to hold that because both parties were under a mutual obligation to prevent delay and to keep the arbitration moving it was not open to the sellers to do nothing themselves and then rely on the buyers' delay as amounting to repudiation of the arbitration agreement by the buyers. He went on, however, to hold that the length of delay was such that the arbitration agreement had been frustrated because a fair trial of the issues was no longer possible. The buyers appealed.

Held (Griffiths LJ dissenting) – The appeal would be dismissed for the following reasons—

(1) Applying the principle that the ratio decidendi of a case was to be ascertained by an analysis of the material facts of that case, the Court of Appeal was only bound by House of Lords authority to the effect that the respondent to an arbitration was not entitled to rely on the claimant's delay in applying for directions in order to keep the arbitration moving as a ground for repudiation of the arbitration agreement if the respondent himself was under an obligation to apply for directions. However, if the delay was caused by the claimant before any obligation arose on the part of the respondent to apply for directions the respondent was then entitled to rely on the claimant's delay as being a repudiation of the agreement. Since, on the facts, the failure to proceed had been entirely the fault of the buyers who had never taken the initiative so as to bring any duty of mutual co-operation into play (as evidenced by the fact that they never took steps to

have a third arbitrator appointed, so that it was impossible for the sellers to apply for
a directions), the sellers were entitled to rely on the buyers' delay as amounting to
repudiation of the arbitration agreement (see p 401 *d e h* to p 403 *b*, p 404 *c d*, p 410 *a b f*
g, p 411 *b* to *g*, p 412 *c d* and p 414, *c* to *e*, post); dictum of Lord Simon in *F A & A B Ltd
v Lupton* [1971] 3 All ER at 964 applied; dicta of Lord Diplock in *Bremer Vulkan Schiffbau
Und Maschinenfabrik v South India Shipping Corp* [1981] 1 All ER at 301, 302 explained;
dicta of Roskill LJ and of Lord Scarman in *Bremer Vulkan Schiffbau Und Maschinenfabrik v*
b *South India Shipping Corp* [1980] 1 All ER at 442, [1981] 1 All ER at 310 followed.

(2) (Per Kerr LJ) A party to a contract was entitled to rely on the doctrine of frustration
if a contractual obligation had become incapable of being performed and he himself was
not at fault in causing the frustrating event. The party relying on the doctrine did not
have to show that that neither party was at fault, nor did mere inaction on the party
relying on the doctrine necessarily amount to fault on his part giving rise to self-induced
c frustration. Accordingly (Lord Denning MR concurring), since the delay had been so
great as to make a fair trial of the arbitration impossible and since the sellers had not been
responsible for the delay, the agreement to arbitrate had been frustrated and the sellers
were entitled to rely on that frustration as putting an end to the agreement (see p 403 *f*
to *j*, p 404 *c d*, p 409 *e* to *g*, p 413 *g h* and p 414 *a* to *h*, post); dicta of Lord Radcliffe in
Davis Contractors Ltd v Fareham UDC [1956] 2 All ER at 160 applied; *Bremer Vulkan*
d *Schiffbau Und Maschinenfabrik v South India Shipping Corp* [1981] 1 All ER 289 distinguished.

Observations on the doctrine of precedent (see p 400 *a* to p 401 *c*, post).

Decision of Staughton J [1982] 1 All ER 197 affirmed.

Notes

For termination of an arbitration agreement, see 2 Halsbury's Laws (4th edn) paras 547–
e 554, and for cases on the subject, see 3 Digest (Reissue) 104–118, 545–646.

For the doctrine of frustration, see 9 Halsbury's Laws (4th edn) paras 450–453, and for
cases on the subject, see 12 Digest (Reissue) 482–511, 3426–3535.

For repudiation of contract, see 9 Halsbury's Laws (4th edn) paras 546–549, and for
cases on the subject, see 12 Digest (Reissue) 411–416, 3032–3049.

f **Cases referred to in judgments**

*Allen v Sir Alfred McAlpine & Sons Ltd, Bostic v Bermondsey and Southwark Group Hospital
Management Committee, Sternberg v Hammond* [1968] 1 All ER 543, [1968] 2 QB 229,
[1968] 2 WLR 336, CA, Digest (Cont Vol C) 1091, 2262*b*.
American Cyanamid Co v Ethicon Ltd [1975] 1 All ER 504, [1975] AC 396, [1975] 2 WLR
316, HL, Digest (Cont Vol D) 536, 152*a*.
g *André & Cie SA v Marine Transocean Ltd, The Splendid Sun* [1981] 2 All ER 993, [1981] QB
694, [1981] 3 WLR 43, CA.
A/S Awilco v Fulvia SpA di Navigazione, The Chikuma [1981] 1 All ER 652, [1981] 1 WLR
314, HL.
Bank Line Ltd v Arthur Capel & Co [1919] AC 435, [1918–19] All ER Rep 504, HL, 41
Digest (Repl) 233, 563.
h *Bremer Vulkan Schiffbau Und Maschinenfabrik v South India Shipping Corp* [1981] 1 All ER
289, [1981] AC 909, [1981] 2 WLR 141, HL; *rvsg* [1980] 1 All ER 420, [1981] AC 909,
[1980] 2 WLR 905, CA; *on appeal from* [1979] 3 All ER 194, [1981] AC 909, [1979] 3
WLR 471.
Cassell & Co Ltd v Broome [1972] 1 All ER 801, [1972] AC 1027, [1972] 2 WLR 645, HL,
17 Digest (Reissue) 82, 17.
j *Chaplin v Boys* [1969] 2 All ER 1085, [1971] AC 356, [1969] 3 WLR 322, HL, 30 Digest
(Reissue) 272, 787.
Constantine (Joseph) Steamship Line Ltd v Imperial Smelting Corp Ltd, The Kingswood [1941] 2
All ER 165, [1942] AC 154, HL, 12 Digest (Reissue) 482, 3428.
Crawford v A E A Prowting Ltd [1972] 1 All ER 1199, [1973] 1 QB 1, [1972] 2 WLR 749,
3 Digest (Reissue) 116, 637.

Davis Contractors Ltd v Fareham UDC [1956] 2 All ER 145, [1956] AC 696, [1956] 3 WLR
37, HL, 12 Digest (Reissue) 507, *3518*.

a

Denmark Productions Ltd v Boscobel Productions Ltd [1968] 3 All ER 513, [1969] 1 QB 699,
[1968] 3 WLR 841, CA, 28(2) Digest (Reissue) 677, *147*.

Denny, Mott & Dickson Ltd v James B Fraser & Co Ltd [1944] 1 All ER 678, [1944] AC 265,
HL, 12 Digest (Reissue) 500, *3495*.

DPP v Smith [1960] 3 All ER 161, [1961] AC 290, [1960] 3 WLR 546, HL, 14(1) Digest
(Reissue) 18, *41*.

b

F A & A B Ltd v Lupton [1971] 3 All ER 948, [1972] AC 634, [1971] 3 WLR 670, HL,
Digest (Cont Vol D) 441, *207*.

Federal Commerce and Navigation Ltd v Molena Alpha Inc, The Nanfri, The Benfri, The Lorfri
[1979] 1 All ER 307, [1979] AC 757, HL, Digest (Cont Vol E) 109, *3036a*.

Heyman v Darwins Ltd [1942] 1 All ER 337, [1942] AC 356, HL, 3 Digest (Reissue) 88,
453.

c

Howard Marine and Dredging Co Ltd v A Ogden & Sons (Excavations) Ltd [1978] 2 All ER
1134, [1978] QB 574, [1978] 2 WLR 515, CA, Digest (Cont Vol E) 425, *115a*.

Kodros Shipping Corp v Empresa Cubana de Fletes, The Evia (No 2) [1982] 1 Lloyd's Rep 334,
CA.

Lim Poh Choo v Camden and Islington Area Health Authority [1979] 2 All ER 910, [1980] AC
174, [1979] 3 WLR 44, HL, Digest (Cont Vol E) 457, *1285a*.

d

Maritime National Fish Ltd v Ocean Trawlers Ltd [1935] AC 524, [1935] All ER Rep 86, 12
Digest (Reissue) 428, *3100*.

NWL Ltd v Woods, NWL Ltd v Nelson [1979] 3 All ER 614, [1979] 1 WLR 1294, HL,
Digest (Cont Vol E) 612, *1457a*.

Pioneer Shipping Ltd v BTP Tioxide Ltd, The Nema [1981] 2 All ER 1030, [1982] AC 724,
[1981] 3 WLR 292, HL.

e

Rookes v Barnard [1964] 1 All ER 367, [1964] AC 1129, [1964] 2 WLR 269, HL, 17 Digest
(Reissue) 81, *14*.

Universal Cargo Carriers Corp v Citati [1957] 2 All ER 70, [1957] 2 QB 401, [1957] 2 WLR
713, 12 Digest (Reissue) 419, *3057*.

Woodar Investment Development Ltd v Wimpey Construction UK Ltd [1980] 1 All ER 571,
[1980] 1 WLR 277, HL.

f

Cases also cited

Banca Popolare di Novara (Cooperative Society with Ltd Liability) v John Livanos & Sons Ltd
(1973) 117 SJ 509.

Estia Compania Navigacion SA v Deutsche Genussmitter GmbH, The Estia [1981] 1 Lloyd's Rep
541.

g

Hare v Murphy Bros Ltd [1974] ICR 603.

IRC v Blott [1921] 2 AC 171.

Mertens v Home Freeholds Co [1921] 2 KB 526.

Turriff Ltd v Richards & Wallington (Contracts) Ltd [1981] Com LR 39.

Appeal

h

The defendants, Partenreederei Hannah Blumenthal (the buyers), appealed against the
decision of Staughton J ([1982] 1 All ER 197, [1981] 3 WLR 823) on 7 July 1981 granting
the plaintiffs, Paal Wilson & Co A/S (the sellers), a declaration that an arbitration
agreement contained in a contract dated 23 September 1969 between the buyers and the
sellers for sale of the vessel Pinto (later renamed the Hannah Blumenthal) was discharged
by frustration. The facts are set out in the judgment of Lord Denning MR.

j

John Hobhouse QC and *Timothy Wormington* for the buyers.
David Johnson QC and *Jonathan Sumption* for the sellers.

Cur adv vult

26 March. The following judgments were read.

a
LORD DENNING MR. The Pinto was built in 1965 in Spain. She was a small ship of 3,700 gross tons. In 1969 she was owned by Norwegian sellers. After lengthy negotiations through brokers the Norwegian sellers agreed to sell her to German buyers for DM 4,600,000. The agreement was in writing, dated 23 September 1969. It was on the Norwegian sale form and contained a clause for arbitration in London. There was also
b this express provision:

> 'The vessel with everything belonging to her shall be at Sellers' risk and expense until she is delivered to the Buyers . . . the vessel with everything belonging to her shall be delivered and taken over as she is at the time of delivery, after which the Sellers shall have no responsibility for possible faults or deficiencies of any description.'

c
The vessel was inspected by the German buyers before delivery. They had competent engineers who thoroughly examined her. On her last voyage before delivery, from Huelva in Spain on the Gulf of Cadiz to Rotterdam in Holland, the marine superintendent of the buyers sailed with the ship together with the marine superintendent of the sellers. So the buyers knew all about her performance. The buyers took delivery of her in
d Rotterdam on 9 December 1969. They changed her name from Pinto to Hannah Blumenthal. She was operated by the German buyers, but let back on time charter to the Norwegian sellers. In 1970 and 1971 the German buyers had extensive repairs done to her engines at much expense, but they made no complaint that it was due to any fault of the Norwegian sellers.

If they had any genuine cause for complaint, you would have thought that they would
e have made it at once, but they did nothing for over two years.

Period A : two years and two months
Then on 28 January 1972, that is two years and two months after the delivery, the German buyers wrote saying they had a number of complaints about the vessel. Their solicitors wrote:

f
'"Hannah Blumenthal"
We are acting for Messrs. Partenreederei Hannah Blumentahl of Hamburg in connection with their purchase of the m.s. "PINTO" from yourselves under sale contract dated 23rd September 1979. Under line 72 of the sale contract it is provided that the sellers shall at the time of delivery hand to the buyers the vessel's log books, unless otherwise agreed. Our clients have a number of complaints about the vessel
g and in order for us to investigate these complaints fully it is necessary for us to sight the deck and engine room log books for the period during which the vessel was in your ownership. As these should apparently have been handed over on delivery of the vessel under the sale contract, we hereby call upon you to now produce these documents.'

h
Two arbitrators are appointed
In August 1972 the German buyers appointed Mr R E Kingsley as their arbitrator. In December 1972 the Norwegian sellers appointed Mr Cedric Barclay as their arbitrator. Nothing more was done by either side in the arbitration. Under the arbitration clause a third arbitrator should have been appointed. But this was never done. So the arbitration
i never got under way. No application was made by either side to the arbitrators for directions. Neither side sought to get a third arbitrator appointed. But each side was represented by experienced solicitors in the City of London. They seem to have assumed that pleadings could be delivered and discovery given without asking anyone for directions. Even so, the German buyers took an undue time to prepare their points of claim.

Period B: one year and two months
   Then on 22 February 1974, that is, one year and two months after the arbitrators were   *a*
appointed, the German buyers delivered their points of claim. They alleged that in
August 1969 (4½ years before): 'Prior to the execution of the contract of sale the
Norwegian sellers represented to the German buyers that the vessel had a service speed
of 12·5 knots and that the vessel's engine had a service speed of 230 rpm.' The German
company alleged that, relying on the said representations they entered into the contract
of sale, that the representations were untrue and that they had suffered damages of over   *b*
DM 1,000,000. Alternatively, they relied on the representations as a collateral warranty.
They gave particulars of the representations. They were all oral, save for a telex on 18
August 1969. They were all in the preliminary stages in the negotiations long before the
contract of sale was concluded on 23 September 1969.

The demerits of the claim   *c*
   If this claim had rested on the old common law of England, it would have been bound
to fail. The contract was in writing and contained all the terms including the term
excluding any liability of the sellers. The representations, if made, were all innocent and
would not give rise to any claim for damages. They were not collateral warranties being
made so long before the contract was signed: see the principles stated in *Howard Marine
and Dredging Co Ltd v A Ogden & Sons (Excavations) Ltd* [1978] 2 All ER 1134, [1978] QB   *d*
574. If the claim was to have any warrant at all, it could only be by reason of s 2 of the
Misrepresentation Act 1967; and that would have been very difficult to maintain, seeing
that the Norwegian sellers could rely on the exclusion clause as being fair and reasonable
in the circumstances of the case (see s 3 of the 1967 Act).
   I cannot think that the German buyers had much confidence in their claim. That is, I
suspect, why they proved to be so dilatory about it. It makes one feel that it was a 'try   *e*
on'. The Norwegian sellers delivered their defence in June 1974. They denied that the
representations were made. They said that the man who sent the telex on 18 August
1969 was not their agent. Then there came from the German buyers this letter of 25
September 1974:

      'We are considering whether a reply to the defence is required, but in the   *f*
      meanwhile perhaps you could ensure that you are in a position to effect discovery of
      documents within the near future.'

Period C: two years and nine months
   From that time onward, from 25 September 1974 to 8 July 1977 (two years and nine
months) nothing happened at all. The German buyers sold the vessel to someone else.   *g*
They forgot all about their claim. The file must have been left in the bottom drawer.
The buyers' arbitrator, Mr R E Kingsley, thought the matter might have died. He wrote
to the buyers' solicitors in January 1975 and February 1977 asking if he should keep the
file open. They asked him to do so. Then the solicitors for the German buyers wrote this
apologetic letter on 8 July 1977 to the solicitors for the Norwegian sellers: *h*

                        '"Hannah Blumenthal"
      As you will be aware, this matter has, to say the least, not progressed very rapidly
      since we were last in contact. The reason for this is that we have been obtaining
      further evidence and we have been obtaining a number of translations which has
      been very time consuming. We have also been obtaining Further Advice from
      Counsel which has proved to be a very protracted business. Having said the above,   *j*
      we are now in a position to make some progress in this matter and, from a review
      of our file, it seems as though the next step in the Reference will be for the parties
      to give mutual disclosure of documents. *In view of the length of time which has elapsed
      since the last step in the Reference was taken,* we would be glad to have your views as to
      the time within which you think that disclosure might take place . . . Counsel has

a advised that, in the light of your Points of Defence, it may be that we will *need to amend our Points of Claim* in respect of the contentions which have been made as to who the various brokers involved were acting for. We mention this only to put you on notice that we may be seeking to do so at *some stage in the future*.'

Thereafter there were over 15 months some fitful attempts at discovery. These were much hampered by the length of time since the sale of the ship in 1969, eight years earlier. In October 1978, however, the Norwegian sellers made available the log books of b the vessel for the period preceding the selling. If the German buyers had been really serious, you would have thought they would have had them examined at once. But no.

Period D: one year and eight months
There then followed a period from December 1978 to July 1980 (one year and eight months) in which the buyers' solicitors appointed an expert to examine the log books. c Then on 30 July 1980 they wrote, strangely enough, from their Hong Kong office:

'"*Hannah Blumenthal*"
. . . We enclose a copy of a detailed analysis of the performance of the ship over the period covered by the Deck and Engine Logs disclosed by your clients. The claims made by our clients have been fully detailed in the pleadings. The enclosed d analysis entirely supports the contentions which have been made by our clients: in particular the following:—(1) The ship had never maintained the represented speed; (2) The ship had never maintained the represented revolutions; (3) The ship had on several occasions experienced problems with her main engine . . . We think that the time has now come when a hearing date for this arbitration should be fixed. However, in view of the content of the pre-delivery logs, we would invite you now e to advise your clients to meet their obligations.'

Adding up
Adding up the periods of delay during which nothing had happened, they were: period A, two years and two months; period B, one year and two months; period C, two years and nine months; and period D, one year and eight months. In all, seven years and f nine months.

The result was that in July 1980 (the sale had taken place in September 1969) 11 years had passed.

The Norwegian sellers retorted on 5 August 1980:

g 'Thank you for your letter of the 30th July with enclosure. We are proceeding to issue an Originating Summons to have your clients' claim struck out for want of prosecution.'

This was followed on 15 August 1980 by a writ by the Norwegian sellers in which they sought a declaration and injunction to stop any further proceedings in the arbitration. In support of it the Norwegian sellers filed an affidavit which showed that, for good reasons, no one of their witnesses would be available to give evidence. Some had h left their employ. Some had been ill. None could remember anything of what had happened at conversations 11 years before.

The German buyers made an affidavit in reply. Staughton J said ([1982] 1 All ER 197 at 204–207, [1981] 3 WLR 823 at 829–832):

'I take the simpler and more robust view that there can inevitably scarcely ever j be a fair trial about the ordinary oral transaction of business more than 11 years after they occurred. That is something which in my judgment the law might do well to acknowledge . . . I hold that the arbitration agreement is frustrated.'

He made a declaration that 'The arbitration agreement contained in a memorandum of agreement made between the parties dated 23 September 1969 has been discharged by reason of frustration'.

The law
The doctrine of precedent

At the outset there is this point: is this court bound by the decision of the House of Lords in *Bremer Vulkan Schiffbau Und Maschinenfabrik v South India Shipping Corp* [1981] 1 All ER 289, [1981] AC 909? That was very like this. It was a case between German shipbuilders and Indian buyers. The contract there was governed by German law but provided for arbitration in London. It included a time bar, barring any claim for defects. It barred them after 12 months. The claim went to arbitration in London. The alleged defects appeared in 1966. The arbitration was not started for five years. The buyers sought to overcome the time bar by saying that it did not apply to the arbitration in London. The arbitration dragged on so long that after 12 years the German shipbuilders applied to stop the arbitration from going any further. Donaldson J stopped it (see [1979] 3 All ER 194, [1981] AC 909). So did this court consisting of myself, Roskill and Cumming-Bruce LJJ (see [1980] 1 All ER 420, [1981] AC 909). Yet the House of Lords reversed us. It was by three against two. In a single judgment the three allowed the arbitration to go on. It is, we are told, still going on, though it is now 16 years past.

I remember, of course, the rebuke which Lord Hailsham LC gave to us in *Cassell & Co Ltd v Broome* [1972] 1 All ER 801 at 809, [1972] AC 1027 at 1054 when he said that 'in the hierarchical system of courts which exists in this country, it is necessary for each lower tier, including the Court of Appeal, to accept loyally the decision of the higher tiers'. But that raises at once the question: what do you mean by the 'decision' of the higher courts? Presumably the reason for the decision. The ratio decidendi as the classicists call it. The reason which is necessary for the decision. It is binding on the lower courts. It is to be distinguished from the obiter dicta. These are the reasons which are not necessary for the decision. They are not binding on the lower courts. The task of distinguishing between them is formidable. Especially when there are four or five speeches and they each give different reasons, as in *Chaplin v Boys* [1969] 2 All ER 1085, [1971] AC 357. Then the ratio decidendi of the case must be somewhat speculative (see *Dicey and Morris on the Conflict of Laws* (10th edn, 1980) vol 2, p 942); and the lower court can choose which it likes. To avoid this embarrassment there has been a marked tendency in recent years in the House of Lords for one of their Lordships to give a single speech and the others to concur. The object is, no doubt, to avoid the difficulties caused by different reasons given by different judges. This object is laudable enough. It is much to be commended in some cases. But it is apt to give rise to problems in others.

It may be presumptuous of me to criticise but I make so bold as to indicate to their Lordships the problems to which a single judgment may give rise. Not often, but just occasionally, it makes it exceedingly difficult to discover what is the ratio decidendi of a case, as distinct from the obiter dicta. It is so difficult that often times the lower courts do not even attempt the task. They treat the words of the single judgment as binding authority. They treat them almost as if they were the words of a statute. So treated, the words are apt to lead lower courts astray. Whereas if there had been, not one single judgment, but three or four or five it would have been much easier to separate the wheat from the chaff and to discover what was really the ratio decidendi and therefore binding, as distinct from obiter dicta and not binding.

As an instance of the problems created by a single judgment, I would draw attention to a few recent cases in which the obiter dicta have been treated as binding and have afterwards been discovered to be erroneous or to have given rise to an infinity of trouble. First, of course, *DPP v Smith* [1960] 3 All ER 161, [1961] AC 290 (on criminal intent), where I would have liked to have delivered a separate judgment but was discouraged from doing so. The reasoning was at once much criticised by academic writers and was reversed by Parliament by s 8 of the Criminal Justice Act 1967. Next, *Rookes v Barnard* [1964] 1 All ER 367, [1964] AC 1129, where there was one single judgment on exemplary damages (see [1964] 1 All ER 367 at 407–413, [1964] AC 1129 at 1221–1231); it gave rise to the controversy in *Cassell & Co Ltd v Broome* [1972] 1 All ER 801, [1972] AC 1027, where Lord Wilberforce gave a reasoned dissent from it (see [1972] 1 All ER 801 at 860–

866, [1972] AC 1027 at 1113–1121). To these I would add the single judgment in
a American Cyanamid Co v Ethicon Ltd [1975] 1 All ER 504, [1975] AC 396, on interlocutory
injunctions, which has given rise to ceaseless misunderstandings in the lower courts, and
had to be explained in NWL Ltd v Woods, NWL Ltd v Nelson [1979] 3 All ER 614 at 625,
[1979] 1 WLR 1294 at 1306. Then to Lim Poh Choo v Camden and Islington Area Health
Authority [1979] 2 All ER 910, [1980] AC 174, where the House of Lords in a single
judgment admitted that a radical reappraisal of the law was needed, but not one of them
b undertook the task, and it looks as if it never will be. There is also the single judgment
in A/S Awilco v Fulvia SpA di Navigazione, The Chikuma [1981] 1 All ER 652, [1981] 1 WLR
314, which has been severely criticised in the Law Quarterly Review (see (1981) 97 LQR
379).

By contrast in the Court of Appeal, if we reverse the judgment of a judge below, our
custom (save in exceptional cases) is for each member of the court to give his own reasons
c in his own words. We do it out of courtesy to him. But it is, in truth, not mere courtesy.
It helps the judges of first instance to discover the ratio decidendi of the case.

All this makes me regret very much that in the Bremer Vulkan case there was only one
single judgment in the House of Lords, concurred in by two others, as against two fully
reasoned judgments in the House, three in the Court of Appeal, and one at first instance.

d The ratio decidendi of Bremer Vulkan

I turn, therefore, to the principal task: to find out the ratio decidendi of the single
judgment in Bremer Vulkan [1981] 1 All ER 289, [1981] AC 909. I take as my starting
point the words of Lord Simon in F A & A B Ltd v Lupton [1971] 3 All ER 948 at 964,
[1972] AC 634 at 658:

e   '. . . what constitutes binding precedent is the ratio decidendi of a case, and this is
        almost always to be ascertained by an analysis of the material facts of the case, that
        is, generally, those facts which the tribunal whose decision is in question itself holds,
        expressly or implicitly, to be material.'

I find the material facts in Bremer Vulkan [1981] 1 All ER 289 at 302, [1981] AC 909 at
987 in the concluding words of Lord Diplock:

f   'In the instant case, however, as in Crawford v A E A Prowting Ltd [1972] 1 All ER
        1199, [1973] 1 QB 1, the respondents, Bremer Vulkan were content to allow the
        claimants, South India, to carry out voluntarily the preparation of detailed points of
        claim. They never made an application for directions to the arbitrator and none
        were made by him. For failure to apply for such directions before so much time had
        elapsed that there was a risk that a fair trial of the dispute would not be possible,
g   [both claimant and respondent were in my view in breach of their contractual
        obligations to one another; and neither can rely on the other's breach as giving him
        a right to treat the primary obligations of each to continue with the reference as
        brought to an end]. Respondents in private arbitrations are not entitled to let sleeping
        dogs lie and then complain that they did not bark.' (My emphasis.)

h   In that passage I would ask you to note the emphasis placed on the breach by the
respondents, on their failure to apply for directions. That is the real ratio decidendi of the
case. To illustrate this I have put brackets round the words which I suggest are obiter
dicta. The reasoning in the passage would be just as cogent if there was substituted there
these words: '. . . the respondents were in my view in breach of their contractual
obligations and cannot rely on the claimant's breach as giving them the right to treat the
j arbitration as at an end.' This shows that the material facts (to use the test of Lord Simon)
were that the respondents had failed to apply for directions and were thus in breach of
their contractual obligations. The respondents were not entitled to let sleeping dogs lie.

It was quite immaterial that the claimants had failed to apply for directions. The
sleeping dog was not bound to wake up and bark. But if it was bound to wake up and
bark, meaning that, if the claimants were bound to apply for directions, then it was not

as a *mutual obligation* binding on both jointly. It was a *separate obligation* binding on each
separately. Like the separate obligation on each side of a contract of sale. If one side is **a**
guilty of a repudiatory breach, the other can accept it, and vice versa.

On this analysis I regard the ratio decidendi, the essential reason for the decision, as
being that, on the facts of that case, the respondents were at fault themselves. They had
not applied for directions as they should have done. They were disentitled, by their own
conduct, from asking for an injunction to stop the arbitration.

If I am right in regarding this as the ratio decidendi of the case, it follows that the **b**
observations about there being a 'mutual obligation' on each party were obiter dicta.
They are not binding on lower courts. I have given my reasons in *André & Cie SA
v Marine Transocean Ltd, The Splendid Sun* [1981] 2 All ER 993 at 996–997, [1981] QB 694
at 700–702 for believing them to be erroneous, and in this I am reinforced by the
judgment which Kerr LJ is about to give.

c

The result in this case

The present case on its facts is quite distinguishable from the facts in *Bremer Vulkan*. I
see no fault whatever, no failure whatever, of the Norwegian sellers or their solicitors. I
can see no reason why they should have tried to awaken the sleeping dog. No reason at
all why they should have applied for directions. In point of law they could not have done
so until a third arbitrator was appointed; and he never was appointed. It was not any **d**
failure of the Norwegian sellers, but the failure of the German buyers, which has made a
fair trial impossible. The German buyers allowed over two years to elapse before they
made any claim at all. Another eight months before they appointed an arbitrator. They
never took any steps to appoint a third arbitrator. For three years they forgot all about
the case. And the last word from them was when they said that they 'may need to amend
our Points of Claim at some stage in the future'.

I cannot help thinking that these failures on their part were because they had no **e**
confidence in their claim. The exclusion clause is in all probability a complete answer to
it.

Seeing that there was no failure at all by the Norwegian sellers, but failure over many
years by the German buyers, making a fair trial impossible, I am clearly of opinion that
the case comes within the principle stated by Roskill LJ in *Bremer Vulkan* [1980] 1 All ER **f**
420 at 442, [1981] AC 909 at 954:

'. . . I see little or no difficulty in attaching to an agreement to arbitrate as a legal
incident of such a contract an implied obligation in point of law on the claimant
who, like a plaintiff in the action, has the conduct of the case not to be guilty of such
dilatory conduct in the prosecution of his claim as will defeat the whole purpose of
the agreement to arbitrate by making a fair hearing before the arbitration tribunal **g**
impossible because of the lapse of time involved. This is merely another way of
saying that a claimant must in such circumstances not be guilty of frustrating delay
of a repudiatory character . . .'

In the House of Lords Lord Fraser and Lord Scarman expressed the same principle in
similar words. Lord Scarman said ([1981] 1 All ER 289 at 310, [1981] AC 909 at 998): **h**

'Where parties agree to refer present or future differences to arbitration, they
enter into a contract, an implied term of which is that each has a right to a fair
arbitration . . . It follows that obstruction of the right will be a breach of contract
and may be a repudiatory breach, and that frustration of the right, ie conduct of a
party making the fair arbitration of a dispute impossible, will be a repudiatory
breach at least of the agreement to refer that dispute to arbitration.' **i**

I see no flaw in the principle there stated. I prefer the reasoning of the dissenting two
in the Lords to the obiter dicta of the majority one.

Applying this principle here, I think the German buyers were guilty of frustrating
delay which made a fair trial impossible. It was a repudiatory breach which the
Norwegian sellers accepted by issuing these proceedings.

I realise that this breach was not intentional on the part of the German buyers. They
a assumed that there was no obligation on them to make any move towards getting the
arbitration under way, either by themselves alone or jointly with the Norwegian sellers.
They thought they could delay as long as they liked with impunity, and that they could
revive the arbitration whenever they liked. In that respect they were under a complete
misapprehension. No matter how innocent their intention, no matter that they thought
they were only doing what they had a right to do, nevertheless, if they were guilty of a
b breach which went to the very root of the contract, the other party is entitled to accept it
as a repudiation, and to treat the contract as at an end. That proposition is amply
established by the decision of the House of Lords in *Federal Commerce and Navigation Ltd
v Molena Alpha Inc, The Nanfri, The Benfri, The Lorfri* [1979] 1 All ER 307, [1979] AC 757.
The principle of that case is not in the least shaken by *Woodar Investment Development Ltd
v Wimpey Construction UK Ltd* [1980] 1 All ER 571, [1980] 1 WLR 277, which was decided
c on the ground that the vendors were entitled to rely simply on the terms of the contract.

Frustration
In case I be wrong on repudiatory breach, however, I turn to frustration proper. It
must always be remembered that we are considering, not frustration of the original
contract of sale, but frustration of the severable contract contained within it, the contract
d to refer disputes to arbitration: see *Heyman v Darwins Ltd* [1942] 1 All ER 337, [1942] AC
356. The contract for arbitration can itself be brought to an end by frustration, as Lord
Diplock himself acknowledged.
I do not think that the decision in *Bremer Vulkan* [1981] 1 All ER 289, [1981] AC 909
excludes us from considering frustration, for the simple reason that in *Bremer Vulkan* in
the House of Lords it was not submitted that the contract for arbitration was brought to
e an end by frustration. It was only argued that the claimants had been guilty of
repudiatory breach because of their frustrating delay, which is a very different thing. I
think it is open to us, therefore, to consider whether this contract for arbitration was
brought to an end by frustration.
When parties agree that any dispute between them shall be referred to arbitration, it
is, I think, implicit that the dispute will be determined by the arbitrators in a fair trial. I
f realise, of course, that often there are delays by one side or the other, or both. Sometimes
they are at fault. Sometimes not. Witnesses may become ill or die. Documents may be
lost or destroyed. These do not by themselves cause a contract for arbitration to be
frustrated. They are everyday occurrences, both in actions at law and in arbitrations, and
the parties have to do the best they can. But there may come a time in arbitrations when
the delays become so great that the courts feel bound to say: 'This has gone on far too
g long. If an arbitration were to be held at this distance of time, it would be a mockery of
justice. There cannot possibly be a fair trial now. The situation now is so radically
different that the arbitration should not now be revived.' In the words of Lord Radcliffe
in *Davis Contractors Ltd v Fareham UDC* [1956] 2 All ER 145 at 160, [1956] AC 696 at
729: 'Non haec in foedera veni. It was not this that I promised to do.' The Norwegian
sellers here can quote this and say with all justice: 'This was not the arbitration to which
h we agreed.'
A parallel can be drawn for delays by strikes or by war or by requisitioning. There are
numerous cases which draw a distinction between those delays which are not so great as
to amount to frustration, and those which do amount to it such as *Pioneer Shipping Ltd v
BTP Tioxide, The Nema* [1981] 2 All ER 1030, [1982] 2 AC 724 and *Kodros Shipping Corp v
Empresa Cubana de Fletes, The Evia (No 2)* [1982] 1 Lloyd's Rep 334. The line between
j them is to be drawn by the tribunal of first instance so long as it does not misdirect itself
in law or in fact. In this case the judge has found that the arbitration agreement was
frustrated. I see no reason to interfere with his decision.

Another point
Whilst preparing my judgment in this case, another point occurred to me. It was this:
the arbitration has never been commenced, because the third arbitrator has never been

appointed. The claim is, therefore, statute-barred. Under s 27 of the Limitation Act 1939
the arbitration should have been commenced within six years. The cause of action
accrued in December 1969. In 1972 each side appointed an arbitrator, but those two had
no jurisdiction at all by themselves. Under the arbitration clause it was necessary for a
third arbitrator to be appointed, not by the parties nor by the two arbitrators, but by a
third person: the Baltic and International Maritime Conference in Copenhagen. In order
to commence the arbitration, the German buyers ought to have requested the Baltic and
International Maritime Conference in Copenhagen to appoint the third arbitrator. They
never did so. The arbitration has, therefore, never been commenced.

But this point was not taken before us. Nor was it argued. So all that I have said on it
is obiter dicta and can, if desired, be discarded.

Conclusion

All the difficulty in this case has been caused by the *Bremer Vulkan* case, but I would
hold that the buyers by their conduct have been guilty of a repudiatory breach which has
been accepted by the sellers. Alternatively, I would hold that there has been so long a
delay as to make a fair trial quite impossible, and on that ground the arbitration
agreement has been frustrated.

I would dismiss the appeal accordingly.

GRIFFITHS LJ. The facts set out in the judgment of Lord Denning MR reveal a
lamentable state of affairs. As a result of the dilatory conduct of the claimant buyers'
solicitors and also, but to a much lesser extent, the respondent sellers' solicitors, if this
arbitration proceeds the arbitrator will be faced with the task of attempting to decide the
dispute on oral conversations alleged to have taken place in 1969. I entirely agree with
counsel for the sellers that as a matter of common sense the arbitration ought not to be
allowed to proceed because after a lapse of 12 years it is a totally unrealistic exercise to
attempt to decide with any precision what was said so long ago, and consequently there
is a grave risk that justice will not be done.

If this dispute had been commenced as an action in the High Court, I have no
hesitation in saying that it would have been struck out for want of prosecution. The
delay has been inordinate and inexcusable, the sellers must be prejudiced in attempting
to meet the buyers' allegations so long after the event, and there is a serious risk that
there cannot be a fair trial of the issue in the sense that justice cannot be done between
the parties after this lapse of time.

If I had not had the advantage of reading Lord Diplock's speech in *Bremer Vulkan
Schiffbau Und Maschinenfabrik v South India Shipping Corp* [1981] 1 All ER 289, [1981] AC
909, I should have fallen into the same error as the judge at first instance (see [1979] 3 All
ER 194, [1981] AC 909), the Court of Appeal (see [1980] 1 All ER 420, [1981] AC 909),
and the two of their Lordships who expressed dissenting opinions in the House of Lords
in that case. It would have appeared to me to be wholly divorced from reality and the
expectation of commercial men that those facing claims should be under the same
obligation to keep the claims moving against them as was imposed on those who made
the claims. Take the present case: the contract under which the ship was sold expressly
excluded any 'responsibility for possible faults or deficiency of any description'; yet here
are the buyers seeking to avoid the consequences of that express term by saying they
were induced to enter into the contract by an oral representation which they first notified
to the sellers some three years after the sale. The sellers might well be excused for
thinking it was just a 'try on' and be reinforced in that view by the apparent lack of
enthusiasm of the buyers' solicitors to bring the matter before the arbitrator. Against this
background, if the sellers' solicitor had written to the sellers to say that as the buyers'
solicitors were proceeding so slowly he was going to prod them into action, I again agree
with their counsel that the sellers would probably have said to their solicitor, 'Whose side
are you on?'

However this may be, I understand the decision in the House of Lords to impose

mutual obligations on the parties to an arbitration to put an end to delay and that the
a respondents in an arbitration are not entitled to complain of the complainants' delay as a
ground for repudiating the arbitration. Lord Diplock ended his speech with these words
([1981] 1 All ER 289 at 302, [1981] AC 909 at 988): 'Respondents in private arbitrations
are not entitled to let sleeping dogs lie and then complain that they did not bark.'

It may by now have appeared that my enthusiasm for the decision of the House of
Lords in *Bremer Vulkan* is somewhat less than whole-hearted, but this does nothing to
b diminish my determination to follow it loyally unless it can legitimately be distinguished.
From time to time every judge will be confronted with the decision of a higher court
with which he does not agree, but there are limits to the judicial ingenuity which it is
permissible to employ to avoid the consequences of the unpopular decision, particularly
when it is a decision of the House of Lords. Staughton J in his judgment made it
abundantly clear that he viewed the decision in *Bremer Vulkan* with disapproval but, like
c me, he declared that he would follow it loyally. However, he concluded that he could
avoid its consequences and stop this arbitration by applying the doctrine of frustration.
The ground on which he held the arbitration agreement to be frustrated was that it was
no longer possible to have a fair trial after such an inordinate delay. But, if this was a
good ground for holding that the arbitration agreement in this case was frustrated, it
would also have been a good ground for finding frustration in *Bremer Vulkan*, because
d Lord Diplock's speech proceeds on the assumption that the judge had found that there
could not be a fair trial within the meaning of that phrase in *Allen v Sir Alfred McAlpine
& Sons Ltd* [1968] 1 All ER 543, [1968] 2 QB 229. It is true that it was not argued that the
arbitration agreement was frustrated in *Bremer Vulkan*; but frustration as a doctrine in
relation to arbitrations was specifically referred to by Lord Diplock: speaking first in
general terms he said ([1981] 1 All ER 289 at 297, [1981] AC 909 at 980):

e   'I would accept that the unperformed primary obligations of the parties under an
      arbitration agreement, like other contracts, may be brought to an end by frustration,
      or at the election of one party when there has been a repudiatory breach of that
      agreement by the other party.'

And at a later passage he gave a particular example of frustration; he said ([1981] 1 All
f ER 289 at 298 [1981] AC 909 at 981):

      '... if the arbitration agreement is restricted to the submission of an identified
      existing dispute to a named arbitrator, the agreement is frustrated if the arbitrator
      turns out not to be impartial.'

And Lord Scarman in his dissenting speech referred to frustration in the following
g passage ([1981] 1 All ER 289 at 310–311, [1981] AC 909 at 998):

      'In a contract of arbitration I accept that there are mutual obligations to be implied
      into the parties' agreement not to obstruct or frustrate the purpose of the agreement,
      ie a fair arbitration to be conducted in accordance with the terms of their agreement.'

These passages show that frustration was present to the minds of their Lordships. I should
h be very slow to assume that even in the absence of argument Lord Diplock would
overlook the fact that the application of the doctrine of frustration would in that case
have led to the opposite result to that which he found, particularly when the path of
strict legal reasoning led to the somewhat unhappy result that an arbitration was to take
place in which a fair trial of the dispute might not be possible. Nor would I readily
assume that Lord Scarman would not have pointed out that, even accepting Lord
j Diplock's analysis of the contractual position, justice could nevertheless be done by
applying the doctrine of frustration. Of course, it is for the party who wishes to rely on
frustration to raise it, but the argument in the House of Lords took five days and if there
is any merit in the point it seems astonishing to me that it should have apparently been
overlooked by all concerned with the argument.

But I must, I suppose, rid myself of these doubts and turn to consider the argument

that has been so persuasively presented by counsel for the sellers. The first step in his
argument is that the doctrine of frustration applies to an arbitration agreement; for this   *a*
he has the authority of *Bremer Vulkan*. Then he says that the central purpose of the
arbitration is to provide for a fair trial of the dispute, that is a trial that takes place before
such delay has occurred that would justify striking out the claim on *Allen v McAlpine*
principles. Once such delay has occurred, says counsel for the sellers, the passage of time
has destroyed the subject matter of the contract, namely a fair trial, and the contract is
frustrated by operation of law. To hold an arbitration 12 years after the event would, he   *b*
says, be something radically different from that which the parties contracted to do,
namely to submit to an arbitration in which there could be a fair trial of the issue. He
cited in support of his submission the well-known passage from Lord Radcliffe's speech
in *Davis Contractors Ltd v Fareham UDC* [(1965)] 2 All ER 145 at 160, [1965] AC 696 at
729.
    The doctrine of frustration has been developed as a judicial device to relieve a   *c*
contracting party in certain limited circumstances where it would be harsh to hold him
to the apparent terms of the contract. It applies when circumstances have so radically
altered from the state of things when the contract was made that the court can say that
the parties cannot have intended their contractual obligations to apply in such altered
circumstances.
    In all the cases to which the doctrine has been applied it is possible to point to some   *d*
supervening event which has had a catastrophic effect on the contract and has occurred
without the fault of the parties; examples are to be found conveniently collected in *Chitty
on Contracts* (24th edn, 1977) paras 1412–1413; they include the outbreak of war, the
cancellation of an expected event, the destruction of the object that was the subject
matter of the contract, seizure of a ship by a foreign government, an explosion and so
forth. Reference is also made to extraordinary delay sufficiently long to frustrate the   *e*
commercial adventure of the parties. But in every case the delay has been due to some
unexpected external cause beyond the control of the parties. No case has been cited, and
I know of none, in which delay arising solely because the parties have failed to carry out
their contractual obligations has been held to have put an end to the contract by the
application of the doctrine of frustration. It is, of course, important to distinguish
between 'frustrating delay', in which the delay of a contracting party in carrying out his   *f*
obligations under a contract is so grave as to enable the other party to rescind, from the
doctrine of frustration: see the judgment of Devlin J in *Universal Cargo Carriers Corp
v Citati* [1957] 2 All ER 70, [1957] 2 QB 401. There can in this case be no finding of
frustrating delay on the part of the buyers as is made clear by the following passage in
Lord Diplock's speech ([1981] 1 All ER 289 at 302, [1981] AC 909 at 987):

> 'For failure to apply for such directions before so much time had elapsed that   *g*
> there was a risk that a fair trial of the dispute would not be possible, both claimant
> and respondent were in my view in breach of their contractual obligations to one
> another; and neither can rely on the other's breach as giving him a right to treat the
> primary obligations of each to continue with the reference as brought to an end.'

    Throughout all the cases on frustration it is constantly asserted by the judges that it   *h*
can only be invoked when it occurs without default of the parties. To cite but a few
examples, in *Bank Line Ltd v Arthur Capel & Co* [1919] AC 435 at 452 Lord Sumner said:

> 'I think it is now well settled that the principle of frustration of an adventure
> assumes that the frustration arises without blame or fault on either side.'

In *Denny, Mott & Dickson Ltd v James B Fraser & Co Ltd* [1944] 1 All ER 678 at 681, [1944]   *j*
AC 265 at 272 Lord Macmillan adopted the following statement from *Bell's Principles of
the Law of Scotland* (10th edn, 1899) s 29:

> 'When by nature of the contract its performance depends on the existence of a
> particular thing or state of things, the failure or destruction of that thing or state of
> things, without default on either side, liberates both parties.'

a In *Davis Contractors Ltd v Fareham UDC* [1956] 2 All ER 145 at 160, [1956] AC 696 at 729
     Lord Radcliffe said:

> '. . . frustration occurs whenever the law recognises that, without default of either
> party, a contractual obligation has become incapable of being performed because
> the circumstances in which performance is called for would render it a thing
> radically different from that which was undertaken by the contract.'

b In *Denmark Productions Ltd v Boscobel Productions Ltd* [1968] 3 All ER 513 at 523, [1969] 1
     QB 699 at 725 Salmon LJ said:

> 'This [frustration] was a doctrine evolved by the courts to meet the case in which
> a contract became impossible of performance through some supervening event, not
> reasonably foreseeable when the contract was made and for which neither
> contracting party was in any way responsible.'

c

And Harman LJ said ([1968] 3 All ER 513 at 533, [1969] 1 QB 699 at 736):

> 'The frustrating event is something altogether outside the control of the parties—
> a war, a famine, a flood or some event of that sort—so that if the parties had thought
> to provide for it they would at once have agreed that on its happening the contract
> must come to an end. I have never heard the doctrine applied to an event such as
> this which depends on the action of one of the parties in connection with their
> contractual duty of the other of them to a third party.'

d

     This last case best illustrates what is meant by default in the context of frustration. The
essence of frustration is that it is caused by some unforeseen supervening event over
which the parties to the contract have no control, and for which they are therefore not
e responsible. To say that the supervening event occurs without the default or blame or
responsibility of the parties is in the context of the doctrine of frustration but another
way of saying it is a supervening event over which they had no control. The doctrine has
no application and cannot be invoked by a contracting party when the frustrating event
was at all times within his control; still less can it apply in a situation in which the parties
owed a contractual duty to one another to prevent the frustrating event occurring.
f   In the present case both parties are responsible for the delay. The sellers, if they wished,
could at any time have taken steps to have brought the delay to an end. It is
understandable that they elected not to do so; no doubt they hoped that the buyers would
abandon the arbitration. But this does not alter the fact that they had control over the
situation if they chose to exercise it. In *Maritime National Fish Ltd v Ocean Trawlers Ltd*
[1935] AC 524 at 530, [1935] All ER Rep 86 at 89 Lord Wright said: 'The essence of
g "frustration" is that it should not be due to the act or election of the party.' In a later
passage in his speech Lord Wright accepted frustration as being a matter caused by
something for which neither party was responsible. In the present case the sellers or their
solicitors, with whom for this purpose the sellers are identified, elected to let the
arbitration proceed at a snail's pace and are at least in part responsible for the delay that
has occurred. In these circumstances, I find it quite impossible to say that the doctrine of
h frustration can be applied to stop this arbitration, and I respectfully agree with the
judgment of Fox LJ to the like effect in *André & Cie SA v Marine Transocean Ltd, The
Splendid Sun* [1981] 2 All ER 993, [1981] 1 QB 694.
     Generally, when there has been inordinate delay in the performance of a contract, the
party who has been prejudiced by the delay will be able either to rely on frustrating delay
by showing that the delay is due to breach by the other contracting party entitling him
j to repudiate the contract or to rely on abandonment. It so happens that because of the
nature of the contractual obligations which the House of Lords have said are undertaken
by the parties to an arbitration agreement and because the facts of this case do not support
abandonment that neither remedy is available to the sellers. This is a misfortune for
them, but it would do a disservice to the orderly development of precedent on which the
common law is founded to apply the doctrine of frustration to a situation which the
overwhelming weight of authority shows it was never intended to cover. The effect of

Lord Diplock's speech in *Bremer Vulkan* is to decide that in arbitrations, unlike actions at law, the parties are not entitled to sit back and do nothing and then complain that delay *a* prevents them from having a fair hearing; and it is not permissible to stand that decision on its head by employing the doctrine of frustration.

I comfort myself, however, with the reflection that the buyers may have an uncommonly hard task to persuade any arbitrator that they have discharged the burden of proving an oral representation said to have been made over 12 years ago, and wholly inconsistent with the express terms of a written contract. All is not lost; justice may yet *b* be done.

I agree with Staughton J that for the reasons he gave the sellers are not able to establish either a repudiatory breach or abandonment and, as, apart from frustration, the sellers have not sought to uphold his decision on any other ground, I would for my part allow this appeal.

c

KERR LJ. In agreement with Lord Denning MR and Griffiths LJ I have no doubt that 'a fair trial' of the issues in this case is no longer possible in the light of the history which has already been stated. I use the term 'a fair trial' in the same sense as it would be used by a businessman knowing the allegations which would have to be determined by the tribunal in this case, and in the sense in which the expression 'fair trial' has constantly been used in cases where inordinate and inexcusable delay has raised the question *d* whether actions in the courts should be struck out for want of prosecution. This was also the sense in which Lord Diplock approached the question of a fair trial in *Bremer Vulkan Schiffbau Und Maschinenfabrik v South India Shipping Corp* [1981] 1 All ER 289 at 301–302, [1981] AC 909 at 986–987: 'a substantial risk that justice cannot be done', 'a risk that a fair trial of the dispute would not be possible'. I accordingly reject the submission of counsel for the buyers that this fundamental concept can be limited to what he says is *e* still possible, viz a fair hearing in accordance with the rules of natural justice and those of the laws of procedure and evidence. A fair trial clearly includes these, but it is not limited to the hearing itself. We are here concerned with a dispute about what various people are alleged to have said, and if so in what capacity, about $12\frac{1}{2}$ years ago in relation to what was for them a routine transaction. These issues are not covered by any contemporary records, and the availability of some of the witnesses at this time is itself *f* in doubt. In my view no one could reasonably consider that a dispute of this kind could still be determined fairly in these circumstances after the lapse of so much time.

On the arguments addressed to us it is in my view unnecessary to consider what would have been the position if the present issue had arisen within the six-year limitation period, or if in some other hypothetical cases all the material witnesses had been killed in an air crash, or all the relevant documents destroyed in a fire, soon after the reference to *g* arbitration. None of these or similar facts have arisen in the unfortunately numerous stale and long-dormant arbitrations which are known to exist and of which the present case is but one example. The very serious problems for the 'credibility' of our arbitral processes which are raised by this and similar cases should in my view not be determined by reference to arguments which are remote from such cases, or even fanciful.

It follows that the stark issue which faces the court is whether parties to an arbitration *h* agreement are to be held to their agreement to arbitrate in such circumstances, whereas an action based on the same dispute would in the same circumstances unhesitatingly be struck out. Unless rigorously compelled by binding authority, I cannot accept that such an extraordinary dichotomy must follow as a matter of law, when our systems of litigation and arbitration are both basically adversarial in their nature, and when both are obviously directed to the common end of doing justice. It hardly needs emphasising that *j* a fundamental characteristic of our common law system has always been the development of legal doctrine with the flexibility of pragmatic common sense, but the acceptance of this dichotomy would to my mind be wholly out of line with this tradition. In the present connection it should also be borne in mind that the recent legislative reforms to improve our laws of arbitration by means of the Arbitration Act 1979 do not touch the

resolution of this dichotomy, if it is one which is really inherent in our law. Had s 5 of
that Act been in force throughout the history of this case, it would have done nothing to
prevent the present situation, since it only comes into operation once an arbitral tribunal
has made an order and since it (rightly) does not compel the tribunal to make any order
in the absence of any application by any of the parties.

The reality, I feel bound to say, is that until the decision by a majority of the House of
Lords in *Bremer Vulkan*, in January 1981, I do not think that it would have occurred to
any practitioner, arbitrator or businessman familiar with arbitrations that our law is
powerless in situations such as the present. I think that I can also properly say that from
my own knowledge this decision has been received with the greatest concern, not only
in the City and the Temple, but also abroad among practitioners and institutions who
look to this country as an important venue for international commercial arbitrations. It
is not surprising, as we were told by counsel, that it has already resulted in attempts to
take advantage of references to arbitration which were thought to be long defunct by
seeking to make capital out of their revival. It is also not surprising that the new Hong
Kong Arbitration Ordinance which has been introduced into the Legislative Council as
the result of proposals by the Hong Kong Law Reform Commission, and which will (I
understand) be shortly enacted, includes a provision which neutralises this decision by
empowering the court to order the termination of arbitrations, and prohibit further
proceedings, where there has been undue delay by a claimant in instituting or prosecuting
his claim, if the court is satisfied that the delay will give rise to a substantial risk that it is
not possible to have a fair trial of the issues.

In my view, however, a close analysis of *Bremer Vulkan* on the basis of our doctrine of
stare decisis does not compel the conclusion that, given that the essence of arbitration
agreements is the parties' intention to resolve their disputes fairly, our law insists on
enforcing such agreements when it is no longer possible to give effect to the parties'
intention. To do so would be a contradiction in terms of justice and common sense
which the decision does not in my view compel. The conclusion which I have reached is
that this arbitration agreement is frustrated by the passage of time and by the
impossibility which has now in fact supervened of resolving this dispute fairly. In the
classic phrase of Lord Radcliffe in *Davis Contractors Ltd v Fareham UDC* [1956] 2 All ER
145 at 160, [1956] AC 696 at 728, it is 'the anthropomorphic conception of justice', in
the figure of the fair and reasonable man, which itself in my view compels this
conclusion, whether on the basis that the subject matter of the arbitration agreement, a
fair trial, has disappeared, or that an arbitration of this dispute after this passage of time
would be something radically different from what was in the contemplation of the
parties when they each appointed an arbitrator for this purpose in 1972. I will return to
this issue in the context of the principles of the doctrine of frustration, but I must first
deal with the ratio of *Bremer Vulkan*.

What is said on behalf of the buyers is that the majority decision in that case precludes
the foregoing conclusion in limine for two reasons. First, because the possibility of the
frustration of an arbitration agreement by inordinate and inexcusable delay on the part
of the parties, or, more accurately, their legal advisers, and in this case overwhelmingly
so on the side of the buyers, is inconsistent with that decision. Second, because, and also
as the result of that decision, the sellers' solicitors' failure to put an end to the ordinate
delays on the part of the buyers' solicitors disentitles the sellers from invoking the
doctrine of frustration in any event on the ground that it would have been 'self-induced'.
However, in my view neither of these arguments stands in the way of the resolution of
the present and similar cases on the basis of what justice and common sense appear to me
to require.

The ratio and scope of the decision in *Bremer Vulkan* have already been considered by
this court in *André & Cie SA v Marine Transocean Ltd, The Splendid Sun* [1981] 2 All ER
993, [1981] QB 694, which revealed a clear difference of opinion between Lord Denning
MR and Fox LJ on which Eveleigh LJ expressed no view. Staughton J said that in the
present case it was unavoidable to choose between this difference of view and concluded

in the upshot, to put it shortly, that *Bremer Vulkan* precluded a respondent to an
arbitration from relying on delay by the claimant as a breach capable of being treated as   *a*
a repudiation of the arbitration agreement, but that it did not preclude him from relying
on the doctrine of frustration in such circumstances. I respectfully agree; thus, the
possibility of an arbitration agreement being frustrated was expressly recognised by Lord
Diplock (see [1981] 1 All ER 289 at 297–298, [1981] AC 909 at 980–981). However, I
cannot avoid express my own views about the ratio and limits of that decision for present
purposes.   *b*

The main issue decided in *Bremer Vulkan*, which requires no elaboration here, is that
there is no inherent jurisdiction, either in the arbitral tribunal or in the courts, to put an
end to an arbitration by, in effect, striking out the claimaint's claim and dismissing it for
want of prosecution with reasonable dispatch. So far as the powers of the arbitral tribunal
are concerned, this had already been decided by Bridge J in *Crawford v A E A Prowting
Ltd* [1972] 1 All ER 1199, [1973] 1 QB 1. The second issue, which was the only other   *c*
submission advanced by the respondents in that case and the only other issue which was
decided, was that the nature of an arbitration agreement, and the obligations of the
parties and the functions of the tribunal thereunder, preclude either party from relying
on inordinate delay by the other party as a ground for treating the agreement as
terminated by its repudiation. In reaching this conclusion the speech of Lord Diplock
analysed, and in turn rejected, a number of suggested implied terms on a breach whereof   *d*
repudiation could have been grounded. Precisely this, and in my view no more, was the
ratio of the decision on this second aspect, and everything said by Lord Diplock was
directed to this submission and to no wider issue. This must be borne in mind when one
considers to what extent his remarks give rise to binding authority in the present context.
Thus, I respectfully agree with the analysis of this aspect of the decision in *Bremer Vulkan*
by Eveleigh LJ in *The Splendid Sun* [1981] 2 All ER 993 at 1002, [1981] QB 694 at 709,   *e*
when he said:

   '... whatever obligation might be implied, for example to co-operate with the
   other party, there was no obligation fundamental to the arbitration agreement
   which had been broken.'

A *mutual obligation of co-operation* between both parties is in my view the only positive   *f*
obligation which the speech of Lord Diplock intended to lay down. The ratio of the
decision on this aspect, given the existence of this mutual obligation, was accordingly
that there was no implied unilateral obligation on the part of the claimaints to proceed
with reasonable dispatch, or any similar obligation on the breach whereof the respondents
could treat the claimants as being in repudiation of the arbitration agreement. This is
clearly expressed in the following passage ([1981] 1 All ER 289 at 301, [1981] AC 909 at   *g*
986):

   '... but, if what is done voluntarily by way of preparation is done so tardily that
   it threatens to delay the hearing to a date when there will be a substantial risk that
   justice cannot be done, it is in my view a necessary implication from their having
   agreed that the arbitrator shall resolve their dispute that both parties, respondent as
   well as claimant, *are under a mutual obligation to one another to join in applying to the*   *h*
   arbitrator for appropriate directions to put an end to the delay. Even if an application
   to the arbitrator for directions in such circumstances were a matter of right only
   and not, as I think it is, *a mutual obligation*, it provides a remedy to the party who
   thinks that the proceedings are not progressing fast enough voluntarily, which
   renders unnecessary the implication in the arbitration agreement of any such term
   as was suggested by Donaldson J or Roskill LJ.' (My emphasis.)   *j*

This, I think, is a key passage and there is also an express reference to co-operation (see
[1981] 1 All ER 289 at 299, [1981] AC 909 at 983). The buyers relied in particular on the
following further passage at the end of the judgment ([1981] 1 All ER 289 at 302, [1981]
AC 909 at 987–988):

a
'For failure to apply for such directions before so much time had elapsed that there was a risk that a fair trial of the dispute would not be possible, both claimant and respondent were in my view in breach of their contractual obligations to one another; and neither can rely on the other's breach as giving him a right to treat the primary obligations of each to continue with the reference as brought to an end. Respondents in private arbitrations are not entitled to let sleeping dogs lie and then complain that they did not bark.'

b
However, in the context of the issues, this can only have been intended to negate the possibility of unilateral repudiation by the claimants; it cannot have been intended to detract from the mutual nature of the obligations stated in the passages referred to above.

It follows in my view that all that was decided in *Bremer Vulkan*, and solely in the context of negativing the possibility of unilateral repudiation by the claimants, was that

c
both parties to an arbitration to which no other rules apply are under a duty of mutual co-operation with each other. However, co-operation still requires an initiative from one party or the other, such as by suggesting, or unilaterally initiating, an application to the tribunal. One side or the other must lift the telephone or write a letter. Co-operation must be called for before it can be given, or before it can be seen not to be forthcoming. Without some initiative by one side or the other, co-operation cannot be a duty which

d
simply exists in the air. The question must therefore always be: whose duty is it at any time to take the initiative and thereby to bring the duty to co-operate into play?

I think it is clear that the question where the duty to take the initiative lies at any particular time must depend on the issues in the arbitration and on the state of the proceedings. It must depend on the circumstances as they exist from time to time. Generally speaking, however, in an arbitration without a counterclaim, which is not

e
governed by any procedural rules to the contrary, and when the respondents are not in mora as regards pleadings, discovery or anything else, the duty to take and maintain the initiative must naturally lie on the side of the claimants. In such cases the respondents will only be in breach of their duty of co-operation if they fail to respond to an initiative by the claimants. They *may* of course at any time themselves take the initiative by calling on the claimants to take some step which it is then incumbent on the claimants to take

f
or they *may* apply to the tribunal for an appropriate order, in either of which cases the claimants will be bound to co-operate. But in my judgment the respondents are in such cases under no positive obligation, either to the claimants or to the tribunal, to assume the initiative. I therefore respectfully do not accept that Lord Diplock's speech is to be interpreted as going so far as to decide the contrary. Had it done so, however, the decision would in my view have been obiter, since the only issue was as to the existence of some

g
unilateral obligation on the claimants which could ground repudiation in favour of the respondents, and nothing more.

If this analysis is correct, then I respectfully decline to accept the buyers' argument that Lord Diplock's speech in *Bremer Vulkan* compels either of two conclusions, which would, as I see it, fly in the face of the realities and good sense and of our adversarial procedures, and which I cannot accept were intended to be laid down by Lord Diplock as

h
a matter of law. Both of these would greatly damage English arbitration if they were the law. I can illustrate both of them by reference to the facts of this case.

First, I do not accept that, when the buyers' solicitors and their chosen expert were as dilatory as they clearly were over long periods in this case, the sellers were in breach of the arbitration agreement towards the buyers, or failing in their duty to the tribunal, by not applying to the arbitrators for directions, or, more accurately, by not initiating the

j
appointment of the full contractual tribunal for this purpose. The duty of the sellers' solicitors was to handle the arbitration in accordance with their clients' legitimate interests, and, if these involved leaving it to the buyers to pursue their claim or not to pursue it, then neither the sellers nor their solicitors were in any manner in breach of contract or of professional duty in leaving the initiative to their respective opponents. Many arbitrations, as indeed many actions, are not pursued, or are not pursued

energetically, for the simple reason that the claimants or plaintiffs come to appreciate the difficulties of going on, and many become dormant and are ultimately in effect allowed to die, with only a faint hope that the continuing formal existence of the proceedings may have a nuisance value which may one day lead to a formal burial without too much loss of face. It seems to me that on the history of this case this may well have been the impression on the side of the sellers, and indeed this was clearly so when nothing whatever happened after the buyers' solicitors' letter of 25 September 1974 for nearly three years, and the files were closed and even counsel's fees were paid, until 8 July 1977 when the matter was suddenly revived with the possibility of amending the points of claim 'at some stage in the future'. I cannot believe that the sellers or their solicitors were under any duty to anyone to take any initiative in such circumstances. To do so might only stir up a dormant and apparently dead hornets' nest in a way which would be bound to cause expense and strife, and which quite possibly would not even be desired by the buyers themselves. It would certainly have been contrary to the interests of the sellers to do so, and it would in practice place the solicitors for respondents (whether to a claim or counterclaim) in an impossible position vis-à-vis their clients if they were under some professional duty to act contrary to their clients' natural and legitimate wishes. In my view Lord Diplock's speech cannot properly be interpreted as laying down that there was any contractual obligation on the sellers, nor any professional duty on their solicitors, which obliged them to take any initiative in the present case. The initiative lay on the side of the buyers; but, since they did nothing, the sellers' obligation to co-operate did not come into play.

The second argument on behalf of the buyers which I cannot accept is that Lord Diplock intended to lay down any rule that it is the duty of the tribunal on its own initiative to coerce the parties into any action, timetable or expense which runs counter to the parties' then common wishes concerning the conduct of the arbitration or which runs counter to what the tribunal is reasonably entitled to conclude represents the common wishes of the parties at any time. As I understood the buyers' argument, they contended that there was some such duty in order to suggest that, apart from initiatives by the parties themselves, arbitration agreements are by law subject to some regime in the nature of a perpetuum mobile, so that they are immune to death because they are subject to a continuous obligation of artificial respiration, or even forced feeding, by the tribunal when the parties are inactive. It was suggested that this was the crucial difference between a purely consensual resolution of disputes by arbitration and the subjection of litigants in the courts to non-consensual rules which have the force of law. However, in my view an arbitral tribunal is under no duty to take any initiative when inactivity represents the apparent common wishes of the parties. Thus, it is no part of the duty of the tribunal to go against the joint wishes of the parties, who may wish to consider the negotiation of a settlement in their own way and at their own pace. The duty of the tribunal is certainly no higher than to keep in touch with the parties' legal advisers to ensure that the parties' common wishes concerning the progress of the arbitration at any time are duly met. The extent to which the tribunal may take the initiative for this purpose will vary according to the circumstances, and is clearly likely to be greater in arbitrations submitted to a jointly and fully constituted tribunal ad hoc than in run-of-the-mill Baltic arbitrations such as the present, where each party and their legal advisers generally nominate their arbitrator in the knowledge that both arbitrators may at any time literally have hundreds of nominations on their books, and to be quite unable to monitor the progress or lack of progress in all these arbitrations on their own initiative.

All this is clearly recognised in the speech of Lord Diplock. Although he said (see [1981] 1 All ER 289 at 301, [1981] AC 909 at 985) that 'the parties make the arbitrator the master of the procedure to be followed in the arbitration', he also said ([1981] 1 All ER 289 at 300, [1981] AC 909 at 984):

'In requiring particular steps to be taken by any party he is entitled to act not only on the application of a party to the arbitration but also on his own initiative; but he a is not under any duty to do the latter, for in the absence of any application he is justified in assuming that *both* parties are satisfied with the way in which the proceedings leading up to his making an award are progressing.' (Lord Diplock's emphasis.)

b I can now leave the majority decision in *Bremer Vulkan* except to point out that its ratio on this aspect involved the conclusion that an arbitration agreement is subject to the ordinary incidents of the law of contract, including the application of the doctrine of frustration where this is appropriate. The application of this doctrine would clearly be appropriate where the intended arbitration becomes simply impossible, such as in cases of a reference to a particular arbitrator, without power of substitution by any means, who dies or otherwise becomes incapable of acting, and indeed also if the named arbitrator 'turns out not to be impartial' (see [1981] 1 All ER 289 at 298, [1981] AC 909 at 981). It would also apply if the arbitration agreement becomes illegal. The question in c the present case, however, is whether an arbitration agreement can also be frustrated by so much delay that a fair trial, in the sense in which I have explained this, is no longer possible. In this connection I do not accept the sellers' submission that Lord Diplock must have had this possibility in mind when he referred to frustration; but nor do I accept the buyers' contention that his speech excludes this possibility. In my view, this was a problem which was left untouched by *Bremer Vulkan*.

d I have already expressed my conclusion on this issue in relation to the present and similar cases. I recognise that frustration by delay in relation to arbitration agreements is 'novel', but so is the problem itself, in the sense that it appears only to have arisen recently, albeit in relation to cases of relative antiquity. However, sudden spurts in novel forensic situations are no novelty in themselves; a single surfacing in the courts of an underlying problem which has not attracted attention before will often produce a spate e of cases. The now classic definition of the doctrine of frustration is to be found in the speech of Lord Radcliffe in *Davis Contractors Ltd v Fareham UDC* [1956] 2 All ER 145 at 160, [1956] AC 696 at 729, to which I have already referred. Without taking up space to set out the whole of this well-known passage, its essence is that frustration occurs when—

f 'without default of either party a contractual obligation has become incapable of being performed because the circumstances in which performance is called for would render it a thing radically different from that which was undertaken by the contract.'

Subject to the words 'without default of either party', to which I return in a moment, I think that this definition of the doctrine applies to the reference of a dispute to arbitration once the fair resolution of the dispute is no longer possible. The essence of such a g reference is 'a fair trial', and the impossibility of having a fair trial renders the performance of the agreement radically different from what was undertaken by the agreement. Similarly, though this was not the issue in *Davis Contractors Ltd v Fareham UDC*, one can say that a fair trial is the subject matter of an agreement to refer a dispute to arbitration, and when this is no longer possible the subject matter of the agreement has gone.

However, the buyers in the present case contest this on two grounds, quite apart from h the effect of the decision in *Bremer Vulkan* with which I have already dealt.

First, they say that delay has never by itself been held to be a ground of frustration, but that the frustration has in all such cases been the event which has caused the delay. In my view this is simply wrong: there are many classic cases where the doctrine of frustration has been successfully invoked because, without default by the party which invokes the doctrine, the passage of time has brought about a radical change in the nature j of the contractual obligation. Several were mentioned by Lord Radcliffe before he stated his definition, and references to the main ones can be found in *Chitty on Contracts* (24th edn, 1977), para 1413, note 69. In all such cases the ground of frustration was in fact the passage of time and not the event, as such, which caused the delay. To say that 'justice delayed is justice denied' has almost become a cliché, but it demonstrates that an agreement, which by its nature is designed to resolve disputes fairly, can by its nature also be overtaken by the passage of so much time that the agreement ceases to be fairly applicable to a particular dispute. For the reasons already explained, this has in my view happened in the present case.

The real issue raised by this submission, however, is whether the sellers are precluded from relying on the passage of time as a ground of frustration because this did not occur without default on their part, a situation which is commonly expressed by the question whether or not the frustration was 'self-induced'. This, as I see it, is the crucial issue. I think that it can be stated quite simply by asking: was it any way the fault of the sellers that a fair determination of this dispute is now no longer possible? If not, then default by the buyers which causes frustrating delay cannot preclude the sellers from relying on the doctrine of frustration if the doctrine otherwise applies. The word 'either' in the words 'without default of either party' does not in my view compel the contrary conclusion as a matter of binding authority. Authority merely requires that the frustrating event must not be due to the default of the party which seeks to invoke the doctrine.

To my mind the answer to the foregoing question is obviously: no, it was the fault of the buyers, or at any rate fault on the side of the buyers. The cause of the delay was not fault on the side of the sellers, because the duty to take and to maintain the initiative in getting on with the arbitration lay throughout on the side of the buyers. The sellers' duty by virtue of *Bremer Vulkan* to co-operate with the buyers never came into play, and was never broken, so as to make the sellers in any way responsible for the delay. True, it lay within the sellers' power to put an end to the delay, or, more accurately, to attempt to do so, by themselves taking some initiative. They could have tried to procure the appointment of a third arbitrator by the Baltic and International Maritime Conference in Copenhagen, and they could then have applied to the tribunal for orders against the buyers; or they could in the first instance have threatened to do so unless the buyers got on with their claim. But there was no obligation or duty on the sellers to take any such initiative. On the contrary, in the circumstances of this case it was natural and understandable that they did not do so. They had no sensible reason for doing anything other than to wait and see. We were referred to all the classic authorities on self-induced frustration such as *Maritime National Fish Ltd v Ocean Trawlers Ltd* [1935] AC 524, [1935] All ER Rep 86 and *Joseph Constantine Steamship Line Ltd v Imperial Smelting Corp Ltd* [1941] 2 All ER 165, [1942] AC 154, but none of them goes anywhere near suggesting that inaction is to be equated with fault or default when there is no obligation or duty to act. On the contrary, while avoiding any precise definition, they suggest that self-induced frustration requires some deliberate or positive act which renders the performance of the contract impossible, or impossible in the way in which performance had been intended. There was no such act, nor any default, on the side of the sellers here.

For these reasons I agree with the conclusion of Staughton J and I would dismiss this appeal. I also agree with him about the only other two issues on which the sellers relied before us, viz that there was no abandonment of the arbitration by the buyers, let alone by mutual consent, and that the sellers cannot rely on repudiation by the buyers, however dressed up, because this is barred by the decision in *Bremer Vulkan*.

Appeal dismissed. Leave to appeal to the House of Lords granted.

Solicitors: *Holman, Fenwick & Willan* (for the buyers); *Sinclair, Roche & Temperley* (for the sellers).

Frances Rustin   Barrister.

a
Hytrac Conveyors Ltd v Conveyors International Ltd and others

COURT OF APPEAL, CIVIL DIVISION
LAWTON, TEMPLEMAN AND FOX LJJ
26 JULY 1982

b

Action – Dismissal – Failure to deliver statement of claim – Plaintiff seeking interlocutory relief – Plaintiff bringing action for alleged breach of copyright and breach of confidence – Plaintiff failing to deliver statement of claim within time specified in rules – Plaintiff applying for Anton Piller order and interlocutory injunction pending trial – Defendants seeking to have action dismissed because no statement of claim had been served – Whether action should be dismissed – RSC Ord
c *19, r 1.*

On 30 April 1982 the plaintiff company issued a writ against the first defendant company and various of their shareholders claiming injunctions restraining them from infringing the plaintiffs' industrial copyrights. The personal defendants had all been or were employees of the plaintiffs and it was alleged that they had acted in breach of either an express or an implied covenant to act faithfully in the course of their employments. On
d the same day the plaintiffs executed an Anton Piller order restraining the first defendants from, inter alia, destroying certain articles, documents or goods, ordering their delivery up and granting the plaintiffs permission to search the first defendant's premises for them. On 6 May a group of the defendants obtained the discharge of part of that order and some of the documents were returned to them. On 11 May a number of the
e defendants gave notice of intention to defend the proceedings. Instead of delivering a statement of claim within the period of 14 days laid down by RSC Ord 18, r 1[a] the plaintiffs applied to the High Court for interlocutory injunctions pending trial. There followed an exchange of affidavits on a very large scale and allegations of conspiracy were introduced. On 20 July as a result of pressure on the plaintiffs by the defendants, some of whom were in ignorance of what was being alleged against them, the plaintiffs applied for an extension of time in which to deliver a statement of claim. Meanwhile, the first
f seven defendants applied under Ord 19, r 1[b] for the action against them to be dismissed on the ground of inordinate delay, no statement of claim having been served on them. The judge granted their application and refused the plaintiffs leave to appeal. The plaintiffs applied ex parte to the Court of Appeal for leave to appeal against the order.

g **Held** – Since the nature of the common law procedure for civil litigation was not inquisitorial but accusatorial those who made charges had to state right at the beginning what those charges were and on what facts they were based. They could not use Anton Piller orders as a means of finding out what sort of charges could be made but had to deliver their statement of claim within the time specified in the rules, unless the court ordered otherwise. Moreover, in a case concerning copyright and breach of confidence,
h it was most important that the ambit of the plaintiff's claims was made known, and if a charge of conspiracy was to be raised it was wholly inappropriate to bring it in at a later stage if it could have been properly pleaded in the first instance. Furthermore, on a motion for an interlocutory injunction it was essential for the purpose of seeing whether the interlocutory injunction should be granted for the court to know the nature of the

j   a   Rule 1 is set out at p 417 d e, post
    b   Rule 1 provides: 'Where the plaintiff is required by these Rules to serve a statement of claim on a defendant and he fails to serve it on him, the defendant may, after the expiration of the period fixed by or under these Rules for service of the statement of claim, apply to the Court for an order to dismiss the action, and the Court may by order dismiss the action or make such other order on such terms as it thinks just.'

allegations which the plaintiff was making, for until at least a statement of claim had been delivered the court could seldom know what the matters in question in the action were. It was not right, therefore, for the plaintiffs to commence their action without knowing what form their statement of claim would take until after the interlocutory proceedings were completed and their application for leave to appeal against the striking out of their action would accordingly be refused (see p 417 *f* to *j* and p 418 *b* to *e*, post).

Dictum of Lawton LJ in *RHM Foods Ltd v Bovril Ltd* [1982] 1 All ER at 677 followed.

Notes

For judgment in default of service of statement of claim, see 37 Halsbury's Laws (4th edn) para 404, and for cases on the subject, see 50 Digest (Repl) 140–142, *1230–1238*.

For Anton Piller orders, see 37 Halsbury's Laws (4th edn) para 372.

Case referred to in judgment

RHM Foods Ltd v Bovril Ltd [1982] 1 All ER 673, [1982] 1 WLR 661, CA.

Application for leave to appeal

By a writ issued on 30 April 1982 the plaintiffs, Hytrac Conveyors Ltd, sought as against the defendants, Conveyors International Ltd, Eric Leslie Wright, Dennis Raymond Griggs, N F Bradshaw, Carl Unwin, Peter Hopwood, F M Nicholson (Materials) Handling Ltd, Rodney Edward Lloyd, Graham Watts, John Patrick Bates and Ian Catto, an injunction restraining them from infringing the plaintiffs' industrial copyright in certain drawings, converting to their own use any infringing copies or plates used for making such copies, using or disclosing any confidential information the property of the plaintiffs, and procuring or attempting to procure directors, servants or agents of the plaintiffs to act in breach of their respective contracts with the plaintiffs, delivery up or destruction on oath of all infringing copies, plates, documents containing confidential information the property of the plaintiffs and documents and articles the property of the plaintiffs, and an inquiry as to damages or, at the plaintiffs' option, an account of profits. As against the second, third, fourth, fifth, sixth and eleventh defendants the plaintiffs sought a declaration that they held their shares in the first defendant company on trust for the benefit of the plaintiffs, an order that they assign their shares in the first defendant company to the plaintiffs and an inquiry as to damages suffered by the plaintiffs by reason of those defendants' breach of their fiduciary duties or, alternatively, an account of profits. As against the eighth, ninth and tenth defendants, the plaintiffs sought an inquiry as to damages suffered by the plaintiffs by reason of the defendants' breach of their respective contract of employment. Against all defendants the plaintiffs claimed further and other relief and costs. On 22 July 1982 the first seven defendants applied to the court under RSC Ord 19, r 1 for an order to dismiss the action against those defendants, no statement of claim having been served on them. Whitford J granted their application and refused the plaintiffs leave to appeal. The plaintiffs applied ex parte to the Court of Appeal for leave to appeal against the judge's order. The facts are set out in the judgment of Lawton LJ.

Alastair J D Wilson for the plaintiffs.
John Fitzgerald for the first, second and third defendants.
W B Spalding for the fourth, fifth, sixth and seventh defendants.
Nicolas Bragge for the eighth, ninth and tenth defendants.
The eleventh defendant did not appear.

LAWTON LJ. This is an application made ex parte but with notice to the first, second, third, fourth, fifth, sixth and seventh defendants, on behalf of Hytrac Conveyors Ltd as plaintiffs, for leave to appeal against an order made by Whitford J on 22 July 1982 whereby he dismissed the plaintiffs' action against those defendants and ordered them to pay the costs on a common fund basis and also ordered an inquiry as to damages on the plaintiffs' undertakings.

This application raises a point of principle on which it is desirable to make some
a comments. The plaintiffs allege that the first defendants, who are a limited liability
company, and various of their shareholders, have infringed the plaintiffs' industrial
copyright. The personal defendants have all been, or still are, employees of the plaintiffs
and it is alleged that they have acted in breach of either an express or an implied covenant
to act faithfully in the course of their employments. It may well be that there is a solid
foundation for those allegations. That will be decided in any trial which may take place
b hereafter. It is the course of events in this case which has caused this court some concern.

It has become a common practice nowadays when men leave an employment and set
up as business rivals to their old employers for those employers to allege that they have
acted in breach of an implied covenant of confidentiality and that they have either
infringed their former employers' industrial copyright or that they have taken away lists
of customers. When that belief is held the employers often apply to a judge for an Anton
c Piller order.

In this case the plaintiffs applied for an Anton Piller order on 29 April 1982 and it was
granted. On 30 April 1982 they issued their writ against the eleven defendants and
executed the order. On 6 May 1982 a group of the defendants, but not all, applied to
discharge the Anton Piller order. In part they were successful and a number of documents
were returned to them; some were retained by the plaintiffs. On 11 May a number of
d the defendants gave notice of intention to defend. As soon as that notice was given, RSC
Ord 18, r 1 came into operation and it is pertinent to remind practitioners of what the
rule says:

> 'Unless the Court gives leave to the contrary or a statement of claim is indorsed
> on the writ, the plaintiff must serve a statement of claim on the defendant or, if
> there are two or more defendants, on each defendant, and must do so either when
e > the writ is served on that defendant or at any time after service of the writ but
> before the expiration of 14 days after that defendant gives notice of intention to
> defend.'

It follows that, if that rule was to be complied with, the plaintiffs, if they found they
could not deliver a statement of claim within 14 days, that is before 25 May, should have
f applied to the court for an extension of time. What they did was to apply to the court for
interlocutory injunctions pending trial.

We have been told by counsel that there has grown up in the Chancery Division a
practice that, when an application is made for an interlocutory injunction, a statement of
claim is not served. It may be that an application for an interlocutory injunction is a good
reason why the court should give an extension of time, but it is not a good reason why
g the rules of court should be disregarded.

As a result of applications by the plaintiffs for interlocutory injunctions against the
defendants, there was an exchange of affidavits on a very large scale. We have been
informed that something like 1,000 pages of documents were exchanged. It was then
said by the plaintiffs, who had not delivered a statement of claim, that it was difficult for
them to do so because of the difficulty of going through the various affidavits making up
h this huge bundle of documents in order to find out what should be put in it. Indeed,
Whitford J, in the course of his judgment, referred to the fact that a statement had been
made to him by counsel (not Mr Wilson who has appeared before us today) that counsel
had advised that delivery of a statement of claim was premature. If the idea is getting
around that, as the result of service of a notice of motion asking for an interlocutory
injunction, no statement of claim should be delivered, then the sooner that idea is
j dissipated the better, because often it is essential for the purposes of seeing whether an
interlocutory injunction should be granted that the court should know what is the nature
of the allegations which the plaintiff is making. In *RHM Foods Ltd v Bovril Ltd* [1982] 1
All ER 673 at 677, [1982] 1 WLR 661 at 665, I pointed out that until at least a statement
of claim has been delivered the court can seldom know what are the matters in question
in the action.

In this case, as a result of the attempt to get an interlocutory injunction before the delivery of the statement of claim, weeks passed and by the middle of July still no statement of claim had been delivered. This was particularly unfortunate from the point of view of the fourth, fifth, sixth and seventh defendants, who said that they were on the fringes of the case and did not know what allegations were being made against them at all. As a result of pressure put on the plaintiffs by the defendants, the plaintiffs asked at long last for extension of time in which to deliver a statement of claim. By this time the first seven defendants had applied under Ord 19, r 1 for the action to be dismissed on the ground of inordinate delay. Whitford J granted that application.

In the note of the judgment which we have (it has not been verified by him but we have no reason to think that it is not accurate) he said:

> 'It is not right that the plaintiff should start this action without knowing what form his statement of claim will take until after the interlocutory proceedings are completed. It is very important in a case concerning copyright and breach of confidence that the exact ambit of the plaintiffs' claims be made known and if charges of conspiracy are to be raised it is wholly inappropriate that it be brought in at a later stage if it could properly be pleaded in the first instance.'

For my part, I agree with that approach. It has to be remembered by all concerned that we do not have in this country an inquisitorial procedure for civil litigation. Our procedure is accusatorial. Those who make charges must state right at the beginning what they are and what facts they are based on. They must not use Anton Piller orders as a means of finding out what sort of charges they can make. They must deliver their statement of claim within the time specified in the rules, unless the court orders otherwise.

I would refuse this application.

TEMPLEMAN LJ. I agree.

FOX LJ. I also agree.

Application for leave to appeal refused.

27 July. The court dismissed an application by the plaintiffs for leave to appeal to the House of Lords.

Solicitors: *Rooks, Rider & Co*, agents for *Stone & Simpson*, Leicester (for the plaintiffs); *Robbins, Olivey & Blake Lapthorn*, agents for *Ironsides*, Leicester (for the first, second and third defendants); *Wrigley, Claydon & Armstrongs*, Oldham (for the fourth, fifth, sixth and seventh defendants); *Harvey, Ingram*, Leicester (for the eighth, ninth and tenth defendants).

Mary Rose Plummer   Barrister.

a ## Inland Revenue Commissioners v Stype Investments (Jersey) Ltd
Re Clore (deceased)

b COURT OF APPEAL, CIVIL DIVISION
TEMPLEMAN, WATKINS AND FOX LJJ
29, 30, 31 MARCH, 1, 7 APRIL 1982

Capital transfer tax – Liability for tax – Persons liable as executor or trustee – Executor de son
tort – Intermeddling – Company selling land as bare nominee for beneficial owner – Company
resident in Jersey – Owner dying before completion of sale – Steps not taken to obtain grant of
c *representation – Company remitting purchase money to its own bank account in Jersey – Whether*
intermeddling – Whether acting as executor de son tort – Finance Act 1975, s 25(6)(a).

Executor and administrator – Administrator – Appointment in special circumstances – Will
naming executors resident abroad – No steps taken to obtain probate in England – Assets
transferred out of jurisdiction – Crown claiming executors liable for capital transfer tax – Official
d *Solicitor appointed administrator ad colligenda bona – Whether Official Solicitor properly*
appointed – Supreme Court of Judicature (Consolidation) Act 1925, s 162(1) proviso (b).

On 23 May 1979 C conveyed land in England to S Ltd, a company resident in Jersey. A
declaration of trust made on the same day between S Ltd and C recited that S Ltd was to
hold the land as a bare nominee for C and would at his request at any time convey it
e either to C personally or to any purchaser from him in the event of the land being sold.
S Ltd undertook to account to C for the net proceeds of sale of the land and the net rents
and profits until sale. S Ltd was entitled to pay out of such proceeds any outgoings or
charges in respect of the sale and to be indemnified against any liability which it incurred
as a result of entering into the contract at the request of C. On 25 May S Ltd, at the
request of C, agreed to sell the land to P Ltd, an English company, for £20·5m. C died
f on 26 July before completion of the sale had taken place. When the sale was completed
on 29 September no grant of representation had been obtained in respect of C's estate.
However, S Ltd arranged for the proceeds of sale of the land to be remitted to its bank
account in Jersey. By his will C had given all his free property to the trustees of his
personal settlement made by him in his lifetime on trust for certain specified foreign
foundations. The executors appointed under his will were foreign residents and were
g also directors of S Ltd and trustees of the personal settlement. C's son, who disputed the
will and opposed the grant of probate to C's executors in England and Jersey, had obtained
injunctions in Jersey restraining the executors and S Ltd from transferring C's money in
Jersey to England. The Crown claimed that the proceeds of sale were C's property situate
in England and that by transferring them to Jersey S Ltd had intermeddled with C's
property and had thus become liable as an executor de son tort within s 25(6)(a)[a] of the
h Finance Act 1975. On that basis, the Crown sought and was granted leave under RSC
Ord 11, r 1(1)[b] to issue and serve an originating summons against S Ltd in Jersey claiming
(i) delivery by S Ltd of an account for the purposes of capital transfer tax of all property
comprised in C's estate at his death and (ii) an injunction restraining S Ltd from removing
or dealing with its other assets within the jurisdiction of the court until the account had

j ---

a Section 25(6), so far as material provides: 'For the purposes of this section [which specifies the
persons liable for capital transfer tax]—(a) any person who takes possession of or intermeddles
with, or otherwise acts in relation to, property so as to become liable as executor or trustee . . . shall
be treated as a person in whom the property is vested.'
b Rule 1, so far as material, is set out at p 422 e f, post

been delivered and any tax and interest due from S Ltd had been paid. S Ltd applied to have the order set aside. Goulding J granted the application on the grounds that S Ltd, *a* by reason only of taking the money to its place of residence before grant of representation had been obtained in England, was not to be treated as an executor de son tort and accordingly the case was not a proper one for service out of the jurisdiction under RSC Ord 11. The Crown appealed. Pending the determination of the appeal, the injunction restraining S Ltd from removing its assets from the jurisdiction of the court was continued. In subsequent proceedings, a grant ad colligenda bona under s 162(1) proviso *b* (b)ᶜ of the Supreme Court of Judicature (Consolidation) Act 1925 was issued to the Official Solicitor on the application of the Crown. The executors named in C's will appealed against the grant, contending that it should have been given to them instead. Ewbank J dismissed the appeal, holding that there were special circumstances which justified the court in exercising its discretion to pass over the executors. The executors appealed.

c
Held – (1) Immediately after the conveyance of the land to S Ltd and the execution of the declaration of trust, the land belonged in equity to C in fee simple and his interest constituted property situate in England. Immediately after the contract for sale had been entered into by S Ltd with P Ltd, C was entitled in equity to the land in fee simple, subject to and with the benefit of the contract. He was therefore entitled in equity to the purchase price payable by P Ltd, to the benefit of the rights of S Ltd to enforce in England *d* the obligations of P Ltd and to be paid damages for breach of those obligations, and those interests were property situate in England. Furthermore, since the land was in England and the rights to specific performance and damages under the contract were enforceable and only enforceable in England, it followed that the purchase price was an obligation or debt which would fall to be performed and paid in England, and which was therefore also situate in England. Accordingly, the interests of C in the land and in the purchase *e* price were therefore property situate in England at the date of his death and belonged to the personal representatives of C when constituted in England. By procuring payment of the proceeds of sale in Jersey, S Ltd had transferred the right to the proceeds from the personal representatives constituted in England to the personal representatives constituted in Jersey, and that act constituted an intermeddling with the English estate and constituted S Ltd executor de son tort, which rendered it liable to capital transfer tax in *f* respect of those proceeds. In the circumstances, the case was a proper one for service out of the jurisdiction pursuant to RSC Ord 11, r 1(1), and the Crown's appeal in relation to the notice served on S Ltd would accordingly be allowed (see p 427 *g* to p 428 *b* and *j* to p 429 *f* and p 430 *h j*, post); *New York Breweries Co v A-G* [1899] AC 62 applied.

(2) The grant ad colligenda bona issued to the Official Solicitor was properly made for it would have been inappropriate to grant representation to executors who, as directors *g* of S Ltd, shared responsibility for removing C's assets from the jurisdiction of the English courts and had strenuously opposed the payment by S Ltd of any tax which might be found to be due on the English estate. The executors' appeal would therefore be dismissed (see p 431 *a* to *f*, post).

Decision of Goulding J [1981] 2 All ER 394 reversed.
Decision of Ewbank J [1982] 2 WLR 314 affirmed.

h

Notes
For intermeddling with the estate and the executor de son tort, see 17 Halsbury's Laws

---

c Section 162(1), so far as material, provides: 'In granting administration the High Court shall have regard to the rights of all persons interested in the estate of the deceased person or the proceeds of *j* sale thereof ... Provided that ... (b) if, by reason of the insolvency of the estate of the deceased or of any other special circumstances, it appears to the court to be necessary or expedient to appoint as administrator some person other than the person who, but for this provision, would by law have been entitled to the grant of administration, the court may in its discretion ... appoint as administrator such person as it thinks expedient ...'

a
(4th edn) paras 753–762, and for cases on the subject, see 23 Digest (Reissue) 69–81, 846–1012.

For the liability for capital transfer tax of persons who take possession of or intermeddle with the property of the deceased and become executors de son tort, see 19 Halsbury's Laws (4th edn) para 830.

For special circumstances enabling the court to pass over a person otherwise entitled to a grant of administration, see 17 ibid para 955, and for cases on the subject, see 23 Digest

b
(Reissue) 251–259, 3041–3122.

For the Finance Act 1975, s 25, see 45 Halsbury's Statutes (3rd edn) 1805.

For the Supreme Court of Judicature (Consolidation) Act 1925, s 162, see 13 ibid 101.

As from 1 January 1982 s 162(1) proviso (b) of the 1925 Act has been replaced by s 116 of the Supreme Court Act 1981, but the reference to insolvency as being a reason for passing over a claim to a grant of administration has been omitted.

c
Case referred to in judgment
New York Breweries Co v A-G [1899] AC 62, HL, 23 Digest (Reissue) 78, 967.

Cases also cited
Baker v Archer-Shee [1927] AC 844, HL.
d
Bayne v Slack (1857) 3 CBNS 363, 140 ER 781.
Berchtold, Re, Berchtold v Capron [1923] 1 Ch 192.
Dodd's Case (1858) 2 De G & J 510, 44 ER 1087, LC.
Ferguson (decd), Re [1935] IR 21.
Haque v Haque (No 2) (1965) 114 CLR 98.
Hole Estate, Re [1948] 4 DLR 419.
e
Hoyles, Re, Row v Jagg [1911] 1 Ch 179, CA.
Philipson-Stow v IRC [1960] 3 All ER 814, [1961] AC 727, HL.
Taylor v London and County Banking Co, London and County Banking Co v Nixon [1901] 2 Ch 231, CA.

Appeals
f
IRC v Stype Investments (Jersey) Ltd

The Commissioners of Inland Revenue appealed against an order of Goulding J ([1981] 2 All ER 394, [1981] Ch 367) dated 12 March 1981 whereby he set aside an order of Dillon J made on 12 December 1980 granting (1) leave to the commissioners to issue an originating summons against the defendant, Stype Investments (Jersey) Ltd (Stype Investments), (2) leave to serve the summons in Jersey and (3) an injunction restraining
g
Stype Investments from removing any of its assets from the jurisdiction of the English court. The facts are set out in the judgment of the court.

Re Clore (decd)

Nathan V Meyohas and Joseph Kasierer, two of the executors named in the will of Sir Charles Clore (deceased), appealed against an order of Ewbank J ([1982] 2 WLR 314)
h
made on 4 December 1981 confirming an order made, on the application of the Commissioners of Inland Revenue, by Mr Registrar Bayne-Powell on 3 August 1981 granting letters of administration ad colligenda bona to the Official Solicitor in respect of the estate of the deceased. The facts are set out in the judgment of the court.

Peter Millett QC and *John Mummery* for the commissioners.
j
Leolin Price QC and *P W E Taylor QC* for Stype Investments and the executors.

Cur adv vult

7 April. **TEMPLEMAN LJ** read the following judgment of the court: By notices of determination dated 11 September 1980 the Commissioners of Inland Revenue

determined that capital transfer tax chargeable on the death of Sir Charles Clore on 20 July 1979 amounted to £21,924,864·50 and that Stype Investments (Jersey) Ltd (Stype Investments) and each of the executors named in the last will of Sir Charles is liable for that tax with interest. Notices of appeal against all these determinations have been lodged but have not yet been heard by the Special Commissioners or by the court.

By an order of Dillon J, made ex parte on 12 September 1980, the commissioners were given leave to serve proceedings on Stype Investments in Jersey and Stype Investments was restrained from removing any of its assets from the jurisdiction of the English court.

An originating summons was served on Stype Investments in Jersey and claimed an account with supporting papers of all the property which formed part of the estate of Sir Charles Clore and an injunction restraining Stype Investments from removing any of its assets from the jurisdiction of the English court until it had paid any capital transfer tax shown by the account to be due from Stype Investments to the Inland Revenue.

By an order of Fox J dated 7 October 1980 Stype Investments was restrained from removing from the jurisdiction of the English court certain specific assets worth about £9m pending the hearing of the summons.

By notice of motion dated 14 November 1980 Stype Investments applied for the proceedings to be discharged on the grounds that leave to serve process out of the jurisdiction ought not to have been given by Dillon J under RSC Ord 11, r 1, having regard to the privileges and immunities of the inhabitants of Jersey or because a good arguable case had not been made out for the relief sought by the commissioners or for other reasons to be advanced.

By an order on that motion dated 12 March 1981 Goulding J (see [1981] 2 All ER 394, [1981] Ch 367) discharged the order of Dillon J and set aside the originating summons and the order made by Fox J. The commissioners appeal to this court. Pending the determination of the appeal, the injunctions restraining Stype Investments from removing its assets from the jurisdiction were continued.

Order 11, r 1(1) provides that service out of the jurisdiction is permissible with the leave of the court where, inter alia, the proceedings are—

'(o)... brought against a defendant... in respect of a claim by the Commissioners of Inland Revenue for estate duty or capital transfer tax.'

The present proceedings are brought by the commissioners against Stype Investments in respect of a claim by the Inland Revenue for capital transfer tax.

By Ord 11, r 4(2) leave to serve out of the jurisdiction shall not be granted unless it shall be made sufficiently to appear to the court that the case is a proper one for service out of the jurisdiction. In the present circumstances well-established principles require that leave be granted to the Commissioners of Inland Revenue if they establish 'a good arguable case' on the merits.

Sir Charles Clore died on 26 July 1979 possessed of a personal fortune in England and abroad which Messrs Titmuss, Sainer & Webb, the solicitors acting for Stype Investments and for the executors named in the will of Sir Charles, now estimate to be worth £23·7m after providing for liabilities and taxes except capital transfer tax.

By the Finance Act 1975 capital transfer tax became payable on the value of all the property of Sir Charles at his death, whether that property was situate in the United Kingdom or elsewhere, provided that Sir Charles was domiciled in the United Kingdom after 27 July 1976, that is to say at any time within the three years immediately preceding his death. An affidavit sworn after the date of the order of Goulding J by Mr Sainer, the personal solicitor of Sir Charles, furnishes indications that Sir Charles did not lose his English domicile of origin (if he lost it at all) until after 27 July 1976, but the domicile of Sir Charles cannot be determined on this appeal. Messrs Titmuss, Sainer & Webb now estimate that the capital transfer tax payable in respect of the free estate of Sir Charles if he was domiciled in the United Kingdom after 26 July 1976 could amount to £15m. Stype Investments and the executors do not admit that any capital transfer tax became payable in respect of that free estate by reason of the domicile of Sir Charles. The a estimated £15m capital transfer tax is concerned only with the free estate of Sir Charles and does not include tax claimed by the commissioners on the trust fund comprised in a personal settlement made by Sir Charles during his lifetime. Further large sums of capital transfer tax running into millions could prove to be payable by the trustees of that settlement who include the executors.

If Sir Charles was not domiciled in the United Kingdom after 26 July 1976, nevertheless capital transfer tax became payable on the value of all the property of Sir Charles situate

b in the United Kingdom at his death. Messrs Titmuss, Sainer & Webb now estimate that the capital transfer tax payable in respect of the property of Sir Charles situate in the United Kingdom at his death could amount to £8·8m. If, however, as Stype Investments maintains, a sum of £20m payable and paid to Stype Investments after the death of Sir Charles did not represent property of Sir Charles situate in the United Kingdom at his death, then no capital transfer tax will be payable or, at any rate, the amount of the tax

c will be reduced to less than £4m, a sum which appears almost trivial in the present context.

The solicitors also estimate that the assets of Sir Charles now situate in the United Kingdom are worth £4·4m. These assets may not suffice to pay capital transfer tax on the free estate of Sir Charles which, on the solicitors' estimate, might be £15m. The commissioners complain that £20m representing property of Sir Charles situate in the

d United Kingdom were spirited away to Jersey by Stype Investments after his death. Hence these proceedings, which are designed to compel and secure payment of capital transfer tax, so far as may be, out of the assets in the United Kingdom of Stype Investments now estimated by the solicitors to be worth £28m.

The commissioners have not withdrawn their claim for £21,924,864·50 and have not agreed any of the estimates of value or schedules of assets which were furnished by the

e solicitors at the request of this court during the hearing of this appeal.

By s 25(5)(a) of the Finance Act 1975 the personal representatives of Sir Charles constituted in England are liable to pay the capital transfer tax attributable to the value of his property at his death. By s 27(1)(a) that liability is limited to the assets which they receive as personal representatives or might have received but for their neglect or default.

By ss 25(5)(a) and (6)(a) and 51 of the 1975 Act a personal representative includes an

f executor de son tort. The commissioners claim, and Stype Investments denies, that Stype Investments intermeddled with the English estate of Sir Charles and became an executor de son tort by spiriting away to Jersey £20m which in the due course of administration could only have been lawfully remitted to Jersey by personal representatives duly constituted in England after the payment of all liabilities in the United Kingdom including the capital transfer tax for which such personal representatives are liable. A

g person who lawfully receives the proceeds of sale of property forming part of the English estate of the deceased does not thereby become an executor de son tort, but if he transfers or procures the payment of the proceeds of sale outside the jurisdiction and cannot thereafter procure them to be paid over on demand to the personal representatives of the deceased duly constituted in England, then he interferes with the due administration of the English estate and is liable as executor de son tort; so runs the argument for the

h commissioners. Stype Investments is, therefore, it is said, liable to pay capital transfer tax which, on the information now supplied by their solicitors, may be £15m. Stype Investments should therefore be restrained from transferring out of the jurisdiction the property belonging to Stype Investments which is now situate in the United Kingdom and within the jurisdiction and estimated to be worth £28m. If that property is transferred out of the United Kingdom the Inland Revenue will, it is submitted, stand

j little chance of being paid more than £4·4m, being the assets of the estate of Sir Charles now admitted to be situated in England to satisfy the claim put forward by the commissioners for £21,924,864·50.

By s 25(5)(c) and (6)(a) of the Finance Act 1975, so far as capital transfer tax is attributable to the value of any property, any person in whom the property is vested (whether beneficially or otherwise) at any time after the death, including an executor de son tort, is liable for the tax. The commissioners claim that Stype Investments is liable in respect of property forming part of the free estate of Sir Charles which was vested in Stype Investments immediately after the death of Sir Charles and is now represented by the sum of £20m in the hands of Stype Investments in Jersey. Capital transfer tax is attributable to the value of that property either because Sir Charles was domiciled in the United Kingdom after 26 July 1976 or because the property in question was situate in the United Kingdom at his death.

In these proceedings the commissioners claim from Stype Investments as executor de son tort an account which every personal representative is bound to deliver to the best of his knowledge and belief of all the property which forms part of the estate of Sir Charles and the value of that property. The commissioners also claim payment of the capital transfer tax shown to be payable by the account, and an injunction restraining Stype Investments from transferring out of the jurisdiction any property of Stype Investments which is now within the jurisdiction.

Stype Investments challenges the jurisdiction of this court over a Jersey corporation, and seeks to set aside the order of the English court authorising service of the present proceedings in Jersey. Stype Investments does not admit that any capital transfer tax is attributable to the value of any property of Sir Charles at his death other than property situate in the United Kingdom. Stype Investments denies that the £20m diverted to Jersey represents property of Sir Charles situated in England at his death and denies acting as an executor de son tort.

Goulding J decided that Stype Investments was not an executor de son tort, discharged the order for service in Jersey and brought the commissioners' claim against Stype Investments to a halt. The commissioners will not be able to recover capital transfer tax in excess of the value of the assets of Sir Charles now admitted to be situate in England of a value of £4·4m.

We turn, therefore, to the events which, according to the available affidavits, gave rise to the present controversy. On 2 April 1974 Sir Charles gave a general power of attorney to his solicitor, Mr Sainer; the power was expressed to be irrevocable for 12 months.

In 1978 Sir Charles transferred out of the United Kingdom property now thought by the Inland Revenue to be worth £19m. In April 1979 Sir Charles still owned the Guy's estate, the Hungerford estate and other property in the United Kingdom.

By his Monaco will dated 4 April 1979 Sir Charles appointed M Meyohas to be executor and gave all his property in Monaco to his daughter, Mrs Duffield.

By a general will dated 9 April 1979 Sir Charles appointed a French lawyer, M Meyohas, a Swiss banker, Mr Karlweis, and an Israeli accountant, Mr Kasierer, to be his executors and gave all his property, except his property in Monaco, to the trustees of his personal settlement dated 20 February 1978. By that personal settlement the trust fund from time to time subject thereto was settled on trust for Sir Charles for life with remainder in the events which happened for certain specified foundations established outside the United Kingdom. The trustees of the personal settlement after the death of Sir Charles were the executors and another Jersey company, Stype Trustees Ltd.

By a conveyance dated 23 May 1979, executed by Mr Sainer in exercise of the 1974 power of attorney, Sir Charles conveyed the Guy's estate to Stype Investments. The conveyance was not expressed to be for value, did not create any trust for sale or settlement and stamp duty was adjudicated at 50p, consistent with the implication that Stype Investments held the legal estate in fee simple on a resulting trust for Sir Charles.

A declaration of trust also dated 23 May 1979 and made between Stype Investments of the one part and Sir Charles, by his attorney Mr Sainer, of the other part recited that, notwithstanding anything contained in the conveyance of the Guy's estate, 'it is intended that no beneficial interest in the property should pass' to Stype Investments, but that Stype Investments should hold the estate 'as a bare nominee' for Sir Charles. By cl 1 of the declaration of trust it was agreed and declared and Stype Investments acknowledged that the Guy's estate would 'continue to remain in the beneficial ownership of Sir Charles' and that Stype Investments 'will hold the same as his nominee and to his order and that

it will at any time at his request convey the said property either to [Sir Charles] personally
a or ... to any purchaser from him in the event of the property being sold'. By cl 2 Stype
Investments undertook to account to Sir Charles for the net proceeds of sale of the estate
and the net rents and profits until sale 'but shall be entitled out of such proceeds or net
rents and profits to pay any outgoings or charges arising in respect of the property so far
as the same shall not have been paid and discharged' by Sir Charles personally.

Stype Investments was incorporated in Jersey and its directors at the date of the
b declaration of trust were the executors, Sir Charles and Mr Dobbs, who was the Jersey
manager of Lloyds Bank Trust Co (Channel Islands) Ltd. Of the 100,000 issued shares of
Stype Investments, 99,988 were registered in the name of Lloyds Bank Trust Co (Channel
Islands) Ltd, of which Mr Dobbs was the manager. All the shares were held for the
trustees of the personal settlement.

In the events which have happened, the beneficiaries ultimately interested in the assets
c of Stype Investments, in the estate of Sir Charles wherever situated and in the personal
settlement are foreign foundations, the assets are effectively under the control of the
executors save for the assets composing the free estate of Sir Charles now in England and
the next of kin of Sir Charles also appear to be resident abroad. In these circumstances,
no one will be willing or anxious for English capital transfer tax to be paid.

After the declaration of trust Mr Sainer orally directed Stype Investments to sell the
d Guy's estate to the Prudential Assurance Co Ltd for £20·5m. On 25 May 1979 Stype
Investments entered into two contracts. By those contracts it agreed to sell the Guy's
estate to the Prudential for an aggregate purchase price of £20·5m. The Prudential paid
a deposit of £1,025,000 to Mr Sainer's firm, Messrs Titmuss, Sainer & Webb, the vendor's
solicitors, as stakeholders. Completion was fixed for 29 September 1979. The National
Conditions of Sale (19th edn, 1976) were incorporated and by condition 5(2) it was
e provided that 'Save where the respective solicitors agree to complete by post, completion
shall take place at such office or place as the vendor's solicitors shall reasonably require'.
Condition 5(3) was amended to provide that where completion was by post, the date of
actual completion should be the day on which the vendor's solicitors received a banker's
draft or, if payment was made by a direct transfer to the vendor's solicitors, the day the
amount was credited to their client's bank account. This provision would seem to point
f to the contemplation of completion in England.

Sir Charles died on 26 July 1979. On 13 August 1979 the Capital Taxes Office of the
Inland Revenue wrote to Messrs Titmuss, Sainer & Webb, who had been acting for Sir
Charles in the past and have acted for Stype Investments and for the executors ever since
the death of Sir Charles. Mr Sainer is a consultant with Messrs Titmuss, Sainer & Webb
and for many years acted as personal solicitor for Sir Charles up to the time of his death.
g Mr Sainer and the directors of Stype Investments, who include the executors nominated
by Sir Charles, and trustees of the personal settlement had been engaged, under the
instruction of Sir Charles, in mitigating English taxes payable in his lifetime and after
his death by transferring out of the United Kingdom property for the benefit of Sir
Charles and the beneficiaries interested in his estate after his death. In their letter dated
13 August 1979 the Inland Revenue referred to previous correspondence and to the death
h of Sir Charles and inquired: 'Can you say who will be acting in connection with the
extraction of a grant of representation to his estate, please?' The letter proceeded to claim
that capital transfer tax was chargeable in respect of the property comprised in the
personal settlement made by Sir Charles and said that the Inland Revenue would be
pleased to learn that Messrs Titmuss, Sainer & Webb were instructed to deliver an account
of the property on behalf of the trustees. The Inland Revenue asked for full particulars of
j all property which had been transferred to the trustees of the personal settlement by way
of addition to the trust fund and of any exercise by the trustees of the powers conferred
on them by the settlement. The letter also asked for information concerning the Charles
Clore Jersey Foundation, which was a settlement established by Sir Charles on the same
day as the personal settlement.

Messrs Titmuss, Sainer & Webb replied to the Inland Revenue on 21 August 1979

saying that 'we will take the instructions of the executors and of the trustees and we hope
to be in a position to write to you shortly'. It should not have taken them long to obtain
the instructions or to supply the information required by the Inland Revenue, but
further prevaricating letters were sent to the Inland Revenue until on 3 June 1980 a
misleading and inaccurate memorandum of the activities of Sir Charles and of his assets
was supplied. Meanwhile much had happened.

On 11 September 1979 Mr Dobbs, on behalf of Stype Investments, wrote to Messrs
Titmuss, Sainer & Webb in the following terms:

> 'We shall be obliged if you will kindly instruct the Prudential Assurance Company
> to remit the monies due from them on completion day by telegraphic transfer to
> Lloyds Bank Limited (Jersey Trust Branch) . . . for the account of Stype Investments
> (Jersey) Limited. Will you please remit to us in the same manner the balance of the
> deposit which we understand you are holding as stake holder less of course your
> outstanding costs and expenses.'

On 12 September Messrs Titmuss, Sainer & Webb wrote to the solicitor acting for the
Prudential, and in answer to one of the requisitions on title said:

> 'It is intended that completion will take place in London but it is requested that
> the payment of monies be dealt with by telegraphic transfer to the Vendor's Bank
> Account in the Channel Islands. The title deeds will be handed over upon
> confirmation from the Bank that the money had arrived there. If this is acceptable
> we will let you have details of the Bank Account.'

A resolution signed by each of the directors of Stype Investments and dated 27 September
1979 authorised Mr Dobbs, as director, and Lloyds Bank Trust Co (Channel Islands) Ltd,
as secretary, to execute all the documents necessary to complete the sale of the Guy's
estate to the Prudential. It was further resolved—

> 'to deposit the proceeds of sale of the GUYS ESTATE with [Lloyds Bank International]
> Finance (Jersey) Limited for such periods as shall be decided by the Secretary of the
> Company after consultation with the executors of the estate of Sir Charles Clore and
> thereafter to renew such deposit(s) as the Secretary and the said executors deem fit.'

By a resolution bearing the same date, namely 27 September 1979, the directors of Stype
Investments resolved to lend to—

> 'the Executors of the estate of the late SIR CHARLES CLORE such sums they may from
> time to time require to pay the debts and expenses of the estate and ex gratia
> payments of £500 a month (these are to continue payments made by Sir Charles
> during his lifetime).'

The resolution did not specify the source from which the loans were to be made. The
directors of Stype Investments were Mr Dobbs and the executors. The executors had not
taken out a grant in England.

Completion of the sale of the Guy's estate took place on 29 September 1979 in the
manner directed by Stype Investments. The Prudential paid £19,499,420·78 to Stype
Investments in Jersey. Messrs Titmuss, Sainer & Webb paid all the costs and expenses of
the sale in England except, we are told, the estate agents' fees for some reason, and
transmitted the balance of the deposit of £1,025,000 to Stype Investments in Jersey.

Mr Alan Clore, a son of Sir Charles, lodged caveats against the grant of probate to the
executors in England and Jersey and put forward a claim that the trusts of the will and
personal settlement were invalid and that the estate of Sir Charles devolved, partly at any
rate, on his next of kin ascertained in accordance with the law of Monaco. The next of
kin appear to be Mr Alan Clore and Mrs Duffield, both of whom appear to be resident
outside the United Kingdom. Mr Alan Clore obtained injunctions in Jersey which
prevent the executors and Stype Investments from transferring property belonging to
the estate of Sir Charles to England. We have been informed that all the creditors of Sir

a Charles in England and all the liabilities of the estate in England have nevertheless been discharged, but no capital transfer tax has been paid. The only, or principal, effect of the injunctions in Jersey is to restrain the executors and Stype Investments from transferring money from Jersey to the United Kingdom in order to pay capital transfer tax. There is no reason to think that Stype Investments or the executors are embarrassed by such injunctions and there is every reason to think that all the beneficiaries interested in the estate of Sir Charles Clore, whether under or by virtue of his will or on his intestacy, will

b strenuously and not unnaturally oppose any payment being made for capital transfer tax other than payment out of assets situate in England and, therefore, subject to the jurisdiction of the English courts. Since all persons in a fiduciary capacity, including Stype Investments, are resident abroad and hold their assets on trust for residents abroad, it does not appear that anyone other than the Inland Revenue can come to any harm if capital transfer tax is not paid.

c   On 3 June 1980 the Inland Revenue were supplied by the executors' solicitors with a memorandum which contains a partial and incomplete account of the affairs of Sir Charles. On 29 June the Inland Revenue asked for an undertaking that the assets of the estate of Sir Charles and of Stype Investments would not be transferred out of the United Kingdom. On 1 August that undertaking was refused. On 11 September the Inland Revenue made their determination that capital transfer tax chargeable on the death of

d Sir Charles was £21,924,864·50 and then instituted the proceedings which have led to this appeal.

We can deal summarily with the submission made on behalf of Stype Investments that this court has no jurisdiction over Stype Investments, which is a Jersey company, or, alternatively, that this court should not exercise jurisdiction over Stype Investments because by doing so the English court would flout the privileges and the immunities

e granted by the Crown to the courts and inhabitants of Jersey. The Jersey courts have jurisdiction over causes of action which arise in Jersey. The English courts have jurisdiction over causes of action which arise in England. In the present case Stype Investments voluntarily came to England, accepted a conveyance of English land as nominee for Sir Charles and, if the Inland Revenue are correct, incurred personal liabilities to the Crown for capital transfer tax which became payable as the result of the

f death of Sir Charles. In these circumstances, the English court has power to determine the dispute between the Inland Revenue and Stype Investments over capital transfer tax. The exercise by the English court of its powers will not cause any affront to the courts or the inhabitants of Jersey.

The first question which falls for determination is whether the £20m which at the behest of Stype Investments was paid by the Prudential and Messrs Titmuss, Sainer &

g Webb to Stype Investments in Jersey in September 1979 represented property which at the death of Sir Charles formed part of his estate situate in England.

Immediately after the conveyance of the Guy's estate to Stype Investments and the execution of the declaration of trust which acknowledged that the Guy's estate would 'continue to remain in the beneficial ownership of Sir Charles', the Guy's estate belonged in equity to Sir Charles in fee simple and his interest constituted property situate in

h England. Stype Investments was entitled to be paid any outgoings or charges in respect of the estate, but this entitlement did not affect the nature, quality or situation of the interest of Sir Charles in the estate.

Immediately after the contract for sale had been entered into by Stype Investments with the Prudential, Sir Charles was entitled in equity to the Guy's estate in fee simple subject to, and with the benefit of, the contract. He was entitled in equity to the purchase

j price payable by the Prudential and to the benefit of the rights of Stype Investments to enforce in England the obligations of the Prudential and to be paid damages for breach of those obligations. Whether those interests of Sir Charles ought to be classified as immovables, as the Inland Revenue assert, or as movables, as Stype Investments claims, is immaterial. Those interests were property situate in England. The Guy's estate was land in England, the rights to specific performance and damages were enforceable, and only enforceable, in England, and the purchase price was an obligation or debt which would fall to be performed and paid by the Prudential, an English company, and this obligation or debt was therefore also situate in England. Stype Investments was entitled to retain or be paid any outgoings and charges in respect of the sale and to be indemnified against any liability which Stype Investments incurred as a result of entering into the contract at the request of Sir Charles, but this entitlement did not affect the nature, quality or situation of the interests of Sir Charles in the estate and in the purchase price. Nor did it affect liability for capital transfer tax. The interests of Sir Charles were property situate in England.

Counsel for Stype Investments submitted that, after the contract, the only property of Sir Charles was the right to an account and payment by Stype Investments in Jersey. Sir Charles could not prevent Stype Investments completing the contract. Sir Charles could not prevent Stype Investments requiring the Prudential to pay the purchase price of £20m in Jersey. Sir Charles could only require an account and payment of the balance of the £20m in Jersey after deduction of the outgoings and charges of Stype Investments in respect of the sale. The relevant property of Sir Charles at his death was a debt of an uncertain amount which would become due from Stype Investments, a Jersey company, and which was therefore property situate in Jersey.

We do not accept this analysis of the rights of Sir Charles. Completion of the sale had not taken place when Sir Charles died, and might never have taken place. There was no debt due from Stype Investments to Sir Charles when he died and there might never have been any such debt. Sir Charles during his lifetime and his personal representatives duly constituted in England after his death could at any time before completion of the sale have required Stype Investments to instruct the Prudential to pay the purchase price of the Guy's estate in England and could have forbidden Stype Investments either to receive the purchase price in Jersey or to transfer the purchase price to Jersey. If Stype Investments refused to accept the instructions of Sir Charles or his personal representatives duly constituted in England with regard to the mode and place of payment of the purchase price, those instructions could have been enforced by an order obtainable by Sir Charles or his personal representatives duly constituted in England from an English court. The order would have directed the Prudential to pay the purchase price into court, directed Stype Investments to convey the Guy's estate to the Prudential on such payment into court being made, directed an account of any unpaid outgoings and charges due to Stype Investments, directed payment out of court to Stype Investments of the sum found due to Stype Investments on the taking of the account, and directed payment to Sir Charles or his representatives duly constituted in England of the balance of the moneys in court.

The executors named in the will of Sir Charles could have obtained the same relief even if they had not proved the will of Sir Charles in England. Any creditor of the estate of Sir Charles in England and any beneficiary interested in the estate of Sir Charles could have obtained the same relief. The only difference would have been that the order of the court would have required the balance of the purchase price paid into court by the Prudential, after payment out of the costs and charges of Stype Investments, to remain in court to the account of the personal representatives of Sir Charles when constituted in England. An order by any interested party ensuring that £20m remained in England would have been made because the interests of Sir Charles in the purchase price was property situate in England at the date of his death.

If the Inland Revenue had known what was going on they could have obtained an order for the payment into court of the purchase price. Counsel for Stype Investments impressed on us that the Inland Revenue had no statutory or other charge on the purchase price or on the free estate of Sir Charles for payment of capital transfer tax. But the Inland Revenue had an interest in the purchase price because the English personal representatives when constituted were liable to pay capital transfer tax. The English personal representatives when constituted were bound to collect, and were entitled to indemnify themselves against the payment of capital transfer tax out of, the English estate of Sir

Charles, including the £20m purchase price. On proceedings being taken by the
a   commissioners in these circumstances, the English court would have ensured that the
purchase price remained in England so that £20m was preserved in England for the
persons entitled thereto, namely the personal representatives when constituted in
England, and so that £20m would be available for the personal representatives to pay
English capital transfer tax found to be payable.

The property of Sir Charles which at the date of his death was situate in England vests
b   automatically in his personal representatives constituted in England by virtue of an
English grant: see Dicey and Morris on the Conflict of Laws (10th edn, 1980) vol 2, p 596.

Executors have power to act before they take out probate, but if they act in relation to
English assets they cannot thereafter renounce but may be cited to take probate and may
be peremptorily ordered to do so. Thus, if the executors in the present case received,
whether within or outside the United Kingdom, £20m representing property of Sir
c   Charles situate in England at his death, the executors would be liable to pay capital
transfer tax just as if they had proved the will of Sir Charles in England.

Similarly, it seems to us that, if a stranger so deals with proceeds of sale of English
property belonging to a deceased in such manner as to submit the proceeds of sale to
another jurisdiction and is unable to pay and account for the proceeds of sale to the
English representatives when constituted in England, the stranger has intermeddled
d   with the estate and constituted himself an executor de son tort, liable to pay capital
transfer tax in England.

After the death of Sir Charles, Stype Investments was entitled and bound to complete
the contract with the Prudential and to receive the purchase price of £20m. But the right
in equity to the purchase price was property situate in England at the death of Sir Charles
and the £20m therefore belonged to the personal representatives of Sir Charles when
e   constituted in England and to nobody else for the purpose of carrying out and completing
administration of the English estate. By procuring payment of the £20m in Jersey, Stype
Investments transferred the right to the £20m from the personal representatives
constituted in England to the personal representatives constituted in Jersey. If this were
not the case, Stype Investments would have no difficulty now in transferring the £20m
from Jersey to England where it belongs. The act of transferring title from English
f   personal representatives to Jersey personal representatives constituted an intermeddling
with the English estate and constituted Stype Investments executor de son tort.

In New York Breweries Co v A-G [1899] AC 62 an English company transferred shares in
the company from the name of a deceased domiciled American into the names of his
executors, who had proved his will in New York but, to the knowledge of the company,
had not obtained, and did not intend to obtain, probate in England. The company also
g   paid dividends and interest to the executors. It was held that the company had 'taken
possession of and administered' part of the testator's estate, that the company was executor
de son tort and that the company was personally liable to deliver an account and pay such
duty as would have been payable if probate had been obtained in England.

Goulding J said that payment of the £20m in Jersey did not affect any such change of
title as founded the decision in the New York Breweries case. But just as the intermeddling
h   in the New York Breweries case transferred title from the English representatives when
constituted to the American representatives already constituted, so in the present case
Stype Investments transferred title from the English representatives when constituted to
the Jersey representatives when constituted.

Counsel for Stype Investments says that it will be open to personal representatives
constituted in England to apply for a grant in Jersey. That only illustrates the fact that
j   title to the money has changed hands. Moreover, it does not lie in the mouth of an
intermeddler to argue that the English personal representatives who have been deprived
of an English asset can undo the mischief caused by the intermeddler by seeking to cloak
themselves with title in a foreign jurisdiction. The English personal representatives could
only obtain a grant in Jersey by accepting all the rights and liabilities of a Jersey personal
representative. The English personal representatives are only bound to collect and

administer English assets according to English law. In any event, an application by the
English personal representatives in Jersey would be certain to be opposed by foreign   *a*
beneficiaries understandably opposed to the payment of capital transfer tax. No one other
than the Inland Revenue is anxious for capital transfer tax to be paid. The estate of Sir
Charles can be made to suffer to the extent of the assets of the estate now situate in
England. But the shares of Stype Investments and the assets of the estate in England are
held on trust for the same foreign beneficiaries. In the result, no one except the Revenue
will suffer if capital transfer tax is not wholly or partly recovered.   *b*

Finally and most vehemently counsel for Stype Investments reiterated the submission
which found favour with Goulding J, that Stype Investments is not to be blamed and is
not to be treated as an executor de son tort because the decision of Stype Investments to
require payment of £20m in Jersey was, in his words and in the words of the judge, 'the
natural act of taking the money to be held in suspense at the place of residence of Stype
Investments, namely Jersey'. We are not impressed with this explanation or with the   *c*
explanations proffered by the affidavit of Mr Dobbs for the decision which was taken to
direct the Prudential to pay Stype Investments in Jersey. No explanation has been
vouchsafed by the other directors of Stype Investments or Mr Sainer.

In the 12 months preceding his death Sir Charles had been engaged in transferring
property out of England with the object of avoiding the onerous burden of English taxes
on himself during his lifetime and on his estate after his death. Sir Charles was assisted   *d*
in that endeavour by Mr Sainer and by the three executors named in his will. Those three
gentlemen were also trustees of his personal settlement and directors of Stype Investments.
The only other director of Stype Investment was Mr Dobbs, the manager of a Jersey trust
company.

Mr Sainer deposes that the death of Sir Charles was unexpected. It was certainly
untimely so far as the avoidance of tax was concerned. Mr Sainer, the executors and Mr   *e*
Dobbs must have been acutely conscious of the difficulties caused by the untimely death
of Sir Charles. The letter from the Capital Taxes Office dated 13 August 1979, written a
little more than a fortnight after the death of Sir Charles and received six weeks before
the Prudential were due to pay £20m, clearly foreshadowed a claim for capital transfer
tax in respect of the free estate of Sir Charles. On any footing the £20m to be paid by the
Prudential was part of the free estate of Sir Charles. We do not know what discussions   *f*
took place between Mr Sainer, the executors and Mr Dobbs, or any of them, between the
date of the death of Sir Charles on 26 July 1979 and the date when the Prudential paid
£20m on 29 September 1979. It does not seem credible that no discussion took place or
that no investigation was made of the capital transfer tax position. Despite the magnitude
of the sum involved, no evidence has been produced that the advice of English counsel
was sought after the death of Sir Charles. In these circumstances there is a grave possibility   *g*
that the object of directing the Prudential to pay £20m in Jersey was to evade tax on
£20m. If this was in fact the object, it may have been the product of a criminal conspiracy
to defraud the Revenue. This court feels very strongly that the Inland Revenue should
ask the Director of Public Prosecutions to investigate. For present purposes it suffices that
the motives of the participants cannot alter or excuse the unlawfulness of the act of Stype
Investments in giving directions whereby £20m, part of the English estate of Sir Charles,   *h*
was diverted to Jersey out of the reach of personal representatives constituted in England
and unlawfully lost to the Treasury. In our judgment, Stype Investments is liable for
intermeddling with the English estate. At the very least, the Inland Revenue establish a
'strong arguable case'.

We allow the appeal and discharge the order made by Goulding J.

We turn to consider the grant of letters of administration to the estate of Sir Charles.   *j*

On 3 August 1981 the senior registrar of the Family Division, at the request of the
Inland Revenue, authorised a grant ad colligenda bona to the estate of Sir Charles to be
issued to the Official Solicitor, under s 162(1) proviso (b) of the Supreme Court of
Judicature (Consolidation) Act 1925. The executors named in the will of Sir Charles
appealed to Ewbank J who dismissed the appeal on 4 December 1981 (see [1982] 2 WLR
314). The executors appeal to this court.

The grant should have been issued to the executors in the absence of special
circumstances. We agree with the judge that there were special circumstances. There are
no grounds for interfering with his decision.

The executors contend that the administration of the estate will be cheaper and more
expeditious if they are given a grant. They do not intend to make provision or offer
security for the payment of any capital transfer tax which may be found to be due and
payable by the executors. Nor do they intend to pay or offer security for the capital
transfer tax which may be found to be due and payable by them as trustees of the
personal settlement of Sir Charles.

The executors as directors of Stype Investments share responsibility for the fact that
£20m of the English assets are now locked up in Jersey. The executors as directors of
Stype Investments share responsibility for opposing strenuously the efforts of the Inland
Revenue to obtain payment by Stype Investments at least to the extent of its assets now
in England of any capital transfer tax which may be found to be payable in respect of the
English estate of Sir Charles. The executors, for reasons which are paltry and disingenuous,
have opposed a grant to the Official Solicitor and have thus delayed investigation into the
affairs of the estate of Sir Charles.

The appointment of the Official Solicitor will render academic the dispute whether
Stype Investments constituted itself executor de son tort. If the £20m now in Jersey
represents property of Sir Charles situated in the United Kingdom at his death, the
Official Solicitor, as personal representative of Sir Charles constituted in this country, will
be able to sue Stype Investments in this country for failing to collect the debt owed by
the Prudential in this country and for failing to retain the £20m in this country available
to be paid over to the Official Solicitor as personal representative of Sir Charles constituted
in England. At the request of the Inland Revenue the English court would grant an
injunction restraining Stype Investments from transferring any of its assets out of the
jurisdiction until the Official Solicitor has taken a grant, instituted proceedings against
Stype Investments and obtained an interlocutory injunction in those proceedings.

In the circumstances, the appointment of the executors as personal representatives
duly constituted in this country would be bizarre. The appeal of the executors against
the decision of Ewbank J is a sinister and time-wasting exercise and must be dismissed.

*First appeal allowed with costs in the Court of Appeal and below. Second appeal dismissed; costs
in the Court of Appeal to be borne by the executors personally; order for costs in court below
affirmed. Application for leave to appeal to the House of Lords refused. Application for stay of
proceedings on originating summons refused.*

*17 June. The Appeal Committee of the House of Lords (Lord Fraser of Tullybelton, Lord Scarman
and Lord Bridge of Harwich) dismissed a petition by Stype Investments for leave to appeal.*

Solicitors: *Solicitor of Inland Revenue; Titmuss, Sainer & Webb* (for Stype Investments and
the executors).

Edwina Epstein   Barrister.

Attorney General of New Zealand v Ortiz and others

QUEEN'S BENCH DIVISION (COMMERCIAL COURT)
STAUGHTON J
2, 3, 4, 5 JUNE, 1 JULY 1981

COURT OF APPEAL, CIVIL DIVISION
LORD DENNING MR, ACKNER AND O'CONNOR LJJ
29, 30, 31 MARCH, 1, 2 APRIL, 21 MAY 1982

Conflict of laws – Foreign law – New Zealand statute providing that historic articles unlawfully removed 'shall be forfeited' to Her Majesty – Whether goods so removed automatically forfeited on removal from New Zealand – Whether forfeiture dependent on seizure of goods – Whether Crown's title accruing only on seizure – Historic Articles Act 1962 (NZ), s 12(2) – Customs Act 1913 (NZ), s 251 – Customs Act 1966 (NZ), s 274.

Conflict of laws – Foreign law – Enforcement – New Zealand statute providing for forfeiture of historic articles unlawfully removed from New Zealand – Claim by New Zealand Attorney General in England for return of article unlawfully removed – Whether claim unenforceable in English courts as being a foreign penal, revenue or public law – Historic Articles Act 1962 (NZ), s 12(2).

New Zealand – Statute – Enforcement of New Zealand statute in England – New Zealand statute providing for forfeiture of historic articles unlawfully removed from New Zealand – Whether statute enforceable in England – Historic Articles Act 1962 (NZ), s 12(2).

New Zealand – Statute – Interpretation – New Zealand statutes deemed to be 'remedial' – Whether all statutes to receive purposive construction – Acts Interpretation Act 1924 (NZ), s 5(j).

In 1973 the third defendant, an art dealer, purchased a valuable Maori carving in New Zealand, which was a historic article within the meaning of the New Zealand Historic Articles Act 1962. By s 5(1) of that Act, it was unlawful to remove such an article from New Zealand without a certificate of permission from the Minister of Internal Affairs. Section 12(2)[a] of the Act further provided that 'an historic article knowingly exported . . . shall be forfeited to Her Majesty' and that the provisions of the New Zealand Customs Act 1913 relating to forfeited goods were to apply 'subject to the provisions' of the Historic Articles Act 1962. Section 251[b] of the 1913 Act provided that 'forfeiture [was] to take effect on seizure' and was then 'for all purposes [to] relate back to the date' when the cause of forfeiture arose. Section 251 of the 1913 Act was replaced by s 274[c] of the Customs Act 1966, which provided that when any goods were forfeited and the goods were seized 'the forfeiture [was] for all purposes [to] relate back to the date of the act or event from which the forfeiture accrued'. The third defendant exported the carving to New York without obtaining a certificate of permission and sold it to the first defendant, a collector of Polynesian art. In 1978 the first defendant placed the carving for sale by auction in London with the second defendant. The plaintiff, the Attorney General of New Zealand suing on behalf of Her Majesty in right of New Zealand, applied to the Commercial Court of the Queen's Bench Division for an injunction restraining the sale of the carving and for an order for its delivery up, on the ground that it had been forfeited

---

a   Section 12(2) is set out at p 454 f, post
b   Section 251 is set out at p 453 j, post
c   Section 274 is set out at p 455 a, post

to Her Majesty by its removal from New Zealand in breach of s 5(1) of the 1962 Act. By
a an order of a master, subsequently affirmed by the Court of Appeal, two preliminary
issues were ordered to be determined by the Commercial Court, namely (i) whether Her
Majesty had become the owner of, and was entitled to possession of the carving pursuant
to the 1962 Act and the 1913 and 1966 Acts, and (ii) whether in any event the provisions
of the three Acts were unenforceable in England as being foreign penal, revenue or
public laws. The plaintiff contended that the words 'shall be forfeited' in s 12(2) of the
b 1962 Act meant that forfeiture occurred automatically when the forfeiting act or event
took place (ie the export of the article without a certificate) and that title to an article so
forfeited passed to Her Majesty at the same time and therefore the Crown was not seeking
to enforce foreign penal or public laws but was merely claiming possession of an article
to which it had title. The plaintiff further contended that since s 12(2) provided that the
provisions in the 1913 and 1966 Acts relating to forfeiture were to apply 'subject to the
c provisions of this Act', ie the 1962 Act, those provisions in the 1913 and 1966 Acts were
to be interpreted in the same way. The plaintiff also contended that since the overall
purpose of the 1962 Act was to preserve articles relating to the heritage of New Zealand
in New Zealand, the forfeiture provisions were incidental to that main purpose and did
not bring the Act within the category of foreign penal or public law. The judge in the
Commercial Court accepted the plaintiff's contentions and held that Her Majesty had
d become the owner of the carving and was entitled to possession of it, and that while there
was no specific category of public law of foreign states which could not be enforced in
England, s 12(2) of the 1962 Act was neither revenue nor penal in character and
consequently was enforceable in England. The defendants appealed to the Court of
Appeal.

e **Held** – (1) The words 'shall be forfeited' in s 12(2) of the 1962 Act were to be construed
in the light of s 251 of the 1913 Act and s 274 of the 1966 Act, both of which provided
that forfeiture was not automatic when the forfeiting act or event took place but only
occurred when the goods had been seized. Accordingly, on the true construction of s
12(2) of the 1962 Act, the words 'shall be forfeited' did not mean that there was automatic
forfeiture but that forfeiture took place only when the goods had been seized, whereupon
f title related back to the time when the cause of forfeiture arose. It followed that since
there had been no seizure of the carving, there had been no forfeiture and accordingly
title had not passed to Her Majesty. Furthermore (per Lord Denning MR), even if the
1962 Act provided for automatic forfeiture such forfeiture would take place and would
come into effect as soon as the historic article was exported (ie as soon as it left the
territorial jurisdiction of New Zealand) and since such an interpretation would infringe
g the rule of international law that no country could legislate so as to effect rights of
property when that property was situated beyond the limits of its own jurisdiction and
since the 1962 Act was to be construed according to the presumption that the New
Zealand Parliament would not legislate in a manner which infringed international law,
s 12(2) could not be construed to mean that there was automatic forfeiture (see p 45 h j,
p 455 d, p 456 b to d, p 463 e f, p 465 b c and p 468 e to g, post).
h   (2) Even if s 12(2) of the 1962 Act did provide for automatic forfeiture it infringed
the principle that English courts would not enforce a law which was penal or (per Lord
Denning MR) public in character because—
      (a) (Per Lord Denning MR) English courts would not enforce any public laws of a
foreign sovereign state by which that state purported to exercise sovereignty beyond the
limits of its authority, and that that included legislation prohibiting the export of works of
j art and providing for their automatic forfeiture if they were exported (see p 457 e and
p 459 , post); *Don Alonso v Cornero* (1611) Hob 212, *King of Italy v Marquis Cosimo de Medici
Tornaquinci* (1918) 34 TLR 623, *Brokaw v Seatrain UK Ltd* [1971] 2 All ER 98 followed;
Paley (Princess Olga) v Weisz [1929] All ER Rep 513 distinguished.
      (b) (Per Ackner and O'Connor LJJ) Although the general purpose of the 1962 Act was
to preserve in New Zealand its historic articles, the substance of the right which the
plaintiff sought to be enforced was a public right which a foreign state sought to be

vindicated by confiscation and it therefore amounted to a penal measure by a foreign
state (see p 467 *b* to *f* and p 468 *g*, post); *Huntington v Attrill* [1893] AC 150 applied.   *a*

Per Ackner LJ. Section 5(j)*d* of the New Zealand Acts Interpretation Act 1924 providing
that New Zealand statutes were to be deemed to be 'remedial' and were to receive 'such
fair, large and liberal construction and interpretation as will best ensure the attainment
of the object of the Act' does no more than abolish the old distinction between remedial
and penal Acts and does not mean that the courts are required to adopt a purposive rather
than a literal construction in every case (see p 464 *a b*, post).   *b*

Notes

For the general rights of the Crown in relation to property, see 8 Halsbury's Laws (4th
edn), paras 1076–1082, and for cases on the subject, see 11 Digest (Reissue) 776–777,
891–900.

For the enforcement or otherwise of foreign law in England, see 8 Halsbury's Laws   *c*
(4th edn) paras 417–420, 663–664, and for cases on the subject, see 11 Digest (Reissue)
340–346, 1–25.

Cases referred to in judgments

A-G v Parsons [1956] 1 All ER 65, [1956] AC 421, [1956] 2 WLR 153, HL, 10 Digest
(Reissue) 1393, 8945.   *d*
Aksionairnoye Obschestvo A M Luther v James Sagor & Co [1921] 3 KB 532, [1921] All ER
Rep 138, CA, 11 Digest (Reissue) 344, 23.
Anglo-Iranian Oil Co Ltd v Jaffrate, The Rose Mary [1953] 1 WLR 246, 11 Digest (Reissue)
730, 491.
Annandale, The (1877) 2 PD 218, CA; *affg* 2 PD 179, 42 Digest (Repl) 678, 4316.
Antelope, The (1825) 10 Wheat 66.   *e*
Apollon, The (1824) 9 Wheat 362.
Banco de Vizcaya v Don Alfonso de Borbon y Austria [1935] 1 KB 140, [1934] All ER Rep
555, 11 Digest (Reissue) 341, 11.
Boucher v Lawson (1735) Lee temp Hard 85, 95 ER 53; *subsequent proceedings* (1736) Lee
temp Hard 194, 95 ER 125, 11 Digest (Reissue) 481, 376.
Brokaw v Seatrain UK Ltd [1971] 2 All ER 98, [1971] 2 QB 476, [1971] 2 WLR 791, CA,   *f*
11 Digest (Reissue) 344, 21.
Cable (Lord) (decd), Re, Garratt v Waters [1976] 3 All ER 417, [1977] 1 WLR 7, Digest
(Cont Vol E) 89, 21a.
Chapman v Chapman [1954] 1 All ER 798, [1954] AC 429, [1954] 2 WLR 723, HL, 47
Digest (Repl) 329, 2973.
Compania Espanola de Navegacion Maritima SA v The Navemar (1938) 303 US 68.
Don Alonso v Cornero (1611) Hob 212, 80 ER 359.   *g*
Foster v Driscoll, Lindsay v Attfield, Lindsay v Driscoll [1929] 1 KB 470, [1928] All ER Rep
130, CA, 6 Digest (Reissue) 66, 578.
Fothergill v Monarch Airlines Ltd [1980] 2 All ER 696, [1981] AC 251, [1980] 3 WLR 209,
HL.
Helbert Wagg & Co Ltd, Re, Re Prudential Assurance Co Ltd [1956] 1 All ER 129, [1956] Ch   *h*
323, [1956] 2 WLR 183, 11 Digest (Reissue) 345, 25.
Huntington v Attrill [1893] AC 150, PC, 11 Digest (Reissue) 600, 1466.
I Congreso del Partido [1981] 2 All ER 1064, [1981] 3 WLR 328, HL; *rvsg* [1981] 1 All ER
1092, CA.
India (Government), Ministry of Finance (Revenue Division) v Taylor [1955] 1 All ER 292,
[1955] AC 491, [1955] 2 WLR 303, HL, 11 Digest (Reissue) 341, 8.   *j*
IRC v Ayrshire Employers Mutual Insurance Association Ltd [1946] 1 All ER 637, HL, 28(1)
Digest (Reissue) 138, 414.

---

d   Section 5, so far as material, is set out at p 463 *j*, post

Isaack v Clark (1615) 2 Bulst 306, 80 ER 1143, 46 Digest (Repl) 457, 53.

a *Italy (King) v Marquis Cosimo de Medici Tornaquinci* (1918) 34 TLR 623, 28(2) Digest (Reissue) 1096, 965.

Jabbour v Custodian of Israeli Absentee Property [1954] 1 All ER 145, [1954] 1 WLR 139, 8(2) Digest (Reissue) 492, 26.

Kahler v Midland Bank Ltd [1949] 2 All ER 621, [1950] AC 24, HL, 3 Digest (Reissue) 675, 4156.

b *Levy's Trusts, Re* (1885) 30 Ch D 119, 5 Digest (Reissue) 712, 6155.

Lockyer v Offley (1786) 1 Term Rep 252, 99 ER 1079, 29 Digest (Reissue) 188, 1626.

Loucks v Standard Oil Co of New York (1918) 224 NY 99, 120 NE 198.

Paley (Princess Olga) v Weisz [1929] 1 KB 718, [1929] All ER Rep 513, CA, 11 Digest (Reissue) 717, 412.

R v Nat Bell Liquors Ltd [1922] 2 AC 128, [1922] All ER Rep 335, PC, 8(2) Digest (Reissue)
c 711, 252.

Ralli Bros v Compañia Naviera Sota y Aznar [1920] 2 KB 287, [1920] All ER Rep 427, CA, 11 Digest (Reissue) 476, 843.

Raulin v Fischer [1911] 2 KB 93, 11 Digest (Reissue) 601, 1468.

Regazzoni v K C Sethia (1944) *Ltd* [1956] 1 All ER 229, [1956] QB 490, [1956] 2 WLR 204; *affd* [1956] 2 All ER 487, [1956] 2 QB 490, [1956] 3 WLR 79, CA; *affd* [1957] 3 All ER
d 286, [1958] AC 301, [1957] 3 WLR 752, HL, 11 Digest (Reissue) 484, 892.

Skylark The, Atle Marine (a firm) v Owners of Ship Skylark, Comrs of Customs and Excise (interveners) [1965] 3 All ER 380, [1965] P 474, [1965] 3 WLR 759, 1(1) Digest (Reissue) 283, 1692.

e **Cases also cited**

Austria (Emperor) v Day and Kossuth (1861) 3 De GF & J 217, 45 ER 861, CA.

Folliott v Ogden (1789) 1 Hy Bl 123, 126 ER 75; *affd* (1790) 3 Term Rep 726, 100 ER 825; *on appeal* (1792) 4 Bro Parl Cas 111, 2 ER 75, HL.

Frankfurther v Exner Ltd [1947] Ch 629.

Hellenes (King) v Brostrom (1923) Ll L Rep 167.
f *Lepage v San Paulo Copper Estates Ltd* (1917) 33 TLR 457.

Lorentzen v Lydden & Co Ltd [1942] 2 KB 202.

Oppenheimer v Cattermole (Inspector of Taxes) [1975] 1 All ER 538, [1976] AC 249, HL.

Schemmer v Property Resources Ltd [1974] 3 All ER 451, [1975] Ch 273.

g

Preliminary issues

By a writ issued on 26 June 1978 the plaintiff, the Attorney General of New Zealand suing on behalf of Her Majesty the Queen in right of New Zealand, sought as against the first defendant, George Ortiz, the second defendant, Sotheby Parke Bernet & Co, and the
h third defendant, Lance Entwhistle, (1) a declaration that a Maori artifact, namely a carving, was the property of the plaintiff, (2) an order for the return and delivery up to the plaintiff of the carving, and (3) an injunction restraining the defendants and each of them whether by themselves, their servants or agents howsoever from selling, exposing or offering for sale disposing of or otherwise dealing with the carving. By an order dated 25 February 1980 Master Warren ordered the trial of two preliminary issues, namely (i)
j whether on the facts alleged in the statement of claim, Her Majesty the Queen became owner and was entitled to possession of the carving within the provisions of the New Zealand Historic Articles Act 1962 and the Customs Acts of 1913 and 1966 and (ii) whether in any event the provisions of those Acts were unenforceable in England as being foreign penal, revenue and/or public laws. On 26 March 1980 Comyn J allowed the appeal of the plaintiff against the order of Master Warren. On appeal by the

defendants, the Court of Appeal, on 10 July 1980 restored the order of Master Warren. The facts are set out in the judgment of Staughton J.   *a*

Charles Gray and *Nicholas Paines* for the Attorney General of New Zealand.
Paul Baker QC and *Nicholas Patten* for the first defendant.
Presiley Baxendale for the second defendant.
Gerald Levy and *Hugo Page* for the third defendant.

Cur adv vult *b*

1 July. **STAUGHTON J** read the following judgment: For a hundred years and more it was the practice for people of this country to go abroad and to return with works of art or antique objects. But now many countries are concerned about their cultural heritage and have enacted legislation that works of art or antique objects may not be exported without permission of the government. This is sometimes done to protect the store of *c* native objects; and also (as in this country) on other occasions to protect the stock of works of art originally acquired from overseas.

This case relates to a Maori carving which is some 150 years old and was discovered a few years ago by a farm labourer in New Zealand. In 1978 it was entered for auction at the house of the second defendants, Messrs Sotheby Parke Bernet and Co.

This action was then commenced by the Attorney General of New Zealand, suing on *d* behalf of Her Majesty the Queen in right of the Government of New Zealand, seeking first, an injunction restraining the sale and second, an order for the return and delivery up of the carving.

By an order of Master Warren, which was subsequently affirmed by the Court of Appeal, I am required to try two preliminary issues. Those issues are to be tried on the facts alleged in paras one to six in the statement of claim. Those facts are not all admitted *e* and may yet be in issue in further proceedings. But I proceed to state them as facts because that is what they are for the purposes of these preliminary issues:

'(1) The Plaintiff brings this action on behalf of Her Majesty The Queen in right of the Government of New Zealand. Her Majesty The Queen is the owner and entitled to possession of a valuable Maori artifact being a series of five Maori carved *f* wood totara wood panels that formed the front of a food store carved in the Taranaki style. The said artifact is hereinafter referred to as "the carving".
(2) The carving was found by one Manukonga in a swamp near Waitara in the province of Taranaki, New Zealand in or about 1972.
(3) In or about March 1973 the said Manukonga sold the carving to the Third Defendant, who was at all material times a dealer in primitive works of art.
(4) At all times material hereto there was in force in New Zealand the Historic *g* Articles Act, 1962. The carving is an historic article within the meaning of the said Act. Accordingly by virtue of section 5(i) of the said Act it was unlawful for any person to remove or to attempt to remove the carving from New Zealand, knowing it to be an historic article, otherwise than pursuant to the authority and in conformity with the terms and conditions of a written certificate of permission *h* given by the Minister of Internal Affairs for New Zealand under the said Act.
(5) On a date which the Plaintiff is unable to specify precisely before discovery herein the carving was removed from New Zealand by or on behalf of the Third Defendant, *who knew that the carving was an historic article within the meaning of the said Act and that the carving was being exported or attempted to be exported.*
(6) No certificate of permission authorising the removal of the carving from New Zealand has been granted by the Minister of Internal Affairs. Accordingly by virtue *j* of Section 12 of the said Act the carving became and was forfeited to Her Majesty.'

In para (1) of the statement of claim I have just read it is said that: 'Her Majesty The Queen is the owner and entitled to possession of a valuable Maori artifact.' That is not one of the facts that I must assume but one of the very issues that I am required to try.

Similarly in para (6) of the statement of claim set out above it is said that the carving
a   became and was forfeited to Her Majesty. That also is, in part, one of the issues which I
have to try.
The preliminary issues as ordered by the Court of Appeal are as follows:

'(1) whether on the facts alleged in paragraphs (1) to (6) inclusive of the Statement
of Claim herein as amended Her Majesty The Queen has become the owner and is
entitled to possession of the carving as therein defined pursuant to the provisions of
b   the Historic Articles Act 1962 and the Customs Acts 1913 and 1966; and (2) whether
in any event the provisions of the said Acts are unenforceable in England as being
foreign penal revenue and/or public laws.'

From the facts I have stated it will be observed that it is the third defendant who is
alleged to have removed the carving from New Zealand with knowledge that it was an
c   historic article and that it was being exported. It is pleaded, but not in the facts that I am
required to assume, that the first defendant bought the carving from the third defendant
and some years later entered it for sale at Sotheby's, the second defendants. They are not
taking any part in this action. For the purposes of the preliminary issues there was no
dispute between the first and third defendants, and although both were represented
before me they were, in effect, making common cause.
d   I was given by counsel for the plaintiff some figures for the prices at which the carving
was first bought by the third defendant in New Zealand, secondly sold by him to the first
defendant, and thirdly expected now to be sold in England. These figures were not all
admitted, or proved, or to be assumed; so I do not pay any regard to them. However, it
does seem right to assume that the carving is of some substantial value.
The first issue which I am required to try is one of the interpretation of a domestic
e   New Zealand statute, the Historic Articles Act 1962. On this issue I had the advantage of
expert evidence, that is to say the evidence of Dr Inglis QC given on behalf of the plaintiff,
and the evidence of Mr Thomas QC given on behalf of the first defendant and adopted
by the third defendant. These witnesses considered whether the principles of statutory
interpretation in New Zealand differ from those prevailing in England and Wales, and
went on to give me valuable assistance in discussing the construction of the statute.
f   The second issue is one of English private international law on which evidence was not
required. The parties were agreed before me that the characterisation of the New Zealand
legislation, as to whether it is penal or revenue or public law, and as to whether in this
action the court is being asked to enforce it, is a matter for English private international
law alone. The parties were also agreed that New Zealand law is for the purposes of this
action to be treated as foreign law, notwithstanding that New Zealand is part of the
g   Commonwealth and that the claim in this action is brought in the name of Her Majesty
The Queen in right of the Government of New Zealand.
On the first issue as to the interpretation of New Zealand law, the statute with which I
am primarily concerned is the Historic Articles Act 1962. Section 5 of that Act provides:

'Restrictions on export of historic articles—(1) It shall not be lawful after the
h   commencement of this Act for any person to remove or attempt to remove any
historic article from New Zealand, knowing it to be an historic article, otherwise
than pursuant to the authority and in conformity with the terms and conditions of
a written certificate of permission given by the Minister under this Act.
(2) Every person who contrary to the provisions of this section removes or
attempts to remove any article from New Zealand, knowing it to be an historic
j   article, commits an offence, and shall be liable on summary conviction to a fine not
exceeding two hundred pounds . . .'

Section 12 of that Act provides:

'Application of Customs Act 1913—(1) Subject to the provisions of this Act, the
provisions of the Customs Act 1913 shall apply to any historic article the removal

from New Zealand of which is prohibited by this Act in all respects as if the article were an article the export of which had been prohibited pursuant to an Order in Council under section 47 of the Customs Act 1913.

(2) An historic article knowingly exported or attempted to be exported in breach of this Act shall be forfeited to Her Majesty and, subject to the provisions of this Act, the provisions of the Customs Act 1913 relating to forfeited goods shall apply to any such article in the same manner as they apply to goods forfeited under the Customs Act 1913.

(3) Where any historic article is forfeited to Her Majesty pursuant to this section, it shall be delivered to the Minister and retained in safe custody in accordance with his directions:

Provided that the Minister may, in his discretion, direct that the article be returned to the person who was the owner thereof immediately before forfeiture subject to such conditions (if any) as the Minister may think fit to impose.'

The issue that arises is whether the words 'shall be forfeited' in s 12(2) have the effect that the ownership of an article is immediately transferred to Her Majesty by operation of law, or whether such transfer only takes effect when the article is seized pursuant to provisions of the Customs Acts or is later condemned pursuant to those Acts. The issue is important because the carving in this case never was seized pursuant to the Customs Acts nor condemned; nor can it now be siezed or condemned, firstly because it is outside New Zealand, and secondly, because (as will be seen later) there is a time limit of two years after which seizure cannot take effect from the date of export or attempt to export. If the former construction is correct, and the Act provides for automatic forfeiture when an article is exported or attempted to be exported, then it is conceded that at any rate by the domestic law of New Zealand the carving became the property of Her Majesty the Queen. It was within the territorial jurisdiction of the New Zealand legislature at the moment when the forfeiture took effect, albeit very soon to leave that jurisdiction. If on the other hand forfeiture under s 12 of the Historic Articles Act 1962 only takes effect either on seizure or later on condemnation, then the plaintiff can have no claim in the present action because neither seizure nor condemnation has occurred.

It was agreed before me that the words 'shall be forfeited', are capable of either meaning. I was told that the definition of 'forfeit' in the *Oxford English Dictionary* is: 'To lose, lose the right to; to render oneself liable to be deprived of (something) . . .' Further definitions are cited in *In Re Levy's Trust* (1885) 30 Ch D 119 at 124. So the Act may be providing for automatic forfeiture, or it may merely be providing that the goods shall be liable to be forfeited if some further step is taken to that end. As I read the speech of Lord Porter in *A-G v Parsons* [1956] 1 All ER 65 at 72, [1956] AC 421 at 443, his Lordship considered the more usual meaning to be, 'liable to be forfeited'. However his Lordship went on: '. . . unless there is something in surrounding expressions which necessitates a contrary implication'. In this case there are substantial matters to be considered under two headings: firstly, other legislative provisions prevailing in New Zealand; and secondly, the purposes of the Historic Articles Act 1962. These point in different directions; but either by itself would in my judgment be sufficient to override the slight preference expressed by Lord Porter on the mere use of the English language alone.

I therefore turn first to the other legislative provisions in New Zealand. The earliest of these to which I was referred was the Maori Antiquities Act 1908. Section 4 of that Act provides:

'*Maori antiquities to be offered for sale before exportation*—It shall not be lawful to remove from New Zealand any Maori antiquities without first offering the same for sale to some person authorised in that behalf by the Governor-General in Council for the benefit of New Zealand.'

Section 6(1) provides for a fine in the case of contravention of the Act and s 6(3) provides:

'Any Maori antiquities entered for export contrary to this Act shall be forfeited,

a   and shall vest in His Majesty for the use of the people of New Zealand: Provided
that the Minister may, after inquiry, cancel the forfeiture if he thinks fit.'

It was agreed before me that s 6(3) provided for automatic forfeiture when a Maori
antiquity was entered for export contrary to the provisions of the Act; and that it did not
merely make the object liable to forfeiture. This subsection was the predecessor of s 12(2)
and (3) of the Historic Articles Act 1962. One notices that it applies to articles 'entered
for export' and not to articles which are exported or attempted to be exported as the 1962
b   Act does. It also applies to a narrower class of articles than the 1962 Act. Neither of these
differences provides any explanation why the legislature of New Zealand, having in 1908
provided for automatic forfeiture, should in 1962 seek to provide that articles exported
without a permit should only be liable to forfeiture. On the other hand it can be argued
that since the wording of the 1908 Act was changed when the 1962 Act was enacted, the
legislature must have intended some different effect. I do not regard either of these
c   considerations as of any great significance, but, in my judgment, the more powerful of
the two is the view that the New Zealand legislature is unlikely to have wanted to change
the provision for automatic forfeiture which existed in the 1908 Act.

Next there is the Customs Act 1913, which is expressly referred to in s 12 of the
Historic Articles Act 1962. A number of the provisions of the Customs Act 1913 were
referred to before me, but the most important was s 251 which provided:
d

'Forfeiture to take effect on seizure—When it is provided by this Act or any other
Customs Act that any goods are forfeited, the forfeiture shall take effect without suit
or judgment of condemnation so soon as the goods have been seized in accordance
with this Act or with the Act under which the forfeiture has accrued, and any such
forfeiture so completed by seizure shall for all purposes relate back to the date of the
e   act or event from which the forfeiture accured.'

At the end of the evidence it was, I think, the common view of both experts, and in
any event I find, that this section did not provide for automatic forfeiture, but merely
provided how forfeiture should take effect on seizure. There is nothing surprising about
that in Customs legislation, and I was told that the United Kingdom Customs and Excise
f   Act 1952 so provides. The position from 1962 until 1966 was thus that s 12 of the
Historic Articles Act 1962 expressly referred to the Customs Act 1913, including s 251 to
which I have just referred. However it may still be that during that period the Historic
Articles Act 1962 provided for automatic forfeiture, for it contained the words 'subject
to the provisions of this Act'. Those words do not in my judgment show that there is
necessarily any distinction between the provisions of the Historic Articles Act 1962 and
those of the Customs Act 1913, but they do show that there may be a difference.
g
In 1966 the Customs Act 1913 was replaced by a new Customs Act of that year. The
long title of that Act is: 'An Act to consolidate and amend certain enactments of the
General Assembly relating to Customs and Excise and to the importation and exportation
of goods.'

A question arose before me whether the reference in s 12 of the Historic Articles Act
h   1962 to the Customs Act 1913 must after 1966 be treated as a reference to the Customs
Act 1966. In this connection I was referred to s 21 of the Acts Interpretation Act 1924
which reads:

'Reference to repealed Act in unrepealed Act—(1) In every unrepealed Act in which
reference is made to any repealed Act such reference shall be construed as referring
to any subsequent enactment passed in substitution for such repealed Act, unless it
j   is otherwise manifested by the context . . .'

Dr Inglis gave it as his opinion that the Customs Act 1966 was 'passed in substitution'
for the Customs Act 1913, so that references in the Historic Articles Act 1962 to the
Customs Act 1913 should now be treated as references to the Customs Act 1966. Mr
Thomas for the first defendant agreed with this view, provided that (as he thought) the

1966 Act made no change in the relevant provision of the 1913 Act, that is to say provided that the 1966 Act made goods liable to forfeiture rather than imposing *a* automatic forfeiture, just as the 1913 Act had made goods liable to forfeiture. On this point I definitely prefer the view of Dr Inglis and find that the 1966 Act was 'passed in substitution' for the 1913 Act, whether or not it made any different provision for when forfeiture should take effect. It follows that references in the Historic Articles Act 1962 to the Customs Act 1913 must now be treated as references to the Customs Act 1966; but it is legitimate to bear in mind that the 1913 Act had provided that goods should be *b* liable to forfeiture and not that they should be forfeited automatically.

Next I must consider whether the Customs Act 1966 provides for automatic forfeiture or whether it merely provides that goods shall be liable to forfeiture as its predecessor did. There was considerable dispute about this between the expert witnesses, and a number of provisions of the 1966 Act were referred to and contrasted with the provisions of the 1913 Act. I must now set out some of these provisions, together with comments *c* on them. Part XII of the 1966 Act comprises ss 269 to 288 and is headed FORFEITURES. It has four sub-headings, of which *Forfeiture* is applicable to ss 270 to 274, *Seizure* to ss 275 to 278 and *Condemnation* to ss 279 to 283. The fourth sub-heading is *Miscellaneous Provisions*, applying to ss 284 to 288.

Section 270 provides that the goods therein referred to 'shall be forfeited to the Crown'. Section 272 provides that certain boats, vehicles and animals 'shall be forfeited'. Section *d* 273 provides:

> '*Equipment of forfeited boats, vehicles, and animals*—When any boat, vehicle, or animal has become liable to forfeiture under the Customs Acts, whether by virtue of section 272 of this Act or otherwise, all equipment thereof shall also be liable to forfeiture.'
>
> *e*

It will be noticed that this section uses the expression 'liable to forfeiture' in contrast to s 272 which says 'shall be forfeited'. A possible explanation, although it does not provide much assistance by way of elucidation, is that s 273 is derived from the United Kingdom Customs and Excise Act 1952, s 277(2), where the words 'liable to forfeiture' were correctly used because other provisions of the United Kingdom Customs and Excise Act 1952 also used those words. *f*

Section 274 provides:

> '*Forfeiture to relate back*—When it is provided by this Act or any other of the Customs Acts that any goods are forfeited, and the goods are seized in accordance with this Act or with the Act under which the forfeiture has accrued, the forfeiture shall for all purposes relate back to the date of the act or event from which the *g* forfeiture accrued.'

This replaced s 251 of the Customs Act 1913, which I have already quoted. There is a difference in wording which may or may not be significant. Dr Inglis was constrained to admit that the section appeared to be unnecessary, introduced out of an abundance of caution. Mr Thomas, in contrast, was of the opinion that forfeiture was no longer to be *h* effective on seizure, but only at the later stage of condemnation. Those are the provisions of the 1966 Act which were said to be relevant under the sub-heading *Forfeiture*.

I now turn to those under the sub-heading *Seizure*. First there is s 275 which reads:

> '*Seizure of forfeited goods*—(1) Any officer of Customs or member of the Police may seize any forfeited goods or any goods which he has reasonable and probable cause for suspecting to be forfeited . . . *j*
>
> (4) No goods shall be so seized at any time except within two years after the cause of forfeiture has arisen.'

It would be odd if the power of seizure through the customs officers and police were limited to a period of two years after the cause of forfeiture had arisen, but the Crown a were thereafter able to exercise any other proprietary right, such as an action claiming delivery up in the courts of New Zealand.

Section 277 provides:

'*Rescue of seized goods*—Every person who, without the permission of the Collector or other proper officer of Customs, whether pretending to be the owner or not, either secretly or openly, and whether with or without force or violence, takes or carries away or otherwise converts to his own use any goods that have been seized as
b forfeited, at any time before they have been declared by competent authority to have been seized without due cause, shall be deemed to have stolen the goods as if they were the property of the Crown and shall be guilty of theft accordingly.'

It was suggested that this showed that goods which by the Act 'shall be forfeited' were not as of that moment the property of the Crown; and a contrast was drawn with s 254
c of the Customs Act 1913 which had provided that anybody taking such goods 'shall be deemed to have stolen such goods being the property of His Majesty'. However a possible explanation of both sections is that they were dealing with goods which were initially thought to have been lawfully seized by the customs or police, but in the event turned out not to be liable to forfeiture. Hence I attach no importance to this section, nor to the contrast which it presents with s 254 of the 1913 Act.

d Sections 279 to 283 deal with condemnation, and I need not set them out but merely record that they deal with a number of methods by which condemnation can come into effect. Turning to the *Miscellaneous Provisions* at the end of Part XII of the 1966 Act, the most important are ss 285 and 286 which provide:

'285. *Sale of perishable articles seized*—(1) When any living creature or anything which, in the opinion of the Collector, is of a perishable nature has been seized as
e forfeited the Collector at or nearest to the place of seizure may, if he thinks fit, sell the thing so seized before its condemnation.

(2) The net proceeds of such sale shall be deemed to be substituted for the thing so sold, and all the provisions of this Act with respect to notice of claim and condemnation shall apply to those proceeds accordingly.

286. *Disposal of forfeited goods*—All forfeited goods shall, on forfeiture, become
f the property of the Crown, and shall be sold, destroyed, or otherwise disposed of as the Comptroller or the Minister may direct.'

There was also some discussion of s 287, which provides:

'When any forfeiture has accrued under the Customs Acts the Governor-General may, whether before or after seizure or condemnation, waive the forfeiture . . .'

g Dr Inglis attached considerable importance to s 286. He said that it provided the answer to the very question that has to be determined, by its use of the words 'shall, on forfeiture, become the property of the Crown'. Mr Thomas said that in his view the words 'on forfeiture' in s 286 meant when forfeiture became effective by condemnation. He pointed to the contrast with s 285 which empowers the collector to sell the goods
h before condemnation. This would not be necessary if the goods were already the property of the Crown, except in the case of goods which later turned out not to have been liable to forfeiture.

I prefer the reasoning of Mr Thomas on this last point to that of Dr Inglis. I am also impressed by the point that was taken on s 275(4), that goods could no longer be seized after two years so that it was odd if it was still open to the Crown to enforce a proprietary
j right by any other means. I am impressed again by the difficulty and uncertainty which would ensue, as Mr Thomas pointed out, if the title to goods passed automatically to the Crown upon any of the various events which gave rise to forfeiture. This point was supported by a manuscript treatise of Hale CJ which was found amongst his papers and published in *Hargrave's Law Tracts* in 1787. This was brought to my attention by counsel for the first defendant. It includes this passage (at 226):

'Though a title of forfeiture be given by the lading or unlading the custome not paid, yet the King's title is not compleat, till he hath a judgment of record to *a* ascertain his title; for otherwise there would be endless suits and vexations; for it may be, 10 or 20 years hence there might be a pretence of forfeiture now incurred.'

Finally, I have to consider whether it can have been the intention of the New Zealand legislature to provide that all sorts and kinds of goods should automatically be forfeited to the Crown in certain circumstances, notwithstanding that the goods might be of an *b* onerous nature.

Considering both the provisions of the Customs Act 1966 and its predecessor, the 1913 Act, and its purpose, I prefer the evidence of Mr Thomas that it does not provide for automatic forfeiture but does provide that goods shall be liable to forfeiture in certain circumstances, with the effect that title passes to the Crown only on seizure or later on condemnation.

I now must turn to s 12 of the Historic Articles Act 1962. It uses the words 'shall be *c* forfeited'. Immediately thereafter it has a reference to the Customs Act 1913. The same words occur in that Act and in the 1966 Act which has replaced it. There they have the meaning 'shall be liable to forfeiture'. Linguistic considerations therefore point to the view that in the 1962 Act they have the same meaning, and do not mean shall be forfeited automatically. But that is not conclusive, since s 12(2) also contains the words *d* 'subject to the provisions of this Act'. Furthermore the nature of the articles dealt with by the Historic Articles Act 1962 may be wholly different from those within the purview of the Customs Acts. Automatic forfeiture is not likely, in the case of the Historic Articles Act 1962, to impose any onerous burden on the Crown. On the contrary it may well have been contemplated that the articles dealt with are such as would be invariably beneficial for the Crown to enjoy.

There was considerable attention given in the evidence to a provision of the New *e* Zealand Acts Interpretation Act 1924 which was said to be relevant in this context. It is s 5(j) which reads:

'Every Act, and every provision or enactment thereof, shall be deemed remedial, whether its immediate purport is to direct the doing of anything Parliament deems to be for the public good, or to prevent or punish the doing of anything it deems *f* contrary to the public good, and shall accordingly receive such fair, large, and liberal construction and interpretation as will best ensure the attainment of the object of the Act and of such provision or enactment according to its true intent, meaning and spirit.'

Dr Inglis attached considerable importance to this section. Mr Thomas, on the other *g* hand, felt that it did no more than abolish the old distinction between penal and remedial Acts, and said that it was very rarely cited in New Zealand. I am inclined to prefer the view of Mr Thomas on this point. I doubt whether s 5(j) was an early recognition in 1924 of the power of the courts to disregard the literal meaning of an Act and to give it a purposive construction. However I need not finally decide this point since both witnesses were of the view that the courts in New Zealand will now adopt the purposive approach *h* to statutes. In particular Mr Thomas agreed that the law of New Zealand as it now stands accords with two passages that are to be found in the speeches in the House of Lords in *Fothergill v Monarch Airlines Ltd* [1980] 2 All ER 696, [1981] AC 251. The first is in the speech of Lord Wilberforce ([1980] 2 All ER 696 at 700, [1981] AC 251 at 272):

'I start by considering the purpose of art 26, and I do not think that in doing so I *j* am infringing any "golden rule". Consideration of the purpose of an enactment is always a legitimate part of the process of interpretation, and if it is usual, and indeed correct, to look first for a clear meaning of the words used it is certain, in the present case, both on a first look at the relevant text and from the judgments in the courts below, that no "golden rule" meaning can be ascribed.'

The second is in the speech of Lord Diplock ([1980] 2 All ER 696 at 705, [1981] AC
a 251 at 280) which after referring to the 'traditional, and widely criticised, style of
legislative draftsmanship which has become familiar to English judges during the
present century and for which their own narrowly semantic approach to statutory
construction, until the last decade or so, may have been largely to blame,' continues:

'That approach for which Parliamentary draftsmen had to cater can hardly be
better illustrated than by the words of Lord Simonds LC in *Inland Revenue Comrs v*
b   *Ayrshire Employers Mutual Insurance Association Ltd* [1946] 1 All ER 637 at 641: "The
section . . . sect. 31 of the Finance Act, 1933, is clearly a remedial section . . . It is at
least clear what is the gap that is intended to be filled and hardly less clear how it is
intended to fill that gap. Yet I can come to no other conclusion than that the
language of the section fails to achieve its apparent purpose and I must decline to
insert words or phrases which might succeed where the draftsman failed." The
c   unhappy legacy of this judicial attitude, although it is now being replaced by an
increasing willingness to give a purposive construction to the Act, is the current
English style of legislative draftsmanship.'

Mr Thomas agreed that the courts of New Zealand would follow and apply these
passages, at any rate in a case where there was no clear meaning which emerged from the
d words of the statute. That condition is in my judgment fulfilled in this case, since the
words 'shall be forfeited' are fairly capable of either of two meanings. However Mr
Thomas considered that the purpose of the Historic Articles Act 1962 did not require
that those words meant that the article should automatically be forfeited. He considered
that the purpose of the 1962 Act was firstly the protection of historic articles, and
secondly the control of their removal from New Zealand. In his view the automatic
e forfeiture of articles exported or attempted to be exported without a permit would not
advance those purposes. Dr Inglis disagreed, and on this point I prefer his evidence. It
seems to me an unduly narrow construction of the purposes of the 1962 Act which
would lead to the conclusion that automatic forfeiture would not advance them. In my
view the purpose of the 1962 Act is to secure the enjoyment of historic articles for the
people of New Zealand in the territory of New Zealand; that purpose is plainly advanced
f if articles exported or attempted to be exported become automatically the property of
the Crown and can if necessary be recovered by the Crown. Mr Thomas observed that
the use of the words 'knowingly' and 'attempted to be exported' in s 12 resulted in an
imprecise and unsatisfactory test if automatic forfeiture were to result. That is certainly
true to some extent; but I have no reason to suppose that it was on that account contrary
to the purpose and intent of the New Zealand legislature.
g   My conclusions on this issue are therefore as follows: (1) the words 'shall be forfeited'
are equally capable of meaning shall be forfeited automatically or shall be liable to
forfeiture; (2) the reference to the Customs Act 1913 and now to the Customs Act 1966
where the same words mean 'shall be liable to be forfeited', points to the words having
that meaning in the 1962 Act; (3) that it is not conclusive because s 12 of the Historic
Articles Act 1962, when it refers to the Customs Act, does so 'subject to the provisions of
h this Act'; (4) the purpose of the 1962 Act may properly be taken into account by a New
Zealand court and points firmly in favour of automatic forfeiture. On these grounds I
accept the evidence of Dr Inglis that it does so provide.
I now turn to the second main issue, that is to say whether the court is being asked to
enforce and should enforce a foreign penal, revenue or public law. First I must consider
whether the court is being asked to enforce the Historic Articles Act 1962, or merely to
j recognise it. There is plainly a difference in English private international law between
enforcement and recognition for this purpose. This emerges for example from the speech
of Viscount Simonds in *Regazzoni v K C Sethia (1944) Ltd* [1957] 3 All ER 286 at 292,
[1958] AC 301 at 322:

'It does not follow from the fact that today the court will not enforce a revenue law at the suit of a foreign state that today it will enforce a contract which requires the doing of an act in a foreign country which violates the revenue law of that country. The two things are not complementary or co-extensive. This may be seen if for revenue law penal law is substituted. For an English court will not enforce a penal law at the suit of a foreign state, yet it would be surprising if it would enforce a contract which required the commission of a crime in that state.'

So also in *Re Helbert Wagg and Co Ltd, Re Prudential Assurance Co Ltd* [1956] 1 All ER 129 at 138–139, [1956] Ch 323 at 345–346 Upjohn J stated three propositions:

'(1) No state will enforce the fiscal laws, however proper, of another state, nor penal statutes, using that phrase in the strict sense of meaning statutes imposing penalties recoverable by the state for infringement of some law ... (ii) English law will not recognise the validity of foreign legislation intended to discriminate against nationals of this country in time of war by legislation which purports to confiscate wholly or in part movable property situated in the foreign state ... (3) English courts will not recognise the validity of foreign legislation aimed at confiscating the property of particular individuals or classes of individuals.'

When the problem is one of recognition, then a different and possibly a stricter test is applied than in the case of enforcement, before the application of foreign law is excluded. Thus in *Aksionairnoye Obschestvo A M Luther v James Sagor and Co* [1921] 3 KB 532, [1921] All ER Rep 138, foreign legislation expropriating property was recognised. So also in *Princess Paley Olga v Weisz* [1929] 1 KB 718, [1929] All ER Rep 513. On the other hand in *Anglo-Iranian Oil Co Ltd v Jaffrate, The Rose Mary* [1953] 1 WLR 246, foreign legislation expropriating property was not recognised. I need not enter upon the distinction between these cases. As I understand the position it is agreed before me that if the question in this case is one of recognising the Historic Articles Act 1962, then it is a law which the English courts will recognise. If the customs officers of New Zealand had seized the carving and it had been condemned and reduced into the possession of the New Zealand government, then that government would have been entitled to defend its title in proceedings in this country by reference to the Historic Articles Act 1962.

Counsel for the Attorney General of New Zealand submits that the position is the same in these proceedings although it is the Attorney General of New Zealand who seeks delivery up of the carving. He says that the Attorney General is suing to enforce a proprietary title, and not to enforce the statute. In my judgment that submission is ill founded. In order to make good his title in these proceedings the Attorney General has to rely on the Historic Articles Act 1962, since he cannot rely on any previous possession or other root of title. *Brokaw v Seatrain UK Ltd* [1971] 2 All ER 98, [1971] 2 QB 476, is exactly in point. There the United States Treasury had served a notice of levy with a view to collecting tax on goods at sea on board an ocean going vessel. When the ship docked at Southampton both the former owner of the goods and the United States government claimed possession from the shipowners. Lord Denning MR said ([1971] 2 All ER 98 at 100, [1971] 2 QB 476 at 483):

'If the United States government had taken these goods into their actual possession, say in a warehouse in Baltimore, or may be by attornment of the master to an officer of the United States government, that might have been sufficient to enable them to claim the goods. But there is nothing of that kind here. The United States government simply rely on this notice of levy given to the shipowners, and that is not, in my view, sufficient to reduce the goods into their possession. Apart from this point, it appears to me that the United States government are seeking the aid of these courts. They come as claimants in these interpleader proceedings. By so doing they are seeking the aid of our courts to collect tax ... It comes within the prohibition of our law whereby we do not enforce directly or indirectly the revenue law of another country.'

Since this is a case of enforcement, I have to consider what are the principles on which
a this court will enforce foreign law relating to chattels. In general the transfer of title to a
movable thing is governed by the law of the place where the thing is at the time when
the transfer is said to take effect: see r 79 in *Dicey and Morris on the Conflict of Laws* (10th
edn, 1980) p 555:

'The validity of a transfer of a tangible movable and its effect on the proprietary
rights of the parties thereto and of those claiming under them in respect thereof are
b governed (in general) by the law of the country where the movable is at the time of
the transfer (*lex situs*).'

But that is subject to another principle the formulation of which is not by any means
clear. It is set out as r 3 in *Dicey and Morris* p 89:

'English courts have no jurisdiction to entertain an action:—(1) for the
c enforcement, either directly or indirectly, of a penal, revenue, or other public law
of a foreign State; or (2) founded upon an act of State.'

I have to consider whether this is indeed the correct formulation of the principle, and
secondly whether this case comes within it. The first aspect of the problem is whether
one looks at the foreign statute as a whole, or at the particular provision of it (in technical
d language, the enactment) which it is sought to enforce. There is high authority which
might be taken to suggest that one must look at the statute as a whole. For example in
Regazzoni v K C Sethia (1944) Ltd [1956] 1 All ER 229, [1956] 2 QB 490 at first instance,
Sellers J observed that the penalty for a breach of the Sea Customs Act 1878 of India was
three times the value of the goods. However he said ([1956] 1 All ER 229 at 233, [1956]
2 QB 490 at 499):

e 'I reject counsel for the plaintiff's submission that the prohibiting Regulation is
to be regarded as either a penal or a revenue enactment (although infringement of
the Regulation might involve penalties and fines which would enhance the
revenue) . . .'

Similarly in the same case in the Court of Appeal Parker LJ said ([1956] 2 All ER 487 at
f 496, [1956] 2 QB 490 at 524):

'Finally counsel for the plaintiff took the point that the Indian law was a revenue,
penal or political law, to which the courts of this country will pay no attention. It is
clearly in my view not a penal or a revenue law . . .'

In the House of Lords Lord Reid said ([1957] 3 All ER 286 at 293, [1958] AC 301 at 324):

g 'The Indian law prohibiting exports to South Africa does not appear to me to be a
revenue or penal law any more than was the law of exchange control considered by
this House in *Kahler* v. *Midland Bank, Ltd* ([1949] 2 All ER 621, [1950] AC 24).'

If, however, the Indian government had been suing in the courts of this country to
enforce and recover a penalty of three times the value of the goods, in a case where goods
h had been exported contrary to the provisions of that Act, I do not have the slightest doubt
that the English courts would have refused to enforce the claim. It follows in my
judgment that it cannot be right simply to categorise the statute sought to be enforced as
a whole. No such point arose in *Regazzoni v K C Sethia (1944) Ltd*, and none of the
judgments or speeches were directed to it. I consider that the court must pay regard only
to the particular provision or enactment of the foreign law which it is sought to enforce.
j Support for this is to be found in *Raulin v Fischer* (1911) 2 KB 93. That case was concerned
not with the enforcement of a foreign law but with the enforcement of a foreign
judgment; but I do not think that the principle to be applied is different. There a
criminal court in France had to try an American lady on a charge of criminal negligence,
in that while recklessly galloping her horse in the Avenue du Bois de Boulogne in Paris
she ran into the plaintiff, a French officer, and seriously injured him. The defendant was

convicted and sentenced to one month's imprisonment and a fine of 100 francs. At the same time the court awarded compensation to Monsieur Raulin of 5,000 francs. He sought to enforce that judgment in England and was held entitled to do so.

In *Huntington v Atrill* [1893] AC 150 at 155–156 Lord Watson, delivering the judgment of their Lordships, said:

'The general law upon this point has been correctly stated by Mr. Justice Story in his "Conflict of Laws", and by other text writers; but their Lordships do not think it necessary to quote from these authorities in explanation of the reasons which have induced courts of justice to decline jurisdiction in suits somewhat loosely described as penal, when these have their origin in a foreign country. The rule has its foundation in the well-recognised principle that crimes, including in that term all breaches of public law punishable by pecuniary mulct or otherwise, at the instance of the State Government or of some one representing the public, are local in this sense, that they are only cognizable and punishable in the country where they were committed. Accordingly no proceeding, even in the shape of a civil suit, which has for its object the enforcement by the State, whether directly or indirectly, of punishment imposed for such breaches by the lex fori, ought to be admitted in the Courts of any other country.'

This passage in my judgment shows that the precise test is one of characterisation of the English suit. Is it a penal suit, or a revenue suit, or a public law suit? I advance this solution with some diffidence, as it was not supported by counsel on either side. But it seems to me with respect to be more satisfactory than either the characterisation of the foreign statute as a whole or the characterisation of any particular enactment in it. After all, there may well be countries elsewhere in which, as in England, some offences are defined and punishable only by the common law.

It was not disputed before me that the English courts will not enforce a foreign penal law or a foreign revenue law. The third category was in dispute, that is to say 'public' law as it is called by *Dicey*.

First I have to consider whether in this action the court is being asked to enforce a foreign penal law. It is no doubt an unpleasant consequence for the owner of an historic article, if he is found to have exported or attempted to export it without a permit and it is thereby forfeited to the Crown. In one sense the statute therefore provides for punishment. However the passage that I have already read from the judgment of Upjohn J in *Re Helbert Wagg & Co Ltd* [1956] 1 All ER 129 at 138, [1956] Ch 323 at 345 shows that the word 'penal' has a somewhat restricted meaning in this context.

Forfeiture may be in certain circumstances, and often is, a penalty: see for example *R v Nat Bell Liquors Ltd* [1922] 2 AC 128, [1922] All ER Rep 335, where forfeiture of whisky to the Crown in the province of Alberta was held to be a penalty, no doubt because the object was to punish those who dealt in it unlawfully rather than to benefit the province of Alberta. So also in *Banco de Vizcaya v Don Alfonso de Borbon y Austria* [1935] 1 KB 140, [1934] All ER Rep 555, a decree expropriating all the property of the defendant on the ground that he was guilty of high treason was held to be a penal law, and unenforceable in this country.

In my judgment the true meaning of a penal suit is best illustrated by a decision of the Court of Appeals of New York: *Loucks v Standard Oil Co of New York* (1918) 120 NE 198. That case was concerned with the enforcement in New York of a Massachusetts statute which provided for the recovery on behalf of the widow or children or next of kin of any person killed by negligence of damages 'in the sum of not less than $500, nor more than $10,000, to be assessed with reference to the degree of . . . culpability [of the wrongdoer]'. Cardozo J said (at 198):

"The courts of no country execute the penal laws of another." The Antelope ((1825) 10 Wheat 66 at 123). The defendant invokes that principle as applicable here. Penal in one sense the statute indisputably is. The damages are not limited to compensation; they are proportioned to the offender's guilt. A minimum recovery a of $500 is allowed in every case. But the question is not whether the statute is penal in some sense. The question is whether it is penal within the rules of private international law. A statute penal in that sense is one that awards a penalty to the state, or to a public officer in its behalf, or to a member of the public, suing in the interest of the whole community to redress a public wrong. [Then some authorities are quoted and the learned judge continues]: The purpose must be, not reparation to one aggrieved, but vindication of the public justice.'

b I apply that test to the present case. Section 5 of the Historic Articles Act 1962 provides for a fine, albeit not a very large one. That is unquestionably penal. But the purpose of the provision for forfeiture in s 12 is not, in my judgment, the vindication of the public justice. Its purpose is to preserve as the property of the people of New Zealand an historic article. It is not therefore a penal provision.

Next I consider whether this is a revenue law. I suspect that an old-fashioned sense of
c the word 'revenue' at one time included or comprised the control over the export and import of goods. That view is consistent with a passage in the speech of Lord Somervell in *Regazzoni's* case [1957] 3 All ER 286 at 297, [1958] AC 301 at 330:

'The statement that in this field one country takes no notice of the revenue laws of another seems to have been based on the principle that smuggling and freedom
d "gang thegither" and had its high-water mark in *Boucher* v. *Lawson* ((1735) Lee *temp* Hard 85, 95 ER 53). Scrutton L.J., in *Ralli Brothers* v. *Compañia Naviera Sota y Aznar* ([1920] 2 KB 287 at 300, [1920] All ER Rep 427 at 435) reserved the issue for consideration should it arise. It was submitted that prohibition in the present case of export to a particular destination was a revenue law, and one can imagine such a prohibition being a revenue law. On the evidence in the present case it would seem
e not to fall within the ordinary meaning of the phrase, but in any event I myself think that the courts of this country should not today enforce a contract to smuggle goods into or out of a foreign and friendly state.'

But whatever the position may once have been, I consider that the present rule as to not enforcing a foreign revenue law applies only to what may more or less accurately be described as taxes. In the plain language of Denning LJ in *Regazzoni's* case [1956] 2 All
f ER 487 at 490, [1956] 2 QB 490 at 515, approved by Viscount Simonds in the House of Lords ([1957] 3 All ER 286 at 289, [1958] AC 301 at 318): 'These courts do not sit to collect taxes for another country or to inflict punishments for it . . .' The demands of the revenue authorities of a foreign state are not given an effect which is exorbitant, in the sense of that word sometimes used by international lawyers. A list of cases in which foreign law has not been enforced on the ground that it was revenue law is set out in
g 8 Halsbury's Laws (4th edn) para 420, note 1. The cases concern capital gains tax, customs duty, rates, succession duty, income tax, profits tax and national insurance contributions. The forfeiture provision in s 12 of the Historic Articles Act 1962 is in my judgment not a foreign revenue law.

Next I turn to the most difficult issue in the whole case, whether there is a third category of foreign laws which this court will not enforce, namely public law, and if so
h what it comprises. In finding the point difficult I am in good company. Dr F A Mann in his lecture on 'Prerogative Rights of Foreign States and the Conflict of Laws' (1954) 40 *Transactions of the Grotius Society* 25 at 33, said:

'It would be of considerably greater value if it were possible to suggest an accurate and comprehensive definition of the rights which come within the scope of these
j descriptions. But at no stage of the historical development and in no country have lawyers succeeded in satisfactorily determining what is meant by "public law" or "matters *jure imperii*" or, as the phrase went in the early 17th century, by "government" and what comes under the heading of "private law" or "matters *jure gestionis*", or "property". Yet the inability of the human mind and vocabulary to explain and contain all cases by an all-embracing form of words does not disprove the reality of a distinction which, with respect, must be considered as indispensable,

though in another connection, Prof. Lauterpacht has recently described it as
"impracticable and productive of uncertainty" (see "The Problem of Jurisdictional
Immunities of Foreign States" (1951) 28 BYIL 240).'

The plaintiff was concerned that the argument on this head might be affected by the
terms of the law in question, and in particular by whether it provided for compensation
when an article was forfeited. He accordingly applied to Robert Goff J for leave to call
additional evidence. That application was dismissed, without prejudice to the right to
renew it before the trial judge, on the first and third defendants making admissions as
follows:

'The great majority of countries have legislation to forbid or control the export of
antiquities and in many cases the sanction for any attempt to export an antiquity
illegally is that the object may be confiscated, and most countries have legislation
broadly similar in effect to the Historic Articles Act 1962 of New Zealand.'

The application was renewed before me. A further concession was made on behalf of
the first and third defendants. This was that, so far as concerned the point of 'public' law
(but not penal law, which I have already considered), the argument was the same whether
the statute did or did not provide for compensation. In the light of that concession, the
plaintiff did not pursue his application for leave to call additional evidence.

Of the English authorities, I start with the textbooks. In *Dicey on Conflict of Laws*, from
at any rate the sixth edition, the third category was described as 'political' laws. That
description was questioned by Birkett LJ in the course of the argument in *Regazzoni's*
case [1956] 2 QB 490 at 506, and in his judgment he found it very difficult to attach to it
any special or particular meaning; Parker LJ shared that difficulty (see [1956] 2 All ER
487 at 493, 496, [1956] 2 QB 490 at 520, 524). In the House of Lords Viscount Simonds
said ([1957] 3 All ER 286 at 289, [1958] AC 301 at 318): '. . . There is still a question how
far, if at all, the doctrine extends to laws which are described as having a "political" or
"public" character.' It was perhaps in consequence of these observations that the
formulation in *Dicey* was changed. Rule 3 now reads, as I have already said:

'English courts have no jurisdiction to entertain an action:—(1) for the
enforcement, either directly or indirectly, of a penal, revenue, or other public law
of a foreign State.'

That is the proposition which the first and third defendants now seek to maintain.
Oppenheim's International Law (8th edn, 1955) vol 1, p 328 states:

'. . . the courts of many countries, including British and American courts, decline
to give effect to the public law, as distinguished from private law, of foreign states.
In particular they refuse to enforce foreign revenue laws as well as penal and
confiscatory legislation of other States.'

In 8 Halsbury's Laws (4th edn) paras 417–420, in the title Conflict of Laws (which is
contributed by, amongst others, Dr Morris and Mr North) the general rule is said to be
that the English court will apply foreign law—'even though the result may be contrary
to a policy of English law which the court would apply in a purely domestic case'. The
exceptions of penal law and revenue law are stated, and a third category is laid down as
follows:

'*Public policy.* Exceptionally, the English court will not enforce or recognise a right
conferred or a duty imposed by a foreign law where, on the facts of the particular
case, enforcement or, as the case may be, recognition,. would be contrary to a
fundamental policy of English law.'

In *Cheshire and North's Private International Law* (10th edn, 1979) pp 131, 135, 137, 145,
there are four categories: foreign revenue laws, foreign penal laws, foreign expropriatory
legislation, and foreign law which 'is repugnant to the distinctive policy of English law'.

a I was referred also to the American Law Institute's Restatement, Conflict of Laws, Second, ch 4, §§ 89–90. This deals first with a foreign penal cause of action (again characterising the suit rather than the foreign law or enactment) and taxes, and then provides in § 90: 'No action will be entertained on a foreign cause of action the enforcement of which is contrary to the strong public policy of the forum.' Turning to the cases, I leave out of account those concerned with foreign expropriatory legislation. Where the problem before the court was one of recognition (as in *Aksionairnoye Obschestvo*

b *A M Luther v James Sagor & Co* [1921] 3 KB 532, [1921] All ER Rep 138, *Princess Paley Olga v Weisz* [1929] 1 KB 718, [1929] All ER Rep 513 and *Anglo-Iranian Oil Co v Jaffrate, The Rose Mary* [1953] 1 WLR 246), the test applied does not appear to have depended on whether the foreign law was political or public law, but on other considerations. Where the problem was one of enforcement, as in *Banco de Vizcaya v Don Alfonso de Borbon y Austria* [1935] 1 KB 140, [1934] All ER Rep 555, the claim failed because the foreign law

c was a penal law, and also possibly because it could not be given extraterritorial operation so as to affect the title to property situate in England. Neither side contended before me that the expropriation cases as a class were relevant to the problem in this case.

There is, however, one expropriation case to which I have been referred which is said to be directly relevant. That is the decision of Pearson J in *Jabbour v Custodian of Israeli Absentee Property* [1954] 1 All ER 145, [1954] 1 WLR 139. The case is acknowledged in

d *Dicey and Morris* p 94, note 20, to be against the principle stated in their text. Likewise Dr Mann in his lecture (at 41–42) considered that it was a case where the judge 'contrary to principle . . . allowed a foreign State to enforce a prerogative right in England'. And counsel for the Attorney General in this case, founded on *Jabbour's* case as inconsistent with the arguments of the first and third defendants.

The issue in that case arose on interpleader, as to which of the parties could recover

e moneys admittedly due from the Yorkshire Insurance Co, consequent on damage by fire to a garage owned by Jabbour Brothers in Haifa. The plaintiffs sued to enforce the contract of insurance; they failed, because by the lex situs the title to their claim had been transferred to the custodian. It followed that the custodian, the only other person with a claim to the insurance moneys, was entitled to them, and a declaration was made to that effect.

f The foreign law, by which the custodian obtained title, was certainly recognised, because thereby the plaintiffs' claim was defeated. Only in a limited sense was it enforced: there being no other claimant left in the field, the custodian succeeded. I cannot regard this case as a firm foundation for the view that foreign confiscatory legislation will be enforced in this country.

In my judgment only two cases of those cited to me are directly relevant to the

g question whether an English court will enforce foreign public laws which are neither penal nor revenue laws. The first is *Re Lord Cable (decd)* [1976] 3 All ER 417, [1977] 1 WLR 7. In that case the plaintiffs, who were beneficiaries under a will but not resident in India, sought to restrain the will trustees and an Indian company which the trustees had formed from remitting the proceeds of some English investments made by the company back to India. Failure to remit the proceeds would have been a breach of Indian

h exchange control legislation on the part of the Indian company. The Union of India applied to be joined as a party, on the ground that it was interested in the action in order to protect its exchange control legislation. Slade J refused the application for joinder. Although it had been held in *Kahler v Midland Bank Ltd* [1949] 2 All ER 621, [1950] AC 24 that foreign exchange control legislation might be recognised in England, the learned judge was not satisfied 'that the English court would ever entertain proceedings by the

j Government of India, or any other foreign government, of which the sole acknowledged purpose was directly to enforce its currency control regulations' (see [1976] 3 All ER 417 at 422–423, [1977] 1 WLR 7 at 13). I accept that this was a decision that exchange control legislation is in a similar category to foreign penal and revenue law. But it does not go so far as to establish a general category of public law.

The other case which is directly relevant, and on the facts closest to the present case, is *King of Italy v Marquis Cosimo di Medici Tornaquinci* (1918) 34 TLR 623. Dr Mann in his lecture (at 34) cited this case as authority for the following proposition: a

'It is also free from doubt that if works of art cannot be exported from Italy without a special licence, the State of Italy cannot come to the English Courts to recover a painting wrongfully exported from Italy.'

The decision was an interlocutory one, and the facts are not fully reported. There were apparently two classes of papers concerned, both forming part of the Medici archives. b The first comprised Italian state papers; the second, historical documents. Peterson J granted an interlocutory injunction restraining the sale of the state papers, on the ground that they were and always had been the property of the Italian state. It is not altogether clear whether the learned judge found that they were or ever had been in the possession of the Italian state; and in consequence it is not clear whether he enforced Italian law, or c merely recognised it. The most that can be said on that part of the case is that no distinction was apparently drawn between enforcement and recognition: it was sufficient that Italian law had vested title in the Italian state before the papers left Italy.

The historical documents, on the other hand, had been exported in breach of Italian Law. Peterson J did not restrain their sale. It does not appear from the report whether the Italian law in question had any provision for forfeiture, similar to s 12 of the Historic d Articles Act 1962 of New Zealand. It may be that the case was decided on the simple ground that, although the historical documents had been exported illegally, they did not thereby cease to be the property of their former owners. Manifestly it would not be right, on that hypothesis, to restrain the sale in England. (It was stated in the argument, 34 TLR 623, that Italian law granted the state a first option to purchase the historical documents. If that is right, could it have been enforced by action in England? Peterson J e did not mention the point.)

I have considered also *Don Alonso v Cornero* (1611) Hob 212, 80 ER 359, since *Dicey and Morris* p 94, note 22, state that it 'remains the only reported English case which approaches the problem'. The case was concerned with 3,000 lb of tobacco, worth £800. The Court of Common Pleas held that: 'if any subject of a foreign prince bring goods into the kingdom, though they were confiscate before, the property of them shall not f here be questioned but at the common law.' On its facts the case was clearly concerned with a penal law.

I can thus detect no support in the English cases for a category of foreign public law, but equally nothing of great weight against it. The most that can be said (of the cases since *Regazzoni v K C Sethia* (1944) *Ltd*, when 'political' law disappeared as a candidate), is that Slade J in *Re Lord Cable (decd)*, accepted foreign exchange control law as an instance g of a foreign law that was neither revenue nor penal, but would not be enforced here.

Dr Mann described the class of claims which would not be enforced here as foreign prerogative rights, or claims jure imperii; *Dicey and Morris*, p 93, as those 'which are enforced as an assertion of the authority of central or local government'. With the greatest respect, I do not accept that any such general principle exists in English law; nor do I consider that it would be right for me to establish it. The kinds of law which would h be comprised in such a wide class are so many and so various, that some should properly be enforced in this country while others perhaps should not. The right of a state to succeed to heirless property as bona vacantia, mentioned by Dr Mann, may be one instance where public policy provides no easy answer. It is a better solution, in my judgment, to follow the treatment of Halsbury's Laws, *Cheshire and North* and the *Restatement*, considering in each individual case whether there is any special ground of j public policy which requires the law in question not to be enforced here.

Dr Mann in his lecture (at 45) cited Lord Asquith in *Chapman v Chapman* [1954] 1 All ER 798 at 819, [1954] AC 429 at 470:

'Nor, speaking more generally, does English jurisprudence start from a broad principle and decide cases in accordance with its logical implications. It starts from

a clean slate, scored over, in course of time, with ad hoc decisions. General rules are
arrived at inductively, from the collation and comparison of these decisions: they
do not pre-exist them.'

From an examination of the slate as it presently stands, I cannot by process of inductive
reasoning arrive at the conclusion that foreign public laws, as a whole, will not be
enforced here.

If the test is one of public policy, applied to the foreign law in question in this
particular case, there is in my judgment every reason why the English courts should
enforce s 12 of the Historic Articles Act 1962 of New Zealand. Comity requires that we
should respect the national heritage of other countries, by according both recognition
and enforcement to their laws which affect the title to property while it is within their
territory. The hope of reciprocity is an additional ground of public policy leading to the
same conclusion.

I therefore give judgment for the plaintiff on the preliminary issues.

Order accordingly. Leave to appeal.

Solicitors: *Allen & Overy* (for the Attorney General of New Zealand); *Joelson, Wilson & Co*
(for the first defendant); *Herbert Smith & Co* (for the second defendant); *Manches & Co* (for
the third defendant).

K Mydeen Esq   Barrister.

Appeal
The first and third defendants appealed to the Court of Appeal.

Paul Baker QC and *Nicholas Patten* for the first defendant.
Colin Ross-Munro QC and *Gerald Levy* for the third defendant.
Charles Gray and *Nicholas Paines* for the Attorney General of New Zealand.

Cur adv vult

21 May. The following judgments were read.

LORD DENNING MR.

The door of the treasure house
Years ago in New Zealand a great chief of the Maoris had a treasure house. In it there
were stored such things as dried fish, special foods and valuables. At the entrance there
was a great door. It was made of totara wood which is light, durable, tough, and of a dark
red colour. This great door was four feet high and nearly five feet wide. It had five panels
carved with exquisite skill. These depicted human figures with serpentine bodies and
wide pointed heads.

This great door was lost for centuries in a swamp near Waitara in the province of
Taranaki in North Island. Then in 1972 a Maori tribesman called Manukonga, whilst
cutting a track through the swamp, came upon it and carried it to his home.

In the next year, 1973, there came to New Zealand Lance Entwistle. He was from
London and was a dealer in primitive works of art. He got to know of this carving and
went to see it. He realised at once that it was of much value. It was of the highest
importance to the study of Maori art and civilisation and Polynesian sculpture. He
persuaded Manukonga to sell it to him for the sum of $6,000. He took it up to Auckland
and then across to New York. From there he telephoned to George Ortiz who lived in
Geneva. Now George Ortiz was a collector of African and Oceanic works of art. His
collection was one of the finest in the world. Lance Entwistle asked George Ortiz to
inspect this carving. George Ortiz went to New York to see it. Lance Entwistle told him

that it had been exported from New Zealand without a permit but nevertheless he was the owner of it and could pass a good title to it. Thereupon, on 23 April 1973, George *a* Ortiz bought this carving from Lance Entwistle for US $65,000. It was sent to Geneva by air and was kept by George Ortiz in his collection there.

In October 1977 the daughter of George Ortiz was kidnapped. In order to raise money for her release, he sent his art collection to Sothebys in London for sale by auction. Sothebys prepared an attractive catalogue. It contained a fine coloured picture of this carving. It was the principal item in the sale. Sothebys announced that the auction was *b* to be held on Thursday, 29 June 1978.

This came to the notice of the New Zealand Government. Their Attorney General at once on 26 June 1978, three days before the sale, issued a writ claiming a declaration that this carving belonged to the New Zealand government and an injunction to prevent the sale or disposal of it. In the face of this writ it was agreed that Sothebys would not include this carving in the sale but would hold it pending trial or further order.

The sale was held without this carving. Enough was realised from the other items to *c* pay the ransom. So George Ortiz does not propose to sell it now. It is said to be worth £300,000.

The case may eventually require a hearing on disputed points of fact. But meanwhile this court has ordered that these two points be tried as preliminary issues: (1) whether Her Majesty The Queen has become the owner and is entitled to possession of the carving *d* under the New Zealand Acts entitled the Historic Articles Act 1962 and the Customs Acts 1913 and 1966, and (2) whether in any event the provisions of the said Acts are unenforceable in England as being foreign, penal, revenue and/or public laws. The defendants have also made the following concessions: 'the great majority of countries have legislation to forbid or control the export of antiquities and in many cases the sanction for any attempt to export an antiquity illegally is that the object may be *e* confiscated.'

Although this case concerns New Zealand law, I propose to consider first the English law. This is because New Zealand has inherited the common law of England: and also because its statutes and methods of interpretation are on much the same lines as our own. We use the same language, the English language, to express the same principles, to define the same concepts, and to give the same meaning. *f*

The law of England

So far as England is concerned, whenever there is legislation providing that goods are to be forfeited for one cause or another, the law has always said that the forfeiture does not take effect until the goods are seized and that the title then relates back to the cause of forfeiture. If the owner or anyone else disputes the forfeiture, there are proceedings *g* for condemnation. After condemnation, the title is perfected and can no longer be disputed by anyone.

That was settled in the great case of *Lockyer v Offley* (1786) 1 Term Rep 252, 99 ER 1079. The master of the sailing vessel Hope smuggled 60 gallons of brandy into London. The customs officers, a month later, seized the ship and claimed her as forfeited. Willes J said (1 Term Rep 252 at 260, 99 ER 1079 at 1083): *h*

'... it has been said that under the 24 Geo. 3, c.47, and the Excise laws, the forfeiture attaches the moment the act is done ... but I think the actual property is not altered till after the seizure, though it may be before condemnation ... Till the seizure of the ship, it was not certain that the officers of the Crown knew of the illicit trade carried on by the master, or whether they would take advantage of the forfeiture.' *i*

In *Manning's Exchequer Practice* (1827) pp 142, 181, it is said:

'Seizures for non-payment of customs, and the like, are grounded upon *a principle of the common law, applied to acts of parliament creating a forfeiture* ... The property in goods, forfeited under the excise laws, is not altered until after seizure ... For some

purposes, as to avoid intermediate alienations and incumbrances, etc., the forfeiture
seems to relate to the act done.' (My emphasis.)

From that time onwards there were many Customs Acts. In most of them, the statute
simply said that on breach the goods 'shall be forfeited' (see the Customs Consolidation
Act 1876, ss 106, 130 and 138); and that on seizure notice is to be given to the owner of
the goods (see s 207). In accordance with the law as laid down in *Lockyer v Offley*, the
forfeiture was not automatic. It did not take effect until the goods were seized. Indeed,
when a fresh consolidation act was passed in 1952, Parliament did not use the words
'shall be forfeited'. It used instead the words 'shall be liable to forfeiture' (see the Customs
and Excise Act 1952, ss 47 to 56, and ss 275 to 280). Paragraph 1 of Sch 7 to the 1952 Act
says:

> 'The Commissioners shall give notice of the seizure of any thing as liable to
> forfeiture and of the grounds therefor to any person who to their knowledge was at
> the time of the seizure the owner or one of the owners thereof.'

Likewise in the Merchant Shipping Act 1854 it was enacted that on certain wrongs
being done 'such ship shall be forfeited to Her Majesty'. Here too it was held that the
forfeiture took effect on seizure, but that the title then related back to the time of the
wrongful act done which was the cause of the forfeiture (see *The Annandale* (1877) 2 PD
179 at 185 per Sir Robert Phillimore), so that any disposal of the ship in the interim was
invalid and of no effect (see the same case in the Court of Appeal 2 PD 218).

So also in the Mortmain and Charitable Uses Act 1888 the words 'shall be forfeited'
were held to mean 'shall be liable to be forfeited': see *A-G v Parsons* [1956] 1 All ER 65,
[1956] AC 421.

Works of art

So far as works of art are concerned, the law of England rests on a statute passed on the
outbreak of the 1939–1945 war. It is the Import, Export and Customs Powers (Defence)
Act 1939. It gave the Board of Trade power by order to prohibit the import or export of
goods of any specified description. The present order is the Export of Goods (Control)
Order, SI 1981/1641. It prohibits the export (unless permitted by licence) of (amongst
other things): 'Any goods manufactured or produced more than 50 years before the date
of exportation', except personal property, letters, and so forth.

Section 3 of the 1939 Act provided that if any goods are imported or exported in
contravention of an order under the Act 'those goods shall be deemed to be prohibited
goods and shall be forfeited'. Section 9(2) said that it was to be construed as one with the
Customs Consolidation Act 1876. So the words 'shall be forfeited' bear the same meaning
as in the 1876 Act. So the forfeiture is not automatic. It does not take effect until the
goods are seized.

It is clear therefore that if works of art more than 50 years old are exported from
England without permission they are not automatically forfeited. They are only 'liable
to be forfeited'. The title does not pass to the Crown until they are seized.

The New Zealand Customs Act 1913

The Customs Act 1913 of New Zealand is much more detailed and precise than the
United Kingdom Act of 1876. For present purposes it is important to notice that it
enacted in express terms the principle of *Lockyer v Offley* (1876) 1 Term Rep 252, 99 ER
1079. It said in s 251:

> '*Forfeiture to take effect on seizure*—When it is provided by this Act or any other
> Customs Act that any goods are forfeited, the forfeiture shall take effect without suit
> or judgment of condemnation so soon as the goods have been seized in accordance
> with this Act or with the Act under which the forfeiture has accrued, and any such
> forfeiture so completed by seizure shall for all purposes relate back to the date of the
> act or event from which the forfeiture accrued.'

It also gave a time bar of one year (s 252(4)):

'*Seizure of forfeited goods* . . . No goods shall be so seized at any time except within one year after the cause of forfeiture has arisen.'

And it also gave a territorial limitation (s 253):

'*Where goods may be seized*—Goods may be seized as forfeited wherever found, whether on land in New Zealand or in the territorial waters of New Zealand.'

The New Zealand Historic Articles Act 1962

The Historic Articles Act 1962 is far more detailed and comprehensive than the United Kingdom Act of 1939 and the orders thereunder.

Section 5 makes it unlawful to remove any historical article without a permit:

'*Restrictions on export of historic articles*—(1) It shall not be lawful after the commencement of this Act for any person to remove or attempt to remove any historic article from New Zealand, knowing it to be an historic article, otherwise than pursuant to the authority and in conformity with the terms and conditions of a written certificate of permission given by the Minister under this Act.

(2) Every person who contrary to the provisions of this section removes or attempts to remove any article from New Zealand, knowing it to be an historic article, commits an offence, and shall be liable on summary conviction to a fine not exceeding two hundred pounds.

(3) Nothing in this section shall apply to any historic article lawfully taken and normally kept outside New Zealand but temporarily within New Zealand.'

Section 12 is the section which most concerns us. So I set it out in full:

'*Application of Customs Act 1913*—(1) Subject to the provisions of this Act, the provisions of the Customs Act 1913 shall apply to any historic article the removal from New Zealand of which is prohibited by this Act in all respects as if the article were an article the export of which had been prohibited pursuant to an Order in Council under section 47 of the Customs Act 1913.

(2) An historic article knowingly exported or attempted to be exported in breach of this Act shall be forfeited to Her Majesty and, subject to the provisions of this Act, the provisions of the Customs Act 1913 relating to forfeited goods shall apply to any such article in the same manner as they apply to goods forfeited under the Customs Act 1913.

(3) Where any historic article is forfeited to Her Majesty pursuant to this section, it shall be delivered to the Minister and retained in safe custody in accordance with his directions:

Provided that the Minister may, in his discretion, direct that the article be returned to the person who was the owner thereof immediately before forfeiture subject to such conditions (if any) as the Minister may think fit to impose.'

The interpretation of s 12(2)

The crucial words are those in s 12(2), 'shall be forfeited to Her Majesty'. Seeing that those words come within a section which is headed 'Application of Customs Act 1913', it seems to me that those words are to be construed as one with the Customs Act 1913. The words 'shall be forfeited' are to be construed in the light of s 251 of the 1913 Act which is, in turn, only an express statement of the principle in *Lockyer v Offley*. They do not mean there is to be an automatic forfeiture. Forfeiture only takes place when the goods are seized; but the title then relates back to the time when the cause of forfeiture arose.

The Customs Act 1966 of New Zealand

Much of the 1966 Act is a re-enactment of the 1913 Act. But there is one section which

changes the wording. Section 251 of the 1913 Act (on which I have placed so much
a stress) is replaced by s 274 of the 1966 Act which says:

> '*Forfeiture to relate back*—When it is provided by this Act or any other of the
> Customs Acts that any goods are forfeited, and the goods are seized in accordance
> with this Act or with the Act under which the forfeiture has accrued, the forfeiture
> shall for all purposes relate back to the date of the act or event from which the
> forfeiture accrued.'

b

Then s 275(4) extends the time from one year to two years:

> '*Seizure of forfeited goods* . . . No goods shall be so seized at any time except within
> two years after the cause of forfeiture has arisen.'

And s 276 keeps the territorial jurisdiction:

c
> '*Where goods may be seized*—Goods may be seized as forfeited wherever found
> within the territorial limits of New Zealand.'

I do not think the change of wording in s 274 of the 1966 Act imputes any change in
sense from s 251 of the 1913 Act. Section 274 shows that the important thing is seizure.
When it says that 'the forfeiture shall for all purposes relate back', that means that the
d forfeiture did not operate automatically. The phrase 'relate back' shows that the title does
not accrue until the seizure: and that it then relates back to the cause of forfeiture. In
short, it is another affirmation of the principle in *Lockyer v Offley*.

The judge's view

Staughton J analysed the Customs Acts 1913 and 1966 of New Zealand and came to
e the conclusion (see p 442, ante):

> '. . . it does not provide for automatic forfeiture but does provide that goods shall
> be liable to forfeiture in certain circumstances, with the effect that title passes to the
> Crown only on seizure or later on condemnation.'

I come to the same conclusion on the Customs Acts.
f   The judge then considered the Historic Articles Act 1962 of New Zealand. He took
the view that it had no clear meaning and that he should adopt the 'purposive' approach
to statutes as indicated perhaps by s 5(j) of the New Zealand Acts Interpretation Act 1924
and the speeches in the House of Lords in *Fothergill v Monarch Airlines Ltd* [1980] 2 All
ER 696, [1981] AC 251. The judge held that the purpose of the 1962 Act 'points firmly
in favour of automatic forfeiture'. He said (see p 443, ante):

g
> '. . . the purpose of the Act is to secure the enjoyment of historic articles for the
> people of New Zealand in the territory of New Zealand; that purpose is plainly
> advanced if articles exported or attempted to be exported become automatically the
> property of the Crown and can if necessary be recovered by the Crown.'

I can well follow the judge's reasoning, but I think it is open to this fatal objection: if
h accepted, it means that the Historic Articles Act 1962 would have effect beyond the
territory of New Zealand. It would have extra-territorial effect. That would be contrary
to international law. To this I now turn.

The territorial theory of jurisdiction

j   It was said long ago by Story J in the Supreme Court of the United States in *The Apollon*
(1824) 9 Wheat 362 at 370: 'The laws of no nation can justly extend beyond its own
territories, except so far as regards its own citizens.' And in his book ten years later on
Conflict of Laws (1835) pp 21–22, he said that 'no state or nation can, by its laws, directly
affect, or bind property out of its own territory' or bind 'persons not resident therein',

except that 'every nation has a right to bind its own subjects by its own laws in every other place'.

In our present case the New Zealand government invite us to interpret s 12(2) of the Historic Articles Act 1962 as if it said: 'An historic article [which has been] knowingly exported [from New Zealand] in breach of this Act shall be [automatically] forfeited to Her Majesty': and Her Majesty can recover it in any other country into which it may be imported.

So interpreted, the Act seems to me to infringe the rule of international law which says that no country can legislate so as to affect rights of property when that property is situated beyond the limits of its own territory. It is a direct infringement of the territorial theory of sovereignty which is most ably discussed by Dr F A Mann in his *Studies in International Law* (1973) pp 1–139.

If this Historic Articles Act 1962 provided for *automatic* forfeiture, that forfeiture would take place and would come into effect as soon as the historic article was *exported*, ie as soon as it left the territorial jurisdiction of New Zealand. That would be a piece of extra-territorial legislation which is invalid by international law.

Rather than suppose that the New Zealand Parliament would infringe international law, or would go beyond the limits of its own jurisdiction, I am quite clear that we should read s 12(2) as not providing for automatic forfeiture, but meaning 'shall be liable to forfeiture'.

A point of vast importance

The next preliminary point proceeds on the assumption that the Historic Articles Act 1962 provided for automatic forfeiture and then asks: should this law be enforced by the courts of England?

This point may become real when it is remembered that the 1962 Act applies not only to *actual export* of an historic article, but also to *attempted export*. An *attempt* might be made to export an historic article. It might be taken to the airport and then prevented at the last moment from being loaded on to the aircraft. A New Zealand statute could well provide (within its territorial jurisdiction) for automatic forfeiture to the Crown on such an attempt being made. The owner makes a second attempt. Then, before it is seized by the authorities, he manages to export it. He gets it to England. The New Zealand government seeks to recover it. Will the English courts enforce its claim?

This second point is of vast importance. Most countries have legislation to prevent the export of their historic articles unless permitted by licence. This legislation may provide for automatic forfeiture on export or attempted export. It might be very desirable that every country should enforce every other country's legislation on the point: by enabling such articles to be recovered and taken back to their original home. But does the law permit of this?

Recognition and enforcement

At the outset I must point out that we are here concerned with a suit by a foreign state to enforce its laws. I hope our New Zealand friends will forgive me calling them a 'foreign state'. I only use the term so as to bring home the fact that we are concerned with an independent sovereign government which exercises sovereign authority over its own territory: and which, by international law, has no right to exercise sovereign authority beyond its own territorial limits.

This suit by a foreign state to enforce its laws is to be distinguished altogether from a suit between private firms or individuals which raises a question whether a contract has been broken by one or the other or whether a wrong has been done by one to the other. In such a suit our courts will often recognise the existence of the laws of a foreign state. We will recognise the foreign law so much that we will refuse to enforce a contract which is in breach of the laws of the foreign state: see the prohibition case of *Foster v Driscoll* [1929] 1 KB 470, [1928] All ER Rep 130, and the jute case of *Regazzoni v K C Sethia* (1944) a *Ltd* [1956] 2 All ER 487, [1956] 2 QB 490, CA, and [1957] 3 All ER 286, [1958] AC 301, HL.

This present case is different. It is a suit by a foreign state brought in the English courts here to enforce its laws. No one has ever doubted that our courts will not entertain a suit brought by a foreign sovereign, directly or indirectly, to enforce the penal or revenue laws of that foreign state. We do not sit to collect taxes for another country or to inflict punishments for it. Now the question arises whether this rule extends to 'other public

b laws'. *Dicey and Morris on the Conflict of Laws* (10th edn, 1980) p 90, r 3, say it does. I agree with them. The term 'other public laws' is very uncertain. But so are the terms 'penal' and 'revenue'. The meaning of 'penal' was discussed in *Huntington v Attrill* [1893] AC 150 and *Loucks v Standard Oil Co of New York* (1918) 224 NY 99. The meaning of 'revenue' was discussed in *Government of India Ministry of Finance (Revenue Division) v Taylor* [1955] 1 All ER 292, [1955] AC 491. But what are 'other public laws'? I think they are laws which are

c ejusdem generis with 'penal' or 'revenue' laws.

Then what is the genus? Or, in English, what is the general concept which embraces 'penal' and 'revenue' laws and others like them? It is to be found, I think, by going back to the classification of acts taken in international law. One class comprises those acts which are done by a sovereign jure imperii, that is, by virtue of his sovereign authority. The others are those which are done by him jure gestionis, that is, which obtain their

d validity by virtue of his performance of them. The application of this distinction to our present problem was well drawn by Dr F A Mann 27 years ago in an article on 'Prerogative Rights of Foreign States and the Conflict of Laws' (1955) 40 *Transactions of the Grotius Society* 25, and reprinted in his *Studies in International Law* (1973) pp 492–514.

Applied to our present problem the class of laws which will be enforced are those laws which are an exercise by the sovereign government of its sovereign authority over

e property within its territory or over its subjects wherever they may be. But other laws will not be enforced. By international law every sovereign state has no sovereignty beyond its own frontiers. The courts of other countries will not allow it to go beyond the bounds. They will not enforce any of its laws which purport to exercise sovereignty beyond the limits of its authority.

If this be right, we come to the question: what is meant by the 'exercise of sovereign

f authority'? It is a term which we will have to grapple with, sooner or later. It comes much into the cases on sovereign immunity and into the State Immunity Act 1978, ss 3(3)(c) and 14(2)(a). It was much discussed recently in *I Congreso del Partido* [1981] 1 All ER 1092, CA; [1981] 2 All ER 1064, [1981] 3 WLR 328, HL, and by Hazel Fox in (1982) 98 LQR 94. It can provoke much difference of opinion as is shown by the differences amongst the Law Lords on the facts of that very case. But, difficult as it is, it

g must be tackled.

I suggest that the first thing in such a case as the present is to determine which is the relevant act. Then to decide whether it is of a sovereign character or a non-sovereign character. Finally, to ask whether it was exercised within the territory of the sovereign state, which is legitimate; or beyond it, which is illegitimate.

In solving the question, we can get guidance from the decided cases. I will take

h therefore the cases decided in the English courts about tangible things which have been confiscated, or attempted to be confiscated, by a sovereign government.

Don Alonso v Cornero (1611) Hob 212, 80 ER 359.

This case was decided in 1611. According to *Dicey and Morris* p 94, it is the only reported English case which approaches the problem. Sir Walter Raleigh had recently introduced tobacco into Europe. It was a growth industry. Senor Cornero, a Spanish subject, committed crimes in Spain and fled in a ship to England, carrying with him 3,000 pounds-weight of tobacco. His very flight was in Spanish law a cause of forfeiture of his goods, as it was in English law at that time: see 4 Bl Com 387. So these goods were 'forfeited upon the High Sea' to the King of Spain. On arrival in England, Cornero unloaded the tobacco and sold it to Sir John Watts for £800.

The Spanish ambassador then on behalf of the king took proceedings in rem in the Court of Admiralty on the grounds that the cargo was the property of the King of Spain. *a* (This procedure in Admiralty for forfeiture is well recognised to this day: see s 1(1)(s) of the Administration of Justice Act 1956 and *The Skylark* [1965] 3 All ER 380, [1965] P 474). The Admiralty marshal served the warrant of arrest on the cargo in the hands of Sir John Watts. Sir John Watts then moved the Court of Common Pleas for a writ of prohibition to prevent the Spanish ambassador from proceeding any further with the arrest. The court granted his application. Prohibition was granted. The goods were *b* released. Sir John Watts kept the tobacco and sold it; or smoked it. The King of Spain took nothing.

The report of the case in Hobart 212 tells us that the judges were quite willing to allow the Spanish ambassador to bring proceedings on behalf of the King of Spain: '. . . they would not let [ie prevent] the embassador from prosecuting his master's subject.' As to the goods, the judges said that:

c

'. . . if any subject of a foreign prince bring goods into the kingdom, though they were confiscate before, the property of them shall not here be questioned but at the common law.'

As I understand it, that means that the courts of this country would not enforce the forfeiture. Our courts would not enforce the title claimed by the Spanish king. Our *d* courts of 'common law' would enforce a possessory title by trespass or trover, but this would not avail the King of Spain because he never had possession: see *Isaak v Clark* (1615) 2 Bulst 306, 80 ER 1143.

The confiscation was an act done in the exercise of sovereign authority outside the territory of Spain; it was done on the High Seas. So our court would not enforce it. So also when many centuries later the Spanish Constituent Cortes passed a decree confiscating *e* all the private property of the ex-king, it was held that it would not be enforced against his property in England: see *Banco de Vizcaya v Don Alfonso de Borbon y Austria* [1935] 1 KB 140, [1934] All ER Rep 555.

King of Italy v Marquis Cosimo de Medici Tornaquinci (1918) 34 TLR 623
In Italy the Marquis of Medici had a most valuable collection of historical manuscripts *f* covering a period of 700 years. They were known as the Medici archives. Some of them were official communications and belonged to the Italian state. The government had allowed the marquis to hold them on behalf of the state. Others were family papers coming down in the Medici family. They belonged to the marquis himself. In 1909 the Italian government passed a law by which the state papers were to be kept in Italy. They belonged to the state. By the same law the Italian government prohibited the export of *g* the family papers without a permit and there was a heavy export duty when a permit was granted. The state also had the right to purchase the family papers. The marquis brought these Medici archives to England and put them into the hands of Christies for sale. Peterson J held that the state papers belonged to the state of Italy and granted an injunction to prevent their being disposed of. But he refused to grant any injunction (at the suit of the Italian government) in respect of the family papers. It was only at the *h* interlocutory stage. Peterson J said (at 624):

'Article 9 prohibited their exportation, but it was manifest that this only applied so long as they remained in Italy. The question arose whether there was any probability, at the trial of the action, that these documents, apart from the State papers, would be ordered to be returned to Italy. He did not think that the Court would undertake such a burden.'

j

The prohibition of export of the family papers was an exercise of sovereign authority by the King of Italy. It would not be enforced in our courts.

Princess Paley Olga v Weisz [1929] 1 KB 718, [1929] All ER Rep 513
Princess Paley Olga was the widow of Grand Duke Paul of Russia. She occupied the

Paley Palace near St Petersburg, full of valuable furniture, pictures and objets d'art. In
a 1918 the revolutionaries took possession of it. The princess fled to England. The Soviet
government passed decrees declaring all of its contents to be the property of the Soviet
Republic. They turned it into a state museum. In 1928 the Soviet government sold some
of the articles to Mr Weisz for £40,000. He brought them to England. The princess
claimed that they belonged to her. She sued Mr Weisz to recover them. She failed.
Scrutton LJ said ([1929] 1 KB 718 at 725, [1929] All ER Rep 513 at 517):

b
'Our Government has recognized the present Russian Government as the de jure
Government of Russia, and our Courts are bound to give effect to the laws and acts
of that Government *so far as they relate to property within* that jurisdiction when it
was affected by those laws and acts.' (My emphasis.)

The confiscation by the Soviet government was an exercise of sovereign authority
c within its own territory. It would therefore be enforced in England. If the princess had
removed the articles from the museum in St Petersburg and brought them to England,
the English courts would have made her give them up to the Soviet government.

Brokaw v Seatrain UK Ltd [1971] 2 All ER 98, [1971] 2 QB 476
Mr and Mrs Shaheen were United States citizens living in the United States. Their
d daughter married Mr Brokaw, an Englishman. The parents determined to send to their
daughter their furniture and household effects so as to set up house in England. They
were shipped on an American ship for delivery in England. While the vessel was on the
high seas, the United States government served a notice of levy on the shipowners. They
claimed possession of the goods on the ground that Mr and Mrs Shaheen owed them
money for taxes and that they were entitled by United States law to levy on all the
e property of Mr and Mrs Shaheen. This court held that the United States government had
no right to the goods. I said ([1971] 2 All ER 98 at 100, [1971] 2 QB 476 at 482–483):

'If this notice of levy had been effective to reduce the goods into the possession of
the United States government, it would, I think, have been enforced by these courts,
because we would then be enforcing an actual possessory title. There would be no
need for the United States government to have recourse to their revenue law. I
f would apply to this situation some words of the United States Supreme Court in *The
Navemar* (1938) 303 US 68 at 75 in an analogous case: ". . . since the decree was *in
invitum*, actual possession by some act of physical dominion or control on behalf of
the Spanish Government, was needful."'

The notice of levy was an act done in the exercise of sovereign authority. It was not
g done in the territory of the United States but outside it. It would not be enforced by our
courts. But if the United States government had actually reduced the goods into their
possession in the United States, that act would have been done within its own territory.
It would therefore have been enforced in our courts.
I have not gone into any of the cases on intangible things or on foreign exchange
regulations, such as *Kahler v Midland Bank Ltd* [1949] 2 All ER 621, [1950] AC 24 and *Re
h Lord Cable (decd)* [1976] 3 All ER 417, [1977] 1 WLR 7: but I would suggest that they
might be solved by adopting the distinction between acts done in the exercise of a
sovereign authority within its own territory, and those outside it.

Conclusion
j Returning to our present case, I am of opinion that if any country should have
legislation prohibiting the export of works of art and providing for the automatic
forfeiture of them to the state should they be exported, then that falls into the category
of 'public laws' which will not be enforced by the courts of the country to which it is
exported or any other country: because it is an act done in the exercise of sovereign
authority which will not be enforced outside its own territory.
On this point, therefore, I differ from the judge; but I would express my gratitude to

him for his most valuable contribution to this important topic. He held that our courts should enforce the foreign laws about works of art by ordering them to be delivered up a to the foreign government. He hoped that if we did this the courts of other countries would reciprocate and enforce our laws which prohibit the export of works of art. I regard this as too sanguine. If our works of art are sold to a dealer and exported to the United States without permission, as many have been, I doubt very much whether the courts of the United States would order them to be returned to England at the suit of our government, on the ground of forfeiture. b

The retrieval of such works of art must be achieved by diplomatic means. Best of all, there should be an international convention on the matter where individual countries can agree and pass the necessary legislation. It is a matter of such importance that I hope steps can be taken to this end.

I would answer the first preliminary issue No, and the second preliminary issue Yes. I would allow the appeal accordingly. c

ACKNER LJ. The most helpful and detailed submissions by counsel have ultimately satisfied me that this apparently complex case is not as difficult as it initially appeared. The appeal raises two main questions, although if the first is decided adversely to the respondent, the Attorney General of New Zealand, he fails in his claim and the resolution d of the second question becomes unnecessary.

1. *Is an historic article knowingly exported or attempted to be exported in breach of the New Zealand Historic Articles Act 1962 automatically forfeited so that title there and then passes to Her Majesty in right of the Government of New Zealand, or must seizure first take place before the property vests in the Crown?*

An Act may provide for automatic forfeiture, or it may provide merely that the goods e shall be liable to forfeiture if some further step is taken to that end. For example, the English Customs and Excise Act 1952, which was in force at the material time (now the Customs and Excise Act 1979) provided in the material sections, not for automatic forfeiture where various offences were committed, but that the goods 'shall be liable to forfeiture'. By contrast the Maori Antiquities Act 1908, which remained in force until 1962 when it was repealed by the Historic Articles Act 1962, made special provision for f a limited category of antiquities, namely those entered for export. Section 6(3) of the 1908 Act provided that:

> 'Any Maori antiquities entered for export contrary to this Act shall be forfeited, and shall vest in His Majesty for the use of the people of New Zealand: Provided that the Minister may, after inquiry, cancel the forfeiture if he thinks fit.'
> g

Antiquities which had been entered for export would not only have come to the attention of Customs, but would have been reduced into the possession of the Crown. Thus, the provision for such goods to vest in the Crown without the necessity for some further action, such as seizure, was a practicable course clearly open to the legislature. However, in respect of Maori antiquities which were not entered for export, there was no provision for automatic forfeiture. Forfeiture could only be achieved under the h Customs Act 1913, and, as appears hereafter, it is indisputable that such forfeiture was not automatic.

When the Maori Antiquities Act 1908 was repealed, the New Zealand legislature did not choose to repeat the wording of s 6(3) referred to above. It adopted the drafting technique of incorporating the provisions of the Customs Act 1913, which had by then been in force for nearly 50 years. Section 12 of the Historic Articles Act 1962 provided as j follows:

> 'Application of Customs Act 1913—(1) Subject to the provisions of this Act, the provisions of the Customs Act 1913 shall apply to any historic article the removal from New Zealand of which is prohibited by this Act in all respects as if the article

were an article the export of which had been prohibited pursuant to an Order in
Council under section 47 of the Customs Act 1913.

(2) An historic article knowingly exported or attempted to be exported in breach
of this Act shall be forfeited to Her Majesty and, subject to the provisions of this Act,
the provisions of the Customs Act 1913 relating to forfeited goods shall apply to any
article in the same manner as they apply to goods forfeited under the Customs Act
1913.

(3) Where any historic article is forfeited to Her Majesty pursuant to this section,
it shall be delivered to the Minister and retained in safe custody in accordance with
his directions:

Provided that the Minister may, in his discretion, direct that the article be
returned to the person who was the owner thereof immediately before forfeiture
subject to such conditions (if any) as the Minister may think fit to impose.'

Section 47 of the Customs Act 1913 referred to in s 12(1) set out above, provided inter
alia for a liability to a penalty of £200 and, by sub-s (5), made this provision:

'All goods shipped on board any ship for the purpose of being exported contrary
to the terms of any such prohibition in force with respect thereto and all goods
waterborne for the purpose of being so shipped and exported shall be forfeited.'

However, any possible ambiguity as to the meaning of the phrase 'shall be forfeited' in
the 1962 Act was resolved, beyond all doubt, by s 251 which provided:

'*Forfeiture to take effect on seizure*—When it is provided by this Act or any other
Customs Act that any goods are forfeited, the forfeiture shall take effect without suit
or judgment of condemnation so soon as the goods have been seized in accordance
with this Act or with any Act under which the forfeiture has accrued, and any such
forfeiture so completed by seizure shall for all purposes relate back to the date of the
Act or event from which the forfeiture accrued.'

It will of course be appreciated that the section not only provided for forfeiture to take
effect on seizure, but that the title thus acquired should, for all purposes, relate back to
the date of the act or event from which forfeiture accrued.

Leading counsel for the Attorney General, to whose able argument I should like to
express a particular tribute, contended in his initial submission that it is clear from the
language of s 12 that forfeiture takes place under the 1962 Act and not under the
Customs legislation. This submission is not referred to by the learned judge in his
judgment, it is barely taken in the respondents' notice and, in my judgment, it is quite
unsustainable. The very purpose of s 12, as its heading indicates, is to apply the Customs
Act 1913 to any historic article the removal of which from New Zealand is prohibited by
the Historic Articles Act. Such application is, as specifically enacted, 'subject to the
provisions of this Act'. Thus, where there is within the 1962 Act a special provision
which conflicts with the Customs Act, the 1962 Act takes precedence. Thus, specific
provision is made in s 12(3) for delivery to the Minister and for his discretion as to the
return of the goods, whereas s 252(3) of the Customs Act 1913 provided for the goods to
be taken 'to a King's warehouse or such other place of security as the Collector or other
proper officer directs'.

If the forfeiture provisions of the Customs Act 1913 applied, as the learned judge in
my judgment rightly so held, it is then common ground that so long as the 1913 Act was
in force the forfeiture was not automatic. Before title could pass to the Crown, the goods
had to be seized. Since s 252(4) provided that no goods shall be seized at any time except
within one year after the cause of forfeiture had arisen, and no such seizure ever took
place, then if the Customs Act 1913 alone regulated the forfeiture, the Attorney General
would fail in his claim.

On 1 January 1967 the Customs Act 1913 was replaced by a new Customs Act, the
Customs Act 1966, and it is common ground that references in the Historic Articles Act

1962 to the Customs Act 1913 must now be treated as references to the Customs Act 1966. Thus, the next question is whether the Customs Act 1966 still required seizure to *a* take place before forfeiture could take effect, or whether it fundamentally changed the position by providing for the automatic vesting in the Crown of the title to the goods, immediately the prohibitive act took place.

Before contrasting s 251 of the 1913 Act with its successor, s 274 of the 1966 Act, it is important to note the marked similarities in the material sections. In both Acts 'forfeited goods' are defined as meaning any goods in respect of which a cause of forfeiture has *b* arisen under the Customs Act. In both Acts there is a time bar in relation to seizure, expressed in the same terms as I have quoted above, except that the period of one year is increased in the 1966 Act to two years. I agree with the learned judge that it does appear odd that goods could no longer be seized after two years and yet, if the Attorney General is right, it is still open to the Crown to enforce a proprietary right by any other means. Moreover, if a significant change was intended it seems strange that the same words, *c* 'cause of forfeiture', should be adopted (see s 252(4) and s 275(4)). The provisions governing notice of seizure are the same (ss 255 and 278) as are the provisions for condemnation (ss 259 and 282). In s 262 of the Customs Act 1913 it is provided that all forfeited goods shall, on forfeiture, become the property of His Majesty. It is common ground that under that Act 'on forfeiture' means on seizure. The only change made in its counterpart, s 286 of the 1966 Act, is that 'the Crown' takes the place of 'His Majesty *d* The King'. The provisions as to waiving the forfeiture are identical (ss 264 and 287). Under the 1913 Act the phrase 'when any forfeiture has accrued' must mean cause of forfeiture. Presumably it would have the same meaning in the 1966 Act. The application of the forfeiture provisions are the same in each Act (ss 265 and 288).

I now set out s 274 of the Customs Act 1966. This provides:

> 'Forfeiture to relate back—When it is provided by this Act or any other of the *e* Customs Acts that any goods are forfeited, and the goods are seized in accordance with this Act or with the Act under which the forfeiture has accrued, the forfeiture shall for all purposes relate back to the date of the act or event from which the forfeiture accrued.'

Thus the heading to s 251 of the 1913 Act, 'Forfeiture to take effect on seizure', has been *f* removed from the section as has the provision that the forfeiture shall take effect without suit or judgment of condemnation so soon as the goods have been seized and any such forfeiture so completed by seizure. It accordingly appears that the intention was that forfeiture should no longer take effect and be completed on seizure. This, however, still leaves unanswered the question: when is it to take effect? The legislature clearly thought it important to continue to provide that forfeiture should relate back, hence the very *g* heading to the section, using the terms of the old s 251. If forfeiture was to be automatic in its effect, so that title passed there and then to the Crown, this specific provision for relating back is clearly superfluous. Moreover, the further question arises: why should there be any reference in the new section to: 'and the goods are seized in accordance with this Act', if seizure was no longer of any relevance?

Counsel for the Attorney General can provide no real explanation for the existence of *h* s 274 of the 1966 Act. Counsel on behalf of the first defendant, Mr Ortiz, does offer this explanation. Section 283 of the 1966 Act provides for a new cause of condemnation of forfeited goods, namely the conviction of an offence which involved forfeiture. The conviction itself shall have effect as condemnation, without suit or judgment, of any goods that have been seized or in respect of which forfeiture has accrued. He submits that if s 251 of the 1913 Act had been left in its original form, then there would have *j* been a conflict, since that section provides for forfeiture to take place on seizure. Thus he submits that under the new Act seizure set in train the process of the alteration of title, but this did not in fact take place until condemnation, and thus it was necessary to retain the provisions in s 251 relating back the title. This, he submitted, explained the slight alteration in s 277 of the 1966 Act dealing with the rescue of seized goods as compared a   to its predecessor, s 254. The words 'as if they were' the property were used instead of 'being the' property because the property passed on condemnation and not on seizure.

I do not find the explanation of counsel for the first defendant a wholly satisfying one, but it is better than nothing at all. It is clear that the draftsman was borrowing language from the 1913 Act, as well as from Australian and English legislation. This may well explain the oddity of the provision (s 272 of the 1966 Act) that every boat, vehicle or animal used in smuggling goods 'shall be forfeited', whereas in the next section it is

b   provided, 'when any boat, vehicles or animal *has become liable* to forfeiture under the Customs Acts, whether by virtue of section 272 of this Act or otherwise, all equipment thereof shall *also be liable to forfeiture*' (my emphasis).

The learned judge was impressed by the apparent inconsistency of forfeiture being automatic and yet there being the time bar on seizure. He was also, in my judgment, rightly concerned about the difficulty and uncertainty which would ensue, as Mr Thomas

c   QC who gave expert evidence for the defendants, pointed out, if title to goods passed automatically to the Crown on any of the various events which gave rise to forfeiture. In this respect he referred to a manuscript treatise of Hale CJ, which was found amongst his papers and published in *Hargrave's Law Tracts* in 1787, and which was brought to the learned judge's attention by counsel for the first defendant. It included this passage:

d   'Though a title of forfeiture be given by the lading or unlading the customs not paid, yet the King's title is not compleat, till he hath a judgment of record to ascertain his title; for otherwise there would be endless suits and vexations; for it may be, 10 or 20 years hence there might be a pretence of forfeiture now incurred.'

To have provided that all sorts and kinds of goods to which the Customs Act 1966 applied should automatically be forfeited to the Crown in certain circumstances could

e   have cast on the Crown a very onerous and burdensome obligation. Thus, considering both the provisions of the Customs Act 1966 and its predecessor, the Act of 1913, and its purpose, the learned judge preferred the evidence of Mr Thomas that it did not provide for automatic forfeiture, but that it provided that goods shall be liable to forfeiture in certain circumstances, with the effect that title passes to the Crown only on seizure or later on condemnation. I respectfully agree. If the legislature had intended to make the

f   very significant change in the 1966 Act for which counsel for the Attorney General contends, then not only would one have reasonably expected clear language to that effect, but also the absence of the apparently inconsistent provision for relation back in s 274, with its reference to the seizure of the goods.

The learned judge thus reached this provisional view. Having regard to the fact that the words in s 12 of the Historic Articles Act 1962 'shall be forfeited' are immediately

g   followed by a reference to the Customs Act 1913 and the same words occur in that Act and in the Act of 1966, where they have the meaning 'shall be liable to forfeiture', linguistic consideration therefore pointed to the view that in the 1962 Act they have the same meaning. Accordingly, they do not mean 'shall be forfeited automatically'. I have used the word 'provisional' because he, that is, the learned judge, then considered the words in s 12(2) 'subject to the provisions of this Act'. Having observed that the nature

h   of the articles dealt with by the Historic Articles Act 1962 were unlikely to impose any onerous burdens on the Crown, he then turned to the provisions of the New Zealand Acts Interpretation Act 1924, which the Attorney General's expert, Dr Inglis, considered to be of considerable importance. This provide in s 5(j):

        'Every Act, and every provision or enactment thereof, shall be deemed remedial, whether its immediate purport is to direct the doing of anything Parliament deems to be for the public good, or to prevent or punish the doing of anything it deems contrary to the public good, and shall accordingly receive such fair, large, and liberal construction and interpretation as will best ensure the attainment of the object of the Act and of such provision or enactment according to its true intent, meaning and spirit.'

Mr Thomas's view that s 5(j) was not an early recognition in 1924 of the power of the courts to disregard the literal meaning of an Act and to give it purposive construction *a* was preferred by the judge. Mr Thomas considered that the section did no more than abolish the old distinction between remedial and penal Acts and said that it was very rarely cited in New Zealand. Counsel for the Attorney General has failed to persuade me that the learned judge was wrong to have preferred Mr Thomas's evidence. The very terms of the section, deeming every Act to be remedial irrespective of whether it is a penal Act, is clearly designed to abolish the distinction. *b*

The learned judge, who had appeared in *Fothergill v Monarch Airlines Ltd* [1980] 2 All ER 696, [1981] AC 251, drew the attention of the experts on New Zealand law to two passages in the speeches in that case. The first was in the speech of Lord Wilberforce ([1980] 2 All ER 696 at 700, [1981] AC 251 at 272):

'I start by considering the purpose of art 26, and I do not think that in doing so I am infringing any "golden rule". Consideration of the purpose of an enactment is *c* always a legitimate part of the process of interpretation, and if it is usual, and indeed correct, to look first for a clear meaning of the words used it is certain, in the present case, both on a first look at the relevant text and from the judgments in the courts below, that no "golden rule" meaning can be ascribed.'

The second passage was in the speech of Lord Diplock ([1980] 2 All ER 696 at 705, *d* [1981] AC 251 at 280) where after referring to the 'traditional, and widely criticised, style of legislative draftsmanship which has become familiar to English judges during the present century and for which their own narrowly semantic approach to statutory construction, until the last decade or so, may have been largely to blame', continued:

'That approach for which parliamentary draftsmen had to cater can hardly be better illustrated than by the words of Lord Simonds LC in *Inland Revenue Comrs v* *e* *Ayrshire Employers Mutual Insurance Association Ltd* [1946] 1 All ER 637 at 641: "The section . . . sect. 31 of the Finance Act, 1933, is clearly a remedial section . . . It is at least clear what is the gap that is intended to be filled and hardly less clear how it is intended to fill that gap. Yet I can come to no other conclusion than that the language of the section fails to achieve its apparent purpose and I must decline to insert words or phrases which might succeed where the draftsman failed." The *f* unhappy legacy of this judicial attitude, although it is now being replaced by an increasing willingness to give a purposive construction to the Act, is the current English style of legislative draftsmanship.'

Fothergill's case concerned an international convention where the essential words were ambiguous and had to be resolved by reference to their French meaning. Both the New *g* Zealand experts said that the courts in New Zealand would follow and apply the passages referred to above. Such an agreement cannot be disassociated from the nature of that case, where there was no clear meaning which emerged from the words in the statute. The learned judge having, in my judgment, correctly concluded that the clear provisions of s 251 of the Customs Act 1913, which provided *against* automatic forfeiture, had been in substance re-enacted in the 1966 Act by making seizure or perhaps even condemnation *h* the sine qua non to the vesting of the property of the goods in the Crown, was not entitled to conclude that the words 'shall be forfeited' were capable of either of the two meanings contended for. Having, in my respectful judgment, wrongly concluded that there was this ambiguity, he then expressed the view (see p 443, ante):

'. . . the purpose of the 1962 Act is to secure the enjoyment of historic articles for the people of New Zealand in the territory of New Zealand; that purpose is plainly *j* advanced if articles exported or attempted to be exported become automatically the property of the Crown and can if necessary be recovered by the Crown.'

The purpose of the Act is set out in its title: 'An Act to provide for the protection of historic articles and to control their removal from New Zealand.' However, I accept the a well-argued submission of counsel for the third defendant that what the learned judge was seeking to do was to interpret the words 'subject to the *provisions* of this Act', in s 12(2) of the Historic Articles Act 1962, as 'subject to the *purpose* of this Act' (my emphasis). Having correctly concluded, after a proper consideration of the Customs Act, that there was no ambiguity in the words 'shall be forfeited' there was no warrant for embarking on a search for the 'purpose' of the Act.

b I therefore reach the clear conclusion that an historic article knowingly exported or attempted to be exported in breach of the New Zealand Historic Articles Act 1962 is *not* automatically forfeited, so that the title there and then passes to Her Majesty in right of the Government of New Zealand. Seizure must first take place and, in view of the time bar contained in s 275(4) of the Customs Act 1966, the Attorney General falls at the first fence.

c *2. Are the provisions of the Historic Articles Act 1962 and the Customs Acts 1913 and 1966 unenforceable in England as being foreign revenue, penal and/or public laws?*

The learned judge answered this question in the negative. I have no difficulty in agreeing with him that the forfeiture provisions in s 12 of the Historic Articles Act 1962 are not a foreign revenue law. He correctly stated that the rule as to not enforcing a foreign law applies only to what may more or less accurately be described as taxes. He d followed the observations of Denning LJ in *Regazzoni v K C Sethia (1944) Ltd* [1956] 2 All ER 487 at 490, [1956] 2 QB 490 at 515, approved by Viscount Simonds in the House of Lords ([1957] 3 All ER 286 at 289, [1958] AC 301 at 318): 'These courts do not sit to collect taxes for another country or to inflict punishment for it . . .' A list of cases in which foreign law has not been enforced on the ground that it was revenue law is set out in 8 Halsbury's Laws (4th edn) para 420, note 1; these are cases concerning capital gains tax, customs duty, stamp duty, rates, succession duty, income tax, profits tax and national e insurance contributions. I do not think it would be overstating the position if I said that, certainly by the end of the appellants' submissions, all criticism of the learned judge's decision on this aspect of the case was virtually abandoned, although technically the point has been kept open.

f *Are the English courts being asked to enforce a foreign penal law?*

It is common ground that if the question in this case was one of *recognising* the Historic Articles Act 1962, then it is a law which the English courts would recognise. Thus, if the carving had been seized and condemned in New Zealand, thereby being reduced into the possession of the New Zealand government, then that government would have been entitled to enforce its proprietary title in this country by reference to the Historic Articles Act. In *Brokaw v Seatrain UK Ltd* [1971] 2 All ER 98, [1971] 2 QB 476, goods said to be g household effects were shipped in a United States ship from Baltimore in the United States to London, via Southampton. While the ship was on the high seas the United States Treasury served a notice of levy in respect of unpaid tax on the shipowners in the United States, demanding the surrender of all property in their possession belonging to two United States taxpayers. When the ship docked at Southampton, both the former owner of the goods and the United States government claimed possession from the shipowners. h Lord Denning MR said this ([1971] 2 All ER 98 at 100, [1971] 2 QB 476 at 482–483):

'If this notice of levy had been effective to reduce the goods into the possession of the United States government, it would, I think, have been enforced by these courts, because we would then be enforcing an actual possessory title. There would be no need for the United States government to have recourse to their revenue law . . . If j the United States government had taken these goods into their actual possession, say in a warehouse in Baltimore, or maybe by attornment of the master to an officer of the United States government, that might have been sufficient to enable them to claim the goods. But there is nothing of that kind here. The United States government simply rely on this notice of levy given to the shipowners, and that is not, in my view, sufficient to reduce the goods into their possession.'

Thus, counsel for the Attorney General cannot validly contend that he is suing to enforce a proprietary title and not to enforce a statute. In order to make good his title in *a* these proceedings, he has to rely on the Historic Articles Act, since he cannot rely on any previous possession or other root of title.

The question whether a foreign law is penal must be decided by the English court. It must determine for itself, in the first place, the substance of the right sought to be enforced; and in the second place whether its enforcement would, either directly or indirectly, involve the execution of the penal law of another state. The rule has its *b* foundation in the well-recognised principle that crimes, including in that term all breaches of public law, punishable by pecuniary mulct, or otherwise, at the instance of the state government, or someone representing the public, are local in this sense, that they are only cognisable and punishable in the country where they were committed. Accordingly, no proceeding, even in the shape of a civil suit, which has for its object the enforcement by the state, whether directly or indirectly, of punishment imposed for *c* such breaches by the lex fori, ought to be admitted in the courts of any other country (per Lord Watson in *Huntington v Attrill* [1893] AC 150 at 155–156). Lord Watson continued (at 157–158):

> 'A proceeding, in order to come within the scope of the rule, must be in the nature of a suit in favour of the State whose law has been infringed . . . But foreign *d* tribunals do not regard these violations of statute law as offences against the State, unless their vindication rests with the State itself, or with the community which it represents. Penalties may be attached to them, but that circumstance will not bring them within the rule, except in cases where these penalties are recoverable at the instance of the State, or of an official duly authorized to prosecute on its behalf, or of a member of the public in the character of a common informer.'

e

It was thus held that the action by the appellant in an Ontario court on a judgment of a New York court against the respondent under New York State laws, being by a subject to enforce in his own interest a liability imposed for the protection of his private rights, was remedial and not penal. It was a suit for a penalty by a private individual in his own interest, and not a suit brought by the government or people of a state for the vindication of public law. *f*

Huntington's case makes it clear that the first part of counsel for the Attorney General's definition of foreign penal law, namely that it must be part of the criminal code of a foreign country, is not sustainable. The right which it is sought to enforce may be a right which arises under legislation which is essentially designed to regulate commercial activities such as company legislation which may well contain a penal provision. I agree with the learned judge that it cannot be right simply to categorise the statute sought to *g* be enforced as a whole. The court must pay regard to the particular provision of the foreign law which it is sought to enforce.

It was readily accepted that forfeiture may, in certain circumstances, be a penalty. In *R v Natbell Liquors Ltd* [1922] 2 AC 128, [1922] All ER Rep 335, forfeiture of whisky to the Crown in the Province of Alberta was held to be a penalty; so also in *Banco de Vizcaya v Don Alfonso de Borbon y Austria* [1935] 1 KB 140, [1934] All ER Rep 655, a decree *h* expropriating all property of the defendant on the ground that he was guilty of high treason was held to be a penal law and unenforceable in this country. But, urges counsel for the Attorney General, the whole scheme of the Historic Articles Act 1962 is to preserve in New Zealand articles to which the Act applies. The provisions for forfeiture are but a deterrent by-product. The fact that it carries with it unpleasant consequences no more makes it penal than does the Massachusetts statute which was the foundation of *j* the dispute in the case in the Court of Appeal of the State of New York, *Loucks v Standard Oil Co of New York* (1918) 224 NY 99. That statute provided for the recovery, on behalf of the widow or children or next of kin of any person killed by negligence, of damages 'in the sum of not less than $500, nor more than $10,000, to be assessed with reference to the degree of culpability' of the wrongdoer. It thus provided for penal damages. To my mind, this decision, so far from assisting the Attorney General, does the contrary.

a Cardozo J, giving the judgment of the court, followed *Huntington v Attrill* [1893] AC 150 by repeating that a penal statute is one which awards a penalty to the state, or to a public officer on its behalf, or to a member suing in the interest of the whole community, to redress a public wrong. The purpose must be, not reparation to one aggrieved but vindication of the public justice. Mrs Loucks was not a member of the public suing in the interests of the whole community. She was suing in her own interest. Nor was she

b suing to redress a public wrong, to vindicate the public justice. She was suing to vindicate a private right: reparation owed to one who was aggrieved.

In the instant submission, the claim is made by the Attorney General on behalf of the state. It is not a claim by a private individual. Further, the cause of action does not concern a private right which demands reparation or compensation. It concerns a public right, the preservation of historic articles within New Zealand, which right the state

c seeks to vindicate. The vindication is not sought by the acquisition of the article in exchange for proper compensation. The vindication is sought through confiscation. It is of course accepted that the provisions of s 5(2) of the Historic Articles Act 1962, which provide for a fine not exceeding £200 for the same offence as gives rise to forfeiture, are penal provisions. However, in the majority of cases, forfeiture is a far more serious consequence. This case is a dramatic example. The current value of the carving is asserted

d by one of the parties to these proceedings to be in the region of £300,000. It seems to me to be wholly unreal to suggest that when a foreign state seeks to enforce these forfeiture provisions in another country, it is not seeking to enforce a foreign penal statute. No doubt the general purpose of the 1962 Act is to preserve in New Zealand its historic articles. However, this does not mean that a suit to enforce the forfeiture provisions contained in s 12 is not a suit by the state to vindicate the public justice. I therefore

e cannot agree with the learned judge that s 12 is not a penal provision. Accordingly, if I am wrong in the answer I have given to the first question raised in this action, I would still dismiss the Attorney General's claim on this point of public international law.

In these circumstances it is unnecessary for me to consider the question of whether there is a third category of foreign laws which our courts do not enforce, namely public law, and if so, what it comprises. Without reaching any firm conclusion, I am impressed

f by the reasoning of the learned judge that there is no such vague general residual category and, that if the test is one of public policy, there is no reason why English courts should not enforce s 12 of the Historic Articles Act 1962 of New Zealand.

I accordingly would also allow this appeal.

g **O'CONNOR LJ** (read by Ackner LJ). In June 1978 the defendant George Ortiz sent part of his collection of Polynesian and Maori artefacts to London for sale by auction at Sothebys. Among the treasures was a carved wooden panel, a Maori rarity from New Zealand estimated by some to be worth £300,000. The auction was to take place on the 29 June. On 26 June the writ in this action was issued and the plaintiff applied for and obtained an injunction to prevent the sale of the Maori carving on the ground that it was

h owned not by Mr Ortiz but by Her Majesty in the right of the Government of New Zealand. The basis of the claim was that the carving had been illegally exported from New Zealand in 1973 and had thus been forfeited to the Crown.

There is no dispute that the defendant Entwistle had exported the carving from New Zealand in 1973 without permission knowing that it was an historical article the export of which was prohibited by the New Zealand Historic Articles Act 1962 unless permission

j under that Act had been obtained. In due course an order was made for the trial of two preliminary issues of law: (1) whether Her Majesty The Queen has become the owner and is entitled to possession of the carving under the New Zealand Acts entitled the Historic Articles Act 1962 and the Customs Acts 1913 and 1966, and (2) whether in any event the provisions of the said Acts are unenforceable in England as being foreign penal, revenue and/or public laws.

Staughton J held that the plaintiff succeeded on both issues. The defendants appeal to this court.

The first issue depends on the true construction of s 12(2) of the New Zealand Historic Articles Act 1962. I set out the whole of s 12 so that the crucial subsection can be seen in its context:

> 'Application of Customs Act 1913—(1) Subject to the provisions of this Act, the provisions of the Customs Act 1913 shall apply to any historic article the removal from New Zealand of which is prohibited by this Act in all respects as if the Article were an article the export of which had been prohibited pursuant to an Order in Council under section 47 of the Customs Act 1913.
>
> (2) An historic article knowingly exported or attempted to be exported in breach of this Act shall be forfeited to Her Majesty and, subject to the provisions of this Act, the provisions of the Customs Act 1913 relating to forfeited goods shall apply to any such article in the same manner as they apply to goods forfeited under the Customs Act 1913.
>
> (3) Where any historic article is forfeited to Her Majesty pursuant to this section, it shall be delivered to the Minister and retained in safe custody in accordance with his directions:
>
> Provided that the Minister may, in his discretion, direct that the article be returned to the person who was the owner thereof immediately before forfeiture subject to such conditions (if any) as the Minister may think fit to impose.'

The question is whether sub-s (2) makes forfeiture automatic on export or attempted export or whether as a result of the Customs Act 1913 forfeiture depends on seizure.

The Customs Act 1913 had been repealed and re-enacted in the Customs Act 1966 so that for this case the 1962 Act must be read with the 1966 Act. Section 251 of the 1913 Act expressly provided that forfeiture was to take place on seizure. That section has been replaced by s 274 in the 1966 Act. Counsel on behalf of the Attorney General submitted that a radical change in the law had been made by the difference in wording between the two sections and that from 1967 when the 1966 Act came into force forfeiture was automatic. Like Lord Denning MR and Ackner LJ and Staughton J I cannot agree with this submission for the reasons given by them.

I can find no ambiguity in s 12(2) of the 1962 Act. The incorporation of the Customs Act 'subject to the provisions of this Act' requires that the same meaning be given to the phrase 'shall be forfeited' in both Acts unless by express provision or necessary implication a different meaning is required under the 1962 Act. There is no express provision and I can find nothing in that Act which requires that a different meaning be given to the phrase. Forfeiture under the 1962 Act is not automatic and the first issue must be decided in favour of the defendants.

Once that decision is reached it is not necessary to decide the second issue. Lord Denning MR and Ackner LJ have however dealt with the issue. I agree the claim fails on this issue as well as the first because this is a penal law which our courts will not enforce.

Appeal allowed. Leave to appeal to the House of Lords granted.

Solicitors: *Joelson, Wilson & Co* (for the first defendant); *Manches & Co* (for the third defendant); *Allen & Overy* (for the Attorney General of New Zealand).

Diana Procter   Barrister.

a # Riley and others v Attorney General of Jamaica and another

PRIVY COUNCIL

LORD HAILSHAM OF ST MARYLEBONE LC, LORD DIPLOCK, LORD SCARMAN, LORD BRIDGE OF HARWICH AND LORD BRIGHTMAN

b 26 APRIL, 28 JUNE 1982

Jamaica – Constitutional law – Human rights and freedoms – Constitution prohibiting inhuman or degrading punishment – Prohibition not extending to punishment which was lawful immediately prior to Constitution coming into force – Sentences of death for murder passed under pre-existing law – Long delay in execution of sentences – Whether execution of sentences after such delay
c *constituting inhuman or degrading punishment – Whether exception for punishment under pre-existing law applicable – Jamaica (Constitution) Order in Council 1962, Sch 2, s 17.*

Each of the five appellants was convicted of murder in Jamaica on dates between March 1975 and October 1976. The appellants were sentenced to death, that being the mandatory sentence for murder under s 3(1) of the Jamaican Offences against the Person
d Act 1864. In each case an appeal against conviction was dismissed by the Court of Appeal of Jamaica. From April 1976 until early 1979 political factors in Jamaica led to the suspension of all sentences of death, but on 30 January 1979 the Jamaican House of Representatives resolved that capital punishment should be retained. Thereafter warrants were issued for the sentences passed on the appellants to be carried out, the dates set for the executions being 29 May 1979 in three cases and 12 June 1979 in the remaining two
e cases. The appellants applied to the Supreme Court of Jamaica for declarations that the executions would be illegal on the grounds that they would be contrary to s 17(1)ᵃ of the Constitution of Jamaica which prohibited 'inhuman or degrading punishment'. However, s 17(2) of the Constitution provided that anything done 'under the authority of any law' was not to be held to be inconsistent with or in contravention of s 17(1) to the extent that the law in question authorised '. . . the infliction of any punishment which was lawful in
f Jamaica immediately before the [coming into force of the Constitution on 6 August 1962]'. The appellants contended that the prolonged delay in the execution of their sentences, which was substantially due to factors outside their control, had caused them sustained mental anguish, thereby rendering the punishment inhuman and degrading. The Crown contended that, although delayed, the actual sentences were authorised by the pre-existing law immediately before the Constitution came into force and therefore
g fell within s 17(2) of the Constitution. The applications were dismissed both at first instance and by the Jamaican Court of Appeal. The appellants appealed to the Privy Council.

Held (Lord Scarman and Lord Brightman dissenting) – A punishment fell within the exception contained in s 17(2) of the Constitution if it satisfied three related conditions,
h namely (a) that it was done by the authority of law, (b) that it involved the infliction of punishment which was authorised by that law and was lawful in Jamaica immediately before the coming into force of the Constitution on 6 August 1962, and (c) that it did not exceed in extent the description of the punishment so authorised. In regard to a delayed execution which satisfied the first two conditions the test to be applied was whether, if the same description of punishment had been inflicted in the same circumstances before
j 6 August 1962, that punishment would have been authorised by law. Since the legality of a delayed execution of a sentence lawfully imposed under s 3(1) of the 1864 Act could not have been questioned before 6 August 1962, the delay could afford no ground for

---

a   Section 17 is set out at p 471 *d*, post

holding the executions to be in contravention of s 17(1). Accordingly, the appeals would
be dismissed (see p 472 j to p 473 d, post).   *a*

Notes
For the Constitution of Jamaica, see 6 Halsbury's Laws (4th edn) paras 970, 971.

                                                                                                b
Cases referred to in judgment
Abbott v A-G of Trinidad and Tobago [1979] 1 WLR 1342, PC.
de Freitas v Benny [1976] AC 239, PC, Digest (Cont Vol D) 111, *132a*..
DPP v Nasralla [1967] 2 All ER 161, [1967] 2 AC 238, [1967] 3 WLR 13, PC, 14(1) Digest
   (Reissue) 441, 3786.
Ediga Anamma v State of Andhra Pradesh [1974] 3 SCR 329.   *c*
Furman v Georgia (1972) 408 US 238.
Maharaj v A-G of Trinidad and Tobago (No 2) [1978] 2 All ER 670, [1979] AC 385, [1978]
   2 WLR 902, PC, Digest (Cont Vol E) 49, 563a.
Minister of Home Affairs v Fisher [1979] 3 All ER 21, [1980] AC 319, [1979] 2 WLR 889,
   PC, Digest (Cont Vol E) 49, *1213a*.
Olivier v Buttigieg [1966] 2 All ER 459, [1967] 1 AC 115, [1966] 3 WLR 310, PC, 8(2)   *d*
   Digest (Reissue) 759, 351.
People v Anderson (1972) 493 P 2d 880.
People v Chessman (1959) 341 P 2d 679.
Rajendra Prasad v State of Uttar Pradesh [1979] 3 SCR 78.
Tyrer v United Kingdom (1978) 2 EHHR 1, E Ct HR.

                                                                                                e

Appeals
Noel Riley, Anthony Forbes, Clifton Irving, Elijah Beekford and Errol Milles appealed
with leave of the Court of Appeal of Jamaica against the decision of the Court of Appeal
(Zacca JA (AG), Melville JA and Carberry JA) on 28 July 1980 dismissing their appeals
against the judgment of the Full Court of the Supreme Court (Parnell, Ross and Carey JJ)   *f*
dismissing their applications by notices of motion for declarations that the executions of
the appellants would be unconstitutional and illegal being contrary to s 17(1) of the
Constitution of Jamaica. The facts are set out in the judgment of the Board.

R N A Henriques QC and *Dennis V Daly* (both of the Jamaican Bar) for the appellants.
The Solicitor General for Jamaica (Kenneth Rattray QC), *The Senior Assistant Attorney General* *g*
   for Jamaica (Ranse Langrin) and *George Warr* for the Attorney General of Jamaica.

LORD BRIDGE OF HARWICH. The five appellants are all under sentence of death
following their several convictions for murder. It is convenient at the outset to indicate
in tabular form the dates of the relevant criminal proceedings in Jamaica.   *h*

Appellant	*Date of Conviction*	*Date of dismissal of appeal to the Court of Appeal of Jamaica*
Noel Riley	7 March 1975	23 February 1976
Anthony Forbes	7 March 1975	23 February 1976
Clifton Irving	22 March 1976	10 January 1977
Elijah Beckford	9 May 1975	6 November 1975
Errol Miller	28 October 1975	5 February 1976

j

Petitions for special leave to appeal to Her Majesty in Council were submitted on behalf
of Riley, Irving and Miller. Miller's petition was dismissed on 9 December 1976, Riley's
on 18 July 1978 and Irving's was abandoned in October 1978.

Warrants for the execution of the appellants were issued in 1979. The dates set for the execution were, in the cases of Riley, Forbes and Irving, 29 May 1979, in the cases of Beckford and Miller, 12 June 1979. Thereupon application was made by each of the appellants to the Supreme Court of Jamaica pursuant to s 25(1) of the Constitution of Jamaica, as embodied in Sch 2 to the Jamaica (Constitution) Order in Council 1962, SI 1962/1550 (hereinafter referred to as 'the Constitution'), seeking in each case:

> 'A declaration that the execution of [the appellant] at this time and in the circumstances leading up to and surrounding the issue of the death warrant, would be unconstitutional and illegal being contrary to section 17(1) of the Constitution ...'

The applications were dismissed by the Full Court on 19 March 1980 and appeals from these decisions to the Court of Appeal of Jamaica were dismissed on 28 July 1980. The present appeals to Her Majesty in Council are brought pursuant to leave granted by the Court of Appeal of Jamaica on 25 September 1980.

The appellants contend that to execute the sentences of death passed on them in 1975 and 1976 would now be, and indeed would have been at any time after the issue of the warrants in 1979, by reason both of the length and of the circumstances of the delay between sentence and execution, 'inhuman or degrading punishment or other treatment'. Section 17 of the Constitution provides:

> '(1) No person shall be subjected to torture or to inhuman or degrading punishment or other treatment.
> (2) Nothing contained in or done under the authority of any law shall be held to be inconsistent with or in contravention of this section to the extent that the law in question authorises the infliction of any description of punishment which was lawful in Jamaica immediately before the appointed day.'

Apart from the delays necessarily occasioned by the appellate procedures pursued by the appellants (of which it could hardly lie in any appellant's mouth to complain), it is also the fact that political factors in Jamaica led to the execution of sentences of death being held in abeyance from April 1976 until early 1979 during a period of acute controversy over capital punishment. This was eventually resolved on 30 January 1979 by a vote by the narrow majority of 23 to 20 in the House of Representatives that capital punishment be retained, coupled with a recommendation that all outstanding sentences of death be reviewed. A resolution of the Senate on 9 February 1979 that 'capital punishment be suspended for a period of eighteen months pending a detailed study, assessment and report of the sociological and psychological effect of capital punishment in today's Jamaican society' was carried by 10 votes to 5, but appears to have had no effect on the further policy pursued by the executive, as the issue of the warrants for the execution of the present appellants demonstrates.

Section 90 of the Constitution provides for the prerogative of mercy to be exercised by the Governor-General, 'in Her Majesty's name and on Her Majesty's behalf', acting on the recommendation of the Privy Council of Jamaica. Their Lordships infer that the review recommended by the House of Representatives was carried out in the case of each appellant but that in no case was it decided to grant a reprieve.

Clearly the appellants cannot base their complaint on the prolongation of their lives by the delay in execution of their sentences. The only proposition capable of sustaining the contention that the execution of the sentences would now contravene s 17 of the Constitution must be that to carry out a death sentence *after* a certain delay, not occasioned by the appeal process invoked by the prisoner, would contravene the provisions of sub-s (1) and could properly be held to do so notwithstanding the provisions of sub-s (2).

Their Lordships fully accept that long delay in the execution of a death sentence, especially delay for which the condemned man is himself in no way responsible, must be an important factor to be taken into account in deciding whether to exercise the prerogative of mercy. But it is not for this Board to usurp the function allocated by s 90 of the Constitution to the Governor-General acting on the recommendation of the Privy Council of Jamaica. The sole question for their Lordships' decision is whether the execution of sentence of death on any of the appellants would contravene s 17 of the Constitution.

In the last analysis this question must depend on the language of s 17. But it is not to be construed in isolation. As was pointed out by Lord Hailsham, in his dissenting opinion in *Maharaj v A-G of Trinidad and Tobago (No 2)* [1978] 2 All ER 670 at 681, [1979] AC 385 at 402, the constitutions of former British dependencies, based on conferences held prior to the enactment of independence, bear a strong family resemblance to each other, and both the Constitution of Jamaica and that of Trinidad and Tobago have come under scrutiny by this Board in contexts which called for consideration of the relationship between the entrenched rights conferred by the Constitution and the rights secured by the law in force immediately before independence. In *DPP v Nasralla* [1967] 2 All ER 161 at 165, [1967] 2 AC 238 at 247–248 Lord Devlin, delivering the judgment of the Board, said of Ch III of the Constitution of Jamaica, which is headed 'Fundamental Rights and Freedoms', and includes s 17:

> 'This chapter . . . proceeds on the presumption that the fundamental rights which it covers are already secured to the people of Jamaica by existing law. The laws in force are not to be subjected to scrutiny in order to see whether or not they conform to the precise terms of the protective provisions. The object of these provisions is to ensure that no future enactment shall in any matter which the chapter covers derogate from the rights which at the coming into force of the Constitution the individual enjoyed.'

In *de Freitas v Benny* [1976] AC 239 at 244 Lord Diplock, delivering the judgment of the Board, pointed out that the corresponding chapter of the Constitution of Trinidad and Tobago proceeded on a similar presumption. In that case the Board rejected an argument that sentence of death, which was the mandatory sentence for murder in Trinidad and Tobago before independence, had become unconstitutional since independence, on the ground, inter alia, that delay in carrying it out rendered it a 'cruel and unusual punishment'.

In Jamaica sentence of death is the mandatory sentence for murder under s 3(1) of the Offences against the Person Act which has not been amended in any respect material to the issue under consideration since its enactment in 1864. The manner of execution of the sentence authorised by law is by hanging, and the passing of the sentence also provides lawful authority for the detention of the condemned man in prison until such time as the sentence is executed. Quite apart from s 17 of the Constitution the continuing constitutional validity of the death sentence is put beyond all doubt by the provision of s 14(1):

> 'No person shall intentionally be deprived of his life save in execution of the sentence of a court in respect of a criminal offence of which he has been convicted.'

The question, therefore, is whether the delayed execution of a sentence of death by hanging, assuming it could otherwise be described as 'inhuman or degrading punishment or other treatment', a question on which their Lordships need express no opinion, can escape the unambiguous prohibition imposed by the words in s 17(2) emphasised as follows:

> '*Nothing* contained in or done under the authority of any law *shall be held to be inconsistent with or in contravention of this section* to the extent that the law in question authorises the infliction of any description of punishment which was lawful in Jamaica immediately before the appointed day.'

An act will fall within this prohibition if it satisfies three related conditions, viz: (a) it must be an act done under the authority of law; (b) it must be an act involving the infliction of punishment of a description authorised by the law in question, being a

description of punishment which was lawful in Jamaica immediately before the
a appointed day; (c) it must not exceed in extent the description of punishment so
authorised.

There can be no doubt whatever that a delayed execution would satisfy conditions (a)
and (b). The only words in s 17(2) that are even arguably ambiguous are the words 'to
the extent that'. It seems to their Lordships that in their context these words pose the
question: to what extent did the law in Jamaica before independence authorise the
b description of punishment which is under challenge? This question can only be answered
by asking in turn the further question: if the like description of punishment had been
inflicted in the like circumstances before independence, would this have been authorised
by law? An obvious instance of a description of punishment exceeding in extent that
authorised by law would be the execution of a death sentence by burning at the stake.
But since the legality of a delayed execution by hanging of a sentence of death lawfully
c imposed under s 3(1) of the Offences against the Person Act could never have been
questioned before independence, their Lordships entertain no doubt that it satisfies
condition (c). Accordingly, whatever the reasons for, or length of, delay in executing a
sentence of death lawfully imposed, the delay can afford no ground for holding the
execution to be a contravention of s 17(1). Their Lordships would have felt impelled to
this conclusion by the language of s 17 alone, but they are reinforced by the consideration
d that their decision accords fully with the general principle stated in *DPP v Nasralla* [1967]
2 All ER 161, [1967] 2 AC 238 and *de Freitas v Benny* [1976] AC 239.

Accordingly, their Lordships will humbly advise Her Majesty that these appeals must
be dismissed.

Dissenting opinion by **LORD SCARMAN** and **LORD BRIGHTMAN**. These five
e appeals raise questions of importance as to the protection afforded by the Constitution of
Jamaica to persons under sentence of death.

It is with great regret that we find it necessary to express our dissent from the majority
opinion of their Lordships' Board. We do so only because of the constitutional importance
of the matters in issue. The first question of constitutional importance is whether the
carrying out after prolonged delay of a death sentence which has been lawfully passed by
f a court of competent jurisdiction can be a contravention of the convicted man's
constitutional rights. If this question be answered in the affirmative, a second question,
almost as important as the first, arises, namely the criterion for determining whether a
punishment is inhuman or degrading. Finally, there is the question whether the
appellants have proved a delay of such length and in such circumstances as to render
their execution a contravention of their constitutional rights.

g The specific point of law in the five cases is as to the true meaning and effect of s 17 of
the Constitution. Subsection (1) provides that 'No person shall be subjected to torture or
to inhuman or degrading punishment or other treatment': language which is almost
identical with art 3 of the European Convention on Human Rights and Fundamental
Freedoms (signed by the United Kingdom on 4 November 1950 and subsequently
ratified) (TS 71 (1953), Cmd 8969). Subsection (2), however, restricts the generality of
h sub-s (1) by providing that nothing done under the authority of any law shall be held to
be in contravention of the section—

'to the extent that the law in question authorises the infliction of any description
of punishment which was lawful in Jamaica immediately before the appointed day.'

The appointed day for the entry into force of the Constitution was 6 August 1962. These
j appellants were sentenced to death under the authority of a law in force before the
appointed day, namely the (Jamaica) Offences against the Person Act 1864; ss 2 and 3 of
the Act make murder a felony for which the mandatory penalty is death. It is submitted
by the respondent and, as we understand it, accepted by the majority opinion that s 17(2)
of the Constitution makes it impossible to hold that the infliction of the death penalty
required by that Act for murder can be an inhuman punishment or treatment within
sub-s (1) because the punishment was of a description authorised by a law which was in

force prior to the appointed day. With respect, we believe this view to arise from a wrong approach to the interpretation of a constitutional instrument and a failure to recognise that the act of the state which is challenged in these proceedings is not the sentence of the court but its execution after prolonged delay. The appellants' case is that this delay, which arose from the exercise of a power conferred not by the pre-existing law but by the Constitution, rendered subsequent execution a contravention of the Constitution.

The Constitution of Jamaica was brought into force on 6 August 1962 by an Order in Council made pursuant to an Act of Parliament of the United Kingdom: The Jamaica (Constitution) Order in Council 1962, SI 1962/1550 made under the West Indies Act 1962. It is one of a family of constitutions (the family includes those of Trinidad and Tobago, Bermuda and many other countries which were previously British colonies) granted by Parliament, which embody a Bill of Rights or Charter of Fundamental Rights and Freedoms drafted on the model of the European Convention on Human Rights. We have no doubt that the proper approach to the interpretation of such constitutions is as described by Lord Wilberforce when he delivered the opinion of the Judicial Committee in *Minister of Home Affairs v Fisher* [1979] 3 All ER 21, [1980] AC 319. He drew a distinction between Acts of Parliament concerned with specific subjects and constitutional enactments, and then considered the Bermuda Constitution, which was in issue in that appeal. He said ([1979] 3 All ER 21 at 25–26, [1980] AC 319 at 328):

'Here, however, we are concerned with a Constitution, brought into force certainly by Act of the United Kingdom Parliament, the Bermuda Constitution Act 1967 but established by a self-contained document set out in Sch 2 to the Bermuda Constitution Order 1968 [UK SI 1968/182]. It can be seen that this instrument has certain special characteristics. (1) It is, particularly in Chapter I, drafted in a broad and ample style which lays down principles of width and generality. (2) Chapter I is headed "Protection of Fundamental Rights and Freedoms of the Individual". It is known that this chapter, as similar portions of other constitutional instruments drafted in the post-colonial period, starting with the Constitution of Nigeria, and including the constitutions of most Caribbean territories, was greatly influenced by the European Convention for the Protection of Human Rights and Fundamental Freedoms. That convention was signed and ratified by the United Kingdom and applied to dependent territories including Bermuda. It was in turn influenced by the United Nations Universal Declaration of Human Rights 1948. These antecedents, and the form of Chapter I itself, call for a generous interpretation avoiding what has been called "the austerity of tabulated legalism", suitable to give to individuals the full measure of the fundamental rights and freedoms referred to. (3) Section 11 of the Constitution forms part of Chapter I. It is thus to "have effect for the purpose of affording protection to the aforesaid rights and freedoms" subject only to such limitations contained in it "being limitations designed to ensure that the enjoyment of the said rights and freedoms by any individual does not prejudice . . . the public interest".'

He elaborated what he meant by 'a generous interpretation'. It was—

'to treat a constitutional instrument such as this as sui generis, calling for principles of interpretation of its own, suitable to its character as already described, without necessary acceptance of all the presumptions that are relevant to legislation of private law.'

(See [1979] 3 All ER 21 at 26, [1980] AC 319 at 329.)

As we shall endeavour to show, we believe that the majority opinion is in error because it has adopted in its construction of the Constitution an approach more appropriate to a specific enactment concerned with private law than to a constitutional instrument declaring and protecting fundamental rights. An austere legalism has been preferred to the generous interpretation which in *Fisher's* case was held to be appropriate. The Jamaican charter of fundamental rights and freedoms is to be found in Ch III of the

Constitution. It consists of 14 sections. Section 13 declares the fundamental rights and
a   freedoms, which include, subject to respect for the rights of others and for the public
interest, the right to life and the protection of the law. Sections 14 to 24 are the protective
provisions, their purpose being to protect the rights and freedoms declared in s 13. The
protection offered by these sections is to be enforced judicially. Section 25 enables any
person who alleges a contravention of any of the protective provisions in relation to him
to apply to the Supreme Court for redress. The court may make such order or give such
b   directions as it considers appropriate for the constitutional protection of the applicant.
But it shall not exercise its protective power if satisfied that adequate means of redress are
or have been available under any other law.
　　It is, of course, clear, as Lord Devlin pointed out in *DPP v Nasralla* [1967] 2 All ER
161, [1967] 2 AC 238 and as Lord Diplock later emphasised in *de Freitas v Benny* [1976]
AC 239, that Ch III of the Constitution proceeds on the presumption that the fundamental
c   rights and freedoms which it declares and protects were already recognised and
acknowledged by the law in force at the commencement of the Constitution. It is further
true that, generally speaking and subject to adaptations and modifications, the law was
the law of England. The contribution which the Constitution makes to the jurisprudence
of Jamaica is that it offers to every person in Jamaica the protection of a written
constitution in respect of the rights and freedoms recognised and acknowledged by the
d   law; and 'law' means both the pre-existing law so far as it remains in force (see s 4(1) of
the Jamaica (Constitution) Order in Council 1962) and the new law arising from the
Constitution itself and from future enactment. However, the Constitution's introduction
of a new judicial remedy negatives any presumption that the remedies available under
the pre-existing law were necessarily sufficient: indeed, the enactment of new protection
suggests that they needed strengthening. In summary, the Constitution declares the
e   fundamental rights and freedoms of every person in Jamaica and provides for their
judicial protection if no adequate means of redress are available to the person concerned
under any other law. Thus the Constitution ensures that in Jamaica 'ubi jus, ibi
remedium'. The 'jus' is the substantive law of fundamental rights and freedoms
recognised by the law and practice of the state and now embodied by statute in ss 13 to
24 of the Constitution: the remedy is their judicial protection under s 25, if no means of
f   redress is available to the victim under any other law. It is also plain that the primary
purpose of Ch III of the Constitution, as too of the European Convention on which it is
modelled, is the protection of the individual against abuse of power by act of the state,
whether the act be legislative, judicial or executive. It follows that the fact that in these
five cases the death sentence when passed was in accordance with law cannot be
determinative of the appeals. The challenge is not to the judicial sentence but to the
g   decision of the executive to carry it out at the time fixed and in the circumstances which
had arisen.
　　Adopting the principle of a generous interpretation and in the light of the objects of
Ch III of the Constitution, we do not find any real difficulty in determining the true
effect of s 17(2) in the circumstances of these five appeals. Trimmed of words inessential
for present purposes, sub-s (2) provides:

h
　　'Nothing ... done under the authority of any law shall be held to be ... in
　　contravention of this section to the extent that the law in question authorises the
　　infliction of any description of punishment which was lawful in Jamaica immediately
　　before [6 August 1962].'

The execution of the appellants, had it taken place, would have been done under the
j   authority of s 3 of the Offences against the Person Act, which enacts '(1) Upon every
conviction for murder the court shall pronounce sentence of death, and the same may be
carried into execution as heretobefore has been the practice . . .' Section 3 of the Offences
against the Person Act is therefore 'the law' in question for the purposes of s 17(2) of the
Constitution. That law authorises the infliction of a 'description of punishment', namely,
death. That 'description of punishment' was lawful in Jamaica immediately before 6
August 1962.

The problem which arises is this: given the premise that no person may lawfully be subjected to 'inhuman treatment', and given the premise that the execution of sentences *a* of death after the prolonged delays which have here taken place would have subjected and would now subject the appellants to 'inhuman treatment', is such 'treatment' cleared of inhumanity for the purposes of the section and thus legalised because 'the law', namely s 3 of the Offences against the Person Act, authorises the death sentence and the death sentence was a lawful punishment in Jamaica immediately before the appointed day? With profound respect to those who take the opposite view, we consider that the question *b* posed should be answered in the negative. The 'treatment' which has to be considered is not the death penalty in isolation. The 'treatment' which is prima facie 'inhuman' under sub-s (1) is the execution of the sentence of death as the culmination of a prolonged period of respite. That species of 'treatment' falls outside the legalising effect of sub-s (2). Subsection (2) is concerned only to legalise certain descriptions of punishment, not to legalise a 'treatment', otherwise inhuman, of which the lawful punishment forms only *c* one ingredient. Subsection (1) deals with 'punishment' and 'other treatment'. In the instant case the punishment is the execution of the death sentence. Subsection (2) is directed both to 'punishment' and to 'other treatment'. The 'other treatment', if inhuman, is not validated by sub-s (2), in our opinion, merely because lawful punishment is an ingredient of the inhuman treatment.

Accordingly, in our opinion, the execution of the respective death sentences in May *d* and June 1979, against the background of the lapse of time since conviction, would have been 'inhuman treatment' within the meaning of sub-s (1) of s 17 and would not have been saved from being unconstitutional and illegal by sub-s (2).

As we have indicated, it is necessary to identify the act of the state which is challenged. It is not the judicial sentence of death: that was and remains a lawful judicial act. If these proceedings were directed towards establishing the proposition that sentence of death is *e* in itself a contravention of the Constitution as being an inhuman or degrading punishment, sub-s (2) would be a complete answer. In Jamaican law a convicted man cannot be heard to say that sentence of death is itself a contravention of the Constitution, since it is authorised by a law which was in force when the Constitution came into effect and still remains in force. But that is not the purpose of these proceedings. The challenge is to the duty of the Governor General in the exercise of the powers conferred on him by *f* ss 90 and 91 of the Constitution. Though they derive as a matter of history from the Crown's prerogative of mercy, they are now statutory in character. They are part of the written Constitution. Significantly the sections appear in a chapter entitled 'Executive Powers'. Their effect is to require the Governor General in every capital case (save in emergency) to seek the advice of the Privy Council of Jamaica so that he may be advised as to the exercise of his power to delay or commute the sentence: and he is obliged to act *g* on the recommendation of the Privy Council. It is to be noted that this is an executive power subject to the sort of safeguard, ie the confidential advice of a distinguished independent body, which is a familiar feature in administrative and public law. The condemned man, though the power exists for his protection as well as for the protection of the public interest, has no right to be heard in the deliberations of the Privy Council and the Governor General (who shall, so far as practicable, attend and preside at all its *h* meetings: see s 87 of the Constitution). In short, the exercise of this executive power is a classic illustration of an administrative situation in which the individual affected has a right to expect the lawful exercise of the power but no legal remedy: that is to say, no legal remedy unless the Constitution itself provides a remedy.

In our view it is exactly the sort of situation with which the Constitution is concerned: what has been called a 'de facto right' exists but there is no remedy available to the *j* individual. Two recent cases before the Judicial Committee reveal how a written Constitution incorporating a charter of fundamental rights operates when a right exists but the individual has no remedy other than by invoking the Constitution. Both cases arose under the Constitution of Trinidad and Tobago, which is similar, though not identical with, the Constitution of Jamaica. Both constitutions are, however, members

of the family of which Lord Wilberforce spoke in *Minister of Home Affairs v Fisher* [1979]
a 3 All ER 21, [1980] AC 319. The facts in the earlier of the two cases, *Maharaj v A-G of
Trinidad and Tobago (No 2)* [1978] 2 All ER 670, [1979] AC 385, are not material. It was a
case in which the Board considered whether a right existed under the law before the
Constitution came into force. Their Lordships' Board, allowing the appeal by a majority,
said in the course of judgment ([1978] 2 All ER 670 at 677, [1979] AC 385 at 397):

b   'Some of the rights and freedoms described in s 1 are of such a nature that, for
        contraventions of them committed by anyone acting on behalf of the state or some
        public authority, there was already at the time of the Constitution an existing
        remedy, whether by statute, by prerogative writ or by an action for tort at common
        law. But for others, of which "(c) the right of the individual to respect for his private
        and family life" and "(e) the right to join political parties and express political views"
        may be taken as examples, all that can be said of them is that at the time of the
c   Constitution there was no enacted law restricting the exercise by the individual of
        the described right or freedom. The right or freedom existed de facto. Had it been
        abrogated or abridged de facto by an executive act of the state there might not
        necessarily have been a legal remedy available to the individual at a time before the
        Constitution came into effect, as, for instance, if a government servant's right to join
        political parties had been curtailed by a departmental instruction. Nevertheless de
d   facto rights and freedoms not protected against abrogation or infringement by any
        legal remedy before the Constitution came into effect are, since that date, given
        protection which is enforceable de jure under s 6(1) (cf *Olivier v Buttigieg* [1966] 2
        All ER 459, [1967] 1 AC 115).'

In our view, the right of these appellants to the proper exercise of the discretion vested
e by the Constitution in the Governor General may be described as a 'de facto' right in the
sense used by their Lordships in *Maharaj*'s case: it is a right for which no remedy exists,
unless its infringement can be shown to be a contravention of one or more of the
protective provisions in Ch III of the Constitution.

The second case is *Abbott v A-G of Trinidad and Tobago* [1979] 1 WLR 1342. In that case
the appellant sought constitutional redress by moving for a declaration that execution of
f sentence of death upon him would contravene his fundamental right to life protected by
the Constitution. The ground alleged was inordinate delay between sentence and the
issue of the death warrant. The period between the last judicial act (dismissal by the
Judicial Committee of appeal against conviction) and the warrant was less than eight
months. The period between sentence and warrant was somewhat less than four years.
The total period between sentence and the Judicial Committee's decision on the
g constitutional motion was five years eleven months. In their judgment dismissing the
condemned man's appeal from a refusal by the courts of Trinidad and Tobago to grant
him relief, their Lordships made this comment (at 1345) on the total period of waiting
in that case:

h   'That so long a total period should have been allowed to elapse between the
        passing of a death sentence and its being carried out is, in their Lordships' view,
        greatly to be deplored. It brings the administration of criminal justice into disrepute
        among law-abiding citizens.'

Later in the judgment their Lordships analysed the period of delay and found that the
period for which the appellant could in no way be said (ie by appeal or other legal
proceedings) to be responsible was one of less than eight months. The critical provision
j in the Trinidad and Tobago Constitution was that the right to life is 'the right not to be
deprived thereof except by due process of law': Ch I, s 4(a) of the Constitution. After
commenting that '"due process of law" does not end with the delivery of judgment in a
civil matter or the pronouncement of sentence in a criminal matter; it includes
enforcement of judgments and the carrying out of sentences', their Lordships said (at
1347–1348):

'So unless the applicant can establish that his execution after a lapse of time of
between seven and eight months from the lodging of his petition for reprieve would
be unlawful under the Criminal Procedure Ordinance read with sections 87 to 89 of
the Constitution, he cannot point to any contravention of his rights and freedoms
under section 4(a) of the Constitution for which he is entitled to apply for redress
under section 14. In their Lordships' view the proposition that, in the circumstances
of the instant case, the fact that seven or eight months elapsed before the applicant's
petition for reprieve was finally disposed of by the President made his execution at
any time thereafter unlawful, is quite untenable. Their Lordships accept that it is
possible to imagine cases in which the time allowed by the authorities to elapse
between the pronouncement of a death sentence and notification to the condemned
man that it was to be carried out was so prolonged as to arouse in him a reasonable
belief that his death sentence must have been commuted to a sentence of life
imprisonment. In such a case, which is without precedent and, in their Lordships'
view, would involve delay measured in years, rather than in months, it might be
argued that the taking of the condemned man's life was not "by due process of law",
but since nothing like this arises in the instant case, this question is one which their
Lordships prefer to leave open.'

Thus in *Abbott's* case the Judicial Committee recognised that inordinate delay might
mean that the taking of the condemned man's life would not be 'by due process of law'.
Significantly they commented that a case of delay so prolonged as to arouse a reasonable
belief that he might be spared was 'without precedent'. *Abbott's* case, therefore, confirms
us in the view not only that the period and circumstances of delay may be such as to put
the taking of the man's life outside the due process of law (in other words, it is no longer
justified by law) but also that the acknowledged proper practice of the state, so as to
ensure due process of law, is not to allow execution after prolonged delay.

We are, therefore, of the opinion that the respondents cannot rely on s 17(2). First,
what is challenged is not the judicial sentence authorised by pre-existing law but the
exercise by the executive of a power conferred on it by the Constitution itself. Second,
the appellants are able to show a 'de facto' right to the proper exercise of that power.

We turn, therefore, to consider s 17(1). Clearly, it would be an improper exercise of
the power conferred by ss 90 and 91 if it should result in subjecting a condemned man
to inhuman or degrading punishment or treatment. Indeed it would be a travesty of the
law if powers intended to enable mercy to be shown in appropriate cases were so used. It
becomes necessary, therefore, to look closely at the practice which has developed and the
views which have become recognised as to the proper use of the delaying power in the
execution of the death sentence. We have already referred to *Abbott's* case, where
inordinate delay was considered to be an affront to the administration of criminal justice
and might become a denial of due process of law, but was said to be (fortunately) 'without
precedent'.

British practice and thinking were to the same effect. It is well known that it was the
practice of the Home Secretary, who had the duty of advising Her Majesty as to the
execution of sentence of death, to ensure that a decision was taken and, if it was to allow
execution, that the punishment was inflicted within a period of weeks after the last
judicial act. The usual period was of the order of three weeks. Indeed, there is a
formidable case for suggesting that execution after inordinate delay would have infringed
the prohibition against cruel and unusual punishments to be found in s 10 of the Bill of
Rights 1688.

Such research as we have been able to conduct shows that many judges in other
countries have recognised the inhumanity and degradation a delayed death penalty can
cause. We cite four instances (but there are many others). In *Furman v Georgia* (1972) 408
US 238 Brennan J, who concluded that capital punishment was unconstitutional in the
United States of America (a conclusion with which we are not concerned and on which
differing opinions are held), commented (at 288) that 'the prospect of pending execution

exacts a frightful toll during the inevitable long wait between the imposition of sentence
a and the actual infliction of death'. The Supreme Court of California has acknowledged in
two cases the cruel and degrading effect of delay: *People v Chessman* (1959) 341 P 2d 679
at 699, and *People v Anderson* (1972) 493 P 2d 880 at 894. In the latter case the court
expressly mentioned the dehumanising effects of lengthy imprisonment prior to
execution. Krishna Iyer J of the Indian Supreme Court has expressed a similar view,
when the delay after sentence was six years: *Rajendra Prasad v State of Uttar Pradesh*
b [1979] 3 SCR 78 at 130, with which should be read the comment of the same judge in an
earlier Supreme Court case on the 'brooding horror of hanging' which had haunted a
prisoner for over two years: *Ediga Anamma v State of Andhra Pradesh* [1974] 3 SCR 329 at
355. There is also a relevant case under the European Convention: *Tyrer v United Kingdom*
(1978) 2 EHHR 1 (the Isle of Man case). It was a case of corporal punishment. The
European Court of Human Rights noted a considerable delay of several weeks in carrying
c out the sentence of the juvenile court and commented that 'Mr. Tyrer was subjected to
the mental anguish of anticipating the violence he was to have inflicted on him': para 33.
It is interesting also to note the point made in the dissenting judgment of Judge
Fitzmaurice that most of the delay was due to the time taken on Mr Tyrer's appeal.

It is no exaggeration, therefore, to say that the jurisprudence of the civilised world,
much of which is derived from common law principles and the prohibition against cruel
d and unusual punishments in the English Bill of Rights, has recognised and acknowledged
that prolonged delay in executing a sentence of death can make the punishment when it
comes inhuman and degrading. As the Supreme Court of California commented in
People v Anderson it is cruel and has dehumanising effects. Sentence of death is one thing:
sentence of death followed by lengthy imprisonment prior to execution is another.

It is, of course, true that a period of anguish and suffering is an inevitable consequence
e of sentence of death. But a prolongation of it beyond the time necessary for appeal and
consideration of reprieve is not. And it is no answer to say that the man will struggle to
stay alive. In truth, it is this ineradicable human desire which makes prolongation
inhuman and degrading. The anguish of alternating hope and despair, the agony of
uncertainty, the consequences of such suffering on the mental, emotional and physical
integrity and health of the individual are vividly described in the evidence of the effect
f of the delay in the circumstances of these five cases. We need not rehearse the facts,
which are not in dispute. We do not doubt that the appellants have proved that they
have been subjected to a cruel and dehumanising experience. But whether this experience
involves the further conclusion that it would have been inhuman and degrading to kill
them at the time fixed by the warrants for their execution is another matter. The answer
depends on the true interpretation of the words of s 17(1).

g The true interpretation of the subsection turns on the criterion to be used in
determining what is meant by subjection to inhuman or degrading punishment or
treatment. Is the test the effect of the delay in all the circumstances, or is it the
reasonableness of the decision to delay execution? And, if effect be the test, is it actual
effect or likely effect?

The Attorney General submitted that the criterion was the reasonableness or otherwise
h of delaying execution: and he relied on the prolonged political and national debate as to
the future of capital punishment in Jamaica. We accept that in the circumstances it was
reasonable, while the debate continued, to refrain from executing the sentences. But
whether it was reasonable ultimately to carry them out is another matter. We would
think it clear, as their Lordships certainly recognised in *Abbott's* case, that a time will
come when the delay is such that it would be intolerable and wrong in law to carry out
i the sentence. And we note that, if the criterion be the effect of the delay on those
subjected to it, the uncertainty engendered by the debate was an aggravating factor in
the cruelty imposed on them.

We therefore reject the Attorney General's submission. It is not the 'generous
interpretation' the law requires of the Constitution. It is too austere because it fails to
give priority to the suffering of the victim in the interpretation of the terms 'inhuman'

and 'degrading'. They are plainly terms apt to describe the effect of the punishment or other treatment on him who is subjected to it. We therefore would adopt as the criterion the effect of the delay in all its circumstances on those subjected to it.

The cruel and dehumanising experience suffered by these appellants does meet the test. But we doubt whether *actual* effect should be the test. It would be quite unacceptable to differentiate in the application of s 17 between victims of strong character and those of weaker character. The test must be, in our view, that of the likely effect of the experience to which they have been subjected. Evidence, of course, of actual effect will be very relevant and, indeed, necessary in order to reach a conclusion as to likely effect.

We answer, therefore, the question as to the meaning and effect of s 17(1) as follows. Prolonged delay when it arises from factors outside the control of the condemned man can render a decision to carry out the sentence of death an inhuman and degrading punishment. It is, of course, for the applicant for constitutional protection to show that the delay was inordinate, arose from no act of his, and was likely to cause such acute suffering that the infliction of the death penalty would be in the circumstances which had arisen inhuman or degrading. Such a case has been established, in our view, by these appellants.

Accordingly in our opinion these appeals should be allowed.

Appeal dismissed.

Solicitors: *Simons, Muirhead & Allan* (for the appellants); *Charles Russell & Co* (for the respondents).

Diana Procter   Barrister.

McLorie v Oxford

QUEEN'S BENCH DIVISION
DONALDSON LJ AND WEBSTER J
17, 25 MAY 1982

Police − Right of search and seizure − Entry to private premises − Power to enter and remove instrument of crime − Police entering private premises without warrant and removing instrument of crime after defendant charged − Occupier of premises objecting to entry and resisting removal − Extent of police powers to enter premises without warrant in order to seize instrument of crime.

Following an incident in which a person was seriously injured by a car, the driver was arrested later that evening and some time later charged with attempted murder, the alleged weapon being the car. The arrest took place at the house where the driver lived with his father and brother who were not involved in the alleged offence. When the police arrested the driver the car was apparently not at the house but a few hours later it was seen in the rear yard of the house by two police officers who were patrolling the area searching for the car. One of the officers, an inspector, asked the father for permission to remove the car, the plain inference being that it was required for forensic examination and as material evidence in connection with the alleged offence, but the father refused permission unless the police produced a warrant for the removal. Later the inspector returned to the house with four police officers and, the father having again refused permission to remove the car, the officers forcibly entered the house and removed the car. The brother resisted the entry, using no more force than was necessary, and in the course of doing so assaulted one police officer and obstructed another. He was charged in a magistrates' court with assault and obstruction of the respective officers in the execution of their duty. The magistrates held that in entering the house to seize the car the police

were acting in the execution of their duty, and convicted the brother of the charges. He
a appealed. On the appeal the chief constable (the prosecutor) submitted that at common
law a police officer had the right to enter private premises without a warrant in order to
seize an instrument used by an offender who had been arrested on the premises for a
serious crime of violence, even though the entry and seizure took place after completion
of the arrest.

b **Held** – Once a person had been arrested on private premises for a serious offence and the
arrest was completed, a police officer had no right at common law subsequently to enter
the premises without a warrant in order to search for or seize an instrument of the crime
known to be on the premises. Accordingly, the police had not been acting in the
execution of their duty and thus within the limits of their lawful authority when they
entered the house in order to seize the car. It followed that the brother had not committed
c the offences of which he was convicted and the convictions would accordingly be quashed
(see p 485 *f* to *j*, post).

Davis v Lisle [1936] 2 All ER 213, R v Waterfield [1963] 3 All ER 659 and dictum of
Lord Widgery CJ in Jeffrey v Black [1978] 1 All ER at 558 considered.

Per curiam. (1) If the police follow a person to a house in 'hot pursuit' they can enter
the house without a warrant for the purpose of removing an instrument of crime which
d is still in possession of the person pursued, despite any objection raised by the occupier.
Furthermore, in such a case the police may postpone the removal of the instrument if
they have good reason for doing so, eg because they wish to take fingerprints first, and
provided they remove the instrument as soon as possible. Any later re-entry for the
purposes of removal in such circumstances is valid (see p 485 *c* to *e* and *h*, post).

(2) A warrant to enter and search for something authorises entry and seizure of an
e article notwithstanding that its whereabouts are not precisely known (see p 483 *c d*, post).

Notes
For a constable's right of entry into private property to obtain evidence or to search,
without a warrant, see 11 Halsbury's Laws (4th edn) paras 122–123.

f **Cases referred to in judgment**
Chic Fashions (West Wales) Ltd v Jones [1968] 1 All ER 229, [1968] 2 QB 299, [1968] 2
    WLR 201, CA, 14(1) Digest (Reissue) 215, 1573.
Davis v Lisle [1936] 2 All ER 213, [1936] 2 KB 434, DC, 15 Digest (Reissue) 985, 8553.
Ghani v Jones [1969] 3 All ER 1700, [1970] 1 QB 693, [1969] 3 WLR 1158, CA, 11 Digest
    (Reissue) 744, 608.
g Jeffrey v Black [1978] 1 All ER 555, [1978] QB 490, [1977] 3 WLR 895, DC, Digest (Cont
    Vol E) 131, 1370a.
Morris v Beardmore [1980] 2 All ER 753, [1981] AC 446, [1980] 3 WLR 283, HL.
R v Waterfield, R v Lynn [1963] 3 All ER 659, [1964] QB 164, [1963] 3 WLR 946, CA, 15
    Digest (Reissue) 986, 8554.
Semayne's Case (1604) 5 Co Rep 91a, [1558–1774] All ER Rep 62, 77 ER 194, 21 Digest
h (Reissue) 393, 2895.
Swales v Cox [1981] 1 All ER 1115, [1981] 2 WLR 814, DC.

Cases also cited
Barnett and Grant v Campbell (1920) 21 NZLR 484.
Dillon v O' Brien and Davies (1887) 16 Cox CC 245.
j McFarlane v Sharp [1972] NZLR 64.

Case stated
Malcolm McLorie appealed by way of case stated against the decision of the justices for
the Metropolitan County of Merseyside, acting in and for the petty sessional division of
St Helens, in respect of their adjudication as a magistrates' court sitting at St Helens,

whereby they convicted the appellant of assaulting a police constable of the Merseyside Police in the execution of his duty and of obstructing a police constable in the execution of his duty. The respondent was Kenneth Gordon Oxford, the Chief Constable of Merseyside. The questions for the opinion of the High Court were (1) whether there was a right of search and/or seizure of material evidence from the scene of an arrest after that arrest had been completed and (2) did the police act in the execution of their duty in entering private property to obtain material evidence of serious crime that was being withheld from them. The facts are set out in the judgment of the court.

Christopher Rose QC and John Dowse for the appellant.
Michael Morland QC and Timothy R A King for the respondent.

Cur adv vult

25 May. **DONALDSON LJ** read the following judgment of the court: This appeal is said to raise the question 'An Englishman's home: his castle, or a sanctuary for weapons used in crime?' Certainly it raises a point of importance and difficulty.

The facts were these. On the evening of 1 June 1981 there was a motor accident in Newton-le-Willows as a result of which someone was injured. We know little of the circumstances, save that they must have been somewhat unusual. We say that because the police later charged the driver with attempted murder, the motor car being the weapon. Furthermore, at his trial he pleaded guilty to causing grievous bodily harm and was sentenced to two years' imprisonment, although that sentence was varied on appeal.

The driver was Marcus McLorie, a brother of the appellant, Malcolm McLorie. Marcus, the driver, was arrested late on the evening of 1 June at 141 Alder Street, Newton-le-Willows. This was a house occupied by George McLorie, the father of Marcus and Malcolm and the home of all three.

A few hours later, in the early hours of 2 June, Inspector Davies and a police constable were on patrol in Alder Street searching for the weapon used in the attack, namely the motor car. In due course they saw it in the rear yard of 141 Alder Street. Why they did not find it when they arrested Marcus is not disclosed, but presumably it was not there at that time. The inspector asked George McLorie, the father, for permission to remove the car, the plain inference being that it was required for forensic examination and as material evidence. The appellant, Malcolm, was present. The inspector was told by George that he was a trespasser and that the car could not be removed by the police without a warrant. The first part of this statement was inaccurate. The inspector was not a trespasser at that stage, but he might have become one if he had not thereupon left the premises, which he did. The accuracy or otherwise of the second part of the statement, namely that the car could not be removed by the police without a warrant, lies at the heart of this appeal. We would add that it is common ground that there is no power to issue a warrant to enter private property and seize a weapon used in crime unless the weapon happens to be stolen property.

A little later the inspector returned with reinforcements in the form of a sergeant and three constables. Once again he asked for permission to remove the car and once again this was refused. The police officers then entered the premises and removed the car. The appellant resisted this entry and, using no more force than was necessary, assaulted the sergeant and obstructed a constable. He was charged with assaulting the sergeant in the execution of his duty and obstructing the constable in the execution of his duty. He was convicted by the St Helen's justices on both charges and fined. He now appeals by case stated.

As has been more than once pointed out, the offence of assaulting a constable in the execution of his duty, contrary to s 51(1) of the Police Act 1964, is liable to be misunderstood. 'In the execution of his duty' is not the same as 'on duty'. The essence of the offence is that the police constable is assaulted while he is acting within the limits of his lawful authority. It has also been pointed out that where this charge is brought, the

accused has almost always used more force than was reasonably necessary, and that a
more appropriate charge, or at least one giving rise to less legal argument, is often one of
common assault or, according to circumstances, assault occasioning actual bodily harm,
to which there would be no defence that the constable had technically exceeded his
authority. However, in the present case no excessive force was used and the charge under
s 51(1) was wholly appropriate. The officers were without doubt 'on duty' and were
purporting to act within the limits of their authority as police constables. The justices
have held that they were so acting and the question is whether they were right.

The police officers had no search warrant or warrant of arrest which authorised their
entry on the premises at 141 Alder Street and they claim no statutory right to enter the
premises without a warrant. Their authority, if any, is to be found in the common law.
Counsel who appeared for the respondent Chief Constable of Merseyside suggested that
the appeal is concerned with rights of seizure rather than search or arrest, because the
officers knew of the whereabouts of the 'weapon' and had already arrested the only
person alleged to have committed the offence. For our part, while we agree that the
appeal is concerned with a right of seizure, we think that this right is comprised within
a right of search and that a warrant to enter and search for something would authorise
entry and seizure of an article notwithstanding that its whereabouts were known
precisely. However, as we have said, there was no warrant in this case. It is also important
to remember that, although on the particular facts the appellant, the driver of the car and
the occupier of the house were all members of the same family, the appellant and the
occupier were in no way involved in the alleged attempted murder.

The justices expressed their opinion on the law in the following terms:

> 'We were of the opinion that although on the face of the matter it appeared that
> the constables were trespassers, they were acting in the execution of their duty
> because: Firstly, a person had been arrested from the premises (admittedly some
> hours earlier) and it would seem reasonable for the police to return to the scene of
> the arrest should material evidence subsequently come to light. Secondly, the
> constables were under a duty at common law to bring offenders to justice and in
> these circumstances they were to be excused from entering onto private property as
> their duty required them to obtain important material evidence of a serious crime
> that was being unreasonably withheld from them.'

The questions submitted for the opinion of the court are: (1) whether there is a right
of search and/or seizure of material evidence from the scene of an arrest after that arrest
has been completed? (2) did the police act in the execution of their duty in entering
private property to obtain material evidence of serious crime that was being withheld
from them?

'An Englishman's home is his castle' is one of the few principles of law known to every
citizen and was affirmed as early as 1604 in *Semayne's Case* 5 Co Rep 91a, [1558–1774]
All ER Rep 62 and reaffirmed as recently as 1980 in *Morris v Beardmore* [1980] 2 All ER
753, [1981] AC 446. The rule is, of course, subject to exceptions, but they are few and it
is for the police to justify a forcible entry.

Counsel for the respondent submits that at common law there is a right to seize, by
force if necessary, the instrument used by an arrested criminal which he has used in the
perpetration of a serious crime of violence when the whereabouts of that instrument is
known. In support of this submission counsel argues that no man can make his home a
sanctuary for weapons used in serious crimes of violence or for the perpetrator. He points
out that at common law a constable and a member of the public each has a right and
duty to arrest the perpetrator of a serious crime of violence and may force entry so long
as he first makes a request. Furthermore, at common law, a constable has the same right
and duty to seize the weapon if found in the same premises and at the same time as the
person arrested. Leaving the common law, counsel for the respondent submits that the
various statutes which authorise entry into private premises with or without warrants
are either concerned with prevention of crime or with crimes which are not of a serious

nature. At common law the only warrant which could be issued was a warrant to search
for stolen goods. He says that in 1600 a warrant could be obtained for some purposes but
there was no authority to issue a warrant to search for weapons. The inference, he
submits, is that no such warrant was needed. It was the citizen's duty to go and find the
criminal. If he had the right to pursue the criminal, he must have been able to pursue
the weapon. The case of stolen goods, for which a warrant was required, is distinguishable
for there the searcher was acting on behalf of the owner rather than the King.

Counsel for the respondent submitted that if the driver had been pursued by two
constables they could have entered the house without warrant and one constable could
have arrested the driver and the other seized the car. But suppose there had only been
one constable. Could it really be said that if he arrested the driver he could not come
back for the car? It would be absurd if in such circumstances the constable could be
prevented from seizing the car if the occupier of the house refused to allow him to re-
enter.

The common law power of entry to effect an arrest without warrant appears to be, and
to always have been, extremely limited. In *Swales v Cox* [1981] 1 All ER 1115, [1981] 2
WLR 814 it was conceded to be limited to four cases only, namely in order to prevent
murder, if a felony had been committed and the felon followed to a house, if a felony
was about to be committed and would be committed unless prevented and if an offender
was running away from an affray. Counsel for the respondent does not accept that this
list is exhaustive, but he has been unable to produce any authority to suggest that it is or
ever was more extensive.

Semayne's Case confirms the right to enter in hot pursuit of a felon, but, apart from
that, the case is concerned with the rights of a sheriff to enter a house on the King's
business. This, to our mind, implies that the sheriff had the King's warrant rather than
that he was entering under common law powers.

In *Chic Fashions (West Wales) Ltd v Jones* [1968] 1 All ER 229, [1968] 2 QB 299 the Court
of Appeal held that a constable is entitled at common law to seize and retain goods which
he finds in the possession of a person whom he has arrested if he has reasonable grounds
for believing that the goods are stolen. The justification for this power is said to be to
enable the goods to be produced as material evidence at the trial and to make them
available for restitution to the rightful owner. However, this decision has nothing to do
with rights of entry.

In *Ghani v Jones* [1969] 3 All ER 1700, [1970] 1 QB 693 the Court of Appeal extended
the principle to some degree in holding that a power of seizure exists where a constable
reasonably believes that a serious offence has been committed, that the article concerned
is the instrument by which the crime was committed and that the person in possession
of it has himself committed the crime, or is implicated in it, or is accessory to it, 'or at
any rate his refusal must be quite unreasonable'. The passage quoted is no doubt binding
on us although the House of Lords may at some stage wish to consider whether it is
correct. However, once again this is a decision which has nothing to do with rights of
entry.

Perhaps the most helpful citation from authority from the point of view of the police
is the remark of Lord Widgery CJ in *Jeffrey v Black* [1978] 1 All ER 555 at 558, [1978] QB
490 at 497:

'. . . if the police officers in the instant case had any sort of reason for thinking
that the respondent's theft of the sandwich required an inspection of his premises,
they might very well have made that inspection without further authority.'

Clearly it was this which led the justices to form the second part of their opinion. The
defendant and the sandwich, which had been stolen from a public house, were both
outside the defendant's house and the defendant refused permission for a search of that
house. It was held that the police officers, who did not suggest that their desire to search
the premises related to the theft of the sandwich, had acted unlawfully in entering. The
basis of Lord Widgery CJ's dictum is not disclosed and it was wholly unnecessary for the
decision in the case. We fear, therefore, that it does not advance the matter any further.

a There are two other authorities which, if anything, suggest that the submissions of counsel for the respondent are incorrect. The first is *Davis v Lisle* [1936] 2 All ER 213, [1936] 2 KB 434 which decides that a police constable has no right to question a suspect on private premises if he has no warrant justifying his presence and has been told to leave. The second is *R v Waterfield* [1963] 3 All ER 659, [1964] 1 QB 164. This decides that a police constable has no right at common law to detain a motor car for use as evidence of a crime when the car is in the street and the owner, who was not under arrest

b or charged with any offence, wishes to remove it.

The submission of counsel on behalf of the appellant is brief but powerful. He says that it is not credible that the common law power alleged should have existed for centuries without trace of it appearing in the books. He further submits that, although the common law is a flexible instrument, capable of evolution, the power for which counsel for the respondent contends involves going too far and too quickly and would

c usurp the functions of Parliament.

We have no doubt that the constables could have entered 141 Alder Street without a warrant and despite objection by the occupier if, but only if, they had followed the driver to that address, ie, if it was a 'hot pursuit' case. In such circumstances they could also have seized and removed the car which, on this hypothesis, would still have been in the possession of the driver. Furthermore, if, as might well have been the case, they had good

d reason to postpone removing the car, for example, they might have wished to fit a ring to the steering wheel in order to preserve finger prints and had no ring available or they might have been unable to spare a constable to remove it immediately, they would have been entitled to tell the householder that they were seizing the car and would return as soon as possible to remove it. If they had then returned and were refused entry, they would have been entitled to use such force as was necessary in order to re-enter.

e But that is not this case. When the police officers left 141 Alder Street, presumably they did not know that the car was there. In all probability it was not there. The fact that that was its location when it was later found is in a sense coincidental and certainly irrelevant. It might have been found almost anywhere, in a repair garage, for example.

Such is the importance attached by the common law to the relative inviolability of a dwelling house that we cannot believe that there is a common law right without warrant

f to enter one either in order to search for instruments of crime, even of serious crime, or in order to seize such an instrument which is known to be there. Certainly if there were, we would expect it to be reflected in the books and it is not.

Counsel for the respondent submits correctly that the common law evolves, or is discovered, in relation to changing social conditions. However, evolution, or discovery, is a delicate process and what he proposes would, in our judgment, constitute a violent

g change. For our part, we are unable to agree to it.

It may well be that the Home Office or the police can make a good case for being given the power to apply to a justice for a warrant to enter and seize in circumstances such as are revealed in this case. This is less draconian than the right claimed in this case. If so, in our judgment, this is a matter for Parliament rather than the courts.

We would answer the questions posed by the justices as follows: (1) there is no right of

h search and/or seizure of material from the scene of an arrest after that arrest has been completed. However a timely seizure may allow a postponed removal if the postponement is as short as possible; (2) the police were not acting in the execution of their duty in entering private property to obtain material evidence of serious crime that was being withheld from them in the circumstances set out in the case stated.

We would allow the appeal and quash the convictions.

j *Appeal allowed ; convictions quashed.*

The court refused leave to appeal to the House of Lords but certified, under s 1(2) of the Administration of Justice Act 1960 that the following points of law of general public importance were involved in the decision: (1) where a person had been lawfully arrested from the premises of a third party and subsequently charged with a serious offence of violence, whether at common law a police constable was acting in the execution of his duty when he returned to the premises and entered the same contrary to the express wishes of the third party in order to seize (i) an instrument which he believed on reasonable grounds to have been used in the commission of the offence or (ii) other evidence which he believed on reasonable grounds to be material evidence to prove the commission of the offence, which instrument or other evidence he knew or believed on reasonable grounds to be on the premises; (2) whether the answer to question (1) would be different in either or both of the following circumstances: (i) where the person had been arrested elsewhere than on the premises of the third party; (ii) where the third party had not been given an opportunity voluntarily to deliver the instrument or other evidence to the constable.

Solicitors: *John Spittle & Frank Howard*, Warrington (for the appellant); *B H Crebbin*, Manchester (for the respondent).

Dilys Tausz   Barrister.

Dennis and another v Charnwood Borough Council

COURT OF APPEAL, CIVIL DIVISION
LAWTON, TEMPLEMAN AND FOX LJJ
14, 15, 19, 20, 29 JULY 1982

Negligence – Duty to take care – Statutory powers – Act performed in exercise of powers – Local authority – Building operations – Legislation giving authority control over building operations – Plans – Building byelaws requiring approval of plans – Plans disclosing that house to be supported by concrete raft – Local authority passing plans on assumption that concrete raft would be adequate for its purpose – Raft constructed partly on natural soil and partly on fills of mixed composition – Raft inadequate and badly constructed – Raft and foundations constructed in breach of building byelaws – Subsequent damage to structure of building resulting from inadequate foundations – Extent of local authority's duty in considering and approving plans – Whether local authority liable for breach of duty to owner of building at time damage occurs.

Limitation of action – When time begins to run – Actions in tort – Accrual of cause of action – Negligence – Damage – Lapse of time between negligent act and occurrence of damage – Action against local authority for breach of duty to take reasonable care in considering and approving plans of house – Plans showing house to be constructed on raft foundations – Raft and foundations inadequate – Cracks appearing in brickwork of house more than six years before action brought – Writ issued within six years of discovery of cause of cracks – Whether limitation period running from date when damage first appeared or when cause of cracks discovered – Limitation Act 1939, s 2(1)(a).

In 1955 the plaintiffs commissioned a local builder to build a house on the site of a former sand pit. The plan was submitted to and duly passed by the local authority pursuant to building byelaws made by regulations under s 61 of the Public Health Act 1936. The approved plan disclosed that the house was to be supported by a concrete raft. The house was completed in 1956 and the plaintiffs moved in. In 1961 cracks appeared in the brickwork and in 1966 further more serious cracks appeared which were diagnosed by a builder as being comparatively trivial, localised and not affecting the main foundations of the house. Thereafter there were no indications of serious defects until 1976, when, following further cracks, investigations showed that the concrete raft was inadequate and badly constructed and that the house was or was likely to be unsafe. The raft and foundations were inadequate for their purpose because the raft was constructed partly on natural soil and partly on fills of mixed composition thereby causing uneven

settlement and subsidence. The raft did not sustain the load of the house so that there
was settlement which impaired the stability of the building in breach of byelaw 18(1)(a)
and the foundations were not taken down to such depth and were not so designed and
constructed as to safeguard the building, as required by byelaw 18(1)(b), against damage
by swelling and shrinking of the subsoil. In 1978 the plaintiffs issued a writ against the
local authority claiming damages for loss and expense caused by the local authority's
negligence in approving the plan of the house. The local authority denied liability on the
grounds, inter alia, that (i) since it was only concerned to carry out its role under the 1936
Act it was entitled, as against the building owner, to assume that, if a plan made provision
for the installation of a concrete raft, then such a raft would be adequate for its purpose,
particularly since it believed that the ground had been filled in with hard material, and
(ii) in any event, the claim was time-barred because more than six years had elapsed since
1966 when the defects manifested themselves and the cause of action arose. The judge
held that the local authority was liable for negligence in approving the plan and that the
action was not time-barred because, on the evidence, the fault did not emerge and could
not reasonably have been discovered until June 1977. The local authority appealed.

Held – The appeal would be dismissed for the following reasons—

(1) A local authority was under a duty to take reasonable care in considering and
approving plans required by the building regulations and if it failed to exercise reasonable
care in the performance of its statutory functions and as a result allowed the erection of a
building which had defects likely to cause damage or discomfort to the occupiers, being
defects which a prudent local authority exercising its statutory powers would have
required to be eliminated, it was liable for negligence at the suit of an owner or occupier
who suffered damage as a result of the breach of duty. However, it was not liable if the
defects were not discoverable by reasonable care or if the defects did not constitute a
likely threat to the safety or comfort of the occupiers for the normal lifespan of the
building because its statutory duty was of a supervisory nature only (see p 489 e, p 493 d
to h and p 495 c, post); Anns v Merton London Borough [1977] 2 All ER 492 applied.

(2) The local authority had been negligent in passing the plan of the plaintiffs' house
because the provision for the installation of a concrete raft revealed that the house was to
be built on made-up ground, and since the dangers of building on made-up ground were
known in 1955 that revelation cast on the local authority the duty to consider whether
the raft would be adequate for its purpose and it was not entitled to assume, when it did
not know the nature of the fill, that a concrete raft would be adequate for its purpose.
The local authority was therefore liable to the plaintiffs (see p 490 b to f and j to p 491 f
and p 495 c, post).

(3) Where it was alleged that a local authority was in breach of its duty to take
reasonable care in considering and approving plans of a building required by building
regulations time began to run under s 2(1)(a)[a] of the Limitation Act 1939 in favour of
the local authority either when, as a result of the breach, the building suffered damage
which caused danger or discomfort to the occupiers or when, before such damage
occurred, the building suffered damage or an event occurred which revealed the local
authority's breach of duty or which would cause a prudent owner or occupier to make
investigations which, if properly carried out, would reveal the local authority's breach of
duty. On the evidence the judge had been right to conclude that the fault which gave
rise to the plaintiffs' cause of action had not emerged and could not reasonably have been
discovered until June 1977. It followed that the plaintiffs' action had been commenced
within the limitation period (see p 493 e to g and p 495 a to c, post); Sparham-Souter v
Town and Country Developments (Essex) Ltd [1976] 2 All ER 65 and Anns v Merton London
Borough [1977] 2 All ER 492 applied; Cartledge v E Jopling & Sons Ltd [1963] 1 All ER 341
distinguished.

---

a   Section 2(1), so far as material, provides: 'The following actions shall not be brought after the
     expiration of six years from the date on which the cause of action accrued, that is to say:—(a)
     actions founded on simple contract or on tort . . .'

Notes

For negligence in relation to statutory functions and the duty to take care, see 34 *a*
Halsbury's Laws (4th edn) paras 4–5, and for cases on the subject, see 36(1) Digest
(Reissue) 17–55, 34–177.

For when a limitation period begins to run, see 28 Halsbury's Laws (4th edn) paras
622–623, and for cases on the subject, see 32 Digest (Reissue) 486–487, 503–509, 3737–
3745, 3842–3869.

For the Limitation Act 1939, s 2, see 19 Halsbury's Statutes (3rd edn) 61.	*b*

As from 1 May 1981 s 2(1)(*a*) of the 1939 Act was replaced by s 2 of the Limitation Act
1980.

Cases referred to in judgments

Anns v Merton London Borough [1977] 2 All ER 492, [1978] AC 728, [1977] 2 WLR 1024,
HL, Digest (Cont Vol E) 449, 99*b*.	*c*

Cartledge v E Jopling & Sons Ltd [1963] 1 All ER 341, [1963] AC 758, [1963] 2 WLR 210,
HL, 32 Digest (Reissue) 503, 3844.

Darley Main Colliery Co v Mitchell (1886) 11 App Cas 127, [1886–90] All ER Rep 449, HL,
32 Digest (Reissue) 504, 3846.

Dutton v Bognor Regis United Building Co Ltd [1972] 1 All ER 462, [1972] 1 QB 373, [1972]
2 WLR 299, CA, 36(1) Digest (Reissue) 30, 98.	*d*

Sparham-Souter v Town and Country Developments (Essex) Ltd [1976] 2 All ER 65, [1976]
QB 858, [1976] 2 WLR 493, CA, 32 Digest (Reissue) 507, 3865.

Cases also cited

Bagot v Stevens Scanlon & Co [1964] 3 All ER 577, [1966] 1 QB 197.

Batty v Metropolitan Property Realizations Ltd [1978] 2 All ER 445, [1978] QB 554, CA.	*e*

Eames London Estates Ltd v North Hertfordshire District Council (1980) 259 EG 491.

Pirelli General Cable Works Ltd v Oscar Faber & Partners (a firm) [1982] CA Bound
Transcript 31.

Appeal

By a writ issued on 8 August 1978 the plaintiffs, James Reginald Dennis and his wife	*f*
Evelyn Doris Ada Dennis, claimed against the defendants, Charnwood Borough Council,
damages for loss and expense caused by the negligence and/or breach of statutory duty of
the defendants, their servants or agents, as the successors of the person empowered to
inspect and approve building works carried out on the plaintiffs' land at 32 Curzon
Avenue, Birstall, Leicestershire in or about 1956. The defendants by their defence denied
liability but pleaded that, if the damage to the plaintiffs' property was caused by their	*g*
negligence or breach of statutory duty, the plaintiffs' action was barred by the Limitation
Act 1939, s 2. On 21 December 1981 Forbes J held that the damage to the plaintiffs'
property was caused wholly by the negligence and breach of statutory duty of the
defendants, their servants or agents, and that the claim was not time-barred and he
ordered the defendants to pay the plaintiffs damages of £23,498·57 and interest. The
defendants appealed. The facts are set out in the judgment of Templeman LJ.	*h*

Igor Judge QC and *Nigel Baker* for the defendants.
Richard Tucker QC and *Rex Tedd* for the plaintiffs.

Cur adv vult
	j
29 July. The following judgments were read.

TEMPLEMAN LJ (delivering the first judgment at the invitation of Lawton LJ). By
s 61 of the Public Health Act 1936, as originally enacted, a local authority had power to
make regulations which might include provisions for the deposit of plans of buildings
and for the inspection of building work. By s 64 the local authority must reject the plans

if they are defective or show that the proposed work would contravene any of the
a building regulations.

In 1953 the Rural District Council of Barrow-upon-Soar, the predecessors of the
appellant defendants, the Charnwood Borough Council, made building byelaws by
regulations under s 61 of the 1936 Act. Byelaw 2(3) and Part C of Sch 1 require every
person who intends to erect a building, other than certain exempt buildings not here
material, to give notice of his intention and to deposit plans and particulars. Byelaw 6
b requires a builder to give prior notice in writing to the council of the date and time of
the commencement of building operations and before the covering up of, inter alia, any
foundation. If a builder fails to give the requisite notice the surveyor of the council may
require him to cut into, lay open or pull down so much of the building works as prevents
the surveyor from ascertaining whether any of the byelaws have been contravened.

In 1955 the respondent plaintiffs, Mr and Mrs Dennis, commissioned a local builder
c to build a house and the plan was duly submitted to and passed by the council.

The first question is whether the council, when they considered and passed the plan of
the house, owed any duty of care to Mr Dennis. In *Anns v Merton London Borough* [1977]
2 All ER 492, [1978] AC 728 the House of Lords decided that under the 1936 Act local
authorities owe a duty to give proper consideration to the question whether they should
inspect the carrying out of any building work. If they decide to inspect, they are under a
d duty to use reasonable care in carrying out their supervisory function of ensuring
compliance with the building byelaws but only within the limits of discretion bona fide
exercised as to the time and manner of inspection (see [1977] 2 All ER 492 at 501, [1978]
AC 728 at 755 per Lord Wilberforce). The duty is owed to the owner or occupier at the
date when damage occurs as a result of a breach of duty by the local authority. The duty
is not owed to a negligent building owner who is the source of his own loss (see [1977] 2
e All ER 492 at 504, [1978] AC 728 at 758 per Lord Wilberforce).

In my judgment, if local authorities are liable within the limits prescribed in the *Anns*
case for negligence in connection with the discretionary inspection of building works,
they must similarly be liable for negligence in failing to use reasonable care in considering
and approving plans.

There is no suggestion that Mr and Mrs Dennis, the building owners, were negligent
f or the source of their own loss. They were entitled to trust the builder and the council.
They were entitled to claim damages against the builder if he was negligent. They were
entitled to claim damages against the council if the council were negligently in breach of
their duty to take reasonable care in the consideration of the plan of the house or in the
exercise of their supervisory and discretionary power of inspection.

Byelaw 18(1)(*a*) provides that the foundations of every building shall be so designed
g and constructed as to sustain the relevant loads and to transmit those loads to the ground
in such a manner that the pressure on the ground shall not cause such settlement as may
impair the stability of the building. Byelaw 18(1)(*b*) provides that the foundations of
every building shall be taken down to such a depth, or be so designed and constructed, as
to safeguard the building against damage by swelling or shrinking of the subsoil. Byelaw
19(1) provides that the foundations of a domestic building constructed as strip foundations
h of plain concrete situated centrally under the walls or piers shall be deemed to satisfy the
requirements of byelaw 18(1)(*a*) if, inter alia, there is no wide variation in the type of
subsoil over the loaded area and no weaker type of soil exists below that on which the
foundation rest within such a depth as may impair the stability of the structure.

The plan for the house to be built for Mr and Mrs Dennis disclosed that the house was
to be supported by a concrete raft. Experience proved that the raft was an inadequate
j foundation for the house. The raft did not sustain the load of the house so that there was
settlement which impaired that stability of the building which was required by byelaw
18(1)(*a*). The foundations of the house were not taken down to such a depth and were
not so designed and constructed as to safeguard the building, as required by byelaw
18(1)(*b*) against damage by swelling or shrinking of the subsoil. There were four reasons
why the raft and the foundations of the house were inadequate for their purpose. First,
the raft was constructed partly on natural soil and partly on soil which filled in the site of

sand extraction. This caused uneven settlement and subsidence which in turn caused the
raft to tilt and crack. Second, the infilling soil was clay which contracts and expands and
reacts differently from natural sand soil. Third, the infilling soil included quantities of
inorganic matter which occasioned uneven settlement and subsidence. Fourth, when the
raft came to be installed, it was constructed by the builder in two halves and those halves
were not properly welded together. This defect was concealed from the council. It was a
defect which, in the circumstances, further impaired the stability of the building.
Although the judge, Forbes J, did not make any express finding on this aspect of the
matter, I deduce from the evidence that the raft would have been inadequate to sustain
the building even if it had been properly constructed. At any rate, the council have not
argued the contrary.

The second question which arises on this appeal is whether the council were negligent
in passing the plan of the house. In 1955 it was known that the house was to be erected
on the site of a former sand pit. The builder's son gave evidence that 'we all thought it
had been filled with hard material'. In these circumstances the council's surveyor insisted
on a raft foundation.

It was submitted on behalf of the council that, in view of the fact that the council were
only concerned to carry out their role under the 1936 Act, they were entitled as against
the building owner to assume that, if a plan made provision for the installation of a
concrete raft of the nature disclosed in the present case, then such a raft would be
adequate for its purpose. But the very proposal to install a concrete raft revealed that the
house was to be built on made-up ground. In my judgment that revelation cast on the
council the duty of considering whether the raft would in fact be adequate for its purpose.
If the council were not satisfied that the raft was adequate for its purpose then they must
reject the plan as being defective or as failing to comply with the byelaws.

It was then submitted that the dangers of building on made-up ground were not
appreciated in general in 1955 and are only apparent in the present case with hindsight.
It was said that it is too much to expect a busy council surveyor to have been conscious of
all the possible dangers in 1955. But the evidence was that the dangers of building on
made-up ground were appreciated as early as 1949 when the Building Research Station
published a report for the guidance of surveyors (see Building Research Station Digest no
9, August 1949: Building on Made-up Ground or Filling). That report pointed out that
in the past the control exercised in filling waste ground had not been such as to ensure
that the site would be suitable for the support of building with normal type foundations.
The time required for a fill to reach a sufficient degree of natural consolidation to make
it suitable as a foundation depended mainly on the following factors: the nature of the
material comprising the fill, the depth of the fill, the method of placing, the nature of
the underlying natural ground and the drainage conditions. It was not possible to lay
down general rules and each case needed to be considered on its merits. Fills containing
a large proportion of very fine grade materials like clay took a very long time to
consolidate sufficiently. The actual time depended mainly on the method of placing and
the depth of the fill. Fills of mixed compositions, especially if they were loosely tipped in
random fashion, were likely to give variable support to foundations. Unless it was known
that the fill was composed of the best type of material or had been placed by rolling in
thin layers, it was always advisable to put test pits down into the fill and by inspection of
the sides to estimate the extent to which natural compaction had proceeded. The
foundation must then be designed to suit the conditions revealed. Special care should be
taken with buildings sited near the edges of filled ground; in particular, placing a
building partly on the natural ground and partly on fill should be avoided. Instead of
this the foundations should be carried down to the natural ground by piers or piles.

On behalf of the council, counsel emphasised that portion of the report which said:
'Where some degree of uneven bearing cannot be avoided, even though the fill has
undergone a certain amount of consolidation, a concrete raft reinforced top and bottom
is particularly suitable for light structures such as houses'.

In my judgment, however, the thrust of the article is that nothing should be done
without full information. The article does not support the submission that the council

in the present case were entitled to assume that the raft would be adequate for its purpose.

a   Next it was submitted that the council were entitled to accept the raft as being adequate having regard to the belief that the sand pit had been filled up with hard material. In my judgment, on proof that the raft was inadequate for its purpose, the onus lies on the council to show that it was reasonable for the council to accept the plan in the light of the information which the council sought and possessed. Unfortunately for the council, the lapse of time has destroyed all their records and we only know that they thought the sand

b   pit had been filled up with hard material. We do not know on what evidence this belief was based. We do know that the belief was unfounded. Moreover, it appears from the article published by the Building Research Station that many other factors ought to have been considered as well as the nature of the material used for filling. If the council had no further information they should have insisted that further information be supplied by the owner, information sufficient to enable the council to be satisfied that the plan

c   was not defective in the circumstances.

At the trial Forbes J came to the conclusion on the evidence available that the council had been negligent in passing the plan when they did not know that the house was to be constructed partly on natural ground and partly on filled ground and they did not know anything about the nature of the fill save that they believed, inaccurately, that it consisted of hard material and they did not know anything about the manner in which the filling

d   had been carried out. In my judgment the judge reached a correct conclusion.

The judge also reached the conclusion that the council had been negligent in not discerning that the concrete raft had been constructed of two halves badly welded together. The only justification for this conclusion is that the council's inspector ought to have realised that the raft was covered by a thin screed which could only have been designed to conceal the true facts from inspection. I am not wholly convinced that it was

e   the duty of the surveyor to inspect the raft unless he had reason to distrust the builder and I am not wholly convinced that inspection would or should have led the inspector to realise that deception was being practised on him. But in all the circumstances I do not feel able to reject the findings and conclusions of the judge on this aspect of the matter. In any event, the council cannot escape liability having regard to the conclusion reached by the judge, and with which I have expressed agreement, namely the conclusion that

f   the council were negligent in passing the plan.

The third question which arises on this appeal is whether the plaintiff's action is barred by the Limitation Act 1939. Section 2(1)(a) of that Act provides that actions founded on tort shall not be brought after the expiration of six years from the date on which the cause of action accrued. Where, as in the present case, the tort is actionable only on proof of damage, time runs only from the date of damage: see *Darley Main Colliery Co v Mitchell*

g   (1886) 11 App Cas 127, [1886–90] All ER Rep 449. Time still runs even though the plaintiff is unaware either of the commission of the tort or the fact of damage until after the period of limitation has expired. By s 26 the period of limitation does not begin to run in cases of fraud or mistake until the plaintiff has discovered the fraud or mistake or could with reasonable diligence have discovered it. In the present case there being neither fraud nor mistake the period of limitation began to run from the date of damage. Thus

h   in *Cartledge v E Jopling & Sons Ltd* [1963] 1 All ER 341, [1963] AC 758 a workman suffered substantial injury to his lungs. Before that injury could be discovered by any means known to medical science the limitation period expired. He was unable to recover damages from his employer because—

'the cause of action accrues at the date of the loss or damage when there has been a wrongdoing by the defendant from which loss or damage (not being insignificant)

j   is suffered by the plaintiff, irrespective of his knowledge of such loss or damage' (see [1963] AC 758 at 759).

The plaintiff's lungs had been damaged, although he was unaware of any damage, more than six years before the date of the writ and, therefore, the plaintiff's action was barred by the Limitation Act 1939. Lord Pearce said ([1963] 1 All ER 341 at 349, [1963] AC 758 at 779):

'It is a question of fact in each case whether a man has suffered material damage by any physical changes in his body. Evidence that those changes are not felt by him and may never be felt tells in favour of the damage coming within the principle de minimis non curat lex. On the other hand evidence that in unusual exertion or at the onslaught of disease he may suffer from his hidden impairment tells in favour of the damage being substantial. There is no legal principle that lack of knowledge in the plaintiff must reduce the damage to nothing or make it minimal'.

In *Cartledge v E. Jopling & Sons Ltd* the House of Lords was dealing with a wrongful act which caused physical damage to the human body. Damage is sustained when the body is materially affected by the tort although the plaintiff may not be aware of the symptoms and if he is aware of the symptoms may not be aware of the cause.

In *Sparham-Souter v Town and Country Developments (Essex) Ltd* [1976] 2 All ER 65, [1976] QB 858 this court dealt with a tort which at the time when the tort was committed did not cause any damage. The tort consisted of building a house with defective foundations. Until the defect manifested itself the occupiers of the house were not put to any expense or inconvenience. Until the defect manifested itself the owner did not suffer because he did not have to carry out remedial works and he could sell the house on the open marker at a price which was not affected by the unknown tort or the unknown defect. Once a defect becomes manifest the occupiers may suffer loss or damage or inconvenience and the owner may suffer loss or damage by being forced to pay for remedial works or being forced to accept a lower price for his property.

The distinction between damage caused to the owner of the human body as in *Cartledge v E Jopling & Sons Ltd* and damage caused to the owner of a house as in *Sparham-Souter v Town and Country Developments (Essex) Ltd* may seem delicate and surprising. In *Cartledge's* case the House of Lords recognised that a hardship was caused to a plaintiff whose body is injured and whose claim is barred because he continues in ignorance of his condition. That hardship was alleviated in the case of personal injuries by the Limitation Act 1963, which prevents time from running until the plaintiff has knowledge actual or constructive of the commission of a tort and the existence of a reasonable cause of action.

In *Sparham-Souter's* case this court expressed views as to the date when a cause of action accrues in connection with the negligent construction of a house with defective foundations. Lord Denning said that a cause of action—

'accrued not at the time of the negligent making or passing of the foundations, nor at the time when the latest owner bought the house, but at the time when the house began to sink and the cracks appeared. That was the first time when any damage was sustained.'

(See [1976] 2 All ER 65 at 69, [1976] QB 858 at 868.)

Roskill LJ said that a plaintiff in the position of a first or subsequent purchaser 'suffers the damage which is the second prerequisite of his cause of action in tort when, but only when, the defective state of the property first appears' (see [1976] 2 All ER 65 at 75–76, [1976] QB 858 at 875). It seems to me this must also apply to a plaintiff in the position of a building owner who has not himself been negligent. It has not been argued that a building owner who employs a builder as his agent can only recover against the negligent builder and not against the negligent local authority which approved the plans or inspected the building work. Geoffrey Lane LJ, dealing with a plaintiff purchaser, said ([1976] 2 All ER 65 at 79–80, [1976] QB 858 at 880):

'If the defects in the building had not become apparent during his ownership he would have suffered no damage. It is the emergence of the faults not the purchase of the house which has caused him the damage. There is no proper analogy between this situation and the type of situation exemplified in *Cartledge v E Jopling & Sons Ltd* where a plaintiff due to the negligence of a defendant suffers physical bodily injury which at the outset and for many years thereafter may be clinically a unobservable. In those circumstances clearly damage is done to the plaintiff and the cause of action accrues from the moment of the first injury, albeit undetected and undetectable. That is not so where the negligence has caused unobservable damage not to the plaintiff's body but to his house. He can get rid of his house before any damage is suffered. Not so with his body'.

b In *Anns v Merton London Borough* the views of the Court of Appeal in *Sparham-Souter* were approved and Lord Wilberforce said that the cause of action 'can only arise when the state of the building is such that there is present or imminent danger to the health or safety of persons occupying it' (see [1977] 2 All ER 492 at 505, [1978] AC 728 at 760). Lord Salmon in expressing approval of the views of the Court of Appeal in *Sparham-Souter* accepted 'that the true view was that the cause of action in negligence accrued at the time when damage was sustained as a result of negligence, ie when the building c began to sink and the cracks appeared' (see [1977] 2 All ER 492 at 513, [1978] AC 728 at 770). Lord Salmon also said that the plaintiff would be statute-barred 'If it could be proved that the building suffered damage ... which endangered the safety of its occupants or visitors' more than six years before the issue of the writ (see [1977] 2 All ER 492 at 514, [1978] AC 728 at 770).

d From the guidance afforded by the authorities I conclude that the present state of the law is as follows. First, a local authority is under a duty to take reasonable care in deciding whether plans required by the building regulations are defective. Second, a local authority is under a duty to take reasonable care to decide whether and when to exercise its discretionary powers to inspect buildings and to take reasonable care in carrying out any inspection. Third, a local authority is only liable for breach of duty if it fails to exercise reasonable care in the performance of its statutory functions and as a result e allows the erection of a building which has defects likely to cause damage or discomfort to the occupiers, being defects which a prudent local authority exercising its statutory powers would have required to be eliminated. Fourth, a local authority can be made liable for breach of duty at the suit of an owner or occupier who suffers damage as a result of the breach. Fifth, time begins to run under the Limitation Act 1939 in favour of a local authority when as a result of the failure of the local authority to use reasonable care f in the performance of its statutory functions the building suffers damage which causes danger or discomfort to the occupiers. And, sixth, time begins to run in favour of a local authority before danger or discomfort ensues to the occupiers of the building if the building suffers damage or an event occurs which reveals the breach of duty by the local authority or which would cause a prudent owner-occupier to make investigations which, if properly carried out, would reveal the breach of duty by that local authority.

g It is not every failure by a local authority to discover a defect in a plan or a defect in a building which imposes liability on the authority. If the defect is not discoverable by reasonable care in the exercise by the local authority of its statutory functions or if the defect does not constitute a likely threat to the safety or comfort of the occupiers then the local authority is not in breach of its statutory duty which is of a supervisory nature only. The builder may be liable for defects for which the local authority is not liable. h Moreover, if the defect is such that the building is not likely to be a danger or source of discomfort for the normal lifespan of the building, then I consider that the local authority is not liable. The present case illustrates the very great difficulties under which local authorities labour when their breach of duty is said to date back 20 years or more.

In the present case damage was suffered by the house when cracks appeared in 1961, when further cracks appeared in 1966 and when further more serious cracks appeared in j 1976. The evidence showed that no unusual cracks or warning indications appeared in the house until 1966 and thereafter there were no indications of serious defects until about 1976 when investigations showed that the concrete raft was inadequate and badly constructed and that the house was or was likely to become unsafe for four reasons which were recorded by the judge. Those reasons were: first, that the house was sited partly on natural soil and partly on filled soil; second, the use of clay as a filling agent; third, the

dumping in parts of inorganic matter; and, fourth, the construction of the raft in two
halves imperfectly welded together. The writ was issued in 1978 and the action by the   *a*
plaintiffs is therefore time-barred if by 1966 the house had suffered damage which
indicated the possibility that the foundations were defective.

The only witnesses as to what took place in 1966 were Mr Dennis and a jobbing
builder, Mr Adams, who was employed by Mr Dennis. Their recollections in 1981 were
inevitably imperfect. Forbes J dealt with their evidence in four parts of his judgment.
He said: *b*

'In 1966 further cracks developed and Mr Dennis called in Mr Adams again. This
time it was more serious. Mr Adams thought that part of the foundations were
sinking where the garage extended forward of the house itself. He knew that the
house was built on a raft, and he dug down to see what the foundations were made
of. He broke a bit off by the garage to see whether the proper reinforcement was   *c*
there. He discovered it was. But because he thought the pieces of foundations which
supported the garage had sunk a bit he poured in some concrete and put in a few
angle irons to hold it up. He was quite satisfied that the main foundations were
sound and told Mr Dennis so . . .

Mr Adams was also called in on the second occasion in 1966. Here the position
was more serious. The cracks occurred at the corner of the house in the angle   *d*
between the face of the house and the garage, whose wall was at right angles to and
projected forward of that face. These cracks, I find, did affect the brickwork but
only at this point. Mr Adams cut out the cracked bricks and replaced them.
Interestingly, he said: 'If it had been lime mortar the bricks would not have cracked,
but as it was cement mortar they did.' He had no fears for the foundations as such
but thought they needed a little reinforcement in way of the angle between the   *e*
house and the garage. He dug down to make sure the raft was there and broke away
some of the concrete to make sure there was reinforcement. He satisfied himself
about both these matters but decided to pour in some concrete in this area and to
place a few angle irons for reinforcement . . . It was a small job and cost £40 to £50.
Mr Adams said that he did not think there was any question mark about the stability
of this house, that he was satisfied with the raft as he saw it, and that there was no   *f*
concern about the cracks he saw. And that is what he told Mr Dennis . . . I feel
satisfied, on consideration of all the evidence about the 1966 cracks, that Mr Adams
realised it had something to do with the foundations of the house but thought, and
thought reasonably, that it was a comparatively trivial matter, localised and not
affecting the foundations of any other part of the house. I am also satisfied that Mr
Adams, as a competent small builder of experience, told Mr Dennis so and that Mr   *g*
Dennis in good faith accepted that advice . . .

The 1966 cracks present a different picture. There seems no doubt that Mr Adams
recognised that the crack in the angle of the house and garage was due in some way
to settlement of the foundations. Within his competence as a small builder he
considered that any settlement did not affect the main foundations of the house,
which in his view were sound. His attempt at underpinning was, again within his   *h*
competence, reasonable and intended to stabilise locally what he reasonably saw as a
local problem. I could not accept that Mr Dennis, having been given the advice he
was given by Mr Adams, should as a reasonable and prudent house-owner have
sought further advice from a surveyor, much less from engineers expert in
foundation work . . . it is my considered opinion that any surveyor called in by Mr
Dennis in 1966 would in all probability have reached the same conclusion and   *j*
tendered the same advice. On the other hand, I am satisfied that if engineers, expert
in foundation works, had been called in in 1966 they, in all probability, would have
been able to attribute the 1966 cracks to defective foundations and discovered the
existence of the hinged raft.'

After consideration of the authorities to which I have referred Forbes J concluded:

a

'I am satisfied on the evidence that a competent surveyor, the expert whom one would reasonably expect to diagnose a fault of this kind if anyone could, would not have discovered the defect from the symptoms which occurred until at the earliest 1977 . . . the fault did not emerge and could not reasonably have been discovered until . . . June 1977. The action was therefore started within the limitation period.'

b
The action was tried by Forbes J at Lincoln in October 1981 and he delivered a reserved judgment on 21 December 1981. The judgment is lucid and clear and contains a careful and perceptive analysis of the relevant authorities. I agree with the findings and conclusions of the judge and would dismiss the appeal.

FOX LJ. I have had the advantage of reading in draft the judgment which Templeman
c LJ has just delivered. I agree with it and I would dismiss the appeal.

LAWTON LJ. I too agree that this appeal should be dismissed. Our decision ensures that an elderly couple who 27 years ago got bad service from a builder will not suffer loss; but what they gain will be at the expense of the ratepayers of the Charnwood Borough Council because of a regrettable but probably uncharacteristic and casual failure
d to take care in 1955 by the building inspectorate of a small local authority now absorbed into a larger authority. That authority have no relevant records of what happened all those years ago. This result has come about as a result of three decisions of the courts within the past ten years, two in this court (*Dutton v Bognor Regis United Building Co Ltd* [1972] 1 All ER 462, [1972] 1 QB 373 and *Sparham-Souter v Town and Country Developments (Essex) Ltd* [1976] 2 All ER 65, [1976] QB 858) and one in the House of Lords (*Anns v*
e *Merton London Borough* [1972] 2 All ER 492, [1978] AC 728).

For my part, I find reconciling *Sparham-Souter* with the reasoning in an earlier House of Lords case, *Cartledge v E Jopling & Sons Ltd* [1963] 1 All ER 341, [1963] AC 758, difficult despite the seeming approval, at least in part, of the former case by the House of Lords in the *Anns* case. If this were not enough, the period of limitation as formulated in the *Sparham-Souter* case in relation to the liability of builders for defective work for or in
f connection with dwellinghouses is different from that enacted by Parliament in the Defective Premises Act 1972 (see s 1(5)), which applies the same approach as *Cartledge v E. Jopling & Sons Ltd* did before the law was changed by the Limitation Act 1963 in respect of personal injuries but not in respect of other kinds of damage, including the kind suffered by the plaintiffs in this case.

In the *Anns* case [1972] 2 All ER 492 at 511, [1978] AC 728 at 767 the opinion was
g expressed by Lord Salmon that that decision was not likely to lead to a flood of litigation. His optimism is not, so I understand, the experience of some local authorities. Building companies, particularly those doing bad work, have a propensity to go into liquidation and when this happens house-owners now look to local authorities for compensation. When defective foundations are put down, a building time-bomb is hidden under the house built on them which may years later go off bringing financial disaster to the owner
h or occupier. It is, in my opinion, unfortunate that in such situations relief for those who suffer loss should, as in this case, turn on memories of what happened and what was noticed years ago and the chances of litigation. A compulsory insurance scheme for builders of houses might provide better justice than the uncertainties of litigation.

Appeal dismissed. Leave to appeal to House of Lords granted on undertakings as to costs.

Solicitors: *Browne, Jacobson & Roose*, Nottingham (for the defendants); *Owston & Co*, Leicester (for the plaintiffs).

Mary Rose Plummer   Barrister.

Robert Baxendale Ltd v Davstone (Holdings) Ltd
Carobene v John Collier Menswear Ltd

COURT OF APPEAL, CIVIL DIVISION

WALLER, ACKNER AND MAY LJJ

17, 21, 22 JUNE, 7 JULY 1982

County court – Practice – Service of documents relating to application for new tenancy of business premises – Failure to serve documents within prescribed time limit – Failure to apply for extension of time within currency of time limit – Jurisdiction to extend time – Exercise of discretion to extend time where jurisdiction – Tenant required to show exceptional or unusual circumstances accounting for failure to serve in time and failure not entirely his fault before jurisdiction to enlarge time – Factors to be taken into consideration in exercising discretion – Relative hardship of landlord and tenant – Tenant's remedy against his solicitors for failure to serve documents in time – CCR 1981 Ord 7, r 20, Ord 13, r 4, Ord 43, r 6(3).

Landlord and tenant – Business premises – Application for new tenancy – County court procedure – Failure to serve documents relating to application within prescribed time limit – Jurisdiction to enlarge time for service – Exercise of discretion to enlarge time where jurisdiction – CCR 1981 Ord 7, r 20, Ord 13, r 4, Ord 43, r 6(3).

Where a tenant of business premises who has applied in the county court for a new tenancy under s 24 of the Landlord and Tenant Act 1954 fails to serve a copy and a notice of the application on the landlord within the time limit prescribed by CCR 1981 Ord 43, r 6(3)[a], applying Ord 7, r 20[b], and fails also to apply for an extension of time within the currency of the prescribed time limit, the court has no jurisdiction to extend the time under Ord 13, r 4[c] (which confers jurisdiction on the court to enlarge any period of time fixed by the rules even where the application for extension of time is made after expiry of the prescribed time limit) unless the tenant can establish that there were exceptional or unusual circumstances accounting for the failure to serve the documents in time and that he was not entirely at fault in regard to the failure to serve in time. Therefore, it is insufficient, in order to establish jurisdiction to exercise the discretion under Ord 13, r 4, for the tenant merely to show that his legal advisers overlooked the time limit or misunderstood the rules as to service, or that unless time is extended the tenant will suffer hardship by being deprived of the right under the 1954 Act to apply for a new tenancy, because those are not unusual circumstances in relation to failure to serve the documents in time. However, once the tenant has established that there were unusual

---

a   Rule 6(3) provides: 'The provisions of Order 7, rule 20, shall apply to an originating application under this rule with the substitution of references to two months for the references therein to 12 months.'

b   Rule 20 provides:

    '(1) The time within which a summons may be served shall, unless extended under paragraph (2), be limited to a period of 12 months beginning with the date of issue of the summons.

    (2) The court may extend the period for service of a summons from time to time for such period, not exceeding 12 months at any one time, beginning with the day next following that on which it would otherwise expire, as the court may specify, if an application for extension is made before that day or such later day (if any) as the court may allow.'

c   Rule 4 provides:

    '(1) Except as otherwise provided, the period within which a person is required or authorised by these rules or by any judgment, order or direction to do any act in any proceedings may be extended or abridged by consent of all the parties or by the court on the application of any party.

    (2) Any such period may be extended by the court although the application for extension is not made until after the expiration of the period.'

circumstances accounting for the failure to serve the documents in time and that he was
a not entirely at fault, there is jurisdiction to exercise, albeit sparingly, the discretion under
Ord 13, r 4, and, in considering whether the discretion under Ord 13, r 4 should be
exercised by extending the time for service, the court can take into account the degree of
hardship the tenant will suffer if the application for extension of time is refused and he
loses the right to apply for a new tenancy, and, in balancing the tenant's hardship against
the hardship the landlord will suffer if the application is granted, can take into account
b any remedy the tenant may have against his legal advisers for their failure to serve the
documents in time, but the weight to be given to that remedy will depend on the
particular circumstances (see p 499 *c* to *f*, p 501 *e f j*, p 502 *a b e*, p 504 *e* to p 505 *d* and *j*
and p 506 *a*, post).

   Heaven v Road and Rail Wagons Ltd [1965] 2 All ER 409, *Lewis v Wolking Properties Ltd*
[1978] 1 All ER 427 and *Joan Barrie Ltd v GUS Property Management Ltd* (1981) 259 EG
c 628 applied.

   Dicta of Lord Diplock and of Lord Edmund-Davies in *Birkett v James* [1977] 2 All ER
at 809, 819 and of Geoffrey Lane LJ in *Lewis v Wolking Properties Ltd* [1978] 1 All ER at
433 considered.

   Where a landlord is a company and its estate agents are handling negotiations with a
tenant in regard to his application in the county court for a new tenancy under the 1954
d Act, neither service of the documents relating to the tenant's application on the estate
agents nor the forwarding by the estate agents to the landlords of a copy of the tenant's
originating application is good service of the application on the landlord within s 437[d] of
the Companies Act 1948 (see p 499 *f g*, p 505 *f g* and p 506 *a*, post).

   Per Waller LJ. The 1954 Act, in the interests of tenants, has seriously interfered with a
landlord's right to possession of his property and therefore it is only fair that a tenant
e should strictly adhere to the timetable for applying for a new tenancy contained in that
Act and the rules of court so as not to prolong the landlord's period of uncertainty (see
p 501 *f* to *h*, post).

Notes

For the county court procedure on an application for a new tenancy of business premises,
f see 27 Halsbury's Laws (4th edn) para 493.

   As from 1 September 1982 CCR 1981 Ord 7, r 20, Ord 13, r 4 and Ord 43, r 6(3) took
the place of CCR 1936 Ord 8, r 35, Ord 13, r 5 and Ord 40, r 8(1A).

Cases referred to in judgments

Barrie (Joan) Ltd v GUS Property Management Ltd (1981) 259 EG 628, CA.
g *Battersby v Anglo-American Oil Co Ltd* [1944] 2 All ER 387, [1945] KB 23, CA, 50 Digest
   (Repl) 292, 336.
Birkett v James [1977] 2 All ER 801, [1978] AC 297, [1977] 3 WLR 38, HL, Digest (Cont
   Vol D) 666, 2698b.
Heaven v Road and Rail Wagons Ltd [1965] 2 All ER 409, [1965] 2 QB 355, [1965] 2 WLR
   1249, 50 Digest (Repl) 292, 337.
h *Kammins Ballrooms Co Ltd v Zenith Investments (Torquay) Ltd* [1970] 2 All ER 871, [1971]
   AC 850, [1970] 3 WLR 287, HL, 31(2) Digest (Reissue) 953, 7757.
Lewis v Wolking Properties Ltd [1978] 1 All ER 427, [1978] 1 WLR 403, CA, Digest (Cont
   Vol E) 122, 3808a.

Appeals

j   *Robert Baxendale Ltd v Davstone (Holdings) Ltd*

Robert Baxendale Ltd, the tenants of business premises in Dominion House, Queen
Street, Cardiff, appealed against (i) the order of Honour Judge Wallis-Jones made in the
Cardiff County Court on 15 March 1982 whereby he allowed the appeal of Davstone

---

d   Section 437, so far as material, is set out at p 499 *f g*, post

(Holdings) Ltd, the landlords of the premises, against two orders made by the registrar, dated 28 October and 11 December 1981, extending the time for service of the tenant's *a* originating application for a new tenancy of the premises, on the ground that it would be wrong to extend the time for serving the originating application and (ii) against the order of the same judge made on 20 April 1982 refusing the tenants' application for a new trial of their application for an extension of time for service of the originating application. The facts are set out in the judgment of Waller LJ.

b

Clemente Carobene v John Collier Menswear Ltd

John Collier Menswear Ltd (the landlords) appealed from the order of his Honour Judge Braithwaite made in Bath County Court on 10 May 1982 whereby he dismissed their application to strike out an originating application by Clemente Carobene (the tenant) for a new tenancy of business premises at 30 Westgate Buildings, Bath, although the tenant had failed to serve the originating application on the landlords within the *c* prescribed time limit, and granted a cross application by the tenant for an extension of the time for service by extending the time for service for 48 hours from the date of the order. The facts are set out in the judgment of Waller LJ.

Michael Barnes QC and David Holgate for the tenants, Robert Baxendale Ltd.
Eian Caws for the landlords in both cases.   *d*
Alan Steynor for the tenant, Clemente Carobene.

Cur adv vult

7 July. The following judgments were read.

e

WALLER LJ. These are, in form, two appeals from decisions of Judge Wallis-Jones given on 15 March and 20 April 1982 respectively. In the former appeal the judge held that the tenants Robert Baxendale Ltd, had lost their right to a new tenancy of their shop premises at Dominion House, Queen Street, Cardiff, because their originating application was not served in time and in the latter appeal the judge refused to order a new trial. The effective appeal, however, is the first one. The appellants have been the tenants of shop *f* premises in Cardiff for 38 years. Their last lease was a 21-year lease expiring on 11 November 1981, and the respondents are the successors in title to the landlords in that lease. The Landlord and Tenant Act 1954 provided certain rights to both tenants and landlords at the termination of the lease and if on the one hand the landlord does not take certain steps the tenant will acquire certain rights in relation to the holding and if on the other hand the tenant does not take certain steps he may lose his right to remain *g* in possession as a tenant with a new lease. Section 24 of the 1954 Act provides for the continuation of tenancies unless terminated under the Act and s 29 lays down the procedure for applying for a new tenancy. Section 25 of the Act provides for the landlord giving notice to the tenant to terminate the lease and on 8 May 1981 the landlords served the appropriate notice stating that they would not oppose the application to the court for a new lease. Section 26 of the act provides for the tenant serving a counter-notice and on *h* 2 July 1981 the tenants served such a notice stating that they were not willing to give up possession at the termination of the lease. On 18 August 1981 (ie not less than two months and not more than four months after the landlords' notice (s 29(3) of the Act)) the tenants issued an originating application under s 24 of the 1954 Act which was filed on 21 August. By virtue of the combined provisions of CCR 1936 Ord 40, r 8, and Ord 8, r 35 the originating application had to be served on the landlords within two months, *j* ie by 21 October. It was not served in time but on 23 October 1981 the originating application was served on the landlords' surveyor, who sent a photocopy to the landlords on 28 October. An application for an extension of time was granted for seven days on 28 October and later there was a further extension granted in December, as a result of which, for the first time, on 15 December, there was service direct on the landlords. On

appeal to the judge both these decisions to grant extensions of time were reversed. The
a tenants now appeal against that decision and also against the refusal of the judge to order
a new trial of the application for an extension of time.

Council for the tenants submitted that the judge had a discretion to grant an extension
in all the circumstances of the case, relying on the decision of this court in *Lewis v Wolking*
Properties Ltd [1978] 1 All ER 427, [1978] 1 WLR 403 and that this court could review
the exercise of that discretion. He further submitted that the judge wrongly took into
b account the remedy which the tenants had, or might have, against their solicitors.
Further, he submitted that the judge had wrongly come to the conclusion that there was
no service on the landlords until 15 December, when a proper examination of the facts
showed that there was service on 28 October by reason of the forwarding by Mr Caddick
of a photocopy of the originating application.

Were it necessary to decide the relevance of the claim against the solicitors I would be
c of the opinion that in a case like the present where relative hardships might have to be
considered but where the effect of the decision, unlike that in a personal injury claim,
was clear, it would be right to take into consideration as an element for consideration the
existence of a claim against the solicitor. In a case like *Birkett v James* [1977] 2 All ER 801,
[1978] AC 297, quite apart from the question of a possible claim against the solicitor,
there were other imponderables such as the question of whether the delay was inordinate
d and inexcusable and whether when the action was ultimately fought the plaintiff would
win or lose. The same considerations apply to personal injury claims.

In this case if the decision is that the service is good the tenants will win. If the service
is bad then the landlords will win. In deciding whether to exercise discretion to extend
the time and make an otherwise bad service good it must, in my view, be relevant to
consider the tenant's rights against his solicitor: see, for example, *Joan Barrie Ltd v GUS*
e *Property Management Ltd* (1981) 259 EG 628.

In *Birkett v James* the House of Lords was considering only the prejudice to the
defendant by reason of inordinate delay, whereas, as I have already indicated, the question
is one of balance of hardship. I see nothing in the observations of Lord Diplock or Lord
Edmund-Davies (see [1977] 2 All ER 801 at 809, 819, [1978] AC 297 at 324, 335–336)
which would rule out consideration of rights against the solicitor in a case such as the
f present.

I would also be of opinion, were it necessary to come to a conclusion about the events
of 28 October, that the forwarding of a photocopy of the originating application by Mr
Caddick to the landlords did not amount to service on the landlords. The submission of
counsel for the tenants was that the requirements of s 437 of the Companies Act 1948
were met. Section 437 requires service on a company to be made 'by leaving it at or
g sending it by post to the registered office of the company'. Counsel's submission
depended in part on the judge's finding that Mr Caddick had a duty to inform his
principals and that sending a photocopy of the originating application was in pursuance
of that duty.

I now come to the question of the extent of the discretion of the judge. The rules
which have to be considered are the following: CCR Ord 40, r 8, which appears under
h the cross-heading 'Part III. Security of Tenure for Business Tenants under Part II of the
Act of 1954' provides:

> '(1) An application for a new tenancy under section 24 of the Act of 1954 shall be
> made by originating application in Form 335.
> (1A) Order 8, Rule 35, shall apply in relation to an originating application under
> this Rule as it applies in relation to a default summons but with the substitution for
j the references to 12 months of references to two months . . .'

Order 8, r 35, provides:

> '(1) The time within which a default summons may be served shall, unless
> extended under the next succeeding paragraph, be limited to a period of 12 months
> from the issue of the summons.

(2) Where reasonable efforts have been made to serve the summons within the said period and service has not been effected, the registrar may, on application, order *a* that the time be extended for a further period not exceeding 12 months or for successive periods not exceeding 12 months each: Provided that the time shall not be extended for any period unless the application is made within the currency of the last preceding period . . .'

At first sight this would appear to make any question of extension once a period of two months has passed impossible. There is, however, another rule, Ord 13, r 5, which *b* provides:

'(1) Subject to the provisions of these Rules, any of the times fixed by these Rules or by any judgment, order or direction for doing any act may be enlarged or abridged by consent of all parties or by the court on the application of any party.
(2) An order enlarging time may be made although the application therefor is *c* not made until after the expiration of the time allowed or appointed.'

Counsel for the tenants submitted that the judge should take into account all the circumstances and not only the circumstances concerning the failure to serve the application within time. The contrary submission was that only the circumstances relating to the failure to serve in time were relevant.

In *Lewis v Wolking Properties Ltd* the court had to consider a case where reasonable *d* efforts had been made to serve within the specified period and had to consider whether the proviso to Ord 8, r 35 prevented the court from extending the period because the application was not made 'within the currency of the last period'. The failure to serve in that case was entirely caused by the landlord moving without informing the tenant. The tenant having made reasonable efforts to serve the landlord, this court came to the conclusion that Ord 13, r 5, permitted the court to grant an extension after the currency *e* of the period. Orr LJ said ([1978] 1 All ER 427 at 430, [1978] 1 WLR 403 at 407):

'I would add, that it is a necessary consequence of counsel for the landlords' argument that, if it is right, no relief at all could be obtained by an applicant for a new lease who, for reasons quite beyond his control, has been unable to serve notice of his application on the landlord within the permitted time; and for this reason, *f* quite apart from authority, I should for my part have been reluctant to adopt the construction which counsel for the landlords advances unless compelled to do so by the language of the rules. I do not, for the reasons I have indicated, find myself so compelled.'

Geoffrey Lane LJ, after referring to the speech of Lord Reid in *Kammins Ballrooms Co Ltd v Zenith Investments (Torquay) Ltd* [1970] 2 All ER 871 at 875, [1971] AC 850 at 860, *g* said([1978] 1 All ER 427 at 43, [1978] 1 WLR 403 at 410):

'That was a decision under s 29(3) of the Landlord and Tenant Act 1954. It is not directly in point, but it is indicative of the view of their Lordships' House that the parties have power to alter by consent statutory times laid down, and if that is the case it seems difficult, to my mind, to argue that those times are mandatory rather *h* than directory (to use the appropriate jargon). I can see no reason for doubting that CCR Ord 13, r 5(1) and (2), applies to these provisions. No doubt the power to extend the time is a power which must be very sparingly used, in the light of the words in CCR Ord 8, r 35. But it is conceded in this case and, if I may say so, properly conceded, by counsel for the landlords that if there is the jurisdiction in the court to extend the time this is indeed a proper case in which that jurisdiction *j* should be exercised.'

That was a case where reasonable efforts to serve had been made. In construing these rules it is important to bear in mind the equivalent High Court rule because it would be surprising if the effect of the rules were different. By RSC Ord 97, r 6, which deals with applications for new tenancies under s 24 of the 1954 Act, provision is made for an originating summons, and by r 6(3), Ord 6, r 8, is to apply to such sumons as it does to a writ but with substitution of 2 months for 12 months.

RSC Ord 6, r 8 reads:

> *Duration and renewal of writ.*—(1) For the purpose of service, a writ (other than a concurrent writ) is valid in the first instance for twelve months beginning with the date of its issue and a concurrent writ is valid in the first instance for the period of validity of the original writ which is unexpired at the date of issue of the concurrent writ.
>
> (2) Where a writ has not been served on a defendant, the Court may by order extend the validity of the writ from time to time for such period, not exceeding twelve months at any one time, beginning with the day next following that on which it would otherwise expire, as may be specified in the order, if an application for extension is made to the court before that day or such later day (if any) as the Court may allow.'

Megaw J in *Heaven v Road and Rail Wagons Ltd* [1965] 2 All ER 409 at 413, [1965] 2 QB 355 at 361 said:

> '... the principle, or the general rule, to be applied is that leave will not be given to extend the validity of a writ when application is made retrospectively after the period of twelve months prescribed by the rules has expired, if the effect of so doing would be to deprive the defendant of a defence which he would have had under the relevant statute of limitation, supposing that leave to extend were not given and the plaintiff were thus compelled to serve a fresh writ.'

Although Megaw J was there considering a case under RSC Ord 6, r 8, where the effect of extending the writ retrospectively would be to defeat a limitation defence, in my opinion, the present case is analagous in that once the time has passed, the landlord is no longer under an obligation to provide his tenant with a new lease. In the present case no effort to serve within the time limited had been made. If an extension is not granted, the tenant will have to vacate his holding and the landlord will make a substantial profit. On the other hand if an extension is granted even though the tenant has not complied with the rules, the landlord will lose his profit. It has to be remembered that the Landlord and Tenant Act 1954 made provision for the continuation and renewal of tenancies which altered very considerably the contractual rights of the parties under a tenancy agreement or lease. Whereas under the lease in the present case the tenants were obliged to leave on 11 November 1981, by virtue of the provisions of the 1954 Act, provided that the tenants took the proper steps, they did not have to leave, and if the landlords did not wish to occupy the premises themselves the tenant could have a new lease on terms decided by the court (see ss 24 ff) but the proper steps involved a timetable, part of which was in the statute and part of which was comprised by CCR Ord 40, r 8 and Ord 8, r 35. I do not see anything unfair in that timetable being strictly adhered to.

The 1954 Act, in the interests of tenants, has seriously interfered with the landlord's right to possession of his property and it is only fair that the period of uncertainty should not be prolonged. No doubt it is for this reason that CCR Ord 40, r 8 adopts the strict default summons procedure set out in CCR Ord 8, r 35.

Accepting, as I do, the decision of this court that these rules are directory and not mandatory, albeit that, as Geoffrey Lane LJ said, the discretion should be used very sparingly, it was a decision made in the context of a case where the tenant had done his best. In the present case the failure to serve the originating application was entirely the fault of the tenant or his advisers. Having regard to the wording of the rules I find it difficult to visualise any facts where it would be permissible to extend time after it had expired and the fault lay entirely on the tenant's side. In my opinion the tenants had to show that there were exceptional circumstances relating to the non-service of the application. Unless there were exceptional circumstances the provisions of CCR Ord 13, r 5, would not arise.

In *Lewis v Wolking Properties Ltd* Geoffrey Lane LJ came to consider Ord 13, r 5, after looking at Ord 8, r 35. It was only in the exceptional circumstances that he went on to consider Ord 13, r 5, and applied it subject to the comment that it should only be used very sparingly.

I have accordingly come to the conclusion that the judge was right to allow the appeal against the registrar, and that this was a case where, time having gone by, the tenant had lost his rights. I would dismiss the appeal in *Robert Baxendale Ltd v Davstone (Holdings) Ltd.*

I now come to *Carobene v John Collier Menswear Ltd.* In that case the applicant is the tenant of property known as 30 Westgate Buildings, Bath, under the terms of a lease dated 23 July 1968, a 14-year lease expiring in December 1981. The tenant carried on a hairdressing business at the property. On 23 June 1981 the landlords served notice on the tenant terminating the lease and saying that an application to the court for the grant of a new tenancy would not be opposed. On 13 August 1981 a counter-notice was served and on 22 October 1981 an originating application for a new lease was made to the county court. No further steps were taken until 12 February 1982, seven weeks after the time for the originating application to be served. The landlords applied to the judge, Judge Braithwaite, for the application to be struck out and the tenant applied to the judge for an extension of time for the service of the application. The judge dismissed the application to strike out the originating application and granted an extension time for seven days. The landlords now appeal.

I do not here set out the arguments for the landlords and the tenant on the facts of this case, because I have taken those arguments into account in the judgment I have just delivered. The fact is that no excuse of any kind was given for the failure to serve the originating application within time and all the arguments were directed to the effect of that failure on the tenant. It is unnecessary to set out the arguments put forward on behalf of the tenant because the facts of this case are clearly covered by the judgment which I have just completed. There were no exceptional circumstances to explain the failure to serve in time and accordingly it was not open to the judge to grant the extension which he did after that time had expired. Accordingly in my judgment the appeal should be allowed.

ACKNER LJ. In both these appeals the landlords gave notice under s 25 of the Landlord and Tenant Act 1954 to terminate the tenancies. In both cases there were no grounds on which they could validly oppose the grant of new tenancies. Accordingly, by virtue of s 25(6) the notices which they served stated, in terms, that they would not oppose an application to the court for the grant of a new tenancy. In those circumstances the fair inference is that the notices were given in each case because the landlords concluded that the rent that they were being paid was less than the market rent. Accordingly, the formal notice under s 25 was but a prerequisite to their obtaining the market rent, either by agreement or by order of the court.

In each of these appeals the tenants, within the requisite period of two months, gave a counter-notice that they would be unwilling to give up possession of the property at the date of termination. Moreover, in both these appeals the tenants made application to the court for the grant of a new tenancy within the period provided by s 29(3) of the 1954 Act. Thus, the tenants in each appeal complied with the statutory time provisions laid down by the 1954 Act.

These appeals are both occasioned by the tenants' failure to comply with the relevant county court rules as to the service of the relevant documents on the landlords. Special provision is made by CCR Ord 40, r 8, where applications are made for a new tenancy under s 24 of the 1954 Act. They shall be made by originating application in Form 335. Further, CCR Ord 8, r 35 is specifically made to apply in relation to an originating application under Ord 40, r 8 as it applies in relation to default summonses, but with the substitution for the reference to 12 months of references to 2 months.

Order 6, r 4 governs originating applications. Rule 4(2)(c) provides that on the filing of the application:

'(i) the registrar shall enter the application in the books of the court, and fix a day for the hearing of the application, and deliver to the applicant a plaint note in Form 14; and (ii) a copy of the application and a notice in Form 26 shall be served on each respondent (if any) in the manner prescribed by these Rules for service of an ordinary summons.'

Form 26 bears the seal of the county court. It gives notice when the matter is to be heard and that if the respondent does not attend such order will be made as the court thinks just. It also states that a sealed copy of the originating application is annexed to the notice.

Order 8, r 35, to which Ord 40, r 8 makes the specific reference referred to above, provides as follows:

'(1) The time within which a default summons may be served shall, unless extended under the next succeeding paragraph, be limited to a period of 12 months from the issue of the summons.

(2) Where *reasonable efforts have been made to serve* the summons within the said period and service has not been effected, the registrar may, on application, order that the time be extended for a further period not exceeding 12 months or for successive periods not exceeding 12 months each: Provided that the time shall not be extended for any period unless the application is made within the currency of the last preceding period.

(3) A note of any extension of the time allowed for service shall be endorsed on the summons and on any copy and shall be entered in the books of the court.

(4) Where the summons has not been served within the time allowed for service by this Rule, the action shall be struck out.'

In neither appeal were reasonable efforts made to serve the summons within the period of two months specified in Ord 40, r 8, and in neither case was an application made to extend time within the currency of that period. Accordingly, if the power of the court to extend time was to be found solely within Ord 8, r 35, no extension could be granted and the originating application would have to be struck out.

However, CCR Ord 13, r 5 provides:

'(1) *Subject to the provisions of these Rules,* any of the times fixed by these Rules or by any judgment, order or direction for doing any act may be enlarged or abridged by consent of all parties or by the court on the application of any party.

(2) An order enlarging time may be made although the application therefor is not made until after the expiration of the time allowed or appointed.'

In *Lewis v Wolking Properties Ltd* [1978] 1 All ER 427, [1978] 1 WLR 403 this court decided that a county court judge is empowered to extend time by virtue of Ord 13, r 5, notwithstanding the provisions of Ord 8, r 35. Having set out the terms of Ord 13, r 5, Geoffrey Lane LJ said ([1978] 1 All ER 427 at 432, [1978] 1 WLR 403 at 409):

'On the face of it, that rule appears to apply to CCR Ord 8, r 35. Does it make any difference that the words "Subject to the provisions of these Rules" are to be found at the outset of CCR Ord 13, r 5? I think not. They cannot mean "except where the Rules specify a particular time within which some steps should be taken". Of course, if it meant that, it would emasculate the rule entirely and deprive it of any potency. All that this exception does, to my mind, is to make it clear that where you get plain words inconsistent with CCR Ord 13, r 5, then that rule shall not apply; and an instance of that is to be found in CCR Ord 10, r 7(ii), which reads as follows: "Where 12 months have expired from the date of service of a default summons, and . . . (ii) an admission has been delivered but no notice of acceptance or non-acceptance has been received by the registrar, the action shall be struck out and no extension of time shall be granted beyond the 12 months, *notwithstanding Order 13, Rule 5*." I can see no reason why the draftsman of the 1954 Act and the orders which apply to this

case should not, if such had been the intention, have included such words as are
found in CCR Ord 10, r 7. The words of CCR Ord 8, r 35, are, in my judgment, not *a*
of a sufficiently mandatory nature to oust the effect of CCR Ord 13.'

He concluded by saying ([1978] 1 All ER 427 at 433, [1978] 1 WLR 403 at 410):

'I can see no reason for doubting that CCR Ord 13, r 5(1) and (2), applies to these
provisions. No doubt the power to extend the time is a power which must be very
sparingly used, in the light of the words in CCR Ord 8, r 35.'
b

In that case the landlords conceded, and in the view of this court properly conceded,
that if there was jurisdiction to extend the time, it was a proper case because the conduct
of the landlords created the very difficulties which had resulted in service being out of
time.

There is of course jurisdiction in the High Court to entertain applications for new
tenancies under s 24 of the 1954 Act. It is, therefore, appropriate to have in mind the *c*
provisions of the Rules of the Supreme Court, since it would obviously be undesirable
for there to be any significant difference in important procedural matters. RSC Ord 97,
r 6, provides that RSC Ord 6, r 8 shall apply to the originating summons as it applies to a
writ, but with the substitution for the reference to 12 months to references to 2 months.
Accordingly, by virtue of the provisions of Ord 6, r 8:

'(i) The originating summons is valid for two months beginning with its date of *d*
issue. (ii) Where the originating summons has not been served within this period,
the Court may by Order extend its validity from time to time for such period not
exceeding two months at any one time.'

It is well settled that if an application is made for renewal the discretion to extend the
validity of the writ ought to be exercised with caution and renewal is not to be granted *e*
as a matter of course: *Battersby v Anglo-American Oil Co Ltd* [1944] 2 All ER 387, [1945]
KB 23. There must be sufficient or good reason to justify the exercise of the court's
discretion and exceptional circumstances need to be shown for the renewal when the
claim has become statute barred: see *Heaven v Road and Rail Wagons Ltd* [1965] 2 All ER
409, [1965] 2 QB 355.

Counsel for the respondent tenant, Clemente Carobene, has accepted that the failure *f*
to serve the landlords with Form 26 and notice of the application for the new lease until
some seven weeks after time had expired was quite inexcusable. His client's own affidavit
concedes that his solicitors made no attempt to serve the landlords until seven weeks
after time had expired. He has therefore been obliged boldly to submit that Lane LJ was
in error when he said that the power to extend time is a power which must be very
sparingly *used*. In his submission the power should be sparingly *refused*. This submission *g*
to my mind must inevitably totally disregard CCR Ord 8, r 35, to which Lane LJ made
specific reference, and would introduce a very significant difference between practice in
the High Court and in the county court in a jurisdiction which is concurrent.

I therefore cannot accept counsel's submission that an extension of time to serve the
application is, except in a wholly unusual case, there for the asking, as if a party was
applying for extra time to deliver a pleading. In my judgment, the cases in which the *h*
discretion can be validly exercised to extend time for the service of the application will
be rare, because sufficient and good reason accounting for the failure to serve the
application in time needs to be established by the applicant. It is not enough to show that
the legal advisers overlooked the time limits, or misunderstood the rules as to service and
that unless time is extended, the tenant will lose his right to a new lease with the sort of
hardship which would normally result. Such a case would have no unusual feature about *j*
it. It would be a common form situation where the rules of court are overlooked or not
properly considered.

If the tenant fails to establish that there are unusual circumstances relating to his
failure to serve the application in due time, then he cannot, in my judgment, base his
application merely on the hardship which he will suffer as a result of being deprived of

a the right to a new lease. The establishment of the unusual circumstances relating to the failure to serve in time is the first fence which he must clear. Having done so, the court is then in a position to consider exercising its discretion and will no doubt then have regard to the degree of hardship which the tenant will suffer if an adverse decision is made against him.

In evaluating the tenant's hardship it is, in my judgment, permissible to have regard to the existence or absence of a claim by the tenant against his solicitors for failing to
b serve in time. In some cases a claim may be cast iron and extensive compensation may be recoverable. In others, while there may be no dispute about liability, there may be difficulty, either in law or in fact, in recovering the whole or a greater part of the damage which has been suffered. In other cases there may be a serious issue as to liability. Thus, the weight to be given to a potential claim by the tenant against his legal advisers can vary greatly, but the tenant's rights against his solicitor are a relevant consideration: see
c *Joan Barrie Ltd v GUS Property Management Ltd* (1981) 259 EG 628.

Like Waller LJ, I consider that *Birkett v James* [1977] 2 All ER 801, [1978] AC 297 was concerned only with the prejudice to the defendant by reason of inordinate delays and not with the evaluation of hardship. I accordingly agree that the observations of Lord Diplock and Lord Edmund-Davies (see [1977] 2 All ER 801 at 809, 819, [1978] AC 297 at 324, 335–336) do not rule out consideration of the tenant's rights against his solicitor
d in a case such as the present.

I have said enough about the facts in the *Carobene* appeal to conclude that it must be allowed.

The facts in the appeal of *Baxendale Ltd* are somewhat different. The tenants' solicitors were two days late in serving the originating application and then they failed to serve the landlords, Davstone Holdings Ltd, as required by s 437 of the Companies Act 1948, 'by
e leaving it at, or sending it by post, to the registered office of the company'. They served the originating application on the landlords' estate agents, who had been handling the negotiations for a new lease. The judge found (and there is no challenge to this finding) that those estate agents were not duly authorised to accept service.

Some five days after service had been effected on the estate agents, they sent a copy of the originating application to the landlords. There was no evidence that they had the
f notice, or even a copy, in Form 26. What the agents were doing, and rightly so, was to provide for the information of their principals a copy of the document in which the tenants had set out the terms on which they were claiming a new lease. They were not purporting to act as process servers. In my judgment there never was good service on the landlords via the agents. On the day the agents were served the tenants' solicitors applied ex parte to the registrar for a seven-day extension to serve the originating application and
g Form 26. Following the registrar's order, the solicitors again served the agents and not the landlords. Following objections by the landlords' solicitors and an appeal against the registrar's order, a further application for extension of time was made to the registrar and a further order, notwithstanding the pending appeal, was made on 11 December. It was only on 15 December that service was effected on the company, that is over seven weeks late.

h Counsel for the tenants, in a well sustained argument, has been unable to point to any exceptional circumstances surrounding the delay and failure to serve. In fact he accepted that there were no exceptional circumstances to account for the delay. His clients too had made no reasonable or any efforts to serve within the time limited by the order, and their attempts to serve after time had expired were, as indicated above, ill-directed. The main burden of his submission was that substantially greater hardship would be suffered by
j his clients than by the landlords, if time was not extended to their favour. As already stated, in my judgment, if the tenant fails to establish unusual circumstances relating to his failure to serve the application in due time, then he cannot base his application merely on the hardship that he will suffer as a result of being deprived of the right to a new lease.

I accordingly agree that the appeal in *Baxendale* be dismissed, and the appeal in *Carobene* be allowed.

MAY LJ. I have had the advantage of reading in advance the judgments of Waller and Ackner LJJ, with which I respectfully agree, and have nothing to add.

Robert Baxendale Ltd v Davstone (Holdings) Ltd: Appeal dismissed. Leave to appeal to the House of Lords refused.

Carobene v John Collier Menswear Ltd: Appeal allowed. Landlords' application to strike out allowed.

Solicitors: *Ellis, Wood, Bickersteth & Hazel*, agents for *Phillips & Buck*, Cardiff (instructed only on the appeal) (for the tenants, Robert Baxendale Ltd); *Thornton, Lynne & Lawson* (for the landlords in both cases); *Lawrence & Co*, Bristol (for the tenant, Clemente Carobene).

Diana Brahams   Barrister.

Wakefield City Council v Box and another

CHANCERY DIVISION AT MANCHESTER
HIS HONOUR JUDGE FITZHUGH QC SITTING AS A JUDGE OF THE HIGH COURT
12, 18, 21 AUGUST 1981

Markets and fairs – Disturbance – Levying a rival market – Common law remedy – Disturbance of statutory market by levying a rival market – Whether common law remedy available to protect a statutory market – Markets and Fairs Clauses Act 1847, s 13.

In several towns in a council's area there were markets which had been set up under various statutes, including the Markets and Fairs Clauses Act 1847. They were operated either by the council itself or under licence from the council. The defendants wished to establish a market in Featherstone, another town in the council's area. On three occasions they held a market there on a site which was less than 6⅔ miles away from the other markets and they advertised that they would be holding another one there. The council, fearing that the defendants' market would rival their own, brought an action against the defendants seeking an injunction to restrain them from holding a market on the site, and applied for an interlocutory injunction in similar terms. At the hearing of the application, the defendants contended that, unlike franchise markets, statutory markets were not protected at common law against disturbance by the levying of a rival market less than 6⅔ miles away, that such markets had to rely for their protection solely on the terms of the statute under which they were established, that the Acts creating the markets in the council's area did not prohibit the holding of a market in Featherstone, and that, accordingly, the defendants could not be restrained from holding a market there.

Held – (1) Whether the common law remedy for disturbance remained in whole or in part depended on the terms of the statute under which the market was created. Where the statute was the 1847 Act, the common law remedy was still available because the protection given by s 13[a] of that Act to a statutory market was additional to, and not a substitute for, the protection against disturbance given to a market by the common law (see p 510 j and p 511 e f, post).

(2) The council's claim against the defendants was a serious one and, on balance, an

---

a Section 13 is set out at p 510 *a b*, post

a order should be made restraining the defendants, until judgment in the action or further order, from holding a market on the site (see p 511 *h* and p 512 *h*, post).

Notes
For the protection of a statutory market against disturbance by sales outside the market, see 29 Halsbury's Laws (4th edn) paras 653, 659, and for cases on the subject, see 33 Digest (Repl) 476–477, 319–324.

b For the Markets and Fairs Clauses Act 1847, s 13, see 21 Halsbury's Statutes (3rd edn) 438.

Cases referred to in judgment
Northampton BC v Midland Development Group of Cos Ltd (1978) 76 LGR 750.
Tamworth BC v Fazeley Town Council (1978) 77 LGR 238.

c
Interlocutory application
The plaintiffs, Wakefield City Council, brought an action against the defendants, John and Thelma Box, and, by a notice of motion dated 6 August 1981, applied for an injunction restraining them (until the trial of the action or further order), whether by themselves, their servants or otherwise howsoever, from (i) using or causing or permitting
d to be used the land at Wakefield Road, Featherstone in the county of West Yorkshire, in such manner as to interfere with or prejudicially affect the rights of the plaintiffs to their markets, (ii) using or permitting the land, the subject of a lease between the plaintiffs and the defendants dated 16 September 1980, to be used for the purpose of holding markets. The facts are set out in the judgment.

e *John Muir* for the council.
John M Collins for the defendants.

Cur adv vult

21 August. **HIS HONOUR JUDGE FITZHUGH QC** read the following judg-
f ment: This is a motion in which the plaintiff council, the council of the city of Wakefield, seeks an interlocutory injunction to restrain the defendants, Mr and Mrs Box, from holding a market on land situate in Wakefield Road, Featherstone, in the county of West Yorkshire.
Prior to the coming into operation on 1 January 1974 of the Local Government Act 1972, the land lay within the administrative area of the former Featherstone urban
g district, but then it was taken into the larger administrative area of the newly constituted council, along with the respective areas of a number of other former authorities, namely the county borough of Wakefield, the borough of Castleford, the borough of Pontefract, the urban district of Normanton and the urban district of Hemsworth.
This land is in part freehold and in part leasehold. The freehold land comprises an area of about two acres and it fronts Wakefield Road. The leasehold land comprises an area of
h approximately five acres, lying immediately behind the freehold land.
At all material times, the freehold land has been vested in Mr and Mrs Box, and they have thereon carried on a business of motor auctioneers under the style or firm name of 'Strand Motor Auctions and Car Sales' with a small vehicle service depot dealing with car tyres and exhaust systems.
In August 1979 Mr Box made an application to the council (as the relevant planning
j authority) to hold a market on the freehold land. In a letter dated 10 August 1979 Mr Box wrote to the council:

'With regard to the proposed Public Market at Strand Motor Auctions, Wakefield Road, Featherstone we have now acquired in principle a further 1.5 acres of land to the rear, part of which will act as Public Car Parking.'

That was part of the land later demised by the lease to which I shall refer.

On 4 March 1980 planning permission was refused; the reason for the refusal being
declared to be, in the words of the refusal: *a*

'In the opinion of the District Planning Authority the establishment of a public
market on this site, which is located outside of the recognised Featherstone shopping
centre, would prejudice the policy of the District Planning Authority in securing
well-planned development.'

Then, on 16 September 1980, the council granted a lease to the defendants in respect *b*
of leasehold land for a term of 99 years from the date thereof. By the lease the defendants
covenanted that they would, within 12 months from the date thereof or such extended
period as the council might permit, develop the land for use as a storage area to be used
in conjunction with and for the purposes of the business of motor car auctions situated
on the adjoining land and any purposes ancillary to the said business, and to carry out a
scheme of landscaping on the areas which would not be built on. By cl 4(15) they further *c*
covenanted not to use or permit or suffer to be used the demised premises or any part
thereof for any purpose other than as a storage area and for ancillary purposes in
conjunction with and for the purposes of the business of motor car auctions situated on
the adjoining land without the written consent of the council.

Nevertheless, on 23 April 1981, notwithstanding the restrictions in the lease, the
defendants submitted a further application for the use of the freehold land and part of *d*
the land demised by the lease as a public market. Planning permission was granted on
15 June 1981 subject to conditions, namely: by condition 1, that the development should
be completed in accordance with the plans/specifications thereby approved by the district
planning authority before the use commenced; by condition 3, that the use of the site
should be restricted to Mondays between the hours of 9 am and 4 pm; and, by condition
4, that before the development was brought into use that part of the site to be used by *e*
vehicles should be properly marked and laid out, drained, surfaced and sealed in a
manner to be approved by the district planning authority.

Even before that planning permission had been granted, the defendants had operated
a market on the site on Monday, 25 May 1981, and after the planning permission had
been granted the defendants held further markets, namely on Saturday, 26 June and
Wednesday, 29 July 1981.   *f*

The further markets were held without the authority of the council and no effort was
made by the defendants to comply with the conditions of the planning permission or to
seek any variations of the provisions of the lease.

The defendants have advertised their intention to hold yet another public market on
Monday, 31 August 1981 and Tuesday, 1 September 1981. Their intention was at first to
hold it on both the freehold land and part of the leasehold land. They advertised that the *g*
market would be held on a 'massive site of seven acres in conjunction with a horse show/
gymkhana of twelve events and the provision of toilets and refreshments'; that there
would be 'massive car parking', that it would cover 'a large catchment area and no
competition' and that it would be supported by 'massive advertising [by] press and radio'.
They have since said, and now assert before me, that they intend to confine the market
solely to the freehold land and they offer an undertaking to the court that they will not *h*
make any use of the leasehold land for that purpose, although it is quite apparent that if
the site were reduced from about seven acres to only two acres the activities involved
would be somewhat different in kind from those which they have advertised.

The defendants assert that the council does not have any right in law to restrain the
holding of a public market, and I turn now to the question of whether the council has or
may have any such right.   *j*

There are a number of markets held in the administrative area of the council and they
are operated by the council itself or under licence from the council. Those markets are:

(a) The Wakefield market. This was acquired under power conferred on the former
county borough of Wakefield by the Wakefield Corporation Market Act 1900 to purchase
an undertaking of the Wakefield Borough Market Co established under an 1847 Act.

This market comprises two market halls with about 150 stalls, one hall being a separate
a fish and meat market. Between the two halls there is a large open area, and in that area
there is an open market of about 250 stalls. The two halls are open daily. The open
market is in part open daily and in full use on Mondays, Tuesdays, Thursdays, Fridays
and Saturdays. The distance between the Wakefield market and the defendants' land is
6·4 miles.

(b) The Castleford market. This was established in 1880 under the Market and Fairs
b Clauses Act 1847. It comprises a market hall with about 100 stalls and an adjoining open
market with over 100 stalls. The open market is in use on Mondays, Fridays and
Saturdays, and the hall is in use daily. The distance between the defendants' land and the
Castleford market is 4·8 miles.

(c) The Pontefract market. This was established under a number of royal charters, the
first charter being granted in 1194 and a charter in 1484 granted and confirmed to the
c mayor of the authority of Pontefract that they and their successors may have in the
authority or borough one market to be held there on every seventh day for ever on every
Saturday. The Pontefract market comprises a market hall of 37 stalls open daily and an
open market of approximately 140 stalls held on Wednesdays and Saturdays. The distance
between the market and the defendants' land is 3·2 miles.

(d) The Normanton market. This was formerly a private market and was acquired by
d the former Normanton urban district council in 1960. It is now operated by the plaintiff
council under the provisions of Part III of the Food and Drugs Act 1955. It comprises 15
lock-up stalls and 48 open market stalls, and it is in use on Tuesdays and Saturdays each
week. The distance between the Normanton market and the defendants' land is 3·5
miles.

(e) The Hemsworth market. The origin of this market is uncertain, but it was in
e existence and controlled by the former Hemsworth urban district council in 1928. It
comprises 70 open market stalls, which are in use on Tuesdays, Fridays and Saturdays
each week. The distance between the Hemsworth market and the defendants' land is 6·6
miles.

I should refer to the West Yorkshire Act 1980, which applies in the area with which I
am concerned and s 19 reads:

f
'Any market carried on by a district council within their district which was not
established or acquired under section 49 of the Act of 1955 or any of the enactments
mentioned in subsection (2) of that section shall be deemed to have been acquired
by the district council under the said section 49'

The council is concerned to develop its market undertakings. It is pursuing questions
g of the provision of an additional extra market day at Pontefract, the establishment of a
market at Featherstone and/or Knottingley and the provision of additional market
facilities throughout the area. In particular, it proposes to establish in the centre of
Featherstone a market of some 30 stalls for use twice weekly. The council is greatly
concerned at the threat to its existing markets from the activities of the defendants,
which activities might well be copied by others. It fears that trade will be drawn from
h the stallholders of its existing markets with the loss of income to the stallholders and the
reduction of its own income from stallage charges.

As I understand him, counsel for the defendants accepts that the council has succeeded
to the benefit of all the markets of the former local authorities which existed within the
area which it now administers. But he submits that prior to the commencement of the
Local Government Act 1972 none of those former authorities, with the doubtful
j exception of the borough of Pontefract, could ever have had the right to prevent the
holding of a market at Featherstone. Even with regard to the former borough of
Pontefract, he says the 1484 charter only authorises a market on Saturdays and so it
would have had to rely on the Food and Drugs Act 1955 for protection of its market on
any day other than Saturday. The council of the county borough of Wakefield could not
have prevented the holding of a market at Featherstone because s 4 of the Wakefield

Corporation Market Act 1900 expressly confined its operation to the city and in s 3 'the city' was declared to be the city of Wakefield.

As regards the former borough of Castleford, s 13 of the Markets and Fairs Clauses Act 1847 provides:

'After the market place is opened for public use every person other than a licensed hawker who shall sell or expose for sale in any place within the prescribed limits, except for his own dwelling place or shop, any articles in respect of which tolls are by the special Act authorised to be taken in the market, shall for such offence be liable to a penalty not exceeding [£25].'

The 'prescribed limits' are the borough of Castleford.

As regards the former urban district of Normanton, its market was acquired pursuant to the provisions of s 49(1)(b) of the Food and Drugs Act 1955, and s 51 of that Act provides:

'A market authority may, with the approval of the Minister of Housing and Local Government, appoint the days on which, and the hours during which, markets are to be held.'

There is no evidence that any byelaw was ever made.

The submissions of counsel for the defendants amount, I think, to this: that when statutory markets are set up their protection depends on the provisions contained in the relevant statute for their protection, and those provisions constitute an entire and exclusive code in the enforcement of the market protection; that the former Featherstone urban district council never had any authority to restrain the establishment of any market within its area; that although the council has succeeded to all the rights previously vested in the former authorities, it has no greater powers than the powers which those authorities themselves could have exercised and so it too cannot now restrain the establishment of any market in Featherstone; and that there can be no disturbance of any statutory market of the council by reason of a market established in the area of Featherstone, even if the new market lies within the common law distance of $6\frac{2}{3}$ miles from any of the council's existing markets. I hope I have summarised the submissions of counsel for the defendants sufficiently.

In considering this point, I am assisted by *Pease and Chitty's Law of Markets and Fairs* (2nd edn, 1958) p 72, where the editor writes:

'REMEDIES FOR DISTURBANCE OF STATUTORY MARKETS AND FAIRS

Acts which would amount to a disturbance of a market established by royal grant may also constitute a disturbance of a market established by statute, and persons disturbing a statutory market may be liable to an action for damages or an injunction. The law with regard to disturbance is not altered, in the case of any particular market, by the mere fact that the charters of the market were granted with the consent of Parliament, or has subsequently become merely statutory. But it may nevertheless be altered by the express or implied terms of the provisions which Parliament has inserted in the charters or statutes regulating the market. The statute may amount to an enactment of the franchise market rights with modifications and additions or be in such terms as to extinguish the franchise market and substitute a statutory one.'

In other words, it is a question of whether by the terms of the statute, the common law remedy, remains in whole or in part. The editor then went on to consider s 13 of the Markets and Fairs Clauses Act 1847, and continued (at pp 73–74):

'. . . the position appears to be as follows: 1.—It cannot be said that the market rights are infringed, or that the market is disturbed, merely because a person sells tollable articles in his own dwelling-place or shop, although it be within the prescribed limits. *A fortiori*, it is not a ground of complaint that a person sells such articles in his own dwelling-place or shop outside the prescribed limits. 2.—If an offence be committed against the section, the penalty thereby imposed may be recovered in a court of summary jurisdiction. So far however as the offence also amounts to an injury to a right of property an injunction to prevent a commission of the offence or its repetition will be granted by a court of competent jurisdiction. But it seems probable also that for a mere offence against the section no action for damages lies. The section appears to create a liability not existing at common law, and, as it prescribes the particular remedy for enforcing it, that remedy must be adopted. 3.—If, on the other hand, the market be disturbed by the unlawful levying of a rival market in a manner which does not constitute any offence against the section, an action lies for damages, as well as for an injunction. It will be observed that a person may set up a rival market without committing an offence under the section, for the section only prohibits selling and exposing for sale, acts which a person who sets up a market does not necessarily commit. Consequently, if the remedy by action did not exist, the market-owner might be without remedy against very serious infringements of his rights. 4.—It is probable that, on similar grounds, an action is maintainable against persons who disturb the market by wrongful acts other than that of setting up a rival market, provided that the wrongful acts complained of amount to more than the commission of an offence under the section. But there seems to be no authority directly on this point. 5.—The effect of the section on the market-owner's rights of action is in some cases complicated by the fact that the section has to be read in conjunction with other sections of the special Act which incorporates it, and when so read its effect may be considerably altered and a particular form of rival market which escapes the section may be excluded from prohibition by another section. In the foregoing observations, it has been assumed that the protection given by s. 13 of the Markets and Fairs Clauses Act is given, not in substitution for, but by way of addition to, the protection against disturbance by levying a rival market, which a market enjoys at common law. It cannot, however, be regarded as finally determined whether this assumption is correct.'

I respectfully agree with the views of the editor of *Pease and Chitty* and I do not accept that s 13 constitutes an entire and exclusive code of the enforcement of rights to statutory markets.

Turning to the intentions of the defendants, it is clear that those are to establish a rival market in Featherstone. One of the documents in the proceedings is a photograph taken from Wakefield Road and it shows the front of the building on the defendants' land. The building is identified by large black lettering as 'Featherstone Market', and below those letters are 'Car Sales Monday and Thursday evening'. The business style or name of 'Strand Motor Auction and Car Sales' does not appear.

The expression 'Featherstone Market' also appears in press advertising in connection with the holding of markets on the land. From that I infer that the defendants look on their activities on the land as the activities of proprietors of a market, namely Featherstone market, a business which they consider already in existence. Such a market being established by the defendants within the common law distance of 6⅔ miles from the council's markets can, in my view, be a rival to those markets and may be presumed to be a nuisance to those markets.

There is a serious question to be tried in this action. There is nothing frivolous or vexatious about the council's claim. The powers claimed by the council are under attack by the defendants.

Counsel for the defendants asks that on the balance of convenience I should not grant the interlocutory injunction sought by the council. He says that earlier markets were held without objection from the council, that the proposed market has been advertised for about two months and that efforts have been made continuously by the defendants to co-operate with the council. He claims further that the grant of an interlocutory injunction would cause considerable financial loss to the defendants.

I am not impressed by the assertion of the anxiety on the part of the defendants to co-operate with the council. Indeed, it appears to me that the only real anxiety felt by the *a* defendants is to establish a market for themselves, and that they have a firm and continuing intention to achieve that purpose. It is to be inferred from the letter of 10 August 1979 that the defendants well knew that the provision for car parking facilities at any market would be considered a significant factor by the planning authority. That was the purpose or one of the purposes for which they acquired the leasehold land, even though it was not a purpose authorised by the lease. The defendants appear to have a *b* blatant disregard of planning regulations. Of course, this is not a planning dispute but planning considerations affect the dispute and I consider that I am entitled to take them into account. Furthermore, I think there would be no difficulty at all in quantifying any loss which they might suffer if, on the full hearing, it should appear that an interlocutory injunction ought not to have been granted. The defendants have advertised space at the proposed market for '50p. per foot and £2 for advertising'. It appears that they do not *c* intend to embark on any capital expenditure of any kind. The registrar would have an easy task in assessing any financial loss suffered by the defendants. Indeed, since it appears that the proposed activities of the defendants would be carried on in breach of planning regulations, the registrar would have to consider whether any damage at all could be recovered by the defendants.

On the other hand, the defendants have known since May last that the council has *d* been greatly concerned about the defendants' intentions. It has recognised that these intentions raise legal difficulties for it and it has proceeded with proper care. If I were to refuse to grant the injunction, then there might be substantial loss to the council and that loss might be extremely difficult to prove.

The point was considered by Walton J in *Northampton BC v Midland Development Group of Cos Ltd* (1978) 76 LGR 750, where the defendant proposed to use one floor of a *e* shopping centre by granting licences to traders to trade from booths to be erected on that floor. After finding there was a triable issue on whether the activities proposed constituted a market, the judge went on to say that a question, partly of fact and partly of law, which arose was whether the borough would suffer any damage, and, if not, whether it was necessary to show such damage. Any flagrant invasion of a market holder's rights was bound to cause damage, though it might take some time to appear. He said: 'It is a very *f* serious matter from the point of view of the person holding the franchise.'

In *Tamworth BC v Fazeley Town Council* (1978) 77 LGR 238 an interlocutory injunction had been refused on the grounds that the plaintiff council had not shown that they had suffered any damage, but at the trial Mr Vivian Price QC, sitting as a deputy judge of the Chancery Division, granted an injunction holding that there was an irrebuttable presumption that a new market set up to be held on the same day as a franchise market *g* within the common law distance was a nuisance, unless licensed by the franchise owner or the subject of a concurrent market franchise, and actionable without proof of damage.

Accordingly, I order that the defendants, and each of them, be restrained until judgment in this action or futher order from holding any market on the land, freehold land or leasehold land, vested in and situate at Wakefield Road, Featherstone in the county of West Yorkshire, and being the land in respect of which planning permission *h* was given on 15 June 1981, or any part of that land.

Injunction granted.

Solicitors: *Lawrence A Tawn*, Wakefield (for the council); *David Collins & Co*, Leeds (for the defendants).

John M Collins Esq Barrister.

Re Overmark Smith Warden Ltd

CHANCERY DIVISION
SLADE J
4, 5, 10 MARCH 1982

b

Limitation of action – Acknowledgment – Debt – Acknowledgment of company's indebtedness – Acknowledgment contained in company's statement of affairs and summaries thereof made in company's receivership and subsequent winding up – Whether statement of affairs and summaries thereof capable of constituting acknowledgment – Whether acknowledgment in documents an acknowledgment of indebtedness only as at date to which statement of affairs relates and not as at later date when documents signed – Whether creditors' claims statute-barred in liquidation – Limitation Act 1939, ss 23(4), 24.

c

In 1968 and 1970 a company granted debentures to its banker. On 20 August 1971 the bank appointed a receiver and manager of the company's assets under the debentures. Under the debentures the receiver was to act as the company's agent. The company had a large number of unsecured creditors all of whose debts were contractual, the causes of action to recover the debts having originally accrued in all cases before 24 May 1972. On 23 December 1981 a director and the secretary of the company submitted to the receiver, pursuant to s 372(1)(b)^a of the Companies Act 1948, a statement of the company's affairs (the first statement of affairs) as at the date of the receiver's appointment (ie 20 August 1971) which contained, inter alia, a list of the unsecured creditors, their names and addresses, the amount of each debt and the total amount of the debts (£339,704). The receiver made a summary of that statement of affairs showing the total amount of the unsecured debts but not the names of the creditors or the individual amounts of their debts, and on 10 January 1972 he wrote a letter to all the company's creditors enclosing a copy of the summary and pointing out that the statement of affairs showed insufficient assets to pay the unsecured creditors' debts. In a further letter to the unsecured creditors dated 12 October 1972 the receiver stated that the realisation of the assets had proved insufficient to meet the prior claims of the bank as debenture holder and therefore no surplus assets were available for the unsecured creditors. On 24 May 1978 the company presented a petition for its compulsory winding up and on 26 June 1978 it was compulsorily wound up by the court. On 6 September 1978 a liquidator was appointed. A director of the company, in an affidavit sworn by him on 12 September 1978 pursuant to s 235^b of the 1948 Act, submitted to the Official Receiver a second statement of the company's affairs as at 20 August 1971 (the date directed by the Official Receiver) which contained a list of the unsecured creditors similar to the list contained in the first statement of affairs. On 15 August 1979 the Official Receiver signed a document the first part of which contained a summary of the second statement of affairs, in terms similar to the receiver's summary of the first statement of affairs, and the second part of which contained the Official Receiver's observations which included the statement that after discharging the bank's debentures there was a surplus of some £84,000 available for distribution to the unsecured creditors, subject to the cost of the winding up. In the course of the winding up the liquidator discovered that because the original causes of action to recover the unsecured debts had accrued before 24 May 1972, ie more than six years before the commencement of the winding up on 24 May 1978, the unsecured creditors' debts would be statute-barred and unenforceable in the liquidation unless there had been sufficient acknowledgment of their debts for the purpose of ss 23 and 24^c of the Limitation Act 1939 within six years of the commencement of the winding up. The

d

e

f

g

h

j

---

a   Section 372(1), so far as material, is set out at p 516 c, post
b   Section 235, so far as material, is set out at p 517 e, post
c   Sections 23 and 24, so far as material, are set out at p 519 h j, post

liquidator applied to the court for the determination of the question whether five specified documents constituted a sufficient acknowledgment of the unsecured debts for the purpose of the 1939 Act, namely (i) the receiver's summary of the first statement of affairs, (ii) the receiver's letter to all the creditors dated 10 January 1972, (iii) the receiver's further letter to the unsecured creditors dated 12 October 1972, (iv) the second statement of affairs made in the director's affidavit sworn on 12 September 1978 and (v) the observations of the official receiver in the document he signed on 15 August 1979.

Held – Assuming in favour of the unsecured creditors that a statement of a company's affairs produced in the company's receivership or liquidation pursuant to the statutory obligation to do so was capable of constituting an effective acknowledgment of indebtedness for the purpose of ss 23 and 24 of the 1939 Act, and that the five documents in question were capable of constituting an effective acknowledgment of the company's indebtedness for the purpose of the 1939 Act, the documents in question only amounted to an admission of the company's indebtedness as at 20 August 1971, and did not amount to an acknowledgment of indebtedness at the later dates on which the documents were signed because, properly construed, the first and second statements of affairs and the summaries of them purported to do no more than show the company's liabilities to creditors as at 20 August 1971, since that was the date to which the statement of affairs specifically related, and the admission by the signatories of the documents that the company was under liability to the unsecured creditors at 20 August 1971 could not amount to an admission that those debts were still liabilities of the company at the later dates on which the signatories signed the documents. It followed that the causes of action to recover the debts accrued, pursuant to s 23(4) of the 1939 Act, on 20 August 1971 (the date the debts were acknowledged), and since that date was more than six years before the commencement of the liquidation on 24 May 1978, the unsecured creditors' claims were therefore statute-barred in the liquidation (see p 521 *d e*, p 522 *b* to *d f* to p 523 *b* and p 524 *b* to *d g*, post).

Jones v Bellegrove Properties Ltd [1949] 2 All ER 198, *Re Gee & Co (Woolwich) Ltd* [1974] 1 All ER 1149 and *Re Compania de Electricidad de la Provincia de Buenos Aires Ltd* [1978] 3 All ER 668 distinguished.

Notes

For documents amounting to acknowledgment of a debt, see 28 Halsbury's Laws (4th edn) para 888, and for cases on the subject, see 32 Digest (Reissue) 517–518, 522–525, 3930–3945, 3983–4007.

For the Limitation Act 1939, ss 23, 24, see 19 Halsbury's Statutes (3rd edn) 82, 84.

For the Companies Act 1948, ss 235, 372, see 5 ibid 300, 384.

As from 1 May 1981 ss 23 and 24 of the 1939 Act were replaced by ss 29 and 30 of the Limitation Act 1980.

Cases referred to in judgment

Art Reproduction Co Ltd, Re [1951] 2 All ER 984, [1952] Ch 89, 10 Digest (Reissue) 1154, 7182.

Beavan, Re, Davies, Banks & Co v Beavan [1912] 1 Ch 196, [1911–13] All ER Rep 793, 23 Digest (Reissue) 444, 5228.

Bowring-Hanbury's trustee v Bowring-Hanbury [1943] 1 All ER 48, [1943] Ch 104, CA, 32 Digest (Reissue) 524, 4001.

Compania de Electricidad de la Provincia de Buenos Aires Ltd, Re [1978] 3 All ER 668, [1980] Ch 146, [1979] 2 WLR 316, Digest (Cont Vol E) 75, 7185a.

Consolidated Agencies Ltd v Bertram Ltd [1964] 3 All ER 282, [1965] AC 470, [1964] 3 WLR 671, PC, 32 Digest (Reissue) 545, *2339.

Courtenay v Williams (1844) 3 Hare 539, 67 ER 494; *affd* (1846) 15 LJ Ch 204, [1843–60] All ER Rep 755, LC, 32 Digest (Reissue) 533, 4074.

Everett v Robertson (1858) 1 E & E 16, 28 LJQB 23, 120 ER 813, 32 Digest (Reissue) 533,
a   4071.
Flynn (decd), Re, (No 2), Flynn v Flynn [1969] 2 All ER 557, [1969] 2 Ch 403, [1969] 2
    WLR 1148, 32 Digest (Reissue) 543, 4153.
Gee & Co (Woolwich) Ltd, Re [1974] 1 All ER 1149, [1975] Ch 52, [1974] 2 WLR 515, 32
    Digest (Reissue) 544, 4164.
Jones v Bellegrove Properties Ltd [1949] 2 All ER 198, [1949] 2 KB 700, CA, 32 Digest
b   (Reissue) 544, 4162.
Kamouh v Associated Electrical Industries International Ltd [1980] QB 199, [1979] 2 WLR
    795.
Levey, Re, ex p Topping (1865) 4 De GJ & Sm 551, [1861–73] All ER Rep 952, 46 ER 1033,
    LC, 32 Digest (Reissue) 551, 4194.
Lyall v Fluker [1873] WN 208, 32 Digest (Reissue) 468, 3603.
c *Surrendra Overseas Ltd v Government of Sri Lanka* [1977] 2 All ER 481, [1977] 1 WLR 565,
    32 Digest (Reissue) 549, 4185.

Cases also cited
Barrett v Birmingham (1842) 4 I Eq R 537.
d *Blair v Nugent* (1846) 3 Jo & Lat 658.
Browne (a bankrupt), Re, ex p Official Receiver v Thompson [1960] 2 All ER 625, [1960] 1
    WLR 692.
Chinnery v Evans (1864) 11 HL Cas 115, 11 ER 1274.
Clendinning, Re, ex p Thomas Anderson (1859) 9 I Ch R 284.
Dungate v Dungate [1965] 3 All ER 393, [1965] 1 WLR 1477.
e *Edwards, Ex p, re Tollemache* (1884) 14 QBD 415.
Good v Parry [1963] 2 All ER 59, [1963] 2 QB 418, CA.
Hanan v Power (1845) 8 ILR 505.
Lloyd v Coote & Ball [1915] 1 KB 242.
M'Donnell v Broderick (1896) 2 IR 136.
Morrogh v Power (1842) 4 ILR 494.
f *Pott v Clegg* (1847) 16 M & W 321, 153 ER 1212.
Prendergast v O'Gorman [1933] IR 460.
Revell, Ex p, re Tollemache (No 1), (1884) 13 QBD 720.
Smallcombe v Bruges (1824) 13 Price 136, 147 ER 944.
Tristram v Harte (1841) 3 I Eq R 386.
Wandsworth Union v Worthington [1906] 1 KB 420.
g *West's Estate, Re* (1879) 3 LR Ir 77.

Originating summons
By an originating summons issued on 10 August 1981, as amended at the hearing of the
summons, Norman Leverton, the liquidator of Overmark Smith Warden Ltd (the
h company), sought determination of the question whether on their true construction and
in the events which had happened certain documents or any of them constituted a
sufficient acknowledgment for the purposes of the Limitation Act 1939 of debts owed to
unsecured creditors of the company. By an order dated 14 May 1981 the Treasury
Solicitor was appointed to act on behalf of the Department of Employment as representing
one of 15 creditors whose debts were not statute-barred and were admissible in the
j liquidation. The facts are set out in the judgment.

Michael Crystal for the liquidator.
John Mummery for the Department of Employment.

                                                    Cur adv vult

10 March. **SLADE J** read the following judgment: This is an application for directions
by Mr Norman Leverton, the liquidator of Overmark Smith Warden Ltd (which I will
call 'the company'). It was incorporated on 12 September 1968. At all material times it
had an issued share capital of £100 divided into 100 ordinary shares of £1 each, of which
99 shares were held by a company called Overmark Ltd and one share by Mr J W H
Hobbs.

On 18 November 1968 and 21 November 1970 the company granted debentures to
its bankers, who are now known as Williams & Glyns Bank Ltd (the bank). On 20 August
1971 Mr D G W Ballard was appointed by the bank to be receiver and manager of the
property and assets of the company. Though this is not formally in evidence, it is
common ground that, under the terms of the debentures, he was expressed to act as agent
for the company.

Paragraph (a) of s 372(1) of the Companies Act 1948 placed on the receiver the
obligation forthwith to send notice to the company of his appointment. Paragraph (b) of
that subsection required that there should, within the period there specified, 'be made
out and submitted to the receiver in accordance with the next following section a
statement in the prescribed form as to the affairs of the company'.

Section 373(1) provides:

> 'The statement as to the affairs of a company required by the last foregoing section
> to be submitted to the receiver (or his successor) shall show as at the date of the
> receiver's appointment the particulars of the company's assets, debts and liabilities,
> the names, residences and occupations of its creditors, the securities held by them
> respectively, the dates when the securities were respectively given and such further
> or other information as may be prescribed.'

Section 373(2) read with s 373(4) contains a general requirement that, in a case where
the receiver is appointed under the powers contained in an instrument, the statement
shall be submitted by and be verified by a statutory declaration of one or more of the
persons who were at the date of the receiver's appointment the directors and by the
person who was at that date the secretary of the company.

Pursuant to the obligations imposed by ss 372(1)(b) and 373(2) of the 1948 Act, Mr
M S Ashworth, a director of the company, and Mr B F Kingsley, its secretary, on 23
December 1971 made a statutory declaration by which they declared that 'the statement
made overleaf' and the several lists annexed to it marked A, C, D, E, F and G, were to the
best of their knowledge and belief a full and complete statement as to the affairs of the
company on 20 August 1971, being the date of the appointment of the receiver. The
'statement made overleaf' was headed 'Statement as to the affairs of Overmark Smith
Warden on the 20th day of August 1971, the estimated realisable values and liabilities
expected to rank'. List E annexed to the statutory declaration was a list of unsecured
creditors. It contained a large number of names and addresses. It also specified the
amount of the relevant debt in the case of each creditor, the amounts totalling
£339,704·04. The statement of affairs showed an estimated deficiency even as regards
debenture holders of £16,706. So it looked at that stage as if no assets at all would be
available for the unsecured creditors.

On 10 January 1972 Mr Ballard wrote a letter to all the creditors of the company
enclosing a copy of a summary of the statement of affairs, together with his comments
thereon. He signed the letter, expressing himself to do so 'for Overmark Smith Warden
Limited (In Receivership)'. The letter pointed out that the statement of affairs showed a
deficiency of £16,706 as regards the debenture holder, with no surplus available for the
unsecured creditors. It informed the creditors that Mr Ballard had advised the directors
that there was no alternative to a liquidation of the company.

The summary of the statement of affairs prepared by Mr Ballard and enclosed with
this letter was described in its heading thus: 'On the 20th August 1971 the date of the
appointment of the Receiver and Manager showing assets at estimated realisable values.'
It showed a total sum of £339,704 as being due to unsecured creditors, without stating
the names of the creditors or particularising the amounts of their debts.

There was also enclosed with Mr Ballard's letter of 10 January 1972 one page consisting
a of his comments on the statement of affairs. He signed this page, but nothing turns on
its contents for present purposes.

On 12 October 1972 Mr Ballard wrote a letter to all unsecured creditors of the
company. It was headed in the matter of 'Overmark Smith Warden Limited (In
Receivership)'. It stated:

b
> 'I have now almost completed the realisation of the above company's assets and I
> regret to inform you that the realisations have proved insufficient to meet the prior
> claim of the debenture holder, Williams & Glyns Bank Limited, by whom I was
> appointed. There is, therefore, no surplus available for unsecured creditors.
>
> Yours faithfully
>
> for Overmark Smith Warden (In Receivership).'

c   There then followed Mr Ballard's manuscript signature. Beneath the typewritten
subscription of his name were the words 'Receiver and Manager'.

On 28 November 1975 Overmark Ltd went into voluntary liquidation and in 1977 it
was dissolved.

On 26 June 1978 this court made a compulsory winding-up order in respect of the
company on the company's own petition, which had been presented on 24 May 1978.
d On 6 September 1978 Mr Leverton, the applicant, was appointed to be the company's
liquidator.

Where a winding-up order has been made, s 235(1) of the Companies Act 1948
requires the making out and submission to the Official Receiver of—

e
> 'a statement as to the affairs of the company in the prescribed form, verified by
> affidavit, and showing the particulars of its assets, debts and liabilities, the names,
> residences and occupations of its creditors, the securities held by them respectively,
> the dates when the securities were respectively given, and such further or other
> information as may be prescribed or as the official receiver may require.'

Subsection (2), read together with sub-s (8), requires the statement to be submitted and
verified by one or more of the persons who were at the date of the winding-up order the
f directors and by the person who was at that date the secretary of the company.

The prescribed form for the purpose of s 235(1) of the 1948 Act is Form 22 in the
appendix to the Companies (Winding-up) Rules 1949, SI 1949/330. On 12 September
1978 Mr S E Sherring, a director of the company, swore an affidavit deposing that 'the
statement made overleaf and the several lists hereunto annexed marked A, C, D, E, G, H,
and I' were to the best of his knowledge and belief a full, true and complete statement as
g to the affairs of the company on 20 August 1971, the date directed by the Official
Receiver. Though the statement of affairs annexed to this affidavit (which I will call 'the
second statement of affairs') is not in evidence, it is common ground that list E annexed
to it corresponded with list E to the statement of affairs made by Mr Ashworth and Mr
Kingsley in 1971 (which I will call 'the first statement of affairs'). Thus it showed an
aggregate sum of £339,704 as being due to unsecured creditors of the company as at 20
h August 1971, giving particulars of the names of the individual creditors and the amounts
of their respective debts.

Subsequently the Official Receiver prepared and signed a document dated 15 August
1979, of which the first part contained a summary of the second statement of affairs and
the second part contained his observations thereon. The first part was headed 'Summary
of the statement of affairs as at 20 August 1971, the date of the appointment of a receiver
j and manager by the debenture holder, submitted on 14 September 1978 by Samuel
Ernest Sherring, a director'. This summary was in much the same form as the summary
of the first statement of affairs referred to earlier in this judgment. Again it showed an
aggregate sum of £339,704 as being due to unsecured creditors of the company as at 20
August 1971, though it did not particularise the individual debts or the names of the
creditors. The observations, inter alia, gave certain details of the receiver's receipts and
payments and stated:

'The surplus in the receivership is therefore £84,462 which is available for
distribution to the unsecured creditors (subject to the cost of the winding-up).'

    a

Though at an earlier stage it appeared that the unsecured creditors of the company
would not receive any dividend, realisations have now been made totalling £91,062.
None of this sum is required to discharge any indebtedness of the company to the bank,
whose claims have been discharged in full. There are therefore some assets available for
distribution to unsecured creditors.

The liquidator, Mr Leverton, however, according to his evidence has discovered in the
course of his investigations that the debts of a considerable number of the company's
unsecured creditors may have become statute-barred before the date of the liquidation of
the company, in default of any sufficient acknowlegment of such debts by or on behalf
of the company. He has been advised that the creditors of the company interested in its
liquidation fall into two categories. The first category comprises 15 creditors, whose
debts total £18,618·83 and whose names are set out in the second schedule to the
summons now before the court. The applicant has been advised that the debts of these
creditors (whom I will call 'the 15 creditors') on any footing are not statute-barred and
should be admitted in the liquidation. The second and much larger category consists of
several hundreds of creditors with claims in excess of £300,000. The liquidator has been
advised that there is some doubt whether this category can claim in the liquidation, since
their claims may be statute-barred. These were the circumstances in which he issued the
summons which is now before the court. Before doing so, however, he obtained an order
from Mr Registrar Bradburn dated 14 May 1981 that the Treasury Solicitor on behalf of
the Department of Employment, which is one of the 15 creditors, should be appointed
to represent all the others of these creditors.

On 10 August 1981 the liquidator issued the summons which is now before the court.
The substantial relief sought by the summons in its original form was as follows:

'1. A direction as to whether the assets of the Company available for distribution
amongst its creditors in its compulsory liquidation should be distributed pari passu
amongst all the creditors of the Company whose names appear in the First Schedule
hereto.
2. *Alternatively*, a direction as to whether the assets of the Company available for
distribution amongst its creditors in its compulsory liquidation should be distributed
amongst the creditors of the Company whose names appear in the Second Schedule
hereto and, to the extent to which there is any surplus on payment of such creditors
in full, a direction as to whom such surplus is payable.
3. Such further or other directions for the payment of the assets of the Company
available for distribution amongst its creditors in its compulsory liquidation as may
be just.'

The second schedule to the summons includes the names of the 15 creditors already
referred to. The first schedule includes the names not only of the 15 creditors but of all
other persons who are known by the liquidator to be unsecured creditors, subject only to
any question of the claims of some of them being statute-barred.

After the matter had been opened, I told counsel that I would not on any footing be
able to grant relief precisely in the form of para 1 or para 2 of the summons because this
would involve an investigation of the details of each individual creditor's debt and there
was not sufficient evidence before the court to make such an investigation possible. In
any event, as counsel explained on the liquidator's behalf, he does not in truth seek such
an investigation. What he requires is the determination of the relevant question of
principle, that is to say whether all or any of the various documents signed by Mr Ballard,
Mr Sherring or the Official Receiver (as the case may be) have constituted sufficient
acknowledgments for the purpose of the Limitation Act 1939 so as to prevent the debts
of the general body of unsecured creditors from being statute-barred, even in the case of
those creditors whose claims would otherwise be defeated by the statute.

In these circumstances I asked counsel to formulate a draft amendment to the
a summons so as to add a paragraph asking substantially for determination of the question
whether all or any of the relevant documents constitute a sufficient acknowledgment of
debts owed to unsecured creditors of the company for the purpose of the 1939 Act. This
they have done. By agreement they suggest that a new para 3 be added to the summons
by amendment in the following form:

b
> 'That it may be determined whether, on their true construction and in the events
> which have happened, the following documents or any of them constitute a
> sufficient acknowledgment for the purposes of the Limitation Act 1939 of debts
> owed to unsecured creditors of the company: (1) the summary of the statement of
> affairs of the company as at 20 August 1971 and made by Mr D G W Ballard as
> receiver and manager of the company; (2) a letter dated 10 January 1972 signed by
> the said Mr Ballard and addressed to all creditors of the company; (3) a letter dated
c
> 12 October 1972 signed by the said Mr Ballard and addressed to all unsecured
> creditors of the company; (4) the summary of the statement of affairs of the
> company as at 20 August 1971 as sworn to in an affidavit made by Samuel Ernest
> Sherring on 12 September 1978 and the exhibits thereto and the observations of the
> Official Receiver dated 15 August 1979.'

d   This proposed amendment seems to me in satisfactory form. I accordingly now direct
amendment of the summons by the addition of a new para 3 in this form, which will
necessitate a consequential renumbering of the later paragraphs.
    I now proceed to consider the question of principle put to me. For this purpose I will
refer collectively to those unsecured creditors whose debts are statute-barred in the
absence of a sufficient written acknowledgment as 'the relevant creditors'. I have had the
e benefit of helpful argument from counsel for the liquidator on their behalf and from
counsel on behalf of the 15 creditors.
    In the case of a compulsory winding up, s 257(1) of the 1948 Act requires the assets of
the company to be collected and applied in discharge of its 'liabilities'. For this purpose,
liabilities include enforceable liabilities and therefore do not include statute-barred debts:
see *Re Art Reproduction Co Ltd* [1951] 2 All ER 984, [1952] Ch 89. Accordingly, the
f liquidator is entitled to allow only those creditors who establish that their debts are not
statute-barred to participate in the distribution of the company's assets.
    All the claims of the relevant creditors are founded on contract. Section 2(1)(*a*) of the
1939 Act provides that actions founded on simple contract shall not be brought after the
expiration of six years from the date on which the cause of action accrued. The
commencement of a liquidation stops time running in favour of the creditors of a
g company. The liquidation in the present case must be deemed to have commenced on
24 May 1978 when the company presented its petition. However, the cause of action to
recover all the relevant debts originally accrued before 24 May 1972. Prima facie,
therefore, all the relevant debts are statute-barred.
    However, s 23(4) of the 1939 Act, so far as material, provided:

h
> 'Where any right of action has accrued to recover any debt . . . and the person
> liable or accountable therefor acknowledges the claim . . . the right shall be deemed
> to have accrued on and not before the date of the acknowledgment . . .'

Section 24(1) provided:

j
> 'Every such acknowledgment as aforesaid shall be in writing and signed by the
> person making the acknowledgment.'

Section 24(2), so far as material for present purposes, provided:

> 'Any such acknowledgment . . . as aforesaid may be made by the agent of the
> person by whom it is required to be made under the last foregoing section, and shall
> be made to the person, or to an agent of the person, whose title or claim is being
> acknowledged . . .'

Section 6 of the Limitation Amendment Act 1980, which came into force on 1 August
1980, amended s 23 of the 1939 Act, but did not affect the operation of the 1939 Act in   *a*
relation to any acknowledgment made before 1 August 1980: see sub-s (5). It is likewise
common ground that the Limitation Act 1980, which came into force on 1 May 1981
and was intended to consolidate the 1939 Act and the Limitation Amendment Act 1980,
has no relevance in the present context.

As Kerr J pointed out in *Surrendra Overseas Ltd v Government of Sri Lanka* [1977] 2 All
ER 481 at 487, [1977] 1 WLR 565 at 573: 'To acknowledge a claim, as a matter of   *b*
ordinary English, signifies an admission that it is due.' In that case he summarised the
pre-1939 history relating to acknowledgments, beginning with the Limitation Act 1623
and tracing it through the Statute of Frauds Amendment Act 1828 (Lord Tenterden's
Act) and the Mercantile Law Amendment Act 1856. He pointed out that before 1939 a
creditor who wished to bring himself outside the Limitation Acts in reliance on a written
acknowledgment had to show that this was a document from which there could be   *c*
implied a promise to pay the debt in question. Since the passing of the 1939 Act,
however, the relevant sections of which omit the word 'promise', this is no longer
necessary. Kerr J, having reviewed the authorities, summarised the present position thus
([1977] 2 All ER 481 at 489, [1977] 1 WLR 565 at 575):

> 'What I draw from these authorities, and from the ordinary meaning of
> "acknowledges the claim", is that the debtor must acknowledge his indebtedness   *d*
> and legal liability to pay the claim in question. There is now no need to go further
> to seek for any implied promise to pay it. That artificiality has been swept away.
> But, taking the debtor's statement as a whole, as it must be, he can only be held to
> have acknowledged the claim if he has in effect admitted his legal liability to pay
> that which the plaintiff seeks to recover.'
>   *e*

The correctness of this summary of the present law has not been challenged in the
present case.

The question whether a statement made by or on behalf of a debtor in a written
document constitutes an admission of his legal liability to pay the debt in question must
of course depend on the terms of the particular document and its proper interpretation
in its context. It is, however, common ground that, provided an acknowledgment is (i)   *f*
in writing, (ii) signed by the person liable or his agent and (iii) made to the creditor or his
agent, it need not be in any particular form.

In *Jones v Bellegrove Properties Ltd* [1949] 2 All ER 198, [1949] 2 KB 700 the facts as
stated in the headnote to the report were as follows ([1949] 2 KB 700):

> 'A balance sheet presented to the shareholders at an annual general meeting of a
> limited liability company signed by chartered accountants, the agents of the   *g*
> company and by two directors, contained the statement: "To sundry creditors
> 7,638*l*. 6*s*. 10*d*." The plaintiff attended that meeting as a shareholder. The company
> owed the plaintiff 1,807*l*., the balance of moneys lent to it by him. This debt did
> not accrue within six years of an action brought by the plaintiff against the company
> to recover the debt. The annual general meeting was held within that period. At
> the hearing of the action a witness from the firm of chartered accountants which   *h*
> had signed the balance sheet testified that the debt of 1,807*l*. owed by the company
> to the plaintiff was included in the sum of 7,638*l*. 8*s*. 10*d*. stated in the balance sheet
> to be due to sundry creditors.'

The Court of Appeal held that the balance sheet (which had been signed by the
chartered accountants as agents of the company and by two of its directors) constituted   *j*
an acknowledgment to the plaintiff, in writing, signed by the company's agents that the
debt of £1,807 at the date of the annual general meeting remained unpaid and due to
the plaintiff. Accordingly it held that by virtue of ss 23 and 24 of the 1939 Act the debt
was not statute-barred.

Lord Goddard CJ, with whose judgment the other two members of the court agreed,
said ([1949] 2 KB 700 at 704–705; cf [1949] 2 All ER 198 at 201):

'For the defendant company it was contended that a balance sheet is not such a document as can contain or amount to an acknowledgment within the meaning of ss. 23 and 24 of the Limitation Act, 1939. I do not see why that is so. Whether a document is or is not an acknowledgment must depend on what the document states; and a balance sheet presented to a shareholder creditor at a meeting of the company, as these balance sheets were presented to the plaintiff, fulfills all the requirements of ss. 23 and 24 of the Limitation Act, 1939. That statute does not extinguish debts: it merely bars the right to recover them after the lapse of the specified time from the accrual of the cause of action. If a claim is made for payment of a debt many years after it has been incurred, there may be difficulty in proving that the debt ever was in fact incurred or that it has not already been paid and so forth. That is why the law bars the right of action after a certain period has elapsed from the accrual of the cause of action, but then if there is an acknowledgment of the debt within the terms of ss. 23 and 24 of the Act, the right shall be deemed to have accrued on and not before the date of that acknowledgment. I can see no reason why a balance sheet should not contain a good acknowledgment within the meaning of the Act. The acknowledgment was only of a sum due to a number of unnamed persons; but the plaintiff established by evidence that he was one of the sundry creditors and that his debt of 1,807l. was included in the total sum acknowledged to be due to those creditors. In my view, therefore, the claim was not barred.'

That case is significant for two reasons in the present context. First, it shows that a balance sheet of a company signed by its directors is capable of constituting an acknowledgment for the purpose of the Limitation Act 1939. Second, it shows that, provided a document contains a clear admission of indebtedness, it may constitute a sufficient acknowledgment for such purpose even if it does not specify the amount of the debt, provided that this amount is capable of being ascertained by extrinsic evidence. Further support for this latter proposition is to be found in the recent decision of Parker J in *Kamouh v Associated Electrical Industries International Ltd* [1980] QB 199. The first of these two propositions, namely that a balance sheet of a company duly signed by the directors is capable of constituting an acknowledgment, has been confirmed by Brightman J in *Re Gee & Co (Woolwich) Ltd* [1974] 1 All ER 1149, [1975] Ch 52 and by myself in *Re Compania de Electricidad de la Provincia de Buenos Aires Ltd* [1978] 3 All ER 668, [1980] Ch 146.

Counsel for the liquidator forcefully submitted that, despite dicta to the contrary in certain modern textbooks and in Halsbury's Laws of England (see, for example, 28 Halsbury's Laws (4th edn) para 888), there is no reason why by analogy with cases such as *Jones v Bellegrove Properties Ltd* a statement of affairs signed by a duly authorised person on a bankruptcy or in the course of the liquidation or receivership of a company should not constitute a perfectly valid acknowledgment. Nevertheless he very properly referred me to a large number of pre-1939 cases which seem to support a contrary proposition. Clear examples of such cases are *Everett v Robertson* (1858) 28 LJQB 23 and *Re Levey, ex p Topping* (1865) 4 De G J & Sm 551, [1861–73] All ER Rep 952. Though numerous other pre-1939 cases (both English and Irish) were cited, I do not find it necessary to refer to them. I believe for present purposes the position can be adequately summarised as follows. At least the principal ground on which these pre-1939 cases were decided appears to have been that, under the law as it then stood, there could be no effective acknowledgment without an express or implied promise to pay, and a statement of affairs on a bankruptcy could not import any such promise. Lord Campbell CJ put the point very clearly in his judgment in *Everett v Robertson* (at 24):

'It has been decided over and over again that there must have been, within six years of action brought, what is in law a promise to pay; that is, either an express promise or an absolute unconditional admission of the debt, from which the law infers a promise to pay; and it is clear that, if the admission be coupled with some qualification or condition as to paying, inasmuch as the law cannot infer such a promise to pay as would be inconsistent with the qualification or condition expressly attached to the promise, it is insufficient; when a debtor, while acknowledging the debt, says, "I am in difficulties, but if time be given me," or "if my creditors will make a compromise or take a composition, I will pay," the law will not infer an unconditional promise to pay, which is inconsistent with what is said by the debtor.'

In so far as these pre-1939 cases were based on the premise that there can be no effective acknowledgment without an express or implied promise to pay, their ratio decidendi clearly no longer applies in the light of the 1939 Act. In these circumstances, while not conceding the point, counsel for the Department of Employment accepted that as the law now stands, in the light of decisions such as *Jones v Bellegrove Properties Ltd*, there are substantial difficulties in contending that a statement of affairs on a bankruptcy or liquidation can never be an effective acknowlegment.

I prefer to express no concluded view on this point because I do not find it necessary to do so. I should, however, refer in passing to one or two points which have been ventilated in the course of argument and may still conceivably render a statement of affairs distinguishable from a balance sheet for the relevant purposes, even under the post-1939 law. First, it may be said that a statement of affairs is by its nature not a document by which the debtor or his agent admits to any personal liability on the part of the debtor to pay the debt in question, but that it is merely a statement that the creditor is entitled to be paid out of a particular fund: compare, for example, *Courtenay v Williams* (1844) 3 Hare 539 at 550, 67 ER 494 at 499 per Wigram V-C and *Lyall v Fluker* [1873] WN 208 at 209. Second, it may be said that a statement of affairs cannot be an acknowledgment because it is made under compulsion of law: see *Courtenay v Williams* 3 Hare 539 at 550, 67 ER 494 at 499, though if this point has any force, it would apply prima facie to a company's balance sheet. Third, it may be said that a statement of affairs cannot constitute an acknowledgment on the grounds that it is not addressed to the creditor or his agent. On this ground it has been held that the inclusion of a debt by a personal representative in an affidavit sworn for probate purposes is not a sufficient acknowledgment: see, for example, *Re Beaven, Davies, Banks & Co v Beavan* [1912] 1 Ch 196, [1911–13] All ER Rep 793 and *Bowring-Hanbury's trustee v Bowring-Hanbury* [1943] 1 All ER 48, [1943] Ch 104.

Having touched on these points, however, I do not think that, for reasons which will appear, it is useful to prolong this judgment by examining them further. For present purposes I am content to assume in favour of the relevant creditors, without so deciding, that a statement produced on a company receivership or on a company liquidation, albeit in pursuance of a statutory obligation, is capable of constituting an effective acknowledgment for the purpose of the Limitation Act 1939.

On this assumption, there seems to me no reason in principle why any of the documents referred to in para 3 of the amended summons should not be equally capable of constituting an effective acknowledgment if it can properly be said that such document on its true construction expressly or by necessary implication admits the correctness of either the first statement of affairs or the second statement of affairs as at the relevant date. It is true that none of these documents, if read in isolation, would suffice to identify the relevant creditors and the amounts of their debts. On the authority of cases such as the *Kamouh* case, however, this would not matter, since these identities and amounts could be ascertained by extrinsic evidence. Mr Ballard's summary of the first statement of affairs, in my judgment, by necessary implication admitted the correctness of that statement of affairs. So did his letter of 10 January 1972, which enclosed that statement. Though this is more debatable, on the whole I think that his letter of 12 October 1972 should be read together with his earlier letter of 10 January 1972 and thus again as constituting an admission of the correctness of the first statement of affairs. Mr Sherring's affidavit expressly admitted and affirmed the correctness of the second statement of affairs. I think that the Official Receiver's summary of the second statement of affairs and his observations thereon by necessary implication constituted an admission of its correctness.

For these reasons I am again content to assume in favour of the relevant creditors,

without deciding, that all of the documents referred to in para 3 of the amended
a summons are capable of constituting an effective acknowledgment for the purpose of the
Limitation Act 1939. Nevertheless, even on this assumption, there is in my judgment
one short point which inevitably prevents such acknowledgments from rescuing the
relevant creditors from the operation of the Act on the particular facts of the present case.

The short point as advanced by counsel for the Department of Employment may be
summarised thus. Even on the assumption just mentioned in favour of the relevant
b creditors, each of the documents referred to in para 3 of the amended summons can only
at most amount to an admission of past indebtedness on the part of the company *as at 20
August 1971*. Accordingly, even on this footing the causes of action would be deemed to
have accrued on the latter date, ie more than six years before the commencement of the
company's liquidation, and would thus be statute-barred.

In this context counsel for the Department of Employment relied on the decision of
c Brightman J in *Re Gee & Co (Woolwich) Ltd* [1974] 1 All ER 1149, [1975] Ch 52. In that
case the question arose whether a balance sheet showing the position of a company as at
31 December 1965 which had been signed by the directors on 25 November 1966 was
an effective acknowledgment for the purpose of the Limitation Act 1939. The liquidator
contended that it was not, principally on the grounds that an acknowledgment cannot
be effective unless it purports to be an acknowledgment of a debt which was subsisting
d at the date when the acknowledgment was made. A mere acknowledgment of past
liability, it was submitted, would not suffice. Though the report of the argument shows
that reliance was also placed on the decision of Buckley J in *Re Flynn (decd) (No 2), Flynn
v Flynn* [1969] 2 All ER 557 at 562, [1969] 2 Ch 403 at 412, the contention was principally
founded on the Privy Council decision in *Consolidated Agencies Ltd v Bertram Ltd* [1964] 3
All ER 282, [1965] AC 470. Brightman J, after a careful and detailed analysis of this
e decision, rejected this main contention and came to the conclusion that there is no
requirement of English law that an acknowledgment to be effective must be of a debt
which is actually existing at the date when the acknowledgment is written. He concluded
on this point ([1974] 1 All ER 1149 at 1160, [1975] Ch 52 at 70–71):

> 'In my judgment there is nothing in the decision in the *Consolidated Agencies* case
> *f* which entitles me to depart from the clear current of English authority. I shall
> accordingly decide this case on the footing that a balance sheet, if duly signed by the
> directors, is capable of being an effective acknowledgment of the state of indebtedness
> as at the date of the balance sheet, and that, in an appropriate case, the cause of action
> will be deemed to have accrued at the date of the balance sheet, being the date to
> which the signatures of the directors relates. In my judgment the balance sheet of
> the company as at 31st December 1965, signed by the directors on 25th November
> *g* 1966, would have been an effective acknowledgment as at 31st December 1965 of
> the liability of the company so as to take the matter out of the [Limitation Act
> 1939], if the acknowledgment had not been made by the directors in favour of one
> of themselves.'

Thus, in the final outcome, in the *Gee & Co* case the balance sheet failed to qualify as
h an acknowledgment solely because it would have constituted an acknowledgment by
one of the directors in favour of themselves. But for this fact it would have qualified.
Significantly for present purposes, however, it would have qualified not as at the date on
which it was actually signed by the directors or received by the creditor but as at the date
of the balance sheet, being the date to which the signature of the directors related; and
the cause of action would be deemed to have accrued at that date.

I summarised the effect of this part of the *Gee & Co* decision in terms such as this in
j the *Compania de Electricidad* case [1978] 3 All ER 668 at 702, [1980] Ch 146 at 194, and
neither counsel in the present case disputed the correctness of this summary.

In these circumstances, counsel for the liquidator submitted, as I think he had to
submit, that the documents referred to in para 3 of the amended summons on their true
construction constituted not only an admission of indebtedness of the company as at 20

August 1971 but also an admission of continuing indebtedness as at the date of their
respective signatures. He pointed out that the balance sheet of a company is by its very
nature only capable of constituting an admission of the company's indebtedness at one
date, that is to say the date as at which the balance sheet is prepared. In contrast, he
submitted that the documents respectively referred to in para 3 of the amended summons
are capable of being read and should be read as an admission of the company's
indebtedness both as at 20 August 1971 and as at the date of the signature of such
documents.

I find it impossible to read any of them as bearing this sense. Each of the first statement
of affairs and the second statement of affairs and the respective summaries of those two
statements did not purport to do more than show the liabilities of the company to
unsecured creditors as at 20 August 1971, the date specifically mentioned in each of those
documents. By admitting in 1972 or 1978 or 1979 (as the case may be) that a company
which went into receivership on 20 August 1971 and into compulsory liquidation on 24
May 1978 was under a specified liability to a specified unsecured creditor as at 20 August
1971, a person does not, in my judgment, expressly or implicitly admit that the debt in
question is still a liability of the company at the date of the admission. In my judgment,
none of the signatories of the relevant documents can properly be said to have admitted
that any of the relevant debts were still liabilities of the company as at the date of the
signature or indeed to have represented that no defence would be taken on behalf of the
company which might be open to it under the Limitation Act 1939.

In my judgment therefore, counsel for the Department of Employment's overriding
submission is a good one and it is not necessary to decide the further questions whether
the alleged acknowledgments were (a) made by an agent of the company and (b) to the
creditor, within the meaning of the statute. In this context, however, I should record
that, while I think counsel for the Department of Employment accepted that Mr Ballard,
in signing the documents to which he was a party, was acting as agent for the company,
he did not make the like concession in regard to Mr Sherring, because he submitted that,
by the time when Mr Sherring swore his affidavit of 12 September 1978, his powers as a
director of the company had already ceased by virtue of the prior appointment of a
liquidator: see the cases cited in *Buckley on the Companies Acts* (14th edn, 1981) vol 1,
p 673, under note (b) to s 285(2) of the Companies Act 1948.

In the event, I do not propose to answer the questions raised by para 3 of the amended
summons in the precise form in which they are formulated. Subject to any further
submission of counsel, I propose simply to declare that none of the documents respectively
referred to in this para 3 constitutes an acknowledgment within the meaning of ss 23
and 24 of the Limitation Act 1939 by virtue of which the cause of action of any creditor
of the company to recover any debt is deemed to have accrued at a date later than 20
August 1971. I believe that a declaration in this form will suffice to give the liquidator
all the guidance which for practical purposes he requires on this application. I do not
propose to make any declaration in answer to paras 1 and 2 of the summons.

Declaration accordingly.

Solicitors: *Durrant Piesse* (for the liquidator); *Treasury Solicitor*.

Jacqueline Metcalfe   Barrister.

Haslemere Estates Ltd and another v Baker and others

CHANCERY DIVISION

SIR ROBERT MEGARRY V-C

29, 30 OCTOBER, 11 DECEMBER 1981, 10 MARCH 1982

Land charge – Vacation of entry in register – Contract registered as estate contract – Conditional contract relating to land – Condition to be satisfied not by parties but by some extraneous person – Motion to vacate entry.

Land charge – Pending action – Registration – Pending land action – Meaning – Action relating to land or any interest in or charge on land – Action in respect of expenditure incurred by plaintiff in hope of obtaining contract relating to land and in furtherance of that contract when made – Plaintiff claiming payment of fair sum in respect of such expenditure and an order that until payment such sum should be a charge on the land – Whether 'an action relating to an interest in the land' – Land Charges Act 1972, s 17(1).

Charity – Proceedings – Parties – Permissible parties – Charity or charity trustees or any person interested in the charity – Person interested in the charity – Whether party to contract with charity trustees relating to property of charity 'a person interested in the charity' – Charities Act 1960, s 28(1).

The defendant charity trustees had a site which, by virtue of s 29(1)[a] of the Charities Act 1960, they could not sell, lease or otherwise dispose of without an order of the court or the Charity Commissioners. By an order of the Secretary of State, dated 6 January 1971, they were, however, excepted from the provisions of s 29(1) as regards 'any lease' which was executed by them on or before 31 December 1980. In January 1979 they began negotiations with the plaintiffs, a property development company, with a view to entering into an agreement with them under which, in exchange for a premium paid to the defendants, the plaintiffs would build houses and flats on the site and when the houses and flats were completed and sold, the plaintiffs could require the defendants to grant leases of the houses and flats direct to the purchasers thereof. During the course of the negotiations the surveyor advising the defendants pointed out to the plaintiffs that it was his duty to certify to the Charity Commissioners that the price obtained for the site was the best obtainable in the open market. The plaintiffs prepared detailed plans for the development of the site and in November 1979 submitted a formal offer of a premium of £450,000. The defendants accepted the offer, subject to contract and to obtaining planning permission, and warned the plaintiffs that the Charity Commissioners' consent would be required to the transaction. After a draft contract had been prepared the defendants told the plaintiffs that they would exchange contracts only on the basis that the term 'planning permission' in the contract was to include the grant by the Charity Commissioners of an order under s 29 of the 1960 Act authorising the defendants to enter into and complete the agreement and leases. The plaintiffs agreed to that, and the contract was executed on 31 March 1980. The contract was stated to be subject to and conditional on the grant of planning permission before 31 March 1982 and that if planning permission was not granted before that date then the contract was to be 'null and void and of no further effect'. The contract provided for the payment by the plaintiffs of £450,000 within 28 days of their receiving notification of the grant of planning

---

a   Section 29(1) provides: 'Subject to the exceptions provided for by this section, no property forming part of the permanent endowment of a charity shall, without an order of the court or of the Commissioners, be mortgaged or charged by way of security for the repayment of money borrowed, nor, in the case of land in England or Wales, be sold, leased or otherwise disposed of.'

permission, for a further payment of £500 per annum until the whole development was
let and for the grant of leases (unit leases) by the defendants to the purchasers of the
houses and flats when completed. The final clause in the contract stated that neither the
contract nor anything contained in it or done in pursuance of it 'except the granting of a
unit lease' was to 'operate as an actual or present demise of the site or any part thereof or
create any leasehold interest therein or tenancy thereof'. The plaintiffs received planning
permission on 20 May 1980 and on 13 June registered the contract as an estate contract
within the meaning of s 2(4)[b] of the Land Charges Act 1972. Meanwhile the Charity
Commissioners told the defendants on 7 May 1980 that in their opinion the 1971 order
of the Secretary of State did not cover the proposed transaction with the plaintiffs, that
they had received on 22 April 1980 a report by the defendants' surveyor which stated
that although £450,000 appeared to be the best price obtainable from the plaintiffs it
was not in his opinion the best price that could be obtained on the open market, and that
consequently they wished to discuss the matter with the defendants before deciding
whether to authorise the transaction with the plaintiffs. After further negotiations it was
decided that the defendants should use the plaintiffs' plans for the purpose of inviting
tenders from other developers as well as the plaintiffs for the development of the site and
that if a better offer than the plaintiffs' was accepted the defendants should pay the
plaintiffs £100,000. A contract to that effect was executed by the plaintiffs and the
defendants on 15 September with the approval of the Charity Commissioners. Offers
were received from other developers.

On 12 March 1981, while the offers were under consideration, the defendants asked
the plaintiffs to have the registration of the estate contract vacated. The plaintiffs refused
and brought an action against the defendants seeking (i) a declaration that on the true
construction of the 1971 order and, inter alia, s 29(1) of the 1960 Act, the order was
sufficient consent for the purpose of s 29(1) and that the contract of 31 March 1980 had
become unconditional on the grant of planning permission on 20 May 1980 and ought
to be performed and carried into execution by the defendants, (ii) alternatively, an order
under s 29(1) of the 1960 Act authorising the defendants to perform their part of the
contract and grant the leases to be granted under it, (iii) alternatively, an order that the
defendants pay the plaintiffs such sum as the court considered represented the fair value
of the time, trouble and expenditure incurred by the plaintiffs in relation to the
negotiations for planning permission and for the contract (on the ground that the
plaintiffs had been encouraged by the defendants to expend the time and money involved
in the expectation that the plaintiffs would obtain an interest in the site), and an order
that until payment such sum should be a charge on the site. The plaintiffs registered the
action as a 'pending land action' within the meaning of s 17[c] of the 1972 Act. The
defendants applied by motion for an order (i) for the vacation of the entry of the estate
contract in the Land Charges Register, (ii) for the vacation of the entry in the same
register of the pending land action, and (iii) for the plaintiffs' alternative claim for relief
under s 29(1) of the 1960 Act to be struck out as disclosing no cause of action in 'charity
proceedings' as defined in s 28[d] of that Act.

Held – (1) The Secretary of State's order of 1971 did not cover the contract because it was
not a 'lease' or even an agreement for a lease within the terms of the 1971 order and so
did not become registrable as an unconditional contract on the grant of planning
permission, because it still required authorisation under s 29(1) of the 1960 Act. Although
it was arguable that, as the outstanding condition had to be satisfied not by the parties to
the contract but by an outside body, the contract was a 'conditional contract relating to
land' and as such might be registrable as an estate contract within the meaning of s 2(4)
of the 1972 Act, that was a matter which should be decided not on a motion but at the

---

b   Section 2(4), so far as material, is set out at p 531 c, post
c   Section 17, so far as material, is set out at p 534 e, post
d   Section 28, so far as material, is set out at p 535 e to j, post

trial of the action, and therefore the application to vacate the entry of the estate contract
would be dismissed (see p 531 g to j and p 533 a b and j to p 534 d, post); *Milner v*
Staffordshire Congregational Union (Inc) [1956] 1 All ER 494, *Manchester Diocesan Council for*
Education v Commercial and General Investments Ltd [1969] 3 All ER 1593 and *Michael*
Richards Properties Ltd v St Saviour's Parish, Southwark [1975] 3 All ER 416 considered.

(2) The plaintiffs' claim, based on proprietary estoppel, in respect of the time spent and
expenditure incurred by them in respect of planning permission and the contract was a
claim to money and was not a 'claim relating to . . . an interest in . . . land', and it did not
become a 'pending land action' within s 17(1) of the 1972 Act merely because the
plaintiffs were seeking an order that until payment the money should be a charge on the
land. Accordingly, an order would be made for the vacation of the entry of the pending
land action (see p 534 j to p 535 b, post); dictum of Lord Denning MR in *Hussey v Palmer*
[1972] 3 All ER at 747–748 considered.

(3) The plaintiffs' alternative claim for an order of the court under s 29(1) of the 1960
Act would be struck out because, by virtue of s 28(1) of that Act, the court could make
such an order only in proceedings which were brought by the charity or the charity
trustees 'or by any person interested in the charity' and the plaintiffs were not persons so
interested (see p 536 j to p 537 d, post).

Notes

For statutory restrictions on the disposal of property belonging to a charity, see 5
Halsbury's Laws (4th edn) para 804.

For the Charities Act 1960, ss 2, 28, 29, see 3 Halsbury's Statutes (3rd edn) 591, 627,
629.

For the Land Charges Act 1972, ss 2, 17, see 42 ibid 1593, 1618.

Cases referred to in judgment

Davis v Nisbett (1861) 10 CBNS 752, 142 ER 649, 31(2) Digest (Reissue) 704, 5752.
Hussey v Palmer [1972] 3 All ER 744, [1972] 1 WLR 1286, CA, Digest (Cont Vol D) 1007,
814b.
Lehmann v McArthur (1868) LR 3 Ch App 496, 28(2) Digest (Reissue) 1022, 479.
London and South Western Rly Co v Gomm (1882) 20 Ch D 562, [1881–5] All ER Rep 1190,
CA, 11 Digest (Reissue) 318, 2018.
Manchester Diocesan Council for Education v Commercial and General Investments Ltd [1969]
3 All ER 1593, [1970] 1 WLR 241, 12 Digest (Reissue) 82, 429.
Milner v Staffordshire Congregational Union (Inc) [1956] 1 All ER 494, [1956] Ch 275, [1956]
2 WLR 556, 8(1) Digest (Reissue) 422, 1560.
Pritchard v Briggs [1980] 1 All ER 294, [1980] Ch 338, [1979] 3 WLR 868, CA; *rvsg*
[1978] 1 All ER 886, [1980] Ch 338, [1978] 2 WLR 317.
Rawlplug Co Ltd v Kamvale Properties Ltd (1968) 20 P & CR 32, Digest (Cont Vol C) 829,
926d.
Rendall v Blair (1890) 45 Ch D 139, CA, 8(1) Digest (Reissue) 461, 2153.
Richards (Michael) Properties Ltd v St Saviour's Parish, Southwark [1975] 3 All ER 416,
Digest (Cont Vol D) 800, 1088a.
Smith v Butler [1900] 1 QB 694, CA, 40 Digest (Repl) 266, 2232.
Thomas v Rose [1968] 3 All ER 765, [1968] 1 WLR 1797, Digest (Cont Vol C) 827, 925aa.
Turley v Mackay [1943] 2 All ER 1, [1944] Ch 37, 38 Digest (Repl) 882, 925.
Williams v Burlington Investments (1977) 121 SJ 424, HL.

Cases also cited

Aberfoyle Plantations Ltd v Cheng [1959] 3 All ER 910, [1960] AC 115, PC.
Benthall v Kilmorey (Earl) (1883) 25 Ch D 39, CA.
Brewer Street Investments Ltd v Barclays Woollen Co Ltd [1953] 2 All ER 1330, [1954] 1 QB
428, CA.
Calgary and Edmonton Land Co Ltd v Dobinson [1974] 1 All ER 484, [1974] Ch 102.

Holme v Guy (1877) 5 Ch D 901, CA.
Lipmans Wallpaper Ltd v Mason & Hodghton Ltd [1968] 1 All ER 1123, [1969] 1 Ch 20.   *a*
Prenn v Simmonds [1971] 3 All ER 237, [1971] 1 WLR 1381, HL.
Willmott v Barber (1880) 15 Ch D 96.

Motion
On 15 May 1981 the plaintiffs, Haslemere Estates Ltd and Carlos Estates Ltd, brought an
action against the defendants, Charles William Baker (sued on his own behalf and on   *b*
behalf of all the other estates governors of the charity known as Alleyn's College of God's
Gift at Dulwich) and Montagu Evans (a firm), seeking as against the first defendants: (1)
a declaration that on the true construction of an order of the Secretary of State for
Education and Science dated 6 January 1971 and of ss 2(1) and 29(1) of the Charities Act
1960 and in the events that had happened an agreement dated 31 March 1980 between
the plaintiffs and the first defendants had become unconditional and ought to be   *c*
performed and carried into execution by the first defendants; (2) alternatively, (a) an
order under s 29(1) of the 1960 Act authorising the first defendants to perform their part
of the agreement dated 31 March 1980 and to grant the leases to be granted pursuant
thereto or (b) an inquiry whether it would be for the benefit of the charity that such an
order should be made and, if so, an order accordingly; (3) alternatively, (a) an order that
the first defendants pay to the plaintiffs such sum as the court should find represented   *d*
the fair value of the time and trouble of the plaintiffs and the expenditure incurred by
them in and for the purpose of the negotiations for the agreement of 31 March 1981 and
for planning permission, from such date as the court thought proper, (b) interest thereon,
(c) an order that until payment such sum and interest should be a charge on the land
referred to in the agreement; (4) alternatively, damages for misrepresentation and interest
thereon; claiming against the second defendants damages for negligence and interest   *e*
thereon; and against both defendants further or other relief. On 20 May 1981 the
plaintiffs registered the action under the Land Charges Act 1972 as a 'pending land
action'. By a notice of motion dated 10 July 1981 the first defendants sought (i) an order
for the vacation of an entry of an estate contract registered by the plaintiffs in the Land
Charges Register on 13 June 1980, (ii) an order for the vacation of the entry in the same
register of the pending land action and (iii) an order that the claim for a declaration in   *f*
the plaintiffs' statement of claim and their alternative claim for relief under s 29(1) of the
1960 Act should be struck out as disclosing no cause of action. The facts are set out in the
judgment.

Leolin Price QC and *Gordon Nurse* for the first defendants.
Richard Scott QC and *David Burton* for the plaintiffs.   *g*

Cur adv vult

10 March. **SIR ROBERT MEGARRY V-C** read the following judgment: This is a
motion by the first defendants in an action. In it, they seek the vacation of the entry of
an estate contract registered in the Land Charges Register on 13 June 1980, and of the   *h*
entry in the same register of a pending land action registered on 20 May 1981. In
addition, they ask for an order striking out a paragraph in the statement of claim and the
corresponding prayer for relief, seeking relief under the Charities Act 1960, s 29(1). The
proceedings relate to a building which stands in a conservation area and is known as
Hambledon House, Dulwich Common. The house and the grounds are nearly 5 acres in
extent. I shall refer to this as 'the site', as it is in the pleadings. The site is vested in the   *j*
first defendants, the Estates Governors of Alleyn's College of God's Gift at Dulwich: I
shall call them 'the governors'. They are the trustees of a well-known charity: and under
s 29(1) of the Charities Act 1960, the site cannot be 'sold, leased or otherwise disposed of'
without an order of the court or the Charity Commissioners. The second defendants are
a firm of chartered surveyors who were advising the governors: I shall call them 'the

a surveyors'. The plaintiffs make a money claim against them, and they play a part in the history of the case, but they are not directly involved in the motion, and were not represented before me. The plaintiffs are two companies which specialise in the refurbishing of buildings of historic and special architectural importance. The second plaintiffs are the wholly-owned subsidiary of the first, and it is not necessary to distinguish between them. Mr Scott and Mr Burton appeared for the plaintiffs and Mr Price and Mr Nurse for the first defendants.

b Hambledon House has not been occupied for some ten years, and it is in a dilapidated condition, aggravated by the operations of vandals. Some scheme for the comprehensive redevelopment of the site by someone is plainly desirable, and it is out of such a proposed scheme that this litigation has arisen. Early in 1979 negotiations between the plaintiffs and the governors began. At that time there was in existence an order of the Secretary of State for Education and Science, dated 6 January 1971, which excepted the governors c from s 29(1) of the Charities Act 1960 as regards 'any Lease which is executed by the Estates Governors on or before 31st December 1980'; and see s 29(4). The initial correspondence was between the plaintiffs and the governors, but soon the governors brought the surveyors into the picture. A letter to the plaintiffs from the surveyors dated 8 June 1979 refers to the duty of the surveyors to certify to the Charity Commissioners that the price obtained for the site was the best obtainable in the open market; and on 26 d June this duty was mentioned again after the plaintiffs had said that their maximum offer would be £350,000. A letter from the plaintiffs dated 17 July 1979 which set out the mixture of houses and flats proposed to be erected also confirmed a formal offer of this figure for a building lease, with a quarter of the net development proceeds, as defined; and on 23 July the surveyors informed the plaintiffs that they had recommended this offer to the governors. On 27 July the surveyors wrote to the plaintiffs to say that the e governors had accepted the proposals on certain terms there set out. This, of course, like the rest of the correspondence, was subject to contract. A letter from the plaintiffs dated 30 July affirms this, and states that the agreement is subject to obtaining planning consent.

At this stage the plaintiffs' architects were preparing some detailed drawings for discussion with the governors. After some revisions to the proposals, on 9 November f 1979 the plaintiffs made an improved offer of a premium of £450,000 and a further payment of £15,000 as fees for the governors' architect; and this the governors accepted on 19 November, again, of course, subject to contract. By this stage the solicitors for the parties were in correspondence with each other on a draft contract; and on 12 December the governors' solicitors informed the plaintiffs' solicitors that they understood from the Charity Commissioners that their consent would be required to the development g agreement and form of lease; and a week later the governors' solicitors repeated this. A letter to them from the Charity Commissioners dated 31 December 1979 confirmed that this was the view of the Charity Commissioners; and on 11 January 1980 the plaintiffs' solicitors noted the contents of this letter, expressing the hope that the Charity Commissioners would be content with approving the agreement and standard form of leases.

h On 11 March 1980 the governors' solicitors wrote to the Charity Commissioners, seeking approval of the terms of the draft development agreement with the plaintiffs, and the form of draft lease. On 14 March the governors' solicitors wrote to the plaintiffs' solicitors saying that the governors wished to exchange agreements only on the basis that the definition of 'planning permission' in cl 1.9 of the agreement was to 'include the granting by the Charity Commissioners of an order under section 29 of the Charities Act j 1960 authorising our clients to enter into and complete the development agreement and the leases'; and on 28 March the plaintiffs' solicitors agreed to this. On 31 March the agreement was executed. In it, the governors are called 'the landlords' and the second plaintiffs are called 'the builder'.

Clause 1 of the agreement consists of definitions. 'Unit' is defined as meaning a self-contained flat, maisonette or house forming part of the development, and 'unit lease' as a

lease for 99 years at a ground rent of £50 a year in one of the agreed forms of lease, with
such variations as are agreed by the builder and the landlords and, if necessary, approved   *a*
by the Charity Commissioners. There is an elaborate definition of planning permission
which does not refer to the provision as to the Charity Commissioners' order that had
been agreed in correspondence. 'Operative date' means 28 days after the builder receives
a copy of the notification of the grant of planning permission, and the 'conditional date'
is two years after the date of the contract, and so is 31 March 1982. The 'building period'
is four years from the operative date.   *b*

There is then cl 2.1 of the agreement: 'The following provisions of this Agreement are
subject to and conditional upon the grant of Planning Permission before the Conditional
Date.' Clause 2.2 provides for a joint application for planning permission to be made
forthwith, and cl 2.3 states that if planning permission 'is not granted before the
Conditional Date then this Agreement shall be and become null and void and of no
further effect', without prejudice to any accrued rights. By cl 3 the builder is to pay the   *c*
landlords £450,000 on the operative date, with a further £500 a year during the building
period and until the whole of the development is let. On request by the builder's
solicitors, the landlords are to enter into an agreement for a unit lease 'and/or a unit lease'
on the first sale of any unit, and duly execute it (or them), with the builder joining in
and receiving the whole of any deposit and premium paid for any lease (cl 13). Finally,
by cl 17, neither the contract nor anything contained in it or done in pursuance of it   *d*
('except the granting of a unit lease') is to 'operate as an actual or present demise of the
Site or any part thereof or create any leasehold interest therein or tenancy thereof'.

On 7 May the Charity Commissioners wrote to the governors' solicitors. They
expressed the view that the order of the Secretary of State dated 6 January 1971 did not
cover the transaction proposed, and that the prior consent of the Charity Commissioners
was requisite for it. They then referred to a report by the governors' surveyors dated 22   *e*
April 1980 which stated that although £450,000 appeared to be the best price obtainable
from the plaintiffs, in their opinion it was not the best price that could be obtained on
the open market. The Charity Commissioners then sought further information on
various matters, including the advertising which had resulted in the offer made by the
plaintiffs, and said that a meeting with the governors to discuss the matter could be
arranged. This, of course, came as a blow to the plaintiffs, who had spent considerable   *f*
sums of money in preparing plans for the development. The surveyors' report, I may
say, is the subject of complaint by the plaintiffs against the surveyors.

On 20 May 1980 the Southwark London Borough Council sent the plaintiffs' architect
a notice that the proposed development would be permitted, subject to certain conditions.
This satisfied cl 2.1 of the contract as executed, though not, of course, the addition to it
about an order of the Charity Commissioners that had been agreed in correspondence.   *g*
On 13 June the plaintiffs registered the contract as a class C(iv) land charge. After much
discussion by the governors with those concerned, it was decided that the governors
would invite tenders for the proposed development from a number of other possible
developers in addition to the plaintiffs, but on the basis of the grant of a building lease
for 125 years at a premium and ground rent. For this purpose, the plans prepared by the
plaintiffs were to be used, and if the plaintiffs' tender was not successful, the governors   *h*
would pay them £100,000. With the approval of the Charity Commissioners a contract
to this effect between the governors and the plaintiffs was made on 15 September 1980.
In the event, a better offer than the plaintiffs' was made, though this was for a form of
development which differed from that proposed by the plaintiffs; and the Charity
Commissioners required the governors to explore certain conditional offers made by
certain developers who had not submitted a tender. An undated letter from the Charity   *j*
Commissioners to the chairman of the governors, sent towards the end of January 1981,
shows that, subject to planning permission, two firms were willing to offer £750,000,
with one of them offering a further £200,000 on completion of the houses.

By March 1981 the governors had been to leading counsel; and on 12 March the
governors' solicitors wrote asking the plaintiffs' solicitors to have the registration of the

estate contract vacated forthwith. On 30 March the plaintiffs' solicitors wrote a reasoned
a reply, refusing to do this; and they issued the writ on 15 May and registered it as a
pending land action on 20 May. The governors' notice of motion was dated 10 July, and
after various vicissitudes it came before me on 29 October. Despite my warning at the
outset that I was available for only two days, counsel for the first defendants elected to
proceed with the motion; and ultimately it proved impossible to arrange the third day
that the hearing was found to require before 11 December.

b   I shall take first the question whether the contract dated 31 March 1980 is registrable
as a class C(iv) land charge. By s 2(1) of the Land Charges Act 1972, 'If a charge on or
obligation affecting land' falls into one of the classes described in s 2 it is registrable as a
land charge; and by s 2(4)(iv)—

c   'an estate contract is a contract by an estate owner . . . to convey or create a legal
          estate, including a contract conferring either expressly or by statutory implication a
          valid option to purchase, a right of pre-emption or any other like right.'

In this case there has been much argument about the word 'contract' in the subsection,
and whether the contract in dispute is an unconditional contract, or whether it is merely
conditional, and if it is, whether as such it is registrable. I am not sure that on this motion
it is strictly necessary to resolve all that has been argued, but it may help the parties if I
d say something about the major contentions.
       The primary contention of counsel for the plaintiffs is that in the events which have
occurred there is an unconditional contract. His argument ran on the following lines. By
cl 2.1 of the contract all the operative provisions of the contract were 'subject to and
conditional upon the grant of Planning Permission' before 31 March 1982; and by virtue
of the letters of 14 and 28 March 1980, the grant of planning permission was to include
e the making of an order of the Charity Commissioners authorising the governors to 'enter
into and complete' the contract. This sub-clause, however, must be read as if the words
'if necessary for compliance with s 29 of the Charities Act 1960' had been added to it,
since the purpose of the sub-clause in its revised form was to ensure that the section was
complied with. In fact, no such order by the Charity Commissioners was necessary, for
at the date of the contract the order of the Secretary of State of 6 January 1971 was still
f operative, and this excepted the governors from s 29(1) as regards 'any Lease which is
executed by the Estates Governors on or before 31st December 1980'. This provision was
wide enough to apply to any agreement for a lease executed by that date, and the contract
fell within that description.
       That is the contention; but I cannot accept it. First, I can see no real reason for
construing the word 'lease' in the 1971 order as including an agreement for a lease. The
g order in terms refers to s 29(1) as requiring that certain charity land 'shall not be leased'
without an order of the court or the Secretary of State, and then exempts the governors
as regards 'any lease which is executed' by them before 1981. Thus out of the statutory
words 'sold, leased or otherwise disposed of' the order has selected the one word 'leased'.
There is no question of the order being nugatory if it does not include any agreement for
a lease, for many leases are granted without there being any antecedent agreement for a
h lease. As a letter from the Charity Commissioners dated 7 May 1980 shows, the governors
own over 4,000 income-producing properties, and it is readily understandable that there
should be an order which freed the governors from the recurrent obligation to obtain
from the Charity Commissioners an order in respect of every lease which, being granted
for over 22 years or wholly or partly in consideration of a fine, stood outside the exception
in s 29(3)(*b*).
j   There are further difficulties. Even if the word 'leased' in the order includes an
agreement for a lease, I cannot see that the contract in this case is an agreement for a lease
in any real sense of the word. There is no agreement that the governors should grant the
plaintiffs any sort of lease or tenancy of the site, since cl 17 expressly excludes this. The
most that can be said is that the governors have agreed with the plaintiffs that on request
by the plaintiffs' solicitors the governors will enter into agreements and leases for units

yet to be built with unidentified persons at unascertained dates. The contract is essentially
a building agreement and not an agreement for a lease. Furthermore, the construction *a*
for which counsel for the plaintiffs contends would render the limitation of date on the
order ineffective to a greater or lesser degree. Provided any agreement for a lease was
entered into before 1981 (as this contract was), the leases themselves could be granted
years after 1980 had ended. I would not construe the order as authorising this. In my
judgment there is no unconditional contract in existence.

On that footing, the question is whether the contract is a conditional contract which is *b*
registrable as an estate contract. Counsel for the first defendants contended that it was
not, for a variety of reasons. First, the contract was void, or at least ineffective, because it
had been made without the approval of the Charity Commissioners. Second, even if
initially it was valid, it had come to an end because the Charity Commissioners had
refused to approve it. Third, even if it continued to exist as a valid conditional contract,
such contracts were not registrable as estate contracts. I shall take the three heads in turn. *c*

For his contention that the contract was void, counsel for the first defendants
understandably relied on *Milner v Staffordshire Congregational Union (Inc)* [1956] 1 All ER
494, [1956] Ch 275. The Charitable Trusts Amendment Act 1855, s 29, provided that 'It
shall not be lawful' for charity trustees 'to make or grant . . . any sale, mortgage, or charge
of the charity estate', unless this was done under certain authorisations or with the
consent of the Charity Commissioners. Charity trustees made an unconditional contract *d*
to sell some charity land at a time when they lacked any authority or consent under s 29.
The purchaser then repudiated the contract, and subsequently the Charity Commissioners
gave their consent to the sale. Danckwerts J, a little hesitantly, held that the 'sale' had
been made when the contract had been entered into, and that as this had been done in
breach of s 29, no lawful contract had been made, and the purchaser was not bound. That
decision, however, was distinguished by Buckley J in *Manchester Diocesan Council for* *e*
Education v Commercial and General Investments Ltd [1969] 3 All ER 1593, [1970] 1 WLR
241, where the somewhat different wording of a scheme gave authority for the governing
body of a charity to sell land, though the sale was to be conditional on approval of the
price by the Minister of Education. Buckley J held that the absence of ministerial
approval did not invalidate the contract for sale, although it would invalidate the
conveyance if not obtained in time. In *Michael Richards Properties Ltd v St Saviour's Parish,* *f*
Southwark [1975] 3 All ER 416 the question arose under the Charities Act 1960, s 29(1),
in relation to a contract which was expressed to be 'subject to the approval of the Charity
Commissioners'. This point had been reserved by Danckwerts J in the *Milner* case [1956]
1 All ER 494 at 498, [1956] Ch 275 at 282. Goff J had little difficulty in distinguishing
the *Milner* case. He held that the contract was not invalidated by s 29(1) of the Charities
Act 1960. He said ([1975] 3 All ER 416 at 421): 'Such a condition is precedent and *g*
therefore either the consent is not forthcoming when cadit quaestio, or if it be, the
contract becomes effective only when the consent is given.'

In the present case, the effect of the exchange of letters in March 1980 was that cl 2.1
of the contract operated to make all the provisions of the contract, apart from the opening
words, cl 1, and cl 2.1 itself, 'subject to and conditional upon' the Charity Commissioners
making an order under s 29 of the Charities Act 1960, authorising the governors to enter *h*
into and complete both the contract and the leases. There is a curious element of
circularity here: the parties enter into an agreement that nearly all the agreement is
subject to an order being made authorising the governors to do what they have done,
namely, enter into the agreement. But looking at the substance, it seems plain to me that
it is the *Michael Richards* case that applies rather than the *Milner* case, so that I do not
think that the contract is invalidated by s 29(1) of the Charities Act 1960. I should say *j*
that counsel for the plaintiffs said that he could not ask me not to follow the *Milner* case,
but he did want to keep the point open so that in a higher court he could contend that it
was wrong.

That, however, is not the end of the *Michael Richards* case; for there are the words of
Goff J saying that if the consent is forthcoming, 'the contract becomes effective only
when the consent is given'. From this flows the contention that where, as here, there has

been no consent, the contract, though not struck down by s 29(1), remains nevertheless

a ineffective until the consent is given. On that footing there is no more than an ineffective contract, and an ineffective contract is not, it is said, registrable as an estate contract. Counsel for the plaintiffs said that Goff J cannot have meant that there was no contract, or no registrable contract; but he was hard put to it to find any understandable reason for saying this. I think that Goff J meant what he said in this characteristically closely-reasoned passage in his judgment. The whole basis of the escape from s 29(1) is that there

b is no contract in existence which offends against the subsection.

The second submission of counsel for the first defendants was that when the Charity Commissioners refused to approve the contract, the contract thereupon ceased to exist. He took as an analogy a lessee who sold his lease subject to obtaining the lessor's consent to the assignment. Once the lessee had made a genuine attempt to obtain this consent, and it had failed, the result was that the contract to assign the lease was at an end. It could

c not be said that there was still a conditional contract in existence, with the lessee remaining under an obligation to make repeated efforts to persuade the lessor to change his mind and consent to the assignment.

I do not find this analogy persuasive. If the Charity Commissioners not only had refused to approve the contract with the plaintiffs but also had approved some other disposition to some other party, then there would be great force in counsel for the first

d defendants' submission. But as the evidence stands this is not the case. If after investigation no other proposal is approved by the Charity Commissioners, then the contract with the plaintiffs might still emerge as the best that the governors can obtain, and so the Charity Commissioners might authorise it after all. Counsel for the first defendants referred to *Smith v Butler* [1900] 1 QB 694, a very different case; but if the test is whether or not the parties are justified in treating a refusal of consent as being final, I

e would say that this has not been established in the present case. I did not find much assistance in *Davis v Nisbett* (1861) 10 CBNS 752, 142 ER 649 or *Lehmann v McArthur* (1868) LR 3 Ch App 496, which were also cited.

Third, there is the question whether a conditional contract is registrable as an estate contract at all. Counsel for the plaintiffs contended that it was. His argument was that a conditional contract to dispose of land created an interest in that land, and was certainly

f an 'obligation affecting land' within the Land Charges Act 1972, s 2(1), if the landowner had put it out of his power to determine whether or not the condition was satisfied. If that test was applied to the present case, the contract fell into that category, and was registrable. This submission was primarily based on *London and South Western Rly Co v Gomm* (1882) 20 Ch D 562 at 580–581, [1881–5] All ER Rep 1190 at 1193 and *Pritchard v Briggs* [1980] 1 All ER 294, [1980] Ch 338. In the latter case it was held that whereas an

g option over land created an interest in it, a right of pre-emption did not, and this, it was said, provided a parallel for conditional contracts which did and did not create an interest in land. Here, the conditions which had to be satisfied were not within the control of the governors, so that by making the conditional contract they had created an interest in land, or at any rate an 'obligation affecting land'. Counsel for the plaintiffs further contended that a contract was registrable as a land charge even if, without requiring any

h legal estate to be conveyed or created, it was capable of requiring this. For this purpose he relied on the concluding words of s 2(4)(iv) of the Land Charges Act 1972, namely, 'including a contract conferring either expressly or by statutory implication a valid option to purchase, a right of pre-emption or any other like right'. In their context, the last five words included a conditional contract, he said, whereas counsel for the first defendants contended that these last words should be construed not widely but narrowly. However,

j counsel for the plaintiffs cited *Williams v Burlington Investments Ltd* (1977) 121 SJ 424, putting before me a print of the speeches in the House of Lords. This case concerned an agreement by a purchaser of land that on the vendor's request he would enter into a legal charge on whatever part of the land he was purchasing remained unsold at the time of the request; and this was held registrable as an estate contract. This certainly provides some support for counsel for the plaintiffs.

I have to remember that this is a motion, and not the trial of the action. There was no

issue between counsel for the plaintiffs and counsel for the first defendants as to the
proper approach of the court on a motion to vacate entries on the Land Charges Register. *a*
I remain of the view that because registration of a land charge is so easy, and it is such a
potent weapon, the court ought, on motion, to have a certain robustness of approach
when an order to vacate an entry is sought; but if there is a fair, arguable case in support
of the registration, the matter must stand over until the trial of the action: see *Rawlplug
Co Ltd v Kamvale Properties Ltd* (1968) 20 P & CR 32 at 40. In this case, there is no doubt
about the parties having made an agreement in relation to the site; it is not one of the *b*
common cases where the existence of any agreement at all is in dispute. I feel no doubt
about holding that no unconditional contract exists, but I am far from having the
requisite degree of assurance that the conditional contract is not registrable. Indeed, as at
present advised I incline to the view that a conditional contract relating to land is
registrable as an estate contract if the condition is one that is to be satisfied not by the
parties but by some extraneous person or event. I say nothing about other conditional *c*
contracts. Such a contract is one of which third parties ought to be warned by registration;
and I bear in mind the wide construction put on the language of class C(iv) in *Turley v
Mackay* [1943] 2 All ER 1, [1944] Ch 37: see *Thomas v Rose* [1968] 3 All ER 765, [1968] 1
WLR 1797. Further, the *Milner* point is certainly not beyond argument, nor is it beyond
possibility that the Charity Commissioners will approve the contract before 31 March
1982. Accordingly, I reject the application to vacate the entry of the estate contract. If *d*
when 31 March arrives the Charity Commissioners have still made no Order authorising
the governors to enter into and complete the contract and the leases, I cannot at present
see how the registration could any longer be maintained; but this has not been argued
out, and I decide nothing on it.

I turn to the registration of the pending land action. What is registrable is 'any action
or proceeding pending in court relating to land or any interest in or charge on land': see *e*
the Land Charges Act 1972, s 17(1). Counsel for the plaintiffs says that this requirement
is satisfied by the claim in the statement of claim based on proprietary estoppel. This
claim is in respect of the plaintiffs' waste of time and their expenditure incurred in
relation to the negotiations for the planning permission and for the contract, or for the
part of it wasted and incurred after 7 August 1980 or 20 November 1980, as having been
spent and incurred at the request of the governors, in the expectation, created and *f*
encouraged by them, that the plaintiffs would obtain the interest in the site conferred by
the contract. The prayer is for payment to the plaintiffs of the fair value of this time and
trouble and the expenditure, and for 'An order that until payment such sum and interest
shall be a charge upon the Site'. It is common ground that there is an arguable case that
the money was spent under encouragement from the governors, and it is also clear that
the expenditure was made not on the site but on plans and so on in relation to the site. *g*

The contention of counsel for the plaintiffs opens a very wide door. Many a developer
spends much time and trouble in putting forward schemes for the development of land
in the hope, often encouraged by the landowner, of obtaining a contract and planning
permission; and in many cases neither contract nor planning permission is obtained.
Here, it seems plain that much of the plaintiffs' expenditure was incurred before the
conditional contract was signed on 31 March 1980. It would be remarkable if every *h*
developer who did this were to be held to be entitled to reimbursement and a charge on
the land until payment. Counsel for the plaintiffs relied on some words in *Hussey v
Palmer* [1972] 3 All ER 744 at 747–748, [1972] 1 WLR 1286 at 1290 for some far-
reaching contentions which would raise a proprietary estoppel whenever justice and
good conscience require it.

I do not think that the subject is as wide and as indefinite as that. Here the expenditure *j*
was made in the hope of obtaining a contract relating to the land, and in furtherance of
that contract when it had been made. There was no legitimate hope or expectation of
obtaining any interest in the land at all; the contract was to yield premiums to the
plaintiffs when the leases were granted, but not estates or interests in the land. In my
view, a right to money remains a right to money and does not become a claim to an
interest in land just because when the claim to the money is launched the plaintiffs seek

an order that until payment the money shall be a charge on the site. I cannot see that the
a statement of claim puts forward any claim which relates 'to land or any interest in or
charge on land'. The claim relates to money, and to a charge on the land which does not
exist but which the plaintiffs hope the court will create if the money claim succeeds; and
such a claim does not appear to me to be even arguably a pending land action. The only
hesitation I feel on the point is that the arguments put before me did not explore the
subject in any great depth; but on the arguments that were advanced, and on my
b reflections on the matter, I have reached the conclusion that the claim that there is a
pending land action is altogether too tenuous to support the registration, and that the
entry should be vacated.

That brings me to the third head, the governors' claim that para 24 of the statement of
claim and the second prayer for relief should be struck out as disclosing no cause of action
in these proceedings. Under para 24 the plaintiffs say that if they are wrong in their
c contention that the order of the Secretary of State dated 6 January 1971 is a sufficient
consent under the Charities Act 1960 (as I have held that they are) then they ask—

> 'for an Order of the Court pursuant to Section 29(1) of the above Act authorising
> the governors to perform their part of the said Agreement dated 31st March 1980
> and grant the leases to be granted pursuant thereto: alternatively, for an inquiry
> *d* whether it would be for the benefit of the said Charity that such an Order should be
> made and an Order accordingly, if it should be so found.'

The second prayer for relief substantially repeats para 24.

This application raises questions as to the effect of s 28 of the Charities Act 1960.
Subsection (1) is as follows:

> *e* 'Charity proceedings may be taken with reference to a charity either by the
> charity, or by any of the charity trustees, or by any person interested in the charity,
> or by any two or more inhabitants of the area of the charity, if it is a local charity,
> but not by any other person.'

Subsection (8) provides:

> *f* 'In this section "charity proceedings" means proceedings in any court in England
> or Wales brought under the court's jurisdiction with respect to charities, or brought
> under the court's jurisdiction with respect to trusts in relation to the administration
> of a trust for charitable purposes.'

The plaintiffs accept that their claim constitutes 'charity proceedings' and that s 28
applies. Then subsection (2) provides:
g
> 'Subject to the following provisions of this section, no charity proceedings relating
> to a charity (other than an exempt charity) shall be entertained or proceeded with in
> any court unless the taking of the proceedings is authorised by order of the
> Commissioners.'

It is common ground that the proceedings have not been authorised by any order of the
h Charity Commissioners, so that in this respect they are not properly constituted as they
stand. Then by subsection (3):

> 'The Commissioners shall not, without special reasons, authorise the taking of
> charity proceedings where in their opinion the case can be dealt with by them under
> the powers of this Act.'

j I need not read subsection (4); but subsection (5) provides:

> 'Where the foregoing provisions of this section require the taking of charity
> proceedings to be authorised by an order of the Commissioners, the proceedings
> may nevertheless be entertained or proceeded with if after the order had been
> applied for and refused leave to take the proceedings was obtained from one of the
> judges of the High Court attached to the Chancery Division.'

Counsel for the first defendants contended, first, that an order of the court will not satisfy the contract. What the letters of 14 and 28 March 1980 added onto cl 1.9 of the contract was a provision that 'planning permission' was to include 'the granting by the Charity Commissioners of an order under Section 29 of the Charities Act 1960' authorising the governors to enter into and complete the agreement and the leases. The letters did not make any provision for an order of the court in place of an order by the Charity Commissioners. Literally, of course, counsel for the first defendants is right; but I do not see why the greater authority of an order of the court should not be held to satisfy the lesser requirement of an order of the Charity Commissioners for exactly the same purpose.

Second, counsel for the first defendants submitted that the plaintiffs did not fall within the term 'any person interested in the charity' in s 28(1), and so were caught by the concluding phrase of the subsection, namely, 'but not by any other person'. Both counsel for the first defendants and counsel for the plaintiffs accepted that the meaning of the expression 'any person interested in the charity' is far from clear: see also 5 Halsbury's Laws (4th edn) para 923, note 3. Counsel for the plaintiffs, of course, submitted that the term should not be construed narrowly, and that it was intended only to exclude officious intermeddlers. He contended that the contract with the governors sufficed to bring the plaintiffs within the expression; and he referred to certain authorities on the law as it stood before the Charities Act 1960 came into force. Junior counsel for the plaintiffs, who was permitted to address the court after counsel for the first defendants had concluded his reply, developed these submissions somewhat, and ended by contending that if charity proceedings related to property, any person interested in the property was a person 'interested in the charity'.

Counsel for the first defendants, on the other hand, pointed to the old law, under which strangers to the charity could not take charity proceedings under the Charities Procedure Act 1812 (Romilly's Act): see *Tudor on Charities* (5th edn, 1929) p 361. Like counsel for the plaintiffs, he drew some comfort from *Rendall v Blair* (1890) 45 Ch D 139, though the language of the statute there in issue was very different from that of s 28. Counsel for the first defendants contended that a person whose only connection with the charity was that he had a contract with the trustees relating to property of the charity was not a person who could be said to be 'interested in the charity' in any real sense of that expression.

In the essentials I think that counsel for the first defendants is right in his submissions. The central question, of course, is the meaning of s 28. The language is quite different from the language of the previous statutory provisions on the point, and the Charities Act 1960 is 'An Act to replace with new provisions the Charitable Trusts Acts, 1853 to 1939 . . .' One may look at the old law to see what the new statute was replacing, but what really matters is what s 28 says. When sub-ss (1), (2) and (8) of s 28 are put together, it is clear, first, that what is being dealt with is a special type of proceedings, namely, those brought under the age-old equitable jurisdiction over charities and charitable trusts, and known as 'charity proceedings'. There is no question of the provisions relating to proceedings in general, whatever the type. Second, those proceedings are contemplated as being taken 'with reference to a charity' or as 'relating to a charity'. Third, the phrase is 'any person interested in the charity', not any person who 'has an interest in the charity's property', or any person who 'has a claim against the charity'. Fourth, that phrase is to be construed not on its own, but in relation to those who are to be permitted to take the special type of proceedings known as 'charity proceedings'.

Now I do not aspire to define the meaning of the phrase 'any person interested in the charity' in this context. That I shall leave for others; I am merely concerned to find a safe resting place for my decision in this case. In my judgment the phrase, in its context, does not bear the wide meaning for which counsel and junior counsel for the plaintiffs contend. Many a person may be interested in the property of a charity without, for this purpose, being interested in the charity. I do not think that to contract with the trustees of a charity turns the contractor into a 'person interested in the charity', even if the contract relates to land or other property of the charity. I do not think that the phrase a   includes every tenant of charity land, or those who have easements or profits or mortgages or restrictive covenants over charity land, or those who contract to repair or decorate charity houses, or those who agree to buy goods from the charity or sell goods to the charity. An interest which is adverse to the charity is one thing, an interest in the charity is another. Those who have some good reason for seeking to enforce the trusts of a charity or secure its due administration may readily be accepted as having an interest in the charity, whereas those who merely have some claim adverse to the charity, and seek to b   improve their position at the expense of the charity, will not. The phrase, I think, is contemplating those who are on the charity side of the fence, as it were, however much they may disagree with what is being done or not being done by or on behalf of the charity. The phrase does not refer to those who are on the other side of the fence, even if they are in some way affected by the internal affairs of the charity.

In the result, I hold that the plaintiffs do not fall within the phrase 'any person c   interested in the charity', and so they are caught by the prohibition at the end of s 28(1). The claim made by the statement of claim in para 24 and the second prayer is therefore prohibited by s 28(1), and so should be struck out. No question therefore arises on counsel for the plaintiffs' subsidiary plea that this was not a 'striking out matter', and that the claim should be left intact in the hope that the Charity Commissioners might yet authorise it under s 28(2); for its seems clear that no authorisation by the Charity d   Commissioners under s 28(2) can validate a claim invalidated by s 28(1). Accordingly I strike out para 24 and the second prayer in the statement of claim.

Order accordingly.

Solicitors: *Lovell, White & King* (for the plaintiffs); *Druces & Attlee* (for the first defendants).

e   Azza M Abdallah   Barrister.

Burton v British Railways Board
f   ## (Case 19/81)

COURT OF JUSTICE OF THE EUROPEAN COMMUNITIES
JUDGES BOSCO (ACTING PRESIDENT), TOUFFAIT, DUE (PRESIDENTS OF CHAMBERS), PESCATORE, LORD
MACKENZIE-STUART, O'KEEFFE, KOOPMANS, CHLOROS AND GRÉVISSE
ADVOCATE-GENERAL VERLOREN VAN THEMAAT
7 OCTOBER, 8 DECEMBER 1981, 16 FEBRUARY 1982

g
European Economic Community – Equality of treatment of men and women – Social security – Minimum pensionable age – Different age for men and women – Whether prohibited sex discrimination.
European Economic Community – Equality of treatment of men and women – Equal working conditions – Redundancy benefit – Voluntary redundancy – Access to voluntary redundancy
h   *benefit – Age limit – Different age limit for men and women – Age limit determined by reference to minimum pensionable age fixed by national social security legislation – Different minimum pensionable age for men and women – Whether different age limit for voluntary redundancy benefit amounting to prohibited sex discrimination – Whether age limit a 'working condition' – EEC Council Directive 76/207, art 5.*

j   The determination of a minimumm pensionable age for social security purposes which is not the same for men as for women does not amount to discrimination prohibited by Community law (see p 550 *a b*, post).

The principle of equal treatment contained in art 5[a] of EEC Council Directive 76/207 applies to the conditions of access to voluntary redundancy benefit paid by an employer

_____
a   Article 5, so far as material, is set out at p 542 *c*, post

to a worker wishing to leave his employment. However, the fact that access to voluntary redundancy is available only during a specified period preceding the minimum *a* pensionable age fixed by national social security legislation and that that age is not the same for men as for women cannot in itself be regarded as discrimination on grounds of sex within art 5 (see p 550 *c* to *h*, post).

Per the Advocate-General. An age limit operating as a condition for the enjoyment of benefits such as the right to specific wages, access to voluntary redundancy benefit or other consideration in respect of employment is a 'working condition' within art 5(1) of *b* EEC Council Directive 76/207 (see p 547 *a* to *c*, post); *Defrenne v Sabena* [1978] ECR 1365 applied.

Notes

For equal treatment of men and women in respect of employment under EEC law, see 16 Halsbury's Laws (4th edn) para 521.   *c*

Cases cited

Defrenne v Belgian State Case 80/70 [1971] ECR 445, CJEC.
Defrenne v Sabena Case 43/75 (1976) [1981] 1 All ER 122, [1976] ECR 455, CJEC, 20 Digest (Reissue) 587, 4488.
Defrenne v Sabena Case 149/77 [1978] ECR 1365, CJEC, 20 Digest (Reissue) 592, 4510.   *d*
Garland v British Rail Engineering Ltd Case 12/81 [1982] 2 All ER 402, [1982] 2 WLR 918, CJEC and HL.
Jenkins v Kingsgate (Clothing Productions) Ltd Case 96/80 [1981] 1 WLR 972, [1981] ECR 911, CJEC.
Macarthys Ltd v Smith Case 129/79 [1981] 1 All ER 111, [1981] QB 180 [1980] 3 WLR 929, [1980] ECR 1275, CJEC and CA.   *e*
Worringham v Lloyds Bank Ltd Case 69/80 [1981] 2 All ER 434, [1981] 1 WLR 950, [1981] ECR 767, CJEC.

Reference

The Employment Appeal Tribunal referred certain questions (set out at p 539 *e* to *g*, post) as to the interpretation of art 119 of the EEC Treaty and EEC Council Directives 75/117 *f* and 76/207 to the Court of Justice of the European Communities for a preliminary ruling under art 177 of the Treaty. The questions arose as a result of the decision of the appeal tribunal to suspend, pending the preliminary ruling, the hearing of an appeal by Arthur Burton against the dismissal of his complaint to an industrial tribunal that his employer, the British Railways Board, had discriminated against him, contrary to the Equal Pay Act 1970, as amended by the Sex Discrimination Act 1975, in rejecting an application by *g* him for voluntary redundancy under a scheme operated by the board. Mr Burton, the board, the United Kingdom government, the Danish government and the Commission of the European Communities submitted observations to the court. The language of the case was English. The facts are set out in the decision of the Advocate-General.

Anthony Lester QC for Mr Burton.   *h*
N E Beddard for the board.
Peter Scott QC for the United Kingdom.
John Forman, agent for the EC Commission, for the Commission.

8 December. **The Advocate-General (P VerLoren van Themaat)** delivered the following opinion[1]: Mr President, Members of the Court,   *j*

1. *Introduction*

    Mr Arthur Burton is the first to confront the court with the fact that the principle that men and women should receive equal pay for equal work laid down in art 119 of the

_____
1   Translated from the Dutch

EEC Treaty and put into effect in EEC Council Directive 75/117 logically implies that
a not only should women enjoy the same benefits as men but conversely that men may
not be treated worse than women.

As an employee of the British Railways Board he believes that for that reason he is
entitled at 58 years of age to avail himself of the opportunity, which female employees
have when they attain 55 years of age, offered by a voluntary redundancy scheme and
the benefits which it confers. He submitted an application to that effect in August 1979.
b However, as a male employee he was not eligible for voluntary redundancy under the
relevant rules of British Railways until the age of 60. British Railways therefore rejected
his application. To put it somewhat simply, the advantages accompanying voluntary
redundancy consisted chiefly but not exclusively in the enjoyment of benefits equal to
the pension payable at pensionable age for a maximum period of five years prior to the
attainment of that age.

c Mr Burton complained to an industrial tribunal against the decision to refuse to grant
him the benefit payable under the voluntary redundancy scheme. He relied on the Equal
Pay Act 1970 as amended by the Sex Discrimination Act 1975. Once it emerged that the
1970 Act did not apply because the payments under the voluntary redundancy scheme
were non-contractual he based his appeal on the 1975 Act alone. That Act applies to
discrimination as regards non-contractual payments, which according to the national
d court also include voluntary redundancy payments. By virtue of s 6(4), however, the Act
does not apply to provision in relation to pensions. I shall return to that provision of the
Act later. The industrial tribunal dismissed the complaint, whereupon Mr Burton
appealed to the Employment Appeal Tribunal. It was before that tribunal that he claimed
that the 1975 Act must be construed in accordance with art 119 of the EEC Treaty and
EEC Council Directives 75/117 and 78/207.

e The Employment Appeal Tribunal then submitted the following questions of
interpretation to the court under art 177 of the EEC Treaty:

'(1) Is a voluntary redundancy benefit, which is paid by an employer to a worker
wishing to leave his employment, within the scope of the principle of equal pay
contained in Article 119 of the EEC Treaty and Article 1 of Council Directive 75/
f 117/EEC of 10 February 1975?
(2) If the answer to Question (1) is in the affirmative, does the principle of equal
pay have direct effect in Member States so as to confer enforceable Community
rights upon individuals in the circumstances of the present case?
(3) If the answer to Question (1) is in the negative: (i) is such a voluntary
redundancy benefit within the scope of the principle of equal treatment for men
and women as regards "working conditions" contained in Article 1(1), Article 2(1)
g and Article 5(1) of Council Directive 76/207/EEC of 9 February 1976? (ii) if so, does
the said principle have direct effect in Member States so as to confer enforceable
Community rights upon individuals in the circumstances of the present case?'

Written observations have been submitted on those questions in accordance with art
20 of the Protocol on the Statute of the Court of Justice by Mr Burton, the British
h Railways Board, the government of the United Kingdom, the Danish government and
the Commission of the European Communities.

Further matters which it might be useful to mention at this point are that when he
made his application in 1979 Mr Burton had worked for British Railways for 42 years
and that by virtue of s 30 of the Transport Act 1962 the British Railways Board is neither
a servant nor an agent of the Crown.

j At this point I refer to the report for the hearing for the rest of the facts and for a
summary of the written observations. Where necessary I shall return to the facts and the
observations made in the written and oral procedure in the rest of my opinion, which
will be constructed as follows: after this introduction I shall first indicate the previous
decisions of the court which may be relevant to this case; that will be followed by a
summary of the provisions of the directives relied on; I shall then analyse the questions
submitted in the light of the case file and the court's previous decisions; finally, I shall

then formulate my opinion on the questions submitted, taking into account the written observations which have been made.

2. The relevant decisions of the court

2.1   In the first *Defrenne* judgment (*Defrenne v Belgian State* Case 80/70 [1971] ECR 445 at 453) the court ruled that:

'A retirement pension established within the framework of a social security scheme laid down by legislation does not constitute consideration which the worker receives indirectly in respect of his employment from his employer within the meaning of the second paragraph of Article 119 of the EEC Treaty.'

That decision makes it desirable for me to examine the relationship between the voluntary redundancy scheme in question and statutory pension schemes. The government of the United Kingdom in particular bases its view of the case primarily on this relationship, which it considers to be of vital importance. It claims that the relationship affects both the amount and the duration of the voluntary redundancy benefits. Mr Burton however denies that there is such a relationship.

2.2   In the second *Defrenne* judgment (*Defrenne v Sabena* Case 43/75 (1976) [1981] 1 All ER 122 at 138) the court ruled, inter alia, that:

'the principle that men and women should receive equal pay, which is laid down by art 119, may be relied on before the national courts. These courts have a duty to ensure the protection of the rights which that provision vests in individuals, in particular in the case of those forms of discrimination which have their origin in legislative provisions or collective labour agreements, as well as where men and women receive unequal pay for equal work which is carried out in the same establishment or service, whether private or public.'

That judgment is cited not only by Mr Burton, whose view is supported by the Commission, but also by British Railways and the government of the United Kingdom, in order to support opposite conclusions. In this regard the term 'pay' and the difference between 'direct and overt discrimination' on the one hand and 'indirect and disguised discrimination' on the other are important in these proceedings. The prohibition of discrimination contained in art 119 is directly applicable to the first kind of discrimination but not to the second. In later judgments, most recently in *Jenkins v Kingsgate (Clothing Productions) Ltd* Case 96/80 [1981] 1 WLR 972, the court has repeatedly emphasised the significance of this distinction as regards the direct applicability of art 119.

2.3   In the third *Defrenne* judgment (*Defrenne v Sabena* Case 149/77 [1978] ECR 1365 at 1379–1380) the court ruled that:

'Article 119 of the EEC Treaty cannot be interpreted as prescribing, in addition to equal pay, equality in respect of the other working conditions applicable to men and women. At the time of the events which form the basis of the main action there was, as regards the relationships between employer and employee under national law, no rule of Community law prohibiting discrimination between men and women in the matter of working conditions other than the requirements as to pay referred to in Article 119 of the Treaty.'

As regards the events forming the basis of the main action, the question submitted to the court in that case referred in particular to the age limit for the termination of a female employee's contract of employment, an age limit which the contracts of employment of comparable male staff did not contain. Mr Burton and the government of the United Kingdom cite that judgment to support opposite conclusions. Although the Employment Appeal Tribunal has not raised any explicit question on this point, the difference in age limits is in fact of crucial importance in this case also, albeit not in the same way as in the third *Defrenne* judgment. The Commission therefore rightly devoted much attention to this point in its written observations. It believes that the second sentence of that judgment

of the court implies that the decision on the age limit would have been different if EEC
a Council Directive 76/207 had been in force at that time. I shall come back to the details
of the Commission's observations concerning the significance of this when I consider the
relevant provisions of Directive 76/207.

2.4   The court's judgment of 29 July 1979 in *Macarthys Ltd v Smith* Case 129/79 [1981]
1 All ER 111, [1981] QB 180 concerned unequal ordinary wages and does not appear to
be relevant to this case.

b   2.5   However, the court's judgment in *Worringham v Lloyds Bank Ltd* Case 69/80
[1981] 2 All ER 434 at 448, [1981] 1 WLR 950 at 971 is relevant to this case. In that
judgment the court ruled, inter alia, that:

'a contribution to a retirement benefits scheme which is paid by an employer in
the name of employees by means of an addition to the gross salary and which
therefore helps to determine the amount of that salary constitutes "pay" within the
c   meaning of the second paragraph of art 119 of the EEC Treaty.'

It appears from that judgment that not all benefits conferred on employees which are
related to a pension scheme fall outside the ambit of art 119 just because they are so
related.

2.6   Finally, in *Jenkins v Kingsgate (Clothing Productions) Ltd* Case 96/80 [1981] 1 WLR
d 972 the court made it clear that the distinction drawn in the second *Defrenne* judgment
between overt and disguised discrimination, which is important in determining whether
or not art 119 is directly applicable, does not coincide with a factual distinction between
direct discrimination or discrimination in form, on the one hand, and indirect
discrimination or discrimination in substance, on the other. The court put it in the
following words (at 984):

e   '1. A difference in pay between full-time workers and part-time workers does not
amount to discrimination prohibited by article 119 of the Treaty unless it is in
reality merely an indirect way of reducing the pay of part-time workers on the
ground that that group of workers is composed exclusively or predominantly of
women. 2. Where the national court is able, using the criteria of equal work and
equal pay, without the operation of Community or national measures, to establish
f   that the payment of lower hourly rates of remuneration for part-time work than for
full-time work represents discrimination based on difference of sex the provisions
of article 119 of the Treaty apply directly to such a situation.'

According to a recent interesting study by A W Govers (Gelijkheid van vrouw en man
in het europees sociaal recht, Geschriften van de Vereniging voor Arbeidsrecht No 6,
g Alphen aan de Rijn, 1981), in making the distinction in para (1) between direct and
indirect discrimination the court was subscribing to a well-established international
tradition, besides confirming its previous decisions on this subject. The distinction drawn
in the second *Defrenne* judgment between overt and disguised discrimination is, however,
related to the distinction between direct and indirect applicability, as the second
paragraph of the *Jenkins* judgment once again shows. Since the terminology of both
h distinctions is virtually identical in some Community languages, use of the terminology
contained in the second *Defrenne* judgment might lead to misunderstanding following
the judgment in the *Jenkins* case. In the rest of my opinion, therefore, I shall use other
terminology where necessary. Perhaps a distinction between 'discrimination directly
ascertainable by the courts' and 'discrimination not directly ascertainable by the courts'
might be adequate for present purposes to clarify the terminology used in para 18 of the
j second *Defrenne* judgment (1976) [1981] 1 All ER 122 at 134.

2.7   The case now before the court is the first in which questions on the interpretation
of directives concerning equal treatment of men and women must also be answered.

3. *Some comments on the directives concerning equal treatment of men and women*

3.1   The parties to the main action are agreed that art 1 of EEC Council Directive 75/

117 has nothing material to add to art 119 of the EEC Treaty for the purposes of this case. Bearing in mind the court's earlier decisions on equal treatment, that directive may *a* therefore be ignored.

3.2   That is not the case with EEC Council Directive 76/207 on the implementation of the principle of equal treatment for men and women as regards, inter alia, working conditions. Article 1 explains that the purpose of the directive is to put into effect the principle of equal treatment for men and women as regards working conditions, and art 2(1) provides: *b*

'For the purposes of the following provisions, the principle of equal treatment shall mean that there shall be no discrimination whatsoever on grounds of sex either directly or indirectly by reference in particular to marital or family status.'

Article 5(1) of the directive provides:

'Application of the principle of equal treatment with regard to working conditions, *c* including the conditions governing dismissal, means that men and women shall be guaranteed the same conditions without discrimination on grounds of sex.'

The third question of the Employment Appeal Tribunal seeks to ascertain whether, should art 119 not apply, voluntary redundancy benefits come under the principle, thus defined, of equal treatment for men and women as regards their working conditions. *d*

3.3   Finally, EEC Council Directive 79/7 on the progressive implementation of the principle of equal treatment for men and women in matters of social security is perhaps indirectly relevant. Referring to art 1(2) of Directive 76/207, which envisages a separate directive on this subject, this third directive, provides, inter alia, in art 7(1):

'This Directive shall be without prejudice to the right of Member States to exclude from its scope: (a) the determination of pensionable age for the purposes of granting *e* old-age and retirement pensions and the possible consequences thereof for other benefits . . .'

Although that directive does not have to be implemented until 1984 it is clear from its terms that at the time of Mr Burton's application the Council had already reached the conclusion that under Community law a difference in age limits in schemes such as those *f* contemplated by art 7(1) of Directive 79/7 is not contrary to the principle of equal treatment. Moreover, member states are of course empowered to make use of that provision before 1984. I shall come back later to the question whether the provision is also relevant to the redundancy payments at issue in these proceedings. Counsel for Mr Burton denied this at the hearing on the ground that by its nature the power given to the member states in art 7 can apply only to social security matters covered by that directive. *g*

4. *Examination of the questions submitted*

In order to answer preliminary questions in a manner useful to the national court it is almost always important to give consideration to the facts relevant to the main dispute. What is more, previous decisions may throw more light on aspects of the questions *h* submitted which require particular attention.

That is certainly true when the national court has framed its questions in very general terms, as in this case. In question 1 the Employment Appeal Tribunal asks the court whether a voluntary redundancy benefit, which is paid by an employer to a worker wishing to leave his employment, is within the scope of the principle of equal pay contained in art 119 of the EEC Treaty and art 1 of EEC Council Directive 75/117 of 10 *j* February 1975. It appears from the facts forming the basis of the dispute, from the arguments put forward in the written and oral procedure and from the court's other decisions that as far as such benefits are concerned a distinction must be drawn between their nature and composition or the method of calculating them, on the other hand, and the duration of and access to them, on the other.

The nature and composition or method of calculating the voluntary redundancy

benefits in question did not become clear until the oral procedure. The benefits concerned
a are those referred to in paras 24 and 25 of the document entitled 'Redundancy, Transfer
and Resettlement Arrangements for Railway Staff—Salaried and Conciliation' dated 20
September 1978. That document was produced by the government of the United
Kingdom at a late stage in the written procedure after reference was made only to an
extract at an earlier stage.

The actual redundancy payments are dealt with in para 24 of the document and
b comprises: (i) the statutory lump-sum redundancy payment under the Redundancy Act
1965 (now replaced by the Employment Protection (Consolidation) Act 1978, Part VI,
ss 81 to 120); (ii) a supplementary severance payment (equal to one week's standard pay
for each year of service in excess of 15 years or after 45 years of age); and (iii) an amount
equal to 25% of the sum of the other two payments.

Paragraph 25 deals with: (i) a special early retirement pension scheme. Where an
c employee is retired on grounds of redundancy within five years prior to minimum
pension age (60 in the case of men and 55 in the case of women) and has an entitlement
to pension the British Railways Board pays a pension equal to the pension from the
minimum pension age; and (iii) An advance for men aged 55 or over and for women
aged 50 or over equal to the amount of the lump-sum retirement benefit on the
attainment of the normal pensionable age; however, the advance falls due for repayment
d when the minimum pensionable age is attained and is thus in the nature of a loan. But
by investing it the employee receives interest during the relevant period and by spending
it he has the advantage of enjoying the benefit earlier, which at a time of high inflation
provides greater purchasing power.

Further details of the two schemes are set out in a memorandum of 9 March 1979
agreed on by the British Railways Board and the trade unions. Paragraph 6 of that
e memorandum states:

'Staff aged 60/65 (Male/Female) may leave the service under the Redundancy and
Resettlement arrangements when the Function in which [they are] employed has
been dealt with under Organization Planning.'

It follows in particular from that additional stipulation that the different age limits for
f access to the payments also apply to the payments referred to in para 24 of the main
document. Although we were told at the hearing that the special early retirement
pension scheme is no longer at issue, the dispute forming the basis of the reference
related both to the payments provided for by para 24 and to those provided for by para
25 of the main document. Since the substantive connection with pension schemes is
especially relevant in the case of the early retirement pension scheme, I shall consider it
g separately in my opinion.

As regards access to, or the duration of, the payments in question it may be observed
first of all that the dispute in fact revolves around this aspect of the voluntary redundancy
benefits on which the court's ruling is sought. Furthermore, the arguments put forward
during the written and oral procedure show that the court's answer on this aspect of the
reference need not necessarily be the same as its answer as regards the nature and
h composition of the payments or the method of calculating them. I refer here in particular
to the Commission's arguments.

I have already given a summary of the relevant previous decisions of the court. In
addition to the exception which the court made in the *Defrenne* judgment [1971] ECR
445 for statutory pension schemes, it seems to me that the exception which the court
made in the third *Defrenne* judgment [1978] ECR 1365 for working conditions other
j than pay is especially important in this case. In the latter judgment the other working
conditions also concerned in particular a difference in age limits for male and female
employees. On balance I think that the judgment in the *Worringham* case [1981] 2 All
ER 434, [1981] 1 WLR 950 is relevant only in so far as it makes the point that not all
schemes which are directly related to a pension scheme fall outside the scope of art 119
for that reason alone.

An answer to question 1 which draws a careful distinction between the different aspects of the benefit scheme may also affect the court's answer to question 2. Unlike question 1, the wording of question 2 gives express consideration to the facts of the actual *a* case and thus, in my view, to the age limit aspect which I have mentioned. For an analysis of EEC Council Directive 76/207, which is relevant for the purposes of question 3(i), I refer to my previous observations on that directive.

With regard to question 3(ii), I think, in the first place, that it may be relevant that the question asks, not whether a particular provision of Directive 76/207 has direct effect, but whether the *principle* of equal treatment contained therein as regards working *b* conditions has direct effect. In using those words perhaps the Employment Appeal Tribunal was indicating that Directive 76/207 might be regarded as putting into effect a generally recognised fundamental or human right. Moreover, since the Commission believes that the question whether the directive has direct effect can be avoided by construing the relevant provisions of the Sex Discrimination Act 1975 in accordance with the directive, I think that it would be useful to cite here the relevant provisions of *c* that Act.

Section 6(2) of the 1975 Act reads as follows:

'It is unlawful for a person, in the case of a woman employed by him at an establishment in Great Britain, to discriminate against her—(*a*) in the way he affords her access to opportunities for promotion, transfer or training, or to any other benefits, facilities or services, or by refusing or deliberately omitting to afford her *d* access to them, or (*b*) by dismissing her, or subjecting her to any other detriment.'

Section 6(4) provides: 'Subsections (1)(*b*) and (2) do not apply to provision in relation to death or retirement.'

In my opinion those provisions taken on their own are indeed no bar to the solution proposed by the Commission. In my view, too, the question whether 'other benefits' also *e* include voluntary redundancy benefits and the question whether those benefits are related to 'death or retirement', as referred to here, could certainly both be answered in the light of Community law. In my judgment there is no question here of manifest departure from Community law, as laid down or defined in directives or in the court's decisions. Even the fact that the section cited at first sight appears to deal only with discrimination against women does not prevent the approach proposed by the *f* Commission from being adopted, for s 2(1) of the 1975 Act provides:

'Section 1, and the provisions of Parts II and III relating to sex discrimination against women, are to be read as applying equally to the treatment of men, and for that purpose shall have effect with such modifications as are requisite.'

Section 6 belongs to Part II of the 1975 Act. Nevertheless in my opinion that solution *g* could only be adopted if the second part of the question raised were reformulated or interpreted to some degree. That reformulation or interpretation might read as follows: 'If so, may the principle put into effect in the said directive be relied on before the national court applying national legislation intended or partly intended to implement that directive.' An answer to the question formed in that way could have regard to the possibility, which emerged during these proceedings, that implementing legislation *h* might depart appreciably from the terms of the relevant directive.

5. Conclusions on the questions submitted

5.1 *Question 1* Let me remind the court that the first question put to it reads:

'Is a voluntary redundancy benefit, which is paid by an employer to a worker *j* wishing to leave his employment, within the scope of the principle of equal pay contained in Article 119 of the EEC Treaty and Article 1 of Council Directive 75/ 117/EEC of 10 February 1975?'

In examining this question I have already indicated that in order for the court's answer to be of practical help in resolving the dispute in the main action a clear distinction must

be drawn in these proceedings between different aspects of the benefit scheme at issue. It
a has been sufficiently established in the written and oral procedure that all the payments
at issue are made directly by the employer to the worker and are mostly for the
employer's account. Only in the case of that part of the benefits which is dealt with in
para 24 of the relevant scheme can 41% of the expenditure at present be reclaimed from
a fund in which employers participate and which is administered by the government.

Moreover, it is clear that the payments are not due under a statutory scheme but under
b voluntary agreements between the employers and workers. This is true both for the
payments made under para 24 and for those made under para 25 of the relevant scheme.
I do not think that it is relevant, for the purpose of determining whether art 119 applies,
that the method of calculating the amount of the benefits partly depends on statutory
provisions. As was rightly pointed out in the course of the proceedings, such a criterion
would mean that statutory minimum wages which discriminated between the sexes
c would not fall under art 119 either. Such a criterion was clearly rejected in the second
Defrenne judgment [1981] 1 All ER 122 at 138, where the court held that 'forms of
discrimination which have their origin in legislative provisions or collective labour
agreements' are contrary to art 119. The parties also agreed at the hearing that in order
to answer the question it does not matter whether or not the relevant payments are based
on a contract.

d It is clear from what I have just said that the voluntary redundancy benefits under the
scheme operated by British Railways are not pension rights in the context of a statutory
social security scheme which, according to the court's judgment in the first *Defrenne*
judgment [1971] ECR 445, are not subject to art 119. A consideration relevant to the
court's decision in the present case is the fact that it based its decision in that judgment
on the finding in paras 6 to 10 that art 119 does not apply to 'schemes ... directly
e governed by legislation without any element of agreement within the undertaking or
the occupational branch concerned, which are obligatorily applicable to general categories
of workers' and are financed from contributions which are 'determined less by the
employment relationship between the employer and the worker than by considerations
of social policy' (see [1971] ECR 445 at 451, paras 7–8). In the present case it is a question
of a direct connection between employers and workers and of a retirement scheme
f introduced voluntarily by the employer with the agreement of, or at any rate after
consultation with, the trade unions concerned.

In order to determine whether the nature of the voluntary redundancy benefits in
question or the method of calculating them renders art 119 inapplicable it is necessary to
begin by examining the wording of the second paragraph of that article. If those benefits
are not ordinary wages they may be other consideration in cash or in kind which the
g worker receives (a) directly or indirectly, from his employer, (b) in respect of his
employment. On the basis of the information before the court it seems indisputable that
the payments in question are received directly or indirectly from the employer. As
regards the required connection with the employment, I would consider that in the light
of the passages which I have cited from the decision in the first *Defrenne* judgment the
decisive question is whether the benefits are received by the worker concerned from his
h employer owing to his employment. The French and Italian texts of art 119 containing
the words 'en raison de l'emploi' and 'in ragione dell' impiego' also show that the test is
not whether the payment is consideration for work performed. Only the English text of
art 119, which contains the words 'in respect of his employment', might perhaps point
to a more restrictive meaning. What is required for the purposes of the final words of
the second paragraph of art 119, and what incidentally I believe is also required by the
j English text logically construed, is rather an unseverable casual link between the payment
and a worker's employment. In my judgment that requirement of an unseverable causal
link between payment and employment is certainly fulfilled in the case of voluntary
redundancy benefits; if he has no such employment a worker cannot lay claim to such
benefits. Consequently the question whether art 119 applies to consideration provided
in respect of employment in the past need not be answered in the present case. As regards
that question I refer to my opinion in *Garland v British Rail Engineering Ltd* Case 12/81

[1982] 2 All ER 402 at 409–411, [1982] 2 WLR 918 at 920–923. As I said earlier, the fact
that the amount of the benefits referred to in paras 24 and 25 of the scheme in question   *a*
is determined in whole or in part by statutory pension rules cannot in my judgment
shake those conclusions reached on the basis of the wording of art 119. My opinion on
this aspect of the first question is therefore that voluntary redundancy benefits paid
voluntarily, or otherwise than by contract, by an employer to a worker do not fall outside
the ambit of art 119 by reason of their nature or the fact that their composition or the
method of calculating them is partly dependent on statutory rules. That conclusion   *b*
means that, subject to the points to be made concerning the other aspect of the dispute,
discrimination on the basis of sex in the granting or the calculation of such benefits is
contrary to art 119.

The case before the court is, however, concerned solely with the other aspect of the
benefit scheme which I mentioned in my analysis of the questions. That other aspect
concerns the alleged discrimination on grounds of sex in the provisions on the duration   *c*
of, or access to, the benefit scheme. Given the wording of art 119 and considering the
third *Defrenne* judgment [1978] ECR 1365, I think it is beyond argument that art 119
does not cover this aspect. As the Commission seems to have implicitly conceded in its
written submissions, the stipulation of the age limit which must be attained in order to
qualify for access to the voluntary redundancy scheme is, at most, to be included amongst
the working conditions referred to in EEC Council Directive 76/207.   *d*

Consequently, my examination of the first question submitted to the court leads me
to the ultimate conclusion that this question must be answered as follows: 'The principle
of equal pay contained in art 119 of the EEC Treaty and art 1 of EEC Council Directive
75/117 of 10 February 1975 applies to voluntary redundancy benefits paid by an
employer to a worker wishing to leave his employment and to the method of calculating
them, but not to age limits placed on qualification for such payments.'   *e*

5.2   *Question 2*   This question presupposes an affirmative answer to question 1 and
reads as follows:

'If the answer to Question (1) is in the affirmative, does the principle of equal pay
have direct effect in Member States so as to confer enforceable Community rights
upon individuals in the circumstances of the present case?'   *f*

Bearing in mind the second *Defrenne* judgment (1976) [1981] 1 All ER 122, the *Jenkins*
judgment [1981] 1 WLR 972 and the answer I have proposed to question 1, I consider
that the answer to question 2 might read as follows: 'Where the national court is able,
using the criteria of equal work and equal pay, without the operation of Community or
national measures, to establish that the benefits in question and the method of calculating
them being determined, whether or not by reference to statutory provisions, by a   *g*
voluntary redundancy scheme applied by the employer voluntarily or otherwise than by
contract, constitute discrimination on the basis of sex, the provisions of art 119 apply
directly to such a situation.'

5.3   *Question 3*   As my answer to question 1 is in the negative on the crucial point of
the age limit, I cannot avoid examining question 3 also. I shall start with the first part of
that question, which, I would remind the court, assumes a negative answer to question 1   *h*
and runs:

'is such a voluntary redundancy benefit within the scope of the principle of equal
treatment for men and women as regards "working conditions" contained in Article
1(1), Article 2(1) and Article 5(1) of Council Directive 76/207/EEC of 9 February
1976?'   *j*

It follows from my answer to question 1 that I should now examine this question
solely in relation to the age limit, for I infer from the third *Defrenne* judgment [1978]
ECR 1365 that an age limit which is a condition for the enjoyment of benefits such as
those in question cannot as such be regarded as falling under art 119.

On closer examination question 3(i), with its scope thus restricted, divides into two

parts. The first part comprises the question whether an age limit operating as a condition
a for the enjoyment of benefits such as those in question comes under the term 'working
conditions' contained in Directive 76/207. Given the customary distinction in labour law
between wages and comparable consideration, on the one hand, and other working
conditions, on the other hand, I consider that an affirmative answer to this question is,
for one thing, logical if a balanced system is to be arrived at. Age limits relating to the
right to specific wages or other consideration in respect of employment are of such
b concern to workers that a negative answer to this part of the question would create an
incomprehensible and illogical gap in the additional guarantees of equal treatment for
men and women as regards their employment which Directive 76/207 seeks to secure.
On no account does the very general term 'working conditions' call for any other answer
either. Last but not least, however, I can refer to the third *Defrenne* judgment [1978]
ECR 1365 at 1377 in which the court expressly described the age limit in question as a
c 'working condition'. Because of that judgment I need not for the purposes of this part of
my opinion place reliance on the use of the phrase 'including the conditions governing
dismissal' contained in art 5(1) of Directive 76/207. Besides, to my mind this case is not
concerned with conditions governing dismissal but with working conditions relating to
the receipt of consideration within the meaning of art 119.

However, I think that it is much more difficult to answer the *second part* of question
d 3(i), namely the question of the interpretation of the principle of equal treatment in a
case such as this. I have already referred to Article 7(1)(a) of EEC Council Directive 79/7.
I would remind the court that that provision states that the directive is to be without
prejudice to the right of member states to exclude from its scope 'the determination of
pensionable age for the purposes of granting old-age and retirement pensions and the
possible consequences thereof for other benefits'. It follows from that provision that the
e difference in pensionable age which member states fix for men and women and the
effects which that may have on other benefits do not constitute a prohibited form of sex
discrimination under Community law.

Where a private scheme is tied to or derived from the statutory difference in
pensionable age such a difference in the private scheme can hardly be regarded as being
contrary to the principle of equal treatment under Community law if a similar provision
f in a statutory scheme must be regarded as being unprohibited discrimination on the
basis of sex under Community law. Moreover, in my opinion it is perfectly possible to
argue that, for the purposes of the application of the principle of equal treatment for
men and women to benefits such as those in question, it is not just the date from which
they are payable which is important but also, perhaps even primarily, the way in which
that date is determined and the duration of the relevant benefits in practice. As both the
g qualifying age for all the types of benefits at issue and their duration are determined
according to criteria which are identical for men and women, there is no question of
conflict with the principle of equal treatment.

For those reasons I suggest that the court should answer question 3(i) as follows:
'Although the age limit for access to a voluntary redundancy scheme such as that in
question and the determination of the duration of the relevant benefits fall within the
h term "working conditions" contained in art 1(1), 2(1) and 5(1) of EEC Council Directive
76/207 of 9 February 1976, such a benefits scheme is not contrary to the last-mentioned
provision if the qualifying age for all the benefits in question and their duration in
practice is derived from the pensionable age in the same way for men and women.'

On account of the similarities between the two types of benefit referred to in paras 24
and 25 of the scheme I do not think that they call for separate consideration in this
respect.

The answer which I have proposed to question 3(i) makes it unnecessary to examine
question 3(ii).

5.4   To sum up therefore I propose that the court should answer the questions put to
it as follows: (1) The principle of equal pay contained in art 119 of the EEC Treaty and
art 1 of EEC Council Directive 75/117 of 10 February 1975 applies to voluntary

redundancy benefits paid by an employer to a worker wishing to leave his employment and to the method of calculating them, but not to age limits placed on qualification for such payments; (2) where the national court is able, using the criteria of equal work and equal pay, without the operation of Community or national measures, to establish that the benefits in question and the method of calculating them, being determined, whether or not by reference to statutory provisions, by a voluntary redundancy scheme applied by the employer voluntarily or otherwise than by contract, constitute discrimination on the basis of sex, the provisions of art 119 apply directly to such a situation; (3) (i) although the age limit for access to a voluntary redundancy scheme such as that in question and the determination of the duration of the relevant benefits fall within the term 'working conditions' contained in art 1(1), 2(1) and 5(1) of EEC Council Directive 76/207 of 9 February 1976, such a benefits scheme is not contrary to the last-mentioned provision if the qualifying age for all the benefits in question and their duration in practice is derived from the pensionable age in the same way for men and women; (ii) this question does not need to be answered.

16 February. **THE COURT OF JUSTICE** delivered its judgment which, having summarised the facts, procedure and submissions of the parties, dealt with the law as follows:

1. By an order of 16 January 1981 which was received at the court on 4 February 1981 the Employment Appeal Tribunal referred to the court for a preliminary ruling under art 177 of the EEC Treaty three questions concerning the interpretation, with regard to payment of voluntary redundancy benefit, of art 119 of the EEC Treaty, art 1 of EEC Council Directive 75/117 of 10 February 1975 on the approximation of the laws of the member states relating to the application of the principle of equal pay for men and women and arts 1(1), 2(1) and 5(1) of EEC Council Directive 76/207 of 9 February 1976 on the implementation of the principle of equal treatment for men and women as regards access to employment, vocational training and promotion, and working conditions.

2. According to the case file Mr Burton, the plaintiff in the main action, is an employee of the British Railways Board (hereinafter referred to as 'the board'), a body established by the Transport Act 1962 and responsible for operating the railway system in Great Britain.

3. As a result of an internal reorganisation the board made an offer of voluntary redundancy to some of its employees. A memorandum was drawn up embodying the terms of a collective agreement between management and the recognised trade unions on the terms on which certain aspects of the reorganisation were to be carried out. Paragraph 6 of the memorandum provides as follows:

'Staff aged 60/55 (Male/Female) may leave the service under the Redundancy and Resettlement arrangements when the Function in which [they are] employed has been dealt with under Organization Planning.'

4. In August 1979 Mr Burton applied for voluntary redundancy but his application was rejected on the ground that he was under the minimum age of 60 specified for male employees by the above-mentioned memorandum. Mr Burton therefore claimed that he was treated less favourably than female employees inasmuch as the benefit would have been granted to a woman of his age (58).

5. After the rejection of his application Mr Burton complained to an industrial tribunal under the provisions of the Equal Pay Act 1970, as last amended by the Sex Discrimination Act 1975. The industrial tribunal rejected Mr Burton's claim and he appealed to the Employment Appeal Tribunal. In the course of the appeal it was conceded on his behalf that by virtue of s 6(4) of the Sex Discrimination Act 1975 it is not contrary to the Act for an employer to treat a male employee less favourably than he treats a female employee as regards access to voluntary redundancy benefit. However, Mr Burton contended that s 6(4) must be construed as subject to the enforceable Community rights

conferred by art 119 of the EEC Treaty, art 1 of EEC Council Directive 75/117 on equal
a pay and arts 1, 2 and 5 of EEC Council Directive 76/207 on equal treatment.
   6. In order to resolve the issue the Employment Appeal Tribunal referred to the court
three questions worded as follows:

   '(1) Is a voluntary redundancy benefit, which is paid by an employer to a worker
   wishing to leave his employment, within the scope of the principle of equal pay
   contained in Article 119 of the EEC Treaty and Article 1 of Council Directive 75/
b 117/EEC of 10 February 1975?
   (2) If the answer to Question (1) is in the affirmative, does the principle of equal
   pay have direct effect in Member States so as to confer enforceable Community
   rights upon individuals in the circumstances of the present case?
   (3) If the answer to Question (1) is in the negative: (i) is such a voluntary
c redundancy benefit within the scope of the principle of equal treatment for men
   and women as regards "working conditions" contained in Article 1(1), Article 2(1)
   and Article 5(1) of Council Directive 76/207/EEC of 9 February 1976? (ii) if so, does
   the said principle have direct effect in Member States so as to confer enforceable
   Community rights upon individuals in the circumstances of the present case?'

   7. The principal issue raised by those questions is whether the requirement that a
d male worker should have reached the age of 60 in order to be eligible for payment of a
voluntary redundancy benefit whereas women workers become eligible at the age of 55
amounts to discrimination prohibited by art 119 of the EEC Treaty or by art 1 of Council
Directive 75/117 or, at least, by Council Directive 76/207 and, if so, whether the relevant
provision of Community law may be relied on in the national courts.
   8. Consequently the question of interpretation which has been referred to the court
e concerns not the benefit itself, but whether the conditions of access to the voluntary
redundancy scheme are discriminatory. That is a matter covered by the provisions of
Council Directive 76/207 to which reference was made by the national court, and not by
those of art 119 of the EEC Treaty or Council Directive 75/117.
   9. According to art 5(1) of Council Directive 76/207 application of the principle of
equal treatment with regard to working conditions, including the conditions governing
f dismissal, means that men and women are to be guaranteed the same conditions without
discrimination on grounds of sex. In the context of the directive the word 'dismissal'
must be widely construed so as to include termination of the employment relationship
between a worker and his employer, even as part of a voluntary redundancy scheme.
   10. In deciding whether the difference in treatment of which the plaintiff in the main
action complains is discriminatory within the meaning of that directive account must be
g taken of the relationship between measures such as that at issue and national provisions
on normal retirement age.
   11. Under United Kingdom legislation the minimum qualifying age for a state
retirement pension is 60 for women and 65 for men.
   12. From the information supplied by the United Kingdom government in the course
of the proceedings it appears that a worker who is permitted by the board to take
h voluntary early retirement must do so within the five years preceding the normal
minimum age of retirement, and that he may receive the following benefits: (1) the
lump sum calculated in accordance with the provisions of the Redundancy Payments Act
1965; (2) a lump sum calculated on the basis of the total length of his employment with
the board; and (3) 25% of the sum of the first two amounts. In addition he is entitled up
to the minimum retiring age to an early retirement pension equal to the pension to
j which he would have been entitled had he attained the minimum statutory retirement
age and to an advance, repayable at the minimum retiring age, equal to the sum to which
he becomes entitled at that age.
   13. EEC Council Directive 79/7 of 19 December 1978 on the progressive
implementation of the principle of equal treatment for men and women in matters of
social security, which was adopted with particular reference to art 235 of the EEC Treaty,

provides in art 7 that the directive shall be without prejudice to the right of member
states to exclude from its scope the determination of pensionable age for the purposes of *a*
granting old-age and retirement pensions and the possible consequences thereof for other
benefits.

14. It follows that the determination of a minimum pensionable age for social security
purposes which is not the same for men as for women does not amount to discrimination
prohibited by Community law.

15. The option given to workers by the provisions at issue in the present instance is *b*
tied to the retirement scheme governed by United Kingdom social security provisions. It
enables a worker who leaves his employment at any time during the five years before he
reaches normal pensionable age to receive certain allowances for a limited period. The
allowances are calculated in the same manner regardless of the sex of the worker. The
only difference between the benefits for men and those for women stems from the fact
that the minimum pensionable age under the national legislation is not the same for *c*
men as for women.

16. In the circumstances the different age conditions for men and women with regard
to access to voluntary redundancy cannot be regarded as discrimination within the
meaning of Council Directive 76/207.

17. In the light of that answer to the first part of the third question it is not necessary
to give a reply to the second part. *d*

18. The answers to be given to the questions which have been raised by the
Employment Appeal Tribunal are therefore as follows: (1) the principle of equal
treatment contained in art 5 of EEC Council Directive 76/207 of 9 February 1976 applies
to the conditions of access to voluntary redundancy benefit paid by an employer to a
worker wishing to leave his employment; (2) the fact that access to voluntary redundancy
is available only during the five years preceding the minimum pensionable age fixed by *e*
national social security legislation and that that age is not the same for men as for women
cannot in itself be regarded as discrimination on grounds of sex within the meaning of
art 5 of EEC Council Directive 76/207.

Costs

19. The costs incurred by the government of the United Kingdom, the government *f*
of the Kingdom of Denmark and the Commission of the European Communities, which
have submitted observations to the court, are not recoverable. As the proceedings are, in
so far as the parties to the main action are concerned, in the nature of a step in the
proceedings before the national court, the decision as to costs is a matter for that court.

On those grounds, the court, in answer to the questions referred to it by the Employment *g*
Appeal Tribunal by order of 16 January 1981, hereby rules: (1) the principle of equal
treatment contained in art 5 of EEC Council Directive 76/207 of 9 February 1976 applies
to the conditions of access to voluntary redundancy benefit paid by an employer to a
worker wishing to leave his employment; (2) the fact that access to voluntary redundancy
is available only during the five years preceding the minimum pensionable age fixed by
national social security legislation and that that age is not the same for men as for women *h*
cannot in itself be regarded as discrimination on grounds of sex within the meaning of
art 5 of EEC Council Directive 76/207.

Agents: *Elaine Donnelly* (for Mr Burton); *Evan Harding* (for the board); *R D Munrow*,
Treasury Solicitor's Department (for the United Kingdom); *John Forman*, Legal Service of
the EC Commission (for the Commission).

Mary Rose Plummer   Barrister.

a   # International Sales and Agencies Ltd and another v Marcus and another

QUEEN'S BENCH DIVISION
LAWSON J
7, 8, 9, 10, 15 APRIL 1981

b

Trust and trustee – Constructive trust – Cheque drawn by director on company's account – Director appropriating company's funds to settle personal debt incurred by deceased director – Creditor knowing that payment made in breach of trust – Whether creditor a constructive trustee for company of money received.

c   *Company – Dealing with company – Person dealing with company in good faith – Transaction decided on by directors deemed to be within company's capacity – Person dealing with company in good faith not bound to inquire into company's capacity – Whether person receiving money from company in breach of trust protected from being a constructive trustee of money received – European Communities Act 1972, s 9(1).*

d   The defendants, who were registered moneylenders, made personal loans of £30,000 to F, who was the major shareholder in the two plaintiff companies. F became seriously ill and told the defendants that his friend M would see that they were repaid if he died. M was also a shareholder in and director of the plaintiff companies and helped F to run them. F later died insolvent, leaving his shares in the plaintiff companies to his widow and children. However, the companies were thereafter effectively controlled by M, who
e   arranged for the £30,000 to be repaid to the defendants by five cheques drawn on the plaintiff companies' bank accounts. Following M's death, F's beneficiaries directed the plaintiff companies to bring proceedings against the defendants to recover the £30,000. The companies accordingly claimed the return of the £30,000 on the ground, inter alia, that it was money had and received. The defendants contended, inter alia, that they were protected by s 9(1)[a] of the European Communities Act 1972, which provided that as
f   regards a person dealing with a company in good faith any transaction decided on by the directors was deemed to be within the company's capacity to enter into and that the person dealing with the company was not bound to inquire into the capacity of the company to enter into the transaction or whether there was any limitation on the powers of directors.

g   **Held** – The plaintiff companies were entitled to the return of the £30,000, for the following reasons—
   (1) The money had been paid to the defendants by M in breach of his fiduciary duty as constructive trustee of the money in the bank account of the companies over which he had control. Furthermore, the payments were ultra vires the objects clauses in the memoranda of association of the companies, since the mere fact that the objects clauses contained express power by the companies to draw cheques did not prevent the court
h   from inquiring into the nature and purpose for which the cheques were drawn. It followed that the defendants became constructive trustees of the money received by them, since they had actual notice that the money received was the property of the plaintiffs and that in arranging for the payment M had acted in breach of trust (see p 556 *j* to p 557 *e* and *h* to p 558 *c* and p 560 *h j*, post); dicta of Ungoed-Thomas J in *Selangor*
j   *United Rubber Estates Ltd v Cradock (a bankrupt) (No 3)* [1968] 2 All ER at 1093, of Lord Dunpark in *Thompson v J Barke & Co (Caterers) Ltd* 1975 SLT at 75 and *Belmont Finance Corp v Williams Furniture Ltd (No 2)* [1980] 1 All ER 393 applied.
   (2) The defendants' liability to account to the plaintiffs for the money received by them

---

a   Section 9(1) is set out at p 558 *j* to p 559 *a*, post in breach of trust was not affected by s 9(1) of the 1972 Act, since the purpose of s 9(1) was to protect innocent third parties who entered into transactions with companies which might otherwise avoid their obligations by relying on the ultra vires doctrine. Section 9(1) therefore did not affect the operation of a constructive trust if the facts gave rise to such a trust (see p 559 *f* to *h* and p 560 *a b*, post).

Notes

For directors' liability as trustees of a company's property, see 7 Halsbury's Laws (4th edn) para 505, and for cases on the subject, see 10 Digest (Reissue) 1335, 8531–8533.

For constructive trusts arising out of the acquisition of property, see 38 Halsbury's Laws (3rd edn) 858, para 1446, and for liability as a constructive trustee, see ibid 860, para 1449, and for cases on the subjects, see 47 Digest (Repl) 184–188, 192, 1525–1565, 1595–1609.

For the European Communities Act 1972, s 9, see 42 Halsbury's Statutes (3rd edn) 60.

Cases referred to in judgment

Belmont Finance Corp v Williams Furniture Ltd (No 2) [1980] 1 All ER 393, CA.
Carl-Zeiss-Stiftung v Herbert Smith & Co (a firm) (No 2) [1969] 2 All ER 367, [1969] 2 Ch 276, [1969] 2 WLR 427, CA, 1(1) Digest (Reissue) 34, 237.
Fibrosa Spolka Akcyjna v Fairbairn Lawson Combe Barbour Ltd [1942] 2 All ER 122, [1943] AC 32, HL, 12 Digest (Reissue) 495, 3479.
Karak Rubber Co Ltd v Burden (No 2) [1972] 1 All ER 1210, [1972] 1 WLR 602, 3 Digest (Reissue) 585, 3730.
Lee, Behrens & Co Ltd, Re [1932] Ch 46, [1932] All ER Rep 889, 9 Digest (Reissue) 571, 3419.
Nelson v Larholt [1947] 2 All ER 751, [1948] 1 KB 339, 47 Digest (Repl) 187, 1554.
Reckitt v Barnett, Pembroke & Slater Ltd [1929] AC 176, [1928] All ER Rep 1, HL, 1(1) Digest (Reissue) 459, 3206.
Selangor United Rubber Estates Ltd v Cradock (a bankrupt) (No 3) [1968] 2 All ER 1073, [1968] 1 WLR 1555, 9 Digest (Reissue) 403, 2379.
Sinclair v Brougham [1914] AC 398, [1914–15] All ER Rep 622, HL, 3 Digest (Reissue) 543, 3545.
Thompson v J Barke & Co (Caterers) Ltd 1975 SLT 67.

Action

By a writ issued on 29 August 1978 the plaintiffs, International Sales and Agencies Ltd (ISA) and Janthorpe Properties Ltd (Janthorpe) claimed from the defendants, Sidney Marcus and Bentinck Securities Ltd, the sum of £30,000, being £10,000 as money had and received to the use of Janthorpe and £20,000 as money had and received for the use of ISA, or alternatively damages for conversion in respect of both amounts, a tracing order and/or an account of the proceeds of the payments. The facts are set out in the judgment.

Mark Potter QC for the plaintiffs.
Patrick Milmo for the defendants.

Cur adv vult

15 April. **LAWSON J.** I would like to say before I commence delivering my judgment that I am very grateful indeed for all the assistance I had from counsel in this case. I am not going to cite at great length from authorities in the course of my judgment, but I have, of course, read again the authorities and particularly the passages cited to me. The second thing I would like to say is that I am grateful to the solicitors for having arranged the documentation in the case in such a clear and easily accessible manner. It is not always that this happens.

a
The plaintiffs, International Sales and Agencies Ltd and Janthorpe Properties Ltd (I shall call International Sales and Agencies 'ISA' and Janthorpe Properties 'Janthorpe'), by a writ issued on 29 August 1978, claim against the first defendant, Mr Sidney Marcus, and the second defendants, Bentinck Securities Ltd, as to ISA £20,000 and as to Janthorpe £10,000 as moneys lent repayable on demand, alternatively as money had and received to their use. There are also claims for the same amount at common law and in equity. All these claims arise out of dealings by a Mr Munsey (who died on 4 March 1978) with

b
the defendants during the period November 1973 to April 1974. They relate to the payment to the second defendants of one Janthorpe cheque for £10,000 and four ISA cheques each for £5,000. All these cheques were drawn by Mr Munsey purportedly as director of Janthorpe and ISA.

It is necessary to set out in some detail the background to the issue and payment of these cheques. The plaintiff companies were the main vehicles through which the late

c
Mr Aziz Fancy transacted his business and financial affairs. Mr Fancy who was of the Ishmaeli Muslim faith, had a long and chequered career. He was reputedly a rich man and indeed, on some occasions, he may well have been. ISA was a company mainly engaged in commodity and steel dealings. The deceased, Mr Fancy, held all but one of the 325,000 issued £1 shares in ISA; the remaining one was held by Mr Munsey. Both were directors of ISA. Janthorpe was mainly a property-owning company in which Mr

d
Fancy and his widow (who took no part in the operation or administration of the company's affairs and was in no sense a woman of business) held some 90% of the equity and Mr Munsey held about 5%. Again, both Mr Fancy and Mr Munsey were directors together with a Mr Day. Mr Fancy and Mr Munsey were close friends of long standing and both were actively and fully engaged in the businesses of the companies.

Mr Sidney Marcus, who is a director of, and controls, Bentinck Securities, the second

e
defendants, who are registered moneylenders, is a man whose main and lengthy business experience through another of his companies was dealing in cars of the more prestigious types. Bentinck Securities Ltd carried out some four or five moneylending transactions a year; some of them were in substantial sums. Mr Marcus had been for many years a close friend of Mr Munsey's, who introduced him some years ago to Mr Fancy. Early in 1973 it is clear that Mr Fancy, to Mr Munsey's knowledge (but not to the knowledge of his

f
widow or his son Ismat, nor to that of his solicitor, Mr Crowe of Gouldens, or of his accountant, a Mr Hawkins) was in serious financial difficulties. On behalf of Mr Fancy, Mr Munsey approached Mr Marcus and proposed that Bentinck Securities, Mr Marcus's moneylending company, should lend Mr Fancy £30,000 for six months. This loan was arranged at 14% per annum, interest payable monthly for six months. The transaction was duly recorded in the necessary statutory memorandum which was specifically prepared for the transaction by Mr Marcus's solicitor, a Mr Kenyon, of Philip Evans &

g
Co. Mr Fancy received Bentinck Securities' cheque for £30,000 on 23 April 1973 and on that occasion Mr Fancy paid Mr Marcus, on behalf of the second defendants, £2,100 interest in advance.

In the summer of 1973 Mr Fancy became seriously ill. Mr Marcus heard of this and after Mr Fancy left hospital, being concerned about his loan, he went to see Mr Fancy,

h
who, in the presence of Mr Munsey, told Mr Marcus that he need not be worried as Mr Munsey would see he was repaid if anything happened. On 7 August 1973 Mr Fancy made a will appointing Mr Munsey, his accountant and bank manager executors. By his will Mr Fancy left his shares in Janthorpe and the rest of his estate, including his ISA shares, in trust for his widow and children. On 23 October 1973 Mr Fancy died. Gouldens, his solicitors, were consulted by the nominated executors, who appraised the

j
situation and concluded that Mr Fancy's estate was substantially, at least to the extent of £200,000, insolvent.

Mr Marcus, shortly after Mr Fancy's death, was informed by Mr Munsey, who also told him that the £30,000 was in jeopardy. I find that in early November Mr Munsey and Mr Marcus called on Mr Fancy's elder son, Ismat Fancy (I say elder son; there was another son, but he was a boy at this time, whereas Ismat Fancy was in his very early twenties). Mr Ismat Fancy on this occasion was, for the first time, told of his late father's debts and I find that Mr Marcus was told on this occasion that the family had no money, *a* but that Mr Munsey would see if anything could be done about repayments. I find that Mr Munsey suggested that the only possibility was through the deceased's companies, but said on that occasion that nothing could be done at the time. Mr Marcus instructed his solicitor, Mr Kenyon, who spoke to Mr Crowe of Gouldens. Mr Crowe told Mr Kenyon that the estate was probably insolvent, but that Mr Munsey would see if it were feasible that the £30,000 debt could be repaid. After receiving this letter, I find that Mr *b* Marcus, with his accountant, a Mr Graham, called on Mr Munsey to discuss the question of the £30,000 debt. Mr Munsey said he would use his best endeavours to see that Bentinck Securities were repaid. I am sure this was in no way a promise, but a mere assurance of Mr Munsey's goodwill. After this meeting Mr Marcus told his solicitors to take no further action for the time being. It is clear that from then on Mr Marcus did not consult his solicitors as to the legal position or seek their advice concerning the means of *c* repayment of the £30,000 Aziz Fancy loan. On 26 November 1973 Gouldens sent a letter to all the known creditors of Aziz Fancy, informing them that his estate was insolvent and that the nominated executors had, as was the fact, renounced probate. A copy of this letter was sent to Mr Marcus's solicitors who informed Mr Marcus of its contents. The renunciations of probate were filed on 26 November 1973. As far as I am aware no letters of administration were ever taken out. *d*

Some time before this, in November 1973, Mr Munsey sought Mr Crowe's advice as to whether the plaintiff companies could pay the debt owed by Mr Fancy's estate to Bentinck Securities. Mr Crowe told Mr Munsey that there was no way in which that could be done. Mr Crowe did not know any of the later dealings between Mr Munsey and Mr Marcus relating to the cheques and moneys of the plaintiffs until the late spring of 1974 after these dealings were completed. Mr Munsey then told Mr Crowe, as he also *e* told Ismat Fancy, that the moneys which had passed to the defendants on the plaintiffs' cheques were loans repayable when the moneys were needed by the plaintiffs or by the Fancy family. Mr Munsey maintained this pretence so far as the plaintiffs' auditors were concerned.

On 27 November 1973 Mr Munsey handed Mr Marcus an ISA cheque for £10,000. It is common ground that the proceeds of this cheque were to be a temporary loan to Mr *f* Marcus until 31 December 1973 (and Mr Marcus later signed a receipt dated 27 November 1973 to that affect). This cheque was paid into Bentinck Securities' bank account on 29 November 1973. At the time no one except Mr Munsey and Mr Marcus knew of this transaction. Mr Marcus's explanation in evidence was that the £10,000 was to be a temporary loan as Mr Munsey did not want the payment to appear in ISA's accounts for the year ending 31 December 1973. Mr Marcus went on to testify that he *g* and Mr Munsey agreed that Mr Marcus was to give Mr Munsey a cheque in repayment dated 31 December 1973 and that he, Mr Munsey, would give Mr Marcus a cheque for £10,000 in exchange dated 1 January 1974. This exchange of cheques duly took place. The cheque which Mr Marcus received from Mr Munsey in exchange for the Bentinck Securities' cheque for £10,000 payable to ISA was in fact drawn by Mr Munsey on Janthorpe's account and represents the first item in the plaintiffs' claim in this case. There *h* followed another cheque for £5,000 drawn by ISA payable to Mr Marcus paid into Bentinck Securities' bank account on 4 January 1974. Mr Marcus gave no evidence concerning this incident which apparently occurred whilst he was away over the Christmas and New Year holiday in Bournemouth. On 16 January 1974 Mr Marcus wrote a letter to Mr Munsey, which I will read. It is written to Mr Munsey at his home address, not at a business address. *j*

'Dear Michael [which is Mr Munsey's first name],
Many thanks for your cheque. [This would, I think, be the cheque of 4 January.] Should your conscience prick you and you feel like sending me some more funds, I should be most grateful. The simplest solution to this would be for you to send it direct to my Bank which is Barclays, 56 Great Portland Street, to the account of

a Bentinck Securities Ltd. Look forward to meeting you upon my return when we will get together.'

There is nothing sinister about the proposal that any more money should be sent direct to Mr Marcus's bank for the account of Bentinck Securities because that letter was written on the eve of Mr Marcus's departure on a cruise to West Africa. A day or so later he went to West Africa and in his absence on 22 January 1974 a further ISA cheque for £5,000 was paid into the second defendant's banking account. There were two further payments
b of ISA cheques each for £5,000 payable to Mr Marcus and paid into Bentinck Securities' banking account on 7 March and 1 April respectively. All these ISA cheques, as was the Janthorpe cheque, were drawn by Mr Munsey as a director of the respective companies. Mr Marcus gave no evidence throwing any further particular light on any of these dealings in 1974. He apparently spoke to his solicitors on 24 May 1974 and Mr Kenyon's record of this conversation with Mr Marcus reads as follows: 'Sidney Marcus told me on
c Monday last the 20th May, that he had recovered so far from Mr Fancy's estate £25,000.' I attach importance to the fact, as I find, that Mr Kenyon was not told that anything had been paid by or received from the plaintiffs. On 22 July 1974 Mr Marcus's solicitors wrote to him again a letter which said:

d 'The Late Aziz Fancy. I assume that there are no further steps that I should take in this matter on your behalf and that my file may now be marked as dead. Is this correct?'

After that Mr Marcus's solicitors entirely vanished from the scene.

Shortly after Mr Fancy's death his widow and his elder son, Ismat, were appointed directors of the plaintiff companies, but from then on until his death in March 1978 the
e business of the plaintiff companies was conducted wholly and solely by Mr Munsey who took all the business decisions and who had full and unfettered authority to act on behalf of the companies. From time to time, as I find, he told Mr Ismat Fancy in broad terms how the businesses were going. I am satisfied, and so find, that at no time did Mr Munsey tell Mr Ismat that the deceased's debt to Bentinck Securities had been paid and I reject Mr Marcus's evidence that he thanked Ismat Fancy in that regard. Mr Marcus may well also
f have made a passing remark of gratitude to Mrs Fancy, but I am quite sure that, being a woman wholly unacquainted with business, it would have meant nothing whatever to her. I am satisfied that until after Mr Munsey's death no one connected with the plaintiff companies had any idea that the payments made to the defendants in January to March 1974 were otherwise than loans repayable on demand when the money was required. The plaintiff companies' records consistently treat them as loans; conversely, Bentinck
g Securities' records treat all the payments, including the temporary loan in November 1973, as repayments to Bentinck Securities of the April 1973 loan to Mr Fancy except that in the second defendants' records there is no record of the £10,000 Janthorpe cheque paid in on 1 January 1974.

After Mr Munsey's death Mrs Fancy, Ismat and others held a meeting with the plaintiff companies' solicitor, Mr Crowe, and the accountant, Mr Hawkins, in which it was
h decided to take steps to recover the 1974 payments. The first move came on 28 March 1978. Mr Marcus took advice with the result that his accountants wrote a letter which was settled in consultation with him. It is dated 9 May 1978 from Wallace, Catch & Co.

j 'Our client has no knowledge of a loan of £30,000 made to him by your clients. In fact, Mr Marcus' company, Bentinck Securities Ltd., made an advance to Mr. Aziz Fancy on the 12th April 1973 as a loan to him. Also on that date, Mr. Fancy paid to Bentinck Securities Ltd. £2,100, being six months advance interest as agreed between the parties. The sum of £30,000 was repaid by instalments as follows.'

And then it sets out: 29 November 1973 the £10,000 which was in fact repaid by Mr Marcus by his cheque of 31 December; £5,000 on 4 January; £5,000 on 22 January; £5,000 paid in on 7 March; and £5,000 on 1 April.

'We understand that at the time the loan was made to Mr. Fancy in April 1973, he was the Managing Director of International Sales & Agencies Limited. Our client *a* [and this is an important passage] informs us that neither he nor his Finance Company, Bentinck Securities Ltd., have transacted any other business, other than that shown above with Mr. Fancy and/or International Sales & Agencies Limited.'

The matters then passed to the parties' solicitors and letters were exchanged between them. There was further correspondence, but those further letters add really nothing to *b* the history of the matter and so it came about that the writ was issued on 29 August 1978.

The first question which I have to decide is as to the nature of the dealings under review, that is, the issue and payment of the cheques totalling £30,000, the subject of the claim, to the defendants. I can dispose briefly of any suggestion that these loans were repayable on demand, as clearly Mr Munsey represented them to be. I am quite satisfied *c* that Mr Marcus never regarded himself or his company as borrowers in relation to the moneys which passed in the January to March 1974 dealings.

It is clear and I am satisfied that these dealings were to further Mr Munsey's assurance that he would use his best endeavours to see that the defendants recovered the £30,000 lent to Aziz Fancy in the situation that, to Mr Marcus's knowledge, from early November 1973, the deceased's estate was insolvent. There is no evidence that either of the plaintiff *d* companies had ever had other business transactions with the defendants (see the passage in the letter of 9 May 1978 from the defendants' accountants to which I have already referred). The January to March 1974 dealings were not in the context that the plaintiff companies, or either of them, had any interest, present or prospective, in seeing that the defendants were paid or that the discharge of the deceased's estate's liability could or would be of any benefit to the plaintiffs. Such considerations were never at any time *e* discussed between Mr Munsey and Mr Marcus. Mr Marcus in his evidence frankly conceded that neither of the plaintiffs nor Mr Munsey had any obligations to the defendants in relation to the loan to Mr Fancy.

The only conclusion it is possible to draw is that Mr Munsey for no consideration handed over the plaintiffs' moneys to the defendants without any obligation. One can only speculate as to the motive but it may well be, as Mr Marcus suggested in evidence, *f* that as Mr Munsey had introduced Mr Fancy to Mr Marcus and he, Mr Munsey, himself, had first suggested the £30,000 loan to Mr Marcus, Mr Munsey felt morally obliged to an old friend to make these payments.

It is important to consider the consequences of these dealings because this has bearing on the other questions I have to consider. Remembering that at all material times from early November Mr Marcus, as I find, knew that Mr Fancy's estate was insolvent, the *g* effect of the dealings under review was not only to deprive the plaintiff companies of their moneys and the use of their moneys, but the other consequences were to the extent that there was any value in the estate's shareholdings in the plaintiff companies (the shares were in fact charged to secured creditors) this would be diminished and to that extent the assets falling into the estate would be smaller in value. Secondly, the defendants would get priority over all the other creditors of the deceased's estate. Thirdly, the *h* defendants would get their loan repaid in full whereas the other creditors of the estate would receive a dividend, if only a small one.

Mr Marcus in his evidence said that these matters did not occur to him at the relevant time. He was speaking of course of 1974 and now he is older and he is a sick man. I am unable to rely on his evidence now as to his state of mind then.

I am quite satisfied, and I hold, that the issue of the cheques by Mr Munsey with intent *j* that they should be cashed by the defendants and taken in repayment of their loan to the deceased, Aziz Fancy, was a clear breach of Mr Munsey's duty to the plaintiffs as their director. It is, to my mind, unarguable that a director who gives away his company's money without the consent of the shareholders is not in breach of his fiduciary duty as constructive trustee of the money in the banking accounts of the companies over which he has control. I make a reference to a passage in Ungoed-Thomas J's judgment in

Selangor United Rubber Estates Ltd v Cradock (a bankrupt) (No 3) [1968] 2 All ER 1073 at
a   1093, [1968] 1 WLR 1555 at 1577 and the authorities to which he there refers.
     The nature of the dealings should also be approached from the aspect of the vires of
the company which may be important. I earlier indicated the nature of each of the
plaintiff companies' main businesses. Their respective memoranda of association, in
addition to setting out their main objects, contained common-form exhaustive lists of
ancillary objects, including, for example, lending money and giving credit, giving
b   guarantees and indemnities, making, drawing and so forth negotiable instruments and
doing all such things as may be deemed incidental or conducive to the attainment of the
companies' objects. I find it impossible to form a view that the handouts, as I shall now
call them, with which I am concerned, could conceivably fall under the umbrella of the
objects clause of either of these plaintiffs. But counsel for the defendants submits that in
considering the question of ultra vires the court is not concerned with the *nature* of any
c   transactions in question, but merely to inquire whether the form in which it is clothed
(for example, the drawing and the issue of cheques) is one covered by the objects clause
which would be the case here. I was referred to the Scottish case of *Thompson v J Barke &
Co (Caterers) Ltd* 1975 SLT 67, a decision of the Outer House given by Lord Dunpark. It
was there contended on behalf of the pursuer, the plaintiff (suing on dishonoured
company cheques issued to settle a director's personal debts), that as the company's objects
d   clause contained an express power to draw cheques, no inquiry should be made as to the
purpose for which they were drawn. Lord Dunpark rejected this submission and referred
to the issue of the cheques in the course of his judgment (at 70) as an 'attempted unlawful
application of company funds . . . which no sane director could genuinely believe . . . was
desirable in the interests of the company'. I will not cite any more from this judgment,
which I have studied very carefully, and I respectfully adopt Lord Dunpark's reasoning
e   since I find this a persuasive authority. I have also, in this context, read the judgment of
Eve J in *Re Lee, Behrens & Co Ltd* [1932] 2 Ch 46, [1932] All ER Rep 889, which reinforces
my conclusion that the 'handouts' were ultra vires.
     The next question follows from my conclusion that the handouts constituted breaches
by Mr Munsey of his fiduciary duty to the plaintiff companies as constructive trustee of
their moneys and the admitted fact that the defendants were the recipients of those
f   moneys. In my judgment, the effect of the authorities, subject to some further
consideration of recent cases, is accurately stated in 38 Halsbury's Laws (3rd edn) 858–
859, paras 1446–1557 and in the passages in *Snell's Equity* (27th edn, 1973) p 186. These
passages were approved by Danckwerts LJ in *Carl-Zeiss-Stiftung v Herbert Smith & Co (No
2)* [1969] 2 All ER 367 at 372, [1969] 2 Ch 276 at 290. It is important to bear in mind
that there are two categories of persons, recipients of company's money who are treated
g   as constructive trustees or may be treated as constructive trustees. The first category is
the person who receives moneys held by a constructive trustee and receives those moneys
for his own benefit; that is the present case. The second category is the constructive
trustee who acts as a channel through which funds disposed of in breach of constructive
trust reach other quarters, and it is clear from the authorities and from the passages in
Halsbury's Laws and *Snell* that different considerations relate to the state of mind of the
h   persons in the two categories. I think it is necessary to say that because the authorities do
not always entirely make it clear which category they are dealing with when they discuss
such questions as knowledge, constructive knowledge, imputed knowledge, and so forth.
Applying these passages, I conclude that the defendants in this case became constructive
trustees of the moneys received if Mr Marcus had actual or constructive notice (i) that the
money received was the property of the plaintiffs and (ii) that the issue of the cheques to
j   the defendants was a breach of trust and duty on Mr Munsey's part.
     So far as the first point is concerned, it is beyond argument that the defendants had
actual notice that the moneys received from paying in the plaintiffs' cheques were the
plaintiffs' moneys. As to the second matter, after considering the authorities cited to me,
in particular *Selangor United Rubber Estates Ltd v Cradock (No 3)* [1968] 2 All ER 1073,
[1968] 1 WLR 1555, *Nelson v Larholt* [1947] 2 All ER 571, [1948] 1 KB 339, *Carl-Zeiss-
Stiftung v Herbert Smith & Co* [1969] 2 All ER 367, [1969] 2 Ch 276, *Karak Rubber Co Ltd v*

Burden (No 2) [1972] 1 All ER 1210, [1972] 1 WLR 602, and the most recent authority, *Belmont Finance Corp v Williams Furniture Ltd (No 2)* [1980] 1 All ER 393, a decision of the *a* Court of Appeal, in my judgment, the knowing recipient of trust property for his own purposes will become a constructive trustee of what he receives if either he was in fact aware at the time that his receipt was affected by a breach of trust, or if he deliberately shut his eyes to the real nature of the transfer to him (this could be called 'imputed notice'), or if an ordinary reasonable man in his position and with his attributes ought to have known of the relevant breach. This I equate with constructive notice. Such a *b* position would arise where such a person would have been put on inquiry as to the probability of a breach of trust. I am satisfied that in respect of actual recipients of trust property to be used for their own purposes the law does not require proof of knowing participation in a fraudulent transaction or want of probity, in the sense of dishonesty, on the part of the recipient. That is a test which relates, not to knowing recipients of trust property for their own use, but to those who knowingly participate by assisting in *c* a breach of trust. (They may be acting, of course, as a channel through which money is passed to other persons.)

I now come to my finding on notice so far as the defendants are concerned. Mr Marcus gave some very candid answers in cross-examination. He agreed that he knew that directors of companies had to run the businesses in the interests of the shareholders and must not give the company's money away. He knew that if the companies paid Fancy *d* deceased's debt they were giving away the companies' money. He knew that Fancy's estate was insolvent and after his death no one was liable for his debts, except his estate. In answer to me he said, it was true that as long as he got his debt paid he did not mind where the money came from. He also said that these matters, together with the matters to which I earlier referred (getting paid 100% in priority to all the other creditors at the expense of the deceased's estate) never occurred to him at the time, and that had he *e* thought there was anything wrong about the dealings under review he would not have taken part in them. I regret to say I do not accept these last answers as rightly reflecting his state of mind in November 1973 through to 1 April 1974. I find it most striking that, having initially consulted his solicitors about the recovery of the debt, and having had meetings and discussions with Mr Munsey, he stayed his hand and had no further recourse to his solicitors or to his accountants about whether the arrangements he had *f* reached with Mr Munsey were 'legally feasible', to use the language of his solicitors' letter. I am sure the financial benefit he was going to derive in the circumstances, from his arrangements with Mr Munsey, overbore the impropriety of these arrangements which were I find obvious to him. I notice also that he does not appear to have told his solicitors in May 1974 that what he had recovered had come from the plaintiff companies and I find that he told his solicitor that it had come from the estate which, as Mr Marcus *g* knew, was clearly untrue. I conclude then that the defendants became constructive trustees of the £30,000 which they received on the ground that they, through the first defendant, had actual notice that this receipt was a consequence of Mr Munsey's breach of trust. In *principle* therefore the defendants are accountable to the plaintiffs for the £30,000 they received. I would add that at the very least Mr Marcus was turning a blind eye to the obvious, but I have been forced to a more unfavourable view, that is to say that *h* he actually knew of Mr Munsey's breach of trust and duty.

I now turn to the question raised by the amended defence, which is whether the defendants' liability to the plaintiffs to account for the moneys they knowingly received in breach of trust is affected by the provisions of s 9(1) of the European Communities Act 1972. This Act was passed to give effect in England to EEC Council Directive 68/151 of 9 March 1968. Section 9(1) of the 1972 Act reads as follows: *j*

> 'In favour of a person dealing with a company in good faith, any transaction decided on by the directors shall be deemed to be one which it is within the capacity of the company to enter into, and the power of the directors to bind the company shall be deemed to be free of any limitation under the memorandum or articles of association; and a party to a transaction so decided on shall not be bound to enquire

a   as to the capacity of the company to enter into it or as to any such limitation on the powers of the directors, and shall be presumed to have acted in good faith unless the contrary is proved.'

It is to be observed that the section (indeed the Act in which it is set) does not in fact reproduce, first, the statement of purposes which precedes the text of the actual articles in the directive; second, the heading of Section II of the directive (this is the section of the directive which contains art 9, which is the ancestor of s 9(1) of the 1972 Act) is:

b   'Validity of obligations entered into by a company'; third, there is an important qualification in the first paragraph of art 9 of the directive (which broadly corresponds with s 9(1) of the 1972 Act) which appears in the second paragraph of art 9. The introductory words of Directive 68/151 make it clear that what the directive is concerned with is the obligations of companies. For example, one of the recitals provides:

c   'Whereas the co-ordination of national provisions concerning disclosure, the validity of obligations entered into by, and the nullity of, such companies is of special importance . . . [and further on:] whereas the protection of third parties must be ensured by provisions which restrict to the greatest possible extent the grounds, on which obligations entered into in the name of the company are not valid . . .'

d   In my judgment, those passages and the heading of Section II of the directive are reflected effectively in the words: 'In favour of a person dealing with a company in good faith, any transaction decided on . . .' This is directed at transactions with companies which obviously will result in the companies being under obligations which before the enactment of the 1972 Act they might have been able to avoid by the application of the old ultra vires doctrine. The other passage in the directive which is not reflected in s 9(1) relates to the state of mind of the person dealing with the company. The second

e   paragraph of art 9(1) reads:

'However, Member States may provide that the company shall not be bound where such acts are outside the objects of the company, if it proves that the third party knew that the act was outside those objects . . . [and it goes on:] or could not in view of the circumstances have been unaware of it . . .'

f   Whilst art 9(1) reflects, if it proves that the third party knew the act was outside those objects, it does not directly reflect or reflect in so many words, the alternative, 'or could not in view of the circumstances have been unaware of it'. Which seems to me very close to turning a blind eye. In my judgment I am entitled to look at the Council's directive as an aid to the interpretation of s 9(1) of the 1972 Act. I conclude, first, that s 9(1) relates only to legal obligations of the company under transactions with third parties, whether

g   or not they be within or without its powers; second, that s 9(1) is designed to give relief to innocent third parties entering into transactions with companies against the operation in England of the old ultra vires doctrine; third, that the test of lack of good faith in somebody entering into obligations with a company will be found either in proof of his actual knowledge that the transaction was ultra vires the company or where it can be shown that such a person could not in view of all the circumstances, have been unaware

h   that he was party to a transaction ultra vires.

It seems to me, so far as the amended defence is concerned, I have to ask a number of questions. First, does s 9(1) of the 1972 Act at all affect the principles of constructive trust in relation to the recipients of companies' moneys knowingly paid in breach of trust, as happened, I find, in this case? Second, if the answer to the first question be No, then there is no need to go any further; but, if the answer to the first question were Yes, one

j   must then answer a number of further questions and these, in my judgment, are: were the defendants in this case '*dealing*' with the plaintiff companies (I emphasise the word 'dealing'); if so were the 'handouts', the result of these dealings, decided on by the directors of the plaintiff companies, to use the terms of s 9(1). Third, if so, has it been proved by the plaintiffs in this action that the defendants were not acting in good faith in relation to the 'handouts' which they received.

The onus of proof is on the defendants in relation to dealing with the companies in relation to the decision of the directors, but it is on the plaintiffs in relation to the absence *a* of good faith. The first question: does s 9(1) of the 1972 Act affect the application of the principles of constructive trust in cases like the present? In my judgment, the answer to this question is No. Constructive trust situations may or may not arise in an ultra vires context. The basic principles governing the two doctrines are, I find, quite different. I am satisfied that s 9(1) of the 1972 Act was designed to deal not with the operation of the doctrine of constructive trust, but only with the effect of the doctrines of ultra vires. In *b* my judgment, in the light of the EEC Council's directive, this conclusion is a plain one.

In the absence of any decided cases on the point (although I have referred to the text books, particularly Goff and Jones *The Law of Restitution* (2nd edn, 1978) and *Gower's Principles of Modern Company Law* (4th edn, 1979), which discuss this section) it is necessary for me to consider the further questions which would arise if my judgment that s 9(1) of the 1972 Act has no effect on the application of the doctrines and principles *c* of constructive trusts. I may be wrong. So I ask whether the defendants in this case were dealing with the plaintiff companies. In my judgment, the answer to this is No. The payments here did not arise from dealings with the plaintiff companies; they arose clearly from dealings with Mr Munsey. Although the companies' cheques and moneys were used by Mr Munsey, they were used by him as a vehicle for his generosity to the defendants. Mr Marcus conceded that the plaintiff companies had no obligations to him *d* in relation to the debt of Aziz Fancy's estate to the second defendants for £30,000 arising out of the April 1973 transaction.

Should I be wrong in my last conclusion, I have to answer the question whether these dealings were decided on by the plaintiffs' directors. In my judgment, although at the material times there were two other directors of the first plaintiffs (Mrs Fancy and Ismat Fancy) and three other directors of the second plaintiffs (the two Fancys and Mr Day), it *e* is clear on the evidence that Mr Munsey was the sole effective director to whom all actual authority to act for the companies was effectively delegated. I conclude therefore that these dealings, if they were in fact dealings with the companies, were in fact decided on by the directors within the terms of s 9(1) of the 1972 Act.

The last question relating to the application of s 9(1) is whether the plaintiffs have proved that the defendants did not act in good faith as that expression in the 1972 Act is *f* to be construed. My earlier findings are that the defendants had actual knowledge that the payments to them were in breach of duty and trust and were ultra vires the companies (and according to Mr Marcus's evidence, for example, he said specifically that he knew that company directors must not give away a company's money); alternatively, at the lowest, that the defendants could not in all the circumstances have been unaware of the unlawful nature of the payments that they received.

So, the final question on liability is whether, assuming Mr Munsey's dealings with the *g* defendants were ultra vires, the plaintiffs, they being, through Mr Munsey, parties to the transactions, are disentitled to recover in this action. Counsel for the defendants relies on *Sinclair v Brougham* [1914] AC 398, [1914–15] All ER Rep 622. He cited extensively from speeches in that case. Counsel for the plaintiffs also referred me to important parts of the speech of Lord Parker in that case, to a passage in the speech of Lord Wright in *Fibrosa* *h* *Spolka Akcyjna v Fairbairn Lawson Combe Barbour Ltd* [1942] 2 All ER 122 at 136–137, [1943] AC 32 at 63–64, and finally to Goff and Jones *The Law of Restitution* (2nd edn, 1978) pp 363–364 and the authorities there referred to. My conclusion is that on my finding that Mr Munsey handed out the plaintiffs' moneys to the defendant without any obligation on his or their parts, the defendants gave no consideration for these moneys and received the moneys with notice that they were the companies' moneys paid over in *j* breach of trust in order to implement Mr Munsey's assurance of 'using his best endeavours' to help an old friend, the decided cases in no way preclude the plaintiffs from recovery at common law or in equity. I base my conclusion, primarily, on my finding of the accountability of the defendants as constructive trustees, but I would reach the same conclusion if the plaintiffs' claims were based solely on the defendants' receipt (in the circumstances I find here) of the moneys paid ultra vires.

I now turn to the question of remedy. Counsel for the plaintiffs concedes that he is not

a in a position to seek a tracing order or to substantiate a claim for conversion of the plaintiffs' cheques or moneys. The remedy he seeks is to recover the plaintiffs' £30,000 as money had and received at common law or by way of restitution in equity. He submits that the defendants were virtually in the same position, so far as relief is concerned, as the defendants in *Reckitt v Barnett, Pembroke & Slater Ltd* [1929] AC 176, [1928] All ER Rep 1 and I agree with him. It follows that the first plaintiffs are entitled

b to judgment against the defendants for £20,000 and the second plaintiff, Janthorpe, are entitled to judgment against the defendants, for £10,000.

Judgment for the plaintiffs.

Solicitors: *Gouldens* (for the plaintiffs); *Jacobson Ridley* (for the defendants).

c

K Mydeen Esq   Barrister.

Habib Bank Ltd v Tailor
d

COURT OF APPEAL, CIVIL DIVISION
CUMMING-BRUCE, DUNN AND OLIVER LJJ
25 MAY 1982

Mortgage – Order for possession of mortgaged property – Suspension of execution of order –
e *Mortgagor permitted to defer payment of principal sum but provision also made for earlier*
payment in event of default by mortgagor – Mortgagor charging dwelling house to secure
repayment of bank overdraft on current account – Mortgage containing covenant by mortgagor
to repay principal sum secured by charge on bank's written demand for payment – Mortgagor
exceeding overdraft and bank making written demand for repayment of principal sum and
interest – Whether court entitled to exercise discretion to postpone order for possession to give
f *mortgagor reasonable time to repay sums due – Whether mortgage permitting mortgagor 'to*
defer payment' of principal sum – Whether mortgage providing for 'earlier payment' in event of
default – Administration of Justice Act 1970, s 36(1) – Administration of Justice Act 1973,
s 8(1).

In 1978 a bank agreed to allow the defendant an overdraft of up to £6,000 on his current
g account. The overdraft was secured by a charge on the defendant's dwelling house. The charge contained a covenant in the usual bankers' form by which the defendant agreed to pay the bank, on demand being made in writing, the balance due in respect of all moneys owing to the bank. By July 1980 the defendant had exceeded the overdraft limit. He failed to reduce his indebtedness to the bank and on 8 July 1981 the bank made a written demand for payment of all the moneys then owed by the defendant, amounting
h to £6,570, made up of principal, interest and bank charges. The defendant did not comply with the demand and on 16 October 1981 the bank commenced proceedings against him in the county court for possession of the house. By the date of hearing the defendant owed the bank £7,212. The deputy registrar found on the facts that the defendant would not be able to pay off the whole of that sum within a reasonable time and therefore held that he was not entitled to exercise the discretion under s 36[a] of the
j Administration of Justice Act 1970 to delay making a possession order of a dwelling house in favour of a mortgagee in order to give the mortgagor reasonable time to pay the sums due under the mortgage. Accordingly, he made an order for possession in favour of the bank. On appeal by the defendant, the judge held that, because s 8[b] of the

---

a   Section 36, so far as material, is set out at p 563 *j* to p 564 *c*, post
b   Section 8, so far as material, is set out at p 564 *g* to p 565 *a*, post

Administration of Justice Act 1973 extended the discretion under s 36 of the 1970 Act to
cases where the mortgage provided for the mortgagor to be permitted 'to defer payment'   *a*
of the principal sum and also provided 'for earlier payment in the event of any default by
the mortgagor', there was discretion under s 36 to postpone the making of a possession
order against the defendant because an indefinite loan (such as that made to the defendant)
by definition provided for the mortgagor to be permitted to defer payment and further
provided for earlier payment in the event of default. The judge accordingly held that
possession should be postponed to give the defendant a reasonable time to pay the   *b*
amount by which the overdraft had been exceeded together with interest thereon. The
bank appealed. On the appeal the defendant conceded that the discretion under s 36 of
the 1970 Act was exercisable only if s 8 of the 1973 Act applied to the charge.

Held – The bank's appeal would be allowed for the following reasons—

(1) For a mortgage, or an agreement under it, 'to defer payment' of the principal sum   *c*
secured by the mortgage, within s 8(1) of the 1973 Act, there had to be an express term
in the mortgage or agreement deferring payment of the principal sum after it had
become due, ie deferring the legal liability to pay the principal sum. In the case of a
normal bank mortgage to secure an overdraft the principal did not become due and
could not be sued for by the bank until a written demand had been made, and up until
that time there was no due date from which any deferment of payment could be made.   *d*
Since the charge did not provide for the defendant to defer payment of the principal after
demand had been made, s 8(1) did not apply to the charge (see p 566 *j* to p 567 *j* and
p 568 *a*, post); *Lloyds Bank Ltd v Margolis* [1954] 1 All ER 734 applied; *Centrax Trustees
Ltd v Ross* [1979] 2 All ER 952 distinguished.

(2) Furthermore, since payment of the principal sum was not due from the defendant
until a demand for payment was made, there was no provision in the charge for payment   *e*
to be made earlier than the date of the demand, and therefore the charge did not provide
for 'earlier payment' in the event of default by the defendant within s 8(1) (see p 567 *b c
d e h* and p 568 *a*, post).

Notes
For the discretion to postpone the date for delivery of possession in an action by a   *f*
mortgagee for possession of a dwelling house, see 32 Halsbury's Laws (4th edn) para 836.

For the Administration of Justice Act 1970, s 36, see 40 Halsbury's Statutes (3rd edn)
1060.

For the Administration of Justice Act 1973, s 8, see 43 ibid 755.

Cases referred to in judgments   *g*
Centrax Trustees Ltd v Ross [1979] 2 All ER 952, Digest (Cont Vol E) 443, *3393b*.
Halifax Building Society v Clark [1973] 2 All ER 33, [1973] Ch 307, [1973] 2 WLR 1, Digest
    (Cont Vol D) 700, *1559b*.
Joachimson v Swiss Bank Corp [1921] 3 KB 110, [1921] All ER Rep 92, CA, 3 Digest
    (Reissue) 571, *3676*.
Lloyds Bank Ltd v Margolis [1954] 1 All ER 734, [1954] 1 WLR 644, 3 Digest (Reissue)   *h*
    707, *4268*.

Appeal
The plaintiffs, Habib Bank Ltd (the bank), appealed against the judgment of his Honour
Judge Owen given on 16 December 1981 in Willesden County Court whereby he allowed
an appeal by the defendant, Gulabhai Naginbas Tailor, from the order of Mr Deputy   *j*
Registrar Israel, dated 2 December 1981, ordering the defendant to give up possession of
his house at 142 Walton Avenue, Harrow, Middlesex, to the bank within 56 days. The
grounds of the appeal were, inter alia, that the judge misdirected himself in law in
holding that s 8 of the Administration of Justice Act 1973 applied to a legal charge dated

a 25 October 1978 made between the bank and the defendant for the purpose of exercising the discretion conferred on the court under s 36 of the Administration of Justice Act 1970. The facts are set out in the judgment of Oliver LJ.

John Wilmers QC and *Diana Adie* for the bank.
Christopher Cutting for the defendant.

b **OLIVER LJ** delivered the first judgment at the invitation of Cumming-Bruce LJ. This is an appeal from the decision of his Honour Judge Owen at the Willesden County Court on 16 December 1981, by which he reversed a decision of the deputy registrar ordering the defendant to give up possession of a property known as 142 Walton Avenue, Harrow, which was the defendant's dwelling house.

The defendant, Mr Tailor, is a customer of the plaintiffs, Habib Bank Ltd, which
c maintains a branch at 334 Kilburn High Road, London.

In 1978 the bank appears to have arranged with the defendant to allow him an overdraft facility of up to £6,000. I say 'appears' because there is no specific finding of fact about this, but it emerges from the particulars of claim which have been verified by an affidavit. That overdraft was secured by a charge on the dwelling house that I have referred to, and which has a rateable value of only some £207. The charge which is dated
d 25 October 1978 is what I take to be the bank's ordinary form for an 'all accounts' charge. Clause 1 is a covenant for payment in the usual bankers' form, under which the mortgagor covenants, on demand in writing, to pay to the bank the balance due in respect of all moneys which may become owing to the bank from the mortgagor. By cl 2, the mortgagor, as beneficial owner, charges the property which I have mentioned with payment of all moneys covenanted to be paid. There is nothing out of the ordinary,
e I think, in any of the other provisions of the charge to which I need refer.

Mr Tailor availed himself fully of his facility with the bank, but by July 1980 he seems to have trespassed a little too far on the bank's goodwill by exceeding the limit of £6,000 which he had been set, and he failed or refused to reduce his indebtedness. Accordingly, on 8 July 1981 the bank, pursuant to the charge, made a written demand for payment of the whole sum owing, which then amounted to £6,570·37. That was made up of £6,000
f principal, £12 bank charges and £558·37 interest outstanding up to the date of demand. That demand was not complied with and on 16 October 1981 the bank commenced proceedings for obtaining possession. By that time the indebtedness had risen to some £6,871, and by the time the matter came before the deputy registrar it had further increased to some £7,212. We are told that it is now something of the order of £7,737.

The deputy registrar ordered possession within eight weeks, but the defendant
g appealed to the judge who reversed his decision. Counsel for the defendant tells us that the matter was fairly perfunctorily dealt with by the deputy registrar, because he took the view, and indeed counsel does not really quarrel with this, that it was fairly obvious that the defendant could not pay off the whole overdraft within a reasonable time. The deputy registrar took the view that in those circumstances he ought not to exercise his discretion to postpone possession under s 36 of the Administration of Justice Act 1970.
h The ground of appeal to the judge was that the deputy registrar had misdirected himself in thinking that this was not a case for the application of his discretion under s 36 of the 1970 Act, because it was said that s 8 of the Administration of Justice Act 1973 applied to this charge and brought that discretion into operation. I think it would be desirable at this stage that I should refer to these sections because they are crucial to the appeal which is before us.
j First of all, s 36 of the 1970 Act provides:

'(1) Where the mortgagee under a mortgage of land which consists of or includes a dwelling-house brings an action in which he claims possession of the mortgaged property, not being an action for foreclosure in which a claim for possession of the mortgaged property is also made, the court may exercise any of the powers conferred on it by subsection (2) below if it appears to the court that in the event of its *a* exercising the power the mortgagor is likely to be able within a reasonable period to pay any sums due under the mortgage or to remedy a default consisting of a breach of any other obligation arising under or by virtue of the mortgage.

(2) The court—(*a*) may adjourn the proceedings, or (*b*) on giving judgment, or making an order, for delivery of possession of the mortgaged property, or at any time before the execution of such judgment or order, may—(i) stay or suspend *b* execution of the judgment or order, or (ii) postpone the date for delivery of possession, for such period or periods as the court thinks reasonable.

(3) Any such adjournment, stay, suspension or postponement as is referred to in subsection (2) above may be made subject to such conditions with regard to payment by the mortgagor of any sum secured by the mortgage or the remedying of any default as the court thinks fit . . .'　　　　　　　　　　　　　　　　　　　　　　　　　　*c*

As originally framed that section suffered from certain defects. It suffered in the first place from a defect that it did not apply to proceedings for foreclosure where possession was also sought, and it became the practice, I think, for quite a number of mortgagees to seek foreclosure and add a claim for possession when their real object was to obtain possession. That was a matter which was dealt with by the subsequent legislation to which I shall refer in a moment. That does not matter for present purposes, but the other *d* defect was this: the idea of s 36 was to mitigate the severity of the legal rule that a mortgagee, as the owner of an estate in land, is entitled as against the mortgagor to possession of the property, and it was to give some protection to mortgagors who had had the misfortune to fall into difficulties with paying their instalments and to allow them a reasonable time to make good their default.

By definition, the cases in which it was likely to be invoked were cases where the *e* whole principal sum had become due by deafult, because most mortgages contain a provision making the whole principal sum due in the case of default. The reference in the section to 'a reasonable period to pay any sums due under the mortgage' had therefore the effect of confining the operation of the section to relatively few cases, for, if the mortgagor was already in difficulties with his instalments, the chances of his being able to pay off the whole principal as well in a reasonable time must be considered fairly slim. *f* That difficulty came to light in *Halifax Building Society v Clark* [1973] 2 All ER 33, [1973] Ch 307. Following that case a further provision was made in s 8 of the Administration of Justice Act 1973. It is in these terms so far as is material for the purpose of this case:

'(1) Where by a mortgage of land which consists of or includes a dwelling-house, or by any agreement between the mortgagee under such a mortgage and the *g* mortgagor, the mortgagor is entitled or is to be permitted to pay the principal sum secured by instalments or otherwise to defer payment of it in whole or in part, but provision is also made for earlier payment in the event of any default by the mortgagor or of a demand by the mortgagee or otherwise, then for purposes of section 36 of the Administration of Justice Act 1970 (under which a court has power to delay giving a mortgagee possession of the mortgaged property so as to allow the *h* mortgagor a reasonable time to pay any sums due under the mortgage) a court may treat as due under the mortgage on account of the principal sum secured and of interest on it only such amounts as the mortgagor would have expected to be required to pay if there had been no such provision for earlier payment.

(2) A court shall not exercise by virtue of subsection (1) above the powers conferred by section 36 of the Administration of Justice Act 1970 unless it appears *j* to the court not only that the mortgagor is likely to be able within a reasonable period to pay any amounts regarded (in accordance with subsection (1) above) as due on account of the principal sum secured, together with the interest on those amounts, but also that he is likely to be able by the end of that period to pay any

a further amounts that he would have expected to be required to pay by then on account of that sum and of interest on it if there had been no such provision as is referred to in subsection (1) above for earlier payment . . .'

So, without seeking to construe the section at this stage, one can see that the intent of it was, in the case of instalment mortgages, to enable the court to defer possession if it was satisfied that there was a reasonable prospect of the mortgagor paying off, within a reasonable period, not the whole of the principal sum, but the outstanding instalments.

b It is this section which is the only one which helps the defendant in this case. Section 36, of course, applies to any mortgage of a dwelling house, and no doubt if the defendant could satisfy the court that he was able, within a reasonable time, to pay off the whole of his overdraft, that section would have enabled the court to postpone the date for delivery of possession, but his counsel agrees that there is no serious question of that. If therefore the powers conferred by s 36(2) of the 1970 Act are to be exercisable in this case, it can c only be because s 8 of the 1973 Act applies to the mortgage which is in question here.

When the matter came before the judge, he considered himself bound to apply s 8 to this mortgage, and he accordingly reversed the decision of the deputy registrar and he remitted the matter to him for consideration of a period which the defendant should be given to allow him to catch up, not with the whole of the overdraft, but simply with the amount of the outstanding interest. It was clear, as I say, that if the principal had not d been paid the defendant could not in any event do it, but it was probable that if, as the judge held, all that he had to repay for the purposes of this section, or what had to be taken into account for the purposes of s 36, was the outstanding interest, there was a reasonable prospect of his being able to do so, and the actual period was a matter which, quite rightly, the judge held ought to be determined by the registrar.

The reasoning by which the judge arrived at his conclusion that the section applied e was that he was referred to a decision of Goulding J in *Centrax Trustees Ltd v Ross* [1979] 2 All ER 952. It was a case in which there was a mortgage with a fixed date for repayment six months ahead of the date of the mortgage, the classic case in effect of the old type of fixed mortgage where the legal date for redemption is fixed at six months after the date of the execution of the mortgage, but there was a clear intention from other provisions in the mortgage, notably the provision for the payment of interest (which was clearly f envisaged as extending beyond the period of six months limited for the repayment of the principal) which indicated that the common intention of the parties was that the mortgage would be allowed to stay out indefinitely and that the mortgagor would be entitled to defer payment of the principal sum beyond the date fixed so long as he paid interest on that principal sum.

Goulding J, in the course of his judgment, read s 8 of the 1973 Act and said (at 955):

g 'Given a mortgage of a dwelling-house, there are two provisions which, as counsel for the plaintiffs pointed out, must be present if s 8 is to apply. One is a provision that the mortgagor is entitled or is to be permitted to pay the principal by instalments or otherwise to defer payment thereof. The second is a provision for earlier payment in the event of any default by the mortgagor or of a demand by the h mortgagee or otherwise. Both provisions must be terms of the contract between the parties, for they must be made either by the mortgage or by an agreement between mortgagee and mortgagor. In the present case, in my judgment, the provisions can be found only in the mortgage itself. [Then he dealt with an exchange of letters, and continued:] Section 8 is not drawn in formal conveyancer's language. I do not find it easy to see exactly what is meant by the phrase "is to be permitted to pay" as j an alternative to "is entitled to pay"; nor is the term "earlier payment" altogether apt in relation to an indefinite and merely permissive deferment of payment. However, it is clear from the words "or otherwise", twice repeated, that Parliament has attempted to give legislative shelter to a wide class of owner-occupiers, and it is unlikely that in what may be called social legislation of this sort Parliament intended an occupier's situation to depend on distinctions in conveyancing. Therefore, in my opinion, notwithstanding that the Acts restrict the rights of lenders without giving *a* compensation, the language used must receive a reasonably liberal interpretation.'

He went on to hold that the section applied in that case.

That of course was a very different case from the instant case. It was a case where there was a fixed date for repayment of the principal sum and it was a case where it was quite clearly intended that the actual payment of the principal sum should be deferred beyond that fixed date. And it was a case also where, if default was made in payment of interest, *b* the mortgage contained a provision for calling in the whole sum.

Counsel for the bank in this case has forcibly submitted that the reasoning of that case cannot apply here. In my judgment he is right in making that submission. I say nothing about the correctness of the decision in *Centrax Trustees* on the construction of the section. It is indeed difficult, I think, to escape from the conclusion that the section did apply to that case, even though I, for myself, rather question whether it was intended by *c* the legislature to do so. But the instant case is really quite a different case. As counsel for the bank pointed out, and indeed as was pointed out by Goulding J in *Centrax Trustees*, there are two necessary conditions for the application of the section: first, either the mortgage itself or some agreement made under it must have the effect that (I will quote only the relevant words) 'the mortgagor . . . is to be permitted . . . otherwise to defer payment of' the principal sum 'in whole or in part'; second, provision must be made in *d* the mortgage or agreement 'for earlier payment in the event of any default by the mortgagor or of a demand by the mortgagee or otherwise'. Counsel for the bank's first submission is that there is no permission to defer payment. As he points out, this is a simple case of a bank mortgage to secure an overdraft. It is quite clear on the authority that in these circumstances the money is not capable of being sued for by the bank until demand has been made. Indeed, the mortgage itself so provides, because it is to secure *e* the moneys covenanted to be paid and the moneys are covenanted to be paid on demand having been made in writing. This nowhere more clearly appears than from *Lloyds Bank Ltd v Margolis* [1954] 1 All ER 734, [1954] 1 WLR 644. I think it is only necessary to read briefly from the judgment of Upjohn J ([1954] 1 All ER 734 at 738, [1954] 1 WLR 644 at 649):

f

'In my judgment, where there is the relationship of banker and customer and the banker permits his customer to overdraw on the terms of entering into a legal charge which provides that the money which is then due or is thereafter to become due is to be paid "on demand", that means what it says. As between the customer and banker, who are dealing on a running account, it seems to me impossible to assume that the bank were to be entitled to sue on the deed on the very day after it *g* was executed without making a demand and giving the customer a reasonable time to pay. It is indeed a nearly correlative case to that decided in *Joachimson* v. *Swiss Bank Corpn.* ([1921] 3 KB 110, [1921] All ER Rep 92) where the headnote was this: "Where money is standing to the credit of a customer on current account with a banker, in the absence of a special agreement a demand by the customer is a necessary ingredient in the cause of action against the banker for money lent." In *h* this case the agreement has provided quite clearly what is to be done before the bank can sue. They must demand the money.'

When one looks at the charge in the instant case, one asks immediately: 'Where is the agreement to be found that the mortgagor is to be permitted otherwise to defer payment of the principal?' because, by definition, the principal does not become due, and cannot *j* be sued for by the bank, until a written demand has been made. Deferment, I think, involves the deferment of payment after it has become due, and quite clearly in this case there appears to me to be no provision, either in the agreement between the parties or in the mortgage itself, by which, on any realistic construction, it can be said that payment by the customer was to be 'deferred', or that the customer was permitted to 'defer'

payment. Counsel for the defendant has in fact submitted that every case where the
a principal money does not become payable immediately the mortgage is executed is a
case where the mortgagor is entitled to defer payment. That is a submission which I find
is impossible to accept.

It seems to me that the defendant's case on the application of s 8 of the 1973 Act fails
at that point, but it also fails, I think, on the other condition too, because, as counsel for
the bank pointed out, the section requires that provision must be made for earlier
b payment, and one has to ask oneself: 'Earlier than what?' In the instant case the payment
was not due until the demand was made, and there is no provision for any payment
earlier than that. It is the demand itself which makes the payment due.

For both those reasons, it seems to me that this is clearly a case where s 8 cannot apply
to this mortgage, and that really concludes the case. I think it unnecessary to elaborate
the matter further. If there had been some reasonable prospect of the defendant repaying
c the whole of the principal sum, then no doubt it would have been appropriate for the
judge to have remitted the matter back to the registrar for a determination of whether
he should exercise his power under s 36(2) of the 1970 Act to adjourn the proceedings or
to postpone the date for the delivery of possession, but that, as counsel for the defendant
accepts, does not arise. Section 8 does not apply. There is then no further room for the
operation of the discretion under s 36, and accordingly in my judgment the decision of
d the judge must be reversed and the decision of the deputy registrar restored. I would
therefore allow the appeal.

DUNN LJ. I entirely agree and only add a few words of my own because we are
disagreeing with the judge.

It seems to me that the judge overlooked the fact that the relationship between the
e plaintiff and the defendant was that of banker and customer. He also overlooked the
express terms of the covenant itself. Unlike a borrower under a simple loan, who borrows
money payable on demand (in which case the loan is repayable as soon as it is made
without the necessity of a formal demand) the customer of a bank who borrows money
on current account is not liable to repay that money unless and until the bank makes
demand. That proposition is nowhere more clearly stated than in the passage of
f Upjohn J's judgment which Oliver LJ has cited in *Lloyds Bank Ltd v Margolis* [1954] 1 All
ER 734 at 738, [1954] 1 WLR 644 at 649. This relationship of banker and customer is
reflected in this case in the covenant, in the mortgage deed, which is the subject of the
charge, because the covenant by the mortgagor (the defendant) is that he will, on demand
in writing, pay to the bank the balance for the time being due or owing to the bank. So
there is nothing payable under that covenant until demand is made, and I find it to be
g straining the language of s 8(1) of the Administration of Justice Act 1973 to say that a
mortgagor in the situation of this defendant is, and I quote from the material words of
this section, 'to be permitted . . . otherwise to defer payment'. Those words seem to me
to presuppose an existing legal liability to pay which is deferred by the terms of the
mortgage or the covenant. That is not the situation here. The situation here is that there
is no liability to pay at all until demand is made, and therefore in my view it is impossible
h to say that payment is deferred by the demand which is itself a precondition of any
liability.

For those reasons, and for the reasons given by Oliver LJ, I, too, would allow this
appeal.

CUMMING-BRUCE LJ. I agree. If the judge had been right, the unexpected effect of
j the language of s 8(1) of the Administration of Justice Act 1973 would have been to
deprive bankers who use the usual charge for security for an overdraft of any right of
enforcement, as long as the debtor continued to pay the interest on the capital lent.
Experience has shown that from time to time the language selected by the draftsmen has
unexpected effects, but for my part it is with some relief that we find that, on a scrutiny
of this very ordinary form of charge, taken in conjunction with the language of s 8, that

an unexpected but necessary revolution in banking practice is not called for. I agree that
the appeal should be allowed.   *a*

Appeal allowed. Order below reversed. Order for possession within 28 days.

Solicitors: *Gillhams*, Willesden (for the bank); *Ivor Levy & Co*, Wembley (for the
defendant).

Henrietta Steinberg   Barrister.   *b*

R v Hereford City Justices, ex parte O

                                                                                                 c

QUEEN'S BENCH DIVISION (CROWN OFFICE LIST)
REEVE J
10 JUNE 1982

*Affiliation – Affiliation order – Appeal – Appeal on question of quantum only – Procedure –
Whether appeal lies to Crown Court or to Divisional Court by way of case stated – Affiliation*   *d*
Proceedings Act 1957, s 8(1).

The mother of an illegitimate child made a complaint to magistrates under s 1 of the
Affiliation Proceedings Act 1957 alleging that B was the father of the child. The
magistrates adjudged that he was and ordered him to pay the mother £1 per week. She
wished to appeal to the Crown Court against the order solely on the ground that the   *e*
amount which the father was ordered to pay was too small, but was advised by Crown
Court officials that s 8(1)[a] of the 1957 Act gave a right of appeal only in respect of 'an
order under this Act' and that, because the adjudication as to paternity was 'the order'
under the Act, she could not appeal purely on a question of quantum. She was further
advised that the proper procedure was to appeal to the Divisional Court by way of case
stated. Accordingly, she asked the magistrates to state a case and when the magistrates   *f*
refused, she applied to the court for an order of mandamus requiring them to do so.

Held – The mother was entitled to appeal to the Crown Court solely on the ground of
quantum because the order for the payment of money was at least part of the 'order'
referred to in s 8(1) of the 1957 Act, and that was the proper course for the mother to
adopt if she wished to appeal against the amount of the award. Accordingly, the   *g*
application for mandamus requiring the magistrates to state a case was misconceived and
would be dismissed (see p 570 *b* to *d*, post).
  Oldfield v National Assistance Board [1960] 1 All ER 524 followed.
  R v Ipswich Crown Court, ex p Smith (1973) 143 JP 586 not followed.

Notes   *h*
For affiliation proceedings, see 1 Halsbury's Laws (4th edn) paras 621, 624, 631.
  For the Affiliation Proceedings Act 1957, ss 1, 8, see 1 Halsbury's Statutes (3rd edn) 76,
84.

Cases referred to in judgment
Oldfield v National Assistance Board [1960] 1 All ER 524, [1960] 1 QB 635, [1960] 2 WLR   *j*
  423, DC, 35 Digest (Repl) 815, 97.
R v Ipswich Crown Court, ex p Smith (1973) 143 JP 586, DC.

---

a   Section 8(1), so far as material, is set out at p 569 *h*, post

Application for judicial review

a The applicant applied by motion for an order of mandamus directed to the Hereford City justices requiring them to state a case so that she could appeal, by way of case stated, against an order which they had made on 1 July 1981 on the hearing of a complaint by her under s 1 of the Affiliation Proceedings Act 1957. The motion came before Woolf J in the Queen's Bench Division on 10 February 1982. He gave leave for the application to proceed and to be heard by a judge attached to the Family Division. The facts are set out
b in the judgment.

Brendan Shiner for the applicant.
The justices did not appear.

REEVE J. On 30 June 1980, the applicant, who lives in Hereford, gave birth to a child.
c In due course, she made complaint before the Hereford City Magistrates' Court alleging that B was the father of that child. Her complaint was heard before the justices on 1 July 1981.

The justices, on B's own admission, were satisfied that he was the father of that child. Having made that adjudication, they proceeded to consider whether they should make financial provision, and they ordered B to pay to the applicant the sum of £1 per week.
d Those advising the applicant sought to appeal from that order in regard to quantum. They were first minded to take that appeal before the Crown Court.

On seeking to enter that appeal, they were advised by officials at the Crown Court that that was not the proper procedure and that no such appeal lay to the Crown Court when a question of quantum only was involved. Such advice was based on a note to s 8 of the Affiliation Proceedings Act 1957 to that effect in *Stone's Justices' Manual* (114th edn, 1982)
e vol 1, p 2070 which cites as authority for the proposition the case of *R v Ipswich Crown Court, ex p Smith* (1973) 143 JP 586. The note goes on to say: 'Presumably a party may appeal by way of case stated to challenge the amount of the order.' So those advising the applicant had to change their tactics, and they sought to appeal by way of case stated.

The justices on being asked to state a case refused to do so, apparently taking the view that the matter was too trivial. The advisers to the applicant then took steps to obtain an
f order of mandamus requiring the justices to state a case. That matter came before Woolf J on 10 February 1982, and he gave leave to the applicant to proceed with her application and for the application to be heard by a Family Division judge. That expression is to be read as meaning a judge allotted to the Family Division; but for jurisdictional purposes, such judge would sit as a Queen's Bench judge to hear the application. In those circumstances, the matter comes before me.

g In *Smith's* case Lord Widgery CJ gave the judgment of the Divisional Court with which Ashworth and Willis JJ agreed. They held that there was no power for either party to appeal against an affiliation order on the ground only of the amount of the payment directed in the order. The provision which the court was considering in s 8 (1) of the Affiliation Proceedings Act 1957, which reads, as amended by the Courts Act 1971, as follows: 'An appeal shall lie to the Crown Court from the making of an order under this
h Act, or from any refusal by a Magistrates' Court to make such an order . . .'

Lord Widgery CJ, after frankly stating that he thought that the point was very largely a matter of first impression, based his judgment on the consideration that a finding that a man was or was not the putative father of the child alone constituted 'an order under this Act'. No cases were referred to in the judgment and there is no indication that any cases were cited in argument. It is, to my mind, unfortunate that the case of *Oldfield v*
j *National Assistance Board* [1960] 1 All ER 524, [1960] 1 QB 635, which was also decided by a Divisional Court of the Queen's Bench Division, was not drawn to his attention. Lord Parker CJ gave the judgment with which Cassels and Ashworth JJ agreed. After considering the provisions of s 4 of the Bastardy Laws Amendment Act 1872, s 7 of the Affiliation Orders Act 1914, and s 8 of the Affiliation Proceedings Act 1957, he observed that in all those three Acts the words used are a little different. But, he went on to say ([1960] 1 All ER 524 at 528, [1960] 1 QB 635 at 644):

'As will be seen, in the Act of 1872 there is no definition but it was contemplated that there should be, as it were, two stages, an adjudication and then what is called *a* an order for the payment of money. In the Act of 1914, the adjudication and the order for the payment of money are together treated as the affiliation order, and in the Affiliation Proceedings Act, 1957, the order for the payment of money alone is treated as the affiliation order. For my part, however, the significant fact is that under all those three statutes adjudication alone is not an order.'

It seems to me to be inevitable that had the judgment of Lord Parker CJ in *Oldfield's* *b* case been drawn to the attention of the court in *Smith's* case, it would have come to a different conclusion, and it would not have held that the adjudication that a man was or was not the putative father was itself the order under the 1957 Act. I feel that in those circumstances I am not bound to follow the decision in *Smith's* case and can adopt the reasoning in *Oldfield's* case. Once it is accepted, as I do, that the order for payment of money is, at the least, part of the order under the 1957 Act, I do not see how it can be *c* argued that an appeal lies only against the making or refusal of an order and not against the amount ordered to be paid. In those circumstances, I hold that the application made before me is entirely misconceived; and that the proper course for the applicant to adopt, if she wishes to appeal against the order for the payment of £1 a week, is to go to the Crown Court.

I dismiss the application. *d*

Application dismissed.

Solicitors: *Beaumont, Smith & Davies*, Hereford (for the applicant).

Bebe Chua   Barrister. *e*

Clay v Pooler

QUEEN'S BENCH DIVISION AT BIRMINGHAM *f*
HODGSON J
25 JUNE, 23 JULY 1982

Fatal accident – Damages – Loss of future earnings – Survival of claim for benefit of estate – Measure of damages – Principles of assessment – Deductions to be made from estimated net future earnings in arriving at surplus earnings on which award to be based – Living expenses – Method of calculating – Same method to be used as under Fatal Accidents Act – Living expenses restricted *g* *to deceased's own living expenses.*

Fatal accident – Damages – Deduction from damages – Award under Fatal Accidents Act – Effect of intestacy on amount of damages under Law Reform (Miscellaneous Provisions) Act 1934 – Effect of intestacy on amount deductible from dependant's award under Fatal Accidents Act *h* *and on total award under both Acts – Whether effect of intestacy making defendant directly interested in division of damages under Fatal Accidents Act between deceased's dependants – Law Reform (Miscellaneous Provisions) Act 1934 – Fatal Accidents Act 1976.*

Fatal accident – Damages – Division of damages between widow and children – Effect on division of claim under Law Reform (Miscellaneous Provisions) Act 1934 for deceased's loss of future *j* *earnings in lost years where deceased died intestate – Fatal Accidents Act 1976.*

Fatal accident – Damages – Benefits excluded in assessing damages – Insurance money paid as a result of the death – Claim under Law Reform (Miscellaneous Provisions) Act 1934 and under Fatal Accidents Act – Deduction of Law Reform Act damages from Fatal Accidents Act damages a *– Deceased dying intestate – Point at which insurance moneys to be excluded from dependant's damages under Law Reform Act – Fatal Accidents Act 1976, s 4(1).*

In calculating damages under the Law Reform (Miscellaneous Provisions) Act 1934 for a deceased's loss of earnings in the lost years, the deceased's probable living expenses in the lost years, which have to be deducted from his probable earnings in arriving at the damages to be awarded, are the same as, and no more than, the deceased's personal living

b expenses which have to be deducted from his probable earnings in calculating the amount of any dependency under the Fatal Accidents Act 1976 (see p 574 *d f* and p 576 *c*, post); *Pickett v British Rail Engineering Ltd* [1979] 1 All ER 774 applied; *Benson v Biggs Wall & Co* (1980) [1982] 3 All ER 300 followed.

Where a deceased dies intestate, different rules will govern the distribution of (i) the damages for loss of earnings in the lost years awarded under the 1934 Act, which, since

c they form part of the deceased's estate, will be distributed according to the rules of intestacy, and (ii) the damages awarded under the 1976 Act, which will be calculated according to the amount of the dependency. Furthermore, a dependant's damages under the 1934 Act, eg those of a dependent wife, may be less than the amount of the dependency under the 1976 Act because of the intestacy rules and therefore the defendant will, in effect, have to make up the difference, since he must pay to the dependant not

d only the damages under the 1934 Act but also the amount of the dependency under the 1976 Act (after deducting the damages under the 1934 Act) and therefore the total damages under both Acts for which the defendant may be liable may exceed the amount of the damages payable under each Act taken separately. It follows that where the deceased dies intestate a defendant has a direct interest in the way in which the award under the 1976 Act is distributed between each dependant because the amount of each

e dependency will determine, after deducting therefrom the dependant's entitlement under the 1934 Act, the amount (if any) payable by the defendant under the 1976 Act (see p 573 *e* to *h*, post); *Eifert v Holt's Transport Co Ltd* [1951] 2 All ER 655n not followed.

If a deceased dies intestate and his estate consists partly of damages awarded under the 1934 Act and partly of insurance money payable as a result of the deceased's death (which insurance money is, by virtue of s 4(1)[a] of the 1976 Act, to be disregarded in assessing

f damages under that Act), the amount of a dependant's entitlement under the 1934 Act, and therefore the amount which has to be deducted from his damages under the 1976 Act in ascertaining the amount of the damages (if any) payable to him under the 1976 Act, is to be calculated by applying the intestacy rules to the whole of the deceased's estate. Accordingly, the appropriate procedure in such a case is to apply the intestacy rules to the amount of the award under the 1934 Act plus the insurance money, then

g divide the whole estate among the beneficiaries and then deduct from each beneficiary's share a proportion of the insurance money in proportion to the amount of his share of the estate, rather than deduct the insurance money from a notional estate before applying the intestacy rules (see p 576 *e* to p 577 *d*, post).

Notes

h For damages for loss of earnings in the lost years, see 12 Halsbury's Laws (4th edn) para 1154.

For damages under the Fatal Accidents Act 1976 generally, see 34 ibid para 14, and for deductions from those damages, see ibid para 97.

For the Law Reform (Miscellaneous Provisions) Act 1934, see 13 Halsbury's Statutes (3rd edn) 115.

j For the Fatal Accidents Act 1976, s 4 see 46 ibid 1122.

Cases referred to in judgment
Benson v Biggs Wall & Co (1980) [1982] 3 All ER 300.

---

a   Section 4(1), so far as material, is set out at p 576 *g h*, post

Davies v Powell Duffryn Associated Collieries Ltd [1942] 1 All ER 657, [1942] AC 601, HL, 36(1) Digest (Reissue) 368, *1484.*

Eifert v Holt's Transport Co Ltd [1951] 2 All ER 655n, CA, 36(1) Digest (Reissue) 376, *1512.*

Gammell v Wilson [1981] 1 All ER 578, [1982] AC 27, [1981] 2 WLR 248, HL.

Lawrence v John Laing Ltd (5th May 1982, unreported), QBD.

Nutbrown v Rosier (1982) Times, 1 March.

Oliver v Ashman [1961] 3 All ER 323, [1962] 2 QB 210, [1961] 3 WLR 669, CA, 36(1) Digest (Reissue) 313, *1267.*

Pickett v British Rail Engineering Ltd [1979] 1 All ER 774, [1980] AC 136, [1978] 3 WLR 955, HL, Digest (Cont Vol E) 459, *1314b.*

Skelton v Collins (1966) 115 CLR 94, Aust HC.

Sullivan v West Yorkshire Passenger Transport Executive (17 December 1980, unreported), QBD.

Thompson v Price [1973] 2 All ER 846, [1973] QB 838, [1973] 2 WLR 1037, 36(1) Digest (Reissue) 365, *1482.*

White v London Transport Executive [1982] 1 All ER 410, [1982] QB 489, [1982] 2 WLR 791.

Action

By a writ issued on 10 July 1981 the plaintiff, Patricia Ann Clay, the widow of and administratrix of the estate of Daniel Joseph Clay deceased, claimed against the defendant, Robert Pooler, (i) damages under the Fatal Accidents Act 1976 on behalf of herself and her two daughters as dependants of the deceased and (ii) damages under the Law Reform (Miscellaneous Provisions) Act 1934 on behalf of the deceased's estate, in consequence of the deceased's death as a result of a road accident on 5 September 1980. The defendant admitted liability and the only issue was the quantum of the damages. The facts are set out in the judgment.

Peter Weitzman QC for the plaintiff.
Harry Wolton QC for the defendant.

Cur adv vult

23 July. **HODGSON J** read the following judgment: On 5 September 1980 Mr Clay was killed in a road accident. For that accident the defendant admits liability. Mr Clay left a widow and two children. His widow, as administratrix of his estate, claims damages on behalf of herself and the children of the marriage under the Fatal Accidents Act 1976 and on behalf of the deceased's estate under the Law Reform (Miscellaneous Provisions) Act 1934.

At the date of his death the deceased was 35 years of age. His widow was exactly the same age, being born on the same day as he was. There are two children: Adelle, born on 6 March 1967, and Julie, born on 17 May 1968.

The deceased was a systems engineer employed by Pye Telecommunications. He was a valued servant and a competent, reliable and skilful man. His prospects for promotion to regional technical adviser were good, limited only by his wish to continue living where his home was, which meant that promotion had to await a vacancy in the actual depot where he worked.

Based on the earnings of a man in the same position as himself, his earnings would today have been £5,933 per annum. In fact, in the months before his death the deceased earned 5·44% more than his comparator and an attempt was made to establish that this pattern would have continued. This actual difference was due to the deceased working more overtime than the other man in those months, but I am satisfied that that was purely a matter of luck. There was no difference in willingness or competence between him and the other man.

a   In addition, the deceased was provided with a car by his employers. The car was a Ford Escort. It was replaced with a new car every two years. The deceased was permitted to use it for his own purposes when not working. It is agreed that this usage would amount to 5,000 miles per annum. Nearly all of this usage was with his family, providing the service demanded by teenage girls and their friends, and taking the family on holidays and for outings. All the expenses of running and maintaining the car were paid for by his employers, save only the cost of petrol for private use.

b   The deceased was a frugal man whose only hobby, apart from his family, was fishing. He spent most of his time with his family, was a moderate drinker, usually going out with his wife, rarely alone. He smoked a pipe occasionally.

He was a very good handyman. Indeed, 'DIY' was his main hobby. The family moved into a new council house some years ago, which they intended to buy. He did a great deal of work of improvement both inside the house and in the garden. He did all the c   decorating. He was able to do most repairs necessary to the services in the house. When central heating was installed he assisted the contractors and became competent enough to envisage himself extending, unaided, the system to the bedrooms in the near future.

The deceased bought few clothes for himself, preferring to spend money on clothes for his wife and children. He took a packed lunch to work. Since his death, the plaintiff has used insurance money to purchase the house and a car which she now herself drives.

d   The children are still at school. The elder girl takes her O level examinations in 1983 and intends to stay on at school to take A level biology with the intention of making a career somewhere in the obstetric side of medicine. The younger girl is at present attracted by the idea of making a career in child care.

On those facts the calculation of damages under the Fatal Accidents Act and its distribution between the three dependants presents no undue difficulty. The difficulty e   which does arise in this case is the calculation of the deceased's claim which enures to his estate under the provisions of the Law Reform (Miscellaneous Provisions) Act 1934, and the reason why this question is or may be of importance to the parties in this case is because, the deceased having died intestate, his estate has to be divided according to the rules governing intestacy, which, of course, give a different distribution to that made by the court under the Fatal Accidents Act. Money coming to a dependant from the f   deceased's estate is taken into account in computing the damages to be awarded to him under the Fatal Accidents Act. It follows that if, for example, a dependent child gets more from his father's estate than the damages to which he would be entitled under the Fatal Accidents Act, his Fatal Accidents Act claim is swallowed up completely. However, this may mean that the dependent wife gets less from the estate than her entitlement under the Fatal Accidents Act, so that the defendant has in effect to make up the g   difference.

Therefore, because different rules govern the distribution of the two funds (the dependency fund and the estate fund) a defendant may find himself having to pay more in damages than he would if the award of damages was made only in relation to one of the claims against him and not both.

It follows also that a defendant has a direct interest not only in the computation of the h   two claims which he faces but also in the distribution between dependants of the Fatal Accidents Act fund, and the decision to the contrary in *Eifert v Holt's Transport Co Ltd* [1951] 2 All ER 655 can no longer be considered good law.

There are two ways in which a claim under the Fatal Accidents Act can be presented. The first and more cumbersome way is to build up the dependency item by item and then cross-check it against the deceased's net annual income at the date of his death. The j   second, the method adopted in this case, is that stated by Lord Wright in the well-known passage from his speech in *Davies v Powell Duffryn Associated Collieries Ltd* [1942] 1 All ER 657 at 665, [1942] AC 601 at 617:

> 'The starting point is the amount of wages which the deceased was earning . . .
> Then there is an estimate of how much was required or expended for his own

personal or living expenses. The balance will give a datum or basic figure which will generally be turned into a lump sum by taking a certain number of years' purchase.' *a*

In Kemp and Kemp *The Quantum of Damages* (4th edn, 1975) vol 1, pp 235–236 this method is expressed thus:

'Start with the deceased's net income at the date of his death: estimate how much of this he spent on himself: then, if his pattern of life justifies the assumption, take *b* the remainder of his net income as being spent for the benefit of his dependants.'

In estimating how much the deceased spent on himself, no account is of course taken of expenditure on things and services the cost of which continue unabated after his death, such as mortgage payments, rates, lighting and heating, although in one sense the moneys spent on such things before his death were part of his personal or living expenses. In *Pickett v British Rail Engineering Ltd* [1979] 1 All ER 774, [1980] AC 136 the House of *c* Lords overruled *Oliver v Ashman* [1961] 3 All ER 323, [1962] 2 QB 210 and held that an injured plaintiff was entitled to recover damages for loss of earnings during the years lost by the reduction of his expectation of life, but that those damages should be computed after deduction of his probable living expenses during that period. In that case the plaintiff had been alive at the date of trial but died before his appeal could be heard. His widow as administratrix of his estate carried on the proceedings. *d*

In this case counsel contends on behalf of the plaintiff that the computation of the deceased's 'probable living expenses' is precisely the same calculation as that used in the Fatal Accidents Act claim to arrive at his 'personal living expenses'. Counsel for the defendant contends that the two calculations are different and that, in arriving at a figure for the deceased's 'probable living expenses' when calculating the value of the lost years claim, one should take into account not only those items of expenditure included in the *e* Fatal Accidents Act claim but also the other items of expenditure which, although part of his 'living expenses', continue to be necessary expenses of his dependants after his death.

If this is correct, then the lost years claim is decreased to a figure below the dependency assessed under the Fatal Accidents Act, and the defendant escapes in whole or in part at least having to pay both the lost years claim for the benefit of the estate and the additional *f* sum to bring the widow's claim up to full dependency.

The method contended for by counsel for the plaintiff was adopted by Peter Pain J in *Benson v Biggs Wall & Co* [1982] 3 All ER 300, a case decided in June 1980. In *Nutbrown v Rosier* (1982) Times, 1 March, Mr Aubrey Myerson QC, sitting as a deputy judge of the High Court, adopted the method contended for by counsel for the defendant. In arriving at his decision, Mr Myerson cited *White v London Transport Executive* [1982] 1 All ER 410, *g* [1982] QB 489 and a case decided by Mustill J, *Sullivan v West Yorkshire Passenger Transport Executive* (17 December 1980, unreported). I have not seen a transcript of Mustill J's judgment and know nothing of the facts of that case. In *White's* case Webster J was concerned with an unmarried man killed in an accident at work and the decision of Peter Pain J in *Benson v Biggs Wall & Co* was not cited to him.

Neither in *Pickett v British Rail Engineering Ltd* nor in the later case of *Gammell v Wilson* *h* [1981] 1 All ER 578, [1982] AC 27 did the House of Lords go into any detail as to what precisely should be included in 'probable living expenses'. In *Pickett's* case [1979] 1 All ER 774 at 781–782, [1980] AC 136 at 150–151 Lord Wilberforce said:

'The judgments [in the Australian case of *Skelton v Collins* (1966) 115 CLR 94], further, bring out an important ingredient, which I would accept, namely that the *j* amount to be recovered in respect of earnings in the "lost" years should be that amount after deduction of an estimated sum to represent the victim's probable living expenses during those years. I think that this is right because the basis, in principle, for recovery lies in the interest which he has in making provision for dependants and others, and this he would do out of his surplus. There is the *a* additional merit of bringing awards under this head into line with what could be recovered under the Fatal Accidents Acts.'

It seems clear from that passage that Lord Wilberforce was saying that, where there were dependants of a deceased, necessary expenditure on them, although also on items enjoyed by the deceased, should be excluded from the calculation of the victim's probable living expenses.

Lord Salmon said ([1979] 1 All ER 774 at 784, [1980] AC 136 at 154):

b 'I think that in assessing those damages, there should be deducted the plaintiff's own living expenses which he would have expended during the "lost years" because these clearly can never constitute any part of his estate. The assessment of these living expenses may, no doubt, sometimes present difficulties, but certainly no difficulties which would be insuperable for the courts to resolve, as they always have done in assessing dependency under the Fatal Accidents Acts.'

c Lord Edmund-Davies said ([1979] 1 All ER 774 at 792, [1980] AC 136 at 163):

'The only guidance I can proffer is that, in reaching their final figure, the court should make what it regards as a suitable deduction for the total sum which Mr Pickett would have been likely to expend on himself during the "lost years". This calculation, too, is by no means free from difficulty, but a similar task has to be performed regularly in cases brought under the Fatal Accidents Act.'

d Finally, Lord Scarman said ([1979] 1 All ER 774 at 798, [1980] AC 136 at 171):

'I conclude, therefore, that damages for loss of future earnings (and future expectations) during the lost years are recoverable, where the facts are such that the loss is not too remote to be measurable. But I think, for the reasons given by Lord Wilberforce, Lord Scarman and Lord Edmund-Davies, that a plaintiff (or his estate) should not recover more than that which would have remained at his disposal after meeting his own living expenses.'

From these passages it seems to me to be clear that the House of Lords was saying that, in cases where a victim had dependants, money expended on those dependants was not *f* to be taken to be part of his own living expenses.

In *Gammell v Wilson* the House of Lords had to consider two cases where awards of damages for lost earnings in the lost years had been made to the estates of two young unmarried men whose deaths had been caused by the negligence which gave rise to the causes of action subsisting to their estates. In his speech, Lord Diplock dealt with the case where a middle-aged married man in steady employment was the victim of a fatal *g* accident and this passage, albeit obiter, seems to me to be conclusive in favour of counsel for the plaintiff's argument. Having referred to the facts of *Oliver v Ashman*, Lord Diplock continued ([1981] 1 All ER 578 at 583, [1982] AC 27 at 65):

'Here was an obvious injustice which this House remedied by overruling *Oliver v Ashman* and holding that a living plaintiff could recover damages for loss of earnings *h* during the lost years, but that in assessing the measure of such damages there should be deducted from the total earnings the amount that he would have spent out of those earnings on his own living expenses and pleasures since these would represent an expense that would be saved in consequence of his death. In the case of a married man of middle age and of a settled pattern of life, which was the case of Mr Pickett, the effect of this deduction is to leave a net figure which represents the amount which he would have spent on providing for his wife and any other dependants, *j* together with any savings that he might set aside out of his income. If one ignores the savings element, which in most cases would be likely to be small, this net figure is substantially the same as the damages that would have been recoverable by the widow under the Fatal Accidents Acts: it represents the dependency. So, in the particular case of Mr Pickett's widow the result was to do substantial justice. My

Lords, if the only victims of fatal accidents were middle-aged married men in steady employment living their lives according to a well-settled pattern that would have been unlikely to change if they had lived on uninjured, the assessment of damages for loss of earnings during the lost years may not involve what can only be matters of purest speculation. But, as the instant appeals demonstrate and so do other unreported cases which have been drawn to the attention of this House, in cases where there is no such settled pattern (and this must be so in a high proportion of cases of fatal injuries) the judge is faced with a task that is so purely one of guesswork that it is not susceptible to solution by the judicial process. Guesses by different judges are likely to differ widely, yet no one can say that one is right and another wrong.'

I conclude accordingly that the reasoning of Peter Pain J in *Benson v Biggs Wall & Co* was correct, and I do not follow Mr Myerson's judgment in *Nutbrown v Rosier*.

There is another question concerning tax which may require answering before I come to the decisions of fact which I have to make. In this case the deceased's estate included what must have been substantial sums of insurance money, and these moneys, together with the conventional sum for loss of expectation of life, will swell the deceased's estate which will not consist solely of the damages awarded for the lost years. But of course insurance moneys are, by statute, not to be taken into account in assessing damages under the Fatal Accidents Act.

The question which may arise is carefully considered in Kemp and Kemp *The Quantum of Damages* (4th edn, 1975) vol 1, p 226. In this case, however, I am told there will be no capital transfer tax to pay on the deceased's estate, so no difficulty of this sort will arise. If this is not the position then there is liberty to apply and address further argument on this point.

Lastly, there is a problem of a not dissimilar nature which will arise in this case. Subject to statutory exceptions, the general rule is that the damages to be awarded to dependants of a deceased person under the Fatal Accidents Act must take into account any net pecuniary benefit accruing to that dependant in consequence of the death of the deceased: see *Davies v Powell Duffryn Associated Collieries Ltd* [1942] 1 All ER 657 at 659, [1942] AC 601 at 609 per Lord Macmillan and the cases cited in Kemp and Kemp *The Quantum of Damages* (4th edn, 1975), vol 1, p 222, footnote 19. If a dependant receives the benefit of sums awarded to the deceased's estate for loss of expectation of life and for earnings in the lost years, such benefit will be deducted in full from the dependant's damages. This deduction is confined to the net pecuniary benefit after allowing for tax and the expenses of administration incurred as a result of the estate benefiting from the damages awarded for the claim, the benefit of which survives to the estate; but s 4(1) of the 1976 Act provides:

'In assessing damages in respect of a person's death in an action under this Act, there shall not be taken into account any insurance money . . . which has been or will or may be paid as a result of the death.'

In this case there are insurance moneys which have been paid to the deceased's estate under a contract or contracts of insurance. The estate therefore consists in part of damages on the deceased's surviving claim, and in part of insurance moneys which must not be taken into account. The problem is the point at which they are excluded from the calculation of the various dependants' pecuniary benefit where, as here, the deceased died intestate.

The rules of law governing the distribution of a deceased's estate apply, of course, to the whole estate so that the amount of deductible gain from a dependant's damages made under the Fatal Accidents Act will depend on when the insurance money is excluded.

A simple example demonstrates the problem. Suppose in this case the Law Reform Act claim amounts to £50,000 and insurance moneys to an equal amount. Ignoring interest and administration expenses, the widow takes £25,000, leaving a residue of

£75,000. As to half, she takes a life interest, a sum of £37,500, the value of which to her
a is perhaps £35,000. The other half is divided between the children in two sums of
£18,750 to which must be added their reversionary interest in the widow's life interest,
a figure of say £1,250 each, making total of £20,000. So from the estate, the widow gets
£60,000 and each child £20,000. If, for the purpose of the Fatal Accidents Act claim, the
insurance moneys are now deducted proportionately, the amount deductible from the
widow's claim will reduce it to £30,000 and each child's deductible amount will be
b £10,000. If, however, the sum of £50,000 for insurance money is deducted from the
estate before the rules on intestacy are notionally applied, the widow's deductible amount
will be £36,500 and each child's £6,750.

As the sum by which each child benefits will, on either calculation, clearly extinguish
completely the Fatal Accidents Act claim, the way in which insurance moneys are taken
into account may be of importance to the defendant.
c   So far as I am aware, this question has not previously called for decision, but I think
that the first solution must be the correct one. It would be wholly artificial to apply the
rules governing the distribution of an estate on intestacy to a notional estate, and there
does not seem to me to be any justification for deducting the insurance moneys otherwise
than proportionately among the beneficiaries.

Since writing this judgment I have seen a decision of Cantley J, *Lawrence v John Laing*
d *Ltd* (5th May 1982, unreported), and I am reinforced in my decision on the question of
living expenses by that judge's findings in that case. After similar reasoning he came to
the same conclusions as I have done.

I now turn to the assessment of damages under the Fatal Accidents Act claim. The
multiplicand in cases where the claim is presented as it has been here consists of a
proportion of the deceased's net earnings divided between the loss before and after trial,
e together with items which increase the value of the dependency but do not come from
the deceased's net income, here, the value of the company car and the deceased's
substantial contribution as a handyman.

In this case the net earnings are £5,933 and, on the facts of this case, I do not think
that it would be right to reduce them by more than 25%. On the evidence, the deceased's
expenditure on himself for his own personal or living expenses was as low as it reasonably
f could be.

So far as the value of the company car is concerned, I have been provided with evidence
as to the estimated standing and running costs per annum of a comparable motor car.
The total for licence, insurance, depreciation and interest on capital is £1,342·67. The
running costs for 5,000 miles per annum, excluding petrol, amount to £228·15, giving
a total of about £1,570 per annum.
g   Counsel for the plaintiff contends that I should take 75% of this sum as an addition to
the multiplicand. Counsel for the defendant contends that it is unrealistic to take the
figures for a car which no doubt because belonging to a company fleet is replaced every
two years, for a family car doing only 5,000 miles per annum. I think this is correct. The
loss is undoubtedly substantial but for a car doing 5,000 miles per annum a depreciation
based on a car doing 10,000 miles per annum, which is the basis on which the figures
h given to me are calculated, must, I think, be wrong; nor do I think I ought to compensate
the dependants for the loss of use of a car replaced by a new one every two years, though
whether that will make very much difference to the figure for interest on capital I doubt.
The company car is replaced every two years presumably because that is the most
economical way of doing it. Nor would the running costs for a car doing 5,000 miles per
annum be as much as they would be for a car doing 10,000 miles. The annual figure
j contended for by counsel for the plaintiff, based on 75% of the total costs, is nearly
£1,200. For the reasons I have given, this seems to me to be too high. An accurate
calculation is impossible, but I think a figure of £800 to be added to the multiplicand
would be fair.

The value of the 'DIY' services of the deceased were clearly very substantial and there
is no doubt that it will require quite heavy expenditure per annum to replace them. I

think a reasonable sum to be awarded would be £200 per annum. Like the main pecuniary dependency, these two figures have to be divided between pre-trial and future *a* loss.

I have decided that the multiplier which should be applied to these sums is 15. In arriving at that figure I take into account the substantial prospects of promotion which the deceased enjoyed. In arriving at the figure I have also taken into account the comparative security of his employment and the regard in which he was held by his employers, as well as the normal discounts such as the dangers of ill-health or of losing *b* his job.

The total sum as damages under the Fatal Accidents Act, excluding interest accrued before trial, is therefore (subject to my arithmetic being correct) £66,600 for pecuniary loss of dependency, £12,000 for the loss of use of a motor car, and £3,000 for loss of 'DIY' services, making a total of £81,600.

So far as apportioning this sum between the dependants, I do not differentiate between *c* the two girls, both of whom will, whilst they stay at home, continue to be provided for by their mother. Following *Thompson v Price* [1973] 2 All ER 846, [1973] QB 838, I also have regard to the possibility that their mother will remarry. The award to the children must be only in respect of the benefits they might have expected to receive from the deceased over and above their keep. Taking these things into consideration, I award each child the sum of £2,500. The widow's share is therefore £76,600. For the sake of *d* completeness, I should add that all interest will go to the widow, together with the sum of £218 funeral expenses.

Computation of the Law Reform Act claim presents no difficulties following my decision on law. Damages for loss of earnings in the lost years are £66,600, being, in my opinion, precisely the same as the damages under the Fatal Accidents Act dependency claim. To this has to be added the conventional sum for loss of expectation of life which *e* I assess at £1,500, making a total of £68,100. For that sum the plaintiff is entitled to judgment. The calculation of its distribution between the widow and children is not an exercise which I have the information to undertake. Clearly, when the net benefit after deduction of the insurance moneys in the way I have indicated is calculated, the claims of the two children under the Fatal Accidents Act will be extinguished. To what extent the widow's claim is reduced by her share of the Law Reform Act part of the estate must *f* await detailed calculation. No doubt there are actuarial calculations which can be used to arrive at the values respectively of the widow's life interest and the children's reversionary interests therein.

Now, are there any findings of fact I ought to have made and have not?

[Counsel for the plaintiff invited his Lordship to deal specifically, in regard to the claim under the Law Reform (Miscellaneous Provisions) Act 1934, with the loss of the *g* use of the company car used by the deceased. Counsel contended that that loss should be treated as part of the deceased's loss of earnings because had he lived he would have had the use of the car in addition to his monetary earnings. His Lordship ruled that in assessing the damages for loss of earnings in the lost years under the 1934 Act the court should not, in the present case, take into account the fact that the deceased had had the use of a company car because the use of the car for his work could not be regarded as part *h* of his earnings. Furthermore, so far as concerned the use of the car by the deceased for his personal enjoyment, that also should not be included in the Law Reform Act claim as part of the deceased's lost earnings.]

Judgment accordingly.

Solicitors: *Robin Thompson & Partners,* Birmingham (for the plaintiff); *Godfrey, Diggines & McKay,* Birmingham (for the defendant).

K Mydeen Esq   Barrister.

a   # Earl of Lonsdale v Attorney General

CHANCERY DIVISION
SLADE J
9–13, 16–20, 23–25 NOVEMBER 1981, 15 JANUARY 1982

b   *Mine – Minerals – Reservation – Implied term – Right to work implied in reservation –
Reservation in respect of petroleum and natural gas – Grant by Crown in 1880 of right to coal,
culm, ironstone and fireclay and 'all other mines and minerals (if any)' in or under certain land –
Whether grant including oil and natural gas.*

*Petroleum rights – Crown – Rights vested in Crown – Petroleum and natural gas situated inside
and outside territorial waters – Rights included in mineral grant made by Crown – Whether
c   rights to oil and natural gas statutorily revesting in Crown – Petroleum (Production) Act 1934 –
Continental Shelf Act 1964.*

By a conveyance made in 1880 a predecessor in title of the plaintiff purchased from the
Crown, for the sum of £50,000, 'the mineral substances' and 'also all other mines and
d   minerals (if any)' in or under a tract of sea bed adjacent to the Cumberland coast, part of
which extended beyond the 3-mile limit of territorial waters. The 'mineral substances'
were defined, by reference to a prior lease and agreement, as 'ALL and every the Mines
veins seams and beds of coal culm ironstone and fireclay'. The grant was expressly
conditional on the grantees 'in no way injuring or interfering with . . . the surface of the
lands' under which the mineral substances lay. In 1973, when it became apparent to the
e   plaintiff that the Crown might include the tract of sea bed in an oil exploration licence
issued under the Petroleum (Production) Act 1934, he issued a writ seeking a declaration
that he was entitled to any oil or natural gas in or under the tract of sea bed. The plaintiff
contended that the ordinary, primary meaning of the term 'minerals' was every substance
which could be obtained from underneath the surface of the earth for the purpose of
profit, and therefore included oil and natural gas, which were accordingly included in
f   the term 'all other mines or minerals (if any)' used in the 1880 conveyance, even though
the parties might not have specifically directed their minds in 1880 to the possibility of
oil and natural gas being present under the sea bed. The Crown contended that the term
'minerals' was to be construed according to its vernacular meaning in 1880 and the
express terms of the grant, neither of which included oil and natural gas, and further
contended that even if the 1880 grant included rights to oil and natural gas those rights
had since become revested in the Crown by virtue of the operation of the 1934 Act and
g   the Continental Shelf Act 1964.

Held – The claim would be dismissed for the following reasons—
    (1) The term 'mines and minerals' was not a definite term which had a primary or
literal meaning and, although the term might in the appropriate context mean every
h   substance which could be obtained from under the earth's surface for profit, the actual
meaning depended, unless the meaning was clear from the instrument of grant itself, on
the factual matrix of the grant and the vernacular meaning used in the mining world,
the commercial world and by landowners at the time of the grant (see p 589 *f*, p 590 *d e*,
p 609 *d* to p 610 *d* and p 628 *a b* and *e*, post); dictum of James LJ in *Hext v Gill* [1861–73]
All ER Rep at 396–397, *North British Rly Co v Budhill Coal and Sandstone Co* [1910] AC 116,
j   dicta of Lord Porter in *Borys v Canadian Pacific Rly Co* [1953] 1 All ER at 454–455 and of
Lord Wilberforce in *Reardon Smith Line Ltd v Hansen-Tangen* [1976] 3 All ER at 574–575
applied; *Darvill v Roper* (1855) 3 Drew 294, *Glasgow Corp v Farie* [1886–90] All ER Rep
115, *Barnard-Argue-Roth-Stearns Oil and Gas Co Ltd v Farquharson* [1911–13] All ER Rep
190 and *O'Callaghan v Elliott* [1965] 3 All ER 111 considered.
    (2) However, since the evidence was inconclusive whether the vernacular usage of the

term 'mines and minerals' in 1880 included oil or natural gas, the question whether petroleum or natural gas were included in the 1880 grant ultimately depended on the construction of the grant itself, construed in the light of the surrounding circumstances. Having regard to the fact that the grant specifically referred to solid substances such as coal, culm, ironstone and fireclay which could be extracted by means of underground mining and also required the grantee not to injure or interfere with the surface of the sea bed, it was to be inferred that the parties in 1880 did not contemplate that the grant would include the extraction of oil and natural gas extracted by drilling involving disturbance of or interference with the sea bed, and the grant was to be construed accordingly (see p 612 *f* and *j* to p 613 *a* and *g* to p 614 *h*, p 615 *c* to *h*, p 616 *c* and p 628 *b c* and *e*, post).

Per curiam. The 1934 Act does not revest in the Crown the rights to any oil or natural gas situated inside territorial waters which has been previously included in a grant of minerals made by the Crown. However, the effect of the 1964 Act is to revest in the Crown the rights to any oil or natural gas situated outside territorial waters which has been included in a mineral grant previously made by the Crown (see p 626 *c* to *f*, p 627 *e* to *h* and p 628 *c d*, post).

Notes

For minerals, see 31 Halsbury's Laws (4th edn) paras 8–11, and for cases on the subject, see 33 Digest (Repl) 727–731, 38–90.

For territorial jurisdiction, see 10 Halsbury's Laws (4th edn) para 727, and for cases on the subject, see 16 Digest (Reissue) 145–146, 1476–1483.

For the Petroleum (Production) Act 1934, see 22 Halsbury's Statutes (3rd edn) 86.

For the Continental Shelf Act 1964, see ibid 587.

Cases referred to in judgment

A-G v Ewelme Hospital (1853) 17 Beav 366, 51 ER 1075, 11 Digest (Reissue) 759, 721.

A-G v Salt Union Ltd [1917] 2 KB 488, 33 Digest (Repl) 730, 72.

A-G for British Columbia v A-G for Canada [1914] AC 153, PC, 8(2) Digest (Reissue) 711, 255.

A-G for the Isle of Man v Mylchreest (1879) 4 App Cas 294, PC, 33 Digest (Repl) 729, 56.

Barnard-Argue-Roth-Stearns Oil and Gas Co Ltd v Farquharson [1912] AC 864, [1911–13] All ER Rep 190, PC, 33 Digest (Repl) 729, 59.

Borthwick-Norton v Gavin Paul & Sons Ltd 1947 SC 659.

Borys v Canadian Pacific Rly Co [1953] 1 All ER 451, [1953] AC 217, [1953] 2 WLR 224, PC, 33 Digest (Repl) 802, 721.

Brown v Chadwick (1857) 7 ICLR 101, 33 Digest (Repl) 752, *201.

Caledonian Rly Co v Glenboig Union Fireclay Co [1911] AC 290, [1911–13] All ER Rep 307, HL, 33 Digest (Repl) 727, 38.

Charrington & Co Ltd v Wooder [1914] AC 71, HL, 17 Digest (Reissue) 377, 1418.

Darvill v Roper (1855) 3 Drew 294, 61 ER 915, 33 Digest (Repl) 723, 1.

Fagernes, The [1927] P 311, CA, 16 Digest (Reissue) 145, 1477.

Feather v R (1865) 6 B & S 257, 122 ER 1191, 17 Digest (Reissue) 339, 1063.

Fitzhardinge (Lord) v Purcell [1908] 2 Ch 139, 47 Digest (Repl) 728, 727.

Glasgow Corp v Farie (1888) 13 App Cas 657, [1886–90] All ER Rep 115, HL, 33 Digest (Repl) 724, 12.

Great Western Rly Co v Carpalla United China Clay Co Ltd [1910] AC 83, HL, 33 Digest (Repl) 729, 67.

Hext v Gill (1872) LR 7 Ch App 699, [1861–73] All ER Rep 388, LJJ, 33 Digest (Repl) 727, 44.

Jersey (Earl) v Neath Poor Law Union Guardians (1889) 22 QBD 555, CA, 33 Digest (Repl) 726, 27.

Johnstone v Crompton & Co [1899] 2 Ch 190, 33 Digest (Repl) 728, 53.

Kirkness v John Hudson & Co Ltd [1955] 2 All ER 345, [1955] AC 696, [1955] 2 WLR 1135, HL, 28(1) Digest (Reissue) 463, 1668.

Linlithgow (Marquis) v North British Rly Co 1912 SC 1327; affd [1914] AC 820, HL, 11 Digest (Reissue) 192, 453.

Listowel v Gibbings (1858) 9 ICLR 223, 33 Digest (Repl) 752, *202.

a   *Lord Advocate v Clyde Navigation Trustees* (1891) 19 R (SC) 174, 47 Digest (Repl) 702, *516.

Lord Advocate v Wemyss [1900] AC 48, 33 Digest (Repl) 740, 185.

Midland Rly Co v Checkley (1867) LR 4 Eq 19, 11 Digest (Reissue) 181, 388.

North British Rly Co v Budhill Coal and Sandstone Co [1910] AC 116, HL, 33 Digest (Repl) 728, 46.

O'Callaghan v Elliott [1965] 3 All ER 111, [1966] 1 QB 601, [1965] 3 WLR 746, CA, 31(2)

b   Digest (Reissue) 942, 7713.

Ontario Natural Gas Co v Smart (1890) 19 OR 591.

Pianka v R [1979] AC 107, [1977] 3 WLR 859, PC, Digest (Cont Vol E) 131, *721a.

Post Office v Estuary Radio Ltd [1967] 3 All ER 663, [1968] 2 QB 740, [1967] 1 WLR 1396, CA, 14(1) Digest (Reissue) 163, 1150.

R v Keyn (1876) 2 Ex D 63, CCR, 16 Digest (Reissue) 146, 1478.

c   *Reardon Smith Line Ltd v Hansen-Tangen* [1976] 3 All ER 570, [1976] 1 WLR 989, HL, Digest (Cont Vol E) 545, 183a.

Rhondda's (Viscountess) Claim [1922] 2 AC 339, HL, 17 Digest (Reissue) 343, 1103.

Robertson v French (1803) 4 East 130, 102 ER 779, 17 Digest (Reissue) 298, 643.

Secretary of State for India v Chelikani Rama Rao (1916) LR 43 Ind App 192, PC, 47 Digest (Repl) 702, 478.

d   *Southland Frozen Meat and Produce Export Co Ltd v Nelson Bros Ltd* [1898] AC 442, PC, 17 Digest (Reissue) 317, 846.

Waring v Foden, Waring v Booth Crushed Gravel Co Ltd [1932] 1 Ch 276, [1931] All ER Rep 291, CA, 33 Digest (Repl) 801, 720.

Cases also cited

e   *Blackpool Pier Co v Fylde Union Assessment Committee* (1877) 46 LJMC 189.

Carr v Fracis Times & Co [1902] AC 176, HL.

Dudley's Settled Estates, Re (1882) 26 Sol Jo 359.

Harris v SS Franconia (owners) (1877) 2 CPD 173.

Knight Sugar Co Ltd v Alberta Rly and Irrigation Co [1938] 1 All ER 266, PC.

Leda, The (1856) Sw 40, 166 ER 1007.

f   *Marker v Kenrick* (1853) 13 CB 188, 138 ER 1169.

Menzies v Breadalbane and Holland (Earl) (1822) 1 Sh Sc App 225.

Midland Rly Co and Kettering, Thrapston and Huntingdon Rly Co v Robinson (1890) 15 App Cas 19, HL.

Quebec Fisheries, Re [1917] 35 DLR 1.

R v Kent Justices, ex p Lye [1967] 1 All ER 560, 1967] 2 QB 153.

g   *River Wear Comrs v Adamson* (1877) 2 App Cas 743, [1874–8] All ER Rep 1, HL.

Sabally v A-G [1964] 3 All ER 377, [1965] 1 QB 273, CA.

Trinidad Asphalt Co v Ambard [1899] AC 594, PC.

United States v California (1947) 332 US 19.

West Rand Central Gold Mining Co Ltd v R [1905] 2 KB 391.

h   ### Action

By a writ issued on 16 February 1973 the plaintiff, James Hugh William, seventh Earl of Lonsdale, sought against the defendants, the Attorney General and Ultramar Exploration Ltd, a declaration that the ownership of any oil or natural gas in or under certain tracts of land forming part of the bed of the Irish Sea adjacent to the coast of Cumberland, referred to as 'the Lonsdale off-shore areas', down to the bottom of the coal measures in

j   and under such areas was vested in the plaintiff as the life tenant of a settlement dated 5 October 1936. At the hearing of the action the plaintiff did not seek a declaration against the second defendant, Ultramar Exploration Ltd, which accordingly took no part in the proceedings and was not represented.

Donald Rattee QC and *Roger Horne* for the plaintiff.
Leonard Bromley QC and *John Mummery* for the Crown.

Cur adv vult

15 January. **SLADE J** read the following judgment: In this action, the Right Honourable James Hugh William, seventh Earl of Lonsdale, as plaintiff, seeks a declaration that the *a* ownership of any oil or natural gas in or under certain tracts of land which form part of the bed of the sea adjacent to the Cumbrian coast and are referred to in the pleadings as 'the Lonsdale off-shore areas', down to the bottom of the coal measures in and under such areas, is vested in him as tenant for life under a settlement dated 5 October 1936. The two defendants are H M Attorney General and Ultramar Exploration Ltd (Ultramar). On 4 August 1969 the Crown granted or purported to grant to Ultramar a licence to search *b* and bore for and get oil and natural gas in an area forming part of the Lonsdale off-shore areas. The prayer to the statement of claim seeks also a declaration that this licence is not binding on the plaintiff, Lord Lonsdale, or his successors in title. However, I have been told that this licence has now been determined. Accordingly, he seeks no declaration as against Ultramar, which itself has not been represented before me. The contest is now one between Lord Lonsdale and the Crown. *c*

The action raises questions on the construction and legal effect of a lease of 1860, articles of agreement of 1880, a conveyance of 1880 and a deed of exchange of 1935. Most particularly, it concerns the proper interpretation to be given to a provision contained in the conveyance of 1880 whereby the Crown granted to predecessors'in title of Lord Lonsdale its interest in all of certain specified mineral substances within or under certain tracts of land and also 'all other mines and minerals (if any) down to the bottom *d* of the coal measures in and under the same tracts of land'. The interpretation of the words just quoted is the first principal issue in the action. If, contrary to the Crown's contention, the effect of one or more of the four instruments was to vest any oil or natural gas in Lord Lonsdale's predecessors in title, the further question arises whether all or any part of the oil or natural gas claimed by him has in the event vested again in the Crown by virtue of subsequent legislation, that is to say the Petroleum (Production) *e* Act 1934 and the Continental Shelf Act 1964 or one of them. This is the other principal issue in the action.

Though the two principal issues may thus be stated quite shortly, they give rise to difficult questions, which have involved a trial of some 13 days and the citation of over 80 statutes and reported cases.

The title of Lord Lonsdale as tenant for life is a somewhat complicated one. It is, *f* however, accepted by the Crown that, subject to the operation of any divesting legislation and of the deed of exchange of 1935, Lord Lonsdale, in his capacity as tenant for life under the settlement of 1936, is, in the events which have happened, entitled to such rights (if any) to oil or natural gas as may have been granted by the Crown under any of the four relevant instruments. It is not, therefore, necessary to trace his title. For the purpose of deciding the issues in the action, his position is the same as if he himself was *g* the original grantee under the 1880 conveyance or the 1935 deed of exchange, as the case may be.

For ease of reference, a plan showing the relevant area has been agreed between the parties. It is shown marked 'Plan B' and I will so refer to it. I understand that, rather confusingly, it is not the same plan as one referred to in the statement of claim by a similar title. Neither side has committed itself to accepting it as precisely accurate. I now *h* turn to the documentation.

The 1860 lease

The 1860 lease was an indenture dated 27 August 1860 made between The Queen's Most Excellent Majesty (1), the Hon Charles Alexander Gore, the Commissioner of Her Majesty's Woods, Forests and Land Revenues (the commissioner) (2), and The Right *j* Honourable William, second Earl of Lonsdale (3). By this lease the commissioner on behalf of Her Majesty granted and demised to the second Earl of Lonsdale for a term of 31 years from 5 July 1859 at the yearly rents and royalties thereby reserved and subject to various covenants and conditions—

'ALL and every the Mines veins seams and beds of coal culm ironstone and fireclay

hereinafter called "Mineral Substances" within under or upon ALL THAT tract of land
a   forming part of the bed of the Sea belonging to Her Majesty below low water mark
to a distance of three miles therefrom and situate adjacent to the Townships or
Parishes of Moresby Parton Preston Quarter Whitehaven Sandwich Rottington and
St Bees in the County of Cumberland and which said tract of land is more
particularly described as follows . . .'

The 1860 lease then contained a more particular description of the area of the bed of
b   the sea within under or on which the 'mineral substances' were thereby demised. The
boundaries of this area, which I will call 'the 1860 lease area', are shown delineated with
a green dotted line on plan B. They were bounded on the east by low-water mark and on
the west by an imaginary line at a distance of three miles from low-water mark. No part
of them, therefore, extended beyond the territorial waters of Great Britain.

The 1860 lease, having defined these boundaries, then proceeded to grant to the
c   grantee—

> 'full power and authority to make such levels headings staples tunnels and other
> works (without interfering with the surface of the land under which the said
> mineral substances lie) as may be necessary for the searching for working getting
> raising and carrying away of the said mineral substances or any of them and to
d   > search for work get raise and carry away the same accordingly . . .'

I pause to comment that the definition of 'mineral substances' in the 1860 lease
included no substance except the specific items of coal, culm, ironstone and fireclay, and
it is not suggested that this deed operated to convey any rights in oil or natural gas.

The 1880 articles
e   The articles of agreement of 1880 (the 1880 articles) were made between The Queen's
Most Excellent Majesty (1), the commissioner (2) and the fourth Earl of Lonsdale (3).
They recited the effect of the 1860 lease, the recitals expressly adopting the definition of
'mineral substances' contained in the 1860 lease. By the 1880 articles, the commissioner
on behalf of Her Majesty agreed to grant to the fourth earl for a term of 42 years from 5
July 1880, at the yearly rent and royalties therein stated, a lease of—
f

> 'ALL such estate right and interest as Her Majesty may possess in and to ALL and
> every the mineral substances within or under ALL that tract of land described in and
> the mineral substances under which were demised by the hereinbefore recited
> Indenture of Lease and within or under ALL that other tract of land forming part of
> the Bed of the Sea called the Irish Sea adjoining the tract of land described in the
g   > hereinbefore recited Indenture of Lease and bounded on the east . . .'

The 1880 articles then proceeded to give a more detailed description of the additional
tract of land, forming part of the bed of the sea, within or under which the 'mineral
substances' were thereby agreed to be demised. The whole of this additional tract, which
I will call 'the 1880 lease area', was situated adjoining the 1860 lease area on its western
boundary, so that it was all situated outside the three mile limit of territorial waters. The
h   whole of the 1860 lease area and of the 1880 lease area is shown delineated with a red
hatched line on plan B.

The 1880 articles, having defined the boundaries of the 1880 lease area, then proceeded
to define the rights of working etc which were to be expressly granted to the lessee over
the 1860 lease area and the 1880 lease area under the contemplated lease, as follows:

j   > 'Together with full power and authority for the Lessee (subject to the provision
> hereinafter contained for reserving certain barriers in the mineral substances) to
> make such levels headings staples tunnels and other works in the mineral substances
> and to and from the adjacent lands of the Lessee situate in the said County of
> Cumberland (without in any way injuring or interfering with and making full
> compensation to Her Majesty her heirs and successors and all other persons entitled
> thereto for all injury or damage done or occasioned to the surface of the lands under

which the said mineral substances lie and any buildings or erections at any time standing and being thereon) as may be necessary for the searching for working getting raising and carrying away of the said mineral substances or any of them and to search for work get raise and carry away the same accordingly (Subject nevertheless as regards such parts of the premises hereinbefore described as are subject thereto to the hereinbefore recited Indenture of Lease) for the terms of Forty two years from the fifth day of July One thousand eight hundred and eighty at the yearly rent of One pound and at the several royalties following videlicet . . .'

Thus far in the 1880 articles, the only substances in respect of which the Crown had agreed to grant rights of any kind whatsoever had been coal, culm, ironstone and fireclay. However, having stated the subject matter (including rights of working etc), the term of the lease agreed to be granted and the rent and royalties to be paid by the lessee, they contained an important proviso to the following effect. The contemplated lease was not to be granted until after 10 October 1880. If the lessee should desire to purchase 'the premises hereinbefore agreed to be demised' and of such desire should before 10 October 1880 give the commissioner written notice, then, instead of granting the proposed lease, the commissioner should sell to the lessee and the lessee should purchase from Her Majesty for £50,000—

'all the premises hereinbefore agreed to be demised and also all other mines and minerals (if any) down to the bottom of the Coal Measures in and under the tracts of land hereinbefore described together with all such rights and powers as are hereinbefore agreed to be granted but subject nevertheless as aforesaid . . .'

The 'rights and powers' thus referred to were clearly the specified powers and authorities for the lessee (subject to the barrier provision) to make such works in the 'mineral substances', as defined in the 1880 articles, and to and from the adjacent lands of the fourth earl situate in Cumberland as might be necessary for the searching for, working, getting, raising and carrying away of the 'mineral substances' (as so defined), which were to be comprised in the contemplated lease of these 'mineral substances', and to search for, work, get, raise and carry away the same accordingly. I do not read the phrase 'together with all such rights and powers as are hereinbefore agreed to be granted' as including anything more than the totality of the rights and powers which the Crown had agreed to grant by the earlier provisions of the 1880 articles, which earlier provisions related exclusively to 'mineral substances' as therein defined. Accordingly, as I read the 1880 articles, the Crown did not thereby agree to confer on the fourth earl, even in the event of his exercising the option to purchase, any express rights to search for, work, get, raise and carry away mines and minerals other than coal, culm, ironstone and fireclay. Though counsel for the Crown submitted that the powers of working etc granted by the subsequent 1880 conveyance should be given a wide sense, I did not understand him to dispute this construction of the 1880 articles themselves.

I now revert to the actual provisions of the 1880 articles. Having thus defined the subject matter of the option to purchase thereby conferred on the fourth earl, they then set out in seven numbered clauses certain conditions and stipulations subject to which the contemplated lease or sale, as the case might be, should be effected. I need only refer to two of these conditions and stipulations. Clause 3 provided (inter alia) that the lease or conveyance, as the case might be, would be prepared by the solicitor to the commissioners, but would 'so far as relates to such parts of the premises hereinbefore described as are subject thereto' be made subject to the 1860 lease. Clause 4 provided:

'THE Lease or Conveyance as the case may be will reserve to Her Majesty Her Heirs and Successors walls or barriers of the said Mines Minerals and Mineral substances of the width of One hundred yards in each and every vein seam or bed thereof and along the entire northern and southern boundaries respectively thereof.'

The reference in this clause to 'the said Mines, Minerals and Mineral substances' was plainly wide enough to include, and was intended to include, the entirety of those

substances which were to be the subject of the contemplated option to purchase, not
a merely the 'mineral substances' as defined in the 1880 articles (coal, culm, ironstone and
fireclay) which were to be the subject of the contemplated lease.

The 1880 conveyance

The option to purchase conferred by the 1880 articles was duly exercised by notice
given by the fourth earl. To give effect to it, on 21 December 1880 a conveyance ('the
b 1880 conveyance') was executed by the commissioner, the fourth earl and Mr W S S
Crawford and Mr J Lowther, the trustees of the settlement under which the fourth earl
was at that time tenant for life. The 1880 conveyance contained lengthy recitals. I need
only mention one or two points on them. The first recital, in describing the subject
matter of the 1860 lease, referred to 'All and every the mines, veins, seams and beds of
coal, culm, ironstone and fireclay (thereinafter and also hereinafter called "mineral
c substances")'. In the tenth recital the draftsman of the 1880 conveyance recited with care,
and more or less verbatim and seriatim, all the operative provisions of the 1880 articles
relating to the agreement for the grant of a lease, save that details of the yearly rent and
royalties were not given. In the part of this recital which described the rights of working
which had been agreed to be included in such lease, the draftsman precisely echoed the
language used by the draftsman of the 1880 articles by using, successively, the phrase
d 'the mineral substances' (twice) and 'the said mineral substances' (twice).

Having recited the agreement for the grant of a lease, the 1880 conveyance then (in
the same recital) proceeded with precise accuracy to recite the proviso in the 1880 articles
which gave the fourth earl an option to purchase. In this recital, the description of the
subject matter of this option was reproduced more or less verbatim from the 1880 articles
and was stated to be—

e
> 'all the premises thereinbefore agreed to be demised and also all other mines and
> minerals (if any) down to the bottom of the coal measures in and under the tracts of
> land thereinbefore described together with all such rights and powers as were
> thereinbefore agreed to be granted but subject nevertheless as aforesaid . . .'

The only possibly material divergence from the wording of the 1880 articles in this
f part of the recital was the reproduction of the phrase 'coal measures', which had been
written with a capital 'C' and capital 'M' in the equivalent part of the 1880 articles
without any capital letters.

The draftsman of the 1880 conveyance then proceeded accurately to summarise the
provisions of cl 1 of the 1880 articles, containing provisions for the payment of the
purchase price in the event of the exercise of the option, and cl 4, relating to the
g reservation of 'walls or barriers of the said mines minerals and mineral substances'. He
then recited the Lonsdale Settled Estates Act 1880, which had empowered Mr Crawfurd
and Mr Lowther to exercise the option and to obtain the benefit of the 1880 articles, and
the subsequent exercise of that option by the fourth earl.

The operative part of the 1880 conveyance (so far as material) reads as follows:

h
> 'NOW KNOW YE that in consideration of the sum of £50,000 so paid by the said
> William Stuart Stirling Crawfurd and James Lowther as aforesaid the said Charles
> Alexander Gore under the powers of an act passed in the tenth year of the reign of
> His Late Majesty King George Fourth chapter 50 and of another act passed in the
> fifteenth year of the reign of Her present Majesty chapter 42 and of all other powers
> in anywise enabling him in this behalf and with the consent of the Lords
> Commissioners of Her Majesty's Treasury signified by their warrant dated the 8th
j > day of April, 1880 DOTH by these presents grant and convey unto the said William
> Stuart Stirling Crawfurd and James Lowther and their heirs ALL such estate right
> and interest as Her Majesty may possess in and to ALL AND EVERY the mineral
> substances within or under the tracts of land described of mentioned in the said
> recited Articles of Agreement of the 2nd day of February, 1880 AND also all other
> mines and minerals (if any) down to the bottom of the coal measures in and under

the same tracts of land TOGETHER with all such powers of searching for working getting raising and carrying away the said mineral substances as are by the same *a* Articles agreed to be granted And all other if any the premises thereby agreed to be demised and the said William Stuart Stirling Crawfurd and James Lowther their heirs and assigns nevertheless in no way injuring or interfering with and making full compensation to Her Majesty her Heirs and Successors and all other persons entitled thereto for all injury or damage done or occasioned to the surface of the lands under which the said mineral substances lie and any buildings or erections at *b* any time standing or being thereon. EXCEPT nevertheless and reserving unto Her Majesty Her Heirs and Successors out of the Conveyance hereby made walls or barriers of the said mines minerals and mineral substances of the width of 100 yards in each and every vein seam or bed thereof along the entire northern and southern boundaries respectively of the mines minerals and mineral substances Her Majesty's interests wherein is intended to be hereby conveyed TO HOLD exercise and enjoy the *c* said minerals hereditaments rights privileges and powers and all and singular other the premises hereby granted and conveyed or intended so to be with the appurtenances (except as aforesaid and subject to the provisions of the Crown Lands Act, 1866 and also as regards such parts of the premises hereinbefore described as are subject thereto to the said recited Indenture of Lease of the 27th day of August, 1860) Unto the said William Stuart Stirling Crawfurd and James Lowther and their *d* heirs to such of the uses . . .'

By the 1880 conveyance the commissioner was expressed to make the conveyance under the powers of the two Acts mentioned in it and of 'all other powers in anywise enabling him in this behalf'. For the record I should mention that no point has been taken before me relating to the nature and extent of these powers.

In defining the subject matter of the 1880 conveyance, the draftsman had demonstrably *e* paid very close attention to the equivalent provisions of the 1880 articles relating to the grant of the option. He had, neverthless, somewhat amplified the description of the rights of searching for, working, getting, raising and carrying away, which were to be granted. In the relevant part of the 1880 articles these rights had simply been described as 'all such rights and powers as are hereinbefore agreed to be granted'. In the 1880 conveyance they are described as 'all such powers of searching for working getting raising *f* and carrying away the said mineral substances as are by the same Articles agreed to be granted'. Counsel for the Crown pointed out that the grant of these powers immediately followed a grant of the Crown's interest first in 'the mineral substances' within or under the 1860 lease area and the 1880 lease area and second in 'all other mines and minerals (if any) down to the bottom of the coal measures' in and under these areas.

He submitted that, in order to give the transaction business efficacy, the 1880 *g* conveyance must be construed as conferring express powers of searching etc wider than those which the Crown had expressly agreed to grant under the 1880 articles and thus as extending to all the premises conveyed by the 1880 conveyance, including the 'mines and minerals (if any)'. He submitted that in the 1880 conveyance the phrase 'all such powers of searching' etc identified merely the nature and quality of the rights of recovery and that the draftsman referred in this context to 'the said mineral substances' for the *h* purpose of identifying not the premises in respect of which the express powers of recovery were to be exercisable, but merely the nature of the relevant powers, doing so by reference to the 1880 articles.

Essentially, I think, the construction which the Crown seeks to place on the relevant phrase in the 1880 conveyance involves reading it as meaning 'the like powers of searching for, working, getting, raising and carrying away the said mineral substances, *j* mines and minerals as are by the same Articles agreed to be granted in respect of the said mineral substances'. Such a construction of the phrase would seem to me to involve a complete distortion of the language used and I cannot accept it for at least five reasons.

(1) In my judgment, as counsel for the Crown himself accepted, the 1880 articles had bound the Crown, on the exercise by the grantee of the option to purchase, to grant

rights of searching etc in respect of 'mineral substances' as thereby defined, but not in
a respect of any other mines or minerals. The wording of the material phrase in the 1880
conveyance thus accurately reflected, and I think was intended to reflect, the agreement
relating to grants of rights of recovery embodied in the 1880 articles.

(2) The grant of the relevant powers of searching etc in the 1880 conveyance
immediately followed a grant of the Crown's interest first in 'the mineral substances'
within or under the 1860 and 1880 lease areas, and second in 'all other mines and
b minerals (if any) down to the bottom of the coal measures in and under' those areas.
Only an incompetent or casual draftsman would have failed to insert a reference to mines
and minerals in the immediately succeeding definition of the powers of searching etc if
these express powers had been intended to extend beyond 'mineral substances', as defined
earlier in the 1880 conveyance.

(3) Though counsel for the Crown suggested otherwise, the 1880 conveyance appears
c to me on the whole a document well and carefully drafted by someone who well knew
what he was doing. One significant example is that, after a second accurate reference in
the parcels clause to 'the said mineral substances', he proceeded to include an exception
and reservation of walls or barriers of 'the said mines, minerals and mineral substances'.
This was correct, because it precisely reflected the provisions of cl 4 of the 1880 articles.
He thus showed himself quite capable of introducing express references to mines and
d minerals where this was appropriate.

(4) As has been submitted by the Crown in another context, it is a general principle of
construction that where two interpretations may be given to a grant by the Crown and
both these interpretations are arguable, that which is more favourable to the Crown is to
be preferred. I shall refer later to some of the relevant authorities. If, contrary to my
view, the relevant words in the 1880 conveyance give rise to a real ambiguity involving
e two possible constructions, the application of the general principle points to the adoption
of the narrower construction, so as to confer on the grantee express rights of recovery
only in respect of the 'mineral substances' as provided by the 1880 articles.

(5) I do not accept that an express grant of rights of recovery would have been
necessary to give business efficacy to the grant of 'other mines and minerals (if any)'
contained in the 1880 conveyance. Any grant or reservation of minerals is ordinarily
f deemed to carry with it an implied grant of the right to work them: see, eg *Borys v
Canadian Pacific Rly Co* [1953] 1 All ER 451 at 457–458, [1953] AC 217 at 227–228, to
which I will revert. The use of the words '(if any)' shows that the parties to the 1880
conveyance were apparently not aware of the existence of any mines and minerals in and
under the relevant tracts of land except for coal, culm, ironstone and fireclay. The proper
inference, I think, is that they were content to leave any questions relating to rights of
g recovery in respect of 'other mines and minerals' to be dealt with by implication of law.
Later in this judgment, I shall have to consider the nature and extent of the rights which
thus fall to be implied.

The 1935 deed of exchange

It is common ground that by January 1935 the mines and minerals, if any, conveyed
h by the 1880 conveyance had become vested in Lowther Estates Ltd (the Lowther
company) in fee simple subject to certain incumbrances. On 17 January 1935 a deed of
exchange (the 1935 deed of exchange) was executed, expressed to be made between the
King's Most Excellent Majesty (1), the Commissioners of Crown Lands (2), the Lowther
company (3), Mr W G F Cavendish Bentinck and the Hon A J B Lowther (4) and the
Right Hon James William Viscount Ullswater, the Hon C W Lowther and Mr W G F
j Cavendish Bentinck (5). The deed referred to all the parties of the fourth and fifth parts
collectively as 'the incumbrancers'.

The 1935 deed of exchange (which referred to the 1880 conveyance as 'the deed poll
of 1880') contained three provisions material for present purposes.

By cl 1 the Commissioners of Crown Lands, by the direction of the Lowther company,
charged the above-mentioned incumbrances on all the interest of the Crown in 'All and

every the mines veins seams and beds of coal culm ironstone and fireclay . . . and also all
other mines and minerals (if any) down to the bottom of the coal measures' within or *a*
under a designated strip of land or barrier 100 yards wide forming part of the bed of the
sea belonging to the Crown 'together with powers of working getting raising and
carrying away the mines veins seams and minerals charged by this clause similar to the
powers for the like purposes contained in the Deed Poll of 1880'. This strip of land
(which I will call 'the old barrier') was further defined in cl 1 of the 1935 deed of exchange
and constituted part of the northern barrier excepted and reserved to the Crown by the *b*
1880 conveyance.

By cl 2 of the 1935 deed of exchange the commissioners conveyed to the Lowther
company the premises charged by cl 1 in fee simple—

> 'subject to the charges hereinbefore created and subject also to provisions for
> compensation for injury or damage to the surface similar to those reserved by and
> contained in the Deed Poll of 1880 with respect to the mines and minerals thereby *c*
> conveyed and subject to the provisions of the Crown Lands Act 1866.'

By cl 3 the Lowther company and the incumbrancers surrendered and released to the
Crown 'All and every the mines veins seams and beds of coal culm ironstone and fireclay
and also all other mines and minerals (if any) down to the bottom of the coal measures'
within or under a strip of land or barrier of varying widths as shown on a plan annexed *d*
to the deed, forming part of the bed of the sea and foreshore below high-water mark.
Clause 3 defined the strip of land as 'the new barrier' and I will so refer to it.

In the rest of this judgment any references to 'the Lonsdale off-shore areas' are intended
to include together the 1860 lease area and the 1880 lease area, with the subtraction of
the new barrier which had been conveyed to the Crown by the 1935 deed of exchange,
but with the addition of the old barrier, which had been conveyed to the Lowther *e*
company by that deed. The definitions of these various areas accord with those employed
by the pleaders in the statement of claim.

As I have already indicated, it is common ground that, subject to the operation of any
divesting legislation, Lord Lonsdale, in his capacity as tenant for life under the 1936
settlement, is now entitled to such rights (if any) to oil or natural gas in or under the
Lonsdale off-shore areas as may have been granted by the Crown under the 1880 *f*
conveyance and the 1935 deed of exchange.

The 1969 licence

On 4 August 1969 the Minister of Power, acting on behalf of the Crown, granted or
purported to grant to the second defendant, Ultramar, a licence under the Petroleum
(Production) Act 1934 (the 1969 licence) to search, bore for and get oil and natural gas in *g*
a tract of the Irish Sea and adjoining land, which is shown approximately delineated with
a black line on plan B. As appears from this plan small parts of this tract fell respectively
within the 1860 lease area and the 1880 lease area. It was granted without the prior
knowledge or consent of the plaintiff, though the Attorney General asserts that no such
consent was required. I understand that, though it has now been surrendered, its grant
gave rise to the present proceedings. *h*

The issues

The plaintiff contends that, on their true construction, the words 'mines and minerals',
as used in the phrase 'all other mines and minerals (if any) down to the bottom of the
coal measures', which appeared in the parcels clauses of the 1880 conveyance and the *i*
1935 deed of exchange, include oil and natural gas and that this is what entitles him to *j*
the declaration which he seeks. The Attorney General's principal answers to this claim
are to be found summarised in a few sentences in his re-reamended defence. Paragraph
9 of this pleading contains the following passage:

> 'Oil and natural gas are by their nature a fluid and a gas respectively which flow
> or permeate and are not mined. Natural gas in the form of firedamp at the respective

times of the 1860 Lease and the 1880 Conveyance created hazards in a mine. Neither
oil nor natural gas would at either of those times have been regarded as a mineral
substance or mine or mineral to be conveyed for value by a conveyance of a
Cumberland mine. In the premises and on its true construction the 1880 Conveyance
conveyed no interest in oil or natural gas. If and so far as necessary this Defendant
will rely on the Crown Lands Act 1866.'

Paragraph 10 begins as follows:

'Alternatively the oil and natural gas claimed by the Plaintiff is petroleum within
the meaning of the Petroleum (Production) Act 1934 and the Crown has title thereto
under that Act and the Continental Shelf Act 1964 or one of them.'

It is common ground that the oil and natural gas claimed by the plaintiff are
'petroleum' within the meaning of the 1934 Act. The Attorney General has, I think,
placed no substantial reliance on the Crown Lands Act 1866 in argument. In the premises
the three principal issues that now fall to be decided (though the second is subsidiary to
the first) are these.

(1) Does the phrase 'mines and minerals' as used in the 1880 conveyance and the 1935
deed of exchange on its true construction include oil and natural gas or either of them?

(2) If the answer to question (1) is Yes, what is the meaning of the phrase 'down to the
bottom of the coal measures' in the relevant grants?

(3) If the answer to question (1) is Yes, were the rights in oil and natural gas or either
of them which had been granted by the 1880 conveyance and the 1935 deed of exchange
or either of them revested in the Crown by virtue of the Petroleum (Production) Act
1934 and the Continental Shelf Act 1964 or one of them?

General principles of construction

Before turning to the evidence and to some of the countless authorities dealing with
the interpretation of particular grants or statutory provisions relating to mines and
minerals, I think it convenient to refer to three unconnected, general principles of
construction, which are in no way confined to grants of this nature.

The first of them is of particular importance in the present case, which primarily
concerns the interpretation of a grant made not in 1982 but in 1880. In construing any
commercial document, the court must do its best to place itself in thought in the same
factual background as the parties were at the time when they entered into the transaction.
As Lord Wilberforce said in *Reardon Smith Line Ltd v Hansen-Tangen* [1976] 3 All ER 570
at 574, [1976] 1 WLR 989 at 995–996:

'No contracts are made in a vacuum: there is always a setting in which they have
to be placed. The nature of what is legitimate to have regard to is usually described
as 'the surrounding circumstances' but this phrase is imprecise: it can be illustrated
but hardly defined. In a commercial contract it is certainly right that the court
should know the commercial purpose of the contract and this in turn presupposes
knowledge of the genesis of the transaction, the background, the context, the market
in which the parties are operating.'

A little later Lord Wilberforce said ([1976] 3 All ER 570 at 574, [1976] 1 WLR 989 at
996):

'It is often said that, in order to be admissible in aid of construction, these extrinsic
facts must be within the knowledge of both parties to the contract, but this
requirement should not be stated in too narrow a sense. When one speaks of the
intention of the parties to the contract, one is speaking objectively—the parties
cannot themselves give direct evidence of what their intention was—and what must
be ascertained is what is to be taken as the intention which reasonable people would
have had if placed in the situation of the parties. Similarly when one is speaking of
aim, or object, or commercial purpose, one is speaking objectively of what reasonable
persons would have in mind in the situation of the parties.'

In the course of his speech Lord Wilberforce referred to three of the speeches in *Charrington & Co Ltd v Wooder* [1914] AC 71, summarising their effect as follows ([1976] *a* 3 All ER 570 at 575, [1976] 1 WLR 989 at 997):

'I think that all of their Lordships are saying, in different words, the same thing— what the court must do must be to place itself in thought in the same factual matrix as that in which the parties were. All of these opinions seem to me implicitly to recognise that, in the search for the relevant background, there may be facts, which form part of the circumstances in which the parties contract, in which one or both *b* may take no particular interest, their minds being addressed to or concentrated on other facts, so that if asked they would assert that they did not have these facts in the forefront of their mind, but that will not prevent those facts from forming part of an objective setting in which the contract is to be construed.'

A similar approach is to be found in the decision of the Judicial Committee of the *c* Privy Council in *Southland Frozen Meat and Produce Export Co Ltd v Nelson Bros Ltd* [1898] AC 442. Lord Herschell in delivering the judgment said (at 444) that the commercial agreement there in issue—

'must be construed in a business fashion, and that the words must not be applied to everything that might be said to come within a possible dictionary use of them, but must be interpreted in the way in which business men would interpret them, *d* when used in relation to a business matter of this description.'

Thus, in construing the relevant words of the 1880 conveyance, it will, I think, be necessary to attempt to do so in the way in which commercial men would have interpreted them in 1880 when used in relation to a commercial transaction of this kind.

The second general principle of construction relevant to the present case is that, *e* contrary to the ordinary rule applicable to grants by a subject, grants by the Crown usually fall to be construed in the manner most favourable to the grantor: see *A-G v Ewelme Hospital* (1853) 17 Beav 366 at 385, 51 ER 1075 at 1083 per Romilly MR and the other cases cited in 8 Halsbury's Laws (4th edn) para 1049. The editors of Halsbury's Laws suggest at para 1050 that the principle does not apply to grants for valuable consideration, but counsel did not feel able to advance this proposition on behalf of the *f* plaintiff in this case.

Cockburn CJ expressed the principle very clearly in *Feather v R* (1865) 6 B & S 257 at 283–284, 122 ER 1191 at 1201:

'It is established on the best authority that, in construing grants from the Crown, a different rule of construction prevails from that by which grants from one subject to another are to be construed. In a grant from one subject to another, every *g* intendment is to be made against the grantor, and in favour of the grantee, in order to give full effect to the grant; but in grants from the Crown an opposite rule of construction prevails. Nothing passes except that which is expressed, or which is matter of necessary and unavoidable intendment in order to give effect to the plain and undoubted intention of the grant. And in no species of grant does this rule of construction more especially obtain than in grants which emanate from, and operate *h* in derogation of, the prerogative of the Crown.'

Though this case happened to concern the grant of a patent, the observations of Cockburn CJ were in general terms.

Viscount Birkenhead LC reaffirmed the principle in *Viscountess Rhondda's Claim* [1922] 2 AC 339 at 353, saying that a grant by the Crown— *j*

'is construed most strictly against the grantee and most beneficially for the Crown, so that nothing will pass to the grantee but by clear and express words.'

The effect of these cases, as I read them, is that, if the wording of a grant by the Crown is clear and unequivocal, the grantee is entitled to rely on it as much as if the grantor had

been any other subject of the Crown; if, on the other hand, the wording is obscure or
a equivocal, the court must lean towards the construction more favourable to the Crown,
unless satisfied that another interpretation of the relevant words in their context is the
true one.

The third general principle of construction which may be relevant in the present case
is that if a particular word employed in a written instrument bears an 'ordinary sense',
the burden of displacing this ordinary sense will fall on any person who seeks to assert
b that, in a particular context, the word does not bear such meaning (see, eg 12 Halsbury's
Laws (4th edn) para 1463, where 'ordinary sense' is explained in a footnote as meaning
'plain, ordinary, and popular sense' by reference to the judgment of Lord Ellenborough
C J in *Robertson v French* (1803) 4 East 130 at 135, 102 ER 779 at 781).

Of many, perhaps the majority, of the words used by English speakng people there
can be little doubt as to the ordinary meaning, or 'literal' or 'primary' meaning, as it is
c often called: see 12 Halsbury's Laws (4th edn) para 1464. To take an example at random,
the court would not, I conceive, find much difficulty in attaching a literal or primary
meaning to the word 'elephant', if it found it in a written instrument. In contrast,
however, some English words and phrases fall into a second, quite different category.
There are words and phrases which are readily capable of bearing two or more alternative
meanings and to which the court is not willing to ascribe a prima facie meaning, so as to
d impose on any party the onus of displacing it. In any such case the court finds itself
obliged to construe the word in its particular context, having regard to the admissible
evidence, without any predisposition to give it one meaning in preference to another. In
the present case it has been a matter of dispute whether the word 'minerals' in the context
of the 1880 conveyance and the 1935 deed of exchange falls into the first of these two
categories, as is submitted on behalf of Lord Lonsdale, or into the second of them, as is
e submitted on behalf of the Crown.

The background of the transactions of 1880

Counsel on both sides have, I think, accepted that in principle those facts which
constitute the factual matrix (to use Lord Wilberforce's phrase) of the transactions of
1880 are admissible in evidence in construing the 1880 articles and the 1880 conveyance,
f as forming part of the objective setting against which these contractual arrangements fall
to be construed. With this in mind they have placed before me a large volume of
documentary evidence. The plaintiffs have adduced oral evidence from Mr D L L
Maclachlan, who is a Fellow of the Geological Society of London and has wide-ranging
experience of the exploration and development of petroleum beneath the sea. The
Attorney General has called two witnesses. One of them was Dr R S Collins, who was a
g principal scientific officer with the Ministry of Defence from 1966 to 1968 and from
1968 until 1980 a principal scientific officer in the mineral intelligence unit of the
Institute of Geological Sciences. The other was a lawyer, Mr S J Youngman, who has
worked in the legal department of the National Coal Board since 1951.

The pleadings, however, give little indication as to the particular features of all this
abundance of evidence on which the parties intend respectively to rely. And, with all
h respect to their otherwise most helpful arguments, counsel on neither side have made
much attempt to collate or categorise those essential facts which in their submission
constitute the factual matrix of the transactions. I have, therefore, found some difficulty
in extracting from all the available material those features of the factual matrix which
may be the most relevant for present purposes. However, I think there are relatively few
disputed issues of fact and, with this preface, will now state findings of fact on certain
j matters which I regard, or a higher court might regard, as relevant.

(1) Though there is no formal evidence to this effect, it is common ground that, at the
date of the 1880 articles and the 1880 conveyance, the grantee, the fourth earl, was the
owner of the land immediately adjacent to the relevant parts of the sea bed above low-
water mark. The 1880 articles themselves refer to 'the adjacent lands of the Lessee in the
said County of Cumberland'. As appears from R W Moore *Historical Sketch of the*

Whitehaven Collieries (1894) p 16 the submarine coal beneath these parts of the sea bed
was being worked between 1860 and 1880 and indeed Sir James Lowther had sunk a pit   *a*
close to the seashore for this purpose as early as about 1729 (see p 12).

(2) Natural gas and oil are, like coal, hydrocarbon substances. They occur naturally in
interstices, cracks and joints of underground rocks. Natural gas is more fluid than oil and
some varieties of oil are much thicker and more waxy than others. But, in general, both
natural gas and oil can move for considerable distances horizontally and vertically
through the interstices, cracks and joints of rocks. They are always seeking a way to the   *b*
surface. Accordingly, in order that there should be an economic deposit of oil or natural
gas, there must also be an impermeable layer of rock which prevents it from rising to the
surface and being lost. Because of the fluidity and migratory nature of oil and natural
gas, it is difficult to ascribe to it a precise location in the earth; the place from which it is
recovered may well not be the place from which it emanated.

(3) Though some natural gases are rich in nitrogen and others contain small quantities   *c*
of helium, natural gas is ordinarily composed mainly of the hydrocarbon known as
methane or firedamp. Firedamp may be spontaneously evolved during the working of
coal. It can be ignited by a naked flame. It caused a number of injuries by burning in the
Whitehaven colliery in the eighteenth century. Its partial combustion will also give rise
to carbon monoxide, a poisonous gas, the inhalation of which may cause death among
miners. It is therefore necessary to remove firedamp from coal mines as far as possible.   *d*
Both the existence and the degree of firedamp were well known by the end of the
eighteenth century. Sir James Lowther had given a written account of its existence in his
coal pit to the Royal Society in 1733. At this time and at the beginning of the nineteenth
century it was removed by exploding the gas in situ every few hours as it accumulated.
Later, techniques were evolved for draining the gas off to a surface vent, where it could
be safely burnt off.   *e*

(4) As at 1880, the existence in many countries of the liquid bituminous substance
now commonly known as petroleum was well known and had been well known in
England for very many years (see, for example, the entry under the heading 'Petroleum'
in the Encyclopaedia Britannica (1796) and Sir Boverton Redwood *A Treatise on Petroleum*
(1913) where there are numerous examples). By 1880 it had been discovered in certain
parts of England. Examples are to be found at pp 32–36 of the latter work. A report   *f*
given in 1838 by a Professor Johnson, Fellow of the Royal Society, referred to the
obtaining of petroleum from the mass overlying three seams of coal in the neighbourhood
of Whitehaven.

(5) Furthermore, by 1880 it was well known in England that petroleum had
considerable potentialities for commercial use, in particular for lighting purposes. So far
as the evidence shows, the first person to attempt to extract it as a commercial venture in   *g*
England was a Mr James Young. Having in 1847 learned of the existence of a petroleum
spring in Derbyshire, he subsequently obtained a patent relating to methods of obtaining
oil and solid paraffin on a commercial scale in England (see the entry in *Chambers
Encyclopaedia* (1874) under the heading 'Naptha'). An extract from the *Transactions of the
Institute of Mining Engineers* (1907–08) vol 35, p 560, attributes the origin of the petroleum
industry directly to Mr Young's discovery of a process for obtaining paraffin and paraffin   *h*
oils by the distillation of oil and shale. In about the 1860's massive oil supplies had been
discovered in Pennsylvania and substantial quantities were imported into the United
Kingdom. As explained in the same entry in *Chambers Encyclopaedia*, the rapid increase
in these imports and some accidents connected with them led to legislation. In 1862 and
1871 there were passed two Petroleum Acts, which contained a number of provisions
designed to ensure the safe keeping of petroleum. The fact that this legislation was   *j*
considered necessary lends support to the inference that oil was widely used in this
country by 1871, particularly for lighting purposes. Furthermore, a petroleum-distilling
industry had been established here before 1880.

(6) On the evidence, however, I find that the extraction and production of oil in
England was of little commercial significance at that date. *A Report on the Production
Technology and Uses of Petroleum and its Products* (1885) p 30 by S F Peckham quotes a letter

a written in 1881 by Mr E W Binney FRS, who is there described as 'the distinguished geologist', in answer to an inquiry in relation to the occurrence of petroleum in England. The writer mentioned a few places in Lancashire, Shropshire and Derbyshire where it had been discovered but, as he said, 'none to my knowledge in commercial quantities', and went on to add that the greatest supply that he had ever seen had not been more than 50 gallons a day. In 1872 there were passed the Coal Mines Regulation Act, which was intended to consolidate and amend the Acts relating to the regulation of mines of coal,
b stratified ironstone, shale or fireclay, and also the Metalliferous Mines Act, of which the expressed purpose was 'to amend the law relating to the regulation and inspection of mines other than mines to which the Coal Mines Regulation Act 1872 applies'. Neither of these 1872 Acts, however, contained anything regulating the extraction of oil or natural gas. Dr Collins in his proof said that liquid petroleum was of little commercial significance in England in the nineteenth century. In his oral evidence-in-chief, he
c corrected this statement by explaining that he had meant to say that production of liquid petroleum was of little commercial significance; he had not meant to say that its use or consumption was of no significance. As so corrected, I am satisfied that his evidence was correct. Dr Collins stated in re-examination that he was not aware of any right to petroleum in Cumberland having been expressly granted in the nineteenth century and no evidence has been adduced to suggest the contrary.

d (7) There are two ways in which oil can be extracted from the reservoir rock. One is by digging a shaft down to the oil strata; the other is by drilling a well, that is to say making a more or less vertical hole, relatively narrow in diameter, until a satisfactory flow is obtained. Up to the early 1890s dug shafts furnished practically the only means of tapping supplies in Europe, though during the course of the next fifteen years or so this method largely fell into disuse (see *Transactions of the Institute of Mining Engineers*
e (1907–08) vol 35, p 564). While the mining of coal situated beneath the sea bed had become quite common by 1880, there is no evidence before me that by 1880 floating drilling rigs had been developed anywhere in the world or indeed that any satisfactory commercial method had yet been developed by which oil could be safely conducted from underneath the bed of the sea to land-based installations. The earliest reference to any satisfactory method of extracting oil from beneath the sea bed was to a method that was
f employed off the coast of California early in the twentieth century; Dr Collins refers to it in his proof.

(8) Firedamp, as was well known in mining circles by the end of the eighteenth century, had its potential uses as well as its dangers, as was appreciated by Mr Carlisle Spedding, who managed the Whitehaven collieries during part of the first half of the eighteenth century. He offered to supply the harbour at Whitehaven with whatever gas
g was required to light the town. Though this offer was refused, he conducted gas from an adjacent pit through a lead pipe to the laboratory of Dr Brownrigg, a scientist who resided at Whitehaven. Natural gas had also been used on a small scale for street lighting in Italy during the nineteenth century. The decision in *Ontario Natural Gas Co v Smart* (1890) 19 OR 591, to which I shall refer later in a different context, clearly indicates that, at least by 1890, the right to bore for natural gas in Ontario was regarded as being of
h commercial value and significance. It appears, however, that, though natural gas had long been known in Ontario, it did not begin to have any commercial significance until about that date (see Sir Boverton Redwood *A Treatise on Petroleum* (1913) p 65).

(9) I am satisfied on the evidence that, as at 1880, for all its potential uses, the presence of firedamp in a mining area in England was regarded as a hazard, rather than an asset which increased the value of the property. An entry in the *National Encyclopaedia*
j (c 1881), under the heading 'Firedamp', described it as 'this terrible scourge of our coal-mines'. There is no evidence before me that firedamp or natural gas under any other description, situated in Cumberland or beneath the sea bed adjacent thereto, had ever been specifically bought or sold before 1880. On the evidence, I accept the correctness of Dr Collins's evidence that, as at that date, natural gas in the Whitehaven area would have been regarded as a dangerous nuisance and not as a vendable commodity.

(10) As at 1880, no method had yet been devised by which natural gas could be

extracted commercially from beneath the sea bed and safely conducted to land-based installations. The example of Mr Spedding's arrangements for the benefit of Dr *a* Brownrigg does not seem to have been generally followed in this country until some years after 1880.

(11) As at 1880, no one knew whether oil or natural gas existed below the relevant tracts of land and indeed, so far as the evidence shows, no one has this knowledge even today.

These factors clearly indicate that, as at 1880, the potential commercial importance *b* and value of a right to search for and extract oil and natural gas in England or in the bed of the sea adjacent thereto were not nearly so fully appreciated as they are today, in 1982.

Submissions on the construction of the documents of 1880

Nevertheless, as counsel for the plaintiff correctly emphasised, the mere fact that the parties to the 1880 articles and the 1880 conveyance may not have specifically directed *c* their minds to oil and natural gas would not necessarily have prevented these items from passing to the grantees. If the wording of the grant of 'all other mines and minerals (if any)' is, on its true construction, apt to include oil and natural gas, these items will have passed, even though the parties may not have thought about them at all. The words '(if any)' clearly showed that any substances properly falling within the description of 'mines and minerals' were intended to pass to the grantees, even though the existence of such *d* substances was unknown to the parties.

To summarise his argument very briefly, counsel for the plaintiff submitted in effect that the authorities establish that the word 'minerals', whether in a statute or deed, has an ordinary, primary meaning, which will apply unless the court can be satisfied that there is some special reason for excluding that primary meaning. The primary meaning which he ascribed to the word 'minerals' was '*every substance which can be got from beneath* *e* *the surface of the earth for the purpose of profit*'. This was the meaning attributed to the word by Lord Denning MR in the Court of Appeal (in the particular context of a definition of a 'mining lease' contained in s 25(1) of the Landlord and Tenant Act 1927) in *O'Callaghan v Elliott* [1965] 3 All ER 111, [1966] 1 QB 601, a case on which counsel for the plaintiff heavily relied. He accepted that what he termed the 'wide, normal meaning' *f* of the word 'minerals' can be treated by the court as cut down in the context of a particular document, for example, if the draftsman makes it plain by the words used that he is using the word in a special sense or if the evidence shows that, at the date of the relevant instrument, the word was used in a particular, vernacular meaning by persons conversant with the class of commercial transaction to which it related. One very clear example of the vernacular test being applied by the House of Lords is *Caledonian Rly Co v* *Glenboig Union Fireclay Co* [1911] AC 290, [1911–13] All ER Rep 307. Nevertheless, *g* counsel submitted, the vernacular test is only relevant where the evidence shows that, at the date of the instrument in question, a particular vernacular meaning was attributed to the word in question by the relevant class of persons under similar circumstances: see *Borys v Canadian Pacific Rly Co* [1953] 1 All ER 451 at 454–455, [1953] AC 217 at 223 per Lord Porter. The common vernacular meaning attributed to the word 'minerals' today by the mining world, the commercial world and landowners is in his submission *h* undoubtedly wide enough to include oil and natural gas. In these circumstances, he contended, the court should assume that its vernacular meaning in 1880 was the same, unless sufficient evidence was adduced to prove the contrary: cf *Caledonian Rly Co v* *Glenboig Union Fireclay Co* [1911] AC 290 at 299, [1911–13] All ER Rep 307 at 308 per Lord Loreburn LC. In his submission, the Crown has neither proved the existence of a special vernacular meaning in 1880, nor shown the existence of a special context sufficient *j* to cut down the wide, normal meaning attributed by him to the word 'minerals'. Thus, he submitted, the wide normal meaning applies and oil and natural gas are included.

Counsel for the Crown submitted a different mode of approach to the problem of construction as the correct one. In essence, his argument on the question of principle was to the following effect. Having emphasised the importance of ascertaining the factual

matrix of the 1880 transactions, in accordance with the principles stated by Lord
a Wilberforce in *Reardon Smith Line Ltd v Hansen-Tangen* [1976] 3 All ER 570, [1976] 1
WLR 989, he submitted that it would be wrong for the court to treat the word 'minerals'
as having any primary ordinary meaning at all. It is a word which is capable of bearing
many different meanings in many different contexts. The court's duty, in his submission,
is objectively to ascertain the meaning of the word 'minerals' as used in the particular
context of the 1880 articles and the 1880 conveyance at that particular time. It must
b construe the wording of these documents as a whole, having regard to the usage of
language at that time by businessmen dealing with commercial transactions of this
nature, and having regard to the purpose which the parties appear to have sought to
achieve. Counsel for the Crown submitted that it would be a wholly erroneous approach
for the court to treat the word 'minerals' as bearing a prima facie meaning, which results
in the onus of proof falling on any person who seeks to ascribe to it a different meaning.
c Thus, he submitted, no onus whatever falls on the Crown in the present case to show
that the word did *not* include natural gas or oil; the court must approach the question of
construction quite neutrally. On such approach the proper meaning to attach to the
word 'minerals', in the context of the 1880 articles and the 1880 conveyance, is in his
submission *those solid substances which are dug out of the earth by underground working*. If,
however, having considered the matter in the light of the wording of the two deeds and
d the relevant admissible evidence, the court should be of the opinion that the wording is
ambiguous, then, in accordance with ordinary principles of construction applicable to
Crown grants, it should, in counsel for the Crown's submission, construe the grant in the
manner more favourable to the Crown, that is to say, narrowly.

These conflicting arguments will necessitate a long journey through some of the many
conflicting authorities relating to grants or reservations of mines and minerals. Before
e embarking on this, however, I think it convenient to refer to a few dictionary definitions
of the words. Their admissibility in evidence has not been disputed, though their
usefulness for present purposes is questioned.

Some dictionary definitions of mines and minerals
    Dr Johnson's Dictionary (1786 edn) gives as its primary definitions of the verb 'mine':
f 'To dig mines or burrows; to form any hollows under ground' and of the noun 'mine': 'A
place or cavern in the earth which contains metals or minerals'. The primary definition
given by this dictionary to the adjective 'mineral' is 'consisting of fossile bodies' and to
the noun 'mineral': 'Fossile body; matter dug out of mines. All metals are minerals, but
all minerals are not metals'. A similar use of language is to be found in the *Encylopaedia
Britannica* (1797 edn) and in Hensleigh Wedgwood's *Dictionary of English Etymology* (1872),
g which defines the verb 'mine' as 'to dig underground' and the noun 'mineral' as 'what is
brought out of mines or obtained by mining'. A similar usage is also reflected in the *New
Oxford Dictionary* (1908). It gives the primary definition of the noun 'mine' as being 'an
excavation made in the earth for the purpose of digging out metals or metallic ores or
certain other minerals as coal, salt, precious stones (in 16th–17th century occasionally
building stones, sand). Also, the place from which such minerals may be obtained by
h excavation'. The primary definition given by this dictionary to the verb 'mine' is 'to dig
in the earth; esp. in a military sense, to dig under the foundations of a wall etc. for the
purpose of destroying it. Also to make subterraneous passages'. The primary definition
given by this dictionary to the noun 'mineral' is 'Any substance which is obtained by
mining; a product of the bowels of the earth'.

However, an alternative meaning in a wider, scientific sense is given by the last
j mentioned dictionary to the word 'mineral', namely, 'A material substance that is neither
animal nor vegetable; a substance belonging to the mineral kingdom'. The following
definition or description of the term 'mineral kingdom' is to be found in *Chambers
Encyclopaedia* (1874 edn):

    'Mineral Kingdom, the inorganic portion of nature. Under this term, however,
    are not included the inorganic products of organic beings, as sugar, resins &c.,

although substances more remotely of vegetable or even animal origin are reckoned among minerals, as coal, fossils, &c. To the Mineral Kingdom belong liquid and gaseous, as well as solid substances; water, atmospheric air, &c., are included in it. All the chemical elements are found in the Mineral Kingdom, from which vegetable and animal organisms derive them; but many of the compounds which exist in nature belong entirely to the vegetable and animal kingdoms, and are produced by the wonderful chemistry of life.'

A correspondingly wide use of the term 'mineral' is to be found in *Dr Ure's Dictionary* (1829), where petroleum is referred to as a 'bituminous mineral'.

The authorities relating to grants or reservations of 'mines and minerals'
If the scientific sense is ascribed to the word 'mineral', so that it includes any inorganic substance that is not animal or vegetable, it is apparent that it can have an extremely wide compass. It is, therefore, not surprising that the courts have shown a certain reluctance to attribute to it as wide a sense as this, in construing statutes and other instruments. However, as the authorities show, they have in many cases shown an almost equal reluctance to attribute the etymological meaning to the word 'minerals', so as to include within it inorganic substances that can be got by mining, but no other substances. In some cases they have regarded such a meaning as being too wide, in that it would include even substances which are not of any use to man. In other cases, they have regarded it as being too narrow, in that it would exclude those substances which can only be got by quarrying, as opposed to mining.

After this introduction, I will begin by referring to an early authority which well illustrates the difficulties which may face any court which has to construe a grant of 'minerals'.

In *Darvill v Roper* (1855) 3 Drew 294, 61 ER 915 Kindersley V-C had to consider an agreement for the partition of certain lands, under which each party conveyed land to the other with an exception of the mines of coal and lead and other minerals. The question was whether this exception extended to include limestone rocks, which were only worked by quarrying. Certain well-known scientists gave evidence to the effect that the proper definition of 'minerals' included any crystalline or earthy substance, whether metalliferous or otherwise, existing in or forming part of the earth and which might be worked by means of a mine or quarry. The plaintiff contended that the scientific interpretation was the proper one to put on the word 'minerals' in the documents and, that being so, the limestone rocks were included in the exception. The defendants pointed out that, if the scientific designation put before the court was followed, the result would be to include within the exception every particle of the earth, except the mere herbage and surface and that this could not have been the intention of the parties. Kindersley V-C accepted this contention. Early in his judgment he drew an important distinction between 'mines' and 'quarries' (3 Drew 294 at 298–299, 61 ER 915 at 917–918):

'Now, with regard to the terms mines and minerals, there can be no doubt that the term "mines" may be used in several different senses. But as to the term mines, if there were no other word used, I do not think there can be any fair doubt of its meaning here. Is a mine and a quarry the same thing? According to the ordinary sense of the term mine, does it mean a quarry? I apprehend clearly not. The meaning of the term does not depend on the nature of the fossil body obtained, it depends on the nature of the mode of working it. Some mines may be worked by means of mining, others by means of quarrying, and, upon the case here shown, the limestone was worked by quarrying. They were not limestone mines, but limestone quarries. That which is worked by mines is by a means of working in which the surface is not disturbed, and when limestone is so worked then it is a limestone mine. It is clear that in the popular, and, I think, in the just and accurate sense of the distinction between mines and quarries, the question is, whether you are

working so as to remove the surface, including perhaps portions of the lateral
surfaces so as not to leave a roof. Mining is when you begin only on the surface,
and, by sinking shafts, or driving lateral drifts, you are working so that you make a
pit or a tunnel, leaving a roof overhead. As to the word mines, therefore, there
would not be much difficulty.'

Kindersley V-C set out various senses in which the word 'minerals' might be used (see
3 Drew 294 at 299–301, 61 ER 915 at 917–919). The first was the scientific sense. The
second was that of metalliferous substances. He continued (3 Drew 294 at 300–301, 61
ER 915 at 918):

'There is then a third sense in which the word minerals may be used, viz., all such
substances as are dug out of the earth by means of a mine, a meaning which, without
being opposed to the other senses, is in accordance with the derivation and etymology
of the word; for whatever may be the origin of the word *mine*, *minerals* is clearly
derived from mines.'

Kindersley V-C went on to refer to a fourth possible sense to be attributed to the word
'minerals', namely such meaning as may be put on it by local usage, but concluded that
the evidence as to local usage before him was so conflicting as to be valueless. He said
that he did not find it necessary to determine the primary meaning of the word 'minerals'
and that, if he was compelled to do so, he would have the greatest difficulty in so
determining. Having discarded the scientific sense, he regarded the contest as being
between the second and third of the senses referred to by him. In the end he adopted the
third sense, namely minerals worked by mines. He regarded this as the construction
which gave best effect to the intentions of the parties to the transaction, as appearing
from the language of the deeds, and to the nature of the transaction itself. He therefore
dismissed the plaintiff's claim.

The Irish Court of Common Pleas in *Brown v Chadwick* (1857) 7 ICLR 101 and the Irish
Court of Queen's Bench in *Listowel v Gibbings* (1858) 9 ICLR 223 referred with approval
to *Darvill v Roper* and drew a similar distinction between mines and quarries.

In *Midland Rly Co v Checkley* (1867) LR 4 Eq 19 Lord Romilly MR had to consider
whether stone was a mineral within the context of a Canal Act, by which 'the mines and
minerals lying and being within or under the said lands or ground' on which the canal
was to be made were reserved to the owner. The plaintiffs contended that stone which
was used only for making roads did not come within the reservation and that the
reservation did not entitle the owner to work open quarries. As in *Darvill v Roper*, the
contention was that the word 'minerals' did not include substances which could only be
won by quarrying, as opposed to digging. However, in the context of the Act in question,
Lord Romilly MR rejected this contention. He said (at 25):

'Stone is, in my opinion, clearly a mineral; and in fact everything except the mere
surface, which is used for agricultural purposes; anything beyond that which is
useful for any purpose whatever, whether it is gravel, marble, fire-clay, or the like,
comes within the word mineral, when there is a reservation of the mines and
minerals from a grant of land; every species of stone, whether marble, limestone, or
ironstone, comes, in my opinion, within the same category.'

A little later, having referred to the wording from the Canal Act which I have already
quoted, he said (at 25):

'In my opinion that includes every species of mineral which is *within* the land, as
distinguished from *under* it, and clearly includes quarrying as well as mining, using
both of those words in their special sense.'

It is not clear whether in this case Lord Romilly MR was intending to assert any
general principle relating to the construction of the word 'mineral' when found in a deed
or statute. However, in *Hext v Gill* (1872) LR 7 Ch App 699, [1861–73] All ER Rep 388

the Court of Appeal in Chancery clearly did assert such a principle. In this case the Duke of Cornwall, as lord of a manor, had granted the freehold in a copyhold tenement to the copyholder, reserving—

' "all mines and minerals within and under the premises with full and free liberty of ingress, egress and regress, to dig and search for, and to take, use, and work the said excepted mines and minerals," the deed not containing any provision for compensation.'

(See LR 7 Ch App 699.)

A question arose whether china clay fell within the exception. It was contended on behalf of the grantee, in reliance on *Darvill v Roper* and the two last mentioned Irish cases, that a reservation of mines and minerals had been commonly understood as applying only to substances got by mining, as distinguished from quarrying. Mellish LJ, giving the first judgment of the Court of Appeal, said (LR 7 Ch App 699 at 712, [1861–73] All ER Rep 388 at 392):

'Is this china clay reserved under the exception of "mines and minerals?" There was a great deal of discussion before us as to the meaning of the word "mines", whether it is confined to underground working, or may possibly extend to open working, or whether it does not apply to the workings at all, but in this sort of reservation means the metal, the veins, and seams themselves, which are in a secondary sense called "mines". I think that it is not necessary here to go into those questions, for whatever may be the meaning of the word "mines" when used alone, it is here combined with the more general word "minerals", and the authorities seem to shew that where there is an exception of "mines and minerals", the putting the word "mines" before "minerals" does not restrict the meaning of the word "minerals". Many authorities, some at law and some in equity, have been brought before us to shew what is the meaning of the word "minerals". But the result of the authorities, without going through them, appears to be this: that a reservation of "minerals" includes every substance which can be got from underneath the surface of the earth for the purpose of profit, unless there is something in the context or in the nature of the transaction to induce the court to give it a more limited meaning.'

Mellish LJ went on to consider the circumstances of the parties to the transaction. A little later he concluded (LR 7 Ch App 699 at 713, cf [1861–73] All ER Rep 388 at 393):

'The position of the parties, therefore, furnishes no reason for restricting the meaning of the word "minerals", and there being no special words before "mines and minerals" which might furnish an argument for restricting them to things *ejusdem generis*, I am of opinion that the surface, and all profit that can be got from cultivating the surface, or building on it, or using the surface, is intended to be conveyed, but that the right to everything under the surface, and to all profit that can be got from digging anything out from under it, is intended to be reserved. I am therefore of opinion that china clay is included in the reservation.'

Mellish LJ, however, went on to hold that the owner of the clay had no right to injure the surface of the land in the course of getting it.

James LJ adopted the same approach as the basis of his decision. He said (LR 7 Ch App 699 at 719, [1861–73] All ER Rep 388 at 396–397):

'I entirely concur both with the conclusions and reasoning of the Lord Justice. The long and uniform series of authorities appear to me to have established a very convenient and consistent system giving the mineral owner every reasonable profit out of the mineral treasures, and at the same time saving the land-owner's practical enjoyment of his houses, gardens, fields, and woods, without which the grant to him would have been illusory.'

James LJ, however, went on to say in a passage which has since been much quoted:

'But for these authorities I should have thought that what was meant by "mines and minerals" in such a grant was a question of fact what these words meant in the vernacular of the mining world and commercial world and landowners at the end of the last century; upon which I am satisfied that no one at that time would have thought of classing clay of any kind as a mineral.'

As will appear, it is James LJ's alternative test that has since received the approval of the House of Lords.

The Court of Appeal in *Hext v Gill* thus approached the construction of the word 'minerals' on the footing that prima facie a reservation of 'minerals' includes every substance which can be got from underneath the surface of the earth for the purpose of profit, unless there is something in the context and the nature of the transaction to induce the court to give it a more limited meaning. It did not, however, suggest that Kindersley V-C had been wrong in deciding, in *Darvill v Roper*, that the context and nature of the transaction in the case led to the word being construed as including merely those substances that are dug out of the earth by means of a mine.

That such remained (even after *Hext v Gill*) a possible construction of the word 'minerals', in an appropriate context, is clearly illustrated by the Privy Council decision in *A-G for the Isle of Man v Mylchreest* (1879) 4 App Cas 294. That case concerned the effect of an exception in the Act of Settlement 1703 of 'mines and minerals, of what kind and nature soever, quarries and delfs of flagg, slate or stone . . .' The Crown contended that the word 'minerals' in this context included clay and sand. The Judicial Committee in its opinion referred without disapproval to *Darvill v Roper* and also to *Hext v Gill*. It considered that the intention of the Act was—

'to except two classes of things, first, mines, and all substances of whatever kind and nature got by mining and, secondly, quarries and delfs, not of all substances which might be got by quarrying or open pits, but of those only which are specifically described.'

(See 4 App Cas 294 at 308.)

It not being disputed that clay and sand were got from open workings, the Judicial Committee rejected the appellants' argument based on *Hext v Gill* that 'minerals' in the particular context of that Act included sand and clay.

The next important landmark in the development of the authorities on this point was the decision in *Glasgow Corp v Farie* (1888) 13 App Cas 657, [1886–90] All ER Rep 115. Section 18 of the Waterworks Clauses Act 1847 provided:

'the undertakers shall not be entitled to any mines of coal, ironstone, salte or other minerals under any land purchased by them . . .'

The appellants purchased from the respondents a piece of land near Glasgow for the purpose of erecting waterworks. The conveyance contained a reservation of the 'whole coal and other minerals in the land in terms of the Waterworks Clauses Act 1847'. The House of Lords (Lord Herschell dissenting) held that common clay, forming the surface and subsoil of the land, was not included in the reservation. Though I need not analyse the speeches, a few extracts from them will show the differences of approach. Lord Macnaghten regarded both the word 'mines' and the word 'minerals' as having a primary meaning. Thus he said (13 App Cas 657 at 687, [1886–90] All ER Rep 115 at 126):

'Now the meaning of the word "mines" is not, I think, open to doubt. In its primary signification it means underground excavations or underground workings. From that it has come to mean things found in mines or to be got by mining, with the chamber in which they are contained. When used of unopened mines in connection with a particular mineral it means little more than veins or seams or strata of that mineral. But however the word may be used, when we speak of mines in this country, there is always some reference more or less direct to underground working.'

A little later Lord Macnaghten said (13 App Cas 657 at 689–690, [1886–90] All ER Rep 115 at 128):

'Now the word "minerals" undoubtedly may have a wider meaning than the word "mines". In its widest signification it probably means every inorganic substance forming part of the crust of the earth other than the layer of soil which sustains vegetable life. In some of the reported cases it seems to be laid down, or assumed, that to be a mineral a thing must be of commercial value, or workable at a profit. But it is difficult to see why commercial value should be a test, or why that which is a mineral when commercially valuable should cease to be a mineral when it cannot be worked at a profit. Be that as it may, it has been laid down that the word "minerals" when used in a legal document, or in an Act of Parliament, must be understood in its widest signification, unless there be something in the context or in the nature of the case to control its meaning. It has also been held that the use of the word "mines" in conjunction with "minerals" does not of itself limit the meaning of the latter word. At the same time, it cannot be disputed that the term "minerals" is not unfrequently used in a narrower sense, and one, perhaps, etymologically more correct, as denoting the contents or products of mines.'

In the end, Lord Macnaghten concluded that in the particular context of the 1847 Act the term 'minerals' was used in this narrow sense, sufficient to displace what (in the light of reported cases such as *Hext v Gill*) he regarded as the primary meaning, referred to by him as its 'widest signification'.

The approach to the problem by Lord Halsbury LC was a different one. He said (13 App Cas 657 at 669, [1886–90] All ER Rep 115 at 117):

'I cannot help thinking that the true test of what are mines and minerals in a grant was suggested by James, L.J., in the case of *Hext v Gill*, which I shall have occasion hereafter to refer to, and although the Lord Justice held himself bound by authority so that he yielded to the technical sense which had been attributed to those words I still think (to use his language) that a grant of "mines and minerals" is a question of fact "what these words meant in the vernacular of the mining world, the commercial world, and landowners," at the time when they were used in the instrument.'

Lord Watson, like Lord Halsbury LC, regarded the words 'mines' and 'minerals' as not having any primary meaning. Thus he said (13 App Cas 657 at 674–675, [1886–90] All ER Rep 115 at 120):

'Nor have I been able to obtain much light from *Hext v. Gill* and other English cases referred to in the opinion of Lord Shand, which his Lordship seems to regard as almost decisive of the present question. The only principle which I can extract from these authorities is this; that in construing a reservation of mines or minerals, whether it occur in a private deed or in an Inclosure Act, regard must be had, not only to the words employed to describe the things reserved, but to the relative position of the parties interested, and to the substance of the transaction or arrangement which such deed or act embodies. "Mines" and "minerals" are not definite terms: they are susceptible of limitation or expansion, according to the intention with which they are used.'

The decision in *Farie's* case thus illustrated, but did not solve, the problems to which *Hext v Gill* had given rise.

In *Earl of Jersey v Neath Poor Law Union Guardians* (1889) 22 QBD 555 all three members of the Court of Appeal (Lord Esher MR, Bowen and Fry LJJ) treated *Hext v Gill* as having laid down a rule of construction which had not been overruled by the decision of the House of Lords in *Farie's* case.

So too did Byrne J in *Johnstone v Crompton & Co* [1899] 2 Ch 190 at 197. He explained the so-called rule as laid down in *Hext v Gill* as follows:

'I understand the true rule to be this: you inquire what the substances are; and
then you ask, Are these "minerals" in the sense that they form or belong to a class or
kind of substances of which it can be said that when separated from the soil they are
valuable either for the purposes of sale or for other purposes?'

Meantime, during this somewhat uncertain period of the relevant law, a case
concerning natural gas itself had been heard in Canada. In *Ontario Natural Gas Co v Smart*
(1890) 19 OR 591 the question arose whether a reference to "minerals" in a section of a
municipal Act included natural gas. The section read:

'The corporation of any township or county, wherever minerals are found, may
sell, or lease, by public auction or otherwise, the right to take minerals found upon
or under any roads over which the township or county may have jurisdiction, if
considered expedient so to do.'

Street J (at 594) referred to Mellish LJ's definition of 'minerals' in *Hext v Gill*. He pointed
out that this definition, although criticised by Lord Halsbury LC in *Farie's* case, received
Lord Herschell's support and was afterwards 'warmly' approved by the Court of Appeal
in the *Earl of Jersey* case. He continued (at 594):

'It appears therefore that the word is capable of a construction which would make
it include natural gas; and the question is whether it is to be taken to have been so
used in section 565 of the Municipal Act in its widest, or in a more restricted sense.'

His conclusion was (at 595):

'There is absolutely nothing in this enactment which appears to control or restrict
what the Legislature expressed or to explain what they meant when they gave the
corporations mentioned in it the right to deal with "minerals".'

He therefore concluded that he was bound by the authorities to give to the word, when
used in the Act, its widest signification and to hold that it included natural gas.

The relevant law appears to have received little further clarification until *North British
Rly Co v Budhill Coal and Sandstone Co* [1910] AC 116. However, in this case the House of
Lords in my judgment affirmed a common principle which finally negatived the
existence of any definite rule of construction, such as had been thought to result from
the decision in *Hext v Gill*. The point which the House of Lords had to consider was
whether or not sandstone is a 'mineral' within the meaning of s 70 of the Railway Clauses
Consolidation (Scotland) Act 1845 which reserved from railway companies buying land
'any mines of coal, ironstone, slate or other minerals under any land purchased by them.'
Lord Loreburn LC, delivering the first speech and having referred to a number of
authorities, said (at 125):

'I have thought it right to summarize these cases (and I might have added a few
others) lest it be supposed they are lost sight of. It is not possible to extract any
uniform standard. The same is true of the opinions expressed by different learned
judges. A variety of tests have been propounded, which are discussed by Lord
Gorell. I agree with him both in his enumeration and in his criticism. Is the
substance in common parlance a mineral? Is it so considered by geologists? Is it a
substance of any peculiar value? No one principle has been accepted, and every
principle appears to have its friends. In these circumstances it would be quite
unprofitable to expect a solution by piecing together the dicta of even the most
eminent authorities. They are contradictory. Your Lordships find the matter at
large, so far as this House is concerned.'

Lord Loreburn LC then pointed out that the purpose of the section was to enable a
railway company to acquire land and build a railroad thereon to carry passengers and
goods. He then expressed the opinion that any exception of minerals inconsistent with

this purpose would fall to be construed strictly and would not extend beyond what the words of exception would clearly cover. He pointed out that if the respondents were *a* entitled to work sandstone under this railway, the same had to be true of chalk or clay or granite or any other rock which formed the crust of the earth. He said (at 126):

> 'I am aware that there are expressions of great judges favourable to such a contention. There are also other expressions in a diametrically opposite sense. Speaking for myself, I will not adopt so startling a conclusion unless I am compelled by a decision of this House, from which there is no escape. There is no such decision.' *b*

Lord Loreburn LC said that he could not believe Parliament ever intended that the common rock of the district should be included in the words of reservation. He concluded by saying (at 127–128):

> 'It is impossible to give an exhaustive definition of the meaning of the much debated words that are to be found in s. 70. But I hope your Lordships may assist in *c* their interpretation. In the first place, I think it is clear that by the words "or other minerals" exceptional substances are designated, not the ordinary rock of the district. In the second place, I think that in deciding whether or not in a particular case exceptional substances are minerals the true test is that laid down by Lord Halsbury in *Lord Provost of Glasgow* v. *Farie*. The Court has to determine "what these words meant in the vernacular of the mining world, the commercial world, and *d* landowners" at the time when the purchase was effected, and whether the particular substance was so regarded as a mineral. Accordingly I move your Lordships to allow this appeal.'

Lord Atkinson agreed with the speeches of Lord Loreburn LC and of Lord Gorell.

Lord Gorell (at 129) said that if the question were considered by inquiring into the *e* object of the section and the succeeding sections and the language used, it seemed reasonably clear that the word 'minerals' must receive some limitation. Having referred to the object of the section, he said (at 130):

> 'Bearing these considerations in mind, it has to be ascertained in what sense the indefinite term "minerals" has been used in the section. Several interpretations *f* either have been or may be suggested.'

Lord Gorell then proceeded to set out six such interpretations, of which the third was that suggested by Mellish LJ in *Hext v Gill*, and the sixth was—

> 'that these words are used in the ordinary sense in which they are understood and used by landowners and those engaged in mining and commerce.'
g

Eventually (at 133) he indicated that in his opinion this sixth test represented the true test of what the section meant by 'mines or minerals', commenting (at 134) that James LJ in *Hext v Gill* would, but for prior authority, have adopted the same interpretation of the phrase 'mines and minerals' reserved in a grant.

Lord Shaw said (at 139–140):

> 'A true interpretation, when it takes the form of a definition, may be open to *h* danger, but for practical purposes I respectfully agree with Lord Halsbury in his adoption of the language of James L.J. in *Hext* v. *Gill* . . .'

Thus, in the *Budhill* case, the House of Lords conclusively rejected the proposition that there was any ordinary or primary meaning to be attached to the word 'minerals', a word described by Lord Gorell as being 'an indefinite term'. *j*

A year or so later the House of Lords, in *Caledonian Rly Co v Glenboig Union Fireclay Co* [1911] AC 290, [1911–13] All ER Rep 307, again had to consider s 70 of the Railways Clauses Consolidation (Scotland) Act 1845. In this instance the question was whether certain fireclay constituted 'minerals' within the section, so as to be excepted from the conveyance of land purchased by railway companies. Lord Loreburn LC, with whose

speech Lord Macnaghten, Lord Shaw and Lord Robson agreed, said ([1911] AC 290 at
299, [1911–13] All ER Rep 307 at 308):

> 'My Lords, the principle of the decision in this House in [*North British Rly Co v
> Budhill Coal and Sandstone Co* [1910] AC 116] and [*Great Western Rly Co v Carpalla
> United China Clay Co* [1910] AC 83] seems to me to have been this: the Court has to
> find what the parties must be taken to have bought and sold respectively,
> remembering that no definition of "minerals" is attainable, the variety of meanings
> which the use of the word "minerals" admits of being itself the source of all the
> difficulty. It must be taken that what the railway company intended to get and the
> landowner intended to give was the land under the line, for the object was to give,
> not a wayleave, but a support. I say this speaking generally. Upon the other hand, if
> anything exceptional in use, character, or value was thereunder, that was reserved,
> provided it could be included under the word "minerals" as understood in the
> vernacular of the mining world, and the commercial world, and the landowner.'

A little later Lord Loreburn LC said:

> '. . . the evidence given as to common meaning is evidence given of the common
> meaning at the present day; I should assume that it was the same at the time of the
> sale, unless sufficient ground was given for coming to a contrary conclusion.'

He pointed out that, on the evidence, the seam of fireclay in question was certainly of
an exceptional character as to its properties and value. On the basis of this evidence and
the evidence as to the vernacular meaning, he held that the seam of fireclay was a
'mineral' within the meaning of the relevant section. The House of Lords thus reapproved
the test originally suggested by James LJ.

The next authority is an interesting and significant one, because it concerned natural
gas. In *Barnard-Argue-Roth-Stearns Oil and Gas Co Ltd v Farquharson* [1912] AC 864, [1911–
13] All ER Rep 190 the Judicial Committee of the Privy Council had to construe a deed,
by which the appellant company had granted to the respondents' predecessor certain land
in Canada, but the deed had contained a reservation in the following terms ([1912] AC
864 at 868, [1911–13] All ER Rep 190 at 192):

> 'Excepting and reserving to the said company their successors and assigns, all
> mines and quarries of metals and minerals, and all springs of oil in or under the said
> land, whether already discovered or not, with liberty of ingress, egress, and regress
> to and for the said company, their successors, lessees, licensees, and assigns, in order
> to search for, work, win, and carry away the same, and for those purposes to make
> and use all needful roads and other works, doing no other unnecessary damage, and
> making reasonable compensation for all damage actually occasioned.'

The question at issue was whether the reservation included the right to search and
bore for natural gas. The Judicial Committee held that it did not. Lord Atkinson,
delivering its judgment, said ([1912] AC 864 at 868–869, [1911–13] All ER Rep 190 at
192):

> 'The sole question for decision in the present case is what is the true construction
> of this clause. Does it or does it not except from the grant the natural gas which
> impregnates certain underlying strata of these lands? The case does not require that
> their Lordships should lay down a definition of minerals, nor even draw the line
> between what are and what are not minerals; the only question for decision is, what,
> having regard to the time at which this instrument was executed, and the facts and
> circumstances then existing, the parties to this deed intended to express by the
> language they have used, or, in other words, what was their intention touching the
> substances to be excepted as revealed by that language?'

Lord Atkinson observed that in one sense natural gas, like rock oil, is a mineral, in that it
is neither an animal nor a vegetable product, and all substances to be found on, in or

under the earth must be included in one or other of the three categories of animal, vegetable or mineral substance. However, he said it was obvious that, in this clause of *a* the grant, the word 'minerals' was not used in this wide and general sense, for these four reasons ([1912] AC 864 at 869, [1911–13] All ER Rep 190 at 192–193):

> 'First, because two substances are expressly mentioned in the clause which would be certainly covered by the word "minerals" used in its widest sense, namely, "metals", and "springs of oil in or under the said land"; secondly, because the words *b* "all mines and quarries of metals and minerals", coupled with the words "search for, work, win, and carry away the same", do not seem to be applicable to a thing of the nature of this gas, obtainable in the way it is obtained; thirdly, because of the nature of the relation which exists between this gas and rock oil, or "the springs of oil in or under the said land", excepted in the grant and of the function which the gas performs in winning, working, or obtaining the oil from these springs; and *c* fourthly, because of the state of knowledge at the date of this deed and the way in which gas of this kind was then regarded and treated. As Lord Watson said in *Lord Provost and Magistrates of Glasgow* v. *Farie* (13 App Cas 657 at 675, [1886–90] All ER Rep 115 at 120) "the words 'mines' and 'minerals' are not definite terms, they are susceptible of limitation or expansion according to the intention with which they are used."'
d

Lord Atkinson went on to express the view that, on the evidence, it could not be contended successfully that the words 'springs of oil' covered natural gas. He pointed out that, at the date of the deed in 1867, the winning of mineral oil through wells was a comparatively new industry. He continued ([1912] AC 864 at 870–871, [1911–13] All ER Rep 140 at 193):
e

> 'This natural gas, according to the witness Mr. W. H. Dowd, did not become commercially valuable till the year 1880. And, according to the evidence of Mr. Coste and others, the accuracy of which does not appear to have been questioned, though gas might be found without the presence of oil, some gas was always found where oil was found, but the gas was regarded as a dangerous and destructive element to be got rid of as it best could. It did not begin to be utilized till the year *f* 1890, over twenty years after the date of the deed. The inference to be drawn from this evidence appears to their Lordships to be that the idea of preserving the ownership of this product, whose presence was regarded in the year 1867, and for many years after, as a dangerous nuisance, never occurred to the parties to the deed of January 22, 1867. If, in the attempt to exclude from the grant and preserve to the granting company what was then esteemed a valuable subject of property believed *g* to be in the soil parted with, namely oil, a term was used which in its wide sense would cover this then worthless product, gas, the parties never intended, their Lordships think, to use that term in this wide sense.'

The decision in *Barnard v Farquharson* is, I think, significant for present purposes, not only because it implicitly approved and applied the 'vernacular' test, but also because, in *h* applying that test, the Judicial Committee paid attention to the state of knowledge at the date of the deed of 1867 and to the way in which gas at that time was regarded and treated. In particular, it drew the inference that it would never have occurred to the parties to that deed to reserve natural gas, which, on the evidence, did not become commercially valuable until 1880 and was still regarded as a dangerous nuisance in 1867. The Judicial Committee, however, did interpret the word 'minerals', when used in its *j* 'widest sense', as including springs of oil.

In *Marquis of Linlithgow v North British Rly Co* 1912 SC 1327, the Court of Session construed a private Act passed in 1817, which had authorised the construction of a canal and had reserved to the owners of any lands through which the canal should be made 'the mines and minerals lying within or under the said lands'. It held that what was

denoted by the term 'mineral' fell to be ascertained as at 1818, the date when possession
a of the land passed to the defendants and not as at 1862, the date of the subsequent
statutory conveyance. It also held that in 1818 oil shale was not described as a 'mineral'
according to the vernacular test, which the Court of Session treated as being the relevant
test. The House of Lords affirmed its decision in the result, but did not find it necessary
to express an opinion on the question whether oil shale was a 'mineral' within the Act
(see [1914] AC 820).

b   A decision of Lush J in A-G v Salt Union Ltd [1917] 2 KB 488, which concerned s 20 of
the Finance (1909–10) Act 1910, may be said to have marked a temporary resurgence of
something like the so-called rule in Hext v Gill, though that case was not referred to by
name in the judgment. However, I do not think I need dwell on it because it was
followed by a decision of the Court of Appeal, which I think clearly confirmed that the
rule no longer exists.

c   In Waring v Foden [1932] 1 Ch 276, [1931] All ER Rep 291 the Court of Appeal had to
consider whether a reservation of 'all mines, minerals and mineral substances' in a
conveyance of 1925 included sand or gravel. Counsel for the appellant argued that it did.
They submitted (see [1932] 1 Ch 276 at 279) that the cases dealing with the construction
of expressions such as 'mines and minerals' in Acts of Parliament had no application to
the case and (see [1932] 1 Ch 276 at 280) that the true view was that expressed by Mellish
d LJ in Hext v Gill which was good law, so far at any rate as the construction of conveyances
was concerned. The Court of Appeal unanimously held that sand and gravel were not
included.

      Romer LJ (see [1932] 1 Ch 276 at 299, [1931] All ER Rep 291 at 299–300) referred to
the definition of the word 'minerals' given by Mellish LJ in Hext v Gill, which he described
as being 'probably as favourable to the plaintiff as any that can be found in the books
e within the last sixty years' and to the alternative definition which James LJ in that case
would have preferred but for earlier authority. Romer LJ said that both these definitions
had been considered in many earlier cases and each of them had found eminent adherents.
Having mentioned a number of authorities, including Farie's case and the Budhill case, he
said it was unnecessary to refer to them in detail, since he had concluded that, whichever
of them applied in the case before the court, the beds of sand and gravel were not within
f the exception. Romer LJ thus expressed no view on the issue of principle. Lord Hanworth
MR, however, in the course of his judgment by necessary implication made it clear that
he did not accept the appellant's argument, in so far as it was based on any supposed
primary meaning to be attached to the word 'minerals' in default of a contrary context.
He rejected the argument that the so-called 'code' cases were to be differentiated in their
meaning and effect from those that were decided on conveyances between private owners
g and purchasers. He referred to the speeches of Lord Halsbury and the other law Lords in
Farie's case as containing many observations that were germane to the present case.
Among the observations thus referred to by Lord Hanworth MR was the observation of
Lord Watson in Farie's case 13 App Cas 657 at 675, [1886–90] All ER Rep 115 at 120,
which I have already quoted. He referred to the Budhill case as demonstrating the futility
of trying to extract a principle which will determine the problems of what is being
h granted and what is being excepted. He did, however, note what he termed a useful
canon of construction added by Lord Gorell in the Budhill case [1910] AC 116 at 134—

      '"The enumeration of certain specified matters tends to shew that its object was
      to except exceptional matters, and not to include in its scope those matters which
      are to be found everywhere in the construction of railways, such as clay, sand, gravel,
      and ordinary stone": see also on this point Caledonian Ry. Co. v. Glenboig Union Fireclay
j   Co. ([1911] AC 290 at 299, [1911–13] All ER Rep 307 at 308) per Lord Loreburn.'

(See [1932] 1 Ch 276 at 291, [1931] All ER Rep 291 at 296.)
      On turning to the exception in the conveyance before him and referring to the
evidence, Lord Hanworth MR said ([1932] 1 Ch 276 at 291, [1931] All ER Rep 291 at
296):

'I think the grant and the exception must be construed in reference to this district and this area, in which open quarrying for sand and gravel was to the knowledge of *a* both parties exercised. Regard must be had, as Lord Watson said, to the relative position of the parties interested and to the substance of the transaction or arrangement embodied.'

Applying these considerations, Lord Hanworth MR held that sand and gravel were not included in the exception.

In thus adopting the principle expressed by Lord Watson in *Farie's* case, Lord *b* Hanworth MR thus implicitly rejected the argument of the appellants based on the definition of 'minerals' given by Mellish LJ in *Hext v Gill*.

Lawrence LJ was more explicit in rejecting this argument, when reaching the same conclusion as the other members of the court. Having referred to some of the authorities, and having adopted the principle stated by Lord Watson in *Farie's* case, he summed up the position as follows ([1932] 1 Ch 276 at 294, [1931] All ER Rep 291 at 297): *c*

'The decision in *Hext v. Gill* was followed by a sharp difference of judicial opinion on the question whether the true principle was that laid down by Mellish L.J. or that suggested by James L.J. This difference of opinion was finally settled by the *Budhill* and *Glenboig* cases, in which the House of Lords definitely decided that the view suggested by James L.J. was the right view. In my judgment it is not necessary *d* to travel beyond the pronouncements in these two last-mentioned cases in order to ascertain the principles upon which the present cases fall to be determined. The two main principles to be gathered from these pronouncements are, first, that the word "minerals" when found in a reservation out of a grant of land means substances exceptional in use, in value and in character (such as, for instance, the china clay in *Great Western Ry. Co. v. Carpalla United China Clay Co.*), and does not mean the *e* ordinary soil of the district which if reserved would practically swallow up the grant (such as, for instance, the sandstone in the *Budhill* case); and, secondly, that in deciding whether or not in a particular case exceptional substances are "minerals" the true test is what that word means in the vernacular of the mining world, the commercial world and landowners at the time of the grant, and whether the particular substance was so regarded as a mineral: see per Lord Loreburn L.C. in the *f* *Budhill* case.'

In *Borthwick-Norton v Gavin Paul & Sons Ltd* 1947 SC 659 the Court of Session in Scotland in effect applied Lawrence LJ's analysis of the earlier authorities. The question in that case was whether sand was included in a reservation of minerals contained in a conveyance. The Court of Session held that it was not, because the defenders, who claimed the benefit of the reservation, had failed to show (a) that the sand was exceptional *g* in use, character or value and other than a part of the ordinary subsoil of the district, and (b) that at the time of the conveyance it was known as a mineral in the vernacular of mining engineers, commercial men and landowners. The court thus regarded the onus of proof, so far as questions of fact were involved, as falling on the defenders (see, e g per Lord Jamieson at 688). Lord Mackay (at 675) went so far as to say that, excepting certain *h* observations in *Farie's* case, 'all intermediate cases before *Budhill* may be set aside as of little help, or even of no value'.

In *Borys v Canadian Pacific Rly Co* [1953] 1 All ER 451, [1953] AC 217 the Judicial Committee of the Privy Council accepted, with a cautionary qualification, the importance of evidence as to a particular vernacular meaning in cases where such evidence is available. This case concerned a reservation of 'all coal, petroleum and valuable stone' contained in a conveyance of land in Alberta. The substantial question was whether the reservation of *j* petroleum included gas in solution in the liquid, as it existed in the earth. The Judicial Committee held that it did. This conclusion on the question of construction as to the meaning of the word 'petroleum' was reached on the basis of the particular facts given in evidence. Two passages from the judgment of the Board delivered by Lord Porter are significant for present purposes. First ([1953] 1 All ER 451 at 454–455, [1953] AC 217 at 223):

a 'The proper approach, says the appellant, is to ascertain the meaning of the word
in the mouths of those non-scientific persons who are concerned with its use, such
as landowners, business men and engineers, and to be guided by them as to the true
construction of the reservation. The vernacular, not the scientific, meaning is, he
maintains, the true one, and in support of this contention he calls attention to the
observations of LORD HALSBURY, L.C., in *Glasgow Corpn.* v. *Farie* ((1888) 13 App Cas
657 at 669, [1886–90] All ER Rep 115 at 117) when he said of mines and minerals
b that in construing the expression it has to be determined what these words mean in
the vernacular of the mining world, the commercial world and landowners at the
time when the grant is made. This method of interpretation has been repeated and
accepted more than once, and their Lordships agree that where it can be ascertained
that a particular vernacular meaning is attributed to words under circumstances
similar to those in which the expression to be construed is found, the vernacular
c meaning must prevail over the scientific. But the distinction is not a rigid one to be
applied without regard to the circumstances in which the word is used. It was said
by LORD WATSON in the same case (13 App Cas 657 at 675, [1886–90] All ER Rep
115 at 120): "'Mines' and 'minerals' are not definite terms: they are susceptible of
limitation or expansion, according to the intention with which they are used." In
their Lordships' view the same observations are true of the meaning of petroleum.
d It may vary according to the circumstances in which it is used.'

Later in the judgment Lord Porter dealt with an argument of the appellants based on the
absence of any specific reservation of a right to work the petroleum contained in the
conveyance. He said ([1953] 1 All ER 451 at 457, [1953] AC 217–228):

e 'In their Lordships' opinion, the absence of any clause giving a right to work does
not abrogate or limit the powers of the respondents. Inherently the reservation of a
substance, which is of no advantage unless a right to work it is added, makes the
reservation useless unless that right follows the grant.'

Though the judgment in this case did not specifically refer to either the *Budhill* or the
Glenboig decisions, it did not, I think, in any way cast doubt on the authority of those
decisions. It merely added the warning that the distinction between the vernacular and
f the scientific meaning is not a rigid one to be applied without regard to the circumstances.

Thus the authorities stood before *O'Callaghan v Elliott* [1965] 3 All ER 111, [1966] 1
QB 601, a case on which counsel laid much stress in argument on behalf of the plaintiff.
In that case the Court of Appeal had to consider whether a tenancy was protected by Part
II of the Landlord and Tenant Act 1954. The answer to this question depended on
whether the tenancy was created by a 'mining lease', within the definition contained in
g s 25(1) of the Landlord and Tenant Act 1927. Section 43(1) of the 1954 Act provides that
Part II shall not apply to a tenancy created by a 'mining lease' and s 46 incorporates the
definition contained in s 25(1) of the 1927 Act, which so far as material provides:

'The expression "mining lease" means a lease for any mining purpose or purposes
connected therewith, and "mining purposes" include the sinking and searching for,
h winning, working, getting, making merchantable, smelting or otherwise converting
or working for the purposes of any manufacture, carrying away, and disposing of
mines and minerals, in or under land, and the erection of buildings, and the
execution of engineering and other words suitable for those purposes . . .'

The lease in question provided for the extraction of sand and gravel by the tenant. The
landlord for this reason claimed that it was a 'mining lease' within the relevant definition.
j The 1927 Act contained no definition of the phrase 'mines and minerals', which appeared
in the latter definition, so that many cases and statutes were cited in which the words had
been used. The Court of Appeal decided that the sand and gravel which the tenant had
the right to extract were 'minerals' within the relevant definition and that accordingly
his lease was a 'mining lease' which was not protected by the 1954 Act.

Lord Denning MR said ([1965] 3 All ER 111 at 113–114, [1966] 1 QB 601 at 608–
609):

'In this particular statute, I think that the words "mines and minerals" are used in the wide sense which was given to them by LORD ROMILLY, M.R., in *Midland Ry. Co.* ***a***
v. *Checkley* ((1867) LR Eq 19 at 25) and by MELLISH, L.J., in *Hext* v. *Gill* ((1872) LR 7 Ch App 699 at 712, [1861–73] All ER Rep 388 at 392). The words "mines and minerals" include every substance which can be got from underneath the surface of the earth for the purpose of profit. In many cases, the wide meaning of "mines and minerals" is cut down by the context. It often does not include the ordinary rock or subsoil of the district. For instance, if a railway company acquires land on which to ***b***
build a railway, it does not acquire the mines or minerals under the land. They are reserved to the previous owner. In such a case the previous owner can claim exceptional substances, but he cannot claim the ordinary rock of the district; see *North British Ry. Co.* v. *Budhill Coal & Sandstone Co.* ([1910] AC 116). Similarly when a man sold a piece of land where the subsoil was sand and gravel, but reserved to himself the "minerals", it was held that he did not reserve to himself all the sand ***c***
and gravel; for the purchaser could not even build a house without cutting into the sand and gravel (see *Waring* v. *Foden* ([1932] 1 Ch 276, [1931] All ER Rep 291)). In this statute, there are no such circumstances to cut down the meaning of the words "mines and minerals". I think they include all substances capable of being worked for profit below the top surface of the land. They include sand and gravel and clay but not, I think, peat. This view is borne out by the object which the legislature had ***d***
in mind in giving a right to a new lease. An ordinary tenant who builds up his own business and creates a goodwill in it should be entitled to a new lease. But a mining tenant does not do this. He is not creating a new capital asset adherent to the land. Quite the reverse. He is taking away part of the landlord's capital assets. He should not be entitled to a new lease, no matter whether it is coal, clay, sand or gravel. In my opinion, therefore, this was a mining lease within the Act of 1927.' ***e***

Davies LJ in his judgment adopted a broad approach to the problem. He began by pointing out that the tenant's counsel admitted that in certain cases gravel, possibly gravel and sand, could be minerals. He referred briefly to *Waring v Foden* and then the *Budhill* case, and suggested that he regarded each decision as having been a decision on its special facts. He then said ([1965] 3 All ER 111 at 115, [1966] 1 QB 601 at 610): ***f***

'It seems to me, looking at the two leases in this case, that it is as plain as anything can be that they were mining leases and that the substance intended to be taken out by the lessee was mineral. It may be difficult to lay down a precise general definition of what a mine is or what a mineral is. One does not get very much help from the OXFORD ENGLISH DICTIONARY. It may be, if one may be for a moment frivolous, that the difficulty of definition in this case is the same as the difficulty of defining ***g***
"elephants", but you recognise them at once when you see them. So here I think it is plain on these documents that they were mining leases.'

Russell LJ in his judgment referred to no decided cases, observing ([1965] 3 All ER 111 at 115, [1966] 1 QB 601 at 610):

'The cases on exceptions and reservations from a grant do not, I think, help at all. ***h***
They are to be related to the circumstances of the particular case.'

He pointed out that it was accepted that gravel and sand could be regarded as minerals and that the inquiry under the Landlord and Tenant Act 1954 was necessarily a totally different inquiry from that under an exception and reservation, but concluded that there was 'no reason for saying that this lease to work, win and get sand and gravel was not a ***j***
mining lease as defined.'

Counsel for the plaintiff submitted that the *O'Callaghan* case is clear authority for the proposition that, in the absence of a contrary context, there is a normal primary meaning which attaches to the word 'minerals', that is to say every substance which can be got from underneath the surface of the earth for the purpose of profit.

I am unable to read the decision in this way. It is clearly authority for the propositions

(i) that the phrase 'minerals' in a proper context is *capable* of including every such

a substance and (ii) that, in the particular context of the definition of a 'mining lease' in
s 25(1) of the Landlord and Tenant Act 1927, the phrase 'mines and minerals' includes
gravel and sand. While isolated sentences could be read as suggesting the contrary, I do
not think that, when Lord Denning MR's judgment is read as a whole, he was intending
to enunciate any general rule that the wide sense must always be given to the words
'mines and minerals', in the absence of a contrary context. All he was saying was that 'in

b this particular statute' (to use his words) the words are used in the wide sense given to
them by Lord Romilly MR and Mellish LJ. Still less did Davies LJ enunciate any such
general rule. In his judgment he specifically referred to the difficulty of laying down a
precise general definition of what a mine or mineral is, and by necessary implication
declined the attempt. His decision was manifestly limited to the proposition that the
sand and gravel intended to be taken by the lessee was a mineral within the meaning of

c the relevant legislation and that the two leases were accordingly 'mining leases'. So too
was the decision of Russell LJ, who derived no assistance at all from the authorities.

Conclusions from the authorities concerning mines and minerals
    At the end of this long investigation of the authorities, the conclusions which I reach
from them may be quite briefly summarised.

d (1) Though the wide sense given to the phrase 'mines and minerals' by Lord Romilly
MR in *Midland Rly Co v Checkley* and by Mellish LJ in *Hext v Gill* is a sense which the
phrase is capable of bearing and can still be attributed to it in a proper context (see e g
O'Callaghan v Elliott), it cannot now properly be regarded as a primary or literal sense
which is always to be applied in the absence of a sufficiently clear contrary context (see
e g the *Budhill* case and *Waring v Foden*).

e (2) The phrase 'mines and minerals' is not a definite term, but is one that is capable of
bearing a wide variety of meanings (see e g the *Budhill* case [1910] AC 116 at 130 per Lord
Gorell and the *Glenboig* case [1911] AC 290 at 299, [1911–13] All ER Rep 307 at 308 per
Lord Loreburn LC). One possible meaning that had been attributed to the word
'minerals' in *Darvill v Roper* (1855) 3 Drew 294, 61 ER 915 and other pre-1880 authorities
was 'all such substances as are dug out of the earth by means of a mine'. This remains a

f possible meaning in a proper context.
    (3) Unless the meaning is clear from the four corners of the relevant instrument itself,
the first duty of the court in construing a grant of mines and minerals is to try to ascertain
what the phrase meant in the vernacular of 'the mining world, the commercial world
and landowners at the time of the grant', in accordance with the test suggested by
James LJ in *Hext v Gill* and approved by the House of Lords in the *Budhill* case. The

g common link between the three categories of persons referred to by James LJ is, I think,
that they are all persons who may ordinarily be expected to have both some knowledge
of mines and minerals and also some experience of dealing with them in the course of
commerce in this country.
    (4) The meaning of the phrase in this vernacular sense may be derived either from
direct evidence as to the vernacular meaning at the relevant time or by inference drawn

h by the court (as in *Barnard v Farquharson*). If there is clear evidence as to the vernacular
meaning at the date of the trial, then, in the absence of evidence to the contrary, the
court may be justified in assuming that there was a similar vernacular usage at the date
of the grant (see the *Glenboig* case [1911] AC 290 at 299, [1911–13] All ER Rep 307 at 308
per Lord Loreburn LC).
    (5) Where it is clearly established that at the date of the grant a particular vernacular

j meaning was attributed to the phrase 'mines and minerals' by 'the mining world, the
commercial world and landowners', the court will be predisposed to adopt that meaning.
The vernacular test, however, is not a rigid test to be applied without regard to all the
other terms of the instrument in question and the circumstances in which it is used (see
Borys v Canadian Pacific Railway Co [1953] 1 All ER 451 at 455, [1953] AC 217 at 223 per
Lord Porter). The court must never overlook the commercial background and apparent
commercial purpose of the transaction.

(6) One pointer to the parties' intentions may be to consider whether or not the substances in question are exceptional in use, in value and in character (see e g *Waring v* **a** *Foden* [1932] 1 Ch 276 at 294, [1931] All ER Rep 291 at 297 per Lawrence LJ). Another pointer is the evidence as to the general state of knowledge of the relevant substance at the date of the grant and the way in which it was then regarded and treated as a commercial matter (see e g *Barnard v Farquharson* [1912] AC 864 at 869, [1911–13] All ER Rep 190 at 193 per Lord Atkinson). A third significant pointer may be derived from any express powers of working that are conferred by the instrument in question (see e g **b** *Barnard v Farquharson* [1912] AC 864 at 869, [1911–13] All ER Rep 190 at 193 per Lord Atkinson).

(7) In considering whether a grant or reservation of mines and minerals includes a specified substance, it is irrelevant that the parties did not actually have that substance in mind. The test of their intention is an objective one (see e g *Reardon Smith Line Ltd v Hansen-Tangen* [1976] 3 All ER 570 at 574, [1976] 1 WLR 959 at 996 per Lord **c** Wilberforce).

(8) With only a few exceptions, the cases cited deal with solid substances and not with liquid or fugacious substances, such as oil or natural gas. In considering the latter substances, cases which dealt with solid substances should be approached with some caution, because different considerations may apply, in particular relating to methods of working and the effects of working on adjacent land.   **d**

Evidence as to vernacular usage in 1880

Though the draftsman of the 1880 conveyance gave his own definition of the phrase 'mineral substances', he did not correspondingly define the phrase 'minerals'. The meaning which he intended to attach to the phrase is not made explicitly clear by the deed itself. In accordance with the principles just stated, it is therefore necessary to try to **e** ascertain what substances this word was understood to include in the vernacular of the mining world, the commercial world and landowners at the time of the grant in 1880.

Mr Maclachlan, in his proof given on behalf of the plaintiff, began by stating his opinion that oil and gas are properly termed minerals. He said:

'The relationship that oil and gas bear to coal is that they are all hydrocarbon **f** substances and I consider that oil and gas can be regarded as minerals in the same way that coal is regarded as a mineral . . . Coal is a hydrocarbon substance mainly of vegetable origin. Oil is a hydrocarbon substance generally considered as of mainly animal origin, although some of the more waxy oils often found in association with coal-bearing rock sequences are thought to be of partly vegetable origin. Some gas is derived from coal, some is formed in association with oil and some may be derived **g** from other sources.'

In his proof Mr Maclachlan went on to express the opinion that oil and gas were known and considered to be of use in 1880. I accept this evidence within the limits appearing from an earlier part of this judgment.

In para 2(2) of his proof he proceeded to state the view that 'oil and gas were believed to be minerals in 1880'. However, I did not derive much assistance from the examples **h** which he gave to support this view. Two of them were derived from *Dr Johnson's Dictionary* (1786). One of these entries had described naphtha as being 'a mineral oil or bitumen'. The other had described it as being 'a very pure clean and thin mineral fluid'. Another example came from Macquer's *Chemistry* (1764), which had defined bitumen as a mineral substance yielding on distillation 'a great deal of oil very like petroleum'. Another came from Samuel Phillips's *An Elementary Introduction to the Knowledge of* **j** *Mineralolgy* (1816), which had described naphtha and petroleum as being included under the heading 'mineral oil'. In each of these four examples, however, the word 'minerals' had been used in an adjectival sense, as meaning 'of the mineral kingdom'. I do not think they give much guidance whether a commercial man in 1880, taking or receiving a grant of 'minerals' under a certain piece of land, would have regarded it as including petroleum or natural gas.

One rather more pertinent example of pre-1881 usage of the word 'mineral' as a noun
a given by Mr Maclachlan was of an entry in *Chambers Encyclopaedia* (1864) which had
referred to 'naptha, petroleum, bitumen, asphalt etc.' as being included under the
description 'minerals'. Similarly, Dr Ure, in his *Dictionary* (1829), had referred to
petroleum as included in 'the whole class of bituminous minerals occurring in nature'.

The *Encyclopaedia Britannica* (1883) under the heading 'Mining', in setting out a
number of statistics relating to minerals, treated petroleum as a mineral for this purpose.
b The documentary evidence contains a number of further examples of oil or natural gas
being referred to as a 'mineral' in twentieth century writings. Petroleum is frequently so
referred to in the *Transactions of the Institute of Mining Engineers* (1907–08) vol 35, pp 144–
145. Sir Boverton Redwood, in his *Treatise on Petroleum* (1913), likewise frequently
referred to petroleum and, from time to time, to natural gas as a mineral. Much more
recently, *United Kingdom Mineral Statistics*, published by Her Majesty's Stationery Office
c in 1979, treats petroleum and natural gas as minerals and give statistics relating to them,
along with statistics relating to such substances as iron, ore, chalk, clays, sand and gravel,
limestone etc.

Counsel for the plaintiff submitted in the first alternative that reference to vernacular
usage was unnecessary, in view of the primary meaning which he asserted should be
attached to the word 'minerals' in the light of decisions such as *Hext v Gill* (1872) LR 7 Ch
d App 699, [1861–73] All ER Rep 388. However, if and so far as the vernacular meaning
may be relevant, he submitted that it is not incumbent on the plaintiff to prove
affirmatively that such meaning did include petroleum and natural gas in 1880. In his
submission the recently published *United Kingdom Mineral Statistics* show that those
responsible for compiling the statistics in Her Majesty's Stationery Office thought it
appropriate to refer to these two substances as minerals. In his submission, I should, in
e the absence of clear evidence to the contrary, assume a similar usage in 1880. Furthermore,
he pointed out, the deeds of 1880 were executed only a few years after the decision in
Hext v Gill. In his submission, it is reasonable to infer that the draftsman of these deeds
would have known of that decision and would have appreciated that, in accordance with
its principles, a grant of minerals in and under certain land would be construed as
including all substances which could be got from underneath the surface of the land for
f the purpose of profit. Such in his submission is the vernacular usage which should be
imputed to the parties.

I am far from convinced that, as at 1880, even conveyancing lawyers would have
regarded the word 'minerals' as including oil and natural gas. The earlier line of cases
exemplified by *Hext v Gill* had all been concerned with solid substances and not with
liquid or fugacious substances. Furthermore, a precedent for a grant of 'coal and ironstone
g and other mines and minerals whatsoever' to be found in Key and Elphinstone's
Compendium of Precedents in Conveyancing (1878) vol 1, p 404, while containing full and
detailed powers of working that were manifestly appropriate to solid substances,
contained none that were manifestly directed to liquid or fugacious substances such as
oil or natural gas. Even if conveyancing lawyers must be taken to have known of the
decision in *Hext v Gill*, they must likewise be taken to have known of the line of cases
h exemplified by *Darvill v Roper* (1855) 3 Drew 294, 61 ER 915 which, so far as I know,
has never been overruled, and to have foreseen that the durability of the rule in *Hext v
Gill* was somewhat doubtful, particularly in the light of the comments of James LJ.

In any event, subsequent House of Lords decisions such as *North British Rly Co v Budhill
Coal and Sandstone Co* [1910] AC 116 have established that the relevant inquiry is not so
much how the word 'minerals' was understood by conveyancing lawyers at the time of
j the grant, but how it was understood by the mining world, the commercial world and
landowners at that time. As to this crucial point, the evidence adduced by the plaintiffs,
in my judgment, gives no clear guidance. There is not in my judgment even any clear
evidence that a grant of 'mines and minerals' in general terms would today, in 1982, be
understood by the relevant category of persons as including petroleum and natural gas.
The recent government statistics on which the plaintiff heavily relied in this context do
not, I think, establish this. As Dr Collins pointed out in cross-examination, it may be

convenient for compilers of statistics or for government legislation to treat these two
substances as minerals, but this does not prove the sense which is attributed to the word
'minerals' by the relevant class of persons. His own opinion, as expressed in his oral
evidence, was that, while petroleum and natural gas can properly be referred to as
'mineral resources', they are not 'minerals' in the true sense. Minerals according to the
true meaning of the word, are in his opinion still solid substances which can be obtained
by mining by means of a bucket and spade.

Dr Collins's opinion as to the proper modern usage of the word 'minerals' derives some
support from an entry in the *Encyclopaedia Britannica Macropaedia* (15th edn, 1981) vol
12, which begins its description of 'minerals' with the words: 'A mineral is a solid formed
by natural processes; generally it is crystalline and inorganic.' This, however, was an
entry in a learned scientific article and Dr Collins himself was speaking as a scientist who,
as appeared from his oral evidence, regards himself as a purist in speech. I regard his
evidence and the other evidence adduced by the Attorney General as no more sufficient
than that of the plaintiff to establish any clear vernacular usage of the word 'minerals'
among the relevant class of the mining world, the commercial world and landowners,
either at the present day or in 1880. While I do not propose to analyse this evidence in
detail, I will nevertheless quote one example. J H Collins in his work *Principles of Metal
Mining* (1875) specifically referred to the vernacular usage common among miners as
follows:

'Any natural substance which is not of animal or vegetable origin and which is in
all parts of the same composition called a mineral. Among miners, however, the
term is only applied to such substances as are usually obtained from mines. These
are more properly called ores. Coal, also, although of vegetable origin and therefore
excluded by the strict application of the above definition, must be here included
with them.'

This passage, while not by itself strong enough to establish a contrary proposition, well
illustrates the difficulty of inferring the vernacular usage in 1880 which the plaintiff, so
far as necessary, invites me to infer.

In the end, I find that the evidence as to vernacular usage is quite inconclusive. It does
not clearly establish that the word 'minerals' was in the vernacular of the relevant class,
either as at 1880 or as at 1935, understood to include petroleum or natural gas or either
of them. Nor does it clearly establish the contrary.

The absence of clear evidence on this point is not surprising, since all the available
evidence seems to suggest that, at least until recently, it has not been common practice to
make specific grants of rights to petroleum and natural gas in and under the soil of Great
Britain or the bed of its adjacent seas. Mr B J Youngman, who is a member of the Bar and
has worked in the legal department of the National Coal Board since 1951, has given
evidence for the defendant that, throughout his employment, he has been concerned
with mining law (among other things) and has examined scores of mineral reservations
contained in conveyances which have been made to effect severance of the ownership of
surface land from underlying strata in all the main coalfields in Great Britain, including
the Cumberland coalfield. He is certain that none of the mineral reservations which he
has seen has contained any specific reference to petroleum or natural gas. He estimates
that he has also examined some hundreds of mining leases, which have come from all
the main coalfields in Great Britain, and have included leases of undersea coal and other
minerals in and off the former county of Cumberland. He is certain that none of the
leases which he has seen has contained any specific reference to petroleum or natural gas.
All this evidence suggests that, at least until recently, rights to petroleum and natural gas
were not given much discussion or thought by the parties to such reservations or leases,
because they were considered to have little or no potential value.

The absence of any clear evidence as to a vernacular usage among the relevant class
makes it necessary to fall back on the wording of the documents themselves, read in the
light of the surrounding circumstances, with the aid of dictionary definitions and the

principles of construction which I have tried to summarise. I therefore revert to a final
examination of the wording of the 1880 conveyance.

The construction of the relevant grants of 1880 and 1935

In the light of the definition of 'mineral substances' contained in the recitals to the
1880 conveyance, the parcels clause in that deed in my judgment falls to be read and
construed as if the longer phrase 'coal, culm, ironstone and fireclay' were substituted for
the phrase 'mineral substances', wherever the latter phrase occurs. Accordingly, the
parcels clause falls to be read as follows:

> 'All and every the coal culm ironstone and fireclay within or under the tracts of
> land described or mentioned in the said recited Articles of Agreement of the 2nd
> day of February 1880 AND also all other mines and minerals (if any) down to the
> bottom of the coal measures in and under the same tracts of land together with all
> such powers of searching for working getting raising and carrying away the said
> coal culm ironstone and fireclay as are by the same Articles agreed to be granted
> And all other if any the premises thereby agreed to be demised and the said William
> Stuart Stirling Crawfurd and James Lowther their heirs and assigns nevertheless in
> no way injuring or interfering with and making full compensation to Her Majesty
> her Heirs and Successors and all other persons entitled thereto for all injury or
> damage done or occasioned to the surface of the lands under which the said coal
> culm ironstone and fireclay lie and any buildings or erections at any time standing
> or being thereon except nevertheless and reserving unto Her Majesty Her Heirs and
> Successors out of the Conveyance hereby made walls or barriers of the said mines
> minerals and coal culm ironstone and fireclay of the width of 100 yards in each and
> every vein seam or bed thereof along the entire northern and southern boundaries
> respectively of the mines minerals and coal culm ironstone and fireclay Her Majesty's
> interests wherein is intended to be hereby conveyed.'

I have already concluded that, on the proper construction of this parcels clause, no
express powers of working and recovery were granted in respect of 'other mines and
minerals (if any)', but that the grant of rights in these 'other mines and minerals (if any)'
necessarily implies the existence of *some* rights to work and recover, without which the
grant would be purposeless (cf *Borys v Canadian Pacific Rly Co* [1953] 1 All ER 451 at 457–
458, [1953] AC 217 at 227–228). It is now necessary to consider further the nature and
extent of these rights.

In this context, one point in my judgment is clear. Any powers to work and recover
'other mines and minerals', which might fall to be implied, could not extend to any acts
which would occasion injury or damage to the surface of the land under which they lay.
Counsel for the plaintiff, if I understood him rightly, submitted that, on the true
construction of the clause, the grantee is entitled to injure or interfere with the surface of
the land under which the coal, culm, ironstone and fireclay lie, provided only that he
makes full compensation for any injury or damage done. On this premise he submitted
that a similar right could be implied in favour of the grantee in respect of 'other mines
and minerals'. I cannot, however, accept the correctness of the premise. In my judgment
the words 'in no way injuring or interfering with' make it plain that the grantee is not
entitled *deliberately* to injure or interfere with the surface of the land, even for the purpose
of recovering coal, culm, ironstone and fireclay. The reference to compensation in my
judgment is inserted simply to cover the contingency of accidental damage to the surface
being occasioned in the course of such recovery. In these circumstances, the court in my
judgment could not and should not imply rights of working and recovery in respect of
'all other mines and minerals', which involved the one thing that the parties to the 1880
conveyance plainly contemplated should not be permitted, namely injury or interference
with the surface of the land.

This conclusion leads on to what I regard as five crucial points in the construction of
the grant of 'all other mines and minerals (if any)' in the particular context of the 1880
conveyance.

(1) In my judgment, it was manifestly not intended to include substances which could only be worked by quarrying, drilling, boring or other work involving disturbance with *a* the surface of the land. It was only intended to include substances which could be won by means of underground works, beginning on the adjacent lands of the grantee.

(2) So far as the evidence shows, oil and natural gas are not and never have been capable of being extracted from the earth on a commercial basis by means of underground mining, whether by tunnels or excavation. The available methods of extraction are either by means of drilling or (in the case of oil) by means of a shaft dug from the surface. As at *b* 1880 the latter, more primitive, method was the one more commonly used in Europe. However, in the case of oil situated beneath the bed of the sea, as opposed to dry land, extraction by means of a dug shaft would not have been practical. Mr Maclachlan in cross-examination said that, so far as he was aware, no shafts were dug down to the bed of the sea in the 1880's. If, therefore, it had been contemplated that the grantee was to have the right to extract oil and natural gas (if any), it must also have been contemplated *c* that he should have the right to drill holes in the bed of the sea for the purpose of such extraction. However, as I have already pointed out, any such last-mentioned right would have been quite inconsistent with the express provisions of the 1880 articles and conveyance. These provisions show clearly that the grantee was not intended to have the right to interfere with the surface of the sea bed for the purpose of extracting any minerals. They clearly contemplated that the coal, culm, ironstone and fireclay would be *d* won by means of underground works beginning on the adjacent lands of the grantee, followed by tunnelling or other excavation. The express powers of working granted by the 1880 conveyance, namely powers of 'searching for, working, getting, raising and carrying away', contemplated a sequence of events connected with solid substances, not with liquid or fugacious substances. The reasonable inference, I think, is that the parties contemplated that the 'other mines and minerals (if any)' granted by the 1880 conveyance *e* would be solid substances won (if at all) in the course of searching for, working, getting, raising and carrying away coal, culm, ironstone or fireclay. This, I infer, is the reason why they thought it unnecessary that the grantee should be given any specific power of recovery in relation to 'other mines and minerals'.

(3) The third point is closely bound up with the second. In the parcels clause to the 1880 conveyance, the words 'other mines and minerals (if any)' closely follow a reference *f* to 'coal, culm, ironstone and fireclay', all of which have the common characteristics that they are solid substances, which are capable of being won by means of underground working beginning on the adjacent land of the grantee followed by digging. This point by itself distinguishes the facts of the present case from those in *Hext v Gill*, where Mellish LJ (LR 7 Ch App 699 at 713, [1861–73] All ER Rep 388 at 393) pointed out that in that case there were no special words before 'mines and minerals' which might furnish *g* an argument for restricting them to things ejusdem generis. In the present case the proper inference seems to me that the draftsman of the 1880 articles and 1880 conveyance did indeed use the phrase 'minerals' in the sense of solid substances belonging to the category to which I have just referred.

(4) This inference is strengthened when attention is directed to the 'barrier' provisions in the two documents under which the Crown reserved 'walls or barriers of the said *h* mines, minerals and mineral substances of the width of 100 yards in each and every vein, seam or bed thereof along the entire northern and southern boundaries respectively of the mines, minerals and mineral substances'. The parties thus contemplated that the 'mines and minerals' in question would (a) have 'veins', 'seams' and 'beds' in which the notional walls or barriers would subsist, and (b) be capable of having notional 'boundaries'. The plaintiff's expert witness, Mr Maclachlan, accepted under cross-examination that the *j* term 'bed' is not appropriate for use in connection either with gas in its natural state, or with petroleum in its fluid state, not in a rock. The terms 'veins' and 'seams' likewise do not seem appropriate to fugacious substances such as gas and petroleum, and Mr Maclachlan under cross-examination accepted that they were not usually so applied. The idea of these substances having notional 'boundaries' is even less appropriate. Mr Maclachlan in his proof suggested that the barrier provisions might have been partly

a intended to prevent the grantee from winning any minerals which might have 'flowed in' from adjacent properties and partly as a safety measure to prevent any flooding of the Lonsdale mines from under any adjoining properties. Dr Collins in chief roundly described the first part of this suggestion as 'nonsense' and I myself found it unconvincing. I accept Dr Collins's explanation of the general purpose of a barrier, given in his proof and in chief. He explained that it is normal mining practice to leave areas of unmined rock as barriers. They perform a number of functions. Their primary purpose is to

b preserve the integrity of the areas adjacent to the relevant minerals, in particular to prevent the escape of foul air or water into those areas from the areas where the minerals are being or have been worked and, at least as to mines under land, to give support for the surface. They may also serve to prevent the illicit working of minerals retained by the grants from nearby areas. Though one *consequence* of the barrier provisions in the present case could have been to prevent flooding of the Lonsdale mines from under

c adjoining properties, I cannot accept that this was their *purpose* or indeed that they were in any sense intended for the protection of the plaintiff's predecessor in title. The proper intention to impute to the parties is, in my judgment, that they were intended solely for the protection of the Crown, in whose favour the reservation was made. In the light of all the evidence, I infer that the primary purpose of the Crown in reserving barriers under the 1880 conveyance was to protect its interests in case it should wish itself to

d exploit any mineral resources under the bed of the sea, to the north or the south of the Lonsdale off-shore areas. In my judgment, it is reasonably plain, both as a matter of language and having regard to the purpose of the provision, that it contemplated that the barriers would be notional barriers in solid, as opposed to gaseous or liquid, substances. This again lends support to the conclusion that the 'mines, minerals and mineral substances' in which the barriers were to exist would be of a solid nature.

e (5) On the authority of *Barnard v Farquharson* [1912] AC 864 at 869, [1911–13] All ER Rep 190 at 193 per Lord Atkinson, I think I am entitled to take into account the state of knowledge of petroleum and natural gas in 1880 and the way in which they were then regarded and treated. The evidence in that case was that, as at the date of the relevant deed (1867), gas in Canada was regarded as a dangerous nuisance, that it did not become commercially valuable till 1880 and that it did not begin to be utilised until 1890. The

f Judicial Committee inferred from this evidence that 'the idea of preserving the ownership of this product, whose presence was regarded in the year 1867, and for many years after, as a dangerous nuisance, never occurred to the parties to the deed of January 22, 1867'.

Applying a similar objective test in the present case, on the evidence before me, I infer that the parties to the two deeds of 1880 never intended that rights to extract oil and natural gas (if any) should pass to the grantee. As at that date, I infer from the evidence

g that neither category of rights would have been regarded as having any use or commercial value by persons dealing with the sale of minerals in the relevant area of Cumberland and indeed that the existence of gas (if any) would have been regarded as a dangerous nuisance.

These five points in my judgment make it reasonably plain that, in the context of the 1880 articles and 1880 conveyance, the phrase 'mines and minerals (if any)' was not

h intended to include anything except solid substances, capable of being dug out of the earth by means of a mine, and in particular was not intended to include oil and natural gas.

Further or alternatively, these five points in my judgment at the very least establish that the phrase 'mines and minerals', which has no definite meaning (see the *Glenboig* case [1911] AC 290 at 299, [1911–13] All ER Rep 307 at 308 per Lord Loreburn LC), is in this

j particular context an ambiguous one. In accordance with the principle applicable to grants by the Crown, the words must in my judgment therefore be construed in the manner most favourable to the grantor, by the exclusion of everything except solid substances capable of being dug out of the earth by means of a mine. Etymologically such a conclusion presents no difficulty. The meaning accorded to the verb 'mine' by the nearly contemporary *Dictionary of Etymology* by Hensleigh Wedgwood (1872) was to 'dig underground' and to the word 'mineral' was 'what is brought out of mines or obtained by mining'. By 1880 the word had been construed in this sense in a number of cases which I have already mentioned, including *Darvill v Roper* (1855) 3 Drew 294, 61 ER *a* 915 and *A-G for the Isle of Man v Mylchreest* (1879) 4 App Cas 294. If the grantee under the 1880 conveyance had wished and intended the grant to him to include rights in liquid and fugacious substances such as petroleum and natural gas in situ, the rights in which were not commonly dealt with commercially in this country at that time, it would in my judgment have been incumbent on him to procure such grant to be effected in his favour by 'clear and express words': see *Viscountess Rhondda's Claim* [1922] 2 AC 339 at *b* 353 per Lord Birkenhead LC. Counsel for the plaintiff referred in argument to the principle of construction applicable to grants by the Crown as a rule of 'last resort'. I accept that in many cases it will have little practical significance. In the present case, however, it has real significance and the court must attach to it its due weight.

I can see no reason for reaching a conclusion in relation to the construction of the 1935 deed of exchange different from that which I have reached in relation to the 1880 *c* conveyance. On the first of the three main issues in this case, my conclusion therefore is that the phrase 'all other mines and minerals (if any)', as used in those two deeds, does not include oil and natural gas.

This conclusion makes it strictly unnecessary to consider the second issue in the case, relating to the meaning of the phrase 'down to the bottom of the coal measures', and the third issue, relating to the effect of the Petroleum (Production) Act 1934 and the *d* Continental Shelf Act 1964. I feel some hesitation in expressing any opinions on these matters, not only because these opinions will be obiter and will substantially prolong my judgment, but also because the third issue raises questions that could be important in other cases besides this one. Nevertheless, since I have had the benefit of full argument on them, I think I should attempt to deal with them, in case this may be of assistance to the parties or a higher court. *e*

The second issue: the meaning of 'coal measures'

According to the terms of the relevant grants, the plaintiff is entitled to 'mines and minerals' in and under the Lonsdale off-shore areas 'down to the bottom of the coal measures' in and under such areas. If, contrary to my view, the grants have conferred on the plaintiff rights to oil and natural gas, a question arises as to the meaning of the phrase 'bottom of the coal measures' in this context. *f*

Evidence as to the meaning attributed to this phrase in the vernacular of the mining world, the commercial world and landowners in 1880 is clearly both admissible and relevant. The report of the commissioners appointed to inquire into the several matters relating to coal in the United Kingdom, presented to both Houses of Parliament in 1871, gives a general indication as to the usage of the word at that date. It contained the following explanatory paragraph: *g*

> 'Coal consists of mineralised vegetable matter occurring in seams, interstratified with beds of sandstone, shale and ironstone and more rarely of limestone, and these together are called the Coal-measures, which in some coalfields attain a thickness of many thousand feet.'

A little further on, it was explained that there is no further growth of coal in the coal *h* measures. In using the phrase 'coal measures', the report employed a capital 'C' and a small 'm'.

As it happened, the draftsman of the 1880 conveyance did the same thing in the habendum clause, but his usage of capital and small letters was by no means consistent throughout this deed. Mr Maclachlan in his proof suggested that the phrase 'coal measures', with no capital letters, has a less precise and technical meaning than the phrase *j* when written with a capital 'C' and a capital 'M'. But in the end neither side placed any reliance at all on this point in argument, so that it will not be necessary further to mention the many inconsistent usages of capital and small letters in this context, throughout the documents and learned works which are in evidence. In using the phrase 'coal measures', I will henceforth employ small letters throughout.

The evidence in my judgment establishes that as at 1880 this phrase was a term used
in the United Kingdom and other parts of Europe as denoting a certain coal-bearing rock
sequence in the upper carboniferous system.

In about 1884 an attempt (apparently the first attempt) to fix finally the base of the
coal measures in Cumberland and North Lancashire was made by Mr J D Kendall, who
presented a paper, entitled 'The Carboniferous Rocks of Cumberland North Lancashire
or Furness', to the North of England Institute of Mines and Mechanical Engineers in
about 1884 (see *Transactions of the Institute of Mining Engineers*, vol 34, p 135). In that
paper he divided the carboniferous system in West Cumberland into six descending
categories, namely (1) Whitehaven sandstone or Upper coal measures; (2) Middle coal
measures; (3) Lower coal measures, including what he termed 'the four-feet coal' and 'the
Udale Band'; (4) Millstone grit; (5) Yoredale rocks; (6) carboniferous limestone; (7) lower
limestone shale. Mr Kendal selected the Udale seam as the base of the coal measures,
immediately under which was situated the Millstone grit. Mr Maclachlan considered
that this reflected the use of the term coal measures in 1880.

However, he explained that the situation has been somewhat complicated because the
classification employed by Mr Kendall was revised by the Geological Survey of England
and Wales in 1931, when terminology based on other parts of the United Kingdom was
introduced in relation to Cumberland. Following this revision, the term 'coal measures'
came to include approximately the first and second of Mr Kendall's seven categories,
namely the Upper and Middle coal measures. The term 'Millstone grit series' came to
include approximately Mr Kendall's third category, his 'Lower coal measures'. The term
'Udale coal' came to refer to the base of this newly termed Millstone grit series. What was
known as 'The Harrington four-feet coal', situated towards the top of Mr Kendall's Lower
coal measures, came to be regarded as the base of the coal measures (see generally, *The
Geology of the Whitehaven and Workington District* by Eastwood and others, pp 95–97, 106–
108, 116–119). The term 'the Hensingham Group' came to include approximately what
Mr Kendall had called the 'Millstone grit'.

Dr Collins in the course of his cross-examination said that a yet further reclassification
took place in about 1956 or 1957, which involved among other things another name
being given to what was at that time known as Millstone grit.

However, I do not think I need further pursue all these niceties for these reasons. As
Mr Maclachlan pointed out in his proof, the Udale seam, as referred to by Mr Kendall,
was the lowest seam that had been worked at the time when he wrote his book.
Accordingly, Mr Kendall selected what he termed 'the Udale seam' as the base of the coal
measures, calling the underlying rocks 'Millstone grit'.

Counsel for the Crown told me that if I were minded to make a declaration in favour
of the plaintiff, the Crown would accept that his rights extended down to the bottom of
the Udale seam as referred to by Mr Kendall. However, if it had been appropriate to
make a declaration in favour of the plaintiff, I would not have contemplated making it
by reference to the Udale seam, at least unless this term were further defined. It is a term
which is itself fraught with potential ambiguity, for reasons which will have already
appeared. For present purposes, the most important feature of Mr Kendall's work, in my
judgment, is that it shows that, in the 1880's, the phrase 'coal measures' was used by
persons conversant with mining matters to include *those identifiable seams of coal which
were or might be worth mining*. He divided such seams into the three categories 'Upper coal
measures', 'Middle coal measures' and 'Lower coal measures', but all three categories
shared this common characteristic. Nothing that lay below them was worth mining. In
my judgment, having regard to the factual matrix of the transactions of 1880 and 1935
and their objective purpose, the proper intention to impute to the parties, in using the
phrase 'down to the bottom of the coal measures', was to grant to the plaintiff's
predecessors rights in the relevant minerals down to the bottom of the lowest identifiable
seam of coal that would or might be worth mining. This would have been the sense
which I would have wished to achieve in making any declaration in favour of the
plaintiff. Its precise terminology would have required further consideration, but the

evidence before me suggests that, if necessary with some further assistance from the
experts, this would have presented no insuperable difficulty.   *a*

I now turn to the third principal issue in the case.

The effect of the 1934 and 1964 Acts

Section 1(1) of the Petroleum (Production) Act 1918, so far as material, provided:

> 'No person other than a person acting on behalf of His Majesty or holding a
> licence under this Act for the purpose shall search or bore for or get petroleum *b*
> within the United Kingdom . . .'

The statute did not define the phrase 'the United Kingdom', but s 5(1) defined the
expression 'petroleum' for the purposes of the Act, as meaning—

> 'all petroleum and its relative hydrocarbons (except coal and bituminous shales
> and other stratified deposits) from which oil can be extracted by distillation and
> natural gas existing in its natural condition in strata.'   *c*

The expression thus included oil and natural gas.

The Royal and Parliamentary Titles Act 1927 then followed. Section 2(2) provided,
inter alia, that in every subsequent Act the expression 'United Kingdom' should, unless
the context otherwise required, mean Great Britain and Northern Ireland.

There then followed the Petroleum (Production) Act 1934, which described itself as— *d*

> 'An Act to vest in the Crown the property in petroleum and natural gas within
> Great Britain and to make provision with respect to the searching and boring for
> and getting of petroleum and natural gas, and for purposes connected with the
> matters aforesaid.'

Section 1 provided:
                                                                                           e
> '(1) The property in petroleum existing in its natural condition in strata in Great
> Britain is hereby vested in His Majesty, and His Majesty shall have the exclusive
> right of searching and boring for and getting such petroleum: Provided that nothing
> in this subsection shall apply to petroleum which at the commencement of this Act
> may lawfully be gotten under a licence in force under the Petroleum (Production)
> Act, 1918, being a licence specified in the Schedule to this Act, so long as that licence *f*
> remains in force.
>
> (2) For the purpose of this Act the expression "petroleum" includes any mineral
> oil or relative hydrocarbon and natural gas existing in its natural condition in strata,
> but does not include coal or bituminous shales or other stratified deposits from
> which oil can be extracted by destructive distillation.'

It is not disputed that the oil and natural gas claimed by the plaintiff in the present *g*
action is 'petroleum' within the meaning of the 1934 Act. Section 2 provided:

> '(1) The Board of Trade, on behalf of His Majesty, shall have power to grant to
> such persons as they think fit licences to search and bore for and get petroleum.
>
> (2) Any such licence shall be granted for such consideration (whether by way of
> royalty or otherwise) as the Board of Trade with the consent of the Treasury may *h*
> determine, and upon such other terms and conditions as the Board of Trade think
> fit.'

Section 3 empowered persons holding licences under the Act to acquire certain
ancillary rights.

Section 5 made provision as to receipts and expenditure under the Act. Sub-section (2)
provided, inter alia, that all moneys received by the Board of Trade under the Act should *j*
be paid into the Exchequer.

Section 6 obliged the Board of Trade, before granting any licence under the Act, to
make regulations prescribing a number of specified matters.

Section 11(2) repealed the 1918 Act, subject to a proviso, the effect of which was that
the validity of three specified licences, which had previously been granted by the Board
of Trade, was not to be affected by the repeal.

Section 11(3) of the 1934 Act provided that the Act should not extend to Northern
a Ireland.

Sections 1(1) and 11(3) of the 1934 Act thus make it plain that the act is to apply to oil
and natural gas existing in their natural condition in strata in 'Great Britain', whatever
'Great Britain' may mean, but the Act unfortunately contains no further definition of
this crucially important phrase. The Crown, as its primary submission in this context,
claimed that in the 1934 Act the expression includes not only the land comprised within
b the geographical limits of Great Britain, as shown on the map, but also the sea bed and
subsoil of its territorial waters. Thus, it submitted, even if the 1880 conveyance operated
to grant to the fourth earl rights in oil or natural gas, the rights in any such substances
situated below those parts of the relevant tracts of land which lay within territorial waters
became revested in the Crown by virtue of the 1934 Act. It further contended that it was
empowered by that Act to grant licences of the nature which it did in fact grant to
c Ultramar.

It is not in dispute that Parliament, in enacting the 1934 Act, would have had the
power to legislate in regard to the territorial waters of Great Britain and all that lay
beneath them, including oil and natural gas: see e g *Pianka v R* [1979] AC 107. Counsel
for the Crown submitted that any municipal statute of the United Kingdom Parliament,
in the absence of limiting words, extends to the whole of the territory of the United
d Kingdom and to all persons within it (see [1979] AC 107 at 122 per Lord Wilberforce).

In the present case, however, s 1(1) of the 1934 Act does contain an express limiting
provision, inasmuch as it is expressed to apply to petroleum 'existing in its natural
condition in strata in Great Britain'. The question is: what does the expression 'Great
Britain' mean in this context?

I have been referred to no general statutory provision which attaches a definition to
e this expression wherever it appears in a statute. The duty of the court in construing any
statute is, of course, to ascertain the intention of the legislature as expressed in the words
used by it. If these words are clear and unambiguous, they must be deemed to represent
Parliament's intention, whatever their effect. Furthermore, as in the case of other
instruments, if there is nothing to alter or qualify the meaning of the words used, they
must be construed according to their ordinary and natural meaning.

f Nevertheless, it has to be borne in mind that s 1(1) of the 1934 Act, so far as it applies
at all in the present case, would have had the effect of expropriating rights of the
plaintiff's predecessors in title without compensation. It is, I think, well established by
authority that an intention to divest private citizens of rights in property without
compensation is not to be imputed to the legislature, unless that intention is expressed in
clear and unambiguous terms. In my judgment therefore the onus must fall on the
g Crown to satisfy the court that s 1(1) of the 1934 Act was capable of applying to any
rights of the plaintiff's predecessors in title in oil and natural gas situated beneath
territorial waters, as well as beneath dry land.

Counsel for the Crown, in submitting that the phrase 'Great Britain' has an ordinary
meaning which includes 'territorial waters', cited a number of dicta in which judges have
referred to territorial waters as if they are part of the realm. I will take a few examples of
h his citations. In *R v Keyn* (1876) 2 Ex D 63 at 155, Lord Coleridge CJ, albeit one of the
dissenting minority of the court, said:

'Furthermore, it has been shewn that English judges have held repeatedly that
these coast waters are portions of the realm. It is true that this particular point does
not seem ever distinctly to have arisen. But Lord Coke, Lord Stowell, Dr. Lushington,
Lord Hatherley, L.C., Erle, C.J., and Lord Wensleydale (and the catalogue might be
j largely extended) have all, not hastily, but in writing, in prepared and deliberate
judgments, as part of the reasoning necessary to support their conclusions, used
language, some of them repeatedly, which I am unable to construe, except as
asserting, on the part of these eminent persons, that the realm of England, the
territory of England, the property of the State and Crown of England over the water
and the land beneath it, extends at least so far beyond the line of low water on the
English coast as to include the place where this offence was committed.'

In *Lord Advocate v Clyde Navigation Trustees* (1891) 19 R (SC) 174 at 183 Lord Young said: 'My opinion is, and, I confess, without doubt or hesitation that Loch Long is part of the territory of Scotland.'

In *Lord Advocate v Wemyss* [1900] AC 48 at 66 Lord Watson said:

'I see no reason to doubt that, by the law of Scotland, the solum underlying the waters of the ocean, whether within the narrow seas, or from the coast outward to the three-mile limit, and also the minerals beneath it, are vested in the Crown.'

In *Lord Fitzhardinge v Purcell* [1908] 2 Ch 139 at 166–167 Parker J said:

'Clearly the bed of the sea, at any rate for some distance below low-water mark, and the beds of tidal navigable rivers, are prima facie vested in the Crown, and there seems no good reason why the ownership thereof by the Crown should not also, subject to the rights of the public, be a beneficial ownership.'

In *A-G for British Columbia v A-G for Canada* [1914] AC 153 at 174–175 Viscount Haldane LC, delivering the judgment of the Judicial Committee of the Privy Council, specifically declined to reach any decision on the question whether the shore below low-water mark to within three miles of the coast forms part of the territory of the Crown or is merely subject to special powers necessary for protective and police purposes. He further gave a warning against municipal tribunals purporting to pronounce on it before the topic had been examined at an international conference. Nevertheless, shortly afterwards in *Secretary of State for India v Chelikani Rama Rao* (1916) LR 43 Ind App 192 at 201 the Judicial Committee of the Privy Council, without expressly referring to the last-mentioned decision, held that the Crown was the owner, and the owner in property, of islands arising in the sea within the territorial limits of the Indian Empire.

For present purposes, particularly in the light of the *Chelikani* decision, I am content to assume in favour of the Crown that, as counsel for the Crown submitted, by 1918 the English courts had come to recognise the sovereignty of the Crown (including beneficial ownership) over the three-mile territorial belt of Great Britain and what lies beneath it. I also accept that, by that time, there were many judicial dicta referring to this subject matter as part of the territory or realm of Great Britain.

In none of the cases relied on by the Crown, however, did the court have to consider whether the expression 'Great Britain', when used in a geographical sense, either in a statute or any other instrument, is apt to include territorial waters. In my judgment it cannot possibly be maintained that, as at 1934, the expression had a clear, ordinary meaning which included territorial waters, if only because no previous statute that has been referred to in argument demonstrably employed the phrase in this sense, while at least two earlier, well-known statutes had employed the phrase 'the United Kingdom' in a sense which demonstrably did *not* include territorial waters.

This latter statement requires some explanation, beginning by reference to the decision of the Court for Crown Cases Reserved in *R v Keyn* (1876) 2 Ex D 63. In that case the majority of the court (seven judges out of thirteen) held that the Central Criminal Court had no jurisdiction to try a foreign subject for an offence (in that case manslaughter) committed by means of a foreign ship in British territorial waters. The grounds of the decision and its validity have been the subject of much controversy. I need not, however, pursue this question. What is relevant is that it was closely followed by the enactment of the Territorial Waters Jurisdiction Act 1878. This Act began by reciting that—

'the rightful jurisdiction of Her Majesty, her heirs and successors extends and has always extended over the open seas adjacent to the coasts of the United Kingdom and of all other parts of Her Majesty's dominions to such a distance as is necessary for the defence and security of such dominions . . .'

Then it recited that—

'it is expedient that all offences committed on the open sea within a certain distance of the coasts of the United Kingdom and of all other parts of Her Majesty's Dominions, by whomsoever committed, should be dealt with according to law . . .'

Section 2, in amending the law as to the Admiralty's jurisdiction accordingly referred
a to 'An offence committed by a person . . . on the open sea within the territorial waters of
Her Majesty's dominions . . .'

Section 7 defined the United Kingdom as including 'the Isle of Man, the Channel
Islands and other adjacent islands', and 'the territorial waters of Her Majesty's dominions',
in reference to the sea, as meaning—

b
> 'such part of the sea adjacent to the coast of the United Kingdom, or the coast of
> some other part of Her Majesty's dominions, as is deemed by international law to be
> within the territorial sovereignty of Her Majesty . . .'

The 1878 Act in my judgment thus provides a clear indication that, while Parliament,
in enacting it, regarded territorial waters of the United Kingdom as being within the
territorial sovereignty of the Crown, it did not regard them as being actually part of the
c United Kingdom in a geographical sense.

A similar use of language is, I think, to be found in the Merchant Shipping Act 1894.
Section 511(1), which deals with the duty of a receiver of wrecks, begins with the words:

> 'Where a British or foreign vessel is wrecked, stranded or in distress at any place
> on or near the coasts of the United Kingdom or any tidal water within the limits of
> the United Kingdom . . .'
d

The Act thus recognised the distinction between territorial waters and internal waters.
Internal waters are those areas of water, including some tidal waters, which by reason of
their location are under the full sovereignty of the territorial state. They differ from
territorial waters in that they are subject to no right of passage for foreign vessels. The
legislature thus treated internal tidal waters, but not territorial waters, as falling within
e the limits of the United Kingdom. A similar use of terminology is to be found in s 519(1)
of the same Act.

Counsel for the Crown drew my attention to the Coal Mines Act 1911, which was an
Act intended to consolidate and amend the law relating to coal mines and certain other
mines. He submitted that, on its true construction, it extended to, inter alia, mines
situated underneath territorial waters. At least the great majority of such mines would
f presumably be approached by openings on dry land and would be situated at least partly
under dry land. I therefore readily accept that this Act might be capable of applying to
mines part of which were situate under the sea bed. But I can find nothing in it which
assists in the construction of the phrase 'Great Britain', as used in the 1934 Act.

Counsel also referred to the Mining Industry Act 1920, the expressed purpose of which
was—

g
> 'to provide for the better administration of mines, and to regulate the coal
> industry, and for other purposes connected with the mining industry and the
> persons employed therein.'

Section 1 of that Act began with the words:

> 'For the purpose of securing the most effective development and utilisation of the
h mineral resources of the United Kingdom and the safety and welfare of those
> engaged in the mining industry, there shall be established a department of the
> Board of Trade (to be known as the Mines Department) . . .'

Counsel for the Crown submitted that this Act, on its true construction, extended to
mines beneath the sea. However, the phrase 'the mineral resources of the United
Kingdom' is prima facie quite capable of bearing the meaning 'the mineral resources
j over which the United Kingdom has sovereignty'. In my judgment this section and the
Act as a whole are of no help in construing the phrase 'petroleum existing in its natural
condition in strata in Great Britain' in a statutory provision where the phrase 'Great
Britain' in its context plainly has a solely geographical significance.

On behalf of the Crown I was also referred to the Mines (Working Facilities and
Support) Act 1923, s 18(3) of which provided that it should 'extend to Great Britain'. The
expressed purpose of this Act was—

'to make provisions for facilitating the working of minerals and for imposing restrictions on the working of minerals required for the support of railways, buildings and works'.

Again I accept that this Act might be capable of applying to mines, of which parts are situated under the sea bed. I am, however, by no means certain that it requires a construction of the phrase 'Great Britain' in s 18(3) as including the sea bed and subsoil of territorial waters, particularly when it is borne in mind that at least the great majority of mines, of which parts are situated under the sea bed, would have openings on the adjacent dry land.

It follows that, by the time that the 1918 and 1934 Acts became law, there were at least two statutes in force (namely the Territorial Waters Jurisdiction Act 1878 and the Merchant Shipping Act 1894) in which the legislature, in using the phrase 'the United Kingdom' in a geographical sense, had quite plainly not included within its ambit either territorial waters themselves or their sea bed and subsoil, but in contrast had thought it necessary to make express reference to such waters. On the other hand, so far as I am aware, the legislature had never used the phrase 'the United Kingdom' or 'Great Britain' in a geographical sense as including territorial waters or the bed of the sea and subsoil beneath them. In these circumstances I cannot accept that as at 1918 or 1934 the phrase 'Great Britain' had any clear, ordinary meaning such as is contended for by the Crown.

Nevertheless, I accept that the phrase in the particular context of s 1(1) of the 1934 Act is an ambiguous phrase, capable of more than one interpretation. Counsel for the Crown drew my attention to the decision of the House of Lords in *Kirkness v John Hudson & Co Ltd* [1955] 2 All ER 345, [1955] AC 696, which illustrates that, where an earlier statute contains a phrase which is fairly open to two or more meanings, later legislation on the same subject may be looked at, for the purpose of construing the earlier provision (see e g [1955] 2 All ER 345 at 350, 366, [1955] AC 696 at 710–711, 735–736 per Viscount Simonds and Lord Reid). He submitted that, if I properly thought that there was any ambiguity in s 1(1), I could properly look at two later statutes for the purposes of resolving it.

The first of these statutes was the Ministry of Fuel and Power Act 1945, the expressed purposes of which were—

'to make further provision with respect to the appointment and functions of the Minister of Fuel and Power, and for purposes connected therewith.'

Section 1(1) of this Act provided:

'It shall be lawful for His Majesty to appoint a Minister of Fuel and Power (in this Act referred to as "the Minister") who shall be charged with the general duty of securing the effective and co-ordinated development of coal, petroleum and other minerals and sources of fuel and power in Great Britain, of maintaining and improving the safety, health and welfare of persons employed in or about mines and quarries therein, and of promoting economy and efficiency in the supply, distribution, use and consumption of fuel and power, whether produced in Great Britain or not.'

Section 6(1) of the Act provided that, for the purposes of s 1(1), the expressions 'coal' and 'petroleum' respectively included products of coal and products of petroleum. Section 7(1) repealed s 8 of the 1934 Act. The Act thus contemplated that there would be imposed on the minister a general duty of co-ordinating the development of coal, petroleum and other minerals and sources of fuel and power (including natural gas) in 'Great Britain'. The phrase 'Great Britain' in this context is plainly used in a geographical sense, but the wording of the Act, unlike the wording of two later statutes of 1966 and 1972, itself gives no direct indication whether the phrase is intended to include the sea bed and subsoil of territorial waters. Again, particularly bearing in mind that at least most mines of which parts are situated under the sea bed would have openings on the adjacent dry land, it would not appear to be demonstrably essential to construe the phrase 'Great Britain' in the extended sense in order to give effect to the intention of the legislature. I do not therefore think this Act affords much guidance in the construction of the 1934

a Act.

The same observation may be made in relation to the next statute on which the Crown relies. This is the Continental Shelf Act 1964, one of the expressed purposes of which was 'to make provision as to the exploration and exploitation of the continental shelf'.

The Convention on the Continental Shelf (Geneva, 29 April to 31 October 1958; TS 39 (1964); Cmnd 2422) (which I will call 'the first convention of 1958'), to which the United

b Kingdom was a party, came into force on 10 June 1964. Article 1 defined the term 'continental shelf' for the purpose of the convention as referring—

> '(a) to the seabed and subsoil of the submarine areas adjacent to the coast but outside the area of the territorial sea, to a depth of 200 metres or, beyond that limit, to where the depth of the superjacent waters admits of the exploitation of the natural resources of the said areas; (b) to the seabed and subsoil of similar submarine
c areas adjacent to the coasts of islands.'

Article 2.1 provided:

> 'The coastal State exercises over the continental shelf sovereign rights for the purpose of exploring it and exploiting its natural resources.'

d Article 2.2 provided:

> 'The rights referred to in paragraph 1 of this article are exclusive in the sense that if the coastal State does not explore the continental shelf or exploit its natural resources, no one may undertake these activities, or make a claim to the continental shelf, without the express consent of the coastal State.'

e Article 2.4 defined 'natural resources' in terms clearly wide enough to include petroleum and natural gas.

The 1964 Act became law on 15 April 1964. Section 1 was, I think, manifestly intended to procure, inter alia, that any rights which would be exercisable by the United Kingdom as a coastal state under international law, pursuant to the first convention of 1958, should vest in the Crown under municipal law. This section provided:

f > '(1) Any rights exercisable by the United Kingdom outside territorial waters with respect to the sea bed and subsoil and their natural resources, except so far as they are exercisable in relation to coal, are hereby vested in Her Majesty.
> (2) In relation to any coal with respect to which those rights are exercisable the Coal Industry Nationalisation Act 1946 shall apply as it applies in relation to coal in Great Britain, but with the modification that the National Coal Board shall not
g engage in any operations for the purpose of working or getting the coal without the consent of the Minister of Power, which may be given on such terms and subject to such conditions as he thinks fit.
> (3) In relation to any petroleum with respect to which those rights are exercisable sections 2 and 6 of the Petroleum (Production) Act 1934 (which relate to the granting of licences to search and bore for, and get, petroleum) shall apply as they
h apply in relation to petroleum in Great Britain, and section 3 of that Act (which enables persons holding licences under that Act to acquire ancillary rights) and section 5 of that Act (which makes provision as to receipts and expenditure under that Act) shall have effect as if this subsection were part of that Act.
> (4) Model clauses prescribed under section 6 of the Petroleum (Production) Act 1934 as applied by the preceding subsection shall include provision for the safety,
j health and welfare of persons employed on operations undertaken under the authority of any licence granted under that Act as so applied.
> (5) The Minister of Power shall for each financial year prepare and lay before Parliament a report stating—(a) the licences under the said Act of 1934 granted in that year in respect of areas beyond low-water mark and the persons to whom and the areas in respect of which they were granted, and the like information as respects such licences held at the end of that year; (b) the total amount of natural gas and of

other petroleum gotten in that year in pursuance of licences held in respect of such areas; and (c) the method used for arriving at the amounts payable by way of *a* consideration for such licences.

(6) The general duty of the Minister of Power of securing the effective and co-ordinated development of such resources in Great Britain as are mentioned in section 1(1) of the Ministry of Fuel and Power Act 1945 shall extend to any such resources outside Great Britain with respect to which the said rights are exercisable.

(7) Her Majesty may from time to time by Order in Council designate any area *b* as an area within which the rights mentioned in subsection (1) of this section are exercisable, and any area so designated is in this Act referred to as a designated area.

(8) In this section "coal" has the same meaning as in the Coal Industry Nationalisation Act 1946 and "petroleum" has the same meaning as in the Petroleum (Production) Act 1934.'

In terms, s (1) of the 1964 Act was thus explicitly dealing only with rights exercisable *c* by the United Kingdom *outside* territorial waters with respect to the sea bed and subsoil. Counsel for the Crown, however, submitted in effect that, in enacting this section, Parliament was proceeding on the implicit assumption that the rights exercisable by the Crown *inside* territorial waters with respect to the sea bed and subsoil had already been dealt with by the three Acts referred to in this section, namely the 1934 Act, the Coal Industry Nationalisation Act 1946 and the Ministry of Fuel and Power Act 1945. He *d* pointed out that s 1 of the 1964 Act had the effect of extending the three earlier Acts to the sea bed and subsoil *outside* territorial waters. He submitted that it cannot have been Parliament's intention to omit the sea bed and subsoil *inside* territorial waters from the ambit of all this legislation. Section 1(5)(a) of the 1964 Act, he submitted, made it plain that such was not Parliament's intention, because it refers to 'licences under the said Act of 1934 granted in that year in respect of areas beyond low-water mark . . .' I see force in *e* the latter point, but do not find it compelling. The reference to 'that year' in s 1(5)(a) is clearly intended as a reference to future financial years following the 1964 Act, during which licences under the 1934 Act, as applied by s 1(3) of the 1964 Act, would fall to be granted in respect of areas outside territorial waters. It is possible that the legislature, in using the phrase 'in respect of areas beyond low water mark' in s 1(5), merely had such licences in mind. More generally, it is possible that, throughout the 1964 Act, it *f* proceeded on erroneous assumptions as to the true construction of the 1934 Act and the other statutes to which it referred. It is even possible, if perhaps less likely, that it was content deliberately to leave areas beneath territorial waters outside the ambit of all this legislation. Speculation, however, is fruitless in regard to these matters. On any footing, in my judgment the 1964 Act gives no clear guidance as to the true construction of the phrase 'Great Britain' as used in s 1 of the 1934 Act. *g*

A far clearer pointer to the true construction of this phrase is in my judgment to be found in the National Coal Board (Additional Powers) Act 1966 and the Mineral Exploration and Investment Grants Act 1972. The expressed purpose of the 1966 Act was—

'to confer on the National Coal Board certain powers with respect to petroleum *h* within the meaning of the Petroleum (Production) Act 1934 and for connected purposes.'

For present purposes it will suffice to read s 1(1) of the Act:

'In addition to their duties and powers under the Coal Industry Acts 1946 to 1965, but subject to the provisions of the Petroleum (Production) Act 1934 and the Continental Shelf Act 1964, the National Coal Board (hereafter in this Act referred *j* to as "the Board") shall have power—(a) to search and bore for and get petroleum within the meaning of the said Act of 1934 in the sea bed and subsoil of the territorial waters of the United Kingdom adjacent to Great Britain and of any area for the time being designated under section 1(7) of the said Act of 1964 . . .'

The 1972 Act was a statute of which the expressed purpose was—

'to authorise the giving of financial assistance in connection with mineral exploration and to clarify or extend certain exceptions from the abolition of investment grants.'

Section 1(1) provided:

'Subject to the following subsections, there shall be defrayed out of money provided by Parliament any payments made by the Secretary of State by way of contribution towards expenditure incurred on searching for, or on discovering and testing, mineral deposits in Great Britain or in the sea bed and subsoil of the territorial waters of the United Kingdom adjacent to Great Britain or in that of any area for the time being designated under section 1(7) of the Continental Shelf Act 1964.'

Section 1(8) provided that in the section the phrase 'mineral deposits' should include any natural deposits capable of being lifted or extracted from the earth.

The legislature in drafting s 1(1) of the 1966 Act and s 1(1) of the 1972 Act thus quite clearly differentiated between (i) Great Britain itself, (ii) the sea bed and subsoil of the territorial waters of the United Kingdom adjacent to Great Britain, and (iii) the sea bed and subsoil of any area of waters outside territorial waters for the time being designated under s 1(7) of the 1964 Act. Thus, in my judgment, the legislature in both the 1966 Act and 1972 Act used the phrase 'Great Britain' in a geographical sense which manifestly did not include the sea bed and subsoil of territorial waters. The 1966 and 1972 Acts both dealt with the same subject matter as the 1934 Act, though the 1972 Act went a little further by dealing with all mineral deposits, as therein defined. If and so far as the meaning of the phrase 'Great Britain' in the context of the 1934 Act can properly be said to be ambiguous, the use of the same phrase 'Great Britain' in the 1966 Act and the 1972 Act, in a sense which plainly does *not* include the sea bed or subsoil of territorial waters, provides an obvious pointer to the conclusion that the phrase 'Great Britain' in the 1934 Act is similarly limited. Consistency in the use of terminology in legislation dealing with broadly the same subject matter is, I think, to be presumed in the absence of clear indication to the contrary. In my judgment the provisions of the 1945 and 1964 Acts relied on by the Crown afford no such clear indication.

As an alternative argument on this part of the case, counsel for the Crown submitted that the phrase 'Great Britain', in the context of s 1(1) of the 1934 Act, means 'Great Britain' as from time to time defined by the Crown, whether by statute or in exercise of the royal prerogative. The relevant principle is to be found set out in Diplock LJ's judgment in *Post Office v Estuary Radio Ltd* [1967] 3 All ER 663 at 680, [1968] 2 QB 740 at 753–754 as follows:

'It still lies within the prerogative power of the Crown to extend its sovereignty and jurisdiction to areas of land or sea over which it has not previously claimed or exercised sovereignty or jurisdiction. For such extension the authority of Parliament is not required. The Queen's Courts, on being informed by Order in Council or by the appropriate minister or law officer of the Crown's claim to sovereignty or jurisdiction over any place, must give effect to it and are bound by it. (See *The Fagernes* [1927] P 311.) So, when any Act of Parliament refers to the United Kingdom or to the territorial waters adjacent thereto those expressions must prima facie be construed as referring to such area of land or sea as may from time to time be formally declared by the Crown to be subject to its sovereignty and jurisdiction as part of the United Kingdom or the territorial waters of the United Kingdom, and not as confined to the precise geographical area of the United Kingdom or its territorial waters at the precise moment at which the Act received the royal assent.'

By the Convention on the Territorial Sea and the Contiguous Zone (Geneva, 29 April 1958; TS 3 (1965); Cmnd 2511) (which I will call 'the second convention of 1958'), to which the United Kingdom was a party, the parties agreed (inter alia) as follows. Article 1.1 provided:

'The sovereignty of a State extends, beyond its land territory and its internal waters, to a belt of the sea adjacent to its coast, described as the territorial sea.'

Article 2 provided that the sovereignty of a coastal state extends to the air space over the territorial sea as well as to its bed and subsoil. Subsequent provisions of the convention defined the limits of the territorial sea and dealt with other such matters as the right of innocent passage. The convention came into force on 10 September 1964.

By the Territorial Waters Order in Council 1964, made on 25 September 1964, which was promulgated to give effect to this convention, the Crown, in the exercise of its prerogative powers, established the baseline from which 'the breadth of the territorial sea adjacent to the United Kingdom' falls to be measured.

Counsel for the Crown confirmed on instructions that the Crown claims that, whatever the position may have been before 1964, as a result of ratification by virtue of the Crown's prerogative and the entry into force of the second convention of 1958, and as confirmed by the 1964 Order in Council, the United Kingdom has sovereignty over territorial sea and the sea bed and subsoil thereof, within the limits resulting from the 1964 order.

I accept that the United Kingdom does indeed have sovereignty over the territorial sea and the sea bed and subsoil thereof within these limits. However, it does not in my judgment follow that the expression 'Great Britain', in the context of the 1934 Act, should now be construed as including territorial waters and the sea bed and subsoil beneath them. First, the 1964 order did not itself purport to incorporate territorial waters within the expression 'the United Kingdom'. Article 2(1) referred to 'the territorial sea adjacent to the United Kingdom', thus reproducing the clear differentiation between the United Kingdom and its territorial waters, which is to be seen in both earlier and later legislation. Second, I have already referred to the general rule that a statute should not be construed so as to impute to the legislature an intention to expropriate property in favour of the Crown, without giving the legal right to compensation, unless the intention is expressed in clear, unequivocal terms. In my judgment, in construing the 1934 Act, it would not be right to impute the intention that it should be open to the Crown thereafter to extend the operation of its expropriating provisions by applying them to substances situated beneath territorial waters merely by an exercise of the royal prerogative.

For all these reasons, in my judgment the 1934 Act on which the Crown relies would not on any footing have divested the title of the plaintiff or his predecessors to any oil or natural gas lying *within* territorial waters, if (contrary to my view) he or they had obtained any title to oil or natural gas under the 1880 conveyance.

However, in my judgment very different considerations would apply to oil or natural gas lying *outside* territorial waters, for these short reasons. Section 1(1) of the 1964 Act, which I have already read, provides:

'Any rights exercisable by the United Kingdom outside territorial waters with respect to the sea bed and subsoil and their natural resources, except so far as they are exercisable in relation to coal, are hereby vested in Her Majesty.'

Section 1(3), read in conjunction with s 1(8) of the 1964 Act and s 1(2) of the 1934 Act make it plain, if there were otherwise any doubt, that the natural resources thus referred to include oil and natural gas. One effect of s 1(1) of the 1964 Act was to extend the expropriation effected by s 1(1) of the 1934 Act, so that it would apply to 'any rights exercisable by the United Kingdom outside territorial waters' with respect to the sea bed and subsoil and their oil and natural gas (if any). The dispute in the present context has centred round the meaning of the phrase 'any rights exercisable by the United Kingdom'. Counsel for the plaintiff has contended, simply and forcefully, that in the present case any relevant rights in respect of oil and natural gas situate in the sea bed outside territorial waters were not 'exercisable by the United Kingdom', on the grounds that such rights had been granted to and were excercisable by the plaintiff or his predecessors. Counsel for the Crown submitted in effect that any relevant rights of the plaintiff or his predecessors in respect of such oil and natural gas did fall within the ambit of the subsection, on the grounds that they were included among the rights exercisable by the state of the United Kingdom as a matter of international law.

No doubt some international lawyers might seek to contend that, as a matter of international law, at the date of the 1880 conveyance and the 1935 deed of exchange the *a*   Crown possessed no rights which were both (a) exercisable in respect of natural resources in the sea bed outside territorial waters, and (b) capable of being effectively granted to the plaintiff's predecessors in title. Nevertheless, in my judgment it would not profit the plaintiff, who derives his title (if any) to the relevant natural resources from the Crown itself, to put forward either of these contentions and I do not think that counsel on his behalf sought to do so. Essentially what he has sought to argue is that the relevant rights (if any) in respect of the sea bed outside territorial waters were *no longer* 'exercisable by

b   the United Kingdom' as at the date of the 1964 Act, because such rights had been granted to the plaintiff's predecessors by the 1880 conveyance and the 1935 deed of exchange.

     The phrase 'rights exercisable by the United Kingdom', which appears in s 1(1) of the 1964 Act, is at first sight an odd one. I have not been referred to any other statute which refers to rights being exercisable or exercised by 'the United Kingdom' or which employs similar phraseology. Nevertheless, the meaning of the phrase becomes reasonably clear

c   when reference is made to the first convention of 1958. Article 2 of this convention had provided (inter alia) that the coastal state exercises over the continental shelf sovereign rights for the purpose of exploring it and exploiting its natural resources and that such rights are exclusive in the sense that, if the coastal state does not explore the continental shelf or exploit its natural resources, no one may undertake these activities or make a claim to the continental shelf without the express consent of the coastal state. The

d   purpose of the legislature in enacting s 1(1) of the 1964 Act was, in my judgment, clearly to entitle the Crown to claim for itself, as a matter of municipal law, the exclusive rights which art 2 would confer on it under international law as soon as the first convention of 1958 came into force and, correspondingly, to divest in favour of itself any such rights so far as they might be vested in other persons. In my judgment, in the context of s 1(1) of the 1964 Act, the phrase 'any rights exercisable by the United Kingdom' can bear only

e   one meaning, that is to say, any rights exercisable by the state of the United Kingdom as against other states under international law, in particular having regard to the first convention of 1958.

     In the present case, notwithstanding the 1880 conveyance, the relevant rights in the relevant parts of the sea bed and subsoil outside territorial waters were, in my judgment, as at the date of the 1964 Act, manifestly exercisable by the state of the United Kingdom under international law, having regard to the provisions of art 2 of the first convention

f   of 1958. It follows in my judgment that the 1964 Act would have operated to expropriate all or any rights in any oil and natural gas in relevant parts of the sea bed and subsoil outside territorial waters which (contrary to my view) might have previously been vested in the plaintiff's predecessors in title, and to vest them in the Sovereign, in her political capacity in right of the Crown. The fact that any such expropriation would have been

g   effected without compensation to the former owners of the rights does not prevent such a conclusion, since the wording of the 1964 Act is in my judgment clear and inescapable. The 1934 Act afforded an equally clear example of the legislature effecting without compensation the expropriation of oil and natural gas in Great Britain, in so far as these substances are situated in or below dry land. The crucial difference between that Act and the 1964 Act is that the earlier Act did not in my opinion clearly and unequivocally deal

h   with substances situated in or beneath the bed and subsoil of the sea.

     These obiter conclusions as to the interpretation of these two Acts may be thought to involve certain anomalies in that, if correct, they mean that the Crown can claim a statutory title to oil and natural gas situated beneath the continental shelf, but not to those substances when situated beneath territorial waters. But I have been unable to find an escape from them.

j

Summary of conclusions

     Counsel on both sides have referred in argument to the theoretical possibility that different conclusions could apply in respect of oil and of natural gas. I have throughout this judgment borne in mind this possibility. Neither side, however, has invited me to draw any distinction between the two substances or has directed my attention to any points which in my judgment make it necessary to draw any such distinction.

     To summarise my conclusions, they are as follows.

(1) The 1880 conveyance and the 1935 deed of exchange did not operate to pass any rights to oil or natural gas to the plaintiff's predecessors in title, principally because (a) the phrase 'mines and minerals' is an indefinite term which may bear many different meanings in different contexts and there is no rule of construction which requires that it should be construed as including oil or natural gas in the absence of a sufficient indication to the contrary, (b) there is no clear evidence that, in the vernacular of the mining world, landowners or commercial men as at 1880 or 1935, the phrase included oil or natural gas, (c) there are a number of indications to be derived from the 1880 conveyance itself which suggest that the phrase was not intended to include anything except solid substances dug out of the earth by means of a mine or mines opened on the adjacent land of the grantee, (d) the phrase is at least an ambiguous one and, since these were grants by the Crown, it was incumbent on the grantees to require the inclusion of explicit words including oil and natural gas, if it was their intention that these substances should be included in the grant.

(2) The phrase 'down to the bottom of the coal measures' in the relevant grants refers to the bottom of the lowest identifiable seam of coal that is or might be worth mining.

(3) If it had become necessary to decide the points, I would have held (a) that the rights in any oil and natural gas situated in the Lonsdale off-shore areas *outside* territorial waters which may have been granted to the plaintiff's predecessors became revested in the Crown by virtue of the Continental Shelf Act 1964, but (b) the rights in any oil and natural gas situated in the Lonsdale off-shore areas *inside* territorial waters which may have been granted to the plaintiff's predecessors did not become revested in the Crown by virtue of the Petroleum (Production) Act 1934 or any other legislation.

However, in view of my decision on the first issue, these second and third issues do not arise.

As things are, I must dismiss this action.

Action dismissed.

Solicitors: *Gregory Rowcliffe & Co*, agents for *Dickinson Dees*, Newcastle upon Tyne (for the plaintiff); *Treasury Solicitor*.

Jacqueline Metcalfe Barrister.

Pennine Raceway Ltd v Kirklees Metropolitan Council

COURT OF APPEAL, CIVIL DIVISION
STEPHENSON, EVELEIGH AND KERR LJJ
12, 13, 14, 28 MAY 1982

Town and country planning – Permission for development – Revocation – Compensation – Expenditure in carrying out work which is rendered abortive by order – Expenditure incurred by person interested in the land – Person interested in the land – Whether 'person interested in the land' limited to person having a legal interest in the land – Whether a licensee capable of being a 'person interested in the land' – Town and Country Planning Act 1971, s 164(1).

A landowner and the claimant company agreed that the landowner would grant the company the sole right to use his land for motor racing events and the company would pay him a percentage of the profits from the events during the first year and thereafter a fee per meeting which would be reviewed every five years. Pursuant to the agreement the company carried out a substantial amount of work on the land to make it suitable for motor racing. At the time the use of the land for motor racing purposes was permitted by the respondent local planning authority but it subsequently revoked that permission by an order made under s 45 of the Town and Country Planning Act 1971. The company applied to the planning authority for compensation under s 164(1)[a] of the 1971 Act on

---

a Section 164(1), so far as material, is set out at p 631 c, post

a the ground that it was 'a person interested in the land [who had] incurred expenditure in carrying out work which [was] rendered abortive by the revocation' of the planning permission. The planning authority contended that the phrase 'a person interested in the land' in s 164(1) referred to a person who had an 'interest in the land' in the strict conveyancing sense and that since the company was merely a licensee and had no true proprietary interest in the land it could not claim compensation under s 164(1).

b **Held** – The phrase 'a person interested in the land' in s 164(1) of the 1971 Act was wide enough to include a person who was granted a right to use land for a permitted purpose and who, after incurring expenses in carrying out work on the land so that it could be used for that purpose, suffered loss or damage as a result of a subsequent revocation of permission by a planning authority. The company was such a person and accordingly it could claim compensation from the respondent planning authority under s 164(1) (see p *c* 632 h to p 633 b g h, p 634 c f j, p 636 b to j, p 637 f, p 638 f to h and p 639 b, post).
   Plimmer v Mayor of Wellington (1884) 9 App Cas 699 and *Frank Warr & Co Ltd v London County Council* [1904] 1 KB 713 considered.

Notes
For compensation for refusal of planning permission, see 8 Halsbury's Laws (4th edn) *d* paras 101, 285.
   For the Town and Country Planning Act 1971, ss 45, 164, see 41 Halsbury's Statutes (3rd edn) 1638, 1772.

Cases referred to in judgments
Barrell v Fordree [1932] AC 676, HL, 31(2) Digest (Reissue) 982, 7893.
e *Bearmans Ltd v Metropolitan Police District Receiver* [1961] 1 All ER 384, [1961] 1 WLR 634, CA, 22 Digest (Reissue) 276, 2506.
DHN Food Distributors Ltd v London Borough of Tower Hamlets [1976] 3 All ER 462, [1976] 1 WLR 852, CA, Digest (Cont Vol E) 84, 165a.
Edinburgh Street Tramways Co v Torbain (1877) 3 App Cas 58, HL, 44 Digest (Repl) 231, 507.
f *Gartside v IRC* [1968] 1 All ER 121, [1968] AC 553, [1968] 2 WLR 277, HL, 26 Digest (Reissue) 17, 66.
Greaves v Tofield (1880) 14 Ch D 563, CA, 35 Digest (Repl) 314, 303.
Hill v Tupper (1863) 2 H & C 121, [1861–73] All ER Rep 696, 159 ER 51, 31(1) Digest (Reissue) 201, 1685.
Inwards v Baker [1965] 1 All ER 446, [1965] 2 QB 29, [1965] 2 WLR 212, CA, 20 Digest *g* (Reissue) 800, 5927.
Ives (E R) Investments Ltd v High [1967] 1 All ER 504, [1967] 2 QB 379, [1967] 2 WLR 789, CA, 21 Digest (Reissue) 5, 47.
King v David Allen & Sons, Billposting, Ltd [1916] 2 AC 54, [1916–17] All ER Rep 268, HL, 31(1) Digest (Reissue) 223, 1821.
Plimmer v Mayor of Wellington (1884) 9 App Cas 699, PC, 11 Digest (Reissue) 129, *98.
h *Walton Harvey Ltd v Walker & Homfrays Ltd* [1931] 1 Ch 274, [1930] All ER Rep 465, CA; affg [1931] 1 Ch 145, 12 Digest (Reissue) 463, 3337.
Ward v Kirkland [1966] 1 All ER 609, [1966] 1 WLR 601, 19 Digest (Reissue) 48, 326.
Warr (Frank) & Co v London County Council [1904] 1 KB 713, CA, 31(1) Digest (Reissue) 213, 1754.
Wilson v Tavener [1901] 1 Ch 578, 31(1) Digest (Reissue) 222, 1811.
j *Wood v Leadbitter* (1845) 13 M & W 838, [1843–60] All ER Rep 190, 153 ER 351, 31(1) Digest (Reissue) 224, 1830.

Cases also cited
Colonial Sugar Refining Co Ltd v Melbourne Harbour Trust Comrs [1927] AC 343, PC.
Hounslow London Borough v Twickenham Garden Developments Ltd [1970] 3 All ER 326, [1971] Ch 233.
Jervis v Lawrence (1882) 22 Ch D 202.

Lee v Risden (1816) 7 Taunt 188, 129 ER 76.

Thomas v Jennings (1896) 66 LJQB 5.

Wallis v Harrison (1838) 4 M & W 538, [1835–42] All ER Rep 284.

Webb v Paternoster (1619) Poph 151, 79 ER 1250.

Willingdale v Islington Green Investment Co [1972] 3 All ER 849, [1972] 1 WLR 1533.

Winter Garden Theatre (London) Ltd v Millennium Productions Ltd [1947] 2 All ER 331, [1948] AC 173, HL.

Appeal

Pennine Raceway Ltd (the company) appealed, by way of case stated, against a decision of the Lands Tribunal, given on 2 February 1981 on a preliminary question of law, to the effect that the company was not entitled to make a claim against the respondent, Kirklees Metropolitan Council, for compensation under s 164(1) of the Town and Country Planning Act 1971. The facts are set out in the judgment of Eveleigh LJ.

John Stuart Colyer QC and *Michael Brooke* for the company.
Alan Fletcher for the council.

Cur adv vult

28 May. The following judgments were read.

EVELEIGH LJ (delivering the first judgment at the invitation of Stephenson LJ). On 2 October 1974 a Mr Witham, the owner of Crosland Moor Airfield, Huddersfield, West Yorkshire, and the appellant company executed a deed which read as follows:

'WHEREAS it is agreed as follows:—

1. The Owner hereby grants to the Company sole rights to promote motor and motor cycle events on the Airfield at Crosland Moor.

2. The Company shall carry out all works fixtures and fittings necessary for the safe-guard of the public at the Airfield at the Company's own expense and shall be fully responsible for all payments as to future maintenance of such fixtures and fittings or the removal reinstatement or addition to the same.

3. The Company covenants with the Owner to insure with an Insurance Company to be approved by the Owner against any claim against the Owner in any way relating to public liability or otherwise in connection with the events.

4. The consideration to be paid to the Owner shall be the sum of Five hundred pounds per meeting except for the first full year which shall be treated as a trial year and during this year the Owner shall be entitled to receive Thirty per cent of the net profits of each event from the Company.

5. Upon ceasing to hold Meetings as detailed above, the Company hereby covenants to return the Airfield to its previous condition and remove all fixtures and fittings barriers or otherwise at the Company's expense. This work shall be carried out to the satisfaction of the Owner and if dispute shall arise shall be referred to a single arbitrator to be appointed by the Surveyor for the Owner whose decision shall be final and binding to all parties.

6. The said sum of Five hundred pounds per meeting shall be reviewed every five years but shall never be less than the said sum of Five hundred pounds.'

The company thereafter erected about 400 yards of substantial safety barriers which were set in the ground. It cleared an area of land for pits and for a competitors' car park and laid a tarmacadam surface for these places. It moved 3,000 cubic metres of soil and created a bank for spectators. It attached nylon cable to existing posts in order to provide fencing.

At that time art 3 of the Town and Country Planning General Development Order 1973, SI 1973/31, and class IV, para 2 of Sch 1 thereto permitted use for—

'any purpose or purposes except as a caravan site on not more than 28 days in total in any calendar year (of which not more than 14 days in total may be devoted to use for the purpose of motor car or motor-cycle racing or for the purpose of the holding

of markets), and the erection or placing of moveable structures on the land for the
a   purposes of that use: Provided that for the purpose of the limitation imposed on the
     number of days on which land may be used for motor car or motor-cycle racing,
     account shall be taken only of those days on which races are held or practising takes
     place.'

     Although two trial races had taken place before the execution of the deed, no further
b   events had been held before 8 November 1974 when the council made a direction under
     art 4 of the 1973 order that the use of the airfield for motor car or motor cycle racing
     should no longer be permitted.
     Section 165 of the Town and Country Planning Act 1971 provides that in such
     circumstances the provisions of s 164 of the Act shall apply. Section 164, so far as is
     material, reads:

c   '(1) Where planning permission is revoked or modified by an order under section
         45 of this Act, then if, on a claim made to the local planning authority within the
         time and in the manner prescribed by regulations under this Act, it is shown that a
         person interested in the land—(a) has incurred expenditure in carrying out work
         which is rendered abortive by the revocation or modification . . . the local planning
         authority shall pay to that person compensation in respect of that expenditure, loss
d   or damage . . .'

     The respondent council, the local planning authority, denied liability to pay
     compensation on the grounds that the company was not 'a person interested in the land'.
     The company applied to the Lands Tribunal for determination of a preliminary point of
     law, namely whether it was entitled to make a claim for compensation. The Lands
e   Tribunal held that it was not 'a person interested in the land' and the sole question raised
     in the stated case is whether that decision was correct.
     For the council it is argued as follows. The phrase 'a person interested in the land' is
     shorthand for 'a person having an interest in the land'. The company had only a licence.
     A licence is not an interest in land: Wood v Leadbitter (1845) M & W 838, [1843–60] All
     ER Rep 190 and Hill v Tupper (1863) 2 H & C 121, [1861–73] All ER Rep 696 were relied
f   on.
     We were referred to s 18 of the Lands Clauses Consolidation Act 1845 and s 39(1) of
     the Land Compensation Act 1961 and ss 5 and 10 of the Compulsory Purchase Act 1965
     in support of the submission that for a person to be interested in land it is necessary to
     show that that person has a proprietary interest in the land. Counsel submitted that such
     an interest must be one of the interests in land referred to in the Law of Property Act
g   1925, or at least it must have the character of a proprietary interest. The company's
     interest was only a contractual one. In other words, counsel submits that the phrase has a
     technical meaning.
     In Maxwell on the Interpretation of Statutes (12th edn, 1969) p 28 we read:

         'The first and most elementary rule of construction is that it is to be assumed that
h   the words and phrases of technical legislation are used in their technical meaning if
         they have acquired one, and otherwise in their ordinary meaning . . .'

     It has, however, not been possible to refer us to a line of authority to show that the
     phrase 'a person interested in the land' has acquired a technical meaning. The phrase 'a
     person interested in' is employed quite frequently in legislation in a wide variety of
     contexts. For example, the Public Health Act 1875, Sch II, r 64, the Metalliferous Mines
j   Regulations Act 1872, s 313, the Administration and Probate Act 1958 (Vict), s 15, the
     Marine Insurance Act 1906, s 5 and the Law of Property Act 1925, s 84.
     As Devlin LJ said in Bearmans Ltd v Metropolitan Police District Receiver [1961] 1 All ER
     384 at 391, [1961] 1 WLR 634 at 655:

         'The word "interested" is not a word which has any well-defined meaning, and
         anybody who was asked what it meant would at once want to know the context in
         which it was used before he could venture an opinion . . . Just as in ordinary speech

one would require to know the context, so in construing the word in an Act of
Parliament it is essential . . . to look at the scope and purpose of the Act . . .'

In my opinion before turning to other statutes and other cases we should look at the
words of the section itself. We should construe them, if their meaning is not plain, in
accordance with the policy and objects of the statute with which we are concerned and
only then if we are uncertain whether they apply to the facts of our particular case should
we seek help elsewhere. In *Barrell v Fordree* [1932] AC 676 at 682 Lord Warrington said:

'. . . the safer and more correct course of dealing with a question of construction
is to take the words themselves and arrive if possible at their meaning without, in
the first instance, reference to cases.'

He might have added 'without reference to other statutes'.

I appreciate that light may be thrown on the meaning of a phrase in a statute by
reference to a specific phrase in an earlier statute dealing with the same subject matter,
and such an aid to construction is permissible where there is an ambiguity. Even so we
are unlikely to find much help unless the statute is in pari materia.

In *Greaves v Tofield* (1880) 14 Ch D 563 at 571 James LJ said:

'. . . if an Act of Parliament uses the same language which was used in a former
Act of Parliament referring to the same subject, and passed with the same purpose,
and for the same object, the safe and well-known rule of construction is to assume
that the Legislature when using well-known words upon which there have been
well-known decisions use those words in the sense which the decisions have attached
to them.'

The circumstances there referred to do not exist in our case. We are dealing with a phrase
which has not acquired a technical meaning and moreover is one of widely different
capabilities, so that previous legislation or judicial decisions are of little help when the
statutes, although dealing with compensation, are not dealing with compensation for
loss arising in parallel circumstances.

We are concerned with that part of the statute whose subject matter is planning control
in relation to the use of land or activities (ie operations) in, on, over or under it: see s 22
of the 1971 Act. Section 164 is one of several sections contained in Part VIII of the 1971
Act which provide for compensation for planning restrictions where broadly speaking
existing permission is revoked. Part VII of the Act provides for compensation in respect
of planning decisions whereby permission for the carrying out of new development is
refused, or granted subject to conditions. It is only in Part VI that we see a link with the
Lands Clauses Consolidation Act 1845, for Part VI deals with compulsory acquisition of
land itself or buildings (not with restrictions on use), although this of course is acquisition
in pursuance of planning control.

Therefore I approach s 164 on the basis that it is a section designed to compensate those
who have incurred expenditure in reliance on a permitted use only to find that they now
face loss because the planning authority has revoked permission. The subject matter of
the compensation is not the compulsory acquisition of land, but the restriction on use.
Clearly some limit has to be placed on the right to claim compensation because many a
person may be affected by a change in the permitted use of land while not themselves
being directly concerned to make any use of it. In the present case, for example, an
omnibus company might have planned to lay on transport facilities to and from the
airfield. In my opinion this section envisages as deserving of compensation a person who
had a right in relation to the land, which right is adversely affected by the restriction on
use.

I now consider the company's position under the deed of 2 October 1974. Under it the
owner for a pecuniary consideration gives to the company the right to use the land for a
specific purpose for at least a year. This in my opinion is the effect of cl 4 which speaks of
the 'first full year'. Clause 6, which provides for revision of the fee after five years, shows
that this arrangement was regarded as one of indefinite but substantial duration. I see in

a these clauses similarities to a yearly tenancy. It is not necessary for me to decide all of the incidents of the agreement, but in my opinion, while of course it is determinable, it must be subject to reasonable notice, and by analogy with a yearly tenancy I would think that six months is probably the correct length of notice.

I therefore think that the appellant company has a substantial right in relation to the land.

b In support of his argument that the phrase 'a person interested' is shorthand for 'a person having an interest in land' counsel for the council referred to s 52 of the 1971 Act. Subsection (1) reads as follows:

c 'A local planning authority may enter into an agreement with any person interested in land in their area for the purpose of restricting or regulating the development or use of the land, either permanently or during such period as may be prescribed by the agreement; and any such agreement may contain such identical and consequential provisions (including provisions of a financial character) as appear to the local planning authority to be necessary or expedient for the purposes of the agreement.'

Subsection (2) reads:

d 'An agreement made under this section with any person interested in land may be enforced by the local planning authority against persons deriving title under that person in respect of that land, as if the local planning authority were possessed of adjacent land and as if the agreement had been expressed to be made for the benefit of such land.'

e Counsel says that the reference in s 52(2) to 'persons deriving title under that person' indicates that the person interested is a person with an interest in land so that it is possible for someone to derive title under him. I cannot read sub-s (2) as saying that a person can only be interested in land under sub-s (1) if it is possible for someone to derive title under him. I read it as saying that if in a particular case the person interested had such an interest which was transferable and had transferred it, then the agreement may be enforced against the transferee. I cannot read sub-s (2) as limiting the meaning of sub-s *f* (1) so as to make sub-s (1) apply only to persons who have an interest in land in a strict conveyancing sense. We are dealing with a statute which controls use and operations on land and provides compensation. It is not a conveyancing statute.

The 1971 Act refers to an 'interest in land' in other sections and to my mind the change to the less technical language of 'interested in the land' in s 164 is deliberate. I cannot see that it was dictated by the desire to achieve economy of language, for the saving between 'a person interested in the land' and 'a person with an interest in the land' is minimal.

g I therefore feel free to interpret the phrase without regard to technical terms. In the context of the 1971 Act, and s 164 in particular, a person who, like the company, has an enforceable right as against the owner to use the land in the way which has now been prohibited is 'a person interested in the land' within s 164.

h Although I have reached my conclusion on the basis that I do not have to regard s 164 as requiring the claimant to establish that he is a person with an interest in the land, I would none the less have come to the conclusion that the company was entitled to compensation even if the words in s 164 had been 'a person with an interest in the land'. I find little difference in principle between the present case and that of *Plimmer v Mayor of Wellington* (1884) 9 App Cas 699. In that case an occupier of land had incurred expense in doing work at the request of the government, the owners of the land. Subsequently *j* the land became vested by statute in the respondents. The question arose whether the occupiers would have been entitled to compensation under a statute, the New Zealand Public Works Act 1882, s 4, which enacted:

'Every person who immediately before the passing of the said Act had any estate or interest in, to or out of the lands by the said Act vested in the corporation . . . shall be entitled to receive full compensation from the corporation . . .'

Sir Arthur Hobhouse said (at 712–713):

'Their Lordships will not be the first to hold, and no authority has been cited to them to shew that after such a landowner has requested such a tenant to incur *a* expense on his land for his benefit, he can without more and at his own will take away the property so improved . . . the question still remains as to the extent of the interest which Plimmer acquired by his expenditure in 1856. Referring again to the passage quoted from Lord Kingsdown's judgment, there is good authority for saying what appears to their Lordships to be quite sound in principle, that the equity arising from expenditure on land need not fail merely on the ground that the *b* interest to be secured has not been expressly indicated.'

In that case Plimmer's right did not rest on a specific agreement, because there was none. It rested on the equity resulting from the fact that he had expended money at the owner's request. In our case the owner has specifically contracted to grant the right to use the land and in addition the appellant company has also incurred expense under the *c* agreement. In each case one sees an enforceable right to use the land.

In *Plimmer's* case (at 714) we read:

'In this case their Lordships feel no great difficulty. In their view, the licence given by the Government to John Plimmer, which was indefinite in point of duration but was revocable at will, became irrevocable by the transactions of 1856, because those transactions were sufficient to create in his mind a reasonable *d* expectation that his occupation would not be disturbed; and because they and the subsequent dealings of the parties cannot be reasonably explained on any other supposition. Nothing was done to limit the use of the jetty in point of duration. The consequence is that Plimmer acquired an indefinite, that is practically a perpetual, right to the jetty for the purposes of the original licence, and if the ground was afterwards wanted for public purposes, it could only be taken from him *e* by the legislature.'

The licence in the present case is irrevocable. It is true that it is not perpetual but the emphasis in *Plimmer's* case is on irrevocability. In that case the licence was to occupy, but it was for a particular use, namely for the purpose of a jetty or wharf. In the present case there is a licence to occupy and use for the purposes of motor racing. It seems to me that *f* the company's right is just as much an interest in land as was Plimmer's right. I do not have to say that the company's interest is an interest in land in a strict conveyancing sense. In *Plimmer's* case (at 714) Sir Arthur Hobhouse said:

'There are perhaps purposes for which such a license would not be held to be an interest in land. But their Lordships are construing a statute which takes away private property for compensation, and in such statutes the expression "estate or *g* interest in, to or out of land" should receive a wide meaning.'

Of course it is a wide meaning which has its limits. As Lord Reid said in *Gartside v IRC* [1968] 1 All ER 121 at 125, [1968] AC 553 at 602:

'That does not mean . . . that everything which the man in the street might call an interest is covered by the word "interest" in these sections. A man might say that *h* a son and heir has an interest in his father's property to which he might reasonably expect to succeed; but one can discard that meaning: the son not only has no right in or over his father's property but he has no right to prevent his father from dissipating it. The Crown admit that, to be an interest under these provisions, it must give to the holder of it some right.'

As I have said, the possession by the company of an enforceable right to use the land is *j* sufficient in my opinion to make them 'a person interested in the land' for the purposes of s 164 of the Town and Country Planning Act 1971.

I think I should add a few words out of respect for the careful argument of counsel for the council. I have said that I do not think it appropriate in the present case to turn to other decided cases as an aid to construction. However, as counsel has relied on a number of other cases, I think it right that I should mention four of them. The first is *Wilson v*

Tavener [1901] 1 Ch 578. There was an agreement permitting the plaintiff to erect a
a hoarding for a billposting station on the defendant's land at the rent of £10 per year
payable quarterly. The defendant gave the plaintiff three months' notice to quit. The
sole question was whether the plaintiff was entitled to six months' notice on the basis
that the agreement created a tenancy from year to year and not a licence. It was held that
there was no tenancy from year to year and that three months' notice was a reasonable
notice to terminate the licence. It is true that Joyce J said (at 518) that the document did
b not confer on the plaintiff any right to the exclusive possession of any property, but this
cannot be taken to indicate that exclusive possession is necessary for the existence of an
interest in land. He was considering whether or not there was a lease. I do not regard
that case as an authority on the meaning of 'interest in land'.

In *Frank Warr & Co Ltd v London County Council* [1904] 1 KB 713 it had been agreed
that the plaintiff should have the exclusive right for term of years to supply refreshments
in a theatre, and for that purpose should have the necessary use of the refreshment rooms
c and other accommodation. It was held that the contract did not confer on the plaintiff an
interest in land which could form the subject of compensation under the Lands Clauses
Consolidation Act 1845, s 68. Collins MR took the view that the agreement was drafted
so as to exclude the idea that any interest in land was to be given. He said (at 718–719):

> 'It seems to me that the agreement in this case is carefully framed so as to exclude
d the notion that there was to be anything like a demise of any part of the premises.'

Romer LJ said (at 721):

> 'There was no such right created, either at law or in equity, as constitutes any
known estate or interest in land.'

Mathew LJ, referring to s 68 of the Lands Clauses Consolidation Act 1845, said (at
e 724):

> 'That section speaks of "compensation in respect of any lands, or of any interest
therein, which shall have been taken for, or injuriously affected by the execution of
the works".'

The word 'taken' involves that the person to be compensated has had and has been
f deprived of the land or some interest therein; and it seems to me impossible to doubt
that the section contemplates as the subject matter of compensation land or some estate
or interest in it, and not a mere licence or contractual privilege such as was conferred by
the agreement in the present case. He went on to say that the use of the accommodation
was only ancillary to the general purpose of the agreement. In my opinion the decision
in that case was arrived at on the basis that 'an estate or interest in land' such as was
already known to the law had to be shown. Furthermore, it seems to me that the decision
g was influenced by the fact that the right to claim compensation arose out of the
compulsory taking of the land. They were not considering a case of compensation in the
context of legislation prohibiting a particular use. I do not think that a decision under a
differently worded Act of 1845 compels me to take the same approach to the phrase
'interested in land' in s 164 of the 1971 Act.

h In *Edinburgh Street Tramways v Torbain* (1877) 3 App Cas 58 at 68 Lord Blackburn said:

> 'I quite agree that in construing an Act of Parliament we are to see what is the
intention which the Legislature has expressed by the words, but then the words
again are to be understood by looking at the subject-matter they are speaking of and
the object of the Legislature, and the words used with reference to that may convey
an intention quite different from what the self-same set of words used in reference
j to another set of circumstances and another object would or might have produced.'

I would accept that the phrase 'a person interested' involves having an interest of some
kind but it does not follow that it is limited to the same class of interests as is required by
other legislation. There has been a considerable development in the law in relation to
equitable interests and I do not think that it is right to regard the category as closed.

We were referred to *King v David Allen & Sons, Billposting, Ltd* [1916] 2 AC 54, [1916–
17] All ER Rep 268. In that case the defendant had given the plaintiff permission to affix

posters to the flank walls of a picture house proposed to be erected on his property by a
company about to be formed. The permission was 'for a period of four years as from   *a*
November 1st 1913 or the first day the picture house should be open for business . . .' It
was held that the agreement did not create an interest in land but merely a personal
obligation. The issue in the case was whether the obligation under the agreement was
such that it could be enforced against a purchaser of the land with notice of it.
Consequently the words 'interest in land' were used in a restricted sense.

Finally *Walton Harvey Ltd v Walker & Homfrays Ltd* [1931] 1 Ch 274, [1930] All ER   *b*
Rep 465 was another case concerned with a claim for compensation under the Lands
Clauses Acts following the compulsory acquisition of land. And my comments on *Frank
Warr & Co Ltd v London County Council* apply here.

For these reasons I would allow this appeal.

KERR LJ. My mind has wavered during the argument, but I have ultimately reached   *c*
the clear conclusion, in agreement with Stephenson and Eveleigh LJJ that this appeal
should be allowed.

It seemed to me that one starts with the following considerations in construing the
words 'a person interested in the land' in s 164(1) of the Town and Country Planning Act
1971. The section provides for compensation for the revocation or modification of
planning permission in circumstances in which any person interested in the land has   *d*
incurred expenditure in carrying out works which are thereby rendered abortive, or has
otherwise sustained loss or damage which is directly attributable to the revocation or
modification. The words 'interested in' are wide and are generally capable of a wide
application in whatever context they may appear. But, whatever may be their limits, as
a matter of ordinary language sub-s (1) would appear to be directly applicable to persons
in the position of the appellant company in this case. Thus, it is conceded that if the   *e*
abortive expenditure had been incurred by the landowner, Mr Witham, he would have
an undeniable right to compensation under this provision, because, as the owner of the
land, he was clearly a person interested in the land. So be it. However, for the purposes
of sub-s (1) his interest would not be as owner of the land, but as the person who would
have done work on the land and incurred expenditure in so doing, both of which would
have been rendered abortive by the revocation of the permission to use the land for the   *f*
purpose for which the work was done and the expenditure incurred. It is *that* interest for
which the subsection provides compensation. In these circumstances, should it make any
difference that the work has been done, and the expenditure incurred, not by Mr
Witham, but by the company in consideration of the contract made with him? In the
context of a statute which recognises the just need for compensation when planning
permission has been revoked or modified, I should be reluctant so to conclude unless   *g*
compelled by authority or by other provisions of the 1971 Act which compel a restricted
construction of sub-s (1). For the purposes of this subsection, and as a matter of ordinary
language, it seems to me that the company would clearly be properly describable as
persons interested in the land in the same way as Mr Witham, if he had done the work
and incurred the expenditure.

Is there then anything which compels a narrower construction of the words 'a person   *h*
interested in the land' in sub-s (1) so as to exclude the company?

It is conceded on behalf of the council that there is no authority where the meaning of
these words has been considered as such, either in relation to this statute or any other
statute. What is relied on by counsel for the council in his lucid argument is the repeated
reference by the draftsman in other provisions of the 1971 Act to an 'interest in land',
coupled with the hallowed meaning of those words in the law of real property and the   *j*
language of conveyancing. However, on the authorities it seems clear that (i) even the
expression 'interest in land' is not necessarily to be interpreted in its narrow technical
sense in the context of statutes providing for compensation and (ii) an interest in land
may in practice result from the application of equity to situations analogous to that in
the present case. Illustrations of the former are *Plimmer v Mayor of Wellington* (1884) 9
App Cas 699 and *DHN Food Distributors Ltd v London Borough of Tower Hamlets* [1976] 3
All ER 462, [1976] 1 WLR 852. Illustrations of the latter are *Inwards v Baker* [1965] 1 All

ER 446, [1965] 2 QB 29 and *Ward v Kirkland* [1966] 1 All ER 609 at 621–626, [1966] 1
a WLR, 601 at 626–632, where Ungoed-Thomas J reviewed the authorities on this aspect,
and his decision was approved by this court in *E R Ives Investment Ltd v High* [1967] 1 All
ER 504, [1967] 2 QB 379. On the other hand, in statutes such as the Lands Clauses
Consolidation Act 1845 and its related modern successor, the Compulsory Purchase Act
1965, where the expression 'interest in land' generally appears in the context of references
to an estate in land, this expression may require to be interpreted in its narrow technical
b sense, as illustrated by *Frank Warr & Co Ltd v London County Council* [1904] 1 KB 713 on
which counsel for the council strongly relied.

The questions which then ultimately arise, on this analysis, are whether the words 'a
person interested in the land' in s 164(1) of the 1971 Act require to be construed as being
synonymous with 'a person having an interest in land', and, if so, whether the references
in this Act to 'an interest in land', as for instance in s 164 itself in sub-ss (2) and (3), are to
c be construed in the narrow technical sense which is illustrated by *Frank Warr & Co Ltd v
London County Council*. As to this, I do not think that it is necessary for present purposes to
form any view on the latter question, since I am not persuaded that the former question
should be answered in the affirmative. It seems to me that, in construing the words 'a
person interested in the land' in a provision dealing with compensation, one is entitled to
say that *if* the draftsman had intended that s 164(1) should only apply to persons who
d have an interest in land, *and if* the draftsman had also intended that the latter expression
should bear its narrow technical meaning wherever it appears in the 1971 Act, then he
would have been most unlikely to use the more general words 'a person interested in the
land' in s 164(1). For 'draftsman' it would no doubt be more correct, but less realistic, to
substitute 'Parliament'.

I am also not persuaded that a contrary conclusion in relation to s 164(1) must be
e drawn from the reference to a person's 'enjoyment of the land' in s 170(2). Counsel for
the council strongly relied on this as showing that protection may be given to persons
who may be 'interested in land' without having 'an interest in land' proprio sensu.
However, the appellant company in this case is only concerned with the question whether
it can bring itself within s 164(1). It is not concerned with the question whether it could
also bring itself within any other provisions of the 1971 Act which refer specifically to
f interests in land. In my judgment, it is able to say that it falls within s 164(1) because
there is no sufficiently compelling reason to exclude it from the section as a matter of
necessary construction.

I therefore agree that this appeal should be allowed.

STEPHENSON LJ. Who is a person interested in the land, who has incurred
g expenditure in carrying out work rendered abortive by the revocation or modification of
planning permission, or who has sustained loss or damage directly attributable to the
revocation or modification? Is the appellant company such a person?

It is common ground that the company has incurred such expenditure and sustained
such damage. But is it a person interested in the land to which the revoked or modified
planning permission related? A wide variety of persons might be said in common
h parlance to be interested in that land; a prospective purchaser, for instance, interested in
buying it, a neighbour interested in seeing what use it is to put to, a geologist or an
agricultural expert interested in the soil of it. Though some such would be ruled out by
not having incurred expenditure or sustained loss or damage, all such could be said to be
interested in the land in the ordinary meaning of those words. In their context what
more precise meaning must they have? What interest in the land must a person have to
j be entitled to compensation from the local planning authority in respect of that
expenditure, loss or damage under s 164(1) of the Town and Country Planning Act 1971?

It is natural to test the meaning of 'interested' by asking 'what interest?' and to find
references in other provisions of the same part of the Act to an interest in land and
persons who have it or are entitled to it: ss 164(3) and (4), 166(1) and (6), 167(3), 169(2),
170(2), 171(2) and 177(1). The same change is to be found from a person interested in a
building to a person who has an interest in a building, again a distinction without a
difference: ss 172(1) and 173(3). Differing, I fear, from Eveleigh and Kerr LJJ in this

respect with due diffidence, I cannot see any difference between a person who has an interest in the land, a person entitled to an interest in it and 'a person interested in the land', and I regard the last expression as shorthand for the others, or synonymous with them.

Any lawyer asking what interest in the land a person must have to entitle him to compensation must be conscious that 'interests in land' have a long legal history and have been the subject of judicial and statutory reference and exposition. And counsel have taken us to perhaps the first appearance in a statute of a person interested in land authorised to be purchased by statute, who qualifies for compensation, in s 18 (and s 19) of the Lands Clauses Consolidation Act 1845. It is clear from the language of s 18 that the phrase has there a technical meaning; a person to be entitled to claim compensation under that Act must have either an estate or an interest in the land required of which he can give particulars on demand. And those interested in the land are coupled and contrasted with those who have the power to sell and convey or release the land.

Estates and interests in land are now distinguished and defined in s 1 of the Law of Property Act 1925. Section 5 of the Compulsory Purchase Act 1965 maintains the distinction between persons interested in the land and those who have the power to sell and convey or release it, and maintains also the requirement of particulars of estate or interest in the land, of estate from freeholders and leaseholders under s 1 of the 1925 Act and of interest from all those others who have equitable interests under that section.

Section 164 of the Town and Country Planning Act 1971, which we have to interpret and apply, makes no reference to estates or estate owners with power to sell and convey or release, but they must, I think, now be included in this section, and in ss 33(1) and 52, with those who have interests, in the comprehensive 'person interested in the land', as ss 45(3) indicates. To my mind the only open question on the interpretation of s 164(1) is whether the context of a planning statute extends the meaning of the words to other interests of a novel kind. Such an extension may be unnecessary if the interest of the company in this case falls within those interests in land which the real property lawyer now recognises, however reluctantly, as having been evolved or extracted by legitimate development of the law and equity by judicial authority binding on this court.

The company's connection with the land in question is close and special. Is it enough to give the company an interest in it, either as an interest already identified by binding authority, or as an interest required by the context to be recognised as entitling the person who has it to compensation?

The authorities cited by counsel for the council for the planning authority, especially *Frank Warr & Co Ltd v London County Council* [1904] 1 KB 713 and *Walton Harvey Ltd v Walker & Homfrays Ltd* [1931] 1 Ch 274, [1930] All ER Rep 465 persuaded me that the company's interest could not amount to an equitable interest in the land, but junior counsel for the company's reply has left me in doubt. I am, however, satisfied that even if the company's interest is one not yet recognised by authority it is one which no authority forbids us to recognise and one which should be recognised as qualifying the company for this statutory compensation. With the permission of the owner the company had erected about 400 yards of substantial safety barriers, had moved about 3,000 cubic metres of top soil to erect a spectator bank, had put up fencing to a height of 5 feet over a length of three-quarters of a mile by attaching two strands of barbed wire and two strands of nylon cable to existing posts and had tarmacked a race track. To reinstate the land before the expiry of the year for which the company had a right to use it, irrevocable by the owner, in consequence of the revocation of planning permission has put the company to expenditure which cannot be less than £16,100, which was the sum offered and accepted before it was withdrawn, and may be nearer £40,000, which was approximately the amount of the company's claim at its highest. That permitted development of the land would seem to give the company a substantial interest in the land requiring compensation under s 164. If not, the planning authority has been given and has exercised a statutory power to take away the company's valuable right to use the land in the manner permitted by the owner without compensation, a consequence which should not lightly be attributed to Parliament.

In my opinion we ought not to decide the question whether ss 45 and 164 have that *a* consequence by answering such questions as whether the company's licence from the owner was revocable or irrevocable or whether the fixtures and fittings which the company had to remove at its own expense were annexed to the land.

So also I do not think it necessary to decide whether the categories of equitable interests in land are closed or whether every development of land, of whatever character and extent, which is permitted under the Town and Country Planning General Development Order 1973, SI 1973/31, or otherwise, is an interest in land entitling a person who has it *b* to statutory compensation under Part VIII of this Act. But I am of opinion that this development of this land is of such a character and extent as to make this company interested in this land for the purposes of this section.

I too would accordingly allow the appeal.

Appeal allowed. Leave to appeal to House of Lords refused.

c

Solicitors: *Ward Bowie*, agents for *Booth & Co*, Leeds (for the company); *M R G Vause*, Huddersfield (for the council).

Sophie Craven   Barrister.

d
Practice Direction

CHANCERY DIVISION
QUEEN'S BENCH DIVISION

e *Practice – Queen's Bench Division and Chancery Division – New practice and procedure – Issue of writ – Postal facilities – Issue of originating summons – Service out of jurisdiction – Acknowledgment of service – Costs on default judgments – Appeal from district registrars – Evidence by deposition – Enforcing arbitration awards – RSC (Amendment No 2) 1982.*

This Practice Direction, which is issued with the concurrence of the Chief Master, *f* Chancery Division, amends a number of Masters' Practice Directions consequent on the coming into operation of RSC (Amendment No 2) 1982, SI 1982/1111, on 1 October 1982 and makes certain other minor amendments.

[Directions 9, 9A, 9B, 11 and 12, which are the subject of the amendments contained in paras C to G below, were substituted by the Practice Direction of 12 June 1980 ([1980] 3 All ER 822). The references in square brackets which follow the titles of the directions are to the paragraphs and pages of *The Supreme Court Practice 1982* vol 2, Part 4, where *g* the directions are set out.]

4 *Assignment of causes and matters in Chancery Division* (see RSC Ord 4, r 1) [para 905, p 204]
This direction is revoked.

h
8 *Title of writs and originating summonses in Chancery Division* (see RSC Ords 6 and 7) [para 908, p 205]
This direction is revoked.

9 *Issue of writ of summons* (see RSC Ord 6) [para 908B, p 208]
j After the words 'Chancery Division' in para 1(i) delete the semi-colon and insert a full stop. Add immediately thereafter a new sentence: 'In the case of a writ issued out of the Chancery Division what amendments to Forms App A nos 1, 8, 10, 11, 11A, 14 and 15 apply.'

9A *Postal facilities for issue of writs etc* (see RSC Ord 1, r 10) [paras 909D, 909F, pp 210, 211]
Paragraph 3(vi) is revoked and the existing para 3(vii) renumbered 3(vi).

9B *Issue of originating summons* [para 910, pp 211–212]

Delete the figure '1' at the commencement of the first paragraph.

Paragraph 2 is revoked.

11 *Service out of the jurisdiction* (see RSC Ord 11) [para 912, p 212]

The words 'or notice thereof' in paras 2 and 3(*a*) shall be deleted wherever they occur.

12 *Acknowledgment of service* (see RSC Ord 12) [paras 913G, 913H, p 214]

The second sentence of para 8 beginning with the word 'This' to the end of that paragraph shall be omitted.

Paragraph 9(3) and (4) shall be revoked and in place thereof shall be substituted:

'(3) He must make a copy of the acknowledgment of service showing the stamped date of receipt and send it to the plaintiff or his solicitor.'

21 *Costs on judgments in default of appearance or defence* [para 922, p 221]

The word 'Appearance' in the title of this direction and in para (1) shall be amended to 'notice of intention to defend'.

25 *Appeal from district registrars* (see RSC Ord 58, r 4) [para 924, p 222]

Paragraph (1) shall be revoked and in place thereof there shall be substituted:

'(1) When papers are sent up to the High Court from a district registry for the purposes of an appeal in the Queen's Bench Division from a district registrar to the judge in chambers, they shall be sent to the Chief Clerk to the Judge in Chambers, Room 128, Royal Courts of Justice, Strand, London WC2A 2LL if the hearing is to take place there and shall be returned to the district registrar by that officer.'

28 *Obtaining evidence for foreign courts* (see RSC Ord 70) [para 929, p 224]

In place of the existing direction there shall be substituted:

'28 *Obtaining evidence by deposition* (see RSC Ord 39, r 17 and Ord 70, r 4(3))

When an order is made for the examination of a witness before an examiner of the court, the name of the examiner must be inserted in the order before it is sealed.

The affidavit or summons bearing the indorsement of the master's or judge's order shall be presented to the masters' secretary, room 118, who is the proper officer for the purposes of RSC Ord 39, r 17, where the name of an examiner will be marked on the affidavit or summons and the order drawn up accordingly in the Action Department.

If for any reason the order is not drawn up or the examination is not proceeded with after an examiner has been allotted, the solicitor shall inform the masters' secretary in room 118.'

30 *Enforcing awards under Arbitration Act 1950* (see RSC Ord 73) [para 931, p 224]

Direction 30 and the title thereto shall be deleted and in substitution there shall be inserted:

'30 *Enforcing awards under the Arbitration Acts 1950 and 1975* (see RSC Ord 73)

An application for leave to enforce an award under s 26 of the Arbitration Act 1950 or s 3(1)(*a*) of the Arbitration Act 1975 should ordinarily be made ex parte to a master in chambers.

The applicant shall leave the affidavit and documents required by RSC Ord 73, r 10(3) to be exhibited to such affidavit in room 122 entitled "In the matter of an arbitration between *AB* and *CD*". The award shall be filed subsequently (without fee) on issuing execution.'

JOHN RITCHIE

24 September 1982   Senior Master, Queen's Bench Division.

a   # Bennett v Markham and another

QUEEN'S BENCH DIVISION
DONALDSON LJ AND WEBSTER J
11, 21 MAY 1982

b   *Weights and measures – Sale by measurement – Causing to be delivered to buyer lesser quantity
than that purported to be sold – Sale of beer for consumption on premises – Sale of one pint (20 fl
oz) of beer in pint brim measure glass in Leeds area – Glass containing 18·25 fl oz of liquid beer
with rest of contents consisting of froth – Whether proper delivery of full quantity purported to be
sold – Weights and Measures Act 1963, s 24(1).*

c   An inspector of weights and measures ordered two pints of bitter beer at the licensee's
public house in Leeds. A pint was 20 fl oz and the barmaid served the beer in two 20 fl
oz stamped brim measure glasses (ie glasses containing 20 fl oz when filled to the brim,
as distinct from pint line measure glasses which were capable of holding more than 20
fluid ounces but were marked with a line to indicate 20 fl oz). The glasses were full but
the beer had a head of froth of about half an inch and the liquid content of each glass was
only 18·25 fl oz. Informations were preferred against the licensee and the barmaid
d   alleging that, in selling bitter beer by measurement, they had 'delivered' to a customer a
lesser quantity of bitter beer (18·25 fl oz) than that purported to be sold (20 fl oz),
contrary to s 24(1)[a] of the Weights and Measures Act 1963. At the hearing of the
informations the magistrate found that customers in the Leeds area demanded beer with
a tight creamy head, served within the glass, that the licensee's brewers specially brewed
a type of bitter beer intended to carry and retain a head of froth in order to meet the
e   preference of customers in the area, that the licensee had instructed the barmaid to serve
beer with a creamy head in order to satisfy the demand of his customers and that beer
was often sold in 20 fl oz brim measure glasses, as opposed to pint line measure glasses,
in Leeds public houses. The magistrate dismissed the informations on the grounds (i)
that the head of froth formed an integral part of the pint as expected and demanded by
customers in the Leeds area and (ii) that the amount of the head in the two glasses served
f   to the inspector was not excessive or unreasonable. The prosecutor appealed, contending
that the head on the beer could not be taken into account when measuring, for the
purposes of s 24(1) of the 1963 Act, the quantity of beer to be supplied, because it was
clear from the wording of s 21(1)[b] of, and paras 1 and 2 of Part VI of Sch 4[c] to, the 1963
Act and s 1(1) and (3)[d] of the Alcoholic Liquor Duties Act 1979 that 'beer' meant 'liquid
beer' and that it had to be sold in a capacity measure of the quantity in question.
g

Held – The appeal would be dismissed for the following reasons—
(1) On the true construction of the 1963 and 1979 Acts 'beer', for the purposes of
s 24(1) of the 1963 Act, did not have to consist wholly of liquid, and furthermore the
requirements of Sch 4, Part VI, para 2, to the 1963 Act (which governed the sale, as
distinct from the delivery, of intoxicating liquor) although relevant to the provisions
h   relating to the sale of beer contained in s 22(1)[e] of that Act were not relevant to the
provisions relating to the 'delivery' of beer contained in s 24(1) (see p 644 c to f, post).

---

a   Section 24(1), so far as material, is set out at p 642 j, post
b   Section 21(1), so far as material, is set out at p 643 j, post
c   Schedule 4, so far as material, is set out at p 643 j and p 644 a b, post
j   d   Section 1, so far as material, is set out at p 644 a, post
e   Section 22(1), so far as material, provides: '. . . in the case of any goods which, when not pre-packed,
are required . . . to be sold only by quantity expressed in a particular manner or only in a particular
quantity, any person shall be guilty of an offence who—(a) whether on his own behalf or on behalf
of another person, offers or . . . sells . . . or (b) causes or suffers any other person to offer or . . . sell
. . . on his behalf, those goods otherwise than by quantity expressed in that manner or, as the case
may be, otherwise than in that quantity.'

(2) On the facts the magistrate was correct in holding that the head of froth on the beer
delivered to a customer in Leeds was an integral part of what was purported to be sold **a**
there, the question of whether the head of froth was excessive or unreasonable being a
question of fact for the magistrate to determine (see p 644 *j* to p 645 *c*, post).

Observations on the meaning and effect of s 22(1) of the 1963 Act (see p 645 *e* to *h*,
post).

Notes   **b**
For offences relating to illegal sales of intoxicating liquor, in particular to measure, see 26
Halsbury's Laws (4th edn) para 373, and for cases on measures, see 47 Digest (Repl) 782–
784, 27–44.

For the Weights and Measures Act 1963, ss 21, 22, 24, Sch 4, Pt VI, see 39 Halsbury's
Statutes (3rd edn) 747, 750, 753, 806.

For the Alcoholic Liquor Duties Act 1979, s 1, see 49 ibid 678.   **c**

Case referred to in judgment
Marshall v Searles [1964] Crim LR 667, DC.

Case stated
John Bennett, the director of trading standards for West Yorkshire, appealed by way of   **d**
case stated by F D L Loy Esq, stipendiary magistrate acting in and for the petty sessional
division of Leeds in the county of West Yorkshire, in respect of his adjudication as a
magistrates' court sitting at the Town Hall, Leeds on 13 October 1981 whereby he
dismissed (i) two informations preferred by the appellant against the first respondent,
Dennis Markham, alleging that on two occasions on 10 March 1981 he had committed
in Leeds an offence under s 24(1) of the Weights and Measures Act 1963 and (ii) two   **e**
informations preferred by the appellant against the second respondent, Barbara Nancy
King, alleging that on two occasions on 10 March 1981 she had committed in Leeds an
offence under s 24(1) of the 1963 Act. The facts are set out in the judgment of the court.

R M Harrison for the appellant.
Timothy Hirst for the respondents.
                                                                                               f
                                                                            Cur adv vult

21 May. **WEBSTER J** read the following judgment of the court: This is an appeal by a
prosecuting authority, the director of trading standards for West Yorkshire, by way of
case stated by the stipendiary magistrate sitting in Leeds, who dismissed four informations
preferred by the appellant against the respondents under s 24(1) of the Weights and   **g**
Measures Act 1963. The first respondent is the licensee of the Nag's Head public house
in Leeds and the second respondent, at the material time, was a barmaid at that public
house. There were two informations preferred by the appellant against the first
respondent, both in identical terms, namely that on 10 March 1981, in selling goods,
namely bitter beer by measurement, he had caused to be delivered to the buyer a lesser
quantity, namely 18·25 fl oz, than that purported to be sold, namely 20 fl oz, contrary to   **h**
s 24(1) of the 1963 Act. Two identical informations were preferred against the second
respondent.

Section 24(1), so far as material, provides:

> 'Subject to the provisions of this Part of this Act, any person who, in selling or
> purporting to sell any goods by ... measurement ... delivers or causes to be
> delivered to the buyer a lesser quantity than that purported to be sold ... shall be   **j**
> guilty of an offence.'

The facts found by the stipendiary magistrate were as follows. On 10 March 1981 a
Mr Lawrence, an inspector of weights and measures, accompanied by an assistant
inspector, ordered, in the Nag's Head public house, two pints of bitter beer. He was

served by the second respondent, who drew the beer into two 20 fl oz (ie pint) stamped
a brim measure glasses and delivered the drinks to Mr Lawrence. A pint brim measure
glass contains 20 fl oz when filled to the brim. It is to be distinguished from a pint line
measure glass, which is capable of holding more than 20 fl oz and is marked with a line
to indicate 20 fl oz.

Mr Lawrence estimated that both glasses had a head of froth, each of approximately
half an inch. He identified himself to the respondent and, in the respondent's presence,
b after waiting a short while for the froth to settle, he measured the liquid contents of the
glasses by pouring each in turn into a graduated measuring vessel. Each glass was found
to contain 18·25 fl oz of liquid. We note, in passing, that Mr Lawrence before identifying
himself to the respondent did not object to the amount of froth in either of the glasses or
ask for more beer to be put into them.

In some parts of the country there is a demand for beer with no head at all, or with
c very little head; but in the North of England, and particularly in the Leeds area,
customers demand a beer with a tight creamy head, served within the glass, so that it
does not disappear but follows the liquid down the inside of the glass as the liquid is
drunk. Samuel Smith's Brewery, the brewers who produced the beer sold at the Nag's
Head, specially brewed a type of bitter beer intended to carry and retain such a head in
order to meet the preference of customers in that area and to meet competition from
d other breweries in the region which brew beers carrying similar heads.

The first respondent had instructed the second respondent to dispense the beer by
drawing it through a tight sparkler, to ensure that the beer was served with a creamy
head in order to satisfy the demands of his customers. If a customer were to object to the
depth of the head, the drink would be topped up with liquid.

A survey carried out on 100 public houses selected at random in the West Yorkshire
e area by a weights and measures inspector revealed an average delivery of 19·7 fl oz on the
purported sale and delivery of a pint of beer. The largest excess was 2·2 fl oz and the
largest deficiency was 2·2 fl oz. Both line glasses and brim glasses were used in the
deliveries. In the 30 instances in which the deliveries were made from free flow (ie hand
operated as distinct from electrically operated metered) pumps into brim glasses the
average quantity of beer delivered was 19·2 fl oz. In the 6 instances in which deliveries
f were made from free flow pumps into line measure glasses the average quantity of beer
delivered was 21·4 fl oz.

The stipendiary magistrate was of the opinion that the head of froth was an integral
part of the pint and was so regarded by the customer, the publican and the brewer; and
that that was what was expected by and demanded by the customer and supplied by the
respondents. He was also of the opinion that the amount of head on the two glasses
g served by the respondent was not excessive or unreasonable and he accordingly dismissed
the information.

The questions which he asks for the opinion of the court are (a) whether the foaming
head on the purported pints of beer sold and delivered should be taken into account in
measuring the quantity of the beer so supplied and (b) whether, in the circumstances of
this case, it was open to the court to dismiss the said informations when the purported
h pints of beer sold and delivered measured 18·25 fl oz and 18·25 fl oz respectively.

Counsel for the appellant submits that the stipendiary magistrate was wrong in his
opinion that the head of froth was an integral part of the pint and that the two questions
should be answered in the negative.

He draws our attention to the following statutory provisions. Section 21(1) of the 1963
Act provides that, inter alia, Sch 4 to that Act 'shall have effect for the purposes of
j transactions in the goods therein mentioned'. Part VI of Sch 4 is headed 'Intoxicating
liquor'. Paragraph 1 (as substituted by the Alcoholic Liquor Duties Act 1979, s 92(1), Sch
3, para 4) provides:

'In this Part of this Schedule—(a) the expressions "beer" ... have the same
meanings respectively as in the Alcoholic Liquor Duties Act 1979 ...'

By s 1(1) and (3) of the 1979 Act beer is defined to include ale, porter, stout and any other description of beer, 'and any liquor which is made or sold as a description of beer . . .'   *a*
Paragraph 2 of Part VI of Sch 4 to the 1963 Act provides:

'Unless pre-packed . . . and except when sold as a constituent of a mixture of two or more liquids, beer . . . shall be sold by retail—(a) only in a quantity of one-third of a pint, half a pint or a multiple of half a pint; and (b) where sold for consumption on the premises of the seller, only in a capacity measure of the quantity in question.'

b

In reliance on those provisions counsel for the appellant makes two short and simple submissions. First he submits that it is plain that, since 1963, or at least since 1979, beer means liquor or liquid; and he emphasises the word 'liquor' in s 1(3) of the Alcoholic Liquor Duties Act 1979 and the word 'liquids' in para 2 of Pt VI of Sch 4 to the 1963 Act. As to that submission, in our view those two words in the context in which they appear are not sufficient to have the effect that, for the purposes of s 24 of the 1963 Act, beer   *c*
must consist wholly of liquor or liquid.

His second submission is that Parliament has specified precisely the measures in which beer is to be sold and has prohibited the sale of beer in any other measures. As to this submission it is necessary, in our view, to distinguish between the provisions and effect of s 22(1) of the 1963 Act on the one hand and those of s 24(1) of the Act on the other. As has been seen, s 24(1) creates an offence where a person delivers to the buyer a lesser   *d*
quantity than that purported to be sold. Section 22(1), on the other hand, creates an offence where goods, required by or under the Act to be sold only by quantity expressed in a particular manner or only in a particular quantity, are sold otherwise than by quantity expressed in that manner or, as the case may be, otherwise than in that quantity. In our judgment, therefore, the difference between ss 22(1) and 24(1) is that s 22(1) relates to the terms or manner in which a sale is made, whereas s 24(1) relates to short delivery   *e*
under a sale.

Although we recognise that the marginal note is not normally to be regarded as an aid to construction, we observe that the marginal note to s 22 is 'Offences in transactions in particular goods'. In our judgment the requirements of para 2 of Pt VI of Sch 4, which are expressed to govern the sale (as distinct from the delivery) of intoxicating liquor, are requirements relevant to the provisions of s 22(1) but not to those of s 24(1). In particular,   *f*
we reject the submission that, by reason of those provisions, the delivery of 18·25 fl oz of liquid under a purported sale of a pint of beer concludes, adversely to the respondents, the question whether, for the purposes of s 24(1), a lesser quantity than that purported to be sold was delivered.

As we have been asked to provide some guidance on the construction of each of these two sections, however, we will, later in this judgment, return to a consideration of s 22(1)   *g*
in the context of a case of this kind. For the moment, however, we confine ourselves to s 24(1) under which the informations in question were preferred.

On the facts found, there can be no doubt but that the respondents purported to sell a pint of something. The question is: of what? If all pint glasses normally used in public houses were pint line measure glasses, that is to say glasses capable of holding 20 fl oz of beer as well as some froth on top, it might be the case that when any customer orders a   *h*
pint of beer the publican purports to sell him a pint of liquid beer, with any additional froth there may be. But according to the facts found, at least in West Yorkshire where the survey was carried out, not all glasses normally used are pint line measure glasses; many of them are pint brim measure glasses which can only hold either a pint of liquid beer without any froth, or less than a pint of liquid beer with some froth. The glasses used in this case were, as we have said, pint brim measure glasses. Moreover, on the facts   *j*
found, 'customers' demand a beer with a head. It is not entirely clear from the facts as found whether the reference is to all customers or to the normal customer. But it can certainly not be taken as a reference to some only, or a few, customers. In our judgment, in the light of those facts, when a customer in that area orders a pint of beer which is offered in a pint brim glass, the publican or his barmaid purports to sell not a pint of

liquid beer but a full pint glass containing liquid beer and tight creamy head. On the
a evidence it was the practice of the respondent to top up the glass if the customer so
required, but this involves a recognition that in such a case the customer's order had been
misinterpreted and not an admission that less liquid had been delivered than was
purported to be sold.

There is no suggestion in this case that the two glasses delivered were not full. There is
no suggestion that Mr Lawrence asked for the beer to be topped up. In our judgment,
b therefore, that which was delivered was that which was sold, so that the stipendiary
magistrate was right in his opinion that, when it was delivered, the head of froth was an
integral part of what was purported to be sold.

As to the question whether or not the head of froth was excessive or unreasonable, in
our judgment that depends on what, when he orders his pint, the customer is to be taken
as ordering. This is a matter for the tribunal of fact to determine. If the head of froth is
c excessive or unreasonable in the light of what the customer is to be taken as ordering, an
offence under s 24(1) is proved.

Before leaving s 24(1) we would only add two matters. The first is that this conclusion
is consistent with the decision of this court in *Marshall v Searles* [1964] Crim LR 667,
when a similar question fell to be considered in relation to s 1 of the Sale of Food (Weights
and Measures) Act 1926. Second, the Weights and Measures Act 1979 contains, in s 19, a
d provision which has not yet been brought into force but which would be unnecessary if
our conclusion were to be wrong and counsel for the appellant's submissions were to be
right. That section provides:

> 'In ascertaining the quantity of any beer or cider for any of the purposes of Part
> VI of Schedule 4 to the principal Act or section 22 or 24 of that Act (which
> respectively regulate particular transactions and penalise short weight etc.) [note
e > those words in parenthesis], the gas comprised in any foam on the beer or cider shall
> be disregarded . . .'

We return to s 22(1). In our view the effect of that section is straightforward, and is
that where beer or cider are sold, or where beer with a head is sold where beer with a
head is taken to be ordered, then that beer (or beer with a head) may only be sold in
f quantities of a third of a pint or a half of a pint or multiples of a half of a pint and, when
sold for consumption on the premises, only in a capacity measure of the quantity in
question. Regulation 23 of the Weights and Measures Regulations 1963, SI 1963/1710,
provides that liquid capacity measures made of glass shall have their maximum purported
values defined either by the brim of the measure or by a line not less than two inches in
length and distant not less than half an inch nor more than one and a half inches from
g the brim. In our view, therefore, the effect of s 22(1) is that where, for instance, a pint of
beer, or of beer with a head, is sold it may only be sold in a pint brim measure or a pint
line measure complying with that last requirement. We note, finally, that if counsel for
the appellant's submissions are right it would never be legal for a publican to sell, in a
pint brim measure glass, beer with any frothy head on top. We do not think that this
was either the intention or the effect of s 22(1) of and Pt VI of Sch 4 to the 1963 Act,
h although it could probably be given that effect if s 19 of the Weights and Measures Act
1979 were to be brought into force.

Appeal dismissed.

Solicitors: *Hewitt, Woollacott & Chown* agents for *M D Shaffner*, Wakefield (for the
appellant); *J Levi & Co*, Leeds (for the respondents).

April Weiss   Barrister.

SEDAC Investments Ltd v Tanner and others

CHANCERY DIVISION

MICHAEL WHEELER QC SITTING AS A DEPUTY JUDGE OF THE HIGH COURT

20 APRIL, 6 MAY 1982

Landlord and tenant – Breach of covenant to repair – Leave to institute proceedings – Conditions to be satisfied before leave may be given – Service by lessor of notice requiring compensation for breach of covenant – Notice served by lessor after he had caused repairs to be executed – Validity of notice – Whether court having jurisdiction to give leave to institute proceedings – Law of Property Act 1925, s 146(1) – Leasehold Property (Repairs) Act 1938, s 1.

The landlords granted a tenant a lease of certain premises. The lease contained the usual repairing covenant on the part of the tenant. At a time when the lease had more than three years to run, the front of the premises became in urgent need of repair. The landlords caused the repairs to be done and then purported to serve on the tenant a notice under s 146(1)[a] of the Law of Property Act 1925 to the effect that the repairs had been necessitated by the tenant's breach of the repairing covenant and that the tenant was required to compensate the landlords for the cost, failing which the landlords intended to claim damages for breach of covenant. When the tenant refused to pay and the landlords applied to the court for leave to bring proceedings against him, under the Leasehold Property (Repairs) Act 1938, the tenant contended that the notice was not a valid notice under s 146(1) of the 1925 Act because (i) it had been served after the repairs had been carried out, whereas s 146(1) provided that a landlord could not enforce his rights 'unless and until' he served notice on the tenant and the tenant failed, within a reasonable time thereafter, to remedy the breach', and (ii) under s 1(2)[b] of the 1938 Act service of a valid s 146 notice was an essential precondition to the landlord claiming damages for a breach of the repairing covenant. On the question whether the landlords' notice under s 146(1) of the 1925 Act was valid for the purposes of s 1 of the 1938 Act,

Held – On the true construction of s 146(1) of the 1925 Act and s 1 of the 1938 Act, a notice under s 146(1) of the 1925 Act was valid for the purposes of s 1 of the 1938 Act only if it was served before the breach complained of was remedied. It followed that, because the landlords had executed the repairs before they served the notice, the notice was void for the purposes of s 1. Accordingly, as the whole operation of s 1 of the 1938 Act depended on the service of a valid notice by the landlords under s 146(1) of the 1925 Act, the court had no jurisdiction to grant the landlords leave to bring proceedings see p 650 c to p 651 g and p 652 g h, post).

Notes

For tenants' obligations towards landlords under repairing covenants in leases, see 27 Halsbury's Laws (4th edn) para 275.

For the Law of Property Act 1925, s 146, see 27 Halsbury's Statutes (3rd edn) 563.

For the Leasehold Property (Repairs) Act 1938, s 1, see 18 ibid 473.

Case referred to in judgment

Sidnell v Wilson [1966] 1 All ER 681, [1966] 2 QB 67, [1966] 2 WLR 560, CA, 31(2) Digest (Reissue) 832, 6888.

---

a   Section 146(1) is set out at p 650 a to c, post

b   Section 1(2), so far as material, provides: 'A right to damages for a breach of [a repairing covenant] shall not be enforceable by action commenced at any time at which three years or more of the term of the lease remain unexpired unless the lessor has served on the lessee not less than one month before the commencement of the action such a notice as is specified in subsection (1) of section one hundred and forty-six of the Law of Property Act, 1925 . . .'

Case also cited

a *Jacob v Down* [1900] 2 Ch 156.

Adjourned summons

By a summons dated 3 June 1981 the plaintiffs, SEDAC Investments Ltd (the lessors), applied for an order giving them leave to take proceedings against the defendants, Arthur Derek Powell Tanner, Michael Armstrong and Martin Edward Portch (sued as Michael

b Edward Portch) (the lessees), for damages for a breach of the covenants to repair contained in a lease dated 18 November 1974 of premises known as the first and second floors of 91 High Street, West Malling, Kent and made between the lessors of the one part and Beverley Denis Malcolm Hicks and Robert Clive Beswarick of the other part who, by a licence made on 19 November 1975 assigned all their estate and interest in the lease to the lessees as trustees of the Tonbridge and Malling Conservative Association. The facts

c are set out in the judgment.

Robert Pryor for the lessors.
Richard Fernyhough for the lessees.

Cur adv vult

d
6 May. **MICHAEL WHEELER QC** read the following judgment: This is a procedure summons which gives rise to a short but difficult question of law, namely whether the plaintiffs, who are lessors under a lease dated 18 November 1974, are, on the facts of the case, now entitled to leave to commence proceedings against the lessee defendants for damages under s 1(2) of the Leasehold Property (Repairs) Act 1938 for breach of a repairing covenant, notwithstanding that the lessors had themselves remedied the breach

e before purporting to give the lessees a notice such as is specified in s 146(1) of the Law of Property Act 1925.

The facts are relatively simple. The lease in question was for a term of 14 years from 24 August 1974. In cl 2(2) there was a general repairing covenant by the lessees, and in cl 2(4) the lessors had a right to call on the lessees to remedy a breach and if the lessees failed to do so the lessors could themselves remedy it. It is common ground that no attempt

f was made by the lessors to invoke the machinery of that latter sub-clause.

On 25 April 1980 a representative of the lessees, a Mr Fisher, noticed that some of the stonework on the front wall of the demised premises (which were used by the local Conservative Association) was loose and that fragments of the front wall at first floor level were falling onto the pavement below. Accordingly, he immediately informed the lessors (through a Mr Tidball) to enable them to ascertain whether their insurance

g provided adequate cover against any claim for injury which might be sustained as a result of the falling stonework. Mr Fisher's evidence is that he did not at that time know whether the lessees were under any legal obligation to maintain or repair the wall.

Mr Tidball took prompt action and on the very same day instructed a Mr Laker, who was a chartered engineer, to make an immediate inspection of the front wall of the

h premises.

As to what happened next, I cannot do better than quote from Mr Laker's affidavit:

'3. On the 25th April 1980 I was instructed by Mr. J. Tidball, a director of the Plaintiff Company, to make an inspection of the front door of the building at No. 91 High Street, West Malling. He told me that he had received a telephone call from the tenants to the effect that the stonework on the front of the building appeared to be loose. I made an immediate inspection of the front wall of the building the same

j day. My inspection revealed that the stonework facing on the righthand side of the window to the main first floor office, as viewed from the High Street had moved out from the main face of the wall by half an inch at sill level and 1½ inches at its head. Furthermore, above the head of the window was a 10 inch high void. Much of the mortar jointing had perished and there was movement in the stonework under hand pressure and from vibration caused by passing lorries. I formed the

view that the stonework might fall if subjected to any unusual vibration, and that if
that happened severe injury might be caused to a passing pedestrian. I therefore *a*
telephoned Mr. Tidball and advised him of the state of the building, the danger to
pedestrians and that his insurance might not protect him against liability for any
damage caused by falling stonework.

4. Mr. Tidball thereupon instructed me to arrange for the wall to be repaired and
instructions were given to proceed. The builders, having obtained permission to
erect the scaffold across the public footpath, erected it on the 1st May 1980. The *b*
work was completed by the 9th May. I supervised the work of repair in the course
of which it became apparent how unsafe the wall had been. In particular as soon as
a start was made on taking down the stone facing, much of it fell away down onto
the scaffold boards. This included stonework up to the string course about three feet
above the window head. It was found that the mortar joints had perished . . .

6. In my opinion it was essential in April 1980 for the front wall of the said *c*
building to be repaired as a matter of the utmost urgency in order to prevent danger
both to the general public and to occupiers of and visitors to the above-mentioned
building.'

The cost to the lessors of getting this remedial work carried out was £2,754·25 and the
total cost (including Mr Laker's fees and solicitors' fees) was just under £3,000. *d*

The lessors made no claim against the lessees in respect of this expenditure until 5
January 1981, when the lessors' solicitors served on the defendants (who are the trustees
of the Tonbridge and Malling Conservative Association) what was described in the
heading as a 'Section 146 Notice' under which the solicitors, as agents for the lessors, gave
notice as follows. It is addressed to the tenants and refers to the lease under which they
hold the premises, and continues: *e*

'WE . . . Solicitors and Agents for the Landlord, hereby give you notice as follows:

1. By the above-mentioned lease the Lessee covenanted "throughout the term to
keep the demised premises and all additions thereto and the Landlord's fixtures
thereon and the boundary walls thereof and the drains soil and other pipes and *f*
sanitary and water apparatus thereof in tenantable repair and condition".

2. In breach of the above-mentioned covenant you allowed the front wall of the
said premises to fall into disrepair.

3. The afore-mentioned breach has been remedied by the Landlord and we
require you to make compensation of the following sums to the Landlord being the
cost to them of remedying the said breach [and those costs are set out, totalling, as I
have said, just under £3,000]. *g*

4. If you fail to comply with this Notice it is the intention of the Landlord to
claim damages against you for breach of the said covenant.

5. You are entitled under the Leasehold Property (Repairs) Act 1938 to serve on
the Landlord a Counter-notice claiming the benefit of the said Act.

6. Such Counter-notice must be served within twenty eights days of the date of
service upon you of this Notice. *h*

7. Such Counter-notice must be in writing and must be served upon the Landlord
by handing the same to him personally. Such Counter-notice shall also be sufficiently
served if it is left at the last known place of abode or business of the Landlord in the
United Kingdom. Such Counter-notice shall also be sufficiently served if it is sent
by post in a registered letter addressed to the Landlord by name at the aforesaid *j*
place of abode or business and if that letter is not returned through the post
undelivered; and that service shall be deemed to be made at the time at which the
registered letter would in the ordinary course be delivered.'

Paragraph 8 gives the name and address for service of the landlord.

On 20 January 1981 the lessees' solicitors sent a counter-notice under the Leasehold
Property (Repairs) Act 1938 as follows:

a 'COUNTER-NOTICE UNDER THE LEASEHOLD PROPERTY (REPAIRS) ACT 1938. AS SOLICITORS for [the lessees] upon whom you have served a Notice under Section 146 of the Law of Property Act, 1925 in respect of premises situate at 91, High Street, West Malling, Kent WE HEREBY GIVE YOU NOTICE that the said [lessees] claim the benefit of the Leasehold Property (Repairs) Act 1938.'

It is dated 20 January 1981.

b This counter-notice was sent under cover of a letter which made it clear that the giving of the counter-notice was to be without prejudice to the lessees' contention that the so-called 'Section 146 Notice' was void. There is therefore no question of the sending of the counter-notice acting as some form of waiver or estoppel.

Two last-minute affidavits were introduced during the hearing on behalf of the lessees, without objection. The first was by a Mr Davies, who is the managing director of a firm of builders, who gave his views as to what his firm would have quoted if they had been c asked to produce an estimate for the repairs in April 1980. Mr Davies asserted that this would have produced a substantially lower figure than that which the lessors have in fact incurred. Mr Davies also made the point that he would have recommended the customer to make an application for a local authority grant towards the cost of the repairs. I understand that it is now too late to make such an application. The second affidavit, by a clerk in the lessees' solicitors, amplified Mr Davies's evidence on the aspect of a local d government grant, but it was, I think, eventually agreed that these two affidavits took the matter little further having regard to the fact that on this summons I am solely concerned with an interlocutory application for leave to *commence* an action for damages and not with the merits or outcome of that action as such. For present purposes I am prepared to assume that an application for a local authority grant might have been made in April 1980 and that such an application might have been successful.

e The summons in the present case was issued on 3 June 1981 and was heard by the district registrar on 10 August 1981. Having heard argument, he indicated that he would grant the lessors leave to commence proceedings under s 1(5)(e) of the 1938 Act, but at the lessees' request he adjourned the summons into court. Thus it is that it comes before me.

So much for the facts. I must now turn to the law. Section 1(2) of the Leasehold f Property (Repairs) Act 1938 (as amended) provides that a right to damages for breach of a repairing covenant in a lease to which that Act applies (such as the lease in the present case) is not to be enforceable unless the lessor has served on the lessee within the time there mentioned 'such a notice as is specified in subsection (1) of section one hundred and forty-six of the Law of Property Act, 1925'; and where such a notice is served the lessee has 28 days in which to serve a counter-notice on the lessor claiming the benefit of the g 1938 Act. Under s 1(3) of the 1938 Act the effect of the lessee serving a counter-notice is to preclude the lessor from taking any proceedings for damages for breach of the repairing covenant otherwise than with the leave of the court.

The purpose of the 1938 Act was conveniently summarised by Lord Denning MR in *Sidnell v Wilson* [1966] 1 All ER 681 at 683, [1966] 2 QB 67 at 76. He said:

h 'The notice . . . did not comply with the Leasehold Property (Repairs) Act, 1938, as amended by s. 51(2) of the Landlord and Tenant Act, 1954. The Act of 1938 was passed shortly before the war because of a great mischief prevalent at that time. Unscrupulous people used to buy up the reversion of leases and then bring pressure to bear on the tenants by an exaggerated list of delapidations. The Act of 1938 applied to leases of seven years or more which had three years or more to run. In j such cases Parliament enacted that the landlord, when he gave a notice under s. 146 of the Law of Property Act, 1925, to make good delapidations, must state on the notice that the tenant is entitled to give a counter-notice.'

But, as Harman LJ pointed out ([1966] 1 All ER 681 at 685, [1966] 2 QB 67 at 79):

'Like most remedial Acts of that sort, it catches the virtuous in the net which is laid for the sinner.'

I should stress at the outset that in the present case nothing that the lessors have done comes within a mile of the type of mischief which the 1938 Act was designed to stop.   *a*

Section 146(1) of the Law of Property Act 1925 provides as follows:

> 'A right of re-entry or forfeiture under any proviso or stipulation in a lease for a breach of any covenant or condition in the lease shall not be enforceable, by action or otherwise, unless and until the lessor serves on the lessee a notice—(a) specifying the particular breach complained of; and (b) if the breach is capable of remedy, requiring the lessee to remedy the breach; and (c) in any case, requiring the lessee to make compensation in money for the breach; and the lessee fails, within a reasonable time thereafter, to remedy the breach, if it is capable of remedy, and to make reasonable compensation in money, to the satisfaction of the lessor, for the breach.'   *b*

It will be seen (i) that s 146(1) relates to a breach of *any* covenant and not merely to a breach of a repairing covenant, (ii) that the section is primarily concerned with claims   *c* for and relief against forfeiture and (iii) that the notice which it requires the lessor to give is one which must contain the information referred to in paras (a), (b) and (c) of s 146(1). The concluding lines of the subsection clearly contemplate that the breach complained of has not been remedied at the time when the lessor serves his notice because, in effect, they give the lessee a reasonable time *after* service of the lessor's notice in which to remedy the breach. Moreover, this concept of the lessor's notice having been served at a   *d* time when the breach still requires to be remedied is, in my judgment, consistent with the natural interpretation of the language used in paras (a), (b) and (c).

This conclusion is, I think, reinforced by consideration of s 18 of the landlord and Tenant Act 1927. That is a section which, by sub-s (3), is to be construed as one with s 146 of the 1925 Act and relates to provisions regarding covenants to keep or put premises in repair. By sub-s (2) a right of re-entry or forfeiture for breach of a repairing covenant   *e* is not to be enforceable unless the lessor proves (i) that the fact 'that such a notice as is required by section one hundred and forty-six of the Law of Property Act, 1925, had been served on the lessee was known' to the lessee, under-lessee or person who last paid the rent, *and* (ii) 'that a time reasonably sufficient to enable the repairs to be executed had elapsed'. Here, too, as it seems to me, the legislature is assuming that at the time when the lessor serves what I will call his 's 146 notice' the breach of the repairing covenant   *f* will not have been remedied.

Not every breach of covenant is capable of being remedied in law, as para (b) of s 146(1) of the 1925 Act recognises; for examples, see *Woodfall on the Law of Landlord and Tenant* (28th edn, 1978) vol 1, p 863. But leaving that type of breach aside it is clear from s 146(1) that before a lessor can enforce a right of re-entry or forfeiture two conditions must have been satisfied, namely (i) that the lessor must have served a s 146 notice on the   *g* lessee and (ii) that the lessee must have failed, within a reasonable time thereafter, to remedy the breach and make reasonable monetary compensation for it.

That being the position under s 146(1) itself, what is meant by the reference in s 1(2) of the 1938 Act and s 18(2) of the 1927 Act to 'such a notice as is required in section [146(1)] of the Law of Property Act, 1925'? In my judgment it means, and means only, a notice which contains the information required by paras (a), (b) and (c) of s 146(1). As I   *h* have already stated, the natural meaning of those paragraphs is that they relate to a breach which, at the date of the service of the notice, has not yet been remedied; and if that is the correct construction of s 146(1) it is difficult to avoid the conclusion that the s 146 notice which the lessor has to serve under s 1(2) of the 1938 Act as a prerequisite to enforcing a right to damages for breach of a repairing covenant is similarly a notice which relates to a breach which at the date of service has not yet been remedied.   *j*

If this be so, it would seem to follow that a lessor is no longer in a position to give a valid s 146 notice if the breach in respect of which he desires to claim damages has already been remedied.

In construing s 1 of the 1938 Act the following points appear to me to be relevant. (i) Under s 1(2) the lessee's right to give a counter-notice claiming the benefit of the Act does not arise unless and until the lessor has duly served a s 146 notice on the lessee.

(ii) Under s 1(3), once the lessee has given the counter-notice, the lessor can only take
a   proceedings for forfeiture or damages for breach of the repairing covenant in question
with the leave of the court. (iii) The importance which the Act attaches to the lessee's
right to give a counter-notice is underlined by s 1(4), which requires the lessor's s 146
notice to contain a conspicuous statement of the lessee's right to give a counter-notice
and relevant details of the manner and time of service; and a notice which does not give
that information is a bad notice: see *Sidnell v Wilson* [1966] 1 All ER 681, [1966] 2 QB 67.

b   (iv) Under s 1(5), leave of the court is not to be given unless the lessor brings himself
within one or more of five separate heads; of these, the last (set out in s 1(5)(e)) is that the
lessor proves 'special circumstances which in the opinion of the court, render it just and
equitable that leave should be given'. It was under this head that the district registrar
would have been prepared to act in the present case. (v) Each of the first four of the
separate heads in s 1(5) imposes on a lessor who seeks leave of the court to commence
c   proceedings the need to prove that the immediate remedying of the breach *is* required
(my emphasis) for the purpose there stated. Thus in sub-s (5) also the draftsman appears
to be contemplating that the breach will not yet have been remedied at the time when
the lessor seeks the leave of the court.

In the light of the foregoing, it seems to me that the scheme of s 1 as a whole
contemplates a series of consecutive steps which must be taken before the court can give
d   leave to a lessor to enforce a claim for damages for breach of a repairing covenant,
namely: (i) the lessor must have served a s 146 notice which complied with ss 1(2) and
(4); (ii) the lessee must then have served a counter-notice which also complied with s
1(2); (iii) the lessor must then have brought himself within one or more of the heads set
out in s 1(5).

If this be so, the power of the court to give a lessor leave to commence proceedings as
e   contemplated by s 1(3) arises, and arises only, where the lessor has duly served a s 146
notice and the lessee has then duly served a counter-notice. The whole scheme of s 1
appears to commence with, and to hinge on, the service of a valid lessor's s 146 notice;
and, if, therefore, I am right in holding that a s 146 notice, to be effective, must be served
before the breach is remedied, I am forced to the conclusion that in a case such as the
present, where the lessor remedied the breach before attempting to serve a notice under
f   s 146(1), he has thereby put it out of his power to serve a valid s 146 notice at all, with
the result that he has deprived the lessee of his right to serve a counter-notice, and the
consequence of this seems inevitably to be that the court has no jurisdiction to give the
lessor leave to commence proceedings for damages because that jurisdiction arises, as I
have already indicated, only where (and because) the lessee has served a valid counter-
notice.

g   I frankly confess that I have reached this conclusion with surprise and regret.
Surprise, because the scheme of s 146(1) itself (and more particularly as applied by s 18
of the 1927 Act and s 1 of the 1938 Act) appears to make no provision whatsoever for the
situation where the consequences of the breach of the repairing covenant require (or
might reasonably be thought to require) urgent attention and where, for example, the
lessor takes immediate remedial action either of his own volition or, perhaps, because the
h   lessee is unable or unwilling to take the necessary action sufficiently promptly.

Regret, because I can see no reason why, in such circumstances, the lessor should (as I
have felt bound to hold) be unable to apply to the court for leave to commence
proceedings for damages merely because of his failure to serve a notice which, on the
facts of the present case, would be unlikely to have had any effect other than, perhaps, to
produce a request by the lessee that the lessor should put in hand the necessary repairs
j   and that they should sort out the question of the quantum of damages once that had
been done. I see no merit in the argument that by remedying the breach himself the
lessor has thereby prevented the lessee from doing so, possibly at less cost. That is a point
which might well be argued in the action for damages itself if the lessor got leave to
commence such an action; so, too, could the more difficult question whether the lessor
could establish a claim for damages having regard to the limitation on damages imposed
by s 18(1) of the 1927 Act. But I see no reason in principle why the court should be

unable to give leave to commence proceedings for damages in any circumstances
whatsoever (and even, it would seem, in a 'special circumstances' case which might *a*
otherwise come within s 1(5)(e) of the 1938 Act) merely because a valid s 146 notice had
not been served before the breach complained of had been remedied.

It is true that, although under s 1(2) a claim for damages for breach of a repairing
covenant cannot be enforced by an action commenced prior to the last three years of the
lease except with leave of the court, the lessor ceases to be under this restriction once the
three-year period has been reached *provided* (and that will be the position in the case *b*
before me) the claim for damages will not by then have become statute-barred. But I am
bound to say that this possible impact (or lack of impact) of statutory limitation on the
circumstances of any particular case seems to be undesirably and unsatisfactorily
fortuitous.

It is also true, as was pointed out in argument, that in the present case the lessors might
have protected their position in other ways. For example, (1) they might have invoked *c*
cl 2(4) of the lease and called on the lessees to remedy the breach; and they could have
reinforced this by seeking, or threatening to seek, a mandatory injunction on the lessees
to undertake the necessary remedial work; alternatively, (2) they might have served a
notice under s 146(1) (however general and imprecise the terms of that notice might, in
the circumstances, have had to be) and might have also stated that in view of the urgency
they regarded it as essential (and, ex hypothesi, as reasonable) that the lessees should at *d*
least commence to remedy the breach within, say, 48 hours.

As to these alternatives, they must, if they are valid, apply to any similar situation
whether more or less urgent than in the present case. Suffice it to say that I do not
consider either of them to be of any practical value in a case of real emergency.

In the present case, the basic trouble has arisen partly from the urgency of the repairs
which were undoubtedly required (Mr Laker's evidence on this score is uncontroverted *e*
and is accepted as correct by counsel for the lessees) and partly from the fact that at the
time when the damage to the wall was first noticed neither side (and I state this as a fact
rather than as a criticism) was apparently aware of their respective legal rights and
obligations. The lessees were unaware of the nature and extent of their liabilities under
the repairing covenant in the lease; and the lessors were unaware of their rights under cl
2(4) of the lease. *f*

So it was that when the emergency arose (an emergency which the lessees themselves
first brought to the attention of the lessors) it was the latter who (rightly as the factual
position was to prove) took immediate emergency action. True it is that they did so really
on their own initiative and without, as their counsel accepted, first giving the lessees the
opportunity to take remedial action themselves. But the fact remains that the emergency
basically arose as a result of the lessees' failure to comply with their obligations under the *g*
repairing covenant in the lease.

Nevertheless, for the reasons which I have given, I feel bound to conclude that in the
present case the lessees are correct in arguing that the purported s 146 notice given by
the lessors did not (and on the facts could not) comply with the requirements of s 1(2) of
the 1938 Act and accordingly that I have no jurisdiction to give leave to the lessors as
contemplated by that section to take proceedings to enforce their claim for damages for *h*
breach of the repairing covenant. But, in case this matter should go further, I wish to
make it clear that, if I felt that as a matter of law I had such jurisdiction, I would, on the
facts of this case, unhesitatingly exercise my judicial discretion in favour of the plaintiff
lessors.

Order accordingly. *j*

Solicitors: *Argles & Court*, Maidstone (for the lessors); *Warners*, Tonbridge (for the lessees).

Hazel Hartman   Barrister.

R v Grays Justices, ex parte Graham

QUEEN'S BENCH DIVISION

MAY LJ AND STEPHEN BROWN J

27 APRIL, 12 MAY 1982

Criminal law – Time – Time limit for bringing prosecution – Delay – Delay in holding committal proceedings – Defendant suspected in January 1980 of having committed offence – Prosecution unprepared to proceed on date fixed for committal proceedings – Magistrates finally refusing to adjourn proceedings in August 1981 – Defendant discharged because no evidence offered by prosecution – Prosecution commencing fresh proceedings in December 1981 in respect of same offence – Whether delay on part of prosecution rendering fresh proceedings vexatious and abuse of process of court.

On 28 occasions between 14 and 16 January 1980 goods were obtained by the use of a stolen cheque book and cheque guarantee card. The police suspected that the applicant was responsible and interviewed her on 27 January 1980. She denied that she was involved. On 5 June 1981, 29 informations were preferred against her, one alleging that she had stolen the cheque book and card, and the remaining 28 alleging that she had obtained property by deception by means of the cheque book and card. Summonses based on those informations were issued against the applicant. On 7 July she appeared before magistrates, who decided that the case was not suitable for summary trial and adjourned it until 5 August so that the prosecution could serve the necessary papers for committal proceedings. The prosecution failed to do so by that date and requested an adjournment until 20 August. The prosecution were still not ready to proceed on that date and when the magistrates refused to grant a further adjournment the prosecution offered no evidence and the applicant was discharged. In December 1981, 29 identical informations were preferred against the applicant by the prosecution and identical summonses were served on her. In February 1982 the applicant appeared before the magistrates to answer the summonses and they again decided that a summary trial would not be appropriate. The case was adjourned and the applicant applied to the High Court for an order prohibiting the magistrates from continuing as examining magistrates in respect of the alleged offences, on the ground that the two-year delay between the alleged commission of the offences and the continued prosecution was vexatious and an abuse of the process of the court. The prosecution submitted that delay by itself could not be a ground for prohibition since there had to be some element of mala fides on the part of the prosecution to cause the delay to be an abuse of process, and that in any event the delay was excusable because the case was such that it took a long time to investigate.

Held – Although delay in bringing criminal proceedings could of itself render the proceedings both vexatious and an abuse of the process of the court where the delay after the events alleged to constitute an offence occurred was sufficiently prolonged, the court would not normally prohibit the further prosecution of the proceedings in the absence of some improper use of the court's procedure. In all the circumstances the delay between the alleged commission of the offences and the bringing of proceedings against the applicant was not sufficient to render the proceedings vexatious or an abuse of process. Accordingly, the application would be dismissed (see p 658 *h* and p 659 *a b*, post).

R v Brentford Justices, ex p Wong [1981] 1 All ER 884 distinguished.

DPP v Humphrys [1976] 2 All ER 497 and *R v Manchester City Stipendiary Magistrate, ex p Snelson* [1978] 2 All ER 62 considered.

Notes

For preliminary inquiry before magistrates, see 1 Halsbury's Laws (4th edn) para 136.

Cases referred to in judgment

DPP v Humphrys [1976] 2 All ER 497, [1977] AC 1, [1976] 2 WLR 857, HL, 21 Digest (Reissue) 81, 531.

Mills v Cooper [1967] 2 All ER 100, [1967] 2 QB 459, [1967] 2 WLR 1343, DC, 21 Digest (Reissue) 80, 530.

R v Brentford Justices, ex p Wong [1981] 1 All ER 884, [1981] QB 445, [1981] 2 WLR 203, DC.

R v Horsham Justices, ex p Reeves [1981] Crim LR 566, DC.

R v Manchester City Stipendiary Magistrate, ex p Snelson [1978] 2 All ER 62, [1977] 1 WLR 911, DC, Digest (Cont Vol E) 134, 1700a.

Application for judicial review

Hazel Marie Graham applied, with the leave of Woolf J given on 18 February 1982, for an order prohibiting the Grays Justices from inquiring further as examining justices into offences under ss 1 and 15 of the Theft Act 1968 alleged to have been committed by the applicant on or about 14, 15 and 16 January 1980. The facts are set out in the judgment of the court.

Michael Wood for the applicant.
Andrew Collins for the prosecutor.
The justices did not appear.

At the conclusion of argument the court announced that, for reasons to be given later, the application would be dismissed.

12 May. **MAY LJ** read the following judgment of the court: On 27 April 1982 this court dismissed an application made by counsel on behalf of Mrs Hazel Marie Graham for judicial review of certain proceedings of the Grays Justices, and in particular for an order prohibiting any such justices sitting as a magistrates' court in Grays from inquiring further into various offences under ss 1 and 15 of the Theft Act 1968 alleged to have been committed by the applicant on or about 14, 15 and 16 January 1980. After we had heard counsel both in support of and against that application we dismissed it and said that we would give our reasons for so doing at a later date. This we now do.

The facts of this case can be briefly stated. A Mrs Goldsmith is a sister of the applicant. She has a current bank account at the National Westminster Bank Ltd in Grays, Essex. To enable her to operate that account she has the usual cheque book and cheque guarantee card. On 14 January 1980, in the course of shopping in Grays, she discovered that her cheque book and card were missing from her handbag. She forthwith reported her loss both to the bank and also to the police. Despite her prompt actions, it seems clear that on or about 14, 15 and 16 January 1980 someone forged cheques from the stolen cheque book and with them and the stolen cheque guarantee card obtained goods from different shops, principally in Essex and Kent, on at least 28 occasions. The total sum involved is of the order of £1,600.

For reasons which we do not know, suspicion fell on the applicant. She was interviewed by police officers on 27 January 1980. She at once denied being in any way involved in the alleged deceptions and has maintained her denial ever since. In answer to a specific question from a police officer she denied ever touching her sister's then current cheque book or any of the cheques in it. In the course of the police investigations, the applicant's finger prints were taken and it is alleged that prints which can only be hers have been found and can be demonstrated on 4 out of the 28 forged cheques which were involved. On her solicitor's advice the applicant declined to stand on any identification parade and there is no other evidence physically identifying her as the person concerned. The police allege that they found on her premises, when these were searched at the outset of their investigations, a green roll-neck woollen jumper which was referred to by one witness involved in one of the occasions on which a forged cheque was passed. In addition, the investigating police officer obtained from the applicant, with her consent, various

specimens of her writing, but there seems little if any evidence in the papers before us
a connecting these specimens with any of the writing on any of the disputed cheques.

After the conclusion of the police interview on 27 January 1980, the applicant was
bailed under s 38(2) of the Magistrates' Courts Act 1952 to return to Grays police station
on 2 April 1980. The police officer concerned, however, was at this time too busy on
other allegedly more important matters. The applicant was accordingly told that her
obligation to attend at the police station was withdrawn and that she would be seen at a
b later date by police officers. It is only right that we should mention at this stage that
apparently at the time when these frauds were being investigated the members of the
police force in the relevant area were severely overstretched in the investigation of serious
crimes which needed more immediate attention.

Be that as it may, it was not until 5 June 1981, that is to say some 16 months after the
applicant had been interviewed by police at the end of January 1980, that 29 informations
c were laid before the justices alleging, in so far as the first was concerned, that the applicant
had stolen the cheque book and cheque card, and, in so far as the remaining 28 were
concerned, that it had been she who had obtained the relevant property by deception by
forged cheques supported by that stolen cheque card. Twenty-nine summonses founded
on those informations were served on the applicant on the same date or very shortly
afterwards. The summonses were originally returnable on 23 June 1981, but as the
d matter was to be contested this date was vacated and the hearing fixed for 7 July 1981.
On that date the magistrates decided that the matter was not one which was suitable for
summary trial. Accordingly, the case was adjourned to 5 August 1981 so that the
prosecution could serve the necessary papers for committal proceedings. By this later
date, however, the prosecution had still not served the relevant statements and they
requested a further adjournment. Despite objection on the part of the solicitors acting
e for the applicant, the case was adjourned to 20 August 1981. On this date the prosecution
again requested an adjournment and this was again objected to by the applicant's
solicitors. The magistrates, for their part, were not prepared to grant a further
adjournment, and accordingly the prosecution offered no evidence and the applicant was
discharged.

On 15 December 1981, a further four months later, 29 identical fresh informations
f were laid before the court and 29 summonses were served on the applicant with return
dates of 6 January 1982. When she attended court on that occasion, she asked that the
matter should be adjourned to 11 February 1982 so that counsel could be instructed on
her behalf. On that day, the magistrates again decided that the matter was not one
suitable for summary trial and counsel on behalf of the applicant then applied that the
summonses should be further adjourned in order that he might apply on her behalf to
g this court for an order of prohibition.

The grounds which counsel for the applicant put before us in support of his application
were that, because of the delay of two years since the alleged original offences, the
continued prosecution of the applicant for them was in the circumstances vexatious, an
abuse of the process of the court, the delay being in no way due to any fault on the part
of the applicant herself, and that in all the circumstances of the case such continued
h prosecution was contrary to natural justice.

On behalf of the prosecutor, counsel submitted that this type of case involved a
substantial amount of detailed travelling and expenditure of time on the part of the
police, which in part explained the passage of time. In any event, delay by itself is not
sufficient, he contended, to entitle this court to make any order for judicial review in the
nature of prohibition; there was, unfortunately, nothing very extraordinary in the
j Crown Court having to try a 'stale' case. Before there can properly be said to be an abuse
of the process of the court, there must be some element of mala fides on the part of the
prosecuting authority.

We were referred to four decided cases. First, the decision of this court in *R v
Manchester City Stipendiary Magistrate, ex p Snelson* [1978] 2 All ER 62, [1977] 1 WLR
911. The point in that case was whether, where a defendant had been discharged on
committal proceedings, there was any settled practice that in order to restart a criminal

prosecution against him this should be done by way of a voluntary bill of indictment
rather than by fresh committal proceedings. In delivering the judgment of the court, *a*
Lord Widgery CJ held that although in the majority of cases a voluntary bill might well
be the convenient course, nevertheless, there certainly was jurisdiction for the justices to
hear and examine fresh committal proceedings. At the end of his judgment he said
([1978] 2 All ER 62 at 64, [1977] 1 WLR 911 at 913):

> '... the only aspect of the whole case which has troubled me is the feeling that if *b*
> the prosecution are right in their argument there seems to be a risk that a defendant
> might be prejudiced by repeated committal proceedings all failing, resulting in a
> committal being repeated time after time by further similar attempts. I am satisfied
> that that particular difficulty is overcome ... by saying that this court has a
> discretionary power to see that the use of repeated committal proceedings is not
> allowed to become vexatious or an abuse of the process of the court. If that point is *c*
> reached (and whether or not it is reached is a matter of degree), then I have no doubt
> that it would be right for us to step in by way of prohibition to prevent the repeated
> use of this procedure. We have not come to that point by a very long way ...'

The delay in that case was only a matter of months. Nevertheless, although his dictum
was obiter, it seems clear that Lord Widgery CJ took the view that a point might come,
after the passage of time and a number of committal proceedings, when an abuse of the *d*
process of the court could exist and when it would be right for the justices to refuse to
consider the matter further.

In *DPP v Humphrys* [1976] 2 All ER 497, [1977] AC 1 the principal question before the
House of Lords related to the doctrine of issue estoppel. In connection with this question,
however, reference was made at various points in the speeches to the question of double
jeopardy, oppression and abuse of the process of the court. Both Viscount Dilhorne and *e*
Lord Salmon referred to a short dictum of Lord Parker CJ in *Mills v Cooper* [1967] 2 All
ER 100 at 104, [1967] 2 QB 459 at 467, where he said:

> '... every court has undoubtedly a right in its discretion to decline to hear
> proceedings on the ground that they are oppressive and an abuse of the process of
> the court.'
> *f*

Viscount Dilhorne doubted whether this was a correct statement of the law in relation
to magistrates' courts. Lord Salmon, on the other hand, thought that there was powerful
authority to support it, and in his speech said ([1976] 2 All ER 497 at 527–528, [1977]
AC 1 at 46):

> 'I respectfully agree with my noble and learned friend, Viscount Dilhorne, that a
> judge has not and should not appear to have any responsibility for the institution of *g*
> prosecutions; nor has he any power to refuse to allow a prosecution to proceed
> merely because he considers that, as a matter of policy, it ought not to have been
> brought. It is only if the prosecution amounts to an abuse of the process of the court
> and is oppressive and vexatious that the judge has the power to intervene.
> Fortunately, such prosecutions are hardly ever brought but the power of the court
> to prevent them is, in my view, of great constitutional importance and should be *h*
> jealously preserved. For a man to be harassed and put to the expense of perhaps a
> long trial and then given an absolute discharge is hardly from any point of view an
> effective substitute for the exercise by the court of the power to which I have
> referred. I express no concluded view whether courts of inferior jurisdiction possess
> similar powers.'
> *j*

In *R v Brentford Justices, ex p Wong* [1981] 1 All ER 884, [1981] QB 445 the prosecutor
laid an information under s 104 of the Magistrates' Courts Act 1952 shortly before the
six months' time limit for doing so had expired. No decision had then been taken to
prosecute, and the information was laid merely as a protective measure. The decision to
prosecute was taken three months later, and the defendant applicant was informed by

letter of that decision. The actual summonses were not served for another two months.

a When they came on before the justices for hearing, the applicant's counsel invited the court to decline to hear them on the grounds that the delay was prejudicial and that for a prosecutor to lay an information on the last possible day to give him longer than the statutory period to decide whether to prosecute amounted to an abuse of the process of the court. The justices, while accepting the merits of the application, decided that they had no power to exercise a discretion not to hear a case when all the statutory requirements

b had been complied with. Thereupon, they adjourned the hearing to enable the applicant to apply to the Divisional Court for an order by way of prohibition. The court, in a judgment delivered by Donaldson LJ held, first, that it was open to the justices to conclude that it was an abuse of the process of the court for a prosecutor to lay an information when he has not reached a decision to prosecute, that they did have discretion to decline jurisdiction; and accordingly remitted the case to them to decide the point on

c the merits. In addition to the fact that the information had been laid before a decision to prosecute had been taken, by the time the matter came before the Divisional Court, two years had elapsed since the original alleged offence, and Donaldson LJ made it quite clear in his judgment that, were it a matter for him, he would unhesitatingly exercise his discretion against the prosecution and dismiss the summons.

. The most recent decision on this type of case is that of *R v Horsham Justices, ex p Reeves*

d [1981] Crim LR 566, which was heard by a Divisional Court presided over by Ackner LJ on 1 December 1980, and of which we and counsel had the benefit of a full transcript of the judgments. That case bore considerable similarities to the one which we have to consider. In May 1977 the applicant's premises were searched by police officers, who seized a quantity of equipment and fittings. On 4 October 1977 12 charges of theft and 12 alternative charges of handling were preferred against him by way of summonses.

e On 22 August 1978 he appeared before the justices who decided that the matter was not fit for summary trial and would have to be committed for trial at the Crown Court. The committal proceedings lasted three days. At the conclusion the defence submitted that there was no case to answer. The essence of the submission was that the prosecution had failed to disclose the necessary ingredients of the offence; it was not a case in which it was alleged that the evidence called by the Crown had been so discredited by cross-

f examination that it was not to be relied on. Having retired to consider their decision, the justices found the defence submissions well-founded, and that there was no prima facie case to answer on any of the 24 charges. They therefore discharged the applicant under s 7 of the Magistrates' Courts Act 1952. After those committal proceedings, the prosecution refused to release to the applicant the property which had been seized from his premises and indicated to his solicitors that they were then minded to apply for a

g voluntary bill of indictment. However, they did not follow this course, and on 2 January 1979, a little more than 18 months after the applicant's premises had originally been searched, the prosecution preferred five fresh charges against the applicant defendant by way of summonses. In three of such cases, if not four, they were identical to the first three or four of the 24 original charges. In the fifth case, it was identical to one part of one of the original charges and to another part of another. Two further witness statements

h were also served on the applicant's solicitors. In these circumstances, counsel for the defendant submitted that the fresh summonses were an abuse of the process of the court and that the justices should not hear them. The justices considered that they had a discretion to decide whether or not what was proposed amounted to an abuse of the process of the court, but decided that in the circumstances of the case before them it was not. Consequently, after the applicant's plea had been taken, the matter was adjourned

j to enable him to apply to the Divisional Court for judicial review of the nature of prohibition, just as has occurred in the present case.

In the *Horsham Justices* case the question arose why the matter had not proceeded in the ordinary course by way of an application for a voluntary bill. Having considered the facts and the affidavits before the court, Ackner LJ concluded that the reason for not applying for a voluntary bill was simply because there was, in the material before the

magistrates on the committal proceedings, so much that was either irrelevant or of little
probative value that it would have been difficult on the basis of that material to pinpoint *a*
the real foundation of the prosecution charges. Ackner LJ thought that in such
circumstances a judge, reading such a body of material of that kind, would have shown
little patience for such an application and would probably have dismissed it. He took the
view that the course of applying to the justices on a fresh committal was looked on by
the prosecution as one more likely to succeed than the alternative procedure of applying
for a voluntary bill. His judgment then continued: *b*

> 'Should the prosecution be entitled, as they seek, to treat the first committal
> proceedings for all practicable purposes as a dummy run and, having concluded that
> they over-complicated them, bring virtually the same proceedings but in a form in
> which they should have been brought if proper thought had been given by the
> prosecution to them in the first place? In my judgment, to allow such a course in
> the particular circumstances of this case would be vexatious to the applicant, and for *c*
> that reason it would, in my judgment, be an abuse of the process of the court. There
> has been considerable anxiety no doubt experienced by the applicant in having to
> deal with the three-day trial. There has been a considerable passage of time since his
> arrest in May 1977 and January 1979, when the second run of the prosecution was
> to take place. There has been considerable expense incurred by him which he will
> be unable to recover. The suggestion now of course is that he should face yet a *d*
> second batch of proceedings. To grant such an indulgence would, in my judgment,
> encourage poor preparation with a resultant waste of time and money. To allow
> prohibition in this case should bring home to the prosecution the desirability of
> following the advice which appellate courts have given again and again. The
> prosecution must direct its energies to the simplification of cases they desire to
> present . . . I would allow this application and order the relief sought on the grounds *e*
> that the prosecution's conduct in seeking to bring on again what were basically the
> same charges, although simplified and shortened, is vexatious and oppressive and
> can therefore be properly categorised as an abuse of the process of the court.'

Skinner J agreed and had no doubt not only that the court had a discretion to prohibit
the proceedings before the justices but that it should do so in the circumstances of that *f*
particular case. For his part, however, he reserved the question whether justices
themselves have a discretion to allow a prosecution to proceed in the circumstances
outlined, having regard to passages in *Humphrys* and *Mills v Cooper*, to which we have
already referred.

It seems to us that in each of the two most recent cases which we have mentioned
there was, in addition to mere delay, an element of mala fides on the part of the *g*
prosecution sufficient to justify the description of the renewed committal proceedings
on each occasion as vexatious and an abuse of the process of the court. In this respect, we
think that the facts of the *Horsham Justices* case can clearly be distinguished from those
before us. Certainly there must be some abuse of the process of the court, some at least
improper and it may be mala fide use of its procedure, before an order of judicial review
in the nature of prohibition will be made. In our opinion, although delay of itself, with *h*
nothing more, if sufficiently prolonged, could in some cases be such as to render criminal
proceedings brought long after the events said to constitute the offence both vexatious
and an abuse, we do not think that delay of the order that there has been in and in the
circumstances of this case can be so described.

Clearly, as a matter of policy, prosecutions should be brought and heard as quickly as
practicable. We think that in the majority of cases excessive delay is likely to prejudice *j*
the prosecution just as much as, if not more than, the defence. We are well aware that
there is today a substantial amount of delay and inefficiency in criminal proceedings,
both before and at trial. This is to be deplored, and all concerned must do their utmost
to bring criminal proceedings to trial and to verdict as swiftly and efficiently as possible.
But we do not think that this court should create any form of artificial limitation period
for criminal proceedings where it cannot truly be said that the due process of the criminal

a courts is being used improperly to harass a defendant. Although we appreciate that it will not be easy for the Crown to present its case, or for the applicant to meet it, in these proceedings because of the delay that there has been, there has been no instance of mala fides on the prosecution's part.

In all the circumstances, on the facts that we have outlined, and provided that the proceedings are now carried on with the necessary urgency, we do not think that it can be said to be vexatious to require this applicant to stand her trial later this year on the

b allegations of theft and obtaining property by deception which have been made against her.

It was for these reasons that we dismissed her application for judicial review.

Application dismissed.

c Solicitors: *Weight, Wolny & Trusler*, Chelmsford (for the applicant); *Sharpe, Pritchard & Co*, agents for *T Hambrey Jones*, Chelmsford (for the prosecutor).

Sepala Munasinghe Esq   Barrister.

d
Re Creehouse Ltd

COURT OF APPEAL, CIVIL DIVISION
LAWTON, TEMPLEMAN AND FOX LJJ
27, 28 JULY 1982

e *Solicitor – Withdrawal – Application for order that solicitor has ceased to act for party to litigation – Service of application – Whether application must be served on every party to the litigation or merely on party for whom solicitor was acting – Whether if improper motive suspected on part of litigant in withdrawing instructions court may insist on solicitor remaining on record to provide address for correspondence with litigant – RSC Ord 32, r 3, Ord 67, r 6(2).*

f The general rule contained in RSC Ord 32, r 3[a] requiring a summons to be 'served on every other party' does not apply to an application by a solicitor under Ord 67, r 6[b] for an order that he has ceased to act for a party to litigation because a summons under Ord 67, r 6(2) is not a summons inter partes in the litigation but a summons dealing with the relationship between the solicitor and his client and nothing more. Accordingly an application under Ord 67, r 6 need not be served on other parties to the litigation and

g such parties have no right to apply to set aside an order made under r 6 on the ground that the application for the order was not served on them. Furthermore, the fact that there is reason to suspect that there is an improper motive on the part of a litigant in withdrawing instructions from a solicitor is no ground for the court to refuse to make an order under r 6 or to insist that the solicitor remains on the record merely in order to provide a convenient address for correspondence with a litigant, since a solicitor on the

h record is shown to the world to be in charge of the litigation and it would be wholly inconsistent with his position in relation to his duties to be shown as being in charge of litigation and responsible for it when he was not (see p 662 g h and p 663 j to p 664 e, post).

Semble. There is a gap in the Rules of the Supreme Court arising from the fact that although parties to litigation when they issue writs or enter appearances are obliged by

j the rules to give an address which can be used for the service of documents, they can avoid service later by changing their address and not giving any notification of the new address (see p 662 c to e, post).

Decision of Vinelott J [1982] 2 All ER 422 affirmed.

a   Rule 3 is set out at p 662 *f g*, post
b   Rule 6, so far as material, is set out at p 663 *b* to *e*, post

Notes
For application by a solicitor for an order terminating his position as solicitor on the *a*
record, see 36 Halsbury's Laws (3rd edn) 72, para 102.

Cases cited
De La Pole (Lady) v Dick (1885) 29 Ch D 351, CA.
De Mora v Concha, Re Ward, Mills, Witham & Lambert [1887] WN 194.
Initial Services Ltd v Putterill [1967] 3 All ER 145, [1968] 1 QB 396, CA.   *b*
Myers v Elman [1939] 4 All ER 484, [1940] AC 282, HL.

Interlocutory appeal
The applicants, (1) Rochem Group SA (formerly Taulay SA), a Panamanian company, (2)
Chalvey Ltd, a Cayman Islands company, and (3) Techem Laboratories LP, a limited
partnership established under the law of Delaware, USA, the plaintiffs by counterclaim *c*
to a petition presented by a Swiss company, Rochem Group SA (the Swiss Rochem), for
the compulsory winding up of an English company, Creehouse Ltd, appealed against the
decision of Vinelott J ([1982] 2 All ER 422, [1982] 1 WLR 710) on 8 February 1982
dismissing their application, inter alia, for an order setting aside orders made by Mr
Registrar Bradburn on 3 February 1982, on summonses issued pursuant to RSC Ord 67,
r 7(1) by solicitors, Messrs Payne, Hicks Beach & Co, declaring that the solicitors had *d*
ceased to be solicitors acting for the Swiss Rochem. The orders were served on the
applicants on 4 February 1982 and on the same day the solicitors were taken off the
record. The facts are set out in the judgment of Lawton LJ.

C A Brodie QC and *Ian Geering* for the applicants.
Donald Nicholls QC and *Edwin Glasgow* for the solicitors.   *e*

LAWTON LJ. This is an appeal by three companies, Rochem Group SA (formerly
known as Taulay SA), Chalvey Ltd and Techem Laboratories LP (the applicants), against
an order made by Vinelott J refusing those parties leave to be joined in a summons issued
in some litigation at the instance of Messrs Payne, Hicks Beach & Co, solicitors, seeking *f*
leave to come off the record as the solicitors to the defendants by counterclaim in those
proceedings, and dismissing the three companies' application that an order dated 3
February 1982 made by Mr Registrar Bradburn, allowing those solicitors' name to be
taken off the record, be set aside.
    The appeal raises a most unusual point, namely when a solicitor to a party to litigation
has his retainer withdrawn and applies to the court for his name to be removed from the *g*
record, pursuant to RSC Ord 67, r 6, should he give notice to the other parties to the
litigation that he is asking to be taken off the record, and should those other parties be
allowed to show cause why his name should not be taken off the record?
    Counsel for the applicants, when opening the appeal, accepted that in modern times
at least it has not been the practice for solicitors applying to the court under Ord 67, r 6
to give notice to the other parties to the litigation. He boldly submitted that, although *h*
that was undoubtedly the modern practice, it was wrong and in breach of the Rules of
the Supreme Court. Further, he submitted that, on the unusual facts of this case, the
solicitors should not have been allowed to take their name off the record, because, if they
were allowed to do so, the consequences would be most inconvenient for the three
companies whose names I have mentioned, because they would have considerable
difficulty in serving the other party to the litigation, which is a corporation domiciled in *j*
the canton of Zurich, and under the laws of that canton considerable problems are likely
to arise about the service of any summonses and the like in the course of English
litigation.
    The story starts in 1974, when two companies, Gamlen Chemical Co (UK) Ltd and
Sybron Corp, an American corporation, started proceedings in England against a number
of persons and a company called Rochem Ltd for conspiracy to defraud. The trial took

place in 1980 before Walton J and lasted 91 days. Walton J gave judgment for the
a plaintiffs. When the plaintiffs tried to get in the fruits of their judgment they discovered
that Rochem Ltd had made away (so it was said) with all its assets, including the assets of
a number of subsidiary companies. Those subsidiary companies included the three
companies whose names I have mentioned. As a result of complicated litigation in many
parts of the world, in the end the successful litigants obtained control of those three
companies in such a way as to enable them, through those three companies, to trace the
b assets of which they were said to have been stripped by Rochem International. The
allegation has been that the assets which those three companies lost have found their way
to Switzerland where they are said to be under the control of another company called
Rochem SA. The only assets which at the present time are known to be in England are
those belonging to a company called Creehouse Ltd. Creehouse Ltd is a £100 company
but it is said to own leasehold property worth just under £100,000. The Swiss company
c says that it is entitled to the assets of Creehouse Ltd and that Creehouse Ltd is one of its
debtors. The three companies say that they are entitled to these assets and they are
creditors of Creehouse Ltd.
  The Swiss company presented a petition for the winding up of Creehouse Ltd. The
three companies opposed that winding up. It became clear when the matter was gone
into in the Companies Court that there was an issue as to whether the Swiss company
d really was a creditor of Creehouse Ltd, and in turn the Swiss company alleged that the
three companies were not creditors of Creehouse Ltd. All this had to be sorted out before
any further steps could be taken in the winding up of Creehouse Ltd.
  In the summer of 1981 Vinelott J made an order that the issues which arose between
the Swiss company and the three companies should be dealt with as a preliminary to the
further hearing of the petition for the winding up of Creehouse Ltd. One of the steps
e which he ordered to be taken was to allow the three companies to counterclaim against
the Swiss company for what they said were the losses they had sustained as a result of the
activities of the Swiss company. In all this litigation in the Companies Court the Swiss
company was represented by Messrs Payne, Hicks Beach & Co. The order made by
Vinelott J was the subject matter of an appeal by the Swiss company to this court. That
appeal was heard on 3 December 1981 and dismissed. The Swiss company applied for
f leave to appeal to the House of Lords but this court refused leave. The Swiss company
then petitioned the House of Lords for leave to appeal. The petition was heard on 21
January 1982 and refused. Messrs Payne, Hicks Beach & Co were still the solicitors.
  By a telex sent on 26 January 1982 the Swiss company withdrew Messrs Payne, Hicks
Beach & Co's retainer. As a result, Messrs Payne, Hicks Beach & Co were of the opinion
that they would have to get their name off the record. As a result, they served a notice on
g their Swiss clients that they were proposing to apply to the court for their name to be
taken off the record. One of the partners in that firm swore an affidavit exhibiting the
telex which they had received from their clients. On 3 February 1982 Mr Registrar
Bradburn allowed them to remove their name from the record.
  Pursuant to the rules to which I shall be referring in detail later Messrs Payne, Hicks
Beach & Co then served the other parties to the litigation with notice of the fact that they
h had ceased to be solicitors to the Swiss corporation. Understandably in the circumstances,
there was considerable disquiet amongst the advisers of the three companies. The reason
was this, that the Swiss company no longer had any address in England where summonses
and the like could be served. There could perhaps be substituted service in Switzerland,
but that is not a matter into which we went in the course of hearing this appeal. It was
accepted that there would be difficulty in serving the Swiss company. It was suggested
j on behalf of the three companies that what had happened was a deliberate move by the
Swiss company, whose conduct had been the subject matter of considerable complaint
and justifiable suspicion, to make it as difficult as they possibly could for the three
companies to get justice and to regain some of the assets which those companies alleged
had got under the control of the Swiss company. For the purposes of this judgment I am
prepared to accept that that is a fair inference to be drawn from the conduct of the Swiss
company. The only gloss I would make on that is to say that Messrs Payne, Hicks Beach

& Co, without any question at all, have not been parties to, nor have they connived at, any such device for avoiding service of documents. They have acted with the utmost *a* propriety in all matters relating to this dispute.

Having discovered that this situation had arisen, the advisers of the three companies then put their minds to the question as to how they could safeguard their clients' interests. The decision they seem to have come to is that, if it could be said that they should have had notice of the intention of Messrs Payne, Hicks Beach & Co to take their name off the record, then they would have pointed out to Mr Registrar Bradburn that *b* they had an interest in seeing that those solicitors should remain on the record as a safeguard for the three companies. It was appreciated that, if the solicitors remained on the record, they would have no duty to their Swiss client save perhaps to give them notice of any hearings which the court might order. It was accepted that they would be under no duty to transmit documents that were served on them to Switzerland, save for the original order of the court removing their name from the record. But it was said that, by *c* being on the record, they would be providing a postbox into which the three companies could put summonses and documents.

In the course of his submission, counsel for the applicants invited our attention to the fact that there does seem to be a gap in the Rules of the Supreme Court arising from the fact that, although parties to litigation when they issue writs or enter appearances are obliged by the rules to give an address which can be used for the service of documents, *d* they can avoid service later by changing their address and not giving any notification of the new address. This is a matter which might perhaps be drawn to the attention of the Rule Committee. It is also relevant for us to remind ourselves that in this case the Swiss company, being a corporation, cannot take any step in this litigation without the aid of a solicitor of the Supreme Court. In other words, by withdrawing Messrs Payne, Hicks Beach & Co's retainer, they have deprived themselves, although they may not know it, *e* of their ability to contest this litigation any further. But perhaps they take the view that it is in their interests not to be further involved in this litigation.

In all those circumstances, counsel for the applicants has submitted that, on the true construction of the Rules of the Supreme Court, his clients were entitled to be served by Messrs Payne, Hicks Beach & Co with notice that they were going to apply for their name to be taken off the record. He based his argument primarily on the provisions of *f* Ord 32, r 3, which, under the heading 'Service of summons', is as follows:

> 'A summons asking only for the extension or abridgment of any period of time may be served on the day before the day specified in the summons for the hearing thereof but, except as aforesaid and unless the Court otherwise orders or any of these rules otherwise provides, a summons must be served on every other party not less than two clear days before the day so specified.' *g*

In my judgment that rule applies to summonses inter partes in the litigation. A summons under Ord 67, r 6 is not, in my opinion, a summons inter partes at all. It is a summons dealing with the relationship between a party and his solicitor and nothing more. As counsel for Messrs Payne, Hicks Beach & Co pointed out, Ord 67 is a code regulating the position of solicitors who are acting as such in litigation. The first four *h* rules deal with the position where a party to litigation changes his solicitors by agreement. It provides what in those sort of circumstances is to be done and what notices are to be given to the other parties to the litigation. Rule 5 deals with a situation where, for a number of reasons, a solicitor is unable to go on acting as a solicitor in the litigation or there has been a change of solicitors or a party to litigation has decided to act in person and to dispense with his solicitor, but no notice of change of any kind has been given to *j* the other parties. Rule 6 deals with the situation where the party to litigation either dispenses with his solicitor, as in this case, or, as can happen, the solicitor decides that he will no longer act for the party. In those circumstances, as the solicitor is an officer of the court, it is only right that the court should investigate whether, in all the circumstances of the case, it is appropriate for the solicitor to withdraw. It may be that the solicitor has been over-hasty in refusing to go on acting for a client. He may by his action have put

the client in difficulty and therefore it is appropriate, as I understand r 6, that the court
a should be apprised of the reason why the solicitor wishes to withdraw, so that the court
can consider whether the reasons for withdrawal are adequate and can give protection to
the client if it is necessary to do so.

Rule 6 is a fairly lengthy rule and it should be read as a whole: parts of it should not be
separated from other parts. The rule starts in this way:

b   '(1) Where a solicitor who has acted for a party in a cause or matter has ceased so
to act and the party has not given notice of change in accordance with rule 1, or
notice of intention to act in person in accordance with rule 4, the solicitor may apply
to the Court for an order declaring that the solicitor has ceased to be the solicitor
acting for the party in the cause or matter, and the Court or the Court of Appeal, as
the case may be, may make an order accordingly, but unless and until the solicitor—
c   (a) serves on every party to the cause or matter (not being a party in default as to
acknowledgment of service) a copy of the order, and (b) procures the order to be
entered in the district registry or other appropriate office mentioned in rule 1(2),
and (c) leaves at that office a copy of the order and a certificate signed by him that
the order has been duly served as aforesaid, he shall, subject to the foregoing
provisions of this Order, be considered the solicitor of the party till the final
conclusion of the cause or matter, whether in the High Court of Court or Appeal.'
d
It is clear from that paragraph that it is only after a decision has been reached that the
other parties to the litigation are to be given notice of what has happened.

Paragraph (2) is in these terms:

'An application for an order under this rule must be made by summons or, in the
case of an application to the Court of Appeal, by motion, and the summons or notice
e   of motion must, unless the Court of Appeal, as the case may be, otherwise directs,
be served on the party for whom the solicitor acted. The application must be
supported by an affidavit stating the grounds of the application.'

The argument of counsel for the applicants was that para (1) uses the word 'may' and
he submits that para (2) provides for service on the party for whom the solicitor has been
f acting, because unless there was such a rule, there would not be any provision in the rules
for service on the former client, because Ord 32, r 3 merely deals with service of
summonses and the like on the other parties to the litigation.

In my judgment, when r 6 is read as a whole, it is clear what is intended. The solicitor
must serve his own client. That is what Messrs Payne, Hicks Beach & Co did. He must
then bring the matter before the court. That is what they did. The application must be
g supported by an affidavit. Their application was so supported. The court then decides
what shall be done. It is appropriate, so it seems to me, that this should be done without
bringing the other parties into the matter at all, because in many cases the contents of
the affidavits may reveal matters which are confidential between solicitor and client. A
typical example is where the client feels that it would not be right for a solicitor to go on
acting for him when the solicitor by his advice has shown that he has no confidence in
h the client's case. Many clients in those circumstances feel that a change of solicitor would
be to their advantage. That sort of information clearly ought not to be brought to the
attention of the other side. It is true, as counsel for the applicants pointed out, that the
court, in the exercise of its discretion, can always exclude confidential matter from the
attention of another party to litigation if it is so minded. Nevertheless, the whole purport
of this rule is to see what is the best thing to be done as between solicitor and client.
j There is really no room whatsoever for third parties to be brought in.

It follows, in my judgment, that the rule itself makes no provision at all for the other
parties to be served with notice that it is the intention of a solicitor to ask the court for
leave to remove his name from the record. That is the end of this appeal but it is right
that I should go on to deal with the second ground on which counsel for the applicants
based his case.

He said that in a case such as this, where there is reason to think that there is an improper motive on the part of a litigant in withdrawing instructions from a solicitor, the court should insist that the solicitor remains on the record in order to provide a *a* convenient postbox. In my judgment, that would be a wrong approach to the relationship between a solicitor, his former client and the court. A solicitor on the record is shown to the world to be in charge of the litigation. If he is in charge of the litigation he is responsible for its proper conduct and it would be wholly inconsistent, in my opinion, with the position of a solicitor in relation to his duties, that he should be shown as being in charge of a litigation and responsible for it when in fact he was nothing more than a *b* convenient postbox.

Even if there had been jurisdiction in the court to allow the three companies to make representations about the removal of a solicitor's name from the record, in the circumstances of this case, and similar kinds of cases, it would, in my judgment, have been wholly inappropriate to have refused the solicitor's application to be removed from the record. *c*

I would dismiss the appeal.

TEMPLEMAN LJ. I agree, and would only add this, that when RSC Ord 32, r 3 requires a summons to be 'served on every other party not less than two clear days before the day so specified' it means, in my judgment, every other party to the summons, not necessarily every other party to the litigation in the course of which the summons is *d* issued. If the relief sought by the summons does not affect certain parties to the litigation then there is no need to serve them, but if a party is served with a summons he must have two clear days' notice.

Subject to that, I agree entirely with the reasons given by Lawton LJ.

FOX LJ. I also agree. I have some sympathy with the applicants in the difficulties in *e* which they may find themselves if the judge's order is upheld, but it seems to me that the cure is quite unacceptable. It produces a situation which is essentially false. First of all, although Messrs Payne, Hicks Beach & Co have ceased to act for Swiss Rochem and have proved it, the court is to refuse a declaration to that effect under RSC Ord 67, r 6. The purpose of r 6 is, I think, the protection of the client and to refuse a declaration where the client has determined the retainer in such circumstances as the present seems *f* to me to be unsatisfactory. Second, the result of refusing a declaration is, under the provisions of Ord 67, r 1, that Messrs Payne, Hicks Beach & Co are (in the language of that rule) 'to be considered the solicitors of Rochem until the final conclusion of the cause or matter'. But, as contemplated by the applicants, Messrs Payne, Hicks Beach & Co will be nothing of the sort. They would write to Rochem and say that their name remains on the record but, although they will recieve the various documents in the case, they will do *g* nothing and will forward no documents. Yet all the essential documents will have to be served on Messrs Payne, Hicks Beach & Co, and not Rochem and Messrs Payne, Hicks Beach & Co would be free, as I understand the applicants' view of the matter, to burn the documents as they arrive, having initially told the clients what their position was, and that would be so even though Rochem ask for the documents to be forwarded.

I think one need have no sympathy, in the circumstances of this case, with Rochem, *h* who can put things right by instructing new solicitors at any time. But, it seems to me that the result for which the applicants contend would make a complete mockery of the rules. The consequences of making a declaration may be to some extent inconvenient to the applicants but, in my view, it represents the reality of the position and the true effect of the rules.

I would dismiss the appeal. *j*

Appeal dismissed.

Solicitors: *Herbert Smith & Co* (for the applicants); *Payne, Hicks Beach & Co.*

Mary Rose Plummer   Barrister.

Victoria Housing Estates Ltd v Ashpurton Estates Ltd

COURT OF APPEAL, CIVIL DIVISION

LORD BRIGHTMAN, LAWTON AND OLIVER LJJ

8, 9, 10, 11, MARCH, 7 MAY 1982

Company – Charge – Registration – Extension of time – Matters to be considered – Imminence of liquidation when application for extension of time before registrar – Company in liquidation when matter before judge – Whether chargee entitled to extension of time – Whether registrar and judge right to refuse extension of time – Companies Act 1948, s 101.

In April 1976 a housing association (Victoria) advanced money to a company (Ashpurton), which was part of a group of companies, to purchase some 50 dwellings in Norfolk. The loan was secured by a legal charge which was registered against title on 19 May 1978. In October 1980 the ultimate holding company of Ashpurton (ILI) went into liquidation and Victoria was so informed by letter dated 7 November. On 20 November Victoria formally demanded repayment of the money outstanding under the legal charge, amounting to about £68,000, but repayment was not forthcoming. On 6 January 1981 Victoria appointed a receiver and manager of the properties charged to it. On 27 February Victoria discovered that by mistake the legal charge had never been registered under s 95(1)ᵃ of the Companies Act 1948. On discovering the mistake Victoria decided to proceed with sales of the properties rather than apply under s 101ᵇ of the 1948 Act to extend the time for registering the charge since it feared that to do so would alarm the company and precipitate a liquidation. On 15 May the board of Ashpurton gave notice convening an extraordinary general meeting of the company for 23 June to consider a resolution to wind up. Notice was also sent out pursuant to s 293(1)ᶜ of the 1948 Act convening a meeting of creditors for the same day, which Victoria received on 20 May. On 4 June Victoria issued proceedings under s 101 to extend the time allowed by s 95 for registering the charge. Ashpurton owed ILI £353,499 and Victoria £69,000. The ILI group was insolvent and most of the constituent companies were in liquidation. If Victoria were allowed to register out of time its debt would absorb all the assets of Ashpurton and it would recover 96p in the pound, but if it ranked pari passu with the other creditors it would receive a dividend of about 16p in the pound. On 11 June the companies registrar dismissed the application to extend time on the ground that it was made at a time when Ashpurton was insolvent and its winding up was imminent. Moreover, he was not satisfied that the omission to register the charge within due time was due to inadvertence. On 12 June Ashpurton went into voluntary liquidation. On 23 June the judge upheld the registrar's decision, holding that as a matter of discretion the court would not, save in exceptional circumstances, make an order extending time for

---

a   Section 95(1) provides: 'Subject to the provisions of this Part of this Act, every charge created after the fixed date by a company registered in England and being a charge to which this section applies shall, so far as any security on the company's property or undertaking is conferred thereby, be void against the liquidator and any creditor of the company, unless the prescribed particulars of the charge together with the instrument, if any, by which the charge is created or evidenced, are delivered to or received by the registrar of companies for registration in manner required by this Act within twenty-one days after the date of its creation, but without prejudice to any contract or obligation for repayment of the money thereby secured, and when a charge becomes void under this section the money secured thereby shall immediately become payable.'

b   Section 101 is set out at p 667 j to p 668 a, post

c   Section 293(1) provides: 'The company shall cause a meeting of the creditors of the company to be summoned for the day, or the day next following the day, on which there is to be held the meeting at which the resolution for voluntary winding up is to be proposed, and shall cause the notices of the said meeting of creditors to be sent by post to the creditors simultaneously with the sending of the notices of the said meeting of the company.'

registration once a winding-up order had supervened, and that since Victoria had deliberately elected not to seek registration out of time when it discovered its mistake, **a** believing it to be in its own interests, the court should not exercise its discretion in favour of Victoria when subsequently it decided that the opposite course was for its benefit. Victoria appealed, contending, inter alia, that s 101 did not itself impose any restrictions on the exercise of the court's discretion.

Held – The registrar was justified in refusing to grant Victoria an extension of time for **b** registration of the charge under s 95 of the 1948 Act both on the ground of the inadequacy of the evidence before him that Victoria's failure to register the charge in due time was due to inadvertence and on the ground of the imminence of Ashpurton's liquidation, and the judge, when the matter came before him on further evidence, was entitled to exercise his own discretion and take into account, as decisive against Victoria, the then fact of the liquidation, to reject the submission that exceptional circumstances **c** existed which entitled him to give Victoria priority notwithstanding the liquidation and to take into account, as equally decisive against Victoria, the fact that Victoria deliberately chose not to apply for an extension of time when the mistake of non-registration was first discovered. It followed therefore that the appeal would be dismissed (see p 675 f g and p 676 h to p 677 b and d, post).

    Re Resinoid and Mica Products Ltd (1967) [1982] 3 All ER 677 followed. **d**

    Per curiam. When a chargee discovers that, by mistake, he is unregistered, he should apply without delay for an extension of time if he desires to register; and the court, when asked to exercise its discretion, should look askance at a chargee who deliberately defers his application in order to see which course would be to his best advantage (see p 677 b c, post).

 e

Notes

For extending time for registration of charges, see 7 Halsbury's Laws (4th edn) paras 875–876, and for cases on the subject, see 10 Digest (Reissue) 868–871, 4995–5021.

    For the Companies Act 1948, ss 95, 101, 293, see 5 Halsbury's Statutes (3rd edn) 189, 194, 333.

    As from 22 December 1981 s 95(1) of the 1948 Act was substituted by s 106(1) of the **f** Companies Act 1981.

Cases referred to in judgment

Abrahams (S) & Sons, Re [1902] 1 Ch 695, 10 Digest (Reissue) 869, 5004.
Anglo-Oriental Carpet Manufacturing Co, Re [1903] 1 Ch 914, 10 Digest (Reissue) 870, **g** 5020.
Bootle Cold Storage and Ice Co, Re [1901] WN 54, 10 Digest (Reissue) 869, 5002.
Cardiff Workmen's Cottage Co Ltd, Re [1906] 2 Ch 627, 10 Digest (Reissue) 870, 5013.
Centrebind Ltd, Re [1966] 3 All ER 889, [1967] 1 WLR 377, 10 Digest (Reissue) 1133, 7034.
Charles (L H) & Co Ltd, Re [1935] WN 15, 10 Digest (Reissue) 870, 5017. **h**
Ehrmann Bros Ltd, Re, Albert v Ehrmann Bros Ltd [1906] 2 Ch 697, CA, 10 Digest (Reissue) 870, 5018.
Flinders Trading Co Pty Ltd, Re (1978) 3 ACLR 218, S Aust SC.
Johnson (I C) & Co Ltd, Re [1902] 2 Ch 101, CA, 10 Digest (Reissue) 869, 5003.
Joplin Brewery Co Ltd, Re [1902] 1 Ch 79, 10 Digest (Reissue) 870, 5010.
Kris Cruisers Ltd, Re [1948] 2 All ER 1105, [1949] Ch 138, 10 Digest (Reissue) 869, 5006. **j**
Mendip Press Ltd, Re (1901) 18 TLR 38, 10 Digest (Reissue) 868, 4997.
MIG Trust Ltd, Re [1933] Ch 542, CA; *affd* sub nom *Peat v Gresham Trust Ltd* [1934] AC 252, [1934] All ER Rep 82, HL, 10 Digest (Reissue) 870, 5014.
Monolithic Building Co, Re, Tacon v Monolithic Building Co [1915] 1 Ch 643, [1914–15] All ER Rep 249, CA, 10 Digest (Reissue) 840, 4842.

Resinoid and Mica Products Ltd, Re (1967) [1982] 3 All ER 677, CA.

a *Spiral Globe Ltd, Re* [1902] 1 Ch 396, 10 Digest (Reissue) 870, 5011.

Cases also cited

Ayerst (Inspector of Taxes) v C & K (Construction) Ltd [1975] 2 All ER 537, [1976] AC 167, HL.

British Eagle International Airlines Ltd v Compagnie Nationale Air France [1975] 2 All ER

b   390, [1975] 1 WLR 756, HL.

Crew v Cummings (1888) 21 QBD 420, CA.

Gardner v Jay (1885) 29 Ch D 50, CA.

Heathstar Properties Ltd, Re (Nos 1 & 2) [1966] 1 All ER 628, 1000, [1966] 1 WLR 993.

Holmes (Eric) (Properties) Ltd, Re [1965] 2 All ER 333, [1965] Ch 1052.

Mechanisations (Eaglescliffe) Ltd, Re [1964] 3 All ER 840, [1966] Ch 20.

c *Parsons, Re, ex p Furber* [1893] 2 QB 122, CA.

Rolls Razor Ltd, Re (No 2) [1969] 3 All ER 1386, [1970] Ch 576.

Smith, Knight & Co, Re, ex p Ashbury (1868) LR 5 Eq 223.

Southard & Co Ltd, Re [1979] 3 All ER 556, [1979] 1 WLR 1198, CA.

Interlocutory appeal

d Victoria Housing Estates Ltd (Victoria) appealed against the order of Allan Heyman QC, sitting as a deputy judge of the High Court in the Chancery Division on 23 June 1981, whereby he dismissed Victoria's appeal from the order of Mr Registrar Bradburn made on 11 June 1981 refusing Victoria's application to extend under s 101 of the Companies Act 1948 the time for registration of a legal charge dated 18 April 1978 created by Ashpurton Estates Ltd (Ashpurton) over property sold by Victoria to Ashpurton to secure

e the payment of £147,957 and interest thereon. The facts are set out in the judgment of Lord Brightman.

John Lindsay QC and *Geoffrey Vos* for Victoria.
William Blackburne for Ashpurton.

f   *Cur adv vult*

7 May. **LORD BRIGHTMAN** read the following judgment of the court: This is an appeal against the refusal of Mr Allan Heyman QC sitting as a deputy judge of the High Court in the Chancery Division to extend under s 101 of the Companies Act 1948 the time allowed by s 95 for registering a charge created by a company.

g   Under s 95 of the 1948 Act a company is required to register a charge within 21 days of its creation. Nothing turns on the wording of the section. It is sufficient to say that, unless duly registered, the charge will 'so far as any security on the company's property or undertaking is conferred thereby, be void against the liquidator and any creditor of the company'. In this context 'any creditor of the company' does not mean just any creditor, but only a creditor who has acquired a proprietary right to or an interest in the subject matter of the unregistered charge: see *Re Ehrmann Bros Ltd* [1906] 2 Ch 697.

h   Under s 96 the legal duty to register is imposed on the company. However, registration may be effected on the application of any person interested in the charge. If the company makes default, and registration is not effected at the instance of anyone else, the company and every officer implicated is liable to a fine.

Section 101, with which this appeal is concerned, contains machinery for remedying an omission to register and for remedying a faulty registration. It is in the following

j terms:

'The court, on being satisfied that the omission to register a charge within the time required by this Act or that the omission or mis-statement of any particular with respect to any such charge or in a memorandum of satisfaction was accidental, or due to inadvertence or to some other sufficient cause, or is not of a nature to prejudice the position of creditors or shareholders of the company, or that on other grounds it is just and equitable to grant relief, may, on the application of the company or any person interested, and on such terms and conditions as seem to the court just and expedient, order that the time for registration shall be extended, or, as the case may be, that the omission or mis-statement shall be rectified.'

It will be observed that the power of the court under s 101 arises in five cases, namely (1) if the omission or misstatement was accidental, or (2) if it was due to inadvertence, or (3) if it was due to some other sufficient cause, or (4) if it was not of a nature to prejudice the position of creditors or shareholders of the company, or (5) if on other grounds it is just and equitable to grant relief. If one of those conditions is satisfied, then the court has a discretion to order that the time for registration shall be extended, or that the omission or misstatement be recitified, in either case 'on such terms and conditions as seem to the court just and expedient'.

In the instant case the chargee is a company known as Ashpurton Estates Ltd (Ashpurton). The chargor is an industrial and provident society registered in Northern Ireland and known as Victoria Housing Estates Ltd (Victoria). The charge in question was not registered in due time. Victoria applied to the companies' registrar for an extension of time. The application was dismissed. Victoria moved before the deputy High Court judge to vary the registrar's order. The motion was dismissed. Hence this appeal.

We will summarise the facts from the affidavit evidence, which was supplemented before the deputy High Court judge and further supplemented before us.

The property charged consisted of some fifty dwellings at King's Lynn in Norfolk. The title to part was registered at the Land Registry. The land was bought by Ashpurton in April 1976. Part of the purchase price, almost £100,000, was advanced to Ashpurton by Victoria against the deposit of documents. The matter was handled on behalf of Victoria by Mr Tughan, then a member of a firm of Belfast solicitors and a director of Victoria. The matter was handled on behalf of Ashpurton by Messrs Macfarlanes, a firm of solicitors in the City of London.

Towards the end of 1977 Victoria turned its attention towards obtaining a legal charge. A letter was written to Messrs Macfarlanes by one of the directors of Ashpurton at the request of Mr Tughan asking them to 'make the necessary arrangements'. Messrs Macfarlanes prepared a form of legal charge and sent copies to Ashpurton and to Mr Tughan. Correspondence ensued, which proceeded on the basis that Messrs Macfarlanes would see the registration of the charge at the Land Registry. The charge was ultimately executed on 18 April 1978. The amount secured was just under £148,000. The final letter in this part of the correspondence is dated 20 April, and its penultimate sentence reads: 'We will now submit the Deed to the Land Registry for registration against that part of the title that is registered.' There was no mention of registration under s 95. The requirement for such registration was overlooked by both sides.

Registration of the charge against the title of the relevant properties took place on 19 May 1978. The entry in the register contained the note: 'This charge is subject to the provisions of section 95 of the Companies Act 1948'. The title deeds were left with Messrs Macfarlanes, the solicitors for the chargee Ashpurton, although perhaps a correct view would be that the solicitors held them to the order of Victoria as chargor.

In or about November 1978 Mr Tughan ceased regular practice as a solicitor and became chairman of Victoria.

It will be convenient to say a little about Ashpurton. The company was registered in England. Its registered office is in London. It was part of a group of companies headed by International Land Investments Ltd (ILI). Most, but not all, of the companies in the group were 100% subsidiaries or sub-subsidiaries of ILI. Drum Developments Ltd was a 100% subsidiary of ILI. Ulster Land Developments Ltd was a 100% subsidiary of Drum. Ashpurton was a 99% subsidiary of Ulster Land. The shares in ILI were owned by Mr Selwyn Midgen, Mr Michael Curran and Mr William Montgomery. The directors of ILI a were Mr Midgen, Mr Curran, Mr Montgomery and Mr Derek Hayes, a member of the firm of Messrs Macfarlanes. It appears from the correspondence that the directors of Ashpurton were Mr Selwyn Midgen, Mr Michael Curran and (in 1978) Mr Derek Hayes and Mr Dickson. The two latter left the board in or before 1980 and Mr Montgomery joined it.

ILI ceased to trade at the beginning of October 1980 and went into liquidation. Mr Tughan was so informed by a letter dated 7 November from Mr Midgen.

b At regular intervals down to the end of 1980 sales of the King's Lynn properties took place, thus reducing the amount outstanding on the mortgage. At some time during 1980 Messrs Travers Smith were instructed to negotiate the sale of the remaining properties to Anglia and General Developments Ltd, a company which was owned partly by companies in which Mr Tughan was involved and partly by ILI. The sale had been agreed in principle but Mr Tughan took the view that Mr Midgen was dragging his feet c and this precipitated the calling in of the loan.

In November 1980 Victoria consulted Messrs Travers Smith with regard to the money outstanding under the legal charge, then amounting to about £68,000. By a letter dated 20 November 1980 Messrs Travers Smith formally demanded repayment of the money due to Victoria. This was not forthcoming. On 6 January 1981 Victoria appointed a receiver and manager and sent the appropriate form to the Companies Registration d Office for filing. This was received by the office on 8 January, but it was seven weeks before the Companies Registration office replied. On 27 February the form was returned unfiled with an intimation that the legal charge had never been registered.

This was the first moment at which it was appreciated by those advising Victoria or by anyone else that the charge was unregistered.

Victoria then sought advice. The advice given was that two courses were open to e Victoria. One course was to apply under s 101 of the Companies Act 1948 to extend the time for registration. The other course was to proceed with sales of the properties. Quoting from the evidence of Mr Tughan: 'He [counsel] felt that, if an application to extend the time were made, it might alarm the company and precipitate a liquidation . . . Victoria chose, with that advice in mind, to follow the second course and sell the properties.'

f On 6 April 1981 Messrs Travers Smith, who also acted for Anglia, sent to Mr Midgen the engrossment of a contract for sale of the properties by Ashpurton to Anglia, and a form of transfer. However, negotiations still continued with regard to both price and purchaser, and these were still in progress down to 8 May.

On 6 May the board of Ashpurton decided that it was advisable to wind the company up voluntarily, and that they should seek the assistance of Messrs Touche, Ross & Co, the g accountants. On or about 15 May notice was given convening an extraordinary general meeting of Ashpurton for 23 June to consider a resolution to wind up, and notice was also sent out pursuant to s 293 convening a meeting of creditors for the same day. The latter notice was received by Victoria, or at any rate came to the knowledge of Mr Tughan, on 20 May. Thereupon, Mr Tughan wrote to Mr Midgen to the effect that he assumed it was intended to complete the sale by Ashpurton before 23 June, ie before the h commencement of liquidation.

On 4 June Victoria issued proceedings under s 101 to extend the time for registration of the charge. The application came before the registrar on 11 June, the evidence then being far less complete than now. The registrar expressed himself as unconvinced on the then state of the evidence that the omission to register the charge within due time was due to inadvertence; but his principal reason for rejecting the application was that it was j made at a time when Ashpurton was insolvent and its winding up was imminent. He relied on Re L H Charles & Co Ltd [1935] WN 15 and Re Resinoid and Mica Products Ltd (1967) [1982] 3 All ER 677, to which reference is made later.

At 3 pm on 12 June a notice of motion by Victoria to vary the registrar's order was served on Ashpurton's solicitors. At 3.30 pm on the same day a general meeting of Ashpurton was held at short notice, with the consent of the members, at which it was

resolved to wind up voluntarily. The validity of this resolution is not disputed: see *Re*
Centrebind Ltd [1966] 3 All ER 889, [1967] 1 WLR 377.   *a*

It is not in dispute that the ILI group is insolvent. Most of the constituent companies
are in liquidation. It is possible that one or more subsidiaries may be solvent, but any
such subsidiaries will need to be liquidated or the shareholding realised in order to
answer the indebtedness of the parent company.

The financial position of Ashpurton is as follows. The sum of £353,499 is due to ILI
and £69,000 to Victoria. Other debts are only £483 and £300. If Victoria's debt is   *b*
treated as unsecured, the assets are estimated to produce £66,553. On these figures, if
Victoria is allowed to register out of time, its debt will absorb all the assets and it will
recover about 96p in the pound. If, however, Victoria ranks pari passu with the other
creditors, it will receive a dividend of about 16p in the pound. The dividend may, in fact,
be less, because there are also four unquantified claims due from the group, which may
affect Ashpurton but cannot at present be allocated with certainty to particular members   *c*
of the group. As all inter-group credits would be wiped out in the course of the
liquidation of the constituent members of the group the ultimate beneficiaries, if Victoria
cannot register its charge and it has to rank as an unsecured creditor, will be the outside
creditors of ILI, of which by far the largest is Northern Bank Ltd, with a claim in excess
of £1m.

Victoria's motion to discharge the registrar's order came before the deputy High Court   *d*
judge on 23 June 1981 and was dismissed for reasons which we will explain later.

We turn now to a consideration of the authorities. The contents of ss 95 and 101 of
the Companies Act 1948 date back to the Companies Act 1900, which came into force
on 1 January 1901. The wording has not changed significantly. The first reported case of
an application to extend the time for registration was heard by Farwell J two months
later: see *Re Bootle Cold Storage and Ice Co* [1901] WN 54. It is of some interest to observe   *e*
that there was evidence (i) that the company was still carrying on business, (ii) that no
petition to wind up had been presented, (iii) that no notice of a meeting to resolve on a
winding up had been given, and (iv) that no creditor had recovered judgment against the
company. On that evidence the order sought was made without any qualification.

The next reported case is *Re Joplin Brewery Co Ltd* [1902] 1 Ch 79, decided by Buckley J
eight months later. Ever since that case it has been the practice to insert in an order   *f*
extending the time for registration some such words as: 'but that this order be without
prejudice to the rights of parties acquired prior to the time when the debentures shall be
actually registered.' The reason for the proviso is as valid today as it was then. Such an
application would be made either ex parte by the chargor company, which had the
statutory duty to register, or by the chargee, in which case the company would be joined
as the only respondent, if there were any respondent at all. It was not the practice to   *g*
advertise for creditors and to make one of them a respondent. Consequently, it was
necessary to protect persons whose rights would otherwise be overridden in their absence.
See also *Re Mendip Press Ltd* (1901) 18 TLR 38, decided by the same judge a few days after
the *Joplin* case.

It soon became established that, so long as the company was a going concern at the
date of registration, the proviso did not protect, and was not intended to protect, an   *h*
unsecured creditor who had lent money at a time when the charge should have been but
was not registered: see *Re Ehrmann Bros Ltd* [1906] 2 Ch 697 and *Re Cardiff Workmen's*
Cottage Co Ltd [1906] 2 Ch 627. The reason for this was that such unsecured creditor
could not have intervened to prevent payment being made to the lender whose charge
was not registered (whom we will call 'the unregistered chargee'). Nor could such
unsecured creditor have prevented the creation of a new charge, duly registered, to take   *j*
the place of the unregistered charge. The proviso was intended to protect only rights
acquired against, or affecting, the property comprised in the unregistered charge, in the
intervening period between the date of the creation of the unregistered charge and the
registration of such charge. Such persons would include a subsequent chargee of the
relevant property, a creditor who has levied execution against the relevant property, and

an unsecured creditor if, but only if, the company has gone into liquidation before
a registration is effected. Once the company has gone into liquidation, the existing
unsecured creditors are interested in all the assets of the company, since the liquidator is
bound by statute to distribute the net proceeds pari passu among the unsecured creditors,
subject to preferential debts. The assets of the company are at that stage vested in the
company for the benefit of its creditors. The unsecured creditors are in the nature of
cestuis que trust with beneficial interests extending to all the company's property.

b It follows from this approach that the court must invariably refuse to extend the time
for registration once the company has gone into liquidation. If an order extending time
were made and the proviso included, registration would be of no assistance whatever to
the unregistered chargee because the unsecured creditors at that stage would be protected
by the proviso. Such an order after liquidation would be futile and will be refused: see
Re Spiral Globe Ltd [1902] 1 Ch 396, where the order was made, though presumably
c useless to the unregistered chargee; *Re S Abrahams & Sons* [1902] 1 Ch 695, where the
order was refused because it would be useless; *Re Anglo-Oriental Carpet Manufacturing Co*
[1903] 1 Ch 914, which was concerned with the construction of the proviso, but it
illustrates the principle; and the *Ehrmann* case where this court approved *Anglo-Oriental*.

The position accordingly became firmly established that the court (i) invariably adds
to an order extending time the proviso which we have mentioned and (ii) will not make
d an order once liquidation has supervened, because the effect of the proviso would be to
render the order futile. This is a matter of discretion and not of law. It is possible to
imagine a case, for example where fraud is involved, in which the court might extend
the time for registration after the commencement of liquidation and omit the proviso
which would render the order futile; we do not know of such a case in practice, and
certainly the instant case does not fall into the category of fraud.

e At the dates when Victoria's summons was issued (4 June) and heard by the registrar
(11 June) notices to convene a meeting of the company to resolve on liquidation had been
sent out (about 15 May) but the meeting had not been held. In those circumstance we
think that one ought first to consider whether the registrar was correct in dismissing the
summons on the ground that winding up was imminent. On this aspect of the case we
venture to make the following observations.

f (1) The *Spiral Globe* and *Abrahams* cases are not directly in point. In those cases the
applications to the court were made and heard after the commencement of the winding
up.

(2) In the *Anglo-Oriental Carpet* case, which we have already mentioned, the company
was insolvent and the dates were as follows: on 11 October notice was given to convene
meeting of shareholders to be held on 21 October (adjourned to 11 November); on a
g subsequent date in October the application to extend time was made; on 1 November
the time was extended by Joyce J to 15 November, subject to the usual proviso; on 11
November resolution passed to wind up; on 15 November registration was made. It is
apparent from this summary that Joyce J extended the time for registration with the
usual proviso, although a meeting to resolve on liquidation had already been convened.
The matter subsequently came before Buckley J on the construction of the proviso. There
h was, however, no suggestion that the order of Joyce J was wrong. The implication is that,
if the unregistered chargee had registered his charge within ten days of the order of
Joyce J, he would have succeeded in protecting his charge.

(3) In *Re MIG Trust Ltd* [1933] Ch 542 the facts were as follows. The charge was
created on 6 May 1930 but was not registered. By the end of 1930 the company had a
deficiency of about £196,000 and its financial position was described as irredeemable.
j On 4 March 1931 the chargee served notice on the company of an application to extend
the time for registration. The application was heard on 6 March, but was adjourned to
10 March for evidence. On 7 March the company decided that it would withdraw its
instructions to its solicitors to oppose the application and that it would not appear on the
hearing of the motion. The usual order for extension was made on 10 March and the
charge was registered on the same day. On 18 March a petition was presented for winding

up, and on 31 March a compulsory order was made. The point at issue was whether the
company had fraudulently preferred the chargee by suffering the order to be made. Lord
Hanworth MR, however, considered a submission that Maugham J would have made
the order even if he had known the true facts. Lord Hanworth MR's conclusion was (at
559): 'I find it very difficult to say whether Maugham J. would have acted otherwise if
there had been the fullest presentation of the facts relating to the M.I.G. Trust by someone
appearing on its behalf . . .' On the other hand, Romer LJ was emphatic that Maugham J
would have made the order. He said (at 569–572):

> 'It was said by Mr. Tucker [for the respondent liquidator] that if the facts disclosed
> in the brief originally delivered to counsel on behalf of the company, but
> subsequently withdrawn, had been disclosed to Maugham J. he, in the interests of
> the unsecured creditors, would either have refused to make any order at all
> extending the time, or would have inserted words protecting the interests of the
> unsecured creditors, or would have adjourned the matter in order to consult their
> wishes, or might have made an order subject to the consent of all the unsecured
> creditors being obtained. In my opinion he would have done nothing of the kind.
> It is not the practice of the Court, when making orders under s. 85 of the Companies
> Act, 1929, any more than it was the practice of the Court when making orders
> under the sections of the earlier Acts corresponding to s. 85, to insert words
> protecting the interests of unsecured creditors . . . But, said Mr. Tucker, if that is so,
> and if the Court is not going to protect unsecured creditors, why is it that the Court
> always insists on being furnished with evidence to the effect that there has been no
> judgment obtained against a company, that no resolution has been passed or even
> notice sent out convening a meeting of the company to pass a resolution to wind
> up? It is a perfectly pertinent observation, but the answer is this: the Court, as far as
> I know, does not do it. I do not know of any case in which the Court has insisted
> upon having evidence of that kind. It is perfectly true that in practice such evidence
> is nearly always furnished to the Court when application is made under s. 85, but I
> think the reason for that is to be found by reference to *In re Bootle Cold Storage and
> Ice Co.* ([1901] WN 54), which is, as Mr. Tucker tells us, the first reported case of any
> extension made under s. 15 of the Act of 1900. In looking at this report I find a
> statement that, in addition to other relevant facts, "evidence was given that the
> company was still carrying on business, and that no petition to wind up the company
> had been presented, nor had notice of a meeting to pass a resolution to wind up the
> same been given, nor had any creditor recovered judgment against the company."
> Counsel in that case, however, stated to the Court that in the parallel case of an
> application to extend the time for registering a bill of sale under s. 14 of the Bills of
> Sale Act, 1878, it was necessary to show that the grantor was not bankrupt, and that
> no creditor had levied execution on the goods, and that was perfectly true; but the
> affidavit in support set out a good deal more than what was required when an
> application was made under s. 14 of the Bills of Sale Act, 1878. Now Farwell J. said:
> "I think the facts proved bring the case within s. 15 and I therefore extend the time."
> The result of that of course was that any one who made an application under the
> section after that note appeared in the Weekly Notes, if he knew his business, would
> put into his affidavit evidence similar to that in the case before Farwell J., and I
> think in that way the practice has sprung up and is still continuing of putting in
> statements which to my mind are wholly irrelevant; that is to say, statements which
> do not indicate that there is anybody who has obtained any interest in the property
> of the company, but statements dealing with the position of the company so far as
> regards its unsecured creditors.'

Lawrence LJ, the third member of the court, did not deal with the point.

(4) In *Re L H Charles & Co Ltd* [1935] WN 15 the dates, so far as ascertainable, were as
follows: 9 November, notice to convene meeting for 19 November to resolve on
liquidation; 16 November, motion to extend time came before Clauson J, who said:

a
'. . . where liquidation was, as in the present case, in contemplation, the order extending the time for registration ought to be in such a form as to give the liquidator when appointed an opportunity of challenging the right of the applicant to an order extending the time. There would, in the circumstances, be an order extending the time for registering the charge; but, having regard to the evident intention of the company to convene a meeting to consider a resolution to wind up the company, it became necessary to consider what terms and conditions ought to

b
be inserted in the order. It was clear that, if the motion were to be deferred, any order made after the appointment of a liquidator would be useless to the applicant.'

The judge then extended the time for registration until 7 December, but he required the chargee to give an undertaking that, in case a resolution to wind up should become effective on or before 16 December, and in case the liquidator should within 21 days

c
apply to the court to discharge the order which he thereby made, then the chargee would submit to the jurisdiction of the court and would abide by any order that the court might make for the rectification of the register by the removal of any registration effect under the order. On 19 November the resolution to wind up was passed, and on 7 December the liquidator moved on behalf of the company to discharge the order. His motion was, however, dismissed. We find it difficult in the circumstances to cull much wisdom from

d
the report of this case. The bare fact is that an order was made, and stood, despite the imminence of liquidation.

(5) In *Re Kris Cruisers Ltd* [1948] 2 All ER 1105, [1949] Ch 138 the company was held by the judge to be 'very far from solvent' at the time when the application to extend time was made, but no petition had been presented and no notices had been sent out to convene a meeting to resolve on liquidation. Vaisey J, before whom the application to

e
extend time was made, was referred to both the *MIG* case and the *L H Charles* case. *Re L H Charles & Co Ltd* he regarded as exceptional and not to be followed except 'possibly' in a case 'where the facts are precisely identical'. He proposed to 'accept as accurate, and to follow, the observations made in [the *MIG* case] by Romer L.J.' He decided that there should be the usual order.

(6) Judicial views, therefore, down to this date on the relevance of solvency, provided

f
there was no actual liquidation at the date of the proposed order, were divided. In the *Anglo-Oriental Carpet* case, Joyce J extended time, notwithstanding that the company was insolvent and that a meeting of the company to resolve on liquidation had already been convened. In the *MIG* case Romer LJ expressed a strong view that, given no actual liquidation, insolvency was irrelevant. Clauson J in *Re L H Charles & Co Ltd* clearly regarded insolvency as relevant, but the case does not seem to have been pressed to a

g
logical conclusion. In *Re Kris Cruisers Ltd* Vaisey J rejected this view. Two schools of thought had emerged. One view was that, if the facts merited a favourable exercise of the court's discretion, the imminence of liquidation was irrelevant. The order would be made, with the usual proviso, unless the company were actually in liquidation, in which case the order, with the usual proviso, would be futile and would, therefore, not be made. The other view, represented at that time only by *Re L H Charles & Co Ltd* but possibly foreshadowed by the remarks of Buckley J in *Re Cardiff Workmen's Cottage Co Ltd* [1906]

h
2 Ch 627 at 630, was that the court might, in the exercise of its discretion, think it proper to protect the inchoate rights of the unsecured creditors if the emergence of such rights, by process of liquidation, were sufficiently imminent.

(7) Against this background of authority the decision of this court in *Re Resinoid and Mica Products Ltd* (1967) [1982] 3 All ER 677 now falls to be considered. The facts were as follows. The charge was created in 1965. It was not registered. In October 1966 the

j
company convened a meeting with a view to a creditors' voluntary liquidation. It was convened for 27 October. After receipt of this notice, the unregistered chargee applied to extend time. The application came before the registrar on 26 October. He refused it. The company went into voluntary liquidation on 27 October. The matter came before Plowman J. He declined to vary the registrar's order. An appeal was made to this court

and was unanimously dismissed. Lord Denning MR based his decision on two grounds. First, adopting a point made by Russell LJ in argument (at 679):

> '. . . it was too late now to extend the time for registration, for the simple reason that the winding up commenced on 27 October 1966 . . . I do not think it is permissible to extend the time for registration after the winding up has commenced.'

Second:

> 'As long ago as 1935 Clauson J said in *Re L H Charles & Co Ltd* [1935] WN 15 that, before extending the time, his practice was to require evidence that the company was solvent and no winding up of the company was impending. No such evidence could be adduced here . . . The application for extension was only made when the winding up was imminent. That is far too late.'

Lord Denning MR added: 'I think the registrar was amply justified in this discretion in refusing the application to extend the time.' Lord Denning MR, therefore, considered that the appeal should be dismissed on two separate and distinct grounds: (i) the imminence of winding up when the chargee applied to the registrar, and (ii) the fact of winding up by the time the matter came before the judge or (perhaps) the fact of winding up by the time the matter came before the Court of Appeal; it matters not which.

Davies LJ (at 679) expressed himself as in agreement with 'the view taken by the registrar and the judge'. The registrar's view cannot have been based on the fact of winding up, because the company was not then in liquidation. He can only have based his view on the imminence of liquidation. Russell LJ based himself only on the fact of winding up. This analysis of the decision in the *Resinoid* case shows that two members of the Court of Appeal regarded the imminence of liquidation, as distinct from the fact of liquidation, as a proper discretionary ground for refusing an extension of time, thus disagreeing with the observations of Romer LJ, obiter, in the *MIG* case and the view of Vaisey J in the *Kris Cruisers* case. In effect, they upheld the decision of the registrar. It is not possible to tell from the information before us, and it is not essential to know, whether Plowman J declined to vary the registrar's order because liquidation was imminent at the date of the registrar's hearing or because liquidation was a fact at the date of the judge's hearing. The important point is that Davies LJ agreed with the registrar, and the registrar's decision must have been based only on the imminence of the liquidation.

The similarity of the facts in the *Resinoid* case and the instant case are striking. In both cases the company was free of liquidation at the date of the application to extend time, and at the date of the unsuccessful hearing before the registrar. In both cases the company was in liquidation when the application came before the judge on appeal from the registrar. In both cases liquidation was imminent at the date of the application to the registrar. Lord Denning MR and Russell LJ decided that the fact of liquidation before the application reached the High Court or the Court of Appeal (it matters not which) precluded an extension of time for registration (as a matter of discretion). Lord Denning MR and Davies LJ accepted the view that the registrar could properly refuse an extension of time in a case where winding up was imminent.

The latter approach is also one which was adopted by the Supreme Court of South Australia in *Re Flinders Trading Co Pty Ltd* (1978) 3 ACLR 218, to which we were referred in argument. The facts were as follows. The charge was created on 25 October 1976. The application to register was a few days out of time under legislation comparable to that of our own. On 10 February 1977 the company applied ex parte for an extension of time. The application, after adjournments, came on for final hearing before the master on 29 March. By that time the winding up of the company was known to be a distinct possibility and was, in fact, inevitable. The master on 29 March provisionally extended the time for registration until 19 April, but gave the unsecured creditors a five-week period within which to lodge objections. The charge was lodged for registration on 29 March. On 13 April a winding-up petition was presented. On 6 May the master made

his final order, except that it was to be without prejudice to the rights of two of the
a unsecured creditors. On 9 May a winding-up order was made. The liquidator and the
other unsecured creditors appealed the master's order. Sangster J discharged the master's
order and an appeal from him was dismissed by a majority decision. The view of the
majority can be summarised by quoting the following from the judgment of Walters J
(at 235):

b   '. . . if at the date of the hearing of the application for enlargement of time for
      registration of a charge, there is insufficient evidence of the company's solvency, or
      if it be made to appear that the company is unable to pay its debts as they fall due
      and that a winding up order is imminent and inescapable, the Court ought not, in
      the exercise of the discretion conferred by s 106 of the Act, to extend the time for
      registration of the charge.'

c   The view of the minority (at 223) was:

      'No decision has gone so far as to hold that the order should be refused because of
      the insolvency or the imminent insolvency of the company when there is no
      suggestion that anyone has yet acquired any proprietary right in relation to the
      assets covered by the charge which would be adversely affected by the registration.
      We are asked to do that for the first time. I have come to the conclusion that we
d   ought not to take this step. To do so, it seems to me, would be contrary to the spirit
      of the section and to the former practice of the courts, both here and in England.'

We have dealt with the authorities at some length, because it was submitted in
argument that the decision of this court in the *Resinoid* case was in substantial conflict
with prior authority. We do not think that is so. The only prior inconsistent authorities,
e apart from the obiter dicta of one Lord Justice in the *MIG* case, were the unreported
decision of Joyce J in *Anglo-Oriental* and the decision of Vaisey J in *Kris Cruisers*. We do
not regard the *Resinoid* case as inconsistent with *Re I C Johnson & Co Ltd* [1902] 2 Ch 101.
The *Johnson* case was a very special case where there was an actual contract for parity of
security between the chargees seeking registration and the only other creditors affected
by registration.
f   So much for the position when the matter came before the registrar. By the time the
application came before the deputy High Court judge, Ashpurton was already in
liquidation. The judge's view can be summarised as follows. As a matter of discretion
the court will not make an order extending the time for registration once a winding up
has supervened, save in very exceptional circumstances. Victoria deliberately elected not
to seek registration out of time when the mistake was discovered, believing that course
g to be in its interests. The court ought not to exercise its discretion in favour of Victoria
when subsequently Victoria decides that the opposite course is for its benefit.
      Counsel for Victoria argued before us that s 101 does not itself impose any restrictions
on the exercise of the court's discretion, and that the proviso to the order, which protects
unsecured creditors once liquidation has supervened, was a fetter introduced by imperfect
analogy with the Bills of Sale Act 1878, without argument (the application in *Re Joplin*
h *Brewery Co Ltd* [1902] 1 Ch 79 being ex parte) and without adequate thought. In our
opinion this submission, even if it has merit, is 80 years too late. We have not been given
any reason to doubt that the proviso, in one form or another, has been inserted in every
order made under s 101 and its predecessors since 1901. The only exception of which we
are aware is *Re Bootle Cold Storage and Ice Co* [1901] WN 54 decided a few months before
the *Joplin* case. The latter case set the pattern for the future.
j   Counsel for Victoria sought to rely on the fact that the application by Victoria was
initiated (4 June) before the winding-up resolution was passed (12 June). But this was
also the position in the *Resinoid* case.
      He also submitted that the *Resinoid* case was inconsistent with the *MIG* case, which
may or may not have been cited in argument. We have already given our reasons for
rejecting this submission.
      Counsel for Victoria further submitted that in *Re I C Johnson & Co Ltd* this court

interfered with vested rights. We agree. It interfered with the vested rights of the pre-Act debenture holders by allowing the post-Act debenture holders to rank pari passu with them, thus diluting the security of the pre-Act debenture holders. There is, however, an important distinction between that and the instant case, namely the existence of a contract between the two descriptions of creditors in the *Johnson* case that they should rank pari passu. The order of this court gave proper effect to that bargain.

In *Re S Abrahams & Sons* [1902] 1 Ch 695 at 700 Buckley J implied that there might be very exceptional cases in which an order to extend the time for registration would not be qualified by the proviso introduced in the *Joplin* case, with the result that, if a winding up had commenced, registration might properly have the effect of interfering with the vested rights of unsecured creditors. Counsel for Victoria submitted that there were special circumstances in the present case. He relied on the following factors.

(1) He submitted that Victoria should not be prejudiced, as he put it, because matters went wrong before the registrar on 11 June, at which time the company was not in liquidation. We would wish to reserve for later consideration what the position might be if (i) the registrar refused an extension of time without any justification at a time when liquidation was not a foreseeable event, but (ii) subsequently the company's fortunes went into reverse so that liquidation supervened before an appeal inevitably succeeded. That is not this case. In our opinion, the dismissal of the application by the registrar was amply justified on the two grounds which he took: first, the paucity of the evidence before him, consisting only of hearsay evidence from a member of the firm of Messrs Travers Smith, Braithwaite & Co (Mr Tughan swore no affidavit until 16 June 1981, by which time the company was already in liquidation); and, second, because the liquidation of Ashpurton was imminent (on this aspect, the registrar followed the guidelines accepted by the majority in the *Resinoid* case).

(2) The second matter on which counsel for Victoria relied is that Victoria would have been in front of the judge before 23 June, the day for which the meeting of shareholders was originally convened. Ashpurton deliberately blocked Victoria by bringing forward the date of the meeting and thus confronting Victoria with a fait accompli. All this is true, but Ashpurton was doing no more than exercising its statutory rights. Counsel for Victoria submitted that the members of Ashpurton thereby impeded Victoria's attempt to remedy Ashpurton's breach of statutory duty and thus perpetuated the wrongdoing. We do not accept this submission, because the mischief occasioned by non-registration is not worsened by the passage of time once liquidation supervenes. People do not lend money on the strength of the credit of a company which has gone into liquidation.

(3) Ashpurton has only one known unsecured creditor of substance, namely ILI, which had knowledge of the charge at all material times and was run by Mr Midgen, as was Ashpurton. But knowledge is irrelevant: see *Re Monolithic Building Co* [1915] 1 Ch 643, [1914–15] All ER Rep 249. In the end it is not ILI which has to be considered, but the outside creditors of ILI, who are the only persons ultimately interested in ILI.

(4) No unsecured creditor was prejudiced by the non-registration of Victoria's charge. That is correct, but irrelevant in the circumstances of this case.

In our judgment none of the factors submitted by counsel for Victoria are so special as to justify the making of an order without the usual proviso once liquidation has commenced.

We think it is important to emphasise that the *Resinoid* case decided two things, and both aspects of the decision are binding on us: first, that the imminence of liquidation is a relevant factor (per Lord Denning MR and Davies LJ); and, second, that an order extending time will not normally be made after a company has gone into liquidation (per Lord Denning MR and Russell LJ). Each of the decisions is authoritative. We should add that the judgments of Lord Denning MR and Russell LJ on the second point ought not in our opinion to be read as laying down an absolute rule that an exceptional case could not exist where it was justifiable to extend the time for registration after the commencement of winding up, eg where fraud exists.

To sum the matter up, in our judgment the registrar was entitled to exercise his discretion against Victoria on 11 June on the ground of the inadequacy of the evidence a and the imminence of liquidation. As we have already said, the majority of this court in the *Resinoid* case decided that the imminence of liquidation is a relevant factor. When the matter came before the deputy High Court judge on further evidence, he was entitled to exercise his own discretion, and (i) to take into account, as decisive against Victoria, the then fact of the liquidation, (ii) to reject the submission that exceptional circumstances existed which entitled him to give Victoria priority notwithstanding the liquidation and (iii) to take into account, as equally decisive against Victoria, the fact that Victoria

b deliberately chose not to apply for an extension of time when the mistake of non-registration was first discovered.

On this last point, we think that, when an unregistered chargee discovers his mistake, he should apply without delay for an extension of time if he desires to register; and the court, when asked to exercise its discretion, should look askance at a chargee who deliberately defers his application in order to see which way the wind is going to blow.

c In conclusion, we should like to express out gratitude to both counsel for Victoria for the carefully reasoned reply which they submitted in writing after this court was compelled to adjourn before their argument was concluded. We found their submissions of great assistance in writing our judgment. We have not commented on every point made, but we would not like it to be supposed that any point has not been considered.

For the reasons we have indicated we dismiss this appeal.

d *Appeal dismissed. Leave to appeal to the House of Lords refused.*

Solicitors: *Travers Smith, Braithwaite & Co* (for Victoria); *William F Prior & Co* (for Ashpurton).

e   Mary Rose Plummer   Barrister.

Note

f # Re Resinoid and Mica Products Ltd

COURT OF APPEAL, CIVIL DIVISION
LORD DENNING MR, DAVIES AND RUSSELL LJJ
3 MAY 1967

g *Company – Charge – Registration – Extension of time – Matters to be considered – Imminence of liquidation when application for extension of time before registrar – Company in liquidation when matter before judge – Whether registrar and judge right to refuse extension of time – Whether imminence of liquidation relevant – Companies Act 1948, s 101.*

In 1965 a company (Bradleys) sold a factory to another company (Resinoid) for £5,000,

h £2,000 of which was left outstanding on mortgage repayable over two years by six-monthly instalments. On 1 February 1965 Resinoid gave Bradleys a legal charge over the property to secure the amount. The charge was not registered within 21 days as required by s 95[a] of the Companies Act 1948. The first instalment was paid but the subsequent

---

a   Section 95(1) provides: 'Subject to the provisions of this Part of this Act, every charge created after
j   the fixed date by a company registered in England and being a charge to which this section applies
        shall, so far as any security on the company's property or undertaking is conferred thereby, be void
        against the liquidator and any creditor of the company, unless the prescribed particulars of the
        charge together with the instrument, if any, by which the charge is created or evidenced, are
        delivered to or received by the registrar of companies for registration in manner required by this
        Act within twenty-one days after the date of its creation, but without prejudice to any contract or
        obligation for repayment of the money thereby secured, and when a charge becomes void under
        this section the money secured thereby shall immediately become payable.'

instalments were not. On 6 October 1966 Resinoid issued a notice convening a meeting
of creditors with a view to a creditors' voluntary winding up. On 25 October, after *a*
receiving that notice, Bradleys applied to the court under s 101[b] of the 1948 Act to extend
the time for registering the charge on the ground that the omission to do so was due to
inadvertence. On 26 October the registrar refused the application. On 27 October
Resinoid went into voluntary liquidation. An appeal by Bradleys to the judge against the
refusal of the registrar to extend the time was dismissed. Bradleys appealed.

b

Held – The appeal would be dismissed for the following reasons—
(1) (Per Lord Denning MR and Russell LJ) The court ought not to extend time for
registering a charge over property of a company under s 101 of the 1948 Act after the
company had gone into liquidation because the rights of all parties were determined at
that date and those rights should not be prejudicially affected by subsequent registration
of a charge. It followed therefore that the registrar and the judge had been right to refuse *c*
the application (see p 679 *f* to *j* and p 680 *c d*, post).
(2) Furthermore (per Lord Denning MR and Davies LJ) even if an extension was
permissible by reason of the fact that Resinoid was free of liquidation at the date of the
application to extend the time and at the date of the hearing before the registrar, the
registrar was justified in exercising his discretion in refusing to grant the extension
because the application was only made when the winding up of Resinoid was imminent *d*
(see p 679 *g* to *j*, post); *Re L H Charles & Co Ltd* [1935] WN 15 considered.

Notes
For extending time for registration of charges, see 7 Halsbury's Laws (4th edn) paras 875–
876, and for cases on the subject, see 10 Digest (Reissue) 868–871, 4995–5021.
For the Companies Act 1948, ss 95, 101, see 5 Halsbury's Statutes (3rd edn) 189, 194. *e*
As from 22 December 1981 s 95(1) of the 1948 Act was substituted by s 106(1) of the
Companies Act 1981.

Case referred to in judgments
Charles (L H) & Co Ltd, Re [1935] WN 15, 10 Digest (Reissue) 870, 5017.

f

Interlocutory appeal
Bradley & Son Ltd (Bradleys) appealed against the decision of Plowman J on 15 November
1966 dismissing an appeal by Bradleys against the order of Mr Registrar Berkeley made
on 26 October 1966 whereby he dismissed Bradleys application for extension of time
under s 101 of the Companies Act 1948 for the registration of a legal charge created by
Resinoid and Mica Products Ltd (Resinoid) over factory premises which Bradleys had *g*
sold to Resinoid. The facts are set out in the judgment of Lord Denning MR.

P M Mottershead for Bradleys.
Martin Jacomb for Resinoid and the liquidator.

LORD DENNING MR. In 1965 Bradley & Son Ltd (Bradleys) sold a factory to *h*
Resinoid and Mica Products Ltd (Resinoid) for £5,000 but only £3,000 was paid in cash.
The balance of £2,000 was left outstanding on mortgage payable by £500 every six

---

b   Section 101 provides: 'The court, on being satisfied that the omission to register a charge within
the time required by this Act or that the omission or mis-statement of any particular with respect
to any such charge or in a memorandum of satisfaction was accidental, or due to inadvertence or *j*
to some other sufficient cause, or is not of a nature to prejudice the position of creditors or
shareholders of the company, or that on other grounds it is just and equitable to grant relief, may,
on the application of the company or any person interested, and on such terms and conditions as
seem to the court just and expedient, order that the time for registration shall be extended, or, as
the case may be, that the omission or mis-statement shall be rectified.'

months over two years with interest. On 1 February 1965 Resinoid gave Bradleys a legal
a charge over the property to secure the amount. It was necessary that particulars of that
legal charge should be registered within 21 days else it would be void: see ss 95 and 96 of
the Companies Act 1948. It was not registered within 21 days. It was the duty of the
company, Resinoid, to register it. But it did not do it. It was open to the mortgagees,
Bradleys, themselves to do it. They did not do it either. It seems that the solicitors on
each side left it to the other to do it and neither did it. So by inadvertence the charge was
b not registered within the 21 days. The result is that the charge is void, unless the time is
extended by the court under s 101 of the 1948 Act. That section gives the court power,
on being satisfied that the omission to register is due to inadvertence, to extend the time
'on such terms and conditions as seem to the court just and expedient'.

So this charge ought to have been registered by 22 February. Months and months
passed. It was not registered. The first instalment of £500 was paid; but the subsequent
c instalments were not paid. Still the charge was not registered. Twenty months passed.
Then in October 1966, Resinoid found itself in a parlous condition. On 6 October
Resinoid issued a notice convening a meeting of creditors with a view to a creditors'
voluntary winding up. The meeting was to be held on 27 October 1966. When the
mortgagees received this notice, they woke up. They realised that they ought to register
this charge. They hurriedly took out an application to extend the time. On 25 October
d they made their application to extend the time. They got leave to serve it on short notice
returnable on 26 October. On 26 October the application came before Mr Registrar
Berkeley. That was one day before the meeting. Mr Registrar Berkeley refused to extend
the time. The very next day, 27 October, the meeting of the creditors was held. A
resolution for voluntary winding up was passed, a liquidator was appointed and the
winding up commenced, all on that day with no charge having been registered. Bradleys
e appealed to Plowman J. He refused to extend the time. Now Bradleys appeal to this
court.

In the course of the argument Russell LJ suggested that it was too late now to extend
the time for registration, for the simple reason that the winding up commenced on 27
October 1966. The rights of all parties are to be determined as at that date. The rights
could not, and should not, be prejudicially affected by subsequent registration of a charge.
f In cases where time is extended before the winding up has commenced, it is the invariable
practice of the court to insert words saving the rights of parties acquired prior to the time
when registration is in fact made. If registration were allowed after the winding up has
commenced, it would affect the rights of parties accrued beforehand. That cannot be
allowed. I do not think it is permissible to extend the time for registration after the
winding up has commenced.

g But, apart from that point, even if extensions were permissible, it seems to me that it
should not be granted here. As long ago as 1935 Clauson J said in Re L H Charles & Co Ltd
[1935] WN 15 that, before extending the time, his practice was to require evidence that
the company was solvent and no winding up of the company was impending. No such
evidence could be adduced here. There was a period from February 1965 to October
1966, that is 20 months, when nothing was done. The application for extension was only
h made when the winding up was imminent. That is far too late.

I think the registrar was amply justified in his discretion in refusing the application to
extend the time. I agree with the judge. I would dismiss this appeal.

DAVIES LJ. I agree with the view taken by the registrar and the judge and have
nothing to add.

j **RUSSELL LJ.** I agree. It has always I think been the practice under s 101 to make sure
that the order extending the time for registration of the charge does not have the effect
of postponing to that charge rights in respect of the property of the company which have
been acquired prior to the time when registration is actually effected pursuant to the
extension order. Moreover, on the commencement of the winding up all creditors of the

company acquired rights in respect of the company's property. On these points I refer to the notes to s 101 in *Buckley on the Companies Acts* (13th edn, 1957) pp 236–237 and the authorities there referred to.

Here the winding up commenced on 27 October 1966 and a reservation in the usual form in the order would wholly stultify any extension of time. The suggested minutes of order seek to avoid this by saving not rights acquired before registration but rights acquired before the winding up date. It was argued by counsel for Bradleys that the registrar should have extended the time at the hearing on 26 October when the ordinary form of saving clause in the order would have had the effect of the order now suggested, assuming registration on 26 October. In those circumstances it is said that the court should accept the suggested order as containing terms and conditions that are just and expedient, although it would in fact displace pro tanto rights already acquired by all the creditors of the company in respect of the company's property. Even if it were correct to say that the registrar ought to have made the order on 26 October, the second part of the proposition cannot in my judgment follow. The fact is that the court will never in my view consider it just and expedient to make an order that will have the effect of postponing to the charge in question previously acquired rights in the property of the company. I am content to rest my support for the dismissal of this appeal on that one point, but I must not be taken to be saying or thinking that either the registrar or the judge were wrong in the order they made on the other point that has been argued by counsel for Bradleys.

Appeal dismissed.

Solicitors: *Field, Roscoe & Co*, agents for *Brain & Brain*, Reading (for Bradleys); *Cameron, Kemm, Nordon & Co* (for Resinoid and the liquidator).

Mary Rose Plummer　Barrister.

O'Reilly v Mackman and others and other cases

QUEEN'S BENCH DIVISION
PETER PAIN J
25 FEBRUARY, 5 MARCH 1982

COURT OF APPEAL, CIVIL DIVISION
LORD DENNING MR, ACKNER AND O'CONNOR LJJ
6, 7, 20 APRIL, 30 JUNE 1982

Judicial review – Declaration – Circumvention of procedure for application for judicial review – Action for declaration circumventing procedure for judicial review – Plaintiffs found guilty of disciplinary offences and penalties imposed by board of prison visitors – Plaintiffs commencing action by writ and originating summons for declaration that board's findings and awards null and void by reason of breach of natural justice – Application by board to strike out actions as abuse of court's process – Whether judicial review the only remedy to impugn adjudications by prison visitors – Supreme Court Act 1981, s 31 – RSC Ord 53.

While serving sentences in prison for serious crimes four prisoners took part in riots at the prison. All four were charged with offences against prison discipline contrary to the Prison Rules 1964. In each case the board of prison visitors held an inquiry into the charges and in each case found the charges proved and imposed penalties, including loss

of remission of sentence. Each prisoner began proceedings against the board of visitors
a by way of an action commenced by writ or originating summons seeking declarations
that the board's findings and awards of penalties were null and void by reason of alleged
breaches of natural justice. The board of visitors applied to have the proceedings struck
out as an abuse of the process of the court on the ground that an adjudication of a board
of prison visitors could be challenged only by judicial review under RSC Ord 53*ᵃ* and not
by writ or originating summons seeking declaratory relief. The prisoners chose to seek
b relief by actions rather than by applications for judicial review because in three of the
cases their delay in seeking relief meant that there was little chance that leave to apply
for judicial review would be granted under Ord 53, and because in each case there was
likely to be a substantial dispute on the facts and in proceedings for judicial review
evidence was usually on affidavit without cross-examination of the deponents whereas in
the actions there would be oral evidence and cross-examination as a matter of course.
c The judge refused to strike out the proceedings as an abuse of process, and the board of
visitors appealed.

Held – Having regard to the constitution of a board of prison visitors, to the rules of
procedure before it, and to the severity of offences with which it dealt, proceedings before
a board of prison visitors were not administrative proceedings but judicial proceedings
of the same character as those before a magistrates' court, and, by analogy with the
d protection against actions afforded to magistrates as a matter of public policy, no action
lay against a board of prison visitors for declaratory relief in respect of its adjudication.
Furthermore, because prior to the coming into force of RSC Ord 53 in 1977 the only
remedy available to a prisoner aggrieved by a decision of the board was to apply for an
order of certiorari to quash the board's decision, it followed that after 1977 the only
method of challenging a decision of a board of prison visitors was to apply for judicial
e relief by way of certiorari under Ord 53. Moreover (per O'Connor LJ), that was the only
appropriate remedy because wider relief was available under Ord 53 than in an action for
declaratory relief. Accordingly, the prisoners' proceedings would be struck out as an
abuse of the court's process, and the board's appeal would be allowed (see p 690 *c* to *j*,
p 691 *c* to *e*, p 692 *e f*, p 695 *c* to *e*, p 696 *a b f*, p 698 *g h*, p 699 *c* to *e*, p 701 *a e f h j* and
p 702 *a*, post).
f Dictum of Lord Goddard in *Pyx Granite Co Ltd v Ministry of Housing and Local
Government* [1959] 3 All ER at 8 and *R v Hull Prison Board of Visitors, ex p St Germain*
[1979] 1 All ER 701 applied.

Per curiam. RSC Ord 53 and s 31*ᵇ* of the Supreme Court Act 1981 (which gives
statutory force to Ord 53) do not have the effect of excluding the remedy of an action for
declaratory relief which was available prior to 1977 to control the exercise of
g administrative power. However, that remedy is discretionary and (per Ackner LJ) may
be refused if it is sought merely to circumvent the procedural safeguards under Ord 53
(see p 693 *g*, p 695 *c d*, p 699 *h*, p 700 *h j* and p 701 *j* to p 702 *a*, post).

Notes
For bodies amenable to certiorari, see 1 Halsbury's Laws (4th edn) paras 148–153, and for
h cases on the subject, see 16 Digest (Reissue) 402–409, 4442–4493.

For the Supreme Court Act 1981, s 31, see 51 Halsbury's Statutes (3rd edn) 625.

For the Prison Rules 1964, see Halsbury's Statutory Instruments (3rd reissue) 13.

Cases referred to in judgments
Air Canada v Secretary of State for Trade, (1982) Times, 25 September, CA.
Anisminic Ltd v Foreign Compensation Commission [1969] 1 All ER 208, [1969] 2 AC 147,
j   [1969] 2 WLR 163, HL, 16 Digest (Reissue) 395, 4357.
Arenson v Casson, Beckman, Rutley & Co [1975] 3 All ER 901, [1977] AC 405, [1975] 3
    WLR 815, HL, Digest (Cont Vol D) 1016, 26a.

---

a Order 53, so far as material, is set out at p 699 *e* to *g*, post
b Section 31, so far as material, is set out at p 700 *d* to *f*, post

Barnard v National Dock Labour Board [1953] 1 All ER 1113, [1953] 2 QB 18, [1953] 2
WLR 995, CA, 30 Digest (Reissue) 208, *310*.

Becker v Home Office [1972] 2 All ER 676, [1972] 2 QB 407, [1972] 2 WLR 1193, CA,
Digest (Cont Vol D) 729, *33b*.

Bousfield v North Yorkshire DC (1982) Times, 4 March.

De Falco v Crawley BC [1980] 1 All ER 913, [1980] QB 460, [1980] 2 WLR 664, CA.

Din v Wandsworth London Borough [1981] 3 All ER 881, [1981] 3 WLR 918, HL.

Dyson v A-G [1911] 1 KB 410, CA, 50 Digest (Repl) 65, *515*.

George v Secretary of State for the Environment (1979) 38 P & CR 609, CA.

Grunwick Processing Laboratories Ltd v Advisory, Conciliation and Arbitration Service [1978] 1
All ER 338, [1978] AC 655, [1978] 2 WLR 277, HL, Digest (Cont Vol E) 606, *1199d*.

Heywood v Hull Prison Board of Visitors [1980] 3 All ER 594, [1980] 1 WLR 1386.

Home Office v Dorset Yacht Co Ltd [1970] 2 All ER 294, [1970] AC 1004, [1970] 2 WLR
1140, HL, Digest (Cont Vol C) 807, *3a*.

Hunter v Chief Constable of West Midlands [1981] 3 All ER 727, [1982] AC 529, [1981] 3
WLR 906, HL.

IRC v National Federation of Self-Employed and Small Businesses Ltd [1981] 2 All ER 93,
[1982] AC 617, [1981] 2 WLR 722, HL.

IRC v Rossminster Ltd [1980] 1 All ER 80, [1980] AC 952, [1980] 2 WLR 1, HL, Digest
(Cont Vol E) 316, *2153f*.

Lambert v Ealing London Borough Council [1982] 2 All ER 394, [1982] 1 WLR 550, CA.

Lyme Regis Corp v Henley (1834) 1 Bing NC 222, 131 ER 1103, 38 Digest (Repl) 57, *306*.

Meade v Haringey London Borough [1979] 2 All ER 1016, [1979] 1 WLR 637, CA, Digest
(Cont Vol E) 195, *41a*.

Payne v Lord Harris of Greenwich [1981] 2 All ER 842, [1981] 1 WLR 754, CA.

Prescott v Birmingham Corp [1954] 3 All ER 698, [1955] Ch 210, [1954] 3 WLR 990, CA,
33 Digest (Reissue) 44, *135*.

Pyx Granite Co Ltd v Ministry of Housing and Local Government [1959] 3 All ER 1, [1960]
AC 260, [1959] 2 WLR 346, HL, 30 Digest (Reissue) 202, *277*.

R v Albany Prison Board of Visitors and Parkhurst Prison Board of Visitors, ex p Fell (8 July
1981, unreported).

R v Bolton (1841) 1 QB 66, [1835–42] All ER Rep 71, 113 ER 1054, 16 Digest (Reissue)
413, *4552*.

R v Crown Court at Sheffield, ex p Brownlow [1980] 2 All ER 444, [1980] QB 530, [1980] 2
WLR 892, CA.

R v Greater London Council, ex p Blackburn [1976] 3 All ER 184, [1976] 1 WLR 550, CA,
Digest (Cont Vol E) 587, *183a*.

R v Hull Prison Board of Visitors, ex p St Germain [1979] 1 All ER 701, [1979] QB 425,
[1979] 2 WLR 42, CA; *rvsg* [1978] 2 All ER 198, [1978] QB 678, [1978] 2 WLR 598,
DC, Digest (Cont Vol E) 488, *6a*.

R v Nat Bell Liquors Ltd [1922] 2 AC 128, [1922] All ER Rep 335, PC, 16 Digest (Reissue)
415, *4572*.

R v Northumberland Compensation Appeal Tribunal, ex p Shaw [1952] 1 All ER 122, [1952]
1 KB 338, CA, 16 Digest (Reissue) 425, *4686*.

R v Senate of the University of Aston, ex p Roffey [1969] 2 All ER 964, [1969] 2 QB 538,
[1969] 2 WLR 1418, DC, 16 Digest (Reissue) 325, *3398*.

R v Speyer [1916] 2 KB 858, CA, 2 Digest (Reissue) 186, *1115*.

Raymond v Honey [1982] 1 All ER 756, [1982] 2 WLR 465, HL.

Sirros v Moore [1974] 3 All ER 776, [1975] QB 118, [1974] 3 WLR 459, CA, Digest (Cont
Vol D) 736, *572a*.

Thornton v Kirklees Metropolitan BC [1979] 2 All ER 349, [1979] QB 626, [1979] 3 WLR 1,
CA, Digest (Cont Vol E) 254, *152Aa*.

Uppal v Home Office (1978) Times, 11 November, CA.

Cases also cited

Birkett v James [1977] 2 All ER 801, [1978] AC 297, HL.

Gouriet v Union of Post Office Workers [1977] 3 All ER 70, [1978] AC 435, HL.

a   Imperial Tobacco Ltd v A-G [1980] 1 All ER 866, [1981] AC 718, HL.

John v Rees [1969] 2 All ER 274, [1970] Ch 345.

Mohamed v Secretary of State for the Home Department [1981] CA Bound Transcript 215.

R v Barnet London Borough Council, ex p Shah [1982] 1 All ER 698, [1982] QB 688, CA.

R v Hull Prison Board of Visitors, ex p Luciano (15 December 1979, unreported).

R v Hull Prison Board of Visitors, ex p St Germain (No 2) [1979] 3 All ER 545, [1979] 1 WLR

b   1401, DC.

R v Hillingdon London Borough, ex p Royco Homes Ltd [1974] 2 All ER 643, [1974] QB 720, DC.

R v Nottingham Justices, ex p Davies [1980] 2 All ER 775, [1981] QB 38.

Ridge v Baldwin [1963] 2 All ER 66, [1964] AC 40, HL.

Royal College of Nursing of the United Kingdom v Department of Health and Social Security

c   [1981] 1 All ER 545, [1981] AC 800, HL.

*United Kingdom Association of Professional Engineers v Advisory, Conciliation and Arbitration
Service* [1979] 2 All ER 478, [1979] 1 WLR 570, CA.

Summonses to strike out

d   By three writs issued on 8 July 1980 and three statements of claim the first three plaintiffs, Christopher Noel O'Reilly, Alexander Vernon John Derbyshire and David Martin Dougan, former prisoners at Hull Prison, claimed against the defendants, Mr E W Mackman, Mr J A Rundle and Mr C Brady, the Board of Visitors of Hull Prison at the relevant times, declarations that the findings and awards made by the board after inquiries into charges brought against the respective plaintiffs for offences against discipline contrary to the Prison Rules 1964 were void and of no effect by reason of

e   breach of the rules of natural justice. The fourth plaintiff Anthony Millbanks, who was also a former prisoner at Hull Prison, by an originating summons issued on 1 September 1980 sought against the defendants, the Home Office and the Board of Visitors of Hull Prison, a declaration that the adjudications made against him by the board on 30 May 1979 were void for want of natural justice. The defendants in each case issued a summons to strike out the three statements of claim and the originating summons respectively on

f   the grounds (i) that they disclosed no reasonable cause of action and (ii) were an abuse of the process of the court. The summonses to strike out were heard in chambers but judgment was given in open court. The facts are set out in the judgment.

David Pannick for the plaintiffs O'Reilly, Derbyshire and Dougan.
Stephen Sedley for the plaintiff Millbanks.

g   *Simon D Brown* for the defendants.

Cur adv vult

5 March. **PETER PAIN J** read the following judgment: I have before me four matters. Three of them are actions in each of which a former prisoner of Hull prison is suing

h   members of the board of visitors at the prison. In each case the plaintiff appeared before the board of visitors in respect of charges alleging offences against discipline in the riots at Hull prison in December 1976. In each case the allegation is that the board acted in breach of the Prison Rules 1964, SI 1964/388, and in breach of natural justice, and a declaration is sought that the findings against the plaintiffs and the penalties awarded were void and of no effect. The fourth matter is an originating summons in which the plaintiff seeks a

j   declaration that the adjudication made against him by the board of visitors at Hull prison in 1979 is void for want of natural justice. This relates to disciplinary proceedings arising out of a riot at Hull prison in April 1979 and the basic allegation is that the chairman of the board of visitors was biased.

As questions of some constitutional importance are in issue and as it is probable that the unsuccessful party will appeal, I have thought it right to adjourn the matters into open court for formal judgment. In all four matters counsel for the defendants has sought an order that the statement of claim or originating summons be struck out on the grounds that (1) it discloses no reasonable cause of action and (2) it is an abuse of the process of the *a* court. For the purposes of these proceedings all four matters fall to be dealt with in exactly the same way.

At the beginning of the proceedings counsel for the defendants agreed that it could not be said that no reasonable cause of action was disclosed and the only matter I had to consider was whether there was an abuse of the process of the court. No criticism was made of the way in which each of the plaintiffs has conducted his case save for the *b* contention that to bring these proceedings by way of writ and/or originating summons, instead of applying under RSC Ord 53 for judicial review is an abuse of process.

The decision of the Court of Appeal in *R v Hull Prison Board of Visitors, ex p St Germain* [1979] 1 All ER 701, [1979] QB 425, made it clear for the first time that an allegation that disciplinary proceedings before a board of prison visitors had not been conducted in accordance with law was justiciable. This decision inevitably leads to further problems as *c* to how such proceedings should be handled by the court.

The cases before me are clearly on all fours with *Heywood v Hull Prison Board of Visitors* [1980] 3 All ER 594, [1980] 1 WLR 1386, in which Goulding J decided that such an action should be struck out as being an abuse of the process of the court. The problem was neatly defined by Goulding J in this way ([1980] 3 All ER 594 at 598, [1980] 1 WLR 1386 at 1391):

d

> 'I think I have to ask myself in the end this question: is the impropriety of using the procedure of an action in the present case so gross that the court, in exercising its undoubted power to regulate its own business and avoid abuse of its process, can stop an action that is within the court's jurisdiction to determine and that might conceivably succeed, stop it at the earliest stage, when the issues have not yet been defined by pleadings, nor elucidated by particulars or discovery, simply in order to *e* force the plaintiff to use the proper machinery in the light of the [Rules of the Supreme Court] considered as a whole?'

After careful consideration of the authorities, and in particular *Uppal v Home Office* (1978) Times, 11 November, and, after a cogent exposition of the practical difficulties which might flow if the plaintiff were permitted to proceed by way of writ, Goulding J *f* said ([1980] 3 All ER 594 at 602, [1980] 1 WLR 1386 at 1395):

> '... judicial discipline requires me to follow the view of the whole [Court of Appeal] in *Uppal*'s case whether technically binding or not.'

I trust that I shall not be found lacking in judicial discipline if I take the view that the authorities constrain me to the opposite conclusion.

g

In *Uppal v Home Office* Sir Robert Megarry V-C at first instance said:

> 'First, [counsel for the Home Office] said that these were the wrong proceedings in the wrong division; the plaintiffs ought to have sought some prerogative order by way of judicial review in the Queen's Bench, and so no declaration should be granted. I do not accept this; nor do I accept counsel's watered-down version, seeking that I should make some obiter pronouncement that such cases ought to be brought *h* in the Queen's Bench. Where two or more different types of proceedings are possible in the same court (and of course the Chancery Division and the Queen's Bench Division are both parts of the High Court) then I do not see why the plaintiffs should not be free to bring whatever type of proceeding they choose. I readily accept that the Queen's Bench Division has had a far greater experience of immigration cases than the Chancery Division has had; but that cannot require a plaintiff to proceed *j* for judicial review in the Queen's Bench if he wishes to proceed for a declaration in the Chancery Division. I do not think the Chancery Division can be regarded as being avid for this jurisdiction: but it would be wrong to turn away or discourage a plaintiff who elects to bring one form of proceedings instead of the other.'

(See [1980] 3 All ER 594 at 600–601, [1980] 1 WLR 1386 at 1394.)

When the matter came before the Court of Appeal the plaintiffs indicated by their
a counsel that they wished to abandon their appeal. I have had read to me a short transcript
of the discussion in the Court of Appeal in the course of which Roskill LJ expressed
concern about Sir Robert Megarry V-C's views but there was no argument whether they
were correct or not (the transcript in fact occupies only 1½ pages). After that Roskill LJ
made the following observations:

b   'With the greatest respect to Sir Robert Megarry V-C I find myself unable to agree
with the latter part of that passage. There is no doubt, and [counsel for the Home
Office] before us had not sought to say otherwise, that in theory the Chancery
Division has jurisdiction to entertain an application of this kind. But, as I said a
moment ago, this application is in principle indistinguishable from an application
for judicial review; and, where an application for judicial review is sought, then as
c   [RSC] Ord 53, r 3(1) provides, that application must be made to the Divisional
Court. I feel bound to say that I find it not a little surprising that this form of
procedure has been chosen rather than an application to the Divisional Court
for judicial review. It is the Divisional Court which is equipped by reason of its
experience, expertise and long practice to deal with these matters and to deal with
them expeditiously; and I express the hope that in future it is the Divisional Court
d   to which this type of problem will be submitted and that the temptation to deal
with immigration problems by way of an originating summons in proceedings for
a declaration in the Chancery Division will be avoided.'

(See [1980] 3 All ER 594 at 601, [1980] 1 WLR 1386 at 1394.)
Then Roskill LJ said further:

e   'There is, as I said a moment ago, and [counsel] has not argued otherwise,
jurisdiction in the Chancery Division to hear an application of this kind, but it
would be wrong that this procedure should be adopted in order to bypass the need
for getting leave from the Divisional Court to move for the relevant order where
what in truth is sought is judicial review. As this is a matter of some general
f   importance, I venture to make that criticism of what Sir Robert Megarry V-C said
with the greatest respect to him.'

(See [1980] 3 All ER 594 at 601, [1980] 1 WLR 1386 at 1395.)
It appears to me that these observations were made obiter. I take it that the court was
indicating that had the appeal been pursued it would in any event have been dismissed
g on the ground that the Court of Appeal thought the plaintiffs should have proceeded by
way of Ord 53 and that it therefore exercised its discretion to refuse a declaration in an
action begun by writ. Since a declaration is an equitable remedy it is always open to the
court to exercise a judicial discretion to refuse it. But to exercise discretion in this way at
trial is very different from denying a plaintiff the opportunity of pursuing his action at
all on the ground that he has been guilty of an abuse of the process of the court. I do not
h read Uppal v Home Office as authority for the proposition that to sue by writ for a
declaration is an abuse of the process where the alternative of applying under Ord 53 for
judicial review is available, but merely as authority that a plaintiff's failure to proceed
under Ord 53 where such procedure is plainly appropriate is one of the matters that may
be weighed in the scales against the plaintiff when the court is deciding how to exercise
its discretion.
j   Prior to the institution of the application for judicial review there was a long line of
authority to the effect that a plaintiff could choose whether to apply for a prerogative
writ or to sue for a declaration. In Pyx Granite Co Ltd v Ministry of Housing and Local
Government [1959] 3 All ER 1 at 8, [1960] AC 260 at 290 Lord Goddard said:

'It was also argued that, if there was a remedy obtainable in the High Court, it
must be by way of certiorari. I know of no authority for saying that, if an order or

decision can be attacked by certiorari, the court is debarred from granting a
declaration in an appropriate case. The remedies are not mutually exclusive though,   *a*
no doubt, there are some orders, notable convictions before justices, where the only
appropriate remedy is certiorari.'

In *Anisminic Ltd v Foreign Compensation Commission* [1969] 1 All ER 208, [1969] 2 AC
147, the principal remedy sought by the plaintiffs was a declaration that certain
determinations by the defendants were void. They might have applied for an order of
certiorari. Lord Reid, Lord Pearce and Lord Wilberforce ([1969] 1 All ER 208 at 211,   *b*
234, 249–250, [1969] 2 AC 147 at 169, 196, 214) made it clear in terms that the plaintiff
was entitled to proceed in the way he had and indeed Lord Wilberforce took the view
that the remedy the plaintiff sought was the most suitable in the circumstances of the
case.

In 1977 RSC Ord 53 was substantially amended to provide for the application for
judicial review and I have to consider whether the changes made affect the plaintiff's   *c*
right of choice. In *IRC v Rossminster Ltd* [1980] 1 All ER 80 at 104, [1980] AC 952 at
1025–1026 Lord Scarman said this about the new procedure:

'The application for judicial review is a recent procedural innovation in our law.
It is governed by RSC Ord 53, r 2, which was introduced in 1977. The rule made no
alteration to the substantive law; nor did it introduce any new remedy. But the   *d*
procedural reforms introduced are significant and valuable. Judicial review is now
the procedure for obtaining relief by way of prerogative order, ie mandamus,
prohibition or certiorari. But it is not confined to such relief: an applicant may now
obtain a declaration or injunction in any case where in the opinion of the court "it
would be just and convenient for the declaration or injunction to be granted on an
application for judicial review". Further, on an application, the court may award   *e*
damages, provided that the court is satisfied that damages could have been awarded,
had the applicant proceeded by action. The rule also makes available at the court's
discretion discovery, interrogatories and cross-examination of deponents. And,
where the relief sought is a declaration, an injunction, or damages but the court
considers it should not be granted on an application for judicial review, the court
may order the proceedings to continue as if they had been begun by writ. Thus the   *f*
application for judicial review, where a declaration, an injunction, or damages are
sought, is a summary way of obtaining a remedy which could be obtained at trial in
an action begun by writ; and it is available only where in all the circumstances it is
just and convenient. If issues of fact, or law and fact, are raised which it is neither
just nor convenient to decide without the full trial process, the court may dismiss
the application or order, in effect, a trial.'   *g*

Lord Diplock also made these observations ([1980] 1 All ER 80 at 94, [1980] AC 952 at
1013):

'In the same way, it would not in my view be open to a person claiming to have
been injured by the purported but unlawful exercise by a public officer of statutory
powers to circumvent the public interest immunity against premature disclosure of   *h*
the grounds on which the officer's exercise of the power was based by applying
under RSC Ord 53 for judicial review instead of bringing a civil action. RSC Ord 53
amends and simplifies the procedure for obtaining on a single application the kind
of relief that was formerly obtainable only in an ordinary civil action against a
public officer or authority and the kind of relief that was formerly obtainable only
on an application for a prerogative order of mandamus, prohibition or certiorari;   *j*
but it does not alter the differing roles played by the court in applications for these
two categories of relief.'

These observations seem to me to point clearly to the conclusion that their Lordships
thought that the plaintiff's choice remained as before. The matter was dealt with

explicitly by the Court of Appeal in *De Falco v Crawley BC* [1980] 1 All ER 913, [1980]
a   QB 460. Although the plaintiffs in that case were represented by the same counsel as the
plaintiffs in *Uppal v Home Office*, it does not appear from the report that the views of the
court in *Uppal v Home Office* were brought to the attention of the court. Lord Denning
MR said ([1980] 1 All ER 913 at 920, [1980] QB 460 at 476):

'During the hearing, a point was raised about the procedure adopted by the
plaintiffs. They issued writs in the High Court claiming declarations and an
b   injunction. It was suggested that they should have applied for judicial review,
because that was the more appropriate machinery. Now the interesting thing is that
this new Act, the Housing (Homeless Persons) Act 1977, contains nothing about
remedies. It does not say what is to be done if the local authority fails to perform
any of the duties imposed by the statute. It has been held by this court that, if the
council fails to provide accommodation as required by s 3(4), the applicant can claim
c   damages in the county court . . . I am very ready to follow that decision and indeed
to carry it further, because this is a statute which is passed for the protection of
private persons, in their capacity as private persons. It is not passed for the benefit of
the public at large. In such a case it is well settled that, if a public authority fails to
perform its statutory duty, the person or persons concerned can bring a civil action
for damages or an injunction [He referred to various authorities and continued:] No
d   doubt such a person could, at his option, bring proceedings for judicial review under
the new RSC Ord 53. In those proceedings he could get a declaration and an
injunction equally well. He could get interim relief also. So the applicant has an
option. He can either go by action in the High Court or county court, or by an
application for judicial review.'

e   The other judgments do not deal expressly with the point but I feel it must follow by
implication that the other Lords Justices shared Lord Denning MR's view. Goulding J in
Heywood v Hull Prison Board of Visitors [1980] 3 All ER 594 at 599–600, [1980] 1 WLR
1386 at 1392–1393 made the following observation on the *De Falco* decision:

'That conclusion, that the plaintiffs in the *De Falco* case had rightly proceeded by
way of action for declarations and an injunction, was shared by the other two
f   members of the Court of Appeal who decided the case . . . It is only, I think, of
limited assistance to the plaintiff in the present case, because Lord Denning MR
founded his observations on the hypothesis that the proceedings with which he was
concerned were for the enforcement of a statute passed for the protection of private
persons, and not passed for the benefit of the public at large. Also I think the Court
of Appeal, in considering that the applicant had an option, were not concerned how
g   far in the preliminary stages of the proceedings the court can interfere with initial
freedom of choice. So far as they go, the observations in the *De Falco* case reinforce
the suggestion in Professor de Smith's book [*Judicial Review of Administrative Action*
(3rd edn, 1973), p 459] that it ought not to make any difference to judges through
which door the petitioner enters the forum.'

h   It seems to me that the provisions of the Prison Rules, which are made under the
provisions of the Prison Act 1952, are for the protection of private persons just as much
as the remedies under the Housing (Homeless Persons) Act 1977. A person who wishes
to bring proceedings for breach of statutory duty has to show (a) that the matter is
justiciable, and (b) that he has locus standi. He will have locus standi if the statutory duty
was imposed for the benefit of a limited class of people of whom the plaintiff is one and
j   there is no other remedy for its breach. I hold that the plaintiff in such a case is a member
of such a limited class, that is to say convicts who appear before the board of prison
visitors on disciplinary charges. There is no right of appeal against the decision of the
board of visitors so the plaintiff has no right to have their decision reviewed. It therefore
seems to me that the weight of authority is clearly against striking out the plaintiff's case.
It might be thought that the plaintiffs have made their choice of procedural route

capriciously. This is not so. I was told by their counsel that they anticipate in each case that there will be a substantial dispute as to fact and they have therefore chosen a route *a* that provides for oral evidence as a matter of course rather than a route in which the evidence is nearly always taken on affidavit. This is clearly a rational choice. It is not for me to say whether it is a wise choice.

Goulding J made this observation in *Heywood v Hull Prison Board of Visitors* [1980] 3 All ER 594 at 598, [1980] 1 WLR 1386 at 1391:

'. . . in proceedings seeking a review of a judicial or quasi-judicial determination, *b* the machinery of an action as to discovery and giving of evidence may result in placing members of the tribunal concerned in a position not really compatible with the free and proper discharge of their public functions, or at least in attempts to put them in that position. In the present case counsel for the plaintiff has contemplated the possibility (though he by no means says it will be a necessity) of cross-examining members of the board of visitors. In principle, that seems to me an undesirable way *c* of dealing with such questions.'

I do not feel that I ought to allow that consideration to influence my decision, and indeed with the amendments that have been made under Ord 53, it is plain that one might get discovery, cross-examination, and so on, even in proceedings under Ord 53, though no doubt the court would be more reluctant to grant them. It may well be that *d* following the decision in *R v Hull Prison Board of Visitors, ex p St Germain* [1979] 1 All ER 701, [1979] QB 425, the boards of visitors will require some special protection. If this be so then it would be provided for in a change in the substantive law or in the rules of the court. I do not think it is for individual judges to effect such a change by striking out the case of a plaintiff who does not proceed by Ord 53. The law recognises no limitation on the right of a convict or ex-convict to sue for what he conceives to be his rights, and an *e* example of that is afforded by *Raymond v Honey* [1982] 1 All ER 756, [1982] 2 WLR 465.

Counsel for the defendants contended that, since the appropriate remedy here would be certiorari to quash, the appropriate procedure is by way of judicial review. The answer to that lies in the *Anisminic* case to which I have already referred.

For the purposes of completeness I will add that since this matter was argued before me the decision of Dillon J in *Bousfield v North Yorkshire DC* (1982) Times, 4 March has *f* been given. In that case Dillon J held that where it was claimed that a decision of an inferior tribunal ought to be quashed for error on the face of the record the appropriate procedure was by way of an application for judicial review before the Queen's Bench Divisional Court: he struck out an originating summons seeking a declaration as to such a decision as being an abuse of the process of the court. The judge made it plain in his judgment that there was a distinction to be drawn between a case of error of law on the *g* face of the record and a case where it was contended that the proceedings before the inferior tribunal were a nullity. I take the view therefore that his decision has no bearing on the matters which are before me.

With the greatest respect to Goulding J in *Heywood v Hull Prison Board of Visitors*, I feel that the overwhelming weight of authority compels me to differ from him. I can well understand the force of the practical considerations which he set out so cogently but I do *h* not feel myself constrained by the decision in *Uppal* in the way that he felt himself to be. Once that constraint disappears, the authorities are all one way. The law offers the plaintiff a choice. If it is inconvenient for the choice to be exercised in a particular way, then the choice should be withdrawn or limited. But while the choice continues to exist it seems to me to be an abuse of language to say that the plaintiff is abusing the process of the court because he exercises the choice in the way he thinks best in his own interest. *j*

All the summonses are dismissed.

Summonses dismissed. Leave to appeal granted.

K Mydeen Esq　　Barrister.

Appeal

a The defendants in each case appealed against the judgment of Peter Pain J on the grounds that the judge was wrong in law (1) in deciding that it was not an abuse of the process of the court for the plaintiffs to bring proceedings by way of writ and by originating summons claiming declaratory relief instead of under RSC Ord 53, and (2) in holding that those who wished to challenge the legal validity of adjudications of prison boards of visitors could do so at their option by proceedings other than under Ord 53.

b

Simon D Brown for the defendants.
Michael Beloff QC and *David Pannick* for the plaintiffs O'Reilly, Derbyshire and Dougan.
Stephen Sedley for the plaintiff Millbanks.

c   *Cur adv vult*

30 June. The following judgments were read.

LORD DENNING MR. Four men were in prison in Hull. They were all serving long
d sentences for serious crimes. O'Reilly is typical. He was serving 15 years for robbery.
Over four days in September 1976 there was a riot in the prison, coupled with extreme
violence. Men got onto the roof and stayed there day and night. They threw missiles and
slates off the roof. They ransacked the canteen. They assaulted prison officers and staff.
After the riot was quelled, many men were charged with offences against discipline
contrary to the provisions of the Prison Rules. In each case the board of visitors held an
e inquiry. Take O'Reilly as an example. The board found him guilty on all charges. They
ordered him to be kept in solitary confinement for 196 days and to lose remission of 510
days. Likewise with others.

Many of the men complained about the conduct of the board of visitors. They said
that the board had failed to comply with the rules of natural justice. Seven of them
applied for judicial review to quash the decision of the board. The Divisional Court held
f that judicial review was not available to them. The Court of Appeal reversed the
Divisional Court and held that it was available. The case is reported under the name of *R
v Hull Prison Board of Visitors, ex p St Germain* [1979] 1 All ER 701, [1979] QB 425. As a
result there were several cases of judicial review in which some of the men succeeded in
having the decisions quashed. I presume there were fresh hearings.

g *Ordinary writs are issued*
Now these four men join in these proceedings. They are long out of time for judicial
review. But they have issued ordinary writs in the High Court. They have got legal aid
for the purpose. Take O'Reilly again as typical. He issued a writ on 8 July 1980. That is
nearly four years since the riot took place. He has issued a writ against three gentlemen
who were the board of visitors and heard his case: Mr Mackman, Mr Rundle and Mr
h Brady. He has served with the writ a statement of claim. In it he has set out the finding
and award of the board and has said:

'... the Board failed to give the Plaintiff an opportunity to call alibi witnesses in
his defence notwithstanding that he requested them to do so and that the evidence
thereof was relevant and material to his said defence.'

j He claims simply 'a declaration that the said finding of and award by the Board was
void and of no effect'.

Thereupon the Treasury Solicitor applied to strike out the statement of claim on the
ground that it is an abuse of the process of the court.

Now the interesting thing is this. Two years ago another of these prisoners issued a
similar writ and statement of claim against the board of visitors: see *Heywood v Hull Prison*

Board of Visitors [1980] 3 All ER 594, [1980] 1 WLR 1386. Goulding J struck it out. Now
this case about our four men was heard by Peter Pain J on 5 March 1982. He differed *a*
from Goulding J and refused to strike out the statement of claim. Now there is an appeal
to this court.

This looks as if it were merely a point of procedure. But it brings into play some of the
fundamentals of our administrative law. I will divide my judgment into three parts. The
first is concerned with an action against the board of visitors. The second is more general.
It is concerned with actions against public authorities. The third part with modern *b*
machinery.

PART I

The board of visitors

It is as well to bear in mind the constitutional position of the board of visitors. It is set
out in the Prison Act 1952 and the Prison Rules made thereunder. The visitors are *c*
appointed by the Secretary of State. At least two of them must be justices of the peace.
When a prisoner is charged with a serious offence against discipline, the rules require the
hearing to be conducted on the self-same lines as a hearing before magistrates. The
accused is to be asked whether he pleads guilty or not guilty. Witnesses are called,
examined and cross-examined. He makes his defence and calls his witnesses, and so forth.
In all essentials, it is a judicial proceeding of the same character as a magistrates' court. *d*
The only difference is in the description of the offence and the kind of punishment.

No action lies against them

Such being the constitutional position, it is clear to my mind that the board of visitors
are entitled to be protected from having actions at law brought against them. They are
in the same position as magistrates. They owe a duty to the state to do their work to the *e*
best of their ability: see *Arenson v Casson, Beckman, Rutley & Co* [1975] 3 All ER 901 at
918, [1977] AC 405 at 431 per Lord Kilbrandon. But this is not a duty owed by them to
the parties before them. It is not a duty which a prisoner can enforce by action. Be they
careless, ignorant or mistaken. Be they guilty of want of natural justice. Be they malicious
or biased. Go they to sleep and do not heed the evidence. Nevertheless, no action lies
against them. As I said of any judge, high or low, in *Sirros v Moore* [1974] 3 All ER 776 *f*
at 785, [1975] QB 118 at 136:

'He is not to be plagued with allegations of malice or ill-will or bias or anything
of that kind. Actions based on such allegations have been struck out and will
continue to be struck out.'

The reason lies in public policy. No judge should be harassed by the thought that 'if I *g*
do this or that, I may be sued by this or that prisoner or this or that litigant'. Rather than
subject a judge to influences of that kind, the law says that no litigant can bring an action
against him for anything done by him in his judicial capacity.

Nevertheless certiorari was available

This does not means that nothing can be done by anyone. Any unjust judge, of an *h*
inferior court or tribunal, is not free from control. Although he does not owe any duty
to the prisoner or to the litigant, he does owe a duty to the state; and the state can call
him to account. For this purpose our old books regarded the king as the state, and the
state as the king. 'L'Etat c'est moi', as Louis XIV said in 1655. It was for the king to call
on a judge of any inferior court and ask him to account for his actions. The king did it
by the prerogative writ of certiorari. I gave its origin and described the nature of it in *R* *j*
v Northumberland Compensation Appeal Tribunal, ex p Shaw [1952] 1 All ER 122 at 128–
129, [1952] 1 KB 338 at 347–348. The very words 'prerogative writ' show that it was
issued by the royal authority of the king. No subject could issue it on his own. He had
no right to issue it as of course as he could for trespass or trover. All that the subject could
do was to inform the king's judges of his complaint. He could tell them about the unjust

judge of any inferior court. The king's judges would then authorise the issue of the writ
a in the king's name.

The very titles of the proceedings show the difference. It goes from the earliest times
down to the present day. When the prisoners at Hull told the judges of their complaint
against the board of visitors, and they allowed certiorari to issue, the case was entitled
Regina v Hull Prison Board of Visitors, ex p St Germain. Regina means the Queen. The
Queen brought the proceedings. The title shows that the prisoners had made an ex parte
b application to the court and that the court had given leave for proceedings to be brought
in the Queen's name against the board of visitors. But, when a prisoner sought to bring
an action on his own (without the leave of the sovereign), the case was entitled *Heywood
v Hull Prison Board of Visitors.* Heywood means the man Heywood. He himself brought
the proceedings. The title shows that the prisoner had brought an action on his own
cause, as of right, without leave, against the visitors.

c

No declaration against the board

In those circumstances, I see no difference between an action for damages and an action
for a declaration. If a prisoner or litigant is not allowed to sue a justice of the peace for
damages, neither should he be allowed to sue him for a declaration. Have you ever heard
of an action against a magistrate asking for a declaration that he was biased? Or was
d guilty of any other kind of misconduct? I have not. Nor has anyone else. I am quite sure
that no such action lies. That was the view of Lord Goddard in *Pyx Granite Co Ltd v
Ministry of Housing and Local Government* [1959] 3 All ER 1 at 8, [1960] AC 260 at 290
when he said: '... no doubt, there are some orders, notably convictions before justices,
where the only appropriate remedy is certiorari.'

If such be true of justices of the peace, so it is of all other judges of inferior courts and
e of persons appointed under statute to carry out judicial duties. The like principle applies
to each. No action lies. But is there a remedy by judicial review? This brings me to
recent developments in administrative law.

The black-out

f At one time there was a black-out of any development of administrative law. The
curtains were drawn across to prevent the light coming in. The remedy of certiorari was
hedged about with all sorts of technical limitations. It did not give a remedy when
inferior tribunals went wrong, but only when they went outside their jurisdiction
altogether. The black-out started in 1841 with *R v Bolton* (1841) 1 QB 66, [1835–42] All
ER Rep 71 and became darkest in 1922 with *R v Nat Bell Liquors Ltd* [1922] 2 AC 128,
[1922] All ER Rep 335. It was not relieved until 1952, in *R v Northumberland Compensation
g Appeal Tribunal, ex p Shaw.* Whilst the darkness still prevailed, we let in some light by
means of a declaration. The most notable cases were *Barnard v National Dock Labour Board*
[1953] 1 All ER 1113, [1953] 2 QB 18, and *Anisminic Ltd v Foreign Compensation Commission*
[1969] 1 All ER 208, [1969] 2 AC 147. I sat in the preliminary hearings of both of them.
We allowed each of those cases to go forward. It was because otherwise persons would be
h without a remedy for an injustice: see eg [1953] 1 All ER 1113 at 1120, [1953] 2 QB 18
at 43. In effect it was only *by leave* that the action for a declaration was allowed to proceed.

Judicial review

In 1977 the black-out was lifted. It was done by RSC Ord 53. The curtains were drawn
back. The light was let in. Our administrative law became well-organised and
j comprehensive. It enabled the High Court to review the decisions of all inferior courts
and tribunals and to quash them when they went wrong. And what is more, it enabled
the High Court to award damages and grant declarations. No longer is it necessary to
bring an ordinary action to obtain damages or declarations. It can all be done by judicial
review. This new remedy (by judicial review) has made the old remedy (by action at law)
superfluous.

Does declaration still lie against the board?

The Law Commission in its Report on Remedies in Administrative Law in March *a*
1976 (Law Com no 73, Cmnd 6407) suggested that the new remedy by judicial review
should not exclude any of the former remedies: see paras 34 and 58(a). But that
suggestion does not appeal to me, at any rate so far as the remedy by action for a
declaration is concerned. It was invented so as to avoid the technical limitations on
certiorari. Now that those limitations have been swept away by Ord 53, the remedy by
an *action* for a declaration should be scrapped. Especially as it was contrary to principle, *b*
by which no action at law lay against an inferior court or the members thereof for
anything done in their judicial capacity. The action for a declaration had many defects.
It could be started, as of right, without the leave of the court. It could be started years
and years after the event. It could involve long trials with discovery, cross-examination,
and so forth. So many defects were present in that remedy by action that I am quite clear
that now that the new procedure has been introduced, there should no longer be recourse *c*
to the remedy by action for a declaration. If a complaint is brought by ordinary writ,
without leave, it can and should be struck out as an abuse of the process of the court.

Abuse of process

Some point was made about the scope of 'abuse of process'. Reference was made to the
opening paragraph of Lord Diplock's speech in *Hunter v Chief Constable of West Midlands* *d*
[1981] 3 All ER 727 at 729, [1982] AC 529 at 531. But that should not be regarded as a
statutory definition. Suppose a prisoner applied under Ord 53 for judicial review of the
decision of a board of visitors, and the judge refused leave. It would, to my mind, be an
abuse of the process of the court for him to start afresh an action at law for a declaration,
thereby avoiding the need for leave. It is an abuse for him to try and avoid the safeguards
of Ord 53 by resorting to an action at law. So also if he deliberately omits to apply under *e*
Ord 53 so as to avoid the necessity of obtaining leave. Where a good and appropriate
remedy is given by the procedure of the court, with safeguards against abuse, it is an
abuse for a person to go by another procedure, so as to avoid the safeguards.

PART II

Public authorities *f*

Thus far I have regarded the board of visitors as in a special category. I have treated
them like justices of the peace. But, in case I am wrong about this, I would go on to
consider them simply as a public authority who can be supervised by means of judicial
review. This raises a point of much importance. Does a complainant have an option?
Can he go by judicial review, or by ordinary action, as he pleases?

g

Private law and public law

In modern times we have come to recognise two separate fields of law, one of private
law, the other of public law. Private law regulates the affairs of subjects as between
themselves. Public law regulates the affairs of subjects vis-à-vis public authorities. For
centuries there were special remedies available in public law. They were the prerogative *h*
writs of certiorari, mandamus and prohibition. As I have shown, they were taken in the
name of the sovereign against a public authority which had failed to perform its duty to
the public at large or had performed it wrongly. Any subject could complain to the
sovereign; and then the king's courts, at their discretion, would give him leave to issue
such one of the prerogative writs as was appropriate to meet his case. But these writs, as
their names show, only gave the remedies of quashing, commanding or prohibiting. *j*
They did not enable a subject to recover damages against a public authority, nor a
declaration, nor an injunction.

This was such a defect in public law that the courts drew on the remedies available in
private law, so as to see that the subject secured justice. It was held that if a public

authority failed to do its duty and, in consequence, a member of the public suffered
a particular damage therefrom, he could sue for damages by an ordinary action in the
courts of common law: see *Lyme Regis Corp v Henley* (1834) 1 Bing NC 222, 131 ER 1103,
Home Office v Dorset Yacht Co Ltd [1970] 2 All ER 294, [1970] AC 1004. Likewise, if a
question arose as to the rights of a subject vis-à-vis the public authority, he could come to
the courts and ask for a declaration (see *Dyson v A-G* [1911] 1 KB 410, *Pyx Granite Co v
Ministry of Housing and Local Government* [1959] 3 All ER 1, [1960] AC 260), or against a
b local authority (see *Prescott v Birmingham Corp* [1954] 3 All ER 698, [1955] Ch 210, *Meade
v Haringey London Borough* [1979] 2 All ER 1016, [1979] 1 WLR 637). And this remedy
has been applied right up to the present time in ordinary actions brought without leave:
see eg *Grunwick Processing Laboratories Ltd v Advisory, Concilation and Arbitration Service*
[1978] 1 All ER 338, [1978] AC 655, *Payne v Lord Harris of Greenwich* [1981] 2 All ER
842, [1981] 1 WLR 754.

c
Section 31 of the 1981 Act
But now we have witnessed a break-through in our public law. It is done by s 31 of
the Supreme Court Act 1981, which came into force on 1 January 1982. This is, to my
mind, of much higher force than RSC Ord 53. That order came into force in 1977, but it
had to be construed in a limited sense, because it could not affect the substance of the
d law: see *IRC v National Federation of Self-Employed and Small Businesses Ltd* [1981] 2 All ER
93 at 111, [1982] AC 617 at 650 per Lord Scarman. Rules of court can only affect
procedure: whereas an Act of Parliament comes in like a lion. It can affect both procedure
and substance alike.

I always thought that this great reform should be done by statute as the Law
Commission recommended. When the Rule Committee made Ord 53, some of us on
e the committee had doubts about whether some of it was not ultra vires, but we took the
risk because it was so desirable. Now that the statute has been passed, I may say that it
has in several respects altered the substance of the law for the better. For instance, s 31(2)
of the 1981 Act uses the significant words 'having regard to', thus expanding the kind of
bodies against whom relief can be obtained. It includes all public authorities and public
officers, and indeed anyone acting in exercise of a public duty, including a university,
f (see *R v Senate of the University of Aston, ex p Roffey* [1969] 2 All ER 964, [1969] 2 QB 538).
It also enlarges the scope of a declaration and injunction so as to apply wherever it is 'just
and convenient'. And s 31(3) gives the remedy to anyone who has 'a sufficient interest',
which is very wide in its scope. Those provisions rid us of a whole mass of technical
limitations which were thought previously to exist.

g
High constitutional principle
Now that judicial review is available to give every kind of remedy, I think it should be
the normal recourse in all cases of public law where a private person is challenging the
conduct of a public authority or a public body, or of anyone acting in the exercise of a
public duty. I am glad to see that in *IRC v National Federation of Self-Employed* Lord
Diplock endorsed the principle which I ventured to set out in *R v Greater London Council,
h* *ex p Blackburn* [1976] 3 All ER 184 at 192, [1976] 1 WLR 550 at 559:

> 'I regard it as a matter of high constitutional principle that, if there is good ground
> for supposing that a government department or a public authority is transgressing
> the law, or is about to transgress it, in a way which offends or injures thousands of
> Her Majesty's subjects, then any one of those offended or injured can draw it to the
> attention of the courts of law and seek to have the law enforced, and the courts in
j > their discretion can grant whatever remedy is appropriate.'

To this I would add the valuable lecture by Patrick Neill QC on 'Locus Standi and the
Mere Busybody' (Denning Lecture 1982), especially his references to *R v Speyer* [1916] 1
KB 595 at 613.

Safeguards against abuse
When considering the merits of judicial review, as against an ordinary action, it is *a*
important to notice that judicial review has some safeguards against abuse, which are not
available in ordinary actions.

(i) *Leave to be obtained*
In the first place, the applicant has to get *leave* of a High Court judge in order to start
the proceedings. Lord Diplock emphasised the importance of it in *IRC v National* *b*
Federation of Self-Employed. Speaking of the need for leave, he said ([1981] 2 All ER 93 at
105, [1982] AC 617 at 642–643):

'Its purpose is to prevent the time of the court being wasted by busybodies with
misguided or trivial complaints of administrative error, and to remove the
uncertainty in which public officers and authorities might be left whether they
could safely proceed with administrative action while proceedings for judicial *c*
review of it were actually pending even though misconceived.'

And as Lord Scarman said ([1981] 2 All ER 93 at 113, [1982] AC 617 at 653):

'The curb represented by the need for an applicant to show, when he seeks leave
to apply, that he has such a case is an essential protection against abuse of legal
process. It enables the court of prevent abuse by busybodies, cranks, and other *d*
mischief makers.'

(ii) *Discovery limited*
Another safeguard against abuse is the need to have a special order for discovery. As
Lord Scarman said in *IRC v National Federation of Self-Employed* [1981] 2 All ER 93 at 114,
[1982] AC 617 at 654: *e*

'On general principles, discovery should not be ordered unless and until the court
is satisfied that the evidence reveals reasonable grounds for believing that there has
been a breach of public duty, and it should be limited strictly to documents relevant
to the issue which emerges from the affidavits.'

f

(iii) *Cross-examination limited*
Another safeguard is to control the use of cross-examination. This can roam unchecked
in ordinary actions, but is kept within strict bounds in judicial review. It is rarely allowed
(see *George v Secretary of State for the Environment* (1979) 38 P & CR 609, *R v Albany Prison
Board of Visitors and Parkhurst Prison Board of Visitors, ex p Fell* (8 July 1981, unreported)).

g

PART III

Modern machinery: no safeguards otherwise
None of these safeguards against abuse are available in an ordinary action issued as of
course, without leave, against a public authority or a public body. Some complainants,
or their advisers, have seized on this. They have brought actions at law instead of for *h*
judicial review. Instances are ready to hand. An action was brought in the county court
for damages against a local authority for breach of the Housing (Homeless Persons) Act
1977: see *Thornton v Kirklees Metropolitan BC* [1979] 2 All ER 349, [1979] QB 626. An
action was brought in the Chancery Division for a declaration against the Home Office
under the Immigration Act: see *Uppal v Home Office* (1978) Times, 11 November. If such
actions were to be permitted (as an alternative to judicial review) it would open the door *j*
to great abuse. Nearly all these people are legally aided. If they were allowed to proceed
by ordinary action, without leave, I can well see that the public authorities of this country
would be harassed by all sorts of claims, long out of time, on the most flimsy of grounds.
So much so that I pray in aid (in cases under the Housing (Homeless Persons) Act 1977)
the reservations made by Lord Wilberforce in *Din v Wandsworth London Borough* [1981] 3

All ER 881 at 885, [1981] 3 WLR 918 at 922, to which I would add my own words in
a *Lambert v Ealing London Borough Council* [1982] 2 All ER 394 at 399, [1982] 1 WLR 550 at
557: 'The only way in which a local authority's decision in these cases can properly be
interfered with is by way of judicial review . . .' Also in immigration cases the words of
Roskill LJ in *Uppal v Home Office*:

> 'I express the hope that in future it is the Divisional Court to which this type of
> problem will be submitted and that the temptation to deal with immigration
> **b** problems by way of an originating summons in proceedings for a declaration in the
> Chancery Division will be avoided . . . There is . . . jurisdiction in the Chancery
> Division to hear an application of this kind, but it would be wrong that this
> procedure should be adopted in order to bypass the need for getting leave from the
> Divisional Court to move for the relevant order where what in truth is sought is
> judicial review.'

c
(See [1980] 3 All ER 594 at 601, [1980] 1 WLR 1386 at 1394–1395).

The end result
In the light of these observations I make this suggestion: that, wherever there is
available a remedy by judicial review under s 31 of the Supreme Court Act 1981, that
remedy should be the normal remedy to be taken by an applicant. If a plaintiff should
d bring an action, instead of judicial review, and the defendant feels that leave would never
have been granted under Ord 53, then he can apply to the court to strike it out as being
an abuse of the process of the court. It is an abuse to go back to the old machinery instead
of using the new streamlined machinery. It is an abuse to go by action when he would
never have been granted leave to go for judicial review.

Alternatively, if the defendant feels that leave would have been granted under Ord 53,
e he can apply for the action to be transferred to the Ord 53 list, and the case can then
proceed under Ord 53 just as if leave had been granted. The High Court has sufficient
control over its proceedings to enable all this to be done. Just as an action in the ordinary
list can be transferred to the commercial list, so it can be transferred to the Ord 53 list,
which I would like to see called the administrative list. If this be thought to be too
venturesome, the Rule Committee might make a rule to enable it to be done.
f So also if it is brought in the Chancery Division, it should be transferred to the Queen's
Bench Division under s 65 of the Supreme Court Act 1981 to be heard as on an application
for judicial review. Likewise if it is brought in the county court.

If this suggestion is acceptable, then it means that most cases will proceed under Ord
53, as they should do. There may be some cases where the action for a declaration is
allowed to proceed. One such is at present being heard in this court: *Air Canada v*
g *Secretary of State for Trade* (1982) Times, 25 September. But these should be regarded as
exceptional.

Procedure
For the sake of completeness I should add that I am here speaking only of *civil* causes
h or matters. The Rules of the Supreme Court, in Ords 53, 55 and 56, draw a distinction
between a 'criminal cause or matter' and a civil cause or matter. Criminal cases usually
go to a Divisional Court and thence to the House of Lords. Civil cases go usually to a
single judge and thence to the Court of Appeal and House of Lords. This distinction has
often given us headaches: see *R v Hull Prison Board of Visitors, ex p St Germain* [1979] 1 All
ER 701, [1979] QB 425, *R v Crown Court at Sheffield, ex p Brownlow* [1980] 2 All ER 444,
j [1980] QB 530. All I am speaking of here is the civil jurisdiction of the Court of Appeal
which is entrusted to the Civil Division of which the Master of the Rolls is the President:
see s 1(2) of the Criminal Appeal Act 1966 and s 3 of the Supreme Court Act 1981.

This new procedure means that we now have an administrative court. It is a division
of the High Court which might well be called the Administrative Division. It is manned
by judges specially versed in administrative law with an appeal to the Civil Division of

the Court of Appeal, in which I myself have taken much interest in the past, and in which the Lord Chief Justice will in future be much interested.

a

Conclusion

My conclusion is that the only appropriate remedy in this case was by judicial review under Ord 53. If leave had been sought, it would certainly have been refused. No judge would have granted it. It is far too late. I would, therefore, allow this appeal and strike out this action as being an abuse of the process of the court.

b

Postscript

I cannot refrain from referring to a few words I said in 1949 at the end of my Hamlyn Lecture on Freedom under the Law (1949) p 126:

'Just as the pick and shovel is no longer suitable for the winning of coal, so also *c* the procedure of mandamus, certiorari, and actions on the case are not suitable for the winning of freedom in the new age. They must be replaced by new and up to date machinery, by declarations, injunctions, and actions for negligence ... We have in our time to deal with changes which are of equal constitutional significance to those which took place 300 years ago. Let us prove ourselves equal to the challenge.'

d

Now, over thirty years later, we do have the new and up-to-date machinery. I would say with Lord Diplock in *IRC v National Federation of Self-Employed* [1981] 2 All ER 93 at 104, [1982] AC 617 at 641:

'To revert to technical restrictions ... that were current thirty years ago or more would be to reverse that progress towards a comprehensive system of administrative *e* law that I regard as having been the greatest achievement of the English courts in my judicial lifetime.'

So we have proved ourselves equal to the challenge. Let us buttress our achievement by interpreting s 31 of the 1981 Act in a wide and liberal spirit. By so doing we shall have done much to prevent the abuse or misuse of power by any public authority or *f* public officer or other person acting in the exercise of a public duty.

I would allow the appeal.

ACKNER LJ. These appeals are concerned with determinations by the Board of Visitors of Hull Prison (the defendants) of alleged breaches of the Prison Rules 1964, SI 1964/388, by the plaintiffs. In *R v Hull Prison Board of Visitors, ex p St Germain* [1979] 1 All ER 701, *g* [1979] QB 425, this court decided that the decision of the visitors, when exercising their disciplinary powers under the Prison Act 1952 and the rules made thereunder is subject to judicial review by way of certiorari. The question which this appeal raises is whether such decisions by the visitors are justiciable only by judicial review under RSC Ord 53, as the defendants contend, or whether prisoners, such as the plaintiffs, may at their option apply for declaratory relief under Ord 15 by writ or by originating application. *h*

Three of the plaintiffs have proceeded by writs issued in July 1980 in respect of the visitors' adjudiciations at the end of 1976. The fourth plaintiff has proceeded by originating summons issued in September 1980, in respect of an adjudication made in May 1979. All four sets of proceedings seek declarations that the findings and awards are null and void by reason of alleged breaches of natural justice. Judicial review has not been sought under Ord 53, partly because the prospect of obtaining leave, certainly in *j* the first three cases mentioned above, is by reason of the delay exceedingly remote, and partly because the plaintiffs anticipate a substantial dispute on the facts. They have, therefore, chosen a route which provides for oral evidence as a matter of course, rather than affidavit evidence, with little prospect of obtaining the right to cross-examine the deponents.

Counsel for the defendants applied before Peter Pain J to strike out these proceedings a as an abuse of the process of the court, relying in particular on a decision of Goulding J in *Heywood v Hull Prison Board of Visitors* [1980] 3 All ER 594, [1980] 1 WLR 1386 where such a course was successful. Although Peter Pain J accepted that that decision was on all fours, he declined to follow it, concluding that 'the overwhelming weight of authority' compelled him to differ.

I think it is convenient to start by referring to a short statement by Lord Diplock in the recent case of *Hunter v Chief Constable of West Midlands* [1981] 3 All ER 727 at 729,
b [1982] AC 529 at 536 on the power to strike out. At the commencement of his speech he said:

c 'My Lords, this is a case about abuse of the process of the High Court. It concerns the inherent power which any court of justice must possess to prevent misuse of its procedure in a way which, although not inconsistent with the literal application of its procedural rules, would nevertheless be manifestly unfair to a party to litigation before it, or would otherwise bring the administration of justice into disrepute among right-thinking people. The circumstances in which abuse of process can arise are very varied; those which give rise to the instant appeal must surely be unique.
d It would, in my view, be most unwise if this House were to use this occasion to say anything that might be taken as limiting to fixed categories the kinds of circumstances in which the court has a duty (I disavow the word discretion) to exercise this salutary power.'

The position of the board of visitors is dealt with in detail in the *St Germain* case. Section 6(2) of the Prison Act 1952 makes provision for the appointment for every prison of a board of visitors, of whom not less than two shall be justices of the peace. Section 47 of the Act empowers the Secretary of State to make rules for the regulation and
e management of prisons and for the discipline and control of persons required to be detained therein. Section 47(2) provides that rules made under this section shall make provision for ensuring that a person who is charged with any offence under the rules shall be given a proper opportunity of presenting his case. Rule 49 provides that where a prisoner is charged with an offence against discipline he shall be informed of the charge as soon as possible and, in every case, before the time when it is inquired into by the
f governor. It further provides, thus giving effect to s 47(2) of the Act, that at any inquiry into a charge against a prisoner he shall be given a full opportunity of hearing what is alleged against him and of presenting his own case.

When a prisoner is to appear before a board of visitors for the determination of a charge of an offence against discipline, he is provided with a printed form which sets out, in simple language, the procedure which the prisoner can expect to be followed. It shows
g that he will be asked whether he pleads guilty or not guilty to the charge, that there will then be evidence of witnesses in support of the charge whom he may question and that, after the evidence against him, he may make his defence to the charge or, if he has pleaded guilty, offer an explanation. It also explains to him the procedure for obtaining permission to call witnesses. As Megaw LJ observed in the *St Germain case* [1979] 1 All ER 701 at 708, [1979] QB 425 at 444 all this points to a judicial proceeding.
h Rule 50 deals with the governor's awards, and r 51 deals with graver offences and brings in the board of visitors. Rule 51(4) provides that the board shall inquire into the charge and, if they find the offence proved, shall make one or more of eight specified awards, including the forfeiture of remission for a period not exceeding 180 days. Rule 52 is concerned with 'especially grave offences' where the forfeiture of remission award may exceed 180 days. Thus, the offences against discipline with which a board of visitors
j will be required to deal are likely to be substantially more serious than offences with which the governor can deal and the punishment which the board can award is very much more severe.

Megaw LJ agreed with the view expressed by Lord Widgery CJ in the Divisional Court that the act which the board of visitors perform under this jurisdiction is a judicial act (see [1978] 2 All ER 198 and 202, [1978] QB 678 at 689). He further accepted counsel for the applicants' submission that the board of visitors were 'enjoined to mete out

punishment only after a formalised inquiry and/or hearing'. Thus, the awards which a
board of visitors make are properly to be regarded as punishments. It was common   *a*
ground in the *St Germain* case, and it is equally so accepted before us, that the Prison
Rules do not confer on a prisoner any rights which may be enforced by an action for
damages on the ground that any statutory duty was owed to them (see *Becker v Home
Office* [1972] 2 All ER 676 at 682, [1972] 2 QB 407 at 418).

One of the main authorities relied on by the respondents is *Pyx Granite Co Ltd v
Ministry of Housing and Local Government* [1959] 3 All ER 1, [1960] AC 260. In that case   *b*
the question which arose was whether planning permission was required for carrying
out certain quarrying in the Malvern Hills and, if so, whether conditions which had been
imposed by the minister were valid. The time limit for certiorari had expired, and the
quarrying company therefore asked instead for a declaration as to its rights. The
respondents particularly rely on this case because the declaration was granted by the
House of Lords who rejected the minister's argument that the right remedy, if any, was   *c*
certiorari. Part of Lord Goddard's speech is of particular relevance. He said ([1959] 3 All
ER 1 at 8, [1960] AC 260 at 290):

> 'It was also argued that if there was a remedy obtainable in the High Court it
> must be by way of certiorari. I know of no authority for saying that if an order or
> decision can be attacked by certiorari the court is debarred from granting a
> declaration in an appropriate case. The remedies are not mutually exclusive, though   *d*
> no doubt there are some orders, notably convictions before justices, where the only
> appropriate remedy is certiorari.'

No one doubts the correctness of the observation that 'there are some orders, notably
convictions before justices, where the only appropriate remedy is certiorari'. Thus, the
first essential question is whether or not certiorari is the only appropriate remedy in   *e*
respect of an award of a board of visitors which is alleged to be null and void by reason of
breaches of natural justice. If it is the only appropriate remedy, it would clearly be an
abuse of the process of the court to seek the remedy of a declaratory judgment.

Counsel for the fourth plaintiff contends that the reasons why a declaration cannot be
obtained in respect of a conviction by justices is clear. He argues that it is contrary to
public policy and therefore an abuse of the process of the court for there to be collateral   *f*
litigation attacking a court of competent jurisdiction. A magistrates' court is such a court.
It is subject to appeal or control by judicial review. The board of visitors is not a court of
law and therefore the same considerations do not apply.

The analogy between proceedings before justices and those before a board of visitors is
too close to be dismissed so lightly. True, a board of visitors is not any ordinary court,
but it is a statutory body set up to act as a disciplinary tribunal and to administer   *g*
punishment where appropriate. A number of the members are likely to be justices of
the peace. The procedure is virtually identical. There is a charge, to which a plea is made,
following which, where the charge is contested, witnesses are called and cross-examination
takes place. True, there is no appeal in the strict sense, but the board's decisions are
subject to review on petition to the Home Secretary (see r 7 of the 1964 rules).

As a matter of public policy certiorari should, in my judgment, be held to be the only   *h*
appropriate remedy in respect of the visitors' decisions. The process of judicial review
provides a number of restraints which have particular relevance to the determination of
a judicial tribunal:

1. Leave is required to bring proceedings. In a field where there is bound to be
numerous disgruntled persons, whose real complaint is more likely to be directed to the
correctness of the punitive decision (which is not justiciable) than the fairness of the   *j*
procedure which was followed (which is justiciable), a 'filter' is most desirable. The
requirement of affidavit evidence in support of the application thus serves a very useful
purpose.

2. Terms may be imposed as to costs and the giving of security (Ord 53, r 3(9)). This
can be a useful form of control over the potentially frivolous application.

3. There is a time bar of three months, although the court has power, for good reason,

to extend this. In relation to judicial determinations, where there may be considerable
a difficulty in recollection of what exactly took place at the hearing, this is particularly
important. Moreover, if the order of certiorari is granted, because of a failure to adhere
to the correct procedure, a new hearing will, or should, often follow. This could be quite
unreal if it was to take place years after the initial hearing.

4. The court retains firm control over discovery and cross-examination, the latter
being rarely permitted. It is clearly most undesirable to place members of a tribunal in a
b position which is not really compatible with the free and proper discharge of their
functions, and such would be the case if cross-examination were a matter of course.

Counsel for the fourth plaintiff strongly urged that it is manifestly unfair to compel
his client, who is alleging bias against the chairman of the board, to seek judicial review
where a bare denial of his client's allegation, which forms the basis of his assertion of bias,
will mean defeat. However, the court has always had power to order cross-examination
c of a deponent, and this power is specifically spelt out in Ord 53, r 8. Although cross-
examination may be rarely ordered, if the interests of justice require it to be allowed it
would be an erroneous exercise of discretion to refuse it.

I would, therefore, conclude that certiorari is the only proper remedy where it is
sought to attack a decision of a board of visitors for want of natural justice.

If the views expressed above are correct, I have said sufficient to justify allowing these
d appeals. I have not, in doing so, felt obliged to go into the question which was much
debated as to the effect of the new Ord 53, which came into force in 1977, on the pre-
existing right to apply for declaratory relief, since, in my judgment, if, as I have found,
the only proper remedy before 1977 was to apply for an order of certiorari, that is an end
of the matter. However, out of deference to the able submissions addressed to us, my
views can be summarised as follows:

e 1. Order 53, r 1, is headed 'Cases appropriate for application for judicial review'. It
provides:

'(1) An application for—(*a*) an order of mandamus, prohibition or certiorari, or
(*b*) an injunction under section 9 of the Administration of Justice (Miscellaneous
Provisions) Act 1938 restraining a person from acting in any office in which he is
not entitled to act, shall be made by way of an application for judicial review in
f accordance with the provisions of this Order.

(2) An application for a declaration or an injunction (not being an injunction
mentioned in paragraph (1)(*b*)) may be made by way of an application for judicial
review, and on such an application the court may grant the declaration or injunction
claimed if it considers that, having regard to—(*a*) the nature of the matters in respect
of which relief may be granted by way of an order of mandamus, prohibition or
g certiorari, (*b*) the nature of the persons and bodies against whom relief may be
granted by way of such an order, and (*c*) in all the circumstances of the case, it would
be just and convenient for the declaration of injunction to be granted on an
application for judicial review.'

In my judgment it is clear that this order does not, either expressly or by necessary
h implication, provide an exclusive remedy for the control of the exercise of administrative
power. To quote Lord Scarman in *IRC v Rossminster Ltd* [1980] 1 All ER 80 at 104, [1980]
AC 952 at 1025–1026:

'The rule made no alteration to the substantive law; nor did it introduce any new
remedy. But the procedural reforms introduced are significant and valuable. Judicial
j review is now the procedure for obtaining relief by way of prerogative order, ie
mandamus, prohibition or certiorari. But it is not confined to such relief: an
applicant may now obtain a declaration or injunction in any case where in the
opinion of the court "it would be just and convenient for the declaration or
injunction to be granted on an application for judicial review". Further, on an
application, the court may award damages, provided that the court is satisfied that
damages could have been awarded, had the applicant proceeded by action. The rule

also makes available, at the court's discretion, discovery, interrogatories, and cross-examination of deponents. And, where the relief sought is a declaration, an injunction, or damages but the court considers that it should not be granted on an application for judicial review, the court may order the proceedings to continue as if they had begun by writ. Thus, the application for judicial review, where a declaration, an injunction, or damages are sought, is a summary way of obtaining a remedy which could be obtained at trial in an action begun by writ; and it is available only where in all the circumstances it is just and convenient. If issues of fact, or law and fact, are raised which it is neither just nor convenient to decide without the full trial process, the court may dismiss the application or order, in effect, a trial.'

2. If Parliament had desired that by reason of the reforms contained in Ord 53 the remedy by way of judicial review should exclude the pre-existing remedy by way of an action for declaratory relief to control the exercise of administrative power, it could have simply so provided in the recent Supreme Court Act 1981. It would, however, have been somewhat of a surprise if it had done so, in view of the contrary recommendation made in 1976 by the Law Commission, who were responsible for the production of the new Ord 53 (see Law Com no 73, Cmnd 6407 (1976)). Section 31 of the 1981 Act does, however, make specific provisions for applications for judicial review. It provides:

'(1) An application to the High Court for one or more of the following forms of relief, namely—(a) an order of mandamus, prohibition or certiorari; (b) a declaration or injunction under subsection (2); or (c) an injunction under section 30 restraining a person not entitled to do so from acting in an office to which that section applies, shall be made in accordance with rules of court by a procedure to be known as an application for judicial review.

(2) A declaration may be made or an injunction granted under this subsection in any case where an application for judicial review, seeking that relief, has been made and the High Court considers that, having regard to—(a) the nature of the matters in respect of which relief may be granted by orders of mandamus, prohibition or certiorari; (b) the nature of the persons and bodies against whom relief may be granted by such orders; and (c) all the circumstances of the case, it would be just and convenient for the declaration to be made or the injunction to be granted, as the case may be . . .'

As the note in the supplement to para [3332] of *The Supreme Court Practice 1982* correctly state, s 31 is a statutory codification of Ord 53. I cannot construe that section, and in particular the subsections set out above, as providing that declarations against public authorities when exercising their public law functions can only be obtained by application for judicial review under Ord 53.

3. I accept that by reason of the radical procedural reforms in the supervisory jurisdiction of the court and the safeguard against abuse built into Ord 53, that where the conduct of a public authority is to be challenged, then as a general rule it is more appropriate that it be done by a process of judicial review and not by way of an action. But, unless and until the law is amended, the litigant still has the option. Accordingly, it cannot in my judgment be said to be an abuse of the process of the court to seek the alternative route rather than to proceed by way of an application under Ord 53.

4. However, it is common ground that declaratory relief is a discretionary remedy. Accordingly, it may be refused for undue delay. It may be also refused if in reality it is sought merely in order to circumvent the procedural safeguards contained in Ord 53 and which the courts consider should attend the process of challenging a particular area of administrative activity, eg immigration control: see the observations of Roskill LJ in *Uppal v Home Office* [1978] CA Transcript 719 quoted by Lord Denning MR in his judgment. I can see no objection, in an appropriate case, to the trial of the preliminary issue: would the court in the exercise of its discretion grant the declaration sought by the plaintiff if the facts he alleges were proved? The purpose of trying such a preliminary issue would, of course, be to avoid the expense and potential oppression which could

result from the obligation to give extensive discovery and to submit to wide-ranging
a cross-examination.

I also would allow the appeal.

O'CONNOR LJ (read by Lord Denning MR). The four plaintiffs in these proceedings
were all at some date prisoners in Hull Prison. The first three took part in a major riot at
that prison in the summer of 1976. The fourth took part in a riot in April 1979. In due
b course all four men were charged with offences before the Board of Visitors of Hull
Prison and various penalties were imposed. In 1980 they began proceedings, the first
three by writs, the fourth by originating summons, claiming declarations that the
adjudications of the visitors were null and void by reason of breaches of natural justice.
The visitors applied to have the proceedings struck out as an abuse of the process of the
court. Peter Pain J refused the applications. They appeal to this court.

c Counsel for the defendants submits that the only way a person aggrieved by an
adjudication of the visitors can challenge it is by asking for judicial review; that means
in this case certiorari to bring up and quash the decision.

Even during the period after the decision in *R v Northumberland Compensation Appeal
Tribunal, ex p Shaw* [1952] 1 All ER 122, [1952] 1 KB 338, when the courts were
developing the use of declarations and injunctions in administrative law, it was recognised
d that decisions of justices could not be challenged by this route. In *Pyx Granite Co Ltd v
Minister of Housing and Local Government* [1959] 3 All ER 1 at 8, [1960] AC 260 at 290,
Lord Goddard said: '. . . no doubt, there are some orders, notably convictions by justices,
where the only appropriate remedy is certiorari.' Lord Goddard was only using the
justices as an example, for he recognised that there could be others.

Once it had been decided by this court in *R v Hull Prison Board of Visitors, ex p St
e Germain* [1979] 1 All ER 701, [1979] QB 425 that judicial review was available to
challenge the decision of boards of visitors, then in my judgment it became clear that
those decisions could not be challenged by actions for declarations. I think that there are
two main reasons why this is so; the constitution of boards of visitors and the limits of
any suggested relief by way of declaration.

As to the first reason, I gratefully adopt what has been said on this topic by Lord
f Denning MR and Ackner LJ.

As to the second reason, I start by looking at the relief claimed, and I take O'Reilly as
an example. Five charges of offences against discipline were proved against him and he
was awarded a total of 196 days' solitary confinement and 510 days' loss of remission of
sentence. The statement of claim alleges that the board of visitors acted in breach of the
Prison Rules and of the requirements of fairness and/or the rules of natural justice. So it
g is alleged that the finding and award of the board were made invalidly, improperly, and
were null and void and of no effect. The prayer is for 'a declaration that the finding of,
and award by, the Board was void and of no effect'. The real purpose of claiming this
relief years after the event is to quash the award of loss of remission. If the action claiming
the declaration went to trial, the court hearing the case would have no power to do more
than to grant or refuse the declaration; contrast the power of the court under RSC Ord
h 53, r 9, if minded to quash the award, to consider the propriety of remitting the matter
for rehearing and in its discretion deciding whether to remit or not. Here was a prisoner
charged before the visitors with very serious offences, which the visitors found proved;
if that finding was to be set aside, it seems to me that it should only be as a result of
judicial review. The time limits, coupled with the power to remit, make judicial review
the only appropriate remedy, and point unerringly to show that an action for a declaration
j should not be permitted.

That is sufficient for the decision of the present appeals, but counsel for the defendants
invited us to say that the effect of the Supreme Court Act 1981, which has given statutory
backing to Ord 53, is that judicial review is the only way in which decisions of
administrative tribunals can be challenged. For my part I am not prepared to accede to
that submission. I see the force of the argument that if an applicant applies within time
for judicial review and is refused leave, he ought not to be permitted to escape the
safeguard by starting an action by writ for a declaration. It may well be that the facts of

such a case may show that the later action is an abuse of the process of the court, but that is quite different from saying that the right to bring an action for a declaration where *a* judicial review lies has been abolished. The real check on the action for a declaration is to remember that it is a discretionary relief.

I would allow this appeal.

Appeals allowed. Leave to appeal to the House of Lords granted.

b

Solicitors: *Treasury Solicitor; Mincoff, Science & Gold*, Newcastle upon Tyne (for the plaintiffs O'Reilly, Derbyshire and Dougan); *Seifert, Sedley & Co*, agents for *Millers*, Manchester (for the plaintiff Millbanks).

Frances Rustin   Barrister.

c

R v Crown Court at Wolverhampton, ex parte Crofts

QUEEN'S BENCH DIVISION   *d*
DONALDSON LJ AND WEBSTER J
19 MAY 1982

*Certiorari – Fraud – Perjury – Acquittal obtained as a result of perjured evidence – Defendant convicted in magistrates' court – Defendant appealing against conviction to Crown Court – Crown Court quashing conviction as a result of evidence given by defendant – Evidence given by *e* defendant false – Prosecutor applying for order of certiorari to quash decision of Crown Court – Whether jurisdiction to grant the order of certiorari – Whether making of order of certiorari would conflict with principle that no one should be put in peril of conviction twice for same offence.*

The defendant failed to appear at a magistrates' court to answer a charge of driving a car after having consumed an excessive amount of alcohol. As a result he was convicted on *f* the uncontroverted evidence of the prosecution. He appealed to the Crown Court, contending that it was not he but his passenger who had been driving at the material time. His evidence was believed and the Crown Court allowed the appeal and ordered his conviction to be quashed. His evidence was in fact false and he was subsequently convicted of perjury. Thereafter the prosecutor applied for an order of certiorari to bring up and set aside the decision of the Crown Court quashing the conviction on the ground *g* that it had been obtained as a result of perjured evidence. The questions arose whether the court could grant an order of certiorari in view of the fact that the Crown Court had quashed the conviction and whether setting aside the Crown Court's decision would conflict with the basic principle of English criminal law that no one should be put in peril of conviction twice in respect of the same offence.

h

Held – Where there was a conflict between the principle that no one should be put in peril of conviction twice for the same offence and the principle that the court should intervene to quash a decision of an inferior court obtained by fraud, the former principle should prevail. But in the defendant's case no such conflict arose because, if the decision of the Crown Court were quashed on the ground that it had been obtained by fraud, the defendant would not be put in peril of conviction twice, since the result would be that *j* he remained convicted as a result of the first and only occasion on which he was put in peril. It followed that there was jurisdiction to quash the decision of the Crown Court and an order of certiorari would be granted (see p 704 g to j, post).

R v Recorder of Leicester, ex p Wood [1947] 1 All ER 928 and *R v West Sussex Quarter Sessions, ex p Albert & Maud Johnson Trust Ltd* [1973] 3 All ER 289 applied.

R v Simpson [1914] 1 KB 66 distinguished.

Notes

a For certiorari to quash an order of the Crown Court quashing conviction of defendant before justices, see 11 Halsbury's Laws (4th edn) paras 1529–1530, and for cases on the subject, see 16 Digest (Reissue) 402–429, 4442–4724 and 33 Digest (Repl) 351, 1637–1640.

Cases referred to in judgment

b *Colonial Bank of Australasia v Willan* (1874) LR 5 PC 417, PC, 16 Digest (Reissue) 165, 1640.

  R v Alleyne (1854) 4 E & B 186, 119 ER 72.

  R v Gillyard (1848) 12 QB 527, 116 ER 965, 16 Digest (Reissue) 428, 4713.

  R v Recorder of Leicester, ex p Wood [1947] 1 All ER 928, [1947] KB 726, DC, 16 Digest (Reissue) 428, 4715.

c *R v Simpson* [1914] 1 KB 66, DC, 16 Digest (Reissue) 429, 4721.

  R v West Sussex Quarter Sessions, ex p Albert & Maud Johnson Trust Ltd [1973] 3 All ER 289, [1974] QB 24, CA, 16 Digest (Reissue) 415, 4573.

Cases also cited

  R v Clare Justices [1905] IR 510, DC.

d *R v Galway Justices* [1906] 2 IR 499.

Application for judicial review

Chief Inspector Ralph John Crofts of the West Midlands Police Force applied for an order of certiorari to bring up and quash an order of the Crown Court at Wolverhampton on 21 October 1981 allowing an appeal by Andrew Whitehouse against his conviction, on

e 27 July 1981 by Wolverhampton Magistrates' Court, of driving a motor vehicle after having consumed an excessive amount of alcohol and driving without 'L' plates. The facts are set out in the judgment of Donaldson LJ.

Andrew Urquhart for the applicant.

f The respondent did not appear.

DONALDSON LJ. In this case Mr Crofts, a chief inspector of police of the West Midlands Police, moves for judicial review of an order of the Crown Court sitting at Wolverhampton, made on 21 October 1981, whereby that court allowed the appeal of Andrew Whitehouse against his convictions on 27 July 1981, by the Wolverhampton

g Magistrates' Court, of driving a motor vehicle after having consumed excess alcohol and with driving without 'L' plates.

  The facts are, happily, unusual. Mr Whitehouse was charged with having consumed excess alcohol and with driving without 'L' plates following his arrest by a police constable. At that time there was a passenger in his car. When he should have appeared before the Wolverhampton Magistrates' Court, he failed to do so, and the prosecution

h evidence was uncontroverted. He then saw fit to appeal to the Crown Court. In that court he was not content to rely on such merits as he might have had, but he did two further things, both of which are now admitted. First, he alleged that it was not he but a lady who had been driving, a Miss Noon. Second, he called Miss Noon to give evidence that she was driving. In fact, as is now admitted, Mr Whitehouse was the driver and Miss Noon was not with him on that night. He was in fact accompanied by another lady. It

j would appear that he persuaded Miss Noon to give this evidence by offering her various sums of money. Mr Whitehouse has subsequently been convicted of perjury.

  The question which now arises is whether this court can (and if it can, whether it should) grant certiorari to quash the decision of the Crown Court, which, in effect, substituted an acquittal for the conviction before the magistrates' court.

  The simplest general statement of the law is to be found in 11 Halsbury's Laws (4th edn) para 1529, where it says:

'Certiorari does not lie to remove a decision of justices to commit or refuse to commit a defendant for trial; nor does it lie, it seems, to remove an acquittal, for an order of an inferior court, even though defective for errors on its face or for want of jurisdiction, is not void but only voidable, and therefore to quash an acquittal would be to put a man in peril twice for the same offence. Where, however, a defendant is convicted by justices, and the conviction is quashed on appeal to the Crown Court, it seems that certiorari lies on the application of the prosecutor to remove the order of the Crown Court quashing the conviction.'

The jurisdiction to quash a decision of an inferior tribunal which has been obtained by fraud is clear. It is sufficient if I refer to two cases only. The first is the decision in *R v Recorder of Leicester, ex p Wood* [1947] 1 All ER 928, [1947] KB 726. There a recorder heard an appeal against a bastardy order made by justices and the appellant gave perjured evidence, as a result of which the appeal was successful. The leading judgment was given by Lord Goddard CJ. Having referred to the leading case of *R v Gillyard* (1848) 12 QB 527, 116 ER 967 he said ([1947] 1 All ER 928, [1947] KB 726 at 727):

'The court held that where a decision of an inferior court resulting in a conviction had been obtained by fraud *certiorari* was a remedy which was open to the subject who had been convicted, and the rule was made absolute and the conviction quashed. That seems to have been followed in other cases; see *R. v. Alleyne* ((1854) 4 E & B 186, 119 ER 72) and in *Colonial Bank of Australasia v. Willan* ((1874) LR 5 PC 417, the Judicial Committee obviously admitted the principle that, if the court was satisfied that there had been fraud in the proceedings, the remedy of *certiorari* would lie.'

The same proposition is supported by a decision of the Court of Appeal, in *R v West Sussex Quarter Sessions, ex p Albert & Maud Johnson Trust Ltd* [1973] 3 All ER 289 at 296, 298, 301, [1974] QB 24 at 36, 39, 42 per Lord Denning MR, Orr and Lawton LJJ.

Thus far it would appear that there is no difficulty in the way of the applicant. Such difficulty as arises, if any, must be based on the decision of this court in *R v Simpson* [1914] 1 KB 66. There a Divisional Court, composed of Ridley, Scrutton and Bailhache JJ, refused to make an order of certiorari quashing a decision of magistrates, dismissing an information charging an offence under the Coal Mines Act 1911. They did so on the basis, not that there was no jurisdiction to quash a conviction, or an acquittal, come to that, which was obtained by fraud, but on the basis that there was an overriding principle of English law that no one should be put in peril of conviction twice in respect of the same offence. For my part I accept that that principle is one of the most important principles of English criminal law and that if there is a conflict between that principle and the principle that courts will intervene in order to quash the decisions of inferior courts which are obtained by fraud, it is the former principle (that no one should be put in peril twice) which should prevail. But in my judgment that does not apply where a court is concerned with an acquittal by the Crown Court on appeal from magistrates, for this reason. If the Crown Court decision is quashed, and this will only occur when it is the beneficiary of the Crown Court decision who has been guilty of the fraud, the result will be not that the defendant is twice put in peril, but that he remains convicted as a result of the first and only occasion on which he was put in peril. That seems to me to be the distinction between this case and *R v Simpson*. Accordingly I would order that the decision be quashed.

WEBSTER J. I agree.

Certiorari granted.

Solicitors: *I S Manson*, Birmingham (for the applicant).

N P Metcalfe Esq   Barrister.

Perry v Sidney Phillips & Son (a firm)

COURT OF APPEAL, CIVIL DIVISION
LORD DENNING MR, OLIVER AND KERR LJJ
13, 14 JULY 1982

Damages – Measure of damages – Negligence – Building – Surveyor's report to purchaser negligently failing to disclose defects – Substantial repairs required to remedy defects – Purchaser of building intending to occupy property and repair defects – Whether appropriate measure of damages cost of repairs or difference between purchase price and value of property as it should have been described.

Damages – Assessment – Date at which damages assessed – Surveyor's report to purchaser negligently failing to disclose defects in building – Substantial repairs required to remedy defects – Purchaser not having money to carry out repairs – Whether damages to be assessed as at date of report or date of hearing.

Damages – Mitigation of loss – Impecuniosity – Defendant's conduct – Surveyor's report to purchaser negligently failing to disclose defects in building – Substantial repairs required to remedy defects – Purchaser unable to afford cost of repairs – Surveyor's conduct causing purchaser to conclude that surveyor would not accept liability – Whether purchaser's impecuniosity and surveyor's conduct reasonably foreseeable causes of purchaser's failure to carry out repairs – Whether purchaser required to mitigate loss by carrying out repairs as soon as possible.

The plaintiff purchased a house property for £27,000 in reliance on a survey report prepared by the defendants, a firm of chartered surveyors. The report stated that most of the house and outbuildings were in good order, that the property was an attractive property and that it was a reasonable buy for £27,000. After completing the purchase and taking possession, the plaintiff discovered that the roof leaked and was in poor condition and that the septic tank was inefficient and caused a nuisance by reason of its smell. The plaintiff brought an action against the defendants alleging negligence and breach of contract. The defendants at all times denied liability. At the hearing of the action some five years after the defendants made their report, the judge found that the defendants were liable both in negligence and for breach of contract. On the question of the appropriate measure of damage the judge held that the plaintiff was entitled to damages assessed according to the cost of repairing the defects as at the date of hearing, on the basis that since he intended to remain in the house he was entitled to the cost of repair or reinstatement. The plaintiff also claimed that he was entitled to damages for the distress and discomfort of living in a house which was in a defective condition. The plaintiff had not carried out the repairs required because, he claimed, he had not been in a financial position to do so, and the defendants' denial of liability deterred him from doing so. The defendants contended that the plaintiff was under a duty to mitigate the damages by carrying out the repairs as soon as possible after discovery of the defects in the house, that his inability to do so because of his impecuniosity was irrelevant and that his failure to do so disentitled him from damages for vexation and discomfort. The judge held that the plaintiff was entitled to damages for vexation. After the hearing the plaintiff sold the house for £43,000 without doing the repairs. The defendants appealed, contending (i) that the correct measure of damages was the difference between the price actually paid by the plaintiff and the market value at the date of purchase, and (ii) that the plaintiff was not entitled to damages for vexation caused by his own impecuniosity. The plaintiff conceded that the sale of the house meant that the cost of the repairs was no longer an appropriate measure of damages, but contended that he was entitled to the difference, as at the date of hearing, between the actual value of the house and the value it would have had at that date if the defendants' report had been correct.

Held – The appeal would be allowed in part for the following reasons—

(1) Where the prospective buyer of a house was misled by a negligent survey report *a*
into paying more for a property than the property was actually worth, the correct
measure of damages payable by the negligent surveyor was the difference between the
price actually paid and the market value assessed as at the date of purchase, together with
interest until the payment of damages, and not the notional difference in value as at the
date of hearing. The plaintiff was therefore entitled to damages on that basis, regardless
of whether he might have intended to remain in the property or whether he cut his *b*
losses by immediately reselling it (see p 708 *d* to *j*, p 709 *f* to *j*, p 710 *g h* and p 711 *e f* and
j to p 712 *c*, post); *Philips v Ward* [1956] 1 All ER 874 and *Ford v White & Co* [1964] 2 All
ER 755 followed; *Dodd Properties (Kent) Ltd v Canterbury City Council* [1980] 1 All ER 928
distinguished.

(2) The plaintiff was entitled to damages for vexation if it was a reasonably foreseeable
result of the defects which the defendants negligently failed to disclose in their report *c*
that the plaintiff would suffer distress and discomfort until the repairs were carried out
and if it was reasonable in all the circumstances for the plaintiff not to carry out the
repairs immediately. Since the plaintiff's impecuniosity was not the only reason for his
not carrying out the repairs and since in the face of the defendants' denial of liability it
was reasonable for the plaintiff not to carry out the repairs immediately, he was entitled
to damages for inconvenience, distress and discomfort (see p 709 *b* to *d* and *g*, p 711 *d* to *d*
f and p 712 *j* to p 713 *b*, post); *The Edison* [1933] All ER Rep 144 distinguished.

Per Oliver and Kerr LJJ. A surveyor's report does not in law amount to a warranty of
the value of the property surveyed or (per Lord Denning MR) a warranty that there are
no defects other than those in the report (see p 708 *e*, p 710 *a* to *c* and p 713 *b*, post).

Decision of Patrick Bennett QC [1982] 1 All ER 1005 reversed in part.

Notes   *e*
For the general principles relating to the measure of damages, see 12 Halsbury's Laws
(4th edn) paras 1127–1144, and for cases on the subject, see 17 Digest (Reissue) 101–119,
109–208.

For the impecuniosity of the plaintiff, the measure of damages for torts affecting land
and the plaintiff's duty to mitigate, see 12 Halsbury's Laws (4th edn) paras 1144, 1168,
1193–1196, and for cases on the subject, see 17 Digest (Reissue) 131–133, 287–302.   *f*

Cases referred to in judgments
Cory (William) & Son Ltd v Wingate Investments (London Colney) Ltd (1980) 17 Build LR
    104, CA.
Dodd Properties (Kent) Ltd v Canterbury City Council [1980] 1 All ER 928, [1980] 1 WLR
    433, CA.   *g*
Ford v White & Co [1964] 2 All ER 755, [1964] 1 WLR 885, Digest (Cont Vol B) 659,
    1083a.
Heywood v Wellers (a firm) [1976] 1 All ER 300, [1976] QB 446, [1976] 2 WLR 101, CA,
    Digest (Cont Vol E) 567, 1098c.
Hutchinson v Harris (1978) 10 Build LR 19, CA.
Jackson v Horizon Holidays Ltd [1975] 3 All ER 92, [1975] 1 WLR 1468, CA, Digest (Cont *h*
    Vol D) 113, 259a.
Jarvis v Swan Tours Ltd [1973] 1 All ER 71, [1973] QB 233, [1972] 3 WLR 954, CA, 17
    Digest (Reissue) 111, 166.
Liesbosch (owners) v Edison (owners), The Edison [1933] AC 449, [1933] All ER Rep 144, HL,
    17 Digest (Reissue) 103, 113.
Miliangos v George Frank (Textiles) Ltd [1975] 3 All ER 801, [1976] AC 443, [1975] 3 WLR *j*
    758, HL, Digest (Cont Vol D) 691, 64c.
Philips v Ward [1956] 1 All ER 874, [1956] 1 WLR 471, CA, 47 Digest (Repl) 564, 35.
Radford v De Froberville [1978] 1 All ER 33, [1977] 1 WLR 1262, Digest (Cont Vol E) 173,
    141a.
Simple Simon Catering Ltd v Binstock Miller & Co (1973) 228 EG 527, CA, Digest (Cont Vol
    D) 844, 1098b.

Cases also cited

a *Brandeis Goldschmidt & Co Ltd v Western Transport Ltd* [1982] 1 All ER 28, [1981] QB 864, CA.

   Compania Financiera Soleada SA v Hamoor Tanker Corp Inc, The Borag [1981] 1 All ER 856, [1981] 1 WLR 274, CA.

   Johnson v Agnew [1979] 1 All ER 883, [1980] AC 367, HL.

   Livingstone v Rawyards Coal Co (1880) 5 App Cas 25, HL.

b *Simpson v Grove Tomkins & Co* (1982) Times, 17 May, CA.

Appeal

The defendants, Sidney Phillips & Son (a firm), appealed against the decision of Patrick Bennett QC sitting as a deputy judge of the High Court ([1982] 1 All ER 1005) on 13 April 1981 whereby he gave judgment for the plaintiff, Ivan H Perry, and ordered the
c defendants to pay damages to be assessed in respect of their negligence. The facts are set out in the judgment of Lord Denning MR.

John Hicks QC and *John L Powell* for the defendants.
Peter Latham for the plaintiff.

d
LORD DENNING MR. In 1976 the plaintiff, Mr Perry, was minded to buy a house. He saw what looked like a very attractive property. It was Kyre Bank Cottage, Kyre, near Tenbury Wells, in Worcestershire. He made an offer of £27,000 subject to survey and contract. He employed a firm of surveyors, Messrs Sidney Phillips & Son, to carry out the survey. They surveyed the property and prepared a report. Mr Perry read the report. On
e the faith of it, although it did disclose some defects in the property, he was satisfied that the cottage was a sound buy. So, on 2 July 1976 he completed the contract of sale for £27,000.

Unfortunately, after Mr Perry took possession, he found many defects. They had not been mentioned in the report. In particular, there were serious defects in the roof and in the septic tank. The surveyors had not noticed them. The roof leaked and the rain came
f in. The septic tank gave off an offensive odour. Mr Perry consulted a different firm of surveyors. They made a report showing that there were many defects which had not been mentioned by Messrs Sidney Phillips & Son in their report. Mr Perry instructed solicitors. They wrote to Messrs Sidney Phillips & Son listing the defects. Messrs Sidney Phillips & Son instructed their own solicitors. The upshot was that the surveyors denied any liability.

g This placed Mr Perry in a quandary. He simply did not have the money to undertake major repairs. He carried out what minor repairs he could on a 'do-it-yourself' basis. As Messrs Sidney Phillips & Son were denying liability, he could not risk doing the repairs on borrowed money.

On his solicitors' advice, Mr Perry brought an action against Messrs Sidney Phillips & Son for damages for their negligence in making their report. The claim was put both in
h breach of contract and in negligence. In 1981 the case was tried by Patrick Bennett QC sitting as a deputy High Court judge. He dealt with liability before considering the quantum of damages. At that stage Mr Perry and his wife were still living in the cottage.

The deputy judge found that the surveyors were negligent in making their report. He held that damages should be assessed according to the cost of repairing the defects in 1981 when the action was tried. He also held that Mr Perry ought to be awarded damages
j for vexation, that is the worry, discomfort and distress which he had suffered by reason of the house being in the poor condition. Messrs Sidney Phillips & Son appeal to this court.

But then the unexpected happened. After the trial and pending the appeal, Mr Perry decided to sell the house. After the trial in April 1981 Mr Perry found himself in financial difficulties. He had received bills from his solicitors for £4,788 costs. He could not get any assurance as to the date when damages would be assessed. He was faced with the prospect of the appeal and long-drawn-out hearings as to damages. So Mr Perry put the cottage on the market without doing any of the repairs. He sold it for £43,000.   *a*

Mr Perry made an affidavit to explain why he had found it necessary to sell the cottage. In August 1981 he had been offered a job as a clerk with stockjobbers on the London Stock Exchange. It was necessary that he should live nearer to his new place of work. So he sold the cottage and brought a house at Fittleworth in Sussex.

We now have to consider how the damages are to be assessed. The cases show up many differences. I need only draw attention to the following.   *b*

First, where there is a contract to build a wall or a house, or to do repairs to it, then if the contractor does not do the work or does it badly, the employer is entitled, by way of damages, to recover the reasonable cost of doing such work as is reasonable to make good the breach. The cost is to be assessed at the time when it would be reasonable for the employer to do it, having regard to all the circumstances of the case, including therein any delay due to a denial of liability by the contractor or the financial situation of the *c* employer. The work may not have been done even up to the date of trial. If the cost has increased in the meantime since the breach, owing to inflation, then the increased cost is recoverable, but no interest is to be allowed for the intervening period (see *Radford v De Froberville* [1978] 1 All ER 33, [1977] 1 WLR 1262, *William Cory & Son Ltd v Wingate Investments (London Colney) Ltd* (1980) 17 Build LR 104); likewise if a wrongdoer damages *d* his neighbour's house by nuisance or negligence, and the neighbour is put to expense in the repairing of it (see *Dodd Properties (Kent) Ltd v Canterbury City Council* [1980] 1 All ER 928, [1980] 1 WLR 433).

Second, where there is a contract by a prospective buyer with a surveyor under which the surveyor agrees to survey a house and make a report on it, and he makes it negligently and the client buys the house on the faith of the report, then the damages are to be assessed at the time of the breach, according to the difference in price which the buyer *e* would have given if the report had been carefully made from that which he in fact gave owing to the negligence of the surveyor. The surveyor gives no warranty that there are no defects other than those in his report. There is no question of specific performance. The contract has already been performed, albeit negligently. The buyer is not entitled to remedy the defects and charge the cost to the surveyor. He is only entitled to damages for the breach of contract or for negligence. That was so decided by this court in *Philips v* *f* *Ward* [1956] 1 All ER 874, [1956] 1 WLR 471, followed in *Simple Simon Catering Ltd v Binstock Miller & Co* (1973) 228 EG 527.

The former case was concerned with breach of contract by surveyors. It is their duty to use reasonable care and skill in making a proper report on the house. In our present case Messrs Sidney Phillips & Son failed in that duty in 1976 when they made the negligent report. Mr Perry acted on the report in 1976 when he bought the house in July *g* 1976. The general rule of law is that you assess the damages at the date of the breach: so as to put the plaintiff in the same position as he would have been in if the contract had been properly performed. Even if the claim be laid in tort against the surveyor, the damages should be on the same basis.

So you have to take the difference in valuation. You have to take the difference between what a man would pay for the house in the condition in which it was reported to be and *h* what he would pay if the report had been properly made showing the defects as they were. In other words, how much more did he pay for the house by reason of the negligent report than he would have paid had it been a good report? That being the position, the difference in valuation should be taken at the date of the breach in 1976. We were given some approximate figures of the difference in the valuation. The plaintiff's figure was £6,000. The defendants' figure was £2,250.   *j*

I would go on to say, and this is important, that although the date for the assessment of damages is 1976, there is some compensation for inflation because those damages carry interest. Probably 9%, 10% or even 11% would be awarded nowadays from 1976 until the date when the damages are paid, or, at least, up until judgment is given and then afterwards at the judgment rate.

The second point is as to the distress, worry, inconvenience and all the trouble to
a which Mr Perry was put during the time when he was in the house. Counsel for the
defendants sought to say before us that damages ought not to be recoverable under this
head at all. He referred to the case of *Liesbosch (owners) v Edison (owners), The Edison* [1933]
AC 449, [1933] All ER Rep 144. In that case Lord Wright said that the loss due to the
impecuniosity of the plaintiffs was not recoverable. I think that that statement must be
restricted to the facts of the *Liesbosch* case. It is not of general application. It is analysed
b and commented on in this court in *Dodd Properties (Kent) Ltd v Canterbury City Council*
[1980] 1 All ER 928, [1980] 1 WLR 433. It is not applicable here. It seems to me that Mr
Perry is entitled to damages for all the vexation, distress and worry which he has been
caused by reason of the negligence of the surveyor. If a man buys a house for his own
occupation on the surveyor's advice that it is sound and then finds out that it is in a
deplorable condition, it is reasonably foreseeable that he will be most upset. He may, as
c here, not have the money to repair it and this will upset him all the more. That too is
reasonably foreseeable. All this anxiety, worry and distress may nowadays be the subject
of compensation. Not excessive, but modest compensation. That appears from such cases
as *Jarvis v Swan Tours Ltd* [1973] 1 All ER 71, [1973] QB 233, *Jackson v Horizon Holidays
Ltd* [1975] 3 All ER 92, [1975] 1 WLR 1468, *Heywood v Wellers* [1976] 1 All ER 300,
[1976] QB 446 and *Hutchinson v Harris* (1978) 10 Build LR 19.
d   In our present case, the deputy judge said ([1982] 1 All ER 1005 at 1016–1017):

'I think it was reasonably foreseeable that, if Mr Perry bought the house in such a
condition that he was exposed to the incursion of water, the anxiety resulting from
the question of when the repairs should be done and the odour and smell from the
defective septic water tank would cause him distress and discomfort which I have
gathered together under the term 'vexation' . . . In my view the plaintiff is entitled
e   . . . to damages for such discomfort, distress and the like which he has suffered as a
result of the defendants' negligence in, in effect, giving this house a clean bill of
health . . . I am satisfied that he has not acted unreasonably and he has not failed to
mitigate his damage and that the consequences which have flowed from the
defendants' breach of contract and/or negligence were foreseeable, are direct and
have not been diminished or extinguished by any failure on the part of Mr Perry to
f   mitigate his loss.'

Mr Perry is entitled to damages on that score also. The quantum of damages is to be
assessed by an official referee later on.
In the circumstances, I think that the appeal must be allowed in so far as it affects the
date at which damages are to be assessed, but dismissed on the question of vexation.
g
OLIVER LJ. I agree with the order which Lord Denning MR has proposed. It is not
now suggested that the measure of damages which was proposed by the learned deputy
judge ought to be sustained in its totality, not because of any error in his reasoning,
although no doubt the defendants would have wished to challenge that if the matter had
proceeded on that basis, but because it has been overtaken by events, the house having
h now been sold by the plaintiff at a price very considerably in excess of that which the
plaintiff paid for it in 1976. In these circumstances, the cost of repairs, which have not in
fact been carried out, cannot any longer be an appropriate measure; and the debate before
us had concentrated on two points. The first is the question whether the appropriate
measure of damage on the basis of what the deputy judge described as 'differential in
valuation' is, as counsel for the defendants submits, the difference between the price paid
j by the plaintiff and the value at the date of its acquisition, the property which he actually
got, or whether it is, as counsel for the plaintiff suggests, the difference between the value
of the house at the date of the trial in its defective condition and the value which it would
then have had if it had been in the condition in which on the basis of the surveyor's
report it should have been. Speaking for myself, I have no doubt whatever that the basis
suggested by counsel for the defendants is the right one. What counsel for the plaintiff

contends for in effect makes the surveyors warrant the value of the property surveyed, and indeed the deputy judge seems so to have thought. He said this in his judgment *a* ([1982] 1 All ER 1005 at 1011):

> 'Counsel for the defendants, in the course of an extremely helpful address, warned me against putting the surveyor into the shoes of the vendor, that is warranting the condition of the property and requiring, if that warranty is breached, the surveyor to pay compensation to the purchaser. [I interpose to say that I do not believe for a moment that vendors normally do do that and it may be that this is a misprint for *b* 'valuer'. The learned judge then goes on to say:] In reality the surveyor is not far removed from that situation. The purchaser is relying on his skill, his expertise and his care to ensure that what he, the purchaser, is buying is worth what he is paying for it. In that sense, the surveyor is describing the property which is being bought.'

c

With the greatest respect to the deputy judge, I cannot agree with that. The position, as I see it, is simply this, that the plaintiff has been misled by a negligent survey report into paying more for the property than that property was actually worth. The position, as I see it, is exactly the same as that which arose in *Philips v Ward* [1956] 1 All ER 874, [1956] 1 WLR 471, to which Lord Denning MR has already referred, and in the subsequent case of *Ford v White & Co* [1964] 2 All ER 755, [1964] 1 WLR 885. It is said *d* by counsel for the plaintiff that this proposition is supported in some way by the more recent case of *Dodd Properties (Kent) Ltd v Canterbury City Council* [1980] 1 All ER 928, [1980] 1 WLR 433. That was a case in which the plaintiffs were claiming damages in tort against the defendants, they having removed a support to the plaintiffs' premises. It could not be suggested in that case that there was any other measure of damages than the cost of repair, the only question being the date at which the repairs ought to have been *e* carried out; and the debate there was as to the date at which it was reasonable for the plaintiffs to have carried out the repairs. As I read the case, it merely exemplifies the general principle which is set out in the headnote to the case ([1980] 1 WLR 433 at 434):

> '... the fundamental principle as to damages was that the measure of damages *f* was that sum of money that would put the injured party in the same position as that in which he would have been if he had not sustained the injury'

and the question was what loss the plaintiff, acting reasonably, had actually suffered.

I see nothing in that case which justifies the proposition, for which counsel for the plaintiff contends, that damages are to be assessed on the basis of some hypothetical value at the date of the trial because the plaintiff has chosen, as he did in this case, to retain the *g* property and not to cut his loss by reselling it. I therefore am of the same view as Lord Denning MR that the right measure of damage is the measure suggested in both *Philips v Ward* and *Ford v White & Co*, which is simply the difference between what the plaintiff paid for the property and its value at the date when he obtained it.

The other question which has been much debated is whether the deputy judge was right in awarding damages for vexation, that is the discomfort and so on suffered by the *h* plaintiff as a result of having to live for a lengthy period in a defective house which for one reason or another was not repaired over the period between the acquisition by the plaintiff and the date of the trial.

Counsel for the defendants has challenged the recoverability of damage under this head on two grounds. First of all, he says that the valuation of the property as at the date of its acquisition would, as a matter of valuation, take into account any discomfort which *j* a prospective purchaser would suffer as a result of defects in the property. With the greatest respect to counsel, I do not think that that is a realistic view at all, and I should be extremely surprised to find any valuer who is prepared to say that that is a factor which he took into account in making his valuation.

The second ground on which counsel for the defendants contends that damages under a this head ought not to be recovered is, he says, that the discomfort suffered by the plaintiff was due to the plaintiff's own failure to carry out the repairs which would otherwise have avoided the discomfort. The reason assigned by the plaintiff in his evidence for not carrying them out was that he was too poor to do so by reason of the fact that he had paid too much for the property and had not got the money to put the house in proper repair. Counsel for the defendants suggested, on the basis of the well-known case of *Liesbosch (owners) v Edison (owners), The Edison* [1933] AC 449, [1933] All ER Rep

b 144, that this is simply an attempt to create additional damage as a result of the poverty referred to, and that it is too remote.

If counsel for the defendants were right, that is to say if the only reason why these repairs were not carried out was the poverty of the plaintiff, then I think that something could be said for this proposition. But it seems to me that the real question, and it was one which was grasped by the deputy judge, was this: was it reasonable in all the

c circumstances for the plaintiff not to mitigate his damage by carrying out the repairs which were required? One reason, no doubt, was the plaintiff's poverty. As I said, if that were the only reason, the *Liesbosch* case might well provide an answer for the defendants. But in fact the plaintiff's conduct in not carrying out the repairs was quite reasonable for a number of other reasons; and one of the reasons why he did not do them was because the defendants were strenuously resisting any liability at all for the repairs and denying

d that they were responsible. The deputy judge found that the plaintiff's conduct in all the circumstances was reasonable. I think that is a finding of fact and is a matter which cannot be challenged in this court and, in my judgment, it provides the answer to the contention of counsel for the defendants. I think that damages, they may not be very substantial, under this head are recoverable, and I would therefore concur with the view which Lord Denning MR has expressed.

e For these reasons, therefore, I agree that the appeal should be allowed on the point of valuation; and as far as the deputy judge's decision on the other question is challenged by counsel for the defendants, that challenge fails.

KERR LJ. I also agree, and there is only a little which I wish to add.

Before the deputy judge this case was conducted on the basis that the plaintiff had

f bought the house as his permanent home, and that he was going to continue to occupy it as his permanent home, with the result that he would have to do the repairs which were the subject matter of the dispute, because the necessity for these had not been noticed by the defendants, and, in that respect, the defendants were negligent. It was on that basis that the deputy judge concluded that the right approach to the question of damages was to take the cost of the repairs as the basis. In this court counsel for the plaintiff has rightly

g abandoned that approach because of the events to which Lord Denning MR has referred, which have occurred since the trial. The plaintiff has sold the house and has changed his life by moving to another job and living in another locality. So the question of doing the repairs, and of the actual cost of the repairs, has never arisen. In these circumstances, this appeal has proceeded on both sides on the basis that the cost of the repairs as such, let alone the question as at what date, did not arise. For myself, I am not in any way

h expressing any dissent from the approach of the deputy judge, but I would say that I would reserve my view whether in a case like this the approach by way of cost of repairs is necessarily right. We have not heard the point argued and it does not arise for decision.

Given the fact that that approach to the measure of damages falls away on this appeal, it seems to me abundantly clear that this case is governed by a trilogy of similar cases where property has been bought in reliance on negligent professional advice. Those cases

j are *Philips v Ward* [1956] 1 All ER 874, [1956] 1 WLR 471, the decision of Pennycuick J in *Ford v White & Co* [1964] 2 All ER 755, [1964] 1 WLR 885 and, finally, the approval of both those cases in this court in the case of *Simple Simon Catering Ltd v Binstock Miller & Co* (1973) 228 EG 527. The effect of those three decisions can be summarised in the way in which it was conveniently stated by Pennycuick J in *Ford v White & Co* [1964] 2 All ER 755 at 758, [1964] 1 WLR 885 at 888:

'In the simple case of the purchase of property at a price in excess of its market value as a result of wrong advice, the relevant measure of damage must be the difference between [for convenience I will reverse the order in which he put it] (i) the price actually paid, and (ii) the market value of the property at the date of purchase.'

To that I would only add, as Lord Denning MR has done, that interest is of course awarded on that difference. It seems to me that the present case is entirely concluded by those authorities, subject only to the argument which counsel for the plaintiff has put forward to the effect that, because of what has happened in relation to the discharge of foreign money obligations, and because of the vicissitudes of sterling which culminated in the decision of the House of Lords in *Miliangos v George Frank (Textiles) Ltd* [1975] 3 All ER 801, [1976] AC 443 it is said that these authorities no longer apply. I cannot accept this, and no authority has been cited by counsel which begins to bear this out. He relied mainly on *Dodd Properties (Kent) Ltd v Canterbury City Council* [1980] 1 All ER 928, [1980] 1 WLR 433, and this is the only case to which I need refer. That was a case where a building occupied by the plaintiff suffered damage by reason of adjacent building operations, so that the cost of repairing the building could provide the only possible measure of damages. That was common ground. It was then held that the date for assessing the cost of repairs was to be taken as at the date when the repairs should reasonably have been done. There is nothing in that case which has any bearing on the cases to which I have referred. However, one point was mentioned in that case on which counsel for the plaintiff relied, because of a few sentences at the end of the judgment of Denning LJ in *Philips v Ward* [1956] 1 All ER 874 at 876, [1956] 1 WLR 471 at 474, where he had referred to the assumption that sterling was to be taken as having a constant value; and it was said that to that extent *Philips v Ward* could no longer be treated as an authority.

While it is perfectly right that those sentences have been overtaken by the fate of sterling and the decision in *Miliangos v George Frank (Textiles) Ltd*, this was only one of the reasons given by Denning LJ for arriving at the decision in *Philips v Ward*; but the same result, without referring to that point, was reached by the other members of this court. Therefore, while the authority for those sentences has been overtaken by the passage of time, this does not in my view afford the slightest reason for going behind the basic approach of the three cases to which I have referred. There is nothing else which counsel for the plaintiff put before us which would justify a departure from the principle of those cases.

So far as the question of damages for vexation and inconvenience is concerned, it should be noted that the deputy judge awarded these not for the tension or frustration of a person who is involved in a legal dispute in which the other party refuses to meet its liabilities. If he had done so, it would have been wrong, because such aggravation is experienced by almost all litigants. He awarded these damages because of the physical consequences of the breach, which were all foreseeable at the time. The fact that in such cases damages under this head may be recoverable, if they have been suffered but not otherwise, is supported by the decision of this court in *Hutchinson v Harris* (1978) 10 Build LR 19.

For the reasons given by Oliver LJ, it seems to me that in this case it was reasonable for the plaintiff not to do any repairs by the time of the trial, and those reasons went beyond his lack of means. In any event, it seems to me that the authority of what Lord Wright said in *Liesbosch (owners) v Edison (owners), The Edison* [1933] AC 449, [1933] All ER Rep 144 is consistently being attenuated in more recent decisions of this court, in particular in *Dodd Properties (Kent) v Canterbury City Council* [1980] 1 All ER 928, [1980] 1 WLR 433 and what was there said by Donaldson LJ. If it is reasonably foreseeable that the plaintiff may be unable to mitigate or remedy the consequence of the other party's breach as soon as he would have done if he had been provided with the necessary means to do so from the other party, then it seems to me that the principle of the *Liesbosch* case no longer applies in its full rigour. In the *Liesbosch* case, as I see it, it was not reasonably foreseeable

that the plaintiff would be put into the difficulties in which he was put by the other
a party's breach of duty. Accordingly, I agree with the deputy judge's assessment in
principle and also as regards the date for the assessment of the damages for vexation.

The final matter I would add relates to the passage which Oliver LJ has read from the
deputy judge's judgment (see [1982] 1 All ER 1005 at 1011). I can only understand that
passage if, instead of the word 'vendor', the deputy judge had intended to say 'valuer';
but, even if he did, I agree with what Oliver LJ has said.
b

*Appeal allowed in part. Official referee to deal with quantum of damages. Application for leave
to appeal to the House of Lords refused.*

Solicitors: *Reynolds Porter Chamberlain* (for the defendants); *Turner Peacock*, agents for
Humfrys & Symonds, Hereford (for the plaintiff).
c

Diana Procter   Barrister.

d Champagne Perrier-Jouet SA v H H Finch Ltd and others

CHANCERY DIVISION
WALTON J
20, 21, 22, 26 APRIL 1982
e

*Company – Shares – Lien – Articles of association giving company paramount lien over shares of
shareholder indebted to it – Company also given right to sell shares subject to lien – Proceeds of
sale received by company to be applied in payment of sum due from shareholder – Shareholder
indebted to company – Equitable charge over his shares given by shareholder to third party –
Whether company entitled to exercise power to sell shares and gain priority over equitable charge.*

f

The defendant company's articles of association provided that the regulations in Part I of
Table A in the Companies Act 1948 were to apply to the company except in so far as they
were modified or excluded by the articles. Regulation 10[a] of Part I of Table A prohibited
the company from making any loans on the security of its shares, and reg 11[b] provided
that the company was to have a first and paramount lien over the shares of any
g shareholder indebted to it. Regulation 12[c] stated that the company could sell any shares
in respect of which it had a lien, but that no sale could be made unless the sum in respect
of which that lien existed was presently payable, nor until the expiry of a notice in
writing demanding payment of such part of the amount in respect of which the lien
existed as was presently payable. Regulation 13 empowered the directors to authorise a
person to transfer to the purchaser the shares which had been sold. Regulation 14
h provided that the proceeds of sale received by the company were to be applied in payment
of such part of the amount in respect of which the lien existed as was presently payable,
and that the residue was to be paid to the person entitled to the shares at the date of the
sale. Article 5 of the articles of association stated that the lien conferred by reg 11 was to
attach to all shares registered in the name of any person indebted or under liability to the
company, and art 7 prohibited any member of the company from transferring his shares,
j whether by sale or otherwise, without first offering them to other members of the
company at a fair value to be fixed by the auditor.

A life director of the company, J, held 12,292 of the 113,250 issued shares in the

---

a   Regulation 10 is set out at p 716 *h*, post
b   Regulation 11 is set out at p 720 *b c*, post
c   Regulations 12 to 14 are set out at p 722 *f* to *h*, post

company. Between 1972 and 1976 he became greatly indebted to the company as a result
of the payment by the company of numerous bills on his behalf. He was also allowed to   *a*
take supplies of wine from the company's stocks and pass them on to I Ltd, a company
which he controlled. These transactions were recorded in what was described as a 'loan
account'. In 1976 his life directorship was terminated by a deed under which he
undertook to repay his loan account with the company at the rate of not less than £52
per annum. If he defaulted in the payment of the instalments, the outstanding amount
was to become payable forthwith. In 1979 I Ltd ran into financial difficulties and J gave   *b*
the plaintiffs, who were suppliers of I Ltd, a guarantee that he would pay all sums due
from time to time to them in return for the grant of credit facilities to I Ltd. At the same
time he mortgaged his shares in the defendant company to the plaintiffs as security for
the payment of the sums due under the guarantee. The defendant company was duly
notified of that equitable charge. J paid the defendant company £52 each year in
accordance with the 1976 deed until 1981, when he failed to do so. The company   *c*
brought an action against him claiming £27,776, being the outstanding amount due
under the 1976 deed. Judgment was entered for the company. When the money was not
paid, the company gave J notice, under reg 12 of Table A, that it proposed to exercise the
lien which it had under reg 11 over his shares by selling them in accordance with art 7 of
the articles of association. Shortly afterwards the plaintiffs demanded from J payment of
the sums due under the guarantee. Questions then arose as to the respective rights of the   *d*
plaintiffs and the defendant company. The plaintiffs took the view that J's indebtedness
to the defendant company arose from a loan, and that since the company was prohibited
by reg 10 of Table A from making a loan it had no enforceable lien on his shares. The
plaintiffs accordingly brought an action against the defendant company seeking, inter
alia, (i) a declaration that the plaintiffs' rights under the equitable charge took priority
over any rights of the defendant company, (ii) an injunction restraining the defendant   *e*
company from selling the shares without the plaintiffs' agreement and/or without giving
effect to the plaintiffs' prior rights, and (iii) in the event that the defendant company had
a lien over the shares which took priority over the plaintiffs' charge, a declaration that it
would be contrary to the company's duties to sell the shares at a fair value fixed in
accordance with art 7 without taking reasonable steps to sell them at the highest price
possible.   *f*

Held – The defendant company had at no stage made a 'loan' to J within the meaning of
reg 10 of Part I of Table A in the 1948 Act since he had not been lent a sum of money but
was simply indebted to the company in respect of the bills paid on his behalf and the
stocks of wine passed over to a third party, I Ltd. Therefore by virtue of reg 11 the
company had at all material times a lien over his shares, and that lien took priority over   *g*
the plaintiffs' equitable charge. Furthermore, the lien conferred on the defendant
company the right to sell a sufficient number of J's shares, through the machinery of art
7 of its articles of association, to discharge J's liability to the company and all incidental
costs and expenses of the sale. The sale could only be effected through the machinery
prescribed by art 7 because, on the true construction of the company's articles, the
provisions of regs 12 to 14 of Table A did not override the scheme laid down in art 7 for   *h*
the sale of shares. Declarations to that effect would be made accordingly (see p 717 *d e*,
p 718 *b c g*, p 720 *h j* and p 726 *a b f*, post).
   Potts's Exors v IRC [1951] 1 All ER 76 applied.

Notes
For a company's lien on a member's shares, see 7 Halsbury's Laws (4th edn) para 342, and   *j*
for cases on the subject, see 9 Digest (Reissue) 350–356, 2073–2104.
   For the Companies Act 1948, Sch 1, Table A, see 5 Halsbury's Statutes (3rd edn) 438.

Cases referred to in judgment
Bradford Banking Co Ltd v Briggs, Son & Co Ltd (1886) 12 App Cas 29, HL, 9 Digest
   (Reissue) 353, 2091.

Everitt v Automatic Weighing Machine Co [1892] 3 Ch 506, 9 Digest (Reissue) 351, 2079.

a *Greenhalgh v Mallard* [1943] 2 All ER 234, CA, 9 Digest (Reissue) 356, 2108.

Hunter v Hunter [1936] AC 222, HL, 9 Digest (Reissue) 223, 1344.

Moodie v W & J Shepherd (Bookbinders) Ltd [1949] 2 All ER 1044, HL, 9 Digest (Reissue) 424, 2506.

Potts's Exors v IRC [1951] 1 All ER 76, [1951] AC 443, HL, 28(1) Digest (Reissue) 429, 1551.

b
Cases also cited

Amalgamated Investment and Property Co Ltd (in liq) v Texas Commerce International Bank Ltd [1981] 3 All ER 577, [1982] QB 84, CA.

Belmont Finance Corp Ltd v Williams Furniture Ltd (1977) [1979] 1 All ER 118, [1979] Ch 250, CA.

c *Borland's Trustee v Steel Bros & Co Ltd* [1901] 1 Ch 279.

Crabb v Arun DC [1975] 3 All ER 865, [1976] Ch 179.

Mackereth v Wigan Coal and Iron Co Ltd [1916] 2 Ch 293.

Ogdens Ltd v Weinberg (1906) 95 LT 567, HL.

Pizzolati & Chittaro Mfg Co Ltd v May (1972) 26 DLR (3d) 274.

Rainford (James) v Keith & Blackman Co Ltd [1905] 2 Ch 147, CA.

d *Rearden v Provincial Bank of Ireland* [1896] 1 IR 532.

Selangor United Rubber Estates Ltd v Cradock (a bankrupt) (No 3) [1968] 2 All ER 1073, [1968] 1 WLR 1555.

Smith & Fawcett Ltd, Re [1942] 1 All ER 542, [1942] Ch 304, CA.

Stockton Malleable Iron Co, Re (1875) 2 Ch D 101.

Taylor Fashions Ltd v Liverpool Victoria Trustees Co Ltd [1981] 1 All ER 897, [1982] QB 133.

e *Wallersteiner v Moir, Moir v Wallersteiner* [1974] 3 All ER 217, [1974] 1 WLR 991, CA.

Webster v Webster (1862) 31 Beav 393, 54 ER 1191.

Action

The plaintiffs, Champagne Perrier-Jouet SA, brought an action against the defendants (1) H H Finch Ltd (the company), (2) James Michael Lynch and (3) David Theodore Welch,
f seeking (i) a declaration as to whether the company had any rights, and if so what rights, over the second defendant's shares in the company, (ii) a declaration that the plaintiffs' rights under its equitable charge over the second defendant's shares took effect in priority to the rights (if any) of the company over the shares under its lien, (iii) further or alternatively, a declaration as to the respective rights of the plaintiffs and the company in or over the second defendant's shares and each of them, (iv) a declaration that the
g plaintiffs' equitable charge was security for the payment of all sums due from time to time from James Lynch (Inns) Ltd to the plaintiffs, (v) an injunction restraining the company, whether by its officers, agents, servants or otherwise howsoever, from selling, disposing of or registering any transfer of the shares or any of them except with the agreement of the plaintiffs and/or to give effect to the plaintiffs' prior rights, (vi) in the event that it be found that the company's lien had priority over the plaintiffs' equitable
h charge (a) a declaration that it would be contrary to the company's duties as mortgagee to sell the second defendant's shares under the lien in accordance with art 7 of the company's articles of association or under any restrictive condition or otherwise without taking all reasonable steps to sell at the highest price possible and without attempting to find the person, whether a member or not, prepared to pay the highest price possible, (b) a declaration that it would be contrary to the company's duties as mortgagee to sell less
j than the complete block of the second defendant's shares if by splitting them the price realisable (whether by the company, plaintiffs or second defendant) for any of the shares (whether those retained or those sold) would be lower as a result, (c) an injunction restraining the company, whether by its officers, agents, servants or otherwise howsoever, from selling the shares at the fair value fixed in accordance with art 7 or under any restrictive condition or otherwise without taking all reasonable steps to sell at the highest price possible and without attempting to find the person, whether a member of the

company or not, prepared to pay the highest price possible, (vii) all such inquiries, accounts and directions as the court should think fit and (viii) further or other relief. The *a* facts are set out in the judgment.

Michael Lyndon-Stanford QC and *John Martineau* for the plaintiffs.
Allan Heyman QC and *Anthony Bompas* for the company.
Richard Fawls for the third defendant.
The second defendant did not appear. *b*

Cur adv vult

26 April. **WALTON J** read the following judgment: The first defendant, H H Finch Ltd (the company) is a private company incorporated under the Companies Act 1948, with an authorised capital of £120,000 divided into as many shares of £1 each, whereof *c* 113,250 have been issued. The second defendant, James Michael Randall Lynch (James), who has, for reasons which will become obvious from a recital of the relevant facts, taken no part whatsoever in the present proceedings, is the holder of 12,292 of such shares. Until recently, he held a further 100 of such shares, but these, in order to test what might be the fair value ascribed thereto by the auditor of the company under fairly common form pre-emptive provisions contained in the articles of the company, have been sold at *d* the price so ascertained of £2·50 per share.

Under the provisions of an agreement of 9 October 1972 James was a life director of the company. For whatever reason, towards the end of his period as a director the affairs of the company did not appear to be prospering, and so by a deed of 14 December 1976 made between James of the first part, the company of the second part, and another company wholly controlled by James, James Lynch (Inns) Ltd (which I shall call 'Inns'), *e* of the third part, James's directorship was terminated. I suspect that the deed had been under negotiation for some little time, as it in fact provided (what is strictly wholly impossible) for James's life directorship terminating at an antecedent date, namely 19 June 1976.

During the course of James's directorship he became greatly indebted to the company, such indebtedness being recorded (as is indeed fairly common in such cases) in what was *f* denominated a 'loan account'. It has not been suggested by counsel who appeared for the plaintiffs that the provisions of s 190 of the 1948 Act, which prohibit the making by a company of a loan to a director, in any way affect the ability of the company to recover such sums from James, whatever may be their true nature. Instead, he takes a rather different point on the articles of the company.

Those articles embody regs 10 and (as somewhat significantly altered) 11 of Table A to *g* the 1948 Act. Regulation 10 provides as follows:

'The company shall not give, whether directly or indirectly, and whether by means of a loan, guarantee, the provision of security or otherwise, any financial assistance for the purpose of or in connection with a purchase or subscription [of shares] made or to be made by any person of or for any shares in the company or in *h* its holding company nor shall the company make a loan for any purpose whatsoever on the security of its shares or those of its holding company, but nothing in this regulation shall prohibit transactions mentioned in the proviso to section 54(1) of the Act.'

The vital words are '. . . nor shall the company make a loan for any purpose whatsoever *j* on the security of its shares'. Regulation 11 then provides, as so altered and as relevant, inter alia, as follows:

'The company shall have a first and paramount lien on every share (whether fully paid or not) standing registered in the name of a person (whether solely or jointly with others) indebted or under liability to the Company . . .'

I pause at this point in this clause as altered, because there is another and totally
a   different point thereon which arises later.

Putting these two provisions together, *Buckley on the Companies Acts* (14th edn, 1981)
p 918, repeating a comment first made in the first edition after the 1948 Act had come
into force, says:

> 'The first part of this Article follows the language of s 54. The article goes beyond
> the section in prohibiting loans for any purpose on the security of the company's
b   > shares, whereas the section only relates to loans made by way of financial assistance
> to pay for shares. The effect of this article is presumably to prohibit any loan to a
> member which would result in the company having a lien upon any of his shares.'

Then reference is made to s 38 of the 1980 Act, which is not material for present
purposes.
c   The answer of counsel for the company to this was a complex one, which I think I
must take in a rather different order from that in which he submitted it. Logically, I
think the first question is whether, at any stage, there really was a loan by the company
to James. Of course, James was very considerably indebted to the company, but such
indebtedness did not arise, except in very small part, from any actual cash advanced by
the company to James. What happened basically was that the company paid a great many
d   bills for James, and James took for Inns (doubtless at a proper price) supplies of wines and
possibly spirits from the stocks of the company. But, in the context of a prohibition in
s 190 and the use of the same word 'loan' in reg 10 of Table A, I am clearly of opinion
that the correct meaning thereof is that to be found in the Shorter Oxford English
Dictionary: 'A sum of money lent for a time to be returned in money or money's worth,'
from which it follows that money paid to B at the request of A is quite definitely not a
e   loan. If authority for such an obvious proposition is required it is, of course, to be found
in *Potts's Exors v IRC* [1951] 1 All ER 76, [1951] AC 443.

The next submission of counsel for the company was that, in any event, the
indebtedness of James to the company had ceased to be in the nature of a loan and had
become an indebtedness due by virtue of the deed of 14 December 1976 already referred
to. It is, accordingly, appropriate to look at the relevant contents thereof next. I have
f   already indicated the parties. It recites that:

> 'WHEREAS (1) By an Agreement dated 9th October 1972 Mr. Lynch was appointed
> a director of the Company for life ("Life Agreement").
> (3) Mr. Lynch has consented to the termination of the Life Agreement with the
> Company on the terms and conditions hereinafter appearing.
> (3) Mr. Lynch has been given the opportunity to disclose in writing to the Board
g   > such guarantees and indemnities as have been given by him.
> NOW THIS DEED WITNESSETH as follows:—
> 1. Mr. Lynch's Life Agreement will by mutual agreement terminate without
> further action being required by either party with effect from 19th June 1976.
> 2. Mr. Lynch shall tender his resignation from the Board of Directors of the
> Company such resignation to take effect from 19th June 1976 . . .
h   > 3. Subject to Clause 8 hereof Mr. Lynch shall repay his loan account with the
> Company being £27,000 (subject to audit confirmation) at the date of this Deed
> (hereinafter called "the Loan") at the rate of not less than £52.00 per calendar year
> such payments to be made to the Company not later than the 25th day of March
> each year the first payment to be made on 25th day of March 1977.
j   > 4. With effect from 19th June 1976 Mr. Lynch's private account for wines spirits
> and liqueurs with the Company shall be closed and the debit balance thereon shall
> be added to and shall form part of the Loan.
> 5. The parties hereto agree that following the termination of the Life Agreement
> pursuant to Clause 1 hereof each of them will absolutely waive any claims that
> either of them may have against the other of them on the date hereof either on
> account of the Life Agreement or Mr. Lynch's directorship of the Company or on

any other account whatsoever PROVIDED THAT this clause shall not apply in any way
to Mr. Lynch's obligations in respect of the Loan which are expressed in Clauses 3   *a*
and 8 hereof or to Mr. Lynch's claim for any accrued salary . . .

8. If Mr. Lynch should die or fail to pay any instalments of the Loan become
bankrupt or make any composition or Deed of Arrangement with his creditors or
give any bill of sale of his personal effects the outstanding amount of the Loan shall
become due and payable forthwith.'

I regret that I am unable to accept the submissions of counsel for the company on this   *b*
point, just as I am equally unable to accept the contra-submissions of counsel for the
plaintiffs that, if the prior position was not one of loan, this deed transformed the
situation into one of loan. In my judgment, it did nothing of the kind; it left the matter
precisely where it was before. It did not in any way alter the status of James's indebtedness
to the company which, as I have already indicated, in my view (apart from a very small
amount anyway) was simple indebtedness but not by way of loan.   *c*

The next submission of counsel for the company was that the situation suffered a sea
change when James, having surprisingly defaulted in making the very modest minimum
payments of £52 per year provided for by the deed by failure to pay on 25 March 1981,
the company recovered judgment for the sum of £27,766·87 and £103 costs on 18 May
1981, James having indicated on the form of acknowledgment of service of the writ that   *d*
he did not intend to contest the proceedings.

But, once again, it seems to me that, if the initial loan, by virtue of reg 10 of Table A,
fell outside the provisions of reg 11, the situation could not be improved by obtaining a
judgment therefor. It would be something which could be enforced against James, in
any of the usual ways in which judgments can be enforced, but, if the company had no
right to exercise its lien in respect of a particular loan, I do not see that the lien would   *e*
attach by virtue of the fact that a judgment had been recovered in respect thereof.

Finally, counsel for the company submitted that, at the highest, all that had happened
was that there had been a breach of a contractual provision contained in reg 10, and that
the only person who could properly take the point was a shareholder. I do not think this
is correct; the question here is whether the company has lien on James's shares in respect
of the money owed by him to the company. If the company, by virtue of its constitution,   *f*
was prohibited from taking such a lien, then no such lien has attached. The situation
might well be different if there had been an express lien granted or taken; but clearly
this did not happen. And, once a lien has failed to attach to an initial debt, it does not
seem to me that any acknowledgment of that debt, or judgment recovered therefor,
makes any difference. No initial lien, no subsequent lien without a transformation of the
initial liability into something completely different, if that be possible.

Accordingly, at the end of the day I decide this matter in favour of counsel for the   *g*
company, but on the basis that the vast bulk of James's indebtedness to the company did
not arise out of any transaction of loan, and leaving the position that, in so far as it did so
arise, the company is not entitled to any lien in respect thereof.

James's own company, Inns, did not in the event prosper. And, in consequence, on 9
June 1979 James gave to the plaintiffs, who are, of course, the well-known champagne   *h*
house, and who were suppliers to Inns, a guarantee in the following terms:

'In consideration of your giving at my request time credit and facilities to James
Lynch (Inns) Limited (hereinafter called "the Principal"), I, the undersigned hereby
Guarantee the payment or discharge to you, of all sums from time to time due to
you from the Principal, and I further undertake that I will on demand in writing
made by you on me pay or discharge to you all monies and liabilities which shall,   *j*
for the time being, be due owing or incurred by the Principal to you, including any
expenses you may incur in taking action against the Principal.

2. I hereby agree to pay you all costs and expenses (on a full indemnity basis)
arising out of or in connection with recovery by you of the monies due to you under
this Guarantee.

a
3. A demand for payment or other demand or notice under this Guarantee may be made by letter addressed to me and sent by post or left at my last known place of business or abode.'

I do not think the other clauses matter.

On the same date he executed a mortgage of his shares in the company to the plaintiffs by an agreement made between them. That recited that Inns was indebted to the plaintiffs in a sum exceeding $1\frac{1}{2}$ million French francs—

b

'and the Surety as Surety has executed a guarantee for the payment to the Lender of all sums due to it from the Borrower.

The Surety has agreed to transfer to the Lender 12,392 £1 shares (the shareholding) in H. H. Finch Limited as security for the payment of the sums due under the said guarantee and the Surety has, on or before the execution hereof, deposited with the Lender the certificates in respect of the said shares, together with a transfer in blank duly signed by the Surety.

c

3. It is hereby agreed between the Lender and the Surety that the Lender will use its best endeavours to sell the shareholding as soon as possible at the best price reasonably obtainable and use the net proceeds of sale to reduce the amount due from the Borrower to the Lender.

d
NOW IT IS HEREBY AGREED AS FOLLOWS:

(1) In consideration of the premises the Surety hereby charges the shareholding to the Lender as security for the payment of all sums due to the Lender from the Borrower or the Surety provided that if the Borrower or the Surety pays to the Lender all sums due to them together with any costs, the Lender will thereafter at the request and cost of the Borrower re-deliver the certificates and transfer so deposited as aforesaid to the Surety or as he shall direct.

e
(2) The Surety hereby irrevocably appoints the Lender and its duly appointed agent his Attorney to complete any share transfers on behalf of the Surety.

(3) The Statutory Power of Sale shall be exercised at any time after the 1st day of June 1979 and Section 103 of the Law of Property Act 1925 shall not apply to this security.

f
(4) In the event of the Lender obtaining or receiving an offer for the purchase of the shareholding it will forthwith notify the Surety in writing of such offer. If the Surety shall serve a counter-notice in writing on the Lender's Solicitors . . . within 14 days stating that the Surety or a third party is prepared to purchase the shareholding at a price of at least 10% above the price stated in the Lenders notice the Lender shall sell the shareholding to the Surety or as he shall direct in writing,

g
provided that the Surety completes the purchase within 14 days of his counter-notice by presenting at the offices of the said [lender's solicitors] a Bankers draft for the purchase price, together with any necessary Bank of England consent. Time shall be of the essence for the provisions of this Clause.'

h
It is quite astonishing that the plaintiffs' solicitors should have let them enter into such an agreement, displaying as it does such abysmal ignorance of the constitution of the company; but no matter. That the document validly taken together with the deposit of the share certificates creates a valid equitable mortgage of the shares, nobody now doubts.

Counsel for the company, however, took the point that there was nothing secured by the equitable mortgage so constituted until the sums due from James under the guarantee had been called up, which took place only on 16 July 1981. It is true that the letter calling for payment refers to previous demands, but no previous demand has been disclosed by the plaintiffs.

j
However, I think this was well answered by counsel for the plaintiffs, who pointed out that the agreement of 9 June 1979 secured the indebtedness of Inns to the plaintiffs by the mortgage, as well as the indebtedness of James himself under the guarantee, so that there were sums immediately due thereunder as from its date.

In these circumstances, it appears to me that the relevant date, so far as the question of priority is concerned, must be the date when notice was actually given to the company *a* of the existence of the plaintiffs' equitable charge, and this was by letter of 23 November 1979.

And as at that date, submitted counsel for the plaintiffs, the company did not in fact have any lien over James's shares. The matter arises in this way. Regulation 11 of Table A reads as follows:

> 'The company shall have a first and paramount lien on every share (not being a *b* fully paid share) for all moneys (whether presently payable or not) called or payable at a fixed time in respect of that share, and the company shall also have a first and paramount lien on all shares (other than fully paid shares) standing registered in the name of a single person for all moneys presently payable by him or his estate to the company; but the directors may at any time declare any share to be wholly or in part exempt from the provisions of this regulation. The company's lien, if any, on a *c* share shall extend to all dividends payable thereon.'

This is modified so far as the articles of the company are concerned by art 5, which reads as follows:

> 'The lien conferred by Clause 11 in Part I of Table "A" shall attach to fully paid shares and to all shares registered in the name of any person indebted or under *d* liability to the Company whether he be the sole registered holder thereof or one of two or more joint holders.'

Apart from the obvious changes (a) including fully paid shares and (b) the case of shares held in joint names, what changes does this modification introduce? Counsel for the plaintiffs submitted that the sole effect of the change of wording from 'all moneys *e* presently payable by him' to 'indebted or under liability to the company' was to include unliquidated sums as well as liquidated. Counsel for the company, on the other hand, submitted that it covered all cases of indebtedness or liability to the company, whether such indebtedness or liability was presently dischargeable or not. Counsel for the plaintiffs said that one must still read the words 'presently payable by him or his estate to the company' as being included in the modified clause. *f*

On this point I am against the contentions of counsel for the plaintiffs. I quite agree that the way in which the clause has been sought to be modified is inartistic in the extreme. However, by substituting a completely different concept, namely a lien on shares of 'any person indebted or under liability to the company' for a lien in respect of 'all moneys ... payable by [a person] to the company', it appears to me that the modification effected has been effected in such a way that it is not proper to extract a *g* qualification which applied to the latter formulation and attach it (highly inartistically) to the former formulation. For, if one added it as it stood, i e so that it read 'on all shares registered in the name of a person indebted or under liability to the company for all moneys presently payable by him to the company', these last words conflict with the extension from monetary payments to payments which are at any rate at the moment unquantifiable in money. That is to say, to retain these words would conflict with the *h* express purpose of the extension of the clause.

Hence, it appears to me that, so far as priority is concerned, at all times the company has had a lien on James's shares for the moneys properly payable by him to the company, although, as a result of the deed of 14 December 1976, immediate payment of such moneys was very considerably deferred.

I should, merely for completeness on this issue, record that an argument raised in the *j* defence of the company to the effect that, by reason of reg 7 of Table A which also finds its place in the company's articles and which read as follows:

> 'Except as required by law, no person shall be recognised by the company as holding any share upon any trust, and the company shall not be bound by or be compelled in any way to recognise (even when having notice thereof) any equitable,

contingent, future or partial interest in any share or any interest in any fractional part of a share or (except only as by these regulations or by law otherwise provided) any other rights in respect of any share except an absolute right to the entirety thereof in the registered holder,'

any notice of the plaintiffs' mortgage on James's shares could safely be ignored by the company. It is well established that, where what is in issue are the rights of the company itself in relation to the shares in question, the priority of its own rights is governed by the general rules relating to the question of priority. For this I need do no more than refer to *Bradford Banking Co Ltd v Briggs, Son & Co Ltd* (1886) 12 App Cas 29.

I now come to what I conceive to be the real nub of the present case, namely if the company chooses to exercise its right to sell the shares comprised in its lien, is it bound to do so through the fairly common form transfer articles which the company has adopted, or is at liberty so to do, or, on the other hand, has it a freedom not possessed by James himself, namely to sell his shares in the open market to whomsoever it pleases?

For this purpose it is necessary to refer to other articles of the company, in particular art 7, which far as material, provides as follows:

'(A) Save as otherwise hereinafter provided no member (hereinafter called "the retiring member") shall be entitled to transfer any shares whether by way of sale or otherwise, without first causing the same to be offered to the other members of the Company at the fair value in accordance with the provisions of this Clause.

(B) In order to ascertain whether any other members of the Company are willing to purchase the shares at the fair value, the retiring member shall give a notice in writing (hereinafter referred to as a "sale notice") to the Company that he desires to sell the same. Every sale notice shall specify the denoting numbers (if any) of the shares which the retiring member desires to sell, and shall constitute the Company the agent of the retiring member for the sale of such shares to the other members of the Company at the fair value. No sale notice shall be withdrawn except with the sanction of the Directors.

(C) The Directors shall, with a view to finding members willing to purchase the shares (hereinafter referred to as "purchasing members"), offer the shares comprised in a sale notice to the persons then holding the remaining shares in the Company as nearly as may be in proportion to their holdings of shares in the Company, and shall limit a time within which such offer, if not accepted, will be deemed to be declined; and the Directors shall make such arrangements as they shall think just and reasonable as regards the finding of purchasing members for any shares not accepted by members to whom they shall in the first instance have been so offered as aforesaid.

(D) If the Company shall within twenty-eight days after service of a sale notice find purchasing members in respect of all or any of the shares comprised therein it shall give notice thereof to the retiring member and the retiring member shall be bound upon payment of the fair value to transfer the shares to such purchasing members, who shall be bound to complete the purchase within seven days from the service of such last-mentioned notice.

(E) The fair value shall be fixed by the Auditors for the time being of the Company and the sum so fixed shall, for the purposes of this Clause, be deemed to be the fair value of any share comprised in such notice.

(F) In the event of the retiring member failing to carry out the sale of any shares which he shall have become bound to transfer as aforesaid, the Directors may authorise some person to execute a transfer of the shares to the purchasing members and may give a good receipt for the purchase price of such shares, and may register the purchasing members as holders thereof and issue to them certificates for the same, and thereupon the purchasing members shall become indeafeasibly entitled thereto. The retiring member shall in such case be bound to deliver up his certificate for the said shares, and on such delivery shall be entitled to receive the said purchase

price, without interest, and if such certificate shall comprise any shares which he has
not become bound to transfer as aforesaid the Company shall issue to him a balance　*a*
certificate for such shares.

(G) If the Directors shall not, within the space of twenty eight days after service
of a sale notice, find purchasing members for all of the shares comprised therein, or
if, through no default of the retiring member, the purchase of any shares shall not
be completed within twenty one days after the service on the retiring member of
the notice provided for by sub-clause (D) hereof, the retiring member shall, at any　*b*
time, within six months after the expiry of the said twenty eight days or the service
on him of the said notice as the case may be, be at liberty, subject to the provisions
of Clause 3 of Part II of Table A, [and that, of course, provides that the directors may
in their absolute discretion and without assigning any reason therefor decline to
register any transfer of any share whether or not it is a fully paid share] to transfer
to any person as he may wish (and, in the case of a sale, at any price) the shares in　*c*
respect of which no purchasing member was found or in respect of which the sale
was not completed as aforesaid.

(H) The provisions of Clause 3 of Part II of Table A shall not apply to any transfer
to a purchasing member in accordance with the provisions of this Clause.

(I) The provisions of this Clause shall apply mutatis mutandis to any person
becoming entitled to a share in consequence of the death or bankruptcy of a member　*d*
and who wishes either to transfer such share or himself to be registered in respect
thereof.

(J) Notwithstanding anything hereinbefore contained in this Clause a share may
be transferred (subject to the provisions of Clause 3 of Part II of Table A) to the
spouse or lineal descendant or brother or sister of a member or deceased or bankrupt
member without first being offered to the other members of the Company in　*e*
accordance with the provisions of this Clause.'

The provisions for sale under the company's lien are contained in regs 12 to 14 of Table
A. They read as follows:

'12. The company may sell, in such manner as the directors think fit, any shares
on which the company has a lien, but no sale shall be made unless a sum in respect　*f*
of which the lien exists is presently payable, nor until the expiration of fourteen
days after a notice in writing, stating and demanding payment of such part of the
amount in respect of which lien exists as is presently payable, has been given to the
registered holder for the time being of the share, or the person entitled thereto by
reason of his death or bankruptcy.

13. To give effect to any such sale the directors may authorise some person to　*g*
transfer the shares sold to the purchaser thereof. The purchaser shall be registered as
the holder of the shares comprised in any such transfer, and he shall not be bound
to see to the application of the purchase money, nor shall his title to the shares be
affected by any irregularity or invalidity in the proceedings in reference to the sale.

14. The proceeds of the sale shall be received by the company and applied in
payment of such part of the amount in respect of which the lien exists as is presently　*h*
payable, and the residue, if any, shall (subject to a like lien for sums not presently
payable as existed upon the shares before the sale) be paid to the person entitled to
the shares at the date of the sale.'

Now, the respective contentions on behalf of the parties are, first, on behalf of the
plaintiffs, that there is nothing in regs 12 to 14 which in any way meshes with the
provisions of art 7 and, in particular, there is no provision whatsoever whereby a sale　*j*
notice, as required by art 7(B), can be served (noting that this is not a mere formality
since, by virtue of art 7(G), the precise time of service may be of considerable significance),
that reg 13 does not mesh well with art 7(D), and, finally, that neither does reg 14.

It is, of course, conceded by counsel for the plaintiffs that, if the plaintiffs as mortgagees
themselves had to effect a sale, either through James or, if James would not co-operate,

by going to the court, such a sale would have to pass through the machinery of art 7.
a Such a concession, in view of the decision in *Hunter v Hunter* [1936] AC 222, was, of course, inevitable.

On the other side, counsel for the company and counsel for the third defendant take a completely different view. I have not, so far, adverted to the third defendant; he is there as a representative shareholder, in view of the fact that the true construction of the company's articles is decidely in question in this action.

b They start from the position that what James has to offer by way of security to anybody, whether the plaintiffs or the company, are his shares. Those shares constitute a bundle of rights and obligations, and one of the obligations is that transfers may only be made in a particular manner. They point to art 7(A) which prohibits any transfer of shares by a member, whether by way of sale or otherwise, without the same being first offered to other members in accordance with the provisions of art 7, and say in substance that it is
c absurd to think that the provisions of regs 12 to 14 should be read in such a manner as to override the scheme of art 7 (plus reg 3 of Part II of Table A) which is to preserve the company in family control so far as possible. These clauses must, so far as is necessary, be regarded as 'modified' by the actual articles of the company, as set out in art 1.

Before discussing this point further I think I should clear out of the way a submission by counsel for the plaintiffs to the effect that, if the language of the relevant provisions is
d doubtful, I should be bound to construe them in such a way as to provide that the company had a completely unfettered power of sale over the shares. For this proposition he cited basically two cases. The first is *Greenhalgh v Mallard* [1943] 2 All ER 234 at 237, where Lord Greene MR undoubtedly said:

e 'Questions of construction of this kind are always difficult, but in the case of the restriction of transfer of shares I think it is right for the court to remember that a share, being personal property, is *prima facie* transferable, although the conditions of the transfer are to be found in the terms laid down in the articles. If the right of transfer, which is inherent in property of this kind, is to be taken away or cut down, it seems to me that it should be done by language of sufficient clarity to make it apparent that that was the intention.'

f The second is *Moodie v W & J Shepherd (Bookbinders) Ltd* [1949] 2 All ER 1044 at 1051, 1052, 1054, where there are similar expressions of opinion in the speeches of Lord Normand, Lord MacDermott and Lord Reid.

But these expressions are directed to a situation where the court is looking at the initial rights of the shareholder himself; prima facie a shareholder has a right to transfer his shares to whomsoever he pleases so that, for any form of restriction to be applicable, it
g must be clearly expressed. So much may be taken for granted. But that is not the situation with which I have to deal. I have to deal with a situation in which there can be no doubt whatsoever about the restrictions placed on the shareholder himself; what is in issue is the vastly different question whether the company, as the holder of an equitable lien over the shares of James, shares which are subject beyond all question to the restrictions set out in art 7, has nevertheless the power under regs 12 to 14 of Table A to
h sell those shares without paying any regard to such provisions. This is not only a totally different situation; it is one in which the more natural answer would be in favour of the restrictions applying than the other way.

I think that some general considerations are here appropriate. I was warned by counsel for the plaintiffs against utilising such considerations for the purpose of determining the true construction of the provisions of the articles in the present case but, although I
i intend to pay full regard to that fully justified warning, I do consider that such considerations do form the background to the case, and hence part of the setting in which I must construe them.

Let it be supposed that the company, for whatever reason, decided not to utilise the power of sale conferred by reg 12: after all, it is only one which the company 'may' not 'must' use. There is no doubt at all that it has an equitable charge on James' shares and, if any authority is wanted for that proposition, it is to be found in *Everitt v Automatic Weighing Machine Co* [1892] 3 Ch 506. The company could, therefore, go to the court and ***a*** say, 'Please provide for a sale of these shares to answer our equitable charge.' This the court could do, as I see it, in one and only one way, namely by ordering James to give a transfer notice. And, if James was unwilling so to do, then under s 30 of the Supreme Court Act 1981 some other person could be authorised to give it on his behalf. But there could be no conceivable doubt but that the sale would be subject to the provisions of art 7; there is no other possibility.   ***b***

Alternatively, let us assume that the company, having its judgment unsatisfied, were to make James bankrupt. Then his trustee in bankruptcy, in order to realise the shares, would have to give a transfer notice as provided by art 7(I) and, once again, the provisions of that article generally would apply. Similarly if James were to die and his executors wished to realise his shares (or, indeed, be registered as the holders of such shares themselves, which might well present problems for the plaintiffs, who have indicated ***c*** that, if all else failed, they would in substance be content to retain the shares as an investment).

Accordingly, if the articles of the company are to be construed in such a manner that the company itself, in exercise of its lien, can sell in disregard of art 7, there will, as counsel for the third defendant submitted, be a major breach in what is otherwise a coherent system, and, moreover, a breach for the sole benefit of James, who has done ***d*** nothing to merit such consideration but, on the contrary, will have earned such tender consideration by failing to discharge the debts he owes to the company.

Counsel for the plaintiffs submitted that this might indeed be in the best interests of the company, for its claim against the shareholder concerned might well exceed the 'fair price' valuation of the shares by the auditors. In my view, it would be a breach of duty on the part of the directors, if this is indeed the limit of the lien, to allow any member to ***e*** become indebted to the company in any greater sum. In any event, I do not think that this is a proper consideration to take into account when construing the articles as a whole.

I pause here to dissent from one submission of counsel for the company; I do not think that the provisions of reg 12, referring to 'such manner as the directors think fit', would authorise the directors to effect a sale under art 7 if they were not otherwise bound so to do. A discretion of this nature would be an impossible one for them to exercise, because ***f*** there would be no possible means of balancing the duty to the mortgagor shareholder against their duty to the other members of the company. Fortunately, there is ample scope for the application of a discretion, as counsel for the third defendant pointed out, in that there may very well be occasions when art 7(G) would fall to be activated.

And this throws up the real difficulty in the way of counsel for the company and counsel for the third defendant, namely the essential part played by the sale notice in the ***g*** working out of art 7, and the absence of any immediately obvious provision for the giving of such a notice when a sale by the company under its lien is contemplated. As counsel for the company pointed out, however, this is by no means fatal to the company's position; all it would entail is that in every case the company would have to resort to the court in the manner already noticed.

Nevertheless, construing the articles as a whole with the background I have already ***h*** mentioned, I think it is right to reach the conclusion that it is not necessary for the company to apply to the court in this manner. The opening words of reg 13 are: 'To give effect to any such sale the directors may authorise some person to transfer the shares sold to the purchaser thereof.' Now, as counsel for the plaintiffs pointed out, perfectly accurately, the more natural meaning of these words is that the person so appointed is a person to complete, not to initiate, a sale. However, I see no reason why the person so ***j*** nominated should not be alpha as well as being omega. Although not expressly so stated, the person so nominated must, in the end, be transferring the shares on behalf of the member concerned, and so I see no difficulty in his also giving notice on behalf of the member concerned that he desires to sell the shares. In this way, the whole of the provisions of the articles, read together and construed as one, make substantial

and interlocking sense. And I do not consider that I am really making any implication in
a the articles beyond such as is quite clearly required to ensure that the provisions of art
7(A) are fully given effect to.

There is one final reflection on all this, and that is that, of course, there is no compulsion
on the company to exercise its power of sale; it may simply rest content with its lien, and
simply not allow any transfer of the shares otherwise than expressly subject thereto.

The final question which, in my view, no longer arises is whether a mortgagee of a
b block of property, such as a block of shares, is bound to sell the whole of such property as
a block, so as to obtain a better pro rata price than would be obtained by a sale only of a
portion thereof, or whether, on the other hand, he may simply sell sufficient of such
shares to satisfy his claim, even although that means that the total purchase price realised
by or on behalf of the mortgagor will be less than it would have been if the whole parcel
had been sold.

c Having regard to my conclusions on the other points, which will produce a uniform
'fair value' for all shares, no such difficulty can arise. The company need not sell any
more shares than is sufficient to discharge its lien, since there would be no bonus in
respect of any parcel of shares, irrespective of size. But, had counsel for the plaintiffs been
correct in his submission that the company was entitled to sell the shares at the open
market price and, of course, that that price was higher than the fair value price as fixed
d by the auditors, then his submission would have led to the astonishing position that the
company would have been bound to have sold *all* James's shares at the higher price, thus
rewarding James, and possibly rewarding him very handsomely, for having become
indebted to the company. This cannot, I suspect, be correct.

That there is no general obligation on a mortgagee to sell the whole of the mortgaged
property if he does not choose so to do is quite apparent from the terms of the Law of
e Property Act 1925, s 101(1). As regards chattels, in *Fisher and Lightwood on the Law of
Mortgage* (8th edn, 1969) p 303 the editor speaks of the duty on the mortgagee to 'return
any unsold part of the security to the debtor'. I, therefore, myself think that the true rule
is probably this: that the mortgagee must not, in selling what he does sell, deliberately
destroy its value by failing to sell what would normally and naturally form part of what
he does sell, for example, he could not properly sell seven of a set of eight antique chairs,
f and so on, because nobody would give pro rata for the seven chairs actually sold the same
as they would give for these same chairs if sold with the missing one.

However, I do not, in the light of my previous findings, need to decide this point and
do not do so. I would, however, point out that any such debate is, on the facts of the
present case, particularly sterile; because, whatever may be the general position, under
the terms of reg 11 the directors may at any time declare any share to be wholly, or in
g part, exempt from the provisions of that article. Hence, all the directors would have to
do would be to declare that all James's shares (except for the number which they really
required to satisfy the liability to the company) were free from any lien in respect of that
existing liability (but without prejudice to any other liability), so that the only shares
standing charged to the company were the precise number with which they wished to
deal. Thereafter, there could be no possible question but that, if the company sold all
h those shares at whatever was the proper price, it would have discharged all the obligations
which the ingenuity of counsel for the plaintiffs has been able to suggest rest on it.

I have not found it necessary to refer to the pleadings in this action, which was
commenced by the plaintiffs on learning that the company, having given the notice
required by reg 12, was in fact proposing to exercise its lien over James's shares by a sale
under art 7, because both parties have co-operated to ensure that all essential facts have
j been placed before me in a simple form, and that all unnecessary issues have been
eliminated. I must, however, finally turn to the relief sought by the reamended statement
of claim herein for the purpose of ascertaining the extent to which it is right to accede
thereto.

The first head of relief sought is as follows: 'A Declaration whether the Company has
any rights, and if so what rights, over the said shares of the Second Defendant.' I answer

this by saying that the company has, and has at all material times had, a lien over James's　*a*
shares conferred by its articles of association, such lien in the events which have happened
conferring on it the right to sell sufficient shares of James through the machinery of its
art 7 as will suffice to discharge James's liability to the company, and all incidental costs
and expenses of the sale.

The second head of relief is: 'A declaration that the rights of the Plaintiff under its said
equitable charge over the Second Defendant's said 12392 shares take effect in priority to
the rights (if any) of the Company over the said shares under its said lien.' I answer this　*b*
by saying that the lien of the company takes priority to the equitable charge of the
plaintiffs.

The third head of relief is: 'Further or alternatively a declaration as to the respective
rights of the Plaintiff and of the Company in or over the said shares and each of them.'
Nothing further on this head occurs to me, but I shall be open to representations from
counsel later.　*c*

Head 3(a) reads: 'A declaration that the Plaintiff's said equitable charge is security for
payment of all sums due from time to time from James Lynch (Inns) Limited to the
Plaintiff.' As I understand that Inns has gone into liquidation, I am uncertain as to the
precise form in which this should now be expressed, but the substance is, I think,
undoubted.

The fourth head of relief is: 'An injunction restraining the Company whether by its　*d*
officers agents servants or otherwise howsoever from selling disposing of or registering
any transfer of the said shares or any of them except with the agreement of the Plaintiff
and/or to give effect to the Plaintiff's rights in priority as aforesaid.' No such injunction
falls to be granted.

The fifth head is split up into a number of sub-heads. The overriding sentence is: 'In
the event that it be found that the Company's lien has priority over the Plaintiff's　*e*
equitable charge', as is the position, and (i) reads: 'A declaration that it would be contrary
to the Company's duties as mortgagee to sell the Second Defendant's said shares under
the lien in accordance with Article 7 of the Company's Articles of Association or under
any restrictive condition or otherwise without taking all reasonable steps to sell at the
highest price possible and without attempting to find the person, whether a member or
not, prepared to pay the highest price possible.' Instead, of course, I shall declare that the　*f*
company has the right and the obligation to sell the shares through and only through the
machinery prescribed by art 7.

Paragraph 5(ii) reads: 'A declaration that it would be contrary to the Company's duties
as mortgagee to sell less than the complete block of the Second Defendant's said shares if
by splitting the said block of shares the price realisable (whether by the Company the
Plaintiff or the Second Defendant) for any of the said shares (whether those retained or　*g*
those sold) would be lower as a result.' That, I think, no longer falls for comment.

Paragraph 5(iii) reads: 'An injunction restraining the Company whether by its officers
agents servants or otherwise howsoever from selling the said shares at the fair value fixed
in accordance with Article 7 or under any restrictive condition or otherwise without
taking all reasonable steps to sell at the highest price possible and without attempting to
find the person, whether a member of the Company or not, prepared to pay the highest　*h*
price possible.' That relief, of course, equally falls to be refused.

I do not think I need deal with the usual claims for ancillary relief which, in my view,
in any event now no longer arise.

Declarations accordingly.

j

Solicitors: *David Alterman & Sewell* (for the plaintiffs); *Ashurst, Morris, Crisp & Co* (for the
company and the third defendant).

Hazel Hartman　Barrister.

R v Waveney District Council, ex parte Bowers

COURT OF APPEAL, CIVIL DIVISION
WALLER, DONALDSON AND GRIFFITHS LJJ
6, 7, 21 JULY 1982

Housing – Homeless person – Duty of local authority to provide accommodation – Duty to provide accommodation to person they have reason to believe may be homeless and have priority need – Priority need – Priority need by reason of being vulnerable 'as a result of old age, mental illness ... or other special reason' – Applicant 59 years and alcoholic – Applicant suffering head injury and unable to find accommodation – Applicant applying for accommodation on ground of priority need – Whether applicant vulnerable – Whether vulnerability as a result of head injury entitling applicant to priority – Whether vulnerability as result of alcoholism alone entitling applicant to priority – Housing (Homeless Persons) Act 1977, s 2(1)(c).

The applicant, who was 59 years old, was an alcoholic. In 1980 he suffered a severe head injury which left him in a disorientated and confused state. On discharge from hospital, he was unable to find anyone willing to offer him accommodation and he became homeless. In 1981 he applied to the local authority for accommodation. Under s 4(5)^a of the Housing (Homeless Persons) Act 1977, the authority had a duty to secure accommodation for a person if the authority was satisfied that the person was homeless, that he had a priority need and that he had not become homeless intentionally. By s 2(1)(c)^b of the 1977 Act a homeless person had a priority need for accommodation where he was 'vulnerable as a result of old age, mental illness or handicap or physical disability or other special reason'. Guidance as to the approach to be adopted by housing authorities when considering priority was given by the code of guidance issued by the Department of Health and Social Security under s 12 of the 1977 Act. To ascertain the degree of vulnerability, the code suggested that a man above the age of 65 should be treated as vulnerable, and that frailty, poor health or vulnerability for any other reason should be reasons for treating a man as being vulnerable by reason of old age even though he was below the age of 65. The code also suggested that local authorities should take a wide and flexible view of what constituted substantial disability, and to recognise that that would depend on individual circumstances. The authority rejected the applicant's application for accommodation on the ground that he was not homeless and that even if he were homeless he would not be a person in priority need within s 2(1)(c). In 1982 the authority again considered his application and rejected it. On an application for judicial review by way of a declaration, inter alia, that the applicant was a homeless person and that he had priority need for accommodation within s 2(1)(c), the judge held that, although the applicant was homeless and there was a measure of vulnerability, the decision of the authority that the applicant had not established a priority need for accommodation was not unreasonable. The applicant appealed to the Court of Appeal, contending that he was homeless, that he was 'vulnerable' within s 2(1)(c) and therefore had a priority need, and that the authority had wrongly applied the provisions of s 2. The authority contended that the words 'substantially disabled mentally and physically' in the code meant that accommodation only had to be provided for those in substantial need, and furthermore that the case had to be brought within one or other of the categories within s 2(1)(c).

---

a Section 4(5), so far as material, provides: 'Where—(a) [a housing authority] are satisfed—(i) that [a person who has applied for accommodation] is homeless, and (ii) that he has a priority need, but (b) they are not satisfied that he became homeless intentionally, their duty ... is to secure that accommodation becomes available for his occupation.'

b Section 2(1) is set out at p 729 c, post

Held – The code of guidance issued by the Department of Health and Social Security, although issued in accordance with s 12 of the 1977 Act, was to be read within the framework of s 2(1) of that Act. Therefore the proper approach to be taken by a local authority in deciding whether a person was in priority need for accommodation under s 2(1)(c) was to consider whether there was vulnerability on the part of the applicant and if so whether it arose from the matters set out in s 2(1)(c). Although the applicant's vulnerability by reason of his alcoholism would not normally have given him priority need, his brain injury, whether it was described as a mental handicap or as other special reason, had increased his vulnerability to such an extent that he had a priority need for accommodation within s 2 of the 1977 Act. Accordingly the appeal would be allowed (see p 730 *a d e* and *h* to p 731 *a*, post).

Notes
For priority need for accommodation, see 22 Halsbury's Laws (4th edn) para 510.
   For the Housing (Homeless Persons) Act 1977, ss 1, 2, 4, 6, see 47 Halsbury's Statutes (3rd edn) 316–319, 321.

Case cited
Padfield v Minister of Agriculture, Fisheries and Food [1968] 1 All ER 694, [1968] AC 997, HL.

Appeal
By notice of appeal dated 30 June 1982 the applicant, Douglas Gordon Bowers, appealed against the decision of Stephen Brown J dated 24 May 1982 whereby he dismissed the applicant's application for judicial review of the the decision of Waveney District Council by way of a declaration that the applicant was a homeless person and that he had priority need of accommodation within s 2(1)(c) of the Housing (Homeless Persons) Act 1977. The facts are set out in the judgment of the court.

Andrew Arden for the applicant.
Graham Stoker for the council.

Cur adv vult

21 July. **WALLER LJ** read the following judgment of the court: In the summer of 1981 the applicant, Douglas Gordon Bowers, applied to the respondent authority, the Waveney District Council, for accommodation. By letter dated 4 August 1981 the district health and housing officer of the council informed the applicant that they were not prepared to accept an application for registration on the housing waiting list because in the council's contention the applicant was not homeless and even if he were homeless their contention was that he would not be a person in priority need within the terms of the Housing (Homeless Persons) Act 1977.
   The council were asked to reconsider the applicant's application and having done so wrote by letter dated 23 February 1982, from the district secretary to the applicant's solicitors, informing them that the council did not consider the applicant to be homeless, and that even if he could be considered to be homeless he did not have priority need within the meaning of s 2 of the 1977 Act. On an application for judicial review Stephen Brown J on 24 May 1982 held that the applicant was homeless, found that it was quite plain that there was a measure of vulnerability, but came to the conclusion that he could not find that the decision of the council that the applicant had not established a priority need for accommodation was an unreasonable decision.
   The applicant now appeals to this court, submitting that he is homeless and is vulnerable within the meaning of s 2(1)(c) and therefore has a priority need and that although it is a question of fact for the authority this is a case where this court can interfere because the council were in error in the manner in which they applied the

a   provisions of s 2, supplemented as it was by the code of guidance given by the Secretary of State under the provisions of s 12 of the 1977 Act.

Section 1 of the 1977 Act sets out the provisions relating to homelessness, and s 4 sets out the duties of housing authorities to homeless persons. Those duties vary according to the circumstances, but by sub-s (5) if the authority is satisfied that the person is homeless and has a priority need and did not become homeless intentionally the duty is 'to secure that accommodation becomes available for his occupation'. Section 6 sets out ways in

b   which the authority may perform its duty under s 4. Section 2 provides the conditions for priority need, and s 2(1) reads as follows:

c

> 'For the purposes of this Act a homeless person or a person threatened with homelessness has a priority need for accommodation when the housing authority are satisfied that he is within one of the following categories:—(*a*) he has dependent children who are residing with him or who might reasonably be expected to reside with him; (*b*) he is homeless or threatened with homelessness as a result of any emergency such as flood, fire or any other disaster; (*c*) he or any person who resides or might reasonably be expected to reside with him is vulnerable as a result of old age, mental illness or handicap or physical disability or other special reason.'

d   The applicant's contention is that he has a priority need because he comes within the provisions of s 2(1)(*c*) and is vulnerable as a result of old age, mental illness or handicap or physical disability or other special reason. The code of guidance, in para 2.12, gives guidance as to the approach to be adopted when considering priority need.

The evidence before the council consisted of a housing welfare report dated 8 May 1981, a report from Dr McEvett, a psychiatrist, dated 9 December 1981, and a report from the divisional social services officer of the Suffolk County Council, dated 10

e   February 1982. There is also before us an affidavit from the applicant which supplements to some extent the facts set out in those reports. The reports reveal that in the early 1970s the applicant was suffering from alcoholism and was an in-patient in hospital from 1971 to 1974. Thereafter he lived in lodgings until the early summer of 1980 when he suffered a severe head injury resulting in treatment in hospital. In September 1980 he was still disorientated for time and place and very confused. He was discharged in December

f   1980, from hospital having been an in-patient for some six months. According to his affidavit he then returned to the lodgings at which he had resided for at least six years before his accident but his drinking became too much for the landlady and he had to leave. Since then he has been homeless but sleeping most nights at the night centre.

The housing welfare report reveals that Lorraine Humphries, the hospital social worker, was of opinion that the applicant was vulnerable because of ill health. It appears

g   that Mrs Pearce, the community sister at the hospital, gave some support to this view. The report also shows that Mr Easton, the warden at the night centre felt that the applicant was a danger to himself; he had broken his nose three times due to falling on his face at the night centre and needed a lot of help before he could be independent. Dr McEvett, after describing a serious head injury thought there had been a continual, gradual, improvement from the state of disorientation which existed up to six months

h   after the accident. His view was that the applicant had received a serious head injury with some persistent disability made worse by his drinking habits. He thought that because of his present disability problems relating to heavy drinking were likely to continue. He thought that the applicant would cope better in a flat by himself and that an ideal placement would be where there was some degree of shelter.

The view of the social services officer was that the slight brain damage coupled with

j   his drinking pattern made him vulnerable at certain times and that although he was able to care for himself he did need some supervision. Further that, because of the applicant's vulnerability to accidents, there should be sheltered accommodation with a warden to supervise. The report concluded that, since the applicant is homeless and vulnerable as a result of his disability, sheltered accommodation might be more appropriate to his needs.

The question we have to consider is whether or not the applicant is vulnerable and secondly whether the vulnerability is as a result of old age, mental illness or handicap or physical or other special reason. Dealing first with the meaning of 'vulnerable', vulnerable *a* literally means 'may be wounded ... susceptible of injury' (see the Concise Oxford Dictionary). In our opinion, however, in the context of this legislation vulnerable means less able to fend for oneself so that injury or detriment will result when a less vulnerable man will be able to cope without harmful effects.

To ascertain the degree of vulnerability guidance is provided by the code. The code of guidance suggests that a man above the age of 65 should be treated as vulnerable. Taken *b* literally this would mean that a healthy man of 64 would not be vulnerable while the same man at 65 would be. It is of course merely a guide but it is an indication of the degree of vulnerability which is contemplated by the 1977 Act.

The guide goes on to indicate frailty, poor health or vulnerability for any other reason as reasons for treating a man as vulnerable by reason of old age even below the age of 65. The code then considers mental illness or handicap or physical disability and says: *c*

'This includes those who are blind, deaf, dumb or otherwise substantially disabled mentally or physically. Authorities are asked to take a wide and flexible view of what constitutes substantial disability, recognising that this will depend on individual circumstances.'

This paragraph starts by stating forms of disability which would necessarily create *d* vulnerability of a much greater degree than reaching the age of 65, but then goes on to recommend a flexible approach. The code of guidance is of great assistance to those who have to make decisions under these provisions, but although it is authorised under s 12 of the 1977 Act it must be read within the framework of s 2(1).

There can be no question here but that the applicant is vulnerable. The judge accepted that there was a degree of vulnerability. Furthermore it is reasonably clear that the degree *e* of vulnerability increased as a result of a serious accident with severe brain injury in the early summer of 1980. Before that, although he had a drink problem, the applicant was able to cope, living in lodgings. Since the accident nobody will give him lodging and all those who have considered his case take the view that he needs either 'support' or 'help' or 'a degree of shelter' or 'sheltered accommodation'.

When approaching the test of vulnerability it is necessary to look at other examples. A *f* pregnant woman is an obvious example, old age is another, although the vulnerability of a man aged 65 is not quite so obvious. An individual who is deaf or dumb is another. In this case, if the applicant's problems arose solely because of his drink problem, it would be very difficult to say that his condition arose from mental illness or handicap etc; but it is not the sole cause.

It would appear from the affidavit of the council that particular reliance was placed on *g* the words 'substantially disabled mentally or physically' in the code of guidance and that led them to the conclusion that accommodation only had to be provided for those in substantial need. It was also suggested in the course of argument that the case had to be brought within one or other of the categories mentioned in s 2(1)(c).

In our judgment this was not the correct approach. The first question which has to be considered is whether or not there is vulnerability. If there is vulnerability, then whether *h* it arises from those matters which are set out within para (c)? It may not arise from any single one but it may arise from a combination of those causes.

In this case, the applicant's age was a factor but the brain injury was another important factor. Whether the brain injury is described as mental handicap or whether it is to be put into the category of other special reason is immaterial. If it had not been for the accident the applicant would not have had a priority need, at any rate until he reached *j* the age of 65, but the accident made, in our judgment, the whole difference. We have no doubt that if the case had been approached in this way by the council they would have come to the conclusion that the applicant did have a priority need. We have great sympathy with the council in applying this section and the code of guidance to the facts of this case. It is important to draw a distinction between those cases solely due to the a problems of drink, where the case will normally not come within the provisions of s 2, and the facts of this case, where an accident causing brain damage to a man of 59 has been an important factor.

We allow this appeal and hold that the applicant is homeless and has a priority need within the meaning of s 2 of the 1977 Act.

Appeal allowed. Declaration accordingly.

b
Solicitors: *Nicholson, Cadge & Gilbert,* Lowestoft (for the applicant); *I W Madin,* Lowestoft (for the council).

Diana Brahams   Barrister.

c

Leith Properties Ltd v Springer

COURT OF APPEAL, CIVIL DIVISION
ORMROD, GRIFFITHS AND SLADE LJJ
d 26, 27 MAY, 24 JUNE 1982

Rent restriction – Possession – Dwelling subject to protected or statutory tenancy – Effect on subtenancy of determination of superior tenancy – Subtenant to whom dwelling has been lawfully sublet – Lawfully sublet – Extent of subtenant's right to remain in possession – Dwelling lawfully sublet without landlord's consent – Tenant's tenancy terminated – Landlord bringing proceedings
e *for possession against subtenant – Whether subletting by original tenant without landlord's consent entitling landlord to possession as against subtenant – Rent Act 1977, ss 98(1)(b), 137, Sch 15, Case 6.*

In 1975 the landlords let a flat to the tenant on a quarterly tenancy. The tenancy agreement contained no covenant against subletting and later in 1975, without asking the landlords for their consent, the tenant sublet the whole of the flat to a subtenant on a
f weekly tenancy. For some years after that the tenant went to great lengths to make the landlords believe that she still had an interest in it. By the time the landlords served a notice to quit on her in December 1980 her contractual tenancy had become a statutory tenancy within the meaning of the Rent Act 1977. When the notice expired on 26 March 1981, the landlords brought an action in the county court against her and against the subtenant who was still living in the flat, claiming an order for possession under s 98(1)(b)[a]
g of the 1977 Act and relying on Case 6[b] of Sch 15 to that Act, namely that 'the tenant' had sublet the flat without the landlords' consent. The judge made an order for possession (i) against the tenant on the ground that she had, within the meaning of Case 6, sublet the flat without the landlords' consent and it was reasonable that the order should be made, and (ii) against the subtenant on the ground that he was not entitled, on the termination of the tenant's statutory tenancy, to retain possession by virtue of s 137[c] of the 1977 Act
h as a person to whom the dwelling had been 'lawfully sublet', since the flat would only have been lawfully sublet if it had not been sublet in contravention of a covenant in a lease or of a statutory provision whereas the flat had in fact been sublet without the landlords' consent. The subtenant appealed against the order.

j **Held** – (1) Since at the time the subletting was effected the tenant was still holding the tenancy on the terms of her contractual tenancy, which contained no prohibition on

---

a   Section 98(1) is set out at p 733 j to p 734 a, post
b   Case 6, so far as material, is set out at p 734 b, post
c   Section 137, so far as material, is set out at p 734 c to e, post

subletting, the subtenancy was valid at common law. Furthermore, Case 6 of Sch 15 to the 1977 Act did not implicitly prohibit a subletting without the landlord's consent, so as to render it unlawful for the purposes of s 137. It followed, therefore, that the flat had been 'lawfully sublet' within s 137(2) (see p 735 *a f* and p 736 *b c*, post); dictum of Andrews LCJ in *Enniskillen UDC v Bartley and Lynch* [1947] NI at 181 applied; *Roe v Russell* [1928] All ER Rep 262 distinguished.

(2) However, the fact that the subtenant was, within the meaning of s 137 of the 1977 Act, a person to whom the dwelling had been 'lawfully sublet' did not necessarily preclude the court from making an order for possession against him under s 98(1)(*b*), because the protection afforded to him by s 137 was not absolute and the subtenant, on the termination of the tenant's statutory tenancy, was only deemed to become the tenant of the landlords 'subject to [the 1977] Act', and under that Act the landlords could bring proceedings against him for possession under Case 6 of Sch 15 because the subletting by 'the tenant' without consent referred to in Case 6 was a subletting by the landlord's immediate tenant (who, in the circumstances, was the original tenant) and not merely a subletting by a subtenant who was deemed to become a lawful tenant by virtue of s 137(2) of the Act. Any other construction would render Case 6 useless to landlords and defeat the purpose of the legislation. Since the landlords' immediate tenant had sublet the flat without consent, the landlords were therefore entitled, subject to the court considering it reasonable, to an order for possession against the subtenant under Case 6 even though he was not the person who had sublet the flat without the landlords' consent. However, since the judge had not considered whether it was reasonable to make the order, the case would be remitted to him to consider that aspect, and to that extent the appeal would be allowed (see p 736 *e* to *h*, p 737 *f j* and p 738 *a* to *h*, post); *Lord Hylton v Heal* [1921] 2 KB 438 and *Enniskillen UDC v Bartley and Lynch* [1947] NI 177 applied.

Notes

For determination of tenancies and recovery of possession generally, see 27 Halsbury's Laws (4th edn) paras 419–421, and for cases on landlord's right to possession, see 31(2) Digest (Reissue) 906–907, 7500–7510.

For the Rent Act 1977, ss 98, 137, Sch 15, Case 6, see 47 Halsbury's Statutes (3rd edn) 504, 539, 600.

Cases referred to in judgments

Enniskillen UDC v Bartley and Lynch [1947] NI 177, 31(2) Digest (Reissue) 1106, 2834.
Hylton (Lord) v Heal [1921] 2 KB 438, DC, 31(2) Digest (Reissue) 1103, 8566.
Regional Properties Co Ltd v Frankenschwerth [1951] 1 All ER 178, [1951] 1 KB 631, CA, 31(2) Digest (Reissue) 1087, 8483.
Roe v Russell [1928] 2 KB 117, [1928] All ER Rep 262, CA, 31(2) Digest (Reissue) 1029, 8167.

Appeal

Metropolitan Properties Co (FGC) Ltd, the predecessors in title of the respondent landlord, Leith Properties Ltd, brought an action against five defendants, Mrs I Byrne, Miss Helen Dawson, Mrs Ergin, Alan Springer and Miss Rose Codling, claiming possession of the premises known as the First Floor Flat, 72 Leith Mansions, Grantully Road, London W9, and mesne profits until possession was yielded. On 5 October 1981 in the Bloomsbury and Marylebone County Court his Honour Judge Hammerton made an order for possession against the first, second, fourth and fifth defendants and for mesne profits against the first and fourth defendant. The fourth defendant, Mr Springer, appealed against the order so far as it concerned him. The facts are set out in the judgment of the court.

David Watkinson for Mr Springer.
David Neuberger for the landlord.

Cur adv vult

24 June. **SLADE LJ** read the following judgment of the court: This is an appeal by Mr
a Alan Springer from part of an order of his Honour Judge Hammerton given at the
Bloomsbury and Marylebone County Court on 5 October 1981. The judgment was given
in possession proceedings in which the plaintiffs were Metropolitan Properties Co (FGC)
Ltd and the five defendants were, respectively, Mrs Byrne, Miss Dawson, Mrs Ergin, Mr
Springer and Miss Codling. The proceedings concerned premises known as the First
Floor Flat, 72 Leith Mansions, Grantully Road, Maida Vale, London W9, which we will
b call 'the flat'. By his order the judge made a possession order in favour of the plaintiffs
against the first, second, fourth and fifth defendants, the third defendant having already
vacated the property, and further awarded mesne profits against the first and fourth
defendants.

The fourth defendant, Mr Springer, appeals from the order. The second and fifth
defendants, whose rights (if any) to occupation of the flat depend on his rights, have not
c been represented on this appeal; neither have the first and third defendants. The
respondents are Leith Properties Ltd, the successors in title of the plaintiff company in
the court below. They are now the leasehold owners of the flat.

The short history of the matter is as follows. In 1975 the first defendant, Mrs Byrne,
was the tenant of the flat under a contractual tenancy agreement, holding on a quarterly
tenancy. It was alleged in the plaintiffs' particulars of claim that there was a term of such
d tenancy which prohibited subletting. But this contention was not pursued before the
judge and it is now common ground that there was no provision in the tenancy
agreement prohibiting subletting. In December 1975 Mrs Byrne sublet the whole of the
flat to Mr Springer at weekly rent of £44 per week so that he became a weekly tenant.
This subletting was effected without the landlords' consent. Mr Springer continued to
pay Mrs Byrne the rent, first on a weekly basis, and later fortnightly. She made a
e handsome profit out of him, because she herself was only paying £30 per week, though
she was continually in arrears.

From 1976 to 1978 Mrs Byrne wrote a number of letters purporting to come from the
flat, as if she was still living there, which she was not. At the end of 1978 she went to live
in Australia. After an investigation in 1978, the landlords' porter reported to them that
Mr Springer and a Miss Astbury were living in the flat. The landlords however continued
f to accept rent paid by or on behalf of Mrs Byrne up to at least August 1979. Before the
judge it was argued that by such acceptance, coupled with the porter's knowledge, the
landlords had approbated or acquiesced in the subletting by Mrs Byrne to Mr Springer.
However, the judge rejected this submission and it has not been pursued in this court.
He found that Mrs Byrne or someone on her behalf went to great lengths to make the
landlords believe that she was still interested in the flat. His conclusions were that they
g took no action as a direct result of the deception practised on them by her, that Mr
Springer himself was her innocent dupe and was treated shabbily by her.

The judge found that Mrs Byrne's contractual tenancy had become a statutory tenancy
by 1979. In due course the landlords served a notice to quit which expired on 26 March
1981. On that day they issued proceedings for possession joining Mrs Byrne, Miss
Dawson, Mrs Ergin and Mr Springer as defendants. Miss Codling was subsequently
h added as a defendant by amendment. In their particulars of claim the landlords pleaded
that, by reason of the matters pleaded, none of the defendants were entitled to the
protection of the Rent Act 1977. In alternative they claimed possession pursuant to one
or more of Cases 1, 6 and 10 of Sch 15 to that Act.

Mr Springer continued to pay rent to Mrs Byrne up to September 1981. On 5 October
1981 the judge heard the action. He found that Mrs Ergin had left the flat but that Mr
j Springer, Miss Dawson and Miss Codling remained in occupation.

Section 98(1) of the 1977 Act provides:

'Subject to this Part of this Act, a court shall not make an order for possession of a
dwelling-house which is for the time being let on a protected tenancy or subject to
a statutory tenancy unless the court considers it reasonable to make such an order
and either—(a) the court is satisfied that suitable alternative accommodation is

available for the tenant or will be available for him when the order in question takes effect, or (*b*) the circumstances are as specified in any of the Cases in Part I of Schedule 15 to this Act.'

Case 6 of Part I of Sch 15 to the 1977 Act reads, so far as material for present purposes:

'Where, without the consent of the landlord, the tenant has, at any time after . . . (*d*) 8th December 1965, in the case of any other tenancy, assigned or sublet the whole of the dwelling-house or sublet part of the dwelling-house, the remainder being already sublet.'

The judge made an immediate order for possession of the flat against Mrs Byrne. The notes of his judgment refer to the order being made under s 98(1)(*a*) but counsel have told us that the order was made under s 98(1)(*b*), presumably read in conjunction with Case 6.

Mr Springer's defence to the proceedings was based on s 137 of the 1977 Act. Section 137(1), so far as material, provides:

'If a court makes an order for possession of a dwelling-house from—(*a*) a protected or statutory tenant . . . and the order is made by virtue of section 98(1) . . . of this Act . . . nothing in the order shall affect the right of any sub-tenant to whom the dwelling-house or any part of it has been lawfully sublet before the commencement of the proceedings to retain possession by virtue of this Part of this Act, nor shall the order operate to give a right to possession against any such sub-tenant.'

Section 137(2) provides:

'Where a statutorily protected tenancy of a dwelling-house is determined, either as a result of an order for possession or for any other reason, any sub-tenant to whom the dwelling-house or any part of it has been lawfully sublet shall, subject to this Act, be deemed to become the tenant of the landlord on the same terms as if the tenant's statutorily protected tenancy had continued.'

Section 137(4) defines the expression 'statutorily protected tenancy' in terms wide enough to include a protected or statutory tenancy.

It was submitted to the judge on behalf of Mr Springer, as it has been submitted to this court, that he is a 'sub-tenant to whom the dwelling-house . . . has been lawfully sublet' within the meaning of s 137(2), and that accordingly, by virtue of that subsection, he is deemed to have become the tenant of the landlords on the same terms as if Mrs Byrne's tenancy had continued. These submissions are necessarily founded on the contention that there has been a 'lawful' subletting.

Before this court and also in the court below, counsel for the landlords sought to refute this contention, essentially on the following ground. He pointed out that the landlords' consent to the subletting was not obtained. He submitted that, having regard to the wording of Case 6, premises cannot be said to be 'lawfully sublet' within the meaning of s 137(2) in any case where they have been sublet without the landlords' consent. The judge accepted this submission. Having referred to Case 6, he said:

'[Counsel for the landlord's] argument has the merit of consistency. It protects the landlord against having an unlawful subtenant foisted on him. The landlord has no chance of choosing him. As there was no covenant against subletting in this case, Springer should not be in a different position from where there is a covenant against assignment or subletting. There should be consistency between the two and I take the view that against Springer the premises were not lawfully sublet.'

The judge accordingly made an order for delivery of possession of the flat against Mr Springer and against Miss Dawson and Mrs Ergin, whose rights (if any) to occupation depended on Mr Springer's rights.

On the evidence, it seems clear that Mrs Byrne was still holding as a protected tenant

on the terms of her contractual tenancy at the time when she sublet the flat to Mr
a Springer on a weekly tenancy in 1975.

At common law, if a lease is silent on the matter, the tenant may grant an effective
sublease without the landlord's consent. Since Mrs Byrne's tenancy agreement did not in
any way expressly restrict her rights to sublet, we can see no reason why the subletting to
Mr Springer should not have been perfectly lawful and valid at common law.

Counsel for the landlord, however, has sought to argue that in the context of s 137(2)
b the phrase 'lawfully sublet' bears a special meaning. He has contended in effect that,
having regard to Case 6, a subletting must be deemed to be unlawful for the purpose of
s 137(2) in any case where it constitutes a subletting of the whole of the dwelling house
without the landlord's consent, even though it was effected at a time when the contractual
tenancy still subsisted and the tenancy agreement contained no prohibition against
subletting. In this context, he relied on a dictum of Eve J in *Roe v Russell* [1928] 2 KB 117
c at 141, [1928] All ER Rep 262 at 271, where he said this in relation to the Increase of
Rent and Mortgage Interest (Restrictions) Act 1920 and the Rent and Mortgage
Restrictions Act 1923:

> 'Reliance was naturally placed by the [landlord] on the expression "lawfully
> sublet," which occurs in both Acts, but the presence of the qualifying word is, I
> *d* think, explained by this, that there are at least two forms of subletting which are
> not lawful under the Acts; one, a subletting which sublets the whole of the dwelling-
> house, or sublets a part the remainder being already sublet, and the other a subletting
> made after the commencement of proceedings for recovery of possession, or
> ejectment.'

However, that case concerned a subletting by a statutory tenant, which gives rise to
e quite different considerations from those applicable to a subletting by a tenant still
holding on a contractual tenancy, such as Mrs Byrne in the present case. The dictum of
Eve J was, in our judgment, solely directed to subletting by statutory tenants and is of no
assistance in the present context.

The very restricted construction which counsel for the landlord seeks to place on the
phrase 'lawfully sublet' in s 137(2) essentially involves the proposition that Case 6
f implicitly prohibits a subletting of the whole dwelling house without the consent of the
landlord, and therefore renders it unlawful. With due respect to the argument, in our
judgment it is wholly ill-founded. As Andrews LCJ said in *Enniskillen UDC v Bartley and
Lynch* [1947] NI 177 at 181 in relation to the equivalent provision in the Rent and
Mortgage Interest (Restrictions) Act (Northern Ireland) 1925:

> *g* 'This I would say, in passing, is an entire misconception of the sub-section, which
> is not in form or in fact a prohibition but merely a provision which enables the
> landlord to recover possession where the tenant without such consent has made such
> sub-letting.'

In *Regional Properties Co Ltd v Frankenschwerth* [1951] 1 All ER 178, [1951] 1 KB 631 a
h contractual tenant, who was not prevented by his tenancy agreement from assigning the
premises without the consent of the landlord, was given notice to quit. Three days before
the notice expired, he assigned the property for the remainder of the term with the
intention that the assignee could hold over as statutory tenant. The Court of Appeal held
that the county court judge had had jurisdiction to make an order for possession against
the assignee under para (*d*) of Sch 1 to the Rent and Mortgage Interest Restrictions
j (Amendment) Act 1933 (a predecessor of Case 6), where it considered it reasonable on
the facts to make the order.

The court therefore, albeit affirming the county court judge's order, did not treat the
occupation of the assignee as unlawful; if it had done so questions of reasonableness or
unreasonableness would not have arisen. Danckwerts J, in the course of his judgment,
said ([1951] 1 All ER 178 at 184, [1951] 1 KB 631 at 641):

'A tenant, assignee, or sub-tenant, who continues in possession after the contractual
tenancy has come to an end in the case of a house to which the Rent Restrictions   *a*
Acts apply retains his possession lawfully under s. 15 of the Increase of Rent and
Mortgage Interest (Restrictions) Act, 1920, and he continues to occupy on the terms
of the tenancy so far as applicable to that situation. Sub-section (3) of that section
recognises him as having an interest. In those circumstances it seems to me that the
sum which is awarded to a landlord who is given an order pursuant to the Act to
recover possession should be described more properly as rent rather than as mesne   *b*
profits.'

Danckwerts J would thus clearly have regarded Mr Springer as being a person to whom
the flat had been 'lawfully sublet', on the facts of the present case. This in our view is
plainly the right conclusion, so that, with all respect to the judge, we differ from his
conclusion that Mr Springer does not enjoy the protection of s 137(2) of the 1977 Act.
    It is, however, still necessary to consider the nature of this protection and to deal with   *c*
a further or additional ground on which the landlords now seek to uphold the judge's
judgment. This ground, as set out in the landlord's respondent's notice, is that the
landlords were entitled to possession not only against Mrs Byrne but also against Mr
Springer by virtue of s 98(1)(*b*) of the 1977 Act, coupled with Case 6, on the grounds that
she had sublet the whole of the flat to Mr Springer without the landlords' licence or   *d*
consent. On a quick reading of s 137(2) of the 1977 Act, it might be thought that, since
the 'statutorily protected tenancy' of Mrs Byrne had determined and as Mr Springer is a
person to whom the flat has been lawfully sublet, he, under the subsection, is deemed to
become the tenant of the landlords on the same terms as if the statutorily protected
tenancy had continued and correspondingly to have the continuing protection of the
1977 Act, without regard to anything that Mrs Byrne may have done. But we think this   *e*
conclusion would be an oversimplification of the position. For under s 137(2) the
subtenant is only deemed to become the tenant of the landlord 'subject to this Act'. The
phrase in our judgment merely means that, where the interest of the original tenant has
been determined for any reason, any lawful subtenant *who is entitled to retain possession
under the provisions of the 1977 Act* shall, notwithstanding that the title under which he
derived his interest has come to an end, continue to be the tenant on the terms mentioned   *f*
in the subsection: see *Lord Hylton v Heal* [1921] 2 KB 438 at 449 per Rowlatt J and
Enniskillen UDC v Bartley and Lynch [1947] NI 177 at 181–182 per Andrews LCJ. The two
passages last cited were directed to s 15(3) of the 1920 Act, a predecessor of s 137(2) of the
1977 Act, but we can see no material difference in the wording of the two subsections.
Section 137(2) refers inferentially to s 137(1) of the 1977 Act and defines the legal position
of subtenants who are entitled to protection under it. In s 137(1) the provision that an
order for possession against a tenant shall not affect the right of any subtenant to whom   *g*
the premises have been lawfully sublet, as therein specified, to retain possession is
similarly qualified in its application by the words 'by virtue of this Part of this Act' which
immediately follow. As Andrews LCJ commented in the *Enniskillen UDC* case (at 182) in
relation to the equivalent subsection of the 1920 Act (s 5(5)):

> 'The whole scope and object of this subsection was (whilst recognising the   *h*
> independent and substantive position of the subtenant which, not absolutely, but to
> a limited extent is conferred by the Act) to render it necessary for a landlord seeking
> to dispossess a subtenant to institute proceedings against him. In other words, the
> order or judgment against the tenant would not suffice where the subletting was
> lawful and was made before proceedings for recovery of possession were commenced.'

Thus the rights of the subtenant do not necessarily stand or fall with those of the   *j*
tenant; he is entitled to have his rights independently considered and ascertained.
Nevertheless, even the lawful subtenant in our judgment remains vulnerable to
possession proceedings in a case where the head landlord can establish as against him the
conditions set out in s 98(1) of the 1977 Act: see and compare *Lord Hylton v Heal* [1921] 2

KB 438 esp at 449, the *Enniskillen UDC* case [1947] NI 177 esp at 182–183, 187–189 per
a Andrews LCJ and Black J, the *Regional Properties* case [1951] 1 All ER 178, [1951] 1 KB
631 passim and *Megarry's Rent Acts* (10th edn, 1967) vol 1, p 467. Under s 152(1) of the
1977 Act, except where the context otherwise requires, the expression 'tenant' includes a
subtenant. We can see no reason why the expression 'tenant' in s 98(1)(a) of the 1977 Act
should not include a subtenant in an appropriate context.

   As we understood his argument, however, counsel for Mr Springer submitted that, on
b the particular facts of the present case, the court had no jurisdiction to make an order for
possession against Mr Springer, essentially on the following grounds, although this was
not precisely the way in which he put the point. (1) Though the judge made no finding
to this effect, on the evidence Mrs Byrne's statutory tenancy had determined before the
start of proceedings, when she sublet the whole of the flat and moved to Australia,
abandoning the intention of retaining it as her home. (2) Though Mrs Byrne had been
c joined as a nominal party to the proceedings, the contest was thus essentially one as
between the landlords and Mr Springer. (3) If the court was to have jurisdiction to make
an order for possession against Mr Springer, it thus had to be satisfied both that it was
reasonable to make such an order against him and also that, having regard to s 98(1)(b),
the circumstances were as specified in one or more of the Cases in Part I of Sch 15 to the
1977 Act. (No reliance has been placed by the landlords on s 98(1)(a).) (4) The only case
d relied on by the landlords is Case 6 and that cannot be relied on *as against Mr Springer*
because it is not Mr Springer who has 'without the consent of the landlord . . . sublet the
whole of the dwelling-house'.

   The first three of these four propositions seems to us correct. The fourth gives rise to
rather greater difficulty. The effect of s 137(2) was that, on the determination of Mrs
Byrne's statutory tenancy, Mr Springer was 'subject to this Act . . . deemed to become the
e tenant of the landlord . . .' On a first reading of Case 6, it might therefore appear that, in
any contest for possession as between the landlords and Mr Springer, Mr Springer himself
must be treated as 'the tenant' for the purposes of ascertaining whether the conditions of
Case 6 are satisfied. On this footing the conditions clearly would *not* be satisfied according
to their terms.

   On consideration of Sch 15 as a whole, however, we do not think this is the correct
f way of looking at the matter. Following the reasoning of Rowlatt J in *Lord Hylton v Heal*
[1921] 2 KB 438 at 445ff in regard to the corresponding provisions of the 1920 Act we
think that the term 'tenant' as used in Part I of Sch 15 is a generic term which at least in
some contexts must be read as referring simply to the last immediate tenant of the
landlord and not as including an assignee of the tenancy or a subtenant who has not yet
been accepted by the landlord as a tenant.

g   Thus for example, beyond doubt in our judgment, the word 'tenant' must bear this
meaning in Case 5, which gives the court power to make an order for possession where,
inter alia, 'the tenant has given notice to quit and, in consequence of that notice, the
landlord has contracted to sell or let the dwelling-house . . .' As Rowlatt J pointed out in
Lord Hylton v Heal [1921] 2 KB 438 at 447–448 in relation to the similar provision of the
1920 Act, this provision must be taken to recognise that—

h
     'it is essential to the protection of the landlord, who has received notice to quit
     from his immediate tenant, and in consequence thereof has contracted to let the
     house to another person, that he should be entitled to recover possession of the
     house; and if it were held that, in the case where the house was sub-let, the landlord
     could not recover possession unless he received notice from the sub-tenant also, he
     would in that case be deprived of the protection of that clause.'
j
   In other words, subject always to the court considering it reasonable, an order for
possession may be made against a lawful subtenant in reliance on Case 5 even though the
subtenant himself has not given any notice to quit, because the notice served by the
immediate tenant of the landlord is the relevant notice, even in proceedings as between
landlord and subtenant. This is clearly established by the decision in *Lord Hylton v Heal*.

Other examples of Cases in Sch 15 where the word 'tenant' must be given a restricted meaning are to be derived from Rowlatt J's judgment in that case (see [1921] 2 KB 438 at 445–448). By parity of reasoning, in our judgment the word 'tenant' in Case 6 must be taken as referring to the immediate tenant of the landlord, rather than to any assignee or sublessee against whom possession is sought. Subject to the court considering it reasonable, a landlord may, in our judgment, obtain an order for possession against a lawful subtenant or assignee in reliance on Case 6, even though ex hypothesi the subtenant or assignee will not himself have effected the relevant subletting or assignment. Any other construction of Case 6 would in our judgment render it more or less useless to any landlord. The obvious purpose of the legislature in including Case 6 is that (whether or not the landlord's consent to assignments or subtenancies has been made necessary under the original tenancy agreement) the court should be given a discretion where it considers it reasonable to make an order for possession against any assignee or subtenant who is unknown to and not approved of by the landlord: see the *Regional Properties* case [1951] 1 All ER 178 at 181, [1951] 1 KB 631 at 637 per Evershed MR. In the latter case the person against whom an order for possession was sought was the lawful assignee of the contractual terms of the original tenant. The Court of Appeal, however, did not regard itself as being precluded from making an order for possession against him under the equivalent of Case 6, even though he had not been the person who had effected the assignment.

In our judgment, therefore, the judge would have had jurisdiction to make an order for possession against Mr Springer under Case 6, provided that he considered it reasonable to do so against him. However, having been persuaded that Mr Springer's subtenancy was unlawful, he did not address his mind to the question of reasonableness or otherwise; and, from his notes of the evidence, we doubt whether he would have had the material to form a concluded view on this point. Before this question can be properly decided, it is necessary that both the landlords and Mr Springer should have the opportunity of urging all matters of fact which they may respectively consider relevant in this context, including matters personal as between themselves, which may affect the reasonableness of the landlords' demand for possession, so soon after they have acquired the reversion (cf *Lord Hylton v Heal* [1921] 2 KB 438 at 449 per Rowlatt J).

For the record, we should perhaps mention that the *Regional Properties* case was not cited in argument, but was drawn to the attention of the court through counsel for the landlords after the conclusion of the hearing. However, since it merely reinforces but does not alter the conclusion we would have reached in this case even in its absence, we have not thought it necessary to put the parties to the trouble and expense of requiring counsel to come back and address further argument on it.

For the reasons given, we allow this appeal. We will set aside the judgment of 5 October 1981 in so far as it made an order for possession of the flat against Mr Springer and ordered the payment of sums of money by him to the landlords. We will remit the case to the county court judge to decide (a) whether or not he considers it reasonable to make an order for possession against him, and (b) what sums (if any) should be paid by Mr Springer to the landlords on account of rent, use and occupation or mesne profits.

Appeal allowed Case remitted to the county court.

Solicitors: *Scott, Winter & Co* (for Mr Springer); *Richard Freeman & Co* (for the landlords).

Bebe Chua   Barrister.

Brown v Sparrow

a

COURT OF APPEAL, CIVIL DIVISION
WALLER, SLADE LJJ AND DAME ELIZABETH LANE
9, 10 JUNE 1982

b
County court – Costs – Jurisdiction – Extent of jurisdiction – Judge ordering taxation on particular scale and then limiting amount recoverable thereunder – Whether judge having power to limit amount recoverable under particular scale – CCR 1936 Ord 47.

c
County court – Costs – Landlord and tenant – Discretion as to costs – Action to recover possession of domestic premises – Judge deciding that 'in view of the nature of the case' there should be 'severe limitations as to costs where people's home were at stake' – Judge imposing limit on amount of costs recoverable on taxation – Whether judge enunciating general rule as to costs in possession actions and thereby restricting exercise of discretion – CCR 1936 Ord 47, r 1.

d
The plaintiff brought separate actions in the county court against X, Y and Z claiming an order for possession of the flat in which they were living, on the ground that their licence to occupy it had expired. The three actions were heard together. X defended the proceedings, but the judge found against all three defendants and ordered them to vacate the premises. A dispute as to costs followed. The plaintiff, who estimated that his costs would be about £1,200, asked for costs on the highest scale (scale 4) against each defendant, while the defendant in each case asked for costs to be on a lower scale (scale 2) subject to a ceiling imposed by the judge. The judge stated that he intended in each case to order under CCR 1936 Ord 47, r 1[a] that the costs were to be on scale 2 and that on

e
taxation the total costs in each case were not to exceed £100. The judge stated that his reasons for making the order were (i) that he had allowed the plaintiff to make substantial amendments to his pleadings in order to seek relief not originally claimed and (ii) that 'in view of the nature of the case' he had 'no doubt that there should be severe limitations as to costs where people's homes were at stake'. The plaintiff appealed against the order for costs, contending (i) that the judge had no jurisdiction to make the order because,

f
although he was entitled under Ord 47, r 1 to order taxation on a particular scale, he had no power to limit the amount recoverable thereunder since that undermined the plaintiff's right under Ord 47, r 35[b] to taxation and constituted a de facto assessment of costs prior to taxation, and (ii) that, in any event, even if the judge did have jurisdiction, he had erred in the exercise of his discretion under Ord 47, r 1 by taking into account the amendments to the pleadings which had been made at the invitation of the judge to

g
remedy technical defects, and by restricting his discretion by ruling that the court should always place strict limitations on the plaintiff's right to recover costs in an action for the recovery of possession of domestic premises.

Held – (1) The judge had jurisdiction to make an order that the plaintiff's costs were to be taxed but that if the taxed costs amounted to more than a fixed sum the defendant

h
was only required to pay the fixed sum, since such an order did not infringe the very wide discretion which he had under CCR 1936 Ord 47, r 1 to make orders as to costs (see p 741 h, p 743 h j, p 744 c to e and p 745 j, post); dictum of Darling J in *Golding v Smith* [1910] 1 KB at 464 applied.

(2) The judge had not erred in the exercise of his discretion since he was entitled to take the amendments to the pleadings into account, and it was apparent from his

j
judgment that he was not laying down a general rule in relation to costs in possession actions but was merely referring to the circumstances of the particular case. Accordingly

---

a   Rule 1 is set out at p 741 *g*, post
b   Rule 35 is set out at p 742 *b*, post

there were no grounds for interfering with his decision. It followed that the appeal would be dismissed (see p 744 g, p 745 e to j and p 746 a, post).   *a*

Notes
For costs in the county court, see 10 Halsbury's Laws (4th edn) para 602.

As from 1 September 1982, CCR 1936 Ord 47, rr 1 and 35 were replaced by CCR 1981 Ord 38, rr 1 and 2.

b

Cases referred to in judgments
Baylis Baxter Ltd v Sabath [1958] 2 All ER 209, [1958] 1 WLR 529, CA, 51 Digest (Repl) 889, 4425.
Bourne v Stanbridge [1965] 1 All ER 241, [1965] 1 WLR 189, CA, 13 Digest (Reissue) 496, 4106.
Friedeberg, The (1885) 54 LJP 75, 51 Digest (Repl) 912, 4599.   *c*
Golding v Smith [1910] 1 KB 462, 51 Digest (Repl) 923, 4667.
Nicholson v Little [1956] 2 All ER 699, [1956] 1 WLR 829, CA, 13 Digest (Reissue) 478, 3963.

Case also cited
Perry v Stopher [1959] 1 All ER 713, [1959] 1 WLR 415, CA.   *d*

Appeal
The plaintiff, Arthur Brown, brought three actions in the county court (i) against the defendant, Richard Sparrow, (ii) against Michael Bull and (iii) against Andre Sim, claiming an order for possession of the first floor flat at 25 Dresden Road, London N19, in which they were living, on the ground that their licence to occupy it had expired. The   *e* three actions were heard together by his Honour Judge Dewar in the Clerkenwell County Court. The defendant defended the action against him, contending that the licence agreement was a sham and did not represent the true intention of the parties and that a tenancy had been created. The judge found against him and on 6 May 1981, made an order restraining him, as from 5 June 1981, from entering or re-entering the flat. A dispute as to costs followed. The judge eventually made an order that the defendant   *f* should pay the plaintiff's costs of the action on Scale 2 to be taxed if not agreed, the total on taxation not to exceed £100. The plaintiff appealed against the order as to costs. The facts are set out in the judgment of Slade LJ.

Jeremy Maurice for the plaintiff.
The defendant appeared in person.   *g*

SLADE LJ delivered the first judgment at the invitation of Waller LJ. This is an appeal by Mr Arthur Brown from an order relating to costs made by his Honour Judge Dewar at the Clerkenwell County Court on 6 May 1981, after he had given judgment in an action between the plaintiff, Mr Brown, and the defendant, Mr Sparrow. The action was for the recovery of possession of the first floor flat at 25 Dresden Road, London N19. The   *h* defendant was alleged to have held over after termination of a licence to occupy the flat, and thereby to have become a trespasser. Two other actions by the plaintiff were heard by the judge at the same time. These actions were, respectively, against a Mr Sim and a Mr Bull. The hearing of the three actions extended over two to three days. The defendant defended the action against him essentially on the basis that the licence agreement was a sham and did not reflect the true intention of the parties, and that he was a tenant. We   *j* are told that the evidence and closing speeches by counsel lasted for one and a half days. Judgment was, in due course, reserved but on 6 May 1981 it was delivered in all three actions.

The judge found against the defendant on the substantive issues in the action against him, and on that day he made an order restraining him as from 5 June 1981 from

a entering or re-entering the flat. He also gave judgment for the plaintiff in the sum of
£510 in respect of use and occupation. He further ordered that the plaintiff should
recover against the defendant: 'Costs on Scale 2 to be taxed if not agreed. The total of
such costs inclusive of any costs of taxation not to exceed £100.' This is the order for costs
against which Mr Brown now appeals. He is represented by counsel. The defendant has
appeared before us in person.

b The judge gave a brief judgment in relation to the question of costs. We have the
benefit of a note of this judgment, signed by counsel for both parties (the defendant was
then represented by counsel) and approved by the judge himself. I think that I should
read it in full:

'On the question of costs the parties reached an agreement but it is meaningless
as they did not put forward a scale. Accordingly I do not propose to make an order
in the proposed terms. I indicated this to counsel and gave them an opportunity to
c negotiate further. On this counsel could not agree. I therefore have to adjudicate on
the plaintiff's application. In each case the plaintiff asks for costs on scale 4, while
the defendant asks for costs on scale 2 subject to a ceiling to be imposed by the judge.
There are unusual features in this case. The three cases were all heard together as if
they were one, and they overlapped. I allowed substantial amendments to enable
the plaintiff to seek relief which was not in the terms of what was originally sought.
d The plaintiff estimates his costs at a figure of £1,200. In view of the nature of the
case, I have no doubt that there should be severe limitations as to costs where people's
homes are at stake. Accordingly I order that costs should be on scale 2, to be taxed if
not agreed, and the total on taxation inclusive of any costs of taxation is not to
exceed £100. In Sim's case the only question reserved was that of costs. There
should be an identical order as in Sparrow's case. The order in Bull's case will be in
e the same terms.'

Counsel for the plaintiff attacks the order relating to costs essentially on two grounds:
First, he submitted (I quote from the notice of appeal) that—

'having ordered taxation on a particular scale, the learned Judge has no power to
limit the amount recoverable thereunder, as the same constitutes an infringement
f of the Plaintiff's right to taxation and de facto estimate of costs against the Plaintiff's
will.'

Second, he submitted in effect, that even if, contrary to his first submission, the judge
had the power to make an order for costs in the form in which he did, the exercise of his
discretion was wrong in principle.

g I will begin by dealing with the first of these submissions. Subject to a proviso which
is immaterial for present purposes, CCR 1936 Ord 47, r 1 provides:

'Subject to the provisions of any Act or Rule, the costs of proceedings in a county
court shall be in the discretion of the court.'

The discretion given to the county court by this rule is thus a very wide one. Prima facie,
h it seems to me that it has the power, under this rule, to make an order in the form which
the judge adopted in the present case, and that counsel for the plaintiff has to point to
something in some Act or rule which prevented him from doing so. Counsel relied on
no statutory provision in his argument, which has been based solely on certain subsequent
rules of Ord 47, to which I will refer.

Rule 5(1) and (2) provides:

j '(1) For the regulation of solicitors' charges and disbursements otherwise than
under Rule 37 of this Order there shall be a Lower Scale and four Higher Scales,
namely Scale 1, Scale 2, Scale 3 and Scale 4.
(2) The Higher Scales, which shall be those set out in Appendix B, shall have
effect subject to and in accordance with the Rules of this Order and the directions
contained in the Scales.'

Rule 5(3) sets out the scale of costs applicable to a sum of money only. Rule 6 sets out
certain further rules for determining the scale of costs in an action for the recovery of a   *a*
sum of money only.

Rule 35, to which counsel for the plaintiff next referred and on which he placed great
reliance, reads:

> 'In every action or matter in which one party is liable to pay any costs incurred by
> any other party, then except as provided in the next two succeeding Rules of this
> Order, the costs shall be taxed.'   *b*

The exceptions to the general provision for taxation of costs appear in rr 36 and 37.
Rule 36(1) states:

> 'Appendix D to these Rules shall have effect for the purpose of showing the total
> amount which, in the several cases to which Appendix D applies, shall be allowed to
> the solicitor for the plaintiff without taxation, unless the judge or registrar otherwise   *c*
> orders.'

Appendix D covers a number of specific cases which I think I need not further detail.
Rule 37(1) and (2) provides, inter alia:

> '(1) Where costs are on the Lower Scale, they shall be fixed and allowed without
> taxation and any reference in these Rules to taxation shall, in relation to such costs,   *d*
> be treated as a reference to fixing and allowing them under this paragraph.
> (2) Where in a case to which Appendix D does not apply costs are awarded on
> one of the Higher Scales, the costs may, if the solicitor for the party in whose favour
> the award has been made so desires, be assessed without taxation.'

Although, as counsel for the plaintiff has told us, there is no similar provision in the   *e*
County Courts Act 1959, a provision, rather similar to Ord 37, r 35, was previously
contained in s 118 of the County Courts Act 1888, which provided that all costs and
charges between party and party should be taxed, and that no costs or charges should be
allowed on such taxation which were not sanctioned by the scale then in force. This
section was considered by the Divisional Court in *Golding v Smith* [1910] 1 KB 462. In
that case, the county court judge had made an order for costs in favour of a party simply   *f*
for a fixed sum without any direction for taxation. The Divisional Court allowed an
appeal from his order. Darling J said (at 464):

> 'I am of opinion that this appeal must be allowed. Sect. 113 of the County Courts
> Act, 1888, gives a county court judge power to order that the costs shall be paid by
> or apportioned between the parties in such manner as he shall think just. In my
> judgment the "costs" referred to in that section mean costs which have been taxed,   *g*
> because s. 118 says "all costs and charges between party and party shall be taxed by
> the registrar." If the county court judge had made an order that if the plaintiff's
> costs when taxed amounted to more than £10 the defendant should pay to the
> plaintiff only £10, I think he would be perfectly right. The costs may yet be taxed,
> and if when that is done the plaintiff's costs amount to more than £10, the county
> court judge will, if he thinks proper, be at liberty to apply s. 113 and allow the   *h*
> plaintiff £10 only for costs. In my judgment we cannot hold that the order as made
> was right, because the effect would be to deprive a party of the right which he has
> under s. 118 to have the costs taxed.'

Pickford J, the other member of the court, agreed that there was no power to order a
lump sum for costs, but said he preferred to express no opinion whether the judge could,   *j*
after taxation, direct that a fixed sum should be allowed.

In the present case, the judge has in effect done what Darling J considered would have
been permissible. He has made an order for taxation of the plaintiff's costs but has
directed that, if these costs amount to more than a fixed sum, the defendant should pay
to the plaintiff only a fixed sum.

Counsel for the plaintiff has submitted that the judge had no power to make such an
a order. He accepted, as I think he had to accept in view of Ord 7, r 1, that a county court
judge has a general discretion in relation to an order for costs. However, he submitted,
this power is subject to limitations imposed by the rules, and in a case such as this, which
falls within the higher scales, either party has an absolute right to taxation. He submitted
that the judge's discretion is limited to choosing a particular scale (higher or lower) or
disallowing specific items of costs. He submitted, however, that a party, such as the
b plaintiff in the present case, who has a right to taxation of his costs, can alone waive this
right and that any limitation on the amount of costs recoverable on taxation (such as that
imposed by the judge in the present case) undermines the right to taxation and to costs
on some scale provided by the County Court Rules. Essentially, he submitted in the
present case, the judge was effecting a de facto assessment of the plaintiff's costs and
putting an arbitrary limit on them. Therefore, in the submission of counsel for the
c plaintiff, he was acting ultra vires.

In further support of his general argument, counsel for the plaintiff also referred to a
number of rules which specifically empower the court, in certain circumstances, to award
costs on such a scale as it thinks fit. Order 47, r 13 provides:

> 'In any proceedings in which the judge certifies that a difficult question of law or
> a question of fact of exceptional complexity is involved, he may award costs on such
> *d* scale as he thinks fit.'

Order 47, r 15(1) states:

> 'In any proceedings to which Rules 6, 7, 12, 14 and 36 of this Order do not apply,
> the judge may award costs on such Scale as he thinks fit.'

e Order 47, r 17 states:

> 'Where the costs of any action or matter are on one of the Higher Scales, the judge
> may direct the registrar to allow or disallow on taxation any item in the Scale.'

If the general discretion to award costs conferred on the court by Ord 47, r 1 were an
unfettered discretion, these various substantive provisions, counsel for the plaintiff
f submitted, would be unnecessary: they show, so he contended, that limitations are to be
read into that power.

I see the force of his point, but I do not find it compelling. The decision of the Court
of Appeal in *Bourne v Stanbridge* [1965] 1 All ER 241, [1965] 1 WLR 189 (referred to in
the notes in *The County Court Practice 1981* under Ord 47, r 6) established that the judge
has an overriding discretion under r 1 of the order to award costs on a scale higher than
g that stated in r 6, if he exercises his discretion properly. It seems to me that rr 13, 15(1)
and 17 were included, not in the contemplation that they would be construed as
restricting the generality of Ord 47, r 1, but simply to make it specifically clear that the
court has the power to depart from the normal scales in the circumstances there stated
and, where costs are in the higher scales, to direct the allowance or disallowance of
particular items on taxation. Counsel for the plaintiff accepted that, provided only that
h the judge had exercised his discretion properly, he would have had the power to make
an order for costs in favour of the plaintiff on any scale which he thought fit, high or low,
or indeed to make no order for costs in his favour at all. When the county court judge
would indisputably have had so wide a discretion as this, it would be an odd result if he
did not have the power also to make an order for taxation, coupled with a limit on the
maximum amount recoverable thereunder. I think that there is nothing in the rules
j subsequent to Ord 47, r 1 which compels such a conclusion.

For my part, I would not be inclined to encourage the making of orders in the form
made in this case, save at the invitation of both parties. As counsel for the plaintiff
pointed out, the advantage of making an order simply for costs to be taxed in default of
agreement, according to what the judge considers an appropriate scale (whatever that
appropriate scale may be) is that there is an ascertainable, demonstrable relationship

between the work done by or on behalf of the party seeking to recover costs, and the amount actually recoverable by him. An order in that simple form will mean that every *a* head of expense falling within the appropriate scale, however low that scale may be, will fall to be at least partially recovered. If, however, an upper ceiling limit is attached to the costs recoverable under an order for taxation, a rather more arbitrary element is introduced, particularly since the judge making the order presumably will have no clear knowledge of the aggregate bill for costs which a successful plaintiff is likely ultimately to have to meet in connection with the whole proceedings. Justice perhaps is thus less *b* obviously seen to be done. These, however, are only passing thoughts. No authority has been cited which suggests that the judge did not have jurisdiction to make the order for taxation of costs with a limit placed on the maximum amount recoverable thereunder, and indeed the dictum of Darling J in *Golding v Smith* [1910] 1 KB 462 at 464 suggests quite the contrary. Oddly enough, this decision is not apparently referred to in *The County Court Practice 1981*. *c*

The provisions of Ord 47, r 35, on which counsel for the plaintiff particularly relied, have not in my opinion been infringed in the present case. Though I recognise that it is a right of which he probably will not wish to avail himself, the plaintiff does still have the right to taxation of his costs, if he wishes. So too does the defendant have the right to taxation of the plaintiff's costs. He likewise probably will not wish to avail himself of the right, on the facts of the present case, but if the limiting figure had been set by the judge *d* at substantially higher than £100, the right would have been of real importance, at least to the defendant. Nor, in my opinion, have any of the other rules of Ord 47 been infringed in the present case by the judge's order. They do not, I think, contain anything which prevented him from making the order which he made, under the wide discretion conferred on him by Ord 47, r 1. I would, therefore, hold that he had jurisdiction to make the order which in fact he made. *e*

I now turn more briefly to the question of the exercise of his discretion. It is, I think, clear that this court will not interfere with the exercise of a discretion by a county court judge in relation to costs, unless he has gone wrong in principle: see, for example, *Nicholson v Little* [1956] 2 All ER 699, [1956] 1 WLR 829 to which the defendant referred us. The judge gave two express reasons for making the order for costs in question. The first was that he had allowed the plaintiff to make substantial amendments to his *f* pleading, to seek relief which was not in the terms of that originally sought. There were two such amendments, both made at the invitation of the judge, to remedy what he regarded as technical defects. Counsel for the plaintiff submitted that the amendments were not in fact necessary. I myself think it doubtful whether they were. Nevertheless, whether or not they were technically necessary, the plaintiff accepted the judge's invitation to amend the pleading, and I do not think that the judge can be said to have *g* erred in principle, in so far as he took these amendments into account in making the order for costs which he did make.

The second, and apparently the more important reason given by the judge, was expressed by him in the words: 'In view of the nature of the case, I have no doubt that there should be severe limitations as to costs where people's homes are at stake.' There are two possible ways of reading this sentence. The first is that the judge was enunciating *h* a general principle that in any action for the recovery of domestic premises, the court should always place severe limitations on the plaintiff's rights to recover costs. This was the way in which counsel for the plaintiff invited us to read the sentence. He also submitted that to decide that costs should be limited merely because living accommodation is at stake, where a commercial transaction has been freely entered into, must be a wrong exercise of the court's discretion. He pointed out that the judge had *j* accepted the plaintiff's submission that the relevant document represented the true transaction entered into between the parties and had eventually rejected the defendant's contention that it was a sham; the judge apparently took the view that the defendant had paid inadequate attention to what he was signing. He submitted there was no good reason at all why the plaintiff should not recover costs on scale 4, and that the judge had, a in effect, subjected himself to a self-imposed limitation on the exercise of his discretion as to costs, which was wrong in principle.

On the interpretation which counsel for the plaintiff placed on the relevant sentence in the judge's judgment as to costs, I would think there was much force in his submission. Denning LJ in *Nicholson v Little* [1956] 2 All ER 699 at 700, [1956] 1 WLR 829 at 831, having referred to Ord 47, r 1, said:

b 'In the face of that rule it is impossible for this or any other court to lay down a rule of law as to costs which would fetter the discretion thus given to the judge.'

He went on to cite a sentence from the judgment of Brett MR in *The Friedeberg* (1885) 54 LJP 75, where he said:

c 'The discretion of the court is to be exercised in each individual case; but the moment a hard and fast rule is laid down as to costs, the discretion of the judge is fettered.'

I think that, in view of Ord 47, r 1, a county court judge is no more entitled to lay down a hard and fast rule for himself in relation to costs than this court would be entitled to lay down such a rule for him. Furthermore, even if it were to be regarded as a mere general practice or rule of thumb, I would not for my own part subscribe to the view d that the plaintiff's costs should necessarily be limited where the nature of the action is for the recovery of domestic premises. As is stated in a note in *The County Court Practice 1981* p 878: 'The judicial discretion must be exercised according to rules of reason or justice, not according to private opinion, or benevolence or sympathy.' It should be based on reasons connected with the particular facts of the particular case: see, for example, *Baylis Baxter Ltd v Sabath* [1958] 2 All ER 209, [1958] 1 WLR 529.

e Nevertheless, on my reading of the crucial sentence in the judge's judgment in the present case, he was exercising his discretion on the basis of the facts before him. It will be observed that this sentence is prefaced with the words 'in view of the nature of the case'. While I entirely accept that the phrases are open to two interpretations, I read these words in their context as meaning 'in view of the circumstances of this case', and the words 'where people's homes are at stake' as meaning 'where the homes of Mr Sparrow, f Mr Bull and Mr Sim are at stake'. The judge in his judgment had already referred to the presence of unusual features in the case. He had heard all the evidence. He knew the full background against which these claims for possession were made. If I may respectfully say so, I think that the relevant passages of his extempore judgment in relation to costs could perhaps have been more clearly expressed. For my own part, however, I accept the submission of the defendant, as set out in his respondent's notice, that the judge was g acting on facts connected with, leading up to, and proved during the case and deliberately intended to exercise his discretionary powers in making the order for costs which he did make, and that he did not place any improper, self-imposed fetter on the exercise of the very wide discretion given him by Ord 47, r 1.

Simply on the basis of the facts as appearing in the judge's judgment on the substantive issues, I am not certain that I myself would have made an order for costs as unfavourable h to the plaintiff as the particular order which in fact he made. But this is not enough to justify this court interfering with the exercise of his discretion. Counsel for the plaintiff, in his fair and able argument, for which I am grateful, has failed to convince me that the judge erred in principle in relation to the question of costs. For all the reasons which I have given, I would dismiss the appeal.

j **DAME ELIZABETH LANE.** I agree.

WALLER LJ. I also agree. I would only add that there are some other words in the note of the judgment of the judge which support the view that this was an independent exercise of discretion because it is clear that there had been specific argument before the judge when he said this: 'In each case the plaintiff asks for costs on scale 4, while the defendant asks for costs on scale 2 subject to a ceiling to be imposed by the judge.' Then he goes on with the fact that there are unusual features in the case, and eventually comes *a* to the passage which Slade LJ has already quoted. In my opinion that supports the view that the judge was making a completely independent decision, based on the facts before him, and the nature of the case which he heard.

I agree that this appeal should be dismissed.

Appeal dismissed.   *b*

Solicitors: *N Ramsay Murray & Co*, Chiswick (for the plaintiff).

Diana Brahams   Barrister.

c

Cardshops Ltd v John Lewis Properties Ltd

COURT OF APPEAL, CIVIL DIVISION
WALLER, EVELEIGH AND ACKNER LJJ   *d*
22 APRIL, 24 JUNE 1982

Landlord and tenant – Business premises – Compensation for disturbance – Amount of compensation – Amount altered by amendment of statutory provision – Landlord serving notice to terminate tenancy before amendment coming into force – Landlord entitled to possession after amendment coming into force – Amount of compensation payable by landlord to tenant on quitting *e* *premises – Whether compensation payable according to statutory scale in force at date of landlord's notice or at date tenant quitting holding – Landlord and Tenant Act 1954, s 37(2) – Local Government, Planning and Land Act 1980, Sch 33, para 4(1) – Landlord and Tenant Act 1954 (Appropriate Multiplier) Regulations 1981.*

On 3 January 1980 the landlords of business premises to which s 37(2)(b)[a] of the Landlord *f* and Tenant Act 1954 applied served on the tenants a notice under s 25[b] of that Act to terminate their tenancy of the premises by 25 December 1980. The tenants served a counter-notice on 6 March and on 24 April applied to the court for a new tenancy under s 24 of the 1954 Act. When the application came before the county court on 18 February 1981 the tenants conceded that they could not oppose the landlords' claim for possession. Accordingly, judgment was given for the landlords. The question then arose as to the *g* amount of compensation payable under s 37(1) of the 1954 Act by the landlords to the tenants on quitting the holding, which the tenants were obliged under that Act to do on 29 June 1981. As originally enacted, s 37(2)(b) provided that the amount of compensation was to be 'the rateable value of the holding' but s 37(2)(b) was amended, after the date of the landlords' s 25 notice, by s 193[c] of, and para 4[d] of Sch 33 to, the Local Government, Planning and Land Act 1980, which received the royal assent on 13 November 1980. *h* The amendment altered the amount of compensation by making it the rateable value increased by 'the appropriate multiplier' as prescribed by the Secretary of State by

---

a Section 37(2) is set out at p 748 *j*, post
b Section 25, so far as material, provides:
    '(1) The landlord may terminate a tenancy [of business premises] by a notice given to the tenant *j* in the prescribed form specifying the date at which the tenancy is to come to an end . . .
    (2) . . . a notice under this section shall not have effect unless it is given not more than twelve nor less than six months before the date of termination specified therein . . .'
c Section 193 is set out at p 752 *j* to p 753 *a*, post
d Paragraph 4 is set out at p 748 *j* to p 749 *b*, post

statutory instrument. By virtue of s 47(5)^e of the 1980 Act, however, the amendment
a was not to take effect until the Secretary of State had prescribed the appropriate
multiplier. On 2 January 1981 the Secretary of State made the Landlord and Tenant Act
1954 (Appropriate Multiplier) Regulations 1981^f, which came into operation on 25
March 1981. The regulations provided that the appropriate multiplier for the purposes
of s 37(2)(*b*) was 2¼. The tenants contended that since they would be quitting the premises
after the date on which the regulations came into force they were entitled to 2¼ times the
b rateable value of the premises as compensation. The landlords submitted (i) that since
under s 37(5)(*a*)^g of the 1954 Act the rateable value of the premises was to be determined
by reference to the valuation list in force on 3 January 1980, ie the date the landlords'
served their s 25 notice, that date was the relevant date for the purposes of assessing the
amount of compensation, and (ii) that the amendment of s 37(2)(*b*) of the 1954 Act by
the 1980 Act was not effective until the 1981 regulations came into force and therefore
c was not applicable when the landlords served their s 25 notice. The landlords accordingly
contended, and the judge held, that the tenants were only entitled to the amount of the
rateable value as compensation. The tenants appealed.

Held (Eveleigh LJ dissenting) – Since the 1980 Act and the 1981 regulations made no
provision for suspending the operation of the amendment of s 37(2)(*b*) of the 1954 Act
d effected by the 1980 Act in the situation where a notice had been served by a landlord
before the amendment came into force on 25 March 1981, it was clear that the
amendment was intended to apply in every case where a tenant quit premises after that
date and was entitled to compensation under s 37(1). The relevant date for the purpose
of assessing compensation under s 37 of the 1954 Act was therefore the date on which
the tenant quit the premises (or, if he wrongfully stayed on, the date on which he should
e have quit). It followed that the tenants were entitled to 2¼ times the rateable value of the
holding as compensation (see p 750 *c* to *f* and *h*, p 751 *e f*, p 759 *j* and p 760 *e* to *h*, post).
International Military Services Ltd v Capital and Counties plc [1982] 2 All ER 20 approved.

Notes
For compensation for disturbance on quitting business premises and the amount of
f compensation, see 27 Halsbury's Laws (4th edn) paras 518–519.
    For the Landlord and Tenant Act 1954, ss 25, 37, see 18 Halsbury's Statutes (3rd edn)
559, 576.
    For the Local Government, Planning and Land Act 1980, ss 47, 193, Sch 33, para 4, see
50(2) ibid 1923, 1385, 1421.

g **Cases referred to in judgments**
Athlumney, Re, ex p Wilson [1898] 2 QB 547, [1895–9] All ER Rep 329, 4 Digest (Reissue)
    12, 27.
Carson v Carson and Stoyek [1964] 1 All ER 681, [1964] 1 WLR 511, 27 (1) Digest (Reissue)
    541, 3895.
Garrett v Lloyds Bank Ltd (7 April 1982, unreported), Ch D.
h *Grafton Street (14), London W 1, Re, De Havilland (Antiques) Ltd v Centrovincial Estates
    (Mayfair) Ltd* [1971] 2 All ER 1, [1971] Ch 935, [1971] 2 WLR 159, 31(2) Digest
    (Reissue) 939, 7705.
International Military Services Ltd v Capital and Counties plc [1982] 2 All ER 20, [1982] 1
    WLR 575.
Master Ladies Tailors Organisation v Minister of Labour and National Service [1950] 2 All ER
j   525, 44 Digest (Repl) 383, 2223.

---

e   Section 47(5) is set out at p 753 *d*, post
f   The 1981 regulations, so far as material, are set out at p 749 *c*, post
g   Section 37(5), so far as material, is set out at p 749 *f* to *h*, post

R v Inhabitants of St Mary, Whitechapel (1848) 12 QB 120, 116 ER 811, 44 Digest (Repl)
285, 1144.   *a*
'Wonderland', Cleethorpes, Re, East Coast Amusement Co Ltd v British Rlys Board [1963] 2 All
ER 775, [1965] AC 58, [1963] 2 WLR 1426, HL; *affg* [1962] 2 All ER 92, [1962] Ch
696, [1962] 2 WLR 776, CA; *affg* [1962] 1 All ER 68, [1962] Ch 696, [1962] 2 WLR
165, 31(2) Digest (Reissue) 957, 7768.

Appeal   *b*
Cardshops Ltd, the tenants of a lockup shop known as 160 Above Bar Street, Southampton,
appealed against an order of his Honour Judge Smithies in the Southampton County
Court, dated 18 February 1981, whereby it was ordered that they should recover, under
s 37 of the Landlord and Tenant Act 1954, the sum of £2,763 (being the rateable value
of the holding) from the landlords, John Lewis Properties Ltd, as compensation for
disturbance. The facts are set out in the judgment of Waller LJ.   *c*

Simon Berry for the tenants.
Andrew Geddes for the landlords.

Cur adv vult
d

24 June. The following judgments were read.

WALLER LJ. Cardshops Ltd were by virtue of an underlease dated 1 April 1968 the
tenants of a lockup shop at 160 Above Bar Street, Southampton, from 25 December 1966
for a term of 14 years. On 3 January 1980 the landlords served a notice under s 25 of the
Landlord and Tenant Act 1954 terminating the tenancy and stating that an application   *e*
for a new tenancy would be opposed on the ground that the landlords intended to occupy
the premises for the purpose of a business to be carried on by them in those premises.
The tenants, served a counter-notice on 6 March and on 24 April applied to the
Southampton County Court for a new tenancy commencing on 25 December 1980. This
was opposed by the landlords.
On 18 February 1981 his Honour Judge Smithies gave judgment for the landlords   *f*
refusing a new tenancy and making an order under s 37(1) of the Landlord and Tenant
Act 1954 for compensation. Section 37(1) was amended by the Law of Property Act
1969, s 11. Section 37(1) and (2) reads as follows:

> '*Compensation where order for new tenancy precluded on certain grounds.*—(1) Where
> on the making of an application under section twenty-four of this Act the court is   *g*
> precluded (whether by subsection (1) or subsection (2) of section thirty-one of this
> Act) from making an order for the grant of a new tenancy by reason of any of the
> grounds specified in paragraphs (*e*), (*f*) and (*g*) of subsection (1) of section thirty of
> this Act and not of any grounds specified in any other paragraph of that subsection
> or where no other ground is specified in the landlord's notice under section 25 of
> this Act or, as the case may be, under section 26(6) thereof, than those specified in   *h*
> the said paragraphs (*e*), (*f*) and (*g*) and either no application under the said section
> 24 is made or such an application is withdrawn, then, subject to the provisions of
> this Act, the tenant shall be entitled on quitting the holding to recover from the
> landlord by way of compensation an amount determined in accordance with the
> following provisions of this section.
> (2) The said amount shall be as follows, that is to say,—(*a*) where the conditions   *j*
> specified in the next following subsection are satisfied it shall be twice the rateable
> value of the holding, (*b*) in any other case it shall be the rateable value of the holding.'

However, by para 4 of Sch 33 to the Local Government, Planning and Land Act 1980,
passed on 13 November 1980, s 37(2) was amended as follows:

> '4.—(1) In subsection (2) of section 37 of the Landlord and Tenant Act 1954

a
(compensation where order for new tenancy precluded on certain grounds) the words "the product of the appropriate multiplier and" shall be inserted after the word "be" in paragraphs (a) and (b).

(2) The following subsections shall be added after subsection (7) of that section—

b
"(8) In subsection (2) of this section 'the appropriate multiplier' means such multiplier as the Secretary of State may by order made by statutory instrument prescribe.

(9) A statutory instrument containing an order under subsection (8) of this section shall be subject to annulment in pursuance of a resolution of either House of Parliament.".'

By s 47(5) the provisions of Sch 33 were not to have effect until the power to prescribe multipliers was exercised by the Secretary of State. On 21 January 1981 the Landlord and Tenant Act 1954 (Appropriate Multiplier) Regulations 1981, SI 1981/69, were made but
c they were not to come into operation until 25 March 1981. Regulation 2 provides that:

'The appropriate multiplier for the purposes of paragraphs (a) and (b) of section 37(2) of the Landlord and Tenant Act 1954 shall be 2¼.'

The judge having refused to grant a new tenancy, by s 64 of the 1954 Act the tenancy continued for three months after the date of the hearing and this brought the date of
d quitting (after allowing for time for notice of appeal) to 29 June 1981.

The court had to decide whether the basis should be the rateable value (there was no dispute that it was a s 37(2)(b) case) or whether the basis should be the rateable value times 2¼. The judge decided that the new regulation did not apply and gave judgment for the rateable value. The tenants now appeal against that compensation assessment.

The 1980 Act, by Part V, abolished the statutory requirement for quinquennial
e revisions of rateable values and the provisions of Sch 33 were part of the consequential changes. At the time of the passing of the 1954 Act the quinquennial revision of rateable values should have ensured that the compensation payable on the termination of the tenancy was related to the current value of the holding. Section 37(5) of the 1954 Act provides:

f
'For the purposes of subsection (2) of this section the rateable value of the holding shall be determined as follows:—(a) where in the valuation list in force at the date on which the landlord's notice under section twenty-five or, as the case may be, subsection (6) of section twenty-six of this Act is given a value is then shown as the annual value (as hereinafter defined) of the holding, the rateable value of the holding shall be taken to be that value; (b) where no such value is so shown with respect to the holding but such a value or such values is or are so shown with respect to
g premises comprised in or comprising the holding or part of it, the rateable value of the holding shall be taken to be such value as is found by a proper apportionment or aggregation of the value or values so shown; (c) where the rateable value of the holding cannot be ascertained in accordance with the foregoing paragraphs of this subsection, it shall be taken to be the value which, apart from any exemption from assessment to rates, would on a proper assessment be the value to be entered in the
h said valuation list as the annual value of the holding; and any dispute arising, whether in proceedings before the court or otherwise, as to the determination for those purposes of the rateable value of the holding shall be referred to the Commissioners of Inland Revenue for decision by a valuation officer . . .'

We have to decide whether the compensation has to be assessed under the old law, that
j is to say in this case the rateable value, having regard to the fact that, while the landlords' notice was served in January 1980, the 1980 Act was not passed until November, and the regulations made in January 1981 did not bring the change into effect until 25 March 1981, or, alternatively, whether the change having taken place on 25 March and the tenants not being obliged to quit until 29 June the compensation should be on the basis of the amending regulation, ie 2¼ times the rateable value.

The absence of any transitional provisions has made the construction of this section

difficult because it is possible to argue in favour of more than one date. The judge has
said that the regulations do not apply but has not identified the crucial date. One
possibility is the date of the landlords' notice. Under the old law the rateable value is to
be the rateable value at the date of the notice. On the other hand, under the revised law
it is the rateable value at the date of the notice multiplied by $2\frac{1}{4}$. Another possibility is
the date specified for termination of the tenancy. The view put forward by the tenants
in this case is that the critical date is the date of quitting.

Section 37(1), having set out the conditions which have to be fulfilled, goes on:

> '... then, subject to the provisions of this Act, the tenant shall be entitled on
> quitting the holding to recover from the landlord by way of compensation an
> amount determined in accordance with the following provisions of this section.'

In *International Military Services Ltd v Capital and Counties plc* [1982] 2 All ER 20 at 27,
[1982] 1 WLR 575 at 582–583 Slade J expressed this view about the meaning of those
words:

> 'The word "then" in my judgment merely means "in that event", that is to say if
> the earlier conditions specified in the subsection are fulfilled. The entitlement arises
> on the quitting of the holding (*and not before*). In my judgment, therefore, it is quite
> plain that the amount of the entitlement must be assessed in accordance with the
> law as it stands at the date of the quitting.' (Slade J's emphasis.)

I agree with the words of Slade J. In my opinion, provided that the conditions set out in
the earlier part of the subsection have been fulfilled, the words I have quoted above
indicate that the entitlement only arises 'on quitting' and the natural construction that
would arise is that the entitlement should be assessed in accordance with the law at that
time. The only other possible interpretation of s 37(1) would make the hearing of the
application the relevant date because the subsection starts with the words: 'Where on the
making of an application ... the court is precluded ...' In my opinion the fact that
s 37(5)(a) refers to the valuation list in force at the date of the landlord's notice does not
invalidate this conclusion. It is the valuation list in force at the date of the landlord's
notice which has to be multiplied by $2\frac{1}{4}$ under the new legislation. The giving of the
landlord's notice is simply an initial step in the proceedings.

It was submitted before this court that to adopt the construction that it is the date of
quitting which is crucial would be to adopt a construction with retrospective effect and
we were referred to the decision of Brightman J in *Re 14 Grafton Street, London W 1, De
Havilland (Antiques) Ltd v Centrovincial Estates (Mayfair) Ltd* [1971] 2 All ER 1, [1971] Ch
935. The facts of that case were quite different from the present case. There it was sought
to set aside an indefeasible right to recover possession by virtue of the passing of the Law
of Property Act 1969. In the present case no such right exists. When the matter came on
for trial before the county court judge there were three possibilities: the landlords might
not be able to establish that they intended to occupy the premises for their own business
purposes; the landlords might have changed their mind and have decided that the cost
was too great; or the landlords might establish their intention and be required to pay
compensation on the tenant quitting. I see nothing retrospective in saying that the
compensation would be on the basis of the law current at the date of quitting. In
International Military Services Ltd v Capital and Counties plc, which I have already
mentioned, the landlord's notice was given after the passing of the 1980 Act. In the
course of his judgment Slade J considered an argument based on the suggestion of
retrospective legislation and, quoting *Re 14 Grafton Street, London W 1*, said ([1982] 2 All
ER 20 at 29, [1982] 1 WLR 575 at 586):

> 'Nevertheless, subject to the points arising on s 47(5) of the 1980 Act, with which
> I have already dealt, the language of the relevant statutory provisions seems to me
> plain and unambiguous. When they are read together, ss 47 and 193 of the 1980
> Act, para 4 of Sch 33 to that Act, and the 1981 regulations in my judgment make it
> quite clear that as from 25 March 1981 the new amendments to paras (a) and (b) of

s 37(2) of the 1954 Act are to apply in the case of every tenant who thereafter quits

a a holding, provided only that the other conditions of s 37(1) have been satisfied. It would have been easy for Parliament in the 1980 Act, or for the Secretary of State in the 1981 regulations, expressly to provide that the amending provisions should not apply in cases where the landlord's s 25 notice had been served before 25 March 1981. No such exception was made, and I can see no sufficient grounds for implying one.'

b   We were also referred to an unreported decision of Walton J in *Garrett v Lloyds Bank Ltd* (7 April 1982). That was a case like the present one, where the landlord's notice was given before the 1980 Act was passed and Walton J, dealing with the suggestion that to make the date of quitting crucial would be retrospective legislation, used words apposite to the present case:

c   '... in the *14 Grafton Street, London W 1* case the tenant could not possibly have brought any proceedings for a fresh lease since his time for so doing had expired. Hence, there was no possibility of a fresh lease being granted. In the present case such proceedings were on foot and could very well, in not impossible circumstances, have succeeded; in particular, had such an application been fought out, the defendant would have had to establish that its intention to use the premises for its own

d   purposes persisted at the date of the hearing. It might well have changed its mind before then, or it might have failed to convince the judge that this was really its true intention. I do not see how a right which depends on the landlord having to persuade a court that it has a certain intention can in any way be said to be a vested right unless and until it has persuaded the court that its intention is as it says it is.'

I respectfully agree with both those observations.

e   In my judgment the law to be applied in cases such as the present is the law at the date on which the tenant is obliged to quit, in this case 29 June 1981. I might add that I do not see any injustice to the landlords in such a conclusion. The policy of the Landlord and Tenant Acts is to hold the balance between landlord and tenant with an obligation on the landlord to pay compensation (and I assume fair compensation) when the tenant is dispossessed. If the unamended law was not achieving fairness I do not see that the

f landlord suffers injustice by having to pay what Parliament views as proper compensation.

EVELEIGH LJ. On 3 January 1980 the landlords served on the tenants a notice under the Landlord and Tenant Act 1954 terminating the tenancy on 25 December 1980. They stated that they required possession for their own occupation, which was a ground for

g possession by s 30(1)(g) of the 1954 Act. The tenants served a notice on the landlords stating that they objected to giving up possession and subsequently, on 24 April, they took out an application in the county court for a new tenancy.

On 18 February 1981 when the matter came before the county court judge the tenants conceded that they could not oppose the landlords' claim for possession. Their application for a new tenancy was accordingly refused.

h   As the law stood at that date the situation was governed by s 37 of the 1954 Act, as amended by s 11 of the Law of Property Act 1969. Section 37(1) as thus amended read:

'Where on the making of an application under section twenty-four of this Act the court is precluded (whether by subsection (1) or subsection (2) of section thirty-one of this Act) from making an order for the grant of a new tenancy by reason of any of the grounds specified in paragraphs (*e*), (*f*) and (*g*) of subsection (1) of section

j thirty of this Act and not of any grounds specified in any other paragraph of that subsection or where no other ground is specified in the landlord's notice under section 25 of this Act or, as the case may be, under section 26(6) thereof, than those specified in the said paragraphs (*e*), (*f*) and (*g*) and either no application under the said section 24 is made or such an application is withdrawn, then, subject to the provisions of this Act, the tenant shall be entitled on quitting the holding to recover from the landlord by way of compensation an amount determined in accordance with the following provisions of this section.'

The statutory amount of compensation was laid down by s 37(2), which reads:

'The said amount shall be as follows, that is to say,—(a) where the conditions specified in the next following subsection are satisfied it shall be twice the rateable value of the holding, (b) in any other case it shall be the rateable value of the holding.'

It is agreed that para (b) is the relevant paragraph for the purposes of this case. Therefore, as the law stood when the application for a new tenancy was refused, as the court was precluded from making an order for the grant of a new tenancy, the situation envisaged by s 37(1) had arisen and the tenants would be entitled when they quit the premises to recover the rateable value of the holding. Section 37(5)(a), so far as material, provides:

'For the purposes of subsection (2) of this section the rateable value of the holding shall be determined as follows:—(a) where in the valuation list in force at the date on which the landlord's notice under section twenty-five . . . is given a value is then shown as the annual value (as hereinafter defined) of the holding, the rateable value of the holding shall be taken to be that value.'

So far as the date for quitting the holding is concerned, that is to some degree capable of being lawfully influenced by the tenant. Section 64 of the 1954 Act provides:

'(1) In any case where—(a) a notice to terminate a tenancy has been given under Part I or Part II of this Act or a request for a new tenancy has been made under Part II thereof, and (b) an application to the court has been made under the said Part I or the said Part II, as the case may be, and (c) apart from this section the effect of the notice or request would be to terminate the tenancy before the expiration of the period of three months beginning with the date on which the application is finally disposed of, the effect of the notice or request shall be to terminate the tenancy at the expiration of the said period of three months and not at any other time.

(2) The reference in paragraph (c) of subsection (1) of this section to the date on which an application is finally disposed of shall be construed as a reference to the earliest date by which the proceedings on the application (including any proceedings on or in consequence of an appeal) have been determined and any time for appealing or further appealing has expired, except that if the application is withdrawn or any appeal is abandoned the reference shall be construed as a reference to the date of the withdrawal or abandonment.'

Of course the tenants did not appeal in the present case and therefore the date for vacating the premises was 29 June 1981. In fact the tenants left on 7 July 1981. Between the date of the landlords' notice and 29 June 1981 a significant change in the law had occurred. The Local Government, Planning and Land Act 1980 received the royal assent on 13 November 1980. Part V of that Act is concerned with rating provisions and by s 28 it provides:

'In section 68 of the General Rate Act 1967 ("the 1967 Act") the following shall be substituted for subsection (1) (new valuation lists to be prepared every 5 years)—

"(1) In the case of each rating area, new valuation lists shall be prepared and made by the valuation officer so as to come into force on 1st April in such year as the Secretary of State may by order from time to time specify.

(1A) An order under this section shall have no effect until approved by resolution of each House of Parliament.".'

If that section stood alone the amount of compensation payable to a tenant would in effect be frozen indefinitely when governed by the section notwithstanding the effects of inflation. However s 193 provides:

'The enactments specified in Schedule 33 to this Act shall have effect subject to a   the amendments specified in that Schedule, being *minor* amendments and amendments *consequential* on the foregoing provisions of this Act.'

Paragraph 4 of Sch 33 is headed 'Landlord and Tenant Act 1954' and reads:

'(1) In subsection (2) of section 37 of the Landlord and Tenant Act 1954 (compensation where order for new tenancy precluded on certain grounds) the words "the product of the appropriate multiplier and" shall be inserted after the word "be" in paragraphs (*a*) and (*b*).

b   (2) The following subsections shall be added after subsection (7) of that section—

"(8) In subsection (2) of this section 'the appropriate multiplier' means such multiplier as the Secretary of State may by order made by statutory instrument prescribe.

(9) A statutory instrument containing an order under subsection (8) of
c   this section shall be subject to annulment in pursuance of a resolution of either House of Parliament.".'

If that paragraph had come into operation on 13 November 1980 there would have been a period when no compensation would have been payable because no multiplier would have existed until the Secretary of State so prescribed. Therefore s 47(5) provided:

d   'The provisions of Schedule 33 to this Act which give the Secretary of State power by order to prescribe multipliers and which are specified in subsection (6)(*a*), (*b*) and (*c*) below shall not have effect until he exercises the power conferred by them.'

Paragraph 4 was covered by this section.

On 21 January 1981 the Secretary of State for the Environment made the Landlord and Tenant Act 1954 (Appropriate Multiplier) Regulations 1981, SI 1981/69, which were
e   laid before Parliament on 2 February and came into operation on 25 March 1981. Regulation 2 provides:

'The appropriate multiplier for the purposes of paragraphs (*a*) and (*b*) of section 37(2) of the Landlord and Tenant Act 1954 shall be 2¼.'

Therefore from 25 March 1981 onwards s 37(2) of the Landlord and Tenant Act 1954, so
f   far as is relevant, reads: 'The said amount shall be as follows, that is to say ... (*b*) in any other case it shall be the product of [2¼] and the rateable value of the holding.'

The tenants say that the right to compensation arises only when the tenant quits the holding or alternatively should have quit, that is June or July of 1981. It is said that the law then in force was that laid down by the 1981 regulations which provide that the multiplier shall be 2¼. The landlords argue that the compensation should be assessed in
g   accordance with the law in force at the date of the landlord's notice, or the tenant's notice, or the date of the application for a new tenancy or the date stated in the landlord's notice for the termination of the tenancy. In my opinion s 37 indicates firmly that the date for the assessment of compensation is the date of the landlord's notice. Section 37 envisages a case where the landlord has an indisputable right to possession, although, it is true, the date for possession will depend on the extent of the tenant's opposition and the date of
h   judgment. The right exists by virtue of s 30. Section 37 sets out the consequences which follow from the landlord's assertion of his right on giving notice to the tenant under s 24. Section 37 does not refer to a situation where the tenant has actually been refused a new tenancy by the court. It says: 'Where on the making of an application under section twenty-four the court is precluded ... from making an order for the grant of a new tenancy ...' Alternatively it refers to the situation where 'either no application under the said section twenty-four is made or such an application is withdrawn' and the landlord
j   has specified one of three particular grounds for possession.

Thus the landlord's indefeasible right for possession by virtue of s 30 is incumbered to the extent that s 37 gives the tenant a right to compensation. This incumbrance (that is, the right of the tenant) originally only arose if the tenant made a claim to a new tenancy, but by the amendment in 1969 it is imposed whether or not the tenant asserts such a claim. If the Act had been drafted originally to include the amending words it could have said: 'Where . . . the court is precluded from making an order for the grant of a new tenancy by reason of any of the grounds specified in paragraphs (*e*), (*f*) and (*g*) of subsection (1) of section thirty of this Act . . . then, subject to the provisions of this Act etc.' Section 37, as amended, incumbers the landlord's right to possession under s 30 with an obligation to pay compensation to the tenant no matter what the tenant's attitude to a new tenancy is, provided that the landlord's right depends on s 30(*e*), (*f*) or (*g*).

What then is the amount of the compensation and when is it ascertainable? The 1954 Act as originally drafted stated that that compensation was to be twice the rateable value for premises occupied for 14 years or more and the rateable value itself for other tenancies. Section 37(5) shows that the relevant date for the rateable value is that of the landlord's notice. Section 37(5)(*a*) says so specifically. Section 37(5)(*c*) requires the value to be assessed when none is to be found in the valuation list. It reads:

> 'where the rateable value of the holding cannot be ascertained in accordance with the foregoing paragraphs of this subsection, it shall be taken to be the value which, apart from any exemption from assessment to rates, would on a proper assessment be the value to be entered in the said valuation list as the annual value of the holding.'

The 'said valuation list' is that in force at the date of the landlord's notice and therefore the assessment must be in relation to values contained in that list. If there had been a quinquennial review by which values had increased, the tenant would not have been entitled to claim on that basis and the review would be irrelevant for the purpose of assessment under s 37(5)(*c*). I regard this as an important consideration. In my opinion the result of ss 30 and 37 is that, on giving notice in the circumstances envisaged by s 30(*e*), (*f*) and (*g*), the landlord acquires a right to possession at some future date and incurs an obligation to pay at a future date (when the tenant quits) compensation which is fixed as at the date of that notice.

Section 193 of the 1980 amending Act which I have already quoted states that the amendments are minor amendments and amendments 'consequential on the foregoing provisions of this Act'. The foregoing provisions of the Act (in so far as they are relevant to this case) are the provisions abolishing the quinquennial review. The quinquennial review can have no effect on a case where notice has been given before the review has taken place. The relevant valuation list is always the one already in existence at the date of the notice. The abolition of the quinquennial review cannot therefore affect the determination of the proper compensation in relation to the case where notice has already been given before the amendment takes effect. There is no need for any consequential provision in relation to a notice already given even though the quinquennial review is abolished. However, the abolition of the quinquennial review might well be prejudicial to a tenant in the future. It is therefore, in my opinion, implicit in the amendment that it is designed to operate prospectively and not retrospectively.

If I am wrong in regarding the amendment itself in the context of the compensation scheme as impliedly relating to future notices to terminate the tenancy I would none the less so treat it on the grounds that it must be assumed that Parliament did not intend to introduce retrospective legislation. In *Re 'Wonderland', Cleethorpes, East Coast Amusement Co Ltd v British Rlys Board* [1963] 2 All ER 775, [1965] AC 58 the House of Lords was able to construe the section itself, ie s 34 of the Landlord and Tenant Act 1954, in the landlord's favour, but Viscount Simonds said ([1963] 2 All ER 775 at 778, [1965] AC 58 at 71):

> 'Both PENNYCUICK, J., ([1962] 1 All ER 68, [1962] Ch 696) and the majority of the Court of Appeal ([1962] 2 All ER 92, [1962] Ch 696) were assisted to their conclusion by a consideration that the contention of the tenants would lead to what they called a "quasi-confiscation of rights vested in the landlord long before the passing of the Act by, in effect, retrospective legislation". I, too, my lords, should have been influenced by this consideration if I had felt any real doubt about the true construction of the section. Undoubtedly the Act of 1954 in important respects

a derogates from the common law rights of the landlord: he is no longer master of the situation to grant or deny a new lease to his tenant, but, if there is any ambiguity about the extent of that derogation, the principle is clear that it is to be resolved in favour of maintaining common law rights unless they are clearly taken away . . . Nor can the retrospective operation of the Act of 1954 be ignored. Again it is true that the Act of 1954 operates in the sense that I have mentioned to deprive the landlord of his vested right to dispose as he will of the reversion on the current

b tenancy. But it is carrying it further to deprive him of the benefit of the improvements on his land already vested in him on the grant of that tenancy.'

In our case I would say that it is carrying it further to increase the cost of a right to possession which was already vested in the landlords at that date of their notice. The tenants say that to apply a multiplier of 2¼ as introduced by the 1981 regulations is not retrospectively altering the situation created by s 37(2) as originally enacted because that

c subsection simply laid down the rateable value as a basis for compensation and it still remains the basis. Furthermore, it is argued, to give effect to the 1981 regulations would not be treating them as retrospective because, it is said, the landlords have not been deprived of their right to possession and the only change in the law relates to the price which they must pay. Such a change, it is said, is not truly retrospective and counsel relied on *Master Ladies Tailors Organisation v Minister of Labour and National Service* [1950]

d 2 All ER 525 in support. The Wholesale Mantle and Costume Wages Council (Great Britain) Wages Regulation (Holidays) Order 1949, SI 1949/1402, made provision by para 9 of the schedule for holiday remuneration calculated on the normal wage to 'accrue' from 1 May 1948. The order became operative on 15 August 1949 and further provided that the remuneration would be payable when a worker ceased to be employed after that

e date. It was contended that the order was retrospective and therefore ultra vires seeing that it provided for remuneration to 'accrue' before the order came into force. In para 3 of the schedule to the order it was provided that an employer should before 30 September 1949 and between 1 May and 30 September in future years allow to workers to whom the schedule applied a holiday, the duration of which was to be determined by the period of employment with the employer. Thus the length of the holiday to be granted after

f the specified date might depend up to 15 August 1950 on whether or not the man had been employed prior to the specified date. Counsel for the plaintiffs did not contend that this paragraph was retrospective. Somervell LJ said (at 527):

'I think he was right. The fact that a prospective benefit is in certain cases to be measured by or depends on antecedent facts [and I would emphasise the word 'facts'] does not necessarily, and I think does not in this case, make the provision

g retrospective.'

Somervell LJ then went on to apply similar reasoning to para 9, the paragraph dealing with the amount of the remuneration which counsel did contend was retrospective. He said (at 528):

'The argument for the plaintiffs is based on the use of the word "accrue". It is

h argued that a provision for accrual before the specified date involves the conception of conferring rights before the specified date. The order purports to confer on those to whom payments are to be made rights measured, not merely by, but in respect of, antecedent employment, and to confer liabilities on employers which have been accruing in respect of antecedent employment. There is force in this, and the Attorney-General admitted that the use of the words "accrue" and "accrued" was

j unfortunate. It is clear, to my mind, that the result of para. 9 could have been achieved by words which, if I am right in my conclusion as to para. 3, would not have been retrospective in the sense to be given to the words in this area. If, for instance, the words had been "holiday remuneration to be paid to a man ceasing to be employed after the specified date shall be two weeks' wages if he has been employed forty-eight weeks or more prior to his ceasing to be employed" and so on for the lesser periods.'

When the council decided that the amount of remuneration should be related to the normal wage and should accrue from 1 May 1948, it was in effect laying down machinery *a* for the calculation of a benefit which a worker could obtain because he had ceased to be employed. It is similar to Parliament saying today that if a man in the future ceases work through personal injury then irrespective of fault the employer shall pay him damages equivalent to his earnings over the period of his service with the employer but commencing not earlier than six years before the Act was passed.

In our case, *before the amendment came into force*, the amount of the landlords' obligation *b* to pay had been fixed as the rateable value at the date of notice. The landlords themselves had given a notice knowing, or thinking that they knew, the price of so doing. The price had been fixed by s 37(2). It cannot be said that in the present case the amount to be paid on quitting in the future is fixed by reference to a past event. The past event, ie the giving of the landlords' notice, is one of the matters on which depends the landlords' obligation to pay compensation. It is a matter material to liability.   *c*

The fact that the landlords still had the right to obtain possession does not help us to decide whether the statute is retrospective. In *Maxwell on the Interpretation of Statutes* (12th edn, 1969) p 215 we find the following statement of the law:

> 'Upon the presumption that the legislature does not intend what is unjust rests the leaning against giving certain statutes a retrospective operation. They are construed as operating only in cases or on facts which come into existence after the *d* statutes were passed unless a retrospective effect is clearly intended. It is a fundamental rule of English law that no statute shall be construed to have a retrospective operation unless such a construction appears very clearly in the terms of the Act, or arises by necessary and distinct implication.'

This statement has received judicial approval (see for example *Carson v Carson and* *e* *Stoyek* [1964] 1 All ER 681 at 686, [1964] 1 WLR 511 at 516 per Scarman J). I would emphasise the reference to cases or facts which come into existence after the statutes were passed. The fact that a statute takes away an existing right does not necessarily make it retrospective. Indeed many statutes do this. When, however, Parliament decrees that certain consequences shall follow on the occurrence of certain events, there is a presumption that it is not intended that those consequences shall ensue in relation to *f* events that have already occurred. The presumption is of particular importance when those events are within a person's control so that he may choose whether they occur or not. Where they have been deliberately brought about lawfully with the knowledge of the legal consequences, very clear words are required in a statute to alter the legal consequences which are said to arise from the events. The giving of the landlord's notice is such an event and in my opinion to apply the 1981 regulations, which came into force *g* on 25 March 1981, to this case would be to make the regulations retrospective.

The tenants also relied on *R v Inhabitants of St Mary, Whitechapel* (1848) 12 QB 120, 116 ER 811. There the defendants claimed the right to remove a widow from the parish. Section 2 of the Poor Removal Act 1846 provided:

> '. . . no Woman residing in any Parish with her Husband at the Time of his Death shall be removed . . . from such Parish, for Twelve Calendar Months next after his *h* Death, if she so long continue a Widow.'

The husband had died before that Act was passed but the 12-month period had not expired. It was claimed that the right to remove was a vested right which had accrued on the husband's death and that to deny the power to remove would be to apply the statute retrospectively. Lord Denman CJ, however, said (12 QB 120 at 127, 116 ER 811 at 814): *j*

> '. . . the statute is in its direct operation prospective, as it relates to future removals only, and is not properly called a retrospective statute because a part of the requisites for its action is drawn from time antecedent to its passing.'

In my opinion that case is to be distinguished from our present case. The 1981

regulations are not concerned with the entitlement to possession or to the entitlement to
a compensation but with the assessment of the amount of compensation. That amount
was determinable as a result of an event that was past and on the happening of that event
the amount became a sum certain. In the *Whitechapel* case the amendment was concerned
with the right to remove in the future, as Lord Denman CJ said. It described persons
with whom it was concerned, namely widows, by a status which could have been
acquired by the time the Act was passed. The Act was not concerned with the date of the
b acquisition of the status except in so far as the prohibition against removal expired after
12 months from the husband's death. Lord Denman CJ said (12 QB 120 at 127, 116 ER
811 at 814):

> 'The clause is general, to prevent all removals of the widows described therein
> after the passing of the Act; the description of the widow does not *at all refer to the*
> *time* when she became widow: and we are therefore of opinion that the pauper was
c > irremoveable at the time she was removed.' (My emphasis.)

While s 37 of the Landlord and Tenant Act 1954 is concerned with the future payment
of compensation, the Act does refer in s 37(5) to the time when the rateable value became
the amount of the compensation (i e the date of the landlord's notice).
    In my opinion the present case is similar to that of *Re Athlumney, ex p Wilson* [1898] 2
d QB 547, [1895–9] All ER Rep 329. A creditor proved for a debt which carried interest at
a rate exceeding 5%. Afterwards in the same year the Bankruptcy Act 1890 was passed.
Section 23 provided:

> 'Where a debt has been proved upon a debtor's estate under the principal Act, and
> such debt includes interest, or any pecuniary consideration in lieu of interest, such
> interest or consideration shall, for the purposes of dividend, be calculated at a rate
e > not exceeding five per centum per annum . . .'

The question was whether that enactment operated so as to govern the distribution of a
dividend under a contract made under a scheme which had taken effect before the Act
was passsed or came into operation. Wright J said ([1898] 2 QB 547 at 551–552, [1895–
9] All ER Rep 329 at 331–332):

f > '. . . the only question is whether there is a rule of construction which prevents
> the section from being interpreted as operating retrospectively. Perhaps no rule of
> construction is more firmly established than this—that a retrospective operation is
> not to be given to a statute so as to impair an existing right or obligation, otherwise
> than as regards a matter of procedure, unless that effect cannot be avoided without
> doing violence to the language of the enactment. If the enactment is expressed in
g > language which is fairly capable of either interpretation, it ought to be construed as
> prospective only.'

Those words apply to the present case. The obligation of the landlords to pay compensation
had been determined as to the amount when notice was given. Similarly it could be said
that they had the right to possession on payment of a sum there and then determined.
h To apply the multiplier introduced by the 1981 regulations would impair that right and
increase their obligation.
    I have dealt with the matter of retrospective legislation because it seems to me that to
interpret it in the way the tenants suggest does involve treating the amendment as
though it were retrospective. Furthermore, two recent authorities in the Chancery
Division, *International Military Services Ltd v Capital and Counties plc* [1982] 2 All ER 20,
j [1982] 1 WLR 575 and *Garrett v Lloyds Bank Ltd* (7 April 1982, unreported), decisions of
Slade J and Walton J, have been referred to in which they concluded that the amendment
affected the case where notice had already been given and the subject of retrospective
legislation was referred to. Slade J thought that on the construction of the relevant
sections they were retrospective and that he should give effect to them retrospectively
because if the amendment was not intended to cover the case where notice had already

been given Parliament could easily have said so. Walton J concluded that the amendment
thus applied was not strictly speaking retrospective and he relied on *R v Inhabitants of St*   *a*
Mary, Whitechapel (1848) 12 QB 120, 116 ER 811, and *Master Ladies Tailors Organisation*
v Minister of Labour and National Service [1950] 2 All ER 525, to which I have already
referred and have sought to distinguish.

I would dismiss this appeal.

ACKNER LJ. A tenant of business is entitled to compensation when the court is   *b*
precluded from granting him a new tenancy by reason of any of the grounds set out in
paras (*e*), (*f*) and (*g*) in s 30 of the Landlord and Tenant Act 1954. In the present appeal,
his Honour Judge Smithies, sitting in the Southampton County Court, was precluded
from granting the tenants, Cardshops Ltd, a new tenancy because their landlords, John
Lewis Properties Ltd, were able to rely on the ground in para (*g*), namely that on the
termination of the current tenancy they intended to occupy the holding for the purpose   *c*
of a business to be carried on by them therein. Section 37 of the 1954 Act provides that:

> '. . . subject to the provisions of this Act, the tenant shall be entitled on quitting
> the holding to recover from the landlord by way of compensation an amount
> determined in accordance with the following provisions of this section.'

It is common ground that the right to receive compensation does not accrue until the   *d*
tenant has given up possession of the premises. Then, and only then, can he claim the
compensation to which he is entitled. The issue which this appeal raises is: what is the
relevant date for assessing that compensation? Until recently this gave rise to no problem,
because the scale of compensation was closely defined by reference to the rateable value
of the holding. What can be loosely referred to as the 14-year tenant received twice the
rateable value and in any other case the compensation was limited to the rateable value   *e*
of the holding. Section 37(5)(*a*) provides that, where in the valuation list which is in force
at the date on which the landlord's notice under s 25 or, as the case may be, sub-s (6) of
s 26 of the Act is given a value is then shown as the annual value of the holding, the
rateable value of the holding shall be taken to be that value. Thus, when the landlord
gave his notice of termination, or opposition to his tenant's request for a new tenancy, he
knew, so long as the holding had a rateable value, the amount of compensation which he   *f*
would have to pay to his tenant if he successfully relied on any of the grounds in paras
(*e*), (*f*) and (*g*) of s 30, thereby preventing the court from granting his tenant a new
tenancy. When the holding had no rateable value, s 37 made provision for its
ascertainment by apportionment or assessment. The landlord was also in a position, by
virtue of s 37(7), to establish whether his tenant was a '14-year tenant' since this subsection
prevented the interim continuance of the current tenancy under s 64 from counting   *g*
towards the 14-year period.

The absence of quinquennial revaluations, coupled with the onset of significant
inflation, inevitably involved the need to increase the tenant's scale of compensation. The
compensation for disturbance which may now be claimed has been substantially
increased by the application of an appropriate multiplier to the rateable value (see the
Local Government, Planning and Land Act 1980, s 193 and Sch 33, para 4).   *h*

'The appropriate multiplier' is the multiplier which the Secretary of State for the
Environment may by order made by statutory instrument prescribe. By the Landlord
and Tenant Act 1954 (Appropriate Multiplier) Regulations 1981, SI 1981/69, which came
into force on 25 March 1981, and which had been previously laid before Parliament on
21 January and 2 February 1981, the appropriate multiplier had been fixed at 2¼.

In relation to the tenants' claim for compensation, not being '14-year tenants', their   *j*
entitlement prior to the amending legislation to the rateable value of the holding,
produces a figure of £2,763. If they are entitled to rely on the new legislation, then their
claim for compensation amounts to £6,216·75.

I now come to the relevant dates. (1) The landlords' notice under s 25 of the 1954 Act
was given on 3 January 1980 and it purports to terminate the tenancy on 25 December
1980, being the date provided in the underlease for the expiration of the term thereby

granted. (2) The application for the grant of a new lease was made by the tenants on 24
a April 1980. (3) On 18 February 1981 Judge Smithies dismissed the application for the
new tenancy and was asked to decide what was the relevant date for the assessment of
compensation. He held that the date was that specified in the landlords' notice of
termination of tenancy, namely 25 December 1980. (4) By virtue of s 64 of the 1954
Act, the tenancy did not terminate until 29 June 1981, that is some three months after
the appropriate multiplier regulations came into force. Owing to a misunderstanding,
b the tenants did not leave until 7 July 1981, but nothing turns on this point.

We have had the advantage of considering two recent cases, *International Military
Services Ltd v Capital and Counties plc* [1982] 2 All ER 20, [1982] 1 WLR 575, decided by
Slade J on 10 December 1981, and *Garrett v Lloyds Bank Ltd* (7 April 1982, unreported)
decided by Walton J on 7 April 1982. Walton J accepted and followed the reasoning of
Slade J, from whose judgment I make the following short quotations ([1982] 2 All ER 20
c at 27–29, [1982] 1 WLR 575 at 582–586):

'The entitlement arises on the quitting of the holding (*and not before*). In my
judgment, therefore, it is quite plain that the amount of the entitlement must be
assessed in accordance with the law as it stands at the date of the quitting. I am not
sure that this point is really in dispute . . . the language of the relevant statutory
provisions seems to me plain and unambiguous. When they are read together, ss 47
d and 193 of the 1980 Act, para 4 of Sch 33 to that Act and the 1981 regulations in my
judgment make it quite clear that as from 25 March 1981 the new amendments to
paras (*a*) and (*b*) of s 37(2) of the 1954 Act are to apply in the case of every tenant
who thereafter quits a holding, provided only that the other conditions of s 37(1)
have been satisfied. It would have been easy for Parliament in the 1980 Act, or for
the Secretary of State in the 1981 regulations, expressly to provide that the amending
e provisions should not apply in cases where the landlord's s 25 notice had been served
before 25 March 1981. No such exception was made, and I can see no sufficient
grounds for implying one.' (Slade J's emphasis.)

Walton J considered that the reasons given for the decision by Slade J were well
founded, in that he was focusing not on the landlord's right to recover possession, but on
f the tenant's right to receive compensation. He said:

'If one looks at it from this point of view, then quitting is the only thing which
the tenant is required to do in order to obtain compensation. He is not required to
serve any kind of notice or make any kind of application; and what does he obtain
by way of compensation? He obtains what the legislation then provides. Looked at
from the point of view of the tenant, to substitute the amount which he would have
g received under the prior law would be to introduce a qualification on the change
which is not required or justified by any difficulty or ambiguity in the legislation
whatsoever.'

Counsel for the landlords contended that, although the entitlement arises on the
quitting, it is a non sequitur that the amount of the entitlement must be assessed in
h accordance with the law as it stands at the date of the quitting. He points out that the
date of the quitting may be a date later than the expiration of the interim continuation
of the tenancy provided for by s 64. The tenant may have unlawfully remained in
possession and in such circumstances to choose the date of his quitting as the appropriate
date for the assessment would be unsupportable. I agree. A tenant would not be entitled
to profit from his own wrong and I have no doubt that Slade J was treating the date of
j the quitting as being the date on which the tenancy continued by s 64 expired. Counsel
for the landlords rightly, in my judgment, did not urge on us that the decisions of Slade
J and Walton J could be said to result in new legislation having a retroactive effect. I agree
with Walton J that the 1980 Act does not in any manner purport to take away the right
of a landlord. What it does is to raise the price of exercising that right. Counsel's real
criticism of the proposition that the entitlement must be assessed in accordance with the

law as it stands at the date of the lawful quitting is that it is capable of introducing wholly
arbitrary situations. He instances that delay in the hearing of the application for the new a
tenancy, whether or not such delay is contrived, can result in a landlord finding that the
compensation which he was entitled to assume he would have to pay, if successful in his
opposition to the grant of a new tenancy, had suddenly substantially increased. The same
situation could, he contends, result from the tenant's entry and prosecution of a hopeless
appeal, since s 64 continues his tenancy until three months after the appeal process has
been concluded or abandoned.   b
    There is of course force in these observations. However, the date chosen by the county
court judge, and defended by counsel for the landlords, ie the date of the termination of
the tenancy specified in the landlord's notice, can result in his being hoisted with a new
rate of compensation if, after the service of the notice and before the date for termination
of the tenancy, a new multiplier comes into force. True, if the date of the landlord's
notice is chosen, this of course avoids this problem, but significantly this was not c
suggested in the court below as being the appropriate date. There are two obvious
objections to this date. First, as soon as the landlord knows of a proposed change in the
multiplier he could issue his notice and thus avoid payment of what Parliament thought
was a proper rate of compensation. Second, because of the fact that the landlord can give
a notice of not more than 12 months nor less than 6 months to determine the tenancy,
then the anomaly could arise of tenants who were quitting on the same date receiving d
different rates of compensation.
    Moreover, if the date specified in the landlord's notice for the termination of the
tenancy is to be the appropriate date for the assessment of compensation, or if the
appropriate date is to be the earlier date of the notice itself, then it could properly be
argued that cases will occur where the apparent intention of the legislation will be
frustrated and hardship will be suffered by the tenant. Parliament intended that the e
tenant should be properly compensated for the disturbance in having to vacate the
premises, and the clear inference is that Parliament considered that by the beginning of
1981, if not earlier, the compensation which was then available was far too low.
Accordingly, if for example the tenant succeeded at first instance in obtaining a new
tenancy, but in the Court of Appeal it was established that the court was precluded from
granting that new tenancy on one of the grounds in paras (e), (f) and (g) of s 30, such a f
decision might well have only been made a year or more after a new multiplier had come
into force. When the tenant is then obliged to quit, is his compensation to be on the out-
of-date scale?
    A choice had to be made by Parliament whether the tenant was to be entitled to the
tariff operating on the date when he lawfully quit (or should have quit, if he wrongfully
stayed on) or whether the new tariff should not apply in cases where the landlord's s 25 g
notice had been previously served or where the date for the termination of the tenancy
specified in that notice had passed. Since Parliament could have, but did not, make any
special provision for suspending the operation of the new tariff once it came into force, I
agree with Slade J and Walton J that the tenant is entitled to the prevailing rate of
compensation on his quitting the premises.
    The appellants are, in my judgment, entitled to $2\frac{1}{4}$ the rateable value, ie £6,216·75, h
and I would accordingly allow this appeal.

Appeal allowed. Leave to appeal to the House of Lords granted on terms.

Solicitors: Stuart Hunt & Co, Croydon (for the tenants); *Lithgow, Pepper & Eldridge* (for the
landlords).

                                                            Diana Brahams   Barrister.

a R v Rochdale Metropolitan Borough Council, ex parte Cromer Ring Mill Ltd

QUEEN'S BENCH DIVISION (CROWN OFFICE LIST)
FORBES J
24 NOVEMBER 1981

b

Rates – Overpayment – Refund – Discretion to refund overpayment of rates – Extent of discretion – Whether discretion complete and unfettered – General Rate Act 1967, s 9.

Local authority – Discretion – Exercise – Fetter – Whether local authority entitled to have fixed policy on how it will exercise discretion conferred on it.

c

Rates – Appeal – Appeal to Crown Court – Mode of appeal – Whether appeal by way of judicial review – General Rate Act 1967, s 7.

The applicants carried on business as spinners and weavers at commercial premises within the district of a borough council. The premises were entered in the valuation list, d as from 1 April 1973, at a rateable value of £83,000, that value having been arrived at by agreement between the valuation officer and valuers acting on behalf of the applicants. In August 1978 the appellants ceased to use the premises as a mill and sought a reduction in their rateable value. During the course of negotiations with the council, as the rating authority, it became apparent that the figure of £83,000 that had been entered in the list in 1973 was excessive, and that the appropriate figure was £60,000. The applicants e accordingly asked, under s 9ᵃ of the General Rate Act 1967, for the council to make a refund of the overpaid rates. The valuation officer certified, under s 9(3), that the premises should have been entered in the valuation list with a rateable value of £60,000. The council's treasurer, to whom the council had specifically delegated the power to deal with refunds under s 9, decided, on receiving the valuation officer's certificate, not to exercise the discretion himself but to refer the matter to the council. In so doing, the f treasurer reported to the council that the discretion had been given to rating authorities to alleviate gross unfairness where, for instance, the valuation officer had assessed a garage or outbuilding that was not there or part of a mill that had been demolished, and was not intended to be used where differences of opinion as the value emerged on appeal even though the valuation officer or the valuation court reduced the value to meet the ratepayer's argument. The council rejected the applicants' request for a refund. The g applicants sought an order of certiorari to quash the council's decision and an order of mandamus requiring the council to reconsider the applicants' request, contending that the council had operated a fixed policy with regard to applications for refunds and had accordingly wrongly fettered its discretion under s 9. The chairman of the council's finance committee deposed that, although the council had had regard to the treasurer's report, it had not felt itself bound by the treasurer's explanation of the intention of s 9 h but had reached its decision in what it believed to be the best interests of the borough.

Held – The discretion given by s 9 of the 1967 Act to rating authorities to refund overpayments of rates was complete and unfettered and could be used in cases where there were differences of opinion as to value; the discretion was not limited in the way suggested by the council's treasurer. It followed, therefore, that the treasurer's guidelines j for the exercise of the discretion were misconceived, and, although it was plain that the treasurer may have fettered the discretion delegated to him and that he had not invited the council so to fetter its discretion, it was impossible to conclude that the council had not been substantially influenced in its decision on how it should exercise its discretion

---

a   Section 9, so far as material, is set out at p 763 *f g*, post

by what the treasurer had told it was the intention with which the discretion had been
given to local authorities; and accordingly it was irrelevant that there may have been
other good reasons for the council reaching its decision. The council's decision would
therefore be quashed and the matter remitted to the council to be redetermined (see p
763 *h*, p 766 *b* to *j*, p 770 *a* to *g* and p 771 *a*, post).

Dicta of Denning LJ in *Earl Fitzwilliam's Wentworth Estates Co v Minister of Town and
Country Planning* [1951] 1 All ER at 996 and of Megaw J in *Hanks v Minister of Housing and
Local Government* [1963] 1 All ER at 54–55 applied.

Associated Provincial Picture Houses Ltd v Wednesbury Corp [1947] 2 All ER 680
distinguished.

Per curiam. (1) A local authority is entitled to have a fixed policy on how it will
exercise a discretion conferred on it so long as it allows people to come forward and say
the policy does not apply to them for various reasons; but, if it applies the fixed policy in
such a way as to show that it has left itself no discretion outside the fixed policy, it will
have improperly fettered its discretion (see p 766 *c* to *e*, post); *Sagnata Investments Ltd v
Norwich Corp* [1971] 2 All ER 1441 followed.

(2) An appeal against any rate etc to the Crown Court under s 7 of the 1967 Act is not
by way of a judicial review of the exercise of an administrative discretion; it is only the
High Court that has the power of judicial review (see p 764 *h j*, post).

Notes

For refunds of overpayments of rates, see 39 Halsbury's Laws (4th edn) para 242.

For appeals against rates, see ibid paras 245–251, and for cases on the subject, see 38
Digest (Repl) 729–735, 1582–1625.

For the adoption of rules which fetter a discretion conferred on a public body, see 1
Halsbury's Laws (4th edn) para 33.

For the General Rate Act 1967, ss 7, 9, see 27 Halsbury's Statutes (3rd edn) 81, 85.

Cases referred to in judgment

Associated Provincial Picture Houses Ltd v Wednesbury Corp [1947] 2 All ER 680, [1948] 1
KB 223, CA, 45 Digest (Repl) 215, 189.

Fitzwilliam's (Earl) Wentworth Estates Co v Minister of Town and Country Planning [1951] 1
All ER 982, [1951] 2 KB 284, CA: affd [1952] 1 All ER 509, [1952] AC 362, HL, 45
Digest (Repl) 367, 160.

Hanks v Minister of Housing and Local Government [1963] 1 All ER 47, [1963] 1 QB 999,
[1962] 3 WLR 1482, 26 Digest (Reissue) 794, 5322.

Sadler v Sheffield Corp [1924] 1 Ch 483, 19 Digest (Reissue) 546, 4120.

Sagnata Investments Ltd v Norwich Corp [1971] 2 All ER 1441, [1971] 2 QB 614, [1971] 3
WLR 133, CA, 25 Digest (Reissue) 516, 4465.

Williams (David) Playthings Ltd v Chester City Council (24 January 1980, unreported), Crown
Court at Chester.

Application for judicial review

Cromer Ring Mill Ltd applied, with the leave of Hodgson J granted on 27 July 1981, for
(i) an order of certiorari to quash the determination or purported determination by
Rochdale Metropolitan Borough Council on 27 August 1980 not to make any refund to
the applicants under s 9 of the General Rate Act 1967 of any amount paid in respect of
rates for the premises known as Cromer Ring Mill, Hilton Fold Lane, Middleton, Greater
Manchester for the period 1 April 1973 to 31 March 1978 and (ii) an order of mandamus
directed to the council requiring it to determine according to law whether such refund
and if so of what amount should be made to the applicants under s 9 of the 1967 Act,
application for such refund having been made by the applicants by letter to the council
dated 1 October 1979. The facts are set out in the judgment.

Nicholas Stewart for the applicants.
Charles Cross for the council.

FORBES J. In this case counsel moves the court for judicial review in the form of an
order of certiorari to bring into this court and quash a determination of the respondent,
the Rochdale Metropolitan Borough Council, given on 27 August 1980 and an order of
mandamus directing it to consider afresh the application made by the applicants for a
refund of rates under s 9 of the General Rate Act 1967.

The facts are very brief. The applicants carried on business as spinners and weavers at
a place called Cromer Ring Mill, Hilton Fold Lane, Middleton, within the district of the
respondent borough. Those were commercial premises and they were entered in the
valuation list, as from 1 April 1973, at a rateable value of £83,000. That value had, in
fact, been arrived at by agreement between the valuation officer and valuers acting on
behalf of these applicants. It was because of that agreement that that figure was entered
in the valuation list.

In August 1978 the applicants had ceased to use the premises as a mill and suggested
that a reduction in the rateable value might be arranged. Negotiations proceeded with
the borough council, as the rating authority, and it was agreed that the rateable value of
the premises should be reduced from £83,000 to £41,638, with effect from 18 August
1978. That agreement was, in fact, embodied in a decision of the local valuation court,
dated 19 July 1978. The premises were subsequently shown in the valuation list when
that agreement bore fruit and instead of being a factory it was a warehouse, which, in
fact, is a better description of the premises as they then were being used.

During the course of the negotiations between the applicants and the council it became
apparent that the figure of £83,000 that had been entered in the list in 1973 was excessive
and that figure should not have been entered. The appropriate figure was considerably
less, namely a figure of £60,000. Having regard to that fact and the fact that from
1 April 1973 until 18 August 1978 (and for the purposes of these proceedings to 31
March 1978) the applicants had been paying rates on the premises, whose rateable value
was some £23,000 in excess of what it ought to be, the applicants asked, under s 9 of the
1967 Act, for the rating authority to make a refund in its discretion.

Section 9, so far as is material, reads:

> '(1) . . . where it is shown to the satisfaction of a rating authority that any amount
> paid in respect of rates, and not recoverable apart from this section, could properly
> be refunded on the ground that—(a) the amount of any entry in the valuation list
> was excessive . . . the rating authority may refund that amount or a part thereof . . .
> (3) Before determining whether a refund should be made under subsection (1) of
> this section—(a) in a case falling within paragraph (a) of that subsection . . . the
> rating authority shall obtain a certificate from the valuation officer as to the manner
> in which in his opinion the hereditament in question should have been treated for
> the purposes of the valuation list, and the certificate shall be binding on the
> authority.'

I should, for completeness, refer to s 79(3). That gives a right to a ratepayer, in the case
of an alteration made in a valuation list, to claim back any excess rates which have been
paid because the figure in the valuation list was too high. Of course, that right only goes
back to 1 April in the year when the alteration in the valuation list was made. The
scheme in s 9 seems to be quite clear. It gives to the local rating authority a complete and
unfettered discretion to allow a refund in rates in any case which is not covered by
provisions of the Act, namely s 79 which I have just referred to, where, in fact, the
ratepayer can recover it, as a right, back to 1 April of the year of the alteration.

Of course, that did not apply in this case because there was no alteration in the
valuation list relating to the 1973 value until August 1978. Even then the alteration
which was made was as a result of a change of circumstances and not as a result of a
wrong value being included in the valuation list.

It is clear that the valuation officer took the view that the £83,000 figure, despite the
fact that it had been arrived at by agreement, was a wrong figure and the appropriate
figure was £60,000. He so certified under s 9(3), but he did not do so until some time in

May 1980. In the mean time, the application, by the present applicants, to the local authority for a refund under s 9 was dealt with by the borough treasurer. He was entitled *a* to do so because the council had delegated to him specifically the power to deal with its discretion to grant refunds under s 9 of the 1967 Act. It was the treasurer who was concerned with exercising that discretion on behalf of the council.

The trouble was that he proceeded to exercise that discretion before he got the certificate from the valuation officer. At one stage there was a threat of proceedings to this court because he had not, in fact, got that certificate. It is quite plain from the *b* material provisions of s 9 that you cannot exercise the discretion until you have got the certificate.

However, events overtook the situation because by the time the valuation officer's certificate showing £60,000 had been received the treasurer thought it wise, and I do not blame him, not to exercise his discretion himself but to refer the matter to the finance committee of the council, and that he did. I have affidavits from the treasurer himself, *c* Mr Henderson, and the chairman of the finance committee, Mr Barker, as to what transpired.

The borough treasurer placed before the committee a report, which I have. It is quite clear from the evidence of Mr Barker that the finance committee took into account that report. What he says in his affidavit is this:

> 'To the best of my knowledge and belief the Committee had regard to the *d* guidelines referred to in the report of the Treasurer . . . but, to the best of my knowledge and belief, the Committee did not feel itself bound by those guidelines or any fixed policy. I assuredly did not feel so bound . . . I verily believe that the Committee in reaching its decision acted in good faith and in what it believed to be the interests of the Borough. I verily believe that the decision reached was the right one in the circumstances.' *e*

That is all I have before me to indicate what were the factors and considerations which the finance committee had in mind when they decided not to accede to the request of the applicants to give any refund. I am not, and counsel for the applicants has not asked me to do so, reading the words 'in what it believed to be the interests of the Borough' as indicating that those were the only matters that the finance committee had in mind. I *f* do not for a moment suppose that the chairman meant me to understand that those were the only matters which the committee had in mind.

The applicants, in the belief that they should exhaust every avenue of appeal before coming to this court, took an appeal to the Crown Court under s 7 of the 1967 Act. The Crown Court at Manchester considered the matter and came to the conclusion that it had no jurisdiction to entertain an appeal under s 7. Without going into it, and the point has not been argued, I think that was right. The Crown Court went on to say that the only *g* forum before which the rating authority's discretion could be reviewed was this court, under RSC Ord 53. That, I am certain, is right.

During the course of the proceedings, reference was apparently made to what purported to be a copy of a judgment given in the Crown Court at Chester in 1980 (*David Williams Playthings Ltd v Chester City Council* (24 January 1980, unreported)). If that *h* judgment is correctly reported in the judgment of the Crown Court at Manchester it does cause me to be slightly disturbed. It is said there that the court treated an appeal under s 7 of the 1967 Act as a judicial review of the exercise of an administrative discretion. I am quite sure, and I want to make it plain, that whatever else s 7 may do, it certainly does not confer on the Crown Court that jurisdiction, which is only exerciseable by this court, namely the judicial review of an administrative discretion. It is only this *j* court that has that power of review which is entrusted to it under the terms of Ord 53.

It is plain from that exercise performed by the applicants that they had sought to exhaust all possible remedies and that is the reason why there has been a delay between the decision of 27 August 1980 and today. It is wholly understandable and wholly due to that effort to exhaust alternative remedies. They are now in this court and what they say about the decision is that, first of all, you have to look at the report and consider what it

is that the committee were being advised to do by the treasurer, who was the appropriate
a officer to give them advice. The report properly sets out, in para 3, that although a refund
for that period cannot be legally claimed the rating authority has a discretion to make a
refund under s 9 of the 1967 Act, and that the applicants have made such an application
for a refund. It then goes on to point out that s 9 gives rating authorities discretion to
allow a deduction of rates before the date laid down by law provided the valuation officer
certified what the reduced amount should be.

b   It then goes on in these terms:

'5. This discretion was given to Rating Authorities to alleviate gross unfairness
where, for instance, the Valuation Officer had assessed a garage or outbuilding that
was not there or, say, part of a mill that had been demolished. It was not intended
to be used where differences of opinion as to value emerged on appeal even though
the Valuation Officer or the Valuation Court reduced the value to meet the
c   ratepayer's argument.
6. In Rochdale, the discretion has been exercised by the Treasurer under delegated
powers. Although individual circumstances have always been taken into account,
the guideline outlined in the previous paragraph has been, in the main, followed,
namely, that discretionary refunds are justified in cases of mistake of fact, but less so
in cases of opinion.
d   7. If the guideline were not followed and *all* reductions of assessment were
allowed back to 1st April 1973 as being claimed by [the applicants], this would lead
to a loss of income every year of approximately £¾ million. This could be said to be
unfair to the general body of ratepayers. Ratepayers should examine their
assessments when the new valuation list comes into force, not six years later.'

It then deals with the application of s 9 in the present case. The figures he gives are, in
e fact, wrong. He says:

'8 . . . To allow the discretionary refund for this period would mean a payment of
£66,870·39 in respect of General Rate and £5,854·85 in respect of Sewage charges
which this Authority collected for the Water Authority during this period. It is
unlikely that the Water Authority would agree to reimburse us for the £5,854·85.
f   9. Because of the large amount involved and also because the solicitor acting for
[the applicants] has indicated that he intends to take the matter to the High Court if
the refund is not allowed in full, the matter is being put to committee.

Reason for Allowing the Refund
10. There has been unfairness that the mill has been so overassessed in relation to
other mills leading to such a large overpayment of rates. The Valuation Officer has
g   been unable to account for the discrepancy.

Reasons against Allowing the Refund
11. [The applicants] DID appeal against the assessment in 1973. The professional
surveyor acting for them decided that the £83,000 rateable value was reasonable
and withdrew the appeal. It would appear, therefore, that any action should be
against their advisor rather than against ourselves.
h   12. To bear such a large repayment in one year and especially in a year of such
financial stringency could be said to be unfair to the general body of ratepayers.
13. There is no affect on the Council's industrial policy as the mill is now in
different ownership and is being redeveloped.
14. High Court action against this Authority could only succeed if our decision
j   were "unreasonable". It would be difficult for this to be argued if no refund were
made especially in view of 11 above.
15. The Committee has a discretion to authorise the refund in full, in part or not
at all.'

That report is the report to which the chairman of the finance committee deposed in
his affidavit the committee had had regard and in particular to what he calls the
'guidelines'.

Counsel for the applicants challenges that report in a number of respects. First of all, he says that it is an indication that the finance committee applied a fixed policy, namely that refunds should only be given in cases where there was a mistake of fact, which was not a mistake of opinion as to value. While that had, in fact, quite clearly been the position which the treasurer adopted when he was being asked to exercise his discretion as the person to whom it had been delegated, it is not the attitude which the committee were being invited to adopt under para 6 of that report.

What was there being said was that the treasurer has, in the past, taken individual circumstances into account, but in the main has followed the guidelines, namely that discretionary refunds are justified in cases of mistake of fact but less so in cases of opinion. I can find nothing in this document which indicates that para 6 is telling the committee that they must follow a fixed policy. All it is saying is that the committee may be interested to know that in the past that is the way the treasurer has been operating the discretion under the 1967 Act. Even then it is not an indication that the treasurer has been operating a fixed policy, but an indication that, in the main, he has taken the view that in cases of mistake of facts refunds are justified, but less justified in cases of opinion.

I think counsel's first point, that there is an indication here that the council fettered its discretion by operating a fixed policy, goes. I think *Sagnata Investments Ltd v Norwich Corp* [1971] 2 All ER 1441, [1971] 2 QB 614 seems to cover this case. I cannot find anything in the words of para 6 which go as far as the Court of Appeal in *Sagnata*. It seems to me that what that case is saying, in essence, is that, if the local authority applies a fixed policy in such a way as to show that it left itself no discretion outside the fixed policy, then that is not a proper way to proceed. It is entitled to have a fixed policy so long as it allows people to come forward and to say that the policy does not apply to them for various reasons. It is plain, on the correspondence, that the treasurer had fettered his discretion. He says, in more than one place, that he cannot exercise the discretion because of the policy. That is not what the committee were invited to do and so counsel's first point fails.

His second point is that there is a straightforward misdirection involved in para 5. I think that is right. I am satisfied that s 9 gives a rating authority complete and unfettered discretion. It is not right to say that the discretion was given by Parliament to the rating authority to alleviate gross unfairness and only applies where the valuation officer has assessed a garage or outbuilding that was not there. Nor is it right to say that it was not intended to be used where there were differences of opinion as to value. So this paragraph seems to me to be wholly misconceived as an indication of the intention with which Parliament gave the local authority these discretions.

Counsel for the council seeks to get around that by suggesting that you cannot really read these paragraphs in this way. What he suggests is really being said is that the local authority ought not to exercise its discretion in favour of a ratepayer who, having had an opportunity to appeal, has not taken it or, if he has taken it, has agreed with his adversary and settled on some other valuation. I cannot read those paragraphs as saying that. It seems to me to require an effort of imagination, of which I find myself wholly incapable, to read them in that way. I think they mean just what they say. The borough treasurer is the officer serving the finance committee and is telling his committee that the discretion given to rating authorities ought to be exercised in a particular fashion. I think he was wholly wrong in so suggesting.

Counsel for the council says that if you look at the whole document it can be read in such a way as indicating, nevertheless, that they had an unfettered discretion. I confess I cannot see that. The points which counsel relies on for that assertion are that in para 3 the word 'discretion' is underlined, and in para 15 you have the bald statement that the committee has a discretion to authorise the refund in full, in part or not at all. Despite these indications it seems to me to be wholly impossible to read this document in any other way than to say that in para 3 the treasurer is setting out the existence of the discretion and the section from which it is derived, and in para 5 he is setting out, as I have indicated, the way in which, in his view, Parliament intended that discretion to be exercised by the rating authorities. I think he was fundamentally wrong.

a   Counsel for the applicants suggests that the matter in para 9, that the applicants' solicitors had indicated that he intended to take the matter to the High Court if a refund was not allowed in full, is wrong. I do not think the solicitors ever suggested that he would take it if the refund was not allowed in full. They said he would take it if the treasurer made a decision without having the valuation officer's certificate. To this extent counsel is right, but I do not think that is a material error in fact. All that the treasurer is doing in para 9 is indicating to his committee why it is that he is bothering them with

b   this application instead of dealing with it himself, as he was entitled to do under the delegation arrangement. I do not think that comparatively minor error of fact is material at all.

It is worth indicating that, of course, one is not looking at this report from the treasurer as if one were construing an Act of Parliament; nor is one giving it what Willis J referred to in one case as 'the analytical attention of a medieval schoolman'. One is looking at this

c   and regarding it in an ordinary commonsense way, having regard to the source from whence it came. The treasurer was not a lawyer, and nor were the persons to whom it was addressed, namely the finance committee. I wholly reject any suggestion, which I detected in counsel for the council's submission, that because the treasurer is not a lawyer one must apply some different criterion of logical expression to what he has written. I do not accept that at all. Logic is not the sole province of the legal profession. One can expect

d   logic from this document, but one must not approach it from a legalistic point of view, and I hope I do not.

The principles which one must apply in a case of this kind are very well known. They are the principles in *Associated Provincial Picture Houses Ltd v Wednesbury Corp* [1947] 2 All ER 680, [1948] 1 KB 223. Although *Wednesbury* is frequently quoted as if it was an authority solely for the proposition that a local authority entrusted with powers of this

e   kind must not act unreasonably, that is not the sole matter which can be lifted from the case. The principles are very well known. A local authority, in this position, must not misdirect itself in law or fact. It must not take into account matters which are immaterial, or fail to take into account matters which are material. Lastly, it must not act so unreasonably that no reasonable local authority could imagine that Parliament had given them powers to act in that way.

f   There is a suggestion here, in the grounds, that the council acted so unreasonably. I do not think that suggestion has been persisted in; certainly I can find no trace in this case of what might be called *Wednesbury* unreasonableness in the attitude of the council. All that can be said here is that either it misdirected itself in law or fact, or that it took into account immaterial considerations. It seems to me that what is being said about para 5 is that either it was a misdirection as to the way Parliament had intended the council to

g   operate its discretion and therefore a misdirection in law, or that it was an immaterial fact which the council took into account when it should not have done.

Using the same criteria, I cannot find the small error in para 9 about taking the matter to the High Court to be one which could possibly be said to have affected the mind of the council so that it was either misdirecting itself or taking into account an immaterial consideration.

h   Counsel for the applicants says that when looking at para 14 what is being said there is that nobody could take the council to the High Court unless its decision was unreasonable. If the paragraph says that, that, of course, would be quite wrong. It is not only when a local authority is unreasonable that the matter can be challenged in the High Court. Indeed, this challenge is mounted, so far as is relevant, on grounds other than unreasonableness. The sentence reads: 'It would be difficult for this to be argued if no refund were made especially in view of 11 above.' What counsel suggests is that this is an

j   invitation to the committee, particularly when read with para 15, that the committee have a discretion to authorise refund in full, in part or not at all; when you read that altogether what it amounts to is an invitation to the council to say that if you give them no refund at all then your reason for doing so cannot be challenged in the High Court because it could not be said to be unreasonable if you did that.

I do not read it in that way at all. In para 11 is a reference to the fact that the £83,000

rateable value was an agreed figure as a result of professional advice. What I think is
being said there is that if the committee decided not to make the refund on that ground   *a*
it would be difficult to say that was unreasonable. If that is what it means, I agree with
it.

Then counsel for the applicant says that in para 11 the borough treasurer has said that,
in consequence of the fact that it was the surveyor acting for the applicants who agreed
the £83,000 figure, 'It would appear, therefore, that any action should be against their
advisor rather than against ourselves'. Counsel says that is wholly wrong, because any   *b*
action against the adviser is statute-barred. That, however, is not to say that no action can
be brought: it is a question of whether the adviser would plead the Limitation Act, and,
if he did, whether any postponement of the limitation period was appropriate.

Again, I do not think that is a matter which I could say was a material misdirection. A
misdirection, in order to affect the matter in this court, has to be a misdirection as to a
material matter, either of fact or law. I cannot see that that is material in that sense.   *c*

As I indicated, in para 8, when dealing with the actual figures, the treasurer got them
wrong. He gave the figure as just under £67,000, in respect of general rate, and just
under £6,000 in respect of sewage charges. The real figures are now accepted to be just
under 20% higher than those figures: £79,028, in respect of general rate, and £7,222, in
respect of sewage charges. Counsel for the applicants says that is plainly a misdirection of
fact. I cannot see however that it is material because the error of fact is the wrong way.   *d*

I can see an argument put in this way. If the committee had been told that it was a
very large sum of money which was at stake when, in fact, the amount was comparatively
trivial, that would be a material error which must have affected the mind of the authority
when coming to a decision on the exercise of their discretion. If it were the other way
around, if the committee were being told that it was a comparatively trivial amount
whereas, in fact, it was a very considerable sum, I cannot see that that would be likely to   *e*
have influenced the minds of the committee to come to a decision to refund rather than
not to refund. I cannot see, therefore, that that error is an error in a material fact in this
case.

Counsel for the applicants says that it makes it even more unfair for the unfortunate
ratepayer because he has been kept out of even more money than the committee thought
he was. Looking at it realistically, I do not believe that that fact would have, or could   *f*
have, altered the decision of the committee in coming to the conclusion which they did.

There are, in this document, a number of matters which are perfectly properly brought
to the attention of the finance committee: for instance, the amount of the loss of income
every year; the fact that the water authority is unlikely to agree to reimburse the
overpayment of sewage charges; the fact that the £83,000 was an agreed figure after
professional advice; the suggestion that it might be unfair to the general body of   *g*
ratepayers to allow a very large repayment in one year; those all seem to be very proper
matters which the finance committee could be asked to take into account and for which,
if the committee did take them into account, they could not possibly be faulted. In
addition, a point that has troubled me is that if, in fact, this decision had been taken
solely on the ground that the finance committee thought that as the figure was an agreed
one it was one in relation to which they ought to exercise their discretion not to refund,   *h*
then I think it would be very difficult to say that that was a wrong or unreasonable
reason. It would be difficult to challenge it before this court. That would appear to be a
good reason. But there appears to be a wholly bad reason set out in para 5 of the report,
namely that the discretion was given to the rating authority for the very restricted
purpose and intent set out in that paragraph.

I asked for assistance on this point because, it seems to me, it is a matter of some   *j*
importance. Here you have a decision on the discretionary exercise of a power by a local
authority and, on the face of it, it is possible that that decision was arrived at by taking
into account a number of different matters, some of those matters being bad, as
immaterial or misdirected, and some of those being perfectly good. There seems to be a
very considerable lack of direct authority on the matter.

In the late Professor de Smith's *Judicial Review of Administrative Action* (4th edn, 1980)
a pp 339–340 there is a passage which I think is worth referring to:

> 'If the exercise of a discretionary power has been influenced by considerations
> that cannot lawfully be taken into account, or by the disregard of relevant
> considerations, a court will normally hold that the power has not been validly
> exercised. It is immaterial that an authority may have considered irrelevant matters
> in arriving at its decision if it has not allowed itself to be influenced by those matters;
> b and it may be right to overlook a minor error of this kind even if it has affected an
> aspect of the decision. The influence of extraneous matters will be manifest if they
> have led the authority to make an order that is invalid *ex facie*, or if the authority
> has set them out as reasons for its order or has otherwise admitted their influence.
> In other cases, the courts must determine whether their influence is to be inferred
> from the surrounding circumstances. If the influence of irrelevant factors is
> c established, it does not appear to be necessary to prove that they were the sole or
> even the dominant influence; it seems to be enough to prove that their influence
> was substantial.'

In the notes to that paragraph there appears this sentence:

> '*Semble*, the court has a discretion whether or not to interfere where there is no
> d material either way to show whether the authority was influenced, and a person
> whose interests are adversely affected by the decision claims to be legally aggrieved
> by it.'

I can find no authority for that portion of the note, and nor could counsel for the council.
I think authority for the other part of that statement can be found in part of the
e judgment of Denning LJ in *Earl Fitzwilliam's Wentworth Estates Co v Minister of Town and
Country Planning* [1951] 1 All ER 982 at 996, [1951] 2 KB 284 at 307, which was quoted
with approval by Megaw J in *Hanks v Minister of Housing and Local Government* [1963] 1
All ER 47 at 54–55, [1963] 1 QB 999 at 1018–1019. Denning LJ said:

> 'If Parliament grants to a government department a power to be used for an
> authorised purpose, then the power is only validly exercised when it is used by the
> f department genuinely for that purpose as its dominant purpose. If that purpose is
> not the main purpose, but is subordinated to some purpose which is not authorised
> by law, then the department exceeds its powers and the action is invalid.'

Megaw J in his own judgment, said:

> 'In the latter case [*Sadler v Sheffield Corp* [1924] 1 Ch 483 at 504–505], the learned
> g judge appears to say that, where a power is exercised on "mixed grounds", some
> being proper grounds and others not proper grounds, the exercise of the power is
> bad. I think counsel agreed that, in the judgment in that case, "grounds" meant
> "motives". Counsel for the borough council submitted that the view expressed by
> DENNING, L.J., was to be preferred, and that, unless the dominant purpose was a
> purpose for the achievement of which the power ought not to be exercised, then the
> h exercise of the power was good . . . I am prepared to assume, for the purposes of this
> case, that, if it be shown that an authority exercising a power has taken into account
> as a relevant factor something which it could not properly take into account in
> deciding whether or not to exercise the power, then the exercise of the power,
> normally at least, is bad. Similarly, if the authority fails to take into account as a
> relevant factor something which is relevant, and which is or ought to be known to
> j it, and which it ought to have taken into account, the exercise of the power is
> normally bad. I say "normally", because I can conceive that there may be cases where
> the factor wrongly taken into account, or omitted, is insignificant, or where the
> wrong taking-into-account, or omission, actually operated in favour of the person
> who later claims to be aggrieved by the decision.'

Although it is fair to say that *Hanks's* case is not binding on me, it is a very persuasive

authority and I would undoubtedly follow it, and do. It seems to me Megaw J is there
saying, having been apprised of the argument about dominant purpose, that the exercise a
of a power is bad if it is shown that an authority exercising that power has taken an
irrelevant factor into account, one of many factors, as long as that irrelevant factor is not
insignificant or substantial. To that extent, it seems to me, that that case wholly supports
the formulation in Professor de Smith's book: 'If the influence of irrelevant factors is
established, it does not appear to be necessary to prove that they were the sole or even the
dominant influence; it seems to be enough to prove that their influence was substantial.' b

In this case, it seems clear to me, from the affidavit of the chairman of the finance
committee, that the committee did have regard to para 5 in the report of the treasurer.
It is para 5 to which the treasurer, in that report, refers as the guideline, and it is to the
guideline contained in the report that the chairman of the finance committee refers. It is
true that he goes on to say that he does not feel it is bound by the guideline or any fixed
policy, but it is impossible not to infer from what is said in para 5, and the fact that the c
report was before the committee, that the committee in all probability took the view
that the way in which Parliament intended them to exercise their discretion was as set
out in para 5.

Counsel for the council sought to escape from that by what I thought was a remarkable
as well as illuminating submission. He said that what an officer of a local authority said
to that local authority was the intent of Parliament was not likely to weigh very heavily d
with a local authority, who could make up its own mind to disagree even with the
government if it thought that was the proper way of acting. That does not seem to me to
be the way a local authority works. It is not the intention of the government that matters,
it is the intention of Parliament.

The intention of Parliament is often the clue to what a statutory provision means.
When any local authority is told that the particular provision dealing with a discretion of e
this kind is not intended to be exercised in a particular way but is intended to be exercised
in some other way, it is impossible, in my view, to come to any conclusion other than
that the local authority may well have been substantially influenced in its decision on
how it should exercise its discretion by what it has been told. In doing so in this case the
council would have been wholly wrong because that is not, in my view, the intention
with which this discretion was given to the local authorities. It was a true unfettered f
discretion, and it seems to me the council, amongst other reasons, may well have come
to the conclusion that its discretion was fettered in a way the treasurer had set out. The
fact that there were other good reasons for coming to the same conclusion does not seem
to me to matter, having regard to the formulation of the principle, which I have just
referred to, as set out in the late Professor de Smith's book.

In those circumstances, it seems to me that this is a case which is made out. The matter g
ought to go back to the council to exercise its discretion in this matter unfettered by any
views as to how the treasurer thought the discretion ought to be exercised. I would only
add that it seems to me that, in exercising that discretion, the grounds which these
applicants may have for suggesting that it would be proper for the council to exercise its
discretion in their favour are matters which, if tendered to the council, the council should
have regard. I cannot detect in this case that the applicants ever did tender such grounds h
to the council. I am sure if they had they would have been taken into account. Looking
at it in the round, as it were, it does appear that the only indication of what might be said
in favour of the ratepayer was that which appeared in one short paragraph in the borough
treasurer's report.

I am only saying this because, it seems to me, the applicants were under the
misapprehension that in some way their case for the exercise of the discretion in their j
favour was being put before the council. In fact, I do not think that is so. I am sure that
in reconsidering the matter, as it would be bound to as a result of this order, the council
would wish to bear in mind any matters which the applicants might wish to urge in
their own favour. I want to make it absolutely clear that I am not suggesting that the
council disregarded any such questions; it just seems to me that, in fact, the applicants

a either never tendered any such reasons or, if they did, in some way they were not placed before the council. I think the former is the case.

Be that as it may, I think that certiorari and mandamus should go in this case in the way I have indicated.

Application granted. Order of certiorari to quash council's determination of 27 August 1981. Order of mandamus requiring council to redetermine matter in light of court's judgment.

b

Solicitors: *Alexander, Tatham & Co*, Manchester (for the applicants); *J Malcolm Russum*, Rochdale (for the council).

N P Metcalfe Esq   Barrister.

c

RCA Corp and another v Pollard

COURT OF APPEAL, CIVIL DIVISION
LAWTON, OLIVER AND SLADE LJJ
d 29, 30 JUNE, 1, 22 JULY 1982

Copyright – Infringement – Right of action – Bootlegging – Persons entitled to bring action to prevent bootlegging – Action by record manufacturer and distributor – Record company having exclusive contract to sell performer's records – Whether performer having civil right of action against bootlegger under performers' protection legislation – Whether record company having
e *similar right of action against bootlegger under legislation – Dramatic and Musical Performers' Protection Act 1958, s 1.*

The plaintiffs were record companies engaged in making and distributing records. They brought an action against the defendant alleging in the statement of claim that the first plaintiffs had had an exclusive recording contract with a well-known musical performer
f whereby they were and had been entitled to the exclusive right to record and exploit for profit recordings of all his performances, that the second plaintiffs had been licensed by the first plaintiffs to manufacture, sell and distribute the performer's records in the United Kingdom, and that the defendant had knowingly traded in 'bootleg' records of his performances, ie records made without the performer's consent, in contravention of the Performers' Protection Acts 1958 to 1972[a]. However, it was not alleged that the
g defendant had been directly concerned in making the original unlawful recordings from the bootleg records. The statement of claim concluded with an averment that the plaintiffs had suffered damage and that the defendant threatened and intended to continue the acts complained of. The plaintiffs sought as against the defendant a declaration that his acts were an unlawful interference with the plaintiffs' proprietary rights and injunctions restraining him from making, dealing in or using for public
h performance bootleg recordings of the performer. The defendant applied to strike out the statement of claim and for the action to be dismissed on the ground that the statement of claim disclosed no reasonable cause of action. The judge dismissed the application on the ground that, although the plaintiffs did not have a private civil right of action against the defendant under the Acts for breach of s 1[b] of the 1958 Act because the Acts had been

j a   Ie the Dramatic and Musical Performers' Protection Act 1958, the Performers' Protection Act 1963 and the Performers' Protection Act 1972
   b   Section 1, so far as material, provides: 'Subject to the provisions of this Act, if a person knowingly—
      (a) makes a record, directly or indirectly from or by means of the performance of a dramatic or musical work without the consent in writing of the performers, or (b) sells or lets for hire, or

(Continued on p 772)

passed for the protection of performers only, the plaintiffs might succeed at the trial on the narrower ground that the defendant's acts in dealing with the bootleg records constituted the tort of unlawful interference with the plaintiffs' rights of property under their exclusive recording contracts, and that therefore it could not be said that the statement of claim did not disclose a reasonable cause of action. The defendant appealed.

Held – The appeal would be allowed and the statement of claim struck out for the following reasons—

(1) The right which the plaintiffs had in the commercial advantage obtained from their exclusive recording contracts with the performer was a right to have the contracts performed which could be protected by the court if there was unlawful interference with performance. However, although the defendant had by his acts made the plaintiffs' exclusive recording contracts with the performer less valuable, he had not interfered with the performance of the contracts themselves, and accordingly he could not be held liable to the plaintiffs on the basis of the tort of unlawful interference with contractual relations (see p 775 j to p 776 a, p 778 d j, p 779 c to e, p 782 b to j, p 783 a b f, p 784 e to j and p 785 e to h, post); *Lonrho Ltd v Shell Petroleum Co Ltd* [1981] 2 All ER 456 applied; *Ex p Island Records Ltd* [1978] 3 All ER 824 not followed.

(2) Furthermore, the plaintiffs had no cause of action against the defendant under the Performers' Protection Acts because (a) those Acts did not confer on performers or the recording companies with whom they contracted a private civil right of action against a bootlegger or dealer in bootleg records for breach of s 1 of the 1958 Act, notwithstanding that they had suffered special damage thereby, and (b) those Acts did not create any duty of permission or omission for the benefit of performers or recording companies the interference with which by acts made illegal by s 1 of the 1958 Act could give rise to an action for breach of statutory duty at the suit of a recording company (see p 778 e to j, p 779 j, p 780 c d, p 782 h j, p 783 a b f and p 784 j to p 785 a and h, post); *Ex p Island Records Ltd* [1978] 3 All ER 824 and *Lonrho Ltd v Shell Petroleum Co Ltd* [1981] 2 All ER 456 applied.

Decision of Vinelott J [1982] 2 All ER 468 reversed.

Notes

For protection of performers of, inter alia, musical works, see 9 Halsbury's Laws (4th edn) para 962, and for a case on the subject, see 13 Digest (Reissue) 158, 1332.

For civil actions in respect of a breach of a duty imposed by statute, see 36 Halsbury's Laws (3rd edn) 449–454, paras 684–690, and for cases on the subject, see 4 Digest (Repl) 320, 1510–1512.

For the tort of interference with contractual relations, see 37 Halsbury's Laws (3rd edn) 124, para 216, and for cases on the subject, see 45 Digest (Repl) 303–310, 194–228.

For threatened invasion of a legal right, see 24 Halsbury's Laws (4th edn) para 932, and for cases on the subject, see 28(2) Digest (Reissue) 1010–1011, 378–383.

For the Dramatic and Musical Performers' Protection Act 1958, s 1, see 7 Halsbury's Statutes (3rd edn) 226.

Cases referred to in judgments

Argyll (Margaret), Duchess of v Duke of Argyll [1965] 1 All ER 611, [1967] Ch 302, [1965] 2 WLR 790, 28(2) Digest (Reissue) 1089, 916.

Austria (Emperor) v Day and Kossuth (1861) 3 De GF & J 217, 45 ER 861, LC and LJJ, 1(1) Digest (Reissue) 49, 328.

(Continued from p 771)

distributes for the purposes of trade, or by way or trade exposes or offers for sale or hire, a record made in contravention of this Act, or (c) uses for the purposes of a public performance a record so made, he shall be guilty of an offence under this Act, and shall be liable, on summary conviction, to a fine not exceeding [£20] for each record in respect of which an offence is proved, but not exceeding [£400] in respect of any one transaction or, on conviction on indictment, to imprisonment for a term not exceeding two years, or to a fine, or to both . . .'

Beaudesert Shire Council v Smith (1966) 120 CLR 145, Aust HC.

a *British Industrial Plastics Ltd v Ferguson* [1940] 1 All ER 479, HL, 45 Digest (Repl) 303, *197*.

British Motor Trade Association v Salvadori [1949] 1 All ER 208, [1949] Ch 556, 45 Digest (Repl) 305, *207*.

Coote v Stone [1971] 1 All ER 657, [1971] 1 WLR 279, CA, Digest (Cont Vol D) 863, *1839a*.

b *Cutler v Wandsworth Stadium Ltd* [1949] 1 All ER 544, [1949] AC 398, HL, 25 Digest (Reissue) 504, *4396*.

De Francesco v Barnum (1890) 45 Ch D 430, [1886–90] All ER Rep 414, 34 Digest (Repl) 319, *2372*.

Dyson v A-G [1911] 1 KB 410, CA, 37(1) Digest (Reissue) 284, *1830*.

Exchange Telegraph Co Ltd v Gregory & Co [1896] 1 QB 147, [1895–9] All ER Rep 1116, c 45 Digest (Repl) 305, *208*.

Gorris v Scott (1874) LR 9 Exch 125, Ex Ch, 44 Digest (Repl) 357, *1933*.

Gouriet v Union of Post Office Workers [1977] 3 All ER 70, [1978] AC 435, [1977] 3 WLR 300, HL, 16 Digest (Reissue) 265, *2528*.

GWK Ltd v Dunlop Rubber Co Ltd (1926) 42 TLR 376; *on appeal* 42 TLR 593, CA, 45 Digest (Repl) 307, *213*.

d *Island Records Ltd, Ex p* [1978] 3 All ER 824, [1978] Ch 122, [1978] 3 WLR 23, CA, Digest (Cont Vol E) 339, *1238e*.

Lonrho Ltd v Shell Petroleum Co Ltd [1981] 2 All ER 456, [1982] AC 173, [1981] 3 WLR 33, HL.

Lumley v Gye (1853) 2 E & B 216, [1843–60] All ER Rep 208, 45 Digest (Repl) 304, *198*.

Mogul Steamship Co Ltd v McGregor, Gow & Co (1889) 23 QBD 598, CA; *affd* [1892] AC e 25, [1891–4] All ER Rep 263, 45 Digest (Repl) 275, *6*.

National Phonograph Co Ltd v Edison-Bell Consolidated Phonograph Co Ltd [1908] 1 Ch 335, [1904–7] All ER Rep 116, CA, 17 Digest (Reissue) 91, *51*.

Prudential Assurance Co v Knott (1875) LR 10 Ch App 142, LC and LJJ, 28(2) Digest (Reissue) 1080, *863*.

Springhead Spinning Co v Riley (1868) LR 6 Eq 551, 28(2) Digest (Reissue) 1079, *861*.

f *Thomson (D C) & Co Ltd v Deakin* [1952] 2 All ER 361, [1952] Ch 646, CA, 45 Digest (Repl) 562, *1379*.

Cases also cited

Erven Warnink BV v J Townend & Sons (Hull) Ltd [1979] 2 All ER 927, [1979] AC 731, HL.
PCUK v Diamond Shamrock Industrial Chemicals Ltd [1981] FSR 427.

g **Interlocutory appeal**

The defendant, Geoffrey Pollard, appealed against the judgment and order of Vinelott J ([1982] 2 All ER 468, [1982] 1 WLR 979) on 26 February 1982 whereby he refused to strike out the statement of claim in an action brought against the defendant by the plaintiffs, RCA Corp and RCA Ltd, on the ground that it disclosed no reasonable cause of action. The facts are set out in the judgment of Lawton LJ.

h

Nicholas Pumfrey for the defendant.
Robin Jacob QC and *Mary Vitoria* for the plaintiffs.

Cur adv vult

j

22 July. The following judgments were read.

LAWTON LJ. When opening the plaintiffs' case, counsel stated that the issue raised in the appeal was of the greatest importance to the recording industry, of which both plaintiffs are leading members. Broadly it can be stated in these terms. The recording companies invest large sums in fees to artistes and in paying for high quality recordings of their songs and music and for the marketing of the results of their efforts and expenditure. If the defendant's contentions are right anyone making a recording of an artiste's performance, without his consent, in a theatre or at a concert or elsewhere can market that recording (known in the recording industry as a bootlegging recording) without paying any fee to the artiste and in competition with the recording companies who have paid fees and incurred great expense in marketing their products. This is said to be so notwithstanding that under s 1 of the Dramatic and Musical Performers' Protection Act 1958 making such recordings and selling, letting for hire or distributing them for the purposes of trade is a criminal offence punishable by a fine.

There can be no doubt that the making and distribution of bootlegging records is causing serious economic loss to the recording companies. Until the decision of the House of Lords in *Lonrho Ltd v Shell Petroleum Co Ltd* [1981] 2 All ER 456, [1982] AC 173 the recording companies were confident that English law provided them with remedies by way of injunction and damages against those who made or distributed bootlegging records. This was because of the decision of this court in *Ex p Island Records Ltd* [1978] 3 All ER 824, [1978] Ch 122.

The defendant, by his counsel has submitted that the *Lonrho* case has, by necessary implication, overruled the *Island Records* case and has left the recording companies without a civil remedy against bootleggers. The problem for which we have to find an answer comes before this court by way of an appeal by the defendant from a refusal by Vinelott J on 26 February 1982 to strike out the plaintiffs' statement of claim against him (see [1982] 2 All ER 468, [1982] 1 WLR 979). As striking out is a matter of judicial discretion, at least to some extent, we discussed with counsel whether this procedure was the best way of getting an important point decided. Counsel for the defendant persuaded me that what had to be decided was a matter of law; that there were enough averments of fact in the statement of claim for this court to reach a conclusion; that, even if the statement of claim were not struck out, he would advise the defendant to raise the same issue in his defence and apply under RSC Ord 33 for points of law to be argued; and, finally, that a decision in this appeal would result in a great saving of costs, which was of particular importance because the defendant was legally aided.

The statement of claim starts by defining some of the expressions used in it and in particular the words 'exclusive recording contract'. It is defined as—

> 'a contract between two parties whereby the first party has the right to the exclusion of all others to exploit for profit records of the performances of the second party and whereby the second party has the right to receive, directly or indirectly, royalties or other remuneration or gain the value of which depends on the success of such exploitation and whereby that second party expressly or impliedly contracts not to consent, either in writing or at all, to persons other than the first party or those approved by the first party making records of his performances.'

It goes on in para 2 to aver that the plaintiffs and each of them at all material times have been engaged in the business of making and distributing records of a wide variety of music. Paragraph 3 alleges that at all material times the first plaintiffs, a United States corporation, had the benefit of exclusive recording contracts with the late Elvis Presley whereby they are and have been entitled to the exclusive right to exploit for profit records of all his performances. The second plaintiffs are and have been licensed by the first plaintiffs in respect of the manufacture, sale and distribution in the United Kingdom of all Elvis Presley's performances. Paragraphs 4 and 5 described how and why the plaintiffs made profits from their recording business. Paragraph 6 was in these terms: 'In the premises the plaintiffs have private or proprietary rights and interests which they are entitled to have protected from unlawful interference which causes them damage.' Paragraph 7 alleged that bootlegging, presumably meaning thereby all the acts described in s 1 of the 1958 Act, is unlawful and para 8 describes the extent of bootlegging in the United Kingdom, the damage which it causes to the plaintiffs and others in the recording industry and the steps which have had to be taken by that industry to restrict and stop it.

Paragraph 9 started with these words: 'Prior to the issue of the writ herein the defendant

_a_ has been bootlegging and dealing in bootleg records of performances of Elvis Presley.' There followed lengthy particulars of the defendant's unlawful acts and facts from which it was averred that he must have known that what he was doing was unlawful. The statement of claim ended with an averment that the plaintiffs and each of them had suffered damage and that the defendant threatens and intends to continue the acts complained of. The relief sought was: first, a declaration that the defendant was not

_b_ entitled to make or deal in bootlegging recordings of Elvis Presley's performances; second, an injunction from doing these kinds of acts; third, an order for delivery up of such bootlegging records as he had in his possession; fourth, judgment for £360 and interest or damages; and, fifth, an inquiry as to damages.

In my judgment this appeal calls for a detail analysis as to what was decided in the _Island Records_ and _Lonrho_ cases. In the latter case Lord Diplock made some critical

_c_ comments about what was decided in the other case. The other members of the House agreed with his speech. If his criticisms were part of and necessary for the decision in the _Lonrho_ case then what he said is binding on us and goes a long way, but perhaps not all the way, to deciding this appeal. If, however, his criticisms were obiter, the _Island Records_ case is binding on us.

It will be convenient to start with an analysis of the _Island Records_ case [1978] 3 All ER

_d_ 824, [1978] Ch 122. Thirty plaintiffs, being performers and recording companies with whom the performers had exclusive contracts to record their performances, complained that they were suffering serious damage from the activities of bootleggers and sought an injunction to restrain a named defendant from committing any acts in contravention of s 1 of the 1958 Act. Walton J refused an injunction on the ground that he had no jursidiction to grant the relief claimed because, although the plaintiffs could show that

_e_ they had suffered damage, they had no right of property infringed by the defendant's acts. The plaintiffs appealed.

This court by a majority (Lord Denning MR and Waller LJ, Shaw LJ dissenting) adjudged that there was jurisdiction in the High Court to grant the relief claimed. Lord Denning MR's decision was based on this proposition: '... a man who is carrying on a lawful trade or calling has a right to be protected from any unlawful interference with it'

_f_ (see [1978] 3 All ER 824 at 830, [1978] Ch 122 at 136). Amongst the many authorities quoted as support for that proposition was _Emperor of Austria v Day and Kossuth_ (1861) 3 De GF & J 217, 45 ER 861. That case is one of the foundation stones of the plaintiffs' submission in this case. The unlawful interference may be a tort or a crime. It matters not which it is. Lord Denning MR said ([1978] 3 All ER 824 at 830, [1978] Ch 122 at 136–137):

_g_ '... the courts must allow a private individual himself to bring an action against the offender in those cases where his private rights and interests are specially affected by the breach. This principle is capable of extension so as to apply not only to rights of property or rights in the nature of it, but to other rights or interests, such as the right of a man to his good name and reputation (see _Margaret, Duchess of Argyll v Duke of Argyll_ [1965] 1 All ER 611 at 633, [1967] Ch 302 at 344) and his right to the

_h_ lawful transmission of his mail (see my illustration in _Gouriet's_ case [1977] 1 All ER 696 at 714–715, [1977] QB 729 at 756–757).'

He went on to consider what were the rights and interests which the plaintiffs in that case were entitled to have protected from unlawful interference. He described those rights and interests in these terms ([1978] 3 All ER 824 at 830–831, [1978] Ch 122 at

_j_ 137):

'The recording companies have the right to exploit the records made by them of the performances. The performers have the right to the royalty payable to them out of those records. Those rights are buttressed by the contracts between the recording companies and the performers. They are rights in the nature of rights of property.'

In this case counsel for the defendant has submitted that a right to exploit records is not a right of property anyway. It is nothing more than the economic advantage which a recording company gets from its exclusive contract with the performer. The recording company's right is to have the contract performed. That right can be protected by the court if there is unlawful interference with performance; but a bootlegger does not interfere with the performance of the contract itself even though his acts make the contract less valuable.

Waller LJ founded his decision on a narrower base than Lord Denning MR (see [1978] 3 All ER 824 at 837, [1978] Ch 122 at 144–145). He was of the opinion that—

'in equity there is jurisdiction for a court to grant an injunction to a person who claims that he suffered special damage to a property interest of his by a crime and that in the circumstances of this case both the record company and the performer would be entitled to such injunction.'

In concluding as he did he relied on *Emperor of Austria's* case, *Springhead Spinning Co v Riley* (1868) LR 6 Eq 551 at 560 and *National Phonograph Co Ltd v Edison-Bell Consolidated Phonograph Co Ltd* [1908] 1 Ch 335 at 361, [1904–7] All ER Rep 116 at 120.

It is pertinent to consider Shaw LJ's dissenting judgment. The plaintiffs had put forward two propositions. The first was that s 1 of the 1958 Act had the result of creating a statutory duty to performers (who were included amongst the plaintiffs) which invested them with a cause of action and gave them a right of action for appropriate relief against any person who was in breach of that duty by reason of committing an offence under that section. Shaw LJ said that he could not accept this proposition, as did Waller LJ. If there was no right to relief for performers, there could not have been any for recording companies.

It follows, so it seems to me, that if the *Island Records* case is binding on us, we must accept that the present plaintiffs have a property right, which the law protects, in the economic advantages to be obtained from their exclusive contract with the late Elvis Presley. That means that the statement of claim does disclose a cause of action.

I turn now to the decision of the House of Lords in the *Lonrho* case [1981] 2 All ER 456, [1982] AC 173. The appellants alleged that they had suffered damage through the alleged contravention by two oil companies of the Southern Rhodesia (Petroleum) Order 1965, SI 1965/2140, which made it a criminal offence to supply oil to Southern Rhodesia. The appellants based their claim on three grounds: first, alleged breaches of contract, second, that the alleged breaches of the order had caused them special damage and, third, 'the breaches were an unlawful interference with, and resulted in damage to, the appellants' rights of property . . .' (see [1982] AC 173 at 179, where counsel's argument on this point is summarised).

It is pertinent to remember that the *Lonrho* case started in the court as a special case stated for the decision of the court pursuant to s 1 of the Arbitration Act 1950. A number of questions had to be answered. The relevant one, for the purposes of this appeal, numbered 5(a), being in these terms: 'Even if there were breaches by the respondents of the 1965 and 1968 Orders: (a) *Whether* breaches of those Orders would give rise to a right of action in the claimants for damage alleged to have been caused by those breaches . . .' In my judgment, that question did raise the issue whether damage to a private property right due to a criminal act was recoverable. In their filed case the appellants sought to rely on the *Island Records* case and did so in these terms:

'In addition to the cases mentioned above, the Appellants rely on the decision of the Court of Appeal in *Ex parte Island Records Ltd* ([1978] 3 All ER 824, [1978] Ch 122) in which, although the majority of the court (Shaw and Waller LJJ) held that the relevant Act, the Dramatic and Musical Performers' Protection Act 1958, was not a statute passed for the protection of the public or of a particular section of it such that a breach of it was an actionable breach of duty, nevertheless Lord Denning M.R. and Waller L.J. held that recording companies and performers were entitled to an injunction to restrain third parties from damaging their private interests by making and marketing recordings in breach of the Act. Lord Denning M.R. based

a his decision on the fact that the criminal act caused or threatened to cause special
damage to the plaintiffs (see [1978] 3 All ER 824 at 829, [1978] Ch 122 at 135) and
that the plaintiffs had the right to be protected from any unlawful interference with
the lawful carrying on of their business (see [1978] 3 All ER 824 at 830, [1978] Ch
122 at 136). So here, it is submitted that the Appellants have the right to be
protected, in carrying on their lawful business of operating the Pipeline, from
interference from criminal acts on the part of the Respondents. Waller L.J. based
b his decision on the jurisdiction to restrain unlawful (including criminal) interference
with rights of property or rights akin to the rights of property (see [1978] 3 All ER
824 at 836, [1978] Ch 122 at 144). If that is a correct analysis, the Appellants point
to the unlawful interference, by breaches of the Sanctions Orders, with their
property, namely, the Pipeline and their entitlement to exploit it commercially.'

The respondents answered this contention in their case but were not called on to do so
c orally at the hearing. They submitted that the order did not alter the legal relationship
between them and Lonrho, that *Cutler v Wandsworth Stadium Ltd* [1949] 1 All ER 544,
[1949] AC 398 applied, that if the *Island Records* case could not be distinguished it should
not be applied for two reasons. First, because it would be contrary to the decision in
Cutler's case and of the Court of Appeal itself in *Coote v Stone* [1971] 1 All ER 657, [1971]
d 1 WLR 279. They pointed out that in the first of these cases there was injury to the
plaintiff's business and in the second to his property. Their second reason was that this
case would be inconsistent with the well-established principle that the statute must not
only be for the plaintiff's benefit but the plaintiff's loss must be loss of the particular kind
which it was the object of the statute to prevent. They quoted *Gorris v Scott* (1874) LR 9
Exch 125 in support. It follows, so it seems to me, that the House was being invited to
consider whether what was decided in the *Island Records* case was sound law which could
e be applied in the *Lonrho* case. Neither in the cases as filed nor in the appellants' argument
was any reference made to either *Emperor of Austria's* case or the *Springhead Spinning Co's*
case; but when considering the appellants' submission and in particular when reading
the judgments in the *Island Records* case their Lordships would have seen and taken into
account the quotations from these two cases which Waller LJ relied on for his decision.

I turn now to consider the way in which Lord Diplock, with whose speech the other
f members of the House concurred, answered question 5(a). He considered, first, whether
on their true construction the relevant statutory provisions were imposed for the benefit
of a particular class of persons or whether they created any public right to be enjoyed by
all Her Majesty's subjects and concluded that they did neither (see [1981] 2 All ER 456 at
462, [1982] AC 173 at 186). This disposed of the appellants' submission that the alleged
breaches of the order had caused them special damage. There remained, however, their
g alternative submission about unlawful interference with their property rights. Lord
Diplock did not say specifically that he was going to consider the alternative submission.
What he did do was to say that he was going to mention two cases, one being the *Island
Records* case. That case was relevant because of this court's decision that the plaintiffs
therein were entitled to relief because of the defendant's alleged interference by a crime
with their 'property interest' (I use Waller LJ's words). Lord Diplock pointed out that
h performers under exclusive recording contracts could claim that the 1958 Act was passed
for their protection and that in consequence an Anton Piller order could be granted for
'entirely orthodox reasons'. He continued as follows ([1981] 2 All ER 456 at 462–463,
[1982] AC 173 at 187):

j 'The Act was passed for the protection of a particular class of individuals, dramatic
and musical performers; even the short title said so. Whether the record companies
would have been entitled to obtain the order in a civil action to which the performers
whose performances had been bootlegged were not parties is a matter which for
present purposes it is not necessary to decide. Lord Denning MR, however, with
whom Waller LJ agreed (Shaw LJ dissenting) appears to enunciate a wider general
rule, which does not depend on the scope and language of the statute by which a
criminal offence is committed, that whenever a lawful business carried on by one

individual in fact suffers damage as the consequence of a contravention by another individual of any statutory prohibition the former has a civil right of action against *a* the latter for such damage. My Lords, with respect, I am unable to accept that this is the law . . .'

Clearly Lord Diplock did not accept the wide principle which Lord Denning MR had enunciated ([1978] 3 All ER 824 at 830, [1978] Ch 122 at 136). Waller LJ, however, did not say that he agreed with this way of putting the law. As I have already commented, *b* he based his decision on the narrower ground of the right to the protection of a property interest. Under a cross-heading 'The present case' Lord Denning MR referred specifically to 'rights in the nature of rights of property'. Was Lord Diplock saying that this too was wrong in law? I infer that he was. What he said disposed of the appellants' alternative submission that the respondents had unlawfully interfered with their property which could only have been the commercial benefit which they would have got from the *c* pipeline but for the alleged breaches of the order. The damage which the present plaintiffs allege they have suffered and will continue to suffer is the loss of the commercial benefits which they hope to obtain from their exclusive recording contract with Elvis Presley, whose personal representatives did not join in this action. The defendant's alleged criminal acts did not alter any legal relationship between him and the plaintiffs. None existed either before or after the acts of which complaints were made. It follows, *d* in my judgment, that what Lord Diplock said about the *Island Records* case was not obiter; it was necessary for the determination of one of the issues before the House and by implication overruled the decision of this court in the *Island Records* case on the injury to property point.

That still leaves, however, the question whether on its true construction the 1958 Act was passed for the benefit or protection of recording companies. Lord Diplock did not *e* express any opinion about this; but that very issue was discussed and decided in the *Island Records* case. I have already referred to Shaw LJ's opinion on the effect of the 1958 Act. Waller LJ was of the same opinion. He referred to the submission which had been made on behalf of the plaintiffs that the 1958 Act created a duty of permission or omission for the benefit of a class of persons which included recording companies (see [1978] 3 All ER 824 at 834, [1978] Ch 122 at 142). After considering the terms of the 1958 Act and a *f* number of authorities he concluded as follows: 'I am satisfied therefore that no action can be brought for a simple breach of statutory duty under this section.' It follows that the very point which Lord Diplock was referring to and about which he expressed no opinion had already been decided by this court. The consequences seem to be these. In the *Island Records* case the plaintiffs asked for relief on two grounds. They were adjudged by Shaw and Waller LJJ not to be entitled to it on one ground but by Lord Denning MR *g* and Waller LJ to be entitled to it on another. If my opinion about the effect of the *Lonrho* case is right the present plaintiffs are not entitled to any relief, first, because of what the House of Lords decided in that case and, second, because of what this court decided in the *Island Records* case. It follows, in my judgment, that the *Island Records* case is binding on us on the very point which Lord Diplock did not discuss. This means that the statement of claim should be struck out. This is a result which I find unpleasing; but I *h* remind myself that it is for Parliament, not the judges, to provide new remedies for new wrongs.

Having regard to the opinion I have formed about the effect of the *Lonrho* case on the *Island Records* case it is unnecessary for me to consider whether the *Lonrho* case by implication overrules a long line of equity cases going back to Lord Eldon's time and of which the leading one is *Emperor of Austria's* case. Save in a limited respect, nothing in *j* this judgment should be read as questioning in any way the underlying principles enunciated in those cases. One of the questions in this case has been whether the commercial value of a contractual right is the kind of property which the Court of Chancery did protect and which this court should protect when, as in this case, the defendant has done nothing to interfere with the right itself.

I would allow the appeal.

OLIVER LJ. The action out of which this appeal arises is one in which the plaintiff
a record companies are seeking to restrain the admittedly criminal activity of the defendant
and the only question which this court has to determine is whether they have any
arguable case for so doing which justifies the exercise by the judge of his discretion to
decline to strike out the plaintiffs' statement of claim as disclosing no reasonable cause of
action. For the purposes of this appeal it must be taken as admitted by the defendant that
the plaintiffs have a contract with the personal representatives of the late Elvis Presley
b under which they have been given, so far as it is possible to do so contractually, the
exclusive right to record and exploit recordings of Mr Presley's live performances. It
must also be taken as admitted that the economic value to them of that contractual right
will be diminished if recordings of such live performances not of their manufacture and
not made from their recordings (in which, of course, they have a copyright) are made
and sold by other persons. It is, however, important to bear in mind what their
c contractual right is, for the expression 'exclusive right' can be misleading if it is not
subjected to some analysis. An artiste who performs a dramatic or musical work obtains
no 'right' in relation to his performance except that which arises from the contract with
the entrepreneur under which he performs. There is no copyright in the performance as
such, although of course the owner of the copyrights in the lyrics and music can restrain
unauthorised publications of the performance. Thus the performer has, as the law now
d stands, no cause of action against a person who records his performance or deals in a
recording of it made by somebody else, save to the extent that such a cause of action is
conferred on him by the Performers' Protection Acts 1958 to 1972 or to the extent that
there is some other general principle of law which comes to his assistance. Subject to this,
the 'exclusive right' which he contracts to confer on a recording company is no more
than an undertaking that he will not give consent to a recording by anybody else.
e   Now Mr Pollard, the defendant, is a bootlegger, that is to say he is a person who either
makes or sells (or possibly both) recordings of live performances by theatrical artistes
(and in particular by Mr Presley), and it must be taken for present purposes that he does
so in the knowledge of the contract between the plaintiffs and Mr Presley's representatives.
The recordings which he makes or sells are not recordings reproducing the plaintiffs'
recordings; that would, of course, infringe the plaintiffs' own copyright. They are records
f reproducing recordings made by someone else who was present at the concert at which
Mr Presley performed or who made a recording of a live broadcast of that concert, and it
may be assumed that they were made and are being sold without the consent of Mr
Presley or his personal representatives. So the question is: do the plaintiffs have any right
which will be recognised by the court to restrain the sale of such recordings in a civil
action for an injunction and damages?
g   There are, or to be more accurate there were until comparatively recently, three ways
in which such a claim could be framed. First, there is the argument advanced in the
plaintiffs' statement of claim, that the Performers' Protection Acts 1958 to 1972, although
they do no more on their face than impose criminal penalties, are Acts which in fact
confer a civil right on the plaintiffs to restrain that which is an offence under the Acts.
Second, there is the argument that the Acts confer some general right in the public to
have their provisions enforced and that the plaintiffs, as persons who suffer some special
h damage as a result of a breach of the prohibition, are entitled to bring an action for an
injunction without enlisting the assistance of the Attorney General. Third, reliance is
placed on some wider principle of equity which entitles the court to intervene to prevent
the commission of a crime which causes damage to the property or interests of an
individual.
j   As regards the first of these, the matter is, as I see it, concluded against the plaintiffs by
the decision of this court in *Ex p Island Records Ltd* [1978] 3 All ER 824, [1978] Ch 122,
where it was held that the Performers' Protection Acts conferred no right of action on
the performers or the recording companies with whom they had contracted. That
decision is binding on us and, for my part, it seems to me, if I respectfully say so, to be
well founded. It was suggested by Vinelott J in the instant case that the case had, in some
way, been overruled by the House of Lords, so far as performers are concerned, by *Lonrho*

Ltd v Shell Petroleum Co Ltd [1981] 2 All ER 456, [1982] AC 173, in which Lord Diplock (with whose speech all their other Lordships concurred) expressed the view that the *a* decision in *Island Records* could be justified, so far as the performers were concerned, for what he referred to as 'entirely orthodox reasons'. The Act, he went on to say, was passed for the protection of a particular class of individuals, dramatic and musical performers. This, Vinelott J considered, amount to a holding that the case was wrongly decided in so far as it was based on the proposition that the Act conferred no civil right of action on performers. I do not so read it. What I think Lord Diplock was referring to was the *b* second principle referred to above, namely that, where there is a breach of a statutory provision for the protection of a class of whom the plaintiff is one and he can show that he is specially damaged by the breach, he may bring proceedings to enforce, not his own civil right of action, but the public duty which has been interfered with or not observed. The matter is, however, academic in the instant case, for the performer is not a plaintiff here and Vinelott J was, in my judgment, right to hold that the Act cannot be said either *c* to confer any right on recording companies and that they cannot be said to be persons falling within the class for whose protection it was passed.

Thus, it seems to me, the plaintiffs in this case do not fall into either of the possible classes of persons who can commence in their own names an action for the enforcement of public rights which would otherwise have to be commenced in the name of the Attorney General. If they are to maintain an action at all, therefore, they must, in my *d* judgment, do so by virtue of some other principle enabling them to sue.

It was suggested by Lord Denning MR in the *Island Records* case that there was some broad principle which conferred a cause of action in tort on anyone who was lawfully carrying on a business and whose business has been injuriously affected by a criminal activity carried on by the defendant. That was decisively rejected by the House of Lords in the *Lonrho* case. The plaintiffs, however, argue that authorities which are binding on *e* this court demonstrate the existence of a narrower principle, expressed thus by Lord Alverstone CJ in *National Phonograph Co Ltd v Edison-Bell Consolidated Phonograph Co Ltd* [1908] 1 Ch 335 at 355–356, [1904–7] All ER Rep 116 at 117: '. . . an illegal act causing injury to a person, or to his rights of property, is an actionable wrong and affords ground for an action on the case.' The *National Phonograph* case was one in which the defendants' liability arose out of a conspiracy between the defendants and two of their employees to *f* obtain goods of the plaintiffs by means of fraudulent representations made to factors and it was strictly unnecessary to base the case on the principle so stated. Nevertheless, it is clear that both Buckley and Kennedy LJJ based themselves on the following passage from the judgment of Bowen LJ in *Mogul Steamship Co Ltd v McGregor, Gow & Co* (1889) 23 QBD 598 at 614:

> 'No man, whether trader or not, can, however, justify damaging another in his *g* commercial business by fraud or misrepresentation. Intimidation, obstruction, and molestation are forbidden; so is the intentional procurement of a violation of individual rights, contractual or other, assuming always that there is no just cause for it.'

The case was, however, one of fraudulent conduct aimed specifically at the plaintiffs and *h* those with whom they had contracts and it is doubtful how far it supports the general proposition enunciated by Lord Alverstone CJ.

That proposition is, it is submitted, supported by the earlier decision of this court in *Exchange Telegraph Co Ltd v Gregory & Co* [1896] 1 QB 147, [1895–9] All ER Rep 1116 (which was referred to by Buckley LJ in the *National Phonograph* case) but, again, that case was a simple case of direct inducement to breach of contract and does not, I think, assist in the present context. Nor, for my part, do I derive any assistance from the case of *j* *GWK Ltd v Dunlop Rubber Co Ltd* (1926) 42 TLR 376 cited on behalf of the plaintiffs, for that was simply a case of a direct physical interference with the carrying out of the plaintiffs' contract with a third party.

The proposition on which the plaintiffs rest their case really depends on the majority judgments in the *Island Records* case and on two cases in the last century. The first is

Emperor of Austria v Day and Kossuth (1861) 3 De GF & J 217, 45 ER 861, a decision of
Lord Campbell LC, Knight-Bruce and Turner LJJ, on appeal from Stuart V-C. That case,
save the extent to which it has been overruled either expressly or by necessary implication,
is binding on us. It was, indeed, a very unusual case and it cannot, as I think, be explained
save on some such principle as that relied on by the plaintiffs in the present case, although
the act there complained of, the printing of banknotes in the name of a proposed
revolutionary government of Hungary, does not appear to have been illegal under
English law. The court was unanimous in upholding, at the suit of the Emperor of
Austria, an order of Stuart V-C restraining the further printing and delivery of the notes
and ordering their delivery up, Turner LJ observing (3 De GF & J 217 at 253, 45 ER 861
at 875): 'I agree that the jurisdiction of this Court in a case of this nature rests upon injury
to property actual or prospective . . .' The same principle was adopted in *Springhead
Spinning Co v Riley* (1868) LR 6 Eq 551, where Malins V-C restrained the defendants from
issuing advertisements which had the effect of deterring potential employees from
engaging themselves to work for the plaintiffs. Malins V-C observed (at 558–560):

> 'The jurisdiction of this Court is to protect property, and it will interfere by
> injunction to stay any proceedings, whether connected with crime or not, which go
> to the immediate, or tend to the ultimate, destruction of property, or to make it less
> valuable or comfortable for use or occupation . . . The truth, I apprehend, is that the
> Court will interfere to prevent acts amounting to crime, if they do not stop at crime,
> but also go to the destruction or deterioration of the value of property. That was the
> principle on which the Court restrained the proceedings of M. *Kossuth*, with regard
> to Hungarian notes in the case of *Emperor of Austria* v. *Day*.'

Now the actual decision in the case was subsequently overruled in *Prudential Assurance
Co v Knott* (1875) LR 10 Ch App 142 on the ground that, as the law then stood, the court
would not restrain by injunction the publication of a libel, but the case was treated as still
being authority for the principle stated by Malins V-C by Viscount Dilhorne in *Gouriet v
Union of Post Office Workers* [1977] 3 All ER 70 at 92, [1978] AC 435 at 492.

The principle was expressed thus by Waller LJ in the *Islands Records* case [1978] 3 All
ER 824 at 837, [1978] Ch 122 at 144: '. . . in equity there is jurisdiction for a court to
grant an injunction to a person who claims that he suffered special damage to a property
interest of his by a crime . . .' The same principle, albeit in the context of the enforcement
by an individual of a public duty, is also found in the judgment of Lord Denning MR in
the same case (see [1978] 3 All ER 824 at 829, [1978] Ch 122 at 135), where he adopted
the following submission of Peter Gibson as amicus curiae ([1978] Ch 122 at 130): 'A
review of the cases shows that the Court of Equity would protect property rights by
granting an injunction to prevent a crime which would affect such rights.'

It is on this principle that the plaintiffs are compelled to rely if they are to support this
action. Two questions arise. First, assuming such a principle still to be part of English
law, how far does it extend? Is it restricted to damage which is the direct and intended
result of the act or does it extend to any case where economic damage, whether intended
or not, is in fact occasioned to some property right as the result of a defendant's criminal
activity? It is to be observed that, in all the cases to which reference has been made,
damage to the plaintiff's property or business (using 'property' in, perhaps, a rather loose
sense, having regard to *Emperor of Austria v Day and Kossuth*) was the direct and intended
consequence of the defendant's act. In *Emperor of Austria*'s case, the object and intent of
the defendant Kossuth was to depreciate the official Austrian currency. In the *Springhead*
case the libel was intended to sterilise the plaintiffs' business by depriving it of labour. In
the *Exchange Telegraph Co* case there was a direct and intentional interference with the
contract to which the plaintiff was a party. The same is true of the *National Phonograph*
case and the *GWK* case. No case cited to us has gone so far as to confer a cause of action
where the damage complained of is merely economic damage as an incidental result of
the breach of a prohibition in a statute not designed to protect the interests of a class to
which the plaintiff belongs. If the principle extends thus far, I can, I confess, see no
logical reason why it does not extend to the full extent suggested by Lord Denning MR

in the *Island Records* case. The possibilities are indeed startling. Does an action for an injunction lie at the suit of a householder in Chelsea to restrain a known burglar from robbing houses in the borough because the publicity attached to burglaries in Chelsea depreciates the value of his property? *a*

Furthermore, since s 21(1) of the Copyright Act 1956 makes it an offence to make for sale any article which the defendant knows to be an infringing copy, it would seem that anyone who makes his living by buying and selling material in which copyright subsists (for instance, a bookseller or the owners of a record shop) can apply to the court for an injunction on the footing that the sale of infringing material potentially reduces his profits. Fortunately, such speculation is, in my judgment, rendered unnecessary by the second submission of counsel for the defendant. For myself, I feel the gravest doubt whether, allowing some such principle as that claimed to exist, it extends to a case such as the present where the defendant's conduct involves no interference with the contractual relationships of the plaintiffs but merely potentially reduces the profits which they make as the result of the performance by Mr Presley's executors of their contractual obligations. The 'property' of the plaintiffs here is the benefit of the undertaking given by Mr Presley or his representatives not to consent to reproductions otherwise than by the plaintiffs and the nature of that 'property' is exactly commensurate to the probability or improbability of other people making reproductions without such consent. The defendant's conduct may, of course, result in the plaintiffs selling fewer copies of their recordings of the Elvis Presley album because recordings of the same songs are thus made available from other sources, but it is a little difficult to see how it can be said that the value of the plaintiffs' 'property' in their contractual right to prevent the Presley representatives from giving consent to reproduction is affected. It is, however, unnecessary to decide the point, for counsel for the defendant submits that the rejection by the House of Lords in the *Lonrho* case of Lord Denning MR's wide proposition necessarily involved also the rejection of the more narrowly expressed proposition which appeared elsewhere in Lord Denning MR's judgment and in the judgment of Waller LJ. In my judgment, this submission is well founded. We have looked at the transcript of the judgments in the Court of Appeal in the *Lonrho* case, which are not reported in the law reports, and it is clear that the majority decision of the Court of Appeal in *Ex p Island Records Ltd* was relied on by the plaintiffs in that case. It appears to have been rejected both by Lord Denning MR and by Eveleigh LJ on the ground that, in contrast to the *Island Records* case, the statutory prohibition in *Lonrho* was not one for the protection of private rights. It seems, however, from the judgment of Fox LJ that reliance was also placed on the Australian case of *Beaudesert Shire Council v Smith* (1966) 120 CLR 145 and that this argument too was rejected. As Lawton LJ has mentioned, both this wide *Beaudesert* point and the slightly narrower formulation of Waller LJ, which encapsulates the plaintiffs' submission in the instant case, were distinctly raised in the appellants' case on appeal to the House of Lords, which we have also seen, and were as distinctly challenged in the respondents' case, so that both were clearly before their Lordships' House. The question asked in the consultative case, which was in effect whether the circumstances in which the plaintiffs' property had been injured gave rise to *any* cause of action, necessarily involved the consideration of precisely similar arguments to those advanced in the instant case. The question was answered in the negative and Lord Diplock's remarks with regard to the innominate tort suggested by Lord Denning MR must, in my judgment, equally apply to the innominate tort referred to in the judgment of Waller LJ. I have had the advantage of reading in draft the judgment of Lawton LJ and I respectfully agree with and adopt his analysis of the case. I too would allow the appeal.

This may seem regrettable, for the defendant who makes money out of regular and persistent breaches of the criminal law can scarcely be said to be over-burdened with merit. But that being said, the position of performers of musical and dramatic works has clearly been considered carefully by the legislature not only in the light of this country's domestic requirements but also on its obligations under international convention and it is not, I think, for the courts to strengthen the plaintiffs' business position by a manufacturing for them a new monopoly which the legislature has not seen fit to confer on them.

SLADE LJ. I have had the great advantage of reading in draft the judgment of Lawton LJ. Since I agree with both his conclusion and his reasoning, I wish to add only a few observations of my own, out of deference to Vinelott J.

b First, I am bound to say that my initial reaction to this appeal was to wonder whether this could possibly be a suitable case in which to interfere with the exercise of his discretion in refusing to strike out the plaintiffs' statement of claim. In accordance with well-established principles, a plaintiff should not be driven from the judgment seat by the striking out of his pleading, on the ground that it discloses no reasonable cause of action, unless the court is satisfied that the action as pleaded has no realistic prospect of success at the trial. Furthermore, the decision of this court in *Dyson v A-G* [1911] 1 KB

c 410 at 414 per Cozens-Hardy MR affirmed the general principle that the striking out procedure 'ought not to be applied to an action involving serious investigation of ancient law and questions of general importance'. This case certainly involves a question of general importance and also some reference to old authorities. As it happens, the defendant is legally aided, but I do not think that this factor should make the court any more inclined to grant him relief. I have also been troubled by the fact that in dealing

d with his application the court is bound to proceed on the assumption that at the trial the plaintiffs would be able to prove no less, but no more, than all the material facts asserted in the statement of claim. I wondered whether the answer to the questions of law now placed before the court might not to some extent depend on the manner in which the evidence supporting these bare assertions of fact would emerge at the trial.

However, counsel for the plaintiffs, as I understood his argument, did not seek to rely

e on this latter point. The issues of law raised by the defendant on this application are difficult as well as important, but he did not seek to submit that they would become less difficult by waiting for them to be decided at the trial. In these circumstances, I have been satisfied that, with a view to a possible avoidance of prolonged and expensive litigation, the court should proceed to consider, with due care, the reasons of counsel for the defendant for submitting that the action as pleaded is legally unsustainable and that,

f if convinced by those submission, it should strike out the statement of claim.

Principally for the reasons given by Lawton LJ I have been so convinced. There is only one aspect of the legal issues involved on which I wish to add anything of my own. Vinelott J said in the course of his judgment ([1982] 2 All ER 468 at 478, [1982] 1 WLR 979 at 990):

g 'It must be I think at least strongly arguable that a person who obtains admission to a performance by a pop star, knowing that the performer has entered into an exclusive recording contract with a recording company, and who makes a secret recording with a view to distributing it by way of trade equally commits an unlawful act (indeed one which might be unlawful apart from the Performers' Protection Acts inasmuch as it might be possible to infer that persons admitted to

h the concert impliedly agreed not to make any recording of it) and one which interferes directly with the recording company's contractual rights.'

There is a well-recognised tort which is commonly referred to as interference with contractual relations. Liability under this head can arise in many different situations of which a number of examples were given in a passage which the judge cited from the judgment of Jenkins LJ in *D C Thomson & Co Ltd v Deakin* [1952] 2 All ER 361 at 378,

j [1952] Ch 646 at 694. It reads as follows:

'Direct persuasion or procedurement or inducement applied by the third party to the contract breaker, with knowledge of the contract and the intention of bringing about its breach, is clearly to be regarded as a wrongful act in itself, and where this is shown a case of actionable interference in its primary form is made out: *Lumley v.*

Gye ((1853) 2 E & B 216, [1843–60] All ER Rep 208). But the contract breaker may himself be a willing party to the breach, without any persuasion by the third party, *a* and there seems to be no doubt that if a third party, with knowledge of a contract between the contract breaker and another, has dealings with the contract breaker which the third party knows to be inconsistent with the contract, he has committed an actionable interference: see, for example, *British Industrial Plastics, Ltd.* v. *Ferguson* ([1940] 1 All ER 479), where the necessary knowledge was held not to have been brought home to the third party; and *British Motor Trade Association* v. *Salvadori* *b* ([1949] 1 All ER 208, [1949] Ch 556). The inconsistent dealing between the third party and the contract breaker may, indeed, be commenced without knowledge by the third party of the contract thus broken, but, if it is continued after the third party has notice of the contract, an actionable interference has been committed by him: see, for example, *De Franceso* v. *Barnum* ((1890) 45 Ch D 430, [1886–90] All ER Rep 414). Again, so far from persuading or inducing or procuring one of the *c* parties to the contract to break it, the third party may commit an actionable interference with the contract, against the will of both and without the knowledge of either, if, with knowledge of the contract, he does an act which, if done by one of the parties to it, would have been a breach. Of this type of interference the case of *G.W.K., Ltd.* v. *Dunlop Rubber Co., Ltd.* ((1926) 42 TLR 376, 593) affords a striking example.'

d

Vinelott J in his judgment summarised the facts of *GWK Ltd v Dunlop Rubber Co Ltd* (1926) 42 TLR 376 and also of *National Phonographic Co Ltd v Edison-Bell Consolidated Phonograph Co Ltd* [1908] 1 Ch 335, [1904–7] All ER Rep 116 as examples of cases where the tort of interference with contractual relations was found to have been committed.

If I thought it seriously arguable that, on the basis of the facts pleaded in the statement *e* of claim, the defendant could be liable for the tort of interference with contractual relations as established in the line of cases to which I have referred, I would for my own part allow this action to proceed. But, as I understand the facts of all these cases where liability has been established under this particular head of tort, there has been an interference or attempt to interfere with the *performance* by a third party of his contractual obligations. There is nothing in *this* line of authority which I have been able *f* to discover which suggests that A may be liable to B under this head of tort merely because A does an act (even an illegal act) which he knows is likely to render less valuable certain contractual rights of B as against C, without actually interfering with the performance by C of the contractual obligations owed by him to B.

In these circumstances, with great respect to him, I am not able to agree with the judge's suggestion (see [1982] 2 All ER 468 at 478, [1982] 1 WLR 979 at 990) that in a *g* case such as the present it could be seriously argued that at least the person who actually made the bootleg records would be under a liability to the recording companies on the basis of the tort of interference with contractual relations, as recognised in *D C Thomson & Co Ltd v Deakin*. A fortiori a claim based on this tort would not, in my opinion, be available in the present case where it is not alleged that the defendant had any part in the making of any bootleg records. On the pleaded facts it cannot, I think, be said that he has *h* interfered in any way, directly or indirectly, with the *performance* of the contractual obligations of Elvis Presley or his personal representatives to the plaintiffs. If, therefore, the plaintiffs are to have any hope of success at the trial, they must, in my opinion, point to some other arguable head of liability.

The House of Lords in the *Lonrho* case found it unnecessary to decide whether s 1 of the Dramatic and Musical Performers' Protection Act 1958 created a statutory duty to *j* recording companies, such as the plaintiffs, as well as to performers, and conferred on such companies a right of action. A claim based on an alleged statutory duty of this kind, for what that claim is worth, would therefore be open to the plaintiffs in the House of Lords. However, I agree with Lawton LJ that this very point was decided adversely to recording companies by Shaw and Waller LJJ in the *Island Records* case. The point is not,

therefore, open to the plaintiffs in argument in this court in opposition to the present
a appeal.

The remaining point that has been strongly pressed in argument on behalf of the
plaintiffs in this court is based on the general proposition that the court can grant an
injunction to a person who claims that he has suffered special damage to a right of
property by a crime. As Vinelott J pointed out, this proposition appears to derive some
support from cases decided both before and after the Judicature Acts. Among those cited
b to us have been *Emperor of Austria v Day and Kossuth* (1861) 3 De GF & J 217 at 253–254,
45 ER 861 at 875 per Turner LJ, *Springhead Spinning Co v Riley* (1868) LR 6 Eq 551 at 560
per Malins V-C and the *National Phonograph* case [1908] 1 Ch 335, [1904–7] All ER Rep
116. It is significant that in the latter case Buckley LJ considered that liability had been
established on two grounds, namely interference with contractual relations and what he
termed interference with 'right of property' (see [1908] 1 Ch 335 at 360–361, [1904–7]
All ER Rep 116 at 120). He thus clearly regarded the two heads of liability as separate
c and distinct. Lord Alverstone CJ in that case stated the position even more broadly in
saying ([1908] 1 Ch 335 at 355–356, [1904–7] All ER Rep 116 at 117): 'It is, in my
opinion, clearly established that an illegal act causing injury to a person, or to his rights
of property, is an actionable wrong and affords ground for an action on the case.'

In the *Island Records* case Lord Denning MR and Waller LJ, as I understand their
d decisions, applied this 'injury to property' principle in holding that the recording
companies were entitled to an injunction for the protection of their property rights,
consisting of the benefit of their contracts with the performers.

If the *Island Records* case stood on its own, I think this court would be entitled and
indeed bound to follow it and to hold that the plaintiffs in the present case, on the basis
of the facts pleaded, have established at least a strongly arguable case. In my judgment,
e however, for the reasons given in more detail by Lawton LJ, the observations by Lord
Diplock in the *Lonrho* case about the *Island Records* decision, concurred in, as they were,
by the rest of their Lordships, by necessary implication overruled that decision in so far
as it decided that the plaintiffs had a cause of action based on the 'injury to property'
principle. When Lord Diplock left open the question whether the recording companies
would have been entitled to obtain an injunction in a civil action to which the performers
f whose performances had been bootlegged were not parties, I understand him to have
been merely leaving open the question whether, on the construction of the 1958 Act,
recording companies were included among the persons for whose protection that Act
was passed, so as to give them a civil remedy on this ground. How far the 'injury to
property' principle has in general survived the *Lonrho* decision may be a matter for debate
hereafter. For present purposes it is sufficient to say that, in my opinion, in view of the
g *Lonrho* decision, it cannot avail the plaintiffs in the present case.

Thus, even if this action were to proceed to trial and the plaintiffs were to establish all
the facts alleged by them, the trial judge, in my judgment, would at the end of the day
be bound to dismiss the action.

In all the circumstances, I think that nothing useful can be achieved by allowing the
proceedings to continue. Though some may think that the absence of a remedy for
h recording companies in this situation constitutes an undesirable gap in the law, this is a
gap which can only be filled by the House of Lords or by Parliament. I would allow this
appeal and grant the order sought, by dismissing the action and striking out the statement
of claim.

Appeal allowed. Statement of claim struck out. Action dismissed. Leave to plaintiffs to appeal to
j *the House of Lords granted.*

Solicitors: *George W Mills & Son*, Washington (for the defendant); *A E Hamlin & Co* (for
the plaintiffs).

Mary Rose Plummer   Barrister.

Manuel and others v Attorney General
Noltcho and others v Attorney General

CHANCERY DIVISION

SIR ROBERT MEGARRY V-C

20, 21, 22, 23, 26 APRIL, 7 MAY 1982

Statute – Validity – Public general Act of United Kingdom Parliament – Constitution of independent sovereign state – Jurisdiction of court – Pleadings challenging validity of properly passed Act – Act passed by United Kingdom Parliament to transfer Canadian constitution to Canada – Allegation that Act ultra vires because 'consent' of Canada not properly obtained – Whether court having jurisdiction to inquire into validity of Act – Canada Act 1982.

Crown – Disability – Proceedings against the Crown – Proceedings against the Crown in right of Canada – Whether proceedings against the Crown in right of Canada can be brought against the Crown in right of the United Kingdom – British North America Act 1867 – Statute of Westminster 1931, ss 4, 7.

Commonwealth – Colony or dominion – Governmental obligation – Whether United Kingdom government owing obligations to Canadian Indians.

Canada – Constitutional law – Treaty rights granted to Canadian Indians – Whether treaty rights enforceable against United Kingdom government.

The plaintiffs, who were Canadian Indian chiefs, brought, in their representative capacities, separate actions against the Attorney General of England arising out of the transfer of the Canadian constitution to Canada effected by the enactment of the Canada Act 1982 by the United Kingdom Parliament. The 1982 Act, after reciting that 'Canada has requested and consented' to the Act, provided that the Constitution of Canada set out in Sch B was to have the force of law in Canada and that no Act of the United Kingdom Parliament passed after the Constitution came into force was to extend to Canada as part of Canadian law. The plaintiffs feared that the transfer of the Constitution to Canada would put at risk certain rights granted to the Indians by treaty and set out in the British North America Acts 1867 to 1930. They contended that those rights were entrenched by the fact that under s 7(1)[a] of the Statute of Westminster 1931 power to repeal, amend or alter the British North America Acts was reserved to the United Kingdom Parliament when Canada, along with other self-governing dominions, attained complete independence as recognised by the Statute of Westminster (subject to the reservation contained in s 7).

In the first action the plaintiffs sought, inter alia, declarations (i) that the United Kingdom Parliament had no power to amend the constitution of Canada so as to prejudice the Indian nations of Canada without their consent, and (ii) that the 1982 Act passed by the United Kingdom Parliament was ultra vires. They contended that the consequence of the transfer of power to Canada under the Statute of Westminster was that the United Kingdom Parliament had deprived itself of all power to legislate for Canada (save only as reserved by s 7(1)) unless the legislation 'expressly declared in that Act that [the] Dominion has requested, and consented to, the enactment', as required by s 4[b] of the Statute of Westminster. That request and consent, the plaintiffs contended, required the actual request and consent of the 'Dominion', which in the Canadian context

---

a   Section 7(1) provides: 'Nothing in this Act shall be deemed to apply to the repeal, amendment or alteration of the British North America Acts, 1867 to 1930, or any order, rule or regulation made thereunder.'

b   Section 4 is set out at p 790 c, post

meant not merely the Dominion's Parliament but all the constituent parts of the
a Dominion, namely Parliament, the provincial legislatures and, by virtue of their
protected constitutional status, the Indian peoples, and the consent of all the constituent
parts had not been obtained. Furthermore, it was contended, the 1982 Act could not be
said to have been enacted under the power reserved to the United Kingdom Parliament
by s 7(1) of the Statute of Westminster to enact legislation effecting 'the repeal,
amendment or alteration of the British North America Acts, 1867 to 1930', since the
b 1982 Act, although effectively repealing and amending parts of those Acts, did much
more than that and so went beyond the reserved competence of the United Kingdom
Parliament.

In the second action the plaintiffs sought declarations to the effect that certain
agreements and collateral warranties arising out of various treaties made by the Crown
and the Indian peoples between 1871 and 1907 were still binding on the Crown in right
c of the United Kingdom and that those treaties and warranties were to be permanent in
character, were to enure to succeeding generations of Indians and were to remain binding
on the Crown in right of the United Kingdom until they were assigned or abrogated
with the consent of the Indian peoples.

The Attorney General issued notices of motion under RSC Ord 18, r 19 seeking, inter
alia, orders to strike out the statement of claim in each action as disclosing no reasonable
d cause of action and orders dismissing the actions.

Held – (1) The first action would be dismissed because—
(a) once an instrument was recognised as being an Act of Parliament, no English court
could refuse to obey it or question its validity, and it followed that the court could not
hold any Act of Parliament to be ultra vires. Since the copy of the 1982 Act which was
e before the court purported to be published by Her Majesty's Stationery Office, and since
there was no suggestion that it had not been passed by both Houses or had not received
the royal assent, it was therefore an Act of Parliament and the court could not hold it to
be invalid (see p 793 *g* to p 794 *d* and p 795 *b* to *d*, post); dictum of Lord Campbell in
Edinburgh and Dalkeith Rly Co v Wauchope (1842) 8 Cl & F at 725 and *British Rlys Board v
Pickin* [1974] 1 All ER 609 followed;
f (b) furthermore, in proceedings for a declaration brought against the Attorney General
of England the court had no jurisdiction to make a declaration as to the validity of the
constitution of an independent sovereign state because the court could not give a
declaratory judgment against a party who had no interest in the subject matter of the
declaration, and apart from any case where the question arose merely incidentally the
courts of the United Kingdom could not pronounce on whether the law of an independent
g sovereign state was valid within that state, for to do so would be to assert jurisdiction
over that state (see p 794 *j* to p 795 *d*, post); *Buck v A-G* [1965] 1 All ER 882 followed.
(2) The second action would be dismissed because any obligations which the Crown
had in respect of the Indian peoples of Canada were the responsibility of the Crown in
right of Canada and were not the responsibility of the Crown in right of the United
Kingdom. Accordingly, the Canadian courts and not the English courts alone had
h jurisdiction to determine what those obligations were. When sovereignty over Canada
was transferred, the obligation to do sovereign acts in Canada could no longer remain
with the Crown in right of the United Kingdom because it no longer had sovereignty
over Canada. A promise that treaty obligations would always bind the Crown in right of
the United Kingdom did not prevent the Crown from transferring or altering sovereignty,
nor did it bind the Crown in right of the United Kingdom to carry out obligations when
j it no longer had the power to do so (see p 798 *g* to *j*, p 799 *f* to *j* and p 800 *b*, post); dictum
of Lord Diplock in *R v Secretary of State for Foreign and Commonwealth Affairs, ex p Indian
Association of Alberta* [1982] 2 All ER at 143 applied.

Notes
For the constitution of Canada and the amendment thereof, see 6 Halsbury's Laws (4th

edn) paras 835–836, 926–930, and for the constitution of Canada generally, see ibid paras
926–943.

For the special independent status of Canada, see ibid paras 832–833.

For the reservation of powers by the United Kingdom Parliament, see ibid paras 842.

For the unity and divisibility of the Crown, see ibid para 820.

For the British North America Act 1867, see 4 Halsbury's Statute (3rd edn) 183.

For the Statute of Westminster 1931, ss 4, 7, see ibid 21, 22.

Cases referred to in judgment

A-G v Great Southern and Western Rly Co of Ireland [1925] AC 754, HL, 8(2) Digest (Reissue)
862, 1054.

Blackburn v A-G [1971] 2 All ER 1380, [1971] 1 WLR 1037, CA, 11 Digest (Reissue) 743,
600.

Bribery Comr v Ranasinghe [1964] 2 All ER 785, [1965] AC 172, [1964] 2 WLR 1301, PC,
8(2) Digest (Reissue) 757, 347.

Brickman's Settlement, Re [1982] 1 All ER 336, sub nom *Practice Note (Chancery: Deposition)*
[1981] 1 WLR 1560.

British Coal Corp v R [1935] AC 500, [1935] All ER Rep 139, PC, 8(2) Digest (Reissue) 821,
697.

British Rlys Board v Pickin [1974] 1 All ER 609, [1974] AC 765, [1974] 2 WLR 208, HL,
Digest (Cont Vol D) 862, 1694a.

Buck v A-G [1965] 1 All ER 882, [1965] Ch 745, [1965] 2 WLR 1033, CA, 8(2) Digest
(Reissue) 661, 32.

Dyson v A-G [1911] 1 KB 400, CA, 11 Digest (Reissue) 693, 308.

Edinburgh and Dalkeith Rly Co v Wauchope (1842) 8 Cl & Fin 710, 1 Bell 252, 8 ER 279,
HL, 44 Digest (Repl) 341, 1771.

Ellen Street Estates Ltd v Minister of Health [1934] 1 KB 590, [1934] All ER Rep 385, CA, 11
Digest (Reissue) 327, 2106.

Harris v Minister of Interior 1952 (2) SA 428.

Heresy, The Case of (1601) 12 Co Rep 56, 77 ER 1335.

Hodge v R (1883) 9 App Cas 117, PC, 8(2) Digest (Reissue) 684, 132.

Joyce v DPP [1946] 1 All ER 186, [1946] AC 347, HL, 14(1) Digest (Reissue) 143, 990.

Madzimbamuto v Lardner-Burke [1968] 3 All ER 561, [1969] 1 AC 645, [1968] 3 WLR
1229, PC, 8(2) Digest (Reissue) 663, 34.

Prince's Case, The (1606) 8 Co Rep 1a, 77 ER 481, 11 Digest (Reissue) 661, 28.

R v Secretary of State for Foreign and Commonwealth Affairs, ex p Indian Association of Alberta
[1982] 2 All ER 118, [1982] QB 892, [1982] 2 WLR 641, CA.

Russell (Earl), The Trial of [1901] AC 446, HL, 15 Digest (Reissue) 1026, 8899.

Tito v Waddell (No 2), Tito v A-G [1977] 3 All ER 129, [1977] Ch 106, [1977] 2 WLR 496,
Digest (Cont Vol E) 634, 15a.

Motion

Manuel and others v Attorney General

By a writ issued on 10 December 1981 the plaintiffs, Chief Robert Manuel and 123 other
Indian chiefs of Canada, sought in their representative capacity declarations, inter alia, (i)
that on the proper construction of the Statute of Westminster 1931 and the British North
America Acts 1867 to 1964 no law thereafter made by the United Kingdom Parliament
could extend to Canada other than at the request of and with the consent of the people of
Canada, (ii) that the British North America Act 1930 could only be amended at the
request of and with the consent of the people of Canada expressed by (a) the Federal
Parliament of Canada, (b) all the legislatures of the Provinces of Canada and (c) the Indian
nations of Canada, who had a separate and special status within the Constitution of
Canada, and (iii) that the United Kingdom Parliament had no power to amend the
Constitution of Canada so as to prejudice the Indian nations without the consent of the
Indian nations of Canada. By a notice of motion dated 31 March 1982 the Attorney

General sought, inter alia, an order that the statement of claim be struck out as disclosing
a no reasonable cause of action and an order that the action be dismissed. The facts are set
out in the judgment.

Noltcho and others v Attorney General

By a writ issued on 14 January 1982 the plaintiffs, Chief Jerome Noltcho and 67 other
Indian chiefs of Canada, the plaintiffs, sought in their representative capacities
b declarations, inter alia, (i) that the agreements and/or collateral warranties evidenced in
treaties between 1871 and 1930 made between the Crown and the Indian peoples
remained in full force and were binding on the Crown in right of the United Kingdom,
and (ii) that the Crown in right of the United Kingdom was in wrongful repudiation of
those agreements and/or collateral warranties and/or treaties. By a notice of motion dated
31 March 1982 the Attorney General sought, inter alia, an order that the statement of
c claim be struck out as disclosing no reasonable cause of action and an order that the
action be dismissed. The facts are set out in the judgment.

John Mummery for the Attorney General.
John Macdonald QC and *Colin Braham* for the Manuel plaintiffs.
Mark Saville QC, Rosalyn Higgins and *Gordon Bennett* for the Noltcho plaintiffs.

d
Cur adv vult

7 May. **SIR ROBERT MEGARRY V-C** read the following judgment: Two motions
are before me. In each, the defendant, the Attorney General of England, moves under a
notice of motion dated 31 March 1982 to strike out the statement of claim as disclosing
e no reasonable cause of action justiciable in this court. The plaintiffs in one action, as
amended, are 124 Canadian Indian chiefs, suing on behalf of themselves and all other
members of named Indian bands. In the other action the plaintiffs are 68 Canadian
Indian chiefs, suing in a similar representative capacity. For convenience, I shall refer to
the first action as the Manuel action and to the second as the Noltcho action, from the
names of the respective first plaintiffs. Mr Macdonald appeared for the plaintiffs in the
f Manuel action, Mr Saville appeared for the plaintiffs in the Noltcho action and Mr
Mummery appeared for the Attorney General in both actions.

By agreement, both motions were heard together. Although the relief sought in each
action is a series of declarations, these are very different in their effect. In the Manuel
action, the first five declarations plainly lead up to the last two. These are, first, that the
Parliament of the United Kingdom has no power to amend the Constitution of Canada
g so as to prejudice the Indian nations of Canada without their consent; and second, that
the Canada Act 1982 is ultra vires. The first of these declarations was in the prayer for
relief in the statement of claim when it was served on 22 January last, and the second was
added on Day 3 of the hearing before me, after the Canada Act 1982 had received the
royal assent and had been brought into force by royal proclamation under the Great Seal
of Canada. The action accordingly challenges the legislative omnipotence of Parliament.
h In the Noltcho action, on the other hand, the declarations sought relate to certain
agreements and collateral warranties which are said to be still binding on the Crown in
right of the United Kingdom and to have been wrongfully repudiated, to certain
subsisting trusts which are said to bind the Crown in right of the United Kingdom, and
to the status of these agreements and collateral warranties as being subsisting treaties,
properly so called. The Noltcho action is thus directed not to a frontal challenge to the
j powers of the Parliament of the United Kingdom but to the continued existence of
obligations outside the statute book as being binding on the Crown in right of the United
Kingdom, as distinct from the Crown in right of Canada.

I do not think that I need enlarge on the background of this litigation. The Canada Act
1982 received the royal assent on 29 March 1982, and was brought into force by a royal
proclamation in Canada on 17 April 1982. The preamble to the Act recites that 'Canada
has requested and consented to the enactment of an Act of the Parliament of the United

Kingdom to give effect to the provisions hereinafter set forth', and that the Canadian
Senate and House of Commons have submitted an address to the Queen requesting that   *a*
Her Majesty may graciously be pleased to cause a Bill to be laid before the United
Kingdom Parliament for that purpose. It is then enacted by s 1 that the Constitution Act
1982 set out in Sch B to the Canada Act 1982 'is hereby enacted for and shall have the
force of law in Canada'. By s 2, no Act of the United Kingdom Parliament passed after
the Constitution Act 1982 comes into force 'shall extend to Canada as part of its law'. The
two remaining sections of the Canada Act then provide for the French version of the Act   *b*
and for the short title. That is all: the English and French texts are each barely a half page
long, and the remaining 34 pages are occupied by the English and French texts in Sch B,
setting out the Constitution Act 1982. As is well known, the effect of s 7(1) of the Statute
of Westminster 1931 was to exclude the repeal, amendment or alteration of the British
North America Acts 1867 to 1930 from the legislative powers conferred on Canada by
the statute. By s 4 of the statute: *c*

> 'No Act of Parliament of the United Kingdom passed after the commencement of
> this Act shall extend, or be deemed to extend, to a Dominion as part of the law of
> that Dominion unless it is expressly declared in that Act that that Dominion has
> requested, and consented to, the enactment thereof.'

The preamble of the Canada Act 1982 is plainly framed with s 4 of the Statute of   *d*
Westminster 1931 in mind.

The hearing of the two motions occupied most of five days. At the end, the question
was whether the claim to relief in each of the actions is so plainly bad that it should be
struck out and not allowed to go to trial: see, for example, the notes to RSC Ord 18, r
19(1)(a) in *The Supreme Court Practice 1982* vol 1, pp 346–352 and *Dyson v A-G* [1911] 1
KB 410 at 418–419. A motion to strike out a pleading should not be treated as being the   *e*
trial of a demurrer or a preliminary point of law, to be determined one way or the other
even if the judge is beset by hesitations and doubts. He who moves such a motion must
make out a case that is clear beyond doubt. At the same time, one must beware of any
assumption that because a case takes a long time to argue, the points at issue must be
doubtful. Arguments must be assessed on their quality rather than on their duration,
and sometimes the weaker the case the greater the profusion of ingenuity in supporting   *f*
it.

I shall take the Manuel action first. In this, the writ was issued on 10 December 1981,
and the statement of claim was served on 22 January 1982, and afterwards was amended.
I think that I should read most of the prayer for relief, setting it out in the form in which
it stood after being amended before and during the hearing. Apart from prayers for
representation orders, inquiries, further and other relief, and so on, there is, as I have   *g*
mentioned, a claim for what in effect are seven declarations, since the sixth has two
limbs. They are as follows:

> '1. A Declaration that the Parliament of the United Kingdom has transferred
> sovereignty over Canada to the Dominion of Canada save and in so far as power is
> reserved to the United Kingdom Parliament by law and by the Statute of
> Westminster 1931 and the British North America Acts 1867 to 1964.   *h*
> 2. A Declaration that on the proper construction of the Statute of Westminster
> and the British North America Acts no law hereafter made by the United Kingdom
> Parliament can extend to Canada other than a law made at the request and with the
> consent of the Dominion of Canada.
> 3. A Declaration that the words "Dominion" in the preamble and section 4 of the   *i*
> Statute of Westminster 1931 means in respect of Canada the people of Canada and
> "the consent of the Dominion" means the consent of the people of Canada expressed
> by (a) the Federal Parliament of Canada (b) all the Legislatures of the Provinces of
> Canada and (c) the Indian Nations of Canada who have a separate and special status
> within the Constitution of Canada.
> 4. A Declaration that on its proper construction the British North America Act

1930 (a) confers on the Indians of the Provinces of Manitoba and British Columbia the rights set out in the agreements scheduled to the Act and (b) imposes restraints on the legislative power of the Parliament of Canada to derogate from such rights.

5. A Declaration that the British North American [sic] Act 1930 can only be amended at the request of and with the consent of the people of Canada expressed by (a) the Federal Parliament of Canada (b) all the Legislatures of the Provinces of Canada and (c) the Indian Nations of Canada.

6. A Declaration that in the premises (1) the United Kingdom Parliament has no power to amend the Constitution of Canada so as to prejudice the Indian Nations without the consent of the Indian Nations of Canada; (2) the Canada Act 1982 is ultra vires.'

The statement of claim is a substantial document, and what is pleaded in support of these declarations cannot easily be summarised. The main thrust, however, can be expressed as follows. As matters stood before the Canada Act 1982 was enacted, the Canadian Indian bands had certain special rights which were protected under the constitution of Canada. The term 'bands', I may say, is used in the sense of a body of Indians for whom lands have been set apart or for whom moneys are held, or who have been declared to be a band by the Governor General in Council. The Indian bands acquired their rights under a royal proclamation made on 7 October 1763, and under a series of treaties made with them in the nineteenth century. I need not describe these rights: they include rights in relation to Indian reservations and rights of hunting, trapping and fishing game and fish for food at all seasons of the year on all unoccupied Crown lands and any other lands to which the Indians have rights of access; and see the agreements set out in the schedule to the British North America Act 1930 which by that Act are given the force of law. Under the British North America Act 1867, the power to legislate for Indians and for land reserved for the Indians was reserved to the Canadian Parliament, though the lands were vested in the several provinces, subject to any trusts or other interests (such as those of the Indians) which affected them: see ss 91(24) and 109. By virtue of the Statute of Westminster 1931, s 7(1), these arrangements could not be altered by the Canadian Parliament or the provincial legislatures, and so only the United Kingdom Parliament could do this. In this way the rights of the Indians were entrenched.

Under the Canada Act 1982 this entrenchment goes. In its place the Constitution Act 1982, s 37, provides for the convening of a constitutional conference within a year, composed of the Prime Minister of Canada and the first ministers of the provinces. By sub-s (2), the agenda for this conference is to include an item—

'respecting constitutional matters that directly affect the aboriginal peoples of Canada, including the identification and definition of the rights of those peoples to be included in the Constitution of Canada, and the Prime Minister of Canada shall invite representatives of those peoples to participate in the discussions on that item.'

The 'aboriginal peoples of Canada' are defined by s 35(2) as including 'the Indian, Inuit and Métis peoples of Canada'. By s 35(1), the existing aboriginal and treaty rights of the aboriginal peoples of Canada are 'recognized and affirmed'; and see s 25. The complaint is thus not that any of the subsisting rights have been taken away but that they are no longer entrenched and protected as they once were, and that their future depends on what emerges from the constitutional conference that is to be held, and what effect is given to it. Under Part V of the Constitution Act 1982 there is now power for Canadian amendments to be made to the Constitution of Canada. In general, this can be done by proclamation after authorisation by resolutions of each House of the Canadian Parliament and by resolutions of the legislative assemblies of at least two-thirds of the provinces which have between them at least half the total population of all the provinces. What the plaintiffs are seeking to do in their action is to preserve the pre-existing protection for their rights rather than to enforce them.

On the face of it, a contention that an Act of Parliament is ultra vires is bold in the extreme. It is contrary to one of the fundamentals of the British Constitution: see, for example, 36 Halsbury's Laws (3rd edn) 377, para 559. That, and the contention that the matter was not one for the courts of England (see *R v Secretary of State for Foreign and Commonwealth Affairs, ex p Indian Association of Alberta* [1982] 2 All ER 118, [1982] QB 892, a case which for brevity may be called the *Alberta* case), was the backbone of counsel for the Attorney General's submissions. Not surprisingly, his contentions, like those of counsel for the Manuel plaintiffs, were the subject of development and refinement as the argument proceeded. In the end, counsel for the Attorney General encapsulated his submissions in the proposition that the only question was whether the Canada Act 1982 was an Act of Parliament. If it was, that was the end of the matter; for the courts could not declare that Parliament had no power to pass it, or that it was ultra vires. In particular, counsel for the Attorney General relied on *British Rlys Board v Pickin* [1974] 1 All ER 609, [1974] AC 765. In that case the House of Lords unanimously held that a private Act of Parliament was not open to attack in the courts on the ground that the promoters of the Act had fraudulently inserted a false recital in the preamble. As was said by Lord Morris ([1974] 1 All ER 609 at 619, [1974] AC 765 at 789), it is not for the courts to proceed 'as though the Act or some part of it had never been passed'; there may be argument on the interpretation of the Act, but 'there must be none as to whether it should be on the statute book at all'. Any complaint on such matters is for Parliament to deal with and not the courts: see, for example, *British Rlys Board v Pickin* [1974] 1 All ER 609 at 622, 629, [1974] AC 765 at 793, 800. Accordingly, in that case the paragraphs of a reply which raised such a point were struck out.

Counsel for the Manuel plaintiffs was, of course, concerned to restrict the ambit of the decision in *Pickin*. He accepted that it was a binding decision for domestic legislation, but he said that it did not apply in relation to the Statute of Westminster 1931 or to the other countries of the Commonwealth. He also contended that it decided no more than that the courts would not inquire into what occurred in the course of the passage of a Bill through Parliament, relying on what Lord Reid said (see [1974] 1 All ER 609 at 618, [1974] AC 765 at 787). This latter point is, I think, plainly wrong, since it ignores the words 'what was done previously to its being introduced' which Lord Reid there cited with approval. The wider point, however, is founded on the theory that Parliament may surrender its sovereign power over some territory or area of land to another person or body: see W R Anson on 'The Government of Ireland Bill and the Sovereignty of Parliament' (1886) 2 LQR 427 at 440; Dicey *Law of the Constitution* (8th edn, 1915) pp 66–67, (10th edn, 1959) pp 68–69; Jennings *The Law and the Constitution* (5th edn, 1967) pp 160–172; Wade and Phillips *Constitutional and administrative law* (9th edn, 1977) pp 65–68; *Harris v Minister of the Interior* 1952 (2) SA 428 at 459–460. After such a surrender, any legislation which Parliament purports to enact for that territory is not merely ineffective there, but is totally void, in this country as elsewhere, since Parliament has surrendered the power to legislate; and the English courts have jurisdiction to declare such legislation ultra vires and void.

Before I discuss this proposition, and its application to Canada, I should mention one curious result of this theory which emerged only at a late stage. In response to a question, counsel for the Manuel plaintiffs accepted that as the theory applied only to territories over which Parliament had surrendered its sovereignty, it did not affect territories over which Parliament had never exercised sovereignty. Thus if one adapts an example given by *Jennings* (at pp 170, 171) an English statute making it an offence to smoke in the streets of Paris or Vienna would be valid, though enforceable only against those who come within the jurisdiction, whereas an English statute making it an offence to smoke in the streets of Bombay or Sydney would be ultra vires and void, and an English court could make a declaration to this effect. At this stage I need say no more than that I find such a distinction surprising. I may perhaps interpose that *Wade and Phillips* takes the example of Heligoland, ceded to Germany in 1890 (see the Anglo-German Agreement Act 1890), and observes (at p 67) that 'Parliament could, if it so wished, subsequently repeal the statute by which cession was approved', adding that this would not recover the territory

for the United Kingdom. What the book said in 1977 could be done had in fact already
a been done some 14 years earlier (see the Statute Law Revision Act 1953, s 1, Sch 1), so
that no further repeal is now possible: one cannot slay the slain.

The application of the theory of counsel for the Manuel plaintiffs to Canada is on the
following lines. In 1931, there was a long tradition that the United Kingdom Parliament
would not legislate for Canada or the other Dominions save at the request and with the
consent of the Dominion concerned. That tradition had ripened into law by 1931, and
b the Statute of Westminster 1931, s 4, was merely declaratory of the existing law. I have
already set out that section. The law that had arisen from the long tradition required that
there should be an actual request and consent of the Dominion, so that a mere declaration
in the Act that there had been such a request and consent was not enough. The Act had,
by s 2, transferred sovereignty to Canada, subject to s 7(1), which provided that nothing
in the Act was to be 'deemed to apply to the repeal, amendment or alteration of the
c British North America Acts 1867 to 1930 . . .' With that transfer, the United Kingdom
Parliament deprived itself of all power to legislate for Canada save only as reserved by
s 7(1). On its true construction, nothing save the actual consent and request of the
Dominion would empower the United Kingdom Parliament to legislate for Canada
under this; and 'Dominion' meant not merely the Parliament of the Dominion, but all
the constituent constitutional fractions of the Dominion, namely, that Parliament, the
d provincial legislatures, and the Indians, with their protected constitutional status. The
consent of the Dominion in this sense manifestly had not been given. Furthermore, the
power reserved for the United Kingdom Parliament was merely in relation to 'the repeal,
amendment or alteration of the British North America Acts 1867 to 1930', and the
Canada Act 1982, though repealing and amending parts of those Acts, did much more
than that, and so went beyond the reserved competence of the United Kingdom
e Parliament. The Statute of Westminster 1931 was an instrument which regulated
Parliament's power to make law, and so was a 'constituent instrument' within the
language of the Judicial Committee in *Bribery Comr v Ranasinghe* [1964] 2 All ER 785 at
792, [1965] AC 172 at 197–198, so that no Act was valid if it did not comply with that
instrument.

I hope that this summary fairly indicates the main thrust of the contentions of counsel
f for the Manuel plaintiffs, spread as they were over some two days of court time, and
developing, as they did in their progress, with a number of sallies into side issues. The
subject, of course, is constitutionally fundamental; and it is also susceptible to much
theoretical speculation and contention which would be out of place in a judgment,
however appropriate to textbooks or articles. My duty is merely to reach a decision in
this case and not to explore side issues, however interesting they are. If I leave on one side
g the European Communities Act 1972 and all that flows from it, and also the Parliament
Acts 1911 and 1949, which do not affect this case, I am bound to say that from first to
last I have heard nothing in this case to make me doubt the simple rule that the duty of
the court is to obey and apply every Act of Parliament, and that the court cannot hold
any such Act to be ultra vires. Of course there may be questions about what the Act
means, and of course there is power to hold statutory instruments and other subordinate
h legislation ultra vires. But once an instrument is recognised as being an Act of Parliament,
no English court can refuse to obey it or question its validity.

In the present case I have before me a copy of the Canada Act 1982 purporting to be
published by Her Majesty's Stationery Office. After reciting the request and consent of
Canada and the submission of an address to Her Majesty by the Senate and House of
Commons of Canada, there are the words of enactment:

j   'Be it therefore enacted by the Queen's Most Excellent Majesty, by and with the
      advice and consent of the Lords Spiritual and Temporal, and Commons, in this
      present Parliament assembled, and by the authority of the same, as follows.'

There has been no suggestion that the copy before me is not a true copy of the Act itself,
or that it was not passed by the House of Commons and the House of Lords, or did not

receive the royal assent. The Act is therefore an Act of Parliament and the court cannot hold it to be invalid. The case is not one which raises any question under the Parliament *a* Acts 1911 and 1949. It is also far removed from any case where, apart from those Acts, only one of the two Houses of Parliament had in fact passed the Bill, so that the cryptic wording of the recital was merely that it was 'assented in this present Parliament', and so on: see *The Case of Heresy* (1601) 12 Co Rep 56 at 57–58, 77 ER 1335 at 1336–1337, in relation to 5 Ric 2 Stat 2 c 5 (1382); *The Prince's Case* (1606) 8 Co Rep 1a at 20b, 77 ER 481 at 505. In the words of Lord Campbell in *Edinburgh and Dalkeith Rly Co v Wauchope* *b* (1842) 8 Cl & F 710 at 725, 8 ER 279 at 285:

> 'All that a Court of Justice can do is to look to the Parliamentary roll: if from that it should appear that a bill has passed both Houses and received the Royal assent, no Court of Justice can inquire into the mode in which it was introduced into Parliament, nor into what was done previous to its introduction, or what passed in Parliament during its progress in its various stages through both Houses.' *c*

In *British Rlys Board v Pickin* [1974] 1 All ER 609 at 618, [1974] AC 765 at 787, Lord Reid quoted this passage as it appears in Bell's Reports (1 Bell 252 at 278–279) and said: 'No doubt this was obiter but, so far as I am aware, no one since 1842 has doubted that it is a correct statement of the constitutional position' (and see [1974] 1 All ER 609 at 620, 622–623, 628, 630, [1974] 1 AC 765 at 790, 793, 799–800, 801). The Canada Act 1982 is *d* an Act of Parliament, and sitting as a judge in an English court I owe full and dutiful obedience to that Act.

I do not think that, as a matter of law, it makes any difference if the Act in question purports to apply outside the United Kingdom. I speak not merely of statutes such as the Continental Shelf Act 1964 but also of statutes purporting to apply to other countries. If that other country is a colony, the English courts will apply the Act even if the colony is *e* in a state of revolt against the Crown and direct enforcement of the decision may be impossible: see *Madzimbamuto v Lardner-Burke* [1968] 3 All ER 561, [1969] 1 AC 645. It matters not if a convention had grown up that the United Kingdom Parliament would not legislate for that colony without the consent of the colony. Such a convention would not limit the powers of Parliament, and if Parliament legislated in breach of the convention, 'the courts could not hold the Act of Parliament invalid' (see [1968] 3 All ER *f* 561 at 573, [1969] 1 AC 645 at 723). Similarly if the other country is a foreign state which has never been British, I do not think that any English court would or could declare the Act ultra vires and void. No doubt the Act would normally be ignored by the foreign state and would not be enforced by it, but that would not invalidate the Act in this country. Those who infringed it could not claim that it was void if proceedings within the jurisdiction were taken against them. Legal validity is one thing, enforceability *g* is another. Thus a marriage in Nevada may constitute statutory bigamy punishable in England (*The Trial of Earl Russell* [1901] AC 446), just as acts in Germany may be punishable here as statutory treason (*Joyce v DPP* [1946] 1 All ER 186, [1946] AC 347). Parliament in fact legislates only for British subjects in this way; but if it also legislated for others, I do not see how the English courts could hold the statute void, however impossible it was to enforce it, and no matter how strong the diplomatic protests. *h*

I do not think that countries which were once colonies but have since been granted independence are in any different position. Plainly once statute has granted independence to a country, the repeal of the statute will not make the country dependent once more: what is done is done, and is not undone by revoking the authority to do it. Heligoland did not in 1953 again become British. But if Parliament then passes an Act applying to such a country, I cannot see why that Act should not be in the same position as an Act *j* applying to what has always been a foreign country, namely, an Act which the English courts will recognise and apply but one which the other country will in all probability ignore.

That brings me to a further point. *Buck v A-G* [1965] 1 All ER 882, [1965] Ch 745 makes it clear that in proceedings for declarations brought against the Attorney General of England the court has no jurisdiction to make declarations as to the validity of the

constitution of an independent sovereign state, in that case Sierra Leone. First, the court
a cannot give a declaratory judgment against a party who has no interest in the subject
matter of the declaration; and I cannot see what interest in the present action is vested in
the Attorney General of England, as distinct from the Attorney General of Canada or the
Attorneys General of the Provinces. Second, apart from any case where the question
arises merely incidentally, the courts of England cannot pronounce on whether a law of
an independent sovereign is valid within that state, for to do this would be to assert
b jurisdiction over that state.

For the reasons that I have given, I have come to the conclusion that the statement of
claim in the Manuel action discloses no reasonable cause of action, and that, despite the
persuasions of counsel for the Manuel plaintiffs, this is plain and obvious enough to
justify striking out the statement of claim. Counsel for the Manuel plaintiffs urged that
this is an important case (as indeed it is), and that it ought to be allowed to go to trial,
c where there could be a full argument, informed by all that had emerged during the
hearing of this motion. He also said that the case involved a serious investigation of
ancient law; yet he failed to indicate how that ancient law, when investigated, could alter
the conclusion that the court could not declare an Act of Parliament void. The question
is one of law, there has been a prolonged hearing before me, and I am left in no doubt
that the plaintiffs have disclosed no reasonable cause of action. In those circumstances the
d motion in the Manuel action succeeds and the statement of claim will be struck out. That
being so, I need not explore a number of the points that have been debated in argument.
Nor need I discuss the various dicta and the interesting comments on them that have
been put before me on matters such as Parliament's inability to bind itself: see *Ellen Street
Estates Ltd v Minister of Health* [1934] 1 KB 590 at 597, [1934] All ER Rep 385 at 390. In
particular I shall not refer to the extensive literature on the subject beyond mentioning
e the valuable article on 'The Basis of Legal Sovereignty' by H W R Wade ([1955] CLJ 172).

I must, however, say something about the well-known statement by Viscount Sankey
LC in *British Coal Corp v R* [1935] AC 500 at 520, [1935] All ER Rep 139 at 146. Speaking
for the Privy Council, he referred to the Statute of Westminster 1931 in relation to
Canada and said that 'Parliament could, as a matter of abstract law, repeal or disregard
s. 4 of the Statute. But that is theory and has no relation to realities.' What was said by
f Lord Denning MR in *Blackburn v A-G* [1971] 2 All ER 1380 at 1382, [1971] 1 WLR 1037
at 1040 must, I think, be read in the light of this passage, which he quoted. He referred
to the Statute of Westminster 1931 as taking away the power of Parliament to legislate
for the Dominions, and said:

> 'Can anyone imagine that Parliament could or would reverse that statute? Take
> the Acts which have granted independence to the dominions and territories overseas.
g > Can anyone imagine that Parliament could or would reverse those laws and take
> away their independence? Most clearly not. Freedom once given cannot be taken
> away.'

I think that it is clear from the context that Lord Denning MR was using the word 'could'
in the sense of 'could effectively'; I cannot read it as meaning 'could as a matter of abstract
h law'. Although it was not discussed in argument, I should observe that Parliament has
now in fact repealed s 4 of the Statute of Westminster 1931, and s 7(1) as well, so far as
they apply to Canada: see the Canada Act 1982, s 1, and the Constitution Act 1982, Sch,
item 17.

Perhaps I may add this. I have grave doubts about the theory of the transfer of
sovereignty as affecting the competence of Parliament. In my view, it is a fundamental
j of the English constitution that Parliament is supreme. As a matter of law the courts of
England recognise Parliament as being omnipotent in all save the power to destroy its
own omnipotence. Under the authority of Parliament the courts of a territory may be
released from their legal duty to obey Parliament, but that does not trench on the
acceptance by the English courts of all that Parliament does. Nor must validity in law be
confused with practical enforceability.

I now turn to the Noltcho action. The writ was issued on 14 January 1982 and the statement of claim was served on 18 February. Both the writ and the statement of claim include in the title a number of treaties made between the 'British Crown' (a term used *a* throughout in the sense of the Crown in right of the United Kingdom) and various Indian tribes, between 1871 and 1907. (The names of the 68 plaintiffs, I may say, are inconveniently set out in disregard of the practice statement in *Re Brickman's Settlement* [1982] 1 All ER 336 at 337–338, [1981] 1 WLR 1560 at 1562; but para 1 of the statement of claim removes the difficulty). The statement of claim alleges that in order to induce the Indians to execute the treaties, Indian Commissioners on behalf of the British Crown *b* made certain solemn oral promises to the Indians which became either terms of the treaties or else collateral warranties. These treaties and warranties were, it was promised, permanent in character and would enure to succeeding generations of Indians; and they would remain binding on the British Crown until they were assigned or abrogated with the consent of the Indians, an event which has never occurred. It is also alleged that in certain respects the treaties and warranties had made the British Crown a trustee or *c* fiduciary for the Indians. The British Crown had nevertheless wrongfully evinced an intention not to be bound by the treaties and warranties, on the footing that they had become the responsibility of the government of Canada by the time the Statute of Westminster 1931 was passed, at the latest.

I pause there to say that I have attempted to summarise in a few sentences seven paragraphs of a statement of claim which extends over ten pages, and I do not forget the *d* passages omitted from this summary. Nevertheless, I think I have said enough to make intelligible the relief claimed by the statement of claim. That relief consists of four declarations, and I shall read them as they stand after being informally modified during the argument. If the declarations were to be made, no doubt the words 'British Crown' would be replaced by 'Crown in right of the United Kingdom'; and I trust that the teratoid 'and/or' would be duly expelled. The four declarations are as follows: *e*

'(i) A Declaration that each of the Agreements contained in and/or evidenced by the Instruments particularised in the title to this Action and/or the collateral warranties thereto remain in full force and effect; and are binding upon the British Crown; and/or
(ii) A Declaration that the aforesaid Agreements and/or collateral warranties constitute trusts which remain in full force and effect; and are binding upon the *f* British Crown; and/or
(iii) A Declaration that each of the aforesaid Agreements and/or collateral warranties constitutes a subsisting Treaty properly so-called made with the British Crown; and/or
(iv) A Declaration that the British Crown is in wrongful repudiation of the said Agreements and/or collateral warranties.' *g*

I should add that the third declaration originally ended with the words 'which remains in full force and effect and binding upon the British Crown', though at a late stage counsel for the Noltcho plaintiffs agreed that he could not ask for this.

For the purposes of this motion, counsel for the Attorney General accepted that he had to argue his case on the footing that the allegations in the statement of claim were *h* established. His main submission was that, even so, the *Alberta* case [1982] 2 All ER 118, [1982] QB 892 was conclusive in his favour. Counsel for the Noltcho plaintiffs, on the other hand, contended that the *Alberta* case was obscure in its ratio and in any case fully distinguishable. It will therefore be necessary to examine that case with some care. The central issue is whether the *Alberta* case establishes that the obligations under the treaties, warranties and trusts in this case are obligations of the Crown in right of Canada and not *j* the Crown in right of the United Kingdom. If they are, then the plaintiffs, in suing the Attorney General of England, are suing the wrong defendant. A second issue is the status of the treaties. Counsel for the Attorney General accepted that for the purposes of this motion he had to accept that the so-called treaties were made in the form of treaties properly so called. He objected, however, that the court had no jurisdiction to declare

that a treaty was binding on the Crown, as was initially sought by the third declaration;
a and without such a declaration, he said, it would be a barren exercise to declare that the
treaties were in full force and effect, for to do so would afford the plaintiffs no 'relief',
and declarations will not be granted if they do not give relief. There was also at one stage
what seemed to be a separate contention that no declarations would be made because
they would be useless; but I think that in the end this became merged in the other
submissions. The main issue was plainly that of the ambit and ratio of the *Alberta* case.

b In the *Alberta* case the Indian Association of Alberta sought leave to apply for the
judicial review of a decision of the Secretary of State for Foreign and Commonwealth
Affairs that all treaty obligations entered into by the Crown with the Indian peoples of
Canada became the responsibility of the government of Canada with the attainment of
independence, and at the latest with the Statute of Westminster 1931. The plaintiffs
contended that this decision was wrong, and that the treaty obligations to the Indians of
c Canada were still owed to them by the Crown in right of the United Kingdom. Leave to
apply was refused at first instance, but was granted by the Court of Appeal. The
substantive application was then argued over some five days before, in reserved
judgments, the court dismissed the application. Though the court was unanimous in its
decision, it was far from unanimous in the grounds on which the decision was based;
and there was much discussion before me about the way in which the matter was put by
d each of the members of the court.

Lord Denning MR put matters on the basis of the treaties having been entered into by
the Crown when in law it was one and indivisible, and was the Crown of the United
Kingdom. Then in the first quarter of the nineteenth century this law was changed, not
by statute but by constitutional usage and practice, so that the Crown thereafter was
separate and divisible for each self-governing territory of the Commonwealth. Thereupon
e the existing obligations of the Crown became obligations of the Crown in respect of the
territories to which they related, binding on the Crown only in right of those territories
and no longer in right of the United Kingdom. This, I think, clearly emerges from the
report (see [1982] 2 All ER 118 at 125, 127, 128, [1982] QB 892 at 913, 915, 916, 917).
As was pointed out during the argument, there is nothing to explain just how
constitutional usage and practice changed the law, nor when the change was made, save
f that it was recognised by the Imperial Conference of 1926 (Cmd 2768).

Kerr LJ put matters in a very different way. The basis of his judgment is that as soon
as there is an established government in the territory in question, it is the Crown in right
of that government, and not the Crown in right of the United Kingdom, which has all
the rights and obligations in respect of that territory. It matters not whether that
government is dependent or independent or partly one and partly the other: all that
g matters is that there should be an established government, and in Canada this clearly had
happened by 1867. The question is that of the situs of the Crown's rights and obligations
and the existence of an established government. It is the creation of that government
which, without any express or statutory transfer, causes the rights and obligations of the
Crown in right of the United Kingdom to devolve on the Crown in right of that territory
(see in particular [1982] 2 All ER 118 at 132, 135, [1982] QB 892 at 923, 926, 927). For
h all treaties made since 1867 there was thus no question of any transfer of obligations
from the Crown in right of the United Kingdom to the Crown in right of Canada, for
they were all ab initio obligations of the Crown in right of Canada. For earlier treaties
and for the Royal Proclamation of 1763 there may or may not be some question of a
transfer, depending on the date when there could be said to be an established government
for the territory in question. Indeed, since it was the 1867 Act which provided for the
j union of certain Provinces to form the Dominion of Canada, there may, I think, have
been two transfers, one from the Crown in right of the United Kingdom to the Crown
in right of a Province and then another from the Province to the Dominion. But there
are deep waters here, and the judgment does not explore them.

The third judgment was delivered by May LJ. He reaches the conclusion that any
treaty or other obligation which the Crown had entered into with the Canadian Indians

'had become the responsibility of the government of Canada with the attainment of independence, at the latest with the Statute of Westminster 1931' (see [1982] 2 All ER *a*
118 at 140, [1982] QB 892 at 933). This, it will be observed, is phrased in terms of independence and not merely 'self-government' or 'established government'; and the words 'had become' suggest agreement with Lord Denning MR's view that obligations which had initially been obligations of the Crown in right of the United Kingdom had been transferred to the Crown in right of Canada, instead of being initially obligations of the Crown in right of Canada. I am not sure that this is what the Lord Justice meant, for *b*
previous passages are phrased in terms of self-government to a greater or lesser degree (see [1982] 2 All ER 118 at 136, 137, 139–140, [1982] QB 892 at 928, 929, 932) rather than independence. Further, a subsequent passage ([1982] 2 All ER 118 at 141–142, [1982] QB 892 at 935) states that the rights granted to Indians by the 'relevant treaty' (which seems to be a treaty of 1876: see [1982] 2 All ER 118 at 141, [1982] QB 892 at 934 and cf [1982] 2 All ER 118 at 126, 127, [1982] QB 892 at 914, 916) 'were granted to them *c*
by the Crown in right of Canada and not by the Crown in right of the United Kingdom', thereby pointing to an initial Canadian obligation rather than an initial United Kingdom obligation which was subsequently transferred to Canada. (I may mention that the reporters' footnotes (see [1982] 2 All ER 118 at 139, [1982] 2 WLR 641 at 665) are erroneous. The opinion of the Judicial Committee in *Hodge v The Queen* (1883) 9 App Cas 117 was delivered by Lord FitzGerald, as correctly stated in the text, and not by Sir Barnes *d*
Peacock, as wrongly stated in the footnote: see 9 App Cas v. Sets of law reports in which the errata have not been noted sometimes set traps for the unwary.)

During the argument it was not surprisingly suggested that on this point (a) there was a majority for Lord Denning MR's view, and that Kerr LJ was in a minority, and (b) that there was a majority for the view of Kerr LJ, and that Lord Denning MR was in a minority. A third contention was that May LJ was agreeing with Lord Denning MR in *e*
his general view but with Kerr LJ in his particular application. A variant is that May LJ took the view that the treaty obligations were those of Canada ab initio, but that if instead they were those of the United Kingdom government, they had been transferred to Canada, either with self-government or on independence. However that may be, it was plain that there was unanimity on the obligations in question being today those of the Crown in right of Canada and not in right of the United Kingdom. The divergence was *f*
merely on how that result was achieved.

Leave to appeal to the House of Lords was refused, and a further application to the Appeal Committee of the House of Lords for leave to appeal was also refused. On this occasion, rather unusually, five members of the Appeal Committee sat instead of three, and short reasons for the refusal of leave were given. Lord Diplock, who presided and who announced the decision of the committee, said ([1982] 2 All ER 118 at 143, [1982] *g*
QB 892 at 937) that the refusal of leave was based not on technical or procedural grounds but because in the opinion of their Lordships—

> 'for the accumulated reasons given in the judgment of the Court of Appeal, it simply is not arguable that any obligations of the Crown in respect of the Indian peoples of Canada are still the responsibility of Her Majesty's government in the United Kingdom. They are the responsibility of Her Majesty's government in *h*
> Canada, and it is the Canadian courts and not the English courts that alone have jurisdiction to determine what those obligations are.'

I say nothing about the word 'accumulated' save to draw attention both to its presence and to its eloquence.

It is this comprehensive and emphatic statement by the Appeal Committee, coupled *j*
with the decision of the Court of Appeal, which stands in the path of counsel for the Noltcho plaintiffs. His contention was that the *Alberta* case was distinguishable. In that case there had been no question of any agreements or warranties being given to the Indians that the Indian Commissioners were acting solely on behalf of the British Crown (in the sense of the Crown in right of the United Kingdom) and that the treaties and

warranties would remain binding on the British Crown until assigned or abrogated with
a the consent of the Indians. Furthermore, these engagements of the British Crown were
made after the British North America Act 1867 had been passed, and so were made by
the British Crown after a Canadian government could have entered into them, thereby
emphasising that they were engagements not of Canada but of the British Crown. This
latter point sufficed to distinguish *A-G v Great Southern and Western Rly Co of Ireland*
[1925] AC 754.

b   Counsel for the Noltcho plaintiffs also urged that it could not be said that the British
Crown was incapable of entering into obligations in Canada, for otherwise an agreement
by the British Crown with a Canadian landowner for the use of his land, for example, for
the training of British troops, could not be made. To this the answer of counsel for the
Attorney General was that it was not contended that the British Crown was incapable of
making ordinary contracts concerning Canadian land; the obligations in the present case
c were of a very different nature. In this I agree. Though counsel for the Attorney General
did not analyse the difference, and I shall not attempt to do so either, I can at least say that
the obligations in issue in the present case seem to me to relate to the government of
Canada, and to sovereignty there, in a way that ordinary contracts do not.

Counsel for the Noltcho plaintiffs emphasised that since the statement of claim alleged
that the engagements were engagements of the British Crown, no question arose of the
d engagements having been engagements ab initio of the Crown in right of Canada. The
case, he said, must therefore be dealt with on the basis that the engagements were
originally engagements of the Crown in right of the United Kingdom, so that the
question was whether, and how, they had been changed into engagements of the Crown
in right of Canada. In short, in the Noltcho case any Canadian liability today could not
be an original liability but could only be a transferred liability. He emphasised the
e difficulties in ascertaining the ratio of the *Alberta* case in the Court of Appeal, and not
least in determining how and when any transfer of obligation from the Crown in right
of the United Kingdom to the Crown in right of Canada took place. He also emphasised
the grounds on which he distinguished this case, and especially the promise that the
obligations would remain obligations of the Crown in right of the United Kingdom.

These contentions are forceful. Yet the words of Lord Diplock are singularly emphatic,
f and I cannot see why the suggested distinctions should make all the difference. The
Crown's promises were made by the Crown as sovereign. If sovereignty is transferred,
the obligation to do sovereign acts can no longer remain with the sovereign which no
longer has sovereignty over the territory where the acts are to be performed. No doubt
such cases will often be dealt with by statute, as had been done in *A-G v Great Southern
and Western Rly Co of Ireland* [1925] AC 754. In such cases argument, or at least the
g primary argument, is likely to be advanced on the construction and operation of the
statute, as it was there. But that does not show that nothing save statute will do. The
Alberta case shows that. Just how the doctrine works may seem to be obscure, but that is
no doubt due to our frail vision: what the *Alberta* case shows is that somehow it does
work, and work beyond a peradventure. I cannot read a promise that the treaty obligation
in this case should always bind the British Crown as preventing the British Crown from
h transferring or altering sovereignty, or as binding the British Crown to carry out
obligations when it no longer has the power to do so. If there are any trusts in the
ordinary equitable sense which bind the Crown (as distinct from 'trusts in the higher
sense': see *Tito v Waddell (No 2)* [1977] 3 All ER 129 at 220–221, [1977] Ch 106 at 216), I
do not see why the Crown, as trustee, should not, in the execution of the trusts, choose to
act on the advice of Canadian ministers instead of United Kingdom ministers.

j   In the result, my conclusion is that the *Alberta* case is decisive of the present case,
despite the suggested distinctions, and that the language of emphasis of the Appeal
Committee in that case requires me to strike out the statement of claim in the Noltcho
action, or at the very least justifies me in doing so; and this I do. I do not think that I
need explore the status of the treaties and consider whether or not they were treaties
properly so called. In the *Alberta* case [1982] 2 All ER 118 at 131, [1982] QB 892 at 921,

Kerr LJ said that they were not; and although, of course, this may very well be right, it
was obiter and stands on its own. In any case, as I have said, counsel for the Attorney
General had to accept that for the purposes of this motion he must regard them as
treaties, while for his part counsel for the Noltcho plaintiffs had to accept that he could
not claim a declaration that the treaties were binding on the Crown in right of the United
Kingdom, or that the Crown had wrongfully repudiated the treaties. I decide nothing
about them or about the further point whether a declaration that the treaties are
subsisting treaties properly so called made with the British Crown should be made,
without more, or whether such a declaration would be refused as not amounting to the
grant of any 'relief'. I simply strike out the statement of claim, for the reasons which I
have given.

Order accordingly.

Solicitors: *Herbert Oppenheimer, Nathan & Vandyk* (for the Manuel plaintiffs); *Bindman &
Partners* (for the Noltcho plaintiffs); *Treasury Solicitor.*

Azza M Abdallah   Barrister.

Practice Direction

COURT OF APPEAL

*Judicial review – Appeal – Appeal by leave of Court of Appeal – Hearing of substantive
application – Substantive application normally to be made to Divisional Court.*

A refusal in a non-criminal cause or matter by a Divisional Court of the Queen's Bench
Division or by a single judge to grant leave to apply for judicial review is appealable to
the Court of Appeal. Heretofore the practice has been for the Court of Appeal to hear the
substantive application if it grants leave (*R v Industrial Injuries Comr, ex p Amalgamated
Engineering Union* [1966] 1 All ER 97, [1966] 2 QB 21).
    There were, at the time of its introduction, good reasons for the practice. Those reasons
no longer exist, except in the rare case where the reason for the refusal was that the court
was bound by a previous decision of the Divisional Court or a single judge.
    In future if, following a refusal by the Divisional Court or a single judge, the Court of
Appeal grants leave to apply for judicial review, the substantive application should be
made to the Divisional Court unless the Court of Appeal otherwise orders. The Court of
Appeal will not normally so order unless the court below is bound by authority or for
some other reason an appeal to the Court of Appeal is inevitable.

LANE CJ
2 November 1982   DONALDSON MR

a
Elias v George Sahely & Co (Barbados) Ltd

PRIVY COUNCIL

LORD SCARMAN, LORD SIMON OF GLAISDALE, LORD EDMUND-DAVIES, LORD BRIDGE OF HARWICH
AND LORD BRANDON OF OAKBROOK

17, 18 MAY, 28 JULY 1982

b
*Sale of land – Memorandum of contract – Two documents – Oral agreement for sale of land –
Letter from purchaser's lawyer containing terms of contract and enclosing deposit – Vendor's
lawyer giving receipt for deposit – Receipt containing neither contractual terms nor reference to
letter – Parol evidence admitted to explain transaction referred to in receipt and to identify letter
as relating to transaction – Whether parol evidence rightly admitted – Whether letter and receipt
c together constituting sufficient note or memorandum evidencing oral contract – Statute of Frauds
1762 (Barbados), s 2.*

*Sale of land – Memorandum of contract – Signature of party to be charged – Vendor's lawyer
giving receipt for deposit received – Vendor's lawyer receiving deposit as stakeholder – Whether
stakeholder having authority to sign memorandum on behalf of vendor.*

d
On 10 February 1975 the vendor agreed in a telephone conversation to sell certain
premises in Barbados to the purchaser at an agreed price. On the same day the purchaser's
lawyer wrote to the vendor's lawyer confirming the contract and enclosing a cheque as
deposit, stating that the deposit was 'to be held by you as stakeholder pending completion
of the contract for sale'. The vendor's lawyer replied by sending a receipt for the money
but did not acknowledge the letter. When the vendor failed to complete the contract,
e the purchaser brought an action in the Barbados High Court for specific performance.
At the trial of the action the judge found that there was an oral contract for the sale of
land between the parties and that the letter and the receipt when read together were a
sufficient note or memorandum in writing under s 2[a] of the Barbados Statute of Frauds
1762. The judge accordingly ordered specific performance of the contract. The Barbados
f Court of Appeal allowed an appeal by the vendor on the ground that, although there was
an oral 'consensus' as to the terms under which the land was being sold, no contract of
sale had been completed because there could be no binding or enforceable contract in the
absence of writing. The court further held that there was no memorandum in writing
signed on behalf of the person to be charged (the vendor) and that the two documents
(the letter and the receipt) did not constitute a sufficient memorandum. The purchaser
appealed to the Privy Council. On the appeal the issues arose whether the purchaser had
g established the existence of an oral contract of sale and whether such a contract, if it
existed, was evidenced by a note or memorandum in writing signed on behalf of the
vendor. The vendor contended (i) that it was inadmissible to read the two documents
together because the receipt did not expressly or by necessary implication refer to another
transaction or document, (ii) that the vendor's lawyer had no authority to sign a note or
memorandum of contract because he had received the money for the vendor as a
h stakeholder and not as agent and (iii) that the letter written by the purchaser's lawyer
referred only to an agreement which was subject to contract.

Held – The appeal would be allowed, and a decree of specific performance made, for the
following reasons—

(1) An oral contract for the sale of land which was not evidenced by writing or partly
j performed was not void but merely unenforceable. Accordingly, the parties had

---

a   Section 2, so far as material, provides: 'No action shall be brought whereby to charge the defendant
. . . upon any contract or sale of land . . . unless . . . some memorandum or note thereof shall be in
writing, and signed by the party to be charged therewith, or some other person thereunto by him
lawfully authorised.'

concluded a contract for sale since there was, on the facts, an oral contract concluded by
the telephone conversation in which the terms of sale were agreed and there was nothing   *a*
further to negotiate or agree on. Furthermore, the letter from the purchaser's lawyer
could not be read as indicating that there was to be no binding contract prior to a formal
contract being drawn up and signed (see p 804 *b c*, p 805 *g* to *j* and p 807 *g j*, post);
Steadman and Steadman [1974] 2 All ER 977 followed.

(2) On the issue of the enforceability or otherwise of the contract made between the
parties, if a document signed by the party to be charged referred to some other document   *b*
or transaction then parol evidence was admissible both to explain the reference and to
identify any other document relating to the transaction, and if such other document and
the document signed by the party to be charged when read together contained all the
terms of a concluded contract then there was a sufficient note or memorandum for the
purposes of the Statute of Frauds. Accordingly, the judge at first instance had been right
to admit the oral evidence of the purchaser's lawyer to explain the transaction to which   *c*
the receipt from the vendor's lawyer referred and to identify his own letter as a document
relating to the transaction. Since that letter set out the terms of a concluded bargain
between the parties, the receipt and the letter together constituted a sufficient
memorandum of sale for the purposes of the Statute of Frauds (see p 807 *b* to *j*, post);
dictum of Jenkins LJ in *Timmins v Moreland Street Property Co Ltd* [1957] 3 All ER at 276
applied.   *d*

(3) It did not follow from the fact that a person accepted a deposit as a stakeholder that
he was not authorised to sign as agent a note or memorandum evidencing the existence
of a contract. On the facts, the vendor's lawyer had authority to sign a note or
memorandum of the sale on behalf of the vendor and was therefore not prevented from
doing so because he happened to receive the deposit as a stakeholder (see p 805 *b* to *f* and
p 807 *j*, post).   *e*

Notes

For the necessity for a memorandum in writing in contracts for the sale of land, see 34
Halsbury's Laws (3rd edn) 207–210, paras 346–348, and for cases on the subject, see 40
Digest (Repl) 21–38, 82–205.

Section 2 of the Barbados Statute of Frauds 1762 corresponds to s 40(1) of the Law of
Property Act 1925. For s 40 of the 1925 Act, see 27 Halsbury's Statutes (3rd edn) 399.   *f*

Cases referred to in judgment

Dobell v Hutchinson (1835) 3 Ad & El 355, [1835–42] All ER Rep 238, 111 ER 448, 12
Digest (Reissue) 173, *1025*.

Long v Millar (1879) 4 CPD 450, [1874–80] All ER Rep 556, CA, 12 Digest (Reissue) 177,
1056.   *g*

Maloney v Hardy and Moorshead [1970] CA Transcript 85.

Peirce v Corf (1874) LR 9 QB 210, 12 Digest (Reissue) 174, *1031*.

Sorrell v Finch [1976] 3 All ER 371, [1977] AC 728, [1976] 2 WLR 833, HL, Digest (Cont
Vol E) 534, *2074ad*.

Steadman v Steadman [1974] 2 All ER 977, [1976] AC 536, [1974] 3 WLR 56, HL, Digest
(Cont Vol D) 794, *81a*.   *h*

Stokes v Whicher [1920] 1 Ch 411, [1920] All ER Rep 771, 12 Digest (Reissue) 178, *1067*.

Timmins v Moreland Street Property Co Ltd [1957] 3 All ER 265, [1958] Ch 110, [1957] 3
WLR 678, CA, 12 Digest (Reissue) 179, *1068*.

Winn v Bull (1877) 7 Ch D 29, 12 Digest (Reissue) 107, *571*.

Appeal

Fauzi Elias appealed to the Judicial Committe of the Privy Council, pursuant to leave   *j*
granted by the Board on 15 October 1981, against the decision of the Court of Appeal of
Barbados (Williams ACJ, Husbands and Worrell JJ) on 31 March 1981 allowing the appeal
of the respondent, George Sahely & Co (Barbados) Ltd, against the decision of Douglas CJ
on 23 July 1979 whereby he granted the appellant an order against the respondent for
specific performance of a contract for the sale of land. The facts are set out in the
judgment.

Gavin Lightman QC and *David Simmons* (of the Barbados Bar) for the appellant.

a   *George Newman QC, Fenton Ramsahaye SC* (of the Barbados Bar) and *Mark Strachan* for the respondent.

LORD SCARMAN. This is an appeal from the Court of Appeal of Barbados. The appellant, Fauzi Elias, asserts that he entered into a binding and enforceable oral contract for the sale of land. His case is that he concluded it on 10 February 1975 in a telephone

b   conversation with Mrs Gloria Redman, a director of the respondent company, George Sahely & Co (Barbados) Ltd. He claims, as purchaser, specific performance of the contract and ancillary relief, including damages. There is now no issue as to damages. The only question for their Lordships' consideration is whether he was entitled to specific performance. If he was, the parties are agreed as to the relief to be granted; and counsel have helpfully indicated in a draft of a possible order the terms which they accept as

c   appropriate in the event of the appeal being allowed.

The case was tried at first instance by Douglas CJ. He found as a fact that there was concluded between the parties an oral contract for the sale of land. He held that two documents, to which it will be necessary to refer in detail, were, when read together, a sufficient note or memorandum in writing signed on behalf of the person to be charged within the meaning of s 2 of the Statute of Frauds 1762 (Barbados). Accordingly, he

d   ordered specific performance of the contract.

The respondent appealed. Allowing the appeal, the Court of Appeal accepted the finding of an oral 'consensus' (their word) as to the terms under which the land was being sold. Nevertheless they held that no contract of sale had been completed, and expressed the opinion that there could be no binding contract in the absence of writing. They further held that there was no memorandum in writing signed on behalf of the person

e   to be charged; and, specifically, that the two documents on which the Chief Justice based his judgment did not constitute a sufficient memorandum.

There are two issues outstanding in the appeal. The first is whether the appellant has established the existence of an oral contract of sale. The second is whether such contract, assuming it exists, is evidenced by a note or memorandum in writing signed on behalf of the respondent. The appellant did seek leave to raise before their Lordships a point not

f   adumbrated in his pleading or raised in either of the courts below. Based on *Steadman v Steadman* [1974] 2 All ER 977, [1976] AC 536, it was to the effect that in the circumstances of this case payment of money under the contract constituted a sufficient part performance to entitle the appellant in equity to the relief he claims. Their Lordships refused leave. The Board's practice is well known: save in very exceptional circumstances, points not raised below will not be entertained.

g   The first issue is a question on which in their Lordships' view there are concurrent findings of the decisive facts. The Chief Justice found that on 10 February 1975 the appellant agreed with Mrs Gloria Redman, a director of the respondent company, to buy 19 Swan Street, Bridgetown for the price which she told him she and her sister, also a director, had decided to sell, namely $390,000. The appellant, as tenant of the Sahely family and their company, had carried on the business of 'Everybody's Store' at the

h   premises since July 1960. The sale was to include fixtures and fittings. The Chief Justice had no doubt that the parties there and then concluded a contract of sale. They knew perfectly well from their long association with the premises as landlord and tenant what were the fixtures and fittings, and there was no difficulty in an open contract on the usual terms prevailing in Barbados. Nothing, he found, was left to further negotiation or agreement. The Court of Appeal also found that the parties 'had reached consensus' and

j   that there was 'an oral understanding between the parties as to the terms under which the premises were being sold'. In the view, therefore, of both courts the parties had reached agreement.

The Court of Appeal, however, was not prepared to hold that the existence of a 'consensus' constituted a contract. It gave two reasons. First, it held that in the absence of writing there could be no binding or enforceable contract of sale. This was an error of law. If there is no note or memorandum, a contract may be unenforceable, but it is not

void: see *Steadman v Steadman* [1974] 2 All ER 977 at 981, 996, [1976] AC 536 at 540,
558 per Lord Reid and Lord Simon. And, in the absence of any writing, it will be   *a*
enforceable if there be a sufficient part performance. Second, it held the consensus or
understanding to be 'subject to contract', ie not intended to be binding until incorporated
into a written contract of sale. This view arose from its construction of a letter of 10
February 1975 written by Mr Forde, the appellant's lawyer, confirming the contract. It
will be necessary later to consider the detailed terms of the letter, as it is one of the two
documents on which the appellant relies as constituting a sufficient memorandum in   *b*
writing of the contract. Suffice it to say at this stage that the Chief Justice did not so
construe the letter; and, for reasons which will appear later, their Lordships agree with
him. The appellant, therefore, succeeds on the first issue. He has established the existence
of an oral contract of sale concluded on 10 February 1975.

The second issue is more difficult. The memorandum in writing of the contract on
which the appellant seeks to rely consists of two documents, the letter written by his   *c*
lawyer on 10 February 1975 and a receipt given the same day by the respondent's lawyers
for the deposit paid pursuant to the agreement for sale. The circumstances in which these
documents came into existence were as follows. After his conversation with Mrs Redman
the appellant was telephoned by the respondent's lawyer, Mr Turney. Nothing was said
by Mr Turney to raise any doubt in the appellant's mind that he had concluded a contract
with Mrs Redman; on the contrary Mr Turney appeared to accept that this was so and   *d*
asked him to send him a cheque for $39,000. The appellant made arrangements for a
loan from his bank and then went to see his own lawyer, Mr Forde, taking with him the
bank manager's cheque for $39,000. Mr Forde then wrote to Mr Turney as follows:

'Dear Sirs,
    Re: Purchase of freehold premises known as Everybody's Store at Swan Street,
Bridgetown from your client, Sahely & Co. Ltd. by Fauzi Elias (trading as   *e*
Everybody's Store) or his nominees.
    Further to our conversation of this morning, I now enclose a cheque for
$39,000·00 drawn on Canadian Imperial Bank of Commerce by Fauzi Elias trading
as Everybody's Store and payable to you as stakeholder in respect of the sale and
purchase of the freehold premises, fixtures and fittings known as Everybody's Store.
It is understood that the purchase price is $390,000·00 of which the sum of   *f*
$39,000·00 is paid as a deposit to be held by you as stakeholder pending completion
of the contract for sale. As I have discussed over the telephone the usual terms will
apply.
    I should be pleased if you would forward the Agreement for Sale to be signed by
my client and if the contract will be between your client and Fauzi Elias (trading as
Everybody's Store) or his nominees.   *g*
    Please acknowledge receipt of this letter and let me have your receipt for
$39,000·00.'

Mr Turney received the letter, but did not acknowledge it. He did, however, send his
firm's receipt for the money. It was in these terms:

'BARBADOS 10-2-1975   *h*
    RECEIVED from Fauzi Elias the sum of Thirty nine thousand Dollars and . . . Cents
being deposit on Property at Swan Street B'town agreed to be sold by George Sahely
& Co. B'dos Ltd. to Fauzi Elias and/or his nominees.

                                                    R. G. MANDEVILLE & CO.
                                                    Per E. Clarke.'   *j*

The appellant's case is that, read together, the letter and the receipt constitute a note or
memorandum in writing of the contract signed on behalf of the person to be charged.
The respondent's case is that it is inadmissible to read the two documents together
because the receipt, on its proper construction, does not expressly or by necessary
implication refer to another written transaction or document.

Before dealing with this, the basic point in the appeal, it will be convenient to dispose
a of two further submissions by the respondent on the two documents. First, it is said that
the respondent's lawyer, Mr Turney (or his firm), had no authority to sign a memorandum
of contract: the 'agency point'. Second, it is said that the letter of 10 February 1975 on its
proper construction refers only to an agreement 'subject to contract': the 'point of
construction'.

First, the agency point. The Chief Justice found, or, perhaps more accurately, assumed,
b that Mr Turney had authority to sign. It is doubtful whether at first instance the
respondent was contending otherwise; and the point, if raised at all in the pleadings, was
certainly not raised with the clarity necessary to prevent the other party from being taken
by surprise. But, be that as it may, the Chief Justice was fully justified in his finding (or
assumption). Neither Mrs Redman not her sister, who were the two directors of the
respondent company concerned, gave evidence, though they were available. Mr Turney
c did; but the Chief Justice preferred the evidence of Mr Forde, accepting it on all points of
conflict.

The Court of Appeal, however, added a new twist to the agency point. Because Mr
Turney received the deposit not as agent for the vendor but as stakeholder, it inferred
that he (or his firm) could not be said to have signed the receipt as 'the vendor's agent for
the purpose of the Statute of Frauds'. Its inference was based on a logical fallacy. It does
d not follow that because a person accepts a deposit as stakeholder he is not authorised to
sign a note or memorandum evidencing the existence of a contract. Indeed, as the Court
of Appeal recognised, quoting some words of Lord Edmund-Davies in an unreported
case (*Maloney v Hardy and Moorshead* [1970] CA Transcript 85) to which he referred in
Sorrel v Finch [1976] 2 All ER 371 at 376, [1977] AC 728 at 745, 'The essence of
stakeholding in vendor and purchaser cases is that a *binding* contract of sale has been
e entered into . . .' It is possible that the Court of Appeal was led into its fallacy by its
erroneous view that there can be no binding contract for the sale of land in the absence
of writing. Be that as it may, their Lordships accept the Chief Justice's finding that Mr
Turney's firm had authority to sign a note or memorandum of the sale. It was a reasonable
inference in the circumstances.

Next, the construction point. This point impressed the Court of Appeal, but not the
f Chief Justice, who rejected it. In his letter Mr Forde stipulated that the deposit was to be
held 'pending completion of the contract for sale' and requested that there be forwarded
to him an agreement for sale to be signed by his client. The Chief Justice, noting that the
words 'subject to contract' do not appear in the letter, refused to construe its terms as
revealing that the parties did not intend to be bound until a formal contract was brought
into existence. He relied on a passage in the judgment of Jessel MR in *Winn v Bull* (1877)
g 7 Ch D 29 at 32 where the Master of the Rolls said:

'When it is not expressly stated to be subject to a formal contract it becomes a
question of construction, whether the parties intended that the terms agreed on
should merely be put into form, or whether they should be subject to a new
agreement the terms of which are not expressed in detail.'

h Applying this test, he expressed himself as satisfied that the agreement reached was not
'subject to contract'.

Their Lordships have no doubt that on the findings of fact reached by the Chief Justice
and accepted by the Court of Appeal it is not possible to read Mr Forde's letter as
indicating that there was no binding agreement prior to a formal contract drawn up and
signed. Accordingly, they reject the respondent's point on the construction of the letter
j and accept the Chief Justice's view that the letter sets out the terms of a concluded bargain
between the parties.

The critical question is, therefore, whether it is admissible to read the letter and the
receipt together. If they are so read, they constitute a sufficient memorandum provided,
of course, that the respondent's points on agency and construction are rejected. The
respondent's counsel submits that it is not permissible to place the two documents side

by side and so to construct a memorandum of the terms of the contract. He makes two points: first, that the receipt neither expressly nor by necessary implication refers to the letter; and, second, that to constitute a sufficient memorandum the receipt must refer either to a written transaction or to a document which by acceptance becomes an integral part of the transaction.

The first stage in the respondent's argument is that the receipt itself does not contain the terms of the contract. It can be relied on only if it refers expressly or by necessary implication to another document which was, or to a transaction which is itself, in writing. The words of reference are 'deposit on Property at Swan Street B'town agreed to be sold'. This is a reference, counsel submits, not to Mr Forde's letter but to the oral agreement. And, even if it could be read with the aid of parol evidence as referring to the letter, parol evidence for that purpose is inadmissible: the reference to a written transaction or document must arise by necessary implication, if not expressly, from the terms of the receipt itself, and the receipt does not identify Mr Forde's letter as the document to which it refers.

To accept this submission would, in their Lordships' view, be to take the law back to what it was in the middle of the nineteenth century when *Peirce v Corf* (1874) LR 9 QB 210 was decided.

Counsel's submission is, in essence, a repetition of the principle laid down by Lord Denman CJ in *Dobell v Hutchinson* (1835) 3 Ad & El 355 at 371, [1835–42] All ER Rep 238 at 243 and followed in *Peirce v Corf* (at 217) where Quain J put it in one sentence:

> 'Therefore on the document itself there must be some reference from the one to the other, leaving nothing to be supplied by parol evidence . . .'

Counsel correctly observes that it is not possible to link the receipt with Mr Forde's letter in the absence of parol evidence. If, therefore, the principle stated in *Peirce v Corf* remains good law, the submission succeeds.

The law has, however, developed since *Peirce v Corf*. The watershed decision is *Long v Millar* (1879) 4 CPD 450, [1874–80] All ER Rep 556. The plaintiff signed a document whereby he agreed to purchase three plots of land for £310 and to pay as a deposit and in part payment of the price the sum of £31. The defendant signed a receipt for the £31 as a deposit on the purchase of the three plots of land. The Court of Appeal allowed parol evidence to be given linking the agreement signed by the plaintiff with the receipt signed by the defendant. The linking word in the receipt was 'purchase', and oral evidence was allowed to identify the written document or transaction to which it referred. In *Long v Millar*, once the identification was made and the two documents placed side by side, there was an agreement of sale in writing, and not merely, as in the present case, a memorandum in writing of an oral contract. Counsel submits that this is the distinguishing feature of *Long v Millar*; but neither the language of the judges in that case nor the subsequent case law treats as important the distinction which counsel seeks to draw.

In *Long v Millar* both Bramwell and Baggallay LJJ stated the principle broadly, the latter saying that 'The true principle is that there must exist a writing to which the document signed by the party to be charged *can* refer, but that this writing may be identified by verbal evidence' (4 CPD 450 at 455; my emphasis). And Thesiger LJ found the explanation for the rule as being a particular application of the doctrine as to latent ambiguity (4 CPD 450 at 456, [1874–80] All ER Rep 556 at 559). He added that to enable parol evidence to be given it must be clear that the words of the signed document will extend to the document sought to be identified.

The next case of importance was the decision of Russell J in *Stokes v Whicher* [1920] 1 Ch 411, [1920] All ER Rep 771. Counsel argued in that case that, even if you do not get any reference, inferential or otherwise, in the signed document to the document which contains the terms of the parties' oral contract, the authorities show that, if by placing the two documents side by side they can be seen to be part and parcel of one transaction, they can be read together. Russell J refused to hold that the law had gone so far. He analysed *Long v Millar* as deciding that—

'if you can spell out of the document a reference in it to some other transaction,
a   you are at liberty to give evidence as to what that other transaction is, and, if that
other transaction contains all the terms in writing, then you get a sufficient
memorandum within the statute by reading the two together.'

(See [1920] 1 Ch 411 at 418, [1920] All ER Rep 771 at 774.)

In *Timmins v Moreland Street Property Co Ltd* [1957] 3 All ER 265, [1958] Ch 110 the
Court of Appeal accepted Russell J's view of *Long v Millar*, but took the law a step further.
b Jenkins LJ, with whose judgment Romer and Sellers LJJ agreed, said ([1957] 3 All ER
265 at 276, [1958] Ch 110 at 130):

'... it is still indispensably necessary, in order to justify the reading of documents
together for this purpose, that there should be a document signed by the party to be
charged which, while not containing in itself all the necessary ingredients of the
required memorandum, does contain some reference, express or implied, to some
c   other document or transaction. Where any such reference can be spelt out of a
document so signed, then parol evidence may be given to identify the other
document referred to, or, as the case may be, to explain the other transaction, and to
identify any document relating to it. If by this process a document is brought to
light which contains in writing all the terms of the bargain so far as not contained
in the document signed by the party to be charged, then the two documents can be
d   read together ...'

Their Lordships accept this passage as a correct statement of the modern law. The first
inquiry must, therefore, be whether the document signed by or on behalf of the person
to be charged on the contract contains some reference to some other document or
transaction. The receipt in this case clearly did refer to some other transaction, namely
an agreement to sell the property in Swan Street. Parol evidence can, therefore, be given
e to explain the transaction, and to identify any document relating to it. Such evidence
was led in the present case: it brought to light a document, namely Mr Forde's letter of
10 February 1975, which does contain in writing all the terms of the bargain. It is a
writing which evidences the transaction, though not itself the transaction. This distinction
is, however, not material, whether the rule be as formulated in *Long v Millar* or as in
f *Timmins v Moreland Street Property Co Ltd*. Moreover, it would be contrary to the
intendment of the Statute of Frauds to limit the rule to cases in which the reference in
the signed document must be to a writing intended to have contractual force. The Statute
of Frauds is concerned to suppress not evidence but fraud. In seeking a sufficient
memorandum it is not necessary to shoulder the further burden of searching for a
written contract. Evidence in writing is what the statute requires. For, as *Steadman v
g* *Steadman* [1974] 2 All ER 977, [1976] AC 536 emphasised, an oral contract for the sale of
land is not void but only, in the absence of evidence in writing or part performance,
unenforceable. If, therefore, a document signed by the party to be charged refers to a
transaction of sale, parol evidence is admissible both to explain the reference and to
identify any document relating to it. Once identified, the document may be placed
alongside the signed document. If the two contain all the terms of a concluded contract,
h the statute is satisfied.

Accordingly, their Lordships are of the opinion that the Chief Justice was right to
admit the oral evidence of Mr Forde to explain the transaction to which the receipt
referred and to identify as a document relating to it his letter of 10 February 1975. Their
Lordships also agree with the Chief Justice that the letter contained all the terms of a
concluded contract of sale of land.

j Their Lordships will therefore humbly advise Her Majesty that the appeal should be
allowed with costs to the appellant in the High Court and the Court of Appeal and a
decree of specific performance made (provided that a good title can be made to the
property). The respondent must also pay the costs of this appeal. Their Lordships will
further advise that the case be remitted to the Court of Appeal for appropriate directions
to be given to the High Court so that the court may make such orders or give such
directions as may be necessary in the absence of agreement between the parties to provide

for (1) an inquiry whether a good title can be made to the property, (2) computation of interest at the appropriate rate on the sum of $351,000 being the balance of the purchase price from 10 May 1975, (3) certification of the amount due to the respondent being the balance of the purchase price plus interest but less the amount of rent paid and the taxed costs of these proceedings in the High Court, the Court of Appeal and before this Board and (4) completion of the transaction within a reasonable time.

Appeal allowed.

Solicitors: *Osmond, Gaunt & Rose* (for the appellants); *Ingledew, Brown, Bennison & Garrett* (for the respondents).

Evelyn M C Budd   Barrister.

Leedale (Inspector of Taxes) v Lewis

HOUSE OF LORDS

LORD FRASER OF TULLYBELTON, LORD WILBERFORCE, LORD SCARMAN, LORD ROSKILL AND LORD BRANDON OF OAKBROOK

19, 20, 21, 22 JULY, 14 OCTOBER 1982

Capital gains tax – Settlement – Interest in settled property – Gains accruing to non-resident trustee – Apportionment of gains to beneficiaries – Beneficiaries resident in United Kingdom – Trustee having power to pay income and appoint capital to beneficiaries – Beneficiaries equally entitled to capital contingently on being alive at end of perpetuity period specified in settlement – Whether beneficiaries having 'interests in the settled property' – Whether apportionment of gains to beneficiaries 'just and reasonable' – Finance Act 1965, s 42(2).

On 16 March 1968 the settlor, who was domiciled and resident in the United Kingdom, settled property on discretionary trusts in respect of income and capital, with power to the trustee to accumulate income, for the benefit of such of the settlor's grandchildren, their spouses and their issue as the trustee might appoint. In default of appointment; there was an ultimate trust, arising at the expiry of a defined perpetuity period, for the grandchildren, their spouses or issue then living and, subject thereto, for the settlor's son and daughter absolutely. A non-resident trustee was appointed. On 18 March 1968 a letter of intent, having no binding effect, was addressed to the trustee in which the settlor made it plain that she wished the settlement to be regarded as primarily for the benefit of her grandchildren and that income should be accumulated at least until they reached the age of 21. At all material times the living beneficiaries of the discretionary trusts were the settlor's five minor grandchildren, and no payment of income or capital had been made by the trustee to any of them. The settlor's five grandchildren were assessed to capital gains tax on capital gains that had accrued to the trustee in the years 1968–69 and 1969–70 on the basis that under s 42(2)[a] of the Finance Act 1965 those gains were apportionable among the settlor's grandchildren equally. The taxpayer, who was the guardian of three of the grandchildren, appealed to the Special Commissioners. The commissioners held that the possibility of participation in any distribution of the unappointed residue was so remote and of so little value, if any, that it ought to be ignored, and that the rights of the grandchildren as objects of the trustee's discretionary power did not amount to 'interests' in the settled fund. The commissioners accordingly

---

a   Section 42(2), so far as material, is set out at p 810 *j* to p 811 *b*, post

allowed the taxpayer's appeal. The judge allowed an appeal by the Crown, holding that,
a although the rights of the grandchildren as mere objects of a discretionary trust or power
of appointment did not amount to an interest in the settled property within s 42(2), the
just and reasonable apportionment of the gain under that section among the grandchildren
as persons likely to take income or capital under the settlement was mandatory, and that
the words 'just and reasonable' governed the selection of the persons among whom the
apportionment was to be made, taking into account their prospects under the settlement.
b The Court of Appeal dismissed an appeal by the taxpayer, holding that the grandchildren
in their capacity as discretionary objects did have interests in respect of which
apportionment could be made. The taxpayer appealed to the House of Lords.

Held – (1) The words 'Any beneficiary' in the first part of s 42(2) of the 1965 Act and
'persons having interests in the settled property' in the second part of that subsection
c included persons who were objects of a discretionary trust or power and the amount to
be apportioned between them was the whole amount of the gains on which the trustee
would have been chargeable had he been resident in the United Kingdom; and the word
'interests' in s 42(2) was to be given a wide rather than a narrow technical meaning since
the section applied not only to English settlements but to settlements governed by other
systems of law (see p 812 *g* to p 813 *b* and *g* to *j*, p 815 *b* to *e* and *j*, p 816 *f g*, p 817 *d*,
d p 818 *h j*, p 820 *d g h* and p 821 *d* and *h j*, post); dictum of Lord Reid in *Gartside v IRC*
[1968] 1 All ER at 125 applied.
(2) An apportionment under s 42(2) was not a strict apportionment by reference to
the actuarial or market values of the interests of the beneficiaries under the settlement,
but a much broader apportionment by reference to what was just and reasonable in view
of the real probabilities under the settlement taking into account all the relevant
e considerations, including how the trust fund was likely to be applied (see p 814 *b* to *f*,
p 815 *j*, p 816 *g* to *j*, p 817 *d*, p 818 *h j*, p 819 *j* to p 820 *e* and p 821 *d* and *h j*, post);
Gartside v IRC [1968] 1 All ER 121 distinguished.
(3) In the circumstances, and taking into account the settlor's letter of intent, the
apportionment of the gain equally among the settlor's grandchildren was just and
reasonable and the taxpayer was liable to capital gains tax on the gains apportioned to his
f three children. The appeal would therefore be dismissed (see p 815 *g* to *j*, p 816 *g* to *j*,
p 817 *c d* and p 821 *c d* and *g h*, post).
Per curiam. If fiscal legislation, on its true construction, has the consequences for
which the Crown contends, 'hardship' alleged to be suffered by a taxpayer cannot be a
legitimate ground for giving that legislation some other (ex hypothesi wrong) construction
(see p 814 *a b*, p 816 *j* to p 817 *b*, p 819 *h j*, p 820 *j* and p 821 *d e* and *h j*, post).
g Decision of the Court of Appeal [1982] 2 All ER 644 affirmed.

Notes
For the liability of beneficiaries resident in the United Kingdom to capital gains tax on
gains accruing to non-resident trustees, see 5 Halsbury's Laws (4th edn) para 113.
For the Finance Act 1965, s 42, see 34 Halsbury's Statutes (3rd edn) 912.
h With effect from 6 April 1979, s 42 of the 1965 Act was replaced by s 17 of the Capital
Gains Tax Act 1979, which in turn was replaced by s 80 of the Finance Act 1981.

Cases referred to in opinions
A-G v Farrell [1931] 1 KB 81, CA.
A-G v Heywood (1887) 19 QBD 326, DC.
j *Archer-Shee v Garland* [1931] AC 212, HL, 28(1) Digest (Reissue) 302, *1040*.
Gartside v IRC [1968] 1 All ER 121, [1968] AC 553, [1968] 2 WLR 277, HL, 26 Digest
(Reissue) 17, *66*.
IRC v Clark's Trustees 1939 SC 11, 26 Digest (Reissue) 30, *118*.
Latham (decd), Re, IRC v Barclays Bank Ltd [1961] 3 All ER 903, [1962] Ch 616, [1961] 3
WLR 1154, 26 Digest (Reissue) 44, *189*.

Roome v Edwards (Inspector of Taxes) [1981] 1 All ER 736, [1982] AC 279, [1981] 2 WLR
268, HL.   *a*

Appeal
Thomas Rosling Haselden Lewis (the taxpayer) appealed against the decision of the Court
of Appeal (Lawton, Brightman and Fox LJJ) ([1982] 2 All ER 644) dated 16 December
1981 dismissing the taxpayer's appeal against the order of Dillon J ([1980] STC 679) made
on 8 July 1980 reversing a decision of the Commissioners for the Special Purposes of the *b*
Income Tax Acts on an appeal by the taxpayer by way of case stated (set out at [1980] STC
681–690) against assessments to capital gains tax made on the footing that gains realised
by the trustee of a settlement resident in Bermuda should be deemed to be chargeable
gains accruing to the taxpayer's three minor children under s 42 of the Finance Act 1965.
The facts are set out in the opinion of Lord Fraser.

                                                                                             c
Peter Horsfield QC and *Robert Walker QC* for the taxpayer.
Edward Nugee QC and *C H McCall* for the Crown.

Their Lordships took time for consideration.

14 October. The following opinions were delivered.   *d*

LORD FRASER OF TULLYBELTON. My Lords, this appeal is concerned with the
liability of beneficiaries for capital gains tax on gains realised by trustees of settled
property who are not resident in the United Kingdom. It involves construing s 42 of the
Finance Act 1965. Section 42 is in Part III of the Act, which is the part that introduced
the long-term capital gains tax. Like income tax, it is chargeable on individuals.   *e*
    The main charging section is s 20(1), under which a person is chargeable to the tax 'in
respect of chargeable gains accruing to him in a year of assessment during any part of
which he is resident in the United Kingdom, or during which he is ordinarily resident in
the United Kingdom'. (For brevity, I shall hereafter use 'resident' to include ordinarily
resident.) So far as trustees are concerned, s 25(1) provides that the trustees of a settlement
are to be treated as being a single and continuing body of persons resident in the United *f*
Kingdom, unless the general administration of the trust is ordinarily carried on outside
the United Kingdom and the trustees or a majority of them for the time being are not
resident in the United Kingdom. The case of a United Kingdom settlement the trustees
of which are not resident here is provided for in s 42. Plainly it required special provision
because of the difficulty of recovering the tax from non-resident trustees. The solution
adopted in s 42 is to impose the liability which would have been chargeable on the   *g*
trustees, if they had been resident in the United Kingdom, on the beneficiaries who are
resident here. The beneficiaries are not just made responsible for paying tax which is
chargeable on the trustees: the beneficiaries themselves are made directly chargeable.
That is to say the section provides machinery of charge and not machinery of collection.
The issue in the appeal is whether persons who are merely objects of a discretionary
power vested in the trustees are within the class of persons who are chargeable to the tax *h*
if they are resident in the United Kingdom.
    By s 42(1) it is declared that the section applies to capital gains accruing to trustees of
the settlement if the trustees are not resident and if the settlor, or one of the settlors, is
domiciled and resident in the United Kingdom or was so domiciled and resident when
he made the settlement. There is no dispute that the section applies to the settlement in
this appeal. The most material provisions of s 42 are sub-ss (2) and (3), which are as   *j*
follows:

'(2) Any beneficiary under the settlement who is domiciled and ... resident ...
in the United Kingdom during any year of assessment shall be treated for the
purposes of this Part of this Act as if an apportioned part of the amount, if any, on
which the trustees would have been chargeable to capital gains tax under section

20(4) of this Act, if domiciled and . . . resident . . . in the United Kingdom in that
year of assessment, had been chargeable gains accruing to the beneficiary in that
year of assessment; and for the purposes of this section any such amount shall be
apportioned in such manner as is just and reasonable between persons having
interests in the settled property, whether the interest be a life interest or an interest
in reversion, and so that the chargeable gain is apportioned, as near as may be,
according to the respective values of those interests, disregarding in the case of a
defeasible interest the possibility of defeasance.

(3) For the purposes of this section—(*a*) if in any of the three years ending with
that in which the chargeable gain accrues a person has received a payment or
payments out of the income of the settled property made in exercise of a discretion
he shall be regarded, in relation to that chargeable gain, as having an interest in the
settled property of a value equal to that of an annuity of a yearly amount equal to
one-third of the total of the payments so received by him in the said three years, and
(*b*) if a person receives at any time after the chargeable gain accrues a capital payment
made out of the settled property in exercise of a discretion, being a payment which
represents the chargeable gain in whole or part then, except so far as any part of the
gain has been attributed under this section to some other person who is domiciled
and resident or ordinarily resident in the United Kingdom, that person shall, if
domiciled and resident . . . in the United Kingdom, be treated as if the chargeable
gain, or as the case may be the part of the chargeable gain represented by the capital
payment, had accrued to him at the time when he received the capital payment.'

Later subsections of s 42 have only an indirect bearing on the question in this appeal.
Section 42 has been replaced, for any year of assessment beginning on or after 6 April
1981, by different machinery provided in the Finance Act 1981, s 80, but s 42 continues
to apply to any cases arising in earlier years of assessment.

The trust with which this appeal is concerned is an inter vivos trust set up on 16 March
1968 by a lady who was domiciled and resident in the United Kingdom. Her husband
contributed additional funds to the trust after it had been set up. The sole trustee has
always been a company registered in Bermuda, originally a bank, later a trust company.
The law of Bermuda is expressed to be the law of the settlement. The trust purposes may
be summarised sufficiently for the present appeal as follows. The settlement defines a
specified class consisting of the grandchildren and remoter issue of the settlor and their
spouses, widows and widowers, whether already living or born before a perpetuity day
defined by reference to royal lives. Clause 2 of the settlement confers on the trustees a
power of appointment over the capital and income of the trust fund, exercisable before
the perpetuity day in favour of the members of the specified class. Until the perpetuity
day, and subject to any such appointment, cl 3 of the settlement provides that income
shall be accumulated. By cl 4 the trusts which will come into force on the perpetuity
day, subject to any prior appointment, are in favour of the grandchildren and remoter
issue of the settlor living on the perpetuity day and, subject thereto, in favour of the
children of the settlor living at the date of settlement, in equal shares. No appointment
had been made at the material times under cl 2 of the settlement, nor had any distribution
of capital or income been made. Five grandchildren of the settlor were in life at the
material dates and they were the only members of the specified class then in existence.

During the years 1968–69 and 1969–70 the trustee made certain capital gains on
which it would have been chargeable to capital gains tax if it had been resident in the
United Kingdom. During those years, and at all material times, all five grandchildren
were minors, and all were resident in the United Kingdom. The inspector of taxes
apportioned the gains of the trustee equally among the five grandchildren. Three of
them are children of the taxpayer who, as their parent, is liable for their tax: see the Taxes
Management Act 1970, ss 73 and 77. The question is whether that apportionment was
in accordance with s 42.

The Special Commissioners decided that it was not, and they allowed an appeal by the
taxpayer. They held that the possibility of participation in any distribution of the

unappointed residue under cl 4 of the settlement was so remote and of so little (if any) value that it ought to be ignored, and that the rights of the grandchildren as objects of *a* the trustee's discretionary power did not amount to 'interests' in the settled funds. From that decision Dillon J allowed an appeal by the Crown by way of case stated (see [1980] STC 679). The judge held that, although the rights of the grandchildren as objects of the discretionary power did not amount to 'interests', they were enough to make it just and reasonable to apportion the gains equally among them. The Court of Appeal (Lawton, Brightman and Fox LJJ) ([1982] 2 All ER 644) held that the grandchildren's rights did *b* amount to 'interests' in the settled funds, and they affirmed the order of Dillon J.

The main question is what is the meaning of the word 'interests' in s 42(2). It is a word that is capable of many meanings, the appropriate meaning depending on the context. In *A-G v Heywood* (1887) 19 QBD 326 the settlor had provided that trustees had a discretion to apply the trust income for the benefit of himself and his wife and children or any one or more of them. It was held that he had reserved an 'interest' within the *c* meaning of the Customs and Inland Revenue Act 1881. But in *Gartside v IRC* [1968] 1 All ER 121, [1968] AC 553 this House decided that a beneficiary under a discretionary trust did not have an 'interest' in the sense of s 43 of the Finance Act 1940. Lord Reid expressed approval of the decision in *A-G v Heywood*, but distinguished it because of the different context in which 'interest' was used in the 1940 Act. He said ([1968] 1 All ER 121 at 131, [1968] AC 553 at 612): *d*

> 'If so vague a word as "interest" is used in different Acts dealing with different problems, there is only, in my view, a slender presumption that it has the same meaning in both . . .'

Lord Wilberforce, after referring to *A-G v Heywood* and also to *A-G v Farrell* [1931] 1 KB 81, declined to treat those cases as having settled the meaning of 'interest' in the different *e* setting of the Finance Act 1940. He said ([1968] 1 All ER 121 at 134, [1968] AC 553 at 617):

> 'No doubt in a certain sense a beneficiary under a discretionary trust has an "interest": the nature of it may, sufficiently for the purpose, be spelt out by saying that he has a right to be considered as a potential recipient of benefit by the trustees *f* and a right to have his interest protected by a court of equity.'

I turn therefore to consider the setting in which the word is used in s 42, and particularly in sub-s (2). Subsection (2) is in two parts, separated by a semicolon. The first part refers to an apportioned part of 'the amount, if any, on which the trustees would have been chargeable to capital gains tax . . . if . . . resident . . . in the United Kingdom'. The second part directs that 'any such amount shall be apportioned in such manner as is *g* just and reasonable'. It is, in my opinion, clear that the amount to be apportioned is the whole amount on which the trustees would have been chargeable if they had been resident. Dillon J considered that there could be cases in which justice and reason would require that there should be no apportionment at all because the interests of those with interests were too remote. With respect that does not seem to me to be a sound construction; it involves reading the second part of the subsection as if it provided that *h* the amount was to be apportioned 'if and so far as is just and reasonable', but that is not what the section says. An alternative construction, which appealed to me at one time, would be to treat the subsection as providing for, or at least permitting, apportionment to a group of beneficiaries, such as the objects of a discretionary power, without making an immediate apportionment to any individual member of the group. But I have reached the view that that also would be wrong, both because the second part of sub-s (2) requires *j* the amount to be apportioned between 'persons' having interests in the settled property, and persons in the context of this personal tax must mean individual persons, and also because it would not permit the ascertainment of an apportioned part on which any individual beneficiary in the group could be treated as chargeable under the first part of the subsection in the year of assessment.

a   Although the provision for apportionment of the gain between persons having interests in the settled property comes in the second part of the subsection, it is the first step chronologically and, I think, logically. The first part of the subsection deals with what must be a later step, which is that 'Any beneficiary' who is (reading short) resident in the United Kingdom during any year of assessment shall be treated as if 'an apportioned part of the amount' (that is a part apportioned to him under the second part of the subsection) had been chargeable gains accruing to him in that year of assessment. It is

b   common ground between the parties that non-resident beneficiaries will not be so treated under that subsection even though they may be persons having interests in the settled property and may have had a share of the gains apportioned to them. But the contention for the Crown is that, as regards beneficiaries who *are* resident in the United Kingdom, the words 'any beneficiary' in the first part of sub-s (2) and 'persons having interests in the settled property' in the second part mean the same thing, and that both include

c   persons who are the objects of a discretionary power.

      The contention for the taxpayer is that beneficiaries under trusts fall into two classes. First, there are persons who have fixed interests, typical examples of which are a life interest and an interest in reversion in a definite part of the settled property. Second, there are persons who are merely objects of a discretionary power (discretionary beneficiaries). According to this contention discretionary beneficiaries are not persons

d   having interests in the settled property in the sense of sub-s (2), and therefore not persons to whom any part of the capital gains can be apportioned. They would become chargeable to capital gains tax only if and when they received actual payments of income or capital, in accordance with sub-s (3) which was said to provide a separate code for taxing discretionary beneficiaries. Reliance was placed on the provision in the second part of sub-s (2) to the effect that apportionment is to be 'as near as may be, according to the

e   respective values of [the] interests' and it was argued that, while fixed interests can be, and regularly are, valued by an actuary, the rights of discretionary beneficiaries are in their nature impossible to value, and cannot have been intended to be included in sub-s (2). Further, it was said that the words 'whether the interest be a life interest or an interest in reversion' are to be regarded as indicating the genus of fixed interests, capable of valuation, to which sub-s (2) is intended to apply. Otherwise, it was said, it was difficult

f   to see any reason for those words being included in the subsection, since they cannot have been intended as an exhaustive list of all possible interests, for, as the Court of Appeal pointed out, they do not include, for example, an absolute interest which is subject to defeasance by the exercise of a power or on a specified event, or an immediate contingent interest or a right to income for a term of years certain (see [1982] 2 All ER 644 at 649).

g   I recognise that the taxpayer's contention is a possible one, but I have reached the conclusion that it is not well founded. One indication against the taxpayer's contention is that, if it were correct, I would have expected the second part of sub-s (2) to be in a separate subsection, which would deal only with the case of beneficiaries who had fixed interests. It would balance the present sub-s (3), which would deal only with beneficiaries who had discretionary interests. The fact that the section has not been drafted in that

h   way is, in my view, a pointer which is entitled to some weight in arriving at its true meaning.

      Another fact which I regard as being against the taxpayer's contention is that s 42 was apparently intended to secure, as far as possible, that beneficiaries resident in the United Kingdom of a trust with trustees also resident in the United Kingdom should not be at a disadvantage, in relation to capital gains tax, compared with beneficiaries in a trust with

j   non-resident trustees. Resident trustees are normally bound to pay capital gains tax in the year after the gains have accrued (see s 20(6)), but, if the taxpayer is right, resident beneficiaries in a trust with non-resident trustees would not be taxable on their shares of capital gains until such time as they received actual payment of income or capital. They would then be taxable under sub-s (3)(*a*) or (*b*), but that might be many years later and, apart altogether from the effects of inflation, a tax liability which is deferred is less

onerous than one that is immediate. The possible hardship to discretionary beneficiaries
who are resident in the United Kingdom by being taxed on benefits which they have not
received, and which some of them may never receive, is at least mitigated by the
provision of s 42(5) whereby, if any capital gains tax payable by a beneficiary under s 42
is paid by the trustees, the amount paid shall not for the purposes of taxation (any
taxation) be regarded as a payment to the beneficiary. In any event I agree with my noble
and learned friend Lord Wilberforce that hardship is not a relevant consideration.

The main reason why the Crown's contention is, in my opinion, correct is that in the
second part of sub-s (2) the primary direction is that the amount that would have been
chargeable if the trustees had been resident 'shall be apportioned in such manner as is
just and reasonable'. The later direction that the gain is to be apportioned 'as near as may
be, according to the respective values of [the] interests' is only a qualification of the
primary direction. Accordingly, what is envisaged is not a strict apportionment by
reference to the actuarial or market values of the interests, which would be impossible in
the case of discretionary interests, but a much looser apportionment by reference to what
is just and reasonable in view of the real probabilities under the particular settlement.
That view is fortified by the final direction in sub-s (2) that the possibility of defeasance
of defeasible interests is to be disregarded. Any attempt to arrive at precise values of the
various interests, while disregarding the possibility of defeasance of those which are
defeasible, would be likely to reach results that might well seem unjust and unreasonable
in a case, such as the present, where the settlor's children have interests under cl 4 which
are defeasible and which, according to evidence that was before the Special Commissioners,
are almost valueless.

Accordingly I agree with the Court of Appeal that the present case is not like *Gartside
v IRC* [1968] 1 All ER 121, [1968] AC 553, where the mechanism of the statute could not
be operated unless the precise extent of the interests could be identified. In s 42(2) the
direction is that the gain is to be apportioned only 'as near as may be' according to the
respective values of the interests, and I think the purpose of the direction is to show that
the justice and reasonableness are to be judged by the respective values of the interests,
and not by the relative wealth or poverty of the discretionary beneficiaries, except in a
case where the poverty of the beneficiary might mean that he was likely to have the
trustees' discretion exercised in his favour more generously than if he had been wealthy,
and might thus increase the value of his interest.

Subsection (3) of s 42 is, in my view, only subsidiary to sub-s (2). Paragraph (a) of sub-
s (3) is concerned with the problem of converting a discretionary payment of income
into an annuity to which an approximate value can be attached for the purposes of sub-s
(2). That appears to me to be all the draftsman had in mind as the function of a valuation
under sub-s (3)(a), as is shown by the lack of detailed guidance as to the assumptions to
be made about the annuity. Nothing is said about its duration; is it to be assumed to be
for the lifetime of the annuitant or for the (possibly shorter) period that the discretion
lasts? Is it to have any other conditions? Without more detailed guidance on the nature
of the annuity it cannot be valued accurately, although it may be given some approximate
value which is adequate for the purpose of sub-s (2).

Paragraph (b) of sub-s (3) is intended to secure that tax will be collected from a resident
beneficiary to whom a discretionary payment of capital is made out of the settled
property, if it is a payment which represents previously untaxed chargeable gains. The
paragraph prevents double taxation, in the sense of taxing the same gains twice, by
making an exception of the case where any part of the gain has already been attributed
under the section to some other person who is domiciled and resident in the United
Kingdom (and who will therefore have paid tax on it). It would only have been previously
untaxed if, or in so far as, it had been attributed to a non-resident beneficiary. I think it
is significant that para (b) contemplates that part of the gain may have been attributed to
a non-resident beneficiary, but does not contemplate that it might not have been
attributed to anyone at all. That is a further indication that sub-s (2) requires the whole
amount of the gain to be apportioned. The reason why the exception applies only when
the gain has been attributed to some *other* person is that, if it had been attributed to the

a person to whom the discretionary payment is made, he would already have paid the tax himself and would naturally not be taxable again on the same gain. The draftsman assumed that that was so obvious that express provision against double taxation of the same person was unnecessary. Finally, with regard to para (*b*), I think that the concept of a payment which 'represents' the chargeable gain is somewhat lacking precision, and that the use of that expression gives some support to the Crown's contention as to the meaning of sub-s (2).

b A further reason why the words 'interests' in s 42(2) should receive a wide meaning, and not a narrow technical meaning, is that the section has to apply not only to English settlements but to settlements governed by other systems of law. And by s 42(7) 'settlement' has the extended meaning which is given to it by what is now the Income and Corporation Taxes Act 1970, s 454(3), and it includes any arrangement. Reference was made in argument, by way of example, to *Archer-Shee v Garland* [1931] AC 212, *c* where the evidence was that by the law of New York no beneficiary has any interest in the settled property but has only a claim against the trustees. It would be absurd in s 42, which is dealing with non-resident trustees, to give to the word 'interests' a technical meaning which would apply to an English settlement but not to a settlement governed by the law of New York. It is, indeed, not necessary to go so far afield as New York to make this point; in *IRC v Clark's Trustees* 1939 SC 11 at 24 the Lord President (Normand) *d* referred to the *Archer-Shee* case and said:

> 'My conclusion is that there is no difference between the law of Scotland as regards the beneficiary's rights and the law which is admitted in the record to be the law of the State of New York.'

There is no doubt that s 42, which forms part of a United Kingdom taxing statute, should *e* if possible be construed in such a way as to apply to beneficiaries in a Scottish trust as well as to beneficiaries in an English trust: see *Gartside v IRC* [1968] 1 All ER 121 at 125, [1968] AC 553 at 602 per Lord Reid.

The settlor, and her husband who contributed an addition to the trust fund after it had been set up, wrote a letter to the trustees dated two days after the settlement setting out their 'wishes' as to the exercise of the powers and discretions vested in the trustees. These *f* were, in brief, that the trustees should regard the settlement as existing primarily for the benefit of their grandchildren in equal shares, and should accumulate the income at first. When each grandchild attained the age of 21 years he should receive the income of his prospective share, but he should not receive any large sums of capital before attaining the age of 30 years. The taxpayer contended that the letter, being merely precatory and not binding on the trustees, should be disregarded when apportioning the capital gains. The *g* Crown contended, on the other hand, that it should be taken into account as one relevant factor in making a just and reasonable apportionment of the gains. In my opinion the contention of the Crown on this matter is right. The apportionment is a question of fact for the inspector, subject to a right of appeal to the Special Commissioners (see the Capital Gains Tax Regulations 1967, SI 1967/149), and it should be carried out in the light of all the circumstances, including the practical probabilities of how the trust estate is likely to *h* be applied. Clearly the letter is one such circumstance which may be highly relevant. Even without taking account of the letter, the apportionment of liability equally among the grandchildren would, in my opinion, have been reasonable and proper. In the light of the letter, it appears to me to be the only possible course.

For these reasons I would dismiss the appeal. The Crown must have costs in this House and in the Court of Appeal. In accordance with an agreement between parties which is *j* referred to in the order of Dillon J, there will be no order for costs in the High Court.

LORD WILBERFORCE. My Lords, the Court of Appeal decided this case in favour of the Crown and refused leave to appeal to this House. In my opinion they were right, and since I agree with the single judgment prepared by Fox LJ, with which I understand that your Lordships also concur, I shall be brief.

The key question is as to the meaning of the word 'interests' in s 42(2) of the Finance

Act 1965, the alternatives being whether this word refers only to such interests as can be
assigned a value or whether it is a word of more general significance capable of covering　a
any interest, quantifiable or non-quantifiable, of a beneficiary under a trust. That either
of these is a possible meaning in fiscal legislation is made clear (a) by the general
observations of Lord Reid in *Gartside v IRC* [1968] 1 All ER 121 at 126, [1968] AC 553 at
603 (see also those of Stephen and Wills JJ in *A-G v Heywood* (1887) 19 QBD 326) and (b)
by a comparison of the cases just cited. In *Heywood*, which arose under s 38 of the
Customs and Inland Revenue Act 1881, and where the question was whether the settlor　b
had reserved 'an interest' by including himself among a discretionary class of beneficiaries,
the word 'interest' was given the more general meaning. To require that it meant
something to which an ascertainable value could be assigned would, it was held, be
contrary to the scheme of the statute. In *Gartside*, on the other hand, which arose under
s 43 of the Finance Act 1940, and where the question was whether estate duty could be
charged in respect of the determination of a discretionary interest, this House held that　c
the word must bear the narrower meaning because the statute necessarily required
ascertainment of the quantum of the interest. In *Gartside* I expressed the opinion, from
which the other members of the House did not dissent, that these two cases could stand
together. The word 'interest' is one of uncertain meaning and it remains to be decided
on the terms of the applicable statute which, or possibly what other, meaning the word
may bear.　d
　The taxpayer contends for the narrower meaning, and can find some support in the
section. There is the reference to 'values' in sub-s (2); there is sub-s (3), which, he contends,
sets out a code for assigning values to discretionary interests in income or capital, an
exclusive code within one of whose provisions a case must fall if a charge to tax in respect
of a discretionary trust is to arise. There is, thirdly, the reference, in sub-s (2), to a life
interest or an interest in reversion, but, in my opinion this does not survive a first critical　e
look: the reference is clearly illustrative and nothing more.
　The two main arguments are by no means negligible, but they are, in my opinion,
greatly outweighed by those on the other side. I simply state them as they impressed me;
they are developed in discussion in the Court of Appeal's judgment.
　1. The initial words of sub-s (2) are 'Any beneficiary'. Unless clearly directed otherwise,
I would assume that 'persons having interests' was correlative to these words. Discretionary　f
objects are clearly 'beneficiaries', so I would suppose them also to be included in 'persons
having interests'.
　2. The apportionment to be made under the subsection is mandatory. The amount of
the gains, ie the whole amount, must be apportioned in the relevant year of assessment.
This can only be done if discretionary objects (who may be the only 'beneficiaries' in that
year) can be the objects of apportionment.　g
　3. The words, in sub-s (2), 'in such manner as is just and reasonable' and 'as near as
may be, according to the respective values of those interests' suggest a broad rather than
an actuarial approach in which all relevant considerations may be taken into account.
They permit, inter alia, consideration of the settlor's letter of intent which shows, at least,
that the settlement was to be regarded as for the benefit of the grandchildren, not of the
settlor's two children.　h
　4. That sub-s (3) represents an exclusive code is in my opinion not supported by the
form of the section. On the contrary, the structure of it suggests that sub-s (2) is the main
and general charging provision, sub-s (3) being auxiliary and confined to particular cases.
　These considerations together convince me that an apportionment in respect of
'interests' under a discretionary trust can, indeed must, be made.
　I would only refer to one other argument, that based on the alleged 'hardship' of　j
accepting the Crown's contention. I do not think that this is a relevant consideration at
all. If there were two equally possible constructions of this subsection, it might be correct
to choose that which is the more favourable to the taxpayer, on the basis that subjects can
only be taxed by clear words. This principle cannot apply where there are decisive legal
reasons for preferring one construction rather than another. Once this step has been

taken, considerations of 'hardship' do not enter into the discussion. The 'hardship' (if any)
a consists in imposing a tax on discretionary beneficiaries at a time when they may have
received no benefit from the trust out of which the tax can be paid. But if that is the
effect of the section, it represents the parliamentary intention. We cannot characterise it
as in itself a hardship. Settlors, after 1965, make their settlements with knowledge of the
legislation and of its consequences. They can avoid the use of discretionary trusts, or, if
they decide to use them, make provision to meet hard cases. The section itself (sub-s (5))
b recognises that trustees may take remedial action.

Reference was made in argument to *Re Latham (decd)*, *IRC v Barclays Bank Ltd* [1961] 3
All ER 903, [1962] Ch 616 as supporting a proposition that the taxed beneficiary can,
under the general law, recover any tax he pays from the trustees of the settlement. While
I have no inclination to question the correctness of that decision, it would represent an
extention, I do not say an unjustified extension, but certainly an extension, to apply it to
c this different tax and in relation to this specific section (s 42). Since the argument from
'hardship' can be met without resort to the principle of that case, I prefer to reserve my
decision as to its applicability.

I would dismiss the appeal.

LORD SCARMAN. My Lords, I agree with the reasons for dismissing the appeal
d which have been developed in the speeches of my noble and learned friends Lord Fraser
and Lord Wilberforce. I add some observations of my own only because of the differences
of opinion that have emerged in the courts below.

The appeal is concerned with the incidence of capital gains tax in relation to property
settled on discretionary trusts, the beneficiaries being resident but the trustee being not
resident in the United Kingdom. The question is whether persons who are the objects of
e discretionary trusts but to whom nothing has yet been paid in the exercise of the
discretion have a sufficient interest in the trust fund to be liable to the tax in respect of a
capital gain accruing to the non-resident trustee; and the answer has to be found in the
true construction to be put on s 42 of the Finance Act 1965.

Capital gains tax is charged in respect of chargeable gains computed in accordance
with statute. For the purposes of this appeal the statute is the Finance Act 1965. The
f gains are those accruing in the year of assessment. A person to whom chargeable gains
accrue is liable to tax if during the year of assessment, or any part of it, he is resident in
the United Kingdom, or if during the year he is ordinarily resident in the United
Kingdom. The tax is a percentage tax on gains after deducting losses allowed by the
statute and is payable before the expiration of three months following the year in which
they accrued, or at the expiration of 30 days beginning with the date of making the
g assessment, whichever is the later.

Structurally, it is a simple tax. Three of its general features require to be borne in mind
in this appeal: (1) the tax is levied on the person to whom the chargeable gain accrues,
irrespective of the nature of his interest (see s 19(1)); (2) the tax is levied only on persons
resident, or ordinarily resident, in the United Kingdom during the year in which the
chargeable gain accrued; (see s 20(1)); (3) the tax is immediately payable, ie within a very
h short time after assessment (see s 20(6)).

In adapting the tax to settled property the Act has adhered faithfully to this simple
structure. Lord Wilberforce has described the effect of the Act in relation to settled
property in *Roome v Edwards (Inspector of Taxes)* [1981] 1 All ER 736 at 741, [1982] AC
279 at 295:

j   '. . . it has attached the liability to pay capital gains tax to the trustees of
        settlements, not to funds held on distinct trusts, and (in this in contrast to estate
        duty legislation) has not concerned itself with questions of incidence of the tax
        between beneficiaries or funds within a settlement.'

Section 25 contains the detailed provisions for charging the tax in relation to settled
property. Trustees of the settlement are liable to pay the tax only if they are, or are to be

treated as being, resident or ordinarily resident in the United Kingdom during the year in which the chargeable gain accrues: see s 25(1). Section 42 deals with the problem *a* where there is a United Kingdom settlement the trustees of which are non-resident, but the beneficiaries, or some of them, under the settlement are resident or ordinarily resident in the United Kingdom during the year in which the chargeable gain accrued to the trustees. It is this section which the House is called on to construe in this appeal.

Its formulation is very similar to s 41, which applies as respects chargeable gains accruing to a non-resident 'close' company. Each section provides basically the same *b* answer to the problem of the chargeable gain which, though it accrues to a non-resident person, benefits persons who are resident in the United Kingdom (namely beneficiaries under the settlement and shareholders in the company). The answer is that resident beneficiaries, or shareholders, shall be treated as if part of the gain had accrued to them so that they are liable to pay the tax on the part properly attributable to each of them.

The critical facts in the present case are these: (1) on 16 March 1968 a United Kingdom *c* family settlement was made by a grandmother for the benefit of her grandchildren, their spouses and their issue; (2) property was settled on discretionary trusts in respect of income and capital, with power to the trustee to accumulate income; (3) a non-resident trustee was appointed; (4) the living beneficiaries of the discretionary trusts are now five grandchildren (all of them minors); (5) no payment of income or capital has yet been made by the trustee to any of the grandchildren; (6) in default of appointment, there is *d* an ultimate trust (arising at the expiry of a 'royal lives' perpetuity period) for the grandchildren, their spouses or issue then living, otherwise for the settlor's children absolutely; (7) on 18 March 1968 a letter of intent, having no binding effect, was addressed to the trustee by the settlor and her husband in which she made plain her wishes that the settlement should be regarded primarily for the benefit of her grandchildren and that income should be accumulated at least until they reached the age *e* of 21.

Assessments for capital gains tax were made by the Revenue on each of the five grandchildren for the years 1968–69 and 1969–70. There is no dispute but that chargeable gains accrued to the trustee during these two years of assessment. The two questions which lie at the centre of this dispute are, first, whether the gains were properly treated by the Revenue as accruing to the grandchildren and, second, what, if any, is a just and *f* reasonable apportionment (a zero answer being possible to the second question).

It will be convenient to clear one question out of the way. The grandchildren have an interest in the trust fund which is contingent on default of appointment of the fund and very remote in time; it could arise only at the expiry of the perpetuity period. Its value is, according to the evidence (and in common sense), negligible. The Special Commissioners, therefore, ignored it, taking the view that it would not be 'just and *g* reasonable' to apportion to that interest any part of the capital gains accruing in the years 1968–69 and 1969–70. The decision was for them and, being one of fact, is not appealable. This appeal is concerned, therefore, solely with the problem whether there should be an apportionment between the grandchildren as objects of the discretionary trusts and, if yes, what is a just and reasonable apportionment.

It is no longer disputed that the grandchildren are by reason of their expectation as *h* objects of the discretionary trusts beneficiaries under the settlement. They are, therefore, caught by the opening words of s 42(2). They are liable to apportionment if their expectation constitutes an interest which can be valued by application of the formula contained in the second sentence of the subsection. That sentence directs an apportionment 'in such manner as is just and reasonable between persons having interests in the settled property, whether the interest be a life interest or an interest in reversion'. The taxpayer *j* (the parent of three of the grandchildren) submits that the formula restricts apportionment to fixed interests recognised by the property law. If this be right, it follows that the expectation of the grandchildren is not such as to constitute them persons having interests in the settled property. The submission is reinforced by reference to sub-s (3), which is said to be an exhaustive code governing the apportionability of gains to the objects of

discretionary trusts and basing it on actual payments to them of capital or income in the
a exercise of the discretion.

The taxpayer further submits that, if contrary to the first submission the grandchildren
have an apportionable interest, it falls to be valued on a market basis and in the
circumstances of this case its value is, as the Special Commissioners found, nil. If both
submissions fail, an equal division of the gains between the five grandchildren is accepted
as appropriate.

b The first submission does not accord with what seems to me, on first impression, to be
the most likely interpretation of sub-s (2). I would expect persons who are the objects of
a discretionary trust to be treated under the subsection as persons having an interest in
the settled property. But it is a possible interpretation. A close look at the language and
context of the subsection is, therefore, necessary.

'Interest' is an ordinary English word which takes its meaning from its context. In the
c context of discretionary trusts it has been held that each one of the objects of a
discretionary trust has an 'interest' in the trust fund: see *A-G v Heywood* (1887) 19 QBD
326 and *A-G v Farrell* [1931] 1 KB 81. The word was considered by the House in *Gartside
v IRC* [1968] 1 All ER 121, [1968] AC 553. Being an estate duty case, the decision has no
relevance to this appeal, but there are some general observations of value. Referring to
the use of the word in the Finance Acts 1894 and 1940 Lord Reid observed ([1968] 1 All
d ER 121 at 125, [1968] AC 553 at 602):

> 'The word "interest", as an ordinary word of the English language, is capable of
> having many meanings, and it is equally clear that in these provisions its meaning
> cannot be limited by any technicality of English law. Not only do these provisions
> also apply to Scotland, but they may have to be applied where duty is claimed in
> respect of an interest under deeds which have to be construed under the laws of
e other countries.'

I would observe that in the present case the settlement is to be construed according to the
law of Bermuda until and unless a contrary intention is declared. Lord Wilberforce in
the course of his speech in the *Gartside* case reminded the House that it was invited to
overrule the *Heywood* and *Farrell* cases. He found it unnecessary either to overrule or to
f uphold those decisions, but he added that he thought them to be acceptable in principle
(see [1968] 1 All ER 121 at 136, [1968] AC 553 at 620–621). Discretionary trusts during
the twentieth century featured largely in family settlements. The non-resident trustee
has also become a well-known feature of such settlements. Being, as the Court of Appeal
said in this case, 'potential instruments of tax avoidance' (see [1982] 2 All ER 644 at 652),
they have attracted their fair share of attention in our tax laws. I would expect, for a
g number of reasons, that the objects of discretionary trusts in such settlements would be
treated for the purpose of s 42 as persons having interests in the settled property. First,
by treating their expectation as an interest the legislative purpose of the section is
achieved in that no advantage is gained by United Kingdom beneficiaries with a non-
resident trustee over those whose settlement is in the hands of a resident trustee. Second,
it secures payment of the tax with the immediacy which is an integral feature of capital
h gains taxation. Third, so to treat their expectation is realistic, for the terms of the
settlement make it abundantly plain that the grandchildren (with their spouses and issue,
if and when they arrive) are the true objects of the settlor's provision. Fourth, there is, in
my judgment, as I shall show, no hardship on the grandchildren (always assuming, as I
am not to be taken to assume, that hardship is a ground for avoiding an interpretation of
a taxing statute which on analysis of its language and context appears to be most likely to
j accord with the legislative intention).

Against this general background I turn to consider the formula for apportionment to
be found in s 42(2). The apportionment is to be carried out on a 'just and reasonable'
basis so that 'the chargeable gain is apportioned, as near as may be, according to the
respective values of those interests'. The governing words are 'just and reasonable'; they
confer on the inspector and the commissioners a wide latitude in judgment. The task is

to apportion the chargeable gain, as near as may be, according to respective values. The language is apt to cover a valuation of interests where factors other than the market value *a* of a property interest have to be considered. The only difficulty is the reference to a life interest or one in reversion as illustrating 'interests in the settled property'. I cannot treat these words as intended to restrict the otherwise clear intendment of the subsection that the interests of any beneficiary, a term which everyone is agreed includes persons who are the objects of the discretionary trusts, are to be valued. Admittedly the reference to these two interests in the second sentence of the subsection is obscure. It may be that the *b* draftsman intended to do no more than emphasise specifically that interests in income and reversionary interests must be valued.

When one turns to the provision for valuation, the formula, with its emphasis on what is just and reasonable and its direction to apportion 'as near as may be' according to the respective values of the interests in the settled property, is carefully drafted so as to admit into the valuation interests other than fixed property interests and to require, where *c* appropriate, a valuation not tied to market values. It is a formula apt for the valuation of the interest of an object of discretionary trusts under a settlement where the expectation of future benefit is real, although the discretion to make a payment has not yet been exercised. For the purpose of valuation, the intention of the settlor, as evidenced by the deed and its recitals, is a significant factor to which value is to be attached to the extent that is just and reasonable and in a manner which, as near as may be, reflects the *d* respective interests under the settlement. Further, the letter of intent, though not by itself of great weight, is admissible as supporting the intention manifested in the settlement itself. Accordingly, I reach the view that sub-s (2) is apt to cover the interests of the grandchildren and to require a valuation in the manner I have described so that the capital gain may be apportioned between them.

When I turn to sub-s (3), I find nothing which would compel me to revise the view I *e* have formed as to the most likely interpretation of sub-s (2). Though, no doubt, it is possible to read sub-s (3) as limiting the liability to tax of persons who are the objects of discretionary trusts to situations in which a payment of capital or income has been made in the exercise of the discretion, the language admits of another interpretation which is consistent with the view I have formed as to the meaning of sub-s (2). Subsection (3) can equally well be construed as confined to two specific situations; and, so confined, it is *f* perfectly consistent with the possibility of an apportionment to such persons under sub-s (2). It deals with two situations in which a person who is the object of the discretionary trust has received a benefit in the exercise of a discretion: para (*a*) deals with an income payment and para (*b*) with a capital payment. The subsection can be read as ensuring that in addition to any apportionment of a person's discretionary interest under sub-s (2) he so be 'regarded' (para (*a*)) or 'treated' (para (*b*)) as having an interest for the purpose of the *g* tax. Accordingly, I find nothing in the subsection to compel the interpretation that in no situation other than that of the receipt of an actual payment in respect of income or capital is a person who is the object of discretionary trusts to be subject to apportionment; and, because it is consistent with the view I have formed as to the preferable construction of sub-s (2), I accept the construction which confines sub-s (3) to two specific situations.

There remains the argument of hardship. It was said to be a harsh consequence, so *h* harsh that Parliament could not have intended it, if the object of a discretionary trust were to be made liable to capital gains tax although he had received not a penny of the gain. He might be poor; the chargeable gain might be great. There would be the possibility that he was being made liable for the sum which he could not afford. There are two reasons why I do not find this to be a compelling argument (even if it be a relevant argument, which, as I have already indicated, I doubt). First, the settlement was *j* made in 1968, three years after the capital gains tax was introduced. A settlor, resident in Leatherhead, making provision for her grandchildren resident in the United Kingdom, chose to appoint as trustee a Bermudian corporation. She acted under advice. Presumably, she, or her advisers, saw some advantage in a foreign trustee for a settlement made in the United Kingdom for the benefit of grandchildren living in the United Kingdom. But,

presumably, she was also advised as to the disadvantages. Second, if the grandchildren
a (through their parents) are liable to the tax, the trustee can pay it. For by s 42(5) it is
provided that, if the trustee does pay the tax payable by a beneficiary, the amount paid
'shall not for the purposes of taxation' be regarded as a payment to the beneficiary.
Indeed, though the point was not the subject of full argument, I would, as at present
advised, accept that a beneficiary paying a tax, or part of a tax, properly attributable to
the whole fund has a right of reimbursement either unconditionally or at least so far as is
b necessary to give an equitable balance between those interested in the fund. The principle
was recognised by Wilberforce J in *Re Latham (decd), IRC v Barclays Bank Ltd* [1961] 3 All
ER 903 at 913, [1962] Ch 616 at 641–642, and I would expect it to be recognised in
Bermuda (there is nothing to indicate otherwise).

In my view, therefore, the Special Commissioners erred in law in two respects. First,
they interpreted incorrectly the word 'interest' where used in s 42(2). Second, they erred
c in thinking that the apportionment must be based on market values. Their errors were
errors of law. I think the Court of Appeal was right in holding that the inspector's
assessments must be restored. I would, therefore, dismiss the appeal.

LORD ROSKILL. My Lords, I have had the advantage of reading in draft the speeches
of my noble and learned friends who have preceded me. On the principal issue argued
d before the House, I am in complete agreement with those speeches and with the
judgment of the Court of Appeal delivered by Fox LJ. I only wish to add two observations
of my own. First, in agreement with my noble and learned friend Lord Wilberforce, I
cannot think that the 'hardship' alleged to arise were the Crown's contentions to be
accepted can in any way be a relevant consideration when the question for determination
is the true construction of this or any other fiscal legislation. If that legislation, on its true
e construction, has the consequences for which the Crown contends, it cannot be a
legitimate ground for giving that legislation some other (ex hypothesi wrong) construction
that those consequences involve some 'hardship'. Parliament must be taken to have
intended that that legislation should have those particular consequences.

Second, and again in agreement with my noble and learned friend Lord Wilberforce,
I prefer to reserve until the matter arises for direct decision the possible applicability of
f the principle enunciated by Wilberforce J in *Re Latham (decd), IRC v Barclays Bank Ltd*
[1961] 3 All ER 903 at 913, [1962] Ch 616 at 641 to the position between the beneficiaries
on whom the statute casts this liability to pay capital gains tax and the trustees of the
fund from which the interest of the beneficiaries derives, so as to entitle the former to
claim reimbursement of the tax from the latter. That decision was not concerned with
capital gains tax; indeed it was given some four years before the introduction of that tax
g in this country and different considerations may possibly arise in connection with the
ultimate incidence of that tax.

I would dismiss this appeal.

LORD BRANDON OF OAKBROOK. My Lords, I have had the advantage of
reading in advance the speeches prepared by my noble and learned friends Lord Fraser,
h Lord Wilberforce and Lord Scarman. I would, like Lord Wilberforce, prefer to reserve
my opinion on the question whether the principle on which *Re Latham (decd), IRC v
Barclays Bank Ltd* [1961] 3 All ER 903, [1962] Ch 616 was decided, assuming that decision
to have been correct, is applicable to the present case. Subject to that qualification, I agree
with all three speeches and, for the reasons set out in them, would dismiss the appeal.

j *Appeal dismissed.*

Solicitors: *Norton Rose, Botterell & Roche* (for the taxpayer); *Solicitor of Inland Revenue.*

Rengan Krishnan Esq   Barrister.

Manuel and others v Attorney General   *a*

COURT OF APPEAL, CIVIL DIVISION
CUMMING-BRUCE, EVELEIGH AND SLADE LJJ
13, 14, 15, 30 JULY 1982

Statute – Validity – Public general Act of United Kingdom Parliament – Constitution of   *b*
independent sovereign state – Jurisdiction of court – Pleadings challenging validity of properly
passed Act – Act passed by United Kingdom Parliament to transfer Canadian constitution to
Canada – Allegation that Act ultra vires because 'consent' of Canada not properly obtained –
Whether court having jurisdiction to inquire into validity of Act – Whether declaration in Act that
Canada had requested and consented to legislation conclusive – Canada Act 1982, preamble.

Canada – Constitutional law – Consent of Canada to Act of United Kingdom Parliament extending   *c*
to Canada – Act stating in preamble that it was enacted at request and with consent of Canada –
Whether court entitled to inquire into facts and nature of request and consent of Canada – Statute
of Westminster 1931, s 4 – Canada Act 1982, preamble.

Canada – Constitutional law – Request and consent of Canada to Act passed by United Kingdom   *d*
Parliament – Whether 'Canada' referring to Senate and House of Commons of Canada or having
extended meaning – Statute of Westminster 1931, s 4 – Canada Act 1982, preamble.

By the British North America Act 1867 the United Kingdom Parliament created the
Dominion of Canada and s 3 of that Act empowered the Queen, by and with the advice
of the Privy Council, to declare by proclamation that the provinces of Canada, Nova
Scotia and New Brunswick should 'form and be one dominion under the name of   *e*
Canada'. Section 4[a] of the 1867 Act provided that unless it was otherwise expressed or
implied 'the name Canada shall be taken to mean Canada as constituted under this Act'.
The 1867 Act continued to be the constitution of Canada, alterable only by the United
Kingdom Parliament and subject to amendments subsequently made by that Parliament.
The Dominion of Canada acquired, largely by agreement and convention, increasing   *f*
independence from the United Kingdom over and above that given to it by the 1867
Act, until, by virtue of the Statute of Westminster 1931, it attained complete
independence, subject to the provisions of s 7[b] of the Statute of Westminster which
entrenched the constitution of Canada at Westminster by reserving to the United
Kingdom Parliament power to effect the 'repeal, amendment or alteration of the British
North America Acts'. On 9 December 1981 the Senate and the House of Commons of
Canada submitted an address to Her Majesty requesting that a Bill (the Canada Bill) be   *g*
laid before the United Kingdom Parliament to amend the constitution of Canada by,
inter alia, terminating the remaining responsibility of the United Kingdom Parliament
for amending the Constitution of Canada and conferring all such responsibility on
Canadian institutions. On 10 December the plaintiffs, who were Canadian Indian chiefs,
brought an action against the Attorney General of England on behalf of themselves and   *h*
various Indian tribes seeking declarations, inter alia, (i) that the United Kingdom
Parliament had no power to amend the constitution of Canada so as to prejudice the
Indian people of Canada without the consent of the Indian people, and (ii) that the
Canada Bill, if enacted, would be inconsistent with, and a derogation from, the
constitutional safeguards provided for the Indian people by the Statute of Westminster
and the British North America Acts and would thereby be ultra vires. On 29 March 1982   *j*
the Canada Act 1982 received the royal assent. The long title stated that it was 'An Act to
give effect to a request by the Senate and House of Commons of Canada' and the

---

a   Section 4 is set out at p 825 *e f*, post
b   Section 7, so far as material, is set out at p 826 *d e*, post

preamble stated that 'Canada has requested and consented to the enactment of an Act of
a the Parliament of the United Kingdom to give effect to [the Canada Bill]'. On 31 March
1982 the Attorney General issued a notice of motion for an order that the plaintiffs'
statement of claim be struck out as disclosing no reasonable cause of action and for an
order that the action be dismissed. At the hearing of the motion the plaintiffs conceded
that the 1982 Act had been passed by both Houses of Parliament and had received the
royal assent. The judge held that the 1982 Act was an Act of Parliament and that the
b duty of the court was to obey and apply that Act and that the court had no power to hold
a properly enacted Act of Parliament to be ultra vires. The plaintiffs appealed, contending
that a mere declaration in a subsequent Act that there had been a request and consent by
the relevant dominion for the legislation would not suffice to satisfy the requirements of
s 4*d* of the Statute of Westminster, because the declaration in question had to be a true
declaration and the consent had to be a real consent. The plaintiffs submitted that in the
c Canadian context the consent of the Dominion of Canada meant the consent of the
federal Parliament, all the provincial legislatures and the Indian people, who had a
separate and special status within the constitution of Canada. Since neither the
government or the legislature of the Province of Quebec nor the Indian people had joined
in making the relevant request or in giving the relevant consent in respect of the 1982
Act, the plaintiffs contended that that Act was void as not complying with s 4 of the
d Statute of Westminster. The plaintiffs further submitted that, even if s 4 by itself merely
required a declaration in a subsequent Act that there had been a request and consent by a
dominion, there was a convention that the actual consent and request of the dominion
was required before the United Kingdom Parliament could legislate for Canada or any
other dominion. That convention was, it was submitted, set out in the preamble*e* to the
Statute of Westminster, which stated that it was 'in accord with the established
e constitutional position' that no law thereafter enacted by the United Kingdom Parliament
would extend to a dominion 'otherwise than at the request and with the consent of that
Dominion'. Accordingly, the request and consent of all the constituent parts of Canada,
and not merely the Canadian Parliament, was required, by virtue of the convention set
out in the preamble to the Statute of Westminster, if not by s 4 itself, before the United
Kingdom Parliament could validly enact the 1982 Act. The plaintiffs further contended
f that the 1982 Act could not be said to have been enacted under the power reserved to the
United Kingdom Parliament by s 7(1) of the Statute of Westminster to enact legislation
effecting 'the repeal, amendment or alteration of the British North America Acts' since
the 1982 Act, although effectively repealing and amending parts of those Acts, did much
more than that and so went beyond the reserved competence of the United Kingdom
Parliament.

g
Held – The appeal would be dismissed for the following reasons—
(1) As far as the law of England was concerned, and assuming that the United
Kingdom Parliament was required as a matter of constitutional principle to comply
precisely with the conditions of s 4 of the Statute of Westminster before an Act of the
United Kingdom purporting to extend to a dominion would be valid and effective, s 4
h did not require that a dominion had in fact to request and consent to the enactment but
merely required the new Act to contain an express declaration that the dominion had
requested and consented to the enactment. Furthermore, the express declaration required
by s 4 was the sole condition precedent which had to be satisfied if a law made by the
United Kingdom Parliament was to extend to a dominion as part of its law. It would run
counter to all principles of statutory interpretation if the court were to purport to vary or
j supplement the terms of the stated condition precedent by reference to some supposed

---

c   The preamble is set out at p 827 *a*, post
d   Section 4 is set out at p 826 *c*, post
e   The preamble, so far as material, is set out at p 826 *a b*, post

convention, which, although referred to in the preamble to the Statute of Westminster, was not incorporated in the body thereof (see p 830 c to g and j to p 831 c and j, post).

(2) In determining whether the declaration in the preamble to the 1982 Act that 'Canada has requested and consented' to its enactment fulfilled the requirement of an express declaration imposed by s 4 of the Statute of Westminster, it was clear that the term 'Canada' was used in the sense of the Dominion of Canada throughout the 1982 Act. Accordingly, the condition precedent imposed by s 4 for the enactment of the Canada Act had been duly complied with by the declaration contained in the preamble .to the 1982 Act. It was therefore unnecessary to decide whether the 1982 Act fell within the reserved powers contained in s 7 of the Statute of Westminster since if and so far as the 1982 Act went beyond those reserved powers it was covered by the express declaration of a request and consent required by s 4 (see p 831 c to j, post).

(3) Since the plaintiffs were unable to show that the condition precedent imposed by s 4 of the Statute of Westminster had not been complied with, their claim failed to disclose a reasonable cause of action and the judge had been right to strike it out (see p 832 g to j, post).

Decision of Sir Robert Megarry V-C [1982] 3 All ER 786 affirmed.

Notes

For the constitution of Canada and the amendment thereof, see 6 Halsbury's Laws (4th edn) paras 835–836, 926–930.

For the extension of United Kingdom legislation to dominions, see ibid para 834.

For the reservation of powers by the United Kingdom Parliament, see ibid para 842.

For the British North America Act 1867, see 4 Halsbury's Statutes (3rd edn) 183.

For the Statute of Westminster 1931, preamble, ss 4, 7, see ibid 18, 21, 22.

Cases referred to in judgment

Amendment of the Constitution of Canada, Re (1981) 125 DLR (3d) 1.

Bribery Comr v Ranasinghe [1964] 2 All ER 785, [1965] AC 172, [1964] 2 WLR 1301, PC, 8(2) Digest (Reissue) 757, 347.

British Coal Corp v R [1935] AC 500, [1935] All ER 139, PC, 8(2) Digest (Reissue) 821, 697.

British Rlys Board v Pickin [1974] 1 All ER 609, [1974] AC 765, [1974] 2 WLR 208, HL; rvsg [1972] 3 All ER 923, [1973] QB 219, [1972] 3 WLR 824, CA, Digest (Cont Vol D) 862, 1694a.

Ellen Street Estates Ltd v Minister of Health [1934] 1 KB 590, [1934] All ER Rep 385, CA, 11 Digest (Reissue) 327, 2106.

Cases also cited

A-G v Blackburn [1971] 2 All ER 1380, [1971] 1 WLR 1037, CA.

Brassey's Settlement, Re, Barclays Bank Ltd v Brassey [1955] 1 All ER 577, [1955] 1 WLR 192.

Buck v A-G [1965] 1 All ER 882, [1965] Ch 745, CA.

Dyson v A-G [1911] 1 KB 410.

Harris v Minister of the Interior 1952 (2) SA 428.

Ibralebbe v R [1964] 1 All ER 251, [1964] AC 900, PC.

Macarthys Ltd v Smith Case 129/79 [1981] 1 All ER 111, [1981] QB 180, CJEC and CA.

Madzimbamuto v Lardner-Burke [1968] 3 All ER 561, [1969] AC 645, PC.

Minister of Home Affairs v Fisher [1979] 3 All ER 21, [1980] AC 319, PC.

R v Secretary of State for Foreign and Commonwealth Affairs, ex p Indian Association of Alberta [1982] 2 All ER 118, [1982] QB 892, CA.

Appeal

The plaintiffs, Chief Robert Manuel and 123 other Indian chiefs of Canada, appealed against the order of Sir Robert Megarry V-C ([1982] 3 All ER 786) made on 7 May 1982 *a* whereby it was ordered on the motion of the Attorney General that the plaintiffs' statement of claim be struck out and their action dismissed. The facts are set out in the judgment of the court.

John Macdonald QC and *Colin Braham* for the plaintiffs.
John Mummery for the Attorney General.

b   *Cur adv vult*

30 July. **SLADE LJ** read the following judgment of the court: This is an appeal from an order of Sir Robert Megarry V-C ([1982] 3 All ER 786) made on 7 May 1982 whereby he acceded to an application by Her Majesty's Attorney General that the statement of claim in an action be struck out and the action dismissed. The plaintiffs in the action were 124 *c* Canadian Indian Chiefs, who were respectively expressed to sue on behalf of themselves and named Indian bands. The defendant was the Attorney General. As Sir Robert Megarry V-C explained in his judgment, the term 'bands' is used in the sense of a body of Indians for whom lands have been set apart or for whom moneys are held or who have been declared to be a band by the Governor General in Council.

The case raises issues which are no doubt of great political importance to all the peoples *d* of Canada, particularly the Indians concerned. This court, however, is concerned with the bare question whether the claim to relief in the action is plainly ill-founded in English law. As Sir Robert Megarry V-C recognised in his judgment, if, but only if, the answer to this question is in the affirmative should the action be prevented from proceeding to trial.

Canada emerged as a dominion 115 years ago. Section 3 of the British North America *e* Act 1867 empowered the Queen, by and with the advice of the Privy Council, to declare by proclamation that the provinces of Canada, Nova Scotia and New Brunswick should 'form and be one dominion under the name of Canada'. Section 4 of that Act, as subsequently amended, provided that 'Unless it is otherwise expressed or implied, the name Canada shall be taken to mean Canada as constituted under this Act'.

Section 5 of 1867 Act (which contained many other provisions) provided for the *f* division of Canada into four provinces, to be named Ontario, Quebec, Nova Scotia and New Brunswick. The proclamation envisaged by the Act was duly made and the Dominion was established on 1 July 1867. Since then a number of additional provinces have been created and a number of further British North America Acts have been passed.

The nature of the present action is an unusual one. The gist of the facts alleged in the statement of claim, which give rise to the proceedings, may be very shortly summarised *g* for present purposes. Immediately before the Canada Act 1982 was enacted by the United Kingdom Parliament, the Canadian Indian bands had certain special rights which were protected under the constitution of Canada. These rights were recognised or confirmed by a royal proclamation made on 7 October 1763 and subsequently under a number of treaties made with the Indian bands. They include, inter alia, rights in relation to Indian reservations, rights of hunting, trapping and fishing game and fish for food at all seasons *h* of the year on all unoccupied Crown Lands and any other lands to which the Indians may have a right of access. Such rights are expressly referred to in a number of agreements set out in the schedule to the British North America Act 1930, which, by s 1, expressly provided that these agreements should have the force of law. For many years, the Indians have thus had entrenched rights under the Canadian constitution.

In 1931 the Statute of Westminster 1931 was enacted to give effect to certain *j* resolutions of Imperial Conferences held in the years 1926 and 1930. The Statute of Westminster substantially gave legislative independence to the territories which were specified in s 1 and were there referred to as 'Dominions'. These included the Dominion of Canada. Before the Act became law, an enactment of a dominion legislature such as that of Canada could not have had extra-territorial effect and, further, would have been void if it had been repugnant to an Act of Parliament of the United Kingdom which

extended to the dominion. These two disabilities were removed respectively by ss 3 and
2 of the Statute of Westminster, subject to certain provisions contained in ss 7, 8 and 9   *a*
and to the adoption of ss 2 and 3 by the dominion Parliament, if necessary under s 10.

The third paragraph of the preamble to the Statute of Westminster had recited:

> 'And whereas it is in accord with the established constitutional position that no
> law hereafter made by the Parliament of the United Kingdom shall extend to any of
> the said Dominions as part of the law of that Dominion otherwise than at the
> request and with the consent of that Dominion.'   *b*

Section 4 contained a corresponding provision but with one significant difference,
which will be mentioned later in this judgment. It provided:

> 'No Act of Parliament of the United Kingdom passed after the commencement of
> this Act shall extend, or be deemed to extend, to a Dominion as part of the law of
> that Dominion unless it is expressly declared in that Act that that Dominion has   *c*
> requested, and consented to, the enactment thereof.'

Section 7(1) provided:

> 'Nothing in this Act shall be deemed to apply to the repeal, amendment or
> alteration of the British North America Acts, 1868 to 1930, or any order, rule or
> regulation made thereunder.'   *d*

Section 7(3) provided:

> 'The powers conferred by this Act upon the Parliament of Canada or upon the
> legislatures of the Provinces shall be restricted to the enactment of laws in relation
> to matters within the competence of the Parliament of Canada or of any of the
> legislatures of the Provinces respectively.'   *e*

Section 7 thus preserved intact the existing powers of the United Kingdom Parliament
to legislate by way of 'repeal, amendment or alteration' of the British North America
Acts. At the time when the Statute of Westminster was passed, these powers were very
extensive, since an alteration of the constitutional Acts of Canada could, with certain
minor exceptions, be effected only by an Act of the United Kingdom Parliament. In   *f*
1949, as a result of the amendment of s 91 of the British North America Act 1867 effected
by the British North America (No 2) Act 1949, the Parliament of Canada acquired
exclusive power to amend the constitution of Canada, except as regards matters coming
within a number of classes of subjects specified in the section. Even after 1949, however,
United Kingdom legislation remained necessary in respect of any amendment affecting
these excepted matters. The plaintiffs consider that it remained necessary in respect of   *g*
amendments affecting certain entrenched rights of the Indians embodied in the British
North America Acts.

On 9 December 1981 the Senate and the House of Commons of Canada submitted an
address to Her Majesty the Queen requesting that a Bill (the Canada Bill) be laid before
the United Kingdom Parliament to amend the constitution of Canada in a manner
summarised in the statement of claim as follows: *h*

> 'by (inter alia) (1) terminating the remaining responsibility of the United
> Kingdom Parliament for amending the constitution of Canada and conferring all
> such responsibility on Canadian institutions, and (2) providing for a Canadian
> Charter of Rights and Freedoms.'

On 10 December 1981, before the Canada Bill had become law, the plaintiffs (or more   *j*
accurately some of the plaintiffs, since others were subsequently added by amendment)
issued the writ in the present action. A statement of claim was served on 22 January 1982
and shortly afterwards amended.

On 29 March 1982 the Canada Act 1982 received the royal assent. The long title to the
Act is 'An Act to give effect to a request by the Senate and House of Commons of Canada'.
It contains a preamble in the following terms:

a

'Whereas Canada has requested and consented to the enactment of an Act of the Parliament of the United Kingdom to give effect to the provisions hereinafter set forth and the Senate and the House of Commons of Canada in Parliament assembled have submitted an address to Her Majesty requesting that Her Majesty may graciously be pleased to cause a Bill to be laid before the Parliament of the United Kingdom for that purpose.'

b

Sections 1, 2 and 3 state:

    1. 'The Constitution Act, 1982 set out in Schedule B to this Act is hereby enacted for and shall have the force of law in Canada and shall come into force as provided in that Act.

    2. 'No Act of the Parliament of the United Kingdom passed after the Constitution Act, 1982 comes into force shall extend to Canada as part of its law.

c

    3. 'So far as it is not contained in Schedule B, the French version of this Act is set out in Schedule A to this Act and has the same authority in Canada as the English version thereof.'

The Constitution Act 1982 referred to in the Canada Act 1982 came into force on 17 April 1982 by a proclamation by the Queen pursuant to s 58 of that Act.

d

Part I of the Constitution Act 1982 (ss 1–34) contains the Canadian Charter of Rights and Freedoms. Under s 25 the guarantee in the Charter of certain rights and freedoms is expressed not to abrogate or derogate from any aboriginal, treaty or other rights or freedoms that pertain to the aboriginal peoples of Canada. Section 35(2) defines 'aboriginal peoples of Canada' as including the Indian, Inuit and Métis peoples of Canada. Section 35(1) explicitly recognises and affirms the existing aboriginal and treaty rights of the aboriginal peoples of Canada. It is not, therefore, claimed that the Constitution Act 1982

e

immediately divests the plaintiffs of any of their subsisting rights. Their anxiety appears to stem from a different cause. Section 37 provides for the convening of a constitutional conference within one year after the section comes into force (17 April 1982), which is to have included in its agenda an item respecting constitutional matters that directly affect the aboriginal peoples of Canada. Part V of the Act (ss 38–49) introduces a new procedure for amending the Constitution of Canada. The effect of this new procedure is that the

f

United Kingdom Parliament will henceforth take no part in any such amendment. Under s 53(1), ss 4 and 7(1) of the Statute of Westminster are repealed in so far as they apply to Canada.

In these circumstances, the submission of the plaintiffs, as appearing from their statement of claim, is that the enactment of the Canada Bill is inconsistent with and a derogation from the constitutional safeguards provided for the Indian peoples by the

g

Statute of Westminster and the British North America Acts.

The statement of claim was reamended on 14 May 1982, during the course of the hearing before Sir Robert Megarry V-C, partly to take account of the fact that the Canada Act 1982 had by then become law. The prayer to the reamended pleading seeks a large number of declarations, but as Sir Robert Megarry V-C observed, the first five plainly lead up to the last two, which are declarations that—

h

'(1) the United Kingdom Parliament has no power to amend the Constitution of Canada so as to prejudice the Indian Nations without the consent of the Indian Nations of Canada; (2) the Canada Act 1982 is ultra vires.'

As Sir Robert Megarry V-C commented in his judgment, a contention that an Act of

j

Parliament is ultra vires is, on the face of it, bold in the extreme. It is not suggested that the Canada Act 1982 was not passed by the House of Commons and the House of Lords or that it did not receive the royal assent. On the face of it, the ordinary, elementary rules of English constitutional law leave the court with no choice but to construe and apply the enactments of Parliament as they stand: see *British Rlys Board v Pickin* [1974] 1 All ER 609, [1974] AC 765. As Lord Morris observed ([1974] 1 All ER 609 at 619, [1979] AC 765 at 789):

'It is the function of the courts to administer the laws which Parliament has
enacted. In the processes of Parliament there will be much consideration whether a   *a*
bill should or should not in one form or another become an enactment. When an
enactment is passed there is finality unless and until it is amended or repealed by
Parliament. In the courts there may be argument as to the correct interpretation of
the enactment: there must be none as to whether it should be on the statute book at
all.'

Though Sir Robert Megarry V-C referred to a number of other matters in his judgment,   *b*
in the end he founded himself substantially on this proposition in striking out the
plaintiffs' statement of claim. As he put it ([1982] 3 All ER 786 at 794): 'The Canada Act
1982 is an Act of Parliament, and sitting as a judge in an English court, I owe full and
dutiful obedience to that Act.'

If the matter is as simple as that, that is an end of the plaintiffs' case. But counsel for
the plaintiffs in effect submitted that it is very far from so simple. In his submission, it is   *c*
open to Parliament to give up its sovereignty in whole or in part. In particular, he
contended, it is open to it to provide that any future legislation on a specified subject
shall be enacted only with certain specified consents and that, in default of such consents,
such future legislation shall be void. This, he submitted, is what Parliament did when it
enacted s 4 of the Statute of Westminster.

As we understood his argument before this court, it proceeded on lines which followed   *d*
closely those which were summarised by Sir Robert Megarry V-C (see [1982] 3 All ER
786 at 793). By 1931 a convention had been established by a long-standing tradition that
the United Kingdom Parliament could not legislate for Canada or the other dominions,
save at the request and with the consent of the dominion concerned. Since (so it was
submitted) that convention had ripened into law by 1931, s 4 of the Statute of
Westminster was merely declaratory of the existing law. This convention required that,   *e*
in any case where s 4 applied, there had to be an actual request and consent of the
dominion concerned. A mere declaration in a subsequent Act that there had been such a
request and consent would not suffice to satisfy the requirements of s 4. The declaration
in question, counsel for the plaintiffs strongly and repeatedly emphasised, had to be a
true one and the consent had to be a real consent. Section 7(1) of the Statute of
Westminster which provided that nothing in the Act was to be 'deemed to apply to the   *f*
repeal, amendment or alteration of the British North America Acts' did not remove the
need for the appropriate request and consent of the Dominion of Canada, and declaration
thereof, in respect of the Canada Act 1982, because that Act went beyond a mere 'repeal,
amendment or alteration' of the British North America Acts. The effect of s 4 of the
Statute of Westminster thus was and is that the actual consent and request of the
Dominion of Canada had to be given to the Canada Act 1982, and the appropriate   *g*
declaration of such request and consent had to be contained in that Act itself, if it was to
be a valid statute extending to Canada. Furthermore, for this purpose, so it was submitted,
the consent of the Dominion of Canada means the consent of the federal Parliament, all
the provincial legislatures and the Indian nations, who are said to have a separate and
special status within the Constitution of Canada, or alternatively at very least the consent
of the federal Parliament and all the provincial legislatures. Neither the government nor   *h*
the legislature of the Province of Quebec, nor the Indian nations of Canada have joined
in making the relevant request or giving the relevant consents in respect of the Canada
Act 1982. In these circumstances, it is submitted that this Act is void, as not complying
with s 4 of the Statute of Westminster, or it must at least be arguable that this is so.

If, as we hope and believe, this is an adequate, albeit abbreviated, summary of the
essential features of counsel's full and strenuous argument, the argument will be seen to   *j*
depend on a number of propositions, each one of which would be essential to its success
at the trial of the action. Included among these essential propositions, though they are by
no means the only ones, are the following three, each one of which must be established
as arguable, if the plaintiffs are to succeed on this appeal: (1) that Parliament can
effectively tie the hands of its successors, if it passes a statute which provides that any

a future legislation on a specified subject shall be enacted only with certain specified consents; (2) that s 7(1) of the Statute of Westminster did not absolve the United Kingdom Parliament from the need to comply with the conditions of s 4 of the Statute of Westminster in enacting the Canada Act 1982, if the latter Act was to extend to Canada as an effective Act; (3) that the conditions of s 4 of the Statute of Westminster have not in fact been complied with in relation to the Canada Act 1982.

b At least at first sight, the first of these propositions conflicts with the general statements of the law made by Maugham LJ in *Ellen Street Estates Ltd v Minister of Health* [1934] 1 KB 590 at 597, [1934] All ER Rep 385 at 390:

c 'The Legislature cannot, according to our constitution, bind itself as to the form of subsequent legislation, and it is impossible for Parliament to enact that in a subsequent statute dealing with the same subject-matter there can be no implied repeal. If in a subsequent Act Parliament chooses to make it plain that the earlier statute is being to some extent repealed, effect must be given to that intention just because it is the will of the Legislature.'

Scrutton LJ said much the same thing in that case (see [1934] 1 KB 590 at 595–596, [1934] All ER Rep 385 at 389). In *British Coal Corp v R* [1935] AC 500 at 520, [1935] All ER Rep 139 at 146 Lord Sankey made certain observations specifically directed to the

d Statute of Westminster:

'It is doubtless true that the power of the Imperial Parliament to pass on its own initiative any legislation that it thought fit extending to Canada remains in theory unimpaired: indeed, the Imperial Parliament could, as a matter of abstract law, repeal or disregard s. 4 of the Statute.'

e Lord Sankey went on to observe that that was theory and had no relation to reality, but, if his statement of theory was correct, it would appear to refute the proposition now under consideration. However, a degree of support for the proposition is to be found in the writings of certain academic lawyers, for example W R Anson 'The Government of Ireland Bill and the Sovereignty of Parliament' (1886) 2 LQR 427 at 440 and Dicey *Law of the Constitution* (8th edn, 1915) pp 66–67 and, possibly, in the decision of the Judicial

f Committee of the Privy Council in *Bribery Comr v Ranasinghe* [1967] 2 All ER 785, [1965] AC 172. In the latter case, Lord Pearce, in delivering the advice of the Board, expressed its view that 'a legislature has no power to ignore the conditions of law-making that are imposed by the instrument which itself regulates its power to make law' (see [1964] 2 All ER 785 at 792, [1965] AC 172 at 197). A little later he described as unacceptable the proposition that—

g 'a legislature, once established, has some inherent power, derived from the mere fact of its establishment, to make a valid law by the resolution of a bare majority which its own constituent instrument has said shall not be a valid law unless made by a different type of majority or by a different legislative process.'

h Counsel for the plaintiffs has submitted that the Statute of Westminster was an instrument which itself regulated the power of Parliament to make law for the dominions and so was a 'constituent instrument' within this language. Accordingly, in his submission, no subsequent Act extending to a dominion can be valid unless it complies with the conditions of the Statute of Westminster.

This submission raises points of great interest and fundamental importance to constitutional lawyers but, for reasons which will appear, we do not find it necessary to

j deal with them. For the purposes of this judgment we are content to assume in favour of the plaintiffs that the first of the three propositions to which we have referred is correct, though we would emphasise that we are not purporting to decide it.

As regards the second of them counsel for the plaintiffs submitted that the Canada Act 1982 does not fall within the exempting provisions of s 7(1) of the Statute of Westminster, on the grounds that its provisions go beyond a mere 'repeal, amendment or alteration of

the British North America Acts'. We do not think it has been or could be disputed that at
least a substantial part of the contents of the Constitution Act 1982, if regarded in   *a*
isolation, would amount to no more than a mere 'repeal, amendment or alteration of the
British America Acts', within those exempting provisions. Counsel for the plaintiffs has
submitted that at least some others of its contents (for example, the Charter of Rights and
Freedoms) fall outside such exemption and accordingly make it necessary that the
conditions of s 4 of the Statute of Westminster should be complied with in relation to the
whole of the Canada Act 1982.   *b*

By far the greater part of the plaintiffs' argument on this appeal has been devoted to an
attempt to show that the conditions of s 4 have not been complied with in this context.

In the circumstances we will proceed to consider the third of the propositions referred
to above which relates to s 4 of the Statute of Westminster. We will revert briefly to the
second of them and to s 7 at the end of this judgment.

For the time being, therefore, let it be supposed that Parliament, in enacting the   *c*
Canada Act 1982, had precisely to comply with the conditions of s 4 of the Statute of
Westminster, if that new Act was to be valid and effective. What then are the conditions
which s 4 imposes? It is significant that, while the preamble to the Statute of Westminster
recites that—

> 'it is in accord with the established constitutional position that no law hereafter   *d*
> made by the Parliament of the United Kingdom shall extend to any of the said
> Dominions as part of the law of that Dominion otherwise that at the request and
> with the consent of that Dominion,'

s 4 itself does *not* provide that no Act of the United Kingdom Parliament shall extend to
a dominion as part of the law of that dominion unless the dominion has *in fact* requested
and consented to the enactment thereof. The condition that must be satisfied is a quite   *e*
different one, namely that it must be 'expressly declared in that Act that that Dominion
has requested and consented to the enactment thereof'. Though counsel for the plaintiffs,
as we have said, submitted that s 4 requires not only a declaration but a true declaration
of a real request and consent, we are unable to read the section in that way. There is no
ambiguity in the relevant words and the court would not in our opinion be justified in
supplying additional words by a process of implication; it must construe and apply the   *f*
words as they stand (see *Maxwell on the Interpretation of Statutes* (12th edn, 1969) p 33 and
the cases there cited). If an Act of Parliament contains an express declaration in the
precise form required by s 4, such declaration is in our opinion conclusive so far as s 4 is
concerned.

There was, we think, nothing unreasonable or illogical in this simple approach to the
matter on the part of the legislature, in reserving to itself the sole function of deciding   *g*
whether the requisite request and consent have been made and given. The present case
itself provides a good illustration of the practical consequences that would have ensued if
s 4 had made an actual request and consent on the part of a dominion a condition
precedent to the validity of the relevant legislation in such manner that the courts or
anyone else would have had to look behind the relevant declaration in order to ascertain
whether a statute of the United Kingdom Parliament, expressed to extend to that   *h*
dominion, was valid. There is obviously room for argument as to the identity of the
representatives of the Dominion of Canada appropriate to express the relevant request
and consent. Counsel for the plaintiffs, while firm in his submission that all legislatures
of the provinces of Canada had to join the federal Parliament in expressing them, seemed
less firm in his submission that all the Indian nations had likewise to join. This is a point
which might well involve difficult questions of Canadian constitutional law. Moreover,   *j*
if all the Indian nations did have to join, further questions might arise as to the manner
in which the consents of these numerous persons and bodies had to be expressed and
whether all of them had in fact been given. As we read the wording of s 4, it was designed
to obviate the need for any further inquiries of this nature once a statute, containing the
requisite declaration, had been duly enacted by the United Kingdom Parliament.

a Parliament, having satisfied itself as to the request and consent, would make the declaration and that would be that.

Counsel for the plaintiffs submitted in the alternative that, even if s 4 on its proper construction does not itself bear the construction which he attributed to it, nevertheless, in view of the convention referred to in the third paragraph of the preamble, the actual request and consent of the dominion is necessary before a law made by the United Kingdom Parliament can extend to that dominion as part of its law. Whether or not an
b argument on these lines might find favour in the courts of a dominion, it is in our opinion quite unsustainable in the courts of this country. The sole condition precedent which has to be satisfied if a law made by the United Kingdom Parliament is to extend to a dominion as part of its law is to be found stated in the body of the Statute of Westminster itself (s 4). This court would run counter to all principles of statutory interpretation if it were to purport to vary or supplement the terms of this stated
c condition precedent by reference to some supposed convention, which, although referred to in the preamble, is not incorporated in the body of the Statute of Westminster.

In the present instance, therefore, the only remaining question is whether it is arguable that the condition precedent specified in s 4 of the Statute of Westminster has not been complied with in relation to the Canada Act 1982. Is it arguable that it has not been 'expressly declared in that Act that that Dominion has requested, and consented to, the
d enactment thereof'? In our judgment this proposition is not arguable, inasmuch as the preamble to the Canada Act 1982 begins with the words 'Whereas Canada has requested and consented to the enactment of an Act of the Parliament of the United Kingdom to give effect to the provisions hereinafter set forth'. Counsel for the plaintiffs, as we understood him, attempted to argue that, in the context of this particular recital, the word 'Canada', as a matter of construction, means not the Dominion of Canada, but the
e Senate and House of Commons of Canada. In this context he referred to the long title of the Canada Act 1982: 'An Act to give effect to a request by the Senate and House of Commons of Canada.' Thus, he submitted, even on the interpretation of s 4 which we think is the correct one, the relevant condition has not been complied with in the present case. In our opinion there is no substance in this point. First, the court is not, we think, entitled to look at the long title of the Act for the purpose of construing the contents of
f the Act, except in so far as these contents are themselves ambiguous (see *Maxwell on the Interpretation of Statutes* (12th edn, 1969) pp 5–6). Second, the preamble itself uses the word 'Canada', followed shortly afterwards by the phrase 'the Senate and the House of Commons of Canada', thereby making it plain that 'Canada' is intended to mean something more than the Senate and the House of Commons of Canada. Third, and most importantly, each of ss 1, 2 and 3 uses the word 'Canada' plainly in the sense of the
g Dominion of Canada. It would not, in our opinion, be justifiable to attribute to the word a different meaning in the preamble. Section 3 of the British North America Act 1867 expressly established one dominion under the name 'Canada', and s 4 expressly provided that the name 'Canada' should be taken to mean Canada as constituted under that Act. Manifestly, in our opinion, the word 'Canada' throughout the Canada Act 1982 bears the meaning of the Dominion of Canada. The use of the word 'Canada' in our opinion
h involves no ambiguity at all.

For all these reasons, we conclude that, if and so far as the conditions of s 4 of the Statute of Westminster had to be complied with in relation to the Canada Act 1982, they were duly complied with by the declaration contained in the preamble to that Act.

Consequently, it is unnecessary to consider further the second of the three propositions referred to earlier in this judgment. It is unnecessary to consider whether the Constitution
j Act 1982 contains provisions which go beyond 'the repeal, amendment or alteration of the British North America Acts' so as to fall outside the exempting provisions of s 7(1) of the Statute of Westminster and thus within s 4 of that Act. If it does contain such provisions, the express declaration of a request and consent required by s 4 is duly contained in the Canada Act 1982. If it contains no such provisions (as we understood counsel would have sought to submit on behalf of the Attorney General, though we did

not think it necessary to call on him), no declaration of request and consent was necessary.

Clearly this is not the first time when the relationship of ss 4 and 7 has been under *a* consideration by the legislature in the course of drafting legislation intended to extend to Canada. It will be observed that the preamble to the Canada Act 1982 contains two limbs. The first recites a request and consent on the part of Canada to the enactment of an Act of the United Kingdom Parliament to give effect to the provisions thereinafter set forth. The second recites the submission by the Senate and House of Commons in Canada to Her Majesty of an address requesting that a Bill be laid before the United Kingdom *b* Parliament for that purpose. The second limb of the preamble follows a form of preamble adopted by the legislature in previous instances where the legislation in question has clearly involved no more than a mere amendment of the British North America Acts, falling within s 7(1) of the Statute of Westminster. The British North America (No 2) Act 1949, for example, which was merely intended to amend s 91 of the British North America Act 1867, contained solely the following preamble: *c*

> 'Whereas the Senate and the House of Commons of Canada in Parliament assembled have submitted an Address to His Majesty praying that His Majesty may graciously be pleased to cause a measure to be laid before the Parliament of the United Kingdom for the enactment of the provisions hereinafter set forth.'

The British North America (No 2) Act 1949 contained no express declaration of a *d* request and consent on the part of the Dominion of Canada, no doubt because this was regarded as an Act which fell fairly and squarely within s 7 of the Statute of Westminster, so that s 4 did not apply. The British North America Acts 1940 and 1946 had contained similar preambles. In striking contrast to that of the British North America (No 2) Act 1949 and of the 1940 and 1946 Acts, the preamble to the British North America Act 1949, which was passed a few months earlier, so as to confirm and give effect to the terms of the union agreed between Canada and Newfoundland, contained a two-limbed recital *e* more or less in the same terms as that employed by the legislature in the Canada Act 1982, and beginning with the words 'And whereas Canada has requested, and consented to, the enactment of an Act of the Parliament of the United Kingdom . . .' We infer that the first limb of the recital in the case of the British North America Act 1949 and the Canada Act 1982 must have been intended and was effective to constitute, so far as might *f* be necessary, a declaration of the very nature specified in s 4 of the Statute of Westminster.

For completeness, we should perhaps add that counsel for the plaintiffs referred us to a recent decision of the Supreme Court of Canada, which concerned, among other things, the consents that are requisite under the constitutional law of Canada for an amendment of the constitution of Canada: see *Re Amendment of the Constitution of Canada* (1981) 125 DLR (3d) 1. However, with all deference to the Supreme Court of Canada, this decision, though very important and interesting, does not in our opinion have any direct bearing *g* on the issues of English law which fall to be decided on the present appeal.

For the reasons which we have given, in our judgment the plaintiffs have failed to disclose an arguable case in submitting that the conditions of s 4 of the Statute of Westminster have not been complied with in relation to the Canada Act 1982, even on the assumption that s 7(1) does not render the provisions of s 4 inapplicable. On this ground if no other, we have reached the clear conclusion that, if this action were to *h* proceed to trial, it would be bound to fail. The trial judge, sitting in an English court and applying English law, would on any footing be bound to follow and apply the House of Lords decision in *British Rlys Board v Pickin* [1974] 1 All ER 609, [1974] AC 765 and accordingly to reject the attack on the validity of that Act.

In our judgment, therefore, Sir Robert Megarry V-C was plainly right to strike out the statement of claim in this action and to dismiss the action. We dismiss this appeal. *j*

Appeal dismissed. Leave to appeal to the House of Lords refused.

Solicitors: *Herbert Oppenheimer, Nathan & Vandyk* (for the plaintiffs); *Treasury Solicitor.*

Henrietta Steinberg   Barrister.

Yew Bon Tew v Kenderaan Bas Mara

PRIVY COUNCIL
LORD FRASER OF TULLYBELTON, LORD SCARMAN, LORD LOWRY, LORD BRIDGE OF HARWICH AND LORD BRIGHTMAN
7, 8 JULY, 7 OCTOBER 1982

Limitation of action – Statute – Amendment – Construction – Extension of limitation period – Cause of action time-barred before amendment – Cause of action within limitation period if amendment retrospective – Whether amendment retrospective – Whether classification of amending statute as procedural or substantive relevant to retrospectivity – Whether cause of action revived by amending statute – Public Authorities Protection Ordinance 1948 (Malaysia), s 2(a) – Public Authorities Protection (Amendment) Act 1974 (Malaysia).

On 5 April 1972 in Selangor, Malaysia, a motor bus belonging to the respondents collided with a motor cycle driven by the first appellant with the second appellant as pillion passenger. Both appellants were injured. The respondents were a statutory body and the accident occurred during the course of the respondents' public duties. Consequently, by virtue of s 2(a)[a] of the Malaysian Public Authorities Protection Ordinance 1948, which prescribed a limitation period of 12 months for bringing any action against any person for any negligent act done in the exercise of any public duty, the appellants' cause of action was liable to become statute-barred on 5 April 1973. The appellants' advisers did not appreciate that the respondents were a public authority, and no proceedings were instituted before the expiration of the limitation period. On 13 June 1974 the Malaysian Public Authorities Protection (Amendment) Act 1974 came into force. The 1974 Act amended the 1948 Ordinance by substituting a 36-month limitation period for the original 12-month limitation period. Immediately before the 1974 Act came into force the appellants' cause of action had been statute-barred for 14 months. Nine months later, on 20 March 1975, ie 36 months less three weeks after the date of the accident, the appellants issued a writ against the respondents claiming damages for injuries caused by the negligence of the respondents' servant. The respondents contended that the claim was statute-barred. The High Court of Malaya rejected that contention, holding that the 1974 Act was retrospective, and gave judgment for the appellants. The Federal Court of Malaysia allowed an appeal by the respondents, holding that the 1974 Act was not retrospective and that accordingly the claim was statute-barred. The appellants appealed to the Privy Council, contending that the 1974 Act was merely procedural and therefore prima facie retrospective and consequently on its coming into force the appellants' cause of action had been revived.

Held – The proper approach to determining whether a statute had retrospective effect was not by classifying it as procedural or substantive but by seeing whether, if applied retrospectively to a particular type of case, it would impair existing rights and obligations; and an accrued right to plead a time bar, which was acquired after the lapse of the statutory period, was in every sense a right even though it arose under a statute which was procedural. The plain purpose of the 1974 Act, read with the 1948 Ordinance, was to give a potential defendant who was not possessed of an accrued limitation defence on the coming into force of the 1974 Act a right to plead such a defence at the expiration of the new statutory period; it was not to deprive a potential defendant of a limitation defence which he already possessed. It followed that the appellants' writ had been issued outside the limitation period, and the appeal would accordingly be dismissed (see p 839 d to j and p 840 j to p 841 a, post).

Dictum of Williams J in *Maxwell v Murphy* (1957) 96 CLR at 277–278 followed.

The Ydun [1899] P 236, *R v Chandra Dharma* [1904–7] All ER Rep 570 and *Mitchell v Harris Engineering Co Ltd* [1967] 2 All ER 682 considered.

---

a   Section 2, so far as material, is set out at p 835 c, post

Noor Mohamed Yousoff v Teo Kai Tee (1955) 19 MLJ 188 not followed.

Dictum of Lord Denning MR in *Mitchell v Harris Engineering Co Ltd* [1967] 2 All ER at **a**
686 disapproved.

Per curiam. (1) Apart from the provisions of the interpretation statutes, there is at
common law a prima facie rule of construction that a statute should not be interpreted
retrospectively so as to impair an existing right or obligation unless that result is
unavoidable on the language used. Whether a statute is to be construed in a retrospective
sense, and if so to what extent, depends on the intention of the legislature as expressed in **b**
the wording of the statute, having regard to the normal canons of construction and to
the relevant provisions of any interpretation statute (see p 836 *a b d e*, post).

(2) The whole purpose of a limitation defence is that, when the period of limitation
has expired, a potential defendant should be able to assume that he is no longer at risk
from a stale claim. He should be able to part with his papers if they exist, discard any
proofs of witnesses which have been taken, discharge his solicitor if he has been retained **c**
and order his affairs on the basis that his potential liability has gone (see p 839 *j* to p 840
a, post).

Notes

For retrospective effect of statutes, see 36 Halsbury's Laws (3rd edn) 423–428, paras 643–
647, and for cases on the subject, see 44 Digest (Repl) 284–291, *1132–1218*. **d**

For statutes of limitations generally, see 28 Halsbury's Laws (4th edn) paras 601–621,
and for cases on the subject, see 32 Digest (Reissue) 468–469, *3599–3616*.

Cases referred to in judgment

Harris v Quine (1869) LR 4 QB 653, 32 Digest (Reissue) 501, *3835*.
Maxwell v Murphy (1957) 96 CLR 261, Aust HC. **e**
Mitchell v Harris Engineering Co Ltd [1967] 2 All ER 682, [1967] 2 QB 703, [1967] 3 WLR
447, CA, 37(1) Digest (Reissue) 264, *1733*.
Noor Mohamed Yousoff v Teo Kai Tee (1955) 19 MLJ 188.
R v Chandra Dharma [1905] 2 KB 335, [1904–7] All ER Rep 570, CCR, 44 Digest (Repl)
290, *1208*.
Rodriguez v Parker [1966] 2 All ER 349, [1967] 1 QB 116, [1966] 3 WLR 546, 32 Digest **f**
(Reissue) 726, *5267*.
Whittam v W J Daniel & Co Ltd [1961] 3 All ER 796, [1962] 1 QB 271, [1961] 3 WLR
1123, CA, 32 Digest (Reissue) 727, *5269*.
Wright v Hale (1860) 6 H & N 227, 158 ER 94, 44 Digest (Repl) 298, *1286*.
Ydun, The [1899] P 236, CA, 44 Digest (Repl) 290, *1206*.

g

Appeal

Yew Bon Tew, also known as Yong Boon Tiew, and Ganesan s/o Thaver (an infant) suing
by his guardian and next friend, Yew Bon Tew, also known as Yong Boon Tiew, appealed
by leave of the Federal Court of Malaysia given on 19 May 1980 against the judgment
and order of the Federal Court of Malaysia (Appellate Jurisdiction) (Raja Azlan Shah CJ
(Acting Lord President), Chang Min Tat and Syed Othman FJJ) dated 27 November 1979 **h**
allowing an appeal by the respondents, Kenderaan Bas Mara, from the judgment and
order of the High Court of Malaya (Azmi J) dated 13 April 1977 whereby the respondents'
preliminary objection that the appellants' claims in their writ and statement of claim
dated 20 March 1975 for damages for injuries caused by the alleged negligence of the
respondents on 5 April 1972 was barred by the Public Authorities Protection Ordinance
1948. The facts are set out in the judgment. **j**

Nigel Murray and *K C Cheah* (of the Malaysian Bar) for the appellants.
Robert Gatehouse QC and *Zainur Zakaria* (of the Malaysian Bar) for the respondents.

LORD BRIGHTMAN. This appeal from the Federal Court of Malaysia raises the
question whether claimants, whose cause of action became statute barred in 1973 by

virtue of the Public Authorities Protection Ordinance 1948, can nevertheless issue a writ
a in 1975 in reliance on the Public Authorities Protection (Amendment) Act 1974 which
substituted a limitation period of 36 months for the previous period of 12 months.

On 5 April 1972 a motor bus belonging to the respondents was being driven along a
road in the State of Selangor. It collided with a motor cycle driven by the first appellant
with the second appellant as pillion passenger. Both were injured.

The respondents are a statutory body and the accident occurred during the course of
b the respondents' public duties. Consequently the appellant's cause of action was liable to
become statute-barred on 5 April 1973 pursuant to the 1948 Ordinance, s 2 of which
reads as follows:

> 'Where, after the coming into force of this Ordinance, any suit, action, prosecution
> or other proceeding is commenced in the Federation against any person for any act
> done in pursuance or execution or intended execution of any written law or of any
c > public duty or authority or in respect of any alleged neglect or default in the
> execution of any such written law, duty or authority the following provisions shall
> have effect—(a) the suit, action, prosecution or proceeding shall not lie or be
> instituted unless it is commenced within twelve months next after the act, neglect
> or default complained of or, in the case of a continuance of injury or damage, within
> twelve months next after the ceasing thereof . . .'
d

Unfortunately those advising the appellants did not appreciate that the respondents
were a public authority. As a result time slipped by without the institution of proceedings
before the 12-month limitation expired on 5 April 1973.

On 5 June 1974 the 1974 Act was passed. It came into force on 13 June. It was
expressed to amend the 1948 Ordinance by deleting the words 'twelve months' wherever
e appearing in para (a) of s 2 and substituting the words 'thirty six months'. Immediately
before the 1974 Act came into force the appellants' cause of action had been statute-
barred for 14 months. A further 9 months went by and on 20 March 1975 the appellants
issued a writ claiming damages for personal injuries caused by the negligence of the
respondents' servant. Three weeks later the 36-month period of limitation, if applicable,
expired. The respondents filed a defence in which they pleaded that the appellants were
f barred from bringing the action by virtue of the 1948 Ordinance. By the time the action
came to trial, this had become the only point in the case. Liability was admitted subject
to contributory negligence on the part of the first appellant, and substantial damages
were also agreed. The sole question remained whether the appellants' cause of action was
finally statute-barred in April 1973 or whether it was revived in June 1974.

There are two other statutory provisions which are relevant. Section 13 of the
g Interpretation and General Clauses Ordinance 1948 provided:

> 'Where a written law repeals in whole or in part any other written law, then,
> unless the contrary intention appears, the repeal shall not . . . (c) affect any right,
> privilege, obligation or liability acquired, accrued or incurred under any written
> law so repealed . . .'

h This Act was replaced by the Interpretation Act 1967, s 30(1)(b) of which says the same
thing in different words.

Their Lordships turn to consider the propositions that a Limitation Act which is not
expressed to extinguish a cause of action is procedural and that a statute which is merely
procedural is prima facie retrospective. These two propositions lie at the root of the
appellants' case.
j A statute of limitations may be described either as procedural or as substantive. For
example, in English law, at the expiration of the period prescribed for any person to
bring an action to recover land, the title of that person to the land is extinguished. Such
a limitation therefore goes to the cause of action itself. In most cases however the English
Limitation Act only takes away the remedies by action or by set-off; it goes only to the
conduct of the suit; it leaves the claimant's right otherwise untouched in theory so that,

in the case of a debt, if the statute-barred creditor has any means of enforcing his claim
other than by action or set-off, the Act does not prevent his recovering by those means. *a*
In this sense, the 1948 Ordinance and the 1974 Act are procedural. Cf *Harris v Quine*
(1869) LR 4 QB 653 and *Rodriguez v Parker* [1966] 2 All ER 349, [1967] 1 QB 116.

Apart from the provisions of the interpretation statutes, there is at common law a
prima facie rule of construction that a statute should not be interpreted retrospectively
so as to impair an existing right or obligation unless that result is unavoidable on the
language used. A statute is retrospective if it takes away or impairs a vested right acquired *b*
under existing laws, or creates a new obligation, or imposes a new duty, or attaches a new
disability, in regard to events already past. There is however said to be an exception in
the case of a statute which is purely procedural, because no person has a vested right in
any particular course of procedure, but only a right to prosecute or defend a suit according
to the rules for the conduct of an action for the time being prescribed.

But these expressions 'retrospective' and 'procedural', though useful in a particular *c*
context, are equivocal and therefore can be misleading. A statute which is retrospective
in relation to one aspect of a case (eg because it applies to a pre-statute cause of action)
may at the same time be prospective in relation to another aspect of the same case (eg
because it applies only to the post-statute commencement of proceedings to enforce that
cause of action); and an Act which is procedural in one sense may in particular
circumstances do far more than regulate the course of proceedings, because it may, on *d*
one interpretation, revive or destroy the cause of action itself.

Whether a statute is to be construed in a retrospective sense, and if so to what extent,
depends on the intention of the legislature as expressed in the wording of the statute,
having regard to the normal canons of construction and to the relevant provisions of any
interpretation statute. The sort of problem which can arise is neatly illustrated by *The
Ydun* [1899] P 236. This was an action by the owners of the barque Ydun against the *e*
Corporation of Preston. On 13 September 1893 the barque went aground owing to the
alleged negligence of the Preston Corporation, which was the port authority. On 5
December 1893 the Public Authorities Protection Act 1893 was passed. It came into
force on 1 January 1894. It had the effect of curtailing the period of limitation applicable
to the institution of proceedings in such an action from six years to six months. The
position therefore at the date of the accident was that the owners had until September *f*
1899 to issue their writ; but on 1 January 1894, if the Act applied to this cause of action,
they had only until march 1894. The owners issued their writ in November 1898. By
the time the case reached the Court of Appeal there were two issues: first, whether the
corporation had been acting in pursuance of its public duties when the accident took
place and was therefore entitled to the protection of the Act, and, second, whether the
Act applied to a cause of action which had already accrued when the Act came into force. *g*
The second issue was decided against the owners, and was disposed of in the judgments
with remarkable brevity for so important an issue. A L Smith LJ expressed himself as
follows (at 245):

'The rule applicable to cases of this sort is well stated by Wilde B. in *Wright v Hale*
((1860) 6 H & N 227 at 232, 158 ER 94 at 95), namely, that when a new enactment
deals with rights of action, unless it is so expressed in the Act, an existing right of *h*
action is not taken away. But when the enactment deals with procedure only, unless
the contrary is expressed, the enactment applies to all actions, whether commenced
before or after the passing of the Act. The Act of 1893 is an Act dealing with
procedure only.'

Vaughan Williams LJ was to the same effect (at 246):   *j*

'I also agree that the Act is retrospective . . . and there is abundant authority that
the presumption against a retrospective construction has no application to enactments
which affect only the procedure and practice of the Courts.'

Romer LJ agreed with the conclusion, but expressed no reasons.

Their Lordships will return to this case later. They have cited it at this stage because it was the foundation of the judgment delivered by the trial judge in the High Court in Malaya.

There is a dearth of authority on the particular point which arises on this appeal, namely the re-emergence of a statute-barred right of action. It is a point that was foreshadowed by Channell J in *R v Chandra Dharma* [1905] 2 KB 335, [1904–7] All ER Rep 570, which merits a brief reference. In that case the first defendant was alleged to have committed an offence on 15 July 1904. At that time the Criminal Law Amendment Act 1885 provided that a prosecution for such an offence was to be brought within three months, that is to say by 15 October 1904. On 1 October 1904 this time limit was extended by statute to six months, thus expiring on 15 January 1905. The prosecution was begun on 27 December 1904. Lord Alverstone CJ said ([1905] 2 KB 335 at 338–339; cf [1904–7] All ER Rep 570 at 571):

'The rule is clearly established that, apart from any special circumstances appearing on the face of the statute in question, statutes which make alterations in procedure are retrospective. It has been held that a statute shortening the time within which proceedings can be taken is retrospective (*The Ydun*), and it seems to me that it is impossible to give any good reason why a statute extending the time within which proceedings may be taken should not also be held to be retrospective. If the case could have been brought within the principle that unless the language is clear a statute ought not to be construed so as to create new disabilities or obligations, or impose new duties in respect of transactions which were complete at the time when the Act came into force, [counsel for the prisoner] would have been entitled to succeed; but when no new disability or obligation has been created by the statute, but it only alters the time within which proceedings may be taken, it may be held to apply to offences completed before the statute was passed. That is the case here. This statute does not alter the character of the offence, or take away any defence which was formerly open to the prisoner. It is a mere matter of procedure, and according to all the authorities it is therefore retrospective.'

Channell J, who agreed, added this important rider ([1905] 2 KB 335 at 339):

'If the time under the old Act had expired before the new Act came into operation the question would have been entirely different, and in my view it would not have enabled a prosecution to be maintained even within six months from the offence.'

The case of *Noor Mohamed Yousoff v Teo Kai Tee* (1953) 19 MLJ 188 fell to be decided on comparable legislation to that which exists in the present case. This was an accident case. The accident was alleged to have been caused by the negligence of the first defendant's servant on 9 February 1952. At that time the limitation period would have expired on 9 February 1953. Before that date the plaintiff issued a writ against the first defendant. On a date which is somewhat obscure, but seems to have been either 22 February or 17 March 1953, a statute came into force which extended the limitation period to three years. On 10 April 1953 the plaintiff amended the writ by adding the driver of the vehicle as the second defendant. It was held that proceedings against the second defendant were not barred.

Lastly, there is the Australian case of *Maxwell v Murphy* (1957) 96 CLR 261. In that case a fatal motor car accident had occurred on 19 March 1951. At that date an action could be brought by the family of the victim within 12 months from the death under the Compensation to Relatives Act 1897. The period therefore expired on 19 March 1952. Under an amending Act which came into force on 16 December 1953 the period was extended to six years, which would expire, if the Act applied, on 19 March 1957. On 30 November 1954 the appellant brought her action. The question arose whether the amending Act did or did not revive the right of action. It was held by the High Court of Australia that it did not. This was a decision by four members of the High Court. The fifth member, Fullagar J, dissented. The principal point involved in the case was whether

the limit of time was an ingredient of the cause of action, so that the cause itself was
extinguished when the period expired. The case was however also considered on the   *a*
alternative basis, which is the one relevant to the instant appeal, that time barred only
the remedy, and not the cause of action.

Their Lordships will return later to this case.

With these preliminary observations, their Lordships turn to the instant appeal. The
appellants' claim succeeded in the High Court. The judge decided it on the 'procedural'
test. He said: *b*

'From authorities cited, it is my considered judgment that whether the prospective
or retrospective rule of construction should apply depends on the nature of the new
statute or amending statute. If it is purely a procedural statute and does not deal
with substantive rights then the retrospective rule of construction should apply. But
where the statute deals with substantive rights, or deals with both procedural and
substantive rights, then the prospective rule of construction is applicable . . . From   *c*
the authority laid down in *The Ydun*, I am of the view that the amending Act deals
only in procedure. In the absence of any express provision to the contrary, the
amending Act should, therefore, apply retrospectively.'

The judge added that, if the appellants had begun their action before the 1974 Act came
into force, the respondents would have escaped liability, thus taking the view that the   *d*
Act, though retrospective in relation to a cause of action, was prospective in relation to
an action to enforce that cause of action. Their Lordships mention the judge's comment
only to illustrate the different senses in which a statute can be said to be retrospective or
prospective.

The respondents appealed. The Federal Court adoped a more flexible approach to the
'procedural' test: *e*

'The pertinent question for determination is the nature of [the 1974 Act]: does it
affect rights or procedure? An Act which makes alteration in procedure only is
retrospective: see *The Ydun*. In our view there are no cases on which differences of
opinion may more readily be entertained, or which are more embarrassing to
dispose of, than the cases where the court has to decide whether or not an amending
statute affects procedure and consequently will operate retrospectively or affects   *f*
substantive rights and therefore, in the absence of a clear contrary intention, should
not be read as acting retrospectively. The distinction between procedural matters
and substantive rights must often be of great fineness. Each case therefore must be
looked at subjectively; there will inevitably be some matters that are classified as
being concerned with substantive rights which at first sight might be considered
procedural and vice versa.'   *g*

The Federal Court developed this line of reasoning by referring to part of the judgment
of Williams J in *Maxwell v Murphy* (1957) 96 CLR 261 at 277–278. The passage in the
judgment of Williams J which the Federal Court found of great assistance, as also have
their Lordships, reads as follows:

'Statutes of limitation are often classed as procedural statutes. But it would be   *h*
unwise to attribute a prima facie retrospective effect to all statutes of limitation.
Two classes of case can be considered. An existing statute of limitation may be
altered by enlarging or abridging the time within which proceedings may be
instituted. If the time is enlarged whilst a person is still within time under the
existing law to institute a cause of action the statute might well be classed as
procedural. Similarly if the time is abridged whilst such person is still left with time   *j*
within which to institute a cause of action the abridgment might again be classed as
procedural. But if the time is enlarged when a person is out of time to institute a
cause of action so as to enable the action to be brought within the new time or is
abridged so as to deprive him of time within which to institute it whilst he still has

a   time to do so, very different considerations could arise. A cause of action which can be enforced is a very different thing to a cause of action the remedy for which is barred by lapse of time. Statutes which enable a person to enforce a cause of action which was then barred or provide a bar to an existing cause of action by abridging the time for its institution could hardly be described as merely procedural. They would affect substantive rights.'

b   The Federal Court in the present case accepted the reasoning of Williams J, and concluded by saying:

'On the failure of the respondents to commence action within the specified period the appellants had acquired an "accrued right" which was designed to give them immunity for acts done in the discharge of their public duties. That right was well preserved by the Interpretation Act 1967 ... It therefore seems to us that in the
c   circumstances of this case, the time for the claim was not enlarged by [the 1974 Act]. The Act is not retroactive in operation and has no application to a cause of action which was barred before the Act came into operation.'

With that conclusion their Lordships entirely agree. They would wish to add only a few observations.

d   Whether a statute has a retrospective effect cannot in all cases safely be decided by classifying the statute as procedural or substantive. For example, in *The Ydun* the barque might have grounded on 13 May instead of 13 September 1893 and the 1893 Act might have come into force on 5 December 1893 when it received the royal assent, instead of 27 days later. Had those been the facts the Act would, if its procedural character were the true criterion of its effect, have deprived the owners of their ability to pursue their cause of action on the day the Act reached the statute book. A Limitation Act which had such
e   a decisive effect on an existing cause of action would not be '*merely* procedural' in any ordinary sense of that expression. Their Lordships assume (without expressing an opinion) that *The Ydun* was, on its facts, correctly decided.

Their Lordships consider that the proper approach to the construction of the 1974 Act is not to decide what label to apply to it, procedural or otherwise, but to see whether the statute, if applied retrospectively to a particular type of case, would impair existing rights
f   and obligations. The appellants assert that a Limitation Act does not impair existing rights because the cause of action remains, on the basis that all that is affected is the remedy. There is logic in the distinction on the particular facts of *The Ydun*, because the right to sue remained, for a while, totally unimpaired. But in most cases the loss, as distinct from curtailment, of the right to sue is equivalent to the loss of the cause of action. The Public Authorities Protection Act 1893 can be regarded as procedural on the
g   facts of *The Ydun*, but a slight alteration to those facts would have made it substantive. A Limitation Act may therefore be procedural in the context of one set of facts, but substantive in the context of a different set of facts.

In their Lordships' view, an accrued right to plead a time bar, which is acquired after the lapse of the statutory period, is in every sense a right, even though it arises under an Act which is procedural. It is a right which is not to be taken away by conferring on the
h   statute a retrospective operation, unless such a construction is unavoidable. Their Lordships see no compelling reason for concluding that the respondents acquired no 'right' when the period prescribed by the 1948 Ordinance expired, merely because the 1948 Ordinance and the 1974 Act are procedural in character. The plain purpose of the 1974 Act, read with the 1948 Ordinance, was to give and not to deprive; it was to give to
j   a potential defendant, who was not on 13 June 1974 possessed of an accrued limitation defence, a right to plead such a defence at the expiration of the new statutory period. The purpose was not to deprive a potential defendant of a limitation defence which he already possessed. The briefest consideration will expose the injustice of the contrary view. When a period of limitation has expired, a potential defendant should be able to assume that he is no longer at risk from a stale claim. He should be able to part with his papers if

they exist and discard any proofs of witnesses which have been taken, discharge his
solicitor if he has been retained, and order his affairs on the basis that his potential   *a*
liability has gone. That is the whole purpose of the limitation defence.

Lastly, their Lordships refer to *Mitchell v Harris Engineering Co Ltd* [1967] 2 All ER 682,
[1967] 2 QB 703. The appellants relied on this case in support of the submission that the
1948 Ordinance had conferred no 'right' on the respondents. This was a case of mistaken
identity, similar to *Rodriguez v Parker* [1966] 2 All ER 349, [1967] 1 QB 116, and was
decided in the same way. The plaintiff had suffered an accident on 27 August 1963, for   *b*
which he claimed damages from his employer. On 9 August 1966 he issued a writ. On
27 August the three-year period expired. There were in fact two companies, with almost
identical names. One was an Irish company (Harris Engineering Co Ltd) and the other
was an English company (Harris Engineering Co (Leeds) Ltd). The Irish company, which
was the employer, carried on business from an address which was also the registered
office of the English company. So the opportunity for confusion was manifest. By   *c*
mistake, the defendant named in the writ was the English company. When the mistake
was discovered, which was after the three years had elapsed, the plaintiff sought to amend
the proceedings by substituting the name of the Irish company for the name of the
English company pursuant to RSC Ord 20, r 5, which gave the court power in a case of
mistaken identity to substitute a new defendant for the defendant originally sued,
notwithstanding that a relevant period of limitation had expired. It was submitted on   *d*
behalf of the employer that the rule was ultra vires because it enabled the court to divest
a defendant of an accrued right. The argument failed, rightly in their Lordships' view.
Lord Denning MR said ([1967] 2 All ER 682 at 686, [1967] 2 QB 703 at 718): '. . .
whenever a writ has been issued within the permitted time, but is found to be defective,
the defendant has no right to have it remain defective'; while Russell LJ put the matter
thus ([1967] 2 All ER 682 at 687, [1967] 2 QB 703 at 720):   *e*

> 'It was argued that before the amendment, the Irish company had a sure shield
> under the statute and the amendment removed that shield; but its sure shield under
> the statute was one which was available to it in another action should one be brought
> out of time. Its shield in the present proceedings was not the statute, but the fact
> that it was not yet a defendant in them. That shield could be taken away by the   *f*
> procedural power of permitting amendment of these proceedings.'

Their Lordships consider that there is an alternative, and perhaps preferable, approach
to the *Mitchell* type of case. Not only did the two companies have a common English
address, but they also had common directors and a common secretary. It was obvious to
all who were concerned on behalf of the two companies that the plaintiff intended to sue
his employer and that those advising the plaintiff believed that the name of his employer   *g*
was correctly written as Harris Engineering Co (Leeds) Ltd. It was fortuitous that a
company bearing the latter name actually existed. Had there been no such company in
existence, the plaintiff's right to correct the name of the defendant would have been
beyond argument. No one was misled by the use of the mistaken name in the
proceedings, and the case resolves itself into one of mere misnomer which was clearly
within the court's corrective power under Ord 20, r 5: see *Whittam v W J Daniel & Co Ltd*   *h*
[1961] 3 All ER 796, [1962] 1 QB 271. So analysed the result of the *Mitchell* case is in no
way inconsistent with the view which their Lordships take in the present case. The only
other comment which their Lordships would make on the decision in the *Mitchell* case is
that they do not accept the generality of the proposition stated by Lord Denning MR
([1967] 2 All ER 682 at 686, [1967] 2 QB 703 at 718): 'The statute of limitations does not
confer any right on the defendant. It only imposes a time limit on the plaintiff.' In the   *j*
opinion of their Lordships an accrued entitlement on the part of a person to plead the
lapse of a limitation period as an answer to the future institution of proceedings is just as
much a 'right' as any other statutory or contractual protection against a future suit.

The case of *Noor Mohamed Yousoff* (1955) 19 MLJ 188 may call for further consideration
on an appropriate occasion.

a For the reasons indicated, their Lordships will advise His Majesty the Yang di-Pertuan
Agong that the appeal should be dismissed. The appellants must pay the respondents'
costs.

Appeal dismissed.

Solicitors: *Le Brasseur & Bury* (for the appellants); *Coward Chance* (for the respondents).

b

Evelyn M C Budd   Barrister.

c
Monterosso Shipping Co Ltd v International Transport Workers' Federation

COURT OF APPEAL, CIVIL DIVISION
LORD DENNING MR AND MAY LJ
13, 14, 28 MAY 1982

d

*Conflict of laws – Contract – Proper law of contract – Labour agreement – Crewing of ships –
Agreement between shipowners and seamen's union – Agreement made in Spain for employment
of ships' crews – Agreement in English and made on behalf of international federation of trade
unions based in London – Agreement conclusively presumed by English law not to be intended to
be legally enforceable – Whether proper law of agreement English or Spanish law – Whether*
e *unenforceability of contract in England raising presumption against English law being proper law
– Trade Union and Labour Relations Act 1974, s 18.*

The shipowners, a Maltese registered company, owned a ship which was registered in
Malta. They employed Norwegian officers and a Spanish crew to man the ship, and had
agents in Spain to recruit crews. The crews were members of a Spanish seamen's union
f which was affiliated to the International Transport Workers' Federation (the ITF), a
federation of trade unions with headquarters in London. A dispute arose between the
shipowners and the ITF as to the nationality of crews to be employed on the ship when
making its regular run between Swedish ports. On 3 November 1980 the ITF informed
the shipowners that, unless Swedish crews were employed on that run, the ship would
be 'blacked'. The next day, an agreement was signed in Spain between the crewing agents
g on behalf of the shipowners and an officer of the Spanish seamen's union purporting to
act on behalf of the ITF. The agreement was in English and on a standard printed form
issued by the ITF, and it stated that the ITF would issue a 'blue certificate' for worldwide
trading with Spanish crews. In particular, the agreement did not include a clause
requiring the shipowners to employ Swedish crews on the Swedish run. The ITF
subsequently disowned the agreement, and on arrival at a Swedish port the ship was
h blacked by the Swedish seamen's union and had to proceed to a Norwegian port to
discharge her cargo. In April 1981 the shipowners issued a writ against the ITF in
England seeking, inter alia, a declaration that the shipowners were entitled to the issue
of the blue certificate under the special agreement made between the shipowners and the
Spanish seamen's union on behalf of the ITF and an order that the ITF should issue the
certificate. Before the trial of the action, the question whether the agreement was
j governed by Spanish law or English law was ordered to be tried as a preliminary point of
law. It was common ground that if the proper law was English law the agreement would
not be enforceable by reason of s 18[a] of the Trade Union and Labour Relations Act 1974,
since it did not contain a provision which stated that the parties intended that the

_____

a   Section 18, so far as material, is set out at p 845 *f* to *h*, post

agreement should be a 'legally enforceable contract'. On the trial of the preliminary point the judge considered that the fact that s 18 made the agreement unenforceable in *a* England pointed to Spanish law being the proper law and he so held. The ITF appealed, contending (i) that s 18 was merely a procedural provision which barred any remedies being sought under the contract without extinguishing the contract itself and that therefore there was no presumption against English law being the proper law, (ii) that English law was in fact the proper law because the agreement was in English and the ITF had its headquarters in England, and (iii) that under English law the agreement was *b* unenforceable against the ITF because of the effect of s 18.

Held – The question of what was the proper law of the agreement was to be determined by considering with which country or system of law the agreement had the closest and most real connection. The facts that the agreement was in English and that the ITF had its headquarters in London were of little weight, since English was the language of *c* shipping and the agreement was in a form in use throughout the world. On the other hand, Spain was the country in which the shipowners recruited their crews and in which the agreement had been negotiated. Accordingly, Spain was the country with which the agreement had the closest and most real connection. It followed that the proper law of the agreement was Spanish law, and the appeal would therefore be dismissed (see p 846 g to j, p 847 a and p 849 b, post). *d*

Per curiam. The provisions of s 18 of the 1974 Act to the effect that, unless the parties have specifically stated the contrary, a collective agreement is 'conclusively presumed not to have been intended by the parties to be a legally enforceable contract' are not merely procedural provisions but have the substantive effect that the parties are deemed not to have intended to create legal relations between themselves. Accordingly, a collective agreement to which s 18 applies is not a contract at all in law but merely an arrangement *e* between the parties which is to be enforced (if at all) by other means (see p 846 c to f, p 848 g to j and p 849 a, post).

Per May LJ. Where there is no express or implicit statement by the parties in the terms of the relevant agreement of their intention which particular system of law is applicable to it, the enforceability or unenforceability of the agreement is irrelevant in deciding objectively with which system of law the transaction has its closest and most real *f* connection (see p 848 e, post).

Notes

For the determination of the proper law of a contract, see 8 Halsbury's Laws (4th edn) paras 583–591, and for cases on the subject, see 11 Digest (Reissue) 455–481, 751–875.

For the Trade Union and Labour Relations Act 1974, s 18, see 44 Halsbury's Statutes *g* (3rd edn) 1773.

Cases referred to in judgments

Black-Clawson International Ltd v Papierwerke Waldhof-Aschaffenburg AG [1975] 1 All ER 810, [1975] AC 591, [1975] 2 WLR 513, HL, Digest (Cont Vol D) 109, *1591a.*

Coast Lines Ltd v Hudig & Veder Chartering NV [1972] 1 All ER 451, [1972] 2 QB 34, *h* [1972] 2 WLR 280, CA, 11 Digest (Reissue) 473, *834.*

Compagnie d'Armement Maritime SA v Compagnie Tunisienne de Navigation SA [1970] 3 All ER 71, [1971] AC 572, [1970] 3 WLR 389, HL, 11 Digest (Reissue) 457, *759.*

Harris v Quine (1869) LR 4 QB 653, 11 Digest (Reissue) 648, *1790.*

Huber v Steiner (1835) 2 Bing NC 202, [1835–42] All ER Rep 159, 6 Digest (Reissue) 398, *j* 2860.

Leroux v Brown (1852) 12 CB 801, 138 ER 1119, 12 Digest (Reissue) 203, *1285.*

Maddison v Alderson (1883) 8 App Cas 467, [1881–5] All ER Rep 742, HL, 12 Digest (Reissue) 208, *1289.*

Case also cited

NWL Ltd v Woods [1979] 3 All ER 614, [1979] 1 WLR 1294.

Interlocutory appeal

a   By a writ issued on 15 April 1981 the plaintiffs, Monterosso Shipping Co Ltd, sought as against the defendants, the International Transport Workers' Federation (the ITF), a declaration that the plaintiffs were entitled, in accordance with the terms of a special agreement dated 4 November 1980, to the issue of the ITF's 'blue certificate' certifying that the plaintiffs' vessel Rosso was covered by a collective agreement acceptable to the ITF, an order that the ITF should issue the certificate, an injunction restraining the ITF
b   from obstructing the discharge, free passage or operation of the vessel, and damages. On 12 February 1982 Robert Goff J directed that a question of law should be tried as a preliminary point, namely whether the proper law of the special agreement alleged to have been made between the plaintiffs and the ITF was Spanish law. On 9 March 1982 Mustill J held that the proper law of the agreement was Spanish law. The defendants appealed. The facts are set out in the judgment of Lord Denning MR.

c
Cyril W F Newman QC for the ITF.
Peter Leaver for the shipowers.

Cur adv vult

28 May. The following judgments were read.

LORD DENNING MR. Once more we have before us the International Transport
d   Workers' Federation (ITF). They are a federation of trade unions with affiliated unions all over the world. They have their headquarters in London. They do all they can to ensure that the merchant ships sailing the seas are good, sound, seaworthy ships with competent crews paid proper rates. They take great objection to absentee owners who register vessels under 'flags of convenience', and then under cover of those flags lower the standards of seaworthiness and competence and pay low wages. The ITF have done much
e   to improve conditions by 'blacking' these ships and thus forcing the owners to agree to ITF terms. Once they agree, the owners are given a 'blue certificate' and are free from being blacked.
      We are here concerned with a motor vessel called the Rosso. She is owned by a company registered in Malta called Monterosso Shipping Co Ltd. She is registered in Valletta, Malta. She flies the Maltese flag. It is undoubtedly a flag of convenience. I do
f   not suppose that her owners have anything to do with Malta, or that the vessel has ever been there.
      The vessel is managed by a Norwegian firm. She is manned by Norwegian officers, but with Spanish crews. The owners have crewing agents in Spain called Marispan. They recruit Spanish crews at lower wages than some other crews. These Spanish crews are members of a Spanish seamen's union called Union General de Trabajadores (UGT). It is
g   affiliated to the ITF. It has an official called Augustin Aguirre, who is also an inspector of the ITF.

The Marco agreement for Spanish crews
      The seamen's union, UGT, in Spain has made an agreement with various shipowners regulating the terms and conditions on which Spanish crews are to be engaged on their
h   vessels. It is called the Marco agreement, and is headed: 'Collective Agreement UGT (ITF) for vessels under flag of convenience, with Spanish crews.' It is signed by Mr Aguirre on behalf of UGT and as inspector for ITF.

The special agreement and the blue certificate for worldwide trading
      That agreement was acceptable to the ITF for the mv Rosso in 1979. So in November
j   1979 the ITF agreed to give the vessel a blue certificate to cover its trading all over the world. This was done by a special agreement on a printed form issued by the ITF in London, but executed in Bilbao in Spain. It contained many provisions, of which the most significant for present purposes are:

      'Article 2: The ITF undertakes ... to issue and each year to renew an ITF Blue Certificate ... certifying that the Ship is covered by a Collective Agreement acceptable to the ITF ...

Article 4: This Special Agreement shall remain in force for a period of twelve months from the date hereof and thereafter from year to year, provided that either *a* party may give [one month's notice to end on any anniversary].'

It was signed at Bilbao on 7 November 1979 by Marispan (the crewing agents) on behalf of the owners of the vessel, and by Mr Aguirre on behalf of UGT and inspector for the ITF.

b

The Swedish run

That agreement continued for several months quite satisfactorily. But then a dispute arose. It was because the owners started the vessel on a regular run between two ports on the Swedish coast in the Baltic Sea. Now there is a Swedish seamen's union, which is also affiliated to the ITF. The Swedish union objected to this vessel making this regular run with Spanish crews. They felt that Swedish seamen should be employed on it. So the *c* Swedish union asked the ITF to use their good offices to ensure this.

The special agreement is terminated

This put the ITF in some difficulty, because there was in existence the special agreement made in November 1979. It entitled the owners of the vessel to a blue certificate for worldwide trading. ITF could not cancel the agreement at once. They had *d* to let the agreement continue for the time being, but they gave notice to terminate it at the earliest possible moment. They gave notice to the owners on 17 June 1980 to expire on 7 November 1980.

Negotiations for renewal: a special clause

This gave rise to intense negotiations. The shipowners wanted to continue with the *e* blue certificate. But the ITF would not continue it unless there was a special clause inserted in it to this effect: 'It is agreed that if the ship running regular line between Sweden ports will be obligated to sign Sweden National Agreement.' In short, ITF would not agree to give the shipowners a blue certificate for worldwide trading, unless there was a special clause inserted in it by which the crew would have the benefit of the Swedish seamen's agreement when running between Swedish ports.   *f*

If this special clause was inserted it is obvious that the shipowners would not employ Spanish crews on this run. They would employ Swedish crews. The Swedish seamen's union pressed hard for this special clause to be inserted in any new agreement. They threatened to 'black' this ship if the clause was not inserted. On 3 November 1980 the ITF wired to the shipowners:

'. . . we now inform you that we have promised sympathetic action, in the form *g* of work stoppage from 7 November, 1980, 00.00 hrs. onwards, to the Swedish Transport Workers Union and we have been informed that this will take place.'

The Spaniards will not have a special clause

Now, although that was the attitude of the ITF in London and their affiliates in *h* Sweden, the affiliate UGT in Spain did not like it. It would mean that the Spanish crew would lose their work. They would be replaced on Swedish voyages by Swedish crews. So the Spanish UGT and their inspector, Aguirre, without any authority from ITF in London, signed a special agreement in Bilbao, without including the special clause at all. It was in the English language on a printed form issued by the ITF. It was stated to be between the ITF 'whose headquarters are at Maritime House, Old Town, Clapham, *j* London . . . in the United Kingdom' and 'Monterosso Shipping Co. Ltd . . . Valletta, Malta, in respect of the Malta flag ship "Rosso".' It was the standard form of special agreement used by the ITF when granting blue certificates for worldwide trading. It did not contain a special clause about Swedish ports. It was signed on 4 November 1980 at Bilbao by Marispan on behalf of the shipowners and by UGT and the inspector, Mr Aguirre, on behalf of the ITF.

London is displeased

a   ITF at their headquarters in London were much displeased with UGT and their inspector in Bilbao. They disowned their special agreement because it did not contain the special clause about Sweden. They told their Swedish affiliate about it. Thereupon the Swedish seamen's union decided to 'black' the Rosso on her next trip to Sweden.

The vessel is blacked

b   On 10 November 1980 the vessel arrived at Wallham in Sweden with a cargo to discharge. She was blacked by the Swedish seamen's union. They refused to unload her cargo. She waited for two days, and then had to go north to a Norwegian port, Oslo, in order to discharge her cargo. The blacking meant that she was off-hire for 2·69 days. The shipowners claimed damages from the ITF. They said that the loss was due to a breach of contract by the ITF contained in the written agreement of 4 November 1980.

c

Damages are claimed

On 15 April 1981 the shipowners issued a writ in the High Court of Justice in England against the ITF claiming damages. Pleadings were exchanged. Particulars were given. The trial was fixed. But, before it started, Robert Goff J ordered that this question of law should be tried as a preliminary point:

d

'Whether the proper law of the "Special Agreement" alleged to have been made between the [shipowners] and the [ITF] on 4th November 1980 at Bilbao, Spain, was Spanish law or English law.'

On 9 March 1982 Mustill J held that it was Spanish law. The ITF appeal to this court.

e   *The effect of s 18 of the 1974 Act*

At the outset of the argument before us, counsel for the ITF raised a point of much importance. It was hardly touched on before Mustill J. So we have not got his views on it. Section 18 of the Trade Union and Labour Relations Act 1974 says:

f

'(1) Subject to subsection (3) below, any collective agreement made before 1st December 1971 or after the commencement of this section shall be conclusively presumed not to have been intended by the parties to be a legally enforceable contract unless the agreement—(a) is in writing, and (b) contains a provision which (however expressed) states that the parties intend that the agreement shall be a legally enforceable contract . . .

(3) If any such agreement is in writing and contains a provision which (however expressed) states that the parties intend that one or more parts of the agreement specified in that provision, but not the whole of the agreement, shall be a legally enforceable contract, then—(a) the specified part or parts shall be conclusively presumed to have been intended by the parties to be a legally enforceable contract; and (b) the remainder of the agreement shall be conclusively presumed not to have been intended by the parties to be such a contract, but a part of an agreement which by virtue of this paragraph is not a legally enforceable contract may be referred to for the purpose of interpreting a part of that agreement which is such a contract . . .'

g

h

When that section is applied to the agreement of 4 November 1980 these points are clear: the ITF is a trade union: see s 28(1)(b); the agreement of 4 November 1980 was a collective agreement: see s 30(1). It did not contain any provision to the effect that the parties intended that it should be a legally enforceable contract; so it is conclusively presumed not to have been intended by the parties to be a legally enforceable contract: see s 18.

j

Notwithstanding the provisions of s 18, counsel for the ITF submitted that the collective agreement of 4 November 1980 was a valid agreement, or, at any rate, it was not rendered void or invalid by s 18. He submitted that s 18 was a rule of procedure and not of substance. It was, therefore, to be given effect in the English courts (lex fori), but not in the courts of any other country.

This distinction between matters of procedure and matters of substance is well
established in the conflict of laws. It is discussed in *Dicey and Morris on the Conflict of Laws*
(10th edn, 1980) pp 1175ff. In our present case the words in s 18 are similar to the words
in the Statute of Frauds 1677 and the Statutes of Limitations. Those statutes contained
the words 'no action shall be brought ... unless' or 'no contract shall be allowed to be
good except', and suchlike phrases. They used to be held to be matters of procedure and
not of substance. Counsel for the ITF referred to these cases: *Huber v Steiner* (1835) 2 Bing
NC 202, [1835–42] All ER Rep 159, *Leroux v Brown* (1852) 12 CB 801, 138 ER 1119,
Harris v Quine (1869) LR 4 QB 653, *Maddison v Alderson* (1883) 8 App Cas 467, [1881–5]
All ER Rep 742 and *Black-Clawson International Ltd v Papierwerke Waldhof-Aschaffenburg
AG* [1975] 1 All ER 810, [1975] AC 591.

I would not suggest that those cases are no longer authoritative. They should be
followed in statutes containing the same words. But the reasoning is unsatisfactory. It
seems to me that the true distinction is between the existence of a contract (which is
substantive law) and the remedies for breach of it (which is procedural law). The right
course is to analyse the statute and see whether it negatives the existence of a contract or
not. If there is no contract, then there is nothing to enforce. That is substantive law. If
there is a contract, but the statute says it cannot be enforced (except in writing or within
a stated period) that is procedural law. It is governed by the lex fori.

In this present case, as I construe s 18 of the 1974 Act, it negatives the existence of any
contract at all. The section draws a distinction between an 'agreement' and a 'legally
enforceable contract'. The agreement is 'not intended' to be binding, except in so far as
the parties say it is to be binding. If and in so far as they say it is to be binding, then there
is a legally enforceable contract.

The special agreement

In our present case there is nothing in the special agreement to say it was intended to
be a legally enforceable contract. It is, therefore, conclusively presumed not to be one. In
short, it is not a contract at all. The essence of a contract, as distinct from a mere
agreement, is that a contract is legally enforceable, whereas a mere agreement is not.

The proper law

In any case, whatever the effect of s 18, it does not help us in any way to decide the
preliminary point: what is the proper law of the contract? That is a matter of substance,
not of procedure. It depends on discovering what is the country or system of law with
which the contract has the closest and most real connection: see *Compagnie d'Armement
Maritime SA v Compagnie Tunisienne de Navigation SA* [1970] 3 All ER 71, [1971] AC 572.

No one has suggested that this contract had any connection with Malta, or with
Sweden. The only competitors are England and Spain. Counsel for the ITF, in support of
England, points to the use of the English language. But that carries him very little way.
English is the language of the sea and seafarers, and of shipowners and charterers. He
also points to the fact that the ITF has its head office in London. But that is of little
weight. This 'special agreement' is in use all the world over. It affects ships and crews in
every country. But the agreement has a very close connection with Spain. It was the
country in which the shipowners hoped to recruit their crews. The agreement was
negotiated in Bilbao by plenipotentiaries of the shipowners and of the ITF. They had in
mind the Marco agreement between the UGT and the shipowners in relation to Spanish
crews. All things considered, I find myself in agreement with Mustill J, who held that
'the legal system with which the transaction is most closely connected is that of the
Kingdom of Spain'. On the preliminary point I would dismiss the appeal. The proper
law of the special agreement is Spanish law.

MAY LJ. Lord Denning MR has set out the terms of the preliminary issue which it fell
to the judge below to decide. He has also retailed the relevant facts of this case.
Accordingly there is no need for me to repeat these matters in this judgment.

a   As the actual intention of the parties as to the system of law by which the special agreement was to be governed was not expressly stated therein and cannot be inferred from all the circumstances, the proper law is that system of law with which the transaction has its closest and most real connection. Before considering this particular question from the objective viewpoint which I think should be employed, however, there is one point which formed a substantial part of the argument both before the judge below and before us with which I think that I should first deal.

b   At the hearing of the preliminary issue below and in this court it was and has been treated as common ground that if the special agreement was governed by English law it was rendered at the least unenforceable in this country by s 18(1) of the Trade Union and Labour Relations Act 1974, to the terms of which Lord Denning MR has already referred. In my opinion, however, it is not entirely clear how the respective arguments on this point were developed before the court below, nor was there agreement between counsel c   before us on this point.

Nevertheless, the judge below was persuaded to approach the task of balancing the factors for and against the application of Spanish law on the one hand and English law on the other with a presumption, albeit a weak one, against English law, because of s 18 of the 1974 Act. It seems that he was so persuaded, first, because it was argued that not only was the special agreement unenforceable in England by virtue of the statute, but also d   that it was never intended to be enforceable anywhere, and, second, and by way of corollary, because he could see no reason for inferring an intention on the part of the owners to yield up all their local remedies based on the agreement, which would probably be the first to which they would seek to have recourse, just because they had agreed on terms which made the document unenforceable in England.

In his argument before this court, counsel for the ITF submitted that the effect of s 18 e   of the 1974 Act was not a matter of substantive law, but that it was merely a procedural provision. He contended that s 18 was analogous to the provisions of the Statute of Frauds 1677 and the Limitation Acts, whose effect was considered in such cases as *Leroux v Brown* (1852) 12 CB 801, 138 ER 1119, *Harris v Quine* (1869) LR 4 QB 653 and *Black-Clawson International Ltd v Papierwerke Waldhof-Aschaffenburg AG* [1975] 1 All ER 810, [1975] AC 591. Similarly to those cases, he suggested that the effect of s 18 of the 1974 Act was f   merely to bar the remedy and not to extinguish the right: the special agreement constituted a contract between the ITF and the owners, but it was a contract which was unenforceable by the English courts. The judge below was, therefore, in error in approaching the question of the proper law of the special agreement with any bias against English law founded on any supposition that so to choose that system of law would in fact destroy the contract. Indeed, counsel's argument continued, to adopt this construction g   of the effect of s 18 and to hold that English law was the proper law of the contract had this advantage, that it gave the parties the option (the reality of which might be open to doubt) whether to make such arrangements as the special agreement enforceable or not. This would give the transaction a flexibility which it would not possess if the court were to conclude that the proper law of the special agreement was the law of Spain. Further, English law being the proper law of the contract, as it was submitted, the bargain could h   in fact have been rendered enforceable if the parties had included in it a statement under s 18(1)(b). The parties had chosen not to include one and accordingly this demonstrated, so counsel contended, that they never contemplated or intended that the contract would be enforceable at law. Still less, therefore, should the judge have approached the fundamental question of deciding on the proper law of the contract with any presumption against that being the law of England. Further, if s 18 was procedural only and did not j   have substantive effect, then the argument may be raised hereafter (although it was advanced only circumspectly before us) that the well-known principles of English conflict of laws would in any event prevent the special agreement from being enforced in the English courts, even if it were valid by whatever other country's law may be its proper law and enforceable in the courts of that country.

On behalf of the owners, counsel argued that s 18 was not merely procedural in its effect but struck substantively at any collective agreement to which it applied and which did not contain the provision contemplated by sub-s (1)(b) to which I have already *a* referred. If English law was the proper law of the special agreement, the effect of s 18 on it was to render it no contract at all, not merely one that was unenforceable in English courts. This he submitted could not have been intended by the parties, at least by the owners, and accordingly the judge below was correct to have a bias against English law when he came to determine the fundamental question.

For my part I do not think that these arguments on the proper construction of s 18 of *b* the 1974 Act are of any real assistance in this case on the issue of what is the proper law of the special agreement.

In *Coast Lines Ltd v Hudig & Veder Chartering NV* [1972] 1 All ER 451, [1972] 2 QB 34, where the court was similarly faced with the choice between two possible systems of law, namely English law on the one hand and Netherlands law on the other, under the first of which an exemption clause in the relevant charterparty would have been valid, but *c* invalid under the second, Lord Denning MR in his judgment expressed the view that this was a pointer to the proper law of the charterparty in that case on the basis of the principle expressed by the Latin maxim ut res magis valeat quam pereat. Megaw LJ also adverted to this argument in the course of his judgment but expressly said that he was inclined to think that the consideration was effective only to negative any argument that the terms of the charterparty showed an actual intention of the parties that Netherlands *d* law should govern, not to support a positive argument based on the principle to which I have just referred. The third member of the court, Stephenson LJ, did not express any final view on this particular point. In my judgment this court is not bound by either of the dicta in the two judgments to which I have referred. With great respect, however, were it necessary to decide the point, I would find myself in agreement with the view expressed by Megaw LJ. Where one cannot gather from the terms of the relevant *e* agreement any express or implicit statement by the parties of their intention about which particular system of law was to be applicable to it, I think that the enforceability or unenforceability of the material agreement is irrelevant when, in the absence of any such express or implicit statement of intention, one has objectively to decide with which system of law the transaction has its closest and most real connection.

However, the proper construction of s 18 of the 1974 Act may be vital if it is argued *f* that, whatever the proper law and validity thereunder of the special agreement, it is nevertheless unenforceable in the English courts under the lex fori. I therefore express my view on this point. First, I think that the precise wording of s 18(1) is noticeably different from the statutory provisions in the Statute of Frauds or the Limitation Acts. In the latter two cases the relevant statutes use the phrases either 'no action shall be brought' or 'an action shall not be brought after the expiration of', which are each very different *g* from 'shall be conclusively presumed not to have been intended by the parties to be a legally enforceable contract' and have a much more mere procedural flavour about them than that in the 1974 Act. The subject matter of s 18 is collective agreements as defined by the Act, and these are certainly agreements in the sense that they contain and are intended to contain mutual undertakings between the parties. This being so, when it is then provided that these mutual undertakings are conclusively to be presumed not to *h* have been intended by the parties to be a legally enforceable contract, I think that the correct construction of this phrase in s 18 is that in a collective agreement, unless the parties specifically state to the contrary, they are to be deemed not to have intended to create legal relations between them. If this is the proper approach to the effect of s 18, then the latter is not merely procedural but must have substantive effect. The corresponding provisions in the Statute of Frauds and the Limitation Acts contemplate *j* agreements between the parties intended to create legal relations, but prevent those legal relations being enforced by the courts either because of the absence of some necessary formality, such as writing, or as the result of the passage of time. This I think is a totally different situation from that in which the parties never contemplated that the agreement to which they have come between themselves would create any legal relations at all. In

these circumstances, I think that a collective agreement to which the provisions of
a s 18(1)(*a*) and (*b*) have not been applied is no contract at all in the sight of the law but
merely an arrangement between the parties the enforcement of which is to be achieved,
if at all, by other means. This is not unusual in English industrial relations.

Subject to these points I agree entirely with the analysis by Lord Denning MR of the
other aspects of the relevant transaction which point towards what was its proper law. I
agree with his conclusion that of the two systems of law contended for, that of England
b on the one hand and of Spain on the other, the latter has the closest and most real
connection. I therefore also agree that this appeal should be dismissed.

Appeal dismissed. Application for leave to appeal to the House of Lords refused.

Solicitors: *Clifford-Turner* (for the ITF); *Coward Chance* (for the shipowners).

c

Diana Procter   Barrister.

d
Walton v Egan and others

QUEEN'S BENCH DIVISION
MUSTILL J
2, 29 OCTOBER 1981

e Solicitor – Costs – Non-contentious business – Interest – Right to charge interest on bill of costs –
Date from which interest runs – Solicitor serving notice required under remuneration rules on
client some months after delivery of bill – Bill unpaid and solicitor bringing action to recover
principal sum and interest – Whether solicitor entitled to interest from one month after delivery
of bill or only from service of notice – Solicitors' Remuneration Order 1972, arts 3(2), 5.

f Solicitor – Costs – Non-contentious business – Interest – Agreement as to remuneration – Solicitor
and client making agreement as to principal sum and interest – Action by solicitor to recover
unpaid interest – Whether statutory provisions as to agreements as to remuneration covering
agreement as to interest – Whether agreements as to remuneration subject to restrictions in rules
regarding interest – Solicitors Act 1974, s 57 – Solicitors' Remuneration Order 1972, arts 3, 5.

g Under s 57[a] of the Solicitors Act 1974 provision was made for solicitors to make
agreements with clients for remuneration for non-contentious business by way of 'a gross
sum, or by a commission or percentage, or by a salary, or otherwise'. Section 57 further
provided that such an agreement could be sued and recovered on in the same manner
and on the same grounds as any other agreement. However, before bringing proceedings
to recover costs on a bill for non-contentious business which had not been taxed, a
h solicitor was required, by art 3(2)[b] of the Solicitors' Remuneration Order 1972, to inform
the client in writing of (i) his right under art 3(1) to require the solicitor to obtain a
certificate from the Law Society that the sum charged was fair and reasonable and (ii) the
provisions of the 1974 Act relating to taxation of costs. After the expiry of one month
from the delivery of a bill the solicitor was entitled under art 5(1)[c] of the 1972 order to
'charge interest on the amount of the bill' but before doing so 'the client must have been
j given the information required by article 3(2)'. On 31 August 1979 the plaintiff solicitor
sent to his clients, the defendants, a bill of costs for non-contentious business. The

_____

a   Section 57, so far as material, is set out at p 851 *f* to *j*, post
b   Article 3, so far as material, is set out at p 852 *b* to *d*, post
c   Article 5 is set out at p 852 *d e*, post

defendants failed to pay. In March 1980 the plaintiff agreed to accept payment by instalments and the defendants agreed to pay interest on the running balance, with *a* retrospective effect to 1 October 1979 (ie one month from the date of the delivery of the bill). The defendants failed to pay anything under the agreement, so the plaintiff brought an action against them and, on 21 July 1980, obtained judgment. The judgment was almost immediately set aside by consent, because the plaintiff conceded that the proceedings were barred by the absence of notice under art 3(2) of the 1972 order. He gave notice forthwith under art 3(2), and, at the request of the defendants, applied for *b* and obtained a Law Society certificate under art 3(1) to the effect that the sum charged was fair and reasonable. However, the certificate made no mention of interest. When the defendants failed to pay, the plaintiff brought a fresh action against the defendants claiming the principal sum together with interest from 1 October 1979 pursuant either to the agreement of March 1980 or to art 5 of the 1972 order. The defendants admitted liability for the principal sum but contended that they were only liable for interest from *c* 30 August 1980 (ie one month from the date of the notice under art 3(2)). The defendants submitted that it was a precondition of a solicitor's right to charge interest that he should, in accordance with art 5, notify the client of his rights under the 1974 Act and the 1972 order.

Held – (1) On the true construction of art 5 of the 1972 order a cause of action for *d* interest arose as soon as one month had elapsed from the date of the delivery of a bill, but it did not become enforceable unless and until a valid notice under art 3(2) had been given. Once the notice had been given, a solicitor had a retrospective right to interest one month after the date of the delivery of the bill (see p 853 *h j*, post).

(2) However, the provisions of the 1972 order did not apply where there was an agreement under s 57 of the 1974 Act between a solicitor and client as to the solicitor's *e* remuneration for non-contentious business because that Act prescribed its own procedure in respect of such agreements which was not linked to the requirements of arts 3 and 5 of the order. An agreement under s 57 included an agreement as to interest and thus, on the basis of such an agreement, a solicitor could bring an action under s 57 to recover unpaid interest without having to give notice to a client under art 3(2) (see p 853 *j* and p 854 *b d e* and *h*, post). *f*

(3) On the facts, the agreement between the parties made in March 1980 was an agreement which stood on its own as a compromise of existing rights and therefore neither s 57 of the 1974 Act nor the 1972 order applied to it. Accordingly, it should be enforced according to its own terms and judgment would be entered for the plaintiff (see p 855 *a b*, post).

g

Notes
For the remuneration of solicitors for non-contentious business, see Supplement to 36 Halsbury's Laws (3rd edn) para 160A, and for cases on the subject, see 43 Digest (Repl) 256–273, 2717–2870.

For the Solicitors Act 1974, s 57, see 44 Halsbury's Statutes (3rd edn) 1527.

For the Solicitors' Remuneration Order 1972, arts 3, 5, see 20 Halsbury's Statutory *h* Instruments (4th reissue) 325.

Case referred to in judgment
Jonesco v Evening Standard Co Ltd, Re Undertaking by Wingfields, Halse and Trustram [1932] 2 KB 340, [1932] All ER Rep 678, CA, 43 Digest (Repl) 139, 1262.

j

Action
In January 1981 the plaintiff, Terence Walton, a solicitor practising under the name of Fallons, brought an action against the defendants, (1) Desmond Francis Egan, (2) David O'Brien Twohig and (3) D Egan Ltd, claiming (i) a specified sum (the principal sum) as his professional fees for work done on behalf of the defendants, and (ii) interest on that sum from 1 October 1979 pursuant to an agreement between the parties made in March 1980 or alternatively under art 5 of the Solicitors' Remuneration Order 1972. The

defendants admitted liability for the principal sum but contended that they were only liable to pay interest from 30 August 1980. On a summons under RSC Ord 14 the plaintiff was given leave to enter judgment against them for the principal sum but the defendants were given leave to defend the action in respect of the claim for interest. The second defendant took no part in the proceedings. The facts are set out in the judgment.

Robert Arnold for the plaintiff.

b *Keith Knight* for the first and third defendants.

Cur adv vult

c 29 October. **MUSTILL J** read the following judgment: In this action the plaintiff is a solicitor, and the defendants are former clients. The claim is for interest on an overdue account. Although the sum involved is comparatively small, the points discussed in argument are of some importance to the legal profession.

In order to make the dispute intelligible, it is necessary to set out at some length the relevant provisions of the Solicitors Act 1974 and the Solicitors' Remuneration Order

d 1972, SI 1972/1139.

Solicitors Act 1974

'**56.**—(1) For the purposes of this section there shall be a committee consisting of the following persons . . .

e (2) The committee . . . may make general orders prescribing and regulating in such manner as they think fit the remuneration of solicitors in respect of non-contentious business . . .

(4) An order under this section may prescribe the mode of remuneration of solicitors in respect of non-contentious business . . .

(5) An order under this section may regulate the amount of such remuneration . . .

f (7) So long as an order made under this section is in operation the taxation of bills of costs of solicitors in respect of non-contentious business shall, subject to the provisions of section 57, be regulated by that order . . .

57.—(1) . . . a solicitor and his client may, before or after or in the course of the transaction of any non-contentious business by the solicitor, make an agreement as to his remuneration in respect of that business.

g (2) The agreement may provide for the remuneration of the solicitor by a gross sum, or by a commission or percentage, or by a salary, or otherwise, and it may be made on the terms that the amount of the remuneration stipulated for shall or shall not include all or any disbursements made by the solicitor in respect of searches, plans, travelling, stamps, fees or other matters.

(3) The agreement shall be in writing and signed by the person to be bound by it

h or his agent in that behalf.

(4) . . . the agreement may be sued and recovered on or set aside in the like manner and on the like grounds as an agreement not relating to the remuneration of a solicitor.

(5) If on any taxation of costs the agreement is relied on by the solicitor and objected to by the client as unfair or unreasonable, the taxing officer may enquire

j into the facts and certify them to the court, and if from that certificate it appears just to the court that the agreement should be set aside, or the amount payable under it reduced, the court may so order . . .

69.—(1) Subject to the provisions of this Act, no action shall be brought to recover any costs due to a solicitor before the expiration of one month from the date on which a bill of those costs is delivered . . .

70.—(1) Where before the expiration of one month from the delivery of a solicitor's bill an application is made by the party chargeable with the bill, the High

Court shall, without requiring any sum to be paid into court, order that the bill be taxed and that no action be commenced on the bill until the taxation is completed.'   *a*

Solicitors' Remuneration Order 1972

'2. A solicitor's remuneration for non-contentious business . . . shall be such sum as may be fair and reasonable having regard to all the circumstances . . .

3.—(1) Without prejudice to the provisions of [ss 70, 71 and 72 of the Solicitors   *b* Act 1974] (which relate to taxation of costs) the client may require the solicitor to obtain a certificate from The Law Society stating that in their opinion the sum charged is fair and reasonable or, as the case may be, what other sum would be fair and reasonable, and in the absence of taxation the sum stated in the certificate, if less than that charged, shall be the sum payable by the client.

(2) Before the solicitor brings proceedings to recover costs on a bill for non-   *c* contentious business he must, unless the costs have been taxed, have informed the client in writing—(i) of his right under paragraph (1) of this article to require the solicitor to obtain a certificate from The Law Society, and (ii) of the provisions of [the Solicitors Act 1974] relating to taxation of costs . . .

4.—(1) On the taxation of any bill delivered under this Order it shall be the duty   *d* of the solicitor to satisfy the taxing officer as to the fairness and reasonableness of the sum charged.

5.—(1) After the expiry of one month from the delivery of any bill for non-contentious business a solicitor may charge interest on the amount of the bill (including any disbursements) at a rate not exceeding the rate for the time being payable on judgment debts, so, however, that before interest may be charged the client must have been given the information required by article 3(2) of this Order.   *e*

(2) If an application is made for the bill to be taxed or the solicitor is required to obtain a certificate from The Law Society, interest shall be calculated by reference to the amount finally ascertained.'

Returning to the present case, the history began in 1978 when the plaintiff started to carry out for the defendants various professional services of a non-contentious nature.   *f* These lasted until July 1979. The plaintiff caused a bill of costs to be prepared by an independent costs draftsman. This showed profit costs of £3,815 together with disbursements of £270 and value added tax of £321·21. Certain payments previously made by the defendants reduced the total sum to £4,177·65. On 30 August 1979 the plaintiff sent the bill to the first two defendants, who were the promoters of the third defendant company. The defendants did not pay, and repeated reminders by letter and   *g* telephone produced no result.

Eventually, the plaintiff agreed with the first defendant to accept payment by instalments, on terms that the defendants paid interest of 15% on the running balance, with retrospective effect from 1 October 1979. The first defendant countersigned a letter dated 14 March 1980 recording the agreement. It is not disputed that in doing so he had power to bind the third defendant as well.   *h*

In the event, however, the defendants paid nothing under this agreement, so the plaintiff commenced an action against them, which he brought to judgment on 21 July 1980. The judgment was, however, set aside by consent on 29 August 1980, apparently because the plaintiff accepted that proceedings were barred by the absence of a notice under art 3(2) of the 1972 order. On the same day the plaintiff did give a notice under art 3(2), and subsequently he applied for, and obtained, a Law Society certificate as   *j* contemplated by art 3(1). The certificate stated that he was entitled to the sum of £3,815 referred to in his bill. It said nothing about interest.

On 12 January 1981 the defendant remitted to the plaintiff on account of that bill a cheque for £2,000 signed on behalf of the third defendant. This was dishonoured. Apart from this, none of the defendants took any steps towards payment of the sum claimed. Accordingly, the plaintiff began the present action, claiming alternatively under the

1972 order and the agreement of March 1980. On the issuing of a summons under RSC
a Ord 14, the first and third defendants admitted that one or both of them was liable for
the principal sum, but denied that they were liable for interest in respect of any period
before 30 August 1980, a date one month after the plaintiff gave his notice under art
3(2). At the hearing of the summons, the plaintiff obtained leave to enter judgment for
£4,537·35 but leave to defend was given in respect of the claim for interest. The second
defendant has taken no part in the proceedings.

b   On these facts, four issues were discussed at the hearing. First, does the wording of art
5(1) demonstrate that the fetter on the rate and duration of interest applies only where
there is a unilateral demand of interest by the solicitor, and not where these matters have
been the subject of agreement by the client? Second, if art 5(1) applies to the present case,
does the period of one month run from the date of the bill, or from the date of the notice,
or from the earlier of the two dates? Third, does the mechanism of s 57 of the 1974 Act
c apply to claims for interest? If so is this mechanism available for the enforcement of the
agreement between the plaintiff and his clients? Fourth, can a claim based on the
agreement be maintained independently of s 57 and art 5?

It is convenient to take the first and second issues together, since in each case the
problem stems from an ambiguity in the verb 'to charge'. This may mean either 'impose
a monetary liability upon someone' or 'make a monetary demand upon someone'.

d   For the plaintiff it is contended that the word is used in the former sense when it first
appears in art 5(1), and that since in this sense a charge cannot arise consensually the
article has no application at all where interest is the subject of a special agreement. I do
not regard this argument as well founded, because I cannot accept the premise that a
'charge' is apposite to refer only to a unilateral levy. Many monetary liabilities which are
called 'charges' in common speech result from consensual relationships, albeit in many
e cases they are not negotiated consensual relationships; for example, charges for the supply
of gas, or admission charges, or charges for the provision of services. I do not think that
on this ground alone it can be held that art 5(1) has no application to the present case.

It is, however, still necessary to decide in what sense the word is used when it appears
for a second time in art 5(1). Here, it seems clear enough that the transitive meaning is
intended. The aim is to make the giving of a notice a condition precedent to something,
f and that something must, it would seem, be the act of making a valid demand for the
interest due. But should this meaning be carried back to the first use of the word, so that
what the solicitor is entitled to do is to make a demand any time after one month has
elapsed? On this view there is no reason to give the word any retrospective effect: so that
the interest will start from the time not earlier than one month after the bill, when the
solicitor gives notice under art 3.

g   It must be acknowledged that this is the reading which best accords with the literal
meaning of art 5(1). It does, however, make little practical sense. The purpose of art 3,
and of the inhibition imposed by the reference to it in art 5, is to make sure that the
client does not pay simply because a demand has been made in terms of a bill, in
ignorance of his rights to test whether the bill is fair. He is to be put on notice of his
rights, and given time to consider whether he should exercise them. These objectives can
h be met perfectly well, with fairness to both sides, if the cause of action for interest arises
as soon as one month has elapsed, but does not become enforceable unless and until the
warning notice has been given. There is no need to go further, and punish a solicitor
who delays in giving a notice, by permanently depriving him of his right to interest,
during the intervening period of delay.

In the circumstances, I consider it legitimate to hold that the verb 'charge' has a rather
j different meaning on the two occasions when it appears in art 5(1) and that if a valid
notice was given under art 3, a retrospective right to interest would thereupon arise.

This is not, however, the end of the matter, since it is necessary to go on to consider
whether art 5(1) applies to the present case at all; for in my view, agreements which are
covered by s 57 lie outside the scope of art 5, because they are outside the scope of the
1972 order altogether. The legislation creates two quite different regimes for non-
contentious business.

Where there is no special agreement, the procedure begins with the delivery of a bill. This is followed by a notification to the client that he is entitled to the safeguards of a Law Society certificate and taxation. Thereafter, when the stipulated period has elapsed, the solicitor can sue on the bill. If, however, the client so desires, and if he acts in time, he is entitled to a taxation as of right, and the proceedings cannot go forward until the taxation is complete.

Where there is a special agreement under s 57 the procedure is quite different. The solicitor's right of action is founded on the agreement not the bill; indeed, so far as s 57 is concerned there is no need for the solicitor to render a bill at all. Nor is there any room for taxation under s 70, for this is concerned with bills, not agreements. It is true that s 57(4) seems to contemplate that a taxation may occur, but this is in my view a procedure initiated by the court pursuant to its own inherent powers to supervise solicitors as officers of the court; it is not a procedure exercised as of right by the client. When an action on a special agreement comes before the court, the matter may be sent to the taxing master so that he can inquire into the facts and report back to the court. When doing so, he is acting as a delegate of powers exercised by the court, and he is not exercising his own originating powers of taxation. Furthermore, I do not see any scope for the Law Society to grant a certificate under art 3(1) in cases where the client has made a special agreement with regard to his obligation to remunerate the solicitor. From a practical point of view, the agreement of the client is the strongest evidence that the fee is reasonable; and if it is to be said that the agreement is oppressive, then it is the court under s 57(4) which has the power to put matters right, not the Law Society. All this being so, there is no call for a notice under art 3(2) and no reason for the solicitor to wait for the period prescribed by art 3(3) before bringing his action. In reality, the 1972 order has nothing to do with a solicitor's rights under a special agreement, and I see no reason why art 5 should be read as imposing any clog on the parties' right to agree whatever they choose about interest, and the right of the solicitor to enforce what has been agreed. This conclusion is reinforced by s 56(7) and its predecessor, which is now consolidated in the 1974 Act, which shows that the mechanisms of s 57 were regarded as standing apart from any procedures which the Remuneration Rules Committee might choose to create for cases where there is no special agreement.

Thus, if it is possible to make a valid special agreement in relation to interest, art 5(1) should not prove a bar to its enforcement. But is this in fact possible? The question is not easy. Certainly, there is force in the submission that the words 'or otherwise' in s 57(2) should be read ejusdem generis with what immediately precedes them. I go this far with the argument, that the section seems to be concerned with the ascertainment of the amount of the remuneration, rather than the way in which it is to be paid, so that an agreement as to the source of the funds which are to be used for paying the bill lies outside the scope of the section: see *Jonesco v Evening Standard Co Ltd* [1932] 2 KB 340, [1932] All ER Rep 678, a decision on the rather different words of the earlier legislation. But if a genus can be found at all, it would seem wide enough to include all methods of calculating the money which the solicitor is to receive; and I detect no flavour in the word 'remuneration' itself which would serve to limit the permissible scope of the agreement to the principal sum alone.

Thus, if it were necessary to reach a conclusion on this point, I would hold (contrary to my first impression) that s 57 embraces agreements as to interest, and that accordingly the plaintiff could pursue his claim without regard to art 5(2).

There is, however, another and more direct way of arriving at the same conclusion. This arises from the order of events. What happened here was that since there was no *prior* special agreement, the plaintiff's original cause of action stemmed from his bill of costs, in the ordinary way. Because he had not given the right notice, this was not a cause of action which for the time being he could enforce by a suit. Nevertheless, there was a valid indebtedness, which was subject to adjustment only if the clients exercised their right to taxation; an event which never occurred. I see nothing in the 1974 Act or the 1972 order to prevent a solicitor and his client from coming to an agreement about the a way in which a bill shall be settled, and indeed it would be very inconvenient if they could not. Nor do I see any reason why the accommodation should not be made at a time when, because the period of one month has not expired, or because the solicitor has not yet given a notice, the debt cannot presently be sued on.

If this view is right, there is no need to force the agreement in the present case into the mould of either s 57 or the 1972 order. It stands on its own feet, as a compromise of existing rights. As such, there is no reason why it should not be enforced according to its
b terms. I therefore conclude that the plaintiff's claim is well founded, and there will be judgment against the first and third defendants accordingly. I would record my obligation to the terse but comprehensive submissions of counsel.

Judgment for the plaintiff for interest as claimed.

c Solicitors: *Fallons* (for the plaintiff); *Amhurst, Brown, Martin & Nicholson* (for the first and third defendants).

K Mydeen Esq   Barrister.

d

Cheall v Association of Professional, Executive, Clerical and Computer Staff

e QUEEN'S BENCH DIVISION
BINGHAM J
9, 10, 11, 12, 13, 24 NOVEMBER 1981

COURT OF APPEAL, CIVIL DIVISION
LORD DENNING MR, DONALDSON AND SLADE LJJ
f 4, 5, 6, 7 MAY, 18 JUNE 1982

Trade union – Membership – Termination of membership – No-poaching agreement between unions – Bridlington principles – Admission by union to membership of person recently belonging to another union – Failure of new union to inquire of former union if it objected to member joining new union – TUC disputes committee holding new union to be in breach of Bridlington principles
g *and requiring new union to expel new member – Member concerned not allowed to make personal representations to disputes committee – Union's executive committee purporting to terminate membership without giving member opportunity to be heard – Committee terminating membership under union rule giving it discretion to terminate membership where necessary to comply with decision of TUC disputes committee – Whether termination of membership valid – Whether disputes committee and union's executive committee acting in breach of rules of natural justice.*

h The plaintiff was a member of a trade union (the first union) until May 1974, when he resigned because he was dissatisfied with the conduct of its affairs. He believed that having duly resigned from the first union he was free to join another union of his choice and accordingly applied to join a rival union (the second union). The second union was aware of the plaintiff's recent membership of the first union and that under the code of
j conduct regulating inter-union relations (the Bridlington principles) it was required, before it accepted the plaintiff as a member, to inquire of the first union whether it objected to the plaintiff joining the second union. However, the second union failed to make any such inquiry before admitting the plaintiff to membership. The first union lodged a complaint with the Trades Union Congress (the TUC) that the second union had acted in breach of the Bridlington principles. The TUC set up a disputes committee to

hear the complaint. The plaintiff, who had become an official of the second union, attended the hearing as a member of the second union's team but was not regarded by *a* the committee as a party in his own right and for all practical purposes was not given an opportunity to be heard on his own behalf, the committee taking the view that the only parties were the two unions. Having heard submissions from both unions the committee ruled in June 1977 that the second union had breached the Bridlington principles, that it should exclude the plaintiff from its membership and should advise him to rejoin the first union. On 30 June 1978 the executive committee of the second union, without *b* giving the plaintiff an opportunity to make representations, purported to give him six weeks' notice terminating his membership of the union, pursuant to r 14*a* of its rules under which the executive committee was empowered to terminate the membership of a member if that was 'necessary in order to comply with a decision' of a TUC disputes committee. The plaintiff brought an action against the second union seeking a declaration that the notice was invalid and of no effect, and an injunction restraining the union from *c* asserting the validity of the notice. The judge dismissed the action on the ground that the second union was entitled to terminate the plaintiff's membership under r 14. The plaintiff appealed, contending that r 14 did not entitle the second union to terminate his membership, because, inter alia, (i) the second union could not rely on r 14 as empowering it to terminate membership where it was the union's own conscious breach of the Bridlington principles which had given rise to the decision of the TUC disputes *d* committee requiring the termination, (ii) alternatively, the contract of membership between the plaintiff and the second union constituted by the union's rules was subject to an implied term that the union would not act so as to bring about an adverse award regarding the plaintiff's membership or would not implement such an award if it was brought about by the union's conscious breach of the Bridlington principles, and (iii) the application of r 14 was in all the circumstances contrary to the rules of natural justice *e* because both the decision of the disputes committee and that of the union's executive committee were made without the plaintiff being given an opportunity to make representations.

Held (Donaldson LJ dissenting) – The notice terminating the plaintiff's union membership was invalid, and the appeal would be allowed, for the following reasons—   *f*
    (1) (Per Lord Denning MR and Slade LJ) The second union would not be allowed to shelter from the consequences of its own misconduct in breaching the Bridlington principles by relying on r 14 of its rules to terminate the plaintiff's membership, since the necessity to terminate his membership had arisen as a direct result of the second union's conscious and deliberate breach of the Bridlington principles and it would be contrary to the principle that the law did not permit a person to take advantage of his *g* own wrongdoing if the second union were to be permitted to rely on r 14. Furthermore (per Slade LJ), it was a fundamental principle of the interpretation of contracts (including a contract between a member and his union constituted by the union rules) that an avoiding provision in a contract on the happening of a contingency would not, unless the contract expressly so provided, be construed so as to permit a party who brought about the contingency by his own wrongdoing to take advantage of his wrong and to *h* rely on the provision (see p 881 *c d*, p 892 *e* to *g*, p 893 *c* to *g*, p 894 *b* to *f* and p 896 *d* to *f* and *h j*, post); *New Zealand Shipping Co Ltd v Société des Ateliers et Chantiers de France* [1918–19] All ER Rep 552 applied.
    (2) (Per Lord Denning MR) It followed from the fundamental principle of the common law that a person was entitled to join a union of his choice (which principle was enshrined in art 11(1)*b* of the European Convention for the Protection of Human Rights) *j* that a person was also entitled not to be expelled from the union of his choice except for reasonable cause and in accordance with the requirements of natural justice. Rule 14 did not accord with that principle since it did not provide reasonable cause for a member's

---

a   Rule 14 is set out at p 880 *j* to p 881 *a*, post
b   Article 11(1) is set out at p 878 *g*, post

a expulsion, because (a) it was unreasonable that a member should be expelled because of a decision of a TUC disputes committee when he was not a party to the dispute and was not entitled to be heard by the committee, and (b) it was contrary to natural justice that the executive committee of the union could decide to expel a member under r 14 without giving him the right to be heard (see p 878 *f g*, p 879 *d h j* and p 881 *a* to *c* and *f g*, post); *Nagle v Feilden* [1966] 1 All ER 689 applied.

b Per Lord Denning MR. The rules of a trade union are merely byelaws, and do not constitute a contract between the members and the union. Furthermore, being byelaws the rules are binding only so far as they are reasonable and certain (see p 880 *b* to *e*, post).

c Per Donaldson LJ. (1) Although a TUC disputes committee is required to act fairly in the discharge of its duties with respect to inter-union disputes, it is not unfair for it to refuse to allow a member, or an applicant for membership, of one of the unions involved to make personal representations because, even though he will or might be indirectly affected by the committee's decision, he is not a party to the dispute (see p 883 *d e* and *g h*, post).

d (2) An executive committee of a union is required to act fairly when deciding to terminate membership pursuant to its rules and, since, in that case, the member is directly affected by the committee's decision and is in a position analogous to that of a party to a dispute which the committee is to determine, the duty to act fairly is more onerous and prima facie the member has a right to be heard by the committee before it reaches its decision although the circumstances may be such that the failure to hear the plaintiff before deciding to terminate his membership is not unfair and does not vitiate the decision (see p 884 *d j*, p 885 *a b* and p 886 *d e*, post).

Notes

e For the rules of natural justice, see 1 Halsbury's Laws (4th edn) paras 64–65.

For the rules of a trade union in regard to membership and expulsion, see 38 Halsbury's Laws (3rd edn) 354–357, paras 612–615, and for cases on the subject, see 45 Digest (Repl) 545–546, 1230–1238.

Cases referred to in judgments

f *Abbott v Sullivan* [1952] 1 All ER 226, [1952] 1 KB 189, CA, 45 Digest (Repl) 400, *139.*

Andrew v NUPE (8 July 1955, unreported), Ch D.

Blathwayt v Lord Cawley [1975] 3 All ER 625, [1976] AC 397, [1975] 3 WLR 684, HL, Digest (Cont Vol D) 1030, *2541a.*

Breen v Amalgamated Engineering Union [1971] 1 All ER 1148, [1971] 2 QB 175, [1971] 2 WLR 742, CA, Digest (Cont Vol D) 954, *1249c.*

g *British Actors' Equity Association v Goring* [1978] ICR 791, HL.

Edwards v Society of Graphical and Allied Trades [1970] 3 All ER 689, [1971] Ch 354, [1970] 3 WLR 713, CA, 17 Digest (Reissue) 128, *273.*

Egerton v Earl Brownlow (1853) 4 HL Cas 1, [1843–60] All ER Rep 970, 10 ER 359, HL, 36(1) Digest (Reissue) 554, *133.*

h *Faramus v Film Artistes' Association* [1964] 1 All ER 25, [1964] AC 925, [1964] 2 WLR 126, HL, 45 Digest (Repl) 542, *1228.*

Fender v Mildmay [1937] 3 All ER 402, [1938] AC 1, HL, 12 Digest (Reissue) 325, *2352.*

Ipswich Tailors' Case (1614) 11 Co Rep 53a, 77 ER 1218, 45 Digest (Repl) 391, *86.*

Lawlor v Union of Post Office Workers [1965] 1 All ER 353, [1965] Ch 712, [1965] 2 WLR 579, Digest (Cont Vol B) 718, *1214a.*

j *Lee v Showmen's Guild of Great Britain* [1952] 1 All ER 1175, [1952] 2 QB 329, CA, 45 Digest (Repl) 541, *1221.*

Levison v Patent Steam Carpet Cleaning Co Ltd [1977] 3 All ER 498, [1978] QB 69, [1977] 3 WLR 90, CA, 3 Digest (Reissue) 470, *3120.*

McInnes v Onslow Fane [1978] 3 All ER 211, [1978] 1 WLR 1520, Digest (Cont Vol E) 45, *62a.*

Malloch v Aberdeen Corp [1971] 2 All ER 1278, [1971] 1 WLR 1578, HL, 19 Digest (Reissue) 548, *4128.*

Malone v Comr of Police of the Metropolis (No 2) [1979] 2 All ER 620, [1979] Ch 344, [1979] 2 WLR 700.

Marco v Valente (1953) 162 EG 117; *affd* (1954) 163 EG 190, CA.

Mirams, Re [1891] 1 QB 594, 38 Digest (Repl) 4, 2.

Monkland v Jack Barclay Ltd [1951] 1 All ER 714, [1951] 2 KB 252, CA, 39 Digest (Repl) 676, 1730.

Nagle v Feilden [1966] 1 All ER 689, [1966] 2 QB 633, [1966] 2 WLR 1027, CA, 25 Digest (Reissue) 503, 4388.

New Zealand Shipping Co Ltd v Société des Ateliers et Chantiers de France [1919] AC 1, [1918–19] All ER Rep 552, HL, 39 Digest (Repl) 808, 2744.

Pan American World Airways Inc v Department of Trade [1976] 1 Lloyd's Rep 257, CA, Digest (Cont Vol E) 42, 6Aa.

Radford v National Society of Operative Printers, Graphical and Media Personnel [1972] ICR 484, Digest (Cont Vol D) 953, 1238a.

Richardson v Mellish (1829) 2 Bing 229, 130 ER 294, 12 Digest (Reissue) 295, 2126.

Rothwell v Association of Professional, Executive, Clerical and Computer Staff [1976] ICR 211, Digest (Cont Vol E) 609, 1254a.

Schering Chemicals Ltd v Falkman Ltd [1981] 2 All ER 321, [1981] 2 WLR 848, CA.

United Kingdom Association of Professional Engineers v Advisory, Conciliation and Arbitration Service [1979] 2 All ER 478, [1979] 1 WLR 570, CA, Digest (Cont Vol E) 608, 1199f.

Young, James and Webster v United Kingdom [1981] IRLR 408, E Ct HR.

Cases also cited

A-G v BBC [1980] 3 All ER 161, [1981] AC 303, HL.

Cinnamond v British Airports Authority [1980] 2 All ER 368, [1980] 1 WLR 582, CA.

John v Rees [1969] 2 All ER 274, [1970] Ch 345.

R v Electricity Comrs, ex p London Electricity Joint Committee Co (1920) *Ltd* [1924] 1 KB 171, [1923] All ER Rep 150, CA.

Ridge v Baldwin [1963] 2 All ER 66, [1964] AC 40, HL.

Rigby v Connol (1880) 14 Ch D 482, [1874–80] All ER Rep 592.

Spring v National Amalgamated Stevedores and Dockers Society [1956] 2 All ER 221, [1956] 1 WLR 585.

Wiseman v Borneman [1969] 3 All ER 275, [1971] AC 297, HL.

Wood v Woad (1874) LR 9 Exch 190.

Action

By a writ issued on 7 March 1980 Ernest Dennis Cheall, the plaintiff, brought an action against the Association of Professional, Executive, Clerical and Computer Staff (APEX), seeking (i) a declaration that a notice purporting to terminate the plaintiff's membership of APEX contained in a letter to the plaintiff dated 30 June 1978 was invalid and of no effect, (ii) an injunction restraining APEX by its servants and agents or otherwise from asserting the validity of the notice, and (iii) damages. The facts are set out in the judgment.

George Newman QC and *Stephen Auld* for Mr Cheall.
Frederic Reynold QC and *Cherie Booth* for APEX.

Cur adv vult

24 November. **BINGHAM J** read the following judgment: In this action the plaintiff, Mr Cheall, challenges the validity of a notice given to him by the defendant trade union, the Association of Professional, Executive, Clerical and Computer Staff (APEX), terminating his membership of that union. The situation of the parties is a strange one. Mr Cheall, a long-serving trade unionist of great loyalty and dedication, adamantly wishes to remain a member of APEX. APEX, for its part, would wish, if it properly

could, to keep Mr Cheall as a member. But pursuant to principles accepted by unions
a affiliated to the Trades Union Congress (the TUC), and generally known as the Bridlington
principles, APEX has felt bound to give Mr Cheall the termination notice of which he
now complains. Put in the most general terms Mr Cheall's case is a plea that his right as
an individual to be free to belong to a union of his choice is one that the law should
respect and enforce. APEX replies that the restriction on the right, for which they have
by contract provided, is proper and necessary if order in the field of industrial relations is
b to be preserved or achieved. The case thus raises a question of some general significance.

In order that the detailed facts of the case may be fully understood it is necessary that
the formal background to those facts should be described. APEX has three relationships
relevant for present purposes: a relationship with its members, including Mr Cheall; a
relationship with other trade unions affiliated to the TUC; and a relationship with the
TUC. I will deal with these in turn.

c The relations between APEX and its members (including Mr Cheall) are governed by
the rules of the union. The objects are, among other things:

'(i) to regulate relations between professional, executive, clerical and computer
staff and their employers and between such workers and other workers . . .

(v) to facilitate co-operation among organisations catering for similar grades,
whether included or not within the Union;

d (vi) to promote friendly relationships and further co-operation between the
Union and the organisations representing manual workers . . .

(ix) generally to promote the welfare of its members.'

Any person over 16 whose employment consists mainly of professional, executive,
clerical and computer or allied work may become a member of the union (r 5), having
e first completed an official application form (r 6). Of central importance in this case is
r 14, which reads:

'*Decisions of T.U.C. Disputes Committee.*—Notwithstanding anything in these rules
the Executive Council may, by giving six weeks' notice in writing, terminate the
membership of any member, if necessary, in order to comply with a decision of a
Disputes Committee of the Trades Union Congress.'

f
This is the rule under which notice was given to Mr Cheall, and I shall have to return to
consider it in detail. It is to be contrasted with r 15, which is in these terms:

'*Expulsion.*—Any member acting in a manner inimical to the interests of the
Union may be expelled from the Union, or fined an amount not exceeding £25 by
the Executive Council. Any Branch or Area Council may recommend the expulsion
g of a member by the passing of a motion by a majority of three-fourths of those
voting. In every case the member shall be given by registered letter not less than
one week's notice of any motion for expulsion or the imposition of a fine and he
shall have the right to be heard by the Executive Council before his expulsion or the
imposition of a fine is made operative. Every such member shall have, and be
advised of his right of appeal to Annual Conference, the decision of which shall be
h final.'

The significance of the contrast lies in the detailed provisions in the later rule, but not in
the earlier, for giving the member a right to be heard.

Relations between APEX and other unions affiliated to the TUC are governed by the
contents of a booklet republished from time to time and now entitled 'TUC Disputes
j Principles and Procedures'. An introduction briefly summarises the history of the
Bridlington principles, the text of which follows. But the preface makes plain the status
of these principles.

'The following Principles constitute a code of conduct accepted as morally binding
by affiliated organisations. They are not intended by such organisations or by the

Trades Union Congress to be a legally enforceable contract. The Principles include the main text and the Notes and both are to be read together as having equal status *a* and validity.'

I can go straight to principle 2, which provides:

'No one who is or has recently been a member of any affiliated union should be accepted into membership in another without enquiry of his present or former union. The present or former union shall be under an obligation to reply within 21 *b* days of the enquiry, stating: (a) Whether the applicant has tendered his resignation; (b) Whether he is clear on the books; (c) Whether he is under discipline or penalty; (d) Whether there are any other reasons why the applicant should not be accepted. If the present or former union objects to the transfer, and the enquiring union considers the objection to be unreasonable, the enquiring union shall not accept the applicant into membership but shall maintain the status quo with regard to *c* membership. If the problem cannot be mutually resolved it should be referred to the TUC for adjudication. A union should not accept an applicant into membership if no reply has been received 21 days after the enquiry, but in such circumstances the union may write again to the present or former union, sending a copy of the letter to the head office of the union if the correspondence is with a branch, stating that if no reply is received within a further 14 days they intend to accept the *d* applicant into membership. Where the union to which application is being made is dealing directly with the head office of the present or former union, a copy of this communication may be sent to the TUC.'

A note indicates that 'recently' in the first sentence of principle 2 covers applicants who have been members of an affiliated union within the preceding year, but it is suggested that trouble will be avoided if inquiries are made in all cases where previous trade union *e* membership is known. Principle 3 provides for a written form on which inquiries may be made by the second union of the first. Principle 4 prohibits a union from accepting a member of another union where that union objects to the transfer (see principle 2 above). Principle 5 provides that no union shall commence organising activities at any establishment or undertaking in respect of any grade or grades of workers in which another union has the majority of workers employed and negotiates wages and *f* conditions, unless by arrangement with that union. Principle 6 calls on each union to include in its membership application form a question asking the applicant whether he is or has been a member of any other trade union. Later principles govern the conduct of affiliated unions where there are disputes between them concerning such matters as trade union recognition and demarcation of work.

It will be necessary to revert to the relationships between affiliated unions, but first let *g* me touch on relations between APEX and the TUC. The TUC is itself a trade union (see the Trade Union and Labour Relations Act 1974, s 28(1)(*b*)) and its members are such bona fide trade union organisations as shall be affiliated in the manner prescribed by the rules and standing orders of the TUC. These rules govern relations between the TUC and its affiliated members. The first object of the TUC is to do anything to promote the interests of all or any of its affiliated organisations or anything beneficial to the interests *h* of past and present individual members of such organisations. Rule 12 of these rules contains a number of provisions important for present purposes. These are (so far as material) as follows:

'(a) Where disputes arise or threaten to arise between affiliated organisations, the General Council or the General Secretary of the Congress shall use their or his *j* influence (as the case may be) to promote a settlement . . .
(e) . . . upon the application of an affiliated organisation, or whenever he considers it to be necessary, the General Secretary may investigate cases of dispute or disagreement between affiliated organisations and may decide on the most appropriate method of resolving the issue. Where he considers it appropriate, the

General Secretary may refer any such case to a Disputes Committee of the Congress
for resolution in accordance with the Regulations governing procedure in regard to
disputes between affiliated organisations (as amended by the General Council and
adopted by the Congress from time to time). In the event of such a reference, the
General Secretary may summon affiliated organisations to appear as parties before a
Disputes Committee and shall require such organisations to submit to that
Committee any information which he or the Committee considers to be essential to
enable the Committee to adjudicate upon the case.

(f) If an affiliated organisation refuses or fails to respond to a summons by the
General Secretary to appear before a Disputes Committee, the General Secretary
shall investigate the circumstances of such a refusal or failure by calling
representatives of the organisation into consultation and inviting the organisation
to give reasons for its conduct. If, after such investigation, the General Secretary
does not withdraw his summons and the organisation persists in its refusal or failure
to appear before the Disputes Committee the General Secretary shall report the
matter to the General Council who may deal with the organisation under Clause (h)
of this Rule as if it were a case of failure by that organisation to comply with an
award of a Disputes Committee.

(g) If an organisation which is a party to a dispute fails or refuses to submit its
case to a Disputes Committee as provided by this Rule, the Disputes Committee
may proceed to make an award in the absence of that organisation and in any event
it shall not be permissible for that organisation to raise the dispute at any annual
Congress.

(h) Affiliated organisations summoned by the General Secretary to appear as
parties before a Disputes Committee shall be bound by any award of the Disputes
Committee and shall comply forthwith with such award. Should any such
organisation refuse or fail forthwith to carry into effect such an award (in whole or
in part) the General Council having received the award may report on the matter as
they think fit to all affiliated organisations, and/or may either (i) deal with the
organisation under clauses (b), (c), (d) and (h) of Rule 13; or (ii) report the matter to
the next annual Congress to be dealt with as that Congress may decide.'

Two points may be interjected at this point. First, the regulations governing procedure,
to which reference is made, are those from which I quote relevant extracts below. Second,
the first sentence in (h) was added by amendment in 1976 after Foster J, in deciding
Rothwell v Association of Professional Executive Clerical and Computer Staff [1976] ICR 211,
attached importance to the fact that awards of the TUC Disputes Committee were of no
binding force.

Rule 13 of the TUC rules contains these important provisions:

'(a) If at any time there appears to the General Council to be justification for an
investigation into the conduct of any affiliated organisation on the ground that the
activities of such organisation may be detrimental to the interests of the trade union
Movement or contrary to the declared principles or declared policy of the Congress,
the General Council shall summon such organisation to appear by duly appointed
representatives before them or before such Committee as the General Council
consider appropriate in order that such activities may be investigated. In the event
of the organisation failing to attend, the investigation shall proceed in its absence.

(b) If after an investigation under ... (iv) an investigation by a Disputes
Committee under clauses (e) and (g) of Rule 12 and a refusal or failure to comply
with its award under clause (h) of Rule 12; it appears to the General Council that the
activities of the organisation may be detrimental to the interests of the trade union
Movement or contrary to the declared principles or declared policy of Congress, the
General Council shall notify the organisation of that fact, specifying the grounds on
which that charge is made and inviting the organisation to present its views to the
General Council. If, after considering those views, the General Council decide that

the said activities are detrimental to the interests of the trade union Movement or contrary to the declared principles or declared policy of Congress, the General Council shall direct the organisation to discontinue such activities forthwith and undertake not to engage therein in the future.

(c) Should the organisation disobey such direction, or fail to give such undertaking, the General Council are hereby empowered in their discretion to order that the organisation be forthwith suspended from membership of the Congress until the next annual Congress.

(d) The General Council shall submit a report upon the matter to the next annual Congress . . .

(h) Any affiliated organisation dealt with under this Rule shall have the right to appeal to the next annual Congress and may appoint delegates in accordance with Rules 17 and 18 to represent the organisation upon the appeal and at the annual Congress if the appeal is allowed. Congress shall upon such appeal have final authority to deal with the matter by way of re-admission, further suspension or exclusion from membership of the Congress.'

The regulations governing procedure in regard to disputes between affiliated organisations provide for a disputes committee to consist of at least three members, drawn from a panel of experienced trade unionists, not members of the unions in dispute and under the chairmanship of a member of the general council. Attempts are to be made by the unions to settle the matter themselves. Particulars of its complaint are to be given by the complainant union (including details of any members allegedly poached) and replied to in writing by the respondent union. If the dispute persists, arrangements are to be made for a hearing at the earliest reasonable date convenient to all parties. The secretary may fix a date for the hearing in the event of unnecessary or wilful delay on the part of any disputant. Regulation L lays down that:

'A Disputes Committee shall investigate the causes and circumstances of the dispute and shall give to the disputants a full opportunity to submit factual information and to present their views to the Disputes Committee . . .'

Regulations M and N continue in this way:

'M. The basic approach of the Disputes Committee shall be to seek to obtain an agreed settlement, whether of a permanent or an interim character, which is acceptable to all the disputants; and the Disputes Committee may at any time make such recommendations as it sees fit. But whenever the Disputes Committee considers it to be necessary, it shall make an award. In deciding the dispute the Disputes Committee shall have general regard to the interests of the trade union Movement and to the declared principles or declared policy of Congress but shall in particular be guided by the Principles Governing Relations Between Unions (currently set out in the booklet, *TUC Disputes Principles and Procedures*) as amended by the General Council and adopted by the Congress from time to time.

N. The Secretary shall send copies of the award of the Disputes Committee to all the disputants and to the General Council.'

A further note in the TUC booklet repeats that:

'In respect of cases (a) membership and (b) recognition the Committee will make an award if discussions do not lead to a solution which is acceptable to the unions concerned.'

The booklet also contains the following statement:

'COMPLIANCE WITH DECISIONS. Affiliated unions are required to act in accordance with the procedure set out in Rule 11 and Rule 12 and to abide by decisions of the General Council and Disputes Committees. The General Council will require the union or unions concerned to satisfy them that they have done all that they can *a*   reasonably be expected to do to secure compliance with such a decision, including taking action within their own rules if necessary. Any refusal on the part of an affiliated union to give effect to a decision will be dealt with under Rule 11, 12 or 13 as may be appropriate.'

The quotations I have given are taken from the 1979 edition of the APEX rules, the 1976 edition of TUC Disputes Principles and Procedures and the 1978 Rules and Standing Orders of the TUC. All these documents have been modified from time to time over the

b   period with which I am concerned, but it is not suggested that any of these modifications (other than that to which I have drawn attention) is of significance in the case.

It will readily be seen that the provisions I have referred to form part of a coherent, interlocking scheme. The objects of that scheme are twofold: first, to give the TUC jurisdiction to entertain and decide disputes between its members concerning (among other things) membership (that is, to enforce the Bridlington principles); and second,

c   where the disputes committee rules that members of an affiliated union be excluded, to enable the union validly to exclude such members. Underlying the first of these objects is the belief that the interest of society in the maintenance of good industrial relations is best served if inter-union disputes can be authoritatively resolved by the TUC before they degenerate into unseemly squabbles or result in industrial disruption. This is not a belief confined to trade unions or the TUC: it is reflected in the Industrial Relations Code of

d   Practice promulgated in 1972 under the authority of the Industrial Relations Act 1971 and retained (with slight modifications) since that time (see paras 11(iv) and 85 of the Code of Practice). Behind the second object there lies a little history. In 1952 a disputes committee of the TUC directed a trade union to exclude from membership a number of individuals improperly recruited from another union. A successful action was brought in the Chancery Division by one of the affected members challenging the union's right

e   to do this: it was held in *Andrew v NUPE* (8 July 1955, unreported) that any expulsion was or would be ultra vires and void. The publicity attaching to this decision provoked a rash of similar actions. In order to counteract this challenge to the authority of the TUC there was devised a model rule, designed to give express authority to affiliated unions to exclude members from membership where it was necessary to do so in order to comply with an award of the TUC disputes committee. That model rule is (save possibly for the

f   punctuation) what is now to be found as r 14 in the APEX rules. It is also to be found, I am told, in the rule books of all save a handful of unions affiliated to the TUC, and the exceptions are mostly unions operating in fields where the Bridlington principles could rarely if ever apply in practice. It was, as I have said, under r 14, the model rule, that APEX purported to exclude Mr Cheall. At the heart of this action therefore lies a challenge both to the validity of the model rule and to the manner of its operation in this

g   case. That leads me on to the detailed facts which give rise to this action.

Mr Cheall is now aged 61. He held his first union card at the age of 14 when he became a trainee cinema projectionist. Since then he has worked in a number of different occupations. But almost always, save during his six years of military service, he has been a member of his appropriate trade union, and on more than one occasion he has acted as secretary of his union branch. He is a man deeply imbued with the loyalties and traditions

h   of the trade union movement. In 1965 he joined Vauxhall Motors as a security officer. In due course he became a member of the National Union of Vehicle Builders, and held branch office. When the NUVB merged with the Transport and General Workers Union he became a member of that union, and was secretary of that union's local branch. From the giant TGWU there emerged a subsidiary organisation, a union in its own right but a part of the TGWU, named the Association of Clerical, Technical and Supervisory Staffs

j   (ACTSS). Its name indicates the classes of employee for whom it was intended to cater. Mr Cheall was secretary of his local branch of this union (branch no 1936).

I need not attempt to paint in detail the industrial relations picture within Vauxhall Motors in the early 1970s. It suffices to say that, in contrast with other motor manufacturing plants, there were many staff employees who were members of no union and among those who were there was an exceptionally high incidence of movement between unions. In respect of certain grades whom they traditionally represented the Technical Administrative and Supervisory Section of the Amalgamated Union of Engineering Workers held collective bargaining rights with the employer, but for staff outside those grades the field was open so far as the securing of rights with the employer was concerned. There was thus an obvious incentive for unions operating in the staff area, AUEW/TASS, ACTSS and APEX, to compete for members in order to strengthen their respective claims on the employer for recognition. The recruitment of non-union members presented no problem, since the case was not one to which Bridlington principle 5 would apply. But where potential recruits were or had been members of either of the other two unions there was an obvious case under principle 2, and the other union was not likely to agree to recruitment of its member or former member, at least unless it gained some compensating advantage.

By the spring of 1974 Mr Cheall was highly dissatisfied with ACTSS and the TGWU of which it formed a subsidiary part. This was primarily because he regarded the local full-time official responsible for the affairs of his branch as being utterly ineffective and uninterested. He also resented the TGWU's increasing involvement in political activity and what he regarded as its increasingly left-wing stance. A series of defections from the branch no doubt added to his demoralisation and that of the branch. The matter came to a head at a branch meeting on 6 May 1974 when, without prior arrangement with Mr Cheall or his chairman, all the members of the branch committee submitted their resignations. The chairman accepted these, and then he and Mr Cheall followed suit. The ACTSS rule book gave no guidance on how to resign from the union, but Mr Cheall was meticulous in carrying out the steps which he believed to be required. He finalised the books of the branch which he held, sent these to the union's head office and received a receipt showing that all was in order. He sent to the local district organiser of ACTSS the minutes of the meeting (recording the resignations) and written notice of his own resignation; of these he received no acknowledgement. Little or no effort was made by ACTSS to reorganise this branch until November of that year.

It is worthy of note that at the time when he took this important step of resigning from ACTSS, Mr Cheall had not been the subject of any approach, formal or informal, from APEX. He had, however, been greatly impressed by the performance of Mr Ray Edwards, the assistant general secretary of APEX, whom he had seen in action on behalf of APEX members at a number of joint meetings which both men attended. It was, indeed, Mr Edwards's ability and effectiveness which had pointed the contrast with Mr Cheall's own full-time official. Although never approached, Mr Cheall had naturally wondered from time to time whether he should join APEX. So it was in no way surprising that on 29 May 1974, following his resignation from ACTSS, Mr Cheall attended a recruiting meeting organised by APEX. During the meeting he signed an application form to become a member of APEX, leaving entirely blank the section of the form which asked for details of any other union of which Mr Cheall was or had been a member. His application was accepted by APEX and Mr Cheall became a member, no inquiry being made by APEX of ACTSS.

Mr Cheall gave three reasons for not filling in this section of the form. First of all, he said, the local and other officials of APEX knew very well from their own direct knowledge that he was or had been a member of ACTSS. Whether or not a good reason for not filling in the form, this was undoubtedly true. It has not been challenged that the APEX officials did indeed know this. Mr Cheall's second reason was that it was general practice not to fill in this section. That also I believe to be true, although not very relevant. His third reason was that omission of reference to ACTSS would save the APEX secretary the trouble of making inquiry and also make his acceptance into membership quicker and easier. This last reason requires just a little elaboration. Mr Cheall thought that if APEX made inquiry of ACTSS, the latter would object to his becoming a member of APEX. He also believed that ACTSS would have no right to object or no justification in objecting, because he had duly resigned from that union and was under no disciplinary or financial disability so far as that union was concerned. As clearly emerges from the

wording of principle 2, which I have quoted, this belief was quite wrong. The principle
a applied not only to members but to recent ex-members of the other union. Mr Cheall
did not appreciate this at the time, and he had no copy of the Bridlington principles. I
am sure that until he came to give evidence before me Mr Cheall persisted in this
misconception. During the years which followed, a man of quicker intelligence would, I
think, have grasped the true position (there was ample opportunity to do so) but Mr
Cheall did not. APEX, as one would expect, did not share this misconception. Its omission
b to make inquiry was calculated. It wanted to build up its membership at Vauxhall. If it
made inquiry an objection by ACTSS was certain, and Mr Cheall could not be taken into
membership until the matter was resolved. If it did not make inquiry an objection was
still likely but Mr Cheall would by then have been taken into membership and time
would have been gained; by the time the crunch came, APEX's bargaining position at
Vauxhall might have been strengthened and an agreement might be negotiable with
c ACTSS which would enable APEX to retain Mr Cheall as a member.

     Having joined APEX, Mr Cheall was appointed a representative of that union and
sought to represent it in dealings with Vauxhall Motors. The company was at first
somewhat bewildered to find a man who had recently negotiated with them on behalf
of ACTSS seeking now to do so on behalf of APEX, but the company's attitude hardened
when it found that the transfer was challenged by ACTSS, which as an offshoot of the
d TGWU had the backing of a union very powerful among the company's manual workers.
And it was not long before the ACTSS challenge came, first concerning members who
had left at the same time as Mr Cheall and then (in September 1974) concerning Mr
Cheall himself. APEX's response to the ACTSS challenge was to adopt a policy of inaction,
believing that if the dispute dragged on long enough an accommodation could be reached
concerning representation at Vauxhall Motors which would enable APEX to keep Mr
e Cheall and others in membership. The matter did drag on. At a meeting between the
two unions on 4 March 1975 it appears that a junior APEX official admitted a violation
of the Bridlington principles, but nothing was done to rectify it. A meeting at national
level was arranged for 29 January 1976, but this proved abortive because the TGWU
would not proceed with lay members present and APEX would not proceed without
them. Mr Cheall meanwhile was becoming vexed and frustrated at his inability to
f function satisfactorily as a representative of APEX, and at the delay in resolving his
position. He took the matter up with his member of Parliament and in July 1975 wrote
in outspoken terms to the general secretary of the TUC. Not understanding the
vulnerability of APEX under the Bridlington principles, Mr Cheall did not (I think)
understand its reasons for welcoming delay. In February 1976 the TGWU made a formal
complaint to the TUC and the wheels of the disputes machinery began to turn. But they
g turned very slowly. Mr Cheall thought that the delay was attributable to the TGWU,
which was only partly true, and wrote both to the TUC and to APEX urging that the
matter be sorted out. Eventually a disputes committee hearing was fixed for 17 May
1977. Before that time Mr Cheall had, at APEX's request, done a good deal of work, the
main effect of which was to show that only 11 members had left ACTSS and joined APEX
although complaint was at one time made concerning over 100. Mr Cheall also supplied
h APEX with a typed submission, setting out his version of the facts of the matter, the facts
concerning his resignation, his criticism of the TGWU's conduct and his critical views on
the Bridlington agreement. Mr Edwards of APEX held a meeting in London, attended
by Mr Cheall among others, at which the broad lines of APEX's defence were discussed.
Both the TGWU and APEX submitted written statements of their cases to the TUC, and
these were exchanged. Mr Cheall did not himself receive a copy of the APEX case, but it
j was the subject of discussion between Mr Edwards, Mr Cheall and the other representatives
of APEX immediately before the opening of the disputes committee hearing.

     The disputes committee was constituted in accordance with the regulations I have
referred to. At the hearing Mr Moss Evans, then the national organiser of the TGWU,
opened his union's case. Mr Edwards replied. They were the principal spokesmen for
their respective parties. Mr Evans rested on the simple assertion that APEX had recruited

former members of ACTSS without inquiry. As in the APEX written case, Mr Edwards made the lame and somewhat disingenuous reply that the application forms of Mr Cheall *a* and the others had not disclosed recent membership of ACTSS. But he did also emphasise that Mr Cheall and the others had left ACTSS because they were profoundly dissatisfied with it. Mr Cheall, who himself attended the hearing as did one other of the disputed members, made two interventions. The first was to show by production of copy documents that he had fully resigned from ACTSS before joining APEX, a fact of which Mr Evans seemed to be unaware; Mr Cheall regarded this fact as a conclusive answer to *b* the charge against APEX. The second was to make some scathing criticisms of the Bridlington principles. The other of the disputed members, Mr Arbuthnott, also intervened briefly. The hearing lasted most of the morning.

The disputes committee issued its findings on 20 June 1977. Having summarised the contentions of the two unions the committee concluded—

> 'that APEX should have made inquiries of the TGWU and by not doing so APEX *c*
> therefore acted in breach of Principle 2 of the TUC Disputes Principles and
> Procedures. The Disputes Committee AWARD that APEX should exclude the
> eleven named individuals and advise them to rejoin the TGWU.'

The first that Mr Cheall knew of this award was when, on 28 June 1977, in company with his APEX representatives, he attended a meeting with Vauxhall Motors concerning *d* a personal problem of his own. (His wife had died, and he had a young son to look after; he was anxious to work the afternoon-evening shift so that he would be at home at night and in the early morning. But he did not want to lose the shift allowance payable for working the ordinary three-shift system. The company for a time continued to pay the allowance while permitting Mr Cheall to work the single shift but had now discontinued payment and were putting a limit on the period for which Mr Cheall could work the one *e* shift.) At the outset of the meeting the company's representative took a telephone call, following which he referred to the effect of the award and refused to listen to any representations by APEX on Mr Cheall's behalf.

The following year was an unhappy one for Mr Cheall. APEX could not pursue his personal problem and he made no progress on his own behalf. His domestic situation made it harder for him to attend, or keep in touch with the affairs of, his local branch, *f* from which he became somewhat alienated. He began to feel that APEX was not giving him the support it should and threatened resignation, having it in mind to change his job. He gave vent to his feelings in a bitterly critical letter to the general secretary of the TUC. In March 1978 he issued an originating application before an industrial tribunal against Vauxhall Motors claiming that the company had deterred him from, and penalised him for, being a member of an independent trade union, contrary to s 53 of *g* the Employment Protection Act 1975; ultimately (but much later, in April 1979) he obtained a declaration in his favour, but the compensation awarded was a very small fraction of the costs which he had personally incurred. APEX meanwhile pursued the same policy as before: implementation of the award could not be refused, but it could be delayed, and if the delay were long enough Mr Cheall's membership might be saved as part of an inter-union settlement at Vauxhall. But that was not what happened. In the *h* spring of 1978 the TGWU put increasing pressure on the TUC to secure compliance by APEX with the award; and the TUC put corresponding pressure on APEX. At Vauxhall Motors ACTSS and AUEW/TASS made a spheres of influence agreement, the main effect of which was to squeeze out APEX; to this development the ill-will created by the events involving Mr Cheall and the others may have made some contribution. At last APEX felt it had no choice but to comply with the award. Notice was accordingly given to Mr *j* Cheall on 30 June 1978, and to the other members a little later. In October 1978 the TGWU invited Mr Cheall to apply to rejoin ACTSS. He has not accepted that invitation, and I am satisfied that he has no intention of doing so. He started these proceedings in March 1980. He remains employed in his old job at Vauxhall Motors, now working on the three-shift basis.

The first issue between the parties concerns the construction of r 14 of the APEX rules.
a It is common ground that the rule is permissive, conferring a discretion and not a
mandatory duty: so much is evident from use of the word 'may'. But when does the
discretion become exercisable? Counsel for Mr Cheall laid stress on the words 'if
necessary'. They showed, he said, that the test was whether the practical exigencies of the
union's position were such that there was no realistic alternative to compliance. That
stage would not be reached until the union had exhausted its rights to make
b representations to the TUC general council under TUC r 13, and was not reached here
because matters never advanced to that stage. He therefore contended that the necessity
contemplated by the rule never arose. I cannot accept his construction. In *British Actors'
Equity Association v Goring* [1978] ICR 791 at 794–795 Viscount Dilhorne said:

> *c* '... I do not think that, because they are the rules of a union, different canons of
> construction should be applied to them than are applied to any written documents.
> Our task is to construe them so as to give them a reasonable interpretation which
> accords with what in our opinion must have been intended.'

The reasonable interpretation of this rule is in my judgment that the union is to have a
discretion to terminate the membership of a member where such termination is required
or called for by a decision of a disputes committee. I do not think the effect of the rule
d would be very different if the words 'if necessary' were not there, but the words are not
mere surplusage because they do underline (for the benefit of the member) that no
discretion to terminate arises where there could be compliance with the decision of the
disputes committee without termination.

If, however, the construction of counsel for Mr Cheall is right and mine is wrong, I
would nonetheless hold that there was on the facts here such a practical 'necessity' as the
e rule (on his construction) requires before the discretion arises. If is of course factually
correct that the general council of the TUC were never involved in this matter under
r 13 of the TUC rules. But that rule does not provide for an appeal against the decision of
a disputes committee. There is no provision for such an appeal. The matter will come
before the general council upon information that an affiliated union, in breach of its
obligation under r 12(h), has refused or failed to comply with a decision of the disputes
f committee, for consideration whether that refusal or failure is detrimental to the interests
of the trade union movement or contrary to the principles or policy of the TUC. There
might, no doubt, be cases where a defaulting union could reasonably hope to persuade
the general council or congress that its conduct did not offend in that way; if so, it might
be reasonable to present its views to the general council under r 13(b) and no practical
necessity to comply would exist until it had done so. But the general council's concern is
g not primarily with the merits of the disputes committee decision but with the interests
of the trade union movement, and in the ordinary run of cases the general council would
be bound to regard defiance of the lawfully constituted authority of the TUC as
detrimental to the interests of the movement. Here, APEX rightly judged their chances
of obtaining a favourable decision from the general council to be nil. The union had,
moreover, practical experience of the effects of non-compliance. On an earlier occasion
h (some of the facts of which are summarised in *Rothwell v APEX* [1976] ICR 211) APEX
had failed to comply with a disputes committee award, believing (correctly as it turned
out) that the award was invalid, and the union's conduct was investigated by the general
council. The process was very uncomfortable. Its officials were ostracised and treated
with hostility by other unions. An appeal to congress fell on deaf ears. By the spring of
1978 a necessity to comply with the present award had undoubtedly arisen; to require
j the union to go to the brink of suspension or disaffiliation would be unrealistic and futile.

Counsel for Mr Cheall advanced a further argument on the contractual effect of r 14.
He pointed out that a union might break Bridlington principle 2 either knowingly or
innocently: knowingly where, as here, it knew or was told that an applicant belonged or
had belonged to another union; innocently where it was not told and did not know and
did not suspect that such was the case. Since, counsel submitted, it was a cardinal

principle of the law of contract that a party should not be allowed to take advantage of a
condition which he has himself brought about, r 14 should be so construed or so applied *a*
as to preclude APEX from relying on the rule where the conduct giving rise to the
disputes committee decision involved a default (that is, a breach of the Bridlington
principles which was not innocent) on its part. Alternatively, counsel submitted that a
term was to be implied into the contract between APEX and Mr Cheall that APEX should
not act so as to lead to an adverse award and/or should not implement an award where it
had acted in default (in the sense I have defined).   *b*

In support of the first of these submissions counsel relied on *New Zealand Shipping Co
Ltd v Société des Ateliers et Chantiers de France* [1919] AC 1, [1918–19] All ER Rep 552. The
speeches in that case undoubtedly contain a number of general statements, founded on
old authority, to the effect that no man can take advantage of the existence of a state of
things which he himself has produced. The case itself concerned a shipbuilding contract
which provided that the contract should become void in certain defined events some of *c*
which would and some of which might not be attributable to any act or omission of the
shipbuilder. One of these events occurred, for reasons altogether outside the builder's
control. The owner contended that the contract was voidable only at his option, the
builder that it was voidable at the option of either party. The House of Lords upheld the
builder's contention, making it clear that the builder could not have claimed the benefit
of the clause had he been responsible for bringing about the event in question. It is to be *d*
noted that in that case, and in the authorities referred to in it, the contracts were
unspecific as to which party should be entitled to take the benefit of the clause. The true
ratio of the case is, I think, that where a contract provides that it shall be void on the
happening of a certain event, a party cannot ordinarily avoid the contract if he is himself
the means of bringing about that event. The principle does not in my judgment assist
Mr Cheall here. Rule 14 is quite specific as to where the discretion to terminate is vested *e*
and when it arises, and there is accordingly no scope for the application of the general
principle. An adverse decision of a disputes committee necessarily envisages a violation
of the Bridlington principles by APEX, and the general language of the rule in my view
permits no refinement concerning the quality of APEX's conduct giving rise to the
decision. It would moreover be entirely contrary to the original intention of the rule,
viewed in its historical context, that a union which had violated the Bridlington principles *f*
should be free to keep the poached members where it had committed a conscious or
deliberate violation but not where its violation was inadvertent. Counsel also relied on
Marco v Valente (1953) 162 EG 117, but so far as one can gather from an inadequate
report the case turned on an implied term and does not assist the present argument.

The implied terms contended for seem to me to face two insuperable obstacles. The
first is that they are inconsistent with the language of r 14, which expressly provides, and *g*
only provides, for termination on a disputes committee decision adverse to APEX and is
drawn in terms too general to permit of any distinction between the circumstances
giving rise to the adverse decision. The second obstacle is this. Any term to be implied
must be implied into the contract of membership between the member and the union.
That contract comes into existence when the member is accepted into membership. By
that stage any violation of the Bridlington principles will have occurred. It is difficult to *h*
imply an undertaking by the union that it had not done something which it may be (as
in this case) it knew it had done. It is equally difficult to see how any post-contractual
conduct by the union could lead to an adverse decision. Counsel for Mr Cheall did
suggest that APEX's delaying tactics had reduced its chances of successfully resisting the
TGWU complaint, but there is no ground whatever for suggesting that the outcome
would have been different however speedily the matter had come before the disputes *j*
committee. I am quite sure that APEX dragged its feet in the hope that a better result
could thereby be achieved for Mr Cheall as well as itself. It is not, after all, unusual for a
defendant with no defence to seek refuge in delay.

I now turn to the argument which counsel for Mr Cheall put at the forefront of his
client's case. I fear that I shall do his able presentation injustice in summarising it briefly

as follows. The admission, and even more particularly the expulsion, of members to and
a from trade unions are matters to which the law attaches a special seriousness because of
the important role which unions play in our society and the serious economic, social and
other consequences which membership and expulsion may entail. This is so even where,
in the absence of a closed shop, loss of a union card does not mean loss of livelihood. In
accordance with the rules of natural justice it is accordingly necessary that before a
member is expelled he should have proper notice of the complaint against him and an
b adequate opportunity to make representations on his own behalf. A union cannot validly
confer on itself an arbitrary discretion to expel nor can such a discretion be exercised
capriciously. Those principles counsel for Mr Cheall derived from a well-known line of
authorities, including *Abbott v Sullivan* [1952] 1 All ER 226 at 234–235, [1952] 1 KB 189
at 198, 204–205; *Lee v Showmen's Guild of Great Britain* [1952] 1 All ER at 1180–1181,
1184, [1952] 2 QB 329 at 342–343, 347; *Lawlor v Union of Post Office Workers* [1965] 1 All
c ER 353 at 360, 363, [1965] Ch 712 at 729, 734; *Breen v Amalgamated Engineering Union*
[1971] 1 All ER 1148 at 1154, 1157–1158, [1971] 2 QB 175 at 190–191, 195; *Edwards v
Society of Graphical and Allied Trades* [1970] 3 All ER 689 at 695–696, 700–701, [1971] Ch
354 at 376–377, 382; *Radford v National Society of Operative Printers, Graphical and Media
Personnel* [1972] ICR 484. Here, said counsel, those principles were flouted because Mr
Cheall was given no notice and no opportunity to be heard before his membership was
d terminated by six weeks' notice under r 14. Moreover, the disputes committee hearing
from which the exercise of the powers to terminate under r 14 derived, was itself
conducted in breach of the foregoing principles. True, Mr Cheall was present and made
a couple of interventions. But he was not there as a party, was not given personal notice
of (and did not in fact understand) the TGWU's grounds of complaint and was not treated
or regarded as a person with a right to be heard at the hearing on his own behalf.
e   In answer to this submission counsel for APEX accepted as a matter of fact that Mr
Cheall was given no notice and was accorded no opportunity to be heard before r 14 was
applied by APEX. He argued that Mr Cheall did have adequate notice of the TGWU's
complaint and an opportunity to be heard at the disputes committee hearing, but this I
cannot accept. Mr Cheall did give vent to his personal feelings, and his dissatisfaction
with ACTSS was ventilated; had he sought to say more I think he would have been heard.
f His interests and those of APEX were also, I think, substantially identical. But he was
certainly not regarded as a party to the issue which the disputes committee were there to
resolve, and for that reason I cannot think that anything he would have said on his own
behalf would have carried any significant weight. The disputes committee were
concerned with regulating the conduct of, and the relations between, unions in dispute,
not with considering what was best for individual members. The central question
g therefore is whether the executive council of APEX and the disputes committee of the
TUC were entitled in law to approach the matter as they did. (I should perhaps mention
that although the TUC is not a party to the action, and no relief is claimed against it, it is
fully aware of the action and the issues raised; it has made its views known to counsel for
APEX and has not sought to intervene, confident that its interests and submissions are
identical with those of APEX).
h   On this central question counsel for APEX submitted that the broad statements of
principle in the authorities as to the observance of natural justice were made in and
confined to cases of alleged misconduct. There notice of the alleged misconduct must be
given and an opportunity given to rebut the charge. Here no misconduct was alleged
against Mr Cheall or relied on, either by the disputes committee or the executive council
of APEX, and there was no duty on either body to give him notice or a hearing. The
j only duty of the disputes committee was to resolve the issue between the unions.
The only duty on APEX was to exercise fairly and reasonably the discretion conferred by
the rule, and it was a fair and reasonable exercise if implementation of the award was
insisted on by the complaining trade union and the TUC and if non-compliance (and the
probable consequent involvement of the general council under TUC r 13) would on a
reasonable and honest assessment by the trade union lead to consequences seriously

detrimental to the trade union and its other members. Counsel for APEX placed strong reliance on *Malloch v Aberdeen Corp* [1971] 2 All ER 1278, [1971] 1 WLR 1578, an appeal *a* heard by the House of Lords concerning the dismissal of a teacher otherwise than for misconduct. A majority of their Lordships, on construing the relevant legislation, held that there was an implied statutory right for the teacher to be heard. But for that statutory implication the majority would have agreed with the minority (who construed the legislation differently) that there was no right to be heard. There was also some support for the view that an individual need not be given a right to be heard if there was, *b* in the circumstances, nothing which he could say which could affect the outcome. This, in short, was the argument of counsel for APEX.

I have already indicated my conclusion that if the law required the rules of natural justice to be observed towards Mr Cheall at the disputes committee hearing, that requirement was not met. But I do not consider that that requirement applied to that hearing. The TUC, and the disputes committee, were correct in regarding their function *c* as being the preservation of order and discipline among affiliated organisations; they were not concerned with considering the conduct or accommodating the wishes of individual members of those organisations. It could be assumed that poached members wished to join the new union, otherwise they would not have left or proposed to leave the old. Beyond that I do not think it was incumbent on the disputes committee to go, any more than in a demarcation dispute it would consider the views of individual *d* workers involved in the dispute as opposed to the submissions of their unions. The APEX written case did, it is true, suggest that Mr Cheall and others had failed to disclose previous union associations without going on to admit that disclosure had in the circumstances been unnecessary, but I do not think that this was understood or intended prejudicially to the members; Mr Edwards certainly did not attribute blame to the members at the hearing (had he done so Mr Cheall would undoubtedly have *e* expostulated); the TGWU gave the obvious and inevitable answer and I am quite sure that the award was in no way based on disapproval of the members' behaviour. It would in my judgment be not only extending but distorting the principles of natural justice to hold that Mr Cheall had a personal or individual right to be treated as a party by the disputes committee. It often happens, where an issue is to be determined between bodies corporate, that individuals who are unrepresented have a close interest in the outcome *f* (for example, in the current fares controversy, the non-ratepayer on the Marble Arch underground) but that does not confer a right of individual representation.

I turn to the exercise by the executive council of its discretion under r 14. I regard it as plain beyond argument that although a discretion in wide terms was conferred it was not untrammelled but had to be fairly exercised (per Edmund Davies LJ in *Breen v Amalgamated Engineering Union* [1971] 1 All ER 1148 at 1158, [1971] 2 QB 175 at 195). I *g* also accept that no trade union can give itself an unfettered discretion to expel a member without hearing him (per Lord Denning MR in *Edwards v Society of Graphical and Allied Trades* [1970] 3 All ER 689 at 695–696, [1971] Ch 354 at 376–377), but APEX by this rule does not seek to do so. The rule is so drawn as to permit the union to give the member notice and an opportunity to be heard in an appropriate case. In some cases it might no doubt be appropriate for the executive council to hold an inquiry or *h* investigation with the corollary that the rules of natural justice would fall to be observed (see the approach of Ungoed-Thomas J in *Lawlor v Union of Post Office Workers* [1965] 1 All ER 353 at 360, [1965] Ch 712 at 729), e g if there were reason to doubt whether the complaining union would readmit the member if his current membership were terminated; or if there were local negotiations, of which the member was better informed than the union, which might lead to an accommodation with the complaining union; or *j* if the complaining union's determination to enforce its award were in question or if there were thought to be grounds for challenging the constitution of the disputes committee, or its conduct of the hearing, or the legal or factual soundness of its conclusion. In any of those cases, fairness might be held to require that the member should be told that the executive council was considering the operation of r 14 against

a him and should be invited to make any representation he wished. But would the duty to act fairly, or the requirements of 'fair play in action' as Sachs LJ called it in *Edwards v Society of Graphical and Allied Trades* [1970] 3 All ER 689 at 701, [1971] Ch 354 at 382, always and necessarily require that process to be followed? Might there not be cases where the executive council could act, and appear to act, fairly without following it? I think there might, and I think the present is such a case. Consider the facts. APEX had had ample notice of the TGWU's complaint against it. The disputes committee had been
b properly constituted and the hearing properly conducted. APEX had been given a full opportunity to put its case and had made all the points which were fairly open to it and some which were not. The result was inevitable. The factual findings inherent in the disputes committee's decision were unassailable. Its award was that which, in practice, always followed a finding that Bridlington principle 2 had been violated. There was no known ground for challenging the award. The TGWU was pressing that it be enforced.
c The TUC was indicating, politely but very firmly, that it did not intend its authority to be undermined. The chances of reaching an accommodation with the TGWU which would obviate the need for termination had, as APEX knew, receded to vanishing point. There was no reason to doubt the willingness of ACTSS to readmit Mr Cheall. There was no realistic hope of respite if the matter reached the general council. It was known to APEX that termination was highly unwelcome to Mr Cheall, and indeed it was
d unpalatable to the union also. But Vauxhall Motors was not a closed shop, so termination did not mean loss of livelihood; and it left Mr Cheall little or no worse off than he had been when, of his own accord, he had left ACTSS and when, without any inducement or representation as to continuity of membership, he had chosen to join APEX. As things were turning out at Vauxhall Motors, ACTSS were better able to represent him effectively than APEX. The ultimate alternatives to termination, namely suspension or disaffiliation
e from the TUC, would in the union's informed view have emasculated it as an industrial force and gravely weakened its ability to serve Mr Cheall or any other of its members. In this situation, as it seems to me, APEX could not conceivably have made any other decision than to terminate, no matter what Mr Cheall urged or argued and no matter how vehement his opposition. If any misconduct had been alleged against him it might have been different, but none was. In my view there was here no legal obligation on
f APEX to give Mr Cheall notice or to grant him an opportunity to be heard. To have done so in circumstances where nothing he said could affect the outcome would in my view have been a cruel deception.

Counsel for Mr Cheall lastly contended that r 14 was void as being contrary to public policy. The first ground relied on was that it was in restraint of trade. I have some real doubt whether the rule is in restraint of trade where there is not, as there was in *Faramus*
g *v Film Artistes' Association* [1964] 1 All ER 25, [1964] AC 925, a closed shop. But even if a restraint is assumed in Mr Cheall's favour, I see no means by which he can overcome the provision in s 2(5) of the Trade Union and Labour Relations Act 1974 that no rule of a trade union shall be unlawful and unenforceable by reason only that the same is in restraint of trade. The ancestor of this provision was fatal to *Faramus*; the descendant is in my judgment no less deadly. Counsel for Mr Cheall did rely, as a separate head of
h public policy invalidity, on infringement of the right to work, but I cannot see that in this context that concept raises any different issue.

Counsel for Mr Cheall also made a more far-reaching submission on public policy. Rule 14, he submitted, taken in conjunction with the Bridlington principles, constituted a restriction on the individual's right to belong to a trade union of his choice. As such it was contrary to British public policy and so void. This submission he based on three
j main grounds: English statutory provisions; the European Convention for the Protection of Human Rights and Fundamental Freedoms (TS71 (1953); Cmd 8969); and expert evidence.

The first ground is straightforward: at all material times over the last ten years there has been statutory protection of the right to belong to a trade union, currently contained in s 4 of the Employment Act 1980.

The second ground is more complex. Article 11 of the convention provides (so far as relevant):

'1. Everyone has the right to . . . freedom of association with others, including the right to form and to join trade unions for the protection of his interests.
2. No restrictions shall be placed on the exercise of these rights other than such as are prescribed by law and are necessary in a democratic society . . . for the protection of the rights and freedoms of others . . .'

Counsel for Mr Cheall accepted that the convention was not of itself law in this country but contended that it should be considered as indicating what the law of this country should be, or should be construed as being. This was the approach taken by Scarman LJ in *Pan American World Airways Inc v Department of Trade* [1976] 1 Lloyd's Rep 257 at 261 and by Sir Robert Megarry V-C in *Malone v Comr of Police of the Metropolis (No 2)* [1979] 2 All ER 620, [1979] Ch 344. Assistance was accordingly to be derived from the case of *Young, James and Webster v United Kingdom* [1981] IRLR 408 in the European Court of Human Rights. That case was concerned with three men who joined British Rail at a time when there was no closed shop agreement in force but who were later dismissed because a closed shop agreement was subsequently made and they refused to join the appropriate union otherwise than for religious reasons. The facts were therefore different from the present, but counsel rightly contended that there were observations in the case helpful to Mr Cheall. For example, the majority held (at 417):

'Another facet of this case concerns the restriction of the applicants' choice as regards the trade unions which they could join of their own volition. An individual does not enjoy the right to freedom of association if in reality the freedom of action or choice which remains available to him is either non-existent or so reduced as to be of no practical value . . .'

And other judges, concurring in the majority decision against the United Kingdom, said (at 419):

'Trade union freedom, a form of freedom of association, involves freedom of choice: it implies that a person has a choice as to whether he will belong to an association or not and that, in the former case, he is able to choose the association. However, the possibility of choice, an indispensable component of freedom of association, is in reality non-existent where there is a trade union monopoly of the kind encountered in the present case.'

These dicta clearly indicated, it was submitted, the direction of British public policy.

The third ground was expert evidence from Dr C G Hanson, a lecturer on labour relations in the Department of Economics at the University of Newcastle. He had had some three years experience on the managerial side in industry, but had over the last 20 years or so devoted himself to the academic study of industrial relations. He accepted that there should be some central control over inter-union disputes and recruitment, and accepted that there must be some limitation on the choice of individual members to join a particular union, but he was strongly opposed to the model rule. The necessary control could be exerted, and the wishes of individual members respected, if violations of the Bridlington principles were visited not with directions to terminate membership but by fines on a graduated scale backed up by the ultimate sanctions of suspension and disaffiliation.

Counsel for APEX challenged all these grounds. So far as the intent of Parliament was concerned, that appeared from the code of practice to which I have already referred, adopted by Parliament at a time when the Bridlington principles and the model rule were well known and widely observed.

Counsel for APEX challenged the relevance of the decision in *Young, James and Webster v United Kingdom* [1981] IRLR 408, although referring me to the provisionally translated opinion of one of the majority (at 419):

a
'Yet both the wording of Article 11 s. 1 and the court's case-law demonstrate that trade union freedom is to a large extent determined by its character of a collective right. When attempting to strike a fair balance, account has to be taken of the welfare of the public and of the collective interests of the trade union organisation that are at stake as well as of the individual's freedom of association . . .'

b
The right to join APEX was not for the protection of Mr Cheall's interests, which would be as well or better protected by ACTSS; if it was, then the restriction contended for by APEX was necessary in a democratic society for the protection of the rights and freedoms of others, both employers and union members. If necessary, counsel for APEX submitted that the decision in *Young, James and Webster v United Kingdom* [1981] IRLR 408 was wrong (and certain judicial observations must, I think, have come as a surprise to certain respected commentators: see Professor F G Jacobs, *The European Convention on Human Rights* (1975) pp 157–158); in any event the convention was not directly applicable.

c
Counsel for APEX thirdly relied on the expert evidence of Mr J E Mortimer, best known as the first chairman of the Advisory, Conciliation and Arbitration Service from 1974 to 1981. Before that Mr Mortimer served as a full-time trade union official for over 20 years, as the board member responsible for personnel and industrial relations in London Transport and as a member of several public bodies. He strongly supported the Bridlington principles which in his opinion operated to preserve order in collective bargaining (in the interests of the employer as well as the employee), to reduce the incidence of breakaway unions (with the consequence of competing demands on the employer by different warring groups), and to encourage union amalgamations and mergers, thus taking one small step towards industry-wide unions such as exist in West Germany and Sweden, which he regarded as the ideal industrial structure. Mr Mortimer also strongly supported the model rule: if it were replaced by a system of fines unions would be free to buy members, at whatever price, and he did not think TUC procedures would command acceptance if poaching unions were allowed to keep their ill-gotten members. He also thought that a system of fines would leave the root problem unsolved: an employer might still find that a union which he had recognised and with which he had negotiated agreements had lost its membership to an unrecognised union, subject to no agreements, in the same plant.

d

e

f
I approach this matter bearing in mind the celebrated utterance of Burrough J in *Richardson v Mellish* (1824) 2 Bing 229 at 252, 130 ER 294 at 303. Like Ungoed-Thomas J in *Lawlor v Union of Post Office Workers* [1965] 1 All ER 353 at 364, [1965] Ch 712 at 735:

g
'My duty here is, to the best of my ability, to administer justice according to law. I am not concerned with the political or economic consequences of doing so. To do that would be to dabble in politics, and that is not my function here. I am only concerned with matters of public policy so far as they are expressed in legal principles of general application.'

h
I accept that where the court is presented with alternative formulations of legal principle regard may be paid to the fact that one or other of them may be more consistent with international treaty obligations undertaken by Her Majesty, but I must bear in mind that the obligations assumed and the rights conferred by the European convention are not justiciable in our municipal courts. Mr Cheall starts with this advantage, that the policy of English law is in general, where possible and appropriate, to lean in favour of the liberty of the individual; but the advantage is whittled down somewhat by the countervailing consideration that the law also, in general, leans in favour of upholding

j
contracts, and Mr Cheall became a member of APEX on terms which included r 14 (even if he was unaware of it). But one must look for more specific indications of public policy. It is (I think) significant that although industrial relations have been the subject of much legislation and much controversy in recent years no attempt has been made to modify or restrict the Bridlington principles or the model rule. The code of practice may be taken as some evidence of approval. But I think the course of legislation over the last ten years

deserves somewhat closer study. The Industrial Relations Act 1971 provided, in s 5(1)(a), that every worker should have the right to be a member of such trade union as he might choose, but it was a right 'as between himself and his employer'. I take that qualification to mean that it was not a right as between himself and the trade union of his choice, although by s 65 he was not to be excluded from membership by way of any arbitrary or unreasonable discrimination and his membership was not to be terminated without a reason being given. When most of that Act was swept away by the Trade Union and Labour Relations Act 1974 it was provided, in s 5 of that Act, that a worker should have the right not to be excluded or expelled from membership by way of arbitrary or unreasonable discrimination. But that section was repealed by s 1 of the Trade Union and Labour Relations (Amendment) Act 1976. There had meanwhile been enacted the Employment Protection Act 1975 which, in s 53, gave an employee the right not to have action taken against him by his employer preventing or deterring him from being a member of an independent trade union. This was the section on which Mr Cheall relied against Vauxhall Motors, and the section reappeared as s 23 of the Employment Protection (Consolidation) Act 1978, but it was not a right against another trade union; had it been, Mr Cheall would have been able to air his real complaint, against the TGWU, before the industrial tribunal. The current statutory provision is found in s 4 of the Employment Act 1980, and it confers a right on an employee not to have an application for membership of a trade union unreasonably refused and not to be unreasonably expelled from a trade union. The question whether a trade union has acted reasonably or unreasonably is to be determined in accordance with equity and the substantial merits of the case, and a union is not to be regarded as having acted reasonably only because it acted in accordance with its rules or unreasonably only because it has acted in contravention of them. One cannot of course predict how this provision would be applied in any given case, and it is certainly not a question for me, but the Royal Commission on Trade Unions and Employers' Associations 1965–1968 was inclined to regard refusal of membership to an applicant in compliance with the Bridlington principles as a good reason for refusal (see Cmnd 3623, para 624) and termination of an existing membership for the same reason would not seem very different in kind. In all this I find no hint that a rule in the form of the model rule is necessarily, and irrespective of the circumstances of its operation, to be regarded as mischievous. In *Rothwell v APEX* [1976] ICR 211 the model rule was argued to be void as being contrary to public policy, but Foster J found it unnecessary to decide the question (see [1976] ICR 211 at 222). That apart, the strictures of the courts have been confined to the purported conferment of unfettered discretions and the arbitrary or capricious or unlawful exercise of discretions. Since neither the present rule nor any analogous rule has (save in *Rothwell's* case) been challenged before, the authorities give no guidance on the policy of the law towards such a rule. But this silence is of course unhelpful towards Mr Cheall, who has undertaken the task of showing that the model rule is contrary to public policy. I do not find that the European convention gives a clear lead on this question. The language of art 11 permits of arguments on which it would be idle for me to speculate and wrong for me to express views. Some passages from the judgments, which I have quoted, read helpfully to Mr Cheall, but they arose in a case where the facts were quite different from the present and where the injustice to the individuals involved was much more pronounced than anything Mr Cheall can complain of.

I turn lastly to the expert evidence. Whether the Bridlington principles and the model rule are on balance beneficial or detrimental to British industry and industrial relations is a very large question, the resolution of which would involve much factual research and comparative study. It would be naive to suppose that a reliable view could be formed on the basis of a couple of hours' evidence, from sources however eminent. In order that a court should find the model rule to be contrary to public policy, in the absence of other indications or authority and on the strength of factual evidence, an overwhelming case would have to be made out. It suffices to say that no such case has in my view been made out here. The practical arguments in favour of the model rule are, at the least, serious *a* and substantial. Taking all these matters together I find it quite impossible to conclude that the model rule is void as being contrary to public policy.

It follows that in my judgment the action fails and must be dismissed. I would like to end by expressing my thanks to both sides for the help I have received from them.

Action dismissed.

K Mydeen Esq   Barrister.

b **Appeal**
Mr Cheall appealed.

George Newman QC and *Stephen Auld* for Mr Cheall.
Frederic Reynold QC and *Cherie Booth* for APEX.

c   *Cur adv vult*

18 June. The following judgments were read.

LORD DENNING MR. This case raises a point of the first importance. No less than the right of a man to join a trade union of his choice. It arises out of a struggle between
d two trade unions. They are rivals. Each trade union wants to maintain and increase its membership. It objects to the rival 'poaching' its members. What is to be done?

The Bridlington principles

It is a problem which has vexed the trade union movement for many years. As long ago as 1939 there was a Congress of Trade Unions at Bridlington. It was much concerned
e with membership questions. They agreed on a code of conduct. It was designed to minimise conflict between trade unions. The code has ever since been called the Bridlington principles. These principles are regarded as morally binding on the members of the TUC, but they are not a legally enforceable contract. The most important principle here is principle 2. Shortly stated, it comes to this: if a man who is already a member of one trade union (which I will call 'the first trade union') applies to join another trade
f union (which I will call 'the second trade union'), then the second trade union must not accept him at that stage. It should make an inquiry of the first trade union and ask if it objects to the transfer. If the first trade union does not object, all well and good. The man can join the second trade union. But, if the first trade union does object, the second trade union must consider the grounds of the objection. If the objection is well founded, the second trade union must not accept the man. If the objection is not well-founded, at any
g rate if the second trade union considers it not to be well founded and still desires to accept the man, then the two unions are in dispute. If the dispute cannot be mutually resolved, it is to be referred to the TUC for adjudication. The decision of the TUC is final. The TUC decides whether the man should transfer to the second trade union or remain with the first.

A like principle applies when a man resigns from his first trade union and soon
h afterwards applies to join a second trade union. Again, the second trade union must not accept him without inquiry: and, if it is not mutually resolved, the dispute is to be referred to the TUC for adjudication.

The important thing to notice is that these Bridlington principles apply only to the two trade unions. The man himself is not a party to them. They are not incorporated into his terms of membership. He has no voice in the decision of any dispute between
j the two trade unions. He is a pawn in the struggle between them. They fight for his body.

The two trade unions here

In our present case the first trade union is the Association of Clerical, Technical and Supervisory Staffs (ACTSS), which is itself a subsidiary of one of the largest trade unions

in the country, the Transport and General Workers Union (the TGWU). I will call it
ACTSS(TGWU).   *a*

The second trade union is the Association of Professional, Executive, Clerical and
Computer Staff. I will call it APEX.

These two unions were in dispute over the application of the Bridlington principles to
a man called Ernest Cheall. He had been a member of ACTSS(TGWU), but left them and
joined APEX. ACTSS(TGWU) complained to the TUC. The TUC decided in favour of
ACTSS(TGWU) and against APEX: with the result that APEX terminated his membership   *b*
with them. He was told to rejoin ACTSS(TGWU). He refused to do so. He now sues
APEX claiming that the termination was unlawful.

Mr Ernest Cheall leaves ACTSS(TGWU)

Mr Cheall is now aged 61. He held his first union card at the age of 14. He is deeply
imbued with the loyalties and traditions of the trade union movement. He is employed   *c*
by Vauxhall Motors as a security officer. He was a member of ACTSS(TGWU) and was
secretary of the local branch. In 1974 several members of the branch became dissatisfied
with their local full-time official. So much so that on 6 May 1974 they submitted their
resignations from ACTSS(TGWU). Mr Cheall, the secretary, followed suit. He was
meticulous in doing everything in good order. He finalised the books of the branch and
sent them to the union's head office. He sent in written notice of his own resignation.   *d*
All this operated on and from 6 May 1974.

He applies to join APEX

APEX had nothing to do with Mr Cheall's resignation. He resigned from ACTSS(TGWU)
solely because of his dissatisfaction with them. At various meetings at which he had been
present, he had been impressed with the effectiveness of the secretary of APEX, so much   *e*
so that on 29 May 1974 (three weeks after leaving ACTSS(TGWU)) he attended a
recruiting meeting for APEX and signed an application form. He gave his name and
address, and said he was a security officer with Vauxhall Motors. There was a question
asking whether he had been a member of any other trade union. He left the answer
blank, but that did not matter because APEX well knew that he had been a member of
ACTSS(TGWU). There was a printed clause above his signature, saying: 'I agree to be   *f*
bound by all the Rules of the Union lawfully applicable to me.'

APEX duly accepted his application. So he became a member of APEX. He thought
that he was perfectly entitled to join APEX because he had left ACTSS(TGWU) three
weeks before, and was free to join another union of his choice. That was a view which he
held throughout. It was his sincere belief over the succeeding years. Was he right or not?
That is the root question in this case.   *g*

APEX turn a blind eye

According to the Bridlington principles, however, APEX were not free to accept Mr
Cheall's application, and they knew it. They knew that he had recently left ACTSS(TGWU)
and that they ought to have applied the Bridlington principles. They deliberately turned
a blind eye to them. The judge said (see p 865, ante): 'Its omission to make inquiry was   *h*
calculated. It wanted to build up its membership at Vauxhall.'

APEX accept him

So APEX accepted Mr Cheall with open arms. They appointed him as their
representative in dealings at Vauxhalls. This gave rise to much resentment by
ACTSS(TGWU). Things dragged on for nearly two years until ACTSS(TGWU) made a   *j*
formal complaint to the TUC.

The formal complaint of ACTSS(TGWU)

On 2 February 1976 TGWU(ACTSS) made this formal complaint to Mr Len Murray,
the general secretary of the TUC:

a
'We have to register our complaint that APEX has contravened TUC disputes principles 2 and 3 by accepting into membership without inquiry the following five individuals ... D Cheall ... These persons are longstanding members of the TGWU(ACTSS), and since this poaching was brought to the attention of APEX way back in 1974 there has been nothing but delay and procrastination on their part.'

The disputes committee hear the complaint

b
Over a year later, on 17 May 1977, there was a hearing by a disputes committee of the TUC. The only parties to the proceedings were TGWU(ACTSS) and APEX. Mr Cheall himself was present and made two interventions. These were to the effect that, as he had lawfully ceased to be a member of TGWU(ACTSS), he was free to join APEX. But his point was swept aside. He was not regarded as a party. The judge said (see p 869, ante):

c
'... he was certainly not regarded as a party to the issue which the disputes committee were there to resolve, and for that reason I cannot think that anything he would have said on his own behalf would have carried any significant weight. The disputes committee were concerned with regulating the conduct of, and the relations between, unions in dispute, not with considering what was best for individual members.'

d *The disputes committee determine the dispute*

On 30 May 1977 the disputes committee made this award. They said:

e
'Having carefully considered the written and oral evidence of both unions, the Committee consider that APEX should have made enquiries of the TGWU and by not doing so APEX therefore acted in breach of Principle 2 of the TUC Disputes Principles and Procedures. The Disputes Committee AWARD that APEX should exclude the eleven named individuals and advise them to rejoin the TGWU.'

Mr Cheall's protest to the TUC

On 16 October 1977 Mr Cheall wrote a letter to Mr Murray protesting against the award of the disputes committee. He said:

f
'... I want to point out that the result is unjust, undemocratic and unacceptable ... I appreciate that there is no appeal procedure laid down on the findings of the Disputes Committee, for a union or members concerned. This in itself is not democratic. This proves what I said at the meeting, that Bridlington is totally out of date, and is inadequate to meet present day requirements.'

g *His application to an industrial tribunal*

Meanwhile, Mr Cheall was involved in a dispute with his employers, Vauxhall Motors, about shift pay. It was owing to a personal problem as his wife had just died. He wanted to be represented by APEX, but the employers refused to listen to any representation by APEX on his behalf. He issued proceedings before an industrial tribunal alleging that the employers were in breach of s 53 of the Employment Protection Act 1975. He succeeded.

h
The tribunal found that the employers had taken action against him for the purpose of penalising him for being a member of an independent trade union, APEX. They awarded him £50 damages.

He is expelled by APEX

The award of the disputes committee was made in June 1977. APEX delayed for many

j
months in acting on it. Much pressure was brought to bear on them by the TUC. Eventually on the 30 June 1978 APEX sent this letter to Mr Cheall:

'... You will recall attending the TUC Disputes Committee hearing which dealt with your application for membership of APEX following your resignation from ACTSS. As you know the Disputes Committee subsequently found against APEX on this occasion. In its award the Disputes Committee stated that those persons the subject of the hearing which included yourself should be excluded from membership of APEX and advised to rejoin the TGWU. In the circumstances I regret I have to advise you that your membership of APEX must be terminated. In doing so I would refer you to rule 14 of the APEX Rule Book, which reads as follows: "Notwithstanding anything in these Rules the Executive Council may, by giving six weeks' notice in writing, terminate the membership of any member, if necessary, in order to comply with a decision of the Disputes Committee of the Trades Union Congress".'

In October 1978 the TGWU invited Mr Cheall to apply to rejoin ACTSS, but he has not done so.

The result

The result is that Mr Cheall has been excluded from membership by APEX. He has not rejoined ACTSS. He is not a member of any trade union. He is still employed by Vauxhall. It is not a 'closed shop'. So he has not lost his job. But, if it had been a 'closed shop' or should become a 'closed shop', he would be out of work.

He takes proceedings at law

On 27 February 1980 Mr Cheall, having got legal aid, commenced proceedings against APEX, claiming that their termination of his membership was invalid and of no effect. The case was heard in November 1981 for several days by Bingham J. He dismissed the claim. Mr Cheall appeals to this court.

The salient facts

Mr Cheall was a member of TGWU(ACTSS) for many years. On 6 May 1974 he was dissatisfied with their conduct of affairs and resigned his membership. That he was perfectly entitled to do. On 29 May 1974 he joined a rival union (APEX) and they accepted him. He was not 'poached' by APEX. He joined them without any inducement by them. That he was perfectly entitled to do. But thereafter TGWU(ACTSS) complained to the TUC that there had been a breach by APEX of the Bridlington principles. The TUC so held. They directed APEX to terminate Mr Cheall's membership. APEX did so. On 30 June 1978 after he had been a member for over four years.

The fundamental principle

I start with the fundamental principle which is enshrined in art 11(1) of the European Convention for the Protection of Human Rights and Fundamental Freedoms (TS 71 (1953); Cmd 8969). It says:

'Everyone has the right to freedom of peaceful assembly and to freedom of association with others, including the right to form and to join trade unions for the protection of his interests.'

In *United Kingdom Association of Professional Engineers v Advisory, Conciliation and Arbitration Service* [1979] 2 All ER 478 at 486, [1979] 1 WLR 570 at 582 I stated: 'That article only states a basic principle of English law.'

Freedom of association itself has never been doubted. No matter whether it be a social club, a football club or a cricket club. Nor whether it be a charitable society for the relief of the poor or the prevention of cruelty. Nor whether it be a political party or for the promotion of political ends. So long as their objects are lawful, everyone in England has a right freely to associate with his fellows.

The right to form and to join trade unions needs more proof. But I gave it in *Nagle v Feilden* [1966] 1 All ER 689 at 693, [1966] 2 QB 633 at 644–646, supported by authorities old and new. I there said:

'The common law of England has for centuries recognised that a man has a right to work at his trade or profession without being unjustly excluded from it. He is a   not to be shut out from it at the whim of those having the governance of it. If they make a rule which enables them to reject his application arbitrarily or capriciously, not reasonably, that rule is bad. It is against public policy. The courts will not give effect to it. Such was held in the seventeenth century in the celebrated *Ipswich Tailors' Case* ((1614) 11 Co Rep 53a) where a rule was made that no person was to be allowed to exercise the trade of a tailor in Ipswich unless he was admitted by them to be a sufficient workman. LORD COKE, C.J. held that the rule was bad, because it

b   was "against the liberty and freedom of the subject".'

Buttressed by Parliament

At the material time in this case, 29 May 1974, this basic principle had been buttressed by an Act of Parliament. At that time the Industrial Relations Act 1971 was still in force. It declared in s 5(1):

c
'Every worker shall, as between himself and his employer, have the following rights, that is to say,—(a) the right to be a member of such trade union as he may choose ...'

Enforceable in the courts

d   I know, of course, that on 31 July 1974 Parliament repealed the Industrial Relations Act 1971 and with it s 5(1) and s 7: see s 1(1) of the Trade Union and Labour Relations Act 1974. But that repeal of a statute did not repeal the common law. It did not affect the common law rights of any man. He still retained his common law right to join a trade union of his choice for the protection of his interests. Nor did the repeal affect the fact that our government had adhered to the European Convention for the Protection of Human Rights and Fundamental Freedoms. Every man could by going to the European

e   Court of Human Rights at Strasbourg vindicate his rights under the convention. Just as the three railwaymen did when they were dismissed for refusing to join a trade union. The Court of Human Rights directed that the United Kingdom government should pay compensation to the three railwaymen. That was on 13 August 1981 in *Young, James and Webster v United Kingdom* [1981] IRLR 408. By being vindicated in this way, I reach the

f   conclusion that art 11(1) of the convention is part of the law of England or at any rate the same as the law of England. The courts of England should themselves give effect to it rather than put a citizen to all the trouble and expense of going to the Court of Human Rights. Our courts should themselves uphold the right of every man to join a trade union of his choice for the protection of his interests.

In any case Mr Cheall joined APEX on 29 May 1974 and APEX accepted him. APEX

g   afterwards, four years later, terminated his membership. They seek to justify it, not by any statute, but by reference to their own rules. To these I will turn in a moment.

The consequences

Starting from that fundamental principle, I go on to work out its consequences. If a man has a right to join a trade union for the protection of his interests, it must follow

h   that he has the right not to be expelled from it, or to have his membership terminated, except for reasonable cause and in accordance with the requirements of natural justice. I said as much in *Nagle v Feilden* [1966] 1 All ER 689 at 694, [1966] 2 QB 633 at 646, and I repeat it here. What good is it for a man to have a right to *join* a trade union, if he can be *expelled* the very next day for no cause, or arbitrarily or capriciously without any reasonable cause? And, if there is some cause alleged against him on which it is said to be

j   reasonable to exclude him, surely he must have notice of what the cause is, and be given a reasonable opportunity of dealing with it? These two are therefore the conditions on which he can be expelled or his membership terminated: first, there must be reasonable cause; second, it must be done in accordance with natural justice. Suppose now that a trade union should put a rule into its rule book which is contrary to this fundamental principle. Such as that the council of the union can exclude any man who works too

hard, or works overtime. Or can exclude any man for misconduct, without giving him a
hearing. I should have thought that such a rule was invalid as being contrary to public *a*
policy.

The rules of a trade union

Times out of number I have protested at the notion that the rules of a trade union
constitute a contract between the member and the trade union. It is simply not true. It
is a fiction. Often enough nowadays a man is compelled to join a trade union so as to be *b*
able to earn his living. He signs an application form which purports to bind him to the
rules. But he hardly ever reads them. Or if he did, he would not understand them. They
are dictated to him. He has no choice but to obey. To hold them to be a contract is far
more a fiction than in the common standard form of consumer contract, with exemption
clauses, as to which see *Levison v Patent Steam Carpet Cleaning Co Ltd* [1977] 3 All ER 498
at 502–503, [1978] QB 69 at 79–80. The man is not even told, 'Take it or leave it.' He is *c*
told, 'You've got no choice. You must sign.' As long ago as 1969 the Law Commission
recommended that exemption clauses should not be given effect to except when
reasonable. Their recommendation has now been implemented by the Unfair Contract
Terms Act 1977. This is a welcome change to reality. Cannot we follow suit in regard to
trade union rules? I think we should. Putting aside fiction and coming to the truth, it is
this: the rules of a trade union are nothing more nor less than bye-laws. They are binding *d*
on all the members whether they like them or not. Everyone has to sign on the dotted
line. No member is allowed to strike out a single word or to make any exception to them.
Being bye-laws they are only binding so far as they are reasonable and certain.

Expulsion

No doubt a mere applicant (before being accepted) must abide by the rules so long as *e*
they are reasonable: see *Faramus v Film Artistes' Association* [1964] 1 All ER 25, [1964] AC
925. But once he has been accepted as a member, then if the committee decide to expel
him or to terminate his membership, the rule in that behalf is open to examination by
the courts of law: see *Breen v Amalgamated Engineering Union* [1971] 1 All ER 1148 at
1154, [1971] 2 QB 175 at 190. The rule itself must be confined to cases where there is
reasonable cause for expulsion or termination. If the rule authorised the committee to *f*
expel a man because he had red hair or a woman because she wore trousers, it would be
invalid: see *Edwards v Society of Graphical and Allied Trades* [1970] 3 All ER 689 at 695–
696, [1971] Ch 354 at 376. And even if the cause is reasonable, the committee must
observe the principles of natural justice. They must give him notice of the charge and a
reasonable opportunity of meeting it. Any stipulation to the contrary is invalid. They
cannot stipulate for a power to condemn a man unheard: see *Lee v Showmen's Guild of* *g*
Great Britain [1952] 1 All ER 1175 at 1181, [1952] 2 QB 329 at 342, approved by Lord
Pearce in *Faramus v Film Artistes' Association* [1964] 1 All ER 25 at 33, [1964] AC 925 at
947.

I turn to apply these considerations to the present rules.

The rules of APEX *h*

Rule 15

This says that 'any member acting in a manner inimical to the interests of the Union
may be expelled from the Union or fined an amount not exceeding £25 by the Executive
Council.' That rule seems fair and reasonable enough. The rule goes on to provide for a
right to be heard and for an appeal. That is fair enough, too. *j*

Rule 14

This is the rule on which APEX rely. It says:

'Notwithstanding anything in these rules the Executive Council may, by giving
six weeks' notice in writing, terminate the membership of any member, if necessary,

a in order to comply with a decision of the Disputes Committee of the Trades Union
Congress.'

To my mind that rule does not accord with the fundamental principle that I have stated.
First, I ask myself: is it reasonable that the man should be bound by a decision of the
disputes committee of the TUC? I do not think so. That is a decision which affects him
vitally. It is a decision whether he is to be allowed to be a member or not. It is decided in
a dispute between two rival unions at which the man is not a party; in which he has no
b right to be heard; and in which his protestations are ignored. It makes him and his
livelihood a pawn in a conflict between two unions.

Second, I ask myself: ought he not to be heard by the executive council (of the union)
before they decide to terminate his membership? In every case where misconduct is
alleged against him, he has a right to be heard. Surely he should have a right to be heard
when he has been guilty of no misconduct. At any rate, so as to show that it is not
c 'necessary' to expel him: and to urge that a fine or a reprimand may suffice.

Third, the misconduct here was of his own trade union, APEX. They were charged
with 'poaching' and were found guilty of it. Can they pray in aid their own misconduct
so as to terminate his membership? Or to deprive him of a hearing? Would they not
then be taking advantage of their own wrongdoing? The law always sets its face against
it: see *New Zealand Shipping Co Ltd v Société des Ateliers et Chantiers de France* [1919] AC 1,
d [1918–19] All ER Rep 552. Surely Mr Cheall should be heard so as to be able to assert:
'You were not guilty of poaching. The disputes committee decided wrongly.' Surely he
can be heard when he says: 'There was no poaching. I joined the union of my own free
will without any inducement being offered at all.'

The argument to the contrary is this: it is said that r 14 is necessary so as to keep order
in industrial relations. If it were not for the Bridlington principles there would be chaos.
e Trade union would fight against trade union, poaching members, and so forth. Either
might call a strike. Strikes are common in inter-union disputes. The conflict would do
great damage to our industrial structure. That is a point of view which is entitled to
respect. But it is not accepted even amongst the experts in industrial relations. In this
very case expert evidence was called the other way.

I take my stand on something more fundamental. It is on the freedom of the
f individual to join a trade union of his choice. He is not to be ordered to join this or that
trade union without having a say in the matter. He is not to be treated as a pawn on the
chessboard. He is not to be moved across it against his will by one or other of the
conflicting parties, or by their disputes committee. It might result, when there is a 'closed
shop', in his being deprived of his livelihood. He would be crushed between the upper
and nether millstones. Even though it should result in industrial chaos, nevertheless the
g freedom of each man should prevail over it. There comes a time in peace as in war, as
recent events show, when a stand must be made on principle, whatever the consequences.
Such a stand should be made here today. I hold the trade union APEX was wrong to
terminate the membership of Mr Cheall. I would allow the appeal, accordingly.

h **DONALDSON LJ.** Mr Cheall is not the first person to feel aggrieved that the
Bridlington principles have prevented him from remaining a member of the union of
his choice. A similar problem arose ten years ago at the National Coal Board's bulk
terminal at Immingham (see report no 41 of the Commission on Industrial Relations).
No doubt there have been others in the meanwhile. Nor will it be the last, for there is an
inherent and inevitable conflict between the need of trade unions to avoid competitive
j strife and the wish of individuals to achieve membership of the union which they
consider to be that best able to represent their interests. This conflict is only one of many
intractable problems in industrial relations and it is not one which can be resolved by
judges.

In considering this appeal, our function is quite different. It is to examine Bingham J's
conclusion that APEX was entitled in law to terminate Mr Cheall's membership under

r 14, which formed part of the rules of APEX at the time when he became a member. Counsel for Mr Cheall attacks this conclusion on four grounds: (a) The rule, or the way in which it was applied in Mr Cheall's case, was contrary to the rules of natural justice. (b) APEX cannot rely on the rule because it was its own breach of the Bridlington principles which led the disputes committee of the TUC to award that APEX should exclude Mr Cheall from membership and advise him to rejoin the TGWU. (c) The rule has no application where the award of the disputes committee was itself made in breach of the rules of natural justice. (d) The rule, and the related rules and regulations of the TUC, are contrary to public policy.

Natural justice

'Natural justice' is an emotive phrase, particularly to judges. But, as Sir Robert Megarry V-C pointed out in *McInnes v Onslow Fane* [1978] 3 All ER 211 at 219, [1978] 1 WLR 1520 at 1530, justice is far from being a natural concept. It is rather a term of art meaning a legal duty to act fairly or, as Sachs LJ put it in *Edwards v Society of Graphical and Allied Trades* [1970] 3 All ER 689 at 701, [1971] Ch 354 at 382, 'fair play in action'. I need no persuading to hold that both the disputes committee of the TUC and the executive council of APEX were subject to a paramount obligation to act fairly in reaching their respective decisions. But this conclusion does not advance matters very much, for what is or is not fair must depend on all the circumstances. Since the decision of the disputes committee preceded and precipitated that of the executive council of APEX and since it is accepted that APEX cannot justify its action in terminating Mr Cheall's membership if the decision of the disputes committee cannot stand, it is appropriate to start by examining that decision.

The decision of the disputes committee

Relations between trade unions which are affiliated to the Trades Union Congress are governed by the Bridlington principles which originated in decisions taken at the Bridlington Congress in 1939, but have been amended in the light of experience. The version relevant to the instant appeal was published in 1976. They are said to constitute a code of conduct accepted as morally binding by all affiliates rather than a legally enforceable contract, but for present purposes this distinction is not material.

Disputes between trade unions fall wholly or mainly into one of four categories, namely:

'(a) a difference about the union to which a particular individual or group of workers should belong (membership); (b) a difference about which unions should be recognised (recognition); (c) a difference about which union members should carry out particular work (demarcation); (d) a difference about the policy which should be pursued in respect of terms and conditions of employment (wages and conditions).'

The Bridlington principles are designed to minimise the likelihood of such disputes, to point the way in which they should be resolved and to provide machinery by which they can be determined should the parties be unable to reach a fraternally amicable settlement.

The instant appeal concerns a membership dispute which the parties were unable to resolve and which was accordingly referred to the disputes committee which made an award. The relevant principles are nos 2 and 7.

Principle 2 is designed to prevent one union from poaching the members of another union. However, as it would be wholly ineffective if it had no application to members who have resigned from one union preparatory to joining a different union, it also involves restrictions on accepting new members who have 'recently' been members of another union. 'Recently' is interpreted as meaning within the previous year. The principle requires the union which the applicant seeks to join ('the new union') to ask the applicant's old union whether it has any objection to him joining the new union. If the old union objects, the new union should not allow the applicant to become a member until the old union has withdrawn its objection or the TUC disputes committee has ruled that the new union may admit the applicant to membership.

Principle 7 requires both unions to notify the TUC of any dispute so that it can, if necessary, be dealt with by the disputes committee.

These principles are supplemented by the rules of the TUC which require affiliated unions to comply with any award on pain of possible disaffiliation.

Counsel for Mr Cheall submits that where two unions are in dispute as to membership, natural justice requires that the applicant for membership or members concerned should have a right of audience before the disputes committee. Mr Cheall did indeed attend the hearing before that committee, but he did so as part of the APEX team and not in his own right. Whilst he expressed his personal feelings on two occasions, these were in the nature of infuriated interjections which were probably ignored by the committee as being wholly out of order. Accordingly, I, like the judge, fully accept that for practical purposes Mr Cheall was neither heard by the disputes committee nor given any opportunity of being heard.

Bingham J concluded that if the law required the rules of natural justice to be observed towards Mr Cheall at the disputes committee hearing, that requirement was not met, but he did not think that the law so required. For my part I prefer to think of natural justice as being of universal application, the issue in each case being what, if any, obligation is imposed by the requirements of natural justice in any particular situation.

In my judgment the disputes committee was subject to a requirement to act fairly in and about the discharge of its duties. Its duty was to resolve a dispute between the TGWU and APEX on a complaint that APEX had failed to inquire whether the TGWU objected before it admitted Mr Cheall to membership. It was the conduct of APEX which was being impugned, not that of Mr Cheall. The committee was not concerned to adjudicate on any dispute to which Mr Cheall was a party. Fairness required that it allow both the TGWU and APEX to make such submissions and call such evidence as was relevant to their dispute. If either party wanted to give evidence of Mr Cheall's experience, it should have been allowed to do so, but there is no suggestion that there was any failure in this respect. Mr Cheall was a stranger to this dispute and can only complain if and to the extent that the disputes committee failed to act fairly towards him as a stranger. Thus a finding that Mr Cheall had been guilty of some misconduct would have been unfair if the disputes committee had not at the same time either given Mr Cheall an opportunity of being heard or had made it clear that Mr Cheall had not been heard and that the finding was only binding as between APEX and the TGWU. But again there was no such finding and this is not the nature of Mr Cheall's complaint.

In essence counsel for Mr Cheall submits that whenever a court or other tribunal has to make a decision in a dispute between A and B and this decision will or may indirectly affect C, fairness requires that C be given an opportunity to be heard before a decision is made. It would follow that in any dispute between, for example, a building owner and a main contractor concerning an alleged repudiation of the contract by the latter, all the sub-contractors would be entitled to be heard, because their right to perform their sub-contracts would cease if the main contractor's right to perform were held to be forfeit. This is plainly incorrect. As Bingham J pointed out, it is commonplace for individuals to have a close interest in the outcome of a dispute between bodies corporate, but that does not give them a right of individual representation.

Counsel for Mr Cheall drew attention to RSC Ord 15, r 6, which gives the High Court power to join additional parties between whom and any party to the cause or matter there may exist a question or issue arising out of or relating to or connected with any relief or remedy claimed in the cause or matter which, in the opinion of the court, it would be just and convenient to determine as between him and that party, as well as between the parties to the cause or matter. This, counsel for Mr Cheall submits, is fairness in action. If the TGWU/APEX dispute had come before the court, it could and would have given Mr Cheall an opportunity to be heard by joining him as a party. This may be right, but the position of the disputes committee is essentially different from that of a court. The committee's jurisdiction was consensual and the TGWU would not have consented to Mr Cheall being joined as a party. The court, on the other hand, has an inherent or statutory jurisdiction and has a duty to use that jurisdiction in appropriate circumstances with a view to preventing a multiplicity of disputes.

The reference to the practice of the courts is also instructive in another way. This practice is, in general, not to hear independent representations by those who are not parties. The only exception is where the court is making an order which will bind the stranger, as, for example, is the case where an injunctive order is made freezing assets in the hands of a third party such as a bank. The disputes committee could never have made an order binding Mr Cheall. The most that it could do was to require APEX to take action against Mr Cheall. Whether that action, if taken, would affect Mr Cheall adversely or at all would depend on his rights as against APEX.

I can find no trace of unfairness in the failure or refusal of the disputes committee to allow Mr Cheall to make personal representation.

The decision of the executive committee of APEX

Here again, in my judgment, there was a duty to act fairly, but it was a different and more onerous duty because Mr Cheall would be directly affected by the committee's decision. Mr Cheall was in a position analogous to that of a party to a dispute which the committee was to determine. Prima facie he had a right to be heard and to have his representations considered before a decision was reached. He was not heard and the point now at issue is whether this omission necessarily vitiates the committee's decision or whether the decision should nevertheless be treated as valid.

Counsel for APEX submits that the decision should be treated as valid because in the peculiar circumstances Mr Cheall could not have contributed anything to the facts and matters present to the minds of the executive council. Accordingly, as he submits, giving Mr Cheall an opportunity to make representations would have been an idle formality. Bingham J accepted this submission and said that to have granted Mr Cheall an opportunity of being heard would have been a cruel deception as implying, contrary to the fact, that his representation could be successful.

A similar problem was considered, but not determined, in *Malloch v Aberdeen Corp* [1971] 2 All ER 1278, [1971] 1 WLR 1578, where Lord Reid and Lord Wilberforce (see [1971] 2 All ER 1278 at 1283, 1294, [1971] 1 WLR 1578 at 1582, 1595) both expressed the view that in such circumstances the decision might be valid.

The circumstances were indeed peculiar. Mr Cheall had been the close and trusted ally of APEX throughout the dispute with the TGWU. He had attended the hearing before the disputes committee as a member of the APEX team. APEX had fought long and hard not only on their own behalf but in support of Mr Cheall's wish to remain a member of the union. He was a highly valued member and a branch official. Even when the award was published, APEX still delayed in giving effect to it. There can be no doubt that if it could have thought of any way in which it could have retained Mr Cheall within its membership without incurring the extreme displeasure of the TUC and other affiliated unions, it would have done so. Certainly counsel for Mr Cheall was unable to formulate any suggestion or representation which Mr Cheall would have wished to make to the committee or indeed any representation which he could have made, which could or would have affected its decision. Seldom can there have been a more tardy or reluctant compliance with an award of a TUC disputes committee.

In fact, therefore, there was no actual unfairness to Mr Cheall in not affording him a hearing at the time when the decision whether or not to terminate his membership was eventually to be taken. But natural justice is not always or entirely about the fact or substance of fairness. It has also something to do with the appearance of fairness. In the hallowed phrase, 'Justice must not only be done, it must also be seen to be done'. If I had thought that Mr Cheall could reasonably feel that he had been unfairly treated in not being allowed a special opportunity for putting his point of view (he had been putting it informally and to the most senior officers of the union from the autumn of 1974 until

the spring of 1978), I should have been prepared to hold that the executive committee's
a   decision was unfair, in breach of the rules of natural justice and invalid. But I do not see
how he could feel unfairly treated. I can well see why Mr Cheall considers the decision
itself to be unfair, but I cannot see how he could reasonably regard the way in which it
was reached as being in any way unfair and it is not without significance that at the time
he made no such complaint.

In my judgment, this ground of complaint fails.

b
Can APEX take advantage of its own default?

The next argument advanced on behalf of Mr Cheall is that, in terminating his
membership, APEX was taking advantage of its own default and that this is not
permissible. Whereas APEX knew that it was in breach of the Bridlington principles in
accepting Mr Cheall into membership, Mr Cheall did not. In the submission of counsel
c   for Mr Cheall, it is a basic principle of the law that no man may rely on his own wrong
and that that was precisely what APEX was doing when it invoked r 14 as authority for
terminating Mr Cheall's membership.

Before Bingham J reliance was placed on the decision of the House of Lords in *New
Zealand Shipping Co Ltd v Société des Ateliers et Chantiers de France* [1919] AC 1, [1918–19]
All ER Rep 552. The judge defined the ratio of that decision, correctly I think, as being:
d   'where a contract provides that it shall be void on the happening of a certain event, a
party cannot ordinarily avoid the contract if he is himself the means of bringing about
that event' (see p 868, ante).

The existence of the general principle is undoubted, but I think that it is properly to
be regarded as a principle of construction. Subject to considerations of public policy, the
starting point in any contractual dispute must be a determination of what the parties are
e   to be taken to have intended. Prima facie, where it is agreed that one party is to have
certain rights or privileges or is to be released from certain obligations on the happening
of an event, neither party intends that this shall be the case if the beneficiary of the
provision intentionally causes the event to happen. In other words, the law will seek to
imply a term to this effect. But the parties remain free to make a different agreement
and accordingly this principle of construction, or potential implied term, must give way
f   if inconsistent with a clearly expressed term of the contract.

In the present case r 14 on its face is clearly intended to allow APEX to terminate a
membership if, but only if, this course if necessary in order to comply with a decision of
the disputes committee of the TUC. It is this necessity which is the relevant event. APEX
might indeed be unable to rely on r 14 if it artificially stimulated such a decision. But
where the issue has been fought out and the disputes committee has ruled against APEX,
g   it can only be said that APEX itself caused the relevant event to occur if it is permissible
to look behind the decision of the committee to the breach of the Bridlington principles
on which that decision was based.

For my part, I doubt whether this is permissible but, if it is, two classes of breach of
the Bridlington principles have to be considered. The first may be described as an
'innocent' breach. APEX is deceived by the applicant for membership into thinking that
h   he has never been a member of an affiliated union. It admits him to membership
without giving the old union any opportunity of objecting. The second may be described
as a 'guilty' breach. APEX knows that the applicant is, or has recently been, a member of
an affiliated union, but fails to adopt the appropriate procedure before admitting him to
membership.

It is submitted that adequate scope can be given to r 14 if it is confined to those who
j   are recruited by APEX in innocent breach of the Bridlington principles. Bingham J
dismissed this approach because, as he pointed out, APEX would be able and indeed
obliged to keep poached members, whilst being able to expel members which it had
acquired innocently. It must be remembered that r 14 was introduced by APEX at the
behest of the TUC in order to enable it and other affiliated trade unions to get rid of
poached members and, in TUC terms, a rule which left a union free to plead inability
when ordered to terminate the membership of poached members would be a nonsense.

Furthermore, such a rule might oblige the TUC to disaffiliate a union for a time at least and this is the last thing which the TUC wants.

However, it is possible to approach the matter from a different standpoint, namely that of the member concerned. Here it is submitted that it makes sense that APEX should be able to terminate the membership of members whose own deception has led it to admit them, but should be obliged to keep those who were deliberately admitted to membership in breach of the Bridlington principles, particularly where, as in Mr Cheall's case, the applicant did not know that any such breach was involved. The argument is that if these poached members have to be retained by APEX and, as a result, APEX is disaffiliated, it has only itself to blame.

Ignoring all the realities of industrial relations, I think that there are reasons for rejecting this view. Trade union rules, like the rules of a club, constitute the terms of a contract between the members inter se and the members and the union or club, if it is a legal entity. But in relation to new members it is a contract of a special kind, a contract of adhesion. If the court is construing the rule, it must do so in the context of circumstances as they existed when it was adopted and in the context of the presumed intention of the parties to the contract at that time. The relevant parties were the existing members of APEX and APEX itself. What they were considering was the position of future applicants for membership. It seems to me to have been in the highest degree unlikely that either APEX or its existing members intended to have a rule which, if APEX thereafter indulged in a little poaching, would leave APEX obliged to retain the poached members and thus face disaffiliation without the opportunity of 'purging its own contempt'.

In my judgment, the rule, properly construed, is wholly inconsistent with any implied term that there should be any circumstances in which APEX was unable to comply with a decision of the disputes committee that it must terminate the membership of those admitted in breach of the Bridlington principles whether innocently or otherwise.

Public policy

Finally it is submitted that the Bridlington principles, the award of the disputes committee based on those principles, APEX's r 14 and the decision to terminate Mr Cheall's membership are all void as being contrary to public policy.

The basis of this somewhat surprising proposition is art 11 of the Human Rights convention and the decision of the European Court of Human Rights in *Young, James and Webster v United Kingdom* [1981] IRLR 408.

Neither the convention, nor the decision, have any direct impact on English domestic law. However, as Lord Denning MR pointed out in *Schering Chemicals Ltd v Falkman Ltd* [1981] 2 All ER 321, [1981] 2 WLR 848, in matters of legal policy regard should be had to this country's international obligation to observe the treaty as interpreted by the European Court of Human Rights.

Article 11 of the convention provides as follows:

'1. Everyone has the right to freedom of peaceful assembly and to freedom of association with others, including the right to form and to join trade unions for the protection of his interests.

2. No restrictions shall be placed on the exercise of these rights other than such as are prescribed by law and are necessary in a democratic society in the interests of national security or public safety, for the prevention of disorder or crime, for the protection of health or morals or for the protection of the rights and freedom of others. This article shall not prevent the imposition of lawful restrictions on the exercise of these rights by members of the armed forces, of the police or of the administration of the State.'

The decision of the majority of the European Court of Human Rights was that art 11 involved not only a right to belong to a trade union, but some degree of freedom of choice between unions. However, what degree of freedom of choice was necessary was not spelt out other than in the context of the facts of that case.

In *Blathwayt v Lord Cawley* [1975] 3 All ER 625 at 636, [1976] AC 397 at 426, Lord
a Wilberforce accepted that 'conceptions of public policy should move with the times and
that widely accepted treaties and statutes may point the direction in which such
conceptions, as applied by the courts, ought to move'. So do I. But equally I accept the
view of Lord Atkin in *Fender v Mildmay* [1937] 3 All ER 402 at 407, [1938] AC 1 at 12
that the doctrine of public policy 'should only be invoked in clear cases in which the
harm to the public is substantially incontestable, and does not depend upon the
b idiosyncratic inferences of a few judicial minds'. Above all I think that judges must
beware of confusing political policy with public policy (see *Egerton v Earl Brownlow*
(1853) 4 HL Cas 1, [1843–60] All ER Rep 970, and, lest this be thought to be an outmoded
approach, *Monkland v Jack Barclay Ltd* [1951] 1 All ER 714, [1951] 2 KB 252). In saying
this, I am very far from agreeing with Cave J who in *Re Mirams* [1891] 1 QB 594 said
that 'judges are more to be trusted as interpreters of the law than as expounders of . . .
c public policy,' unless perhaps he was himself falling into the trap of confusing political
with public policy. Whether judges are better or less able than others to assess the merits
and demerits of political policies is beside the point, because that is not their function.
On the other hand, 'public policy' in the true sense is a part of the law and it is wholly
within the province and capacity of the judges to declare it. However, they must be
satisfied that *any* reasonable person would agree that the enforcement of the provision
d under consideration would be 'a harmful thing', to use Lord Atkin's homely phrase in
Fender v Mildmay [1937] 3 All ER 402 at 407, [1938] AC 1 at 12. I have no doubt that
reasonable people could be found in large numbers both to support and to oppose the
proposition that on balance the Bridlington principles and r 14 were harmful things.
This being the case, the issue is very far from being incontestable and we are being
invited to apply considerations of political rather than public policy. This I absolutely
e decline to do.

For these reasons I would dismiss the appeal.

SLADE LJ. At all material times before these proceedings were issued the appellant, Mr
Cheall, had been employed as a security officer by Vauxhall Motors Ltd at their plant at
Dunstable, Bedfordshire. He was described by the judge in the court below as 'a long-
f serving trade unionist of great loyalty and dedication'. For a period up to 1974, whilst
employed by Vauxhalls, he was a member of the trade union known as the Association
of Clerical, Technical and Supervisory Staffs (ACTSS). This is itself a branch of a larger
trade union known as the Transport and General Workers Union (the TGWU). Mr Cheall
was a branch secretary of ACTSS.

However, by May 1974, for a number of reasons immaterial for present purposes, Mr
g Cheall had become disillusioned with both ACTSS and the TGWU. He decided that he
wished to resign from ACTSS and did so during the course of that month. He was, as the
learned judge found, meticulous in carrying out the steps which he believed to be
required to effect this resignation. At least in this court, no suggestion has been made
that this resignation was improper in any way.

On 29 May 1974, after his resignation from ACTSS, Mr Cheall attended a recruiting
h meeting organised by APEX. The judge found as a fact that, at the time when he resigned
from ACTSS, Mr Cheall had not been the subject of any approach, formal or informal,
from APEX. During the course of this meeting Mr Cheall completed, or partially
completed, and signed a printed application form for membership of APEX. This form
provided for the inclusion of certain particulars which he gave. It asked him whether he
had been a member of APEX before. To this question he responded 'No'. In a separate
j section, it asked him the following further questions:

'Are you a member of any other Trade Union? Have you been a member of any
other Trade Union? If YES to (a) or (b) state particulars.'

Mr Cheall signed and submitted his application form without answering these two
questions (a) and (b).

Mr Cheall gave the judge three explanations for not filling in this section of the application form, namely: (1) the local and other officials of APEX very well knew from their own direct knowledge that he was or had been a member of ACTSS (it is not in dispute that these officials did indeed well know this); (2) it was the general practice not to fill in this section; (3) the omission of any reference to ACTSS would save the APEX secretary the trouble of making inquiry of ACTSS and also make his acceptance into membership quicker and easier.

All these three reasons were accepted as true ones by the judge. Furthermore, at least in this court, there has been no criticism of Mr Cheall for his failure to complete this section of the application form when APEX did not insist on it. As the judge found, Mr Cheall did think that if APEX made inquiry of ACTSS the latter would object to his becoming a member of APEX. At the same time, however, he thought genuinely, if mistakenly, that ACTSS would have no valid grounds for any such objection, because he had duly resigned from ACTSS and was under no disciplinary or financial disability so far as that union was concerned. In all these circumstances, I think that if APEX was content to accept the application form without the inquiry as to membership of other trade unions having been answered, Mr Cheall himself cannot be blamed. And, as I have indicated, at least in this court no one has sought to blame him in this context.

The conduct of APEX in admitting Mr Cheall into membership, pursuant to his application, is in my opinion more open to criticism. As the judge found as a fact, APEX was well aware that, even though Mr Cheall had duly resigned from ACTSS and was under no disciplinary or financial disability in relation to the union, ACTSS would or might still have valid grounds for objecting to APEX taking on Mr Cheall as a member. The reason for this lay in the TUC principles governing relations between affiliated unions, which are designed to minimise disputes over membership questions and have come to be known as the Bridlington principles. The opening words of principle 2 state: 'No one who is or has recently been a member of any affiliated union should be accepted into membership in another without enquiry of his present or former union.' Principle 4 begins with the words: 'A union shall not accept a member of another union where that union objects to the transfer . . .' Principle 6 obliges each union to include in its membership forms questions on the lines of the TUC model form in regard to past or present membership of another union.

The membership form presented by APEX to Mr Cheall at the meeting of 29 May 1974 duly included questions on the lines of the TUC model form. In every other respect, however, APEX, in accepting Mr Cheall into membership, was acting in flagrant disregard of the Bridlington principles 2 and 6. Principle 6 by necessary implication clearly contemplates that a union will require answers to the relevant questions before admitting a person to membership. A failure to require answers will, to quote the words of the note to principle 6, 'make it impossible for a union to pursue the course of enquiry laid down'. Accordingly, even if APEX had accepted Mr Cheall into membership without any knowledge of his previous membership of ACTSS, I think that it would have done so in breach of the principles. A fortiori, when the relevant APEX officials had direct knowledge of this previous membership.

The findings of fact of the judge as to the attitude of APEX in accepting Mr Cheall were as follows (see p 865, ante):

'Its omission to make inquiry was calculated. It wanted to build up its membership at Vauxhall. If it made inquiry an objection by ACTSS was certain, and Mr Cheall could not be taken into membership until the matter was resolved. If it did not make inquiry an objection was still likely but Mr Cheall would by then have been taken into membership and time would have been gained; by the time the crunch came, APEX's bargaining position at Vauxhall might have been strengthened and an agreement might be negotiable with ACTSS which would enable APEX to retain Mr Cheall as a member.'

These findings of fact have not been challenged. It is thus, I think, clear that APEX, in accepting Mr Cheall into membership, was acting not only in breach of principle 6, but *a*   also in conscious and deliberate breach of principle 2. It well knew that Mr Cheall had recently been a member of an affiliated union, ACTSS, and that therefore, in accordance with principle 2, it could not properly accept Mr Cheall into membership without prior inquiry of ACTSS. It must be taken also to have known that the failure to make proper inquiry of ACTSS would be likely to lead to its being brought before a TUC disputes committee by ACTSS or the TGWU as soon as those bodies discovered its default. It must further be taken to have known that such deliberate default would be regarded by any

b   disputes committee which dealt with the matter as an important factor in determining any complaint brought against APEX.

Mr Cheall having joined APEX was appointed a representative of that union and sought to represent it in dealings with Vauxhall Motors.

The events that followed could, I think, have been readily foreseen by APEX, though not by Mr Cheall. Soon afterwards, ACTSS learned of APEX's acceptance of Mr Cheall

c   into membership and challenged its propriety. Shortly before that, a similar challenge had been made by ACTSS in regard to a few other persons who had left ACTSS and joined APEX at about the same time as Mr Cheall. In due course, namely on 2 February 1976, the TGWU wrote a letter to the general secretary of the TUC registering a formal complaint that APEX had contravened the Bridlington principles by accepting into membership without inquiry Mr Cheall and four other named individuals employed at

d   the Luton and Dunstable plants of Vauxhalls. This letter asserted:

> 'These persons are longstanding members of the TGWU (ACTSS) and since this poaching was brought to the attention of APEX way back in 1974, there has been nothing but delay and procrastination on their part.'

I mention two points in passing. First and foremost, this complaint by the TGWU was

e   in no sense a complaint about the conduct of Mr Cheall, who was not a party to the Bridlington principles. It was a complaint against APEX. Second, it is at least doubtful whether 'poaching' was in fact an accurate description of APEX's activities, at least in regard to MR Cheall, bearing in mind that before he voluntarily left ACTSS of his own accord he had not been the subject of any approach, formal or informal, by APEX. Nevertheless it is not surprising that the TGWU inferred that poaching had taken place,

f   bearing in mind the somewhat disingenuous manner in which APEX had dealt with the matter.

The lodging of this complaint brought into play the rules which govern the relationship of the TUC and its affiliated members. The general secretary of the TUC, on the application of the TGWU and in accordance with r 12, referred the case of dispute between it and APEX to a disputes committee of the TUC for resolution in accordance

g   with the TUC regulations governing procedure in regard to disputes between affiliated organisations. Also in exercise of the power conferred on him by r 12, the general secretary required APEX and the TGWU to appear as parties before a disputes committee and required them to submit to that committee certain information, which he considered necessary to enable the committee to adjudicate on them. The TUC disputes regulations (reg A) provided, inter alia, for the constitution of a disputes committee. As I read them,

h   they implicitly assume that disputes between unions concerning membership will relate to alleged poaching of members.

The TUC disputes machinery, having thus been set in operation in regard to the dispute between the TGWU and APEX, moved very slowly. At long last, a disputes committee hearing was fixed for 17 May 1977. The committee was constituted in accordance with the TUC disputes regulations. The TGWU and APEX submitted written

j   statements of their cases to the TUC and these were exchanged. At the hearing Mr Cheall, though personally represented along with other representatives of APEX, had been given no adequate notice of the TGWU's complaint and, though he made two interventions, was given no proper opportunity to be heard on his own account; correctly, in my opinion, he was not regarded as a party to the issue which the disputes committee had to resolve. These points the judge found as facts. He also indicated his conclusion that, if the law required the rules of natural justice to be observed towards Mr Cheall at that hearing, that requirement was not met.

At the hearing of the disputes committee Mr Moss Evans, who presented the case on behalf of TGWU, rested it on the simple assertion that APEX had recruited former members of the ACTSS without inquiry. This simple assertion was accepted by the disputes committee. It issued its findings on 20 June 1977. After summarising the contentions of the two unions, it concluded:

'APEX should have made enquiries of the TGWU and by not doing so APEX therefore acted in breach of Principle 2 of the TUC Disputes Principles and Procedures. The Disputes Committee AWARD that APEX should exclude the eleven named individuals and advise them to rejoin the TGWU.'

The judge said 'the result was inevitable'.

In the spring of 1978, the TGWU put increasing pressure on the TUC to secure compliance with the award by APEX; and the TUC put corresponding pressure on APEX. Finally APEX decided that it had no choice but to comply.

On 30 June 1978, without giving Mr Cheall the opportunity to make representations, the area organiser of APEX wrote to him referring to the award of the disputes committee and saying that he regretted to advise him that his membership of APEX must be terminated. This letter referred Mr Cheall to r 14 of the current rules of APEX, which provided:

'Notwithstanding anything in these rules the Executive Council may, by giving six weeks' notice in writing terminate the membership of any member, if necessary, in order to comply with a decision of the Disputes Committee of the Trades Union Congress.'

In October 1978 the TGWU invited Mr Cheall to rejoin ACTSS. He did not accept the invitation, and Bingham J was satisfied that he had no intention of doing so.

On 7 March 1980 Mr Cheall issued proceedings against APEX seeking in effect a declaration that the notice of 30 June 1978 terminating his membership was invalid and of no effect and an injunction to restrain APEX from asserting its validity.

Bingham J decided that APEX was entitled in law to terminate Mr Cheall's membership under r 14.

It appears from his judgment that substantially five points were argued before him on behalf of Mr Cheall. I will set them out in the order in which they are dealt with in the judgment. (1) The termination of Mr Cheall's membership of APEX was not 'necessary' within the meaning of r 14. (2) APEX could not rely on r 14 because it was a conscious breach of the Bridlington principles by APEX which gave rise to the adverse decision of the disputes committee and a party cannot rely on a condition in a contract which purports to entitle him to avoid it in a specified event, in a case where he himself has caused that event to occur. (3) A term should be implied in the contract of membership between APEX and Mr Cheall that APEX should not act so as to lead to an adverse award, and/or should not implement such an award, where it has been brought about through a conscious breach by APEX of the Bridlington principles. (4) In accordance with the rules of natural justice, it is necessary that, before a member is expelled from a trade union, he should have proper notice of the complaint against him and an adequate opportunity to make representations on his behalf. These principles were flouted in the present case because: (a) Mr Cheall was given no notice and no opportunity to be heard before his membership was terminated by the executive council of APEX on six weeks' notice under r 14; (b) moreover the disputes committee hearing, from which the exercise of the power to terminate derived, was itself conducted in breach of the principles of natural justice because Mr Cheall was not present as a party, was given no personal notice of the TGWU's grounds of complaint and was not treated or regarded as a person with a right to be heard at the hearing on his own behalf. (5) Rule 14 is in any event void as being contrary to public policy.

The judge in his very careful judgment rejected all these submissions. In relation to
a the fourth of them, he concluded that, if the law required the rules of natural justice to
be observed towards Mr Cheall at the disputes committee hearing, this requirement was
not met. However, he considered that these rules did not apply to this hearing, because
Mr Cheall had no personal or individual right to be treated as a party by the disputes
committee. As to the exercise of the discretion by the executive council of APEX under
r 14, he concluded that there was no legal obligation on APEX to give Mr Cheall notice
b or grant him an opportunity to be heard.

Substantially the same five points have been argued by counsel for Mr Cheall on this
appeal, though the first has been canvassed only very briefly. The fourth and fifth raise
issues of wide general importance. Despite the forceful submissions of counsel for Mr
Cheall to the contrary, I have found both the reasoning and conclusions of the judge on
these last two issues very persuasive. I hope however that counsel will not think it shows
c any disrespect to their full and interesting arguments on those two issues if I do not deal
with them in this judgment, because I have come to the conclusion that Mr Cheall ought
to succeed on this appeal on the first and second of the five issues, to which I therefore
turn.

Rule 14 of the rules of APEX, which I have already quoted, is followed by r 15 which
provides:
d
> '*Expulsion.*—Any member acting in a manner inimical to the interests of the
> Union may be expelled from the Union, or fined an amount not exceeding £25 by
> the Executive Council. Any Branch or Area Council may recommend the expulsion
> of a member by the passing of a motion by a majority of three-fourths of those
> voting. In every case the member shall be given by registered letter, not less than
> one week's notice of any motion for expulsion, and he shall have the right to be
e > heard by the Executive Council before his expulsion is made operative. Every such
> member shall have, and be advised of, his right of appeal to Annual Conference, the
> decision of which shall be final.'

The powers conferred on APEX by both rr 14 and 15 are powers to terminate a
member's contract of membership. Rule 14, though it does not use the word 'expel', is,
f no less than r 15, a power to expel a member from the union. There is, however, one
significant difference between the power of expulsion conferred by r 14 from that
conferred by r 15. Rule 15 gives the member concerned an express right to be heard by
the executive council before his expulsion is made operative. Rule 14 gives him no such
express right.

For the purpose of this judgment, I am content to assume that APEX is correct in
g contending that (i) a member, such as Mr Cheall, has no right whatever to be heard at
the hearing of a disputes committee of the TUC which may give rise to a decision of the
nature referred to in r 14, and (ii) if a contingency of the nature referred to in r 14 arises,
the executive council has the right unilaterally to determine his membership, without
giving him the opportunity to be heard. If these two contentions are correct, however, it
makes it all the more necessary to consider very carefully the true construction and effect
h of the words in the rule which define the nature of the contingency that brings into
operation this practically unfettered power of the executive council.

The words are: '. . . if necessary, in order to comply with a decision of the Disputes
Committee of the Trades Union Congress.' The reference to a decision of this nature
necessitates reference to the disputes procedure embodied in the TUC rules and in the
Bridlington principles, when one comes to construe the rule. This procedure and these
j principles are an essential part of its matrix. As Bingham J pointed out in his judgment,
an adverse decision of the disputes committee necessarily envisages a breach of the
Bridlington principles by APEX. All these matters must have been in the contemplation
of the makers of the relevant rules of APEX at the time when they were made.

Reference to this disputes procedure and to the Bridlington principles reveals that the
circumstances in which a disputes committee of the TUC will or may (after an appropriate

reference to that committee) require an affiliated union to terminate the membership of a member arise in particular where the union has accepted into membership a person who is or has recently been a member of another affiliated union either (i) without inquiry of his present or former union, in breach of Bridlington principle 2, or (ii) in the fact of an objection to the transfer by the other union, so that the admission is in breach of principles 2 and 4, or (iii) inquiry has shown that the member is under discipline or is engaged in a trade dispute or is in arrears with contributions, so that the admission is in breach of principle 4.

Breaches of the Bridlington principles by the admitting union may fall into one of two categories. They may be innocent breaches, for example where the joining member, by a false entry on his application form, has led the union to believe that he has never been a member of another union. Alternatively they may be conscious breaches, as in the present case, where APEX, in admitting Mr Cheall to membership, well knew that it was doing so in breach of principle 2.

In the present case, a question for decision is whether r 14 on its true construction empowers APEX, after receiving a decision of the disputes committee requiring it to terminate a member's membership, to expel such a member in reliance on r 14, (a) whether the breach by APEX of the Bridlington principles was innocent or conscious or (b) only in cases where the breach was an innocent one. APEX submits that (a) is the correct construction. In its submission the circumstances which lead to the adverse decision of the disputes committee are wholly immaterial. It matters not, in its submission, if the event which gave rise to this decision was its own conscious breach of the Bridlington principles or if the necessity of which r 14 speaks is in any particular case a self-induced necessity. The quality of APEX's conduct which gives rise to the relevant decision and the alleged consequential necessity is, it is submitted, quite irrelevant. I cannot accept these submissions, for the reasons which I will now try to explain.

It is, of course, open to parties to a contract expressly and specifically to stipulate that one party may by his own act bring about an event which will entitle him to elect to avoid the contract. A simple example of such a provision is one expressly entitling a party to avoid the contract by serving a written notice on the other side before a specified date. In the absence of an express specific provision of this nature, however, I understand it to be a fundamental principle of the interpretation of contracts that, if an agreement is expressed to be void or voidable on the happening of a contingency, which a party can by his own act or omission bring about, then the party who has by his own act or omission brought about that contingency cannot ordinarily be permitted to rely on the avoiding words. As Lord Finlay LC said in *New Zealand Shipping Co Ltd v Société des Ateliers et Chantiers de France* [1919] AC 1 at 6, [1918–19] All ER Rep 552 at 555: 'It is a principle of law that no one can in such case take advantage of the existence of a state of things which he himself produced.' Lord Atkinson stated the principle more fully in the following terms (see [1919] AC 1 at 9, [1918–19] All ER Rep 552 at 556):

'It is undoubtedly competent for the two parties to a contract to stipulate by a clause in it that the contract shall be void upon the happening of an event over which neither of the parties shall have any control, cannot bring about, prevent or retard. For instance, they may stipulate that if rain should fall on the thirtieth day after the date of the contract, the contract should be void. Then if rain did fall on that day the contract would be put an end to by this event, whether the parties so desire or not. Of course, they might during the currency of the contract rescind it and enter into a new one, or on its avoidance immediately enter into a new contract. But if the stipulation be that the contract shall be void on the happening of an event which one or either of them can by his own act or omission bring about, then the party, who by his own act or omission brings that event about, cannot be permitted either to insist upon the stipulation himself or to compel the other party, who is blameless, to insist upon it, because to permit the blameable party to do either would be to permit him to take advantage of his own wrong, in the one case directly, and in the other case indirectly in a roundabout way, but in either way putting an end to the contract.'

The application of this principle may well involve attributing to the words of a contract
a something other than their literal meaning. Thus, for example, as Lord Wrenbury
pointed out in the *New Zealand Shipping Co Ltd* case [1919] AC 1 at 15, [1918–19] All ER
Rep 552 at 559:

> 'The rule is that in a contract "void" is to be read "voidable", if the result of reading
> it as "void" would be to enable a party to avail himself of his own wrong to defeat
> his contract. It may be stated either in the form that if one party is in default it is
b "void as against him", or that if one party is in default it is "voidable at the option of
> the other party". The two amount to the same thing. But the contract is not "void"
> in favour of or "voidable at the option of" the party in default. He cannot say that it
> is void, and has no option of avoiding it in his own wrong. Here the contract is, in
> my opinion, voidable at the option of either party provided always that he is not
> seeking to avoid it in his own wrong.'

c
The passage from Lord Atkinson's speech, and indeed the other statements of principle
in the speeches in that case, are directed to the situation where the relevant act or
omission which gives rise to the stated contingency occurs *after* the date of the contract.
What then is the position when, unknown to the other contracting party, the relevant
act has already been done, or omitted to be done, *before* the contract is concluded?
d Without much doubt, I think, the legal position must, mutatis mutandis, be the same.
In my judgment, where a contract is expressed to be voidable at the option of one party
on the happening of a contingency which he can by his own act or omission cause to
happen, then that party cannot ordinarily subsequently rely on that avoiding provision
if (a) before the conclusion of the contract he has already knowingly done or omitted
some act which at the date of the contract he could reasonably foresee is likely to cause
e the occurrence of the contingency, and (b) the other contracting party is unaware of this
act or omission at the time when he enters into the contract, and (c) the stated contingency
subsequently in fact occurs as a result of the relevant act or omission.
These propositions seem to me inevitably to follow from the reasoning of the speeches
in the *New Zealand Shipping Co Ltd* case. That reasoning is not, I think, based on the
implication of an additional term in the original contract. It is based on the more simple
f principle that, unless a contract clearly and specifically so provides, the court will not
construe an avoiding provision contained in it in such manner as to permit a party to
take advantage of his own wrong. To permit a man to invoke the avoiding provision in
a case where conditions (a), (b) and (c) above all apply would be to permit him to take
advantage of his own wrong, no less than if he had done or omitted the relevant act after
the execution of the contract. The point may be illustrated by this hypothetical example.
g A man, for motives best known to himself, agrees to buy a horse for a stated sum,
completion to take place in 14 days' time, subject to an express proviso that the buyer
shall have the right to rescind the contract at any time during that 14-day period if it be
discovered that the horse has suffered an injury which makes it unfit to race. Unknown
to the seller, the buyer, before the conclusion of the contract, has already caused his agent
to maim the horse. The buyer, I would suggest, plainly could not subsequently be
h permitted to rely on the avoiding provision, even though the stipulated contingency
would have occurred according to its precise terms. The seller would not, I think, have
to rely on any implied term in the contract; it may be difficult to imply a promise by
one party to a contract that he has not done something which he knows he has done. His
case would be based on the simple principle affirmed by the House of Lords in the *New
Zealand Shipping Co Ltd* case.
j The judge, having referred to Mr Cheall's submissions based on this principle, said (see
p 868, ante):

> 'The true ratio of the case is, I think, that where a contract provides that it shall be
> void on the happening of a certain event, a party cannot ordinarily avoid the contract
> if he is himself the means of bringing about that event. The principle does not in
> my judgment assist Mr Cheall here. Rule 14 is quite specific as to where the
> discretion to terminate is vested and when it arises, and there is accordingly no scope

for the application of the general principle. An adverse decision of a disputes
committee necessarily envisages a violation of Bridlington principles by APEX, and
the general language of the rule in my view permits no refinement concerning the
quality of APEX's conduct giving rise to the decision. It would moreover be entirely
contrary to the original intention of the rule, viewed in its historical context, that a
union which had violated the Bridlington principles should be free to keep the
poached members where it had committed a conscious or deliberate violation but
not where its violation was inadvertent.'

With great respect to the judge, I think there are three fallacies in this critically
important passage in his judgment. First, though r 14 is quite specific in providing that
the discretion to terminate is vested in the executive council of APEX and that it arises if
this is 'necessary in order to comply with a decision of the Disputes Committee of the
Trades Union Congress', it does not specifically state that a necessity arising as a result of
a conscious and deliberate default on the part of APEX will entitle its executive council
to exercise the discretion. I think there is therefore scope for the application of the
general principle of the *New Zealand Shipping Co Ltd* case.

Second, while I think it is correct that an adverse decision of a disputes committee
necessarily envisages a violation of the Bridlington principles by APEX, it does not by
any means necessarily envisage a conscious and deliberate violation. In a case where a
merely unwitting breach by APEX of the Bridlington principles had given rise to the
relevant decision, the principle of the *New Zealand Shipping Co Ltd* case would in no way
prevent APEX from relying on r 14; the situation would in no sense be one in which
APEX would be relying on its own wrong; it would be just the kind of situation that r 14
is apt to meet. However, in a case where APEX has throughout acted in conscious
violation of the Bridlington principles and the member concerned is not a knowing party
to that violation, the situation seems to me quite different. The application of the
principle of the *New Zealand Shipping Co Ltd* case in my opinion can, should and does
permit a refinement concerning the quality of APEX's conduct giving rise to the decision
of the disputes committee, when r 14 falls to be construed and applied.

The third fallacy, which I venture to suggest is to be found in the critically important
passage from the judgment of Bingham J which I have quoted, lies in his statement that
it would be 'entirely contrary to the original intention of the rule, viewed in its historical
context, that a union which had violated the Bridlington principles should be free to
keep the poached members where it had committed a conscious or deliberate violation
but not where its violation was inadvertent'. In using the phrase 'free to keep', the judge
would appear to be suggesting that the effect of accepting Mr Cheall's submissions in this
context would be that, in a case where a union had committed a conscious or deliberate
violation of the Bridlington principles, it could insist on keeping the member concerned
with complete impunity. But I do not think is correct. The effect of accepting the
submissions would certainly be that the union in such a case would have no right to
expel the member in question. But that is not to say that it would in all senses be free to
keep him. It would still be exposed to the likelihood of being summoned before a
disputes committee of the TUC for its breach of the Bridlington principles and to the risk
of subsequent sanctions as provided for by r 13 of the TUC rules. These sanctions are
wide-ranging and can include temporary or, ultimately, even permanent exclusion from
the TUC. I do not know how the disputes committee or the executive council of the TUC
or congress as a whole would in practice choose to deal with the situation. The difficulties
and embarrassment for the union in meeting the complaints made against it and in
satisfying the requirements of the TUC authorities would no doubt be all the greater if
the union was not in a position to expel the member concerned. But this would be an
embarrassment which the union could fairly be regarded as having brought on its own
head in admitting the member in conscious violation of the Bridlington principles.

For these reasons I do not accept the submission of counsel for APEX that it would be
anomalous if APEX were bound to retain Mr Cheall in the present case even at the

theoretical risk of disaffiliation from the TUC. The greater anomaly would seem to me
a to arise if it were at liberty to rely on r 14 for the purpose of expelling Mr Cheall and
thereby avoid possible sanctions to be imposed against itself by the TUC, when at the
time of originally admitting him, it knew full well that it was in breach of the Bridlington
principles and that, as a result, a future decision of the TUC disputes committee requiring
it to expel Mr Cheall was likely. If Mr Cheall in completing his application form for
membership of APEX and in accepting membership had been a conscious party to the
b breach by APEX of the Bridlington principles, the situation would of course have been
quite different. He could not then have been heard to complain when APEX invoked
r 14. He, no less than APEX, would have been responsible for the occurrence of the
contingency referred to in that rule. However, the findings of the judge, which I have
already mentioned earlier in this judgment, make it plain that Mr Cheall was in no way
a conscious party to the breach by APEX of the Bridlington principles. Counsel for APEX
c contended that these findings showed that Mr Cheall, in submitting his application form,
was aware that 'shortcuts' might be made by APEX. He submitted that Mr Cheall, having
enjoyed the benefit of membership for four years, which he would not have had if APEX
had duly made inquiry of his former union, cannot now legitimately complain if APEX
finds itself obliged to invoke r 14.

I am not convinced that the making of prior inquiries of ACTSS by APEX would
d necessarily have meant that Mr Cheall could not be admitted to membership. Presumably
the procedure envisaged by Bridlington principle 2 would then have been followed.
ACTSS would have objected to the transfer; APEX would have considered the objection
to be unreasonable, but would not for the time being have accepted Mr Cheall into
membership until either ACTSS had withdrawn its objection or the TUC disputes
committee, after a reference to it for adjudication, had decided that the objection of
e ACTSS was unreasonable. I do not know why it should be assumed that such decision
would necessarily have been adverse to APEX, bearing in mind that, for reasons already
mentioned, the admission of Mr Cheall did not amount to poaching in the ordinary sense
of that word, and both the Bridlington principles and the TUC disputes regulations seem
to make it clear that poaching is the matter of concern in disputes concerning
membership.

f Be that as it may, however, I see no sufficient reason why APEX should pray in aid the
benefits of membership enjoyed by Mr Cheall as a result of a breach by APEX of the
Bridlington principles. When it accepted him as a member, it never informed him that
its failure to make prior inquiries of ACTSS constituted a breach of these principles and
could, by itself, well lead to a submission to the disputes committee of the TUC and a
subsequent decision of the very nature referred to in r 14. No doubt due regard must be
g paid to the realities of industrial relations. But, even having regard to these realities, it
does not seem to me unreasonable that APEX, having itself acted in conscious breach of
the Bridlington principles in admitting Mr Cheall into membership, should suffer any
consequences that may as a result fall on it through the operation of these principles and
the TUC disputes procedure (to both of which it is a party) and the various sanctions that
are available thereunder. In contrast, in the circumstances of this case, it would in my
h view be a highly unreasonable conclusion if Mr Cheall (who is not a party to either these
principles and this procedure) should be obliged to surrender his membership at the
instance of the TUC disputes committee after a hearing at which I assume for present
purposes he had no right to be heard. When r 14 is properly construed and applied, the
law does not in my opinion compel such a conclusion.

Donaldson LJ, for reasons which he has explained, has concluded that r 14, properly
j construed, is wholly inconsistent with any implied term that there should be any
circumstance in which APEX should be unable to comply with a decision of the disputes
committee that it must terminate the membership of those admitted in breach of the
Bridlington principles, whether innocently or otherwise. He has pointed out that the
rules of a trade union constitute the terms of a contract between the members inter se
and the members and the union and that, in relation to new members, it is a contract of

adhesion. He has pointed out (and I respectfully agree) that the court must construe r 14 in the context of the circumstances as they existed when the rule was made and that the *a* parties to the contract embodying that rule were the then existing members of APEX and APEX itself. He has expressed the view that it was—

'in the highest degree unlikely that either APEX or its existing members intended to have a rule which, if APEX thereafter indulged in a little poaching, would leave APEX obliged to retain the poached members and thus face disaffiliation without the opportunity of "purging its contempt".' *b*

The point of course is a forceful one, but, with the greatest respect to Donaldson LJ, I do not find it compelling. If and so far as the presumed intentions of the original parties to the introduction of r 14 are relevant, I think these by no means all point in the same direction. At the time when the rule was introduced, the then members of APEX who participated in its introduction may well have included a number of persons like Mr *c* Cheall, who had recently been admitted to membership of APEX in conscious breach of the Bridlington principles on the part of APEX itself, but in innocence on their part. It seems to me very unlikely that any such person would have intended to be a party to the introduction of a rule which would confer on APEX the unfettered right to expel him (without a hearing) at any time thereafter if and when the TUC disputes committee (also without having given him a hearing) required APEX to do so because of a default by *d* APEX for which the member was in no way to blame.

The first three of the five submissions made on behalf of Mr Cheall to which I have referred all really turn on the construction of r 14. In response to the third submission, I do not think it necessary to imply any term in construing it. In response to the first and second of these submissions, however, following the principle of the *New Zealand Shipping Co Ltd* case [1919] AC 1, [1918–19] All ER Rep 552, I would hold that, as a matter of *e* construction of the rule, APEX cannot be heard to say that expulsion of Mr Cheall is 'necessary in order to comply with a decision of the Disputes Committee of the Trades Union Congress', within the meaning of the rule, in a case such as the present where such necessity as there may be has arisen as a direct result of the conscious and deliberate breach by APEX of the Bridlington principles in admitting him to membership.

No doubt another model rule could be devised which clearly and explicitly gave the *f* admitting union the power to expel a member even in such circumstances. I leave open the question whether such a rule would be void as being contrary to public policy, just as I have left this question open in regard to r 14. In my judgment, however, the principle of the *New Zealand Shipping Co Ltd* case would not itself prevent the union from relying on a rule which took this different form. That principle does not prevent a party to a contract from invoking an avoiding clause even where he himself has by his own *g* conscious act brought about the relevant contingency, provided that the clause clearly and explicitly gives him this right. If r 14 had clearly and explicitly given APEX such a right, any joining member would have been put on adequate notice before joining the union, so that he could either ensure for himself that it had duly complied with the Bridlington principles, by making inquiries of his previous union before admitting him, or join with full notice of the personal risks involved. The bare wording of r 14 did not *h* in my opinion suffice to give Mr Cheall any such notice.

On the facts of the present case, for the reasons which I have given, I would allow this appeal and grant a declaration in effect that the notice contained in the letter of APEX to Mr Cheall of 30 June 1978 purporting to terminate his membership of APEX is invalid and of no effect.

j

Appeal allowed. Leave to appeal to the House of Lords granted.

Solicitors: *Boyle & Ormerod*, Aylesbury (for Mr Cheall); *John L Williams* (for APEX).

Frances Rustin   Barrister.

D v M (minor: custody appeal)

COURT OF APPEAL, CIVIL DIVISION
ORMROD, DUNN LJJ AND SIR SEBAG SHAW
22 JUNE, 8 JULY 1982

Appeal – Review of exercise of discretion – Duty of appellate court – Extent of duty – Custody cases – Domestic Proceedings and Magistrates' Courts Act 1978, s 29 – RSC Ord 53, r 3.

In January 1980, when she was only 18, the mother gave birth to an illegitimate child. She was not living with the child's father and looked after the child full-time at home with the aid of her family. She often let the father visit the child. In May 1981 there were affiliation proceedings in which the magistrates awarded her custody of the child and gave the father access. In August 1981 the father asked the magistrates to vary their order by transferring custody of the child to him. He had by then been living for several months with a married woman, who had a young family of her own, and he proposed that the child should come and live with them and that, while they were out working during the day, the child should be looked after by a child-minder and, on one or two days a week, by a relative. He submitted that the child's mother was inadequate and that the child was often dirty and not well cared for. A report by the welfare authorities prepared at the request of the magistrates stated that the child was not lacking in love and affection and recommended that the existing arrangements should continue so that the child's sense of security was not jeopardised. The magistrates decided that custody should be given to the father and stated in their reasons (i) that they had been more impressed by the evidence of the father than that of the mother, (ii) that they felt that the father could provide a more stable background and much better standard of care and welfare for the child, and (iii) that those considerations outweighed any emotional upset which the child might suffer as a result of the transfer of custody. The mother appealed, under s 29[a] of the Domestic Proceedings and Magistrates' Courts Act 1978, to the Divisional Court of the Family Division. The Divisional Court dismissed the appeal on the grounds that on the evidence before them the magistrates were entitled to reach the decision they had and that the Divisional Court was not entitled to usurp the magistrates' function in custody matters by interfering with the magistrates' exercise of their discretionary powers, particularly since the magistrates had had the advantage of seeing and hearing the parties concerned. The mother appealed to the Court of Appeal.

Held – The mother's appeal would be allowed, and the original order giving custody of the child to the mother would be confirmed, for the following reasons—

(1) The Divisional Court had misdirected itself in the way in which it had dealt with the mother's appeal because by virtue of s 29 of the 1978 Act and RSC Ord 55, r 3[b], such an appeal was by way of a rehearing and the court had a statutory duty to hold a full review of the case. The court's powers were not limited by the fact that it was a custody case, since in such a case the appellate court could, and should, still review the way in which the court below had 'balanced' the factors which had to be taken into account and had exercised its discretionary powers. Such cases were not an exception to the general principle that an appellate court should correct the decision of the court below if it was satisfied that the decision of the court below was wrong (see p 900 j to p 901 b and d to j, p 902 c to e h j and p 903 f, post); *Evans v Bartlam* [1937] 2 All ER 646 and *Re F (a minor) (wardship: appeal)* [1976] 1 All ER 417 followed.

---

a   Section 29, so far as material, provides:
    '(1) Subject to section 27 of this Act, where a magistrates' court makes or refuses to make, varies or refuses to vary, revokes or refuses to revoke an order (other than an interim maintenance order) under this Part of this Act, an appeal shall lie to the High Court.
    (2) On an appeal under this section the High Court shall have power to make such orders as may be necessary to give effect to its determination of the appeal . . .'
b   Rule 3, so far as material, is set out at p 900 j, post

(2) The magistrates had not conducted the required 'balancing exercise' properly because they had given too little weight (a) to the need to avoid, if possible, an interruption in the care of a young child, (b) to the fact that the child's care would be divided between three or four adults if he went to live with the father and that the child would see little of the father, and (iii) to evidence which showed that the father would be reluctant to allow the mother access to the child. Those were serious considerations which indicated that the existing arrangements should be maintained and they were not outweighed by the evidence on the father's side (see p 902 *j* to p 903 *f*, post).

Notes

For procedure on appeals to the High Court under RSC Ord 55, see 37 Halsbury's Laws (4th edn) para 674, and for appeals from the exercise of a judge's discretion, see ibid para 656.

     For the Domestic Proceedings and Magistrates' Courts Act 1978, s 29, see 48 Halsbury's Statutes (3rd edn) 779.

Cases referred to in judgment

Associated Provincial Picture Houses Ltd v Wednesbury Corp [1947] 2 All ER 680, [1948] 1 KB 223, CA, 45 Digest (Repl) 215, *189*.

B (an infant), Re [1962] 1 All ER 872, [1962] 1 WLR 550, CA, 28(2) Digest (Reissue) 811, *1285*.

Evans v Bartlam [1937] 2 All ER 646, [1937] AC 473, HL, 50 Digest (Repl) 169, *1458*.

F (a minor) (wardship: appeal), Re [1976] 1 All ER 417, [1976] Fam 238, [1976] 2 WLR 189, CA, Digest (Cont Vol E) 320, *1351a*.

O (infants), Re [1971] 2 All ER 744, [1971] Ch 748, [1971] 2 WLR 784, CA, Digest (Cont Vol D) 1062, *3494a*.

Osenton (Charles) & Co v Johnston [1941] 2 All ER 245, [1942] AC 130, HL, 51 Digest (Repl) 681, *2840*.

Appeal

The mother of an illegitimate child appealed, with the leave of the Court of Appeal, against an order of the Divisional Court of the Family Division (Arnold P and Sheldon J), dated 6 April 1982, dismissing an appeal by her against an order made on 13 January 1982 by the justices sitting at Trafford Metropolitan Magistrates' Court whereby they directed that custody of the child should be transferred from the mother to the child's father. The facts are set out in the judgment of the court.

Geoffrey Tattersall for the mother.
David Berkley for the father.

At the conclusion of the argument the court announced that, for reasons to be given later, the appeal would be allowed and the order for custody confirmed in the mother's favour.

8 July. **ORMROD LJ** read the following judgment of the court: This is an appeal by the mother, with the leave of this court, from a decision of the Divisional Court of the Family Division (Arnold P and Sheldon J) given on 6 April 1982. That court dismissed the mother's appeal from an order made by Trafford Metropolitan Magistrates' Court on 13 January 1982, by which they transferred the custody of a child, S, who was born on 23 January 1980 and was, therefore, not quite two years of age, from the mother to the father.

     The history of the matter is as follows. S is the illegitimate child of the mother and the father. The parties met in 1978 when she was 16 years of age and he was 19. She became pregnant by the father in 1979 and gave birth to the child in January 1980 when she was about 18 years old. She is now about 20 and he is about 24. He was employed in a well-a known social club at Stretford. After the birth the mother and baby lived with her mother and her brothers and sisters. The father saw the child frequently at this stage and their relationship was quite good, although he made it clear before the child was born that he was not ready to marry and had suggested an abortion. They never lived together at any time, but the association continued until December 1980, when it broke down completely. The father began an association about this time with a Mrs C, a married woman of about his own age with a young son. She and her husband had separated and

b she was working in the same social club. They began to live together, and are still living together. The father made voluntary payments to the mother in respect of the child from April 1980 onwards.

Following the breakdown of her relationship with the father, the mother became acutely depressed and, in January 1981, took an overdose of tablets, and was admitted to hospital for a short time.

c In March 1981 a fire occurred at her parents' home where she and the child were living, which meant that the family had to be rehoused, and the mother was allotted a council flat for herself and the baby. She is still occupying this flat, which is very close to her mother's home. Shortly afterwards the child had an accident in the grandmother's new house. This house had a coal fire and while the mother was out of the room for a few moments the child fell into the grate and burned the palms of his hands, necessitating

d for a time frequent attendance at the hospital for dressings. The burns cleared up completely within quite a short time.

In May 1981 an affiliation order was made against the father and he was ordered to pay the mother £8 per week. At the same time, an order was made giving the mother custody of the child, either by consent or without opposition by the father. The father continued to see the child regularly without any objection by the mother. This included

e a holiday in Wales of one or two weeks.

In August 1981, for reasons which do not appear at all clearly from the notes of evidence, the father issued a complaint under the Guardianship of Minors Act 1971 in the Trafford Metropolitan Magistrates' Court, asking for a variation of the order made in May 1981, to give him the custody of the child. A welfare report was ordered and was made by Mr Bolchover on 10 November 1981. The matter came on for hearing before

f the justices on 13 January 1982.

The alternative proposals for the future of this child were as follows. The father proposed that he should come to live with him and Mrs C in their two-bedroom council flat in Stretford and her child, who is a little older than S. The child had frequently visited this home, knew Mrs C well, and got on well with her son. The father complained that the mother was inadequate, and gave evidence that S was often dirty or unwashed and frequently smelt of urine. He also suggested that the child was backward in speech

g compared with Mrs C's son. However, it was clear from the evidence that both he and Mrs C were in full-time employment and that the child would have to be looked after by some third party for five days a week. The proposal was that S and Mrs C's son should be looked after by a registered child-minder (who was already looking after Mrs C's son) on three days a week, and on the other two by Mrs C's mother.

h The mother proposed that the existing arrangements should continue. She was not in work and was available all day to look after S. Her social security payments enabled her to live with S in her flat which was simply, but adequately furnished, and she was able to live, frugally, on the money she was getting from social security. She spent most of her time during the day at her mother's home with S, where there was a family of six of her brothers and sisters, aged 4, 6, 8, 9, 13 and 14. Her mother helped her with washing,

j cooking etc. She also has three other sisters living in the neighbourhood who helped her with baby-sitting in the evening if she went out.

The welfare officer described S as a 'normal boisterous inquisitive toddler' who related well to his father and his mother, and got on well with both Mrs C's son and his uncle aged four. The mother said she had no difficulty coping with S. He had had the usual childhood illnesses. There was ample support from the mother's large and close family.

The welfare officer's conclusion was summarised in these words:

'Both [the father] and [the mother] can offer [S] love and security, and under the present circumstances I would consider that [S's] present sense of security should not be jeopardised. I would respectfully suggest that [the mother] retain custody of [S], and [the father] continue to enjoy access as defined at this court in May 1981.'

The health visitor, an important witness in a case like this, was subpoenaed to attend court by the husband's solicitors, attended court but was not called as a witness and allowed to go. This was unfortunate because all that was known of her views was contained in a paragraph in the welfare report, which reads thus:

'The Health Visitor concerned with [S] stated that [the mother] is an adequate mother, although her standards of hygiene could be improved. [S] definitely does not lack love, but perhaps needs more appropriate stimulation and attention. [The mother] appears anxious to provide a home for [S], but at the same time wishes to enjoy her own life. In pursuit of this, she is prone to mix with what the Health Visitor believes to be the "wrong" sort of person.'

On that material the magistrates decided to transfer the custody of S to the father, a decision which, on the face of it, is surprising. Moreover, they omitted to deal with the question of access by the mother. In their reasons they describe this as an 'oversight', but it is and was an extremely important matter. If a child of this age is to be removed from the mother's care it is essential that adequate arrangements are made to preserve the child's links with the mother.

In their reasons the justices said that they placed greater reliance on the evidence called on behalf of the father than on that called for the mother. They were much impressed by the father and were satisfied that regular contact between the father and the son had forged a bond between them. They said that the mother left the impression that she was 'still rather immature in her ambitions and attitudes'. They referred to the taking of the overdose of drugs and obviously attached much significance to the fact that she had told the welfare officer in November 1981 that she had no serious relationship with anyone, whereas in evidence she said she was engaged to be married. They were not satisfied that the child was receiving the standard of care and instruction to be expected from a parent, although there was no lack of affection on the part of the mother. They were very critical of the mother in relation to the accident in March 1981 when the child's hands were burned. They noted that if the child went to the father he would be looked after by a registered child minder but did not express any concern on this point. They said that they recognised that the move would cause considerable emotional upset to the child, but thought that the father could provide a more stable emotional background, and greatly improved standard of care and welfare which, they thought, outweighed the emotional upset. They made no reference to the welfare officer's recommendation.

On the appeal to the Divisional Court Arnold P, in his judgment, dealt with the case on the footing that there was evidence on which the magistrates could find as they had done in their reasons, and disposed of the appeal by saying:

'They formed clear impressions, not only of their credibility, but of their competence, and it seems to me that if we were to interfere with their conclusions we really would be usurping the proper and rightful functions that Parliament has entrusted to magistrates in this sort of case.'

The Divisional Court did not undertake an evaluation of the evidence, nor apparently, form any view itself what would be the best or wisest course to take in the interests of this little boy.

We think, with respect, that the Divisional Court misdirected itself in the way in which it dealt with the mother's appeal.

By RSC Ord 55, r 3, appeals from, inter alia, magistrates' courts to the High Court, 'shall be by way of rehearing'. The right of appeal to the High Court is given by s 29 of

the Domestic Proceedings and Magistrates' Courts Act 1978, and that section gives the
a High Court all the powers necessary to give effect to its determination. By Ord 55, r 7,
the High Court has power to receive further evidence and to draw any inferences of fact
which might have been drawn in the court below. In other words, the statute provides
for a full review by the High Court of all material available to it on such an appeal. In
this respect, the High Court is in precisely the same position as the Court of Appeal in
relation to appeals from the High Court under s 16 of the Supreme Court Act 1981 and
b RSC Ord 59, r 3.

The duties and powers of appellate courts in relation to appeals in cases relating to the
custody of children have been very carefully considered in two cases in this court within
the last ten years or so, viz Re O (infants) [1971] 2 All ER 744, [1971] Ch 748 and Re F (a
minor) (wardship: appeal) [1976] 1 All ER 417, [1976] Fam 238. In these cases the court
had to consider two schools of thought. One, of which Stamp LJ was the leading
c exponent, supported the view that in cases concerning the future well-being of children,
an appellate court should not interfere with the exercise of the discretion of the court of
first instance, which had had the advantage of seeing and hearing the parties concerned,
unless the decision of the court below was one which no reasonable court could have
reached, or unless it could be shown that the court below had erred in law, or had taken
into account any matter which should not have been taken into account, or failed to take
d into account any matter which ought to have been taken into account (see [1976] 1 All
ER 417 at 430, [1976] Fam 238 at 254 per Stamp LJ). The other school took the view that
was cogently expressed in the following passage in the judgment of Davies LJ in Re O
(infants) [1971] 2 All ER 744 at 748–749, [1971] Ch 748 at 755:

> 'In my considered opinion the law now is that if an appellate court is satisfied that
> the decision of the court below is wrong, it is its duty to say so and to act accordingly.
e > This applies whether the appeal is an interlocutory or a final appeal, whether it is an
> appeal from justices to a Chancery judge or from justices to a Divisional Court of
> the Divorce Division. Every court has a duty to do its best to arrive at a proper and
> just decision. And if an appellate court is satisfied that the decision of the court
> below is improper, unjust or wrong, then the decision must be set aside. I am quite
> unable to subscribe to the view that a decision must be treated as sacrosanct because
f > it was made in the exercise of "discretion": so to do might well perpetuate injustice.'

In Re O (infants) this court decided that the school of thought represented by Davies LJ
was correct in law. But the controversy continued and the views of the other school were
frequently advanced by counsel in argument. Eventually the issue came to a head in Re
F (a minor) (wardship: appeal), and was resolved by the majority (Browne and Bridge LJJ,
g Stamp LJ dissenting) in favour of the opinion expressed by Davies LJ in Re O (infants).
This decision is binding on us but, perhaps because it was a majority decision, it is still
not whole-heartedly accepted, as is clear from the judgments of the Divisional Court in
the instant case.

We are clearly of the opinion that the very careful judgments of Browne and Bridge
LJJ should be regarded as settling the question once and for all. But, as the matter is so
h important, it may be useful to state briefly our own reasons.

In the first place, in cases concerning the custody of children, there is a statutory right
of appeal without leave, and the appellate courts have a statutory duty to rehear such
appeals. There is no statutory justification for restricting or limiting the powers of the
appellate courts in such cases, although practical considerations will lead the appellate
court to adopt a cautious approach. If the minority view were to be accepted, this
j statutory right of appeal would be rendered largely nugatory, and appellants, in many
case, denied a rehearing, or a review of the decision of the court below. In the second
place, the proposition that the powers of appellate courts in appeals from orders made by
lower courts in the exercise of discretionary powers are subject to limitations which do
not apply to appeals from other classes of judgments or orders, was decisively rejected by
the House of Lords in Evans v Bartlam [1937] 2 All ER 646, [1937] AC 473 and again in

Charles Osenton & Co v Johnston [1941] 2 All ER 245, [1942] AC 130. In *Evans v Bartlam*, Lord Wright said ([1937] 2 All ER 646 at 654, [1937] AC 473 at 486):

> 'It is clear that the Court of Appeal should not interfere with the discretion of a judge acting within his jurisdiction, unless the court is clearly satisfied that he was wrong. But the court is not entitled simply to say that, if a judge had jurisdiction, and had all the facts before him, the Court of Appeal cannot review his order, unless he is shown to have applied a wrong principle. The court must, if necessary, examine anew the relevant facts and circumstances, in order to exercise by way of review a discretion which may reverse or vary the order. Otherwise, in interlocutory matters, the judge might be regarded as independent of supervision. Yet an interlocutory order of the judge may often be of decisive importance on the final issue of the case, and may be one which requires a careful examination by the Court of Appeal.'

(See also [1937] 2 All ER 646 at 650, [1937] AC 473 at 480 per Lord Atkin.)

These cases were concerned with the exercise of discretion in procedural matters, but the language used is quite general and must apply to appeals from discretionary orders of all kinds, including cases relating to the welfare of children, unless these are to be regarded as a separate class. Attempts have been made to distinguish them by reference to the indefinite nature of the criteria which have to be applied in such cases, and to the weight to be attached to the advantage which the court of first instance has of direct contact with the individuals concerned. Important as these considerations undoubtedly are, the majority in *Re F (a minor) (wardship: appeal)* [1976] 1 All ER 417, [1976] Fam 238 held that they did not take this class of case out of the general principle laid down by the House of Lords, although they had to be given due weight in applying that principle to the facts of each case. The first point is sufficiently covered by the qualification that the appellate court must be 'satisfied' that the decision under appeal is wrong; the second point must not be made into a dogma. We agree with Browne LJ's comment on it in his judgment (see [1976] 1 All ER 417 at 434, [1976] Fam 238 at 259), and with the passage which he cited from Donovan LJ's judgment in *Re B (an infant)* [1962] 1 All ER 872 at 875, [1962] 1 WLR 550 at 555.

> 'In matters where credibility is an issue, of course that consideration . . . is of great weight. I do not think it is of such weight when one is assessing a person's character and ability to look after a child. The encounter is too brief for any reliable conclusion.'

Stamp LJ's dissenting judgment is really based on the *Wednesbury* principles; his language (at [1976] 1 All ER 417 at 430, [1976] Fam 238 at 254) actually follows almost verbatim the well-known judgment of Lord Greene MR in *Associated Provincial Picture Houses Ltd v Wednesbury Corp* [1947] 2 All ER 680, [1948] 1 KB 223. But Lord Greene MR was not dealing with appeals from orders made by courts in the exercise of a judicial discretion; he was concerned with the quite different problem of the extent to which the High Court, under its supervisory jurisdiction, could interfere with the exercise of an administrative discretion by a non-judicial body. This is more closely related to the problem of vires, than to appeals from lower courts.

We think that the matter can be summarised, using Bridge LJ's words in *Re F (a minor) (wardship: appeal)* [1976] 1 All ER 417 at 440, [1976] Fam 238 at 266, by saying that it is the duty of an appellate court in these cases to review the way in which the court below has conducted the 'balancing exercise', and, if satisfied that it has erred, to correct it.

Since the Divisional Court did not approach this case on those lines, we ourselves, following *Evans v Bartlam*, reviewed the evidence, the welfare report, and the justices' reasons, and came to the conclusion that we were satisfied that they had erred in carrying out the balancing exercise for the following reasons.

In our opinion, the justices attached much too little weight to three important considerations in this case. In the first place, it is generally accepted by those who are a professionally concerned with children that, particularly in the early years, continuity of care is a most important part of a child's sense of security and that disruption of established bonds is to be avoided whenever it is possible to do so. Where, as in this case, a child of two years of age has been brought up without interruption by the mother (or a mother substitute) it should not be removed from her care unless there are strong countervailing reasons for doing so. This is not only the professional view, it is commonly accepted in all walks of life, and was the recommendation of the experienced welfare

b officer.

In the second place, the justices do not seem to have properly appreciated the implications of the father's proposals which were that the child would be looked after, on three days a week, by a child-minder and on, at least, one day by Mrs C's mother. We were told that the child would be with one or other from about 8 am to 4.30 pm each day. The result, inevitably, would be that he would spend most of his waking hours

c away from his father and Mrs C, and that his care would be divided between, at least, three, possibly four, adults. This is a situation which is to be avoided, if it is possible to do so.

The third point is the contrast between the mother's attitude to access by the father which has been co-operative at all times, and the father's which, as his evidence showed, was grudging and reluctant and likely to lead to the ousting of the mother, if he had the

d custody of the child.

To be balanced against these serious considerations was the evidence of the father (which the justices accepted as against the mother) that the child was often unwashed and not provided with clean or adequate nappies and rubbers, and was not sufficiently stimulated by the mother, who was said to be immature and, by implication, lazy. The justices, however, accepted that there was no lack of love and affection on the part of the

e mother and made no finding that she neglected or ill-treated the child. They do not seem to have given any weight to the welfare officer's report that S was 'a normal boisterous inquisitive toddler', or to the fact that the father did not call the health visitor who, so far as the evidence goes, had no serious anxiety about the mother's standard of care.

In these circumstances we came to the conclusion that the evidence was altogether inadequate to displace the serious considerations which indicated that the existing

f arrangements should be maintained. We, therefore, allowed the mother's appeal and confirmed the order for custody in her favour.

Appeal allowed.

Solicitors: *Waterhouse & Co*, agents for *Anthony Clarke & Co*, Partington (for the mother); *Barnett & Barnett*, agents for *Rowlands*, Stretford (for the father).

Bebe Chua   Barrister.

Practice Note

CHANCERY DIVISION
SIR ROBERT MEGARRY V-C
18 NOVEMBER 1982

Practice – Chancery Division – Revenue appeals – New listing procedure – Abolition of Revenue Paper.

SIR ROBERT MEGARRY V-C made the following statement at the sitting of the court: As from the beginning of the Hilary Sittings 1983, revenue appeals in the Chancery Division will no longer be listed in a separate Revenue Paper, to be heard for a fixed period by one judge or by two judges in succession. Instead, such appeals will be entered in a list of revenue appeals, usually with fixed dates, and will be heard by such judges as are available. The dates for hearing will be settled in the usual way on application to the Clerk of the Lists. Where it would assist counsel and solicitors with their other commitments, the Clerk of the Lists, if requested, will endeavour to fix two or more revenue appeals so that they will come on consecutively.

The object of the change is to make a more effective and flexible use of the time of the judges of the Chancery Division, both for revenue appeals and for other work, than is possible when there is a fixed Revenue Paper due to be heard by one judge. It is hoped, too, that the greater flexibility of the new system will assist counsel and solicitors who encounter difficulties in the present system of a fixed period for revenue appeals each term. When the new system has been in operation for a year it will be reviewed, and it may then be amended in the light of experience and the views of the profession.

Azza M Abdallah   Barrister.

The Clifford Maersk

QUEEN'S BENCH DIVISION (ADMIRALTY COURT)
SHEEN J
19, 25 MAY 1982

Writ – Issue – Time – Limitation period prescribed by agreement – Contract incorporating Hague Rules – Agreement extending time prescribed by Hague Rules – Agreed period expiring on day court offices closed – Writ issued on first day thereafter that court offices open – Whether writ issued in time – Carriage of Goods by Sea Act 1971, Sch, art 3, r 6.

By a contract of carriage which by agreement incorporated the Hague Rules, the defendant shipowners carried the plaintiffs' cargo to the port of delivery. The plaintiffs alleged that the cargo was delivered in a damaged state in June or July 1979. Under art 3, r 6[a] of the Hague Rules as set out in the schedule to the Carriage of Goods by Sea Act 1971 an action in respect of damage to cargo had to be brought within one year after delivery. Because the investigations into the cause of the damage took some time, the defendants agreed to grant the plaintiffs several extensions of the one-year limitation period, the last of which extended the limitation period 'up to and including 21st June 1981'. That date was a Sunday but, since a writ could not be issued on a Sunday because the court offices were closed, the plaintiffs issued their writ on Monday, 22 June 1981. The defendants applied to have the writ set aside on the ground that it was not issued within the limitation period prescribed by the Hague Rules as extended by agreement between the parties because, properly construed, the last extension of time was only up to and including Friday, 19 June 1981. The defendants submitted that where time was extended by agreement it could not, unlike an extension of time under a statute or rules of court, be further extended by operation of law merely because the agreed time limit expired on a day when the court offices were closed.

Held – In determining whether an act was done in time under an agreed time limit which expired on a day when the court offices were closed, the same rule applied as that applicable where a time limit prescribed by statute or rules of court expired on such a day. Therefore an agreed time limit which expired on a day when the court offices were closed extended to the next ensuing day on which the offices were open. It followed that the last extension of time granted by the defendants extended the time for issuing a writ up to and including Monday, 22 June 1981. Accordingly, the writ had been served in time (see p 909 *b c*, post).

Pritam Kaur v S Russell & Sons Ltd [1973] 1 All ER 617 and *J Aron & Co Inc v SS Olga Jacob* (1976) 527 F 2d 416 applied.

Per curiam. It is desirable that decisions of the Admiralty Court should be consistent with decisions of the United States courts (see p 909 *c*, post).

Notes
For extension of a limitation period where it expires on a day when the court offices are closed, see 28 Halsbury's Laws (4th edn) para 691n, and for cases on the subject, see 45 Digest (Repl) 268–269, 349–359.

For the Carriage of Goods by Sea Act 1971, Sch, see 41 Halsbury's Statutes (3rd edn) 1318.

---

a Rule 6, so far as material, provides: '. . . the carrier and the ship shall . . . be discharged from all liability whatsoever in respect of the goods, unless suit is brought within one year of their delivery or of the date when they should have been delivered. This period may, however, be extended if the parties so agree after the cause of action has arisen.'

Cases referred to in judgment

Aron (J) & Co Inc v SS Olga Jacob (1976) 527 F 2d 416, US Ct of Appeals, Fifth Circuit.

Astro Amo Compania Naviera SA v Elf Union SA and First National Bank, The Zographia M [1976] 2 Lloyd's Rep 382, Digest (Cont Vol E) 547, 536a.

Pritam Kaur (administratrix of Bikar Singh (decd)) v S Russell & Sons Ltd [1973] 1 All ER 617, [1973] QB 336, [1973] 2 WLR 147, CA, 32 Digest (Reissue) 508, 3869.

Cases also cited

A/S Awilco v Fulvia SpA di Navigazione, The Chikuma [1981] 1 All ER 652, [1981] 1 WLR 314, HL.

Babanaft International Co SA v Avant Petroleum Inc, The Oltenia [1982] 1 Lloyd's Rep 448; affd [1982] 3 All ER 244, [1982] 1 WLR 871, CA.

Consolidated Investment and Contracting Co v Saponaria Shipping Co Ltd, The Virgo [1978] 3 All ER 988, [1978] 1 WLR 986, CA.

Hughes v Griffiths (1862) 13 CBNS 324, 143 ER 129.

Mardorf Peach & Co Ltd v Attica Sea Carriers Corp of Liberia, The Laconia [1977] 1 All ER 545, [1977] AC 850, HL.

NV Stoomv Maats 'De Maas' v Nippon Yusen Kaisha, The Pendrecht [1980] 2 Lloyd's Rep 56.

Siebe Gorman & Co Ltd v Pneupac Ltd [1982] 1 All ER 377, [1982] 1 WLR 185, CA.

Preliminary issue

By a writ issued on Monday, 22 June 1981, and a statement of claim served on 6 November 1981, the plaintiffs, N De Groot Cargadoors en Expeditiebedrijf BV, cargo owners, claimed damages against the defendants, A/S D/S Svendborg and D/S AF 1912 A/S, shipowners, for breach of contract and/or duty in delivering the cargo in a damaged condition. By a notice of motion dated 20 November 1981 the defendants applied to have the writ set aside on the ground that it was not issued within the time required by art 3, r 6 of the Hague Rules (which were incorporated into the contract of carriage between the parties) as extended by agreement between the parties which, it was alleged, expired on Sunday, 21 June 1981. The defendants entered a conditional appearance in order to argue as a preliminary issue before the Admiralty judge the question whether the writ had been issued in time. The facts are set out in the judgment.

Peter Gross for the plaintiffs.
Peter Irvin for the defendants.

Cur adv vult

25 May. **SHEEN J** read the following judgment: In this action the plaintiffs, who are the owners of cargo carried in the ship Clifford Maersk, claim damages from the owners of that ship for damage to their cargo. The parties have agreed that I should determine, as a preliminary point of law, the question whether the carrier is discharged from all liability in respect of that damage because the action was not brought on or before 21 June 1981. There is no dispute as to the facts relevant to this issue. They can be stated briefly.

In June and July 1979 the Clifford Maersk carried a cargo of timber from Japan to Rotterdam and Amsterdam. The plaintiffs allege that when it was delivered to them in Amsterdam it was damaged and that the defendants, as carriers, are liable for that damage. The contract of carriage incorporated the Hague Rules. In July 1980 investigations into the causes of the damage were still proceeding. By then nearly a year had elapsed since the cargo was delivered, and so the cargo owners requested an extension of the limitation period by three months. On behalf of the defendants an extension was granted up to and including 25 October 1980. In October a further extension was requested and granted up to 25 January 1981. In December 1980 a further extension was

granted up to and including 21 April 1981. Finally on 16 March 1981 a letter was written
a on behalf of the defendants in the following terms:

> 'Further to your telephone request of 4.3.81 we inform you that our principals
> have granted you postponement of the time-bar period up to and including 21st
> June 1981.'

The 21 June 1981 was a Sunday. The writ was issued on Monday, 22 June 1981. The
b question which I have to decide is whether that writ was issued in time. Counsel for the
defendants submitted that the effect of the extension of time was to substitute the date
21 June 1981 for the date which was 'one year after delivery of the goods' and that
accordingly the agreement between the parties became (adapting art 3, r 6 of the Hague
Rules): The carrier and the ship shall be discharged from all liability in respect of loss or
damage unless suit is brought on or before 21 June 1981.

c   Counsel for the defendants submitted that this is a clear, unambiguous commercial
contract which leaves no room for doubt as to its meaning, and that I should not hesitate
to give effect to it by deciding the preliminary issue in favour of the defendants. There is
no room for sympathy with a plaintiff who may be deprived of his right to pursue his
claim. It is unwise of a party to grant an extension of time which expires on a Sunday,
and it is likewise unwise of the other party to leave until the last moment the issue of a
d writ, and therefore there is no overriding necessity to 'give an extra day'.

On behalf of the plaintiffs, counsel submitted that the date '21st June 1981' was
inserted in the letter of 16 March 1981 merely as a means of communicating that a
further extension of the limitation period by two months was being granted, and that it
must be inferred that neither party appreciated at the time when the letter was sent and
received that 21 June 1981 was a Sunday. This inference is drawn from the facts (1) that
e suit is brought by the issue of a writ, and (2) a writ cannot be issued on a Saturday or a
Sunday. Accordingly he submitted that the letter contains an ambiguity which would
have become apparent immediately if the wording of the letter had been: 'Our principals
have granted you postponement of the time-bar period up to and including *Sunday*, 21st
June 1981.' The insertion of the word 'Sunday' makes no difference to the terms of the
agreement, but it highlights the ambiguity. Counsel for the plaintiffs asked rhetorically:
f how can effect be given to the words 'up to and including' if in fact Sunday, 21 June 1981
could not be included because the office of the Supreme Court was closed on that day?
The question arises whether the last extension of time was in fact an extension up to and
including 19 June 1981, that is to say the last day on which a writ could be issued before
21 June, or until 22 June, being the next day on which the office of the Supreme Court
was open.

g   There can be no doubt that the plaintiffs would have issued a writ within the period of
one year after the delivery of the goods if the shipowners had not agreed to extend the
limitation period. When investigations are proceeding into the causes of damage to cargo
it is in the interest of both parties that the cost of issuing a writ should be avoided if
possible. I mention this only because counsel for the plaintiffs submitted, and in my
view rightly submitted, that the true view of the letter of 16 March 1981 is that it is a
h contractual agreement to extend the limitation period in consideration of the plaintiffs
refraining from issuing a writ.

In *Pritam Kaur v S Russell & Sons Ltd* [1973] 1 All ER 617, [1973] QB 336 the Court of
Appeal had to consider a case in which a period of limitation prescribed by statute expired
on Saturday, 5 September 1970. The court held that a writ issued on Monday, 7
September was in time. Lord Denning MR said ([1973] 1 All ER 617 at 620, [1973] QB
j 336 at 349):

> 'Those arguments are so evenly balanced that we can come down either way. The
> important thing is to lay down a rule for the future so that people can know how
> they stand. In laying down a rule, we can look to parallel fields of law to see the rule
> there. The nearest parallel is the case where a time is prescribed by the rules of court

for doing any act. The rule prescribed in both the county court and the High Court is this: if the time expires on a Sunday or any other day on which the court office is closed, the act is done in time if it is done on the next day on which the court office is open. I think we should apply a similar rule when the time is prescribed by statute. By so doing, we make the law consistent in itself; and we avoid confusion to practitioners. So I am prepared to hold that, when a time is prescribed by statute for doing any act, and that act can only be done if the court office is open on the day when the time expires, then, if it turns out in any particular case that the day is a Sunday or other dies non, the time is extended until the next day on which the court office is open.'

Counsel for the defendants stressed in his submissions that Lord Denning MR was there dealing with a time prescribed by statute whereas I am concerned with a period of time agreed between the parties. Counsel submitted that when the parties have made an express agreement there is no room for extending that period of time by one day. To this counsel for the plaintiffs replied that he was not asking for any extension of time but inviting me to define the period which was agreed, because that agreement contains a latent ambiguity to which I have already referred.

There is no decision of an English court directly in point, but the same point has arisen in the United States. Counsel for the plaintiffs drew my attention to a decision of the United States Court of Appeals, Fifth Circuit, in *J Aron & Co Inc v SS Olga Jacob* (1976) 527 F 2d 416. The question in issue was whether a complaint filed on Monday, 21 January 1974 was in time. The steamship carrier had extended the shipper's time for suit 'up to and including January 20, 1974' which was a Sunday. The Court of Appeals, reversing the decision of the trial judge, held that where an agreement to extend the time within which to file a suit as provided by the Carriage of Goods by Sea Act expired on a Sunday the person charged with acting has the following day to comply. In the judgment of that court (at 417)—

'Allowing this suit would conform to the spirit of the Rules and would be consistent with the treatment of a [Carriage of Goods by Sea Act] limitation period not modified by agreement between the parties.'

Counsel for the plaintiffs submitted that it is desirable that there should be consistency between the decisions of English and United States courts in cases concerned with matters affecting international trade. He further pointed out that it would be a curious state of the law if on the one hand it were to be held that when the period of one year prescribed by the Hague Rules expires on a Sunday the prospective plaintiff has until the following day to issue his writ, but on the other hand if that period of limitation is extended by agreement to a date which happens to be a Sunday then the prospective plaintiff only has until the preceding Friday to issue his writ.

Counsel for the defendants drew attention to the fact that in the *Pritam Kaur* case the arguments were evenly balanced, and he argued that because in this case the limitation period expired on an agreed date that tilted the balance in his favour. In support of this argument he prayed in aid some words of Ackner J in *Astro AMO Compania Naviera SA v Elf Union SA and First National Bank, The Zographia M* [1976] 2 Lloyd's Rep 382 at 393:

'I ... am not persuaded that the obligation to pay in advance of a certain date, which must mean before a certain date, means after that date where there is some practical difficulty, such as a bank being closed, which prevents payment being made on the very last day before that date.'

To this counsel for the plaintiffs replied with equal force that some effect must be given to the words 'up to and including' and that the granting of an extension of time 'up to and including 21st June 1981' should not be construed as meaning 'only up to and including 19th June 1981'. Counsel contended that the plaintiffs were entitled to the full extension of two months and not two months less two days. If the only reason why the plaintiffs have not been able to issue a writ on the last day of the agreed period is that the

office of the Supreme Court was closed, it would be consistent with the *Pritam Kaur* case
a and RSC Ord 3, r 4 to hold that the agreement entitled the plaintiffs to issue a writ on the
next day on which the court office was open.

Finally counsel for the plaintiffs pointed out that although in this case the Hague Rules
were incorporated by agreement, there are circumstances in which they (or the Hague-
Visby Rules) are incorporated by statute. It would be absurd if that made a difference to
the date by which a writ must be issued.

b   After weighing the arguments which were advanced so attractively by both counsel, I
have reached the conclusion that I must hold that the writ was issued in time, because:
(1) In the *Pritam Kaur* case the Court of Appeal laid down a rule, applicable to time-bars
prescribed by statute, similar to the Rules of the Supreme Court, in order to make the
law consistent and avoid confusion to practitioners. It is desirable to follow that policy.
(2) It is also desirable that the decisions of this court should be consistent with decisions
c of the courts of the United States.

Order accordingly. Leave to appeal granted.

Solicitors: *Bird & Bird* (for the plaintiffs); *Holman, Fenwick & Willan* (for the defendants)

d   N P Metcalfe Esq   Barrister.

R v Secretary of State for the Home
e # Department, ex parte Margueritte

COURT OF APPEAL, CIVIL DIVISION
LORD DENNING MR, OLIVER AND KERR LJJ
15, 19 JULY 1982

f *Citizenship – United Kingdom citizenship – Entitlement – Ordinary residence – Precondition of
five years' ordinary residence prior to application for citizenship – Applicant overstaying leave
to enter and unlawfully resident for part of qualifying period – Whether applicant required to be
lawfully resident in United Kingdom during qualifying period – British Nationality Act 1948,
s 5A(3) – Immigration Act 1971, s 33(2), Sch 1, para 1, App A.*

g   In 1972 the applicant came to England from Mauritius and was granted limited leave to
enter as a visitor. In July 1974 he was granted further leave to remain as a visitor for one
month. At the end of that time he overstayed and remained, without authority, until
June 1978, when he was granted indefinite leave to remain. In September 1979 he
applied for registration as a United Kingdom citizen but his application was refused by
the Home Office on the ground that he did not fulfil the precondition laid down by s
h 5A(3)[a] of the British Nationality Act 1948 that he had been 'ordinarily resident' in the
United Kingdom 'throughout the period of five years' prior to his application. The Home
Office took the view that the applicant's period of residence without permission from
August 1974 until June 1978 did not count towards satisfying the five years' residence
qualification. The applicant applied for judicial review of the Home Office's decision but
his application was refused. He appealed, contending that whether a person was
j 'ordinarily resident' depended solely on the fact of residence and not on the legality or
otherwise of that residence.

Held – Since s 5A of the 1948 Act was added by para 1[b] of, and App A to Sch 1 to, the

___

a   Section 5A(3) is set out at p 915 c d, post
b   Paragraph 1, so far as material, is set out at p 914 j to p 915 a, post

Immigration Act 1971 it was to be regarded as a 'provision of this [ie the 1971] Act' for
the purposes of s 33(2)ᶜ of the 1971 Act and was to be construed subject to s 33(2) which   *a*
expressly provided that a person was not to be treated 'for the purposes of any provision
of this [ie the 1971] Act' as being ordinarily resident in the United Kingdom at a time
when he was in breach of the immigration laws. Accordingly, an applicant for registration
as a United Kingdom citizen was required to be lawfully resident in the United Kingdom
for five years prior to his application in order to fulfil the requirement of five years'
ordinary residence laid down by s 5A(3) of the 1948 Act. Since the applicant had not been   *b*
lawfully resident in the United Kingdom for five years prior to his application, his
application had been rightly refused. The appeal would accordingly be dismissed (see
p 912 *f* to *j*, p 913 *a g h*, p 914 *c g* to *j*, p 915 *e* to *j*, p 916 *d* to *f* and p 917 *e* to *h*, post).

Re Abdul Manan [1971] 2 All ER 1016 followed.

Dictum of Eveleigh LJ in *R v Barnet London Borough Council, ex p Shah* [1982] 1 All ER
at 706 approved.   *c*

Dicta of Lord Wilberforce and of Lord Salmon in *Azam v Secretary of State for the Home
Dept* [1973] 2 All ER at 771, 779 not followed.

Notes

For acquisition of citizenship by registration, see 4 Halsbury's Laws (4th edn) para 912.

For the British Nationality Act 1948, s 5A (as inserted by the Immigration Act 1971,   *d*
s 2, Sch 1, para 1(*a*), App A), see 41 Halsbury's Statutes (3rd edn) 58.

For the Immigration Act 1971, s 33, Sch 1, para 1 see ibid 52, 56.

As from 1 January 1983 fresh provision about citizenship and nationality is made by
the British Nationality Act 1981.

Cases referred to in judgments   *e*

Abdul Manan, Re [1971] 2 All ER 1016, [1971] 1 WLR 859, CA, 2 Digest (Reissue) 198,
1151.

Adlam v Law Society [1968] 1 All ER 17, [1968] 1 WLR 6, Digest (Cont Vol C) 897, 215a.

Azam v Secretary of State for the Home Dept [1973] 2 All ER 765, [1974] AC 18, [1973] 2
WLR 859, HL, 2 Digest (Reissue) 199, 1153.

R v Barnet London Borough Council, ex p Shah [1982] 1 All ER 698, [1982] QB 688, [1982] 2   *f*
WLR 474, CA.

Suthendran v Immigration Appeal Tribunal [1976] 3 All ER 611, [1977] AC 359, [1976] 3
WLR 725, HL, 2 Digest (Reissue) 221, 1234.

Cases also cited

Grant v Borg [1982] 2 All ER 257, [1982] 1 WLR 638, HL.   *g*
MacManaway, Re [1951] AC 161, PC.

Appeal

Louis Mario Margueritte (the applicant) appealed against the decision of Webster J,
hearing the Divisional Court List, on 10 April 1981 dismissing his application for judicial
review of the decision of the Secretary of State for Home Affairs refusing the applicant's   *h*
application for registration as a United Kingdom citizen. The facts are set out in the
judgment of Lord Denning MR.

Louis Blom-Cooper QC and *Ian Macdonald* for the applicant.
David Latham for the Secretary of State.

j

Cur adv vult

---

c   Section 33(2) is set out at p 912 *e*, post

19 July. The following judgments were read.

a **LORD DENNING MR.** It is a proud thing to be a British subject, or, as the British Nationality Act 1948 puts it, to be 'a citizen of the United Kingdom and Colonies'. No wonder then that Louis Margueritte wishes to attain it. He came originally from Mauritius. That island was acquired by Great Britain in 1814 by cession from France. It was a dependent territory under the Crown until 1968 when it became independent **b** under the Mauritius Independence Act 1968.

Louis Margueritte was born in Mauritius in 1952 whilst it was still a British colony. In October 1972, when he was 20 years of age, he came to England and was given leave to enter as a visitor for a few months. He 'overstayed' until June 1974 when he went to France for three weeks. In July 1974 he returned to the United Kingdom and was granted leave to enter as a visitor limited to one month. He again 'overstayed' without leave. He **c** obtained work and was not found out. He lived as if 'ordinarily resident' here. In 1978 he married. His wife had come from Mauritius herself originally but she had been settled here for some years. On marrying her, he became entitled to take advantage of her settlement. He applied for indefinite leave to remain. He was granted it on 1 June 1978 and has resided here ever since.

In September 1979 he and his wife applied to the Home Office for registration as **d** citizens of the United Kingdom and colonies. She was registered, but he was not. He consulted solicitors and applied for judicial review. It was refused by Webster J. Mr Margueritte now appeals to this court.

The law

The law as to British nationality is contained in a principal Act, the British Nationality **e** Act 1948. Mr Margueritte's application comes under an amendment to it which was made by the Immigration Act 1971, Sch 1, which added a new s 5A, which says, so far as material, that the Secretary of State may cause to be registered as a citizen of the United Kingdom and colonies any person of full age and capacity who satisfies the Secretary of State of five conditions (see s 5A(2)). The relevant condition here is set out in s 5A(3), which says that 'throughout the period of five years ending with the date of his **f** application to be registered . . . he has been ordinarily resident in the United Kingdom . . .'

Mr Margueritte's application was made on 12 September 1979, so the relevant five years were from 12 September 1974 to 12 September 1979. During that time he was an 'overstayer' from 12 September 1974 to 1 June 1978, but from 1 June 1978 to 12 September 1979 he was here on indefinite leave.

g It appears that at one time the Home Office would have regarded Mr Margueritte as satisfying the condition of being 'ordinarily resident' for five years. They used to hold that if an 'overstayer' improved his position by getting indefinite leave to enter he could count the whole of his time here as being 'ordinarily resident' here. This was acknowledged in a letter of 31 July 1980 to Mr Margueritte's solicitors in which the Home Office said:

h   'Until recently, the Secretary of State was able to regard a person who had remained here, without permission, as having satisfied the 5 years' ordinary residence requirement for the purpose of an application for registration providing that person's stay was eventually regularised. However, in a recent House of Lords' judgment it was established as a matter of principle that a person who remains in this country after the period for which he was granted permission cannot be lawfully **j**   resident here.'

We asked what was that House of Lords judgment. We were told it was *Suthendran v Immigration Appeal Tribunal* [1976] 3 All ER 611, [1977] AC 359. But on examining it, it is plain that it had nothing whatever to do with the words 'ordinarily resident' at all. It

was concerned only with the effect of the words 'a person who has a limited leave'. The
Home Office were quite mistaken in thinking that it had any application here at all.   *a*

So we come to the words 'ordinarily resident'. Counsel for Mr Margueritte submitted
to us that this depended solely on the facts of the man's residence here and not on the
legality or illegality of it. He suggested that an 'illegal entrant' who came into this
country clandestinely in a little boat was qualified to apply for citizenship as soon as he
had been living here and working here openly for five years. Likewise, he said, an
'overstayer'. He supported this by reference to some observations of Lord Wilberforce   *b*
and Lord Salmon in *Azam v Secretary of State for the Home Dept* [1973] 2 All ER 765 at
771, 779, [1974] AC 18 at 62, 72. But those observations are to be explained by
remembering that before 1 January 1973 it was only landing here which was an offence.
Once a person got in, however unlawfully, and lived openly here he was to be regarded
as lawfully here and could not be removed. I described the position myself in those
periods in my judgment in the Court of Appeal in *Azam's* case [1973] 2 All ER 741 at   *c*
748–749, [1974] AC 18 at 28–29. So it seems to me that those observations of Lord
Wilberforce and Lord Salmon are not applicable to the present case and we have got to
come back to the words of the statute itself, 'ordinarily resident'.

When those words were first used in the 1948 Act there were no such persons in
existence such as 'illegal entrants' or 'overstayers'. So I do not think we should construe
the words 'ordinarily resident' as at that time in 1948. It was in 1973 that those persons   *d*
first came into being and started living in England. I think those words should be
construed in their new setting. They have to be applied in a new setting and should be
construed accordingly. In this new setting the Immigration Act 1971 contains specific
provisions whether such a person is to be regarded as 'ordinarily resident' here. There is
a general provision in s 33(2) of the 1971 Act, which says:

> 'It is hereby declared that, except as otherwise provided in this Act, a person is not   *e*
> to be treated for the purposes of any provision of this Act as ordinarily resident in
> the United Kingdom or in any of the Islands at a time when he is there in breach of
> the immigration laws.'

There is also a special provision in para 2 of Sch 1 to the same effect.

Although that declaration is itself only 'for the purposes of any provision of this Act' I   *f*
think it is permissible to have regard to it when considering the new s 5A of the 1948
Act. It is part of the new setting in which the words 'ordinarily resident' have to be
construed.

Applying it, I am of opinion that an 'illegal entrant' or an 'overstayer' is not to be
treated as 'ordinarily resident' here at a time when he is in breach of the immigration
laws. Furthermore, I think the broad principle which we stated in this court in *Re Abdul*   *g*
Manan [1971] 2 All ER 1016 at 1017, [1971] 1 WLR 859 at 861 still applies. I said:

> 'The point turns on the meaning of "ordinarily resident" in these statutes. If this
> were an income tax case he would, I expect, be held to be ordinarily resident here.
> But it is not an income tax case. It is an immigration case. In these statutes
> "ordinarily resident" means *lawfully* ordinarily resident here. The word "lawfully"
> is often read into an Act . . . It should be read into these Acts.'   *h*

I would apply that principle here. Mr Margueritte was not lawfully resident here
during those five years which I have mentioned.

I would put it on an even wider ground. It is still a privilege to be a national of this
country, to be registered as a citizen of the United Kingdom and colonies, and to hold a
British passport. This privilege should not be accorded to a person who has come into   *j*
this country unlawfully or has stayed here unlawfully in breach of our laws. He may,
and often does, redeem his fault so as to get indefinite leave to remain. But that is as far
as we should go for him. We need not give him British nationality as well.

Then we were referred to the recent British Nationality Act 1981, but I need not
consider those provisions today because they do not come into consideration in this case.
I would dismiss the appeal accordingly.

OLIVER LJ. I agree that this appeal fails. The question which has been much debated
a is: what is the natural meaning of the words 'ordinarily resident'? Does it mean merely
habitually resident or does it import some quality beyond mere habit and, in particular,
that residence to be 'ordinary' must also be regular in the sense of lawful? It was construed
in the latter sense by this court in *Re Abdul Manan* [1971] 2 All ER 1016, [1971] 1 WLR
859 in the context of the Commonwealth Immigration Acts 1962 and 1968, but in *Azam
v Secretary of State for the Home Dept* [1973] 2 All ER 765, [1974] AC 18 both Lord
b Wilberforce (with whom Lord Hodson, Lord Pearson and Lord Kilbrandon agreed) and
Lord Salmon (who dissented) were at one in expressing the view that, apart from the
special provisions of s 33 of the Immigration Act 1971, all the appellants in that case, one
of whom at least had entered illegally and whose continued presence in this country
constituted an offence, were ordinarily resident here.

Manan's case was cited in argument in *Azam's* case but was not expressly disapproved;
c and there may be room for debate about (a) whether it applies to anything except the
Commonwealth Immigration Acts 1962 and 1968 (which have now been repealed) or
(b) the extent to which the observations of Lord Wilberforce and Lord Salmon were ratio
or merely obiter, and (c) how far, in any event, they are applicable to a case where
ordinary residence is the essential foundation for some privilege which is claimed by the
propositus.

d Our attention has been drawn to the judgment of Eveleigh LJ in the recent case of *R v
Barnet London Borough Council, ex p Shah* [1982] 1 All ER 698 at 706, [1982] QB 688 at
722–723 where he said:

> 'It is quite clear, therefore, that in so far as the Immigration Act 1971 is concerned
> the expression "ordinarily resident" is something less than that of having the right
> of abode. None the less when a person asserts a claim on the basis of being "ordinarily
e > resident" he must also be in a position lawfully to claim that status. A person,
> therefore, who would appear to be "ordinarily resident" to anyone observing the
> way in which he is living will not be able to substantiate his claim if he is not
> entitled lawfully so to live. It may well be that for the purposes of taxation he will
> not be allowed to deny his apparent status. When he seeks to claim a benefit from
> the state, however, the position will be different. Then it will be necessary to show
f > that he has the right or permission to live here in the manner which has led to the
> conclusion that he is living as any ordinary member of the community may live.'

This, although in the quite different context of the Education Act 1962, appears to me,
if I may say so respectfully, to be good common sense and accords with the decision of
this court in *Manan's* case. It is, however, unnecessary in the instant case to resolve the
g point, for the question which we are called on to answer is not, in my judgment, what is
the natural or normal meaning of the expression in general, but what is its meaning in
s 5A of the British Nationality Act 1948.

In my judgment, the words as used in that section do import the notion that the
propositus is lawfully here, and, in order to explain the reason why I have reached that
conclusion, it is necessary to say a word about the legislative history and about the way in
h which s 5A came to be inserted into the 1948 Act.

Section 6(1) of the 1948 Act provided a system under which citizens of Commonwealth
countries had a right, on applying to the Secretary of State, to be registered as citizens of
the United Kingdom and colonies if they satisfied the Secretary of State that they were
ordinarily resident in the United Kingdom and had been so resident for 12 months
immediately preceding the application. Looking at the matter at the date of that
j enactment there was no context for reading 'ordinarily resident' as 'normally and lawfully
resident', for the Commonwealth Immigration Acts were not yet in being and there was
no reason why a citizen of a Commonwealth country who was resident here should not
have been lawfully so resident.

The Immigration Act 1971, however, by Sch 6, repealed s 6(1) of the 1948 Act and,
from the coming into force of the 1971 Act, there were only two machineries provided
for the registration of Commonwealth citizens as citizens of the United Kingdom and

colonies. Both arise under the provisions of Sch 1 to the 1971 Act. The first is under para 2 of Sch 1, which provides that, subject to certain exceptions which do not matter for present purposes, a person who would, but for the provisions of the 1971 Act, have been entitled to be so registered if s 6(1) of the 1948 Act had not been repealed, shall be entitled to be so registered if he satisfies the Secretary of State that, at the date of his application, he has, throughout the last five years or, if it is more than five years, throughout the period since the coming into force of the 1971 Act, been ordinarily resident in the United Kingdom without being subject, by virtue of any law relating to immigration, to any restriction on the period for which he might remain.

This then is the transitional provision which preserves the *right* of the person who could have applied for registration under the repealed section when the 1971 Act came into force, but extends the qualifying period to five years instead of 12 months, and excludes from computation any period during which he was subject to a restriction on the period during which he was entitled to remain here. On the face of this provision standing alone, there is nothing that necessarily suggests that 'ordinarily resident' has any different meaning from that which was borne by the same words in the repealed section. But that it does in fact have a different meaning must, I think, inevitably follow from the provisions of the 1971 Act to which I will now refer. These provisions are in s 33. First of all s 33(1) provides that:

'... "immigration laws" means this Act and any law for purposes similar to this Act which is for the time being or has (before or after the passing of this Act) been in force in any part of the United Kingdom and Islands.'

Section 33(2) provides:

'It is hereby declared that, except as otherwise provided in this Act, a person is not to be treated for the purposes of any provision of this Act as ordinarily resident in the United Kingdom or in any of the Islands at a time when he is there in breach of the immigration laws.'

The reference to 'otherwise provided' is, I think, clearly a reference to s 7, which provides exemption from deportation to certain Commonwealth citizens who were ordinarily resident in the United Kingdom when the 1971 Act came into force. Section 7(2) is in the following terms:

'A person who has at any time become ordinarily resident in the United Kingdom or in any of the Islands shall not be treated for the purposes of this section as having ceased to be so by reason only of his having remained there in breach of the immigration laws.'

The important words in s 33(2) for present purposes, however, are the words 'for the purposes of any provision of this Act'. The schedules are part of the Act and it cannot, in my judgment, be doubted that the transitional provisions in para 2 of Sch 1 are 'provisions of this Act'. So the right which the Commonwealth citizen had under s 6(1) of the 1948 Act has been qualified not only by an extension of the period but also by a revision of the meaning of 'ordinarily resident'. One asks, therefore, whether there is any logical or readily explicable reason why the legislature, which plainly intended to qualify the rights of those with existing entitlements, should have intended to exclude the same qualifications from the rights of those who had no existing entitlement, but might apply for registration in the future. For my part, I can think of none.

I turn, then, to see how the legislature set about dealing with future applications. Having repealed s 6(1) of the 1948 Act and dealt with transitional cases, it did so by the device of inserting into the 1948 Act an entirely new section, and it is quite clear that, in doing so, it can hardly have looked at the matter through 1948 eyes, for the new section itself contains a reference to the 1971 Act.

Paragraph 1 of Sch 1 to the 1971 Act reads, for relevant purposes, as follows:

'The law with respect to registration as a citizen of the United Kingdom and a Colonies shall be modified as follows:—(*a*) in the British Nationality Act 1948, immediately before section 6, there shall be inserted as section 5A the provisions set out in Appendix A to this Schedule, and no person shall be entitled to be registered under or by virtue of section 6(1) of that Act except in the transitional cases allowed for by paragraph 2 below . . .'

b I need not read the remaining two sub-paragraphs. Their only significance in the present context is that, under sub-paragraph (*b*)(ii), the reference which originally appeared in s 8 of the 1948 Act to a person being 'ordinarily resident' is now replaced by a somewhat circuitous reference to the new s 5A set out in App A.

The new s 5A deals with two classes of persons, that is to say 'patrials' under the 1971 Act (who are *entitled* to registration if they satisfy the condition set out in s 5A(3)) and others who *may* be registered at the discretion of the Secretary of State if they satisfy him that they comply with a number of conditions, the important one for present purposes c being the condition set out in s 5A(3). That reads as follows:

'The condition that a person is required by subsection (1)(*b*) or (2)(*b*) above to fulfil is that throughout the period of five years ending with the date of his application to be registered, or such shorter period so ending as the Secretary of State may in the special circumstances of any particular case accept, he has been ordinarily resident d in the United Kingdom, or engaged in relevant employment, or partly the one and partly the other.'

So here again we have the reference to being 'ordinarily resident'; and what counsel for the applicant has to suggest, and he has done so with his characteristic valour, is that this expression, which is contained in the same schedule to the same Act as para 2, here bears a quite different meaning from the meaning which it bears in that paragraph.

e For my part, I find myself unable to accept this either as a matter of sense or as a matter of construction. In the ultimate analysis one has to ask oneself: what is the intention evinced by the legislature as it appears from the language used? I find it quite impossible to suppose that the legislature, which has gone out of its way to exclude from computation the period of unlawful residence in the case of an applicant who is entitled to register under the transitional provisions, should have intended that the same applicant should f nevertheless be able to qualify for registration under the new section by residence for the same period of five years but including the period of unlawful residence. As a matter of ordinary common sense it seems to me that the expression must have the same meaning both in para 2 of Sch 1 and in App A to the same schedule.

But it also seems to me that the result ensues as a matter of construction. The argument is that the new s 5A set out in App A to Sch 1, which is headed 'Provisions to have effect g as Section 5A of the British Nationality Act 1948', are simply a part of the 1948 Act and, therefore, have to be treated as if they had originally been inserted in that Act in 1948 and not in the Immigration Act in 1971. They are not, therefore, the argument would run, a 'provision of this Act' for the purposes of s 33(2) of the 1971 Act and thus are not subject to the qualification imposed by that subsection on the meaning of the words 'ordinarily resident'.

h I am unable to accept this. Section 2(5) of the 1971 Act provides: 'The law with respect to registration as a citizen of the United Kingdom and Colonies shall be modified as provided by Schedule 1 to this Act.' That is clearly a 'provision of this Act' for the purposes of s 33(2). So, in my judgment, is the schedule itself, and the new section which is 'to have effect as Section 5A' of the 1948 Act is no less a part of the schedule because it is contained in an appendix to it.

j In my judgment, therefore, the applicant cannot claim to include in his period of ordinary residence any of the time during which he was here in breach of the immigration laws. Although the matter has been argued in this court in a way very different from that in which it appears to have been argued before the judge, I am persuaded that in fact he came to the right conclusion and I agree, therefore, that the appeal should be dismissed.

KERR LJ. On 14 July 1974 the applicant came to this country as a visitor with permission to stay for one month. He did not leave on 14 August 1974 and was therefore liable to prosecution under s 24(1)(b)(i) of the Immigration Act 1971 for being what has become known as an 'overstayer'. It is clear that he was thereafter in this country unlawfully: see the remarks of Viscount Dilhorne in *Suthendran v Immigration Appeal Tribunal* [1976] 3 All ER 611 at 615, [1977] AC 359 at 366. The expiry of the period for the prosecution of his offence under s 28 cannot in itself have caused the unlawfulness of his presence in this country to have 'dropped away': see per Lord Wilberforce in *Azam v Secretary of State for the Home Dept* [1973] 2 All ER 765 at 772, [1974] AC 18 at 63. He therefore remained here unlawfully until he was given indefinite leave to remain on 1 June 1978. However, it has not been seriously contended that this permission had the effect of retrospectively rendering his presence lawful as from 15 August 1974, and I cannot see any justification for such a conclusion. On 11 September 1979 he then applied for registration under s 5A(2) of the 1948 Act, as set out in App A to Sch 1 to the 1971 Act. As stated in the heading, this was 'to have effect as Section 5A of British Nationality Act 1948'. His entitlement thereunder depended, inter alia, on his having been ordinarily resident in this country throughout a period of five years prior to 11 September 1979: see s 5A(3). The issue is whether he complied with this requirement of ordinary residence despite the fact that from 15 August 1974 to 1 June 1978 his presence in this country was unlawful.

As a matter of first impression it seems to me that someone who has no right to be in this country at all cannot be said to be 'ordinarily' resident here, at any rate in a statutory context in which ordinary residence is a requirement for the purpose of qualifying for some benefit, whether as a matter or right or of discretion. This was the view of Eveleigh LJ in *R v Barnet London Borough Council, ex p Shah* [1982] 1 All ER 698 at 706, [1982] QB 688 at 722–723. Another way of expressing, or arriving at, the same conclusion is to say that in such cases Parliament must have intended that the prima facie entitlement to the qualification in question must have been earned lawfully and unlawfully. That was the clear view of Pennycuick J in a different context in *Adlam v Law Society* [1968] 1 All ER 17, [1968] 1 WLR 6 and of this court in the context of 'ordinary residence' in *Re Abdul Manan* [1971] 2 All ER 1016, [1971] 1 WLR 859. As a matter of first impression I would unhesitatingly reach the same conclusion on the ground that Parliament cannot have intended that a person should be able to take advantage of his own wrong.

However, the argument for the applicant in this court has centred on the submission that in *Azam's* case, in an earlier statutory context which is not easily distinguishable in substance from the present one, the reasoning of the speeches in the House of Lords clearly included a step which accepted that the words 'ordinarily resident' refer to a purely factual state of affairs, irrespective of the lawfulness of the residence in question (see [1973] 2 All ER 765 at 771, [1974] AC 18 at 62 per Lord Wilberforce, with whose speech the remainder of the majority agreed, and [1973] 2 All ER 765 at 779, [1974] AC 18 at 72 per Lord Salmon, dissenting, who was to the same effect on this step in the reasoning). Although, with respect, I do not regard these remarks in their then context as authoritative for present purposes, I feel on safer ground in relation to the present appeal by asking myself the following question: on the true construction of the words 'ordinarily resident' in App A to Sch 1, viewed in the context of the 1971 Act as a whole, did Parliament intend that a period should count towards the qualifying period of five years if the person in question was then in this country unlawfully?

The first part of the answer to this question is that there is nothing whatever in the 1971 Act which would positively justify such a conclusion, and this is perhaps not surprising. The second part of the answer is that s 33(2) is prima facie a clear expression of intent to the contrary effect. This provides:

'It is hereby declared that, except as otherwise provided in this Act, a person is not to be treated for the purposes of any provision of this Act as ordinarily resident in the United Kingdom or in any of the Islands at a time when he is there in breach of the immigration laws.'

The words 'except as otherwise provided in this Act' were no doubt intended to refer
a in particular to s 7(2), which provides for exemption from liability to deportation in
certain cases. But there is nothing to suggest that these words were also intended to
qualify the words 'ordinarily resident' in s 5A(3) set out in App A to Sch 1 to the 1971
Act, which was to take effect as s 5A(3) of the British Nationality Act 1948. The kernel of
the applicant's argument, as it seems to me, must be the words 'for the purposes of any
provision of this Act' in s 33(2), on the ground that App A to Sch 1 does not form part of
b the 1971 Act because it amends the 1948 Act.

I cannot accept this argument. In the first place, it seems to me to rest on the purely
technical difficulties which no doubt faced the draftsman of the Act. Since the provision
in question relates more to nationality than to immigration, he presumably considered
that this provision had to be enacted by way of amendment of the 1948 Act and not as a
substantive provision of the 1971 Act. But in the context of the 1948 Act it would have
c been impossible to qualify the words 'ordinarily resident' on the same lines as in s 7(2)
and para 2 of Sch 1 to the 1971 Act, where it is made clear that these words are
respectively subject to 'the immigration laws' and to 'any law relating to immigration'.
The reason is that these laws were not yet in existence in 1948, and that the then existing
laws in the same field have long ago been repealed and superseded by a great deal of
subsequent legislation. I therefore attach no real weight, in seeking to ascertain the
d intention of Parliament in 1971, to the argument that the words in s 33(2) of the 1971
Act 'for the purposes of any provision of this Act' should be regarded as some indication
that Parliament did not intend s 33(2) also to govern the words 'ordinarily resident' in
the new s 5A(3) which was then inserted into the 1948 Act.

Furthermore, it seems to me that s 5A(3) set out in App A to Sch 1 to the 1971 Act,
which is to have effect as s 5A(3) of the 1948 Act, is in itself to be regarded as a provision
e which was enacted for the purposes of the 1971 Act. Section 2(5) of the 1971 Act
provides: 'The law with respect to registration as a citizen of the United Kingdom and
Colonies shall be modified as provided by Schedule 1 to this Act.' Paragraph 1(*a*) of Sch 1
provides:

'The law with respect to registration as a citizen of the United Kingdom and
Colonies shall be modified as follows:—(*a*) in the British Nationality Act 1948,
f   immediately before section 6, there shall be inserted as section 5A the provisions set
out in Appendix A to this Schedule, and no person shall be entitled to be registered
under or by virtue of section 6(1) of that Act except in the transitional cases allowed
for by paragraph 2 below . . .'

Then, finally, in the transitional cases referred to in para (2) of Sch 1, which are subject
g to the exceptions in para (3) to which Oliver LJ has referred, the meaning of the words
'ordinarily resident' is clearly qualified by the criterion of legality, so as to make it
impossible to conclude that Parliament intended in 1971 that these words should have a
purely factual meaning without regard to the lawfulness of the presence in this country
of the persons referred to. Accordingly, as it seems to me, the whole of Sch 1, including
(for present purposes) App A in particular, was enacted 'for the purposes of' the 1971 Act
h and is governed by s 33(2).

It follows, since the applicant was here 'in breach of the immigration laws' from 15
August 1974 to 1 June 1978 within the terms of s 33(2), that he cannot claim that he was
'ordinarily resident' for five years prior to 11 September 1979.

I therefore agree that this appeal must be dismissed.

j   *Appeal dismissed. Leave to appeal to the House of Lords refused.*

Solicitors: *Bernard Sheridan & Co* (for the applicant); *Treasury Solicitor.*

Diana Procter   Barrister.

R v Bouch

a

COURT OF APPEAL, CRIMINAL DIVISION
LORD LANE CJ, THOMPSON AND LEONARD JJ
15 JULY 1982

Explosives – Offence – Making explosive substance with intent to endanger life or cause serious
injury to property – Explosive substance – Whether petrol bomb an 'explosive substance' –
Explosives Act 1875, s 3 – Explosive Substances Act 1883, ss 3(1)(b), 9(1).

b

The applicant was charged with making an explosive substance, namely petrol bombs,
with intent to endanger life or cause serious injury to property, contrary to s 3(1)(b)[a] of
the Explosive Substances Act 1883. A petrol bomb was a bottle containing petrol with a
lighted wick in the top. When it was thrown and broke, the petrol spilt, vaporised, c
mixed with the air in the atmosphere and was ignited by the wick, causing a fireball and
possibly a blast. The extent of the fireball and whether there was a blast depended on
whether there was instantaneous ignition. By s 9(1)[b] of the 1883 Act an 'explosive
substance' included 'any materials for making any explosive substance' and by s 3[c] of the
Explosives Act 1875 (which, on legal authority, applied to the 1883 Act) the definition of
'explosive' included any substance used with a view to producing an 'explosion or a d
pyrotechnic effect'. The only question in issue at the applicant's trial was whether a petrol
bomb qualified as an 'explosive substance'. The judge directed the jury that it did and
the applicant was convicted and sentenced. He applied for leave to appeal against
conviction, contending that the judge had misdirected the jury because (i) an 'explosive'
was something which blew up, making a loud noise and producing a direct physical
effect, and (ii) an explosion was a necessary ingredient of a 'pyrotechnic effect' for the e
purposes of s 3 of the 1875 Act.

Held – A petrol bomb was an 'explosive substance' for the purposes of ss 3 and 9 of the
1883 Act because (a) it produced an 'explosion' when it landed in that it produced a
fireball and all the characteristics of an explosion, and the fact that it did not produce a f
blast effect on every occasion was irrelevant, (b) the bottle, the petrol and the wick were
'materials for making any explosive substance' because they produced a mixture of petrol
vapour and air in explosive proportions, and (c) the fireball produced was a 'pyrotechnic
effect'. The application would accordingly be refused (see p 921 f to h, p 922 b to e and g
h and p 923 d to f, post).

The Orion [1891] P 307 and *R v Wheatley* [1979] 1 All ER 954 applied.

g

Notes
For doing an act with intent to cause an explosion, see 18 Halsbury's Laws (4th edn) para
108.

For the Explosives Act 1875, s 3, see 13 Halsbury's Statutes (3rd edn) 160.

For the Explosive Substances Act 1883, s 3 (as substituted by the Criminal Jurisdiction h
Act 1975, s 7(1)), see 45 ibid 528, and for s 9 of the 1883 Act, see 8 ibid 224.

Cases referred to in judgment
Orion, The [1891] P 307, 42 Digest (Repl) 826, 6024.
R v Wheatley [1979] 1 All ER 954, [1979] 1 WLR 144, 68 Cr App R 287, CA, Digest (Cont
Vol E) 157, 1036*1a*.

j

---

a   Section 3(1), so far as material, is set out at p 919 *f g*, post
b   Section 9(1), so far as material, is set out at p 919 *h*, post
c   Section 3, so far as material, is set out at p 920 *f*, post

Application for leave to appeal

a Malcolm Alan Bouch applied for leave to appeal against his conviction in the Crown Court at Leeds on 16 December 1981 before his Honour Judge Chapman QC and a jury, on a charge of making an explosive substance with intent to endanger life or cause serious injury to property, contrary to s 3(1)(b) of the Explosive Substances Act 1883. The facts are set out in the judgment of the court.

b *Nigel Fricker QC* and *Jonathan Crabtree* (assigned by the Registrar of Criminal Appeals) for the applicant.
Paul Kennedy QC and *John W Mellor* for the Crown.

LORD LANE CJ delivered the following judgment of the court: This is an application
c for leave to appeal against conviction by Malcolm Alan Bouch. On 16 December 1981 at the Crown Court at Leeds before his Honour Judge Chapman QC and a jury he was convicted of making an explosive substance with intent, contrary to s 3(1)(b) of the Explosive Substances Act 1883, and he was sentenced to four years' imprisonment.

The charge arose out of events in July 1981 in Leeds when there were civil disturbances. The case for the prosecution was that the applicant, having been present at some of these
d disturbances, then returned to the house or flat where he was living on the evening of Monday, 13 July, and there made some 36 petrol bombs. The petrol bombs, according to the evidence, consisted of bottles, mostly milk bottles, with some petrol contained in them. Into the mouth of the bottle was rammed a wick made from torn-up sheeting, with some of the wick hanging outside the bottle. The object was to set fire to the wick hanging outside and to throw the missile, with results which will have to be more closely examined in a moment. In the upshot, the applicant admitted that he had made these
e missiles, and the only live issue, at any rate in this court, is whether they qualified, within the meaning of the 1883 Act, to be called explosive substances.

It is first of all necessary to read the relevant provisions in the two statutes which are involved. First of all the statute under which he is charged, the Explosive Substances Act 1883. Section 3 of that Act (as substituted by s 7(1) of the Criminal Jurisdiction Act 1975)
f reads as follows:

> '(1) A person who in the United Kingdom or a dependency or . . . elsewhere unlawfully and maliciously . . . (b) makes or has in his possession or under his control an explosive substance with intent by means thereof to endanger life, or cause serious injury to property, whether in the United Kingdom or the Republic of Ireland, or to enable any other person so to do, shall, whether any explosion does
g or does not take place, and whether any injury to person or property is actually caused or not, be guilty of an offence . . .'

The only other section of the 1883 Act which requires reading and is relevant, as will become plain in a moment, is s 9, which reads as follows:

> '(1) In this Act, unless the context otherwise requires—The expression "explosive
h substance" shall be deemed to include any materials for making any explosive substance; also any apparatus, machine, implement, or materials used, or intended to be used, or adapted for causing, or aiding in causing, any explosion in or with any explosive substance; also any part of any such apparatus, machine, or implement . . .'

Further help is derived in defining the word 'explosive' from the Explosives Act 1875.
j It is necessary first of all to lay the foundation to show why that Act has any relevance to the 1883 Act. The reason for that is a decision of this court in *R v Wheatley* [1979] 1 All ER 954, [1979] 1 WLR 144. That was a case where a man had been charged under the Explosive Substances Act 1883. He was charged under ss 3 and 4, and the question of the meaning of 'explosive' arose for decision. This court, the judgment being delivered by Bridge LJ, held as follows (see 68 Cr App R 287):

'... the definition of the word "explosive" found in the Explosives Act 1875 was available to be adopted and applied under the provisions of the Act of 1883; thus, *a* the trial judge had come to the right conclusion and on the evidence he was right to withdraw the issue from the jury and rule that the substances in question were explosive substances, the definition aforesaid including a substance used to produce a pyrotechnic effect.'

The relevant passage of the judgment reads as follows ([1979] 1 All ER 954 at 957, [1979] 1 WLR 144 at 147): *b*

'Looking at the two statutes, at the nature of the provisions which they both contain, and in particular at the short and long titles of both statutes, it appears to this court that clearly they are in pari materia, and that conclusion alone would seem to us to be sufficient to justify the conclusion which the judge reached that the definition of the word "explosive" found in the 1875 Act is available to be adopted *c* and applied under the provisions of the 1883 Act. But if that conclusion were in any way in doubt, it is, in our judgment, put beyond doubt by the express provisions of s 8 of the 1883 Act which is in these terms: "(1) Sections seventy-three, seventy-four, seventy-five, eighty-nine and ninety-six of the Explosives Act, 1875 (which sections relate to the search for, seizure and detention of explosive substances, and the forfeiture thereof, and the disposal of explosive substances seized or forfeited), *d* shall apply in like manner as if a crime or forfeiture under this Act were an offence or forfeiture under the Explosives Act 1875 ..." Here is Parliament in terms providing that certain powers in relation to explosive substances under the 1875 Act shall be applied for the purposes of the 1883 Act. That, as it seems to us, shows Parliament assuming of necessity that what is an explosive substance essentially under the one Act will be the same as under the other.' *e*

In the light of that decision, which is binding on us, we turn to the terms of the provisions of the Explosives Act 1875, and particularly s 3, which reads as follows:

'... The term "explosive" in this Act—(1) Means gunpowder ... coloured fires, and every other substance, whether similar to those above mentioned or not, used or manufactured with a view to produce a practical effect by explosion or a *f* pyrotechnic effect; and (2) Includes fog-signals, fireworks, fuzes, rockets, percussion caps, detonators, cartridges, ammunition of all descriptions, and every adaptation or preparation of an explosive as above defined.'

It is now necessary, before we turn to the submissions which have been made by counsel for the applicant, to see what the basis of fact was on which the jury had to decide whether they were satisfied so as to feel sure or not that these particular devices were *g* explosives. The judge dealt with it in a compendious and succinct way as follows:

'Well, what is the evidence about petrol bombs? It is a bottle containing petrol with a wick in the top. It is thrown, the bottle breaks, the petrol is spilt; it vaporises, it mixes with the air in the atmosphere; then the wick sets it alight and it goes off. Normally, says Mr Harrison [he was the expert called on behalf of the prosecution], *h* it goes off in under one-hundreth of a second. If it goes off then, that is instantaneously, the blast effect is very little, and he agreed that it would not cause injury to a man in an asbestos suit, and if you found that a petrol bomb was thrown at you and hit your chest and dropped to your feet and went off, you would not be blown over by the blast. However, sometimes ignition is not instantaneous; there may be a delay of a second or two, and then you have got a bigger area of petrol and *j* air vapour, and then when it goes off there will be a blast, which, he thought, could be sufficient possibly to break a window. So the blast effect is either minimal or it is not guaranteed. The pyrotechnic effect, though, is this; with instantaneous ignition there is a fireball, 2 to 3 feet in diameter, which spreads to 10 to 15 feet in diameter, bigger than a man.'

Those were the facts of the matter on which the jury eventually had to reach their
a conclusion.

Counsel for the applicant makes the following submissions to this court. He submits
that the word 'explosive' means something which blows up; it requires a loud noise, a
bursting or a flying into pieces or a violent projection of a pressure wave or fragments. It
must, he submits, produce a direct physical practical effect. Basing himself on those
submissions he suggests that the way in which the judge dealt with it before the jury was
b inadequate.

This is how the judge dealt with it. First of all he read out the section of the 1875 Act
defining 'explosive'. He then went on:

'Well, we had a lot of discussion about all those substances and about the use of
chemical terms in 1875. But it is a matter for me and I did rule on it, and I direct
c you that the law is this. First of all, an explosive is something that goes off; it is
something that produces a sudden release of energy as distinct from a gradual release
of energy. Second, a practical effect by explosion means blast, fast moving air. When
I say "blast", I mean something that you feel, more than a gale or a storm force 10.
You know what blast means. [The section continues] "or a pyrotechnic effect".
"Pyrotechnic effect" means fire. It means fire produced by the sudden triggering of
d a device, not a torch, and as a matter of law, members of the jury, I direct you that
it does not matter where the oxygen comes from.'

It is with regard to that latter direction on pyrotechnic effect that counsel for the
applicant makes his next submission, which he regarded as his stronger point of the two.
He agrees that pyrotechnic effect is wider than a firework effect, and he is very careful in
e this definition which he submitted to us: 'Pyrotechnic means an explosive substance or
device for achieving a visual or audible effect by light, sound or smoke', and he went on
to suggest that the judge, by not predicating an 'explosion' as a necessary ingredient of
pyrotechnic, was wrong.

It must be observed that one of the difficulties facing counsel for the applicant on that
basis is that he is including in his definition of 'explosive' the very word he is seeking to
f define, which is a shaky basis for any definition. We have come to the conclusion that
those submissions of counsel for the applicant are not sustainable.

We accede to the submissions of counsel for the Crown, which were as follows. He
submitted to us that a jury properly directed could find that these devices (I shall call
them petrol bombs for the purpose of convenience) were explosive substances and there
were three possible bases for that conclusion. First of all, these bombs could and did
g explode within the meaning of that word in the 1883 Act; second, these bombs consisted
of material for making an explosive substance, that is to say a mixture of petrol and air,
within the explosive limits; and, third, that they were used, or manufactured, with a
view to produce a pyrotechnic effect. And he points out, correctly as we have already
observed from a reading of the judge's direction, that the judge directed the jury on the
basis of his first and third contention but did not direct the jury on the basis of his second
h contention, although, let it be said in fairness to the judge, he must have had that
particular basis in mind, because he had adverted to it when he was dealing with the
submissions made to him at an earlier stage of the case. It is not necessary for us to read
that part of the transcript which deals with that.

First, then, did these bombs explode? When the bomb landed, is it proper to say that
what happened thereafter was an explosion? The expert, Mr Harrison, on behalf of the
j prosecution contended that a loud noise was not necessary, though the defence expert
disagreed in so far as this was a matter for experts to deal with.

We have had our attention directed to a passage in the Encyclopaedia Britannica (9th
edn, 1886) vol 8, p 807, which was only three years after this particular Act was passed.
That extract precisely sets out the basis on which the jury should have approached this
problem:

'... "explosion" may for our purpose be defined as the sudden or extremely rapid conversion of a solid or liquid body of small bulk into gas or vapour, occupying very many times the volume of the original substance, and, in addition, highly expanded by the heat generated during the transformation. This sudden or very rapid expansion of volume is attended by an exhibition of force, more or less violent according to the constitution of the original substance and the circumstances of explosion. Any substance capable of undergoing such a change upon the application of heat, or other disturbing cause, is called "explosive".'

We do not think that for this purpose that particular passage can be improved on. We do not think in those circumstances that it was really necessary for the judge to go on to say anything about a blast effect. What always happens is a fireball, and what the author of that particular passage in the Encyclopaedia Britannica was describing was, amongst other things, quite plainly a fireball, which is the inevitable concomitant of a successful petrol bomb. Consequently the reaction, in our judgment, in every case of a petrol bomb which ignites is an explosion within the proper meaning of that word.

The reason why we say it was not necessary for the judge to go into the question of a blast is primarily based on this further fact. Even if a great blast is required to constitute an 'explosion', the evidence shows that if the petrol bomb on landing does not immediately ignite there is a pause, maybe a very slight pause, and then there may, as the judge in his summing up pointed out, be a sufficient blast to break a window. The fact that such devices do not on every occasion have a blast effect seems to be neither here nor there. It does not make the devices any less explosive substances, that is things liable to explode. It follows that the passage read from the judge's directions was, in so far as it went, correct.

There appears a further passage of the directions as follows:

'It is a matter for you whether you think the blast is sufficient to make a petrol bomb an explosive substance. But, even if you do not, you must ask yourselves whether the fireball effect, a fireball 2 or 3 feet in diameter of blazing petrol and air vapour that expands to 10 to 15 feet in diameter, is not indeed a pyrotechnic effect.'

It seems to us, in so far as the judge is there dealing with the blast, he is being, if anything, perhaps too favourable to the defendant.

Counsel for the Crown's second point, with which the judge did not deal, is based on the terms of s 9 of the 1883 Act, which I have read but will repeat for the purposes of clarity: 'The expression "explosive substance" shall be deemed to include any materials for making any explosive substance . . .' Petrol mixed with air in certain proportions is an explosive substance. Petrol in a milk bottle in the sort of concentration which existed in the present case and usually exists in the case of petrol bombs is not an explosive mixture, because it is too rich: there is too much petrol and too little air for it to be explosive. But, when that mixture is thrown and the bottle breaks, then the explosive substance is created, because the mixture of air and petrol vapour becomes suitable for explosion; hence the fireball. Therefore it seems to us that counsel for the Crown is correct when he submits that the petrol and the bottle and the wick are materials for making that explosive substance within s 9.

The judge could have left the matter to the jury in that way. But he did not, and he is not to be criticised for that. But it may well be that this would have been the simplest and the most easily comprehensible, and therefore the best way of leaving the matter to the jury.

Finally one comes to the question of pyrotechnic effect and once again we look at the words of s 3(1) of the 1875 Act, which include the expression, '. . . every other substance, whether similar to those above mentioned or not, used or manufactured with a view to produce a practical effect by explosion or a pyrotechnic effect . . .' What is a pyrotechnic effect? At one stage we thought that perhaps counsel for the applicant was confining pyrotechnic effect to fireworks pure and simple. But he concedes that the word must go beyond that.

a We have been referred to numerous dictionary definitions in the late eighteenth century, to which we do not propose to make reference, but by the early nineteenth century it was not confined to the narrow definition; it was certainly not confined to something which could merely amuse or entertain. For support for that one can turn to the Oxford English Dictionary (1933) meaning: '2. Of or pertaining to fireworks, or the art of making or managing them; of the nature of a firework.' A note under that reads: '1873 *Board of Trade Notice* in Bedford *Sailor's Pocket Bk*. iii. (1875) 68 The Pyrotechnic *b* Light, commonly known as a Blue Light, every 15 minutes.'

It may be convenient at this stage to make reference to a decision in 1891, *The Orion* [1891] P 307. That was a case dealing with regulations for preventing collisions at sea. By those regulations—

c 'a British sailing trawler in the North Sea, having her trawl in the water, and carrying the prescribed white light, is to be supplied with red pyrotechnic lights, and shall shew "one of the red pyrotechnic lights . . . on being approached by another . . . vessel in sufficient time to prevent collision".'

So an object which might perhaps be described as a flare is, quite plainly, at the end of the nineteenth century being used under the heading 'pyrotechnic', and indeed counsel for the applicant conceded, properly, that a flare is a pyrotechnic device. He goes on, as already indicated, to insist that it would be quite improper to describe as pyrotechnic, in *d* the terms of either of those two cases, anything which did not, at the same time as being pyrotechnic, explode. For the reasons already stated we reject that contention.

It seems to us that what emerges from the petrol bomb, namely the fireball already described, comes within the definition of pyrotechnic effect. It is not dissimilar indeed to a flare, albeit a flare burning very quickly. On this basis too we think that the judge *e* was correct and this direction to the jury is not to be faulted.

Counsel for the applicant concluded by suggesting that, if the Crown's contentions were correct, then all sorts of innocent people would find themselves in difficulties, such as those carrying tins of petrol in the boot of their car, who would be likely to be charged under the 1883 Act. We think that these alarming suggestions are not realistic. There are all sorts of safeguards in the Act, not least the fact that before anyone can proceed to *f* charge or prosecute under this Act, the Attorney General's fiat must be obtained.

In all it seems to us that there is no legitimate criticism of the way in which the judge dealt with the matter, and there is nothing unsafe and unsatisfactory about the conviction. Accordingly the application must be refused.

Application refused.

Solicitors: *Director of Public Prosecutions.*

Jacqueline Charles   Barrister.

Practice Note

COURT OF APPEAL, CIVIL DIVISION
DONALDSON MR, WATKINS AND MAY LJJ
5 NOVEMBER 1982

Practice – Inspection of property – Property subject matter of action or in respect of which question arising – Appeal – Appeals normally to be heard in open court – Counsel to give written reasons where hearing in camera is sought.

DONALDSON MR made the following statement at the sitting of the court: We have been discussing how this court should deal with Anton Piller orders. The applications are made ex parte in the court below. They are by their nature applications whose purpose could in some circumstances be frustrated if an appeal was heard in open court, although experience has shown that it is often possible to consider the matter in open court, relying on the great responsibility and discretion which is always shown by those who report the cases on a regular basis (the members of the High Court Journalists' Association). Accordingly, something out of the ordinary has to be shown before it would be right for the court to go into camera. We would like it to be known that, where counsel forms the view that it is necessary in the interests of justice that a preliminary application for an appeal against an ex parte refusal of an Anton Piller or similar order should be heard in camera, he should approach the registrar indicating his view. The reasons should be put into writing, signed by counsel and handed to the registrar. In so doing, it should be understood that counsel is expressing his personal professional view and is not making a submission on behalf of his client. This will enable the court to make a preliminary decision on whether the application should initially be made in camera or in open court. This procedure will avoid the problem which arises where the very reasons which justify a hearing in camera must themselves be put forward in camera if they are to be put forward at all.

Diana Procter   Barrister.

Leeds Permanent Building Society v Procter (Inspector of Taxes)

CHANCERY DIVISION
GOULDING J
28, 29, 30 JULY 1982

Income tax – Capital allowances – Plant – Apparatus used by taxpayer for purposes of business – Building society – Decorative screens – Society installing decorative screens in windows of its branch offices with a view to attracting custom from passers-by – Whether screens plant – Finance Act 1971, s 41(1).

A building society installed movable decorative screens, incorporating the society's name and sometimes its crest, in the windows of its branch offices. The screens were individually made for the particular premises and were readily removable. The purpose of the screens was to attract the attention of the passer-by in the hope that he might notice the society's display cards, giving particulars of investments and other facilities offered by the society, placed in front of or beside the screens. In addition, the screens provided some degree of privacy for those doing business inside the premises and performed a minor security function by shielding the society's activities and the cash it received from public gaze. When the society vacated any of its premises, it always removed the screens. In assessing the society to corporation tax, the Revenue rejected the society's claim that the screens were plant and that the expenditure incurred on them qualified for a first-year allowance under s 41(1)[a] of the Finance Act 1971. The society appealed, contending, inter alia, that the screens were movable chattels forming an important part of the visual presentation of its branches and performing a distinct business function of attracting customers to its branch offices and accordingly were plant for the purposes of the allowance claimed. The General Commissioners determined that the screens formed part of the setting in which the society's business was carried on and did not perform any function in connection with the society's business and were accordingly not plant. The society appealed.

Held – Although the functional test that an article which was part of the setting of a business and which did not perform any function in connection with that business was not plant was applicable to every kind of subject matter, it was not to be applied to any and every item used in a business without regard to the character of the item and its relation to the particular business. Accordingly, the commissioners' findings of fact that the screens were part of the setting in which the society's business was carried on and that their purpose was to attract the attention of the passer-by and so bring business to the society were inconsistent with the commissioners' conclusions that the screens did not perform any function in connection with the society's business and that expenditure on them was not incurred in the provision of plant for the purposes of the society's trade. Rather, the screens were part of the apparatus employed in the commercial activities of the society's business and were not the structure within which the business was carried on. They were an adjunct to the carrying on of the business and not the essential site or core of the business itself. They were not used as premises, but as part of the means by which the relevant trade was carried out. It followed therefore that the expenditure incurred by the society in respect of the screens was expenditure incurred in the provision of plant and as such qualified for a first-year allowance under s 41(1) of the 1971 Act. The appeal would therefore be allowed (see p 935 *j* to p 936 *f* and *j*, p 937 *e f* and *j* and p 938 *b*, post).

Dicta of Buckley, Shaw and Templeman LJJ in *Benson (Inspector of Taxes) v Yard Arm Club Ltd* [1979] 2 All ER at 343–345, 346, 348 and of Lord Lowry in *IRC v Scottish and Newcastle Breweries Ltd* [1982] 2 All ER at 238, 240 applied.

---

a   Section 41(1), so far as is material, is set out at p 930 *f*, post

Benson (Inspector of Taxes) v Yard Arm Club Ltd [1979] 2 All ER 336 distinguished.

Per curiam. It is not legitimate to take a number of reported judgments and to establish inductively by comparing the facts and the decisions a complex proposition never itself enunciated by authority but tailored to the facts of a new case. The proper approach is to look at the statements of principle in the authorities and to apply them directly to the case under scrutiny (see p 938 *a b*, post).

Notes

For first-year allowances, see 23 Halsbury's Laws (4th edn) para 426.

For the meaning of plant, see ibid para 416, and for cases on the subject, see s 28(1) Digest (Reissue) 214–216, 637–643.

For the Finance Act 1971, s 41, see 41 Halsbury's Statutes (3rd edn) 1459.

Cases referred to in judgment

Benson (Inspector of Taxes) v Yard Arm Club Ltd [1979] 2 All ER 336, [1979] 1 WLR 347, CA; *affg* [1978] 2 All ER 958, [1978] 1 WLR 1217, Digest (Cont Vol E) 309, 1676e.

Cole Bros Ltd v Phillips (Inspector of Taxes) [1982] 2 All ER 247, HL; *affg* [1981] STC 671, CA.

Cooke (Inspector of Taxes) v Beach Station Caravans Ltd [1974] 3 All ER 159, [1974] 1 WLR 1398, Digest (Cont Vol D) 456, 640a.

Dixon (Inspector of Taxes) v Fitch's Garage Ltd [1975] 3 All ER 455, [1976] 1 WLR 215, Digest (Cont Vol D) 493, 1676c.

Edwards (Inspector of Taxes) v Bairstow [1955] 3 All ER 48, [1956] AC 14, 28(1) Digest (Reissue) 566, 2089.

IRC v Barclay Curle & Co Ltd [1969] 1 All ER 732, [1969] 1 WLR 675, HL, 28(1) Digest (Reissue) 465, 1676.

IRC v Scottish and Newcastle Breweries Ltd [1982] 2 All ER 230, [1982] 1 WLR 322, HL.

Lyons (J) & Co Ltd v A-G [1944] 1 All ER 477, [1944] Ch 281, 17 Digest (Reissue) 542, 324.

St John's School (Mountford and Knibbs) v Ward (Inspector of Taxes) [1974] STC 69; *affd* [1975] STC 7, CA, Digest (Cont Vol D) 493, 1676d.

Yarmouth v France (1887) 19 QBD 647, DC, 20 Digest (Reissue) 515, 4005.

Case stated

1. At a meeting of the Commissioners for the General Purposes of the Income Tax for the division of Leeds held on 13 and 14 June 1979 Leeds Permanent Building Society appealed against the following assessment to corporation tax: year ended 30 September 1975: profits chargeable to corporation tax £4,700,000.

2. Shortly stated the question for determination was whether expenditure in respect of certain items referred to during the hearing as 'screens' qualified for allowance in the assessment as expenditure incurred in the provision of plant for the purposes of the society's business under the Finance Act 1971, Part III, Chapter 1.

[Paragraphs 3 and 4 identified the witness who gave evidence and listed the documents proved or admitted before the commissioners.]

5. The commissioners were invited by counsel for the society to view a number of the branch offices of the society in order to see examples of the types of screens which were the subject of the claim for allowance in respect of plant. The commissioners inspected such examples at the following branch offices in the Leeds area: Harehills Lane, Roundhay Road, Moortown, King Edward Street and City Square. During this view they were accompanied by counsel for the society, instructing solicitor and representatives of the society and also by the inspector and his officers. They had been informed by the society that it would arrange for the screens which they inspected to be available in the High Court. The screens occupied in the branch offices concerned positions similar to those shown in photographs produced in evidence.

6. The following facts were admitted or found from the evidence, both oral and

documentary, adduced before the commissioners: (1) It was the practice of the society to
a install decorative screens, incorporating the society's name and sometimes its crest, in the
windows of its branch offices. The commissioners described the historical evolution
leading to this practice in sub-paras (3)ff below. Currently nearly all of the screens used
by the society were of five types, listed in the table below. The commissioners also
indicated the particular type of which the photographs and the screens inspected by them
were examples.

b

Type of screen	Maker/designer	Examples
1. Painting	Design Partnership	Photograph A Moortown branch
2. Embroidered collage	Janet Rawlins	Photographs B and BB King Edward Street branch
3. Metallic sculpture	Jan Kepinski	Photograph C Roundhay Road branch
4. Wood with glazed panels	Shopfitters	Photographs D and DD Harehills Lane branch
5. Engraved glass	Various artists	Photograph E

d In one or two cases, usually because of a special lay-out of premises or because of
requirements of lessors, an individually designed type of screen not falling within the
five normal types was used. The screen at the City Square branch, designed by a Leeds
artist and consisting of glass transparencies mounted on a metal frame, was an example.
(2) It was common ground that the screens which the commissioners saw, either in
photographs or in the course of their view, were typical. Although only one of them
e happened to be included in the allowances claimed for the particular accounting period
before them, it was accepted that they fairly provided representative examples of the
disputed items. It was also common ground that the case was an 'all or nothing' one:
either all the society's screens were 'plant' or none of them were. In the circumstances,
although in the accounting period under appeal not every kind of screen currently in use
was included in the disputed items, the society thought it right to show examples of all
f the kinds. (3) The society was established in 1848. Its purpose was to supply finance to
help people buy their own homes and to provide this service it therefore needed to attract
investment money. Originally the society consisted of a single group of people who
contributed to a central fund and drew lots to see in what order they could use this fund
to finance the building of a house for each member of the group. All building societies
commenced in a similar manner and terminated once all the members had acquired a
g house. The society was one of the first to depart from this practice by inviting investment
and mortgage applications from the public at large, hence the use of the word 'Permanent'
in its name. The society needed to attract investors to deposit money and borrowers to
apply for mortgages. There had been periods when the society had been short of
borrowers rather than investors but usually this was not the case. The business of the
society's branches was mainly the paying in of cash for investment or mortgage
h repayment and the processing of mortgage applications, which took time. The society
now had to be very competitive to obtain funds, and considered it important that the
public should be attracted into its branch offices. (4) In the 1930s the business was
carried on as in earlier years, mainly through local agents in various parts of the country
together with a few branch offices. A typical branch office would have wooden doors and
frosted windows. Photographs were produced to illustrate typical branch offices of the
j society in the 1930s. It was in the pre-shopfront era and they were similar to the head
office and banks. A photograph, was produced of the head office and it was explained
that was taken in 1965 and was not materially different from how the premises were in
the 1930s. Although the functions of a branch office were similar to those of today the
appearance of the office did little to attract business. (5) The changes in appearance of
the offices commenced after the 1939–45 war. Competition intensified and the society

decided that the appearance of its offices must be made more attractive as it needed more and more investors to satisfy the ever-growing demand for mortgages. Thus a new concept was introduced of moving into the market place by acquiring shop units to sell the society and its services. The format was a shopfront boxed in with a heavy wooden window frame and opaque glass, intended to be attractive but retaining privacy. Photographs of two offices, at Bournemouth (1955) and Wolverhampton (1956), were produced illustrating that style. (6) In the Leeds area the society had opened small sub-offices before the 1939–45 war but most of those had since been closed. The society had subsequently moved back into the suburbs and now had 14 branches in the area. The Roundhay Road branch was the only branch which had remained open throughout the entire period. (7) In the late 1950s the society decided that its shopfronts were still not eye-catching enough. A new design with a free standing low screen inside the window was introduced in place of the boxed-in style. The society now had 313 branches and the number was increasing by about 40 per year. In the year for which the capital allowances claim was being considered, there were 50 screens placed in 30 offices. Of these 30 offices, 7 had had replacement screens with which the hearing was not concerned. That left 23 offices which had received screens of the following types: 2, collage (Janet Rawlins); 9, painting (Design Partnership); 7, metallic sculpture (Kepinski); 5, wood with glazed panels (Shopfitters). (8) Capital allowances had not been claimed on the shop-window styles depicted in photographs of the two offices at Bournemouth and Wolverhampton but the design introduced in 1959 was thought by the society to be fundamentally different and a claim was accordingly made for capital allowances on that expenditure. The then inspector of taxes called at the society's Harrogate branch office of his own volition. A photograph of that office was produced to illustrate the specific screen inspected. After inspecting the screen the inspector accepted that it could be regarded as plant and capital allowances were accordingly granted for all screens until the inspector's successor refused them for the accounting period with which we were concerned. (9) By coincidence the screen at Harrogate, seen by the then inspector, became the 'standard' for screens in subsequent branch offices, as indicated in a letter dated 12 April 1960 to the architect concerned. The society regarded the new style as a success. An illuminated screen containing the society's coat of arms had been fitted in the window of the Blackpool branch as a prototype. The commissioners were shown a letter from the branch manager in which he stated that he believed that 50% of his new accounts came from passers-by after seeing the window display. The management were convinced of the value of the new free-standing screen, which was considered as having the same effect as a display cabinet. The concept of the screens was a major departure from the previous policy, and the policy had been followed ever since. The society felt it had a winner and no other society had the same window effect. (10) The screens were now highly decorative and had evolved over the years from the plain style of the 1960s; all still contained the society's name in a prominent position and their purpose was still the same; they did not however make any specific reference to the nature of the society's business or to the particular advantages which it offered to its customers. Their sizes varied to match the shops frontage, usually at eye height, about 4 ft 6 in, and generally covered 80% to 90% of the available width of the window. The society tried to make its branches as much like retail shops as possible. The purpose of the screens was to attract the attention of the passer-by; then the passer-by might notice the society's display cards, giving particulars of investments and other facilities offered by the society, placed in front of or beside them. The screens were attached by screws or placed in slots. They were therefore readily removable and could be replaced. They were also capable of being repositioned in the same office or elsewhere, but (as mentioned in sub-para (11) below) that was only rarely done. (11) All screens were individually made for the particular premises. Also, with the exception of the Shopfitters-type each screen was individually designed to attract local people. That meant that often items of local interest were depicted. Screens in one area could be moved to another nearby location, but that was not the society's general practice and only rarely happened. The screens had often aroused considerable local interest, for example in Ripon and Tooting as adduced in evidence.

The general manager of the society recounted in evidence that at a recent conference of
a the Building Societies Association someone had asked him whether he could buy the
screen in the Eastbourne branch or a copy of it. (12) The society considered that there
was no specified evidence as to the effect of the screens as they formed part of its general
advertising policy. They were, however, a very important part of the society's visual
presentation of its branches, together with the high-level fascia signs and projecting signs.
Over the past 20 years, building societies as a whole had grown 15-fold. The society had
b grown 19-fold and considered the screens to be one of the major reasons for that success.
All the major building societies advertised but no other had that style of screen. (13) The
average life of a screen was 10 to 15 years, after which it was usually scrapped, although
occasionally some were moved to an agent's office or another branch office and sometimes
the inserts were removed or changed round. (14) When the society vacated any of its
premises, it always removed the screens as well as the fascia signs and any projecting
c signs, unlike electric wiring and light fittings which always remained. Occasionally the
society might sell the office counter and fitments to the new occupier but never the
screens in the window. (15) The society considered that the screens served five main
purposes as follows: (a) to sell the society's name, by attracting attention in the same way
as high-level fascia and projecting signs, i e, short range rather than long-range; (b) to sell
the society's products; by having the particular style of screen as a back cloth the attention
d of passers-by was directed to the society's products and the type of business conducted in
the premises; (c) to foster a corporate image; being unique and distinctive, without
gimmick, the screens established an image of the society, and hopefully a society with
which the passer-by would wish to do business; (d) to preserve some degree of privacy;
although members had become accustomed to the previous style, times changed and a
calculated risk was taken by the society that people would accept less secrecy; privacy was
e no longer complete but the inside of the office was masked from direct and casual vision.
(e) To provide a minor security function, by shielding the society's activities and routines
concerning cash from the gaze of the public and potential thieves. (16) There could be
seen in photographs produced in evidence the high level fascia signs and projecting signs
referred to in sub-paras (12) and (14) above. It was common ground that those signs were
plant qualifying for capital allowances.
f   7. The following cases were referred to in argument before the commissioners: *Benson
(Inspector of Taxes) v Yard Arm Club Ltd* [1979] 2 All ER 958, [1978] 1 WLR 1217; *Cooke
(Inspector of Taxes) v Beach Station Caravans Ltd* [1974] 3 All ER 159, [1974] 1 WLR 1398;
Dixon (Inspector of Taxes) v Fitch's Garage Ltd [1975] 3 All ER 455, [1976] 1 WLR 215;
IRC v Barclay Curle & Co Ltd [1969] 1 All ER 732, [1969] 1 WLR 675, HL; *Jarrold
(Inspector of Taxes) v John Good & Sons Ltd* [1963] 1 All ER 141, [1963] 1 WLR 214, CA;
g *Lyons (J) & Co Ltd v A-G* [1944] 1 All ER 477, [1944] Ch 281; *Munby v Furlong (Inspector
of Taxes)* [1977] 2 All ER 953, [1977] Ch 359, CA; *St John's School (Mountford and Knibbs) v
Ward (Inspector of Taxes)* [1974] STC 69; *affd* [1975] STC 7, CA; *Yarmouth v France* (1887)
19 QBD 647, DC.
8. It was contended on behalf of the society as follows. (1) The screens were not parts
of the premises, but were rather chattels forming part of the contents of the premises.
h (2) They were not normal appurtenances of any premises, such as light fittings, but on
the contrary were specially designed for the society's premises, and were only suitable to
be used in the society's premises. (3) The screens were indistinguishable in principle
from the high-level fascia signs and projecting signs affixed to the society's premises,
which were admitted to be plant. (4) The screens were designed to perform and did
perform several functions in connection with the society's trade. To perform a function
i it was not necessary for a chattel to contain moving parts or to be the subject of physical
handling or use. (5) It followed that on the basis of the criteria laid down in the
authorities the screens were plant, and the appeal should be allowed.
9. It was contended on behalf of the Crown as follows. (1) The screens fixed in the
society's offices were part of the setting in which the society's business was carried on
rather than apparatus with which it was carried on. (2) The screens did not qualify to be
regarded as plant or machinery and allowances were not therefore due under ss 41 and

42 of the Finance Act 1971. (3) The corporation tax assessment should be determined
for the year ending 30 September 1975 at £5,179,977.

10. The commissioners who heard the appeal came to the following conclusion:

'... the screens on which the expenditure claimed had been incurred were part
of the setting in which the Society's business was carried on and did not perform
any function in connection with the said business and accordingly we held that the
expenditure was not incurred in the provision of plant for the purposes of the trade.
We determined the Appeal against the assessment in the sum of £5,179,977.'

11. Immediately after the determination of the appeal the society expressed
dissatisfaction therewith as being erroneous in point of law and required the
commissioners to state a case for the opinion of the High Court pursuant to s 56 of the
Taxes Management Act 1970.

12. The question of law for the opinion of the High Court was whether, on the facts
found by them and set out in the case, the commissioners were entitled to reach the
decision set out in para 10 above.

Andrew Park QC and *John Gardiner QC* for the society.
Robert Carnwath for the Crown.

GOULDING J. This is an appeal from a decision of the General Commissioners for the
Leeds division. Those commissioners in 1979 heard and determined an appeal by the
Leeds Permanent Building Society (which I shall refer to simply as 'the society'), against
an assessment to corporation tax for the year ending 30 September 1975. The
commissioners decided that appeal in favour of the Crown and the society now appeals
by way of case stated to this court.

The question before the commissioners was whether expenditure by the society in
respect of certain articles in the form of screens, which the society places in the windows
of its branch offices, qualified for a capital allowance as being expenditure incurred by
the society in the provision of plant for the purpose of the society's business. The relevant
statutory provision is in the Finance Act 1971, where s 41(1) enacts as follows:

'Subject to the provisions of this Chapter, where—(a) a person carrying on a trade
incurs capital expenditure on the provision of machinery or plant for the purposes
of the trade, and (b) in consequence of his incurring the expenditure, the machinery
or plant belongs to him at some time during the chargeable period related to the
incurring of the expenditure, there shall be made to him for that period an allowance
(in this Chapter referred to as "a first-year allowance") which shall be of an amount
determined in accordance with section 42 below . . .'

and the effect of s 42 for the relevant period was that a first-year allowance should be
equal to the whole of the expenditure in respect of which it was made.

The appeal, as argued before the commissioners and here, turns simply on the
interpretation of the statutory word 'plant' in relation to the screens on which the society
had made the expenditure in question. The commissioners hearing the appeal visited a
number of the society's branch offices to see examples of the screens which the society
had acquired. They found that they were for the most part of five distinct types as regards
construction and appearance, but it is common ground that nothing turns on the variety
displayed by the articles.

Among the facts found by the commissioners were the following: It is the practice of
the society to install decorative screens incorporating the society's name and sometimes
its crest in the windows of its branch offices. 'Crest' I think should be interpreted in a
broad sense as including the whole coat of arms of the society. The commissioners
further found that as a building society the society needs to attract investment money
and now has to be very competitive to obtain funds and considers it important that the
public should be attracted into its branch offices. After the end of the war in 1945

competition intensified and the society decided that the appearance of its offices must be
made more attractive as it needed more and more investors to satisfy the ever-growing
demand for mortgages. Later, in the late 1950s, the society decided that its shopfronts
were still not, in the words of the commissioners, 'eye-catching enough'. Accordingly a
new design with a free-standing low screen inside the window was introduced in place
of the boxed-in style of shopfront previously employed. It is those low screens which are
the subject matter of the litigation.

The screens, as the commissioners found, are now highly decorative; all still contain
the society's name in a prominent position and their purpose is still the same. They do
not however make any specific reference to the nature of the society's business or to the
particular advantages which it offers to its customers. Their sizes vary to match the shop
frontage, which is usually at eye height, about 4 ft 6 in, and generally covering 80% to
90% of the available width of the window. The society tries to make its branches as much
like retail shops as possible. The purpose of the screens is to attract the attention of the
passer-by; then the passer-by may notice the society's display cards, giving particulars of
investments and other facilities offered by the society, placed in front of or beside them.
The screens are attached by screws or placed in slots. They are therefore readily removable
and can be replaced. They are also capable of being repositioned in the same office or
elsewhere, but this is only rarely done. All screens are individually made for particular
premises and many of the screens are individually designed to attract local people.

The society, so the commissioners found, considers that there is no specific evidence as
to the effect of the screens as they form part of its general advertising policy. They are
however a very important part of the society's visual presentation of its branches together
with the high-level fascia signs and projecting signs. The average life of a screen is 10 to
15 years, after which it is usually scrapped although occasionally some are moved to an
agent's office or another branch office and sometimes the inserts in the screen are moved
or changed round. When the society vacates any of its premises it always removes the
screens as well as the fascia signs and any projecting signs, unlike electric wiring and light
fittings which always remain. Occasionally the society might sell the office counter and
fitments to the new occupier but never the screens in the window.

The commissioners stated in their case that the society considers the screens serve five
main purposes. Three of those are advertising purposes, attracting the attention of the
public in one way or another, one was to preserve some degree of privacy for those doing
business inside and the fifth was to provide a minor security function by shielding the
society's activities and cash it receives from public gaze. It was common ground before
the commissioners that the high-level fascia signs and the projecting signs used at the
society's branch offices were plant qualifying for capital allowance.

That will be a sufficient extract for the purpose of this judgment from the facts as
found by the commissioners. They gave their decision concisely in the following
sentence:

'WE the Commissioners who heard the Appeal came to the conclusion that the
screens on which the expenditure claimed had been incurred were part of the setting
in which the Society's business was carried on and did not perform any function in
connection with the said business and accordingly we held that the expenditure was
not incurred in the provision of plant for the purposes of the trade.'

It is from that decision that the society now appeals.

I shall not conduct yet another review of the numerous reported authorities on the
meaning of the word 'plant' in this context, although it will be necessary for me to refer
to particular passages in several. On the general principles of the law all I need say is, first,
that the classicial statement regarding the word 'plant', which has never been disapproved
of and has repeatedly been applied, is that of Lindley LJ in *Yarmouth v France* (1887) 19
QBD 647 at 658. It was a decision in fact not on a revenue question but on the Employers'
Liability Act 1880 and the Lord Justice said:

'There is no definition of plant in the Act: but, in its ordinary sense, it includes
whatever apparatus is used by a business man for carrying on his business,—not his   *a*
stock-in-trade which he buys or makes for sale; but all goods and chattels, fixed or
moveable, live or dead, which he keeps for permanent employment in his business
. . .'

Second, in applying that conception of the apparatus used by a businessman for carrying
on his business, it was found convenient to draw a distinction between the setting in
which a business is carried on and the apparatus with which a business is carried on,   *b*
though subsequent developments have shown that there are overlapping cases where the
distinction is not in itself decisive because one object may partake of both characters.
Leaving those overlapping cases to one side, that which is the setting in which the trader
performs his trade is not plant; the apparatus with which he performs it is plant.

An early example of that distinction is to be found in *J Lyons & Co Ltd v A-G* [1944] 1
All ER 477, [1944] Ch 281. That was a case relating to the war damage legislation in the   *c*
1939–45 war. The articles in question were electric lamps for the lighting of a tea-shop.
Uthwatt J decided the case. He put on one side nine lamps, being six counter lamps, two
lamps directly over the service bar, and the window lamp, because he thought they
might stand in a different position from the other lamps as they might be connected
with the needs of a particular trade carried on on the premises. Of all the rest he said this   *d*
([1944] 1 All ER 477 at 479–480, [1944] Ch 281 at 287):

'In the present case, the question at issue may, I think, be put thus: Are the lamps
and fitments properly to be regarded as part of the setting in which the business is
carried on, or as part of the apparatus used for carrying on the business? In this case
the lamps and their fitments are owned by a caterer and used in premises exclusively
devoted to catering purposes. But the presence of lamps in this building is not   *e*
dictated by the nature of the particular trade there carried on, or by the fact that it is
for trade purposes that the building is used. Lamps are required to enable the
building to be used where natural light is insufficient. The actual lamps themselves,
so far as the evidence goes, present no special feature either in construction, purpose
or position and, being supplied with electricity from public suppliers, they form no
part of an electric lighting plant in or on the hereditament. In my opinion, these   *f*
lamps are not, in these circumstances, properly described as "plant," but are part of
the general setting in which the business is carried on.'

Third, the use of the distinction between setting and apparatus for the purpose of
identifying plant has led to the growth, to deal with difficult or borderline cases, of what
has been called the functional test. It is conveniently and shortly expressed by Oliver LJ
in *Cole Bros Ltd v Phillips (Inspector of Taxes)* [1981] STC 671 at 677 where he said: *g*

'. . . it seems to me that the authorities, with one possible exception, demonstrate
that the question (however expressed) which the court must ask itself is whether the
particular subject matter under consideration either itself performs, or is a necessary
or integral part of that which performs, simply and solely the function of "housing"
the business or whether, as its sole function or as an additional function, it performs   *h*
some other distinct business purpose.'

On the same topic I refer also to the report of the same case of *Cole Bros Ltd v Phillips
(Inspector of Taxes)* [1982] 2 All ER 247 at 251 in the House of Lords where Lord
Hailsham LC said:

'If "plant" is to be contrasted with the place in which the business is carried on,   *j*
the line must be drawn somewhere . . . There must therefore be a criterion (or
criteria) by which the courts define the frontier between the two. Thus arises the
analysis of the function in the authorities . . . If the plant is to be distinguished from
the housing of the plant ("the place where the business is carried on" as distinct from
the means by which it is to be carried on) it is necessary before it is possible to decide

a   whether the disputed object is apparatus or not to look at it in order to see what it is and then consider what, in the context of the business actually being carried on, is its function.'

A week earlier in another appeal on the same topic decided by the House of Lords, that of *IRC v Scottish and Newcastle Breweries Ltd* [1982] 2 All ER 230 at 233, [1982] 1 WLR 322 at 325, Lord Wilberforce had said:

b   'Another much used test word is "functional". This is useful as expanding the notion of "apparatus"; it was used by Lord Reid in *IRC v Barclay Curle & Co Ltd* [1969] 1 All ER 732, [1969] 1 WLR 675. But this, too, must be considered, in itself, as inconclusive. Functional for what? Does the item serve a functional purpose in providing a setting? Or one for use in the trade? . . . In the end each case must be resolved, in my opinion, by considering carefully the nature of the particular trade
c   being carried on, and the relation of the expenditure to the promotion of the trade.'

Those I think are sufficient examples from authority to indicate the established principles on this subject.

Counsel for the society, proceeded to examine the particular articles in question. He said that these screens are movable chattels. They are not parts of the buildings in which
d   they are used. They are not standard appurtenances of those buildings. They are special to the society, bearing its name and often its heraldic device. They are individually designed for each branch office of the society. They are taken away by the society when it vacates the branch office. They perform a business function, namely attracting custom to the branch offices. They are indistinguishable for this purpose, in counsel's submission, from the fascia boards and projecting signs used to proclaim the identity of the society's offices which are, or were treated before the commissioners as being, confessedly plant.
e   On that basis of fact as found by the commissioners counsel for the society submitted that the screens are, for the purpose of the legislation in question, certainly plant. In Lindley LJ's words he said they are chattels which the society keeps for permanent employment in its business; in Uthwatt J's words they are part of the apparatus used for carrying on the business and not part of the general setting in which the business is
f   carried on; and in Oliver LJ's words they are not a necessary or integral part of that which performs simply and solely the functions of housing the business but they do perform some other distinct business purpose, namely that of attracting the public.

Such, as I understand them, are the submissions made on behalf of the society.

Counsel for the Crown has submitted arguments which, as I have recorded them, really fall under three heads. First of all he emphasises, and rightly emphasises, that the appellate function of this court under the Taxes Management Act 1970 is confined to the
g   correction of decisions erroneous in point of law. Matters of fact are for the commissioners and are finally decided by their own opinion.

I can conveniently amplify that point by reference to the speech of Lord Lowry in the *Scottish and Newcastle Breweries* case [1982] 2 All ER 230 at 234, [1982] 1 WLR 322 at 327, where his Lordship propounded five points as follows:

h   '(1) it is a question of law what meaning is to be given to the word "plant", and it is for the courts to interpret its meaning, having regard to the context in which it occurs; (2) the law does not supply a definition of plant or prescribe a detailed or exhaustive set of rules for application to any particular set of circumstances, and there are cases which, on the facts found, are capable of decision either way; (3) a decision in such a case is a decision on a question of fact and degree and cannot be
j   upset as being erroneous in point of law unless the commissioners show by some reason they give or statement they make in the case stated that they have misunderstood or misapplied the law in some relevant particular; (4) the commissioners err in point of law when they make a finding which there is no evidence to support; (5) the commissioners may also err by reaching a conclusion which is inconsistent with the facts which they have found.'

Lord Lowry then referred to the well known passage by Lord Radcliffe in *Edwards
(Inspector of Taxes) v Bairstow* [1955] 3 All ER 48 at 58, [1956] AC 14 at 36.   *a*

If one looks here at the sentence expressing the decision of the commissioners, where
they found that the screens were part of the setting in which the society's business was
carried on and did not perform any function in connection with the business and
accordingly were not plant, it is clear that (although not explicit) the proposition of law
accepted by the commissioners is that an article which is part of the setting in which a
business is carried on and does not perform any function in connection with the business   *b*
cannot be plant. That proposition, said counsel for the Crown, is clearly right on the
authorities. The rest, the findings that these screens were part of the setting and did not
perform any function in connection with the business, he would say are findings of fact
and I cannot interfere with them because they do not disclose any error of law. I shall of
course return to that later, but for the moment I will continue with the other ways in
which counsel for the Crown put his case.   *c*

The second branch of his submissions was founded on the judgment of Buckley LJ, an
expository judgment, as Lord Hailsham LC said of it with evident approval in *Cole Bros
Ltd v Phillips* [1982] 2 All ER 247 at 254, in *Benson (Inspector of Taxes) v Yard Arm Club Ltd*
[1979] 2 All ER 336, [1979] 1 WLR 347. That was a case relating to a floating vessel,
called the Hispaniola, kept alongside the Victoria Embankment in London and used for
the purpose of a restaurant. The General Commissioners in that case considered that the   *d*
vessel was plant for the purposes of claiming a capital allowance. They were held to be
wrong by this court and again in the Court of Appeal. To do justice to counsel for the
Crown's argument I must read some passages from what Buckley LJ there said. After
referring to several of the reported cases, his Lordship continued ([1979] 2 All ER 336 at
342–344, [1979] 1 WLR 347 at 354–356):

> 'In all these cases the court had regard to the use which was made of the subject-   *e*
> matter under consideration. To an extent this was necessitated by the statutes, for to
> qualify for capital allowances the subject-matter must have been provided "for the
> purposes of the trade". This, however, is not the end of the matter, for stock-in-trade
> is provided for the purposes of the trade but is admittedly not "plant". The building
> in which a business is carried on may accurately be described as "provided for the
> purposes of the business", but again admittedly is not for that reason alone to be   *f*
> held to be plant. A structure attached to the soil may be plant. The dry dock in
> *Inland Revenue Comrs v Barclay Curle & Co Ltd* [1969] 1 All ER 732, [1969] 1 WLR
> 675 was such, as also were the pools in *Cooke (Inspector of Taxes) v Beach Station
> Caravans Ltd* [1974] 3 All ER 159, [1974] 1 WLR 1398. On the other hand, a
> structure of the nature of a building which was not attached to the soil was held not
> to be plant in *St John's School (Mountford and Knibbs) v Ward (Inspector of Taxes)* [1974]   *g*
> STC 69; *affd* [1975] STC 7. The distinction, I think, is that in the one case the
> structure is something by means of which the business activities are in part carried
> on; in the other case the structure plays no part in the carrying on of those activities,
> but is merely the place within which they are carried on. So, in the case at any rate
> of a subject-matter which is a building or some other kind of structure, regard must   *h*
> be paid to the way in which it is used to discover whether it can or cannot be
> properly described as plant. This is what has been referred to as the functional test.
> Indeed I think that this test is applicable to every kind of subject-matter. In some
> cases the effect of the functional test may be so immediately apparent that the
> character of the subject-matter as plant goes without saying and the test need not be
> consciously applied. But in cases nearer the line, in my opinion, the functional test   *j*
> provides the criterion to be applied. Is the subject-matter the apparatus, or part of
> the apparatus, employed in carrying on the activities of the business? If it is, it is no
> matter that it consists of some structure attached to the soil. If it is not part of the
> apparatus so employed, it is not plant, whatever its characteristics may be. [Buckley
> LJ examined a particular authority and argument based on it, and continued:] The
> General Commissioners decided the present case on the analogy of the pools in *Cooke*

(*Inspector of Taxes*) v *Beach Station Caravans Ltd*. In my judgment Megarry J was clearly right in regarding the pools in that case as part of the apparatus employed in carrying on the caravan site business; the pools as a whole, and not merely their mechanical parts, provided an attractive service or amenity for patrons of the caravan site; they were part of the facilities provided for patrons and as such formed part of the commercial activity of the business. That part of the taxpayer's enterprise could not have been carried on by the use of the mechanical parts alone unassociated with the structure of the pools, which was consequently an essential part of the apparatus or equipment employed in the business. In my judgment, the same cannot be said of the vessel in the present case. The business of the company is that of restaurateurs, that is to say, the preparation and service of meals to the public, as well, no doubt, as the sale of alcoholic liquors and other beverages. Such a business must, at least in our climate, be conducted in the shelter of a building of some kind. It is not disputed that, if such a business were carried on in the normal way in a building attached to the soil, the building would not constitute plant; it would be no more than the structure within which the business was carried on. Why is the vessel in the present case anything other than the structure within which the company's business is carried on? Counsel for the taxpayer company has of course laid stress on the fact that, as he says, the business is not that of merely a restaurant, but that of a floating restaurant. No doubt the fact that it is situated on the river is an attraction to patrons, and that it has the appearance of being a ship may also be an attractive feature. The commissioners found that patrons came to the vessel "to get good food, somewhere different with views of the river etc, and a shipboard feeling". But these features do not differ in quality from the advantages of having a restaurant in a building on dry land which enjoys an attractive view over countryside or a lake or, as in the case of the restaurant at the top of the Post Office Tower, over a great city. They may serve to attract custom, but they play no part in the conducting of the business. The circumstance that the use of a particular building is commercially desirable to enable the taxpayer to conduct his business profitably does not import that the building is part of the apparatus used for carrying on the business; it merely imports that that building is a good venue at which to carry on the business: see in this connection the observations of Brightman J in *Dixon (Inspector of Taxes) v Fitch's Garage Ltd* [1975] 3 All ER 455, [1976] 1 WLR 215.'

From those passages counsel for the Crown expresses two propositions: first, the attracting of customers is not of itself a sufficient business function to stamp an article as plant; and, second, the functional test is applicable to every kind of subject matter. Accordingly, he says, the function of the screens here has to be judged in the same way as the function of the floating vessel in *Benson's* case. Here, as there, the function of the article is in substance simply to attract customers. Accordingly, like the Hispaniola, the screens are not plant.

The third branch of counsel for the Crown's submissions consisted of a proposition which he had composed in order to reconcile, as he submitted, the decisions in a number of authoritative cases on their particular facts. The proposition was this: that items used to make the setting of a business more attractive do not satisfy the functional test so as to qualify as plant unless either the provision of an attractive setting is itself found to be part of the trade processes or alternatively the item or form of the attraction is dictated by the nature of the trade processes. That proposition he submitted as reconciling a number of authorities otherwise difficult to subsume under a single rule, and having set it up he submitted that in the present case the provision of the screens as an attractive setting was no part of the trade of obtaining investments from the public and lending money on mortgage, nor did those activities in any way determine the appearance or form of the screens. Therefore they were not plant.

I am unable to accept those respective contentions by counsel for the Crown and I will examine them now under the three heads in which I cited them. First of all, as to the fundamental question whether the commissioners can be said to have committed any

error of law, I agree with counsel that the implicit proposition of law is correct, namely
that an article which is part of the setting of a business and does not perform any function *a*
in connection with the business is not plant; but, given that proposition, in my judgment
the determination which the commissioners arrived at is not consistent with the facts
which they have found. In the sense in which the word 'setting' is used in the authorities
the facts do not show, and there is nothing in them to my mind that tends to show, that
these screens are part of the setting. They are not part of or inseparably annexed to the
structure of the branch office. They are not capable of use without considerable *b*
modification for any business but that of the society and indeed some of them are of such
a character that they are really only of use in the particular branch. As found by the
commissioners, they are removed by the society when it leaves a branch office and are
designed specifically for the society's business. The facts found go in my judgment to
identify the screens as part of the shop furniture with which the trade of the society is
carried on in a branch office. Accordingly, the finding that the screens are part of the *c*
setting is to my mind an inference which the primary facts do not support and show
plainly to be wrong. Similarly, a statement that the screens did not perform any function
in connection with the business contradicts what the commissioners have themselves
found, that their purpose is to attract the attention of the passer-by and so bring business
to the society.

Where the tribunal, starting with a correct idea of the law, reaches conclusions *d*
inconsistent with the facts which it has found on the evidence, it does commit an error
in point of law. In my view, on the legal principle recognised by the commissioners and
the facts as found by them, only one conclusion was possible and it is not that to which
the commissioners have come. Accordingly, in my judgment they have erred in point
of law.

Now I come to the particular argument based on Buckley LJ's judgment in the *Benson* *e*
case. The fallacy of that argument in my view is that when Buckley LJ said, as he did,
that the functional test was applicable to every kind of subject matter, he did not say and
did not mean that it was to be applied to any and every item used in a business without
regard to the character of the item and its relation to the particular business. Counsel for
the Crown himself shrank from saying that no article whose function was advertising to
attract customers to a business could rank as plant for the purpose of capital allowance. *f*
Yet, so far as I can see, that must logically be the effect of his submissions. The farthest he
went in that direction was to hint that perhaps the Commissioners of Inland Revenue
might not hitherto have taken full advantage of the law.

Let me just go back for a moment to the *Benson* case. What Buckley LJ said of the
functional test was ([1979] 2 All ER 336 at 343–345, [1979] 1 WLR 347 at 355–357):

> 'I . . . think that this test is applicable to every kind of subject-matter. In some *g*
> cases the effect of the functional test may be so immediately apparent that the
> character of the subject-matter as plant goes without saying and the test need not be
> consciously applied . . . They may serve to attract custom, but they play no part in
> the conducting of the business. [The pronoun there referred back to the facts that
> patrons came to the vessel to get good food and a shipboard feeling, and his
> conclusion was this:] . . . I have reached the conclusion that on the facts found in *h*
> this case the vessel and the barge, although chattels and although used in connection
> with the business of the taxpayer company as restaurateurs, were not part of the
> apparatus employed in the commercial activities of those businesses, but were the
> structure within which the business was carried on.'

So that while he applies the functional test he applies it with considerable regard to the *j*
subject matter and the underlying distinction between setting and apparatus.

Similarly, Shaw LJ in the same case said ([1979] 2 All ER 336 at 346, [1979] 1 WLR
347 at 358):

> 'The context of the subject-matter which is said to be plant cannot be ignored,

a

and this is made plain by the citation from Lindley LJ's definition. Although because of its buoyancy the Hispaniola hulk was used to make a floating restaurant possible, it cannot merely for that reason be regarded as apparatus which achieved that result. It was, in actuality, restaurant premises which by a conjunction of construction and situation, rode on the water instead of standing on land. If the hulk were obliterated, there would be no business of a restaurant left at all; there would not survive any restaurant floating or not. A characteristic of plant appears to me to be that it is an adjunct to the carrying on of a business and not the essential site or core of the business itself.'

b

The third member of the court, Templeman LJ, said ([1979] 2 All ER 336 at 348, [1979] 1 WLR 347 at 360–361):

c

'It plainly appears, therefore, that if, and only if, land, premises or structures in addition to their primary purpose perform the function of plant, in that they are the means by which a trading operation is carried out, then for the purposes of income tax and corporation tax the land, premises or structures are treated as plant. It is quite true, as junior counsel for the taxpayer company in the present case forcefully submitted, that the authorities do not illustrate the converse proposition, namely that if a chattel capable of being plant in many circumstances, only performs the function of premises by providing accommodation for a business and does not perform any function in carrying on that business, then such a chattel is not plant. But in my judgment this proposition must hold good. If land, premises or structures operate as the means by which a trading operation is carried out, then they rank as plant. If chattels are used as premises and are not part of the means by which the relevant trade is carried out, then those chattels do not rank as plant.'

d

e

That being the ratio decidendi of the *Benson* case, it seems to me to lend support to the argument of counsel for the society in the present case. In my judgment, using the respective words of the three different Lords Justices in their conclusions, the screens here were part of the apparatus employed in the commercial activities of the society's business and were not the structure within which the business was carried on. They were an adjunct to the carrying on of the business and not the essential site or core of business itself. They were not used as premises but were part of the means by which the relevant trade was carried out.

f

I am fortified in my notion that the *Benson* case is helpful to the society's argument rather than the Crown's by what is said about it by Lord Lowry in the *Scottish and Newcastle* case [1982] 2 All ER 230 at 240, [1982] 1 WLR 322 at 333. Of *Benson's* case he said:

g

'... the distinction is that the ship, although a chattel, was the *place in which* the trade was carried on and was therefore the equivalent of the various premises in which the present taxpayer company carry on their trade and not of the apparatus used as an adjunct of the trade carried on in those premises.' (Lord Lowry's emphasis.)

h

It is also instructive to notice what Lord Lowry said a little earlier ([1982] 2 All ER 230 at 238, [1982] 1 WLR 322 at 332):

'It is correct, as the Crown contends, that the setting, for example a beautiful house or garden, may attract custom and create atmosphere without being plant. That does not mean that a chattel or movables used (as part of the setting) to create atmosphere is *not* plant.'

j

Accordingly, once it is accepted that the functional test, though applicable to every kind of subject matter, is none the less applicable with due regard to the character of the subject matter and its relation to the business in question, I see no difficulty in distinguishing the society's screens from the ship Hispaniola.

Of the third branch of counsel for the Crown's argument I would say only this, that in my respectful view he does not use authority in the correct way. It is not, I think, legitimate to take a number of reported judgments and to establish inductively by comparing the facts and the decisions a complex proposition never itself enunciated by authority but tailored to the facts of a new case. The proper thing surely is to look at the statements of principle in the authorities and apply them directly to the case under scrutiny as I have, under the guidance of counsel, sought to do in the present case with the statements by Lindley LJ and the subsequent principal authorities.

On that test in my view the society's case prevails and the appeal must be allowed.

Appeal allowed.

Solicitors: *Kingsford Dorman* (for the society); *Solicitor of Inland Revenue.*

Nirmala Harlow   Barrister.

Standard Chartered Bank Ltd v Walker and another

COURT OF APPEAL, CIVIL DIVISION

LORD DENNING MR, WATKINS AND FOX LJJ

14, 15, 16, 17 JUNE 1982

Company – Receiver – Duty – Duty to guarantor of company's debts – Sale of company's assets – Receiver appointed by debenture holder selling company's assets to repay debt – Debenture providing that receiver deemed to be agent of company – Debenture holder instructing receiver to hold sale of assets as soon as possible and in consequence sale negligently conducted – Assets sold at undervalue – Whether receiver owing duty of care to guarantor in realising assets – Whether receiver acting as debenture holder's agent in realising assets.

In 1977 a company borrowed money from a bank on the security of a debenture which gave the bank a floating charge on the company's assets and empowered it on default of repayment on demand to appoint a receiver to take possession of the assets and to sell them. The debenture provided that the receiver was to be deemed to be the agent of the company. The bank also required the company's two directors (the guarantors) personally to guarantee the company's indebtedness to the bank up to a limit of £75,000, with interest thereon. In 1978 the company's business declined and by November 1980 its overdraft with the bank had increased to £80,000. In April 1981 the bank demanded repayment of the amount outstanding and on 6 November appointed a receiver under the debenture. There was evidence that the bank instructed the receiver to realise the company's assets as soon as possible and that in accordance with those instructions the receiver instructed an auctioneer to hold a sale of the company's stock as soon as possible. The guarantors claimed that in consequence of the bank's instructions the sale was held at the wrong time of the year, that it was poorly advertised and therefore poorly attended, and that the stock was sold for £42,800 which was considerably less than its real value. The amount realised was barely sufficient to cover the costs of realisation, and after payment of preferential creditors nothing remained to pay off the bank's overdraft. The bank issued a writ against the guarantors claiming the full amount of their guarantee (£75,000) together with interest, and applied for summary judgment under RSC Ord 14. The registrar made an order for summary judgment. On appeal by the guarantors, the judge upheld the order on the ground that any claim which the guarantors had in

a respect of the incompetent conduct of the sale lay against the receiver and not against the
   bank. The guarantors appealed to the Court of Appeal, submitting that they ought to be
   given leave to defend the bank's claim, on the grounds (i) that a receiver under a
   debenture owed to a guarantor of the debt secured by the debenture a duty to exercise
   reasonable care in realising the company's assets and (ii) that the receiver had acted as the
   agent of the bank, and not of the company, in realising the assets and therefore the bank
   was liable as principal for the receiver's negligence in conducting the sale.

b
   Held – The appeal would be allowed for the following reasons—
       (1) The duty of care owed by the receiver of a company under a debenture in disposing
   of the company's assets was owed not only to the company but also to a guarantor of the
   company's liability under the debenture, since the liability of the guarantor depended on
   the amount which was realised by the assets and he was therefore within the test of
c sufficient proximity to the receiver for him to owe the guarantor a duty to use reasonable
   care to obtain the best possible price in the circumstances (see p 942 g to j, p 943 d e,
   p 944 a f and p 945 e, post); Barclays Bank Ltd v Thienel (1978) 247 EG 385 and Latchford v
   Beirne [1981] 3 All ER 705 disapproved.
       (2) On the evidence filed, there were triable issues of law and fact, namely (a) whether
   the bank could be liable for the conduct of the receivership, (b) whether the bank had
d interfered, by giving instructions to the receiver, in the conduct of the receivership in
   respect of the sale of the company's assets, so as to make the receiver its agent, and (c)
   whether the receiver had been negligent in the conduct of the sale so that the bank, on
   the basis of principal and agent, was liable for his negligence. The guarantors would
   therefore be given unconditional leave to defend the bank's claim (see p 943 f to j, p 944
   a and c to f and p 945 c to g, post).

e
   Notes
   For the effect of appointment of a receiver, see 7 Halsbury's Laws (4th edn) para 880.
       For a receiver's liability, see ibid para 886, and for cases on the subject, see 10 Digest
   (Reissue) 881–882, 5098–5106.

f **Cases referred to in judgments**
   Anns v Merton London Borough [1977] 2 All ER 492, [1978] AC 728, [1977] 2 WLR 1024,
       HL, Digest (Cont Vol E) 451, 99b.
   Barclays Bank Ltd v Thienel (1978) 247 EG 385.
   Cuckmere Brick Co Ltd v Mutual Finance Ltd [1971] 2 All ER 633, [1971] Ch 949, [1971] 2
       WLR 1207, CA, 1(2) Digest (Reissue) 914, 5941.
g Donoghue (or M'Alister) v Stevenson [1932] AC 562, [1932] All ER Rep 1, HL, 36(1) Digest
       (Reissue) 144, 562.
   Gillespie Bros & Co Ltd v Roy Bowles Transport Ltd [1973] 1 All ER 193, [1973] QB 400,
       [1972] 3 WLR 1003, CA, 8(1) Digest (Reissue) 53, 300.
   Gosling v Gaskell [1897] AC 575, [1895–9] All ER Rep 300, HL; rvsg [1896] 1 QB 669, 10
       Digest (Reissue) 876, 5072.
h Home Office v Dorset Yacht Co Ltd [1970] 2 All ER 294, [1970] AC 1004, [1970] 2 WLR
       1140, HL, 36(1) Digest (Reissue) 27, 93.
   Latchford v Beirne [1981] 3 All ER 705.

   Cases also cited
   Brown (S) & Son (General Warehousemen) Ltd, Re [1940] 3 All ER 638, [1940] Ch 961.
j Eastern Counties Building Society v Russell [1947] 2 All ER 734, CA.
   Farrar v Farrars Ltd (1888) 40 Ch D 395, CA.
   Henry Roach Petroleum Pty Ltd v Credit House (Vic) Pty Ltd [1976] VR 309.
   Kennedy v De Trafford [1897] AC 180, [1895–9] All ER Rep 408, HL.
   Mercantile Credit v Edge [1969] CA Transcript 221.
   Miles v Bull [1968] 3 All ER 632, [1969] 1 QB 258.
   Mutual Loan Fund Association v Sudlow (1858) 5 CBNS 449, 141 ER 183.

Pendlebury v Colonial Mutual Life Assurance Society Ltd (1912) 13 CLR 676.
TC Trustees Ltd v J S Darwen (Successors) Ltd [1969] 1 All ER 271, [1969] 2 QB 295, CA.   *a*
Taylor v Bank of New South Wales (1886) 11 App Cas 596, PC.
Tomlin v Luce (1889) 43 Ch D 191, CA.
Wood, Re [1940] 4 All ER 306, [1941] Ch 112.
Wulff v Jay (1872) LR 7 QB 756.

Interlocutory appeal   *b*

The defendants, Johnny Walker and his wife Greta Gloria Walker (the guarantors), who had guaranteed up to the limit of £75,000 the liabilities under a debenture of a company, Johnny Walker (Developments) Ltd, appealed against the order of Bristow J made on 14 January 1982 affirming the order of Mr Deputy Registrar Sykes made in the Bristol District Registry on 1 July 1981 giving leave to the plaintiffs, Standard Chartered Bank Ltd (the bank), which was the debenture holder, to sign summary judgment under RSC *c* Ord 14 against the guarantors in the sum of £77,712·16, following a written demand made by the bank on 3 April 1981 that the company repay the amount owing to the bank and the subsequent failure of the company to make repayment. The grounds of the appeal were (i) that the judge was wrong in law in holding that the bank as debenture holder owed no duty of care towards the guarantors in respect of the disposal of the company's assets by the receiver appointed under the debenture and (ii) in the alternative, *d* that the judge was wrong in law in holding that the receiver was not to be regarded as the bank's agent for the purpose of conducting the sale of the company's assets. The facts are set out in the judgment of Lord Denning MR.

Michael Lyndon-Stanford QC and *David G M Marks* for Mr and Mrs Walker.
John Lindsay QC and *John Higham* for the bank.   *e*

LORD DENNING MR. When a bank lends money to a private company, it usually insists on the overdraft being guaranteed by the directors personally; especially when a husband and wife are the directors and shareholders of the company. Then, when the company crashes and is unable to meet its liabilities, the bank puts in a receiver. He realises the assets of the company. But not enough to pay off the overdraft. The bank *f* then comes down on the directors on the guarantee. Have they any defence? The directors here say that the assets were sold at a gross undervalue. How far does that give them any defence?

The directors here are Johnny Walker and his wife Gloria. They have been concerned with several private companies using the name 'Johnny Walker', but nothing to do with whisky. We are here concerned with the latest one, John Walker (Developments) Ltd. *g* They carried on a very specialised business. They had a large workshop and warehouse in Gloucestershire. It was called Vortex Works at Tetbury. They bought huge metal presses and moulding machines secondhand and stored them there. They resold them to buyers all over the world. They did it on money borrowed from the Standard Chartered Bank. The bank insisted on a debenture. It was dated 25 October 1977. It gave the bank a fixed and floating charge on the assets of the company. It gave the bank power to appoint a *h* receiver who was to have power to take possession of the assets and to sell them. It contained an express provision:

   'Any receiver or receivers so appointed shall be deemed to be the agent or agents of the Company and the Company shall be solely responsible for his or their acts or defaults and for his or their remuneration.'   *j*

The bank also insisted on a personal guarantee by Johnny Walker and his wife. It was dated 12 December 1978. It guaranteed the payment by the company of all its indebtedness to the bank provided that the total amount recoverable from Johnny Walker and his wife was not to exceed £75,000 together with interest thereon.

From 1978 onwards the business was badly hit by the slump in trade which was

worldwide. In order to meet wages, rent and other expenses, the company incurred a
a large overdraft. At one time it was over £275,000. The bank pressed the company to
reduce it. They took stringent measures. They cut down the staff greatly and reduced
expenses on all sides. By April 1980 the overdraft had got down to £65,751. The bank
urged its further reduction to £50,000. Johnny Walker constantly told them of his
efforts. He told them of the sales he hoped to make. But, despite his efforts, the overdraft
went somewhat higher. The bank thought of appointing a receiver. On 1 September
b 1980 Johnny Walker wrote:

> 'To put a receiver in at the moment, when the company has done so well in
> streamlining itself, "digging it's heels in" and preparing to combat the recession,
> would mean, literally economic suicide ... If commonsense prevails and we are
> allowed to continue to trade, which I may add now is profitably so, it will not be
> long before we can reduce down within the £50,000 but it is going to take a little
c longer in time.'

Despite Johnny Walker's hopes, things got no better. They got rather worse. The
overdraft came to over £80,000. So much so that on 6 November 1980 the bank
appointed a receiver. He was Mr Heaford of the well-known firm of chartered
accountants, Touche Ross & Co of Bristol. Johnny Walker saw Mr Heaford and asked if
d he could continue to trade through another of his companies. The receiver said: 'As from
now, Mr Walker, you are out of business. My instructions are to be out of here as quickly
as possible', and that he intended to hold an auction sale as quickly as possible.
The receiver instructed well-known auctioneers Edward Rushton & Co. They
examined the stock and estimated that at an auction sale they might sell the whole of the
stock for £90,000. They proposed to hold the auction on 21 January 1981. Johnny
e Walker afterwards thought this was too soon and asked for it to be postponed. It was
then fixed for Wednesday, 4 February 1981 at the works at Tetbury.
The auctioneers got to work preparing for the auction. They numbered all the lots.
They made up a catalogue containing a description of all the machines. They did some
advertising.
On Wednesday, 4 February the auction was held. It was a disaster. Only about 70
f persons attended, nearly all from places round about, and only one buyer from overseas,
although the market for these machines was worldwide. It was a bitterly cold day. They
had a few heating stoves, but these made such a noise that the auctioneer could not make
himself heard. So they were turned off; and many prospective buyers left. The result in
outline was this.
The stock only realised £42,864. The expenses of realisation came to £42,718. That
g left hardly anything for the preferential creditors who came to £37,139. And nothing at
all for the bank whose debt was £88,432. So the result was a disaster for everyone. The
receiver had got enough to pay the expenses of the sale and so forth, but nothing for the
preferential creditors, and nothing for the bank.
Soon afterwards, on 8 April 1981 the bank issued a writ against Johnny Walker and
his wife as guarantors claiming the whole sum of £75,000 and interest at £30 a day.
h They issued a summons for judgment under RSC Ord 14. The registrar and the judge
gave judgment in favour of the bank. Johnny Walker and his wife appeal to this court.
It is interesting to see that the only affidavit put in by the bank throughout was the
formal affidavit under Ord 14, which just said that in their belief the defendant
guarantors were justly indebted in those sums. There were affidavits in answer. I will
not go into all of them. Mr Johnny Walker set out his defence. The bank never replied
j to his affidavits. I will read a passage from one of his affidavits. He said:

> 'It is apparent from the Affidavits referred to that the prices achieved at auction
> were much lower than could reasonably have been expected and, indeed, were less
> than half of the conservative valuation made by the Auctioneer. There were many
> reasons for this. The main reasons are, in my opinion, that the auction was held at

the wrong time of the year, that it was insufficiently advertised, that no notice was
given to the prospective customers on my Company's mailing list by direct mailing, *a*
that the viewing arrangements were inadequate and the attendance poor . . . It will
be apparent that the decision by the Receiver to hold an auction quickly and without
adequate publicity was taken by him as a result of an instruction received from the
[bank]. Messrs Touche Ross & Company of Bristol made a Report to the [bank] on
the financial affairs of [the company] on 20th October 1980. At about that time, I
had a telephone conversation with Roger Bailey who was then the Manager of the *b*
Branch of the [bank] in Bristol. Mr. Bailey told me during the conversation that the
Bank had already made provision to write off the entire . . . overdraft as a bad debt,
that the [bank] had decided to appoint a Receiver under its debenture and that the
Receiver would be instructed to sell off the stock of [the company] as quickly as
possible so that the [bank] could recover quickly some of the loss incurred from
writing off the overdraft of [the company].'   *c*

   As I read that defence, it contains an allegation that the assets of the company were
sold at a gross undervalue: and, if reasonable care had been taken all the way through,
they could have been realised at a much higher value; probably double, if not more,
maybe up to £130,000; in which case, the company's debt would have been very much
reduced. In consequence the guaranteed figure of £75,000 would have been reduced *d*
greatly. Such are the facts of the case.
   We have had much discussion on the law. So far as mortgages are concerned the law is
set out in *Cuckmere Brick Co Ltd v Mutual Finance Ltd* [1971] 2 All ER 633, [1971] Ch 949.
If a mortgagee enters into possession and realises a mortgaged property, it is his duty to
use reasonable care to obtain the best possible price which the circumstances of the case
permit. He owes this duty not only to himself (to clear off as much of the debt as he can) *e*
but also to the mortgagor so as to reduce the balance owing as much as possible, and also
to the guarantor so that he is made liable for as little as possible on the guarantee. This
duty is only a particular application of the general duty of care to your neighbour which
was stated by Lord Atkin in *Donoghue v Stevenson* [1932] AC 562, [1932] All ER Rep 1 and
applied in many cases since: see *Home Office v Dorset Yacht Co Ltd* [1970] 2 All ER 294,
[1970] AC 1004 and *Anns v Merton London Borough* [1977] 2 All ER 492, [1978] AC 728. *f*
The mortgagor and the guarantor are clearly in very close 'proximity' to those who
conduct the sale. The duty of care is owing to them, if not to the general body of creditors
of the mortgagor. There are several dicta to the effect that the mortgagee can choose his
own time for the sale, but I do not think this means that he can sell at the worst possible
time. It is at least arguable that, in choosing the time, he must exercise a reasonable
degree of care.   *g*
   So far as the receiver is concerned, the law is well stated by Rigby LJ in *Gosling v Gaskell*
[1896] 1 QB 669, a dissenting judgment which was approved by the House of Lords (see
[1897] AC 575, [1895–9] All ER Rep 300). The receiver is the agent of the company, not
of the debenture holder, the bank. He owes a duty to use reasonable care to obtain the
best possible price which the circumstances of the case permit. He owes this duty not
only to the company (of which he is the agent) to clear off as much of its indebtedness to *h*
the bank as possible, but he also owes a duty to the guarantor, because the guarantor is
liable only to the same extent as the company. The more the overdraft is reduced, the
better for the guarantor. It may be that the receiver can choose the time of sale within a
considerable margin, but he should, I think, exercise a reasonable degree of care about it.
The debenture holder, the bank, is not responsible for what the receiver does except in so
far as it gives him directions or interferes with his conduct of the realisation. If it does so, *j*
then it too is under a duty to use reasonable care towards the company and the guarantor.
   If it should appear that the mortgagee or the receiver have not used reasonable care to
realise the assets to the best advantage, then the mortgagor, the company, and the
guarantor are entitled in equity to an allowance. They should be given credit for the
amount which the sale should have realised if reasonable care had been used. Their
indebtedness is to be reduced accordingly.

a   The only doubt on those propositions is cast by two cases at first instance. The first is *Barclays Bank Ltd v Thienel* (1978) 247 EG 385. It is only reported in the Estates Gazette, but we have been provided with a transcript of the judgment. That was a case of a mortgagee. The amount realised was only £6,500 to meet a debt of £11,000. The allegation on the part of the guarantor was that the sale was at a gross undervalue, and that there had been a want of care in the realisation. Thesiger J said that the guarantor could not rely on that want of care because of a very wide clause in the form of guarantee. b But it seems to me that, if a clause in a guarantee makes the guarantor liable for a larger sum than the mortgagor, that clause is unenforceable. The guarantor is only under a secondary obligation to guarantee the debt of the principal debtor. If the principal debtor's debt is reduced for good reason, equally the guarantor's obligation is reduced. If there is a term in the contract to the contrary, it should be rejected as being repugnant or unreasonable: see *Gillespie Bros & Co Ltd v Roy Bowles Transport Ltd* [1973] 1 All ER 193, c [1973] QB 400 and the cases cited therein. But nowadays we do not have to look at those cases. The Unfair Contract Terms Act 1977 applies to this contract. The terms of a contract are only good in so far as they are fair and reasonable. So I would reject Thesiger J's reliance on the contract.

    The second case is *Latchford v Beirne* [1981] 3 All ER 705. That was a case of a receiver. A debenture holder had put in a receiver. The receiver sold the property. Again the d guarantor sought to say that there had been want of reasonable care in the disposal of the assets. Milmo J went so far as to say that there was no duty of care towards the guarantor. He said that there was no duty of care towards the creditor. He treated the guarantor as though he was simply a creditor. I cannot agree with that either. Clearly the guarantor's liability is dependent on the company's. He is in a very special position. The amount of his liability depends entirely on the amount that the stock realises when sold with proper e care. To my mind he is well within the test of 'proximity'. The receiver owes a duty not only to the company, but to the guarantor, to exercise reasonable care in the disposal of the assets. I say nothing about creditors. We are not concerned with them today.

    Neither counsel before us sought to support the decisions in those two cases. In so far as those decisions hold that the guarantor is liable for a larger amount than the principal debtor they are erroneous and should not be followed. I am afraid that those cases may f have misled the bank in this case. That may be the reason why those who first advised the bank thought they need only rely on their own formal affidavit: and that they did not have to worry about all the affidavits put in on behalf of Mr and Mrs Walker. Putting those two cases on one side, it seems to me that on the facts of this case there are these triable issues:

    There is a triable issue whether or not the bank did interfere with the sale in such a g way as to take away some of the receiver's discretion, not only by directing him to sell as quickly as possible but also in regard to publicity and so forth. On reading the affidavit of Mr Walker it seems to me that, until there has been discovery, there is an arguable case for saying that the bank did interfere not only in the timing of the sale, but also in other respects. So the matter should be investigated to determine the liability of the bank.

h   I will not go into whether or not the receiver would be liable for any negligence of the auctioneer; but there is certainly a triable issue whether or not the sale was conducted with the proper degree of care which is owed to all those interested in the proceeds of it. It is clear that it was a disastrous sale which realised far less than any of the experts had anticipated. There is a triable issue whether that was due to any fault in the arrangements for the sale.

j   Those are triable issues of fact which ought to go for trial. There should be unconditional leave to defend. That being given, it is for the advisers of Mr and Mrs Walker to consider whether they should put in a counterclaim and bring in other parties to their counterclaim, the receiver and the auctioneers. They should consider whether they should make an application to put in a counterclaim. It is undesirable that there should be a subsequent action brought by Mr and Mrs Walker against the receiver or the auctioneers separately. All should be dealt with in one action.

All I would say at the moment is that, in my opinion, the appeal should be allowed with unconditional leave to defend; and the defendants should take such steps on the *a* pleadings and interlocutory matters as they are advised.

WATKINS LJ. The question before this court is whether the defendant guarantors, Mr and Mrs Walker, ought to have been granted leave firstly by the deputy registrar and secondly by Bristow J to defend the bank's claim which it sought successfully to bring to judgment under the RSC Ord 14 procedure.   *b*

The defendants' application for leave to defend was amply supported by affidavits especially when it was heard by the judge. The allegations contained in those affidavits were not replied to in any shape or form by the bank, which has contented itself throughout by seeking to defeat the application almost exclusively by legal arguments supported by such inferences arising out of the uncontested facts as it contended favoured it. This was, I think, a dangerous course for it to have adopted, seeing that the relevant *c* law to be applied to the issues arising here is to some extent unclear.

There are, in my opinion, three triable issues involved in this litigation. First, as to the state of the law governing the liability, if any, of a bank in any circumstances in the conduct of a receivership initiated by that bank. Second, in the present case, whether the bank so interfered in the receivership which it initiated so as to be liable both in law and in fact to have been responsible for the conduct of it. Third, whether there was negligence *d* shown by the auctioneers and possibly by the receivers in the conduct of the auction itself for which the bank, on the basis of principal and agent, can be said to be properly liable in damages provided that the defendants can show (and this too, of course, is a question of fact) that they have sustained damage for which they are entitled to be recompensed.

It would have been a simple matter for the bank to have replied in very short form by *e* affidavit to the central contention made by the defendants in this case, that contention being that the bank unwarrantably and inappropriately interfered in the receivership which it had set up by instructing the receivers to hold a quick action. From that much of the trouble, if not all of it, which eventually ensued is said to have flowed.

For the reasons provided by Lord Denning MR I too would allow this appeal with the consequences which he has stated.   *f*

FOX LJ. On the evidence which is before us it seems clear that the auction sale on 4 February 1981 was a sad failure. The auctioneers' prior estimate of the value of the assets was about £90,000. The sale fetched less than half that amount. Mr Walker, the first defendant, would say that the position is far worse than that since he regards £90,000 as being much too low anyway. Allowing for the fact that the two figures are possibly not *g* truly comparing like with like, nevertheless the defendants' evidence suggests that far more could have been realised.

That, however, does not impose liability on the bank. The sale is by the receiver under the debenture, and the debenture provided in terms that the receiver is the agent of the company and not of the bank. The defendants were perfectly well aware of the debenture when they gave the guarantee.   *h*

Two further matters, however, emerge from the evidence as it stands. First, there is evidence that the sale was incompetently organised. Thus Mr Fenton, the managing director of a Manchester engineering firm, said that in his opinion the sale was badly organised at short notice and received the minimum of publicity. Second, Mr Walker deposed that he had many conversations with the receiver's manager Mr Mallett, after the receiver was appointed, and protested at the haste with which the receiver was acting. *j* He said that during one of their conversations Mr Mallett told him that the receiver was acting throughout on the express instructions of the bank.

Apart from intervention in the conduct of receivership, the bank can rely on the provisions of the debenture making the receiver the agent of the company. But, it is said, if the bank gave directions to the receiver as to the conduct of the sale, the receiver a   became the agent of the bank; and, it is said, in such an event, if the receiver was negligent, the bank was liable. It is not disputed that a mortgagee can choose his own time for sale but, say the defendants, the sale must be a proper sale and must be properly organised. The auction, it is alleged, was nothing of the sort.

The bank has put in no evidence at all apart from a largely formal affidavit in support of the RSC Ord 14 summons. Counsel for the bank has told us of the circumstances in which the case developed, and he says that having regard to the lateness in which the

b   defendants put in their evidence on the previous hearing the bank decided not to answer it itself but to proceed on the evidence as it stood. I follow that, but nevertheless the fact remains that in the period between the decision of the judge and the hearing in this court the bank had ample time and the fullest opportunity to explain to the court exactly what instructions, if any, it gave to the receiver.

The evidence as it stands suggests that the receiver was acting on the directions of the

c   bank and that the bank at any rate directed the receiver to proceed with haste. That is the first thing. There is also on the evidence, it seems to me, a clear issue to be tried whether the sale was negligently conducted. But for present purposes there is then a gap, and one is left with the question, was the conduct of the auction the consequence of instructions from the bank? On the evidence, we do not know. The bank has given us no information about it at all. That is evidence which is peculiarly within the knowledge of the bank

d   and not of the defendants. It seems to me, as the evidence stands, that it is certainly a possibility that, if the auction was negligently conducted, it was the direct consequence of instructions by the bank to the receiver not merely to proceed with haste but as to the actual conduct of the sale. I think there is a triable issue as to that and that it would be wrong to prevent it from being fully investigated by the court on trial. I bear in mind that despite express allegations of interference the bank has filed no evidence.

e   That assumes that a surety could have a cause of action at all in such circumstances. I think that he could. I agree with Lord Denning MR in his view that the decisions in *Barclays Bank Ltd v Thienel* (1978) 247 EG 385 and in *Latchford v Beirne* [1981] 3 All ER 705 in so far as they decide, in principle, the contrary, cannot be supported. I should add that neither counsel before us in fact attempted to support them.

There is one further matter to which I should refer. Counsel for the bank, in an

f   attractive argument based on the arithmetic, suggested that even if the auction sale had produced the full amount of £90,000 it would make no difference because there would still be an indebtedness to the bank in excess of the guaranteed amount. I do not think that this court can safely rely on the evidence which is before it on such a matter as this; we simply do not know with any assurance whether £90,000 is a reliable figure at all.

In the circumstances, my view of the matter is that there are triable issues of fact and

g   law on the evidence as it was presented to us, and accordingly that leave to defend should be given.

Appeal allowed ; unconditional leave to defend.

Solicitors: *William F Prior & Co* (for Mr and Mrs Walker); *Donald Bennett & Legat*, Bristol (for the bank).

Diana Procter   Barrister.

Coates and another v Modern Methods and Materials Ltd

COURT OF APPEAL, CIVIL DIVISION
STEPHENSON, EVELEIGH AND KERR LJJ
27, 28 MAY, 1 JULY 1982

Unfair dismissal – Dismissal in connection with strike or other industrial action – Dismissal not unfair unless relevant employee not dismissed – Relevant employee – Relevant employee meaning employee who took part in strike – Employee who refused to go into factory to work during strike for fear of abuse from strikers not dismissed – Whether that employee a 'relevant employee' – Employment Protection (Consolidation) Act 1978, s 62.

After weeks of unrest among the employer's workforce following the closure of one factory and the transfer of employees between other factories, the employer made a request on 8 February 1980 for volunteers for further transfers from one factory. The workforce at the factory refused to accept further transfers. On 11 February the employer dismissed nine employees. The following morning the workforce held a meeting outside the factory gates and nearly all of them decided not to go in to work. Among those who decided not to go in was Mrs L, who was not prepared to face the abuse which the rest of the workforce directed towards those who did go in. After waiting for an hour to see what was going to happen Mrs L went to keep a pre-arranged appointment with her doctor, who certified that she was unfit for work. Mrs L sent the doctor's certificate to the employer and remained off work until 25 April, during which time she attended strike meetings of the workforce to find out what was happening, but without drawing strike pay because she considered that she was sick and not on strike. On 25 March the applicants, who were both members of the workforce, were dismissed for taking part in a strike. On 25 April Mrs L returned to work. The applicants filed a complaint with an industrial tribunal claiming that they had been unfairly dismissed. The question arose whether the industrial tribunal had jurisdiction to hear the complaint. The employer contended that under s 62[a] of the Employment Protection (Consolidation) Act 1978 an industrial tribunal had no jurisdiction to hear a complaint of unfair dismissal made by an employee who was taking part in a strike at the time of his dismissal unless another employee (the 'relevant employee') who took part in the strike had not been dismissed, and that there was no such relevant employee. The applicants contended that Mrs L had taken part in the strike and had not been dismissed and was therefore a relevant employee. The industrial tribunal found that irrespective of what her later actions might have been Mrs L had taken part in a strike on the morning of 12 February when she decided, along with most of the workforce, not to go in to work. The industrial tribunal accordingly held that they had jurisdiction to hear the applicants' complaints. The employer appealed to the Employment Appeal Tribunal, which upheld the appeal on the ground that Mrs L did not take part in a strike on the morning of 12 February because the reason she did not go into work was her fear of being abused and not because of any trade union principles. The applicants appealed to the Court of Appeal.

Held (Eveleigh LJ dissenting) – Participation in a strike was to be judged by an employee's actions and not by the reasons behind them. If, for whatever reason, an employee stopped work when other employees came out on strike, and said nothing to indicate disagreement with the strike and did nothing which amounted to a refusal to join the strike, he 'took part in it', within s 62 of the 1978 Act. The industrial tribunal

---

a   Section 62, so far as material, is set out at p 948 *b c*, post

a had not given those words an unnatural meaning by applying them to the actions of Mrs L on the morning of 12 February, and accordingly they had been entitled to conclude on the evidence that Mrs L was a 'relevant employee' within s 62. The appeal would therefore be allowed, the decision of the Employment Appeal Tribunal set aside and the decision of the industrial tribunal restored (see p 954 *g h*, p 955 *c* to *e* and p 959 *c f* to p 960 *c e* to *g*, post).

McCormick v Horsepower Ltd [1981] 2 All ER 746 considered.

b
Notes

For dismissal in connection with industrial action, see 16 Halsbury's Laws (4th edn) paras 633–633:1.

For the Employment Protection (Consolidation) Act 1978, s 62, see 48 Halsbury's Statutes (3rd edn) 514.

c As from a day to be appointed s 62 of the 1978 Act is to be amended by s 9(1) to (4) of the Employment Act 1982.

Cases referred to in judgments

Brutus v Cozens [1972] 2 All ER 1297, [1973] AC 854, [1972] 3 WLR 521, HL, 15 Digest (Reissue) 910, 7807.

d Edwards (Inspector of Taxes) v Bairstow [1955] 3 All ER 48, [1956] AC 14, [1955] 3 WLR 410, HL, 28(1) Digest (Reissue) 566, 2089.

McCormick v Horsepower Ltd [1981] 2 All ER 746, [1981] 1 WLR 993, CA; affg [1980] ICR 278, EAT, 20 Digest (Reissue) 412, 3388.

Pedersen v Camden London Borough Council [1981] ICR 674, CA.

Stock v Frank Jones (Tipton) Ltd [1978] 1 All ER 948, [1978] 1 WLR 231, HL, 20 Digest e (Reissue) 412, 3389.

Tramp Shipping Corp v Greenwich Marine Inc [1975] 2 All ER 989, [1975] 1 WLR 1042, CA, Digest (Cont Vol D) 826, 2450c.

W (an infant), Re [1971] 2 All ER 49, [1971] AC 682, [1971] 2 WLR 1011, HL, 28(2) Digest (Reissue) 832, 1389.

Woods v WM Car Services (Peterborough) Ltd [1981] ICR 666, EAT.

f
Appeal

The applicants, Iris Coates and Jeanette Ann Venables, appealed against the decision of the Employment Appeal Tribunal (Bristow J, Mrs D Lancaster and Mr J G C Milligan) on 13 March 1981 allowing an appeal by the respondents, Modern Methods and Materials Ltd (the employers), against a decision of an industrial tribunal (chairman Mr R H g Boyers) sitting at Sheffield on 3 October 1980 whereby the tribunal decided that they had jurisdiction under s 62 of the Employment Protection (Consolidation) Act 1978 to hear the applicants' complaints of unfair dismissal. The facts are set out in the judgment of Stephenson LJ.

Stephen Sedley for the applicants.
h *Christopher Clarke* for the employers.

Cur adv vult

1 July. The following judgments were read.

j **STEPHENSON LJ.** This appeal, by leave from a decision of the Employment Appeal Tribunal given on 13 March 1981, raises one question: was the decision of the industrial tribunal given on 25 September 1980 that Mrs Doreen Leith took part in a strike, in which the applicants, Mrs Iris Coates and Mrs Jeanette Venables, took part, a decision which on the evidence no reasonable tribunal properly directing itself could come to? If it was, the Employment Appeal Tribunal was right to reverse it and we should dismiss the applicants' appeal. If the decision was one which a reasonable tribunal properly directing itself on the evidence could come to, the Employment Appeal Tribunal was *a* wrong and we should allow the appeal and restore the decision of the industrial tribunal.

The issue arises in this way. Section 62 of the Employment Protection (Consolidation) Act 1978 provides:

'(1) The provisions of this section shall have effect in relation to an employee who claims that he has been unfairly dismissed by his employer where at the date of dismissal . . . (b) the employee was taking part in a strike or other industrial action. *b*

(2) In such a case an industrial tribunal shall not determine whether the dismissal was fair or unfair unless it is shown—(a) that one or more relevant employees of the same employer have not been dismissed, or (b) that one or more such employees have been offered re-engagement, and that the employee concerned has not been offered re-engagement . . .

(4) In this section . . . (b) "relevant employees" means . . . (ii) in relation to a strike *c* . . . employees who took part in it . . .'

In effect an industrial tribunal has no jurisdiction to entertain a complaint of unfair dismissal from an employee dismissed for taking part in a strike unless he or she has been victimised by one or more other employees who took part in the strike being kept on or given the chance of coming back. The employers dismissed the applicants when they *d* were taking part in a strike. The industrial tribunal had no jurisdiction to entertain their complaints unless they could find a 'relevant employee' who had also taken part in the strike but had not been dismissed. They contended that they had found one, and only one, in Mrs Leith. She had not been dismissed: had she taken part in the strike? The industrial tribunal said, 'Yes, she had,' so they had jurisdiction; the appeal tribunal, by a majority, said, 'No, she had not,' so the industrial tribunal should have rejected the *e* applicants' complaints. The member of the appeal tribunal who dissented held that the industrial tribunal's conclusion was one they were entitled to draw from what they had heard and seen during the hearing and they have not, therefore, erred in law.

It cannot be stated too emphatically or too often that appeals to the Employment Appeal Tribunal, and from that tribunal, lie only on questions of law: see s 136(1) and (4) of the 1978 Act. The industrial tribunal's findings of fact are therefore final unless they *f* have no evidence to support them, and the inferences they draw from those facts and the conclusions they base on them cannot be reversed simply because the appellate tribunal or court thinks them wrong, and the appellate tribunal or court cannot replace them by its own inferences or conclusions unless the industrial tribunal's decision is unsupported by any evidence or inconsistent with the evidence or contradicted by the true and only conclusion, which the appellate tribunal or court can and must then substitute: see the *g* classic statement of Lord Radcliffe in *Edwards (Inspector of Taxes) v Bairstow* [1955] 3 All ER 48 at 57, [1956] AC 14 at 36. It is only if the first tribunal reaches its determination without evidence or without reason or by misdirecting itself as to the law that there can be any error of law for correction on appeal.

It was accepted by counsel, and stated by Lawton and Waller LJJ with the concurrence of Sir David Cairns, that the questions on appeal in *Pedersen v Camden London Borough* *h* *Council* [1981] ICR 674, reported in a note to *Woods v WM Car Services (Peterborough) Ltd* [1981] ICR 666, whether the evidence was sufficient to prove there was a breach of contract and that the breach was fundamental were matters of fact for the industrial tribunal to decide and that there was evidence on which they could conclude that there was a fundamental breach of contract. That decision of this court led the appeal tribunal in the *Woods* case to change its mind and, applying *Edwards v Bairstow*, to decide not to *j* substitute for the conclusion of the industrial tribunal its own conclusion of mixed fact and law on what was a repudiatory breach.

In *McCormick v Horsepower Ltd* [1981] 2 All ER 746, [1981] 1 WLR 993 an industrial tribunal held that Mr Brazier was not a relevant employee; the appeal tribunal held that he was a relevant employee; this court upheld the decision of the appeal tribunal, but on

the ground that Mr Brazier had been dismissed. All three members of the court, however,
a expressed the opinion that he was not a relevant employee on the further ground that he
did not take part in the applicant's strike, Lawton LJ stating ([1981] 2 All ER 746 at 751,
[1981] 1 WLR 993 at 999):

> 'In my judgment there was evidence on which the industrial tribunal could find,
> as it did, that he was not taking part in the strike and in consequence was not a
> relevant employee.'
b

In my judgment the question for this court in this case, as also for the appeal tribunal,
can accordingly be put in this way: was there evidence on which the industrial tribunal
could find that Mrs Leith was not taking part in the strike, giving those words a meaning
of which they are reasonably capable? Or, adapting Lord Reid's oft-quoted words in
Brutus v Cozens [1972] 2 All ER 1297 at 1299. [1973] AC 854 at 861, was their decision
c unreasonable in the sense that no tribunal acquainted with the ordinary use of language
could reasonably reach that decision? This was the approach of Mrs Lancaster, the
minority member of the appeal tribunal. I am by no means sure that it was the approach
of the majority. They began well but appear to me to have fallen into error as they
proceeded. In their judgment they said:

> 'In our judgment, what the tribunal found Mrs Leith said and did and what the
d > circumstances were are the matters of primary fact on which their findings, if there
> is evidence to support them and they are not perverse, are binding on this court. It
> is on those findings that the conclusion has to be drawn: was she or was she not
> taking part in a strike? That is just as much a conclusion of law as is the question
> whether a man is an independent contractor or an employee so that he has the right
> not to be unfairly dismissed by virtue of s 54 of the Employment Protection
e > (Consolidation) Act 1978. The situation is quite different from that which arises
> under s 57(3) of the 1978 Act where the industrial tribunal is charged by the statute
> with the task of making a value judgment on the fairness of the employer's conduct.
> That value judgment is not a conclusion of law and is properly treated as (and
> generally called) a finding of fact with which this court cannot interfere unless there
> is no evidence to justify it or it is "perverse". Whether an employer's conduct over
f > dismissal is fair is an "industrial jury" question: whether you are an employee or
> taking part in a strike depends not on a value judgment based on evidence but
> depends on the proper logical conclusion which follows from the application of
> legal concepts to the primary facts found on the evidence. What then is the proper
> conclusion on the primary facts? Was Mrs Leith taking part in a strike or was she
> not? The 1978 Act contains no definition of what "taking part in a strike" within
g > the meaning of s 62(2) involves. Each case must be decided on the proper conclusions
> to be drawn from its own primary facts, but some help is to be had from a
> consideration of the judgment of this court in *McCormick v Horsepower Ltd.*'

They then correctly summarised the decision of the appeal tribunal in *McCormick's*
case, the Court of Appeal having not then given their judgments dismissing that
h employee's appeal. Had the appeal tribunal had the judgment of Lawton LJ in that case
or the judgment of Browne-Wilkinson J in *Wood's* case, which had also not then been
given, they might have agreed with the opinion of the minority member. That is,
however, doubtful in the light of the concluding words of their judgment:

> 'On the facts of this case, therefore, and by reason particularly of the tribunal's
> express finding that they accepted Mrs Leith's evidence, in the judgment of the
j > majority of this court the only conclusion that the industrial tribunal could properly
> have reached was that Mrs Leith did not take part in the strike which started on 12
> February 1980 and at no time thereafter took part in that strike.'

There they leave off asking (incorrectly) what is the proper conclusion on the primary
facts, to consider (correctly) the *only* proper conclusion, and we have to decide whether

the appeal tribunal's is the only proper conclusion or whether the industrial tribunal's conclusion is within the bounds of possible reasonable decisions which are exempt from appellate interference: see *Re W (an infant)* [1971] 2 All ER 49 at 56, [1971] AC 682 at 700 per Lord Hailsham LC.

The facts which were proved in evidence before the industrial tribunal are in a small compass. I cannot do better than take them from the majority judgment of Bristow J and Mr Milligan, read by the latter. I read from the judgment, quoting the evidence of Mrs Leith in chief and in re-examination:

'In the second week of February 1980, weeks of unrest among the workforce employed by Modern Methods and Materials Ltd (the company) came to a head. One of the company's three factories had been closed and some employees had been transferred to another. Management had then decided that there must be further transfers between the remaining two. Ten volunteers were asked for. None was forthcoming. Management gave the works committee ten names on Friday, 8 February. On that day at 1630 hrs it was decided among the workforce that none would go. On Monday, 11 February everyone, including the named ten, went to work. At lunchtime they were told that, because the named ten would not transfer, nine workers were to be dismissed, and nine girls were taken to the office one by one and dismissed. The works director, Mr Fraser, refused to address a mass meeting in the canteen at 1500 hrs and the workforce decided to meet outside the factory gate next morning. Mrs Leith was an employee of the company of $7\frac{1}{2}$ years' standing. She had a history of trouble with her back. She hurt her back at work on Monday, 11 February and on Monday evening made an appointment to see her doctor. She had previously hurt her back on Sunday at home. She was present during what happened on the Monday. The industrial tribunal, in their decision and reasons, expressly state that they accepted Mrs Leith's evidence. If that means anything, they found as a fact that in giving evidence before them she was telling them the truth. On Tuesday morning the workforce, including Mrs Leith, met together outside the factory gate. Nearly all remained outside, taking the view that if they went into work their grievances about what had happened over the proposed transfers, dismissals and threatened redundancies would remain unredressed. At about 0810 hrs, before anyone had gone in, Mr Raistrick, the managing director, was at the gate trying to persuade them all to go in. Mrs Leith says that she turned up on that Tuesday morning fully expecting to go in to work. Mrs Jessop, an employee of five years' standing, had gone to the factory in Mrs Leith's car. When Mr Raistrick tried to persuade all the workforce to go in, Mrs Jessop asked those who like herself had been subjected to a transfer already, including Mrs Leith, to go in to work with her. Only two did so. Mrs Jessop says: "We got some abuse. They called us 'scabs'." This was from the crowd of employees at the gate who, though not a "picket line", were by then performing the picket line function of seeking to dissuade anyone from going in to work. Bearing in mind that the industrial tribunal expressly accepted Mrs Leith's evidence (that is to say, were satisfied that she was telling the truth), we quote two passages of question and answer on the note of her examination-in-chief by Mr Farmeary, the GMWU official who conducted the applicants' case and who called her to give evidence, having ensured her attendance by a witness order: "Q. Why didn't you go in with Mrs Jessop when she asked you? A. Because I did not want the abuse that the other two were getting when they went in . . . Q. Why did you not go in to work with Mrs Jessop? A. Because I did not want all that abuse." After this Mrs Leith says she stayed for about an hour. She says at that time that "it was not a picket line. I do not think anybody operated as a picket. We were trying to find out what was happening." Then she went home. Either on that day or next day, Mrs Leith went to her doctor, who gave her a sick note saying "I examined you today" and certifying that she was unable to attend work from 13 February 1980. The note is dated 13 February 1980. Mrs Leith sent the sick note to

a

the company, as the industrial tribunal found, "to excuse her attendance [sic] from work".'

Mrs Leith remained off work sick until 25 April, when she managed five hours only, but later resumed normal work. While off work she went to strike meetings, but she did not draw strike pay. She did not call them strike meetings and did not regard herself as a striker. Her evidence-in-chief with regard to that was:

b

'Q. Why didn't you go in with Mrs Jessop when she asked you? A. Because I did not want the abuse that the other two were getting when they went in.

Q. Did you return on Wednesday? A. No.

Q. Why not? A. I had an appointment with the doctor on Tuesday and when I told him how bad I was with my nerves he gave me a sick note. I thought I saw him on Tuesday. I made my appointment two nights before I saw him . . .

c

Q. Between 12 February and 18 April did you know that strike pay was made up for you? A. I had already told Mr Brearley that I was on the sick panel. I was not on strike.

Q. Why did you turn up at the strike meetings then? A. I am in the union. I am entitled to know what is going on. I was never dismissed by the company.'

d

Her evidence in cross-examination was: 'Mr Brearley suggested I take strike pay. I declined on the grounds that I was sick and was not on strike.'

Now that evidence was not contradicted and the industrial tribunal accepted it. The crucial matter is their interpretation of what, according to Mrs Leith's evidence and the other evidence consistent with it, Mrs Leith said and did, and perhaps did not do, for at least an hour between 8.00 and 10.30 on the morning of Tuesday, 12 February 1980. Her evidence as to later events is in my judgment only relevant in so far as it throws light

e

on the events of that morning. If she did not take part in the strike then, she could not continue to take part in it later. Mrs Coates gave evidence that at the works gates Mrs Jessop invited Mrs Leith to go in with her and said, 'Our job is not in jeopardy.' She stayed about one hour at the gates as 'Everybody was confused, including Mrs Leith. But she knew everything that was happening.' Mrs Venables put the time Mrs Leith went home at between 10.30 and 11. Mrs Jessop said:

f

'I spoke to Mrs Leith. She did not want to pass the pickets. All the women were on the gate. Three of us went in. We got some abuse. They called us "scabs". They said everybody pleases themselves. I said to Mrs Leith would she come in to work with me? She didn't want to pass the pickets.'

g

The reasons given by the industrial tribunal for being unanimously satisfied that on Tuesday, 12 February 1980 Mrs Leith took part in the strike outside the works gates were these:

'(a) Mrs Leith went to work at the usual time intending to go in to work. (b) Mrs Leith did not go in to work, although Mrs Jessop tried to persuade her to do so. (c) Mrs Leith was not prepared to defy the pickets. (d) There was no good reason for

h

Mrs Leith to withhold her labour apart from the decision which she took while she was standing with the other striking workers outside the works gates, that she would not break the strike. (e) Mrs Leith was with the other strikers when Mr Raistrick spoke to them, but his arguments did not persuade her to go in to work. (f) Mrs Leith stayed outside the gates until she went home at about 10.30 a m. (g) Mrs Leith did not receive any strike pay because her certificated sickness disqualified her from entitlement thereto. (h) Mrs Leith attended some strike meetings.'

j

In refusing the employers a review on 3 October 1980 the chairman of the industrial tribunal referred to those reasons and stated:

'The weight of evidence showed that Mrs Leith was taking part in industrial action during the morning of 12 February 1980. Mrs Leith's evidence was not

inconsistent with this finding of fact. Even if it had been, where some evidence
conflicts with other evidence it is the duty of a tribunal to decide which evidence it   *a*
will accept and which it should reject.'

The last sentence is either irrelevant or inconsistent with the statement in para 3 of their
decision that Mrs Leith's evidence was accepted by the tribunal.

The grounds on which the appeal tribunal majority based the opposite conclusion are
contained in the following two paragraphs: *b*

'The primary facts, as we have set them out, were (except in so far as they depend
on Mrs Leith's evidence) not in dispute. The industrial tribunal tell us that they
accepted Mrs Leith's evidence (so, we repeat, their finding of primary fact in that
respect is that what Mrs Leith told them was the truth). The reason she did not go
in to work with Mrs Jessop was that she did not want to be abused. She did not
refuse to go in, like Brazier in *McCormick's* case, by reason of trade union principles.   *c*
The reason that she refused strike pay from Mr Brearley was that she was away sick
and was not on strike, not that, being away sick, she was not entitled to strike pay.

In some respects her behaviour while she was away sick might, in the absence of
other factors, have led to the inference, just as Brazier's did in *McCormick's* case, that
she was on strike. She stayed at the gate for 1½ hours. She went to the strike meetings
at the Mexborough Civic Hall. When questioned at the tribunal about this she said,   *d*
however, that this was because she wanted to know what was going on and what
was going to happen. On the other side, she sent her sick note to the company and
the documents are consistent with the company treating her throughout as being
off sick, not off on strike. She was not dismissed on 5 March. She resumed work
later, before the strike ended, without any reinstatement or re-engagement
operation. She in fact took steps to show the union that she was sick, not striking.'   *e*

The minority member based her dissenting opinion that the industrial tribunal's
decision should be upheld on the evidence of all these witnesses. She said:

'From all these testimonies the industrial tribunal concluded that there was no
reason why Mrs Leith should withold her labour in so far as it related to her personal
employment circumstances. They clearly gave full weight to her reason for not   *f*
facing her workmates and going into the factory but concluded that none the less
she had not broken the strike or other industrial action. Their unanimous finding
from the facts given in evidence was that Mrs Leith was on strike on Tuesday, 12
February 1980. It was a conclusion they were entitled to draw from what they had
heard and seen during the hearing and they have not, therefore, erred in law.'

It is to be observed that the industrial tribunal's decision rests partly on the view that   *g*
there was no good reason why Mrs Leith should withhold her labour and that she decided
not to back the strike or did not break it. They must have held that to refuse to pass the
pickets because she did not want the abuse meted out to Mrs Jessop and to stay outside
the works gates in consequence with the others (some 40 in number according to the
evidence), instead of going in to work with Mrs Jessop and (according to the evidence)
one other, constituted taking part in the strike. There is no reference in their decision to   *h*
Mrs Leith's reason, expressed to Mr Brearley, for declining strike pay not because she was
disqualified by certificated sickness but because she was not on strike; and they cannot
have regarded that or her explanation for attending strike meetings as of importance, if
indeed they accepted her evidence on those two matters.

Can Mrs Leith reasonably be said to have taken part in this strike by yielding to her   *j*
fear of abuse, and so withholding her labour (a dignified paraphrase of 'not working') and
not breaking the strike either by braving the pickets and going to work, or by some
protest or expression of dissent? There is no binding authority defining what constitutes
taking part in a strike, but there is authority defining the essentials of a strike. Paragraph
24(1) of Sch 13 to the 1978 Act, which is concerned with computation of an employee's
period of employment, provides:

'In this Schedule, unless the context otherwise requires . . . "strike" means the cessation of work by a body of persons employed acting in combination, or a concerted refusal or a refusal under a common understanding of any number of persons employed to continue to work for an employer in consequence of a dispute, done as a means of compelling their employer or any person or body of persons employed, or to aid other employees in compelling their employer or any person or body of persons employed, to accept or not to accept terms or conditions of or affecting employment . . .'

In *Tramp Shipping Corp v Greenwich Marine Inc* [1975] 2 All ER 989 at 991–992, [1975] 1 WLR 1042 at 1046 Lord Denning MR said:

'. . . I think a strike is a concerted stoppage of work by men done with a view to improving their wages or conditions, or giving vent to a grievance or making a protest about something or other, or supporting or sympathising with other workmen in such endeavour. It is distinct from a stoppage which is brought about by an external event such as a bomb scare or by apprehension of danger.'

And I said much the same thing (see [1975] 2 All ER 989 at 992, [1975] 1 WLR 1042 at 1047).

In *McCormick's* case [1981] 2 All ER 746 at 751, [1981] 1 WLR 993 at 998 Lawton LJ, with the fact of Brazier's refusal to cross the boilermaker's picket lines in mind, gave his view of what constitutes taking part in a strike. He said:

'The statutory words "who took part in it" (that is, the strike) mean giving help by acting in concert with each other and in withdrawing their labour for a common purpose or pursuant to a dispute which they or a majority of them or their union have with their employer and staying away from work as long as the strike lasts. Some help by standing on picket lines or by doing organising work in committee rooms. Evidence of Mr Brazier's refusal to cross the boilermaker's picket lines even though, as the industrial tribunal found, his refusal was not brought about by fear, was not in my judgment enough to prove that he was taking part in the boilermakers' strike. He was not shown to have had a common purpose with them or any interest in their dispute with their employers. He was not acting in concert with them as was shown by the fact that he returned to his work on 13th November 1978 whilst they were still on strike. In my judgment there was evidence on which the industrial tribunal could find, as it did, that he was not taking part in the strike and in consequence was not a relevant employee.'

Counsel for the applicants and counsel for the employers take something from these definitions of a strike for the meaning which they submit should be given to the words 'was taking (or took) part in a strike or other industrial action'. For they must mean the same in sub-ss (1)(*b*) and (4)(*b*)(ii) of s 62. Counsel for the applicants accepts counsel for the employers' submission that for an employee to come within the words there must be a concerted stoppage of work done as a means of compelling the employer to accede to certain demands and that there must be in existence at the time the strike is called a common purpose of compelling the employer to accede to the demand. But they differ as to what is required of the employee when there is such a concerted cessation of work or withdrawal of labour and a common purpose to put pressure on the employer. Counsel for the employers submits that the employee must support the strike by sharing the common purpose of compelling the employer to accede to the demand. Counsel for the applicants, on the other hand, contends that, once there is an attempt to persuade all workers affected to join in withdrawing their labour, the individual worker affected can take part in the attempt without supporting, or even fully appreciating, the purpose or the cause. The individuals may be ignorant or confused. Their motives may be mixed. But motivation and intention are irrelevant; provided the effect of what they do adds to the pressure on the employer, they take part in the strike. Mere withdrawal of labour when or after others do so will usually contribute to achieving the object of the strike; if

it does so, that is taking part in it. Counsel for the applicants submits that on this interpretation of the statutory words the industrial tribunal reasonably held that Mrs   *a*
Leith had taken part in the strike by withdrawing her labour and not breaking the strike on 12 February 1980. If she had been unable to go in to work because she was prevented physically or by such threats or violence as might have deprived her of her freedom of choice, she might not have taken part. But the pressure or constraint put on her by the threat of being abused, as Mrs Jessop was, was not enough to prevent her from making a voluntary decision to stay out of the factory and so take part, however unwillingly, in the   *b*
strike of those who stayed out with her. That is the view expressed in the industrial tribunal's decision. Fear of abuse was not a good reason; she had the power to decide whether or not to break the strike, she did decide not to do so and it matters not why.

On counsel for the employers' construction of the statutory words he submits that no reasonable tribunal could have found that Mrs Leith took part in the strike without rejecting her evidence. But the industrial tribunal accepted her evidence that she did not   *c*
go into the factory because of the abuse and so it was not open to them to find, and they did not find, that she supported the strike or acted in concert with the strikers or shared their purpose. On her accepted evidence she did not share in the strikers' purpose or agree with it, and acted not in pursuance of it but in apprehension of what others might say in pursuance of it. Her intention in going to work on 12 February 1980, knowing that strike action was being taken, was to work, not strike; and it was never suggested   *d*
that she changed her mind that morning or indeed right up to the time when she was fit enough to return to work. Counsel for the employers points out that nowhere does the industrial tribunal attempt to state what meaning they give to the statutory phrase nor for that matter does the appeal tribunal; and it can only be by misinterpreting the phrase and giving it an unnatural meaning that the industrial tribunal have held that it applied to Mrs Leith's actions on 12 February 1980. That is a misdirection in law which entitled   *e*
the appeal tribunal to review the industrial tribunal's decision and required it to correct it. It would, he submits, be most unreasonable to conclude from a strained construction of the statutory words that Mrs Leith was on strike with the others; the employer and the majority of the appeal tribunal were right to hold that she was not.

I have found this a difficult case. It ought to be easy to decide what 'taking part in a strike' means and whether on proved or accepted facts a particular employee was or was   *f*
not taking part in a strike. The industrial tribunal seem to have found it easy, because they unanimously decided that Mrs Leith was taking part, and on an application for review the chairman thought the weight of the evidence showed that she was taking part and a review had no reasonable prospect of success. I know that the construction of a statute is a question of law; but the meaning of ordinary words is not, and the meaning of 'taking part in a strike' seems to me to be just the sort of question which an industrial   *g*
jury is best fitted to decide. No member of either tribunal has spelt out its meaning, perhaps because it was thought unwise or impossible to attempt a paraphrase of plain words. But I should be very reluctant to assume that any of them attributed to the words an unnatural meaning which they were incapable of bearing in their context, or to differ from their conclusion that Mrs Leith took part in the strike. Only the plainest error in law would enable me to differ from them on such a finding, particularly when the   *h*
majority of the appeal tribunal, whose decision convicts them of such error, appear themselves to be influenced by an erroneous conception of their power to interfere with the industrial tribunal's decision.

On the other hand, I think that on the evidence without argument and reflection I should have taken the view which Mrs Leith's employers appear to have taken that she was not on strike or striking or taking part in the strike. That view takes into account   *j*
her state of mind, her intention, her motive, her wishes. Some support for doing that is to be found in what Talbot J said in giving the judgment of the appeal tribunal in *McCormick v Horsepower Ltd* [1980] ICR 278 at 283 about Mr Brazier not being motivated by fear in refusing to cross the picket line and withdrawing his labour to aid the strikers; and also in what Lawton LJ in the passage I have quoted from his judgment in the Court of Appeal in the same case said obiter about giving help generally and about Mr Brazier

not being shown to have had a common purpose with the striking boilermakers.
Furthermore, it seems hard on an employer who takes the trouble to investigate an employee's motives and reasons for stopping work to be told, 'You were wrong to accept what she told you; you ought to have dismissed her and so prevented two other strikers from complaining to the industrial tribunal of unfair dismissal.'

On the other side it is said that it would be intolerable to impose on employers the burden, which these employers undertook with one employee, of looking into the mind of every employee withholding his or her labour before deciding whether to dismiss, in order to see if each had some reason for stopping work unconnected with the object of the strike.

I have come to the conclusion that participation in a strike must be judged by what the employee does and not by what he thinks or why he does it. If he stops work when his workmates come out on strike and does not say or do anything to make plain his disagreement, or which could amount to a refusal to join them, he takes part in their strike. The line between unwilling participation and not taking part may be difficult to draw, but those who stay away from work with the strikers without protest for whatever reason are to be regarded as having crossed that line to take part in the strike. In the field of industrial action those who are not openly against it are presumably for it.

This seems to be the thinking behind the industrial tribunal's decision. If the words in question are capable of bearing that meaning, they are capable of being applied to Mrs Leith's actions on the morning of 12 February 1980, though her time outside the factory gates with the strikers was short and her reason for not entering the factory was accepted. In my judgment a reasonable tribunal could give that meaning to the statutory words and could apply them to Mrs Leith. The industrial tribunal did not, therefore, go wrong in law and it was the majority of the appeal tribunal who did.

I would accordingly allow the appeal, set aside the decision of the Employment Appeal Tribunal and restore the decision of the industrial tribunal.

EVELEIGH LJ. Section 62 of the Employment Protection (Consolidation) Act 1978 reads, so far as is immediately relevant, as follows:

> '(1) The provisions of this section shall have effect in relation to an employee who claims that he has been unfairly dismissed by his employer where at the date of dismissal . . . (b) the employee was taking part in a strike . . .
>
> (2) In such a case an industrial tribunal shall not determine whether the dismissal was fair or unfair unless it is shown—(a) that one or more relevant employees of the same employer have not been dismissed . . .
>
> (4) In this section . . . (b) "relevant employees" means . . . (ii) in relation to a strike . . . employees who took part in it . . .'

It is to be noted that the employee who is the claimant and the relevant employees with whom the claimant is to be compared are both similarly described as employees who take part in a strike. Furthermore the section clearly indicates that they are employees who take part in the same strike. This is apparent from the last ten words.

The object of s 62 is, as Viscount Dilhorne said in *Stock v Frank Jones (Tipton) Ltd* [1978] 1 All ER 948 at 951, [1978] 1 WLR 231 at 234—

> 'to prevent victimisation by an employer of persons who took part in a strike or other industrial action. The dismissal of all who took part in such action was not to be regarded as unfair, but discrimination between those who took part either by not dismissing some of those who took part or by re-engaging some, but not the claimant for compensation, of those who had been dismissed rendered the dismissal unfair if it was for an inadmissible reason.'

The 1978 Act then is designed to prevent intimidation or preferential treatment between people taking part in the same strike. It is to prevent discrimination between equals, that is those engaged in similar behaviour. Unaided by authority I would have thought that a strike meant concerted withdrawal of labour for the purpose of enforcing the

determination of an industrial dispute. Those who take part in it would be strikers as I
understand that word. They may display varying measures of enthusiasm and perhaps
even reluctance, but they must all be treated equally. The section is thus in some measure
a protection even for a ringleader. I would therefore regard all of the employees referred
to in s 62 as quoted above as people who are making the same protest and for that purpose
are withdrawing their labour. In fact, however, there is a more detailed definition of a
strike in para 24(1) of Sch 13 to the 1978 Act. It reads:

> 'In this Schedule, unless the context otherwise requires . . . "strike" means the
> cessation of work by a body of persons employed acting in combination, or a
> concerted refusal or a refusal under a common understanding of any number of
> persons employed to continue to work for an employer in consequence of a dispute,
> done as a means of compelling their employer or any person or body of persons
> employed, or to aid other employees in compelling their employer or any person or
> body of persons employed, to accept or not to accept terms or conditions of or
> affecting employment . . .'

Those words very closely correspond to the definition suggested by Lord Denning MR
in *Tramp Shipping Corp v Greenwich Marine Inc* [1975] 2 All ER 989 at 991–992, [1975] 1
WLR 1042 at 1046:

> '. . . I think a strike is a concerted stoppage of work by men done with a view to
> improving their wages or conditions, or giving vent to a grievance or making a
> protest about something or other, or supporting or sympathising with other
> workmen in such endeavour. It is distinct from a stoppage, which is brought about
> by an external event such as a bomb scare or by apprehension of danger.'

Stephenson LJ said ([1975] 2 All ER 989 at 992, [1975] 1 WLR 1042 at 1047):

> '. . . what kind of concerted stoppages are properly called strikes today? It must
> be a stoppage intended to achieve something or to call attention to something, as
> Lord Denning MR has said; a rise in wages, improvement of conditions, support for
> other workers or for political changes; an expression of sympathy or protest.'

In my opinion the word 'strike' has achieved a technical meaning and it is that which
appears in para 24 of Sch 13. I appreciate that we do not find it in the main body of the
1978 Act. However this legislation began by adopting the method of laying down
principles which were to govern industrial relations in schedules and the schedules are of
very great importance. Schedule 13 is dealing with the financial consequences of a strike
to those who take part in it and I would find it strange if a strike for the purpose of s 62
was something different from a strike for the purpose of Sch 13.

The claimant, being a person who took part in a strike, is subject to certain disabilities
both under s 62 and also as laid down in Sch 13. The relevant person is also subject to the
disabilities in Sch 13. Consequently in my opinion the expression 'to take part in a strike'
should be strictly and not widely construed. I remind myself that both the claimant and
the relevant person are described by the same expression.

There are many different ways in which a person can be involved in a strike. There are
many ways in which a person's actions may be of assistance to the strikers. It does not
follow that they are taking part in a strike. In my opinion for a person to take part in a
strike he must be acting jointly or in concert with others who withdraw their labour,
and this means that he must withdraw his labour in support of their claim. The fact that
a man stays away from work when a strike is on does not lead inevitably to the conclusion
that he is taking part in the strike. This was firmly the view of the Court of Appeal in
McCormick v Horsepower Ltd [1981] 2 All ER 746, [1981] 1 WLR 993, and also of the
Employment Appeal Tribunal in the same case ([1980] ICR 278). In the Court of Appeal
two grounds for the decision were stated. The first was that it was sufficient to defeat the
claim if the dismissal of the 'relevant employee' took place before the date of the hearing.
The second ground was that the alleged 'relevant employee' did not take part in the same
strike as the complainant because although he decided not to cross the picket line he was

not acting in concert with the strikers. It is true that Templeman LJ said that it was
a strictly unnecessary to determine whether the man was a 'relevant employee'. None the
less he, Lawton and O'Connor LJJ were unanimous in the test which they applied to
determine whether or not a person was a 'relevant employee'. I regard both grounds for
the decision as being of equal force. If, as has been submitted, the second ground was
obiter and therefore not binding on us, I would feel the greatest reluctance in not
following it unless of course it could be shown to have been arrived at per incuriam.
b Templeman LJ said ([1981] 2 All ER 746 at 750, [1981] 1 WLR 993 at 997):

> 'The boilermakers went on strike and agreed or were instructed to come out
> together and they were under a mutual obligation to stay out together and go back
> together. Mr Brazier did not become under any obligation to come out or stay out
> with the boilermakers. Mr Brazier did not take part in any sympathetic strike by
> the engineers or any other body of persons because there was no sympathetic strike.
c > Mr Brazier did not agree with any other person or become under any obligation to
> come out or stay out with the boilermakers, the engineers or any other person. Mr
> Brazier was an individual who voluntarily decided not to work on 9th October 1978
> because the boilermakers were on strike and voluntarily decided to resume work on
> 13th November 1978 although the boilermakers were still on strike.'

d Lawton LJ said ([1981] 2 All ER 746 at 751, [1981] 1 WLR 993 at 998):

> 'He was not a relevant employee unless he took part in the same strike as Mr
> McCormick. The statutory words "who took part in it" (that is, the strike) mean
> giving help by acting in concert with each other and in withdrawing their labour
> for a common purpose or pursuant to a dispute which they or a majority of them or
> their union have with their employers and staying away from work as long as the
e > strike lasts. Some help by standing on picket lines or by doing organising work in
> committee rooms. Evidence of Mr Brazier's refusal to cross the boilermakers' picket
> lines even though, as the industrial tribunal found, his refusal was not brought
> about by fear, was not in my judgment enough to prove that he was taking part in
> the boilermakers' strike. He was not shown to have had a common purpose with
> them or any interest in their dispute with their employers. He was not acting in
f > concert with them as was shown by the fact that he returned to his work on 13th
> November 1978 whilst they were still on strike. In my judgment there was evidence
> on which the industrial tribunal could find, as it did, that he was not taking part in
> the strike and in consequence was not a relevant employee.'

In that case the industrial tribunal had held that the workman was not a 'relevant
g employee'. The Employment Appeal Tribunal, applying the same test, decided that the
workman's actions can only be explained in terms that he withdrew his labour in order
as a minimum to give sympathy and support to the boilermakers in their action against
their employer (see [1980] ICR 278 at 283). The Court of Appeal restored the decision of
the industrial tribunal because it shared the industrial tribunal's view of the evidence. It
would of course have been sufficient to say that the industrial tribunal's decision was one
h which they were entitled to arrive at on the evidence.

The facts of *McCormick*'s case are of interest. The workman was a fitter's mate who
arrived at the employer's premises on returning from holiday to find a picket line set up
by boilermakers who were on strike. He refused to cross it. He went each week to the
employer's office with the striking boilermakers in order to receive whatever income tax
rebates were due to him. In the majority decision of the industrial tribunal it was stated
j (at 281):

> 'We are not satisfied that Mr. Brazier was acting in combination with the
> [employees] or that there was a concerted refusal or a refusal under a common
> understanding between him and the [employees] not to continue to work for the
> [employers] in consequence of a dispute. We are satisfied that the [employees] were
> in dispute with the [employers] but we are not satisfied that Mr. Brazier was so in

dispute. What is clear is that Mr. Brazier would not cross the picket line, which at
the most can mean that as a trade unionist he felt that he must not cross the picket
line. It would have been a simple matter for him or his trade union representative
to have told the [employers] that Mr. Brazier was not coming into work because he
was taking part in a strike but he did not do so and that fact satisfies us that he did
not regard himself as in dispute with the [employers] and consequently was not on
strike. We do not regard the fact that he would not cross the picket line as being an
attempt to compel the [employers] to agree to the [employees'] demands. Nor do
we regard it as giving aid to [them]. For all we know he may have been entirely
unsympathetic to the [employees] but because of his principles he would not cross
the picket line. Furthermore we find it significant that if he was taking part in the
strike he was, during its existence, allowed to return to work by the [employees]
and therefore cross the picket line daily without any trouble being caused.
Accordingly in answering the second question we find that Mr. Brazier was not a
relevant employee as defined by the Act.'

In reading the judgment of the appeal tribunal, Talbot J said (at 283):

'The finding of fact that Mr. Brazier would not cross the picket line between
October 6, and November 13, and that he was not motivated by fear in this refusal,
must, we believe, mean that he was withdrawing his labour to aid the strikers; that
thereby he took part in the strike, and in consequence he was a "relevant employee"
as defined in the Act.'

It seems clear that if the workman had been deterred by fear the appeal tribunal would
have had no difficulty in finding that the workman was not a 'relevant employee'.

In this context I do not regard the word 'fear' as indicating a threat of violence to the
extent necessary to sustain a defence of coercion in the criminal law. Indeed we are not
concerned with defences. The explanation that a worker stayed away through fear would
simply be some evidence to indicate that he was not acting in concert with the other
strikers.

In the present case Mrs Leith (the alleged 'relevant employee'), whose evidence was
expressly accepted by the industrial tribunal, was asked why she did not go in to work
when she arrived at the employers' premises and when asked to do so by a Mrs Jessop.
She replied: 'Because I did not want the abuse that the other two were getting when they
went in.' The question was repeated: 'Why did you not go in to work with Mrs Jessop?'
She replied: 'Because I did not want all that abuse.'

In the present case counsel for the applicants accepts, or indeed contends, that we are
concerned to determine whether or not the evidence can support a finding that Mrs
Leith took part in the strike at the time when she decided not to cross the picket line and
returned home. As her evidence was accepted, and as she stated that her reason for not
returning to work the following day was sickness, the applicants are unable to contend
that if she did not take part in a strike on the first day a subsequent absence made her a
'relevant employee'.

Mrs Jessop's evidence was as follows:

'Three of us went in, but not Mrs Leith. I was standing with Mrs Leith ... I
spoke to Mrs Leith. She did not want to pass the pickets. All the women were on
the gate. Three of us went in. We got some abuse. They called us "scabs". They said
everybody pleases themselves. I said to Mrs Leith would she come in to work with
me? She didn't want to pass the pickets.'

That evidence to my mind clearly establishes that Mrs Leith's reason for not going in
to work that afternoon was her unwillingness to expose herself to abuse. As she saw it,
she could not cross the picket line without suffering the abuse. She did not have the
courage to go to work when she wanted to. The presence of the picket line hurling abuse
was enough to deter Mrs Leith. I feel sure that she is not the only lady who would have
been deterred and who would have turned back even though wholly out of sympathy

with the strikers. It seems to me to be completely wrong to say that such a person is
a herself a striker and must suffer the disabilities which result under the industrial relations
legislation.

I am unable to find in this case any route by which the industrial tribunal could have
accepted Mrs Leith's evidence and none the less come to the conclusion that she acted in
concert with the other strikers.

I can only conclude that the industrial tribunal wrongly approached the question
b whether or not Mrs Leith took part in the strike. The tribunal seem to have treated as
conclusive against Mrs Leith that she was not prepared to defy the pickets and 'that she
would not break the strike'. I would dismiss this appeal.

KERR LJ (read by Stephenson LJ). Subject to one point mentioned by Stephenson LJ in
his judgment, to which I refer below but which does not affect the primary issue, I agree
c that this appeal should be allowed for the reasons stated by him. My main reasons for
adding to what he has said are that we are differing by a majority from a majority
decision of the Employment Appeal Tribunal, and that I respectfully differ from Eveleigh
LJ in his analysis of the ratio of the decision of this court in *McCormick v Horsepower Ltd*
[1981] 2 All ER 746, [1981] 1 WLR 993.

The primary issue raised by this appeal is whether the industrial tribunal could
d reasonably conclude on the evidence before them that Mrs Leith was taking part in a
strike on the morning of Tuesday, 12 February 1980. However, on reading the decision
of the majority of the appeal tribunal, it seems to me to be clear that this is not the basis
on which they approached the appeal to them. Stephenson LJ has already drawn attention
to the difference in approach which is reflected in various passages of their decision. In
the ultimate analysis, however, I think it is clear from the two paragraphs in which they
e state their reasons for reaching the opposite conclusion from that of the industrial
tribunal, which Stephenson LJ has read, that they substituted their own conclusion on
the effect of the evidence for that of the industrial tribunal. To this extent, as it seems to
me, they fell into error in their approach.

Turning then to what I have referred to as the primary issue, it seems to me, for the
reasons already stated by Stephenson LJ, that there was ample material on which the
f industrial tribunal could reasonably conclude that Mrs Leith was taking part in a strike
on that Tuesday morning. Indeed, I would go further and say that I would have reached
the same conclusion as the industrial tribunal as a matter of first impression, and that I
remain of this view after having heard the arguments on this appeal. To this extent,
accordingly, I am inclined to differ from Stephenson LJ's views in that regard. Since there
has been so much argument and so many references in the judgments as to what
g constitutes 'taking part in a strike', I propose briefly to add my own view on this question,
although this is not strictly necessary for the decision of the primary issue.

Whatever definition of a strike one may adopt, such as that in para 24 of Sch 13 to the
Employment Protection (Consolidation) Act 1978, it is common ground that there was a
strike in progress on that Tuesday morning. The only issue is whether Mrs Leith was
among the persons who took part in it, and it is also common ground that in the ultimate
h analysis this falls to be decided by reference to the events of that morning. As to this
issue, and on this basis, it seems to me, given that there was then a strike, that all those,
including Mrs Leith, who chose to remain outside and not to go to work were taking
part in that strike, and only those, like Mrs Jessop, who chose to go in were not taking
part in it.

In this connection I do not think that it would be correct, or practicable, to differentiate
j between those who chose to remain outside by reference to their reasons for doing so.
They were all free to go in, in the sense that the gate was open and that Mr Raistrick, the
managing director, was urging them to do so. The fact that they had to cross the picket
line to go in, and thereby suffer some abuse at the time, and quite possibly some
unpopularity, or worse, among their fellow employees thereafter, and that feelings of
this kind, as in the case of Mrs Leith, may have deterred them from going in, does not
appear to me to make any difference. Nor would it make any difference, in my view,

that their reason for staying out was that they were in sympathy with the strike. As it seems to me, their reasons or motives cannot be regarded as relevant; nor would it be relevant to consider whether their utterances or actions, or silence or inaction, showed support, opposition or indifference in relation to the strike.

When it is necessary to determine the question whether an employee does or does not take part in a strike which is admittedly in progress, but which does not prevent the employee from going to work in defiance of the manifold pressures which the existence of the strike is bound to exert, then it seems to me that this question can in practice only be answered on the basis of his or her action by either staying out or going in. Of course, if the employee does not go to work for reasons which have nothing to do with the strike, such as illness or being on holiday, then the position would be different. But when the employee's absence from work is due to the existence of the strike in some respect, because he or she chooses not to go to work during the strike, then I think that the employee should be regarded as taking part in the strike.

If this were not so, it seems to me that s 62 of the 1978 Act would be unworkable in practice. To take one example which I mentioned in the course of the argument, suppose that there is a meeting of the workforce to decide whether there should be a strike or not, in circumstances where the employers make it clear that they hope that everyone will continue to work whatever may be the outcome and that it will be open to everyone to do so. At the meeting there are then speeches for and against, and then 60% vote in favour of the strike and 40% against. A strike is then declared to exist, whether official or unofficial, and then everyone goes home and no one goes back to work, with some maintaining their support, others their opposition, and many saying nothing. How is it possible in practice to differentiate between them? Or suppose that some of those opposed to the strike go back to work, but that others decide not to do so because they fear the consequences, or because they will not, or fear to, cross a picket line, but nevertheless remain opposed to the strike, with some of them perhaps expressing their opposition by action or words, while the majority do and say nothing. As it seems to me, the issue who takes part in the strike in such commonplace occurrences can only be determined on the basis of who stays out and who does not.

I then turn finally to *McCormick v Horsepower Ltd*. Assuming that the judgments in this court are to be taken as having decided a second issue apart from the decision that the relevant time is the date of the hearing for the purposes of determining whether or not any 'relevant employee' has been dismissed, it seems to me that the judgments are only authority for the proposition that anyone who may or may not have been a 'relevant employee' must on any view have taken part in the same strike as those employees who were dismissed. This was clearly what Templeman LJ decided (see [1981] 2 All ER 746 at 750, [1981] 1 WLR 993 at 997) and O'Connor LJ agreed with him. Lawton LJ also agreed with this conclusion (see [1981] 2 All ER 746 at 751, [1981] 1 WLR 993 at 998) and I think that his remarks in that passage were directed to this issue and that they should not be treated as authority for present purposes.

For these reasons I would allow this appeal.

Appeal allowed; order of the Employment Appeal Tribunal set aside and order of the industrial tribunal restored. Liberty to apply for leave to appeal to the House of Lords.

16 July. *The Court of Appeal dismissed an application by the employers for leave to appeal to the House of Lords.*

14 October. *The Appeal Committee of the House of Lords (Lord Diplock, Lord Bridge of Harwich and Lord Brightman) dismissed a petition by the employers for leave to appeal.*

Solicitors: *Tess Gill*, Claygate (for the applicants); *Taylor & Emmet*, Sheffield (for the employers).

Sophie Craven   Barrister.

a
Ronex Properties Ltd v John Laing Construction Ltd and others (Clarke, Nicholls & Marcel (a firm), third parties)

COURT OF APPEAL, CIVIL DIVISION

b STEPHENSON, DONALDSON LJJ AND SIR SEBAG SHAW

1, 2, 22 JULY 1982

Pleading – Striking out – No reasonable cause of action – Defendant having defence under statute of limitations – Whether pleading may be struck out as disclosing no reasonable cause of action merely because defendant may have limitation defence – RSC Ord 18, r 19.

c
Tort – Contribution between joint tortfeasors – Survival of claim for contribution on death of one joint tortfeasor – Joint tortfeasor's liability to plaintiff in main action not established or admitted at date of death – Joint tortfeasor not having subsisting cause of action for contribution at date of death – Whether joint tortfeasor's claim for contribution a defined inchoate right at date of death – Whether claim for contribution extinguished on claimant's death – Whether rule that a cause of
d *action in tort dies with the person in whom cause vested applying to joint tortfeasor's claim – Whether claim for contribution preserved for benefit of claimant's estate – Law Reform (Miscellaneous Provisions) Act 1934, s 1(1) – Law Reform (Married Women and Tortfeasors) Act 1935, s 6(1).*

The plaintiffs brought an action against, inter alios, an architect (the second defendant)
e claiming damages for breach of contract and negligence in the design of a building. The second defendant began third party proceedings against the firm of consulting engineers (the third parties) who had advised him, claiming an indemnity or contribution under s 6(1)[d] of the Law Reform (Married Women and Tortfeasors) Act 1935 on the grounds that the third parties had been in breach of contract and negligent in their advice to the second defendant. The second defendant also served a defence to the plaintiffs' claim
f denying the claim. Shortly thereafter the second defendant died. The plaintiffs obtained an order to carry on their action against the second defendant's personal representatives. The personal representatives proposed to obtain an order to carry on the third party proceedings but before they did so the third parties applied to strike out the third party proceedings as disclosing no reasonable cause of action, on the grounds (i) that any right to recover a contribution against them under the 1935 Act was extinguished on the
g second defendant's death and (ii) that the second defendant's causes of action against the third parties were time-barred under s 2(1)[b] of the Limitation Act 1939 at the time the third party proceedings were commenced. The judge dismissed the application to strike out the third party proceedings. The third parties appealed.

Held – The appeal would be dismissed for the following reasons—
h   (1) Since statutes of limitations merely barred a plaintiff's remedy and not his cause of action, and since a limitation defence when pleaded might be subject to exceptions, a defendant could never apply under RSC Ord 18, r 19[c] to strike out a claim against him as

a   Section 6(1), so far as material, provides: 'Where damage is suffered by any person as a result of a tort . . . (a) judgment recovered against any tortfeasor liable in respect of that damage shall not be a bar to an action against any other person who would, if sued, have been liable as a joint tortfeasor
j   in respect of the same damage . . . (c) any tortfeasor liable in respect of that damage may recover contribution from any other tortfeasor who is, or would if sued have been, liable in respect of the same damage, whether as a joint tortfeasor or otherwise, so, however, that no person shall be entitled to recover contribution under this section from any person entitled to be indemnified by him in respect of the liability in respect of which the contribution is sought.'

b   Section 2(1), so far as material provides: 'The following actions shall not be brought after the expiration of six years from the date on which the cause of action accrued, that is to say:—(a) actions founded on simple contract or on tort . . .'

disclosing no reasonable cause of action merely because he might have a good limitation defence. It followed that the third parties' possible defence under s 2 of the 1939 Act was not a good reason for striking out the third party proceedings as disclosing no reasonable cause of action (see p 965 *e* to *g*, p 966 *a b* and p 968 *a* to *h*, post); *Dismore v Milton* [1938] 3 All ER 762 followed.

(2) Assuming (a) that a cause of action for contribution under the 1935 Act arose only when the plaintiff in the contribution suit had been held liable or had admitted liability to the plaintiff in the main action and the amount of his liability had been ascertained and (b) that at the date of the second defendant's death there was no subsisting cause of action for contribution against the third parties, because at that date the second defendant had neither been held liable nor admitted liability to the plaintiffs in the main action, it could not be said that the second defendant's right to claim contribution under the 1935 Act had been preserved for the benefit of his estate by s 1(1)^d of the Law Reform (Miscellaneous Provisions) Act 1934, because s 1(1) only applied to a cause of action which subsisted and was vested in the deceased at his death. However, the second defendant's cause of action for contribution, being at his death a defined inchoate right, passed to his personal representatives for the benefit of his estate under the general law of succession unaffected by the common law maxim that a cause of action in tort died with the person in whom it was vested, because, although the maxim had not been abrogated by the 1934 Act, it did not apply to a cause of action for contribution under the 1935 Act since such a cause of action, although arising out of tortious rights, namely those of the plaintiff in the main action against the parties to the contribution suit, was not, as between the parties to the contribution suit, a claim in tort but was a right sui generis which (per Sir Sebag Shaw) resembled a plaintiff's claim for money paid by him (ie to the plaintiff in the main action) to the use of the defendant in the contribution suit. Accordingly, the second defendant's claim to contribution under the 1934 Act had not been extinguished on his death and the third party proceedings could not be struck out on that ground (see p 967 *a* to p 968 *d*, post); dictum of McNair J in *Harvey v R G O'Dell Ltd* [1958] 1 All ER at 668 applied.

Per Stephenson and Donaldson LJJ. Where a defendant considers that he has a good limitation defence his proper course is either to plead the defence and seek trial of the defence as a preliminary issue or, in a very clear case, to apply to strike out the claim on the ground that it is frivolous, vexatious and an abuse of the court's process (see p 965 *j* to p 966 *a* and p 968 *e*, post).

Notes

For striking out a pleading as showing no reasonable cause of action, see 36 Halsbury's Laws (4th edn) para 73, and for cases on the subject, see 37(1) Digest (Reissue) 272–286, 1782–1837.

For survival of causes of action, see 17 Halsbury's Laws (4th edn) paras 1563–1572.

For the right of contribution between joint tortfeasors, see 37 Halsbury's Laws (3rd edn) 137–139, para 247.

For the Law Reform (Miscellaneous Provisions) Act 1934, s 1, see 13 Halsbury's Statutes (3rd edn) 115.

For the Law Reform (Married Women and Tortfeasors) Act 1935, s 6, see 35 ibid 543.

For the Limitation Act 1939, s 2, see 19 ibid 61.

As from 1 January 1979 new provision for contribution between persons jointly or severally, or both jointly and severally, liable for the same damage is made by the Civil Liability (Contribution) Act 1978, which repealed s 6 of the 1935 Act.

As from 1 May 1981 s 2 of the 1939 Act was replaced, so far as relevant, by ss 2 and 5 of the Limitation Act 1980.

---

c Rule 19, so far as material, is set out at p 965 *d e*, post

d Section 1(1), so far as material, provides: 'Subject to the provisions of this section, on the death of any person after the commencement of this Act all causes of action . . . vested in him shall survive . . . for the benefit of, his estate . . .'

Cases referred to in judgments

a *Dismore v Milton* [1938] 3 All ER 762, CA, 32 Digest (Reissue) 744, 5355.
Harvey v R G O'Dell Ltd [1958] 1 All ER 657, [1958] 2 QB 78, [1958] 2 WLR 473, 45 Digest (Repl) 293, 129.
Riches v DPP [1973] 2 All ER 935, [1973] 1 WLR 1019, CA, Digest (Cont Vol D) 1038, 520a.
Wimpey (George) & Co Ltd v British Overseas Airways Corp [1954] 3 All ER 661, [1955] AC
b 169, [1954] 3 WLR 932, HL, 45 Digest (Repl) 292, 128.

Cases also cited

D (J) v D (S) [1973] 1 All ER 349, sub nom *D'Este v D'Este* [1973] Fam 55.
Dean v Wiesengrund [1955] 2 All ER 432, [1955] QB 120, CA.
Phillips v Homfray (1883) 24 Ch D 439, CA; *on appeal* sub nom *Phillips v Fothergill* (1886)
c 11 App Cas 466, HL.
Post Office v Official Solicitor [1951] 1 All ER 522.
Sparham-Souter v Town and Country Developments (Essex) Ltd [1976] 2 All ER 65, [1976] QB 858, CA.
Stott v West Yorkshire Road Car Co Ltd [1971] 3 All ER 534, [1971] 2 QB 651, CA.
Sugden v Sugden [1957] 1 All ER 300, [1957] P 120, CA.

d
Appeal

Clarke, Nicholls & Marcel (a firm), the third parties in an action brought by Ronex Properties Ltd against the first defendant, John Laing Construction Ltd and (under an order to carry on) against the second defendants, Mr Alan James Palmer and Mr Michael John McCloughlin, as administrators of the estate of Mr Derek Stephenson deceased, who
e in effect was the original second defendant in the action and who had issued the proceedings against the third parties, appealed against the order of his Honour Judge Newey QC sitting as an official referee made on 2 November 1981 dismissing the third party's summons applying (1) to strike out the third party proceedings for want of prosecution and for an order for judgment for the third parties against the second defendants, and (2) alternatively applying to strike out the third party notice on the
f ground that it disclosed no reasonable cause of action (i) because any right to recover contribution against the third parties under s 6 of the Law Reform (Married Women and Tortfeasors) Act 1935 was extinguished by Mr Stephenson's death and (ii) because at the time the third party proceedings were issued the alleged causes of action against the third parties in contract and tort were time-barred by s 2 of the Limitation Act 1939. The grounds of the appeal were (1) that the judge misdirected himself in law in dismissing
g the third parties' applications and (2) alternatively, if he had a discretion in the matter, he exercised it on wrong principles. By a respondent's notice the respondents to the appeal, the second defendants, whilst seeking to uphold the judge's judgment on the grounds stated in his judgment, gave notice that on the appeal they would seek to uphold his judgment on the further ground that the judge ought to have held that the right of the second defendants as Mr Stephenson's administrators to claim a contribution against
h the third parties pursuant to s 6 of the 1935 Act passed to the second defendants under s 1(1) of the Law Reform (Miscellaneous Provisions) Act 1934, alternatively under the general law of succession. The facts are set out in the judgment of Donaldson LJ.

William Crowther QC and *Timothy Lamb* for the third parties.
Richard Fernyhough for the second defendants.

j
                                                                        Cur adv vult

22 July. The following judgments were read.

DONALDSON LJ (read, in his Lordship's absence, by Sir Sebag Shaw at the invitation of Stephenson LJ). The late Mr Derek Stephenson was an architect. Before his death he

had the misfortune to be sued by Ronex Properties Ltd (Ronex), who alleged that he had
been negligent in the design of Heron House, Bothwell Street, Glasgow. Ronex also sued   *a*
the contractors, John Laing Construction Ltd (Laings). Mr Stephenson thereupon issued
a third party notice against Clarke, Nicholls and Marcel, consulting engineers. He then
died. Herein lies the problem. It is said by the third parties that, owing to a lacuna in the
law, Mr Stephenson's death, occurring when it did, destroyed any rights which he might
have had against them. The issue is whether they are right. The form in which it arises
is an application to strike out the third party notice on the ground that it discloses no   *b*
reasonable cause of action. His Honour Judge John Newey QC refused the application
and the third parties now appeal.

The relevant facts were these. The building was completed in 1972. It was built by
Laings to designs prepared by the architects, Derek Stephenson & Partners (Stephensons),
who were assisted by Clarke, Nicholls & Marcel (Clarkes). Ronex claim that the building
has leaked since its completion and continues to do so despite certain remedial work   *c*
carried out in 1974 by Laings, advised by Stephensons. Ronex issued a writ in May 1978
naming Laings and Stephensons as defendants and claiming damages for breach of
contract and for negligence. It was served in May 1979 and a statement of claim was
delivered in June 1979. On 14 September 1979, and before serving a defence on Ronex,
Stephensons exercised their right under RSC Ord 16, r 1, to issue without leave a third
party notice addressed to Clarkes. This claimed an indemnity or contribution in respect   *d*
of the plaintiffs' claim and the costs of the action both at common law and under s 6 of
the Law Reform (Married Women and Tortfeasors) Act 1935. The grounds alleged were
breach of contract and/or negligence. Stephensons' defence to Ronex's claim was served
three days later, on 17 September 1979.

There was then a hiatus caused in part by an attempt to have the dispute referred to
arbitration. However, on 17 June 1980 Stephensons served the third party notice on   *e*
Clarkes. Thereupon Clarkes became parties to the action 'with the same rights in respect
of his defence against any claim made against him in the notice and otherwise as if he
had been duly sued in the ordinary way by the defendant by whom the notice is issued'
(see RSC Ord 16, r 1(3)).

Mr Stephenson died on 17 August 1980. By RSC Ord 15, r 7(1):

> 'Where a party to an action dies or becomes bankrupt but the cause of action   *f*
> survives, the action shall not abate by reason of his death or bankruptcy.'

In such a case the rule empowers the court to make orders for the proceedings to be
carried on by personal representatives of the deceased party. At the time of his death Mr
Stephenson was the sole partner of Derek Stephenson & Partners and was not bankrupt.
His estate was, however, insolvent and this produced further delay. However, in April   *g*
1981 Mr Palmer and Mr McLoughlin took out letters of administration to Mr
Stephenson's estate and on 15 May 1981 Ronex obtained an order that the action be
carried on against Laings as first defendants and Messrs Palmer and McLoughlin as
second defendants in their capacity as administrators of the estate of the late Mr
Stephenson. This order did not in terms extend to the third party proceedings, and on 25
September 1981 Messrs Palmer and McLoughlin obtained an order that the third party   *h*
proceedings be carried on as between them and Clarkes. At some stage the proceedings
were transferred to the official referees' court and allocated to his Honour Judge Newey
QC.

Thus far the proceedings were unremarkable, albeit leisurely even by construction
industry standards. However, on 13 August 1981, before the carry-on order had been
made in relation to the third party proceedings, the third parties had issued a summons   *j*
in those proceedings. In it they sought an order (1) dismissing the third party proceedings
for want of prosecution and entering judgment for the third parties against Stephensons,
or, alternatively, (2) striking out the third party notice on the ground that it disclosed no
cause of action since (a) any right to recover contribution under s 6 of the Law Reform
(Married Women and Tortfeasors) Act 1935 had been extinguished by the death of Mr
Stephenson and (b) the alleged causes of action in contract and tort were barred by s 2 of

the Limitation Act 1939 at the time of the issue of the third party proceedings. The judge dismissed both applications on 2 November 1981.

Clarkes accept the judge's decision in so far as he refused to dismiss the third party proceedings for want of prosecution. However, they appeal against his refusal to strike out on the grounds that the third party notice discloses no cause of action. No third party statement of claim has yet been delivered and accordingly the claim is still indicated in only the broadest terms. The third party notice could embrace (a) a claim for damages for breach of contract, (b) a claim for damages for negligence (that is to say, breach of a duty of care owed by the third parties to Stephensons) and (c) a claim to contribution under the 1935 Act. Counsel for the third parties says that the claim in negligence is so widely stated at this stage that it is difficult to submit that no arguable claim could be formulated. However, he makes no such concession in relation to the other two heads, breach of contract and contribution. The appeal has proceeded on the sensible basis that, if it succeeds, the order which the third parties will seek must preserve such limited rights as the personal representatives of Mr Stephenson may have to claim damages for negligence from the third parties. In these circumstances, the argument resolved itself into two separate compartments, namely 'limitation' and 'actio personalis moritur cum persona'.

Limitation

Under RSC Ord 18, r 19(1) the power to strike out any pleading or the indorsement of any writ in the action or anything contained therein is exercisable—

> 'on the ground that—(a) it discloses no reasonable cause of action or defence, as the case may be; or (b) it is scandalous, frivolous or vexatious; or (c) it may prejudice, embarrass or delay the fair trial of the action; or (d) it is otherwise an abuse of the process of the court . . .'

In the case of an application under para (1)(a), which is the present case, no evidence is admissible.

Authority apart, I would have thought that it was absurd to contend that a writ or third party notice could be struck out as disclosing no cause of action merely because the defendant may have a defence under the Limitation Acts. Whilst it is possible to have a contractual provision whereby the effluxion of time eliminates a cause of action and there are some provisions of foreign law which can have that effect, it is trite law that the English Limitation Acts bar the remedy and not the right, and furthermore that they do not even have this effect unless and until pleaded. Even when pleaded, they are subject to various exceptions, such as acknowledgment of a debt or concealed fraud which can be raised by way of reply. Concealed fraud has, we are told, been pleaded by the plaintiffs in this case as against the defendants, but whether the personal representatives will or can adopt a similar attitude vis-à-vis the third parties can only really emerge if ever they get to the stage of delivering a reply in the third party proceedings. Accordingly, authority apart, I would have unhesitatingly dismissed the application to strike out on this ground. The answer might well have been different if the third parties had relied on any ground other than failure to disclose a reasonable cause of action, but in that event all concerned could have adduced evidence and we would have been able to explore the factual basis on which it is said the Limitation Acts do, or as the case may be do not, apply.

The matter is not in fact free from authority. It was considered in *Riches v DPP* [1973] 2 All ER 935, [1973] 1 WLR 1019, in which the earlier cases are reviewed. There the grounds put forward in support of the application to strike out included an allegation that the claim was frivolous and vexatious and an abuse of the process of the court. Accordingly, the court was able to consider evidence and it is understandable that the claim could be struck out. Of the cases referred to, it seems that only in *Dismore v Milton* [1938] 3 All ER 762 was an attempt made to strike out solely on the grounds that the Limitation Acts applied and accordingly no cause of action was disclosed. Greer and Slesser LJJ held that such an application must fail for the reasons which I have already indicated and contrasted the effect of the statute of limitations with that of the real

property limitation Acts. That being a two-judge court, we are not strictly bound by its
decision, but I have no doubt that it was right. Where it is thought to be clear that there   *a*
is a defence under the Limitation Act, the defendant can either plead that defence and
seek the trial of a preliminary issue or, in a very clear case, he can seek to strike out the
claim on the ground that it is frivolous, vexatious and an abuse of the process of the court
and support his application with evidence. But in no circumstances can he seek to strike
out on the ground that no cause of action is disclosed.

The judge refused to strike out on this ground both for the reasons given in *Dismore v*   *b*
Milton and because, in the exercise of his discretion, he thought that the application was
premature in that at that stage he was not satisfied that no reasonable cause of action was
disclosed. In my judgment, he was absolutely right in so refusing.

Actio personalis moritur cum persona
In 1913 Professor Goudy in his *Essays in Legal History* p 216 wrote: *c*

'Though this is one of the most familiar maxims of English law, the veil of
obscurity covers not only its origin but its true import and significance.'

Something of its history is set out in Sir William Holdsworth's *History of English Law*
(1938) vol 1, pp 576–583, but its relevance, if any, to this appeal must depend on the law
as it was immediately prior to the passing of the Law Reform (Miscellaneous Provisions)   *d*
Act 1934. The general rule then was that an action for tort had to be begun in the joint
lifetime of the wrongdoer and the person injured. If, after it had been so begun, either
of the parties died before a verdict could be obtained, the action abated and could not be
continued or recommenced by or against the representatives of the deceased: see *Salmond
on Torts* (8th edn, 1934) p 74. The rule was subject to exceptions, but only one is here
material, namely that the rule did not apply to breaches of contract, even if they were   *e*
also torts, which resulted in pecuniary damage, though it did apply to breach of contract
which resulted in personal injuries unaccompanied by pecuniary damage.

The 1934 Act did not simply abrogate the rule, although it made comprehensive
provision for what was to happen and what conditions were to apply over the whole field
of law to which the rule had applied. Section 1(1) provided that, subject to immaterial
exceptions, all causes of actions subsisting against or vested in the deceased on his death   *f*
should survive against or for the benefit of his estate. This left the problem of those torts
where damage is an essential element in the cause of action. The act or omission
complained of might occur before death and the damage be suffered afterwards. In such
circumstances there would be no cause of action subsisting and vested in the deceased at
the time of death. This is dealt with by s 1(4), which backdates the damage so as to
produce a deemed cause of action vested in the deceased and subsisting at the time of   *g*
death.

In the instant case it is common ground that Ronex's cause of action against Mr
Stephenson for negligence is unaffected by his death, and subsists against his estate. Both
the alleged negligence and at least some of the damage, occurred before Mr Stephenson's
death, thereby giving rise to a complete cause of action. If and in so far as damage
occurred after his death, either it is capable of forming part of the claim in respect of that   *h*
subsisting cause of action or, by operation of s 1(4), it is deemed to have produced a cause
of action subsisting at his death.

However, counsel for the third parties submits that the position is quite different
when it comes to Mr Stephenson's claim over against the third parties for contribution
under the 1935 Act. The claim in negligence is, of course, covered by the 1934 Act and
that in contract is not affected by the rule. The starting point of this submission is that a   *j*
cause of action for contribution under the 1935 Act arises at the earliest when the
claimant tortfeasor has been held liable, or has admitted liability to the plaintiff, and the
amount of that liability has been ascertained by judgment or admission. This proposition
is supported by dicta in *George Wimpey & Co Ltd v British Overseas Airways Corp* [1954] 3
All ER 661 at 663, 667, 674, [1955] AC 169 at 177, 182, 193 per Viscount Simonds, Lord

Porter and Lord Keith. It is also in accordance with the dictum of McNair J in *Harvey v R*
a G *O'Dell Ltd* [1958] 1 All ER 657 at 669, [1958] 2 QB 78 at 108, and it is consistent with
the approach of Parliament in s 4 of the Limitation Act 1963. For my part I am content
to assume that it is right.

Counsel for the third parties then goes on to submit that, since at the time of his death
Mr Stephenson had neither been held liable to the plaintiffs nor admitted any such
liability, there was at that time no subsisting cause of action for contribution from the
b third parties under s 6 of the 1935 Act. Again I assume that that is right.

However, it is in my judgment at the next and final stage of the argument that counsel
for the third parties gets into difficulties. Apart from the operation of the actio personalis
rule, Mr Stephenson's right to claim contribution from the third parties, contingent on
his liability to the plaintiffs being established, would have passed to his personal
representatives. It was a defined inchoate right and not a mere hope or expectation.
c Accordingly, counsel for the third parties has to establish that the rule applies.

For my part I see no reason why it should. The rule, emerging from the mists of
history, has been subject to progressive restriction culminating in the 1934 Act.
Parliament's intention, as manifested by that Act, was that it should only continue to
apply to causes of action for defamation, seduction, inducing one spouse to leave or
remain away from another and damages for adultery (see s 1(1) proviso). This is not, of
d course, conclusive, because the statutory right to contribution between tortfeasors did
not exist at that date and Parliament did not in terms abrogate the rule, but provided a
statutory escape from its effects in all known situations other than those which I have
mentioned. However, that said, it would require an expanded redefinition of the rule if
it were to apply to this statutory right. The rule applied to causes of action based on a
breach of a tortious obligation owed by the plaintiff to the defendant. If in 1935
e Parliament had created a new tortious obligation by statute in a form to which the 1934
Act would not have applied, and if it had failed to make special provision for the benefit
and burden of that obligation to pass to the estate of those who died before judgment, no
doubt the rule would have applied. But the statutory right of contribution created by the
1935 Act is not based on a breach of any obligation, whether tortious or otherwise, owed
to the claimant in the contribution suit by the respondent in that suit. It is based on
f breaches of tortious duties owed by both parties to the contribution suit, whether jointly
or severally, to a third party and stranger to that suit, the plaintiff in the main action. As
it was put in geometrical terms in argument, the rights of those concerned are triangular,
the sides AB and AC representing the tortious rights and causes of action, and the base
BC representing rights which are sui generis, not being tortious but arising out of tortious
rights: see dicta of McNair J in *Harvey v R G O'Dell Ltd* [1958] 1 All ER 657 at 668, [1958]
g 2 QB 78 at 107. Accordingly, in my judgment, the rule has no application to Mr
Stephenson's right to claim contribution under the 1935 Act and that right has passed to
his personal representatives for the benefit of his estate under the law of succession.

The judge arrived at the same conclusion by a different route, holding that Mr
Stephenson's right to claim contribution was preserved for the benefit of his estate by the
operation of s 1(1) of the 1934 Act, supplemented if need be by s 1(4) of that Act. I have
h some difficulty in accepting this reasoning, because it seems to me that s 1(1) can only
apply to a cause of action which subsisted and was vested in the deceased at the time of
his death, ie was actionable at that date. Although it is true that RSC Ord 16 permitted
Mr Stephenson to start proceedings claiming contribution before his death and that he
had indeed done so, there was no perfected cause of action subsisting and vested in him
at that stage. That stage would not be reached until he had been held liable to the
j plaintiff. Indeed, it has not yet been reached. It would therefore be necessary to pray in
aid s 1(4), the wording of which is inappropriate to a claim for contribution under the
1935 Act. The missing factor in Mr Stephenson's suggested cause of action is not the
suffering of damage but being held liable and the amount of that liability being
ascertained by judgment (or the equivalent processes by way of admission). It may be
said that ascertainment of a liability involves suffering damage, but this is not necessarily

true: it depends on whether the liability is discharged. In a word, the 1934 Act does not fit with, and in my judgment has no application to, a claim for contribution under the 1935 Act.

I would dismiss the appeal.

SIR SEBAG SHAW. I agree that this appeal should be dismissed for the reasons given by Donaldson LJ in the course of his judgment. As he points out, the statutory right of contribution created by the Law Reform (Married Women and Tortfeasors) Act 1935 is not in the nature of a claim in tort. It derives from a liability in tort to some third party who could have sued any or all of the tortfeasors concerned. As between them, a claim for contribution resembles a claim by a plaintiff for money paid by him to the use of the defendant who has been relieved, pro tanto, of his direct liability to the victim of the tort.

As to striking out a writ or other initiating process on the ground that it discloses no reasonable cause of action, I would regard this power as properly exercisable only when it is manifest that there is an answer immediately destructive of whatever claim to relief is made, and that such answer can and will be effectively made. In such a case it would, as I understand Stephenson LJ will observe in the course of his judgment, be a waste of time and money to allow the matter to be pursued so as to give rise to what would be an abuse of the process of the court.

STEPHENSON LJ. I agree, and desire only to add a few observations on the limitation point.

There are many cases in which the expiry of the limitation period makes it a waste of time and money to let a plaintiff go on with his action. But in those cases it may be impossible to say that he has no reasonable cause of action. The right course is therefore for a defendant to apply to strike out his claim as frivolous and vexatious and an abuse of the process of the court, on the ground that it is statute-barred. Then the plaintiff and the court know that the statute of limitation will be pleaded, the defendant can, if necessary, file evidence to that effect, the plaintiff can file evidence of an acknowledgment or concealed fraud or any matter which may show the court that his claim is not vexatious or an abuse of process and the court will be able to do in, I suspect, most cases what was done in *Riches v DPP* [1973] 2 All ER 935, [1973] 1 WLR 1019, strike out the claim and dismiss the action.

That cannot be done here because the third parties' summons alleged only no reasonable cause of action and an amendment would have given the second defendants the opportunity of meeting the plea of the statute with a plea of concealed fraud which has been raised in the plaintiffs' reply to the amended defence of the first defendants served shortly before the hearing of this appeal.

The judge was clearly justified in not striking out the claim on the ground that the question whether the second defendants' claims were statute-barred should be decided after 'a proper analysis of the damage suffered and full argument as to the law, both of which cannot occur without a trial'. And the further possibility that there may be an answer to a plea of the statute in s 26(b) of the Limitation Act 1939 makes it even plainer that they should not be struck out now.

Appeal dismissed. Leave to appeal to the House of Lords refused.

Solicitors: *Beale & Co* (for the third parties); *Hewitt, Woollacott & Chown* (for the second defendants).

Sophie Craven　Barrister.

a

R v Khan and another

COURT OF APPEAL, CRIMINAL DIVISION
DUNN LJ, TALBOT AND TUDOR EVANS JJ
6 AUGUST 1982

b *Sentence – Forfeiture order – Forfeiture of property – Property – Real property – Defendant convicted of drug offences – Court ordering forfeiture of house belonging to defendant – Whether court having jurisdiction to order forfeiture of real property – Whether jurisdiction to order forfeiture of property limited to personal property – Powers of Criminal Courts Act 1973, s 43.*

Section 43[a] of the Powers of Criminal Courts Act 1973, which empowers the court to make a forfeiture order depriving an offender of property used, or intended for use, for *c* the purposes of crime, does not extend to the forfeiture of real property, since it is clear from s 43(4) that the 'property' to which the section refers is only property in the possession of the police by virtue of s 43, thereby necessarily confining it to personal property (see p 971 *f* and p 972 *b c*, post).

R v Beard (Graham) [1974] 1 WLR 1549 and dicta of Lord Diplock and of Lord Scarman in *R v Cuthbertson* [1980] 2 All ER at 405, 407 applied.
d

Notes

For forfeiture of property used for crime, see 11 Halsbury's Laws (4th edn) para 568.

For the Powers of Criminal Courts Act 1973, s 43, see 43 Halsbury's Statutes (3rd edn) 337.
e

Cases referred to in judgment

R v Beard (Graham) [1974] 1 WLR 1549, 14(2) Digest (Reissue) 864, 7487.
R v Cuthbertson [1980] 2 All ER 401, [1981] AC 470, [1980] 3 WLR 89, HL.
R v Waterfield (17 February 1975, unreported), CA.
f

Appeal

On 12 October 1982 at the Crown Court at St Albans, following his conviction on one count and plea of guilty to two counts of possession of a controlled drug with intent to supply, the appellant, Sultan Ashraf Khan, was sentenced by his Honour Judge Watling

g

---

a   Section 43, so far as material, provides:

'(1) Where a person is convicted of an offence punishable on indictment with imprisonment for a term of two years or more and the court by or before which he is convicted is satisfied that any property which was in his possession or under his control at the time of his apprehension—(*a*) has been used for the purpose of committing, or facilitating the commission of, any offence; or (*b*)
h was intended by him to be for that purpose; the court may make an order under this section in respect of that property . . .

(3) An order under this section shall operate to deprive the offender of his rights, if any, in the property to which it relates, and the property shall (if not already in their possession) be taken into the possession of the police.

(4) The Police (Property) Act 1897 shall apply, with the following modifications, to property which is in the possession of the police by virtue of this section—(*a*) no application shall be made
j under section 1(1) of that Act by any claimant of the property after the expiration of six months from the date on which the order in respect of the property was made under this section; and (*b*) no such application shall succeed unless the claimant satisfies the court either that he had not consented to the offender having possession of the property or that he did not know, and had no reason to suspect, that the property was likely to be used for the purpose mentioned in subsection (1) above . . .'

QC to a total of 10 years' imprisonment, a fine of £10,000 and was ordered to forfeit a Ford Cortina motor car under s 27 of the Misuse of Drugs Act 1971 and the property at 4 Burnham Road, St Albans under s 43 of the Powers of Criminal Courts Act 1973. The appellant appealed against sentence. On 16 November 1981 at the same court following her plea of guilty to five counts of possession of a controlled drug the appellant, Pauline Susan Crawley, was sentenced by Judge Watling to a total of three years' imprisonment. She appealed against sentence. The case is only reported in respect of the appeal of the appellant Khan. The facts are set out in the judgment of the court.

Peter Thornton for the appellant Khan.
Kieran Coonan (assigned by the Registrar of Criminal Appeals) for the appellant Crawley.
Ian Kennedy QC and *Douglas Hogg* for the Crown.

DUNN LJ delivered the following judgment of the court: On 12 October 1981, in the Crown Court at St Albans before his Honour Judge Watling QC, the appellant Khan was sentenced as follows, having been convicted on 8 October 1981: on a count of possessing cannabis with intent to supply, 3 years' imprisonment; on two counts of possessing heroin with intent to supply, 5 years' imprisonment on each count concurrent. An order was made under s 27 of the Misuse of Drugs Act 1971 for the forfeiture of a Ford Cortina motor car.

On the same day he was further sentenced, having pleaded guilty, to a second indictment, on two counts of supplying heroin, one count of possessing heroin with intent to supply and one count of possessing heroin, to 5 years' imprisonment on each count concurrent; those sentences to be consecutive to the sentences passed on the first indictment; making a total of 10 years' imprisonment. He was further ordered to pay a fine of £10,000, and an order was made under s 43 of the Powers of Criminal Courts Act 1973 for the forfeiture of the property known as 4 Burnham Road, St Albans.

On 16 November 1981, before the same court, the appellant Crawley was sentenced as follows, having pleaded guilty on 5 October: on a count of possessing cannabis with intent to supply, 2 years' imprisonment; on a count of possessing cannabis, 12 months' imprisonment concurrent; on a count of possessing heroin with intent to supply, 3 years' imprisonment concurrent; on two counts of possessing heroin, 12 months' imprisonment concurrent on each count; making a total sentence of 3 years' imprisonment.

Both appellants now appeal against sentence by leave of the single judge.

The facts of the matter were that between 15 January and 21 February 1980 police officers kept observation at an address, 180 London Road, St Albans, where the appellants were cohabiting in the top flat. There were numerous visitors each day, and some people were arriving regularly. Their identity appeared to be checked on each occasion by one or other appellant looking out before they were admitted.

On 21 February 1980 the police unsuccessfully tried to stop the appellants in a car. Later that day a search warrant was executed at 180 London Road, where quantities of heroin, cannabis resin and scales bearing traces of heroin and cocaine were seized.

The appellants were arrested on 25 February 1980. The appellant Khan declined to answer questions. The appellant Crawley, after an initial silence, admitted that she had been a heroin addict for two years and that she had supplied it to others.

The second indictment, which related to Khan only, arose out of these facts. On 21 May 1981, some 11 months after his committal for trial on bail in the first case, in furtherance of a plan conceived by the police, one Lahl Khan obtained 195 milligrammes of heroin from the appellant. On 31 May 1981 a meeting took place in a motor car outside 4 Burnham Road, St Albans, a property owned and occupied by the appellant. Present were the appellant, Lahl Khan and a police constable, who was an undercover agent and who was wired up with a tape recorder. The appellant told the police constable that he dealt in heroin and cannabis on a large scale and also had some cocaine. During this meeting Lahl Khan purported to purchase 498 grammes (about one pound) of heroin

from the appellant for £13,000, and a cigarette containing heroin was partly smoked as
a a test of the quality of the heroin. The appellant said that his share of the money was no
more than £750. At this point the police, who had been waiting in the vicinity, arrested
the appellant, and 4 Burnham Road was searched. A number of articles consistent with
the marketing of heroin were found and in two suitcases was found a total of £6,500 in
cash, which the judge said he was quite satisfied was the proceeds of the sale of drugs. He
referred to it as 'drug money'. When interviewed, the appellant admitted that he supplied
b drugs on a large scale, after being told that his conversation in the car had been recorded.

Khan is 32 years old. He was born in Pakistan. He came to this country in 1964. He
has two previous convictions for drug offences, both spent.

Crawley is now aged 29. Since 1977 she had been employed in good employment. She
has two previous convictions for drug offences, one in Sri Lanka, and one in St Albans, an
offence of unlawfully possessing heroin and cannabis in 1978, when she was put on
c probation for 12 months. She apparently started using drugs at the age of 16 and became
addicted to heroin. Her relationship with Khan began and was sustained by her need for
drugs. According to the social inquiry report, she said that the extent of her personal
supplying of drugs was the supplying of friends and she expressed fear at one moment at
the reaction of the appellant if he discovered that she was selling drugs cheap to her
friends. She became pregnant by the appellant in 1980 and she was very fearful of the
d effect that her drug-taking might have on the unborn child. Accordingly, while she was
still living with the appellant, in January 1981, she went voluntarily to the Hill End
Hospital to cure herself of her addiction.

There are reports before the court, which were before the judge. A report from Hill
End Hospital states that she was successfully withdrawn, and discharged on no medication.
In May 1981 she gave birth to the child and the evidence is that she has stopped taking
e heroin since she left hospital. It was she, according to what was said in court, who
persuaded Khan to surrender to the police in early 1980 after they had evaded arrest on a
previous occasion.

So far as the appeal of Khan is concerned, a number of points have been taken. Firstly,
as to the forfeiture of the house, it is conceded by the Crown that s 43 of the Powers of
Criminal Courts Act 1973, which was the section under which the judge purported to
f order the forfeiture of the house, does not apply to real property. It is true that the section
uses the word 'property' in sub-s (1) without any qualification, but sub-s (4), which makes
the Police Property Act 1897 applicable, refers to property which is in the possession of
the police by virtue of the section, thus confining it to personal property and not real
property.

There are also two cases which were decided under s 27 of the Misuse of Drugs Act
g 1971, which indicate that under that section the powers of the court to forfeit property
are confined to personal property and not to real property. The ambit of s 27 of the 1971
Act is wider than that of s 43 of the 1973 Act.

In *R v Beard (Graham)* [1974] 1 WLR 1549 Caulfield J held that a house was not
included in the word 'anything' in s 27 of the 1971 Act. In *R v Cuthbertson* [1980] 2 All
ER 401 at 405, [1981] AC 470 at 483 Lord Diplock said:
h

'I would apply a purposive construction to the section considered as a whole [that
is s 27 of the 1971 Act]. What does it set out to do? Its evident purpose is to enable
things to be forfeited so that they may be destroyed or dealt with in some other
manner as the court thinks fit. The words are apt and, as it seems to me, are only apt
to deal with things that are tangible, things of which physical possession can be
j taken by a person authorised to do so by the court and which are capable of being
physically destroyed by that person or disposed of by him in some other way. To
ascribe to the section any more extended ambit would involve putting a strained
construction on the actual language that is used, and so far from there being any
grounds for doing so, it seems to me that if it were attempted to extend the subject
matter of orders of forfeiture to choses in action or other intangibles, this would

lead to difficulties and uncertainties in application which it can hardly be supposed that Parliament intended to create.'

Lord Scarman said ([1980] 2 All ER 401 at 407, [1981] AC 470 at 486):

'Counsel for the appellants put it correctly, though strangely, when he suggested that forfeiture was limited to "the accoutrements of crime", by which I took him to mean, in workaday English, the tools, instruments, or other physical means used to commit the crime.'

Although the matter has never been considered before, or if it has been considered has never been reported, in view of the concession by the Crown and in view of the construction that we have put on the section and in view of the two cases to which we have referred, we accept that the order for forfeiture of the house must be set aside, the judge having no jurisdiction to make it.

It is not suggested that there was any error in the judge making an order for forfeiture of the Cortina car. What is suggested is that grave as these offences were, the sentence of 10 years' imprisonment in total was excessive and that the sentences on the two indictments should have been made concurrent, making a total of 5 years' imprisonment.

It was submitted, first of all, that the judge, having heard in full the evidence on the first indictment, was wrong to accept the evidence of a police officer who gave evidence after the pleas on the second indictment, that Khan was in effect the main supplier of drugs in the county of Hertford, and that the evidence on the first indictment, which was contested, indicated that this was almost entirely local and confined to St Albans. It was also said that the second indictment related only to one isolated sale of heroin and that, albeit that sale was effected at a time when Khan was on bail, nonetheless the judge should have looked at the whole course of dealing over the period and that the sentence of 5 years' imprisonment on the second indictment should accordingly have been made concurrent.

It is quite plain that whatever the precise territorial extent of Khan's operation, he was supplying drugs on a substantial scale from his premises. He was supplying this lethal drug heroin. The courts have always taken the view that very substantial periods of imprisonment are required for people who commit that offence because of the terrible social consequences of what they do. Having said that, however, it is important to remember that this was not a case of importation and there must be room in the graduation of sentences for the importer and large scale wholesaler of these very dangerous drugs. The courts must take that into account in considering the proper sentence for a supplier such as Khan was.

We have come to the conclusion that the proper total sentence, having regard to the activities in which Khan engaged, is one of 7 years' imprisonment. He gets no discount or credit for assisting the police or for a plea of guilty so far as the first indictment is concerned, which was the principal one. We think that the sentence of 7 years can conveniently be made up by reducing the sentence on the second indictment from 5 years' imprisonment to 2 years' imprisonment and making that run consecutively to the 5 years' imprisonment on the first indictment. We think that that adequately reflects his own assessment of himself as having been supplying drugs on a large scale.

There remains to consider the fine. On reflection, notwithstanding the length of this sentence and its effect on this man, we have come to the conclusion that a substantial fine was appropriate in this case. We bear in mind what Lawton LJ said in *R v Waterfield* (17 February 1975, unreported), which was a case relating to the commercial exploitation of pornography. Lawton LJ said:

'The first thing the law should do is to ensure that those who break it in the sort of way this appellant has broken it should not make any money out of their wrongdoing. It follows that the fines totalling £7,000, in so far as they were a calculation by the learned judge of the profit this appellant had been making, cannot be criticised. They could, on the evidence, have been larger. Perhaps they should

a have been. This court is finally of the opinion that if those who take part in this
kind of trade know that on conviction they are likely to be stripped of every penny
of profit they make and a good deal more then the desire to enter it will be
diminished.'

We think that those observations equally apply to those who take part in the supply of
heroin. Counsel for Khan has submitted that as the fine was imposed on the second
indictment and as the total value of the heroin involved in the second indictment was
b only £13,000, that a fine of £10,000 was out of scale. We regard that as a technical
matter. The judge plainly was looking at the whole picture of the profits which this man
was likely to have made out of his drug-trafficking as a whole and there was the evidence
of the £6,500 in the two suitcases. We have come to the conclusion that the fine of
£10,000 was not excessive in the circumstances, and we uphold it.

c Accordingly the appeal of Khan will be allowed to the extent that the order for
forfeiture of the house will be quashed and the sentence on the second indictment will
be reduced to 2 years' imprisonment to run consecutively to the 5 years on the first
indictment.

[The court then considered the sentence imposed on the appellant Crawley and
reduced the sentence to two years' imprisonment suspended for a period of two years.]

d *Appeals allowed in part.*

Solicitors: *Offenbach & Co* (for the appellant Khan); *Director of Public Prosecutions.*

Sophie Craven   Barrister.

e

Badry v Director of Public Prosecutions of Mauritius

f
PRIVY COUNCIL
LORD HAILSHAM OF ST MARYLEBONE LC, LORD SCARMAN, LORD ROSKILL, LORD BRANDON OF
OAKBROOK AND LORD TEMPLEMAN
4, 5 OCTOBER, 15 NOVEMBER 1982

g *Contempt of court – Court – Commission of inquiry – Inquiry into allegations of fraud and
corruption by appellant – Supreme Court judge appointed as sole commissioner to conduct inquiry
– Abusive and scurrilous remarks made by appellant about judge in his capacity as a commissioner
– Whether contempt of court.*

*Mauritius – Public authorities – Commission of inquiry – Contempt of court – Whether law of
h contempt applying to commission of inquiry – Commissions of Inquiry Ordinance (Mauritius).*

The appellant was a well-known public figure in Mauritius who had been a minister in
the government of Mauritius. On 21 December 1978 a judge of the Supreme Court of
Mauritius was appointed as a sole commissioner under the Commissions of Inquiry
Ordinance (Mauritius) to conduct an inquiry into allegations of fraud and corruption
j made against the appellant in his capacity as a minister. On 2 May 1979 the judge
produced a report which was adverse to the appellant on the matters inquired into. On
18 May 1980 the appellant delivered a public speech in the French Creole dialect in
which (i) he stated that a Creole employee's claim for compensation for industrial injury
had been dismissed by the Supreme Court simply because the other party to the action
was a wealthy company, (ii) he uttered words directed against the tribunal judge which

were vulgar, scurrilous, abusive and lacking in respect to the person of the judge, and (iii)
he said that the judge's report was being used to destroy the appellant and that it *a*
contained a number of misstatements. Three motions were issued to commit the
appellant for contempt of court. The Supreme Court held that the remarks made by the
appellant relating to the dismissal of the Creole employee's claim for compensation
constituted a serious accusation of bias against the Supreme Court which were clearly
meant to shake the public's confidence in the administration of justice in Mauritius and
were therefore a contempt of court. As to the other words spoken by the appellant, the *b*
court, although deciding that they were directed against the judge in his capacity as a
commissioner and not against him in his judicial capacity, further decided that at
common law the law of contempt applied to a commissioner appointed under the
Ordinance as it did to a court of justice, and accordingly held that the words complained
of constituted a contempt of court. The appellant appealed to the Privy Council.

c
Held – The accusation of bias levelled against the Supreme Court clearly constituted
contempt of court and the appeal in respect thereof would be dismissed. However, with
respect to the other statements made by the appellant, it was well established that, in the
absence of statutory provision to the contrary, the law of contempt of court applied by
definition only to courts of justice properly so called and to judges of such courts of
justice. Since the statements complained of were made against the judge in his capacity *d*
as a commissioner and not against him in his judicial capacity, the Supreme Court had
erred in finding that they constituted a contempt of court and the appeals in respect
thereof would be allowed. Furthermore, the criticisms of the judge's report could not, in
the absence of any finding of maliciousness or lack of good faith, amount to contempt
(see p 979 *e* to *j*, p 980 *h j* and p 981 *d* to *h*, post).

Ibrahim v R [1914–15] All ER Rep 874 and *Practice Note* (1932) 48 TLR 300 applied. *e*
R v Gray [1900–3] All ER Rep 59 and *A-G v BBC* [1980] 3 All ER 161 approved.

Notes
For what constitutes a court, see 10 Halsbury's Laws (4th edn) paras 701–702, and for
cases on the subject, see 16 Digest (Reissue) 136–138, *1373–1394.*
For scandalising the court, see 9 Halsbury's Laws (4th edn) para 27, and for cases on *f*
the subject, see 16 Digest (Reissue) 45–47, *434–455.*

Cases referred to in judgment
A-G v BBC [1980] 3 All ER 161, [1981] AC 303, [1980] 3 WLR 109, HL.
Ambard v A-G for Trinidad and Tobago [1936] 1 All ER 704, [1936] AC 322, PC, 16 Digest
    (Reissue) 46, *436.*
g
Deeming, Ex p [1892] AC 422, PC, 8(2) Digest (Reissue) 835, *820.*
Dillet, Re (1887) 12 App Cas 459, 8(2) Digest (Reissue) 835, *817.*
DPP v Masson [1972] Mauritius Rep 47.
Ibrahim v R [1914] AC 599, [1914–15] All ER Rep 874, PC, 14(2) Digest (Reissue) 562,
    4583.
Macrea, Ex p [1893] AC 346, PC, 8(2) Digest (Reissue) 836, *829.* *h*
McLeod v St Aubyn [1899] AC 549, PC, 16 Digest (Reissue) 45, *434.*
Practice Note (1932) 48 TLR 300, PC, 16 Digest (Reissue) 196, *1958.*
R v Bertrand (1867) LR 1 PC 520, PC, 14(1) Digest (Reissue) 406, *3436.*
R v Freeman (1925) Times, 18 November.
R v Gray [1900] 2 QB 36, [1900–3] All ER Rep 59, DC, 16 Digest (Reissue) 47, *452.*
R v New Statesman (editor), ex p DPP (1928) 44 TLR 301, DC, 16 Digest (Reissue) 47, *449.* *j*
R v Wilkinson (1930) Times, 16 July.
Read and Huggonson, Re (1742) 2 Atk 469, 26 ER 683, LC, 16 Digest (Reissue) 1, *1.*
Reil v R (1885) 10 App Cas 675, PC, 8(2) Digest (Reissue) 835, *816.*
Shaw v DPP [1961] 2 All ER 446, [1962] AC 220, [1961] 2 WLR 897, HL, 14(1) Digest
    (Reissue) 139, *965.*

Consolidated appeals

a Lutchmeeparsad Badry appealed with leave of the Supreme Court of Mauritius granted by order dated 23 October 1980 and final leave to appeal granted on 9 February 1981 against two judgments of the Supreme Court of Mauritius (Espitalier-Noel J and Ahmed AJ) delivered on 23 October 1980 whereby the appellant was found guilty of contempt of court, as alleged in three motions each dated 7 July 1980. The three appeals were consolidated by order of the Judicial Committee of the Privy Council dated 28 June 1982.

b The facts are set out in the judgment of the Board.

John Platts-Mills QC, Dabi Simon Kumalo and *Ewam Juggernauth* (both of the Mauritian Bar) for the appellant.
Mark Strachan for the respondent.

c
LORD HAILSHAM OF ST MARYLEBONE LC. These three consolidated appeals (Privy Council appeals nos 4, 5 and 6 of 1981) from the Supreme Court of Mauritius arise from three motions to commit the appellant for contempt of court. These three motions will be referred to hereafter as no 4, no 5, and no 6. All three motions arose out of words alleged to have been spoken by the appellant in the course of a single speech on
d 18 May 1980 to a regional congress of the Labour Party of Mauritius at the Social Welfare Centre of Mare d'Albert. There were three separate records before their Lordships, one in respect of each speech, but the motions were heard together and resulted in two separate judgments of the Supreme Court (Espitalier-Noel J and Ahmed AJ) delivered on 23 October 1980. In each of these judgments the appellant was found guilty of contempt. In the first, that relating to no 4, the appellant was sentenced to six weeks' imprisonment.
e In the second, the appellant was sentenced to six weeks' imprisonment in respect of each of nos 5 and 6. The sentences in respect of nos 5 and 6 were to be served concurrently with one another, but consecutively to the sentence imposed in respect of no 4, so that the total term of imprisonment imposed on the appellant was 12 weeks. There has been a stay of execution pending the appellant's appeal to Her Majesty in Council, leave to prosecute which was granted by the Supreme Court (on terms since complied with).
f The appellant is a person well known in the public life of Mauritius. At the material times he was a member of the Legislative Assembly and until a date in 1978 or 1979 had been Minister of Social Security in the government of Mauritius. In order to understand what follows it is necessary to state that on 21 December 1978 Glover J, of the Supreme Court of Mauritius, was appointed as sole commissioner under the commissions of Inquiry Ordinance to inquire into allegations of fraud and corruption made against the
g appellant in his former capacity as Minister of Social Security and against another and on 2 May 1979 Glover J, in his capacity as sole commissioner, produced a report adverse to the appellant on the matters inquired into.

On the hearing of the three motions it was not disputed that the appellant had attended the meeting of 18 May 1980, and together with others, had made a speech to the assembled audience in the local Creole dialect of French. The affidavits in support of the
h three notices of motion attributed to the appellant the Creole words which follow, and which were found to constitute contempt of court. The words attributed to the appellant in the notices of motion were:

Motion no 4

j (1) 'Ainan aine dimoune fine touyer, li pas fine gagne narien parcequi li ainan galette li fine aller-aine zenfant fine mort.'

(These words attributed murder to an unnamed person but may be disregarded, since the Supreme Court held that they were not in fact a contempt of court since the court was 'not satisfied . . . that the respondent must have been referring and been understood to refer to a court case'. There is no appeal in respect of this decision.)

(2) 'Aine creole travaille F.U.E.L., fine gagne aine accident travail, li fine vine 50% infirme, zaffaire fine alle en Cour Supreme, case fine dismiss, parcequi li *a* F.U.E.L. parcequi Missie Series qui la-bas, aine sou li pas fine gagne. Alla la justice ici.'

The translation of these words supplied to their Lordships (slightly altered), which for this purpose may be treated as accurate, is as follows:

'A creole working at F.U.E.L. [sc Flacq Limited Estates Ltd., a well-known *b* commercial concern in Mauritius] met with an accident at work. He is now 50% incapacitated. The case went (or "was referred") to the Supreme Court. The case was dismissed. Because it is F.U.E.L. Because it is M Series who is there [it is admitted that M Series was an important person in the management of FUEL], he did not get a sou (a "penny") in compensation. This is the kind of justice we have here.'

On the part of the appellant it was pointed out that the punctuation of the translation did *c* not correspond with the punctuation of the French, and that the words "in compensation" did not appear in the original French at all. In the opinion of their Lordships, nothing turns on this.

Motion no 5
The words attributed to the appellant in the affidavits supporting no 5 differed slightly *d* from one another, but in the version of the main witness in support of the motion were:

'Quand zenfants coolies pou prendre so vengeance, est-ce qui missie Glover qui pou dirige ca pays la, nous bisin dechire so calecon dans ca pays la.'

The translation supplied to their Lordships was:
e
'When the children of the coolies take their revenge is it M. Glover who is going to run this country? We must teach him a lesson, in this country, and expose him for what he is.'

It is evident that this is a mistranslation, no doubt introduced to spare their Lordships' feelings. The correct translation, to anyone with even a modest acquaintance with the French language, obviously concludes with the words 'We must tear off his trousers in *f* this country' and not 'We must teach him a lesson and expose him for what he is'. In passing, it must be pointed out that the typed copy of the record supplied to their Lordships is innocent alike of all accents and the cedilla.

A slightly different and rather longer version was supplied by a supporting witness, but it was to the same effect. It referred to the taking of vengeance by the coolies and included the critical phrase: 'bisoin [sic] dechire calecon missie Glover dans ca pays la.' *g*

Motion no 6
The words deposed to in support of no 6 were as follows:

'Ape utilise rapport Glover pour detruire moi-pas tout ce qui li fine ecrire qui vrai—ainan aine paquet quiquechose qui li pas fine prend en consideration.' *h*

The supplied translation of this, which their Lordships are content to accept as correct, is as follows:

'The Glover report is being used to destroy me—it is not everything he said that is true—there are a lot of things he has not taken into consideration.'

At the hearing of the three motions the deponents to the supporting affidavits were *j* sworn and tendered for cross-examination and cross-examined. The appellant gave evidence and was cross-examined at length and two witnesses spoke on his behalf. He offered no innocent explanation of any of the words in question, but swore firmly that he had never uttered them at all. At the hearing before their Lordships it was argued strongly that the prosecution had failed to discharge the burden on them to prove that

the words in question were in fact spoken or bore the meanings alleged, and other
a questions were raised as to the admissibility of certain evidence introduced at the stage of
re-examination. It may be necessary in part of the case to examine more closely the
construction to be put on some of the words, but in general their Lordships, on the
principles on which their Lordships' Board invariably acts and which will be shortly
stated in greater detail, find themselves bound by the findings of fact of the Supreme
Court, who, after all, saw the witnesses and observed their demeanour. These findings
b on no 4 were as follows:

> 'We have considered the evidence of Mr Ombrasine [the principal witness in
> support of the motion] and the complete denials by the respondent and find that
> the issues of fact raised in the present case are clear cut. The question of Mr
> Ombrasine having possibly misunderstood or mistakenly reported what the
> respondent would have said, we find just does not arise. Either the respondent did
c > utter the incriminated words or he did not, and Mr Ombrasine would have
> deliberately fabricated evidence against him.'

Earlier the Supreme Court dismissed the two witnesses called in support of the appellant
in these words:

> 'We have found them to be thoroughly unconvincing and unreliable and we have
d > no hesitation in discarding their evidence.'

On Mr Ombrasine himself the primary fact found by the court was as follows:

> 'We . . . are fully satisfied of the good faith of Mr. Ombrasine. The absence, in the
> circumstances, of corroborating witnesses has not shaken our unreserved belief that
> Mr. Ombrasine has spoken the truth and we are satisfied that the [appellant] did
e > utter the incriminated words.'

Similar findings of primary fact were made in nos 5 and 6 by the Supreme Court. After
discarding the witnesses supportive of the appellant's denials, they said:

> 'We are satisfied that the [appellant] did utter the words which are the subject
> matter of the two motions before us.'
f

By these findings of primary fact, on the ordinary principles which actuate this Board,
their Lordships consider themselves bound, and since this appeal may be the first to be
heard under the legislation (Courts (Amendment) Act 1980, s 7) extending the right of
appeal to the Judicial Committee in appeals from Mauritius, their Lordships feel it right
to reiterate the general principles on which they will continue to feel bound to tender
g their advice in criminal matters.

The locus classicus in which these principles are stated are the passages in the opinion
of the Board given by Lord Sumner in *Ibrahim v R* [1914] AC 599 at 614–615, [1914–15]
All ER Rep 874 at 880, where he said:

> 'Their Lordships' practice has been repeatedly defined. Leave to appeal is not
> granted "except where some clear departure from the requirements of justice"
h > exists: *Riel v. Reg.* (1885) 10 App Cas 675); nor unless "by a disregard of the forms of
> legal process, or by some violation of the principles of natural justice or otherwise,
> substantial and grave injustice has been done": *Dillet's Case* ((1887) 12 App Cas 459).
> It is true that these are cases of applications for special leave to appeal, but the Board
> has repeatedly treated applications for leave to appeal and the hearing of criminal
> appeals as being upon the same footing: *Riel's Case; Ex parte Deeming* ([1892] AC
i > 422). The Board cannot give leave to appeal where the grounds suggested could not
> sustain the appeal itself; and, conversely, it cannot allow an appeal on grounds that
> would not have sufficed for the grant of permission to bring it. Misdirection as such,
> even irregularity as such, will not suffice: *Ex parte Macrea* ([1893] AC 346). There
> must be something which, in the particular case, deprives the accused of the
> substance of fair trial and the protection of the law, or which, in general, tends to

divert the due and orderly administration of the law into a new course, which may be drawn into an evil precedent in future: *Reg.* v. *Bertrand* ((1867) LR 1 PC 520).'   *a*

By these words their Lordships, notwithstanding any new legislation in the territories of the Commonwealth from which appeals may be brought in criminal matters, continue to feel themselves bound and, in the instant appeals, their Lordships consider that they have been guided by them. Their Lordships also desire to repeat the practice direction issued by Lord Dunedin (see *Practice Note* (1932) 48 TLR 300) as follows:

'Their Lordships have repeated *ad nauseam* the statement that they do not sit as a   *b*
Court of Criminal Appeal. For them to interfere with a criminal sentence there must be something so irregular or so outrageous as to shake the very basis of justice. Such an instance was found in *Dillet's Case* ((1887) 12 App Cas 459), which has all along been held to be the leading authority in such matters. In the present case [an Indian petition for special leave to appeal against conviction and sentence of death   *c*
for murder] the only real point is a point for argument on a section of a statute, and all that the petitioners can say is that it was wrongly decided. That is to ask the Board to sit as a Court of Criminal Appeal and nothing else.'

In all that their Lordships say hereafter in discussing the merits of the instant consolidated appeals their Lordships believe that they remain bound by, and have stayed within, the confines of these precepts.   *d*

Contempt of court may consist of conduct of different kinds. The classical description relevant to this class of contempt is contained in the judgment of Lord Russell CJ in *R v Gray* [1900] 2 QB 36 at 40, [1900–3] All ER Rep 59 at 62 when he said:

'Any act done or writing published calculated to bring a Court or a judge of the Court into contempt, or to lower his authority, is a contempt of Court. That is one   *e*
class of contempt. Further, any act done or writing published calculated to obstruct or interfere with the due course of justice or the lawful process of the Courts is a contempt of Court.'

In the United Kingdom the latter class must now be considered as modified in a liberal direction by the Contempt of Court Act 1981. Lord Russell CJ went on:

'The former class belongs to the category which Lord Hardwicke LC characterised   *f*
as "scandalising a Court or a judge" (*In re Read and Huggonson* ((1742) 2 Atk 469, 26 ER 683)). That description of that class of contempt is to be taken subject to one and an important qualification. Judges and Courts are alike open to criticism, and if reasonable argument or expostulation is offered against any judicial act as contrary to law or public good, no Court could or would treat that as a contempt of Court. The law ought not to be astute in such cases to criticise adversely what under such   *g*
circumstances and with such an object is published; but it is to be remembered that in this matter the liberty of the press is no greater and no less than the liberty of every subject of the Queen.'

This qualification must be considered to have been amplified and emphasised, though not altered, by the famous passage in Lord Atkin's opinion when he gave the advice of   *h*
the Board in *Ambard v A-G for Trinidad and Tobago* [1936] 1 All ER 704 at 709, [1936] AC 322 at 335:

'But whether the authority and position of an individual judge or the due administration of justice is concerned, no wrong is committed by any member of the public who exercises the ordinary right of criticising in good faith in private or   *j*
public the public act done in the seat of justice. The path of criticism is a public way: the wrong headed are permitted to err therein: provided that members of the public abstain from imputing improper motives to those taking part in the administration of justice, and are genuinely exercising a right of criticism and not acting in malice or attempting to impair the administration of justice, they are

a
immune. Justice is not a cloistered virtue: she must be allowed to suffer the scrutiny and respectful even though outspoken comments of ordinary men.'

Their Lordships' attention was drawn to many cases before and after the decision in *R v Gray*, including *McLeod v St Aubyn* [1899] AC 549, where Lord Morris's statement that the first class of contempt had in this country become obsolete unfortunately proved incorrect (see *R v Gray* [1900] 2 QB 36, [1900–3] All ER Rep 59, *R v New Statesman (editor), ex p DPP* (1928) 44 TLR 301, *Ambard v A-G for Trinidad and Tobago, R v Freeman*

b
(1925) Times, 18 November, *R v Wilkinson* (1930) Times, 16 July and others). But, whilst nothing really encourages courts or Attorneys General to prosecute cases of this kind in all but the most serious examples, or courts to take notice of any but the most intolerable instances, nothing has happened in the intervening eighty years to invalidate the analysis by the first Lord Russell of Killowen CJ in *R v Gray*.

This leads inevitably to the conclusion that the instant appeal on no 4 falls to be

c
dismissed. On this matter, the Supreme Court reached the conclusion:

'By his latter remarks [ie excluding those relating to the dead child], on the other hand, relating to the man who had been incapacitated at 50% we have no doubt that the [appellant] meant and could only have been understood to mean that this man's claim for damages or compensation had been unjustly dismissed by the Supreme

d
Court because the other party to the case happened to be a wealthy company. It was, we find, nothing else but a serious accusation of bias being levelled at the Supreme Court and can in no way be possibly considered, as was suggested by counsel, as having been a comment on the difficulties poor litigants may encounter in having their cases adequately presented in Court.'

e
In spite of earnest endeavours by the appellant's counsel to pursue before their Lordships the line of alternative interpretation suggested in the last sentence, their Lordships find it impossible to accompany him in this journey. It seems impossible to attribute any meaning to the words spoken other than attribution to an actual case, real or ficititious, and the worse if fictitious, in which the justice of the case was overborne by bias and the overweening influence alleged to have been exerted by FUEL and their

f
powerful official, M Series. Even if their Lordships were not disposed to this view by the internal logic of the words, the fact that the Supreme Court, with knowledge of the conditions local to Mauritius and the nuances of the Creole expressions, is in a position far more qualified to understand its meaning than their Lordships, situated in the United Kingdom and bound by the self-denying ordinance formulated by Lord Sumner in *Ibrahim v R* and in Lord Dunedin's practice direction, would make them hesitate to differ

g
from their conclusion. As it is, their Lordships can only confirm the conclusion of the Supreme Court when they said:

'The fact remains that we find that the grave and unwarranted accusation which he [the appellant] chose to level at the Supreme Court on the 18th May was clearly meant to shake public confidence in the administration of justice in Mauritius.'

h
It follows that the appeal in respect of no 4 should be dismissed.

The situation is quite different in respect to the appeals in respect of motions nos 5 and 6 and, in their Lordships' view, these appeals must be allowed. In their Lordships' opinion, the easier of these two to determine is no 6. Quite apart from considerations common both to nos 5 and 6, the words complained of in no 6 appear to mean no more than that the appellant's opponents had used the Glover report to destroy him (an

j
assertion, false or true, which cannot on any view be construed as contemptuous of Glover J), and that the Glover report contained a number of statements which were incorrect, and failed to take into account a whole bundle of considerations which ought to have been considered relevant. In the absence of any express finding by the Supreme Court that these criticisms were made maliciously or made otherwise than in good faith by the person impugned by the report (which may or may not have been the fact) their

Lordships find it quite impossible to say that these words by themselves do not come squarely within the 'important qualification' postulated by Lord Russell CJ in *R v Gray* [1900] 2 QB 36 at 40, [1900–3] All ER Rep 59 at 62.

This leads their Lordships to a discussion of the appeal on no 5, the reasons for which are contained in the same judgment as that on no 6. It must be said at once that the words found to have been uttered by the appellant in either variant version are vulgar, scurrilous, abusive and lacking in respect to the person of a judge which would be expected, though, were they uttered in this country, it may be doubted whether they would be calculated to lower the authority of the judge rather than the reputation of any public man who uttered them so as to bring them within the condemnation of Lord Russell's definition of contempt. Nevertheless, bearing in mind the self-denying ordinance accepted in this Board by *Ibrahim v R* and the practice direction of Lord Dunedin, it may be doubted whether, if the Supreme Court had simply said that in the circumstances prevailing in Mauritius these words were 'calculated to bring a judge of the Court into contempt or to lower his authority', this Board would have felt it proper to differ from their opinion.

Unhappily, although there are words in the judgment which could be construed in this sense if taken by themselves, a more careful reading of the judgment leads their Lordships to the conclusion that these words are taken simply as aggravation of an offence which the Supreme Court treated as having been established on wholly different grounds which their Lordships can only describe as based on a fundamental error of law.

Put simply, in their judgments on nos 5 and 6 (the latter of which has now been disposed of separately) the Supreme Court decided that the words in both cases were directed against Glover J not in his judicial capacity, but as a commissioner, indeed the sole commissioner, in the inquiry into the appellant's conduct and that, at common law, the law of contempt applied to such a commission and a commissioner, appointed under the Ordinance as amended, as it would have done to a court of justice. They did so on the supposed authority of *DPP v Masson* [1972] Mauritius Rep 47, where the point was neither argued nor expressly decided, but simply assumed. In the view of their Lordships this doctrine, for which no other authority exists, is plainly untenable. That commissions of inquiry do require some protection of this nature is, of course, not to be doubted. But such protection only exists when conferred by statute. A limited protection of this kind is indeed conferred in Mauritius by s 11(3) of the amended Ordinance. But this is limited to contempts at any sitting of the commission, and to a fine not exceeding Rs500 to be imposed by the commissioners, and levied as if it were a fine of the district magistrate of Port Louis. Since the appellant's speech was delivered long after the commission was functus officio, it need not be said that this disciplinary power was not, and could not have been, used in the present case. The corresponding United Kingdom statute, the Tribunals of Inquiry (Evidence) Act 1921, by s 1(2)(c), accords a wider power of committal on certification by the chairman of the tribunal to be exercised by the High Court in England and by the Court of Session in Scotland, and the value of this extended power was expressly indorsed both by the Report of the Royal Commission on Tribunals of Inquiry 1966 (Cmnd 3121; ch 13) and that of the interdepartmental committee, under the chairmanship of Salmon LJ, on the law of contempt as it affects tribunals of inquiry in 1969 (Cmnd 4078; ch 7), to the latter of which reference is made in the judgment of the Supreme Court. These statutory provisions, however desirable as they may be, only serve to illustrate the fact that, without them, commissions and committees of inquiry are not protected at common law. Driven up against this difficulty, it was seriously argued for the respondent that their Lordships should extend the law of contempt to such bodies by a bold act of judicial legislation. This their Lordships resolutely decline to do, particularly as the sole authority relied on in support of the invitation was the Ladies' Directory case, *Shaw v DPP* [1961] 2 All ER 446, [1962] AC 220 where, so far from purporting to indulge in such legislative activities, the majority in the House of Lords claimed to be following a line of authority in the Court of King's Bench as far back as the

tenure of office of Best CJ. Happily, though not in time to be cited before the Supreme
Court, their Lordships find themselves sustained in their view, to which in any case they
would have adhered, by the conclusive authority of the House of Lords in *A-G v BBC*
[1980] 3 All ER 161, [1981] AC 303. In that case, to which in their Lordships' view the
present appeal succeeds a fortiori, the House of Lords refused to apply the law of contempt
to a local valuation court, which at least enjoyed the designation, if not all the functions,
of a court of law. In their Lordships' view it is plainly established by this authority that,
in the absence of statutory provision to the contrary, the law of contempt of court applies
by definition only to courts of justice properly so called and to the judges of such courts
of justice. It would be invidious to supply quotations at length. but reference may be
made to the speeches of Viscount Dilhorne, Lord Salmon, Lord Edmund-Davies, Lord
Fraser and Lord Scarman (see [1980] 3 All ER 161 at 165, 166, 168–169, 172, 175, 176,
183, [1981] AC 303 at 337, 339, 342, 347, 351, 352, 362). It accordingly follows that,
when in their judgments on nos 5 and 6 the Supreme Court founded their opinion on an
affirmative answer to the question whether the law of contempt applies to a commission
or commissioner appointed to hold an inquiry under the Commissions of Inquiry
Ordinance (as amended), they erred in a respect which, to quote Lord Sumner in *Ibrahim
v R* [1914] AC 599 at 615—

'deprives the accused of the substance of a fair trial and the protection of the law
(and) which in general tends to divert the due and orderly administration of the law
into a new course which may be drawn into an evil precedent in future.'

In the view of their Lordships, both the decision on no 6, which they have already
disposed of on other lines, and that on no 5, with which they are now concerned, were
infected with this error, and therefore cannot stand. If confirmation were required of
this view in relation to no 5, their Lordships would find it in the finding of the Supreme
Court that the words complained of as spoken by the appellant constituted '. . . scurrilous
abuse of Mr Justice Glover *as commissioner*' and, as regards no 6, in the findings that the
words complained of there were a 'clear attack on the integrity and impartiality *of the
Commissioner*' (emphases added).

There remains the disposal of these appeals. Since the conclusion reached by their
Lordships involves the dismissal of the appeal on no 4, and allowing those on nos 5 and
6, logic would seem at first sight to involve that the sentence on no 4 should stand and
those on nos 5 and 6 should be quashed. But sentencing is a delicate matter and in their
Lordships' view it is possible that the Supreme Court imposed a custodial sentence on
motion no 4 on the footing that it was one of a sequence of three offences of which two
have now disappeared, and their Lordships are therefore of the opinion that the better
course would be to refer back the question of the appropriate sentence on no 4 to be
considered by the Supreme Court in the light of the advice tendered to Her Majesty on
all three appeals. The appeal on no 4 should therefore be dismissed as regards the
conviction but their Lordships will humbly advise Her Majesty that the question of
sentence be remitted to the consideration of the Supreme Court in the light of this appeal,
and that the appeals in relation to nos 5 and 6 be allowed and the convictions and
sentences set aside.

So far as regards costs, the costs of the hearing before the Supreme Court should follow
the event, those of no 4 being awarded to the Director of Public Prosecutions, those of
nos 5 and 6 being awarded to the appellant. The appellant already has to bear the cost of
a short adjournment granted at his request owing to the lateness of his instructions to
counsel. As regards the costs of the hearing before this Board, in principle, of course, the
questions are severable, and in principle costs could be awarded with mutual set-offs on
the issues on which the respective parties have succeeded. In the event, however, their
Lordships conclude that substantial justice will be done if each party be left to bear their
own respective costs.

Their Lordships will humbly advise Her Majesty accordingly.

Appeal on motion no 4 dismissed, appeals on motions nos 5 and 6 allowed. Case remitted to Supreme Court of Mauritius for reconsideration of sentence.

Solicitors: *Donald Nelson & Co* (for the appellant); *Charles Russell & Co* (for the respondent).

Mary Rose Plummer   Barrister.

Re Hurren (a bankrupt), ex parte the trustee v Inland Revenue Commissioners

CHANCERY DIVISION
WALTON J
26, 27 JULY 1982

Bankruptcy – Debts provable in bankruptcy – Penalty – Penalties in respect of income tax offences – Whether penalties 'debts provable in bankruptcy' – Bankruptcy Act 1914, s 30(3) – Taxes Management Act 1970, ss 93, 95.

Income tax – Penalty – Proceedings – Compromise – Power of Revenue to compromise proceedings to recover penalty – Bankruptcy – Compromise by trustee in bankruptcy of penalties in proceedings pending before General Commissioners – Whether trustees may agree or compromise penalties – Whether prior consent of bankrupt required – Taxes Management Act 1970, ss 93, 95.

On 6 October 1981 proceedings were instituted against the bankrupt for the recovery of penalties under ss 93 and 95 of the Taxes Management Act 1970 in respect of fraudulent or negligent delivery of incorrect returns or accounts of his income. On 24 November, when the proceedings were still pending before the General Commissioners, the bankrupt was adjudged bankrupt on the presentation of his own petition. Apart from a small claim by the Department of Health and Social Security, the Revenue was the only creditor, claiming tax unpaid on back duty assessments which had been agreed. Sufficient funds were available to the trustee to satisfy those claims. The trustee sought (1) the determination by the court of the question whether the penalties that might be awarded or agreed between the trustee and the Revenue, after the making of the receiving order, were debts provable in the bankruptcy, (2) an order that penalty proceedings be stayed permanently or until further order and (3) if the penalties were provable in the bankruptcy, the leave of the court to agree or compromise the amount of the penalties with the Revenue in such sum as he should think fit or the court should direct without the prior consent of the bankrupt.

Held – (1) The penalties incurred by the bankrupt under ss 93 and 95 of the 1970 Act were contingent liabilities to which he was subject at the date of the receiving order and which, with enough information, could be quantified, or, alternatively, were liabilities to which he might become subject before his discharge. In either case they were liabilities to which the bankrupt had become subject by reason of an obligation incurred before the date of the receiving order. Accordingly, the penalties were provable debts under s 30(3)[a] of the Bankruptcy Act 1914 (see p 985 c d and j to p 986 b and p 987 e f, post).

(2) There was no reason why the Revenue's claim for penalties should not be compromised, but any compromise agreed to by the trustee had also to be agreed to by the bankrupt because, particularly having regard to the fact that the bankrupt's only creditor was the Revenue and that, when the ordinary claims for tax had been satisfied, there might be a surplus for the bankrupt, the issue was in reality one between the bankrupt and the Revenue (see p 986 f to j and p 987 f g, post).

---

a   Section 30(3), so far as material, is set out at p 984 j, post

Notes

a   For debts provable in bankruptcy, see 3 Halsbury's Laws (4th edn) para 710, and for cases on the subject, see 4 Digest (Reissue) 282–284, 2532–2547.

For the power of the Commissioners of Inland Revenue to compound proceedings to recover a penalty, see 23 Halsbury's Laws (4th edn) para 1567, and for cases on the subject, see 28(1) Digest (Reissue) 579, 2154–2155.

For the Bankruptcy Act 1914, s 30, see 3 Halsbury's Statutes (3rd edn) 78.

b   For the Taxes Management Act 1970, ss 93, 95, see 34 ibid 1330, 1333.

Cases referred to in judgment

Ellis & Co's Trustee v Dixon-Johnson [1924] 1 Ch 342; *affd* [1924] 2 Ch 451, CA; *affd* [1925] AC 489, [1925] All ER Rep 715, HL, 4 Digest (Reissue) 447, 3878.

Pascoe, Re, Trustee in bankruptcy v HM Treasury's Lords Comrs [1944] 1 All ER 593, [1944]
c   Ch 310, DC, 4 Digest (Reissue) 284, 2546.

Adjourned summons

By an originating summons dated 15 July 1982 the trustee in bankruptcy of Frank Robert Hurren (the bankrupt) applied to the court seeking (1) the determination of the question whether the Commissioners of Inland Revenue might prove in the bankruptcy

d   of the bankrupt for the amount of penalties which might be awarded against the bankrupt under ss 93 and 95 of the Taxes Management Act 1970 in consequence of proceedings commenced against the bankrupt prior to the making of the receiving order, (2) an order that the proceedings for the recovery of penalties might be stayed permanently or until further order and (3) subject to (1) and (2) above an order granting the trustee leave to agree or compromise the amount of the penalties with the Inland

e   Revenue in such sum as he should think fit or otherwise as the court should direct without the necessity for the prior consent of the bankrupt. The Commissioners of Inland Revenue and the bankrupt were respondents to the summons. The facts are set out in the judgment.

Roger Kaye for the trustee.
f   *Michael Hart* for the Crown.
Marcus Jones for the bankrupt.

WALTON J. This is an unusual summons taken out by the trustee of the property of the bankrupt in the present case. It asks:

g
'(1) That it may be determined whether [the Commissioners of Inland Revenue] may prove in the bankruptcy of the . . . Bankrupt for the amount of penalties (if any) claimed by the Inland Revenue from the Bankrupt under Sections 93 and 95 of the Taxes Management Act 1970 in consequence of proceedings commenced against the Bankrupt on the 6th October 1981 for the recovery of such penalties in the

h   circumstances which have happened and in the following period or any of the next following two events, that is to say: (a) in the period prior to the ascertainment or determination of the amount of such penalties; (b) in the event of the determination of the amount of such penalties by the appropriate Tribunal having jurisdiction in the matter; (c) in the event of the Trustee and the Inland Revenue agreeing or compromising the amount of such penalties.

j   (2) Further or alternatively an Order that the proceedings for the recovery of the said penalties presently before the Commissioners for the General Purposes of the Income Tax for the Division of Surbiton in the County of Surrey instituted against the Bankrupt by a Summons dated the said 6th October 1981 may be stayed permanently or until further order or upon such other terms or conditions or otherwise as this Honourable Court shall direct.

(3) Subject to (1) and (2) above, an Order granting the Trustee leave to agree or compromise the amount of the said penalties with the Inland Revenue in such sum as he shall think fit (or otherwise as the Court shall direct) without the necessity for the prior consent of the Bankrupt.

(4) Further or alternatively directions as to how the Trustee should deal in the bankruptcy with the claims of the Inland Revenue for the recovery of and proof for the said penalties.'

The case is remarkable in a large number of ways, which is why the trustee has taken out this unusual summons. The bankrupt has had a history of not getting on very well with the Commissioners of Inland Revenue, to the extent that there have in fact been no less than two investigations into his affairs, and it is I think reasonably clear that he has not made all the returns which he ought to have made. There have consequently been back duty assessments, and those are now agreed and are final and binding on him.

Following those assessments the Revenue instituted, on 6 October 1981, proceedings against the bankrupt before the Commissioners for the General Purposes of the Income Tax for the division of Surbiton in the county of Surrey for the recovery of penalties under ss 93 and 95 of the Taxes Management Act 1970 in respect of fraudulent or negligent delivery of incorrect returns or accounts of his income for the years ending 5 April 1956 to 5 April 1979, thus covering a very long period indeed. The maximum amount of the penalties which could be awarded under the main section, that is s 95, would appear to be £65,439·15.

The bankrupt in fact has a large number of assets which he has given away within the statutory period, or made over to others, and the trustee has on foot various proceedings for recovering those; and before this present application was moved in front of me I approved minutes of another application whereunder a sum of something like £60,000 is being made immediately available to him on account of such claims. The situation is that in the bankruptcy of the bankrupt there are only at the' moment, and quite apart from any question of penalties, two creditors: the Department of Health and Social Security for the comparatively trifling sum of £61·20; and the Inland Revenue, in respect of all the unpaid tax, for the sum of £59,042·64.

The reason perhaps why the present situation has never arisen before is that where there are other creditors (and there are normally other creditors in a bankruptcy) it is not the practice of the Revenue to apply for penalties, because in substance they will only be able to prove for those penalties, if they can prove for them, in competition with the outside creditors, and that is something which the Inland Revenue do not normally wish to do. But here the situation is different. They are virtually the only creditor, and, having regard to the assets which may be available to the trustee in bankruptcy, there may be more than sufficient to pay their simple claim for tax. So these proceedings were instituted on 6 October 1981, and as a counter to those proceedings the bankrupt was adjudged bankrupt on 24 November 1981 on the presentation of his own petition.

Now the first question which arises, and it is really a fundamental one, is whether the penalties can be proved for in the bankruptcy. There is no doubt that had the penalties in fact been awarded by the date of the bankruptcy then they could have been proved for, and there is the case of *Re Pascoe, trustee in bankruptcy v HM Treasury's Lords Comrs* [1944] 1 All ER 593, [1944] Ch 310, which establishes that fact beyond all question. However, that was not the situation, of course, at the commencement of the bankruptcy, and one therefore has to look at the section dealing with debts provable in bankruptcy to see whether the claims for the penalties here are so provable. I think it is agreed that if they are it is because under s 30(3) of the Bankruptcy Act 1914 it is provided, after dealing with various other matters, that:

'. . . all debts and liabilities, present or future, certain or contingent, to which the debtor is subject at the date of the receiving order, or to which he may become subject before his discharge by reason of any obligation incurred before the date of the receiving order, shall be deemed to be debts provable in bankruptcy.'

Before I consider that any further, it is perhaps interesting to note that under s 28 of
the 1914 Act it is provided:

'(1) An order of discharge shall not release the bankrupt—(a) from any debt on a
recognizance nor from any debt with which the bankrupt may be chargeable at the
suit of the Crown or of any person for any offence against a statute relating to any
branch of the public revenue . . . and he shall not be discharged from such excepted
debts unless the Treasury certify in writing their consent to his being discharged
therefrom . . .'

Then it goes on in sub-s (2): 'An order of discharge shall release the bankrupt from all
other debts provable in bankruptcy', thus suggesting very strongly that the debts firstly
referred to are in fact provable in bankruptcy. But it seems to me that in any event the
claim for penalties is a liability (which, of course, as at the date of the receiving
order, was only contingent) to which the debtor was subject at the date of the receiving
order, and which might very well become quantified before his discharge, by reason of
an obligation which he incurred before the date of the receiving order, he having satisfied
the conditions (if he has in fact satisfied them) which enabled the General Commissioners
to award the penalties.

One of the difficulties concerning the matter is this. Supposing there had not been
these proceedings on foot, or supposing that these proceedings were to be stayed, how
would one ascertain the amount of the liability? Reading on, s 30(4) says:

'An estimate shall be made by the trustee of the value of any debt or liability
provable as aforesaid, which by reason of its being subject to any contingency or
contingencies, or for any other reason, does not bear a certain value.'

And, of course, one can never be absolutely certain of the value of the penalties; one can
only be certain what the maximum will be. Then, sub-s (6):

'If, in the opinion of the court, the value of the debt or liability is incapable of
being fairly estimated, the court may make an order to that effect, and thereupon
the debt or liability shall, for the purposes of this Act, be deemed to be a debt not
provable in bankruptcy.'

There are examples in the books of debts which are not provable in bankruptcy, but
they are such debts (as, for example, future maintenance) as cannot be ascertained on any
known principle of valuation by reason of the fact that the court in charge of the order
has power to vary its own order. So one is dealing with a protean subject matter which,
therefore, cannot be valued. Here, the difficulty is not that one is dealing with a protean
subject matter. It is accepted on all hands that, once the General Commissioners, if the
matter is fought out in front of them, have in fact decided on the amount of the penalties,
that is that. There is a power in the Inland Revenue to remit them, but that power is
nothing more than the power of any creditor, if he is so minded, to remit the liability
which the debtor owes to him. So there is nothing in that; but the difficulty lies in the
initial ascertainment.

However, it is in my judgment most illuminating and material to notice that under
s 100(5) of the Taxes Management Act 1970, where a person who has incurred any
penalty has died, any proceedings which have been or could have been commenced
against his personal representatives, and any penalty awarded in proceedings so continued
or commenced, shall be a debt due from and payable out of his estate, but nothing in the
subsection shall extend the time for commencing proceedings against the personal
representatives. That is most illuminating, because it suggests that there is really an
absolute standard based on the General Commissioners being placed in possession of all
the relevant facts which might conceivably be material. That being so, it seems to me
that it must be theoretically possible, at any rate, for bodies other than the General
Commissioners, if the matter comes to the crunch, to estimate the likely value of any
penalties under the relevant sections.

So it seems to me that the penalties which are here in question under ss 93 and 95 of
the Taxes Management Act 1970 are liabilities, contingent, to which the debtor was at   *a*
the date of the receiving order liable and which can, if given enough information, be
quantified. As an alternative, certainly I would think they were liabilities to which he
might very well become subject before his discharge. In either case it is by reason of an
obligation incurred before the date of the receiving order, and so they are debts provable
in the bankruptcy.

That being so, the question then arises: what next ought to be done? Counsel for the   *b*
Crown suggests that, since the ordinary duty of the trustee is to make an estimate under
s 30(4) of the value of that liability because it is subject to a contingency, that is precisely
what he should do, and he and the Revenue should try to agree a value for the liability
which the trustee should then admit. Of course, if the Revenue and the trustee cannot
agree, why, then, the Revenue would have to put in a proof, the proof would have to be
referred to this court, and what would happen then? It seems to me that what would   *c*
happen then is undoubtedly that the court would say that the proper body to determine
the amount in the present circumstances is undoubtedly the General Commissioners
before whom the proceedings are at the moment pending. It is not that this court,
properly instructed, would not be in at least as good a position as the General
Commissioners to determine the penalties, but this court would have to be properly and
thoroughly instructed in the whole matter. That would require a very great deal of   *d*
evidence and would occupy a very great deal of time, whereas the General Commissioners
are accustomed to dealing with these matters and, if I may borrow a notion from a totally
different branch of the law, they are well aware of the tone of the list, in which this court
would have to be instructed in some little detail.

Counsel for the bankrupt, while conceding that the penalties are recoverable in the
bankruptcy, properly provable, has argued very strongly that these proceedings are quasi-   *e*
criminal proceedings and they cannot really expect to be got on foot until the
presumption of innocence of his client is displaced. I accept that in general, but I think
that in the particular circumstances of the present case, where his client has been, not
once, but twice, the subject of investigation by the Inland Revenue for failure to deal
properly with his tax affairs, it must be taken with a considerable pinch of salt, and I
think that if the matter had to be dealt with by this court it would take it with rather   *f*
more than a pinch.

But, however that may be, it seems to me, especially having regard to the fact that
after what I may term the ordinary claims of the Revenue have been satisfied there may
be a surplus for the bankrupt, that this is a particular case where the real battle is and
should be between the bankrupt and the Inland Revenue, and that to bring the trustee
into the matter is only complicating the issue. Because the trustee does not feel very   *g*
happy about having to make up his mind what would be a proper compromise, and one
can well see that it is going to be difficult for him, being pressed on one side by the
bankrupt, who will of course threaten to appeal any decision to which the trustee comes
under s 180, and, on the other hand, being borne down on by the Revenue, who will say
that of course there cannot be any doubt that the maximum ought to be awarded.

It seems to me that in the present case the matter is capable of very simple and very   *h*
just resolution. It seems to me that there can be no reason at all why the matter should
not be compromised (because claims for penalties frequently are compromised by the
Revenue anyway), but that the compromise must be one to which not only the trustee
in bankruptcy agrees but to which the bankrupt also agrees, and if the bankrupt agrees I
cannot really see that the trustee in bankruptcy will have any grounds for holding out.
So in substance it is really a question between the bankrupt and the Revenue, with the   *j*
trustee holding a watching brief to see that neither of them makes any fatal errors, which
seems to me, advised as they are on both sides, extraordinarily unlikely.

That, if it can be done, will, I think, achieve the greatest possible saving of costs all
ways round; but if it is going to be done then it should be done quickly. It seems to me
that it would not be right to make any order staying the proceedings for the recovery of

a the penalties before the commissioners for any greater time than will enable that possibility to be explored. I will discuss with counsel in a moment what the length of the stay should be, but I would have in mind a period of something like three months, bearing in mind that the long vacation is on us, and that if there is no agreement within that period then the Inland Revenue should be free to restore the matter before the commissioners for final determination. Alternatively, if within the three months period there is such an agreement, then the matter should be stayed permanently.

b It will be seen that I have not dealt with a large number of the very interesting cases which have been cited to me, but it seems to me that this is really a very simple and a very plain case, and one really does not need to go too deeply at all into any of the more esoteric branches of the law. But it does seem to me that the approach of P O Lawrence J in *Ellis & Co's Trustee v Dixon-Johnson* [1924] 1 Ch 342 at 356–357 is the correct approach. All he is saying there is that, where you have a contingent claim which is going to sort *c* itself out, the best thing to do is to stand back and let it sort itself out. That does not mean that if there are other contingencies one assumes that the contingencies have in fact happened at the date of the receiving order, but that where the only contingency is the amount of the claim the best thing to do is to stand back and wait and see what happens. Then, as P O Lawrence J said, there will be no difficulty in arriving at the amount of the claim. He went on:

d '. . . if the contingency happens after the proof is lodged and it appears that the amount at which [he mentions 'the damages', but 'the liabilities' will do] have been estimated is below the true value, the creditor will be allowed to amend his proof or lodge a fresh proof at any time during the continuance of the bankruptcy, but not so as to disturb prior dividends . . .'

e Although some of the judge's remarks were criticised in the Court of Appeal in that case, I do not think the criticisms were really directed towards that simple 'wait and see' approach in a case such as the present.

For those reasons, therefore, I propose to declare that the penalties are provable debts in the bankruptcy of the bankrupt, that the proceedings to recover those penalties pending before the Commissioners for the General Purposes of the Income Tax for the *f* division of Surbiton in the county of Surrey instituted against the bankrupt by the summons dated 6 October 1981 should be stayed for a period of three months (although I will discuss the precise length of time in a moment), and that, if agreement between the bankrupt, the trustee and the Commissioners of Inland Revenue as to the quantum at which the proof for those penalties is to be admitted is arrived at within that period of three months, then the proceedings should be stayed permanently. In so far as it is *g* necessary, there will also be an order granting the trustee leave to agree or compromise the amount of the penalties with the Inland Revenue in the manner which I have already indicated.

Order accordingly.

Solicitors: *Booth & Blackwell* (for the trustee in bankruptcy); *Solicitor of Inland Revenue*; *David Lewis & Co* (for the bankrupt).

Edwina Epstein   Barrister.

Practice Direction

FAMILY DIVISION

Divorce – Practice – Children – Custody – Applications for custody and access – Contested applications – Conciliation – Conciliation before registrar and court welfare officer – Subsequent applications – Legal aid.

As from 1 January 1983 the Principal Registry of the Family Division will operate a pilot scheme of conciliation in contested applications in matrimonial proceedings for custody, access and variation thereof. The object of the scheme is to give an opportunity for agreement to be reached without the bitterness and exchange of recriminations which often develops between the parties when these issues remain in dispute. It may sometimes also result in considerable saving of time and expense both to the parties and to the court.

General experience has shown that the earlier a conciliation effort is deployed the more likely is the prospect of success. It is emphasised that it is extremely important that no affidavit should be filed or exchanged until after an unsuccessful conciliation appointment or until the registrar has so directed.

When such an application is lodged, the return date which is given will be that on which the conciliation appointment will take place before a registrar. It is intended that two registrars will be available on each of two days each week. Each registrar will be attended by a court welfare officer. It is essential that both the parties and any legal advisers having conduct of the case attend. The nature of the application and the matters in dispute will be outlined to the registrar and the welfare officer. If the dispute continues, the parties and their advisers will be given the opportunity of retiring to a private room together with the welfare officer to attempt to reach agreement. These discussions will be privileged and will not be disclosed on any subsequent application. Anything which is said before the registrar on such appointments will also remain privileged.

Any application to vacate a conciliation appointment must be made in writing to the registrar at least seven days before the return date.

If the conciliation appointment is successful, the registrar will make such orders as are agreed between the parties. If the appointment does not result in agreement being reached, any other subsequent application to a registrar will normally be dealt with by a different registrar and any further inquiry by a court welfare officer will be made by a different officer. Conciliation appointments which have been adjourned will be brought back before the same registrar whenever possible. Applications for variation of custody or access orders made as a result of conciliation will generally be dealt with by the same registrar who dealt with the initial conciliation appointment.

If the conciliation appointment is unsuccessful the registrar will give such directions as he considers appropriate as to the obtaining of welfare officer's reports and the filing of affidavits.

The party who has living with him or her any child aged 11 years or over in respect of whom the dispute exists should bring that child to the conciliation appointment, because it will sometimes be appropriate for the child to be seen by the registrar or the welfare officer.

Any party on whom a summons is served and who wishes to apply for legal aid should do so immediately. The Law Society will consider applications for emergency certificates in appropriate circumstances.

Urgent applications made by summons will be referred to the registrar for the day to determine whether they are outside the scope of the conciliation scheme.

B P TICKLE
Senior Registrar.

2 November 1982

European Grain and Shipping Ltd v Johnston

COURT OF APPEAL, CIVIL DIVISION
LORD DENNING MR, OLIVER AND KERR LJJ
19, 20 JULY 1982

Arbitration – Award – Setting aside award – Misconduct – Award signed by three arbitrators although award determined by only two members – Third arbitrator absent during determination but signing blank award form – Whether award defective.

Arbitration – Award – Defective award – Claimant accepting favourable part of award but seeking to set aside unfavourable part of award – Whether claimant waiving right to set aside defective award by accepting part of award.

The buyer agreed to purchase from the sellers 600 tonnes of wheat to be delivered in three equal monthly instalments of 200 tonnes. The contract of sale was subject to the arbitration rules of the United Kingdom Agricultural Supply Trade Association (UKASTA). The first two instalments were duly delivered, but on the third instalment only 100 tonnes were delivered. A dispute arose as to the third instalment, the sellers claiming payment for the 100 tonnes delivered and the buyer cross-claiming for the delivery of the outstanding 100 tonnes. The matter went to arbitration. The UKASTA arbitration rules provided for each party to appoint an arbitrator and for a third arbitrator to be appointed by agreement. They further provided for the arbitrators to proceed on documentary evidence and submissions, unless either party to the arbitration wished otherwise. The parties each appointed an arbitrator, who together appointed a third arbitrator as chairman. Before all the submissions had been made, the arbitrator appointed by the sellers, who was going abroad, wrote a letter to the chairman stating his views as to what the award should be and he signed a blank award form. The other two arbitrators took a different view from the arbitrator appointed by the sellers and, on agreeing the award, they filled in the blank award form with their own decision and added their signatures after that of the arbitrator appointed by the sellers already on the form. The award ordered the buyer to pay the sellers for the 100 tonnes received and further ordered, on the cross-claim, the sellers to pay the difference between the market price and the contract price in respect of the 100 tonnes undelivered. The buyer, in accordance with the first part of the award, paid the amount due, which the sellers accepted. However, the sellers then issued a notice of motion seeking to set aside the second part of the award, claiming, inter alia, that the arbitrators had wrongly purported to determine the buyer's claim in the buyer's favour without giving the sellers or the arbitrator appointed by them an opportunity to consider any evidence or documents in support of the claim. The judge dismissed the motion and the sellers appealed.

Held – An arbitration conducted by a tribunal of several arbitrators necessarily required a joint process of full and complete adjudication by all of them, so that the ultimate award represented the state of mind of all of them at the time when they signed it. Although it was not necessary for the arbitrators themselves to sign the award at the same time and place, the award could only be determined after the arbitrators had each considered the facts in dispute and had mutually reached an agreement as to the form the award should take. It followed that since the arbitrator appointed by the sellers had not actually participated in the award, although on the face of it he appeared to be a party to it, there were grounds for setting aside the whole award. However, since the sellers had accepted the benefit from the first part of the award, they could not afterwards dispute the award by challenging the second part. The appeal would therefore be dismissed (see p 992 *f* to p 993 *e* and *h* to p 994 *g*, post).

Dictum of Scrutton LJ in *Dexters Ltd and Hillcrest Oil Co (Bradford) Ltd* [1925] All ER Rep at 278 applied.

Lord v Lord (1855) 5 E & B 404 and *Re Beck and Jackson* (1857) 1 CBNS 695 distinguished.

Notes

For the conduct of an arbitration, see 2 Halsbury's Laws (4th edn) para 590, for misconduct of an arbitrator, see ibid para 587, and for cases on the subject, see 3 Digest (Reissue) 155–177, 897–1078.

Cases referred to in judgments

Beck and Jackson, Re (1857) 1 CBNS 695, 140 ER 286, 3 Digest (Reissue) 190, *1161.*
Dexters Ltd v Hill Crest Oil Co (Bradford) Ltd [1926] 1 KB 348, [1925] All ER Rep 273, CA, 3 Digest (Reissue) 189, *1148.*
Lord v Lord (1855) 5 E & B 404, 119 ER 531, 3 Digest (Reissue) 123, *665.*

Cases also cited

Alpine Shipping Co v Vinbee (Manchester) Ltd, The Dusan [1980] 1 Lloyd's Rep 400.
British Metal Corp Ltd v Ludlow Bros (1913) Ltd [1938] 1 All ER 135, CA.
Myron (owners) v Tradax Export SA Panama City RP [1969] 2 All ER 1263, [1970] 1 QB 527.

Interlocutory appeal

European Grain and Shipping Ltd (the sellers) appealed against the order of Parker J ([1982] 1 Lloyd's Rep 414) made on 4 November 1981 dismissing their notice of motion dated 3 March 1981 seeking to set aside that part of the award of Mr W H Defoe, Mr L M Lawrence and Mr D T Little made on 12 February 1981 whereby they held that the sellers were in default of their contract of sale with Richard Johnston (the buyer) on an arbitration of a dispute under a contract dated 8 April 1980 in accordance with the terms of the United Kingdom Agricultural Supply Trade Association (UKASTA) Contract 2/77 for the sale of 600 tonnes of denaturable wheat, 5% more or less, to the buyer. The facts are set out in the judgment of Lord Denning MR.

Anthony Havelock-Allan for the sellers.
Jeffrey Gruder for the buyer.

LORD DENNING MR. This case raises some points about the proper conduct of arbitrations. In particular whether the arbitrators must meet together to sign their award or whether they can each sign it separately. The dispute arose out of the sale of wheat. The sellers were a London firm called European Grain and Shipping Ltd of London. The buyer was a Norfolk grain merchant called Richard Johnston. In April 1980 there was a contract of sale between them whereby 600 tonnes of wheat, 5% more or less, were to be delivered to the buyer: 200 tonnes in May 1980, another 200 tonnes in June 1980 and another 200 tonnes in July 1980. The price was £98·25 per thousand kilos. It was subject to the arbitration rules of UKASTA (the United Kingdom Agricultural Supply Trade Association).

The first two batches of 200 tonnes were satisfactorily delivered. But when it came to the 200 tonnes in July 1980, the first 100 tonnes were delivered all right. But the second 100 tonnes were not delivered at all. There was a question about times and notices and so on which I need not go into. The upshot of it was that a dispute arose between the parties as to the last 200 tonnes. The sellers said that they wanted payment for the 100 tonnes which had been delivered. The buyer said he had a cross-claim in respect of the other 100 tonnes which had not been delivered. The price had gone up and he claimed damages for non-delivery accordingly. So there was claim and cross-claim.

When the sellers said that they wanted payment for the first 100 tonnes, the buyer deducted his cross-claim. It came to £2,775. He said he was deducting that sum from

the price of the first 100 tonnes because of his claim on the second 100 tonnes. The sellers
a objected. They said that the buyer ought to pay the whole amount of the first 100 tonnes
and that, if he had a cross-claim, he should go to arbitration on the other 100 tonnes.
That was the dispute between the parties.

I will not go into the details. The UKASTA arbitration rules were shown to us. These
provided for the arbitrators to proceed on documentary evidence and submissions, unless
either party wished otherwise. They also provided for each party to appoint an arbitrator
b and a third arbitrator to be appointed by agreement. The sellers appointed a Mr Defoe as
their arbitrator. The buyer appointed a Mr Lawrence as his arbitrator. Those two
arbitrators appointed a third, a Mr Little, who, in accordance with ordinary practice,
would be the chairman.

But then this question arose. The sellers were saying to the arbitrators, 'Only deal with
our claim on the first 100 tonnes. Do not deal with the cross-claim at all.' That was quite
c untenable. The dispute was as to both matters: whether payment should be made for the
first 100 tonnes and whether there was a cross-claim on the second. Quite clearly all those
matters came within the arbitration. There is no doubt whatever about it. It could not
be severed into two separate contracts. It was all one running contract.

The point of interest which has arisen is this. Mr Defoe was going to Australia before
all the submissions were made. He told the other two arbitrators that he was going.
d Before he left, he signed in blank a form of award, and left the award itself to be filled in
by the others. The form was completely blank save for Mr Defoe's own signature. He
then wrote a letter to the chairman stating his own views as to what the award should be,
but also realising that there could be alternative views.

The other two arbitrators did not agree with Mr Defoe's views. They differed from
him. They agreed, the two of them, what the award should be. They filled in the blanks
e with their own views. They then put their own signatures below that of Mr Defoe. The
result was that, after Mr Defoe had gone to Australia, on 12 February 1981 the other two
arbitrators filled in the award. They left Mr Defoe's signature on in ink, and they added
their own signatures. I will read the award. It was in two parts:

'WE, the undersigned, having been appointed to arbitrate in a dispute that has
arisen between EUROPEAN GRAIN & SHIPPING LTD. . . . and Richard Johnston (Grain
f Merchants) . . . in respect to 200 tonnes DNQ Wheat delivery July 1980 . . . have
considered the case of each of the disputing parties respectively, and DO HEREBY
AWARD . . .'

Then this is the first part:

'that buyers shall pay to sellers the sum of £2,775 wrongfully deducted from
their invoice No. 04470 due for payment on 29th August 1980 and shall pay interest
g on that amount at the rate of 16% per annum from 30th August 1980 until the date
of this award. Payment to be made within 14 days from date of this award . . .'

There it is. They decided on the first 100 tonnes that the buyer wrongfully deducted
£2,775. He ought to have paid the full amount, and he should pay interest on the
h amount outstanding. That is the first part. Then on to the second part:

'. . . and do further award that sellers are in default on 103·05 tonnes not delivered
against contract, settling price on 1st August 1980 to be £126 per tonne and shall
pay to buyers the sum of £2859·64 being the difference between buying price of
£98·25 per tonne and settling price of £126 per tonne . . .'

j So there it is. On the second part they ordered that the sellers had to pay the difference
between the market price and the contract price. Those are the two parts of the award.

The buyer accepted the whole of the award, both parts of it. He paid to the sellers the
sum of £2,775 and interest awarded in the first part, and the sellers accepted it. But the
sellers took exception to the second part, in which they were held liable. I need not go
through all of the technical points which were taken on behalf of the sellers. The judge

disposed of them fully and faithfully. There are only two points which I need mention.
The first is this: what is the effect of Mr Defoe signing the award in blank, and then   *a*
going off to Australia? He left the other two arbitrators to come to a decision, to fill in
the blanks, and to issue the award.

In *Russell on Arbitration* (19th edn, 1979) p 247 it is said:

> '*All must make award together*. Where there are two or more arbitrators, all should
> execute the award at the same time and place. If they do not, the award may be
> invalidated, but as the objection is one of a formal character, if no other objection is   *b*
> shown, the court may remit the award to the arbitrators for correction.'

That statement is amply supported by the old cases which are cited in *Russell*. In
particular by *Lord v Lord* (1855) 5 E & B 404, 119 ER 531, where each of two arbitrators
signed the award but did so at a different time and place. The Court of Queen's Bench
upset it. But Coleridge J said (5 E & B 404 at 406, 119 ER 531 at 532):   *c*

> 'It is now clearly established that every judicial act, to be done by two or more,
> must be completed in the presence of all who do it: for those who are to be affected
> by it have a right to the united judgment of all up to the very last moment.'

That principle was accepted as correct by the Court of Common Pleas in *Re Beck and
Jackson* (1857) 1 CBNS 695, 140 ER 286.   *d*

Those cases are not binding on this court. I think the time has come when we should
lay down a different rule. Business convenience requires it. Nowadays, whenever an
agreement or award or any other document is to be done by two or three jointly, the
practice is for one or the other to draw up a draft and send it to the other or others for
their consideration and comments. One or other may suggest amendments and send it
back. So it goes to and fro until the draft is agreed. Once the draft is agreed, all that   *e*
remains is for it to be copied out in a legible form ready for signature. If it is already
legible, it need not even be copied out. It is then sent round and signed by each separately.
Once all have signed it becomes the final document. It is quite unnecessary for them all
to meet together to sign it. When each appends his signature, he expresses his assent to it
and then, as soon as the others sign, it becomes final. In short, whenever all have signed,
each must be regarded as having assented to it, even though each signed it at a different   *f*
time or place from the others. That principle applies to an award of arbitrators just as it
does to a written agreement or any other document to be executed by two or three
people.

It is true, as Coleridge J said, that 'those who are to be affected by it have a right to the
united judgment of all up to the very last moment', but that is easily secured. If one of
those who sign first should change his mind, then he can in these days by telephone or   *g*
telex tell the others about it before they sign. The document is then held up. Any
necessary amendments are made until, by correspondence, by telephone or by telex, all
are agreed. Once they agree, the document is signed by the last one. It is then final, even
though each have signed separately at a different time and place.

In this case, however, the principle does not apply. Mr Defoe never did agree a draft
award. He never saw it. He signed a form in blank not knowing what it would contain.   *h*
He signed before any agreement had been reached. He signed, both literally and
figuratively, carte blanche. He left the decision to the others, without himself taking his
proper part in it. That will never do. It was misconduct on his part to sign in this way,
and for the others to indorse it as they did. That would be a ground for setting aside the
award, the whole award and not part, if it is going to be set aside for misconduct.

But there is this further point which emerged in the course of discussion: namely that   *j*
in this particular case the sellers took advantage of the first part of the award, because the
buyer paid over the sum of £2,775. He paid that and the interest which had been
awarded on it, and the sellers received that payment. Thereby they affirmed that part of
the award. They accepted the benefit of it plus the interest. It seems to me quite
impossible for them to say, 'Oh, well; we like that part of the award but we do not like

a the other part where we were ordered to pay damages. We do not like that and therefore we want it set aside.'

That certainly cannot be done. The principle was stated long ago in *Dexters Ltd v Hill Crest Oil Co (Bradford) Ltd* [1926] 1 KB 348 at 358; cf [1925] All ER Rep 273 at 278, where Scrutton LJ said that a person could not reap the fruits of an award, because that infers that the award was right, and afterwards say that the award was wrong. He said:

b 'That is the same thing as saying first: "I approbate this award and claim a benefit, 2000*l.*, under it; pay me that 2000*l.*"; and then when he has got it, saying: "I reprobate this award and say it is wrong and ask you to substitute another award ..."'

Those observations apply exactly to this case. The judge put it as a form of waiver: he did not cite the cases. But in substance it is all the same thing. Having accepted the
c benefit, as the sellers did, from the first part of the award, they cannot afterwards dispute the award and say they do not like the second part.

I think the judge was quite right, and I would dismiss the appeal.

OLIVER LJ. The appellants (the sellers) in this case are well-known grain merchants.
d They do not, I think, supply straw. At any rate, they did not supply any to their counsel, and I have watched and listened with awe and admiration as counsel for the sellers has striven with courage, with frankness and with skill to make bricks without that essential commodity. That he has failed is no fault of his, for in my view this appeal was and is hopeless; and I am content, for my part, to adopt the judgment of the judge in the court below (see [1982] 1 Lloyd's Rep 414).

e The only point on which I would wish to add anything at all is the question to which Lord Denning MR has already adverted, which is how far in an arbitration by three arbitrators it is essential that all three should participate in the hearing and the award. The principle is stated in *Russell on Arbitration* (19th edn, 1979) p 247, where it is said:

'*All the arbitrators must act together.* As they must all act, so they must all act together. They must each be present at every meeting; and the witnesses and the
f parties must be examined in the presence of them all.

"*All must make award together.* Where there are two or more arbitrators, all should execute the award at the same time and place.'

The only query that I would have on that is whether in modern conditions, and in particular in international arbitrations where arbitrators and jurisdictions are often
g widely separated geographically, it is essential that the award should be signed by all at the same time and place. The old cases certainly so state, and *Re Beck and Jackson* (1857) 1 CBNS 695, 140 ER 286 is a case in point. The reasoning on which the principle is based is the sound one that right up to the last moment one or other of the three might wish to change his mind. But those old cases, of course, were decided at a time when communications were very much more leisurely than they are today, at any rate on the
h assumption that those methods of communication are free from disruption by industrial action, and one can readily see that this consideration is a valid one in a case, for instance, where an award was signed by one arbitrator in York and then was consigned to another by the slow stage to Bristol. But I cannot think that the principle can be a valid reason in modern conditions. The point does not directly arise for decision in this case, but one thing I think which is quite clear is that an arbitrator cannot properly become a party to
j an award if he does not even know, as Mr Defoe did not know in this case, what the award is. But for my part I doubt whether, assuming that the arbitrators are agreed on what the award is going to be, it is necessary that they should all sign the award at the same time and place.

I agree, therefore, with the views which Lord Denning MR has expressed. I also agree that the appeal should be dismissed.

KERR LJ. I also agree with the judgment of Parker J ([1982] 1 Lloyd's Rep 414) and there is little I wish to add.

In this case there was one dispute. It was referred to a tribunal of three arbitrators, the third being the chairman, and they made one award, to my mind, one indivisible award.

The only point on which it is perhaps desirable to add something is with reference to the last part of the judgment (see [1982] 1 Lloyd's Rep 414 at 420–421). We were told that in relation to that part, which deals with the fact that Mr Defoe signed a blank form of award in advance, the judge did not have the advantage of argument. We were referred to some of the relevant authorities, including *Re Beck and Jackson* (1857) 1 CBNS 695, 140 ER 286. What I think the authorities show, as must be right, is that an arbitration conducted by a tribunal of several arbitrators necessarily requires a joint process of full and complete adjudication by all of them, so that the ultimate award represents the state of mind of all of them at the time when they sign it.

What Mr Defoe did in the present case, although of course he did it perfectly openly and everybody knew what he was doing, in my view constitutes a very serious instance of technical misconduct. He did not participate in this award, although, looking at it and at the signature below it, he appears to be a party to every word of it. But, as has been pointed out, not a single word of the award was on that piece of paper when he signed it, and he was therefore simply not a party to that award. In my view this award should unhesitatingly be set aside, were it not for the fact that it is not open to the sellers in this case to ask the court to exercise its discretion to do so. The sellers have taken the benefit of this award, they have taken the benefit of that part of it which they like, and they cannot possibly now come to the court and ask the court to set the award aside.

In regard to what Lord Denning MR and Oliver LJ have said about the passages in *Russell on Arbitration* (19th edn, 1979) p 247 and the authorities that arbitrators must meet in one place at the same time and all sign the award together and in the presence of each other, I agree with what has been said. I would only add that in some arbitral rules, particularly, I think, of the International Chamber of Commerce, it is provided that this must happen, and that it is a requirement of the validity of the award that it should have been done. I regard that as unnecessary and undesirable. I have myself been party to cases where the arbitrators were in different countries and took many important decisions by correspondence or by telephone. This would be in the interests of all parties in saving costs. Therefore, like Lord Denning MR and Oliver LJ, I do not regard the coincidence in time and place for the purely formal purposes of signing the award as something which is essential, unless it is prescribed by rules which govern the arbitration.

I agree that this appeal must be dismissed.

Appeal dismissed.

Solicitors: *Middleton, Potts & Co* (for the sellers); *Greene & Greene*, Bury St Edmunds (for the buyer).

Frances Rustin   Barrister.

Corpus Christi College, Oxford v Gloucestershire County Council

a

COURT OF APPEAL, CIVIL DIVISION
LORD DENNING MR, OLIVER AND KERR LJJ
5, 6, 23 JULY 1982

b

Commons – Registration – Common land and rights of common – Effect of registration – Conclusive evidence of matters registered – Registration as common land – Land subject to rights of common – Registration in consequence of registration of rights – Owner objecting to registration of rights but not to registration of land – Registration of land becoming final – Commons commissioner refusing to confirm registration of rights – Registration of rights avoided and
c cancelled – Owner applying to amend register by removal of registration of land – Whether land 'ceasing' to be common land on cancellation of registration of rights – Whether registration of land conclusive that land common land even though no rights of common existing over it – Commons Registration Act 1965, ss 10, 13(a).

For centuries the residents of a parish had grazed cattle on a meadow in the parish. In
d February 1968 the parish council applied under the Commons Registration Act 1965 to have that right of common registered and on 5 June 1968 the registration authority (i) provisionally registered the right of common in the rights section of the commons register and (ii) pursuant to s 4(2)(b)^a of the 1965 Act provisionally registered the meadow as common land in the land section of the register, that entry stating that it was made 'in consequence of' the registration of the right of common. The owners of the meadow
e objected to the registration of the right of common in the rights section but did not lodge any objection to the registration of the land as common land in the lands section because they knew that it was common land and that some persons had rights of common over it; the owners merely wished to assert that not all the residents of the parish had a right of common over the meadow. Since there was no objection to the registration in the land section, that registration became final under s 7 of the 1965 Act
f on 1 October 1970 and, under s 10^b of that Act, the registration was conclusive evidence of the matters registered. In February 1976 the commons commissioner, having held an inquiry into the objection to the registration of the right of common in the rights section, refused to confirm that registration and in consequence it became void and was cancelled. However, the entry of the land as common land in the land section of the register remained. The owners applied under s 13^c of the 1965 Act to the registration authority
g to have the register amended by the removal from the land section of the register of the entry relating to the land being common land, on the ground that since the entry in the land section was consequential on the entry in the rights section the avoidance and cancellation of the entry in the rights section caused the land to 'cease' to be common land within s 13(a) thus enabling the register to be amended. The authority refused to amend the register and their decision was upheld by the county court. The owners
h appealed to the Court of Appeal. It was common ground that the land had never been waste land of a manor for the purposes of the definition of common land in s 22(1)^d of the 1965 Act.

Held – The appeal would be dismissed for the following reasons—
(1) (Per Lord Denning MR) Since under s 10 of the 1965 Act the final registration of
j land as common land was conclusive evidence that it was common land, and since the definition of common land in s 22(1) of that Act included both (a) land which was subject

---

a   Section 4(2), so far as material, is set out at p 1003 *g*, post
b   Section 10, so far as material, is set out at p 1005 *a b*, post
c   Section 13, so far as material, is set out at p 1005 *d*, post
d   Section 22(1), so far as material, is set out at p 1001 *j*, post

to rights of common and (b) land which was waste land of a manor not subject to rights
of common, the final registration of land as common land where no rights of common   *a*
were registered over it had the effect under s 10 that the land was conclusively presumed
to have been in the past and to continue to be waste land of a manor not subject to rights
of common and as such to be common land. Accordingly, the meadow had not ceased to
be common land and the owners were not entitled to have the register amended under
s 13 (see p 1001 *h* to p 1002 *c* and *f g*, post); *Central Electricity Generating Board v Clwyd CC*
[1976] 1 All ER 251 and *Box Parish Council v Lacey* [1979] 1 All ER 113 doubted.   *b*

(2) (Per Oliver and Kerr LJJ) The meadow could not 'cease' to be common land for the
purposes of amending the register under s 13(*a*) of the 1965 Act, because such a cessation
postulated that the meadow was common land at the date of the final registration,
whereas the commons commissioner's decision that the registration of the right of
common was void had the effect that the right of common never existed. Consequently
(and assuming that the meadow had never been waste land of a manor), the meadow was   *c*
not common land at the date of final registration and therefore could not, within s 13(*a*),
'cease' to be so. Furthermore, the effect of s 10 was to preclude the owners from showing
that any other rights had at some time existed in order to prove that they had
subsequently 'ceased'. Accordingly, the fact of the registration of the meadow as common
land in the land section of the register was conclusive of the fact that the land was
common land (see p 1004 *j* to p 1005 *c e f*, p 1008 *h j*, p 1009 *a* to *e*, and p 1010 *e* to *g* and   *d*
j to p 1011 *e*, post).

Per Lord Denning MR (Oliver LJ not concurring). A hearing before a commons
commissioner should not be treated as civil litigation in the nature of a lis inter partes in
which the applicant has to prove his case, but should be regarded as an administrative
inquiry to get the register right rather than as a legal contest (see p 1000 *d* to *f*, post); *Re
Sutton Common, Wimborne* [1982] 2 All ER 376 doubted.   *e*

Per Oliver LJ. None of the documents issued under the 1965 Act draws attention in
terms to the importance, in a case where the only reason for the registration of land is the
provisional registration of rights over it, of the landowner registering an objection not
only to the registration of the rights but also to the consequential registration of the land
as common land (see p 1004 *c*, post).

f

Notes
For the requirement of registration of common land and the effect of registration, see 6
Halsbury's Laws (4th edn) para 504, for the amendment of the register, see ibid para 683,
and for cases on the subject, see 11 Digest (Reissue) 92–93, *1101–1104*.

For the Commons Registration Act 1965, ss 4, 7, 10, 13, 22, see 3 Halsbury's Statutes
(3rd edn) 922, 924, 926, 928, 933.

g

Cases referred to in judgments
Box Parish Council v Lacey [1979] 1 All ER 113, [1980] Ch 109, [1979] 2 WLR 177, CA,
    Digest (Cont Vol E) 81, *366a*.
Central Electricity Generating Board v Clwyd CC [1976] 1 All ER 251, [1976] 1 WLR 151,
    Digest (Cont Vol E) 83, *1101a*.   *h*
Chewton Common, Christchurch, Re, Borough of Christchurch v Milligan [1977] 3 All ER 509,
    [1977] 1 WLR 1242, Digest (Cont Vol E) 81, *282c*.
Delacherois v Delacherois (1864) 11 HL Cas 62, 11 ER 1254, 13 Digest (Reissue) 4, *1*.
R v Duchess of Buccleugh (1704) 6 Mod Rep 150, 87 ER 909, 13 Digest (Reissue) 11, *82*.
Smith v East Sussex CC (1977) 76 LGR 332.
Sutton Common, Wimborne, Re [1982] 2 All ER 376, [1982] 1 WLR 647.   *j*
Swayne's Case (1608) 8 Co Rep 63a, 77 ER 568, 28(2) Digest (Reissue) 672, *98*.
Yately Common, Hampshire, Re, Arnold v Dodd [1977] 1 All ER 505, [1977] 1 WLR 840,
    Digest (Cont Vol E) 83, *791a*.

Appeal
By an application dated 4 November 1980 the applicants, the president and scholars of
Corpus Christi College in the University of Oxford (the college), applied in the

a Cheltenham County Court for a declaration that the land known as and situated at Temple Ham Meadow, Little Rissington, Gloucestershire had ceased to be common land for the purposes of s 13 of the Commons Registration Act 1965. The respondent to the application was Gloucestershire County Council (the registration authority). By a judgment given on 31 March 1981 his Honour Judge Bulger rejected the college's claim. The college appealed. The grounds of the appeal were that the judge erred in law (1) in construing s 10 of the 1965 Act as providing that registration under the 1965 Act of any

b land as common land was conclusive evidence that on and after the date the registration became final the land was common land, even where there were no registered rights of common in respect of it, (2) in failing to construe s 10 as providing that, in the events which happened, there was conclusive evidence only that the land was common land as at 5 June 1968 (the date of its provisional registration as common land) and not as at any other time, (3) in failing to construe s 1(2)(b) of the 1965 Act as providing that, in the

c events which happened, all rights of common over the land were extinguished by operation of law on 1 August 1970, (4) in holding that land registered under the 1965 Act could not cease to be common land for the purposes of s 13 by virtue of the processes and procedures of registration itself because that would nullify the effect of s 10, and that (5) the judge ought to have found that, on (i) the refusal of the commons commissioner (Mr C R Settle QC) on 6 March 1976 to confirm the registration by the Parish Council of

d Little Rissington of rights of common over the land and the expiry of the time for appealing against that refusal without any appeal therefrom and (ii) the failure to register any other rights of common before the expiry of the period laid down for registration, the land had ceased to be common land for the purposes of s 13. By a respondent's notice the registration authority stated that it would contend on the appeal that the judge's judgment should be affirmed on the additional grounds (1) that the college having failed

e to object to the registration of the land as common land were estopped by the operation of ss 7 and 10 of the 1965 Act from subsequently adducing evidence about the status of the land at the date of its registration, (2) that the effect of s 10 was that land which was finally registered as common land was deemed to be within the definition of common land within s 22 of the 1965 Act even if that was or might be factually incorrect, and (3) that to bring the land within s 13(a) of the 1965 Act the college had to prove that since

f the date of final registration an event had occurred which had altered the status of the land so that it was outside the definition of common land contained in both s 22(1)(a) and (b) of the 1965 Act, and that on the facts the college were unable to discharge that burden. The facts are set out in the judgment of Lord Denning MR.

Jules Sher QC and *M Keenan* for the college.
g *Sheila Cameron* for the registration authority.

Cur adv vult

23 July. The following judgments were read.

h **LORD DENNING MR.** In the lovely Cotswold country there is the old parish of Little Rissington not far from Bourton-on-the-Water. It is a small place with only a few houses and the church. In the parish there is a meadow called Temple Ham meadow of nearly 26 acres. It has been grazed by the residents of the parish for centuries. They have put their cattle or sheep on it each year, for half of the year only, from 1 August to 28

j February or thereabouts. None of them knew the origin of the right but that they had it there was no doubt in any of their minds.
. So, when Parliament required a register to be made of all the rights of common in England, the parish council applied to the Gloucestershire County Council for this right of the residents to be registered. It was made on 27 February 1968, the very first of all the applications to be made to the county council under the Commons Registration Act 1965. The clerk said in the application that he made it 'On behalf of the residents for the time being of the Parish of Little Rissington, Gloucestershire'. He described their right

as: 'The right to graze animals: 50 cattle or 100 sheep: 1st August each year to 28th
February of the following year.' He said further: 'The right is exercisable by residents of
the Parish of Little Rissington owning cattle or sheep.'

On receiving that application, the clerk to the county council marked out the meadow
on a map and described it as 'Register Unit CL95'. He made an entry in the rights section
of the register containing the claim made by the parish council. He made a corresponding
entry in the land section describing the meadow and adding that it was 'Registered in
consequence of the application' for the rights section.

So far so good. But it then appeared that the meadow was owned by an Oxford college,
called Corpus Christi College. And this college objected to the entry in the rights section.
They did not object to the entry in the land section for this very good reason. The college
knew that Temple Ham meadow was common land and that some persons had rights of
common over it. So it was properly entered in the land section. But they objected to it
being entered in the rights section. Their grounds of objection I will set out in full:

> '1. Only the tenants of the Manor of Little Rissington have rights over the land
> and so far as the modern Civil Parish is inconsistent as to Parish Boundaries with the
> boundaries of the Manor, Landowners in the Civil Parish should be excluded.
> 2. The Registration does not refer to land to which the Common Rights are
> attached and is, therefore, bad, unless it is shown that all property in the Civil Parish
> has Common Rights attached to it. Residence in the Parish, or indeed in the Manor,
> is irrelevant in this context.
> 3. The field will not carry 50 head of cattle or 100 sheep for the period registered.
> Serious damage to the land would occur if this number of stock were grazed.
> Reasonable stocking rates in our opinion are 20 cattle or 60 sheep; furthermore, the
> period during which such Rights as exist may be exercised is from 1st August to
> 24th December, and not as Registered.'

The tenants of the manor

In order to understand that objection, you should know what is meant by the 'tenants
of the Manor of Little Rissington'. I ought to know myself because by statute 'All
manorial documents shall be under the charge and superintendence of the Master of the
Rolls' and he is entitled to make all inquiries about them and to see that they are properly
preserved: see the Law of Property Act 1922, s 144A(1). Further, for over 20 years I lived
in a lane called Copyhold Lane, in Cuckfield, Sussex.

The bald statement in the objection that 'Only the tenants of the Manor of Little
Rissington have rights over the land' has since been amplified in an agreed statement of
facts, which says:

> 'Temple Ham Meadow ("Temple Ham") comprises approximately 25·8 acres of
> grazing land. At all times since 1665 (if not before) it has been held by the applicants
> as part of the demesne lands of the Manor of Guiting. It has never been waste land
> of the Manor.'

That statement is brief in the extreme. I suppose it has been got out by one of the
college historians. I will endeavour to supplement it by my own researches. As Thomas
Scrutton (afterwards Scrutton LJ) said in his essay on *Commons and Common Fields* (1887)
p 1: 'The origin and history of common lands in England are insuperably bound up with
the history of the manor.'

The nature of the manor

In medieval times the manor was the nucleus of English rural life. It was an
administrative unit of an extensive area of land. The whole of it was owned originally by
the lord of the manor. He lived in the big house called the manor house. Attached to it
were many acres of grassland and woodlands called the park. These were the 'demesne
lands' which were for the personal use of the lord of the manor. Dotted all round were
the inclosed homes and land occupied by the 'tenants of the manor'. They held them by

copyhold tenure. Their titles were entered in the court rolls of the manor. They were
nearly equivalent to freehold, but the tenants were described as 'tenants of the manor'.
The rest of the manorial lands were the 'waste lands of the manor'. The tenants of the
manor had the right to graze their animals on the waste lands of the manor. Although
the demesne land was personal to the lord of the manor, nevertheless he sometimes
granted to the tenants of the manor the right to graze their animals on it, or they
acquired it by custom. In such case their right to graze on the demesne land was
indistinguishable from their right to graze on the waste lands of the manor, so long as it
remained open to them and uncultivated, although there might be hedges and gates to
keep the cattle from straying. So much so that their rights over it became known as a
'right of common' and the land became known as 'common land'.

In the course of time, however, the lordship of the manor became severed from the
lands of the manor. This was where the lord of the manor sold off parcels of the land to
purchasers. He might, for instance, sell off the demesne lands and convey them as a
distinct property. Thenceforward the land ceased to form part of the manor and was held
by a freeholder: see *Delacherois v Delacherois* (1864) 11 HL Cas 62 at 102–103, 11 ER 1254
at 1269–1270 per Lord St Leonards. But no such conveyance could adversely affect the
rights of common of those who were entitled to them as tenants of the manor or
otherwise. No lord of the manor could, by alienation, deprive those entitled to their
rights over it or in respect of it: see *Swayne's Case* (1608) 8 Co Rep 63a, 77 ER 568 and *R
v Duchess of Buccleugh* (1704) 6 Mod Rep 150, 87 ER 909.

Nowadays there are few, if any, manors left intact. The lords of the manor have sold
off the house and lands to strangers. Nothing remains in the lordship except the title of
lord of the manor and the right to hold the manorial documents. This bare title and
right is sometimes put on the market and sold for a nominal figure of £200 or £300.

The one point of principle of all this is that no lord of the manor could, by selling the
manorial lands, deprive the tenants of the manor of their rights of common over them,
no matter whether those lands were originally part of the demesne lands or the waste
land of the manor.

Enfranchisement

In the 1922 legislation every parcel of copyhold land was enfranchised. It ceased to be
copyhold and became freehold. But there was a special provision preserving the right of
common. The previous tenants of the manor, now freeholders, remained entitled to
exercise their right of common. It was provided in the Law of Property Act 1922, Sch
12, para (4) that:

> 'An enfranchisement by virtue of this Act shall not deprive a tenant of any
> commonable right to which he is entitled in respect of the enfranchised land, but
> where any such right exists in respect of any land at the commencement of this Act
> it shall continue attached to the land notwithstanding that the land has become
> freehold.'

This little piece of history shows clearly that, when the Parish Council of Little
Rissington applied in 1968 to register the right of common, there were undoubtedly
several freeholders of land in and about Little Rissington who were successors to the
former tenants of the manor and as such had the right to graze their animals in Temple
Ham meadow. I will call them the 'commoners'.

The hearing before the commissioner

In February 1976 Mr Settle QC, the commons commissioner, held an inquiry.
Unfortunately for the commoners, he refused to confirm the entry in the rights section.
I will set out his decision in full:

> 'This dispute relates to the registration at Entry No. 1 in the Rights Section of
> Register Unit No. CL.95 in the Register of Common Land maintained by the

Gloucestershire County Council and is occasioned by Objection No. 119 made by
the President and Scholars of Corpus Christi College and noted in the Register on
10th May 1971. I held a hearing for the purpose of inquiring into the dispute at
Gloucester on 18th February 1976. The hearing was attended by Mr. H. R. Tillett of
Messrs. Cole and Cole on behalf of Little Rissington Parish Council, and by Mr. R.
C. Metcalfe, articled clerk to Messrs Morrell Peel and Gamlen on behalf of Corpus
Christi. The rights registration was made by Little Rissington Parish Council. Mr.
Tillett conceded at an early stage that the Parish Council had no title to any grazing
rights and that there had been no corporate activity on its part as regards the exercise
of any grazing rights and his research into the minutes of the parish council revealed
no such corporate activity. *The land has always been grazed though by what if any right
is unknown and Mr. Tillett stated that the parish council took the view that only it could
protect such rights as existed.* While I have sympathy for the Parish Council's effort to
maintain on behalf of some parishioners a long-standing practice I can find no
justification in law for confirming the Registration. For these reasons I refuse to
confirm the registration.' (My emphasis.)

A commentary on the decision

I regret that decision of the commons commissioner. He seems to have regarded the
case as a piece of civil litigation between the Parish Council of Little Rissington on the
one hand and Corpus Christi College on the other hand, and that, as the parish council
could prove no title in themselves, the registration ought not to be confirmed.

That was to my mind a mistake. I cannot think it correct for the commons
commissioners to treat these cases as if they were pieces of civil litigation, such as a lis
inter partes, in which the applicants have to prove their case. Often enough the persons
concerned are the inhabitants of a parish or persons grazing land, without any legal
advice. They know they have a right of common and that their predecessors have
exercised it for hundreds of years, but they do not know the origin of it. If they do
consult lawyers, those lawyers do not do the necessary research or do not have the means
of research available to them. The hearing by the commissioner should be regarded more
as an administrative matter, to get the register right, rather than as a legal contest. The
commons commissioner should inquire carefully whether any land is common land,
and, if it is, register it in the land section accordingly. If it appears that there are
commoners who have rights of common, he should take all necessary steps to register
their rights in the rights section. He should make any amendments that are necessary or
desirable for this purpose. I feel confident that this was the intention of the legislature. It
was to see that all the common land in England and Wales should be registered and, in
addition, that all the commoners' rights should be registered so that in the future
everyone should know what the position was.

I notice that in the recent case of *Re Sutton Common, Wimborne* [1982] 2 All ER 376,
[1982] 1 WLR 647 Walton J put the burden of proof on the person making the
registration. I do not think that was right. It treats the case far too much as a lis inter
partes.

Take this very case. It is apparent from the documents that there have been rights of
common over Temple Ham meadow for centuries. These rights had previously subsisted
in the hands of the tenants of the manor. They now subsist in their successors, that is the
freeholders of the manorial lands. It might have been difficult to ascertain the boundaries
of the manor and the precise extent of the right of the commoners. But that is a difficulty
which the commons commissioner is there to resolve. The application was made by the
parish council who said they were making it on behalf of the 'residents of Little
Rissington owning cattle and sheep'. That was quite a sufficient basis on which the
commons commissioner could have and should have acted. He should have confirmed
the application in the rights section, but modified it so as to state the rights as disclosed
by the evidence.

The problem before us

a   This erroneous decision by the commons commissioner has created a real problem. This is because (as he refused confirmation) the registration in the rights section became void: see s 6(1)(a) of the Commons Registration Act 1965. So there is no entry of any rights of common in the rights section. But there is still an entry of the land as common land in the land section. This was, however, expressly consequential on the entry in the rights section; and, as that entry has been avoided, there are no rights of common b   whatever over this land: see s 1(2)(b). On this account the college say that the entry in the land section should be amended under s 13 of the 1965 Act so as to strike out the land as common land altogether. They say that the entry in the land section was expressly consequential on the entry in the rights section. So when it became void (by reason of the decision of the commons commissioner) the land 'ceased' to be comon land, and thus the entry in the land section was able to be amended under s 13.

c   This raises a very important point under the 1965 Act. You have a registration in the land section which says that it is common land, but there is no entry in the rights section to say that anyone has any rights over that common land. Then there is s 10, which says:

'The registration under this Act of any land as common land . . . or of any rights of common over any such land, shall be conclusive evidence of the matters registered . . .'

d
The letter of the department

On 25 September 1973 the Department of the Environment sent a circular letter to all county councils stating their views. They analysed the various sections and concluded:

'Where land has attained final registration as common land, the effect of section 10 of the 1965 Act is to make the registration conclusive evidence of "the matters e   registered, as at the date of registration". The registration system created by Parliament allows for commons to be on the register unsupported by rights of common, even where the land is not manorial waste. This seems clear from the case of a common which is not objected to but where all the rights thereover are objected to and are struck down. The common itself is entitled to final registration without regard to whether or not it is waste of the manor. This is apparent from the absence f   of any converse provision to section 5(7) of the Act which provides for an objection to a registration of land to be treated as an objection to any registration of rights over the land. As the subject is of general interest . . . the Department [are] sending a copy of this letter for information to all county councils.'

The Clwyd case

g   That letter was considered by Goff J in *Central Electricity Generating Board v Clwyd CC* [1976] 1 All ER 251, [1976] 1 WLR 151. He declined to accept the view of the department. Mr Hugh Francis QC, sitting as a commons commissioner, had confirmed the registration of the Dee Marsh saltings as common land. But Goff J overruled him. I must say that I prefer the ruling of the department and Mr Hugh Francis to the ruling of Goff J.

h
My view

To my mind the ultimate question is: what is the effect in law of land registered in the land section as 'common land' but with no 'rights of common' registered in the rights section and that entry becoming conclusive under s 10? This must be judged by the effect the entry would have on a reader examining the register, who wanted to know what the position was. He is not to be credited with any knowledge of the previous j   history of the land. He ought to have by his side the definition of 'common land' in s 22(1) of the 1965 Act, namely: '(a) land subject to rights of common . . . (b) waste land of a manor not subject to rights of common . . .'

Seeing that no rights of common are entered on the register, the person examining the register would at once assume that the land must be 'waste land of a manor'. That is the only way of reconciling the entry in the land section with the non-entry in the rights section. As the land is conclusively to be regarded as 'common land', it follows that it must conclusively be deemed to be waste land of the manor.

Now in this case it is said that, on the agreed statement of facts, this land was never waste land of the manor. But our reader of the register is not to know this. He is entitled to go by the register itself.

This is a most just result as is shown by this very case. The tenants of the manor had the undoubted right to graze Temple Ham meadow then it was part of the demesne lands of the manor. Now they have the same rights but under the deemed description of waste land of the manor. As I have said in the passage about the history of the manor, these parcels of land, demesne land and waste land of the manor, became in the course of time virtually the same, so far as the commoners were concerned. It was all common land. So there is no harm done to anyone by holding that wherever common land is registered conclusively in the land section as common land, and no rights are registered in anyone in the rights section, the common land is deemed conclusively to be waste land of the manor.

The Box Common case

I have read with some dismay the decision of this court in *Box Parish Council v Lacey* [1979] 1 All ER 113, [1980] Ch 109. It seems to me that the decisions of Foster J in *Re Yately Common, Hampshire* [1977] 1 All ER 505, [1977] 1 WLR 840, of Slade J in *Re Chewton Common* [1977] 3 All ER 509, [1977] 1 WLR 1242 and of Foster J in the *Box Hill Common* case (13 October 1977, unreported) were far more in accordance with the intention of Parliament than the decision of this court. I feel that if this court had been more fully informed of the history of manors it would have come to a different decision. I hope that it may soon be reconsidered.

Conclusion

The common lands scattered all about England and Wales are part of our heritage from the past. They have enabled considerable areas of land to be preserved intact and unspoilt. Wherever they are registered as 'common land' they should be preserved intact, even though there is no entry against them of any particular rights of any particular commoners. The conclusive presumption from such an entry is that in time past they were waste land of the manor and have never lost that character even though now separated from the lordship of the manor. For this reason I think the county court judge was right and I would dismiss the appeal.

I cannot part from this case without an expression of regret. It was nearly 100 years ago that Thomas Scrutton (afterwards Scrutton LJ) pleaded for legislation so as to preserve our commons (see *Commons and Common Fields* (1887) pp 152–176). The Commons Registration Act 1965 was an attempt to preserve them but it has sadly failed in its purpose. It is ill-drafted and has given rise to many difficulties. It has been interpreted by the courts so as to put an unduly heavy burden of proof onto commoners. It set down an unduly rigid timetable for registration of common land and of rights of common. It made the register too conclusive. The power to amend the register is too narrowly confined. I should like to see provisions made by which past registrations, or references of them, can be reopened, where the circumstances require it. After all our common land has been with us for hundreds of years. Modern legislation should be aimed at preserving it and not reducing it. Our comon land should not be cut down any further or any more.

OLIVER LJ. It is one of the pitfalls for the unwary landowner provided by the Commons Registration Act 1965 that he may find that his land has been irrevocably registered as common land without the matter ever having been brought to his attention. The case of *Smith v East Sussex CC* (1977) 76 LGR 332 is an example.

The present case brings to light yet another pitfall, namely that a successful objector to

the registration of common rights against his land may nevertheless find himself still
a saddled with an irremovable registration of the land as common land. That result may
seem to be of very little practical significance if no one is capable of exercising any rights
over the land, but it clearly affects the value of the land and subjects it to whatever
consequences may be provided for common land in the future by the legislature.

It comes about in this way. Common land is defined in s 22(1) of the 1965 Act as
embracing two mutually exclusive types of land, that is to say '(*a*) land subject to rights
b of common . . . (*b*) waste land of a manor not subject to rights of common'.

Section 1(1) of the 1965 Act (so far as relevant) provides for the registration of—

'(*a*) land in England or Wales which is common land . . . (*b*) rights of common
over such land; and (*c*) persons claiming or found to be the owners of such land . . .'

Section 1(2) effectively produces the extinguishment of any unregistered common rights
c by providing that after the end of a given period (which, in the event, expired on 31 July
1970)—

'no rights of common shall be exercisable over any such land unless they are
registered either under this Act or under the Land Registration Acts 1925 and 1936.'

Sections 2 and 3 impose on local authorities the obligation of keeping registers and
d s 19 provides for regulations to be made prescribing the form of the registers. It is the
prescribed form and the statutory provisions governing registration which have given
rise to the problem presented by this case, which we are told is but one of a number of
similar problems which have arisen in various parts of the country. The relevant
regulations for present purposes, and there have been a number of statutory instruments
made under the powers in s 19, are the Commons Registration (General) Regulations
e 1966, SI 1966/1471. Regulation 4(5) provides that the register units shall be prepared in
accordance with reg 10 and that such register shall consist of three sections, called
respectively the land section, the rights section and the ownership section, and reg 4(6)
provides that the land section—

'shall be in Form 2 and shall contain the registration of the common land . . . and
such other information as may by any regulation . . . be required or authorised to
f be entered therein.'

Returning now to the 1965 Act, s 4(1) imposes on the registration authority a duty to
register any land as common land or any rights of common over or ownership of such
land on an application duly made. Section 4(2) authorises an application for the
registration of any land as common land to be made by *any* person and provides that the
g registration authority—

'(*a*) *may* so register any land notwithstanding that no application for that
registration has been made, and (*b*) *shall* so register any land in any case where it
registers any rights over it under this section.'

Thus the automatic result of an application for the registration of common rights over
h land, however well- or ill-founded, is that the land over which the rights are claimed is
registered as common land in the land section of the register. Initially, however, the
registration is provisional only. That is provided by s 4(5), and under s 4(6) no application
can be entertained unless made within the period specified by ministerial order (again,
in the event, by 31 July 1970).

Curiously, neither the Act nor the regulations make any provision for direct notification
j to the owner of the land that his land has been registered as common land. The
registration map and the register are open to public inspection but the landowner is
apprised of the registration only if his attention is drawn to it from public notice or if his
own industry prompts him to search. Section 5 of the 1965 Act prescribes a period for
the notification of objections to registration and that period, so far as the instant case is
concerned, expired on 30 September 1970. The authority is obliged, on receipt of an

objection, to note it on the register and to notify any applicant for registration. If the
objection is not withdrawn, the matter must be referred to a commons commissioner. *a*
Section 5(7) provides that an objection to the registration of land as common land is to be
treated also as an objection to the registration of any rights. That is, of course, logical
because if the registration of rights is allowed to stand it necessarily follows that, by
definition, the land over which the rights are claimed is common land. Thus a successful
objection to the land registration and the cancellation of that entry necessarily means that
the land is not subject to common rights. It is also logical, however, that the converse *b*
should not apply because, since common land by definition includes manorial waste land
not subject to any common rights, a successful objection to the registration of rights
would not necessarily conclude the question of whether the land was common land. It
might still be registrable as manorial waste if the facts justified such registration. This
has important consequences in the present case and in similar cases, for none of the
documents issued under the 1965 Act draw attention in terms to the importance, in a *c*
case where the only reason for the registration of the land is that an application has been
made for the registration of rights over it, of registering an objection not only to the
registration of the rights but also to the consequential registration of the land. The critical
importance of this from the landowner's point of view appears from the next two
sections. Under s 6, the commons commissioner to whom the matter of an objection is
referred has to inquire into it and either confirm or refuse the registration. If confirmed, *d*
it becomes final. If it is not confirmed, it is avoided, and in that event the registration
authority is obliged to cancel it. Here lies the concealed trap. What is to be cancelled is
the registration against which the objection has been lodged, for that is the matter which
has been referred to the commissioner. Going back for one moment to the 1966
regulations, reg 10(1) provides that in making a registration the registration authority
shall follow as closely as possible such of model entries 4 to 12 as may be applicable, with *e*
such variations as circumstances may require, and shall mark every registration as
provisional. Those model entries are set out in Sch 2 to the 1966 regulations, and model
entry 4 is for the land section of the register where the entry is pursuant to an application
for registration of land as common land. The register consists of a date column and a
column headed 'Description of the land, reference to the register map, registration
particulars, etc.' In that column is to be entered a short description of the land by *f*
reference to area and parish—

'as marked with a green verge line inside the boundary on sheet 8 of the register
map and distinguished by number of this register unit. Registered pursuant to
Application No. 14 made the 2nd January 1967 by . . . (Registration Provisional).'

There is an important note in the schedule to the regulations which is in these terms:
  g
'In the case of a registration under Section 4(2)(b) of the Act [that is, where the
registration is the automatic consequence of a rights registration] the phrase
"pursuant to application No. 14" would be replaced by "in consequence of application
No. 14 (rights)".'

The land registration which was effected in the instant case was such an automatic *h*
consequence and it followed the prescribed form. Now anyone not fully instructed in
the obscurities of this legislation could be pardoned for thinking that, where he finds a
registration of land in the land section which is described as being there 'in consequence
of' an application for the registration of rights and which is described as 'provisional', if
he objects successfully to the registration of the rights in consequence of which the land
has been registered so that that registration is cancelled, that will result also in the *j*
cancellation of the consequential registration of the land. He would however be wrong,
for the application of common sense to the registration of common land is altogether too
naive an approach. Returning to the 1965 Act, s 7 provides that if no objection is made
to a registration under s 4 (which, of course, includes the automatic consequential
registration) the registration shall become final at the end of the period during which
such objection could have been made under s 5 of the Act. So the failure to lodge an

objection to the consequential registration of the land in the land section of the register
a results in that registration becoming final even though the only thing that supports such
registration is the (still provisional) registration of rights over the land, and, that having
occurred, s 10 of the Act comes into play. Section 10 provides that:

> 'The registration under this Act of any land as common land . . . or of any rights
> of common over any such land, shall be conclusive evidence of the matters
> *b* registered, as at the date of registration, except where the registration is provisional
> only.'

So the land is now conclusively presumed to be common land although it is not
conclusively presumed to be land subject to rights of common, since those rights have
not yet been established.

The facts in the instant case have already been adverted to in the judgment of Lord
c Denning MR and it is not in dispute that the consequences outlined above ensued as
regards the registration of this land in the land section of the register on 30 September
1970, that being the last date by which objection to that registration had to be lodged.
The only question then is whether that registration ought to be cancelled. Again, it is not
in dispute that the only provisions under which it can be cancelled, if it can be cancelled
at all, are to be found in s 13 of the 1965 Act and the regulations therein referred to.
d Section 13 provides:

> 'Regulations under this Act shall provide for the amendment of the registers
> maintained under this Act where—(a) any land registered under this Act ceases to
> be common land . . . or (c) any rights registered under this Act are apportioned,
> extinguished or released, or are varied or transferred in such circumstances as may
> *e* be prescribed . . .'

Regulations 27 and 29 provide for the procedure to be followed where any of the
contemplated events has occurred. In the end the short question on this appeal is whether
the effect of the commons commissioner's refusal to confirm the registration of common
rights was an event which either caused the land entered in the land register to 'cease to
be common land' or 'extinguished rights registered under this Act'. If it was not, then
f the registration stands and the land is and continues to be common land, even though
everyone knows perfectly well that there are no common rights any longer exercisable
over it and that it is not and never was waste land of the manor.

The argument of counsel on behalf of the college starts from the undoubted proposition
that, on the period available for registration of rights expiring, any rights of common
which did exist necessarily became no longer exercisable unless they were registered.
g That follows from s 1(2). The only rights which were registered were the rights claimed
by the Parish Council of Little Rissington and, that registration having become void and
been cancelled as a result of the commons commissioner's decision, the land has now
ceased to be common land. This problem was in fact foreshadowed some time ago by
Goff J in *Central Electricity Generating Board v Clwyd CC* [1976] 1 All ER 251, [1976] 1
WLR 151, although that case was concerned with a different situation in which the
h applicants had registered the land as common land although there was no supporting
registration of common rights and no suggestion that it was or ever had been manorial
waste not subject to common rights. Goff J held that, in so far as any common rights had
existed, they had ceased to be exercisable under s 1(2) of the 1965 Act and were therefore
extinguished and that since the only title to register the land was that it was land subject
to rights of common the registration of the land as common land could not be supported.
j It was argued before him that, since, when the land was registered, the last date for
registration of any rights had not yet arrived, the land was then still capable of being
common land and thus the registration could properly be confirmed. That argument,
however, he rejected. He said ([1976] 1 All ER 251 at 255, [1976] 1 WLR 151 at 156):

> 'It appears to be suggested that it was right for the commissioner to look only at
> the date of registration, because if he confirmed the registration it could stand,

notwithstanding the failure to register any rights of common, and could not be
amended under s 13 of the 1965 Act because that could only be applied if there was
some change of circumstance or something outside [which caused] the failure to
register rights of common. I cannot accept that view. It seems to me that if the
commissioner were right in looking at that date and therefore confirming the
registration, it would become conclusive evidence that the land was common land
at the time of registration but nothing more. And accordingly, when the rights
ceased to be exercisable, it would cease to be common land and therefore it would
lead inevitably to an application, an unanswerable application, to amend the register.
Of course, land may be registered as common land though there are no rights of
common over it, because the definition [in s 22(1)] includes 'waste land of a manor
not subject to rights of common', but that is not this case.'

That, counsel for the college submits, is precisely what has happened in this case. He
agrees that one has to look for the occurrence of some event since the registration which
has caused the land to cease to be common land, but that, he submits, is to be found here
in the decision of the commons commissioner and the consequent cancellation of the
rights registration. It is true, he says, that on 1 October 1970 (the last date for lodging an
objection) the registration of the land as common land in the land section of the register
became final; and it is true that the result of that is that under s 10 the registration is
conclusive evidence of the matters registered as at the date of registration; but that, he
submits, does not detract from, indeed it reinforces, his central submission that the case
falls squarely within s 13(a). There is only one date of registration, and that is the date
when the registered entry is made, even though it was, at that time, provisional only.
There is no room, as a matter of construction, for treating 'the date of registration' as the
date on which the registration ceases to be provisional. What, then, are 'the matters
registered' as to which the evidence is conclusive? The first is that the land described is
common land. The second is that the registration was effected under s 4(2)(b), since it is
described as 'consequent on' the rights registration. Thus, counsel for the college argues,
it is to be conclusively presumed that on 5 June 1968 (the date of registration) the land
was common land and it was common land because it was land subject to rights of
common, since it was not waste land of the manor and no one has ever suggested that it
was. Now it might be, at that date, common land because of the rights which had been
registered and whose registration gave rise to the entry in the land section, if those rights
in fact existed and their existence was subsequently conceded or confirmed by the
commons commissioner; or it might be common land because of some other rights of
common which had not yet been registered. But, whichever it was, it has, since 5 June
1968, ceased to be subject to any common rights. As to the registered rights, it so ceased
on 15 May 1976 (the date of the commons commissioner's decision) when the rights
registration became void, and in so far as it was subject to other rights, it ceased to be so
subject on 31 July 1970, the last day for registration: see *Central Electricity Generating
Board v Clwyd CC*. Therefore, says counsel, it has actually and literally ceased to be
common land since the date of registration and the register can now be properly amended
under s 13.

This is a persuasive argument and it has the merit of having common sense behind it.
If, for instance, an applicant applies to register the right to graze sheep in common with
the landowner and the landowner does not object to the registration, then when it
becomes final the land is common land and it is common land only because it is subject
to the registered common right. If then the landowner buys out the commoner's right,
the only right capable of being exercised, it follows that the land has now ceased to be
common land and the land section of the register falls to be amended under s 13. Why,
asks counsel for the college, should it make any difference that the right which has been
extinguished has been extinguished by operation of law rather than act of the parties?
Speaking for myself, I see no answer to this, so long, and only so long, as the
extinguishment does in fact cause an existing state of affairs to 'cease'. There was a

suggestion in *Central Electricity Generating Board v Clwyd CC* that the cessation referred to had, in some way, to be a cessation independently of the provisions of the 1965 Act, but, as has already been mentioned, Goff J rejected this and, if I may say so respectfully, for my part I think that he was right to do so in the case before him, where registration had not yet become final, an objection had been lodged and it was clear that the land was not waste land of a manor and no longer subject to any rights. There is no context in the 1965 Act for limiting the word 'cease' to any particular method of cessation. I do not however think that it follows that the objector in that case would, as Goff J suggested, have had an unanswerable case for rectification if registration had in fact become final.

I confess to a considerable sympathy with the argument of counsel for the college for I find it offensive that the accidental failure to lodge an objection to the registration of the land at the same time as objection was lodged to the registration of the rights should lead to a conclusive and immutable status of the land as common land which is entirely contrary to the facts, the more so when there is nothing in the 1965 Act itself or in any of the documents issued under it to lead any but the most skilled and attentive reader to see the importance of lodging a dual objection.

Counsel for the registration authority, however, submits that there is a fatal flaw in the argument, which arises from the combination of ss 13 and 10. What s 13 envisages is that the land has 'ceased to be common land', not that it never was common land. It therefore postulates that at the date of registration the land was common land within the statutory definition but that something has happened since which has caused it no longer to be so. Thus far she is not, I think, propounding anything with which counsel for the college would disagree. If, she argues, the real case of the applicant for amendment of the register is that the land never was common land, so that it ought never to have been registered, his only remedy lies under s 14, where he is effectively restricted to proving fraud. The intention of the 1965 Act is that, subject to the power to amend where there has been some relevant change since registration, the registration is final and this, counsel for the registration authority submits, is the importance of s 10.

Counsel for the registration authority does not shrink from the proposition that 'the matters registered' under that section embrace all the material appearing on the register, including the entry that the registration was made under s 4(2)(b) consequent on the registration of rights. But that entry, she submits, in no way restricts the possible nature of the common land which is registered. The registration of the land as common land means, in effect, that you write out the statutory definition in s 22(1) and apply it to the registered land, so that in effect the register says 'this land is (a) land subject to rights of common ... (b) waste land of a manor not subject to rights of common'. It cannot, counsel agrees, be both, but it may be either and therefore, if you are going to establish, as you have to, to succeed under s 13, that something has happened whereby the land has 'ceased' to be common land, you have to show something or some things which negative both branches of the definition and you have to show that those things have occurred *since* the registration. You cannot negative any part of the statutory definition by calling evidence to show that *before* or at the time of registration the land did not qualify for that part, for that would be to contradict the statutory presumption appearing from s 10 which makes it conclusive that the land did then fall within the definition. To demonstrate that the land has ceased to be subject to any exercisable common rights, therefore, does not go far enough, for the land might equally well have been waste of the manor not subject to common rights, its actual status never having been determined because nobody raised any objection to the registration. It is not enough to show that no one claimed that this was so prior to registration. Any such claim would have fallen to be investigated if an objection had been raised to the registration of the land, but no objection was raised and it must be assumed that potential claims that the land was, contrary to what was asserted by the claimants to the common rights, common land within the other branch of the definition must be taken to have been conceded.

Thus, in order to succeed under s 13, you would have to show either that there was something in the registered entries themselves which demonstrated not just a probability but a certainty that the registration was attributable, and attributable only, to the existence of common rights (which rights have now ceased) or that something had occurred since registration which negatived both branches of the definition. The mere fact that the registered entries show the registration to have been effected in consequence of the rights registration does not, counsel for the registration authority submits, demonstrate that the existence of common rights was the only justification for the registration. It would only do so if the position were this, that had objection been raised to the registration the only matter into which the commissioner could have inquired on the reference to him of 'the matter' (ie the matter of the registration) would have been the validity or existence of the rights of common registered in the rights section of the register. But the recent decision of Walton J in *Re Sutton Common* [1982] 2 All ER 376, [1982] 1 WLR 647 shows that this is not so. There was a registration of the land as 'common land' (made, it is true, consequent on a rights registration) and on a reference to the commissioner of an objection to that registration it would have been open to him to receive all relevant evidence in relation to 'the matter' of whether the registration should or should not stand. Thus it would, I apprehend, have been open to the applicants, if they failed to establish their rights, to seek to prove, if they could, an alternative case that the land concerned was waste land of the manor.

Although I found the argument of counsel for the registration authority extremely persuasive, I am not sure that I fully agree with this way of putting it, for to assert as a general proposition that an applicant for amendment of the register cannot adduce evidence of a state of affairs existing prior to the registration of the land and which might have been inquired into on a reference to the commissioner would mean in many, if not all, cases that the land register could never be amended consequent on the extinguishment of registered rights. It has to be borne in mind that there are potentially three and not merely two categories of common land, for the first category of land subject to rights of common may include land which is waste land of the manor but which is so subject. It was unnecessary for definition purposes to specify this as a separate class of land since it would be included in para (*a*) of the definition in s 22(1), but it is inherent in the definition that the extinguishment of rights in such a case would not result in the land ceasing to be common land but would merely transfer it from one branch of the definition to the other. Thus, if there is supposed a case where, as here, the land registration is allowed to go unchallenged but there is a registration of common rights which is confirmed by the commissioner, the effect of the land registration, at the date when that registration is effected, will be that the common land may be either subject to rights (at that stage unconfirmed) or manorial waste. If then the landowner and the commoners agree on a release of the rights, the land ceases to be common land under the first branch of the definition, but there remains the possibility that it may be waste land of the manor and that, since it is now waste land not subject to common rights, it remains common land under the second branch of the definition. In order to make sense of s 13 at all in such a case, it must, as it seems to me, be open to the landowner to demonstrate by evidence which could have been brought before an inquiry if one had taken place that the land never was waste of the manor, for this is a critical part of the demonstration that it has indeed 'ceased' to be common land. But the fact that counsel for the registration authority has, as I think that she may have done, sought to cast her net a little too wide does not detract from what I apprehend is the main burden of her submission that to 'cease' postulates a beginning, and that ceasing to be is not the same thing as never having been. Counsel for the college, she would say, simply by demonstrating that there are no longer any rights now capable of being exercised over the land, does not demonstrate that is has 'ceased' to be common land since it was registered. Looking at the position of the land at the date of its registration, there were four possibilities: (1) it was waste land of the manor not subject to any rights of common; (2) it was land (including, possibly, manorial waste land) subject to the rights of common which had been registered but which had not yet been finally established; (3) it was land subject to other rights not yet registered (either in addition to or in substitution for the registered rights); (4) it was land other than manorial waste which was not subject to any rights at all.

a Into which of these four categories it fell would depend on whether there was any further registration of rights and on the result of an inquiry into any objections lodged to registered rights. Once the time for registration of rights had passed, there was no longer any possibility of the land being subject to any unregistered common rights, but that does not mean that it has 'ceased' to be common land. It merely means that land which might or might not have been subject to rights of common and which might, therefore, possibly not be common land within the first branch of the definition, now *b* definitely is not within the first branch of the definition. The possibility remains that it never was subject to any such rights at all, registered or not, at the date of its registration. If that was so, the cancellation of the rights register effected no change in the position. Effectively the commons commissioner's decision meant that the rights claimed did not exist and thus that, if there had been an objection to the land registration on this ground, it would have succeeded. But that does not demonstrate a 'cessation'; if it demonstrates *c* anything, it demonstrates only that the land (assuming it not to have been waste land of the manor) was not common land at the date of its registration and that the registration should never therefore have been permitted to become final. But that, as I read s 10, is what that section puts beyond challenge.

To put it another way, in order to show that the cancellation of registered rights or the failure to register rights has caused land to 'cease' to be common land, you must show *d* that those rights did in fact exist but have now ceased. But so far as the registered rights are concerned, that has already been determined against the college by the commissioner, and, so far as any other rights are concerned, proof of their existence or non-existence is the very thing that the finality of registration is designed to avoid.

This case reveals what I cannot but think is yet another most unsatisfactory state of affairs created by this Act which, if I may say so, is crying out for amendment; but in the *e* end I have found the submissions of counsel for the registration authority persuasive and I have felt bound to arrive, though possibly by a slightly different route, at the same conclusion as the judge. I agree, therefore, that the appeal should be dismissed.

I would only add this, that I respectfully differ from the view expressed by Lord Denning MR with regard to the correctness of the commissioner's decision in this case. It may well be that commons commissioners, who have the difficult task of inquiring *f* into matters which are frequently presented by laymen, may properly allow greater latitude both as regards proof and procedure than a judge deciding a civil dispute inter partes. But in my judgment, where rights are registered and asserted and challenged, the burden of demonstrating the existence of the rights registered and what they are must rest in the ultimate on those who assert it.

g **KERR LJ.** The only issue in this case, but a difficult one, is whether Temple Ham meadow has ceased to be common land for the purposes of s 13(*a*) of the Commons Registration Act 1965 and reg 27 of the Commons Registration (General) Regulations 1966, SI 1966/1471. Since the registration of the land as common land, which had been made pursuant to s 4(2)(*b*) in consequence of a registration of alleged rights of common, was not the subject of any objection under s 5, this registration became final on 30 *h* September 1970 by virtue of ss 4(5) and 7(1) read with reg 4(2) of the Commons Registration (Objections and Maps) Regulations 1968, SI 1968/989. However, when the commons commissioner refused to confirm the provisional registration of the rights on 6 March 1976 without there being any appeal against his decision, that registration became void and was cancelled pursuant to s 6(1) and (3). The argument is, in effect, that, since this registration had been the sole basis for the registration of the land, its *j* disappearance and the extinction of all rights of common over the land by virtue of s 1(2)(*b*) have the effect that the land ceased to be common land, and that the land section of the register falls to be amended accordingly.

There is nothing in the scheme or wording of the Act or regulations which provides for this consequence, either expressly or by necessary implication. Under the definition of common land in s 22, land can be common land without being subject to rights of common, ie if it is waste land of a manor. This, no doubt, is the reason why a distinction is drawn throughout the legislation between the registration of rights of common and the registration of land as common land: see, for example, s 1(1)(a) and (b); s 1(2)(a) and (b); s 4(1), (2)(a) and (2)(b); s 13(a) and (c); reg 4(6) and (7); regs 27 and 29 of the 1966 regulations. The two types of registration are therefore treated as being independent of each other, and this is indeed stated expressly in para 4 of the schedule to the Commons Registration (Objections and Maps) (Amendment) Regulations 1970, SI 1970/384. Only two exceptions to this independence of the two kinds of registration are to be found in the legislation. Both of these follow from the fact that, since rights of common cannot exist in the air, a registration of rights must necessarily entail a registration of the land which is alleged to be subject to the rights (see s 4(2)(b)), and an objection to a registration of the land as common land must necessarily also be treated as an objection to any registration of alleged rights over the land (see s 5(7)). But the converse does not follow and is nowhere indicated: a registration of the land is treated as being independent from the existence or absence of any registration of rights over the land; and an objection to any registration of rights is treated as being independent from any objection to the registration of the land in question.

It is against this background that one then comes to s 10. For present purposes this provides, in effect, that the final registration of any land as common land is 'conclusive evidence of the matters registered, as at the date of registration'. Whatever may be the precise point of time denoted by the words 'as at the date of registration', it is clear that this time is now long past; in the present case it cannot have been later than 30 September 1970. The purpose of these words was presumably to contrast the time of registration with that of some subsequent event, as referred to in s 13, which is to entail an amendment of the register: in the present case the alleged cessation of Temple Ham meadow as being common land on the avoidance and cancellation of the provisional registration of rights of common over it.

The clear prima facie effect of s 10, as it seems to me, must be that it is not now open to anyone to dispute the fact that Temple Ham meadow is common land, and, further, that to this extent it is now irrelevant whether it be common land because it is subject to rights of common or whether it is waste land of a manor. Furthermore, subject to the final argument of the college as mentioned below, this conclusion could not possibly be affected by any investigation whether any provisional registration of alleged rights of common over this land had ever been made pursuant to ss 1 and 4, and, if so, whether such registration subsequently became final under s 6 or s 7 or became void under s 6. Thus, if the land had been registered by A as alleged waste land of a manor, and there had then been a registration by B of alleged rights of common over it, the ultimate avoidance and cancellation of B's registration could not have any possible effect on A's registration if this achieved finality, whether under s 6 or s 7.

The argument of the college, however, is that this is not the position in the present case, because the land was only registered pursuant to s 4(2)(b) in consequence of the registration of the alleged rights of common over it, and because this fact appears on the face of the register, as was indeed required by reg 10 of the 1966 regulations and model entry 4 of Part I of Sch 2 thereto. The college accordingly contend, since s 10 provides that the registration is to be conclusive evidence 'of the matters registered', that the latter include the fact that the registration of the land had only been made in consequence of the registration of alleged rights of common over the land. Accordingly, the college say, the land cannot have been registered as waste land of a manor: any further application for registration of the land on this basis, if there had been one, would have had to be noted on the register under s 4(4); but there is no such notation. Therefore, the college say, proof of the subsequent avoidance and cancellation of the provisional registration of the alleged rights of common does not contradict anything which is deemed to be conclusive by virtue of s 10, and such avoidance and cancellation must have removed the only foundation for the registration of Temple Ham meadow as common land, so that the land must thereupon have ceased to be common land for the purposes of s 13(a).

At first sight this seems a formidable line of argument. But I have not been convinced *a* by it, because in my view it does involve a conflict with s 10, both in relation to its wording and its purpose. I think that the argument reads more into the words 'of the matters registered' than these words and their purpose will bear. Section 10 deals compendiously with the registration of (a) land as common land, (b) town or village greens and (c) rights of common over such land. The particulars of the registration of any or all of these are then compendiously referred to as 'the matters registered'. In my view these words have no wider effect than this. For present purposes their effect is that

b the registration of Temple Ham meadow as common land is now conclusive.

Nor do I think that the college can succeed by saying, as they do, 'The register shows that Temple Ham meadow was registered as common land in consequence of a registration of alleged rights of common over it, and not as waste land of a manor. Moreover, we can prove that it was never waste land of a manor; indeed, this is accepted by the registration authority.' The irony of this argument in the present case is that there

c is no doubt that Temple Ham meadow is in fact land which has been subject to rights of common for centuries, although (unfortunately) not those which were registered by the parish council, so that this registration became void in 1976; and any other registration of rights of common had already previously become impossible as from 31 July 1970: see the Commons Registration (Time Limits) (Amendment) Order 1970, SI 1970/383. However, in my view none of this makes any difference. In the face of s 10 it is not now

d open to the college to seek to show that Temple Ham meadow has ceased to be common land except by reference to some subsequent event or transaction which concerned the land itself and which had this effect. But nothing of the kind has happened in this case. As is pointed out by Oliver LJ, the college's application to amend the register in effect involves them in seeking to show that the land had never been common land (because it had never been waste land of a manor), but this is clearly precluded by s 10.

e I therefore agree that this appeal fails.

Appeal dismissed. Leave to appeal to the House of Lords granted.

Solicitors: *Morrell, Peel & Gamlen*, Oxford (for the college); *D A Dean*, Gloucester (for the registration authority).

Diana Procter   Barrister.

R v Governor of Pentonville Prison, ex parte Passingham and another

QUEEN'S BENCH DIVISION

GRIFFITHS LJ AND FORBES J

22 JUNE 1982

Extradition – Committal – Evidence – Evidence sufficient to justify committal – Evidence relied on not given under oath or by way of affirmation in requesting state – Affirmation– Witness acknowledging that he was aware of need to tell truth when making statement – No penal sanction for perjury if witness made false statement – Whether an 'affirmation' has to be supported by sanction of penalty for perjury – Whether witness's statement amounting to affirmation and therefore admissible – Extradition Act 1870, s 14 – Extradition Act 1873, s 4.

In the course of his interrogation by the Swedish police in connection with certain drug offences allegedly committed there, an informant incriminated the applicants, who lived in England. The Swedish government applied for their extradition under the Extradition Acts 1870 and 1873 and the extradition treaty between Sweden and the United Kingdom to answer drugs charges there. At the extradition proceedings the evidence which was admitted under the Extradition Acts by the metropolitan stipendiary magistrate included a copy of the informant's statement to the police and a record of the proceedings in a Swedish court. The record of those proceedings showed that the informant was asked whether his statement to the police about the applicants was correct and that, before the applicant answered the question, the judge informed him that, although under the Swedish Code of Judicial Procedure it was an offence punishable by imprisonment to make a false statement to the police during interrogation, it was not an offence under Swedish law to make a false statement in court regarding a crime committed by another person. The judge had gone on to tell the informant that he should none the less tell the truth when replying to the question. By Swedish law his reply was not given on oath. The informant's reply confirmed that the particulars which he had given to the police were correct and that he understood the implications of the judge's reminder of the law. The metropolitan stipendiary magistrate found that there was a case to answer and committed the applicants to prison to await extradition to Sweden. The applicants applied for a writ of habeas corpus, contending that the magistrate had erred in admitting the statement made by the informant to the police because the record of the proceedings in the Swedish court showed that, although the informant had acknowledged its veracity in court, he had not done so on oath or by way of 'affirmation' in accordance with s 14[a] of the 1870 Act, as extended by s 4[b] of the 1873 Act, since the informant's statement in court could not amount to an 'affirmation' because it was not supported by the sanction of a penalty for perjury.

Held – For a statement to be received in evidence under the Extradition Acts in extradition proceedings it did not have to be made under the sanction of a penalty for perjury: it was sufficient if it was made in circumstances of sufficient gravity and formal solemnity for the witness to appreciate fully the importance of telling the truth. On the evidence, the informant had realised the importance of that when acknowledging in the

---

a   Section 14 provides: 'Depositions or statements on oath, taken in a foreign state, and copies of such original depositions or statements, and foreign certificates of or judicial documents stating the fact of conviction, may, if duly authenticated, be received in evidence in proceedings under this Act.'

b   Section 4 provides: 'The provisions of the principal Act relating to depositions and statements on oath taken in a foreign state, and copies of such original depositions and statements, do and shall extend to affirmations taken in a foreign state, and copies of such affirmations.'

a   Swedish court the veracity of his statement to the police and that was sufficient to constitute an 'affirmation' of his statement for the purpose of the Extradition Acts. Accordingly, the magistrate was entitled to act on the basis of his statement. The applicants' request for a writ of habeas corpus would therefore be refused (see p 104 *j* to p 105 *c* and p 1016 *a* to *d*, post).

R v Governor of Brixton Prison, ex p Twema (27 November 1980, unreported, DC).

b   **Notes**
For evidence required for extradition, see 18 Halsbury's Laws (4th edn) paras 225, 233–235, and for cases on the subject see 24 Digest (Reissue) 1136–1138, 12055–12074.
    For the Extradition Act 1870, s 14, see 13 Halsbury's Statutes (3rd edn) 259.
    For the Extradition Act 1873, s 4, see ibid 270.

c   **Cases referred to in judgments**
R v Governor of Brixton Prison, ex p Twema (27 November 1980, unreported), DC.
R v Governor of Pentonville Prison, ex p Singh [1981] 3 All ER 23, [1981] 1 WLR 1031, DC.

Application
d   Stephen Passingham and Neil Dowse applied for a writ of habeas corpus directed to the Governor of Pentonville Prison, where the applicants were detained, in respect of a warrant of committal issued by the metropolitan stipendiary magistrate at Bow Street on 17 February 1982. The government of Sweden, which was also a respondent to the application, had sought the applicants' extradition under the Extradition Acts 1870 and 1873, and the extradition treaty between Sweden and the United Kingdom, so that the applicants could answer drugs charges there. The facts are set out in the judgment of
e   Griffiths LJ.

Clive Stanbrook for the applicants.
Ann Goddard QC for the respondents.

f   **GRIFFITHS LJ.** The applicants apply for a writ of habeas corpus in respect of a warrant of committal by the metropolitan magistrate, sitting at Bow Street Magistrates' Court on 17 February 1982, to await the directions of the Secretary of State for extradition to Sweden under the Extradition Act 1870.
    The government of Sweden wish to extradite the applicants to face trial in Sweden on charges of possession, supplying and smuggling of heroin. The application is made on
g   the ground that the magistrate wrongly admitted in evidence against both accused statements made by an accomplice in Sweden which were not taken on oath, nor by way of affirmation, contrary to the conditions of s 14 of the Extradition Act 1870, as extended by s 4 of the Extradition Act 1873.
    To understand the basis on which this ground has been argued, it is necessary to recite some of the evidence placed before the Bow Street magistrate on behalf of the government
h   of Sweden. The evidence included the following statement of Swedish law contained in a statement of the public and district prosecutor of the Huddinge district of prosecutions:

'Under Swedish law "false incrimination" implies the following: a co-defendant may not swear an oath when he is examined before a court in a case in order to substantiate an indictment against a co-defendant. This means that he cannot be punished for his statements before a court. On the other hand, according to Chapter
j   15, Section 7 of the Swedish Code of Judicial Procedure a person may be punished if during a police interrogation in a pre-trial investigation or before a prosecutor falsely states that another person has committed a criminal act.'

Part of the evidence against the accused was that of an accomplice, Richard Florian Michalski, and it is this witness whose evidence is said to be inadmissible. The record of

the Huddinge district court, dated 9 November 1981, contains the following record of
evidence given by Michalski before that court:

> 'RICHARD Florian Michalski, born 11 February, 1959, came before the court. He
> was informed by the Judge that if the statement he had made about the involvement
> of other persons in narcotic drugs trafficking were untrue, he could be sentenced
> under Swedish law for false incrimination to imprisonment for a maximum of two
> years. He was also reminded that it was not an offence under Swedish law to make
> false statements before a court concerning a crime committed by another person if
> the statements were not made on oath. Finally, he was told that notwithstanding he
> should keep to the truth in his statements before the court. The interpreter read out
> the translation into the English language of the following police interrogations of
> Michalski at Visby . . .'

The interrogations took place on 28 October, 2 November, and 3 November 1981. I
interpose to say that those interrogations were before the Bow Street magistrate and they
contained material which shows that Michalski was alleging that the applicants were
deeply implicated in the heroin trafficking. The record continues:

> 'When asked, Michalski confirmed that the particulars he had given at the police
> interrogation were correct and that one of the signatures on each page of the
> interrogation record was his. [The prosecutor] asked Michalski: "Have you during
> these proceedings understood that if you have lied at the police interrogations about
> Passingham's and Dowse's complicity in crime, that you are guilty of an offence
> under Swedish law? Have you been aware of this?" Michalski answered: "Yes".
> Michalski was shown one copy of the enclosed photographs (A and B) and stated that
> one was a photograph of Dowse (A) and the other a photograph of Passingham (B),
> and wrote on the back of both photographs the place, date and his signature.'

It appears, therefore, that under Swedish law if Michalski made untrue statements
about the involvement of the applicants in the face of the district court he would not be
committing an offence. Nevertheless, he would have committed an offence if he had told
untruths to the police in the interrogations referred to in the district court proceedings.
Common sense dictates that having been warned of that he would realise that he would
compound that offence, making punishment more likely and more grave, if he
untruthfully repeated in the face of the court that he had told the police the truth about
the applicants when, in fact, he had been lying.

It is submitted on behalf of the applicants that the statement of Michalski to the police,
even though acknowledged before the district court to be true, does not amount to an
affirmation within the meaning of s 4 of the Extradition Act 1873, and art 13 of the
extradition treaty between the United Kingdom and Sweden.

Under English law, if a witness giving evidence in a court of law chooses to affirm
rather than take the oath, he is liable to be prosecuted for perjury if he gives false evidence
in precisely the same way as if he gives false evidence on oath. Thus, say the applicants,
an essential feature of an affirmation in English law is that it is supported by the sanction
of a prosecution for perjury. It must therefore have been intended that the procedure
referred to as an affirmation in the Extradition Act was one that was supported by the
sanction of punishment. As Michalski could neither take the oath nor be punished for
anything he said about the applicants in the Swedish district court, the evidence before
that court could not amount to an affirmation within the meaning of the Extradition
Acts.

I cannot accept this argument. In my view, the object of enabling statements to be
received, if made on oath or affirmation, is to enable the procedure of extradition to
operate without the cumbrous necessity of bringing witnesses from abroad to this
country if the evidence that they have given in their own country had been made in
circumstances of such formal solemnity as to make it likely that the witnesses fully
appreciated the gravity of the occasion and the importance that they should give true

testimony. If evidence has been given under such conditions in their own country, it can
a be assumed with reasonable confidence that if brought to this country they would be
likely to give similar evidence to our court and it is therefore safe to act on the evidence
given in their own country.

I am afraid a lifetime's experience makes me somewhat sceptical of the value of the
threat of a prosecution for perjury acting as an inducement to tell the truth in legal
proceedings. If a witness is determined to lie, the threat of perjury is unlikely to deter
b him. On the other hand, people on less formal occasions do, all too frequently, make
casual statements to which they have not applied their minds with sufficient detail to be
safely acted on. If, on the other hand, they are called on to make a statement under
circumstances of grave formality such as will bring home to their minds the importance
that their testimony should be the truth, it will as a general rule be safe to rely on it and,
for my part, I think the sanction of the possibility of a prosecution for perjury would add
c little, if anything, to that safeguard.

This question of the meaning of an affirmation has been considered by this court in
two fairly recent decisions. It was considered by a Divisional Court consisting of
Donaldson LJ and Hodgson J in *R v Governor of Brixton Prison, ex p Twena* (27 November
1980, unreported). In the course of giving his judgment in that case, Donaldson LJ said:

d
> 'It seems to me that that is a document which is evidence of Tsim having affirmed
> in open court that the contents of the police record of his statement to them were
> correct, but that it is not an affirmation, because an affirmation in this context must
> be a document which is in some way acknowledged by the witness as being his
> solemn declaration. He can acknowledge it in a number of ways. The most obvious
> way to acknowledge it is to sign it. Next, although it may be less usual, he could
> have written it in his own handwriting without signing it, but that is not, in my
e > judgment, the limit of the number of ways in which someone may acknowledge a
> document as his affirmation. I have come to the conclusion in the light of the
> further argument since the adjournment that the affirmation here is the statement,
> or the record of the statement, made by the police officers, appearing within
> inverted commas, which was not originally an affirmation at all but became an
> affirmation when adopted by Tsim before the examining magistrate.'

f
That is really on all fours with this case save only this: that the point was not taken
before the Divisional Court in that case that Tsim could not have been prosecuted for
perjury. Indeed, we do not know from the transcript whether he could have been or not,
but it certainly does not appear to have occurred to Donaldson LJ that a sanction was
necessary before a statement could amount to an affirmation.

g The matter was also considered in the reported decision of *R v Governor of Pentonville
Prison, ex p Singh* [1981] 3 All ER 23 at 27, [1981] 1 WLR 1031 at 1036. In that case
Ackner LJ put the matter thus:

> 'The right to affirm was introduced in 1838 for the benefit of Quakers and
> Moravians and the essential part of the declaration is still retained today, namely
> "I . . . do solemnly, sincerely, and truly declare and affirm". Although neither party
h > suggests that this or any closely comparable formula has to be used, it is agreed that
> the mere signature to a document or the verbal acknowledgement that its contents
> are correct cannot amount to an affirmation. Where then is the line to be drawn?
> The answer cannot be precise: it must be a matter of fact and degree dependent on
> the particular circumstances of the case. I do not consider that the affirmation need
> take place prior to the making of the statement. [Here come the vital words:] What
j > is required, where the statement has been made, is its adoption in circumstances
> which recognise the gravity and importance of the truth being told on the particular
> occasion.'

It is true that in that case the provisions of s 168 of the Norwegian Penal Code would
have involved the witness exposing himself to the risk of a prosecution if the evidence he

gave, albeit not on oath, had subsequently proved to be untrue. Ackner LJ drew attention to that fact, but there is nothing in his language to show that he considered that the fact of that sanction was an essential ingredient contributing to the statement being regarded as an affirmation. It was merely one of the matters which pointed towards the solemnity of the occasion on which the statement was made.

In this case this witness had been told by the judge that although he did not immediately expose himself to prosecution, it was a matter of importance that he should speak the truth and he was reminded of the fact that if he had lied to the police interrogators he had already exposed himself to a prosecution, and I have already adverted to the way that that would, as a matter of common sense, have been likely to act on his mind.

In my view, this evidence given in these circumstances did have all the necessary attendant solemnity and gravity to constitute an affirmation within the meaning of the Extradition Act, and it was accordingly material on which the magistrate was entitled to act. In my judgment, therefore, this application must be refused.

FORBES J. I agree.

Application dismissed. Leave to appeal to House of Lords refused.

Solicitors: *Simons, Muirhead & Allan* (for the applicants); *Director of Public Prosecutions.*

April Weiss   Barrister.

Re Halt Garage (1964) Ltd

CHANCERY DIVISION
OLIVER J
2, 3, 4, 5, 9, 12, 25 MAY 1978

Company – Director – Remuneration – Express power of company in general meeting to award renumeration – Test of company's capacity to award remuneration – Payment to director out of capital – Husband and wife sole shareholders and directors of company – Husband and wife drawing remuneration out of capital after company suffering trading loss – Husband working full-time in business but wife ceasing to be active because of illness – Wife remaining a director – Liquidator claiming to recover remuneration on ground of misfeasance – Whether drawings by husband and wife while company suffering loss ultra vires company – Whether company's capacity to award renumeration under express power dependant on benefit to company – Whether genuine award of remuneration intra vires regardless of benefit to company – Companies Act 1948, s 333, Sch 1, Table A, Part I, reg 76.

In 1964 the husband acquired a ready-made company and thereafter carried on a garage business through the company. He and his wife owned the only issued share capital in the company and at all material times were the only directors of the company. The company's articles incorporated reg 76[a] of Part I of Table A in Sch 1 to the Companies Act 1948, which gave the company an express power to award remuneration to a director, the remuneration to be determined by the company in general meeting. The company's articles also included express power for the company to determine and pay directors' remuneration for the mere assumption of the post of director. The husband and wife built up the company together and drew weekly sums from the business as

---

a   Regulation 76, so far as material, provides: 'The remuneration of the directors shall from time to time be determined by the company in general meeting. Such remuneration shall be deemed to accrue from day to day.'

their director's remuneration. In 1967 the wife became ill. She remained a director of
a the company but from December 1967 it became apparent that she would not be active
again in the business. The husband continued to work virtually full-time in the business
until 1971, apart from two periods of three and six months, when he was away from the
business because of his wife's illness and an accident he sustained. By the year ended 30
April 1967 the business had a turnover of £106,000 and was making a substantial trading
profit. However, in the year 1967–68 the profits began to decline and by the year 1968–
b 69 the accounts showed that despite an increase in turnover the company was insolvent.
In March 1971 the company went into voluntary liquidation and was subsequently
compulsorily wound up. Throughout the period from January 1968 to March 1971 the
husband drew director's remuneration of some £2,500 per annum rising to £3,500 per
annum, and the wife drew director's renumeration of £1,500 per annum decreasing to
some £500 per annum even though during that period she took no active part in the
c business. Throughout that period the drawings of remuneration were mainly out of
capital because the company was suffering a trading loss. The liquidator in the winding
up brought proceedings against the husband and wife under s 333(1)[b] of the Companies
Act 1948 claiming to recover from them jointly and severally the whole of the
remuneration drawn by the wife from January 1968 onwards and such part of the
husband's renumeration as exceeded the market value of his services to the company, on
d the ground that the husband and wife were guilty of misfeasance and breach of trust in
making the drawings. The liquidator submitted that, although the amounts drawn by
the husband and wife were either formally determined by the company in general
meeting as directors' remuneration or were otherwise sanctioned as such by the company
and although they were made in good faith, nevertheless they were ultra vires the
company as being gratuitous payments made out of capital otherwise than for
consideration, unless it could be shown that they were made for the benefit of the
e company and to promote its prosperity. The liquidator further submitted that, having
regard to the amount of the drawings, they could not have been made for the company's
benefit when it was suffering a loss and the money was needed for the business.

Held – (1) Where payments of remuneration to a director were made under the
f authority of the company acting in general meeting pursuant to an express power in its
articles to award director's remuneration and there was no question of fraud on the
company's creditors or on minority shareholders, the competence of the company to
award the remuneration depended on whether the payments were genuinely director's
remuneration (as opposed to a disguised gift out of capital) and not on an abstract test of
benefit to the company. The amount of remuneration awarded in such circumstances
was a matter of company management and, provided there had been a genuine exercise
g of the company's power to award remuneration, it was not for the court to determine if,
or to what extent, the remuneration awarded was reasonable (see p 1038 c d, p 1039 c e
to j and p 1043 a to c, post); dictum of Astbury J in *Parker & Cooper Ltd v Reading* [1926]
All ER Rep at 328 applied; *Hampson v Price's Patent Candle Co* (1876) 45 LJ Ch 437, *Hutton
v West Cork Rly Co* (1883) 23 Ch D 654, *Henderson v Bank of Australasia* (1888) 40 Ch D
170, dictum of Lindley LJ in *Re George Newman & Co* [1895] 1 Ch at 685–686, *Re Lee,*
h *Behrens & Co Ltd* [1932] All ER Rep 889, *Parke v Daily News Ltd* [1962] 2 All ER 929,
Ridge Securities Ltd v IRC [1964] 1 All ER 275, *Re W & M Roith Ltd* [1967] 1 All ER 427
and *Charterbridge Corp Ltd v Lloyds Bank Ltd* [1969] 2 All ER 1185 considered.

---

b   Section 333(1), so far as material, provides: 'If in the course of winding up a company it appears
j   that any person who has taken part in the formation or promotion of the company, or any past or
present director ... has misapplied or retained or become liable or accountable for any money or
property of the company, or been guilty of any misfeasance or breach of trust in relation to the
company, the court may, on the application of the ... liquidator ... examine into the conduct of
the ... director ... and compel him to repay or restore the money or property or any part thereof
respectively with interest at such rate as the court thinks just, or to contribute such sum to the
assets of the company by way of compensation in respect of the misapplication, retainer,
misfeasance or breach of trust as the court thinks just.'

(2) There was no evidence that, having regard to the company's turnover, the
husband's drawings were patently excessive or unreasonable as director's remuneration, *a*
or that they were disguised gifts of capital rather than genuine awards of remuneration.
Accordingly, the court would not inquire into whether it would have been more
beneficial to the company to have made lesser awards of remuneration to him, since that
was a matter for the company. It followed that the claim for misfeasance in regard to the
husband's drawings failed (see p 1040 *b* to *d* and *f* to *j*, p 1041 *c d* and p 1045 *b*, post).

(3) In regard to the wife's drawings, although the company's articles included power *b*
to award remuneration for the mere assumption of the office of director even where the
director was not active in the conduct of the company's business, that power predicated
that a director would receive remuneration for services rendered or to be rendered and
the mere fact that the label of 'director's remuneration' was attached to the drawings did
not preclude the court from examining their true nature. Having regard to the wife's
inactivity during the period in question, it could not be said that the whole of the *c*
amounts drawn by the wife in that period were genuine awards of remuneration to her
for holding office as a director. That part of her drawings in excess of what would have
been a reasonable award of remuneration for holding office as a director amounted to a
disguised gift of capital or payment of dividends in recognition of her co-proprietorship
of the business and was ultra vires the company and repayable to the liquidator (see
p 1042 *f* to *j*, p 1043 *c* to *e* and *j* to p 1044 *c* and *e* to p 1045 *b*, post); *Ridge Securities Ltd v* *d*
IRC [1964] 1 All ER 275 applied.

Notes

For remuneration of directors, see 7 Halsbury's Laws (4th edn) paras 488–489, and for
cases on the subject, see 9 Digest (Reissue) 480–483, 2857–2879.

For the Companies Act 1948, s 333, Sch 1, Table A, Part I, reg 76, see 5 Halsbury's *e*
Statutes (3rd edn) 362, 448.

Cases referred to in judgment

Allen v Golds Reefs of West Africa Ltd [1900] 1 Ch 656, [1900–3] All ER Rep 746, CA, 9
Digest (Reissue) 624, 3716.
British Seamless Paper Box Co, Re (1881) 17 Ch D 467, CA, 9 Digest (Reissue) 524, 3132. *f*
Charterbridge Corp Ltd v Lloyds Bank Ltd [1969] 2 All ER 1185, [1970] Ch 62, [1969] 3
WLR 122, 9 Digest (Reissue) 492, 2942.
Clemens v Clemens Bros [1976] 2 All ER 268, Digest (Cont Vol E) 59, 4083a.
Cyclists' Touring Club v Hopkinson [1910] 1 Ch 179, 8(2) Digest (Reissue) 627, 79.
Dunston v Imperial Gas Light Co (1831) 3 B & Ad 125, 110 ER 47, 10 Digest (Reissue) 1334,
8527.   *g*
Duomatic Ltd, Re [1969] 1 All ER 161, [1969] Ch 365, [1969] 2 WLR 114, 9 Digest
(Reissue) 483, 2879.
Express Engineering Works Ltd, Re [1920] 1 Ch 466, CA, 9 Digest (Reissue) 557, 3331.
Greenhalgh v Arderne Cinemas Ltd [1950] 2 All ER 1120, [1951] Ch 286, CA, 9 Digest
(Reissue) 610, 3639.
Hampson v Price's Patent Candle Co (1876) 45 LJ Ch 437, 10 Digest (Reissue) 1349, 8641. *h*
Henderson v Bank of Australasia (1888) 40 Ch D 170, 9 Digest (Reissue) 582, 3468.
Hindle v John Cotton Ltd (1919) 56 Sc LR 625.
Hutton v West Cork Rly Co (1883) 23 Ch D 654, CA, 9 Digest (Reissue) 685, 4077.
Introductions Ltd, Re, Introductions Ltd v National Provincial Bank Ltd [1969] 1 All ER 887,
[1970] Ch 199, [1969] 2 WLR 791, CA; *affg* [1968] 2 All ER 1221, 9 Digest (Reissue)
75, 336.   *j*
Kaye v Croydon Tramways Co [1898] 1 Ch 358, CA, 10 Digest (Reissue) 1179, 7341.
Lee, Behrens & Co Ltd, Re [1932] 2 Ch 46, [1932] All ER Rep 889, 9 Digest (Reissue) 571,
3419.
Lundy Granite Co Ltd, Re, Lewis's Case (1872) 26 LT 673, LJJ, 9 Digest (Reissue) 177, 1085.
National Funds Assurance Co, Re (1878) 10 Ch D 118, 9 Digest (Reissue) 656, 3926.

Newman (George) & Co, Re [1895] 1 Ch 674, CA, 9 Digest (Reissue) 528, 3168.

a   *Parke v Daily News Ltd* [1962] 2 All ER 929, [1962] Ch 927, [1962] 3 WLR 566, 9 Digest
     (Reissue) 690, 4097.

Parker & Cooper Ltd v Reading [1926] Ch 975, [1926] All ER Rep 323, 9 Digest (Reissue)
515, 3076.

Payne (David) & Co Ltd, Re, Young v David Payne & Co Ltd [1904] 2 Ch 608, CA, 9 Digest
(Reissue) 511, 3058.

b   *Phillips v Manufacturers' Securities Ltd* (1917) 86 LJ Ch 305, CA, 9 Digest (Reissue) 420,
2483.

Ridge Securities Ltd v IRC [1964] 1 All ER 275, [1964] 1 WLR 479, 28(1) Digest (Reissue)
178, 536.

Roith (W & M) Ltd, Re [1967] 1 All ER 427, [1967] 1 WLR 432, 9 Digest (Reissue) 571,
3420.

c   *Smith (Howard) Ltd v Ampol Petroleum Ltd* [1974] 1 All ER 1126, [1974] AC 821, [1974] 2
WLR 689, PC, 9 Digest (Reissue) 496, *1352.

Tomkinson v South-Eastern Rly Co (1887) 35 Ch D 675, 10 Digest (Reissue) 1349, 8639.

Case also cited

Wallersteiner v Moir (No 2), Moir v Wallersteiner (No 2) [1975] 1 All ER 849, [1975] QB
d   373, CA.

Summons

By a summons dated 18 January 1974 the liquidator of Halt Garage (1964) Ltd (the
company) claimed against the respondents, Robert Charlesworth and his wife, Margaret
Gwendoline Charlesworth, the directors of the company, a declaration under s 333 of the
e   Companies Act 1948 that the respondents were guilty of misfeasance and breach of trust
in relation to the company in misapplying money and assets of the company (i) by paying
any sum by way of director's remuneration to Mrs Charlesworth from 1 March 1967
onwards, and (ii) in paying excessive remuneration to Mr Charlesworth from January
1968 onwards. The facts are set out in the judgment.

f   *W A Blackburne* for the liquidator.
David A Smith for the respondents.

Cur adv vult

25 May. **OLIVER J** read the following judgment: This is a summons by a liquidator
g   under s 333 of the Companies Act 1948, claiming against the respondents, Mr and Mrs
Charlesworth, who were formerly directors of the company in liquidation, the repayment
of sums paid to them respectively by way of directors' remuneration in the years 1967–
68, 1968–69, 1969–70 and 1970–71. The company went into voluntary liquidation on
15 March 1971 and was subsequently wound up compulsorily. Originally there was a
claim for relief under s 332 of the 1948 Act, based on allegations of fraudulent trading,
h   but those have not been pursued and the only live claim is that in respect of the payments
of directors' remuneration, the major part of which was voted by the company in general
meeting but which the liquidator claims was ultra vires. This absolves me from the
necessity of giving more than a summary account of the company's trading history.

The respondent Robert Charlesworth acquired in 1964 a garage site near Woburn
Sands in Bedfordshire, which was a prime site because of its proximity to the M1
j   motorway. The freehold was acquired with the aid of Continental Oil Co (which I shall
refer to as Conoco) and it was done in this way. A sum was paid to Mr Charlesworth as a
premium for the grant of a lease of the premises for 50 years by him to Conoco at a
peppercorn rent. There was also a loan of a sum of £5,000, with which he was required
at his own expense to carry out certain works of development and renovation. Conoco at
the same time granted a sublease to Mr Charlesworth at a rent of £1,000 per annum for

21 years, and he personally entered into a service agreement with Conoco for 50 years, tying the garage to accept only Conoco petrol.

Although these arrangements were made with Mr Charlesworth personally and envisaged that the business would be carried on by him personally, he in fact acquired the £2 issued capital of the company, which was a ready-made company, changed its name to Halt Garage (1964) Ltd and thereafter carried on the garage business at the premises through the medium of the company. He and his wife were registered as the holders of the only two issued shares and they were at all material times the only directors. At the end of 1965 a Mr Gore became, and was at all material times thereafter, the secretary.

The company held no estate in the premises. Its occupation can, I think, only have been that of a licensee; the underlease prohibited, or purported to prohibit, assignment or underletting. It paid the rent under the underlease, which appears to have been well below the full market rent, and, although no doubt Mr Charlesworth could legitimately have charged a profit rental to the company (a letter from Jackson-Stops & Staff, estate agents, in March 1968 indicates that this might have been as much as a further £2,000 per annum) he never in fact did so. Indeed, it would have been disadvantageous to him personally, from an income tax point of view, to receive from the company moneys which could not qualify as earned income. I mention this because it is the submission of counsel on behalf of the respondents that it has some importance in relation to the liquidator's claim.

From 1964 till January 1967 Mr and Mrs Charlesworth built up the business with considerable success. Mr Gore's evidence is that they both worked extremely hard in the business from early morning until late at night and at weekends as well. The garage was one which was utilised extensively by the AA, the RAC and the police for the collection of wrecks and breakdowns from the M1 and, although the garage was closed for petrol at night, its breakdown service was, I understand, on 24-hour call.

In its first 13 months of operation it achieved a turnover of £80,000, but made a small net loss, £160-odd, after charging directors' remuneration of £1,350. At that stage Mr and Mrs Charlesworth were drawing between them only £30 per week, the amount drawn by each being considerably less than the wages of the fitters employed at the garage. In the following year the turnover increased to £87,000, and the business was able to show a small profit. It is to the third and subsequent years of the company's operations that the present claim relates. The turnover in the year to 30 April 1967 increased substantially to some £106,000, and there was a substantial trading profit amounting to over £10,000. During this year the company's wage books show regular weekly payments to Mr and Mrs Charlesworth at first at a rate of £30 gross between them, then £42·10, then £60 and finally £90, split as to £60 to Mr Charlesworth and £30 to Mrs Charlesworth. Those payments continued throughout until April 1969, when the payments to Mr Charlesworth were reduced to £50 gross, those to Mrs Charlesworth remaining unaltered, so that thereafter they were drawing between them regular weekly amounts of £80. That continued unaltered up to 15 March 1971, when the company went into liquidation, save that in May 1970 the proportionate split between them was varied, apparently as a result of the accountant's advice that it might be difficult to justify payments of £30 per week to Mrs Charlesworth to the Revenue. Thereafter Mr Charlesworth was paid £70 and his wife £10. Throughout, these payments appear to have been made after deduction of tax and national insurance contributions.

Audited accounts for the years 1966–67, 1967–68 and 1968–69 were, according to the company's minute book, presented to general meetings of the company and approved and signed, and at directors' meetings held at the same time formal resolutions were passed that the amounts of the directors' remuneration were correct. I cannot in fact reconcile the amounts of the remuneration shown in the company's accounts with the drawings of Mr and Mrs Charlesworth shown in the wages book and it may be that part of those drawings, for some reason known only to the company's accountants, is shown under the heading of 'Wages and National Insurance'. It is not, however, alleged that a other directors' remuneration was paid in addition to the drawings shown in the company's wages book.

In February 1967 Mrs Charlesworth was taken seriously ill and was removed to hospital. The prognosis was most unfavourable and she was not expected to survive the next two years, although happily, though still very ill, she is still alive. Mr Charlesworth was advised that he must move to the south coast for the benefit of her health and in December 1967 they moved to the Isle of Wight where they still live. From the time
b when she was taken ill she took no further part in running the business of the company, because she was not able to, and although she remained a director she was able to contribute nothing to the company's prosperity beyond, perhaps, the occasional discussion with her husband and the formal signature of documents.

I am satisfied on the evidence that throughout 1967 up to the end of the first week in December, when they moved, Mr Charlesworth devoted his full time and attention to
c the business, working extremely long and unsocial hours and taking about three hours a day off in order to visit his wife in hospital. Having made up his mind to move, however, he was anxious to sell the business and when he did take up residence in the Isle of Wight he ceased full-time attendance, leaving Mr Gore in charge of the business but in telephonic contact when circumstances required.

The business had been valued by a well-known firm of valuers at £125,000 and it
d seems that a purchaser interested at that price was found but withdrew. Mr Charlesworth was, however, in a very disadvantageous position for bargaining, because he had to look after his wife, and Mr Gore, who was a bookkeeper without any mechanical qualifications, could hardly carry on indefinitely in sole charge. Negotiations accordingly ensued with another purchaser at £60,000 and these continued until March 1968 when that purchaser withdrew. Mr Gore felt unable to carry on and Mr Charlesworth then returned to take
e personal day-to-day charge of the business, coming up each Monday and returning to the Isle of Wight on Fridays. In the meanwhile, efforts to find a purchaser for the business continued.

It may perhaps be appropriate to mention here a matter which troubled me a good deal when this case was opened. In going through the documents counsel ascertained that some nine years ago I myself, as leading counsel, had advised Mr Charlesworth in
f connection with the question whether the premises could be disposed of free from the tie to Conoco, and there are references in the correspondence with prospective purchasers to an opinion on that matter which I had written. I confess to very little recollection of the matter beyond the fact that a sale was then urgently required because of Mrs Charlesworth's state of health and it has no bearing on the matters which I am now called on to decide, but I would have been more at ease if the matter could have been transferred
g to another judge. I have continued to hear the case only on the urgent representations of both parties, who were anxious to avoid the adjournment which would otherwise have been necessary and the costs which would have been thus thrown away, and I have found myself in fact unembarrassed in doing so. I think, however, that it is right that I should mention it.

To continue with the history, Mr Charlesworth continued in overall charge of the
h business and actively working in it until the end of September 1970, when he had an accident in which he broke both ankles and which precluded further activity. From August 1968 until March 1969 a Mr Axall was engaged as manager, but the evidence is that Mr Charlesworth himself continued to attend the garage during the week, coming up on Monday and leaving on Friday, save that one weekend in four he would stay over to give the manager a break. It seems that, as a result of the business brought in from the
j M1, the weekends tended to be the busiest time.

Mr Gore's recollection is that Mr Charlesworth's attendance was less frequent than this, but he confesses to some difficulty in remembering, and Mr Charlesworth's own evidence and that of his son is that he was putting in four days a week at the garage. Mr Axall proved unsatisfactory and in March 1969 his employment was terminated and the management was taken over by Mr Charlesworth's son, Andrew, who seems to have

continued to run the business in much the same way, having sole charge three weekends
out of four and sharing the management with his father on Monday afternoons to Friday
mornings.   *a*

The profitability of the business, however, declined drastically. The year 1966–67
showed a net profit of £2,179 after charging directors' remuneration of over £7,000
(which Mr Charlesworth says was never in fact drawn, his and his wife's drawings being
the weekly sums of £60 and £30 shown in the wages book). In 1967–68, however, the
turnover dropped and the company made a loss of £961 after charging remuneration of   *b*
£3,900, which again seems to have been merely an accountant's figure. The bank
overdraft, which was guaranteed by Mr Charlesworth and secured on the freehold, had
risen by £2,000, but there is no reason to think that the company was not still solvent.

In the following year, 1968–69, however, things took a decisive turn for the worse.
This seems to have been due in part, if not primarily, to some roadworks which interfered
with convenient access to the garage and with the traffic flow over the critical seasonal   *c*
period of April, May and June. In order to get the business back, an expensive advertising
campaign was launched involving the giving of extra Green Shield stamps, and Mr
Charlesworth's evidence as to this is that there was an arrangement with Conoco that that
company and the stamp suppliers would pay the cost, an obligation which they failed to
fulfil. Whether this is right or not, the company was in difficulties in paying its suppliers
in early 1969. At Whitsun in that year Conoco failed to supply and, disregarding the tie,   *d*
Mr Charlesworth started to take his supplies from Ultramar, which continued to be the
company's supplier until the latter part of 1970.

The accounts for the year 1968–69 showed that, despite an increase in turnover from
£98,000-odd to £108,000-odd, a heavy trading loss of over £9,000 had been incurred
and the balance sheet, with a capital deficit of over £7,900, showed the company to be
insolvent, a matter which was drawn to the attention of Mr Charlesworth by the   *e*
accountants when the accounts were sent for signature in August 1970.

Unaudited accounts for 1970 show that the losses still continued during that year. The
business, however, continued and Mr Charlesworth's evidence is, and I see no reason to
disbelieve him, that he still hoped to pull it round, although he was really pinning his
hopes on a sale, efforts to effect which continued. Towards the middle of 1970 a Mr
Sharpe was on the verge of purchasing, but apparently withdrew for health reasons.   *f*
Efforts were made to raise the finance for a purchase by Andrew Charlesworth, but they
came to nothing. Finally, arrangements were made for the purchase by a Mr Bills, who
had previously been the managing director of Ultramar and who, through his own
company, had been supplying petrol to the garage from January 1971 onwards, at which
date the company owed Ultramar something over £16,000.

As a result of the accident to which I have referred, Mr Charlesworth was away from   *g*
the garage from the end of September 1970 to December of that year, when he returned
for about two or three weeks, still on crutches, but had to leave again as a result of a fall
on the forecourt causing a dislocated shoulder. He never thereafter returned to take an
active part in the business.

Heads of agreement were signed in February providing for the purchase of the freehold
by Mr Bills, the discharge of the bank overdraft by Mr Charlesworth out of the proceeds,   *h*
and the transfer of the shares in the company to Mr Bills for a nominal consideration.
That transaction was completed on 15 March 1971 and on that very day Mr Bills procured
the company to be put into voluntary liquidation, although it was subsequently
compulsorily wound up on the petition of Ultramar. There was an acute controversy
between Mr Charlesworth and Mr Bills whether Mr Charlesworth knew that it was
intended to liquidate the company, his contention being that, although the agreement   *j*
concluded with Mr Bills does not so state, Mr Bills was going to assume responsibility for
the discharge of the company's liabilities other than the bank overdraft. It is, however,
unnecessary for me to resolve this, because counsel for the liquidator is prepared,
helpfully, to accept, for the purposes of these proceedings, that Mr Charlesworth was
unaware of Mr Bill's intention in relation to the liquidation.

Those are the salient facts. The liquidator now claims to recover from Mr and Mrs
a Charlesworth jointly and severally the whole of the remuneration paid to Mrs
Charlesworth from January 1968 onwards and such part of the remuneration paid to
Mr Charlesworth over the same period as was in excess of the value of the services which
he performed, which the liquidator puts at £30 per week.

As I mentioned at the outset, the claim originally made under s 332 of the Companies
Act 1948 has not been proceeded with and the present claim is restricted to a claim for
b misfeasance and breach of trust under s 333. So it has to be shown that in making these
payments the directors were in breach of some fiduciary duty which they owed to their
beneficiary, which either was not or could not be sanctioned by that beneficiary. In
relation to this claim, although it is alleged that the respondents (and that means,
effectively, Mr Charlesworth) knew that the company was making losses and was unable
to pay its debts without at least a further injection of funds or a measure of forbearance
c on the part of its major creditors, there is no allegation of fraud. What is said, quite
simply, is that the payments made to Mrs Charlesworth from the date on which it was
known that she was incurably ill and would not return and those made to Mr
Charlesworth from December 1967 onwards, so far as they exceeded £30 per week, were
presents which the company had no power to make and which could not, therefore, be
ratified by the shareholders. The claim has, however, been limited in the summons and
d the pleadings to the period from January 1968 onwards, because counsel then acting
thought that some limitation point arose; and counsel for the liquidator has, very
properly, not sought to go beyond the pleaded claim, although his submissions involve
the consequence that he would be strictly entitled to do so if a suitable amendment were
made.

The company's articles in the present case incorporate reg 76 of Table A, Part I (see Sch
e 1 to the 1948 Act), which provides that the remuneration of the directors shall from time
to time be determined by the company in general meeting and shall be deemed to accrue
from day to day. The directors, qua directors, are not, therefore, entitled as of right to
any remuneration for their services, and in so far as remuneration has been drawn
without the proper authority, they are bound to account to the company for it or to pay
damages.

f Obviously in the case of a lady who is as ill as Mrs Charlesworth is and whose illness,
so far as the evidence goes, appears to have been contributed to by the long hours of work
and irregularity of meals which she underwent whilst working up the business, the
claim is not a very attractive one, but a liquidator has no discretion about the performance
of his duties and if the claim is good in law it must succeed. If charity has, to use the
words of Bowen LJ in *Hutton v West Cork Rly Co* (1883) 23 Ch D 654 at 673, no business
g to sit at the board of directors, equally sympathy has no voice at the Bar of the court.

Counsel for the respondents takes his stand on the fact that the company has, by its
constitution, an express power to determine and pay directors' remuneration, a power,
moreover, which is recognised expressly in the case of every limited company by the
Companies Act 1948 (see, for instance, ss 189 and 196). While it is true that a director,
under an article in this form, has no entitlement to remuneration, nevertheless his
h agreement with the company when he accepts office is, impliedly, to serve the company
as a director and to take the responsibilities which that office entails at whatever
remuneration the company in general meeting may choose to vote to him, be it mean or
generous, liberal or illiberal. It may vote nothing. But, if it votes him something, he is
entitled to have it and it cannot be recovered from him in misfeasance proceedings, even
if it is very greatly in excess of any possible value attributable to his services.

j In the absence of fraud on the creditors or on minority shareholders, the quantum of
such remuneration is a matter for the company. There is no implication or requirement
that it must come out of profits only and, indeed, any requirement that it must be so
restricted would, in many cases, bring businesses to a halt and prevent a business which
had fallen on hard times from being brought round.

There is, counsel for the respondents submits, no principle of law which establishes that the payment of a scale of remuneration which the court may consider overgenerous, having regard to the services performed by a particular director, is ultra vires the company, either in toto or pro tanto, and indeed it is not for the courts to decide how far remuneration is reasonable, absente some plea that its payment is a fraud on the creditors or on minority shareholders. As long as it is acting within its express powers, a company may be unwise, at least so long as it is honest, and, as I have said, there is now no suggestion of mala fides here.

In this context counsel relies on this passage from the judgment of North J in *Henderson v Bank of Australasia* (1888) 40 Ch D 170 at 181. The judge, having reviewed the cases, said:

'I do not fail to notice that the sums which were the subject of discussion in the two last cases were considerably less than the sum which is the subject of the present application, but that is a matter with which I conceive I have nothing to do. It is not for a Judge to express any opinion upon such matters as whether the amount is too large or too small. In the first place he has no means of forming any opinion about that: the directors of the company know a great deal more about these matters than he can possibly do: and in the next place the persons who have power to bind the dissentients are the other members of the company, and they are the persons who have passed the resolution in the present case.'

Counsel goes on to submit that if, contrary to his primary submission, the payments have to be submitted to some further tests of validity beyond that of mere formal compliance with an express power, then they satisfy those tests. It will, however, be convenient if I deal with his first submission which, if correct, concludes the matter against the liquidator's claim as it is now framed.

Counsel for the liquidator concedes, as he has to, that the payments of remuneration were formally determined by the company at general meetings held to consider the accounts for the years 1967–68 and 1968–69 and that even in relation to the subsequent years he would, having regard to the fact that Mr and Mrs Charlesworth were the only shareholders, have difficulty in arguing that it had not been sanctioned by the company in the light of the decision of Buckley J in *Re Duomatic Ltd* [1969] 1 All ER 161, [1969] 2 Ch 365. But, he argues, those determinations and that sanction were ineffective so far as they purported to sanction or ratify the payments to Mrs Charlesworth or excess payments to Mr Charlesworth, either because they were ultra vires or, if not ultra vires, such as were, on the authorities, incapable of ratification by a general meeting. The shareholders, acting as a body and subject to the rights of minority shareholders, may, he submits, make such disposition as they think fit of that part of the funds of the company which consists of profit available for distribution by way of dividend. But when profits have been exhausted so that the company is dealing with its capital, whether share capital or loan capital, any disposition of the company's assets, otherwise than for consideration and whether made by directors alone or directors acting with the sanction of a general meeting, must, in order to be valid, satisfy the three tests set out in the judgment of Eve J in *Re Lee, Behrens & Co Ltd* [1932] 2 Ch 46, [1932] All ER Rep 889. The payment of a director's remuneration in the absence of a service agreement and under articles such as those applicable in the present case is a gratuitous payment which the company is under no obligation to resolve on, and the cases show that any voluntary and gratuitous disposition by a company of its assets which does not satisfy the three tests mentioned is ultra vires. The acts of the directors who make such a disposition by paying themselves remuneration are not, therefore, capable of ratification.

There is not, so far as I am aware and so far as the industry of counsel has been able to discover, any reported authority in which the competence of a general meeting, while the company is a going concern, to vote remuneration to a director under an article in the form of reg 76 of Table A has formed the subject matter of direct decision, but counsel for the liquidator justifies his propositions by reference to a familiar line of

authorities, starting with *Hutton v West Cork Railway Co* (1883) 23 Ch D 654. I must, I
think, look at that case in a little detail.

It was a case where the powers of the company were subject to the provisions of a
special Act, which provided in terms that the proceeds of sale of the undertaking, which
was transferred to another company, should be applied in making particular payments
to debenture holders and shareholders, subject only, for relevant purposes, to 'paying off
any revenue debts or charges' so far as the same had not already been paid out of revenue.
The Act went on to provide that on payment of the purchase price the company should
be dissolved—

> 'excepting for the purpose of regulating their internal affairs and winding-up the
> same, and of applying the said purchase-money in accordance with the provisions of
> this Act.'

The question which the court had to determine was whether, in the light of these
provisions, a resolution of a general meeting authorising the payment of gratuities to
former employees and to the directors was binding on dissentient debenture holders and
shareholders.

The company had, whilst a going concern, a power to fix directors' remuneration in
general meeting, which had never in fact been exercised, but it could not be contended
that the resolution in question was in exercise of that power or that it constituted
anything but an act of spontaneous generosity, having regard to the directors' past
services which they had given free of charge. So the case was concerned not with the
construction of express powers applicable while the company was a going concern but
with what power still remained, having regard to the provisions of the special Act and
whether a power to pay gratuities could be implied as one reasonably incidental to the
internal regulation of the company's affairs during its winding up. The members of the
court approached the problem in different ways. Cotton LJ's approach was to consider
whether what had been done was intra vires in the true sense of the term having regard
to the provisions of the special Act. After reciting the sections of the special Act and
summarising the effect of the resolution, he said this ((1883) 23 Ch D 654 at 664):

> 'It was said that it is within the powers of the directors of a trading or business
> company to grant gratuities to its servants, and this case comes within that principle,
> as the directors of this company retained such powers as were incident to a company
> of this kind, notwithstanding that its railway had been handed over to the purchasing
> company—the *Bandon Company*. I think that the directors did continue to have
> powers, so far as they were necessary for or incidental to the winding-up of the
> company. But, in my opinion, they had not such powers as only are impliedly given
> to general meetings or to directors because they are carrying on a business for the
> purpose of carrying on its business, and for the purpose of making a profit from it.'

A little later he said (at 665–666):

> 'But here the company was gone as a company carrying on business for the
> purpose of making profit, and the sums paid, therefore, to its officials and managing
> directors, could not be looked upon as an inducement to them to exert themselves
> in the future, or as an act done reasonably for the purpose of getting the greatest
> profit from the business of the company, but must be looked upon simply as a
> gratuity, perhaps reasonable in itself, but without any prospect of its in any way
> reasonably conducing to the benefit of the company. In my opinion, therefore,
> under these circumstances, neither the directors nor the general meeting had any
> power in the circumstances which are before us, as I understand the facts of the case,
> of granting that compensation to the officials and other servants.'

As regards remuneration of directors for past services he specifically refrained from
laying down any general rule as to the exercise of the company's powers to remunerate
directors while it was a going concern. He said (at 666–667):

'I do not propose to lay down any general rule as to how far a general meeting could, under the powers of sect. 91 of the *Companies Clauses Act* [1845] in a going concern and where they are not bound by any special clause in their articles as to the application of their funds, give remuneration to directors not only for the current year or the first year, but for past years during which they have acted apparently without intending to receive any remuneration at all.'

A little later he went on to say (at 667):

'I quite agree with what [counsel for the company] said that during the first year of a parliamentary company which comes under the *Companies Clauses Act* directors must be acting without any fixed salary, but merely in expectation of receiving such a salary as the general meeting may grant them, and that therefore it must be in expectation. But then I think that would negative the idea that they had agreed to act without any remuneration. They were agreeing to act for such remuneration during that time at least as the general meeting at the end of the first year should grant them.'

He said later (at 667–668):

'I do not however mean to decide—in fact my opinion is rather the other way—that a general meeting of this company could not in the winding-up, and in exercising for the purpose of winding-up the powers given by sect. 91 of the *Companies Clauses Act*, give to the directors what may be considered a fair remuneration for their services to the company after the railway and the undertaking had been taken over by the *Bandon Company*, and all that was being done was being done for the purposes not of carrying on the railway as a going concern but for the purposes of doing that which was incidental to and connected with the winding-up of the company.'

He concluded (at 668):

'But I think on the evidence the necessary inference is that this sum of £1500 was agreed to or voted to be paid to them not as a reasonable sum for remuneration for their services during that term, but as a sum which might with reasonable generosity be paid to them taking into consideration the fact that they never received anything during the years when they carried on the railway. That, I think, was beyond the powers which the company preserved under sect. 14, and the powers of the *Companies Act* incidental to carrying on the winding-up of the company, and therefore would be *ultra vires*.'

The case is, however, chiefly notable for the classical 'cakes and ale' judgment of Bowen LJ. Although he agreed with Cotton LJ, he approached the problem in a rather different way. Cotton LJ had considered whether, having regard to the restrictive provisions of the sections of the special Act, any power had been expressly or impliedly preserved to the company to make payments of this type. Bowen LJ engaged on a rather wider consideration of whether, even in the case of a going concern, the resolution was the sort of resolution which could be forced on a dissentient minority. He said (at 670): 'Now the directors in this case have done, it seems to me, nothing at all wrong.' A little later he said:

'Not only have they done nothing wrong, but I confess I think the company have done what nine companies out of ten would do, and do without the least objection being made. They have paid, perhaps liberally, perhaps not at all too liberally, persons who have served them faithfully. But that, of course, does not get rid of the difficulty. As soon as a question is raised by a dissentient shareholder, or by a person standing in the position of a dissentient shareholder [I pause there to remark that he is clearly referring to the debenture holders who had also voting rights] sympathy must be cut adrift, and we have simply to consider what the law is. In this particular a instance the Plaintiff is a person who stands *primâ facie* in the condition of those who are bound by the vote of a general meeting acting within the powers of a general meeting, but he complains that the majority propose to expend certain purchase-money which the company are receiving from the *Bandon Company* in two ways which he thinks are beyond their powers.'

Then, he postulated this question (at 671):

b 'Now can a majority compel a dissentient unit in the company to give way and to submit to these payments? We must go back to the root of things. The money which is going to be spent is not the money of the majority. That is clear. It is the money of the company, and the majority want to spend it. What would be the natural limit of their power to do so? They can only spend money which is not theirs but the company's, if they are spending it for the purposes which are c reasonably incidental to the carrying on of the business of the company. That is the general doctrine. *Bona fides* cannot be the sole test, otherwise you might have a lunatic conducting the affairs of the company, and paying away its money with both hands in a manner perfectly *bonâ fide* yet perfectly irrational. The test must be what is reasonably incidental to, and within the reasonable scope of carrying on, the business of the company.'

d Dealing specifically with directors' remuneration, he said (at 671–672):

'But what is the remuneration of directors? I think it is pretty clear that, like the compensation for loss of the services of the managing director, it is a gratuity. A director is not a servant. He is a person who is doing business for the company, but not upon ordinary terms. It is not implied from the mere fact that he is a director, e that he is to have a right to be paid for it.'

A little later he said:

'If there is a special provision for the way in which they are paid, you must look to the special provision to see how to deal with it. But if there is no special provision their payment is in the nature of a gratuity, as was pointed out in the case cited by f [counsel for the debenture holder] of *Dunston* v. *Imperial Gas Light and Coke Company* ((1831) 3 B & Ad 125, 110 ER 47). Directors, under those circumstances, often do get money. But whenever they get it it is in the nature of a gratuity voted. That does not get rid of the difficulty, because one must still ask oneself what is the general law about gratuitous payments which are made by the directors or by a company so as to bind dissentients.'

g Later he said (at 672–673):

'The test there again is not whether it is *bonâ fide*, but whether, as well as being done *bonâ fide*, it is done within the ordinary scope of the company's business, and whether it is reasonably incidental to the carrying on of the company's business for the company's benefit. Take this sort of instance. A railway company, or the h directors of the company, might send down all the porters at a railway station to have tea in the country at the expense of the company. Why should they not? It is for the directors to judge, provided it is a matter which is reasonably incidental to the carrying on of the business of the company . . .'

He then said (at 673):

j 'A company could not always go on if the moment the directors had served six weeks or months, or a year, they insisted on their immediate remuneration for the past period. That is not the way to do business. The past remuneration of directors seems to me like the gratuitous wages in *Hampson* v. *Price's Patent Candle Company* ((1876) 45 LJ Ch 437), to be justifiable, provided it is within the scope of the business and secures advantage to the company.'

He then considered how those principles could be applied in the circumstances created by the special Act, and said (at 675):

> 'It had a special and limited business, and that business was to preside at its own funeral, to wind itself up and carry on its own internal affairs until it had distributed the purchase-money in the way the Act of Parliament prescribed. If that be so, when one is applying the general test whether what has been done is incident to the business of the company, we have this further matter to recollect—what the business of this company is—and we have to ask ourselves whether these payments were necessary for that kind of limited business or could reasonably be said to be part of the business.'

He concluded (at 678):

> 'I do not understand Lord Justice *Cotton* to say that no remuneration can be granted to the directors out of the purchase-money which is reasonably measured by the services they have rendered in winding up this company and in connection with the completion of the dissolution and transfer; but this resolution is couched in much wider terms and is evidently based upon the idea that they might be charitable with reference to past services done for the company at the time it was a going company, and I think a willing majority has no right to bind a dissentient minority by any resolution so conceived.'

So, if I may pause there for a moment, Bowen LJ is clearly considering the question in the context of whether a majority could bind a dissentient minority. Indeed, this last passage shows that he clearly contemplated that there was nothing necessarily improper or wrong with paying reasonable remuneration, albeit it could not be said to be for the benefit of the company, since the business at that time was defunct and the services which the directors had rendered were past.

Now this was one of the cases applied and relied on by Eve J in *Re Lee, Behrens & Co Ltd* [1932] 2 Ch 46, [1932] All ER Rep 889. This was a case which dealt with the question of the exercise by directors, not by a general meeting, of an implied power of a trading company, it being held that, as a matter of construction of the memorandum, the company's express powers did not extend to what had been done in that case. It was conceded that a trading company had power to make grants for rewarding those who served it well, but the first ground of Eve J's decision rests on the tests to be applied for the valid exercise of such a power. It has, however, to be borne in mind that what Eve J was concerned with was a grant made on the authority of a resolution of the directors only, a matter which very clearly emerges from the report of the argument (see [1932] 2 Ch 46 at 48). Eve J propounds the test for a valid exercise of powers in a passage so well known that I need hardly, I think, refer to it ([1932] 2 Ch 46 at 51–52, [1932] All ER Rep 889 at 890–891):

> 'But whether they be made under an express or implied power, all such grants involve an expenditure of the company's money, and that money can only be spent for purposes reasonably incidental to the carrying on of the company's business, and the validity of such grants is to be tested, as is shown in all the authorities, by the answers to three pertinent questions: (i.) Is the transaction reasonably incidental to the carrying on of the company's business? (ii.) Is it a bona fide transaction? and (iii.) Is it done for the benefit and to promote the prosperity of the company? Authority for each of the foregoing propositions is to be found in the following cases: *Hampson* v. *Price's Patent Candle Co.* ((1876) 45 LJ Ch 437); *Hutton* v. *West Cork Ry. Co.* ((1883) 23 Ch D 654); and *Henderson* v. *Bank of Australasia* ((1888) 40 Ch D 170).'

It is interesting to see that Eve J in fact carries the matter one stage further than *Hutton's* case, where Bowen LJ had postulated (at 671) the test as 'what is reasonably incidental to, and within the reasonable scope of carrying on, the business of the company', or (at 672) 'reasonably incidental to the carrying on of the company's business *a* for the company's benefit'. The test of whether the power is exercised 'for the benefit and to promote the prosperity of the company' is added by Eve J as a separate and distinct matter and must, I think, be derived from the judgment of North J in *Henderson v Bank of Australasia*, and from the line of cases relating to the power of a company in general meeting to alter its articles. It is, of course, wholly appropriate to a consideration of the propriety of the exercise of a fiduciary power and, indeed, it appears from the report that it is in relation to an exercise of the power by directors that Eve J is considering the

b question. He said ([1932] 2 Ch 46 at 52, [1932] All ER Rep 889 at 891):

> 'The conclusion to which in my opinion such evidence as is available irresistibly points is that the predominant, if not the only, consideration operating in the minds of the directors, was a desire to provide for the applicant, and that the question what, if any, benefit would accrue to the company never presented itself to their minds.'

c He then went on to the alternative ground of decision, namely that this being, as he put it ([1932] 2 Ch 46 at 53, [1932] 2 All ER Rep 889 at 891), 'a gift or reward given out of the company's assets by the directors to one of their own body', it could be done only under an express power (of which there was none) or with the sanction of a general meeting (which had not been obtained). The applicant was not in fact 'one of their own body' but the widow of a former director, but that does not affect the principle.

d Applying these principles to the instant case, the propositions of counsel for the liquidator may be summarised thus:

1. It is not claimed that the payments of £60 and £30 (or later £50 and £30 or £70 and £10) to Mr and Mrs Charlesworth respectively were payments made under contract or that they purported to be anything other than directors' remuneration.

2. They were therefore gratuitous payments made out of the company's assets.

e 3. *Re Lee, Behrens & Co Ltd* shows that such dispositions of the company's assets are valid only if they satisfy the three stated tests set out in Eve J's judgment.

4. Accepting that they were bona fide and, as payments to the directors for acting as such, incidental to the company's business, they were not, in the case of Mr Charlesworth, so far as they exceeded a reasonable sum for services performed, and in the case of Mrs Charlesworth as to any part, payments made for the benefit of the company or to promote

f its prosperity. Indeed, the reverse, for they resulted in the company being deprived of funds which it badly needed for its business and the company got nothing in return.

5. Therefore the resolutions of the general meetings sanctioning those payments were ultra vires or pro tanto ultra vires or, alternatively, they were not such as could stand against a dissentient shareholder, if there had been one, and they cannot now stand against the liquidator.

g I confess that I have not found it easy to understand the logical basis for the doctrine which emerges from *Re Lee, Behrens & Co Ltd* as it was applied in that case and has been applied in subsequent cases. It is frequently spoken of as a facet of the ultra vires doctrine, but I doubt whether that is strictly correct. If it were, it would involve this, that every power, express or implied, would have to be read and qualified by some such words as 'if (but only if) it is for the benefit of the company's business and to promote its interests';

h and if that has to be read into every power, it is difficult to see how the company (at least in the case of a company whose affairs are not public knowledge and whose status or credit could not be affected by its dividend record) could ever declare a dividend, which must necessarily reduce the assets available for the promotion of the company's business.

I cannot help thinking, if I may respectfully say so, that there has been a certain confusion between the requirements for a valid exercise of the fiduciary powers of

j directors (which have nothing to do with the capacity of the company but everything to do with the propriety of acts done within that capacity), the extent to which powers can be implied or limits be placed, as a matter of construction, on express powers, and the matters which the court will take into consideration at the suit of a minority shareholder in determining the extent to which his interests can be overridden by a majority vote. These three matters, as it seems to me, raise questions which are logically quite distinct

but which have sometimes been treated as if they demanded a single, universal answer
leading to the conclusion that, because a power must not be abused, therefore, beyond　*a*
the limit of propriety it does not exist.

Nevertheless, it cannot, I think, be doubted that, whether it be logically defensible or
not and whether it be labelled an application of the ultra vires doctrine or the protection
of minorities, the courts have over the past hundred years evolved a series of principles
which have been stated to be of general application to gratuitous dispositions of the
property of trading companies. These principles were expressed by Plowman J in *Parke v*　*b*
Daily News Ltd [1962] 2 All ER 929 at 942, [1962] Ch 927 at 954, when, after reviewing
the cases, he said:

> 'The conclusions which, I think, follow from these cases are: first, that a company's
> funds cannot be applied in making ex gratia payments as such; secondly, that the
> court will inquire into the motives actuating any gratuitous payment, and the ob-
> jectives which it is intended to achieve; thirdly, that the court will uphold the　*c*
> validity of gratuitous payments if, but only if, after such inquiry it appears that
> the tests enumerated by EVE, J., are satisfied; fourthly, that the onus of upholding
> the validity of such payments lies on those who assert it.'

But it is said that *Parke*'s case and the cases which preceded it were all cases where what
the court had to consider was the test to be applied where reliance was being placed,　*d*
either by directors or by a general meeting, on an implied power, whereas the power in
the instant case, which is written into the company's constitution and is not subject to
any expressed limitation, is an express power.

So far as express powers are concerned, there has been, at least in the context of dealings
for value between the company and an outsider, a clear rejection of the *Lee, Behrens & Co*
test in *Charterbridge Corp Ltd v Lloyds Bank Ltd* [1969] 2 All ER 1185, [1970] Ch 62, a case　*e*
concerned with the exercise by directors of an express power in a company's articles to
guarantee liabilities either of the company or of other persons falling within a given
description. I can take the effect of the decision from the headnote ([1970] Ch 62 at 63)—

> 'that where, as here, a company was carrying out the purposes expressed in its
> memorandum, and did an act within the scope of a power expressed in it, that act
> was within the powers of the company; that the memorandum of a company set　*f*
> out its objects and proclaimed them to persons dealing with the company and it
> would be contrary to the whole function of a memorandum if objects unequivocally
> set out in it should be subject to some implied limitation by reference to the state of
> mind of the parties concerned; and that the state of mind of officers of C. Ltd. and
> the bank as to whether the transaction was intended to benefit the company was
> irrelevant on the issue of ultra vires.'　*g*

I turn now to the judgment, where Pennycuick J said ([1969] 2 All ER 1185 at 1189–
1191, [1970] Ch 62 at 69–71):

> 'Apart from authority, I should feel little doubt that where a company is carrying
> out the purposes expressed in its memorandum, and does an act within the scope of
> a power expressed in its memorandum, that act is an act within the powers of the　*h*
> company. The memorandum of a company sets out its objects and proclaims them
> to persons dealing with the company and it would be contrary to the whole function
> of a memorandum that objects unequivocally set out in it should be subject to some
> implied limitation by reference to the state of mind of the parties concerned. Where
> directors misapply the assets of their company, that may give rise to a claim based
> on breach of duty. Again, a claim may arise against the other party to the transaction,　*j*
> if he has notice that the transaction was effected in breach of duty. Further, in a
> proper case, the company concerned may be entitled to have the transaction set
> aside. But all that results from the ordinary law of agency and has not of itself
> anything to do with the corporate powers of the company. The plaintiff company's
> contention is formulated under two heads, namely: (i) that the guarantee and legal

a   charge were created for purposes outside the scope of Castleford's business; and (ii) that the guarantee and legal charge were created for purposes which were not for the benefit of Castleford. This second contention is intended to mean and is accepted as being intended to mean that the directors of Castleford in creating these obligations were not acting with a view to the benefit of the company ... The second head, namely that the guarantee and legal charge were not created for the benefit of Castleford in the sense which I have indicated, formed the real basis of the

b   argument of counsel for the plaintiff company. As I have said, he founded that argument primarily on the decision in *Re Lee, Behrens & Co Ltd* and I will now turn to that case ... [Then, after reading the headnote of that case and particularly the last sentence of the headnote, which was in these terms, 'The grant of the pension was therefore void and ultra vires the company', Pennycuick J continued:] I think it is really clear that the last sentence does not fully reflect the content of the judgment.

c   The liquidator rejected the proof so far as now material on two distinct grounds: (i) that it was ultra vires the company and void: (ii) alternatively, that it could only be authorised by the company in general meeting and that no such meeting was summoned or held. Neither in the arguments as reported nor in the judgment are these two grounds kept clearly distinct ... It seems to me, on the best consideration I can give to this passage [which is the passage from *Re Lee, Behrens & Co Ltd* [1932]

d   2 Ch 46 at 51–52, [1932] All ER Rep 889 at 890–891, which I have already read] that the learned judge must have been directing his mind to both the issues raised by the liquidator, without differentiating them. In truth (i), the first of the three pertinent questions which he raises, is probably appropriate to the scope of the implied powers of a company where there is no express power. Question (ii) is appropriate in part again to the scope of implied powers, and in part, and perhaps

e   principally, to the duty of directors. Question (iii) is, I think, quite inappropriate to the scope of express powers, and notwithstanding the words "whether they be made under an express or implied power" at the beginning of the paragraph, I doubt very much whether the judge really intended to apply this last question to express powers. None of the cases cited by him ... would support such an application. If he did so intend, his statement is obiter, and with great diffidence I do not feel bound

f   to follow it. Finally, I would observe that the whole passage ([1932] 2 Ch 46 at 53, [1932] All ER Rep 889 at 891) proceeds on the footing that the transaction might have been ratified, which would not be possible if it had been ultra vires the company.'

Pennycuick J then dealt with *Re David Payne & Co Ltd* [1904] 2 Ch 608 which was relied on by counsel for the plaintiff, and cited from the judgment of Buckley J in that

g   case. There are, I think, two further passages which it would be convenient to refer to at this point, although they relate to matters which I shall have to consider later in this judgment. They indicate that, in the absence of evidence that a separate consideration was actually given to the question of the company's benefit, the third limb of the *Lee, Behrens & Co* test is to be applied objectively. Pennycuick J than referred to *Re Introductions Ltd, Introductions Ltd v National Provincial Bank Ltd* [1968] 2 All ER 1221 and said ([1969]

h   2 All ER 1185 at 1193–1194, [1970] Ch 62 at 73–74):

'In that case [*Re Introductions Ltd*] the company concerned was carrying on a single business, pig-breeding, which was not authorised by its memorandum and was consequently ultra vires. BUCKLEY, J., held ([1968] 2 All ER 1221 at 1225, 1227) that the borrowing under an express power was likewise ultra vires. Those passages are

j   directed to the particular case before him, where the company was not carrying on any authorised business, and he held that the power to borrow was not a power which could subsist in isolation from a business. That case, I think, throws no light on the position where, as here, the company concerned is carrying on a business authorised by its memorandum ... Counsel for the plaintiff company contended that in the absence of separate consideration they must, ipso facto, be treated as not

having acted with a view to the benefit of Castleford. That is, I think, an unduly
stringent test and would lead to really absurd results, i.e., unless the directors of a
company addressed their minds specifically to the interest of the company in
connection with each particular transaction, that transaction would be ultra vires
and void, notwithstanding that the transaction might be beneficial to the company
... The proper test, I think, in the absence of actual separate consideration, must be
whether an intelligent and honest man in the position of a director of the company
concerned, could, in the whole of the existing circumstances, have reasonably
believed that the transactions were for the benefit of the company. If that is the
proper test, I am satisfied that the answer here is in the affirmative.'

I would add parenthetically that I think that that must be read in context. It applies
where there is no evidence of what the directors did consider, but it does not absolve the
court from inquiry whether there was any consideration of the company's interest or
entitle it to ignore evidence of actual motives. That, I think, is clear from the speech of
Lord Finlay in *Hindle v John Cotton Ltd* (1919) 56 Sc LR 625, which was cited with approval
in *Howard Smith Ltd v Ampol Petroleum Ltd* [1974] 1 All ER 1126 at 1133, [1974] AC 821
at 835.

Returning to the consideration of the impact of the *Charterbridge* case on the
construction or exercise of express powers, counsel for the liquidator submits that it
cannot stand with the decision of Buckley J in *Re Introductions Ltd* [1968] 1 All ER 1221,
referred to by Pennycuick J and subsequently affirmed in the Court of Appeal ([1969] 1
All ER 887, [1970] Ch 199). But I see no conflict between the two cases. *Re Introductions
Ltd* was not, and did not purport to be, an application of the *Lee, Behrens & Co* principle,
but was a question of construction and does not appear to me to bear at all on the rejection
in the *Charterbridge* case of the *Lee, Behrens & Co* test as the test of the company's capacity
to exercise an express power where the question arises as between the company and an
outsider dealing with the company without knowledge and for value. That point has, in
any event, now been overtaken by s 9 of the European Communities Act 1972.

But it does not appear to me, in any event, that the *Charterbridge* case assists very much
in the present context. It does not, as I see it, relate at all to the distinctive principles
which the courts have established in relation to gratuitous dispositions of companies'
assets. The decision of Plowman J in *Re W M Roith Ltd* [1967] 1 All ER 427, [1967] 1
WLR 432, to which counsel for the liquidator drew my attention and in which Plowman
J again applied the *Lee, Behrens & Co* test to what he found, as a fact, was a sham transaction
for the purpose of conferring a gratuity on the principal shareholder's widow, was a case
of an express power and, indeed, one introduced by the company in general meeting for
the very purpose of enabling the transaction to be effected, although the actual exercise
of the power which was attacked by the liquidator was an exercise by the directors, as it
was in the *Charterbridge* case, without any endorsement by a general meeting.

Furthermore, I do not think that Pennycuick J himself envisaged his observations in
the *Charterbridge* case as affecting the application of the *Lee, Behrens & Co* test to gratuitous
dispositions by the directors of a company's assets, certainly so far as made under implied
powers. In *Ridge Securities Ltd v IRC* [1964] 1 All ER 275, [1964] 1 WLR 479 he applied
the principle to the purported exercise by directors of a power to issue debentures
carrying an obviously sham rate of so-called 'interest'. There does not appear to have been
any evidence either as to the funds from which this came or as to the powers, whether
express or implied, which the directors had purported to exercise. I think that the real
ground for the decision was simply that no one had sought to justify the application
either as being made under an express power or, if made under some implied power, as
having any connection at all with anything that the companies were incorporated to do
and that it may, indeed, have been an illegal return of capital to the shareholders. Counsel
for the appellants, however, relied on the *Lee, Behrens & Co* test in support of an argument
that it would not be right to decide the matter in the absence of the companies the
exercise of whose powers was in question. That submission was rejected by Pennycuick
J, who did apply the test but pointed out that he had not been asked to look at the
companies' express powers in their respective memoranda of association.

Pennycuick J commented on this decision in the *Charterbridge* case, and his observations
as to this make it, I think, clear that his view of the applicability of the test to the situation
with which he was confronted in the *Ridge* case, namely that of a gratuitous disposition
by directors under an implied power, remained unchanged. He said ([1969] 2 All ER
1185 at 1193, [1970] Ch 62 at 73–72):

> 'The relevant transaction in [the *Ridge* case] was a dressed-up gift of a large sum
> by certain companies to another company which had acquired their shares. In the
> absence of a power in the memorandum of those companies, the transaction was
> clearly ultra vires, and, I so held ([1964] 1 All ER 275 at 287–288, [1964] 1 WLR
> 479 at 495). In this passage I referred to *Re Lee, Behrens & Co., Ltd.* and I must plead
> guilty to citing the whole passage ([1932] 2 Ch 46 at 51, [1932] All ER Rep 889 at
> 890) in that case without entering on the distinctions which have become important
> in the present case but which were not important in [that] case.'

However, as I have already mentioned, counsel for the liquidator has not been able to
point to any reported case in which the principle has been applied to the determination
and payment of directors' remuneration by a company in general meeting while the
company is a going concern, and I was at first rather startled by his submissions, which
appeared to me to have surprising and very far-reaching consequences. If it is really the
case that such a payment is ultra vires unless it be, whether viewed subjectively or
objectively, for the benefit of the company and to promote its prosperity as a corporate
entity, then it must logically be ultra vires from whatever funds the payment is made
and whatever be the company's financial position. But it is a commonplace in private
family companies, where there are substantial profits available for distribution by way of
dividend, for the shareholder directors to distribute those profits by way of directors'
remuneration rather than by way of dividend, because the latter course has certain fiscal
disadvantages. But such a distribution may, and frequently does, bear very little relation
to the true market value of the services rendered by the directors and if one is to look at
it from the point of view of the benefit of the company as a corporate entity, then it is
wholly unjustifiable, because it deprives the company of funds which might otherwise
be used for expansion or investment or contingency reserves.

Yet unless it is to be said that the *Lee, Behrens & Co* test is to be applied also even to a
unanimous exercise of the power of the company in general meeting to distribute profits
by way of dividend (which I should hardly have thought was arguable) it is very difficult
to see why the payment of directors' remuneration, on whatever scale the company in
general meeting chooses, out of funds which could perfectly well be distributed by way
of dividend, should be open to attack merely because the shareholders, in their own
interests, choose to attach to it the label of directors' remuneration. After all, the close
company provisions of the Income Tax Acts are specifically designed to compel
distributions and deem them to have taken place if they fall short of the standard
required. Is it then to be said that subsequently, perhaps years later, the company, by its
liquidator or possibly at the instance of a purchaser of the shares, can come along and
demand back profits paid out as remuneration with the active assent and concurrence of
all the shareholders at the time because their payment was ultra vires?

Counsel for the liquidator avoids this particular difficulty by a submission that the *Lee,
Behrens & Co* test is one which is to be applied not to all gratuitous payments but only to
those made otherwise than out of divisible profits, and he cites *Re George Newman & Co*
[1895] 1 Ch 674 in support of that proposition. That was a case of a blatant and dishonest
misuse of the directors' powers by dispensing, by way of gratuitous payment to one of
the directors, moneys borrowed for the purpose of the company's business. Lindley LJ,
delivering the judgment of the court, said (at 685–686):

> 'But in this case the presents made by the directors to Mr. *Newman*, their chairman,
> were made out of money borrowed by the company for the purposes of its business;
> and this money the directors had no right to apply in making presents to one of
> themselves. The transaction was a breach of trust by the whole of them; and even if
> all the shareholders could have sanctioned it, they never did so in such a way as to

bind the company . . . An incorporated company's assets are its property and not the property of the shareholders for the time being; and if the directors misapply those a assets by applying them to purposes for which they cannot lawfully be applied by the company itself, the company can make them liable for such misapplication as soon as anyone properly sets the company in motion . . . Directors have no right to be paid for their services, and cannot pay themselves or each other, or make presents to themselves out of the company's assets unless authorized so to do by the instrument which regulates the company or by the shareholders at a properly b convened meeting. The shareholders, at a meeting duly convened for the purpose, can, if they think proper, remunerate directors for their trouble or make presents to them for their services out of assets properly divisible amongst the shareholders themselves. Further, if the company is a going concern, the majority can bind the minority in such a matter as this. But to make presents out of profits is one thing and to make them out of capital or out of money borrowed by the company is a c very different matter. Such money cannot be lawfully divided among the shareholders themselves, nor can it be given away by them for nothing to their directors so as to bind the company in its corporate capacity.'

This certainly appears to support the submission of counsel for the liquidator and indicates that, when it comes to paying gratuities out of profits, there is no necessary requirement of a consideration of the interests of the company's business. The d shareholders may do as they please. What they cannot do, at least without the leave of the court, is to return capital to themselves.

But if counsel is right in limiting the application of the doctrine in this way, how is one to account for the decision in *Parke v Daily News* [1962] 2 All ER 929, [1962] Ch 927, where the funds intended to be dispensed by way of gratuity were in fact funds which represented profits on the sale of part of the company's business and could properly have e been divided among the shareholders? And what would have been the position in that case if the payment had been sanctioned by the unanimous vote of all the shareholders? If it is truly beyond a company's capacity to make any gratuitous payment out of its funds that is not, viewed objectively, for the benefit of the company and to promote its business, then such a payment cannot logically be sanctioned or ratified even by all the shareholders acting in unison and it cannot logically matter how the company came by f the funds. Company funds are company funds whether they are in the form of cash and representing profits earned by trading or in the form of credit from suppliers or moneys drawn on loan from the company's bankers. They do not belong to the shareholders unless and until they are paid to them by way of a properly declared dividend.

I do not find it altogether easy to reconcile the cases or to extract the principle from them, and it is not in this case of merely academic interest to seek to do so, because the g payments under attack here were expressly sanctioned by all the shareholders and the liquidator's claim relates in part to a period when there were divisible profits from which the payments could be made and in part to a period when there were not.

I must therefore attempt, although I do so with some unease, some analysis of what I conceive to be the principles which underlie the cases. Part of the difficulty, I think, arises from the fact that Eve J in *Re Lee, Behrens & Co* combined together, in the context h of an inquiry as to the effective exercise of directors' powers, two different concepts which have since been regarded as a single composite test of the corporate entity's capacity. In fact, however, as it seems to me at any rate, only one of the three tests postulated in *Lee, Behrens & Co* is truly applicable to that question. The court will clearly not imply a power, even if potentially beneficial to the company, if it is not reasonably incidental to the company's business (see *Tomkinson v South-Eastern Rly Co* (1887) 35 Ch D j 675) and express powers are to be construed as if they were subject to that limitation (see *Re Introductions Ltd*, particularly the judgment of Russell LJ ([1969] 1 All ER 887 at 890, [1970] Ch 199 at 211). But the test of bona fides and benefit to the company seems to me to be appropriate, and really only appropriate, to the question of the propriety of an exercise of a power rather than the capacity to exercise it.

a The cases really divide into two groups: those such as *Hampson v Price's Patent Candle Co, Hutton's* case, *Henderson v Bank of Australasia* and *Parke v Daily News*, where the question was not so much that of the company's capacity to do a particular act as that of the extent to which a majority in general meeting could force a particular measure on a dissentient minority; and those such as *Lee, Behrens & Co* itself, *Re W & M Roith Ltd, Ridge Securities v IRC* and the *Charterbridge* case, where the question was as to the validity of an exercise of the powers, express or implied, by directors. Although the test of benefit to

b the company was applied in both groups of cases, I am not at all sure that the phrase 'the benefit of the company' was being employed in quite the same sense in each.

In the latter group, where what was in question was whether an exercise of powers by directors was effective, the benefit regarded seems to have been that of the company as a corporate entity (see the phrase 'to promote the prosperity of the company') whereas in the former group it was, I think, used in the same sense as that in which it was used in

c the line of cases dealing with, for instance, the power of the majority to alter the articles of association. In *Allen v Gold Reefs of West Africa Ltd* [1900] 1 Ch 656 at 671, [1900–3] All ER Rep 746 at 749 Lindley MR observed that such a power must—

> 'be exercised subject to those general principles of law and equity which are applicable to all powers conferred on majorities and enabling them to bind minorities. It must be exercised, not only in the manner required by law, but also

d > bonâ fide for the benefit of the company as a whole . . .'

And in *Greenhalgh v Arderne Cinemas Ltd* [1950] 2 All ER 1120 at 1126, [1951] Ch 286 at 291 Evershed MR said:

> '. . . it is now plain that "*bona fide* for the benefit of the company as a whole" means not two things but one thing. It means that the shareholder must proceed on

e > what, in his honest opinion, is for the benefit of the company as a whole. Secondly, the phrase, "the company as a whole", does not (at any rate in such a case as the present) mean the company as a commercial entity, distinct from the corporators. It means the corporators as a general body. That is to say, you may take the case of an individual hypothetical member and ask whether what is proposed is, in the honest opinion of those who voted in its favour, for that person's benefit.'

f That was specifically adopted by Plowman J in *Parke v Daily News* [1962] 2 All ER 929 at 948, [1962] Ch 927 at 963 as being applicable in that case.

In my judgment the true rationale of this group of cases is not that what was proposed was ultra vires in the sense that it could not be confirmed by a general meeting where there was no dissentient minority, but that they were concerned with a very different

g question, namely the circumstances in which the court will interfere to prevent a majority from overriding the rights of a dissentient minority to have the company's property administered in accordance with its constitution. I think that, in truth, neither group properly falls to be regarded as exemplifying applications of the ultra vires doctrine. Both, as it seems to me, more properly belong to the sphere of abuse of power, and part of the confusion has, I think, arisen from the fact that in *Hutton's* case, which

h contains the classical judgment of Bowen LJ always cited in this context, the determination of the question of the majority's power to bind the minority did, because the affairs of the company were being conducted under, and only under, the provisions of a special Act conferring very limited powers, necessarily also involve a consideration of the extent of those powers, which was, indeed, a true ultra vires question.

The distinction clearly emerges from the judgment of Vaughan Williams LJ in *Kaye v*

j *Croydon Tramways Co* [1898] 1 Ch 358 at 374–375, where he said:

> 'Then it is said that another ground acted upon by the learned judge was that the entering into such a contract was ultra vires of the company. I am not quite sure that the learned judge meant so to decide, although he may have said some things in the judgment which point in that direction. It is plain that if you speak of something as being ultra vires of the company, and something else as being ultra

vires of the directors or officers of the company, you have not exhausted all the
possible cases, because there is another case which may arise, and frequently does
arise, that is to say, the majority of the shareholders meet together, and they by
resolution purport to bind the minority to do something as to which it is not
competent for the majority to bind the minority. Now, such a resolution is not ultra
vires in the sense in which that word is properly used—it is not ultra vires in the
sense in which counsel for the plaintiff asked us to say that the words of ss. 85 and
86 of the Companies Clauses Act [1845] made this resolution ultra vires, because
when anything is ultra vires in that sense the vote of all the shareholders, every one
of them who were present assenting, would not make the matter one which it was
competent for the company to carry through. There is another sense in which it
might be said that the matter was ultra vires which is not ultra vires in the proper
sense of the words "ultra vires of the company", nor ultra vires in the much more
limited sense of the words "ultra vires of the directors", but ultra vires of the
majority of the shareholders.'

It may be, of course, that where the particular power in question is totally divorced
from any conceivable connection with the company's activities, it cannot be ratified even
by the unanimous vote of all the corporators. This was a situation envisaged by Rigby LJ
in the *Croydon Tramways* case, where he said (at 371):

'What is the meaning of an ultra vires contract? It is one which the company has
no legal power to carry into effect at all, even although in the opinion of each and
every shareholder it is a contract advantageous to the company and to them, and
though each individual shareholder, being fully competent to agree for himself,
approves of and agrees with it.'

Possibly *Tomkinson v South Eastern Rly Co* (1887) 35 Ch D 675 was such a case, although
the action there was in fact brought at the suit of a minority shareholder.

Subject to that, however, it does not appear to me that the group of cases culminating
in *Parke v Daily News* really has much bearing on a case where what has been done is
something expressly authorised by the company's constitution and has been expressly
sanctioned by the unanimous vote of all the shareholders in general meeting. Counsel
for the liquidator, however, submits that the liquidator is, in effect, in the position of a
minority shareholder. Suppose, he suggests, that the directors of a company vote
themselves a present and then use their majority votes as shareholders to override a
dissentient minority. Suppose that before the minority can act to challenge this the
company is wound up. Can it be said, he asks, that the liquidator cannot pursue a claim
on their behalf? That may be perfectly right, but it does not seem to me that it really is
of any help in the context of a case where there is not and never has been any minority
shareholder.

Is there then anything in the other group of cases which leads to the conclusion that a
unanimous vote in general meeting approving directors' remuneration is incompetent,
unless it complies with the whole of the composite *Lee, Behrens & Co* test? On what
ground, in the absence of fraud or any consideration of minority interests, are the votes
of shareholders in general meeting to be treated as if they were, like the powers of
directors, exercisable in a fiduciary capacity? The shareholder is under no fiduciary duty
to the company as to the manner in which he exercises his vote (see *Phillips v
Manufacturers' Securities Ltd* (1917) 86 LJ Ch 305), although the court may in appropriate
circumstances, such as oppression or fraud on a minority, restrain the company from
acting on the resolution resulting from the exercise (see, for instance, the case of *Clemens
v Clemens Bros* [1976] 2 All ER 268).

Lee, Behrens & Co itself does not, in my judgment, provide any support for such a
proposition. If Eve J had considered that the transaction in that case was incapable of
ratification by a general meeting except subject to the same tests as those which affected
the exercise of the directors' powers, then the last part of his judgment which forms the

a alternative ground for the decision is really inexplicable. He clearly considered that that which, in the directors, was a breach of their fiduciary duty (because he was treating the applicant, whether rightly or wrongly, as if she herself were a director) could be endorsed by a properly convened meeting of the shareholders. Equally, it does not appear to me that very much guidance is obtained from *Re W & M Roith Ltd*. That was again a case of an exercise of power by the directors, and it is clear from the report that the applicability of the *Lee, Behrens & Co* test in those circumstances was there conceded, and, I think,

b rightly conceded (see [1967] 1 All ER 427 at 430, [1967] 1 WLR 432 at 437).

No doubt the effectiveness even of a resolution in general meeting will depend on its bona fides. Fraud opens all doors and the court will not uphold or permit the fraudulent exercise of a power. *Re George Newman & Co* [1895] 1 Ch 674 was a clear case of dishonesty, and it is not surprising to find in the judgment of the court the doubt expressed whether what was done there could have been sanctioned even by all the

c shareholders, although the point was not actually decided. But there is no suggestion of bad faith in this case and, as is shown by *Re British Seamless Paper Box Co* (1881) 17 Ch D 467, which is referred to in the judgment of Lindley LJ in the *George Newman* case, the position is quite different where the transaction is honest and is sanctioned by all members of the company at the time (see also *Re Express Engineering Works Ltd* [1920] 1 Ch 466). It is perhaps worth noting, in this context, that the test of benefit to the

d company was impliedly rejected in the case of unanimous consent by Astbury J in *Parker and Cooper Ltd v Reading* [1926] Ch 975 at 984, [1926] All ER Rep 323 at 328. After referring to the two cases last cited, he said:

> 'Now the view I take of both these decisions is that where the transaction is intra vires and honest, and *especially* if it is for the benefit of the company, it cannot be upset if the assent of all the corporators is given to it.' (Emphasis mine.)

e He could hardly have expressed this view if he regarded the notion of benefit to the company as already comprehended in the question of whether the transaction was intra vires.

Counsel for the liquidator submits, however, that, even given a bona fide unanimous resolution in general meeting, it still must be a resolution to do something which the

f company can lawfully do. It cannot, for instance, lawfully return money to its shareholders out of capital. That is plainly right, and *Ridge Securities Ltd v IRC* [1964] 1 All ER 275, [1964] 1 WLR 479 illustrates the proposition. That was a case of what Pennycuick J in the *Charterbridge* case described as 'a dressed-up gift' of a company's funds to its parent company. Counsel for the liquidator has referred me to the passage in the judgment in the *Ridge Securities* case [1964] 1 All ER 275 at 287–288, [1964] 1 WLR 479

g at 495 where Pennycuick J said:

> 'The Special Commissioners have found that none of the companies had any reason to issue a debenture unless the taxpayer company caused it to do so and that the Marlborough companies and Anthracite had no reason at all for borrowing. Indeed, the terms of each debenture indicate on the face of it that the so-called interest represented in fact a gratuitous disposition of an enormous sum by the
>
h > company concerned in favour of the taxpayer company. On these facts and in the absence of any further material, it seems to me to follow that it was not within the powers of the company to enter into the covenant or to make the payment. A company can only lawfully deal with its assets in furtherance of its objects. The corporators may take assets out of the company by way of dividend or, with leave of the court, by way of reduction of capital, or in a winding up. They may of course
>
j > acquire them for full consideration. They cannot take assets out of the company by way of voluntary disposition, however described, and, if they attempt to do so, the disposition is ultra vires the company.'

He then went on to deal with the *Lee, Behrens & Co* test which, as I have mentioned already, the appellants asserted did apply in that case.

Of course, when Pennycuick J referred in that passage to the corporators taking money
out, he was referring to payments to them qua corporators and I do not for one moment
think that he could have had in mind the payment of directors' remuneration as a result
of a vote passed in accordance with the express provisions of the company's constitution.
In the context of the instant case, however, counsel for the liquidator submits that since
(at any rate during most of the material time) there were no profits available in the
company for distribution and since directors' emoluments are always gratuities, except
where payable under contract, and since the directors were shareholders as well, every
payment to them constituted an illegal reduction of capital except to the extent to which
it can be justified by the test of benefit to the company. One difficulty about that, even
accepting the submission for the moment, is that if 'the benefit of the company' means,
as Plowman J suggested in *Parke v Daily News*, 'the benefit of the shareholders as a whole',
it leads him nowhere.

I accept entirely the submission of counsel for the liquidator that a gratuitous payment
out of the company's capital to a member, qua member, is unlawful and cannot stand,
even if authorised by all the shareholders. What I find difficulty in accepting is that,
assuming a sum to be genuinely paid to a director-shareholder as remuneration under an
express power, it becomes an illegal return of capital to him, qua member, if it does not
satisfy some further test of being paid for the benefit of the company as a corporate
entity. If he genuinely receives the money as a reward for his directorship, the question
whether the payment is beneficial to the company or not cannot, as I see it, alter the
capacity in which he receives it: see, for instance, *Cyclists' Touring Club v Hopkinson* [1910]
1 Ch 179 at 188.

Now, there is no presumption that directors' remuneration is payable only out of
divisible profits. That appears clearly from *Re Lundy Granite Co Ltd, Lewis's Case* (1872) 26
LT 673, where an alternative ground for the decision was that the company in general
meeting had indeed sanctioned the payment of directors' remuneration out of capital,
the company never having made any profits. James LJ said (at 675):

> '. . . independently of that construction, I think it would be mischievous, after
> four years' transactions that have been conducted honestly, there being no suggestion
> of fraud or concealment as against the directors—to open up transactions which had
> been submitted to the auditors and shareholders of the company who have passed
> the accounts, which were then submitted to the general meeting, and of which
> there was distinct notice given to everybody. It is true that the directors' fees appear
> in the accounts among a number of other items, but everything appears there.
> Shareholders, like other persons, must be supposed to read the accounts given to
> them of their own matters, and therefore there was distinct notice on the face of the
> reports that the directors' fees were paid, although no profits had been made . . . It
> appears to me that it would be most mischievous to suggest that the company could
> have filed a bill under these circumstances to recover back the money, the payment
> of which they had assented to in that way. I am of opinion that creditors can be in
> no better position than the company itself would be in if it were a solvent company,
> and had raised this question with its directors.'

Mellish LJ said (at 675):

> 'The only question is whether that must necessarily be implied—whether it is so
> much the ordinary course, that directors should be paid only out of profits that that
> must necessarily be implied, and was intended, although it is not expressed. I am
> not aware that there is any such rule. If people want the services of directors, I
> presume directors are entitled to say, we will not serve unless we are paid for our
> services. If directors are appointed and act on that understanding, I do not see any
> reason why they should not be paid.'

Counsel for the liquidator does not go to the extent, in fact, of suggesting that when a
company has fallen on bad times the directors must either close the business down

immediately or go on trying to pull it round for nothing. If that were right, I cannot

a   think that the remuneration sanctioned in *Re Duomatic Ltd* [1969] 1 All ER 161, [1969] Ch 365 would have been allowed to stand. The report does not make it entirely clear, but I infer from the facts that an injection of new capital was required in August 1964 and that the company went into liquidation three months later that it must have been in considerable financial difficulties for some time.

What I think counsel's submission comes to is this, that while the company has

b   divisible profits remuneration may be paid on any scale which the shareholders are prepared to sanction within the limits of available profits, but that, as soon as there cease to be divisible profits, it can only lawfully be paid on a scale which the court, applying some objective standard of benefit to the company, considers to be reasonable. But assuming that the sum is bona fide voted to be paid as remuneration, it seems to me that the amount, whether it be mean or generous, must be a matter of management for the

c   company to determine in accordance with its constitution which expressly authorises payment for directors' services. Shareholders are required to be honest but, as counsel for the respondents suggests, there is no requirement that they must be wise and it is not for the court to manage the company.

Counsel for the liquidator submits, however, that if this is right it leads to the bizarre result that a meeting of stupid or deranged but perfectly honest shareholders can, like

d   Bowen LJ's lunatic director, vote to themselves, qua directors, some perfectly outlandish sum by way of remuneration and that in a subsequent winding up the liquidator can do nothing to recover it. It seems to me that the answer to this lies in the objective test which the court necessarily applies. It assumes human beings to be rational and to apply ordinary standards. In the postulated circumstances of a wholly unreasonable payment, that might, no doubt, be prima facie evidence of fraud, but it might also be evidence that

e   what purported to be remuneration was not remuneration at all but a dressed-up gift to a shareholder out of capital, like the 'interest' payment in the *Ridge Securities* case which bore no relation to the principal sums advanced.

This, as it seems to me, is the real question in a case such as the present. I do not think that in circumstances such as those in the instant case the authorities compel the application to the express power of a test of benefit to the company which, certainly

f   construed as Plowman J held that it should be construed, would be largely meaningless. The real test must, I think, be whether the transaction in question is a genuine exercise of the power. The motive is more important than the label. Those who deal with a limited company do so on the basis that its affairs will be conducted in accordance with its constitution, one of the express incidents of which is that the directors may be paid remuneration. Subject to that, they are entitled to have the capital kept intact. They have

g   to accept the shareholders' assessment of the scale of that remuneration, but they are entitled to assume that, whether liberal or illiberal, what is paid is genuinely remuneration and that the power is not used as a cloak for making payments out of capital to the shareholders as such.

It may well be that one way of ascertaining the true nature of the payment made in purported exercise of such an express power is by subjecting it to the three tests postulated

h   in the *Lee, Behrens & Co* case, but it cannot, I think, be conclusive that the court, looking at the matter with hindsight, concludes that a particular application was not beneficial to the company as a corporate entity or that the shareholders in considering it did not have that in mind. If benefit in that sense were the conclusive test, it is difficult to see how the directors in *Hutton v West Cork Rly Co* (1883) 23 Ch D 654 could have been paid for their past services in connection with the winding up. Such a payment, as I have pointed out,

j   could not have been of any possible benefit to the company which was in the course of winding up. Yet both Cotton and Bowen LJJ clearly contemplated that this could quite properly be paid.

I ought perhaps to add that it has not been suggested that the payments made, if otherwise beyond the powers of a general meeting, were validated by s 9 of the European Communities Act 1972. In any event, the view is expressed in *Gore-Browne on Companies*

(43rd edn, 1977) para 3–16, that the recipient of a corporate gift is not 'a person dealing with a company' within the meaning of the section and that those words contemplate a   *a*
contractual relationship. Since counsel for the respondents does not rely on that section, however, it is not necessary for me to decide the point.

Turning now to the facts of the instant case, it seems to me that the question which I have to determine is whether, on the evidence before me, I can say that the payments made to Mr Charlesworth and to Mrs Charlesworth were genuinely exercises of the company's power to pay remuneration, and counsel for the liquidator very properly   *b*
concedes that he is in some difficulties as regards the case of Mr Charlesworth. Despite some rather confusing statements made by Mr Charlesworth to the Official Receiver which indicate the contrary (at any rate as regards part of the relevant time), I am satisfied on the evidence that, except for the period from December 1967 to March 1968 when Mr Gore was in charge and the period from September 1970 to March 1971 when he was away (save for two weeks or so in December), he was working more or less full-time in   *c*
the business. This was a business with a turnover of the order of £100,000 per annum and the director's remuneration for a full-time working director on a scale of £3,500 per annum does not, I am bound to say, appear to me to be over-generous or unreasonable. It has to be borne in mind, in addition, that Mr Charlesworth, although indemnified by the company against the rent under the lease, was not charging, as he might legitimately have done, any profit rental and that he had personally guaranteed the company's   *d*
overdraft with its bankers. But counsel for the liquidator submits that, at least from December 1970 onwards when he had his second accident and when he was on the eve of selling the business to Mr Bills, Mr Charlesworth ought to have ceased to draw anything at all, since he was no longer working at the garage. I do not see why, and I do not see why those payments ceased, because he was not actually at the garage, to be remuneration properly so-called. He remained a director and retained the overall   *e*
responsibility for the company's affairs. He remained the guarantor of the company's overdraft. It was by no means certain that the sale to Mr Bills would not have gone off as other previous anticipated sales had. Once bona fides is conceded, there seems to me to be nothing unreasonable in his continuing, as the person with the responsibility, both legal and financial, for the running of the business, to draw remuneration on the same scale as that which had been established and accepted in the past and, according to Mr   *f*
Gore's evidence, discussed with the company's accountants.

There is nothing, in my judgment, in the circumstances of Mr Charlesworth's absence from the business over this period following his accidents, the latter of which was directly attributable to his work at the garage, to lead me to conclude that his drawings are to be regarded in some different light from those made while he was able to work actively at the garage or to hold that the moneys were not genuinely paid as director's remuneration.   *g*
The suggestion seems to be that because the payments were drawn weekly it therefore follows that they were not remuneration as regards any week not worked. But that cannot, I think, be right. In my judgment, the remuneration has to be looked at as a whole against the background of the company's practice that drawings were made weekly and that wages continued to be paid during sickness. Mr Charlesworth was a working director over the whole year and the fact that for part of the time, even a   *h*
substantial part of the time, he was disabled from attending to the business cannot, I think, alter the quality of the payments made. He was throughout the man ultimately in charge.

Even if I am wrong in the view which I take of the applicability and conclusiveness of the composite *Lee, Behrens & Co* test to these premises, those tests were, in my judgment, satisfied, at any rate up to the time when Mr Charlesworth ceased to be there. But, as I   *j*
say, I do not think that that is the real question. I have to look to see whether the payment, in my judgment, was a true payment of remuneration under the power in the articles. I bear in mind that Mr Charlesworth, having in April 1969 reduced his weekly drawings to £50, increased them in May 1970 to £70, and there is really no dispute about the reason for this. He had no other means of livelihood apart from the business

a and the increase was a direct result of and coincided with the corresponding decrease in the sums paid to his wife. Mr Gore's evidence was that the latter was effected as a result of advice from the company's accountant that it might be difficult to justify to the Inland Revenue payments of more than £10 a week to a non-working director, and I have no doubt that the increase was intended to ensure that their joint earnings from the enterprise remained the same. It meant that Mr Charlesworth's remuneration as, in effect, managing director was increased from £2,500-odd a year, which might be thought

b to be on the low side having regard to the company's turnover, to £3,500-odd. That is not, in itself, an unreasonable figure and Mr Gore's evidence was that in his view Mr Charlesworth earned every penny of it; but the decision to do this is one which is obviously open to the criticism that it was unwise. The accounts for the year 1969 had not then been completed, but Mr Charlesworth knew that the business was going through a difficult time and was heavily indebted to its suppliers.

c But I do not think that, in the absence of evidence that the payments made were patently excessive or unreasonable, the court can or should engage on a minute examination of whether it would have been more appropriate or beneficial to the company to fix the remuneration at £X rather than £Y, so long as it is satisfied that it was indeed drawn as remuneration. That is a matter left by the company's constitution to its members. In my judgment, a general meeting was competent to sanction the

d payments which he in fact drew and the claim in misfeasance against Mr Charlesworth under this head must fail.

I have felt considerably greater difficulty over the payments to Mrs Charlesworth. If, contrary to the view which I have formed, it be right to apply to them the test of benefit to the company as a corporate entity and if, as counsel for the liquidator submits, they have to be regarded as entirely separate and divorced from her husband's services to the

e company, it is very difficult indeed to justify them by any rational application of that test and it would follow that the directors' act in paying them could not be ratified by the unanimous consent of all the shareholders, whether or not at a formal general meeting.

It should perhaps be mentioned that even on this footing counsel's own formulation of the applicability of the test would restrict the liquidator's claim to payments made after 30 April 1968. It is true that in the year ending on that date the drawings reduced

f the trading profit to a loss on the profit and loss account, but the balance sheet of the company shows that, even allowing for this loss, there was a substantial reserve of profit from the previous year, which could quite properly have been distributed by way of dividend. But subject to that and putting aside the sympathy that must inevitably be felt for Mrs Charlesworth, it is really not possible to see how the business can be said to have derived any benefit at all from the payments nor how anyone could reasonably suppose

g that it could.

It was known from, at the latest, December 1967 onwards, that Mrs Charlesworth could never return to render any services in the actual conduct of the company's business, and she was never thereafter called on, nor was she ever expected, to fulfil any function save that of being a director and carrying out such minimal formal acts as the holding of that office entailed. Mr Charlesworth in his evidence admitted that the company derived

h no benefit at all from the payments made to her, save such as may be thought to flow from the fact that she held office. She was incurably ill and living at a distance of several hundred miles from the company's place of business. Yet in each of the years 1968–69 and 1969–70 she received a sum of some £1,500 and in the year 1970–71 something over £500. It is true that Mr Charlesworth said in his evidence that it had always been the company's practice to continue the payment of full wages to employees who were off sick, and indeed the company's memorandum of association contains a wide express

j power in these terms:

'To pay gratuities or pensions or allowances on retirement to any directors who have held any other salaried office or place of profit with the company or to their widows or dependants and to make contributions to any fund and to pay premiums for the purchase or provision of any such gratuity, pension or allowance and to promote or assist, financially, whether by way of contributions, donations, the payment of premiums or otherwise, any fund or scheme for the benefit, wholly or in part, of directors, ex-directors, or employees, or ex-employees, of the company, or their dependants or relatives, or for charitable purposes generally.'

But it cannot be contended, I think, that Mrs Charlesworth came within that clause. She had never held any office other than that of director and that she retained. Moreover, Mr Charlesworth was not prepared to say that this practice of the company to which he referred had, or was thought to have, any effect on the loyalty of his staff.

The fact is that, however valuable and exacting may have been the services which Mrs Charlesworth had rendered in the past, her continued directorship contributed nothing to the company's future, beyond the fact that she was and remained responsible as a director and was able to make up the necessary quorum for directors' meetings (of which remarkably few took place if the minutes are any accurate guide).

On the other hand, it is said that the Companies Act 1948 imposes on every company incorporated under its provisions an obligation to have a director and it contemplates that those who assume the responsibilities of office, whether they carry them out well or ill, may be paid for that service in such way and in such measure as the company's regulations prescribe or permit. Here the company's constitution conferred on it in express terms a power to award to a director a reward or remuneration for the bare fact of holding office, and that power the company purported to exercise. If it be legitimate for the company to award some remuneration, however nominal, to Mrs Charlesworth for acting as a director and taking on herself, for good or ill, the responsibilities which that office entails, at what point, counsel for the respondents asks, does it become beyond the company's power to do that which its constitution permits it to do and how can the court take on itself the discretion as to quantum which is vested in the shareholders, there being, ex concessis, no mala fides? I have not found the point an easy one, but on the view that I take of the law the argument of counsel for the respondents is very difficult to meet *if* the payments made really were within the express power conferred by the company's constitution.

But of course what the company's articles authorise is the fixing of 'remuneration', which I take to mean a reward for services rendered or to be rendered; and, whatever the terms of the resolutions passed and however described in the accounts or the company's books, the real question seems to me to be whether the payments really were 'directors' remuneration' or whether they were gratuitous distributions to a shareholder out of capital dressed up as remuneration.

I do not think that it can be said that a director of a company cannot be rewarded as such merely because he is not active in the company's business. The mere holding of office involves responsibility even in the absence of any substantial activity, and it is indeed in part to the mere holding of office that Mrs Charlesworth owes her position as a respondent in these proceedings. I can see nothing as a matter of construction of the article to disentitle the company, if the shareholders so resolve, from paying a reward attributable to the mere holding of the office of director, for being, as it were, a name on the notepaper and attending such meetings or signing such documents as are from time to time required. The director assumes the responsibility on the footing that he will receive whatever recompense the company in general meeting may think appropriate. In this case, however, counsel for the liquidator is entitled to submit that the sums paid to Mrs Charlesworth were so out of proportion to any possible value attributable to her holding of office that the court is entitled to treat them as not being genuine payments of remuneration at all but as dressed-up dividends out of capital, like the dressed-up payments of 'interest' in the *Ridge Securities* case.

The difficulty that I felt about this at first was that there is, in relation to the misfeasance claim, which is the only claim with which I am concerned, no allegation of fraud or mala fides in relation to these payments. The liquidator's case has been argued

throughout on the footing that they were payments of remuneration but were also
a payments which could not be sanctioned by a general meeting because it was not for the
benefit of the company to resolve on payments on this scale. For the reasons which I have
endeavoured to state, I think that in circumstances such as exist in this case, where
payments are made under the authority of a general meeting acting pursuant to an
express power, the matter falls to be tested by reference to the genuineness and honesty
of the transaction rather than by reference to some abstract standard of benefit. I do not,
b however, think that bona fides (in the sense of absence of fraudulent intention) and
genuineness are necessarily the same thing. It is not suggested here that there was any
intent to defraud, but that cannot be conclusive. As Jessel MR remarked in *Re National
Funds Assurance Co* (1878) 10 Ch D 118 at 128, to say that something is done bona fide is
not the same thing as merely to say that the actor had no intention to commit a fraud.
The real question is, were these payments genuinely director's remuneration? If your
c intention is to make a gift out of the capital of the company, you do not alter the nature
of that by giving it another label and calling it 'remuneration'.

As it seems to me, the submission of counsel for the respondents involves the notion
that where there is a purported exercise of an express power by a general meeting the
court is slave to whatever form of words the members may have chosen to use in the
resolution which they pass. I do not think that can be so. I agree with counsel for the
d liquidator that it cannot be right that shareholder directors acting in unison can draw
any sum they like out of the company's capital and leave the liquidator and the company's
creditors without remedy in the absence of proof of intent to defraud merely because
they choose to dignify the drawing with a particular description. The cases show, I think,
that the mere fact that the company is in low financial water does not prevent the
payment of a proper director's remuneration even though it may be technically a
e gratuity. But equally, the court is not, in my judgment, precluded from examining the
true nature of the payments merely because the members choose to call them
remuneration.

Now, looking at the payments made to Mrs Charlesworth, I was at first inclined to
regard them merely as part of a global (but, on the face of it, not unreasonable)
remuneration for Mr Charlesworth's service which, as a matter of convenience, were
f allocated to his wife. But that, I think, cannot be. Mr Charlesworth himself did not claim
it to be so. They were the same sums as were paid to her when she was genuinely
working in the business, and Mr Gore in his evidence made it quite clear that they were,
and were intended to be, her own separate money.

Mr Gore gave evidence of a meeting with a representative of the company's auditors,
Mr Marshall, in May 1970, following which the payments to Mrs Charlesworth were
g reduced. Mr Marshall pointed out that the company was carrying too high a proportion
of administrative wages as compared with productive wages and suggested that the scale
of Mrs Charlesworth's remuneration should be reduced because, according to my note of
Mr Gore's answer, 'it was difficult to say that she was earning that class of money'. This
shows, I think, first that the amount being paid as remuneration to a non-working
director was considered by Mr Marshall (who, after all, was well acquainted with the
h company's affairs) to be excessive, but it also shows that nobody had previously given any
real consideration to the services or responsibilities in respect of which it was allegedly
paid. Mr Gore admitted that he had simply gone on paying the weekly sums to Mrs
Charlesworth because he could not bring himself to reduce them while she was so ill.

I find it really impossible on the facts to hold that the whole of these sums, amounting
to £1,500 per annum, drawn during the years 1968–69 and 1969–70, can be treated as
j genuine director's remuneration in any real sense of the term. They were, as it seems to
me, simply a recognition that, as a co-proprietor of the business with her husband, she
ought to be getting out of the business what she had had before and that 'director's
remuneration' was a convenient label to attach to these sums and one which, it was
thought, would enable them to be properly paid. The mere attachment of that label
cannot, in my view, alter the fact that they were in truth, from 1 April 1968 onwards,

paid out of capital, which, so far at any rate as they exceeded anything which could reasonably be called remuneration for acting as a director, the company had no power to sanction.

I was troubled in the course of the argument by the question whether, logically, a payment made in these circumstances could be apportioned. Accepting counsel for the liquidator's premise that directors' remuneration under an article in this form is a gratuitous payment, can part be, as it were, more gratuitous than the rest? The answer is, I think, that what the article authorises is the making of a gratuitous payment which is related to the services rendered or to be rendered, be it actually working in the business or merely holding an office and taking responsibility. It does not authorise what, for want of a better term, I may call a 'pure gift', however described, although if it is to come out of divisible profits the shareholders can, as Lindley LJ said in the *George Newman* case, do what they like, and it cannot, I think, be right that, where a payment is made out of capital which is described as remuneration but which is so manifestly beyond any possible justifiable reward for that in respect of which allegedly it is paid, it has to be treated as valid in whole simply because a part of it (which may be difficult to quantify) can be genuinely related to some service or office. Counsel for the liquidator, indeed, does not submit that there can be no apportionment, because the whole of his case in respect of Mr Charlesworth's remuneration was based on the premise that that part which genuinely represented a reasonable reward for services rendered was intra vires and the balance ultra vires. Thus, for instance, if a dividend is paid in part out of capital and in part out of profits, it is, I apprehend, only pro tanto ultra vires and can be recovered to that extent from the directors responsible for its payment.

Counsel for the liquidator submits here, however, that the entirety of the payments to Mrs Charlesworth over the relevant period are recoverable because she should and could have been paid nothing at all since she was not actively working in the business at the garage. That I feel unable to accept. As I have said, a sum paid simply for the assumption of the responsibility of being a director is, in my view, properly described as remuneration. The difficulty must necessarily be to know where to draw the line between what could reasonably be described as a genuine reward for service and what could not. Remuneration does not cease to be remuneration because it is generous or even, perhaps, unwisely generous, but there is an obvious difficulty about fixing any point at which it can be said that a purported exercise of the power to pay ceases to be genuine. In the absence of any evidence of actual motive, the court must, I think, look at the matter objectively and apply the standard of reasonableness.

In the instant case, however, there is some evidence of a standard in the interview with Mr Marshall to which I have referred. The sum of £10 per week, which may seem rather on the generous side even in these inflationary days, was the sum which the company's accountant, a partner in a very well-known firm of chartered accountants, thought was a justifiable sum to pay in May 1970 for Mrs Charlesworth's presence on the board of directors, and it was the sum in fact paid from then on. I do not think that the court can proceed on a minute examination of whether that did or did not conform to the average sum paid by companies of this size to non-working directors. It was the sum which the company was professionally advised could legitimately be regarded as remuneration, and I find it difficult, therefore, to say that it was not genuinely paid as such or that to vote it was beyond the power of a general meeting. Accepting, however, that there was no intention to defraud anyone, I cannot regard the payments made to Mrs Charlesworth in excess of this weekly amount, however well intentioned, as being anything more than disguised gifts out of capital. In my judgment, even the sanction of the shareholders in general meeting could not, simply by calling the payments remuneration, validate the acts of the directors in making them, and to this extent the liquidator's summons must succeed in respect of the period from 30 April 1968 to May 1970, subject only to a claim for relief under s 448 of the 1968 Act.

I have not felt able to accede to the submission of counsel for the respondents that the respondents ought to be excused under this section. Mr Charlesworth was well aware of a the difficulties which the company was exercising, although, according to Mr Gore's evidence, he felt that the accountants were being too pessimistic, and both respondents were told in August 1970 in unmistakable terms that the accounts to the end of the year 1969 showed a state of insolvency. While Mr Charlesworth may well have thought that he would be able to pull the business round, prudence would, I think, have dictated a reduction in overall drawings. Accepting that they have acted honestly, therefore, I do not think that they can be said to have acted reasonably.

b   Accordingly, so far as the claim in respect of Mr Charlesworth's drawings is concerned, the summons fails; but as regards those of Mrs Charlesworth, I feel bound to hold that it must succeed to the extent which I have indicated.

Order accordingly.

c Solicitors: *William F Prior & Co* (for the liquidator); *Poole, Bairstow & Co*, Bedford (for the respondents).

Evelyn M C Budd   Barrister.

d

Re Horsley & Weight Ltd

COURT OF APPEAL, CIVIL DIVISION
BUCKLEY, CUMMING-BRUCE AND TEMPLEMAN LJJ
16, 17, 18, 19, 20 JUNE, 30 JULY 1980

e

Company – Objects clause – Construction – Power to provide pensions for directors and employees – Whether power capable of being substantive object of company – Whether merely an ancillary or incidental power – Whether grant of pension to director/employee ultra vires company.

Company – Director – Unauthorised act – Misfeasance – Ratification – Purchase of pension for
f *director/employee by two directors of company without authority of board of directors or company in general meeting – Two directors the sole shareholders of company – Purchase of pension unauthorised but intra vires company and effected in good faith – Whether assent to purchase by the two directors ratifying transaction – Whether directors who are sole shareholders and who commit misfeasance by an act of gross negligence which inflicts loss on creditors can ratify their own negligence – Companies Act 1948, s 333(1).*

g A company which carried on the business of shopfitters had as one of its objects (set out in cl 3(o) of its memorandum of association) to 'grant pensions to employees and ex-employees and directors and ex-directors'. Clause 3 also contained a 'separate objects clause' which provided that all the objects specified in cl 3 were to be read and construed as separate and distinct objects. There were five directors of the company. One director
h was the respondent, but he was a director in name only and took no part in the company's financial affairs, his true position being that of an employee of the company. Two other directors were C and F, who were the sole shareholders of the company and the only authorised signatories on the company's bank account. The remaining two directors were their wives, who took no part in the company's affairs. In 1975, shortly before the respondent was due to retire, C told him that in recognition of his service the company would grant him a retirement pension of £1,176 per annum which would be secured by
j the company taking out a pension policy with an insurance company, the premium for which was £10,000. C and F, without the authority of the board of directors or of the company in general meeting, effected the policy and signed cheques for the premium of £10,000. In effecting the policy C and F acted in good faith, after considering whether it was proper to take out the policy in the light of the company's financial state, and the

evidence did not establish that they ought to have appreciated that payment of the
premium would cause loss to the company's creditors. The respondent retired from the
company in 1976. In 1977 the company was compulsorily wound up owing sums to
creditors. The liquidator applied to the court under s 333(1)ᵃ of the Companies Act 1948
for declarations that the procurement of the pension policy by C and F was ultra vires the
company and a misfeasance on their part and that, because the respondent had knowledge
of the misfeasance, he held the policy in trust for the company. The judge dismissed the
application and held that the policy was not available as an asset in the winding up on the
grounds (i) that the purchase of the pension was intra vires the company and (ii) that the
purchase of the policy was not misfeasance on the part of C and F. The liquidator
appealed.

Held – The appeal would be dismissed for the following reasons—

(1) The doing of an act which was expressed in the memorandum of a company to be,
and which was capable of being, an independent or substantive object of the company,
rather than a mere power which was ancillary or incidental to a substantive object, could
not be ultra vires the company, because by definition it was something which the
company was formed to do. The power to grant a pension, set out in cl 3(o) of
the company's memorandum, was capable of subsisting as a substantive object of the
company, and not merely as an incidental power, and, having regard to the separate
objects clause, was therefore to be construed as being a substantive object of the company.
Since the power to grant a pension was a substantive object it was irrelevant whether the
grant of a pension pursuant to that power would benefit or promote the commercial
prosperity of the company. It followed that the procurement of the pension policy by C
and F had been intra vires the company (see p 1051 *d*, p 1502 *d* to *f*, p 1054 *a* to *c*, p 1055
f g j and p 1056 *a f*, post); dictum of Eve J in *Re Lee, Behrens & Co Ltd* [1932] All ER Rep
at 890–891 explained.

(2) Since a company or its directors could properly expend contributed capital for any
purpose which was intra vires the company, and since the purchase of the pension policy
was intra vires the company and in the circumstances had been done in good faith, the
purchase of it was not misfeasance on the part of C and F. It was, however, an
unauthorised act, since it had been done without the consent of the board of directors or
of the company in general meeting, and unless effectually ratified it could not bind the
company. Nevertheless, C and F's assent to the transaction, being assent by the only
shareholders of the company to an intra vires act, had the effect of ratifying the
transaction. It followed that the purchase of the pension was binding on the company
and could not be assailed by the liquidator (see p 1054 *c* to *e* and *j* to p 1055 *j* and p 1056 *f*,
post); dictum of Lord Davey in *Salomon v Salomon & Co Ltd* [1895–9] All ER Rep at 51,
Re Express Engineering Works Ltd [1920] 1 Ch 466 and *Parker & Cooper Ltd v Reading*
[1926] All ER Rep 323 applied.

Per Templeman LJ. Quaere whether directors who hold all the issued shares in a
company and who commit misfeasance by an act of gross negligence which inflicts loss
on the creditors of the company can, as the sole shareholders, ratify their own gross
negligence (see p 1056 *f g*, post).

Notes

For the construction of the objects clause of a memorandum of association, see 7
Halsbury's Laws (4th edn) para 703, for acts ultra vires a company, see ibid paras 705–
708, and for cases on the construction of the objects clause of a memorandum, see 9

---

a   Section 333(1), so far as material, provides: 'If in the course of winding up a company it appears
    that . . . any past or present director . . . has misapplied . . . any money . . . of the company, or been
    guilty of any misfeasance or breach of trust in relation to the company, the court may, on the
    application . . . of the liquidator . . . compel him to repay or restore the money . . . by way of
    compensation in respect of the misapplication . . . misfeasance or breach of trust as the court thinks
    just.'

Digest (Reissue) 75, *334–339*, and for cases on ultra vires acts, see ibid 672–673, *4012–4017*.

For ratification of directors' acts which are not ultra vires, see 7 Halsbury's Laws (4th edn) para 504, and for cases on the subject, see 9 Digest (Reissue) 515–516, *3075–3085*.

For the Companies Act 1948, s 333, see 5 Halsbury's Statutes (3rd edn) 362.

Cases referred to in judgments

Charterbridge Corp Ltd v Lloyds Bank Ltd [1969] 2 All ER 1185, [1970] Ch 62, [1969] 3 WLR 122, 9 Digest (Reissue) 492, *2942*.

Exchange Banking Co, Re, Flitcroft's Case (1882) 21 Ch D 519, CA, 9 Digest (Reissue) 534, *3194*.

Express Engineering Works Ltd, Re [1920] 1 Ch 466, CA, 9 Digest (Reissue) 557, *3331*.

German Date Coffee Co, Re (1882) 20 Ch D 169, [1881–5] All ER Rep 372, CA, 9 Digest (Reissue) 75, *337*.

Hampson v Price's Patent Candle Co (1876) 45 LJ Ch 437, 10 Digest (Reissue) 1349, *8641*.

Henderson v Bank of Australasia (1888) 40 Ch D 170, 9 Digest (Reissue) 582, *3468*.

Hutton v West Cork Rly Co (1883) 23 Ch D 654, CA, 9 Digest (Reissue) 685, *4077*.

Introductions Ltd, Re, Introductions Ltd v National Provincial Bank Ltd [1969] 1 All ER 887, [1970] Ch 199, [1969] 2 WLR 791, CA, 9 Digest (Reissue) 75, *336*.

Lee, Behrens & Co Ltd, Re [1932] 2 Ch 46, [1932] All ER Rep 889, 9 Digest (Reissue) 571, *3419*.

Newman (George) & Co, Re [1895] 1 Ch 674, CA, 9 Digest (Reissue) 528, *3168*.

Parker & Cooper Ltd v Reading [1926] Ch 975, [1926] All ER Rep 323, 9 Digest (Reissue) 515, *3076*.

Payne (David) & Co Ltd, Re, Young v David Payne & Co Ltd [1904] 2 Ch 608, CA, 9 Digest (Reissue) 511, *3058*.

Ridge Securities Ltd v IRC [1964] 1 All ER 275, [1964] 1 WLR 479, 28(1) Digest (Reissue) 178, *536*.

Roith (W & M) Ltd, Re [1967] 1 All ER 427, [1967] 1 WLR 432, 9 Digest (Reissue) 571, *3420*.

Salomon v Salomon & Co Ltd [1897] AC 22, [1895–9] All ER Rep 33, HL, 9 Digest (Reissue) 19, *10*.

Cases also cited

British Seamless Paper Box Co, Re (1881) 17 Ch D 467, CA.

Kaye v Croydon Tramways Co [1898] 1 Ch 358, CA.

Simpson v Westminster Palace Hotel Co (1860) 8 HL Cas 712, 11 ER 608, HL.

Appeal

By a summons dated 23 May 1978 issued by the liquidator of Horsley & Weight Ltd under s 333 of the Companies Act 1948, the liquidator claimed against the respondent, Stephen Albert Horsley, a former director of the company, (1) a declaration that he was guilty of misfeasance and breach of trust in relation to the company by procuring it to take out for his benefit a pension policy with Hambro Life Assurance Ltd and to pay therefor a single premium of £9,000 and one annual premium of £1,000, and (2) a declaration that the respondent held the policy or its proceeds on trust for the company, or alternatively that he was bound to repay to the company the amount of the premiums and interest. By an order made on 4 December 1979 Oliver J dismissed the liquidator's summons. The liquidator appealed on the grounds (1) that the judge erred in law in holding, on the facts he found, that the purchase of the policy and the payment of premiums were intra vires the company, and (2) if he was correct in holding that the purchase of the policy was intra vires, he erred in law in holding that the act of the two directors who procured its purchase was capable of being ratified or alternatively had been ratified by them as the sole shareholders of the company. By a respondent's notice the respondent contended, inter alia, that the judgment should be affirmed on the additional ground that, having regard to r 68 of the Companies (Winding-up) Rules

1949, the liquidator was only entitled to rely on the ground stated in his summons, that the respondent procured the company to take out a pension policy for his benefit. The facts are set out in the judgment of Buckley LJ.

E C Evans-Lombe QC and *John Higham* for the liquidator.
Philip Goodenday and *Nigel Clifford* for the respondent.

Cur adv vult

30 July. The following judgments were read.

BUCKLEY LJ. The appellant liquidator of Horsley and Weight Ltd (the company) claims in proceedings under s 333 of the Companies Act 1948 against the respondent, Mr Stephen Albert Horsley (the respondent), a declaration that the respondent was guilty of misfeasance and breach of trust in relation to the company in respect of the acquisition by the company of a pension policy for the respondent's benefit. The policy in question was taken in the name of the company and is held by the company, and consequently the question is whether that policy is held by the company for the benefit of the respondent, or is an asset applicable in the liquidation of the company for the benefit of the company's creditors. Oliver J rejected the liquidator's claim in a judgment delivered on 4 December 1979, and the liquidator appeals from that decision.

The company was incorporated in 1950 to take over a business of shopfitters then being carried on by the respondent and a Mr Weight in partnership. The issued and paid-up share capital has at all material times been £1,200, divided into 1,200 shares of £1 each. Originally the respondent held 450 shares and his wife held 150; Mr Weight held 450 and his wife 150. In 1972 Mr Weight and his wife retired and their 600 shares were acquired by a Mr Campbell-Dick, who then became a director. At the end of 1973 the respondent and his wife transferred their 600 shares to their son, Mr Frank Stephen Horsley. Thenceforth Mr Campbell-Dick and Mr Frank Horsley were the only shareholders, each holding 600 shares. The respondent remained a director and continued to work in the business until his retirement in 1976. The other directors from the end of 1973 were Mr Campbell-Dick, Mr Frank Horsley and their two wives. The two ladies took no active part in the business or the company's affairs.

Among the objects for which the company was established, set forth in cl 3 of its memorandum of association, is the following:

'(o) To grant pensions to employees and ex-employees and directors and ex-directors or other officers or ex-officers of the company, their widows, children and dependants, and to subscribe to benevolent and other funds for the benefit of any such persons and to subscribe to or assist in the promotion of any charitable benevolent or public purpose or object.'

Clause 3 contains the following paragraph, which has of recent years become regrettably common notwithstanding that it is often in some respects inappropriate, if not actually misleading:

'All the foregoing objects shall be read and construed as separate and distinct objects and the generality of any such objects shall not be abridged or cut down by reference to any other object of the company.'

I shall use the expression 'separate objects clause' to describe any clause to this effect.

During 1973, 1974 and 1975 the business of the company expanded in consequence of Mr Campbell-Dick and Mr Frank Horsley acquiring control of, or interests in, certain other companies in a similar line of business to the company's business, for which the company acted as sub-contractor and supplier.

The affairs of the company seem to have been conducted with the utmost informality. The judge found that no board meetings were held. The respondent acted as assistant

production manager, and although he remained a director in name his position was
a really that of an employee of the company. His trade was that of a carpenter and his
responsibility was to estimate for contracts to be carried out by the company. The
financial policy was directed by Mr Campbell-Dick. The respondent had no control over
the financial affairs of the company and knew very little about them. At the relevant
time Mr Campbell-Dick and Mr Frank Horsley were the only authorised signatories on
the company's bank account. The respondent had no contract of service with the
b company. He, like the other directors, including the two ladies who took no part in the
company's affairs, was remunerated at rates which varied from year to year, fluctuating,
as it would seem, with the amount which was thought suitable to be drawn out of the
company having regard to the fluctuating fortunes of the business. No dividends seem
to have been declared.

The events which give rise to the liquidator's claim are described as follows in the
c respondent's affidavit:

'9. Ever since I had parted with my shares as aforesaid I had made it clear that it
was my intention to retire on my 65th birthday on 2nd May 1976 and my said
intention was well known, but the idea that I should receive from the Company a
retirement policy or other retirement benefit had never occurred to me. The events
disclosed in the next paragraph hereof came as a complete surprise to me.

d 10. On a date which I verily believe must have been 30th September 1975
(judging from the date on the application form hereinafter mentioned) I was
working in my office on the ground floor of the Company's said premises. I
remember that I was working at the time on the preparation of estimates to be
submitted to intending customers. Whilst I was thus engaged, Mr. Campbell-Dick
came into the room and asked me to accompany him to his room on the 1st floor
e which I accordingly did. Waiting in his room was a gentleman whom I had not
previously met and who was then introduced to me as Mr. Pope, a representative of
Hambro Life Assurance Limited. I remember saying "What's this all about?". Mr.
Campbell-Dick then told me that having regard to my intending retirement and
because of my service to the Company over a period of 23 years the Directors had
decided that the Company would spend £10,000 in providing me with a retirement
f pension policy. I have in fact now been advised that the policy provides for payment
of a single premium of £9,000 and annual premiums of £1,000 and that the said
single premium plus the first annual premium of £1,000 has been paid to Hambro,
but I do not remember that being explained to me at the time. I was simply told
that the Company would pay the sum of £10,000. I saw no reason to refuse this
gesture by the Company and I was very glad to accept the same. Mr. Pope had with
g him a form which he produced and which had already been partly filled in by him
and which he then completed in my presence and I then at his request and in his
presence and in the presence of Mr. Campbell-Dick at the said interview signed the
same. Looking now at exhibit "GAA1" which is a photostat of the said application
form, I notice that the document is also initialled by my son and Mr. Campbell-
Dick on behalf of the Employer (i.e. the Company). I regret that I do not know at
h what stage those initials were put on the form and my son was not present at the
said interview. Presumably the said initials must have already been on the said form
because the form having been thus completed as aforesaid the same was then handed
by Mr. Campbell-Dick to Mr. Pope together with a cheque for £10,000 and Mr.
Pope took the same away with him. I did not examine the cheque but it must have
been signed by Mr. Campbell-Dick and my son as directors on behalf of the
j Company. That interview was the beginning and end of the transaction so far as I
was concerned; before then I did not have the slightest inkling of any intention that
the Company should thus provide for me. I did not receive the policy as the same
was presumably in due course received and held by the Company as trustee.'

Oliver J accepted that evidence. The amount of the pension secured by the policy was
£1,176 per annum, payable from 1 October 1975.

In his summons the liquidator described the respondent's alleged misfeasance and breach of trust as being:

a

'... by procuring that the company take out for his benefit an executive pension plan policy with Hambro Life Assurance Ltd. and pay therefor a single premium of £9,000 and one yearly premium of £1,000 on or about the 1st October 1975.'

In the light of the respondent's evidence which I have read, that charge obviously cannot prevail. However, before the summons came on, the liquidator widened his *b* grounds in two respects. In para 3 of an affidavit sworn on 27 November 1978 the liquidator gave notice that he would contend that, if the respondent did not procure the company to take out the policy—

'nonetheless that policy was procured to be taken out by the company in circumstances of misfeasance and breach of trust by the responsible directors of the company ... the respondent has had or alternatively now has knowledge of such *c* misfeasance and breach of trust by the responsible directors and accordingly now holds the policy in trust for the company.'

By a further affidavit sworn on 16 November 1979 the liquidator further deposed:

'With further reference to paragraph 3 of my affidavit of 27th November 1978, I should make clear that it will be contended on my behalf that the circumstances of *d* misfeasance and breach of trust referred to include the disposition of the company's property ultra vires the company.'

Counsel for the respondent contends that the liquidator's summons fails to comply with the requirements of r 68 of the Companies (Winding-up) Rules 1949, SI 1949/330, which requires an application under s 333 of the 1948 Act to be by summons stating the *e* grounds of the application. In my view, this submission is not without justification. An application alleging misfeasance should, in my judgment, give sufficient particulars, either in the summons or in the supporting affidavits, of the alleged misfeasance to enable the respondent to know what case he will be expected to meet. In the present case there is a conspicuous absence of particulars of the misfeasance said to have been committed by 'the responsible directors'. I take this expression to refer to Mr Campbell- *f* Dick and Mr Frank Horsley. Neither of those two gentlemen was made a respondent to the summons and neither of them was called as a witness by the liquidator. It seems not impossible that, if the liquidator's allegations against them had been particularised in greater detail, the respondent might have been advised to call one or both of them. But the respondent was offered an adjournment in the court below and declined to take it. The matter was fully canvassed before Oliver J and also in this court, and in my judgment *g* we should not refuse on purely procedural grounds to deal with it.

Counsel for the liquidator has presented his argument under two broad heads: first, that the purchase of the pension policy was ultra vires the company, and second, that if it was intra vires the company, the purchase was effected by Mr Campbell-Dick and Mr Frank Horsley without the authority of the board of directors or of the company in general meeting, and was an act of misfeasance which was not validated as against the *h* company's creditors by virtue of the fact that Mr Campbell-Dick and Mr Frank Horsley were the only shareholders.

I will first consider the ultra vires point. The Companies Act 1948, s 2, requires the memorandum of association of a company incorporated under that Act to state the objects of the company. A company has no capacity to pursue any objects outside those which are so stated. It does not follow, however, that any act which is not expressly *j* authorised by the memorandum is ultra vires the company. Anything reasonably incidental to the attainment or pursuit of any of the express objects of the company will, unless expressly prohibited, be within the implied powers of the company. It has now long been a common practice to set out in memoranda of association a great number and variety of 'objects' so called, some of which (for example, to borrow money, to promote

the company's interests by advertising its products or services, or to do acts or things
a conducive or incidental to the company's objects) are by their very nature incapable of
standing as independent objects which can be pursued in isolation as the sole activity of
the company. Such 'objects' must, by reason of their very nature, be interpreted merely
as powers incidental to the true objects of the company and must be so treated
notwithstanding the presence of a separate objects clause: see *Re Introductions Ltd,
Introductions Ltd v National Provincial Bank Ltd* [1969] 1 All ER 887, [1970] Ch 199. Where
b there is no separate objects clause, some of the express 'objects' may on construction fall
to be treated as no more than powers which are ancillary to the dominant or main objects
of the company: see, for example, *Re German Date Coffee Co* (1882) 20 Ch D 169, [1881–
5] All ER Rep 372.

Ex hypothesi an implied power can only legitimately be used in a way which is
ancillary or incidental to the pursuit of an authorised object of the company, for it is the
c practical need to imply the power in order to enable the company effectively to pursue
its authorised objects which justifies the implication of the power. So an exercise of an
implied power can only be intra vires the company if it is ancillary or incidental to the
pursuit of an authorised object. So also, in the case of express 'objects' which, on
construction of the memorandum or by their very nature, are ancillary to the dominant
or main objects of the company, an exercise of any such power can only be intra vires if
d it is in fact ancillary or incidental to the pursuit of some such dominant or main object.

On the other hand, the doing of an act which is expressed to be, and is capable of
being, an independent object of the company cannot be ultra vires, for it is by definition
something which the company is formed to do and so must be intra vires. I shall use the
term 'substantive object' to describe such an object of a company.

The question, therefore, is whether cl 3(o) of the company's memorandum of
e association in the present case contains a substantive object or merely an ancillary power.
Having regard to the presence of the separate objects clause, the former of these
alternatives must be the case unless the subject matter of cl 3(o) is of its nature incapable
of constituting a substantive object.

We are not concerned here with whether the pension policy is a valid enforceable
contract between the company and the insurers. It has been assumed in argument on
f both sides that this is the case. The question with which we are concerned is whether as
between the company (now acting by its liquidator), and the respondent, the respondent
can be made liable on the ground that he knowingly participated in an act of misfeasance
by Mr Campbell-Dick and Mr Frank Horsley by expending the company's money in a
way which was ultra vires the company, or which, if not ultra vires the company, was
nevertheless a misfeasance which was incapable of ratification by Mr Campbell-Dick and
g Mr Frank Horsley as the only shareholders.

Counsel for the liquidator, relying principally on the judgment of Eve J in *Re Lee,
Behrens & Co Ltd* [1932] 2 Ch 46, [1932] All ER Rep 889 submits that, properly construed,
para (o) should be read as conferring merely an ancillary power. In that case the directors
of a company procured that the company should enter into a deed of covenant to pay to
the widow of a former director a life annuity. The company subsequently went into
h liquidation and the annuitant lodged a proof in the winding up for the capitalised value
of the annuity. The liquidator rejected the proof on, among other grounds, the ground
that the deed was ultra vires the company. Eve J held that, although the company's
memorandum contained an express power to pension widows of ex-employees of the
company, this did not extend to pensioning widows of ex-directors. Accordingly, the
transaction in question had to be justified, if at all, under an implied power to pension
j widows of ex-directors. Eve J said ([1932] 2 Ch 46 at 51–52, [1932] All ER Rep 889 at
890–891):

'But whether they be made under an express or an implied power, all such grants
involve an expenditure of the company's money, and that money can only be spent
for purposes reasonably incidental to the carrying on of the company's business, and
the validity of such grants is to be tested, as is shown in all the authorities, by the

answers to three pertinent questions: (i.) Is the transaction reasonably incidental to the carrying on of the company's business? (ii.) Is it a bona fide transaction? and (iii.) Is it done for the benefit and to promote the prosperity of the company? Authority for each of the foregoing propositions is to be found in the following cases: *Hampson v. Price's Patent Candle Co.* ((1876) 45 LJ Ch 437); *Hutton v. West Cork Ry Co.* ((1888) 23 ChD 654); and *Henderson v. Bank of Australasia* ((1888) 40 ChD 170).'

Those three cases all depended on whether the transactions there in question were within the implied powers of the companies or (which I think comes to the same thing) whether the transaction in question was within an express general power to conduct the company's business.

Counsel for the liquidator submits that that passage from the judgment of Eve J is applicable to the present case and provides, as he submits, an aid to construction of any memorandum of association which contains a paragraph such as we have in cl 3(o) of the company's memorandum. It is true that Eve J's observation expressly refers to both express and implied powers, but in relation to the former it was no more than an obiter dictum. It is worthy of note that the judge used the word 'power', not the word 'object'. Counsel for the liquidator, however, submits that the decision indicates that a capacity to grant pensions to employees or ex-employees, or to directors or ex-directors, is of its nature a power enabling the company to act as a good employer in the course of carrying on its business, and as such is an incidental power which must be treated as though it were expressly subject to a limitation that it can only be exercised in circumstances in which a grant of a pension will benefit the company's business. I do not feel able to accept that contention. Clause 3(o) must be read as a whole. It includes not only pensions and other disbursements which will benefit directors, employees and their dependants, but also making grants for charitable, benevolent or public purposes or objects. The objects of a company do not need to be commercial; they can be charitable or philanthropic; indeed, they can be whatever the original incorporators wish, provided that they are legal. Nor is there any reason why a company should not part with its funds gratuitously or for non-commercial reasons if to do so is within its declared objects.

Counsel for the liquidator relies on the finding of Oliver J that there is no evidence that the company did or could derive any benefit or that the question was considered by anyone connected with the transaction. He says that the provision of the pension must accordingly be accepted as having been purely gratuitous, that is to say, a gift which could and did confer no consequent benefit on the company. Accepting this to have been the case, the transaction none the less falls, in my view, precisely within the scope of cl 3(o) and, in my judgment, the purposes referred to in that clause are such as to be capable of subsisting as substantive objects of the company and, having regard to the separate objects clause, must be so construed. For these reasons the liquidator fails, in my view, on the ultra vires point.

We were referred to a number of authorities in this connection, but I do not think that I need go through them in detail. Several of them were cases of implied powers.

Re George Newman & Co [1895] 1 Ch 674 was a case in which a director received what were in effect presents out of his company's funds or out of moneys borrowed by the company for the purposes of its business. There is no suggestion that the company was in any way expressly empowered to make such gifts. The company being insolvent, the shareholders were held incompetent to approve such gifts, even by unanimous approval. The director was accordingly held accountable to the company in a winding up. That case was quite different from the present case.

Re David Payne & Co Ltd, Young v David Payne & Co Ltd [1904] 2 Ch 608 was a case in which moneys were borrowed on mortgage under an express power to borrow, but for a purpose ultra vires the borrowing company. The company's liquidator sought a declaration that the mortgage was ultra vires. The lenders were held to have been ignorant of the proposed misapplication of the money. The mortgage was held to be a valid security as between the lenders and the company, the lenders being under no

obligation to inquire how the money was to be applied. Quite different considerations
arose from those which arise in the present case.

In *Ridge Securities Ltd v IRC* [1964] 1 All ER 275, [1964] 1 WLR 479 the plaintiff
company procured four associated companies to enter into onerous obligations to the
plaintiff for purposes unrelated to their own objects, which amounted to gratuitous
dispositions of large sums of money. Pennycuick J held these transactions to have been
ultra vires the four companies (see [1964] 1 All ER 275 at 287, [1964] 1 WLR 479 at 495).
That decision does not, in my view, assist in the present case.

In *Re W & M Roith Ltd* [1967] 1 All ER 427, [1967] 1 WLR 432 the controlling
shareholder and a director of the company, R, entered into a service agreement with the
company whereby he agreed to serve the company as general manager and director
throughout the remainder of his life at such salary as should be agreed between them
from time to time, to devote the whole of his time and abilities to the business of the
company, and to use his best endeavours to promote its interests. The company
covenanted that in the event of R's death during his retention of office the company
would pay his widow, if she should survive him, a pension of £1,040 per annum during
the remainder of her life. R was in poor health at the time, but was unaware that he had
a fatal disease. About two months later he died. Some four years later the company went
into liquidation. The widow proved for the value of the pension and the liquidator
rejected her proof. Plowman J upheld the liquidator's decision, drawing the inference
from the facts that really the whole object of the plan was to benefit, not the company,
but the widow. The company's memorandum of association included a paragraph
authorising the grant of a pension to any person who might have served the company or
its predecessors in business, or to the wife of any such person. The memorandum does
not appear to have included a separate objects clause. It was treated as common ground
that the tests enunciated by Eve J in *Re Lee, Behrens & Co Ltd* were applicable. It appears
from the judgment that there was no evidence of lack of good faith on the part of anyone
concerned, but the judge evidently took the view that the service agreement was a facade.
If the judge was justified in taking that view, and if the paragraph in the company's
memorandum of association relating to the grant of pensions ought to have been
construed merely as an ancillary power, Plowman J may have been justified in his
conclusion, but not, in my view, otherwise.

In *Charterbridge Corp Ltd v Lloyds Bank Ltd* [1969] 2 All ER 1185, [1970] Ch 62 a
company referred to as Castleford had created a legal charge on certain of its assets to
secure a guarantee of the liability of another company, referred to as Pomeroy, to Lloyds
Bank. Pomeroy and Castleford were companies comprised in a group of which Pomeroy
was the principal company; the other companies in the group, including Castleford,
were not subsidiaries of Pomeroy but had a common shareholding, directorate and
offices. The trade of the group was property development. Castleford's objects expressly
included—

> 'To secure or guarantee by mortgages, charges or otherwise the performance and
> discharge of any contract, obligation or liability of [Castleford] or of any other
> person or corporation with whom or which [Castleford] has dealings or having a
> business or undertaking in which [Castleford] is concerned or interested whether
> directly or indirectly.'

The memorandum of association included a separate objects clause. Castleford sold the
subject matter of the legal charge to the plaintiff company Charterbridge. The bank
sought to enforce the security and Charterbridge sued to establish the alleged invalidity
of the legal charge as having been ultra vires Castleford. Charterbridge contended (1)
that the guarantee and legal charge were created for purposes outside the scope of
Castleford's business, and (2) that the guarantee and legal charge were created for purposes
which were not for the benefit of Castleford. Pennycuick J held that the first of these
contentions failed (see [1969] 2 All ER 1185 at 1189, [1970] Ch 62 at 69). He then
proceeded to consider the second. In doing so he referred to Eve J's decision in *Re Lee,*

Behrens & Co Ltd. In the course of doing so he said that he thought that Eve J's third test
(viz, is the act done for the benefit and to promote the prosperity of the company?) was
quite inappropriate to the scope of express powers (see [1969] 2 All ER 1185 at 1191,
[1970] Ch 62 at 71). In that view I concur. Of course, if the memorandum of association
expressly or by implication provides that an express object only extends to acts which
benefit or promote the prosperity of the company, regard must be paid to that limitation;
but, where there is no such express or implied limitation, the question whether an act
done within the terms of an express object of the company will benefit or promote the
prosperity of the company or of its business is, in my view, irrelevant. In the present case
cl 3(o) contains no such express limitation, and I see no grounds for implying such a
limitation; the provision of the pension was within the terms of the clause, and
consequently it was, in my judgment, intra vires the company.

I now turn to the second head of counsel for the liquidator's argument, viz that the
purchase of the pension was effected by Mr Campbell-Dick and Mr Frank Horsley
without the authority of the board of directors or of the company in general meeting,
and was an act of misfeasance which was not validated as against the company's creditors
by virtue of the fact that Mr Campbell-Dick and Mr Frank Horsley were the only
shareholders. Ignoring for the moment that Mr Campbell-Dick and Mr Frank Horsley
were the only shareholders, the transaction in question was indeed carried out by them
without the sanction of any board resolution, whether antecedent, contemporary or by
way of subsequent ratification. It was an unauthorised act which they were, as two only
of the company's five directors, incompetent to carry out on the company's behalf. It
therefore cannot stand unless it has in some way been ratified. The question is whether
the fact that Mr Campbell-Dick and Mr Frank Horsley were the only shareholders of the
company has the effect of validating the transaction.

Counsel for the liquidator has submitted that there is a general duty incumbent on
directors of a company, whether properly described as owed to creditors or not, to
preserve the company's capital fund (which he identifies as those assets which are not
distributable by way of dividend) and not to dispose of it otherwise than for the benefit
or intended benefit of the company. He submits that creditors dealing with the company
are entitled to assume that directors will observe that duty; and that creditors, although
they are not entitled to interfere in the day-to-day management of a company which is
not in liquidation, are entitled through a liquidator to seek redress in respect of a breach
of the duty. Consequently counsel for the liquidator submits, the members of the
company cannot, even unanimously, deprive the creditors of any remedy so available to
them.

On this part of the case counsel for the liquidator mainly relies on *Re Exchange Banking
Co, Flitcroft's Case* (1882) 21 Ch D 519. In that case dividends were declared and paid at a
time when the directors of the company knew, but the shareholders did not know, that
there were no profits available out of which to pay them, with the consequence that the
dividends were paid out of contributed capital. The directors were held liable to repay to
the company the amounts distributed in dividends notwithstanding that the dividends
had been declared by resolutions of the company in general meeting. It was held that the
company in general meeting had not ratified the improper payment of the dividends
because the shareholders were ignorant of the circumstances which rendered the
dividends improper; but it was also held that, even if all the shareholders individually
had assented to the payments, this would not have relieved the directors from liability,
or have bound the company, because the payments were illegal and ultra vires the
company and so were incapable of ratification by the shareholders. The facts of that case
were very different from those of the present case and the principles applicable were, in
my opinion, also different. A company cannot legally repay contributed capital to the
contributors otherwise than by way of an authorised reduction of capital. Nothing of
that kind occurred in the present case. There is nothing in the statute or in the general
law which prevents a company or its directors expending contributed capital in doing
anything which is an authorised object of the company. In the present case the cost of

effecting the pension policy was, in my view, incurred in the course of carrying out an
express object of the company.

It is a misapprehension to suppose that the directors of a company owe a duty to the
company's creditors to keep the contributed capital of the company intact. The company's
creditors are entitled to assume that the company will not in any way repay any paid-up
share capital to the shareholders except by means of a duly authorised reduction of
capital. They are entitled to assume that the company's directors will conduct its affairs
in such a manner that no such unauthorised repayment will take place. It may be
somewhat loosely said that the directors owe an indirect duty to the creditors not to
permit any unlawful reduction of capital to occur, but I would regard it as more accurate
to say that the directors owe a duty to the company in this respect and that, if the
company is put into liquidation when paid-up capital has been improperly repaid, the
liquidator owes a duty to the creditors to enforce any right to repayment which is
available to the company. On the other hand, a company, and its directors acting on its
behalf, can quite properly expend contributed capital for any purpose which is intra vires
the company. As I have already indicated, the purchase of the pension policy was, in my
view, intra vires the company. It was not, however, within the powers of Mr Campbell-
Dick and Mr Frank Horsley acting not as members of the board of directors but as
individual directors. Unless the act was effectually ratified it cannot bind the company.
They were, however, the only two shareholders. A company is bound in a matter which
is intra vires the company by the unanimous agreement of its members (per Lord Davey
in *Salomon v Salomon & Co Ltd* [1897] AC 22 at 57, [1895–9] All ER Rep 33 at 51; and see
Re Express Engineering Works Ltd [1920] 1 Ch 466) even where that agreement is given
informally (see *Parker and Cooper Ltd v Reading* [1926] Ch 975, [1926] All ER Rep 323).
That both Mr Campbell-Dick and Mr Frank Horsley assented to the transaction in
question in the present case is beyond dispute. They both initialled the proposal form
and they both signed the cheques for the premiums. Their good faith has not been
impugned, nor, in my view, does the evidence support any suggestion that in effecting
the policy they did not honestly apply their minds to the question whether it was a fair
and proper thing for the company to do in the light of the company's financial state as
known to them at the time. In my judgment, their assent made the transaction binding
on the company and unassailable by the liquidator.

For these reasons this appeal in my view fails and should be dismissed.

CUMMING-BRUCE LJ (read by Buckley LJ). I agree with the reasons just given by
Buckley LJ for holding that the grant of a pension was within the powers of the company
whose memorandum gave an express and independent power in that regard. The third
test formulated by Eve J in *Re Lee, Behrens & Co Ltd* [1932] 2 Ch 46, [1932] All ER Rep
889 is not relevant to the exercise of a power expressly made an independent object on a
proper construction of the memorandum.

The ratification by the shareholders was effective unless the decision of the directors
was proved to have been misfeasance on their part. Their good faith was not questioned.
The evidence gives rise to suspicion that at the time of the decision by the directors and
of the purported ratification the company was not in a position to pay £10,000 to the
respondent. But that evidence fell far short of proof that the directors should at the time
have appreciated that the payment was likely to cause loss to creditors.

On these facts it is unnecessary to decide whether, had misfeasance by the directors
been proved, it was open to them in their capacity as shareholders to ratify their own
negligence and so to prejudice the claims of creditors. It would surprise me to find that
the law is to be so understood.

I agree that the appeal should be dismissed.

TEMPLEMAN LJ. I too agree that the appeal should be dismissed.

Clause 3(o) of the memorandum of association authorises the grant of a pension to a
director. Mr Horsley senior was a director. The pension was granted to him. The scope

of an object of a company as expressed in its memorandum must depend on the true construction of that memorandum read as a whole, but in view of the plain language of cl 3(o) I fail to understand how the grant of a pension to Mr Horsley senior could be ultra vires the company.

There remains the question whether the grant of the pension was in the circumstances a misfeasance committed by the two directors who procured the grant and by Mr Horsley senior, the director who accepted the grant. If the company had been doubtfully solvent at the date of the grant to the knowledge of the directors, the grant would have been both a misfeasance and a fraud on the creditors for which the directors would remain liable. But the good faith of the directors is not impugned.

In the absence of fraud there could still have been negligence on the part of the directors. If the company could not afford to spend £10,000 on the grant of a pension, having regard to problems of cash flow and profitability, it was negligent of the directors to pay out £10,000 for the benefit of Mr Horsley senior at that juncture. There could have been gross negligence, amounting to misfeasance. If the company could not afford to pay out £10,000 and was doubtfully solvent so that the expenditure threatened the continued existence of the company, the directors ought to have known the facts and ought at any rate to have postponed the grant of the pension until the financial position of the company was assured.

The findings of the judge are sufficient to support the suspicion that the company could not afford to pay out £10,000 for the benefit of Mr Horsley senior, but this suspicion is largely based on hindsight. The accounts show that business was expanding, that there were no discernible cash flow problems and that past profits were sufficient to absorb half of the payment for the pension, leaving the other half to be absorbed in the future. There seemed to be every indication that with the profits anticipated, and the possibility of reducing directors' salaries if necessary, the remainder of the payment for the pension could be absorbed by the company. In these circumstances it is difficult to convict the directors of negligence. It is impossible to convict them of gross negligence amounting to misfeasance because the allegation was never clearly levied, the directors were not even accused by the receiver and did not give evidence, and the judge therefore made no sufficient finding.

I would dismiss the appeal on the grounds that the payment was intra vires the company and on the grounds that misfeasance by the directors was not proved.

If, however, there had been evidence and a finding of misfeasance and it appeared that the payment of £10,000 in the event reduced the fund available for creditors by that sum, or by a substantial proportion of that sum, I am not satisfied that the directors convicted of such misfeasance, albeit with no fraudulent intent or action, could excuse themselves because two of them held all the issued shares in the company and as shareholders ratified their own gross negligence as directors which inflicted loss on creditors. I should be sorry to find the scope of s 333 of the Companies Act 1948 so restricted and need not do so on this occasion.

Appeal dismissed.

Solicitors: *Titmuss, Sainer & Webb* (for the liquidator); *Harry I Alkin & Co* (for the respondent).

Diana Procter   Barrister.

a   # Rolled Steel Products (Holdings) Ltd v British Steel Corp and others

CHANCERY DIVISION

VINELOTT J

9–13, 16–19, 23–26, 30, 31 MARCH, 1, 2, 6, 7 APRIL, 2 DECEMBER 1981

b

Company – Objects clause – Construction – Borrowing power declared as an object – Power to lend money and give guarantees – Company owing debt to second company which owed much larger debt to third party – Debt to third party personally guaranteed by director of company – Company giving guarantee of payment of debt owed to third party in return for loan to pay off its debt to second company – Company thereby assuming liability under guarantee for amount

c *greater than debt owed by it – Whether guarantee within company's objects clause – Whether guarantee given for unauthorised purpose – Whether guarantee should be set aside.*

The plaintiff was a company which carried on business as wholesalers of steel, mainly to motor vehicle manufacturers. The two directors were S and his father, S being the majority shareholder. Clause 3(k) of the company's memorandum of association

d empowered it to 'lend and advance money or give credit to such persons, firms or companies and on such terms as may seem expedient, and . . . to give guarantees or become security for any such persons, firms or companies'. S formed another company (SSS Ltd) in which he held all the shares, and on behalf of that company entered into an agreement with a steel producing company (C Ltd) for SSS Ltd to act as distributor of coil and cut steel for C Ltd. Under the agreement C Ltd agreed to supply SSS Ltd with coil

e and cut steel and SSS Ltd agreed to set up a steel service centre from which customers would be supplied. S arranged for the plaintiff company to set up the steel service centre with some £400,000 borrowed from SSS Ltd. The plaintiff company purchased a site (the Rainham site) for the centre but did not proceed with development there because of the cost and instead purchased another site where erection of the steel service centre was commenced. The plaintiff company meanwhile retained the Rainham site. SSS Ltd

f commenced purchasing coil and cut steel on credit from C Ltd. C Ltd was later taken over by the British Steel Corp (BSC). SSS Ltd's debt to C Ltd increased to a sum substantially in excess of its only significant asset, namely the loan from SSS Ltd to the plaintiff company, and C Ltd began to press for its debt to be reduced. When SSS Ltd failed to reduce the debt, BSC suggested that S execute a personal guarantee of SSS Ltd's debt to C Ltd, which then amounted to some £860,000. S accordingly entered into

g a guarantee but BSC then had doubts whether the combined assets of SSS Ltd and S under his personal guarantee were sufficient to cover the debt due to C Ltd. BSC accordingly desired to obtain a further guarantee of payment from the plaintiff company, which was known to have sufficient assets (including the Rainham site valued at £850,000) to meet the debt. As a result a scheme was devised whereby C Ltd agreed not to press SSS Ltd for repayment of the debt and further agreed to lend the plaintiff company the amount

h required to pay its debt to SSS Ltd (which SSS Ltd was in turn to repay to C Ltd) in return for the plaintiff company agreeing to guarantee the debt from SSS Ltd to C Ltd and to sell the Rainham site by a specified date and use the proceeds to repay the debt, failing which the plaintiff company would issue a debenture over all its assets in favour of C Ltd. A board meeting of the plaintiff company was held at which S and his co-director passed the necessary resolution approving and authorising the execution of the guarantee

j and debenture. Following the passing of the resolution and various payments by banker's draft, the debt owed to C Ltd was effectively passed from SSS Ltd to the plaintiff company, which executed a guarantee in favour of C Ltd. When the Rainham site was not sold by the specified date the plaintiff company executed a debenture in favour of C Ltd, and when a demand for repayment of the debt was not met C Ltd appointed a receiver under the debenture. The receiver eventually managed to sell the Rainham site for sufficient to pay to BSC the amount secured by the debenture and interest, the total payment being £1,148,078. However, after payment of other preferential debts there was insufficient left to meet the unsecured liabilities of the plaintiff company. In those circumstances the plaintiff company brought an action against, among others, BSC seeking a declaration that the guarantee and debenture were void and claiming repayment of the sum paid over to BSC by the receiver. The plaintiff company contended (i) that it had no capacity to enter into the scheme by which it guaranteed the debt due to C Ltd and therefore the guarantee and, to the extent of the sum guaranteed, debenture were ultra vires the plaintiff company, because the scheme was not for the benefit or purposes of the plaintiff company but for the benefit of both C Ltd (because it would obtain greater security for its debt) and S (because it was to be assumed that C Ltd would look to the plaintiff company for the satisfaction of its debt before looking to S under his personal guarantee), and (ii) alternatively, that the giving of the guarantee by the plaintiff was an improper exercise of its powers and ought to be set aside, since it was done by the directors of the plaintiff company in bad faith and in breach of their duties, and C Ltd and BSC were aware or ought to have been aware that it was an improper exercise of the plaintiff company's powers.

Held – (1) In construing the objects clause of a memorandum of association the stated objects were not to be construed independently. Instead, 'objects' properly so called, which stated the purposes which the company was authorised to pursue, were to be distinguished from objects which were merely powers to be exercised in the furtherance of those purposes and which either added to or possibly limited the powers which would otherwise be implied as being reasonably incidental to the substantive objects of the company. On the facts, cl 3(k) of the plaintiff company's memorandum of association empowering the company to lend money and give guarantees was not an independent object but merely a power ancillary to the objects of the company to be exercised when expedient in furtherance of those objects (see p 1075 g to j and p 1078 b c, post); dictum of Buckley LJ in *Re Horsley & Weight Ltd* [1982] 3 All ER at 1050–1051 followed.

(2) A transaction which, although within the scope of the express or implied powers of the company, was entered into in furtherance of a purpose which was not authorised by the memorandum of association could be described as being ultra vires the company, since the members were not entitled to authorise the use of the company's property for purposes other than those authorised by the memorandum of association and therefore a transaction for an unauthorised purpose was incapable of being made binding on the company even by the assent of all the members. However, in contrast to a transaction which was strictly ultra vires, a transaction for an unauthorised purpose could confer rights on a third party if the third party could show that he dealt with the company in good faith for valuable consideration without notice of the fact that the transaction, although ostensibly within the express or implied powers of the company, was entered into in furtherance of an unauthorised purpose (see p 1076 a to d and p 1077 c to e, post); dictum of Buckley J in *Re Introductions Ltd, Introductions Ltd v National Provincial Bank Ltd* [1968] 2 All ER at 1225 applied.

(3) On the issue, therefore, whether the guarantee and, to the extent of the sum guaranteed, the debenture were given by the plaintiff company in furtherance of its substantive objects or for an unauthorised purpose, an independent board would not have decided that it was in the plaintiff company's interest to enter into the transaction. Furthermore, the directors and advisers of the plaintiff company were aware that to the extent that the guarantee was for a liability which exceeded the amount of the debt due from the plaintiff company to SSS Ltd the guarantee amounted to a gratuitous disposition on the part of the plaintiff company which could not be justified as being for its purposes or in its interests, and the directors and advisers of the plaintiff company were further aware that the giving of the guarantee was an act of gross misfeasance by the directors. On the issue whether C Ltd and BSC had notice of that fact, the evidence was that their purpose in obtaining a personal guarantee from S was to put C Ltd in a position to exert pressure on S to arrange for the plaintiff company's assets to be made available for

payment of the debt owed by SSS Ltd to C Ltd, and that they were aware that the
a guarantee and the debenture amounted to a gratuitous disposition of the plaintiff
company's property for the benefit of SSS Ltd and S personally rather than the plaintiff
company itself. The plaintiff company was accordingly entitled to have the guarantee set
aside and the sum paid under it repaid by BSC with interest (see p 1087 *d*, p 1079 *e* to *h*,
p 1080 *b e f h*, p 1082 *h* and p 1085 *e f*, post).

Notes
b For general principles affecting powers and duties of directors, see 7 Halsbury's Laws (4th
edn) paras 496–510, for liabilities of directors, see ibid paras 516–527, and for cases on
the subject, see 9 Digest (Reissue) 490–494, 2927–2962.

For the meaning of 'ultra vires', see 7 Halsbury's Laws (4th edn) para 705, for acts ultra
vires a company, see ibid paras 706–708, and for cases on the power of companies in
regard to guarantees, see 9 Digest (Reissue) 682–683, 4058–4062.
c
Cases referred to in judgment
Allen v Gold Reefs of West Africa Ltd [1900] 1 Ch 656, [1900–3] All ER Rep 746, CA, 9
Digest (Reissue) 624, 3716.
Belmont Finance Corp v Williams Furniture Ltd (No 2) [1980] 1 All ER 393, CA.
Charterbridge Corp Ltd v Lloyds Bank Ltd [1969] 2 All ER 1185, [1970] Ch 62, [1969] 3
d WLR 122, 9 Digest (Reissue) 492, 2942.
Duomatic Ltd, Re [1969] 1 All ER 161, [1969] 2 Ch 365, [1969] 2 WLR 114, 9 Digest
(Reissue) 483, 2879.
Durham County Permanent Investment Land and Building Society, Re, Davis's Case (1871) LR
12 Eq 516, 7 Digest (Reissue) 507, 2876.
German Date Coffee Co, Re (1882) 20 Ch D 169, [1881–5] All ER Rep 372, CA, 9 Digest
e (Reissue) 75, 337.
Greenhalgh v Arderne Cinemas Ltd [1950] 2 All ER 1120, [1951] Ch 286, CA, 9 Digest
(Reissue) 610, 3639.
Halt Garage (1964) Ltd, Re (1978) [1982] 3 All ER 1016.
Hampson v Price's Patent Candle Co (1876) 45 LJ Ch 437, 10 Digest (Reissue) 1349, 8641.
Henderson v Bank of Australasia (1888) 40 Ch D 170, 9 Digest (Reissue) 582, 3468.
f *Horsley & Weight Ltd, Re* (1980) [1982] 3 All ER 1045, [1982] 3 WLR 431, CA.
Hutton v West Cork Rly Co (1883) 23 Ch D 654, CA, 9 Digest (Reissue) 685, 4077.
Imperial Mercantile Credit Association (liquidators) v Coleman (1873) LR 6 HL 189, 47 Digest
(Reissue) 483, 4342.
Introductions Ltd, Re, Introductions Ltd v National Provincial Bank Ltd [1968] 2 All ER 1221;
affd [1969] 1 All ER 887, [1970] Ch 199, [1969] 2 WLR 791, CA, 9 Digest (Reissue)
g 75, 336.
Jon Beauforte (London) Ltd, Re [1953] 1 All ER 634, [1953] Ch 131, [1953] 2 WLR 465, 10
Digest (Reissue) 1053, 6470.
Lee, Behrens & Co Ltd, Re [1932] 2 Ch 46, [1932] All ER Rep 889, 9 Digest (Reissue) 571,
3419.
Newman (George) & Co, Re [1895] 1 Ch 674, CA, 9 Digest (Reissue) 672, 4009.
h *North-West Transportation Co Ltd v Beatty* (1887) 12 App Cas 589, PC, 9 Digest (Reissue)
515, 3079.
Parke v Daily News Ltd [1962] 2 All ER 929, [1962] Ch 927, [1962] 3 WLR 566, 9 Digest
(Reissue) 690, 4097.
Payne (David) & Co Ltd, Re, Young v David Payne & Co Ltd [1904] 2 Ch 608, CA, 9 Digest
(Reissue) 511, 3058.
j *Ridge Securities Ltd v IRC* [1964] 1 All ER 275, [1964] 1 WLR 479, 28(1) Digest (Reissue)
178, 536.
Roith (W & M) Ltd, Re [1967] 1 All ER 427, [1967] 1 WLR 432, 9 Digest (Reissue) 571,
3420.
Royal British Bank v Turquand (1856) 6 E & B 327, [1843–60] All ER Rep 435, 119 ER 886,
Ex Ch, 9 Digest (Reissue) 91, 425.
Tomkinson v South-Eastern Rly Co (1887) 35 Ch D 675, 10 Digest (Reissue) 1349, 8639.

Wenlock (Baroness) v River Dee Co (1887) 10 App Cas 354, HL, 13 Digest (Reissue) 307, 2695.

Cases also cited

D'Arcy v Tamar, Kit Hill and Callington Rly Co (1867) LR 2 Ex 158.
De Bussche v Alt (1878) 8 Ch D 286, [1874–80] All ER Rep 1247, CA.
EBM Co Ltd v Dominion Bank [1937] 3 All ER 555, PC.
Morris v Kanssen [1946] 1 All ER 586, [1946] AC 459, HL.
Nelson v Larholt [1947] 2 All ER 751, [1948] 1 KB 339.
Simms, Re, ex p trustee [1934] Ch 1, [1933] All ER Rep 302, CA.
Smith (Howard) Ltd v Ampol Petroleum Ltd [1974] 1 All ER 1126, [1974] AC 821, PC.
Thompson v J Barke & Co (Caterers) Ltd 1975 SLT 67.
Transvaal Lands Co v New Belgium (Transvaal) Land and Development Co [1914] 2 Ch 488, CA.
Underwood (A L) Ltd v Bank of Liverpool and Martins [1924] 1 KB 775, [1924] All ER Rep 230, CA.

Consolidated actions

By a writ issued on 25 March 1975 and a statement of claim served on 31 December 1975 the plaintiff, Rolled Steel Products (Holdings) Ltd (RSP), brought an action against the defendants, British Steel Corp (BSC), Vivian Rupert Vaughan Cooper, the trustees of the property of Alexander Ilytch Shenkman (Mr Shenkman), a bankrupt, who had been adjudged bankrupt on 18 March 1970, and Ilya M Shenkman, seeking inter alia, (1) as against BSC and Mr Cooper, a declaration that a guarantee dated 22 January 1969 made between RSP and Colvilles Ltd (Colvilles), a company engaged in the production of steel whose property rights, liabilities and obligations were now vested in BSC, and a debenture granted by RSP to Colvilles pursuant to the guarantee, and the purported appointment on 2 April 1969 by Colvilles of Mr Cooper as receiver and manager of the property charged by the debenture, was in each case void and of no effect, (2) payment to RSP of £1,148,078·15 as money had and received to the use of RSP, with interest, (3) alternatively, against all the defendants, a declaration that BSC, Mr Cooper, Mr Ilya Shenkman and Mr Shenkman were jointly and severally liable to repay to RSP with interest thereon the sum of £1,148,078·15 as moneys of the plaintiffs RSP which had been misapplied, (4) an order (a) in the case of BSC, Mr Cooper and Ilya Shenkman, for payment and (b) in the case of Mr Shenkman, leave to prove in the bankruptcy for such sum as he might be declared liable to repay to RSP. By their defence served on 2 March 1976, BSC and Mr Cooper, inter alia, denied that the execution of the guarantee and debenture was of no effect, that Mr Cooper's appointment was void and of no effect, and that RSP was entitled to the relief claimed or any relief. The fourth defendant, Mr Ilya Shenkman died in 1976 and his personal representatives, the fifth defendant, Olga Shenkman, and the sixth defendant, Gregory Alexander Shenkman, were added as defendants by order to carry on dated 18 January 1977 but took no part in the proceedings. The third defendant also took no part in the proceedings but agreed to be bound by any order that was made.

On 11 December 1976 RSP issued a writ against the trustee in bankruptcy of Mr Shenkman seeking similar relief. By order dated 3 November 1977 the two actions were consolidated, it being ordered that the plaintiff should be the plaintiff and the defendants the defendants in the consolidated action, and the statement of claim served on 31 December 1975 should stand as the statement of claim in the consolidation.

RSP was incorporated on 27 September 1954 under the Companies Act 1948 as a company limited by shares and at all material times its memorandum of association empowered it by art 3(k): 'To lend and advance money or give credit to such persons, firms, or companies and on such terms as may seem expedient, and in particular to customers of and others having dealings with the Company, and to give guarantees or

become security for any such persons, firms, or companies.' The articles of association
a provided:

'17. Provided the Director declares his interest in a contract or arrangement or
proposed contract or arrangement with the Company in manner provided by
Section 199 of the Act he shall be counted in the quorum at any meeting of Directors
at which the same is considered and shall be entitled as a Director in respect thereof.
b 18(a). *Proceedings of directors.* The quorum necessary for the transaction of the
business of the Directors may be fixed by the Directors, and unless so fixed, shall be
two . . .'

The facts are set out in the judgment of Vinelott J.

Andrew Morritt QC and *Charles Aldous* for RSP.
c *Allan Heyman QC* and *Eben Hamilton* for the defendants.

Cur adv vult

2 December. **VINELOTT J** read the following judgment: On 22 January 1969 the
d plaintiff in these consolidated actions, Rolled Steel Products (Holdings) Ltd (RSP),
executed or purportedly executed two documents. By the first document (the guarantee)
it was recited that another company, Scottish Steel Sheet Ltd (SSS), owed Colvilles Ltd
(Colvilles) the sum of £383,084 15s 4d and RSP thereby guaranteed to Colvilles the
repayment by SSS of all moneys and liabilities then due or becoming due to Colvilles by
SSS. By the second document (the agreement) it was recited that RSP was indebted to
e Colvilles in the sum of £401,448 and that RSP had guaranteed the debt of £383,084 15s 4d
due from SSS to Colvilles and RSP thereby agreed that unless it had before 17 February
1969 entered into a binding contract for the sale of the freehold interest in certain land
owned by it at Rainham in Essex for a sum, which after discharging any existing charges,
would leave the sum of £784,532 15s 4d (the aggregate of the sums owed to Colvilles by
RSP and SSS) with interest and unless all the sums due from RSP and SSS to Colvilles had
f been paid before 1 March 1969 it would issue to Colvilles a debenture in the form of an
annexed draft. The agreement and the debenture provided for interest to be paid on the
aggregate sum of £784,532 15s 4d at 1% above bank rate for the time being. The land
referred to in the agreement was not sold before 17 February 1969 and on that date a
debenture in the terms of the agreed draft (which had also been executed on 22 January
and delivered to RSP's solicitors as an escrow) was delivered to Colvilles. Colvilles
g appointed a receiver under powers conferred by the debenture on 2 April 1969. By virtue
of the Steel Companies (Vesting) Order 1970, SI 1970/430, the British Steel Corp (BSC)
succeeded on 29 March 1970 to all the assets and obligations of Colvilles. Between the
appointment of the receiver and 31 December 1973 the receiver received in respect of
property of RSP and paid to BSC in discharge of the moneys secured by the debenture
(including interest) sums amounting in the aggregate to £1,005,347. In addition the
h receiver accounted to the Inland Revenue for the sum of £92,731·15 in respect of tax
deducted from interest paid to BSC making, with the £1,005,347 paid to Colvilles, a total
of £1,098,078. He retained the sum of £50,000 in respect of his fees and expenses as
receiver and manager. The balance of the moneys received by the receiver in respect of
property of RSP charged by the debenture (which created a fixed and floating charge
over all the assets of RSP) are insufficient to meet other unsecured liabilities of RSP.
j Before outlining the claims made in these consolidated actions an explanation of the
origin of the debt secured by the debenture and of the relationship between RSP and SSS
is necessary. At all material times a Mr Alexander Ilytch Shenkman (Mr Shenkman)
owned the entire issued share capital of SSS. He also held 51% of the issued share capital
of RSP. The remaining 49% of the issued share capital of RSP was held by the trustees of
a settlement made by Mr Shenkman for the benefit of his children. In April 1968 SSS

owed Colvilles and certain subsidiaries of Colvilles substantial sums which it was believed exceeded £800,000 in the aggregate although the precise amount was in dispute. On 2 May 1968 Mr Shenkman executed a guarantee whereby he guaranteed the payment to Colvilles and its subsidiaries of all moneys then due or becoming due from SSS. It was provided that payment should be made by Mr Shenkman within 90 days after notice by Colvilles and that interest would be paid at 1% above bank rate from the expiry of any notice calling for payment of the debt or part thereof, but that the total payable by virtue of any notice or notices given before 1 August 1968 was not to exceed £400,000. By 22 January 1969 notices had been given calling on Mr Shenkman to pay the whole of the indebtedness of SSS. On 22 January 1969 the total liability of SSS to Colvilles had been agreed to be £784,532 15s 4d. In April 1968 RSP owed SSS a substantial sum then thought to be approximately £360,000 but which was later agreed to be £401,448. The sum owed by RSP to SSS did not carry interest.

On 22 January there was a meeting of the board of directors of RSP attended by its only directors, who were Mr Shenkman and his father, Mr Ilya Michael Shenkman (Mr Ilya Shenkman). Mr Ilya Shenkman was also the secretary of RSP. The articles of association of RSP provided, by art 17, that, if a director declared his interest in a proposed contract or arrangement in accordance with s 199 of the Companies Act 1948, he should be counted in the quorum at any meeting of the directors at which the proposed contract or arrangement was considered and entitled to vote as a director in respect of it. The articles of association also fixed, by art 18(a), the quorum necessary for the transaction of the business of the directors at two. The minutes of the meeting of the directors of RSP on 22 January 1969 record that it had been reported to the board that RSP had agreed with Colvilles, first, that, 'in consideration of Colvilles not demanding immediate repayment of all sums due to it from' SSS, RSP could guarantee SSS's liability to Colvilles and, second, that Colvilles had agreed to advance £401,448 to SSS. Engrossments of the guarantee, the agreement and the debenture were then put before the directors. The minutes record a resolution that the transactions reported to the board be approved and that the documents put before the board be approved and executed by RSP as to the guarantee of the agreement for delivery to Colvilles on receipt of the advance and as to the debenture to be held in escrow for delivery in the circumstances described in the agreement.

On the same day, an account was opened with Midland Bank Ltd, RSP's bankers, in the name of its solicitors, Messrs Montague Cox & Cardales, entitled 'Re Rolled Steel' and a bankers draft for £401,448 drawn on Colvilles was paid into that account. That sum was immediately transferred to an account also with Midland Bank as bankers to SSS in the name of Messrs Montague Cox & Cardales, the account being entitled 'Re Scottish Steel'. A bankers draft was drawn on that account in favour of Messrs Lovell, White & King, who were Colvilles's solicitors. The guarantee and the agreement were then delivered to them.

It was clearly for Mr Shenkman's benefit that transactions approved at the meeting of the board should be approved. In particular the advance of £401,448 to RSP, which, under arrangements already made, could only be used to discharge the liability of RSP to SSS and in turn could only be used by SSS towards payment of the sum owed by SSS to Colvilles, would indirectly reduce Mr Shenkman's liability under the guarantee of 2 May 1968. However, the minutes of the meeting of the board of directors of RSP do not record any declaration or disclosure by Mr Shenkman of this guarantee.

The first claim in these consolidated actions is that no such declaration or disclosure was in fact made by Mr Shenkman, that in consequence he was not entitled to vote on the resolutions purportedly passed at that meeting and that accordingly the meeting of the board was inquorate. On that footing no authority was given by the board for the acceptance of the advance by Colvilles or for the execution by RSP of the guarantee, the agreement and the debenture. Thus RSP claim against BSC and Mr Vivian Rupert Vaughan Cooper, the receiver appointed under the debenture (who is the second defendant), that RSP is now entitled at its election either to recover from BSC and the

receiver all sums received by the receiver in respect of property of RSP with interest as
a moneys had and received to the use of RSP or to recover damages from the receiver for
trespass and conversion. In his opening counsel for RSP elected to claim on the footing
of money had and received.

The second claim is that the guarantee and the debenture, if only authorised by RSP,
were ultra vires and void. The ground of this claim set out in the statement of claim is
that the guarantee and the debenture were not made for the purposes or for the benefit
b of RSP but for the purposes and for the benefit of Mr Shenkman, SSS and Colvilles. In his
opening counsel for RSP made it clear that, if the first claim failed, there could be no
objection to the advance by Colvilles to RSP of the sum of £401,448 or to the use of that
money to discharge the debt owed by RSP to SSS and that on that footing the debenture
(and in consequence the appointment of the receiver thereunder) would be valid to the
extent of that advance.

c In the alternative it is said that, if the guarantee and the debenture was not ultra vires,
none the less the giving of the guarantee was and was known by Colvilles and the receiver
to have been an act done in bad faith and in breach of the duties of the directors of RSP
(being something done to the detriment of RSP and for the purposes and benefit of Mr
Shenkman, SSS and Colvilles) and that the guarantee and (to the extent of the sum
guaranteed) the debenture ought to be set aside and the sum of £383,084 15s 4d repaid
d to RSP with interest.

The defendants to these claims, in addition to BSC and the receiver, are the trustee in
bankruptcy of Mr Shenkman (who was adjudicated bankrupt on 18 March 1970) and the
personal representatives of Mr Ilya Shenkman (who died in 1976). Neither the trustee in
bankruptcy of Mr Shenkman nor the personal representatives of Mr Ilya Shenkman have
taken any part in these proceedings, though the trustee in bankruptcy of Mr Shenkman
e has agreed to be bound by any order which is made. An order for the compulsory
winding up of SSS was made on 16 March 1970. The assets of SSS are wholly insufficient
to meet its liabilities even if the potential liability to BSC is disregarded. An order for the
compulsory winding up of RSP was made on 29 October 1973. Its liabilities, apart from
any liability to RSC or SSS, amount to approximately £373,000. Of this sum £250,000
is owed to the Inland Revenue, which is a preferential creditor.

f [His Lordship then dealt with the background and the relationship between Mr
Shenkman and Colvilles. He said that RSP had been formed in 1954 by Mr Shenkman
and its business was the importation and sale of steel in the United Kingdom. Its main
customers were motor manufacturing companies, in particular the Ford Motor Co. In
July 1961 RSP approached Colvilles, a company engaged in the production of steel, with
a proposal that SSS, which had been formed by Mr Shenkman for the purpose, would act
g as sole distributor in Southern England of coil and cut steel sheet produced by Colvilles.
Mr Shenkman planned to develop a steel service centre, which SSS would operate and
Colvilles would supply with coil in standard guages. The centre would supply the
customer. RSP acquired a site for the steel centre at Rainham, Essex, but its erection
there was not proceeded with because it proved too costly. Instead in 1964 RSP acquired
a site at Andover and began to build the new steel service centre there with moneys
h borrowed from SSS amounting to £401,448. The centre was to be operated by a company
formed for the purpose.

Meanwhile SSS's business with Fords increased, with the result that the amount
outstanding by SSS to Colvilles on credit terms also increased. By the middle of 1966 the
sums owed by SSS to Colvilles had increased to about £500,000. Between 1961 and 1966
SSS incurred losses on a merchanting and stockholding business of over £200,000. The
j account of SSS with Colvilles fell into arrears and in October 1966 Mr Shenkman agreed
that the amount owed by SSS would be reduced to and kept below £400,000 overdue,
that is as additional to any sums in respect of which SSS was entitled to credit. In July
1967 Colvilles was renationalised and its shares vested in BSC. In November 1967 it
became clear that the new steel centre would not be completed until July 1968 at the
earliest. Colvilles became increasingly concerned at the delay and the continuing

indebtedness of SSS, which in November amounted to £820,000, £420,000 of which
was overdue. Colvilles began to press SSS to reduce its indebtedness. In December 1967 *a*
Mr Shenkman was told that the arrangements by which the sheet steel was sold through
SSS would be terminated and in future Colvilles would sell to Fords direct and he must
take immediate steps to reduce the indebtedness of SSS to £400,000 and to produce a
programme for the elimination of the balance after 60 days' credit had expired. Once the
Ford arrangements came to an end SSS would have no income until the new steel service
centre became operative. Mr Shenkman made proposals for the repayment of the debt *b*
of SSS but they were not acceptable to Colvilles. He also promised to reduce the
indebtedness to £400,000 by 10 April, but the promised reduction did not materialise.
Colvilles reported the position to the legal services department of BSC. Mr Edwards, the
head of the department, decided that the best solution for Colvilles and BSC would be to
persuade Mr Shenkman to execute an immediate and binding guarantee of the whole
indebtedness of SSS, which at that time was of the order of £860,000. Mr Shenkman *c*
calculated that the realisation of the assets held by RSP and of his personal assets would
raise some £810,000. On 2 May 1968 he signed the guarantee. When he executed the
guarantee he mistakenly believed that Colvilles and BSC, though not prepared to enter
into a legally binding commitment, had agreed that if SSS's debt could be reduced to
£400,000 within the near future they would not press for the balance of £400,000 until
the steel service centre was in full operation, and he was confident that he could reduce *d*
the debt to £400,000.

On 17 May 1968 Colvilles served on SSS a statutory demand for payment of the sum
of £868,875 1s 2d then claimed to be due from SSS, the purpose of which was to enable
Colvilles to take advantage of s 222 of the Companies Act 1948 should it be deemed
necessary. Meanwhile, it became apparent to BSC that Mr Shenkman's 51% interest in
RSP, together with other assets, was insufficient to meet the debt due from SSS. It was *e*
decided to seek a compulsory winding-up order unless Mr Shenkman would come to
some arrangement for the voluntary winding up of SSS and the payment off of Colvilles's
debt. A meeting was arranged for 11 September 1968 to reappraise the whole approach
to the problem of the repayment of the debt owing to Colvilles. Shortly before the
meeting it occurred to Mr Hands (the assistant to Mr Edwards in the legal services
department of BSC) that the solution was to persuade Mr Shenkman to procure RSP to *f*
guarantee the debt due from SSS and on 4 September he wrote to Mr Shenton, a partner
in Messrs Lovell White & King, BSC's solicitors, and explained that BSC had it in mind
to propose to Mr Shenkman's advisors that BSC would agree to the liquidator not
pursuing his claim against RSP on terms that RSP would guarantee SSS's debt, the debt if
necessary to be phased over an agreed period. The only significant asset of SSS was the
debt due to it from RSP and RSP had assets sufficient to meet that debt. After consulting *g*
counsel, Mr Arthur Figgis, Mr Shenton pointed out that, if SSS was put into liquidation,
the liquidator could not enter into an arrangement with RSP under which RSP guaranteed
the debt to Colvilles unless Colvilles was prepared to ensure that all other creditors of SSS
were paid in full. He put forward an alternative proposal, namely, that Colvilles should
offer to defer the presentation of a petition for the winding up of SSS in consideration of
a guarantee by RSP of an amount in excess of the £360,000 then thought to be owed by *h*
RSP to SSS, the excess over the amount of the debt being justified as the price of BSC's
forbearance in relation to SSS, which would benefit RSP inasmuch as it would gain time
in which to realise its assets without pressure from a liquidator of SSS. At the meeting of
11 September this proposal was put to Mr Dyson of Messrs Montague Cox & Cardales,
Mr Shenkman's solicitors, and it was explained to him that the consideration for the
giving of the guarantee was the forbearance of Colvilles from taking steps to place SSS in *j*
liquidation during the period of the repayment programme. Mr Shenton again consulted
Mr Figgis, who confirmed Mr Shenton's advice that if SSS were put into liquidation it
would not be open to the liquidator to obtain a guarantee of the kind contemplated.
With respect to the validity of the guarantee, Mr Figgis advised that it would be within
the powers conferred by RSP's memorandum of association to give a guarantee even for
a sum larger than the debt owed by RSP to SSS on the ground that it was in RSP's interests

that Colvilles should hold its hand against SSS provided that the sum guaranteed should

a not be so large as to make plain that RSP could not meet its obligations under the guarantee and pay its other creditors 20s in the pound. Mr Figgis added that he did not think that the directors of RSP would be advised by their legal advisers to grant a guarantee considerably in excess of the debt due to SSS and suggested that the guarantee should be limited to £400,000, ie £40,000 more than the debt then thought to be owed by RSP to SSS. The reason he recommended a limit of £400,000 being placed on the

b guarantee was that that appeared to be the limit of RSP's excess of assets over liabilities on the basis of the information he had been given as to the value of the Rainham land. He was concerned about inducing RSP to give a guarantee of such an amount as would clearly have the effect of making its liabilities exceed its assets. He added that what he was concerned with was that BSC should not be a party to inducing RSP's directors to do that which on the figures known to BSC it would be a breach of RSP's directors duty to

c do.

On 9 October 1968 Mr Edwards wrote to Mr Dyson stating that he could only advise Colvilles to refrain from taking immediate action if the following three conditions were complied with: (1) prompt payment was to be made on the due dates (17 October and 17 November) of the two sums of £100,000 which had been claimed from Mr Shenkman under his guarantee; (2) the giving by RSP before 17 November of a guarantee by RSP of

d the full amount owing by SSS with a limit to liability of £400,000, payments to be made at a minimum rate of £50,000 per month starting on 17 December but on the footing that claims for the same amounts would also be made against Mr Shenkman under his guarantee and that, if he paid, RSP would not be expected to pay as well; and (3) a nominee of Colvilles should be appointed to the board of RSP within one week after, but not before, the giving of the guarantee by the company. Various meetings took place

e and Mr Dyson in the mean time sought the advice of Mr A J Balcombe QC whether RSP could properly enter into the guarantee. Mr Dyson reported to Mr Hands the advice he had been given by Mr Balcombe, namely that for RSP to give a guarantee of a debt in an amount in excess of the amount owed by RSP to SSS would be an act of gross misfeasance on the part of the directors of RSP and that RSP could properly give a guarantee not in excess of the amount it owed to SSS provided that RSP was given some consideration

f which could only be the imposition of a timetable for payment under the guarantee. Mr Dyson also reported that Mr Balcombe had expressed surprise at the suggestion that the appointment of a director nominated by BSC to the board of RSP should be deferred until after the guarantee had been given.

On 13 November 1968 Colvilles obtained summary judgment under RSC Ord 14 against Mr Shenkman for £100,000 which was then due on 17 October. On 21

g November it gave Mr Shenkman notice to pay the balance of approximately £485,000 due from SSS, after taking into account the three sums of £100,000 called for under the earlier demands. A further writ was issued against Mr Shenkman for the payment of the £100,000 then due on 18 November and Colvilles also issued a bankruptcy notice against him. On 28 November Messrs Foster & Cranfield valued the Rainham land and advised that it would not be unreasonable to anticipate obtaining a price in the region of

h £850,000 for the freehold interest. If that sum could be obtained by sale before the end of January 1969 RSP would be in a position to pay off the debt it owed to SSS before any effective steps could be taken by a liquidator of SSS to launch a petition for the winding up of RSP and would be left with ample money to finance the completion of the steel service centre at Andover. A scheme was considered whereby Mr Shenkman would sell his shares in SSS to RSP at par, RSP would repay its debt to SSS and guarantee the balance

j of the debt due from SSS to Colvilles, RSP would sell its lease of the Andover factory for full value and RSP would then be put into liquidation, and in that liquidation the assets would be so distributed that the trustees of the settlement to the scheme would get the proceeds of sale of the Andover lease and the shares of SSS, while Mr Shenkman received the benefit of the debt of £400,000 due from SSS to RSP against which would be set off his debt of £200,000 to SSS.

The scheme could not be put into operation in the time available but the trustees decided to give their consent to the execution of the guarantee in exchange for an indemnity by Mr Shenkman secured by a charge on his shares of RSP. On 22 January *a* 1979 there was a board meeting of RSP at which its two directors (Mr Shenkman and Mr Ilya Shenkman) passed a resolution approving the execution of the guarantee and debenture. The Rainham land had not been sold when on 14 February 1969 a debenture creating a floating charge over all the assets of RSP was delivered to Colvilles under which Colvilles was entitled to give notice demanding immediate payment of the moneys thereby secured on or after 1 April and if the moneys were not paid to appoint a receiver. *b*

A demand was made on 12 March for a payment on 1 April of the full amount secured by the debenture and on the same day a writ was issued by Colvilles against Mr Shenkman claiming the balance of the sum due under his guarantee which was followed by an application for summary judgment under RSC Ord 14 on 25 March. On 2 April Mr Cooper the second defendant was appointed receiver and manager of RSP. Shortly after 14 November a bankruptcy notice was served on Mr Shenkman, who was adjudicated *c* bankrupt on 8 March 1970. After protracted efforts the receiver sold the Rainham land in October 1972 for £1,025,000. His accounts showed receipts totalling £1,281,660 (including £122,500 for the lease of the Andover factory) out of which he paid Colvilles £858,772 capital and £239,306 interest and after other payments including his remuneration of £50,000 he accounted to the liquidator of RSP for the surplus of £47,778. *d*

His Lordship then examined the claims made in the proceedings and dealt with the argument addressed to him on the validity of the resolution passed at the board meeting of 22 January 1969, which was challenged on the ground that Mr Shenkman had not declared the nature of his interest in the proposed transaction in compliance with s 199 of the 1948 Act, and accordingly, by art 17, was not entitled to be counted in the quorum at the meeting. His Lordship having considered *Imperial Mercantile Credit Association* *e* *(liquidators) v Coleman* (1873) LR 6 HL 189 held that there was no sufficient evidence that Mr Shenkman had made a declaration of his interest as required by art 17, that he was accordingly not entitled to vote on the resolution put to the meeting of the directors of RSP on 22 January 1969, and that the resolution was accordingly not validly passed, there being no quorum. His Lordship also gave leave for an amendment to raise the defence that Colvilles was entitled to assume that the resolution had been passed at a properly *f* constituted meeting of the directors of RSP at which a proper disclosure of Mr Shenkman's interest had been made and that RSC was entitled (under the rule in *Royal British Bank v Turquand* (1856) 6 E & B 357, [1843–60] All ER Rep 435) to rely on that defence, and continued:]

Ultra vires   *g*

In para 11 of the statement of claim it is alleged that the arrangements constituted by the transactions and documents specified in paras 6 and 7 [ie the loan by Colvilles to RSP of £401,448 and the authorisation of the guarantee and debenture by the directors of RSP] 'were made not for the purposes or benefit of RSP but for the purposes and benefit of Mr Shenkman and Colvilles and were not and could not have seemed to be expedient in the interests of RSP'. It is claimed that the guarantee and, to the extent of the sum *h* guaranteed, the debenture were accordingly ultra vires. It is claimed in the alternative that the borrowing of £401,448 and the execution of the guarantee and the debenture were acts done in bad faith and in breach of Mr Shenkman's and Mr Ilya Shenkman's respective duties as directors and that Colvilles and that the receiver knew or ought to have known that the borrowing and the execution of the guarantee and the debenture were acts done otherwise than for the benefit of RSP and in bad faith and in breach of the *j* directors' duties. As I have said, the claim that the borrowing of £401,448 and its subsequent application in paying off RSP's indebtedness to SSS was ultra vires or an act done in bad faith and in breach of the directors' duties was not pursued at the hearing and it is accepted that the debenture was a valid security to the extent of this sum.

In support of the first claim, counsel for RSP relied mainly on the decision of the Court

of Appeal in *Re Introductions Ltd, Introductions Ltd v National Provincial Bank Ltd* [1969] 1
a All ER 887, [1970] Ch 199, confirming the decision of Buckley J ([1968] 2 All ER 1221).
Counsel for the defendants relied mainly on the decision of Pennycuick J in *Charterbridge
Corp v Lloyds Bank Ltd* [1969] 2 All ER 1185, [1970] Ch 62. The decision of Buckley J in
Re Introductions Ltd had been reported when Pennycuick J decided *Charterbridge*. The
decision of Pennycuick J in *Charterbridge* was given on 5 November 1968 and had not
been reported when the decision of the Court of Appeal in *Re Introductions Ltd* was given
b on 28 January 1969.

In *Re Introductions Ltd* the company's principal object was the provision of
entertainments services and facilities for foreign visitors. It had an express power in its
memorandum of association to borrow or raise money in such manner as it should think
fit and the objects clause in the memorandum of association included a common form
declaration that each sub-clause of the clause setting out the objects of the company
c should be construed independently of and be in no way limited by reference to any other
sub-clause and that the objects set out in each sub-clause were independent objects of the
company. The company's business came to an end in 1958. Thereafter there was a change
of control and in 1960 the company embarked on a new business, that of pig breeding
which was not a business it was authorised to carry on. The company's bank account
became overdrawn in 1961 and it gave the bank debentures on its assets to secure the
d overdraft. The bank was fully aware that the only business of the company was that of
pig breeding. Buckley J held that the debentures were ultra vires and void. He said
([1968] 2 All ER 1221 at 1225):

> 'Where a company incorporated under the Companies Act, 1948, has the power
> to borrow, that fact must be discovered from its memorandum of association. The
e > power may be one which has to be inferred from the objects of the company, or it
> may be one that is expressly conferred on the company by the terms of its
> memorandum. If the power to borrow is one which is inferred, it naturally follows
> that the borrowing is only within the power of the company in relation to those
> matters in respect of which the inference arises. Where the memorandum is one in
> which those sub-clauses of the objects clause, which confer what are truly powers
f > rather than objects, are to be read as subsidiary to the main and real objects of the
> company, in such a case also the borrowing power must be read as confined to
> borrowing for the purposes for which the company is formed. Moreover, borrowing
> for any purpose other than the legitimate activities of the company will be ultra
> vires, and if the lender is aware of the circumstances which render the borrowing
> ultra vires he will be unable to recover the moneys as moneys lent.'

g He went on to observe that the separate objects clause was incapable of elevating what
was in truth a power ancillary to the purposes which the company was authorised to
pursue into an independent object which the company could carry on as its sole activity.
As I have said, that decision was confirmed in the Court of Appeal. I do not propose to
recite extensively from the judgments of the Court of Appeal. Harman LJ said ([1969] 1
All ER 887 at 889, [1970] Ch 199 at 210):
h

> 'It was argued that the only obligation of the defendant bank was to satisfy itself
> that there was an express power to borrow money and that this power was converted
> into an object by the concluding words [of the objects clause] which I have read. It
> was said that if this was so not only need the defendant bank enquire no further but
> they were unaffected by the knowledge that they had that the activity on which the
j > money was to be spent was one beyond the company's powers. The judge rejected
> this view, and I agree with him. He based his judgment I think, on the view that a
> power or an object conferred on a company to borrow cannot mean something in
> the air: borrowing is not an end in itself and must be for some purpose of the
> company; and as this borrowing was for an ultra vires purpose that is an end of the
> matter.'

Russell LJ said ([1969] 1 All ER 889 at 890, [1970] Ch 199 at 211):

'If the borrowing clause had expressly stated that it did not include borrowing for *a* use in an undertaking ultra vires the company, it would have been plainly unarguable that the defendant bank's security was valid, the bank being fully aware that the borrowing was only for use in the pig-breeding business and being at least deemed to be aware that such business was wholly ultra vires the company. But in every borrowing clause that which I have stated as having been expressly stated is implicit, whether or not the objects clause contains the proviso that is contained *b* here. Putting the matter round the other way, supposing the borrowing clause had purported expressly to include borrowing for use in a business ultra vires the company, no lender could conceivably rely upon such a provision, which would have to be ignored as mere nonsense.'

Charterbridge Corp v Lloyds Bank Ltd concerned a legal charge granted by a company *c* referred to in the judgment as 'Castleford'. The main object of Castleford was to acquire land for investment. It had power under its memorandum of association—

'To secure or guarantee by mortgages, charges or otherwise the performance and discharge of any contract, obligation or liability of [Castleford] or of any other person or corporation with whom or which [Castleford] has dealings or having a business or undertaking in which [Castleford] is concerned or interested whether *d* directly or indirectly.'

The objects clause in the memorandum of association also included a common form separate objects clause.

In 1961 Castleford guaranteed the overdraft of another company referred to in the judgment as 'Pomeroy'. Castleford and Pomeroy were members of the same group, *e* Pomeroy standing at the head of the group, in that, in conjunction with a number of other companies, they had a common shareholding, directorate and office. But Castleford was not a subsidiary of Pomeroy. In March 1962 Castleford gave a legal charge over leasehold property which it owned, subject to a mortgage in favour of another company in the group, to secure its indebtedness to its bank including any indebtedness arising under the guarantee it had given in favour of Pomeroy. The evidence of a Mr Pomeroy, *f* accepted by Pennycuick J, was that in causing Castleford to enter into the guarantee and the legal charge he and the officer at the bank concerned—

'looked to the group as a whole. They believed the transactions to be proper ones. They likewise did not at the time of the transactions take into consideration the interest of Castleford separately from that of the group.'

g

The claim by the plaintiff company which had purchased Castleford's leasehold property was that the guarantee and the charges were ultra vires. The claim was formulated under two heads. The first was that the guarantee and charge were created for purposes outside the scope of Castleford's business; the second was that the guarantee and charge were created for purposes which were not for the benefit of Castleford. As regards the first head, Pennycuick J said at ([1969] 2 All ER 1185 at 1190, [1970] Ch 62 at 69): *h*

'But where as here a company is carrying on the purposes authorised by its memorandum and a transaction is effected pursuant to an express power conferred by the memorandum, counsel for the plaintiff company found difficulty in attaching any significant meaning to the expression "purposes outside the scope of Castleford's business" in the first head. He suggested as alternatives: (i) not for the purpose of *j* carrying on Castleford's business; (ii) not reasonably connected with Castleford's business; and (iii) not done for the benefit of and to promote prosperity of Castleford. But (i) is tautology; (ii) could not be asserted on the facts of the present case; and (iii) is a paraphrase of the second head. I think I need to say no more about the first head.'

He went on to consider the second head, which was founded on the decision of Eve J in
a the well-known case of *Re Lee, Behrens & Co Ltd* [1932] 2 Ch 46, [1932] All ER Rep 889.
In that case the memorandum of association of the company authorised the directors to
provide for the welfare of employees and their widows and children. Pursuant to a
resolution of the directors, the company entered into a deed of covenant granting a
pension to the widow of a former director payable for five years after his death. In the
liquidation of the company the liquidator rejected a proof of the value of the annuity
b first on the grounds that the grant of the annuity was ultra vires the company and,
alternatively, on the ground that it could only be authorised by the company in general
meeting. The widow, of course, was not an object of the power to provide for the welfare
of employees and their widows.

Eve J said ([1932] 2 Ch 46 at 51–52, [1932] All ER Rep 889 at 890–891):

c
> 'It is not contended, nor in the face of a number of the authorities to the contrary
> effect could it be, that an arrangement of this nature for rewarding long and faithful
> service on the part of the persons employed by the company is not within the power
> of an ordinary trading company such as this company was, and indeed, in the
> company's memorandum of association is contained (clause 3) an express power to
> provide for the welfare of persons in the employment of the company or formerly
d
> in its employment, and the widows and children of such persons and others
> dependent upon them by granting money or pensions, providing schools, reading
> rooms or places of recreation, subscribing to sick or benefit clubs or societies or
> otherwise as the company may think fit. But whether they be made under an
> express or implied power, all such grants involve an expenditure of the company's
> money, and that money can only be spent for purposes reasonably incidental to the
> carrying on of the company's business, and the validity of such grants is to be tested,
e
> as is shown in all the authorities, by the answers to three pertinent questions: (i) Is
> the transaction reasonably incidental to the carrying on of the company's business?
> (ii) Is it a bona fide transaction? (iii) Is it done for the benefit and to promote the
> prosperity of the company? Authority for each of the foregoing propositions is to
> be found in the following cases: *Hampson* v. *Price's Patent Candle Co.* ((1876) 45 LJ
> Ch 437); *Hutton* v. *West Cork Ry. Co.* ((1883) 23 Ch D 654); and *Henderson* v. *Bank of*
f
> *Australasia* ((1888) 40 Ch D 170):

Eve J concluded ([1932] 2 Ch 46 at 52, [1932] All ER Rep 889 at 891) that the evidence
pointed irresistibly to the conclusion that—

> 'the predominant, if not the only, considerations operating in the minds of the
> directors was a desire to provide for the applicant, and that the question what, if
g > any, benefit would accrue to the company never presented itself to their minds.'

He accordingly upheld the liquidator's rejection of the proof. But he added ([1932] 2 Ch
46 at 53, [1932] All ER Rep 889 at 891):

> 'The alternative of getting authority from the shareholders at a meeting duly
h
> convened for the purpose was never thought of, or, if thought of, was dismissed as
> superfluous, inasmuch as the shares were in the hands of so few, and so far as was
> known nobody was likely to object.'

In *Charterbridge* Pennycuick J, having referred to the first passage from the judgment
of Eve J which I have cited, said ([1969] 2 All ER 1185 at 1191, [1970] Ch 62 at 70):

j
> 'It seems to me, on the best consideration I can give to this passage, that the
> learned judge must have been directing his mind to both the issues raised by the
> liquidator, without differentiating them. In truth (i), the first of the three pertinent
> questions which he raises, is probably appropriate to the scope of the implied powers
> of a company where there is no express power. Question (ii) is appropriate in part
> again to the scope of implied powers, and in part, and perhaps principally, to the

duty of directors. Question (iii) is, I think, quite inappropriate to the scope of express
powers, and notwithstanding the words "whether they be made under an express or
implied power" at the beginning of the paragraph, I doubt very much whether the
judge really intended to apply this last question to express powers. None of the cases
cited by him ([1932] 2 Ch 46 at 52, [1932] All ER Rep 889 at 891) supports such an
application. If he did so intend, his statement is obiter and with great diffidence I
do not feel bound to follow it. Finally, I would observe that the whole passage
([1932] 2 Ch 52 at 53, [1932] All ER Rep 889 at 891) proceeds on the footing that
the transaction might have been ratified, which would not be possible if it had been
ultra vires the company.'

He distinguished the decision of Buckley J in *Re Introductions Ltd* on the ground that
the observations of Buckley J to which I have referred were—

'directed to the particular case before him, where the company was not carrying
on any authorised business, and he held that the power to borrow was not a power
which could subsist in isolation from the business. That case, I think, throws no
light on the position where, as here, the company concerned is carrying on a business
authorised by its memorandum'.

(See [1969] 2 All ER 1185 at 1193, [1970] Ch 62 at 73.) He also distinguished his own
decision in *Ridge Securities Ltd v IRC* [1964] 1 All ER 275, [1964] 1 WLR 479 on the
footing that the transaction which he held ultra vires in that case amounted to no more
than a 'dressed-up gift of a large sum by certain companies to another company which
had acquired their shares'. He accordingly rejected the claim under the second head and
concluded that the state of mind of the directors of Castleford and of the bank's officers
was irrelevant on the issue of ultra vires. He added, though it was unnecessary in view of
his conclusion as to the law, that a director of Castleford taking an objective view in the
exclusive interest of Castleford at the date of the guarantee could reasonably have
concluded that the transaction was for the benefit of Castleford. The ground of that
conclusion was that the collapse of Pomeroy which was threatened by demands from the
bank would have been a disaster for Castleford since although it would have remained
solvent and could have realised the value of its land it would have been deprived of the
opportunity of developing and realising the land at the most favourable price in
conjunction with the group.

The decisions in *Re Introductions Ltd* and *Charterbridge* have been considered in two
subsequent cases. They are, first, the decision of Oliver J in *Re Halt Garage (1964) Ltd*
(1978) [1982] 3 All ER 1016 and, second, the decision of the Court of Appeal, affirming
a decision of Oliver J, in *Re Horsley & Weight Ltd* (1980), [1982] 3 All ER 1045, [1982] 3
WLR 431.

Re Halt Garage (1964) Ltd concerned a claim made by the liquidator of a company,
which was being compulsorily wound up, to recover remuneration paid to the directors
of the company, a Mr and Mrs Charlesworth, in the accounting years (which ended on
30 May) 1967–68, 1968–69, 1969–70 and 1970–71. The application was made under s
333 of the Companies Act 1948. Mr and Mrs Charlesworth were the only shareholders
of the company. The remuneration paid to them as directors for the years 1967–68 and
1968–69 had been approved by the company in general meeting and it was conceded by
the liquidator that, in the light of *Re Duomatic Ltd* [1969] 1 All ER 161, [1969] 2 Ch 365,
the remuneration paid in the last two years also fell to be treated as if it had been
sanctioned by the company in general meeting. In the year 1967–68 the company traded
at a loss but it had a reserve on profit and loss account distributable as dividend greater
than the remuneration paid in that year. In the year 1968–69 and subsequent years there
was a deficit on profit and loss account even after taking into account the reserve on profit
and loss account for the earlier years and, accordingly, the sums paid to the directors by
way of remuneration in those years could not be treated as paid out of moneys which, if
the remuneration had not been paid, could have been distributed to Mr and Mrs
Charlesworth by way of dividend. It was conceded by counsel who appeared for the

a liquidator that while a company 'has divisible profits remuneration may be paid on any scale which the shareholders are prepared to sanction within the limits of available profits'. The question was whether the remuneration paid in the last three years, when there were no distributable profits, to the extent that it exceeded reasonable remuneration, could be recovered by the liquidator. The proposition contended for by the liquidator was that any disposition of a company's assets made otherwise than for full consideration was invalid unless the disposition satisfied the test set out in the judgment of Eve J in *Re*

b *Lee, Behrens & Co Ltd* [1932] 2 Ch 46, [1932] All ER Rep 889 and that, to the extent that the disposition was made otherwise than out of the profits available for distribution by way of dividend, the invalidity could not be cured by the sanction of the company in general meeting. I should mention that the company's articles incorporated reg 76 of Part 1 of Table A in Sch 1 to the Companies Act 1948.

The judgment of Oliver J contains an exhaustive review of the decisions cited by Eve J

c in the *Lee, Behrens & Co* case, of the cases in which the decision in the *Lee, Behrens & Co* case has been followed, in particular *Parke v Daily News Ltd* [1962] 2 All ER 929, [1962] 1 Ch 927, *Re W & M Roith Ltd* [1967] 1 All ER 427, [1967] 1 WLR 43 and *Ridge Securities Ltd v IRC* [1964] 1 All ER 275, [1964] 1 WLR 479 and of *Re Introductions Ltd* and *Charterbridge*. He summarised his conclusions in these terms ([1982] 3 All ER 1016 at 1034–1035):

d
'I must therefore attempt, although I do so with some unease, some analysis of what I conceive to be the principles which underlie the cases. Part of the difficulty, I think, arises from the fact that Eve J in *Re Lee, Behrens & Co* combined together, in the context of an inquiry as to the effective exercise of directors' powers, two different concepts which have since been regarded as a single composite test of the corporate entity's capacity. In fact, however, as it seems to me at any rate, only one

e of the three tests postulated in *Lee, Behrens & Co* is truly applicable to that question. The court will clearly not imply a power, even if potentially beneficial to the comany, if it is not reasonably incidental to the company's business (see *Tomkinson v South-Eastern Rly Co* (1887) 35 Ch D 675) and express powers are to be construed as if they were subject to that limitation (see *Re Introductions Ltd*, particularly the judgment of Russell LJ ([1969] 1 All ER 887 at 890, [1970] Ch 199 at 211). But the

f test of bona fides and benefit to the company seems to me to be appropriate, and really only appropriate, to the question of the propriety of an exercise of a power rather than the capacity to exercise it. The cases really divide into two groups: those such as *Hampson v Price's Patent Candle Co, Hutton's* case, *Henderson v Bank of Australasia* and *Parke v Daily News Ltd*, where the question was not so much that of the company's capacity to do a particular act as that of the extent to which a majority

g in general meeting could force a particular measure on a dissentient minority; and those such as *Lee, Behrens & Co* itself, *Re W & M Roith Ltd, Ridge Securities v IRC* and the *Charterbridge* case, where the question was as to the validity of an exercise of the powers, express or implied, by directors. Although the test of benefit to the company was applied in both groups of cases, I am not at all sure that the phrase "the benefit of the company" was being employed in quite the same sense in each. In the latter

h group, where what was in question was whether an exercise of powers by directors was effective, the benefit regarded seems to have been that of the company as a corporate entity (see the phrase "to promote the prosperity of the company") whereas in the former it was, I think, used in the same sense as that in which it was used in the line of cases dealing with, for instance, the power of the majority to alter the articles of association.'

j
Then after citing from *Allen v Gold Reefs of West Africa Ltd* [1900] 1 Ch 656 at 671, [1900–3] All ER Rep 746 at 749 and *Greenhalgh v Arderne Cinemas Ltd* [1950] 2 All ER 1120 at 1126, [1951] Ch 286 at 291, he continued:

'In my judgment the true rationale of this group of cases is not that what was proposed was ultra vires in the sense that it could not be confirmed by a general

meeting where there was no dissentient minority, but that they were concerned
with a very different question, namely the circumstances in which the court will   *a*
interfere to prevent a majority from overriding the rights of a dissentient minority
to have the company's property administered in accordance with its constitution. I
think that, in truth, neither group properly falls to be regarded as exemplifying
applications of the ultra vires doctrine. Both, as it seems to me, more properly
belong to the sphere of abuse of power, and part of the confusion has, I think, arisen
from the fact that in *Hutton's* case, which contains the classical judgment of Bowen   *b*
LJ always cited in this context, the determination of the question of the majority's
power to bind the minority did, because the affairs of the company were being
conducted under, and only under, the provisions of a special Act conferring very
limited powers, necessarily also involve a consideration of the extent of those powers,
which was, indeed, a true ultra vires question.'

Later, having pointed out that there is no rule that directors' remuneration is payable   *c*
only out of divisible profits, he stated his conclusion as to the application of the principles
he had explained to the payment of remuneration in the following terms (at 1039):

> 'I do not think that in circumstances such as those in the instant case the
> authorities compel the application to the express power of a test of benefit to the
> company which, certainly construed as Plowman J held that it should be construed,   *d*
> would be largely meaningless. The real test must, I think, be whether the transaction
> in question was a genuine exercise of the power. The motive is more important
> than the label. Those who deal with a limited company do so on the basis that its
> affairs will be conducted in accordance with its constitution, one of the express
> incidents of which is that the directors may be paid remuneration. Subject to that,
> they are entitled to have the capital kept intact. They have to accept the shareholders'   *e*
> assessment of the scale of that remuneration, but they are entitled to assume that,
> whether liberal or illiberal, what is paid is genuinely remuneration and that the
> power is not used as a cloak for making payments out of capital to the shareholders
> as such. It may well be that one way of ascertaining the true nature of the payment
> made in purported exercise of such an express power is by subjecting it to the three
> tests postulated in the *Lee, Behrens & Co* case, but it cannot, I think, be conclusive   *f*
> that the court, looking at the matter with hindsight, concludes that a particular
> application was not beneficial to the company as a corporate entity or that the
> shareholders in considering it did not have that in mind. If benefit in that sense
> were the conclusive test, it is difficult to see how the directors in *Hutton v West Cork
> Rly Co* (1883) 23 Ch D 654 could have been paid for their past services in connection
> with the winding up. Such a payment, as I have pointed out, could not have been of   *g*
> any possible benefit to the company which was in the course of winding up. Yet
> both Cotton and Bowen LJJ clearly contemplated that this could quite properly be
> paid.'

This last sentence is a reference to the last paragraph of the judgment of Bowen LJ in
the *Hutton* case (1883) 23 Ch D 654 at 678, as to which Oliver J had earlier observed that
it showed that Bowen LJ—   *h*

> 'clearly contemplated that there was nothing necessarily improper or wrong with
> paying reasonable remuneration, albeit it could not be said to be for the benefit of
> the company, since the business at that time was defunct and the services which the
> directors had rendered were past.'

(See [1982] 3 All ER 1016 at 1028.)   *j*

Turning to the facts of that case Oliver J held that the payments to Mr Charlesworth
were not so blatantly excessive or unreasonable as to compel the conclusion that the
payments were not really remuneration but gratuitous distributions to a shareholder out
of capital dressed up as remuneration. As regards the payments to Mrs Charlesworth

(who in the last three years was so seriously ill that 'she was able to contribute nothing to
a the company's prosperity beyond, perhaps, the occasional discussion with her husband
and the formal signature of documents' (see [1982] 3 All ER 1016 at 1021)) he held that
payments in excess of a modest weekly sum could not be regarded 'as being anything
more than disguised gifts out of capital' (see [1982] 3 All ER 1016 at 1044). He therefore
held that the liquidator succeeded to that extent.

In *Re Horsley & Weight Ltd* [1982] 3 All ER 1045, [1982] 3 WLR 431 the liquidator of
b a company which was in compulsory liquidation claimed under s 333 that the respondent
held a retirement pension policy, which had been effected by the company with Hambro
Life Assurance Ltd, on trust for the company. The respondent had been a director of the
company although at the material time a director in name only, his position being
substantially that of an employee. At the material time there were four other directors, a
Mr Campbell-Dick, a Mr Frank Horsley, and their respective wives; Mr Campbell-Dick
c and Mr Frank Horsley were the only shareholders. Shortly before the respondent attained
65 he was introduced to a representative of the insurance company. Mr Campbell-Dick
told the respondent that, having regard to his intending retirement and his long service,
the directors had decided to purchase a retirement pension policy for him. The
representative of the insurance company produced a form which the respondent and Mr
Campbell-Dick signed. The company gave the representative of the insurance company
d a cheque for £10,000, being a single premium of £9,000 and a single annual premium
of £1,000. The objects of the company set out in its memorandum of association
included a paragraph in the following terms:

> '(c) To grant pensions to employees and ex-employees and directors and ex-
> directors or other officers or ex-officers of the company, their widows, children and
> dependants, and to subscribe to benevolent and other funds for the benefit of any
e > such persons and to subscribe to or assist in the promotion of any charitable
> benevolent or public purpose or object.'

The objects clause also contained a common form of separate objects clause.

The liquidator's case was that the policy was procured to be taken out in circumstances
of misfeasance and breach of trust by the directors and that the respondent had at the
f time or at the date of the proceedings knowledge of such misfeasance and breach of trust
and held the policy in trust for the company. Buckley LJ said ([1982] 3 All ER 1045 at
1050–1051, [1982] 3 WLR 431 at 437):

> 'It has now long been a common practice to set out in memoranda of association
> a great number and variety of "objects" so called, some of which (for example, to
> borrow money, to promote the company's interests by advertising its products or
g > services, or to do acts or things conducive or incidental to the company's objects) are
> by their very nature incapable of standing as independent objects which can be
> pursued in isolation as the sole activity of the company. Such "objects" must, by
> reason of their very nature, be interpreted merely as powers incidental to the true
> objects of the company and must be so treated notwithstanding the presence of a
> separate objects clause: see *Re Introductions Ltd, Introductions Ltd v National Provincial
h > Bank Ltd* [1969] 1 All ER 887, [1970] Ch 199. Where there is no separate objects
> clause, some of the express "objects" may on construction fall to be treated as no
> more than powers which are ancillary to the dominant or main objects of the
> company: see, for example, *Re German Date Coffee Co* (1882) 20 Ch D 169, [1881–5]
> All ER Rep 372. Ex hypothesi an implied power can only legitimately be used in a
> way which is ancillary or incidental to the pursuit of an authorised object of the
j > company, for it is the practical need to imply the power in order to enable the
> company effectively to pursue its authorised objects which justifies the implication
> of the power. So an exercise of an implied power can only be intra vires the company
> if it is ancillary or incidental to the pursuit of an authorised object. So also, in the
> case of express "objects" which, on construction of the memorandum or by their

very nature, are ancillary to the dominant or main objects of the company, an exercise of any such power can only be intra vires if it is in fact ancillary or incidental to the pursuit of some such dominant or main object. On the other hand, the doing of an act which is expressed to be, and is capable of being, an independent object of the company cannot be ultra vires, for it is by definition something which the company is formed to do and so must be intra vires. I shall use the term "substantive object" to describe such an object of a company.'

Then, having referred to the passage in the judgment of Eve J in *Re Lee, Behrens & Co Ltd* which I have cited, he said ([1982] 3 All ER 1045 at 1052, [1982] 3 WLR 431 at 438–439):

'Clause 3(o) must be read as a whole. It includes not only pensions and other disbursements which will benefit directors, employees and their dependants, but also making grants for charitable, benevolent or public purposes or objects. The objects of a company do not need to be commercial; they can be charitable or philanthropic; indeed, they can be whatever the original incorporators wish, provided that they are legal. Nor is there any reason why a company should not part with its funds gratuitously or for non-commercial reasons if to do so is within its declared objects. Counsel for the liquidator relies on the finding of Oliver J that there is no evidence that the company did or could derive any benefit or that the question was considered by anyone connected with the transaction. He says that the provision of the pension must accordingly be accepted as having been purely gratuitous, that is to say, a gift which could and did confer no consequent benefit on the company. Accepting this to have been the case, the transaction none the less falls, in my view, precisely within the scope of cl 3(o) and, in my judgment, the purposes referred to in that clause are such as to be capable of subsisting as substantive objects of the company and, having regard to the separate objects clause, must be so construed. For these reasons the liquidator fail, in my view, on the ultra vires point.'

As regards the decision of Plowman J in *Re W & M Roith Ltd* [1967] 1 All ER 427, [1967] 1 WLR 43 Buckley LJ said ([1982] 3 All ER 1045 at 1053, [1982] 3 WLR 431 at 440):

'It appears from the judgment that there was no evidence of lack of good faith on the part of anyone concerned, but the judge evidently took the view that the service agreement was a facade. If the judge was justified in taking that view, and if the paragraph in the company's memorandum of association relating to the grant of pensions ought to have been construed merely as an ancillary power, Plowman J may have been justified in his conclusion, but not, in my view, otherwise.'

Buckley LJ then went on to cite without disapproval the decision of Pennycuick J in *Charterbridge Corp Ltd v Lloyds Bank Ltd* [1969] 2 All ER 1185, [1970] Ch 62 and expressly affirmed the view expressed by Pennycuick J that Eve J's third test was inappropriate to the scope of express powers. He continued ([1982] 3 All ER 1045 at 1054, [1982] 3 WLR 431 at 440–441):

'Of course, if the memorandum of association expressly or by implication provides that an express object only extends to acts which benefit or promote the prosperity of the company, regard must be paid to the limitation; but, where there is no such express or implied limitation, the question whether an act done within the terms of an express object of the company will benefit or promote the prosperity of the company or of its business is, in my view, irrelevant. In the present case cl 3(o) contains no such express limitation, and I see no grounds for implying such a limitation; the provision of the pension was within the terms of the clause, and consequently it was, in my judgment, intra vires the company.'

He then turned to the liquidator's alternative argument that the purchase of the pension was effected by Mr Campbell-Dick and Mr Frank Horsley without the authority of the

board or of the company in general meeting. He pointed out that the transaction, having
been carried out without the sanction of a board resolution, could not stand unless
ratified; he turned to consider the further submission by the liquidator—

> 'that there is a general duty incumbent on directors of a company, whether
> properly described as owed to creditors or not, to preserve the company's capital
> fund (which he identifies as those assets which are not distributable by way of
> dividend) and not to dispose of it otherwise than for the benefit or intended benefit
> of the company.'

Buckley LJ held ([1982] 3 All ER 1045 at 1054, [1982] 3 WLR 431 at 441–442):

> 'There was nothing in the statute or in the general law which prevents a company
> or its directors expending contributed capital in doing anything which is an
> authorised object of the company.'

He accordingly held that as Mr Campbell-Dick and Mr Frank Horsley were the only
shareholders their assent made the transaction binding on the company and unassailable
by the liquidator. Cumming-Bruce LJ agreed with the judgment of Buckley LJ, as did
Templeman LJ. I need only mention one point in those judgments. Templeman LJ
questioned whether:

> 'If the company had been doubtfully solvent at the date of the grant to the
> knowledge of the directors, the grant would have been both a misfeasance and a
> fraud on the creditors for which the directors would remain liable ... If the
> company could not afford to pay out £10,000 and was doubtfully solvent so that the
> expenditure threatened the continued existence of the company, the directors ought
> to have known the fact and ought at any rate to have postponed the grant of the
> pension until the financial position of the company was assured.'

(See [1982] 3 All ER 1045 at 1056, [1982] 3 WLR 431 at 443.)
He concluded on the evidence that it was impossible to convict the directors of 'gross
negligence amounting to misfeasance' but concluded ([1982] 3 All ER 1045 at 1056,
[1982] 3 WLR 431 at 443–444):

> 'If, however, there had been evidence and a finding of misfeasance and it appeared
> that the payment of £10,000 in the event reduced the fund available for creditors
> by that sum, or by a substantial proportion of that sum, I am not satisfied that the
> directors convicted of such misfeasance, albeit with no fraudulent intent or action,
> could excuse themselves because two of them held all the issued shares in the
> company and as shareholders ratified their own gross negligence as directors which
> inflicted loss on creditors.'

Before turning to the detailed arguments which have been addressed to me, I should
make three observations on these authorities. First, in *Re Horsley & Weight Ltd,* Buckley
LJ stressed the distinction (which he had drawn in *Re Introductions Ltd*) between 'objects'
properly so called which state the purposes which a company is authorised to pursue and
provisions which though described as 'objects' can be seen on construction of the
memorandum of association as a whole and notwithstanding a 'separate objects clause' to
be powers to be exercised in the furtherance of those purposes and which add to, or may
in some circumstances, limit the powers that would otherwise be implied as reasonably
incidental to them. The question whether a stated 'object' is truly an independent object
or purpose is always a question of construction. Even borrowing and lending moneys are
activities capable of being pursued as independent objects, for instance, in the case of a
bank or finance company; but commonly, where a sub-clause of the memorandum of
association of a company states that one of the objects of the company is 'to lend or
advance' or 'to borrow and raise' money it is artificial to construe the sub-clause as
anything other than a power conferred for the furtherance of what are in truth its
'substantive objects' or purposes. That may be so notwithstanding that the memorandum
of association includes a separate objects clause.

The second observation is that the phrase 'ultra vires' is used, even in cases where what is in question is the capacity of a company to enter into a given transaction and not the extent of the powers of the directors or of the power of a majority of the shareholders to bind the minority, in a narrow and in a wider sense. It is used in a narrow sense to describe a transaction which is outside the scope of the powers expressed in the memorandum of association of a company or which can be implied as reasonably incidental to the furtherance of the objects thereby authorised. For instance, an express power to borrow may, on construction of a memorandum of association or of the Act of Parliament governing the purposes and powers of a company, be found to restrict and not enlarge the power of borrowing that would otherwise be implied. A borrowing in excess of the stated limit will then be ultra vires the company in this narrow sense (see *Baroness Wenlock v River Dee Co* (1885) 10 App Cas 354). The phrase 'ultra vires' is also used to describe a transaction which, although it falls within the scope of the powers of a company, express or implied, is entered into in furtherance of some purpose which is not an authorised purpose. Buckley J, in the passage I have cited from his judgment in *Re Introductions Ltd*, described a borrowing which prima facie fell within the scope of the express powers conferred by the memorandum of association of the company but which was made for an unauthorised purpose as ultra vires. Oliver J, in *Re Halt Garage (1964) Ltd* [1982] 3 All ER 1016 at 1030, expressed doubt whether such a transaction should not properly be classified as an abuse of power rather than as an ultra vires transaction and commented that it does not follow that 'because a power must not be abused, therefore, beyond the limits of propriety it does not exist'. This approach is, I think, consistent with a decision of the Court of Appeal in *Re Introductions Ltd* where Harman and Russell LJJ refer to the borrowing as 'made for the purposes of an ultra vires business' but do not describe the borrowing itself as ultra vires. It is also supported by the decision of the Court of Appeal in *Re David Payne & Co Ltd, Young v David Payne & Co Ltd* [1904] 2 Ch 608. In that case a company borrowed money from another company for a purpose outside the scope of its authorised business but the lender company did not know the purpose for which the moneys were borrowed. Buckley J said (at 612): 'A corporation cannot do anything except for the purposes of its business, borrowing or anything else; everything else is beyond its power, and is ultra vires'. This observation taken in isolation suggests that a borrowing, even under an express power, otherwise than for the purposes of the company's authorised business is ultra vires. But Buckley J continued (at 613):

'If this borrowing was made, as it appears to me at present it was made, for a purpose illegitimate so far as the borrowing company was concerned, that may very well be a matter on which rights may arise as between the shareholders and directors of that company. It may have been a wrongful act on the part of the directors. But I do not think that a person who lends to the company is by any words such as these required to investigate whether the money borrowed is borrowed for a proper purpose or an improper purpose. The borrowing being affected, and the money passing to the company, the subsequent application of the money is a matter in which the directors may have acted wrongly; but that does not affect the principal act, which is the borrowing of the money . . . I think here the power to borrow was a power resting in the directors.'

Pennycuick J in *Charterbridge* found it difficult to reconcile these two passages. He pointed out that in the Court of Appeal Vaughan Williams LJ distinguished the transaction in that case from a transaction that 'was ultra vires altogether', such as a borrowing in excess of the amount authorised by an express power and disapproved the decision in *Re Durham County Permanent Investment, Land and Building Society, Davis's Case* (1871) LR 12 Eq 516 in so far as that case suggested that a borrowing within the powers of a company is invalid and the security a nullity if there is an intention on the part of the borrowing company to apply the moneys for an improper purpose, although the lending company has no knowledge of that intention. The Court of Appeal affirmed the decision of Buckley J that a lender lending money to a company which has a general *a*   power to borrow is not bound to inquire into the purpose for which the money is intended to be applied and that the misapplication of the money does not avoid the loan in the absence of knowledge on the part of the lender that the money was intended to be misapplied. The explanation of the apparent inconsistency in the judgment of Buckley J in *Re David Payne & Co Ltd* is, I think, that in the first of the passages I have cited he was using the words 'ultra vires' in this wider sense. That is, I think, also the sense in which Roxburgh J described the transaction in question in *Re Jon Beauforte (London) Ltd* [1953] 1

b   All ER 634 at 635, [1953] Ch 131 at 135 as 'ultra vires'. For he specifically left open the question what the position would have been if the third party dealing with the company had not had clear notice that goods supplied to the company were not required for any authorised purpose of the company.

   The reason why a transaction which is within the powers, express or implied, of a company but which is entered into for a purpose which is not authorised by its memorandum of association is equated with one which is ultra vires in the narrow sense

c   is, I think, that such a transaction like a transaction which is ultra vires in the narrow sense is incapable of being made binding on the company even by the assent of all the members. The members cannot authorise the use of the company's property for a purpose other than the purposes which the company is authorised to pursue by its memorandum of association. The difference between a transaction which is ultra vires

d   in the narrow sense and one which is ultra vires in the wider sense is, of course, that a transaction which is ultra vires in the narrow sense is altogether void and cannot confer rights on third parties whereas a transaction which is ultra vires in the wider sense may confer rights on a third party who can show that he dealt with the company in good faith and for valuable consideration and did not have notice of the fact that the transaction, while ostensibly within the powers, express or implied, of the company, was entered into

e   in furtherance of a purpose which was not an authorised purpose. But in the past the distinction has only been of practical importance in those cases where a third party dealing with a company in good faith and for value has been able to show that he did not have notice of the purpose for which the transaction was entered into by the company and the distinction is of even less practical importance now that, under s 9(1) of the European Communities Act 1972, a transaction decided on by the directors of a company

f   is to be treated in favour of a third party dealing with the company in good faith as within the capacity of the company.

   Thirdly, it is now clear in the light of *Charterbridge, Re Halt Garage Ltd* and *Re Horsley & Weight Ltd* that the answer to the question whether a disposition of the property of a company was made for the benefit and to promote the prosperity of the company, though directly relevant to the question whether that disposition if made by the directors without the sanction of the company in general meeting was either an excess or abuse of

g   their powers, is not conclusive nor always even relevant to the question whether the disposition was ultra vires the company whether in the narrow or the wider sense. In particular it may be within the power of a company to make a gratuitous disposition of its property which is not calculated to confer any indirect benefit on the company. Thus, if a company has power in general meeting to 'vote' remuneration to its directors in

h   respect of a past period it can validly resolve to pay remuneration even if at the time of the resolution the company's business has come to an end (as in *Hutton v West Cork Rly Co* (1883) 23 Ch D 654) so that the payment cannot be said to have been made to promote the prosperity of the company; and a gratuitous payment may also be authorised by a specific provision in the memorandum of association if, on construction, the provision falls to be construed otherwise than as a power conferred for the furtherance of its

j   commercial purposes (as in *Re Horsley & Weight Ltd*). On the other hand, if a transaction is entered into in purported reliance on a provision in the memorandum of association of a company which on construction can be seen to be a power conferred for the furtherance of the company's commercial objects, the question whether the transaction was ultra vires in the wider sense as being an abuse of the power, and the question whether the transaction was entered into for the benefit and to promote the prosperity of the company in large measure overlap if they do not coincide. It is difficult to see how a transaction apparently within the scope of such a power but which was clearly detrimental to the company's commercial interests could be said to be one entered into in pursuance of its commercial purposes.

Turning to the present case I have already referred to cl 3(k) of the memorandum of association of RSP. Counsel for RSP submitted that the effect of the words 'as may seem expedient', like the limit on the power of borrowing in *Baroness Wenlock v River Dee Co*, limits the scope of the power and that a transaction apparently within the scope of the power but which could not be considered expedient in the interests of the company is ultra vires in the narrow sense. It is not, to my mind, clear that the words 'as may seem expedient' do govern the last part of sub-cl (k) 'to give guarantees or become a security for any such persons, firms or companies'. But I think that counsel's submission is open to the more fundamental objection that if the words 'as may seem expedient' are construed as governing and qualifying the power conferred by sub-cl (k) they do not limit the scope of the power, but make clear what might otherwise be open to doubt that, notwithstanding the separate objects provision at the end of cl 3, sub-cl (k) is a power ancillary to and to be exercised when expedient in furtherance of the objects of the company and is not to be construed as an independent object.

The main question, therefore, which I have to consider is whether the guarantee and, to the extent of the sum guaranteed, the debenture were given by RSP in furtherance of the objects of RSP, in the sense of its substantive objects or purposes, or for some purpose not authorised by the memorandum of association of RSP; and, if the latter is the case, whether Colvilles and BSC had notice of that fact.

The first submission of counsel for the defendants was that RSP entered into the arrangements and executed the documents resolved on at the meeting of the directors on 22 January in order to obtain time for RSP to sell the land at Rainham in an orderly way and to avoid the risk that Colvilles would present a petition for the winding up of SSS, that in due course the liquidator of SSS would present a petition for the winding up of RSP and that RSP would be unable to realise sufficient moneys to pay its debt to SSS in time to avoid a compulsory winding up. On the facts of this case, that submission seems to me quite unreal. Even if the validity of the transactions is judged by reference to the situation on 19 December 1968 (when Mr Dyson in a telephone conversation with Mr Hoare of Messrs Lovell, White & King told him that the proposals in Mr Shenton's letter of 17 December were acceptable) rather than on 22 January, the position then was that RSP had been advised by no less than four experienced estate agents that the land at Rainham was worth more than double the debt owed by RSP to SSS and although, at an earlier stage, the agents then concerned had advised that the realisation of the full value of the Rainham land might take some time, by the end of November Mr Dyson had had the advice of Messrs Foster & Cranfield that the land might be expected to realise £850,000 if sold by tender with a closing date at 30 January (later extended to 12 February). Instructions to sell the land by tender had been given to Fosters and their associate firm Alsop & Co. Everyone concerned expected that the sale by tender would produce a figure if not of £850,000 only a little less and on any view far in excess of the £400,000 or thereabouts owed by RSP to SSS. At that date, therefore, RSP were not confronted with any real risk that a liquidator of SSS would present a winding-up petition. Even if Colvilles could have obtained an order for the compulsory winding up of SSS and the appointment of a liquidator before the end of January (which I doubt), it is inconceivable that the liquidator could or would have presented a petition for the winding up of RSP before the end of January knowing that the sale of the Rainham land was under way and would most probably produce sufficient for the payment of the debt due to SSS within a matter of a few weeks at the most. Of course, looking at the matter on 19 December, a cautious adviser or director of RSP might have taken the view that it would be in the interests of RSP to enter into an arrangement with Colvilles under which, if the sale at Rainham did not go as planned, RSP would give a guarantee of a sum in excess of the debt owed by it to SSS in consideration of an agreement by Colvilles to defer the payment of the debt owed by SSS for a period which would enable RSP to

explore other means of realising the value of the Rainham land (and possibly the Andover
site), in particular, as regards the Rainham land over the five-year period contemplated
in a valuation obtained by Mr Shenkman in August 1968 from Glenny & Son, a firm
with local experience who had acted for Fords in acquiring land. But that was not done.
Counsel for RSP commented that under the arrangements agreed on 19 December in so
far as RSP got time it did not need it, and in so far as it might need time it did not get it.

The alternative submission of counsel for the defendants was that on 19 December the
directors of RSP were faced with a business decision. On the one hand, they could refuse
to give any guarantee in excess of the sum owed to SSS in the expectation that the
Rainham land would be sold and that the debt due to SSS could be paid off in the near
future; RSP would still own the Andover factory and it would have sufficient moneys to
complete it and finance its operation; on the other hand, Colvilles would then present a
petition for the winding up of SSS and would take immediate steps to make Mr
Shenkman bankrupt; further, if Colvilles were not paid, RSP might not be allowed to
purchase steel from Colvilles or possibly BSC on normal credit terms and might be
compelled to resort to the import of steel from abroad; thus the venture in which Mr
Shenkman had so much confidence would be hamstrung. The alternative was to use the
expected proceeds of the sale of the Rainham land to pay off Colvilles; normal trading
would be resumed with Colvilles; Mr Shenkman was confident that he would then be
able to 'make a go' of the Andover project; Mr Shenkman would be of greater value to
RSP if he was not made bankrupt; furthermore, if the trustees developed and ran the
Andover factory with the assistance of Mr Shenkman and after normal trading had been
resumed with Colvilles, the profits to be expected from the Andover venture would (it
was thought) more than outweigh the cost to RSP of meeting the debt due from SSS to
Colvilles in excess of its liability to SSS.

This is a more formidable argument. But it is, I think, remote from the facts and the
events as they unfolded. It is quite clear that the directors of RSP did not, in fact, decide
that it would be in the interests of RSP to enter into the proposed transaction in order to
obtain the benefits I have outlined. Moreover, if an independent board had been faced
with the suggested choice it could not, as I see it, have decided that it was in the interests
of RSP to enter into the proposed transaction without any commitment on the part of
Mr Shenkman to develop the Andover project for the benefit of RSP or of any
commitment on the part of Colvilles to supply Andover (which started one shift
production in January 1969) with steel on normal credit terms if the debt due to them
was paid in full. Colvilles had, it is true, indicated that it would give favourable
consideration to the resumption of normal trading terms with RSP or the Andover
company if SSS's debt were paid in full; but Colvilles had been careful to make it clear
that it was not entering into any commitment.

The true position, as I see it, is as follows. Even before Fosters' advice had been received,
the directors of RSP had been advised by Mr Balcombe that a guarantee which in effect
cast on RSP, by whatever means, a liability to pay to Colvilles a sum in excess of the debt
due to SSS would be an act of gross misfeasance on their part. I have already summarised
the instructions given to Mr Balcombe [his Lordship's summary of the instructions
occurs in a portion of his judgment not reproduced in this report]. Mr Edwards in his
evidence criticised those instructions. He said that Mr Balcombe should have been given
the statement of affairs and accounts of SSS and should have been told of Mr Shenkman's
personal position, of the demands made on him and of his possible bankruptcy; he said
that he should have been told that without the then proposed guarantee the Andover
project would founder, and he should have been told that if SSS went into liquidation
there was a strong possibility that RSP would also go into liquidation. I do not think that
there is any substance in those criticisms. Mr Balcombe was given instructions which, in
my view, were quite adequate for the general questions on which he was asked to advise.
He was given the draft balance sheet of RSP with notes bringing its position up to date;
he was told that it was solvent, that it owed SSS £400,000 and that SSS owed Colvilles
£750,000; he was told that arrangements had been made under which RSP might be
able to realise £250,000 in the near future; he was told the relationship of Mr Shenkman

to both companies. Mr Dyson originally intended to ask Mr Balcombe for a written opinion. In his evidence he said, and I accept, that he did not ask Mr Balcombe for a written opinion because events moved so quickly that there was not time to obtain one and, more importantly, because a subsequent development made it even more plain that the transaction envisaged would involve a disposition of assets of RSP for no consideration, which could not be justified as being for the purposes or in the interests of RSP. The subsequent development is, of course, that when Fosters' advice was received at the end of November, RSP had for the first time a reasonable assurance that it would be able to meet any demand that might be made on it to meet its debt to SSS. Thereafter, everybody on the RSP side proceeded on the footing that the transactions proposed would not only not be for the purposes or in the interests of RSP but would be positively injurious to it. When Mr Dyson proposed at the meeting on 29 November that he would consult counsel 'as to the best method of implementing the proposals', his proposal was not that he should go back to Mr Balcombe for further advice whether the implementation of the proposals would be a misfeasance on the part of the directors of RSP; he proposed to put a scheme before the trustees and before counsel instructed on behalf of the trustees, designed to compensate the trustees for the injury which the trust holding would suffer indirectly if RSP entered into the proposed transaction. In his letter to Mr Shenkman, cited in the letter to a trustee of the settlement, Mr Perkins, of 3 January, he stressed that it would be necessary that the trustees 'somehow be properly compensated for an otherwise unwarrantable depreciation in the value of one of the trust assets'. The reason for proposing a scheme which would give the trustees compensation in one of the ways suggested in the letter of 3 January was, of course, that the transaction was not one which could be justified as carried out for the purposes or in the interests of RSP but would, on the contrary, be detrimental to it.

In my judgment the conclusion is inescapable that of the directors of RSP Mr Shenkman at least knew that the proposals accepted on behalf of RSP on 19 December and implemented on 22 January involved, to the extent of the guarantee of the liability of SSS in excess of the debt due from RSP to SSS and to that extent the debenture, a gratuitous disposition on the part of RSP which could not be justified as something done for the purposes or in the interests of RSP.

Colvilles's knowledge

The further question is whether Colvilles knew or must be taken as having known that the transaction was not one carried out for the purposes or in the interests of RSP. To answer this question it is, I think, necessary to go back to 2 May when Mr Shenkman first gave his personal guarantee. At that time Mr Shenkman had made it clear to Colvilles that he 'did not have an orthodox view of limited liability companies' and that he regarded all assets held by all companies of which he had control as available to meet the debt due to Colvilles. When he was induced to enter into a personal guarantee, it was with the knowledge on the part of Colvilles and BSC that his personal assets including his shares of RSP would be wholly insufficient to meet the liability. The purpose of obtaining a guarantee from Mr Shenkman was, in my judgment, to put Colvilles in the position where it could exert pressure on Mr Shenkman personally to honour his professed intention of making available for payment of the debt, amongst other things, the assets of RSP. Throughout the summer of 1968 Colvilles expected that assets of RSP would be sold and the proceeds made available to meet the debt. The proposal that RSP should give a guarantee emerged towards the end of September. Mr Figgis's advice was sought. Mr Figgis advised that it would be intra vires RSP to give a guarantee in an amount equal to or greater than its debt to SSS but it is important to observe that he also expressed the view that it was doubtful whether the directors could be advised by their legal advisers to grant a guarantee considerably in excess of the debt due to SSS and that, if a guarantee were given of a figure £40,000 in excess of that debt, it would have to be tied with a timetable for repayment which would give some compensating advantage to RSP. He also advised that the guarantee would have to be limited to a sum such that if RSP was called on it would remain solvent. When Mr Figgis later elaborated his advice by suggesting that the guarantee could be in a form which would leave RSP liable to pay

Colvilles £400,000, even after RSP had paid SSS and SSS in turn had paid Colvilles
£360,000, his advice must, I think, have been based on the assumption that, while it
would be a breach of duty by the directors to give the guarantee, the only risk would be
a risk of attack by a liquidator of RSP in a compulsory winding up of RSP. He must have
assumed that Mr Shenkman would be able to persuade the trustees to consent to the
giving of a guarantee (as had been suggested in Mr Hands's original letter of instruction
to Mr Shenton) and that the transaction could be made invulnerable (except in the event
of insolvency) either because the shareholders acting unanimously could ratify it or
because RSP would be wound up voluntarily and its reduced assets distributed to its
shareholders. Mr Dyson of course, learning of this proposal, took alarm and consulted
Mr Balcombe. In my view Mr Balcombe's advice when reported to Mr Edwards in Mr
Dyson's letter of 6 November came as no surprise to Mr Edwards. I think the view he
took at that time was that Colvilles and BSC were not concerned with whether the giving
of a guarantee in the form proposed would be a breach of duty by the directors and that
it was up to Mr Shenkman to persuade the trustees to assent to it. That is, I think, why
BSC suggested that the director nominated by BSC, who Mr Dyson and Mr Shenkman
had agreed to appoint to the board of RSP, should be appointed after the proposed
guarantee had been given, a suggestion which, not surprisingly, was adversely
commented on by Mr Balcombe. The reason for delaying the appointment of the
nominated director can only have been to ensure that he was not a party to a breach of
duty by the board. Mr Edwards thought that the only risk which need concern Colvilles
and BSC was the risk that, if RSP was called on to pay what it owed SSS and in addition to
pay £400,000 to Colvilles, the guarantee might be attacked by a liquidator if, as a result,
RSP became insolvent. There is direct confirmation that that was the attitude of Mr
Edwards in BSC's notes of the meeting on 29 November. I have already summarised
those notes but I should, I think, at this stage refer again to one passage. Mr Dyson having
expressed the view that part only of the proceeds of the sale of the Rainham land should
be paid over, a reserve being kept for tax, said that he had in mind 'the possible risk of a
subsequent claim by a liquidator that such a payment was a fraudulent preference or
perhaps even misfeasance'. Mr Edwards is recorded as having said that he would 'prefer
that the debt to Colvilles were wholly discharged notwithstanding these possibilities, on
the assumption that everything possible would be done to reduce the risk'. The risk of
attack by a liquidator in an insolvent winding up of RSP was the only one which, he
thought, concerned Colvilles and BSC.

Mr Edwards in his evidence said that he was throughout anxious that there should be
no impropriety on the part of the directors of RSP and that he made this clear to Mr
Dyson and pressed him to provide him with his instructions to Mr Balcombe and for a
written opinion. I regret to say that after the most anxious consideration I have come to
the conclusion that I cannot accept that that was Mr Edwards's attitude at the time. It is,
I fear, a reconstruction of events which, after all, took place very many years ago. There
is no reference in the voluminous correspondence and notes of telephone conversations
to any request to Mr Dyson to provide a copy of Mr Balcombe's instructions and Mr
Dyson was not pressed to obtain a written opinion. On and after 29 November Mr Dyson
made it clear that he proposed to go to counsel not to advise whether the transaction was
a proper transaction in the interests of RSP, but to advise on a scheme which he proposed
to work out in detail which would provide compensation to the trustees if they assented
to, or, at least, did not take any steps to prevent the implementation of, a transaction
which would involve the use of RSP's assets for purposes other than any legitimate
purposes of RSP. It is significant that there is no reference in the correspondence between
BSC and Mr Dyson or in notes of telephone conversations to the fact that BSC had
obtained advice from Mr Figgis. Mr Edwards in his evidence said that he though he
must have mentioned this to Mr Dyson in a telephone conversation at the time when Mr
Dyson obtained advice from Mr Balcombe. Again I regret that I cannot accept that Mr
Dyson was told at any time that BSC had obtained advice from counsel. The suggestion
that he was so told was not put to Mr Dyson when he gave evidence. The initial claim
for privilege was maintained until after Mr Dyson had given evidence and was only
waived in the course of Mr Edwards's evidence. I have no doubt that if Mr Dyson had

been told that BSC had obtained advice from counsel he would have pressed vigorously
for a sight of the instructions to counsel and of any opinion or note of conference that
had been obtained. He had, of course, earlier suggested that he and BSC should both
consult counsel and should agree the instructions to be sent to their respective counsel in
advance. I find myself compelled to the conclusion that the fact that BSC had obtained
advice from counsel was not only not disclosed to Mr Dyson but was quite deliberately
not revealed. If Mr Dyson had known that Colvilles had instructed counsel, he would
have asked to see a note of the advice given by counsel and his instructions. If he had
seen Mr Figgis's original note he would have seen that Mr Figgis had expressed doubt
whether the directors of RSP would be advised to grant a guarantee considerably in excess
of the debt due to SSS and had suggested that the consideration for the assumption by
RSP of a liability in excess of the debt due to SSS should be the acceptance by Colvilles of
a timetable for repayment over a period (advice which was not inconsistent with though
not as categorical as the advice given by Mr Balcombe) and he might have relied on it in
the negotiations. Indeed, I think the explanation of Mr Edwards's failure to ask Mr Dyson
for a copy of the instructions given to Mr Balcombe and for a written opinion to be
obtained is that he knew that, if he asked Mr Dyson for them, Mr Dyson in turn might
well ask whether Colvilles had sought advice. That would have been an embarrassing
question for him to answer.

Counsel for the defendants also relied on the fact that it appears from the instructions
given to Mr Figgis on 19 March 1969 that he had advised BSC in conference 'on 15th
January 1969, and subsequently'. He invited me to infer that Mr Figgis must have given
the same advice as he gave in his written opinion on 27 March 1969 and submitted that
in the light of that advice Colvilles was entitled to assume that the guarantee was
something which RSP was entitled to give as being for the benefit of RSP in that in Mr
Figgis's words 'it was in RSP's interest that time might be given by Colvilles and time
was obtained'. He stressed that I should not draw any adverse inference from the fact
that BSC had maintained its claim for privilege in respect of the instructions given to Mr
Figgis before the conference on 15 January and of the note of the advice he gave at that
and possibly at a subsequent conference. I accept that it would be wrong to draw any
adverse inference from the fact that a claim to legal professional privilege is made even
where, as here, counsel is asked to advise in respect of a transaction on more than one
occasion and privilege is waived in respect of some but not all the instructions, opinions
and notes of conference. The privilege afforded to communications between a citizen
and his legal advisers is of fundamental constitutional importance and it is not to be
whittled down. But equally it would be wrong for me to draw any inference favourable
to Colvilles and BSC. I think I must disregard altogether the fact that Mr Figgis gave
further advice in conference on 15 January. Moreover, if Colvilles had been advised that
the transaction was a proper one and not (in the wider sense) ultra vires or an abuse of the
directors' powers, that advice would not have exempted them from liability if, as I think,
they knew the facts which made the transaction improper (see *Belmont Finance Corp v
Williams Furniture Ltd (No 2)* [1980] 1 All ER 393 at 404 per Buckley LJ).

In my judgment, Colvilles and BSC knew that the guarantee and, to the extent of the
sum guaranteed, the debenture were not entered into by RSP for any purpose of RSP but
were a gratuitous disposition of the property of RSP and were entered into by RSP for
the benefit of SSS and Mr Shenkman personally. I do not propose to refer again to all the
occasions when Colvilles or BSC or their solicitors were told that a scheme to compensate
the trustees for the damage to their shareholding consequent in the implementation of
the proposed guarantee and debenture was being worked out. It is sufficient to refer to
the note of Messrs Lovell, White & King of the telephone conversation with Mr Dyson
on 6 January when he recorded that Mr Dyson said that 'he was being asked to do an act
which was probably ultra vires and would constitute a misfeasance by its directors' and
which could only be carried into effect with the consent of all the shareholders.

Ratification

The defence as originally pleaded contains no trace of any claim that the transactions
and documents entered into or executed on 22 January were entered into or executed

with the authority and approval of all the shareholders in RSP. Counsel for RSP drew
attention to this fact in his opening. No application was then made for leave to amend
the defence. After the evidence had been called, counsel for the defendants in his address
submitted that, if the guarantee and the debenture were executed without the authority
of the board (the board being inquorate) or if the execution of those documents was an
abuse by the directors of their powers, the debenture and the guarantee were none the
less binding on RSP because the execution of those documents had been approved by the
trustees before 22 January. Counsel for RSP objected that that argument was not open to
counsel for the defendants on the pleadings. At the hearing I upheld that objection.
Counsel for the defendants then applied to amend the defence by adding to para 11
(where it is averred that the guarantee and debenture were duly executed by RSP) a
further sentence:

> 'In support of such averment these defendants will rely on the fact that the
> granting of the guarantee and the debenture had been approved by all the
> shareholders in RSP prior to the execution thereof.'

I do not think that it would be right to allow this amendment. There are many matters
which RSP might have wished to investigate and on which counsel for RSP might have
wished to call evidence if this claim had been pleaded before the evidence was heard. Mr
Dyson in his evidence said that he thought that all the trustees were present at the
meeting with him on 21 January. But it appears from the correspondence that shortly
before then one of the trustees, Mr Hibbert, was away in Switzerland. Mr Dyson's
recollection of events in 1968 was, not surprisingly, far from clear. Inquiries might have
shown that Mr Hibbert was not there. Further, Mr Dyson, reporting to Mr Maunsell of
Messrs Lovell, White & King on 22 January, told him that the trustee had 'agreed to the
arrangements provided that Mr Shenkman gave him certain personal obligations secured
on his shares'. That, of course, was not what Mr Dyson had proposed in his letter of 3
January. There had been no time in which to formulate in detail and carry into effect the
elaborate scheme for the protection of the trustees which Mr Dyson proposed. It is not
clear from the brief note of Mr Dyson's conversation with Mr Maunsell whether the
trustees agreed to the arrangements conditionally on Mr Shenkman first giving an
indemnity secured on his shares, nor is it clear what the terms of the indemnity were to
be. In fact, no indemnity was ever given. Lastly, but I think most important of all, it is
vital that directors who seek the approval of shareholders to a transaction in which the
directors are personally interested should make proper disclosure of all relevant facts.
While I have no doubt that Mr Dyson when he wrote to the trustees on 3 January (when
he was acting as Mr Shenkman's solicitor) did his best to give a fair account of the
situation which had arisen, there are some matters which are not referred to, in particular
the trustees were not told that the sale of the Rainham land would give rise to a substantial
tax liability and that after allowing for that liability the payment by RSP of the whole
debt due from SSS might result in RSP's insolvency (which would effectively destroy any
prospect of its benefiting from the Andover project). Further, the statement at the end of
that letter that refusal by the trustees to give their consent to his scheme would 'result in
the certain collapse of the Companies, in a very short space of time' was not justified as
regards RSP in the light of the expectation at the time that the sale of the Rainham land
would produce ample funds to pay off its debt to SSS and leave a substantial surplus. It is
conceivable that if the matter had been properly pleaded the question whether there was
a full disclosure to the trustees and whether this last paragraph in Mr Dyson's letter was
misleading would have been put in issue.

However, as the point has been fully argued I should say that it is in my judgment
clear that, even if BSC had alleged in its defence and proved that the transactions entered
into and the documents executed on 22 January had been entered into or executed with
the assent of all the shareholders, then (subject to one possible qualification) the assent of
the shareholders would not have founded any defence to RSP's claim. Shareholders, even
acting unanimously, cannot authorise a transaction which is ultra vires in the wider sense
of being an application of the company's assets for purposes other than those which the
company is authorised to pursue and cannot ratify or excuse such a transaction if entered

into by the directors in the purported exercise of their powers as directors. Of course, shareholders exercising their votes in general meeting do not owe any fiduciary duty to a company (see *North-West Transportation Co Ltd v Beatty* (1887) 12 App Cas 589). It does not follow that shareholders can exercise their votes without regard to the purposes for which the powers conferred on the company by its memorandum of association were conferred. Thus, in exercising their power to vote remuneration to directors, shareholders are not bound to consider whether it is for the benefit of the company that the proposed remuneration be paid; but what is voted and paid must be something which can genuinely be considered a remuneration and if the proposed payments exceed what can fairly be considered remuneration 'even the sanction of the shareholders in general meeting could not, simply by calling the payments remuneration, validate the acts of the directors in making them' (see *Re Halt Garage (1964) Ltd* [1982] 3 All ER 1016 at 1044) per Oliver J). Similarly, if a power, like the power conferred by cl 3(k) of the memorandum of association of RSP, is conferred for the furtherance of the company's commercial purposes, the shareholders cannot sanction and make binding on the company a purported exercise of that power which they know to be detrimental to the company's commercial interests. In the present case, the fact that the trustees gave their consent conditionally on Mr Shenkman giving an indemnity and in the expectation that in a subsequent liquidation of RSP the trustees would take the whole assets available for distribution or, if RSP was not liquidated, would be compensated in some other way for the 'watering down of their assets by 49% of approximately £400,000' (see the letter of 24 January 1969 from Mr Wills, a trustee) is to my mind fatal to the submission that the guarantee and debenture could have been made binding on the company by the assent of all the shareholders.

The principle that shareholders, even acting unanimously, cannot ratify or make binding on a company a transaction which is ultra vires whether in the narrow or in the wider sense is subject to one exception. In *Re Halt Garage Ltd* Oliver J accepted that a concession by counsel for the liquidator that he could not attack payments of remuneration to the extent that when they were made the company had a reserve on profit and loss account capable of being distributed by way of dividend was rightly made. Having referred to the decision of the Court of Appeal in *Re George Newman & Co Ltd* [1895] 1 Ch 674, he said ([1982] 3 All ER 1016 at 1034) that the observations of Lindley LJ indicate that—

'when it comes to paying gratuities out of profits, there is no necessary requirement of a consideration of the interests of the company's business. The shareholders may do as they please.'

Earlier in his judgment ([1982] 3 All ER 1016 at 1033) he observed that it is—

'a commonplace in private family companies, where there are substantial profits available for distribution by way of dividend, for the shareholder directors to distribute those profits by way of directors' remuneration rather than by way of dividend, because the latter course has certain fiscal disadvantages. But such a distribution may, and frequently does, bear very little relation to the true market value of the services rendered by the directors and if one is to look at it from the point of view of the benefit of the company as a corporate entity, then it is wholly unjustifiable, because it deprives the company of funds which might otherwise be used for expansion or investment or contingency reserves.'

The extent of this exception, whether it applies to any disposition of a company's assets which could have been accomplished by a distribution to shareholders and a disposition by them of the moneys or assets distributed by the company, and the fiscal consequences of a disposition of a company's assets which is ultra vires either in the narrow or in the wider sense and which is justified on this ground are matters which I do not think it necessary or desirable to explore. A defence to an action to set aside a transaction if founded on this ground would require to be very specifically pleaded. In particular the a defence would have to state what assets could have been distributed to the shareholders and at what time and by reference to what accounts of the company. However, I should say that on the evidence before me it appears that RSP did not have profits available for distribution to its shareholders equal to the amount of the guarantee given of the indebtedness of SSS. The latest balance sheet of RSP is not in evidence but it is common ground that the draft statement of affairs was based on it. In that statement of affairs the value of the Rainham land is taken in at cost plus expenditure on it and, attributing that

b value to the Rainham land, RSP's available reserves fell far short of £400,000. In the light of Glenny & Sons' valuation it might have been open to the directors to have resolved to substitute a higher figure for the value of the Rainham land and (as the law then stood) RSP could then have distributed by way of dividend the larger surplus that would have been thrown up. But they did not do so, and if the directors had resolved to substitute a higher value for the Rainham land they would clearly have been advised by the auditors

c that a proper reserve would have to be made for the development gains tax or corporation tax that would be payable on the disposal of the Rainham land. Of course, Mr Shenkman believed that RSP would be entitled to roll-over relief. But there was no foundation for that belief, which would, I think, have been easily dispelled by the auditors. Equally, the proposal that RSP should repay the whole debt due from SSS and look to future profits to meet the liability to development gains tax or corporation tax on the Rainham land

d would not have been accepted by them as a basis on which accounts could properly be drawn. Whether Colvilles or BSC can maintain a claim against Mr Shenkman or the trustees to the extent of any surplus assets which may come into their hands as a result of the repayment of the sum guaranteed by RSP with interest is a question which cannot be decided in these proceedings.

e *Conclusion*

In my judgment, therefore, the guarantee and, to the extent of the sum guaranteed, the debenture were executed by RSP to the knowledge of Colvilles for a purpose other than the purposes authorised by the memorandum of association of RSP and RSP is entitled to have the guarantee set aside and to require BSC to repay the sum guaranteed with interest. In the statement of claim RSP alleges that the receiver when he took up his

f appointment had actual or constructive knowledge that the guarantee and, to the extent of the sum guaranteed, the debenture were invalid. It is accepted by counsel for RSP that, if Colvilles was entitled to rely on the resolutions at the meeting of the board of RSP on 22 January as resolutions of a board validly constituted, the debenture was a valid debenture to the extent of the sum paid to RSP by Colvilles to enable RSP to repay its debt to SSS. No criticism is made of the conduct of the receivership or of the remuneration

g charged by the receiver. In these circumstances the question whether the receiver had notice that the guarantee and, to the extent of the sum guaranteed, the debenture were invalid is devoid of any practical consequence. But in case the point does become material I should say that in my judgment Mr Cooper, when he took possession of the assets of RSP as receiver, had knowledge of facts from which it should have been apparent to him that the giving of the guarantee was ultra vires RSP in the wider sense and also a breach

h of duty by the directors of RSP. My Dyson told him on 22 May that he had entered into arrangements with the trustees, the effect of which was that 'in exchange for not complaining about the giving of the Guarantee, they would, in due course, be "cut into" the Andover Group' and that a reorganisation then under consideration would have to be carried out in such a way that the trustees were compensated for what they had 'permitted to be given away from the value of their Holdings Shares'.

j *Order accordingly.*

Solicitors: *Herbert Smith & Co* (for RSP); *Lovell, White & King* (for the defendants).

Jacqueline Metcalfe   Barrister.

R & T Thew Ltd v Reeves (No 2)   *a*

COURT OF APPEAL, CIVIL DIVISION
LORD DENNING MR, DUNN AND O'CONNOR LJJ
7 JULY, 24 SEPTEMBER 1982

Solicitor – Disciplinary proceedings – Jurisdiction of court – Extent of court's jurisdiction –
Exercise of court's jurisdiction – Jurisdiction of court to order solicitor to pay costs – Nature of   *b*
conduct justifying court in exercising jurisdiction – Conduct required to be inexcusable and such
as to merit reproof – Mistake, error of judgment or mere negligence insufficient – Solicitors Act
1974, s 50.

The jurisdiction of the Supreme Court over solicitors as officers of the court, which is
preserved by s 50ᵃ of the Solicitors Act 1974, is both punitive (in which case it can strike   *c*
a solicitor's name off the roll or suspend him) and compensatory (in which case it can
order a solicitor to pay the costs of his own client, those of the opposite party or those of
both). In so far as it is punitive it is usually inappropriate for the court to exercise the
jurisdiction of its own motion, such matters generally being reported by the court to the
Law Society for the consideration of the Solicitors Disciplinary Tribunal. In so far as the
jurisdiction is compensatory, however, it is retained by the court itself, and the court   *d*
may act on its own motion or on the application of the party who has incurred useless
costs as a result of the conduct of the solicitor of which complaint is made. To warrant
the exercise of the jurisdiction the solicitor's conduct must be inexcusable and such as to
merit reproof; mistake, error of judgment and mere negligence are not generally
sufficient to call into operation the exercise of the court's jurisdiction (see p 1088 *e* to
p 1089 *d* and p 1090 *d e g,* post).   *e*
Myers v Elman [1939] 4 All ER 484 followed.

Notes
For the jurisdiction of the Supreme Court over solicitors, see 36 Halsbury's Laws (3rd
edn) 192, 219, paras 263, 303, and for cases on the subject, see 43 Digest (Repl) 350–352,
3651–3690.   *f*
  For the Solicitors Act 1974, s 50, see 44 Halsbury's Statutes (3rd edn) 1522.

Cases referred to in judgments
Balogh v Crown Court at St Albans [1974] 3 All ER 283, [1975] QB 73, [1974] 3 WLR 314,
  CA, 16 Digest (Reissue) 12, *109.*
Edwards v Edwards [1958] 2 All ER 179, [1958] P 235, [1958] 2 WLR 956, 43 Digest   *g*
  (Repl) 376, *3995.*
Maroux v Sociedade Comercial Abel Pereira da Fonseca SARL [1972] 2 All ER 1085, [1972] 1
  WLR 962, Digest (Cont Vol D) 849, *3995a.*
Myers v Elman [1939] 4 All ER 484, [1940] AC 282, HL, 43 Digest (Repl) 375, *3981.*
R v Smith (Martin) [1974] 1 All ER 651, [1975] QB 531, [1974] 2 WLR 495, CA, 16 Digest
  (Reissue) 238, *2349.*   *h*
Stephens v Hill (1842) 10 M & W 28, 152 ER 368, 43 Digest (Repl) 429, *4532.*
Thew (R & T) Ltd v Reeves [1981] 2 All ER 964, [1982] QB 172, [1981] 3 WLR 190, CA.

---

a Section 50 provides:
     '(1) Any person duly admitted as a solicitor shall be an officer of the Supreme Court.
     (2) Subject to the provisions of this Act, the High Court, the Crown Court and the Court of
   Appeal respectively, or any division or judge of those courts, may exercise the same jurisdiction in   *j*
   respect of solicitors as any one of the superior courts of law or equity from which the Supreme
   Court was constituted might have exercised immediately before the passing of the Supreme Court
   of Judicature Act 1873 in respect of any solicitor, attorney or proctor admitted to practise there.
     (3) An appeal shall lie to the Court of Appeal from any order made against a solicitor by the
   High Court or the Crown Court in the exercise of its jurisdiction in respect of solicitors under
   subsection (2).'

Cases also cited

a   *Davies v Davies* [1960] 3 All ER 248, [1960] 1 WLR 1004, CA.
Kyle v Mason (1963) Times, 3 July, CA.
Solicitors, Re, re Taxation of Costs [1982] 2 All ER 683, [1982] 1 WLR 745.
Weston v Courts Administrator of the Central Criminal Court [1976] 2 All ER 875, [1977] QB
    32, CA.

b   **Summons**
Pursuant to the order of the Court of Appeal (Lord Denning MR, Dunn and O'Connor
LJJ) on 19 June 1981 (see [1982] QB 172 at 207) and following submissions as to costs in
R & T Thew Ltd v Reeves [1981] 2 All ER 964, [1982] QB 172 and the reading of a letter
from the solicitors for the plaintiffs therein to the Law Society dated 16 December 1980,
the plaintiffs' solicitors attended before the court for the purposes of enabling the court
c   to consider whether they should be ordered to pay personally costs from 16 August 1977
to 7 March 1980 in the High Court action on the ground that such costs were incurred
and occasioned as a result of a mistake of their clerk or articled clerk, such costs not being
recoverable from the Law Society under the Legal Aid Act 1974. The Attorney General
was invited to consider the appointment of amicus curiae to assist the court. The facts are
set out in the judgment of Lord Denning MR.
d

Arthur Mildon QC and *Rupert Jackson* for the solicitors.
Michael Wright QC and *Anna Shaw* for the Law Society.
Simon D Brown as amicus curiae.

Cur adv vult
e

24 September. The following judgments were read.

LORD DENNING MR.
The 'unacceptable face' of British justice
f   In *R & T Thew Ltd v Reeves* [1981] 2 All ER 964, [1982] QB 172 I delivered a dissenting
judgment. Towards the end of it I summarised the position ([1981] 2 All ER 964 at 976,
[1982] QB 172 at 193–194):

'So here we have presented to us at its most ugly the "unacceptable face" of British
justice. The Thews came to the courts of law to obtain sums from a debtor which
g   were undoubtedly due to them. They were baulked by the grant of legal aid to the
defendant. Their own costs came to £7,000. When they sought to recover those
costs from the legal aid fund, they were met by the plea: "You cannot recover them
because a mistake was made in the legal aid certificate and it cannot be corrected."
That plea has succeeded. I hang my head in shame that it should be so.'

h   *A remedy is suggested*
After the hearing, this court itself suggested a remedy. It appeared to be possible that
the disaster to the Thews was caused, not by anything done by their own solicitor, but by
a mistake made by the solicitors for Mr Reeves on the other side. It was the mistake of
their articled clerk which led to all the trouble. He had applied only for legal aid to
'defend', whereas he should have applied for legal aid to 'defend and counterclaim'. So
j   why should they not compensate the Thews, especially as they would be insured against
liability for negligence?
Despite this suggestion by the court, counsel for the Thews declined to make any
application against those other solicitors. He refused for good reason. The Thews had
expended all their money already. They could not get legal aid. If they took proceedings
against the solicitors for the other side, they might lose and have to pay all the costs. So
they decided to cut their losses and do nothing.

The court acts on its own

This court then decided to act of its own motion. It ordered the solicitors for Mr *a*
Reeves to attend—

'for the purposes of considering whether or not they should be ordered to pay
personally costs from August 16, 1977, to March 7, 1980, in the High Court action
on grounds that such costs were incurred and occasioned as a result of a mistake of
their clerk or articled clerk such costs not being recoverable from The Law Society
under the provisions of the Legal Aid Act 1974. The Attorney-General was asked to *b*
consider the appointment of amicus curiae to assist the court.'

(See [1982] QB 172 at 207.)

The motion was heard last term. We had the benefit of submissions by Mr Arthur
Mildon QC for the solicitors for Mr Reeves, by Mr Michael Wright QC for the Law
Society and by Mr Simon Brown as amicus curiae. We are most grateful for the assistance *c*
of all of them. I will state the law as I understand it.

The jurisdiction over solicitors

The jurisdiction of the court over solicitors was much considered by the House of
Lords in *Myers v Elman* [1939] 4 All ER 484, [1940] AC 282. It originated in early days
because a solicitor was an officer of the court. His name was entered on the rolls of the *d*
court. He was subject to the discipline of the court. This disciplinary jurisdiction was
exercisable in two ways: either by punishing him or by making him pay compensation.

In so far as it was *punitive*, the court could strike a solicitor off the roll of the court or it
could suspend him. In so far as it was *compensatory*, it could order him to pay costs;
sometimes the costs of his own client, sometimes those of the opposite party, sometimes
it may be of both (see [1939] 4 All ER 484 at 508, [1940] AC 282 at 318 per Lord Wright). *e*

Both these disciplinary powers are preserved by s 50 of the Solicitors Act 1974.

The punitive jurisdiction

The *punitive* jurisdiction of the court itself is now rarely if ever exercised. It is left to
the Solicitors Disciplinary Tribunal. If a judge thinks that a solicitor may have been
guilty of conduct deserving punishment, he reports the matter to the Law Society. It will *f*
then be considered by the Professional Purposes Committee. They will decide whether
to charge him before the Solicitors Disciplinary Tribunal or not. The tribunal can strike
him off the roll, suspend him or fine him; see s 47 of the 1974 Act.

Nowadays it would usually be inappropriate for any judge to exercise this punitive
jurisdiction of his own motion. He would have to give notice to the solicitor so as to give
him an opportunity of answering the charge: see *R v Smith (Martin)* [1974] 1 All ER 651, *g*
[1975] QB 531. And then, when the charge was heard, the judge would appear to be
both prosecutor and judge. That is a role which does not become him well: see *Balogh v
Crown Court at St Albans* [1974] 3 All ER 283 at 288, [1975] QB 73 at 85. It should be
avoided in all but the most exceptional cases.

h

The compensatory jurisdiction

The *compensatory* jurisdiction is also preserved, but with this difference; it is retained
by the courts themselves. The Solicitors Disciplinary Tribunal has no power to award
compensation to anyone. Our old books all show that if a solicitor for one side has done
something wrong, which has caused useless costs to the other party, he could be ordered
personally to compensate the other party. That other party made his application at the *j*
conclusion of the case or soon after it. He would apply to the court for an order that the
solicitor on the other side do pay the costs. He would do it by motion in the Chancery
court or by a motion or application for a rule in the courts of common law. It was a
summary jurisdiction without pleadings. All that was necessary was a notice telling the
solicitor what was alleged against him and giving him an opportunity of answering it.

This is all described by Lord Wright in *Myers v Elman* [1939] 4 All ER 484 at 508, [1940]
a   AC 282 at 318. This jurisdiction still exists in full force. As a rule the party who has
incurred useless costs will himself make the application. But this is not invariable.
Sometimes the court may act of its own motion. As we did in this very case.

What conduct is sufficient?
This *compensatory* jurisdiction still retains, however, a disciplinary slant. Just as officers
b   in the services are subject to military discipline (see ss 64 and 69 of the Army Act 1955),
so are solicitors, as officers of the court, subject to judicial discipline. If they are guilty of
'any act, conduct or neglect to the prejudice of good order and [judicial] discipline' or
which is 'unbecoming the character of an officer and a gentlemen', causing loss or damage
to another, they can be ordered personally to compensate him. The cases show that it is
not available in cases of mistake, error of judgment or mere negligence. It is only
c   available where the conduct of the solicitor is inexcusable and such as to merit reproof.
In *Myers v Elman* [1939] 4 All ER 484 at 490, 498, 509, [1940] AC 282 at 292, 304, 319
Viscount Maugham put it as 'a serious dereliction of duty', Lord Atkin spoke of 'gross
negligence', and Lord Wright said that 'gross neglect or inaccuracy' may suffice. Lord
Wright's definition included 'a failure on the part of a solicitor . . . to realise his duty to
aid in promoting, in his own sphere, the cause of justice'. Lord Porter said that the
d   solicitor there had been 'grossly negligent' (see [1939] 4 All ER 484 at 522, [1940] AC
282 at 338). Useful illustrations are to be found in *Edwards v Edwards* [1958] 2 All ER
179 at 193, [1958] P 235 at 258 (holding the solicitor liable to pay the costs of the other
side because of his 'oppressive procedure') and *Mauroux v Sociedade Comercial Abel Pereira
da Fonseca SARL* [1972] 2 All ER 1085, [1972] 1 WLR 962 (holding the solicitor not liable
for an 'oversight').

e
Applied to this case
Applying this test, it seems to me that the conduct of the articled clerk was not
sufficiently serious to warrant the court in exercising its compensatory jurisdiction. It
was at most a mere slip. As I said in my judgment ([1981] 2 All ER 964 at 971, [1982]
QB 172 at 187), the articled clerk 'botched up the application, so that it did not correctly
f   state the description of the legal aid desired'. It omitted the words 'and counterclaim'.
But everyone treated it as containing those words, and it was corrected as soon as it was
discovered.
In any case, it may not have been the cause of the disaster. It may have been due to the
mistake of the clerk in the legal aid office. As I said in my judgment ([1981] 2 All ER
964 at 974, [1982] QB 172 at 190): '. . . a mistake was made by the clerk who drew up
g   the offer of legal aid. He bungled it by copying out the words of the botched application
form . . .'

Fresh evidence
On this application we have had more evidence than we had before. We have an
affidavit by the articled clerk himself. On reading it I would myself acquit him of any
h   negligence, and it is only fair to him that I should say so. When he submitted his
application form, he attached to it the pleadings. These made it quite clear, clear beyond
all question, that there was *no defence* to the action and the sole dispute was on *the
counterclaim*. The clerks in the legal aid office so read it. They made it quite clear in their
synopsis. The area committee simply said, 'Granted.'
All these documents must be construed together. On their true construction I should
j   have thought that, when the application form asked for legal aid to 'defend', that meant
to 'defend' in accordance with the pleaded case of the defendant. His pleaded case was
confined to the counterclaim. It follows that, on *its true construction*, the application was
for legal aid on the counterclaim. It is impossible to construe it as legal aid to 'defend'
strictly so-called when he admitted he had no defence. The clerk put the point succinctly
in his affidavit:

'... my conclusion ... was that ... after reading the facts of the case as given by
the pleadings the legal aid would be applied to the correct case. It did not occur to   *a*
me that the counterclaim could be considered as anything other than Mr. Reeves'
substantial defence in case number 77 R 33 in the Oldham District Registry.'

I am sorry that this point was not submitted to this court at the hearing of the appeal
([1981] 2 All ER 964, [1982] QB 172). Everyone then assumed that the application was
only for legal aid 'to defend' (strictly) and was only granted 'to defend' (actually). So that
it was necessary for it to 'be amended', as it was 'amended' afterwards to include 'to   *b*
counterclaim'. But in truth no amendment was needed, because on its true construction
'to defend' in this context included 'to counterclaim'. All that was needed was elucidation,
not amendment.

If this point had been taken in this court, the result might have been quite different. I
say might, because I only speak for myself. I cannot say how it might have affected my
brethren. But there it is. It was not taken. And we have to accept the consequences.   *c*

Conclusion

It was in the hope of helping the Thews that this court suggested that a remedy might
be available. It has proved to be abortive. We are left to weep over the 'unacceptable face
of British justice'.

We are grateful to Mr Simon Brown for his help as amicus curiae. We hope that Mr   *d*
Reeves's solicitors are insured, so that they get their costs from their insurers. But we can
make no order in their favour. There is no one to make it against.

Dunn LJ tells me he is unable to be present today, but he agrees with the judgment
about to be delivered by O'Connor LJ.

O'CONNOR LJ. On 19 June 1982 this court ordered that the defendant's solicitors   *e*
should attend before this court on a date to be arranged for the purpose of considering
whether or not they should be ordered to pay personally costs from 16 August 1977 to 7
March 1980 in the High Court action on grounds that such costs were incurred and
occasioned as a result of a mistake of their articled clerk, such costs not being recoverable
from the Law Society under the provisions of the Legal Aid Act 1974. The Attorney
General was asked to consider the appointment of an amicus curiae to assist the court.   *f*

The reasons for which the court made this order will be found in the judgments of
this court (see [1981] 2 All ER 964, [1982] QB 172).

The solicitors duly appeared by counsel on 7 July 1982. The Law Society also appeared
and the court had the help of Mr Simon Brown as amicus. Lord Denning MR in his
judgment has explained the nature of the power of the court to discipline solicitors; I
agree with that part of his judgment and do not wish to add anything of my own.   *g*

In the present case the question is: should the solicitors be ordered to pay compensation
by way of costs to the Thews? The cases show that such an order ought not to be made
unless it is shown that the Thews have suffered loss as a result of serious misconduct by
the solicitors in the case. In *Myers v Elman* [1939] 4 All ER 484 at 490, [1940] AC 282 at
292 Viscount Maugham said:

'... I entirely agree with the contention that the jurisdiction in question ought to   *h*
be exercised only when there has been established a serious dereliction of duty as a
solicitor, either by himself or by his clerks.'

Lord Wright said ([1939] 4 All ER 484 at 508–509, [1940] AC 282 at 318–319):

'The cases of the exercise of this jurisdiction to be found in the reports are   *j*
numerous, and show how the courts were guided by their opinion as to the character
of the conduct complained of. The underlying principle is that the court has a right
and a duty to supervise the conduct of its solicitors, and visit with penalties any
conduct of a solicitor which is of such a nature as to tend to defeat justice in the very
cause in which he is engaged professionally, as was said by LORD ABINGER, C. B., in

Stephens v. *Hill* ((1842) 10 M & W 28, 152 ER 368). The matter complained of need not be criminal. It need not involve peculation or dishonesty. A mere mistake or error of judgment is not generally sufficient, but a gross neglect or inaccuracy in a matter which it is a solicitor's duty to ascertain with accuracy may suffice. Thus, a solicitor may be held bound in certain events to satisfy himself that he has a retainer to act, or as to the accuracy of an affidavit which his client swears. It is impossible to enumerate the various contingencies which may call into operation the exercise of this jurisdiction. It need not involve personal obliquity. The term "professional misconduct" has often been used to describe the ground on which the court acts. It would perhaps be more accurate to describe it as conduct which involves a failure on the part of a solicitor to fulfil his duty to the court and to realise his duty to aid in promoting, in his own sphere, the cause of justice. This summary procedure may often be invoked to save the expense of an action. Thus, it may, in proper cases, take the place of an action for negligence, or an action for breach of warranty of authority brought by the person named as defendant in the writ. The jurisdiction is not merely punitive, but compensatory. The order is for payment of costs thrown away or lost because of the conduct complained of. It is frequently, as in this case, exercised in order to compensate the opposite party in the action.'

There are many authorities to the same effect, but in view of the speeches in *Myers v Elman* I do not find it useful to refer to them.

The basis of the inquiry as to the possible exercise of the jurisdiction of the court was the incompetence of the solicitors by their articled clerk in making application for legal aid which, if granted, as it was, would lull the non-assisted opponent into the belief that the financial hardship of fighting a case against a legally-aided opponent might be relieved by an order against the legal aid fund. Now that I have seen the account given by the articled clerk of exactly what occurred I find it quite impossible to say that it discloses the kind of misconduct spoken of in the speeches in *Myers v Elman* which I have cited. I find it unnecessary to say more because I do not wish to express any opinion which might affect any issue between the solicitors and their own client should there be one. It follows that, in my judgment, there are no grounds for ordering the solicitors to pay any part of the Thews' costs.

I have only one thing to add; I regret that I cannot agree with the view of Lord Denning MR that, if the information now available to the court had been available to us when the appeal of the Law Society was heard, I might have come to a different conclusion. For my part, I find nothing in the evidence which has been adduced on this issue which makes me question my judgment in the appeal. I would have come to the same conclusion even if this evidence had been before the court.

I agree with the order proposed by Lord Denning MR.

No order on the appeal. No order for costs.

Solicitors: *Reynolds, Porter, Chamberlain* (for the solicitors); *J L Bowron*, Secretary-General (for the Law Society); *Treasury Solicitor.*

Diana Procter   Barrister.

R v Williams (Carl)

COURT OF APPEAL, CRIMINAL DIVISION

LORD LANE CJ, MICHAEL DAVIES AND HOBHOUSE JJ

24 JUNE 1982

Sentence – Binding over – Appeal – Right of appeal against binding-over order – Whether binding-over order a 'sentence' – Criminal Appeal Act 1968, ss 9, 50(1).

Crown Court – Binding over – Powers of court – Terms of order – Defendant bound over on condition that he go with his mother to Jamaica and not return for five years – Defendant a British subject born and brought up in England who had never lived in Jamaica – Defendant reluctantly consenting to terms of order on learning that alternative a custodial sentence – Whether order appropriate.

The appellant, an 18-year-old British subject, was convicted in the Crown Court of theft. He already had a bad criminal record and the judge indicated that his intention was to sentence him to borstal training. The appellant's counsel asked the judge not to impose a custodial sentence because the appellant's mother, a Jamaican, was planning to take the appellant with her to Jamaica so that he could make a fresh start there. Counsel made it clear to the judge that he did not know how long she would be able to stay there. The judge told the appellant that in view of what his counsel had said he planned to make an order binding him over in his own recognisance conditional on the appellant accompanying his mother to Jamaica and not returning to England for five years. The appellant replied that since he had been born and brought up in England and had never lived in Jamaica he had no wish to spend five years there. When the judge pointed out to him that the alternative was a custodial sentence, he reluctantly consented to the terms of the order. He subsequently appealed under s 9[a] of the Criminal Appeal Act 1968 to the Court of Appeal against the 'sentence' contending that it was too severe and that he had not consented to it freely but only under the threat of a custodial sentence. The questions arose whether a binding-over order, being by way of a respite of judgment, was a 'sentence' which the court could review under s 9 and, if it was, whether the order was appropriate in the circumstances.

Held – (1) Since the binding-over order was contingent on conviction and could not be made otherwise than on conviction, it was a 'sentence' within s 50(1)[b] of the 1968 Act and therefore the court had jurisdiction to entertain the appeal (see p 1095 c, post); R v Dwyer (1975) 60 Cr App R 39 distinguished.

(2) The Crown Court could only make a binding-over order conditional on the defendant leaving the jurisdiction for a specified period if the defendant consented to the imposition of the condition or acknowledged that he was bound by its terms, and the fact that the defendant gave his consent under the threat of imprisonment did not invalidate that consent. On the facts, however, the binding-over order and the condition attached to it was not an appropriate order to make and it would therefore be quashed and an order of conditional discharge for a period of 12 months substituted (see p 1095 g j, p 1096 b to d and g to j and p 1097 b to d, post); R v McCartan [1958] 3 All ER 140, R v Ayu [1958] 3 All ER 636, R v Hodges (1967) 51 Cr App R 361 and Veater v G [1981] 2 All ER 304 considered.

Per curiam. The power to make a binding-over order conditional on the defendant leaving the jurisdiction for a specified period should be used very sparingly, and in all but the most exceptional cases the power should only be used to ensure that the defendant goes to a country of which he is a citizen or in which he is habitually resident or which is prepared in special circumstances to accept him for his well-being (see p 1096 d to f, post).

---

a   Section 9 is set out at p 1095 a, post

b   Section 50(1) is set out at p 1095 b c, post

Notes

a For binding over to keep the peace, see 11 Halsbury's Laws (4th edn) paras 521–522. For appeal therefrom to the Court of Appeal, see ibid para 521.

For appeal against sentence and meaning of sentence, see 11 ibid paras 481, 615, 617, and for cases on sentence generally, see 14(2) Digest (Reissue) 770–771, 6444–6461.

For the Criminal Appeal Act 1968, ss 9, 50, see 8 Halsbury's Statutes (3rd edn) 695, 719.

b

Cases referred to in judgment

R v Ayu [1958] 3 All ER 636, [1958] 1 WLR 1264, CA, 14(2) Digest (Reissue) 701, 5882.

R v Dwyer (1975) 60 Cr App R 39, CA.

R v East Grinstead Justices, ex p Doeve [1968] 3 All ER 666, [1969] 1 QB 136, [1969] 3 WLR 920, DC, 2 Digest (Reissue) 212, 1207.

c   *R v Flaherty* [1958] Crim LR 556, CCA.

R v Hodges (1967) 51 Cr App R 361, [1967] Crim LR 375, CA, 14(2) Digest (Reissue) 700, 5871.

R v McCartan [1958] 3 All ER 140, [1958] 1 WLR 933, CCA, 14(2) Digest (Reissue) 706, 5930.

R v Vincent (13 November 1981, unreported), CA.

d   *Veater v G* [1981] 2 All ER 304, [1981] 1 WLR 567, DC.

Cases also cited

R v Abrahams (1952) 36 Cr App R 147, CCA.

R v Edgehill [1963] 1 All ER 181, [1963] 1 QB 593, CCA.

R v Marquis [1974] 2 All ER 1216, [1974] 1 WLR 1087, CA.

e   *R v Tucker* [1974] 2 All ER 639, [1974] 1 WLR 615, CA.

R v Wehner [1977] 3 All ER 553, [1977] 1 WLR 1143, CA.

Appeal against sentence

On 8 February at the Crown Court at Croydon before his Honour Judge Clay and a jury

f the appellant, Carl Williams, was convicted by a majority verdict of 10 to 2 on two counts of theft. Sentence was postponed until 5 March 1982 when the appellant was bound over to come up for judgment on his own recognisance of £20 on terms that he accompany his mother to Jamaica and not return to England for five years. He appealed to the Court of Appeal against the 'sentence' contending, inter alia, that it was too severe and that he had not consented to it freely but only under the threat of a custodial sentence. The facts

g are set out in the judgment of the court.

Ian Macdonald and *Arthur James* for the appellant.
Allan Green and *Daphne Wickham* for the Crown.

LORD LANE CJ delivered the following judgment of the court: On 8 February 1982

h in the Crown Court at Croydon the appellant, to whom we have now given leave to appeal, was convicted by a majority verdict on two counts of theft, and the jury were discharged from giving verdicts on the other counts. With the consent of counsel who appears on behalf of the appellant, we propose to deal with the matter as the hearing of the appeal.

The judge postponed sentence until 5 March 1982. That was a day before the

j appellant's mother proposed to take the appellant to live in Jamaica in order to give him a fresh start, and he was remanded on bail on certain terms. On 5 March he came before the same court and was then bound over to come up for judgment in his own recognisance of £20 on terms that he accompany his mother to Jamaica within ten days and not return to this country for five years.

In fairness to the judge who made that order, the way in which these matters came to be considered should be explained in a little more detail. The first suggestion came from

Mr Arthur James, who was then representing the appellant. He told the judge that Mrs
Williams, the appellant's mother, proposed to go back to Jamaica shortly and to take the *a*
appellant with her. He said:

> 'It is proposed, because of the husband's ill health, that they will live in Jamaica. I
> understand a flight has been booked for 6 March of this year. Mrs Williams has
> been saving up to buy tickets for that flight. There is no doubt that up till 1981, and
> up until the time of this offence, that Carl Williams was going further and further *b*
> downhill and his parents realised that they had to make a fresh start for him and
> that that would be best for him. He is a citizen of this country, he was born here
> and is British by birth and not Jamaican at all.'

He then went on to deal with the remainder of the facts.

All of that has to be read against the unpleasant history of this young man's criminal *c*
career. He was born on 30 November 1963, so that at the time those matters were being
considered he was about 18 years of age. He has acquired an astonishing number of
convictions since 1979, and there is no need to read all of them. They include several
thefts and burglaries, criminal damage and robbery. He has had a supervision order
imposed on him; he has been to a detention centre; he has been conditionally discharged;
he has had sentence deferred; he has been fined, and he has been ordered to do 100 hours *d*
of community service. There is no doubt, as the judge made perfectly plain, and as he
was entitled to do, that he had very much in mind sentencing the appellant to a period
of borstal training, though quite clearly and properly minded to avoid doing so if he
possibly could.

In the interests of the appellant, in the upshot the judge made up his mind to make
the order which has already been described. But it seems that by that time the appellant *e*
himself had suffered a change of heart, and as soon as the judge made it clear that five
years was the period that he had in mind during which the appellant should not come
back to this country, the appellant was disinclined to consent to that order being made.
Counsel for the appellant then said:

> 'Your Honour, he only wishes to make this point through me: a period of five *f*
> years seemed in your Honour's mind in your Honour's bind-over. He has never
> lived in Jamaica and he is a British subject, born here. He has only known life in
> this country and he feels at the moment that a period of five years' compulsory
> extradition, as it were, from this country he does not want to face at all.'

The judge said: 'If he does not want to, the alternative is a custodial sentence.' A little
later counsel said: *g*

> 'The difficulty is, as I explained to your Honour the last time, that the father is
> quite ill and his wife cannot make further arrangements with that situation. She is
> going to Jamaica for an extended stay. ['Stay' is different from the expression 'live',
> which was used on the previous occasion. Counsel continued:] She may very well
> have to come back for her husband may not be able to travel. Her husband is not *h*
> going with her, so it may not be an arrangement that will last as long as five years;
> it might last for a shorter period.'

In the result the judge made the order already mentioned.

This appeal really raises a number of separate points. First of all, is there jurisdiction
in this court to hear the appeal? It is suggested, somewhat tentatively, by counsel for the *j*
Crown that there is not. As has been so frequently said, this court is a court of statute,
and we have to determine whether, in the light of the provisions of the Criminal Appeal
Act 1968, this common law binding over is a matter which is subject to review by this
court. There are two sections of the 1968 Act which are involved; first of all s 9, which
reads:

a
'A person who has been convicted of an offence on indictment may appeal to the Court of Appeal against any sentence (not being a sentence fixed by law) passed on him for the offence, whether passed on his conviction or in subsequent proceedings.'

There is no doubt that this appellant was convicted of an offence on indictment.

The only question that remains is therefore whether the order made by the judge was a 'sentence'. On the face of it, without further definition of the word 'sentence', it was not of course a sentence; it was deliberately not passing a sentence. It was, so to speak, a respite of judgment for the time being. But the matter is not as simple as that, because

b
s 50(1) of the 1968 Act defines 'sentence' in the following terms:

'In this Act, "sentence", in relation to an offence, includes any order made by a court when dealing with an offender (including a hospital order under Part V of the Mental Health Act 1959, with or without an order restricting discharge) and also

c
includes a recommendation for deportation.'

It seems to this court that plainly that includes the order that the judge made in this case, namely the order of binding over, which was contingent on the conviction and could not have been made otherwise than on conviction.

It was suggested as an alternative by counsel for the appellant that if his argument failed on that point there was another method by which this court could have jurisdiction,

d
that is on the basis that the order made by the judge in this case was in effect a nullity, which would give this court power to review it. There is no need in the circumstances for us to embark on an examination of that proposition.

The only doubt cast on the conclusion that we have reached is to be found in *R v Dwyer* (1975) 60 Cr App R 39. In delivering the judgment of the court, Roskill LJ

e
described it as one in which almost everything that could possibly go wrong had gone wrong. It is true that certain observations were made by Roskill LJ about the nature of the court's powers to bind over a defendant and the possibility of such orders being subject to review by this court. Having read that judgment, it seems to this court that the issue which arises in this case was not properly before the court which considered that case; and we do not feel in any way constrained by anything that appears in that

f
decision from reaching our conclusion on the question of jurisdiction.

It now remains for us to consider whether the order made by the judge was in fact an appropriate order in the circumstances of the case. We have already dealt with the background of the appellant and the nature of his previous criminal record. The nature of the offences of which he was found guilty was this. They took place at the time of the trouble in the summer of 1981. He stole from shops during the time of the trouble certain electrical apparatus of some £80 in value. Those offences were committed against

g
the background of the antecedent history to which we have already referred.

There is no doubt that there exists in the Crown Court power to bind over convicted persons to come up for judgment. That is made perfectly plain by s 79 of the Supreme Court Act 1981, which preserves the old common law power. That section provides:

'(1) All enactments and rules of law relating to procedure in connection with indictable offences shall continue to have effect in relation to proceedings in the

h
Crown Court.
(2) Without prejudice to the generality of subsection (1), that subsection applies in particular to . . . (b) the release, after respite of judgment, of a convicted person on recognizance to come up for judgment if called on, but meanwhile to be of good behaviour.'

j
Likewise there is no doubt that it is open to the court to impose as a condition of the binding over a term that the defendant leave this jurisdiction for his own country and not return to this country for a specified period of time. That emerges from a number of cases to which we have been referred: *R v McCartan* [1958] 3 All ER 140, [1958] 1 WLR 933 per Lord Goddard CJ, *R v Ayu* [1958] 3 All ER 636, [1958] 1 WLR 1264, *R v Flaherty*

[1958] Crim LR 556, and perhaps of most interest *R v Hodges* (1967) 51 Cr App R 361, in which a defendant of bad character was bound over to give him a last chance to reform. *a* The order obliged him to attend a Carmelite organisation in the Republic of Ireland which was prepared to take him, although he was a citizen of this country and, it seems, apart from that offer by the Carmelite organisation, had no connection with Ireland. Then there is the more recent case of *R v Vincent* (13 November 1981, unreported), in which a young man was anxious to return to Trinidad, where his parents were in a comfortable way of business, and a similar order, to last for ten years, was made in respect *b* of him.

It is a power which can be exercised only if the subject of the order consents to its being made or acknowledges himself to be bound by its terms. But the fact that the consent has been given under threat of imprisonment does not invalidate the consent. If that requires authority it is to be found in the recent decision in *Veater v G* [1981] 2 All ER 304, [1981] 1 WLR 567, where the court examined the history of this kind of order *c* and set out the basis of the principle which we have just endeavoured to explain.

The matter is given point by this: it may very well be that the only power in the court which it is proper for the court to exercise on the defendant declining to give his consent is the power to imprison or to impose some custodial sentence. Consequently the way in which the judge acted in the present case was technically entirely proper. However, this power to keep a defendant out of the jurisdiction on pain of imprisonment is one which *d* plainly should be used very sparingly. Counsel for the appellant has invited our attention to the provisions of the Immigration Act 1972, and in particular to ss 1, 3(5) and 7. He has also invited our attention to *R v East Grinstead Justices, ex p Doeve* [1963] 3 All ER 666, [1969] 1 QB 136. It is plain that there are many other methods of producing this sort of result, and that the occasions on which the power to bind over on these terms are appropriate are likely to be very few and far between. It is certainly very seldom to be *e* done if the defendant does not freely give his consent; and, save in exceptional circumstances such as those in *R v Hodges* (1967) 51 Cr App R 361, it should be used only to ensure that the defendant goes to a country of which he is a citizen or in which he is habitually resident, or where there are very special circumstances in which the receiving country is prepared to take him for his own well-being. Those last few words cover the situation in *R v Hodges* and also to some extent that in the recent case of *R v Vincent*. *f*

We are indebted to counsel for the appellant, not only for that form of words, with which we agree, but also for the rest of his arugument, which has been presented with admirable conciseness and clarity.

Here, as already indicated, the judge was not making a threat; he was only stating correctly what the probable alternative, namely borstal training, would be if the defendant failed to give his consent to the formal order which the judge proposed to *g* make. In the present case however it is plain that eventually the appellant was unwilling to give his consent, although in fact he gave it. It was on the express invitation of counsel for the appellant that the matter was considered and that going to Jamaica was ever broached as a subject, and, as has been said, the judge was only trying to do what he could to help the appellant.

But it was made clear, at least in the end, by counsel to the judge that the appellant *h* had been born in England, was a British citizen, and had never lived for any length of time, if at all, in Jamaica, and apparently did not wish to do so. Eventually likewise it was made clear to the judge that the chances of the appellant's mother, on whom he was dependent, staying for any length of time in Jamaica were, owing to the physical condition of the father, very slender.

In those circumstances we think that the order should not have been made and that *j* this was not an appropriate case in which to make an order of binding over in those terms. The appellant could not at the time, let it be added, have complained for a moment if he had been sent to borstal.

The only other point that remains is what this court should do. We are to some extent possibly inhibited by the terms of s 11(3) of the Criminal Appeal Act 1968, viz:

a

'On an appeal against sentence the Court of Appeal, if they consider that the appellant should be sentenced differently for an offence for which he was dealt with by the court below may—(a) quash any sentence or order which is the subject of the appeal; and (b) in place of it pass such sentence or make such order as they think appropriate for the case and as the court below had power to pass or make when dealing with him for the offence; but the court shall so exercise their powers under this subsection that, taking the case as a whole, the appellant is not more severely

b

dealt with on appeal than he was dealt with by the court below.'

The way in which the appellant was dealt with by the court below was by the imposition of the order which has already been described and which, by the definition in s 50, is a 'sentence'. We have to determine what sentence can properly be passed now on this man, with the setting aside of the binding-over order, which will not be dealing with him more severely than he was dealt with by the court below.

c

We are assisted to a considerable extent by the fact that, if the up-to-date social inquiry report is to be believed, which of course it is, there is every indication that this appellant is at last seeing the error of his ways in the past. Quite apart from the proviso to s 11(3) of the 1968 Act which has just been read, we think that the proper course is to impose a sentence of conditional discharge in the place of the order, which we quash.

d

Accordingly we substitute an order of conditional discharge for a period of 12 months from today.

Appeal allowed. Order appealed quashed. Sentence varied.

Solicitors: *H C L Hanne & Co*, Battersea (for the appellant); *Director of Public Prosecutions.*

N P Metcalfe Esq   Barrister.

R v West Yorkshire Coroner, ex parte Smith   *a*

COURT OF APPEAL, CIVIL DIVISION
LORD LANE CJ, WALLER AND DONALDSON LJJ
28, 29, 30 JULY 1982

Coroner – Inquest – Jurisdiction – Death occurring abroad – Body brought to England and lying   *b*
within coroner's district – Reasonable cause to suspect violent or unnatural death – Whether
coroner having jurisdiction to hold inquest – Coroners Act 1877, ss 3(1), 7(1).

In May 1979 the appellant's daughter, a British subject who was employed as a nurse at a
hospital in Jeddah, Saudi Arabia, died. It was said that she fell to her death from a balcony
in a block of flats in Jeddah, but the circumstances of her fall and death were unclear.
The appellant, who wished to have those circumstances formally examined in order to   *c*
remove some of the obscurity and to determine, if possible, the cause of his daughter's
death, had her body brought back to England and then asked the coroner in whose
district the body was lying to hold an inquest on the body. The coroner refused, stating
that he had no jurisdiction to hold an inquest because the daughter's death had occurred
outside the jurisdiction of the English courts. The Divisional Court refused an application   *d*
for judicial review of the coroner's decision, holding that where the cause of death of a
person and the death itself occurred outside the jurisdiction of the English courts a
coroner had no jurisdiction under the Coroners Act 1887 (which consolidated earlier
legislation) to hold an inquest merely because the body had been brought into and was
lying within the coroner's district and there was reasonable cause to suspect that the
person died a violent or unnatural death. In reaching that conclusion the Divisional   *e*
Court had regard to the common law and the earlier legislation which the 1887 Act
replaced. The appellant appealed to the Court of Appeal.

Held (Waller LJ dissenting) – The appeal would be allowed and an order of certiorari
quashing the coroner's decision not to hold an inquest would issue for the following
reasons—   *f*
   (1) A coroner's duty under s 3(1)*[a]* of the 1887 Act was mandatory and he had no
discretion; thus, when he was informed that a dead body of a person was lying within
his geographical area of jurisdiction and there was reasonable cause to suspect that the
death fell into one of the categories specified in s 3(1), he was required to hold an inquest
'whether the cause of death arose within his jurisdiction or not'. There was no ambiguity
or obscurity in the words of s 3 nor were they fairly susceptible of bearing more than one   *g*
meaning in their context, and consequently it was not permissible to have regard to
earlier legislation as an aid to the construction of s 3. Furthermore, s 7(1)*[b]* of the 1887 Act
did not in any way cast doubt on or cause to be ambiguous the provisions of s 3(1), but
merely made it clear which coroner had the duty to hold an inquest (see p 1101 *h*, p 1102
f to *h*, p 1104 *g h*, p 1105 *c*, p 1106 *d*, p 1107 *b c e f* and p 1108 *c*, post); dicta of Lord
Herschell in *Bank of England v Vagliano Bros* [1891–4] All ER Rep at 113, of Lord Simon   *h*
in *Maunsell v Olins* [1975] 1 All ER at 27, *Farrell v Alexander* [1976] 2 All ER 721 and
dicta of Lord Simon and Lord Scarman in *Stock v Frank Jones (Tipton) Ltd* [1978] 1 All ER
at 953–954, 955 applied.
   (2) Section 3 did not confer any extra-territorial jurisdiction on a coroner since the
territoriality of the jurisdiction was provided by the presence of the body in the coroner's
area of jurisdiction. The coroner was required to inquire about the reasons for the death,   *i*
which might have happened elsewhere, but he was not required to inquire into the *j*
reasons for the death of a body which was outside England and Wales (see p 1105 *a c*,
p 1106 *d j* to p 1107 *a e f j* and p 1108 *c*, post).

---

a   Section 3(1) is set out at p 1100 *f* to *h*, post
b   Section 7(1) is set out at p 1101 *j* to p 1102 *a*, post

Per Donaldson LJ. (1) Once an inquest on a body has been held by a coroner pursuant
a to the 1887 Act, no other coroner will have jurisdiction to hold a further inquest in
relation to that body unless and until the verdict of the first inquest has been set aside
(see p 1108 b, post).

(2) The purpose of a coroner's verdict is to inform the community of how a dead body
came to be within its midst rather than to initiate any action, save to the extent of
authorising its disposal. Accordingly, to require a coroner to hold an inquest into a death
b where he is powerless to take any action would not result in a verdict that would be a
mere brutum fulmen (see p 1108 c, post).

Decision of the Divisional Court of the Queen's Bench Division [1982] 2 All ER 801
reversed.

c **Notes**
For a coroner's jurisdiction, see 9 Halsbury's Laws (4th edn) paras 1011, 1013, for his
duty to hold an inquest, see ibid para 1036, and for cases on the subject, see 13 Digest
(Reissue) 171–172, 1436–1452.

For the Coroners Act 1887, ss 3, 7, see 7 Halsbury's Statutes (3rd edn) 242, 246.

d **Cases referred to in judgments**
Bank of England v Vagliano Bros [1891] AC 107, [1891–4] All ER Rep 93, HL, 44 Digest
(Repl) 377, 2177.
Brandling v Barrington (1827) 6 B & C 467, 108 ER 523, 44 Digest (Repl) 272, 992.
Farrell v Alexander [1976] 2 All ER 721, [1977] AC 59, [1976] 3 WLR 145, HL, Digest
e (Cont Vol E) 382, 8375b.
Maunsell v Olins [1975] 1 All ER 16, [1975] AC 373, [1974] 3 WLR 835, HL, Digest (Cont
Vol D) 596, 8565a.
R v City of London Court Judge and Payne [1892] 1 QB 273, CA, 1(1) Digest (Reissue) 219,
1240.
R v Great Western Rly Co (1842) 3 QB 333, 114 ER 533, 13 Digest (Reissue) 171, 1444.
f *Stock v Frank Jones (Tipton) Ltd* [1978] 1 All ER 948, [1978] 1 WLR 231, HL, 20 Digest
(Reissue) 412, 3389.
Sutherland Publishing Co Ltd v Caxton Publishing Co Ltd (No 2) [1937] 4 All ER 405, [1938]
Ch 174, CA; *rvsd* [1938] 4 All ER 389, [1939] AC 178, HL, 13 Digest (Reissue) 146,
1201.
Vacher & Sons Ltd v London Society of Compositors [1913] AC 107, [1911–13] All ER Rep
g 241, HL, 44 Digest (Repl) 193, 56.

Cases also cited
Hunter v Chief Constable of West Midlands Police [1981] 3 All ER 727, [1982] AC 529, HL.
Macmanaway, Re [1951] AC 161, PC.
Ormond Investment Co Ltd v Betts [1928] AC 143, [1928] All ER Rep 709, HL.
h *R v Berwick-on-Tweed Coroner* (1843) 7 JP 676.
R v Ingham (1864) 5 B & S 257, 122 ER 827.
R v Surrey Coroner, ex p Campbell [1982] 2 All ER 545, [1982] QB 661, DC.
Royal College of Nursing of the UK v Dept of Health and Social Security [1981] 1 All ER 545,
[1981] AC 800, QBD, CA and HL.

j **Appeal**
Ronald Smith appealed against the decision of the Divisonal Court of the Queen's Bench
Division (Ormrod LJ and Forbes J) ([1982] 2 All ER 801, [1982] 2 WLR 1071) on 2 April
1982 dismissing the appellant's application for judicial review of the decision of the
coroner for the Eastern District of the Metropolitan County of West Yorkshire, Mr Philip

S Gill, not to hold an inquest on the body of Helen Linda Smith, the appellant's daughter.
The facts are set out in the judgment of Lord Lane CJ.   *a*

Stephen Sedley for the applicant.
Simon D Brown as amicus curiae.

LORD LANE CJ. This is an appeal from a judgment of the Divisional Court on 2   *b*
April 1982 dismissing an application for judicial review, in the shape of orders of
certiorari and mandamus directed to one of Her Majesty's coroners who had refused to
hold an inquest (see [1982] 2 All ER 801, [1982] 2 WLR 1071).

The facts are as follows. Helen Linda Smith was the daughter of Ronald Smith, the
appellant. At the material times she was employed as a nurse at a hospital in Jeddah,
Saudi Arabia. She died on 20 May 1979. It is said that she fell to her death from one of   *c*
the balconies in a block of flats in that city. The circumstances of her fall and death are
by no means clear. Her father wished to have those circumstances formally examined in
order to remove some of the obscurity and to determine, if possible, the cause of the girl's
fall and death. He has filed a lengthy affidavit setting out, amongst other things, his
complaints and his difficulties.

On 17 June 1980 the body was brought back to England, and at all material times was   *d*
lying in a place over which Mr Philip S Gill, as Her Majesty's Coroner for the Eastern
District of the Metropolitan County of West Yorkshire, has jurisdiction. The appellant
requested Mr Gill to hold an inquest on the body of his daughter for the reasons already
stated, but Mr Gill, in a letter to the appellant on 3 August 1981, refused to hold an
inquest, saying, '... her death occurred outside the jurisdiction of the English Courts,
and I am satisfied that this case does not fall within my jurisdiction for the holding of an   *e*
Inquest.'

The Divisional Court came to the conclusion that the coroner's view was correct and
from that conclusion Mr Smith now appeals. Our sole task in this court is to determine
whether in the circumstances which I have described the coroner is obliged to hold an
inquest or not.

The cornerstone of the submission of counsel for the appellant is s 3(1) of the Coroners   *f*
Act 1887. That reads as follows:

'Where a coroner is informed that the dead body of a person is lying within his
jurisdiction, and there is reasonable cause to suspect that such person had died either
a violent or an unnatural death, or has died a sudden death of which the cause is
unknown, or that such person has died in prison, or in such place or under such
circumstances as to require an inquest in pursuance of any Act, the coroner, whether   *g*
the cause of death arose within his jurisdiction or not, shall, as soon as practicable,
issue his warrant for summoning not less than twelve nor more than twenty-three
good and lawful men to appear before him at a specified time and place, there to
inquire as jurors touching the death of such person as aforesaid.'

There have been, by subsequent enactments, amendments to the numbers of jurors   *h*
required. These amendments are irrelevant for the purposes of the present appeal.

In the present case the coroner was informed that the body of a dead person was lying
within his jurisdiction. There was reasonable cause to suspect that the person had died
an unnatural death and counsel for the appellant submits that accordingly the coroner is
obliged (this is by the word 'shall' employed in the subsection) to conduct an inquest as
soon as possible. To the objection that the death took place outside the jurisdiction of the   *j*
courts of this country counsel replies that the words of the section are 'whether the cause
of death arose within his jurisdiction or not', and accordingly it is unnecessary for the
death to have occurred in England or Wales for him to have jurisdiction.

It may first of all be helpful to see what the textbook writers have said about this
particular section. First of all 9 Halsbury's Laws (4th edn) para 1011 reads:

'Extent of jurisdiction The local jurisdiction of a coroner is normally limited to the area for which he is appointed coroner; it is immaterial for this purpose where the cause of death arose or where the death occurred; whenever an inquest ought to be held it is sufficient to give the coroner jurisdiction to hold such inquest that the body should be lying within the area of his jurisdiction . . .'

Paragraph 1013 reads:

'Deaths abroad. Where a death has occurred abroad and the body has been brought into England or Wales for disposal, the coroner for the district in which it is lying has jurisdiction. If the death appears to have been natural or to have been properly investigated at the place where it occurred the coroner does not usually make further inquiry. If there seems to be good reason for inquiring into the death, such as suspicion of homicide, complaint by relatives or apparent failure to make full investigation, the coroner may assume jurisdiction . . .'

There is then a footnote which reads as follows:

'The difficulties of obtaining evidence concerning a death which has occurred abroad are considerable. The coroner has no power to summon witnesses from foreign countries or to require the production of documents. In these circumstances there is very little prospect of an adequate inquiry.'

Dr Gavin Thurston was the contributor who supplied that passage to Halsbury's Laws of England, and perhaps not surprisingly in his own book *Coronership* (2nd edn, 1980) p 39 he takes the same view as there expressed.

The other text book to which I refer is *Jervis on Coroners* (9th edn, 1957) p 69, under the heading 'Death abroad', where it says:

'Where a death has occurred at sea or abroad and the body has been moved into his area, the coroner should treat the case in the same way as any other case of death which occurs in his area. Provided that the death has been adequately investigated abroad, it may not normally serve any useful purpose for the coroner to make fresh inquiries concerning it. There may be circumstances, however, in which an inquest should be held; for instance, where the relatives of a deceased serviceman were of opinion that his death had not been properly investigated abroad or where they had not been informed of the results of the investigation. In other cases where the coroner is of opinion that the cause of death should be investigated, the same procedure should be followed that would be followed if the death had taken place in his area. Unless an order is made by the coroner, the death is not required to be registered . . .'

It will be observed that those passages indicate the writers' view that a discretion exists in the coroner in these circumstances. Before us, as before the Divisional Court, counsel for the appellant and counsel whom we have had as amicus curiae are both agreed that the textbooks are wrong so far as discretion is concerned. Whatever the words of the section may mean, the coroner's duty is mandatory and he has no discretion.

Counsel as amicus has greatly assisted us. His first submission is that, despite the apparently clear meaning of s 3(1) of the 1887 Act taken on its own, it is not permissible to take it on its own in that way. It must be read with s 7 of that Act. Section 7(1) reads as follows:

'The coroner only within whose jurisdiction the body of a person upon whose death an inquest ought to be holden is lying shall hold the inquest [I interpolate that I propose to read the rest of the section, although it has been repealed, because the fact that it has been repealed is irrelevant to the consideration of these submissions. The section went on as follows:] and where a body is found dead in the sea, or any creek, river, or navigable canal within the flowing of the sea where there is no deputy coroner for the jurisdiction of the Admiralty of England the inquest shall be

held only by the coroner having jurisdiction in the place where the body is first
brought to land.'　　　　　　　　　　　　　　　　　　　　　　　　　　　　　　　**a**

The submission of counsel is that, if one reads s 3(1) together with that part of s 7
which I have read, the real and substantial difficulty or ambiguity becomes apparent.
That ambiguity in its turn entitles one to examine earlier legislation as an aid to resolving
the ambiguity and, so the submission went, if one does that, it becomes clear that what
the draftsman intended was to restrict the obligation to hold an inquest to those cases
where either the cause of death or the death itself took place in England or Wales, but　**b**
where both the cause of death and the death itself occurred outside this jurisdiction of
England and Wales, the coroner has no jurisdiction.

The way he puts the argument before us is this. Although s 3 taken in isolation
requires, in circumstances such as the present, only two circumstances to be fulfilled
before the coroner's mandatory duties arise, that is to say that the dead body of a person
is in the coroner's territorial area and, secondly, that there is reasonable cause to suspect　**c**
that such person had died a violent or an unnatural death, yet s 7 has further preconditions
which have to be satisfied before an inquest 'has to be held under s 3. The two
requirements in s 3 are not enough on their own. Section 7 demands also, by using the
words 'upon whose death an inquest ought to be holden', that there must be jurisdiction
to hold an inquest and that, in order for that to happen, either the injury which caused　**d**
death or the death itself must have taken place in England or Wales.

Counsel then turns to the second half of s 7(1), and suggests that that too operates as a
further rider to s 3(1).

That is not the way in which the Divisional Court approached this matter. It came to
the conclusion that the results of giving to s 3 the meaning contended for by counsel for
the appellant would lead to such absurdity that 'the wide language of this section must
be read subject to some form of limitation' (see [1982] 2 All ER 801 at 803, [1982] 2　**e**
WLR 1071 at 1073). As to most of the examples of the alleged absurdities given by the
Divisional Court, counsel as amicus agrees with counsel for the appellant that they are
not apposite. As I understand it, he did not seek to base his submission on the argument
that the results of adopting the appellant's construction would lead to absurdity. He
prefers to describe such examples as there are as oddities and difficulties themselves. That
leaves s 7(1) and its effect as being the sole basis for the alleged ambiguity.　　　　　**f**

I do not accept counsel's arguments on this point. It seems to me that s 3(1) is setting
out the circumstances under which a coroner has to act, namely when he is informed
that a dead body is lying in his area, and so on, whereas s 7(1) is making it clear which
coroner has the duty so to act after the matters in s 3(1) have taken place. The suggestion
implicit in counsel's submission that the words 'upon whose death an inquest ought to
be holden' casts on the coroner some duty to ensure that either the death or the injury　**g**
took place in England or Wales I find unacceptable. So far as the second part of s 7(1)
(which has now been repealed) is concerned, this is simply, in my judgment, to deal with
the particular case of a body found in the sea or other waters, and was no doubt designed,
amongst other things, to avoid disputes between coroners in such circumstances. I do
not consider s 7(1) in any way casts doubts on or causes to be ambiguous the provisions　**h**
in s 3(1). Those provisions are, to my mind, clear.

It is said that if one examines the earlier history of legislation in respect of coroners it
can be seen that s 3(1) does not bear the meaning which the words contained in it seem
to indicate. It is therefore necessary to see what guidance there is on the subject of
statutory interpretation in these circumstances.

The Coroners Act 1887 is expressed to be a consolidating statute, though, it is fair to　**j**
say, one has to look no further than s 6 of the Act (which provides a whole new method
of redress) to realise that consolidation was not the only aim of the statute. I start off by
examining *Bank of England v Vagliano Bros* [1891] AC 107 at 144–145, [1891–4] All ER
Rep 93 at 113, where Lord Herschell said:

'I think the proper course is in the first instance to examine the language of the
statute and to ask what is its natural meaning, uninfluenced by any considerations

a
derived from the previous state of the law, and not to start with inquiring how the
law previously stood, and then, assuming that it was probably intended to leave it
unaltered, to see if the words of the enactment will bear an interpretation in
conformity with this view. If a statute, intended to embody in a code a particular
branch of the law, is to be treated in this fashion, it appears to me that its utility will
be almost entirely destroyed, and the very object with which it was enacted will be
frustrated. The purpose of such a statute surely was that on any point specifically
b
dealt with by it, the law should be ascertained by interpreting the language used
instead of, as before, by roaming over a vast number of authorities in order to
discover what the law was, extracting it by a minute critical examination of the
prior decisions, dependent upon a knowledge of the exact effect even of an obsolete
proceeding such as a demurrer to evidence. I am of course far from asserting that
resort may never be had to the previous state of the law for the purpose of aiding in
c
the construction of the provisions of the code. If, for example, a provision be of
doubtful import, such resort would be perfectly legitimate. Or, again, if in a code
of the law of negotiable instruments words be found which have previously acquired
a technical meaning, or been used in a sense other than their ordinary one, in
relation to such instruments, the same interpretation might well be put upon them
in the code. I give these as examples merely; they, of course, do not exhaust the
d
category. What, however, I am venturing to insist upon is, that the first step taken
should be to interpret the language of the statute, and that an appeal to earlier
decisions can only be justified on some special ground.'

The next case to which I wish to make reference is *Maunsell v Olins* [1975] 1 All ER 16
at 27, [1975] AC 373 at 392–393. The passage I should like to read is from the speech of
Lord Simon which runs thus:

e
'It is only where the actual words used in the consolidation Act are ambiguous (in
the sense of being fairly susceptible of bearing more than one meaning in their
context and register) that recourse may be had to any difference in phraseology of
the corresponding provision in the repealed enactment as an aid to their construction.
Even in such a case the corresponding provision of the repealed enactment is capable
of being an aid to the construction of the consolidation Act only if its own wording
f
is unambiguous and its sole meaning is one of those which the words in the
consolidation Act can fairly bear.'

The next is *Farrell v Alexander* [1976] 2 All ER 721, [1977] AC 59. All I need read there
are the last words of the headnote ([1977] AC 59 at 60):

g
'Held ... Per Lord Wilberforce, Lord Simon of Glaisdale and Lord Edmund-
Davies. When the words of a consolidation Act are clear, the court in construing it
should treat it as standing on its own feet and it is not necessary to examine its
legislative antecedents.'

Finally, there is *Stock v Frank Jones (Tipton) Ltd* [1978] 1 All ER 948 at 953–954, [1978]
1 WLR 231 at 237. First of all I wish to read a passage from the speech of Lord Simon
h   which reads as follows:

'... the Parliamentary draftsman knows what objective the legislative promotor
wishes to attain, and he will normally and desirably try to achieve that objective by
using language of the appropriate register in its natural, ordinary and primary sense;
to reject such an approach on the ground that it gives rise to an anomaly is liable to
encourage complication and anfractuosity in drafting ... Parliament is nowadays in
j
continuous session, so that an unlooked-for and unsupportable injustice or anomaly
can be readily rectified by legislation; this is far preferable to judicial contortion of
the law to meet apparently hard cases with the result that ordinary citizens and their
advisers hardly know where they stand.'

The other passage is from the speech of Lord Scarman, which reads as follows ([1978]
1 All ER 948 at 955, [1978] 1 WLR 231 at 238–239):

'I wish, however, to add a few words of my own on the "anomalies" argument. Counsel for the appellants sought to give the words a meaning other than their plain *a* meaning by drawing attention to what he called the "anomalies" which would result from giving effect to the words used by Parliament. If the words used be plain, this is, I think, an illegitimate method of statutory interpretation unless it can be demonstrated that the anomalies are such that they produce an absurdity which Parliament could not have intended, or destroy the remedy established by Parliament to deal with the mischief which the Act is designed to combat. It is not enough that *b* the words, though clear, lead to a "manifest absurdity": per Lord Esher MR in *R v City of London Court Judge* [1892] 1 QB 273 at 290. Lord Atkinson put the point starkly in *Vacher & Sons Ltd v London Society of Compositors* [1913] AC 107 at 121, [1911–13] All ER Rep 241 at 248: "If the language of a statute be plain, admitting of only one meaning, the Legislature must be taken to have meant and intended what it has plainly expressed, and whatever it has in clear terms enacted must be *c* enforced though it should lead to absurd or mischievous results." The reason for the rule was given by Lord Tenterden CJ in *Brandling v Barrington* (1827) 6 B & C 467 at 475, 108 ER 523 at 527 in a passage in which he was considering the so-called "equity of a statute"; he commented—" ... that it is much safer and better to rely on and abide by the plain words, although the Legislature might possibly have provided for other cases had their attention been directed to them." As Lord *d* Moulton said in *Vacher's* case [1913] AC 107 at 130, [1911–13] All ER Rep 241 at 252: "The argument ab inconvenienti is one which requires to be used with great caution. There is a danger that it may degrade into mere judicial criticism of the propriety of the acts of the Legislature." If the words used by Parliament are plain, there is no room for the "anomalies" test, unless the consequences are so absurd that, without going outside the statute, one can see that Parliament must have made a *e* drafting mistake. If words "have been inadvertently used", it is legitimate for the court to substitute what is apt to avoid the intention of the legislature being defeated: per MacKinnon LJ in *Sutherland Publishing Co Ltd v Caxton Publishing Co Ltd (No 2)* [1937] 4 All ER 405 at 421, [1938] Ch 174 at 201. This is an acceptable exception to the general rule that plain language excludes a consideration of "anomalies", ie mischievous or absurd consequences. If a study of the statute as a *f* whole leads inexorably to the conclusion that Parliament has erred in its choice of words, eg used "and" when "or" was clearly intended, the courts can, and must, eliminate the error by interpretation. But mere "manifest absurdity" is not enough: it must be an error (of commission or omission) which in its context defeats the intention of the Act.'

g

Applying those various considerations then to the words of s 3, I am unable to find any ambiguity or obscurity. I do not think that the words used are fairly susceptible of bearing more than one meaning in their context. Consequently it is not permissible to have regard, in my judgment, to any earlier statutory enactment as an aid to construction. No aid is required save the words themselves. It should perhaps be added that the interpretation of s 3 suggested by counsel as amicus would itself require extensive *h* wording being read into the section, which, on its own, perhaps provides an argument against such an interpretation being adopted.

It was at one stage suggested that the appellant's interpretation of s 3 would confer some extra-territorial power on the coroner which he did not enjoy before. Of course every statute, as pointed out by Donaldson LJ in the course of argument, has to be read against an accepted background, and of course one of the features of that background is *j* that as a general rule that statute will only apply to activities within the jurisdiction of the court. If a statute, for example, says that you must not sell chocolates on Sunday, that will, generally speaking, apply to England and Wales and will not apply to anyone selling chocolates on Sundays in France.

Can it be said that the plain interpretation of s 3 contravenes that principle and therefore must be read subject to the proviso that it only applies to injuries abroad resulting in death in England, or injuries in England resulting in death abroad? I think

a not. The territoriality is provided by the presence of the body in the coroner's area of jurisdiction. The coroner is inquiring about the reasons for the death which may have happened elsewhere. What he is not being asked to do is to inquire into the reasons for the death of a body which is outside England and Wales. In any event it has been since 1729 the duty of a coroner in certain circumstances to inquire into the death in England of a body, the death having been caused by injuries suffered outside the jurisdiction

b abroad and vice versa, provided of course the body is in his geographical area. Inevitably a coroner conducting an inquisition into a death abroad will be faced with difficulties of evidence and so on, but that must have been so ever since the statute 2 Geo 2 c 21 (murder). Such difficulties are indeed by no means confined to death occurring overseas. Coroners are well experienced in dealing with such problems. Indeed the same difficulties would have arisen if Miss Smith had survived her fall long enough to be brought back to

c England to hospital and had died in hospital or elsewhere in England.

For these reasons I would allow this appeal.

WALLER LJ. With some hesitation, because I am differing both from Lord Lane CJ and I understand also from Donaldson LJ, I would dismiss this appeal. I will very briefly set out my reasons.

d I do not find the words of s 3(1) of the Coroners Act 1887 clear. There is no difficulty about the first part of the subsection. The use of the phrase 'his jurisdiction' is a clear reference to the district in which the coroner operates. However, when one comes to the words 'the coroner, whether the cause of death arose within his jurisdiction or not', the words may be contrasting his jurisdiction with the jurisdiction of other coroners, that is to say in England and Wales, or may be contrasting his jurisdiction with the rest of the

e world, something which was not so likely in 1887.

Consideration of s 7 of the 1887 Act before it was amended to some extent supports the more restricted meaning, because in the part now repealed, in certain circumstances as set out therein, there is substituted 'another coroner' for 'the coroner' in s 3. Furthermore, the words at the beginning of s 7 appear to be mere repetition of s 3. Unless there is some special meaning to be attached to the phrase 'upon whose death an inquest

f ought to be holden', it is difficult to understand why there should be a repetition, and therefore this raises further doubts about the effect of s 3(1).

This being a consolidating Act, I bear in mind that the court should not look at legislation which this Act replaces, unless there is some ambiguity or real or substantial difficulty which needs resolving (see *Maunsell v Olins* [1975] 1 All ER 16, [1975] AC 373, *Farrell v Alexander* [1976] 2 All ER 721, [1977] AC 59 and the other cases to which Lord

g Lane CJ has referred). However, in my opinion there is such an ambiguity and difficulty, and accordingly I have felt free to look at the statute 6 & 7 Vict c 12 (1843) (coroners), which was passed as a result of the decision in *R v Great Western Rly Co* (1842) 3 QB 333, 114 ER 533. But first I should mention that under the statute 9 Geo 4 c 31 (1828) (offences against the person) a charge of murder or manslaughter by one of His Majesty's subjects was made triable in England wherever it was committed. This, however, did

h not give a similar jurisdiction where the death was not felonious.

R v Great Western Rly Co decided that, unless the coroner suspected murder or manslaughter, the coroner of the place where a dead body was lying had no jurisdiction to inquire into the death. In that case the Reading coroner was seeking to hold an inquest on a man who had been killed on the railway outside Reading. But s 1 of the 1843 Act said:

j 'That the Coroner only within whose Jurisdiction the Body of any Person upon whose Death an Inquest ought to be holden shall be lying dead shall hold the Inquest, notwithstanding that the Cause of Death did not arise within the Jurisdiction of such Coroner . . .'

and so reversed the effect of the *Great Western Rly* decision.

The words 'upon whose death an inquest ought to be holden', which words are in s 7

of the 1887 Act, come straight from the 1843 Act, whose object was to deal with
jurisdiction as between two different coroners, the one in whose jurisdiction the death *a*
was caused and the other in whose jurisdiction the body was lying. In either case there
was territorial jurisdiction.

It is difficult to see how the 1843 Act could possibly give jurisdiction to the coroner to
deal with a case such as the present. If the effect of s 3(1) is to give jurisdiction to a coroner
to investigate a violent death caused and occurring anywhere in the world, provided only
that the body lies in his jurisdiction, it is surprising that the change was made in such a *b*
way as in this section.

In my opinion s 3(1) of the 1887 Act does not make such a radical change in
jurisdiction. It is simply making clear that the coroner is obliged to hold an inquest on a
body lying within his jurisdiction, where death has occurred within the jurisdiction of
some other coroner, that is to say where there is territorial jurisdiction within England
and Wales, where an inquest ought to be holden.   *c*

In my opinion, which I have set out very briefly, s 3(1) should not be construed so as
to give jurisdiction to a coroner where the body has been brought from abroad where
both the death and the cause of death took place.

DONALDSON LJ. I agree with the judgment of Lord Lane CJ, but as we are differing *d*
from the Divisional Court, and as we are not ourselves unanimous, I would like to add a
few words.

It is the highly unusual nature of this case which has, as I think, led the Divisional
Court into error. We know that Helen Smith was a British subject. We know that she
died in Jeddah in May 1979. We know that her death does not appear to have been due
to natural causes. These facts, without more, would give rise to public sympathy and *e*
concern. However, without more, neither in terms of the common law nor in terms of
statute law do they give rise to any right or obligation in a coroner to inquire into the
circumstances of Miss Smith's death. Given those facts and no more, that would be a
matter for the Saudi Arabian authorities, and for them alone.

We then have the fact that Miss Smith's body has been flown to this country, partly no
doubt in order that she may be buried here, but partly in order that one of Her Majesty's *f*
coroners may inquire into the circumstances of her death. The Divisional Court
was convinced that the mere removal of her body to this country could not make any
difference and that Parliament could never have intended that it should. Starting with
that premise the Divisional Court concluded that the words of s 3(1) of the Coroners Act
1887, which read literally seem to produce this result, must be subject to some limitation.
Going on from there, the court considered and rejected the possibility that the coroner *g*
might have a discretion whether or not to hold an inquest. It then turned to the rules
relating to the construction of consolidating statutes and concluded that it was permissible
to examine the earlier statutes and the common law. It thought that it had found the
solution to its dilemma in the words 'upon whose death an inquest ought to be holden'
which appear in s 7(1) of the Act and held—

> 'that jurisdiction to hold an inquest requires something more than the fact that *h*
> the body is lying within the geographical limits of the coroner's jurisdiction, and
> there is reasonable cause to suspect a violent or unnatural death. There is no warrant
> in any of the legislation or at common law to support the proposition that an inquest
> can be held where both the cause of death and the death itself occurred out of the
> jurisdiction of the English courts.'
>   *j*
(See [1982] 2 All ER 801 at 805, [1982] 2 WLR 1071 at 1076.)

With all respect to the judges of the Divisional Court, I do not accept their premise.
The presence of a dead human body in this country is a factor of significance. It creates a
very real and legitimate public interest in holding an inquiry, and this interest is in no
way extra-territorial. In the absence of a death certificate by an appropriate authority in

a this country, it may well be considered essential at the very least to ascertain where the body came from, whether the deceased died in this country and, if so, how. The public interest centres on the body which is in this country, on the cause of the death of that body and only incidentally on where that cause or the death itself occurred.

Section 3(1) of the 1887 Act seems to me to be both unambiguous and entirely consistent with this approach. Where a coroner is informed that a dead body of a person is lying within the geographical area of his jurisdiction, and there is reasonable cause to
b suspect that the death fell into one of the specified categories, he has to make inquiries, to hold an inquest, 'whether the cause of death arose within his jurisdiction or not'. Section 3(3) then instructs the coroner on the nature of his inquiries. Subject to the relevant rules, he has to try to ascertain who the deceased was and how, when and where the deceased came by his death. Of course Parliament could have added a rider that, if the death occurred abroad other than on the high seas, the coroner need not, or even
c should not, inquire into the cause of death, but it has not done so. Section 7(1) then resolves demarcation disputes between coroners who wish to, or are in doubt which coroner should, officiate when 'an inquest ought to be holden', that being a reference back to s 3(1), which defines when this situation arises.

The Divisional Court seems to have struggled to import a territorial limitation. In my judgment this obscured the issue. Every parliamentary draftsman writes on paper which
d bears the legend, albeit in invisible ink, 'this Act shall not have extra-territorial effect save to the extent that it expressly so provides'. The courts know this and they read it into every statute. If Parliament ordained that there shall be no night baking, this would mean that there should be no night baking in this country. If Parliament ordained that all deaths shall be reported to the police, it would be referring to all deaths occurring in this country. And if it ordained that certain inquiries should be made about dead bodies,
e prima facie it would mean dead bodies present in this country. In fact Parliament has said so expressly in the case of the 1877 Act, but it need not have done so.

The words of s 3(1) are clear and wholly free from ambiguity. Once it is appreciated that it is the dead body lying within the jurisdiction which gives rise to the need for inquiry and which is the subject of the inquiry, the section is free from any possible objection that it creates what the Americans call a 'long-arm jurisdiction'.

f There will be some who say that this is all very well, but in the circumstances of this case the coroner will be inquiring into matters which occurred in Saudi Arabia and that the rulers, and indeed the courts of that country, will be justifiably affronted. I do not agree. I would expect the Saudi Arabian authorities to make similar inquiries in relation to a dead body in their country and I would not expect them to feel under any obligation to desist because those inquiries led them to believe that the deceased had met his death
g in England. Although national governments and courts are usually only concerned with inquiring into matters which occurred exclusively within their own territories, this is by no means always the case. The starting point will always be a problem arising within their own territory, but resolving that problem may well involve them in asking what happened elsewhere.

This case is concerned with the finding of a body in this country. The appellant has
h told us where it came from and of course I do not doubt his assertion. But neither the Divisional Court nor this court is the appropriate authority to accept or test his assertion. That is the function of a coroner. In another case the English courts might be faced with a claim by a Saudi Arabian citizen that a British citizen had injured him by negligent driving in Saudi Arabia. The English courts would have to investigate what happened in Saudi Arabia and, having done so, would award the claimant damages if his case was
j proved. Similarly the Saudi Arabian courts might well be called on to investigate negligent acts alleged to have occurred in this country. None of this offends against comity between nations and courts or against the territorial integrity of those nations.

The Divisional Court seemed to fear that a decision favourable to the appellant might lead to bodies being brought to this country for the sole purpose of obtaining the benefit of an inquest by a British coroner. I do not share their fears. If they are well founded, the remedy lies not in seeking to place a limitation on the plain words of the statute but in restricting the right to bring dead bodies to this country.

The court also feared that if s 3 was construed so as to give a coroner jurisdiction based on a body being found in his area, bodies could be moved from area to area with a view to having further and better inquests, but it was rightly conceded in argument that this fear was misconceived. Once an inquest has been held pursuant to the statute, no other coroner will have jurisdiction to hold a further inquest in relation to that body unless and until the verdict of the first inquiry has been set aside.

Finally the Divisional Court asserted that it was anomalous that a coroner should be required 'to hold an inquest into a death where he is powerless to take any action, so that the verdict would be a mere brutum fulmen' (see [1982] 2 All ER 801 at 803, [1982] 2 WLR 1071 at 1073). This involves a misunderstanding of the purpose of the coroner's verdict, which is to inform the community of how a dead body comes to be within its midst rather than to initiate any action, save to the extent of authorising its disposal. In no sense could a verdict in the present case be properly described as 'brutum fulmen'.

For these reasons and for those given by Lord Lane CJ, I would allow the appeal and make the order which he proposes.

Appeal allowed; order of certiorari to go. No order as to costs.

Solicitors: *Bindman & Partners,* agents for *Howard Cohen & Co,* Leeds (for the appellant); *Treasury Solicitor.*

Sepala Munasinghe Esq   Barrister.

Mandla v Dowell Lee and another

COURT OF APPEAL, CIVIL DIVISION
LORD DENNING MR, OLIVER AND KERR LJJ
21, 22, 23, 29 JULY 1982

Race relations – Discrimination – Discrimination against racial group – Sikhs – Racial group defined by reference to colour, race, nationality or ethnic or national origins – Ethnic or national origins – Ethnic – Headmaster refusing to admit Sikh boy to school unless he removed his turban and cut his hair – Whether unlawful discrimination – Whether Sikhs a 'racial group' – Whether Sikhs a group defined by reference to 'ethnic or national origins' – Race Relations Act 1976, ss 1(1)(b), 3(1).

The headmaster of a private school refused to admit to the school a boy who was an orthodox Sikh, and who therefore wore long hair under a turban, unless he removed his turban and cut his hair, on the ground that the wearing of a turban would accentuate religious and social distinctions in the school which, being a multiracial school based on the Christian faith, the headmaster desired to minimise. The boy, suing by his father, sought a declaration in the county court that the refusal to admit him unless he removed his turban and cut his hair was discrimination under s 1(1)(b)[a] of the Race Relations Act 1976 against a member of a 'racial group' within s 1(1)(b) and was therefore unlawful. Damages were also claimed. The evidence before the court was that Sikhism originated as a religion among Hindus in the Punjab area of India, that it also became a militant political movement within the Punjab, that its adherents were not a separate race but were Punjabis whose common language was Punjabi, that they represented only a

_____

a   Section 1(1), so far as material, is set out at p 1115 c d, post

fraction of the population of the Punjab, and that the outstanding distinction between
a Sikhs and the other peoples of India was the religion of Sikhism and its accompanying
culture, which manifested itself in distinctive social customs such as the wearing of long
hair and a turban. The judge dismissed the claim on the ground that Sikhs were not a
'racial group' within the definition of that term contained in s 3(1)^b of the 1976 Act since
Sikhs were not a group of persons who could be 'defined by reference to . . . ethnic or
national origins' (although as Punjabis or Indians they might be so defined). The boy and
b his father appealed, submitting that Sikhs were a group of persons defined by reference
to 'ethnic origins' since the word 'ethnic' embraced more than a merely racial concept
and meant a cultural, linguistic or religious community. It was common ground that
Sikhism was a religion, that the adherents of a religion were not as such a 'racial group'
within the 1976 Act and that discrimination in regard to religious practices was not
unlawful.

c

Held – (1) A group was able to be defined by reference to its 'ethnic origins', within s
3(1) of the 1976 Act, only if the group could be distinguished from other groups by a
definable racial characteristic with which members of the group were born, that is by
some fixed or inherited characteristic. It followed that communities or movements
whose members or adherents merely shared a common religion or common social
d customs or political aspirations and whose members could freely move into or out of the
community or movement could not be described as a group defined by its 'ethnic
origins'. It also followed that such communities or movements did not fall within the
alternative meaning of 'racial group' in s 3(1), namely a group defined by reference to
'national origins', since that meant a group defined by descent from the people of a
particular country or nation (see p 1112 j, p 1113 b c, p 1115 g, p 1116 c j to p 1117 b,
e p 1121 h to p 1122 a and p 1123 c, post).

(2) Since Sikhs were merely a distinct religious and cultural community to which
anyone might belong, and who could not be distinguished from other peoples of the
Punjab by reference to any racial characteristic, they were not, as Sikhs, a group of
persons defined by reference to 'ethnic or national origins' within s 3(1) of the 1976 Act.
It followed that they were not a racial group within s 1(1)(b) of the 1976 Act and that it
f was not unlawful under that Act to discriminate against them. Accordingly, the appeal
would be dismissed. (See p 1114 d to j, p 1115 a g, p 1117 c d j, p 1118 j, p 1122 b c and
p 1123 g, post.)

Dicta of Lord Simon and of Lord Cross in *Ealing London Borough v Race Relations Board*
[1972] 1 All ER at 116, 117 applied.

Notes
g For the general meaning of unlawful discrimination on ground of ethnic or national
origins, see 4 Halsbury's Laws (4th edn) para 1035.

For the Race Relations Act 1976, ss 1, 3, see 46 Halsbury's Statutes (3rd edn) 395, 397.

Cases referred to in judgments
Clayton v Ramsden [1943] 1 All ER 16, [1943] AC 320, HL; rvsg [1941] 3 All ER 196,
h [1942] Ch 1, CA, 48 Digest (Repl) 320, 2774.
Commission for Racial Equality v Genture Restaurants Ltd [1981] CA Bound Transcript 227.
Ealing London Borough v Race Relations Board [1972] 1 All ER 105, [1972] AC 342, [1972]
2 WLR 71, HL, 2 Digest (Reissue) 316, 1783.
Kingston and Richmond Area Health Authority v Kaur [1981] ICR 631, EAT.
Panesar v Nestlé Co [1980] ICR 144, CA.
j *Price v Civil Service Commission* [1978] 1 All ER 1228, [1977] 1 WLR 1417, EAT, Digest
(Cont Vol E) 407, 72Ab.
Tuck's Settlement Trusts, Re, Public Trustee v Tuck [1978] 1 All ER 1047, [1978] Ch 49,
[1978] 2 WLR 411, CA, Digest (Cont Vol E) 540, 89a.

b   Section 3(1), so far as material, is set out at p 1111 f, post

Cases also cited

Singh v Rowntree Mackintosh Ltd [1979] ICR 554, EAT.
Steel v Union of Post Office Workers [1978] 2 All ER 504, [1978] 1 WLR 64, EAT.

Appeal

By amended particulars of claim the plaintiffs, who were Sikhs, Sewa Singh Mandla and his son Gurinder Singh Mandla, an infant suing through his father, claimed against the first defendant, Mr A G Dowell Lee, the headmaster of Park Grove Private School Ltd, which was the second defendant, damages limited to £500 and a declaration that the defendants had committed an act of unlawful discrimination against the plaintiffs within the Race Relations Act 1976 by refusing to offer the second plaintiff a place at the school unless he removed his turban and cut his hair to conform with the school rules. By a judgment delivered on 10 December 1980 his Honour Judge Gosling, sitting in the Birmingham County Court, dismissed the plaintiffs' claim. The plaintiffs appealed. The grounds of the appeal were, inter alia, (1) that on the evidence before him the judge should have held that the defendants discriminated against the plaintiffs within s 1(1)(b) of the 1976 Act; (2) that the judge misinterpreted and misapplied s 3(1) of the Act in holding that Sikhs were not a racial group by reference to either 'ethnic or national origins'; (3) that he construed the words 'can comply' in s 1(1)(b)(i) too narrowly as meaning 'can comply without practical difficulty' and (4) he wrongly applied the test of 'justifiable' in s 1(1)(b)(ii). The facts are set out in the judgment of Lord Denning MR.

Alexander Irvine QC and *Harjit Singh* for the plaintiffs.
The first defendant appeared in person.
The second defendant was not represented.

Cur adv vult

29 July. The following judgments were read.

LORD DENNING MR. How far can Sikhs in England insist on wearing their turbans? A turban is their distinctive headgear. They do not cut their hair but plait it under their turbans. Some of them feel so strongly about it that, when they are motor cyclists, they do not wear crash helmets; and when they are barristers they do not wear wigs.

Sewa Singh Mandla is a Sikh and rightly proud of it. He is a solicitor of the Supreme Court, practising in Birmingham. In 1978 he applied to send his son Gurinder to a private school in Birmingham called the Park Grove School. Gurinder was then aged 13. The school was very suitable for him. It had a high reputation. It took boys of all races. There were 305 boys altogether. Over 200 were English, but there were many others. Five were Sikhs, 34 Hindus, 16 Persians, six Negroes, seven Chinese and about 15 from European countries.

Mr Mandla took his son to see the headmaster. Both he and his son were wearing their turbans The headmaster felt that it might give rise to difficulties if Gurinder wore his turban in school. He asked the father: 'Will you consent to his removing his turban and cutting his hair?' The father said: 'No. That is completely out of the question.' The headmaster said that he would think about it. Then on 24 July 1978 he wrote:

'Thank you for bringing your son to see me. As I promised, I have given much thought to the problem and I have reluctantly come to the conclusion that on balance it would be unwise to relax the School Rules with regard to uniform at the moment. I do not see any way in which it would be possible to reconcile the two conflicting requirements. May I wish you well in your efforts to promote harmony and peace, and I hope you find a suitable school for Gurinder without difficulty.'

a Mr Mandla did find another school for Gurinder where he is allowed to wear his turban. So all is now well with them. But Mr Mandla reported the headmaster to the Commission for Racial Equality. They took the matter up with the headmaster. On 19 September 1978 the headmaster wrote this letter:

'To make my position quite clear, the boy was not rejected because he was a Sikh since we do not make racial distinctions and we have several Sikhs in the School. It was the turban that was rejected, and I believe your Acts cover people, not clothes.'

b
The commission, however, did not let the matter rest. They pursued the headmaster relentlessly. They interviewed him. They demanded information from him. Eventually they decided to assist Mr Mandla in legal proceedings against him. With their assistance in money and advice Mr Mandla issued proceedings against the headmaster of the school in the Birmingham County Court. He claimed damages limited to £500 and a declaration *c* that the defendants had committed an act of unlawful discrimination. The county court judge heard the case for five days in February and June 1980, with many witnesses and much argument. The judge dismissed the claim. The Commission for Racial Equality, in Mr Mandla's name, appeal to this court.

The headmaster appeared before us in person. He has not the means to instruct counsel and solicitors. He put his case moderately and with restraint. He has himself done much *d* research in the India Office library and elsewhere. It must have taken him many hours and many days. Now we have to consider what it all comes to.

The law

The case raises this point of great interest: what is a 'racial group' within the Race Relations Act 1976? If the Sikhs are a 'racial group' no one is allowed to discriminate *e* against any of their members in the important fields of education and employment and so forth. No matter whether the discrimination is direct or indirect, it is unlawful. But, if they are not a 'racial group' discrimination is perfectly lawful. So everything depends on whether they are a 'racial group' or not.

The statute in s 3(1) of the 1976 Act contains a definition of a 'racial group'. It means a 'group of persons defined by reference to colour, race, nationality or ethnic or national *f* origins'. That definition is very carefully framed. Most interesting is that it does not include religion or politics or culture. You can discriminate for or against Roman Catholics as much as you like without being in breach of the law. You can discriminate for or against Communists as much as you please, without being in breach of the law. You can discriminate for or against the 'hippies' as much as you like, without being in breach of the law. But you must not discriminate against a man because of his colour or *g* of his race or of his nationality, or of 'his ethnic or national origins'. It is not suggested that the Sikhs are a group defined by reference to colour or race or nationality. Nor was much stress laid on national origins. But it is said most persuasively by counsel for the plaintiffs that the Sikhs are a group of persons 'defined by reference to ethnic origins'. It is so important that I will consider each word of that phrase.

h *'Ethnic'*

The word 'ethnic' is derived from the Greek word 'ἔθνος' which meant simply 'nation'. It was used by the 72 Palestinian Jews who translated the Old Testament from Hebrew into Greek (in the Septuagint). They used it to denote the non-Israelitish nations, that is, the Gentiles 'τὰ ἔθνη'. When the word 'ethnic' was first used in England, it was used to denote peoples who were not Christian or Jewish. This was the meaning attached to it in *j* the great *Oxford English Dictionary* itself in 1890.

But in 1934 in the *Concise Oxford Dictionary* it was given an entirely different meaning. It was given as: 'pertaining to race, ethnological'. And 'ethnological' was given as meaning: 'corresponding to a division of races'. That is the meaning which I, acquiring my vocabulary in 1934, have always myself attached to the word 'ethnic'. It is, to my mind, the correct meaning. It means 'pertaining to race'.

But then in 1972 there was appended a second supplement of the *Oxford English Dictionary*. It gives a very much wider meaning than that which I am used to. It was *a* relied on by counsel for the plaintiffs:

'Also, pertaining to or having common racial, cultural, religious or linguistic characteristics, especially designating a racial *or other group* within a larger system; hence (U.S. colloquial), foreign, exotic.'

As an example of this new meaning, the second supplement refers to a book by Huxley *b* and Haddon called *We Europeans* (1935). It mentions 'the non-committal terms *ethnic group*' and refers to the 'special type of *ethnic* grouping of which the Jews form the best-known example' (my emphasis). This reference to the Jews gives a clue to the meaning of ethnic.

Why are 'the Jews' given as the best-known example of 'ethnic grouping'? What is their special characteristic which distinguishes them from non-Jews? To my mind it is a *c* racial characteristic. The Shorter Oxford Dictionary describes a Jew as 'a person of Hebrew race'. Some help too can be found in our law books, especially from *Clayton v Ramsden* [1941] 3 All ER 196, [1942] Ch 1; [1943] 1 All ER 16, [1943] AC 320 and *Re Tuck's Settlement Trust* [1978] 1 All ER 1047, [1978] Ch 49. If a man desires that his daughter should only marry 'a Jew' and cuts her out of his will if she should marry a man who is not 'a Jew', he will find that the court will hold the condition void for uncertainty. The *d* reason is because 'a Jew' may mean a dozen different things. It may mean a man of the Jewish faith. Even if he was a convert from Christianity, he would be of the Jewish faith. Or it may mean a man of Jewish parentage, even though he may be a convert to Christianity. It may suffice if his grandfather was a Jew and his grandmother was not. The Jewish blood may have become very thin by intermarriage with Christians, but still many would call him 'a Jew'. All this leads me to think that, when it is said of the Jews *e* that they are an 'ethnic group', it means that the group as a whole share a common characteristic which is a racial characteristic. It is that they are descended, however remotely, from a Jewish ancestor. When we spoke of the 'Jewish regiments' which were formed and fought so well during the war, we had in mind those who were of Jewish descent or parentage. When Hitler and the Nazis so fiendishly exterminated 'the Jews', it was because of their racial characteristics and not because of their religion. *f*

There is nothing in their culture of language or literature to mark out Jews in England from others. The Jews in England share all of these characteristics equally with the rest of us. Apart from religion, the one characteristic which is different is a racial characteristic.

'Origins'
g
The statute uses the word 'ethnic' in the context of 'origins'. This carries the same thought. I turn once again to the *Shorter Oxford Dictionary*. Where the word 'origin' is used of a person it means 'descent, parentage'. I turn also to the speech of Lord Cross in *Ealing London Borough v Race Relations Board* [1972] 1 All ER 105 at 117, [1972] AC 342 at 365:

'To me it suggests a connection subsisting at the time of birth . . . The connection *h* will normally arise because the parents or one of the parents of the individual in question are or is identified by descent . . .'

So the word 'origins' connotes a group which has a common racial characteristic.

'Ethnic origins'
j
If I am right in thinking that the phrase 'ethnic origins' denotes a group with a common racial characteristic, the question arises: why is it used at all? The answer is given by Lord Cross in the *Ealing London Borough* case ([1972] 1 All ER 105 at 117–118, [1972] AC 342 at 366):

a 'The reason why the words "ethnic or national origins" were added to the words "racial grounds" which alone appear in the long title was, I imagine, to prevent argument over the exact meaning of the word "race".'

In other words, there might be much argument whether one group or other was of the same 'race' as another, but there was thought to be less whether it was a different 'ethnic group'.

b *'Racial group'*

This brings me back to the definition in the statute of a 'racial group'. It means 'a group of persons defined by reference to colour, race, nationality or ethnic or national origins'.

The word 'defined' shows that the group must be distinguished from another group by some definable characteristic. English, Scots or Welsh football teams are to be c distinguished by their national origins. The Scottish clans are not distinguishable from one another either by their ethnic or national origins, but only by their clannish or tribal differences. French Canadians are distinguished from other Canadians by their ethnic or national origins. Jews are not to be distinguished by their national origins. The wandering Jew has no nation. He is a wanderer over the face of the earth. The one definable characteristic of the Jews is a racial characteristic. I have no doubt that, in using the words d 'ethnic origins', Parliament had in mind primarily the Jews. There must be no discrimination against the Jews in England. Anti-Semitism must not be allowed. It has produced great evils elsewhere. It must not be allowed here.

But the words 'ethnic origins' have a wider significance than the Jews. The question before us today is whether they include the Sikhs.

e *The Sikhs*

The word 'Sikh' is derived from the Sanskrit 'Shishya', which means 'disciple'. Sikhs are the disciples or followers of Guru Nanak, who was born on 5 April 1469. There are about 14m Sikhs, most of whom live in the part of the Punjab which is in India. Before the partition of the province in 1947 half of them lived in that portion which is now Pakistan; but on the partition most of them moved across into India. There was tragic f loss of life.

There is no difference in language which distinguishes the Sikhs from the other peoples in India. They speak Punjabi or Hindi or Urdu, or whatever the vernacular may be. There is no difference in blood which distinguishes them either. The people of India are largely the product of successive invasions that have swept into the country. They have intermingled to such an extent that it is impossible now to separate one strain from g the other. The Sikhs do not recognise any distinction of race between them and the other peoples of India. They freely receive converts from Hinduism, or vice versa. Not only from outside, but even within the same family. The outstanding distinction between the Sikhs and the other peoples of India is in their religion, Sikhism, and its accompanying culture.

This is so marked that Dr Ballard, who is a lecturer in race relations in the University h of Leeds, thought it was an ethnic difference. But, if you study his evidence, it is plain that he was using the word 'ethnic' in a special sense of his own. For him it did not signify any racial characteristic at all. These are some illuminating passages from his evidence:

'Sikhs, most obviously, are not a race in biological terms. Their origins are extremely diverse, probably more diverse than us English . . . I think they are a j classic example of an ethnic group because of their distinctive cultural traditions . . . We are busy coining lots of new words here. I think ethnicity is the proper word to coin . . .'

The evidence shows that the Sikhs as a community originate from the teaching of Guru Nanak. About the fifteenth century he founded the religious sect. There were a

series of gurus who followed Nanak, but the tenth and last is most important. Early in
the nineteenth century he instituted major social and cultural reforms and turned the *a*
Sikhs into a community. He laid down the rules by which the hair was not to be cut and
it was to be covered by a turban. By adopting this uniform Sikhs made their communal
affiliation very clear, both to each other and to outsiders. But they remained at bottom a
religious sect.

It is sometimes suggested that the Sikhs are physically a different people. But that is
not so. In an important book on *The People of Asia* (1977) p 327 Professor Bowles of *b*
Syracuse University, New York, says:

'The difference [between Muslims, Sikhs and Hindus] are mainly cultural, not
biological. Much has been written about the tallness . . . and excellent physique of
the Sikh, qualities often attributed to their well-balanced vegetarian diet. In part
this may be true, but the Skihs are matched in physique by several other Punjab
populations—meat-eating as well as vegetarian, Muslims as well as Hindus. Some *c*
of the neighbouring Pathan tribesmen are even taller. The Sikh physique is probably
due to the fact that many have entered professions that have given them an
economic advantage over their compatriots, Indians or Pakistans. A correlation
between nutrition and physique holds throughout the entire subcontinent, but it
may be more noticeable in the Punjab, where there is such a variety of merchants
and traders . . .' *d*

On all this evidence, it is plain to me that the Sikhs, as a group, cannot be distinguished
from others in the Punjab by reference to any racial characteristic whatever. They are
only to be distinguished by their religion and culture. That is not an ethnic difference at
all.

e

Conclusion

I have dealt with the evidence at length because of the differences on the point in the
lower courts and tribunals. In our present case the evidence has been more fully canvassed
than ever before. It has been most well and carefully considered by his Honour Judge
Gosling here. I agree with his conclusion that Sikhs are not a racial group. They cannot
be defined by reference to their ethnic or national origins. No doubt they are a distinct *f*
community, just as many other religious and cultural communities. But that is not good
enough. It does not enable them to complain of discrimination against them.

You must remember that it is perfectly lawful to discriminate against groups of people
to whom you object, so long as they are not a racial group. You can discriminate against
the Moonies or the skinheads or any other group which you dislike or to which you take
objection. No matter whether your objection to them is reasonable or unreasonable, you *g*
can discriminate against them, without being in breach of the law.

No doubt the Sikhs are very different from some of those groups. They are a fine
community upholding the highest standards, but they are not a 'racial group'. So it is not
unlawful to discriminate against them. Even though the discrimination may be unfair
or unreasonable, there is nothing unlawful in it.

In our present case the headmaster did not discriminate against the Sikhs at all. He has *h*
five Sikh boys in his school already. All he has done is to say that, when the boy attends
school, he must wear the school uniform and not wear a turban. The other Sikh boys in
the school conform to this requirement. They make no objection. Mr Mandla is, I expect,
strictly orthodox. He feels so strongly that he insists on his son wearing his turban at all
times. But that feeling does not mean that the headmaster was at fault in any way. He
was not unfair or unreasonable. It is for him to run his school in the way he feels best. *j*
He was not guilty of any discrimination against the Sikhs, direct or indirect.

I cannot pass from this case without expressing some regret that the Commission for
Racial Equality thought it right to take up this case against the headmaster. It must be
very difficult for educational establishments in this country to keep a proper balance
between the various pupils who seek entry. The statutes relating to race discrimination

and sex discrimination are difficult enough to understand and apply anyway. They
a should not be used so as to interfere with the discretion of schools and colleges in the
proper management of their affairs.

In the circumstances I need say nothing as to the contentions about the word 'can' or
'justifiable' in the statute. They do not arise.

I would dismiss the appeal.

b **OLIVER LJ.** Although the notice of appeal challenges the decision of the judge as
regards direct discrimination under s 1(1)(*a*) of the Race Relations Act 1976 (a point
which counsel for the plaintiffs wishes to keep open) this aspect of the case has not been
pressed before us and the argument has centred entirely on whether the defendants'
refusal to admit the second plaintiff to their school unless he is willing to dispense with
the wearing of the turban during school hours constitutes indirect discrimination under
c s 1(1). Under this subsection—

'A person discriminates against another . . . if . . . (*b*) he applies to that other a
requirement or condition which he applies or would apply to persons not of the
same racial group as that other but—(i) which is such that the proportion of persons
of the same racial group as that other who can comply with it is considerably smaller
than the proportion of persons not of that racial group who can comply with it.'
d

Sikhs are rightly honoured and respected, and one can well understand the importance
which the more orthodox adherents of Sikhism attach to the outward manifestation of
their faith. But leaving aside for the moment the question whether, as they contend, any
inhibition which the plaintiffs may feel against appearing in public without a turban is
of so fundamental and compelling a nature as to justify the conclusion that the defendants'
e requirement is one with which they *cannot* comply, it is fundamental to their case that
the requirement is one with which they cannot comply by reason of their membership
of a racial group. It is conceded that the only reason why they cannot, if they cannot,
accept the requirement imposed by the defendants is that they are Sikhs, and the case
thus raises directly for decision the question whether Sikhs *as such* are a racial group in
the sense in which that term is used in the 1976 Act. That depends on s 3(1) of the Act
f where 'racial group' is defined as 'a group of persons defined by reference to
colour . . . nationality or ethnic or national origins'. There is no question that Sikhs are
not a group defined by reference to colour or nationality and the only question is whether
they can as a group be said to be defined by reference to ethnic or national origins, and in
particular as to the meaning, in this context, of the word 'ethnic'.

I have had the advantage of reading in draft the judgment to be delivered by Kerr LJ
g and am in entire agreement with his analysis. I add some observations of my own only
because the case is an important one and one which has given me some concern.

It is worth noting, at the outset, how this matter was pleaded by the plaintiffs
themselves who may be supposed to know best how they put their own case. They were
asked for particulars of the allegation of discrimination stating what racial group they
alleged that they belonged to (to which the answer was originally 'Indian Sikhs born in
h Kenya', subsequently amended simply to 'Sikhs') and 'how the said racial group is defined
by reference to colour, nationality or ethnic or national origins', to which the answer
was:

'The said racial group is defined by reference to its colour (brown) and/or ethnic
(the Sikhs belong to a non-Christian faith) and/or national origins (the Sikhs originate
from the Punjab in Northern India).'
j

Now we have been treated to a fascinating and instructive educational excursion into
the origins, development and tenets of the Sikh faith, from which it is evident that
although Sikhism, as has so often happened in the past with other movements, started
life as a purely religious teaching, it evolved into a political movement as well,
symbolising resistance to the Mogul invaders of the Punjab. It is also evident that

historically the turban was adopted not so much as a symbol of religious faith as a mark of political protest. There was, indeed, a brief period under Ranjit Singh at the beginning *a* of the nineteenth century when it could be said that their political and military hegemony in the Punjab was such that they could be said to command or even to represent the Punjabi nation. There is also evidence that in the reconstituted state of the Punjab they constitute the majority (estimates vary between 51% and 60%) of the indigenous population. It would, however, be a misuse of language in its ordinary meaning to say that the Sikhs are a group defined by reference to their national origins. That their *b* membership is and has always been drawn primarily from the Punjab (in its former sense before reconstitution) is no doubt true, but that local association appears to have arisen from the locality of the founder and to have formed no essential part of the faith any more than did, for instance, birth or residence in Palestine form an integral part of the Christian faith. Nor have they ever represented more than a fraction of the whole population of the Punjab; and certainly there is no evidence to suggest that derivation *c* from any particular tribal or national group was ever regarded as any sort of qualification. The discussion before us, therefore, has centred (and, in my judgment, rightly centred) on the word 'ethnic'. A glance at the dictionary is sufficient to show both that this is a term of very uncertain meaning and that the sense in which the word is used has altered considerably with the passage of time so that it is now long removed from that borne by the Greek 'ἔθνος' from which it is derived. For my part, I doubt whether one can obtain *d* anything but the most general assistance from dictionaries. We have to construe an Act of Parliament and it is permissible and indeed essential to construe the words used in the light of what the legislature was obviously seeking to achieve. The one thing that must surely be clear is that Parliament cannot have intended to create (as it did in this Act) a criminal offence which involves an extensive etymological research before any member of the public can determine whether he is offending or not. The word must, I infer, have *e* been used in its popularly accepted meaning; but, having said that, one is faced with the difficulty of discovering what the popularly accepted meaning is. Counsel for the plaintiffs submits that it imports no more than a state of being united by common features such as language, race, culture, religion, literature and habit of life. No one aspect is necessarily essential: one has to look at the matter in the round and ask whether the combination of features which one finds constitute an identifiable 'community' in *f* the loose sense of the word. If they do, then a member of that community is a member of an ethnic group. Here, he points out, the Sikhs display a large number of common features. They have a common religion; they have common customs, such as the wearing of the turban and the comb; they have a common language, for most of them hail from the Punjab and speak Punjabi; a substantial proportion is literate in a script (Gurmukhi) which, whilst not peculiar to the Sikhs, is read by many more Sikhs than Hindus; and *g* there is, so the evidence shows, a Sikh literature.

There appears to me to be a number of difficulties about this. In the first place, it is evident that their customs, whilst widespread, are by no means common to all Sikhs. A substantial proportion do not assume the turban, and, indeed, the evidence shows that there are two sects within Sikhism with differing customs and, to some extent, differing philosophies. The proportion of all Sikhs literate in the Gurmukhi script is small, and it *h* is read by a much smaller number of Hindus, both men and women, who nevertheless form a sizable minority of Gurmukhi readers. Moreover, counsel for the plaintiffs' test of an ethnic group would, as it seems to me, be equally applicable to any number of organisations, religious, political or social. Furthermore, one must not lose sight of the terms of the definition. What the statute directs us to look for is not membership of an ethnic group but membership of a group which (that is the group, not the individual) is *j* defined by reference to '*its* ethnic *origins*'. Counsel for the plaintiffs may be right in saying that 'ethnic', as a word on its own, embraces more than a merely racial concept (why otherwise, he asks, does the legislature use the word as an alternative to 'racial' or 'national'?) and I would accept that it embraces, perhaps, notions of cultural or linguistic community. Nevertheless, in its popular meaning, it does, in my judgment, involve *a* essentially a racial concept: the concept of something with which the members of the group are born; some fixed or inherited characteristic. I do not believe that the man in the street would apply the word 'ethnic' to a characteristic which the propositus could assume or reject as a matter of choice. No one, for instance, in ordinary speech, would describe a member of the Church of England or the Conservative Party as a member of an ethnic group.

b Now that is a fortiori the case, as it seems to me, when one uses the expression 'ethnic origins'. What is embraced in that expression, to my mind, is the notion of a group distinguished by some peculiarity of birth, perhaps as a result of intermarriage within a community, but lacking any element of free will. It seems to me entirely inappropriate to describe a group into and out of which anyone may travel as a matter of free choice; and freedom of choice (to join or not to join, to remain or to leave) is inherent in the whole philosophy of Sikhism.

c It is true, of course, that the great majority of the individual members of the Sikh faith have a common ethnic origin which is generically Indian (as have a great many Muslims and Hindus), but that, in my judgment, does not mean that Sikhs, Muslims or Hindus are groups 'defined by reference to their ethnic origins'. They are, in my judgment, groups defined by reference to their religious and philosophical tenets to which anyone may belong but which are primarily composed of persons of Indian birth or descent. I,

d therefore, reach the same conclusion as that reached by the judge and Lord Denning MR.

That is a conclusion which renders it strictly unnecessary to consider the two further arguments addressed to us and also decided by the judge in the defendants' favour. We were referred to the decision of the Employment Appeal Tribunal in *Price v Civil Services Commission* [1978] 1 All ER 1228, [1977] 1 WLR 1417 in which, on precisely similar wording in the Sex Discrimination Act 1975 the word 'can' was construed as meaning

e 'can practically' so that a requirement that an applicant for a post should be between the ages of 17½ and 28 was held to discriminate against married female applicants, since family commitments in that age group resulted in fewer married women being able to take on full-time employment. I say nothing about that decision in the context of that Act, but I am not, for my part, convinced that the word 'can' should necessarily be accorded the same extended meaning in the legislation with which this appeal is

f concerned. Section 1(1)(b) of the 1976 Act seems to me to be aimed at indirect discrimination by the imposition of requirements with which it is, in general, impossible for persons of a particular racial group to comply, such, for instance, as height, pigmentation, or linguistic or educational qualifications which the majority of that group will not ordinarily have and, like the judge, I entertain some doubt whether it can be read as extending to conditions which anyone can fulfil but which some individual

g members of a group are unwilling to fulfil or may find unacceptable by reason of religious or conscientious scruple. It is, however, unnecessary to decide the point as it equally is unnecessary to decide the further question whether, as the judge held, the first defendant's insistence on the absence of any distinguishing headgear among the boys at his school was a justifiable requirement. Mr Dowell Lee, the first defendant, has put forward a number of considerations of varying cogency to justify his decision, including

h the not unreasonable one that, all other considerations apart, the school curriculum includes participation in sports such as swimming and rugby football which, almost of necessity, involve the removal of the turban. In the light of the conclusion stated above, however, I need say no more than that, for my part, I am far from persuaded that the judge was wrong in concluding that the condition was, in any event, a justifiable one.

In the result, I agree that the appeal fails. I would add only this. Without in any way

j minimising the great assistance which counsel for the plaintiffs have given the court in this difficult case, it is right that some tribute should be paid to the courtesy, skill and patience with which Mr Dowell Lee has conducted in person a case which must have caused him immense personal distress and anxiety. I cannot help observing that the events of which complaint has been made took place as long ago as the summer of 1978, four years ago. Throughout Mr Dowell Lee appears to have behaved with the greatest courtesy and restraint. After an entirely courteous correspondence with the first plaintiff, he found himself the subject of a visitation from a representative of the Commission for *a* Racial Equality and the papers before us contain the notes of an interview with him at which he appears to have been deliberately interrogated with a view to extracting admissions of racial bias and at which barely concealed threats of 'investigation' were made unless he modified the stance which he had adopted. Thereafter he, whose proper business was running his school in a way which to him seemed most suited to the needs of his students, found himself involved in an action fostered and supported by the *b* commission. The proceedings were commenced two years later and have throughout been maintained by the commission in the name of better race relations, although it emerged, ironically, at the trial, that the first plaintiff would not, if the matter of his son's entry had been pursued, have been willing in any event for him to go to a school where he would have been expected to attend religious classes in the Christian faith as part of the normal curriculum. There is, and this should be made, I think, entirely clear, *c* absolutely no foundation, in my judgment, for the suggestion that Mr Dowell Lee is seeking or has sought to exclude children from the school either on racial or religious grounds. In fact, as Lord Denning MR has mentioned and the judge found, out of 305 children the school contained 34 Hindus, 16 Persians, 6 Negroes, 7 Chinese and some 15 other non-English students of European extraction. In addition there was at the material time a number of Sikhs in the school whose parents did not insist, as the first plaintiff *d* did, on their sons wearing their distinctive religious headgear. Indeed Mr Dowell Lee's objection to the wearing of the turban at school is precisely, as I understand it, because he feels that it would tend to accentuate those very religious and social distinctions which it is his desire to minimise in trying to effect a homogenous school community. Whether that is an objection which all or any of the members of this court would equally feel is immaterial. It is, in my judgment, a perfectly respectable viewpoint and is the sincerely *e* held and responsible opinion of a man who is running a multiracial school in a difficult area. I have to say that, speaking entirely for myself, I regard it as lamentable that Mr Dowell Lee's entire livelihood and the future of his school should have been put at risk at the instance of a publicly financed body designed to foster better racial relations. Anything less likely to achieve that result than this case I find it difficult to imagine. As it is Mr Dowell Lee has been compelled to waste a great deal of his time and the resources *f* of the school in defending himself against charges which could hardly have been levelled at any target less deserving of them. He has been dragged through two courts at enormous expense in order, apparently, to establish a point which no doubt is a difficult and important one, but is now entirely academic for both plaintiffs. It seems to me a great pity that it should have been thought necessary to test it at the expense of an entirely blameless individual who has done no more than to seek in the best way that he *g* knows how to run his own business in his own way. What makes it, perhaps, particularly ironic is the evidence of the plaintiffs' expert Mr Indarijit Singh:

> 'Tolerance is the willingness, and a Sikh should be willing, to fight in every way including, if need be, eventually to give his life, to upholding the next person's right to determine his own particular way of life.'
> *h*

For my part, I find it regrettable that this unimpeachable sentiment should not have been applied here and that machinery designed specifically for the protection of the weak and disadvantaged should have operated as, it seems to me, it has in this case, albeit no doubt with the loftiest of motives, as an engine of oppression.

I should only add that, in saying this, I am making no criticism whatever of counsel for the plaintiffs or those instructing him, who have conducted the appeal in accordance *j* with their clients' instructions with the most punctilious fairness and propriety.

I too would dismiss the appeal.

KERR LJ. This is a difficult and troubling case. Many members of the Sikh community are strict or orthodox in the sense that their religious beliefs prohibit the men from cutting their hair. This has the consequence that they wear beards which should strictly

be untrimmed, though may undoubtedly trim them. It also means that for reasons of
a tidiness and hygiene they tie their hair into a topknot and wear a turban. This has come
to assume a distinctive shape, and has also come to be a symbol of Sikhism. In the present
case the effect of this custom falls to be considered by reference to the Race Relations Act
1976 in relation to a 13-year-old boy who was refused admission to a private school unless
he removed his turban.

In the fields of employment generally, even where turbans conflict with the prescribed
b headgear for particular occupations, the right of Sikhs to wear turbans has been widely
recognised out of respect for their beliefs. Thus, Sikhs wear turbans in the armed forces,
in the police, as traffic wardens; Sikh barristers do not wear wigs; and the crash-helmet
regulations for motor cyclists have been expressly relaxed for them. It is only when their
beards have caused problems in employment, for instance in the processing of food, that
it has been held justifiable to object to these: see e g *Panesar v Nestlé Co* [1980] ICR 144.
c Sikh women traditionally wear trousers, and their right to do so, despite the normal
uniform of nurses, was ultimately accepted administratively without having to be
decided in this court: see *Kingston and Richmond Area Health Authority v Kaur* [1981] ICR
631. Apart from cases before industrial tribunals, the general position under the 1976
Act has only once been considered in depth, and then only at the level of a county court.
It was there held that the Sikhs constitute a 'racial group' for the purposes of the 1976 Act
d on the ground that they are a 'group of persons defined by reference to . . . ethnic origins'
within s 3(1). In the result, the owner and manager of a night club, who did not allow
men to wear headgear on the premises, were held to have discriminated unlawfully
against Sikhs when they refused to admit them wearing their turbans. When that case
reached this court, though not on this point, two members of the court expressed
reservations about the decision: see *Commission for Racial Equality v Genture Restaurants*
e *Ltd* [1981] CA Bound Transcript 227. In the present case the same point has now been
decided in the contrary sense by Judge Gosling in the Birmingham County Court, and
this is the main point which arises for decision on the present appeal.

Basically, Sikhism is undoubtedly a religion; and this was not in dispute. The question
is whether Sikhs are also 'a group of persons defined by reference to . . . ethnic or national
origins', and I will have to refer to the history and features of Sikhism later on. First, it is
f necessary to say something about the policy of the 1976 Act and about the circumstances
in which this issue arises in the present case.

As the title of the 1976 Act indicates, its object was to outlaw discrimination against
anyone on the ground of their race. However 'race' is an elusive term. Some scientists
and social anthropologists deny that it has any meaning. But it clearly has a meaning for
Parliament and ordinary people. However, recognisable racial differences and character-
g istics can become so diffused as the result of generations of mixed marriages that the
term may in any event become largely meaningless when it is sought to apply it to
individuals. If it is to be used in a legal context at all, it therefore needs to be defined; and
the obvious and first element of the statutory definition is by reference to colour. The
original definition in the Race Relations Acts 1965 and 1968 only added to the word
'colour' the words 'race or ethnic or national origins'. Whatever these latter words may
h mean, as discussed hereafter, they clearly refer to human characteristics with which a
person is born and which he or she cannot change, any more than the leopard can change
his spots. This is important, because it has a considerable bearing on the words 'can
comply' in s 1(1)(b)(i) of the 1976 Act to which I turn later. Indeed, it was precisely
because of the natural abhorrence of right-minded people of discrimination against
others on the ground of their having been born with features and characteristics which
j are unalterable, that this legislation unfortunately became necessary.

Subsequent to its enactment, when the House of Lords had decided that 'national
origins' was not to be equated with 'nationality' in *Ealing London Borough v Race Relations
Board* [1972] 1 All ER 105, [1972] AC 342 the word 'nationality' was added in the 1976
Act to the definition of 'racial group'. 'Nationality' differs from the other parts of the
definition to the extent that people can change their nationality, though only with
difficulty. But discrimination on the grounds of nationality undoubtedly exists, as shown

by that case, and is equally to be condemned. In the context of the policy of the legislation it was therefore logical and necessary, in the light of that decision, to extend the definition   *a* accordingly. However, the definition of 'racial group' remains confined to human attributes which, save for changes of nationality, are unalterable.

In the present case the allegation of discrimination arises mainly in the context of religion. The first defendant is the headmaster of a private school, and the school is the second defendant. His objection to the turban is primarily that it is an outward and distinct manifestation of a religious creed, and that he therefore regards it as divisive and   *b* undesirable in a school which, although in fact multiracial, bases its religious teaching and general education on the Christian faith, which is also the religion of the great majority of the pupils. At the same time, the school's aim is clearly to provide a multiracial approach to the education of all its pupils for life in the present-day multiracial society of this country. The pupils, who go up to the age of 16, are required to wear uniforms, and the purpose of this requirement is set out in the school rules as follows: *c*

> 'The purpose of School Uniform is to minimise the divisive differences of race, class or creed, and to serve as a good advertisement for the School.'

To make it clear that this is in no way a school which infringes the letter or spirit of the 1976 Act, or merely pays lip-service to it (unless the objection to the wearing of turbans is in itself an infringement) it should be emphasised that out of the 305 pupils   *d* there are 34 Hindus, 16 Persians, 6 Negroes, 7 Chinese and about 15 children of various non-British European nationalities. The objection to the turban is therefore not based on chauvinism, or on racial discrimination, or on religious intolerance. All reliance on direct discrimination under s 1(1)(*a*) of the 1976 Act was abandoned on this appeal. However, since the objection to the turban has arisen mainly in the context of religion, it is necessary to say something about religion in relation to the 1976 Act.   *e*

In this regard it is common ground between the parties, and indeed self-evident, that adherents to a certain religion or creed are not as such within the definition of 'racial group' in s 3. Despite the ugly overtones of the word 'discrimination', discrimination is not prohibited by the 1976 Act in relation to religious beliefs or practices. Nor is religion made the subject matter of the criminal offence of stirring up racial hatred which, by s 70 of the Act, was inserted into the Public Order Act 1936 on the basis of the same   *f* definition of 'racial group' (see s 5A(6) of the 1936 Act as inserted by s 70(2) of the 1976 Act). Whether one agrees with this or not, it is so; and, since this point concerning the 1976 Act is not in issue, it is permissible to note that the decision to exclude religion was a matter of deliberate legislative policy (see Offences against Religion and Public Worship, (1981; Law Com no 79) paras 5.9–5.11, 8.5). Thus, it seems clear beyond doubt that there is nothing in the 1976 Act which precludes schools and other establishments only   *g* to admit persons of a particular religion, whether it be Christian, Muslim, Jewish etc, or to exclude particular religions (though this would rarely happen in practice), or to admit or exclude persons of particular denominations within a certain religion, such as Protestants or Catholics.

Moreover, religions and religious practices frequently involve acceptance of, or insistence on, social and other customs on the part of those who strictly observe whatever   *h* tenets may thereby be prescribed: such as not to eat pork, or not to drink wine, or not to work on the Sabbath; or, as in the present case, not to cut one's hair and therefore to wear a turban. To discriminate against such customs or habits, in the sense that others may decline to alter or adapt their own ways of life to them, or may even decline to accept them in organisations or establishments where they are regarded as unsuitable or unwelcome, may be intolerant or even bigoted; but this is not unlawful under the 1976   *j* Act. To that extent the right not to be discriminated against must give way to the beliefs and free will of others. If persons wish to insist on wearing bathing suits, then they cannot reasonably insist on admission to a nudist colony; similarly, people who passionately believe in nudism cannot complain if they are not accepted on ordinary bathing beaches. Further, as with religion and religious or other social customs, the 1976 Act is not concerned with politics. It operates only in the field of 'race', and only on the

a
basis of the definition which Parliament has given to this word. As Lord Simon said in *Ealing London Borough v Race Relations Board* [1972] 1 All ER 105 at 114, [1972] AC 342 at 362:

b
> 'Secondly, for the general legal conspectus. The Race Relations Acts 1965 and 1968 do not provide a complete code against discrimination of socially divisive propaganda. The Acts do not deal at all with discrimination on the grounds of religion or political tenet. It is no offence under the Acts to stir up class hatred. It is, therefore, unquestionably with a limited sort of socially disruptive conduct that the Acts are concerned; and it is, on any reading, within a limited sphere that Parliament put its ameliorative measures into action.'

All this is crucial to the issues which arise in this case. However, these issues have to be decided by reference to groups of persons 'defined by reference to ethnic or national origins', since it is contended that Sikhs fall within this part of the definition of a 'racial group', in particular on the basis of the word 'ethnic'.

c
Parliament must accept responsibility for the difficulties which this word has created for the courts.

The word 'ethnic' derives from the Greek 'ethnos', meaning something akin to 'nation' or 'tribe'. Later it came to refer to people who were neither Christians nor Jews, and who were therefore regarded as heathen or pagan. At one time it was believed that 'heathen'

d
had its etymological source in this word, but all these meanings of the word 'ethnic' are now obsolete. The primary modern meaning, as shown by the *Oxford English Dictionary*, is 'pertaining to race; peculiar to a race or nation; ethnological'. More recently, however, the sense of the word has become further diluted and to some extent changed. The 1972 Supplement to the *Oxford English Dictionary* adds—

e
> 'Pertaining to or having common racial, cultural, religious or linguistic characteristics; esp. designating a racial or other group within a larger system.'

It also adds that, colloquially in the United States, 'ethnic' can mean 'foreign or exotic; un-American or plain quaint'. So Parliament has used this word in a statute to be interpreted by our courts when across the Atlantic, and perhaps even here, people may

f
already be using it in the sense of saying of someone that, 'He seems a pretty ethnic sort of a guy!'

However, we are fortunately not concerned with this further linguistic advance, but only with the modern usage of 'ethnic' to be found, for instance, in *Collins' English Dictionary* (1979), where 'Bosnian ethnic dances' is given as an illustration. It is this extended modern meaning on which the plaintiffs rely, and which they maintain to be

g
descriptive of Sikhs and Sikhism.

But in the context of the 1976 Act, this is not the correct approach. The Act does not define a racial group by reference to its members forming part of some 'ethnic' community. It defines it as 'a group of persons defined by reference to ethnic origins'. The word 'origin', as pointed out by Lord Simon in the *Ealing London Borough* case 'in its ordinary sense, signifies a source, someone or something from which someone or

h
something else has descended' (see [1972] 1 All ER 105 at 116, [1972] AC 342 at 363). We are therefore concerned with the interpretation of 'ethnic' in this restricted context.

It follows that the definition of a group by reference to its 'ethnic origin' requires the investigation of the 'ethnic' ancestry and provenance of the group in question, in the sense of considering whether the group has characteristics which are primarily 'pertaining to or peculiar to race'. The definition is not concerned with communities or movements

j
whose members or adherents merely share a common religion, or common social customs, or common political aspirations. These will often be concomitants derived from a common ethnic origin. But, for the purpose of the definition of a 'racial group' within the terms of the 1976 Act, any such communal features will not by themselves be sufficient. Ethnic origins are not to be equated with what may be called 'current ethnicity' in the wide sense of the term.

In relation to the alternative expression of a group defined by reference to 'national origins' the position is the same. 'National' means 'peculiar to the people of a particular country; characteristic or distinctive of a nation'. A nation, whether in the anthropological *a* or political sense of the word, is even less to be equated with communities or movements which merely share religious, social or political beliefs or practices, than any form of 'ethnic' grouping. The definition of 'nation' in the *Oxford English Dictionary* is—

> 'an extensive aggregate of persons so closely associated with each other by common descent, language or history as to form a distinct race or people, usually organised as a separate political state and occupying a definite territory.' *b*

It is accordingly on this basis that the words 'national origin' fall to be applied.

When these definitions are then considered in relation to the Sikhs and Sikhism, I am left in no doubt on the evidence that Sikhs do not constitute a 'racial group defined by ethnic or national origins'. Sikhs can only be described as a 'racial group' within the 1976 *c* Act in the wider sense of colour, or by reference to descent from the peoples of the Indian subcontinent or (predominantly) from what is now the Republic of India, or, possibly, by reference to the region or state of the Punjab or the Punjabi people. Counsel for the plaintiffs was expressly invited to put the plaintiffs' case on any of the latter wider bases; but he declined to do so.

We have been taken through a great deal of evidence concerning the origins, history and customs of Sikhism and Sikhs. This evidence has already been referred to in some *d* detail in the judgment of Lord Denning MR, and I therefore only summarise my conclusions on it. Sikhism originated as a religion among the Hindus of the Punjab in the middle of the fifteenth century. Having started as something in the nature of a school of sectarian reform as the result of the teachings of Guru Nanak, under the nine gurus who succeeded him Sikhism became a militant political movement within the Punjab against the Muslims. Its adherents were in no way a separate race, which has not been *e* suggested, but its militancy attracted the sturdiest of the Punjabis; and Sikhism rejected the system of caste. The religious and political features of the movement then bred distinctions in social customs, including in particular the wearing of the turban as a symbol of defiance; and it also led to a measure of individual development in literature and art, a common characteristic of religious, political and social movements. One particular feature of Sikhism is that adherence to it has ebbed and flowed (mainly the *f* latter) as Hindus have responded to it for political, militant or social reasons. This is clearly shown by the figures and comments on the Sikhs, to be found in the Indian censuses from 1853 to 1931 to which we were referred. Sikhism is a religion, but a religion which appears to have particularly highly developed political and social overtones among its adherents and converts.

However, apart from religion, politics and social customs, none of which have in *g* themselves anything to do with the 1976 Act, Sikhs are Punjabis. Their language is Punjabi in common with that of the majority of the inhabitants of that region, past and present. The Gurmukhi script originally came to be used for writing the scriptures of the Sikh religion; but for long its usage has not been confined to Sikhs. Within the Punjab, Sikhs have predominated in certain regions, and they are now predominant in East Punjab as the result of partition and of its dreadful consequences for them. In the *h* Britain of today the Sikhs form a respected religious and social community, within the English-born or immigrant part of the population stemming from the Indian subcontinent, who are proud of their history and traditions. The wearing of the turban is the symbol of religious and social distinctiveness among strict or orthodox Sikhs, but a very large number of Sikhs cut their hair and do not wear turbans or beards. Viewed as a group which falls to be defined by 'ethnic or national origins', the Sikhs are Indians, and *j* in particular Punjabis; they are not a people or a group having any ethnic or national origin.

It follows in my judgment that Sikhs and Sikhism do not as such fall within the Race Relations Act 1976 at all, any more than members of the Church of England, Catholics, Muslims, Quakers, or Jehovah Witnesses; or any other groups which are only distinctive because they adhere to distinct religious, political or social beliefs and customs.

In these circumstances I am reluctant to express any opinion on the application to the
a present case of the problems raised by s 1(1)(b) (i) and (ii) of the 1976 Act, and I say no
more about these issues than for the purpose of explaining why, in my view, they do not
arise, and cannot properly be determined, in the context of the issues on this appeal.

The issues raised by s 1(1)(b) (i) and (ii) can be summarised as follows, but only if Sikhs
were properly to be regarded as a racial group for the purposes of the 1976 Act, which in
my view they are not. As regards the defendants' requirement that the second plaintiff,
b the Sikh boy, should remove his turban and cut his hair before being admitted as a pupil
to this school, the issues are (i) was this a requirement with which a proportion of Sikhs
can comply, in the sense that such proportion is considerably smaller than the proportion
of non-Sikhs who can comply with it? and, if so, (ii) can the defendants show that this
requirement is justifiable irrespective of the fact that the boy is a Sikh? The reason why I
am reluctant to attempt to express any views on these questions is that in the present case
c they can only be raised in a false context to which the 1976 Act was never intended to
apply. I have already explained that, apart from the possibility of a change of nationality,
the definition of 'racial group' is based on characteristics or attributes which are by their
nature unalterable. In this statute, accordingly, the word 'can' in para (b)(i) was in my
view intended to be contrasted with something approaching impossibility. It was not
intended to be measured against criteria of free-will, choice, or conscience. In one sense,
d Sikhs can obviously refrain from wearing a turban, either by choosing not to be orthodox
to this extent or by ceasing to be orthodox. This, however, is a matter of religious or
social choice and therefore one with which the 1976 Act was never intended to be
concerned at all. It follows that I find it impossible to consider the application of the
word 'can' in this context. Similarly, I cannot properly express any view in this context
about the word 'justifiable' in para (b)(ii) which in its turn depends on the applicability of
e para (b)(i). The difficulty of applying these provisions in the present case merely
demonstrates that the case lies in a context which is solely one of religious and social
choice on the part of the plaintiffs, and of a corresponding freedom of choice on the part
of the defendants, to which the wording of the 1976 Act has no application and cannot
be applied.

Meanwhile the boy has gone to another school, wearing his turban. In this connection
f it appears from the evidence, and should be emphasised, that many other headmasters
disagree profoundly with the decision taken by this defendant. Many people would no
doubt prefer their views to his. But he is entitled to decide for himself how his school
should be run in relation to the wearing of turbans by his pupils, and the 1976 Act does
not curtail his freedom of decision in this regard.

For these reasons I would dismiss this appeal. However, I would add my disquiet to
g what Lord Denning MR and Oliver LJ have already said about the events which have led
up to these proceedings. The Commission for Racial Equality is clearly highly motivated
and does useful work in cases where there is clear evidence, or real ground for suspicion,
that racial discrimination exists and is practised. But this is not such a case. This school
was demonstrably conducted harmoniously on a multiracial basis. I have read in the
evidence the notes of the interview of the headmaster by an official of the commission.
h In parts this reads more like an inquisition than an interview, and I can see no basis
whatever for what I can only describe as harassment of this headmaster. All that the
commission has achieved in this case, as it seems to me, is to create racial discord where
there was none before.

Appeal dismissed. Leave to appeal to the House of Lords refused.

18 November. *The Appeal Committee of the House of Lords granted the plaintiffs leave to appeal.*

Solicitors: *Bindman & Partners* (for the plaintiffs).

Frances Rustin   Barrister.

O'Reilly v Mackman and others
and other cases

a

HOUSE OF LORDS

LORD DIPLOCK, LORD FRASER OF TULLYBELTON, LORD KEITH OF KINKEL, LORD BRIDGE OF
HARWICH AND LORD BRIGHTMAN

11, 12, 13 OCTOBER, 25 NOVEMBER 1982

b

*Judicial review – Declaration – Circumvention of procedure for judicial review – Action for
declaration circumventing procedure for judicial review – Plaintiffs found guilty of disciplinary
offences and penalties imposed by board of prison visitors – Plaintiffs commencing actions by writ
and originating summons for declaration that board's findings and awards null and void by
reason of breach of natural justice – Application by board to strike out actions as abuse of court's
process – Whether judicial review the only remedy to impugn adjudications by prison visitors –
RSC Ord 53.*

c

A person seeking to establish that a decision of a public authority infringes rights which
he is entitled to have protected under public law must as a general rule proceed by way
of an application for judicial review under RSC Ord 53, r 1(1)^a rather than by way of an
ordinary action. Since a prisoner's right that a board of prison visitors should act within
its jurisdiction and observe the rules of natural justice when conducting a hearing
concerning him is a right protected only under public law and not by private law, a
prisoner who seeks to challenge a decision of a board of prison visitors must do so by way
of an application under Ord 53 for judicial review of the board's decision (see p 1133 c to
e and j and p 1134 e to p 1135 a, post).

d

e

R v Electricity Comrs, ex p London Electricity Joint Committee Co (1920) Ltd [1923] All ER
Rep 150, *R v Northumberland Compensation Appeal Tribunal, ex p Shaw* [1952] 1 All ER
122, *Ridge v Baldwin* [1963] 2 All ER 66 and *Anisminic Ltd v Foreign Compensation
Commission* [1969] 1 All ER 208 considered.

Decision of the Court of Appeal [1982] 3 All ER 680 affirmed.

f

Notes

For bodies amenable to certiorari, see 1 Halsbury's Laws (4th edn) paras 148–153, and for
cases on the subject, see 16 Digest (Reissue) 402–409, 4442–4493.

Cases referred to in opinions

Anisminic Ltd v Foreign Compensation Commission [1969] 1 All ER 208, [1969] 2 AC 147,
[1969] 2 WLR 163, HL; *rvsg* [1967] 2 All ER 986, [1968] 2 QB 862, CA, 16 Digest
(Reissue) 395, 4357.

g

Edwards v Bairstow [1955] 3 All ER 48, [1956] AC 14, [1955] 3 WLR 410, HL, 28(1)
Digest (Reissue) 566, 2089.

George v Secretary of State for the Environment (1979) 38 P & CR 609, CA.

Padfield v Minister of Agriculture, Fisheries and Food [1968] 1 All ER 694, [1968] AC 997,
[1968] 2 WLR 924, HL, 16 Digest (Reissue) 349, 3659.

h

Pyx Granite Co Ltd v Ministry of Housing and Local Government [1959] 3 All ER 1, [1960]
AC 260, [1959] 2 WLR 346, HL, 30 Digest (Reissue) 202, 277.

R v Electricity Comrs, ex p London Electricity Joint Committee Co (1920) Ltd [1924] 1 KB 171,
[1923] All ER Rep 150, CA, 16 Digest (Reissue) 385, 4176.

R v Hull Prison Board of Visitors, ex p St Germain [1979] 1 All ER 701, [1979] QB 425,
[1979] 2 WLR 42, CA, Digest (Cont Vol E) 488, 6a.

j

---

a Rule 1(1), so far as material, provides: 'An application for—(a) an order of mandamus, prohibition
or certiorari . . . shall be made by way of an application for judicial review in accordance with the
provisions of this Order.'

a *R v Hull Prison Board of Visitors, ex p St Germain (No 2)* [1979] 3 All ER 545, [1979] 1 WLR
     1401, DC.
     R v Northumberland Compensation Appeal Tribunal, ex p Shaw [1952] 1 All ER 122, [1952]
     1 KB 338, CA; *affg* [1951] 1 All ER 268, [1951] 1 KB 711, DC, 16 Digest (Reissue) 425,
     4686.
     R v Stokesley (Yorkshire) Justices, ex p Bartram [1956] 1 All ER 563, [1956] 1 WLR 254, DC,
     16 Digest (Reissue) 434, 4790.
b *Racecourse Betting Control Board v Secretary for Air* [1944] 1 All ER 60, [1944] Ch 114, CA,
     17 Digest (Reissue) 498, 157.
     Ridge v Baldwin [1963] 2 All ER 66, [1964] AC 40, [1963] 2 WLR 935, HL, 37 Digest
     (Repl) 195, 32.
     Vine v National Dock Labour Board [1956] 3 All ER 939, [1957] AC 488, [1957] 2 WLR
     106, HL, 30 Digest (Reissue) 208, 310.

c
Appeal

The appellants, Christopher Noel O'Reilly, Alexander Vernon John Derbyshire, David
Margin Dougan and Anthony Millbanks, appealed, with leave of the Court of Appeal
granted on 30 June 1982, against the decision of the Court of Appeal (Lord Denning MR,
Ackner and O'Connor LJJ) ([1982] 3 All ER 680, [1982] 3 WLR 604) on 30 June 1982
d allowing the appeals of the respondents, E W Mackman, J A Rundle, C Brady, C R
Wainhouse, and S A Streets, who comprised the Board of Visitors of Hull Prison at the
relevant times, and the Home Office, from the judgment of Peter Pain J ([1982] 3 All ER
680, [1982] 3 WLR 604) given on 5 March 1982 by which he dismissed summonses
severally issued by the respondents seeking orders striking out the statements of claim
served by the appellants O'Reilly, Derbyshire and Dougan and the originating summons
e served by the appellant Millbanks on the grounds that the same disclosed no reasonable
cause of action and/or were an abuse of the process of the court. The facts are set out in
the judgment of Lord Diplock.

Michael Beloff QC and *David Pannick* for the appellants O'Reilly, Derbyshire and Dougan.
Stephen Sedley for the appellant Millbanks.
f *Simon D Brown* and *John Laws* for the respondents.

Their Lordships took time for consideration.

25 November. The following opinions were delivered.

g **LORD DIPLOCK.** My Lords, at the time of the commencement by the appellants of
the actions in which these consolidated appeals are brought each of the appellants was
serving a long sentence of imprisonment which even now has not expired. By those
actions, which were commenced in 1980, in the case of the appellant Millbanks by
originating summons, and in the case of the other appellants by writ, each appellant
seeks to establish that a disciplinary award of forfeiture of remission of sentence made by
h the Board of Visitors of Hull prison (the board) in the exercise of their disciplinary
jurisdiction under r 51 of the Prison Rules 1964, SI 1964/338, is null and void because
the board failed to observe the rules of natural justice. Millbanks in the indorsement to
his originating summons alleges bias on the part of the member of the board who
presided over the hearing of the disciplinary proceedings against him. The other
appellants in their statements of claim allege that they were not given by the board a fair
j opportunity to present their respective cases.
   The board applied to the High Court (Peter Pain J) ([1982] 3 All ER 680, [1982] 3 WLR
604) that all the actions be struck out as being an abuse of the process of the court. The
judge refused the applications but, on appeal to the Court of Appeal (Lord Denning MR,
Ackner and O'Connor LJJ) ([1982] 3 All ER 680, [1982] 3 WLR 604), the actions were
struck out.

My Lords, it is not contested that if the allegations set out in the originating summons or statements of claim are true each of the appellants would have had a remedy obtainable *a* by the procedure of an application for judicial review under RSC Ord 53, but to obtain that remedy, whether it took the form of an order of certiorari to quash the board's award or a declaration of its nullity, would have required the leave of the court under Ord 53, r 3. That judicial review lies against an award of the board of visitors of a prison made in the exercise of their disciplinary functions was established by the judgment of the Court of Appeal (overruling a Divisional Court) in *R v Hull Visitors, ex p St Germain* *b* [1979] 1 All ER 701, [1979] QB 425, a decision that was, in my view, clearly right and which has not been challenged in the instant appeals by the respondents.

In the *St Germain* case the only remedy that had been sought was certiorari to quash the decision of the prison visitors; but the alternative remedy of a declaration of nullity if the court considered it to be just and convenient would also have been available on an application for judicial review under Ord 53 after the replacement of the old rule by the *c* new rule in 1977. In the instant cases, which were commenced after the new rule came into effect (but before the coming into force of s 31 of the Supreme Court Act 1981), certiorari would unquestionably have been the more appropriate remedy, since r 5 of the Prison Rules 1964, which provides for remission of sentence up to a maximum of one-third, stipulates that the 'rule shall have effect subject to any disciplinary award of forfeiture . . .' Rule 56, however, expressly empowers the Secretary of State to remit a *d* disciplinary award and, since he would presumably do so in the case of a disciplinary award that had been declared by the High Court to be a nullity, such a declaration would achieve, though less directly, the same result in practice as quashing the award by certiorari.

So no question arises as to the 'jurisdiction' of the High Court to grant to each of the appellants relief by way of a declaration in the terms sought, if they succeeded in *e* establishing the facts alleged in their respective statements of claim or originating summons and the court considered a declaration to be an appropriate remedy. All that is at issue in the instant appeal is the procedure by which such relief ought to be sought. Put in a single sentence the question for your Lordships is: whether in 1980, after RSC Ord 53 in its new form, adopted in 1977, had come into operation, it was an abuse of the process of the court to apply for such declarations by using the procedure laid down by *f* the rules for proceedings begun by writ or by originating summons instead of using the procedure laid down by Ord 53 for an application for judicial review of the awards of forfeiture of remission of sentence made against them by the board which the appellants are seeking to impugn?

In their respective actions, the appellants claim only declaratory relief. It is conceded on their behalf that, for reasons into which the concession makes it unnecessary to enter, *g* no claim for damages would lie against the members of the board of visitors by whom the awards were made. The only claim was for a form of relief which it lies within the discretion of the court to grant or to withhold. So the first thing to be noted is that the relief sought in the action is discretionary only.

It is not, and it could not be, contended that the decision of the board awarding him forfeiture of remission had infringed or threatened to infringe any right of the appellant *h* derived from private law, whether a common law right or one created by a statute. Under the Prison Rules remission of sentence is not a matter of right but of indulgence. So far as private law is concerned all that each appellant had was a legitimate expectation, based on his knowledge of what is the general practice, that he would be granted the maximum remission, permitted by r 5(2) of the Prison Rules, of one-third of his sentence if by that time no disciplinary award of forfeiture of remission had been made against *j* him. So the second thing to be noted is that none of the appellants had any remedy in private law.

In public law, as distinguished from private law, however, such legitimate expectation gave to each appellant a sufficient interest to challenge the legality of the adverse disciplinary award made against him by the board on the ground that in one way or

another the board in reaching its decision had acted outwith the powers conferred on it
a by the legislation under which it was acting; and such grounds would include the board's
failure to observe the rules of natural justice: which means no more than to act fairly
towards him in carrying out their decision-making process, and I prefer so to put it.

The power of boards of visitors of a prison to make disciplinary awards is conferred on
them by subordinate legislation, i e the Prison Rules 1964 made by the Secretary of State
under ss 6 and 47 of the Prison Act 1952. The charges against the appellants were of
b grave offences against discipline falling within r 51 of the Prison Rules. They were
referred by the governor of the prison to the board under r 51(1). It thereupon became
the duty of the board under r 51(3) to inquire into the charge and decide whether it was
proved and if so to award what the board considered to be the appropriate punishment.
Rule 49 is applicable to such inquiry by the board. It lays down expressly that the
prisoner 'shall be given a full opportunity of hearing what is alleged against him and of
c presenting his own case'. In exercising their functions under r 51 members of the board
are acting as a statutory tribunal, as contrasted with a domestic tribunal on which powers
are conferred by contract between those who agree to submit to its jurisdiction. Where
the legislation which confers on a statutory tribunal its decision-making powers also
provides expressly for the procedure it shall follow in the course of reaching its decision,
it is a question of construction of the relevant legislation, to be decided by the court in
d which the decision is challenged, whether a particular procedural provision is mandatory,
so that its non-observance in the process of reaching the decision makes the decision itself
a nullity, or whether it is merely directory, so that the statutory tribunal has a discretion
not to comply with it if, in its opinion, the exceptional circumstances of a particular case
justify departing from it. But the requirement that a person who is charged with having
done something which, if proved to the satisfaction of a statutory tribunal, has
e consequences that will, or may, affect him adversely, should be given a fair opportunity
of hearing what is alleged against him and of presenting his own case, is so fundamental
to any civilised legal system that it is to be presumed that Parliament intended that a
failure to observe it should render null and void any decision reached in breach of this
requirement. What is alleged by the appellants other than Millbanks would amount to
an infringement of the express r 49; but even if there were no such express provision a
f requirement to observe it would be a necessary implication from the nature of the
disciplinary functions of the board. In the absence of express provision to the contrary,
Parliament whenever it provides for the creation of a statutory tribunal must be
presumed not to have intended that the tribunal should be authorised to act in
contravention of one of the most fundamental rules of natural justice or fairness, namely:
audi alteram partem.

g In the appellant Millbanks's case, there is no express provision in the Prison Rules that
the members of the board who inquire into a disciplinary offence under r 51 must be
free from personal bias against the prisoner. It is another fundamental rule of natural
justice or fairness, too obvious to call for express statement of it, that a tribunal exercising
functions such as those exercised by the board in Millbanks's case should be constituted
of persons who enter on the inquiry without any pre-conceived personal bias against the
h prisoner. Failure to comply with this implied requirement would likewise render the
decision of the tribunal a nullity.

So the third thing to be noted is that each of the appellants, if he established the facts
alleged in his action, was entitled to a remedy in public law which would have the effect
of preventing the decision of the board from having any adverse consequences on him.

My Lords, the power of the High Court to make declaratory judgments is conferred
j by what is now RSC Ord 15, r 16. The language of the rule, which was first made in
1883, has never been altered, though the numbering of the rule has from time to time
been changed:

'No action or other proceeding shall be open to objection on the ground that a
merely declaratory judgment or order is sought thereby, and the Court may make

binding declarations of right whether or not any consequential relief is or could be claimed.'

This rule, which is in two parts separated by 'and', has been very liberally interpreted in the course of its long history, wherever it appeared to the court that the justice of the case required the grant of declaratory relief in the particular action before it. Since 'action' is defined so as to have included since 1938 an originating motion applying for prerogative orders, Ord 15, r 16 says nothing as to the appropriate procedure by which declarations of different kinds ought to be sought. Nor does it draw any distinction between declarations that relate to rights and obligations under private law and those that relate to rights and obligations under public law. Indeed the appreciation of the distinction in substantive law between what is private law and what is public law has itself been a latecomer to the English legal system. It is a consequence of the development that has taken place in the last thirty years of the procedures available for judicial control of administrative action. This development started with the expansion of the grounds on which orders of certiorari could be obtained as a result of the decision of the Court of Appeal in *R v Northumberland Compensation Appeal Tribunal, ex p Shaw* [1952] 1 All ER 122, [1952] 1 KB 338, it was accelerated by the passing of the Tribunals and Inquiries Act 1958, and culminated in the substitution in 1977 of the new form of RSC Ord 53 which has since been given statutory confirmation in s 31 of the Supreme Court Act 1981.

The importance of the *Northumberland Compensation Appeal Tribunal* case is that it re-established, largely as a result of the historical erudition of Lord Goddard CJ displayed in the judgment of the Divisional Court ([1951] 1 All ER 268, [1951] 1 KB 711), a matter that had long been forgotten by practitioners and had been overlooked as recently as 1944 in *Racecourse Betting Control Board v Secretary for Air* [1944] 1 All ER 60, [1944] Ch 114, a judgment given per incuriam by a Court of Appeal of which Lord Goddard had himself been a member. What was there rediscovered was that the High Court had power to quash by an order of certiorari a decision of any body of persons having legal authority (not derived from contract only) to determine questions affecting the rights of subjects, not only on the ground that it had acted outwith its jurisdiction but also on the ground that it was apparent on the face of its written determination that it had made a mistake as to the applicable law.

However, this rediscovered ground on which relief by an order of certiorari to quash the decision as erroneous in law could be obtained, was available only when there was an error of law apparent 'on the face of the record' and so was liable to be defeated by the decision-making body if it gave no reasons for its determination.

In 1958 this lacuna, so far as statutory tribunals were concerned, was largely filled by the passing of the first Tribunals and Inquiries Act, now replaced by the Tribunals and Inquiries Act 1971. This Act required the giving of reasons for their determinations by the great majority of statutory tribunals from which there is no express statutory provision for an appeal to the Supreme Court on a point of law. But boards of visitors of prisons have never been included among those tribunals that are covered by that Act. The 1971 Act also in effect repealed, with two exceptions, what had become to be called generically 'no certiorari' clauses in all previous statutes, by providing in s 14(1) as follows:

'As respects England and Wales . . . any provision in an Act passed before [the commencement of the Act] that any order or determination shall not be called into question in any court, or any provision in such an Act which by similar words excludes any of the powers of the High Court, shall not have effect so as to prevent the removal of the proceedings into the High Court by order of certiorari or to prejudice the powers of the High Court to make orders of mandamus . . .'

The subsection, it is to be observed, says nothing about any right to bring civil actions for declarations of nullity of orders or determinations of statutory bodies where an earlier Act of Parliament contains a provision that such order or determination 'shall not be called into question in any court'. Since actions begun by writ seeking such declarations *a* were already coming into common use in the High Court so as to provide an alternative remedy to orders of certiorari, the section suggests a parliamentary preference in favour of making the latter remedy available rather than the former. I will defer consideration of the reasons for this preference until later.

Fortunately for the development of public law in England, s 14(3) contained express provision that the section should not apply to any order or determination of the Foreign Compensation Commission, a statutory body established under the Foreign Compensation *b* Act 1950, which contained in s 4(4) an express provision:

> 'The determination by the Commission of any application made to them under this Act shall not be called in question in any court of law.'

It was this provision that provided the occasion for the landmark decision of this House in *Anisminic Ltd v Foreign Compensation Commission* [1969] 1 All ER 208, [1969] 2 *c* AC 147, and particularly the leading speech of Lord Reid, which has liberated English public law from the fetters that the courts had theretofore imposed on themselves so far as determinations of inferior courts and statutory tribunals were concerned, by drawing esoteric distinctions between errors of law committed by such tribunals that went to their jurisdiction, and errors of law committed by them within their jurisdiction. The breakthrough that *Anisminic* made was the recognition by the majority of this House that *d* if a tribunal whose jurisdiction was limited by statute or subordinate legislation mistook the law applicable to the facts as it had found them, it must have asked itself the wrong question, ie one into which it was not empowered to inquire and so had no jurisdiction to determine. Its purported 'determination', not being a 'determination' within the meaning of the empowering legislation, was accordingly a nullity.

Anisminic was an action commenced by writ for a declaration, in which a minute of *e* the commission's reasons for their determination adverse to the plaintiff company did not appear on the face of their determination, and had in fact been obtained only on discovery: but, as appears from the report of my own judgment when *Anisminic* was in the Court of Appeal (see [1967] 2 All ER 986 at 996, [1968] 2 QB 862 at 893), the case had been argued up to that stage as if it were an application for certiorari in which the minute of the commission's reasons formed part of the 'record' on which an error of law *f* appeared. In the House of Lords the question of the propriety of suing by writ for a declaration instead of applying for certiorari and mandamus played no part in the main argument for the commission. It appears for the first time in the report of counsel for the commission's reply (see [1969] 2 AC 147 at 167), where an argument that the court had no 'jurisdiction' to make the declaration seems to have been put forward on the narrow ground, special to the limited functions of the commission, alluded to of my own *g* judgment in the Court of Appeal ([1967] 2 All ER 986 at 1007, [1968] 2 QB 862 at 910–911) that the House overruled; but I did not purport to decide the question because, in the view that I had (erroneously) taken of the effect of s 4(4) of the 1950 Act, it appeared to me to be unnecessary to do so.

My Lords, *Anisminic* was decided by this House before the alteration was made to Ord 53 in 1977. The order of the Rules of the Supreme Court dealing with applications for *h* the prerogative orders of mandamus, certiorari and prohibition in force at the time of *Anisminic* was numbered Ord 53 and had been made in 1965. It replaced, but in substance only repeated, the first twelve rules of what had been Ord 59 and which had in 1938 itself replaced the former Crown Office Rules of 1906. The pre-1977 Ord 53, like its predecessors, placed under considerable procedural disadvantage applicants who wished to challenge the lawfulness of a determination of a statutory tribunal or any other body *j* of persons having legal authority to determine questions affecting the common law or statutory rights or obligations of other persons as individuals. It will be noted that I have broadened the much-cited description by Atkin LJ in *R v Electricity Comrs, ex p London Electricity Joint Committee Co (1920) Ltd* [1924] 1 KB 171, [1923] All ER Rep 156 of bodies of persons subject to the supervisory jurisdiction of the High Court by prerogative remedies (which in 1924 then took the form of the prerogative writs of mandamus, prohibition, certiorari, and quo warranto) by excluding Atkins LJ's limitation of the bodies of persons to whom the prerogative writs might issue, to those 'having a duty to act judicially'. For the next forty years this phrase gave rise to many attempts, with *a* varying success, to draw subtle distinctions between decisions that were quasi-judicial and those that were administrative only. But the relevance of arguments of this kind was destroyed by the decision of this House in *Ridge v Baldwin* [1963] 2 All ER 66, [1964] AC 40, where again the leading speech was given by Lord Reid. Wherever any person or body of persons has authority conferred by legislation to make decisions of the kind I have described, it is amenable to the remedy of an order to quash its decision either for *b* error of law in reaching it or for failure to act fairly towards the person who will be adversely affected by the decision by failing to observe either one or other of the two fundamental rights accorded to him by the rules of natural justice or fairness, viz to have afforded to him a reasonable opportunity of learning what is alleged against him and of putting forward his own case in answer to it, and to the absence of personal bias against him on the part of the person by whom the decision falls to be made. In *Ridge v Baldwin* *c* [1963] 2 All ER 66 at 76, [1964] AC 40 at 72 it is interesting to observe that Lord Reid said: 'We do not have a developed system of administrative law—perhaps because until fairly recently we did not need it.' By 1977 the need had continued to grow apace and this reproach to English law had been removed. We did have by then a developed system of administrative law, to the development of which Lord Reid himself, by his speeches in cases which reached this House, had made an outstanding contribution. To the *d* landmark cases of *Ridge v Baldwin* and *Anisminic* I would add a third, *Padfield v Minister of Agriculture, Fisheries and Food* [1968] 1 All ER 694, [1968] AC 997, another case in which a too-timid judgment of my own in the Court of Appeal was (fortunately) overruled.

Although the availability of the remedy of order to quash a decision by certiorari had in theory been widely extended by these developments, the procedural disadvantages under which applicants for this remedy laboured remained substantially unchanged *e* until the alteration of Ord 53 in 1977. Foremost among these was the absence of any provision for discovery. In the case of a decision which did not state the reasons for it, it was not possible to challenge its validity for error of law in the reasoning by which the decision had been reached. If it had been an application for certiorari those who were the plaintiffs in *Anisminic* would have failed; it was only because by pursuing an action by writ for a declaration of nullity that the plaintiffs were entitled to the discovery by which *f* the minute of the commission's reasons which showed that they had asked themselves the wrong question, was obtained. Again under Ord 53 evidence was required to be on affidavit. This in itself is not an unjust disadvantage; it is a common feature of many forms of procedure in the High Court, including originating summonses; but in the absence of any express provision for cross-examination of deponents, as your Lordships who are familiar with the pre-1977 procedure will be aware, even *applications* for leave to *g* cross-examine were virtually unknown, let alone the grant of leave itself, save in very exceptional cases of which I believe none of your Lordships has ever had actual experience. Lord Goddard CJ, whose experience was at that time unrivalled, had so stated in *R v Stokesley (Yorkshire) Justices, ex p Bartram* [1956] 1 All ER 563 at 564, [1956] 1 WLR 254 at 257.

On the other hand, as compared with an action for a declaration commenced by writ *h* or originating summons, the procedure under Ord 53 both before and after 1977 provided for the respondent decision-making statutory tribunal or public authority against which the remedy of certiorari was sought protection against claims which it was not in the public interest for courts of justice to entertain.

First, leave to apply for the order was required. The application for leave, which was ex parte but could be, and in practice often was, adjourned in order to enable the proposed *j* respondent to be represented, had to be supported by a statement setting out, inter alia, the grounds on which the relief was sought and by affidavits verifying the facts relied on; so that a knowingly false statement of fact would amount to the criminal offence of perjury. Such affidavit was also required to satisfy the requirement of uberrima fides, with the consequence that failure to make on oath a full and candid disclosure of material

facts was of itself a ground for refusing the relief sought in the substantive application
a for which leave had been obtained on the strength of the affidavit. This was an important
safeguard, which is preserved in the new Ord 53 of 1977. The public interest in good
administration requires that public authorities and third parties should not be kept in
suspense as to the legal validity of a decision the authority has reached in purported
exercise of decision-making powers for any longer period than is absolutely necessary in
fairness to the person affected by the decision. In contrast, allegations made in a statement
b of claim or an indorsement of an originating summons are not on oath, so the
requirement of a prior application for leave to be supported by full and candid affidavits
verifying the facts relied on is an important safeguard against groundless or unmeritorious
claims that a particular decision is a nullity. There was also power in the court on
granting leave to impose terms as to costs or security.

Furthermore, as Ord 53 was applied in practice, as soon as the application for leave had
c been made it provided a very speedy means, available in urgent cases within a matter of
days rather than months, for determining whether a disputed decision was valid in law
or not.

A reduction of the period of suspense was also effected by the requirement that leave
to apply for certiorari to quash a decision must be made within a limited period after the
impugned decision was made, unless delay beyond that limited period was accounted for
d to the satisfaction of the judge. The period was six months under the pre-1977 Ord 53;
under the current Ord 53 it is further reduced to three months.

My Lords, the exclusion of all right to discovery in applications for certiorari under
Ord 53, particularly before the passing of the Tribunals and Inquiries Act 1958, was
calculated to cause injustice to persons who had no means, if they adopted that procedure,
of ascertaining whether a public body, which had made a decision adversely affecting
e them, had done so for reasons which were wrong in law and rendered their decision
invalid. It will be within the knowledge of all of your Lordships that, at any rate from
the 1950s onwards, actions for declarations of nullity of decisions affecting the rights of
individuals under public law were widely entertained, in parallel to applications for
certiorari to quash, as a means of obtaining an effective alternative remedy. I will not
weary your Lordships by reciting examples of cases where this practice received the
f express approval of the Court of Appeal, though I should point out that of those cases in
this House in which this practice was approved, *Vine v National Dock Labour Board* [1956]
3 All ER 939, [1957] AC 488 and *Ridge v Baldwin* involved, as well as questions of public
law, contracts of employment which gave rise to rights under private law. In *Anisminic*
the procedural question was not seriously argued, while *Pyx Granite Ltd v Ministry of
Housing and Local Government* [1959] 3 All ER 1, [1960] AC 260, which is referred to in
g *The Supreme Court Practice 1982*, vol 1, p 252, para 15/16/1 as an instance of the approval
by this House of the practice of suing for a declaration instead of applying for an order of
certiorari, appears on analysis to have been concerned with declaring that the plaintiffs
had a legal right to do what they were seeking to do without the need to obtain any
decision from the minister. Nevertheless I accept that having regard to the disadvantages,
particularly in relation to the absolute bar on compelling discovery of documents by the
h respondent public authority to an applicant for an order of certiorari, and the almost
invariable practice of refusing leave to allow cross-examination of deponents to affidavits
lodged on its behalf, it could not be regarded as an abuse of the process of the court,
before the amendments made to Ord 53 in 1977, to proceed against the authority by an
action for a declaration of nullity of the impugned decision with an injunction to prevent
the authority from acting on it, instead of applying for an order of certiorari; and this
j despite the fact that, by adopting this course, the plaintiff evaded the safeguards imposed
in the public interest against groundless, unmeritorious or tardy attacks on the validity
of decisions made by public authorities in the field of public law.

Those disadvantages, which formerly might have resulted in an applicant being unable
to obtain justice in an application for certiorari under Ord 53, have all been removed by
the new rules introduced in 1977. There is express provision in the new r 8 for

interlocutory applications for discovery of documents, the administration of interrogatories and the cross-examination of deponents to affidavits. Discovery of documents *a*
(which may often be a time-consuming process) is not automatic as in an action begun
by writ, but otherwise Ord 24 applies to it and discovery is obtainable on application
whenever, and to the extent that, the justice of the case requires; similarly Ord 26 applies
to applications for interrogatories; and to applications for cross-examination of deponents
to affidavits Ord 28, r 2(3) applies. This is the rule that deals with evidence in actions
begun by originating summons and permits oral cross-examination on affidavit evidence *b*
wherever the justice of the cases requires. It may well be that for the reasons given by
Lord Denning MR in *George v Secretary of State for the Environment* (1979) 38 P & CR 609,
it will only be on rare occasions that the interests of justice will require that leave be
given for cross-examination of deponents on their affidavits in applications for judicial
review. This is because of the nature of the issues that normally arise on judicial review.
The facts, except where the claim that a decision was invalid on the ground that the *c*
statutory tribunal or public authority that made the decision failed to comply with the
procedure prescribed by the legislation under which it was acting or failed to observe the
fundamental rules of natural justice or fairness, can seldom be a matter of relevant
dispute on an application for judicial review, since the tribunal or authority's findings of
fact, as distinguished from the legal consequences of the facts that they have found, are
not open to review by the court in the exercise of its supervisory powers except on the *d*
principles laid down in *Edwards v Bairstow* [1955] 3 All ER 48 at 57–58, [1956] AC 14 at
36; and to allow cross-examination presents the court with a temptation, not always
easily resisted, to substitute its own view of the facts for that of the decision-making body
on whom the exclusive jurisdiction to determine facts had been conferred by Parliament.
Nevertheless, having regard to a possible misunderstanding of what was said by Geoffrey
Lane LJ in *R v Hull Visitors, ex p St Germain (No 2)* [1979] 3 All ER 545 at 553–554, [1979] *e*
1 WLR 1401 at 1410, your Lordships may think this an appropriate occasion on which
to emphasise that, whatever may have been the position before the rule was altered in
1977, in all proceedings for judicial review that have been started since that date the
grant of leave to cross-examine deponents on applications for judicial review is governed
by the same principles as it is in actions begun by originating summons; it should be
allowed whenever the justice of the particular case so requires. *f*

Another handicap under which an applicant for a prerogative order under Ord 53
formerly laboured (though it would not have affected the appellants in the instant cases
even if they had brought their actions before the 1977 alteration to Ord 53) was that a
claim for damages for breach of a right in private law by the applicant resulting from an
invalid decision of a public authority could not be made in an application under Ord 53.
Damages could only be claimed in a separate action begun by writ; whereas in an action *g*
so begun they could be claimed as additional relief as well as a declaration of nullity of
the decision from which the damage claimed had flowed. Rule 7 of the new Ord 53
permits the applicant for judicial review to include in the statement in support of his
application for leave a claim for damages and empowers the court to award damages on
the hearing of the application if satisfied that such damages could have been awarded to
him in an action begun by him by writ at the time of the making of the application. *h*

Finally r 1 of the new Ord 53 enables an application for a declaration or an injunction
to be included in an application for judicial review. This was not previously the case;
only prerogative orders could be obtained in proceedings under Ord 53. Declarations or
injunctions were obtainable only in actions begun by writ or originating summons. So a
person seeking to challenge a decision had to make a choice of the remedy that he sought
at the outset of the proceedings, although when the matter was examined more closely *j*
in the course of the proceedings it might appear that he was not entitled to that remedy
but would have been entitled to some other remedy available only in the other kind of
proceeding.

This reform may have lost some of its importance since there have come to be realised
that the full consequences of *Anisminic*, in introducing the concept that if a statutory

decision-making authority asks itself the wrong question it acts without jurisdiction,
a have been virtually to abolish the distinction between errors within jurisdiction that
rendered voidable a decision that remained valid until quashed, and errors that went to
jurisdiction and rendered a decision void ab initio provided that its validity was challenged
timeously in the High Court by an appropriate procedure. Failing such challenge within
the applicable time limit, public policy, expressed in the maxim omnia praesumuntur
rite esse acta, requires that after the expiry of the time limit it should be given all the
b effects in law of a valid decision.

Nevertheless, there may still be cases where it turns out in the course of proceedings to
challenge a decision of a statutory authority that a declaration of rights rather than
certiorari is the appropriate remedy. The *Pyx Granite* case [1959] 3 All ER 1, [1960] AC
260 provides an example of such a case.

So Ord 53 since 1977 has provided a procedure by which every type of remedy for
c infringement of the rights of individuals that are entitled to protection in public law can
be obtained in one and the same proceeding by way of an application for judicial review,
and whichever remedy is found to be the most appropriate in the light of what has
emerged on the hearing of the application, can be granted to him. If what should emerge
is that his complaint is not of an infringement of any of his rights that are entitled to
protection in public law, but may be an infringement of his rights in private law and
d thus not a proper subject for judicial review, the court has power under r 9(5), instead of
refusing the application, to order the proceedings to continue as if they had begun by
writ. There is no such converse power under the Rules of the Supreme Court to permit
an action begun by writ to continue as if it were an application for judicial review; and I
respectfully disagree with that part of the judgment of Lord Denning MR in the instant
case which suggests that such a power may exist; nor do I see the need to amend the rules
e in order to create one.

My Lords, at the outset of this speech, I drew attention to the fact that the remedy by
way of declaration of nullity of the decisions of the board was discretionary: as are all the
remedies available on judicial review. Counsel for the appellants accordingly conceded
that the fact that by adopting the procedure of an action begun by writ or by originating
summons instead of an application for judicial review under Ord 53 (from which there
f have now been removed all those disadvantages to applicants that had previously led the
courts to countenance actions for declarations and injunctions as an alternative procedure
for obtaining a remedy for infringement of the rights of the individual that are entitled
to protection in public law only) the appellants had thereby been able to evade those
protections against groundless, unmeritorious or tardy harassment that were afforded to
statutory tribunals or decision-making public authorities by Ord 53, and which might
g have resulted in the summary, and would in any event have resulted in the speedy,
disposition of the application, is among the matters fit to be taken into consideration by
the judge in deciding whether to exercise his discretion by refusing to grant a declaration;
but, it was contended, this he may only do at the conclusion of the trial.

So to delay the judge's decision as to how to exercise his discretion would defeat the
public policy that underlies the grant of those protections: viz the need, in the interests
h of good administration and of third parties who may be indirectly affected by the
decision, for speedy certainty as to whether it has the effect of a decision that is valid in
public law. An action for a declaration or injunction need not be commenced until the
very end of the limitation period; if begun by writ, discovery and interlocutory
proceedings may be prolonged and the plaintiffs are not required to support their
allegations by evidence on oath until the actual trial. The period of uncertainty as to the
j validity of a decision that has been challenged on allegations that may eventually turn
out to be baseless and unsupported by evidence on oath, may thus be strung out for a
very lengthy period, as the actions of the first three appellants in the instant appeals show.
Unless such an action can be struck out summarily at the outset as an abuse of the process
of the court the whole purpose of the public policy to which the change in Ord 53 was
directed would be defeated.

My Lords, Ord 53 does not expressly provide that procedure by application for judicial review shall be the exclusive procedure available by which the remedy of a declaration *a* or injunction may be obtained for infringement of rights that are entitled to protection under public law; nor does s 31 of the Supreme Court Act 1981. There is great variation between individual cases that fall within Ord 53 and the Rules Committee and subsequently the legislature were, I think, for this reason content to rely on the express and the inherent power of the High Court, exercised on a case to case basis, to prevent abuse of its process whatever might be the form taken by that abuse. Accordingly, I do *b* not think that your Lordships would be wise to use this as an occasion to lay down categories of cases in which it would necessarily always be an abuse to seek in an action begun by writ or originating summons a remedy against infringement of rights of the individual that are entitled to protection in public law.

The position of applicants for judicial review has been drastically ameliorated by the new Ord 53. It has removed all those disadvantages, particularly in relation to discovery, *c* that were manifestly unfair to them and had, in many cases, made applications for prerogative orders an inadequate remedy if justice was to be done. This it was that justified the courts in not treating as an abuse of their powers resort to an alternative procedure by way of action for a declaration or injunction (not then obtainable on an application under Ord 53), despite the fact that this procedure had the effect of depriving the defendants of the protection to statutory tribunals and public authorities for which *d* for public policy reasons Ord 53 provided.

Now that those disadvantages to applicants have been removed and all remedies for infringements of rights protected by public law can be obtained on an application for judicial review, as can also remedies for infringements of rights under private law if such infringements should also be involved, it would in my view as a general rule be contrary to public policy, and as such an abuse of the process of the court, to permit a person *e* seeking to establish that a decision of a public authority infringed rights to which he was entitled to protection under public law to proceed by way of an ordinary action and by this means to evade the provisions of Ord 53 for the protection of such authorities.

My Lords, I have described this as a general rule; for, though it may normally be appropriate to apply it by the summary process of striking out the action, there may be exceptions, particularly where the invalidity of the decision arises as a collateral issue in a *f* claim for infringement of a right of the plaintiff arising under private law, or where none of the parties objects to the adoption of the procedure by writ or originating summons. Whether there should be other exceptions should, in my view, at this stage in the development of procedural public law, be left to be decided on a case to case basis: a process that your Lordships will be continuing in the next case in which judgment is to be delivered today (see *Cocks v Thanet DC* [1982] 3 All ER 1135). *g*

In the instant cases where the only relief sought is a declaration of nullity of the decisions of a statutory tribunal, the Board of Visitors of Hull Prison, as in any other case in which a similar declaration of nullity in public law is the only relief claimed, I have no hesitation, in agreement with the Court of Appeal, in holding that to allow the actions to proceed would be an abuse of the process of the court. They are blatant attempts to avoid the protections for the respondents for which Ord 53 provides. *h*

I would dismiss these appeals.

LORD FRASER OF TULLYBELTON. My Lords, I have had the advantage of reading in draft the speech prepared by my noble and learned friend Lord Diplock. I agree with it and for the reasons stated in it would dismiss these appeals.

j

LORD KEITH OF KINKEL. My Lords, I have had the advantage of reading in draft the speech prepared by my noble and learned friend Lord Diplock. I agree with it and for the reasons stated in it I would dismiss these appeals.

LORD BRIDGE OF HARWICH. My Lords, I have had the advantage of reading in

a draft the speech of my noble and learned friend Lord Diplock. I entirely agree with it
and for the reasons he gives I would dismiss these appeals.

LORD BRIGHTMAN. My Lords, I also would dismiss these appeals for the reasons
given by my noble and learned friend Lord Diplock.

Appeals dismissed.

b

Solicitors: *Edwin Coe & Calder Woods* (for the appellants O'Reilly, Derbyshire and
Dougan); *Seifert, Sedley & Co* (for the appellant Millbanks); *Treasury Solicitor*.

Mary Rose Plummer   Barrister.

c

Cocks v Thanet District Council

HOUSE OF LORDS
LORD DIPLOCK, LORD FRASER OF TULLYBELTON, LORD KEITH OF KINKEL, LORD BRIDGE OF
d HARWICH AND LORD BRIGHTMAN
6, 7, 25 NOVEMBER 1982

*Housing – Homeless person – Duty of housing authority to provide accommodation – Remedy for
breach of duty – Whether applicant can proceed by way of ordinary action – Whether applicant
restricted to applying for judicial review – Housing (Homeless Persons) Act 1977, s 4(1) – RSC*
e *Ord 53.*

Applying the general rule relating to the procedure for impugning a decision of a public
body which infringes rights that are protected under public law, a person who seeks to
challenge a decision made by a housing authority under s 4(1)[a] of the Housing (Homeless
Persons) Act 1977 that he became homeless intentionally and is therefore not entitled to
f permanent accommodation must do so by way of an application under RSC Ord 53,
r 1(1)[b] for judicial review of the authority's decision (see p 1136 g to j, p 1139 b to f and p
1140 c d and f, post).
   O'Reilly v Mackman [1982] 3 All ER 1124 applied.
   De Falco v Crawley BC [1980] 1 All ER 913 overruled.

g **Notes**
For the general principles relating to judicial review, see 1 Halsbury's Laws (4th edn) para
41.
   For orders of mandamus compelling public bodies to carry out their duties, see ibid
para 100, and for cases on the discretion of the court to grant an order of mandamus, see
16 Digest (Reissue) 323–326, 3378–3415.
h For the Housing (Homeless Persons) Act 1977, s 4, see 47 Halsbury's Statutes (3rd edn)
318.

Cases referred to in opinions
Associated Provincial Picture Houses Ltd v Wednesbury Corp [1947] 2 All ER 680, [1948] 1
   KB 223, CA, 45 Digest (Repl) 215, 189.

j   *a*   Section 4(1), so far as material, provides: 'If a housing authority are satisfied . . . that a person who
        has applied to them for accommodation . . . is homeless or threatened with homelessness, they
        shall be subject to a duty towards him under this section.'
     b   Rule 1(1), so far as material, provides: 'An application for—(*a*) an order of mandamus, prohibition
        or certiorari . . . shall be made by way of an application for judicial review in accordance with the
        provisions of this Order.'

De Falco v Crawley BC, Silvestri v Crawley BC [1980] 1 All ER 913, [1980] QB 460, [1980]
2 WLR 664, CA, 26 Digest (Reissue) 798, 5331.   *a*

Din v Wandsworth London Borough [1981] 3 All ER 881, [1981] 3 WLR 918, HL.

Edwards v Bairstow [1955] 3 All ER 48, [1956] AC 14, [1955] 3 WLR 410, HL, 28(1)
Digest (Reissue) 566, 2089.

Islam v Hillingdon London Borough [1981] 3 All ER 901, [1981] 3 WLR 942, HL.

Lambert v Ealing London Borough Council [1982] 2 All ER 394, [1982] 1 WLR 550, CA.

O'Reilly v Mackman [1982] 3 All ER 1124, HL.   *b*

Thornton v Kirklees Metropolitan Borough Council [1979] 2 All ER 349, [1979] QB 626,
[1979] 3 WLR 1, CA, 26 Digest (Reissue) 799, 5335.

Appeal

The defendants, Thanet District Council, appealed against the order of Milmo J dated 18
May 1982 whereby judgment was entered for the respondent, the plaintiff William   *c*
Charles Cocks, on the preliminary issue ordered by Master Elton on 1 March 1982 to be
tried as such, namely whether the respondent was entitled to proceed against the
appellants by an action brought in the Thanet County Court for a declaration to the effect
that the appellants owed him a duty under the Housing (Homeless Persons) Act 1977 to
provide him with permanent accommodation or whether the respondent was required
to apply for judicial review of the appellants' decision that the respondent had become   *d*
homeless intentionally. On 14 June 1982 an Appeal Committee of the House of Lords
granted the appellants leave to appeal directly to the House, Milmo J having granted
them a certificate pursuant to s 12(3)(b) of the Administration of Justice Act 1969 that a
point of law of general public importance was involved in the decision and that the point
of law was one in respect of which the judge was bound by a previous decision of the
Court of Appeal in previous proceedings and was fully considered in the judgment given   *e*
by the Court of Appeal in previous proceedings. The facts are set out in the opinion of
Lord Bridge.

Anthony Scrivener QC and *Graham Stoker* for the appellants.
The respondent did not appear.
                                                                                                                                    f
Their Lordships took time for consideration.

25 November. The following opinions were delivered.

LORD DIPLOCK. My Lords, I have had the advantage of reading in draft the speech
of my noble and learned friend Lord Bridge. I agree with it and would allow the appeal   *g*
and concur in the order which he proposes.

LORD FRASER OF TULLYBELTON. My Lords, I have had the advantage of
reading in draft the speech prepared by my noble and learned friend Lord Bridge. I agree
with it, and with the order proposed by him.   *h*

LORD KEITH OF KINKEL. My Lords, I have had the benefit of reading in draft the
speech to be delivered by my noble and learned friend Lord Bridge. For the reasons
which he gives I would allow the appeal and concur in the order which he proposes.

LORD BRIDGE OF HARWICH. My Lords, the Housing (Homeless Persons) Act   *j*
1977 has been, and will no doubt continue to be, a fruitful source of litigation. The rights
of an applicant for accommodation under the 1977 Act, and the corresponding duties of
the housing authority, depend on three questions with respect to the applicant. (1) Is he
homeless or threatened with homelessness? (2) If yes, has he a priority need? (3) If yes,
did he become homeless intentionally?

The primary duties of the housing authority are fourfold: (a) If the housing authority
a have reason to believe that the applicant may be homeless or threatened with
homelessness, they must make such inquiries as are necessary to satisfy themselves of the
answers to the three questions indicated above (the duty to inquire): s 3(1) and (2). (b) If
they have reason to believe that he may be homeless and have a priority need, they must
accommodate him pending the outcome of their inquiries (the temporary housing duty):
s 3(4). (c) If they are satisfied that questions (1) and (2) should be answered affirmatively,
b but are not so satisfied as to question (3), they must provide permanent accommodation
for the applicant (the full housing duty): s 4(5). (d) If they are satisfied that all three
questions should be answered affirmatively, they must provide him with interim
accommodation and with advice and assistance (the limited housing duty): s 4(2) and (3).

Normally there will be no room for dispute as to whether or not an applicant is (a)
homeless or threatened with homelessness or (b) has a priority need. But the question
c whether or not a person became homeless intentionally may frequently give rise to
difficulties, as is shown by the many reported cases on the subject, including two in your
Lordships' House: *Din v Wandsworth London Borough* [1981] 3 All ER 881, [1981] 3 WLR
918, *Islam v Hillingdon London Borough* [1981] 3 All ER 901, [1981] 3 WLR 942. Moreover,
it is the resolution of this question, when disputed, which is of crucial importance both
to the applicant and to the housing authority because of the great practical differences in
d effect for both parties between the full housing duty and the limited housing duty. The
rights claimed by the respondent to the present appeal probably turn in the end on the
question of intentional homelessness. But the issue for your Lordships' decision on this
occasion is concerned, not with the substance of that question, but with the procedure by
which that and other questions under the 1977 Act ought properly to be resolved.

The respondent instituted these proceedings in the Thanet County Court on 29 January
e 1982. By his particulars of claim he pleads, in effect, that since 21 December 1981 he and
his family have been homeless (although accommodated at the home of a friend) and in
priority need and that his frequent applications to the appellant housing authority for
accommodation since that date have been refused. The pleading makes no reference to
any decision of the appellants notified to the respondent pursuant to s 8 of the 1977 Act,
but asserts, baldly and boldly, that the appellants owe to the respondent and are in breach
f of both the temporary and the full housing duty. The prayer for relief claims, inter alia,
a declaration to that effect, consequential mandatory injunctions and damages. I mention
in passing that the appellant might well have applied to strike out the pleading as it
stands as disclosing no cause of action, but this would probably only have led to an
amendment of the pleading to identify and particularise the precise issues which the
respondent seeks to litigate. Sensibly, no doubt, the parties sought and obtained a consent
g order from Master Elton which (a) transferred the proceedings to the Queen's Bench
Division of the High Court, and (b) ordered trial of a preliminary issue as to whether the
proceedings were properly brought by action or could only be brought by application for
judicial review. That issue was heard before Milmo J on 30 April 1982, when counsel for
the appellants conceded that the judge was bound by the decision of the Court of Appeal
in *De Falco v Crawley BC* [1980] 1 All ER 913, [1980] QB 460 to decide the issue in favour
h of the respondent. The judge granted an appropriate certificate under s 12 of the
Administration of Justice Act 1969 for appeal direct to your Lordships' House and in due
course leave to appeal was granted.

The procedural issue on which the appeal turns will naturally fall for decision in the
light of the principles expounded in the speech of Lord Diplock in *O'Reilly v Mackman*
[1982] 3 All ER 1124. But before attempting to apply those principles, it is necessary to
j analyse the functions of housing authorities under the 1977 Act. These functions fall
into two wholly distinct categories.

On the one hand, the housing authority are charged with decision-making functions.
It is for the housing authority to decide whether they have reason to believe the matters
which will give rise to the duty of inquiry or to the temporary housing duty. It is for the
housing authority, once the duty of inquiry has arisen, to make the appropriate inquiries

and to decide whether they are satisfied, or not satisfied as the case may be, of the matters which will give rise to the limited housing duty or the full housing duty. These are essentially public law functions. The power of decision being committed by the statute exclusively to the housing authority, their exercise of the power can only be challenged before the courts on the strictly limited grounds (i) that their decision was vitiated by bias or procedural unfairness (ii) that they have reached a conclusion of fact which can be impugned on the principles set out in the speech of Lord Radcliffe in *Edwards v Bairstow* [1955] 3 All ER 48, [1956] AC 14 or (iii) that, in so far as they have exercised a discretion (as they may require to do in considering questions of reasonableness under s 17(1), (2) and (4)), the exercise can be impugned on the principles set out in the judgment of Lord Greene MR in *Associated Provincial Picture Houses Ltd v Wednesbury Corp* [1947] 2 All ER 680, [1948] 1 KB 223. All this is trite law and the contrary has, so far as I know, never been argued in any case which has come before the courts under the 1977 Act.

On the other hand, the housing authority are charged with executive functions. Once a decision has been reached by the housing authority which gives rise to the temporary, the limited or the full housing duty, rights and obligations are immediately created in the field of private law. Each of the duties referred to, once established, is capable of being enforced by injunction and the breach of it will give rise to a liability in damages. But it is inherent in the scheme of the 1977 Act that an appropriate public law decision of the housing authority is a condition precedent to the establishment of the private law duty.

When the Court of Appeal, of which I was a member, decided *De Falco's* case, we did not, of course, have the benefit of Lord Diplock's analysis of the consequences of the introduction in 1977 by the amended RSC Ord 53 of the new public law procedure by way of an application for judicial review. That apart, I believe our decision was influenced by a failure to appreciate the significance of the dichotomy of functions to which I have drawn attention in the two foregoing paragraphs and a consequent misunderstanding of the true effect of the earlier Court of Appeal decision in *Thornton v Kirklees Metropolitan Borough Council* [1979] 2 All ER 349, [1979] 1 QB 626. The view expressed in *De Falco v Crawley BC* [1980] 1 All ER 913 at 920, 923, [1980] QB 460 at 476, 480 by Lord Denning MR and by myself, that an applicant for accommodation under the 1977 Act who wishes to challenge the housing authority's decision that he was intentionally homeless can do so either by action or by application for judicial review, I can now see to have been based on false reasoning. I am the more ready to say so since Lord Denning MR has also subsequently resiled from his previous opinion: see *Lambert v Ealing London Borough Council* [1982] 2 All ER 394 at 399, [1982] 1 WLR 550 at 557.

Thornton v Kirklees Metropolitan Borough Council was an appeal from a decision to strike out the plaintiff's particulars of claim in the county court on the ground that they disclosed no reasonable cause of action. The sole issue canvassed on the appeal was whether a breach of the duty under s 3(4) of the 1977 Act (what I have called the temporary housing duty) gave a cause of action in damages against the housing authority, which was essential to found jurisdiction in the county court. The Court of Appeal held that it did. On such an application to strike out, the court necessarily assumed the truth of the facts pleaded and these were taken sufficiently to allege both the existence and the breach of a duty owed to the plaintiff under s 3(4). On these assumptions the decision was, in my respectful view, correct. But the decision is authority for no more extensive proposition than that once the existence of a duty resting on a housing authority under the 1977 Act to provide accommodation, whether temporary or permanent, has been established, an action for damages for breach of that private law duty lies. It is to be noted that in that case the housing authority did not object to the proceedings in the county court as an abuse of process. If they had done so, they would have been entitled, for the reasons which I am about to develop, to have the action struck out on that ground.

After reference to *Thornton*, I said in *De Falco* [1980] 1 All ER 913 at 923, [1980] QB 460 at 480:

'If an ordinary action lies in respect of an alleged breach of duty, it must follow, it

a   seems to me, that in such an action the plaintiff as well as claiming damages or an injunction as his remedy for the breach of duty can claim any declaration necessary to establish that there was a relevant breach of duty, and, in particular, a declaration that a local authority's decision adverse to him under the Act was not validly made.'

In the light of the dichotomy between a housing authority's public and private law functions, this is a non-sequitur. The fallacy is in the implicit assumption that the court

b   has the power not only to review the housing authority's public law decision but also to substitute its own decision to the contrary effect in order to establish the necessary condition precedent to the housing authority's private law liability.

I have already indicated my agreement with the views of my noble and learned friend Lord Diplock, as expressed in *O'Reilly's* case [1982] 3 All ER 1124 at 1134, and I gratefully adopt all his reasons for the conclusion that:

c

'... it would ... as a general rule be contrary to public policy, and as such an abuse of the process of the court, to permit a person seeking to establish that a decision of a public authority infringed rights to which he was entitled to protection under public law to proceed by way of an ordinary action and by this means to evade the provisions of Ord 53 for the protection of such authorities.'

d   Does the same general rule apply, where the decision of the public authority which the litigant wishes to overturn is not one alleged to infringe any existing right but a decision which, being adverse to him, prevents him establishing a necessary condition precedent to the statutory private law right which he seeks to enforce? Any relevant decision of a housing authority under the 1977 Act which an applicant for accommodation wants to challenge will be of that character. I have no doubt that the same general rule should

e   apply to such a case. The safeguards built into the Ord 53 procedure which protect from harassment public authorities on whom Parliament has imposed a duty to make public law decisions and the inherent advantages of that procedure over proceedings begun by writ or originating summons for the purposes of investigating whether such decisions are open to challenge are of no less importance in relation to this type of decision than to the type of decision your Lordships have just been considering in *O'Reilly's* case. I have

f   in mind, in particular, the need to obtain leave to apply on the basis of sworn evidence which makes frank disclosure of all relevant facts known to the applicant; the court's discretionary control of both discovery and cross-examination; the capacity of the court to act with the utmost speed when necessary; and the avoidance of the temptation for the court to substitute its own decision of fact for that of the housing authority. Undue delay in seeking a remedy on the part of an aggrieved applicant for accommodation

g   under the 1977 Act is perhaps not often likely to present a problem, but since this appeal, unlike *O'Reilly's* case, arises from proceedings commenced after the coming into operation of the Supreme Court Act 1981, it is an appropriate occasion to observe both that s 31 of that Act removes any doubt there may have been as to the vires of the 1977 amendment of Ord 53 and also that s 31(6), by expressly recognising that delay in seeking the public law remedies obtainable by application for judicial review may be detrimental to good

h   administration, lends added weight to the consideration that the court, in the control of its own process, is fully justified in confining litigants to the use of procedural machinery which affords protection against such detrimental delay.

Even though nullification of a public law decision can, if necessary, be achieved by declaration as an alternative to an order of certiorari, certiorari to quash remains the primary and most appropriate remedy. Now that all public law remedies are available to

j   be sought by the unified and simplified procedure of an application for judicial review, there can be no valid reason, where the quashing of a decision is the sole remedy sought, why it should be sought otherwise than by certiorari. But an unsuccessful applicant for accommodation under the 1977 Act, confronted by an adverse decision of the housing authority as to, say, the question of his intentional homelessness, may strictly need not

only an order of certiorari to quash the adverse decision but also an order of mandamus
to the housing authority to determine the question afresh according to law. I have said a
that the court has no power to substitute its own decision for that of the housing
authority. That is strictly correct, though no doubt in practice there will be cases where
the court's decision will effectively determine the issue, as for instance where on
undisputed primary facts the court holds that no reasonable housing authority, correctly
directing itself in law, could be satisfied that the applicant became homeless intentionally.
But it will be otherwise where the housing authority's decision is successfully impugned b
on other grounds, as for instance that the applicant was not fairly heard or that irrelevant
factors have been taken into account. In such cases certiorari to quash and mandamus to
re-determine will, in strictness, be the appropriate remedies and the only appropriate
remedies.

It follows from these considerations that proceedings in which an unsuccessful
applicant for accommodation under the 1977 Act sets out to challenge the decision of the c
housing authority against him will afford another application of Lord Diplock's general
rule and will amount to an abuse of the process of the court if instituted otherwise than
by an application for judicial review under Ord 53.

In view of some technical but significant differences in the approach to the question
raised in this appeal between the law of England and the law of Scotland, which is to be
considered in the next judgment of your Lordships' House to be delivered, and in order d
to dispel any possible doubt, I think it appropriate to emphasise that the conclusion
reached in this appeal arises from the English court's inherent jurisdiction to control its
own process to prevent abuse, and has nothing to do with any limitation on the
jurisdiction of the county court. As Lord Diplock has observed in *O'Reilly's* case, the
validity of a public law decision may come into question collaterally in an ordinary
action. In such a case the issue would have to be decided by the High Court or the county e
court trying the action, as the case might be.

My Lords, I would allow this appeal, set aside the order of the judge and determine the
preliminary issue by declaring that the respondent is not entitled to continue these
proceedings or to seek any of the relief he claims otherwise than by an application for
judicial review.

f

LORD BRIGHTMAN. My Lords, I also would allow this appeal for the reasons given
by my noble and learned friend Lord Bridge.

Appeal allowed.

Solicitors: *Sharpe, Pritchard & Co* (for the appellants).

Mary Rose Plummer   Barrister.

The Hollandia

HOUSE OF LORDS

LORD DIPLOCK, LORD KEITH OF KINKEL, LORD ROSKILL, LORD BRANDON OF OAKBROOK AND LORD BRIGHTMAN

25 OCTOBER, 25 NOVEMBER 1982

Shipping – Carriage by sea – Damages for breach of contract – Loss of or damage to goods – Jurisdiction of English courts – Cargo shipped from United Kingdom port – Bill of lading providing for Dutch court to have exclusive jurisdiction – Carrier's liability limited under bill of lading to £250 – Hague-Visby Rules extending carrier's liability to £11,500 – Damage to cargo during carriage estimated at £22,000 – Whether Hague-Visby Rules applying to contract – Whether exclusive jurisdiction and limitation of liability provisions in bill of lading null and void – Carriage of Goods by Sea Act 1971, Sch, art III, para 8, art X.

In March 1978 an English company (the cargo owners) shipped a large machine on board a vessel belonging to Dutch carriers, for carriage from Scotland to Bonaire in the Netherlands Antilles, under a bill of lading which, by cl 2, provided (i) that the proper law of the contract was to be Dutch law (where the original Hague Rules for the carriage of goods by sea still applied), (ii) that the Court of Amsterdam was to have exclusive jurisdiction and (iii) that the liability of the carriers under the bill of lading was to be limited to 1,250 Dutch florins (about £250) per package. Under art IV, para 5(a) of the Hague-Visby Rules, as set out in the schedule to the Carriage of Goods by Sea Act 1971, the carriers' liability for loss or damage to the machine was limited to some £11,500. The machine was transhipped at Amsterdam onto a Norwegian vessel for carriage to Bonaire. During discharge at Bonaire, the machine was severely damaged, the cost of the damage being estimated at £22,000. The cargo owners brought an action in England against the carriers claiming damages. The cargo owners claimed to be entitled, by virtue of art X*a* of the Hague-Visby Rules, to bring their action in England because the bill of lading was issued in, and the carriage was from a port in, a 'contracting State', ie the United Kingdom. By art III, para 8*b* of the Hague-Visby Rules it was provided that 'Any clause . . . in a contract of carriage . . . lessening [the carrier's] liability . . . shall be null and void and of no effect'. The carriers applied to the English court for, and were granted, a stay of the action on the grounds that the cargo owners were bound by the exclusive jurisdiction clause in the bill of lading and that the action should accordingly proceed in the Netherlands. The cargo owners appealed, contending that the exclusive jurisdiction clause in the bill of lading was null and void under art III, para 8 of the Hague-Visby Rules and that they were thus entitled to bring their action in England. The Court of Appeal upheld that contention, removed the stay and allowed the action to proceed. The carriers appealed to the House of Lords, contending, inter alia, that a choice of forum clause only prescribed the procedure by which disputes arising under the contract of carriage were to be resolved and did not ex facie deal with liability at all and so was not a 'clause . . . lessening . . . liability' which was rendered null and void by art III, para 8.

Held – The description of provisions in contracts of carriage which were rendered 'null and void and of no effect' by art III, para 8 of the Hague-Visby Rules embraced every provision in a contract of carriage which, if it were applied, would have the effect of lessening liability otherwise than as provided by those rules. Accordingly cl 2 of the bill of lading, in so far as it limited liability for loss or damage otherwise than as provided by those rules, was null and void under art III, para 8. Where an exclusive jurisdiction clause in a bill of lading did not ex facie offend against art III, para 8 because it came into

---

a   Article X is set out at p 1145 *a b*, post
b   Paragraph 8 is set out at p 1144 *h*, post

operation only when a dispute arose between the parties, but where also it was established as a fact that the foreign court chosen as the exclusive forum would apply a domestic substantive law which would result in limiting the carriers' liability to a sum lower than that to which they would be entitled if art IV, para 5 of the Hague-Visby Rules applied, an English court was required by the 1971 Act to treat the choice of forum clause as of no effect. Since the Court of Amsterdam was bound to limit the carriers' liability in accordance with the Hague Rules rather than the Hague-Visby Rules, it followed that the English court in exercising its discretion regarding a stay of proceedings was bound to treat the bill of lading as if it had no choice of forum clause and to refuse a stay unless the carriers were able to satisfy it, independently of cl 2 of the bill of lading, that the Court of Amsterdam was a forum conveniens and the English court was not. Since the carriers had not established that the conditions for the granting of a stay had been fulfilled a stay would be refused and the appeal would be dismissed (see p 1145 *f g* and *j* to p 1146 *a* and *f* to p 1147 *c* and p 1148 *a* to *f* and *j* to p 1149 *c*, post).

Dictum of Lord Diplock in *MacShannon v Rockware Glass Ltd* [1978] 1 All ER at 630 and *Castanho v Brown & Root (UK) Ltd* [1981] 1 All ER 143 applied.

Decision of the Court of Appeal [1982] 1 All ER 1076 affirmed.

Notes

For the proper law governing contracts, see 8 Halsbury's Laws (4th edn) paras 583–591, and for cases on the subject, see 11 Digest (Reissue) 455–457, 751–759.

For the Carriage of Goods by Sea Act 1971, Sch, art III, para 8, art IV, para 5, art X, see 41 Halsbury's Statutes (3rd edn) 1322, 1325, 1330.

Cases referred to in opinions

Castanho v Brown & Root (UK) Ltd [1981] 1 All ER 143, [1981] AC 557, [1980] 3 WLR 991, HL.

Compagnie d'Armement Maritime SA v Compagnie Tunisienne de Navigation SA [1970] 3 All ER 71, [1971] AC 572, [1970] 3 WLR 389, HL, 11 Digest (Reissue) 457, 759.

MacShannon v Rockware Glass Ltd [1978] 1 All ER 625, [1978] AC 795, [1978] 2 WLR 362, HL, Digest (Cont Vol E) 99, 1691a.

Stag Line Ltd v Foscolo, Mango & Co Ltd [1932] AC 328, [1931] All ER Rep 666, HL, 41 Digest (Repl) 379, 1698.

Vita Foods Products Inc v Unus Shipping Co Ltd [1939] 1 All ER 513, [1939] AC 277, PC, 11 Digest (Reissue) 456, 755.

Interlocutory appeal

By a writ issued on 26 February 1980 the plaintiffs, the owners of cargo shipped on board the Haico Holwerda, a vessel owned by the defendants (the carriers), and later transhipped on board the vessel Morviken owned by a Norwegian company, brought an action in rem against the Hollandia, a vessel owned by the carriers, in respect of their claim against the carriers for damages arising out of the carriers' alleged negligence in the carriage of the cargo. On 26 June 1980 Sheen J, sitting in the Admiralty Court of the Queen's Bench Division ordered, on the carriers' application, that all further proceedings in the action be stayed on the grounds that the action should proceed in the Netherlands. The cargo owners appealed to the Court of Appeal. On 13 January 1982 the Court of Appeal (Lord Denning MR, Ackner LJ and Sir Sebag Shaw) ([1982] 1 All ER 1076, [1982] 2 WLR 556) allowed the appeal, removed the stay and allowed the action to proceed in England. The carriers appealed to the House of Lords with leave of the Court of Appeal. The facts are set out in the opinion of Lord Diplock.

Johan Steyn QC and *Angus Glennie* for the carriers.
Robert Alexander QC and *Michael Dean QC* for the cargo owners.

Their Lordships took time for consideration.

25 November. The following opinions were delivered.

a

LORD DIPLOCK. My Lords, on 21 March 1978, some nine months after the Carriage of Goods by Sea Act 1971 came into force, the respondents (the cargo owners) shipped from the port of Leith a large machine weighing 9906 kg on a vessel, Haico Holwerda, belonging to the appellants, the Royal Netherlands Steamship Co (the carriers), for carriage to Bonaire in the Netherlands Antilles. In respect of this carriage the carriers *b* issued at the port of Leith a through bill of lading providing for transhipment at Amsterdam.

The cargo owners claim that the machine was damaged during the course of discharge from the carrying vessel at Bonaire as a result of the negligence of the servants of the carrying vessel which for the ocean leg of the voyage was in fact a ship under the Norwegian flag, the Morviken, of which the carriers were charterers.

c On 26 February 1980 the cargo owners commenced an action in rem in the High Court against the Hollandia, a sister ship of the Haico Holwerda, belonging to the carriers. The Hollandia was within the jurisdiction of the Admiralty Court though she was not in fact arrested because, as so often happens, the carriers' solicitors agreed to accept service of the writ without prejudice to their right to move the Admiralty Court for a stay of all further proceedings.

d The only ground on which such stay was sought which it is necessary for your Lordships to consider was based on the incorporation in the bill of lading of a printed clause included among some 16 other clauses appearing under the heading 'Company's Standard Conditions'. The clause relied on was cl 2 which was in the following terms:

e
'*Law of application and jurisdication.* The law of the Netherlands in which the Hague Rules, as adopted by the Brussels Convention of 25th August 1924, are incorporated—with the exception of article 9—shall apply to this contract. The maximum liability per package is D.fl. 1250.—. For goods loaded or discharged at a Belgian port, the rules of art. 91 of chapter 2 of the Belgian Commercial Code shall apply.

f
Whenever the Carrier is not the Owner or Demise Charterer of the Ocean vessel, the Owner or Demise Charterer of such vessel shall, nevertheless, be entitled to avail himself of every exemption, limitation, condition and liberty herein contained, and every right, exemption from liability, defence and immunity of whatsoever nature applicable to the Carrier or to which the Carrier is entitled hereunder as if this Bill of Lading had been issued by the said Owner or Demise Charterer in his own name and on his own behalf.

g
All actions under the present contract of carriage shall be brought before the Court of Amsterdam and no other Court shall have jurisdiction with regard to any such action unless the Carrier appeals to another jurisdiction or voluntarily submits himself thereto.'

The last paragraph of this clause is unquestionably a choice of forum clause, weighted no doubt in favour of the carriers, providing for the exclusive jurisdiction of the Court *h* of Amsterdam unless the carriers elect otherwise. It was submitted on behalf of the carriers that, since they had not waived it, the High Court in England ought to give effect to the choice of forum clause by granting the stay. Although the Admiralty Court in England had undoubted jurisdiction to determine disputes between the parties in the exercise of its in rem jurisdiction over the Hollandia, it would, it was contended, be an unjudicial exercise of that discretion to allow the action to proceed in the High Court in England.

j My Lords, as is apparent from the first paragraph of the clause, the Netherlands at the time of the issue of the bill of lading were parties to the Brussels Convention of 1924, commonly known as the Hague Rules, which were scheduled to the Carriage of Goods by Sea Act 1924; but the Netherlands had not by then ratified the Brussels protocol of 1968, amending the Hague Rules, commonly known as the Hague-Visby Rules, which are scheduled to the 1971 Act. The Hague-Visby Rules modify the Hague Rules in several relevant respects and in particular by the new art IV, para 5 they provide a higher maximum monetary liability of a carrier to a shipper or consignee in damages for any negligence or breach of contract for which the carrier is not relieved from liability under art IV. In the instant case, under the Hague Rules the maximum liability of the carriers would be calculated on the package or unit basis, for which alone the Hague Rules provide, and would amount to about £250; whereas under the Hague-Visby Rules the cargo owners would be entitled to the higher maximum based on weight, which would amount to some £11,000.

It is common ground between the parties that, if the dispute were to be litigated before the Court of Amsterdam, that court would apply the lower maximum applicable under the Hague Rules. Since in English law it is a question of fact what a Netherlands court would decide under Netherlands law, your Lordships must, I think, in determining this appeal accept as accurate the statement of the law that would be applied by the Court of Amsterdam on which the parties are agreed.

The provisions of the 1971 Act that are most directly relevant to the instant appeal are s 1(1) to (3), which reads as follows:

> '**1.**—(1) In this Act, "the Rules" means the International Convention for the unification of certain rules of law relating to bills of lading signed at Brussels on 25th August 1924, as amended by the Protocol signed at Brussels on 23rd February 1968.
>
> (2) The provisions of the Rules, as set out in the Schedule to this Act, shall have the force of law.
>
> (3) Without prejudice to subsection (2) above, the said provisions shall have effect (and have the force of law) in relation to and in connection with the carriage of goods by sea in ships where the port of shipment is a port in the United Kingdom, whether or not the carriage is between ports in two different States within the meaning of Article X of the Rules.'

The provisions of the Hague-Visby Rules set out in the schedule to the 1971 Act, on the meaning of which this appeal mainly turns, are art III, para 8 (read in conjunction with paras 1 and 2 of the same article and art IV, para 5(a)) and art X.

For ease of reference I have set these rules out below.

Article III:

> '1. The carrier shall be bound before and at the beginning of the voyage to exercise due diligence to— (a) Make the ship seaworthy. (b) Properly man, equip and supply the ship. (c) Make the holds, refrigerating and cool chambers, and all other parts of the ship in which goods are carried, fit and safe for reception, carriage and preservation.
>
> 2. Subject to the provisions of Article IV, the carrier shall properly and carefully load, handle, stow, carry, keep, care for, and discharge the goods carried . . .
>
> 8. Any clause, covenant, or agreement in a contract of carriage relieving the carrier or the ship from liability for loss or damage to, or in connection with, goods arising from negligence, fault, or failure in the duties and obligations provided in this article or lessening such liability otherwise than as provided in these Rules, shall be null and void and of no effect. A benefit of insurance in favour of the carrier or similar clause shall be deemed to be a clause relieving the carrier from liability.'

Article IV:

> '5. (a) Unless the nature and value of such goods have been declared by the shipper before shipment and inserted in the bill of lading, neither the carrier nor the ship shall in any event be or become liable for any loss or damage to or in connection with the goods in an amount exceeding the equivalent of 10,000 francs per package or unit or 30 francs per kilo of gross weight of the goods lost or damaged, whichever is the higher . . .'

Article X:

a
      'The provisions of these Rules shall apply to every bill of lading relating to the carriage of goods between ports in two different States if: (*a*) the bill of lading is issued in a contracting State, or (*b*) the carriage is from a port in a contracting State, or (*c*) the contract contained in or evidenced by the bill of lading provides that these Rules or legislation of any State giving effect to them are to govern the contract, whatever may be the nationality of the ship, the carrier, the shipper, the consignee,
b
      or any other interested person.'

My Lords, the provisions in s 1 of the 1971 Act that I have quoted appear to me to be free from any ambiguity perceptible to even the most ingenious of legal minds. The Hague-Visby Rules, or rather all those of them that are included in the schedule, are to have the force of law in the United Kingdom: they are to be treated as if they were part of directly enacted statute law. But since they form part of an international convention
c
which must come under the consideration of foreign as well as English courts, it is, as Lord Macmillan said of the Hague Rules themselves in *Stag Line Ltd v Foscolo, Mango & Co Ltd* [1932] AC 328 at 350, [1931] All ER Rep 666 at 677—

d
      'desirable in the interests of uniformity that their interpretation should not be rigidly controlled by domestic precedents of antecedent date, but rather that the language of the rules should be construed on broad principles of general acceptation.'

They should be given a purposive rather than a narrow literalistic construction, particularly wherever the adoption of a literalistic construction would enable the stated purpose of the international convention, viz the unification of domestic laws of the contracting states relating to bills of lading, to be evaded by the use of colourable devices
e
that, not being expressly referred to in the rules, are not specifically prohibited.

The bill of lading issued to the cargo owners by the carriers on the shipment of the goods at the Scottish port of Leith was one to which the Hague-Visby Rules were expressly made applicable by art X; it fell within both para (*a*) and para (*b*); it was issued in a contracting state, the United Kingdom, and it covered a contract for a carriage from a port in a contracting state. For good measure, it also fell directly within s 1(3) of the
f
1971 Act itself.

The first paragraph of cl 2 of the bill of lading, prescribing as it does for a per package maximum limit of liability on the part of the carriers for loss or damage arising from negligence or breach of contract instead of the higher per kilogramme maximum applicable under the Hague-Visby Rules, is ex facie a clause in a contract of carriage which purports to lessen the liability of the carriers for such loss or damage otherwise than is provided in the Hague-Visby Rules. As such it is therefore rendered null and void
g
and of no effect under art III, para 8. So much indeed was conceded by counsel for the carriers, subject to a possible argument to the contrary which was briefly mentioned but not elaborated on. I shall have to revert to this argument later, but can do so with equal brevity.

The first paragraph of cl 2 of the bill of lading down to the first full stop is ambiguous.
h
It may mean that the general law of the Netherlands (including its private international law) relating to carriage of goods by sea is adopted as the 'proper law' of the contract of carriage or it may mean, as the absence of a comma between 'Netherlands' and 'in which' might suggest, that only that part of the law of the Netherlands which incorporates the Hague Rules is to be applicable to the contract which, in other respects, is to be governed by what the court seised of any claim under the contract would treat as being its 'proper
j
law'. In the case of a contract made in Scotland for the carriage of goods from a port in Scotland, the 'proper law' would, prima facie at any rate, be Scots law, and this, so far as contracts of carriage of goods by sea are concerned, is in all relevant respects the same as English law. But, whether the first paragraph of cl 2 of the bill of lading be given the wider or the narrower meaning, in so far as it purports to lessen, as it expressly does, the liability of the carriers for which art IV, para 5 of the Hague-Visby Rules provides, it

unquestionably contravenes art III, para 8 and by that paragraph is deprived of any effect in English or Scots law.

The Court of Appeal was unanimous in so holding and counsel for the carriers has not argued to the contrary in this House, at any rate so far as the paragraph limits the maximum liability of the carriers to 1,250 Dutch florins instead of the higher maximum for which the Hague-Visby Rules provide. Sheen J, at first instance (see [1981] 2 Lloyd's Rep 61), found it unnecessary to decide this point because he regarded the three paragraphs of cl 2 as severable, since they deal with separate subject matters. Indeed, the second paragraph does not deal with choice of law, whether substantive or curial, at all. It was on the third paragraph of cl 2, which deals only with choice of forum that the judge based his judgment granting the stay. This he felt able to do notwithstanding the fact that, although on the face of the third paragraph it deals only with the choice of curial law which (as was held by this House in *Compagnie d'Armement Maritime SA v Compagnie Tunisienne de Navigation SA* [1970] 3 All ER 71, [1971] AC 572) may be a different law from that chosen as the 'proper law' of the contract, it was common ground between the parties that to give effect to the choice of the Court of Amsterdam as the forum would have the same consequences in limiting the carriers' liability as would the application of the first paragraph of the clause, since the Court of Amsterdam would treat as the applicable substantive law that substantive law for which the first paragraph of cl 2 provides.

Counsel for the carriers sought to justify the judge's decision on this point by putting a narrow literalistic interpretation on art III, para 8 of the Hague-Visby Rules. A choice of forum clause, he contended, is to be classified as a clause which only prescribes the procedure by which disputes arising under the contract of carriage are to be resolved. It does not ex facie deal with liability at all and so does not fall within the description 'any clause, covenant, or agreement in a contract of carriage ... lessening ... liability', so as to bring it within art III, para 8, even though the consequence of giving effect to the clause will be to lessen, otherwise than is provided in the Hague-Visby Rules, the liability of the carrier for loss or damage to or in connection with the goods arising from negligence, fault or failure in the duties and obligations provided in the rules.

My Lords, like all three members of the Court of Appeal, I have no hesitation in rejecting this narrow construction of art III, para 8, which looks solely to the form of the clause in the contract of carriage and wholly ignores its substance. The only sensible meaning to be given to the description of provisions in contracts of carriage which are rendered 'null and void and of no effect' by this paragraph is one which would embrace every provision in a contract of carriage which, if it were applied, would have the effect of lessening the carrier's liability otherwise than as provided in the rules. To ascribe to it the narrow meaning for which counsel contended would leave it open to any shipowner to evade the provisions of art III, para 8 by the simple device of inserting in his bills of lading issued in, or for carriage from a port in, any contracting state a clause in standard form providing as the exclusive forum for resolution of disputes what might aptly be described as a court of convenience, viz one situated in a country which did not apply the Hague-Visby Rules or, for that matter, a country whose law recognised an unfettered right in a shipowner by the terms of the bill of lading to relieve himself from all liability for loss or damage to the goods caused by his own negligence, fault or breach of contract.

My Lords, unlike the first paragraph of cl 2 a choice of forum clause, such as that appearing in the third paragraph, does not ex facie offend against art III, para 8. It is a provision of the contract of carriage that is subject to a condition subsequent; it comes into operation only on the occurrence of a future event that may or may not occur, viz the coming into existence of a dispute between the parties as to their respective legal rights and duties under the contract which they are unable to settle by agreement. There may be some disputes that would bring the choice of forum clause into operation but which would not be concerned at all with negligence fault or failure by the carrier or the ship in the duties and obligations provided by art III; a claim for unpaid freight is an obvious example. So a choice of forum clause which selects as the exclusive forum for

the resolution of disputes a court which will not apply the Hague-Visby Rules, even after
_a_ such clause has come into operation, does not necessarily always have the effect of
lessening the liability of the carrier in a way that attracts the application of art III, para 8.

My Lords, it is, in my view, most consistent with the achievement of the purpose of
the 1971 Act that the time at which to ascertain whether a choice of forum clause will
have an effect that is proscribed by art III, para 8 should be when the condition subsequent
is fulfilled and the carrier seeks to bring the clause into operation and to rely on it. If the
_b_ dispute is about duties and obligations of the carrier or ship that are referred to in that
rule and it is established as a fact (either by evidence or as in the instant case by the
common agreement of the parties) that the foreign court chosen as the exclusive forum
would apply a domestic substantive law which would result in limiting the carrier's
liability to a sum lower than that to which he would be entitled if art IV, para 5 of the
Hague-Visby Rules applied, then an English court is in my view commanded by the
_c_ 1971 Act to treat the choice of forum clause as of no effect.

The rule itself speaks of a proscribed provision in a contract of carriage as a 'clause,
covenant, or agreement in a contract of carriage' and describes the effect of the rule on
the offending provision as being to render it 'null and void and of no effect'. These
pleonastic expressions occurring in an international convention (of which the similarly
pleonastic version in the French language is of equal authenticity) are not to be construed
_d_ as technical terms of legal art. It may well be that if they were to be so construed the
most apt to be applied to a choice of forum clause when brought into operation by the
occurrence of a particular dispute would be the expression 'of no effect', but it is no
misuse of ordinary language to describe the clause in its application to the particular
dispute as being pro tanto 'null' or 'void' or both.

I have mentioned this because counsel for the carriers sought to support his argument
_e_ that a choice of forum clause fell outside the ambit of art III, para 8 because it was
analogous to a foreign arbitration clause which was not a 'domestic arbitration agreement'
within the meaning of the Arbitration Act 1975; and accordingly for the court to refuse
to grant a stay of proceedings brought against the carrier in breach of the foreign
arbitration clause would contravene s 1(1) of that Act. This, it was suggested by counsel,
would give rise to an anomaly which your Lordships' decision in the instant appeal
_f_ should seek to avoid.

My Lords, it is not necessary in the instant appeal to consider what the effect of art III,
para 8 would be on a foreign arbitration clause in a bill of lading and since we have no
actual specimen of any such clause before us it would be unwise to attempt to deal with
the effect of s 1(1) of the 1975 Act on a foreign arbitration clause in a bill of lading issued
in, or for carriage from a port in, the United Kingdom which purported by the wording
_g_ that it used to exclude the application by the arbitrator of the Hague-Visby Rules. I
content myself by saying that I do not accept the analogy nor do I accept the suggested
consequences under s 1(1) of the 1975 Act. An arbitration clause providing for the
submission of future disputes to arbitration is to be distinguished from a clause making
a choice of the substantive law by which the agreement containing the arbitration clause
is to be governed. What the arbitration clause does is to leave it to the arbitrator to
_h_ determine what is the 'proper law' of the contract in accordance with accepted principles
of conflict of laws and then to apply that 'proper law' to the interpretation and the validity
of the contract and the mode of performance and the consequences of breaches of
contract. One, but by no means the only, matter to be taken into consideration in
deciding what is the 'proper law' is a particular choice of substantive law by which the
contract is to be governed, made by an express clause in the contract itself. But if the
_j_ particular choice of substantive law made by the express clause is such as to make the
clause null and void under the law of the place where the contract was made, or under
what, in the absence of such express clause, would be the proper law of the contract, I am
very far from accepting that it would be open to the arbitrator to treat the clause as being
otherwise than null and void, or to give any effect to it.

In the instant appeal, however, your Lordships are not concerned with a foreign arbitration clause or an application for a stay of proceedings in the High Court whether under s 1(1) of the Arbitration Act 1975 or under s 4(1) of the Arbitration Act 1950. Having regard to the nature of the dispute which the carriers asserted brought into operation the choice of forum clause that forms the third paragraph of cl 2 of the bill of lading, Sheen J was, for the reasons that I have given, bound to treat the bill of lading as if it contained neither the first nor the third paragraph of cl 2 and consequently was without any choice of forum clause. That did not deprive the judge of all discretion to grant a stay if the carriers were able to satisfy him that, independently of cl 2, the Court of Amsterdam was a forum conveniens and the Admiralty Court in London was not. But in exercising his discretion to grant the stay the judge gave decisive weight to the fact that by accepting the bill of lading, even though it was a contract of adhesion so far as the 'Company's Standard Condition' were concerned, the cargo owners had agreed not to bring any action under the contract against the carriers in any court other than the Court of Amsterdam. Since by English law he was required to treat the choice of forum clause as null and void and of no effect, it follows that by giving any weight to it in deciding how to exercise his discretion he was taking into consideration a matter which he was not entitled to take into consideration.

The choice of forum clause being eliminated from the contract of carriage, the cargo owners, as plaintiffs, were prima facie at liberty to avail themselves of the right of access to the Admiralty Court. In determining whether to grant a stay that would deny them that prima facie right the principle to be followed became that which I stated in *MacShannon v Rockware Glass Ltd* [1978] 1 All ER 625 at 630, [1978] AC 795 at 812:

> 'In order to justify a stay two conditions must be satisfied, one positive and the other negative: (a) the defendant must satisfy the court that there is another forum to whose jurisdiction he is amenable in which justice can be done between the parties at substantially less inconvenience or expense, and (b) the stay must not deprive the plaintiff of a legitimate personal or juridical advantage which would be available to him if he invoked the jurisdiction of the English court . . .'

That formulation was subsequently accepted by this House in *Castanho v Brown & Root (UK) Ltd* [1981] 1 All ER 143, [1981] AC 557.

It has not been seriously contended that either of these conditions is fulfilled in the instant case if the third paragraph of cl 2 is, like the first paragraph, struck down by the 1971 Act.

As foreshadowed at an earlier point in this speech I must return in a brief postscript to an argument based on certain passages in an article by a distinguished commentator, Dr F A Mann 'Statutes and the Conflict of Laws' (1974) 46 BYIL 117, and which, it is suggested, supports the view that even a choice of substantive law, which excludes the application of the Hague-Visby Rules, is not prohibited by the 1971 Act notwithstanding that the bill of lading is issued in and is for carriage from a port in the United Kingdom. The passages to which our attention was directed by counsel for the carriers I find myself (apparently in respectable academic company) unable to accept. They draw no distinction between the 1924 Act and the 1971 Act despite the contrast between the legislative techniques adopted in the two Acts, and the express inclusion in the Hague-Visby Rules of art X (absent from the Hague Rules), expressly applying the Hague-Visby Rules to every bill of lading falling within the description contained in the article, which article is given the force of law in the United Kingdom by s 1(2) of the 1971 Act. The 1971 Act deliberately abandoned what may conveniently be termed the 'clause paramount' technique employed in s 3 of the 1924 Act, the Newfoundland counterpart of which provided the occasion for wide-ranging dicta in the opinion of the Privy Council delivered by Lord Wright in *Vita Food Products Inc v Unus Shipping Co Ltd* [1939] 1 All ER 513, [1939] AC 277. Although the actual decision in that case would have been the same if the relevant Newfoundland statute had been in the terms of the 1971 Act, those dicta have no application to the construction of the latter Act and this has rendered it no longer necessary to embark on what I have always found to be an unrewarding task of ascertaining precisely what those dicta meant.

I would dismiss this appeal.

a **LORD KEITH OF KINKEL.** My Lords, I have had the advantage of reading in draft the speech delivered by my noble and learned friend Lord Diplock. I agree with it, and for the reasons he gives I too would dismiss the appeal.

LORD ROSKILL. My Lords, I have had the advantage of reading in draft the speech of my noble and learned friend Lord Diplock. I agree with it in all respects and for the reasons he gives I would dismiss this appeal.

b **LORD BRANDON OF OAKBROOK.** My Lords, I have had the advantage of reading in advance the speech prepared by my noble and learned friend Lord Diplock. I agree with it, and for the reasons which he gives I would dismiss the appeal.

LORD BRIGHTMAN. My Lords, I also would dismiss this appeal for the reasons c given by my noble and learned friend Lord Diplock.

Appeal dismissed.

Solicitors: *Middleton, Lewis, Lawrence, Graham* (for the carriers); *Clyde & Co* (for the cargo owners).

d

Mary Rose Plummer   Barrister.

e
Note
Central Electricity Board of Mauritius v Bata Shoe Co (Mauritius) Ltd and another

PRIVY COUNCIL
f LORD KEITH OF KINKEL, LORD ROSKILL AND LORD BRANDON OF OAKBROOK
15, 16, 17, 18, 22, 23 MARCH, 26 MAY 1982

Privy Council – Jurisdiction – Interest – Interest on award of damages – Jurisdiction to award interest – Determination of appropriate rate of interest.

g **LORD BRANDON OF OAKBROOK,** after giving the Board's reasons for advising Her Majesty that an appeal by the Central Electricity Board of Mauritius (the CEB) against the decision of the Supreme Court of Mauritius (Rault CJ and de Ravel J) on 12 June 1978 awarding the respondents, Bata Shoe Co (Mauritius) Ltd and East Africa Bata Shoe Co Ltd (Mauritius Department) (jointly referred to hereinafter as 'Bata'), damages of 1,895,000 rupees for loss suffered by Bata in consequence of a fire in their warehouse h at Plaine Lauzun in the industrial zone of Port Louis in Mauritius, which was caused by the negligence of the CEB, its servants or agents, be dismissed, then dealt with the Board's jurisdiction to award interest on an award of damages as follows: It remains for their Lordships to consider the further question raised by Bata with regard to their right, consequent on the affirmation of the judgment of the Supreme Court, to be awarded interest on the damages awarded to them from the date of such judgment until payment.

j   It was common ground that there was no statute or ordinance in force in Mauritius having an effect comparable to that of the Judgments Act 1838 in England. It was contended, however, for Bata that this Board has now, and has always had, a common law jurisdiction to award interest, or to direct the award of interest, in any case where the doing of complete justice between the parties to an appeal so requires.

In support of that contention counsel for Bata relied mainly on two authorities of long standing. The first authority was *Bank of Australasia v Breillat* (1847) 6 Moo PCC 152 at 206, 13 ER 642 at 662, an appeal from the Supreme Court of New South Wales. The second authority was *Rodger v Comptoir D'Escompte de Paris* (1871) LR 3 PC 465, an application in an appeal from the Supreme Court of Hong Kong.

In the first case it was held that where appellants, having failed in a monetary claim in the courts below, succeeded on appeal to this Board, the latter had a common law jurisdiction to award to the appellants interest on the amount of the moneys finally recovered from the date on which they should have obtained judgment for such amount in the first court below.

In the second case it was held that where appellants, who had satisfied a money judgment of the court below, subsequently succeeded, on an appeal to this Board, in having such judgment reversed this Board had jurisdiction to order that the money paid by the appellants should be repaid to them by the respondents with interest from the date of the original payment.

The present case differs from both of the two cases referred to above in that Bata succeeded in the court below, and have succeeded again in this appeal. The CEB did not obtain a stay of execution of the judgment of the Supreme Court pending their appeal to this Board. It appears, however, that there was an implied agreement or arrangement between the parties or their legal representatives that matters should proceed as if a stay of execution had been granted. The situation is, therefore, that the CEB have had, for a period of nearly four years, the benefit of the use of moneys which should, according to the rights of the case, have been paid by them to Bata at the beginning of that period.

The principle on which the Board acted in the second case referred to above was explained at considerable length by Lord Cairns (at 475–476). It can be summarised as being that, in order to do complete justice between the parties, money paid in satisfaction of a judgment subsequently reversed by this Board should be repaid with interest from the date on which the money concerned was paid.

In their Lordships' view, although the situation in the present case differs, in the respects stated, from the situation in each of the two cases referred to above, the same general principle, founded on the need to do, so far as possible, complete justice between the parties, can and should be applied, by analogy, in the present appeal.

Their Lordships are, therefore, of the opinion that they have jurisdiction, which has in one case at least been described, whether rightly or wrongly, as a common law jurisdiction, to order the CEB, as one of the consequences of the dismissal of the appeal, to pay to Bata interest on the total amount of the damages awarded to them by the Supreme Court from 12 June 1978, the date of the judgment of that Court, until payment. Their Lordships are further of the opinion that, in the circumstances of this case, it would be just for them to exercise that jurisdiction.

Their Lordships, however, take the view that the Supreme Court, by reason of its knowledge of conditions in Mauritius during the period for which interest is to be awarded, is far better placed than they are to determine the appropriate rate or rates at which such interest should be paid, and that the determination of such rate or rates should accordingly be remitted to that court for determination.

In the result, their Lordships will humbly advise Her Majesty that the appeal should be dismissed, and that the CEB should pay to Bata interest on the total amount of the damages awarded from the date of the judgment of the Supreme Court appealed from until payment at such rate or rates as the Supreme Court shall hereafter determine. The CEB must pay Bata's costs of the appeal.

Diana Procter   Barrister.

Practice Direction

QUEEN'S BENCH DIVISION

Practice – Interest – Pleading – Claim – Debt or liquidated sum – Contents of prayer for interest – Contractual interest – Law Reform (Miscellaneous Provisions) Act 1934 – Bills of Exchange Act 1882.

1. *Interest under the Law Reform (Miscellaneous Provisions) Act 1934*

(a) This is in the discretion of the court and is treated as a claim for unliquidated damages.

(b) It should be claimed expressly in the prayer in the statement of claim; 'Interest pursuant to the Law Reform (Miscellaneous Provisions) Act 1934' is sufficient. ('Interest pursuant to statute' is unsatisfactory, for there are several statutes dealing with interest.)

(c) If there is such a claim for interest the indorsement for 14-day costs may be deleted. If the plaintiff wishes to stimulate the defendant to pay promptly, he may leave it in, completing it with the principal sum only; if the defendant pays within the 14 days, the action is stayed and the right to go on for interest is lost.

(d) If the defendant makes default in giving notice of intention to defend, or serving a defence, the plaintiff may *either* (i) sign final judgment for the principal sum and interlocutory judgment for interest to be assessed (costs are dealt with on the assessment; the plaintiff usually then gets the equivalent of the scale costs of the claim plus a moderate additional sum for the assessment) *or* (ii) abandon the claim for interest and sign final judgment for the principal sum and scale costs.

2. *Contractual interest*

(a) The statement of claim must give sufficient particulars of the contract relied on, and, in particular, must show (i) the date from which interest is payable, (ii) the rate of interest fixed by the contract, (iii) the amount of interest due at the issue of the writ.

(b) The interest up to the issue of the writ should be claimed in the prayer and included in the sum entered in the indorsement for 14-day costs. This indorsement must be made; if the defendant pays the principal sum, the interest to the date of the writ and the 14-day costs within the 14 days, the action is stayed and no further interest is payable.

(c) The statement of claim should also contain a prayer for further interest at the contract rate from the issue of the writ or judgment or sooner payment. It is often helpful to work out and show this interest also as a daily rate.

(d) If the defendant makes default in giving notice of intention to defend or in serving a defence, the plaintiff may sign judgment for the principal sum, interest to the date of the writ, further interest calculated to the date of judgment and scale costs. This last calculation is checked by the court when judgment is entered, and it is for this reason that the statement of claim must give sufficient information to enable this to be done quickly.

3. *Interest under the Bills of Exchange Act 1882*

(a) By s 57 of the Bills of Exchange Act 1882 the holder of a cheque (or other bill of exchange) which is dishonoured when duly presented is entitled to recover, in addition to the amount of the cheque, interest as liquidated damages from the date of dishonour until the date of judgment or sooner payment.

(b) There is no prescribed rate of interest; the plaintiff may properly ask for a reasonable rate around or somewhat above base rate. If a high rate is asked, there may be difficulty in entering a default judgment while the matter is referred to the Practice Master (see s 57(3) of the 1882 Act). Short Term Investment Account rate is a safe guide.

(c) The statement of claim should set out the date of dishonour, the rate of interest claimed, a calculation of the interest due at the date of the issue of the writ, and prayers for this interest and further interest until judgment or sooner payment. The procedure is as explained for contractual interest in para 2(b) to (d) above.

Note: The expression 'judgment or sooner payment' is used in this direction because the right to interest after judgment is almost always under the Judgments Act 1838 *only.*

J B ELTON
28 October 1982   Senior Master of the Supreme Court.

Practice Note

COURT OF APPEAL, CRIMINAL DIVISION
LORD LANE CJ, WATKINS LJ AND SIR ROGER ORMROD
25 NOVEMBER 1982

Criminal law – Costs – Magistrates' courts – Indictable offences – Summary trial or inquiry as examining justices – Exercise of powers to award costs – Dismissal of information or decision not to commit accused for trial – Costs of defence normally to be awarded out of central funds – Costs in Criminal Cases Act 1973, ss 1, 2, 12(1).

LORD LANE CJ made the following statement at the sitting of the court: I understand that there is a need for guidance to magistrates in exercising their powers to order costs in indictable offences.

Under s 1 of the Costs in Criminal Cases Act 1973 a magistrates' court dealing summarily with an indictable offence and dismissing the information, or inquiring into any offence as examining justices and determining not to commit the accused for trial, may order the payment out of central funds of the costs of the defence. A similar power exists under s 12(1) of the 1973 Act where an information is not proceeded with.

Whether to make such an award is a matter in the unfettered discretion of the court in the light of the circumstances of each particular case.

It should be accepted as normal practice that such an award be made unless there are positive reasons for making a different order. Examples of such reasons are: (a) where the prosecution has acted spitefully or has instituted or continued proceedings without reasonable cause, the defendant's costs should be paid by the prosecutor under s 2 of the 1973 Act; if there is any doubt whether payment will be forthcoming from the prosecutor the position of the defendant should be protected by making an order for costs from central funds in his favour as well; (b) where the defendant's own conduct has brought suspicion on himself and has misled the prosecution into thinking that the case against him is stronger than it is, the defendant can be left to pay his own costs; (c) where there is ample evidence to support a conviction but the defendant is acquitted on a technicality which has no merit, again the defendant can be left to pay his own costs; (d) where the defendant is acquitted on one charge but convicted on another, the court should make whatever order seems just having regard to the relative importance of the two charges and the conduct of the parties generally.

N P Metcalfe Esq   Barrister.

End of Volume 3